August 20-23, 2017
Boston, MA, USA

I0882058

Association for Computing Machinery

Advancing Computing as a Science & Profession

ACM-BCB'17

Proceedings of the 8th ACM International Conference on Bioinformatics, Computational Biology, and Health Informatics

Sponsored by:

ACM SIGBIO

Supported by:

National Science Foundation

Association for
Computing Machinery

Advancing Computing as a Science & Profession

The Association for Computing Machinery
2 Penn Plaza, Suite 701
New York, New York 10121-0701

Copyright © 2017 by the Association for Computing Machinery, Inc. (ACM). Permission to make digital or hard copies of portions of this work for personal or classroom use is granted without fee provided that copies are not made or distributed for profit or commercial advantage and that copies bear this notice and the full citation on the first page. Copyright for components of this work owned by others than ACM must be honored. Abstracting with credit is permitted. To copy otherwise, to republish, to post on servers or to redistribute to lists, requires prior specific permission and/or a fee. Request permission to republish from: permissions@acm.org or Fax +1 (212) 869-0481.

For other copying of articles that carry a code at the bottom of the first or last page, copying is permitted provided that the per-copy fee indicated in the code is paid through www.copyright.com.

Notice to Past Authors of ACM-Published Articles
ACM intends to create a complete electronic archive of all articles and/or other material previously published by ACM. If you have written a work that has been previously published by ACM in any journal or conference proceedings prior to 1978, or any SIG Newsletter at any time, and you do NOT want this work to appear in the ACM Digital Library, please inform permissions@acm.org, stating the title of the work, the author(s), and where and when published.

ISBN: 978-1-4503-4722-8 (Digital)

ISBN: 978-1-4503-5673-2 (Print)

Additional copies may be ordered prepaid from:

ACM Order Department
PO Box 30777
New York, NY 10087-0777, USA

Phone: 1-800-342-6626 (USA and Canada)
+1-212-626-0500 (Global)
Fax: +1-212-944-1318
E-mail: acmhelp@acm.org
Hours of Operation: 8:30 am – 4:30 pm ET

Message from the ACM-BCB 2017 General Chairs

It is our great pleasure to welcome you to the 8th ACM Conference on Bioinformatics, Computational Biology, and Health Informatics (ACM-BCB 2017). The meeting is the flagship conference of SIGBio, the ACM Special Interest Group in Bioinformatics, Computational Biology, and Biomedical Informatics. Continuing the tradition, the conference focuses on interdisciplinary research linking computer science, mathematics, statistics, biology, bioinformatics, biomedical informatics, and health informatics.

With the help of numerous volunteers but most importantly with the contributions of many researchers like yourself we have put together a program that we hope that everyone will find very interesting and stimulating. The technical program is the centerpiece of our meeting with 42 peer-reviewed full research papers and 28 short research papers, carefully selected from the 132 original submissions to the conference by diligent efforts of the members of program committee. Additionally, we have approximately 60 poster presentations and eight highlights presentations on recently published research. The technical program is enriched by six pre-conference workshops, four tutorials and featured sessions such as the NSF Travel Fellowship Awardee Forum and a panel on Women in Bioinformatics. We are also pleased that the Workshop on Algorithms in Bioinformatics (WABI) is co-located with ACM-BCB this year and will be sharing plenary talks and running parallel sessions alongside ACM BCB.

Such an organization cannot be accomplished without the selfless devotion of numerous volunteers who have tirelessly worked to shape this year's meeting. We are especially grateful to Amarda Shehu, Giuseppe Pozzi and Tamer Kahveci for serving as Program Committee Co-Chairs, and the army of volunteer program committee members who did the bulwark of reviewing the submissions. We similarly thank Jianlin Cheng, Bhaskar DasGupta and Lydia Tapia for putting together yet another strong workshop program; Filip Jagodzinski, Dario Ghersi and Giuseppe Tradigo for selecting four strong tutorials; and Dong Si, A. Ercument Cicek and Noah Daniels for bringing an outstanding set of timely research for display at the conference as poster presentations. Preetam Ghosh, yet again, handled registrations very smoothly, and our proceedings chairs Xinghua Mindy Shi, Yang Shen and Benjamin Hescott diligently and meticulously worked with Sheridan Printing and ACM headquarters to produce the proceedings.

Special thanks go to Aidong Zhang, the Editor-in-Chief of IEEE/ACM Transactions on Computational Biology and Bioinformatics (TCBB), and Dimitrios I. Fotiadis, the Editor-in-Chief of IEEE Journal of Biomedical and Health Informatics for approving ACM-BCB'2017 to have special issues in their journals; and May D. Wang, Zhaohui (Steve) Qin, Anna Ritz, and Ying Sha for selecting the NSF travel grant awardees. We are also grateful to Robert Cottingham and Narayan Ganesan for serving as Demo and Exhibits Chairs, and Pierangelo Veltri, A. Ercument Cicek, Oznur Tastan and Rolf Backofen for serving as Publicity Chairs. Thanks to May D. Wang for organizing the Women in Bioinformatics Panel; Shilpa Nadimpalli Kobren and Jisoo Park for spearheading student activities, and to Jonathan Kho and Ümit V. Çatalyürek for providing web support. Donna Cirelli and all the student volunteers from Tufts and UMass Boston will be providing logistical and operational assistance service during the conference. We also thank the ACM staff, especially Diana Brantuas for budget planning, John Otero for site negotiations, Irene Frawley for conference operations and logistics and Adrienne Griscti (from ACM) and Lisa Tolles (from Sheridan) for their help in printing the proceedings. Our logo for ACM BCB '17 featuring the Boston skyline was created by Barbara Pixton Designs.

A special note of thanks to our Steering Committee Co-Chairs Aidong Zhang and May D. Wang for being a constant source of support we could rely on.

We are truly grateful to the National Science Foundation (NSF) for providing travel support for students and young professionals to attend our conference, to interact with distinguished researchers, present their research, network with peers, and build a community of peers. In addition, we would like to thank ACM and SiGBio who provide this platform for researchers to share their state-of-art work in Bioinformatics and Health Informatics.

It has been a privilege to serve as your general chairs by putting the program in place, and making local and hospitality arrangements. On behalf of the entire team of volunteers and the organizing committee, we wish you four days of learning, engagement, pleasant stay, and fun!

Nurit Haspel
University of Massachusetts Boston

Lenore J. Cowen
Tufts University

ACM-BCB 2017 Program Chairs' Welcome

Welcome from the Program Chairs of the 8th ACM Conference on Bioinformatics, Computational Biology, and Health Informatics (ACM-BCB). The ACM-BCB 2017 conference received 132 paper submissions, 15 submissions in the "Highlight" category, 5 submissions in the "Tutorial" category, 8 submissions in the "Workshop" category, and 62 submissions in the "Poster" category.

The 132 paper submissions were grouped into 16 tracks: Advancing Algorithms and Methods, Automated Diagnosis and Prediction, Applications to Healthcare Processes, Applications to Microbes and Imaging Genetics, Big Data in Bioinformatics, Biological Modeling, Clinical Databases and Information Systems, Cancer Genomics, Genomic Variations and Disease, Inferring Phylogenies and Haplotypes, Knowledge Representation Applications, Protein and RNA Analysis, Structure and Dynamics, Sequence Analysis and Genome Assembly, Systems Biology, and Text Mining and Classification.

Every track was led by 3 track chairs, who with the help of numerous program committee members, performed diligently the task of carefully reviewing submissions. Every submission received between three and five reviews evaluating relevance, novelty, and technical rigor. The Program Chairs, in a close collaboration with the General Chairs, considered the reviewer-based track chair recommendations, and after discussing every submission, made the decision to accept 43 submissions as long papers and 28 submissions as short papers. Out of 15 submissions in the Highlight category, 8 submissions were accepted for oral presentation. Additionally, 6 submissions in the Workshop category and 4 submissions in the Tutorial category were included in the program.

The accepted papers and highlight papers were scheduled in three parallel sessions, spanning the three days of the conference, while accepted tutorials and accepted workshops were scheduled on the first day of the conference.

The authorship of papers, workshops, and tutorials submitted to ACM BCB 2017 was diverse, representing 35 different countries. To reflect the diversity of the ACM SIGBIO community, the program chairs made a conscious decision to have at least one chair of every track represent a non-US country and to have more than 30% of the track chairs be women.

It is with great pleasure that the Program Chairs and General Chairs welcome all attendees of *ACM-BCB 2017* and hope that the conference will be an exciting opportunity for authors to share results with colleagues, advance the state of bioinformatics and computational biology, and contribute to fostering a sense of community among established and junior researchers.

Amarda Shehu
George Mason University
Fairfax, VA, USA

Tamer Kahveci
University of Florida
Gainesville, FL, USA

Giuseppe Pozzi
Politecnico di Milano
Milano, Italy

Table of Contents

Session 12: Systems Biology I

Session Chair: Jérôme Waldispühl *(McGill University)*

Session 13: Knowledge Representation Applications

Session Chair: Pierangelo Veltri *(University Magna Graecia of Catanzaro)*

Session 14: Integrative Methods for Genomic Data

Session Chair: Marco Masseroli *(Politecnico di Milano)*

Session 15: Sdequence Analysis and Genome Assembly

Session Chair: Christina Boucher *(University of Florida)*

Session 16: Applications to Healthcare Processes

Session Chair: Alistair Johnson *(MIT)*

Session 17: Biological Modeling

Session Chair: Naveena Yanamala *(National Institute of Occupational and Safety Health)*

Session 18: Systems Biology II

Session Chair: Xinghua (Mindy) Shi *(University of North Carolina at Charlotte)*

Session 19: Automated Diagnosys and Prediction II

Session Chair: Dong Si *(University of Washington, Bothell)*

Session 20: Big Data in Bioinformatics II

Session Chair: Tom Pollard *(MIT)*

Poster Session

Tutorials

Invited Keynote Talks

Highlights

Computational Structural Bioinformatics Workshop (CSBW)

6th Workshop on Parallel and Cloud-based Bioinformatics and Biomedicine (ParBio)

4th International Workshop on Computational Network Biology: Modeling, Analysis, and Control (CNB-MAC)

6th Workshop on Computational Advances in Molecular Epidemiology (CAME 2017)

Workshop on Microbiomics, Metagenomics, and Metabolomics

ACM-BCB 2017 Organization Committee

General Chairs:
Nurit Haspel, University of Massachusetts Boston, USA
Lenore J. Cowen, Tufts University, USA

Program Chairs:
Amarda Shehu, George Mason University, USA
Tamer Kahveci, University of Florida, USA
Giuseppe Pozzi, Politecnico di Milano, Italy

Workshop Chairs:
Jianlin Cheng, University of Missouri, USA
Bhaskar DasGupta, University of Illinois at Chicago, USA
Lydia Tapia, University of New Mexico, USA

Tutorial Chairs:
Filip Jagodzinski, Western Washington University, USA
Dario Ghersi, University of Nebraska, USA
Giuseppe Tradigo, University Magna Graecia of Catanzaro, Italy

Demo and Exhibit Chairs:
Robert (Bob) Cottingham, Oak Ridge National Laboratory, USA
Narayan Ganesan, Stevens Institute of Technology, USA

Poster Chairs:
Dong Si, University of Washington Bothell, USA
A. Ercument Cicek, Bilkent University, Turkey
Noah Daniels, University of Rhode Island, USA

Registration Chair:
Preetam Ghosh, Virginia Commonwealth University, USA

Publicity Chairs:
Pierangelo Veltri, University Magna Graecia of Catanzaro, Italy
A. Ercument Cicek, Bilkent University, Turkey
Oznur Tastan, Bilkent University, Turkey

Student Travel Award Chair:
May D. Wang, Georgia Institute of Technology and Emory University, USA
Anna Ritz, Reed College, USA
Zhaohui (Steve) Qin, Emory University, GA, USA
Ying Sha, Georgia Institute of Technology, USA

Student Activity Chairs:
Shilpa Nadimpalli Kobren, Princeton University, USA
Jisoo Park, Tufts University, USA

Women in Bioinformatics (WiB) Chair:
May D. Wang, Georgia Institute of Technology and Emory University, USA

Proceedings Chairs:
Xinghua Mindy Shi, University of North Carolina at Charlotte, USA
Yang Shen, Texas A&M University, USA
Benjamin Hescott, Tufts University, USA

Web Admin:
Jonathan Kho, Georgia Institute of Technology, USA

WABI Chairs:
Russell Schwartz, Carnegie Mellon University, USA
Knut Reinert, Freie Universität Berlin, Germany

Steering Committee:
Aidong Zhang, State University of New York at Buffalo, Co-Chair
May D. Wang, Georgia Institute of Technology and Emory University, Co-Chair
Srinivas Aluru, Georgia Institute of Technology
Christopher C. Yang, Drexel University

ACM-BCB 2017 Sponsor & Supporter

Sponsor:

Supporter:

Beyond Perfect Phylogeny: Multisample Phylogeny Reconstruction via ILP

Paola Bonizzoni
Dipartimento di Informatica Sistemistica e Comunicazione
Università degli Studi di Milano–Bicocca
Viale Sarca 336, 20126
Milano
bonizzoni@disco.unimib.it

Simone Ciccolella
Dipartimento di Informatica Sistemistica e Comunicazione
Università degli Studi di Milano–Bicocca
Viale Sarca 336, 20126
Milano
s.ciccolella@campus.unimib.it

Gianluca Della Vedova
Dipartimento di Informatica Sistemistica e Comunicazione
Università degli Studi di Milano–Bicocca
Viale Sarca 336, 20126
Milano
gianluca.dellavedova@unimib.it

Mauricio Soto
Dipartimento di Informatica Sistemistica e Comunicazione
Università degli Studi di Milano–Bicocca
Viale Sarca 336, 20126
Milano
mauricio.sotogomez@unimib.it

ABSTRACT

Most of the evolutionary history reconstruction approaches are based on the infinite site assumption which is underlying the Perfect Phylogeny model. This is one of the most used models in cancer genomics. Recent results gives a strong evidence that recurrent and back mutations are present in the evolutionary history of tumors [19], thus showing that more general models then the Perfect phylogeny are required. To address this problem we propose a framework based on the notion of Incomplete Perfect Phylogeny. Our framework incorporates losing and gaining mutations, hence including the Dollo and the Camin-Sokal models, and is described with an Integer Linear Programming (ILP) formulation. Our approach generalizes the notion of persistent phylogeny [1] and the ILP approach [14, 15] proposed to solve the corresponding phylogeny reconstruction problem on character data.

The final goal of our paper is to integrate our approach into an ILP formulation of the problem of reconstructing trees on mixed populations, where the input data consists of the fraction of cells in a set of samples that have a certain mutation. This is a fundamental problem in cancer genomics, where the goal is to study the evolutionary history of a tumor. An experimental analysis shows that our ILP approach is able to explain data that do not fit the perfect phylogeny assumption, thereby allowing (1) multiple losses and gains of mutations, and (2) a number of subpopulations that is smaller than the number of input mutations.

CCS CONCEPTS

• **Applied computing** → *Bioinformatics*;

Permission to make digital or hard copies of all or part of this work for personal or classroom use is granted without fee provided that copies are not made or distributed for profit or commercial advantage and that copies bear this notice and the full citation on the first page. Copyrights for components of this work owned by others than the author(s) must be honored. Abstracting with credit is permitted. To copy otherwise, or republish, to post on servers or to redistribute to lists, requires prior specific permission and/or a fee. Request permissions from permissions@acm.org.
ACM-BCB '17, August 20-23, 2017, Boston, MA, USA
© 2017 Copyright held by the owner/author(s). Publication rights licensed to Association for Computing Machinery.
ACM ISBN 978-1-4503-4722-8/17/08...$15.00
https://doi.org/10.1145/3107411.3107441

KEYWORDS

phylogeny; clonal reconstruction

ACM Reference format:
Paola Bonizzoni, Simone Ciccolella, Gianluca Della Vedova, and Mauricio Soto. 2017. Beyond Perfect Phylogeny: Multisample Phylogeny Reconstruction via ILP. In *Proceedings of ACM-BCB '17, Boston, MA, USA, August 20-23, 2017*, 10 pages.
https://doi.org/10.1145/3107411.3107441

1 INTRODUCTION

Character-based phylogeny reconstruction is one of the fundamental problems in Bioinformatics, with a large literature [10, 13, 25, 26] focusing on a simple assumption: the input data consists of a set of species (or individuals) for which we know the set of characters that it possesses. In this case, the goal is to compute a phylogeny that explains the set of input species and characters, where each edge of the phylogeny allows characters gains and losses. Character-based phylogenies play a crucial role in modeling the evolution in cancer genomics. Cancer is an uncontrolled evolutionary process of somatic mutations of tumor cells from a single founder cell [11] creating a diverse set of subpopulations [6, 20, 27], each originated from a single *clone*: each clone (and each subpopulation) has a distinctive set of mutations. From this point of view, a tumor progression is a phylogeny where clones and mutations have the same role as species and mutations in the classical phylogeny reconstruction setting as characters.

To fall within the classical framework we would need to obtain data directly from a cell. Unfortunately, single cell sequencing is not cheap [21] and is prone to errors, therefore we have to study *samples* comprising lots of cells belonging to an unknown set of subpopulations. This adds a new complication, since for each sample we know the (approximate) fraction of cells that have a given somatic mutation. More precisely, each read extracted from the sample is mapped against the reference genome, therefore we obtain the mutations of each read. Since reads can be extracted from repeated regions of the genome and the coverage of the reads is not uniform throughout the genome or the cells of the sample, the fraction of reads that have a mutation is only an approximation of the fraction of cells of the sample that have that mutation. In other words, the observed frequencies are an estimate of the actual frequencies of the mutation.

The above argument leads to define a computational problem called *variant allele frequency factorization problem* (VAFFP) [7, 8, 16], where the input is the observed frequencies of the mutation in each sample and the desired output is a phylogeny representing the tumoral evolution, as well as the composition of each sample in terms of the subpopulations or clones. The literature has mainly focused on the binary perfect phylogenies [7], where samples contain mixtures of two-state characters, i.e. where each character/locus is either mutated or not and mutation can be gained only once and never lost in the entire history of the tumor. A possible generalization (that we do not explore in this paper) to the multi-state perfect phylogeny has been recently proposed in order to take into account the effect of copy number aberrations on alleles [8]. Then characters that can assume different states (multi states), but as in the binary case changes to the same state occur only once. This restriction — known as the infinite site assumption — allows to obtain efficient algorithms, but most recent studies refutes it [19] and state that more complex models are needed to describe the tumor evolution. In this paper we describe some efficient approaches that overcome this limitation and allow to reconstruct phylogenies that are more general than perfect phylogeny and are able to capture a likely evolutionary history of the tumor studied.

We will focus on three main character-based models: the Persistent Phylogeny [1] (where each character can be gained once and lost at most once), Camin-Sokal [5] (where each character can be gained several times, but never lost), and Dollo [9] (where each character can be gained at most once, but lost several times). We denote by Camin-Sokal(k) the restriction of the Camin-Sokal model where each character can be gained at most k times in the entire tree. Moreover, we denote by Dollo(k) the restriction of the Dollo model where each character can be lost at most k times in the entire tree. Clearly, the Persistent Phylogeny [1] corresponds to the Dollo(1) model which has been recently investigated in several works aiming to develop efficient solutions for the model [3, 4, 14] since its use is motivated also in other contexts [2, 23]. In particular, in [1] it is proved that the Persistent Phylogeny Problem over a binary matrix M can be formulated as finding a special completion of an extended matrix M_e that is a Perfect Phylogeny. Based on this characterization, an ILP formulation for the Persistent Phylogeny has been developed in [14]. In [7] the approach used to solve the VAFFP problem is a combination of an integer linear programming (ILP) formulation and a clever approach to compute the set of relevant phylogenies, based on the notion of ancestry graph. Since the last component is tightly coupled with the fact that perfect phylogenies have as many species as characters, it is not immediate to extend the approach of [7] to more general models. Starting, from this ILP formulation and the main characterization in [1], we developed a novel approach to the VAFFP problem that is entirely based on ILP and allows to take into account the three evolutionary models presented above. We have experimented our ILP approach on simulated and real data to test whether allowing the models to violate the infinite site assumption leads to better solutions, even when the Perfect Phylogeny model is able to explain the input data. Indeed, our experiments show that the Persistent phylogeny may explain the input data better than the Perfect Phylogeny while requiring a number of clones that is smaller than the number of mutations. Finally, the inferred tree from real data on a Leukemia tumor CLL077 reveals the losses of a mutation, though being the tree mostly consistent with the one reconstructed by other known methods [18].

2 PRELIMINARIES

The character-based phylogeny reconstruction problems we study in this paper are constrained version of the general Incomplete Directed Perfect Phylogeny (IDP) [22], where the input is an $n \times m$ matrix $M_?$, where $M_?(i, j) \in \{0, 1, ?\}$ represents the absence, presence or uncertainty of a character j in the species i respectively. A solution consists of changing each ? into 0 or 1 obtaining a new binary matrix M_s that has a directed perfect phylogeny (since all phylogenies of this paper are directed, we will skip this fact). The unconstrained IDP problem has a $O(mn \log^2(m + n))$-time algorithm [22].

A binary matrix M_s has a perfect phylogeny if and only if there are not two columns containing all the pairs $(0, 0)$, $(0, 1)$, $(1, 0)$ — two columns containing all those pairs are called incompatible or conflicting. The problem of determining if a binary matrix has a perfect phylogeny, and to compute such perfect phylogeny if possible, has a linear-time algorithm [12, 13]. Moreover, there exists an ILP formulation for determining if a binary matrix has a perfect phylogeny [15]. Since finding a perfect phylogeny is easy, the main difficulty in solving the IDP problem consists of determining if each ? must be replaced with a 0 or a 1.

In [1] the Persistent Perfect Phylogeny has been restated as a constrained IDP problem. More precisely, given a binary matrix M, they solve the IDP problem on an extended matrix M_e where each entry $M[s, c]$ is replaced by two entries $M_e[s, c^+]$ and $M_e[s, c^-]$ as follows: if $M[s, c] = 1$ then $M_e[s, c^+] = 1$ and $M_e[s, c^-] = 0$; if $M[s, c] = 0$ then $M_e[s, c^+] = M_e[s, c^-] =?$. The constraint is that, for each pair $(M_e[s, c^+], M_e[s, c^-])$ of ? entries, the corresponding entries in the matrix M_s must be the same, that is $M_e[s, c^+] = M_e[s, c^-]$. This additional constraints make impossible to use the algorithm of [22], but some algorithms have been developed [3, 4], including one based on an ILP formulation [14]. The latter algorithm can be trivially extended to compute the perfect phylogeny with the fewest edges.

A $p \times m$ *frequency* matrix F, contains the frequencies of the mutation in a set of samples. More precisely, each entry $F[t, j]$ indicates the proportion of cells in sample t with the mutation j. A $p \times n$ *usage* matrix U, contains the mixture of cells in each sample. More precisely, each entry $U[t, i]$ is the proportion of the cells in the sample t belonging to the subpopulation i. Finally, the $n \times m$ (clonal) matrix M contains which subpopulation has a given mutation. An evolution model $\mathcal{M}$ consists of a set of constraints that a phylogeny T realizing the clonal matrix M must obey. For example, when the evolution model is the persistent phylogeny, then the phylogeny T cannot have two edges corresponding to two gains or two losses of the same character. The $\mathcal{P}$-VAFF problem can be formally defined as follows.

Definition 2.1. Given a $p \times m$ frequency matrix F, a number of clones n, and an evolution model $\mathcal{P}$, the $\mathcal{P}$-VAFFP (short for $\mathcal{P}$-Variant Allele Frequency Factorization Problem) asks for an $p \times n$ usage matrix U and an $n \times m$ clonal matrix M such that (1) $F = \frac{1}{2}UM$, and (2) M admits a phylogeny under the model $\mathcal{P}$.

The 1/2 factor in the definition is a technical consequence of the fact that the healthy (wild type) cell subpopulation exists, but is not one of the clones of M, and human beings are diploid, that is they have two copies of each chromosome.

We decouple the $\mathcal{P}$-VAFFP problems into two different problems: computing M and U. In fact, once we have computed a clonal matrix M, the problem of finding a composition of samples, i.e. a usage matrix U, compatible with M consists of finding a matrix U such that $\sum_{i=1}^{n} U(t,i)M(i,j) = F(t,j)$ and $\sum_{i=1}^{n} U(t,i) \leq 1 \; \forall t, j$.

In our setting, clonal matrix M is an unknown variable generating two main issues. First, the restrictions regarding the sample proportions become non linear. Second, we must ensure that clones can be represented under parsimony rule $\mathcal{P}$. The first difficulty can be easily resolved since the product of two $\{0, 1\}$ variables can be expressed as a set of linear constraints. We detail this technique in section 4. Second issue is a more daunting task since involves the recognition problem for general parsimony rules. We deal with this issue in section 3 by proposing an ILP formulation for the reconstruction problem.

3 THE $\mathcal{P}$ PHYLOGENY RECONSTRUCTION PROBLEM

This section is devoted to the development of an ILP formulation for the following decision problem:

$\mathcal{P}$ Phylogeny Reconstruction Problem. Given a character-based phylogeny model $\mathcal{P}$ and a binary matrix M, decide if M admits a representation in the phylogeny model $\mathcal{P}$.

In this paper we focus on Dollo(k) and Camin-Sokal(k) models.

Our strategy is based on the approach discussed by Gusfield in [14] for the Persistent Phylogeny reconstruction problem. The formulation presented by Gusfield is founded on two main results:

(1) Every instance of the Persistent Perfect Phylogeny reconstruction problem consisting of a binary matrix M can be reduced to an instance M_e, consisting of a matrix over alphabet $\{0, 1, ?\}$, called *extended matrix*, of an equivalent Incomplete Directed Perfect Phylogeny problem with additional constraints [1].
(2) The Incomplete Directed Phylogeny problem can be stated as an ILP problem by minimizing the number of conflicts between characters [15].

We will extend the aforementioned results to solve the Dollo(k) (Camin-Sokal(k)) Phylogeny Reconstruction Problem by generalizing the construction of the extended matrix proposed in [1] to those more general models. Additionally, we extend the ILP formulation presented in [15] in order to incorporate constraints imposed by our generalization of (1). The later result will allow us to develop an ILP formulation for finding a Dollo(k) or Camin-Sokal(k) tree representation for the input matrix M of the $\mathcal{P}$ Phylogeny Reconstruction Problem.

3.1 Construction of the Extended Matrices

Definition 3.1. Given an incomplete binary matrix M and a set $\mathcal{R} = \{F_i(M) \leq 0\}_{i \in [1,r]}$ of r constraints, the *Modified Incomplete Directed Perfect Phylogeny for the set $\mathcal{R}$*, denoted by MIDPP($M, \mathcal{R}$), asks for finding a completion of matrix M which admits a Perfect Phylogeny and satisfies all constraints in $\mathcal{R}$

Is easy to see that if every constraint in $\mathcal{R}$ can be expressed as a linear constraint in terms of the matrix entries, then the problem MIDPP($M, \mathcal{R}$) admits a ILP formulation. The formulation can be obtained by simply adding the set of (linear) constraint $\mathcal{R}$ to the basic ILP formulation presented in [15].

Therefore, in the following we show the construction of the extended matrices and the set of constraints for Dollo(k) and Camin-Sokal(k) models.

Extended Matrix and constraints for Dollo(k). Let M be a binary matrix with n species and m characters. The extended matrix $M_{e,D(k)}$ for the Dollo(k) model is defined as follows:

- $M_{e,D(k)}$ has n rows and $m \times (k+1)$ columns, where each character j of matrix M is associated to $k+1$ columns in $M_{e,D(k)}$ denoted by $j_0, j_1, \ldots, j_k$.
- If $M(i,j) = 1$ then $M_{e,D(k)}(i, j_0) = 1$ and $M_{e,D(k)}(i, j_l) = 0$, $l \in [1,k]$.
- If $M(i,j) = 0$ then $M_{e,D(k)}(i, j_l) = ?$ for each $l \in [0,k]$.

For a character j, the column j_0 represents the acquisition of character j while each of the following k columns represents a possible loss of the gained character. In every feasible solution, a character can be gained/lost at most once along any path from the root, therefore, if $M(i,j) = 0$ it must hold that $\sum_{1 \leq l \leq k} M_{e,D(k)}(i, j_l) = M_{e,D(k)}(i, j_0)$. Let us define the following set of constraints for the matrix $M_{e,D(k)}$:

$$\mathcal{R}_{D(k)} = \left\{ \sum_{1 \leq l \leq k} M_{e,D(k)}(i, j_l) = M_{e,D(k)}(i, j_0), (i,j) : M(i,j) = 0 \right\} \tag{1}$$

Extended Matrix and constraints for Camin-Sokal(k). Let M be a binary matrix with n species and m characters. The extended matrix $M_{e,CS(k)}$ for the Camin-Sokal(k) model is defined as follows:

- $M_{e,CS(k)}$ has n rows and $m \times k$ columns; each character j of matrix M is associated to k columns in $M_{e,CS(k)}$ denoted by $j_1, \ldots, j_k$.
- If $M(i,j) = 0$ then $M_{e,CS(k)}(i, j_l) = 0$, $l \in [1,k]$.
- If $M(i,j) = 1$ then $M_{e,CS(k)}(i, j_l) = ?$, $l \in [1,k]$.

Every group of columns $j_1, \ldots, j_k$ represent the possible gain of a character in the resulting phylogenetic tree. In every feasible solution, a character can be gained at most once on any path from the root to a leaf, therefore we define the set following set of constrains for the extended matrix $M_{e,CS(k)}$:

$$\mathcal{R}_{CS(k)} = \left\{ \sum_{1 \leq l \leq k} M_{e,CS(k)}(i, j_l) = 1, (i,j) : M(i,j) = 1 \right\} \tag{2}$$

Thus, the Dollo(k) ((Camin-Sokal(k)) Phylogeny Reconstruction Problem is equivalent to solve the MIDPP problem over an extended matrix $M_{e,D(k)}$ and constraints $R_{D(k)}$, as stated in the following Theorem that generalizes the main Theorem in [1].

THEOREM 3.2. *Given a binary matrix M, then M admits a phylogeny under the Dollo(k) model if and only if the decision problem MIDPP($M_{e,D(k)}, \mathcal{R}_{D(k)}$) admits a solution.*

PROOF. ($\Rightarrow$) Let M a matrix, and let T be a Dollo(k) phylogeny representing M. For each character j we relabel T as follows: the edge labeled as j^+ will have label j_0 while edges labeled with j^- are relabeled arbitrarily from the set $\{j_1, \ldots, j_k\}$ (no two edges have the same label). Let $\hat{T}$ be the tree obtained from M after relabeling. It is immediate to notice that $\hat{T}$ is a perfect phylogeny.

Let $\hat{M}$ be the matrix associated with $\hat{T}$. Let s be a generic species, and let c be a character. If s has the character j in M, then the path from s to the root of $\hat{T}$ traverses the edge j_0 but not any of the edges j_h with $h > 0$, that is $\hat{M}(i, j_h) = 0$ for $h > 0$ and $\hat{M}(i, j_0) = 1$. If s does not have the character j in M, then either the path from s to the root of $\hat{T}$ does not traverse the edge j_0, or it traverses the edge j_0 and one of the edges j_h with $h > 0$. In both cases $\sum_{h=1}^{k} \hat{M}(i, j_h) = \hat{M}(i, j_0)$, hence $\hat{M}$ satisfies (1).

($\Leftarrow$) Conversely, let M be a binary matrix whose corresponding instance of MIDPP($M_{e,D(k)}, \mathcal{R}_{D(k)}$) is solved by the extended matrix $\hat{M}$. We will proof that M admits a Dollo(k) representation.

Let $\hat{T}$ be a perfect phylogeny solving $\hat{M}$. Let T be the phylogeny obtained from $\hat{T}$ by replacing each label j_0 with j_+ and any j_h with $h > 0$ with j^-. Just as for the first part of the proof, since the assignment $\hat{M}$ satisfies (1), for each species s and each character j of M, one of the following three cases holds: (1) $\hat{M}(i, j_h) = 0$ for $h > 0$ and $\hat{M}(i, j_0) = 1$, (2) $\sum_{h=1}^{k} \hat{M}(i, j_h) = \hat{M}(i, j_0) = 0$, (3) $\sum_{h=1}^{k} \hat{M}(i, j_h) = \hat{M}(i, j_0) = 1$. The same argument of the first part of the proof shows that in case (1) the path from s to the root of $\hat{T}$ traverses the edge j_0 but not any of the edges j_h with $h > 0$: hence the path from s to the root of T traverses the edge j^+ but not any of the edges j^-. In case (2), the path from s to the root of T does not traverse the edge j^+, while in case (3) the path from s to the root of T traverses the edge j^+ and of the edges j^-. We conclude that the tree T is a Dollo(k) phylogeny for the matrix M. □

Notice that a similar proof shows that the binary matrix M admits a phylogeny under the Camin-Sokal(k) model if and only if the decision problem (MIDPP($M_{e,CS(k)}, \mathcal{R}_{CS(k)}$)) has a solution. Moreover, it is quite natural to observe that every Dollo(k) (Camin-Sokal(k)) phylogeny for the matrix M is uniquely associated to a completion of the extended matrix which is instance to the problem MIDPP.

Theorem 3.2 allows us to reduce the $\mathcal{P}$ reconstruction problem to an ILP problem. As it was already mentioned, our formulation is based on the one presented in [15] for the IDP problem which we detail in the next section.

3.2 ILP formulation for the MIDPP

In this section we revisit the formulation proposed in [15] for the IDP problem.

The input of the problem is an incomplete matrix M. The goal is to decide if there exists a completion of the unknown entries of M in order to obtain a (complete) matrix admitting a Perfect Phylogeny. The main strategy is the minimization of the conflicts between pairs of characters. In virtue of the Perfect Phylogeny Theorem, the IDP problem will have a solution if and only if the optimal value of the problem is zero.

In what follows, we briefly explain the key elements of the ILP and we discuss the required changes for its use in the MIDPP problem.

Variables. We define a binary variable $Y(i, j)$ for each unknown position of M. With abuse of notation, $Y(i, j)$ will be a constant for every known position of the matrix of value $M(i, j)$. Since the objective is to determine if two columns are in conflict, for every pair of columns p, q we define a binary variable $C(p, q)$ that indicates the existence of a conflict between these two columns. To establish if two columns are in conflict, binary variables $B(p, q, a, b)$ are defined

	a	b	c
1	1	0	0
2	0	1	0
3	0	0	1
4	1	1	0
5	0	1	1
6	1	0	1

	a_0	a_1	a_2	b_0	b_1	b_2	c_0	c_1	c_2
1	1	0	0	?	?	?	?	?	?
2	?	?	?	1	0	0	?	?	?
3	?	?	?	?	?	?	1	0	0
4	1	0	0	1	0	0	?	?	?
5	?	?	?	1	0	0	1	0	0
6	1	0	0	?	?	?	1	0	0

Figure 1: Input matrix M (left) and the corresponding Dollo(2) extended matrix (right)

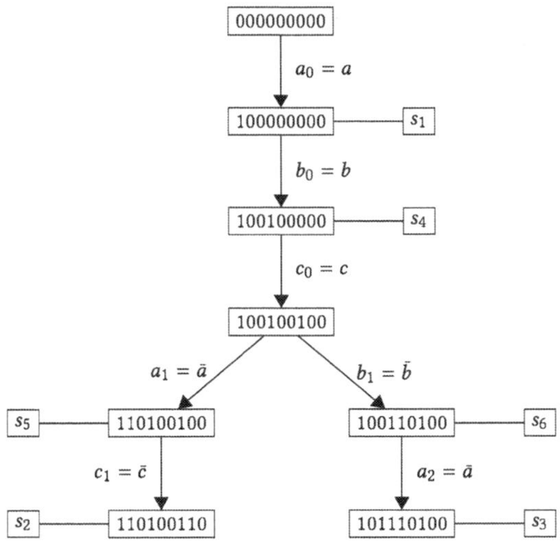

	a_0	a_1	a_2	b_0	b_1	b_2	c_0	c_1	c_2
1	1	0	0	0	0	0	0	0	0
2	1	1	0	1	0	0	1	1	0
3	1	0	1	1	1	0	1	0	0
4	1	0	0	1	0	0	0	0	0
5	1	1	0	1	0	0	1	0	0
6	1	0	0	1	1	0	1	0	0

Figure 2: A phylogeny for the input matrix M of Figure 1 (see Theorem 3.2) and the corresponding completion for the MIDPP($M_{e,D(k)}, \mathcal{R}_{D(k)}$).

for each pair of columns (p, q) and for each possible pair of values $(a, b) \in \{0, 1\}^2$. These variables indicate if for the (ordered) pair of columns (p, q) there exists a row i where $Y(i, p) = a$ and $Y(i, q) = b$. Similarly to the variable $Y(i, j)$, if for a pair (p, q) it already exits among known entries of the matrix a row where $Y(i, p) = a$ and $Y(j, q) = b$ then $B(p, q, a, b)$ will be considered as a constant of value 1.

Inequalities. For every pair of columns (p, q), every binary pair $(a, b) \in \{0, 1\}^2$ and every i, the following set of inequalities

$$B(p, q, a, b) \geq 1 - [a + (-1)^a \cdot Y(i, p)] - [b + (-1)^b \cdot Y(i, q)] \quad (3)$$

force the variable $B(p, q, a, b)$ to be 1 if and only if columns p, q exhibit the pair (a, b) in some rows. On the other hand, the following inequalities forces variables $C(p, q)$ to be 1 when characters p and q are in conflict.

$$C(p, q) \geq B(p, q, 0, 1) + B(p, q, 1, 0) + B(p, q, 1, 1) - 2 \quad (4)$$

Objective Function. Since we aim to minimize the number of conflicts, the objective function is defined as: $\min \sum_{(p,q)} C(p, q)$.

This formulation can be extended to solve the $\mathcal{P}$ phylogeny reconstruction problem under different $\mathcal{P}$ models Section 3 in order to find minimal conflict completions. Nevertheless, in the reconstruction problem we are mainly concern about feasible solutions with no conflicts. For this reason, we consider an alternative version of constraint (4):

$$B(p, q, 0, 1) + B(p, q, 1, 0) + B(p, q, 1, 1) \leq 2 \quad (5)$$

Hence, we can state the Dollo(k) (Camin-Sokal(k)) phylogeny reconstruction problem as any feasible solution of the set of constraints (3), (5) and $\mathcal{R}_{D(k)}$ ($\mathcal{R}_{CS(k)}$).

Additionally, since the number of total negated characters corresponds to $N(M) = \sum_{j=1}^{m} \sum_{l=1}^{k} B(j_0, j_l, 1, 1)$, we can state the problem of finding a parsimony representation with the minimum number of conflicts by considering the solution of the following minimization problem: $\min \sum_{(p,q)} C(p, q)$ s.t. (3), and (4).

4 THE CLONAL RECONSTRUCTION PROBLEM

In this section we present an ILP formulation for the $\mathcal{P}$-VAFFP. Let us recall that a $\mathcal{P}$-VAFFP instance is a $p \times m$ frequency matrix F, a number of clones n and a model $\mathcal{M}$. The objective is to find matrices U and M, defining clone populations and the configuration of different samples, such that $F = \frac{1}{2}UM$ where matrix M admits a phylogeny satisfying rule $\mathcal{P}$.

Variables. Variables are the entries of usage, clonal and extended matrices which we denote by U, M and M_e respectively. Extended matrix is constructed according to Section 3.1 based on the considered phylogeny model.

The formulation is divided in two sets of inequalities. The first part of the formulation deals with the feasibility of sample proportions for a set of clones. The second set of inequalities ensures that clones can be explained by an evolutionary history following a specific phylogeny model using the extended matrix formulation proposed in Theorem 3.2.

On the one hand, the relation between the proportion of the somatic mutations in the samples and the proportion of clones in the samples can be described as:

$$\frac{1}{2} \sum_{i=1}^{n} U(t, i) M(i, j) = F(t, j). \quad (6)$$

That is, for each sample $t \in [1, p]$, clone $i \in [1, n]$ and mutation $j \in [i, m]$ the sum of the proportions of clones present in the sample t which present mutation j must be equal to $F(i, j)$. Since each sample row t in matrix U describe a sample composition then it holds:

$$\sum_{i=1}^{n} U(t, i) \leq 1. \quad (7)$$

The (non linear) product of Equation 6 can be expressed in a linear form by introducing a set of auxiliary binary variables $X(t, i, j)$ as follows:

$$\sum_{i=1}^{n} X(t, i, j) = F(t, j), \quad X(t, i, j) \geq 0, \quad X(t, i, j) \leq M(i, j), \quad X(t, i, j) \leq U(t, i), \quad X(t, i, j) \geq U(t, i) + M(i, j) - 1 \quad (8)$$

On the other hand, we must guarantee that the clonal matrix M admits a phylogeny under the $\mathcal{P}$ model. As it was discussed in Section 3, it is possible to state the $\mathcal{P}$ phylogeny reconstruction problem as a solution for an IDP problem on the corresponding extended matrix (Theorem 3.2).

Notice that the set of constraints $\mathcal{R}_{D(k)}$ and $\mathcal{R}_{CS(k)}$ are defined for a known incomplete matrix M_e, while we have an incomplete matrix that is only described by a set of variables $M(i, j)$. Therefore we have to modify the set of constraints in order to overcome this problem. Namely, for each clone i and mutation j, we define the following set of constraints on the variables Y:

$$M_e(i, j_0) - \sum_{1 \leq l \leq k} M_e(i, j_l) = M(i, j) \text{ for the Dollo}(k) \text{ model, and} \quad (9)$$

$$\sum_{1 \leq l \leq k} M_e(i, j_l) = M(i, j) \text{ for the Camin-Sokal}(k) \text{ model.} \quad (10)$$

Thus, the $\mathcal{P}$-VAFFP corresponds to finding a feasible solution with the linear constraints (7), (8), (9), (3), (5) for the Dollo(k) model, and (7), (8), (10), (3), (5) for the Camin-Sokal(k) model.

Finally, let m_e the number of columns in the matrix M_e, our formulation has $O(nm_e + m_e^2 + mpn)$ variables and $O(m_e^2 + npm)$ constraints.

4.1 Clonal Reconstruction admitting errors

Since frequency matrices are obtained experimentally, they can only contain approximation of the actual frequencies. Hence, we have to incorporate frequency errors in the formulation of the problem, most notably in the construction of the usage matrix U. Let us define the $p \times m$ matrix E, where $E(t, j)$ represents the error of the frequency $F(t, j)$.

The set of constraints bounding the difference between input frequencies and the frequencies associated to our proposed solution (that is, corresponding to the product UM) is:

$$-E(t, j) \leq \sum_{i=1}^{n} X(t, i, j) - F(t, j) \leq E(t, j)$$

Since now our goal is to minimize the overall error introduced in the reconstruction, the objective function is:

$$\min \sum_{(t,j)\in[1,p]\times[1,m]} E(t,j)$$

5 EXPERIMENTAL RESULTS

We implemented our approach with a Python program called gppf that receives a frequency matrix M and outputs the corresponding ILP in a format that is then fed to Gurobi 6.5.2. The program gppf is available at https://github.com/AlgoLab/gppf. All experiments have been performed on an Ubuntu 14.04 server with four 8-core Intel Xeon E5-4610v2 2.30GHz CPUs (hyperthreading was enabled for a total of 16 threads per processor). The proposed ILP formulations have been experimented to test how the proposed general models (Persistent Phylogeny, Dollo(k) and Camin-Sokal(k)) fit the input data w.r.t. the Perfect Phylogeny model. For this purpose we have tested the formulation in both simulated and real data. The size of the instances are typical for real data applications such as liquid cancer and in particular Leukemia for which we show here the inferred (persistent) tree for a real instance (CLL077). For our experiments we have generated different sets of frequency matrices F as follows:

(1) generate a clonal $n \times m$ matrix M by using the tool developed in [17], called ms, obtaining a Perfect Phylogeny on n clones and m mutations.
(2) In order to avoid obtaining only matrices admitting a Perfect Phylogeny, some values of the original are modified randomly from 0 to 1.
(3) Generate a usage matrix U of dimensions $p \times n$ assigning to each clone a proportion in each sample. Those values are chosen randomly, following a Dirichlet distribution. The number p of samples is decided a priori and n is the number of clones imposed by M.
(4) Multiply U and M to generate a $p \times m$ frequency matrix F.

Generated matrices are used as input of our implementation for different formulation settings. Finally, we measure the quality of the predictions for each phylogeny model, by considering the total error. We remark that we do not compare the predicted clonal matrix M with the original, since different models can generate diverse clonal evolution trees.

The parameters of the implementation are the maximum number of clones that a solution can use (expressed as the percentage of the number of mutations), the maximum time permitted for each execution, the maximum number of persistent character allowed, and a parameter k associated to the model Dollo(k) and the Camin-Sokal(k) in the formulation. Moreover, we have introduced a timeout on the running time, since the generated ILP problem is often large and its resolution could require a considerable amount of time. Nevertheless, imposing a timeout allows the ILP solver to compute a solution with a small total error.

We evaluate the obtained solutions according to the following measure:

$$\text{Error}_F(\overline{F}) = \frac{\|F - \overline{F}\|}{\|F\|}$$

Where F is the input frequency matrix, $\overline{F}$ is the frequency matrix inferred by the solution, and $\|A\| = [\sum_{ij} |a_{ij}|^2]^{1/2}$ is the Frobenius norm. This metric give us the ratio between the total error and the optimal value, therefore it is not too dependent on the actual values.

Previous works focused on Perfect Phylogeny as the evolutionary model, thereby restricting the attention to a number of clones equal to the number of mutations. Since more general evolutionary models are allowed, the number of clones might be different, the user can provide the maximum number of clones. We have investigated the effect of choosing different values for such pameter. More precisely, we have explored bounding the number of clones to be at most 100%, 80%, 60% and 40% of the maximum number of clones in the instance, which is a representative set of values. We recall that these values are upper bounds, while the actual number of clones used in the actual solution might be smaller.

5.1 Simulated Data

For the simulated data, we have generated two different data sets:

Exp. 1 contains 100 frequency matrices composed of 6 samples and 10 mutations. Matrices are generated from a 20×20 clonal matrix M. The phylogenetic models tested in this set are: Perfect, Persistent, Dollo(2) and Camin-Sokal(2).

Exp. 2 contains 10 frequency matrices with 12 samples and 25 mutations, generated by a 25×50 clonal matrix M, The models tested in this set are: Perfect, Persistent, Dollo(4) and Camin-Sokal(4).

Figure 3 shows how the error of each solution varies as a function of the running time for both experiments. Analyzing those plots, we note that the total error rapidly stabilizes. Therefore we have decided to set a time limit for the running time equal to 5 minutes for Exp. 1 and 2 hours for Exp.2, since allowing a large time limit results in only marginal improvements of the quality of the solutions computed.

In almost all cases the solver uses the entire available time to find a solution. The only exception is the Perfect Phylogeny model when maximum number of clones is 40% of the mutations. Moreover, we notice that the computed solutions usually use fewer clones than maximum allowed.

Figures 4 and 5 shows the total error of the solutions obtained under different phylogenetic models and different upper bounds on the number of clones for the set Exp. 1 and Exp. 2 respectively. Additionally, Tables 1 and 2 exhibit the number of instances for which the general phylogeny models outperform the Perfect Phylogeny model on both datasets.

As we can see from Figure 4, the obtained solutions have average error smaller than the 15% of the input matrix norm. As expected, we observe that the error of all models increases as we decrease the number of maximum clones allowed. The increase in the total error is larger for the Perfect Phylogeny model, since it is not sufficient to correctly explain the instances for a small number of clones. In fact, Table 2 shows that, in almost all instances, a general phylogeny model outperform the results of the Perfect Phylogeny solution.

In Figure 5 and Table 2 we see that Dollo(4) and Camin-Sokal(4) have worse total error than more restricted models. This effect is due to the much larger size of the ILP formulation for Dollo(4) and

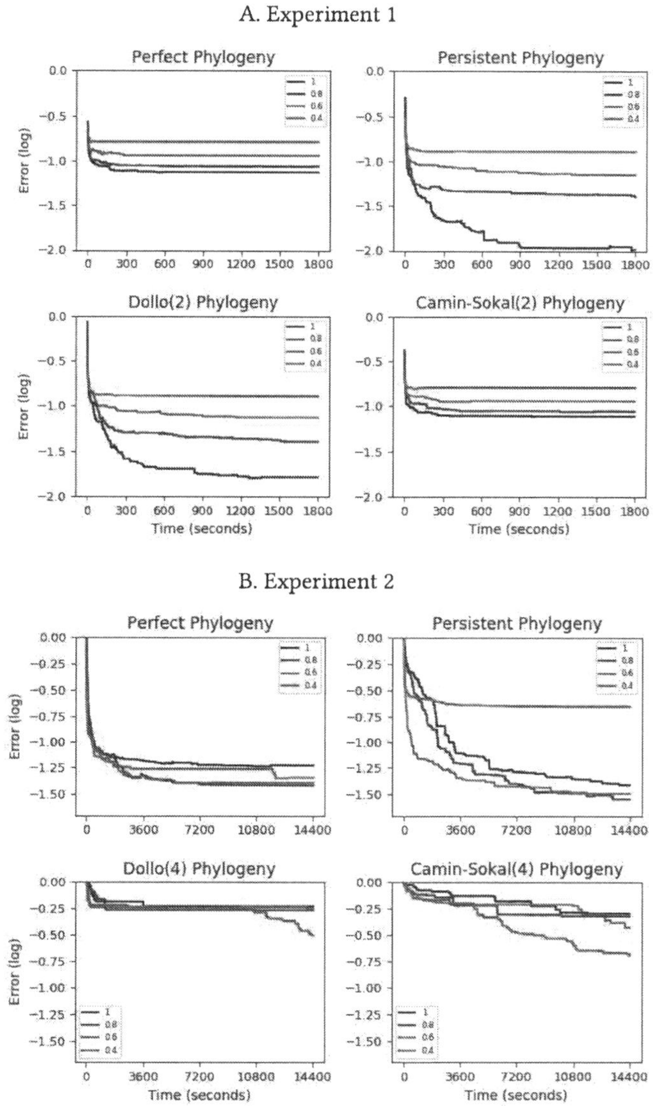

Figure 3: Mean error evolution of solutions in terms of time.

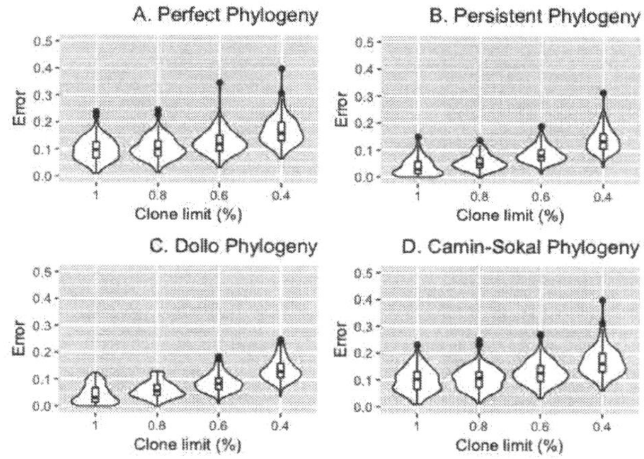

Figure 4: Error for the solutions obtained from Exp. 1 under different evolutionary models

Total error	Persistent	Dollo(2)	Camin-Sokal(2)
Clone limit 100%			
≤ PPE	100/100	94/100	47/100
≤ 90% PPE	99/100	92/100	18/100
≤ 80% PPE	97/100	86/100	10/100
≤ 50% PPE	74/100	66/100	0/100
Clone limit 80%			
≤ PPE	100/100	97/100	53/100
≤ 90% PPE	99/100	91/100	11/100
≤ 80% PPE	89/100	84/100	4/100
≤ 50% PPE	44/100	39/100	0/100
Clone limit 60%			
≤ PPE	98/100	92/100	51/100
≤ 90% PPE	91/100	83/100	2/100
≤ 80% PPE	74/100	62/100	1/100
≤ 50% PPE	13/100	17/100	0/100
Clone limit 40%			
≤ PPE	90/100	93/100	79/100
≤ 90% PPE	70/100	74/100	0/100
≤ 80% PPE	43/100	43/100	0/100
≤ 50% PPE	0/100	0/100	0/100

Table 1: Comparison between evolution models on Exp. 1. Each entry contains the number of instances (out of 100) where the formulations based on the Persistent Phylogeny, Dollo(2), Camin-Sokal(2) models obtain a total error that is smaller than the one obtained with the Perfect Phylogeny model.

Camin-Sokal(4), which does not allow to find a proper solution within the allotted timeout (Figure 3). Nevertheless, we note that Persistent model obtains better results than the Perfect Phylogeny, especially when the allowed number of clones is small. The experimentations and considerations exposed here required a total of 105 CPU hour for Exp. 1 and 120 CPU hour for Exp. 2.

5.2 Real Data

We also tested our models on real cancer data, in particular Leukemia data from [24] because liquid tumors seem to have the fewest somatic mutations, therefore we are able to calculate an optimal solution in a reasonable amount of time. We have been able to compute a clonal evolution for the CLL patient 077[7, 18] under the Persistent Phylogeny model in approximately 3 days of computation.

We cannot directly compare the persistent tree we inferred (Figure 6.A) with AncesTree [7] (Figure 6.C), because the latter infers only seven of the 16 mutations present in the sample. In order to perform such comparison we had to restrict the instance to contain

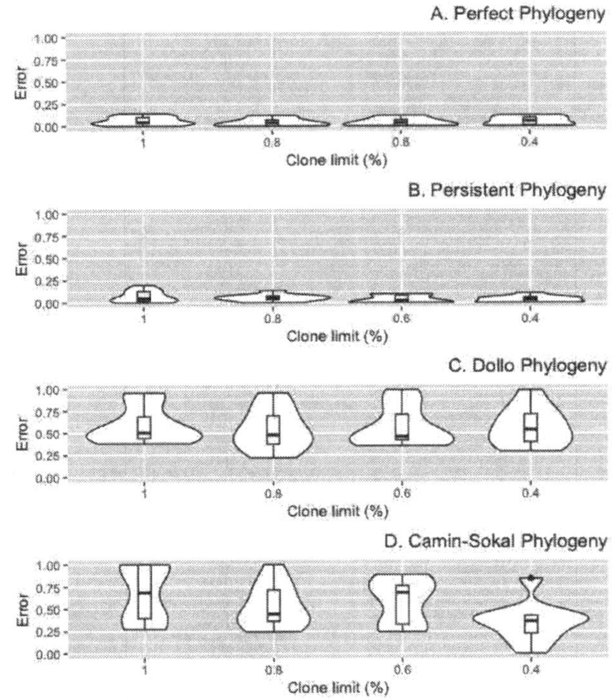

Figure 5: Errors for the solution founded for instances in Exp. 2 for different phylogenetic models.

Total error	Persistent	Dollo(4)	Camin-Sokal(4)
Clone limit 100%			
≤ PPE	3/10	0/10	0/10
≤ 90% PPE	3/10	0/10	0/10
≤ 80% PPE	3/10	0/10	0/10
≤ 50% PPE	2/10	0/10	0/10
Clone limit 80%			
≤ PPE	5/10	0/10	0/10
≤ 90% PPE	3/10	0/10	0/10
≤ 80% PPE	3/10	0/10	0/10
≤ 50% PPE	0/10	0/10	0/10
Clone limit 60%			
≤ PPE	6/10	0/10	0/10
≤ 90% PPE	5/10	0/10	0/10
≤ 80% PPE	4/10	0/10	0/10
≤ 50% PPE	4/10	0/10	0/10
Clone limit 40%			
≤ PPE	7/10	0/10	1/10
≤ 90% PPE	5/10	0/10	1/10
≤ 80% PPE	5/10	0/10	1/10
≤ 50% PPE	4/10	0/10	1/10

Table 2: Comparison between evolution models on Exp. 2. Each entry contains the number of instances (out of 10) where the formulations based on the Persistent Phylogeny, Dollo(4), Camin-Sokal(4) models obtain a total error that is smaller than the one obtained with the Perfect Phylogeny model.

only the mutations that are also in the solution computed by AncesTree. The output is presented in Figure 6.D and shares several structural similarities with the AncesTree solution. Moreover, we would also like to point out that our solution for the restricted instance (Figure 6.D) has zero errors (and is therefore optimal).

We have compared our predictions with those of PhyloSub [18] (Figure 6.B). PhyloSub compacts different mutations in the same clone while we infer a tree in which each mutation correspond to a vertex. The differences between the two are that the cluster of mutations containing NAMPTL, PLAG2616, SLC12A1, BCL2L13 and GPR158 occurs before mutation EXOC6B while in our model the latter occurs first. The main differences are that the clone containing mutation COL24A1 in our model contains also mutation EXOC6B while it doesn't in PhyloSub, on contrary in our model the clone containing LRRPC16A does not contain NAMPTL and in PhyloSub does. The most interesting fact regards the clone that contains NOD1: in PhyloSub it lies on a branch that does not contain EXOC6B, while we have predicted a phylogeny where such clone occurs after the acquisition and the loss of EXOC6B.

From the experiment on CLL077, we can see that our prediction is similar to that obtained with the other available tools, but we incorporated in the evolutionary history two mutations losses, that is our evolutionary history is not consistent with the limitations of the Perfect Phylogeny model.

6 CONCLUSIONS AND FUTURE WORK

In this paper we have proposed a ILP formulation of the problem of reconstructing the evolutionary history of tumors, where the evolutionary tree is character-based and can violate the infinite site assumption of the Perfect Phylogeny model. First, we have proposed an ILP framework for the Dollo(k) and Camin-Sokal(k) models — k is a bound on the number of losses and gains of each mutation. Then we have shown how to extend it for solving the Variant Allele Frequency Factorization Problem under those evolution models. We have performed an experimental analysis on simulated and real data which shows that the Persistent and Dollo(k) model for $k > 1$, allow to obtain phylogenies whose predicted frequencies are closer to the true frequencies than those obtained via the Perfect Phylogeny model. Mainly, our approach achieves good performances when the input data do not fit the Perfect Phylogeny model, but the number of recurrent or back mutations is relatively small. Moreover, our approach allows to relax the constraint that then number of clones is equal to the number of distinct mutations. These promising results have been obtained with ILP formulations that have not been optimized for efficiency.

Future research will be devoted to further investigate our approach on larger instances (more samples and mutations): this will require to improve the computational efficiency of the ILP formulation or adopting some combinatorial strategies to govern the introduction of a small number of mutation losses and gains in the solution, as our initial analysis has not investigated the scalability

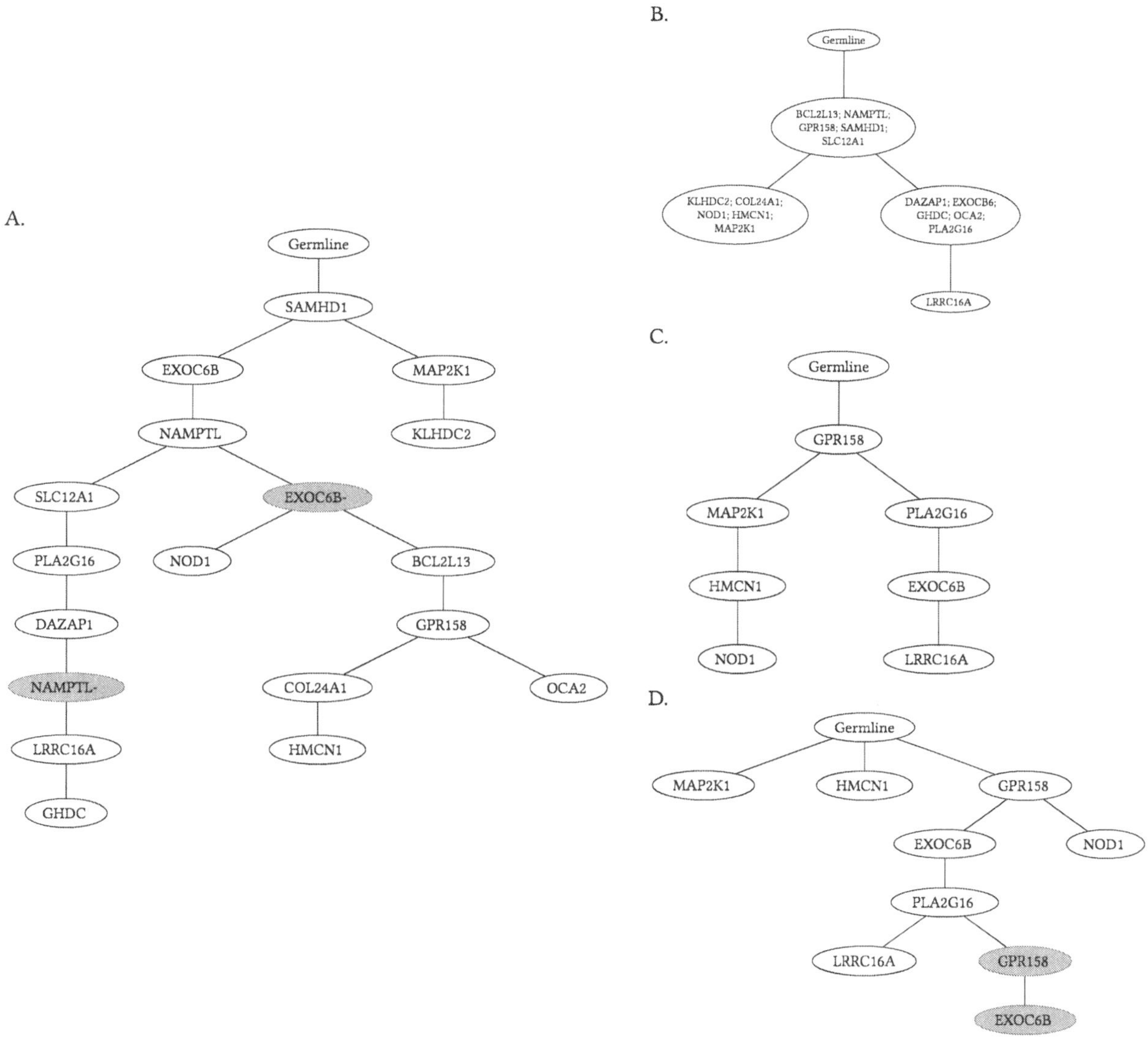

Figure 6: Persistent inferred tree for tumor CLL077 (A) Tree inferred by gppf, the red circular vertices are the losses of a mutation, therefore we have two clonal expansion where mutations *EXOC6B* and *NAMPTL* are lost during the clonal evolutionary history. B. shows the tree inferred by PhyloSub, while C. shows the result of AncesTree. D. shows the solution under the Persistent model for the restricted instance presented in [7] for the AncesTree algorithm.

of the approach. Moreover, we would like to assess the biological soundness of the solutions provided by our approach.

ACKNOWLEDGMENTS

The authors would like to thank Simone Zaccaria for the useful discussion on the VAFFP and ILP formulation. We also wish to thank the reviewers for their valuable comments allowing us to improve the clarity and content of the paper.

We acknowledge the support of the MIUR PRIN 2010–2011 grant "Automi e Linguaggi Formali: Aspetti Matematici e Applicativi" code 2010LYA9RH, of the Cariplo Foundation grant 2013–0955 (Modulation of anti cancer immune response by regulatory non-coding RNAs), of the FA grants 2013-ATE-0281, 2014-ATE-0382, and 2015-ATE-0113.

REFERENCES

[1] Paola Bonizzoni, Chiara Braghin, Riccardo Dondi, and Gabriella Trucco. 2012. The binary perfect phylogeny with persistent characters. *Theor. Comput. Sci.* 454 (2012), 51–63. https://doi.org/10.1016/j.tcs.2012.05.035

[2] Paola Bonizzoni, Anna Paola Carrieri, Gianluca Della Vedova, Riccardo Dondi, and Teresa M. Przytycka. 2014. When and How the Perfect Phylogeny Model Explains Evolution. In *Discrete and Topological Models in Molecular Biology*, Nataša Jonoska and Masahico Saito (Eds.). Springer Berlin Heidelberg, Berlin, Germany, 67–83.

[3] Paola Bonizzoni, Anna Paola Carrieri, Gianluca Della Vedova, Raffaella Rizzi, and Gabriella Trucco. 2017. A colored graph approach to perfect phylogeny with persistent characters. *Theoretical Computer Science* 658 (2017), 60–73. https://doi.org/10.1016/j.tcs.2016.08.015

[4] Paola Bonizzoni, Anna Paola Carrieri, Gianluca Della Vedova, and Gabriella Trucco. 2014. Explaining evolution via constrained persistent perfect phylogeny. *BMC Genomics* 15, Suppl 6 (Oct. 2014), S10. https://doi.org/10.1186/1471-2164-15-S6-S10

[5] Joseph H. Camin and Robert R. Sokal. 1965. A Method for Deducing Branching Sequences in Phylogeny. *Evolution* 19, 3 (Sep 1965), 311–326. https://doi.org/10.2307/2406441

[6] Li Ding, Benjamin J. Raphael, Feng Chen, and Michael C. Wendl. 2013. Advances for Studying Clonal Evolution in Cancer. *Cancer Letters* 340, 2 (2013), 212–219. https://doi.org/10.1016/j.canlet.2012.12.028

[7] Mohammed El-Kebir, Layla Oesper, Hannah Acheson-Field, and Benjamin J. Raphael. 2015. Reconstruction of clonal trees and tumor composition from multi-sample sequencing data. *Bioinformatics* 31, 12 (2015), 62–70. https://doi.org/10.1093/bioinformatics/btv261

[8] Mohammed El-Kebir, Gryte Satas, Layla Oesper, and Benjamin J. Raphael. 2016. Inferring the Mutational History of a Tumor Using Multi-state Perfect Phylogeny Mixtures. *Cell Systems* 3, 1 (2016), 43–53. https://doi.org/10.1016/j.cels.2016.07.004

[9] J. S. Farris. 1977. Phylogenetic Analysis Under Dollo's Law. *Systematic Biology* 26, 1 (Mar 1977), 77–88. https://doi.org/10.1093/sysbio/26.1.77

[10] Joseph Felsenstein. 2004. *Inferring Phylogenies*. Sinauer Associates, Sunderland, MA (USA).

[11] Mel Greaves and Carlo C. Maley. 2012. Clonal Evolution in Cancer. *Nature* 481, 7381 (2012), 306–313. https://doi.org/10.1038/nature10762

[12] Dan Gusfield. 1991. Efficient algorithms for inferring evolutionary trees. *Networks* 21, 1 (1991), 19–28. https://doi.org/10.1002/net.3230210104

[13] Dan Gusfield. 1997. *Algorithms on Strings, Trees and Sequences: Computer Science and Computational Biology*. Cambridge University Press, Cambridge.

[14] Dan Gusfield. 2015. Persistent phylogeny: a galled-tree and integer linear programming approach. In *Proceedings of the 6th ACM Conference on Bioinformatics, Computational Biology and Health Informatics*. ACM, 443–451.

[15] Dan Gusfield, Yelena Frid, and Dan Brown. 2007. Integer Programming Formulations and Computations Solving Phylogenetic and Population Genetic Problems with Missing or Genotypic Data. In *Computing and Combinatorics: 13th Annual International Conference, COCOON 2007, Banff, Canada, July 16-19, 2007. Proceedings*, Guohui Lin (Ed.). Springer Berlin Heidelberg, Berlin, Heidelberg, 51–64. https://doi.org/10.1007/978-3-540-73545-8_8

[16] Iman Hajirasouliha, Ahmad Mahmoody, and Benjamin J. Raphael. 2014. A combinatorial approach for analyzing intra-tumor heterogeneity from high-throughput sequencing data. *Bioinformatics* 30, 12 (June 2014), i78–i86. https://doi.org/10.1093/bioinformatics/btu284

[17] Richard R. Hudson. 2002. Generating samples under a Wright-Fisher neutral model of genetic variation. *Bioinformatics* 18, 2 (2002), 337–338. https://doi.org/10.1093/bioinformatics/18.2.337

[18] Wei Jiao, Shankar Vembu, Amit G. Deshwar, Lincoln Stein, and Quaid Morris. 2014. Inferring clonal evolution of tumors from single nucleotide somatic mutations. *BMC Bioinformatics* 15, 1 (2014), 35. https://doi.org/10.1186/1471-2105-15-35

[19] Jack Kuipers, Katharina Jahn, Benjamin J. Raphael, and Niko Beerenwinkel. 2016. A statistical test on single-cell data reveals widespread recurrent mutations in tumor evolution. *bioRxiv* (Dec. 2016), 094722. https://doi.org/10.1101/094722

[20] Michael S. Lawrence, Petar Stojanov, Paz Polak, Gregory V. Kryukov, Kristian Cibulskis, Andrey Sivachenko, Scott L. Carter, Chip Stewart, Craig H. Mermel, Steven A. Roberts, Adam Kiezun, Peter S. Hammerman, Aaron McKenna, Yotam Drier, Lihua Zou, Alex H. Ramos, Trevor J. Pugh, Nicolas Stransky, Elena Helman, Jaegil Kim, Carrie Sougnez, Lauren Ambrogio, Elizabeth Nickerson, Erica Shefler, Maria L. Cortés, Daniel Auclair, Gordon Saksena, Douglas Voet, Michael Noble, Daniel DiCara, Pei Lin, Lee Lichtenstein, David I. Heiman, Timothy Fennell, Marcin Imielinski, Bryan Hernandez, Eran Hodis, Sylvan Baca, Austin M. Dulak, Jens Lohr, Dan-Avi Landau, Catherine J. Wu, Jorge Melendez-Zajgla, Alfredo Hidalgo-Miranda, Amnon Koren, Steven A. McCarroll, Jaume Mora, Ryan S. Lee, Brian Crompton, Robert Onofrio, Melissa Parkin, Wendy Winckler, Kristin Ardlie, Stacey B. Gabriel, Charles W. M. Roberts, Jaclyn A. Biegel, Kimberly Stegmaier, Adam J. Bass, Levi A. Garraway, Matthew Meyerson, Todd R. Golub, Dmitry A. Gordenin, Shamil Sunyaev, Eric S. Lander, and Gad Getz. 2013. Mutational Heterogeneity in Cancer and the Search for New Cancer-Associated Genes. *Nature* 499, 7457 (2013), 214–218. https://doi.org/10.1038/nature12213

[21] Nicholas E Navin. 2014. Cancer Genomics: One Cell At a Time. *Genome Biology* 15, 8 (2014), 452. https://doi.org/10.1186/s13059-014-0452-9

[22] Itsik Pe'er, Tal Pupko, Ron Shamir, and Roded Sharan. 2004. Incomplete Directed Perfect Phylogeny. *SIAM J. Comput.* 33, 3 (Jan 2004), 590–607. https://doi.org/10.1137/s0097539702406510

[23] Teresa Przytycka, George Davis, Nan Song, and Dannie Durand. 2006. Graph Theoretical Insights into Dollo Parsimony and Evolution of Multidomain Proteins. *Journal of Computational Biology* 13(2) (2006), 351–363.

[24] Anna Schuh, Jennifer Becq, Sean Humphray, Adrian Alexa, Adam Burns, Ruth Clifford, Stephan M. Feller, Russell Grocock, Shirley Henderson, Irina Khrebtukova, Zoya Kingsbury, Shujun Luo, David McBride, Lisa Murray, Toshi Menju, Adele Timbs, Mark Ross, Jenny Taylor, and David Bentley. 2012. Monitoring chronic lymphocytic leukemia progression by whole genome sequencing reveals heterogeneous clonal evolution patterns. *Blood* 120, 20 (2012), 4191–4196. https://doi.org/10.1182/blood-2012-05-433540

[25] C. Semple and M. Steel. 2003. *Phylogenetics*. Oxford University Press, USA.

[26] M. A. Steel. 2016. *Phylogeny: discrete and random processes in evolution*. Number 89 in CBMS-NSF regional conference series in applied mathematics. Society for Industrial and Applied Mathematics, Philadelphia.

[27] B. Vogelstein, N. Papadopoulos, V. E. Velculescu, S. Zhou, L. A. Diaz, and K. W. Kinzler. 2013. Cancer Genome Landscapes. *Science* 339, 6127 (2013), 1546–1558. https://doi.org/10.1126/science.1235122

A Compatibility Approach to Identify Recombination Breakpoints in Bacterial and Viral Genomes

Yi-Pin Lai and Thomas R. Ioerger
Department of Computer Science and Engineering
Texas A & M University
College Station, Texas 77843
{yplai.tw,ioerger}@tamu.edu

ABSTRACT

Recombination is an evolutionary force that results in mosaic genomes for microorganisms. The evolutionary history of microorganisms cannot be properly inferred if recombination has occurred among a set of taxa. That is, polymorphic sites of a multiple sequence alignment cannot be described by a single phylogenetic tree. Thus, detecting the presence of recombination is crucial before phylogeny inference. The phylogenetic-based methods are commonly utilized to explore recombination, however, the compatibility-based methods are more computationally efficient since the phylogeny construction is not required. We propose a novel approach focusing on the pairwise compatibility of polymorphic sites of given regions to characterize potential breakpoints in recombinant bacterial and viral genomes. The performance of average compatibility ratio (ACR) approach is evaluated on simulated alignments of different scenarios comparing with two programs, GARD and RDP4. Three empirical datasets of varying genome sizes with varying levels of homoplasy are also utilized for testing. The results demonstrate that our approach is able to detect the presence of recombination and identify the recombinant breakpoints efficiently, which provides a better understanding of distinct phylogenies among mosaic sequences.

CCS CONCEPTS

•**Applied computing** →*Computational genomics; Bioinformatics;*

KEYWORDS

Phylogeny; Compatibility; Recombination; SNPs; Multiple Sequence Alignments; Bacterial Genomes; Viral Genomes

1 INTRODUCTION

The accurate inference of phylogeny for microorganisms is essential to better understand the evolutionary history of a set of species. A phylogenetic tree will be reconstructed based on polymorphisms of a multiple sequence alignment to present the evolutionary relationships of a set of isolates using methods such as maximum parsimony, maximum likelihood, or minimum evolution, etc. If there exists a single tree topology that can explain all polymorphic sites of an alignment, then the tree represents the evolutionary history of the given set of taxa. In recent decades, studies indicate that some microorganisms are relatively less mosaic because of shorter evolutionary history or complete clonality, for instance, *Mycobacterium tuberculosis*[15] and *Bacillus anthracis*[26]. However, growing evidences have shown that some microbiota exhibit homoplasy in their genomes, that is, they are not monophyletic. The appearance of homoplasy is that polymorphic sites are not from a common ancestor but arise independently in multiple branches[45]. Homoplasy could be caused by horizontal gene transfer (HGT) and homologous recombination. For bacteria, HGT is an evolutionary force that frequently occurs and results in mosaic genomes[17, 44]. The known mechanisms of HGT are transformation, transduction and conjugation. Transformation and transduction acquire a new DNA fragment from environment or other organisms via insertion while conjugation requires intercellular contact to transfer genetic variants from donor to recipient by homologous recombination. Homologous recombination exchanges genetic material between two homologous DNA sequences [4]. For viruses, main mechanisms for driving evolution are point mutation and recombination. Several bacteria and viruses have been reported that suggest recombination events occurred during evolution, including HIV-1[1, 32, 36], *Mycobacterium avium*[18], *Staphylococcus aureus*[13], *Streptococcus pneumoniae*[6] and *Salmonella enterica*[7].

A phylogenetic tree can be misleading if a sequence alignment is mosaic since some recombinant sites cannot be described by a single tree topology. If the microorganisms underwent recombination, it is essential to estimate the extent of homoplasy and identify recombination breakpoints to obtain corresponding phylogenies to model the evolution[27, 35, 40]. Current methods to detect recombination can be categorized into phylogenetic, distance, compatibility and nucleotide substitution distribution methods[33, 34]. Phylogenetic methods are commonly used in existing programs, for instance, Simplot, Plato, GARD, RDP4 and ClonalFrameML[8, 14, 23, 31, 36]. If recombinant regions exist, then the tree topologies that are constructed based on the regions will be discordant with the global topology. Among them, GARD is a phylogenetic-based method that applies a genetic algorithm to build a maximum likelihood model for recombination detection[30, 31]. RDP4 is also a phylogenetic-based method that makes use of a pairwise scanning approach to scan for the alignment[23]. In contrast, distance and compatibility methods do not require the phylogeny. For distance-based methods, pairwise distances will be computed, and distance patterns will be searched along a multiple sequence alignment. PHYPRO uses a sliding window to get the genetic statistics[47] while RAT

Permission to make digital or hard copies of all or part of this work for personal or classroom use is granted without fee provided that copies are not made or distributed for profit or commercial advantage and that copies bear this notice and the full citation on the first page. Copyrights for components of this work owned by others than ACM must be honored. Abstracting with credit is permitted. To copy otherwise, or republish, to post on servers or to redistribute to lists, requires prior specific permission and/or a fee. Request permissions from permissions@acm.org.
ACM-BCB'17, August 20-23, 2017, Boston, MA, USA
© 2017 ACM. 978-1-4503-4722-8/17/08...$15.00
DOI: http://dx.doi.org/10.1145/3107411.3107432

utilizes thresholds of genetic distance and number of sequences to search for possible recombinant regions[12]. In addition, compatibility methods focus on site-to-site congruence and extend pairwise sites to all possible combinations of pairs within a given region. If two sites are compatible, then the relationship of taxa at both sites can be explained by the same tree topology[11, 20, 21, 24]. Nucleotide substitution distribution methods analyze the trends in substitutions or fitting degree in nucleotide distributions across the alignment[39, 43, 48].

With the advancement of next-generation sequencing techniques, the whole genomes of a number of strains can be analyzed at the same time so the size of an alignment may increase as the number of strains scales. Since phylogenetic-based methods require the phylogeny construction, they are less efficient than matrix-based or compatibility-based methods. Also, studies have shown that methods of substitution patterns and compatibility perform better than phylogenetic methods or other general methods in terms of accuracy and efficiency[5, 33, 34, 41]. Yet, only a few studies have applied the compatibility concept[3, 16]. Reticulate is a program to compute neighbor similarity score (NSS) using compatibility matrices to cluster sites that are compatible[16]. The clustering is obtained by shuffling the matrices with Monte Carlo randomization. Another recombination testing program defines a refined incompatibility score as a pairwise homoplasy index (PHI) to test for recombination[3]. The significance of PHI is computed by permutation tests. Both methods are able to detect recombination and report the informative sites, but unable to identify breakpoints to obtain non-overlapping regions.

To better understand different phylogenetic histories of evolution that involve recombination for a given set of taxa in a more computationally efficient way, we develop an average compatibility ratio approach to analyze the multiple sequence alignment of Single Nucleotide Polymorphisms (SNPs) to explore possible recombination breakpoints. The overall compatibility ratio will be calculated first to screen for the presence or absence of recombination. If it presents, then ACR approach will scan for each site along the alignment to identify the site where its upstream sites are incompatible with its downstream sites but the adjacent sites located within the same region are more jointly compatible. The potential breakpoints depending on a given threshold will be reported, and then the alignment will be divided into non-overlapping consecutive segments. The compatibility ratios and changes per site (CPS) information of each segment are also provided. The ACR approach is tested on simulated datasets of two scenarios and three empirical datasets, and the performance is compared with GARD[31] and RDP4[23]. Comparing the results of simulation scenarios with ground truths, we show that ACR approach performs better than other programs. The results of the analyses of bacterial and viral genomes demonstrate that our proposed approach is able to characterize biological sequence alignments and provide segments that reflect distinct phylogenetic histories.

2 METHODS

2.1 Compatibility Score

For a given multiple sequence alignment of n taxa ($n \geq 4$) and m sites ($m \geq 1$), a character χ is a set of states $(A_1, A_2, \ldots, A_n)$ of all strains at a given site of the alignment. The states are elements of $\{A, T, C, G\}$. Hence, for the above alignment, there are m characters and four types of states. Pairwise compatibility is defined as two characters are compatible if and only if there exists a phylogenetic tree that explains both characters. That is, no extra changes of state are required for both characters to evolve with a single tree topology. For a given set of characters, $C = (\chi_1, \chi_2, \ldots)$, all characters are jointly compatible if and only if all pairs of characters are compatible with each other, i.e., a single tree exists and fits for all of the characters[10, 11, 20, 21, 24].

Since the single nucleotide polymorphisms in a multiple sequence alignment are informative for inferring phylogeny, the polymorphic sites are extracted. If the site has an unknown nucleotide, a gap or over two types of nucleotides, it is considered as ambiguous and excluded before determining compatibility. Therefore, each site will contain two types of nucleotides, and then the multiple sequence alignment will be converted to the binary sequence. That is, each character becomes a binary character whose states have two elements, 0 and 1.

Given a site in a binary sequence alignment of length n, the character χ_b is presented as a binary string concatenating the states of all n strains in the same order as the alignment, and the set χ_b' records the indexes of the strains with state 1 in χ_b. Two binary characters χ_1 and χ_2, which represent two sites, are compatible if and only if one of the following conditions is satisfied: $\chi_1' \subseteq \chi_2'$, $\chi_2' \subseteq \chi_1'$, $\overline{\chi_1'} \subseteq \chi_2'$ or $\chi_2' \subseteq \overline{\chi_1'}$. In other words, two binary characters of length n are compatible if and only if the set of pairs of binary states $A \in \chi_1$ and $B \in \chi_2$, $\{(A_1, B_1), (A_2, B_2), \ldots, (A_n, B_n)\}$, has at most three types of binary pairs of states out of four combinations, $\{(0,0), (0,1), (1,0), (1,1)\}$. The compatibility theorem has been proved in [10, 11]. An example of SNP sequences of three characters in $site_i$, $site_j$ and $site_k$ is illustrated for the concept of compatibility. For $site_i$ and $site_j$, they are incompatible according to the definition, so there does not exist any tree that is able to accommodate characters at the $site_i$ and $site_j$. Characters at the $site_i$ and $site_k$ are compatible, so there exists a single tree that is compatible with both sites. As shown in Figure 1(a), the number of changes per site for $site_i$ or $site_k$ is 1, yet it requires at least 2 changes for $site_j$, that is, presence of homoplasy. Characters at the $site_j$ and $site_k$ are also compatible. In Figure 1(b), the tree that is able to describe both $site_j$ and $site_k$ cannot accommodate the character at the $site_i$. Figure 1 demonstrates that there does not exist a tree that is compatible with $site_i$ and $site_j$, therefore there does not exist a tree that is compatible with these 3 sites.

Example for demonstrating compatibility:

$$
\begin{array}{l}
\\
strain_1 \\
strain_2 \\
strain_3 \\
strain_4 \\
strain_5
\end{array}
\begin{array}{c}
\begin{array}{ccc} site_i & site_j & site_k \end{array} \\
\begin{pmatrix}
C & G & C \\
A & T & C \\
C & T & C \\
A & G & G \\
A & G & G
\end{pmatrix}
\end{array}
\begin{array}{r}
\\
strain_1 \\
strain_2 \\
=> strain_3 \\
strain_4 \\
strain_5
\end{array}
\begin{array}{c}
\begin{array}{ccc} site_i & site_j & site_k \end{array} \\
\begin{pmatrix}
0 & 0 & 0 \\
1 & 1 & 0 \\
0 & 1 & 0 \\
1 & 0 & 1 \\
1 & 0 & 1
\end{pmatrix}
\end{array}
$$

2.1.1 Pairwise Compatibility Score of Characters: Suppose that the number of total polymorphic sites in a sequence alignment of n taxa is m, a m x m matrix, *CompatPW*, is generated to record

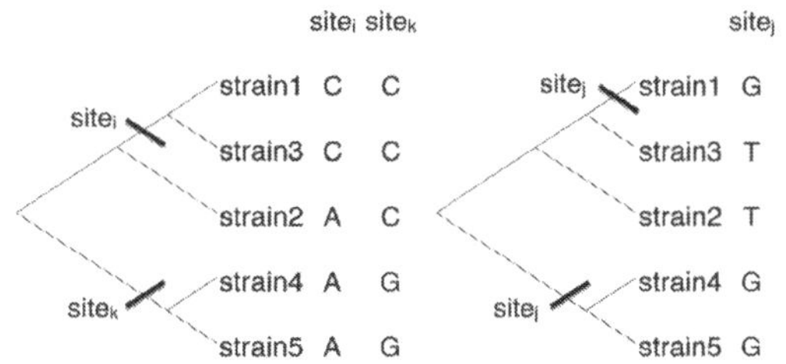

(a) A tree based on SNPs at the $site_i$ and $site_k$

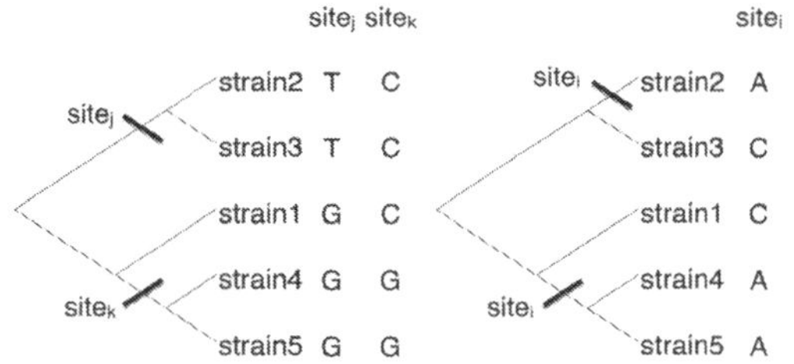

(b) A tree based on SNPs at the $site_j$ and $site_k$

Figure 1: Phylogenetic trees of the example

compatibility information for each pair of sites. That is, the compatibility information of pairwise characters at the $site_i$ and $site_j$, χ_i and χ_j, is recorded in $CompatPW_{ij}$, where $1 \le i, j \le m$. If two characters are compatible, the score is 1; otherwise, 0.

$$CompatPW_{ij} = \begin{cases} 1, & \text{if characters of } \chi_i \text{ and } \chi_j \text{ are compatible} \\ 0, & \text{otherwise} \end{cases}$$

$$CompatPW = \begin{bmatrix} CompatPW_{11} & CompatPW_{12} & \dots & CompatPW_{1m} \\ CompatPW_{21} & CompatPW_{22} & \dots & CompatPW_{2m} \\ \vdots & \vdots & & \vdots \\ CompatPW_{m1} & CompatPW_{m2} & \dots & CompatPW_{mm} \end{bmatrix}$$

2.1.2 Summary of Compatibility Scores of a Given Region: The summary of compatibility of a given region starting from $site_p$ to $site_q$, $CompatSum_{pq}$, where $1 \le p, q \le m$, is the summation of compatibility scores of all pairs within the region. For an alignment of length m, given a length l ($l \le m$), a $m \times l$ matrix $CompatSumMatrix$ represents the summary of compatibility of all pairs within a given region of at most length l starting from each site to its downstream sites. The $CompatSum_{pq}$ could be calculated recursively by summing $CompatSum_{p(q-1)}$ and the compatibility information of additional combinations of pairs that are contributed by adding a downstream site q.

Since the SNP sequence alignment of microorganisms may be cyclic or linear, two conditions are considered during computation. If the genome sequence is cyclic, the next downstream site of the ending site in the alignment will be the first site. For each site, the summary of compatibility will be calculated recursively starting from its next downstream site to the given length l. If the genome sequence is linear, the summary of compatibility will be computed recursively until q reaches to m or the summation of p and l, whichever occurs first.

$$CompatSum_{pq} = \begin{cases} CompatPW_{pq}, \text{if } q = p + 1 \\ CompatSum_{p(q-1)} + \sum_{i=p}^{q-1} CompatPW_{iq}, \text{if } 1 \le p < q \le m \\ CompatSum_{p(q-1)} + \sum_{i=p}^{m} CompatPW_{iq} + \sum_{i=1}^{q-1} CompatPW_{iq}, \\ \text{if } 1 \le q < p \le m \text{ (cyclic)} \end{cases}$$

$$CompatSumMatrix(cyclic) = \begin{bmatrix} CompatSum_{12} & CompatSum_{13} & \dots & CompatSum_{1(1+l)} \\ CompatSum_{23} & CompatSum_{24} & \dots & CompatSum_{2(2+l)} \\ \vdots & \vdots & & \vdots \\ CompatSum_{m1} & CompatSum_{m2} & \dots & CompatSum_{ml} \end{bmatrix}$$

2.1.3 Ratio of Compatibility Scores of a Given Region: The ratio of compatibility score of a given region, $CompatRR_{pq}$, is the summation of compatibility scores of all pairs of sites to the number of all combinations of pairwise sites starting from $site_p$ to $site_q$. The $CompatRR_{pq}$ will be bounded between 0 and 1, which indicates the tendency of compatibility within the regions between $site_p$ and $site_q$. In other words, the higher ratio reflects that more characters are jointly compatible, suggesting more sites are congruent in a tree within the region. In contrast, the lower the ratio is, the less likely the recombination events happened in the region.

$$CompatRR_{pq} = \frac{CompatSum_{pq}}{\binom{r}{2}},$$

$$\begin{cases} r = q - p + 1, & \text{if } 1 \le p < q \le m \\ r = m - p + q + 1, & \text{if } 1 \le q < p \le m \text{ (cyclic)} \end{cases}$$

2.2 Characterization of Recombination Breakpoints

A sliding window size, w, is defined in terms of SNPs, regardless of genomic span (bp) or overall rate of mutations because non-polymorphic sites are non-informative and discarded. That is, the size of a sliding window is the constant number of polymorphic sites instead of nucleotides. It would get better estimates of incompatibility, especially in the regions with sparse SNPs. Given a size w, for each $site_i$, we average all of the compatibility ratios of regions that include $site_i$ and locate within $[i - w, i + w]$, i.e., $avgCompatRR_i$. The total number of combinations of regions that satisfy the criteria is $|w|^2$. If the genome sequence is linear, the sites located in the head and tail regions of size w will be ignored. The sliding window size can be adjusted according to the length of an alignment.

A site with a local minimum represents that its upstream region and downstream region within the length of $|w|$ are less jointly compatible comparing to other regions. So, sites with local minimums are the potential breakpoints for inferring phylogeny incongruence. The default value of the cutoff is the mean minus two standard deviations of all ratios, which is of the one-tailed order of a two-sigma effect. The value can be adjusted for rare recombinant or frequently recombinant sequences. Or top k non-overlapping segments of the entire alignment can be reported by giving an intended number of k. Then, the top k-1 sites that have local minimums will be returned as breakpoints. In addition, the minimum length of a segment can be set to reduce the false positive rate since smaller regions may result in higher compatibility ratio. The consecutive sites between every two adjacent breakpoints construct a non-overlapping segment that is expected to be more congruent with a topology. Thus, a list of top potentially recombinant regions will be obtained.

$$avgCompatRR_i = \begin{cases} \dfrac{\sum_{p=i-w}^{i-1} \sum_{q=i+1}^{w} CompatRR_{pq}}{|w|^2}, \text{ if } w+1 \le i \le m-w \\ \dfrac{(\sum_{p=m-(w+1-i)}^{m} + \sum_{p=1}^{i-1}) \sum_{q=i+1}^{w} CompatRR_{pq}}{|w|^2}, \\ \text{if } i < w+1 \text{ (cyclic)} \\ \dfrac{\sum_{p=i-w}^{i-1} (\sum_{q=i+1}^{m} + \sum_{q=1}^{w-(m-i)+1)}) CompatRR_{pq}}{|w|^2}, \\ \text{if } i > m-w \text{ (cyclic)} \end{cases}$$

2.3 Build the Phylogenetic Trees and Calculate the Homoplasy Ratios for Segments:

Once the recombination segments are identified, the homoplasy ratio will be computed to evaluate the congruence/correctness, and the phylogenetic tree will be plotted for each segment. The polymorphic sites of segments will be extracted and used to build a phylogenetic tree for all strains. The ratio of the required SNPs for constructing a phylogenetic tree to the total number of selected SNPs of a segment will be calculated and defined as homoplasy ratio, that is, changes per site. The PHYLIP package of version 3.695[29] is used to infer the phylogeny of a dataset. The phylogenetic tree is reconstructed using the maximum parsimony method as the default setting. The homoplasy ratio can also be calculated using Sankoff's algorithm[37]. Sankoff's algorithm is a dynamic programming algorithm for counting the minimum cost of a tree using a cost matrix and backtracing approach. Here, the Sankoff score stands for the minimum number of state changes that are required in a given tree topology. The score of 1 represents that the character of a given site is congruent with the tree while the score above 1 stands for the extra number of changes needed for a given tree. The higher the Sankoff score, the higher the extent of incongruence of a given site, i.e., multiple changes are required to explain the tree pattern. Hence, the homoplasy ratio using Sankoff's algorithm is the summation of the Sankoff scores to the number of sites of a given region.

2.4 Computational Complexity

The Algorithms of compatibility determination, average ratio calculation and breakpoints characterization are shown in Algorithm 1 to Algorithm 3.

2.4.1 Time Complexity. Since it has to loop over all SNP sites and all isolates, the time complexity of Algorithm 2 is $O(ml * max(n, l))$, where m is the length of SNPs, n is the number of strains and l is the number of downstream sites. For Algorithm 3, the time complexity is $O(mw)$, where w is the sliding window size.

2.4.2 Space Complexity. The matrix size of Algorithm 2 is $O(ml)$, while the space of Algorithm 3 is $O(m)$.

Algorithm 1 Determination of pairwise compatibility of characters

```
Input: Two binary characters χ_i and χ_j at the site_i and site_j
Let A and B be the states of characters χ_i and χ_j, respectively
A_subset_B ← True, B_subset_A ← True, notA_subset_B ← True,
B_subset_notA ← True
for i = 1 → n do
    if A[i] = 1 && B[i] = 0 then
        A_subset_B ← False
    end if
    if A[i] = 0 && B[i] = 1 then
        B_subset_A ← False
    end if
    if A[i] = 0 && B[i] = 0 then
        notA_subset_B ← False
    end if
    if A[i] = 1 && B[i] = 1 then
        B_subset_notA ← False
    end if
end for
if A_subset_B || B_subset_A || notA_subset_B || B_subset_notA then
    return True
else
    return False
end if
True means χ_i and χ_j are compatible while False means they are incompatible
```

Algorithm 2 Efficient computation of compatibility score and ratio for each site to its downstream sites of length l

```
Input: A binary n x m matrix of an alignment of SNPs with m sites and n strains
Require: A given length of downstream sites, l
if CompatAll ≥ a given threshold (99.5% as default) then
    Print "No recombination event detected in the alignment."
    return
end if
CompatPW[m, l] ← 0
for i = 1 → m do
    for j = i + 1 → l do
        CompatPW[i, j] ← Algorithm 1 (Characters at the site_i and site_j)
    end for
end for
CompatSumMatrix[m, l] ← 0
for p = 1 → m do
    for q = p + 1 → p + l do
        if q = p + 1 then
            CompatSumMatrix[p, 1] ← CompatPW[p, q]
        else if q ≤ m then
            CompatSumMatrix[p, q−p] ← CompatSumMatrix[p, q−
p − 1] + Σ_{i=p}^{q−1} CompatPW[i, q]
        else
            t ← q − m
            CompatSumMatrix[p, q−p] ← CompatSumMatrix[p, q−
p − 1] + Σ_{i=p}^{m} CompatPW[i, t]+ Σ_{i=1}^{t−1} CompatPW[i, t]
        end if
    end for
end for
CompatRR[m, l] ← 0
for r = 1 → l do
    NumCombi[1 : m, r] ← (r+1 choose 2)
end for
CompatRR ← CompatSumMatrix / NumCombi
return CompatRR
```

Algorithm 3 Identification of recombination breakpoints

```
Input: The m x l CompatRR matrix
Require: A given sliding window size of w, targeting k breakpoints or cutoff for local minimums
avgCompatRR[m, 1] ← 0
for i = 1 → m do
    if i ≥ w + 1 && i ≤ m − w then
        avgCompatRR[i, 1] ← (Σ_{p=i−w}^{i−1} Σ_{q=i+1}^{w} CompatRR_pq) / |w|^2
    else if i < w + 1 then
        avgCompatRR[i, 1] ← ((Σ_{p=m−(w+1−i)}^{m} + Σ_{p=1}^{i−1}) Σ_{q=i+1}^{w} CompatRR_pq) / |w|^2
    else
        avgCompatRR[i, 1] ← (Σ_{p=i−w}^{i−1} (Σ_{q=i+1}^{m} + Σ_{q=1}^{w−(m−i)+1}) CompatRR_pq) / |w|^2
    end if
end for
return positions of local minimums that are lower than the given cutoff or top k local minimums as breakpoints
```

3 EVALUATION DATASETS

Four simulated datasets and three empirical datasets of bacterial and viral genomes are used to evaluate the ACR approach. The sequences of all strains are aligned, the sites that have low coverages or gaps are excluded, and then the sites that have polymorphisms are extracted. The input format is the same as fasta files.

3.1 Generation of Simulated Datasets

To generate datasets of recombinant sequences, our simulation algorithm consists of the generation of DNA sequences evolving along a tree topology and the construction of shuffled tree topology. For a given phylogeny, it generates (polymorphic) nucleotide sequences by generating a random ancestral sequence (with equal nucleotide prior probabilities), and then sampling changes on random branches (one per site) with probability proportional to branch length, assuming equal nucleotide transition probabilities. Also, the input tree topology can be modified by swapping any two branches. That is, the algorithm will randomly pick two internal nodes, cut off one node with all its child nodes as a branch, and attach it to another node to get a shuffled tree. Given a non-recombinant phylogenetic topology and a targeting sequence length, the sequences of strains will be simulated till reaching the given length based on the given topology and the shuffled topology, respectively. Next, recombinant sequences will be obtained by concatenating the generated sequences to get the simulated alignment. For each alignment, the positions of region boundaries will be recorded, the homoplasy score for each site will be calculated using the Sankoff's algorithm, and the scores will be averaged to get the extent of genetic diversity.

3.2 Empirical Datasets

The first empirical dataset consists of nine *Staphylococcus aureus (S. aureus)* clinical isolates[13] and aligned with the reference strain of ST8:USA300 (methicillin-resistant *S. aureus*). Mosaic structure has already been reported for these strains. The alignment has 48417 SNP sites. The second one is Human Immunodeficiency virus type 1 (HIV-1) recombinant dataset. Recombination is well-known among HIV-1 genomes. It contains an alignment of gene *pol* (DNA polymerase) of 12 strains and 1593 sites[42]. The third one is composed of 50 strains of *Mycobacterium tuberculosis (M. tuberculosis)* with 10565 SNP sites[46] that is highly congruent and have shown basically no recombination events in previous studies[2, 15].

4 RESULTS

4.1 Evaluations using Simulated Datasets

To evaluate the performance of our compatibility approach, a non-homoplastic phylogenetic tree topology of 73 taxa is utilized from a study of clinical isolates of *M. tuberculosis* in Panama [19] to generate SNP sequence alignments that are assumed cyclic. Two scenarios are set, including different levels of genetic diversity of one recombinant region and datasets of more than one recombinant regions. The first simulated scenario has two datasets of different levels of homoplasy containing 3000 SNP sites where the region[1000, 2000] is reorganized. The alignments of relatively low and high levels of homoplasy and the plot of six kinds of sliding window sizes for averaging the ratios for each site are shown in Figure 2 and Figure 3, respectively. The multiple curves show how sensitivity for detecting breakpoints depends on window size used.

The second simulated scenario has a dataset of two recombined regions with the same reorganizing topology and a dataset of two recombined regions with distinct topologies. Both datasets contain 6000 SNP sites where region[1000, 2000] and region[4000, 4500] are reorganized. Both of them are reconstructed by shuffling some internal branches, that is, these two regions have recombination and may not be described by the original tree topology. The first dataset has two distinct topologies for two recombinant regions, and the second dataset has the same topology for two recombinant regions. The plot of the Sankoff score for each site and the plot of six kinds of sliding window sizes for averaging the ratios for each site are shown in Figure 4 for dataset I and in Figure 5 for dataset II.

The ground truth and the results of using GARD, RDP4 and our approach for four simulated datasets of two scenarios are listed in Table 1. In scenario I, the identified breakpoints are around 1000 and 2000 with differences of at most 25 nucleotides for two datasets for three approaches, showing the capability of recombination detection. In scenario II, GARD only reported one breakpoint around 2000 for both datasets yet the expecting results should be four points that are close to 1000, 2000, 4000 and 4500, suggesting that GARD is unable to detect the recombinant regions for this kind of simulations. The breakpoints characterized by our approach are closer to the ground truth than those by RDP4.

4.2 Evaluations using Empirical Datasets

4.2.1 A Case Study on Recombinant Dataset: Staphylococcus aureus. The phylogenetic tree that is constructed using all SNP sites is shown in Figure 6. It requires a total number of 54157 SNPs to build the tree yet has 48417 SNPs, so its number of changes per site is 1.119 (54157/48417). The overall compatibility ratio is 0.978. The plot of average compatibility ratio of three window sizes is shown in Figure 7. Figure 8 illustrates that 10 breakpoints are identified using default setting and the window size of 500 for the overall alignment. Since the GARD is unable to analyze sequences of length above 12k, the alignments between 10k and 20k are taken out to evaluate three programs in the same base. Top four breakpoints are identified by our ACR approach using the window size of 500 and default cutoff. Five segments are obtained, and

Table 1: Breakpoints of four simulated datasets identified by our approach, GARD and RDP4

Breakpoints	Ground truth	ACR	GARD	RDP4
$ScenarioI - DatasetI$	1000, 2000	989, 2000	1025, 1999	984, 2010
$ScenarioI - DatasetII$	1000, 2000	998, 1998	1003, 1996	989, 1266, 2037
$ScenarioII - DatasetI$	1000, 2000, 4000, 4500	993, 2006, 4005, 4496	2001	978, 2000, 4005, 4515
$ScenarioII - DatasetII$	1000, 2000, 4000, 4500	998, 1995, 4000, 4498	2004	980, 2008, 4014, 4533

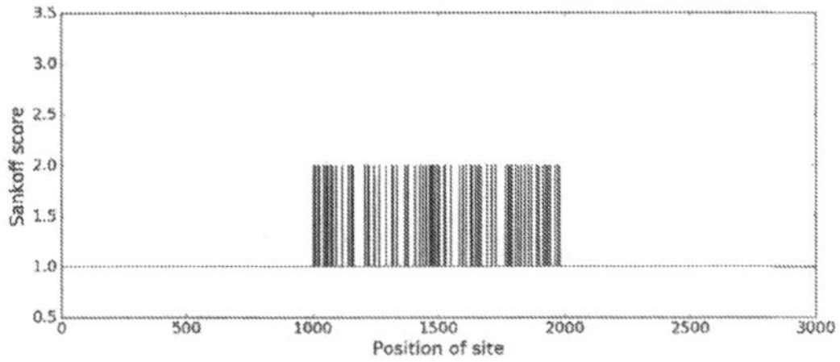

(a) Sankoff score for each site

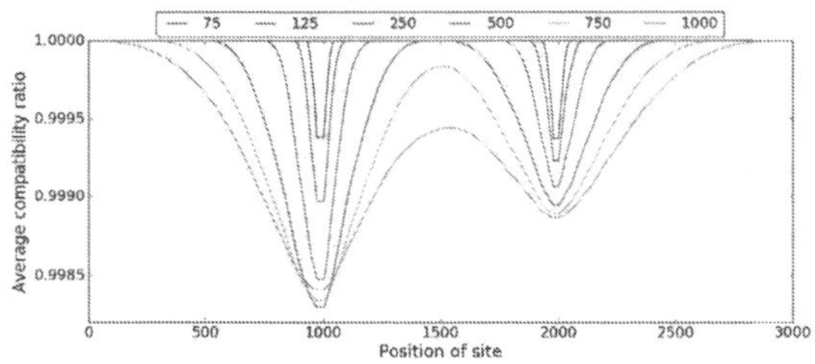

(b) Average compatibility ratio for each site using window sizes of 75, 125, 250, 500, 750 and 1000

Figure 2: Scenario I–Dataset I: Relatively low level of homoplasy

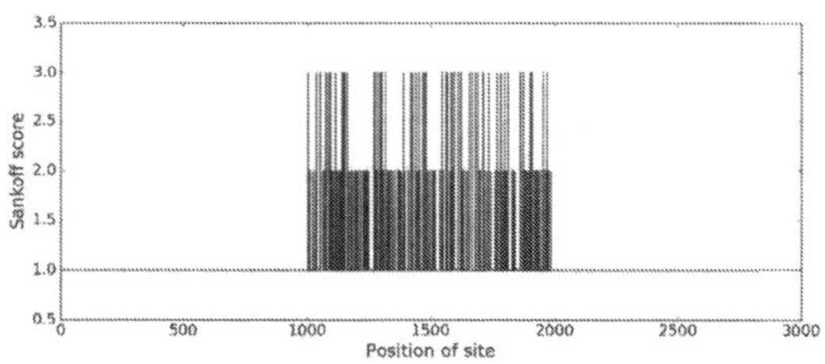

(a) Sankoff score for each site

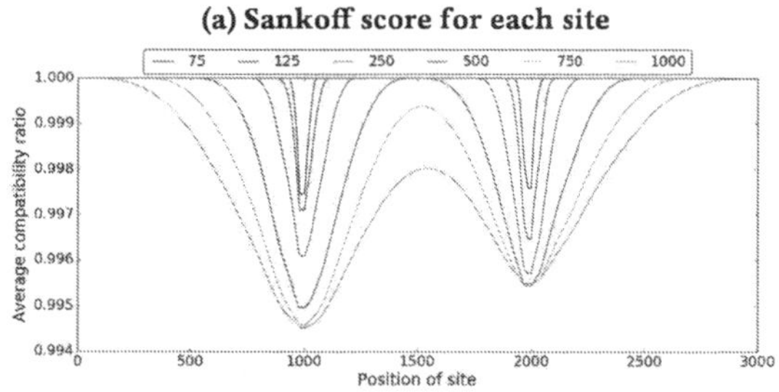

(b) Average compatibility ratio for each site using window sizes of 75, 125, 250, 500, 750 and 1000

Figure 3: Scenario I–Dataset II: Relatively high level of homoplasy

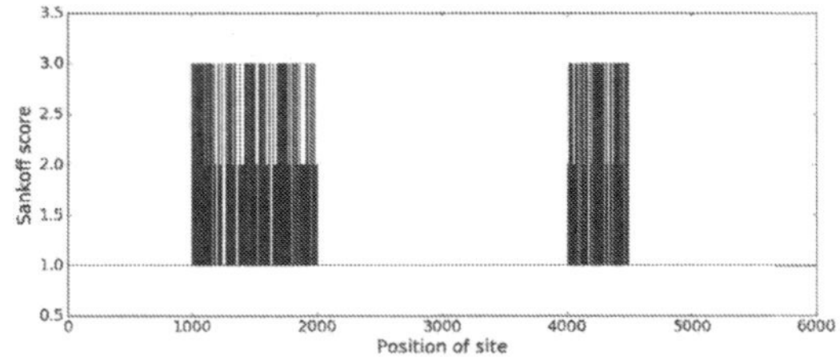

(a) Sankoff score for each site

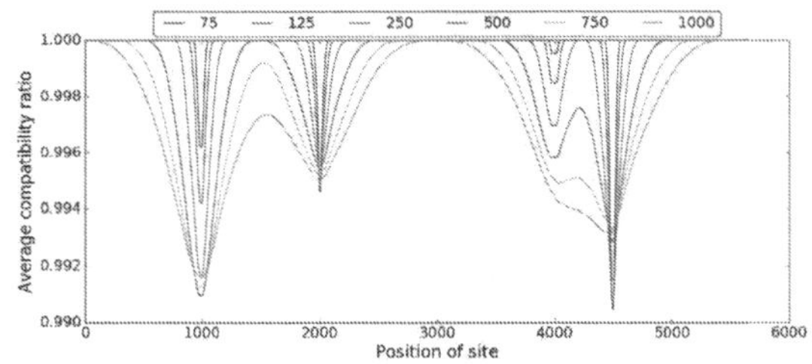

(b) Average compatibility ratio for each site using window sizes of 75, 125, 250, 500, 750 and 1000

Figure 4: Scenario II–Dataset I: Combined regions with distinct tree topologies

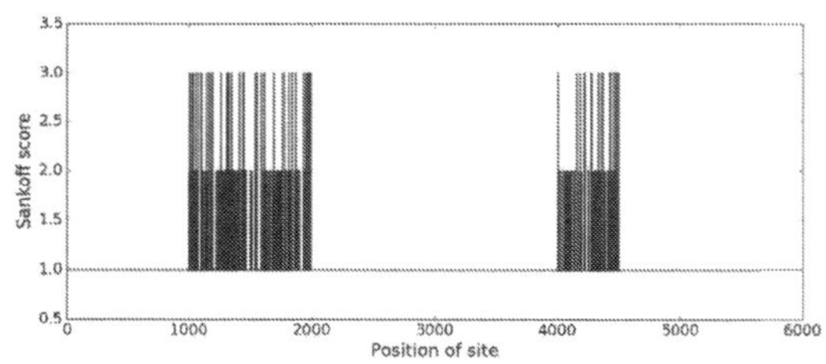

(a) Sankoff score for each site

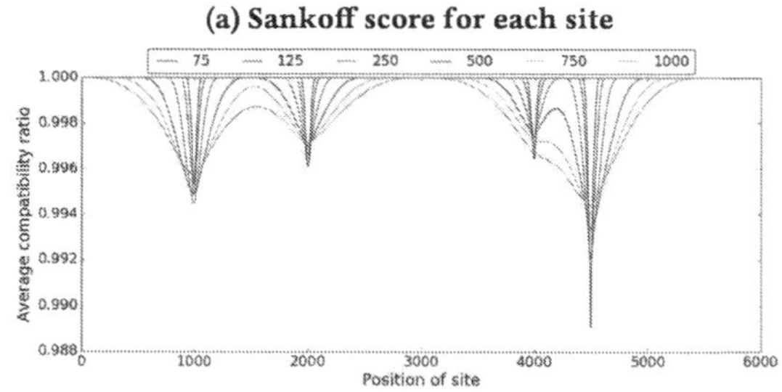

(b) Average compatibility ratio for each site using window sizes of 75, 125, 250, 500, 750 and 1000

Figure 5: Scenario II–Dataset II: Combined regions with the same tree topology

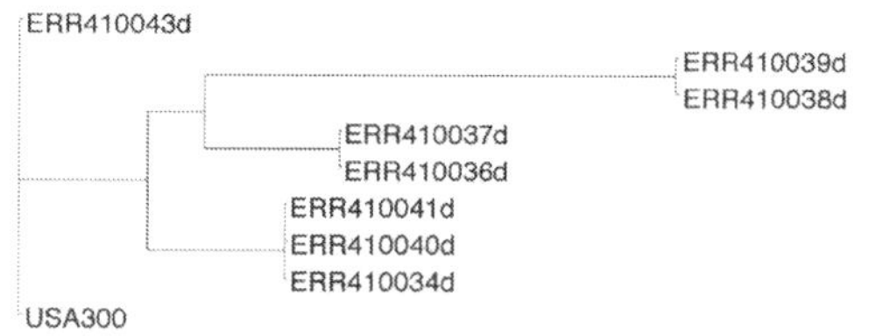

Figure 6: Phylogenetic tree of 9 strains based on all 48417 SNPs for *S. aureus*

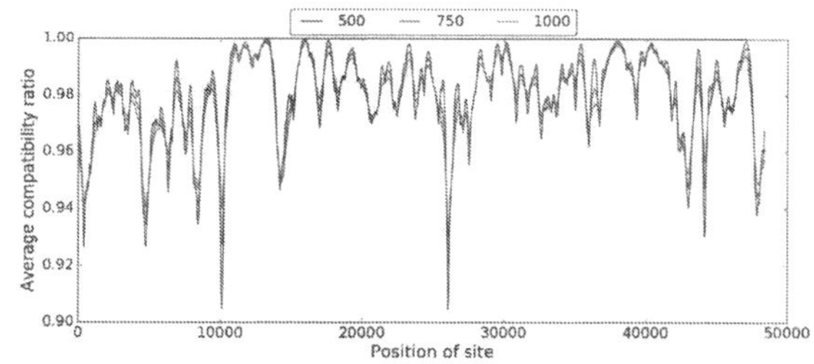

Figure 7: Average compatibility ratio for each site using window sizes of 500, 750 and 1000 for *S. aureus*

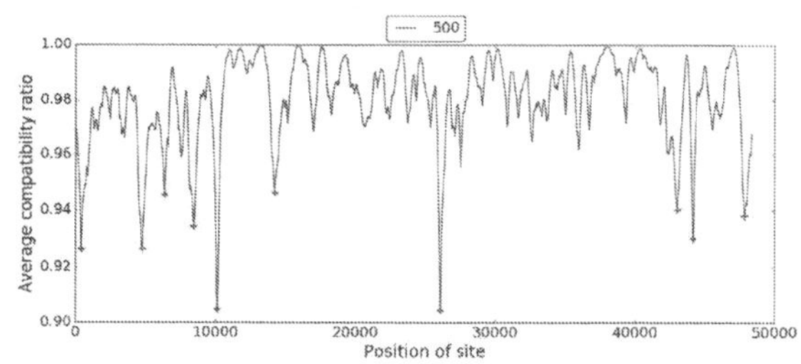

Figure 8: Identified breakpoints using window sizes of 500 for *S. aureus*

their local phylogenetic trees are shown in Figure 9. Comparing to the regional tree, phylogenetic trees of the second, third and fifth segments show that the branch of two strains, ERR410037 and ERR410036, receives the copies from parents of the branch of three strains, ERR410041, ERR410040 and ERR410034. The tree topology of the regional tree is different from the global tree. Additionally, the information of compatibility ratio (CompatRR) and changes per site for 5 segments, local region between 10k and 20k and the entire region are listed in Table 2. The analysis of the alignment using GARD with default setting was stopped before convergence while RDP4 reveals evidence of recombination in this alignment using PHI-test (p-value $< 10^{-5}$). The breakpoint distribution plot using RDP4 is shown in Figure 10. The top six breakpoints are 10147, 14410, 14975, 16990, 17285 and 19485. Besides the first and last sites, the rest are close to the sites identified by ACR, showing similar recombination detection results from ACR and RDP4.

4.2.2 A Case Study on Recombinant Dataset: HIV-1 pol. The HIV-1 *pol* (DNA polymerase) dataset contains 12 strains with 1593 sites and 72 polymorphic sites. The multiple-sequence alignment is

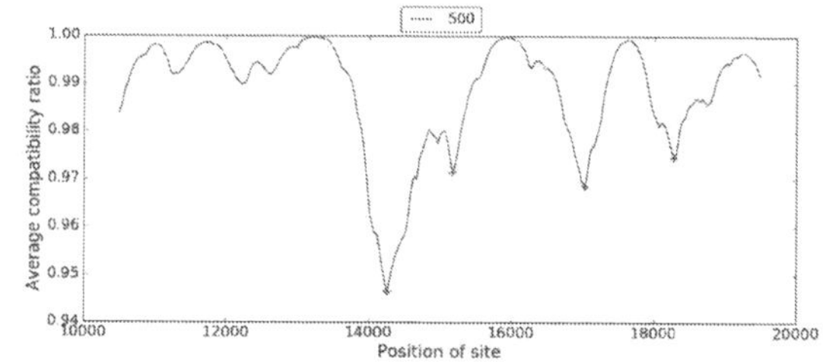

(a) Top four breakpoints of the region[10k, 20k] using window sizes of 500 nucleotides

(b) Phylogenetic tree of the region[10k, 20k]

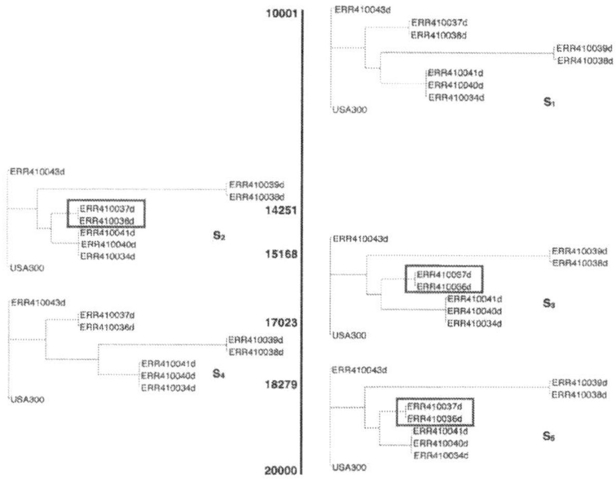

(c) Regional phylogenetic trees of five segments

Figure 9: Recombination segments within the region[10k, 20k] identified by ACR for *S. aureus*

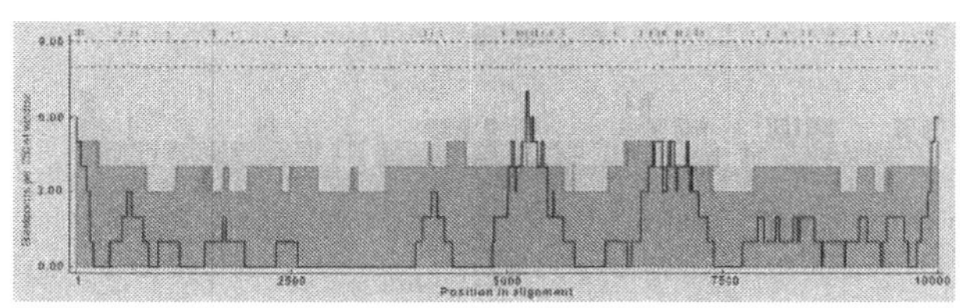

Figure 10: Breakpoints characterized by RDP4 for *S. aureus*

acyclic for the HIV-1 virus. Figure 11 describes the phylogenetic tree of using all polymorphic sites. The number of changes per site is 1.375 (99/72), and the overall compatibility ratio is 0.927. The plot of average compatibility ratio of three window sizes is shown in Figure 12. Two breakpoints, 27 and 61, are identified using default cutoff (mean-2*std) and window size 7. The results

Table 2: Compatibility ratio and changes per site of three segments within the region[10k, 20k] using ACR for *S. aureus*

	Segment	Size	Genes	CompatRR	Required sites	CPS
S_{all}	[1, 48417]	48417	*USA300HOU_0001-USA300HOU_2716*	0.978	105217	1.119
S_{local}	[10001, 20000]	10000	*USA300HOU_0555-USA300HOU_1155*	0.986	10945	1.095
S_1	[10001, 14250]	4250	*USA300HOU_0555-USA300HOU_0810*	0.990	4591	1.080
S_2	[14251, 15167]	917	*USA300HOU_0810-USA300HOU_0903*	0.953	1022	1.115
S_3	[15168, 17022]	1855	*USA300HOU_0903-USA300HOU_0983*	0.992	1987	1.071
S_4	[17023, 18278]	1256	*USA300HOU_0984-USA300HOU_1042*	0.989	1350	1.075
S_5	[18279, 20000]	1722	*USA300HOU_1043-USA300HOU_1155*	0.987	1878	1.091

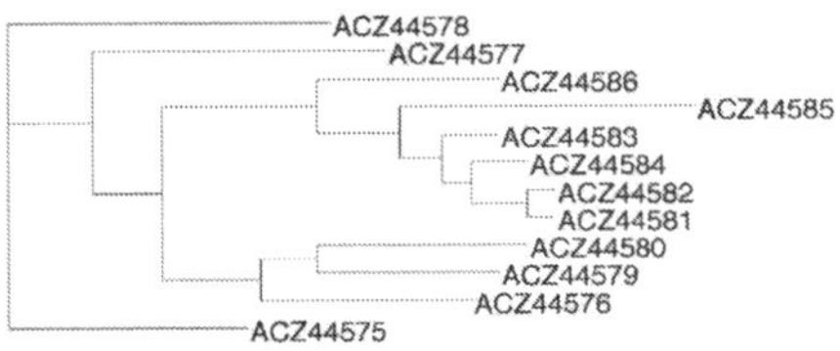

Figure 11: Phylogenetic tree of 12 strains based on all 72 SNPs for HIV-1 *pol*

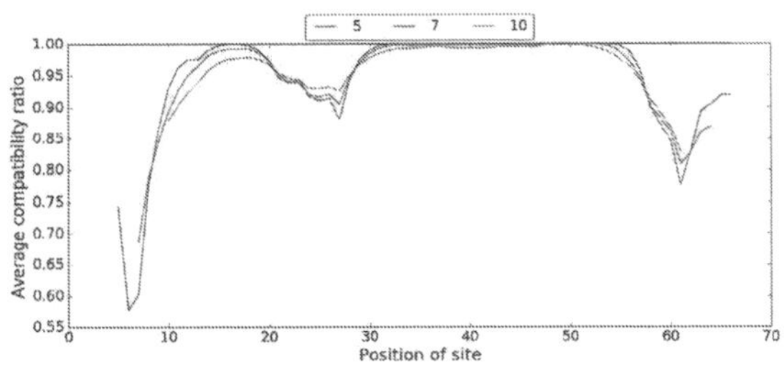

Figure 12: Average compatibility ratio for each site using window sizes of 5, 7 and 10 for HIV-1 *pol*

of three segments are shown in Figure 13 and listed in Table 3. The first segment has the lower number of changes per site and different evolutionary phylogeny. The number of changes per site of the second segment drops down to 1.088, indicating that the sites within this segment are more jointly compatible. The coordinates of 11 sites located in the third segments are from 1325 to 1586 consecutively in the *pol* gene. The polymorphic sites within this region are highly incompatible with each other and incongruent with the global tree. However, both GARD and RDP4 found no evidence of recombination events in this alignment.

4.2.3 A Case Study on Non-recombinant Dataset: Mycobacterium tuberculosis. The dataset contains 50 strains with 10565 SNPs sites. The number of changes per site is 1.006 (10633/10565). The overall compatibility ratio is 0.999, reflecting the clonal nature of *M. tuberculosis* strains worldwide. Hence, we should expect to find no recombination. The plot of average compatibility ratio of three window sizes is shown in Figure 14. Since the average compatibility ratio of the entire alignment is over 99.5%, our approach will report no combination breakpoints. In addition, both GARD and RDP4 reported that no evidence of recombination event was found in the alignment.

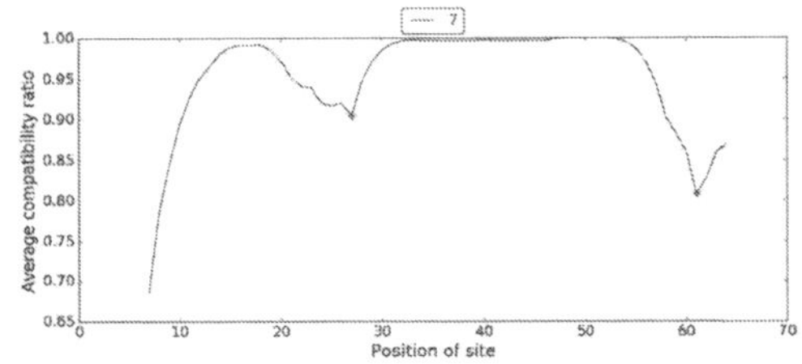

(a) Top two breakpoints using window sizes of 7 nucleotides

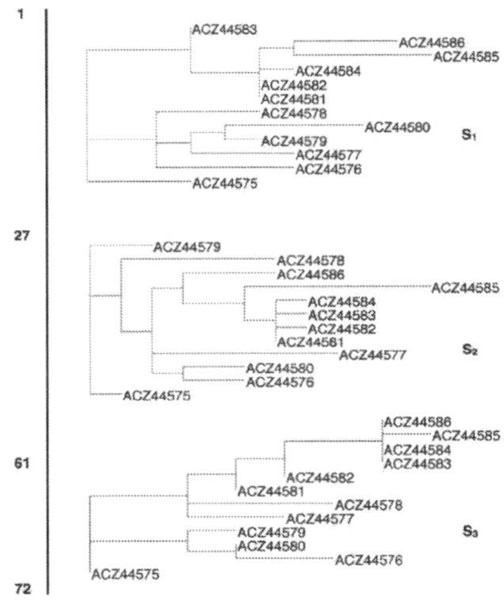

(b) Regional phylogenetic trees of four segments

Figure 13: Recombination segments identified by ACR for HIV-1 *pol*

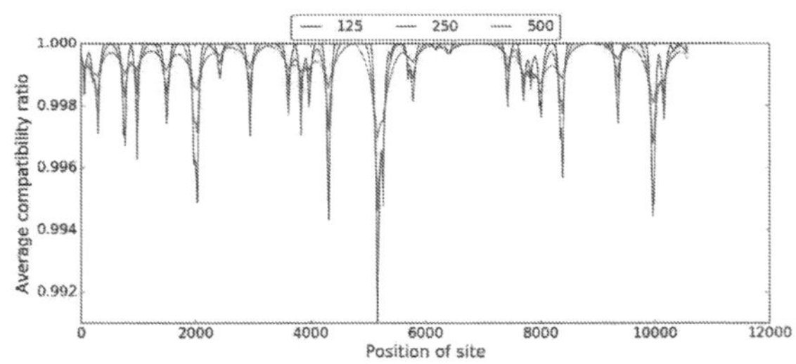

Figure 14: Average compatibility ratio for each site using window sizes of 125, 250 and 500 for *M. tuberculosis*

Table 3: Compatibility ratio and changes per site for window size of 7 using ACR for HIV-1 *pol*

	Segment	Size	CompatRR	Required sites	CPS
S_{all}	[1, 72]	72	0.927	99	1.375
S_1	[1, 27]	27	0.912	36	1.333
S_2	[28, 61]	34	0.989	37	1.088
S_3	[62, 72]	11	0.727	18	1.636

5 DISCUSSION

In the simulations, scenario I provides two levels of sequence divergences within a region in the middle of alignments. GARD, RDP4 and our approaches are all able to detect the presence of recombination. The breakpoints that are identified by our approach are closer to the ground truth than the other two programs. In scenario II, two recombinant regions with the same or distinct phylogenies are simulated. GARD only reports one breakpoint. RDP4 is able to report four breakpoints but deviates more from the ground truth than our method. Default settings of GARD and RDP4 are used for analyzing the alignments, respectively. GARD has three parameters, including nucleotide substitution bias mode, site-to-site rate variation, rate classes. The performance of GARD may be improved by adjusting different settings for parameters. RDP4 contains its own automated RDP program[22] as well as other programs. Automated RDP program and breakpoint distribution plot are applied. No parameter is required for automated RDP program while the windows size can be adjusted for screening for the alignment using breakpoint distribution plot.

Since recombination events are more complex in biological organisms and the genomes of virus are usually smaller than genomes of bacteria, recombinant empirical datasets of bacteria and virus are included for evaluation. In the virus dataset of shorter sequences, GARD and RDP4 report no recombination in the alignment of 72 polymorphic sites. In the bacteria dataset of larger size of sequences, the results of RDP4 and our approach are similar. GARD has the restriction of sequence length of 12k nucleotides. The analysis of the alignment using GARD was stopped before convergence, because the CPU time limit per job was reached.

Evidence of homologous recombination has been reported in the pathogen of *S. aureus*. Examining the polymorphic sequences of a set of isolates throughout the genomes provides an opportunity to profile the genetic exchanges that may be driven by selective forces such as antibiotic usage or drug resistance[9, 28]. The existence of several recombination hotspots has been discovered in *S. aureus*, including transposons, plasmids, phages, the staphylococcal cassette chromosome (SCC), pathogenicity genomic islands and genomic islets [13, 38]. In our analysis, the methicillin-resistance gene *mecA* (*USA300HOU_0956*) is located in the third segment in Figure 9. The *mecA* gene belongs to staphylococcal cassette chromosome *mec* (SCC*mec*) elements that are genomic islands. The third segment has distinct phylogeny, indicating genetic changes occur within the region. Therefore, identifying recombination breakpoints based on the variation of alignment would contribute to uncovering the genomic evolutionary histories in terms of phylogenetic incongruence.

It has been observed that the HIV-1 genome is highly mosaic within the regions of envelope gene (*env*), polymerase gene (*pol*) and *gag* [1, 25]. The highly chimeric genomes of HIV-1 isolates are generated by inter-subtype or inter-group recombination of divergent strains under selective pressures, selective advantages, rapid evolution or immune response after infection[36, 42]. Studies have shown that recombination is responsible for HIV-1 evolution, suggesting that exploration of the recombination patterns and hotspots is crucial for characterization of pathogenesis. In our analysis, 72 sites are polymorphic out of 1593 site of alignment, yet 22 polymorphic sites are not compatible to the global tree topology, showing highly mosaic in the sequences. The alignment is further divided to three segments using our ACR approach. As a result, the changes per site for the first and second segments are lower than the global one, and the phylogenies of them are distinct from the global tree, showing that the evolutionary histories are inconsistent. Furthermore, the last 11 consecutive polymorphic sites located within the third segment are quite incompatible with each other.

6 CONCLUSIONS

The proposed average compatibility ratio approach is able to quickly screen for multiple sequence alignments to detect the presence of recombination and then characterize the breakpoints. Non-overlapping segments divided by the identified breakpoints have higher compatibility ratios, lower homoplasy ratios and distinct phylogenies, showing that adjacent sites within a segment are more jointly compatible and are more likely to be described by a single tree. Our analyses of simulated and empirical datasets and comparisons of two programs demonstrate that our ACR approach is effective and efficient to identify recombinant regions in bacterial and viral genomes. It could potentially provide a better understanding of phylogenetic relationships and evolutionary history among a set of taxa.

REFERENCES

[1] John Archer, John W Pinney, Jun Fan, Etienne Simon-Loriere, Eric J Arts, Matteo Negroni, and David L Robertson. 2008. Identifying the important HIV-1 recombination breakpoints. *PLoS Comput Biol* 4, 9 (2008), e1000178.

[2] C Arnold. 2007. Molecular evolution of Mycobacterium tuberculosis. *Clinical microbiology and infection* 13, 2 (2007), 120–128.

[3] Trevor C Bruen, Hervé Philippe, and David Bryant. 2006. A simple and robust statistical test for detecting the presence of recombination. *Genetics* 172, 4 (2006), 2665–2681.

[4] Josephine Bryant, Claire Chewapreecha, and Stephen D Bentley. 2012. Developing insights into the mechanisms of evolution of bacterial pathogens from whole-genome sequences. *Future microbiology* 7, 11 (2012), 1283–1296.

[5] Cheong Xin Chan, Robert G Beiko, and Mark A Ragan. 2006. Detecting recombination in evolving nucleotide sequences. *BMC bioinformatics* 7, 1 (2006), 412.

[6] Nicholas J Croucher, Simon R Harris, Christophe Fraser, Michael A Quail, John Burton, Mark van der Linden, Lesley McGee, Anne von Gottberg, Jae Hoon Song,

Kwan Soo Ko, and others. 2011. Rapid pneumococcal evolution in response to clinical interventions. *science* 331, 6016 (2011), 430–434.

[7] Xavier Didelot, Rory Bowden, Teresa Street, Tanya Golubchik, Chris Spencer, Gil McVean, Vartul Sangal, Muna F Anjum, Mark Achtman, Daniel Falush, and others. 2011. Recombination and population structure in Salmonella enterica. *PLoS Genet* 7, 7 (2011), e1002191.

[8] Xavier Didelot and Daniel J Wilson. 2015. ClonalFrameML: efficient inference of recombination in whole bacterial genomes. *PLoS Comput Biol* 11, 2 (2015), e1004041.

[9] Elizabeth M Driebe, Jason W Sahl, Chandler Roe, Jolene R Bowers, James M Schupp, John D Gillece, Erin Kelley, Lance B Price, Talima R Pearson, Crystal M Hepp, and others. 2015. Using whole genome analysis to examine recombination across diverse sequence types of Staphylococcus aureus. *PloS one* 10, 7 (2015), e0130955.

[10] George F Estabrook, CS Johnson, and FR McMorris. 1976. A mathematical foundation for the analysis of cladistic character compatibility. *Mathematical Biosciences* 29, 1-2 (1976), 181–187.

[11] George F Estabrook and FR McMorris. 1980. When is one estimate of evolutionary relationships a refinement of another? *Journal of Mathematical Biology* 10, 4 (1980), 367–373.

[12] Graham J Etherington, Jo Dicks, and Ian N Roberts. 2004. Recombination Analysis Tool (RAT): a program for the high-throughput detection of recombination. *Bioinformatics* 21, 3 (2004), 278–281.

[13] Richard G Everitt, Xavier Didelot, Elizabeth M Batty, Ruth R Miller, Kyle Knox, Bernadette C Young, Rory Bowden, Adam Auton, Antonina Votintseva, Hanna Larner-Svensson, and others. 2014. Mobile elements drive recombination hotspots in the core genome of Staphylococcus aureus. *Nature communications* 5 (2014).

[14] Nicholas C Grassly and Edward C Holmes. 1997. A likelihood method for the detection of selection and recombination using nucleotide sequences. *Molecular Biology and Evolution* 14, 3 (1997), 239–247.

[15] Michaela M Gutacker, James C Smoot, Cristi A Lux Migliaccio, Stacy M Ricklefs, Su Hua, Debby V Cousins, Edward A Graviss, Elena Shashkina, Barry N Kreiswirth, and James M Musser. 2002. Genome-wide analysis of synonymous single nucleotide polymorphisms in Mycobacterium tuberculosis complex organisms: resolution of genetic relationships among closely related microbial strains. *Genetics* 162, 4 (2002), 1533–1543.

[16] Ingrid B Jakobsen and Simon Easteal. 1996. A program for calculating and displaying compatibility matrices as an aid in determining reticulate evolution in molecular sequences. *Computer applications in the biosciences: CABIOS* 12, 4 (1996), 291–295.

[17] BG Kelly, A Vespermann, and DJ Bolton. 2009. The role of horizontal gene transfer in the evolution of selected foodborne bacterial pathogens. *Food and Chemical Toxicology* 47, 5 (2009), 951–968.

[18] Elzbieta Krzywinska, Jaroslaw Krzywinski, and Jeffrey S Schorey. 2004. Naturally occurring horizontal gene transfer and homologous recombination in Mycobacterium. *Microbiology* 150, 6 (2004), 1707–1712.

[19] Fedora Lanzas, Petros C Karakousis, James C Sacchettini, and Thomas R Ioerger. 2013. Multidrug-resistant tuberculosis in panama is driven by clonal expansion of a multidrug-resistant Mycobacterium tuberculosis strain related to the KZN extensively drug-resistant M. tuberculosis strain from South Africa. *Journal of clinical microbiology* 51, 10 (2013), 3277–3285.

[20] Walter J Le Quesne. 1969. A method of selection of characters in numerical taxonomy. *Systematic Biology* 18, 2 (1969), 201–205.

[21] Walter J LeQuesne. 1972. Further studies based on the uniquely derived character concept. *Systematic Biology* 21, 3 (1972), 281–288.

[22] Darren Martin and Ed Rybicki. 2000. RDP: detection of recombination amongst aligned sequences. *Bioinformatics* 16, 6 (2000), 562–563.

[23] Darren P Martin, Ben Murrell, Michael Golden, Arjun Khoosal, and Brejnev Muhire. 2015. RDP4: Detection and analysis of recombination patterns in virus genomes. *Virus Evolution* 1, 1 (2015), vev003.

[24] Christopher A Meacham and George F Estabrook. 1985. Compatibility methods in systematics. *Annual Review of Ecology and Systematics* 16, 1 (1985), 431–446.

[25] Adewunmi Onafuwa-Nuga and Alice Telesnitsky. 2009. The remarkable frequency of human immunodeficiency virus type 1 genetic recombination. *Microbiology and Molecular Biology Reviews* 73, 3 (2009), 451–480.

[26] Talima Pearson, Joseph D Busch, Jacques Ravel, Timothy D Read, Shane D Rhoton, Jana M U'ren, Tatum S Simonson, Sergey M Kachur, Rebecca R Leadem, Michelle L Cardon, and others. 2004. Phylogenetic discovery bias in Bacillus anthracis using single-nucleotide polymorphisms from whole-genome sequencing. *Proceedings of the National Academy of Sciences of the United States of America* 101, 37 (2004), 13536–13541.

[27] Hervé Philippe, Henner Brinkmann, Dennis V Lavrov, D Timothy J Littlewood, Michael Manuel, Gert Wörheide, and Denis Baurain. 2011. Resolving difficult phylogenetic questions: why more sequences are not enough. *PLoS Biol* 9, 3 (2011), e1000602.

[28] Paul J Planet, Apurva Narechania, Liang Chen, Barun Mathema, Sam Boundy, Gordon Archer, and Barry Kreiswirth. 2016. Architecture of a Species: Phylogenomics of Staphylococcus aureus. *Trends in Microbiology* (2016).

[29] DOTREE Plotree and DOTGRAM Plotgram. 1989. PHYLIP-phylogeny inference package (version 3.2). *cladistics* 5, 163 (1989), 6.

[30] Sergei L Kosakovsky Pond, David Posada, Michael B Gravenor, Christopher H Woelk, and Simon DW Frost. 2006. Automated phylogenetic detection of recombination using a genetic algorithm. *Molecular biology and evolution* 23, 10 (2006), 1891–1901.

[31] Sergei L Kosakovsky Pond, David Posada, Michael B Gravenor, Christopher H Woelk, and Simon DW Frost. 2006. GARD: a genetic algorithm for recombination detection. *Bioinformatics* 22, 24 (2006), 3096–3098.

[32] Sergei L Kosakovsky Pond, David Posada, Eric Stawiski, Colombe Chappey, Art FY Poon, Gareth Hughes, Esther Fearnhill, Mike B Gravenor, Andrew J Leigh Brown, and Simon DW Frost. 2009. An evolutionary model-based algorithm for accurate phylogenetic breakpoint mapping and subtype prediction in HIV-1. *PLoS Comput Biol* 5, 11 (2009), e1000581.

[33] David Posada. 2002. Evaluation of methods for detecting recombination from DNA sequences: empirical data. *Molecular biology and evolution* 19, 5 (2002), 708–717.

[34] David Posada and Keith A Crandall. 2001. Evaluation of methods for detecting recombination from DNA sequences: computer simulations. *Proceedings of the National Academy of Sciences* 98, 24 (2001), 13757–13762.

[35] David Posada and Keith A Crandall. 2002. The effect of recombination on the accuracy of phylogeny estimation. *Journal of molecular evolution* 54, 3 (2002), 396–402.

[36] MIKA O SALMINEN, JEAN K CARR, DONALD S BURKE, and FRANCINE E McCUTCHAN. 1995. Identification of breakpoints in intergenotypic recombinants of HIV type 1 by bootscanning. *AIDS research and human retroviruses* 11, 11 (1995), 1423–1425.

[37] David Sankoff. 1975. Minimal mutation trees of sequences. *SIAM J. Appl. Math.* 28, 1 (1975), 35–42.

[38] Célio D Santos-Júnior, António Veríssimo, and Joana Costa. 2016. The recombination dynamics of Staphylococcus aureus inferred from spA gene. *BMC microbiology* 16, 1 (2016), 143.

[39] SA Sawyer. 1999. GENECONV: A computer package for the statistical detection of gene conversion. *Distributed by the author, Department of Mathematics, Washington University in St. Louis* (1999).

[40] Mikkel H Schierup and Jotun Hein. 2000. Consequences of recombination on traditional phylogenetic analysis. *Genetics* 156, 2 (2000), 879–891.

[41] Robert W Scotland and Mike Steel. 2015. Circumstances in which parsimony but not compatibility will be provably misleading. *Systematic biology* 64, 3 (2015), 492–504.

[42] Binshan Shi, Christina Kitchen, Barbara Weiser, Douglas Mayers, Brian Foley, Kimdar Kemal, Kathryn Anastos, Marc Suchard, Monica Parker, Cheryl Brunner, and others. 2010. Evolution and recombination of genes encoding HIV-1 drug resistance and tropism during antiretroviral therapy. *Virology* 404, 1 (2010), 5–20.

[43] John Maynard Smith. 1992. Analyzing the mosaic structure of genes. *Journal of molecular evolution* 34, 2 (1992), 126–129.

[44] Christopher M Thomas and Kaare M Nielsen. 2005. Mechanisms of, and barriers to, horizontal gene transfer between bacteria. *Nature reviews microbiology* 3, 9 (2005), 711–721.

[45] David B Wake. 1991. Homoplasy: the result of natural selection, or evidence of design limitations? *The American Naturalist* 138, 3 (1991), 543–567.

[46] Timothy M Walker, Camilla LC Ip, Ruth H Harrell, Jason T Evans, Georgia Kapatai, Martin J Dedicoat, David W Eyre, Daniel J Wilson, Peter M Hawkey, Derrick W Crook, and others. 2013. Whole-genome sequencing to delineate Mycobacterium tuberculosis outbreaks: a retrospective observational study. *The Lancet infectious diseases* 13, 2 (2013), 137–146.

[47] Georg F Weiller. 1998. Phylogenetic profiles: a graphical method for detecting genetic recombinations in homologous sequences. *Molecular Biology and Evolution* 15, 3 (1998), 326–335.

[48] Michael Worobey. 2001. A novel approach to detecting and measuring recombination: new insights into evolution in viruses, bacteria, and mitochondria. *Molecular Biology and Evolution* 18, 8 (2001), 1425–1434.

Phylogenetic Tree based Method for Uncovering Co-mutational Site-pairs in Influenza Viruses

Fransiskus Xaverius Ivan
Biomedical Informatics Lab, Nanyang Technological University, Singapore
fivan@ntu.edu.sg

Xinrui Zhou
Akhila Deshpande, Rui Yin
Biomedical Informatics Lab, Nanyang Technological University, Singapore
xzhou010|akhila004|yinr0002@e.ntu.edu.sg

Jie Zheng*
Chee Keong Kwoh
Biomedical Informatics Lab, Nanyang Technological University, Singapore
zhengjie|asckkwoh@ntu.edu.sg

ABSTRACT

Various computational and statistical approaches have been proposed to uncover the mutational patterns of rapidly evolving influenza viral genes. A problem that draws much attention is to identify pairs of sites that potentially co-mutate to contribute to the overall fitness of the virus. Unlike previous methods that extract the mutations from sequence alignments, here we endeavor a novel method that relies on identifying mutations in the phylogenetic trees that are reconstructed using resampled sequence data. Since the method takes into account the evolutionary structure presents in the sequence data, spurious mutations obtained by comparing sequences from different clades could be removed. Furthermore, this approach does not only allow us to capture site-pairs that potentially co-mutate, but also provides an opportunity to extract the direction of their relationships. By applying network analyses to the set of site-pairs, we could further identify and rank the sites that are likely to be influential or under influence from changes on other sites. We applied the method to the hemagglutinin of influenza H3N2, and interestingly, we successfully recovered mutational sites that are important for cluster antigenic transition of the virus in the top list of our findings. Moreover, we detected a directional relationship that would be interesting for experimental investigation.

1 INTRODUCTION

Influenza A viruses are the most virulent type of influenza partly due to their high mutational rate. A major culprit for the virulence is the hemagglutinin (HA), which is a membrane glycoprotein responsible for the entry of the virus particles to host cells. The cleavage of HA protein into HA1 and HA2 proteins by a cellular enzyme is essential for viral entry [1], with HA1 protein containing the host receptor binding domain and most antigenic sites. The HA has been considered as a primary target for vaccine production recommended by the World Health Organization (WHO). Therefore, identifying antigenic dynamics or mutational patterns of influenza HA is critical to facilitate the recommendation of more effective vaccines. This include finding co-mutational patterns of different sites of the protein, which may have some biological significance such as reported in [2–6].

To assist biological experiments, some computational methods for identifying potential co-mutational patterns of influenza viral genes have been developed. Smith et al. mapped the results of hemagglutinin assays into a phylogenetic tree using a maximum-likelihood approach to analyze the antigenic evolution of the HA protein of influenza A/H3N2 [7]. This work was extended by Bedford et al. by incorporating a diffusion model [8]. Shih et al. conducted statistical analysis on frequency switches of H3N2 HA domain residues, drawing the conclusion that co-mutations at antigenic sites could accumulatively enhance the antigenic drift [9]. Xia et al proposed a mutual information (MI)-based site transition network (STN) to measure the correlation of pair wise mutations and predict future site mutations with 70% accuracy [10]. Machine learning algorithms, such as association rule mining and Naïve Bayes classifiers, are widely used to identify rules of multiple co-mutational sites and to predict antigenic clusters [11, 12].

However, those methods have not yet fully used the chronological and structural information that can be extracted from the phylogenetic tree of the sequence data; they relied on alignment data and thus may give spurious mutational events due to the comparison of sequences from different clades. In this paper, we propose a phylogenetic tree based method to uncover the co-mutational patterns in HA protein during the evolution of A/H3N2. Remarkably, the method may also be used to uncover potential directional or sequential (chronological) relationships between mutational sites, which has been shown to be important in correcting the direction of HA evolution towards a new antigenic cluster [13]. Finally, using each of the co-mutational and sequential-mutational site-pairs that form a network, we proposed the application of network analyses for ranking the mutational sites, which may facilitate the surveillance of the mutations of influenza HA protein as well as guiding further experimental works.

2 METHODS

2.1 Sequence dataset

The coding DNA sequences (CDS) and protein sequences for HA of influenza H3N2 viruses were extracted from influenza genome

*Also with More affiliation: Genome Institute of Singapore, A*STAR, Biopolis, 138672 Singapore, Singapore.

Permission to make digital or hard copies of all or part of this work for personal or classroom use is granted without fee provided that copies are not made or distributed for profit or commercial advantage and that copies bear this notice and the full citation on the first page. Copyrights for components of this work owned by others than ACM must be honored. Abstracting with credit is permitted. To copy otherwise, or republish, to post on servers or to redistribute to lists, requires prior specific permission and/or a fee. Request permissions from permissions@acm.org.
ACM-BCB '17, August 20-23, 2017, Boston, MA, USA
© 2017 Association for Computing Machinery.
ACM ISBN 978-1-4503-4722-8/17/08...$15.00
https://doi.org/10.1145/3107411.3107479

datasets available in NCBI by 28 February 2017. We also downloaded influenza genome datasets from GISAID EpiFlu database and obtained the CDS and protein sequences for HA of H3N2 using Influenza Virus Sequence Annotation Tool [14]. Records with identical HA sequences were collapsed, giving a total of 5977 unique records. Five records whose protein length were different from 566 were removed. Sequences with the collection year 1968-69 were grouped together, as well as for years 1970-72,1973-75, 1976-79, 1980-84, 1985-88, and 1989-90, so that the number of sequences in each year group was more than 20. The numbers of sequences for those year groups were 22, 22, 26, 23, 24, 28, and 25, respectively; while the numbers of sequences for each year group from 1991 to 2017 were 25, 28, 79, 27, 30, 30, 18, 22, 103, 84, 32, 108, 195, 151, 159, 71, 200, 136, 238, 215, 273, 417, 420, 695, 1175, 755, and 121, respectively.

2.2 Phylogenetic tree reconstruction

We repeatedly selected a fixed number of random HA sequences from each year group and aligned their CDS to codon position for phylogenetic tree reconstruction using maximum likelihood method under $GTR+G+I$ substitution model. The muscle package [15] was used to perform the alignments, and the phangorn package [16] was used to reconstruct the trees. Each edge length or distance between two adjacent nodes in the trees was associated with the evolutionary distance or number of nucleotide substitutions per site estimated based on the chosen substitution model. The distance between any two nodes (of interest, between ancestor and predecessor) in the tree was calculated by summing the length of edges in the path connecting the two nodes. Next, due to progressive evolution of HA sequences [17], the trees were rooted using the earliest sequence as an outgroup. The CDS, and subsequently the protein sequence, at each internal node of each tree was inferred using Fitch's algorithm [18]. Amino acid mutations were detected at each node (except for the root) by comparing its protein sequence to its parent's protein sequence. Each mutation was in the form AA1-p-AA2, representing a mutation of a given amino acid AA1 in the parent node to another amino acid AA2 in the child node at a given site p in the sequence. Finally, the distance of each node to the root of the tree was also recorded.

2.3 Identifying dominant amino acid mutations during influenza virus evolution

In order to identify the dominant amino acid mutations during influenza virus evolution, we first mapped each mutation in the phylogenetic trees to a list of real numbers representing the distances between the nodes where the mutation observed and their corresponding root. And then, for each mutation, we smoothed the distribution of its distance data with a Gaussian kernel density estimate [19], followed by the detection of the peaks that were defined as local maxima centered in any interval for the distance. Assuming $h_1, h_2, ..., h_k$ are the heights of the detected peaks for mutation m at distance to the root $d_1, d_2, ..., d_k$, then the strength of the signal for the peak with height h_i, denoted by $S(m_i, d_i)$, was calculated as follows: $S(m_i, d_i) = N * \frac{h_i}{\sum_1^k h_j}$, where N is the number of observations for the mutation of interest. The formula is indicative of the portion of observations that support the observed mutation. Given I is the number of resampled trees, a threshold of $\frac{I}{2}$ for the strength of signal or support was applied to claim whether a mutation at a certain distance was dominant or not.

2.4 Identifying sequential-mutational site-pairs and co-mutational site-pairs with high confidence

For convenience, the identification for highly confident sequential-mutational site-pairs over the course of viral evolution is explained before the identification for highly confident co-mutational site-pairs. Briefly, for each possible pair of mutations observed in two nodes that have ancestor-predecessor relationship and distance below a certain threshold, we mapped the pair of mutations to the distance of the associated ancestor to the root of its tree. The reconstruction of the map can be done while walking from an initial node (any node other than the root), in the direction to the associated root, up to the node whose distance to the initial node is below the threshold. Then, highly confident sequential-mutations were detected from the map in the same way we detected highly confident mutations as described in the previous subsection. Highly confident sequential-mutational site-pairs were obtained by simply extracting the ordered site-pairs from highly confident sequential-mutations and summing the supports for each unique site-pair.

To formalize the process, let $T_i = (V_i, E_i)$ be the i-th resampled tree, with V_i and E_i are the set of nodes and edges in the tree, respectively. In addition, let r_i be the root of T_i and for any node $v_0 \in V_i - \{r_i\}$, $d(v_0, r_i)$ be the distance of v_0 to r_i and M_{v_0} be the set of mutations observed in the sequence at node v_0. Also, let P be a path from v_0 to r_i in T_i, and for $v_k \in P$, d^* be the threshold for distance from v_0 to v_k. Next, let SM be a dictionary that maps sequential-mutations (m_1, m_2) to a set of distances of the nodes associated with m_1 to their respective root. Finally, let $S(m_1, m_2, d)$ be the support for sequential mutations (m_1, m_2) at distance d obtained from SM using the same approach described in previous subsection. Then the formal process of collecting highly confident sequential-mutations (the step for getting the site-pairs is omitted) from the resampled trees to a list named HCSM is given in the pseudocode in Algorithm 1.

The identification of highly confident co-mutational site-pairs was done similarly. But in addition to sequential or chronologically ordered mutations, all possible pairs of mutations observed at each node were also collected. Additionally, the direction of the mutations was ignored.

2.5 Graph analysis for mutational-site networks

The set of each co-mutational and sequential-mutational site-pairs obtained from applying the algorithm described in the previous section basically forms a network. The nodes in the network represent a site of mutation, while the edges represent the relationship between two sites. For co-mutational network (CoMN), the edges are undirected; while for sequential-mutational network (SMN), the edges are directed. For each CoMN and SMN, some network measurements or statistics were calculated. Of our interest, these include the number of connected components (a component is defined as a set of nodes that are all linked one to another through

Algorithm 1: Pseudocode for identifying highly confident sequential-mutations from sampled phylogenetic trees

Input: $d^*, T_i = (V_i, E_i), r_i, \forall v \in V_i, label(v) = (d(v, r_i), M_v),$ $i = 1, 2, ..., I$
Output: $HCSM$
Initialize: Dictionary SM = { } and array HCSM = ()
foreach $i = 1, 2, ..., I$ **do**
  foreach $v_0 \in V_i - \{r_i\}$ **do**
    Find a path P from v_0 to r_i
    foreach $v \in P - \{v_0, r_i\}$ **do**
      if $d(v_0, r_i) - d(v, r_i) < d^*$ **then**
        foreach $(m_1, m_2) \in M_{v_0} \times M_v$ **do**
          $SM[(m_1, m_2)] = (SM[(m_1, m_2)], d(v, r_i))$
foreach $(m_1, m_2) \in keys(SM)$ **do**
  Calculate Gaussian smoothing G for the array of distances $SM[(m_1, m_2)]$
  Find the locations $d_1, d_2, ..., d_k$ of the peaks for G that are local maxima centered in any interval for the distance and their respective height $h_1, h_2, ..., h_k$
  foreach $i = 1, 2, ..., k$ **do**
    Calculate support for (m_1, m_2) at distance d_i:
    $S(m_1, m_2, d_i) = |SM[(m_1, m_2)]| * \frac{h_i}{\sum_1^k h_j}$
    if $S(m_1, m_2, d_i) > \frac{I}{2}$ **then**
      $HCSM = (HCSM, (m_1, m_2, d_i))$
Return $HCSM$

a path) and the number of nodes and edges in all connected components. We also calculated the average degree, network diameter, and the average path length of CoMN and SMN as described in [20]. The direction of SMN was omitted when calculating these network statistics. For CoMN, we also calculated the degree for each node and then divide it by the number of HA sites to obtain the degree centrality for each node; while for SMN, we calculated the indegree and outdegree for each node and then divide it by the number of HA sites to obtain the indegree and outdegree centrality for each node. The division is to allow us to compare the centrality measures for CoMN and SMN obtained using different d^*.

3 RESULTS

3.1 Characteristics of resampled phylogenetic trees for HA genes of influenza H3N2 viruses

For our analyses, we resampled 1000 phylogenetic trees generated from a total of 510 random HA sequences of H3N2, consisting of 15 sequences from each of 36 year groups as described in Methods. The number of resampling was chosen since relatively fewer new mutations were recovered when adding more resampled trees of that size; while the number of sequences was kept at 15 since relatively fewer new sequential mutations were recovered when adding more sequences for reconstructing 1000 resampled trees. As illustrated in Figure 1, the phylogenetic trees typically follow a ladder-like structure, which demonstrates the ability of the virus to

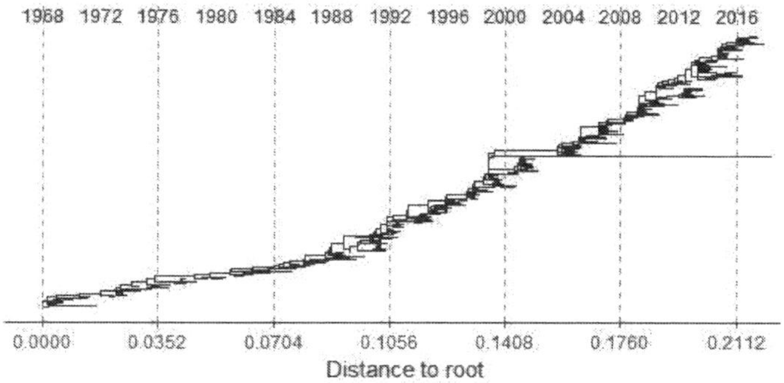

Figure 1: A typical structure for the phylogenetic tree of the HA of influenza H3N2 from the 510 sequences randomly sampled from 34 year groups (as described in Methods.) The years equivalent to the distance to root at the tree is shown at the top.

escape from host immunity [21]. Of a particular note, the tree has a long branch emerging from an internal node at a distance between 0.10 and 0.15 from the root in the resampled trees. The tips of that branch mainly consist of the HAs of influenza H3N2 strains that were circulating in the North America around 2011-2012, which include the A/Iowa/09/2011, A/Ohio/88/2012, and Indiana/103/2012. These HAs contribute to the unusual distance of the furthest node to the associated root in 22 resampled trees, which are more than two standard deviation from the average. Hence, the 22 trees are excluded when estimating the rate of evolution of the HA of influenza that is assumed to be constant [22]. This gives an average and standard deviation of distances of the furthest nodes to the root at 0.218 and 0.003, respectively (with outliers, the values were 0.221 and 0.022). Thus, considering the evolution of H3N2 has undergone for 49 years, distance of 0.0044 is about equivalent to 1 year range. This becomes the basis of the conversion of distance to the range of year in the rest of this paper.

3.2 Uncovering dominant mutations in HA during influenza H3N2 evolution

As mentioned in the Methods, dominant mutations refer to a mutation at certain distance that is supported by >50% resampled trees. Such mutations might contribute to the transition between two dominant influenza clades or two antigenic clusters, and they are expected to accumulate in the epitope regions (epitopes A, B, C, D, and E, as proposed in [23]) located at sites 50-300 (H3 numbering). As a result of our investigation, the number of dominant mutations are more or less uniformly distributed over the years of evolution, and the majority (66% of 773 mutations) were indeed found at the epitope regions. Of interest, 80% of dominant mutations recovered from the longest path of the resampled trees are located at the epitope regions. The percentage is much higher than the overall percentage, which correlates with the expectation that the path contains crucial mutations for the survival of influenza H3N2 viruses. Nonetheless, the portion of the mutations are mainly recovered at distance to root < 0.14 and > 0.21 (i.e., around 1968-1999 and after 2015). The earlier dominant mutations (Table 1) are

Table 1: Dominant amino acid mutations at the longest path of the sampled phylogenetic trees. Mutations associated with antigenic cluster transitions reported in Smith et al [7] are underlined and bolded. The antigenic clusters and the year their sequences circulated are given at the top two rows.

Antigenic cluster	Year	Distance to root	Epitope A	Epitope B	Epitope C	Epitope D	Epitope E	Non-epitope
HK68	1968	0.0000						
	-	-					V78G	N31D D31N
	1970	0.0088						
	-	-			D275G	V242I **R207K**		E479G
	1972	0.0176						
	-	-	**G144D** **T122N**	**T155Y** **N188D**				L3F L331I
EN72	1974	0.0264						
	-	-	T126N **S145N**	S193N **Q189K**	**I278S** **N53D**	**I217V**	D63N T83K	F3L
VI75	1976	0.0352						
	-	-	N137Y	**G158E**	**K50R**		**M260I**	
TX77	1978	0.0440						
	-	-	**G146S**	**K156E** **T160K**	**N54S**	**V244L**	**I62K**	D2N I347V
BA79	1980	0.0528						
	-	-	**N133S** **P143S**	**Q197R**		**D172G** **V217I**		
	1982	0.0616						
	-	-	D144V		K307R	I213V N248T N173K		R453K N2K V384L
	1984	0.0704						
	-	-	**G124D**	V163A S159Y **K189R** **Y155H**				
	1986	0.0792						
	-	-	T131A		K299R		F94Y E82K K83E	
SI87	1988	0.0880						
	-	-	**S133D**	N193S **E156K** **E190D**			**T262N**	
BE89	1990	0.0968						
	-	-	G135K	R189S S157L	T276N	I214T T214I		K450R
	1992	0.1056						
	-	-	D124G **N145K**	R197Q	S278N	L226I I121T G172D		
BE92	1994	0.1144						
	-	-	K135T G124S D133N G142R	**Y196A**	G275D	I226V T121N	N262S	D375N
WU95	1996	0.1232						
	-	-	V144I Y137S	**E158K** **K156Q**	**N276K**		**K62E** R57Q	
SY97	1998	0.1320						
	-	-	I144N	T192I		D172E		R452K
	2000	0.1408						
	-	-						
	2002	0.1496						
	-	-	K145N					
FU02	2004	0.1584						
	-	-						
...	2006	0.1672						
	-	-						
	2008	0.1760						
	-	-		K158N				
	2010	0.1848						

highly overlapped with the mutations associated with antigenic variants reported by Smith et al. [7] for that period of time (38 out of 63 amino acid mutations at epitopes were recovered). The later ones (Table 2) likely correspond to the emergence of new influenza H3N2 strains that have dominated the 2016-2017 seasons (FluNet: www.who.int/flunet). On the other hand, the lack of dominant mutations in the period between 2000 and 2015 might be linked to reduced affinity of influenza H3N2 to human receptors [24].

3.3 Uncovering dominant co-mutational and sequential-mutational site-pairs

Our method successfully identifies a significant subset of dominant single amino acid mutations that has been shown to contribute to antigenic variation of HA. Thus, similar approaches may reliably uncover pairs of HA sites that have co-mutated. Uniquely, our tree-based approach may not only be useful for the identification of co-mutational site-pairs, but it may also allow the identification of the site-pairs potentially showing directional relationships. The site-pairs with either relation can be collected in a certain range of time or distance, notated as d^*, that separating an ancestor node and its predecessor node that are associated with the observed site-pairs. Here, we present results from experiment using $d^* = 0.0011, 0.0022, 0.0033, \ldots, 0.0088$, which correspond to observations within $\frac{1}{4}, \frac{1}{2}, \frac{3}{4}$ ..., and 2 years, respectively. The choice of limiting d^* up to 0.0088 or up to 2 years relates to the fact that influenza vaccines are updated every year by WHO; and thus, a significant influenza drift should be observed within 2 years.

The top 10 co-mutational site-pairs and the top 10 sequential-mutational site-pairs for those d^* values are listed in Table 3. The site-pairs that frequently appear (>4 times) in each case are highlighted. Overall, we obtained 6 frequent co-mutational pairs: 124-145, 145-172, 145-189, 145-226, 189-226, and 226-276, and 3 frequent sequential-mutational pairs: 3->145, 83->145, and 124->145. One interesting observation is the frequent appearance of site 145 in

Table 2: List of dominant single-mutations recovered at distance to root >0.21 (around 2016-2017).

Epitope	Mutations
A	N122Q, N133D, S137Y, T135S, K140R, R142G, K145N
B	H155Y, K158N, A163E, S189K, I192T, S193N, A196V
C	D53N, P273H, G275D, K276E, R299K
D	T117N, N121T, E172D, T203I
E	E62K, G78D, K92T, R261Q
Non epitope	N6S, T10M, N31D, D101Y, S107T, L164Q, P289S, N378T, L384V, E386K, N445S, K452R, K453R, V490I, D493N

the site pairs, and this site seems to be under strong influence from other sites, including site 3 in non-epitope and site 83 and 124 in epitope (E and A, respectively). Another interesting observation is the co-mutations among site 145, 189 and 226. The site-pairs involving these three sites dominates the top 3, and two of them interestingly appears in the column for smaller d^*. Site 145 and site 189 are located in close proximity at the periphery of HA's receptor binding site, and both were involved in the antigenic cluster transition from EN72 to VI75 [7]. The substitutions at this site-pairs were also likely involved in the recent emergence of new dominant H3N2 strains we highlight earlier (Table 2). On the other hand, site 226 has been shown to play a role in determining receptor specificity [25].

3.4 Ranking of the importance of sites

From a list of pairs of sites that co-mutate, we may construct a co-mutational network (CoMN) and characterize it. Similarly, we may construct and analyze a sequential-mutational network (SMN) from a list of pairs of sites that show a sequential order along the paths in the phylogenetic trees. This approach, to our knowledge,

Table 3: List of top 10 co-mutational site-pairs (A) and top 10 sequential-mutational site-pairs (B) for varying distance thresholds between ancestor and predecessor nodes associated with the site-pairs (d^*). The cells for a co-mutational site-pair are given a light gray background if it appears >4 times, and the background color is also applied to the cells containing associated sequential-mutational site-pair. Similarly, the other way around is done from sequential-mutational site-pair to co-mutational site-pair using darker gray background. If a site-pair appears >4 times in both A and B, then the background for its cells is black.

A. Top 10 co-mutational site-pairs

Ranking	d*							
	0.0011	0.0022	0.0033	0.0044	0.0055	0.0066	0.0077	0.0088
1	121-142	137-158	121-122	145-189	145-189	189-226	145-189	145-189
2	137-158	121-142	137-213	3-145	189-226	145-189	189-226	145-226
3	172-197	155-189	145-193	145-193	226-276	226-276	145-172	189-226
4	3-83	121-122	135-145	189-226	145-172	137-144	124-145	145-278
5	156-186	10-62	137-158	226-276	124-145	145-226	121-135	142-225
6	62-144	137-213	145-188	137-144	145-226	145-172	145-226	145-172
7	135-145	62-158	62-158	145-172	3-145	124-145	226-276	142-144
8	145-226	145-193	121-142	145-226	137-144	124-145	121-145	124-145
9	159-225	135-193	226-262	121-122	145-278	145-193	83-145	121-135
10	144-159	145-189	155-189	124-145	137-213	83-145	142-144	226-276

B. Top 10 sequential-mutational site-pairs

Ranking	d*							
	0.0011	0.0022	0.0033	0.0044	0.0055	0.0066	0.0077	0.0088
1	142->196	484->142	3->145	3->145	3->145	189->226	189->145	189->145
2	212->312	406->142	144->220	124->145	83->145	83->145	83->145	83->145
3	121->196	171->142	213->137	144->220	124->145	3->145	124->145	155->145
4	144->213	213->137	276->226	347->220	347->220	189->145	189->226	156->226
5	128->347	248->193	219->145	197->145	106->220	124->145	156->226	225->142
6	142->347	142->347	217->145	106->220	276->226	156->226	144->220	124->145
7	144->3	3->331	278->246	219->145	144->220	276->226	197->145	189->226
8	62->3	188->331	83->189	172->145	156->226	347->220	172->145	144->220
9	156->3	193->50	347->220	83->145	189->226	106->220	3->145	278->145
10	212->45	225->50	144->226	142->45	189->145	219->145	225->142	144->142

is the first attempt to study influenza sequences by network analysis despite its popularity for analyzing biological networks [26].

An overview of some statistics for both CoMN and SMN across different d^* or the range of time is given in Table 4. Of interest, CoMN and SMN quickly become a single connected network; but while CoMN quickly covers most of the 239 sites harboring dominant amino acid mutations detected earlier, SMN only gradually covers them as d^* increases. The number of links or edges between the mutational sites for CoMN is much larger than that for SMN, and similarly for the average degree of the nodes. As d^* increases, the diameter and the average path length of CoMN and SMN converge to 4 and 2, respectively.

Next, our goal is to capture the importance of HA sites by using the information extracted from the CoMN and SMN. An intuitive approach is to calculate the degree centralities for each node in the CoMN and the indegree and outdegree centrality of each node in the SMN. The first measure is highly benefitted from additional site-pairs extracted from a list of mutations observed at the nodes of the trees. Hence, a higher confidence about the structure of the CoMN could be obtained. The other two measures may provide insights into whether a mutation in a specific site of HA is strongly

Table 4: Statistical overview for co-mutational networks (CoMN) and sequential-mutational networks (SMN) for varying distance thresholds between ancestor and predecessor nodes associated with the site-pairs (d^*) used for reconstructing the networks.

Network	d*							
measurements	0.0011	0.0022	0.0033	0.0044	0.0055	0.0066	0.0077	0.0088
1. Connected componets (component with more than one node)								
CoMN	2	1	1	1	1	1	1	1
SMN	9	1	1	1	1	1	1	1
2. Nodes in the connected components								
CoMN	196	207	213	215	218	220	220	220
SMN	58	139	169	183	197	201	203	208
3. Edges								
CoMN	1446	1763	2108	2463	2889	3220	3600	3942
SMN	55	371	768	1141	1688	2122	2631	3090
4. Average degree								
CoMN	14.8	17.0	19.8	22.9	26.5	29.3	32.7	35.8
SMN	1.9	5.3	9.1	12.5	17.1	21.1	25.9	29.7
5. Network diameter								
CoMN	Inf.	7	6	5	4	4	4	4
SMN	Inf.	7	5	5	5	4	4	4
6. Average path length								
CoMN	Inf.	2.5	2.4	2.2	2.1	2.1	2.0	2.0
SMN	Inf.	3.2	2.7	2.5	2.4	2.2	2.1	2.1

under the influence of other mutations in other sites or could drive mutations in other sites over time.

The top 10 results from ranking the HA sites based on these three measurements for the same d^* values used in the previous section are highlighted in Table 5. The sites that frequently appear (>4 times) in the ranking group based on degree centrality from CoMN are of interest. Apparently, almost all sites in that ranking group occur frequently, and they are all located in the epitope area (epitope A: 137, 142, 144, 145; epitope B: 158, 189, 193; epitope D: 121, 226; and epitope E: 62). Four of these sites, i.e., 145, 158, 189, and 193, are out of seven sites (we missed sites 155, 156 and 159 from the top 10 sites) that has been experimentally shown to be responsible for influenza H3N2 antigenic cluster transitions [13]. Hence it would be interesting to investigate the significance of other sites at the top of our list but not yet experimentally tested. Further experiments may also be designed to confirm whether measuring the responsiveness of a site based on the indegree centrality and the influence of a site based on the outdegree centrality would help us to further understand the evolutionary mechanisms of the viruses. For the responsiveness, sites 45, 137, 138, 142, 145, 156, 193, 226, and 229 would be on the top of list for testing, while for the influence, the sites of interest will be 121, 135, 144, 156, 158, 172, 189, 262, and 276.

4 CONCLUSION AND FUTURE WORK

In this paper, we presented a novel method based on reconstructing and analyses of phylogenetic trees to uncover site-pairs that potentially co-mutate as well as determine the direction of their relationships. By rigorously taking into account the evolutionary structures in the sequence data by a resampling method, we could capture most of the HA sites of influenza H3N2 that are known to contribute to major antigenic changes of the virus. Moreover, the method could also uncover a directional relationship that has

Table 5: Top 10 sites ranked by degree centrality in CoMN (A) and indegree and outdegree centralities in SMN (B and C, respectively) for varying distance thresholds between ancestor and predecessor nodes associated with the site-pairs (d^*) used for reconstructing the networks. The sites appears >4 times in A and B are given light gray background, in A and C dark gray background, and in B or C but not in A black background.

		d^*							
	Ranking	0.0011	0.0022	0.0033	0.0044	0.0055	0.0066	0.0077	0.0088
A. Degree-centrality-based ranking	1	137	145	145	145	145	145	145	145
	2	145	137	62	193	62	144	189	62
	3	62	62	193	62	137	62	62	189
	4	142	121	121	137	193	137	144	144
	5	193	193	137	142	121	193	137	137
	6	155	189	142	121	189	189	193	193
	7	261	142	144	189	142	226	226	158
	8	121	158	158	144	144	156	156	156
	9	78	155	189	158	226	121	121	121
	10	189	275	276	226	135	142	158	226
		d^*							
	Ranking	0.0011	0.0022	0.0033	0.0044	0.0055	0.0066	0.0077	0.0088
B. Indegree-centrality-based ranking	1	3	226	145	145	145	145	145	145
	2	261	145	226	226	226	226	138	138
	3	275	137	142	45	229	229	226	226
	4	142	189	193	142	45	45	229	45
	5	144	193	45	229	142	142	45	142
	6	196	233	137	138	137	137	142	229
	7	213	45	138	193	138	138	144	137
	8	45	126	220	137	193	156	137	144
	9	50	159	156	156	156	121	53	193
	10	122	138	92	92	246	193	121	53
		d^*							
	Ranking	0.0011	0.0022	0.0033	0.0044	0.0055	0.0066	0.0077	0.0088
C. Outdegre-centrality-based ranking	1	144	144	144	144	144	144	144	144
	2	189	121	158	158	158	158	189	189
	3	213	158	121	121	62	189	158	158
	4	3	213	62	62	135	276	62	156
	5	62	62	156	156	189	62	124	62
	6	121	156	213	189	172	156	276	276
	7	142	3	276	135	156	135	156	145
	8	156	276	172	172	121	172	135	124
	9	158	262	262	3	262	262	172	172
	10	212	219	3	262	276	145	193	135

been demonstrated experimentally. These findings are quite encouraging and demonstrate the potency of the phylogenetic tree based method and analyses for uncovering the relationships between mutational sites in the proteins of influenza viruses or other rapidly evolving viruses. As part of future work, we aim to investigate the reliability of the method in capturing co-mutational and sequential-mutational site-pairs in the HA of influenza H1N1 and H5N1, and perform more rigorous network analyses on the co-mutational and sequential-mutational networks for those viruses.

ACKNOWLEDGMENTS

This project is supported by AcRF Tier 2 grant MOE2014-T2-2-023, Ministry of Education, Singapore.

REFERENCES

[1] J. J. Skehel and D. C. Wiley. Receptor binding and membrane fusion in virus entry: the influenza hemagglutinin. *Annu. Rev. Biochem.*, 69(1):531–569, 2000.

[2] J. Pu, J. Wang, Y. Zhang, G. Fu, Y. Bi, Y. Sun, and J. Liu. Synergism of co-mutation of two amino acid residues in NS1 protein increases the pathogenicity of influenza virus in mice. *Virus Res.*, 151(2):200–204, 2010.

[3] W. Zhu, Y. Zhu, K. Qin, Z. Yu, R. Gao, H. Yu, J. Zhou, and Y. Shu. Mutations in polymerase genes enhanced the virulence of 2009 pandemic H1N1 influenza virus in mice. *PloS one*, 7(3):e33383, 2012.

[4] A. S. Taft, M. Ozawa, A. Fitch, J. V. Depasse, P. J. Halfmann, L. Hill-Batorski, M. Hatta, T. C. Friedrich, T. J. Lopes, E. A. Maher, E. Ghedin, C. A. Macken, G. Neumann, and Y. Kawaoka. Identification of mammalian-adapting mutations in the polymerase complex of an avian H5N1 influenza virus. *Nat. Commun.*, 6:7491, 2015.

[5] W. S. Choi, Y. H. Baek, J. J. Kwon, J. H. Jeong, S. J. Park, Y. I. Kim, S. W. Yoon, J. Hwang, M. H. Kim, C. J. Kim, R. J. Webby, Y. K. Choi, and M. S. Song. Rapid acquisition of polymorphic virulence markers during adaptation of highly pathogenic avian influenza H5N8 virus in the mouse. *Sci. Rep.*, 7:40667, 2017.

[6] G. F. Rimmelzwaan, E. G. Berkhoff, N. J. Nieuwkoop, D. J. Smith, R. A. Fouchier, and A. D. Osterhaus. Full restoration of viral fitness by multiple compensatory co-mutations in the nucleoprotein of influenza A virus cytotoxic T-lymphocyte escape mutants. *J. Gen. Virol.*, 86(6):1801–1805, 2005.

[7] D. J. Smith, A. S. Lapedes, J. C. de Jong, T. M. Bestebroer, G. F. Rimmelzwaan, A. D. Osterhaus, and R. A. Fouchier. Mapping the antigenic and genetic evolution of influenza virus. *Science*, 305(5682):371–376, 2004.

[8] T. Bedford, M. A. Suchard, P. Lemey, G. Dudas, V. Gregory, A. J. Hay, J. W. McCauley, C. A. Russell, D. J. Smith, and A. Rambaut. Integrating influenza antigenic dynamics with molecular evolution. *Elife*, 3:e01914, 2014.

[9] A. C. Shih, T. C. Hsiao, M. S. Ho, and W. H. Li. Simultaneous amino acid substitutions at antigenic sites drive influenza A hemagglutinin evolution. *Proc. Natl. Acad. Sci. U S A*, 104(15):6283–6288, 2007.

[10] Z. Xia, G. Jin, J. Zhu, and R. Zhou. Using a mutual information-based site transition network to map the genetic evolution of influenza A/H3N2 virus. *Bioinformatics*, 25(18):2309–2317, 2009.

[11] X. Du, L. Dong, Y. Lan, Y. Peng, A. Wu, Y. Zhang, W. Huang, D. Wang, M. Wang, Y. Guo, Y. Shu, and T. Jiang. Mapping of H3N2 influenza antigenic evolution in China reveals a strategy for vaccine strain recommendation. *Nat. Commun.*, 3:709, 2012.

[12] H. Chen, X. Zhou, J. Zheng, and C. K. Kwoh. Rules of co-occurring mutations characterize the antigenic evolution of human influenza A/H3N2, A/H1N1 and B viruses. *BMC Med. Genomics*, 9(3):69, 2016.

[13] B. F. Koel, D. F. Burke, T. M. Bestebroer, S. van der Vliet, G. C. Zondag, G. Vervaet, E. Skepner, N. S. Lewis, M. I. Spronken, C. A. Russell, M. Y. Eropkin, A. C. Hurt, I. G. Barr, J. C. de Jong, G. F. Rimmelzwaan, A. D. Osterhaus, R. A. Fouchier, and D. J. Smith. Substitutions near the receptor binding site determine major antigenic change during influenza virus evolution. *Science*, 342(6161):976–979, 2013.

[14] Y. Bao, P. Bolotov, D. Dernovoy, B. Kiryutin, and T. Tatusova. FLAN: a web server for influenza virus genome annotation. *Nucleic Acids Res.*, 35(suppl_2):W280–W284, 2007.

[15] R. C. Edgar. MUSCLE: multiple sequence alignment with high accuracy and high throughput. *Nucleic Acids Res.*, 32(5):1792–1797, 2004.

[16] K. P. Schliep. phangorn: phylogenetic analysis in R. *Bioinformatics*, 27(4):592–593, 2011.

[17] M. I. Nelson and E. C. Holmes. The evolution of epidemic influenza. *Nat. Rev. Genet.*, 8(3):196–205, 2007.

[18] W. M. Fitch. Toward defining the course of evolution: minimum change for a specific tree topology. *Syst. Zool.*, 20(4):406–416, 1971.

[19] S. J. Sheather and M. C. Jones. A reliable data-based bandwidth selection method for kernel density estimation. *J. R. Stat. Soc. Ser. B*, 53:683–690, 1991.

[20] L. F. Costa, F. A. Rodrigues, G. Travieso, and P. R. V. Boas. Characterization of complex networks: A survey of measurements. *Adv. Phys.*, 56(1):167–242, 2007.

[21] E. M. Volz, K. Koelle, and T. Bedford. Viral phylodynamics. *PLoS Comput. Biol.*, 9(3):e1002947, 2013.

[22] H. Hayashida, H. Toh, R. Kikuno, and T. Miyata. Evolution of influenza virus genes. *Mol. Biol. Evol.*, 2(4):289–303, 1985.

[23] E. T. Muñoz and M. W. Deem. Epitope analysis for influenza vaccine design. *Vaccine*, 23(9):1144–1148, 2005.

[24] Y. P. Lin, X. Xiong, S. A. Wharton, S. R. Martin, P. J. Coombs, S. G. Vachieri, E. Christodoulou, P. A. Walker, J. Liu, J. J. Skehel, S. J. Gamblin, A. J. Hay, R. S. Daniels, and J. W. McCauley. Evolution of the receptor binding properties of the influenza A (H3N2) hemagglutinin. *Proc. Natl. Acad. Sci. U S A*, 109(52):21474–21479, 2012.

[25] G. N. Rogers, J. C. Paulson, R. S. Daniels, J. J. Skehel, I. A. Wilson, and D. C. Wiley. Single amino acid substitutions in influenza haemagglutinin change receptor binding specificity. *Nature*, 304(5921):76–78, 1983.

[26] G. A. Pavlopoulos, M. Secrier, C. N. Moschopoulos, T. G. Soldatos, S. Kossida, J. Aerts, R. Schneider, and P. G. Bagos. Using graph theory to analyze biological networks. *BioData Min.*, 4(1):10, 2011.

Mapping Free Text into MedDRA by Natural Language Processing: a Modular Approach in Designing and Evaluating Software Extensions

Margherita Zorzi
Department of Computer Science
University of Verona, Italy
margherita.zorzi@univr.it

Carlo Combi
Department of Computer Science
University of Verona, Italy
carlo.combi@univr.it

Gabriele Pozzani
Department of Diagnostics and Public Health
University of Verona, Italy
gabriele.pozzani@univr.it

Ugo Moretti
Department of Diagnostics and Public Health
University of Verona, Italy
ugo.moretti@univr.it

ABSTRACT

MagiCoder is a Natural Language Processing application designed to extract MedDRA terms from narrative clinical text. MagiCoder has been developed to support the work of people responsible for pharmacovigilance. Given a narrative description, MagiCoder proposes an automatic encoding; the pharmacologist reviews, (possibly) corrects, and then validates the solution. This drastically reduces the time needed for the validation of reports with respect to a completely manual encoding. In this paper we extend in a modular way and analyse MagiCoder, comparing its different new extensions. We designed a benchmark consisting of a representative set of adverse drug reaction reports that also includes long and badly written descriptions. We measured an average precision and recall of 68.74% and 70.19%, respectively. On descriptions up to 100 characters, both precision and recall exceeded 75%, i.e., 77.97% and 75.78%, respectively.

CCS CONCEPTS

•Information systems → Information extraction; Evaluation of retrieval results; •Applied computing → Health informatics;

KEYWORDS

Healthcare Informatics, Natural Language Processing, Pharmacovigilance

1 INTRODUCTION

Dictionaries are an essential tool in medical tasks as classification and standardisation and in general in clinical research. Main examples of medical dictionaries are MedDRA, a medical terminology used to encode adverse drug reaction information, ICD-9/10[1], the International Statistical Classification of Diseases and Related Health Problems, and SNOMED CT[2], a comprehensive, multilingual clinical healthcare terminology used in clinical documentation and reporting.

A typical research setting in which text annotation plays a crucial role is *pharmacovigilance*, which includes activities aimed to systematically study risks and benefits related to the use of marketed drugs. One of the main methods pharmacovigilance adopts in order to identify adverse drug reactions is spontaneous reporting [6]. Through spontaneous reporting, health care professionals, patients, and pharmaceutical companies can voluntarily send information about suspected adverse drug reactions (ADRs) to the national regulatory authority[3]. This irreplaceable activity provides early alerts and information about every marketed drug and every patient category.

As pointed out in [18], natural language is the most user friendly and expressive way for recording information. Thus, a free-text description is the best way to collect high-quality ADR descriptions. It is definitively simpler with respect to other solutions (based on a direct encoding with MedDRA terms by the reporter, e.g., by an autocompletion form or a menu) and it does not influence the reporter nor limit her expressiveness. Unfortunately, natural language text of spontaneous reports is completely unstructured. Qualified domain experts have to manually revise narrative descriptions and then encode texts according to MedDRA dictionary. The manual annotation of narrative documents with medical terminology is a subtle and expensive task, since the number of reports is increasing day-by-day and an expert possibly encodes hundreds of descriptions in a week. The work clearly becomes unbearable, also for short length reports. Moreover, in Italy, about 300 people (with possibly different experience) are responsible for encoding all Italian reports. The heterogeneity of people involved may lead to differences and inconsistences in encodings. Natural Language Processing (NLP) [13] applications can support this work and help

Permission to make digital or hard copies of all or part of this work for personal or classroom use is granted without fee provided that copies are not made or distributed for profit or commercial advantage and that copies bear this notice and the full citation on the first page. Copyrights for components of this work owned by others than ACM must be honored. Abstracting with credit is permitted. To copy otherwise, or republish, to post on servers or to redistribute to lists, requires prior specific permission and/or a fee. Request permissions from permissions@acm.org.
ACM-BCB'17, August 20-23, 2017, Boston, MA, USA.
© 2017 ACM. 978-1-4503-4722-8/17/08...$15.00
DOI: http://dx.doi.org/10.1145/3107411.3107431

[1]https://www.cdc.gov/nchs/icd/icd9.htm, https://www.cdc.gov/nchs/icd/icd10cm.htm
[2]http://www.snomed.org/snomed-ct
[3]in Italy, AIFA – Agenzia Italiana del FArmaco, http://www.agenziafarmaco.gov.it/

in reducing heterogeneity and inconsistences providing a common and shared encoding.

In [28] we proposed MagiCoder, an NLP algorithm and the related software tool, which automatically assigns one or more dictionary terms to a narrative text. MagiCoder has been first developed for supporting pharmacovigilance supervisors in using VigiFarmaco, a web application designed and implemented for the Italian pharmacovigilance[4]. MagiCoder provides reviewers with an initial automatic MedDRA encoding of ADR descriptions in the reports collected online by VigiFarmaco. Supervisors check the automatically proposed MedDRA terms and may correct or accept them. In this way, the encoding task, previously completely manual, becomes semi-automatic, reducing errors and the required time for accomplishing it. Although originally motivated only by pharmacovigilance needs, MagiCoder has been designed and implemented as an autonomous algorithm and software, usable in all contexts where terms from a dictionary have to be recognized in a free narrative text. With respect to other solutions already available in literature, MagiCoder has been designed to be efficient and unsupervised.

With respect to the version of MagiCoder proposed in [28], here we introduce several new modular extensions to improve the performances of our algorithm. Such extensions have been evaluated and compared in the domain of pharmacovigilance. More precisely, we designed a benchmark to automatically compare human and automatic solutions, based on a data set of 4500 ADR reports collected and manually annotated by experts during 2014 in Regione Veneto (Italy).

The remaining of the paper is organized as follows: in Section 2 we recall related work and some background notions about MedDRA; in Section 3 we describe MagiCoder main features and the different extensions of the software; Section 4 is devoted to the performances analysis of MagiCoder; finally, in Section 5 conclusions and future work are reported.

2 BACKGROUND AND RELATED WORK

Automatic detection of adverse drug reactions from text has recently received an increasing interest in pharmacovigilance research. Narrative descriptions of ADRs come from heterogeneous sources: electronic health records, spontaneous reporting, clinical reports, and social media. In [1, 9, 15] some NLP approaches have been proposed for the extraction of ADRs from text.

In [26] the authors collect narrative discharge summaries from the Clinical Information System at New York Presbyterian Hospital through the NLP system MedLEE[5]. The main aim of the study is to provide a framework for the development of systems which could potentially unveil drug safety profiles throughout their entire market life. The authors identify clinical events and pathologies, which could be potential adverse drug events. Co-occurrence based statistics are used to detect associations between the different types of entities, to calculate the strengths of the associations and support clinical decisions. Seven drugs with known ADRs are selected to evaluate the system. Overall recall and precision were 75% and 31% for known ADRs respectively.

A clear overview about the use of the MedLEE NLP system and statistical methods to automatically discover novel adverse drug events can be found in [7].

In [8] the authors report on the adaptation of a machine learning-based system for the identification and extraction of ADRs in case reports. The role of NLP approaches in optimised machine learning algorithms is also explored in [23], where the authors address the problem of automatic detection of ADR assertive text segments from several sources, focusing on data posted by users on Twitter and DailyStrength, a healthcare-oriented social media. In [27] the authors propose to use association mining and Proportional Reporting Ratio (PRR, a well-known pharmacovigilance statistical index) to mine the associations between drugs and adverse reactions from the user contributed content in social media. In [4] the authors develop an algorithm in order to help coders in the subtle task of auto-assigning ICD-9 codes to clinical narrative descriptions. In [2], authors use machine learning techniques to address the problem of extracting knowledge (e.g., relevant entities such as symptoms, diseases, and treatments) from clinical records written in Italian by physicians. Experiments performed on medical data provided in the context of a regional research project on technologies for health care[6], extending semi-automatically generated corpora and defining ad hoc new sets of annotated documents. In [22], authors evaluate the retrieval performance of an algorithm that automatically categorizes medical documents assigning an International Code of Disease (ICD). The algorithm is based on well-known information retrieval techniques, operates in a fully automatic mode, and requires no supervision or training data. Performances are evaluated on a data set of about 20k documents, and authors reveal the algorithm attains levels of average precision around the 70 – 80% range. In [25], some methods for automatically categorizing clinical documents are described and compared. The authors exploit the PALGA data set[7], a collection of 14 million pathological reports, each of which has been classified by a domain expert. In [20] Finite-State Transducers (FSTs, finite-state machines with a memory tape) are used to classify medical records (written in Spanish language) by their diagnostic terms according to the International Classification of Diseases Clinical Modification (ICD-9-CM) and SNOMED CT[8]. In [10] MEDSYNDIKATE is introduced, a natural language processor that couples grammatical knowledge, semantic knowledge, and conceptual (ontological) knowledge, and automatically acquires medical information from pathology-oriented clinical reports. Other related papers about pharmacovigilance and machine learning or data mining are [11, 18–20].

Let us now consider in some detail the medical terminology we specifically studied in this work. The Medical Dictionary for Regulatory Activities (MedDRA) [12] is a medical terminology used to encode adverse event information associated with the use of biopharmaceuticals and other medical products (e.g., medical devices and vaccines). MedDRA is available in eleven European languages,

[4] Available at https://www.vigifarmaco.it. Through VigiFarmaco, a spontaneous report can be filled out online by both healthcare professionals and citizens. VigiFarmaco provides support also to pharmacovigilance supervisors in reviewing and validating the reports. Finally, thanks to VigiFarmaco, pharmacologists can send reports (actually, XML files [5]) to AIFA by simply clicking a button.

[5] http://www.medlingmap.org/taxonomy/term/80

[6] http://progetto-ris.isti.cnr.it/

[7] http://www.palga.nl/en/public-pathology-database/

[8] http://www.snomed.org/snomed-ct

Chinese, and Japanese. MedDRA terms are organised into a hierarchy. The SOC (System Organ Classes) level includes the most general terms. The LLT (Low Level Terms) level includes more specific terminologies. Between SOC and LLT there are three intermediate levels (HLGT, HLT, and PT). Preferred Terms are Low Level Terms chosen to be the representative of a group of semantically equivalent terms. An example of the hierarchy is the following one: the reaction *Itch* (LLT) is described starting from *Skin disorders* (SOC), *Epidermal conditions* (HLGT), *Pruritus NEC* (HLT), and *Pruritus* (PT). Thanks to MedDRA it is possible to group similar/analogous cases described in different ways (e.g., by synonyms) or with different details/levels of abstraction. The encoding of ADRs through MedDRA is extremely important for report analysis as for a prompt detection of issues related to drug-based treatments.

3 THE NLP ALGORITHM MAGICODER

In [28] we introduced MagiCoder, an NLP algorithm specifically developed for the detection and the classification of free-text description of adverse drug reactions. The main idea of MagiCoder is that a single linear scan of the free-text is sufficient for recognizing MedDRA terms. From an abstract point of view, we try to recognize, in the narrative description, *single words* belonging to LLT terms, where recognised words do not necessarily occupy consecutive positions in the text. This way, we try to *"rebuild"* MedDRA terms, taking into account the fact that in a description the reporter can permute or omit words. MagiCoder does not involve computationally expensive tasks, such as subroutines for permutations and combinations of words. We distinguish five phases of the procedure.

(1) *Preprocessing of the original text.* We perform standard operations such as tokenization (segmentation of the text into syntactical units), elimination of irrelevant words, called *stop-words* (e.g., connectives, numeral adjective and words we know to be uninformative for the specific domain), and, possibly, stemming (reduction of words to their root form)[9].
(2) *Word-by-word linear scan* of the description and "voting task". A word "votes" LLT terms it belongs to. In the following, a voting word is called *voter*. For each term voted by one or more words, we store some information about the retrieved syntactical matching, such as relative position of voters in the original text and in the voted LLT.
(3) *Weights calculation.* Recognised terms (terms voted by at least one word of the text) are weighted according to information about the syntactical matching. Main weights (ordered by priority) are: coverage, i.e., the estimation of the percentage of the LLT recognised in the narrative description; kind of coverage, i.e., the recognition of a word in its non stemmed form receives a better evaluation; density, i.e., the "quality" of the coverage.
(4) *Sorting of voted terms.* Voted LLTs are (multi-valued) sorted by their weights.
(5) *Winning terms release.* A solution, a set of winning terms, is released. The main idea is that the procedure scans the list of ordered terms and try to "cover", as best as possible, the textual description.

The use of suitable data structures is central for MagiCoder efficiency. Data (description tokens, LLTs, and auxiliary information) are all arranged into direct access arrays. The MagiCoder abstract computational complexity is $O(mk)$ for the setting up phase (required only once when the tool starts) and $O(nm)$ for each encoding phase, where n is the input size (in terms of tokens), m is the size of the dictionary (the number of terms), and k is the length (in terms of tokens) of the longest term in the dictionary. An in-depth description of MagiCoder, its pseudocode and full complexity analysis can be found in [28, 30]. MagiCoder computational complexity is strongly related to the size of the considered dictionary. In Section 4.3 we discuss MagiCoder performances. In particular, we briefly focus on *effective* time performances of the procedure, showing that theoretical bounds are strongly pessimistic. This is due to the fact that, during the computation (the five phases described above), MagiCoder works on progressively smaller sub-sets of MedDRA terms. This drastically reduces computation time of (theoretically) expensive subroutines, such as the heuristics Maximality criterion and Relative position described in the following section (both requiring $O(nm)$ time units).

3.1 MagiCoder Extensions

We describe now the new modules of MagiCoder we designed and developed.

M - Maximality criterion. This is a heuristic criterion. Roughly speaking, we erase from the solution each term that can be considered "subset" of other ones (i.e., there exists another term, which extends it with further words).

IT - Exclusion of irrelevant dictionary terms. Some LLTs are irrelevant for the purpose of identifying ADRs (e.g., LLTs describing social conditions). Experts of the domain suggested a list of uninformative PTs. This module instructs MagiCoder to disregard all LLTs related to such PTs.

RP - Relative position criterion. Module RP introduces the order of words in the narrative description as a selection discriminating factor. From the set of selected LLTs, it removes those terms where voters (i.e., tokens in the original free text) appear in the ADR description in a relative order different from that of the corresponding voted tokens in the LLT. The criterion is applied only to LLTs which voters have voted also for other terms.

St - Stemmer. This extension introduces two different versions of stemming procedure. The first is based on Porter's algorithm [21]. Based on a list of predefined suffixes, it remove the last part of words. We call it "aggressive" (and we dub it aSt) because the suffix can involve more syllables. Using it, we note that the recognition of some Italian MedDRA terms is lost. In some sense, this stemming algorithm is too aggressive and, in some cases, counterintuitive. For example, the Italian adjective "psichiatrico" (in English, psichiatric) and its plural form "psichiatrici" have two

[9]In MagiCoder no part-of-speech analysis is performed. Even if speech tagging can be useful in clinical setting, we evaluate that it is not crucial in our case, since spontaneous reports are very informally written and there not exists a formal structure of phrases.

different stems, "psichiatr" and "psichiatric", respectively. Thus, in this case the stemmer fails in recognizing the singular and plural forms of the same word. The second stemmer is based on the algorithm in [24]. It can be considered as a "light" stemmer (and we dub it lSt) because it breaks off only the last letters of the last syllable. This induces a conservative approach and a uniform processing of the whole set of MedDRA words. This should be unsatisfactory for a general problem of text processing, but it is fruitful in our setting.

Syn - Addition of synonyms. Module Syn equips MagiCoder with a set of about 4500 synonyms of MedDRA terms (i.e., locutions semantically equivalent to the official ones). The additional lexicon has been generated in the following ways: a subset of terms has been automatically generated by considering some nouns that frequently occur in MedDRA, and their adjectival form. For each LLT containing one of these nouns (resp., adjectives) an equivalent term taking into account the corresponding adjective (resp., noun) is generated. Moreover, other terms can be easily obtained by replacing words in LLTs with frequently used abbreviations.

Another set of synonyms has been automatically generated with statistical methods for linguistics from a corpus of about 250k narrative ADR reports; this set has been successively validated by an expert of the domain, and finally added to the lexicon. The description of the latter methods for synonyms generation can be found in [29].

Moreover, we addressed three tricky cases. The first problem comes from the Italian MedDRA low level terms "epatite A" (10019618)" and "epatite E" (10019768) (in English, hepatitis A and hepatitis E, respectively). In Italian, letters *a* (a preposition) and *e* (a conjunction) are stopwords: by default, MagiCoder removes them and, processing "epatite A" and "epatite E", returns the more general LLT "epatite". These cases have been separately handled in order to return the more precise adverse reaction. The second and the third tricky cases are related to stemming. The plural of word *mano* (in English, *hand*) is *mani* (in English, *hands*), and their stemmed root is *man*, which is also the stem of *mania* (in English, *mania*). The LLT "Mania"(10026749) is returned whenever words "mano" or "mani" occur in a description and it is clearly a false positive. Similarly, reaction "Vaccinia" (10066048) (in English "Vaccinia") and word *vaccino* (in English, *vaccine*) have the same root and may cause false positives. False positives are a well-know accepted side effects of stemming processing. Notwithstanding we decided to manage these two cases since they frequently occur in narrative ADR descriptions. More precisely, word "mano/i" is very frequent and informative (a number of reports contain signals about suspected limb-related reactions); word *vaccino*, which generates false positive "vaccinia", is an uninformative word as it does not describe an ADR, but is habitually employed by users to describe the clinical scenario of the patient[10]. Notice that these three particular situations described above are related to the use of Italian, but similar cases can be found also in English and other languages.

P - Parent PT criterion. During the release of the solutions, the Parent PT criterion removes an LLT from the list of the winning terms if another term with the same PT already belongs to the solution.

D - Digits management. Digits (e.g., codes and numeral adjective) frequently occur in MedDRA. We try to improve MagiCoder behaviour by adding the capability to deal with digits (digits were treated as irrelevant information in previous versions).

All these extensions may be independently added to the basic version of MagiCoder, here dubbed B (see Figure 1(a)). No additional bases of knowledge or heuristic criteria are exploited in B.

Notice that features M, IT, RP, St, and D, have not been developed ad hoc for our particular setting. They are planly adaptable to the general problem of the text normalization into a (medical/technical) dictionary.

IT and PT are clearly related to the MedDRA structure. Syn requires some further comments. The handling of the three particular case is comprehensibly induced by the Italian language and the MedDRA terminology (but is not related to our specific data set). Moreover, in general, every set of synonyms has to be "tuned" to the particular language and to the technical terminology one tries to encode. The generation of synonyms we adopt is plainly adaptable to other languages and linguistic settings. This holds in particular for the semi-automatic generation proposed in [29], where the techniques we used also work for different languages and different technical terminology (see for example [3]).

4 PERFORMANCE ANALYSIS OF MAGICODER EXTENSIONS

A possible setting for evaluating performances of MagiCoder extensions is to add them one-by-one to B and then measure the increase (or decrease) of some metrics. Figure 1(b) depicts the versions of MagiCoder (and the extensions they involve) that we tested. We started including at least aSt because performances of B were too poor.

Performances are measured by two well-known metrics, namely *precision* and *recall*, both definable in terms of *false positive* (FP) and *false negative* (FN) errors, the two main kinds of error in binary classification [17]. In our setting, an FP error is the inopportune retrieval of a "wrong" LLT, i.e., a term that does not correctly encode the textual description. An FN error is the failure in the recognition of a "good" LLT, i.e., a term that effectively encodes (a part of) the narrative description and that would be selected by a human expert. As dual notions of false positive and false negative, one can define *correct* results, i.e., *true positive* (TP) and *true negative* (TN). In our case, a true positive is a correctly returned LLT, and a true negative is an LLT, which, correctly, is not recognized as a solution.

[10]The application VigiFarmaco offers a dedicated form to point out information such the delivery of vaccination. The narrative part of the spontaneous report should contain only ADR description.

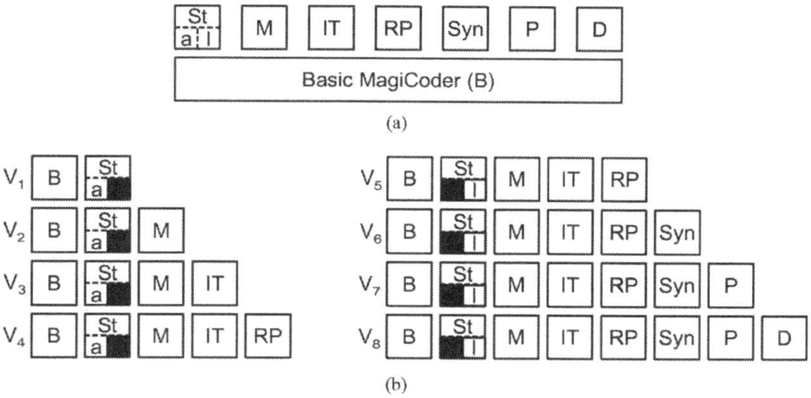

Figure 1: (a) MagiCoder extensions. (b) MagiCoder versions and extensions they involve.

Precision and recall are defined as $\frac{TP}{TP+FP}$ and $\frac{TP}{TP+FN}$, respectively. Informally, precision measures the portion of the returned results (i.e., LLTs) that is actually correct, while recall measures the portion of correct results (w.r.t. the gold reference standard) that is actually returned.

4.1 The Experiment

We exploited a corpus of formerly manually revised and annotated reports. MagiCoder and human solutions have been automatically compared.

The dataset includes 4500 ADR reports concerning Regione Veneto (Italy) from Vigisegn [16], a data warehouse system for the Italian pharmacovigilance activities. We divided reports in five classes according to their length: (0) from 0 to 20 characters (459 reports); (1) from 21 to 40 characters (1012 reports); (2) from 41 to 100 characters (1998 reports); (3) from 101 to 255 characters (1020 reports); (4) more than 255 characters (11 reports). Classes have been selected to reflect in the dataset the actual distribution of text lengths in the whole database. Reports have been manually annotated by pharmacovigilance experts. These manual revisions represent our *reference standard.*

To evaluate MagiCoder performances, we *automatically* compared the output provided by each MagiCoder version with the manual encoding of the ADR reports from the dataset. For each report, we checked which terms belong to both or only one of manual and automatic solutions, and then calculated errors and performance measures. Results are discussed in Section 4.2. It is worth noting that this test simply estimates how much, for each report, MagiCoder behaviour is similar to the manual one. It is *quantitative.* It is able to detect common retrieved terms and terms returned either by the human expert or by MagiCoder. Conversely, it is not able to fairly test *redundancy errors.* Human experts make some encoding choices in order to avoid repetitions. A term returned by MagiCoder that has not been selected by the expert because redundant should not be a false positive. For example, consider the following Vigisegn report (here translated in English): "anaphylactic shock (hypotension) 1 hour after taking the drug." MagiCoder returned both "anaphylactic shock" and "hypotension", while human experts did not encode "hypotension" since it is considered a well-known symptom of "anaphylactic shock". This suggests that we are probably underestimating MagiCoder performances. We know that this kind of semantic information can be extracted from suitable MedDRA ontologies. This is an interesting future work we plan to address to equip MagiCoder with further knowledge bases.

Table 1: MagiCoder overall performances

Version	avg PTs recall	avg PTs precision
V_1	65.88%	61.80%
V_2	65.68%	63.15%
V_3	66.45%	66.43%
V_4	66.17%	66.32%
V_5	66.74%	68.63%
V_6	68.56%	69.62%
V_7	68.75%	69.93%
V_8	68.74%	70.19%

4.2 Results

Table 1 summarises global average (avg) performances on all report descriptions, i.e., without regard to length-based classes, of the considered MagiCoder versions. Figure 2 depicts a graphical representation of the trend of precision and recall, respectively. Extensions involved in MagiCoder versions (from V_1 to V_8) are reported in Figure 1(b).

Results are computed considering terms at PT level, both for the human and the automatic encoding. By moving to PT level, instead of using the LLT level, we group together terms that represent the same medical concept (i.e., the same adverse reaction). In this way, we try to not consider as an error a case in which MagiCoder and the human expert use two different LLTs for representing the same adverse event. The use of the LLT level for reporting purposes and the PT level for analysis is suggested also by MedDRA [12]. As previously indicated, we adopt precision and recall as main statistical measures. Let us now analyze the changes in performances produced by the new features included in the different MagiCoder versions (see Figure 1(b)).

By moving from version V_1 to V_3, we observe a significant increase of the precision (+4.63%). In particular, the maximality criterion M (introduced in version V_2) increases precision from 61.8% to 63.15% (+1.35%), while the exclusion of irrelevant dictionary entries IT (introduced in version V_3) raises precision from 63.15% to 66.43% (+3.28%). In version V_3 we also observe a small increase of the recall (+0.57%).

In version V_4, MagiCoder experiences a little worsening of both recall (−0.28%) and precision (−0.11%). The Relative position criterion RP (main feature of version V_4) behaves well on medium-long descriptions (classes 2, 3, and 4), but does not have an observable good effect on shorter ones. As a consequence, at least on this dataset, global performances are negatively affected by the introduction of the feature. Notwithstanding, such criterion has been introduced in order to address critical and long narrative descriptions, and the worsening can be considered acceptable.

Version V_5 replaces module aSt with a different algorithm for word stemming, lSt. This has a clear effect on the precision (+2.31%), while the recall enjoys a smaller improvement, moving to 66.75% (+0.57%). We will comment on the crucial role of the stemming algorithm below, when we directly compare version V_6 with other different approaches to that problem (the stemming-free version V_6^- and the one including aSt module, V_6^a).

Extension Syn, i.e., the addition of a set of about 4500 synonymical LLTs plus the ad hoc management of "tricky cases" (*hepatithis, mania, and vaccinia*) in version V_6, has an expected visible effect on the recall. With respect to the previous version, we have a global improvement of 1.82%. Also precision enjoys a smaller but significant increase (+0.99%). As expected, an evident benefit can be observed for class 4, where the recall increases from 46.36% to 57.23% (+10.87%) and the precision increases from 49.7% to 61.06% (+11.36%).

In version V_7 the criterion P, returning at most one LLT for each parent PT, is introduced. This feature aims to heuristically avoid redundant solutions, since human experts try to exclude from the encoding overlapping medical concepts. Surprisingly, this feature has a negligible effect on both recall (+0.19%) and precision (+0.31%). Together with some domain experts, we carried out a careful qualitative analysis of the difference between human and automatic solutions. We observed that redundancy is not simply controlled by avoiding repeated PTs. Manual encoding praxis results in not encoding ADRs "implied" by other ones, while encoding, where it is present, only the pathology and not its symptoms. For example, if a narrative text reports *"influenza and fever"*, a pharmacovigilance expert possibly omits from the encoding the term "fever".

Version V_8 extends MagiCoder with the Digits Management module D: MedDRA terminology frequently contains codes, numerical classifications, and numerical acronyms. We observed a negligible worsening of the recall (−0.01%) and a small increase of the precision (+0.26%). These outcomes are related to the dataset we considered and have to be clarified. In MedDRA digits frequently occur, whereas in spontaneous reports the use of digits is often inappropriate. More precisely, description so much precise to contain digits occurring in MedDRA terms are very infrequent. Instead, long spontaneous reports frequently contain "numerical" information such as dates, hours, temperature. These numerical data are misleading for MagiCoder. It is not surprising that class 4 (more than 255 characters) highlights a decrease of both recall and precision. Nevertheless, this feature is potentially useful. For example, it can be used to define new important and frequent synonyms based on numerical values. For example, we may define the locution "febbre superiore a 39" (in English, "fever higher than 39") as synonym of the LLT "Hyperpyrexia".

Summing up, from version V_1 to version V_8, we measured an improvement of +2.86% for the recall and of +8.4% for the precision. Heuristics and improvements we introduced principally act on the precision, since the recall enjoys a good performance also in basic version V_1 and because, as discussed later in this section, precision is more important than recall in our setting.

It is worth noting that short-medium descriptions are easier to handle than the longer ones, which contain long, verbose, and (often) badly written text. On very short reports (class 0, up to 20 characters) MagiCoder reaches a recall of 88.62% and a precision of 90.1%. Taking into account the first three classes, i.e., considering descriptions up to 100 characters, both average precision and average recall exceed 75%. We measure a recall of 75.78% and a precision of 77.97%. Trends of recall and precision for class 2, the most densely populated class of the sample (1900 reports), retrace performances presented above. In version V_8 recall and precision are 64.43% and 66.64%, respectively.

On the basis of version V_6 we studied the effects of different approaches to the stemming problem. For Italian language, we identified four possibilities: (1) do not apply any stemmer, (2) use a stemmer based on Porter's algorithm [21] (that here we call "aggressive" stemmer), (3) use a stemmer based on the algorithm presented in [24] (that here we call "light" stemmer), and (4) use both aggressive and light stemmers.

The first case has been tested in version V_6^- that clearly presents the best performance in terms of precision (70.89%) and the worst in terms of recall (67.11%). Notice also that there is a considerable difference between the values of the two measures. Adding the "aggressive" stemmer in version V_6^a it improves the recall (67.77%), while precision decreases to 67.93%. Indeed, stemming, by improving the number of retrieved matches, introduces false positives. On average, the most satisfactory results can be achieved by adopting a "light" stemmer (case (3)) as in version V_6, which experiences a good increase in recall but a decrease in precision smaller than the aggressive one. We calculated a recall of 68.56% and a precision of 69.62%. Finally, we observed the behavior of the software with the combined use of different stemmers, case (4). This case leads to two possible approaches. In the first one, both light and aggressive stemmers are always used. A word, stemmed by using the two different algorithms may produce two different roots and then votes for different terms. As expected, solution results in higher recall (69.05%) and in decreasing of the precision (68.44%). In the second approach, we eventually apply the aggressive stemmer to a word only if the light one does not produce a root that votes for any dictionary term. This solution seems more cautious, and actually it leads to a smaller increase of recall (68.98%) and a comparable decrease of the precision (69.14%). Figure 3 summarizes recall and precision for all cited solutions.

As already mentioned, among all different possibilities we decided to use only the light stemmer. This is because of the pharmacovigilance application domain. As previously discussed, MagiCoder is used in VigiFarmaco for suggesting a MedDRA encoding of ADR descriptions. Each suggested encoding is then manually reviewed by an expert before confirm the ADR report and send it to the regulatory authority. In VigiFarmaco at most the first six LLTs suggested by MagiCoder are showed to the reviewer, while subsequent ones are discarded and omitted from the user interface. Thus, the presence of false positive errors, if ranked in the first positions, may induce VigiFarmaco to exclude correct LLTs. Moreover, considering the possibility to apply MagiCoder to ADR reports without a subsequent human manual review, pharmacovigilance experts we collaborate with suggested that precision (i.e., reduce false positive errors) is more important than recall (i.e., reduce false negative errors). Indeed, spontaneous ADR reports and their data are collected, aggregated, and analyzed looking for unexpected (w.r.t. already known reactions, severity, or frequency) ADRs. Thus, increasing precision, we aim to provide cleaner data. High quality data generates less false alarms and, as a consequence, experts can focus on really interesting cases.

4.3 MagiCoder computational performances analysis

Now we briefly analyse MagiCoder computational performances.

As discussed in Section 3 MagiCoder abstract computational complexity is $O(mk)$ for the preprocessing phase required only once when the tool starts, in order to build MagiCoder data structures, and $O(nm)$ for each encoding request, where n is the input size (in terms of tokens), m is the size of the dictionary (the number of terms), and k is the length (in terms of tokens) of the longest term in the dictionary. Let us consider the factor $O(nm)$. As previously said, MagiCoder is linear in the scanning of the text, which indeed requires $O(n)$ time units. The bound $O(nm)$ comes essentially from the weighting and heuristics phases.

These complexity bounds are strongly pessimistic. In fact, the Italian version of MedDRA includes 64223 different LLTs built upon about 17400 different words. The average number of characters in the descriptions set is 57.43 while the average number of tokens is 6.71, and the average number of voters (tokens that effectively vote one or more LLT) is only 1.04.

Voted terms (that are successively weighted and sorted) are, on average, 600, and this number is further reduced by modules IT and RP.

The average size of selected terms is 2.17 (2.04 after the application of heuristics M and PT). These heuristics are theoretically quite expensive in term of complexity ($O(nm)$), but, as the previous numbers show, MagiCoder actually works on a very small set of terms. Thus, the real computational complexity of MagiCoder can be rewritten as $O(n) + O(n'm')$. $n' \in O(n)$ represents the size of voters; it is n in the worst case, but it is drastically less than n (~ 1 in our sample) in concrete computations. $m' \in O(m)$ represents the size of voted terms. It is m in worst case, but as suggested by our experiment, it is very smaller in real applications. Finally, we report some statistics about MagiCoder execution time. Tests have been performed implementing MagiCoder in Ruby 2.3.0 (without a multi-processor/multi-thread support) on a desktop PC equipped with a CPU Intel® Core™ i5-4570 @ 3.2 GHz and running Ubuntu Linux 14.04.5. On average, MagiCoder required 2.77ms for encoding the reports in class 0, 5.61ms for reports in class 1, 12.43ms for reports in class 2, 25.72ms for reports in class 3, and 37.57ms for reports in class 4.

5 CONCLUSIONS AND FUTURE WORK

In this paper we evaluated the performances of MagiCoder, an NLP algorithm developed to support the manual encoding of narrative descriptions about ADRs into MedDRA terminology. We showed, step-by-step, how to improve the basic version of the tool, by the addition of heuristics and incremental features, following a modular approach. Our analysis proved how the different extensions act on MagiCoder performances, addressing specific problems coming either from NLP general tasks or from the healthcare terminology we are treating.

Moreover, we briefly focused on the effective execution time, providing some evidence about the efficiency of MagiCoder on a concrete dataset (about 4500 narrative description from spontaneous web reporting).

MagiCoder is an active and work in progress project. We are working both on the improvement of performances and on the definition of a more refined performance test. First, we are equipping MagiCoder with new knowledge bases and new heuristics. As previously said, we are enlarging the set of synonyms by developing and using statistical methods for linguistics. Some initial results can be found in [29]. To find significant synonyms and knowledge bases for Italian language is a non trivial task. Unfortunately, the Unified Medical Language System (UMLS) can not be directly used (there is no Italian version), and reality as National Library of Medicine Medical Subject Headings (MeSH) that includes an Italian section, is not really useful. Second, three "blind" domain experts (two reviewers plus one moderator) are manually revising *ex novo* a significant set of reports, in order to create a *gold reference standard*; the same experts are also comparing their solution with MagiCoder encoding, in order to provide a fair evaluation that will consider redundant term extraction as correct solution.

MagiCoder has been developed and tested for Italian Pharmacovigilance. We are interested to test MagiCoder also on English written narrative descriptions. Even if MagiCoder has been designed to be (as much as possible) independent on the language, knowledge bases and heuristics may be differently "specialized". Up to now, we tested MagiCoder on English language on a small dataset of summary of products characteristics provided by the European Medicines Agency (EMA)[11]. Initial results are promising: we claim we can quickly align MagiCoder performances on English texts to results measured in the experiment we designed and discussed in this work. Once we provided a satisfactory preliminary investigation about the performances of MagiCoder on English texts, we will equip the procedure with some initial heuristics and knowledge bases. We plan to test MagiCoder on the ADR corpus CADEC[12] [14]. This will permit us to compare MagiCoder with other similar software tools on a common dataset. This task

[11] http://www.ema.europa.eu/ema/

[12] Available at http://doi.org/10.4225/08/570FB102BDAD2

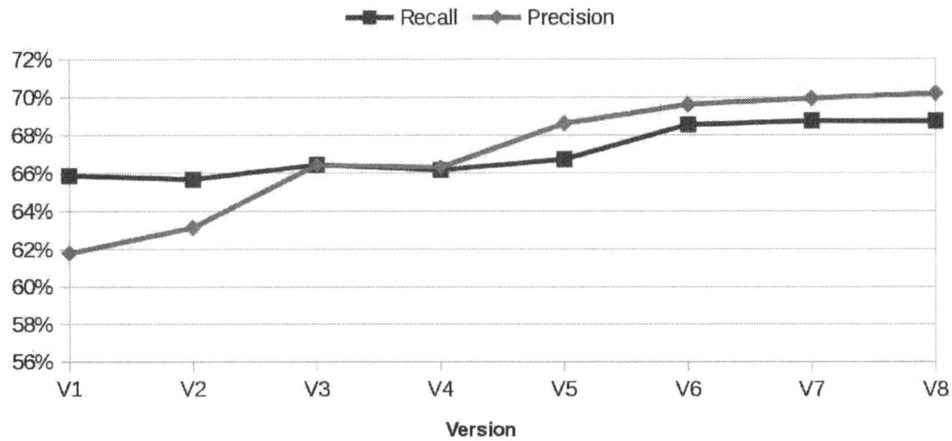

Figure 2: Global trend of recall and precision for MagiCoder

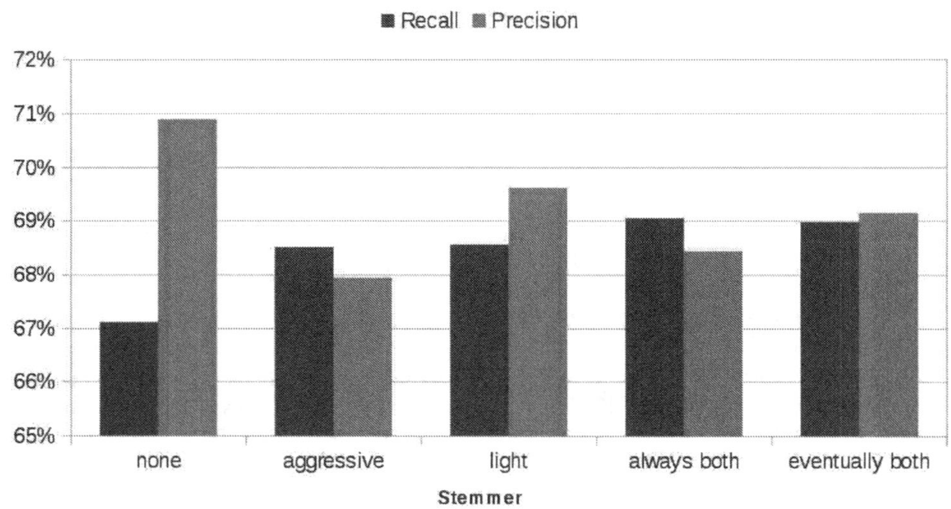

Figure 3: The effect of different stemmers on MagiCoder performances

is difficult for the Italian language, since in Italy clinical data are considered sensitive, difficultly achievable resources.

REFERENCES

[1] E. Aramaki, Y. Miura, M. Tonoike, T. Ohkuma, H. Masuichi, and K. Waki. 2010. Extraction of adverse drug effects from clinical records. *Stud Health Technol Inform* 160, Pt1 (2010), 739–743.

[2] Giuseppe Attardi, Vittoria Cozza, and Daniele Sartiano. 2015. Annotation and Extraction of Relations from Italian Medical Records. In *Proceedings of the 6th Italian Information Retrieval Workshop, Cagliari, Italy, May 25-26, 2015.*

[3] Marco Baroni and Sabrina Bisi. 2004. Using Cooccurrence Statistics and the Web to Discover Synonyms in a Technical Language. In *Proc. of LREC.* http://www.lrec-conf.org/proceedings/lrec2004/pdf/249.pdf

[4] Abe Coffman and Nat Wharton. 2007. Clinical Natural Language Processing: Auto-Assigning ICD-9 Codes. In *Overview of the Computational Medicine Center's 2007 Medical Natural Language Processing Challenge.*

[5] C. Combi, A. Masini, B. Oliboni, and M. Zorzi. 2015. A logical framework for XML reference specification. *Lecture Notes in Computer Science (including subseries Lecture Notes in Artificial Intelligence and Lecture Notes in Bioinformatics)* 9262 (2015), 258–267. DOI: https://doi.org/10.1007/978-3-319-22852-5_22

[6] European Medicines Agency 2014. *Guideline on good pharmacovigilance practices (GVP) - Module VI.* European Medicines Agency. EMA/873138/2011.

[7] Carol Friedman. 2009. Discovering Novel Adverse Drug Events Using Natural Language Processing and Mining of the Electronic Health Record. In *12th Conference on Artificial Intelligence in Medicine, AIME 2009 (LNCS)*, Vol. 5651. Springer, 1–5. DOI: https://doi.org/10.1007/978-3-642-02976-9_1

[8] H. Gurulingappa, A. Mateen-Rajput, and Luca Toldo. 2012. Extraction of potential adverse drug events from medical case reports. *J Biomed Semantics* 3, 15 (2012), 1–10.

[9] M. Gysbers, R. Reichley, P.M. Kilbridge, L. Noirot, R. Nagarajan, W.C. Dunagan, and T.C. Bailey. 2008. Natural language processing to identify adverse drug events. In *AMIA Annu Symp Proc.* 961.

[10] Udo Hahn, Martin Romacker, and Stefan Schulz. 2002. MEDSYNDAKATE natural language system for the extraction of medical information from findings reports. *International Journal of Medical Informatics* 67, 1 (2002), 63 – 74. DOI: https://doi.org/10.1016/S1386-5056(02)00053-9

[11] Rave Harpaz, Herbert S. Chase, and Carol Friedman. 2010. Mining multi-item drug adverse effect associations in spontaneous reporting systems. *BMC Bioinformatics* 11, S-9 (2010).

[12] ICH. 2017. MedDRA data retrieval and presentation: points to consider. (2017).

[13] D. Jurafsky and J. H. Martin. 2000. *Speech and language processing: an introduction to natural language processing, computational linguistics, and speech recognition*

(1st ed.). Prentice Hall PTR, Upper Saddle River, NJ, USA.

[14] Sarvnaz Karimi, Alejandro Metke-Jimenez, Madonna Kemp, and Chen Wang. 2015. CADEC: A corpus of adverse drug event annotations. *Journal of Biomedical Informatics* 55 (2015), 73–81. DOI: https://doi.org/10.1016/j.jbi.2015.03.010

[15] P. M. Kilbridge, L. A. Noirot, R. M. Reichley, and T. C. Bailey. 2009. Computerized Surveillance for Adverse Drug Events in a Pediatric Hospital. *J Am Med Inform Assoc.* 16, 5 (2009), 607–612.

[16] Riccardo Lora, Alberto Sabaini, Carlo Combi, and Ugo Moretti. Designing the Reconciled Schema for a Pharmacovigilance Data Warehouse Through a Temporally-enhanced ER Model. In *2012 Int. Workshop on Smart Health and Wellbeing (SHB 2012).* ACM, 17–24. DOI: https://doi.org/10.1145/2389707.2389711

[17] Christopher D. Manning, Prabhakar Raghavan, and Hinrich Schütze. 2008. *Introduction to Information Retrieval.* Cambridge University Press, New York, NY, USA.

[18] Stéphane Meystre and Peter J. Haug. 2006. Natural language processing to extract medical problems from electronic clinical documents: Performance evaluation. *J Biomed Inform* 39, 6 (2006), 589 – 599. DOI: https://doi.org/10.1016/j.jbi.2005.11.004

[19] N. Nissim, M. Boland, R. Moskovitch, N. Tatonetti, Y. Elovici, Y. Shahar, and G. Hripcsak. 2015. An Active Learning Framework for Efficient Condition Severity Classification. In *Artificial Intelligence in Medicine (AIME'15).* Lecture Notes in Computer Science, Vol. 9105. Springer, 13–24.

[20] Alicia Perez, Koldo Gojenola, Arantza Casillas, Maite Oronoz, and Arantza Diaz de Ilarraza. 2015. Computer aided classification of diagnostic terms in spanish. *Expert Systems with Applications* 42, 6 (2015), 2949 – 2958. DOI: https://doi.org/10.1016/j.eswa.2014.11.035

[21] Martin F Porter. 1980. An algorithm for suffix stripping. *Program* 14, 3 (1980), 130–137.

[22] Berthier Ribeiro-Neto, Alberto H.F. Laender, and Luciano R.S. de Lima. 2001. An experimental study in automatically categorizing medical documents. *Journal of the American Society for Information Science and Technology* 52, 5 (2001), 391–401. DOI: https://doi.org/10.1002/1532-2890(2001)9999:9999⟨::AID-ASI1083⟩3.0.CO;2-1

[23] A. Sarker and G. Gonzalez. 2015. Portable automatic text classification for adverse drug reaction detection via multi-corpus training. *J Biomed Inform* 53 (2015), 196–207.

[24] Jacques Savoy. 2001. *Report on CLEF-2001 Experiments.* Technical Report. Université de Neuchâtel, Switzerland.

[25] Janneke van der Zwaan, Erik Tjong Kim Sang, and Maarten de Rijke. 2007. *An Experiment in Automatic Classification of Pathological Reports.* Springer Berlin Heidelberg, Berlin, Heidelberg, 207–216. DOI: https://doi.org/10.1007/978-3-540-73599-1_28

[26] X. Wang, G. Hripcsak, M. Markatou, and C. Friedman. 2009. Active Computerized Pharmacovigilance Using Natural Language Processing, Statistics, and Electronic Health Records: A Feasibility Study. *J Am Med Inform Assoc.* 16, 3 (2009), 328–337.

[27] C. C. Yang, H. Yang, L. Jiang, and Mi. Zhang. Social media mining for drug safety signal detection. In *2012 Int. Workshop on Smart Health and Wellbeing, SHB 2012.* ACM, 33–40.

[28] Margherita Zorzi, Carlo Combi, Riccardo Lora, Marco Pagliarini, and Ugo Moretti. 2015. Automagically Encoding Adverse Drug Reactions in MedDRA. In *IEEE Int. Conference on Healthcare Informatics, ICHI 2015.* 90–99.

[29] Margherita Zorzi, Carlo Combi, Gabriele Pozzani, Elena Arzenton, and Ugo Moretti. 2017. A Co-occurrence Based MedDRA Terminology Generation: Some Preliminary Results. In *Proceedings of the 16th Conference on Artificial Intelligence in Medicine, AIME 2017 (Lecture Notes in Computer Science),* Vol. 10259. Springer, Vienna, Austria, 215–220. DOI: https://doi.org/10.1007/978-3-319-59758-4

[30] Margherita Zorzi, Carlo Combi, Gabriele Pozzani, Elena Arzenton, and Ugo Moretti. 2017. From narrative descriptions to MedDRA: automagically encoding adverse drug reactions. (2017), 1–38. Journal paper, submitted.

Dependency and AMR Embeddings for Drug-Drug Interaction Extraction from Biomedical Literature

Yanshan Wang
Mayo Clinic
200 1st ST SW
Rochester, MN 55902
wang.yanshan@mayo.edu

Sijia Liu
Mayo Clinic
200 1st ST SW
Rochester, MN 55902
liu.sijia@mayo.edu

Majid Rastegar-Mojarad
Mayo Clinic
200 1st ST SW
Rochester, MN 55902
mojarad.majid@mayo.edu

Liwei Wang
Mayo Clinic
200 1st ST SW
Rochester, MN 55902
wang.liwei@mayo.edu

Feichen Shen
Mayo Clinic
200 1st ST SW
Rochester, MN 55902
shen.feichen@mayo.edu

Fei Liu
University of Central Florida
4000 Central Florida Blvd
Orlando, FL 32816
feiliu@cs.ucf.edu

Hongfang Liu*
Mayo Clinic
200 1st ST SW
Rochester, MN 55902
liu.hongfang@mayo.edu

ABSTRACT

Drug-drug interaction (DDI) is an unexpected change in a drug's effect on the human body when the drug and a second drug are co-prescribed and taken together. As many DDIs are frequently reported in biomedical literature, it is important to mine DDI information from literature to keep DDI knowledge up to date. One of the SemEval challenges in the year 2011 and 2013 was designed to tackle the task where the best system achieved an F1 score of 0.80. In this paper, we propose to utilize dependency embeddings and Abstract Meaning Representation (AMR) embeddings as features for extracting DDIs. Our contribution is two-fold. First, we employed dependency embeddings, previously shown effective for sentence classification, for DDI extraction. The dependency embeddings incorporated structural syntactic contexts into the embeddings, which were not present in the conventional word embeddings. Second, we proposed a novel syntactic embedding approach using AMR. AMR aims to abstract away from syntactic idiosyncrasies and attempts to capture only the core meaning of a sentence, which could potentially improve DDI extraction from sentences. Two classifiers (Support Vector Machine and Random Forest) taking these embedding features as input were evaluated on the DDIExtraction 2013 challenge corpus. The experimental results show the effectiveness of dependency and AMR embeddings in the DDI extraction task. The best performance was obtained by combining word, dependency and AMR embeddings (F1 score=0.84).

*Corresponding author.

Permission to make digital or hard copies of all or part of this work for personal or classroom use is granted without fee provided that copies are not made or distributed for profit or commercial advantage and that copies bear this notice and the full citation on the first page. Copyrights for components of this work owned by others than ACM must be honored. Abstracting with credit is permitted. To copy otherwise, or republish, to post on servers or to redistribute to lists, requires prior specific permission and/or a fee. Request permissions from permissions@acm.org.
ACM-BCB'17, August 20–23, 2017, Boston, MA, USA.
© 2017 ACM. ISBN 978-1-4503-4722-8/17/08...$15.00
DOI: http://dx.doi.org/10.1145/3107411.3107426

CCS CONCEPTS

• **Computing methodologies → Knowledge representation and reasoning**; *Supervised learning by classification*; • **Applied computing** → *Life and medical sciences*;

KEYWORDS

drug-drug interaction; embeddings; dependency; abstract meaning representation; deep learning

1 INTRODUCTION

According to a recent study, medical error has become the third most common cause of death in the United States [27]. A literature review estimated a range of 210,000-400,000 deaths a year was associated with medical errors among hospital patients [17]. Medication error is one of the primary medical errors due to drug-drug interactions (DDIs) [12, 24, 34]. DDI is an unexpected change in a drug's effect on the human body when the drug and a second drug are co-prescribed and taken together. As a matter of fact, many such errors are preventable adverse drug events (ADEs) [30]. In one study at six hospitals, 75% of ADEs were preventable [16]. As a result, detecting DDIs has been crucial in health safety, which may dramatically reduce drug-related harms.

As noted by the Institute of Medicine, a lack of drug knowledge is one of the most frequent proximal causes of medication errors [10]. To enrich the drug knowledge, a number of drug databases, such as DrugBank[1] [21], DailyMed[2], Stockley's Drug Interactions [3],

[1]https://www.drugbank.ca/
[2]https://dailymed.nlm.nih.gov/

National Drug File[3], and WebMD[4], have been initiated. However, there still exists a large amount of hidden DDI information in the vastness of the textual biomedical literature. As the volume of the published literature grows rapidly and greatly, it is challenging and time-consuming to extract DDIs manually. Therefore, automatically extracting DDI information from literature remains an important research topic.

To accelerate the research on automatic DDI extraction, the shared task challenges for DDI extraction were organized in 2011 (DDIExtraction 2011) [37] and 2013 (DDIExtraction 2013) [36]. Many participating systems utilized identical classification models, like Support Vector machines (SVMs) [9, 33, 39]. However, the performance of these systems is highly dependent on feature engineering, and a variety of features has been adopted in each of these systems.

Recently, deep learning has been widely utilized as a feature representation method since it can transform the raw data (such as the pixel values of an image or words in a textual document) into a high level representation or feature vector [22]. Word embeddings are one of the most successful cases in deep learning that can capture high level semantic properties of words. However, the standard word embeddings ignore syntax information. Dependency embeddings have been proposed. For example, Levy and Goldberg [23] proposed dependency-based embeddings (dependency embeddings) that incorporate structural syntactic contexts into the embeddings. A study by Komninos et al. [20] shows that these structural information contributes positively to sentence classifiers. However, dependency embeddings have not been utilized in DDI extraction to the best of our knowledge.

Unlike a dependency-based representation of a sentence, Abstract Meaning Representation (AMR) is a semantic formalism that expresses the logical meanings of English sentences in the form of a directed, acyclic graph [2]. AMR aims to abstract away from syntactic idiosyncrasies and attempts to capture only the core meaning of a sentence. Thus, embeddings based on AMR could encode more information from the sentence, such as semantic roles, named entities, and co-reference information, which is important for DDI extraction. However, we cannot find any study of encoding AMR into embeddings.

In this paper, we utilize dependency and AMR embeddings as features for DDI extraction. We evaluate these embeddings on DDIExtraction 2013 challenge corpus with two different classification methods: SVM and Random Forest. We compare the performance of using different embeddings in a baseline method. The experimental results show that both dependency and AMR embeddings are effective in extracting DDIs. The best performance was obtained by using word, dependency and AMR embeddings.

The paper is organized as follows. In the next section, we briefly introduce the related work of used features for DDI extraction in the literature. In Section 3, we describe the proposed methods for DDI extraction. Experiments and results are reported in Section 4, followed by discussion and conclusion in Sections 5 and 6, respectively.

[3]https://www.pbm.va.gov/NationalFormulary.asp

[4]http://www.webmd.com/

2 RELATED WORK

Since many drug interactions are frequently reported in biomedical literature, Segura et al. [36, 37] organized the DDI extraction challenge tasks in 2011 and 2013 to stimulate research in developing automatic information extraction tools for DDI extraction from literature. The datasets for DDIExtraction 2011 were composed of sentences describing DDIs from the DrugBank database and another dataset including MedLine abstracts was added to DDIExtraction 2013. In the datasets, drug entities and DDIs were annotated at the sentence level and each sentence could contain two or more drugs. There are two subtasks considered, one is to extract DDI drug pairs and the second is to classify the pairs to different DDI types. In this paper, we focused on the first task and utilized the datasets of DDIExtraction 2013.

The top systems in DDIExtraction 2013 utilized diverse features for their classifiers. The system with the highest F1 score (0.80) was proposed by the FBK-irst team [9]. They used shallow linguistic and contextual features to train a binary SVM classifier. The shallow linguistic features include features generated from shallow linguistic processing, such as tokenization, sentence splitting, Part-of-Speech (PoS) tagging and lemmatization [14]. The contextual features are a set of heterogeneous features related to the context of drug entities. The second best system proposed by Rocktaschel et al. [35] investigated the usage of domain-specific features based on handcrafted rules and domain-dependent dictionaries. Bokharaeian and Diaz [7] utilized 49 features, including lexical, morphosyntactic, conjunction, verbs, negation and parse tree features, in their SVM and achieved an F1 score of 0.66. Similarly, Bobic et al. [6] also used lexical features, dependency-based features and semantic features. Björne et al.[5] used The Turku Event Extraction System (TEES), an open source relation extraction system leveraging dependency features, and achieved an F1 score of 0.60. However, the features used in these systems require extensive human efforts to engineer and extract and are usually specific to the datasets.

Representation learning methods, inspired by deep neural network models, transform discrete symbols into representations (usually dense vectors) at higher and abstract level. Word embedding is a word representation that captures semantic and syntactic similarities between words. It has been widely utilized for a variety of tasks, such as sentence classification [42], relation classification [41], and sentiment analysis [38], since the introduction of word2vec software. For DDI extraction from biomedical literature, word embeddings have also drawn researchers' attention recently. Liu et al. [26] deployed word embeddings in a convolutional neural network (CNN) for the DDI classification task (F1 score=0.70). Zhao et al. [43] utilized word embeddings in a syntax convolutional neural network (SCNN) by changing the input of word2vec to the word sequences on the shortest path in the predicate argument sentence structure to extract DDIs (F1 score=0.78). Both systems achieved promising performance. In addition to word embeddings, dependency embeddings exhibit more functional similarity than word embeddings [23] and outperform standard word embeddings for sentence classification tasks [20]. However, dependency embeddings have not been employed for DDI extraction, to the best of our knowledge.

Linguistically, AMR is similar to the dependency structure of a sentence where both describe relations between a head and a child [40]. On the other hand, AMR generally represents function words as relations or omits them if they have no contribution to the sentence. It utilizes multi-layer linguistic analyses including PropBank frames, non-core semantic roles, coreference, named entity annotation, modality, and negation to represent the semantic structure of a sentence and abstracts away its syntax form [15]. The nodes in AMR are entities instead of words, and the edge types are much more fine-grained. Therefore, compared to the conventional dependency parsing, AMR captures deeper and more semantic meaning [25]. However, AMR parse graphs have not been utilized in training embeddings for classification tasks in the literature. Our hypothesis is that AMR-based embeddings might be more informative for DDI extraction than dependency embeddings as AMR could capture syntactic, semantic and abstractive information.

3 METHODS

In this section, we first elaborate the embedding methods, including word embeddings, dependency embeddings, and AMR embeddings, and then briefly introduce the classifiers utilized for DDI extraction, including SVM, and Random Forest.

3.1 Embedding Methods

3.1.1 Word Embeddings. We utilized skipgram model [28, 29], a popular method of learning word embeddings by predicting context words occurring in a window around a target word. Suppose that given a target word w_t and its context word h, the goal of skipgram model is to maximize the log-likelihood on the training data, i.e.,

$$J = \log P(h|w_t). \tag{1}$$

$P(h|w_t)$ is the conditional probability in the neural probabilistic language model [4], which is usually defined as:

$$P(h|w_t) = \sigma(score(w_t,h)) \quad = \frac{e^{score(w_t,h)}}{\sum_{w' \in V} e^{score(w',h)}} \tag{2}$$

where V represents the vocabulary list, $score(w_t,h)$ the compatibility score between w_t and h and $\sigma(z_j) = \frac{e^{z_j}}{\sum_{k=1}^{K} e^{z_k}}, j = 1,2,...,K$ a softmax function that normalizes a K-dimensional real vector into a K-dimensional real vector with summation of all elements equaling to 1. Accordingly, the log-likelihood can be written as:

$$J = score(w_t,h) - \log(\sum_{w' \in V} e^{score(w',h)}). \tag{3}$$

In order to avoid expensive computation of softmax for the whole vocabulary, negative sampling is commonly adopted in the learning algorithm. Then the objective function becomes:

$$J' = \sum_{w_t,h \in D} \log Q_\theta(D = 1|w_t,h) + \sum_{w_t,h \in D'} \log Q_\theta(D = 0|w_t,h), \tag{4}$$

where D is the observed data, D' the unobserved data, θ the embeddings, $Q_\theta(D = 1|w_t,h)$ is the probability of w_t and h being observed and $Q_\theta(D = 0|w_t,h)$ is the probability not being observed. Since the objective function is concave, the embeddings can be learned by setting the derivative of the objective function to 0 with respect to θ, i.e., $\frac{\partial}{\partial \theta}J' = 0$, and using stochastic gradient descent on the training data batches.

As shown by previous studies [18, 33], the neighboring words (i.e., contexts) of target drug entities capture repetitive expression patterns for classifying DDIs. Since the DDI is defined for a pair of drugs in a sentence, we created a feature vector x_w for each drug entity pair by using its associated word context embeddings, i.e.,

$$x_w = \frac{1}{C}\sum_{c}^{C}\theta_c^{e1} \oplus \frac{1}{C'}\sum_{c}^{C'}\theta_c^{e2} \tag{5}$$

where θ_c^{e1} denotes the embeddings for the context word c of drug entity $e1$, θ_c^{e2} is the embeddings for the context word c of drug entity $e2$, C and C' are the number of context words for drug entities $e1$ and $e2$, respectively, and $\oplus$ is the concatenation operator. The reason of selecting the concatenation operator is that Komninos and Manandhar [20] verified its superiority over the linear combination of embeddings.

3.1.2 Dependency Embeddings. Unlike the conventional skipgram embedding model in which the context h of a target word w_t is the words surrounding it in a window, the dependency skipgram model[20, 23] considers w_t's syntactic context (denoted as h_d) in the dependency graph.

Figure 1 illustrates an example showing the word contexts and dependency contexts for the sentence "Acarbose might have a potential side effect when it is given with metformin." As we can see, the dependency contexts include discrete symbols representing syntactically connected words and the dependency relations in a dependency parse graph. For example, *nsubj_inv_have* is a dependency context for target word "acarbose", where "inv" denotes the reverse relation. Here we only consider the dependency contexts within distance one in the graph. Algorithm 1 shows the steps for generating the dependency contextscontexts for a target word.

Training the dependency skipgram model is similar to training the conventional skipgram except that embeddings (θ_d) are optimized to predict the target word's dependency contexts, i.e.,

$$\begin{aligned} \arg\max_{\theta_d} J' = \arg\max_{\theta_d} & \sum_{w_t,h_d \in D} \log Q_{\theta_d}(D = 1|w_t,h_d) \\ & + \sum_{w_t,h_d \in D'} Q_{\theta_d}(D = 0|w_t,h_d). \end{aligned} \tag{6}$$

The dependency feature vector x_d for a pair of drug entities can be written as:

$$x_d = \frac{1}{T}\sum_{t}^{T}\theta_t^{e1} \oplus \frac{1}{T'}\sum_{t}^{T'}\theta_t^{e2} \tag{7}$$

where θ_t^{e1} denotes the dependency embeddings for drug entity $e1$'s dependency context t, and T and T' are the number of dependency contexts for drug entities $e1$ and $e2$, respectively.

3.1.3 AMR Embeddings. Since AMR provides a whole-sentence semantic representation [25], it could capture long-range dependencies among constituent words in a sentence. As shown in Figure 1, the AMR graph for the example sentence is an abstractive representation of the semantic meaning in the sentence. The key word "effect" reflecting the DDI between "acarbose" and "metformin" is an AMR context for "acarbose" (i.e., "ARG1_inv_effect") whereas

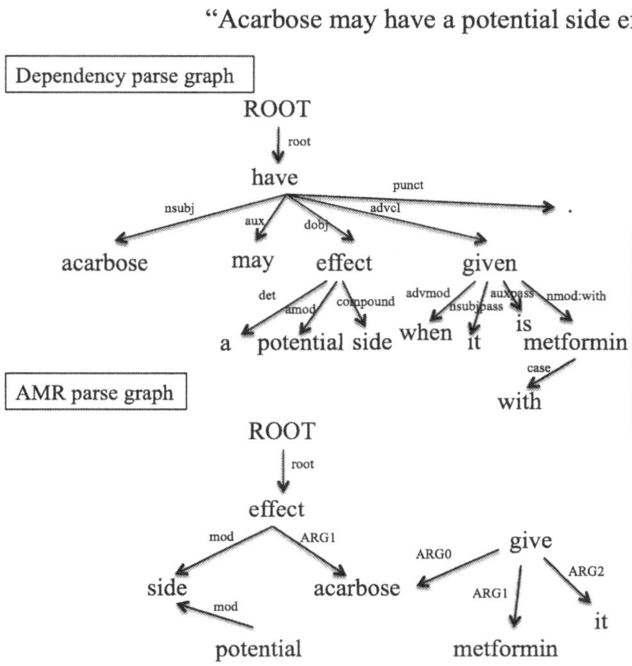

	"acarbose"	"metformin"
Word contexts	may, have, a, potential, side	when, it, is, given, with
Dependency contexts	nsubj_inv_have	case_with, nmod:with_inv_given
AMR contexts	ARG1_inv_effect, ARG0_inv_give	ARG1_inv_give

Figure 1: An example of word contexts, dependency contexts, and AMR contexts for a sentence with drug-drug interactions.

Algorithm 1 Generation of dependency contexts.

Require: dependency dep(head, child)
for target word i in a sentence **do**
  for word i's child **do**
    add dep_child to word i's dependency contexts
  end for
  for word i's head **do**
    add dep_inv_head to word i's dependency contexts
  end for
  return dependency contexts for word i.
end for

neither word contexts nor dependency contexts capture this information.

In our framework, we first parse DDI sentences into AMR graphs, generate the AMR contexts for each target word, and then input the target word and the corresponding AMR contexts into the skigram model. In the first step, we use JAMR [13], a statistical semantic parser trained on AMR bank, for AMR parsing. Similar to many other statistical parsing methods, JAMR also significantly depends on the training data [31]. Considering that many drug names are rarely appeared in the AMR bank and that the contexts of drug entities are crucial for detecting drug-drug relation instead of drug entities themselves, we replace "drug" with "medication", drug entities with "drug" and run the AMR parsing algorithm. Then, after AMR parsing we restore the drug entities and "drug". By doing so, we could parse the drug entities correctly without losing any drug information. Figure 2 shows the procedure of generating AMR contexts for the example sentence.

After obtaining the AMR contexts, we utilize the dependency skipgram model to learn the AMR embeddings and define AMR embeddings feature vector x_a for a pair of drug entities as:

$$x_a = \frac{1}{M}\sum_m^M \theta_m^{e1} \oplus \frac{1}{M'}\sum_m^{M'} \theta_m^{e2} \tag{8}$$

where θ_m^{e1} denotes the AMR embeddings for the AMR context m of drug entity $e1$, and M and M' are the number of AMR contexts for drug entities $e1$ and $e2$, respectively.

3.2 Classification Methods

As mentioned in Section 2, we focus on the DDI extraction for each drug-drug pair. For a given drug pair, we use binary classifiers to detect whether the drug pair has interactions (positive) or not (negative). In this section, we elaborate two classifiers used for this DDI extraction task: SVM and Random Forest.

3.2.1 Support Vector Machines. Given the embedding feature vector x_i of the ith drug entity pair in the training data, we train a linear SVM for detecting DDIs in the testing data. We denote $y_i = 1$ if the interaction of drug entity pair is positive and $y_i = -1$ otherwise. Then the cost function can be written as

$$\min_{w,b} \frac{1}{2} w^T w + C \sum_i^N \max(1 - y_i(w^T x_i + b, 0)). \tag{9}$$

For the drug pair in the testing data with embedding feature vector $\tilde{x}$, the prediction of DDI is defined by the decision function:

$$\tilde{y} = \mathrm{sgn}(w^T \tilde{x} + b). \tag{10}$$

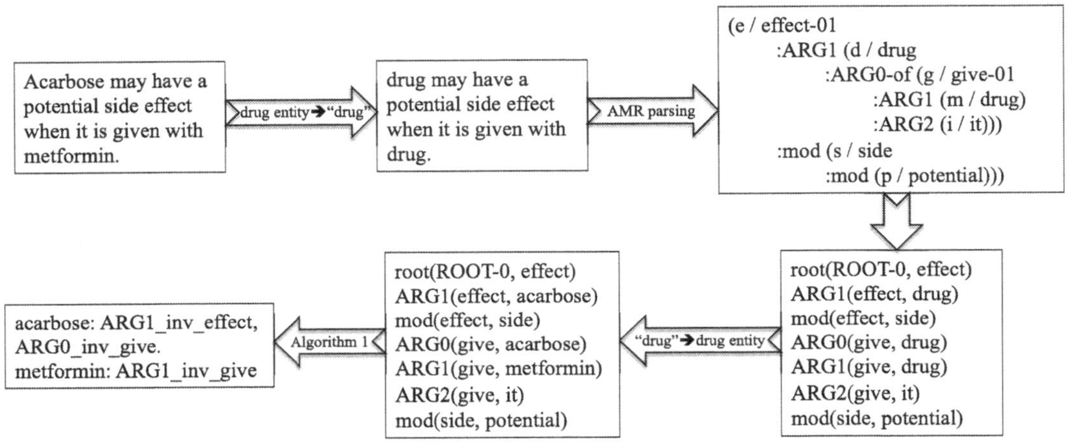

Figure 2: An example of generating AMR contexts.

3.2.2 Random Forest. Random Forest is an ensemble of classification trees, where each tree contributes with a single vote for the assignment of the most frequent class to the input data [8]. Compared to other classifiers, Random Forest usually has high classification accuracy and ability to model complex interactions among input variables. In training, Random Forest creates multiple trees by bootstrap aggregating from the original training data on each drug pair, and splits each node by searching across a randomly selected subset of the input variables. For classification of the unseen embedding feature vector $\tilde{x}$, the prediction of DDI is made by averaging the predictions from all the individual regression trees on $\tilde{x}$:

$$\tilde{y} = \frac{1}{B}\sum_{b=1}^{B} f_b(\tilde{x}). \tag{11}$$

where B is the number of trees and f_b is a trained decision tree at bth step.

4 EXPERIMENTS

The proposed methods were evaluated on the DDI corpus provided by the DDIExtraction 2013 challenge. The corpus contains 142 MedLine abstracts on the subject of DDIs, and 572 documents from the DrugBank database. There are a total of 6976 sentences with annotated drug entities and DDIs. The corpus was randomly split by the organizer into training dataset (77%) and testing dataset (23%). 17.2% of all possible drug pairs are positive pairs, while the rest are negatives. In our problem setting, we assume that all drug entities are provided. Our goal is to detect whether a given drug pair in a sentence has interactions or not. We trained the embeddings on the entire corpus. Using labels in the training dataset and embedding features, we trained the classifiers with 10-fold cross-validation and then evaluated the methods on the testing dataset.

The features used in the baseline method include words and word bigrams with binary values indicating their presence or absence in a sentence, cosine similarity between centroid vector of each class and the instance, negation (three features indicating negation before the first main drug, between two main drugs, and after the two main drugs), and mutual information. Detailed information about these features can be found in [33] and [32].

Let the baseline feature vector for a drug entity pair be x_0. For the same drug entity pair, we calculate word embeddings x_w, dependency embeddings x_d, and AMR embeddings x_a according to Equations 5, 7 and 8, respectively. We compare the results using Baseline (i.e., x_0), Baseline + WordEmbeddings (i.e., $x_0 \oplus x_w$), Baseline + DepEmbeddings (i.e., $x_0 \oplus x_d$), Baseline + AMREmbeddings (i.e., $x_0 \oplus x_a$), Baseline + WordEmbeddings + DepEmbeddings (i.e., $x_0 \oplus x_w \oplus x_d$), Baseline + WordEmbeddings + DepEmbeddings + AMREmbeddings (i.e., $x_0 \oplus x_w \oplus x_d \oplus x_a$). A DDI is considered to be correctly detected only if the system is able to assign the correct prediction label (positive vs. negative) to the candidate drug entity pair. The evaluation is drug-drug relation oriented and based on the micro-average F1 score of both classes.

Appropriate preprocessing could enhance the final performance. Since numbers (digits) occurred frequently in the corpus, we replaced all the digits with "7". Then all tokens were converted to lowercase. For AMR parsing, an additional preprocessing step is the replacement of drug entities with "drug", as shown in Figure 2, due to the fact that many drug names are not in the AMR vocabulary. Note that we used a special symbol to replace "drug" if it appears in the original text before this additional preprocessing and restored "drug" after AMR parsing.

Stanford CoreNLP[5] tools were employed to obtain dependencies and JAMR[6] was used for AMR parsing. We utilized the modified word2vec implementation [20] to generate the dependency and AMR embeddings. The negative-sampling parameter was set to 15, and the dimension of embeddings was set to 100. The machine learning library Scikit-learn[7] 0.18.1 was used for the binary label classification of positive and negative DDI pairs. For SVM, we tried a series of C values, and utilized the optimal value C=0.10. For Random Forest, the number of estimators was tuned and set at the optimal value of 40.

[5] https://stanfordnlp.github.io/CoreNLP/
[6] https://github.com/jflanigan/jamr
[7] http://scikit-learn.org/stable/index.html

Table 1: F1 score on the DDIExtraction 2013 test dataset.

	DrugBank (5265 pairs)		MedLine (451 pairs)		Total (5716 pairs)	
Embeddings	SVM	Random Forest	SVM	Random Forest	SVM	Random Forest
Baseline	0.66	0.59	**0.69**	0.69	0.74	0.76
Baseline+WordEmbeddings	0.73 (+11%)	0.84 (+42%)	0.68 (-1%)	0.70 (+1%)	0.77 (+4%)	0.81 (+7%)
Baseline+DepEmbeddings	0.68 (+3%)	0.84 (+42%)	0.62 (-10%)	**0.72** (+4%)	0.77 (+4%)	0.83 (+9%)
Baseline+AMREmbeddings	0.64 (-3%)	0.82 (+39%)	0.67 (-3%)	0.70 (+1%)	0.77 (+4%)	0.82 (+8%)
Baseline+WordEmbeddings+DepEmbeddings	0.74 (+12%)	0.85 (+44%)	**0.69** (+0%)	**0.72** (+4%)	**0.79** (+7%)	0.83 (+9%)
Baseline+WordEmbeddings+DepEmbeddings+AMREmbeddings	**0.75** (+14%)	**0.86** (+46%)	**0.69** (+0%)	**0.72** (+4%)	0.78 (+5%)	**0.84** (+11%)
Kim et al. [18]	0.80		0.47		0.78	
FBK-irst [9]	0.83		0.53		0.80	
SCNN [43]	–		–		0.78	

The F1 scores of methods are listed in Table 1. As shown in the table, the best performance measures are achieved by Random Forest utilizing baseline and three embedding features together with an F1 score of 0.86 for DrugBank, 0.72 for MedLine, and 0.84 overall. We observe that adding any of three embedding features improves the baseline performance. For DrugBank, Baseline + DepEmbeddings is comparative with Baseline + WordEmbeddings and superior to Baseline + AMREmbeddings when Random Forest classifier is used. For MedLine, Baseline + DepEmbeddings performs the best when only one embedding feature is considered. Though the results of Baseline + AMREmbeddings are similar to those of Baseline + WordEmbeddings and inferior to those of Baseline + DepEmbeddings, adding AMR embeddings always improves the performance when Random Forest classifier is used. It means that AMR embeddings contain alternative useful information for DDI extraction. Compared with the state-of-the-art systems, including the best existing system (FBK-irst [9]) and CNN-based system (SCNN [43]), the proposed method shows better performance.

5 DISCUSSION

Our experiment shows that dependency and AMR embeddings provide valuable information for DDI extraction thus the performance improves when they are added to the baseline. This result indicates that dependency and AMR embeddings should be utilized in conjunction with the word embeddings to obtain the best performance. This is consistent with previous study [20], where syntactic contexts were combined with word contexts for sentence classification.

The results using AMR embeddings alone are not promising as we expected. This might be due to that the pre-trained model we used for JAMR -LDC2014T12 [19]- does not contain sufficient medical terms and documents. Figure 3 shows an example that was misclassified by AMR embeddings. In the sentence "Consequently, the combination of methotrexate with acitretin is also contraindicated.", the word "contraindicated" plays an important role in determining the interaction between "methotrexate" and "acitretin". Since the pre-trained model for AMR parsing does not contain this term, this information could not be captured by AME embeddings. Other misclassified cases are due to the limitations of AMR. For example, AMR does not deeply capture noun-noun or noun-adjective relations [1].

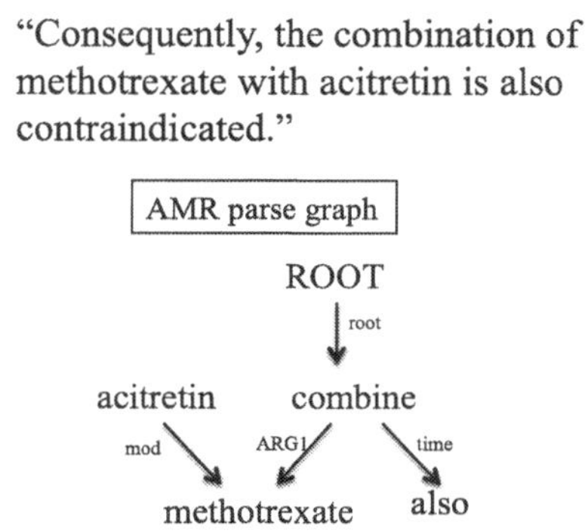

Figure 3: A misclassified example by AMR embeddings.

A limitation associated with both dependency and AMR embeddings is that only contexts within distance one in the dependency or AMR graph are considered. Increasing the distance might include more information in the embeddings but Algorithm 1 should be refined to avoid adding redundant contexts. In addition, another option is to add the nodes at the same level to incorporate more significant words for detecting DDIs. In Figure 1, "effect" would be added if such strategy was taken. However, this strategy will also add redundant contexts. For example, "when", "it" and "may" will also be considered as contexts for the example in Figure 1. Thus, more sophisticated methods are needed to study what are the best contexts in the graph for learning dependency and AMR embeddings.

We observe that Random Forest performs better than SVM except the DrugBank dataset. The reason is that Random Forest could provide a more complex model when dimensionality is less than the sample size. The study conducted by Delgado et al. tested 179 classifiers and found that Random Forest was the best family of classifiers [11]. Our experiments verified this result.

We notice that the proposed methods failed for the sentences that contain multiple drug pairs. The sentence "Before taking this medication, tell your doctor if you are taking a tricyclic antidepressant such as amitriptyline (Elavil), amoxapine (Asendin), doxepin (Sinequan), nortriptyline (Pamelor), imipramine (Tofranil), clomipramine (Anafranil), protriptyline (Vivactil), or desipramine

(Norpramin)." contains 16 drugs and 136 drug pairs. The reason that the dependency embeddings failed to detect these negative DDIs might be that each drug pair was connected by conjunct relation in the dependency graph. Another misclassified example is "Single dose pharmacokinetic studies demonstrated that the metabolism of rivastigmine is not significantly affected by concurrent administration of digoxin, warfarin, diazepam, or fluoxetine.", which consists of 4 drugs and 10 drug pairs. The proposed methods failed to identify the negated interaction between "rivastigmine" and any of "warfarin", "diazepam", and "fluoxetine".

6 CONCLUSION AND FUTURE WORK

In this paper, we proposed dependency embeddings and novel AMR embeddings for detecting DDIs from biomedical literature. We evaluated the proposed methods on DDIExtraction-2013 corpus with two different classification methods. The experiments shows the effectiveness of dependency embeddings and AMR embeddings. The best performance was obtained by using word, dependency and AMR embeddings in the baseline.

In the future work, we would like to utilize more comprehensive classifiers, such as Convolutional Neural Network (CNN) and Long Short Term Memory network (LSTM), for detecting DDIs. Since the dimension of embeddings might impact the classification, we also want to investigate what the best dimension is for the DDI extraction task. Moreover, extending the proposed methods to detect undiscovered DDIs from a large number of biomedical articles is subject to a future study.

ACKNOWLEDGMENTS

This work has been supported by the National Institute of Health (NIH) grants R01LM011934 and R01GM102282.

REFERENCES

[1] Laura Banarescu, Claire Bonial, Shu Cai, Madalina Georgescu, Kira Griffitt, Ulf Hermjakob, Kevin Knight, Philipp Koehn, Martha Palmer, and Nathan Schneider. 2012. Abstract meaning representation (AMR) 1.2 specification. In *Parsing on Freebase from Question-Answer Pairs. In Proceedings of the 2013 Conference on Empirical Methods in Natural Language Processing. Seattle: ACL*. 1533–1544.

[2] Laura Banarescu, Claire Bonial, Shu Cai, Madalina Georgescu, Kira Griffitt, Ulf Hermjakob, Kevin Knight, Philipp Koehn, Martha Palmer, and Nathan Schneider. 2013. Abstract Meaning Representation for Sembanking. In *Proceedings of the 7th Linguistic Annotation Workshop & Interoperability with Discourse*. 178–186.

[3] Karen Baxter and Claire L Preston. 2010. *Stockley's drug interactions*. Vol. 495. Pharmaceutical Press London.

[4] Yoshua Bengio, Réjean Ducharme, Pascal Vincent, and Christian Jauvin. 2003. A neural probabilistic language model. *Journal of machine learning research* 3, Feb (2003), 1137–1155.

[5] Jari Björne, Suwisa Kaewphan, and Tapio Salakoski. 2013. UTurku: drug named entity recognition and drug-drug interaction extraction using SVM classification and domain knowledge. In *Second Joint Conference on Lexical and Computational Semantics (* SEM)*, Vol. 2. 651–659.

[6] Tamara Bobic, Juliane Fluck, and Martin Hofmann-Apitius. 2013. SCAI: Extracting drug-drug interactions using a rich feature vector. In *Second Joint Conference on Lexical and Computational Semantics*. Citeseer, 675.

[7] Behrouz Bokharaeian and Alberto Díaz. 2013. NIL UCM: Extracting Drug-Drug interactions from text through combination of sequence and tree kernels. In *Second Joint Conference on Lexical and Computational Semantics*. 644–650.

[8] Leo Breiman. 2001. Random forests. *Machine learning* 45, 1 (2001), 5–32.

[9] Md Faisal Mahbub Chowdhury and Alberto Lavelli. 2013. FBK-irst: A multi-phase kernel based approach for drug-drug interaction detection and classification that exploits linguistic information. *Atlanta, Georgia, USA* 351 (2013), 53.

[10] Linda R Cronenwett, J Lyle Bootman, Julie Wolcott, Philip Aspden, and others. 2007. *Preventing medication errors: quality chasm series*. National Academies Press.

[11] Manuel Fernández-Delgado, Eva Cernadas, Senén Barro, and Dinani Amorim. 2014. Do we need hundreds of classifiers to solve real world classification problems. *J. Mach. Learn. Res* 15, 1 (2014), 3133–3181.

[12] Noha Ferrah, Janaka J Lovell, and Joseph E Ibrahim. 2017. Systematic review of the prevalence of medication errors resulting in hospitalization and death of nursing home residents. *Journal of the American Geriatrics Society* 65, 2 (2017), 433–442.

[13] Jeffrey Flanigan, Sam Thomson, Jaime G Carbonell, Chris Dyer, and Noah A Smith. 2014. A discriminative graph-based parser for the abstract meaning representation. (2014).

[14] Claudio Giuliano, Alberto Lavelli, and Lorenza Romano. 2006. Exploiting shallow linguistic information for relation extraction from biomedical literature.. In *EACL*, Vol. 18. Citeseer, 401–408.

[15] Lifu Huang, Jonathan May, Xiaoman Pan, and Heng Ji. 2016. Building a Fine-Grained Entity Typing System Overnight for a New X (X= Language, Domain, Genre). *arXiv preprint arXiv:1603.03112* (2016).

[16] Balthasar L Hug, Daniel J Witkowski, Colin M Sox, Carol A Keohane, Diane L Seger, Catherine Yoon, Michael E Matheny, and David W Bates. 2010. Adverse drug event rates in six community hospitals and the potential impact of computerized physician order entry for prevention. *Journal of general internal medicine* 25, 1 (2010), 31–38.

[17] John T James. 2013. A new, evidence-based estimate of patient harms associated with hospital care. *Journal of patient safety* 9, 3 (2013), 122–128.

[18] Sun Kim, Haibin Liu, Lana Yeganova, and W John Wilbur. 2015. Extracting drug–drug interactions from literature using a rich feature-based linear kernel approach. *Journal of biomedical informatics* 55 (2015), 23–30.

[19] Kevin Knight, Lauren Baranescu, Claire Bonial, Madalina Georgescu, Kira Griffitt, Ulf Hermjakob, Daniel Marcu, Martha Palmer, and Nathan Schneifer. 2014. Abstract meaning representation (AMR) annotation release 1.0. *Web download* (2014).

[20] Alexandros Komninos and Suresh Manandhar. 2016. Dependency based embeddings for sentence classification tasks. In *Proceedings of NAACL-HLT*. 1490–1500.

[21] Vivian Law, Craig Knox, Yannick Djoumbou, Tim Jewison, An Chi Guo, Yifeng Liu, Adam Maciejewski, David Arndt, Michael Wilson, Vanessa Neveu, and others. 2014. DrugBank 4.0: shedding new light on drug metabolism. *Nucleic acids research* 42, D1 (2014), D1091–D1097.

[22] Yann LeCun, Yoshua Bengio, and Geoffrey Hinton. 2015. Deep learning. *Nature* 521, 7553 (2015), 436–444.

[23] Omer Levy and Yoav Goldberg. 2014. Dependency-Based Word Embeddings.. In *ACL (2)*. Citeseer, 302–308.

[24] Dingcheng Li, Sijia Liu, Majid Rastegar-Mojarad, Yanshan Wang, Vipin Chaudhary, Terry Therneau, and Hongfang Liu. 2016. A Topic-modeling Based Framework for Drug-drug Interaction Classification from Biomedical Text. In *AMIA Annual Symposium Proceedings*, Vol. 2016. American Medical Informatics Association, 789.

[25] Fei Liu, Jeffrey Flanigan, Sam Thomson, Norman Sadeh, and Noah A Smith. 2015. Toward abstractive summarization using semantic representations. In *Proceedings of the North American Chapter of the Association for Computational Linguistics (NAACL)*.

[26] Shengyu Liu, Buzhou Tang, Qingcai Chen, and Xiaolong Wang. 2016. Drug-drug interaction extraction via convolutional neural networks. *Computational and mathematical methods in medicine* 2016 (2016).

[27] Martin A Makary and Michael Daniel. 2016. Medical error?the third leading cause of death in the US. *Bmj* 353 (2016), i2139.

[28] Tomas Mikolov, Kai Chen, Greg Corrado, and Jeffrey Dean. 2013. Efficient estimation of word representations in vector space. *arXiv preprint arXiv:1301.3781* (2013).

[29] Tomas Mikolov, Ilya Sutskever, Kai Chen, Greg S Corrado, and Jeff Dean. 2013. Distributed representations of words and phrases and their compositionality. In *Advances in neural information processing systems*. 3111–3119.

[30] Teryl K Nuckols, Crystal Smith-Spangler, Sally C Morton, Steven M Asch, Vaspaan M Patel, Laura J Anderson, Emily L Deichsel, and Paul G Shekelle. 2014. The effectiveness of computerized order entry at reducing preventable adverse drug events and medication errors in hospital settings: a systematic review and meta-analysis. *Systematic reviews* 3, 1 (2014), 56.

[31] Xiaochang Peng, Chuan Wang, Daniel Gildea, and Nianwen Xue. 2017. Addressing the Data Sparsity Issue in Neural AMR Parsing. *arXiv preprint arXiv:1702.05053* (2017).

[32] Majid Rastegar-Mojarad. 2013. Extraction and Classification of Drug-Drug Interaction from Biomedical Text Using a Two-Stage Classifier. *Theses and Dissertations* 304 (2013).

[33] Majid Rastegar-Mojarad, Richard D Boyce, and Rashmi Prasad. 2013. UWM-TRIADS: classifying drug-drug interactions with two-stage SVM and post-processing. In *Proceedings of the 7th International Workshop on Semantic Evaluation*. 667–674.

[34] Nancy E Reame, Tammy L Wyman, David J Phillips, David M de Kretser, and Vasantha Padmanabhan. 1998. Net Increase in Stimulatory Input Resulting from a Decrease in Inhibin B and an Increase in Activin A May Contribute in Part to the

Rise in Follicular Phase Follicle-Stimulating Hormone of Aging Cycling Women 1. *The Journal of Clinical Endocrinology & Metabolism* 83, 9 (1998), 3302–3307.

[35] Tim Rocktäschel, Torsten Huber, Michael Weidlich, and Ulf Leser. 2013. WBI-NER: The impact of domain-specific features on the performance of identifying and classifying mentions of drugs. In *Second Joint Conference on Lexical and Computational Semantics*, Vol. 2. 356–363.

[36] Isabel Segura Bedmar, Paloma Martínez, and María Herrero Zazo. 2013. Semeval-2013 task 9: Extraction of drug-drug interactions from biomedical texts (ddiextraction 2013). Association for Computational Linguistics.

[37] Isabel Segura Bedmar, Paloma Martinez, and Daniel Sánchez Cisneros. 2011. The 1st DDIExtraction-2011 challenge task: Extraction of Drug-Drug Interactions from biomedical texts. (2011).

[38] Duyu Tang, Furu Wei, Nan Yang, Ming Zhou, Ting Liu, and Bing Qin. 2014. Learning Sentiment-Specific Word Embedding for Twitter Sentiment Classification.. In *ACL (1)*. 1555–1565.

[39] Philippe Thomas, Mariana Neves, Tim Rocktäschel, and Ulf Leser. 2013. WBI-DDI: drug-drug interaction extraction using majority voting. In *Second Joint Conference on Lexical and Computational Semantics (* SEM)*, Vol. 2. 628–635.

[40] Chuan Wang, Nianwen Xue, Sameer Pradhan, and Sameer Pradhan. 2015. A Transition-based Algorithm for AMR Parsing.. In *HLT-NAACL*. 366–375.

[41] Daojian Zeng, Kang Liu, Siwei Lai, Guangyou Zhou, Jun Zhao, and others. 2014. Relation Classification via Convolutional Deep Neural Network.. In *COLING*. 2335–2344.

[42] Xiang Zhang, Junbo Zhao, and Yann LeCun. 2015. Character-level convolutional networks for text classification. In *Advances in neural information processing systems*. 649–657.

[43] Zhehuan Zhao, Zhihao Yang, Ling Luo, Hongfei Lin, and Jian Wang. 2016. Drug drug interaction extraction from biomedical literature using syntax convolutional neural network. *Bioinformatics* 32, 22 (2016), 3444–3453.

Leveraging Sentiment Analysis for Classifying Patient Complaints

Adel ElMessiry
Utilize Health
700 12th Avenue South
Nashville, Tennessee 37203
Adel_ElMessiry@ncsu.edu

Zhe Zhang
IBM
Research Triangle Park
Raleigh, North Carolina 27606
zzhang13@ncsu.edu

William O. Cooper
Vanderbilt University Medical Center
1211 Medical Center Dr
Nashville, Tennessee 37232
william.cooper@vanderbilt.edu

Thomas F. Catron
Vanderbilt University Medical Center
1211 Medical Center Dr
Nashville, Tennessee 37232
tom.catron@vanderbilt.edu

Jan Karrass
Vanderbilt University Medical Center
1211 Medical Center Dr
Nashville, Tennessee 37232
jan.karrass@vanderbilt.edu

Munindar P. Singh
North Carolina State University
Department of Computer Science
Raleigh, North Carolina 27695
mpsingh@ncsu.edu

ABSTRACT

Unsolicited patient complaints expressed in patients' own words provide an evidential basis for identifying and mitigating patient safety and financial risks associated with physicians and other practitioners. Classifying patient complaints is complicated by the complexity of linguistic representation. Current practice relies upon manual classification, which limits scalability. An automatic approach can potentially improve response time and scale, thereby enhancing opportunities to promote physician accountability for safe and respectful care. This research seeks to automate the classification of patient complaints to improve triage and response. We process a corpus of patient complaints data collected by the Patient Advocacy Reporting System (PARS) developed at Vanderbilt and associated institutions. Our method is to map each complaint to a vector based on enhanced Linguistic Inquiry and Word Count (LIWC) lexicons and to train a Naïve Bayes classifier over those vectors. We compare it to both Term Frequency–Inverse Document Frequency (TF-IDF) and the best case results of any classifier over bag of words features. Our classifier outperforms traditional complaint analysis approaches, which disregard sentiment. Our classifier yields 3% greater accuracy overall than traditional approaches. For the *SAFETY OF ENVIRONMENT* label, our classifier had an accuracy of 84% (compared to 50% for traditional) and a sensitivity of 96% (compared to 0% for traditional). We conclude that patient sentiments conveyed in complaints are often overlooked yet can be valuable in analyzing such complaints to identify and mitigate patient safety and provider financial risks. We demonstrate that inferring the complaint sentiment leads to improved classification accuracy.

Permission to make digital or hard copies of all or part of this work for personal or classroom use is granted without fee provided that copies are not made or distributed for profit or commercial advantage and that copies bear this notice and the full citation on the first page. Copyrights for components of this work owned by others than the author(s) must be honored. Abstracting with credit is permitted. To copy otherwise, or republish, to post on servers or to redistribute to lists, requires prior specific permission and/or a fee. Request permissions from permissions@acm.org.
ACM-BCB '17, August 20-23, 2017, Boston, MA,USA
© 2017 Copyright held by the owner/author(s). Publication rights licensed to Association for Computing Machinery.
ACM ISBN 978-1-4503-4722-8/17/08...$15.00
https://doi.org/10.1145/3107411.3107421

CCS CONCEPTS

• **Computing methodologies** → **Natural language processing; Machine learning approaches;** • **Applied computing** → **Health care information systems; Health informatics;** • **General and reference** → *Cross-computing tools and techniques;* • **Theory of computation** → *Semi-supervised learning;*

KEYWORDS

Patient Complaints, NLP, Text Mining

1 BACKGROUND AND SIGNIFICANCE

Patients are uniquely positioned to make observations about the care they receive, particularly when health care professionals or organizations fail to meet or exceed their expectations. When patients and family members share their observations, in the form of unsolicited patient complaints, service recovery can take place. Put simply, service recovery is the process by which organizations attempt to "make right" what went wrong for patients and families [13]. In this regard, how can we measure, track, and improve healthcare quality of service?

In commerce, customer feedback is a valuable resource for validating the quality of service and improve customer satisfaction [2, 21]. Healthcare is changing through the wealth of user-generated textual artifacts that can be used to support personalized health and wellness by the combination and interoperation of modern technologies [1]. Zhao [43] shows how the sentiment included in healthcare posts can reflect the user emotions at the time of posting. Using Natural Language Processing (NLP) has been demonstrated to be a useful technique for detecting a broad range of adverse events in discharge summaries and has outperformed traditional and previous automated adverse event detection methods [23].

Patient feedback regarding the quality of service has significant ramifications on how patient outcomes are assessed and thus, on healthcare provider financial viability. The most valuable and direct feedback are patient complaints. Patient complaints can help healthcare organizations identify unsafe and dissatisfying behaviors as well as avoidable variability in performance. Reported observations of patients and families to health care organizations in the form of spontaneous complaints of unprofessional behavior exhibited by the surgeon has been shown to be an indication of surgical team performance degradation [4]. The Patient Advocacy Reporting System (PARS) developed at Vanderbilt and used at more than 140 other medical centers is a system used to capture, classify, and address such complaints. Effective and efficient classification is crucial to subsequent responses. Current manual techniques are not easily scaled due to the required effort [10]. We develop an approach that automates the classification and produces human-competitive results.

1.1 Problem and Motivation

The technical obstacle we address is how to take real-life patient complaint data and classify it into one of a small number of categories. The determination of the categories is an essential step in responding to patient complaints. In the current process, this step is carried out manually by extensively trained personnel. The problem we address is to perform the classification automatically with accuracy that is competitive with manual approaches.

This problem is challenging for the following reasons:

- The data come from multiple people from various affiliated institutions. The report authors (patient advocates in different institutions) have different writing styles for reporting the patient complaints as well as the actions taken (if any) in response to a complaint.
- Different users may contribute to the same complaint. These can include the patient, a family member of the patient, a physician, or the nurse. Each user reflects his or her point of view and these points of view can be mutually contradictory.
- Variation in patients' age can lead to discrepancies in the expressions used and the length of the complaint text.
- Size of the data: A typical hospital handles thousands of patients, all of whom can potentially contribute unsolicited feedback. Unlike surveys where the hospital would request the information and control the format, unsolicited feedback is initiated by the patient, the patient's family, and sometimes the provider.
- Time sensitivity in classification: It is important to classify feedback so as to produce a correct intervention plan and respond before the problem escalates leading to a potential malpractice lawsuit.

1.2 Analyzing Sentiment in Text

Our approach is based on the observation that realizing what compels the patient to complain is the key to modeling the patient's concerns. A sentiment can be defined as an attitude, thought, or judgment promoted by a feeling [24]. Attempting to model patient complaints in a nonsentiment approach ignores the fundamental drive behind the complaint inception, which explains why when faced with challenging dataset, we can obtain better classification accuracy incorporating sentiments.

The sentiment analysis of text [20] is challenging because humans express their sentiments in subtle domain-specific ways. We adopt Linguist Inquiry Word Count (LIWC) [31] as a way to determine the sentiment-relevant words in a complaint. LIWC provides dictionaries that have been validated through previous studies. LIWC has been shown to tap into the psychological meaning of words [40]. Additionally, previous studies [16, 37] demonstrate the causal validity of LIWC-based emotive scores by documenting their sensitivity to motive arousal. Measuring consumer satisfaction is shown to be possible through linguistic-based emotion analysis and recognition based on LIWC [34].

2 MATERIALS AND METHODS

PARS is a tool and a process that uses patient comments and complaints about their healthcare experiences to promote a kinder, safer, more reliable healthcare environment while addressing malpractice risk [14, 38].

Patients with unresolved issues contact the Office of Patient Relations or the Office of Patient Affairs at the hospital. A patient advocate helps resolve the issue and documents the complaint in the system. Narratives of patient complaints are sent to Vanderbilt Center for Patient and Professional Advocacy (CPPA). Professional coders mark the relevant parts of the complaint narratives so that they can be shared with the care provider. Examples of the categorizations are as below. (Care and Treatment are the most common complaints.)

Care and Treatment: *I needed to be examined ...Dr. XX never touched me except to shake hands. I feel Dr. XX has put off my surgery too long with no good reason.*

Safety of Environment: *Wife states when nurse started IV that the patient bled and there was a large amount of blood on the floor, and he had blood on his gown.*

No Complaint: *Mr. XX called wanting to speak to someone about the pool hours at Sports Medical Center.*

Single events may often be addressed via an informal "Cup of Coffee" conversation between peers. Further events may require an intervention plan. The intervention plan is created to address the risks through local peers and leadership. In most cases, the plan has three levels [32]:

Level I: Awareness A confidential interaction with the care provider to make sure the provider is aware of his/her pattern of events and the associated.

Level II: Authority If the pattern persists after the Level 1 Awareness intervention, an authority intervention is provided via an authority figure such as the Department Chair.

Level III: Administrative If the pattern persists after the Authority intervention, an administrative disciplinary process is initiated to assure organization risk mitigation.

By implementing the PARS recommendation, the organization can detect and address risk before it escalates [39].

2.1 Human Coders and Classification

CPPA has a team of 10–15 coders who read each individual patient complaint and manually code the complaints according to guidelines set forth in the CPPA manual. *Coding* here means selecting the appropriate category for the complaint. The coding manual was developed in 2000 through a collaboration with a social worker, an educational psychologist, and a biostatistician. The patient complaint coders go through extensive training before they begin to code live. Furthermore, the trainee codes are reviewed by the coding trainer or another coder, and the trainee advised accordingly. Coding trainees are also encouraged and expected to ask multiple questions throughout the training process. After the trainee has been in training for three months, they are given a reliability test; the standard of reliability is the alpha of 0.80 or higher [5, 11]. If a coding trainee scores relatively lower on the test, then their work continues to receive close scrutiny; if they score higher, only a small (random) sample of their reports are reviewed. Again at six months, the coders take another reliability test to verify that they have improved sufficiently, or if they were already coding reliably, that they are not experiencing any significant observer drift. Once coding trainees have been coding for six months and are reliable, they begin to code narratives from hospitals and medical centers whose reports are less straightforward.

For the most recent assessment of patient complaint reports included in the present study (December 2013), the results of the inter-coder agreement reliability had a median alpha of 0.9. The inter-coder agreement is high due to the extensive training the coders undergo on the PARS classification.

2.2 Data Composition

We examined a longitudinal dataset containing 7,400 complaints associated with 457 physicians collected from June 2002 to September 2014. We observed that many complaints have a standard beginning expressing the department, date, and the last person updating the record. Such boilerplate consumes a lot of characters which would not leave room for meaningful information in a very short complaint. For this reason, to ensure that we had substantial information content, we restricted our dataset to comments of 150 characters or more. This dataset contained 3954 complaints with average complaint length of 793 characters, 16 labeled SAFETY, 3504 labeled CARE, and 434 labeled NO COMPLAINT.

2.3 Our Approach

In order to analyze the sentiment content of patient complaints we first enriched the LIWC dimensions with three simple healthcare specific dimensions, then we developed a mapping function using the LIWC lexicon. The simple healthcare specific dimensions help account for the specific domain that we are addressing. The mapping generates a sparse representation of the patient complaint in the form of a vector containing the hits for each of enriched LIWC's 67 dimensions. Attempting to learn a model using all of the 67 dimensions is exhaustive. Our problem can then be viewed as a feature extraction followed by feature reduction, where the extracted features are the LIWC dimensions that we seek to reduce for the purpose of learning a model that can predict the patient complaint classification. The desired solution will need to determine the minimal number of features to obtain the best prediction performance.

. Our approach consists of four steps:

- Enrich with domain-specific dimensions.
- Extract features through mapping to LIWC dimensions.
- Reduce features to select the relevant LIWC dimensions.
- Learning a model to predict the labels.

Next, we describe each step in detail.

2.4 Healthcare Specific Domains

LIWC is based on ordinary language whereas patient complaints tend to use specialized words. We select terms based on their TF-IDF weights [15], additionally selecting medical terms. Our steps are:

- Generate a TF-IDF vector of the entire corpus.
- Select the top 250 TF-IDF weighted terms.
- Remove any term that appeared in the LIWC terms.
- From the data remaining, select words that have medical meaning.

As in LIWC, we retain misspelled words with high TF-IDF weight such as "surgeri". The resulting list partitions into three dimensions:

Patient contains words such as patient, patients, pt
Medical Personnel contains words such as physician, nurse
Treatment contains words such as surgery, procedure, diagnoses

We include these dimensions in the lexicon we use below.

2.5 Feature Extraction: Mapping to LIWC Dimensions

Feature extraction focuses on computing a representation of the input data that facilitates learning a model of it. Using LIWC dimensions for feature extraction has been well established in work done by [28]. We consider the 64 dimensions defined in the LIWC framework as the source of our features. The dimensions, in essence, are lists of words (including their variants and derivatives) organized according to their psycholinguistic significance. For example, the *Negemo (Negative Emotions)* dimension includes words connoting negative emotion, such as "alone," "anger," "stress," "sufferer," "suffering,".... Likewise the *Family* dimension includes family-related words, such as "bro," "brother," "daughter," "ex," "hubby," "husband," ....

We map each patient complaint to the LIWC dimensions. Specifically, our mapping function measures the frequency with which a certain dimension is repeated in a complaint using Equation 1.

$$f_d(C_n) = \sum w_{d,n} \tag{1}$$

where $w_{d,n}$ counts a word that appears both in dimension d and complaint C_n.

Using the above, we generate a compact representation of each complaint as a vector: each element in this vector equals the mapping to a particular LIWC dimension as Equation 1 explains. In general, we would consider not all, but only some selected dimensions.

To understand the mapping, consider the following complaint with respect to six LIWC dimensions, {Posemo (Positive Emotions), Negemo, Family, Money, Relig, Home}:

> My father and hubby almost slipped on the wet floor, even my bro who is well built, had a hard time to control himself. So stupid, especially that we have a huge bill to pay.

The underlined words occur in the selected LIWC dimensions: "father," "hubby," "bro" in *Family*; "stupid" in *Negemo*; and "bill," "pay" in *Money*. Therefore, this complaint maps to the six-element vector (over the selected dimensions):

$$\langle 0, 1, 3, 2, 0, 0 \rangle$$

If we were to append *Relative* and *Space* to our list of dimensions, "room" in *Relative* and "floor" in *Space* would be relevant, producing an eight-element vector

$$\langle 0, 1, 3, 2, 0, 0, 1, 1 \rangle$$

Notice that some words may appear in two or more LIWC dimensions. Our mapping counts such a word in each dimension with the intuition that such a word indicates multiple dimensions are relevant. However, as we explain below, we select the dimensions themselves so as to reduce the features thus countering any systematic redundancy across the dimensions.

2.6 Feature Reduction: Selecting the Relevant LIWC Dimensions

In general, having too many features can lead to an over-fitted model. This problem is exacerbated by features that are mutually correlated. For this reason, we adopt the well-known idea of feature reduction [17, 25].

We adopt a variation of steepest-ascent hill climbing [35] to select a small set of dimensions as our features. Specifically, we identify three LIWC dimensions that yield good prediction as follows. The idea is to compute the accuracy resulting from several sets of three dimensions on the training data and then use the best of those sets on the test data. That is, the objective function for our hill climbing is prediction accuracy using a model based on the selected features.

We maintain five best sets of dimensions. We begin from the five singletons of dimensions that give the best prediction accuracy. For each of these five singletons, we add to it each of the remaining 66 dimensions in turn and evaluate the accuracy of the resulting pairs. From these 5 × 66 pairs, we select the best five pairs. Next, for each of these five singletons, we add to it each of the remaining 65 dimensions in turn and evaluate the accuracy of the resulting triples. From these 5 × 65 triples, we select the best five triples.

Although our algorithm does not ensure finding the optimum set of dimensions, it presents a good tradeoff by producing a good enough set of dimensions without dealing with the combinatorial explosion of considering all possibilities. In general, we could proceed in this manner to find the best five quadruples, and so on. However, we find that having six or more dimensions is not helpful.

We have implemented our method using R [33] and RTextTools [16].

2.7 Predicting the Labels

We divided the dataset into a training and a testing dataset. We used a Naïve Bayes classifier to learn a model over the mapped LIWC dimensions. We then used the testing dataset to validate the accuracy of our classifier. Accuracy is defined by Equation 2, where TP, FP, TN, and FN refer to true and false positive and negative

$$Accuracy = (\text{TP} + \text{TN})/(\text{TP} + \text{FP} + \text{TN} + \text{FN}) \tag{2}$$

Fig. 1 provides an overview of our process.

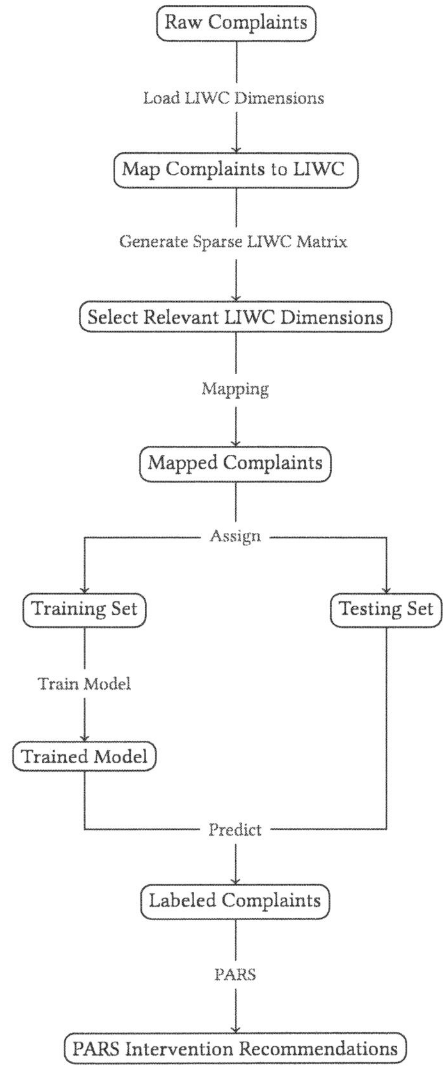

Figure 1: Classification and evaluation process overview.

2.8 Evaluation Methods

We evaluate our work in two parts. We examine the validity of our first hypothesis, namely, that the complaint text carries a sentiment-related meaning. To that end, we investigate the occurrence of LIWC dimensions in the dataset. We map the complaints to the LIWC dimensions as in Equation 1. Then, for every label, we compute the ratio of the occurrences of the Money, Family, Posemo, Negemo, Anx and Anger LIWC dimension to the total number of LIWC dimension occurrences, as described in Equation 3.

$$p_d = \frac{\sum_{n=1}^{n=k} f_d(C_n)}{\sum_{n=1}^{n=k} \sum_{i=1}^{i=m} f_i(C_n)} \tag{3}$$

Where k is the total number of complaints and m is the number of LIWC dimensions. We expect to see a pattern that can be attributed to the underlying meaning.

Next, we compare our approach to an array of classifiers, implemented using RTextTools [16], including:

SLDA or Scaled Linear Discriminant Analysis expresses one dependent variable as a linear combination of other variables similar to ANOVA, but with the difference that SLDA assumes continuous independent variables and categorical dependent labels. SLDA is widely used in image and pattern recognition [22].

SVM or Support Vector Machines divides the dataset via a set of hyperplanes during the learning phase and maps new data to fall behind one of the hyperplanes. SVM has been used for text classification [30].

GLMNET is an implementation of the Lasso and elastic-net regularized generalized linear models. GLMNet is popular for domains with large databases [8].

Max Entropy is a probabilistic classifier that selects the model with maximum entropy from among a set of models and uses it to classify the data [27].

Boosting aggregates a set of weak learners (classifiers that perform slightly better than random) to create a strong learner by weighting them appropriately [36].

Random Forests selects the best performing from among multiple learning algorithms so as to improve predictions.

Neural Networks are inspired by neurons and their interconnections (through which neurons activate other neurons) [19]. Neural networks have been used for medical applications [3], as well as in text classification [12].

We manually select the best performing classifier per label, to obtain the best performance as a baseline and compare it with our LIWC-based model.

Finally, we compare our results to using only TF-IDF (Term Frequency–Inverse Document Frequency) for feature extraction. TF-IDF is designed to emphasize the importance of a word to a document in a collection or corpus [18], for feature extractions.

TF-IDF has been widely used in information classification and retrieval [7]. The idea is simply to combine the TF (Term Frequency) with IDF (Inverse Document Frequency) by multiplying the frequency of a term in a document by the inverse document frequency of this term in the documents of the corpus. A commonly used example is the word "the". If we only use TF, the word "the" will score highly while it does not convey any significant meaning for predicting the label. Now, contrast that with counting the number of documents in the corpus which the word "the" appears in, which is equally high and almost in all documents. IDF for a term takes the logarithm of the total number of documents divided by the number of documents that this word appears in, as shown in Equation 4.

$$TFIDF(t) = tf(t,d) * \log \frac{N}{n_t} \tag{4}$$

where $tf(t,d)$ counts the frequency by which term t appears in document d, while N is the total number of documents in the corpus and n_t is the number of documents in which the term t appears.

In the case of the word "the", and assuming it will appear in all documents, that ratio is 1 and thus will generate an IDF value of 0. The IDF will then cancel the weight of the word "the". Our approach consists of four steps:

- Preprocess the documents to remove stop words, numbers and perform stemming.
- Feature extraction through generating TF-IDF sparse representation of the documents.
- Feature reduction by removing sparse terms.
- Learning a model to predict the labels.

We randomly select the training and testing dataset. The feature selection is performed on the training dataset independently of the testing dataset. We repeat the entire process 10 folds, reselecting the features each time. We take the average prediction of the 10 folds.

IRB Approval

This research was reviewed and approved by the Vanderbilt Medical Center Institutional Review Board and the North Carolina State University Institutional Review Board.

3 RESULTS

Our first hypothesis that complaint text classes emphasize the LIWC dimensions differently was supported. As Fig. 2 shows, *CARE RELATED* is more evenly distributed whereas *SAFETY OF ENVIRONMENT* emphasizes *FAMILY*. Interestingly, *SAFETY OF ENVIRONMENT* emphasizes *Family* more than *NO COMPLAINT does*. We attribute this to the fact that the environment impacts, not the patient, but visitors, who tend to be the patient's family.

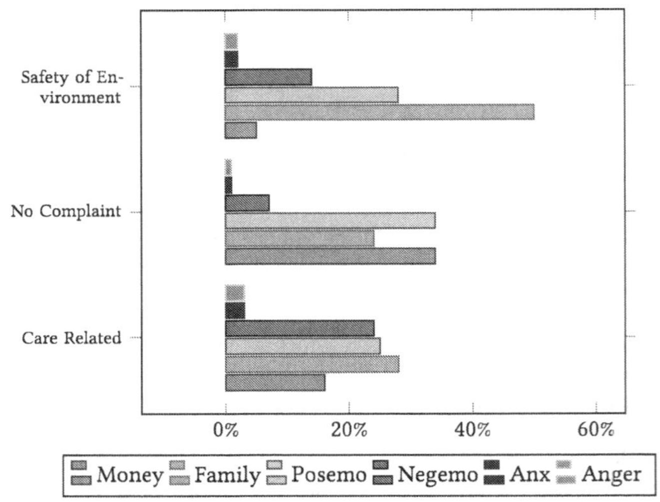

Figure 2: LIWC dimension analysis.

Using TF-IDF alone failed to yield significant improvements in most of the labels, except in the case of "Safety". An explanation for this result is that the bag of words uses term frequency as the base representation of the document, which is ineffective when the terms with the most impact are localized to only a subset of documents. The IDF component helps by emphasizing terms that are more informative. We see that mapping the complaints to LIWC dimensions helps predict complaint labels better than with traditional features, which ignore sentiment and consider only unigrams. Our

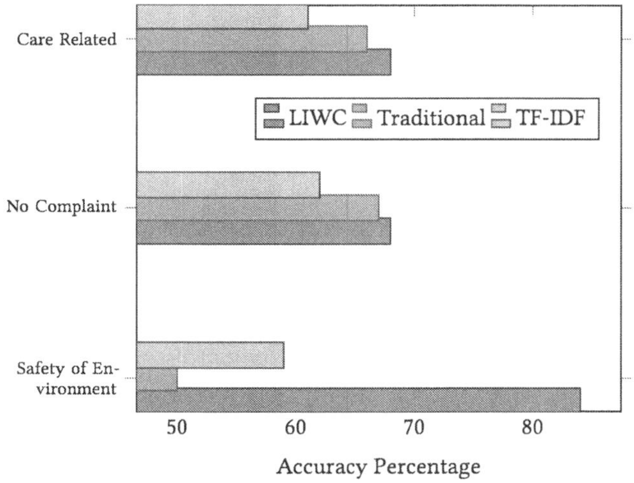

Figure 3: Comparison of LIWC-based, traditional and TF-IDF features.

approach mitigates the shortcomings of using only TF-IDF and further enhances the feature extraction by using the dimension, which unlike unigram terms, combines adjacent words in one dimension that conveys a sentiment. The *SAFETY OF ENVIRONMENT* label shows the most gain in accuracy. Further, the high accuracy associated with *NO COMPLAINT* prediction has a huge impact on scaling PARS as it removes unnecessary processing. These results coupled with the ease of applying our method demonstrate the potential benefits of our work, as Fig. 3 shows.

We hypothesize that our approach yields a higher mean value for the above-mentioned quality metrics (i.e., accuracy, sensitivity, and specificity) than classification approaches that disregard sentiment in a patient complaint. We produce three pairs of hypotheses, one for each metric.

NULL HYPOTHESIS 1. *Our approach using LIWC dimensions yields the same mean metric (accuracy, sensitivity, specificity) as approaches that disregard sentiment.*

ALTERNATIVE HYPOTHESIS 1. *Our approach yields greater mean metric (accuracy, sensitivity, specificity) than approaches that disregard sentiment.*

To evaluate the null hypothesis, we generate Table 1, wherein we use the approaches ignoring sentiments prediction as the expected values for each label and the LIWC predictions as the observed values. Then we conduct the one-tailed Chi-squared test [29]. We set our significance level α to be 0.005. We obtain a p-value of 0.03^{-10}. We thus reject the null hypothesis.

As Table 2 shows, we exceed accuracy achieved by the best traditional approach (SLDA) for each category label. Our approach yields slightly greater accuracy than the best traditional approaches for NO COMPLAINT and CARE RELATED. For SAFETY OF ENVIRONMENT, our approach yields a 68% improvement, from 50% to 84%. For SAFETY OF ENVIRONMENT, a false negative is much riskier than a false positive. For this reason, it helps to compute the

Table 1: Chi-squared test.

Label	Traditional Expected	LIWC Observed
Safety of Environment	9	13
No Complaint	247	308
Care Related	2028	1809

sensitivity of a classifier. Our approach predicts SAFETY OF ENVIRONMENT with a sensitivity of 96%. That is, the probability of a false negative, (1 - Sensitivity), is 4%. For the other two labels, the results are mixed though on balance accuracy favors our approach, as described above. Table 3 shows our Sensitivity and specificity computed over ten folds.

Table 2: Prediction accuracy per label. Accuracy is computed over ten folds.

Label	Accuracy (Ours)	LIWC Dimensions	Accuracy (SLDA)	Gain
SAFETY	0.84	Treatment, MedPerson, Patient, Ipron, Conj, Space	0.5	68%
CARE	0.68	Treatment, MedPerson, Patient, Funct, SheHe, Negemo	0.66	3%
NO COMPLAINT	0.68	Treatment, MedPerson, Patient, Negemo, Inhib, Body	0.67	1.5%

Table 3: Prediction sensitivity and specificity per label, computed over ten folds.

Label	Our Approach		SLDA Approach	
	Sensitivity	Specificity	Sensitivity	Specificity
SAFETY	0.96	0.68	0	1
CARE	0.60	0.75	0.97	0.29
NO COMPLAINT	0.75	0.66	0.30	0.97

4 CONCLUSION

We demonstrate that inferring the complaint sentiment leads to the improved classification accuracy of patient complaints. Our approach is less computationally demanding, but produces better results, than traditional approaches. We attribute the success of our approach to its incorporating the sentiment implicitly conveyed in the complaints. As medicine is adopting evidence-based practices, there are expanding efforts, e.g., pSCANNER [26], on building and using patient-centric clinical databases to support medical research. However, to understand and avoid adverse medical actions, we need not only clinical information but also information about patients' subjective reactions to a treatment and associated interactions with people. PARS is an important such database. The problem of extracting valuable information from it is the topic of this article. An important direction is to build a new healthcare-specific lexicon exploring methods outlined by Tausczik and Pennebaker [40] and Zhang and Singh [42] to further improve the performance and accuracy of our model across all the labels. Another interesting direction is to evaluate the influence of geography: specifically, do patients from different locations express themselves differently? Do their differences in phrasing affect the underlying meaning? A patient complaint or any complaint, for that matter, is an indication of some expectation violation, especially a violation of a social norm in the sense of Von Wright [41]. We conjecture that the study of norms from a computational perspective can provide a theoretical foundation for the study of patient complaints and provider accountability, e.g., as advanced by Ghose and Savarimuthu [9]. Moreover, recent advances in computing techniques help mine norms from a variety of text-based sources [6]. Such techniques may be enhanced for mining complaint text: challenges include tackling the facts that patient complaints are not associated with structured artifacts and are not public (and therefore not commented upon by other patients).

ACKNOWLEDGMENTS

We thank the Center for Patient and Professional Advocacy at Vanderbilt University Medical Center for access to the de-identified dataset for research purposes.

REFERENCES

[1] Oresti Banos, Muhammad Bilal Amin, Wajahat Ali Khan, Taqdir Ali, Muhammad Afzal, Byeong Ho Kang, and Sungyoung Lee. 2015. Mining minds: an innovative framework for personalized health and wellness support. In *Proceedings of the 9th International Conference on Pervasive Computing Technologies for Healthcare (PervasiveHealth)*. Istanbul, 1–8.

[2] Dawn Bendall-Lyon and Thomas L Powers. 2001. The role of complaint management in the service recovery process. *Joint Commission Journal on Quality and Patient Safety* 27, 5 (May 2001), 278–286.

[3] H.B. Burke, D.B. Rosen, and P.H. Goodman. 1994. Comparing artificial neural networks to other statistical methods for medical outcome prediction. In *Proceedings of the IEEE International Conference on Neural Networks*, Vol. 4. IEEE, Orlando, 2213–2216.

[4] Thomas F. Catron, Oscar D. Guillamondegui, Jan Karrass, William O. Cooper, Barbara J. Martin, Roger R. Dmochowski, James W. Pichert, and Gerald B. Hickson. 2016. Patient Complaints and Adverse Surgical Outcomes. *American Journal of Medical Quality* 31, 5 (2016), 415–422.

[5] Jose M. Cortina. 1993. What is coefficient alpha? An examination of theory and applications. *Journal of Applied Psychology* 78, 1 (Feb. 1993), 98–104.

[6] Hoa Khanh Dam, Bastin Tony Roy Savarimuthu, Daniel Avery, and Aditya Ghose. 2015. Mining software repositories for social norms. In *2015 IEEE/ACM 37th IEEE International Conference on Software Engineering*, Vol. 2. IEEE, 627–630.

[7] Susan Dumais, John Platt, David Heckerman, and Mehran Sahami. 1998. Inductive learning algorithms and representations for text categorization. In *Proceedings of the 7th International Conference on Information and Knowledge Management*. Bethesda, MD, 148–155.

[8] Jerome Friedman, Trevor Hastie, and Rob Tibshirani. 2010. Regularization paths for generalized linear models via coordinate descent. *Journal of Statistical Software* 33, 1 (2010), 1.

[9] Aditya Ghose and Tony Bastin Roy Savarimuthu. 2012. Norms as objectives: Revisiting compliance management in multi-agent systems. In *Proceedings of the 14th International Workshop on Coordination, Organizations, Institutions, and Norms in Agent Systems*. Valencia, 105–122.

[10] Michael J Gonzales, Vanice C Cheung, and Laurel D Riek. 2015. Designing collaborative healthcare technology for the acute care workflow. In *Proceedings of the 9th International Conference on Pervasive Computing Technologies for Healthcare*. Istanbul, 145–152.

[11] Kilem Gwet. 2001. *Handbook of Inter-Rater Reliability*. Stataxis Publishing Company, Gaithersburg, MD. 223–246 pages.

[12] F. Harrag and E. El-Qawasmah. 2009. Neural Network for Arabic text classification. In *Proceedings of the 2nd International Conference on the Applications of Digital Information and Web Technologies*. London, 778–783.

[13] Anna C Hayden, James W Pichert, Jodi Fawcett, Ilene N Moore, and Gerald B Hickson. 2010. Best practices for basic and advanced skills in health care service recovery: A case study of a re-admitted patient. *The Joint Commission Journal on Quality and Patient Safety* 36, 7 (2010), 310–318.

[14] Gerald B Hickson, Anna C Caruso-Hayden, and James W Pichert. 2010. The PARS® program: How unsolicited patient comments can be used to promote a safer healthcare environment, address unprofessional conduct and reduce unnecessary malpractice risk. In *Annual Meeting of the American Health Lawyers Association*. Seattle.

[15] Li-Ping Jing, Hou-Kuan Huang, and Hong-Bo Shi. 2002. Improved feature selection approach TFIDF in text mining. In *Proceedings of the 1st International Conference on Machine Learning and Cybernetics*, Vol. 2. Beijing, 944–946.

[16] Timothy P. Jurka, Loren Collingwood, Amber E. Boydstun, Emiliano Grossman, and Wouter van Atteveldt. 2014. *RTextTools: Automatic Text Classification via Supervised Learning*. http://CRAN.R-project.org/package=RTextTools R package version 1.4.2.

[17] Ron Kohavi and George H. John. 1997. Wrappers for feature subset selection. *Artificial intelligence* 97, 1 (1997), 273–324.

[18] Jure Leskovec, Anand Rajaraman, and Jeffrey D. Ullman. 2014. *Mining of Massive Datasets, 2nd Ed.* Cambridge University Press, Cambridge, UK.

[19] Cheng Hua Li and Soon Cheol Park. 2007. Neural Network for Text Classification Based on Singular Value Decomposition. In *Proceedings of the 7th IEEE International Conference on Computer and Information Technology*. Washington, DC, 47–52.

[20] Bing Liu and Lei Zhang. 2012. A Survey of Opinion Mining and Sentiment Analysis. In *Mining Text Data*, Charu C. Aggarwal and ChengXiang Zhai (Eds.). Springer US, New York, Chapter 13, 415–463.

[21] Luigi M De Luca and Kwaku Atuahene-Gima. 2007. Market knowledge dimensions and cross-functional collaboration: Examining the different routes to product innovation performance. *Journal of Marketing* 71, 1 (Jan. 2007), 95–112.

[22] Aleix M. Martinez and Avinash C. Kak. 2001. PCA versus LDA. *IEEE Transactions on Pattern Analysis and Machine Intelligence* 23, 2 (Feb 2001), 228–233.

[23] Genevieve B. Melton and George Hripcsak. 2005. Automated detection of adverse events using natural language processing of discharge summaries. *Journal of the American Medical Informatics Association* 12, 4 (2005), 448–457.

[24] Myriam D. Munezero, C. Suero Montero, Erkki Sutinen, and John Pajunen. 2014. Are They Different? Affect, Feeling, Emotion, Sentiment, and Opinion Detection in Text. *IEEE Transaction on Affective Computing* 5, 2 (April–June 2014), 101âĂŞ–111.

[25] C.M. Nunes, Jr. Britto, Ad.S., C.A.A. Kaestner, and R. Sabourin. 2004. An optimized hill climbing algorithm for feature subset selection: evaluation on handwritten character recognition. In *Proceedings of the 9th International Workshop on Frontiers in Handwriting Recognition*. Kokubunji,Tokyo, 365–370.

[26] Lucila Ohno-Machado, Zia Agha, Douglas S Bell, Lisa Dahm, Michele E Day, Jason N Doctor, Davera Gabriel, Maninder K Kahlon, Katherine K Kim, Michael Hogarth, et al. 2014. pSCANNER: patient-centered Scalable National Network for Effectiveness Research. *Journal of the American Medical Informatics Association* 21, 4 (2014), 621–626.

[27] Miles Osborne. 2002. Using Maximum Entropy for Sentence Extraction. In *Proceedings of the 40th Annual Meeting of the Association for Computational Linguistics (ACL) Workshop on Automatic Summarization*. Philadelphia, 1–8.

[28] Alexander Osherenko and Elisabeth André. 2007. Lexical affect sensing: Are affect dictionaries necessary to analyze affect?. In *Proceedings of the 2nd international conference on Affective Computing and Intelligent Interaction*. Lisbon, 230–241.

[29] Karl Pearson. 1900. On the Criterion that a Given System of Deviations from the Probable in the Case of a Correlated System of Variables is such that it can be Reasonably Supposed to have Arisen from Random Sampling. *Philos. Mag.* 50, 302 (1900), 157–175.

[30] Tao Peng, Wanli Zuo, and Fengling He. 2008. SVM based adaptive learning method for text classification from positive and unlabeled documents. *Knowledge and Information Systems* 16, 3 (Sept. 2008), 281–301.

[31] James W Pennebaker and Laura A King. 1999. Linguistic styles: language use as an individual difference. *Journal of personality and social psychology* 77, 6 (1999), 1296.

[32] James W Pichert, Gerald Hickson, and Ilene Moore. 2008. Using patient complaints to promote patient safety. In *Advances in Patient Safety: New Directions and Alternative Approaches (Vol. 2: Culture and Redesign)*, Kerm Henriksen, James B. Battles, Margaret A. Keyes, and Mary L. Grady (Eds.). Agency for Healthcare Research and Quality (US), Rockville,MD.

[33] R Core Team. 2014. *R: A Language and Environment for Statistical Computing*. R Foundation for Statistical Computing, Vienna. http://www.R-project.org

[34] Fuji Ren and Changqin Quan. 2012. Linguistic-based emotion analysis and recognition for measuring consumer satisfaction: an application of affective computing. *Information Technology and Management* 13, 4 (Dec. 2012), 321–332.

[35] Stuart J. Russell and Peter Norvig. 2010. *Artificial Intelligence - A Modern Approach (3. internat. ed.).* Pearson Education, New Jersey.
[36] Robert E. Schapire. 1990. The Strength of Weak Learnability. *Machine Learning* 5 (July 1990), 197–227.
[37] Oliver C. Schultheiss. 2013. Are implicit motives revealed in mere words? Testing the marker-word hypothesis with computer-based text analysis. *Frontiers in Psychology* 4 (Oct. 2013), 748.
[38] C.J. Stimson, James W. Pichert, Ilene N. Moore, Roger R. Dmochowski, M. Bernadette Cornett, Angel Q. An, and Gerald B. Hickson. 2010. Medical Malpractice Claims Risk in Urology: An Empirical Analysis of Patient Complaint Data. *The Journal of Urology* 183, 5 (May 2010), 1971–1976.
[39] Chunke Su, Meikuan Huang, and Noshir Contractor. 2010. Understanding the structures, antecedents and outcomes of organisational learning and knowledge transfer: A multi-theoretical and multilevel network analysis. *European Journal of International Management* 4, 6 (2010), 576–601.
[40] Yla R. Tausczik and James W. Pennebaker. 2010. The psychological meaning of words: LIWC and computerized text analysis methods. *Journal of Language and Social Psychology* 29, 1 (March 2010), 24–54.
[41] Georg Henrik von Wright. 1963. *Norm and Action.* Routledge & Kegan Paul, London.
[42] Zhe Zhang and Munindar P. Singh. 2014. ReNew: A Semi-Supervised Framework for Generating Domain-Specific Lexicons and Sentiment Analysis. In *Proceedings of the 52nd Annual Meeting of the Association for Computational Linguistics (ACL).* Baltimore, 542–551.
[43] Kang Zhao, John Yen, Greta Greer, Baojun Qiu, Prasenjit Mitra, and Kenneth Portier. 2014. Finding influential users of online health communities: a new metric based on sentiment influence. *Journal of the American Medical Informatics Association* 21, e2 (2014), e212–e218. https://doi.org/10.1136/amiajnl-2013-002282

Identifying Harm Events in Clinical Care through Medical Narratives

Arman Cohan
Information Retrieval Lab, Dept. of Computer Science
Georgetown University
arman@ir.cs.georgetown.edu

Allan Fong
National Center for Human Factors in Healthcare
MedStar Health
allan.fong@medstar.net

Raj Ratwani
National Center for Human Factors in Healthcare
MedStar Health
raj.m.ratwani@medstar.net

Nazli Goharian
Information Retrieval Lab, Dept. of Computer Science
Georgetown University
nazli@ir.cs.georgetown.edu

ABSTRACT

Preventable medical errors are estimated to be among the leading causes of injury and death in the United States. To prevent such errors, healthcare systems have implemented patient safety and incident reporting systems. These systems enable clinicians to report unsafe conditions and cases where patients have been harmed due to errors in medical care. These reports are narratives in natural language and while they provide detailed information about the situation, it is non-trivial to perform large scale analysis for identifying common causes of errors and harm to the patients. In this work, we present a method for identifying harm events in patient care and categorize the harm event types based on their severity level. We show that our method which is based on convolutional and recurrent networks with an attention mechanism is able to significantly improve over the existing methods on two large scale datasets of patient reports.

KEYWORDS

Natural Language Processing; Medical Text; Deep Learning

1 INTRODUCTION

Preventable medical errors have been shown to be a major cause of injury and death in the United States [9, 24, 34]. Medical errors are estimated to be the 3rd leading causes of death in the U.S. [24, 30], which translates to an estimated incidence of 210,000 to 400,000 deaths annually [17, 24]. To address these major concerns, healthcare systems have adopted reporting systems in clinical care to help track and trend hazards and errors in patient care [25, 34]. The data from these systems are later used to identify the causes of harm and actions that should be taken to prevent similar situations. These reporting systems allow frontline clinicians to report events that are relevant to patient care including both near misses and serious safety events. Near misses are events or situations where a hazard was identified before a patient could be harmed. For example, a wrong medication order that was never administered to a patient would be considered a near miss, hence reported as a no-harm event. Serious safety events on the other hand are situations where a patient was harmed. The above example would be considered a patient harm event if the nurse had actually administered the medication causing additional treatment, monitoring, or irreversible effects on the patient.

Although reporting systems have been implemented with the goal of improving patient safety and patient care, hospital staff are faced with many challenges in analyzing and understanding these reports [23, 25]. These reports which are narratives in natural language are generated by frontline staff and vary widely in content, structure, language used, and style. These reports include a textual field where the clinicians describe the safety event and its details in free-form text. While these texts provide valuable information about the safety event, it is challenging to perform large scale analysis of these narratives to identify important safety events. In this paper, we propose and evaluate Natural Language Processing (NLP) methods to identify cases that caused harm to the patient based on medical narratives.

One important aspect in patient care is to identify events that have contributed to or resulted in harm to the patient [34]. There have been many efforts in characterizing harm to the patients based on their severity. The most common is a harm categorical system that indicates the severity of the harm to the patient [1]. These categories range from an unsafe condition (which describes an event where there was no error, but had capacity to cause harm) to death (which is an event where an error has caused or contributed to the death of a patient). These harm categories are described in Table 1 in detail [1].

The patient incident narratives can be complex and it is challenging to identify the cases of harm from these reports. These reports often consist of multiple events. For example, consider a case where a patient is found on the floor in the emergency department (ED) with no physical signs of injury. This is initially entered as a no-harm case. However, later when the patient is transferred to the radiology for an x-ray as a precaution, a small fracture is discovered from the x-ray. Therefore, while the ED staff originally entered the event as a no-harm event, the radiology department would revise this as a harm event.

Permission to make digital or hard copies of all or part of this work for personal or classroom use is granted without fee provided that copies are not made or distributed for profit or commercial advantage and that copies bear this notice and the full citation on the first page. Copyrights for components of this work owned by others than ACM must be honored. Abstracting with credit is permitted. To copy otherwise, or republish, to post on servers or to redistribute to lists, requires prior specific permission and/or a fee. Request permissions from permissions@acm.org.
ACM-BCB'17, August 20-23, 2017, Boston, MA, USA.
© 2017 ACM. 978-1-4503-4722-8/17/08...$15.00
DOI: http://dx.doi.org/10.1145/3107411.3107485

Table 1: Categories of Errors in Patient Care as defined by Agency for Healthcare Research and Quality [1]. The severity of harm increases from top to bottom. Categories {E,F,G,H,I} are harm categories while {A,B1,B2,C,D} are no-harm events.

Cat.	Description	Example
A	No error, capacity to cause error	Confusing equipment
B1	Error that did not reach the patient (due to chance)	Wrong medication label discovered
B2	Error that did not reach the patient (because of active recovery efforts by caregivers)	Mislabeled specimen in a laboratory discovered on a regular checking
C	Error that reached patient but unlikely to cause harm	Multivitamin was not ordered on admission
D	Error that reached the patient and could have necessitated monitoring and/or intervention to preclude harm	Regular release metoprolol was ordered for patient instead of extended-release
E	Error that contributed to or resulted in temporary harm	Blood pressure medication was inadvertently omitted from the orders
F	Error that could have caused temporary harm requiring initial or prolonged hospitalization	Anticoagulant, such as warfarin, was ordered daily when the patient takes it every other day
G	Error that resulted in permanent harm	Immunosuppressant medication was unintentionally ordered at wrong dose
H	Error that necessitated intervention to sustain life	Anticonvulsant therapy was inadvertently omitted
I	Error that contributed to or resulted in death	Beta-blocker was not reordered post-operatively

For these reasons, reporting harm is often miscategorized. While most events are eventually recategorized by a department manager or patient safety officers who have a more global perspective of events, this recategorization incurs additional time, resources, and expenses leading to missed opportunities to address the actual event in a timely fashion. We present a method for identifying the severity of harm from narratives regarding incidents in patient care. While there is a growing number of work in categorizing patient safety reports, none has looked at the modeling of general harm across all event types [12, 26]. Our method is based on a neural network model consisting of several layers including a convolutional layer, a recurrent layer, and an attention mechanism to improve the performance of the recurrent layer. Our method is designed to capture local significant features as well as the interactions and dependencies between the features in long sequences. Traditional methods in general and domain specific NLP rely heavily on engineering a set of representative features for the task and utilizing external knowledge and resources. While these models have been shown to work reasonably well for different tasks, their success relies on the type of features that they utilize. Apart from the feature engineering efforts, these approaches usually model the problem with respect to certain selected features and ignore other indicators and signals that might improve prediction. In contrast, our approach only relies on the text in the patient incident narratives and it does not rely on any features or external resources, making it generalizable. Through extensive evaluation on two large datasets, we show that our proposed method is able to significantly outperform the existing approaches of identifying harm in clinical care. Effective identification of harm can help the hospital staff save time both during analysis and reporting. Furthermore, a more accurate and immediate classification of harm can also help to better prioritize resources to address safety incidents, which subsequently improves general patient care.

2 RELATED WORK

There has been a growing number of work in categorizing patient incident and safety narratives in clinical care. Fong et al. [12] explored both the unstructured free-text and structured data elements in safety reports to identify and rank similar events. They evaluated different search methods utilizing bag of words features, structured elements, and topic modeling features to rank and identify similar events. In another work, Ong et al. [26] explored the similar problem of identifying extreme-risk events in patient safety and incident reports using Naive Bayes and SVM classifiers with bag of words features. In contrast to these works, we focus on the problem of identifying harm and categorizing the harm based on its severity in medical narratives. We present neural network methods that are able to capture information from the complex narratives regarding safety events without utilizing any external features. We compare our results with feature based methods and show that our proposed methods are significantly superior in identifying and classifying harm in patient incident reports.

The problem of identifying harm in patient safety reports is a type of text classification problem. Traditional approaches in text classification include methods to extract features from text and then use the feature vector as an input to a classifier such as SVM [2]. More recently, neural networks have shown success in many NLP tasks including text classification. Two of the more widely used neural network architectures have been Convolutional Neural Networks (CNN) [21] and Recurrent Neural Networks (RNN) [11]. Collobert et al. [7] were one of the first to utilize CNNs in many NLP tasks including text classification. In particular, they proposed a CNN architecture which operated on one-hot encodings of words; their model was based on the original CNN architecture of LeCun et al. [21] with adaptations to the NLP domain and showed improvements on several NLP tasks. Later CNNs were further explored for sentence modeling and classification tasks [10, 18, 19].

In the biomedical domain, there have been many efforts in classifying biomedical text and narratives based on different tasks. Many works have looked at the specific problem of indexing biomedical literature using MeSH[1] terms. These works have mostly used supervised learning frameworks with bag of words features, named-entities, and ontology specific features [37]. More recently, Rios and Kavuluru [28] utilized CNNs for this task; they showed that CNNs are more effective than feature based methods in biomedical indexing. The authors in [6] used a neural network architecture using CNN and RNNs to classify patient safety report. Xu et al. [35] used a CNN architecture, with multiple sources of word embeddings and evaluated its effectiveness on the tasks of biomedical

[1] Medical Subject Heading

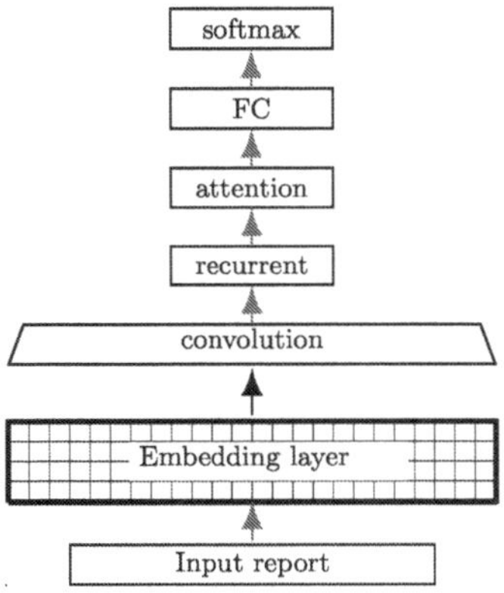

Figure 1: The outline of the proposed model. Input report consists of the raw text of the report, embedding layer does the pre-processing and represents the input as a matrix. FC stands for Fully Connected layers.

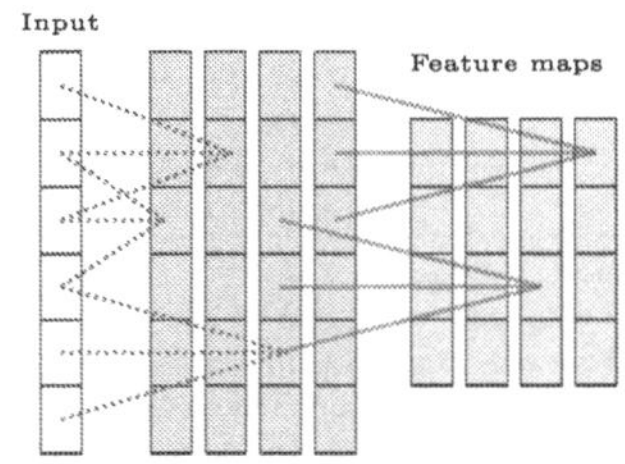

Figure 2: A convolutional layer takes a series of tokens as input and applies l filters of size k (green dotted arrows in the figure) to derive the feature values over a local window of tokens; $l = 4$ and $k = 3$ are shown here (all filters are the same size). To produce the component's output, a max pooling layer (red arrows in the figure) considers region sequences of length n and keeps the highest feature value for the sequence $n = 3$ is shown here.

literature indexing and clinical note annotation. Our method, in contrast, is based on an extension of CNNs with recurrent layer as well as an attention model to improve performance on longer sequences. We compare our methods with a CNN baseline and show that our methods can significantly outperform the baselines. Our focus is on the challenging task of identifying harm in patient incident reports where the incident narratives are often complex, consisting of multiple chained events in a single narrative. Our proposed model, is designed to capture these complexities.

3 METHODS

We present a general neural network architecture for identifying harm in patient safety reports. As explained in §1, the narratives regarding patient safety can be complex and identifying harm to the patient is challenging in these reports. To be able to perform this task effectively, we will need a model that is able to capture both local features as well as the language usage in the entire report. To achieve this goal, we propose a neural network consisting of several layers where each layer is designed to address the aforementioned challenges. Our approach does not require feature engineering and it learns to identify significant features from the raw text automatically. We first describe the general outline of our model and then we describe each component in more detail.

The outline of the model. The proposed architecture is shown in the Figure 1. The input report is first pre-processed and represented as a matrix corresponding to word embeddings. Word emdeddings or distributed representations of words aim to embed (represent) words with dense vectors such that words with similar properties have similar vectors [4]. These embeddings can be general and pre-trained or can be trained according to the task at hand. Then a convolutional layer extracts the significant local features that are helpful for identifying harm in the report. Next, a recurrent layer captures the interactions of the local features along the entire sequence of the words in the report. In the next layer, we propose an attention model which serves to overcome the problem of recurrent networks in compressing an entire sequence in a single vector by focusing the attention to the important timesteps (steps of the sequence) in the recurrent layer. Finally, the output of the attention model is a vector which is passed to a fully connected layer and a softmax classifier identifies the level of harm associated with the report. We now explain each of these layers in detail.

3.1 Embedding layer

This layer pre-processes the raw text corresponding to the medical report and represents it as a matrix of real valued numbers. This matrix consists of embeddings of the words in the report. We tokenize the text using a simple white space tokenizer and we lowercase all the words. We then transform the input sequence of tokens into a sequence of dense distributional vectors. Specifically, given a sequence of tokens W where $W = \langle w_1, w_2, ..., w_n \rangle$ and w_i's are the input sequence tokens, the embedding layer represents each token w_i as a d dimensional vector x_i, and the sequence W will be represented as a matrix of real valued numbers $\mathbf{X}$ with dimensions of $\mathbf{X} \in \mathbb{R}^{(n_{\max} \times d)}$ where $n_{\max}$ is the maximum sequence length. Text inputs with length larger than $n_{\max}$ will be cropped and text inputs shorter than the $n_{\max}$ are padded with zeros. The value of $n_{\max}$ is determined empirically.

3.2 Convolutional layer

Convolutional layer is repsonsible for extracting local features from the input text. Convolutional Neural Networks (CNNs) [21] have been previously used in sentence modeling and classification tasks [18, 19]. A CNN is a neural network that consists of two main operations: convolution and pooling. A convolution is an operation between two functions f and g where f is the primary vector and g is the filter. The convolution operation between f and g, evaluated at entry n is represented as: $(f * g)[n] = \sum_{i=-K}^{K} f[n-i] \times g[i]$ Where $*$ denotes the convolution operation and $L = 2K - 1$ is the length of the filter. Here, f is the input to the convolution (word vectors obtained from the embedding layer).

Features are extracted by convolution of the input text with a number of linear filters, adding a bias term and applying a non-linearity. The result is called a feature map. The trained weights in

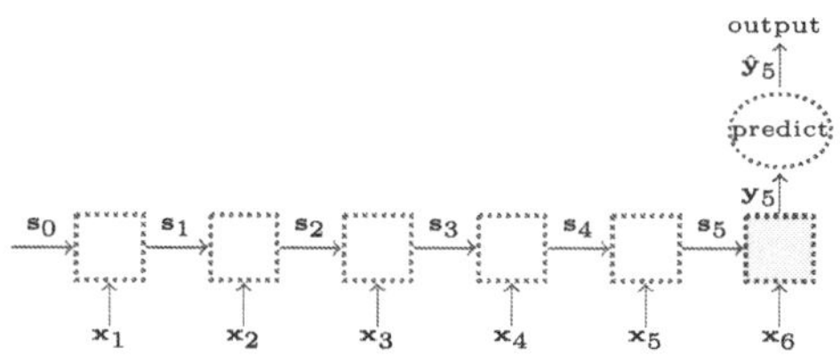

Figure 3: Representing a sequence with an RNN and using it's last hidden state for making predictions.

these filters correspond to a linguistic feature detector that learns to recognize a specific class of n-grams where $L \leq n$. A max-pooling operation is used after the convolution to extract the significant features.

Multiple feature maps. Similar to convolutional networks for object recognition [21], we use multiple feature maps with different filters to capture various aspects of the input sequence. Figure 2 illustrates how the feature maps are constructed from the input. First the convolution and non-linearity are applied to the input and then the max pooling derives the resulting feature maps. The final output of this layer at each time-step is the concatenation of the feature maps at that time-step.

3.3 Recurrent layer

The result of the convolution layer is a sequence of vectors each of which is the concatenation of the feature maps at corresponding time-step. Convolutional layer is able to extract significant local features that are important for our task. However, the interactions between the words are not captured specially if the words are distant from each others. Recurrent Neural Networks (RNNs) are a family of neural networks that are designed to process a sequence of values. We use an RNN on top of the result of the convolution layer to capture interactions along the entire sequence of words. RNNs are an extension of multilayer perceptrons in which the output of each step is used as an additional input to the next step. Specifically, the activations arrive at the hidden layer of the network from both the current external input and the hidden layer activations one step back in time. The general formulation of an RNN is as follows:

$$h(t) = g(W^{(h)}h(t-1) + W^{(x)}x(t)) \tag{1a}$$

$$\hat{y}(t) = \text{softmax}(W^{(s)}h(t)) \tag{1b}$$

Where $h(t)$ shows the hidden state of the RNN in time step t, $x(t)$ is the input sequence at time step t, $W^{(h)}$, $W^{(x)}$, and $W^{(s)}$ are the weights associated with the hidden state, input, and softmax, respectively, and g is an activation function such as RELU [8].

In sequence modeling tasks, the final hidden state of the network can represent the whole sequence and can be used for making predictions [13]. This final hidden state, in theory, can capture all the information in the entire sequence. This is because the output of each timestep is used as an input to the subsequent timestep in the network. Figure 3 illustrates the prediction made at the last hidden state of the network.

3.3.1 *RNN variants.* Training the general formulation of RNNs in practice is difficult due to the exploding and vanishing gradient problems (gradients becoming exceedingly high or become exceedingly close to 0 after only a few timesteps) [27]. For the exploding gradient problem, a common solution is to cap the gradient value at a specific maximum threshold. There has been some variants of RNNs that assist the gradient flow and mitigate the vanishing gradient problem. Most notable are the Long Short Term Memory (LSTM) [16] and Gated Recurrent Unit (GRU) [5].

LSTM adds additional gates to the regular hidden layer of a recurrent network to assist the gradient flow and allow the network to be effectively trained. These gates control the amount of information to be forgotten or preserved throughout the sequence. Concretely, we are referring to the formulation of Graves [15] for LSTM.

GRU proposed by Cho et al. [5] makes each recurrent unit to adaptively capture dependencies of different time scales and similar to LSTM, GRU also has gating units that control the flow of information through the computational graph. The difference with LSTM is that the GRU does not have a separate memory cell. We use the exact formulation of Cho et al. [5] for GRU.

Bidirectional RNNs. In order to also capture the backward dependencies and interactions between different parts of a sequence, a backward RNN is also trained which can encode the information from the future time steps [14, 29]. The hidden states of the backward RNN are then considered along with the corresponding hidden states of the forward RNN (e.g. by concatenation) at each time step and used in the subsequent layers.

Let $\boldsymbol{x} = \langle x_1, ..., x_n \rangle$ be the input to the Recurrent layer. Then the bidirectional RNN over the time steps $t = 1, ..., n$ is as follows:

$$h_t = \langle \overrightarrow{h_t}; \overleftarrow{h_t} \rangle \tag{2}$$

where "$\langle \cdot; \cdot \rangle$" shows the concatenation operation and $\overrightarrow{h_t}$ ($\overleftarrow{h_t}$) is the forward (backward) RNN defined as follows:

$$\overrightarrow{h_t} = \overrightarrow{RNN}(x_t); \quad \overleftarrow{h_t} = \overleftarrow{RNN}(x_t) \tag{3}$$

Where RNN($\cdot$) is the feed forward RNN cell in the general form, LSTM, or GRU.

3.4 Attention model

We use an attention model on top of our recurrent layer to be able to capture the local features that are more important in the task at hand. The limitation of using the regular recurrent network for the classification task is that the last time step of recurrent network loses some information about the sequence, specially when the sequence length becomes large [5]. This will not be a significant problem in short sentence classification tasks, but in our problem, the reports can have several sentences and the sequence length can be long. While in theory, the last step of the RNN is able to encode all the important information in the entire sequence, in practice it tends to focus more on the more recent time steps [31] and therefore loses some information specially about the earlier time steps. Using a bidirectional RNN can partially mitigate this problem where the last state of the backward RNN along with the last state of the forward RNN are able to capture the information in beginning and the end of the sequence. However, bidirectional RNNs are still suffering from the same information loss problem.

Inspired by recent work in machine translation [3] and document modeling [36], we propose to address this problem using a soft attention mechanism. Attention mechanism helps in constructing

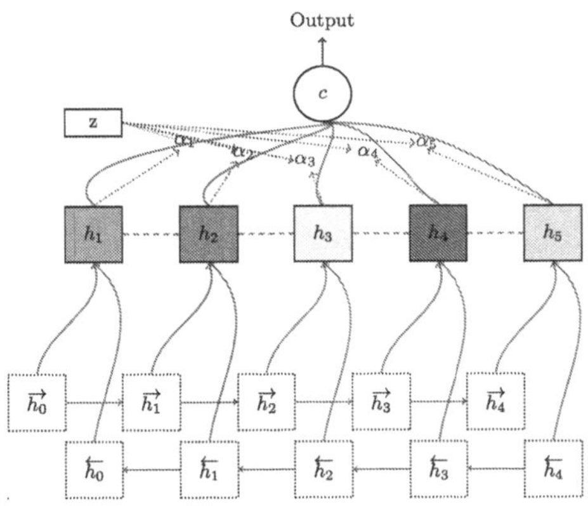

Figure 4: The attention mechanism over the recurrent layer. The states $\overrightarrow{h_i}$ and $\overleftarrow{h_i}$ show forward and backward hidden state of the RNN respectively. h_i's are the concatenation of the forward and backward RNN states. z is a context vector that attends to important time steps and α_i are the weights associated with each hidden state h_i. The figure shows an example where darker colors for the h_i show more importance in constructing c which is used as input to the next layer.

a context vector over the input that automatically incorporates the important parts of the input. The attention mechanism is shown in Figure 4. Particularly, instead of only considering the last hidden state of the RNN (h_n), the attention model attends to the important timesteps by introducing additional weights (α's):

$$c = \sum_{t=1}^{N} \alpha_t h_t \tag{4}$$

where t are the time steps in the input sequence and the weights α are learned according to the following softmax function:

$$\alpha_t = \text{softmax}(u_t^{\intercal} z) \tag{5}$$

where z is a context vector that helps in finding the weight importance of the local states h_t. This context vector can be seen as an input memory representation in memory networks and is jointly trained with the network. u_t is a feed forward function which we will define later and for a set of scores s_i, the softmax function returns a probability distribution over the scores:

$$\text{softmax}(s_i) = \frac{\exp(s_i/\beta)}{\sum_j \exp(s_j/\beta)}; \tag{6}$$

with β being a parameter controlling the smoothness of the resulting distribution.

u_t in equation 5 is the result of applying a regular feed forward network over the hidden state h_t with weights U and biases b:

$$u_t = F(h_t) = \tanh(Uh_t + b) \tag{7}$$

Finally, our model at the top layer has a fully connected layer followed by a softmax non-linear layer that predicts the probability distribution of harm severity given an input report.

Table 2: Dataset characteristics. Avg. refers to the average and std is the standard deviation.

Statistic	Dataset 1	Dataset 2
Number of reports	28,539	248,213
Avg. report length (character)	411.4	239.2
Stdev report length (character)	370.9	187.2

Table 3: Distribution of harm levels across different severity categories. Numbers show percentage of the entire data. The severity increases as we move from A to I. For the definition of the harm severity levels refer to Table 1 at page 2.

	no-harm				harm
Dataset	A	B	C	D	[E-I]
1	39.3	13.8	19.9	13.1	13.9
2	11.7	12.9	40.4	31.6	3.4

3.5 Training

Let Θ denote all the parameters in the network which includes the weights associated with each of the layers described in previous sections. The entire network is then trained to minimize the following loss function:

$$J(\Theta) = -\sum_{c=1}^{C} \mathbf{1}[y^* = c] \log \Pr(Y = c|\mathbf{x}) \tag{8}$$

where C is the number of harm severity classes and y^* is the ground truth label for the input report $\mathbf{x}$, $\mathbf{1}[\cdot]$ is the indicator function, and the probability of each harm severity class is estimated through the network.

4 EXPERIMENTS

4.1 Data

We use two large scale datasets consisting of patient safety and incidents reports sampled from various healthcare systems. These reports are sometimes referred to as "patient safety reports" in the health informatics literature, but in general they are meant to identify and characterize errors in patient care.

This study was approved by the MedStar Health Research Institute Institutional Review Board (protocol 2014-101). The characteristics of the datasets are outlined in Table 2. We observe that one of the datasets (DS2) is larger than the other one (DS1) and the length of reports are rather different between them. Each dataset consists of reports regarding different categories in patient care. The statistics about each of the harm levels are shown in Table 3. The harm events (right side of the Table) are usually much less frequent than the events with no actual harm (left side of the Table). We divide each dataset to 3 subsets of training, validation, and test with respective distribution of 60%, 20%, and 20% of the entire data. The hyper-parameters of the models were chosen empirically based on the performance on the validation set and the test set is preserved for evaluation.

Table 4: The results of identifying harm vs no-harm events. The top part of the Table shows the baselines while the bottom part shows the variants of the models presented in this work. Metrics are precision (P.), recall (R.), F-1 score for the harm category as well as the ROC Area Under the Curve (AUC). The numbers are percentages.

Method	Dataset 1				Dataset 2			
	P	R	F-1	AUC	P	R	F-1	AUC
Baselines								
SVM bow1	81.5	52.4	63.8	89.2	85.1	61.7	71.5	94.0
SVM bow2	81.8	55.7	66.3	89.7	84.8	64.9	73.5	94.6
SVM bow3	81.9	55.1	65.9	89.7	84.5	65.6	73.9	94.8
MNB bow1	81.1	52.8	64.0	83.0	66.6	73.9	70.1	89.3
MNB bow2	86.6	43.1	57.5	79.0	73.9	66.0	69.7	86.9
MNB bow3	**88.3**	37.7	52.9	77.2	77.0	60.0	67.5	85.1
CNN	75.7	63.9	69.3	90.4	80.2	67.2	73.1	94.7
LSTM	76.6	61.9	68.8	90.3	70.1	**75.9**	72.9	94.6
This work								
GRU CNN	75.8	68.3	71.8	91.0	77.9	73.2	75.5	95.0
Bi-GRU CNN	72.3	71.8	72.1	91.1	80.1	71.0	75.3	94.9
LSTM CNN	77.1	67.1	71.8	91.2	77.6	74.0	75.8	95.0
Bi-LSTM CNN	78.7	62.8	69.8	91.1	79.6	70.7	74.9	94.9
ATT GRU CNN	78.1	64.4	70.6	91.0	78.0	75.1	76.5	95.0
ATT Bi-GRU CNN	73.4	69.3	71.3	91.0	**87.3**	70.3	**77.9**	94.8
ATT LSTM CNN	69.4	**76.8**	**72.9**	**91.2**	78.8	74.9	76.8	95.0
ATT Bi-LSTM CNN	83.0	64.0	72.3	91.0	79.9	74.5	77.1	**95.2**

4.2 Evaluation

We evaluate the effectiveness of our models in identifying harm by using standard classification evaluation metrics namely precision, recall, F-1 and Area Under the Curve (AUC).

4.3 Baselines

For comparing the performance of the proposed methods, we consider the following baselines:

- *SVM bow* - SVM with linear kernel with n-gram bag of words (bow) features [33]. We experiment with three types of features, n-grams of size {1}, {1,2}, and {1,2,3} (we respectively abbreviate the resulting models with *bow1*, *bow2*, and *bow3*).
- *MNB bow* - We also experiment with Multinomial Naive Bayes method for classification where Wang and Manning [33] show its effectiveness in many text classification tasks. We used scikit-learn (http://scikit-learn.org/) implementation of SVM and MNB.
- *CNN* - We consider CNN model for text classification which has shown good results in both general domain [18, 19] and biomedical domain [28].
- *LSTM* - We also compare against RNN (LSTM) classifier which is similar to the models used in [22, 32] (see Figure 3).

These methods form strong baselines with which we compare the performance of our models.

4.4 Model variants

We evaluate several variants of our models. The first variant is our model architecture which is the entire model presented in §3 minus the attention model. We consider two types of recurrent networks, GRU and LSTM, as well as their bidirectional variants (Bi-GRU and Bi-LSTM). We then evaluate our complete model which utilizes the attention mechanism. When considering attention, we evaluated both GRU and LSTM as the underlying recurrent layer. We abbreviate these models based on the layers from top to bottom. For example "*ATT GRU CNN*" corresponds to our attention model with GRU unit, while example "*ATT Bi-LSTM CNN*" corresponds to our attention model with bidirectional LSTM in the recurrent layer.

Table 5: The performance of our top model variants in identifying more fine grained types of harm. For the definition of the categories refer to §1 and Table 1. The numbers are F-1 scores percentages in each category.

	Temp./ perm. harm	Didn't reach pt.	Near Miss	Unsafe	Avg
Dataset1					
MNB bow2	41.4	39.7	67.7	77.0	64.1
SVM bow2	53.5	49.8	68.1	77.1	66.6
LSTM CNN	62.5	52.36	67.7	75.8	68.2
CNN	64.0	47.4	65.4	75.4	66.8
ATT Bi-LSTM CNN	64.1	51.6	68.5	76.1	68.7
ATT Bi-GRU CNN	64.5	48.9	69.7	77.0	**68.9**
Dataset2					
MNB bow2	43.4	52.0	82.8	51.8	71.0
SVM bow2	49.3	56.4	82.1	55.7	72.6
LSTM CNN	62.9	55.1	83.8	54.2	73.8
CNN	58.5	54.6	82.7	55.0	72.6
ATT Bi-LSTM CNN	59.3	59.2	83.8	54.6	74.1
ATT Bi-GRU CNN	66.6	60.2	83.4	59.3	**75.3**

Design decisions and hyperparameters. We empirically made the following design choices and hyperparameter selection: We used embedding size of 100 for word vectors and we set the maximum sequence length to 100 words (smaller sequences are padded with zero vectors and larger sequences are cropped). For convolution, we used filters of length 2 to 5 with 128 channels each, max pooling of length 4, and merge the output of the filters by concatenation. For RNN, we use LSTM and GRU with hidden size of 100. We used dropout rate of 0.25 after convolution. Training was done with batch size of 128 and through 2 and 6 epochs for the larger and smaller datasets, respectively. Adam [20] was used as optimizer and early stopping was applied by monitoring accuracy on the validation set.

4.5 Results

We first consider the problem of identifying harm cases in the patient reports. That is, we classify a report as indicating some signs of harm to the patient (a harm case) or not (a no-harm case). The main results of our methods in identifying harm are illustrated in Table 4. The metrics are Precision, Recall, F-1 score for the harm category as well as the Area under the curve. We observe that our attention models (starting with ATT in the Table) are the best performing methods in both datasets evaluated by F-1 scores. In particular, the attention model using an LSTM recurrent unit (ATT LSTM CNN) achieves the highest F-1 of 72.9% on the first dataset and the attention model using a bidirectional GRU (ATT Bi-GRU CNN) achieves F-1 of 77.9% on the second dataset. While the results ranges are similar between the two datasets, in general we can see that the results on the second dataset are slightly higher. This is due to the datasets being generated at different healthcare systems and thus there are qualitative and quantitative difference between the datasets. As far as the baselines, we can see that in general, in terms of F-1 scores, traditional bag of words approaches [33] are not

Table 6: The results of our best method for the 1st dataset (ATT LSTM CNN) on different safety categories. We only show resuls for common categories.

Category	F-1	P	R	Acc
Skin/Tissue	92.9	94.1	91.8	87.2
Surgery/Procedure	76.1	79.4	73	84.2
Restraints/Seclusion Injury	75	75	75	90.9
Airway Management	73.7	70	77.8	81
Blood Bank	71.4	100	55.6	98.1
Lines/Tubes/Drain	66	70	62.5	71.7
Medication/Fluid	63.9	77.5	54.4	93
Safety/Security	56.4	75.9	44.9	73.2
Diagnosis/Treatment	55	56.9	53.2	79.3
Miscellaneous	55	54.5	55.6	83.7
Fall	52.2	63.8	44.1	86.4
Diagnostic Imaging	50	44	57.9	83.7
Patient ID/Documentation	36.4	40	33.3	97
Lab/Specimen	0	0	0	97.2

quite competitive. In terms of precision, the Multinommial Naive Bayes method using up to 3gram features (MNB bow3) achieves the highest overall scores on first dataset; however, its recall is very low, making it relatively ineffective. The SVM baselines work generally better on the second dataset compared with the first dataset, and they outperform the performance of CNN and LSTM baselines. For example, the best F-1 score on the second dataset is 73.9% which is for the SVM bow3 baseline. Our methods are still able to significantly improve over this baseline (compare the performance of *ATT Bi-GRU CNN* with *SVM bow 3*). Another trend that is worth noting is the significantly higher recall performance of our proposed models in comparison with the baselines. Recall is important in the task of harm detection, as any harm case can impact the patient and the method should minimize false negatives. We then compare the result of our method using a recurrent model on top of a convolutional model and observe how it can improve both the CNN and LSTM baselines. This suggests that while CNNs are effective in capturing the information in longer sequences, there is also some additional information that is captured when considering the interactions between the words along the entire sequence. We also observe that using a recurrent layer on top of a convoluational layer improves the performance (compare LSTM with our models in the Table), suggesting that local features captured by CNN are important in the final prediction.

Next, we evaluate the performance of our top models in fine-grain classification of harm severity on patients compared with the top baselines. Table 5 shows the performance on 4 levels of harm: Temporary or permenant harm, event that reached the patient but did not cause harm, near miss events, unsafe events. For description of these categories refer to Section 1 and Table 1. We observe that our method variant *ATT Bi-GRU CNN* achieves the best overall performance with average respective F-1 scores of 68.9% and 75.3% in datasets 1 and 2.

4.6 Analysis

To better evaluate the performance of our system and study the errors that it makes, we analyze the performance on each dataset based on each category of incident reports. The incident reports are categorized into several categories and there are often qualitative

Table 7: The results of harm identification for our best method on the second dataset (ATT Bi-GRU CNN) on different safety categories. Numbers are percentages. P/T/T refers to the category of Procedure/Treatment/Test

Category	F-1	P	R	Acc
Complication of P/T/T	81.8	80.6	83.1	85.7
Fall	79.7	86	74.3	95
Error in P/T/T	71.3	68.8	74	96.3
Miscellaneous	68.4	68.2	68.5	87
Skin Integrity	66.4	75.2	59.4	92.2
Equipment/Supplies/Devices	61.7	62.5	61	95.9
Transfusion	52.4	68.8	42.3	96
Medication error	49.4	69.4	38.3	98.3
Adverse Drug Reaction	46.2	61.5	37	80.8

differences between the narratives in different categories. Tables 6 and 7 show the breakdown of results based on top common categories in dataset 1 and 2, respectively. We report the results of the best performing model variant on each dataset (i.e. *ATT LSTM CNN* for dataset 1 and *ATT Bi-GRU CNN* for dataset 2). On dataset 1 (Table 6) we observe that the model achieves very high scores in identifying harm in Skin/Tissue category with F-1 of 92.9% in identifying harm. Results on some other categories such as *Surgury/Procedure, Seclusion Injury, Airway Management*, and *Blood bank* are also relatively high. However, we observe that on some categories such as *Patient ID/Documentation* and *Lab/Specimen* the performance is low. We attribute the low performance in these categories to three main reasons: the total number of data in each category, the relative number of harm cases in the category, and the diversity of the type of reports in each category. We analyzed the distribution of the harm cases in each category. Some categories are more balanced in terms of harm and no-harm cases, while other categories are extremely unbalanced. We calculate the class ratios of harm in each category and compare the results based on these ratios. Figure 5 illustrates the performance of our method on each category and the ratio of harm cases in that category. Each data point shows the performance results in terms of F-1 based on the ratio of harm cases in that category. We observe that as the ratio of harm cases increases, the performance generally tends to increase. This is expected, as training the model on highly unbalanced datasets prevents the model to learn the appropriate weights associated with the positive class. The two categories at the

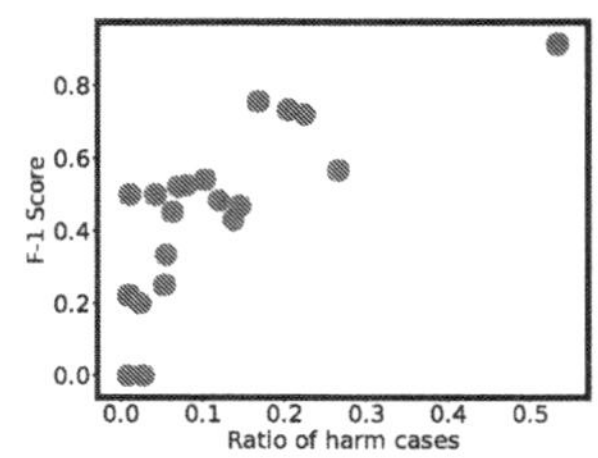

Figure 5: The performance of the our best method on dataset 1 based on each category. Each data point shows the results in a specific category as well as the ratio of harm cases in that category. The x-axis shows the ratio of harm cases.

bottom left side of Figure 5 are the categories with lowest results in Table 6. The respective ratio of harm cases in these categories are 0.009 and 0.027, while the ratio of harm cases in *Skin/Tissue* (the point on top right side of the Figure) is 0.53.

We also performed qualitative analysis on the reports in each category by inspecting the type of incidents in each category. We investigate the types of incidents in the best performing category in dataset 1 *Skin/Tissue* and most of the events are regarding pressure ulcer and wounds. On the other hand, looking at the *Lab/Specimen* category, there are many diverse types of errors and harm in this category such as collection issues, documentation problems, labeling issues, ordering issues, etc, that are very different in description, making it difficult for the model to learn all the nuances in this category. This reason, coupled with relative low number of harm cases in the dataset in this category, results in low performance. We believe that having more data would help improving the performance of the model.

5 CONCLUSIONS

In this paper, we presented a neural network model for identifying harm in safety narratives related to clinical care. We used a multi-layer network with convolutional, recurrent, and soft attention mechanism layers. We argued that convolutional layer is important in finding the local features and the recurrent layer with attention is effective in finding the interactions and dependencies along the sequence. We demonstrated that our methods can significantly improve the performance over existing methods in identifying harm safety cases. The impact of the methods and results presented in this paper is substantial to patient care. More accurate methods in the identification of harm can help the data analysis and reporting process, prevent harm to patients, better prioritize resources to address safety incidents, and subsequently improve general patient care.

ACKNOWLEDGMENTS

We thank the four anonymous reviewers for their helpful comments and suggestions. We gratefully acknowledge the support of NVIDIA Corporation with the donation of the Titan X Pascal GPU used for this research. This project was funded under contract/grant number Grant R01 HS023701-02 from the Agency for Healthcare Research and Quality (AHRQ), U.S. Department of Health and Human Services. The opinions expressed in this document are those of the authors and do not necessarily reflect the official position of AHRQ or the U.S. Department of Health and Human Services.

REFERENCES

[1] Agency for Healthcare Research and Quality. 2012. Categories of Medication Error Classification. *Content last reviewed August* (2012). http://www.ahrq.gov/

[2] Charu C Aggarwal and ChengXiang Zhai. 2012. A survey of text classification algorithms. In *Mining text data*. Springer, 163–222.

[3] Dzmitry Bahdanau, Kyunghyun Cho, and Yoshua Bengio. 2014. Neural machine translation by jointly learning to align and translate. *arXiv preprint arXiv:1409.0473* (2014).

[4] Yoshua Bengio, Aaron Courville, and Pascal Vincent. 2013. Representation learning: A review and new perspectives. *IEEE transactions on pattern analysis and machine intelligence* 35, 8 (2013), 1798–1828.

[5] Kyunghyun Cho, Bart Van Merriënboer, Dzmitry Bahdanau, and Yoshua Bengio. 2014. On the properties of neural machine translation: Encoder-decoder approaches. *arXiv preprint arXiv:1409.1259* (2014).

[6] Arman Cohan, Allan Fong, Nazli Goharian, and Raj Ratwani. 2017. A Neural Attention Model for Categorizing Patient Safety Events. In *Advances in Information Retrieval: 39th European Conference on IR Research, ECIR 2017*. 720–726.

[7] Ronan Collobert, Jason Weston, Léon Bottou, Michael Karlen, Koray Kavukcuoglu, and Pavel Kuksa. 2011. Natural Language Processing (Almost) from Scratch. *J. Mach. Learn. Res.* (2011), 45.

[8] George E Dahl, Tara N Sainath, and Geoffrey E Hinton. 2013. Improving deep neural networks for LVCSR using rectified linear units and dropout. In *ICASSP*. IEEE, 8609–8613.

[9] Molla S Donaldson, Janet M Corrigan, Linda T Kohn, and others. 2000. *To err is human: building a safer health system*. Vol. 6. National Academies Press.

[10] Cícero Nogueira dos Santos and Maira Gatti. 2014. Deep Convolutional Neural Networks for Sentiment Analysis of Short Texts. In *COLING*. 69–78.

[11] Jeffrey L Elman. 1990. Finding structure in time. *Cognitive science* 14, 2 (1990).

[12] Allan Fong, A Zachary Hettinger, and Raj M Ratwani. 2015. Exploring methods for identifying related patient safety events using structured and unstructured data. *Journal of biomedical informatics* 58 (2015), 89–95.

[13] Yoav Goldberg. 2016. A Primer on Neural Network Models for Natural Language Processing. *Journal of Artificial Intelligence Research (JAIR)* 57 (2016), 345–420.

[14] Alex Graves. 2008. Supervised sequence labelling with recurrent neural networks. *Ph.D. thesis, Technische UniversitÃĺat MÃĺunchen* (2008).

[15] Alex Graves. 2013. Generating sequences with recurrent neural networks. *arXiv preprint arXiv:1308.0850* (2013).

[16] Sepp Hochreiter and Jürgen Schmidhuber. 1997. Long short-term memory. *Neural computation* 9, 8 (1997), 1735–1780.

[17] John T. James. 2013. A New, Evidence-based Estimate of Patient Harms Associated with Hospital Care. *Journal of Patient Safety* 9 (2013), 122–128. DOI: http://dx.doi.org/10.1097/PTS.0b013e3182948a69

[18] Nal Kalchbrenner, Edward Grefenstette, and Phil Blunsom. 2014. A Convolutional Neural Network for Modelling Sentences. In *ACL*. 655–665.

[19] Yoon Kim. 2014. Convolutional Neural Networks for Sentence Classification. In *EMNLP*. 1746–1751.

[20] Diederik Kingma and Jimmy Ba. 2014. Adam: A method for stochastic optimization. *arXiv preprint arXiv:1412.6980* (2014).

[21] Yann LeCun, Léon Bottou, Yoshua Bengio, and Patrick Haffner. 1998. Gradient-based learning applied to document recognition. *Proc. IEEE* 86, 11 (1998).

[22] Pengfei Liu, Xipeng Qiu, and Xuanjing Huang. 2016. Recurrent neural network for text classification with multi-task learning. *arXiv preprint arXiv:1605.05101* (2016).

[23] Carl Macrae. 2016. The problem with incident reporting. *BMJ Quality & Safety* 25 (2016), 71–75. DOI: http://dx.doi.org/10.1136/bmjqs-2015-004732

[24] Martin A Makary and Michael Daniel. 2016. Medical errorâĂŤthe third leading cause of death in the US. *Bmj* 353 (2016), i2139.

[25] Imogen Mitchell, Anne Schuster, Katherine Smith, Peter Pronovost, and Albert Wu. 2016. Patient safety incident reporting: a qualitative study of thoughts and perceptions of experts 15 years after âĂŸ To Err is Human '. *BMJ Quality & Safety* 25 (2016), 92–99. DOI: http://dx.doi.org/10.1136/bmjqs-2015-004405

[26] Mei-Sing Ong, Farah Magrabi, and Enrico Coiera. 2012. Automated identification of extreme-risk events in clinical incident reports. *Journal of the American Medical Informatics Association* 19, e1 (2012), e110–e118.

[27] Razvan Pascanu, Tomas Mikolov, and Yoshua Bengio. 2013. On the difficulty of training recurrent neural networks. *ICML* 28 (2013), 1310–1318.

[28] Anthony Rios and Ramakanth Kavuluru. 2015. Convolutional neural networks for biomedical text classification: application in indexing biomedical articles. In *ACM-BCB*. ACM, 258–267.

[29] Mike Schuster and Kuldip K Paliwal. 1997. Bidirectional recurrent neural networks. *IEEE Transactions on Signal Processing* 45, 11 (1997), 2673–2681.

[30] Barbara Starfield. 2000. Is US health really the best in the world? *Jama* 284, 4 (2000), 483–485.

[31] Ilya Sutskever, Oriol Vinyals, and Quoc V Le. 2014. Sequence to sequence learning with neural networks. In *Advances in neural information processing systems*. 3104–3112.

[32] Duyu Tang, Bing Qin, and Ting Liu. 2015. Document Modeling with Gated Recurrent Neural Network for Sentiment Classification.. In *EMNLP*. 1422–1432.

[33] Sida Wang and Christopher D Manning. 2012. Baselines and bigrams: Simple, good sentiment and topic classification. In *ACL*. 90–94.

[34] Huw Williams, Alison Cooper, and Andrew Carson-Stevens. 2016. Opportunities for incident reporting. *BMJ Quality & Safety* 25 (2016), 133–134.

[35] Haotian Xu, Ming Dong, Dongxiao Zhu, Alexander Kotov, April Idalski Carcone, and Sylvie Naar-King. 2016. Text Classification with Topic-based Word Embedding and Convolutional Neural Networks. In *ACM-BCB*. 88–97.

[36] Zichao Yang, Diyi Yang, Chris Dyer, Xiaodong He, Alex Smola, and Eduard Hovy. 2016. Hierarchical Attention Networks for Document Classification. In *NAACL-HLT*. 1480–1489.

[37] Antonio Jose Jimeno Yepes, James G Mork, Dina Demner-Fushman, and Alan R Aronson. 2013. Comparison and combination of several MeSH indexing approaches. In *AMIA annual symposium proceedings*, Vol. 2013. 709.

GOstruct 2.0: Automated Protein Function Prediction for Annotated Proteins

Indika Kahanda
Montana State University
357 Barnard Hall, Montana State University
Bozeman, MT 59717
indika.kahanda@montana.edu

Asa Ben-Hur
Colorado State University
Computer Science Department, 1873 Campus Delivery
Fort Collins, CO 80523-1873
asa@cs.colostate.edu

ABSTRACT

Automated Protein Function Prediction is the task of automatically predicting functional annotations for a protein based on gold-standard annotations derived from experimental assays. These experiment-based annotations accumulate over time: proteins without annotations get annotated, and new functions of already annotated proteins are discovered. Therefore, function prediction can be considered a combination of two sub-tasks: making predictions on annotated proteins and making predictions on previously unannotated proteins. In previous work, we analyzed the performance of several protein function prediction methods in these two scenarios. Our results showed that GOstruct, which is based on the structured output framework, had lower accuracy in the task of predicting annotations for proteins with existing annotations, while its performance on un-annotated proteins was similar to the performance in cross-validation. In this work, we present GOstruct 2.0 which includes improvements that allow the model to make use of information of a protein's current annotations to better handle the task of predicting novel annotations for previously annotated proteins. This is highly important for model organisms where most proteins have some level of annotations. Experimental results on human data show that GOstruct 2.0 outperforms the original GOstruct in this task, demonstrating the effectiveness of the proposed improvements. This is the first study that focuses on adapting the structured output framework for applications in which labels are incomplete by nature.

CCS CONCEPTS

•Theory of computation →Structured prediction; •Computing methodologies →Supervised learning by classification; Structured outputs; Support vector machines; *Cross-validation;* **•Applied computing →Computational proteomics; Bioinformatics;**

KEYWORDS

Automated Protein Function Prediction, Hierarchical Multilabel Classification, Structured Support Vector Machines, incomplete labels.

Permission to make digital or hard copies of part or all of this work for personal or classroom use is granted without fee provided that copies are not made or distributed for profit or commercial advantage and that copies bear this notice and the full citation on the first page. Copyrights for third-party components of this work must be honored. For all other uses, contact the owner/author(s).
ACM-BCB'17, August 20-23, 2017, Boston, MA, USA.
© 2017 Copyright held by the owner/author(s). 978-1-4503-4722-8/17/08...$15.00
DOI: http://dx.doi.org/10.1145/3107411.3107417

1 INTRODUCTION

Identifying the functions of the multitude of proteins encoded by a genome is a key problem in bioinformatics [15, 27]. The Gene Ontology (GO) [1] has emerged as the standard for describing protein function. It is a structured vocabulary with thousands of terms which describes different aspects of protein function using a hierarchy of keywords. It is composed of three independent subontologies for annotating the molecular functions of proteins, the biological processes they participate in, and the cellular components in which these occur. Examples of GO categories in these subontologies include RNA binding (molecular function), chromosome segregation (biological process) and nucleus (cellular component).

Despite the difficulty of experimentally determining function, scientists have been able to annotate a large number of proteins with GO categories through various wet-lab experiments. Currently there are more than 100,000 GO annotations for a large number of proteins across many species. But as the cost of sequencing continues to decline rapidly [24] there is an increasingly larger gap between sequences with and without annotations; therefore it is not realistic to use experimental determination as the sole means of annotation, and computational methods, enabled by the existing data, have emerged as a viable alternative.

In recent years, the bioinformatics community has developed many computational methods for function prediction [27]. Many of the earliest methods performed "transfer of annotation" using amino acid sequence similarity to proteins with known functions [9]. Over the years, discriminative algorithms such as SVMs [12, 25] and decision trees [13, 34], as well as probabilistic models which perform label propagation on graphs [5, 21, 22] have been developed. More recently, structured output methods have demonstrated high accuracy in GO term prediction [33], enzyme function prediction [2], and phenotype ontology term prediction [17]. The success in computationally determining the functions of proteins using a variety of data sources — protein sequence or structure, and various biological network data [8, 27, 33, 36] — has led to the establishment of automated function prediction (AFP) as one of the most important bioinformatics challenges in the last decade. However, according to a community based competition for evaluating automated function prediction methods (CAFA, see below), there is still significant room for improvement in the accuracy of existing methods [27].

Due to the emergence of a multitude of computational methods for GO term prediction, the community has realized the need for a systematic and organized means of comparing the performance of these methods in order to assess how far the area has progressed.

Taking note from critical assessment efforts such as CASP (Critical Assessment of protein Structure Prediction) [23] and CAPRI (Critical Assessment of Prediction of Interactions) [14], the AFP community decided to hold its own competition: CAFA (Critical Assessment of Function Annotation) [27]. The main objective of CAFA is to gather all AFP researchers in one place to fairly assess and compare the latest computational methods using a centralized and independent assessment. In the first CAFA (CAFA1) the participants were provided with a list of protein targets that didn't have any previous GO annotations and were asked to submit computational predictions using their own AFP methods [27]. Once the predictions were submitted, the organizers collected the experimentally validated GO annotations acquired for those target proteins over a period of six months. Finally, the computational predictions were compared against those annotations to compute the accuracy of each AFP method.

The recent CAFA2 challenge had exactly the same setup, except that the list of 100,000 target proteins consisted of both annotated and unannotated proteins [15]. The added requirement of making predictions on currently annotated proteins makes CAFA2 a more realistic representation of the function prediction problem, as it better models the accumulation of annotations over time.

The AFP problem posed in CAFA is more challenging than the typical machine learning problem, as the usual assumption in machine learning is that the distribution of examples in the training set is reflective of that in the test set. In the CAFA AFP problem this assumption likely does not hold because the training is performed on an older set of annotations while testing is performed on newer annotations; and it is known that distribution of GO categories changes over time due to biases in the annotation process [29]. Furthermore, the annotations acquired for annotated proteins and the annotations acquired for unannotated proteins can be expected to be different in frequency and specificity: an annotated protein can be expected to acquire more specific GO categories than an unannotated protein, and perhaps more of them, as the biology community tends to study proteins that are already characterized.

In previous work we identified the CAFA2 requirements as a combination of two subtasks: making predictions on annotated proteins and making predictions on unannotated proteins [18]. In the task of making predictions on annotated proteins, methods are trained using the set of annotations acquired on or before a specific time-stamp t_1, and tested on the set of annotations gathered on the same set of proteins after t_1. In other words, the same set of proteins are used for training and testing, but the training labels are annotations that were available at t_1, while testing labels are annotations made available after t_1. In the task of making predictions on unannotated proteins, methods are trained using the set of annotations acquired on or before t_1 while they are tested on the annotations acquired for proteins that were not annotated on or before t_1. In this setup, the proteins used for training and the proteins used for testing are disjoint sets. This distinction is illustrated in Figure 1.

It turns out that the distinction between these two AFP tasks is an important one. In recent work we have compared the performance of GOstruct, binary support vector machines and guilt-by-association methods on these two tasks with their performance in cross-validation, which is typically used to assess and compare AFP methods. We observed that making predictions for already annotated proteins is challenging for all three methods compared to the task of making predictions on unannotated proteins [18]. This observation can be understood given that none of the methods take into account the incompleteness of existing annotations in their learning and inference procedures.

When it comes to the task of making predictions for annotated proteins, several recent methods use only existing annotations for making predictions. In other words, given the labels associated with a protein, these methods predict additional labels based only on its existing annotations. These methods are based on singular value decomposition [7], autoencoder neural networks [6], probabilistic latent semantic analysis [20] and Latent Dirichlet Allocation [26]. However, all these methods ignore the wealth of information available in all other types of genomic data sources such as sequence and protein-protein interactions. Therefore, it is worth exploring how both existing annotations and other data can be used together for this task; in methods like GOstruct and label reconciliation methods such as described in Guan et al. [12], information on existing annotations can be encoded in the learning or inference procedure itself. In this work, we propose novel improvements to the GOstruct method by taking into consideration that existing annotations are incomplete. We observe that GOstruct 2.0, the new version of GOstruct, has improved performance compared to original in the task of making predictions for annotated proteins, suggesting that better modeling of the problem leads to better performance. To the best of our knowledge, this is the first study that focuses on modeling the incompleteness of the labels in a structured output framework, and may be of use in other applications as well.

2 METHODOLOGY

2.1 Approach

The problem of GO term prediction is a hierarchical multilabel classification problem (HMC) [4], as a given protein can be annotated with multiple labels, and the set of labels have a hierarchy associated with them. Whereas the standard approach is to use multiple classifiers, one for each GO category, GOstruct takes the approach of using a single classifier that learns a direct mapping from inputs to the space of hierarchically consistent labels; this is achieved using structured prediction, which is a framework for learning a mapping from inputs to a label space that has a structure associated with it [35]. This framework can capture information from the inter-relationships between labels and allows the prediction of a set of labels that are hierarchically consistent. It eliminates the need for multiple classifiers, and the need for establishing hierarchical consistency between the predictions.

The key component of GOstruct's structured SVM formulation is the compatibility function, which computes the compatibility between a given protein and a label (i.e., a set of GO annotations). GOstruct learns this compatability by maximizing the margin between the correct label and all incorrect labels [33]. However, while it does allow for the possibility of mis-annotations, it does not explicitly take into account that the existing annotations of a protein are partial, i.e., are only a subset of its true annotations.

Our results from the previous work [18] demonstrate that the AFP task of making predictions on annotated proteins is much

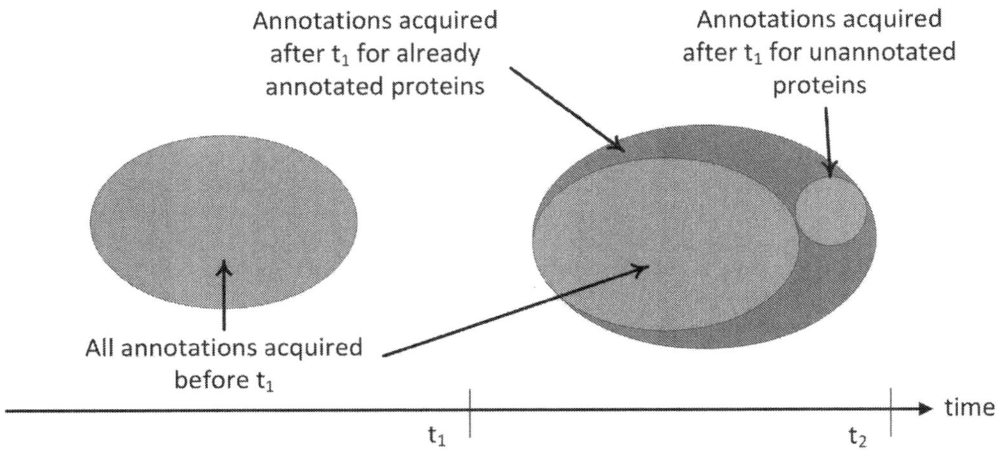

Figure 1: Overview of the two AFP subtasks. We distinguish between three sets of annotations that are used to define the train/test set with respect to the two tasks: making prediction for annotated proteins and making prediction for unannotated proteins. Annotations accumulate until time t_1 and form the set in grey, which is the training set for the task of making prediction for annotated proteins. The set of annotations acquired for those proteins after t_1 form the set in blue, which is the test set in the task of making prediction for annotated proteins. The set of annotations acquired after t_1 for proteins that were un-annotated before t_1 is denoted by the set in green, and is used as the test set in that task.

more difficult than performing well on un-annotated proteins or in cross-validation. This suggested that the task of predicting annotations for already annotated proteins could benefit from algorithms that explicitly leverage existing annotations to better rank novel predicted annotations.

GOstruct 2.0 is a modification of the original structured SVM formulation that reduces the penalty for margin violations involving examples for which the second best candidate label is an extension of its actual label. This allows the model to be more flexible with candidate labels that are extensions of the actual labels. This models the process of annotation whereby a protein might accumulate annotations with increasing level of specificity.

2.2 Models

In this section we present the proposed structured SVM formulation of GOstruct 2.0. Let $\mathcal{X}$ be the input space where proteins are represented, and let $\mathcal{Y}$ be the space of labels (GO categories). The training set consists of labeled training examples $\{(x_i, y_i)\}_{i=1}^n$ where $x_i \in \mathcal{X}$ and $y_i \in \mathcal{Y}$. The set of GO categories annotated to a given protein is collectively referred to as its (structured) label. $\mathcal{Y}$ represents each GO subontology in a vector space where component j represents category j, and a label vector $y \in \{0, 1\}^d$, where d is the number of GO categories has $y_j = 1$ if the corresponding protein is associated with category j, and 0 otherwise. In constructing the label vectors we assume the so-called *true-path rule*: whenever a protein is annotated with a given category, it is also associated with all its ancestors in the hierarchy. This is also known as *hierarchical consistency*. The *compatibility* function $f : \mathcal{X} \times \mathcal{Y} \mapsto \mathbb{R}$ maps input-output pairs to a score that indicates the strength of the association of an input to a set of GO categories. This function is expressed as a linear function in a feature space representing the labels and inputs, i.e. $f(x, y) = w^T\phi(x, y)$, where $\phi(x, y)$ is the joint input-output feature map. The predicted label $\hat{y}$ for an input x can then be obtained using the argmax operator as $\hat{y} = \arg\max_{y \in \mathcal{Y}_c} f(x, y)$ where $\mathcal{Y}_c \subset \mathcal{Y}$ is the set of all candidate labels. GOstruct uses the combinations of all GO categories present in the training set as the set of candidate labels $\mathcal{Y}_c$.

In order to obtain correct classification, the compatibility value of the true label (correct set of GO annotations) of an input protein needs to be higher than that of any other candidate label. This is captured by the following large-margin formulation [35]:

$$\min_{w, \epsilon} \frac{1}{2}||w||_2^2 + \frac{C}{n}\sum_{i=1}^{n} \epsilon_i$$

subject to :

$$f(x_i, y_i) - \max_{y \in \mathcal{Y}_c} f(x_i, y) \geq 1 - \epsilon_i \qquad i = 1, \ldots, n \tag{1}$$

$$\epsilon_i \geq 0 \qquad i = 1, \ldots, n, \tag{2}$$

where w is the weight vector, C is a user-specified soft-margin constant, $\mathcal{Y}_c$ is the set of candidate labels, ϵ_i are the slack variables which allow margin violations, and $|| \cdot ||_2$ is the L^2 norm. The first constraint, Equation (1), ensures that the compatibility score for the actual label of a protein is higher than all other candidate labels, and the use of slack variables allow flexibility in satisfying this constraint. This optimization problem is solved in the dual with a kernel function that is a product of a linear input space kernel and a linear output space kernel as described elsewhere [33].

In this work we propose a modification to the above model in order to help GOstruct better handle the task of making predictions for annotated proteins. For that purpose, we define a label y' as an *extension* of a label y if whenever $y_i = 1$ then $y'_i = 1$. In other words, y' is consistent with y, and might include additional and more specific terms than y. Figure 2 illustrates this concept.

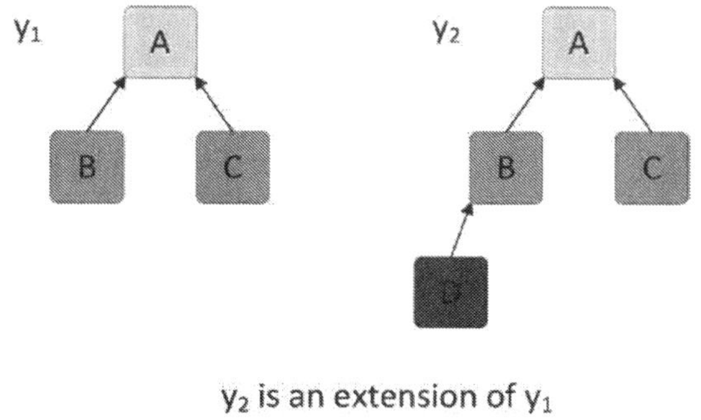

Figure 2: Label extensions: the label y_2 in this toy example is an extension of y_1 because y_2 includes all terms represented by y_1.

The original GOstruct formulation does not take into account that the existing labels represent a snapshot of our knowledge of protein function, which is incomplete [3]. For example, in our dataset, the fraction of human proteins that had new molecular function, biological process and cellular component annotations between January 2009 and December 2013 are approximately 14%, 35% and 28%, respectively. In order to model the fact that an existing label can be incomplete, any second best candidate label that is an extension of the existing annotations should be penalized to a lesser extent. This can be achieved by using a different (and lower) soft-margin constant for the subset of examples for which the second best candidate label is a more specific label. To do this, we partition the examples into two non-overlapping sets based on whether their corresponding second best candidate label are extensions of the known annotations and associate different soft-margin constants with them. We denote these two sets by A^+ and A^-, and their associated soft-margin constants by C^+ and C^-, respectively; A^+ is the set of examples for which the second best candidate label is an extension of its known label, A^- are the rest of the examples. We propose the following modification of the original structured SVM formulation as follows:

$$\min_{w,\epsilon^1,\epsilon^2} \frac{1}{2}||w||_2^2 + \frac{C^+}{n}\sum_{i \in A^+} \epsilon_i^1 + \frac{C^-}{n}\sum_{i \in A^-} \epsilon_i^2$$

subject to:

$$f(x_i, y_i) - \max_{y \in \mathcal{Y}_c} f(x_i, y) \geq 1 - \epsilon_i^1 \qquad \text{for } i \in A^+ \tag{3}$$

$$f(x_i, y_i) - \max_{y \in \mathcal{Y}_c} f(x_i, y) \geq 1 - \epsilon_i^2 \qquad \text{for } i \in A^- \tag{4}$$

$$\epsilon_i^1 \geq 0 \qquad \text{for } i \in A^+ \tag{5}$$

$$\epsilon_i^2 \geq 0 \qquad \text{for } i \in A^-, \tag{6}$$

where ϵ_i^1 and ϵ_i^2 are the slack variables, and $\mathcal{Y}_c$ is the candidate label set. The soft-margin constants C^+ and C^- are hyperparameters specified by the user and should satisfy $C^- \geq C^+$ for a lower penalty on annotations that are more specific than the known ones. The new constraints (inequalities 3 and 4) allow the model to be more flexible towards picking candidate labels that are extensions of the current label. This allows it to use the information of the existing annotations to model the accumulation of annotations over time.

2.3 Experimental setup

We compare the performance of GOstruct 2.0 against the original GOstruct (denoted as 1.0) with respect to the three tasks (a) cross-validation (CV), (b) making predictions on annotated proteins (denoted as NA) and (c) making predictions on unannotated proteins (denoted as NP) on human proteins. Each method was trained/tested using the same set of features and labels.

We extracted GO annotations from the Gene Ontology and UniProt databases on 12/01/2013. We removed all annotations not originating from an experimental assay, and ignored GO categories that were annotated with less than 10 proteins. The number of proteins/annotations in the train/test sets with respect to the three setups are given in Table 1.

We generated three types of sequence features (localization signals, low complexity regions and transmembrane data). BLAST scores were represented using a simpler version of a score used in [8]. We extracted PPI and other functional association data (co-expression, co-occurrence, etc.) from BioGRID 3.2.106, STRING 9.1 and GeneMANIA 3.1.2. To take advantage of the information found in the biomedical literature, an NLP pipeline was utilized to extract the co-occurrence of protein names and GO terms both at the sentence and paragraph level from all full-text publications available in PubMed; the datasets are publicly available [16], and additional details are provided elsewhere [18].

We use 5-fold cross validation for evaluating the performance in the CV task. Here, the folds are generated by partitioning the complete set of annotations randomly without regard to their time-stamps (i.e. all existing annotations of a protein are used as the gold standard). In the NA task, methods are trained using the set of annotations acquired on or before the year 2009, and tested on the set of annotations gathered on the same set of proteins after 2009. In the NP task, methods are trained using the set of annotations acquired on or before the year 2009 while they are tested on the annotations acquired for proteins that were not annotated on or before 2009. Note that the NA and NP tasks share the same training data; for example, in the molecular function subontology, there are 4,305 proteins that had at least one annotation before 2009 (see Table 1) In our experiments we used $C^+ = 1$ and $C^- = 10$ for all our experiments; the value of C^- is the default value of the GOstruct soft-margin parameter on the basis of experiments in other datasets; we have not optimized the value of C^+.

We use *term-centric* AUC [27] as our primary evaluation measure for reporting results. In order to perform a fair comparison across setups we first identified the GO subgraph that consists of only the GO categories common to all three setups (CV, NA and NP). Then we computed the AUC only on this subgraph.

3 RESULTS AND DISCUSSION

Figure 3 and Table 2 show CV, NA, and NP results in human for all three GO namespaces: molecular function, biological process and

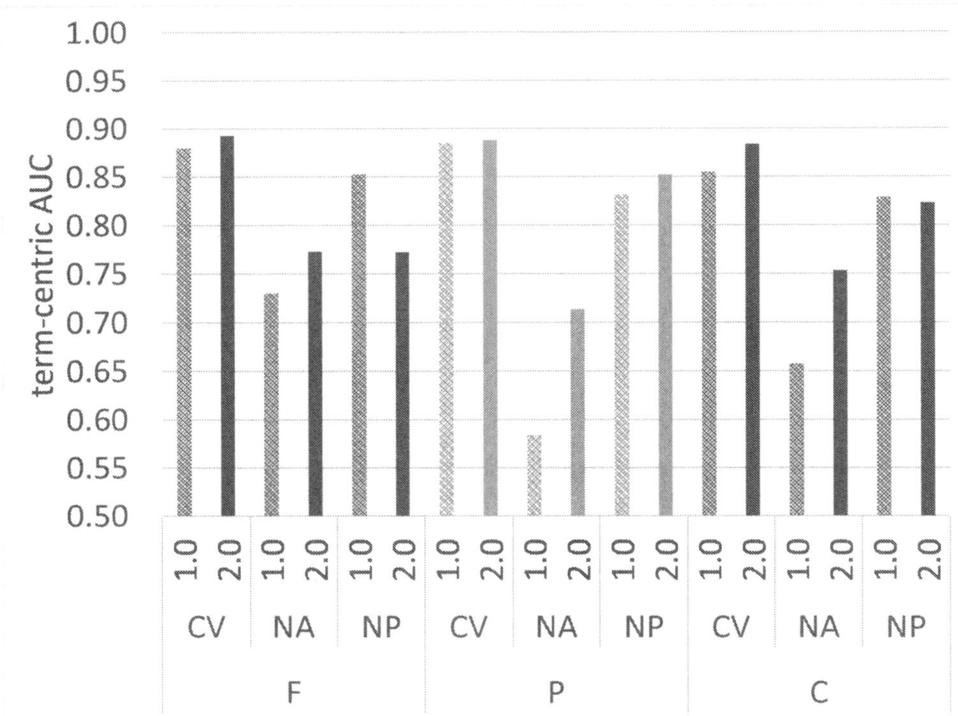

Figure 3: Performance comparison between GOstruct 2.0 and the original GOstruct in CV, NA and NP for human. GOstruct 2.0 (solid fill) and the original GOstruct (denoted as 1.0 and shown in patterned fill) are evaluated in CV (cross-validation), NA (novel-annotation) and NP (novel-proteins) on human. Performance is reported using the term-centric AUC in the molecular function (F), biological process (P) and cellular component (C) subontologies (depicted using red, green, and blue bars, respectively). Higher values indicate better performance.

Table 1: The number of proteins and the number of annotations in the training and test sets for the three setups: CV (cross-validation), NA (novel-annotations) and NP (novel-proteins) in human. Numbers are separately provided for the three subontologies: molecular function (F), biological process (P) and cellular component (C) subontologies. For the CV setup, numbers represent average values computed across train/test folds (5-fold cross-validation).

		Training set		Test set	
Ontology	Setup	Proteins	Annots.	Proteins	Annots.
F	CV	4532	8467	1133	2116
	NA	4305	6898	799	1343
	NP	4305	6898	1344	2174
P	CV	7533	31794	1883	7948
	NA	5824	12196	3301	13192
	NP	5824	12196	3574	12973
C	CV	8440	19196	2110	4799
	NA	5082	8185	2966	5511
	NP	5082	8185	5468	10200

cellular component. First, as noted in our previous work [18], performance for the NA task is much lower. We observe that GOstruct 2.0 outperforms GOstruct 1.0 in the NA task in all subontologies. We also note that it performs as well as or better than GOstruct 1.0 in the molecular function and biological process subontologies in yeast (data not shown). This demonstrates the ability of the new constraints to model the accumulation of annotations over time for improving performance in the NA task.

The largest improvement is in the biological process subontology (a jump from 0.58 to 0.71, see Figure 3). This observation can be attributed to the fact that it is by far the deepest subontology [11] as well as it being the subontology with the highest rate of increase in the number of categories over the years [10]. This makes biological process annotations more incomplete than the other two, thereby providing for more room for improvement. It is also important to note that GOstruct 2.0 produced AUCs above 0.7 for all three subontologies, which is a major improvement over the original GOstruct, which had low values of 0.58 and 0.66 in NA for the BP and CC subontologies, respectively. On unannotated proteins the results are mixed. This not surprising, since the 2.0 constraints are specifically designed for the NA scenario; however, it is always possible to apply the original version for proteins without annotations. In fact,

Table 2: Performance comparison between GOstruct 2.0 and the original GOstruct in CV, NA and NP for human. GOstruct 2.0 and original GOstruct (denoted as 1.0) are evaluated in CV (cross-validation), NA (novel-annotation) and NP (novel-proteins). Performance is reported using the term-centric AUC and the corresponding p-values computed using paired t-tests in the molecular function (F), biological process (P) and cellular component (C) subontologies. P-values < 0.05 are in bold.

Ontology	Setup	1.0	2.0	P-value
	CV	0.88	0.89	**9.90E-03**
F	NA	0.73	0.77	**6.58E-07**
	NP	0.85	0.77	**2.89E-12**
	CV	0.89	0.89	3.06E-01
P	NA	0.58	0.71	**8.10E-200**
	NP	0.83	0.85	**1.54E-11**
	CV	0.85	0.88	**1.15E-04**
C	NA	0.66	0.75	**5.54E-21**
	NP	0.83	0.82	5.74E-01

based on these results, the latest release of the GOstruct library[1] defaults to the 1.0 behavior for the NP task and applies 2.0 behavior for the NA task automatically based on the input annotations.

4 CONCLUSIONS AND FUTURE WORK

In this work we developed GOstruct 2.0, which includes enhancements to the underlying structured SVM formulation of the original GOstruct, allowing it to model the incompleteness of GO annotations. Using human data we showed that GOstruct 2.0 outperforms the original GOstruct, especially for the task of making predictions on annotated proteins. To the best of our knowledge, this is the first study that incorporates explicit modeling of label incompleteness in the context of the structured output framework, and demonstrated the importance of modeling label incompleteness. This idea can be applied in other settings. Several large-scale biological ontologies such as the Human Phenotype Ontology (HPO) [28], the Mammalian Phenotype Ontology (MPO) [31, 32] and the Disease Ontology (DO) [19, 30], are manually curated, and are also known to be incomplete due to the lag between the large volume of information in the published literature and the time-consuming process of manual curation. Therefore, the methodology developed here is directly applicable for the tasks of predicting novel annotations in these ontologies.

Several issues related to this work remain to be solved. An extensive model selection procedure for selecting the optimal soft-margin parameters with respect to the newly introduced constraints could further improve performance. This work only looked at modifying the learning procedure of the original GOstruct to account for incompleteness of labels. Another aspect worth exploring is introducing modifications to the inference rule used in the original GOstruct. GOstruct uses all combinations of labels present in the training set as the candidate label set when making predictions. However, for the task of making predictions on annotated proteins it may be beneficial to restrict the candidate label set to a subset of labels that are consistent to the current label, and further investigation is required to explore how to best incorporate this idea into the framework.

[1] http://sourceforge.net/projects/strut/

ACKNOWLEDGMENTS

The authors would like to thank Dr. Karin Verspoor and Dr. Christopher Funk for providing the literature features used with GOstruct method. This work was supported by the NSF Advances in Biological Informatics program through grant number 0965768.

REFERENCES

[1] Michael Ashburner, Catherine A. Ball, Judith A. Blake, David Botstein, Heather Butler, J. Michael Cherry, Allan P. Davis, Kara Dolinski, Selina S. Dwight, Janan T. Eppig, Midori A. Harris, David P. Hill, Laurie Issel-Tarver, Andrew Kasarskis, Suzanna Lewis, John C. Matese, Joel E. Richardson, Martin Ringwald, Gerald M. Rubin, and Gavin Sherlock. 2000. Gene Ontology: tool for the unification of biology. *Nature Genetics* 25, 1 (May 2000), 25–29. DOI: http://dx.doi.org/10.1038/75556

[2] Katja Astikainen, Liisa Holm, Esa Pitkänen, Sandor Szedmak, and Juho Rousu. 2008. Towards structured output prediction of enzyme function. In *BMC proceedings*, Vol. 2. BioMed Central, S2.

[3] William A. Baumgartner, K. Bretonnel Cohen, Lynne M. Fox, George Acquaah-Mensah, and Lawrence Hunter. 2007. Manual curation is not sufficient for annotation of genomic databases. *Bioinformatics* 23, 13 (2007), i41–i48. DOI: http://dx.doi.org/10.1093/bioinformatics/btm229

[4] Wei Bi and James T. Kwok. 2011. Multi-Label Classification on Tree- and DAG-Structured Hierarchies. In *Proceedings of the 28th International Conference on Machine Learning (ICML-11)*, Lise Getoor and Tobias Scheffer (Eds.). ACM, New York, NY, USA, 17–24.

[5] Yu Chen and Dong Xu. 2004. Global protein function annotation through mining genome-scale data in yeast Saccharomyces cerevisiae. *Nucleic acids research* 32, 21 (2004), 6414–6424.

[6] Davide Chicco, Peter Sadowski, and Pierre Baldi. 2014. Deep Autoencoder Neural Networks for Gene Ontology Annotation Predictions. In *Proceedings of the 5th ACM Conference on Bioinformatics, Computational Biology, and Health Informatics (BCB '14)*. ACM, New York, NY, USA, 533–540. DOI: http://dx.doi.org/10.1145/2649387.2649442

[7] Davide Chicco, Marco Tagliasacchi, and Marco Masseroli. 2012. Genomic Annotation Prediction Based on Integrated Information. In *Computational Intelligence Methods for Bioinformatics and Biostatistics*, Elia Biganzoli, Alfredo Vellido, Federico Ambrogi, and Roberto Tagliaferri (Eds.). Lecture Notes in Computer Science, Vol. 7548. Springer Berlin Heidelberg, 238–252. DOI: http://dx.doi.org/10.1007/978-3-642-35686-5_20

[8] Wyatt T. Clark and Predrag Radivojac. 2011. Analysis of protein function and its prediction from amino acid sequence. *Proteins: Structure, Function, and Bioinformatics* 79, 7 (2011), 2086–2096. DOI: http://dx.doi.org/10.1002/prot.23029

[9] Ana Conesa, Stefan Götz, Juan Miguel García-Gómez, Javier Terol, Manuel Talón, and Montserrat Robles. 2005. Blast2GO: a universal tool for annotation, visualization and analysis in functional genomics research. *Bioinformatics* 21, 18 (2005), 3674–3676.

[10] The Gene Ontology Consortium. 2015. Gene Ontology Consortium: going forward. *Nucleic Acids Research* 43, D1 (2015), D1049–D1056. DOI: http://dx.doi.org/10.1093/nar/gku1179 arXiv:http://nar.oxfordjournals.org/content/43/D1/D1049.full.pdf+html

[11] Olivier Dameron, Charles Bettembourg, and Nolwenn Le Meur. 2013. Measuring the evolution of ontology complexity: the gene ontology case study. *PLoS One* 8, 10 (2013), e75993.

[12] Yuanfang Guan, Chad L Myers, David C Hess, Zafer Barutcuoglu, A Caudy, and O Troyanskaya. 2008. Predicting gene function in a hierarchical context with an ensemble of classifiers. *Genome biology* 9, Suppl 1 (2008), S3.

[13] Boris Hayete and Jadwiga R Bienkowska. 2005. GOtrees: predicting go associations from protein domain composition using decision trees.. In *Pacific Symposium on Biocomputing*, Vol. 10. World Scientific, 127–138.

[14] Jol Janin, Kim Henrick, John Moult, Lynn Ten Eyck, Michael J. E. Sternberg, Sandor Vajda, Ilya Vakser, and Shoshana J. Wodak. 2003. CAPRI: A Critical Assessment of PRedicted Interactions. *Proteins: Structure, Function, and Bioinformatics* 52, 1 (2003), 2–9. DOI: http://dx.doi.org/10.1002/prot.10381

[15] Yuxiang Jiang, Tal Ronnen Oron, Wyatt T Clark, Asma R Bankapur, Daniel DfiAndrea, Rosalba Lepore, Christopher S Funk, Indika Kahanda, Karin M Verspoor, Asa Ben-Hur, and others. 2016. An expanded evaluation of protein function

prediction methods shows an improvement in accuracy. *Genome biology* 17, 1 (2016), 184.
[16] Indika Kahanda, Chris Funk, Fahad Ullah, Karin Verspoor, and Asa Ben-Hur. 2015. Supporting data for "A close look at protein function prediction evaluation protocols". *GigaScience Database* (2015). DOI: http://dx.doi.org/10.1002/prot.23029
[17] Indika Kahanda, Christopher Funk, Karin Verspoor, and Asa Ben-Hur. 2015. PHENOstruct: Prediction of human phenotype ontology terms using heterogeneous data sources. *F1000Research* 4 (2015).
[18] Indika Kahanda, Christopher S. Funk, Fahad Ullah, Karin M. Verspoor, and Asa Ben-Hur. 2015. A close look at protein function prediction evaluation protocols. *GigaScience* 4, 1 (2015), 1–10. DOI: http://dx.doi.org/10.1186/s13742-015-0082-5
[19] Warren A Kibbe, Cesar Arze, Victor Felix, Elvira Mitraka, Evan Bolton, Gang Fu, Christopher J Mungall, Janos X Binder, James Malone, Drashtti Vasant, and others. 2014. Disease Ontology 2015 update: an expanded and updated database of human diseases for linking biomedical knowledge through disease data. *Nucleic acids research* (2014), gku1011.
[20] M. Masseroli, D. Chicco, and P. Pinoli. 2012. Probabilistic Latent Semantic Analysis for prediction of Gene Ontology annotations. In *Proceedings of the International Joint Conference on Neural Networks (IJCNN)*. 1–8. DOI: http://dx.doi.org/10.1109/IJCNN.2012.6252767
[21] Jason McDermott, Roger Bumgarner, and Ram Samudrala. 2005. Functional annotation from predicted protein interaction networks. *Bioinformatics* 21, 15 (2005), 3217–3226.
[22] Sara Mostafavi, Debajyoti Ray, David Warde-Farley, Chris Grouios, Quaid Morris, and others. 2008. GeneMANIA: a real-time multiple association network integration algorithm for predicting gene function. *Genome Biology* 9, Suppl 1 (2008), S4.
[23] John Moult, Jan T. Pedersen, Richard Judson, and Krzysztof Fidelis. 1995. A large-scale experiment to assess protein structure prediction methods. *Proteins: Structure, Function, and Bioinformatics* 23, 3 (1995), ii–iv. DOI: http://dx.doi.org/10.1002/prot.340230303
[24] Paul Muir, Shantao Li, Shaoke Lou, Daifeng Wang, Daniel J. Spakowicz, Leonidas Salichos, Jing Zhang, George M. Weinstock, Farren Isaacs, Joel Rozowsky, and Mark Gerstein. 2016. The real cost of sequencing: scaling computation to keep pace with data generation. *Genome Biology* 17, 1 (2016), 1–9. DOI: http://dx.doi.org/10.1186/s13059-016-0917-0
[25] Guillaume Obozinski, Gert Lanckriet, Charles Grant, Michael I Jordan, and William Stafford Noble. 2008. Consistent probabilistic outputs for protein function prediction. *Genome Biology* 9, Suppl 1 (2008), S6.
[26] P. Pinoli, D. Chicco, and M. Masseroli. 2014. Latent Dirichlet Allocation based on Gibbs Sampling for gene function prediction. In *Proceedings of the IEEE Conference on Computational Intelligence in Bioinformatics and Computational Biology*. 1–8. DOI: http://dx.doi.org/10.1109/CIBCB.2014.6845514
[27] Predrag Radivojac, Wyatt T. Clark, Iddo Friedberg, and others. 2013. A large-scale evaluation of computational protein function prediction. *Nat Meth* 10, 3 (Mar 2013), 221–227. DOI: http://dx.doi.org/10.1038/nmeth.2340
[28] Peter N. Robinson. 2012. Deep phenotyping for precision medicine. *Human Mutation* 33, 5 (2012), 777–780. DOI: http://dx.doi.org/10.1002/humu.22080
[29] AM Schnoes, DC Ream, AW Thorman, PC Babbitt, and I Friedberg. 2012. Biases in the experimental annotations of protein function and their effect on our understanding of protein function space. *PLoS computational biology* 9, 5 (2012), e1003063–e1003063.
[30] Lynn Marie Schriml, Cesar Arze, Suvarna Nadendla, Yu-Wei Wayne Chang, Mark Mazaitis, Victor Felix, Gang Feng, and Warren Alden Kibbe. 2012. Disease Ontology: a backbone for disease semantic integration. *Nucleic acids research* 40, D1 (2012), D940–D946.
[31] Cynthia L Smith and Janan T Eppig. 2009. The mammalian phenotype ontology: enabling robust annotation and comparative analysis. *Wiley Interdisciplinary Reviews: Systems Biology and Medicine* 1, 3 (2009), 390–399.
[32] Cynthia L Smith, Carroll-Ann W Goldsmith, and Janan T Eppig. 2004. The Mammalian Phenotype Ontology as a tool for annotating, analyzing and comparing phenotypic information. *Genome biology* 6, 1 (2004), R7.
[33] Artem Sokolov and Asa Ben-Hur. 2010. Hierarchical classification of Gene Ontology Terms Using the GOstruct Method. *J. Bioinformatics and Computational Biology* 8, 2 (2010), 357–376.
[34] Weidong Tian, Lan V Zhang, Murat Tasan, Francis D Gibbons, Oliver D King, Julie Park, Zeba Wunderlich, J Michael Cherry, and Frederick P Roth. 2008. Combining guilt-by-association and guilt-by-profiling to predict Saccharomyces cerevisiae gene function. *Genome Biology* 9, Suppl 1 (2008), S7.
[35] Ioannis Tsochantaridis, Thorsten Joachims, Thomas Hofmann, and Yasemin Altun. 2005. Large Margin Methods for Structured and Interdependent Output Variables. *J. Mach. Learn. Res.* 6 (Dec. 2005), 1453–1484.
[36] David Warde-Farley, Sylva L. Donaldson, Ovi Comes, Khalid Zuberi, Rashad Badrawi, Pauline Chao, Max Franz, Chris Grouios, Farzana Kazi, Christian Tannus Lopes, Anson Maitland, Sara Mostafavi, Jason Montojo, Quentin Shao, George Wright, Gary D. Bader, and Quaid Morris. 2010. The GeneMANIA prediction server: biological network integration for gene prioritization and predicting gene function. *Nucleic Acids Research* 38, suppl 2 (2010), W214–W220. DOI: http://dx.doi.org/10.1093/nar/gkq537

Identification and Prediction of Intrinsically Disordered Regions in Proteins Using n-grams

Mauricio Oberti
School of Systems Biology
George Mason University
Manassas, Virginia
mobertib@gmu.edu

Iosif I. Vaisman
School of Systems Biology
George Mason University
Manassas, Virginia
ivaisman@gmu.edu

ABSTRACT[1]

Intrinsically disordered proteins (IDPs) play an important role in many biological processes and are closely related to human diseases [1]. They also have the potential to serve as targets for drug discovery, especially in disordered binding regions [2], [3]. Accurate prediction of IDPs is challenging, most methods rely on sequence profiles to improve accuracy making them computationally expensive.

This paper describes a method based on n-gram frequencies using reduced amino acid alphabets, which tries to overcome this challenge by utilizing only sequence information.

Our results show that the described IDP prediction approach performs at the same level as some of the other state of the art ab initio methods. However, the simplicity of n-grams allows to construct decision trees which can provide important insights into common patterns and properties associated with disordered regions.

KEYWORDS

Disordered proteins; machine learning; n-grams

1 INTRODUCTION

It has been the dominant paradigm in structural biology that a well-defined structure determines protein function. Intrinsically disordered proteins (IDPs), which lack a stable three-dimensional structure under normal physiological conditions, are a challenge to the structure-to-function paradigm [4]. Disorder exists in up to half of the amino acids in eukaryotic proteins, and disordered regions are involved in numerous biological functions [5], as a result of their flexibility. Since amino acid sequence is known to determine protein structure, sequence information can be used to identify disordered regions. Protein disorder is involved in the development of many diseases, and identifying disordered regions can help us understand how to use them as potential drug targets [2], [6], [7]. The identified regions can also be used to better understand the pathways of protein folding and provide insights into protein function.

In this study, machine-learning classification techniques will be applied to distinguish between disordered and ordered residues within a sequence based on n-gram frequencies content. Initial results show that using n-gram frequencies is an accurate and computationally inexpensive method to predict disordered regions, based on raw sequence data. This method of prediction can subsequently aid in the development of next-generation treatments for a variety of biomedical applications.

N-grams are a commonly used technique in computational linguistics, probability, text categorization, and biology [8]. In this study, an n-gram has been denoted as a contiguous string of *n* amino acid residues in a protein sequence. The primary structure, or the amino acid sequence, of a protein determines the protein's three-dimensional structure. This implies that disorder, or lack of stable structure, can also be encoded in the sequence. A sequence can be decomposed into a list of overlapping n-grams. N-gram patterns have been previously used to show evolutionary relationships between protein sequences and to predict protein secondary structure [8]. We also successfully used n-gram analysis to predict functional properties of proteins, including drug resistance [9].

Current predictors of protein disorder use multiple sequence alignments, secondary structure analyses, PSI-BLAST sequence profiles, or distinctive residue compositions [5]. These predictors require analyzing and comparing entire sequences, taking relatively longer compared to n-grams, which decompose sequences into smaller pieces, each of which can be readily analyzed quantitatively. Computational techniques used for predictions are generally "black-box" models such as Neural Networks and Support Vector Machines. In addition, the features that these models use are not fully understood. To help with feature selection, n-gram frequency data can also be used to train decision trees, which can provide more insight into how the training data is actually used to create the decision-making process.

[1]Permission to make digital or hard copies of all or part of this work for personal or classroom use is granted without fee provided that copies are not made or distributed for profit or commercial advantage and that copies bear this notice and the full citation on the first page. Copyrights for components of this work owned by others than ACM must be honored. Abstracting with credit is permitted. To copy otherwise, or republish, to post on servers or to redistribute to lists, requires prior specific permission and/or a fee. Request permissions from Permissions@acm.org.
ACM-BCB'17, August 20-23, 2017, Boston, MA, USA
© 2017 Association of Computing Machinery.
ACM ISBN 978-1-4503-4722-8/17/08...$15.00.
DOI: http://dx.doi.org/10.1145/3107411.3107480

2 EXPERIMENTAL AND COMPUTATIONAL METHODS

2.1 Current prediction methods

Over 60 protein disorder prediction servers are currently available, although not all publicly. The methods can be classified in one of the following categories [10]: (i) Ab initio or sequence-based, (ii) clustering, (iii) template based and (iv) meta or consensus. The methods that can't easily be assigned to one of the above categories fall into the hybrid classification. Below is a brief description of the basis of each of the type of method.

Ab initio methods. They rely almost exclusively on amino acid sequence information to make a prediction. Features extracted from the primary sequence, alignment profiles or scoring matrices are used as input for statistical models to make predictions of disorder regions. This class of methods was widely used in the CASP8 [11] and CASP9 [12] experiments. A few examples of it are Disopred [13], ESpritz [14] and PreDisorder [15].

Clustering methods. This approach generates tertiary structure models from the primary sequence. It then superimposes the different models onto each other under the assumption that positions in ordered regions will be conserved across the models [16]. Residues in disordered regions are likely to vary. Since this approach doesn't rely on a training set, it is less likely to be bias by the training data.

Template based methods. Similar to clustering, it predicts disordered regions of proteins by aligning the input sequence to homologous proteins with known structure. Homologous proteins are found by database search or by fold recognition methods. This method is frequently used in combination with other prediction approaches and they generally fall into the hybrid category.

Meta methods. They combine the output of several disordered predictors into a single average, which tends to have a moderate increase in accuracy. This is one of the most popular method and is used by metaPrDOS [17] and GSmetaDisorder [18] among others.

Hybrid methods. These are the methods combining two or more of the previous approaches in order to improve prediction accuracy. PrDOS [19] is one common example, combining ab initio and template based homologous alignment to output a prediction.

2.2 Alphabet Reduction Evaluation and Selection

The 20-letter amino acid alphabet was reduced to a 3-letter alphabet in order to simplify and quicken the machine learning process, as the model would have to analyze fewer n-grams during training and testing. One problem with using the original 20-letter alphabet is that the total number of features (n-grams) would exceed the number of sequences in the training set. By reducing the number of letters in the alphabet to three, and thus decreasing the number of possible n-grams, the number of sequences would be almost 250 times the total number of features. Therefore, it would be highly unlikely for the model to over fit. The reduction of the amino acid space from a 20-letter alphabet to a 3-letter alphabet carries a reduction in the information content. One key hypothesis in our method is that this reduction won't affect the n-gram signal or the method predictive capability.

The reduced alphabets were taken from outside sources (Table 1). Residues can be clustered based on various properties, including chemical and genetic properties. Reduced alphabets cluster residues in ways that prevent the loss of key biochemical information.

Table 1: The six reduced alphabets and their sources. Each letter contains a cluster of amino acid residues (one-letter abbreviations). The residue clusters were denoted by the letters "B", "J", and "U" in this study

Alphabet/ref	Letter 1 (B)	Letter 2 (J)	Letter 3 (U)
a1 [20]	CFILMVWY	AGHPRT	DEKNQS
a2 [21]	CFILMVWY	AGPST	DEHKNQR
a3 [22]	AFGILMPV	DEKR	CHNQSTWY
a4 [23]	DHIMNVY	EFKLQ	ACGPRSTW
a5 [24]	ACGILMPSTV	EKRDNQH	FYW
a6 [25]	CILMVFWY	AGHST	DEKNPQR

2.3 Disorder prediction by n-gram frequencies

2.3.1 Feature Generation. For a given protein sequence of length L and a reduce alphabet of A letters, we extract L feature vectors of size T where T is the total numbers of possible n-grams (T=A^n). In order to calculate the n-gram feature vector for a particular position, we use a centered sliding window of size W.

Each position of the N-size feature vector contains the frequency of a particular n-gram for the current residue centered window. N-gram frequencies are then normalized to prevent frequency of a feature from skewing the decision process. The following shows how the 3-gram BJU was normalized, as an example:

$$q_{BJU} = \frac{f_{BJU}}{f_B \cdot f_J \cdot f_U} \tag{1}$$

Where q is the normalized frequency and f is the frequency of the 3-gram of the reduce residue within the protein sequence. Finally, each feature vector is assigned a label (0=order, 1=disorder) based on the residue annotation and is used as input to a classification algorithm. Random Forest [26] was chosen based on its known performance and ability to provide insight into the mechanism of classification. It follows a decision tree model, which creates different nodes on a tree based on the provided attributes in the training set [26], [27]. The algorithm constructs an ensemble of decision trees, which reduces overfitting, a common issue when only a single decision tree is used.

2.3.2 Parameter Selection. In order to select the reduced alphabet, window size and n-gram that maximize the model predictive value, we construct a simplified classification model for each possible combination of a select group of values. We test each model performance using a dataset containing a combination of CASP8, CASP9 and CASP10 targets [11], [12], [28]. The AUC for each model is calculated and used as main metric to compare performance. Table 2 shows a summary of the parameters tested and Figure 1 shows the results for a selected group of parameters. It was found that 3-grams, alphabets a1, a3 and a6 and $W>71$ have a better overall performance and increase model predictive value. The final implementation of the method uses 3-gram, alphabet 6 and W=101. The window size was derived after experimentation within the final model.

2.3.3 Control Experiments. In order to ensure that the observed AUC values were different from those in a random feature space, controls were created by shuffling the residue labels. Labels were shuffled such that half of the disordered residues and half of the ordered residues were labelled into the incorrect class. The shuffled datasets were used to train the same machine learning algorithm.

Table 2: **Model construction parameters**

Parameter	Tested values
Sliding Window Size (W)	9,11,15,19,23,29,39,51, 71,81
n-gram (n)	3,4
Reduce Alphabet (A)	a1,a2,a3,a4,a5,a6
Classification algorithm	Naïve Bayes

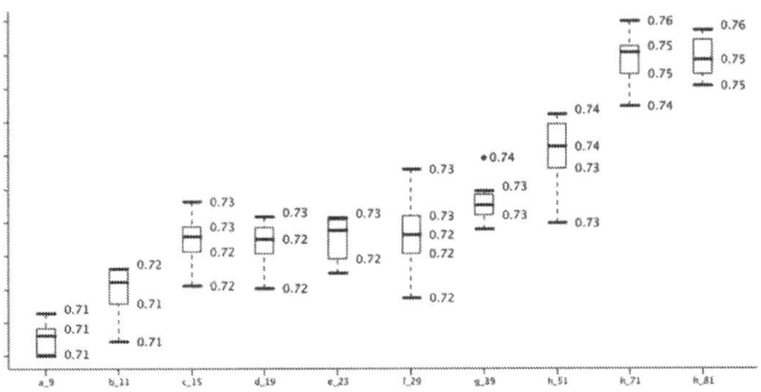

Figure 1: **Sliding window size models performance (3-gram, all alphabets)**

3 RESULTS AND DISCUSSION

3.1 Datasets

Publicly available datasets are used to train and evaluate our method. High resolution X-ray crystal structures from the Protein Data Bank (PDB) [29] are used to construct the training and test data sets while CASP10 [28] and CAMEO [30] (http://www.cameo3d.org) are used for further validation. We use Pisces protein sequence culling server (http://dunbrack.fccc.edu) [31] to extract sequences from PDB to filter for high resolution and reduce redundancy. Parameters selected for culling are: (i) proteins sharing >25% sequence identity (ii) maximum resolution of 1.8 Angstroms (iii) R-value >0.30. In total, 7,119 proteins are retrieved from PDB with an average length of 349 residues. We randomly divide the initial set in two distinct subsets: PDB70 containing 70% of the sequences for training and PDB30 with the remaining 30% for testing.

There is no common agreement on how to define disorder residues from PDB files [32]. For the purpose of this work, we consider a residue to be in a disorder position if it appears in the sequence records but its coordinates are missing from the electron density map. This is not a perfect definition since there are other reasons why a residue can have missing coordinates (i.e.: crystallization artifacts). However, it allows us to use a large number of proteins from PDB without further experimental validation.

CASP10 is the latest dataset available from the series experiments, which released specific targets for protein disorder prediction. The 94 available targets are used for validation and as independent benchmark set. To prevent any redundancy between training and validation sets, we use BLASTClust [33] to filter for sequence identity between the PDB70 (training set) and CASP10 (validation set). Finally, to further assess our method, we tested against CAMEO 6 Months targets released from August 26, 2016 to February 18th, 2017 (504 targets, categorized in 3 groups).

3.2 Program benchmarking

To benchmark our method we selected previous CASP participating programs, in particular a sequence-only method (Espritz) and a sequence profile based method (Disopred3).

Espritz is an ensemble of sequence-only and multiple sequence alignments disorder prediction methods. The sequence-only method has three different versions, depending on the initial set used for training (X-ray, NMR, Disprot). We used X-ray and NMR versions. The X-ray trained version is the one that performs best among the three.

Disopred3 runs a PSI-BLAST search for each of the residues in a 15-residue window. The profile is then used as input to a neural network classifier which outputs a probability estimate of the residue being disordered.

3.3 Metrics and Evaluation Criteria

Disorder data is characterized by high class imbalance, disordered residues account for less than 5% of the data in the PDB set (training and test). Since disordered residues are relatively rare compared to ordered ones, they are harder to predict. Performance metrics should account for this imbalance and reward correct prediction of disordered residues higher than correct prediction of ordered ones [12]. We selected a subset of the metrics commonly used for the assessment of disorder data [34]–[36] that take into account the nature of the imbalanced data: (i) specificity (ii) sensitivity (iii) balanced accuracy (iv) Matthews correlation coefficient and (v) AUC.

Binary metrics

$$\text{Specifity} = \frac{TN}{TN + FP} \tag{2}$$

$$\text{Sensitivity} = \frac{TP}{TP + FN} \tag{3}$$

$$\text{Acc} = \frac{TP}{TP + FN} + \frac{TN}{TN + FP} \tag{4}$$

$$\text{MCC} = \frac{TP.TN - FP.FN}{\sqrt{(TP + FP)(TP + FN)(TN + FP)(TN + FN)}} \tag{5}$$

True positives (TP) and true negatives (TN) are the numbers of correctly predicted disordered and ordered residues.

False positives (FP) and false negatives (FN) are the numbers of incorrectly predicted disordered and ordered residues.

Statistical metrics. The ROC curve is a plot that compares the true positive rate against the false positive rate under various threshold values for a binary classifier.

AUC = Area under the ROC curve plotting 1-specificify and sensitivity (6)

To confirm the robustness of our classifier we perform 10-fold cross validation [37], [38] across our PDB set. Complete data set is divided into ten equally-sized groups. One group is used as a validation set to test the model, while the other groups are used to train it. This process is executed ten times, with a different group used for testing each time. Results for cross validation are shown in Figure 5.

3.4 Method Performance

We compare the performance of our n-gram method against the benchmark programs using CASP10 (Figure 3.), PDB30 (Figure 4.) and CAMEO (hard targets, Figure 5.) sets. Our method performs at the same level than Espritz NMR (sequence only) for PDB30 and CAMEO sets and outperforms it for the CASP10 set. The comparison with Espritz X-ray in the PDB30 set is not relevant since there is a significant overlap between sequences in our test set (PDB30) and Espritz X-ray training set. This overlap explains in part the relative high performance. For the CASP10 dataset, we included results from Disopred3 to have a comparison point with a sequence profile method. Both methods were downloaded and ran locally in a Linux server using the default parameters.

The performance of the method was evaluated on disordered regions of various lengths for the CASP10 dataset. The percentage of residues correctly predicted to be disordered is reported in Table 4. As only disordered residues are considered for each category, the percentage of correctly predicted as disordered corresponds to the recall.

Finally, to evaluate the speed at which our method performs predictions we created a script which takes as input a FASTA file of proteins to predict, performs predictions and saves the results to a file. Average execution time needed to perform predictions in a standard Linux server (4 CPUs/4GB memory) was 5.86s for the CASP10 dataset.

Table 3: Performance of methods predictor against CASP10 targets

Method	Acc.	Sens.	Spec.	MCC	AUC
Espritz (Xray)	0.72	0.54	0.89	0.30	0.81
Espritz (NMR)	0.68	0.56	0.79	0.20	0.73
ngram	0.72	0.61	0.83	0.26	0.80
Disopred3	0.64	0.32	0.97	0.32	0.85

Table 4: Prediction accuracy by region length in CASP10

Method	<10AA	10-30AA	>30AA
Espritz (Xray)	50.5	58.8	48.3
ngram	48.8	46.3	54.7
Disopred3	25.1	33.1	45.2

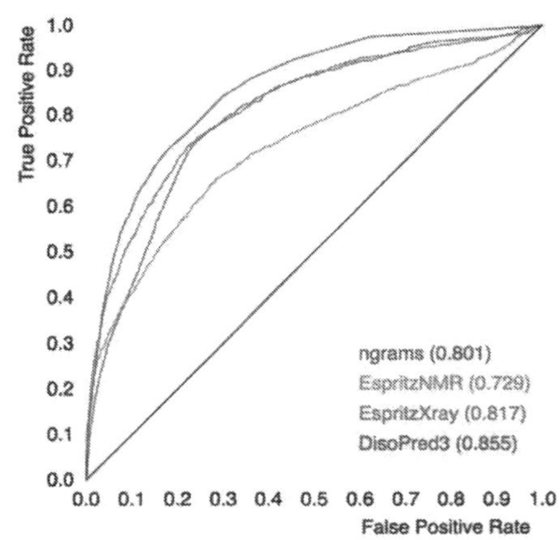

Figure 2: CASP10 performance

Table 5: **Performance of methods predictor against PDB30 targets**

Method	Acc.	Sens.	Spec.	MCC	AUC
Espritz (Xray)	0.83	0.78	0.87	0.39	0.90
Espritz (NMR)	0.78	0.75	0.80	0.27	0.86
ngrams	0.79	0.73	0.86	0.33	0.85

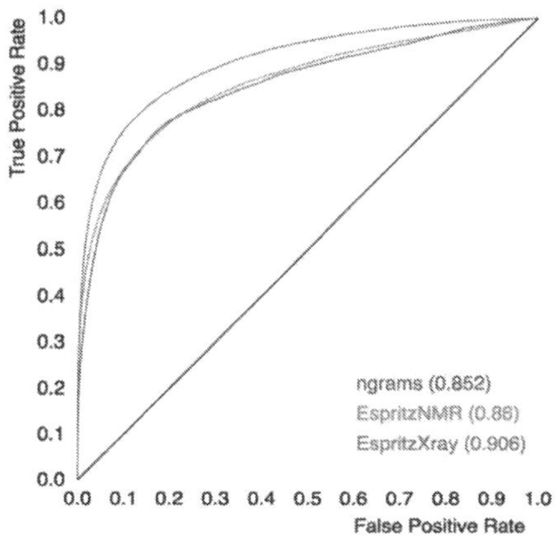

Figure 3: **PDB30 performance**

Table 6: **Performance of methods predictor against CAMEO targets**

Method	Acc.	Sens.	Spec.	MCC	AUC
Espritz (Xray)	0.74	0.74	0.74	0.27	0.80
ngrams	0.73	0.56	0.89	0.34	0.79

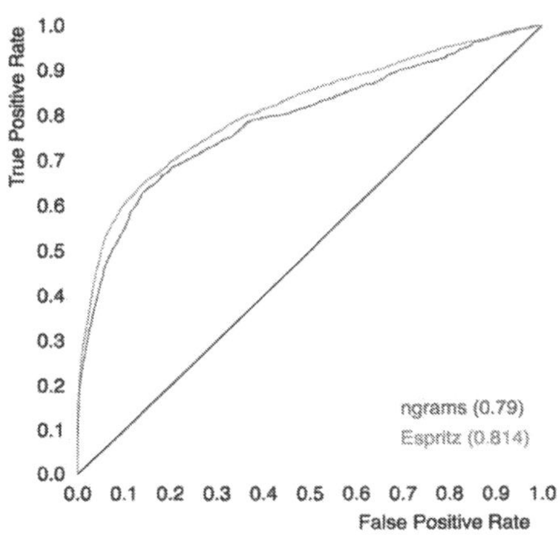

Figure 4: **CAMEO (hard) performance**

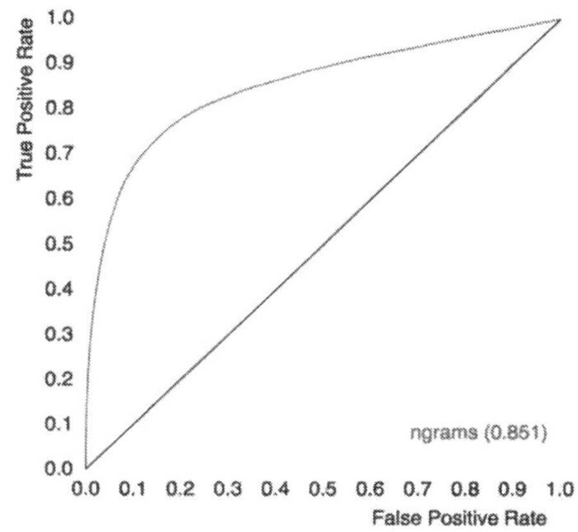

Figure 5: **PDB set 10-fold validation**

3.5 Decision Tree Analysis

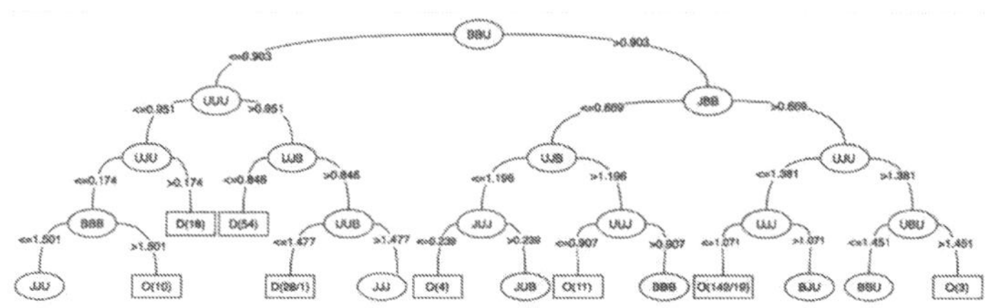

Figure 6: **Visual representation of 3-gram based C4.5 decision tree using reduced alphabet 1. Each circular node represents a 3-gram, and the edges show how the 3-gram frequencies were used in the decision-making process**

Figure 6 provides an example visual representation of the type of trees generated by the random forest algorithm. Trees tended to use n-gram features with polar and charged residues (letter 'U' in the reduced alphabet). Since these n-grams tended to be close to the root of the tree, these features were particularly important in classification. This may imply that the presence of these residues is a key factor in how an n-gram based model differentiates between disorder and order. In fact, disordered sequences are known to contain higher proportions of polar and charged residues than ordered sequences [13]. This suggests a possible link between the importance of such residues in the decision trees and this previously known observation.

4 CONCLUSIONS

This paper presents a new n-gram based classification method for protein disorder prediction. We demonstrated that a combination of an alphabet reduction strategy with n-gram frequency patterns leads to an approach which can successfully compete with more elaborated and computationally expensive algorithms.

Overall and despite its simplicity, our method performs at similar levels as other sequence based algorithms across all tested data sets. It has the additional advantage of providing insight into the mechanism of classification on the supplied data set.

Analysis of the decision trees showed that many n-grams were necessary in the decision-making process. However, the presence of polar and charged residues in the n-grams contributes to how the model differentiates between disorder and order state.

ACKNOWLEDGMENTS

The authors are grateful for the computational facilities provided by NIBR.

REFERENCES

[1] V. N. Uversky, "Wrecked regulation of intrinsically disordered proteins in diseases: pathogenicity of deregulated regulators," *Front. Mol. Biosci.*, vol. 1, Jul. 2014.

[2] G. Hu, Z. Wu, K. Wang, V. N. Uversky, and L. Kurgan, "Untapped potential of disordered proteins in current druggable human proteome," *Curr. Drug Targets*, Jul. 2015.

[3] N. Rezaei-Ghaleh, M. Blackledge, and M. Zweckstetter, "Intrinsically disordered proteins: from sequence and conformational properties toward drug discovery," *Chembiochem Eur. J. Chem. Biol.*, vol. 13, no. 7, pp. 930–950, May 2012.

[4] A. K. Dunker, S. E. Bondos, F. Huang, and C. J. Oldfield, "Intrinsically disordered proteins and multicellular organisms," *Semin. Cell Dev. Biol.*, vol. 37, pp. 44–55, Jan. 2015.

[5] B. He, K. Wang, Y. Liu, B. Xue, V. N. Uversky, and A. K. Dunker, "Predicting intrinsic disorder in proteins: an overview," *Cell Res.*, vol. 19, no. 8, pp. 929–949, Aug. 2009.

[6] C. Y.-C. Chen and W. I. Tou, "How to design a drug for the disordered proteins?," *Drug Discov. Today*, vol. 18, no. 19–20, pp. 910–915, Oct. 2013.

[7] Y. Cheng *et al.*, "Rational drug design via intrinsically disordered protein," *Trends Biotechnol.*, vol. 24, no. 10, pp. 435–442, Oct. 2006.

[8] J. K. Vries, X. Liu, and I. Bahar, "The relationship between N-gram patterns and protein secondary structure," *Proteins Struct. Funct. Bioinforma.*, vol. 68, no. 4, pp. 830–838, Sep. 2007.

[9] I. Vaisman and A. Srinivasan, "Identification and Prediction of Intrinsically Disordered Regions in Proteins Using n-Grams." 2015.

[10] J. D. Atkins, S. Y. Boateng, T. Sorensen, and L. J. McGuffin, "Disorder Prediction Methods, Their Applicability to Different Protein Targets and Their Usefulness for Guiding Experimental Studies," *Int. J. Mol. Sci.*, vol. 16, no. 8, pp. 19040–19054, Aug. 2015.

[11] O. Noivirt-Brik, J. Prilusky, and J. L. Sussman, "Assessment of disorder predictions in CASP8," *Proteins Struct. Funct. Bioinforma.*, vol. 77, no. S9, pp. 210–216, Jan. 2009.

[12] B. Monastyrskyy, K. Fidelis, J. Moult, A. Tramontano, and A. Kryshtafovych, "Evaluation of disorder predictions in CASP9," *Proteins*, vol. 79, no. S10, pp. 107–118, 2011.

[13] J. J. Ward, L. J. McGuffin, K. Bryson, B. F. Buxton, and D. T. Jones, "The DISOPRED server for the prediction of protein disorder," *Bioinformatics*, vol. 20, no. 13, pp. 2138–2139, Sep. 2004.

[14] I. Walsh, A. J. M. Martin, T. D. Domenico, and S. C. E. Tosatto, "ESpritz: accurate and fast prediction of protein disorder," *Bioinformatics*, vol. 28, no. 4, pp. 503–509, Feb. 2012.

[15] X. Deng, J. Eickholt, and J. Cheng, "PreDisorder: ab initio sequence-based prediction of protein disordered regions," *BMC Bioinformatics*, vol. 10, p. 436, Dec. 2009.

[16] X. Deng, J. Eickholt, and J. Cheng, "A comprehensive overview of computational protein disorder prediction methods," *Mol. Biosyst.*, vol. 8, no. 1, pp. 114–121, Jan. 2012.

[17] T. Ishida and K. Kinoshita, "Prediction of disordered regions in proteins based on the meta approach," *Bioinforma. Oxf. Engl.*, vol. 24, no. 11, pp. 1344–1348, Jun. 2008.

[18] L. P. Kozlowski and J. M. Bujnicki, "MetaDisorder: a meta-server for the prediction of intrinsic disorder in proteins," *BMC Bioinformatics*, vol. 13, p. 111, May 2012.

[19] T. Ishida and K. Kinoshita, "PrDOS: prediction of disordered protein regions from amino acid sequence," *Nucleic Acids Res.*, vol. 35, no. Web Server issue, pp. W460-464, Jul. 2007.

[20] J. Wang and W. Wang, "A computational approach to simplifying the protein folding alphabet," *Nat. Struct. Mol. Biol.*, vol. 6, no. 11, pp. 1033–1038, Nov. 1999.

[21] C. Branden, "Introduction to protein structure. By C Branden and J Tooze. pp 302. garland publishing, New York. 1991 ISBN 0-8513-0270-3 (pbk)," *Biochem. Educ.*, vol. 20, no. 2, pp. 121–122, Apr. 1992.

[22] T. Li, K. Fan, J. Wang, and W. Wang, "Reduction of protein sequence complexity by residue grouping," *Protein Eng.*, vol. 16, no. 5, pp. 323–330, May 2003.

[23] L. B. Mekler, *Specific selective interaction between amino acid residues of polypeptide chains.* 1969.

[24] L. R. Murphy, A. Wallqvist, and R. M. Levy, "Simplified amino acid alphabets for protein fold recognition and implications for folding," *Protein Eng.*, vol. 13, no. 3, pp. 149–152, Mar. 2000.

[25] J. Bacardit, M. Stout, J. D. Hirst, A. Valencia, R. E. Smith, and N. Krasnogor, "Automated Alphabet Reduction for Protein Datasets," *BMC Bioinformatics*, vol. 10, no. 1, p. 6, Jan. 2009.

[26] T. K. Ho, "The Random Subspace Method for Constructing Decision Forests," *IEEE Trans Pattern Anal Mach Intell*, vol. 20, no. 8, pp. 832–844, Aug. 1998.

[27] J. R. Quinlan, "Induction of Decision Trees," *Mach Learn*, vol. 1, no. 1, pp. 81–106, Mar. 1986.

[28] B. Monastyrskyy, A. Kryshtafovych, J. Moult, A. Tramontano, and K. Fidelis, "Assessment of protein disorder region predictions in CASP10," *Proteins*, vol. 82, no. 0 2, pp. 127–137, Feb. 2014.

[29] H. M. Berman *et al.*, "The Protein Data Bank," *Nucleic Acids Res.*, vol. 28, no. 1, pp. 235–242, Jan. 2000.

[30] J. Haas *et al.*, "The Protein Model Portal--a comprehensive resource for protein structure and model information," *Database J. Biol. Databases Curation*, vol. 2013, p. bat031, 2013.

[31] G. Wang and R. L. Dunbrack, "PISCES: a protein sequence culling server," *Bioinforma. Oxf. Engl.*, vol. 19, no. 12, pp. 1589–1591, Aug. 2003.

[32] R. Linding, L. J. Jensen, F. Diella, P. Bork, T. J. Gibson, and R. B. Russell, "Protein disorder prediction: implications for structural proteomics," *Struct. Lond. Engl. 1993*, vol. 11, no. 11, pp. 1453–1459, Nov. 2003.

[33] "NCBI News: Spring 2004|BLASTLab." [Online]. Available: https://www.ncbi.nlm.nih.gov/Web/Newsltr/Spring04/blastlab.html. [Accessed: 17-Apr-2017].

[34] S. Wang, J. Ma, and J. Xu, "AUCpreD: proteome-level protein disorder prediction by AUC-maximized deep convolutional neural fields," *Bioinformatics*, vol. 32, no. 17, pp. i672–i679, Sep. 2016.

[35] X. Deng, J. Gumm, S. Karki, J. Eickholt, and J. Cheng, "An Overview of Practical Applications of Protein Disorder Prediction and Drive for Faster, More Accurate Predictions," *Int. J. Mol. Sci.*, vol. 16, no. 7, pp. 15384–15404, Jul. 2015.

[36] T. Huang *et al.*, "A Sequence-based Approach for Predicting Protein Disordered Regions," *Protein Pept. Lett.*, vol. 20, no. 3, pp. 243–248, Jan. 2013.

[37] R. Kohavi, "A Study of Cross-validation and Bootstrap for Accuracy Estimation and Model Selection," in *Proceedings of the 14th International Joint Conference on Artificial Intelligence - Volume 2*, San Francisco, CA, USA, 1995, pp. 1137–1143.

[38] E. Frank, M. Hall, L. Trigg, G. Holmes, and I. H. Witten, "Data mining in bioinformatics using Weka," *Bioinformatics*, vol. 20, no. 15, pp. 2479–2481, Oct. 2004.

Deep Recurrent Conditional Random Field Network for Protein Secondary Prediction

Alexander Rosenberg Johansen
Technical University of Denmark, DTU Compute
alexander@munk.ai

Casper Kaae Sønderby
University of Copenhagen, Bioinformatics Centre
casper.sonderby@bio.ku.dk

Søren Kaae Sønderby
University of Copenhagen, Bioinformatics Centre
soren.sonderby@bio.ku.dk

Ole Winther
Technical University of Denmark, DTU Compute
olwi@dtu.dk

ABSTRACT

Deep learning has become the state-of-the-art method for predicting protein secondary structure from only its amino acid residues and sequence profile. Building upon these results, we propose to combine a bi-directional recurrent neural network (biRNN) with a conditional random field (CRF), which we call the biRNN-CRF. The biRNN-CRF may be seen as an improved alternative to an auto-regressive uni-directional RNN where predictions are performed sequentially conditioning on the prediction in the previous time-step. The CRF is instead nearest neighbor-aware and models for the joint distribution of the labels for all time-steps. We condition the CRF on the output of biRNN, which learns a distributed representation based on the entire sequence. The biRNN-CRF is therefore close to ideally suited for the secondary structure task because a high degree of cross-talk between neighboring elements can be expected. We validate the model on several benchmark datasets. For example, on CB513, a model with 1.7 million parameters, achieves a Q8 accuracy of 69.4 for single model and 70.9 for ensemble, which to our knowledge is state-of-the-art. [1]

CCS CONCEPTS

• **Computing methodologies → Supervised learning by classification**; **Neural networks**; *Batch learning*;

KEYWORDS

Secondary protein structure; Recurrent Neural Network; Conditional Random Field

1 INTRODUCTION

Current approaches to predict secondary protein structures, from amino acid residues and sequence profiles, use machine learning methods [14, 24]. Recently, artificial neural network based methods [18] has emerged and received state of the art performance [6, 19, 26, 29, 31]. These approaches have arisen as the challenge of annotating secondary protein structures is predictable from conformations along the sequence of the amino acid and sequence profiles [29].

Recent methods propose using either; convolutions, which work as fixed-sized sliding windows, combined with variants of auto-regressive models [6, 31], convolutions with a conditional random field (CRF) output layer [29], a bi-directional RNN [26] or convolutions combined with a bi-directional RNN and multi-task learning [19].

Thus, previous work has had a tendency to either focus on integrating information over longer distances with a RNN or modeling the sequence likelihood in secondary structures with auto-regressive or CRF components. We propose to combine these methods in an end-to-end trainable artificial neural network. A method that learns to model temporal information along the entire protein structure, using a bi-directional recurrent neural network (biRNN), as well as inferring the most likely sequence of proteins, using a conditional random field (CRF). We argue that the biRNN part of the model learns a hidden representation that integrates information from formations along the sequence, and the CRF uses that representation to model the joint distribution of the secondary structure for all labels. Furthermore, by modeling the labels jointly rather than independent conditioned on the hidden states of the biRNN means that it will produce predictions closer to what is observed in actual proteins. E.g. a prediction alpha-turn-alpha-turn will be highly unlikely.

The recurrent neural network (RNN), as well as the convolutional neural network (CNN), are modular architectures for spatial feature extraction. Both these methods have proven the preferred way for modelling sequences with deep learning methods [2, 11]. The RNN subjects the network to reuse its weights by recursively applying them across a sequence, based on a prior that the input domain will have a time dependency, e.g. along a series of words or amino acids. Having only one set of parameters for every time-step along the entire sequence lowers the parameter space significantly, as opposed to a standard feed forward network, which reduces overfitting. As the RNN applies the same weights repeatedly a fixed sequences length is not required. [11] Furthermore, modern RNNs use gating mechanisms, such as the long-short term memory cell (LSTM) [13] or the gated recurrent unit (GRU) [7, 9], to exhibit an internal memory state. An internal memory state makes the RNN capable of modeling dynamical temporal behavior over longer

[1]Codebase available at: github.com/alrojo/biRNN-CRF

Permission to make digital or hard copies of all or part of this work for personal or classroom use is granted without fee provided that copies are not made or distributed for profit or commercial advantage and that copies bear this notice and the full citation on the first page. Copyrights for components of this work owned by others than the author(s) must be honored. Abstracting with credit is permitted. To copy otherwise, or republish, to post on servers or to redistribute to lists, requires prior specific permission and/or a fee. Request permissions from permissions@acm.org.
ACM-BCB'17, August 20-23, 2017, Boston, MA, USA.
© 2017 Copyright held by the owner/author(s). Publication rights licensed to ACM.
978-1-4503-4722-8/17/08...$15.00
DOI: http://dx.doi.org/10.1145/3107411.3107489

sequences and enabling the neural network to express long-term dependencies.

When predicting a sequence of labels the probability of a transition between labels may depend not only on the current observation, but also on past and future observations. The Conditional Random Field (CRF) [17] allow us to incorporate transitions between labels by modeling the joint probability of the entire sequence. The CRF uses a transition between neighboring states to achieve such. As each label becomes dependent on the transition of its neighbors, so will the neighbors become dependent on the transition of their neighbors, creating a chain of dependencies that stretches the entire sequence for each label (also known as the Markov assumption).

Despite the attractive qualities of neural network architectures, building state-of-the-art neural networks is prohibitively expensive. Luckily, current graphics processing units (GPUs), paired with optimized implementations of neural network architectures make it convenient to train state-of-the-art neural networks. Furthermore, easy-to-use libraries for wrapping GPU implementations, such as the Python based TensorFlow [1] (our preferred choice) or Keras [8], empowers researchers to quickly iterate and build state-of-the-art neural networks with limited knowledge of GPUs.

The specific contribution of this paper are as follows: we present how a recurrent neural network, with memory cells, and a conditional random field can be successfully combined and trained on secondary protein structure prediction given a sequence of amino acids and sequence profiles. Our results find that using a CRF improves our baseline model and makes it comparable state-of-the-art neural networks with much higher parameter count and complexity.

2 RELATED WORK

The use of deep learning for sequence analysis is not new. Since the break-through of deep learning methods, which came from the increase in available data and computational power [16], new and previously underutilized deep learning methods [3, 4, 13, 23] have achieved significant improvements over state-of-the-art methods within their respective sequential field. Such as Machine Translation [4, 30], Speech Recognition [2] and Audio Generation [28]. Tasks in computational biology that fits well into these deep learning methods have experienced a spill-over, resulting in state-of-the-art improvements as well [25]. More specifically, CRF is a method originally tested on sequential labeling in natural language processing for POS tagging [17], but has later been found useful to the, mathematically, much similar problem of predicting secondary protein structures [29]. In our work, we attempt to accomplish a similar feat. As previous effort in secondary structure prediction has yet to combine the representational power of RNNs with benefits of modeling the joint probability of the entire sequence.

3 MATERIALS AND METHODS

This section describes the datasets used, evaluation metric and the deep learning architecture.

3.1 Dataset

We use four different dataset combinations: 1) the CB6133 with the official train, validation and test split, 2-4) the filtered version of the CB6133 as train and validation set and either the CB513, CASP10 or CASP11 as test set [20, 21, 31] [2].

3.1.1 CB6133. In the CB6133 (non-filtered) dataset [3] we use the amino acid residues (features [0 : 21)) and sequence profiles (features [35 : 56)) giving a total of 42 input features at each time step. For labels, we use the secondary structure notation (features [22 : 30)) at every time step and mask the loss using the NoSeq label (feature [30]). We train and evaluate on the official dataset splits (training: [0 : 5600), validation: [5877 : 6133), test: [5605 : 5877)).

3.1.2 CB6133 filtered with CB513 & CASP10 & CASP11. For training and validation, we use the filtered-CB6133 dataset [4] with the same features as the non-filtered version. As no official validation set is provided we optimized hyperparameters using 256 random samples from the training set. For testing we use CB513 [5], CASP10 and CASP11 [6].

3.2 Evaluation

All models are evaluated using tagging accuracy reporting the following scores: 3-class accuracy (Q3; α-helix, β-strand and coil) and 8-class accuracy (Q8; α-helix={G for 310-helix, H for α'-helix, I for π-helix}; β-strand={E for β'-strand, B for β-bridge} and coil={T for β-turn, S for high-curvature-loop, L for irregular}) tagging accuracy.

3.3 Our Model

The architecture of the network is defined by three different types of learnable layers and one regularization layer, the fully connected, the recurrent layer with gated recurrent unit (GRU) memory cells, a conditional random field (CRF) layer and a Bernoulli dropout regularization layer. Below, we describe the different layer types used for our network in more detail.

3.4 Fully Connected

The fully connected layer, also known as a dense layer or a multi layer perceptron (MLP) [22], is a non-linear transformation of the previous layer, $\ell - 1$. The first layer, $\ell = 0$, is considered the input layer. In our case the input layer is sequence profiles and a one-hot encoding of the amino acid. The standard MLP is defined in the following linear algebraic operation

$$z_t^\ell = h_t^{\ell-1}\theta^\ell + b^\ell, \quad (1)$$

$$h_t^\ell = a(z_t^\ell) \quad (2)$$

where h^l is the current layer, θ^ℓ is the weight matrix and b^ℓ is the bias used to compute the linear combination of the input; z^ℓ. Notice that we subscript t as this is performed individually for every state at all time-steps. A non-linear activation function, $a(z^\ell)$ is applied element-wise to the linear combination of the input, which results in the next layer; h^ℓ.

Most commonly used functions for the element-wise activation function $a(z)$ includes the Logistic Sigmoid $a(z) = 1/(1 + e^{-z})$ and

[2] http://www.princeton.edu/~jzthree/datasets/ICML2014/

[3] http://www.princeton.edu/~jzthree/datasets/ICML2014/cullpdb+profile_6133.npy.gz

[4] http://www.princeton.edu/~jzthree/datasets/ICML2014/cullpdb+profile_6133_filtered.npy.gz

[5] http://www.princeton.edu/~jzthree/datasets/ICML2014/cb513+profile_split1.npy.gz

[6] Generously supplied by the authors of [29] and [19] and formatted identically to CB6133/CB513

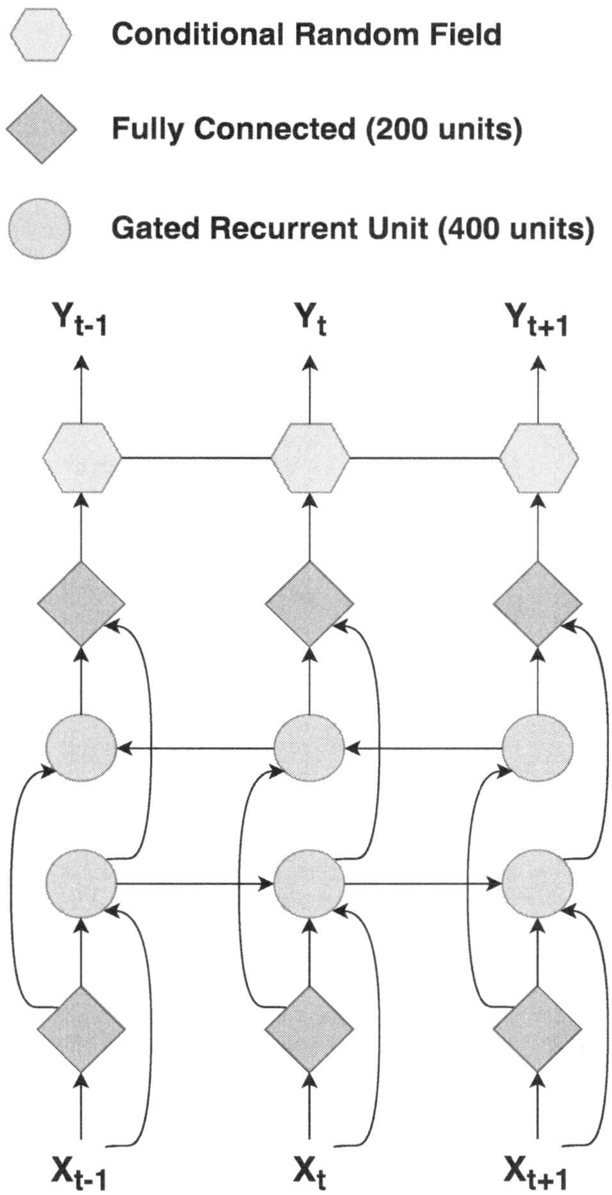

Figure 1: Our proposed model: The biRNN-CRF

the Hyperbolic Tangent $a(z) = (e^z - e^{-z})/(e^z + e^{-z})$. Non-saturating functions such as the Rectifier Linear Unit (ReLU) $a(z) = max(0, z)$ (our preferred choice) has become popular as their gradients do not vanish and it is computationally easier, which makes optimizing the network faster using stochastic gradient descent [10, 16].

As regularization technique, to avoid overfitting, we add Bernoulli dropouts [27], which is a non-trainable layer. Such that

$$h^\ell = h^{\ell-1} \odot p \quad (3)$$

where $p_i \in [0, 1]$ is sampled from a Bernoulli distribution with chance k for $p_i = 0$ and $1 - k$ for $p_i = 1$. Most commonly $k = 0.5$, which is also the case in our Bernoulli dropout layer. The purpose of the Bernoulli Dropout is to introduce noise such that the model becomes less dependent on combinations of specific activations.

3.5 Bi-directional Recurrent Neural Network

A recurrent neural network (RNN) is a type of neural network layer that repeatedly uses the same weights along a sequence of data with a prior that the sequence dimension contains a useful signal [11]. The gated recurrent unit (GRU), which we use, is a type of computational unit for calculating the hidden representation at every time step of the RNN. The GRU uses memory cells to better model long-term dependencies and improve convergence speed. The GRU is defined as described in Chung, 2014 [9].

$$r_t^\ell = \sigma(h_t^{\ell-1} W_r^\ell + h_{t-1}^\ell U_r^\ell + b_r^\ell), \quad (4)$$

$$z_t^\ell = \sigma(h_t^{\ell-1} W_z^\ell + h_{t-1}^\ell U_z^\ell + b_z^\ell), \quad (5)$$

$$\hat{h}_t^\ell = \tanh(h_t^{\ell-1} W_h^\ell + (r \odot h_{t-1}^\ell) U_h^\ell + b_h^\ell), \quad (6)$$

$$h_t^\ell = (1 - z_t^\ell) \odot h_{t-1}^\ell z_t^\ell \odot \hat{h}_t^\ell \quad (7)$$

Where $\sigma(z)$ is the sigmoid function $1/(1 + e^{-z})$, $h_t^{\ell-1}$ is the input at time t and h_{t-1}^ℓ the hidden state at time $t - 1$. The RNN with GRU is only defined in one direction, h_t^ℓ for $t = [1, 2, ..., T]$ where T is sequence length. To utilize information from both directions we compute the backwards RNN with h_t for $t = [T, T-1, ..., 1]$ and h_t^ℓ being dependent on h_{t+1}^ℓ instead of h_{t-1}^ℓ. To combined both directions, we concatenate the hidden states from the forward and backward pass, such as described by [23], where the hidden states are aligned with their index, $t = [1, 2, ..., T]$, such that.

$$h_t^\ell = \begin{bmatrix} \overrightarrow{h_t^\ell} \\ \overleftarrow{h_t^\ell} \end{bmatrix} \quad (8)$$

where $\overrightarrow{h_t^\ell}$ is the forward pass and $\overleftarrow{h_t^\ell}$ the backwards pass. This is known as the bi-directional RNN (biRNN).

3.6 Conditional Random Field (CRF)

The CRF is a joint distribution of the labels in the sequence $y = y_1, \ldots, y_T$ given the input sequence $x = x_1, \ldots, x_T$ on the following restricted form

$$p(y|x) = \frac{1}{Z(h)} \prod_{t=1}^{T} \exp \psi_{y_t}(h_t) \prod_{t=1}^{T-1} \exp \phi_{y_t, y_{t+1}}(h_t, h_{t+1}), \quad (9)$$

where $h = h_1, \ldots, h_T$ is the output of the previous hidden layer, $\psi_t = \psi(h_t)$ is a linear model which takes h_t as input and has the number of classes C ($C = 8$ or $C = 3$ in this paper) outputs, $\phi_t = \phi(h_t, h_{t+1})$ is another linear model with C^2 real-valued outputs

$$\psi_t = W_\psi h_t + b_\psi \quad (10)$$

$$\phi_t = W_\phi \begin{bmatrix} h_t \\ h_{t+1} \end{bmatrix} + b_\phi \quad (11)$$

and $Z(h)$ is the normalization constant of the distribution. Due to the chain structure, inference can be carried out exactly using dynamic programming in $O(TC^2)$ [5]. During training where (x, y) is observed we need to compute $Z(h)$ for each training sequence as part of the likelihood $p(y|x)$. During prediction where only x

Table 1: Q8 accuracy on: CullPDB, CB513, CASP10, CASP11.

Methods	Q8(%)			
	CullPDB	CB513	CASP10	CASP11
Single Model				
GSN	72.1	66.4	N/A	N/A
DCRNN	N/A	69.4	N/A	N/A
Deep Multi-Scale CNN	N/A	**70.0**	N/A	N/A
biRNN (ours)**	μ=72.5, σ=0.15	μ=68.5, σ=0.12	μ=72.8, σ=0.23	μ=70.1, σ=0.32
biRNN-CRF (ours)**	μ=**73.4**, σ=0.13	μ=69.4, σ=0.16	μ=**73.5**, σ=0.38	μ=**70.8**, σ=0.33
Ensemble				
DeepCNF	N/A*	68.3	71.8	72.3
DCRNN	73.2	69.7	**76.9**	**73.1**
Deep Multi-Scale CNN	N/A	70.6	N/A	N/A
biRNN-CRF (ours)***	74.6	70.8	74.7	72.2
biRNN-CRF (ours)****	**74.8**	**70.9**	74.9	72.4

Table 2: Q3 accuracy on: CullPDB, CB513, CASP10, CASP11.

Methods	Q3(%)			
	CullPDB	CB513	CASP10	CASP11
Single Model				
biRNN (ours)**	μ=83.6, σ=0.14	μ=81.8, σ=0.13	μ=84.1, σ=0.20	μ=81.3, σ=0.28
biRNN-CRF (ours)**	μ=**84.2**, σ=0.13	μ=**82.2**, σ=0.16	μ=**84.2**, σ=0.29	μ=**81.7**, σ=0.25
Ensemble				
DeepCNF	N/A*	82.3	84.4	84.7
DCRNN	N/A	**84.0**	**87.8**	**85.3**
biRNN-CRF (ours)***	**85.0**	83.2	85.0	83.2
biRNN-CRF (ours)****	**85.0**	83.3	85.2	82.8

is observed we can calculate either the most probably sequence $\arg\max_y p(y|x)$ (using the Viterbi decoding algorithm) or the marginal probabilities $p(y_t|x)$, $t = 1, \ldots, T$. In all our reported results, we use the maximum marginal probability prediction since this gives the smallest expected element-wise error [5]. Viterbi decoding is relevant when the objective is the lowest possible sequence-wise prediction error.

The most straight forward alternative to the CRF is an auto-regressive model:

$$p(y|x) = p(y_1|x) \prod_{t=2}^{T} p(y_t|y_1, \ldots, y_{t-1}, x) \tag{12}$$

which can be implemented by replacing the CRF layer in figure figure 1 with T independent C-dimensional softmax units and adding y_{t-1} as an extra dimension to $\overrightarrow{h_t}$. The disadvantage of this model compared to the CRF is two-fold: 1) computing the most probable sequences and marginals have exponential complexity in the sequence length and 2) predictions are slow because we need to recompute a large part of the model at each time step.

3.7 Architecture and details of learning

As depicted in figure 1 the network contains five layers. The first layer is a fully connected layer, the second is a bi-directional RNN with GRU memory cells. The third layer is a dropout layer, the fourth is a fully connected layer and the fifth is a conditional random field layer that provides the conditional probability of the 8-way classification problem. Note that the input has a skip connection to the bidirectional RNN. Both of the fully connected layers have 200 hidden units each and use ReLU as their activation function. Both of the recurrent GRU layers have 400 hidden units each. To train the model we minimize the loss which is the negative log likelihood of the model parameters collectively denoted by θ over a training set (X, Y) of n paired input and output sequences $X = x^{(1)}, \ldots, x^{(n)}$ and $Y = y^{(1)}, \ldots, y^{(n)}$:

$$\mathrm{Loss}_\theta(\mathrm{X}, \mathrm{Y}) = - \sum_{(\mathrm{x},\mathrm{y}) \in (\mathrm{X},\mathrm{Y})} \log \mathrm{p}(\mathrm{y}|\mathrm{x}, \theta) \,. \tag{13}$$

We train our model with the first order method: stochastic gradient descent (SGD) with mini batches of size 64. SGD works by utilizing chain ruling to take the partial derivative of the loss function with respect to each weight vector in the network, and use the derivative to update the weights. We use a version of SGD known as Adam [15] with default parameters and a learning rate of $1e-3$. Adam uses historic information to adapt the learning rate for every parameter while training. To avoid exploding gradients [11] we normalize and clip the gradients if its norm exceeds a threshold of 1. We train our neural network on an Nvidia GeForce GTX Titan X GPU using the python built TensorFlow library [1] to compile to CUDA (a GPU interpretable language).

Table 3: Recall and precision of biRNN-CRF**, DeepCNF ensemble and GSN on the CB6133 dataset. SS8 label corresponds to the eight secondary protein structure labels as described in section 3.2**

SS8 label	Recall			Precision		
	biRNN-CRF	DCRNN	GSN	biRNN-CRF	DCRNN	GSN
L	**0.672**	0.662	0.633	**0.606**	0.589	0.541
B	**0.099**	0.049	0.001	**0.614**	0.596	0.500
E	0.853	**0.862**	0.823	**0.803**	0.792	0.748
G	**0.343**	0.311	0.133	**0.530**	0.434	0.496
I	0.000	0.000	0.000	0.000	0.000	0.000
H	**0.936**	0.927	0.935	0.878	0.878	0.828
S	**0.288**	0.275	0.159	**0.537**	0.518	0.423
T	**0.604**	0.572	0.506	**0.589**	0.577	0.548

Table 4: Recall and precision of biRNN-CRF** and DeepCNF ensemble on the CB513 dataset.**

SS8 label	Recall		Precision	
	biRNN-CRF	DeepCNF	biRNN-CRF	DeepCNF
L	0.657	0.657	**0.597**	0.571
B	**0.042**	0.026	**0.515**	0.433
E	**0.835**	0.833	**0.760**	0.748
G	**0.348**	0.260	0.456	**0.490**
I	0.000	0.000	0.000	0.000
H	**0.931**	0.904	0.847	**0.849**
S	**0.265**	0.255	**0.549**	0.487
T	**0.554**	0.528	**0.557**	0.53

4 EXPERIMENTS

We evaluate the Q3 and Q8 performance of our neural network (biRNN-CRF) on the four datasets CB6133 train/val/test, CB6133 filtered with either CB513, CASP10 or CASP11 as test set (elaborated in section 3.1). The Q3 and Q8 accuracy is elaborated in section 3.2.

On the Q8 problem we further supply recall and precision for the CB6133 and the CB6133 filtered + CB513 dataset.

We compute the Q3 for our models by summing over our predictions from the Q8 into their respective Q3 classes: helix (H), strand (E) and coil (C).

The deep learning models we benchmark against are the GSN [31], DeepCNF [29], DCRNN [19] and the Deep Multi-Scale CNN [6].

4.1 Training details

We train two different type of models, the biRNN-CRF as illustrated in figure 1 and the biRNN, which is the exact same setup as the biRNN-CRF, but using the sequence independent cross entropy instead of the CRF layer and loss function.

We train 10 models for both the biRNN and biRNN-CRF to calculate single model mean/standard deviation as well as ensembles. All models are trained with the same setup, only seed for initializing weights differ. We use early stopping, based on the validation set, to pick the optimal set of weights.

4.2 Results

In single model performance, the biRNN-CRF outperforms the baseline biRNN using cross entropy across all datasets with between **0.1-0.9%**, as shown in table 1 and table 2. In our benchmark against state-of-the-art models using deep learning methods, our model achieves a new state-of-the-art performances on the CB6133 Q8: **74.8%(+1.6%)**, CB513 Q8: **70.9%(+0.3%)** and we also achieve **85.0%** on CB6133 Q3. Since we have not found any previously published results using deep learning methods on the CB6133 Q3 dataset we assume that it is also state-of-the-art. However, on the CASP10 and CASP11 datasets the DCRNN model significantly outperforms ours.

Furthermore, precision and recall for the CB6133 and CB513 is illustrated in table 3 and table 4. Here we find that our ensemble model outperforms or equals most previously published deep learning models.

4.3 Notes on models and ensemble

Not all previously published work we use for comparison has provided single model and ensemble results for all datasets. Because of such, we either supply a N/A if one or more results are missing or leave out the method from the table if all results are missing. * The DeepCNF article uses a different test set than the official for their CB6133 results. ** Mean, μ, and standard deviation, σ, are based on our 10 trained models as described in section 4.1. As there is not a single adopted way of ensembling models within the secondary protein structure literature, we employ our own ensembling strategy. Our ensemble is based on averaging predictions from our 10 trained models used for **. For the *** ensemble, we sample the weights from the best performing epoch, based on the validation set. The **** ensemble is the same as ***, but samples the top three weights instead of top one to reduce variance in predictions from each model.

5 DISCUSSION

Our results show that the bi-directional recurrent neural network with a conditional random field (biRNN-CRF) can perform on pair with vastly more advanced architectures. The biRNN model can be seen as a Spartan version of the DCRNN [19] ,which makes the DCRNN interesting for comparison. The biRNN has about a quarter of the parameters of the DCRNN (1.7 million vs. >6 million), no cascading convolutions, only one RNN layer and no multi-task training. Increasing depth and network size has in recent literature proven successful strategy [12], which might point to why our baseline (biRNN) is trailing the DCRNN. However, as we add the CRF layer we close the gap between the models. This result might indicate that the temporal benefits of a recurrent neural network with the conditioning power of a CRF is helpful when tackling sequential problems in computational biology. Moreover, there is no reason to conclude that the benefits obtained from the depth and capacity of the DCRNN are mutually exclusive with the benefits from the CRF layer. However, we will leave combining deep models for secondary protein structure prediction with a CRF layer for future research.

ACKNOWLEDGMENTS

This research was supported by the Novo Nordisk Foundation and the NVIDIA Corporation with the donation of TITAN X and Tesla K40 GPUs.

REFERENCES

[1] M. Abadi, A. Agarwal, P. Barham, E. Brevdo, Z. Chen, C. Citro, G. Corrado, A. Davis, J. Dean, M. Devin, S. Ghemawat, I. Goodfellow, A. Harp, G. Irving, M. Isard, Y. Jia, R. Józefowicz, L. Kaiser, M. Kudlur, J. Levenberg, D. Mané, R. Monga, S. Moore, D. Gordon Murray, C. Olah, M. Schuster, J. Shlens, B. Steiner, I. Sutskever, K. Talwar, P. A. Tucker, V. Vanhoucke, V. Vasudevan, F. Viégas, O. Vinyals, P. Warden, M. Wattenberg, M. Wicke, Y. Yu, and X. Zheng. 2016. TensorFlow: Large-Scale Machine Learning on Heterogeneous Distributed Systems. *CoRR* abs/1603.04467 (2016). https://arxiv.org/abs/1603.04467 Software available from tensorflow.org.

[2] D. Amodei, R. Anubhai, E. Battenberg, C. Case, J. Casper, B. Catanzaro, J. Chen, M. Chrzanowski, A. Coates, G. Diamos, E. Elsen, J. Engel, L. Fan, C. Fougner, T. Han, A. Hannun, B. Jun, P. LeGresley, L. Lin, S. Narang, A. Ng, S. Ozair, R. Prenger, J. Raiman, S. Satheesh, D. Seetapun, S. Sengupta, Y. Wang, Z. Wang, C. Wang, B. Xiao, D. Yogatama, J. Zhan, and Z. Zhu. 2015. Deep Speech 2: End-to-End Speech Recognition in English and Mandarin. *CoRR* abs/1512.02595 (2015). http://arxiv.org/abs/1512.02595

[3] J. Ba, J. Kiros, and G. Hinton. 2016. Layer normalization. *arXiv preprint arXiv:1607.06450* (2016).

[4] D. Bahdanau, K. Cho, and Y. Bengio. 2014. Neural Machine Translation by Jointly Learning to Align and Translate. *CoRR* abs/1409.0473 (2014). https://arxiv.org/abs/1409.0473

[5] C. Bishop. 2006. *Pattern recognition and machine learning*. Springer.

[6] A. Busia, J. Collins, and N. Jaitly. 2016. Protein Secondary Structure Prediction Using Deep Multi-scale Convolutional Neural Networks and Next-Step Conditioning. *CoRR* abs/1611.01503 (2016). http://arxiv.org/abs/1611.01503

[7] K. Cho, B. van Merrienboer, C. Gulcehre, F. Bougares, H. Schwenk, and Y. Bengio. 2014. Learning Phrase Representations using RNN Encoder-Decoder for Statistical Machine Translation. In *Conference on Empirical Methods in Natural Language Processing (EMNLP 2014)*.

[8] F. Chollet. 2015. Keras: Theano-based deep learning library. (2015). https://github.com/fchollet/keras

[9] J. Chung, Ç. Gülçehre, K. Cho, and Y. Bengio. 2014. Empirical Evaluation of Gated Recurrent Neural Networks on Sequence Modeling. *CoRR* abs/1412.3555 (2014). http://arxiv.org/abs/1412.3555

[10] X. Glorot, A. Bordes, and Y. Bengio. 2011. Deep Sparse Rectifier Neural Networks.. In *Aistats*, Vol. 15. 275.

[11] A. Graves. 2012. Supervised sequence labelling with recurrent neural networks. *Springer* (2012).

[12] K. He, X. Zhang, S. Ren, and J. Sun. 2015. Deep Residual Learning for Image Recognition. *CoRR* abs/1512.03385 (2015). http://arxiv.org/abs/1512.03385

[13] S. Hochreiter and J. Schmidhuber. 1997. Long Short-Term Memory. *Neural Comput.* 9, 8 (Nov. 1997), 1735–1780. DOI: http://dx.doi.org/10.1162/neco.1997.9.8.1735

[14] D. Jones. 1999. Protein secondary structure prediction based on position-specific scoring matrices. *Journal of Molecular Biology* 292, 2 (1999), 195 – 202. DOI: http://dx.doi.org/10.1006/jmbi.1999.3091

[15] D. Kingma and J. Ba. 2015. Adam: A method for stochastic optimization. International Conference on Learning Representation.

[16] A. Krizhevsky, I. Sutskever, and G. Hinton. 2012. ImageNet Classification with Deep Convolutional Neural Networks. In *Advances in Neural Information Processing Systems 25*, F. Pereira, C. J. C. Burges, L. Bottou, and K. Q. Weinberger (Eds.). Curran Associates, Inc., 1097–1105. http://papers.nips.cc/paper/4824-imagenet-classification-with-deep-convolutional-neural-networks.pdf

[17] J. Lafferty, A. McCallum, and F. Pereira. 2001. Conditional Random Fields: Probabilistic Models for Segmenting and Labeling Sequence Data. In *Proceedings of the Eighteenth International Conference on Machine Learning (ICML '01)*. Morgan Kaufmann Publishers Inc., San Francisco, CA, USA, 282–289. http://dl.acm.org/citation.cfm?id=645530.655813

[18] Y. LeCun, Y. Bengio, and G. Hinton. 2015. Deep learning. *Nature* 521, 7553 (2015), 436–444.

[19] Z. Li and Y. Yu. 2016. Protein Secondary Structure Prediction Using Cascaded Convolutional and Recurrent Neural Networks. *arXiv preprint arXiv:1604.07176* (2016).

[20] B. Monastyrskyy, A. Kryshtafovych, J. Moult, A. Tramontano, and K. Fidelis. 2014. Assessment of protein disorder region predictions in CASP10. *Proteins: Structure, Function, and Bioinformatics* 82, S2 (2014), 127–137.

[21] J. Moult, K. Fidelis, A. Kryshtafovych, T. Schwede, and A. Tramontano. 2014. Critical assessment of methods of protein structure prediction (CASP)âĂŤround x. *Proteins: Structure, Function, and Bioinformatics* 82, S2 (2014), 1–6.

[22] D. Ruck, S. Rogers, M. Kabrisky, M. Oxley, and B. Suter. 1990. The multilayer perceptron as an approximation to a Bayes optimal discriminant function. *Neural Networks, IEEE Transactions on* 1, 4 (1990), 296–298.

[23] M. Schuster and K. Paliwal. 1997. Bidirectional Recurrent Neural Networks. *Trans. Sig. Proc.* 45, 11 (Nov. 1997), 2673–2681. DOI: http://dx.doi.org/10.1109/78.650093

[24] M. Singh. 2005. Predicting protein secondary and supersecondary structure. *Handbook of Computational Molecular Biology, hapman & Hall CRC Computer and Information Science Series* (2005).

[25] S. Sønderby, C. Sønderby, H. Nielsen, and O. Winther. 2015. Convolutional LSTM networks for subcellular localization of proteins. In *International Conference on Algorithms for Computational Biology*. Springer, 68–80.

[26] S. Sønderby and O. Winther. 2014. Protein secondary structure prediction with long short term memory networks. *arXiv preprint arXiv:1412.7828* (2014).

[27] N. Srivastava, G. Hinton, A. Krizhevsky, I. Sutskever, and R. Salakhutdinov. 2014. Dropout: A Simple Way to Prevent Neural Networks from Overfitting. *J. Mach. Learn. Res.* (2014). http://dl.acm.org/citation.cfm?id=2627435.2670313

[28] A. van den Oord, S. Dieleman, H. Zen, K. Simonyan, O. Vinyals, A. Graves, N. Kalchbrenner, A. Senior, and K. Kavukcuoglu. 2016. WaveNet: A Generative Model for Raw Audio. *CoRR* abs/1609.03499 (2016). http://arxiv.org/abs/1609.03499

[29] S. Wang, J. Peng, J. Ma, and J. Xu. 2016. Protein secondary structure prediction using deep convolutional neural fields. *Scientific reports* 6 (2016).

[30] Y. Wu, M. Schuster, Z. Chen, Q. Le, M. Norouzi, W. Macherey, M. Krikun, Y. Cao, Q. Gao, K. Macherey, and others. 2016. Google's Neural Machine Translation System: Bridging the Gap between Human and Machine Translation. *arXiv preprint arXiv:1609.08144* (2016). https://arxiv.org/abs/1609.08144

[31] J. Zhou and O. Troyanskaya. 2014. Deep Supervised and Convolutional Generative Stochastic Network for Protein Secondary Structure Prediction.. In *ICML*. 745–753.

CERENKOV: Computational Elucidation of the Regulatory Noncoding Variome

Yao Yao*
Oregon State University
EECS
yaoyao@oregonstate.edu

Zheng Liu*
Oregon State University
EECS
liuzhen@oregonstate.edu

Satpreet Singh
Oregon State University
EECS
singhsa@oregonstate.edu

Qi Wei
Oregon State University
EECS
weiq@oregonstate.edu

Stephen A. Ramsey
Oregon State University
Department of Biomedical Sciences
Corvallis, Oregon 97330
stephen.ramsey@oregonstate.edu

ABSTRACT

We describe a novel computational approach, CERENKOV (Computational Elucidation of the REgulatory NonKOding Variome), for discriminating regulatory single nucleotide polymorphisms (rSNPs) from non-regulatory SNPs within noncoding genetic loci. CERENKOV is specifically designed for recognizing rSNPs in the context of a post-analysis of a genome-wide association study (GWAS); it includes a novel accuracy scoring metric (which we call average rank, or AVGRANK) and a novel cross-validation strategy (locus-based sampling) that both correctly account for the "sparse positive bag" nature of the GWAS post-analysis rSNP recognition problem. We trained and validated CERENKOV using a reference set of 15,331 SNPs (the `OSU17` SNP set) whose composition is based on selection criteria (linkage disequilibrium and minor allele frequency) that we designed to ensure relevance to GWAS post-analysis. CERENKOV is based on a machine-learning algorithm (gradient boosted decision trees) incorporating 246 SNP annotation features that we extracted from genomic, epigenomic, phylogenetic, and chromatin datasets. CERENKOV includes novel features based on replication timing and DNA shape. We found that tuning a classifier for AUPVR performance does not guarantee optimality for AVGRANK. We compared the validation performance of CERENKOV to nine other methods for rSNP recognition (including GWAVA, RSVP, DeltaSVM, DeepSEA, Eigen, and DANQ), and found that CERENKOV's validation performance is the strongest out of all of the classifiers that we tested, by both traditional global rank-based measures ($\langle$AUPVR$\rangle$ = 0.506; $\langle$AUROC$\rangle$ = 0.855) and AVGRANK ($\langle$AVGRANK$\rangle$ = 3.877). The source code for CERENKOV is available on GitHub and the SNP feature data files are available for download via the CERENKOV website.

Permission to make digital or hard copies of all or part of this work for personal or classroom use is granted without fee provided that copies are not made or distributed for profit or commercial advantage and that copies bear this notice and the full citation on the first page. Copyrights for components of this work owned by others than the author(s) must be honored. Abstracting with credit is permitted. To copy otherwise, or republish, to post on servers or to redistribute to lists, requires prior specific permission and/or a fee. Request permissions from permissions@acm.org.
ACM-BCB '17, August 20-23, 2017, Boston, MA, USA
© 2017 Copyright held by the owner/author(s). Publication rights licensed to ACM.
978-1-4503-4722-8/17/08... $15.00
DOI: http://dx.doi.org/10.1145/3107411.3107414

CCS CONCEPTS

• **Computing methodologies → Machine learning**; • **Applied computing → Computational biology**; **Bioinformatics**;

KEYWORDS

SNP, GWAS, noncoding, rSNP, SNV, machine learning

1 INTRODUCTION

1.1 The rSNP detection problem

Human genome-wide association studies (GWAS) have led to the discovery of 21,751 unique SNP-trait associations in more than 2,400 studies (based on millions of individuals) that are linked to human traits [55]. However, GWAS functional interpretation has been largely limited to *coding regions* in which single nucleotide polymorphisms (SNPs) can be mapped to functional consequence predictions using well-established methods [45]. This limits the yield of knowledge from GWAS because 90% of human GWAS-identified SNPs are located in noncoding regions [33]. Within noncoding regions, a key roadblock to identifying the molecular mechanisms underlying trait variation is the difficulty of pinpointing the probable causal noncoding SNPs [48]—the so-called *regulatory SNPs* (rSNPs)—that are associated with the trait. Various correlates of rSNPs are known [31], with expression quantitative trait locus (expression QTL, or eQTL) associations being one validated example [36]. But in general, how to computationally integrate various types of genomic, phylogenetic, epigenomic, transcription factor binding site (TFBS), and chromatin-structural rSNP correlates in order to discriminate regulatory SNPs from non-regulatory noncoding SNPs is a fundamental problem in computational biology.

* These authors contributed equally to this work.

Machine learning (ML) classification approaches based on sets of experimentally verified regulatory single nucleotide variants (rSNVs) from databases such as the Human Gene Mutation Database (HGMD), ORegAnno [35] or ClinVar (as well as neighboring "control SNVs" (cSNVs) that are presumed non-functional) have shown promise for advancing the field of computational rSNP recognition.

1.2 Previous approaches

Previous computational approaches to the problem of discriminating functional noncoding SNPs (i.e., regulatory SNPs or rSNPs) from nonfunctional SNPs can be divided into two categories, "rSNV-supervised" approaches that in which ground-truth sets of regulatory single nucleotide variants (rSNVs, such as from HGMD) were used in model training, and "rSNV-unsupervised" approaches that were not trained using ground-truth sets of rSNVs (and were instead trained using other sets of variants, typically much larger than the training sets used in the rSNV-supervised methods).

1.2.1 rSNV-unsupervised approaches. Among the rSNV-unsupervised approaches, various classification models have been proposed including probabilistic graphical models (such as in the fitCons variant scoring method [16]), support vector machine (SVM; such as in the CADD variant scoring method [24] and in the DeltaSVM variant scoring method [29]), deep neural networks (such as in the DANN variant scoring method [41]), and spectral methods (such as in the Eigen-PC method [21]). Somewhat counter-intuitively, some previous studies [21, 29] of rSNV-unsupervised methods have reported greater accuracy than rSNV-supervised methods [43] that were used for comparison, with Eigen-PC appearing to have the strongest such comparative performance results. These previous results suggest that state-of-the-art rSNV-unsupervised scoring methods, such as Eigen-PC, may be useful as *features* within an rSNV-supervised method.

1.2.2 rSNV-supervised approaches. A variety of classification algorithm types and feature-set types have been used for rSNV-supervised methods to identify regulatory variants. Montgomery *et al.* [34] integrated 23 variant annotation features (including transcription factor binding sites, TFBS) within a support vector machine (SVM) model, using a small reference set (104 rSNVs). Torkamani & Schork [51] integrated 28 TFBS, epigenomic, and chromatin features within a naïve Bayes classifier, also using a small reference set (102 rSNVs). Zhao et al. [58] derived 158 variant annotation features from population haplotype, gene annotation, and phylogenetic datasets and employed the Random Forest [4] algorithm, using a larger reference set (445 rSNVs). Ritchie et al. [43] engineered 175 features from several hundred epigenomic, population genetic, phylogenetic, and TFBS datasets; they used Random Forest and a moderate-sized reference set (1,614 rSNVs) to train their classifier, which they called GWAVA. In a method called DeepSEA, Zhou & Troyanskaya [59] employed deep convolutional neural networks (CNNs) in order to reduce the dimension of 1,000 bp of flanking sequence for a SNV to a single allele-dependent score. They trained 919 such CNNs using published epigenomic and chromatin measurements and integrated the allele-dependent scores within a gradient boosted decision tree algorithm, using a moderate-sized reference set (2,997 rSNVs). In a method called DANQ, Quang & Xie [42] used the same 919 chromatin measurements as Zhou & Troyanskaya used for training DeepSEA, but they used a hybrid network architecture combining CNN and deep recurrent neural network (RNN) components. In the RSVP method, Peterson *et al.* [39] derived a set of 2,237 SNP annotation features that was substantially expanded (versus previous approaches) by including a SNP's nearest-gene functional annotations and its nearest-gene multi-tissue expression profile; their feature-set also included SNP annotations based on local genomic replication timing measurements (Repli-chip [19] and Repli-seq [17] assay data from cell lines). Using a moderate-sized ground truth set (1,999 rSNVs), Peterson *et al.* trained an ensemble decision tree classifier. Thus, in terms of supervised methods for rSNP classification, there has been a steady progression in the comprehensiveness of the feature-sets and in the variety of algorithmic approaches that have been used.

1.2.3 DNA shape as a potential feature. Previous computational and experimental studies have demonstrated that local pentameric DNA sequence is predictive of three-dimensional DNA shape distortions (such as roll, propeller twist, and helical twist) [44, 60] and that specific features of the local DNA shape can improve discrimination of regulatory from non-regulatory DNA [57] in general and for transcription factor-specific prediction of TFBS [32]. Montgomery *et al.* have reported [34] that a specific DNA physical parameter (bendability) is beneficial for discriminating regulatory from non-regulatory variants. We have previously developed a computational model, `regshape`, that incorporates four sequence-predicted DNA shape parameters to predict transcription factor binding sites [57], for which allele-dependent scores may be useful within an rSNP detection model.

1.3 Limitations of previous approaches

An important limitation of all of the previous rSNV-supervised approaches to the rSNP recognition problem (of which we are aware) is that none of the models were trained and validated (i) using locus-by-locus assignment of variants to cross-validation (CV) folds and (ii) using a reference set of SNPs that was *selected for relevance to the application of GWAS post-analysis* and assigned to CV folds on a locus-by-locus basis. In the GWAS post-analysis application context, trait-linked SNPs are analyzed within *linkage disequilibrium blocks,* and thus, the SNPs are partitioned into loci and the goal is to identify the functional noncoding variant *within each locus.*[1] Thus, it is the *rank of the classifier's rSNP prediction score within a locus matters more than the global (locus-agnostic) ranking of rSNP prediction scores.* In every previous rSNV-supervised approach to this problem (of

[1] Thus, the rSNP recognition problem for GWAS post-analysis could be described as having a "sparse positive bag" structure [5].

which we are aware), SNVs are assigned to CV folds without regard to the SNVs' genomic positions; such "variant-level sampling", while standard practice, makes it impossible to use CV to measure the accuracy of the method on a per-locus basis and it makes the results not representative of how the method would perform in identifying a candidate causal rSNP within a "new" region identified by a GWAS.

A second limitation of previous approaches concerns selection of reference variants. Intrinsic to the GWAS approach is that the local linkage disequilibrium (LD) block needs to have a sufficiently high minor allele frequency (MAF; greater than 0.05) in order for GWAS to be sufficiently powered to detect an association of the block with the trait at genome-wide significance ($p \leq 5 \times 10^{-8}$). In the previous rSNP recognition methods development efforts of which we are aware, a significant fraction of the variants that were used for training are unrealistic in the context of a GWAS post-analysis application domain, either due to the variant having a low (i.e., less than 0.05) MAF,[2] or due to the variant not being in linkage disequilibrium with any known functional noncoding SNP. Further, no previous approach to this problem has combined a comprehensive SNP annotation feature-set (including replication timing data, chromatin segmentation information, expression quantitative trait locus annotations, and transcription factor binding site (TFBS) information for all available TFBS models) within a high-performance gradient boosted decision trees classification algorithm.

1.4 Our approach

We have developed a method, CERENKOV (Computational Elucidation of the REgulatory NonKOding Variome) for identifying rSNPs within GWAS regions. The method is in the "rSNV-supervised" category of approaches (but we note that it includes SNP scores from a state-of-the-art rSNV-unsupervised method, Eigen-PC). CERENKOV is based on the integration of 246 SNP annotation features (including a novel feature based on allele-dependent difference in a DNA shape score that we have previously shown is predictive of TFBS [57]) within a gradient boosted decision tree classification algorithm. Our approach for training and testing CERENKOV was focused on maximizing the relevance and generalizability of our model and its performance assessments for the specific application of GWAS post-analysis.

1.4.1 New performance measure: AVGRANK. In addition to measuring the performance of our classifiers using traditional locus-independent metrics (area under the receiver operating characteristic (AUROC) curve and area under the precision versus recall (AUPVR) curve), we propose and demonstrate a novel performance metric based on averaging, over all rSNPs, the ranks of the rSNP prediction scores of all ground-truth rSNPs within their loci (defined by LD as described above). Specifically, we define, for the sets $L \subset \mathbb{Z}_+$ of numbered loci, $S \subset \mathbb{Z}_+$ of numbered SNPs, and $R \subset S$ of numbered rSNPs,

$$\text{AVGRANK} = \langle \text{rank}(y_r, \vec{y}_{S_{l(r)}}) \rangle_{r \in R \text{ sth. } |S_{l(r)}|>1}, \quad (1)$$

where $l(r)$ is the locus $l \in L$ for rSNP $r \in R$, $S_l \subset S$ is the set of all SNPs in locus l, y_s is the classifier prediction score for SNP s to be in the rSNP class, $\vec{y}_Q$ is the vector of prediction scores of SNPs $Q \subset S$, $\text{rank}(q, \vec{w})$ is the rank of the score $q \in [0,1]$ in the (length W) vector of scores $\vec{w} \in [0,1]^W$ (with lowest score having rank 1, and with tied scores given identical rank assignments), and $\langle\rangle$ denotes arithmetic mean. We propose that the classifier with the best performance for GWAS post-analysis should minimize the AVGRANK.

1.4.2 The `OSU17` reference SNP set. In order to maximize the relevance of our method to GWAS post-analysis, it is critical to train and test using *common variants*, i.e., SNPs within their local linkage disequilibrium blocks in the genome. Thus, we trained and validated CERENKOV using only SNPs with MAF ≥ 0.05 (as opposed to MAF ≥ 0.01 for the two key previous studies [43, 59]). Further, for the set of control SNPs (cSNPs) that we used as negative examples for training and validation, we used only SNPs that were in strong linkage disequilibrium ($r^2 \geq 0.8$) with, and located no more than 50 kbp distance from, a "positive example" rSNP.

1.4.3 Locus-based sampling. In order to maximize the relevance of our method to GWAS post-analysis as well as enable the assessment of CERENKOV's performance using both global rank-based measures (e.g., AUPVR and AUROC) and the new AVGRANK measure, we trained and tested CERENKOV using a novel (so far as we are aware) method for assigning SNPs to CV folds, which we call *locus-based sampling*. In brief, for each replication of a k-fold CV assessment of CERENKOV's performance, we assign *loci* (i.e., all SNPs together within a given locus) to CV folds, in such a manner that the SNPs overall and the rSNPs are both equipartitioned across the folds. We used the same fold assignments for CERENKOV that we used for the models to which we compared CERENKOV.

2 METHODS

2.1 The `OSU17` reference SNP set

We obtained minor allele frequencies (MAFs) for all SNPs from the dbSNP-based [46] **snp146** SQL table hosted at the UCSC Genome Browser [23] site; for SNPs not in **snp146**, we obtained MAFs from the 1,000 Genomes (1KG) Project Phase 3 [1] Variant Call Format (VCF) file. For the representative set of rSNPs for training/evaluation, we obtained 1,659 SNPs from HGMD (Rel. 2016) that satisfied all of the following criteria: (i) the SNP was marked as **regulatory** in HGMD; (ii) the **disease** field did not not contain **cancer**; (iii) MAF ≥ 0.05; (iv) the SNP was not an indel and not contained within a CDS (based on the complete set of transcripts from the Ensembl 75 gene annotation build); and (v) the SNP was not exclusively mapped to the Y chromosome (due to the lack of phased haplotype data available for proxy SNP searching). For each of these rSNPs, we used the SNP

[2] Databases of rSNVs such as HGMD have an ascertainment bias for low-MAF variants [27], and this can potentially bias the classifier in a way that does not generalize to the GWAS post-analysis application.

Annotation and Proxy Search (SNAP) tool [22] to identify SNPs that are in LD ($r^2 \geq 0.8$ in 1KG Phase 1, with HapMap used instead of 1KG for chromosome X), and we filtered to include only SNPs within 1 kbp of an rSNP, that were not contained within a CDS, that have MAF ≥ 0.05, and that are not themselves on the list of rSNPs. Overall, this filtering procedure produced a list of 13,672 cSNPs. The combined set of 15,331 SNPs (which we call the `OSU17` reference SNP set) was thus designed as an appropriate ground-truth set for the application of GWAS post-analysis. Overall, the class imbalance of `OSU17` is ~8.24 (cSNP/rSNP).

2.2 Extracting the CERENKOV features

The CERENKOV feature extraction software is based on Python and SQL. We extracted 246 SNP features for each of the `OSU17` SNPs, using data from SNP annotation databases, epigenomic and chromatin datasets, phylogenetic conservation scores, and DNA shape-based scores (Table 1).

2.2.1 Features extracted from UCSC. We used the `snp146` UCSC SQL table as the initial source for SNP annotations (GRCh37 assembly coordinate system). We extracted additional SNP annotation information by (i) coordinate-based joins to other genome annotation tracks in the UCSC database; and (ii) by joining with non-UCSC data sources using the SNP coordinate. For triallelic and quadrallelic SNPs, we used the two most frequent alleles, for the purpose of obtaining features that depend on allele-dependent scores. We derived DNase I hypersensitive site (DHS) features from data tracks from published genome-wide assays with high-throughput sequencing-based detection (DNase-seq) from the ENCODE project [50] (the `master` peaks are summary peaks combining data from DHS experiments in 125 cell types; the `uniform` DHS peaks are from DHS experiments in individual cells, processed using the ENCODE uniform peaks analysis pipeline [28]). The `ENCODE_TFBS` feature is presented in the table as a single feature for conciseness, but in fact it is 158 separate binary features, one for each TF for which genome-wide TF binding site data (from chromatin immunoprecipitation with high-throughput sequencing readout, or ChIP-seq) peak data from the ENCODE Uniform Peaks analysis are available [28]. For replication timing features, we processed track-specific BigWig files from UCSC to obtain the timing scores at individual SNP positions. For ChromHMM, Segway and lamina-associated domains (LAD) annotations, we used the SQL tables from UCSC.

2.2.2 Features extracted from Ensembl. We used the BioMart tool to download (i) TFBS motif occurrences (based on the 2014 release of the Jaspar database [40]) and ChromHMM chromatin segmentation labels from Ensembl Regulation 75 and (ii) GENCODE transcription start sites (from Ensembl Genes 75) with which we computed signed TSS distances.

2.2.3 GTEx feature. We obtained SNP-to-gene associations for 13 tissues (adipose, artery/aorta, artery/tibial, esophagus/mucosa, esophagus/muscularis, heart left ventricle, lung, skeletal muscle, tibial nerve, sun-exposed skin, stomach, thyroid, and whole blood) from GTEx Analysis Version 4 from the GTEx project data portal. For each SNP, we selected the minimum association p-value across genes and tissues.

2.2.4 DNA shape feature. We used the `regshape` R package [57] and computed the difference in the regulatory potential scores for the local 11 bp sequence centered on the SNP, for both the major and next-to-major SNP alleles.

2.3 Features for the other classifiers that we compared to CERENKOV

2.3.1 GWAVA. For the 15,331 `OSU17` SNPs, we extracted the 175 GWAVA [43] SNP annotation features using the GWAVA software (version 1.0). For the GWAVA features that overlapped with CERENKOV features, we compared feature vectors directly to verify consistency.

2.3.2 DeltaSVM. For DeltaSVM, we obtained 19 bp sequences centered on each of the `OSU17` SNPs, using the GRCh37 genome assembly and inserting the two possible SNP alleles into the central base position. We used the DeltaSVM software (3/30/2015 version), using the 19mer sequence files as input and using 226 pre-built 19mer-based chromatin models from the DeltaSVM website as input, to produce a 15,331×226 feature matrix.

2.3.3 RSVP. For RSVP, we used the RSVP software [39] version 1.0.1. We mapped the `OSU17` SNPs to their nearest gene using `Annovar` [53] release 2016Feb01. In addition, the flanking five nucleotides on either side of the SNPs were also included in the input to the perl script, `script_RSVP.pl`, which output a 15,331×2,238 feature matrix for RSVP classifier. For analyzing RSVP features with Random Forest, we imputed missing values using the column-wise mean.

2.3.4 DeepSEA. We extracted 1,000 bp haplotype sequences flanking the `OSU17` SNPs (for the two most common alleles for each of the SNPs) using the 1KG Phase 3 VCF data (see Sec. 2.1). For each of the 15,331 pairs of 1 kbp sequences, we obtained scores from the 919 DeepSEA CNN models using the web tool. As in the original publication [59], for each SNP and each of the 919 CNNs, we obtained two features consisting of (i) the absolute difference of scores between the two alleles and (ii) the absolute difference of the logit-transformed scores for each of the two alleles. This overall procedure produced a 15,331×1,838 feature matrix.

2.3.5 DANQ. For DanQ [42], we extracted 919 hybrid CNN-RNN scores for each of the two alleles for each of the 15,331 `OSU17` SNPs, using the DANQ software and bundled model files in HDF5 format (Jan. 13, 2016). For each SNP and each of the 919 CNNs, we obtained two features consisting of the absolute difference of scores between the two alleles and the absolute difference of the logit-transformed scores between the two alleles. This produced a 15,331×1,838 feature matrix which we cross-checked against DeepSEA for consistency.

feature(s)	*feature type*	*raw data src.*	*feature description*
normChromCoord	continuous	UCSC	the SNP coordinate (normalized to chrom. length)
majorAlleleFreq	continuous	UCSC/1KG	the major allele frequency (1KG)
minorAlleleFreq	continuous	UCSC/1KG	the next-to-major allele frequency (1KG)
phastCons	continuous	UCSC	46-way placental mammal phastCons score [47]
GERP++	continuous	UCSC	bp-level GERP++ [10] score
avg_GERP	continuous	UCSC	avg. GERP score [8] in ±100 bp window
DNAShapeScore	continuous	UCSC	diff. of 11 bp **regshape** [57] score between alleles
avg_daf	continuous	1KG	average derived allele frequency in ±1 kbp region
avg_het	continuous	1KG	average heterozygosity rate in ±1 kbp region
maf1kb	continuous	UCSC/1KG	average of the MAF values for all SNPs in ±1 kbp window
eqtlPvalue	continuous	GTEx	$-\log_{10}\min(p)$ for GTEx eQTL for the SNP, across 13 tissues [14]
GC5Content	integer (0-5)	UCSC	GC content in a 5 bp window
GC7Content	integer (0-7)	UCSC	GC content in a 7 bp window
GC11Content	integer (0-11)	UCSC	GC content in a 11 bp window
local_purine	integer (0-11)	UCSC	number of purine bases in local 11 bp window
local_CpG	integer (0-10)	UCSC	number of CpG dinucleotides in 11 bp window
ss_dist	integer	UCSC	signed distance to nearest exon boundary
tssDistance	integer	Ensembl75	signed distance to nearest Ensembl TSS
gencode_tss	integer	GENCODE	signed distance to nearest GENCODE TSS
tfCount	integer	UCSC	sqrt(count) of ENCODE ChIP-seq TFBS overlap. SNP
uniformDhsScore	integer	UCSC	sum scores of ENCODE uniform DHS peaks overlap. SNP
uniformDhsCount	integer	UCSC	count of ENCODE uniform DHS peaks overlap. SNP
masterDhsScore	integer	UCSC	sum scores of ENCODE master DHS peaks overlap. SNP
masterDhsCount	integer	UCSC	count of ENCODE master DHS peaks overlap. SNP
chrom	categorical (23)	UCSC	the chromosome to which the SNP maps
nestedrepeat	categorical (2)	UCSC	SNP is in a RepeatMasker [6] DNA repeat
simplerepeat	categorical (2)	UCSC	SNP is in a Tandem Repeats Finder [2] repeat
cpg_island	categorical (2)	UCSC	SNP is in an epigenome-predicted CpG island [3]
geneannot	categorical (4)	UCSC	classifies SNP location as CDS, intergenic, UTR, or intron
majorAllele	categorical (4)	UCSC/1KG	the major allele for the SNP
minorAllele	categorical (4)	UCSC/1KG	the next-to-major allele for the SNP
pwm	categorical (22)	Ensembl75	ID of the Jaspar 2014 [40] motif in which SNP is a match
chromhmm	6×categ. (26)	UCSC	ChromHMM label in Gm12878, H1hesc, HeLaS3, HepG2, HUVEC and K562 cells
segway	6×categ. (26)	UCSC	Segway label in Gm12878, H1hesc, HeLaS3, HepG2, HUVEC and K562 cells
ch_comb_WEAKENH	categorical (4)	Ensembl75	ChromHMM label in Ensembl Reg. Seg. build
ch_comb_ENH	categorical (6)	Ensembl75	ChromHMM label in Ensembl Reg. Seg. build
ch_comb_REP	categorical (7)	Ensembl75	ChromHMM label in Ensembl Reg. Seg. build
ch_comb_TSSFLANK	categorical (5)	Ensembl75	ChromHMM label in Ensembl Reg. Seg. build
ch_comb_TRAN	categorical (7)	Ensembl75	ChromHMM label in Ensembl Reg. Seg. build
ch_comb_TSS	categorical (7)	Ensembl75	ChromHMM label in Ensembl Reg. Seg. build
ch_comb_CTCFREG	categorical (7)	Ensembl75	ChromHMM label in Ensembl Reg. Seg. build
ENCODE_TFBS	158×categ. (2)	UCSC	158 features for SNP being in an ENCODE TFBS [13] peak
FsuRepliSeq	16×continuous	UCSC	Replication Timing by Repli-chip [19] from ENCODE/FSU
UwRepliSeq	16×continuous	UCSC	Replication Timing by Repli-seq [17] from ENCODE/UW
SangerTfbsSummary50kb	continuous	Ensembl75	Summary of Ensembl TFBS peaks from 18 human cell types
NkiLad	categorical (2)	UCSC	SNP is in a Lamina Associated Domain (NKI study [15], Tig-3 cells)
vistaEnhancerCnt	categorical (2)	UCSC	count of VISTA [52] HMR-Conserved Non-coding Human Enhancers [38] overlap. SNP
vistaEnhancerTotalScore	categorical (2)	UCSC	sum scores of VISTA [52] HMR-Conserved Non-coding Human Enhancers [38]
eigen	continuous	Eigen	Eigen-PC v1.1 raw score [21]

Table 1: The 246 SNP features that are used in CERENKOV. Abbreviations are as follows: UCSC, UC Santa Cruz Genome Browser portal; 1KG, 1,000 Genomes Project; Ensembl75, Ensembl Release 75 [9]; GENCODE, the GENCODE project release 19 [18]; ENCODE, Encyclopedia of DNA Elements [49]; FSU, Florida State University; UW, University of Washington; NKI, Netherlands Cancer Institute; GTEx, the genotype tissue-expression project; GERP, the Genomic Evolutionary Rate Profiling score; CDS, coding DNA sequence; UTR, untranslated region; MAF, minor allele frequency; HMR, human-mouse-rat; TSS, transcription start site.

2.3.6 Eigen, CADD, DANN, fitCons. For Eigen [21], we downloaded genome-wide nucleotide-level scores (version 1.1) and filtered them to obtain the raw Eigen-PC scores for the OSU17 SNPs. For CADD [24], we downloaded genome-wide nucleotide-level scores (version 1.3). For DANN [41], we downloaded genome-wide nucleotide-level scores (released Nov. 13, 2014) and filtered them to obtain scores for the OSU17 SNPs. For fitCons [16], we downloaded genome-wide feature files (version 1.01) for highly significant scores (`fc-hu-0.bw`) and extracted the scores at the locations of the OSU17 SNPs. For all four of these score types, we used the published per-SNP scores directly to rank validation-set SNPs for computing AVGRANK, AUROC, and AUPVR.

2.4 Machine learning

For the machine learning framework, we used the R statistical computing environment (version 3.2) [20] under Ubuntu 16.04.1 LTS running on Amazon EC2 within an m4.16xlarge instance (or across multiple such instances in parallel).

2.4.1 Random Forest. We used the R package **ranger** [56] version 0.6.0. We used **ranger** in decision-tree mode (i.e., not in probabilistic forest mode). For GWAVA [43] and RSVP [39], we used the published hyperparameters. To validate the equivalency of this classification algorithm vs. the original GWAVA python implementation, we cross-checked the AUROC performance of **ranger** (with the GWAVA features and the published GWAVA **region** SNP set) against the **RandomForest** implementation in **scikit-learn** [37] (version 0.14.1) and found nearly identical performance between **ranger** and **scikit-learn**, $\langle \text{AUROC} \rangle = 0.71$.

2.4.2 Gradient Boosted Decision Trees. For the gradient boosted decision trees (GBDT) classifier, we used the R API for **xgboost** [7] version 0.6-4 (hereafter, **xgboost**-GBDT). We used gradient boosted trees (**booster=gbtree**) and binary "logistic" classification as the objective, with the default loss function (**objective=binary:logistic**). We used ten-fold CV [25] with *locus-level sampling* as described in Sec. 3, in which we assigned rSNPs to folds (stratifying on the number of cSNPs per rSNP), and then assigned cSNPs to the *same fold to which it's LD-linked rSNP was assigned.* Thus, in the case of locus-level sampling, an rSNP and its linked cSNPs are always assigned to the same CV fold. For every prediction performance metric we report, the fold composition was exactly the same across all of the rSNP recognition models studied. We used the **xgboost**-GBDT classification algorithm for the studies in Fig. 1b, Fig. 1c, Fig. 2, and for the classifiers CERENKOV, RSVP_XGB, Deepsea_XGB, DANQ_XGB, and deltaSVM_XGB in Fig. 3. We used **base_score** $= 0.1082121$ (the rSNP/cSNP class imbalance). We obtained the feature importance scores using the **xgb.importance** method.

2.4.3 Tuning CERENKOV. We tuned the **xgboost**-GBDT classifier with a hyperparameter septuple grid size of 3,888, with locus-based sampling. The tuning hyperparameter tuple that maximized the validation $\langle \text{AUPVR} \rangle$ was: $\eta = 0.1$, $\gamma = 10$, **nrounds** $= 30$, **max_depth** $= 6$, **subsample** $= 1.0$, **colsample_bytree** $= 0.85$, and **scale_pos_weight** $= 1$; we used these hyperparameter values for all subsequent analyses using **xgboost**-GBDT. [In contrast, the hyperparameter tuple that minimized the validation $\langle \text{AVGRANK} \rangle$ was: $\eta = 0.1$, $\gamma = 100$, **nrounds** $= 30$, **max_depth** $= 6$, **subsample** $= 0.85$, **colsample_bytree** $= 0.85$, and **scale_pos_weight** $= 8$].

2.5 *t*-SNE and Statistical testing

For the unsupervised analysis, we used the *t*-distributed stochastic neighbor embedding (*t*-SNE) implementation in the R package **Rtsne** on the standardized, numeric-encoded feature data; results were consistent across multiple runs of *t*-SNE. For averaging and statistical testing of performance data, we used logit-transformed AUROC and AUPVR values [12]. We compared different combinations of classifiers and feature-sets using 95% confidence intervals (CI) on the average measures, that we estimated using bootstrap with 1,000 iterations.

3 RESULTS

3.1 Comparing AUPVR and AVGRANK

We first analyzed the distributions of two SNP classes (rSNPs and cSNPs) within an unsupervised two-dimensional embedding of their 246-dimensional feature vectors, using *t*-SNE (see Sec. 2.5). This analysis revealed that the majority of rSNPs are located in dense clusters in the embedding space, suggesting that effective machine learning-based discrimination of rSNPs from cSNPs would be possible using this feature-set (**Fig. 1a**). Next, we used a supervised approach to investigate the degree of concordance between the traditional AUPVR accuracy measure and the AVGRANK accuracy measure that we have proposed for the GWAS rSNP detection problem. For this analysis we used the gradient boosted decision trees classification algorithm implementation in **xgboost** [7] and our 15,331×246 matrix of SNP feature data. We trained and tested **xgboost**-GBDT (using 24 independent replications of 10-fold [25] CV with locus-based sampling) for each of 3,888 different tuples of **xgboost** hyperparameters (see Sec. 2.4.3) and for each hyperparameter tuple, we computed $\langle \text{AUPVR} \rangle$ and $\langle \text{AVGRANK} \rangle$ on the validation set SNPs, across the 240 independent samples. We found that while $\langle \text{AVGRANK} \rangle$ and $\langle \text{AUPVR} \rangle$ are strongly correlated on the large scale (Fig. 1b), the relationship between $\langle \text{AVGRANK} \rangle$ and $\langle \text{AUPVR} \rangle$ for the stronger-performing hyperparameter tuples (for which $\langle \text{AUPVR} \rangle > 0.42$) deviates from a linear relationship (Fig. 1c). Specifically, we found that the hyperparameter tuple that maximizes the $\langle \text{AUPVR} \rangle$ has an $\langle \text{AUPVR} \rangle$ of 0.506 (95% CI, 0.500–0.512), whereas the hyperparameter tuple that minimizes the $\langle \text{AVGRANK} \rangle$ has an $\langle \text{AUPVR} \rangle$ of 0.491 (95% CI, 0.485–0.496). Thus, in this example using **xgboost**-GBDT and the CERENKOV features on the **OSU17** SNP set, we found that tuning a classifier to maximize validation AUPVR does not guarantee optimality of the classifier in terms of AVGRANK accuracy (we argue that the latter, AVGRANK, is more relevant to the GWAS application domain).

3.2 CERENKOV feature importance

In order to better understand the contributions of different categories of features to classification accuracy for rSNP recognition, we analyzed the frequencies with which each of the 246 features in CERENKOV was used in a tree split by the **xgboost**-GBDT algorithm, using the hyperparameters that we had selected to maximize validation-set AUPVR (Sec. 3.1). We additively aggregated the feature scores into 14 feature categories such as "SNP-to-gene distances," "chromatin segmentation," and "TFBS annotations." As shown in Fig. 2, and consistent with previous SNP annotation-based studies (all of which used different filtering criteria for cSNP selection than we used in this study), the distance between a SNP and the transcription start site of the nearest genes has the strongest feature importance overall [34, 39, 43, 51], and that SNP annotation based on the gene context (3′ UTR, 5′ UTR, intron, or intergenic) also has high importance [43]. Furthermore, consistent with the Peterson *et al.* study [39],

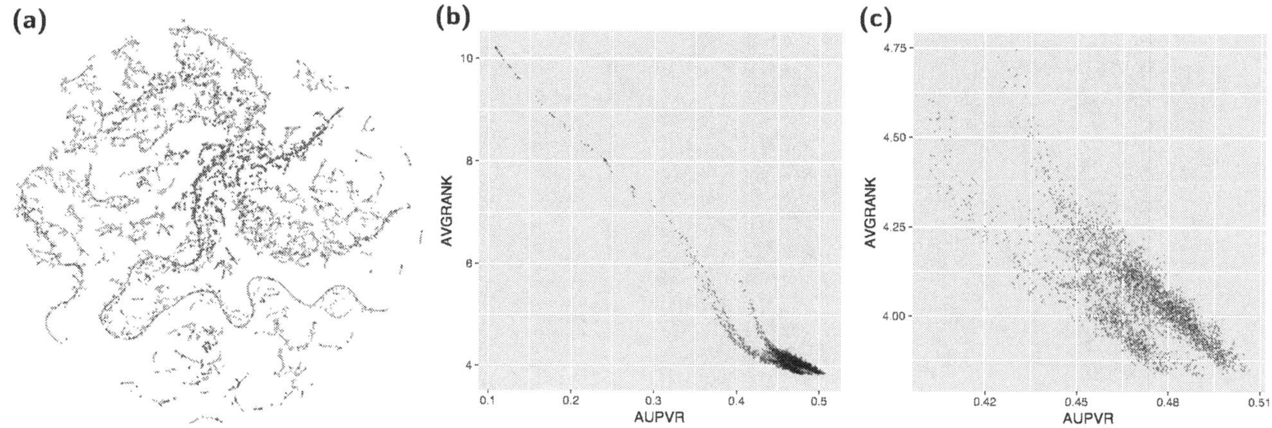

Figure 1: The AUPVR and AVGRANK performance measures are functionally distinct. (a) *t*-SNE embedding of the 246-dimensional featureset for the `OSU17` set of SNPs; rSNPs are colored in red, showing local concentrations of rSNPs. (b) Scatter plot of validation ⟨AVGRANK⟩ and ⟨AUPVR⟩ values for CERENKOV, for 3,888 `xgboost`-GBDT hyperparameter tuples. (c) Zoom of the lower-right of (b), showing that optimizing for average AVGRANK and optimizing for average AUPVR are not equivalent, for the `OSU17` SNPs.

Measure	Mean	95% CI
AUPVR	0.505	0.503–0.508
AUROC	0.855	0.854–0.856
AVGRANK	3.877	3.843–3.909

Table 2: Validation-set performance measures for CERENKOV on the `OSU17` reference SNP set.

we found that SNP annotations based on replication timing experimental measurements ("Replication Timing") had high feature importance. The feature importance analysis also yielded a novel finding, that the Eigen-PC score [21] strongly contributed to CERENKOV's accuracy; ours if the first supervised method (of which we are aware) in which Eigen-PC scores are incorporated with SNP annotations for rSNP recognition. Out of the 246 features, we found that the DNA shape-based score ranked 105 in terms of its feature importance, and nearly as highly as the uniform DNase I hypersensitive site count (`uniformDhsCount`) feature.

3.3 Comparing CERENKOV to other methods for rSNP recognition

Having identified an `xgboost`-GBDT hyperparameter set that maximizes validation-set ⟨AUPVR⟩ for rSNP/cSNP discrimination, we precisely measured the validation-set performance of CERENKOV by AUPVR, AUROC, and AVGRANK, using 200 replications with 10-fold CV, and using bootstrap resampling of the results to obtain 95% confidence intervals (see Sec. 2.5). We found that on the `OSU17` set of SNPs, CERENKOV has a validation-set ⟨AUPVR⟩ of 0.505, an ⟨AUROC⟩ of 0.855, and an ⟨AVGRANK⟩ of 3.877 (Table 2).

Next, we compared CERENKOV to nine other methods for prioritizing functional noncoding SNPs: DeltaSVM [29],

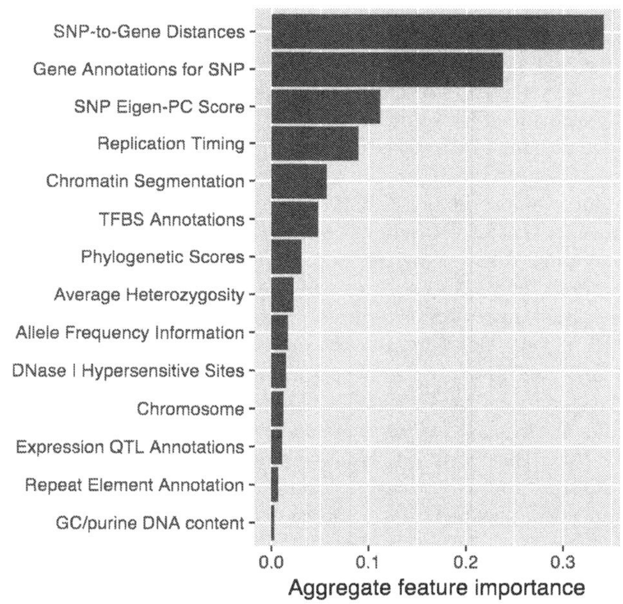

Figure 2: Importance scores for 14 categories of features used in CERENKOV. Bar length represents the aggregate frequency with which all features in the indicated category are used for a tree split.

RSVP [39], DANN [41], fitCons [16], CADD [24], DeepSEA [59], DANQ [42], Eigen [21], and GWAVA [43]. For the single-score-per-SNP methods (CADD, Eigen, DANN, fitCons) that were not trained using ground-truth rSNPs from HGMD in the original reference studies in which the methods were reported, we used the published per-SNP scores directly to

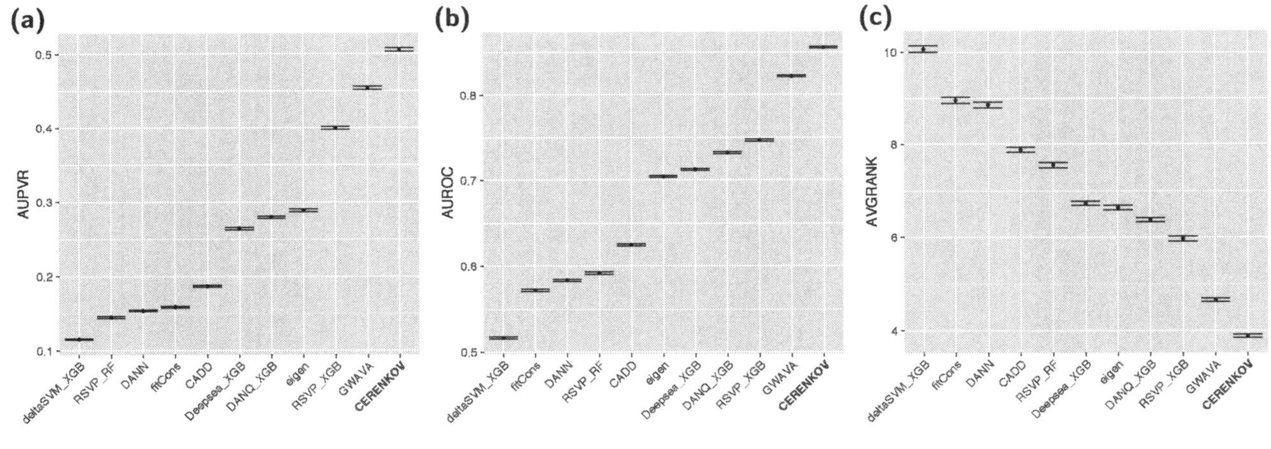

Figure 3: Validation performance of CERENKOV improves upon nine methods for rSNP detection to which we compared it, by both global rank-based measures (AUPVR (a) and AUROC (b)) and our AVGRANK method (c). Marks, average performance in 200 replications of 10-fold CV (2,000 samples); bars, bootstrap 95% confidence interval. XGB means xgboost-GBDT was used; RF means that Random Forest was used.

rank validation-set SNPs for computing AVGRANK and AUPVR. For the multi-feature methods, where possible, we used the classification algorithms as described in the original reference publications for the methods (i.e., for GWAVA, Random Forest; for DeepSEA, `xgboost`-GBDT) using the hyperparameters from the original publications.[3] For RSVP, since we did not have access to the MATLAB `treefit` implementation, we used both Random Forest (with imputed feature values; see Sec. 2.3.3) with hyperparameters matching those in the RSVP article, as well as `xgboost`-GBDT using our optimal set of hyperparameters. For DANQ, based on the high degree of similarity of the DANQ approach to the DeepSEA approach (identical chromatin datasets used for training the deep neural networks), we used the `xgboost`-GBDT method and the DeepSEA hyperparameter values; we post-processed the 919×2 DANQ scores for each SNP exactly as for DeepSEA. On identical assignments of genomic loci to CV folds (based on our locus-sampling approach), and with a 200-fold outer replication loop (thus yielding 2,000 performance samples per classifier), we compared the validation-set performance of the ten classifiers with CERENKOV, based on AUPVR, AUROC, and AVGRANK. We found that the average performance of CERENKOV was superior to the other ten classifiers, by all three performance measures (Fig. 3; bars indicate 95% confidence intervals). Consistent with the observation (Fig. 1b,c) that AUPVR and AVGRANK are closely related but that the relationship is not a simple monotonic function, the rankings of classifiers by AUPVR and AVGRANK in Fig. 3a and Fig. 3c are not identical; for example, Eigen outperforms DANQ_XGB by AUPVR, but DANQ_XGB outperforms Eigen by AVGRANK.

[3] The DeepSEA method produces one probability score for each of 919 convolutional neural network (CNN) models for each of two SNP alleles. We computed absolute score differences and absolute logit-transformed score differences (for the two alleles) for each CNN model and for each SNP, exactly as described in the DeepSEA method publication.

4 CONCLUSION AND DISCUSSION

We report a new framework and classifier, CERENKOV, for scoring noncoding SNPs based on their regulatory potential. CERENKOV—by virtue of its training-set construction criteria (locus-based, MAF $\geq$ 0.05), its novel performance measure (AVGRANK), and its novel CV approach (locus-based sampling)—is specifically designed for the problem of identifying candidate causal noncoding SNPs in GWAS post-analysis. We have demonstrated, using side-by-side comparisons on identical assignments of SNPs to CV folds, that CERENKOV's performance exceeds that of the nine other functional noncoding SNP prioritization methods to which we compared it, by both classical global rank-based measures (AUPVR and AUROC) and by the new GWAS-oriented performance measure (AVGRANK) that we proposed. CERENKOV's validation-set AUROC performance, 0.855 (95% CI of 0.854–0.856), compares favorably with the AUROC[4] (0.84) of the recently published PRVCS rSNP predictor [30].

The source code for CERENKOV is available on GitHub at **`github.com/ramseylab/cerenkov`** under the Apache 2.0 open-source software license, and the feature files that were used in the comparative analysis of CERENKOV with the other published methods are available on the CERENKOV website at **`lab.saramsey.org/cerenkov`**. By making the software, the data files, and in particular the `OSU17` SNP set (with benchmark results) available, we hope to accelerate development of methods for noncoding SNP functional analysis.

We anticipate that CERENKOV's performance may be improved through several possible enhancements that we are investigating, including new features and the use of a custom `xgboost`-GBDT loss function that is specifically designed to minimize AVGRANK. An appealing extension of

[4] The published [30] AUROC for the PRVCS classifier was based on an HGMD-based set of ground-truth SNPs with similar class imbalance (10.7) to that of the `OSU17` set of SNPs used here. Efforts to directly compare these classifiers on on the `OSU17` set of SNPs are ongoing.

CERENKOV would be to combine deep neural network-based approaches based on the local 1 kbp sequence haplotype (recognizing that the local haplotype is important to contextualizing functional SNP alleles [54]), with CERENKOV's current matrix of 246 features; such a hybrid "neural network plus decision trees" approach has shown promise in image classification [26]. It is presently unclear what the minimum attainable validation AVGRANK score would be expected to be, for the OSU17 SNP set; undoubtedly, precision values are dampened by "latent positives" in the training dataset, i.e., high-scoring cSNPs that are simply undiscovered rSNPs. Using machine learning techniques that are specifically designed to address "positives-plus-unlabeled" problems [11] (such as the rSNP detection problem studied here) is another appealing avenue for future investigation.

ACKNOWLEDGMENTS

This work was supported by the NIH (award HL098807 to S.A.R.), the Medical Research Foundation of Oregon (New Investigator Award to S.A.R.), Oregon State University (Health Sciences award to S.A.R.), the Oregon State University Center for Genome Research and Biocomputing (in-kind contribution of compute time to S.A.R.), the PhRMA Foundation (Research Starter Grant in Informatics to S.A.R.) and the NSF (awards 1557605-DMS and 1553728-DBI to S.A.R.).

REFERENCES

[1] 1000 Genomes Project Consortium, Adam Auton, Lisa D Brooks, Richard M Durbin, Erik P Garrison, Hyun Min Kang, Jan O Korbel, Jonathan L Marchini, Shane McCarthy, Gil A McVean, and Gonçalo R Abecasis. 2015. A global reference for human genetic variation. *Nature* 526, 7571 (2015), 68–74.

[2] G Benson. 1999. Tandem repeats finder: a program to analyze DNA sequences. *Nucleic Acids Res* 27, 2 (1999), 573–580.

[3] Christoph Bock, Jörn Walter, Martina Paulsen, and Thomas Lengauer. 2007. CpG Island Mapping by Epigenome Prediction. *PLOS Computat Biol* 3, 6 (2007), e110.

[4] Leo Breiman. 2001. Random Forests. *Machine Learning* 45, 1 (2001), 5–32.

[5] Razvan C. Bunescu and Raymond J. Mooney. 2007. Multiple Instance Learning for Sparse Positive Bags. In *Proceedings of the 24th Annual International Conference on Machine Learning (ICML-2007)*. ACM, Corvallis, OR, 105–112.

[6] Juan Caballero, Arian F A Smit, Leroy Hood, and Gustavo Glusman. 2014. Realistic artificial DNA sequences as negative controls for computational genomics. *Nucleic Acids Res* 42, 12 (2014), e99.

[7] Tianqi Chen and Carlos Guestrin. 2016. XGBoost: A scalable tree boosting system. *arXiv.org* 1603.02754 (2016), 1–13.

[8] Gregory M Cooper, Eric A Stone, George Asimenos, NISC Comparative Sequencing Program, Eric D Green, Serafim Batzoglou, and Arend Sidow. 2005. Distribution and intensity of constraint in mammalian genomic sequence. *Genome Res* 15, 7 (2005), 901–913.

[9] Fiona Cunningham, M Ridwan Amode, Daniel Barrell, Kathryn Beal, Konstantinos Billis, Simon Brent, Denise Carvalho-Silva, Peter Clapham, Guy Coates, Stephen Fitzgerald, Laurent Gil, Carlos García Girón, Leo Gordon, Thibaut Hourlier, Sarah E Hunt, Sophie H Janacek, Nathan Johnson, Thomas Juettemann, Andreas K Kähäri, Stephen Keenan, Fergal J Martin, Thomas Maurel, William McLaren, Daniel N Murphy, Rishi Nag, Bert Overduin, Anne Parker, Mateus Patricio, Emily Perry, Miguel Pignatelli, Harpreet Singh Riat, Daniel Sheppard, Kieron Taylor, Anja Thormann, Alessandro Vullo, Steven P Wilder, Amonida Zadissa, Bronwen L Aken, Ewan Birney, Jennifer Harrow, Rhoda Kinsella, Matthieu Muffato, Magali Ruffier, Stephen M J Searle, Giulietta Spudich, Stephen J Trevanion, Andy Yates, Daniel R Zerbino, and Paul Flicek. 2015. Ensembl 2015. *Nucleic Acids Research* 43, Database issue (2015), D662–9.

[10] Eugene V Davydov, David L Goode, Marina Sirota, Gregory M Cooper, Arend Sidow, and Serafim Batzoglou. 2010. Identifying a High Fraction of the Human Genome to be under Selective Constraint Using GERP++. *PLoS Comput Biol* 6, 12 (2010), e1001025.

[11] C Elkan and K Noto. 2008. Learning classifiers from only positive and unlabeled data. In *Proceeding of the 14th ACM SIGKDD international conference on Knowledge discovery and data mining*. ACM, Las Vegas, NV, 213–220.

[12] Vadim Farztdinov and Fionnuala McDyer. 2012. Distributional fold change test - a statistical approach for detecting differential expression in microarray experiments. *Algorithms Mol Biol* 7, 1 (2012), 29.

[13] Mark B Gerstein, Anshul Kundaje, Manoj Hariharan, Stephen G Landt, Koon-Kiu Yan, Chao Cheng, Xinmeng Jasmine Mu, Ekta Khurana, Joel Rozowsky, Roger Alexander, Renqiang Min, Pedro Alves, Alexej Abyzov, Nick Addleman, Nitin Bhardwaj, Alan P Boyle, Philip Cayting, Alexandra Charos, David Z Chen, Yong Cheng, Declan Clarke, Catharine Eastman, Ghia Euskirchen, Seth Frietze, Yao Fu, Jason Gertz, Fabian Grubert, Arif Harmanci, Preti Jain, Maya Kasowski, Phil Lacroute, Jing Leng, Jin Lian, Hannah Monahan, Henriette O'Geen, Zhengqing Ouyang, E Christopher Partridge, Dorrelyn Patacsil, Florencia Pauli, Debasish Raha, Lucia Ramirez, Timothy E Reddy, et al. 2012. Architecture of the human regulatory network derived from ENCODE data. *Nature* 489, 7414 (2012), 91–100.

[14] GTEx Consortium. 2015. Human genomics. The Genotype-Tissue Expression (GTEx) pilot analysis: multitissue gene regulation in humans. *Science* 348, 6235 (2015), 648–660.

[15] Lars Guelen, Ludo Pagie, Emilie Brasset, Wouter Meuleman, Marius B Faza, Wendy Talhout, Bert H Eussen, Annelies de Klein, Lodewyk Wessels, Wouter de Laat, and Bas van Steensel. 2008. Domain organization of human chromosomes revealed by mapping of nuclear lamina interactions. *Nature* 453, 7197 (2008), 948–951.

[16] Brad Gulko, Melissa J Hubisz, Ilan Gronau, and Adam Siepel. 2015. A method for calculating probabilities of fitness consequences for point mutations across the human genome. *Nature Genetics* 47, 3 (2015), 276–283.

[17] R Scott Hansen, Sean Thomas, Richard Sandstrom, Theresa K Canfield, Robert E Thurman, Molly Weaver, Michael O Dorschner, Stanley M Gartler, and John A Stamatoyannopoulos. 2010. Sequencing newly replicated DNA reveals widespread plasticity in human replication timing. *Proceedings of the National Academy of Sciences* 107, 1 (2010), 139–144.

[18] Jennifer Harrow, France Denoeud, Adam Frankish, Alexandre Reymond, Chao-Kung Chen, Jacqueline Chrast, Julien Lagarde, James G R Gilbert, Roy Storey, David Swarbreck, Colette Rossier, Catherine Ucla, Tim Hubbard, Stylianos E Antonarakis, and Roderic Guigo. 2006. GENCODE: producing a reference annotation for ENCODE. *Genome Biol* 7 Suppl 1 (2006), S4.1–9.

[19] Ichiro Hiratani, Tyrone Ryba, Mari Itoh, Tomoki Yokochi, Michaela Schwaiger, Chia-Wei Chang, Yung Lyou, Tim M Townes, Dirk Schübeler, and David M Gilbert. 2008. Global reorganization of replication domains during embryonic stem cell differentiation. *PLoS Biology* 6, 10 (2008), e245.

[20] Ross Ihaka and Robert Gentleman. 1995. R: A Language for Data Analysis and Graphics. *J Comp Graph Stat* 5, 3 (1995), 299–314.

[21] Iuliana Ionita-Laza, Kenneth McCallum, Bin Xu, and Joseph D Buxbaum. 2016. A spectral approach integrating functional genomic annotations for coding and noncoding variants. *Nature Genetics* 48, 2 (2016), 214–220.

[22] Andrew D Johnson, R E Handsaker, S L Pulit, M M Nizzari, C J O'Donnell, and P I W de Bakker. 2008. SNAP: a web-based tool for identification and annotation of proxy SNPs using HapMap. *Bioinformatics* 24, 24 (2008), 2938–2939.

[23] Donna Karolchik, Angie S Hinrichs, and W James Kent. 2009. The UCSC Genome Browser. In *Cur Protoc Bioinformatics*. John Wiley & Sons, Inc., Hoboken, NJ, USA.

[24] Martin Kircher, Daniela M Witten, Preti Jain, Brian J O'Roak, Gregory M Cooper, and Jay Shendure. 2014. A general framework for estimating the relative pathogenicity of human genetic variants. *Nature Genet* 46, 3 (2014), 310–315.

[25] R Kohavi. 1995. A Study of Cross-Validation and Bootstrap for Accuracy Selection and Model Estimation. In *Proc Int Joint Conf Artif Intel.* ACM, San Francisco, CA, 1137–1143.

[26] P Kontschieder, M Fiterau, and A Criminisi. 2015. Deep neural decision forests. In *Proc Int Conf Comput Vision.* IEEE, Santiago, Chile, 1467–1475.

[27] Gregory V Kryukov, Len A Pennacchio, and Shamil R Sunyaev. 2007. Most rare missense alleles are deleterious in humans: implications for complex disease and association studies. *Am J Hum Genet* 80, 4 (2007), 727–739.

[28] S G Landt, G K Marinov, A Kundaje, P Kheradpour, F Pauli, S Batzoglou, B E Bernstein, P Bickel, J B Brown, P Cayting, Y Chen, G DeSalvo, C Epstein, K I Fisher-Aylor, G Euskirchen, M Gerstein, J Gertz, A J Hartemink, M M Hoffman, V R Iyer, Y L Jung, S Karmakar, M Kellis, P V Kharchenko, Q Li, T Liu, X S Liu, L Ma, A Milosavljevic, R M Myers, P J Park, M J Pazin, M D Perry, D Raha, T E Reddy, J Rozowsky, N Shoresh, A Sidow, M Slattery, J A Stamatoyannopoulos, M Y Tolstorukov, K P White, S Xi, P J Farnham, J D Lieb, B J Wold, and M Snyder. 2012. ChIP-seq guidelines and practices of the ENCODE and modENCODE consortia. *Genome Research* 22, 9 (2012), 1813–1831.

[29] Dongwon Lee, David U Gorkin, Maggie Baker, Benjamin J Strober, Alessandro L Asoni, Andrew S McCallion, and Michael A Beer. 2015. A method to predict the impact of regulatory variants from DNA sequence. *Nature Genet* 47, 8 (2015), 955–961. gkm-SVM.

[30] Mulin Jun Li, Zhicheng Pan, Zipeng Liu, Jiexing Wu, Panwen Wang, Yun Zhu, Feng Xu, Zhengyuan Xia, Pak Chung Sham, Jean-Pierre A Kocher, Miaoxin Li, Jun S Liu, and Junwen Wang. 2016. Predicting regulatory variants with composite statistic. *Bioinformatics* 32, 18 (2016), 2729–2736.

[31] M J Li, B Yan, P C Sham, and J Wang. 2015. Exploring the function of genetic variants in the non-coding genomic regions: approaches for identifying human regulatory variants affecting gene expression. *Brief Bioinformatics* 16, 3 (2015), 393–412.

[32] Anthony Mathelier, Beibei Xin, Tsu-Pei Chiu, Lin Yang, Remo Rohs, and Wyeth W Wasserman. 2016. DNA Shape Features Improve Transcription Factor Binding Site Predictions *In Vivo*. *Cell systems* 3, 3 (2016), 278–286.e4.

[33] Matthew T Maurano, Richard Humbert, Eric Rynes, Robert E Thurman, Eric Haugen, Hao Wang, Alex P Reynolds, Richard Sandstrom, Hongzhu Qu, Jennifer Brody, et al. 2012. Systematic localization of common disease-associated variation in regulatory DNA. *Science* 337, 6099 (2012), 1190–1195.

[34] Stephen B Montgomery, Obi L Griffith, Johanna M Schuetz, Angela Brooks-Wilson, and Steven J M Jones. 2007. A survey of genomic properties for the detection of regulatory polymorphisms. *PLOS Comput Biol* 3, 6 (2007), e106.

[35] Stephen B Montgomery, O L Griffith, M C Sleumer, C M Bergman, M Bilenky, E D Pleasance, Y Prychyna, X Zhang, and S J M Jones. 2006. ORegAnno: an open access database and curation system for literature-derived promoters, transcription factor binding sites and regulatory variation. *Bioinformatics* 22, 5 (2006), 637–640.

[36] Dan L Nicolae, Eric Gamazon, Wei Zhang, Shiwei Duan, M Eileen Dolan, and Nancy J Cox. 2010. Trait-Associated SNPs Are More Likely to Be eQTLs: Annotation to Enhance Discovery from GWAS. *PLOS Genet* 6, 4 (2010), e1000888.

[37] F. Pedregosa, G. Varoquaux, A. Gramfort, V. Michel, B. Thirion, O. Grisel, M. Blondel, P. Prettenhofer, R. Weiss, V. Dubourg, J. Vanderplas, A. Passos, D. Cournapeau, M. Brucher, M. Perrot, and E. Duchesnay. 2011. scikit-learn: Machine Learning in Python. *J Mach Learn Res* 12 (2011), 2825–2830.

[38] Len A Pennacchio, Nadav Ahituv, Alan M Moses, Shyam Prabhakar, Marcelo A Nobrega, Malak Shoukry, Simon Minovitsky, Inna Dubchak, Amy Holt, Keith D Lewis, Ingrid Plajzer-Frick, Jennifer Akiyama, Sarah De Val, Veena Afzal, Brian L Black, Olivier Couronne, Michael B Eisen, Axel Visel, and Edward M Rubin. 2006. *In vivo* enhancer analysis of human conserved non-coding sequences. *Nature* 444, 7118 (2006), 499–502.

[39] Thomas A Peterson, Matthew Mort, David N Cooper, Predrag Radivojac, Maricel G Kann, and Sean D Mooney. 2016. Regulatory Single-Nucleotide Variant Predictor Increases Predictive Performance of Functional Regulatory Variants. *Hum Mutat* 37, 11 (2016), 1137–1143.

[40] E Portales-Casamar, S Thongjuea, A T Kwon, D Arenillas, X Zhao, E Valen, D Yusuf, B Lenhard, W W Wasserman, and A Sandelin. 2009. JASPAR 2010: the greatly expanded open-access database of transcription factor binding profiles. *Nucleic Acids Res* 38, Database (2009), D105–D110.

[41] Daniel Quang, Yifei Chen, and Xiaohui Xie. 2015. DANN: a deep learning approach for annotating the pathogenicity of genetic variants. *Bioinformatics* 31, 5 (2015), 761–763.

[42] Daniel Quang and Xiaohui Xie. 2016. DanQ: a hybrid convolutional and recurrent deep neural network for quantifying the function of DNA sequences. *Nucleic Acids Res* 44, 11 (2016), e107.

[43] Graham R S Ritchie, Ian Dunham, Eleftheria Zeggini, and Paul Flicek. 2014. Functional annotation of noncoding sequence variants. *Nature Methods* 11, 3 (2014), 294–296.

[44] Remo Rohs, Sean M West, Alona Sosinsky, Peng Liu, Richard S Mann, and Barry Honig. 2009. The role of DNA shape in protein–DNA recognition. *Nature* 461, 7268 (2009), 1248–1253.

[45] Marc A Schaub, Alan P Boyle, Anshul Kundaje, Serafim Batzoglou, and Michael Snyder. 2012. Linking disease associations with regulatory information in the human genome. *Genome Res* 22, 9 (2012), 1748–1759.

[46] S T Sherry, M H Ward, M Kholodov, J Baker, L Phan, E M Smigielski, and K Sirotkin. 2001. dbSNP: the NCBI database of genetic variation. *Nucleic Acids Res* 29, 1 (2001), 308–311.

[47] A Siepel. 2005. Evolutionarily conserved elements in vertebrate, insect, worm, and yeast genomes. *Genome Res* 15, 8 (2005), 1034–1050.

[48] Barbara E Stranger, Eli A Stahl, and Towfique Raj. 2011. Progress and promise of genome-wide association studies for human complex trait genetics. *Genetics* 187, 2 (2011), 367–383.

[49] The ENCODE Project Consortium. 2011. A User's Guide to the Encyclopedia of DNA Elements (ENCODE). *PLoS Biology* 9, 4 (2011), e1001046.

[50] Robert E Thurman, Eric Rynes, Richard Humbert, Jeff Vierstra, Matthew T Maurano, Eric Haugen, Nathan C Sheffield, Andrew B Stergachis, Hao Wang, Benjamin Vernot, et al. 2012. The accessible chromatin landscape of the human genome. *Nature* 489, 7414 (2012), 75–82.

[51] Ali Torkamani and Nicholas J Schork. 2008. Predicting functional regulatory polymorphisms. *Bioinformatics* 24, 16 (2008), 1787–1792.

[52] Axel Visel, Simon Minovitsky, Inna Dubchak, and Len A Pennacchio. 2007. VISTA Enhancer Browser–a database of tissue-specific human enhancers. *Nucleic Acids Research* 35, Database issue (2007), D88–92.

[53] Kai Wang, Mingyao Li, and Hakon Hakonarson. 2010. ANNOVAR: functional annotation of genetic variants from high-throughput sequencing data. *Nucleic Acids Res* 38, 16 (2010), e164.

[54] Lucas D Ward and Manolis Kellis. 2012. Interpreting noncoding genetic variation in complex traits and human disease. *Nature Biotechnol* 30, 11 (2012), 1095–1106.

[55] Danielle Welter, Jacqueline MacArthur, Joannella Morales, Tony Burdett, Peggy Hall, Heather Junkins, Alan Klemm, Paul Flicek, Teri Manolio, Lucia Hindorff, and Helen Parkinson. 2014. The NHGRI GWAS Catalog, a curated resource of SNP-trait associations. *Nucleic Acids Res* 42, Database issue (2014), D1001–6. accessed in 2016.

[56] Marvin N. Wright and Andreas Ziegler. 2015. ranger: A Fast Implementation of Random Forests for High Dimensional Data in C++ and R. *arXiv.org* 1508.04409 (2015), 1–17.

[57] Jichen Yang and Stephen A Ramsey. 2015. A DNA shape-based regulatory score improves position-weight matrix-based recognition of transcription factor binding sites. *Bioinformatics* 31, 21 (2015), 3445–3450.

[58] Yiqiang Zhao, Wyatt T Clark, Matthew Mort, David N Cooper, Predrag Radivojac, and Sean D Mooney. 2011. Prediction of functional regulatory SNPs in monogenic and complex disease. *Hum Mutat* 32, 10 (2011), 1183–1190.

[59] Jian Zhou and Olga G Troyanskaya. 2015. Predicting effects of noncoding variants with deep learning-based sequence model. *Nature Methods* 12, 10 (2015), 931–934.

[60] T Zhou, L Yang, Y Lu, I Dror, A C Dantas Machado, T Ghane, R Di Felice, and R Rohs. 2013. DNAshape: a method for the high-throughput prediction of DNA structural features on a genomic scale. *Nucleic Acids Res* 41, W1 (2013), W56–W62.

Exploring Frequented Regions in Pan-Genomic Graphs

Alan Cleary
Indika Kahanda
Brendan Mumey
Montana State University
Gianforte School of Computing
Bozeman, MT 59717, USA

Joann Mudge
Thiruvarangan Ramaraj
National Center for Genome Resources
2935 Rodeo Park Dr E
Santa Fe, NM 87505, USA

ABSTRACT

We consider the problem of identifying regions within a pan-genome de Bruijn graph that are traversed by many sequence paths. We define such regions and the subpaths that traverse them as frequented regions (FRs). In this work we formalize the FR problem and describe an efficient algorithm for finding FRs. Subsequently, we propose some applications of FRs based on machine-learning and pan-genome graph simplification. We demonstrate the effectiveness of these applications using data sets for the organisms *Staphylococcus aureus* (bacteria) and *Saccharomyces cerevisiae* (yeast). We corroborate the biological relevance of FRs such as identifying introgressions in yeast that aid in alcohol tolerance, and show that FRs are useful for classification of yeast strains by industrial use and visualizing pan-genomic space.

CCS CONCEPTS

•Applied computing → Computational biology; Computational genomics; •Computing methodologies → *Feature selection;*

KEYWORDS

Pan-genomics; classification; visualization

1 INTRODUCTION

With the unit cost of DNA sequencing continuing on a downward trajectory, research institutions and genome sequencing consortia have proposed and implemented strategies to sequence multiple genomes per species[1] [12]. This has resulted in a large volume of genome sequences of species that represent major phylogenetic clades [19]. As such, there is a need for novel methods of analysis that can scale to such unprecedented quantities of genomic data [26, 33].

A pan-genome represents the collective genomic information of multiple individuals or organisms from a related group or species [37]. Recently, pan-genomes have been represented using colored de Bruijn graphs [2, 25, 28], which can succinctly capture structural variation within a population by giving each genome's path through the graph a unique color [17].

An important problem in population genomics is the identification of synteny, that is, sequences that are (in)exactly preserved within the population. Though there exist a variety of whole genome pairwise and multiple sequence alignment approaches, these are generally not scalable. In this work we present the Frequented Regions (FR) problem, which mines regions of a graph that are frequently traversed by a set of paths in the graph. By exploiting the structure of the graph we are able to develop an efficient algorithm that effectively mines inexact syntenic regions from pan-genomic graphs.

In Section 2 we discuss work related to the FR problem and in Section 3 we formalize the the FR problem and discuss its computational complexity. In Section 4 we present an efficient algorithm for finding FRs, describe some applications in Section 5 and in Section 6 provide results on two pan-genome test cases. Lastly, in Section 7 we discuss future work and make closing remarks.

2 RELATED WORK

The FR problem is somewhat similar to other data mining problems, especially Frequent Itemset Mining (FI), which identifies sets of items that frequently occur together in a database of transactions. Specifically, the database is a binary matrix where the columns correspond to items and the rows to transactions. If an item occurred in a transaction, then its cell has a 1, otherwise 0. An itemset is considered *frequent* if each of its items occurred together in *minsup* transactions, where minsup is either a fraction of the transactions in the database or a minimum number of transactions. Transactions in which a frequent itemset's items occur together are called *supporting transactions*, since they support the itemset as being frequent. A seminal FI algorithm, Apriori, was introduced in [1]. It works by performing an exhaustive search of the itemset space and has an exponential run-time complexity. There are variations of FI that are tolerant to noise in the data [6, 24, 39]. These require that the supporting transactions in the transaction matrix meet a *row error threshold* constraint and/or the items meet a *column error threshold* constraint. Like exact FI algorithms, these do not consider the structure of the underlying graph and so are likely to generate several false positives.

Also related is Frequent Subgraph Mining, which is concerned with finding subgraphs that frequently occur in a database of graphs [16]. It is a well studied problem [18] commonly applied to biological datasets [13, 14, 20]. It could be applied to paths through a

[1] See http://www.1000genomes.org/, http://www.1001genomes.org/, and http://www.100kgenome.vetmed.ucdavis.edu/.

Permission to make digital or hard copies of all or part of this work for personal or classroom use is granted without fee provided that copies are not made or distributed for profit or commercial advantage and that copies bear this notice and the full citation on the first page. Copyrights for components of this work owned by others than the author(s) must be honored. Abstracting with credit is permitted. To copy otherwise, or republish, to post on servers or to redistribute to lists, requires prior specific permission and/or a fee. Request permissions from permissions@acm.org.
ACM-BCB'17, August 20-23, 2017, Boston, MA, USA.
© 2017 Copyright held by the owner/author(s). Publication rights licensed to ACM.
978-1-4503-4722-8/17/08...$15.00
DOI: http://dx.doi.org/10.1145/3107411.3107427

graph by treating each path as a different graph, but little work has been done with regards to discovering approximate solutions or scalability [22]. Yet another related problem is Frequent Subpath Mining, which is described in [11]. The author shows that the problem of mining exact frequent subpaths is similar to FI, but differs in that the structure of the graph can be exploited to achieve more efficient running time. Unfortunately, the algorithm is incapable of mining frequent subpaths whose supporting paths contain some error. Furthermore, the algorithm is exhaustive and has exponential run-time complexity. In [7] the authors formulate an approximate version of the Frequent Subpath Mining problem and present an efficient algorithm for mining syntenic regions from pan-genome graphs.

There exist a variety of tools for pan-genome analysis [38]. Unfortunately few of these are concerned with mining synteny [21] or scale beyond populations of microbial genomes, both of which are needs of the pan-genomics community [26]. One exception to the lack of synteny-based approaches is Sibelia [27], which determines syntenic regions from pan-genomes by iteratively eliminating bubbles in a de Bruijn graph with the sequence modification algorithm [31]. Since all bubbles are eventually merged into a single syntenic region, regions that are truly divergent will be falsely identified as syntenic, requiring the user to manually differentiate between false and true positives - a tedious task. Furthermore, this method also does not scale beyond populations of microbial genomes, as noted in Section 6.

3 PROBLEM FORMULATION

We assume the following input and parameters are supplied: A graph G and set of paths P within G. In our application, G corresponds to a (compressed) de Bruijn graph (cDBG) of a pan-genome composed of multiple genomic sequences. Nodes in G represent specific k-mers (or $\geq k$-mers if the graph has been compressed). An edge (u, v) is present if and only if the last $k-1$ nucleotides of u match the first $k-1$ nucleotides of v. Each genomic sequence corresponds to a path p in G; P is the collection of these paths.

A *frequented region* (FR) is characterized by a set of nodes C and a set of supporting subpaths from P that pass through the nodes in C. There are two error parameters that we consider: (1) what is the minimum fraction of the nodes in C that each subpath must contain; we call this the *penetrance* parameter α, and (2) if a subpath from P leaves C, how soon must it return to C (measured by the length of the corresponding sequence insertion); we call this the *maximum insertion* parameter κ. With this in mind, we formalize the definition of an FR as follows:

Given a path $p \in P$, let $p = \langle n_1, n_2, \ldots, n_L \rangle$, where n_i is the ith node visited by p and L is the length of the path. We define a subpath as $p[i, j] = \langle n_i, n_{i+1}, \ldots, n_j \rangle$ and $\text{seq}(p[i, j])$ as the genomic sequence corresponding to $p[i, j]$ in the de Bruijn graph.

Definition 3.1. We say $p[i, j]$ is an (α, κ)-supporting subpath for a set of nodes C if and only if

(1) $n_i, n_j \in C$ and between any two consecutive C nodes in $p[i, j]$, any gap of inserted sequence is at most κ in length (see (3) for a computational definition).
(2) $p[i, j]$ is *maximal* in the sense that it cannot be extended to either the left or right, i.e. $\nexists\,(\alpha, \kappa)$-supporting subpath $p[i', j']$ s.t. $[i, j] \subsetneq [i', j']$.
(3) $|p[i, j] \cap C| \geq \alpha |C|$.

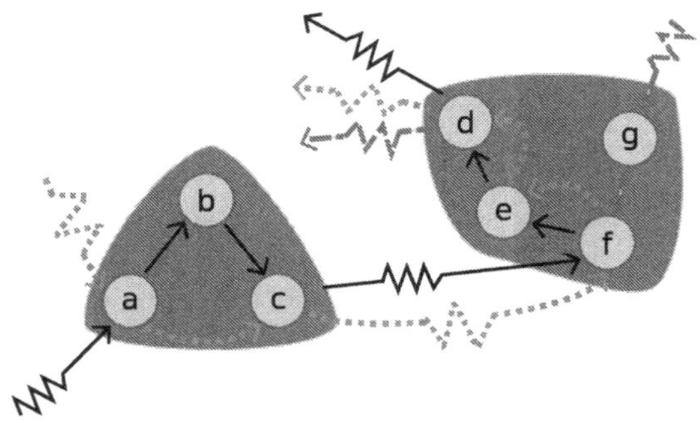

Figure 1: Example FRs: Assuming $\alpha \leq \frac{2}{3}$, the left group of nodes $C_L = \{a, b, c\}$ forms a FR with support 2 (from the black and blue paths). The right group of nodes $C_R = \{d, e, f, g\}$ forms a FR with support 3 (from the back, blue and red paths). If C_L and C_R were merged, the merged FR would have support 2, provided the connecting black and blue path segments between nodes c and f each have at most κ insertions.

Note that (α, κ)-supporting subpaths do not overlap due to the maximality requirement; if they did overlap they could be merged. It is also fairly easy to identify all of the (α, κ)-supporting subpaths for a given path p and node set C; we just need to identify all maximal runs of C nodes in p whose corresponding sequences have insertions of length at most κ and then check if the run contains at least $\alpha|C|$ distinct nodes from C. Algorithm 7 implements this idea.

Definition 3.2. A *frequented region* (FR) is a tuple (C, S), where C is a set of de Bruijn nodes and S is a set of (α, κ)-supporting subpaths of paths from P.

We say C is the *node-set* and S is the *supporting-subpath-set* for the FR. We define the *support* of the FR as

$$\text{support}(C, S) = |S| \tag{1}$$

and also define the *average length* of the FR as

$$\text{average-length}(FR) = \frac{\sum_{p[i,j] \in S} |\text{seq}(p[i, j])|}{|S|}. \tag{2}$$

Fig. 1 provides an example. The computational problem considered is to find FRs that have high support and high average length.

Computational complexity: Counting exact frequent itemsets is known to be #P-complete [40]. It can be seen that the exact frequent itemset problem can be reduced to the FR problem by setting $\alpha = 1, \kappa = \infty$. Thus, just counting the number of FRs is also #P-complete.

4 FINDING FREQUENTED REGIONS

Due to the vast scale of pan-genomic data, we opted for a simple heuristic approach to find interesting FRs. The basic idea of the algorithm is to find FRs in a bottom-up, agglomerative fashion, where each de Bruijn node starts in its own cluster and pairs of clusters

Algorithm 1 Compute supporting path segments

```
1:  function ComputeSupport(C,p)
2:      Let S = ∅
3:      Let m = [i : p[i] ∈ C]
4:      start = 1
5:      while start ≤ |m| do
6:          i = start
7:          while i < |m|, gap(p, m, i) ≤ κ do
8:              i = i + 1
9:          end while
10:         if (i − start + 1) ≥ α|C| then
11:             S = S ∪ p[m[start], m[i]]
12:         end if
13:         start = i
14:     end while
15:     return S
16: end function
```

Algorithm 2 Evaluate FR merge

```
function EvalMerge((C_L, S_L), (C_R, S_R))
    Let C = C_L ∪ C_R.
    Let S = ∅.
    for p ∈ P do
        S = S∪ ComputeSupport(C, p)
    end for
    return S
end function
```

are repeatedly merged. When an FR is created for a set of nodes C, the corresponding set of supporting subpaths S must be found. This is accomplished by the ComputeSupport subroutine shown as Algorithm 1. Note, in line 7, the gap subroutine returns the length of the inserted sequence between the consecutive matching node $m[i]$ and $m[i+1]$ along the path p; each end of $p[m[i], m[i+1]]$ matches a node in C, so the insert gap length is

$$\text{gap}(p, m, i) = |\text{seq}(p[m[i], m[i+1]])| - |\text{seq}(p[m[i]])| - |\text{seq}(p[m[i+1]])|. \quad (3)$$

The idea of the algorithm is to find a pair of existing FRs and merge them such that the newly created FR has the greatest possible support. The procedure terminates when no new FRs with positive support can be found. Pseudocode of the procedure is provided in Algorithm 3. Line 10 can be computed efficiently using a priority queue of possible merges. When a new FR is formed by merging (C_L, S_L) and (C_R, S_R), other potential merges involving either of these FRs remaining in the queue must be updated to be potential merges with the newly formed FR. After Algorithm 3 completes, the FRs will form a *hierarchical clustering* with one or more root FRs. The final step of the algorithm is to filter the FRs with high support. A simple recursive procedure is used to do this, as outlined in Algorithm 4. For each root FR (C, S) found, we call Explore($(C, S, 1)$). This will recursively explore the tree in a depth-first manner and report the FR associated with a tree node t if and only t's support is greater than any of its ancestors (superset FRs). All such reported

Algorithm 3 Agglomerate FRs

```
1:  procedure MergeFRs(G, P)
2:      for n ∈ nodes(G) do
3:          Let S = ∅.
4:          for p ∈ P do
5:              S = S∪ ComputeSupport({n}, p)
6:          end for
7:          Create FR ({n}, S).
8:      end for
9:      repeat
10:         Compute
                (C_L, S_L), (C_R, S_R) =     argmax
                                      (C_L,S_L),(C_R,S_R)
                              |EvalMerge((C_L, S_L), (C_R, S_R))|
11:         Let C = C_L ∪ C_R.
12:         Let S = EvalMerge((C_L, S_L), (C_R, S_R))
13:         Create FR (C, S)
14:         Mark (C_L, S_L), (C_R, S_R) unavailable for subsq. mergers
15:     until EvalMerge((C_L, S_L), (C_R, S_R)) = ∅
16: end procedure
```

Algorithm 4 Report interesting FRs

```
procedure Explore((C, S), m)
    if support(C, S) ≥ m then
        report (C, S).
    end if
    Suppose (C, S) = merge(C_L, S_L, C_R, S_R)
    Let m' = max(m, support(C, S) + 1)
    Explore((C_L, S_L), m')
    Explore((C_R, S_R), m')
end procedure
```

FRs are considered *interesting* FRs (iFRs). We limit the analyses in Section 6 to such FRs.

Time complexity. Suppose the cDBG contains V vertices and E edges and let L be the total length of all the pangenomic paths in P. Algorithm 3 is the main program; it begins with creating a new FR for each node $n \in G$ and finds its support. This can be done in $O(V + L)$ time. Next, we note that there are at most $V - 1$ iterations of the repeat-until loop since each iteration creates an internal node in a binary tree with V leaves. Determining the next FR merger (internal node) can done efficiently using a priority queue data structure. After each FR merger happens, the queue needs to be updated. This can done in $O(V + L + V \lg V)$ time; the $O(V + L)$ accounts for computing the support of all new potential FR mergers with the newly-created FR (there are at most V of them) and the $O(V \lg V)$ accounts for the resulting priority queue updates. The overall running time is thus, $O(LV + V^2 \lg V)$.

5 APPLICATIONS

In this section we discuss some applications for FRs including machine learning methods and an approach for pan-genome graph simplification and visualization.

5.1 Machine learning with FRs

Like other sequence features, such as SNPs, FRs may provide sequence characteristics that can be used to distinguish or categorize groups of genomes. For example, in Section 6 we differentiate between yeast strain genomes based on their industrial origin. In order to evaluate the effectiveness of FRs for this task we model this as a *multi-class classification* problem in which each strain is annotated with one of the industrial-origin class labels, and each iFR is a feature. The problem is then to apply a *supervised learning* algorithm to the feature set, or a subset of the feature set, such that unlabeled strains are labeled with the correct class.

Support Vector Machines (SVMs) [8] have been shown to be an effective approach to classifying genomes based on shared genetic features. Traditionally such classifications are done with Genome Wide Association Studies (GWAS) and/or Principal Component Analysis (PCA) [32], however SVMs been shown to have more classification power than GWAS/PCA [5]. Therefore, in this work we use Support Vector Machines for classifying genomes within a pan-genome based on their FR content as described below.

Specifically, each example (i.e. genome) is represented as an n-dimensional vector (n is the total number of FRs used) in which each individual component of a vector corresponds to the number of times a certain FR occurs with that genome. We use these vectors as input to our SVM model [29] and evaluate its accuracy in predicting the correct industrial origin based on the FRs they are associated with (see Section 6.2.2 for results of this study).

However, depending on the parameters used and size of the pan-genome, a large number of iFRs may be identified by Algorithm 4. These may span a variety of classes, ranging from the pan to strain-specific, among others. As such, *feature selection* is an important task when trying to maximize classification power. An effective feature selection strategy is one that can identify a small number of features that can discriminate classes based on their attributes.

A simple approach based on multinomial distributions which we refer to as *multinomial-filter* is as follows: Suppose that the sequence paths are divided into a set of groups $\{G_1, \ldots, G_k\}$. Let

$$c_{ij} = \sum_{p \in G_i} \text{support}_p(\text{FR}_j), \tag{4}$$

be the total support of FR_j for all sequence paths belonging to group G_i. In other words, c_{ij} is a count of the number of times FR_j occurs in G_i. Let $T_i = \sum_j c_{ij}$ be the total count of iFRs found in group G_i and let $T = \sum_i T_i$ be the total across all groups. The frequency with which a random iFR occurs in G_i is then $f_i = {}^{T_i+1}/_T$ (a pseudo-count of 1 is added to the count for each group.) The probability of observing the group counts for FR_j in a random FR is multinomially distributed with bin probabilities $\langle f_i \rangle$,

$$\Pr(\text{FR}_j) = \frac{n!}{c_{1j}! \cdots c_{kj}!} f_1^{c_{1j}} \cdots f_k^{c_{kj}}, \tag{5}$$

where $n = \sum_i c_{ij}$. The lower the $\Pr(\text{FR}_j)$ value, the less likely that the observed group counts for that FR occurred by random chance. (We note that $\Pr(\text{FR}_j)$ is similar but not identical to a p-value, as the latter includes the probability of at least as extreme data under the null hypothesis.)

5.2 Graph simplification

Visualizing a pan-genome graph is a difficult task, especially when dealing with larger, complex genomes. It is relatively simpler to visualize pan-genomes at the microbial level and with a limited number of genomes, but when the number of genomes and size increases, the result is an indecipherable "hairball", as depicted in the SplitMEM [25] work. To that end, we would like to use iFRs to create visualizations of pan-genomes that are human parsable, meaningful and facilitate knowledge discovery.

One approach is to filter what contents of a pan-genome are visualized by selecting a group of FRs and restrict attention to how the pan-genome traverses the corresponding FR node clusters. If we are given a list $L = \{C_1, \ldots C_n\}$ of disjoint FR clusters, we can create a corresponding graph G_L with n vertices, where each vertex represents one of the FR clusters in L. For each sequence path p in the original cDBG, we can trace a path in G_L according to the order in which p supports the clusters in L. Fig. 3 shows an application of the approach to visualize paths in a yeast pan-genome.

6 EXPERIMENTAL RESULTS

We evaluated the FR-finding algorithm on two datasets, *Staphylococcus aureus* and *Saccharomyces cerevisiae*. The algorithm is implemented in a Java program called `FindFRs` (which first runs Algorithm 3 to construct the FR hierarchy and then runs Algorithm 4 to report iFRs). The *Staphylococcus aureus* dataset was used to compare against Sibelia [27], the only other program currently available for mining synteny from a pan-genome de Bruijn graph. The *Saccharomyces cerevisiae* dataset was used to illustrate the scalability of the FR-finding algorithm and exhibit a variety of FR-based analyses.

We used `E-SplitMem` [2] to construct the cDBGs for each dataset. Our `FindFRs` implementation exploits obvious opportunities for parallelization; e.g. the for loop in Algorithm 2. Besides the main parameters α and κ, we also include two other parameters *minSup* and *minSize* which serve to limit the amount of output generated; only iFRs whose support and size (number of cDBG nodes) are at least these minimums are reported.

Experiments were run on a server with 4 Intel Xeon 2.2GHz 32 core processors and 1 TB of RAM, however most data sets could also run on standard desktop PCs, with longer running times.

6.1 *Staphylococcus aureus*

`FindFRs` algorithm was compared against `Sibelia` [27]. We selected `Sibelia`, a tool for finding synteny blocks in multiple closely related microbial genomes. Four *Staphylococcus aureus* strains (JH1, N315, TW20 and MSSA476), used as an example in the original `Sibelia` paper, were used for comparative purposes. Both programs were run with different $k \in \{25, 100, 500 and 1000\}$ values. Table 1 shows that `FindFRs` reports a higher number of frequented regions compared to `Sibelias` synteny blocks indicating the finer scale of partitioning regions based on biological significance. For this test case, we estimated percent overlap between regions reported by these two algorithms: For all k-mer values, approximately 98% of FindFRs FRs overlapped with Sibelias synteny blocks. Furthermore, we also computed overlap in terms of sequence percentage (i.e. What percentage of the Sibelia block sequences are contained in FindFRs FRs and vice versa). For the aforementioned four *S. aureus* strains with $k = 25$, alignments showed 91% of Sibelia Synteny block sequence base pairs were contained within FindFRs frequented regions and only 82% of FindFRs frequented regions sequence base pairs were contained within Sibelia Synteny blocks indicating FindFRs FRs captured most of Sibelia Synteny blocks at the nucleotide base pair level.

To compare run times of both programs, we tested a slightly larger dataset, consisting of 31 *Staphylococcus aureus* ($\approx$ 90 Mb) strains. For $k = 25$, Sibelia took 186 minutes, whereas FindFRs took 43 minutes, approximately four times faster.

Table 1: Sibelia versus FindFRs comparison

S. aureus (4 Strains)	$k = 25$	$k = 100$	$k = 500$	$k = 1000$
Synteny blocks	142	143	132	132
iFRs	10,740	1,334	2,011	1,351
iFR roots	392	122	97	134

FindFRs: $\alpha = 0.5, \kappa = 0$, minSup = 2, minSize = 2
Sibelia: All set to default, except for k values

6.2 *Saccharomyces cerevisiae*

Yeast (*Saccharomyces cerevisiae*) is a well studied model system with some published comparative genomic and pan-genomic work [4, 10], allowing us to use the existing knowledge base to assess the quality of the FRs found by our algorithm. Furthermore, yeast is highly diverse, economically important, and its multiple industrial applications enable interesting functional genomics. These attributes, compounded with a genome size of approximately 12 Mb, make yeast an interesting and tractable dataset for algorithm testing.

Our yeast pan-genome was built with assemblies from the *Saccharomyces* Genome Database (http://www.yeastgenome.org/). The dataset consisted of 55 assemblies from 48 yeast strains over a wide range of industrial applications and geographic origins; see Table 2. We tested $k \in \{25, 100, 500, 1000\}$, since k-mer size can affect which genomic features are explicitly represented in the topology of the graph and it is not yet well understood how to choose an appropriate k-mer size for pan-genome analysis. We also varied α and κ, as indicated. Running times ranged from a few minutes for $k = 1000$ to approximately an hour for $k = 25$. Table 3 indicates the size of the cDBGs created and the number of iFRs found. Figure 2 shows support versus average length for a sample run. We note that Sibelia was not able to process this data set ($\approx$ 600 Mb), so we do not report a comparison.

6.2.1 *Consistency with Yeast Biology.*

Because yeast is one of the simplest eukaryotes, it has been an important model system, including for genomic research [4, 10]. In addition to being an important laboratory model, yeast is economically important, as it is critical in baking bread, generating

Table 2: The 48 yeast strains with usage and region listed where known.

Strain	Source	Region
AWRI1631	Wine	South Africa
AWRI796	Wine	South Africa
BC187	Wine	California
BY4741	Laboratory	
BY4742	Laboratory	
CBS7960	Bioethanol	Brazil
CEN.PK	Laboratory	
CLIB215	Bakery	New Zealand
CLIB324	Bakery	Vietnam
CLIB382	Ale	Ireland
D273-10B	Laboratory	
DBVPG6044	Wine	West African
EC1118	Wine	
EC9-8	Nature	Israel
FL100	Laboratory	
Foster's B	Ale	
Foster's O	Ale	
FY1679	Laboratory	
JAY291	Bioethanol	Brazil
JK9-3d	Laboratory	
K11	Sake	Japan
Kyokai7	Sake	Japan
L1528	Wine	Chile
LalvinQA23	Wine	Portugal
M22	Fruit/Nectar	Italy
PW5	Wine	Nigeria
Red Star	Bakery	
RM11-1a	Fruit/Nectar	California
SEY6210	Laboratory	
SK1	Laboratory	
T7	Nature	Missouri
T73	Wine	Spain
UC5	Sake	Japan
UWOPS05_217_3	Fruit/Nectar	Malaysia
VIN13	Wine	South Africa
VL3	Wine	France
W303	Laboratory	
X2180-1A	Laboratory	
Y10	Fruit/Nectar	Coconut
Y55	Laboratory	
YJM269	Wine	Austria
YJM339	Pathogen	
YJM789	Pathogen	
YPH499	Laboratory	
YPS128	Nature	Pennsylvania
YPS163	Nature	Pennsylvania
YS9	Bakery	Singapore
ZTW1	Bioethanol	China

alcoholic beverages such as wine, sake, and ale, and is also used in generating biofuels. Yeast is also important in other contexts, being found in natural environmental systems, including as pathogens of humans and other organisms.

The ability to thrive in harsh environments, which is required for industrial specialization in yeast, is often obtained through horizontal transfer of sets of genes [4, 10]. To determine whether we could uncover some of these introgressed regions, we looked at introgressions that have been validated in EC1118. These introgressions introduce genes that allow EC1118, which is used in wine-making, to be able to grow in the presence of alcohol. EC1118

Table 3: Number of cDBG nodes and iFRs
($\alpha = .0.7, \kappa = 0$, minSup = 5, minSize = 5)

k	cDBG nodes	iFRs
25	2,260,767	115,585
100	1,758,760	97,550
500	890,055	29,766
1000	443,764	8,994

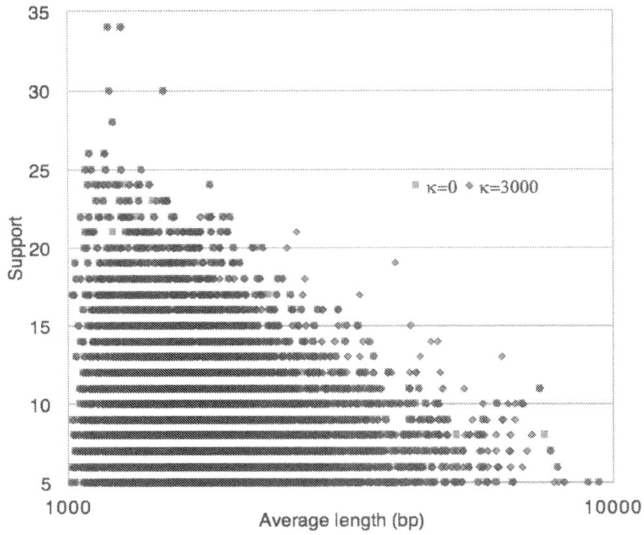

Figure 2: Distribution of iFR support versus average length. Allowing insertions (κ = 3000) creates some longer FRs. (α = .0.7,$\kappa \in \{0, 3000\}$, minSup = 5, minSize = 5)

has three introgressions compared to S288C [30]. Because S288C is not in our dataset, we used FR nodes contained in BY4741 (derived from S288C) to compare to those found in EC1118. All three introgressions were uncovered using our FR approach (Fig 3).

The shortest introgression is a 17kb introgression on chromosome XIV [30]. Five novel genes are inserted near the telomere between S288C genes YNL037C and YNL038W. The introgression likely comes from the species *Zygosaccharomyces bailii*, with the possible exception of EC1118_1N26_0034g which could not be found in *Z. bailii* and has counterparts in the *Saccharomyces* genus. The order of the genes is slightly different in *Z. bailii*, however, with EC1118_1N26_0056g occuring before EC1118_1N26_0012g in *Z. bailii*.

The 17kb introgressed region was found on EC1118 sequence accession FN393084.1 (k = 500, α = 0.7). Although this sequence was only approximately 25kb, it contained the introgression and anchoring sequence on both sides (Fig. 3a). The order of the green nodes reflects their order in EC1118. Multiple alcohol-related strains have versions of this introgression as indicated by the thicker green edges as well as green edges that follow alternate paths through the region. Interestingly, some of the alcohol-related strains appear to have a rearrangement matching that of *Z. bailii* with EC1118_1N26_00056g leading into EC1118_1N26_00012g. None of the laboratory strains, including the five S288C-derived strains, show support any of the introgressed FRs.

Most of the nodes in the introgression occur only in alcohol-related strains (green) (Fig 3a), confirming that this region could be important in determining alcohol tolerance. The two nodes which show "other" (gray) strain support include the EC1118_1N26_00034g gene which is not thought to be from *Z. bailii* but rather to be from a congeneric strain. [30] found a related gene in RM11-1A while we found it in our dataset in M22 and alcohol-related strains. Both

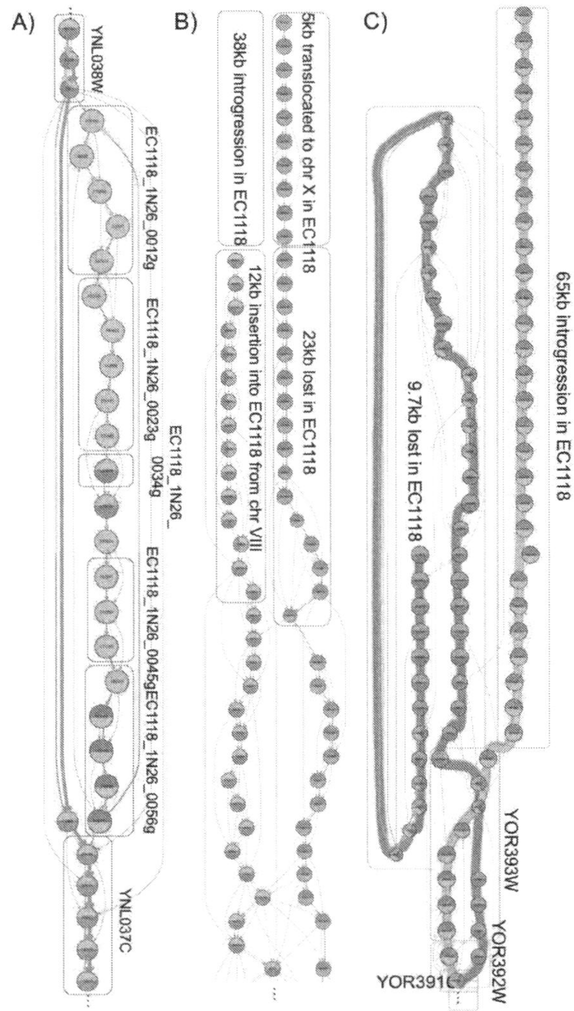

Figure 3: The three introgression regions [30] showing FRs from EC1118 (green) compared to S288C (represented by the S288C-derived strain BY4741, light blue). (A) 17kb introgression on chromosome XIV showing alcohol (green, including wine, sake, ale and bioethanol strains), laboratory (light blue), bakery (brown), and other (gray) strains. (B) A complex introgression event on chromosome VI shows a 12kb translocation in EC1118 from chromosome VIII, a 23kb deletion from in EC1118 and a 5kb region from S288C that is translocated to chrX in EC1118. Strains included were EC1118 (green), S288C-derived (light blue, strains BY4741, BY4742, FY1679, X2180-1A, and YPH499), and other (gray). (C) A 65kb novel introgression replaced 9.7 kb of the chromosome XV telomere in EC1118. Shown are EC1118 (green) and BY4741 (light-blue).

RM11-1A and M22 were isolated from vineyards and might need some alcohol tolerance to survive fermenting fruit, though it is also possible that the gene is unrelated to alcohol tolerance.

The four introgression FRs adjacent to YNL037C, which are part of the EC1118_1N26_00056g gene, appear to be contained in bakery yeasts (brown) as well as alcohol yeasts (green) (Fig 3a). The EC1118_1N26_00056g gene is involved in activating the proline utilization pathway, though whether this foreign version of the gene increases proline utilization or competes with or replaces the native gene resulting in reduced proline utilization is not clear. Nevertheless, proline is important in both the alcohol and bread-making industries. Proline can provide a nitrogen source and is the dominant free amino acid in grapes and grape wine [15]. In addition, proline accumulation can confer tolerance to freezing, dessication, and ethanol stress [34–36]. It is interesting to note that the two bakery yeasts sharing these FRs, CLIB324 (Vietnam) and YS9 (Singapore), are geographically close and likely come from a geographically isolated lineage, which are common in *S. cerevisiae* [23].

The 38kb EC1118 insertion on one of the telomeres of chromosome VI [30] was also uncovered in EC1118 (k = 500, α = 0.7, minSup = 4, minSize = 4). This is a more complicated introgression with some rearrangements also occurring. A 23 kb segment of chromosome VI (genes YFL052W to YFL058W) was deleted in EC1118 while an adjacent segment (genes YFL062W-YFL059W) was translocated to one of EC1118's chromosome X telomeres. The 38kb novel insertion merged onto the end of the chromosome, connecting to a 12kb segment translocated from EC1118's chromosome VIII (genes YHR217C through YHR211W). This segment, in turn, merged with the remaining sequence from chromosome VI, with YHR211W (chromosome VIII) and YFL051C (chromosome VI), which are similar on a sequence level, fusing together.

Many of the EC1118 FRs that were translocated to chromosome VI from chromosome VIII (12kb) are shared by the S288C-derived accessions (light blue). This is not surprising because the S288C-derived accessions have this region on chromosome VIII. As expected, none of the blue edges (S288C-derived) connect the 12kb chromosome VIII translocation with the rest of chromosome VIII. None of the FRs in the 23kb segment lost in EC1118 show support in EC1118, as expected given that it has been deleted in EC1118. However, none of the FRs in the 5kb region that was translocated to chromosome X in EC1118 are contained in EC1118, either, even though this region occurs on chromosome X. Presumably, it has evolved away from the S288C version to make it different enough that our paramaters did not link the two regions into the same set of nodes. The EC1118 FRs stop approximately 38kb from the end of chromosome VI. No FRs were found in the 38kb novel region, presumably because there wasn't enough support to generate FRs. This raises the issue that sometimes it is interesting to look for regions where FRs are absent as they are potentially novel.

The final novel introgression is a 65kb region that replaced the last 9.7 kb (including genes YOR394-C-A (2 copies), YOR394C, and YOR396W, not shown) of chromosome XV [30]. For simplicity, only EC1118 (green) and BY4741 (light blue) compared to all others (gray) are shown in Fig 3C and their chromosome XV paths have been highlighted (k = 500, α = 0.7). The last gene shared by EC1118 and BY4741, YOR393W, has some shared FRs and some FRs having diverged. Thereafter, the paths diverge. The EC1118 65 kb novel insertion is shared with other yeast strains. This region is highly conserved as there are not alternate paths through the region. The 9.7 kb region in BY4741, which was deleted in EC1118 actually has FRs that are shared with EC1118, though EC1118 does not have them on chromosome XV. These are telomeric genes that tend to occur on several yeast telomers. This region is shared with other strains as well. It contains many alternate paths through the region and, though smaller, actually contains more (and smaller) FRs than EC1118's 65 kb introgression. The alternate paths and small FRs indicate divergence and rearrangement between strains.

6.2.2 Using FRs for classification.

As mentioned in Section 5.1, we use SVMs as our supervised learning model. Specifically, we applied a one-against-rest multi-class SVM classifier with degree 2 polynomial kernels. We normalize the data using L1 normalization and then used stratified cross-validation to evaluate the effectiveness of the model. In this work we used this SVM configuration to predict the industrial origin for a given yeast strain.

We implemented the SVM model with the above configuration using the PyML Python library[2]. We then used the model to classify the strains of the yeast dataset by their industrial application, or rather *source* from Table 2. The dataset is composed of 55 examples and they are annotated with nine distinct class labels. Given the distribution of the source labels in the data set, we used two-fold stratified cross-validation. For $\alpha \in \{0.7, 0.75, 0.8, 0.85, 0.9\}$ and $\kappa = 0$, we computed the average Area Under Receiver Operating Characteristic (AUROC) curve [3] for 10 iterations of classifier training. Due to the large number of iFRs (see Table 3), we found it necessary to employ feature-selection to reduce the number of iFRs considered by the classifier in order to improve classification power. This was done using two different methods: (1) iFRs were filtered with minSup $\in \{1, 5, 10, 15, 20\}$ and minSize $\in \{1, 5, 10, 15, 25, 100\}$ which we refer to as the *support/size-filter*, and (2) iFRs were filtered with the *multinomial-filter* feature selection method described in Section 5.1, keeping the top 1000, 500, and 250 iFRs based on $\Pr(FR_j)$-value rank. We chose these feature set sizes to explore if there is an appropriate size for such a classification task. Table 4 reports the highest AUROC for each k-value and filtering method.

As can be seen, both methods of FR filtration provide feature sets that are effective for classifying yeast by their industrial application, though the multinomial-filter is more effective. It is worth noting that there does not appear to be a specific iFR sample size that yields higher AUROC and so Recursive Feature Selection should be employed to maximize the AUROC. This can be much more computationally demanding than trying a variety of sizes as we have done. We have omitted classification results for the unfiltered iFR sets because their AUROCs were seldom better than guessing.

[2]http://pyml.sourceforge.net/

Table 4: Best AUROC for each k-value.

k	support/size-filter	multinomial-filter
25	0.68	0.75
100	0.75	0.79
500	0.72	0.91
1000	0.72	0.9

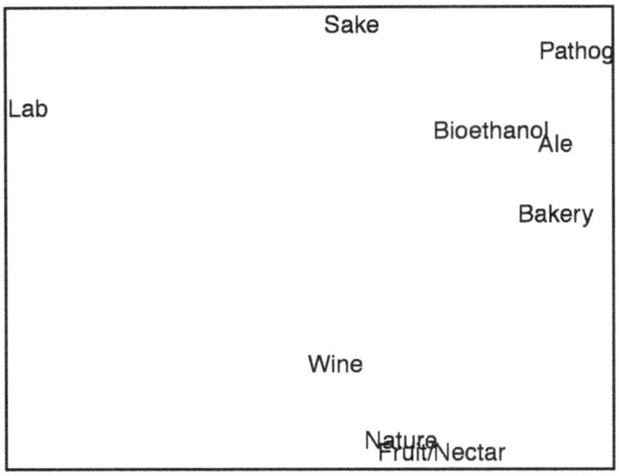

Figure 4: Yeast industrial usage multidimensional-scaling plot based on the top 500 discriminative iFRs found.
($k = 500$, $\alpha = 0.7$, $\kappa = 0$)

6.2.3 Visualizing pangenomic space.
We also applied *multidimensional-scaling* [9], using the isoMDS method in *R*, to provide a visual representation of the industrial uses for yeast. The ranking method described in Section 5.1 was first used to determine the top 500 iFRs by p-value (eqn. 5) for discriminating the nine industrial uses from Table 2. Distances between usages were found using the Canberra method, an appropriate metric for count-based data, provided by R's dist function. As can be seen in Fig. 4, the plot provides a visual interpretation of yeast usages based entirely on the aggregate genomic content of each group.

7 CONCLUSIONS

Frequented regions provide new approaches to analyze pangenomic space. While we have described a few examples showing biological relevance above, there are many other biological problems to which our pangenomic method can be applied [26].

FRs permit analyzing multiple related assemblies simultaneously without reference bias to find patterns both of divergence (novelty) and conservation. Identification of divergent regions (regions that do not fall into FRs even with lenient parameters) allows the detection of novel genes that are not present in the reference sequence and/or in other assemblies from a species. These genes could represent genes obtained through horizontal transfer, hybridization, or strong positive selection, and may have important adaptive functions. On the other hand, identification of regions that are conserved enables the determination of core gene sets that are required for the species. Determining unannotated regions that are conserved across the species is also important. Such conservation could imply that purifying selection has been active to keep important regions conserved. Such regions could also lead to the identification of new genes or important regulatory elements.

Path-based approaches could also be applied at the amino acid level and potentially at the domain, gene, gene family, operon, or molecule (ie. chromosome or plasmid) level. Our FR approach would be best integrated into a visual tool to help researchers understand and explore pan-genomic data, e.g. graph visualizations allowing users to expand iFR nodes into the underlying structure or perform analyses on their genetic content, such as multiple sequence alignment. Furthermore, existing annotation data could be superimposed on the graph to guide the user's inquiry.

Software: Available at github.com/abi-pangenomics/FindFRs

ACKNOWLEDGMENTS

This work was supported by the National Science Foundation, under grant DBI-1542262.

REFERENCES

[1] Rakesh Agrawal, Ramakrishnan Srikant, and others. 1994. Fast algorithms for mining association rules. In *Proc. 20th int. conf. very large data bases, VLDB*, Vol. 1215. 487–499.
[2] Timo Beller and Enno Ohlebusch. 2015. Efficient construction of a compressed de Bruijn graph for pan-genome analysis. In *Combinatorial Pattern Matching*. Springer, 40–51.
[3] Viv Bewick, Liz Cheek, and Jonathan Ball. 2004. Statistics review 13: receiver operating characteristic curves. *Critical care* 8, 6 (2004), 508.
[4] Anthony R Borneman, Brian A Desany, David Riches, Jason P Affourtit, Angus H Forgan, Isak S Pretorius, Michael Egholm, and Paul J Chambers. 2011. Whole-genome comparison reveals novel genetic elements that characterize the genome of industrial strains of Saccharomyces cerevisiae. *PLoS Genet* 7, 2 (2011), e1001287.
[5] Michael Bridges, Elizabeth A Heron, Colm O'Dushlaine, Ricardo Segurado, Derek Morris, Aiden Corvin, Michael Gill, Carlos Pinto, International Schizophrenia Consortium, and others. 2011. Genetic classification of populations using supervised learning. *PloS one* 6, 5 (2011), e14802.
[6] Hong Cheng, Philip S Yu, and Jiawei Han. 2006. Ac-close: Efficiently mining approximate closed itemsets by core pattern recovery. In *Data Mining, 2006. ICDM'06. Sixth International Conference on*. 839–844.
[7] Alan Cleary, Brendan Mumey, Thiruvarangan Ramaraj, and Joann Mudge. 2017. Approximate Frequent Subpath Mining Applied to Pangenomics. In *BICoB*. 59–65.
[8] Corinna Cortes and Vladimir Vapnik. 1995. Support-vector networks. *Machine learning* 20, 3 (1995), 273–297.
[9] Trevor F Cox and Michael AA Cox. 2000. *Multidimensional scaling*. CRC press.
[10] Barbara Dunn, Chandra Richter, Daniel J Kvitek, Tom Pugh, and Gavin Sherlock. 2012. Analysis of the Saccharomyces cerevisiae pan-genome reveals a pool of copy number variants distributed in diverse yeast strains from differing industrial environments. *Genome research* 22, 5 (2012), 908–924.
[11] Sumanta Guha. 2009. Efficiently mining frequent subpaths. In *Proceedings of the Eighth Australasian Data Mining Conference-Volume 101*. 11–15.
[12] David Haussler, Stephen J O'Brien, Oliver A Ryder, F Keith Barker, Michele Clamp, Andrew J Crawford, Robert Hanner, Olivier Hanotte, Warren E Johnson, Jimmy A McGuire, and others. 2009. Genome 10K: a proposal to obtain whole-genome sequence for 10 000 vertebrate species. *Journal of Heredity* 100, 6 (2009), 659–674.
[13] Steven Hill, Bismita Srichandan, and Rajshekhar Sunderraman. 2012. An iterative mapreduce approach to frequent subgraph mining in biological datasets. In *Proceedings of the ACM Conference on Bioinformatics, Computational Biology and Biomedicine*. ACM, 661–666.
[14] Jun Huan, Wei Wang, Deepak Bandyopadhyay, Jack Snoeyink, Jan Prins, and Alexander Tropsha. 2004. Mining protein family specific residue packing patterns from protein structure graphs. In *Proceedings of the eighth annual international conference on Resaerch in computational molecular biology*. ACM, 308–315.
[15] Hoching L Huang and Marjorie C Brandriss. 2000. The regulator of the yeast proline utilization pathway is differentially phosphorylated in response to the quality of the nitrogen source. *Molecular and cellular biology* 20, 3 (2000), 892–899.
[16] Akihiro Inokuchi, Takashi Washio, and Hiroshi Motoda. 2000. An apriori-based algorithm for mining frequent substructures from graph data. In *European Conference on Principles of Data Mining and Knowledge Discovery*. Springer, 13–23.
[17] Zamin Iqbal, Mario Caccamo, Isaac Turner, Paul Flicek, and Gil McVean. 2012. De novo assembly and genotyping of variants using colored de Bruijn graphs. *Nature genetics* 44, 2 (2012), 226–232.
[18] Chuntao Jiang, Frans Coenen, and Michele Zito. 2013. A survey of frequent subgraph mining algorithms. *The Knowledge Engineering Review* 28, 01 (2013), 75–105.
[19] Jaebum Kim, Denis M Larkin, Qingle Cai, Yongfen Zhang, Ri-Li Ge, Loretta Auvil, Boris Capitanu, Guojie Zhang, Harris A Lewin, Jian Ma, and others. 2013.

Reference-assisted chromosome assembly. *Proceedings of the National Academy of Sciences* 110, 5 (2013), 1785–1790.
[20] Mehmet Koyutürk, Ananth Grama, and Wojciech Szpankowski. 2004. An efficient algorithm for detecting frequent subgraphs in biological networks. *Bioinformatics* 20, suppl 1 (2004), i200–i207.
[21] Heng Li and Nils Homer. 2010. A survey of sequence alignment algorithms for next-generation sequencing. *Briefings in bioinformatics* 11, 5 (2010), 473–483.
[22] Ruirui Li and Wei Wang. 2015. REAFUM: Representative Approximate Frequent Subgraph Mining. In *SIAM International Conference on Data Mining*. SIAM, 2167–0099.
[23] Gianni Liti, David M Carter, Alan M Moses, Jonas Warringer, Leopold Parts, Stephen A James, Robert P Davey, Ian N Roberts, Austin Burt, Vassiliki Koufopanou, and others. 2009. Population genomics of domestic and wild yeasts. *Nature* 458, 7236 (2009), 337–341.
[24] Jinze Liu, Susan Paulsen, Xing Sun, Wei Wang, Andrew B Nobel, and Jan Prins. 2006. Mining Approximate Frequent Itemsets In the Presence of Noise: Algorithm and Analysis.. In *SDM*, Vol. 6. 405–416.
[25] Shoshana Marcus, Hayan Lee, and Michael C Schatz. 2014. SplitMEM: a graphical algorithm for pan-genome analysis with suffix skips. *Bioinformatics* 30, 24 (2014), 3476–3483.
[26] Tobias Marschall, Manja Marz, Thomas Abeel, Louis Dijkstra, Bas E Dutilh, Ali Ghaffaari, Paul Kersey, Wigard Kloosterman, Veli Makinen, Adam Novak, and others. 2016. Computational Pan-Genomics: Status, Promises and Challenges. *bioRxiv* (2016), 043430.
[27] Ilya Minkin, Anand Patel, Mikhail Kolmogorov, Nikolay Vyahhi, and Son Pham. 2013. Sibelia: a scalable and comprehensive synteny block generation tool for closely related microbial genomes. In *Algorithms in Bioinformatics*. Springer, 215–229.
[28] Ilia Minkin, Son Pham, and Paul Medvedev. 2016. TwoPaCo: An efficient algorithm to build the compacted de Bruijn graph from many complete genomes. *arXiv:1602.05856* (2016).
[29] William S Noble. 2006. What is a support vector machine? *Nature biotechnology* 24, 12 (2006), 1565–1567.
[30] Maite Novo, Frédéric Bigey, Emmanuelle Beyne, Virginie Galeote, Frédérick Gavory, Sandrine Mallet, Brigitte Cambon, Jean-Luc Legras, Patrick Wincker, Serge Casaregola, and others. 2009. Eukaryote-to-eukaryote gene transfer events revealed by the genome sequence of the wine yeast Saccharomyces cerevisiae EC1118. *Proceedings of the National Academy of Sciences* 106, 38 (2009), 16333–16338.
[31] Son K Pham and Pavel A Pevzner. 2010. DRIMM-Synteny: decomposing genomes into evolutionary conserved segments. *Bioinformatics* 26, 20 (2010), 2509–2516.
[32] Markus Ringnér. 2008. What is principal component analysis? *Nature biotechnology* 26, 3 (2008), 303.
[33] Zachary D Stephens, Skylar Y Lee, Faraz Faghri, Roy H Campbell, Chengxiang Zhai, Miles J Efron, Ravishankar Iyer, Michael C Schatz, Saurabh Sinha, and Gene E Robinson. 2015. Big data: astronomical or genomical? *PLoS Biol* 13, 7 (2015), e1002195.
[34] H Takagi, F Iwamoto, and S Nakamori. 1997. Isolation of freeze-tolerant laboratory strains of Saccharomyces cerevisiae from proline-analogue-resistant mutants. *Applied microbiology and biotechnology* 47, 4 (1997), 405–411.
[35] Hiroshi Takagi, Kuumi Sakai, Kana Morida, and Shigeru Nakamori. 2000. Proline accumulation by mutation or disruption of the proline oxidase gene improves resistance to freezing and desiccation stresses in Saccharomyces cerevisiae. *FEMS microbiology letters* 184, 1 (2000), 103–108.
[36] Hiroshi Takagi, Miki Takaoka, Akari Kawaguchi, and Yoshito Kubo. 2005. Effect of L-proline on sake brewing and ethanol stress in Saccharomyces cerevisiae. *Applied and environmental microbiology* 71, 12 (2005), 8656–8662.
[37] Hervé Tettelin, Vega Masignani, Michael J Cieslewicz, Claudio Donati, Duccio Medini, Naomi L Ward, Samuel V Angiuoli, Jonathan Crabtree, Amanda L Jones, A Scott Durkin, and others. 2005. Genome analysis of multiple pathogenic isolates of Streptococcus agalactiae: implications for the microbial fipan-genomefi. *Proceedings of the National Academy of Sciences* 102, 39 (2005), 13950–13955.
[38] George Vernikos, Duccio Medini, David R Riley, and Herve Tettelin. 2015. Ten years of pan-genome analyses. *Current opinion in microbiology* 23 (2015), 148–154.
[39] Cheng Yang, Usama Fayyad, and Paul S Bradley. 2001. Efficient discovery of error-tolerant frequent itemsets in high dimensions. In *Proceedings of ACM SIGKDD*. 194–203.
[40] Guizhen Yang. 2004. The complexity of mining maximal frequent itemsets and maximal frequent patterns. In *Proceedings of ACM SIGKDD*. 344–353.

Bayesian Hyperparameter Optimization for Machine Learning Based eQTL Analysis

Andrew Quitadamo
University of North Carolina at Charlotte
9201 University City Blvd
Charlotte, North Carolina
aquitada@uncc.edu

James Johnson
University of North Carolina at Charlotte
9201 University City Blvd
Charlotte, North Carolina
jjohn443@uncc.edu

Xinghua Shi
University of North Carolina at Charlotte
9201 University City Blvd
Charlotte, North Carolina
x.shi@uncc.edu

ABSTRACT

Machine learning methods are being applied to a wide range of problems in biology and bioinformatics. These methods often rely on configuring high level parameters, or hyperparameters, such as regularization hyperparameters in sparse learning models like graph-guided multitask Lasso methods. Different choices for these hyperparameters will lead to different results, which makes finding good hyperparameter combinations an important task when using these hyperparameter dependent methods. There are several different ways to tune hyperparameters including manual tuning, grid search, random search, and Bayesian optimization. In this paper, we apply three hyperparameter tuning strategies to eQTL analysis including grid and random search in addition to Bayesian optimization. Experiments show that the Bayesian optimization strategy outperforms the other strategies in modeling eQTL associations. Applying this strategy to assess eQTL associations using the 1000 Genomes structural variation genotypes and RNAseq data in gEUVADIS, we identify a set of new SVs associated with gene expression changes in a human population.

KEYWORDS

hyperparameter optimization, eQTL analysis, Bayesian optimization, graph-guided multitask Lasso

1 INTRODUCTION

Gene expression is a critical intermediate step that genetic variation leads to a particular human trait including diseases. With an unprecedented availability of data at many levels, such as genetic variation and gene expression, it is now possible to combine these cross-layered data for integrative analysis to understand the complex interplay between genetic variants and genes expression. Recently, expression quantitative trait loci (eQTL) analysis has been demonstrated as a powerful method to integrate such cross-layered data to understand many different biological phenomena, from diseases like diabetes to cancer genetics[10, 11, 15, 16]. In general, eQTL analysis aims at studying the impact of genetic variation on gene expression, by treating gene expression quantifications as quantitative traits. A typical eQTL setting is that genotypes of genetic variants, and gene expressions are both assessed for the same set of samples in a population. Particularly, eQTL analysis achieves integrative analysis by identifying significant associations between these genetic variants and gene expressions.

There are many different methods for performing an eQTL analysis, ranging from pairwise association analysis to various machine learning techniques [19]. While pairwise association models tend to be simple, quick, and powerful, they assume independence between the genes and between the genetic variation. Such independence may not reflect the actual underlying biology, as genes are co-regulated and interact with each other, and genetic variations contain correlations due to inheritance patterns. Newer statistical based methods like two graph-guided multitask Lasso (MtLasso2G) and sparse conditional Gaussian graphical models (SCGGM) attempt to model these interactions, and use them to inform the eQTL search[4, 21]. Although these methods capture interactions among biological entities, the results are dependent on model hyperparameters, making it critical to find hyperparameters that optimize the models.

The goal of machine learning is to automatically optimize a set of parameters given a set of inputs. Many machine learning methods also have hyperparameters that need to be chosen before any analysis can be performed. These hyperparameters include learning rates in a neural network and the regularization parameter in Lasso based methods. Different values of these hyperparameters can produce different results from the same input. Hyperparameter optimization is the process of finding a set of hyperparameters that produce the best output. Because of its importance there have been several different methods proposed to address this problem.

A simple method for finding good hyperparameters is a manual search, where an individual picks starting hyperparameters and subsequently changes them in subsequent iterations in an attempt to produce better results. Manual optimization is easy to implement, but is highly dependent on the individual running the analysis and their expertise. This variability makes replication of the optimization very hard, if not impossible. Manual tuning also is hard to parallelize efficiently, as a human needs to evaluate the results after each iteration is complete.

Another method that is easy to implement and commonly used for optimizing hyperparameters is through a grid search. For each individual hyperparameter a list of potential values is determined, and every possible combination of hyperparameter values is used

Permission to make digital or hard copies of all or part of this work for personal or classroom use is granted without fee provided that copies are not made or distributed for profit or commercial advantage and that copies bear this notice and the full citation on the first page. Copyrights for components of this work owned by others than ACM must be honored. Abstracting with credit is permitted. To copy otherwise, or republish, to post on servers or to redistribute to lists, requires prior specific permission and/or a fee. Request permissions from permissions@acm.org.
ACM-BCB'17 August 20-23, 2017, Boston, MA, USA.
© 2017 Association for Computing Machinery.
ACM ISBN 978-1-4503-4722-8/17/08...$15.00
https://doi.org/10.1145/3107411.3107434

to perform an analysis. The results of these analyses are then used to pick the best hyperparameter combination. A grid search is easy to run in parallel, and given the same amount of time as manual tuning, can usually find better hyperparameters[1].

Bergstra and Bengio demonstrated that a random search can yield better results than a grid search, especially on problems that are high dimensional. Like in the grid search, a range of potential values for each hyperparameter is determined for random search. However, instead of moving through all possible combinations, in a random search the potential hyperparameters are picked at random from the range. This randomness allows for hyperparameter combinations to be explored that are missed in a grid search. Similar to grid search, a random search is easy to implement in parallel[1].

Recently, Bayesian optimization has also been applied to the hyperparameter search problem. By treating algorithms as black box functions and using Bayesian optimization, Snoek et al. [14] were able to find hyperparameters that performed as well as, and in some cases better than, hyperparameters found by other methods. Bayesian optimization creates a probabilistic model of the function being optimized and then leverages this model to decide where next to evaluate the function. Other methods like gradient descent and Hessian approximations use local information while Bayesian optimization incorporates information from all previous evaluations of the function. When optimizing a machine learning model, evaluating the function entails running and training the model. The time spent by Bayesian optimization in picking the next model is significantly less than the time required to train and run the model. Bayesian optimization is worthwhile if this trade-off of spending more time to pick better models, reduces the number of models that need to be run.

2 METHODS

To test the different hyperparameter optimization methods on a bioinformatics application we used data from the 1000 Genomes project. We used a subset of the available data to run initial tests of the methods, and then applied them to a larger set of the data. This allowed us to explore the biological implications of the results that were generated using the optimal hyperparameters.

2.1 Data Pre-processing and Sampling

We downloaded the structural variation (SV) genotypes for chromosome 22 for the Yoruba (YRI) population from the 1000 Genomes project [17]. We applied a minor allele frequency cutoff of 5% to the genotypes. For the quantitative trait we used the gene expression data for chromosome 22 from the gEUVADIS project for the YRI population [9]. We used gene based quantile normalization to transform the data into the standard normal distribution.

In order to demonstrate the application of hyperparameter tuning to eQTL mapping, we applied two eQTL analysis models by first sampling a human eQTL dataset and then conducting a final analysis on the full dataset. Sampling of the eQTL datasets was done through randomly sampling a subset of individuals, genetic variants, and genes from the original data from human chromosome 22 on YRI. Groups were chosen from a range of 75 to 150 structural variants and from a range of 75 to 250 genes for a total of 20 different group sizes. Each of these 20 different groups were sampled at random without any repeats ten times to ensure that any outliers would not skew the overall results.

2.2 Machine Learning Methods for eQTL Analysis

As illustrated in Figure 1, a set of samples in a population or cohort is usually assessed for their genotypes of genetic variants, and the expression profiles of genes in the same individuals in eQTL analysis. The genotypes can be categorized by microarrays or DNA sequencing, while gene expression profiles can be quantified by gene expression arrays or mRNA sequencing.

A linear regression model is typically used for eQTL analysis in a machine learning modeling setting. Here, X and Y are the input data, representing the matrix of features (or genotypes of genetic variants) and the matrix of labels (or gene expression traits) respectively. Note that in such modeling, the two data matrices should be organized in a way that the samples correspond to each other in X and Y. The objective of such a linear model is to find a coefficient matrix B that would convert the feature matrix X to label matrix, with some white noise term E. Specifically, X is an $n \times J$ matrix, where each row contains the measurements of the J genetic variants of the corresponding individual, and each column contains n observations for one genetic variant. Y is an $n \times K$ matrix, where each row contains the quantitative profiles of K genes in that individual, and each column contains n observations for one gene. $B_{J \times K}$ is the association coefficient matrix denoting the connection strengths between traits and genetic variants and E is a Gaussian white-noise term with constant variance σ^2. The coefficient matrix B represents the association value between every genetic variant and each gene.

$$Y = BX + E$$

Genomic data is usually high dimensional, i.e., the number of genetic variants or genes is significantly larger than the sample size ($J \gg n$ and $K \gg n$). Therefore, sparse learning models with regularizations fit well with eQTL analysis, where B is sparse and most items are regularized to zeros. Any non-zero value in B indicates that the genetic variant is associated with the corresponding gene, with a weight determined by the value. A widely-used sparse learning method is Least Absolute Shrinkage and Selection Operator (Lasso). Lasso achieves sparse feature selection within a linear model by adding an l_1 term to the objective function (Equation 1), which is the convex surrogate of l_0 penalty. Lasso estimated B is sparse, which means only a small number of positions in B will be nonzero.

$$\min_{\beta} \quad \|Y - XB\|_F^2 + \lambda \|\beta\|_1. \tag{1}$$

The classical Lasso method actually does not use any shared information between tasks. Variants of Lasso, such as multitask Lasso models, fit well with modeling eQTL analysis in which multiple genes are simultaneously considered [?]. A multitask Lasso model assumes a small common subset of features among all tasks, this is done by adding an $l_{2,1}$ term, which makes B share rows of zeros.

In reality, the genotypes of different genetic variants may be highly correlated due to inheritance patterns and shared ancestry, and the expressions of multiple genes can be highly correlated due

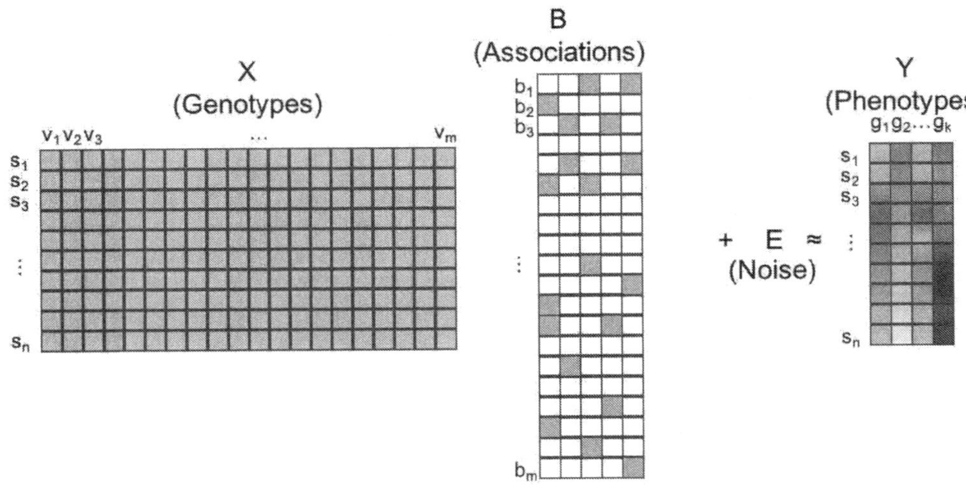

Figure 1: An Illustration of Machine Learning Models for eQTL Analysis.

to co-regulation or co-location in pathways. Therefore, a multitask Lasso model for eQTL analysis can be further improved to incorporate these correlations in the data [4? ? ? ? ? ? ? ?].

Particularly, a two-graph guided multitask Lasso (MtLasso2G) was developed for eQTL analysis[4] with the aim of considering correlations in both features and labels. MtLasso2G achieves this by adding two regularization terms on a graph for the features and a graph for the labels respectively (Equation 2). Specifically, MtLasso2G starts with taking input of the genotypes as the feature matrix X and gene expressions as the label matrix Y. It then uses two graphs G_1 on the labels and G_2 on the features to capture the relationships among labels and features respectively. MtLasso2G model then takes the input matrices X and Y, and the two graphs G_1 and G_2, and generates results in terms of a subset of correlated features that are associated with an interactive subset of labels. Note that the two graphs can be incorporated into MtLasso2G are flexible, and they could be correlation graphs or known pathways or biological networks.

MtLasso2G learns the model by minimizing the following objective function:

$$\min_{\beta} \quad ||Y - XB||_F^2 + \lambda||\beta||_1$$
$$+\gamma_1 \sum_{e_{m,l} \in E_1} w(e_{m,l}) \sum_{j=1}^{J} |b_{jm} - Sign(r_{m,l})b_{jl}| \tag{2}$$
$$+\gamma_2 \sum_{e_{f,g} \in E_2} w(e_{f,g}) \sum_{k=1}^{K} |b_{fk} - Sign(r_{f,g})b_{gk}|.$$

Here, graph $G_1 = (V_1, E_1)$ is a graph that represents the relationships among gene expression profiles. $w(e_{m,l})$ is a weight assigned to the edge $e_{m,l}$ in graph G_1 and $r_{m,l}$ is the correlation between y^m and y^l. Graph $G_2 = (V_2, E_2)$ is a graph that represents the correlation among genetic variants. V_2 is the set of vertices representing genetic variants, and E_2 is the set of edges representing the correlation among these variants. $w(e_{f,g})$ is a weight assigned to the edge $e_{m,l}$ in graph G_2 and $r_{f,g}$ is the correlation between y^f and y^g.

The optimization problem in Equation 2 can be solved by a coordinate-descent algorithm as described in [2]. The results of MtLasso2G depends on three hyperparameters, λ, γ_1, and γ_2. Therefore, we need to tune these three hyperparameters when we apply MtLasso2G to any data set.

2.3 Hyperparameter Optimization

We applied three hyperparameter optimization methods, grid search, random search and Bayesian optimization to MtLasso2G using the sampled datasets with various sizes as inputs. The grid search was implemented with three nested loops, one for each hyperparameter. Both the random search and the Bayesian optimization were run using the Spearmint package[14]. Spearmint is available on GitHub, and provides easy methods for random search and Bayesian optimization. Spearmint can be applied to machine learning applications that are written in either Python and Matlab. It allows users to run the optimizations, and to run them in parallel. Users can write their own custom drivers for their system to execute parallel implementations. Spearmint comes with a local driver, and one for the Sun Grid Compute Engine, and writing drivers for different compute environments is relatively simple. To create an equal comparison between the methods, each was allowed to run for 320 iterations. For each dataset, we conducted 3-fold cross validation to learn the hyperparameters. There are three hyperparameters to be learned in the MtLasso2G model, which are λ, γ_1 and γ_2 in Equation 2. The set of hyperparameters that produced the lowest cross validation error was picked to use for the comparison.

3 RESULTS

3.1 Comparison of Optimization Strategies on Sampling Datasets

We evaluated the three optimization strategies on the randomly sampled datasets based on the pre-processed SV genotypes and gene expression quantifications. We assessed their performances using two metrics, the cross validation error and the number of eQTLs identified, for the three strategies. The overall cross validation error varied by each of the three strategies chosen, with the Bayesian Spearmint having the lowest average error followed by grid search and random search respectively (Figure 2(a), Table 2). The lowest scores were observed for all three methods when looking at groups that had the largest number of genes and structural variants, while the largest scores were seen for the smallest number of genes and structural variants tested. This observation suggested that the MtLasso2G model worked well when the input data is sparse, agreeing with the sparsity assumption of this model.

The number of eQTLs varied by group size although no overall trend could be established from the number of genes and SVs examined (Figure 2(b)). Noticeable dispersion in the number of eQTLs identified was irrespective of method chosen. However, when looking at all SVs and genes from chromosome 22 where the random method performed poorly for identifying eQTLs. Bayesian optimization and Grid Search performed relatively well with Grid Search finding less SVs but still influenced a similar number of genes as the Bayesian Spearmint approach.

Hence, we concluded Spearmint gave us the best results on the sampling sets for eQTL analysis. With that Bayesian hyperparameter optimization implemented by Spearmint outperforms the other two methods for comparison, we therefore chose the Bayesian optimization strategy using Spearmint to analyze the full data.

3.2 SV eQTL Analysis on the Full Dataset

To illustrate the application of our methods to a typical eQTL dataset, we applied Bayesian optimization (i.e. the Bayesian Spearmint algorithm) to MtLasso2G using SV genotypes and gene expression quantifications on chromosome 22 of the YRI population[9, 13]. There were 177 SVs, and 633 genes for 86 samples in the dataset after pre-processing. We chose the hyperparameters that minimized the cross validation error for the Bayesian Spearmint strategy, and used them to perform the eQTL analysis for all three methods.

The number of eQTL associations and genes identified were similar for both Grid Search and Bayesian Spearmint (Figure 3). The random search results were surprisingly even poorer with regard to the observed behavior in the randomly sampling sets in Section 3.1. This observation further confirmed that random hyperparameter optimization didn't perform well comparing with other methods such as Grid Search or Bayesian Spearmint (Figure 3). We observed that there were quite some overlapping between results from Grid Search and Spearmint, which confirmed that these two strategies replicated each other and should capture real signals in SV eQTL analysis on the dataset. Spearmint identified more SV eQTLs as compared to Grid Search. Therefore, Spearmint were shown to outperform the other two methods in comparision, and we chose Spearmint over the other two methods for generating the final results.

With the Spearmint strategy, we identified 124 SV eQTL associations between 50 SVs and 68 genes. These genes whose expressions are identified to be affected by SVs, have important biomedical implications. Of these genes affected by SVs, 9 belonged to the immunoglobulin lambda variable cluster, and 3 belonged to the immunoglobulin constant cluster. The immunoglobulin molecules, also known as antibodies, are an integral part of the immune system. The are made up of light chains and heavy chains. There are two different types of light chains λ and κ, each is found on a different chromosome. The λ light chain is found on chromosome 22, and it is produced by the *IGLC* genes and *IGLV* genes[6].

Other noteworthy cluster included members of the Apolipoprotein L which had 9 eQTLs between the two genes identified (*APOL*1 and *APOL*2). The Apolipoprotein L family primary and first discovered role was in lipid transport[5]. Other roles were slowly discover with *APOL*1 having a diverse roles such as autophagic cell death[20], and apoptosis in cancer cells[12]. *APOL*1 and *APOL*2 have also been linked to upregulation in patients suffering from schizophrenia[18].

We used Enrichr[3, 8] to conduct an gene ontology enrichment analysis for the eQTL genes from the Spearmint results. The top 10 gene ontology terms all involved four genes, *GGT*1, *GGT*2, *GGTLC*2, and *GGTP*3 1. Each of these genes was associated with SV *UW_VH*_8052. Using the eQTL results and the correlation network from the gene expression matrix we constructed a network represented in Figure 4. This network view showed that these genes affected by one SV, might be co-regulated as their gene expressions are highly correlated. Hence, this observation confirmed that our MtLasso2G model can capture the underlining network structure whiling performing eQTL analysis. Each of the genes involved in as affected by SV *UW_VH*_8052 showed a similar pattern of expression as seen in Figure 5. We used the USCS Genome Browser[7] to examine how the genes and the SV *UW_VH*_8052 were arranged, and found that the genes were located a considerable distance from the structural variant (Figure 6). Such observation showed that SVs could not only affect gene expression directly or in close distance, but also bring about distal impact on genes. When we examined functional elements near the SV, we found that the SV overlapped both a DNAse hypersensitivity peak cluster, and a transcription factor binding site for FOXA1 (Figure 7). The cluster included 33 of 95 potential items, and had a score of 676 of 1000. This suggests that *UW_VH*_8052 could have the impact we saw through an intermediate gene or genes.

4 CONCLUSIONS

When using machine learning methods for eQTL analysis, finding hyperparameters that produce good results should be an important and integral part of the process. The number of actual eQTLs differed tremendously between hyperparameter combinations. If a researcher was relying on manual tuning, it is possible that they could never find the hyperparameter combinations that produced lower cross validation error values. Some form of automatic hyperparameter tuning is required to better explore the entire range of possible hyperparameter values. This also increases the level of

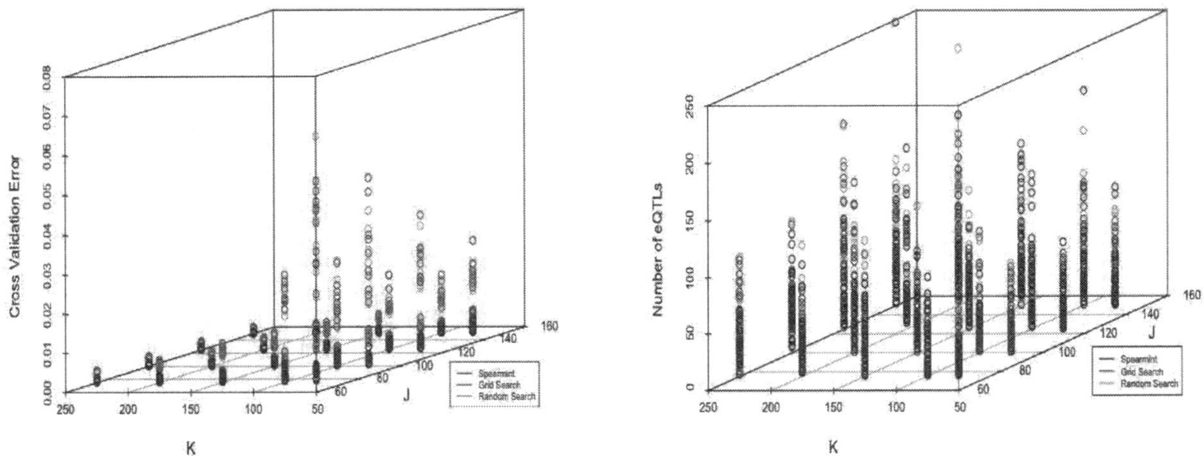

(a) (b)

Figure 2: Results for Grid Search, Random Search, and Bayesian Spearmint on 10 randomly sampled datasets with the number of SVs J=[75,100,125,150] and the number of genes K=[75,100,150,200,250]. (a) CV errors; (b) The number of eQTL associations.

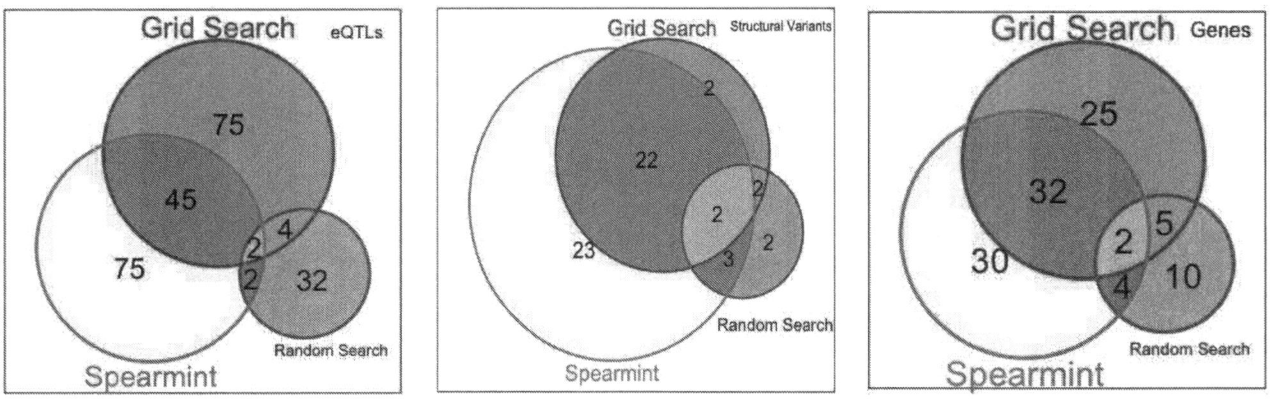

(a) (b) (c)

Figure 3: Results for Grid Search, Random Search, and Bayesian Spearmint. (a) The number of SV-gene eQTL associations; (b) The number of SVs; (c) The number of genes.

reproducibility of the analysis. Biological conclusions are drawn from machine learning results, and if the wrong hyperparameter values are chosen, the wrong conclusions may be reached.

Even when using these automatic hyperparameter tuning methods human intuition and domain knowledge is still required. The range of the potential hyperparameters has to be specified, which creates a space for human judgment and error. One drawback in using these optimization methods is the time costs. Depending on the size of the data, a single eQTL analysis can take hours or even days, which makes running the multiple iterations required for hyperparameter optimization very time consuming. However given the dependence of the results on choosing the correct set of hyperparameters this trade off may be worth the time cost. Bayesian optimization found the best hyperparameter combinations in the same amount of time, making it the more attractive option.

In this paper we applied three optimization methods to one machine learning based method for eQTL analysis, but Bayesian optimization can also be applied to other machine learning eQTL

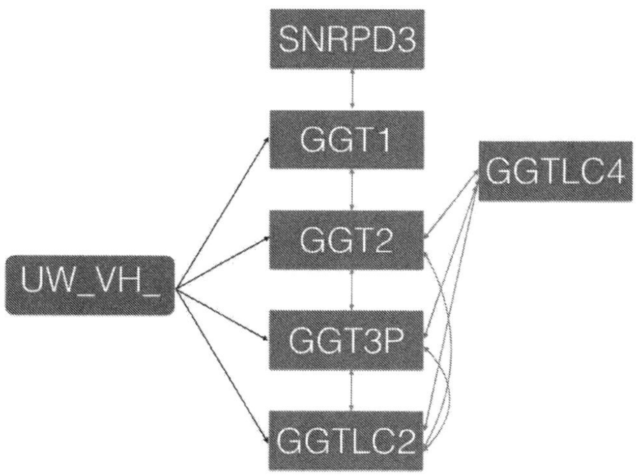

Figure 4: An illustration of the eQTL Network with SV eQTL associations and gene correlations. eQTL associations are represented by black arrows, and gene correlations are in purple.

analysis models, or any hyperparameter dependent method. Using Bayesian optimization of hyperparameters we were able to produce better results and in the same amount of time compared to other optimization methods. Our study is focused on eQTL analysis, but our strategy should be applied to many other applications in analyzing genomics data and many other types of data.

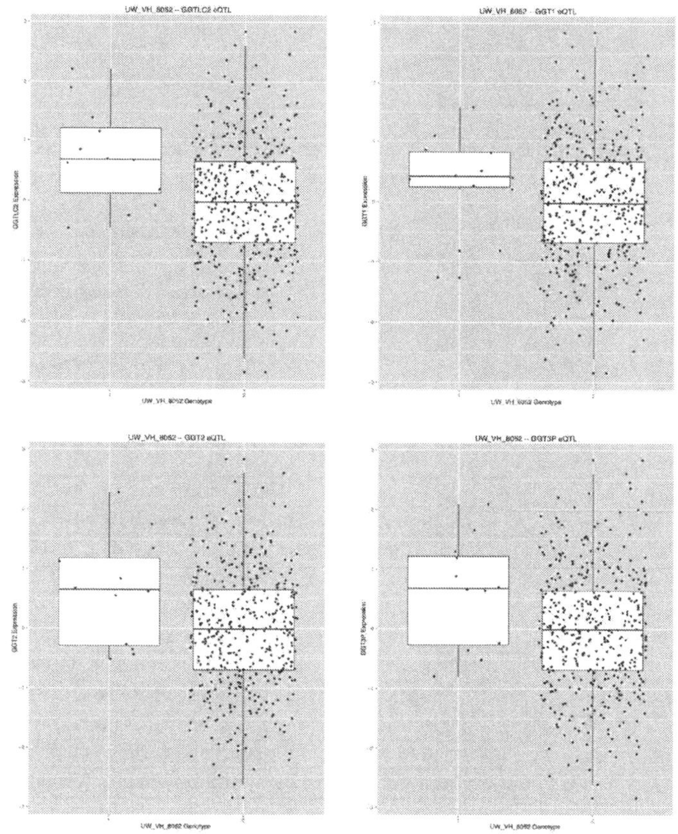

Figure 5: SV-eQTL association boxplots of the SV *UW_VH_*8052 and four associated genes *GGTLC*2, *GGT*1, *GGT*2, and *GGTP*3 respectively. In each boxplot, X axis represents the genotypes of the SV *UW_VH_*8052, and Y axis denotes the expression of each gene affected by this SV.

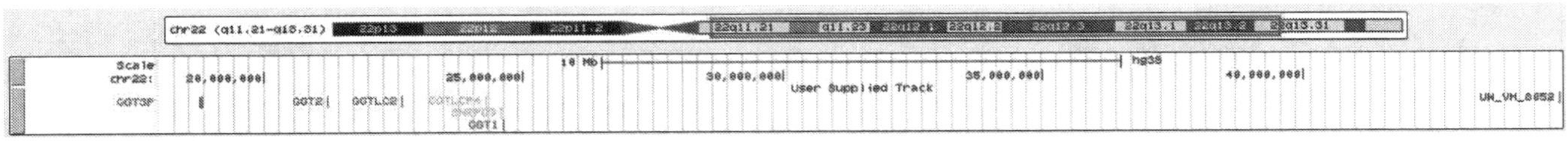

Figure 6: The location of the genes in relationship to a SV $UW_V H_8052$. The genes that are involved in an eQTL with the SV are in red, and those that are found in the correlation network with the eQTL genes are in green.

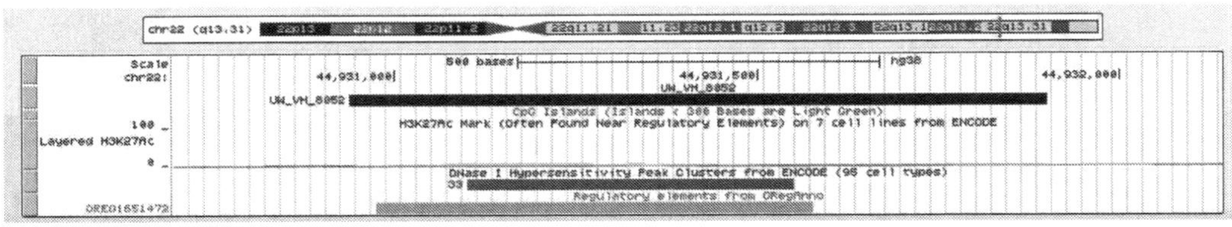

Figure 7: UW_VH_8052 **overlaps with both a DNAse hypersensitivity peak cluster, and a transcription factor binding site.**

GO Term	Adjusted p-value	Genes
leukotriene biosynthetic process (GO:0019370)	0.0003702	GGTLC2 GGT3P GGT1 GGT2
glutathione biosynthetic process (GO:0006750)	0.001055	GGT3P GGT1 GGT2
nonribosomal peptide biosynthetic process (GO:0019184)	0.001055	GGT3P GGT1 GGT2
leukotriene metabolic process (GO:0006691)	0.0009364	GGTLC2 GGT3P GGT1 GGT2
icosanoid biosynthetic process (GO:0046456)	0.0009364	GGTLC2 GGT3P GGT1 GGT2
fatty acid derivative biosynthetic process (GO:1901570)	0.0009364	GGTLC2 GGT3P GGT1 GGT2
peptide biosynthetic process (GO:0043043)	0.002410	GGT3P GGT1 GGT2
glutathione metabolic process (GO:0006749)	0.001055	GGTLC2 GGT3P GGT1 GGT2
unsaturated fatty acid biosynthetic process (GO:0006636)	0.001055	GGTLC2 GGT3P GGT1 GGT2
glutathionederivative biosynthetic process (GO:1901687)	0.003229	GGT1 GSTT2B GGT2

Table 1: Gene Ontology Results.

J	K	N	Minimum CV Error			Maximum eQTLs		
			Random	Grid	Spearmint	Random	Grid	Spearmint
75	75	20	0.002263875	0.002178426	0.000672	87	113	115
75	100	20	0.001476481	0.001407143	0.000463	70	64	88
75	150	20	0.0007904175	0.0007979744	0.000295	82	71	68
75	200	20	0.000549637	0.0005207614	0.000239	57	61	80
75	250	20	0.0005124437	0.0004612196	0.00017	68	70	55
100	75	20	0.001674905	0.001679244	0.000504	79	76	71
100	100	20	0.0009704443	0.000941896	0.000274	99	102	107
100	150	20	0.0005582393	0.0005616887	0.000272	68	71	62
100	200	20	0.000434874	0.0003673215	0.000172	97	89	85
100	250	20	0.0004326509	0.0003785027	0.000141	59	60	96
125	75	20	0.001399957	0.001351829	0.000416	53	59	77
125	100	20	0.0009839088	0.0008747361	0.00029	72	136	129
125	150	20	0.0005089936	0.0004844796	0.000163	122	89	71
125	200	20	0.000374403	0.0003640498	0.000138	90	97	159
125	250	20	0.0002623705	0.0002521929	9.8e-05	94	94	84
150	75	20	0.001236504	0.001152514	0.00038	82	98	104
150	100	20	0.0007058939	0.000666812	0.000271	153	108	188
150	150	20	0.0003559717	0.0003427179	0.000155	132	142	127
150	200	20	0.0003141803	0.0003265179	0.000108	225	114	142
150	250	20	0.0002598214	0.0002243206	8.6e-05	81	82	84
75	75	30	0.008319043	0.008541045000000001	0.0023	77	52	32
75	100	30	0.00488367	0.00492698	0.001388	58	57	59
75	150	30	0.002400051	0.002410782	0.000635	89	82	82
75	200	30	0.001395612	0.001423994	0.00043	87	79	40
75	250	30	0.001029267	0.001017038	0.000339	106	99	103
100	75	30	0.005856966	0.006067522	0.001468	53	38	42
100	100	30	0.002954839	0.003130248	0.000913	55	79	41
100	150	30	0.001654421	0.001673915	0.000526	129	90	86
100	200	30	0.001125418	0.001151942	0.000358	107	130	150
100	250	30	0.0007019076	0.0007021751	0.000248	116	105	71
125	75	30	0.0052363	0.005479655	0.001338	61	67	46
125	100	30	0.002647034	0.002721126	0.000723	71	61	69
125	150	30	0.001454186	0.001431071	0.000391	101	91	63
125	200	30	0.0007954465	0.0007794778	0.00028	142	123	96
125	250	30	0.0005960487	0.0005992738	0.000215	147	143	133
150	75	30	0.003855019	0.004086521	0.001042	84	74	22
150	100	30	0.00233417	0.002411401	0.000682	116	104	59
150	150	30	0.001185388	0.001179248	0.000372	133	122	92
150	200	30	0.0006567205	0.0006540763	0.000238	166	150	167
150	250	30	0.0005173099	0.0005031553	0.000154	128	118	248
75	75	40	0.004142482	0.02269779	0.003245	19	19	36
75	100	40	0.01703015	0.01863552	0.002967	58	59	73
75	150	40	0.006631388	0.007121909	0.001494	120	108	33
75	200	40	0.003403434	0.003544673	0.001105	116	76	99
75	250	40	0.00241831	0.002448667	0.000738	68	75	57
100	75	40	0.01590267	0.01645523	0.002772	38	51	23
100	100	40	0.009850739000000001	0.01015976	0.00207	69	41	43
100	150	40	0.004738836	0.004956501	0.001216	65	54	51
100	200	40	0.00278387	0.002796554	0.00084	112	108	81
100	250	40	0.001847186	0.001858016	0.000465	114	113	68
125	75	40	0.01582753	0.01739386	0.002144	52	63	14
125	100	40	0.009104635	0.01002368	0.001623	30	60	51
125	150	40	0.003997842	0.004210716	0.000694	50	90	63
125	200	40	0.002244411	0.002327737	0.000559	93	96	119
125	250	40	0.001484169	0.001542031	0.000396	178	180	112
150	75	40	0.01088182	0.0117818	0.001731	41	40	43
150	100	40	0.006183828	0.006636154	0.001468	60	57	43
150	150	40	0.003105559	0.003270112	0.000816	128	132	53
150	200	40	0.001884003	0.00189039	0.00053	111	119	120
150	250	40	0.001363623	0.001376554	0.000364	91	93	63

Table 2: CV errors and the number of eQTLs identfied for grid, random and Bayesian optimizations on sampling datasets.Here, J represents the number of SVs, K represents the number of genes, and N is the sample size.

REFERENCES

[1] J. Bergstra and Y. Bengio. Random Search for Hyper-parameter Optimization. *J. Mach. Learn. Res.*, 13:281–305, Feb. 2012.

[2] E. J. Candes, M. B. Wakin, and S. P. Boyd. Enhancing sparsity by reweighted ??? 1 minimization. *Journal of Fourier analysis and applications*, 14(5-6):877–905, 2008.

[3] E. Y. Chen, C. M. Tan, Y. Kou, Q. Duan, Z. Wang, G. V. Meirelles, N. R. Clark, and A. Ma???ayan. Enrichr: interactive and collaborative html5 gene list enrichment analysis tool. *BMC bioinformatics*, 14(1):128, 2013.

[4] X. Chen, X. Shi, X. Xu, Z. Wang, R. Mills, C. Lee, and J. Xu. A two-graph guided multi-task lasso approach for eqtl mapping. In *International Conference on Artificial Intelligence and Statistics*, pages 208–217, 2012.

[5] P. Duchateau, C. Pullinger, M. Cho, C. Eng, and J. Kane. Apolipoprotein l gene family: tissue-specific expression, splicing, promoter regions; discovery of a new gene. *Journal of Lipid Research*, 42(4):620–630, 2001.

[6] K. Kawasaki, S. Minoshima, E. Nakato, K. Shibuya, A. Shintani, J. L. Schmeits, J. Wang, and N. Shimizu. One-megabase sequence analysis of the human immunoglobulin lambda gene locus. *Genome Research*, 7(3):250–261, 1997.

[7] W. J. Kent, C. W. Sugnet, T. S. Furey, K. M. Roskin, T. H. Pringle, A. M. Zahler, and D. Haussler. The human genome browser at ucsc. *Genome research*, 12(6):996–1006, 2002.

[8] M. V. Kuleshov, M. R. Jones, A. D. Rouillard, N. F. Fernandez, Q. Duan, Z. Wang, S. Koplev, S. L. Jenkins, K. M. Jagodnik, A. Lachmann, et al. Enrichr: a comprehensive gene set enrichment analysis web server 2016 update. *Nucleic acids research*, page gkw377, 2016.

[9] T. Lappalainen, M. Sammeth, M. R. Friedländer, P. AC???t Hoen, J. Monlong, M. A. Rivas, M. Gonzàlez-Porta, N. Kurbatova, T. Griebel, P. G. Ferreira, et al. Transcriptome and genome sequencing uncovers functional variation in humans. *Nature*, 501(7468):506–511, 2013.

[10] Q. Li, J.-H. Seo, B. Stranger, A. McKenna, I. Pe??????er, T. LaFramboise, M. Brown, S. Tyekucheva, and M. L. Freedman. Integrative eqtl-based analyses reveal the biology of breast cancer risk loci. *Cell*, 152(3):633–641, 2013.

[11] L. Liang, N. Morar, A. L. Dixon, G. M. Lathrop, G. R. Abecasis, M. F. Moffatt, and W. O. Cookson. A cross-platform analysis of 14,177 expression quantitative trait loci derived from lymphoblastoid cell lines. *Genome research*, 23(4):716–726, 2013.

[12] Z. Liu, H. Lu, Z. Jiang, A. Pastuszyn, and C.-a. A. Hu. Apolipoprotein l6, a novel proapoptotic bcl-2 homology 3-only protein, induces mitochondria-mediated apoptosis in cancer cells. *Molecular Cancer Research*, 3(1):21–31, 2005.

[13] R. E. Mills, K. Walter, C. Stewart, R. E. Handsaker, K. Chen, C. Alkan, A. Abyzov, S. C. Yoon, K. Ye, R. K. Cheetham, et al. Mapping copy number variation by population-scale genome sequencing. *Nature*, 470(7332):59–65, 2011.

[14] J. Snoek, H. Larochelle, and R. P. Adams. Practical Bayesian Optimization of Machine Learning Algorithms. *arXiv:1206.2944 [cs, stat]*, June 2012. arXiv: 1206.2944.

[15] B. E. Stranger, M. S. Forrest, A. G. Clark, M. J. Minichiello, S. Deutsch, R. Lyle, S. Hunt, B. Kahl, S. E. Antonarakis, S. Tavaré, et al. Genome-wide associations of gene expression variation in humans. *PLoS genetics*, 1(6):e78, 2005.

[16] B. E. Stranger, M. S. Forrest, M. Dunning, C. E. Ingle, C. Beazley, N. Thorne, R. Redon, C. P. Bird, A. De Grassi, C. Lee, et al. Relative impact of nucleotide and copy number variation on gene expression phenotypes. *Science*, 315(5813):848–853, 2007.

[17] P. H. Sudmant, T. Rausch, E. J. Gardner, R. E. Handsaker, A. Abyzov, J. Huddleston, Y. Zhang, K. Ye, G. Jun, M. H.-Y. Fritz, et al. An integrated map of structural variation in 2,504 human genomes. *Nature*, 526(7571):75–81, 2015.

[18] S. Takahashi, Y. Cui, Y. Han, J. Fagerness, B. Galloway, Y. Shen, and M. T. ?Tsuang. Association of snps and haplotypes in apol1, 2 and 4 with schizophrenia. schizophrenia research. *Journal of Schizophrenia Research*, 104(0):153–164, 2008.

[19] L. Tian, A. Quitadamo, F. Lin, and X. Shi. Methods for population-based eqtl analysis in human genetics. *Tsinghua Science and Technology*, 19(6):624–634, 2014.

[20] G. Wan, S. Zhaorigetu, Z. Liu, R. Kaini, Z. Jiang, and C. Hu. Apolipoprotein l1, a novel bcl-2 homology domain 3-only lipid-binding protein, induces autophagic cell death. *Journal of Biological Chemistry*, 283(31):21540–21549, 2008.

[21] L. Zhang and S. Kim. Learning gene networks under snp perturbations using eqtl datasets. *PLoS computational biology*, 10(2):e1003420, 2014.

Coal-Miner: A Statistical Method for GWA Studies of Quantitative Traits with Complex Evolutionary Origins

Hussein A. Hejase
Department of Computer Science and Engineering
Michigan State University
East Lansing, Michigan 48824
hijazihu@msu.edu

Natalie Vande Pol
Department of Plant, Soil and Microbial Sciences
Michigan State University
East Lansing, Michigan 48824
vandepo7@msu.edu

Gregory M. Bonito
Department of Plant, Soil and Microbial Sciences
Michigan State University
East Lansing, Michigan 48824
bonito@msu.edu

Patrick P. Edger
Department of Horticulture
Michigan State University
East Lansing, Michigan 48824
edgerpat@msu.edu

Kevin J. Liu*
Department of Computer Science and Engineering
Michigan State University
East Lansing, Michigan 48824
kjl@msu.edu

ABSTRACT

Association mapping (AM) methods are used in genome-wide association (GWA) studies to test for statistically significant associations between genotypic and phenotypic data. The genotypic and phenotypic data share common evolutionary origins – namely, the evolutionary history of sampled organisms – introducing covariance which must be distinguished from the covariance due to biological function that is of primary interest in GWA studies. A variety of methods have been introduced to perform AM while accounting for sample relatedness. However, the state of the art predominantly utilizes the simplifying assumption that sample relatedness is effectively fixed across the genome. In contrast, population genetic theory and empirical studies have shown that sample relatedness can vary greatly across different loci within a genome. This phenomenon – referred to as local genealogical variation – is commonly encountered in many genomic datasets. New AM methods are needed to better account for local variation in sample relatedness within genomes.

We address this gap by introducing Coal-Miner, a new statistical AM method. The Coal-Miner algorithm takes the form of a methodological pipeline. The initial stages of Coal-Miner seek to detect candidate loci, or loci which contain putatively associated markers. Subsequent stages of Coal-Miner perform test for association using a linear mixed model with multiple effects which account for sample relatedness locally within candidate loci and globally across the entire genome. Using synthetic and empirical datasets, we compare the statistical power and type I error control of Coal-Miner against state-of-the-art AM methods. The simulation conditions reflect a variety of genomic architectures for complex traits and incorporate a range of evolutionary scenarios, each with different evolutionary processes that can generate local genealogical variation. Across the datasets in our study, we find that Coal-Miner consistently offers comparable or typically better statistical power and type I error control compared to the state-of-the-art methods.

CCS CONCEPTS

•**Applied computing** → *Computational genomics; Computational biology; Molecular sequence analysis; Molecular evolution; Computational genomics; Systems biology; Bioinformatics; Population genetics;*

KEYWORDS

genome wide association study; GWAS; population stratification; genealogy; coalescent; Arabidopsis

1 INTRODUCTION

Genome-wide association (GWA) studies aim to pinpoint loci with genetic contributions to a phenotype by uncovering significant statistical associations between genomic markers and a phenotypic trait under study. We refer to the computational methods used in a GWA analysis as association mapping (AM) methods. Among the most widely studied organisms in GWA studies are natural human populations and laboratory strains of house mouse. Recently, GWA approaches have been applied to natural populations of other organisms sampled from across the Tree of Life. For example, the 1001 Genomes Consortium study [7] published whole genome sequences for over a thousand samples from globally distributed *Arabidopsis* populations. In combination with phenotypic data, the genomic sequence data was used in a GWA analysis to pinpoint genomic loci involved in flowering time at two different temperatures. Other recent GWA studies such as the study of Porter et al. [24] have focused on bacteria and other microbes (see [6] for a review of relevant literature).

Regardless of sampling strategy – from one or more closely related populations involving a single species to multiple populations from divergent species – it is well understood that sample relatedness can be a confounding factor in GWA analyses unless

*To whom correspondence should be addressed.

This work is licensed under a Creative Commons Attribution-NonCommercial-ShareAlike International 4.0 License.

ACM-BCB'17, August 20-23, 2017, Boston, MA, USA.
© 2017 Copyright held by the owner/author(s).
978-1-4503-4722-8/17/08.
DOI: http://dx.doi.org/10.1145/3107411.3107490

properly accounted for. Intuitively, the genotypes and phenotypes of present-day samples reflect their shared evolutionary history, or phylogeny. For this reason, covariance due to a functional relationship between genotypic markers and a phenotypic character must be distinguished from shared covariance due to common evolutionary origins. A number of AM methods have been developed to address this issue. EIGENSTRAT [26] is a popular AM method which accounts for sample relatedness as a fixed effect. Other statistical AM methods have utilized linear mixed models (LMMs) to capture sample relatedness using random effects; these include EMMAX [17] and GEMMA [31]. Local variation in functional covariance across the genome is a crucial signature that AM methods use to uncover putatively associated markers. In contrast, virtually all of the most widely used state-of-the-art AM methods assume that covariance due to sample relatedness does not vary appreciably across the genome. Sample relatedness is therefore evaluated "globally" across the genome, eliding over "local" genealogical variation across loci. The latter has been observed by many comparative genomic and phylogenomic studies (see [10] for a review of relevant literature). It is now well understood that local genealogical variation within genomes is pervasive across a range of evolutionary divergence – from structured populations within a single species to multiple species at various scales up to the Tree of Life, the evolutionary history of all living organisms on Earth. The evolutionary processes that can contribute to local genealogical variation include genetic drift and incomplete lineage sorting, recombination, gene flow, positive selection, and the combination of all of these processes (and others) [10].

Computational approaches for detecting local genealogical variation are broadly characterized by their modeling assumptions. One class of methods makes use of the Four-Gamete Test [14], which requires the simplifying assumption that sequence evolution can be described by the infinite sites model. The LRScan algorithm [29] belongs to this class of methods. Another class consists of parametric methods that make use of finite-sites models of sequence evolution. These include methods such as RecHMM [30]. More recently, coalescent-based methods such as PhyloNet-HMM [19] have been developed to infer local coalescent histories and explicitly ascribe local genealogical variation to different evolutionary processes.

Building upon these insights, we previously developed Coal-Map [12], an AM method that utilizes a fixed effects model to account for global sample relatedness and, depending upon whether the test marker is located within a locus containing putatively associated markers, local sample relatedness as well. The latter condition is evaluated using model selection criteria. Coal-Map requires local-phylogeny-switching breakpoints as input. We conducted a simulation study which demonstrated that Coal-Map's statistical power and type I error control was comparable or better than other state-of-the-art methods that account for global sample relatedness using fixed effects.

2 METHODS

2.1 Overview of Coal-Miner algorithm

In this study, we introduce Coal-Miner, a new statistical AM method which accounts for local variation of sample relatedness across genomic sequences as well as global sample relatedness. Coal-Miner's contributions relative to the state of the art (including Coal-Map) consist of the following. First, Coal-Miner utilizes an LMM with multiple effects to explicitly capture the genomic architecture of a phenotype, where both genotypic and phenotypic characters are the product of a complex evolutionary history which can cause sample relatedness to vary locally across genomic loci. The LMM captures global sample relatedness as a random effect, in contrast to the fixed-effect approach used by Coal-Map. Second, the pipeline-based design of Coal-Miner incorporates an intermediate stage to infer "candidate loci" for use in the new LMM, where a candidate locus is a locus that is inferred to contain one or more putatively associated SNPs.

We begin by introducing the high-level design of Coal-Miner. The input to the Coal-Miner algorithm consists of: (1) an $n \times k$ multi-locus sequence data matrix $\boldsymbol{X}$, (2) an $n \times 1$ vector $\boldsymbol{y}$ which represents a phenotypic character, and (3) ℓ^*, the number of candidate loci used during analysis. The output consists of an association score for each site $\boldsymbol{x} \in \boldsymbol{X}$.

Coal-Miner's statistical model captures the relationship between genotypic data $\boldsymbol{X}$ and the phenotypic character $\boldsymbol{y}$ in the form of a linear mixed model (LMM). The LMM incorporates multiple effects to capture the phenotypic contributions of and local genealogical variation among multiple candidate loci. A candidate locus is represented by a fixed effect, and a random effect is included to capture global sample relatedness as measured across all loci in $\boldsymbol{X}$. Ideally, the set of candidate loci identified during a Coal-Miner analysis is identical to the set of causal loci (i.e., loci containing causal SNPs) for the trait under study; in practice, the set of candidate loci are inferred as part of the Coal-Miner algorithm, which we discuss in greater detail below. The LMM takes the following form (based on the notation of Zhou and Stephens [31]):

$$\boldsymbol{y} = \boldsymbol{W}\boldsymbol{\alpha} + \boldsymbol{x}\beta + \boldsymbol{u} + \boldsymbol{\epsilon}$$
$$\boldsymbol{u} \sim \mathrm{MVN}_n(0, \lambda\tau^{-1}\boldsymbol{K}_{\mathrm{global}})$$
$$\boldsymbol{\epsilon} \sim \mathrm{MVN}_n(0, \tau^{-1}\boldsymbol{I}_n)$$

The fixed effects are represented by c covariates in the $n \times c$ matrix $\boldsymbol{W}$, which include covariates that capture local sample relatedness within each candidate locus, the $c \times 1$ vector $\boldsymbol{\alpha}$ of corresponding coefficients, and the test SNP is represented by the $n \times 1$ vector $\boldsymbol{x}$ with effect size β. Global sample relatedness (i.e., sample relatedness as measured across all loci in the genotypic data $\boldsymbol{X}$) is specified by the $n \times n$ relatedness matrix $\boldsymbol{K}_{\mathrm{global}}$ computed using $\boldsymbol{X}$, following the approach of state-of-the-art LMM-based AM methods (e.g., GEMMA [31]). The $n \times 1$ vectors $\boldsymbol{u}$ and $\boldsymbol{\epsilon}$ represent random effects which account for global sample relatedness and residual error, respectively. Each of the two random effects follows an n-dimensional multivariate normal distribution (abbreviated "MVN") with mean 0. The random effects $\boldsymbol{u}$ have covariance $\lambda\tau^{-1}\boldsymbol{K}_{\mathrm{global}}$ and the random effects $\boldsymbol{\epsilon}$ have covariance $\tau^{-1}\boldsymbol{I}_n$, where λ is the relative ratio between the two, $\boldsymbol{I}_n$ is the $n \times n$ identity matrix, and the residual errors have variance τ^{-1}.

The design of the Coal-Miner algorithm takes the form of a methodological pipeline. We now discuss each pipeline stage in turn.

Stage one of Coal-Miner: inferring local-phylogeny-switching breakpoints. The input to the first stage of Coal-Miner is the genotypic data matrix $\boldsymbol{X}$. The output consists of a set of local-phylogeny-switching breakpoints $\boldsymbol{b}$ which partition the sites in $\boldsymbol{X}$ into loci $\{\boldsymbol{X}_i\}$, where $1 \leq i \leq \ell$ and ℓ is the number of loci. We require that $\ell^* \leq \ell$. (The ratio of ℓ^* and ℓ depends upon the genomic architecture of the trait corresponding to character $\boldsymbol{y}$.)

The general approach to address this computational problem is to infer local coalescent histories under an appropriate multi-species extension of the coalescent model [18], and then to assign breakpoints based upon gene tree discordance. Each pair of neighboring breakpoints delineates a locus for use in downstream stages of the Coal-Miner pipeline. The specific choice of model/method depends upon the relevant evolutionary processes involved in multi-locus sequence evolution, particularly regarding the source(s) of local genealogical discordance.

In this study, we use one of two different methods, depending upon assumptions about biomolecular sequence evolution. In the simulation study, the simulations make use of the infinite sites model. We therefore used the LRScan algorithm [29] to compute local-topology-switching breakpoints based upon the Four Gamete Test (FGT) [14]. In the empirical study, we did not make use of the infinite sites model and its assumptions about sequence evolution. Furthermore, multiple evolutionary processes were known to be involved in multi-locus sequence evolution, including genetic drift/incomplete lineage sorting (ILS), recombination/gene conversion, gene flow/horizontal gene transfer (HGT), and natural selection. Breakpoint inference under the corresponding extended coalescent model is suspected to be a computationally difficult problem. Existing methods for this problem (e.g., PhyloNet-HMM [19]) did not have sufficient scalability for the dataset sizes examined in our study. As a more feasible alternative, we inferred local-topology-switching breakpoints using Rec-HMM [30]. Rec-HMM performs fixed-species-phylogeny inference of local genealogies under a statistical model that combines a finite-sites substitution model and a hidden Markov model which is meant to capture intra-sequence dependence (such as arises from recombination).

Stage two of Coal-Miner: identifying candidate loci. The input to the second stage of Coal-Miner consists of the genotypic data matrix $\boldsymbol{X}$, the set of breakpoints $\boldsymbol{b}$ which partition $\boldsymbol{X}$ into loci $\{\boldsymbol{X}_i\}$, where $1 \leq i \leq \ell$ and ℓ is the number of loci, the phenotypic character $\boldsymbol{y}$, and ℓ^*, the number of candidate loci to identify. Note that the input $\boldsymbol{b}$ is an output of the preceding stage of Coal-Miner. The output is a set of candidate loci $\{\boldsymbol{X}_j^*\} \subseteq \{\boldsymbol{X}_i\}$ where $1 \leq j \leq \ell^*$.

Our general approach to this problem consists of a search among possible sets of candidate loci $\{X_j^*\}$ using optimization under a "null" version of Coal-Miner's LMM, where we do not consider a test SNP (i.e., $\beta = 0$ in Coal-Miner's LMM) and the phenotypic contributions from putatively associated SNPs in each candidate locus X_j^* is captured by covariates $\{\boldsymbol{w}_j\} \subseteq \boldsymbol{W}$. Since we compare fitted LMMs that may have varying fixed effects, our optimization criterion consists of the LMM log-likelihood $\mathcal{L}(\lambda, \tau, \boldsymbol{\alpha}, \beta) = \frac{n}{2}\log(\tau) - \frac{n}{2}\log(2\pi) - \frac{1}{2}\log|\boldsymbol{H}| - \frac{1}{2}\tau(\boldsymbol{y}-\boldsymbol{W\alpha}-\boldsymbol{x}\beta)^T\boldsymbol{H}^{-1}(\boldsymbol{y}-\boldsymbol{W\alpha}-\boldsymbol{x}\beta)$ where $\boldsymbol{H} = \lambda\boldsymbol{K}_{\text{global}} + \boldsymbol{I}_n$ (reproduced from equation (3) in [31]). Due to the computational difficulty of this optimization problem, numerical optimization procedures are typically used. We obtained estimates of λ in the range of $[10^{-5}, 1]$ using the optimization heuristic implemented in the GEMMA software library [31], which combines Brent's method [5] and the Newton-Raphson method.

For each candidate locus $\boldsymbol{X}_j^*$, local sample relatedness was evaluated using principal component analysis (PCA) [16] of $\boldsymbol{X}_j^*$ – similar to techniques that are widely used by AM methods to account for global sample relatedness as fixed effects [26]. The phenotypic contribution of candidate locus $\boldsymbol{X}_j^*$ was represented using covariates $\{\boldsymbol{w}_j\}$ which consisted of the top five principal components, where the zth principal component corresponds to the sample covariance matrix eigenvector with the zth largest eigenvalue and the number of covariates was based upon a design experiment in [12]. For added computational efficiency, we substituted the following search heuristic in place of set-based search among all possible ℓ^*-size sets of candidate loci. For each locus $\boldsymbol{X}_i$, we used MLE to fit an equivalent LMM, except that the covariates W included only the covariates $\{\boldsymbol{w}_i\}$ for locus $\boldsymbol{X}_i$ (as computed using the above PCA-based procedure). The output set of candidate loci consists of the top ℓ^* loci based upon fitted LMM likelihood.

Stage three of Coal-Miner: SNP-based association testing. The input to the third stage of Coal-Miner consists of the genotypic data matrix $\boldsymbol{X}$, the set of breakpoints $\boldsymbol{b}$ which partition $\boldsymbol{X}$ into loci $\{\boldsymbol{X}_i\}$, where $1 \leq i \leq \ell$ and ℓ is the number of loci, the phenotypic character $\boldsymbol{y}$, and the set of candidate loci $\{\boldsymbol{X}_j^*\}$. Note that the inputs $\boldsymbol{b}$ and $\{\boldsymbol{X}_j^*\}$ are outputs of stages one and two of Coal-Miner, respectively. The output of this stage is Coal-Miner's final output.

Each test SNP $\boldsymbol{x}$ is tested for association under Coal-Miner's LMM. Variation in local sample relatedness across candidate loci $\{\boldsymbol{X}_j^*\}$ is captured by covariates in $\boldsymbol{W}$: specifically, if the test SNP $\boldsymbol{x}$ is located within a candidate locus $\boldsymbol{X}_j^*$, the covariates $\boldsymbol{W}$ include a corresponding covariate $\boldsymbol{w}_j$ which consists of the top principal component from PCA applied to $\boldsymbol{X}_j^*$ (see above discussion of previous stage), and otherwise not. (Stages two and three of the Coal-Miner pipeline utilize different covariates $\boldsymbol{W}$ due to the absence or presence of a test SNP effect in their respective LMMs.) The LMM is fitted using the likelihood-based numerical optimization procedures that are also used in stage two of Coal-Miner, and the association score is computed using a likelihood ratio test of the fitted model against a null model with no SNP effect.

2.2 Simulation study

Neutral simulations of multi-locus sequence data were based upon either tree-like or non-tree-like evolutionary scenarios. The evolutionary scenarios shared a species phylogeny that we used in a prior simulation study (Supplementary Figure S1 in the Supporting Online Materials (SOM)). We used ms [13] to simulate coalescent histories (and embedded gene trees) under an extension of the coalescent model [18] which allows instantaneous unidirectional admixture (IUA) [9]. Under this model, the parameterization of the model phylogeny includes an admixture proportion γ. Appropriate choices of γ allow us to explore the impact of tree-like and non-tree-like evolution in our simulation study, where we set γ to either 0.0 or 0.5, respectively. Each replicate dataset sampled 10 independently and identically distributed loci and 1000 individuals; taxa A, B, and C were represented by 250, 250, and 500 samples, respectively. Bi-allelic sequence evolution was simulated under the infinite sites model to obtain 250 bp per locus, resulting in total sequence length of 2.5 kb per replicate dataset.

As a means to investigate the impact of the genomic architecture of phenotypes, we simulated phenotypic characters using the approach from our previous work [12]. For each synthetic multi-locus sequence dataset in the neutral simulations, we randomly selected either 10%, 20%, or 30% of loci as causal. Twenty causal SNPs were then randomly selected from causal loci such that each causal locus contained at least one causal SNP and causal SNPs had minor allele frequency between 0.1 and 0.3. Given a set of causal SNPs δ, we sampled character y under an extension of the quantitative trait model used by Long and Langley [20]. The trait value for the ith individual is represented as $y_i = \pi \sum_{j \in \delta} \frac{Q_{i,j}}{|\delta|} + (1-\pi)N(0, 0.01)$ where π specifies the ratio between the genotypic contribution and an environmental residual, Q is 1 if sample i has the derived allele at the jth causal SNP and 0 otherwise, and the environmental residual is normally distributed with mean 0 and standard deviation 0.01. Our simulations utilized a ratio π of 0.5.

Our simulation study also included non-neutral simulations that incorporated positive selection. We used msms [11] to conduct forward-time coalescent simulations of genotypic sequence evolution (in place of an otherwise equivalent neutral backward-time coalescent simulation using ms), where causal loci were evolved under deme-dependent positive selection with a finite sites mutation model and all other loci evolved neutrally (as discussed above in the neutral simulation procedure). We used a selection coefficient of $s = 0.56$, which is in line with estimates from prior studies of positive selection in natural *Mus* populations [28]. Quantitative traits were simulated using the above procedure.

The simulation study experiments involving quantitative traits with varying genomic architectures included 12 different model conditions in total. To recap, the model conditions differed in terms of the proportion of causal loci (either 10%, 20%, or 30%), model phylogeny (either tree-like or non-tree-like), and the presence or absence of positive selection. For each model condition, we repeated the simulation procedure to obtain 20 replicate datasets.

Performance evaluation. The other methods in our study consisted of Coal-Map, GEMMA, and EIGENSTRAT. We followed the procedure from [12] to obtain FGT-based local-phylogeny-switching breakpoints and run Coal-Map analyses. For consistency with the other LMM-based AM methods in our study, we ran GEMMA using an IBS kinship matrix as our measure of global sample relatedness and MLE and LRT to obtain association scores. EIGENSTRAT was run with default settings using the top ten principal components from the genotypic data matrix $\boldsymbol{X}$, following the recommendations of Price et al. [26]. Detailed software commands are listed in the SOM Appendix.

We evaluated performance based on statistical power, type I error, and AUROC. To compare AUROC, we performed DeLong *et al.* tests [8] using the Daim v. 1.1.0 package [25] in R [27]. Custom scripts were used to conduct the simulation study. All scripts are provided under an open source license. See SOM Appendix for details and download instructions.

2.3 Empirical study

We re-analyzed an *Arabidopsis* dataset which consists of whole genome sequence (WGS) data and phenotypic data for two quantitative traits: flowering time at 10 °C and 16 °C. A total of 1,135 samples from natural populations across the globe are represented. The phylogeny shown in SOM Supplementary Figure S16 depicts the geographic origins of and evolutionary relationships among the samples. The dataset was originally published and analyzed by the 1001 Genomes Consortium [7], and we obtained genomic sequences and quantitative trait data from the 1001 Genomes Project database (accessible at www.1001genomes.org); the former includes both assembled WGS data and variant calls for a total of 10,707,430 bi-allelic SNPs. (Details about sequencing, assembly, filtering, quality controls, and variant calling are described in the 1001 Genomes Consortium study [7].)

Stage one of the Coal-Miner pipeline made use of RecHMM [30] to infer local-phylogeny-switching breakpoints. For computational efficiency, the breakpoint inference utilized a subset of taxa rather than the full set of taxa. The subset was chosen to maximize evolutionary divergence and was comprised of one sample from each of the following geographic regions: Spain, Sweden, USA, and Russia. For chromosomes 1 through 5, the analysis in stage one resulted in 1876, 991, 783, 559, and 913 loci with an average locus length of 16 kb, 19 kb, 30 kb, 33 kb, and 29 kb, respectively.

Using the loci obtained in stage one as input, the second stage of Coal-Miner was run on both trait characters. The 10 °C analysis identified 179, 99, 108, 109, and 95 candidate loci in chromosomes 1 through 5, respectively. The 16 °C analysis identified 115, 42, 88, 65, and 89 candidate loci in chromosomes 1 through 5, respectively. Coal-Miner also requires that ℓ^*, the number of candidate loci, be provided as an input parameter. In practice, model selection approaches are typically used in this context. Our study utilized the following procedure to determine a suitable value for ℓ^*. We calculated the likelihood score of the fitted "null" LMM for each locus (see above), and we examined the distribution of likelihood scores (Supplementary Figure S15 in the SOM). We then assigned ℓ^* based on the distribution's inflection point.

The inputs to the third stage of Coal-Miner consisted of the set of candidate loci, a quantitative trait character (flowering time at either 10 °C or 16 °C), and the genotypic sequence data matrix which consisted of sites with minor allele frequency threshold of 0.03 (i.e., sites having a minor allele frequency less than or equals to 0.03 were removed). The third stage of Coal-Miner was run using the same settings as in the simulation study.

3 RESULTS

3.1 Simulation study

We conducted experiments that varied the proportion of causal loci as a means to investigate the impact of the genomic architecture of a trait on AM method performance. The model conditions utilized simulations with between 10% and 30% causal loci and either neutral or non-neutral evolution on either tree-like or non-tree-like model phylogenies. The methods under study included Coal-Miner, our new AM method, as well as representative methods from different classes of state-of-the-art methods: Coal-Map, an AM method that accounts for local and global sample relatedness as fixed effects,

GEMMA, a LMM-based AM method that accounts for global sample relatedness as a random effect (but does not account for local sample relatedness), and EIGENSTRAT, an AM method that accounts for global sample relatedness as a fixed effect (but does not account for local sample relatedness). We compared the statistical power and type I error control of each method using receiver operating characteristic (ROC) curves (Supplementary figures S2 through S5 in the SOM), and Table 1 compares the area under ROC curve (AUROC) of each method.

Regardless of the proportion of causal loci and the evolutionary scenario explored in these model conditions, Coal-Miner's AUROC was significantly better than the next best method in our study (either Coal-Map or GEMMA) based upon the corrected test of DeLong et al. [8] (Table 1). A similar observation was made when measuring performance using true positive rate (TPR) at a false positive rate (FPR) of 0.1 (Supplementary Table S2 in the SOM), except that Coal-Miner's performance advantage over the next best method was even more pronounced. The TPR difference was 0.158 on average and ranged as high as 0.248. Across these model conditions, we observed a consistent ranking of AM methods by AUROC (with two minor exceptions): Coal-Miner first, Coal-Map second, GEMMA third, and EIGENSTRAT fourth. The minor exceptions involved the two lowest AUROC values on the neutral, non-tree-like model condition with 10% or 20% causal loci, where GEMMA and EIGENSTRAT swapped rankings. We noted that Coal-Map's AUROC was second best on model conditions with the smallest proportion of causal loci, but its performance tended to degrade as the proportion increased. Coal-Map's AUROC was only marginally better than GEMMA on model conditions with the highest proportion of causal loci.

The impact of varying the proportion of causal loci was similar for all methods: AUROC tended to degrade as the proportion of causal loci increased from 10% to 30%. However, Coal-Miner's performance advantage relative to the other AM methods was flat or improved as the proportion of causal loci increased.

The model conditions included different combinations of genetic drift/incomplete lineage sorting and/or gene flow – evolutionary processes which can generate local variation in sample relatedness. Note that model conditions with non-tree-like model phylogenies incorporated all of these evolutionary processes (including genetic drift/incomplete lineage sorting). The impact of the different evolutionary processes varied across the methods. Coal-Miner's AUROC tended to be larger on model conditions involving both drift/ILS and gene flow as sources of local genealogical variation, and Coal-Map's AUROC was similarly affected. On the other hand, GEMMA's AUROC was comparable (within 0.01) based on this comparison, with the exception of non-neutral model conditions involving 10% or 20% causal loci.

A comparison of model conditions that differed only with respect to neutral versus non-neutral evolution revealed the impact of positive selection on AM method performance. We note that, in our experiments, the evolution of causal loci differed from non-causal loci since positive selection acted only upon the former but not the latter. Coal-Miner and Coal-Map returned comparable AUROC (within 0.025) regardless of neutral versus non-neutral evolution. GEMMA and EIGENSTRAT performed similarly, although slightly greater variability (within 0.035) was observed. For LMM-based methods, there was no obvious trend in terms of direction of change when comparing neutral versus non-neutral experiment results. There was an apparent trend for EIGENSTRAT, however: positive selection tended to reduce EIGENSTRAT's AUROC, with one exception (model conditions with a tree-like model phylogeny and 10% causal loci).

3.2 Empirical study

We used Coal-Miner to re-analyze an *Arabidopsis* dataset which was originally studied by the 1001 Genomes Consortium [7]. The dataset includes samples from 1,135 high quality re-sequenced natural lines adapted to different environments with varying local climates [7]. The sampled data included whole genome sequences and quantitative trait data for two traits: flowering time under high and low temperature – 16 °C and 10 °C, respectively.

A key component of the 1001 Genomes Consortium study was a GWA analysis of the genomic sequences and quantitative trait data using EMMAX [17], another state-of-the-art statistical AM method (see [31] for a comparison of EMMAX and other state-of-the-art statistical AM methods). A major focus of the analysis was a set of five genes which are known to regulate flowering and contribute to flowering time variation at 10 °C in *Arabidopsis* [7]: FLOWERING LOCUS T (FT), SHORT VEGETATIVE PHASE (SVP), FLOWERING LOCUS C (FLC), DELAY OF GERMINATION 1 (DOG1), and VERNALIZATION INSENSITIVE 3 (VIN3). Plants rely on both endogenous and environmental (e.g. temperature and photoperiod) cues to initiate flowering [1, 2]. These five genes encode major components of the vernalization (exposure to the prolonged cold) and autonomous pathways known to regulate the initiation of flowering in *Arabidopsis*. Allelic and copy number variants (CNV) for many of these genes, including FLC, are known to serve important roles in generating novel variation in flowering time and permit plants to adapt to new climates [21–23]. DOG1 is known to be involved in determining seasonal timing of seed germination and influences flowering time in Arabidopsis [15].

Under a conservative Bonferroni-corrected threshold [4], Coal-Miner identified significant peaks associated with flowering time under high and low temperature (16 °C and 10 °C, respectively). In particular, Coal-Miner identified significantly associated markers in all five genes (FT, SVP, FLC, DOG1, and VIN3) for both the 16 °C dataset and the 10 °C dataset (Supplementary Figure S12 in the SOM). Within the five genes, Coal-Miner analyses returned peaks which largely agreed across the 10 °C and 16 °C datasets. Some differences involved association scores that were borderline significant in one dataset but not the other.

Table 2 compares the Coal-Miner analysis with similar analyses using two other state-of-the-art statistical AM methods. The EMMAX analysis in the 1001 Genomes Consortium study [7] identified significant associations for three of the genes at 10 °C, and association score peaks were marginally below a Bonferroni-corrected threshold in the other two genes (SVP and FLC). Furthermore, significant peaks were only detected in DOG1 at 16 °C, but no significant peaks were detected in the other four genes for this dataset. (See Figure 2 in the 1001 Genomes Consortium study [7] for the original Manhattan plot.) GEMMA's performance was qualitatively similar to EMMAX (Supplementary Figure S13 in the SOM). At 10 °C,

Model condition			AUROC				
Neutral vs. non-neutral	Model phylogeny	Percentage of causal loci (%)	Coal-Miner	Coal-Map	GEMMA	EIGENSTRAT	q-value
Neutral	Non-tree-like	10	**0.962 (0.009)**	0.939 (0.009)	0.866 (0.017)	0.871 (0.014)	< 0.00001
		20	**0.921 (0.010)**	0.899 (0.009)	0.849 (0.015)	0.859 (0.012)	< 0.00001
		30	**0.904 (0.013)**	0.882 (0.009)	0.847 (0.017)	0.832 (0.018)	< 0.00001
Neutral	Tree-like	10	**0.943 (0.014)**	0.922 (0.010)	0.870 (0.009)	0.833 (0.019)	0.0053
		20	**0.904 (0.016)**	0.847 (0.011)	0.843 (0.010)	0.813 (0.016)	< 0.00001
		30	**0.904 (0.013)**	0.853 (0.009)	0.844 (0.008)	0.799 (0.022)	0.00003
Non-neutral	Non-tree-like	10	**0.959 (0.009)**	0.933 (0.013)	0.896 (0.014)	0.836 (0.022)	< 0.00001
		20	**0.926 (0.009)**	0.897 (0.009)	0.856 (0.017)	0.847 (0.013)	< 0.00001
		30	**0.894 (0.015)**	0.863 (0.010)	0.832 (0.018)	0.816 (0.014)	< 0.00001
Non-neutral	Tree-like	10	**0.954 (0.014)**	0.922 (0.010)	0.856 (0.012)	0.841 (0.018)	< 0.00001
		20	**0.890 (0.015)**	0.850 (0.013)	0.832 (0.014)	0.796 (0.020)	0.00003
		30	**0.879 (0.014)**	0.836 (0.011)	0.830 (0.009)	0.783 (0.018)	0.0007

Table 1: The impact of the genomic architecture of a quantitative trait on the performance of Coal-Miner and the other AM methods. Multi-locus sequences were simulated under neutral or non-neutral evolution on tree-like or non-tree-like model phylogenies, and quantitative traits were simulated using causal markers sampled from 10%, 20%, or 30% of loci (see Methods section for more details). The performance of each AM method was evaluated based on the area under its receiver operating characteristic (ROC) curve, or AUROC. We report each method's AUROC as an average (and standard error in parentheses) across twenty replicate datasets for each model condition. Coal-Miner's AUROC is shown in bold where it significantly improved upon the AUROC of the most accurate of the other AM methods, based upon the test of DeLong et al. [8] ($n = 20$; $\alpha = 0.05$). We corrected for multiple tests using the approach of Benjamini and Hochberg [3], and corrected q-values are shown. (The corresponding ROC plots are shown in Supplementary Figures S2 through S5 in the SOM.)

GEMMA recovered significant associations in three of the genes but not in the remaining two (SVP and FLC); at 16 °C, no significant peaks were detected in three genes, a peak just above the threshold of significance was detected in FT, and another peak was detected in DOG1.

4 DISCUSSION

Simulation study. For the model conditions that varied the proportion of causal loci with neutral or non-neutral evolution on tree-like or non-tree-like model phylogenies, Coal-Miner had better performance than all of the other state-of-the-art methods in our study, as measured using AUROC and TPR at an FPR of 0.1. This suggests that Coal-Miner's performance advantage is robust to the specific proportion of causal loci that contribute genetic effects to a quantitative trait, which relates to trait architecture, as well as the evolutionary processes involved. We note that, as even more causal loci are added beyond the proportions explored in our study, the effects contributed by any individual locus becomes more diffuse, and global sample structure will become a more reasonable approximation of different causal loci with different local sample structures. In general, we found traits with "diffuse" genomic architecture (i.e., traits with a relatively high proportion of causal loci) to be challenging for all methods. Coal-Miner tended to cope better with the challenge relative to the other methods in our study, which we attribute to the design of the second stage in the Coal-Miner pipeline (i.e., candidate locus detection). Consistent performance trends were observed when comparing neutral versus non-neutral simulations. This suggests that, for the model conditions that we explored in our study, Coal-Miner's performance is robust to the presence or absence of positive selection. A similar outcome was observed when comparing IUA model-based experiments involving two different types of model phylogenies – tree-like and non-tree-like.

Taken together, the model conditions included multiple sources of local genealogical variation, including genetic drift/ILS, gene flow, positive selection, and combinations thereof. The specific evolutionary processes contributing to local genealogical variation did not seem to matter as much as the presence of local genealogical variation, and Coal-Miner's performance advantage was not necessarily predicated on specific evolutionary cause(s) of local genealogical discordance. These findings seem to suggest that Coal-Miner's model and algorithm may be generalized to other evolutionary scenarios, so long as the breakpoint inference method used in the Coal-Miner pipeline suitably accounts for evolutionary processes with first-order contributions to genome evolution. An additional consideration is that the simulations utilized minor allele frequencies of at least 0.1, and future work is needed to understand Coal-Miner's performance in GWA studies involving rare variants.

Empirical study. The empirical datasets in our study were more challenging than the simulated datasets because the former likely involved more complex evolutionary evolutionary scenarios compared to the latter. Additional evolutionary processes which may have played an important role include other types of natural selection and demographic events (e.g., fluctuations in effective population size).

For both of the *Arabidopsis* datasets, Coal-Miner was able to detect significant associations in all five positive control regions. In contrast, neither GEMMA nor EMMAX – the statistical AM method used in the 1001 Genomes Consortium study [7] – were able to do the same. The vernalization requirement for flowering in

Dataset	Positive control gene	Significantly associated markers detected?		
		Coal-Miner	EMMAX	GEMMA
10 °C	FLOWERING LOCUS T (FT)	Yes	Yes	Yes
10 °C	SHORT VEGETATIVE PHASE (SVP)	Yes	No*	No
10 °C	FLOWERING LOCUS C (FLC)	Yes	No*	No
10 °C	DELAY OF GERMINATION 1 (DOG1)	Yes	Yes	Yes
10 °C	VERNALIZATION INSENSITIVE 3 (VIN3)	Yes	Yes	Yes
16 °C	FLOWERING LOCUS T (FT)	Yes	No	Yes
16 °C	SHORT VEGETATIVE PHASE (SVP)	Yes	No	No
16 °C	FLOWERING LOCUS C (FLC)	Yes	No	No
16 °C	DELAY OF GERMINATION 1 (DOG1)	Yes	Yes	Yes
16 °C	VERNALIZATION INSENSITIVE 3 (VIN3)	Yes	No	No

Table 2: A comparison of Coal-Miner and two other state-of-the-art statistical AM methods based upon analyses of the two *Arabidopsis* datasets. The other AM methods are GEMMA and EMMAX, the statistical AM method used in the 1001 Genomes Consortium study [7]. We evaluated whether the three AM methods detected significantly associated markers in five genomic regions centered on positive control genes which are known to regulate flowering time in *Arabidopsis*. We used a Bonferroni-corrected threshold for significance. For two of the five genomic regions in the 10 °C dataset, EMMAX returned association scores that were near the threshold of significance (marked using an asterisk). The corresponding Manhattan plots for the Coal-Miner and GEMMA analyses are shown in Supplementary Figures S12 and S13 in the SOM, respectively. The corresponding Manhattan plot for the EMMAX analysis is shown as Figure 2 in the 1001 Genomes Consortium study [7].

Arabidopsis suggests that the flowering response at 16 °C presents a greater AM challenge than at 10 °C. Our findings were consistent with a need for more statistical power for the former as compared with the latter as well as the overall findings in the simulation study, which suggested that Coal-Miner offered improved statistical power relative to the state of the art. As noted above, the empirical datasets likely involved relatively complex evolutionary histories as compared to the synthetic datasets in our study, and an expanded simulation study would be needed to confirm our initial comparison of performance findings using synthetic and empirical data. Furthermore, Coal-Miner analysis of the *Arabidopsis* dataset identified putatively novel markers (i.e., markers which were not flagged using other AM methods). Additional comparative and functional analyses are needed to interpret these findings.

5 CONCLUSIONS

Across the range of genomic architectures and evolutionary scenarios explored in our study, Coal-Miner had comparable or typically improved statistical power and type I error control compared to state-of-the-art AM methods. The scenarios included different evolutionary processes such as genetic drift and ILS, positive selection, gene flow, and recombination – all of which can generate local genealogical variation that differs from the true species phylogeny. More work needs to be done to explore additional evolutionary processes which have first-order impacts on genome evolution (e.g., gene duplication and loss, other genome rearrangement events, etc.). As more divergent samples are included in a GWA study, more evolutionary processes potentially will become relevant to AM analysis. We fully expect that more algorithmic development will need to be done in this case, particularly regarding the breakpoint inference stage of Coal-Miner.

We conclude with our thoughts on future work. As an alternative to the pipeline-based design of Coal-Miner, simultaneous inference of local coalescent histories and AM model parameters will avoid error propagation across different stages of a pipeline-based algorithm. Furthermore, viewed through the lens of evolution, genotype and phenotype are arguably two sides of the same coin. The same could be said of "intermediate-scale" characters (e.g., interactomic characters). A combination of the extended coalescent models and LMMs could be used to capture evolutionary relatedness of and functional dependence between heterogeneous biological characters across multiple scales of complexity and at higher evolutionary divergences.

6 SUPPORTING ONLINE MATERIALS (SOM)

SOM files are located at https://doi.org/10.6084/m9.figshare.5165470.v1. These materials include: (1) an appendix with supplementary text, tables, and figures, (2) source code for software used in this study, and (3) datasets analyzed in this study. All materials are provided under open and free licenses.

ACKNOWLEDGMENTS

The authors gratefully acknowledge the following support: National Science Foundation Grants No. CCF-1565719 and No. CCF-1714417 (to KJL), grants from the BEACON Center for the Study of Evolution in Action (NSF STC Cooperative Agreement DBI-093954) to KJL and GAB, and Michigan State University faculty startup funds (to KJL, to GAB, and to PPE). The authors would also like to thank the anonymous referees for their valuable feedback and suggestions.

REFERENCES

[1] Richard Amasino. 2010. Seasonal and developmental timing of flowering. *The Plant Journal* 61, 6 (2010), 1001–1013.

[2] Richard M Amasino and Scott D Michaels. 2010. The timing of flowering. *Plant Physiology* 154, 2 (2010), 516–520.

[3] Yoav Benjamini and Yosef Hochberg. 1995. Controlling the false discovery rate: a practical and powerful approach to multiple testing. *Journal of the Royal Statistical Society Series B (Methodological)* 57, 1 (1995), 289–300.

[4] Carlo E Bonferroni. 1936. *Teoria statistica delle classi e calcolo delle probabilita*. Libreria internazionale Seeber.

[5] Richard P. Brent. 1973. *Algorithms for Minimization without Derivatives.* Dover Publications, Mineola, New York. 1–208 pages.

[6] Peter E Chen and B Jesse Shapiro. 2015. The advent of genome-wide association studies for bacteria. *Current Opinion in Microbiology* 25 (2015), 17–24.

[7] 1001 Genomes Consortium. 2016. 1,135 genomes reveal the global pattern of polymorphism in *Arabidopsis thaliana*. *Cell* 166, 2 (2016), 481–491.

[8] Elizabeth R DeLong, David M DeLong, and Daniel L Clarke-Pearson. 1988. Comparing the areas under two or more correlated receiver operating characteristic curves: a nonparametric approach. *Biometrics* 44, 3 (1988), 837–845.

[9] Eric Y. Durand, Nick Patterson, David Reich, and Montgomery Slatkin. 2011. Testing for ancient admixture between closely related populations. *Molecular Biology and Evolution* 28, 8 (2011), 2239–2252.

[10] Scott V Edwards. 2009. Is a new and general theory of molecular systematics emerging? *Evolution* 63, 1 (2009), 1–19.

[11] Gregory Ewing and Joachim Hermisson. 2010. MSMS: a coalescent simulation program including recombination, demographic structure and selection at a single locus. *Bioinformatics* 26, 16 (2010), 2064–2065.

[12] Hussein A Hejase and Kevin J Liu. 2016. Mapping the genomic architecture of adaptive traits with interspecific introgressive origin: a coalescent-based approach. *BMC Genomics* 17, 1 (2016), 41.

[13] Richard R. Hudson. 2002. Generating samples under a Wright-Fisher neutral model of genetic variation. *Bioinformatics* 18, 2 (2002), 337–338.

[14] Richard R Hudson and Norman L Kaplan. 1985. Statistical properties of the number of recombination events in the history of a sample of DNA sequences. *Genetics* 111, 1 (1985), 147–164.

[15] Heqiang Huo, Shouhui Wei, and Kent J. Bradford. 2016. DELAY OF GERMINATION1 (DOG1) regulates both seed dormancy and flowering time through microRNA pathways. *Proceedings of the National Academy of Sciences* 113, 15 (2016), E2199–E2206.

[16] Ian Jolliffe. 2002. *Principal Component Analysis.* Wiley Online Library.

[17] Hyun Min Kang, Jae Hoon Sul, Susan K. Service, Noah A. Zaitlen, Sit-yee Kong, Nelson B. Freimer, Chiara Sabatti, and Eleazar Eskin. 2010. Variance component model to account for sample structure in genome-wide association studies. *Nature Genetics* 42, 4 (Apr 2010), 348–354.

[18] John F. C. Kingman. 1982. On the genealogy of large populations. *Journal of Applied Probability* 19 (1982), pp. 27–43.

[19] Kevin J. Liu, Jingxuan Dai, Kathy Truong, Ying Song, Michael H. Kohn, and Luay Nakhleh. 2014. An HMM-based comparative genomic framework for detecting introgression in eukaryotes. *PLoS Computational Biology* 10, 6 (06 2014), e1003649.

[20] Anthony D Long and Charles H Langley. 1999. The power of association studies to detect the contribution of candidate genetic loci to variation in complex traits. *Genome Research* 9, 8 (1999), 720–731.

[21] Dustin Mayfield, Z Jeffrey Chen, and J Chris Pires. 2011. Epigenetic regulation of flowering time in polyploids. *Current Opinion in Plant Biology* 14, 2 (2011), 174 – 178.

[22] Belén Méndez-Vigo, F. Xavier Picó, Mercedes Ramiro, José M. Martínez-Zapater, and Carlos Alonso-Blanco. 2011. Altitudinal and climatic adaptation is mediated by flowering traits and FRI, FLC, and PHYC genes in *Arabidopsis. Plant Physiology* 157, 4 (12 2011), 1942–1955.

[23] J. Chris Pires, Jianwei Zhao, M. Eric Schranz, Enrique J. Leon, Pablo A. Quijada, Lewis N. Lukens, and Thomas C. Osborn. 2004. Flowering time divergence and genomic rearrangements in resynthesized *Brassica* polyploids (Brassicaceae). *Biological Journal of the Linnean Society* 82, 4 (2004), 675–688.

[24] Stephanie S Porter, Peter L Chang, Christopher A Conow, Joseph P Dunham, and Maren L Friesen. 2017. Association mapping reveals novel serpentine adaptation gene clusters in a population of symbiotic *Mesorhizobium. The ISME Journal* 11, 1 (2017), 248–262.

[25] Sergej Potapov, Werner Adler, Benjamin Hofner, and Berthold Lausen. 2013. *Daim: Diagnostic accuracy of classification models.* R package version 1.1.0.

[26] Alkes L Price, Nick J Patterson, Robert M Plenge, Michael E Weinblatt, Nancy A Shadick, and David Reich. 2006. Principal components analysis corrects for stratification in genome-wide association studies. *Nature Genetics* 38, 8 (2006), 904–909.

[27] R Core Team. 2015. *R: A Language and Environment for Statistical Computing.* R Foundation for Statistical Computing, Vienna, Austria.

[28] Ying Song, Stefan Endepols, Nicole Klemann, Dania Richter, Franz-Rainer Matuschka, Ching-Hua Shih, Michael W. Nachman, and Michael H. Kohn. 2011. Adaptive introgression of anticoagulant rodent poison resistance by hybridization between old world mice. *Current Biology* 21, 15 (2011), 1296 – 1301.

[29] Jeremy Wang, Kyle J. Moore, Qi Zhang, Fernando Pardo-Manual de Villena, Wei Wang, and Leonard McMillan. 2010. Genome-wide compatible SNP intervals and their properties. In *Proceedings of the First ACM International Conference on Bioinformatics and Computational Biology (BCB '10).* ACM, New York, NY, USA, 43–52.

[30] Oscar Westesson and Ian Holmes. 2009. Accurate detection of recombinant breakpoints in whole-genome alignments. *PLoS Computational Biology* 5, 3 (03 2009), e1000318.

[31] Xiang Zhou and Matthew Stephens. 2012. Genome-wide efficient mixed-model analysis for association studies. *Nature Genetics* 44, 7 (2012), 821–824.

Learning Deep Representations from Heterogeneous Patient Data for Predictive Diagnosis

Chongyu Zhou
Department of Electrical and Computer Engineering
National University of Singapore
Singapore
chongyuzhou@u.nus.edu

Yao Jia
Department of Electrical and Computer Engineering
National University of Singapore
Singapore
eleyaj@nus.edu.sg

Mehul Motani*
Department of Electrical and Computer Engineering
National University of Singapore
Singapore
motani@nus.edu.sg

Jingwei Chew†
Octavus Technologies
Singapore
chew.jingwei@gmail.com

ABSTRACT

Predictive diagnosis benefits both patients and hospitals. Major challenges limiting the effectiveness of machine learning based predictive diagnosis include the lack of efficient feature selection methods and the heterogeneity of measured patient data (e.g., vital signs). In this paper, we propose DLFS, an efficient feature selection scheme based on deep learning that is applicable for heterogeneous data. DLFS is unsupervised in nature and can learn compact representations from patient data automatically for efficient prediction. In this paper, the specific problem of predicting the patients' length of stay in the hospital is investigated in a predictive diagnosis framework which uses DLFS for feature selection. Real patient data from the pneumonia database of the National University Health System (NUHS) in Singapore are collected to verify the effectiveness of DLFS. By running experiments on real-world patient data and comparing with several other commonly used feature selection methods, we demonstrate the advantage of the proposed DLFS scheme.

CCS CONCEPTS

• **Applied computing → Health informatics**;

KEYWORDS

Feature selection; predictive diagnosis; classification; heterogeneous patient data

*Corresponding author.
†This work was done when Jingwei Chew was at the Department of Electrical and Computer Engineering, National University of Singapore.

Permission to make digital or hard copies of all or part of this work for personal or classroom use is granted without fee provided that copies are not made or distributed for profit or commercial advantage and that copies bear this notice and the full citation on the first page. Copyrights for components of this work owned by others than ACM must be honored. Abstracting with credit is permitted. To copy otherwise, or republish, to post on servers or to redistribute to lists, requires prior specific permission and/or a fee. Request permissions from permissions@acm.org.
ACM-BCB '17, August 20-23, 2017, Boston, MA, USA
© 2017 Association for Computing Machinery.
ACM ISBN 978-1-4503-4722-8/17/08...$15.00
https://doi.org/10.1145/3107411.3107433

1 INTRODUCTION

Evidence supporting the benefits of predictive diagnosis for both patients and the hospitals has been mounting [10, 17]. For patients, being able to predict the future status not only can help the patients to get preventive treatments, but also can reduce the risk of adverse events, such as hospital-acquired infections, adverse drug events, poor nutritional levels, and other complications caused by prolonged hospital stays [5, 6, 14]. For hospitals, the ability to predict the future status of the patients can improve the patient flow, which facilitates beneficial treatment, minimal waiting and efficient use of hospital resources such as beds, clinical staffs and medical equipments [15].

Recent advance in artificial intelligence and machine learning techniques has boosted the potential of post-analyzing the patient data in order to support clinical decisions. In particular, a hidden Markov model (HMM) has been used in [16] to learn the patterns of the patients from a set of Asthma patient data. A nonnegative matrix factorization (NMF) based algorithm is proposed in [19] for mining temporal signatures from a set of patient data for event detection applications. Furthermore, a compressive sensing (CS) based method is adopted in [9] to detect abnormal events in ECG signals. Despite these successful applications in post-processing of patient data, mining practical patient data to support predictive diagnosis is still facing a lot of challenges [2, 21].

First, as the success of predictive algorithms largely depends on feature selection and data representation [3], an efficient feature selection method is crucial for the predictive accuracies. A common approach in the literature is to specify the features in an ad-hoc manner where some domain experts designate the patterns to look for [8]. This is similar to the techniques used in [9, 16, 19] where a prior on the structure of the data model is assumed to be known. This kind of supervised definitions of the feature space, though appropriate in some situations, scales poorly and does not generalize well. Therefore, an unsupervised manner of feature selection is preferred to learn the feature from the patient data directly.

Another challenge in analyzing patient data is due to their heterogeneity [11]. Due to the differences in the health status of patients, clinicians may decide to monitor the patients based on different schedules. For example, clinicians may decide to monitor a patient more intensively when the patient's health status is deteriorating. As a result, the timestamps, order and frequency of the measurements may be highly different from one patient to another. This kind of irregularity and heterogeneity in the patient data make feature selection and representation learning even more challenging [8, 20].

In this paper, we present a novel feature selection scheme, referred to as DLFS, to learn the representation of patient data for predictive diagnosis through a deep learning approach, which attempts to overcome the limitations of supervised feature selection methods and the difficulties caused by data heterogeneity. The proposed DLFS scheme is an unsupervised feature selection approach that is able to automatically identify patterns and dependencies in the data and learn a compact representation of each patient for easier classification or prediction. Specifically, DLFS uses a deep neural network composed of a stack of denoising autoencoders [18] to learn the patterns and dependencies in the patient data. Despite the success of applying stacked denoising autoencoders in image processing, text mining and marketing problems [3], their application on processing patient data for prediction is limited.

The predictive diagnosis problem considered in this paper is to predict the patients' lengths of stay in the hospital. To prove the effectiveness of the proposed DLFS feature selection scheme, we apply it to select features for predicting the patients' lengths of stay in the hospital using a set of real-world patient data. We show that:

- DLFS achieves fairly good prediction performance (with 80% accuracy) compared to several other commonly used feature selection methods.
- By experimenting with the features selected by DLFS, we find that the features selected by DLFS are consistent with each other, which explains the fundamental reason why DLFS outperforms the other feature selection methods.

The rest of this paper is organized as follows. Section 2 describes the details of the data set used and the problem investigated in this paper. Section 3 introduces the whole predictive diagnosis framework including various interpolation, feature selection and classification methods used in this paper. In Section 4, we carry out a number of experiments to evaluate the performance of the proposed DLFS feature selection scheme and present some interesting discussions on the selected features. Finally, Section 5 concludes the paper.

2 DATA SET & PROBLEM DESCRIPTION

In this section, we introduce the data set used and the problem investigated in our study.

2.1 Data Collection and Preparation

We collaborated with the National University Hospital (NUH), which is a member of the National University Health System (NUHS), an integrated academic health and regional health system in Singapore. We collected medical dockets of patients from their Medical Records Office.

A total of 116 patient's physical medical dockets were collected from January 2016 to March 2016. Our study focused on patients admitted with community acquired pneumonia, and so we eliminated 5 dockets which did not contain medical records related to

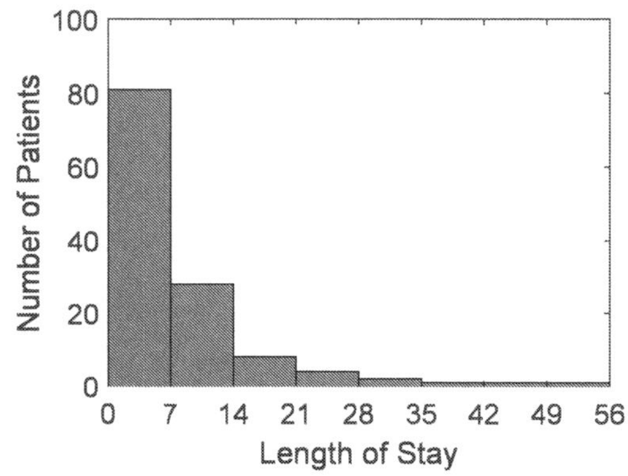

Figure 1: Histogram of patients' lengths of stay.

pneumonia. Eventually, there were a total of 111 patients' physical medical records and the clinical charts from their hospital stay were digitalized for data analysis.

The pneumonia patient data set includes patients' demographic information, clinical charts and intravenous infusion records. Among the 111 patients, 63 of them are male and 48 of them are female, with overall 68 years old in average, and they are of different races. Clinical charts data, which are recorded by assistant nurse, includes vital sign measurements, required oxygenation level, mental state, conscious state and pain score in time series. The intravenous infusion records include different types of intravenous medication and the amounts have been injected that are all recorded in time series.

Some of the patients have multiple health records due to multiple admissions to the hospital. In our study, we consider each different health record as a different patient and try to predict the length of stay of each health record. Therefore, in total, we have 126 different health records, which are considered as 126 different patients in our study.

Hereinafter, we are referring to the corresponding health record when we mention patient. The data set contains the ground truth of the length-of-stay information, which indicates the number of days that each patient stays in the hospital. The histogram of the patients' lengths of stay in the data set is shown in Figure 1. In total, there are 80 patients who stay in the hospital for less or equal to 7 days and 46 patients who stay in the hospital for more than 7 days.

The time series data (e.g., vital signs) contained in the data set are highly heterogeneous. Different patients may be measured at different timestamps and frequencies. Even for the same patient, the time and frequency of the measurements may also vary with time. Furthermore, different types of time series data from the same patient may be measured at different time instances and frequencies.

The data collection for this study was approved by the local institutional ethics committee (DSRB).

2.2 Problem Description

In this paper, we consider the the problem of predicting the patients' lengths of stay in the hospital. Specifically, using the first 24 hours' vital sign data, we would like to predict whether the patients will stay in the hospital for more than a week. The problem is modeled

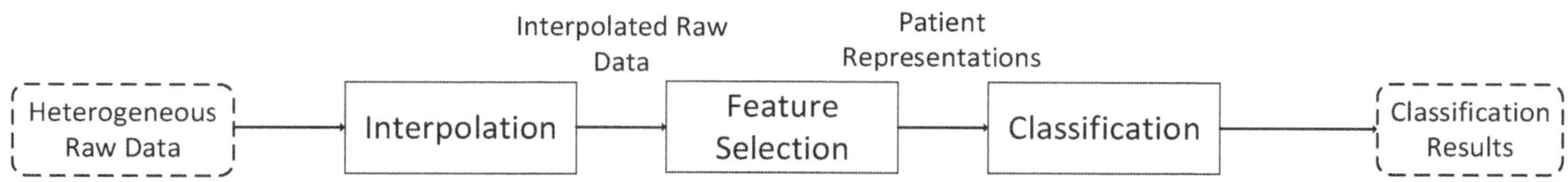

Figure 2: Overview of the predictive diagnosis framework.

as a binary classification problem, where staying for less than or equal to 7 days is assigned to Class 0 and staying for greater than 7 days is assigned to Class 1. We believe this study is important for providing the right patient treatment, improving patient outcomes, and optimizing hospital operations.

The following information was extracted from the data set for analysis. From patients' clinical charts, we selected the first 24 hours' vital sign data of all patients, including respiration rate, SpO2 level, temperature, blood pressure and pulse rate. The vital signs are measured at different time instances and frequencies, with each data point having a timestamp. The delta change of the vital signs between two adjacent measurements was also computed to represent the fluctuation of the vital signs in the time series. In addition to time series vital sign data, we also included patient demographic information, i.e., gender and age, in the analysis.

3 METHODOLOGY

Figure 2 shows an overview of the proposed predictive diagnosis framework. The heterogeneous raw patient data are first passed through an interpolation block where the heterogeneous data are interpolated to make the data from different patients have the same size. Then, a feature selection block is applied to the interpolated raw data to get efficient patient representations (features) for classification. In the end, the obtained patient representations are passed into the classification block to get the predictive decision.

The main contribution of this paper is in the feature selection block where we propose the DLFS feature selection scheme. However, to get the whole picture of the predictive diagnosis framework, we also need to introduce the methods used in the interpolation and classification blocks. In this section, we introduce these three blocks in details.

3.1 Interpolation

One major challenge in analyzing the patient health data is the irregularity of the sampled observations. In the data set that we are using, the vital signs of different patients are monitored and recorded at different timestamps and frequencies. The reason could be the differences in the health status and the symptoms of different patients, which makes the clinicians come up with different monitoring plans. Furthermore, even for the same patient, the measurement frequency of her vital signs may change through time. This kind of heterogeneity in the health records have caused a lot of challenges in the feature selection and classification steps later on.

In this paper, we tackle these challenges by interpolating the heterogeneous patient health records. We would like to virtually make all patients measured at the same frequency and timestamps. For the patients whose measurements are not taken at certain timestamps, we predict those "missing" measurements via interpolation. Two different interpolation methods are applied in this paper.

3.1.1 Spline Interpolation. Spline interpolation is a popular method for interpolating data. By constructing piecewise-cubic polynomials that have continuous second-order derivatives, spline interpolation can efficiently estimates the "missing" measurements at any timestamp and unify the health record of each patient. The detailed formulation of spline interpolation is illustrated in [23].

3.1.2 Gaussian Process Regression. Gaussian process regression (GPR) [13] is another popular method for data interpolation. In particular, we define the data model and the covariance matrix in the following way to fit in our problem here.

Suppose we have N types of health records in a patient's data, where each type of health record covers T time slots. We use $x_{i,t}$ to denote the index of a type i health record at time slot t for a patient. For instance, $x_{1,t}$ could indicate the blood pressure data during time slot t; while $x_{2,t+1}$ could indicate the SpO2 data during time slot $t+1$. Therefore, the health record from a patient can be represented by the matrix $\mathbf{X}_{N,T} = \{\mathbf{x}_{1,T}, \mathbf{x}_{2,T}, ..., \mathbf{x}_{N,T}\}^T$, where each $\mathbf{x}_{i,T} = \{x_{i,1}, x_{i,2}, ..., x_{i,T}\}$ is a vector indicating the whole type i health records of a patient. The measurement $z_{i,t}$ of a certain type of data $x_{i,t}$ during time slot t is modeled by the following process:

$$z_{i,t} = f(x_{i,t}) + \epsilon_{i,t}, \tag{1}$$

where $\epsilon_{i,t}$ is a Gaussian noise with zero mean and covariance $\sigma^2_{i,t}$, noted as $\epsilon_{i,t} = N(0, \sigma^2_{i,t})$. In a Gaussian process (GP) model, the prior distribution of latent variable $f_{i,t} = f(x_{i,t})$ is modeled as a Gaussian; while the prior distribution of multiple latent variables is modeled by a covariance matrix $\mathbf{K} = [k(x_{i,t}, x_{i,t'})]$, where $k(x_{i,t}, x_{i,t'})$ is the kernel function describing the covariance. With a positive-definite covariance matrix $\mathbf{K}$, the joint GP prior distribution of all latent variables $\mathbf{f}_{i,T} = [f_{i,1}, f_{i,2}, ..., f_{i,T}]^T$ is represented as

$$p(\mathbf{f}_{i,T}) = N(0, \mathbf{K}), \tag{2}$$

where the likelihood distribution of the observations $\mathbf{z}_{i,T}$ is

$$p(\mathbf{z}_{i,T}|\mathbf{f}_{i,T}) = N(\mathbf{f}_{i,T}, \mathbf{R}_{i,T}), \tag{3}$$

where $\mathbf{R}_{i,T} = \text{diag}(\sigma^2_{i,1}, \sigma^2_{i,2}, ..., \sigma^2_{i,T})$.

GPR can infer $f_{i,*} = f(x_{i,*})$ for a test point $x_{i,*}$ using $p(f_{i,*}|\mathbf{z}_{i,T})$ given a training data set $(X_{i,T}, \mathbf{z}_{i,T})$. The inference is done by solving the maximum *a posteriori* problem, which is given by

$$p(f_{i,T}|\mathbf{z}_{i,T}) = N(\mu_{i,*}, \Sigma_{i,*}), \tag{4}$$

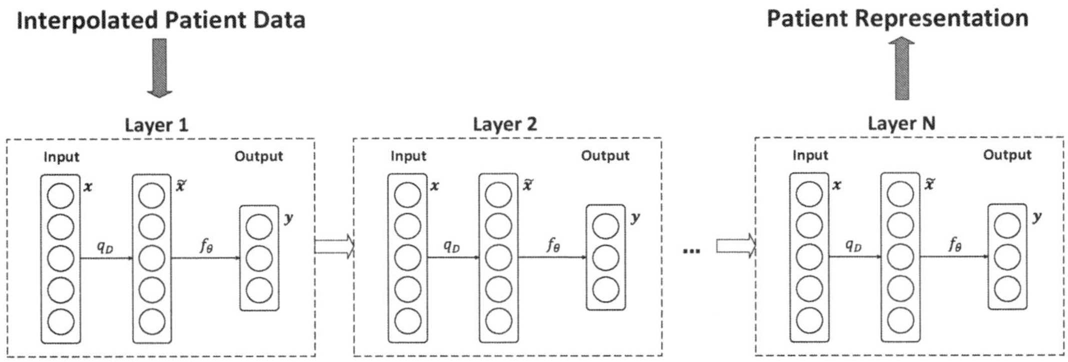

Figure 3: DLFS feature learning using stacked denoising autoencoders.

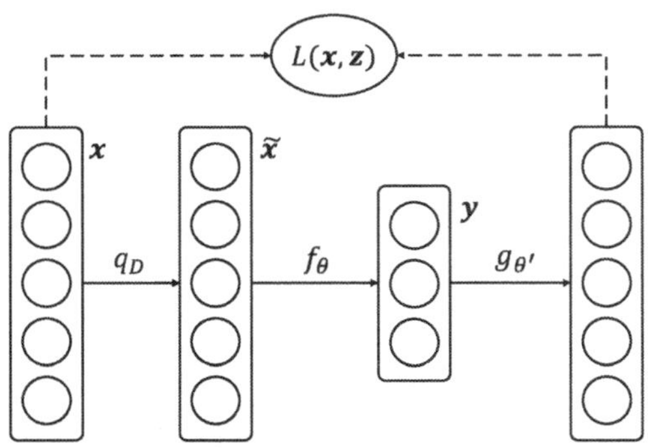

Figure 4: Denoising autoencoder.

where the predictive mean and covariance are calculated as

$$\mu_{i,*} = \mathbf{K}_{*T}(\mathbf{K} + \mathbf{R}_{i,*})^{-1}\mathbf{z}_{i,T} \quad (5)$$

$$\Sigma_{*,t} = \mathbf{K}_{**} - \mathbf{K}_{*T}(\mathbf{K} + \mathbf{R}_{i,*})^{-1}\mathbf{K}_{T*} \quad (6)$$

where $K_{*T} = [k(x_{i,*}, x_{i,1}), k(x_{i,*}, x_{i,2}), ..., k(x_{i,*}, x_{i,T})]$ and $K_{**} = k(x_{i,*}, x_{i,*})$. $K_{T*} = K_{*T}^T$ for symmetrical kernel functions. In this paper, we use radial basis function (RBF) as the kernel functions of the GP.

3.2 DLFS: Deep Learning Feature Selection

We next present a deep learning-based method for feature selection, referred to as DLFS. The interpolated data are passed into DLFS to get a compact representation of each patient. In DLFS, the patient representation is derived using a multi-layer neural network in a deep learning architecture. Each layer of the network is trained to produce a higher-level representation of the observed patterns. This is done by optimizing a local unsupervised criterion based on the data it receives from the previous layer. Therefore, every layer produces a representation of the input pattern that is more abstract than the previous layer.

The proposed deep learning framework is implemented using a stack of denoising autoencoders (SDAs) [18] (see Figure 3), where each layer of the neural network is a denoising autoencoder (DA) (see Figure 4). With such architecture, each DA is independently trained layer by layer. Similar to [18], we assume all the DAs share the same structure and functionalities.

Figure 4 shows the structure of a basic DA. The input signal $\mathbf{x} \in \mathbb{R}^d$ to the DA is first corrupted by a stochastic mapping $\tilde{\mathbf{x}} \sim q_D(\tilde{\mathbf{x}}|\mathbf{x})$. This corruption process is to avoid over-fitting the input data during the training process. In this paper, we obtain the corrupted signal $\tilde{\mathbf{x}}$ by adding Gaussian noise to the input signal $\mathbf{x}$. The corrupted signal $\tilde{\mathbf{x}}$ is then mapped to a hidden representation $\mathbf{y} \in \mathbb{R}^{d'}$ through a deterministic mapping:

$$\mathbf{y} = f_\theta(\tilde{\mathbf{x}}) = s(\mathbf{W}\tilde{\mathbf{x}} + \mathbf{b}), \quad (7)$$

parameterized by $\boldsymbol{\theta} = (\mathbf{W}, \mathbf{b})$ where $\mathbf{W}$ is a weight coefficient matrix, and $\mathbf{b}$ is a bias vector. $s(\cdot)$ is a non-linear transformation, which is also referred to as an activation function. The hidden representation $\mathbf{y}$ is then mapped back to a reconstructed signal $\mathbf{z} \in \mathbb{R}^d$ through a decoder:

$$\mathbf{z} = g_{\theta'}(\mathbf{y}) = s(\mathbf{W}'\mathbf{y} + \mathbf{b}'), \quad (8)$$

parameterized by $\boldsymbol{\theta}' = (\mathbf{W}', \mathbf{b}')$. The parameters $\boldsymbol{\theta}$ and $\boldsymbol{\theta}'$ are trained to minimize the average reconstruction error over a training set, which is measured by some loss function $L(\mathbf{x}, \mathbf{z})$. In this paper, we use *cross-entropy* as the loss function for training the parameters.

Besides minimizing the reconstruction error between $\mathbf{x}$ and $\mathbf{z}$, the DAs also minimize the reconstruction error between $\mathbf{x}$ and $\mathbf{y}$, which is equivalent to maximizing the lower bound of the mutual information between $\mathbf{x}$ and $\mathbf{y}$ [1],[18]. Therefore, $\mathbf{y}$ can be treated as a compact representation of the raw data $\mathbf{x}$ that captures the coordinates along the main factors of variation in the data. After training the parameters of the current DA, the encoded signal $\mathbf{y}$ is returned as the output signal of the current DA, which will be used as the input signal of the DA in the following layer. The whole training process of the SDA is shown in Figure 3. The interpolated raw data are first passed into the DA in the first layer of the SDA. Then after N layers of filtering, the interpolated raw data is transformed into a compact representation, which will be used as features for classification.

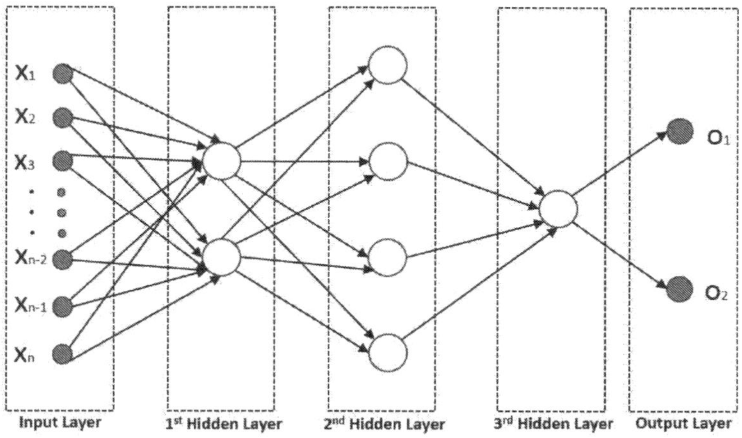

Figure 5: Structure of the ANN classifier.

3.3 Classification

We now discuss the classifiers used in this paper. As the ground truths of the patients' lengths of stay are known, we consider supervised classification algorithms.

3.3.1 Support Vector Machines. Support vector machine (SVM) is a supervised machine learning algorithm for classification modeling. It uses a set of support vectors to represent input data in high-dimensional spaces and constructs hyperplanes to separate the data points into different classes. Specifically, we choose C-Support Vector Classification (SVC) [7] as the classifier. The selection of kernel functions affects the accuracy of the model. In our study, we use a polynomial kernel function to transform the input data, as it is more suitable for nonlinear classification.

3.3.2 Artificial Neural Networks. An artificial neural network (ANN) is a parameterized computational nonlinear algorithm popularly used for supervised classification problems. It feeds input data and desired outputs into a multi-layer perceptron network with several hidden layers to separate data into different classes.

The structure of the ANN affects the classification accuracy. We conducted some experiments in order to find a good structure for the ANN. Based on the experimental results, we decided the structure of the ANN used in this paper to be the one shown in Figure 5. It consists of one input layer, one output layer and 3 hidden layers with 4, 2, and 1 neurons at each of the hidden layers. To create the nonlinearity for the model, we implement different activation functions at each layer, i.e., the sigmoid function, rectified linear function, and the Softmax function are used at the first, second, and third hidden layers, respectively.

4 RESULTS

In this section, we compare the proposed DLFS feature selection scheme with some benchmark feature selection methods, namely, MFS and RFS. MFS is a manual feature selection method which manually picks a set of the features from the raw patient data. RFS uses the interpolated vital sign data as the features for classification. In this paper, we refer to the manually selected feature set as *ManFeat* and refer to the feature set selected by RFS as *RawFeat*.

Figure 6 shows the flow of the testing experiments. For fair comparison, the same set of classifiers are used to compare the performance of different feature selection methods. In the following, we first introduce the competing feature selection methods in detail. Then, we present a comparison of the classification performance.

4.1 Comparison of Feature Selection Methods

4.1.1 Manual Feature Selection (MFS). MFS extracts features from raw heterogeneous patient data, which contains both time-series data, such as vital sign data, and static data, such as gender and age.

For time-series data, MFS extracts features in both time and frequency domains. In the time domain, we compute statistics, including mean (Mean), maximum value (Max), minimum value (Min) and standard deviation (StdDev) of the vital sign time series. Since the patients' vital signs are time series data, which are non-stationary in general, important features from the frequency domain could be useful to describe the distribution of vital sign signals as well. Therefore, in the frequency domain, we compute approximation and detailed coefficients of Discrete Wavelet Transform (DWT) [4]. The maximum approximation coefficient (MAC-DWT) and the maximum detailed coefficient (MDC-DWT) are selected as features since they are considered to be the dominant coefficients in the frequency domain. We also choose the amplitude of the best frequency component in Discrete Fourier Transform (DFT) [22], denoted by BFC-DFT, as a feature. We compute the same metrics in both time and frequency domains for the delta change of the vital signs as features in order to represent those properties of the first derivatives of the vital sign signals.

MFS also extracts static patient data as features, such as total amount of intravenous infusion (an integer value), nurse monitoring frequency (an integer value) and whether oxygenation was required in the first 24 hours (a binary value). Furthermore, MFS

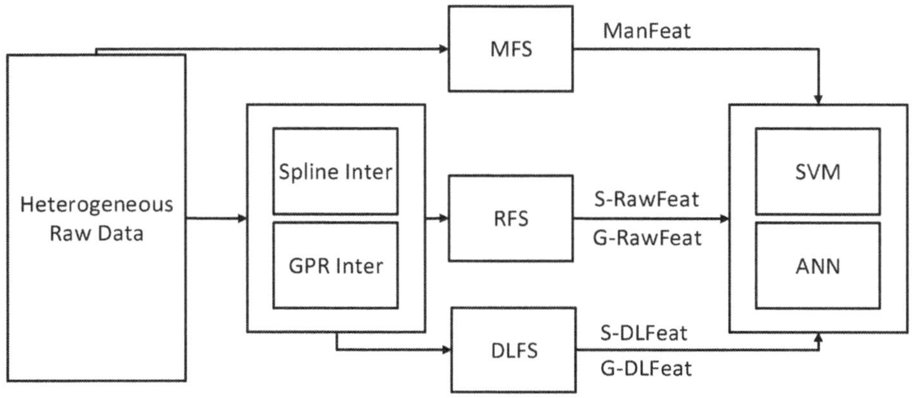

Figure 6: Illustration of the various feature selection systems studied.

Table 1: List of extracted features in ManFeat

		Value	Mean	Max	Min	StdDev	MAC-DWT	MDC-DWT	BFC-DFT
1	**Respiration**	-	X	X	X	X	X	X	X
2	**SpO2**	-	X	X	X	X	X	X	X
3	**Temperature**	-	X	X	X	X	X	X	X
4	**BP Systolic**	-	X	X	X	X	X	X	X
5	**BP Diastolic**	-	X	X	X	X	X	X	X
6	**Pulse**	-	X	X	X	X	X	X	X
7	**Delta_Respiration**	-	X	X	X	X	X	X	X
8	**Delta_SpO2**	-	X	X	X	X	X	X	X
9	**Delta_Temperature**	-	X	X	X	X	X	X	X
10	**Delta_BP Systolic**	-	X	X	X	X	X	X	X
11	**Delta_BP Diastolic**	-	X	X	X	X	X	X	X
12	**Delta_Pulse**	-	X	X	X	X	X	X	X
13	**Oxygenation**	X	-	-	-	-	-	-	-
14	**Intravenous Infusion**	X	-	-	-	-	-	-	-
15	**Monitoring Frequency**	X	-	-	-	-	-	-	-
16	**Gender**	X	-	-	-	-	-	-	-
17	**Age**	X	-	-	-	-	-	-	-

also includes some demographic information such as gender and age in the feature sets.

We use *ManFeat* to denote the feature set selected by MFS. Overall, MFS extracts 89 features in the ManFeat feature set. The list of features in ManFeat is shown in Table 1, where the fields marked with "X" are the fields included as features in the ManFeat. For example, according to Row 1, the Mean, Max, Min, StdDev, MAC-DWT, MDC-DWT and BFC-DFT of the respiration data are selected as features in the ManFeat. One the other hand, according to Row 13, whether the patient has been given oxygenation, which is a binary value, is selected as a feature in the ManFeat. In Table 1, Rows 1-12 are the features representing the statistical information derived from the vital sign time series and Rows 13-17 are single value measurements.

4.1.2 Interpolated Data as features (RFS). RFS aims to use the raw data as features. However, the raw vital sign data cannot be used as feature directly as they are highly heterogeneous. Therefore, we use the interpolated data as the features instead. Using the interpolation methods introduced in Section 3.1, we interpolate the patient data to a finer grain with 1 minute interval between every adjacent data points. After interpolation, we use the first 24 hours' data from each patient as the feature for classification. Let *S-RawFeat* and *G-RawFeat* be the interpolated data from spline interpolation and GPR interpolation, respectively. Therefore, *S-RawFeat* and *G-RawFeat* have feature vectors with size 1440 for each type of vital sign. As the dataset contains 6 types of vital signs, *S-RawFeat* and *G-RawFeat* both have feature vectors of size 8640.

4.1.3 Feature set computed from DLFS. The DLFeat feature set is obtained by passing the interpolated raw data through the deep learning framework, i.e., DLFS, as shown in Figure 3. Let *S-DLFeat* and *G-DLFeat* denote the resulting feature sets from DLFS with spline-interpolated data and GPR-interpolated data as inputs, respectively. The feature set obtained depends on the number of layers in the deep neural network and the dimensions of the input and output of each DA in each layer. Based on some preliminary experimental results, we set the number of layers in the deep neural network to be $N = 3$ and set the dimensions of the input and output of each DA to be (8640, 4320), (4320, 256) and (256, 128), receptively. Therefore, the resulting features *S-DLFeat* and *G-DLFeat* will have sizes of 128 for each patient.

4.2 Prediction Accuracy

In this section, we compare the classification accuracy using the feature sets obtained from different feature selection methods. As shown in Figure 6, there are 5 feature sets generated in this paper, i.e., ManFeat, S-RawFeat, G-RawFeat, S-DLFeat and G-DLFeat. We trained the supervised SVM and ANN classifiers with these 5 feature sets respectively and investigated the classification results. Each feature set has 126 instances representing each patient. As introduced in Section 2, the number of instances from Class 0 and Class 1 are imbalanced as we have 80 patients from Class 0 and 46 patients from Class 1. To reduce the bias in training and testing, during each experiment run, we randomly select 30 instances from both Class 0 and Class 1 as the training set, and randomly select 16 instances from the remaining Class 0 instances and all remaining Class 1 instances as the testing set. In this way, there are an equal number of instances from Class 0 and Class 1 in both training and testing sets. The training dataset is used to train the classifiers and the testing dataset is used to evaluate the classification accuracy. The experiment runs for 100 times with different randomly constructed training and testing sets during each run to avoid biases.

Three metrics are computed to characterize the classification results, namely, classification accuracy, AUC-ROC and F1-Score. Classification accuracy indicates the probability of the classification answer being correct, which is obtained by averaging all accuracy results generated from each experiment run. We also compute Receiver Operating Characteristic (ROC) and F1-score for the classification results. ROC curve is commonly used in the binary classification study to evaluate the quality of a classification model by presenting the true and false positive rate. The quality of a model is measured by the area-under-curve (AUC) of ROC curve. The higher the AUC score, the better the model performs. F1-score computes the harmonic mean of the precision and recalled of a binary classification model. The detailed mathematical expressions of AUC-ROC and F1-score can be found in [12]. All these three metrics are computed as the average over the 100 experiment runs.

The classification results of different feature sets with different classifiers are presented in Table 2 and Table 3, respectively. We name the different test cases in the following way: "Feature Set-Classifier". For example, in Table 2, the row starting with ManFeat-SVM shows the classification results by using ManFeat as the feature set and SVM as the classifier. It can be seen that features extracted from DLFS, especially G-DLFeat, can achieve the highest classification accuracy among all the selected feature sets for both SVM and ANN classifiers, which shows the advantage of the DLFS scheme.

It can be seen from Table 2 that, with the feature set G-DLFeat, the SVM classifier can classify patients' lengths of stay in the hospital with 70.39% accuracy, which is the highest among all 5 feature sets. ManFeat does not perform so well, which only has a accuracy of 53.41%. Moreover, the spline interpolation generally performs worse than GPR interpolation as the accuracy from S-RawFeat is much lower than that of G-RawFeat with a difference of around 15% and the accuracy from S-DLFeat is also much lower than that of G-DLFeat with a difference of around 8%. Even with DLFS, S-DLFeat still performs worse than G-RawFeat. This shows the disadvantage of spline interpolation as it will become unstable when the number of training samples are too small; whereas GPR interpolation is generally stable regardless of the training sample size.

Similar results can be seen from the AUC-ROC comparisons in Table 2. The highest AUC of ROC is achieved by G-DLFeat, which is the highest among all 5 feature sets. Moreover, the F1-score of the G-DLFeat is 0.7011 that is much better than the F1-score achieved by the other 4 feature sets.

The classification results with ANN classifier are shown in Table 3. Similarly, G-DLFeat achieves the best results in all performance metrics. With the ANN classifier, G-DLFeat can achieve a classification accuracy of 80.03%, which is around 20% higher than ManFeat and around 10% higher than the other 3 feature sets. The AUC of ROC and F1-score achieved by G-DLFeat are also the highest among all 5 feature sets, which shows the advantage of G-DLFeat using ANN classifier.

We also compare the performances of the two classifiers. By comparing Table 2 and Table 3, it can be seen that the ANN classifier generally performs better than SVM as it can achieve a higher classification accuracy for all feature sets. Furthermore, the achieved AUC-ROC score and the F1-score by the ANN classifier are also better than those achieved by the SVM classifier. Though ANN classifier performs better than SVM classifier in terms of classification accuracy, it also comes with high complexity. During our experiments, we notice that the computation time for ANN classifier is longer than that of SVM classifier, which shows one disadvantage of the ANN classifier.

4.3 Experimenting with Feature Selection

Feature selection is necessary to remove noise and irrelevant attributes so to optimize machine learning models and to improve the classification performance, as redundant information brought by irrelevant features might affect the accuracy of the classifiers. As shown in Section 4.2, different feature selection methods can cause large discrepancies in classification accuracy. In this section, we would like to explicitly vary the features selected by different feature selection methods and investigate the effects on the classification results.

We start with ManFeat. As discussed in Section 4.1, ManFeat selects 89 features in total including some statistical metrics in the time domain, some coefficients in the frequency domain and some static information. In this section, we would like to manually remove some features from the 89 features and see the effect on the classification accuracy. The results are presented in Table 4.

The classification results tell that removing nurse monitoring frequency, oxygenation required, gender and age from the ManFeat

Table 2: SVM classification results using different feature selection methods

Patient Representation and Classifier	Accuracy	AUC-ROC	F1-score
ManFeat-SVM	0.5341	0.6174	0.5348
S-RawFeat-SVM	0.5313	0.6351	0.5138
G-RawFeat-SVM	0.6814	0.7955	0.6811
S-DLFeat-SVM	0.6319	0.7228	0.6129
G-DLFeat-SVM	**0.7039**	**0.8028**	**0.7011**

Table 3: ANN classification results using different feature selection methods

Patient Representation and Classifier	Accuracy	AUC-ROC	F1-score
ManFeat-ANN	0.6193	0.6854	0.5741
S-RawFeat-ANN	0.6875	0.7151	0.6753
G-RawFeat-ANN	0.7183	0.7951	0.7087
S-DLFeat-ANN	0.7031	0.7361	0.6812
G-DLFeat-ANN	**0.8003**	**0.8519**	**0.7921**

Table 4: Classification accuracy of selective ManFeat feature set

Patient Representation	SVM Accuracy	ANN Accuracy
Original ManFeat	0.5341	0.6193
Exclude Gender and Age	0.5300	0.6192
Exclude Intravenous Infusion	0.5484	0.6192
Exclude Oxygenation	0.5340	0.6193
Exclude Monitoring Frequency	0.5330	0.6193
Exclude features related to delta change of vital-signs	0.5086	0.6193

do not contribute to any increase in the accuracy of the SVM classifier, as the classification accuracy achieved by training the SVM classifier with these sub-feature sets are all around 53%, which only differ by 0.41% to 0.01% as compared to the accuracy obtained from the original ManFeat. However, removing intravenous infusion from the ManFeat allows the classification accuracy of the SVM classifier to improve by 1.43%, achieving 54.84% accuracy instead. It indicates that the total amount of intravenous infused would be an irrelevant feature to the SVM classifier. On the contrary, excluding delta change of the vital-signs from the ManFeat results in a significant drop in the classification accuracy by 2.55%, which indicates that the delta change of the vital signs could be important features. However, manually excluding features from ManFeat does not have any significant effect on the ANN classifier, since its classification accuracy does not change obviously. The reason may be that ANN is a more powerful classifier which is able to recover some of the effects caused by the disappearance of certain features.

It can be seen in the results in Table 4 that such ad-hoc way of removing features may not be efficient in identifying which features are the most important. Therefore, we propose another method to quantify the importance of each feature. Specifically, we compute the *mutual information* (MI) between each feature and the label, and then rank the features according their MI scores. We perform experiments by including the features one by one, starting from the feature with the highest MI score, and investigate the change in classification accuracy as we include more features. The experiments are performed using both the feature sets from ManFeat and G-DLFeat, whose results are shown in Figure 7 and Figure 8 respectively. We use SVM as the classifier for these experiments.

It can be seen from Figure 7 that adding more features from the ManFeat feature set does not always give a better classification result. The highest classification accuracy is obtained when only 32 features are included. After 32 features, as we include more features from the ManFeat feature set, the classification accuracy drops. The reason is that, as ManFeat feature sets are created in an ad-hoc manner, there could be some features in the feature set causing confusion to others. When those features are included together for classification, the accuracy will degrade.

An interesting comparison can be seen in Figure 8, in which we observe that, by including more features from the G-DLFeat feature set, the classification accuracy always improves. The is because, by going through the deep learning framework in DLFS, the features selected by the DLFS are always consistent with each other. In such cases, including more features from the G-DLFeat feature set will always give a better classification result. This highlights one of the advantages of the DLFS feature selection method.

5 CONCLUSIONS

In this paper, we propose DLFS, a novel feature selection scheme for predictive diagnosis based on deep learning. DLFS is an unsupervised feature selection method, which can learn compact representations from heterogeneous patient data automatically for efficient classification and prediction. The problem of predicting the patients' lengths of stay in the hospital is investigated via a

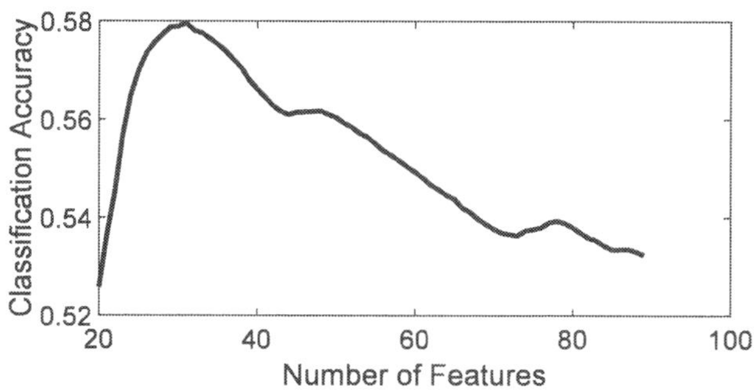

Figure 7: Performance of ManFeat-SVM with Mutual Information feature ranking.

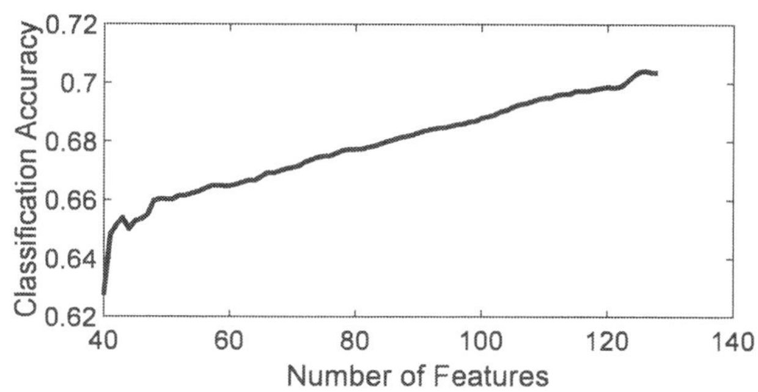

Figure 8: Performance of G-DLFeat-SVM with Mutual Information feature ranking.

predictive diagnosis framework that incorporates DLFS. We verify the advantage of DLFS, in terms of prediction accuracy, by running experiments using real-world patient data and comparing with several other commonly used feature selection methods. Furthermore, by experimenting with feature selection via mutual information ranking, we find that DLFS selects relevant features in a consistent manner.

6 ACKNOWLEDGMENTS

We would like to thank Dr. Leisel Fong, Dr. Jason Phua and Prof. Lawrence Ho from the National University Hospital in Singapore for facilitating DSRB ethics approval, providing patient data access, and generously giving constructive feedback.

This research was supported in part by the Singapore Ministry of Education under grant R-263-000-B57-112 and the Singapore National Research Foundation Competitive Research Programme (CRP Award No. NRF-CRP-8-2011-01).

REFERENCES

[1] Anthony J. Bell and Terrence J. Sejnowski. 1995. An Information-maximization Approach to Blind Separation and Blind Deconvolution. *Neural Comput.* 7, 6 (Nov. 1995), 1129–1159.

[2] Riccardo Bellazzi and Blaz Zupan. 2008. Predictive data mining in clinical medicine: Current issues and guidelines. *International Journal of Medical Informatics* 77, 2 (Apr 2008), 81–97.

[3] Y. Bengio, A. Courville, and P. Vincent. 2013. Representation Learning: A Review and New Perspectives. *IEEE Transactions on Pattern Analysis and Machine Intelligence* 35, 8 (Aug 2013), 1798–1828.

[4] Jaison Bennet, Chilambuchelvan Arul Ganaprakasam, and Kannan Arputharaj. 2014. A Discrete Wavelet Based Feature Extraction and Hybrid Classification Technique for Microarray Data Analysis. *Scientific World Journal* 2014 (06 Aug 2014).

[5] R. Caccialanza, C. Klersy, E. Cereda, B. Cameletti, A. Bonoldi, C. Bonardi, M. Marinelli, and P. Dionigi. 2010. Nutritional parameters associated with prolonged hospital stay among ambulatory adult patients. *CMAJ* 182, 17 (Nov 2010), 1843–1849.

[6] D. B. Chalfin, S. Trzeciak, A. Likourezos, B. M. Baumann, and R. P. Dellinger. 2007. Impact of delayed transfer of critically ill patients from the emergency department to the intensive care unit. *Crit. Care Med.* 35, 6 (Jun 2007), 1477–1483.

[7] Chih-Chung Chang and Chih-Jen Lin. 2011. LIBSVM: A Library for Support Vector Machines. *ACM Trans. Intell. Syst. Technol.* 2, 3 (May 2011), 1–27.

[8] Peter B. Jensen, Lars J. Jensen, and Soren Brunak. 2012. Mining electronic health records: towards better research applications and clinical care. *Nat Rev Genet* 13, 6 (Jun 2012), 395–405.

[9] H. Mamaghanian, N. Khaled, D. Atienza, and P. Vandergheynst. 2011. Compressed Sensing for Real-Time Energy-Efficient ECG Compression on Wireless Body Sensor Nodes. *IEEE Transactions on Biomedical Engineering* 58, 9 (Sept 2011), 2456–2466.

[10] D. B. Neill. 2013. Using Artificial Intelligence to Improve Hospital Inpatient Care. *IEEE Intelligent Systems* 28, 2 (March 2013), 92–95.

[11] Rimma Pivovarov, David J. Albers, Jorge L. Sepulveda, and NoÃĺmie Elhadad. 2014. Identifying and mitigating biases in EHR laboratory tests. *Journal of Biomedical Informatics* 51 (2014), 24 – 34.

[12] David Martin Ward Powers. 2011. Evaluation: from precision, recall and F-measure to ROC, informedness, markedness and correlation. *International Journal of Machine Learning Technology* 2, 1 (2011), 37–63.

[13] Carl Edward Rasmussen and Christopher K. I. Williams. 2005. *Gaussian Processes for Machine Learning*. The MIT Press.

[14] F. Rincon, S. A. Mayer, J. Rivolta, J. Stillman, B. Boden-Albala, M. S. Elkind, R. Marshall, and J. Y. Chong. 2010. Impact of delayed transfer of critically ill stroke patients from the Emergency Department to the Neuro-ICU. *Neurocrit Care* 13, 1 (Aug 2010), 75–81.

[15] F. C. Ryckman, P. A. Yelton, A. M. Anneken, P. E. Kiessling, P. J. Schoettker, and U. R. Kotagal. 2009. Redesigning intensive care unit flow using variability management to improve access and safety. *Jt Comm J Qual Patient Saf* 35, 11 (Nov 2009), 535–543.

[16] Angela Simpson, Vincent Y. Tan, John Winn, Markus Svensen, Christopher Bishop, David Heckerman, Iain Buchan, and Adnan Custovic. 2010. Beyond Atopy: Multiple Patterns of Sensitization in Relation to Asthma in a Birth Cohort Study. *American Journal of Respiratory and Critical Care Medicine* 181 (February 2010), 1200–1206.

[17] Ralph Snyderman. 2012. Personalized health care: From theory to practice. *Biotechnology Journal* 7, 8 (2012), 973–979.

[18] Pascal Vincent, Hugo Larochelle, Isabelle Lajoie, Yoshua Bengio, and Pierre-Antoine Manzagol. 2010. Stacked Denoising Autoencoders: Learning Useful Representations in a Deep Network with a Local Denoising Criterion. *J. Mach. Learn. Res.* 11 (Dec. 2010), 3371–3408.

[19] F. Wang, N. Lee, J. Hu, J. Sun, S. Ebadollahi, and A. F. Laine. 2013. A Framework for Mining Signatures from Event Sequences and Its Applications in Healthcare Data. *IEEE Transactions on Pattern Analysis and Machine Intelligence* 35, 2 (Feb 2013), 272–285.

[20] N. G. Weiskopf and C. Weng. 2013. Methods and dimensions of electronic health record data quality assessment: enabling reuse for clinical research. *J Am Med Inform Assoc* 20, 1 (Jan 2013), 144–151.

[21] Jionglin Wu, Jason Roy, and Walter F. Stewart. 2010. Prediction Modeling Using EHR Data: Challenges, Strategies, and a Comparison of Machine Learning Approaches. 48, 6 (2010), S106–S113.

[22] F. Zhao and R. Yang. 2007. Power-Quality Disturbance Recognition Using S-Transform. *IEEE Transactions on Power Delivery* 22, 2 (April 2007), 944–950.

[23] O. C. Zienkiewicz. 1976. Splines and variational methods. *Internat. J. Numer. Methods Engrg.* 10, 2 (1976), 487–487.

Winnow: Interactive Visualization of Temporal Changes in Multidimensional Clinical Data

Hsueh-Chien Cheng
Department of Computer Science, University of Maryland
College Park, Maryland 20742
hccheng@umd.edu

Rainer von Coelln
Department of Neurology, University of Maryland School of Medicine
Baltimore, Maryland 21201
rvoncoelln@som.umaryland.edu

Ann L. Gruber-Baldini
Department of Epidemiology and Public Health, University of Maryland School of Medicine
Baltimore, Maryland 21201
abaldin@som.umaryland.edu

Lisa M. Shulman
Department of Neurology, University of Maryland School of Medicine
Baltimore, Maryland 21201
lshulman@som.umaryland.edu

Amitabh Varshney
Department of Computer Science and UMIACS, University of Maryland
College Park, Maryland 20742
varshney@umiacs.umd.edu

ABSTRACT

Over the last two decades, an emerging paradigm of Parkinson's disease (PD) research that considers diverse clinical and biological markers in evaluating disease severity has emerged. This can lead to important insights including patterns of disease subtypes and progression. However, identification of disease subtypes and progression across multidimensional longitudinal variables representing diverse biomarkers, outcomes, and demographics remains a challenge. In this paper we present our interactive visual analytics tool, *Winnow™*, to help clinicians understand and interpret inter-relationships between a broad range of outcome measures and patient subgroups. Based on a close collaboration between clinical experts and computer scientists, Winnow is designed to intuitively visualize data from multiple outcome measures to enable users to easily filter and compare patient subgroups. We summarize the challenges in multidimensional clinical data analysis, the visual representations and design of Winnow, and present case studies based on a public PD dataset.

KEYWORDS

Interactive visualization; parallel coordinates; multidimensional visualization; web-based application; clinical visual analytics

1 INTRODUCTION

Parkinson's disease (PD) is a chronic neuro-degenerative disorder characterized by gradual progression. Whereas motor impairments are the most recognized symptoms of PD, there is increasing recognition of the importance of a range of non-motor symptoms including cognitive decline, sleep disturbance, and depression [20]. For example, the presence of inter-relationships between clinical subgroups and disease progression is supported by the discovery that patients with greater postural instability and gait difficulty tend to have faster rates of progression and greater cognitive decline [3]. This paradigm shift has resulted in large datasets with diverse clinical and biologic markers [10]. For example, at the University of Maryland PD Center, we have collected 15 years of heterogeneous and multidimensional data (e.g. clinical and genomics) on 2, 500 PD patients across 20, 000 office visits.

The expanded scope of disease beyond traditional motor symptoms raises the complexity of analysis significantly. These large multidimensional longitudinal datasets need new tools to identify disease subtypes and patterns of disease progression across diverse biomarkers, outcomes, and demographic subgroups. Conducting longitudinal studies of multidimensional data is challenging because of the limited human capacity to comprehend numerous interactions among a large number of variables. The immense cognitive load of such complex tasks causes these analyses to be time-consuming and ineffective. To address this challenge, many computational techniques such as data clustering and dimensionality reduction have been developed [1, 2]. Clustering techniques group similar data points (patients) into clusters based on specific criteria defined in a high-dimensional space. Dimension reduction techniques transform high-dimensional data points into low-dimensional representations while preserving crucial information required to proceed with the intended analysis.

Although these computational techniques provide a data-driven, objective perspective generated mathematically and statistically, they do not generate clinically meaningful results since clinical insight and experience with the domains is disconnected from the analysis. In addition, in some cases the stability of these results is questionable. For example, PD subtypes generated by cluster analysis were found to be inconsistent in various studies [22]. The results generated by pure data-driven approaches can therefore be misleading without proper clinical interpretation. We had a similar experience when we applied computational techniques in our preliminary studies, where the results were inaccessible to clinicians and not clinically relevant. This observation led us to believe that the most useful tools should be intuitive, interactive,

Permission to make digital or hard copies of all or part of this work for personal or classroom use is granted without fee provided that copies are not made or distributed for profit or commercial advantage and that copies bear this notice and the full citation on the first page. Copyrights for components of this work owned by others than ACM must be honored. Abstracting with credit is permitted. To copy otherwise, or republish, to post on servers or to redistribute to lists, requires prior specific permission and/or a fee. Request permissions from permissions@acm.org.
ACM-BCB '17, August 20-23, 2017, Boston, MA, USA
© 2017 Association for Computing Machinery.
ACM ISBN 978-1-4503-4722-8/17/08...$15.00
https://doi.org/10.1145/3107411.3107449

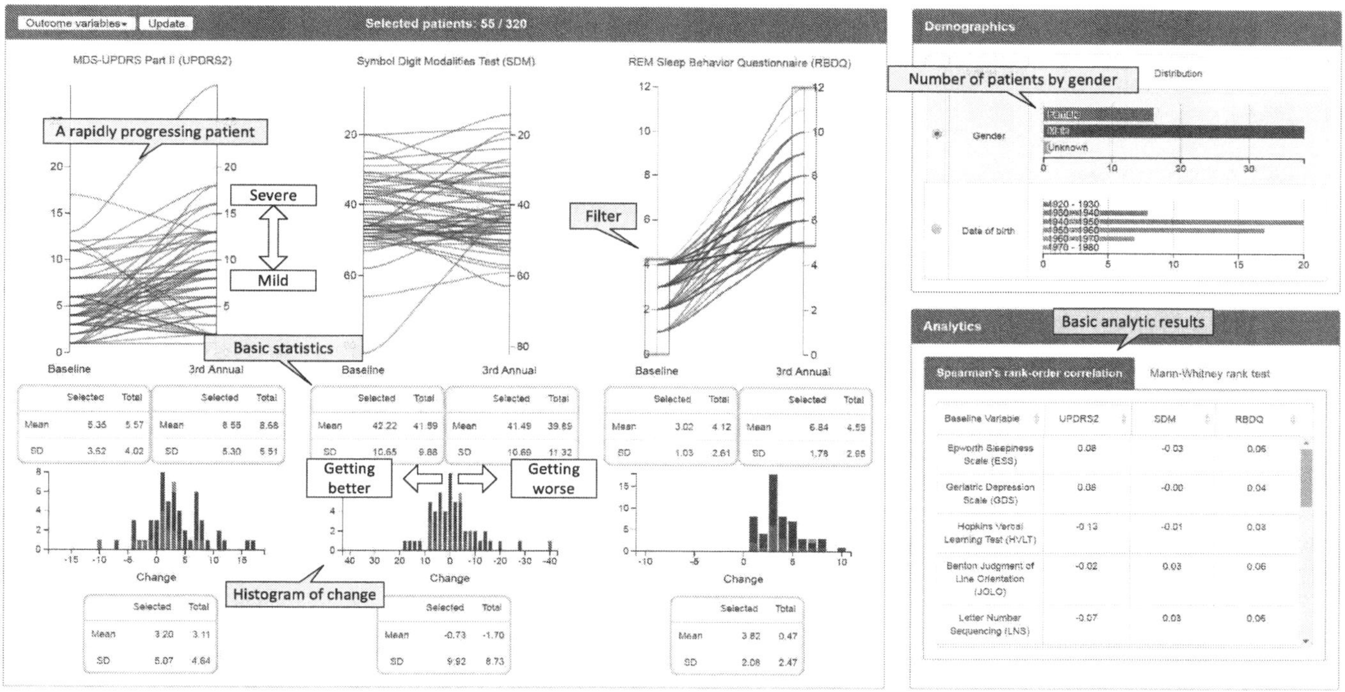

Figure 1: This screenshot of Winnow shows the results based on the Parkinson's Progression Markers Initiative (PPMI) dataset (Section 4). Winnow consists of three panels: the Outcomes panel (left), the Demographics panel (top right), and the analytics panel (bottom right). Here 55 patients (out of 320) with low baseline REM sleep behavior disorder (RBDQ < 5) and high RBDQ (RBDQ ≥ 5) at the third annual visit are selected. The colors represent the gender of patients (magenta for females and blue for males).

and generate results interpretable by clinicians. This tool should allow clinicians to efficiently sift through arrays of longitudinal data, identify patterns, and generate hypotheses, which can then be subjected to rigorous statistical analysis.

In this paper, we present a preliminary analysis of a public PD dataset with our tool Winnow (Figure 1) to study patterns of disease progression between time points. As a visual analytics tool, Winnow presents complex data in a way that facilitates detection of patterns and anomalies by the human eye. In contrast to the fully-automatic analysis conducted with computational techniques, visual analytics tools allow users to interactively explore the data through dynamic filtering and subgrouping. By interacting with intuitive visual representations, users can generate clinically relevant hypotheses and insights that are not easily accessible with conventional approaches.

Winnow visualizes multiple selected outcome measures simultaneously to enable the investigation of inter-relationships across outcome measures in various domains. By representing each patient as a line defined by the values of a selected outcome measure recorded at the first and second time points, the slope of lines indicates the rate of disease progression of the corresponding outcome. We also show a histogram of disease progression to facilitate the selection of fast- and slow-progressing patients. All visualizations are color-coded by demographic characteristics of patients (e.g. gender) to foster understanding of demographic-related questions such as whether female and male patients progress differently with respect to specific outcomes. The panels in Winnow are linked together to provide consistent visualizations during data exploration.

We have made our design choices in Winnow based on the feedback obtained from data scientists and clinicians in a long-term collaboration following the guidelines of Multi-dimensional In-depth Long-term Case studies (MILC) [19]. One example of the design choices we collaboratively made is reducing the complexity of visualization by choosing clinically relevant features, thus improving the usability of the tool. Clinical investigators want the opportunity for "hands-on" experience with clinical datasets to explore data based on experiential intuition. We repeatedly found the interpretability of results to be the top priority for the clinicians.

We make the following contributions in this work:

- A visual analytics tool, Winnow, to help clinicians understand the interactions across multiple disease features and their changes over time.
- A MILC analyzing the needs of clinicians to facilitate the design of a clinician-friendly tool for visualizing multidimensional clinical data.
- A preliminary analysis of a public PD dataset based on 16 outcome measures in multiple domains.

In the following, we first review the work on computational and visualization-based techniques in Section 2. We then summarize our MILC in Section 3. We introduce the dataset used in our study in Section 4, the visual analytics tool Winnow in Section 5, and the example case studies conducted with Winnow in Section 6. Finally, we present conclusions and future extensions of Winnow in Section 7.

2 RELATED WORK

2.1 Data Clustering

Clustering techniques reveal patterns by grouping similar data points together. These techniques create another layer of abstraction on top of the raw high-dimensional data, thus allowing users to inspect the clustering results without directly addressing the high dimensionality of the data. Because the grouping of data points is based on an explicitly defined similarity function, defining a reasonable function is key to the success of clustering analysis. Typical k-means algorithm [11] defines dissimilarity of two high-dimensional points as the Euclidean distance between them. Density-based techniques such as OPTICS [1] rely on a neighborhood function to determine whether two data points are (similar) neighbors. Spectral clustering [18] requires a similarity function in constructing the adjacency graph. In practice, different similarity functions may lead to distinct results.

Nevertheless, the similarity of two data points is subjective, application-dependent, and usually difficult to define especially for high-dimensional data. This difficulty is fundamental because typical distance functions (e.g. Euclidean distance) fail to measure similarity precisely in high-dimensional space, a known problem referred to as the "curse of dimensionality". In an exploratory clinical analysis that lacks a well-defined disease model, the limited interpretability of clustering results also aggravates the generation of clinically relevant, actionable results.

2.2 Dimension Reduction

Dimension reduction techniques reduce data dimensionality while maintaining certain relationships among data points with respect to specific criteria. Principal component analysis (PCA) finds a series of mutually orthogonal principal components that account for the most variance in the data. Locally linear embedding (LLE) [17] and Laplacian Eigenmaps [2] first construct a neighborhood representation, typically based on pairwise Euclidean distances, and then derive a low-dimensional space that preserves local distances among neighboring data points. A neural network that learns to reconstruct the original high-dimensional training data from the derived low-dimensional latent variables can also be used for reducing data dimensionality [7].

All these techniques share similar limitations with clustering techniques such as requiring an explicitly-defined similarity function and limited interpretability of results. Whereas each principal component generated by PCA represents a linear combination of variables, the clinical meaning of adding (or subtracting) two clinically-unrelated features from different domains is unclear. The results generated by LLE and Laplacian Eigenmaps provide little clue for further interpretation. In fact, even extending a low-dimensional space derived by LLE or Laplacian Eigenmaps to include a new data point is non-trivial. The latent variables found by neural-network-based techniques are usually cryptic unless the training data are already labeled, which is not the case for exploratory analysis.

2.3 High-dimensional Data Visualization

High-dimensional data visualization creates a visual abstraction of high-dimensional data such that patterns and anomalies can be detected by the human eye. Several successful visualizations of high-dimensional data such as the scatter plot matrix (SPLOM) [4] and parallel coordinates [8] have been widely applied. A SPLOM organizes scatter plots generated for each dimension pair as the elements inside a matrix; this layout facilitates efficient scanning of correlations between dimension pairs. A parallel coordinates visualization represents dimensions as individual parallel lines (axes); a data point is therefore represented as a segmented line connecting each point in order from the first axis to the last. Clusters of data points can therefore be visually detected as clusters of lines. Spreadsheet-based approaches that associate groups of cells with various types of visual representations can also help understand complex inter-relationships in heterogeneous datasets [23]. In contrast to the automatic analysis of computational approaches, data visualization can be easily combined with user interactions (e.g. brushing and linking) to allow interactive data exploration via filtering and zooming in and out of specific subsets of data.

The amount of information that can be displayed in a single visualization is, however, limited by the screen size and the perceptual capability of the human visual system. Such limitations can cause usability issues that adversely affect the efficacy of visual analytics tools. For example, visualizing all pairs of dimensions in a SPLOM is increasingly unrealistic as dimensionality grows. The parallel-coordinates visualization is incomprehensible even with a moderate number of dimensions. Better visual design strategies such as reordering dimensions [16], subsampling [6], and edge bundling [25] improve visual quality, but in general visualizing high-dimensional data remains a challenging task.

3 PRELIMINARY STUDY: MILC

The Multi-dimensional In-depth Long-term Case studies (MILC) method [19] evaluates the efficacy of visualization tools using various approaches, such as interviews and observations, while collaborating closely with expert users. Here we describe the MILC we conducted as a preliminary study in the development of a clinician-friendly visual analytics tool.

We formed a multi-disciplinary research group of data scientists, database specialists, neurologists, and biostatisticians in 2015, targeting the analysis of the PD data collected at the University of Maryland PD Center. Group members included movement disorder specialists (neurologists) with extensive expertise in PD but little experience with visualization tools. In contrast, other group members with computational backgrounds were only familiar with computational and visualization techniques.

During each group session, a visualization tool or a new version of a tool based on previous group discussion was presented. Users then attempted to apply the tool for routine analysis tasks or confirming/rejecting PD-related hypotheses. The comments and feedback from users were recorded by the observers while they interacted with the tool.

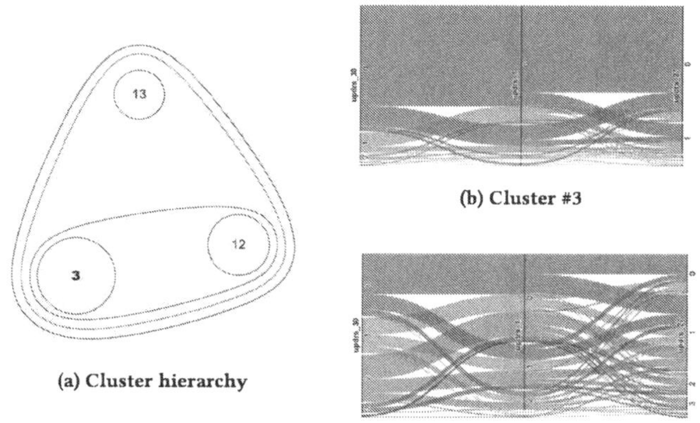

(a) Cluster hierarchy

(b) Cluster #3

(c) Cluster #12

Figure 2: (a) Our early attempt created a hierarchy of clusters to allow splitting and merging of clusters following a pre-generated hierarchy. Nevertheless, the parallel set visualization of two sibling clusters: cluster #3 (figure (b)) and cluster #12 (figure (c)), are difficult to interpret even with three dimensions.

Early in the project, we focused on identifying novel multi-domain PD subtypes to extend the recognized motor-based subtypes [9]. Our first attempt (April, 2015) was an interactive hierarchical clustering method based on OPTICS [1]. We implemented an interactive tool that enables users to explore alternative clustering results in a pre-generated hierarchy of clusters (Figure 2a). We then tried a series of dimension reduction techniques including PCA, LLE [17], Laplacian Eigenmaps [2], and t-Distributed Stochastic Neighbor Embedding [21] to reveal possible low-dimensional representations that lead to visually apparent clusters of patients.

Common issues in all the above attempts were the limited interpretability of the results and the lack of flexibility for clinicians to steer and manipulate the analysis as desired. The goals from the clinician's perspective were to 1) visualize data on patient signs and symptoms in ways that align with their experience and 2) enable a simple hands-on interrogation of data to pose questions and generate hypotheses. We tried to improve user-friendliness by visualizing the constituent patient clusters but without success because of the complexity introduced by high data dimensionality. For example, one of our early attempts created parallel sets visualizations for each cluster. The visualizations containing overlapping lines are, however, difficult to read even with only three dimensions (Figure 2b and 2c). The lack of flexibility is related to the limited capacity for user interventions in these techniques–the only way users can modify the results is through reconfiguring the parameters of the applied computational techniques. Furthermore, these two issues of interpretability and flexibility are related and may exacerbate each other. For example, one would not know how to modify the parameters of OPTICS without a proper interpretation of the results.

Acknowledging the obstacles in our group's process, we developed two key strategies: 1) switching to a simpler PD dataset and 2) organizing two half-day group retreats (July and August, 2016). We chose to use the Parkinson's Progression Markers Initiative (PPMI) dataset (Section 4) because it is a smaller, simpler, and more structured dataset with a well-defined protocol, thus allowing us to find patterns more easily with less interference from noise. Unlike the University of Maryland PD dataset, PPMI patients are more homogeneous (recently diagnosed and untreated at enrollment) and are assessed at more standardized intervals (every six months).

A consultant with expertise in applied biostatistics and modeling (Dr. Søren Bentzen) was invited to attend the retreats for a fresh perspective and to recharge the group dynamic. After a lively discussion, the major result of the first retreat was a preliminary sketch of Winnow, a clear breakthrough to achieve our goals. As compared to the previously developed methods, Winnow's data visualization is clinically intuitive and invites the hands-on experience that clinicians seek. In addition to Winnow's approach, we also discussed the following computational techniques for future extensions.

- Clustering analysis that groups patients by their temporal characteristics (e.g. multiple cross-sectional clustering or clustering the change in clinical features).
- Supervised learning methods that predict a user-defined rate of disease progression based on multiple outcome measures.
- Statistical methods, for example multivariate regression analysis, that prove or disprove hypotheses generated by users.

These techniques provide complementary strength to the visual analytics approach of Winnow. We also reached consensus to add a biomarkers panel in the future to include data from genomics, imaging, serology, and cerebrospinal fluid. Group members had mixed reactions on the importance of interactivity to a successful tool; although most members ranked interactivity high on the list of key components, some prioritized a robust data model or user-friendly interfaces over interactivity.

Based on the results of the first retreat, we designed an interactive visualization tool with the features found to be useful for clinicians. The second retreat was held in August, 2016 to present the first version of Winnow and to review its strengths and weaknesses. The group was unanimous in their positive assessment of the intuitiveness of the data visualization and the capacity for simple interaction with the data by users without intensive training (e.g. selecting patient subgroups and outcomes for analysis). We later developed new features proposed in the second retreat, including statistical tests for group comparisons. We describe the design of Winnow in Section 5.

4 DATA

We present the following examples and case studies using data obtained from the Parkinson's Progression Markers Initiative (PPMI) database [14] (www.ppmi-info.org/data). The PPMI dataset contains patient and clinician-reported outcome measures as well as genetics, imaging and serologic data collected over a five-year period since 2010. As of now, more than 400 PD patients have been enrolled in the study. The PPMI is an ongoing study with patient records being updated on a rolling basis. In this paper, we use the data downloaded on March 2nd, 2017. For up-to-date information on the PPMI study, visit www.ppmi-info.org.

Table 1: List of the 16 outcome measures and six domains of PD in our study.

Domain	Outcome Measure	Description	Range
PD Severity: Motor & Non-Motor	MDS-UPDRS Part I (UPDRS1)	Non-motor aspects of experiences of daily living	0–52
	MDS-UPDRS Part II (UPDRS2)	Motor aspects of experiences of daily living (disability)	0–52
	MDS-UPDRS Part III (UPDRS3)	Motor examination for signs of PD	0–132
	MDS-UPDRS Total Score (T-UPDRS)	General PD severity: sum of MDS-UPDRS Part I-III	0–236
Autonomic	Autonomic Scale for Outcomes in PD (SCOPA-AUT)	Autonomic symptoms in PD	0–75
Cognitive	Hopkins Verbal Learning Test (HVLT)	Verbal short-term memory and new learning	0–12
	Benton Judgment of Line Orientation (JOLO)	Visuospatial perception and orientation	0–30*
	Semantic Fluency (SFT)	Semantic and phonetic memory	> 0
	Letter Number Sequencing (LNS)	Attention, working memory, and visuospatial ability	0–21
	Symbol Digit Modalities Test (SDM)	Processing speed	0–110*
	Montreal Cognitive Assessment (MoCA)	Global cognitive evaluation	0–30*
Sleep	Epworth Sleepiness Scale (ESS)	Daytime sleepiness	0–24
	Rapid Eye Movement Sleep (REM) Behavior Disorder Questionnaire (RBDQ)	Abnormal behaviors during REM sleep	0–13
Behavior	Geriatric Depression Scale (GDS)	Depressive symptoms in the elderly	0–15
	State-Trait Anxiety Inventory (STAI)	State and traits of anxiety in adults	40–160
Disability	Modified Schwab & England Activities of Daily Living (SEADL)	Independent and dependent function of daily activities	0–100*

* Lower score indicates more severe symptom. For all others, higher score indicates more severe symptoms.

We selected the 16 outcome measures listed in Table 1 that were collected when patients were enrolled (BL) and at their third annual follow-up visit (Y3) to study disease progression. The MDS-UPDRS (Movement Disorders Society-Unified PD Rating Scale) measures PD severity and the other measures are selected from the autonomic, cognitive, sleep, behavior, and disability domains. We chose the third instead of the fifth annual visit to generate a representative set of data with a sufficient number of patients. We excluded patients with missing or incomplete data (e.g. enrolled for less than three years) from our analysis. In summary, a total of 320 patients (90 female, 211 male and 19 unknown) born between 1927 and 1979 were included. Each patient is represented by 34 features (16 outcome measures collected at BL and Y3, and two demographic attributes). The outcome measures are aggregated scores calculated from sets of items from validated questionnaires.

5 WINNOW

Figure 1 shows a screenshot of Winnow consisting of three panels: the outcomes panel (left), the demographics panel (top right), and the analytics panel (bottom right). The number near the top shows the total number of selected patients (55 in Figure 1). We also provide the option for descriptions of the selected ranges of the currently applied filters in a tooltip (not shown here).

5.1 Outcomes Panel

Each selected outcome measure corresponds to two plots in the outcomes panel: one showing the values at BL and Y3 (top) for each individual patient, and the other showing the number of patients with a certain amount of change between BL and Y3 as a stacked histogram (bottom). In the top plot, each patient is represented by a line connecting the values of that outcome measure at BL and Y3 for that patient. Using this visual representation, changes in values correspond to the slope of lines, whose differences can be detected efficiently by human eye [13]. We reverse the positive direction of axes in the plots, if needed, such that a positive slope always indicates PD progression (from mild to severe symptoms). Therefore, a line with a steep upward slope shows the corresponding patient is experiencing rapid progression on that outcome measure. This axis reversal is applied to Benton Judgment of Line Orientation (JOLO), Symbol Digit Modalities Test (SDM), Montreal Cognitive Assessment (MoCA), and Modified Schwab & England Activities of Daily Living (SEADL) where higher scores indicate milder symptoms (marked with an asterisk in Table 1).

Although the slope of lines can be easily seen for a moderate number of lines (patients), the difficulty in locating individual lines increases significantly with the degree of occlusion. We therefore also show the number of patients with a certain amount of change between BL and Y3 in a stacked histogram in the bottom plot to provide a summary of disease progression. A similar axis reversal is applied to the histograms such that a bar on the right represents more rapid progression. In both the top and bottom plots, the colors of lines and bars are determined by the selected demographic attribute in the demographics panel (Section 5.2).

Users can select a subset of patients by dragging the target interval on the target axis. During selection, all plots, including the ones in the demographics panel, are updated interactively to reflect the latest selected patients through brushing and linking. We show the mean and standard deviation of the values at BL, Y3, and the changes in between the two for the total sample and for the selected patients to allow for easy comparison.

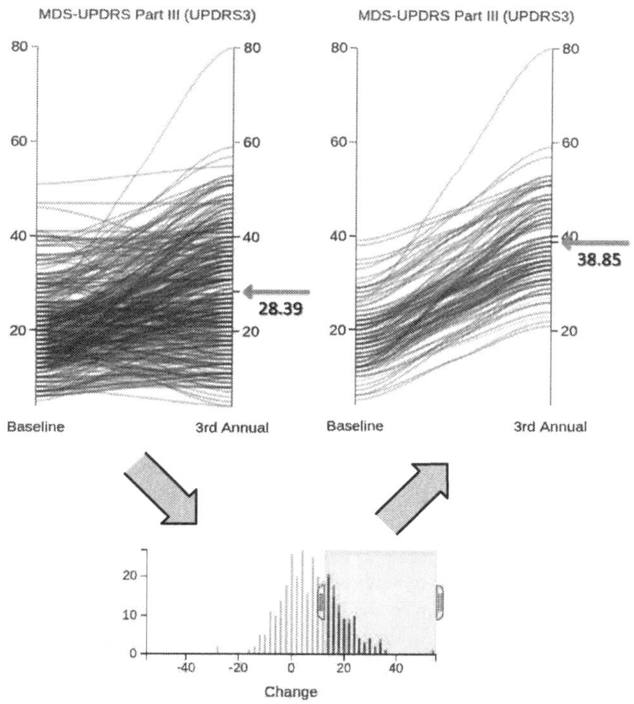

Figure 3: After using the bottom histogram for selecting patients with the most rapid progression in the motor domain (Δ(UPDRS3) > 12), the corresponding plot of UPDRS3 in the outcomes panel shows only the 109 matching patients, represented by the lines with steep upward slopes. The mean UPDRS3 at Y3 of the group of selected patients (right arrow) is greater than that of the total patient sample (left arrow).

For example, users can select the rapidly progressing patients whose UPDRS3 (motor exam) score increased by more than 12 over three years in the bottom histogram (bottom of Figure 3). After applying the filter, the 109 selected patients are represented by lines with steep upward slopes in the top plot (right of Figure 3). The mean UPDRS3 at Y3 for the selected patients (38.85, right arrow in Figure 3), is higher than the mean UPDRS3 at Y3 for the total patient sample (28.39, left arrow in Figure 3).

5.2 Demographics Panel

The demographics panel shows the gender and the year of birth in two individual histograms (top right of Figure 1). Instead of showing every year as a separate bar in the histogram, which would result in a crowded visual display, the years are grouped into decades to facilitate interpretation of age distribution and efficient use of the limited screen space.

The color scheme used in Winnow is determined by the selected demographic attribute. For example, when gender is selected, the lines (top plot) and bars (bottom plot) in the outcomes panel are colored in magenta and blue for female and male patients, respectively. Users select a subset of patients with respect to a particular demographic attribute by clicking the corresponding bar.

For example, users can select the 24 female patients from the previously selected 109 rapidly progressing patients using the demographics panel (left of Figure 4). After applying the gender filter, the mean value of Δ(SDM) is −3.33 (comparable to the decline of −3.36 before filtering by gender); this shows that the female patients in the selected cohort progress similarly to the mean total sample in terms of cognitive function as measured by SDM.

Users can also identify female patients with the most rapid progression in SDM. For example, they can select the four patients with Δ(SDM) < −16.62, which is more than one standard deviation from the mean, represented by lines with significantly steeper slopes when compared with other female patients (center of Figure 4). If we select those four patients and switch from gender to year of birth in the demographics panel, we see that these four patients were born between 1940 and 1960, corresponding to ages between 56 to 76 years (right of Figure 4).

5.3 Analytics Panel

The analytics panel shows the relationships between pairs of variables through statistical analysis (bottom right of Figure 1). The first tab shows the correlation of a pair of outcomes evaluated by the Spearman's rank correlation; a high correlation coefficient for a pair of outcomes indicates that patients with severe symptoms in one outcome are likely to have severe symptoms in the other outcome; similarly, those with low on one outcome are likely to be low on the other. The second tab shows the *p*-values of the Mann-Whitney test comparing the distributions of outcomes in the selected patients and the remainder of the patients in the total sample; an outcome has a low *p*-value when its distributions are different in the selected patients and the remainder of the patients. Both the Spearman's rank correlation and the Mann-Whitney test are non-parametric. The variable tested can be selected from the values at BL, Y3, or the change in values from BL to Y3.

In the following example we use the Mann-Whitney test to compare the changes in values between two groups: The 109 fast-progressing patients with respect to UPDRS3 (selected in Figure 3) and the remainder of the patients ($n = 211$). The result shows, beside the trivial case comparing Δ(UPDRS3) in the two groups, the other two UPDRS sub-scales (Δ(UPDRS1) and Δ(UPDRS2)–non-motor symptoms and disability) have low *p*-values ($p < 0.05$). Other variables with low *p*-values in increasing order are Δ(GDS), Δ(SDM), Δ(SCOPA-AUT), Δ(SEADL), Δ(STAI), and Δ(LNS), associated with a range of domains (behavior, cognitive, autonomic, and disability). In summary, disease progression in motor functions is associated with progression of autonomic dysfunction, cognitive decline, depression, anxiety, and disability.

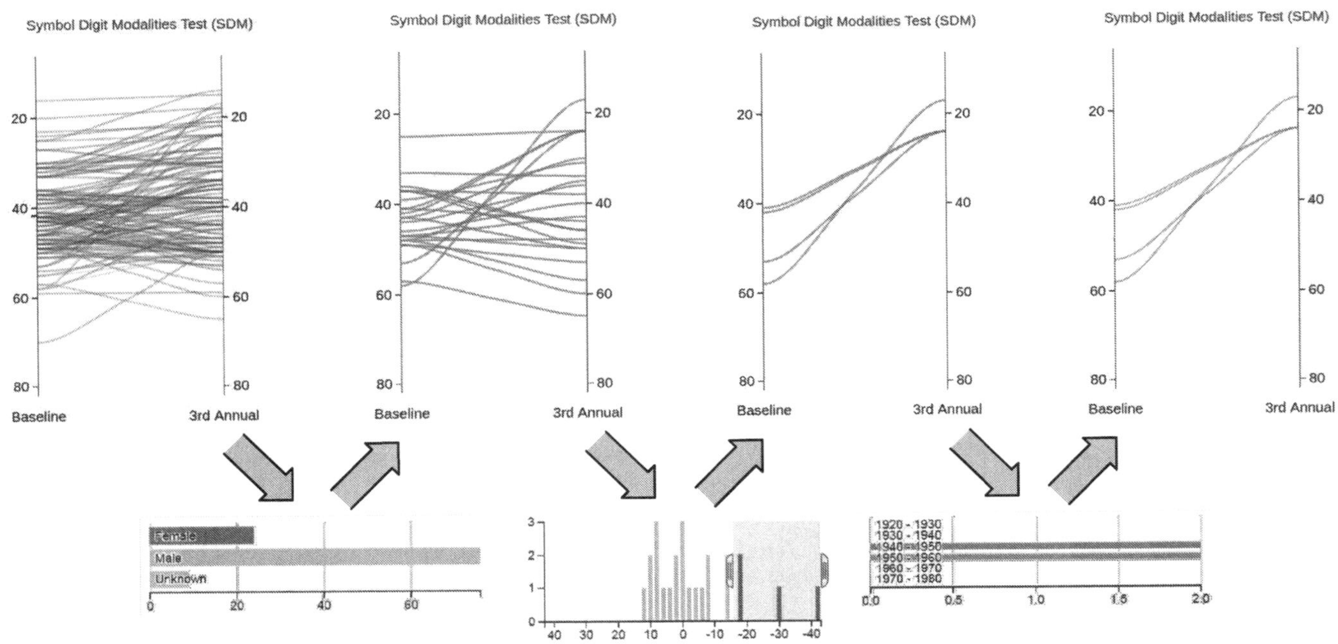

Figure 4: Users can filter the 109 previously selected patients (in Figure 3) by gender by clicking the corresponding bar in the demographics panel. After selecting female patients (left) with unusually rapid changes in cognitive function as measured by SDM (center), users can then change the color scheme to explore the year of birth of the selected patients (right).

5.4 Implementation

Winnow is implemented in JavaScript (frontend) and Python (backend). Users can conveniently run Winnow on modern browsers without installation through a link to the website[1].

6 CASE STUDIES

We now summarize two case studies we conducted with Winnow. The results shown in this section are for demonstration only. Analyses with Winnow are intended to uncover promising relationships between a range of outcome measures for selected patient subgroups. These analyses are for the purpose of generating hypotheses and need to be reproduced in future studies.

6.1 Questions

We have identified two clinically relevant questions about disease progression in PD with input from our clinical experts.

Q1 Does gender affect Parkinson's disease severity at year three?
Q2 Does the baseline severity of REM sleep behavior disorder (RBDQ) affect year three outcomes?

In the following we assess the effect of grouping using the Cohen's d [5], which is the difference between two sample means divided by the pooled standard deviation:

$$d = \frac{\overline{x_1} - \overline{x_2}}{\sqrt{\frac{\sigma_1^2 + \sigma_2^2}{2}}}, \quad (1)$$

[1]http://hccheng.pythonanywhere.com/vis/

where x_i and σ_i are the mean and standard deviation of the i-th group. A Cohen's d of value 0.2, 0.5, or 0.8 suggests a small, medium, or large magnitude of relationship, respectively [5]. We use Cohen's d to provide a different but complementary perspective on group differences in addition to the rank-based Mann-Whitney test.

6.1.1 Q1: Does gender affect Parkinson's disease severity at year three?

Gender differences in PD-related symptoms have been studied in the past. For example, RBD (REM sleep behavior disorder) was shown to be more prevalent in male patients than female patients [24]. A thorough review of gender differences in cognitive functions can be found in [12]. In the following analysis, we first applied a filter in the demographics panel and then used the plots in the outcomes panel to investigate various outcome measures at Y3 (Figure 5).

For UPDRS3 in the motor domain, female patients have a mean value of 25.89 at Y3 (first plot in the top of Figure 5) and males have a mean value of 29.36 at Y3 (first plot in the bottom of Figure 5). Therefore, comparing female with male patients, females have less severe motor symptoms than males at Y3 ($d = 0.27$). The Mann-Whitney test shows a significant difference ($p = 0.003$, shown in Table 2) between the female and male patients. In contrast, female patients have more severe symptoms on semantic fluency (SFT in the cognitive domain) at Y3. Females have mean SFT of 53.13 whereas males have mean SFT of 45.98 at Y3. The difference in mean SFT at Y3 for females and males shows a medium to large magnitude ($d = 0.59$ and $d = 0.63$). The Mann-Whitney test confirms the significance of gender difference in SFT at Y3. Other measures that significantly differ by gender at Y3 are listed in Table 2, including measures in the cognitive, sleep, and disability domains. Male patients have more severe symptoms than females in seven out of the nine outcome measures (marked in bold in Table 2). These seven outcomes are UPDRS2, UPDRS3, and T-UPDRS (general PD severity), MoCA and SDM (cognition), ESS (sleep), and SEADL (disability).

Table 2: Outcome measures that are significantly different ($p < 0.05$) by gender at year three (Y3)

Domain	Outcome Measure	Mean value at Y3 Female	Mean value at Y3 male	p-value
PD Severity: Motor & Non-Motor	UPDRS2	6.98	**9.31**	< 0.001
	T-UPDRS	41.07	**46.71**	0.001
	UPDRS3	25.89	**29.36**	0.003
Cognitive	SFT	**53.13**	45.98	< 0.001
	JOLO*	**11.80**	12.98	< 0.001
	MoCA*	27.08	**25.94**	< 0.001
	SDM*	42.48	**38.19**	0.006
Sleep	ESS	6.49	**7.49**	0.013
Disability	SEADL*	89.06	**87.49**	0.021

* Lower score indicates more severe symptom.

6.1.2 Q2: Does the baseline severity of REM sleep behavior disorder (RBDQ) affect year three outcomes?

In this question, we investigate how the baseline severity of REM sleep behavior disorder (measured by RBDQ) affects the severity of outcomes in other domains over three years. We approached this question by selecting patients with increasingly severe REM sleep behavior disorder (greater values of RBDQ) at BL and comparing the severity of the other outcomes at Y3.

After applying a filter on baseline RBDQ with a cut-off value of four (Figure 6a), the mean values of T-UPDRS (PD severity) at Y3 is 50.17 for the top 50% of patients for RBDQ at BL (left of Figure 6b), and 39.96 for the bottom 50% of patients for RBDQ at BL (not shown here). These results show that for patients with greater baseline REM sleep behavior disorder, their general PD severity (T-UPDRS) is more severe at the third annual follow-up visit ($d = 0.57$).

In fact, if we use the analytics panel to compare the top and bottom 50% of baseline RBDQ ratings, the Mann-Whitney test shows that the distributions of nearly all outcome measures at Y3 are significantly different ($p < 0.05$) between the two groups except for a single cognitive measure, the semantic fluency test (SFT). These results show that the baseline severity of REM sleep behavior disorder is an important predictor of three-year outcomes across all the domains. Further studies are needed to investigate this important finding.

The difference in outcomes at Y3 between patients with more and less baseline REM sleep behavior disorder becomes even more apparent if we adjust the filter to select increasingly greater RBDQ ratings at BL (Figure 6a). The patient groups with the top 50%, 25%, and 10% baseline RBDQ ratings have increasingly greater mean values of T-UPDRS at Y3 (50.17, 53.65, and 58.54 from left to right in Figure 6b). In summary, these results show a positive correlation between the severity of baseline REM sleep behavior disorder and the severity of multiple other domains at year three, indicating that the baseline severity of REM sleep behavior disorder is an important predictor of Parkinson's disease progression.

6.2 Discussion

Winnow enables clinicians and scientists to interactively and flexibly query complex and high-dimensional datasets with minimal training. This hands-on experience is critical for clinicians to generate hypotheses and to discover actionable, clinically-relevant results. Currently hypotheses are investigated with basic statistics; in the future we plan to use Winnow as an interface for complex analytic methods, such as supervised learning. For example, users can define patient subgroups with distinct profiles of progression in Winnow and then use these defined subgroups as the targets for supervised learning methods.

Based on the features of the dataset used in our examples, our analysis is limited to three years of longitudinal data. Whereas Winnow currently supports comparing two groups of patients (selected and unselected), future modification will enable selecting and switching between multiple patient groups to allow more sophisticated comparisons. In addition to the outcome measures used in our preliminary study, biologic data (e.g. genomics and serologic markers) may enable more precise and reliable groupings.

7 CONCLUSIONS

Over the last 25 years, chronic medical conditions have been redefined with an expanding scope of symptoms and biologic disease markers. These advances have resulted in complex multidimensional clinical datasets. Such datasets pose substantial opportunities for discovery, but also pose unique challenges for traditional analysis. Parkinson's disease (PD) is a key example of these challenges–a complex progressive neurodegenerative disorder with rapidly expanding biologic data including genetics, imaging, and serologic markers. Since the diverse symptoms of PD progress over different timeframes, and are likely to vary in different patient subgroups, novel tools and approaches are needed to capitalize on the large, multidimensional, and longitudinal datasets available today.

In this paper we present Winnow, a visual analytics tool that is intuitive, interactive and insightful for both scientists and clinicians. The design of Winnow is based on an intensive long-term collaboration between experts from diverse backgrounds. Winnow is a significant step to conduct complex analysis on existing databases that are necessary to advance the study of chronic medical conditions.

We are designing more concise and scalable visualizations by grouping similar patients in the outcomes panel and creating a graph-based representation summarizing the changes in outcomes [15]. We are also working on extending Winnow to incorporate new emerging biomarkers including genetics, imaging, serology, and biosensor metrics. The extension will also include a machine learning module to perform automatic data analysis.

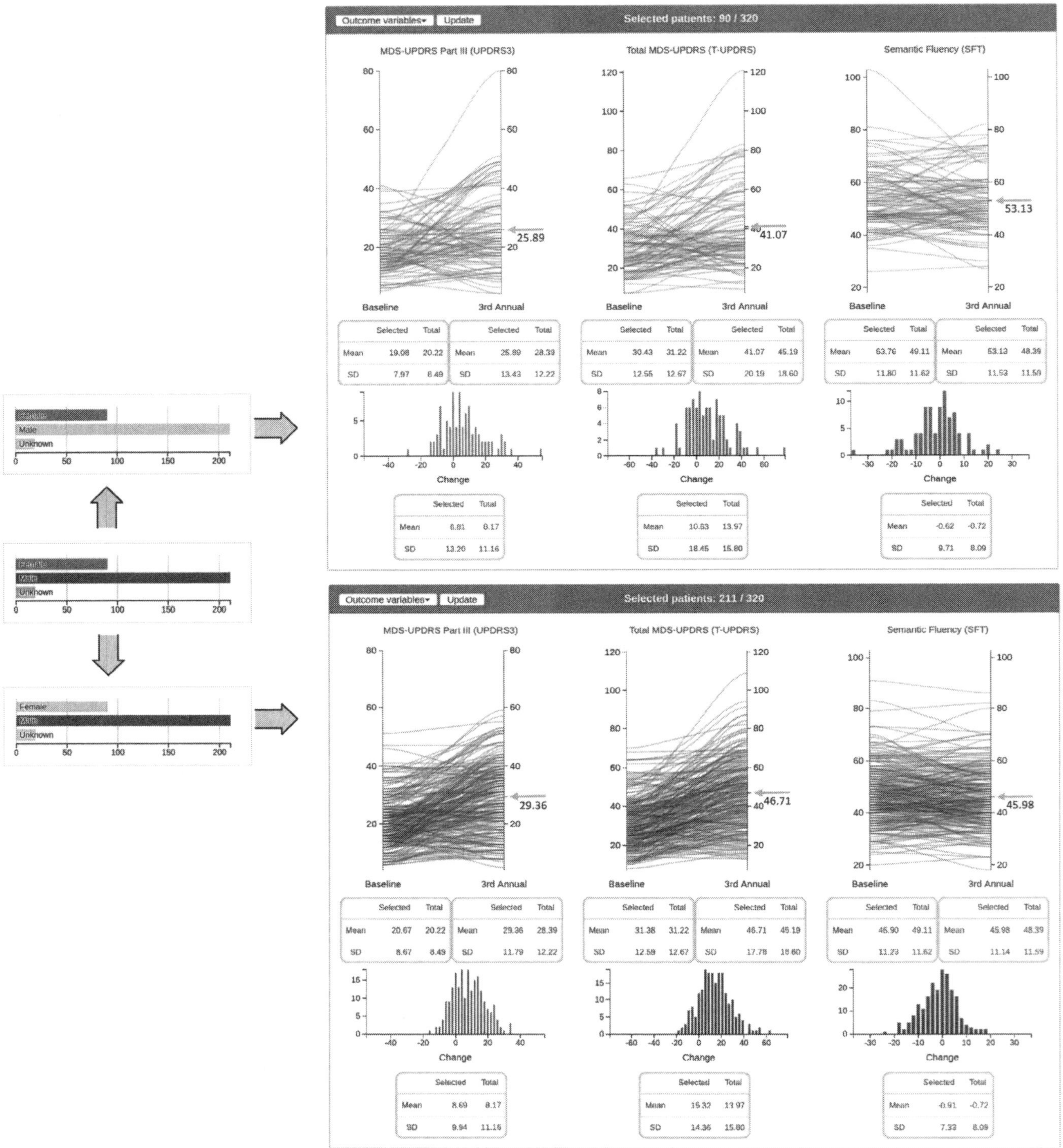

Figure 5: After applying the gender filter, the plots show that female patients (top) have comparable motor symptoms (UPDRS3) and general PD severity (T-UPDRS) at BL and less severe symptoms at Y3 than male patients (bottom). In contrast, female patients have more severe symptoms on semantic fluency (SFT) at Y3. arrows mark the mean values at Y3 for the males and females.

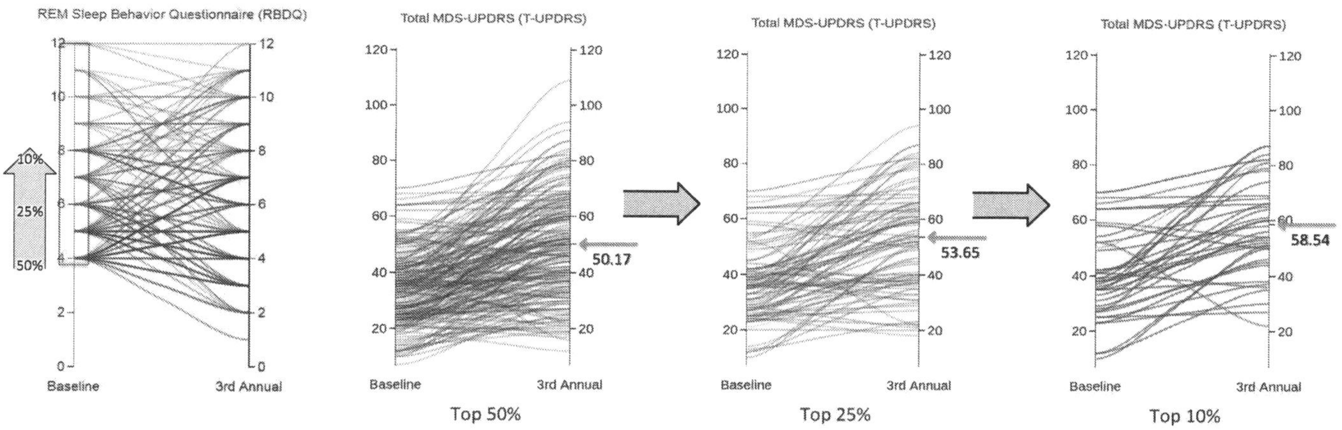

(a) Filtering baseline RBDQ

(b) Increasing mean T-UPDRS at Y3 from 50% to top 10% of patients (left to right)

Figure 6: (a) A filter that selects patients with increasingly greater baseline RBDQ. (b) As the filter moves to select patients with more severe baseline RBDQ (top 50%, 25%, and 10% from left to right), the mean T-UPDRS at Y3 increases from 50.17 to 53.65 and 58.54.

ACKNOWLEDGMENTS

This research is supported in part by the Seed Grant Program of the University of Maryland. We thank Dr. Søren Bentzen for useful advice on data analysis. We also thank PPMI for providing the data used in the case study. The PPMI dataset is a public-private partnership, funded by the Michael J. Fox Foundation for Parkinson's Research and the Fox funding partners- AbbVie, Avid, Biogen, Bristol-Myers Squibb, Covance, GE Healthcare, Genentech, GlaxoSmithKline, Lilly, Lundbeck, Merck, Meso Scale Discovery, Pfizer, Piramal, Roche, Sanofi Genzyme, Servier, Teva, and UCB.

REFERENCES

[1] Mihael Ankerst, Markus M. Breunig, Hans-Peter Kriegel, and Jörg Sander. 1999. OPTICS: Ordering Points to Identify the Clustering Structure. In *Proceedings of ACM SIGMOD International Conference on Management of Data*. ACM, New York, NY, USA, 49–60.

[2] Mikhail Belkin and Partha Niyogi. 2003. Laplacian Eigenmaps for Dimensionality Reduction and Data Representation. *Neural Computation* 15, 6 (2003), 1373–1396.

[3] D. J. Burn, E. N. Rowan, L. M. Allan, S. Molloy, J. T. O'Brien, and I. G. McKeith. 2006. Motor Subtype and Cognitive Decline in Parkinson's Disease, Parkinson's Disease with Dementia, and Dementia with Lewy Bodies. *Journal of Neurology, Neurosurgery, and Psychiatry* 77, 5 (May 2006), 585–589.

[4] William C. Cleveland and Marylyn E. McGill. 1988. *Dynamic Graphics for Statistics* (1st ed.). CRC Press, Inc., Boca Raton, FL, USA.

[5] Jacob Cohen. 1992. Statistical Power Analysis. *Current Directions in Psychological Science* 1, 3 (June 1992), 98–101.

[6] Geoffrey Ellis and Alan Dix. 2006. Enabling Automatic Clutter Reduction in Parallel Coordinate Plots. *IEEE Transactions on Visualization and Computer Graphics* 12, 5 (2006), 717–724.

[7] Geoffrey E. Hinton and Ruslan R. Salakhutdinov. 2006. Reducing the Dimensionality of Data with Neural Networks. *Science* 313, 5786 (July 2006), 504–507.

[8] Alfred Inselberg. 1985. The Plane with Parallel Coordinates. *The Visual Computer* 1, 2 (Aug. 1985), 69–91.

[9] J. Jankovic, M. McDermott, J. Carter, S. Gauthier, C. Goetz, L. Golbe, S. Huber, W. Koller, C. Olanow, I. Shoulson, M. Stern, and C. Tanner. 1990. Variable Expression of Parkinson's Disease: A Base-Line Analysis of the DATATOP Cohort. *Neurology* 40, 10 (Oct. 1990), 1529–1534.

[10] Roxanne E. Jensen, Nan E. Rothrock, Esi M. DeWitt, Brennan Spiegel, Carole A. Tucker, Heidi M. Crane, Christopher B. Forrest, Donald L. Patrick, Rob Fredericksen, Lisa M. Shulman, David Cella, and Paul K. Crane. 2015. The Role of Technical Advances in the Adoption and Integration of Patient-Reported Outcomes in Clinical Care. *Medical Care* 53, 2 (Feb. 2015), 153–159.

[11] Stuart Lloyd. 1982. Least Squares Quantization in PCM. *IEEE Transactions on Information Theory* 28, 2 (1982), 129–137.

[12] Ivy N. Miller and Alice Cronin-Golomb. 2010. Gender Differences in Parkinson's Disease: Clinical Characteristics and Cognition. *Movement Disorders* 25, 16 (Dec. 2010), 2695–2703.

[13] Hans-Christoph Nothdurft. 1993. The Role of Features in Preattentive Vision: Comparison of Orientation, Motion and Color Cues. *Vision Research* 33, 14 (Sept. 1993), 1937–1958.

[14] Parkinson Progression Marker Initiative. 2011. The Parkinson Progression Marker Initiative (PPMI). *Progress in Neurobiology* 95, 4 (Dec. 2011), 629–635.

[15] Robert Patro, Cheuk Yiu Ip, Sujal Bista, Samuel S. Cho, D. Thirumalai, and Amitabh Varshney. 2011. MDMap: A System for Data-Driven Layout and Exploration of Molecular Dynamics Simulations. In *Proceedings of IEEE Symposium on Biological Data Visualization*. 111–118.

[16] Wei Peng, Matthew O. Ward, and Elke A. Rundensteiner. 2004. Clutter Reduction in Multi-Dimensional Data Visualization Using Dimension Reordering. In *Proceedings of IEEE Symposium on Information Visualization*. 89–96.

[17] Sam T. Roweis and Lawrence K. Saul. 2000. Nonlinear Dimensionality Reduction by Locally Linear Embedding. *Science* 290, 5500 (Dec. 2000), 2323–2326.

[18] Jianbo Shi and Jitendra Malik. 2000. Normalized Cuts and Image Segmentation. *IEEE Transactions on Pattern Analysis and Machine Intelligence* 22, 8 (2000), 888–905.

[19] Ben Shneiderman and Catherine Plaisant. 2006. Strategies for Evaluating Information Visualization Tools: Multi-Dimensional in-Depth Long-Term Case Studies. In *Proceedings of the International Conference on Advanced Visual Interfaces*. ACM, 1–7.

[20] Lisa M. Shulman, Robin Leifert Taback, Judy Bean, and William J. Weiner. 2001. Comorbidity of the Nonmotor Symptoms of Parkinson's Disease. *Movement Disorders* 16, 3 (2001), 507–510.

[21] Laurens van der Maaten and Geoffrey Hinton. 2008. Visualizing Data Using T-SNE. *Journal of Machine Learning Research* 9, Nov (2008), 2579–2605.

[22] Stephanie M. van Rooden, Willem J. Heiser, Joost N. Kok, Dagmar Verbaan, Jacobus J. van Hilten, and Johan Marinus. 2010. The Identification of Parkinson's Disease Subtypes Using Cluster Analysis: A Systematic Review. *Movement Disorders: Official Journal of the Movement Disorder Society* 25, 8 (June 2010), 969–978.

[23] Amitabh Varshney and Arie Kaufman. 1996. FINESSE: A Financial Information Spreadsheet. In *Proceedings of IEEE Symposium on Information Visualization*. IEEE, 70–71.

[24] Asako Yoritaka, Hideki Ohizumi, Shigeki Tanaka, and Nobutaka Hattori. 2009. Parkinson's Disease with and without REM Sleep Behaviour Disorder: Are There Any Clinical Differences? *European Neurology* 61, 3 (2009), 164–170.

[25] Hong Zhou, Xiaoru Yuan, Huamin Qu, Weiwei Cui, and Baoquan Chen. 2008. Visual Clustering in Parallel Coordinates. *Computer Graphics Forum* 27, 3 (2008), 1047–1054.

Associating Genomics and Clinical Information by Means of Semantic Based Ranking

Francesca Cristiano
Department of Surgical and Medical Sciences
Magna Graecia University
Catanzaro, Italy
fcristiano@unicz.it

Giuseppe Tradigo
Department of Computer Science, Modeling, Electronics and Systems Engineering
University of Calabria
Rende, Italy
gtradigo@dimes.unical.it

Pierangelo Veltri
Department of Surgical and Medical Sciences
Magna Graecia University
Catanzaro, Italy
veltri@unicz.it

ABSTRACT

Relating genomic data with clinical and disease information is a new challenge for life sciences research. High performance computational platforms allow huge quantity of biological data production with new technologies (e.g. Next Generation Sequencing techniques). Nowadays, genomic ontologies describing genes and functions, as well as databases containing diseases groups, are available. We focus on the problem of enriching genomic datasets containing miRNA genes by adding related disease information. The enrichment is performed by using ontologies to find genes-to-diseases associations. Ontologies are used to describe molecular genomic processes and functions, as well as disease classes and experimental details. International Classification of Diseases (ICD) is used for the classification of diseases and clinical information. Diseases are ranked by using a Google Page Rank based algorithm. An application tool called *Surf App!* has been coded and developed in *R* and tested on a neurological disease dataset.

CCS CONCEPTS

• **Applied computing** → *Life and medical sciences*; *Computational biology*;

KEYWORDS

miRNA; NGS; Google Page Rank; ICD9CM

1 INTRODUCTION

Correlating data from different data sources (e.g., clinical, environmental and genomic data) is becoming crucial for studying diseases, especially chronic ones where patients deal with long treatments and recovery, for which potentially large data is acquired from different sources and for long time windows. Many databases have been developed and attracting an always higher number of researchers and clinicians. The Repository of Molecular Brain Neoplasia Data (*Rembrandt*) [23] is an example of cancer clinical to functional genomic database targeted for brain tumors datasets.

Genotypes, phenotypes and genes-diseases relations are contained in many databases, such as: *OMIM* (Online Mendelian Inheritance in Man [34]), *Gene Cards* [7], *HGMD* (Human Gene Mutation Database) [18], the *NCBI* (National Center for Biotechnology Information) database on gene variations (Single Nucleotide Polymorphism) [12]. Literature and genomics information are contained in *BLAST* [1, 2] that allows to align locally genes and proteins against those present in the *NCBI* system to identify similar sequences and in available databases such as *ENTREZ*, *PubMed*, *EMBL*. These resources can be used to build reliable and high-performance pipelines to enrich large datasets of genes, diseases, clinical treatments and exploit their mutual relations.

One of the most adopted technique is to reduce the big dataset produced by using NGS methods by discarding less relevant information while keeping significant ones, extracting genomic features useful for clinical practice. Ontology-based pipelines have been used to enrich genomic data. For instance, gene lists can be enriched and then reduced by using *Gene Ontology* [3, 9] and *DAVID* [19, 20] selecting only the genes with the desired semantic features.

In this work, we focus on enriching genomic datasets by means of disease related information. We present an algorithm and a software tool which is able to find genes-diseases relations. Using ontologies, semantics rules, and an ad-hoc ranking algorithm, it is able to enrich a genetic input dataset containing microRNA (miRNA) sequences. miRNAs are short portions of non-coding RNA of ~ 20 nucleotides, which have been identified as responsible for gene silencing and post-translational regulatory functions. The aim is to propose a data enrichment approach for miRNA datasets thus to support genomic data integration procedures and to associate *miRNA* sequences to a list of significant diseases, potentially related to the original samples [10], [11]. The method also proposes ranking functions to ranks diseases to *miRNAs* by using a *Google* Page Rank based algorithm and it has been implemented in a web application, called *Surf App!*, developed in *R* using *Shiny* by *RStudio* [21]. *Surf App!* is composed by 18 functions which performs step by step the algorithm implemented in the described method. A screenshot of *Surf App!* is reported in Figure 1, whereas Table 1 shows an example of its output on a miRNA dataset. Both the algorithm and the application are reported in Section 3. The following Section reports related works, while section 4 discusses experimental results.

Permission to make digital or hard copies of all or part of this work for personal or classroom use is granted without fee provided that copies are not made or distributed for profit or commercial advantage and that copies bear this notice and the full citation on the first page. Copyrights for components of this work owned by others than ACM must be honored. Abstracting with credit is permitted. To copy otherwise, or republish, to post on servers or to redistribute to lists, requires prior specific permission and/or a fee. Request permissions from permissions@acm.org.
ACM-BCB'17, , August 20-23, 2017, Boston, MA, USA.
© 2017 Association for Computing Machinery.
ACM ISBN 978-1-4503-4722-8/17/08...$15.00
https://doi.org/10.1145/3107411.3107436

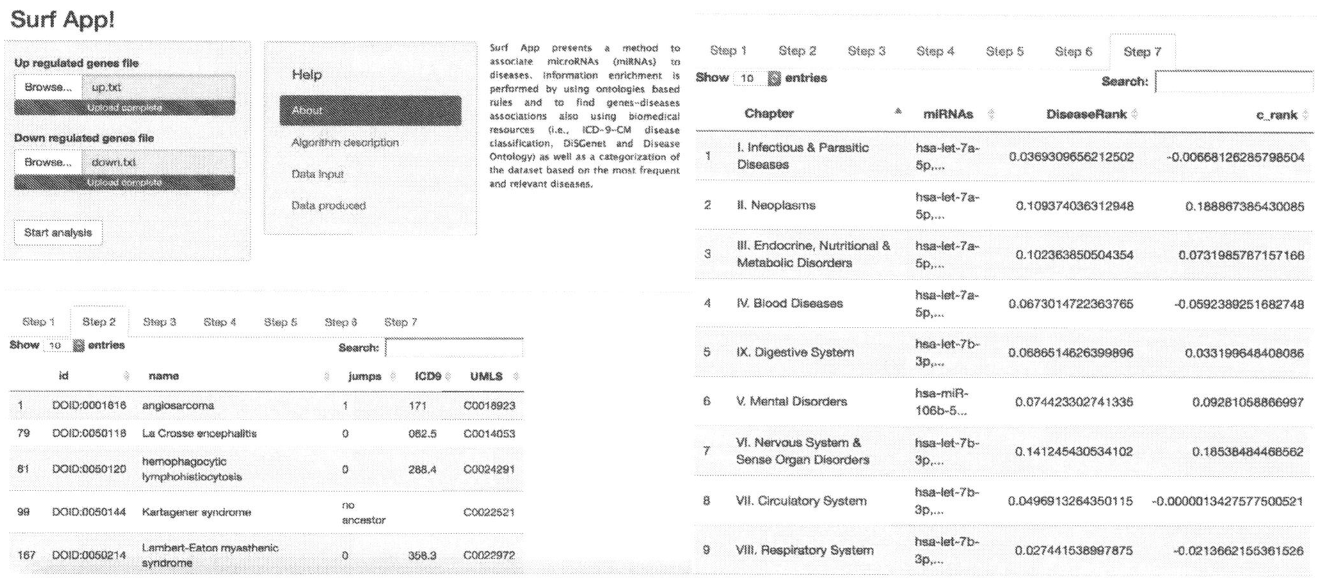

Figure 1: *Surf App!* web application: the upper part on the left side of the figure shows the input form where *miRNAs* are loaded. Gene-disease connections are shown in the bottom part. Results, including the c_{rank} for each *ICD-9-CM* chapter, are reported on the right side.

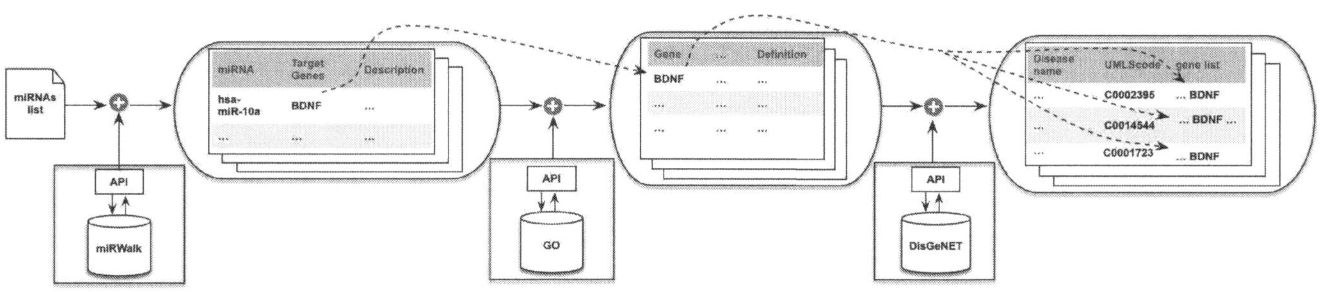

Figure 2: From *miRNAs* to diseases. The designed workflow performs the enrichment step. Dashed lines indicate the attribute used to join tables. Following step by step the methods, the *hsa-miR-10a miRNA* is associated with the *BDNF* target gene; the BDNF target gene is then enriched with gene ontologies in which it results to be involved; the *BDNF* target gene is thus associated to diseases, which are identified by the *UMLS* codes.

2 RELATED WORKS

Genomic resources describing genes and their functions, as well as databases containing diseases groups, are available on the web. Enrichment analysis refers to the annotation of datasets obtained from biological experiments and enriching a list of genes means adding biological functions (or processes) and/or diseases description. The enrichment is performed by using ontologies [5] [16] to find genes-to-diseases associations and *ICD-9-CM* codes for diseases classification. Ontologies are used for information enrichment describing molecular genomic processes and functions, as well as disease classes and experimental details. The International Classification of Diseases (*ICD*) is used for the classification of diseases and clinical information. *Gene Ontology* (*GO*) is a project aiming to unify the gene description for each organism. Structurally *GO* is a directed acyclic graph where each gene is described using terms, annotations, and ontologies. The three ontologies defined in *GO* are cell component, molecular function, and biological process. Queries in *GO* are performed by considering that each term (or list of genes) can be associated with biological processes or pathways. It is possible starting from the biological description of interest to find the set of genes involved in the process. Similarly to *GO*, genes can be also associated by using their relation with diseases. Genes can be used to identify biomarkers related to pathologies. For this aim, it is necessary to associate genes with pathologies by using available

ICD-9-CM	miRNAs	c_{rank}
II Neoplasms	hsa-let-7a-5p, hsa-miR-106b-3p, hsa-let-7b-3p ...	0.1888
VI Nervous, Sense	hsa-let-7b-3p, hsa-miR-1294, hsa-let-7d-5p, ...	0.183
XIII Musculoskeletal, Connective Tissue	hsa-let-7a-5p, hsa-miR-101-3p hsa-let-7b-5p, ...	0.1010
V Mental Dis.	hsa-miR-106b-5p, hsa-let-7a-5p, ... hsa-miR-143-3p, ...	0.0928
III Endocrine, Nutritional, Metabolic	hsa-let-7a-5p, hsa-miR-103a-3p, hsa-let-7b-3p, ...	0.0731
IX Digestive	hsa-let-7b-3p, ...	0.0331
	hsa-miR-4775, ...	0.0331
X Genitourinary Disease	hsa-let-7a-5p, hsa-let-7b-3p, ...	3.263

Table 1: Application of the *C-rank*. Results obtained by using the implemented ranking algorithm on available *miRNAs* dataset. *miRNAs* goes from tens to hundreds.

miRNA	Target genes	Description
hsa-miR-10a	BDNF	brain-derived neurotrophic factor
	KCNA6	potassium voltage-gated channel, shaker-related subfamily, member 6
	RORA	RAR-related orphan receptor A
	TFAP2C	transcription factor AP-2 gamma
	CSMD1	CUB and Sushi multiple domains 1
	...	

Table 2: Associating *miRNA*-to-target genes. An example of the result produced by using *miRWalk*. *MiRWalk* identified 419 target genes for *hsa-miR-10a miRNA* (only the first five target genes are shown.)

databases, also increasing the number of information associated to genes.

In *DAVID*, the functional enrichment analysis can be performed using a large genes list with different gene identifiers (e.g., *Ensembl* and *Entrez* IDs). For large datasets, it is possible to organize data into clusters, where each one contains biologically similar annotations, by using methods such as the *Functional Classification Clustering*. In genomics, there are several analysis techniques that may produce a huge quantity of information from single patient samples, and the challenge is in extracting the most useful ones, possibly related to known investigated pathologies. Enrichment analyses can be performed by using *Disease Ontology* (*DO*) [26, 38], to identify the over-represented genes in a given disease and vice versa. Each disease (or a group of diseases) can be associated with a graph representing the *is_a* relation as a parent/child one. Each disease description is represented in a hierarchical form to allow a simple disease navigation. Also, the graphical user interface allows visualizing diseases and related information such as *Disease Ontology* ID (*DOid*), pathology name, a short description, various synonyms, and other information such as MeSH [27] and ICD-CM codes [35]. For instance, *DisGeNET* [14, 37] is a gene-disease database which allows enriching a gene list by using literature, predictions, and curated dataset, using a score to evaluate the rank of the gene-disease associations.

Software tools such as *i2b2* (Informatics for Integrating Biology and the Bedside) [17], *BTRIS* (Biomedical Translational Research Information System) [8], *IGV* (Integrative Genomics Viewer), and *KEGG* allow to integrate clinical and genomic data. Data extraction and integration techniques may be used to get information from medical documents, as in [25] or in [6]. The system described in [31] allows managing the integration of biomolecular information and patients' clinical data, by using ontologies. Also, *DiseaseConnect* [29] is an example of a tool able to discover interaction networks, allowing to define relationships between genes and diseases. It uses Genome-Wide Associations Studies (*GWAS*) [4] and *OMIM* records.

Many biological and clinical ontologies have been developed and implemented in systems reported in literature, such as: the *NCBO* BioPortal [30], the Unified Medical Language System (*UMLS*) [33], the *NCI Thesaurus* [22], the Generalised Architecture for Languages, Encyclopedia and Nomenclature in Medicine (*GALEN*) [15], the Foundational Model of Anatomy (*FMA*) [39], the Systematized Nomenclature of Medicine (*SNOMED*) [24], the Gene Ontology (*GO*), the Open Biomedical Ontology (*OBO)* [40] and Disease Ontology (*DO*). Biomedical ontologies are used to integrate biomedical resources stored in a number of formats (i.e. *OBO, OWL, SQL, RRF,* and *CSV*) and few systems are able to enrich a reference datasets using more than one ontology. For this purpose, ontology-based data integration should be used in biomedical applications to unify the available information represented for example in the Electronic Health Records.

Ranking algorithms have been also used to classify and enrich biological data, such as microarray data [13, 32], gene expression profiles [41] as well as drugs experimental results [42]. The most famous ranking algorithm is the *Google* Page Rank [36] used to order web pages with the respect to their relevance. The page rank algorithm is used by *Google* to find the relevance of a web page by considering the number of links shown from other pages.

3 SEMANTIC BASED ENRICHMENT ALGORITHM

The proposed method enriches the *miRNAs* dataset with clinical terms integrating genomics and clinical data downloaded by *miRWalk, Gene Ontology, DisGeNet, Disease Ontology* and *ICD-9-CM*. The method starts by associating *miRNAs* with predicted target genes by using *miRWalk* database. *miRBase* nomenclature and the official gene symbols are used to recognize *miRNAs* and genes. The *miRNA*-target genes association is fundamental because there are few validated data that allows associating directly *miRNAs* across medical and clinical databases. The enrichment phase implemented

GOid associated with BDNF gene	Term	Definition
GO:0031553	positive regulation of brain-derived neurotrophic factor-activated receptor activity	Any process that activates or increases the frequency, rate or extent of brain-derived neurotrophic factor-activated receptor activity
GO:0031552	negative regulation of brain-derived neurotrophic factor-activated receptor activity	Any process that stops, prevents, or reduces the frequency, rate or extent of brain-derived neurotrophic factor-activated receptor activity
GO:0031551	regulation of brain-derived neurotrophic factor-activated receptor activity	Any process that modulates the frequency, rate or extent of brain-derived neurotrophic factor-activated receptor activity
GO:0031550	positive regulation of brain-derived neurotrophic factor receptor signaling pathway	Any process that activates or increases the frequency, rate or extent of signaling via the brain-derived neurotrophic factor receptor signaling pathway
GO:0031549	negative regulation of brain-derived neurotrophic factor receptor signaling pathway	Any process that stops, prevents, or reduces the frequency, rate or extent of signaling via the brain-derived neurotrophic factor receptor signaling pathway
GO:0031547	brain-derived neurotrophic factor receptor signaling pathway	The series of molecular signals generated as a consequence of a brain-derived neurotrophic factor receptor binding to one of its physiological ligands
GO:0031548	regulation of brain-derived neurotrophic factor receptor signaling pathway	Any process that modulates the frequency, rate or extent of signaling via the brain-derived neurotrophic factor receptor signaling pathway
GO:1990416	cellular response to brain-derived neurotrophic factor stimulus	A process that results in a change in state or activity of a cell (in terms of movement, secretion, enzyme production, gene expression, etc.) as a result of a brain-derived neurotrophic factor stimulus

Table 3: *Term* and *Definition* associated to the *BDNF* gene as extracted from *Gene Ontology*. Table shows the associations of biological processes, molecular functions or cellular components to the gene via the *GOid*.

Disease name	UMLS code	Genes
Congenital abnormalities	C0000768	ADAMTS1, BDNF, ...
Affective disorders	C0001723	BDNF, COMT, DAOA, ...
Alzheimer disease	C0002395	ABCA1, ABCA12, ABCA2, BDNF, ...
Epilepsy	C0014544	ABCB1, ABCB4, BDNF, ...

Table 4: Associating gene-to-diseases performed by using *DiGeNET*. An example of diseases and corresponding *UMLS* codes that are related to the *BDNF* gene. The number of genes varies from a few numbers to hundreds.

in the workflow is shown in Figure 2 which is composed of three steps.

From left to right: (i) a *miRNA* dataset representing the input of the system; (ii) a query in *miRWalk* allows associating *miRNAs*-to-genes; (iii) the identified genes are associated with biological and molecular processes by using *Gene Ontology*; (iv) each gene is finally associated with diseases uniquely identified by the *UMLS* code by using *DisGeNet*. *UMLS* codes are matched with *ICD-9-CM* codes by using *Disease Ontology*. *DO* represents data as graph structure and adopts the *OBO* format. Each term in *DO* is identified by a unique key, named Disease Ontology-Identifier (*DOid*).

A set of properties is associated with each term, such as the disease definition, synonyms, and *ICD-9-CM* codes. It may happen that some of the *DO* terms are not associated with any *ICD-9-CM* code. In such case, the algorithm navigates through the ancestors in the graph structure until it finds at least one term containing an *ICD-9-CM* code. The number of nodes passed through while moving up in the graph is indicated as *jumps*. The higher number of jumps (i.e., connections) is associated with more general disease definition. Figure 3 shows an example of graph representing *DO*. For istance, considering the *UMLS* code: C0002395 in Figure 3 (that identifies a given disease in which some of the genes are involved) the algorithm searches within each *DO* term (in the *xref* field), the *ICD-9-CM* code associated. In this case, the *DO* term referred to Alzheimer disease already contains the *ICD-9-CM* code (331), thus the number of *jumps* is zero. The *jumps* represent the number of

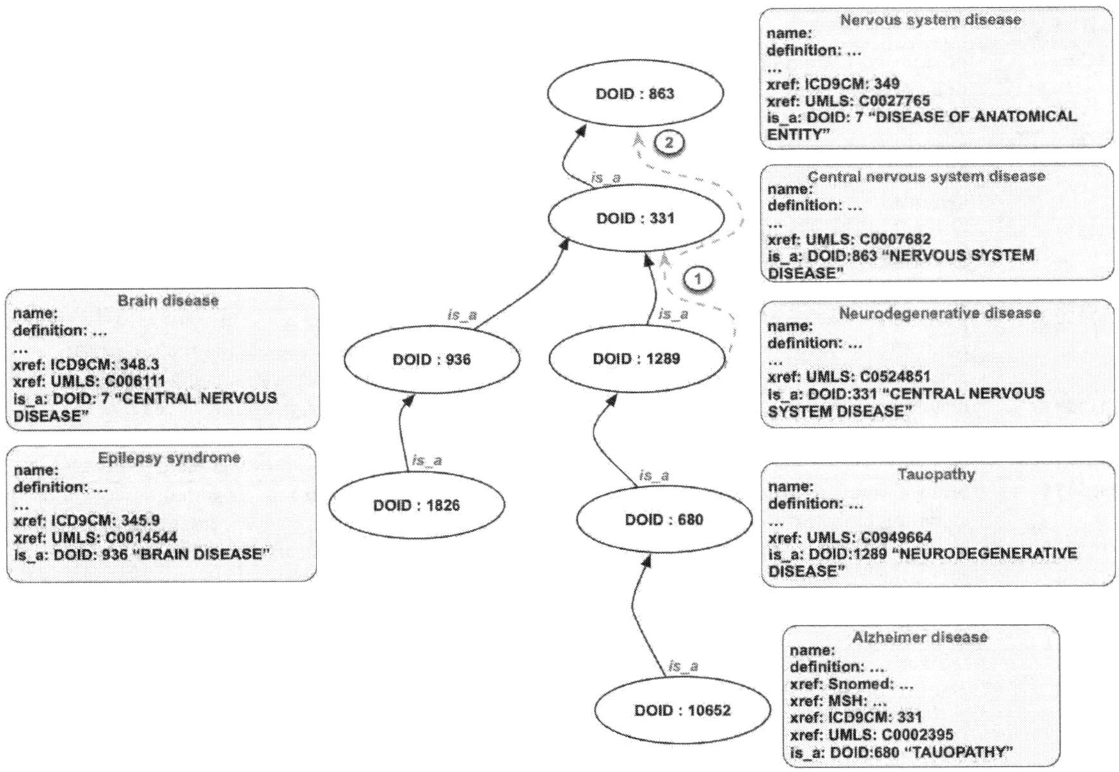

Figure 3: Fragment of *Disease Ontology* graph. Each *DO* term, identified by a *DOid* is associated with metadata. Metadata includes name and definition term. The *xref* field includes multiple vocabularies and ontology codes. Dashed line represents the number of connections (*jumps*) required to reach an *ICD-9-CM* code.

terms which must be exceeded in order to find the closest term that contains the *ICD-9-CM* code. To retrieve the *ICD-9-CM* code for the *UMLS* code: C0524851 in the *DO* instance, the algorithm navigates looking for more general terms, towards the ancestor direction. In fact, the term neurodegenerative disease *is-a* central nervous system disease (first ancestor), but this term does not have the *ICD-9-CM* code, therefore the algorithm visits the node related to nervous system diseases (*ICD-9-CM* code: 349). Dashed line in Figure 3 shows the *jumps* (which are equals to 2) performed by the algorithm. Each retrieved *ICD-9-CM* code is then associated with the respective *ICD-9-CM* chapter in which the code is referred.

The next step in the algorithm flow consists of evaluating the ranking of each *ICD-9-CM* chapter. A modified version of the *Google* Page Rank algorithm is used in the algorithm: (*i*) by considering *ICD-9-CM* chapters and diseases in which the diseases are involved, and (*ii*) by considering *ICD-9-CM* chapters and genes in which the genes are involved. In general, the ranking is used whenever there is a huge number of interactions which have to be sorted in order to highlight the most relevant ones.

The *Google* Page Rank has been adapted and named *Disease Rank* which has been included in the algorithm to assign a significativity to each identified chapter. *DR* formula is definited as follows:

$$DR(n) = \frac{1}{S}(1-\delta) + \delta\left(\sum_{k=1}^{N} \frac{DR(n_k)}{G(n_k)}\right) \tag{1}$$

where the $DR(n)$ function calculates the *Disease Rank* value for a given node n of the graph, δ is the damping factor (0.85 as in the original formula), S is the total number of *ICD-9-CM* chapters in the dataset (currently 17 in the released *ICD-9-CM* version), $DR(n_k)$ is the rank of the k_{th} section and $G(n_k)$ is the total number of diseases (or genes) associated with a chapter n_k. Such a formula is implemented in an *R* package, receiving in input a dataset with two columns: the first contains *ICD-9-CM* sections and the second contains the associated diseases. Similarly it is evaluated the rank of *ICD-9-CM* with the associated genes.

The c_{rank} ranking function has been applied to associate a relevance value to each of the *ICD-9-CM* chapters within the dataset and calculated considering: (*i*) the number of arcs encountered in the graph to find the *ICD-9-CM* code, (*ii*) the number of genes and (*iii*) the number of diseases involved and included in each chapter. The c_{rank} formula is definited as follows:

$$c_{rank}(c) = (G(c) + D(c) - J(c))\, DR(n) \tag{2}$$

Algorithm 1 Data Enrichment Algorithm

```
Input: miRNAs, DO-graph, ICD9-CM
Dataset = ∅
Infos = ∅
for all m ∈ miRNAs do
    m.g ← targetGenes(m)
    m.d ← diseases(m)
    m.o ← ontologies(m)
    Dataset ∪ {m}
    for all dis ∈ m.d do
        dis.ICD9CMcode ← ICD9CM.find(dis.UMLSid)
        if dis.ICD9CMcode is not Null then
            info ← (dis.UMLSid, dis.DOid, dis.ICD9CMcode, 0)
        else
            {a, j} ← DO.searchClosestAncestor(dis)
            info ← (dis.UMLSid, a.DOid, a.ICD9CMcode, j)
        end if
    end for
end for
Tmp ← Infos ⋈ ICD9CM on ICD9id
Mrg ← Tmp ⋈ Dataset on UMLSid
A ← buildGraph(Mrg.ICD9Chapter, Mrg.diseaseNumber)
B ← buildGraph(Mrg.ICD9Chapter, Mrg.geneNumber)
for all n ∈ A.nodes do
    n.dr ← DR(n)
end for
for all n ∈ B.nodes do
    n.dr ← DR(n)
end for
CRank ← Mrg.getChapters()
for all cr_i ∈ CRank do
    s ← cr.ICD9Chapter
    dr ← (A.getNode(s).dr + B.getNode(s).dr)/2
    genes ← Mrg.find(s).numGenes
    jumps ← Mrg.find(s).numJumps
    cr_i ← c_rank(s, genes, jumps, dr)
end for
return CRank
```

where $DR(c)$ is the *Disease Rank* of a given chapter c, $G(c)$ is the number of genes, $D(c)$ the number of diseases and $J(c)$ the number of jumps that have been performed in the *DO* graph to find a match between the disease (*DOid*) and an *ICD-9-CM* entry.

UMLS code	DO id	ICD-9-CM	Jumps
C0025517	0014667	277.9	0
C0002395	10652	331.0	0
C0042995	1245	184.4	0
C0022584	0050428	702	3
C0027822	3309	702	2
C0024299	0060058	199	4
C0949664	680	349	3
C0524851	1289	349	2
C0014868	11963	530.1	0
C0005779	1247	286	0
C0020179	12858	333.4	0
C0007771	13097	442.9	3
C0004659	1412	No Ancestor	NA
C0005967	184	199	4
C0019189	2237	570	0
C0008441	2649	199	4
C0017551	2739	277.9	3
C0010403	2917	279	3
C0010631	3111	199	4
C0022572	3149	Over Limit	NA
C0011303	3213	349.9	3

Table 5: Associating disease-to-*ICD-9-CM* codes. Each *UMLS* code which identifies a unique disease is found in *DO.obo* file. For each term, the respective *DOid* and *ICD-9-CM* code have been retrieved. E.g. the *UMLS* code C0025517 matches with the term *DOid*:0014667 (*Jumps*=0) whereas the *UMLS* code C0022584 requires three jumps to reach the *DOid* and the respective *ICD-9-CM* code. Finally, the *UMLS* code C0004659 is associated to No Ancestor value meaning that no *ICD-9-CM* code related to the term has been found.

Chapter	ICD-9-CM
V: Mental disorder	331.0, 307.1, 301.83, 300.11, 300.4, 300.3, ...
VI: Nervous system and sense disorder	333.31, 430, 372.30, 340, 572.2, 367.1 ...

Table 6: An example of *ICD-9-CM* chapters and some of their corresponding *ICD-9-CM* codes.

4 EXPERIMENTAL RESULTS

The *miRNAs* data have been obtained from [28] in which a small *RNA-seq* of 22 healthy control samples and 48 Alzheimer disease patients has carried out. Authors present a miRNA-based signature for Alzheimer Disease (*AD*) studies. NGS analysis has detected 180 dysregulated *miRNAs* related to neurological diseases. Preliminary results of the method which allows integrating the *miRNAs* dataset with clinical terms show the soundness of the proposed approach. Since each *miRNA* can be regulated by several genes, and each gene can regulate many *miRNAs*, the association operation may produce a large dataset; in fact, for each *miRNA*, 804, 465 *miRNA*-target gene associations has been obtained. Table 2 shows an example of *miRNA* to genes association where some of the genes obtained by querying *miRWalk* and associated to *hsa-miR-10a miRNA*, are reported. Then, by using *GO*, a module associates each target gene (e.g., the target gene *BDNF* associated to *hsa-miR-10a miRNA*) to biological processes, molecular functions and cell components in which the gene is involved. For instance, Table 3 shows the results for the *BDNF* gene.

Linking the genes with *DisGenet*, 334, 321 associations to diseases have been identified and then grouped by the *UMLS* codes. Table 4

Chapter	Disease name	ICD-9-CM	Num. genes
V Mental Disorder	Borderline personality	301.83	70
VI Nervous System and Sense Organ Dis	Multiple Sclerosis	340	957
IV. Blood diseases	Anemia	285.9	290
IX. Digestive System	Barrett's esophagitis	530.85	199

Table 7: Diseases associated with the respective *ICD-9-CM* chapter. The gene count reports the number of genes involved in a given diseases.

Chapter	D.Rank 1	D.Rank 2
IV. Nervous System and Sense Organ Disorders	0.08287	0.0583
II. Neoplasms	0.0146	0.0946
III. Endocrine, Nutritional and Metabolic Disorders	0.0451	0.0571
XIII. Musculoskeletal and Connective Tissue	0.0200	0.0545
V. Mental Disorders	0.0236	0.0507

Table 8: Application of the *Disease Rank* (D.Rank 1 and 2 columns) based on the *Google* Page Rank. The result obtained by using a *Disease Rank* for each chapter considering first the diseases related to a given *ICD-9-CM* chapter and then the genes related to each chapter. The highest value represents the most linked *ICD-9-CM* chapter.

shows an example of additional information related to the *BDNF* gene obtained through *DisGeNET*. To relate genes with *ICD-9-CM* codes, the algorithm navigates through the *DO* graph instance. For istance, to retrieve the *ICD-9-CM* codes associated to the *UMLS* code: C0002395 (i.e. Alzheimer diseases in Table 4), the algorithm searches for the *UMLS* code in the graph to find terms containing the *ICD-9-CM* code. The result is a data structure as the one reported in Table 5.

ICD-9-CM codes are also grouped with respect to the *ICD-9-CM* chapters (see Table 6) in Table 7, in which the total number of genes for each *ICD-9-CM* chapter is calculated.

The algorithm ranks *miRNAs*-to-*ICD-9-CM* chapters by using the ranking function. The rank is used to evaluate the relations between genes and diseases (enrichment phase). The obtained results are reported in Table 8. Finally, a *Disease Rank* calculated as the mean value between *Disease Rank 1* and *Disease Rank 2* is used to obtain the c_{rank} (as in Equation 2). Table 1 presents the results obtained by applying *Surf App!* on the *miRNA* dataset available at [28].

5 CONCLUSION

Annotating *non-coding* molecules to clinical data is a recent trend in bioinformatics research. We propose an enriching strategy for *miRNAs* dataset by using an ontology-based approach. Good results in terms of experimental results confirm that the method is valid. We plan to apply the method on different datasets.

ACKNOWLEDGMENTS

The authors thanks Prof. Pierre Baldi for preliminary discussions on the topic.

REFERENCES

[1] Stephen F Altschul, Warren Gish, Webb Miller, Eugene W Myers, and David J Lipman. 1990. Basic local alignment search tool. *Journal of molecular biology* 215, 3 (1990), 403–410.

[2] Stephen F Altschul, Thomas L Madden, Alejandro A Schäffer, Jinghui Zhang, Zheng Zhang, Webb Miller, and David J Lipman. 1997. Gapped BLAST and PSI-BLAST: a new generation of protein database search programs. *Nucleic acids research* 25, 17 (1997), 3389–3402.

[3] Michael Ashburner, Catherine A Ball, Judith A Blake, David Botstein, Heather Butler, J Michael Cherry, Allan P Davis, Kara Dolinski, Selina S Dwight, Janan T Eppig, et al. 2000. Gene Ontology: tool for the unification of biology. *Nature genetics* 25, 1 (2000), 25–29.

[4] Tim Beck, Robert K Hastings, Sirisha Gollapudi, Robert C Free, and Anthony J Brookes. 2014. GWAS Central: a comprehensive resource for the comparison and interrogation of genome-wide association studies. *European Journal of Human Genetics* 22, 7 (2014), 949–952.

[5] Mario Cannataro, Pietro Hiram Guzzi, and Pierangelo Veltri. 2010. Using ontologies for querying and analysing protein-protein interaction data. *Procedia Computer Science* 1, 1 (2010), 997–1004.

[6] Mario Cannataro, Domenico Talia, Giuseppe Tradigo, Paolo Trunfio, and Pierangelo Veltri. 2008. SIGMCC: A system for sharing meta patient records in a Peer-to-Peer environment. *Future Generation Computer Systems* 24, 3 (2008), 222–234.

[7] GENE CARDS. 2016. The Human Gene Database. (2016). http://www.genecards.org/ Website accessed on Sept. 2016.

[8] James J Cimino, Elaine J Ayres, Lyubov Remennik, Sachi Rath, Robert Freedman, Andrea Beri, Yang Chen, and Vojtech Huser. 2014. The National Institutes of HealthâÅŹs Biomedical Translational Research Information System (BTRIS): design, contents, functionality and experience to date. *Journal of biomedical informatics* 52 (2014), 11–27.

[9] The Gene Ontology Consortium. 2015. Gene Ontology Consortium: going forward. *Nucleic Acids Research* 43, D1 (2015), D1049–D1056.

[10] Francesca Cristiano and Pierangelo Veltri. 2016. Methods and Techniques for miRNA data analysis. *Microarray Data Analysis: Methods and Applications* (2016), 11–23.

[11] Francesca Cristiano, Pierangelo Veltri, Mattia Prosperi, and Giuseppe Tradigo. 2016. On the identification of long non-coding rnas from RNA-Seq. In *Bioinformatics and Biomedicine (BIBM), 2016 IEEE International Conference on*. IEEE, 1103–1106.

[12] dbSNP. 2016. dbSNP Short Genetic Variations. (2016). http://www.ncbi.nlm.nih.gov/SNP/ Website accessed on Sept. 2016.

[13] Eugene Demidenko. 2015. Microarray enriched gene rank. *BioData mining* 8, 1 (2015), 2.

[14] DisGeNET. 2016. Gene-disease association data retrieved from DisGeNET v4.0. (2016). http://www.disgenet.org/ Integrative Biomedical Informatics Group GRIB/IMIM/UPF - Website accessed on Sept. 2016.

[15] Open Galen. 2017. GALEN. (2017). http://www.opengalen.org/ June 2017.

[16] Pietro H Guzzi, Maria Teresa Di Martino, Giuseppe Tradigo, Pierangelo Veltri, Pierfrancesco Tassone, Pierosandro Tagliaferri, and Mario Cannataro. 2011. Automatic summarisation and annotation of microarray data. *Soft Computing* 15, 8 (2011), 1505–1512.

[17] Partner HealthCare. 2016. Informatics for Integrating Biology and the Bedside. (2016). https://www.i2b2.org/ Website accessed on Sept. 2016.

[18] HGMD. 2016. The Human Gene Mutation Database. (2016). http://www.hgmd.org/ Website accessed on Sept. 2016.

[19] Da Wei Huang, Brad T Sherman, and Richard A Lempicki. 2009. Systematic and integrative analysis of large gene lists using DAVID bioinformatics resources. *Nature protocols* 4, 1 (2009), 44–57.

[20] W. Huang et al. 2009. Bioinformatics enrichment tools: paths toward the comprehensive functional analysis of large gene lists. 31, 1 (2009), 1–13.

[21] RStudio Inc. [n. d.]. Shiny - A web application framework for R. ([n. d.]). https://shiny.rstudio.com Website accessed on June 2017.

[22] National Cancer Institute. 2017. NCI Thesaurus. (2017). http://ncit.nci.nih.gov/ Website accessed on June 2017.

[23] NIH National Human Genome Research Institute. 2016. Breast Cancer Information Core. (2016). http://research.nhgri.nih.gov/bic/ Website accessed on Sept.

2016.
[24] Snomed International. 2017. SNOMED - Clinical terms. (2017). http://www.ihtsdo.org/snomed-ct/ Website accessed on June 2017.
[25] Peter B Jensen, Lars J Jensen, and Søren Brunak. 2012. Mining electronic health records: towards better research applications and clinical care. *Nature Reviews Genetics* 13, 6 (2012), 395–405.
[26] Warren A Kibbe, Cesar Arze, Victor Felix, Elvira Mitraka, Evan Bolton, Gang Fu, Christopher J Mungall, Janos X Binder, James Malone, Drashtti Vasant, et al. 2014. Disease Ontology 2015 update: an expanded and updated database of human diseases for linking biomedical knowledge through disease data. *Nucleic acids research* (2014), gku1011.
[27] Rajewsky Lab. 2016. MeSH (Medical Subject Headings) is the NLM controlled vocabulary thesaurus used for indexing articles for PubMed. (2016). https://www.ncbi.nlm.nih.gov/mesh Website accessed on Sept. 2016.
[28] Petra Leidinger, Christina Backes, Stephanie Deutscher, Katja Schmitt, Sabine C Mueller, Karen Frese, Jan Haas, Klemens Ruprecht, Friedemann Paul, Cord Stähler, et al. 2013. A blood based 12-miRNA signature of Alzheimer disease patients. *Genome biology* 14, 7 (2013), R78.
[29] C. Liu et al. 2014. DiseaseConnect: a comprehensive web server for mechanism-based disease–disease connections. *Nucleic acids research* 42, W1 (2014), W137–W146.
[30] Musen MA, Noy NF, Shah NH, Whetzel PL, Chute CG, Story MA, and Smith B. 2012. NCBO team. The National Center for Biomedical Ontology. *J Am Med Inform Assoc.* 19, 2 (2012).
[31] N.S.B. Miyoshi et al. 2013. Computational framework to support integration of biomolecular and clinical data within a translational approach. *BMC Bioinformatics* 14, 180 (2013).
[32] J.L. Morrison et al. [n. d.]. Generank: using search engine technology for the analysis of microarray experiments. *BMC Bioinformatics* ([n. d.]).
[33] U.S. National Library of Medicine. 2017. UMLS - Unified Medical Language System. (2017). http://www.nlm.nih.gov/research/umls/ Website accessed on June 2017.
[34] OMIM. 2016. Online Mendelian Inheritance in Man. (2016). http://www.omim.org Website accessed on Sept. 2016.
[35] World Health Organization. 2016. International Classification of Diseases. (2016). http://www.who.int/classifications/icd/en/ Website accessed on Sept. 2016.
[36] Lawrence Page, Sergey Brin, Rajeev Motwani, and Terry Winograd. 1999. *The PageRank citation ranking: Bringing order to the web.* Technical Report. Stanford InfoLab.
[37] Janet Piñero, Àlex Bravo, Núria Queralt-Rosinach, Alba Gutiérrez-Sacristán, Jordi Deu-Pons, Emilio Centeno, Javier García-García, Ferran Sanz, and Laura I Furlong. 2017. DisGeNET: a comprehensive platform integrating information on human disease-associated genes and variants. *Nucleic acids research* 45, D1 (2017), D833–D839.
[38] Lynn Marie Schriml, Cesar Arze, Suvarna Nadendla, Yu-Wei Wayne Chang, Mark Mazaitis, Victor Felix, Gang Feng, and Warren Alden Kibbe. 2011. Disease Ontology: a backbone for disease semantic integration. *Nucleic acids research* 40, D1 (2011), D940–D946.
[39] School of Medicine University of Washington. 2016. FMA - Foundational Model of Analysis. (2016). http://sig.biostr.washington.edu/projects/fm/AboutFM.html Website accessed on June 2017.
[40] OBO Technical WG. 2017. OBO. (2017). http://www.obofoundry.org/ Website accessed on June 2017.
[41] Christof Winter, Glen Kristiansen, Stephan Kersting, Janine Roy, Daniela Aust, Thomas Knösel, Petra Rümmele, Beatrix Jahnke, Vera Hentrich, Felix Rückert, et al. 2012. Google goes cancer: improving outcome prediction for cancer patients by network-based ranking of marker genes. *PLoS Comput Biol* 8, 5 (2012), e1002511.
[42] Lun Yang, Langlai Xu, and Lin He. 2009. A CitationRank algorithm inheriting Google technology designed to highlight genes responsible for serious adverse drug reaction. *Bioinformatics* 25, 17 (2009), 2244–2250.

Tailoring Training for Obese Individuals with Case-Based Reasoning

Fabiana Lorenzi
Universidade Luterana do Brasil
Canoas, RS, Brazil
florenzi@ulbra.edu.br

Rodrigo G. da Rosa
Universidade Luterana do Brasil
Canoas, RS, Brazil
rodrigo80221@gmail.com

Alessandra Peres
Centro Universitario Metodista IPA, UFCSPA
Porto Alegre, RS, Brazil
aleimuno@hotmail.com

Gilson Pires Dorneles
Centro Universitario Metodista IPA, UFCSPA
Porto Alegre, RS, Brazil
gilsonpd@hotmail.com

Andre Peres
IFRS
Porto Alegre, RS, Brazil
andre.peres@poa.ifrs.edu.br

Francesco Ricci
Free University of Bozen-Bolzano
Bolzano, Italy
fricci@unibz.it

ABSTRACT

Obesity is a complex disease that involves genetic factors, inflammatory patterns, resilience and psycho-social factors. An effective system which is able to recommend adequate training for obese subjects that starts a new protocol would enhance the quality and success of the rehabilitation of these subjects. This paper presents a case-based reasoning system that suggests the most effective type of physical training exercise for obese individuals. The presented system was validated by domain experts and the results of this analysis show that case-based reasoning is a viable approach that can help to improve life of obese people.

1 INTRODUCTION

Obesity is a chronic and multifactorial disease that is spreading worldwide. It is causing an increasing incidence of cardiovascular diseases, cancer, metabolic syndrome, and type 2 diabetes mellitus. Epidemiological studies indicate a strong link between high calorie intake, sedentary lifestyle and obesity. In Brazil, for example, almost half of the population is overweight, which makes obesity a serious public health problem.

There are specific training programs for lean individuals, however, for obese subjects, the correct settings are not yet well known. This calls for the need of managing, treating and manipulating data, with the ultimate goal of defining the most appropriate physical activity for each individual. In fact, although numerous scientific studies have shown large benefits of exercise training for obese individuals, the actual benefit of the exercises depends on numerous variables that can impact positively or negatively, such as genetics, social and cultural influence. For example, a recent study identified that even with a large caloric expenditure in the exercise training (4 kcal/week, 8 kcal/week or 12 kcal/week), a discrete body weight change has occurred only after six months [3]. In fact, individual subjects' variability for a specific physical training must be taken into account, but often subjects are referred to exercise programs without proper knowledge of their needs [10].

This paper presents a case-based reasoning system that suggests an exercise training program to a new patient by reusing the knowledge contained in a set of cases of patients that already were submitted to training programs and where the effect of the program was measured. The implemented tool is able to relate clinical and training data in the history of patients with results, i.e., body weight loss, hence determining the most appropriate training program for a new patient.

This paper is organized as follow. The next section reviews related work on clinical guidelines and case-based reasoning. Section 3 presents the developed tool and section 4 illustrates the experimental evaluation that was conducted with data obtained from a laboratory of exercise and immunology. Finally section 5 presents the conclusions of this research and discusses future work.

2 RELATED WORK

Physical training is a key part of rehabilitation programs for obesity because of its capacity to increase caloric consumption and improve physical fitness as cardiorespiratory capacity, muscular strength, flexibility, balance and muscle power [6]. In addition, physical activity is recommended for weight management, body weight loss and for the prevention of weight regain after body weight loss.

Clinical Guidelines for the identification, evaluation and treatment of overweight and obesity in adults [14] encourage a 10% reduction in weight from physical activity. The American College Sports Medicine supports the recommendation of 150-250 minutes/week of moderate physical exercise to prevent weight gain or obtain a modest weight loss, while a minimum of 250 minutes/week for large reductions in body mass [6]. However, there is still no consensus about the best exercise for each obese individual.

Generally, aerobic exercise with moderate intensity (50-75% of oxygen consumption or 60-75% of maximal heart rate) is recommended for body weight loss, due to great caloric expenditure and

Permission to make digital or hard copies of all or part of this work for personal or classroom use is granted without fee provided that copies are not made or distributed for profit or commercial advantage and that copies bear this notice and the full citation on the first page. Copyrights for components of this work owned by others than ACM must be honored. Abstracting with credit is permitted. To copy otherwise, or republish, to post on servers or to redistribute to lists, requires prior specific permission and/or a fee. Request permissions from permissions@acm.org.
ACM-BCB '17, August 20-23, 2017, Boston, MA, USA
© 2017 Association for Computing Machinery.
ACM ISBN 978-1-4503-4722-8/17/08...$15.00
https://doi.org/10.1145/3107411.3107467

reduction of subcutaneous and visceral fat mass [9]. Another popular prescription is the strength training, a type of exercise that involves concentric-eccentric contractions against some kind of external resistance [7]. The advantage of this type of exercise is the increase of muscle mass and basal metabolic rate, and the reduction of some inflammatory adipokines [4].

Both types of exercises, *aerobic* and *strength*, have great benefits for obese individuals in anthropometrical and biochemical parameters and cardiometabolic risks. For example, the participation to *aerobic* training programs can prevent a number of risk factors, such the lipid profile and cardiovascular parameters, while *strength* training are associated with control of lipid parameters and resting glycemia, but in this case, little reductions in the visceral fat occurs [13].

A very common type of physical training is the combined training, a combination of aerobic and strength exercises in the same training session. A recent meta-analysis has shown that combined training is efficient to reduce anthropometric measurements compared with exclusive aerobic or strength training [15].

We now consider technical approaches to support medical decision making. Case-Based Reasoning (CBR) is an approach that solves new problems by reusing solutions that were successfully applied in previous cases [1]. Case-Based Reasoning has been applied to support human decision making in dealing with health-related problems, such as, hypertension detection [8], liver disease diagnosis [12] and diabetes [12]. In these applications, CBR has been shown to be effective and not brittle, since solutions for a subject could also be reused for another one with a similar profile, hence, enabling the optimization of the treatment time[2]. Hence, CBR provides an easy and fast knowledge acquisition method when compared with model-based approaches.

Obesity is a potential application domain for CBR and some studies have been already conducted. In [16], for instance, the authors present a CBR system for counseling obese children. The system uses CBR for weight management counseling. Another CBR system is presented in [5] where the authors integrated CBR with Bayesian networks (BN) in a probabilistic framework to assist health professionals to share their experiences of obesity exercise prescription online.

3 SYSTEM DEVELOPMENT

This paper presents a Case-Based Reasoning system developed to help experts to recommend the best treatment (exercise training) according to patient clinical and personal data.

The system development was informed by an extensive analysis of the obesity domain. We modelled and created the case base and finally we identified a proper system evaluation method. These stages are described in the next sections.

Figure 1 illustrates the typical interaction with the system: the patient asks to the expert for help; the expert enters patient data in the system; the system processes the received information and suggest the best training exercises, i.e., one treatment that was effective for a patient similar to the current one.

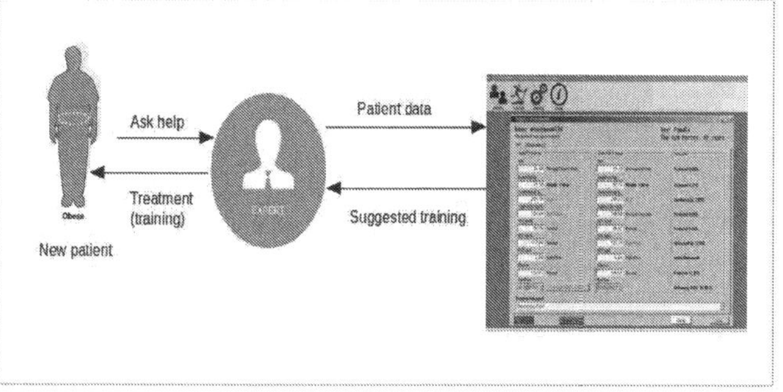

Figure 1: Interaction with the CBR support system

3.1 Case Representation

A case is represented by a set of distinguished features or attributes. The interviewed expert suggested the following attributes as relevant for tailoring training to individuals: Age, Gender, BMI, Body mass, Height, Cholesterol, Triglyceride, HDL, LDL, CRP and Glucose. Moreover, four types of treatment were suggested as suitable for obese patients:

- *Pool*: training in water or swimming;
- *Concurrent*: a combination of aerobic and strength exercises in the same training session;
- *Electrolipolysis*: eletrolipolysis is a technique for the treatment of localized fat, by applying specific electric currents that act directly at the level of adipocytes and lipid accumulated percutaneously or transcutaneously;
- *Electro + Aerobic*: the combination of the electrolipolysis tretament plus aerobic training.

These four types of training were chosen by the experts because they showed positive results in previous experiments with volunteers. However, experts do not know exactly which treatment is more suited to which type of subject. In order to identify this correlation, they analyze previous cases searching for correlations between patients characteristics and the effects of training in order to identify the best training for each individual.

To structure and then populate the case base we followed a study performed by the experts. This was a quantitative experiment involving volunteers recruited by convenience. The inclusion criteria for the participants (volunteers) were: (1) sedentary; (2) body mass index (BMI) between 25 kg/m^2 and 49.9 kg/m^2; (3) older than 18 years old; and (4) a medical certificate approving the practice of physical training. Patients with some disease hindering the practice of physical exercise, such as cancer, chronic infection, or autoimmune disease where not included in the study. Smokers were also excluded. All volunteers participating in this study signed a consent and the study was approved by the Brazilian Research Ethics Committee.

The experts collected 15 mL of peripheral blood by venepuncture (between 7:00AM and 10:00AM) after an overnight fast of 12 hours. The blood samples were divided into tubes without anticoagulant to obtain the serum and into heparinized tubes for whole blood (BD Vacutainer heparin tubes). Serum samples were separated by centrifugation for 10 minutes at 2500 rpm 1048g, divided into aliquots, and frozen at 20C for further analysis. The heparinized whole blood was analyzed within 3 hours of collection. Forty-eight hours after the last concurrent training session, blood samples were collected again. Body weight and height were determined by a semi-analytical scale with a capacity for 200Kg and an attached stadiometer, with accuracies of 0.1Kg and 0.005cm, respectively.

A case is a piece of knowledge in a particular context representing an experience that teaches the essential lesson to reach the goal of the reasoner [11]. In a CBR system a case model the problem to solve and the solution that was applied to solve the problem. In our application, the problem part describes the patient before the treatment while the solution describes the patient after the treatment and the training program. A case is modelled using the key patient attributes identified by the experts and by the prescribed training. Table 1 shows the attributes of a case. Attributes *BMI, Body Mass, Height, Cholesterol, Triglyceride, HDL, LDL, CRP* and *Glucose* store values obtained before and after the training routine. The post-training attributes are not used for searching for similar cases, but they are necessary for the expert to access the full profile of each patient case. All the attributes that represent the problem have weights (used in the retrieval stage). The weights of each attribute were set by the experts and range from 1 to 10 (from less to more important). The attributes that represent the description of the solution do not have weights because they are not used in the similarity calculation and retrieval.

The attributes *Training, Training duration* and *Observation training* represent the case solution. It is important to mention that an expert can make some observations during the training, such as, changes in eating habits of the patient or changes in the exercise intensity during the training). These observations are considered part of the case solution.

Our case base was created with cases obtained from an experiment done by the experts. We must observe that not all treatments described in the acquired cases were "successful". In fact, some of the volunteers did not respond to the treatment and they did not lose weight with the training prescribed by the expert. However, the experts recommended to keep all cases (successful and not successful). The experts collected the information pertaining to 133 patients.

3.2 Case Retrieval

Case retrieval is performed by the system in two steps: 1) retrieving the most similar cases and 2) calculating the efficiency indicator and selecting the case with the highest efficiency among the 10 most similar cases. When the system is requested to suggest a treatment to a new patient her case is matched with the cases in the case base. At this stage, the system uses only the attributes modeling information obtained before the training, plus *age* and *gender*.

To compare a new problem case with the cases stored in the case base, we have introduced a specific similarity function. The attribute similarity function (Equation 1), is applied to each numeric attribute to compute an attribute-level similarity. By summing the similarity values of all the attributes we obtain the similarity of the probe case with each case in the case base. For nominal attributes the similarity is 1 if the compared values are equal and 0 otherwise.

Table 1: The structure of a case

Attribute	Type of description	Weight
Age	problem	2
Gender	problem	2
preBMI	problem	10
preBody mass	problem	4
preHeight	problem	2
preCholesterol	problem	8
preTriglyceride	problem	8
preHDL	problem	8
preLDL	problem	8
preCRP	problem	8
preGlucose	problem	8
posBMI	solution	-
posBody mass	solution	-
posHeight	solution	-
posCholesterol	solution	-
posTriglyceride	solution	-
posHDL	solution	-
posLDL	solution	-
posCRP	solution	-
posGlucose	solution	-
Training	solution	-
Training duration	solution	-
Observation training	solution	-

$$sim(p_f, c_f) = \frac{w_f * (p_f - |p_f - \sqrt{p_f * c_f}|)}{p_f} \qquad (1)$$

where:

- f is an attribute;
- w_f is the weight of the attribute f;
- p_f is the new problem attribute value;
- c_f is the attribute value of a case in the case base;

After the probe is case is matched with all the cases in the case base, the system presents the retrieved cases ordered by decreasing value of similarity. However, the most similar case may not be the most appropriate one, because it may have resulted in a "failure", i.e., the patient had a minor weight reduction or even increased his/her weight. Moreover, the best solution might not come always from the most similar case, i.e., the proposed similarity function may not produce the optimal ranking.

To deal with this issue, the system calculates the efficiency indicator of the 10 most similar cases. According to the expert, a training that reduces the patient BMI in a short period is more efficient than a training that has a similar effect but in a longer period of time. Thus, the efficiency indicator, is a numeric score, that takes into account the patient BMI (pre and pos) and the period of the training (the number of training days). To compute the efficiency indicator we first search in the case-base for the case where the patient has the largest BMI reduction in the shortest time. This case is considered the best case, with 100% efficiency. Knowing this best case, we then calculate with the rule of three (the method for finding the fourth term in a proportion when three terms are given) the efficiency indicator of the 10 most similar cases (retrieved in the first step). Equation 2 shows how the calculation of the efficiency indicator is done for the best case.

$$bcase\_eff = \max_{c \in CB} \{ \frac{preBMI(c) - postBMI(c)}{ntd(c)} \} \quad (2)$$

where:

- *CB* is the full case base and *c* is a case;
- *bcase–eff* is the efficiency of the best case;
- *post BMI(c)* is the BMI value of the case *c* collected after the training;
- *pre BMI(c)* is the BMI value of the case *c* collected before the training;
- *ntd(c)* is the number of training days of case *c*.

After calculating the efficiency indicator of the best case, the system calculates the efficiency indicator for the 10 most similar retrieved cases, as shown in Equation 3.

$$eff(c) = \frac{preBMI(c) - postBMI(c)}{ntd(c)} \quad (3)$$

The last step is to calculate the percentage of the efficiency of the case, represented by *Perc*, as shown in Equation 4.

$$Perc(c) = (eff(c) * 100)/bcase\_eff) \quad (4)$$

Figure 2 shows an example of a retrieved case where the *similarity* of the new problem (new patient) with the case is 90.19%. This was the third most similar case, however it was recommended because its *efficiency indicator* is 79.30% (higher than the other retrieved cases). It means that this retrieved case is similar to new problem and its training was efficient for the patient and for this reason the system can recommend the retrieved case solution to the new patient.

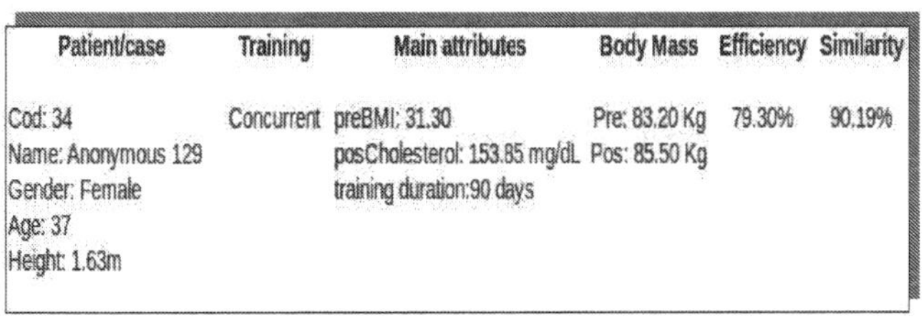

Figure 2: Example of retrieved case

Table 2 shows another example. Here case 46 (in the case base) is compared with a new patient that is being evaluated. The similarity of these two cases is 90.19%.

3.3 Adaptation and Retention of Cases

After the system has found the most effective training among those contained in the 10 most similar cases, the system can reuse this case solution for the new problem. We note that the expert may always adapt the system suggested training and can add observations (about the patient or the training) if needed. However, after a training is selected, the case still lacks the information about post training and the finalization date, which can be obtained only at

Table 2: Comparing case 46 with the new problem

Attributes	Case 46	New Problem
Age	37	46
Gender	female	female
preBMI	31.30	39.60
preBody Mass	83.20	85.14
preCholesterol	170.90.76	175.40
Triglyceride	254.71	261.30
HDL	60.48	56.8
HDL	150.48	156.80
LDL	0	0
CRP	0	0
Glucose	92.30	112.04

the end of the training program. Once the expert has entered this information in the system, a new case is finally created in the base, which makes it possible system learning.

4 SYSTEM VALIDATION AND TESTS

This section presents how the validation was performed and the results obtained in the test. Figure 3 shows the main screen of the system with an example case. The screen is divided in three columns. The first one shows attributes collected before the training; the second column shows attributes collected after the training; and the last column shows the variation of the patient attributes caused by the training. Next to each attribute the system presents the risk level (risk or normal, for example). This helps the expert during the analysis of the patient's profile.

We run the system validation in two scenarios. In the first one we tried to qualitatively analyze the case retrieved by the system for some (40) input cases. In the second one we compared the training that the system would recommend with the one that experts gave.

4.1 Qualitative Evaluation

As mentioned before the experts carried out an experiment with volunteers and they stored in the system 133 patients cases that were solved before by them. Hence, these cases contain both the problem and the solution description.

In this first evaluation we considered 40 patients from these 133 and we run the case retrieval function. These 40 cases were first removed from the case base which then contained 93 cases. The goal was to analyze the characteristics of the retrieved cases, i.e., the case with the largest efficiency among the 10 most similar cases to the probe case.

Figure 4 shows the results screen presented by the system; it is divided in seven columns. The first one shows basic information about the patient in the similar case (name, age, gender, height). The second column presents the training performed by that patient. The third column shows the interval of the training (start and end date). The fourth column shows the main indexes of the patient (BMI, body mass and cholesterol). The fifth column presents the percentage of body mass lost by the patient. The sixth column shows the efficiency indicator and the last column shows the similarity value.

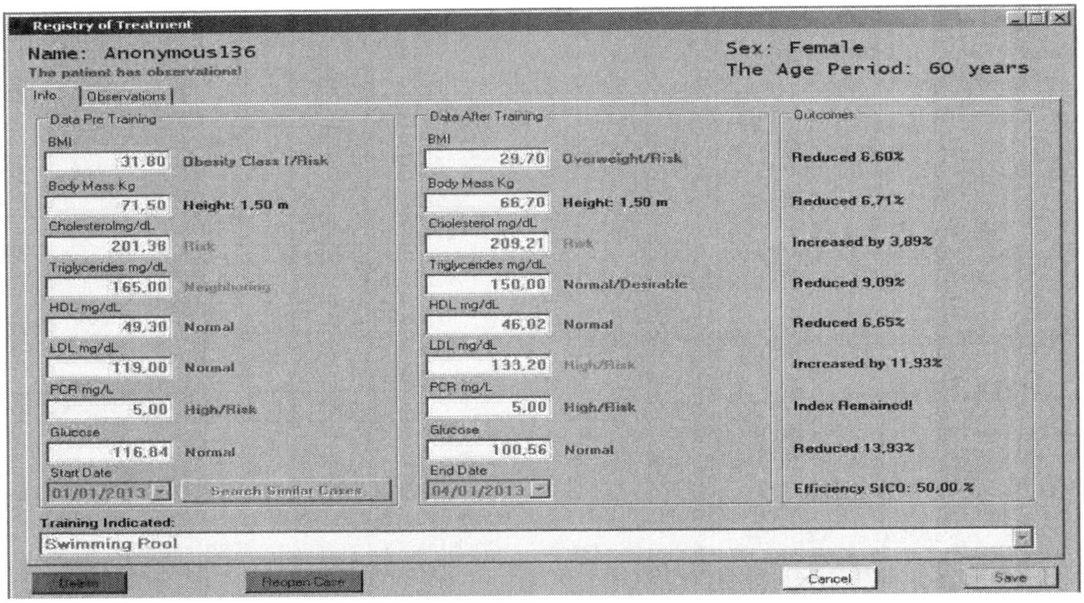

Figure 3: Main screen

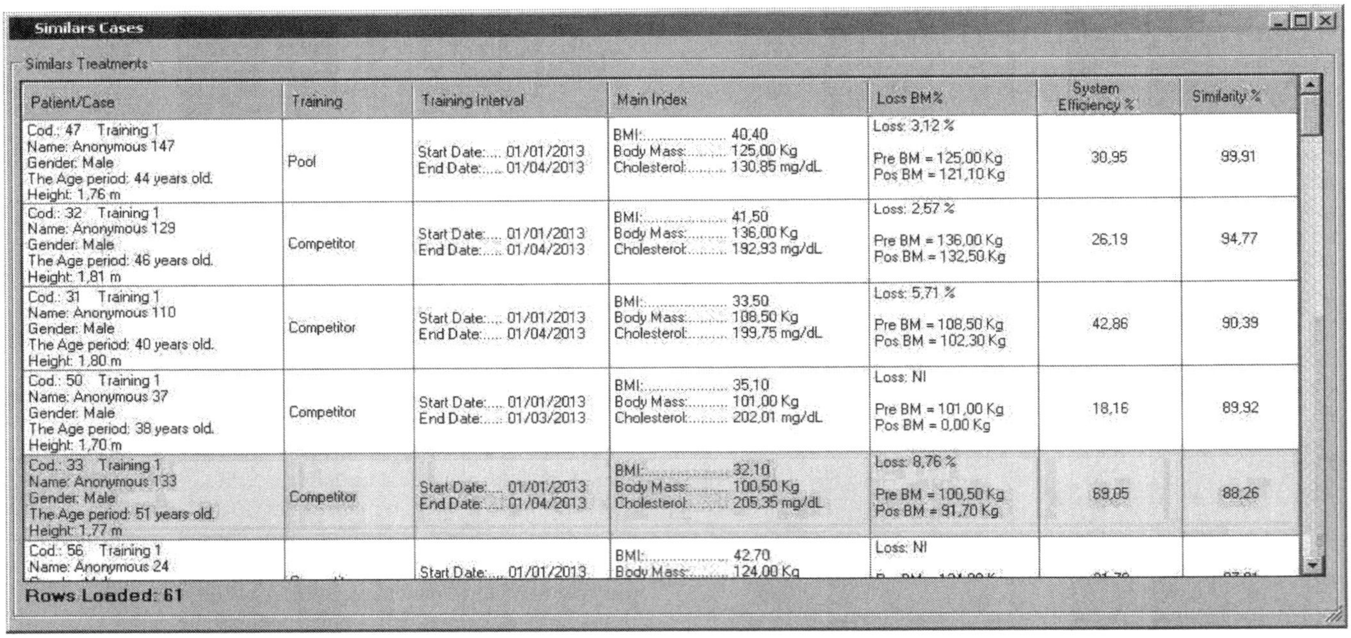

Figure 4: Similar cases retrieved to a new problem

After querying the system with the 40 cases that we considered, we noticed that:

- For each problem the system correctly returned the case with the highest similarity;
- The first five cases presented had always similarity greater than 88%, they were males with ages between 38 and 51 years, and BMI between 32.10 and 41.50;
- The most similar case was not recommended to the new patient. As figure 4 shows, the fifth retrieved case has similarity 88,26%, but has efficiency 69,05%. Analyzing this case we can see that the patient lost 8.8Kg in 3 months while the patient from the most similar case lost only 3.9Kg in the same period. This illustrates that the usage of a simple case similarity in this domain is not enough.

4.2 Reliability Test

As shown in [2], reliability is an important property of a medical CBR system. This measures how trustworthy or dependable a system is. The functionality of a system should be tested to see if it provides an accurate solution when needed. Hence, in a second test we verified if case similarity and efficiency computations do help to retrieve a case with the same training defined by the experts for that case.

In fact, by testing the system on some cases, we found that sometimes the treatment prescribed by the expert was different from that suggested by the system. For this reason, in order to be sure of the correctness of the treatments suggested by the experts, we asked them to re-consider some cases.

The experts were able to solve again 15 cases, without looking at the original solutions, i.e., the treatments assigned to these 15 patients. We then used these 15 patients to query the system and compared the outcome, i.e., the treatment contained in the most effective case among the 10 most similar ones to the probe case, with that suggested by the experts. Before performing the retrieval, these 15 cases were removed from the case base.

Among these 15 problems solved again by the system, 3 had a system suggested treatment different from that identified by the experts. Analyzing these cases we learned that (depending on the patient profile) the experts, in order to chose a treatment, considered as target attributes for the training, in addition to BMI, also other user data, such as, cholesterol, glucose and triglyceride.

In these three cases where the system prescription was different from the expert ones, the patients, after the treatment, reported changes in the levels of cholesterol and glucose. In fact, they gained weight but they reduced the cholesterol and glucose and, according to the experts, this outcome is even better than losing weight.

Hence, in future work, we will take into account these aspects and we will modify the efficiency indicator. However, although in 3 cases out of 15 the system proposed a treatment different from that prescribed by the experts, the experts approved the system, because the task of fully analyzing the patient status is hard and the system proved to be a useful tool to support the experts in this task.

5 CONCLUSIONS AND FUTURE WORK

CBR systems are know to be effective tools to improve decision making in several domains. This is particularly important in the health domain, where the systems results may help to speed several processes that are usually conducted manually by experts. The development of simple and low-cost decision support systems allows extracting, preserving, distributing and reusing existing expert knowledge more effectively.

In the CBR system presented in this paper the cases model obese patients that were invited to participate to a study. Their data were collected before and after the physical exercises prescribed by experts, and then converted into cases. The system was able to support experts to explore the existing case base, containing solutions and treatments, and to search for consistent patterns in the data and to tailor the best type of training for obese people. The system proved to be trustworthy at the same degree of expert level.

The proposed system provides a straightforward solution for supporting experts that deal with obesity. The experts' decisions are stored by the system, which makes possible learning new knowledge in the form of cases.

As future work we plan to share the case base with experts from other institutions to increase its size and to help more experts in the process of suggesting types of training to obese subjects. Also, we will improve the calculation of the efficiency indicator in order to consider additional user attributes that the experts consider informative, in addition to BMI.

REFERENCES

[1] Agnar Aamodt and Enric Plaza. 1994. Case-based reasoning: Foundational issues, methodological variations, and system approaches. *AI communications* 7, 1 (1994), 39–59.

[2] Shahina Begum, Mobyen Uddin Ahmed, Peter Funk, Ning Xiong, and Mia Folke. 2011. Case-based reasoning systems in the health sciences: a survey of recent trends and developments. *Systems, Man, and Cybernetics, Part C: Applications and Reviews, IEEE Transactions on* 41, 4 (2011), 421–434.

[3] TS Church, CK Martin, AM Thompson, CP Earnest, CR Mikus, and SN Blair. 2009. Changes in weight, waist circumference and compensatory responses with different doses of exercise among sedentary, overweight postmenopausal women. *PLoS One* 4, 3 (2009), e4515.

[4] BF De Salles, R SimÃčo, SJ Fleck, I Dias, LG Kraemer-Aguiar, and E. Bouskela. 2010. Effects of resistance training on cytokines. *Int J Sports Med* 31, 7 (2010), 441–450.

[5] Dong Dong, Zhaohao Sun, and Feng Gao. 2010. PCOPM: a probabilistic CBR framework for obesity prescription management. In *Advanced Intelligent Computing Theories and Applications. With Aspects of Artificial Intelligence.* Springer, Heidelberg, 91–99.

[6] JE Donnelly, SN Blair, JM JAKICIC, MM Manore, JW Rankin, and B Smith. 2009. Appropriate Physical Activity Intervention Strategies for Weight Loss and Prevention of Weight Regain for Adults. *Systems, Man, and Cybernetics, Part C: Applications and Reviews, IEEE Transactions on* 41, 2 (2009), 459–471.

[7] CE Garber, B Blissmer, MR Deschenes, BA Franklin, MJ Lamonte, IM Lee, DC Nieman, and Swain DP. 2011. Quantity and quality of exercise for developing and maintaining cardiorespiratory, musculoskeletal, and neuromotor fitness in apparently healthy adults: guidance for prescribing exercise. *American College of Sports Medicine position stand* 43, 7 (2011), 1334–1359.

[8] Kuang-Hung Hsu, Chaochang Chiu, Nan-Hsing Chiu, Po-Chi Lee, Wen-Ko Chiu, Thu-Hua Liu, and Chorng-Jer Hwang. 2011. A case-based classifier for hypertension detection. *Knowledge-Based Systems* 24, 1 (2011), 33–39.

[9] BC Johnston, S Kanters, K Bandayrel, P Wu, F Naji, RA Siemieniuk, GD Ball, JW Busse, K Thorlund, G Guyatt, JP Jansen, and EJ Mills. 2014. Comparison of weight loss among named diet programs in overweight and obese adults: a meta-analysis. *American College of Sports Medicine position stand* 312, 9 (2014), 923–933.

[10] NA King, M Hopkins, P Caudwell, RJ Stubbs, and JE Blundell. 2008. Individual variability following 12 weeks of supervised exercise: identification and characterization of compensation for exercise-induced weight loss. *Int J Obes* 32, 1 (2008), 177–184.

[11] Janet Kolodner. 1993. *Case-based Reasoning.* Morgan Kaufmann Publishers Inc., San Francisco, CA, USA.

[12] Cindy Marling, Jay Shubrook, and Frank Schwartz. 2008. Case-based decision support for patients with type 1 diabetes on insulin pump therapy. In *Advances in Case-Based Reasoning.* Springer, Heidelberg, 325–339.

[13] Carla Pedrosa, BMPM Oliveira, Isabel Albuquerque, Carlos Simões-Pereira, MD Vaz-de Almeida, and Flora Correia. 2011. Markers of metabolic syndrome in obese children before and after 1-year lifestyle intervention program. *European journal of nutrition* 50, 6 (2011), 391–400.

[14] F Xavier Pi-Sunyer, Diane M Becker, C Bouchard, RA Carleton, GA Colditz, WH Dietz, JP Foreyt, RJ Garrison, SM Grundy, BC Hansen, et al. 1998. Clinical guidelines on the identification, evaluation, and treatment of overweight and obesity in adults. *American Journal of Clinical Nutrition* 68, 4 (1998), 899–917.

[15] Lukas Schwingshackl, Sofia Dias, Barbara Strasser, and Georg Hoffmann. 2013. Impact of different training modalities on anthropometric and metabolic characteristics in overweight/obese subjects: a systematic review and network meta-analysis. *PloS one* 8, 12 (2013), e82853.

[16] Sunita Soni Soni and Jyothi Pillai. 2008. An Expert Case-Based System using Decision Tree Induction for Weight Management Counseling To Obese Children. *International Journal Of Computer Science And Applications* 1, 2 (2008), 117–120.

SparkGA: A Spark Framework for Cost Effective, Fast and Accurate DNA Analysis at Scale

Hamid Mushtaq
TU Delft
h.mushtaq@tudelft.nl

Frank Liu
IBM
frankliu@us.ibm.com

Carlos Costa
IBM
chcost@us.ibm.com

Gang Liu
IBM
gliu@us.ibm.com

Peter Hofstee
IBM
hofstee@us.ibm.com

Zaid Al-Ars
TU Delft
z.al-ars@tudelft.nl

ABSTRACT

In recent years, the cost of NGS (Next Generation Sequencing) technology has dramatically reduced, making it a viable method for diagnosing genetic diseases. The large amount of data generated by NGS technology, usually in the order of hundreds of gigabytes per experiment, have to be analyzed quickly to generate meaningful variant results. The GATK best practices pipeline from the Broad Institute is one of the most popular computational pipelines for DNA analysis. Many components of the GATK pipeline are not very parallelizable though. In this paper, we present SparkGA, a parallel implementation of a DNA analysis pipeline based on the big data Apache Spark framework. This implementation is highly scalable and capable of parallelizing computation by utilizing data-level parallelism as well as load balancing techniques. In order to reduce the analysis cost, SparkGA can run on nodes with as little memory as 16GB. For whole genome sequencing experiments, we show that the runtime can be reduced to about 1.5 hours on a 20-node cluster with an accuracy of up to 99.9981%. Moreover, SparkGA is about 71% faster than other state-of-the-art solutions while also being more accurate. The source code of SparkGA is publicly available at https://github.com/HamidMushtaq/SparkGA1.git.

ACM Reference format:
Hamid Mushtaq, Frank Liu, Carlos Costa, Gang Liu, Peter Hofstee, and Zaid Al-Ars. 2017. SparkGA: A Spark Framework for Cost Effective, Fast and Accurate DNA Analysis at Scale. In *Proceedings of ACM-BCB '17, Boston, MA, USA, August 20-23, 2017,* 10 pages.
https://doi.org/10.1145/3107411.3107438

1 INTRODUCTION

The fast reduction in the cost of DNA sequencing is making it an accessible method to use in clinics for diagnosing genetic diseases. However, the computational cost of DNA analysis has become the bottleneck in deploying this technique at scale. DNA analysis is needed to process the generated data to identify mutations in the DNA that could indicate specific susceptibilities to certain diseases. One of the most popular methods for DNA analysis is the GATK best practices pipeline from the Broad Institute [Auwera13]. The data generated by the DNA sequencing platforms is typically hundreds of GBs in size and therefore requires a lot of computational resources to process. This means that for efficient analysis, we require parallelizable solutions which can be easily scaled. While some stages of the analysis pipeline, such as the Burrows-Wheeler Aligner (BWA mem) [Li13], are highly scalable, other stages are not, when executed on a distributed computing infrastructure.

In recent years, a number of big data frameworks have emerged to efficiently manage and process large datasets in an easy way, the most popular of which are MapReduce [Dean08] and Apache Spark [Zaharia10]. Both of these frameworks provide good scalability and fault tolerance. The MapReduce framework has a limitation on programmability though, as it requires the programmer to write code where a map step is always followed by a reduce step. Moreover, it saves intermediate data into disk, which increases disk access overhead. Spark removes those restrictions, allowing programmers to perform many other transformations besides just map and reduce, while keeping data in memory between these transformations.

There are existing big data frameworks that attempt to improve the scalability and efficiency of genomics pipelines. One example is SparkBWA [Abuin16], which implements a Spark API to allow easy cluster scalability of BWA. However, SparkBWA only addresses the first stage of the GATK pipeline. Like SparkBWA, [Al-Ars15] also only deals with the first stage of the pipeline. Other solutions, such as the Churchill DNA analysis pipeline, efficiently utilize the available computational resources using a custom-made tightly-integrated computational pipeline [Kelly15]. The disadvantage of Churchill though is that it combines the different analysis stages into a single tightly-integrated computational pipeline, making it non-generic, meaning that parts of the pipeline cannot be easily replaced. Another solution proposed to solve the scalability challenge of the GATK pipeline is the Halvade framework, which implements the different GATK pipeline stages using a Hadoop-based MapReduce approach [Decap15]. The advantage of the Halvade's approach is that it leaves the pipeline tools unmodified, meaning that one can easily replace a pipeline tool with another one. A drawback of the Halvade framework though is that it is implemented using a classic Hadoop MapReduce based big data framework that is heavily disk oriented, which therefore leads to large disk access overhead due to the large data set sizes of genomics applications.

Permission to make digital or hard copies of all or part of this work for personal or classroom use is granted without fee provided that copies are not made or distributed for profit or commercial advantage and that copies bear this notice and the full citation on the first page. Copyrights for components of this work owned by others than ACM must be honored. Abstracting with credit is permitted. To copy otherwise, or republish, to post on servers or to redistribute to lists, requires prior specific permission and/or a fee. Request permissions from permissions@acm.org.
ACM-BCB '17, August 20-23, 2017, Boston, MA, USA
© 2017 Association for Computing Machinery.
ACM ISBN 978-1-4503-4722-8/17/08...$15.00
https://doi.org/10.1145/3107411.3107438

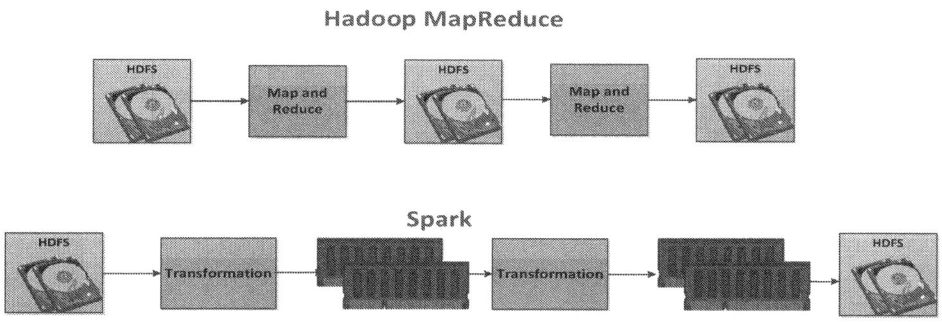

Figure 1: Spark vs Hadoop MapReduce

[Mushtaq15] discusses a Spark implementation of the full GATK DNA analysis pipeline that targets smaller Exome input files. The system described there attempts to process the GATK pipeline fully in memory, which creates memory size bottlenecks resulting in runtime failure for input files of larger sizes. In addition, that framework does not differentiate between the requirements of the various stages of the GATK pipeline, and runs the whole pipeline as a single run, thereby not fully optimizing system utilization for each stage.

In this paper, we propose a new Spark based framework called SparkGA (Spark Genome Analysis) that allows a DNA pipeline to run efficiently and cost-effectively on a scalable computational cluster. SparkGA uses Spark's in-memory computation capabilities to improve performance of the framework. At the same time and depending on available system resources, it can be configured to reduce its memory needs as a trade off for reduced performance. Due to this feature, it can even be run on a single node computer with just 16 GB of RAM. SparkGA implements the genomics computational pipeline as three distinct steps, and therefore allows for optimizing various Spark runtime parameters independently for each step of the framework. Moreover, like Halvade, it uses the pipeline tools unmodified, meaning that one tool can easily be replaced with another one. There has been recent work to accelerate individual stages of the pipeline using accelerators, such as in [Ahmed15] and [Ren15]. Since, like Halvade, SparkGA can also use the individual tools unmodified, such tools can directly rely on SparkGA for a scalable solution.

The contributions of this paper are as follows.

- We implemented SparkGA: a highly scalable, cost-effective, accurate and generic Apache Spark-based framework for a DNA analysis pipeline, which uses the original unmodified tools of a classical DNA pipeline.
- We optimized the framework using a memory-efficient load balancing step to ensure reducing the memory requirements of the compute nodes. Due to this, SparkGA can run even on a single node computer with just 16 GB of RAM.
- We ensured a modular implementation of the framework as three distinct steps that allow us to optimize the Spark runtime parameters for each step.

This paper is organized as follows. In Section 2, we discuss big data techniques, different stages of a DNA analysis pipeline and related work. Section 3 presents the Apache Spark framework we implemented to enable pipeline scalability. This is followed by Section 4, which discusses the performance and accuracy evaluations. We finally conclude the paper with Section 5.

2 BACKGROUND

In this section, first we discuss big data techniques available for executing parallel applications on scalable computational infrastructure, and then we discuss the GATK best practices DNA analysis pipeline. Lastly, we discuss the related work.

2.1 Big data techniques

The MapReduce programming model has been one of the most prevalent approaches used to manage data intensive computational pipelines that need to be processed on multiple compute nodes in a scalable cluster. This model divides the computation into two phases: map and reduce. During the map phase, input data is first formatted as key-value $<K, V>$ pairs followed by performing a specific mapping function on all of these pairs, resulting in a mapping of the input to an output set of $<K, V>$ pairs. The mapping function is executed in a distributed fashion using various mapping tasks that run locally on the data present in the nodes of the cluster. The output is then taken by the reduce tasks which first shuffle the data by grouping all the values that belong to the same key together. Afterwards, the reduce tasks compute a single output from the grouped $<K, V>$ pairs. Apache Hadoop is an open source implementation of the MapReduce programming model, which consists of three components: 1) the Hadoop Distributed File System (HDFS) that allows storing large data files on multiple nodes, 2) a resource manager called YARN that distributes the tasks to be executed to the various nodes in the cluster, and 3) the Hadoop MapReduce framework itself.

One disadvantage of the MapReduce framework is that it stores all data generated between the two phases (map and reduce) on disk, and if multiple map/reduce stages are chained together, it stores the output of each stage on the HDFS. This implies significant overhead due to the intensive disk access. Another disadvantage is that the only transformations allowed are map and reduce. If a different transformation has to be applied, it has to be done by modifying the map and reduce functions, thus making development with this framework very cumbersome.

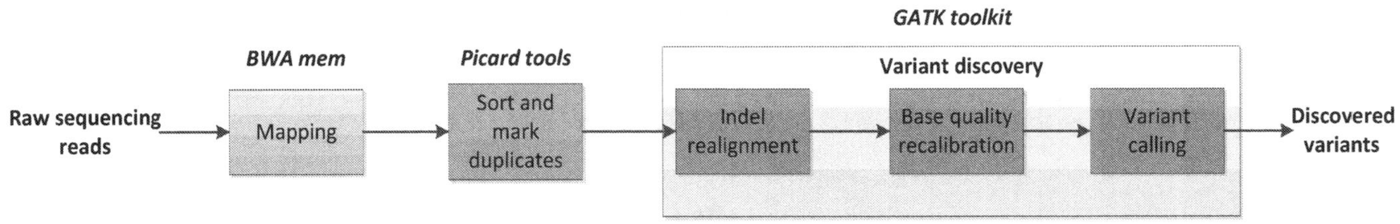

Figure 2: Classical DNA analysis and variant calling pipeline.

Apache Spark is a more recent big data framework that addresses the disadvantages of MapReduce listed above, as illustrated in Figure 1. First, it allows more transformations than mere map and reduce. It provides transformations such as join, cogroup, intersection, distinct and many others as predefined operations. This makes development of programs much easier as compared to the MapReduce framework. Moreover, the output of each transformation is saved in memory, but still allowing disk to be used to save data that does not fit within the available memory size. In this way, Spark avoids the overhead of disk access that is so prevalent in the MapReduce framework. In addition, Spark provides a programming interface to implement algorithms in various programming languages such as Scala, Python and Java, which allows writing programs in the language that is best suitable for the problem.

2.2 DNA analysis pipeline

Figure 2 shows a typical DNA analysis and variant calling pipeline. The input data set to this pipeline are the raw sequencing reads, which are obtained from a DNA sequencing machine. Since the DNA is usually over-sampled by as much as 30x to 100x by the sequencing machine, the number of such reads for a human are very large, and therefore the file storing these reads is of a very large size, typically in the range of several hundreds of gigabytes. One standard file format used today to store these reads is the FASTQ file format [Jones12].

The first step performed in the DNA analysis pipeline is DNA mapping. In this step, raw reads are mapped to a reference genome. Many classic alignment tools can be used in the GATK pipeline, including Bowtie2 [Langmead12] or the popular Burrows-Wheeler Aligner (BWA).

Since the DNA sequencing machine over-samples the DNA, the input data set might have multiple copies of the same raw read. These copies are reduced to a single copy by marking the duplicates. In the GATK best practices pipeline, this is usually done by using the mark duplicates tool from Picard [Picard]. The output of mark duplicates is a compressed file of BAM format.

Finally, the last part of the GATK best practices pipeline is done using tools from the GATK toolkit built by the Broad institute. The final output of the pipeline is a VCF (variant call format) file that contains all of the discovered variants. The first step is the indel realigner, which performs local realignment of reads around indels. The output of this part goes to the base quality recalibrator, which corrects quality scores for those reads which were assigned incorrect quality scores by the sequencing machine. Finally, a variant calling tool, such as the haplotype caller, discovers all the variants and saves them in a VCF file.

While the BWA mem DNA alignment tool of the best practices pipeline can scale well on a multicore system using multi-threading, it is difficult to exploit parallelism for other tools in the rest of the pipeline. In addition, other pipelines, not as well constructed and optimized as the best practices pipeline, are much less able to utilize the available computational infrastructure efficiently. The objective of our framework is to provide a generic method that is easy to use to ensure scalability to many of the various genomics analysis pipelines.

2.3 Related work

Recently, there have been approaches to tackle the scalability problem of a DNA analysis pipeline, by using big data parallelization techniques. One such example is the Churchill [Kelly15] DNA analysis pipeline, which utilizes the available computational resources using a custom-made tightly-integrated computational pipeline. Due to this tight integration, it is not trivial to replace parts of that pipeline. Halvade on the other hand, which uses the Hadoop MapReduce framework, allows the original unmodified pipeline tools to be used, meaning that parts of the pipeline can easily be replaced by new and better tools. The DNA mapping part is done by the map tasks while marking of duplicates and remaining parts of the pipeline are done by the reduce tasks. Within a map task, the unmodified DNA mapping tool is called using the Java's process package. Similarly, marking of duplicates and the remaining parts of the pipeline are done using unmodified original tools. The output of the mapping phase contains mapped reads keyed by chromosomal regions, where each chromosomal region is a part of a chromosome. Each reduce task therefore works on a chromosomal region, and outputs a corresponding vcf file. These vcf files are later combined into a single file.

There are a few limitations with Halvade's approach though. Firstly, it employs the MapReduce framework, which is heavily disk oriented, which leads to disk access overhead due to the large data set sizes of genomics applications. Secondly, it creates chromosomal regions based on the length of the chromosomes, while not checking the actual number of reads. This tends to create unbalanced regions, meaning that some regions may have significantly larger number of reads than other regions. This in turn, slows down the execution time of tasks working on bigger regions significantly, compared to tasks working on smaller regions, thus limiting the overall performance.

Our previous work [Mushtaq15] addressed the problems with MapReduce based solutions like Halvade by having a Spark based implementation of the DNA analysis pipeline. The system described there attempts to process the DNA pipeline fully in memory, and

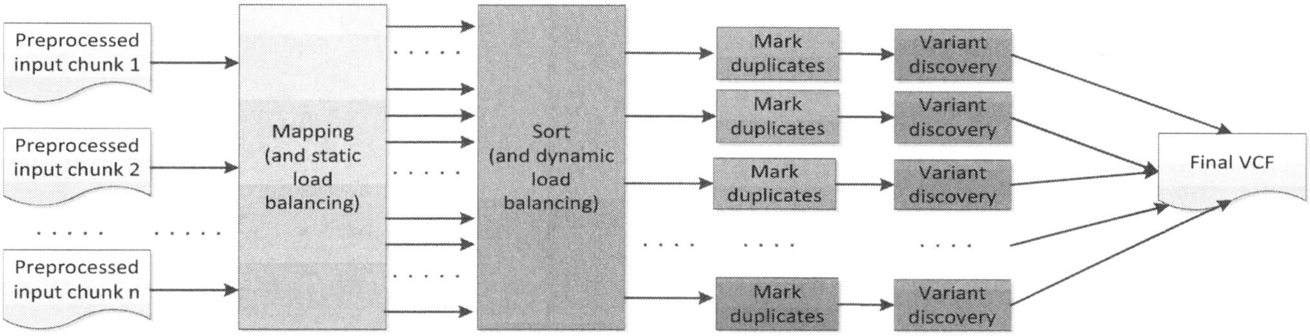

Figure 3: Data flow of the Spark-enabled GATK best practices pipeline using our framework

Table 1: Comparison of tools used in GATK best practices pipeline and SparkGA

Step	GATK best practices	Our framework
Align reads	BWA mem	BWA mem
SAM to BAM	Picard	Picard's Java library
Sort reads	Picard	Sorting in Scala
Mark duplicates	Picard	Picard
Indel realignment	GATK	GATK
Base recalibration	GATK	GATK
Haplotype caller	GATK	GATK

thus is able to create chromosomal regions based on the number of reads. However, since its load balancing step is done fully in memory, it results in out of memory errors for large input files. In addition, that framework does not differentiate between the requirements of the various stages of the GATK pipeline, and runs the whole pipeline as a single run, thereby not fully optimizing system utilization for each stage.

SparkGA, addresses the problem of [Mushtaq15] by implementing a memory efficient load balancing step. Moreover, since the memory and computational requirements for different steps vary, instead of running the whole pipeline with one program, SparkGA runs the pipeline in three different steps: DNA mapping & static load balancing; dynamic load balancing & SAM to BAM; and marking of duplicates and variant discovery. Through an xml configuration file, SparkGA allows the user to tune memory and cores of executors for all those three different steps. It has to be noticed here that Apache Spark does not allow to modify the memory and number of cores for executors at runtime. Therefore, the only way we can achieve this is by running the program in three steps, like SparkGA does.

3 IMPLEMENTATION

We used Apache Spark to implement our framework to parallelize a DNA classical pipeline. We use all the tools of a DNA pipeline unchanged. As shown in Table 1, the only parts of the pipeline that our framework replaces are sorting and SAM to BAM conversion. Those two parts are straightforward to implement anyway and do not require complex tools.

We discuss the overview of our parallelized GATK approach in Section 3.1, followed by our mapping and static load balancing approach in Section 3.2. Next, we discuss our sorting and dynamic load balancing method in Section 3.3 followed by our method to discover the variants in Section 3.4.

3.1 Overview

The dataflow of the execution of SparkGA is shown in Figure 3. In a typical DNA sequencing experiment, two FASTQ files are generated, that represent the two ends of a pair of sequences. These two input FASTQ files are divided into interleaved chunks using a chunks segmentation tool built by us, that also uploads these files to HDFS, thereby making them accessible to all nodes in a distributed cluster. Each chunk is then processed by a separate DNA mapping task that performs DNA alignment of the short reads against a reference genome, using a DNA mapping tool, such as BWA mem. The output of this step represents a list of read alignments (so-called SAM records) that will normally be stored in the SAM file. Since, we already know the length of each chromosome through the given reference file, we can already apply an approximate load balancing by reading the output of the SAM files produced by each BWA mem task. We call this approach static load balancing, since it depends upon information available even before running the program. Later, we apply further load balancing that evenly distributes the data for further computation. We call this approach dynamic load balancing, since it depends upon actual reads, which are only available at runtime. Each load balanced region contains reads from a part of a chromosome. By being able to create regions based on actual reads, rather than just the chromosomal length, like in the case of Halvade, we are able to achieve a better performance, as shown by the evaluation results section (Section 4 of this paper). Moreover, unlike Halvade, our tool is able to run even with less free disk space. Lastly, unlike [Mushtaq15], which consumes too much memory in the load balancing step, and is therefore prone to memory crashes for big data sets, our tool can work even on a single node with just 16 GB of RAM.

Subsequently, for each chromosome region, the aligned reads are sorted using their alignment positions (which replaces the sorting step in the best practices pipeline). Then, the rest of the analysis steps are performed in parallel using a tool for marking duplicates and other tools of the pipeline, such as indel realigner, base recalibration and haplotype caller, by applying those tools on different chromosomal regions separately, resulting in various VCF files. Finally, the contents of those VCF files are sorted and merged into a single file that contains all variants identified in the analysis.

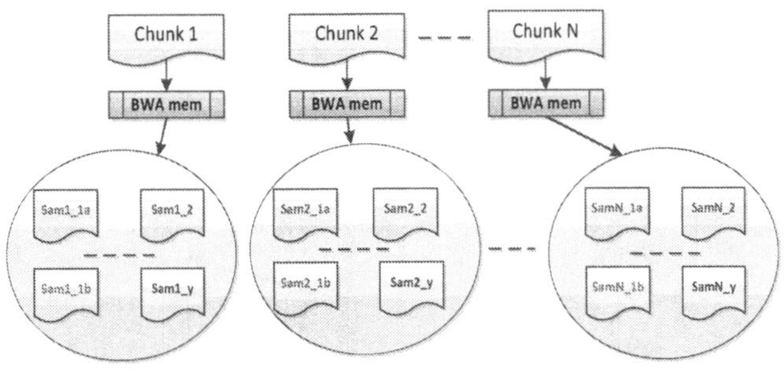

Figure 4: Mapping and static load balancing

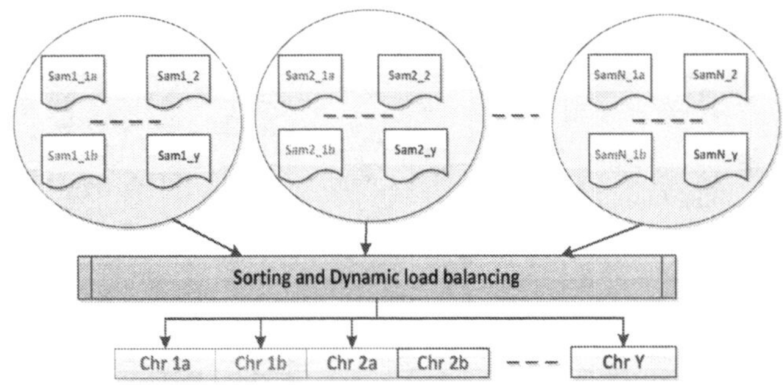

Figure 5: Sorting and dynamic load balancing

We perform the execution in three different steps: mapping and static load balancing; sorting and dynamic load balancing; and mark duplicates and variant discovery. The benefit of this approach is that we can set different optimized Spark execution parameters (such as executor memories and number of executors) for each of these three steps separately. Spark has limitations that do not allow it to change those parameters at runtime.

3.2 Mapping and static load balancing

Figure 4 illustrates this step of our implementation. In this step, each input chunk is fed to a mapping and static load balancing task. Mapping can be done by using a mapping tool, such as BWA mem, while load balancing is done by creating sub-groups (or chromosomal regions) of the resulting mapped reads output by the mapping tool, according to the chromosome number and mapping position. The chromosomal regions are created by equally dividing chromosomes based on their length. This means that longer chromosomes will have more regions than smaller ones. All the SAM files produced by this step are placed into the HDFS in preparation to perform the next step. Each of the mapping and static load balancing tasks creates SAM files that map to any region of the whole genome. For example, it is possible that task 1 produces a SAM file for region $<1, a>$ (Chromosome 1, part a) and task 2 also produces a SAM file for that same region ($<1, a>$). That is why we tag each SAM file with the task number. For example, for task 1, we can name this file as Sam1_1a, while for task 2, name it as Sam2_1a. All the data from SAM files corresponding to the same region will then be grouped together by the next step of the framework, which is the sorting and dynamic load balancing step.

The advantage of static load balancing is that it incurs almost no performance cost, as we rely on the length of the chromosomes which are already known. We notice that after this step, most of the regions made are already balanced according to the number of reads, which reduces the amount of work that needs to be done by the dynamic load balancing part of the next step. Lastly, since we communicate data from this step to the next step through the HDFS, the memory requirement for the nodes is reduced significantly, which enables SparkGA to run on nodes with as little memory as 16 GB.

SparkGA also provides the feature of multiplicating the number of regions after the static load balancing step, through a region multiplicating factor. For example, if the user sets the region multiplication factor of 4, the dynamic load balancing step would create approximately 4 times more regions than created by the static load balancing step. The benefit of that is that fewer number of files would have to be uploaded by the static load balancing step, thus reducing the overhead of accessing HDFS.

3.3 Sorting and dynamic load balancing

Approach. In this step, all the SAM files produced for different regions in the mapping and static load balancing part are combined and sorted to produce BAM and BED files. A BED file is used to restrict the computation in the variant discovery part. The idea is that since a BAM file for a region contains data for only that region, the variant discovery part does not need to scan the whole genome for finding mutations, but instead just inspect within that region. The way SAM files are combined is illustrated in Figure 5. For example, all SAM files produced for region 1a (for example, Sam1_1a, Sam2_1a, etc.) are combined into one BAM file.

The dynamic load balancing step can further divide a region if it has too many reads, since the execution time for several tools in the pipeline depends on the number of reads being processed. We note that after static load balancing, most of the regions during the dynamic load balancing step are already well-balanced. Only a limited number of regions need further division by the dynamic load balancer. The information about the number of reads is already provided by the mapping and static load balancing part, so by reading that information, we already know which regions are too big.

Creating BAM and BED files for a region which is already balanced is simple. The SAM records for such a region are simply sorted and put into a BAM file. Moroever, the BED file is created by looking at the positions of the SAM records in that region.

However, for regions which are not balanced, dynamic load balancing has to be applied. For that purpose, for each SAM chunk produced by the static load balancer, a corresponding file which contains positions of all the reads inside that SAM chunk, is also produced. This is done because otherwise, when dividing a region into sub regions, a dynamic load balancing task would have to collect all the SAM records for that region and sort them first. Sorting the SAM records themselves is memory intensive. That is why, in SparkGA, instead of sorting the SAM records themselves, a dynamic load balancing task just sorts the positions that come from the files containing the positions of those SAM records. Afterwards, as it reads each SAM record from the corresponding chunks, it

Algorithm 1: Dynamic load balancing

```
procedure CREATEBAMFILES
▷ Elements of the RDD are of type <regID, <chunkID, numOfReads>>
    inputData ← readInfoFile(dynLBInfo).cache()
▷ Get the number of reads for each chunk
    readsPerChunk ← inputData.map{case(regID, (chunkID, numOfReads)) => numOfReads}
▷ Get the total number of reads
    totalReads ← readsPerChunk.reduceByKey(_ + _)
▷ Group the input data by region
    chrReg ← inputData.groupByKey()
    chrReg.cache()
▷ Calculate average number of reads per statically load balanced regions
    avgReadsPerRegion ← totalReads/chrReg.count()
▷ makeBAM divides a region further if required, & creates BAM and BED files for each (sub)region
    chrReg.foreach{case(regID, infoList) => makeBAM(regID, infoList, avgReadsPerRegion)}
end procedure
```

checks which subregion that SAM record would go to by finding its position in the sorted positions array, using binary search. After finding out this information, it directly appends that SAM record to the SAM file representing that subregion. To accelerate this step, SparkGA allows to perform this step with multiple threads. In this way, different threads can read the SAM records from the different chunks representing a region, in parallel. Afterwards, all SAM files created by a dynamic load balancing task are read, sorted and converted into BAM files. The BED files are also created in that step. The sorting and conversion from SAM to BAM for subregions can also be done in parallel by using multiple threads.

Algorithm. The main algorithm for dynamic load balancing is shown as algorithm 1. Besides creating the SAM chunks and their corresponding positions files, the static load balancing step also uploads a global information file to help the dynamic load balancer. Each line of this file corresponds to a SAM chunk and contains information about the region ID that chunks belongs to, the ID of that chunk itself, and the number of reads it has. This file is then read by the dynamic load balancing step as shown in algorithm 1. The information from this file is first placed in a Spark's RDD (Resilient Distributed Dataset), which is the basic distributed data structure of Spark. This RDD is transformed into another RDD where each element of the RDD is assigned to the number of reads the corresponding chunk contains. Next, these number of reads are summed up using reduceByKey, giving us the total number of reads. After that, we group the input data by region, so that the information for each region is now contained in a list. The total number of reads divided by the total number of regions then gives us the average number of reads per region. Then for each statically load balanced region, the function *makeBAM* is called which performs the dynamic load balancing. The *makeBAM* function reads all the SAM files pertaining to the region its working on. The information passed to it contains a list of tuples (the 2nd parameter), where each tuple contains the chunk ID and the number of reads that chunk contains. Since the number of reads for each chunk is known as well as the average number of reads per statically load balanced regions (the 3rd parameter), the *makeBAM* function can divide a statically load balanced region into subregions of approximately equal sizes if that region has too many reads. Through a region multiplication factor, the user can also set how many regions the dynamic load balancer step would create. For example, if the user sets a region multiplication factor of 4, the dynamic load balancing step would create approximately 4 times more regions than what the static load balancing step created. The dynamic load balancing tasks can be run with multiple threads to improve the performance, as discussed in the previous paragraph.

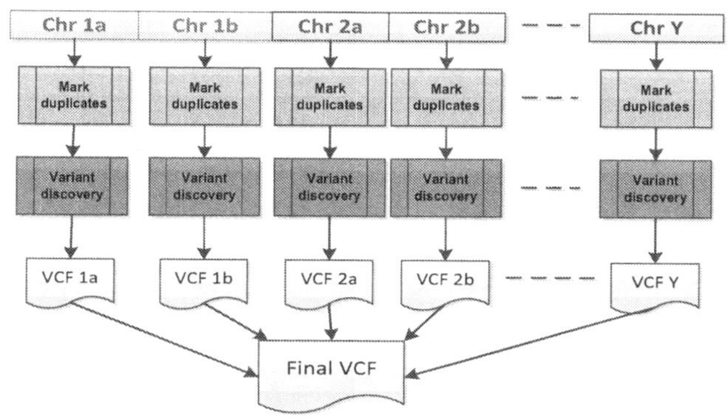

Figure 6: Mark duplicate and variant discovery

3.4 Mark duplicates and variant discovery

In the last step, the BAM and BED files produced by the previous step, are used as an input for the rest of the pipeline. Each task works on a separate set of BAM and BED files, and outputs a VCF file. Later, all these VCF files are combined into one final VCF file. This is illustrated in Figure 6 as discussed next.

Mark duplicates—In this step, all identical short reads mapping to the exact same location in the reference are marked as copies of each other. This is done because allele frequencies and genotype calls can be skewed if certain individual reads are preferentially amplified relative to others.

Table 2: Runtime in minutes on a 4-data node Power7+, and a 5, 10, 15 & 19-data node Power8 (+1 name node) IBM cluster

	4-node P7+		5-node P8		10-node P8		15-node P8		19-node P8	
Step	**Time**	**%**	**Time**	**%**	**Time**	**%**	**Time**	**%**	**Time**	**%**
Mapping and static LB	128	30%	78.7	32%	40.6	29%	29.0	28%	24.4	27%
Sorting and dynamic LB	45	11%	22.1	9%	19.5	14%	18.8	18%	18.7	21%
Variant discovery	249	59%	145.9	59%	77.7	56%	57.2	54%	47.7	52%
Total	422	100%	246.7	100%	137.7	100%	105.0	100%	90.9	100%

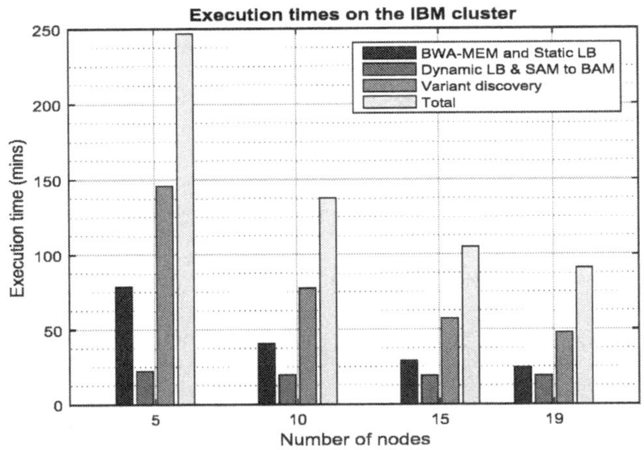

Figure 7: Performance on the IBM cluster

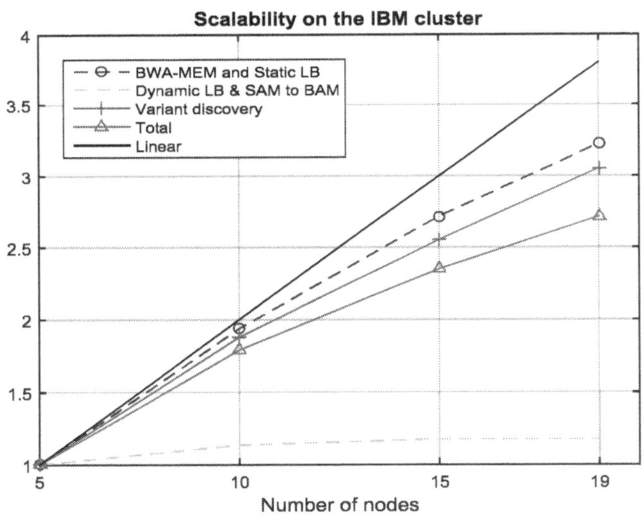

Figure 8: Scalability on IBM cluster

Indel realigner—The indel realigner tool performs local realignment of reads around indels, so as to minimize mismatching bases across all reads.

Base quality recalibration—When a sequencing machine outputs data, it assigns a quality score to each read. This quality score is to signal how much a read can be trusted to be accurate. However, sometimes a sequencing machine can also generate erroneous quality scores. The base quality recalibrator tries to correct this problem by looking at a human genome database. Since it is estimated that 99% of all variants in the Caucasian population have been put in the dbSNP database, the vast majority of mapping differences not in dbSNP should basically be sequencing errors. By using this database and and applying machine learning models on the output from indel realigner, the base recalibrator tries to correct any erroneous quality scores given to the reads.

Haplotype caller—The haplotype caller is the variant discovery tool of choice for the GATK pipeline. Whenever the haplotype caller sees a region which shows signs of variations, it discards the existing mapping information and assembles the reads itself for that region. This helps in making the haplotype caller more accurate for regions which are difficult to call, such as those that contain variants close to each other.

4 EVALUATION RESULTS

We tested the results on three different types of hardware platforms. The first platform is an IBM Power7+ cluster with 4 data nodes + 1 master node. Each node has two sockets that host a Power7+ processor. In total, a node there has 16 physical cores and 128GB of memory. Each Power7+ core is capable of 4-way simultaneous multithreading. Spark is run over YARN in that platform. The second platform consists of 20 IBM Power8 S822LC nodes (19 data nodes + 1 master node), with each node having two sockets, where each socket hosts a Power8 processor. In total, a node there has 20 physical cores and 512GB of physical memory. Each Power8 core can support 8-way simultaneous multithreading. Spark was run using a Spark cluster on that platform. Lastly, the third platform used was the Dutch national e-infrastructure's SURFsara cluster [SURFsara], which allows up to 72 Intel/AMD nodes to be used using YARN as a resource manager. This cluster was used to compare our results with Halvade.

We tested SparkGA with the publicly available whole human genome dataset G15512.HCC1954.1 from Genomics Data Commons (formally Cancer Genomics Hub) [GDC], with the reference genome human_g1k_v37_decoy. The raw reads have 65x coverage with size of over 402GB. SparkGA is able to compute the pipeline in 422 minutes (7 hours and 2 minutes) on the 4-node Power7+ cluster. The breakdown of this runtime for different steps is shown in Table 2, indicating that the variant discovery step consumes most of the time amounting to 59%, followed by the mapping step at 30%, then the sorting at 11%. On the 19-node IBM Power8 cluster, the execution consumed a total of 90.9 minutes, with similar distribution of runtime. However, the table shows that the for this shorter runtime, the sorting step is becoming more dominant, with its share

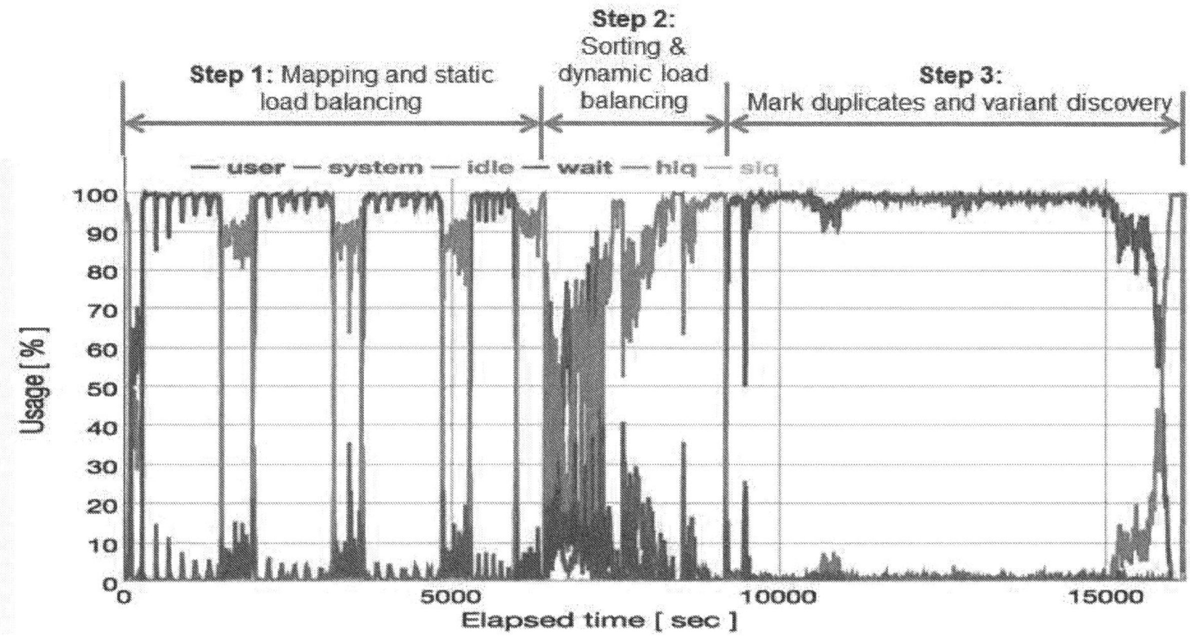

Figure 9: Utilization of the compute resources of a single data node in a 5-node Power8 cluster

increasing to 21%. In the same table, execution times for different sizes of IBM Power8 clusters are also shown.

4.1 Scalability analysis

Figure 7 shows a bar chart of the execution times registered for different steps and the total runtime for the IBM Power8 cluster with an increasing number of data nodes activated, ranging from 5, 10, 15 to 19 data nodes. The corresponding speedup graph is shown in Figure 8. Here, we observe that the BWA mem and variant discovery steps scale quite well, while the load balancing step plateaus. BWA mem was expected to scale well, but here we see that the variant discovery step scales almost as well. The reason it scales so well is that tools such as the haplotype caller can make very efficient use of vector instructions to improve the performance. Moreover, simultaneous multithreading also improves the performance. Each IBM Power8 processor has 8 high quality simultaneous threads for each physical core, which can benefit the workload greatly.

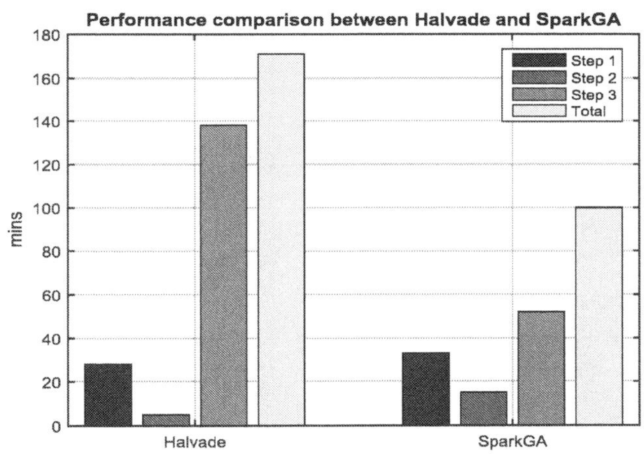

Figure 10: Halvade vs SparkGA performance comparison

4.2 Performance measurements

In order to understand the bottlenecks in the three steps, we plot the utilization of system resources in Figure 9. The figure shows rather high CPU utilization in the mapping as well as in the variant discovery steps. We also observe a drop in the CPU utilization for the mapping step at regular intervals. This is caused by the files that this step needs to upload to the HDFS. In addition, we observe some idle time in the sorting and dynamic load balancing step. This is due to the heavy I/O activity done by the sorting and dynamic load balancing step. This explains the limited scalability of the sorting and dynamic load balancing step as we increase the size of the cluster. However, we see a very high utilization in the last step (mark duplicates and variant discovery). The reason is that in this step there is no interaction with the HDFS, except for when the BAM files from the dynamic load balancing part are read, and when the final output VCF files (which are very small in size anyway) are written.

4.3 Performance comparison with Halvade

We also compared the performance with Halvade on a YARN based cluster. For that purpose, we used the maximum 72 nodes allowed by the SURFsara cluster. The SURFsara cluster nodes have mixed

Table 3: Different steps of Halvade and SparkGA

Steps	Halvade	SparkGA
1	Mapping and static load balancing	Mapping and static load balancing
2	Sorting and grouping of data by regions	Sorting, Dynamic load balancing and SAM to BAM
3	SAM to BAM, Mark duplicates and Variant discovery	Mark duplicates and Variant discovery

Table 4: Performance comparison between Halvade and SparkGA

	Halvade		SparkGA	
Step	**Minutes**	**% of Total**	**Minutes**	**% of Total**
1	28	16%	33	33%
2	5	3%	15	15%
3	138	81%	52	52%
Total	**171**	100%	**100**	100%

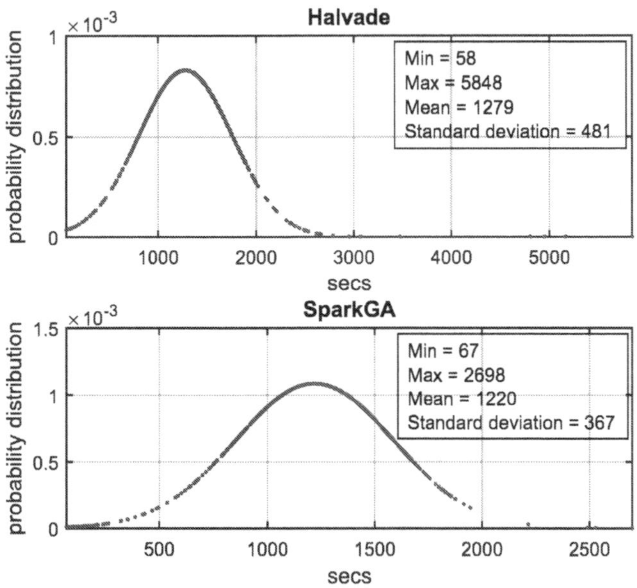

Figure 11: Load balancing of tasks in step 3

Intel and AMD processors, with each processor having 8 processing cores, and each node having 56 GB of RAM. We also tried to run Halvade on the 4 node IBM P7+ cluster, but it exceeded the available disk space. On the other hand, [Mushtaq15] exceeded the memory available on the 4 node IBM P7+ cluster. However, SparkGA is able to run on the 4 node IBM P7+ cluster, despite the low hard disk space and memory on the nodes.

It has to be noted first that the steps taken by SparkGA are not exactly the same as those taken by Halvade. This difference is shown in Table 3. In the second step, Halvade does not perform dynamic load balancing nor it creates the BAM and BED files, which it creates in the third step rather. However, since creation of BAM

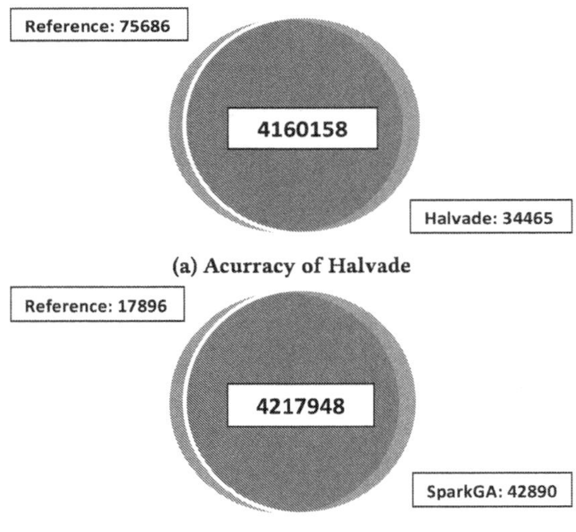

(a) Acurracy of Halvade

(b) Accuracy of SparkGA

Figure 12: Accuracy comparison of SparkGA and Halvade with the classical GATK pipeline

and BED files take on average, just around 5% of a reduce task in Halvade, The execution times of Halvade and SparkGA for the third step can still be compared fairly.

The comparison with Halvade is shown in Table 4 and illustrated in Figure 10. The time for Step 1 is slightly higher for SparkGA because SparkGA also uploads some files required for its next step: sorting and dynamic load balancing part. In Step 2, Halvade performs sorting without dynamic load balancing, that is why it consumes less time than SparkGA. In the variant discovery step (Step 3) however, SparkGA is much faster than Halvade due to its improved load balancing. Overall Spark took 71% less time than Halvade for the selected data set.

The improvement achieved due to better load balancing can be understood from the Figure 11, which shows bell curve of the time taken by the tasks of Step 3. The mean and standard deviations of the execution time of these tasks are also shown in that figure. We can see that the standard deviation for Halvade is poorer (481 as compared to 367 seconds for SparkGA). This is because some of the tasks in Halvade take too much time. On the other hand, the task execution times for SparkGA are concentrated more towards the mean.

Since the cost of using a cluster depends directly on the time spent running the applications, this means that compared to Halvade, our solution is much more cost effective, as it takes significantly less time in comparison.

4.4 Correctness of the results

We evaluate the correctness of our framework by comparing the variants discovered in the VCF files of SparkGA with those resulting from the GATK best practices pipeline as a reference. One obvious concern is that since our method partitions the input dataset into chunks and the reference genome into regions, there is a risk of reduction in accuracy of the results. The correctness analysis is

Table 5: Accuracy comparison of SparkGA and Halvade

Parameter	Formula	Halvade (%)	SparkGA (%)
Sensitivity	TP / (TP + FN)	98.2%	99.6%
Specificity	TN / (TN + FP)	99.999%	99.999%
Precision	TP / (TP + FP)	99.18%	99.0%
False discovery rate	FP / (TP + FP)	0.82%	1.01%
Accuracy	**(TP + TN) / (TP + TN + FP + FN)**	**99.9966%**	**99.9981%**

based on measuring: the true positive (TP) variants detected by the analysis in the sample (those detected by both SparkGA and GATK); the false negatives (FN) detected by GATK but not by SparkGA; the false positives (FP) detected by SparkGA but not by GATK; and the true negatives (TN) representing all possible mutation locations in the genome that are not detected by either pipeline.

We first experiment by varying the number of chunks and regions from 512 to 8192 in powers of 2 and measure the accuracy of the results. Our method achieves a constant accuracy rate of 99.9981% for all experiments, which is better than Halvade's accuracy of 99.9966%. The Venn diagrams of Figure 12 show the comparison results of the VCF output of SparkGA and Halvade with that of the traditional GATK pipeline. The lower Venn diagram in that figure shows that both SparkGA and GATK pipelines detect 4217948 variants (TP). Moreover, SparkGA detects 42890 false positives and 17896 false negatives. In comparison, Halvade detects less variants, meaning it has more false negatives (75686 compared to SparkGA's 17896), as shown by the upper Venn diagram in Figure 12.

Table 5 also compares SparkGA's accuracy with that of Halvade. Moreover, it defines a number of parameters to quantify the correctness. Besides, better accuracy, SparkGA also has better Sensitivity compared to Halvade, due to its ability to detect more variants. Halvade however is slightly better when it comes to precision and false discovery rate.

5 CONCLUSIONS

Next generation sequencing has dramatically increased the speed and throughput of DNA sequencing. However, DNA analysis requires efficient and scalable solutions to ensure high computational performance at an affordable cost. We propose SparkGA, a big data framework based on Apache Spark that runs efficiently on a multi-node cluster. By applying novel static and dynamic load balancing techniques, our framework can spread the input data more uniformly across the computational nodes, hence ensuring better scalability. It also allows to run the framework on lower-cost nodes with as little as 16GB of memory. SparkGA enables scaling up the GATK best practices pipelines, a well accepted industry standard, achieving a high accuracy of up to 99.9981%. Experimental results show that when deployed on a 20-node IBM Power8 cluster, SparkGA can complete the GATK best practices pipeline in about 90 minutes. Moreover, it is 71% faster than the state-of-the-art solution. Having better performance also means that it is more cost-effective.

The source code of SparkGA is publicly available at the GitHub repository (https://github.com/HamidMushtaq/SparkGA1.git).

ACKNOWLEDGMENTS

Special thanks to SURF cooperative for providing support in testing our framework on the Dutch national e-infrastructure's SURFsara cluster [SURFsara].

REFERENCES

[Auwera13] G.A. van der Auwera, M. Carneiro, C. Hartl, R. Poplin, G. del Angel, A. Levy-Moonshine, T. Jordan, K. Shakir, D. Roazen, J. Thibault, E. Banks, K. Garimella, D. Altshuler, S. Gabriel, M. DePristo, "From FastQ Data to High-Confidence Variant Calls: The Genome Analysis Toolkit Best Practices Pipeline", Current Protocols in Bioinformatics, 43:11.10.1-11.10.33, 2013.

[Decap15] D. Decap, J. Reumers, C. Herzeel, P. Costanza and J. Fostier, "Halvade: scalable sequence analysis with MapReduce", *Bioinformatics*, btv179v2-btv179, 2015.

[Picard] https://broadinstitute.github.io/picard/

[GDC] https://gdc.cancer.gov/

[SURFsara] https://www.surf.nl/en/services-and-products/big-data-services/access/index.html

[Dean08] J. Dean and S. Ghemawat, "MapReduce: Simplified Data Processing on Large Clusters", *Commun. ACM*, vol. 51, no. 1, 2008.

[Zaharia10] M. Zaharia, M. Chowdhury, M.J. Franklin, S. Shenker and I.Stoica, "Spark: cluster computing with working sets", *HotCloud'10*, USENIX Association, Berkeley, CA, USA, 10-10.

[Abuin16] J.M. Abuin, J.C. Pichel, T.F. Pena and J. Amigo, "SparkBWA: Speeding Up the Alignment of High-Throughput DNA Sequencing Data" Ed" *PLoS ONE 11.5 (2016)*, e0155461. PMC. Web. 31 Oct. 2016.

[Jones12] D.C. Jones, W.L. Ruzzo, X. Peng and M.G. Katze, "Compression of next-generation sequencing reads aided by highly efficient de novo assembly", *Nucleic Acids Research*, 2012.

[Kelly15] B.J. Kelly, J.R. Fitch, Y. Hu, D.J. Corsmeier, H. Zhong, A.N. Wetzel, R.D. Nordquist, D.L. Newsom and P. White,"Churchill: an ultra-fast, deterministic, highly scalable and balanced parallelization strategy for the discovery of human genetic variation in clinical and population-scale genomics", *Genome Biology*, vol. 16, no. 6, 2015.

[Ahmed15] N. Ahmed, V. M. Sima, E. Houtgast, K. Bertels and Z. Al-Ars, "Heterogeneous hardware/software acceleration of the BWA-MEM DNA alignment algorithm", 2015 IEEE/ACM International Conference on Computer-Aided Design (ICCAD), Austin, TX, 2015, pp. 240-246.

[Ren15] S. Ren, V. M. Sima and Z. Al-Ars, "FPGA acceleration of the pair-HMMs forward algorithm for DNA sequence analysis", 2015 IEEE International Conference on Bioinformatics and Biomedicine (BIBM), Washington, DC, 2015, pp. 1465-1470.

[Al-Ars15] Z. Al-Ars and Hamid Mushtaq "Scalability Potential of BWA DNA Mapping Algorithm on Apache Spark", SIMBig 2015, Cusco, Peru, 2015, pp. 85-88.

[Li13] H. Li, "Aligning sequence reads, clone sequences and assembly contigs with BWA-MEM", arXiv:1303.3997 [q-bio.GN], 2013.

[Mushtaq15] H. Mushtaq and Z. Al-Ars, "Cluster-based Apache Spark implementation of the GATK DNA analysis pipeline", 2015 IEEE International Conference on Bioinformatics and Biomedicine (BIBM), Washington, DC, 2015, pp. 1471-1477.

[Langmead12] B. Langmead and S.L. Salzberg, "Fast gapped-read alignment with Bowtie 2", Nature Methods, vol. 9, no. 4, pp. 357-359, 2012.

Fast and Highly Scalable Bayesian MDP on a GPU Platform

He Zhou
Texas A&M University
Department of Electrical & Computer Engineering
zhouhe@tamu.edu

Sunil P. Khatri
Texas A&M University
Department of Electrical & Computer Engineering
sunilkhatri@tamu.edu

Jiang Hu
Texas A&M University
Department of Electrical & Computer Engineering
jianghu@tamu.edu

Frank Liu
IBM Research, Austin
frankliu@us.ibm.com

Cliff Sze*
IBM Research, Austin
csze@google.com

ABSTRACT

By employing the Optimal Bayesian Robust (OBR) policy, Bayesian Markov Decision Process (BMDP) can be used to solve the Gene Regulatory Network (GRN) control problem. However, due to the "curse of dimensionality", the data storage limitation hinders the practical applicability of the BMDP. To overcome this impediment, we propose a novel Duplex Sparse Storage (DSS) scheme in this paper, and develop a BMDP solver with the DSS scheme on a heterogeneous GPU-based platform. The simulation results demonstrate that our approach achieves a 5× reduction in memory utilization with a 2.4% "decision difference" and an average speedup of 4.1× compared to the full matrix based storage scheme. Additionally, we present the tradeoff between the runtime and result accuracy for our DSS techniques versus the full matrix approach. We also compare our results with the well known Compressed Sparse Row (CSR) approach for reducing memory utilization, and discuss the benefits of DSS over CSR.

CCS CONCEPTS

• **Theory of computation → Data compression**; *Parallel algorithms*; *Sequential decision making*; • **Applied computing →** *Bioinformatics*; • **Mathematics of computing →** Bayesian computation;

KEYWORDS

Duplex Sparse Storage; Data compression; Graphics processing units; Acceleration; Bayesian Markov processes

1 INTRODUCTION

The Markov Decision Process (MDP) has been applied to solve many fundamental optimization problems such as gene regulatory network control [30], robotics [17, 26], inventory management [7], finance [3, 4], etc. The theory of MDP is a natural framework for constructing optimal intervention policies for a system in which the state transition behavior of the system is stochastic.

However, classic MDP requires a prefect knowledge of the system model, which is rarely available due to the inherent complexity and variability of the processes that govern the underlying system behavior. The system model is usually represented by a state transition probability matrix (TPM). To express the uncertainty in the MDP framework, a class of TPMs with a prior probability distribution over this class is assumed. The prior probability distribution indicates the degree of confidence in how much each TPM might represent the hidden underlying true TPM [10]. To search for the optimal non-stationary policy, dynamic programming is repeatedly performed on the expected TPM across the uncertainty class. Throughout the process of policy search, Bayes' rule is applied to update the prior probability distribution of the TPM class and generate the posterior distribution. The MDP in such an uncertainty framework with the Bayesian update is denoted as Bayesian MDP (BMDP).

Such an approach has been applied to the Gene Regulatory Network (GRN) control problem, and is named the Optimal Bayesian Robust (OBR) policy [30]. The GRN can be regarded as a dynamic system, in which the state of the modeled system changes sequentially. The TPM describes the probability of a transition from any current state to any next state. Due to the complexity of the underlying biological mechanisms, the perfect knowledge of the TPM of the GRN is usually unavailable. The goal is to decide an intervention policy to control the GRN so that the long-term accumulated reward is optimal. In [30], it is assumed that both prior and posterior distributions belong to the same family. An example of the distribution family is the Dirichlet distribution, which is the conjugate prior of the multinomial distribution.

Although the OBR approach is an effective approach to overcome the obstacle of partial knowledge of the system model, its computational complexity is exponential. The OBR approach also suffers from the "curse of dimensionality" [6] inherited from the MDP framework and dynamic programming. As a result, when the dimension of the MDP problem increases, the CPU runtime and memory required to compute a solution increases exponentially as a function of the size of state space, the size of action space and the length of horizon. This is because the prior distribution of the TPMs is updated when there is a new observation, and hence the corresponding expected TPM also changes. As a result, we need to track the expected TPM throughout the entire dynamic programming process. Also, the size of the TPM is quadratic with respect

*This research was conducted while this co-author was with IBM. The co-author is currently with Google

Permission to make digital or hard copies of all or part of this work for personal or classroom use is granted without fee provided that copies are not made or distributed for profit or commercial advantage and that copies bear this notice and the full citation on the first page. Copyrights for components of this work owned by others than the author(s) must be honored. Abstracting with credit is permitted. To copy otherwise, or republish, to post on servers or to redistribute to lists, requires prior specific permission and/or a fee. Request permissions from permissions@acm.org.
ACM-BCB'17, August 20-23, 2017, Boston, MA, USA.
© 2017 Copyright held by the owner/author(s). Publication rights licensed to ACM.
978-1-4503-4722-8/17/08...$15.00
DOI: http://dx.doi.org/10.1145/3107411.3107440

to the size of the state space, which is large in many MDP problems of interest, particularly for translation genomics and precision medicine problems.

Parallel computing based on Graphic Processing Units (GPUs) has been used to improve the runtime performance of OBR [31]. The GPU is a high performance computing platform which employs massive multithreading, fast hardware-based context switching as well as high memory bandwidth. A GPU has thousands of small processor cores, and when properly utilized, it can achieve impressive performance gains for several applications compared to traditional multi-core CPUs. However, the GPU platform has its limitations. A single GPU has limited memory storage and operates in a single instruction multiple data (SIMD) manner. Also in a modern GPU platform, the cost of transferring data between the GPU and the main memory is non-negligible. Hence memory utilization often results in the performance bottleneck of GPU-based parallel computing. Alleviating the memory bottleneck for large BMDP problems is a critical problem, and is the key goal of this paper.

In order to solve the memory problem, we exploit the observation that the expected TPMs tend to be sparse, since the expression of one gene usually depends on only a few other genes [12]. This sparsity feature of the TPM motivates us to investigate sparse data storage techniques to address the memory issue. Since both the prior and posterior distributions of the TPM in BMDP are known, we can exploit the sparsity of the TPM. The Compressed Sparse Row (CSR) format is an efficient approach to store a sparse matrix [23]. Compared to full matrix storage, in which every single entry is stored in memory regardless of its value, CSR only stores the non-zero entries of the matrix. The CSR format requires some overhead to store the row/column locations of the non-zero entries. Obviously the overall efficiency of the CSR format heavily depends on the sparsity ratio *SR* (or the percentage of zero entries compared to the matrix size) of the matrix. We propose Duplex Sparse Storage (DSS) scheme to improve over CSR. To address potential accuracy issues, we lump all trivial values (*trivial* values are defined as the smallest $(1 - R) \times 100\%$ of the entries, where R is the percentage of entries the DSS stores) of the TPM into a single average nonzero entry in the CSR format. Furthermore, we enhance the CSR to gain better storage efficiency, by duplex use of the same words of storage.

We use "GPU-based OBR" (or GPU-OBR) to generically refer to the parallel OBR approach for solving the BMDP problem on GPU. The GPU-based OBR using a full matrix to represent the expected TPM in [31] is denoted as "G-Full". We implemented the GPU-based OBR with CSR and our proposed DSS method to represent the expected TPM (called "G-CSR" and "G-DSS" respectively). We have simulated G-DSS on the BMDP-based gene regulatory network (GRNs) control problem defined in [25, 30]. Simulations on 500 synthetic GRNs demonstrated that G-DSS achieves a 5× reduction in memory utilization while introducing only 2.4% "decision difference" in the largest GRN compared with G-Full. The corresponding memory reduction and "decision difference" for G-CSR are 2.1× and 6.3% respectively. Our simulation results of DSS on the GPU exhibit an average speedup of 4.1× compared with using full sparse matrix on the GPU.

The key contributions of this paper is that we developed DSS which is used to alleviate the memory issue in G-Full. Compared to CSR, the DSS scheme has a smaller memory utilization, a better accuracy and a better L^∞ norm. Compared to the full matrix storage scheme, DSS also has a smaller memory utilization, and a better speedup. Moreover, the DSS is designed to enable efficient Bayesian updates in GPU-based OBR, by eliminating the need to reallocate memory during Bayesian updates.

The rest of this paper is organized as follows: In Section 2, we review the background and previous work of the parallel OBR algorithm for the MDP and BMDP problems. In Section 3, we explain the problems of using conventional full matrix to represent the expected TPM in the BMDP problem. The CSR format is then briefly introduced. Next, we describe our proposed DSS method in the context of representing the expected TPM in BMDP. In Section 4, we present the simulation results of runtime, accuracy and peak memory utilization of G-DSS compared with G-Full and G-CSR.

2 PREVIOUS WORK - BAYESIAN MDP AND OBR

2.1 MDP Problem Formulation

The Markov Decision Process (MDP) is a framework for making a sequence of decisions over a stochastic dynamic system. Due to the dynamic characteristics of the system and the intervention of the decision maker, the state of the system changes from time 1 through a sequence of t state transitions. Formally, $Z = \{z_1, d_1, z_2, d_2 ..., d_{t-1}, z_t\}$, where z_t is the state of the system at time t and d_t is the action applied to the system at time t. Systems that can be described as an MDP usually obey the Markov property, which indicates that the probability distribution of the future states of the system only depend on the present state and not on the state transition history [8].

An MDP is described by the 5-tuple (S, A, P, r, λ), where $S = \{s_1, s_2, ..., s_n\}$ describes the set of states of a system. $A = \{a_1, a_2, ..., a_m\}$ is a set of actions which can be applied to the system. $P_{ij}(a_k) = Prob.(z_{t+1} = s_j \mid z_t = s_i, d_t = a_k)$ describes the state transition probability of the system at time t, when the state of the system at time t is s_i, the state of the system at time $t+1$ is s_j, and the action applied to the system at time t is a_k. The reward function $r_{a_k}(s_i, s_j)$ describes the reward that the system receives by transitioning from state s_i to s_j under action a_k. The discount factor $\lambda \in [0, 1]$ expresses the rate of decrease of the importance between present rewards and future rewards.

The fundamental MDP problem is to find a policy $\pi : S \longrightarrow A$ to inform the decision maker which action to take when the system is in a certain state, so that the cumulative reward of the system over horizon T, as defined in Eq. (1) is maximized.

$$\sum_{t=1}^{T-1} (\lambda^t r_{d_t}(z_t, z_{t+1})) \tag{1}$$

The MDP problem can be solved by linear programming [13] or dynamic programming [20]. Algorithms such as value iteration [5], policy iteration [14] and Q-learning [29] are widely used to solve the classic MDP problem.

2.2 Bayesian MDP and OBR Approach

The classic MDP formulation and algorithms require a perfect knowledge of the system. In particular, the transition probability matrix P and the reward function R need to be completely known in order to solve the MDP problem. However, in practical scenarios, a perfect knowledge of P and R (especially P) is not available due to the complicated underlying interactions and dynamic nature of the system. Hence, a statistical characterization of P is often used in order to address the uncertainty of the system [16].

Since only partial prior knowledge of the TPM is known, it is assumed that there is a family of TPMs following a certain distribution $\Omega(P)$, which describes the degree of confidence we place on each TPM. When a new observation is made in which the system transitions from state s_i to s_j under a certain action a, the posterior probability distribution of the TPMs can be computed by following Bayes' rule. In the special case where both the prior and posterior distributions belong to the same distribution family, it can be assumed that the TPM family obeys the Dirichlet distribution. In order to account for the uncertainty of the TPM in the classic MDP formulation, the state s_i of the MDP is extended to a hyperstate $(s_i, \mathcal{P})$, where $\mathcal{P}$ is the expected TPM over $\Omega(P)$.

The policy of an MDP model with hyperstate $(s_i, \mathcal{P})$ defines the action executed at a certain state s_i, so that the long-term accumulated reward $J^*(s_i, \mathcal{P})$ of the system starting from an initial state with an expected TPM $\mathcal{P}$ is maximized. $J^*(s_i, \mathcal{P})$ is defined in Eq. (2), where $g_{ij}(a)$ is the immediate reward obtained when the system transitions from state s_i to s_j under action a, $\mathcal{P}$ is the prior expected TPM, and $\mathcal{P}'$ is the posterior expected TPM.

$$J^*(s_i, \mathcal{P}) = \max_{a \in A}\{\sum_{\forall j \in S} \mathcal{P}_{ij}(a)[g_{ij}(a) + \lambda J^*(s_j, \mathcal{P}')]\} \qquad (2)$$

In Eq. (2), $\mathcal{P}_{ij}(a)$ is the expected state transition probability from s_i to s_j under action a. If the TPM family follows the Dirichlet distribution with a parameter matrix α, $\mathcal{P}_{ij}(a)$ is mathematically defined as follows:

$$\mathcal{P}_{ij}(a) = \frac{\alpha_{ij}}{\sum_{\forall m \in S} \alpha_{im}} \qquad (3)$$

When a new state transition from s_i to s_j is observed, the prior α is updated to the posterior α' as follows [16, 30]:

$$\alpha' = \alpha + \gamma \qquad (4)$$

where γ is a matrix of zeros, except $\gamma_{ij} = 1$. Then the corresponding $\mathcal{P}'$ matrix can be obtained via Eq. (3) with the posterior α'.

In order to solve Eq. (2), an Optimal Bayesian Robust (OBR) approach is proposed in [16] by applying successive approximation. In the OBR scheme, $J^*(s_i, \alpha)$ is approximated recursively by Eq. (5), using K iterations with a set of predefined $J_0(s, \mathcal{P})$.

$$J_{k+1}(s_i, \mathcal{P}) = \max_{a \in A}\{\sum_{\forall j \in S} \mathcal{P}_{ij}(a)[g_{ij}(a) + \lambda J_k(s_j, \mathcal{P}')]\} \qquad (5)$$

In [16], it is proved that $J_{k+1}(s_i, \mathcal{P})$ will converge monotonically to the optimal solution $J^*(s_i, \mathcal{P})$ for a valid $\mathcal{P}$ under certain moderate conditions.

2.3 Parallelization of OBR

Although the Bayesian MDP model and the OBR approach can address the uncertainty of the conventional MDP model, its performance is limited in practical problems, especially when the size of the problem is large. Eq. (5) essentially yields a decision tree computation structure with K horizons. For example, consider such a scenario where $S = \{s_1, s_2, s_3, s_4\}$, $A = \{a_0, a_1\}$ and $K = 2$, and the decision maker wants to know which action to take when the state of the system is s_1. Fig. 1 [31] illustrates the corresponding decision tree obtained by following Eq. (5), starting from the $k = 0$ level. Since the $\mathcal{P}$ matrix needs to be updated by following Eq.(4) and Eq.(3) whenever a state transition is observed, and each circled node in Fig. 1 has a unique state transition path from the root, each circled node in Fig. 1 will have a unique hyperstate. Therefore, the computation needs to traverse every node in the decision tree and compute the $J(s_i, \mathcal{P})$ value in order to make the decision of the action at the root node. In practice, since the size of the tree is $(|S| \times |A|)^K$, this method scales poorly.

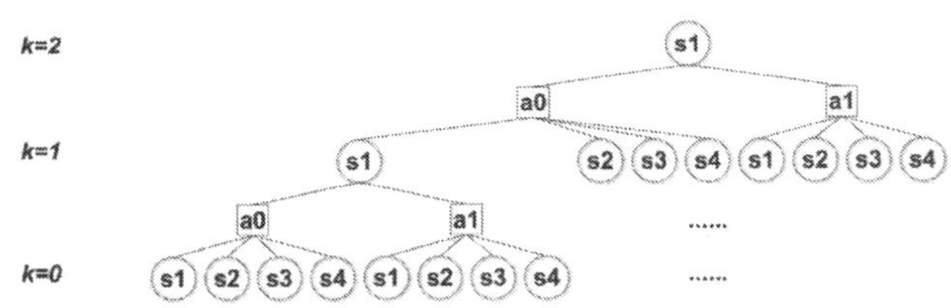

Figure 1: Computational Structure of OBR

A GPU-based parallel approach [31] was proposed to address the runtime of sequential OBR as the problem size increases. The key idea in [31] is that since the $J(s_i, \mathcal{P})$ of the hyperstate nodes at the same level of the tree are independent of each other, the computation of these $J(s_i, \mathcal{P})$ can be performed simultaneously. Sampling-based techniques were introduced to accelerate the computation in [1, 11]. However, when the problem size grows, the performance of these approaches degrades, and their accuracy also becomes an issue. Since the GPU operates in a SIMD fashion and each hyperstate node has a unique $\mathcal{P}$ matrix, the GPU needs to store multiple unique $\mathcal{P}$ matrices at the same time. Hence, memory utilization becomes the bottleneck of the G-Full approach, even though impressive speedups are obtained. To address the memory issue of storing the TPM, a factored MDP model is proposed in [24]. However, the factored MDP requires a knowledge of independence among states in order to construct the model. This knowledge is usually not available in the GRN control problem. Practical MDP problems often have sparse TPMs [21], in which most of the elements are zero or close to zero. The most widely used sparse matrix storage format is Compressed Sparse Row (CSR) [2]. Another commonly used format is the Jagged Diagonal Storage (JDS) format which is particularly suitable for iterative methods [22].

3 OUR APPROACH - DUPLEX SPARSE STORAGE (DSS)

3.1 Overview

In this section, we describe Duplex Sparse Storage (DSS), a new storage format based on CSR, to store the $\mathcal{P}$ matrix for the BMDP problem. We first show how Bayesian updates preserve sparsity. We next describe CSR and DSS along with a comparison between their features.

3.2 Problems of Using Conventional Full Matrix

In general, the expected TPM (i.e., the $\overline{\mathcal{P}}$ matrix) with each element defined in Eq. (3) can be represented by a full floating-point matrix with the size of $|S| \times |S|$. However, in the GPU-based acceleration approach, each action node (the square nodes in Fig. 1) requires a row of the $\overline{\mathcal{P}}$ matrix to perform the computation of Eq. (5). Therefore, using an $|S| \times |S|$ matrix leads to a $(|S| \times |A|)^K$ memory utilization complexity. Such a prohibitively expensive memory complexity limits the applicability of the GPU-based BMDP approach on large problems. In our paper we focus on how to improve the storage cost of the $\overline{\mathcal{P}}$ matrix.

In many practical problems, the $\overline{\mathcal{P}}$ matrix is likely to be sparse due to the natural sparsity of the problem and its large state space. In the context of gene regulatory networks (GRNs) or more general biochemical networks, the structure of the problem tends to be sparse [9, 15, 27, 28]. Hence the corresponding $\overline{\mathcal{P}}$ matrix is also sparse. Generally speaking, for such problems, most elements of each row of the $\overline{\mathcal{P}}$ matrix are close to zero. However, OBR is oblivious to this natural sparsity, and performs the computation in a brute force manner. Before we can employ sparse storage techniques to this problem, we need to ensure that the sparsity is conserved after K Bayesian updates during OBR. Fig. 2 shows the histogram of a randomly selected row in a 16×16 $\overline{\mathcal{P}}$ matrix after 5 Bayesian updates by following 100 different random histories. In this figure, each curve is associated with one Bayesian update history. Note that in Fig. 2, many of these 100 curves overlap. Fig. 2 indicates that if the prior $\overline{\mathcal{P}}$ matrix is sparse, then after K Bayesian updates (usually $K \leq 5$ in practical cases), the posterior $\overline{\mathcal{P}}'$ matrix tends to remain sparse. Due to this feature of sparsity conservation, sparse matrix storage techniques can be effective in alleviating the high memory complexity throughout the entire G-Full approach.

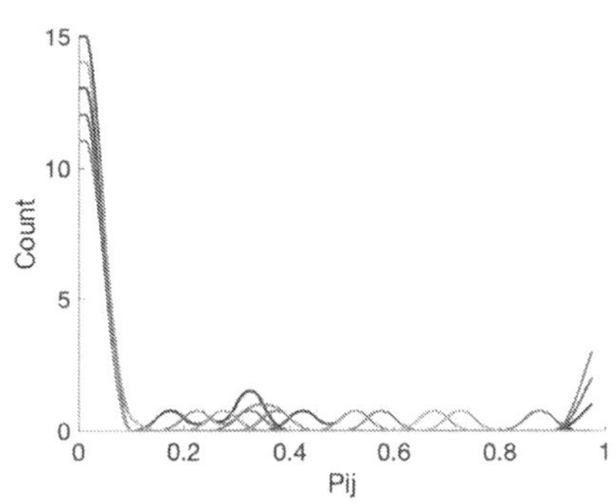

Figure 2: Histogram of P_{ij} after 5 Bayesian Updates

3.3 CSR Storage Format

Compressed Sparse Row (CSR) is a storage format for sparse matrices and is widely used for scientific and engineering computations [2]. Fig. 3 shows an example of CSR. The 4×4 matrix M in Fig. 3 is sparse since most of the elements are zero. The bold italic elements are non-zero elements, and are elements of interest. Clearly, there is no need to store the zero-valued entries. The CSR format stores the sparse matrix using three vectors: the *data* vector, the *colIndex* vector and the *rowPtr* vector. The *data* vector stores the non-zero

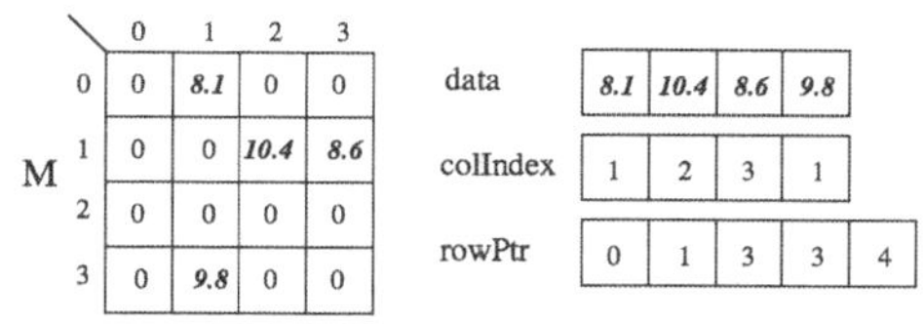

Figure 3: CSR Example

elements in a row-major fashion. In the *colIndex* vector, $colIndex[i]$ stores the column position of $data[i]$ in M. The *rowPtr vector* is defined as follows:

$$rowPtr[0] = 0$$
$$rowPtr[i] = rowPtr[i-1] + NZ(i-1), \qquad i > 0$$

where $NZ(i)$ is the number of non-zero elements in the ith row of the original M matrix. Algorithm 1 shows how to look up M_{ij} in the CSR storage format.

Algorithm 1 Look Up M_{ij} in the CSR Format

```
StartIndex = rowPtr[i];
EndIndex = rowPtr[i+1];
Found = 0;
for k = StartIndex; k < EndIndex; k++ do
    if colIndex[k] == j then
        Found = 1;
        return data[k]
    end if
end for
if Found == 0 then
    return 0
end if
```

In most scientific and engineering computations, the information of interest in M is the value, the row position index and the column position index of the non-zero elements. Although the storage cost per element in CSR is higher, the total storage cost of CSR is significantly smaller than the full matrix when M is sparse. If the size of the original matrix is $N \times N$ and the total number of the non-zero elements is N_{nz}, then the memory utilization of the full matrix is $O(N^2)$. However, in the CSR format, the memory utilization is $O(2N_{nz} + N)$, which is less than that of the full matrix if M is large and sufficiently sparse.

Although the CSR format alleviates the memory utilization compared to the full matrix, the memory utilization can still be large when the original sparse matrix is large, since $rowPtr$ depends on the size of the matrix. Moreover, in BMDP problem settings, the matrix may have many elements close to zero, but not exactly zero. We note that the $\overline{\mathcal{P}}$ matrix in the BMDP problem has the following properties:

$$\begin{cases} 1 > \overline{\mathcal{P}}_{ij} > 0 \\ \sum_{\forall j \in S} \overline{\mathcal{P}}_{ij} = 1 \end{cases} \qquad (6)$$

In such a scenario, there could be a significant number of small values in each row. Storing such small values using the CSR format can often increase the total memory requirement, and hence negate the benefit of CSR. A naive approach is to discard elements that are smaller than a threshold value and store them as zero. By doing so, we can artificially boost the sparsity of the matrix. However such an approach can have a negative impact on the accuracy of the subsequent MDP computation steps. The approach we take in this paper is to use the Duplex Sparse Storage (DSS) format, which is described next.

3.4 DSS Format in BMDP

In DSS, instead of using three vectors, we only use one vector *data_col* to store all the information needed (in a row-major fashion). A DSS for an $N \times N$ matrix is a vector composed by N components, where each component corresponds to one row in the matrix. Each component contains three fields:

(1) X words to save the top X significant entries of its corresponding row. Since we would like to store the matrix elements with relatively large values, we store the top X largest values from every row (such that $R = X/N \times 100\%$, where N is the size of one row of $\overline{\mathcal{P}}$).
(2) $K-1$ words reserved for matrix entries that would change from a "trivial" value to significant value in a future Bayesian update.
(3) One word for storing the average value of the $N-X$ "trivial" entries.
(4) Each significant entry is stored in a duplex fashion, using a single word to store the value of the entry (in 12-bit binary) and its column position (in 20-bit binary).

Suppose a sequence of state transitions $Z_T = (z_1, d_1, z_2, d_2 ..., z_m, ..., z_{M-1}, d_{M-1}, z_M)$ is observed. Assume $z_m = s_i$ and $z_{m+1} = s_j$, and from time step 0 to time step $(m+1)$, there are C state transitions from s_i to other states in Z_T. Then the ith row of the $\overline{\mathcal{P}}'$ matrix at time step $(m+1)$ can be obtained from the $\overline{\mathcal{P}}$ matrix at time step m. The resulting $\overline{\mathcal{P}}'$ can be derived from Eq. (3) and Eq. (4), and is shown in Eq. (7). All the other rows of the $\overline{\mathcal{P}}'$ matrix are unchanged by this Bayesian update.

$$\begin{cases} \overline{\mathcal{P}}'_{ik} = \frac{C \times \overline{\mathcal{P}}_{ik}}{C+1}, & k \neq j \\ \overline{\mathcal{P}}'_{ij} = \frac{C \times \overline{\mathcal{P}}_{ij}+1}{C+1} \end{cases} \tag{7}$$

Eq. (7) indicates that after the Bayesian update $\overline{\mathcal{P}}'_{ij}$ becomes larger, which means that $\overline{\mathcal{P}}'_{ij}$ may qualify to be stored in the DSS format, even though $\overline{\mathcal{P}}_{ij}$ is close to zero. This increase in $\overline{\mathcal{P}}'_{ij}$ caused by the Bayesian update requires DSS to reserve "holes" in order to store the elements which become larger due to Eq. (7). A BMDP problem with a horizon length of K needs to preform $K-1$ Bayesian updates in all. Hence the DSS approach needs to leave exactly $K-1$ "holes" for each row of a $N \times N$ $\overline{\mathcal{P}}$ matrix, and $N \times (K-1)$ "holes" in total for the entire $\overline{\mathcal{P}}$ matrix. This guarantees that no array re-allocations are needed in the DSS approach, for the entire BMDP computation.

Since the $\overline{\mathcal{P}}$ matrix is sparse, with a reasonable choice of R, we are able to represent all the "non-trivial" elements in the $\overline{\mathcal{P}}$ matrix while maintaining a small memory footprint. However, since the size of the $\overline{\mathcal{P}}$ matrix is usually large in practical BMDP problem, the number of trivial elements in the $\overline{\mathcal{P}}$ matrix can still be quite large. Even though we can neglect the contribution of a single "trivial" element to the subsequent computation, we may not be able to neglect the contribution of a large number of trivial elements. Therefore, in the DSS, we use a special cell to store the average value of the trivial elements for each row in the *data_col* vector. From Eq. (6), we can easily compute the sum for the trivial elements by subtracting the sum of the non-trivial elements from 1. Hence the average of the trivial elements is also easy to compute. An intuitive way to understand this approach is that each row represents the "mass" of the probability distribution in each state. Instead of throwing away the entries with small values (which is equivalent to losing mass), we conserve the total "mass" by accumulating the small entries. Even though we keep only an approximated value of each individual small element, we improve the memory efficiency of the BMDP method while not impacting error appreciably. The benefit is clearly demonstrated in the experimental results.

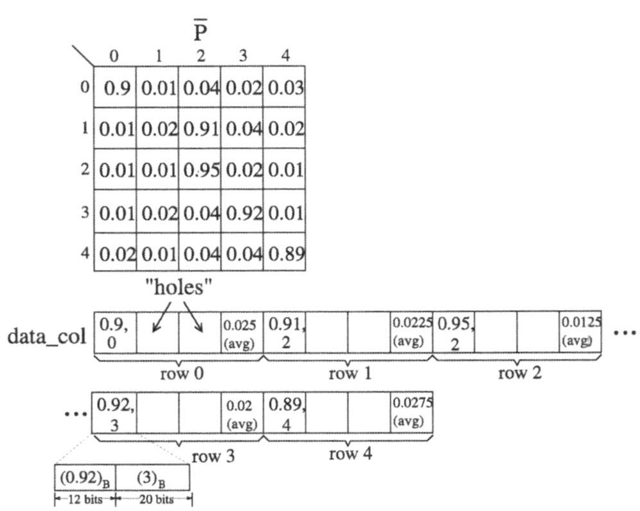

Figure 4: DSS Example

An example of DSS for a 5×5 $\overline{\mathcal{P}}$ matrix is shown in Fig. 4 with $R = 20\%$. Suppose the DSS representation in Fig. 4 is used for a BMDP problem with $K = 3$. Then in the *data_col* vector, there are 2 "holes" reserved for each row (for the Bayesian update). The average of the trivial elements in each row is stored in the cell labeled "avg". In the DSS, $(1 - R) \times 100\%$ of the entries are deemed as "trivial". Since the number of elements to be stored in each row of the $\overline{\mathcal{P}}$ matrix is fixed, the starting position of the ith row of the $\overline{\mathcal{P}}$ matrix in the *data_col* vector is exactly $(i \times (X + K))$. Hence the *rowPtr* vector in the CSR format is no longer needed. The number of bits used to store the entry value and its column position is 12 and 20 respectively, which don't match any standard data type in popular programming languages. 12-bits provides a good resolution for P_{ij} in the TPM, and 20-bits can handle a large matrix (the largest matrix size that DSS can store is $(2^{20})^2 = 2^{40}$). The total number of bits used for every entry of *data_col* is 32, since the native word size of the architecture we used is 32. For other applications, the number of bits used to store the value of the entries and their column position may be different.

We next discuss how a Bayesian update is performed on DSS. Once a state transition from $z_m = s_i$ to $z_{m+1} = s_j$ is observed, we need to go through a component of the *data_col* vector in which the ith row of the $\overline{\mathcal{P}}$ matrix is stored. If $\overline{\mathcal{P}}_{ij}$ doesn't exist in the non-trivial cells of this component (i.e. $\overline{\mathcal{P}}_{ij}$ is not among the $R \times 100\%$ largest entries of row i), we need to use the average value of the trivial elements as $\overline{\mathcal{P}}_{ij}$. Then we compute $\overline{\mathcal{P}}'_{ij}$ using Eq. (7), and store the $\overline{\mathcal{P}}'_{ij}$ in the first empty "hole" in this component. The average value of the trivial elements in the ith row of $\overline{\mathcal{P}}'$ also needs to be updated.

3.5 Parallel DSS-based OBR

As discussed earlier, the G-Full approach presented in [31] is fast but has memory problems. To alleviate the memory utilization issues, we use DSS to store the expected TPM data in GPU-based OBR. To accomplish this, the following extra algorithms were implemented for DSS on the GPU:

- Look up $\overline{\mathcal{P}}_{ij}$
- Bayesian Update

3.5.1 Look Up $\overline{\mathcal{P}}_{ij}$. Algorithm 2 shows how to look up $\overline{\mathcal{P}}_{ij}$ in the DSS format on the GPU. An example of how look-up works in DSS on GPU is shown in Fig. 5. The $\overline{\mathcal{P}}$ matrix and the corresponding

Algorithm 2 Look Up $\overline{\mathcal{P}}_{ij}$ in the DSS Format

```
1:  Found = 0
2:  StartIndex = (X + K) × i;
3:  EndIndex = (X + K) × (i + 1) − 1
4:  Assign (X + K − 1) threads;
5:  for ALL the threads do
6:      tid ← getThreadID;
7:      loc = StartIndex+tid;
8:      if (data_col[loc] AND 0x000FFFFF) == j then
9:          Found = 1
10:         return (data_col[loc] AND 0xFFF00000)>> 20
11:     end if
12: end for
13: if Found == 0 then return data_col[EndIndex]
14: end if
```

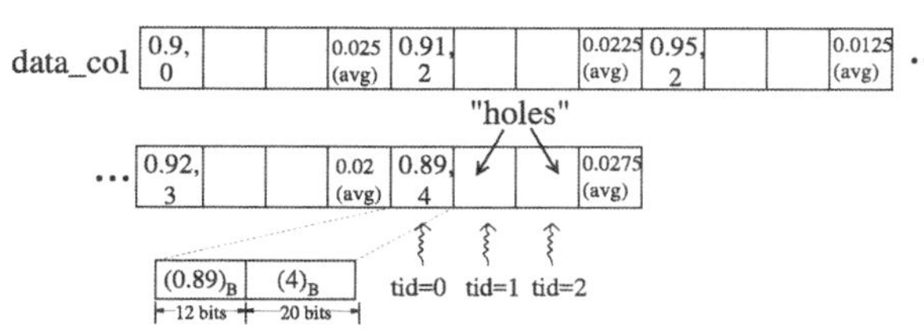

Figure 5: Example of Looking Up $\overline{\mathcal{P}}_{44}$ on GPU

DSS are the same as Fig. 4, where $X = 1$ and $K = 3$. Since some "holes" in DSS might be filled due to the Bayesian update, the $(K-1)$ "holes" also need to be checked in the look-up. Hence a total of $(X+K-1)$ cells in the *data_col* vector need to be checked in parallel to find any $\overline{\mathcal{P}}_{ij}$. Suppose we look up $\overline{\mathcal{P}}_{44}$. In this case, 3 threads are launched by the GPU in Fig. 5 with a *tid* starting from 0. Each thread checks a different cell in the *data_col* vector, and the location of its cell is defined in step 7 in Algorithm 2. In step 8, a bitwise *AND* operation is used to mask the contents of *data_col*[*loc*] so that the value of the element and its column position can be separated. Since the value of the data is located in the most significant 12 bits of *data_col*[*loc*], a bitwise shift operation is needed to return the correct $\overline{\mathcal{P}}_{ij}$. If we neglect the overhead incurred by the thread launching on the GPU, the time complexity of Algorithm 2 is $O(1)$.

3.5.2 Bayesian Update. The GPU-based OBR algorithm proposed in [31] yields a tree computation structure. Fig. 6 shows an example of how the Bayesian update works. For the BMDP in Fig. 6, assume that $S = \{s_0, s_1, s_2, s_3\}$ $A = \{a_0, a_1\}$, and $K = 3$. If we want to compute the J value of the black circled node in Fig. 6 by following Eq. (5), we need to know the 0th row in $\overline{\mathcal{P}}'$ after following the transition $Z_3 = \{s_0, a_0, s_3, a_0, s_0\}$. By following Eq. (4) and Eq. (3), $\overline{\mathcal{P}}_{03}$ needs to be updated. Since for the GPU-based OBR algorithm, the problem is the memory issue instead of runtime, we compute $\overline{\mathcal{P}}'$ from $\overline{\mathcal{P}}$ without storing the internal result of $\overline{\mathcal{P}}$ at the circled node labeled $S3$ in Fig. 6. Algorithm 3 describes how to do Bayesian up-

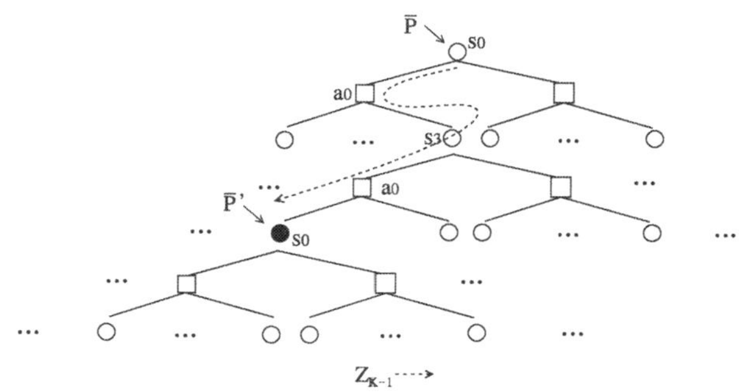

Figure 6: Bayesian Update Example

date on the ith row of the $\overline{\mathcal{P}}$ matrix in DSS when a sequence of state transition Z_M is observed, where $Z_M = \{z_1, d_1, z_2, d_2, ...d_{M-1}, z_M\}$, and $s_i = z_M$. Similar with Algorithm 2, in Algorithm 3, $(X+K)$ threads are launched to update the ith row of the $\overline{\mathcal{P}}$ matrix, and each thread processes one entry whose location in the *data_col* vector is defined in step 7. Each thread goes through the state transition sequence and decides what to do with its own *data_col*[*loc*]. There are 4 possible cases:

- The state transition from z_m to z_{m+1} doesn't contribute to the Bayesian update on the ith row of the $\overline{\mathcal{P}}$ matrix. In such case, Algorithm 3 does nothing.
- The state transition from $z_m = s_i$ to $z_{m+1} = s_j$ contributes to the Bayesian update on the ith row of the $\overline{\mathcal{P}}$ matrix. The current thread processes the DSS entry including $\overline{\mathcal{P}}_{ij}$. In this case, this thread executes step 13 and step 14 in Algorithm 3 to increase its $\overline{\mathcal{P}}_{ij}$ by following Eq. (7).
- The state transition from $z_m = s_i$ to $z_{m+1} = s_j$ contributes to the Bayesian update on the ith row of the $\overline{\mathcal{P}}$ matrix. The current thread doesn't process the DSS cell including $\overline{\mathcal{P}}_{ij}$. In this case, this thread executes step 16 in Algorithm 3 to decrease its $\overline{\mathcal{P}}_{ik}$ by following Eq. (7). Note that the "average" of trivial elements also just needs to decrease as $\overline{\mathcal{P}}_{ik}$ in Eq. (7).
- The state transition from $z_m = s_i$ to $z_{m+1} = s_j$ contributes to the Bayesian update on the ith row of the $\overline{\mathcal{P}}$ matrix. However, $\overline{\mathcal{P}}_{ij}$ was a trivial element in time step m. In this case, the $(X+K)^{th}$ thread executes from step 19 to step 21 in Algorithm 3 to insert a new DSS element to the first available "hole" in *data_col* vector. The most significant 12-bits in this new DSS element notated as $\overline{\mathcal{P}}'_{ij}$ is defined

Algorithm 3 Bayesian update on the ith row of $\overline{\mathcal{P}}$ matrix when a sequence of state transition Z_M is observed.

```
StartIndex = (X + K) × z_M;
AvgIndex = StartIndex + (X + K − 1)
set flag = 0 in global memory.
Assign (X + K) threads;
for ALL the (X + K) threads do
    tid ← getThreadID;
    loc = StartIndex+tid;
    C = 0; j = (data_col[loc] AND 0x000FFFFF);
    for m=1; m<M; m++ do
        if z_m == z_M then
            C = C+1;
            if z_{m+1} == j then
                increase "P_ij" in data_col[loc] using Eq. (7);
                flag =1;
            else
                decrease "P_ik" in data_col[loc] using Eq. (7);
            end if
            wait for all the threads to reach to here;
            if (flag==0 && tid == (X + K)) then
                Insert a new DSS element into the first empty hole in the data_col vector;
                update data_col[AvgIndex];
            end if
        end if
    end for
end for
```

as follows:

$$\overline{\mathcal{P}}'_{ij} = \frac{C \times data\_col[AvgIndex] + 1}{C + 1} \tag{8}$$

And the least significant 20-bits in this new DSS is z_{m+1}. The data_col[AvgIndex] also needs to be updated in order to keep the sum of the ith row to be 1.

The time complexity of Algorithm 3 is $O(M)$. Since M (which is bounded above by K) is usually small in practical BMDP problems, the practical time complexity of Algorithm 3 is nearly $O(1)$. Since the G-Full method in [31] stores the full $\overline{\mathcal{P}}$ matrix, the Bayesian update in G-Full needs to touch N elements for each black circled node in Fig. 6 (where N is the row length of the matrix). This means the GPU has to launch N threads for each black circled node. However, in the DSS method, only $(X + K)$ elements need to be touched, which means the GPU has to launch only $(X + K)$ threads for each black circled node. This gives the G-DSS algorithm the potential to handle more black circled nodes (i.e. more hyperstates in the BMDP) simultaneously, which increases the speedup of the G-DSS algorithm.

3.6 Comparison Between DSS and CSR

Table 1 shows a summary of the differences between DSS and CSR in the context of storing $\overline{\mathcal{P}}$ for the GPU-based OBR. Here we assume that the CSR treats all the trivial elements (smaller than a threshold) as 0 in order to store the $\overline{\mathcal{P}}$ matrix with a small memory utilization. Let N_{th} be the number of such elements.

Let the J value computed in Eq. (5) using the full matrix be called J_m, the J value computed using CSR be called J_{CSR}, and the J value computed using DSS be denoted as J_{DSS}. Then $J_m > J_{DSS} > J_{CSR}$ with an appropriate choice of X. This is because in Eq. (5), every variable is positive and CSR abandons the trivial elements while DSS uses an average value for them. In other words, DSS contains more accurate information about the $\overline{\mathcal{P}}$ matrix compared to CSR.

In Table 1 we also show the L^∞ norm of both CSR and DSS. The L^∞ norm of the original full $\overline{\mathcal{P}}$ matrix is 1 due to Eq. (6). Suppose we reconstruct the $\overline{\mathcal{P}}$ matrix from the DSS format and the CSR format, and denote them as $\overline{\mathcal{P}}_{DSS}$ and $\overline{\mathcal{P}}_{CSR}$ respectively. Since DSS uses an average value to represent the trivial elements, the sum of each row in $\overline{\mathcal{P}}_{DSS}$ is still 1. However, since $\overline{\mathcal{P}}_{CSR}$ abandons some entries of the original full $\overline{\mathcal{P}}$ matrix in order to maintain a small memory utilization, the sum of each row in $\overline{\mathcal{P}}_{CSR}$ is often less than 1. If the CSR doesn't abandon any entry in the full $\overline{\mathcal{P}}$ matrix in extreme cases, then the sum of each row in $\overline{\mathcal{P}}_{CSR}$ will be equal to 1. Therefore, we have the following relationship among the L^∞ norms of $\overline{\mathcal{P}}$, $\overline{\mathcal{P}}_{DSS}$ and $\overline{\mathcal{P}}_{CSR}$:

$$||\overline{\mathcal{P}}_{CSR}||_\infty \leq ||\overline{\mathcal{P}}_{DSS}||_\infty = ||\overline{\mathcal{P}}||_\infty = 1 \tag{9}$$

In other words, the L^∞ norm for P_{CSR} is inaccurate, while that of P_{DSS} matches $||\overline{\mathcal{P}}||_\infty$. We claim that this could be one of the reasons why the J and A values of DSS are more accurate than those of CSR, as shown in our experiments. In addition, in DSS, since the upper-bound of the number of new non-trivial elements introduced by Bayesian update is predefined and DSS reserves "holes" for these new non-trivial elements, we don't have to reallocate memory for the DSS while performing Bayesian updates. In the special case where all the elements in the original $\overline{\mathcal{P}}$ matrix are identical, the DSS method can still handle such matrices without introducing any error for the future computations.

Since the value of each element and its column position are combined in one 32-bit word in DSS, we need to perform bit-wise operations to separate the value of the element from the column position when needed. Although any contemporary computer architecture can perform this type of operation very efficiently through bitwise manipulation instructions, these operations do take up computation cycles. In some cases, when the row length N of the $\overline{\mathcal{P}}$ matrix is small and K is large, DSS may consume more memory than CSR. However, such cases are not interesting when we are considering large BMDP problem instances.

4 EXPERIMENTAL RESULTS

The DSS approach is implemented to store the expected TPM data in the GPU-based OBR algorithm by using Nvidia CUDA Toolkit 8.0 [18]. The element values in DSS are represented using 12-bit fractions, while the full matrix and CSR methods use 32-bit floating point values. We ran the simulations on 500 synthetic GRNs generated following the descriptions in [30]. The main hardware specifications are listed as follows:

- CPU: Intel Core i5-4670, 3.4GHz
- RAM: 8GB DDR2 Memory
- GPU: Nvidia GTX 780, 863MHz Clock Rate, 3GB GDDR5 Memory, 6.0 Gbps Memory Speed [19]

Table 1: Differences Between CSR and DSS

	CSR	DSS
Elements Stored	elements larger than the threshold	X largest elements in each row (where $X/N \times 100\% = R$)
How to deal with trivial elements	Abandon (treat as 0)	Use the average value
Data Structure	3 vectors	1 vector which combines of $\mathcal{P}_{ij}$ and j
Memory Complexity	$O(2N_{th} + N)$	$O(N(X + K))$
L^{∞} Norm	≤ 1	1

In our experiments, we compare the performance among using three different storage methods to store the $\mathcal{P}$ matrix in the GPU-based OBR algorithm: G-DSS, G-CSR and G-Full. Runtime and memory utilization are used to quantify the effectiveness of these three methods. We also include the sequential OBR algorithm using full matrix in the results for reference, which is denoted as S-Full.

We used the differences of J values and final action decisions (denoted as J_{Full}^{DSS} and A_{Full}^{DSS} respectively) between G-DSS and G-Full to assess the accuracy of DSS. J_{Full}^{DSS} and A_{Full}^{DSS} are defined as follows:

$$J_{Full}^{DSS} = \frac{|J_{DSS} - J_{Full}|}{J_{Full}} \times 100\% \qquad A_{Full}^{DSS} = \begin{cases} 100\%, & A_{DSS} \neq A_{Full} \\ 0\%, & A_{DSS} = A_{Full} \end{cases} \tag{10}$$

where J_{DSS} and A_{DSS} are respectively the J value and action decision computed by G-DSS, while J_{Full} and A_{Full} are respectively the J value and action decision computed by G-Full (or S-Full). In some experiments, the G-Full algorithm ran out of memory and didn't terminate. In such a case, we use the J value and action decision computed by S-Full as J_{Full} and A_{Full} respectively. J_{Full}^{CSR} and A_{Full}^{CSR} are defined similarly. Table 2 summarizes the notations used from Fig. 7 to Fig. 10.

Table 2: Summary of Notations Used From Fig. 7 to Fig. 10

Symbol	Meaning
R	the percentage of elements the DSS stores (i.e. X/N)
K	Number of horizons in the OBR framework (i.e. number of the tree levels in Fig. 1)
J_{Full}^{CSR}	The difference of J values between using CSR and using full matrix
A_{Full}^{CSR}	The difference of action decisions between using CSR and using full matrix
T_{G-DSS}	Runtime of GPU-based OBR using DSS
T_{G-CSR}	Runtime of GPU-based OBR using CSR
T_{G-Full}	Runtime of GPU-based OBR using full matrix
T_{S-Full}	Runtime of sequential OBR using full matrix
MEM_{G-DSS}	Peak memory utilization of GPU-based OBR using DSS
MEM_{G-CSR}	Peak memory utilization of GPU-based OBR using CSR
MEM_{G-Full}	Peak memory utilization of GPU-based OBR using full matrix

Fig. 7 compares the differences of the performance between G-CSR and G-DSS. Fig. 7(a) shows that G-DSS uses less memory than G-CSR. When the number of states is larger than 32, G-DSS uses about half the memory compared to G-CSR. This is mainly because DSS stores both $\mathcal{P}_{ij}$ and j in one word.

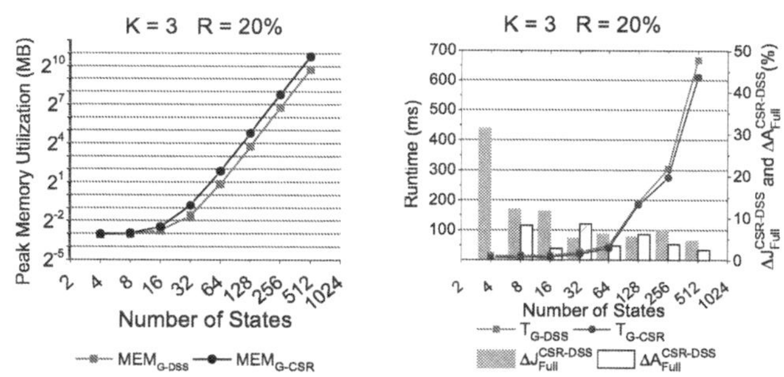

(a) Peak Memory Utilization, $R = 20\%$ (b) Runtime and Accuracy, $R = 20\%$

Figure 7: Performance of G-DSS and G-CSR

In Fig. 7(b), $\Delta J_{Full}^{CSR-DSS}$ and $\Delta A_{Full}^{CSR-DSS}$ are defined as follows:

$$\Delta J_{Full}^{CSR-DSS} = J_{Full}^{CSR} - J_{Full}^{DSS} \tag{11}$$

$$\Delta A_{Full}^{CSR-DSS} = A_{Full}^{CSR} - A_{Full}^{DSS} \tag{12}$$

When $\Delta J_{Full}^{CSR-DSS}$ (or $\Delta A_{Full}^{CSR-DSS}$) is larger than zero, it means that the J value (or the final action decision result) computed by G-DSS is closer to that computed by G-Full, compared to G-CSR. Fig. 7(b) shows that G-DSS has a better accuracy on J value and final action decision compared to G-CSR for all the cases. DSS uses 12-bit fixed-point fractions to represent $\mathcal{P}_{ij}$ (as opposed to 32-bit floats for CSR). This might seem to sacrifice computation accuracy. However, unlike CSR, DSS doesn't abandon the trivial values but instead uses their average value to approximately represent them. Hence its results are closer to the results of G-Full, for both the J value and final action decision. In Fig. 7(b), the runtime of G-DSS is found to be 25.6% higher than G-CSR on average. This is mainly because DSS needs to update the average value of all the trivial entries during Bayesian update, which requires more computations than CSR. Based on these results, we note that DSS is superior to CSR in terms of memory utilization and accuracy with a modest performance penalty.

In Fig. 8, we present the runtime, accuracy and the peak memory utilization of G-DSS and compare these quantities with G-Full, while varying the R value. In some experiments, certain data points of G-Full are missing, because the G-Full algorithm ran out of memory and didn't terminate. In Fig. 8, we focus on how the performance changes with respect to the number of states (the size of the $\mathcal{P}$ matrix). Note that the runtime, peak memory utilization and the

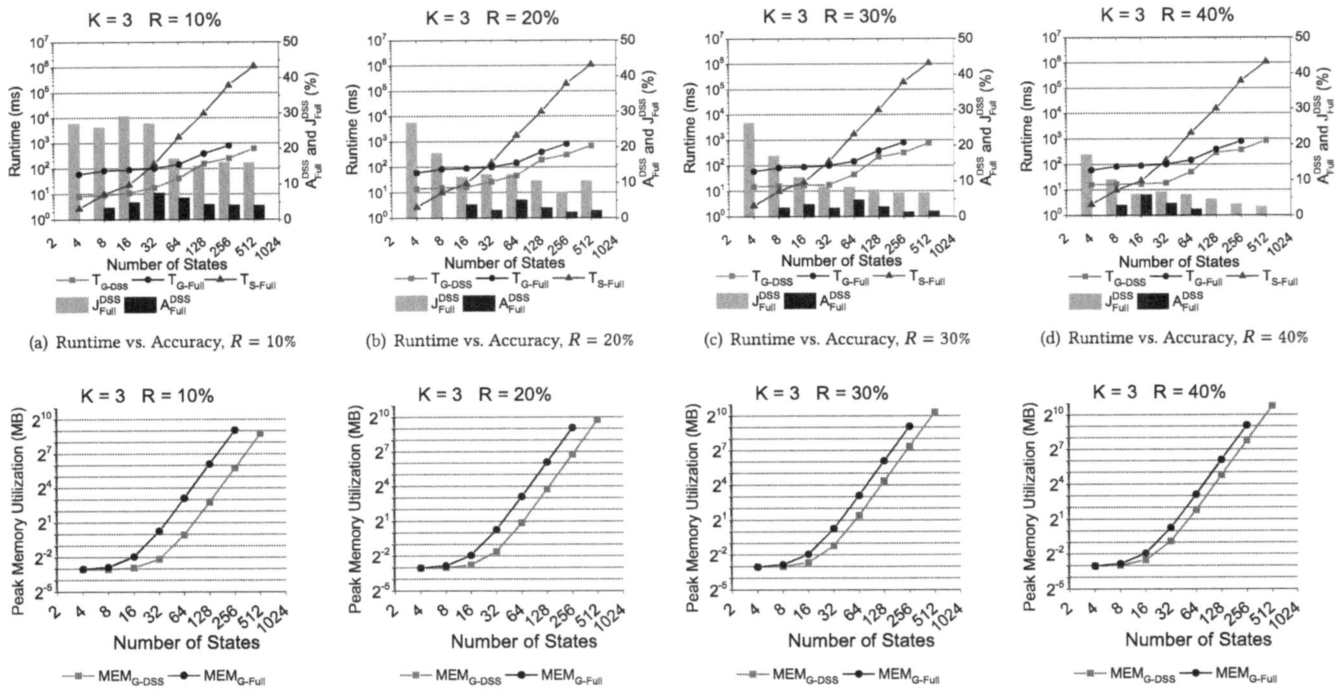

(a) Runtime vs. Accuracy, $R = 10\%$ (b) Runtime vs. Accuracy, $R = 20\%$ (c) Runtime vs. Accuracy, $R = 30\%$ (d) Runtime vs. Accuracy, $R = 40\%$

(e) Peak Memory Utilization, $R = 10\%$ (f) Peak Memory Utilization, $R = 20\%$ (g) Peak Memory Utilization, $R = 30\%$ (h) Peak Memory Utilization, $R = 40\%$

Figure 8: Performance of G-DSS and G-Full when $K = 3$

number of states are represented on a logarithmic scale, with base value of 10, 2 and 2 respectively. From these figures, we notice that the G-DSS is faster than G-Full. In particular, for $R = 10\%$, the G-DSS is faster by 5.7× on average, and this improvement reduces slightly as R increases. As discussed in Section 3.5, the reason why G-DSS is faster is that DSS only stores $(X+K)$ elements for each row instead of G-Full which stores N elements. Hence, in G-DSS, the GPU only needs to launch $(X+K)$ threads for each node in the computation tree shown in Fig. 1 (versus N threads for G-Full). Generally speaking, launching more threads on the GPU will require more hardware resources. Since G-DSS requires less threads than G-Full for each node in the tree, it can process more nodes simultaneously. As R increases from 10% to 40%, the average runtime of G-DSS increases by 47.2%. In general, J^{DSS}_{Full} and A^{DSS}_{Full} improve as the number of states increases and R increases. Note that A^{DSS}_{Full} is not monotonic as the number of states increases. This is mainly because the final decision A_{DSS} depends on the accumulated rewards over multiple actions as described in Eq. (5). The DSS scheme introduces an error to the rewards under different actions in varying amounts, depending on the number and sparsity of the entries in the $\overline{\mathcal{P}}$ matrix. Hence, there is some noise in the trend of A^{DSS}_{Full} as the number of the states increases. The peak memory utilization reduces by 6.3× on average when $R = 10\%$. This improvement reduces as R increases as expected. For $R = 30\%$, the peak memory utilization is 2.4× better for G-DSS on average.

Considering both runtime and peak memory utilization, a practical choice of R could be 20% or 30%. When $R = 20\%$, the average speedup of DSS over full matrix from 4 states to 256 states is about 4.1×. In the largest case (with 512 states), G-Full can't handle such case because it runs out of memory. Hence we use the J value and action decision computed by S-Full as J_{Full} and A_{Full} respectively to calculate the J^{DSS}_{Full} and A^{DSS}_{Full} following Eq. (10). When the number of states is 512, $J^{DSS}_{Full} = 10.3\%$ and $A^{DSS}_{Full} = 2.4\%$.

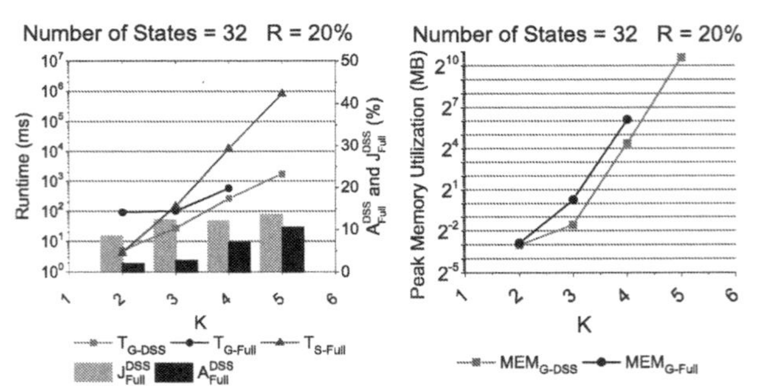

(a) Runtime vs. Accuracy (b) Peak Memory Utilization

Figure 9: Performance of G-DSS when $R = 20\%$ and number of states = 32

Fig. 9 shows the runtime, accuracy and the peak memory utilization of G-DSS compared with G-Full as K is varied. When K increases, the J^{DSS}_{Full} and A^{DSS}_{Full} also increase. This is mainly because the error in the J value at level $(k-1)$ propagates to level k according to Eq. 5. Also, even though $T_{G-DSS} < T_{G-Full}$ for all the cases, the runtime of G-DSS increases at a faster rate than G-Full as K increases in Fig. 9(a). A reason for this is that DSS needs to do more computation for looking up a single $\overline{\mathcal{P}}_{ij}$. Although look-ups are parallelized, the number of extra look-up computations depends heavily on K. Hence when K increases, the total amount of extra look-up work also increases, which means that the GPU needs more time to process these look-ups with its fixed hardware resources. In Fig. 9(b), the peak memory utilization of G-DSS is 1.1× lower than G-Full when $K = 2$. For $K = 4$, G-DSS uses 3.1× less memory than G-Full. When $K = 5$, G-Full runs out of memory.

Fig. 10 shows the split between the lookup and computation time of G-DSS. We also include the total runtime of the full matrix approach for reference. Since DSS requires more computation for lookup compared with full matrix, it's important to quantify the trend in the runtime for lookup operations as the number of states increases. Fig. 10 shows that compared with G-Full, the runtime of G-DSS lookup isn't the dominant component of the total G-DSS runtime for 32 or fewer states. This is mainly because the lookup time of DSS benefits from the parallel processing of GPU. As the number of states increases beyond 32, the lookup becomes a noticeable fraction of the total G-DSS runtime.

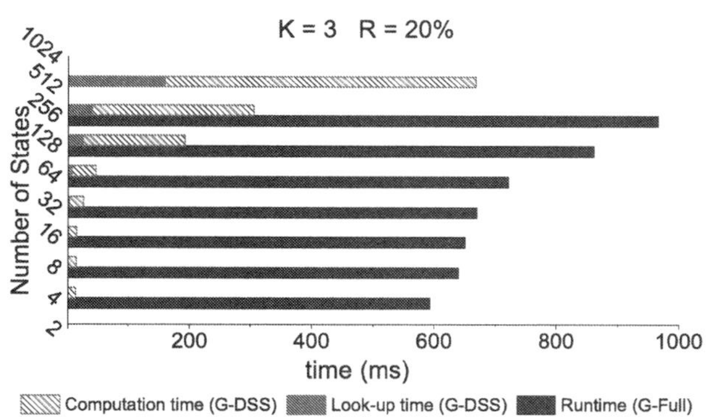

Figure 10: Look-up and computation time of G-DSS

5 CONCLUSION

In this paper, we propose a Duplex Sparse Storage (DSS) format to alleviate the memory growth of the GPU-based OBR algorithm in the context of the GRN control problem. By combining the column position index and the entry value in the same word and using an average value to represent all trivial elements (instead of abandoning them as in CSR), our method significantly reduces the memory utilization compared with both full matrix and CSR. DSS also improves the result accuracy of GPU-based OBR compared with CSR. Our DSS is faster than the full matrix by 4.1× in the context of GPU-based OBR on the GRN control problem when $R = 20\%$. With a fixed memory limitation, our DSS can handle a larger state space and deeper horizons for the GPU-based OBR algorithm. In the future, we plan to focus on testing the DSS scheme on more general sparse matrices, and will also focus on speeding up the look-up function by using caching techniques.

REFERENCES

[1] John Asmuth and Michael L Littman. 2011. Approaching Bayes-optimalilty using Monte-Carlo tree search. In *Proceedings of the 21st International Conference on Automated Planning and Scheduling*.

[2] Zhaojun Bai, James Demmel, Jack Dongarra, Axel Ruhe, and Henk Van Der Vorst. 2000. *Templates for the solution of algebraic eigenvalue problems: a practical guide.* SIAM, Philadelphia, PA.

[3] Nicole Bäuerle and Ulrich Rieder. 2009. MDP algorithms for portfolio optimization problems in pure jump markets. *Finance and Stochastics* 13, 4 (2009), 591–611.

[4] Nicole Bäuerle and Ulrich Rieder. 2011. *Markov decision processes with applications to finance.* Springer Science & Business Media, New York, NY.

[5] Richard Bellman. 1957. *A Markovian decision process.* Technical Report. DTIC Document.

[6] Richard E Bellman and Stuart E Dreyfus. 2015. *Applied dynamic programming.* Princeton university press, Princeton, New Jersey.

[7] Oded Berman and Eungab Kim. 1999. Stochastic models for inventory management at service facilities. *Stochastic Models* 15, 4 (1999), 695–718.

[8] Arthur Earl Bryson. 1975. *Applied optimal control: optimization, estimation and control.* CRC Press, Boca Raton, FL.

[9] Xiaodong Cai, Juan Andrés Bazerque, and Georgios B Giannakis. 2013. Inference of gene regulatory networks with sparse structural equation models exploiting genetic perturbations. *PLOS Computational Biology* 9, 5 (2013), e1003068.

[10] Nir Friedman and Yoram Singer. 1998. Efficient Bayesian parameter estimation in large discrete domains. In *Proceedings of the 11th International Conference on Neural Information Processing Systems.* MIT Press, 417–423.

[11] Arthur Guez, David Silver, and Peter Dayan. 2012. Efficient Bayes-adaptive reinforcement learning using sample-based search. In *Proceedings of Advances in Neural Information Processing Systems.* 1025–1033.

[12] Michael Hecker, Sandro Lambeck, Susanne Toepfer, Eugene Van Someren, and Reinhard Guthke. 2009. Gene regulatory network inference: data integration in dynamic models - a review. *Biosystems* 96, 1 (2009), 86–103.

[13] Arie Hordijk and L. C. M. Kallenberg. 1979. Linear programming and Markov decision chains. *Management Science* 25, 4 (1979), 352–362.

[14] Ronald A Howard and James E Matheson. 1972. Risk-sensitive Markov decision processes. *Management science* 18, 7 (1972), 356–369.

[15] Hawoong Jeong, Sean P Mason, A-L Barabási, and Zoltan N Oltvai. 2001. Lethality and centrality in protein networks. *Nature* 411, 6833 (2001), 41–42.

[16] James John Martin. 1967. *Bayesian decision problems and Markov chains.* John Wiley & Sons, Hoboken, NJ.

[17] Arnab Nilim and Laurent El Ghaoui. 2005. Robust control of Markov decision processes with uncertain transition matrices. *Operations Research* 53, 5 (2005), 780–798.

[18] Nvidia CUDA 2016. CUDA Toolkit Documentation v8.0. (2016). http://docs.nvidia.com/cuda/#axzz4dPkFrRLs

[19] Nvidia GeForce 2015. The Nvidia GeForce Website. (2015). http://www.geforce.com/hardware/desktop-gpus/geforce-gtx-780/specifications

[20] Martin L Puterman. 2014. *Markov decision processes: discrete stochastic dynamic programming.* John Wiley & Sons, Hoboken, NJ.

[21] Martin L Puterman and Moon Chirl Shin. 1978. Modified policy iteration algorithms for discounted Markov decision problems. *Management Science* 24, 11 (1978), 1127–1137.

[22] Yousef Saad. 1989. Krylov subspace methods on supercomputers. *Scientific and Statistical Computing* 10, 6 (1989), 1200–1232.

[23] Yousef Saad. 2003. *Iterative methods for sparse linear systems.* SIAM, Philadelphia, PA.

[24] Brian Sallans and G. E. Hinton. 2004. Reinforcement learning with factored states and actions. *Journal of Machine Learning Research* 5, Aug (2004), 1063–1088.

[25] Ilya Shmulevich and Edward R Dougherty. 2010. *Probabilistic Boolean networks: the modeling and control of gene regulatory networks.* SIAM, Philadelphia, PA.

[26] Olivier Sigaud and Olivier Buffet. 2013. *Markov decision processes in artificial intelligence.* John Wiley & Sons, Hoboken, NJ.

[27] Jesper Tegner, M. K. Stephen Yeung, Jeff Hasty, and J. J. Collins. 2003. Reverse engineering gene networks: integrating genetic perturbations with dynamical modeling. *the National Academy of Sciences* 100, 10 (2003), 5944–5949.

[28] Denis Thieffry, Araceli M Huerta, Ernesto Pérez-Rueda, and Julio Collado-Vides. 1998. From specific gene regulation to genomic networks: a global analysis of transcriptional regulation in Escherichia coli. *Bioessays* 20, 5 (1998), 433–440.

[29] Christopher J. C. H. Watkins and Peter Dayan. 1992. Q-learning. *Machine learning* 8, 3-4 (1992), 279–292.

[30] Mohammadmahdi R Yousefi and Edward R Dougherty. 2014. A comparison study of optimal and suboptimal intervention policies for gene regulatory networks in the presence of uncertainty. *EURASIP Journal on Bioinformatics and Systems Biology* 2014, 1 (2014), 6.

[31] He Zhou, Jiang Hu, Sunil P Khatri, Frank Liu, Cliff Sze, and Mohammadmahdi R Yousefi. 2016. GPU acceleration for Bayesian control of Markovian genetic regulatory networks. In *Proceedings of the 3rd International Conference on Biomedical and Health Informatic.* IEEE, 304–307.

Inferring Microbial Interactions from Metagenomic Time-series Using Prior Biological Knowledge

Chieh Lo
Carnegie Mellon University
Pittsburgh, PA 15213
chiehl@andrew.cmu.edu

Radu Marculescu
Carnegie Mellon University
Pittsburgh, PA 15213
radum@cmu.edu

ABSTRACT

Due to the recent advances in modern metagenomics sequencing methods, it becomes possible to directly analyze the microbial communities within human body. To understand how microbial communities adapt, develop, and interact over time with the human body and the surrounding environment, a critical step is the inference of interactions among different microbes directly from sequencing data. However, metagenomics data is both compositional and highly dimensional in nature. Consequently, new approaches that can accurately and robustly estimate the interactions among various microbe species are needed to analyze such data. To this end, we propose a novel framework called Microbial Time-series Prior Lasso (MTPLasso) which integrates sparse linear regression with microbial co-occurrences and associations obtained from scientific literature and cross-sectional metagenomics data. We show that MTPLasso outperforms existing models in terms of precision and recall rates, as well as the accuracy in inferring the interaction types. Finally, the interaction networks we infer from human gut data demonstrate credible results when compared against real data.

CCS CONCEPTS

•**Applied computing** → *Systems biology; Biological networks; Bioinformatics;* •**Mathematics of computing** → *Differential equations;* •**Computing methodologies** → *Machine learning algorithms;*

KEYWORDS

microbial interaction; metagenomics; prior knowledge; sparse regression; network inference

1 INTRODUCTION

Microbiome plays an important role in determining the human health and well-being [9, 24]. For example, the inflammatory bowel disease (IBD) currently affects approximately 1.8 million Americans. Results show that IBD-affected individuals have 30-50% reduced biodiversity of commensal bacteria, such as significant decrease in *Firmicutes* and *Bacteroidetes* [3]. Consequently, finding new ways to analyze the human microbiome may help better understand, prevent, or cure diseases.

Permission to make digital or hard copies of all or part of this work for personal or classroom use is granted without fee provided that copies are not made or distributed for profit or commercial advantage and that copies bear this notice and the full citation on the first page. Copyrights for components of this work owned by others than ACM must be honored. Abstracting with credit is permitted. To copy otherwise, or republish, to post on servers or to redistribute to lists, requires prior specific permission and/or a fee. Request permissions from permissions@acm.org.
ACM-BCB'17, August 20–23, 2017, Boston, MA, USA.
© 2017 ACM. 978-1-4503-4722-8/17/08...$15.00
DOI: http://dx.doi.org/10.1145/3107411.3107435

Microbial communities exhibit rich dynamics including the way they adapt, develop, and interact with the human body and the surrounding environment. However, the specific way of how human associated microbes affect the human health remains largely unknown. To this end, studies on the microbial interactions can provide a solid foundation to model the interplay between the (host) human body and the microbial populations; this can serve as a key step towards precision medicine [22]. Unfortunately, understanding microbial interactions is difficult, as most microbes cannot be easily cultivated in standard laboratory settings.

To date, various datasets that focus on human niches exist; they can be classified into two different types: cross-sectional and time-series datasets. Cross-sectional data (e.g., Human Microbiome Project [28]) provides microbial co-occurrences collected from different body sites (e.g., gut, mouth) each with multiple individual samples. Several algorithms [13, 20] have been proposed to utilize such data to infer associations (i.e., putative interactions) among microbes. In contrast, time-series data [8, 23, 27] focus on the dynamics of microbial communities over time, typically, for a few individuals. By utilizing dynamical modeling (e.g., ordinary differential equations), specialized algorithms [7, 11, 23] can infer the interactions between microbe species; this is completely different from the associations inferred from the cross-sectional data.

In this paper, we aim at analyzing the *structure* and *dynamics* of networks of interaction among microbes of human microbiome in order to understand how microbes can affect the human health. To this end, there exist several challenges: First, the amount of (time-series) sequencing data that corresponds to human microbiome available from public websites is scarce. For instance, to date, one of the largest published datasets [8] only provides a few hundred time points for one individual, while the number of microbes (p) usually ranges from hundreds to thousands. As a consequence, the number of possible interactions (p^2) is much greater than the number of samples that can be obtained from real datasets (i.e., high-dimensional data). Another big challenge stems from the nature of the data itself. Sequencing data only provides the *relative* abundance of various species; this is because the sequencing results are a function of sequencing depth and the biological sample size [26]. Therefore, from a statistical standpoint, the relative microbial abundance falls into the class of compositional data [1]; this causes statical methods such as Pearson or Spearman correlations (which work with absolute values) to generate spurious results.

To solve the problem caused by high-dimensional data, we propose to integrate multiple levels of biological information to enhance the model accuracy on inferring microbial interactions. To date, an increasing amount of scientific literatures provides data which can be mined not only for the co-occurrence of microbes,

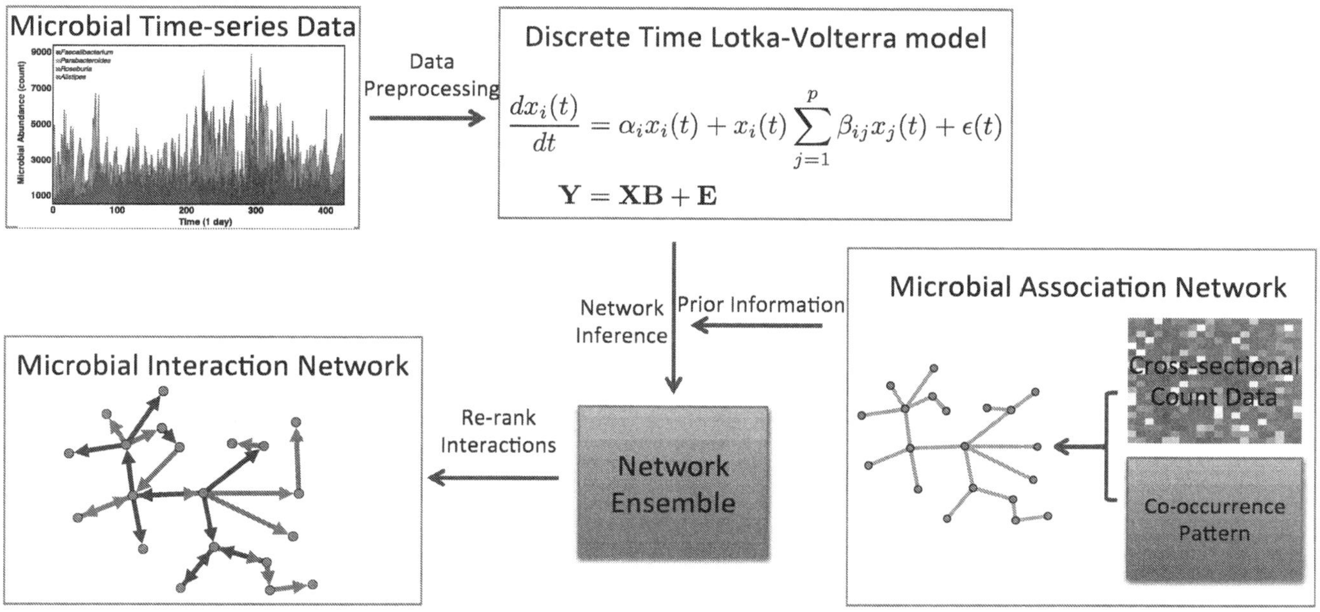

Figure 1: The proposed MTPLasso pipeline. We first preprocess the microbial time-series data and then model it using discrete time Lotka-Volterra model. By incorporating the associations from cross-sectional data and microbial co-occurrences, our proposed algorithms can robustly infer interaction among microbes. Network bagging and interaction re-ranking can further improve robustness and provide credible results. The associations among microbes are represented by green color. The competitive and beneficial interactions are represented by red and blue colors, respectively, while the grey color represents wrongly estimated edges.

but also to predict microbial associations directly. For instance, the pioneering work in [12] considers automated analysis of the co-occurrence of bacterial species through statistical testing approaches (e.g., Fisher's exact test). In [5], the authors show that gut and mouth microbiomes display pronounced universal dynamics (i.e., host independent). As such, by incorporating the microbial co-occurrences with various cross-sectional data into the existing methods [20], the resulting microbial associations can serve as prior information to infer the interactions for microbial time-series; this can truly mitigate the problem of high-dimensionality.

Although several approaches have successfully applied prior biological information to reconstruct gene-interaction networks [15, 21, 29], to the best of knowledge, we are the first to consider multiple levels of biological knowledge as *a priori* information to derive microbial interaction networks. Indeed, as shown in Fig. 1, we first transform the microbial time-series count data into relative abundance data (i.e., compositional data) and then model it by using a discrete time Lotka-Volterra model. Thus, we can easily incorporate the prior information provided by microbial associations to a Lasso regression algorithm and solve for a sparse interaction network; this sparse algorithm can help increase the model performance in terms of precision and recall rates.

To boost the performance and robustness, we further conduct model ensemble and selection through bootstrap aggregating [6] and re-ranking [15], respectively for the inferred interactions; the resulting interactions are robust to different choice of parameters. Overall, the proposed algorithm, the *Microbial Time-series Prior Lasso (MTPLasso)*, turns out to be more accurate than the other existing methods on inferring the microbial interactions [11, 27].

To assess the performance of MTPLasso, we first evaluate and compare it against other previously proposed methods, namely, ridge regression [27] and sparse regression [11], under different graph structures that encode various levels of sparsity. We show that our proposed MTPLasso outperforms all these methods in terms of two metrices, namely, area under the precision-recall curve (AUPR) and interaction type classification accuracy (IACC) of network interactions prediction. Next, we evaluate the dataset available in [8] and compare the inferred results against laboratory settings. Taken together, our contributions are three fold:

(1) First, we integrate the linear Lasso regression with *a priori* knowledge obtained from cross-sectional datasets and the co-occurrence patterns of interacting microbes. To the best of our knowledge, we are the first to integrate these two different components to infer the interaction networks among microbes.
(2) Second, we show that our proposed method, MTPLasso, outperforms all other previously proposed methods for inferring graph structures on different synthetic datasets. Additionally, the AUPR and IACC of MTPLasso are up to 75% and 80%, on average.
(3) Third, we show that MTPLasso can robustly infer the interactions type in real time-series datasets. Additionally, the interactions found by our approach correlate well with the experimental findings reported in the scientific literature.

Symbols	Representations
p, T	Number of microbes and time points
Y, **X**, **B**, **E**	Response, data, parameter, and error matrices.
$\bar{S}$	Mean microbial total abundance
$\boldsymbol{\alpha}, \hat{\boldsymbol{\alpha}}$	True and estimated intrinsic growth rates matrices
$\boldsymbol{\beta}, \hat{\boldsymbol{\beta}}$	True and estimated interaction matrices
λ, ρ	Penalizing parameters for interaction and association
P, **Q**	Prior matrix for interaction and association
γ, **R**	Error of true and predicted model and interaction rank matrix
μ, Σ, Ω	Mean, covariance, and precision matrix of normal distribution
$\hat{\mathbf{C}}$	Empirical covariance of cross-sectional abundance data
θ, b	Weight parameter and bagging size

Table 1: Model and experimental parameters.

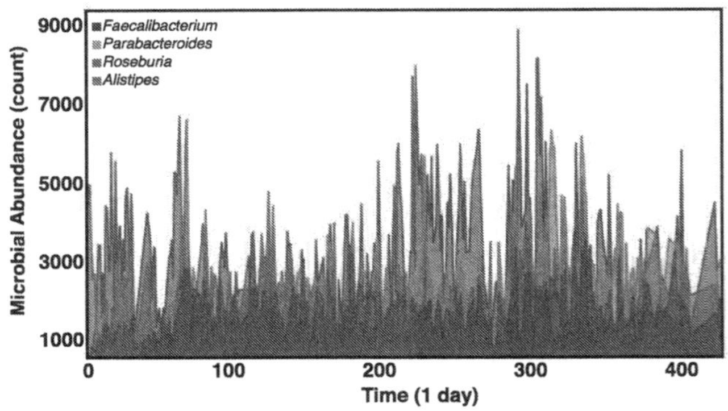

Figure 2: Microbial time-series visualization for individual MALE in daily resolution [8]. The abundance of four most abundant genera in human gut (abundance is represented by different colors).

The remainder of this paper is organized as follows. Section 2 summarizes related work for inferring microbial time-series. Section 3 focuses on the mathematical details of our proposed pipelines as shown in Fig. 1. Section 4 shows the experimental results of our proposed system on synthetic datasets. Section 5 describes the results of applying our proposed method on the real time-series. Section 6 discusses and compares our solution against other existing methods.

2 RELATED WORK

Several algorithms have been developed to infer microbe interactions for both compositional and high-dimensional data. For instance, Stein et al. [27] propose a ridge regression model and extend the generalized Lotka-Volterra equations [23] to infer microbial ecology and predict the temporal dynamics under time-dependent external perturbations. However, the interactions inferred from the ridge regression suffer from low precision and low recall rates under such high-dimensional data. In [7], the authors propose constrained ridge regression and bayesian algorithms that enhance the model performance using the same dataset as in [27]. The inference engine proposed in [7] requires the information of biomass in order to mitigate the problem caused by the compositional nature of data itself. However, most public available data such as [8, 28] only provide the relative abundance of microbes. Fisher et al. [11] propose a sparse linear regression algorithm that selects interactions that minimize the prediction errors in a greedy manner. Although it can circumvent the high-dimensional problem, the algorithm itself still suffers from low precision when recall rates are high.

3 MATHEMATICAL MODELING FOR MICROBIAL TIME-SERIES

In this section, we first describe the mathematical modeling for time-series data based on Lotka-Volterra model. Next, we describe the modeling of our proposed Microbial Time-series Prior Lasso (MTPLasso). We outline the synthetic data generation and real data preprocessing in Appendices A and B, respectively. Model and experimental parameters are summarized in Table 1.

3.1 Discrete Time Lotka-Volterra (LV) Model

Metagenomics data provides the relative abundance for microbes in discrete time intervals (e.g., daily measurements); this makes it possible to infer the interactions among microbes directly from such data. To model the dynamics and interactions among microbes over time, a sensible way is to utilize the discrete time LV model for population dynamics [17].

For *absolute* abundance data (x) that contains p microbes over T time points, the behavior of microbe i at time $t+dt$ is related to other microbes at time t. The LV model explicitly captures the interactions among microbes via the interaction coefficient (β). More precisely, there exist three possible interactions between microbe i and j: beneficial ($\beta_{ij} > 0$), competitive ($\beta_{ij} < 0$), and non-interacting ($\beta_{ij} = 0$). Beneficial interaction means that microbe i can facilitate the growth of microbe j, while competitive interaction inhibits the growth of microbe j.

The change of microbial abundance can also be affected by environment and other noise sources such as measurement errors. To account for such effects, we can directly add a stochastic noise ϵ into the LV model. Specifically, the LV model is as follows:

$$\frac{dx_i(t)}{dt} = \alpha_i x_i(t) + x_i(t)\sum_{j=1}^{p}\beta_{ij}x_j(t) + \epsilon_i(t) \quad (1)$$

where α_i represents the intrinsic growth rate for microbe i.

As indicated by [11] and shown in Fig. 2, the microbiome abundance profiles stay close to the equilibrium values (with some fluctuations). Therefore, we can assume that the LV system of equations have a unique steady-state solution; by setting $dt = 1$ (i.e., unit time measurement), and without loss of generality, we can rewrite Eq. (1) near steady-state as:

$$\frac{dx_i(t)}{x_i(t)} = [\alpha_i + \sum_{j=1}^{p}\beta_{ij}(x_j(t) - \overline{x_j}) + \epsilon_i(t)]dt \quad (2)$$

where $\overline{x_j}$ is the equilibrium abundance of microbe j. To fit the dynamics described by Eq. (2), we can approximate the left hand side by using the relationship: $\frac{dx_i(t)}{x_i(t)} = d\ln x_i(t) \approx \ln x_i(t+1) - \ln x_i(t)$. Additionally, we can combine the intrinsic growth rates ($\boldsymbol{\alpha} \in \mathbb{R}^p$) and interactions ($\boldsymbol{\beta} \in \mathbb{R}^{p\times p}$) matrices to form the parameter matrix $\mathbf{B} = [\boldsymbol{\alpha}; \boldsymbol{\beta}] \in \mathbb{R}^{(p+1)\times p}$. By using the above notations, we can

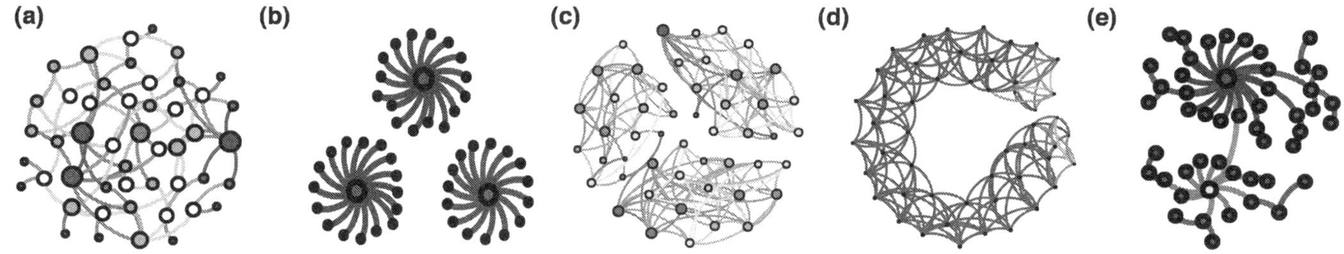

Figure 3: Different types of graphs we consider to generate synthetic data: (a) random (b) hub (c) cluster (d) band and (e) scale-free graphs. Node and edges are represented by round circles and curve lines, respectively. See Appendix A for details.

reformulate Eq. (2) into a compact representation:

$$\mathrm{Y} = \mathrm{XB} + \mathrm{E} \tag{3}$$

where the entry Y_{ti} of the response matrix $\mathrm{Y} \in \mathbb{R}^{T \times p}$ is defined as $Y_{ti} \triangleq \ln x_i(t+1) - \ln x_i(t)$. The entry E_{ti} of the error matrix E is equal to $\epsilon_i(t)$. The data matrix $\mathbf{X} \in \mathbb{R}^{T \times (p+1)}$ is defined as:

$$\mathbf{X} = \begin{pmatrix} 1 & x_1(1) & x_2(1) & \cdots & x_p(1) \\ 1 & x_1(2) & x_2(2) & \cdots & x_p(2) \\ \vdots & \vdots & \ddots & \vdots & \\ 1 & x_1(T) & x_2(T) & \cdots & x_p(T) \end{pmatrix}$$

Eq. (3) can be considered as a standard linear regression problem if the entry in error matrix (E) is assumed to follow normal distribution. In the following analyses, without loss of generality, error terms are considered to follow a normal distribution for both synthetic and real datasets.

To account for relative abundance, we follow the same assumption as in [11], i.e., given time t, the fluctuations of the total abundance ($S(t) = \sum_i^p x_i(t)$) around the mean value $\overline{S} = \sum_i^p \overline{x_i}$ are small. As a result, the dynamics of the relative abundance is described by:

$$\mathrm{Y} \approx \tilde{\mathrm{X}}\tilde{\mathrm{B}} + \mathrm{E} \tag{4}$$

where $\widetilde{X_{ti}} = X_{ti}/\overline{S}$ and $\widetilde{B_{ti}} = \overline{S}B_{ti}$. We can solve Eq. (4) to infer unscaled interactions and then relate them to the true interactions through the mean total abundance $\overline{S}$.

3.2 MTPLasso

The microbial time-series data can be formulated into a linear regression problem as explained in section 3.1. To infer the pairwise interactions among microbes, we can use sparse regression methods and select the interactions that minimize the mean square error (i.e., $||\mathrm{Y} - \mathbf{XB}||_2^2$). More specifically, by applying the L_1 norm on the interaction matrix, the standard Lasso regression can be formulated as follows:

$$\hat{\boldsymbol{\beta}} = \min_{\boldsymbol{\beta} \in \mathbb{R}^{p \times p}} \left\{ ||\mathrm{Y} - \mathbf{XB}||_2^2 + \lambda ||\boldsymbol{\beta}||_1 \right\} \tag{5}$$

where λ is a penalizing parameter and $||\boldsymbol{\beta}||_1$ is the L_1 norm, i.e., the sum of the absolute values of the elements of $\boldsymbol{\beta}$. Note that the optimization problem defined in Eq. (5) does not penalize the intrinsic growth rates $\boldsymbol{\alpha}$ since they are viewed as intercept terms in Lasso regression.

However, microbial data usually come with a limited amount of time points (T) but with high dimensionality (p); this makes the regression problem intractable since the number of interactions (p^2) is far greater than time points (T). To make the problem tractable, we propose to utilize the information obtained from the scientific literature and cross-sectional datasets in order to construct the prior matrix $\mathrm{P} \in \mathbb{R}^{p \times p}$, where each entry $P_{i,j} \in [0, 1]$ represents the prior probability of interactions between microbe i and microbe j. We can impose different penalties on the precision matrix; this is different from the standard formulation where the penalty (λ) imposed on the precision matrix is the same. Therefore, by incorporating the prior information into the prior matrix (P), the proposed MTPLasso can be formulated as follows:

$$\hat{\boldsymbol{\beta}} = \min_{\boldsymbol{\beta} \in \mathbb{R}^{p \times p}} \left\{ ||\mathrm{Y} - \mathbf{XB}||_2^2 + \lambda ||P \otimes \boldsymbol{\beta}||_1 \right\} \tag{6}$$

where $\otimes$ represents component-wise multiplication. When the value of $P_{i,j}$ is large, it directly puts a heavy penalty and represents a weaker interaction between microbes and vice versa. This way, by imposing the prior information, we can accurately infer the interactions among microbes. To select λ, we use n-fold cross validation. We follow standard usage by setting $n = 5$.

3.3 Bootstrap aggregating (Bagging) MTPLasso

Microbial time-series datasets often come with a limited amount of time points. Even with the help of prior information, MTPLasso still operates in a high-dimensional setting; to enhance and stabilize the model performance, we can infer the interaction matrix multiple times and average over the inferred parameters; this is know as bootstrap aggregating or bagging [6]. This ensemble meta-algorithm can not only improve the stability and accuracy of the regression results but also reduce variance. To bag the regression results, we uniformly draw the same amount of samples with replacement; this procedure is repeated b times which results in different estimates for the interaction matrix. The proposed Bagging MTPLasso is summarized in Algorithm 1.

3.4 Re-rank Interactions

The output of the Bagging MTPLasso is the parameter matrix $\hat{\mathbf{B}}$ which contains the estimated intrinsic growth rate ($\hat{\boldsymbol{\alpha}}$) and interaction ($\hat{\boldsymbol{\beta}}$) matrices. We can calculate the confidence score of the inferred interactions and then choose interactions with high confidence scores. However, by simply using the magnitude (i.e., $|\beta_{i,j}|$)

Algorithm 1 Bagging MTPLasso

procedure BAGGING MTPLASSO($\mathbf{Y}, \mathbf{X}, \mathbf{P}, b$)
  $\mathbf{Y} \in \mathbb{R}^{T \times p}, \mathbf{X} \in \mathbb{R}^{T \times (p+1)}, \mathbf{P} \in \mathbb{R}^{p \times p}$
  for $i = 1 : b$ **do** ▷ b: number of bagging
    Draw $\mathbf{Y}'$ from $\mathbf{Y}$ uniformly with replacement
    Draw $\mathbf{X}'$ from $\mathbf{X}$ uniformly with replacement
    Compute $\mathbf{B_i}$ using Eq. (6) including model selection
  end for
  Compute median $\hat{\mathbf{B}}$ from $(\mathbf{B}_1, \mathbf{B}_2, ..., \mathbf{B}_b)$
  return $\hat{\mathbf{B}}$ ▷ The estimated parameter matrix
end procedure

of the inferred parameters as ranking criteria is not the best scheme since it does not account for model performance as pointed out in [15]. We hence modify the scheme proposed in [15] to account for model performance as follows:

$$r_{ij} = 1 - \frac{\gamma_j}{\gamma_{ij}} \qquad (7)$$

where r_{ij} represents the rank for interaction β_{ij}. γ_j is defined as: $\frac{||Y_j - XB_i||^2}{Var(Y_j)}$ where Y_j is the j_{th} column vector of $\mathbf{Y}$. γ_{ij} is the model response *without* interaction β_{ij}. The resulting interaction rank matrix $\mathbf{R} = (r_{ij}) \in \mathbb{R}^{p \times p}$ can be used to select interactions that truly explain the microbial time-series.

3.5 Microbial Prior Knowledge Acquisition

3.5.1 Microbial Co-occurrence. To acquire the prior knowledge of microbial interactions from reported experiments and published papers, we utilize the PubMed database[1] that contains a massive amount of papers with abstracts. For the 16S rRNA data where the taxonomy level can be achieved at the genus-level, we adopt the co-occurrence method [12] that uses statistical testing to identify the pairwise associations among genera.

We modify the code[2] that utilizes the Entrez search system to query all the possible combinations of genus-genus pairs from the data. More specifically, queries for the query term "genus i AND genus j" for genus-level are performed on PubMed database in order to compute the number of papers that contain each genus name, and contains both genera name.

The co-occurrence approach is based on the statistical significance on the number of abstracts obtained from the PubMed database. More specifically, we can create a 2-by-2 contingency table where entries contain: abstracts containing solely genus i or j, abstracts containing both genera i and j, and abstracts containing neither genera i nor j. We use Fisher's exact test and then correct the resulting statistical significance (i.e., p-value) in order to select potentially interacting genus pairs [16].

3.5.2 Cross-sectional Data. Next, we incorporate the prior knowledge obtained from section 3.5.1 into the cross-sectional datasets (i.e., HMP dataset) in order to correctly estimate associations among genera. We briefly summarize the approaches we use in this paper.

Suppose the cross-sectional count data are drawn from a multivariate normal distribution with mean μ and covariance Σ. The inverse covariance matrix (precision matrix) $\Omega = \Sigma^{-1}$ encodes the conditional independence among nodes. More specifically, if the entry (i,j) of the precision matrix $\Omega_{i,j} = 0$, then node i and node j are conditionally independent (given the other nodes) and there is no edge among them.

One suitable algorithm to select the precision matrix under sparsity assumption is to utilize the graphical Lasso proposed previously in [14, 20]. By incorporating the prior information (i.e., microbial co-occurrence) into the prior matrix (Q), we can formulate the graph estimation problem as follows:

$$\hat{\Omega} = \arg\max_{\Omega} \{\log\det(\Omega) - \mathrm{tr}(\Omega\hat{\mathbf{C}}) - \rho|\mathbf{Q} \otimes \Omega|_1\} \qquad (8)$$

where $\hat{\mathbf{C}}$ is the empirical covariance of the microbial data, and Ω is the precision matrix of the estimated associations among genera. ρ is the penalizing parameter. Here det and tr denote the determinant and the trace of a matrix, respectively. When the value of $Q_{i,j}$ is large, this directly puts a heavy penalty and represents a weaker association between genera.

For our proposed MTPLasso, the entry of the prior matrix P_{ij} is set to θ if genus i has an association with genus j (i.e., $\Omega_{ij} = 1$), where $\theta \in [0, 1]$ is the weight parameter. We will examine the effect of the weight parameter of the prior information in section 4.2. Note that the formulation of the prior matrix (Q) for cross-sectional data is different from the prior matrix (P) for time-series data since prior information is obtained from microbial co-occurrences and cross-sectional analyses, respectively.

4 EXPERIMENTS WITH SYNTHETIC DATA

To show the effectiveness of our proposed model, we first compare our model against two regression-based and two baseline methods: ridge regression [27], LIMITS [11], Lasso regression (without prior information), and least square solution on absolute abundances (LSA). We use the package in [30] to generate different graph structures as described in Appendix A and shown in Fig. 3. Given a particular graph (i.e., the vertex and edge sets), we follow the procedure as described in Appendix A.2. For each set of time-series, we consider M initial conditions each with T time points. Additionally, we consider different levels of additive noise ϵ when generating time-series data.

For MTPLasso working on real datasets, the true underlying network is only partially known and contains spurious information. To assess our algorithm performance with imperfect prior information, we consider prior information with different precision levels. The total number of edges in the prior network is set equal to the number of edges in the true underlying network. Therefore, a precision level of 0.1 indicates that 10% of the edges in prior are true edges, whereas the other 90% are spurious ones. We examine different precision levels in section 4.3 and report the 0.5 precision level in the following synthetic experiments.

In the following synthetic experimental analyses, the default parameter setting (without explicit indication) is: $M = 2$, $T = 30$, $\epsilon \sim N(0, 0.1)$, prior percentage = 50%, and precision level = 100%. For each experiment, we average over 20 simulation runs and show standard deviations as error bars in Figs. 4-9[3].

[1] https://www.ncbi.nlm.nih.gov/pubmed/
[2] https://github.com/CSB5/atminter

[3] For plotting purpose, the standard deviation on the figure is one-fifth of the true value.

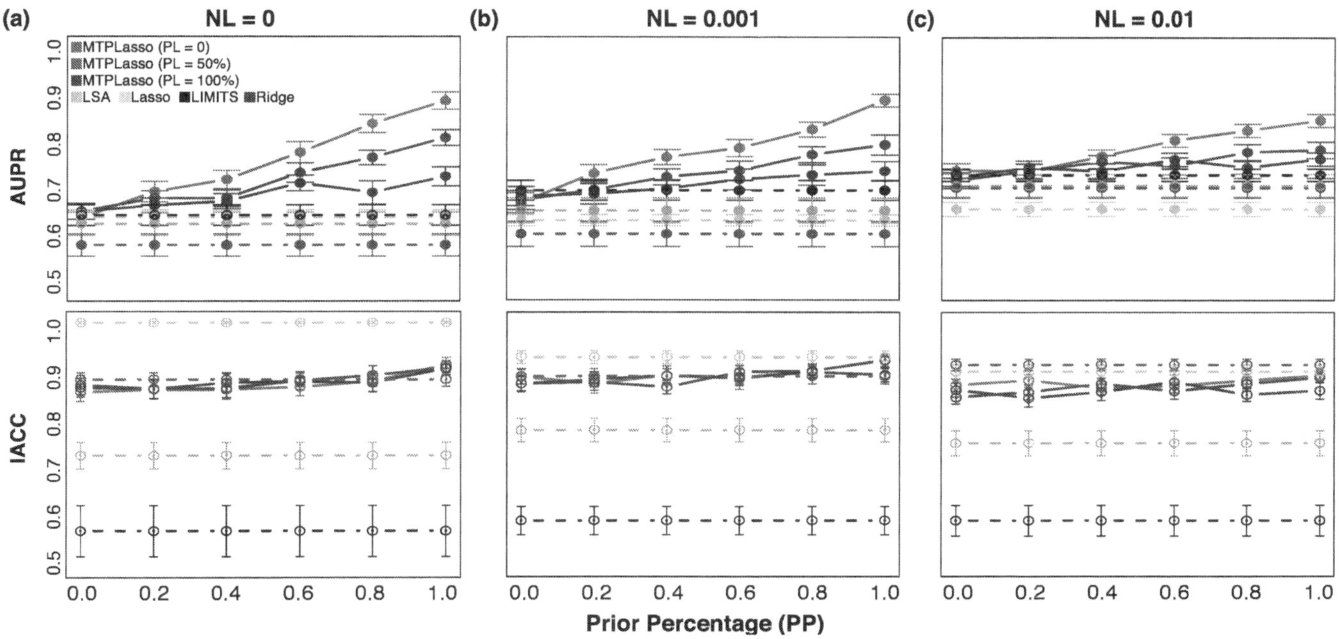

Figure 4: Performance evaluation on random graphs under different combinations of parameters. As prior percentage (PP) increases, both AUPR and IACC increase, as expected. MTPLasso outperforms all other methods, even with high precision level (PL) and high noise level (NL). (a) NL = 0, (b) NL = 0.001, (c) NL = 0.01.

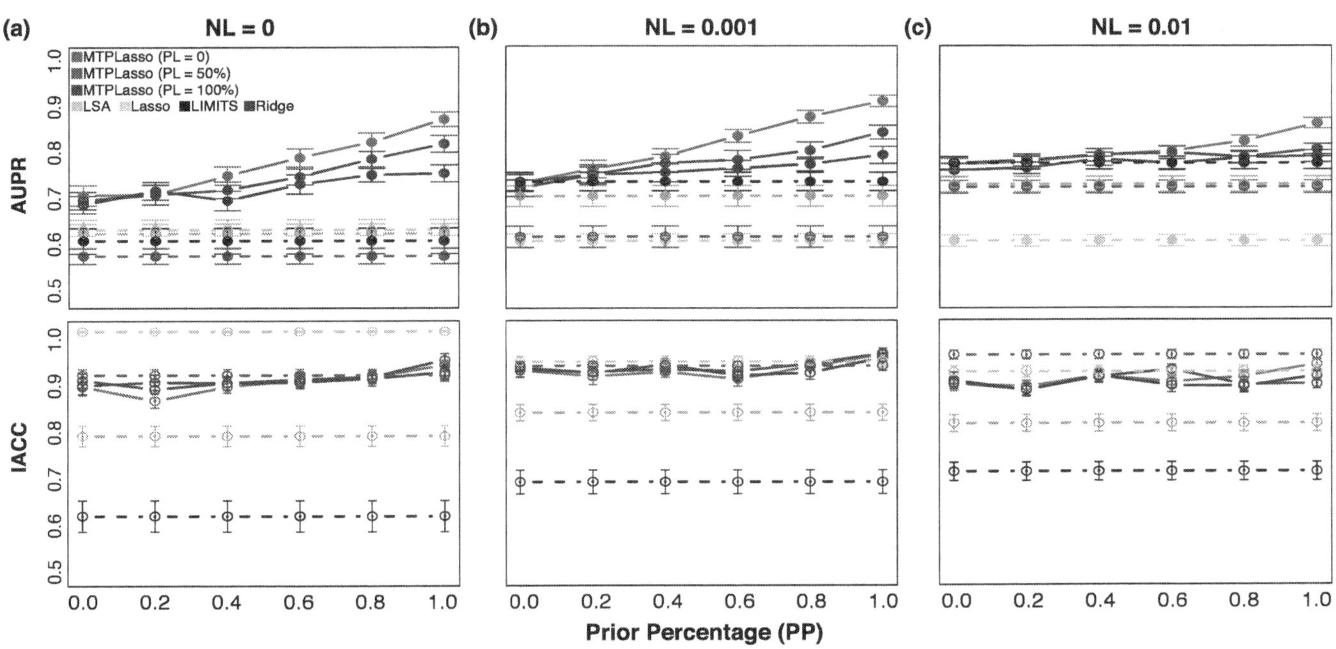

Figure 5: Performance evaluation on scale-free graphs under different combinations of parameters. Similar to the results on random graphs, both AUPR and IACC increase when PP increases. Compared to random graphs, scale-free graphs have better performances for all the methods. As it can be seen, MTPLasso outperforms the other methods even with high precision level (PL) and high noise level (NL). (a) NL = 0, (b) NL = 0.001, (c) NL = 0.01.

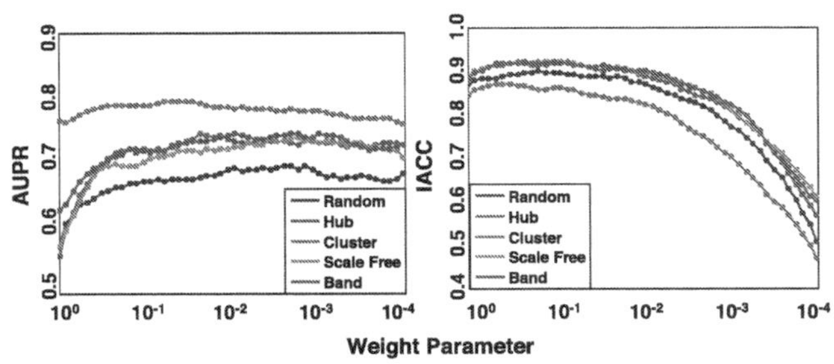

Figure 6: The effect of different weight parameters (θ) on AUPR and IACC for five different graphs. For AUPR, MTPLasso is relative robust to different weight parameters. In contrast, a small weight parameter (θ) can dramatically degrade IACC.

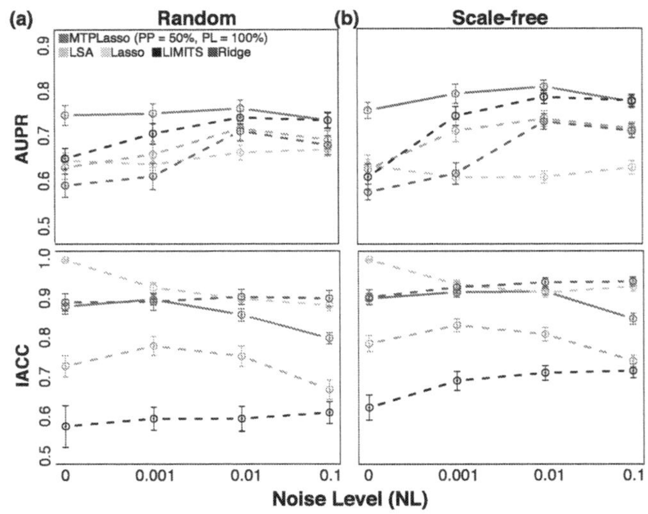

Figure 7: The effect of noise levels on (a) random and (b) scale-free graphs. As noise level increases, our proposed method degrades slightly (~0.05). The performance on scale-free graphs is better than than random graphs.

4.1 Evaluation Metrics

We consider two different metrics as follows:

- Area Under the Precision-Recall Curve (AUPR): We compute the AUPR and ignore the sign of inferred edges. Precision is defined as the number of true positives, divided by the sum of true and false positives, while recall is defined as the number of true positives, divided by the sum of true positive and false negatives.
- Interaction Type Classification Accuracy (IACC): Since interactions can be classified into three types: beneficial ($\beta > 0$), competitive ($\beta < 0$), and non-interacting ($\beta = 0$), we estimate IACC as the fraction of correctly estimated interacting interactions (i.e., $\beta \neq 0$).

4.2 Weight Parameter

To assess the sensitivity of how weight parameter (θ) can affect the performance, we vary the weight parameter within the range $[10^{-4}, 10^{0}]$.[4] We consider the case where we use 50% true interactions (i.e., prior percentage = 50%) and the same amount of false interactions (i.e., precision level = 100%). As can be seen in Fig. 6, when the weight parameter decreases, AUPR increases and achieves similar values after $\theta = 0.1$; this shows that AUPR is quite robust against different choices of the weight parameter. On the contrary, IACC gradually decreases as the weight parameter decreases; this is because MTPLasso prevents solving wrong edges by sacrificing the accuracy. To obtain both high AUPR and IACC, we choose $\theta = 0.01$ that are robust for different graph structures for the following analyses. Additionally, the performance of our proposed method on cluster graph achieves the best results, while the least on random graph in terms of AUPR. Therefore, in the following analyses, we consider the random graph and scale-free graph which is commonly seen in many real-networks including microbial and gene networks.

4.3 Prior Percentage and Precision Level

To quantify the effects of different percentages of prior information and levels of precision, we vary the percentage of prior information that is included into the prior matrix (**P**) and consider three precision levels: 0%, 50%, and 100%. Additionally, we consider one scenario with noiseless data (i.e., $\epsilon(t) = 0, \forall t$) and two scenarios with noisy data where the noise levels are set to 0.001 and 0.01, respectively. We report two graph structures: random and scale-free as discussed in section 4.2.

As shown in Figs. 4 and 5, when the amount of prior information increases, both AUPR and IACC increase as expected. When the noise level increases, although with some degradation in performances (both in AUPR and IACC), our proposed method can still outperform other existing methods in terms of AUPR. For the IACC, ridge regression and LSA perform relatively well. However, they achieve poor results on AUPR since most of the inferred interactions are wrongly estimated. Another observation is that MTPLasso is relatively robust to different precision levels; this can be found with small differences in IACC.

4.4 Noise Level

In the real-world settings, the metagenomic data can contain different types of noise. One main source of noise comes from the measurement errors. For example, genus i may be misclassified as genus j. To quantify such measurement errors, the additive noise included in Eq. (2) is set to different noise levels. More specifically, we consider error ranges from 0.001 to 0.1.[5] As shown in Fig. 7, our proposed method is robust against the measurement errors and outperforms other methods with an average AUPR = 0.75. In terms of IACC, the performance slightly degrades as the noise level increases; this is because noise makes it harder to infer the types of interaction (while we can still infer interacting genera). Overall, our proposed method is quite robust to different levels of noise.

[4] This is a typical range for the penalizing parameter using in standard Lasso regression.

[5] For larger noise levels, the LV dynamical system becomes unstable.

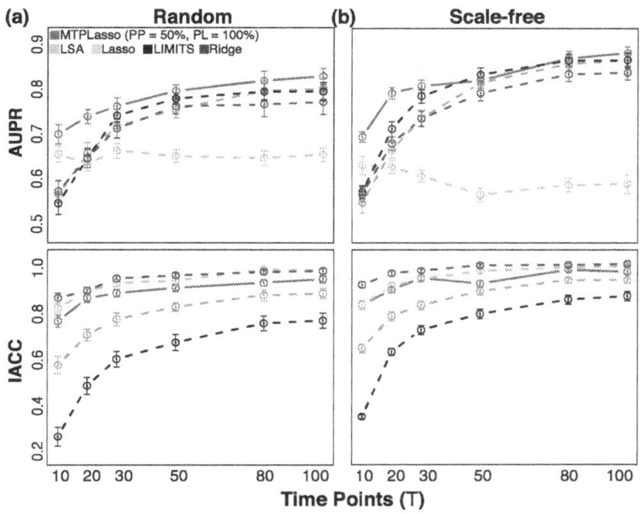

Figure 8: Performance evaluation on different lengths of time for (a) random and (b) scale-free graphs. When the length of time increases, all methods achieve better results for both AUPR and IACC, as expected. We observe that, however, at low length values, MTPLasso can still achieve AUPR = 0.7 and IACC = 0.8.

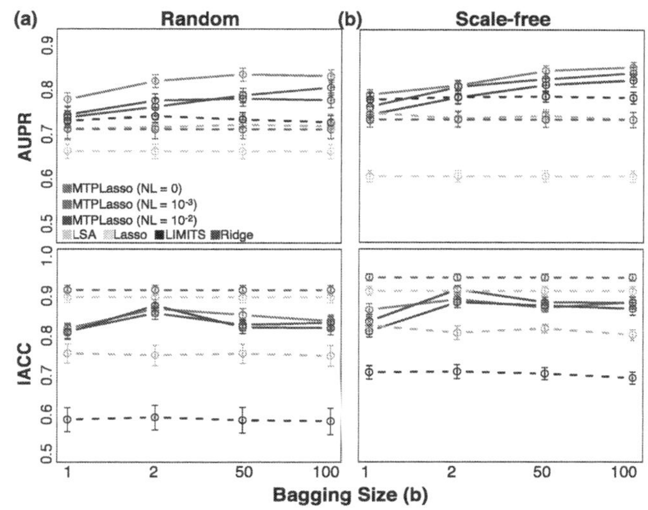

Figure 9: Performance evaluation on different bagging sizes for (a) random and (b) scale-free graphs. As it can be seen for both graphs, bagging can increase the performance and stabilize the inference results.

4.5 Number of Time Points

For a microbial network that contains p genera, the interaction matrix has up to p^2 free parameters. Thus, in general, we would need at least p^2 time points to infer the interactions from p genera. However, in microbial datasets, samples (T) are often less than number of genera (p). To examine the effect of different lengths of time, we vary the sample size from as small as $T = 10$, all the way up to $T = 100$. As we can see in Fig. 8, our proposed method still outperforms the other existing methods in terms of AUPR even at small sample sizes. As the sample size increases, MTPLasso can achieve up to AUPR = 0.8. Although ridge regression can more accurately predict the interaction types, the AUPR is much lower than MTPLasso; over all, MTPLasso can achieve high performances both in random and scale-free graphs.

4.6 Bagging Size

To evaluate the effect of bagging, we vary the bagging size (b), where $b = 1$ represents no bagging at all. As it can be seen in Fig. 9, for both random and scale-free graphs, bagging can increase AUPR with a jump from $b = 1$ to $b = 2$. However, for IACC, there is not much difference when we increase the bagging size; this shows that MTPLasso is quite robust in inferring the type of interaction.

5 EXPERIMENTS ON REAL DATA

To explore the applicability of our proposed framework, we utilize data from [8] to examine the interactions among genera. Acquisitions and pre-processing for genus-level abundance data are described in Appendix B. We utilize the microbial associations found by the HMP cross-sectional datasets as our prior information and set up a precision level = 50% (since it may still contain spurious information). In the end, we report the inferred interactions in the gut microbiomes of two individuals (i.e., MALE and FEMALE); the resulting *directed* interaction networks are shown in Fig. 10.

Based on the node degree, the genus-level interaction networks for individual MALE and FEMALE are dominated by *Escherichia* and *Prevotella*, respectively; these two genera are prevalent in human gut. Notably, *Prevotella* was proposed as one of the three main genera representing the human gut microbiome, namely enterotypes [4]. The number of beneficial and competitive interactions is found to be similar. All interactions found in both graphs in Fig. 10 (e.g., <*Escherichia, Prevotella*>) are inferred to be the same type (i.e., competitive interactions); this shows that MTPLasso is robust at inferring interaction types.

If we take a deeper look, we note that the interaction pair <*Prevotella, Alistipes*> found in individual MALE is classified as beneficial. Additionally, both *Prevotella* and *Alistipes* both have been found abundant in healthy subjects [18]; this may suggest that one of them may be beneficial to another. Another example lies in the competitive interaction pair <*Coprococcus, Roseburia*> found in individual FEMALE. A recent study [10] has shown that *Coprococcus* and *Roseburia* are important promoters for production of certain chemicals. Therefore, there may exist competition among these two genera in order to gain growth advantage over another.

Additionally, we notice that the dominant genera in both individuals are not the most abundant ones. For example, *Prevotella* has the highest node degree in individual MALE, which is only the fifth abundant species. On the contrary, the node degree of the most abundant genus *Faecalibacterium* is only two in the inferred interaction network; this may suggest that abundant genera do not necessary have more interaction with other genera. The key is the trend of interacting time-series that can determine the type and the strength of interactions among genera. Further experimental results are still needed to validate the interactions inferred by our proposed algorithm.

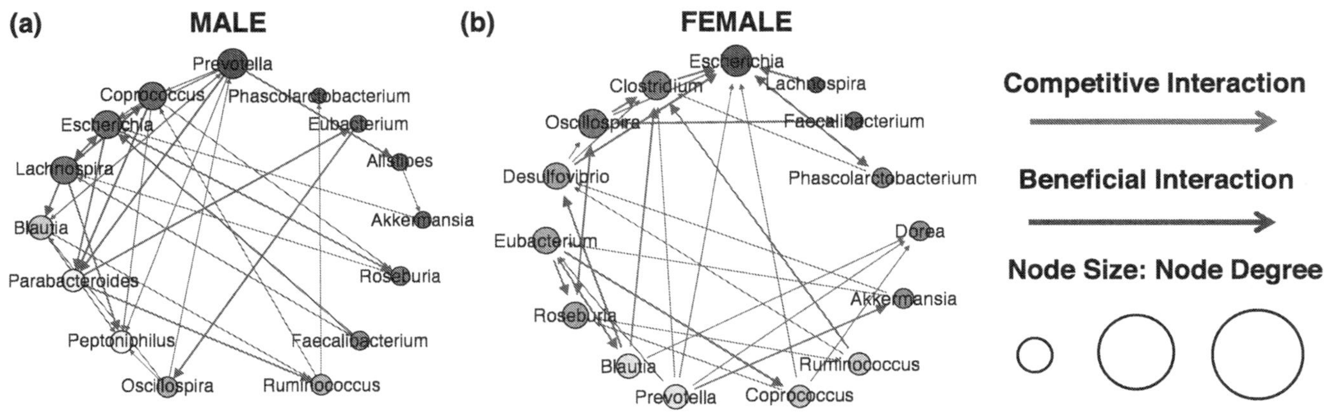

Figure 10: Interaction network visualization for highest degree nodes in the human gut of two individuals: (a) MALE and (b) FEMALE. Node size represents the relative node degree within the association network with counterclockwise layout. The red and blue edges represent competitive and beneficial interactions, respectively. Arrows represent the direction of the interaction.

6 DISCUSSION AND CONCLUSION

Advances of high-throughput sequencing techniques enable us to gather metagenomic sequencing data from different environment and human niches. The available high-throughput experimental data, however, are compositional and high-dimensional in nature. Inferring interactions among microbes and understanding their influence on the human body is an important step towards precision medicine.

Existing microbial interaction network inferring methods either requires the data of biomass or use greedy methods to obtain sparse estimation to overcome problems caused by high-dimensional data. However, all these prior approaches do *not* consider the information that can be obtained from the cross-sectional data and scientific literature to directly describe the associations among microbes and their co-occurrences, respectively.

By integrating multiple levels of biological information into the statistical models, we have shown that one can dramatically increase model's precision and recall rates, as well as interaction type classification accuracy. To the best of knowledge, this is the first work to propose an automated pipeline to infer the interactions on microbial data, show its feasibility, and measure performance metrics on both synthetic and real datasets.

We have also shown that our proposed algorithm *Microbial Time-series Prior Lasso (MTPLasso)* outperforms other existing methods (considered in this paper) in terms of AUPR when using synthetic data with different graph structures which simulate different levels of sparsity. We have also evaluated several different factors including different noise levels, sample sizes, and bagging sizes to demonstrate the applicability of our approach under different conditions; we have also suggested rough guidelines for requisite sample size for the real data for the given assumption of the underlying graph structures.

Embolden by the success of our proposed algorithm on synthetic data, we have applied MTPLasso to infer the genus-level interactions in the human gut of two individuals. Our analyses on real time-series data show that interactions found in both graphs are classified to be the same interaction type. Additionally, we found that *Prevotella* (which represents one of the enterotypes in human gut) is a high degree node of the interaction network. Although some of the inferred interactions have not yet been directly found in laboratory settings, our predictions may still suggest credible directions for possible interactions without exhaustively searching all interaction pairs.

Finally, the estimated microbial interaction networks on real datasets can be used to understand why and how various ecosystems evolve over time. By plugging in the inferred interactions into the dynamic models (such as Lotka-Volterra model), we can even quantify the effects of different types of perturbations from other microbes such as probiotics. Overall, MTPLasso shows promising results. We envision that our model can reveal the underlying dynamics of the microbial compositional data in often high-dimensional settings.

ACKNOWLEDGMENTS

This work was supported in part by the US National Science Foundation (NSF) under Grant CCF-1514206

REFERENCES

[1] J. Aitchison. 1986. *The Statistical Analysis of Compositional Data.* Chapman & Hall, Ltd., London, UK, UK.
[2] R. Albert and A.L. Barabási. 2002. Statistical mechanics of complex networks. *Reviews of modern physics* 74, January (2002).
[3] O.C. Aroniadis and L.J. Brandt. 2013. Fecal microbiota transplantation: past, present and future. *Current opinion in gastroenterology* 29, 1 (Jan. 2013), 79–84.
[4] M. Arumugam, J. Raes, and E. Pelletier et al. 2013. Enterotypes of the human gut microbiome. *Nature* 473, 7346 (2013), 174–180.
[5] A. Bashan, T.E. Gibson, and J. Friedman et al. 2016. Universality of human microbial dynamics. *Nature* 534, 7606 (2016), 259–62. arXiv:NIHMS150003
[6] L. Breiman. 1996. Bagging Predictors. *Machine Learning* 24, 421 (1996), 123–140.
[7] V. Bucci, B. Tzen, and N. Li et al. 2016. MDSINE: Microbial Dynamical Systems INference Engine for microbiome time-series analyses. *Genome Biology* 17, 1 (2016), 121.
[8] J.G. Caporaso, C.L. Lauber, and E.K. Costello et al. 2011. Moving pictures of the human microbiome. *Genome Biology* 12, 5 (2011), R50.
[9] I. Cho and M.J. Blaser. 2012. The human microbiome: at the interface of health and disease. 13, 4 (2012), 260–270.

[10] S.H. Duncan, A. Belenguer, and G. Holtrop et al. 2007. Reduced dietary intake of carbohydrates by obese subjects results in decreased concentrations of butyrate and butyrate-producing bacteria in feces. *Applied and Environmental Microbiology* 73, 4 (2007), 1073–1078.
[11] C.K. Fisher and P. Mehta. 2014. Identifying keystone species in the human gut microbiome from metagenomic timeseries using sparse linear regression. *PLoS ONE* 9, 7 (2014), 1–10. arXiv:1402.0511
[12] S. Freilich, A. Kreimer, and I. Meilijson et al. 2010. The large-scale organization of the bacterial network of ecological co-occurrence interactions. *Nucleic acids research* 38, 12 (July 2010), 3857–68.
[13] J. Friedman and E.J. Alm. 2012. Inferring correlation networks from genomic survey data. *PLoS computational biology* 8, 9 (Jan. 2012), e1002687.
[14] J. Friedman, T. Hastie, and R. Tibshirani. 2008. Sparse inverse covariance estimation with the graphical lasso. *Biostatistics* (2008), 1–14.
[15] A. Greenfield, C. Hafemeister, and R. Bonneau. 2013. Robust data-driven incorporation of prior knowledge into the inference of dynamic regulatory networks. *Bioinformatics* 29, 8 (2013), 1060–1067.
[16] Y. Hochberg. 1988. A sharper bonferroni procedure for multiple tests of significance. (1988), 800–802 pages.
[17] J. Hofbauer, V. Hutson, and W. Jansen. 1987. Coexistence for systems governed by difference equations of Lotka-Volterra type. *Journal of Mathematical Biology* 25, 5 (1987), 553–570.
[18] W. Jiang, N. Wu, and X. Wang et al. 2015. Dysbiosis gut microbiota associated with inflammation and impaired mucosal immune function in intestine of humans with non-alcoholic fatty liver disease. *Scientific reports* 5 (2015), 8096.
[19] J. Kuczynski and J. Stombaugh. 2012. Using QIIME to analyze 16S rRNA gene sequences from Microbial Communities. *Current Protocols in Bioinformatics* (2012), 1–28.
[20] Z.D. Kurtz, C.L. Müller, and E.R. Miraldi et al. 2015. Sparse and compositionally robust inference of microbial ecological networks. *PLoS Computational Biology* (2015), 1–25.
[21] Y. Li and S.A. Jackson. 2015. Gene network reconstruction by integration of prior biological knowledge. *G3: Genes— Genomes— Genetics* 5, 6 (March 2015), 1075–9.
[22] Y.F. Lu and D.B. Goldstein. 2014. Personalized medicine and human genetic diversity. *Cold Spring Harbor Perspectives in Medicine* (2014), 1–12.
[23] S. Marino, N.T. Baxter, and G.B. Huffnagle et al. 2014. Mathematical modeling of primary succession of murine intestinal microbiota. *Proceedings of the National Academy of Sciences of the United States of America* 111, 1 (Jan. 2014), 439–44.
[24] K.J. Pflughoeft and J. Versalovic. 2012. Human microbiome in health and disease. *Annual review of pathology* 7, December 2011 (2012), 99–122.
[25] P.D. Schloss, S.L. Westcott, and T. Ryabin. 2009. Introducing mothur: open-source, platform-independent, community-supported software for describing and comparing microbial communities. *Applied and environmental microbiology* 75, 23 (Dec. 2009), 7537–41.
[26] D. Sims, I. Sudbery, and N.E. Ilott. 2014. Sequencing depth and coverage: key considerations in genomic analyses. *Nature reviews. Genetics* 15, 2 (Feb. 2014), 121–32.
[27] R.R. Stein, V. Bucci, and N.C. Toussaint et al. 2013. Ecological Modeling from Time-Series Inference: Insight into Dynamics and Stability of Intestinal Microbiota. *PLoS Computational Biology* 9, 12 (2013), 31–36.
[28] P.J. Turnbaugh, R.E. Ley, and M. Hamady et al. 2007. The human microbiome project: exploring the microbial part of ourselves in a changing world. *Nature* 449, 7164 (2007), 804–810.
[29] Z. Wang, W. Xu, and F.A.S. Lucas et al. 2013. Incorporating prior knowledge into Gene Network Study. *Bioinformatics* 29, 20 (2013), 2633–2640.
[30] T. Zhao, H. Liu, and K. Roeder. 2012. The huge package for high-dimensional undirected graph estimation in R. *Journal of Machine Learning Research* 13 (2012), 1059–1062.

A SYNTHETIC DATA GENERATION

A.1 Microbial Association Network

Microbial association network consists of p nodes and e edges where each node represents a microbe and each edge represents a pairwise associations between microbes. To evaluate the performance of our model to recover different network structures, we consider five different graph structures (Fig. 3) as discussed in [30] with different precision matrices Ω defined as follows:

- Random Graph: Each pair of off-diagonal elements are set to non-zero with probability $\frac{3}{p}$ which results in about $e = \frac{3}{2}(p-1)$ edges in the graph.
- Hub Graph: Nodes are randomly partitioned into g groups and within each groups, nodes are connected to the center node which result in $e = p - g$ edges in the graph.
- Cluster Graph: Nodes are randomly partitioned into g groups and within each group, nodes are connected with probability Pr which result in $e = p(\frac{p}{g-1})(\frac{Pr}{2})$ edges in the graph.
- Band Graph: Each adjacent pair of off-diagonal elements (i.e., node i and j) are connected if $1 \le |i-j| \le b$ (b is the bandwidth) which result in $e = (2p-1-b)\frac{b}{2}$ edges in the graph. We use $b = 1$ to construct the band graph.
- Scale-free Graph: We generate the graph by using Barabasi-Albert algorithm [2]. The initial graph has two connected nodes and each new node is connected to only one node in the existing graph with the probability proportional to the degree of the each node in the existing graph. It results in $e = p$ edges in the graph.

A.2 Microbiome Time-series Generation

Given the association network, we randomly generate the interaction matrix ($\boldsymbol{\beta}$). To ensure the dynamical system that has stable internal equilibriums, we set up the intrinsic growth rate ($\boldsymbol{\alpha}$) to be within [0.1, 0.3]. For the self-interacting parameters (i.e., β_{ii}), we draw from a uniform distribution over the interval [-0.1, -0.3]. The off-diagonal entries β_{ij} are also draw from uniform distribution over the interval [-0.2, 0.2] except 0. Note that the generated interaction matrix is asymmetric and the generated microbiome abundance at any given time should be greater than zero.

B DATA PREPROCESSING

We consider high-throughput comparative metagenomics data obtained from the next-generation sequencing (NGS) platforms. More specifically, cross-sectional data is obtained from the human microbiome project (HMP) that offers a curated collection of 16S rRNA sequences of microorganisms associated with the human body. The time-series dataset is obtained from [8] via preprocessing as relative abundances instead of raw sequencing data.

For the cross-sectional data, we consider the high-quality sequencing reads in 16S variable regions 3-5 (V35) of HMP healthy individuals from Phase one production study (May 1, 2010). The taxonomy classification of the 16S rRNA are performed using either mothur (HMMCP) (http://hmpdacc.org/HMMCP/) [25] or QIIME (HMQCP) (http://hmpdacc.org/HMQCP/) [19] pipelines. We filter out genera that appear less than 10% of total samples and then apply inference method describe in section 3.5.2 to infer the microbial association networks.

For the time-series dataset which consists of approximately half and one year of daily samples (i.e., daily resolution) for individual MALE and FEMALE, respectively (see Fig. 2). The total number of different genera found for both MALE and FEMALE is around 200. We first filter out genera that are less than 1% in terms of the total abundance count of the top genus; this resulting in around 15 genera of interest. Next, at any given time point t, the abundances of genus are normalized and subjected to unit sum constraint (i.e., $\sum_{i=1}^{p} x_i(t) = 1$).

Secure Cloud Computing for Pairwise Sequence Alignment

Sergio Salinas
Department of Electrical Engineering and Computer Science
Wichita State University
salinas@cs.wichita.edu

Pan Li
Department of Electrical Engineering and Computer Science
Case Western Reserve University
lipan@case.edu

ABSTRACT

Today's massive amount of biological sequence data has the potential to rapidly advance our understanding of life's processes. However, since analyzing biological sequences is a very expensive computing task, users face a formidable challenge in trying to analyze these data on their own. Cloud computing offers access to a large amount of computing resources in an on-demand and pay-per-use fashion, which is a practical way for people to analyze these huge data sets. However, many people are still reluctant to outsource biological sequences to the cloud because they contain sensitive information that should be kept secret for ethical, security, and legal reasons. One of the most fundamental and frequently used computational tools for biological sequence analysis is pairwise sequence alignment (PSA). Previous works for securely solving PSAs at the cloud suffer from poor scalability, i.e., they are unable to exploit the cloud's infrastructure to solve PSAs in parallel because resource-limited users need to be constantly involved in the computations. In this paper, we develop a secure outsourcing algorithm that allows users to solve an arbitrary number of PSAs in parallel at the cloud. Compared with previous works, our algorithm can reduce computing time of a large number of PSAs by more than 50% with as few as 5 computing nodes at the cloud.

1 INTRODUCTION

The exponentially growing amount of biological sequence data holds the potential to rapidly advance scientific knowledge [10, 21]. To efficiently and economically analyze these large-scale data sets, resource-limited users can choose to employ cloud computing. In this computing paradigm, users outsource their computing tasks to a cloud server [19], which contains a large amount of computing resources and offers them on an on-demand and pay-per-use basis [18].

Unfortunately, many people are unwilling to outsource their data to the cloud due to privacy concerns [20]. Specifically, biological sequences are very sensitive and should be kept secret from the cloud for ethical, security, and legal reasons [17]. For example, analyzing plant genetic data at the cloud could disclose an agricultural company's intellectual property. Moreover, since biological sequences often belong to different parties, it is difficult for researchers to perform collaborative analyses at the cloud without compromising the sequence owners' privacy. For instance, to enable collaboratively drug discovery at the cloud, pharmaceutical companies would need to share their sequences, compromising their intellectual property[15]. Therefore, to enable scientists and engineers to collaboratively analyze biological sequences at the cloud, it is important to design secure outsourcing tools that preserve data privacy.

One of the most fundamental mathematical problems in biological sequence analysis is pairwise-sequence alignment (PSA), i.e., finding the least-cost set of edit operations, such as insertion, deletion, and substitution, that transform a sequence into another one. For example, in phylogenetics, scientists compute PSAs to obtain genetic trees that reveal organisms evolutionary relationships; and pharmaceutical companies identify protein functionality for drug discovery by solving many PSAs.

Some existing works on secure outsourcing of large-scale computations may potentially be used to collaboratively solve PSAs at the cloud. In particular, Gennaro et al. [9] propose fully homomorphic encryption (FHE), which allows secure outsourcing of a function to the cloud. Although FHE offers a theoretical privacy guarantee, it requires the user to perform computationally expensive operations and forces the cloud to carry out operations on ciphertexts, which adds significant overhead to already expensive computations at the cloud. Researchers have proposed improvements to the computing time of FHE, e.g., [7], but its overhead remains impractically large for users to analyze large-scale data sets. To avoid the computational complexity introduced by FHE, Wang et al. [22] propose to privately outsource a linear program, which can be used to solve a PSA, by applying a linear algebra-based transformation to the objective and constraints. However, this transformation requires prohibitively expensive matrix multiplications, and results in an optimization problem that prevents users from employing the Simplex algorithm, which is the most efficient solution method for linear programs such as the ones that arise when solving PSAs.

There are some works based on secure multi-party computations (SMC) that allow two users, each holding a private sequence, to compute a PSA by performing local computations and exchanging some data. In the work by Atallah et al. [1], users first protect their privacy with partially homomorphic encryption and then collaborate with each other. Jha et al. [13] further reduce computing times by designing an algorithm where the users first create a custom garbled circuit and then collaboratively evaluate it. Huang et al. [12] achieve further improvements on garbled circuit evaluation times by employing optimizations such as pipelined circuit

Permission to make digital or hard copies of all or part of this work for personal or classroom use is granted without fee provided that copies are not made or distributed for profit or commercial advantage and that copies bear this notice and the full citation on the first page. Copyrights for components of this work owned by others than the author(s) must be honored. Abstracting with credit is permitted. To copy otherwise, or republish, to post on servers or to redistribute to lists, requires prior specific permission and/or a fee. Request permissions from permissions@acm.org.
ACM-BCB '17, August 20-23, 2017, Boston, MA, USA.
© 2017 Copyright held by the owner/author(s). Publication rights licensed to ACM.
978-1-4503-4722-8/17/08...$15.00
DOI: http://dx.doi.org/10.1145/3107411.3107477

execution, and a reduced number of circuit gates. Although SMC-based approaches allow users to collaboratively solve a PSA within a practical amount of time, their performance depends on the quality of the communication link between the users, and it is unclear how they can be applied to securely solve the computation of a two-user PSA at the cloud.

More importantly, we notice that SMC-approaches share a common serious problem, i.e., users actively participate during the solution of the PSA. The need for users to be online during PSA computations significantly limits the scalability of SMC-approaches, and thus are impractical for the analysis of large-scale biological sequence data sets at the cloud. Specifically, since users only have modest computing resources, they are unable to participate in the solution of more than a few PSAs at a time. Therefore, any practical algorithm for large-scale biological sequence analysis should be parallel and scalable, i.e., the cloud should be able to solve an arbitrary number of PSAs in parallel with minimal computing resources, and without having to continuously interact with the users.

In this paper, we develop a practical and efficient secure outsourcing algorithm that allows two users, each holding a private sequence, to collaboratively solve a large amount of PSAs in parallel at the cloud. Specifically, the users protect their data privacy by concealing its sequences with bilinear maps, which is a cryptographic technique that can be efficiently applied by the users. Then, based on the encrypted sequences, the cloud securely formulates a linear program that is equivalent to the user's PSA. Based on the Simplex algorithm, the cloud solves the linear program, and returns the solution to the users, who efficiently retrieve the optimal solution to the original PSA. To preserve the users' privacy, our algorithm restricts the cloud to operate only on the encrypted sequences and randomized values, rather than on the original PSA's values.

The proposed algorithm requires the users to perform computations with only $O(m)$ and $O(n)$ complexity, which is lower than the complexity of solving a PSA, i.e., $O(mn)$, where m and n are the users' sequence lengths. Furthermore, the proposed algorithm only needs one round of communication between the users and the cloud, which is optimal. We implement the user part of the algorithm on a general purpose PC, and the cloud part on the AWS Elastic Compute Cloud (EC2). Compared to previous works, our algorithm can reduce computing time of a large number of PSAs by more than 50% with as few as 5 computing nodes at the cloud.

2 PROBLEM FORMULATION

System Architecture. We consider an asymmetric three-party system architecture formed by two resource-limited users, i.e., Alice and Bob, and a resource-rich cloud server. We show this architecture in Fig. 1. Alice and Bob each hold a character sequence, i.e., $\mathbf{a} = \{a_1, a_2, \ldots, a_{n-1}\}$ and $\mathbf{b} = \{b_1, b_2, \ldots, b_{m-1}\}$, respectively, and intend to calculate the similarity between their sequences by solving a pairwise sequence alignment (PSA). The elements in a and b are taken from a character alphabet $\mathcal{H} = \{h_1, h_2, \ldots, h_p\}$. Let the sequence similarity be defined as the least-cost set of edit operations, such as insertion, deletion, and substitution, needed to transform $\mathbf{x} = \{- \mid \mathbf{a}\}$ into $\mathbf{y} = \{- \mid \mathbf{b}\}$, where $-$ is the null character. Then, the PSA is as follows [8]:

$$\min_{\mathcal{D}} \sum_{[x'_i, y'_j] \in \mathcal{D}} d([x'_i, y'_j]) \tag{1}$$

where the minimum is taken over all edit operation sets $\mathcal{D}$ that transform $\mathbf{x}$ into $\mathbf{y}$, and $[x'_i, y'_j]$ denotes an edit operation based on the characters x'_i and y'_j, and d is the edit operation cost function. If $[x'_i, y'_j]$ denotes a substitution operation, i.e., when $[x'_i, y'_j] = [x_i, y_j]$, then function d outputs a value of matrix $\mathbf{G} \in \mathbb{Z}^{p \times p}$ (e.g., the BLOSUM50 matrix), which stores the substitution cost for pairs of characters in $\mathcal{H}$. In particular, if $[x_i, y_j] = [h_k, h_l]$, then $d([x'_i, y'_j]) = g_{k,l}$, which is the element in the kth row and lth column of G. We denote the substitution costs by $w_{sub}([x'_i, y'_j])$. Further, if $[x'_i, y'_j]$ denotes a deletion or insertion operation, i.e., $[x'_i, y'_j] = [x_i, -]$ or $[x'_i, y'_j] = [-, y_j]$, then d outputs w_{del} or w_{ins}, which are the deletion and insertion costs, respectively.

Due to the large amount of biological sequences, in many applications, Alice and Bob need to collaborate to compute (1) repeatedly many times, and hence, they are unable to solve the PSAs by themselves in a feasible amount of time. For example, in phylogenetic analysis, scientists need to compute a very large amount of PSAs to classify biological sequences, e.g., $\approx 500,000$ PSAs are needed to explore the phylogenetic relationships between viruses within a family [6, 16, 23]. Thus, to solve the PSAs, Alice and Bob need to outsource the most computationally expensive tasks to the cloud.

Threat Model. We consider a semi-honest threat model for all parties in the system, i.e., Alice, Bob, and the cloud. In particular, the cloud attempts to learn Alice's and Bob's private information from their outsourced sequences and from the results of its own computations. Moreover, both Alice and Bob will attempt to extract each others' private information from the results that they receive from the cloud. Therefore, to securely outsource the computation of a PSA problem, the data that Alice and Bob outsource to the cloud should be provably secure [14]. We note that the semi-honest model is a standard threat model for secure computations [11], and it is consistent with previous works in the area of secure multiparty PSA computations, i.e., [12, 13].

Bilinear Map. In our proposed secure PSA outsourcing algorithm, we leverage the properties of pairing-based cryptography (PBC) to conceal Alice and Bob's private sequences. In particular, let $\mathbb{G}_1$ and $\mathbb{G}_2$ be cyclic multiplicative groups of the same prime order q. An admissible bilinear pairing $e : \mathbb{G}_1 \times \mathbb{G}_1 \rightarrow \mathbb{G}_2$ is a map with the following property [5]: $e(u^a, v^b) = e(u, v)^{ab}$, for any $u, v \in \mathbb{G}_1$, and $a, b \in \mathbb{Z}_q$, where $\mathbb{Z}_q$ denotes the integers modulo q. The bilinearity property implies that for any $u_1, u_2 \in \mathbb{G}_1$, $e(u_1 \cdot u_2, v) = e(u_1, v) \cdot e(u_2, v)$. Besides, a bilinear map satisfies the non-degeneracy and computability properties. Such an admissible bilinear pairing $e : \mathbb{G}_1 \times \mathbb{G}_1 \rightarrow \mathbb{G}_2$ can be implemented by the modified Weil/Tate pairings.

3 PRIVACY-PRESERVING TRANSFORMATIONS

To securely upload a PSA to the cloud, Alice and Bob first secure their private information by performing certain computations. In

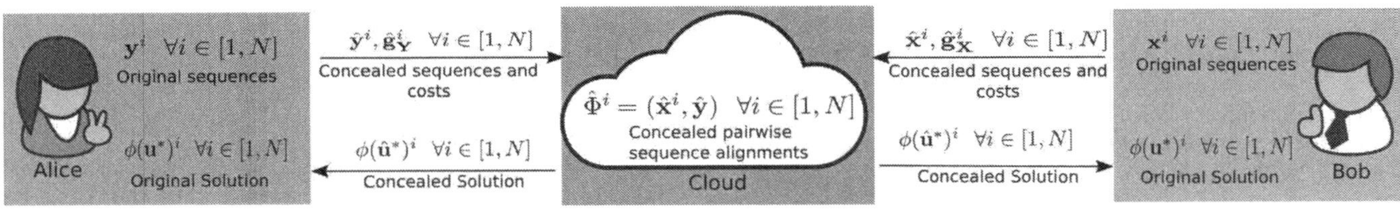

Figure 1: A secure architecture for secure outsourcing of pairwise sequence alignment

this section, we describe an efficient method to conceal a biological sequence and a method to securely obtain a PSA's substitution costs from two concealed sequences. This method can be used by the cloud to securely find the similarity between the sequences.

Privacy-Preserving Sequence Transformation. To conceal its private sequence, a user, e.g., Alice or Bob, first replaces its sequence's characters with integers, and then conceals them through modular multiplications with random numbers. Specifically, let $\mathbf{s} = [s_1, s_2, \ldots, s_m]$ be a private sequence with characters taken from an alphabet $\mathcal{T} = \{t_1, t_2, \ldots, t_p\}$. Then, the user conceals $\mathbf{s}$ as follows:

$$\hat{\mathbf{s}} = \mathbf{V_s}\bar{\mathbf{s}}. \tag{2}$$

The elements of vector $\bar{\mathbf{s}} = [\mathcal{M}(s_1), \mathcal{M}(s_2), \ldots, \mathcal{M}(s_m)]$ are given by a function $\mathcal{M} : \mathcal{T} \to \mathbb{G}_1$ that uniquely maps characters in $\mathcal{T}$ to integers in the multiplicative cyclic group $\mathbb{G}_1$ of prime order q. The matrix $\mathbf{V_s} \in \mathbb{G}_1^{m \times m}$ is diagonal with non-zero elements given by the vector $\mathbf{v_s} = [h^{\sigma_1}, \ldots, h^{\sigma_m}]$, where h is a generator of $\mathbb{G}_1$, and σ_i is a randomly chosen element from the set of integers less than q, which we denote by $\mathbb{Z}_q$ (for all $i \in [1, m]$).

Consequently, the elements of $\hat{\mathbf{s}}$ in (2) are given by $\hat{s}_i = \bar{s}_i h^{\sigma_i} \mod q$ (for all $i \in [1, m]$), where q is a large prime number. Besides, the user calculates a vector of concealed random numbers $\hat{\mathbf{v}}_\mathbf{s} = [e(h, h)^{\nu_1}, \ldots, e(h, h)^{\nu_m}]$, where $\nu_i = q - \sigma_i \mod q$, and $e(\cdot, \cdot)$ is the bilinear map defined in Section 2.

Privacy-Preserving Substitution Cost Transformation. To allow the cloud to securely formulate the substitution costs in the PSA based on the concealed sequences, Alice and Bob need to upload a concealed version of the substitution costs to the cloud.

Specifically, to find integers that represent all possible character pairs in alphabet $\mathcal{T}$, Alice builds a matrix $\mathbf{Z} \in \mathbb{G}_2^{p \times p}$ with elements given by $z_{i,j} = e(\bar{t}_i \cdot \bar{t}_j, h)$ (for all $i, j \in [1, p]$), where h is a generator of $\mathbb{G}_1$, $\bar{t}_i$ and $\bar{t}_j$ are the integer representations of t_i and t_j given by $\mathcal{M}$ as described in (2), respectively, and e is the bilinear map described in Section 2. Besides, we denote a function that maps elements in $\mathbf{Z}$ to substitution costs in G, i.e., $\psi(z_{i,j}) = g_{i,j} = w_{sub}([t_i, t_j])$ (for all $i, j \in [1, p]$).

Alice then forms buckets of elements $z_{i,j}$'s that are mapped by ψ to the same substitution cost in G, that is, $\mathcal{B}_l = \{z_{i,j} \mid \psi(z_{i,j}) = g'_l\}$ for all $l \in [1, p']$, where g'_l is the lth unique substitution cost in G, and p' is the total number of unique substitution costs. We denote a second function $\tilde{\psi}$ that maps $z_{i,j}$ to its corresponding bucket's index l.

Now, after Alice uploads the concealed sequence $\hat{\mathbf{s}} \in \mathbb{G}_1^{m \times 1}$ to the cloud as described in Section 3, she uploads the set of concealed costs for every element s_i which is given by

$$\hat{\mathbf{g}}_{s_i} = \beta^{\frac{1}{2}} \gamma_{s_i} \mathbf{g}'^{\frac{1}{2}} \tag{3}$$

for all $i \in [1, m]$, where $\mathbf{g}'$ is the vector of unique substitution costs in G, and β and γ_{s_i} are random positive integers in $\mathbb{Z}$. Alice uploads $\hat{\mathbf{g}}_{s_i}$ (for all $i \in [1, m]$) to the cloud.

Similarly, Bob can follow the same procedure to find its concealed sequence, and upload his concealed substitution costs, i.e,. $\hat{\mathbf{g}}_{f_i} = \beta^{\frac{1}{2}} \gamma_{f_i} \mathbf{g}'^{\frac{1}{2}}$, where $\mathbf{f}$ is Bob's private sequence. In Section 5, we explain how the cloud can employ the outsourced sequences, and the results of (3) to find the PSA's concealed substitution costs.

Note that the size of vectors $\hat{\mathbf{g}}_{s_i}$ is determined by the number of unique costs p'. In practice, this quantity is small, e.g., 18 for the BLOSUM50 matrix, and thus it only adds a small constant overhead to the user's memory and communication complexities.

4 A LINEAR PROGRAM FOR PAIRWISE SEQUENCE ALIGNMENT

In this section, we reformulate the PSA in (1) as a linear program (LP), i.e., an optimization problem with a linear objective, and affine constraints, that can be efficiently solved by the cloud using the Simplex algorithm. We also show that the solution to the PSA is readily available from the solution of the LP.

We first express (1) as a shortest-path problem on a directed acyclic graph (DAG) $\mathcal{G} = \{\mathcal{V}, \mathcal{E}\}$, where the node set $\mathcal{V}$ and edge set $\mathcal{E}$ are based on the cost of edit operations between sequences $\mathbf{x}$ and $\mathbf{y}$. Specifically, we first store the cost of substituting elements in $\mathbf{x}$ for elements in $\mathbf{y}$ in a matrix $\mathrm{T} \in \mathbb{Z}^{m \times n}$ as follows:

$$t_{i,j} = w_{sub}([x_i, y_j]) \tag{4}$$

for all $i \in [1, m]$ and $j \in [1, n]$, where $w_{sub}(\cdot)$ is as defined in Section 2.

We then form the node set $\mathcal{V}$ by adding a node for each element in T, that is, $\mathcal{V} = \{v_p \mid p = i + m(j-1) \; \forall i \in [1, m], \; \forall j \in [1, n]\}$, where the node v_p corresponds to the element $t_{i,j}$. To form the edge set $\mathcal{E}$, we arrange $\mathcal{V}$'s nodes on a two-dimensional grid according to their positions in T, and add a directed edge from each node to its bottom, right, and bottom-right neighbors, that is, $\mathcal{E} = \mathcal{E}_{del} \cup \mathcal{E}_{ins} \cup \mathcal{E}_{sub}$, where $\mathcal{E}_{del} = \{(v_p, v_q) \mid q = p+1\}$, $\mathcal{E}_{ins} = \{(v_p, v_q) \mid q = p+m\}$, $\mathcal{E}_{sub} = \{(v_p, v_q) \mid q = p+m+1\}$, and (v_p, v_q) is an ordered pair denoting a directed edge from start node v_p to end node v_q.

The weights for edges corresponding to substitutions are given by the elements of T, i.e., $w_l = t_{\pi(v_l)}$, if $e_l \in \mathcal{E}_{sub}$, where e_l is the lth element of $\mathcal{E}$, and v_l is e_l's end node. The function $\pi(v_l)$ returns v_l's two-dimensional index in T, i.e., $\pi(v_l) = (i, j)$, where $i = (l - 1 \mod m) + 1$, and $j = \lceil l/m \rceil$. Weights for edges corresponding to deletion and insertion operations are given by w_{del}, if $e_l \in \mathcal{E}_{del}$ and by w_{ins}, if $e_l \in \mathcal{E}_{ins}$, where w_{del} and w_{ins} are the deletion and insertion costs defined in Section 2, respectively.

Consequently, the shortest-path between v_1 and v_{mn} on $\mathcal{G}$ can be defined by an integer LP as follows:

$$\min_{\mathbf{z}} \phi(\mathbf{z}) = \mathbf{w}^T \mathbf{z} \text{ subject to } \mathbf{A}\mathbf{z} = \mathbf{b},\ \mathbf{z} \geq 0,\ \mathbf{z} \in \mathbb{Z}, \tag{5}$$

where $\mathbf{z} \in \mathbb{Z}^{|\mathcal{E}|}$ is the optimization variable. We form the node-edge incidence matrix $\mathbf{A} \in \mathbb{Z}^{|\mathcal{V}|\times|\mathcal{E}|}$ by placing $a_{i,l} = 1$ if node i is a start node of edge e_l, and $a_{i,l} = -1$, if node i is the end node of e_l. The rest of the elements are set to zero. We set the element that corresponds to the source node in the vector $\mathbf{b} \in \mathbb{Z}^{|\mathcal{V}|}$ equal to 1, i.e., $b_1 = 1$, and the element that corresponds to the destination node equal to -1, that is, $b_{mn} = -1$. We denote the solution of (5) by $\mathbf{z}^*$. Note that due to the particular definitions of $\mathbf{A}$, $\mathbf{b}$, and $\mathbf{c}$, the elements of $\mathbf{z}$ can only take binary integer values, i.e,. $\{0, 1\}$, even though $\mathbf{z}$ is constrained as a non-negative integer in (5).

Since the shortest-path between v_1 and v_{mn} on $\mathcal{G}$ can be interpreted as the least-cost set of edit operations that transforms $\mathbf{x}$ into $\mathbf{y}$, the solution to (1) based on $\mathbf{z}^*$ is given by: $\mathcal{D}^* = \{[x'_i, y'_j] \mid z^*_l > 0 \wedge \pi(v_l) = (i, j)\}$, where $[x'_i, y'_j]$ has a one-to-one mapping to a deletion, insertion, or substitution operation according to whether edge e_l belongs to $\mathcal{E}_{del}, \mathcal{E}_{ins}$ or $\mathcal{E}_{sub}$, respectively.

A Relaxed Optimization Problem for PSA. In general, integer LPs such as (5) are very difficult to solve because they are NP-hard. However, since (5) is defined by integers, i.e., $\mathbf{A}$, $\mathbf{b}$, and $\mathbf{c}$ all have integer values, we can relax (5) to form a continuous LP that can be efficiently solved by the Simplex algorithm in polynomial time, and yields the solution to (5). Specifically, by removing the integrality constraint in (5), we get the following continuous LP, i.e.,

$$\min_{\mathbf{u}} \phi(\mathbf{u}) = \mathbf{w}^T \mathbf{u} \text{ subject to } \mathbf{A}\mathbf{u} = \mathbf{b},\ \mathbf{u} \geq 0, \tag{6}$$

where $\mathbf{u}$ is the optimization variable. We denote the optimal solution of the relaxed problem by $\mathbf{u}^*$.

Since the values in $\mathbf{A}$, $\mathbf{w}$ and $\mathbf{b}$ in the relaxed problem in (6) are all integers, the Simplex algorithm's computations result in integer values, including the solution $\mathbf{u}^*$ [3]. Therefore, the optimal solution of the LP in (6) found by the Simplex algorithm, is also the optimal solution of the integer LP in (5), and ultimately to the PSA in (1). In the following, we describe how the cloud can use the Simplex algorithm to solve a secure version of (6).

5 SECURE OUTSOURCING OF PAIRWISE SEQUENCE ALIGNMENT

In this section, we describe our secure PSA solver (SPSA), which efficiently and securely solves the PSA in (1) in parallel at the cloud. Specifically, Alice and Bob conceal their private sequences and substitution cost matrix with the transformations in Section 3, and collaborate with the cloud to securely formulate the LP in (6). Then, by applying the Simplex algorithm, the cloud solves the secure LP and returns the results to Alice and Bob, who efficiently find the solution to the original PSA.

Secure Computation of the Similarity Matrix. To securely outsource the computation of the similarity matrix T in Section 4, Alice and Bob conceal sequences $\mathbf{y}$ and $\mathbf{x}$ in (1), respectively, compute the secure substitution costs, and then the cloud employs these outsourced data to securely find the edit operation costs. In particular, Alice and Bob conceal their sequences as follows: $\hat{\mathbf{y}} = \mathbf{V}_{\mathbf{y}}\bar{\mathbf{y}}$, $\hat{\mathbf{x}} = \mathbf{V}_{\mathbf{x}}\bar{\mathbf{x}}$, where $\mathbf{V}_{\mathbf{y}}$ and $\mathbf{V}_{\mathbf{x}}$ are computed as in (2), and $\bar{\mathbf{y}} \in \mathbb{G}_1^{m\times 1}$, and $\bar{\mathbf{x}} \in \mathbb{G}_1^{n\times 1}$ are the integer representations of $\mathbf{x}$ and $\mathbf{y}$ as described in Section 3, respectively. In this step, Alice and Bob also find the vectors of concealed random numbers $\hat{\mathbf{v}}_{\mathbf{y}}$ and $\hat{\mathbf{v}}_{\mathbf{x}}$.

Then, Alice forms the buckets $\mathcal{B}_i$ for every unique substitution cost as in Section 3, and securely shares them with Bob using public key cryptography techniques, e.g., RSA cryptosystem. Similarly, Alice and Bob generate the random numbers α and β, respectively, and securely share them with each other.

Next, Alice and Bob generate their concealed cost vectors for $\mathbf{x}$ and $\mathbf{y}$, respectively, that is, $\hat{\mathbf{g}}_{y_i} = \beta^{\frac{1}{2}}\gamma_{y_i}\mathbf{g}'^{\frac{1}{2}}$, $\hat{\mathbf{g}}_{x_j} = \beta^{\frac{1}{2}}\gamma_{x_j}\mathbf{g}'^{\frac{1}{2}}$ (for all $i \in [1, m]$ and $j \in [1, n]$), where γ_{y_i} and γ_{x_j} are computed as in (3). We denote the vectors of random numbers used to conceal the substitution costs by $\boldsymbol{\gamma}_{\mathbf{y}}$ and $\boldsymbol{\gamma}_{\mathbf{x}}$, respectively. Alice and Bob keep $\boldsymbol{\gamma}_{\mathbf{y}}, \boldsymbol{\gamma}_{\mathbf{x}}, \beta$, and α secret.

Alice also conceals the insertion and deletion operation costs as follows: $\hat{w}_{ins} = \beta\gamma_{ins}w_{ins}$, $\hat{w}_{del} = \beta\gamma_{del}w_{del}$, where $\gamma_{ins} \in \mathbb{Z}$ and $\gamma_{del} \in \mathbb{Z}$ are random positive numbers. Besides, both Alice and Bob conceal their respective random numbers, i.e., $\hat{\boldsymbol{\gamma}}_{\mathbf{y}} = \alpha^{\frac{1}{2}}\boldsymbol{\gamma}_{\mathbf{y}}$, $\hat{\boldsymbol{\gamma}}_{\mathbf{x}} = \alpha^{\frac{1}{2}}\boldsymbol{\gamma}_{\mathbf{x}}$, $\hat{\gamma}_\alpha = \alpha\gamma_\alpha$, $\hat{\gamma}_{ins} = \alpha\gamma_{ins}$, $\hat{\gamma}_{del} = \alpha\gamma_{del}$. Once Alice completes her computations, she uploads $\hat{\mathbf{y}}$, $\hat{\mathbf{g}}_{y_i}$ (for all $i \in [1, m]$), $\hat{w}_{ins}, \hat{w}_{del}, \hat{\boldsymbol{\gamma}}_{\mathbf{y}}, \hat{\gamma}_\alpha, \hat{\gamma}_{ins} = \alpha\gamma_{ins}, \hat{\gamma}_{del} = \alpha\gamma_{del}$, and the buckets $\mathcal{B}_l$ (for all $l \in [1, p']$). Similarly, Bob uploads $\hat{\mathbf{x}}$, $\hat{\mathbf{g}}_{x_j}$ (for all $j \in [1, n]$), and $\hat{\boldsymbol{\gamma}}_{\mathbf{x}}$.

After receiving the concealed values, the cloud securely finds the elements of the similarity matrix in (4) by first computing the product of bilinear mappings between characters in $\hat{\mathbf{x}}$ and $\hat{\mathbf{y}}$, and then mapping them to their corresponding buckets. In particular, the cloud first forms the matrix $\bar{\mathbf{T}} \in \mathbb{G}_2^{m\times n}$ with values defined by: $\bar{t}_{i,j} = e(\hat{y}_i\hat{x}_j, h) \cdot \hat{v}_{y_i} \cdot \hat{v}_{x_j}$. We show the correctness of $\bar{t}_{i,j}$ as follows:

$$\begin{aligned}
\bar{t}_{i,j} &= e(\hat{y}_i\hat{x}_j, h) \cdot \hat{v}_{y_i} \cdot \hat{v}_{x_j} \\
&= e(\bar{y}_i h^{\sigma_{y_i}} \cdot \bar{x}_j h^{\sigma_{x_j}}, h) \cdot e(h, h)^{\nu_{y_i}} \cdot e(h, h)^{\nu_{x_j}} \\
&= e(\bar{y}_i\bar{x}_j, h) \cdot e(h^{\sigma_{y_i}+\sigma_{x_j}}, h) \cdot e(h, h)^{\nu_{y_i}+\nu_{x_j}} \\
&= e(\bar{y}_i\bar{x}_j, h).
\end{aligned}$$

where $\nu_{y_i} = q - \sigma_{y_i} \mod q$, and $\nu_{x_j} = q - \sigma_{x_j} \mod q$.

Based on the mapping $\tilde{\psi}$ between elements in $\bar{\mathbf{T}}$ and bucket indexes, the cloud computes the secure substitution cost matrix $\hat{\mathbf{T}} \in \mathbb{Z}^{m\times n}$ as follows: $\hat{t}_{i,j} = \hat{g}'_{y_i,l}\hat{g}'_{x_j,l} = (\beta\gamma_{y_j}\gamma_{x_j})g_l$, (for all $i \in [1, m]$ and $j \in [1, n]$), where l is the index of bucket $\mathcal{B}_l$ that contains $\bar{t}_{i,j}$, and $\hat{g}'_{y_i,l}$ and $\hat{g}'_{x_j,l}$ are the lth elements of $\hat{\mathbf{g}}'_{x_i}$ and $\hat{\mathbf{g}}'_{y_j}$, respectively. Due to the properties of the bilinear map and the finite groups used to conceal the private sequences, the cloud is unable to compute $\mathbf{x}$ and $\mathbf{y}$ based on $\bar{\mathbf{T}}$, $\hat{\mathbf{T}}$, $\hat{\mathbf{x}}$ and $\hat{\mathbf{y}}$.

Secure Formulation of the Linear Program. To securely formulate the LP described in (6), the cloud needs to form the secure weight vector $\hat{\mathbf{w}} \in \mathbb{Z}^{|\mathcal{E}|}$ and the secure constraint matrix $\hat{\mathbf{A}} \in \mathbb{Z}_*^{|\mathcal{V}|\times|\mathcal{E}|}$. To this end, the cloud first forms the secure weight vector $\hat{\mathbf{w}}$ by assigning elements of $\hat{\mathbf{T}}$ to substitution edges, i.e., $w_l = \hat{t}_{\pi(l)}$, if $e_l \in \mathcal{E}_{sub}$, and by assigning the secure insertions and deletion costs to the corresponding edges, i.e., $\hat{w}_l = \hat{w}_{del}$, if $e_l \in \mathcal{E}_{del}$ and $\hat{w}_l = \hat{w}_{ins}$, if $e_l \in \mathcal{E}_{ins}$.

To form $\hat{\mathbf{A}}$, the cloud computes the following matrix of concealed random numbers: $\hat{\mathbf{P}} = (\hat{\gamma}_{\mathbf{y}}^{\top}\hat{\gamma}_{\mathbf{x}})$ and then forms $\hat{\mathbf{A}}'$'s columns vectors by multiplying columns corresponding to substitution edges by elements in $\hat{\mathbf{P}}$, that is, $\hat{\mathbf{a}}_j' = \hat{p}_{\pi(j)}\mathbf{a}_j$ if $e_j \in \mathcal{E}_{sub}$, and columns corresponding to insertion and deletion edges by the concealed weights, that is, $\hat{\mathbf{a}}_j' = \hat{\gamma}_{del}\mathbf{a}_j$, if $e_j \in \mathcal{E}_{del}$, $\hat{\mathbf{a}}_j' = \hat{\gamma}_{ins}\mathbf{a}_j$, if $e_j \in \mathcal{E}_{ins}$, where $\mathbf{a}_j$ is the jth column of $\mathbf{A}$ in (6), $\hat{p}_{\pi(j)}$ is the element in the ith row and jth column of $\hat{\mathbf{P}}$ as defined by $\pi(\cdot)$ in Section 4. Besides, the cloud multiplies the rows of $\hat{\mathbf{A}}'$ by $\hat{\gamma}_{\alpha}$, that is $\hat{\mathbf{A}} = \mathbf{K}\hat{\mathbf{A}}'$ where $\mathbf{K} = \hat{\gamma}_{\alpha}\mathbf{I}$ and $\mathbf{I} \in \mathbb{Z}_*^{|\mathcal{V}|\times|\mathcal{E}|}$ is the identity matrix.

To compute the concealed constraint vector, the cloud computes the following: $\hat{\mathbf{b}} = \hat{\gamma}_{\alpha}\mathbf{b}$, where $\mathbf{b}$ is the constant vector in (6). Note that the cloud can compute $\mathbf{A}$ and $\mathbf{b}$ based on the LP formulation in Section 4 and the length of sequences $\hat{\mathbf{x}}$ and $\hat{\mathbf{y}}$ that Alice and Bob upload.

Secure solution of the Linear Program. Before the cloud can apply the Simplex algorithm to solve the secure LP, it needs to find an initial solution. Specifically, the Simplex algorithm requires a basic feasible starting point $\mathbf{u}$ such that a matrix $\mathbf{B} \in \mathbb{Z}^{|\mathcal{V}|\times|\mathcal{V}|}$ is invertible, and $\mathbf{u}^{\mathrm{B}} > \mathbf{0}$ and $\mathbf{u}^{\mathrm{N}} = \mathbf{0}$. Matrix $\mathbf{B}$ is formed with $|\mathcal{V}|$ columns of $\mathbf{A}$, and $\mathbf{u}^{\mathrm{B}} \in \mathbb{Z}^{|\mathcal{V}|\times 1}$ with the elements of $\mathbf{u}$ that correspond to these columns. Vector $\mathbf{u}^{\mathrm{N}} \in \mathbb{Z}^{(|\mathcal{E}|-|\mathcal{V}|)\times 1}$ is formed with the remaining values of $\mathbf{u}$. Since we are dealing with a shortest-path problem on a DAG, we can form a feasible solution for (6) based on any path between the source node and the sink node. However, since such a path contains less than $|\mathcal{V}|$ edges, its corresponding initial solution is not basic. To obtain an initial basic feasible solution, we find an arbitrary path between all nodes and the destination node, and redefine the constraint vector $\mathbf{b}$ in (6) as $b_i = 1$ (for all $i \in [1, mn-1]$) and $b_{mn} = \sum_{i=1}^{mn-1} -b_i$. Note that the solution to our original problem is still readily available from the solution to the LP with this choice of $\mathbf{b}$.

The cloud can find the initial basic feasible solution for the secure LP by computing the following: $\hat{\mathbf{u}} = \hat{\mathbf{B}}^{-1}\hat{\mathbf{b}}$, where $\hat{\mathbf{B}}$ is the set of basic feasible columns of $\hat{\mathbf{A}}$ based on a path between the source and destination nodes.

After the cloud finds the concealed starting basic feasible solution $\hat{\mathbf{u}}$, it executes the revised Simplex algorithm's main iteration with the secure LP's matrices until convergence [3]. Once the cloud finds the solution to the secure LP, i.e., $\hat{\mathbf{u}}^*$, it calculates a concealed optimal objective value as follows: $\phi(\hat{\mathbf{u}}^*) = \hat{\mathbf{w}}^{\top}\hat{\mathbf{u}}^*$, and transmits it to the users. Finally, both Alice and Bob can recover the original objective value by computing $\phi(\mathbf{u}^*) = \alpha\beta^{-1}\phi(\hat{\mathbf{u}}^*)$. Note that since we are dealing with a shortest path problem on a DAG, the revised Simplex algorithm is guaranteed to converge.

Since Alice and Bob only perform operations with their own sequences, their overall computational complexity in the SPSA algorithm is $O(n)$ and $O(m)$, respectively, which is lower than $O(mn)$, i.e., the complexity for users solving PSAs by themselves.

Also note that the cloud is unable to learn private information about the users because it only has access to the securely transformed sequences, and the securely transformed edit operation costs. In particular, the cloud would need to find the σ_{y_i}'s and σ_{x_i}'s used to transform $\mathbf{x}$ and $\mathbf{y}$ based on the elements of $\hat{\mathbf{x}}$ and $\hat{\mathbf{y}}$. However, finding σ_{y_i}'s or σ_{x_i}'s requires the cloud to break the PBC encryption in Section 2 by solving a discrete logarithm under a multiplicative cyclic group $\mathbb{G}_1$ of order q, which has no known polynomial time solution.

A Parallel Implementation for the SPSA. Since Alice and Bob are interested in solving (1) repeatedly many times as described in Section 2, we propose an scheme for them to solve a large amount of PSAs at the cloud in parallel. Specifically, suppose Alice and Bob hold the private sequence sets $\mathrm{Y} = \{\mathbf{y}^1, \mathbf{y}^2, \ldots, \mathbf{y}^N\}$ and $\mathrm{X} = \{\mathbf{x}^1, \mathbf{x}^2, \ldots, \mathbf{x}^N\}$, respectively, and outsource to the cloud the following PSAs: $\hat{\Phi}^i = (\hat{\mathbf{y}}^i, \hat{\mathbf{x}}^i)$ (for all $i \in [1, N]$), where $(\hat{\mathbf{y}}^i, \hat{\mathbf{x}}^i)$ is a tuple that denotes the alignment problem in (1) with the concealed sequences as inputs, and N is the number of sequence pairs held by Alice and Bob.

Since the sequence transformation and concealed PSAs $\hat{\Phi}^i$'s are independent from each other, they can be computed in parallel. In particular, to conceal their sequences, Alice first finds the buckets $\mathcal{B}_l^i$'s, and random numbers α^i as described in Section (3) for all $i \in [1, N]$, and securely shares them with Bob. Similarly, Bob finds β^i for all $i \in [1, N]$ and securely sends them to Alice. Then, Alice and Bob compute $\hat{\mathrm{Y}}$ and $\hat{\mathrm{X}}$, i.e., the concealed sequences in Y and X, and the concealed substitution costs $\hat{\mathbf{g}}$'s for all characters and for all sequences, and upload them to the cloud. After the cloud receives the concealed values, it can solve $\hat{\Phi}^i$ for all $i \in [1, N]$ in parallel, without interacting with neither Alice or Bob. After solving the PSAs, the cloud returns the results to Alice and Bob, who then retrieve the solution to the original PSA by computing: $\phi(\mathbf{u}^{*(i)}) = \alpha^i\beta^{-1(i)}\phi(\hat{\mathbf{u}}^{*(i)})$. Note that finding the buckets $\mathcal{B}_l$'s and generating random scalars α^i and β^i for a large number of PSAs are one-time operations and can be done efficiently. Besides, the cloud can begin to solve the PSAs as soon as a pair of concealed sequences becomes available, without the need to wait for Alice and Bob to finish concealing their sequences.

6 EXPERIMENT RESULTS

To closely replicate a practical cloud computing scenario, we run Alice and Bob's part of the SPSA algorithm on a laptop with a dual-core 2.6GHz CPU, 8GB RAM memory, and a 150GB solid state drive, and the cloud part on an Amazon Elastic Compute Cloud (EC2) cluster using m4.large instances, which each have 2 CPUs and 8GB RAM. We implement the linear algebra computations on Matlab 2015b, the pairing-based cryptography operations in C using the Pairing-Based Cryptography (PBC) Library, and the Simplex algorithm with IBM's CPLEX. We test the performance of our algorithm with beta protein sequences taken from the Protein Data Bank [2] of the same size, that is $n = m$. We also employ randomly generated sequences to compare the SPSA with previous works.

We first analyze the computing time of our secure outsourcing algorithm SPSA at both the user and at the cloud. In Fig. 2(a), we observe that a user, i.e., Alice or Bob, can transform sequences very quickly, even for large n and m. For example, the computing time of the user when the length of its sequence is 1000 characters is only 9.3s. Besides, in Fig. 2(b), we observe that the computing time of the cloud increases with the length of the sequences.

We also investigate the scalability of our SPSA algorithm by comparing its overall computing time with different cloud cluster sizes with the least computing time that we can expect. To find this theoretical lower bound on the computing time of the cloud, we take the overall computing time with a one-node cluster and divide it by the number of nodes in the cluster. Fig. 2(c) shows both the SPSA's computing time and the lower bound on the computing time for solving 100 PSAs under different cluster sizes. We observe that our algorithm is very close to the lower bound on the computing time. This is due to the ability of the SPSA to independently solve linear programs at different nodes. Therefore, our secure outsourcing algorithm is scalable, which is a crucial requirement to solve a large number of PSAs within a feasible amount of time.

Next, we compare the overall computing time of the SPSA algorithm with different cluster sizes with that of [12] in Fig. 2(d). We observe that our algorithm offers significant time savings compared to [12] with only a modest amount of computing nodes at the cloud. For example, in Fig. 2(d), we observe that for 500 PSAs with input sequences of length $n = m = 200$ the algorithm by [12] takes 183 minutes, while the SPSA algorithm with a 5-node cluster only takes 83 minutes. This is due to the ability of the SPSA to solve many linear programs at the cloud in parallel without having to interact with the users. In contrast, the garbled circuits in [12] require the users to participate in circuit evaluation, which prevents them from solving PSAs in parallel[1].

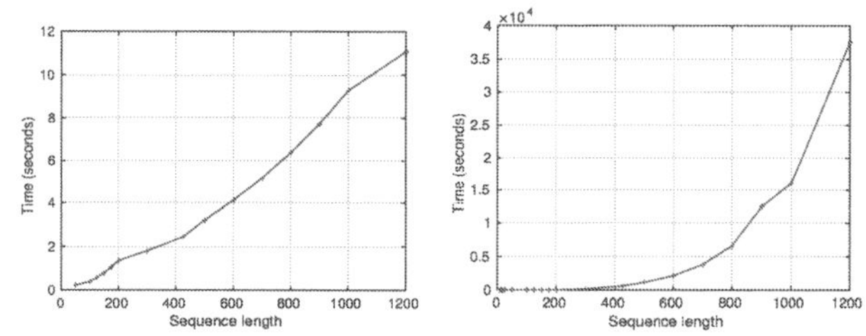

(a) Computing time at the users for problems with sequences of different sizes with $n = m$.

(b) Computing time at the cloud for problems with sequences of different sizes with $n = m$.

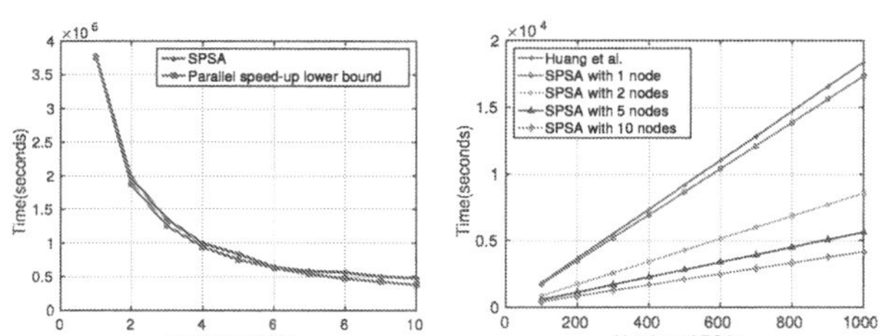

(c) Overall computing time for different number of nodes at the cloud for 100 PSAs with sequence sizes $n = m = 1200$.

(d) Performance comparison of our SPSA with [4] for sequences of size $m = n = 1000$ with different cluster sizes.

Figure 2: Performance evaluation of the proposed secure pairwise sequence alignment (SPSA) algorithm.

7 CONCLUSIONS

In this paper, we have investigated the problem of two users, each holding a private sequence, securely outsourcing pairwise sequence alignments (PSAs) to the cloud. To protect the users' private data, we develop a sequence transformation scheme that has low computational complexity. Then, based on the Simplex algorithm, the cloud solves the PSA under the transformed sequences, and sends the results to the users, who can find the solution to their original PSA with minimal computing resources. Different from previous works, our algorithm can solve an arbitrary number of PSAs at the cloud in parallel, which significantly reduces the computing time. Our results show that the proposed algorithm is scalable and can reduce computing time of a large number of PSAs by more than 50% with as few as 5 computing nodes at the cloud.

[1] The authors in [12] implemented their algorithm on a PC with similar characteristics to the EC2 m4.large instance used in our simulations

REFERENCES

[1] M. J. Atallah, F. Kerschbaum, and W. Du. Secure and private sequence comparisons. In *ACM Workshop on Privacy in the Electronic Society*, WPES '03, Washington, DC, 2003.

[2] H. Berman, J. Westbrook, Z. Feng, G. Gilliland, T. Bhat, H. Weissig, I. Shindyalov, and P. Bourne. The protein data bank. *Nucleic Acids Research*, 28:235–242, 2000.

[3] D. Bertsimas and J. N. Tsitsiklis. *Introduction to Linear Optimization*. Athena Scientific-Dynamic Ideas, Nashua, NH, USA, 1997.

[4] M. Blanton, M. J. Atallah, K. B. Frikken, and Q. Malluhi. Secure and efficient outsourcing of sequence comparisons. In *European Symposium on Research in Computer Security (ESORICS)*, Pisa, Italy, September 2012.

[5] D. Boneh, B. Lynn, and H. Shacham. Short signatures from the weil pairing. In *International Conference on the Theory and Application of Cryptology and Information Security*, pages 514–532. Springer, 2001.

[6] J. K. Brown, F. M. Zerbini, J. Navas-Castillo, E. Moriones, R. Ramos-Sobrinho, J. C. Silva, E. Fiallo-Olivé, R. W. Briddon, C. Hernández-Zepeda, A. Idris, et al. Revision of begomovirus taxonomy based on pairwise sequence comparisons. *Archives of virology*, 160(6):1593–1619, 2015.

[7] C. Costello, C. Fournet, J. Howell, M. Kohlweiss, B. Kreuter, M. Naehrig, B. Parno, and S. Zahur. Geppetto: Versatile verifiable computation. In *IEEE Symposium on Security and Privacy*, pages 253–270. IEEE, 2015.

[8] R. Durbin, S. Eddy, and A. krogh anf G. Mitchison. *Biological Sequence Anlaysis*. Cambridge University Press, Cambridge, UK, 1998.

[9] R. Gennaro, C. Gentry, and B. Parno. Non-interactive verifiable computing: Outsourcing computation to untrusted workers. In *Advances in Cryptology (CRYPTO)*, Santa Barbara, CA, USA, 2010.

[10] D. Gevers, R. Knight, J. F. Petrosino, K. Huang, A. L. McGuire, B. W. Birren, K. E. Nelson, O. White, B. A. Meth, and C. Huttenhower. The human microbiome project: A community resource for the healthy human microbiome. *PLoS Biol*, 10(8):1–5, 08 2012.

[11] O. Goldreich. *Foundations of Cryptography: Volume 2, Basic Applications*. Cambridge University Press, New York, NY, USA, 2004.

[12] Y. Huang, D. Evans, J. Katz, and L. Malka. Faster secure two-party computation using garbled circuits. In *USENIX Conference on Security*, San Francisco, CA, USA, August 2011.

[13] S. Jha, L. Kruger, and V. Shmatikov. Towards practical privacy for genomic computation. In *IEEE Symposium on Security and Privacy*, Oakland, CA, USA, 2008.

[14] J. Katz and Y. Lindell. *Introduction to Modern Cryptography*. Chapman and Hall/ CRC, 2008.

[15] Organisation for Economic Co-operation and Development (OECD). Collaborative mechanisms for intellectual property management in the life sciences. http://www.oecd.org/sti/biotech/48665248.pdf, 2011.

[16] B. M. Muhire, A. Varsani, and D. P. Martin. Sdt: A virus classification tool based on pairwise sequence alignment and identity calculation. *PLOS ONE*, 9(9):1–8, 09 2014.

[17] H. K. Patil and R. Seshadri. Big data security and privacy issues in healthcare. In *IEEE International Congress on Big Data*, Anchorage, AK, USA, June 2014.

[18] S. Sakr, A. Liu, D. Batista, and M. Alomari. A survey of large scale data management approaches in cloud environments. *IEEE Communications Surveys Tutorials*, 13(3):311–336, March 2011.

[19] Y. Simmhan, S. Aman, A. Kumbhare, R. Liu, S. Stevens, Q. Zhou, and V. Prasanna. Cloud-based software platform for big data analytics in smart grids. *Computing in Science Engineering*, 15(4):38–47, July 2013.

[20] F. Stajano, L. Bianchi, P. Liò, and D. Korff. Forensic genomics: Kin privacy, driftnets and other open questions. In *ACM Workshop on Privacy in the Electronic Society*, Alexandria, Virginia, USA, 2008.

[21] Z. D. Stephens, S. Y. Lee, F. Faghri, R. H. Campbell, C. Zhai, M. J. Efron, R. Iyer, M. C. Schatz, S. Sinha, and G. E. Robinson. Big data: Astronomical or genomical? *PLoS Biol*, 13(7):1–11, July 2015.

[22] C. Wang, K. Ren, and J. Wang. Secure and practical outsourcing of linear programming in cloud computing. In *International Conference on Computer Communications*, Shangai, China, 2011.

[23] X. Xia. Phypa: Phylogenetic method with pairwise sequence alignment outperforms likelihood methods in phylogenetics involving highly diverged sequences. *Molecular Phylogenetics and Evolution*, 102:331 – 343, 2016.

Rich Chromatin Structure Prediction from Hi-C Data

Laraib Malik
Stony Brook University
lmalik@cs.stonybrook.edu

Rob Patro
Stony Brook University
rob.patro@cs.stonybrook.edu

ABSTRACT

Recent studies involving the 3-dimensional conformation of chromatin have revealed the important role it has to play in different processes within the cell. These studies have also led to the discovery of densely interacting segments of the chromosome, called topologically associating domains. The accurate identification of these domains from Hi-C interaction data is an interesting and important computational problem for which numerous methods have been proposed. Unfortunately, most existing algorithms designed to identify these domains assume that they are non-overlapping whereas there is substantial evidence to believe a nested structure exists. We present an efficient methodology to predict hierarchical chromatin domains using chromatin conformation capture data. Our method predicts domains at different resolutions, calculated using intrinsic properties of the chromatin data, and efficiently clusters these to construct the hierarchy. At each individual level, the domains are non-overlapping in such a way that the intra-domain interaction frequencies are maximized. We show that our predicted structure is highly enriched for actively transcribing housekeeping genes and various chromatin markers, including CTCF, around the domain boundaries. We also show that large-scale domains, at multiple resolutions within our hierarchy, are conserved across cell types and species. Apart from these, our tool is robust and highly efficient, taking only a few minutes to process each dataset. Our software, Matryoshka, is written in C++11 and licensed under GPL v3; it is available at https://github.com/COMBINE-lab/matryoshka.

KEYWORDS

Chromatin conformation, Hi-C, topologically associating domains, hierarchy

ACM Reference format:
Laraib Malik and Rob Patro. 2017. Rich Chromatin Structure Prediction from Hi-C Data. In *Proceedings of ACM-BCB'17, August 20-23, 2017, Boston, MA, USA.*, 10 pages.
DOI: http://dx.doi.org/10.1145/3107411.3107448

1 INTRODUCTION

The 3D structure and folding of chromatin has been shown to influence many biological processes within the cell. These include cell replication, differentiation and gene expression [5, 9], as well as alterations leading to disease [12, 30]. Recent advances in chromosome conformation capture (3C) technologies [8], that combine chemical cross-linking and high-throughput sequencing, have led to the discovery of densely packed regions of chromatin referred to as topologically associating domains. These domains are found to be conserved across cell types and species, reflecting their biological importance, and their boundaries are known to be enriched for several epigenetic marks, suggesting that these domains play a role in epigenomic regulation of expression [9, 10, 17, 33, 35].

Several methods have been developed to identify these domains using data from Hi-C— a high-throughput experimental assay that allows genome-wide conformation capture [2, 22]. These methods are based on a variety of different approaches, but most focus on exploiting particular statistics and properties of contact frequencies in the resulting data. Dixon et al. [9] introduced the concept of the directionality index, which measures the difference in contact frequency upstream and downstream of a particular chromosomal locus. Treating the directionality index as a spatially-varying statistic over the chromosome, they use a Hidden Markov Model to determine a set of domain boundaries. This statistic was then employed in several other studies [24, 25]. Similarly, the arrowhead algorithm, introduced by Rao et al. [29], performs a transformation on the contact matrix designed to enhance domain boundary signals. The algorithm then determines the positions of high-scoring "corners" to determine domains (thus the algorithm's name). Instead of predicting domains directly, some methods provide change points along the diagonal of the contact frequency matrix [21, 34], but this leaves the question of which chromatin regions are *not* in domains unresolved. Filippova et al.. [11] introduce a dynamic programming approach that predicts domains by maximizing a score based on normalized, intra-domain interaction frequencies. The algorithm is run at multiple resolutions and a consensus domain set is returned with the goal of predicting domains that persist across multiple scales. More recently, Chen et al. [7] developed a method to iteratively apply Laplacian-based graph segmentation in order to obtain domains across the matrix. However, all these algorithms have an underlying assumption that chromatin domains are non-overlapping or are not nested.

There is significant evidence to believe that chromatin folding is hierarchical, wherein sub-domains combine to form larger super-domains, instead of a sequence of non-overlapping or non-nested domains. This was initially predicted in the *Drosophila* genome by Sexton et al. [35]. Further studies across different cell types and species, including humans, have supported this claim [4]. Gibcus et al. [13] went on to explain the possibility of inter-domain interactions, along with the intra-domain interactions, in mammalian genomes, including mouse and human. It was shown by Filippova et al. [11] that domains predicted by their method at different size

Permission to make digital or hard copies of all or part of this work for personal or classroom use is granted without fee provided that copies are not made or distributed for profit or commercial advantage and that copies bear this notice and the full citation on the first page. Copyrights for components of this work owned by others than the author(s) must be honored. Abstracting with credit is permitted. To copy otherwise, or republish, to post on servers or to redistribute to lists, requires prior specific permission and/or a fee. Request permissions from permissions@acm.org.
ACM-BCB'17, August 20-23, 2017, Boston, MA, USA.
© 2017 Copyright held by the owner/author(s). Publication rights licensed to ACM.
978-1-4503-4722-8/17/08...$15.00
DOI: http://dx.doi.org/10.1145/3107411.3107448

scales tend to be more nested (i.e. hierarchical) than what would be expected in a collection of appropriately randomized domains with the same size distribution. There is also theoretical evidence to believe that the chromatin structure is hierarchical as shown by replicating its statistical properties on a heteropolymer chain and observing the structure of the resulting folding pattern [26]. IC-Finder [15] is a recently-published method that also considers the hierarchical structure of chromatin organization when calling domains. However, the tool does not, by default, output hierarchies of chromatin domains, and such a hierarchy has to be constructed by running the algorithm multiple times and tuning the parameter that control how the domains are merged, with the final hierarchy consisting of a union of all outputs. Finally, IC-Finder, like HICSeg [1], outputs a segmentation of the contact matrix rather than a set of domains directly, which requires further processing.

Here, we introduce a new, efficient algorithm to derive a nested hierarchy of domains from chromatin conformation capture data. Initially, our method optimizes an objective function to obtain an optimal set of non-overlapping domains at a collection of different resolutions (i.e. size scales) [11]. The resolution values are then clustered based on the variation of information distance [23] between the corresponding domain sets. This clustering is used to determine discrete levels of the hierarchy, such that interactions are optimized in the overall predicted structure. In order to obtain consensus domains at each level, we use a scoring function that is proportional to the frequency of interactions within the domain but is normalized for variation across domain sizes. We analyze the biological significance of the hierarchical domains predicted by our method, Matryoshka, in a number of ways and also compare our results against the publicly available tool, TADtree, for identifying hierarchical chromatin domains [39]. We show that, across multiple levels of our predicted hierarchy, the boundaries of domains are statistically significantly enriched for chromatin binding factors and modifications known to be associated with domain boundaries. We also test the conservation of multiple levels of the hierarchy across cell types and species, and find that significant conservation occurs at multiple levels. Across a variety of datasets, we demonstrate that our method can efficiently determine a domain hierarchy and can automatically account for variations in nesting and domain sizes in a data-dependent manner.

2 MATERIALS AND METHODS

2.1 Algorithm Overview

In order to find the set of nested domains in Hi-C data, we designed a multi-step algorithm that aims to predict a collection of domains such that inter-domain interaction frequencies are maximized. The algorithm first predicts an optimal set of domains across a wide range of resolutions, and then clusters and nests these domains in a data-driven manner to produce a coherent hierarchy representative of the input contact matrix. The algorithm is illustrated in Fig, 1, and the phases of the algorithm are explained in detail below (corresponding to the order of the pipeline in the figure):

(1) A set of non-overlapping domains is predicted at each resolution, where domain sizes tend to vary across resolutions. The first heatmap in Fig 1, from IMR90 data, made using HiCPlotter [1], gives an idea of the hierarchical structure observed in Hi-C data.
(2) The variation of information between domain sets is calculated. This is used as a distance metric for clustering the sets.
(3) The domain sets are clustered and corresponding γ (resolution) value clusters are used for building the hierarchy of chromatin domains.
(4) A set of consensus domains is obtained based on a quality score using the relevant γ values at each level of the hierarchy. For the first level, the set of consensus domains is across the whole matrix.
(5) For subsequent levels, sub-matrices predicted as domains at the higher level are used and sub-domains are predicted within these using the next set of γ values.

2.2 Working of Matryoshka

2.2.1 Identifying putative domains across resolutions. Matryoshka takes as input an $n \times n$ interaction frequency matrix $\mathbf{A}$, where each entry $\mathbf{A}_{ij}$ represents the interaction frequency between chromosome locations (bins) i and j, and a set of resolution parameters, Γ, satisfying the condition that each $\gamma \geq 0$, where $\gamma \in \Gamma$. Using the method of Filippova et al. [11], a set of non-overlapping domains D_γ is identified for each γ. Each D_γ maximizes the following objective:

$$q(k, l, \gamma) = s(k, l, \gamma) - \mu_s(l - k), \tag{1}$$

where k and l are respective genomic positions along the chromosome, and

$$s(k, l, \gamma) = \frac{\sum_{g=k}^{l} \sum_{h=g+1}^{l} A_{gh}}{(l - k)^{\gamma}}. \tag{2}$$

Here, $\mu_s(l - k)$ is the mean value of $s(k, l, \gamma)$ over all sub-matrices of $\mathbf{A}$ with length $l - k$. Hence, γ is inversely proportional to domain size.

In order to obtain a set of domains in the matrix, the following dynamic program is run over the length of the chromosome. This program enumerates the optimal set of domains (OPT) in the sub-matrix defined by the first l positions on the chromosome, such that the objective function is maximized.

$$OPT(l) = \max_{k<l}\{OPT(k - 1) + \max\{q(k, l, \gamma), 0\}\}. \tag{3}$$

Additionally, we filter the domains based on their boundary indices, as adopted by Weinreb et al. [39]. This filtering is a reflection of the amount of shift in interaction frequencies around the boundary, and we find that it substantially reduces the number of "spurious" domains called by the algorithm. Valid boundaries should have a larger shift and, therefore, we consider domains where at least one of the boundaries has an index value greater than the mean boundary index for the whole matrix $\mathbf{A}$. The boundary index for

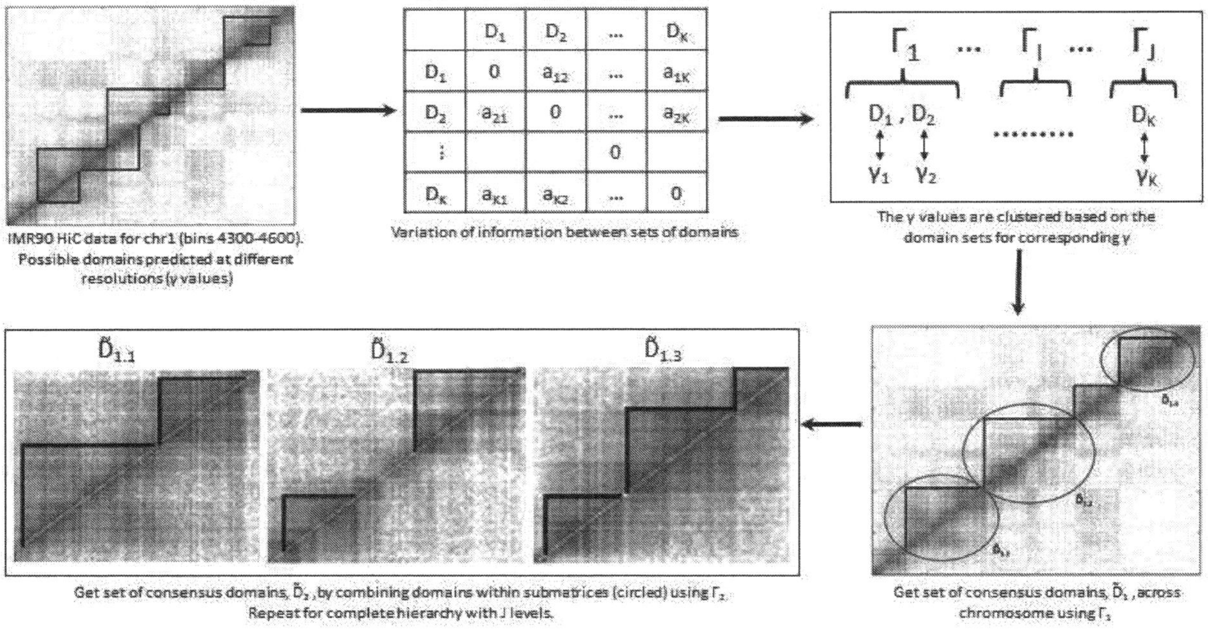

Figure 1: Overview of main steps of the hierarchical domain finding algorithm of Matryoshka. The steps are briefly explained in Section 2.1 with further details in the methods section.

any position i is calculated as follows

$$B_{p,q}(i) = \sum_{l=i-q}^{i+q} \left| \sum_{k=1}^{p} (A_{l,i+k} - A_{l,i-k}) \right|, \tag{4}$$

where p determines the length of the interval containing i and q is the length (i.e. window size) we wish to use for calculating the difference in interaction frequency upstream and downstream of i. Values for p and q are set to 3 and 12, respectively.

Given a collection Γ of resolution parameters with $|\Gamma| = K$, we apply this dynamic program over all $\gamma \in \Gamma$, and obtain K sets of domains. The set of domains returned at each resolution are non-overlapping, but domains across resolutions may overlap. Smaller γ values result in solutions with larger domains and vice versa. These domain sets are then used to cluster similar solutions across resolutions, and the consensus domains of each cluster are used to construct the different levels of the hierarchy.

2.2.2 Clustering domains to generate hierarchy. Domains obtained across resolutions from the first step are clustered based on the variation of information distance between them [23]. For any two domain sets, D_i and D_j, new derivative sets, C_i and C_j, are constructed such that C_i contains all the domains and the inter-domain regions from D_i and similarly C_j is constructed from D_j. The probability of seeing an interval $x_i = [a_i, b_i]$ in a derivative set for chromosome of length L is defined as $p_i = (b_i - a_i + 1)/L$. In the same way, the joint probability is defined as $p_{ij} = \left|[a_i, b_i] \cap [a_j, b_j]\right|/L$.

Using these probabilities, the entropy of a derivative set C_i is computed as

$$H(C_i) = \sum_{x_i \in C_i} p_i \log p_i, \tag{5}$$

and the mutual information is computed as

$$I(C_i, C_j) = \sum_{x_i \in C_i} \sum_{x_j \in C_j} p_{ij} \log \left[p_{ij}/p_i p_j \right]. \tag{6}$$

Finally, the variation of information between two sets is defined as $VI(C_i, C_j) = H(C_i) + H(C_j) - 2I(C_i, C_j)$.

From these distances, the $K \times K$ variation of information matrix $\mathbf{V}$ is constructed. Each entry $\mathbf{V}_{ij}$ of this matrix provides the VI distance between the set of domains at resolutions i and j. Next, we use a clustering procedure to obtain a grouping of the K domain sets into a collection of J clusters, where $J \leq K$. Rather than allowing clusters to consist of groups of domain sets at arbitrary resolutions, we restrict clusters to consist of collections of domain sets at contiguous values of the resolution parameter — this also allows us to employ a simple dynamic program to obtain an optimal set of clusters, by turning the clustering problem into a problem of finding an optimal partitioning of the domain sets across values of γ. Consider a particular partitioning of K domain sets into disjoint intervals, given as $\mathcal{I} = [[0, x_1][x_1 + 1, x_2], \ldots, [x_{t-1} + 1, K]]$. We define a cost for this partition as

$$C(\mathcal{I}) = \sum_{[m,m'] \in \mathcal{I}} \left(\sum_{m \leq i < j \leq m'} V_{ij} \right). \tag{7}$$

We seek a partitioning of our K domain sets into a collection of intervals that minimizes this cost. Given the desired number of intervals, ℓ, we can determine the optimal intervals, OPT^{ℓ}, by finding those that minimize the following objective:

$$\mathsf{OPT}_C^{\ell} = \min_{\mathcal{I} \in I} C(\mathcal{I}) \tag{8}$$

As explained, this objective can be minimized efficiently via dynamic programming. Consider the objective $\mathsf{OPT}_C^{\ell}(x)$, which defines the cost of an optimal set of ℓ intervals that cover domains at resolutions 0 through x. $\mathsf{OPT}_C^{1}(x)$ is trivial (simply the interval $[0, x]$), and

$$\mathsf{OPT}_C^{\ell}(x) = \min_{x'} \left(\mathsf{OPT}_C^{\ell-1}(x') + \sum_{x'<i<j\leq x} V_{ij} \right). \tag{9}$$

If we consider computing $\mathsf{OPT}_C^{\ell}(x)$ for increasing values of x and increasing values of ℓ, the optimal solution for the overall partitioning problem $\mathsf{OPT}_C^{\ell}(K)$ can be computed in $O(K\ell^2)$ time; the actual set of intervals obtaining the optimal score can be recovered via backtracking.

This partitioning is obtained for all possible values of ℓ and the optimal number of clusters is decided based on the maximum silhouette value [32] of the returned clustering. This score is defined as

$$s(i) = \frac{b(i) - a(i)}{max(a(i), b(i))}. \tag{10}$$

Here, i is a particular domain set, value $a(i)$ is the average distance of i from all points within the cluster and value $b(i)$ is the lowest average distance of i from points in a cluster other than its own, called the neighboring cluster of i. The number of clusters for which the average of this value over all domain sets is maximum is chosen as the optimal cluster number. Based on this optimal clustering of the domain sets, the corresponding γ values are used to identify consensus domains at each level of the hierarchy.

2.2.3 Building hierarchy using consensus domains. Given the sized K set of γ values that are split into J clusters, $\{\Gamma_1, \Gamma_2, ..., \Gamma_J\}$ where $1 < J < K$ and γ values are sorted in ascending order, we construct a hierarchy of domains with J levels. Domains at any level i are constructed using γ values from within a cluster Γ_i. A non-overlapping set of domains is derived at each level separately using a quality score independent of γ and domains at any level i completely cover the domains at any level $j > i$. Domains at coarser levels (for example level 1) are identified using larger γ values than those at finer levels (for example level J).

At level 1 of the hierarchy, a multiset of domains D_1 is obtained using the interaction matrix $\mathbf{A}$ as described above. Instead of using the complete γ set, only the first cluster, Γ_1, which has the largest γ values, is used. In order to obtain a set of non-overlapping consensus domains for level 1 of the hierarchy, the problem is reduced to the weighted interval scheduling problem [11, 18], where each domain in D_1 is assigned a quality score that corresponds to its priority as follows:

$$qs(k, l) = \log_{10}\left(\sum_{g=k}^{l} \sum_{h=g+1}^{l} A_{gh} \right) \log_{10}\left(\frac{\text{cov}(D)}{l - k} \right), \tag{11}$$

where cov(D) is simply the length of the chromosome covered by the complete set of domains D obtained in the first step. This quality score normalizes the sum of the interaction frequency A_{gh} between genomic loci k and l, which increases logarithmically with the domain size, against the ratio of length covered by the domain. This ratio is calculated over the complete length covered by domains in D instead of the chromosome length in order to disregard non-domain regions, which may cover a large portion of the chromosome. This quality score gives us the ability to compare domains of vastly different sizes across resolutions so that we can extract a set of non-overlapping consensus domains while reducing bias due to domain sizes. The result of solving the weighted interval scheduling problem with the quality scores defined above is a set of consensus domains, $\tilde{D_1} = \{d_1, d_2, ..., d_n\}$, for the first level of the hierarchy.

Now, for each domain $d_i \in \tilde{D_1}$, we get a submatrix of the interaction matrix $\mathbf{A}[a_i, b_i]$ such that the size of this submatrix is defined by the boundaries of the domain where $d_i = [a_i, b_i]$. On this submatrix, we repeat the steps explained above to get a set of domains at different resolutions defined by the γ values from Γ_2. Then we get a set of non-overlapping consensus domains using weighted interval scheduling that is placed at the second level of the hierarchy. This procedure is repeated for the all the domains within $\tilde{D_1}$. In a similar way, we use $\{\Gamma_3, \Gamma_4, ..., \Gamma_J\}$ in order to get domains at lower levels of the hierarchy, $\{D_3, D_4, ..., D_J\}$ and then extract consensus domains from it for each level, $\{\tilde{D_3}, \tilde{D_4}, ..., \tilde{D_J}\}$, to eventually construct the complete hierarchy of chromatin domains.

2.3 Generating Random Hierarchies

We compared our results against a 1,000 randomized hierarchies which serve to provide expected values of each factor. These hierarchies are generated such that the following features are preserved while shuffling the order of domains and non-domains:

(1) The number of domains at each level of the hierarchy.
(2) Sizes of the domains, as well as the regions between the domains.
(3) The structure of the hierarchy, such that the nesting of the domains is preserved and sub-domains shuffle within the shuffled super-domain.

3 RESULTS

3.1 Hierarchical structure

We ran Matryoshka for all the test genomes using γ value 1. Increased γ values simply result in an insignificant number of smaller domains at the lower levels. The minimum γ value can be set higher to ignore the larger domains. For the rest of the parameters, the default values were used. Decreasing the step size to 0.025 from

0.05 did not alter the domains significantly either since the VI distance between the domains remained consistent. This shows that the resulting domains are robust to changes in the parameters, including the step size.

We extracted hierarchical domains by running Matryoshka on Hi-C data from three different species. For human, major tests were done on the IMR90 cell line data constructed from all read pairs that map with a $MAPQ >= 30$, binned at 5kb and normalized using the KR vector [34]. The mouse data, obtained from cortex cells, was binned at 40kb and normalized using an integrated probabilistic model [9]. For *Drosophila*, Hi-C matrix constructed using reads extracted from Kc167 cells and binned at 20kb was used [37]. The different resolutions are used to show that Matryoshka has the ability to process higher quality data. Tests on this wide variety of datasets prove that Matryoshka results are robust to changes in the input. Where mentioned, randomized hierarchies are generated while preserving certain properties, as explained in the Methods section.

The results from Matryoshka show the hierarchical structure for the three datasets. It is evident that the human genome is folded into a complex hierarchical structure in comparison to the much simpler hierarchy for the fruit fly. The mouse genome, as further results show, has very similar features to the human genome, suggesting that the chromatin folding mechanism may be conserved across mammals, even when the overall complexity of chromatin structure is not. The difference in overall complexity could also, in part, be due to the lower resolution data for mouse and the higher resolution for human.

	IMR90	mCortex	Kc167
Total	14538	2695	866
Level 1	496	2192	418
Level 2	7012	467	214
Level 3	2593	60	116
Level 4	3058	21	48
Level 5	1009	9	39
Level 6	364	9	31

Table 1: Number of TADs at each level of the hierarchy.

3.2 Enrichment of insulator elements

For mammalian genomes, it has been shown that the protein CTCF binds many known insulator or barrier elements in the genome which tend to lie at the borders of chromatin domains [14]. Hence, CTCF binding has been used as a measure of the quality of domains, as predicted by previous works [9, 11]. Similarly, a recent study shows that the *Drosophila* homolog of CTCF, dCTCF, is weakly enriched at domain boundaries [37]. By counting the average number of peaks per 10kb in a 500kb region on each side of a boundary, we show that our hierarchical domains boundaries are highly enriched for CTCF for both the human and mouse datasets (see Fig 2a). Such a pattern is not observed for the *Drosophila* cells, possibly reflecting the weaker enrichment pattern. These results suggest that our hierarchical domains are closely linked with biologically functional sites in the genome.

To further test these hypotheses, we compared the ratio of CTCF sites, overlapping with our domains and boundaries in each dataset against 1000 randomized hierarchies. We also repeated this test for su(Hw) protein, an insulator, binding sites in *Drosophila*. These results are summarized in Fig 2b, showing that the 1000 randomized hierarchies have a significantly lower ratio of sites that overlap with domain boundaries in each case. These proteins restrict trasnscriptional activity across domains in mammals and may have a similar function in the chromatin structure of other organisms. However, despite this bias towards the boundaries, only a small proportion of insulator protein binding sites are present within boundaries, as detailed in prior work [9]. This observation holds true for our hierarchies as well, considering domains only at the level with maximum number of domains for each species (Fig 2c). The weaker enrichment in *Drosophila* is evident from this as well.

3.3 Conservation of hierarchies in mammals

Previous studies have shown that chromatin domains in mammals are conserved across species and cell types [9]. We show that not just the domains we predict, but the hierarchical structure is conserved at each level as well. We do so by comparing domains in the whole genome, as well as those at individual levels of the hierarchy. Since we are comparing data from human fibroblast and mouse cortex, results would reflect conservation across both species and cell type. In order to compare the datasets, we use the UCSC liftover tool to convert domains from one set to the other. We calculate the ratio of overlap between two sets of domains, D_i and D_j, as follows:

$$\text{overlap}(D_i, D_j) = \frac{IS(D_i, D_j)}{\sum\limits_{d_i \in D_i} |d_i| + \sum\limits_{d_j \in D_j} |d_j| - IS(D_i, D_j)} \quad (12)$$

where $d_i = [a_i, b_i]$, $|d_i| = (b_i - a_i + 1)$ and IS calculated by taking the sum of the lengths of the intersecting regions in the two sets, $\sum_{d_i \in D_i} \sum_{d_j \in D_j} \left|[a_i, b_i] \cap [a_j, b_j]\right|$.

We converted domains from the IMR90 data to the mCortex data and calculated the overlap between this new domain set and the domains from mCortex. This liftover was expected to have minimal loss of information due to the much higher resolution of the IMR90 dataset. As control, we used the randomized hierarchical domains from IMR90 and repeated the procedure on these randomized sets. The randomized results presented are an average over the 1000 randomized domain trials. All these results are presented in Table 2. Looking at the complete structure, we see a greater overlap between predicted domains in the whole genome as compared to randomized domains, showing that they are conserved across the datasets. This is also true for the higher (i.e. coarser) levels of the hierarchy.

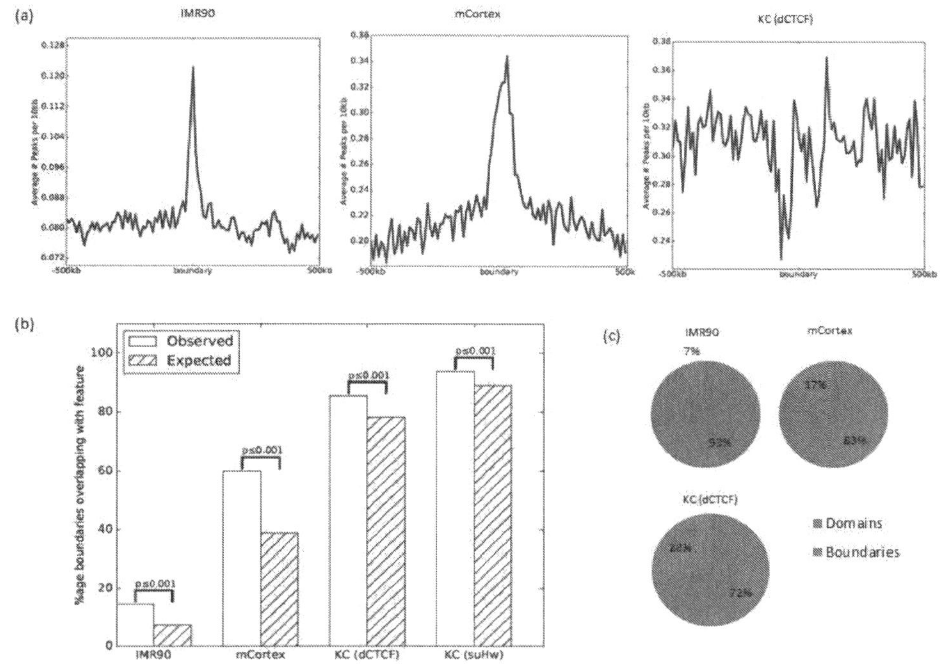

Figure 2: Enrichment of insulator binding sites at chromatin domain boundaries. Plots in (*a*) show the high number of CTCF peaks 500kb upstream and downstream of the domain boundaries for each species. The number of overlapping boundaries and sites is compared against a 1000 randomized hierarchies (*b*) and, although concentrated around boundaries, the actual percentage of overlapping sites is low (*c*). Note that for (*c*) only top level of the hierarchy is considered.

The reason for discrepancy at lower levels could be two-fold. It shows that the superdomains are conserved, whereas the subdomains possibly allow for the phenotypic variation across cell types [27]. It has been predicted that larger domains are stable across cells and changes at a smaller level correspond to differentiation and variation in gene expression [13]. These results reflect the biological significance of chromatin structure and domains that have been conserved across evolution and are an important property of the genomic architecture. However, it is also possible, of course, that the discrepancy comes from the inevitable loss of data when lifting-over between species. To check for this, we repeated the tests for overlap between domains predicted using human B-lymphoblastoid cells (GM12878) data and those from the IMR90 data and also between domains predicted using the mouse embryonic stem cell (mESC) data and those from the mCortex data. For the former pair of datasets, there is statistically-significant conservation even at lower (i.e. finer) levels of the hierarchy, showing that loss of data at lift-over needs to be accounted for during domain comparisons across organisms. For the latter dataset, the lower resolution and, consequently, fewer number of domains at the lower levels does not allow for this comparison. Further testing on higher resolution datasets could provide more insights into the conservation of hierarchical domains and their role in different cell types and species.

3.4 Location of housekeeping genes

We analyzed the pattern of overlap between our predicted domains in the hierarchy and housekeeping genes. The role of topological domains in gene activation in mammals has been analysed before [9, 36, 38] and results show that actively transcribing genes lie at domain boundaries. The complex chromatin architecture and the significance of hierarchical structure is evident from our analysis as well. In both human and mouse, it is observed that housekeeping genes tend to lie within domains at the top-most levels of the hierarchy (level 1 and 2) and outside domains at the lower levels (see Fig 3a, b). While the smaller domains play a part in controlling transcriptional activity, the larger folded structures may have a different role in the biological system. (Note that the mouse data is at much lower resolution, reflected by the p-values.)

On the other hand, a similar test in *Drosophila* reveals that the housekeeping genes are present at domain boundaries with a higher probability, than that expected at random, at each level of the hierarchy (see Fig 3c). Super-domains in the hierarchical chromatin structure of mammals may regulate gene expression differently than that in the less complex genome of *Drosophila*. Further analysis could reveal how chromatin architectures affect the activity of genes in various species.

Projection type	Whole Genome	Level 1	Level 2	Level 3	Level 4
D_mCortex vs. D_IMR90 → mCortex	0.737 (0.001)	0.352 (0.002)	0.175 (0.132)	0.022 (0.856)	0.023 (0.131)
RD_mCortes vs. RD_IMR90 → mCortex	0.677	0.283	0.156	0.031	0.015
D_GM12878 vs. D_IMR90	0.995 (0.001)	0.995 (0.001)	0.973 (0.001)	0.461 (0.001)	0.089 (001)
RD_GM12878 vs. RD_IMR90	0.877	0.877	0.855	0.417	0.085
D_mESC vs. D_mCortex	0.643 (0.001)	0.643 (0.001)	0.065 (0.004)	0 (-)	0 (-)
RD_mESC vs. RD_mCortex	0.531	0.531	0.017	0	0

Table 2: Conservation of domain structure across species and cell types, measured by overlap, calculated using equation 12. The → implies that the dataset was converted using the UCSC liftover tool; D is for domains predicted by Matryoshka and RD for randomized domains. Values in brackets are p-values calculated against a 1000 randomized hierarchies.

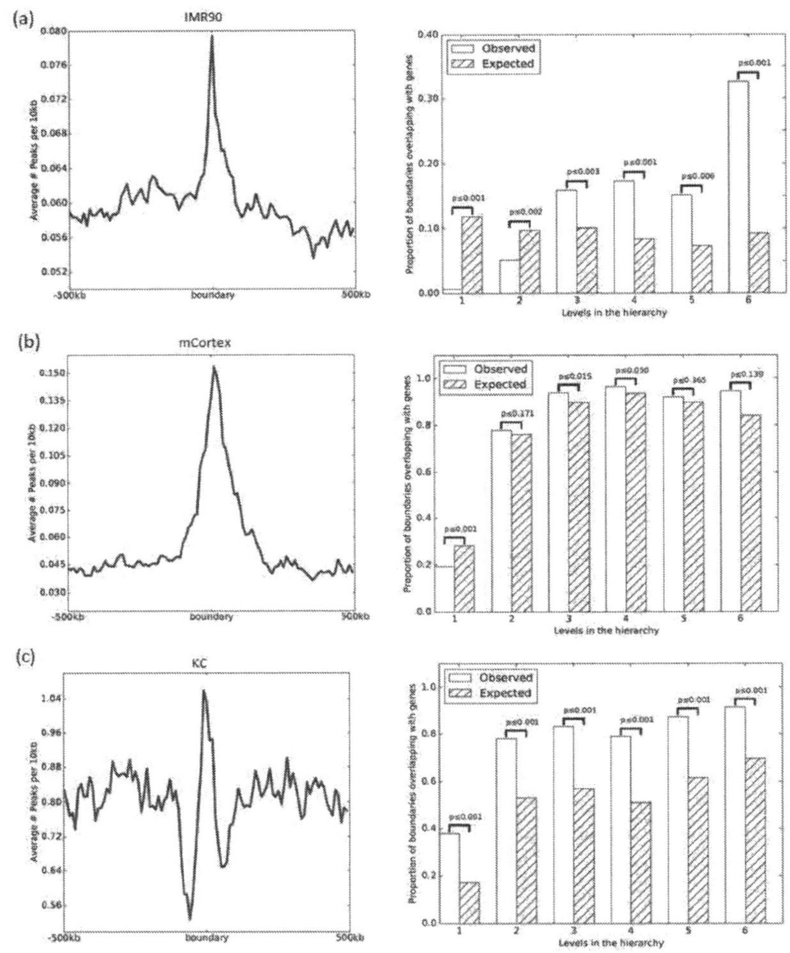

Figure 3: Enrichment of housekeeping genes in the 500kb region on each side of the domain boundaries along with comparison against a 1000 randomized hierarchies. Housekeeping genes tend to lie at boundaries of the smaller domains in mammals (*a*, *b*) and domains across all levels in *Drosophila* (*c*).

3.5 Location of interacting regulatory elements

Enhancers and promoters regulate gene expression but can frequently be at long distances from the genes that they control. It is predicted that associated enhancers and promoters are more likely to interact within the same topological domain as compared to across domains [36]. To test this for our domains at the top most level, we used associated enhancers and promoters in mouse cortex provided by [36] and enhancer-promoter pairs in human predicted by [16]. We compared the ratio of these clusters or pairs that are completely nested within domains predicted by our algorithm against a 1000 randomized hierarchies. For the mouse dataset, we find that 49% of the enhancer-promoter pairs are completely nested within the domains predicted, compared to an average of 22% in the randomized domains ($p \leq 0.043$). Similarly, for the domains in human, 57% of the enhancer-promoter pairs are nested, compared to an average of 12% in the random selection ($p \leq 0.008$). These show a strong correlation between topological domains and regulatory elements in the genome, with more interactions within a domain and relatively greater insulation across domains. These also reflect the functional role that topological domains play in gene expression and regulation. (We were unable to find a concise listing of enhancer and promoter locations in *Drosophila* for similar tests.)

3.6 Comparison with TADtree

We provide a comparison between the domains detected by Matryoshka and TADtree, along with some features of the two softwares. We were able to run TADtree only on the mouse cortex and mouse embryonic stem cell datasets. (It does not properly parse and process the higher resolution and normalized datasets from human and fly.) Predicted hierarchies are dependent on several parameters that are required as input by TADtree. One of these is the maximum domain size allowed, S, and the run-time of the algorithm is $O(S^4)$. For the purpose of this study, we set the maximum domain size to 50 bins, the default suggested by the authors. Note that this is smaller than the maximum size detected by Matryoshka, and could also vary significantly based on the resolution of the data. Apart from this, TADtree also requires the number of domains the hierarchy can contain, N. We ran with multiple values for N and selected the best result using the ratio of duplicate domains detected, which should ideally be around 1 (this selection procedure was suggested by the authors of TADtree). The exact value of N varied between 8 and 70 for each chromosome in the datasets.

In terms of computational power, Matryoshka, using γ values 0 to 1 (inclusive) with a step size of 0.01, was run on a personal computer with 1.8GHz Intel Core *i*7 and 8Gb of RAM. It took only 31 minutes and 11 seconds to process the entire mouse cortex dataset containing 19 chromosomes. On the other hand, TADtree took several (>6) hours to run on data from a *single* chromosome of the mouse. This time could vary a lot depending on the choice of parameters by the user and, in this case, was minimized due to prior tests using a range of parameters on the same dataset. It should also be noted that Matryoshka is able to process much higher resolutions than TADtree and requires only a single parameter as input, signficantly reducing the complexity and making it easier to use. Hence, our method provides an efficient and robust way for predicting hierarchical chromatin structures using Hi-C data.

The total number of domains given by TADtree is 533 and 484 in the mCortex and mESC data, respectively, which is much less than the total number predicted by Matryoshka across all the chromosomes. Testing for enrichment of CTCF binding sites at the boundaries of these domains shows that only 21.2% in the mCortex data and only 44.1% in the mESC data overlap with the known sites,

	Matryoshka	
TADtree	mESC	mCortex
mESC	0.19	0.16
mCortex	0.19	0.2

Table 3: Overlap between domains predicted by the two tools, as calculated using equation 12

where a boundary is considered to be the region between two domains and the result is averaged over all levels of the hierarchy. In comparison, 76.2% and 73.3% of boundaries in mCortex and mESC cells, respectively, given by our tool overlap with these sites. Since chromatin domains are known to be preserved across mammalian cells, we check for overlap within these sets and also with domains predicted by Matryoshka. The overlap ratio, calculated using equation 12, between the two cell type domains given by Matryoshka is 0.643, whereas that given by TADtree is only 0.175. This overlap ratio is much lower than that expected for domains from the same species ($p \leq 0.001$ obtained by comparing against a 1000 randomized hierarchies from these species). Similarly, domains predicted by the two tools have little overlap across cell types, as presented in table 3, showing that the two tools give vastly different outputs. These results show that domains predicted by Matryoshka may be closer to the actual structure of the chromatin than those predicted by TADtree.

4 DISCUSSION AND CONCLUSION

Analysis of chromatin conformation data has revealed the hierarchical nature of chromatin folding but there are no efficient tools that allow the extraction of this hierarchy from raw chromatin conformation capture data. In this paper, we presented a tool, Matryoshka, that predicts the nested structure of chromatin domains from raw Hi-C interaction matrices. Domains are extracted independently across a wide range of different scales using a variant of the method of Filippova et al. [11]. Subsequently, our method effectively predicts the number of levels for the hierarchy based on the variation among domains at multiple resolutions. The distance metric used for clustering reflects the variation in domains at different resolutions and therefore a greater variation implies a larger number of possible nested domains. The algorithm is completely data-driven, and the only input required from the user is the maximum γ value, for which an appropriate value can be set based on properties of the input data. We show, by testing across multiple datasets, that Matryoshka is robust to changes in the nature of the input Hi-C data and is able to efficiently process high resolution Hi-C matrices as well. We also show that the domain boundaries predicted are highly enriched for insulator and regulatory elements. The role of these elements in gene regulation and their relationship with chromatin domains has been previously validated.

Further, we show the relationship between hierarchical domains in mouse and human data and demonstrate that superdomains (the coarse-grained levels of our hierarchy) are conserved. A more extensive study of the complete structure across various species, and not just the set of linear domains, could contribute to our understanding of the evolution of DNA structure. It would help to analyze how gene regulatory mechanisms vary at the super and subdomain levels in different organisms. Previous studies have predicted that stable larger domains may have a role to play in cell-cycle regulation and timing, whereas changes within these domains could control gene expression and differentiation [3, 28]. Our method provides an robust and efficient way to classify the structures of domains at different scales, enabling us to compare them across cell types.

Similarly, the role of hierarchical domains in diseased cells could be analyzed. It is known, for example, that chromatin structure is correlated with the activity of cancerous cells [12, 20, 31]. A comparison of the nested structure in diseased and normal cells could give insights into the regulatory methods employed by healthy cells and how these are perturbed in the disease state. Further analysis would be required to determine if differences are in superdomains or subdomains, and the functions to which the genes in these domains correspond. Our algorithm allows for these studies to be carried out effectively on a large number of datasets.

Apart from these investigations, future work on chromatin structure using higher resolution data would give more insights into how domain hierarchies vary at a finer level and the significance of nested domains may become be more evident. Combining chromatin structure data with other sequencing assays is an interesting direction to explore and will enable us to relate variation in expression levels with topological domains [6, 19]. The relationship between nesting of domains and differential expression can be studied in a similar way. The importance of the 3-dimensional structure of chromatin may only become fully apparent when analyzed in conjunction with other assays, so that we can explore how changes in chromatin architecture correlate with other functional changes in the cell.

ACKNOWLEDGMENTS

This work has been supported by the National Science Foundation (BBSRC-NSF/BIO award 1564917)

REFERENCES

[1] Kadir Caner Akdemir and Lynda Chin. 2015. HiCPlotter integrates genomic data with interaction matrices. *Genome biology* 16, 1 (2015), 1–8.

[2] Ferhat Ay and William S Noble. 2015. Analysis methods for studying the 3D architecture of the genome. *Genome biology* 16, 1 (2015), 183.

[3] Megan S Bodnar and David L Spector. 2013. Chromatin Meets Its Organizers. *Cell* 153, 6 (2013), 1187–1189.

[4] Rasha E Boulos, Nicolas Tremblay, Alain Arneodo, Pierre Borgnat, and Benjamin Audit. 2017. Multi-scale structural community organisation of the human genome. *BMC bioinformatics* 18, 1 (2017), 209.

[5] Giacomo Cavalli and Tom Misteli. 2013. Functional implications of genome topology. *Nature structural & molecular biology* 20, 3 (2013), 290–299.

[6] Haiming Chen, Jie Chen, Lindsey A Muir, Scott Ronquist, Walter Meixner, Mats Ljungman, Thomas Ried, Stephen Smale, and Indika Rajapakse. 2015. Functional organization of the human 4D Nucleome. *Proceedings of the National Academy of Sciences* 112, 26 (2015), 8002–8007.

[7] Jie Chen, Alfred O Hero, and Indika Rajapakse. 2016. Spectral identification of topological domains. *Bioinformatics* (2016), btw221.

[8] Elzo de Wit and Wouter de Laat. 2012. A decade of 3C technologies: insights into nuclear organization. *Genes & development* 26, 1 (2012), 11–24.

[9] Jesse R Dixon, Siddarth Selvaraj, Feng Yue, Audrey Kim, Yan Li, Yin Shen, Ming Hu, Jun S Liu, and Bing Ren. 2012. Topological domains in mammalian genomes identified by analysis of chromatin interactions. *Nature* 485, 7398 (2012), 376–380.

[10] Celso A Espinoza and Bing Ren. 2011. Mapping higher order structure of chromatin domains. *Nature genetics* 43, 7 (2011), 615–617.

[11] Darya Filippova, Rob Patro, Geet Duggal, and Carl Kingsford. 2014. Identification of alternative topological domains in chromatin. *Algorithms for Molecular Biology* 9, 1 (2014), 1.

[12] Geoff Fudenberg, Gad Getz, Matthew Meyerson, and Leonid A Mirny. 2011. High order chromatin architecture shapes the landscape of chromosomal alterations in cancer. *Nature biotechnology* 29, 12 (2011), 1109–1113.

[13] Johan H Gibcus and Job Dekker. 2013. The hierarchy of the 3D genome. *Molecular cell* 49, 5 (2013), 773–782.

[14] Lars Guelen, Ludo Pagie, Emilie Brasset, Wouter Meuleman, Marius B Faza, Wendy Talhout, Bert H Eussen, Annelies de Klein, Lodewyk Wessels, Wouter de Laat, and others. 2008. Domain organization of human chromosomes revealed by mapping of nuclear lamina interactions. *Nature* 453, 7197 (2008), 948–951.

[15] Noelle Haddad, Cédric Vaillant, and Daniel Jost. 2017. IC-Finder: inferring robustly the hierarchical organization of chromatin folding. *Nucleic acids research* 45, 10 (2017), e81–e81.

[16] Bing He, Changya Chen, Li Teng, and Kai Tan. 2014. Global view of enhancer-promoter interactome in human cells. *Proceedings of the National Academy of Sciences* 111, 21 (2014), E2191–E2199.

[17] Chunhui Hou, Li Li, Zhaohui S Qin, and Victor G Corces. 2012. Gene density, transcription, and insulators contribute to the partition of the Drosophila genome into physical domains. *Molecular cell* 48, 3 (2012), 471–484.

[18] Jon Kleinberg and Eva Tardos. 2005. Dynamic Programming. In *Algorithm Design*. Addison-Wesley, 251–260.

[19] Xun Lan, Heather Witt, Koichi Katsumura, Zhenqing Ye, Qianben Wang, Emery H Bresnick, Peggy J Farnham, and Victor X Jin. 2012. Integration of Hi-C and ChIP-seq data reveals distinct types of chromatin linkages. *Nucleic acids research* 40, 16 (2012), 7690–7704.

[20] François Le Dily, Davide Baù, Andy Pohl, Guillermo P Vicent, François Serra, Daniel Soronellas, Giancarlo Castellano, Roni HG Wright, Cecilia Ballare, Guillaume Filion, and others. 2014. Distinct structural transitions of chromatin topological domains correlate with coordinated hormone-induced gene regulation. *Genes & development* 28, 19 (2014), 2151–2162.

[21] Celine Lévy-Leduc, Maud Delattre, Tristan Mary-Huard, and Stéphane Robin. 2014. Two-dimensional segmentation for analyzing Hi-C data. *Bioinformatics* 30, 17 (2014), i386–i392.

[22] Erez Lieberman-Aiden, Nynke L Van Berkum, Louise Williams, Maxim Imakaev, Tobias Ragoczy, Agnes Telling, Ido Amit, Bryan R Lajoie, Peter J Sabo, Michael O Dorschner, and others. 2009. Comprehensive mapping of long-range interactions reveals folding principles of the human genome. *science* 326, 5950 (2009), 289–293.

[23] Marina Meilă. 2003. Comparing clusterings by the variation of information. In *Learning theory and kernel machines*. Springer, 173–187.

[24] Takeshi Mizuguchi, Geoffrey Fudenberg, Sameet Mehta, Jon-Matthew Belton, Nitika Taneja, Hernan Diego Folco, Peter FitzGerald, Job Dekker, Leonid Mirny, Jemima Barrowman, and others. 2014. Cohesin-dependent globules and heterochromatin shape 3D genome architecture in S. pombe. *Nature* 516, 7531 (2014), 432–435.

[25] Natalia Naumova, Maxim Imakaev, Geoffrey Fudenberg, Ye Zhan, Bryan R Lajoie, Leonid A Mirny, and Job Dekker. 2013. Organization of the mitotic chromosome. *Science* 342, 6161 (2013), 948–953.

[26] Leonid I Nazarov, Mikhail V Tamm, Vladik A Avetisov, and Sergei K Nechaev. 2015. A statistical model of intra-chromosome contact maps. *Soft matter* 11, 5 (2015), 1019–1025.

[27] Jennifer E Phillips-Cremins, Michael EG Sauria, Amartya Sanyal, Tatiana I Gerasimova, Bryan R Lajoie, Joshua SK Bell, Chin-Tong Ong, Tracy A Hookway, Changying Guo, Yuhua Sun, and others. 2013. Architectural protein subclasses shape 3D organization of genomes during lineage commitment. *Cell* 153, 6 (2013), 1281–1295.

[28] Benjamin D Pope, Tyrone Ryba, Vishnu Dileep, Feng Yue, Weisheng Wu, Olgert Denas, Daniel L Vera, Yanli Wang, R Scott Hansen, Theresa K Canfield, and others. 2014. Topologically associating domains are stable units of replication-timing regulation. *Nature* 515, 7527 (2014), 402–405.

[29] Suhas SP Rao, Miriam H Huntley, Neva C Durand, Elena K Stamenova, Ivan D Bochkov, James T Robinson, Adrian L Sanborn, Ido Machol, Arina D Omer, Eric S Lander, and others. 2014. A 3D map of the human genome at kilobase resolution reveals principles of chromatin looping. *Cell* 159, 7 (2014), 1665–1680.

[30] Lindsay Rizzardi, Peter Hickey, Varenka Rodriguez, Rakel Tryggvadottir, Colin Callahan, Adrian Idrizi, Kasper Hansen, and Andrew P Feinberg. 2017. Neuronal brain region-specific DNA methylation and chromatin accessibility are associated with neuropsychiatric disease heritability. *bioRxiv* (2017), 120386.

[31] Mathieu Rousseau, Maria A Ferraiuolo, Jennifer L Crutchley, XQ Wang, Hisashi Miura, Mathieu Blanchette, and Josée Dostie. 2014. Classifying leukemia types with chromatin conformation data. *Genome Biol* 15, 4 (2014), R60.

[32] Peter J Rousseeuw. 1987. Silhouettes: a graphical aid to the interpretation and validation of cluster analysis. *Journal of computational and applied mathematics* 20 (1987), 53–65.

[33] M Jordan Rowley and Victor G Corces. 2016. The three-dimensional genome: principles and roles of long-distance interactions. *Current opinion in cell biology* 40 (2016), 8–14.

[34] Michael EG Sauria, Jennifer E Phillips-Cremins, Victor G Corces, and James Taylor. 2014. Hifive: a normalization approach for higher-resolution hic and 5c chromosome conformation data analysis. *bioRxiv* (2014), 009951.

[35] Tom Sexton, Eitan Yaffe, Ephraim Kenigsberg, Frédéric Bantignies, Benjamin Leblanc, Michael Hoichman, Hugues Parrinello, Amos Tanay, and Giacomo Cavalli. 2012. Three-dimensional folding and functional organization principles of the Drosophila genome. *Cell* 148, 3 (2012), 458–472.

[36] Yin Shen, Feng Yue, David F McCleary, Zhen Ye, Lee Edsall, Samantha Kuan, Ulrich Wagner, Jesse Dixon, Leonard Lee, Victor V Lobanenkov, and others. 2012. A map of the cis-regulatory sequences in the mouse genome. *Nature* 488, 7409 (2012), 116–120.

[37] Sergey V Ulianov, Ekaterina E Khrameeva, Alexey A Gavrilov, Ilya M Flyamer, Pavel Kos, Elena A Mikhaleva, Aleksey A Penin, Maria D Logacheva, Maxim V Imakaev, Alexander Chertovich, and others. 2015. Active chromatin and transcription play a key role in chromosome partitioning into topologically associating domains. *Genome research* (2015).

[38] Kylee J Veazey, Haiqing Wang, Yudhishtar S Behdi, William M Skiles, Richard Cheng-An Chang, and Michael C Golding. 2017. Disconnect between alcohol-induced alterations in chromatin structure and gene transcription in a mouse embryonic stem cell model of exposure. *Alcohol* (2017).

[39] Caleb Weinreb and Benjamin J Raphael. 2015. Identification of hierarchical chromatin domains. *Bioinformatics* (2015), btv485.

Cophenetic Median Trees Under the Manhattan Distance

Alexey Markin
Department of Computer Science
Iowa State University
Ames, IA 50011
amarkin@iastate.edu

Oliver Eulenstein
Department of Computer Science
Iowa State University
Ames, IA 50011
oeulenst@iastate.edu

ABSTRACT

Computing median trees from gene trees using path-difference metrics has provided several credible species tree estimates. Similar to these metrics is the cophenetic family of metrics that originates from a dendrogram comparison metric introduced more than 50 years ago. Despite the tradition and appeal of the cophenetic metrics, the problem of computing median trees under this family of metrics has not been analyzed. Like other standard median tree problems relevant in practice, as we show here, this problem is also NP-hard. NP-hard median tree problems have been successfully addressed by local search heuristics that are solving thousands of instances of a corresponding local search problem. For the local search problem under a cophenetic metric the best known (naïve) algorithm has a time complexity that is typically prohibitive for effective heuristic searches. Focusing on the Manhattan norm (Manhattan cophenetic metric), we describe an efficient algorithm for this problem that improves on the naïve solution by a factor of n, where n is the size of the input trees. We demonstrate the performance of our local search algorithm in a comparative study using published empirical data sets.

CCS CONCEPTS

• **Applied computing** → **Molecular evolution**; **Bioinformatics**;

KEYWORDS

Cophenetic distance, median trees, phylogenetics, local search, SPR

ACM Reference format:
Alexey Markin and Oliver Eulenstein. 2017. Cophenetic Median Trees Under the Manhattan Distance. In *Proceedings of ACM-BCB'17, August 20-23, 2017, Boston, MA, USA.*, 9 pages.
DOI: http://dx.doi.org/10.1145/3107411.3107443

Reconstruction of the evolutionary history, commonly modeled as a phylogenetic tree, is one of the central problems in biology. Solutions to this problem have direct applications in almost every discipline of natural sciences including medicine, epidemiology, biochemistry, agronomy, environmental sciences, and linguistics [15, 17, 18, 28, 32]. While the paramount goal of evolutionary biology is the representation of the true phylogenetic tree for millions of existing species, today the computation of phylogenies even for hundreds of species is a greatly challenging problem.

A well-established framework for large-scale phylogenetic tree inference comprises the construction of a species tree, called a *supertree*, from a collection of smaller trees each covering a subset of the species in question. Such collections of trees appear naturally either as so-called *gene trees* – the trees describing the evolution of a gene shared by species [16, 27]; or as trees collected from various sources in an attempt to unify the previously inferred knowledge and present a single phylogenetic tree with high confidence in it [5].

Supertree construction is a challenging problem on its own, since in practice the input trees often appear to be in disagreement, meaning that they suggest discordant evolutionary histories [5]. A classic approach for addressing this problem entails the search for a supertree that *fits* all the input trees as best as possible. The goodness of fit is mathematically assessed by a *cost function* that computes dissimilarity between any two phylogenetic trees. The resulting supertree search problem is called the *median tree problem* under the respective cost function. The problem has been extensively studied both from the theoretical and applications perspectives [5]. While all studied median tree problems of interest are inherently hard, various heuristics estimating median trees, such as the classic maximum representation with parsimony (MRP), hold enormous value for the biological community and have become an essential tool in practice [8, 19, 30, 38, 40].

The recent surge of interest in median trees under one of the oldest and extensively studied metrics in comparative phylogenetics, the path-difference distance [25, 26], opened a promising path for studies of median trees under other vector-based objectives. Perhaps, the most well-established one of them is the *cophenetic distance* [9]. The cophenetic distance was established based on one of the most popular dendrogram (which can be seen to be equivalent to a bijectively labeled weighted phylogenetic tree) comparison methods introduced by Sokal and Rohlf more than 50 years ago [35].

Similarly to the path-difference distance that uses the encoding of trees as path-length vectors, the cophenetic distance uses a vector encoding called a *cophenetic vector.* A cophenetic vector contains information about a distance from the least common ancestor (LCA) of two taxa to the root of the tree for *each* pair of taxa in a given rooted tree. A cophenetic vector *equivalently* encodes a phylogenetic tree [9]; hence one can measure a distance between two trees in the cophenetic vector space. Such distance can be formulated in terms of common vector norms, such as the Manhattan norm (also known as the Taxicab norm) and the Euclidean norm; the corresponding tree metrics are called the *Manhattan cophenetic distance* and the *Euclidean cophenetic distance* respectively. In

Permission to make digital or hard copies of all or part of this work for personal or classroom use is granted without fee provided that copies are not made or distributed for profit or commercial advantage and that copies bear this notice and the full citation on the first page. Copyrights for components of this work owned by others than ACM must be honored. Abstracting with credit is permitted. To copy otherwise, or republish, to post on servers or to redistribute to lists, requires prior specific permission and/or a fee. Request permissions from permissions@acm.org.
ACM-BCB'17, August 20-23, 2017, Boston, MA, USA.
© 2017 ACM. 978-1-4503-4722-8/17/08...$15.00
DOI: http://dx.doi.org/10.1145/3107411.3107443

contrast to other popular comparative metrics, such as Robinson-Foulds, the cophenetic metrics can be similarly defined for weighted phylogenetic trees as well, which gives it an additional perspective advantage.

While both the cophenetic metrics and the path-difference metrics use vector distances, apart from that the two distance families do not bare much similarity. Primarily, the cophenetic distance relies on the LCA-mappings which brings it semantically closer to the classic model-based *deep coalescence* cost function [23] and the related *duplications with losses* cost function [6]. Indeed, in this work we experimentally establish that the cophenetic metrics are more closely correlated with the classic model-based deep coalescence cost function than the path-difference metrics. Further, in contrast to the path-difference metrics, which are only insignificantly perturbed by the rootings of the trees under consideration, the cophenetic metrics rely heavily on the rootings, and therefore, are better suited for the inference of rooted phylogenies.

As most of the other median tree problems are inherently complex, unsurprisingly, here we show that the cophenetic median tree problem is NP-hard. In fact, even the commonly practiced local search estimation approach implemented naïvely turns out to be computationally heavy and already infeasible for an instance of the cophenetic median tree problem involving less than a hundred of species. In our work we move the feasibility bound for the local search heuristic much farther by designing an efficient local neighborhood search algorithm. The algorithm results from (i) an extensive analysis of properties of the cophenetic vectors and (ii) the adapted preprocessing part of the recently developed algorithmic framework targeting the path-difference median tree heuristics. With the efficient heuristic at hand we were able to compute the first large-scale cophenetic median tree estimates and evaluate them against supertrees constructed by other standard supertree methods on benchmark empirical datasets.

Related work. The family of cophenetic metrics has been first extensively studied by Cardona et.al. [9]. Their work, on one hand, addresses the minimum and maximum values as well as distributions of the cophenetic metrics; on the other hand, compares the cophenetic metrics to other popular comparative metrics, such as path-difference distances and the Robinson-Foulds metric. The best known algorithm for computing the cophenetic distance between any two phylogenetic trees of size n requires $O(n^2)$ time.

There has been a large body of work focusing on the biological, mathematical, and algorithmic properties of median trees adopting various definitions of distance measures that have been effectively used in comparative phylogenetics [5]. As most of the studied median tree problems are NP-hard, the classic median tree estimation algorithms, including MRP, effectively employ the local search (hill-climbing) heuristics [2, 10, 22, 24, 39], which have provided credible estimates of large-scale species trees [24, 39]. Local search heuristics typically operate in a search space of all existing supertrees (candidate median trees) for the given collection of input trees. The search starts with a supertree called a *seed* and it maintains the candidate median tree updating it on each iteration. An iteration encompasses a search of a tree with the minimum distance to the input trees in the neighborhood of the current candidate tree. The neighborhood is typically defined in terms of a tree edit operation of choice. One of the most popular such operations is called *subtree prune and regraft (SPR)*, whose respective neighborhood contains $\Theta(n^2)$ trees, where n is the size of a median tree. Consequently, the SPR-neighborhood search problem under the Manhattan cophenetic metric can be solved naïvely in $\Theta(kn^4)$ time, where k is the number of input trees.

The effectiveness of standard local search heuristics is typically highly dependent on the choice of the starting tree. Traditionally, greedy heuristics are employed to efficiently construct well-fitting starting trees; that is, trees that consistently have a significantly smaller distance to the input trees than a randomly chosen tree. An extension of this approach, a *hybrid heuristic*, was introduced as a method to improve the power of the traditional approach by applying the local search heuristic in multiple stages of constructing the starting tree itself [25].

Our contribution. The focus of this work is the development and the applicability study of effective heuristics estimating cophenetic median trees. The design of a heuristic is a necessary component, as we show that the *cophenetic median tree problem* under any vector norm is NP-hard.

Focusing on the Manhattan norm, we reveal that Manhattan cophenetic median trees can be successfully estimated via the local search approach. To make this possible, we propose an efficient algorithm that exploits the properties of the cophenetic vectors and enables the heuristical computation of Manhattan cophenetic median trees for sufficiently large phylogenetic datasets relating hundreds of species. The latter is demonstrated in our first experimental study that explores the runtime of the local search heuristic. The proposed algorithm solves the local SPR-neighborhood search problem in $O(kn^3)$ improving on the naïve runtime by a factor of n.

Further, in our experiments, we use the developed algorithm as a core of the state-of-the-art hybrid heuristic to evaluate cophenetic median trees on published empirical datasets. We evaluate the obtained cophenetic median trees against supertrees constructed by several other classic supertree methods. Finally, motivated by the previous work and our results, we study the correlation of the Manhattan cophenetic metric to the classic model-based cost functions including deep coalescence, duplications, and duplications with losses.

1 BASICS AND PRELIMINARIES

Basic definitions. Throughout this paper we adhere to the definitions and notation introduced in [25]. A *(phylogenetic) tree* T is a rooted binary tree, where each leaf is uniquely labeled with a taxon, each internal node v has exactly two children nodes, denoted by $\mathrm{Ch}_T(v)$, and each node u except for the root has a single parent node denoted by $\mathrm{Pa}_T(u)$. In addition, we denote the node set, edge set and leaf set of T by $V(T)$, $E(T)$ and $\mathsf{L}(T)$ respectively. We denote the root by $\mathrm{Rt}(T)$ and a sibling of each non-root node u by $\mathrm{Sb}(u)$. We also set $T(v)$ to be a subtree of T rooted at $v \in V(T)$, and $\overline{T(v)}$ to be a tree obtained by pruning $T(v)$ from T. Occasionally we use the standard nested parenthesis notation to represent small trees.

We define a partial order $\leq_T$ on the vertex set $V(T)$, such that $u \leq v$, if v is a node on the path from u to $\mathrm{Rt}(T)$. Additionally, we say $u < v$, if $u \leq v$ and $u \neq v$. The *least common ancestor (LCA)* of two nodes $u, v \in V(T)$, $\mathsf{LCA}_T(u, v)$, is the furthest from the root node, w, such that $v \preceq w$ and $u \preceq w$.

A set of leaves $\mathsf{L}(T(v))$ is called a *cluster* of the node v, and is denoted by C_v. Note that for convenience we identify the leaves in a phylogenetic tree with the respective labels (taxa).

Let $L \subsetneq \mathsf{L}(T)$ and T' be the minimal subtree of T with leaf set L. We define the *leaf-induced subtree* $T[L]$ of T to be the tree obtained from T' by successively removing each node of degree two (except for the root) and adjoining its two neighbors (a parent and a child).

Let $\mathcal{P}$ be a set of phylogenetic trees $\{G_1, \ldots, G_k\}$. We extend the definition of a leaf set to a set of trees as follows: $\mathsf{L}(\mathcal{P}) := \cup_{i=1}^{k} \mathsf{L}(G_i)$. A tree S is called a *supertree* of $\mathcal{P}$, if $\mathsf{L}(S) = \mathsf{L}(\mathcal{P})$. A set of trees $\mathcal{P}$ is called *compatible* if there exist a supertree T consistent with every tree in $\mathcal{P}$, and a tree T is *consistent* with a tree G if $T[\mathsf{L}(G)] \equiv G$ up to isomorphism of rooted semi-labeled trees [33].

Cophenetic distance. In this section we follow the definitions presented in [9]. Given a phylogenetic tree T, let the *cophenetic value* of $u, v \in V(T)$, denoted by $\phi_{u,v}(T)$, be the length (measured in the number of edges) of the path from $\mathsf{LCA}_T(u, v)$ to $\mathsf{Rt}(T)$. Additionally, $\delta_u := \phi_{u,u}(T)$ is the *depth* of the node u. Given that, the *cophenetic vector* of T is

$$\phi(T) = (\phi_{i,j}(T))_{1 \le i \le j \le |\mathsf{L}(T)|},$$

for some fixed ordering of leaves in T. The *cophenetic distance* between two trees G and S over the same leaf set is defined as

$$\mathsf{d}_{\phi,p}(G, S) := ||\phi(G) - \phi(S)||_p,$$

where $|| \cdot ||_p$ denotes an L_p norm of a vector for some fixed $p \in [1, \infty)$.

Next, let $\Phi(G, S)$ be the *cophenetic difference matrix* of size $|\mathsf{L}(G)| \times |\mathsf{L}(G)|$, such that for all $i, j \in \mathsf{L}(G)$, $\Phi_{i,j}(G, S) = \phi_{i,j}(G) - \phi_{i,j}(S)$. Note that $\mathsf{L}(G)$ should be equivalent to $\mathsf{L}(S)$.

We further extend the definition of cophenetic distance to a set of trees. Given a set of trees $\mathcal{P}$ and a supertree of $\mathcal{P}$, S, the cophenetic distance between S and $\mathcal{P}$ is

$$\mathsf{d}_{\phi,p}(\mathcal{P}, S) := \sum_{G \in \mathcal{P}} \mathsf{d}_{\phi,p}(G, S[\mathsf{L}(G)]).$$

On practice the input trees are of different sizes and might be involved this different sets of taxa. Consequently, the supertrees are typically larger than the input trees. Note however that we defined the cophenetic distance only for trees over the same taxon set. Hence, in the above equation we use the *minus method* [13] to account for the cophenetic distance between the supertree S and an input tree G (that is, we prune the extra information from S when comparing to G).

Path-induced subtrees. Let $P = (u_0, u_1, \ldots, u_k)$ be a simple path in a tree T, then *i-th exit node*, denoted by $e_i(P)$, for $0 < i < k$ is defined as follows:

(a) **If** $u_{i-1} \prec u_i \prec u_{i+1}$, then $e_i := \mathsf{Sb}_T(u_{i-1})$; Figure 1 depicts an example for this case;
(b) **If** $u_{i+1} \prec u_i \prec u_{i-1}$, then $e_i := \mathsf{Sb}_T(u_{i+1})$.

Additionally, if $u_{k-1} \prec u_k$, then $e_k := \mathsf{Sb}_T(u_{k-1})$; otherwise, $e_k := u_k$. For brevity, $E_i(P) := C_{e_i(P)}$ (*i*-th *exit cluster*), or simply E_i when the path P can be inferred from the context. Figure 2 illustrates the exit nodes induced by two different types of paths.

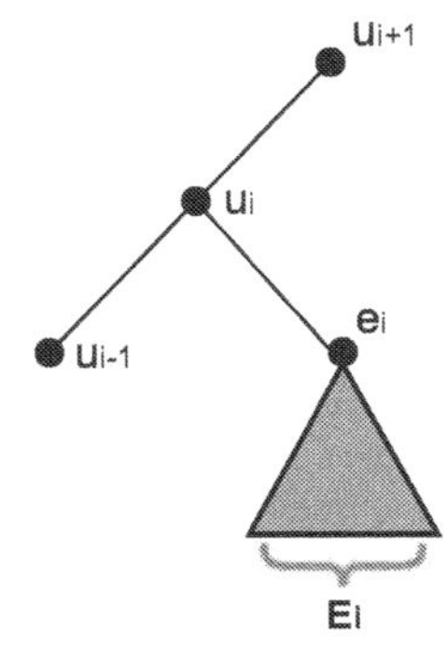

Figure 1: An example of an exit-node and the corresponding subtree

2 COPHENETIC MEDIAN TREE PROBLEMS

In this section we formulate and explore the basic properties of the median tree problems defined for cophenetic distances under different vector norms. Based on the definitions presented in the previous section we introduce a class of *cophenetic median tree problems* as follows:

Problem 2.1 (Cophenetic median tree (for an L_p norm) – decision version).
Instance: A set of input trees $\mathcal{P}$ and a real number q;
Question: Determine whether there exists a supertree S, such that $\mathsf{d}_{\phi,p}(\mathcal{P}, S) \le q$.

2.1 Cophenetic median tree problems are NP-hard

We prove that Problem 2.1 is NP-hard under any L_p vector norm. The proof is based on the NP-hardness proof of the related path-difference median tree problem [26]. To show NP-hardness we provide a reduction from the NP-complete MaxRTC [7].

Problem 2.2 (Maximum Compatible Subset of Rooted Triplets – MaxRTC).
Instance: A set of rooted triplets $\mathcal{R}$ and an integer $0 \le c \le |\mathcal{R}|$;
Question: Is there a subset $\mathcal{R}' \subseteq \mathcal{R}$, such that $\mathcal{R}'$ is compatible and $|\mathcal{R}'| \ge c$.

THEOREM 2.1. *The cophenetic median tree problem under an L_p norm is NP-hard for any $p \ge 1$.*

PROOF. Consider a rooted triplet R and a tree S, such that $\mathsf{L}(R) \subseteq \mathsf{L}(S)$. Note that if S is *consistent* with R, then $\mathsf{d}_{\phi,p}(R, S[\mathsf{L}(R)]) = 0$; otherwise, $\mathsf{d}_{\phi,p}(R, S[\mathsf{L}(R)]) = 4^{\frac{1}{p}}$. The latter relationship can be easily verified by, for example, computing a cophenetic distance between two incompatible triplets $((a, b), c)$ and $((a, c), b)$.

Given that $\mathsf{d}_{\phi,p}(R, S[\mathsf{L}(R)])$ is a constant that depends only on whether S is consistent with R or not, we can map an instance $\langle \mathcal{R}, c \rangle$ of the MaxRTC problem to an instance $\langle \mathcal{R}, (|\mathcal{R}| - c)4^{\frac{1}{p}} \rangle$ of the cophenetic median tree problem. It is not difficult to observe that $\langle \mathcal{R}, (|\mathcal{R}| - c)4^{\frac{1}{p}} \rangle$ is a *yes*-instance if and only if $\langle \mathcal{R}, c \rangle$ is a *yes*-instance of MaxRTC. □

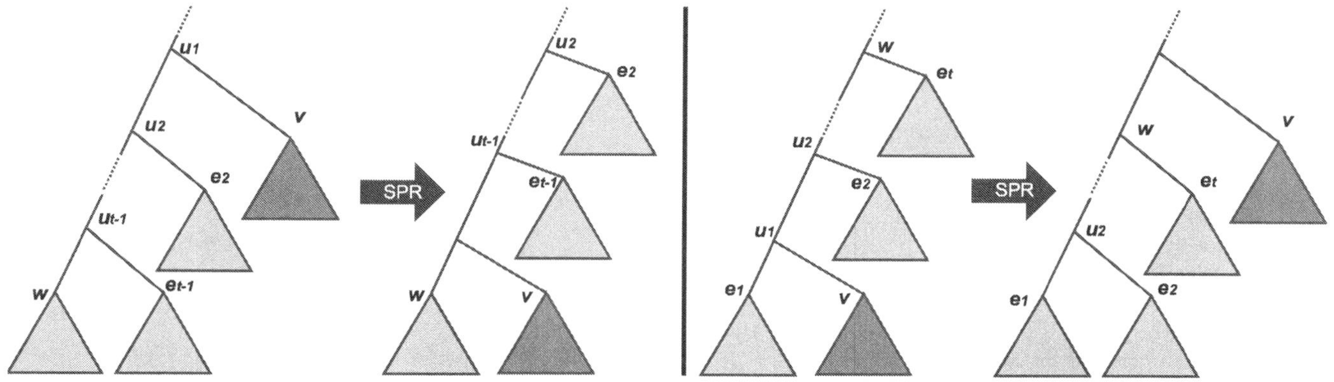

Figure 2: (left) shows how the $SPR(v, w)$ operation changes the tree structure, when w is an descendant of $\mathsf{Sb}(v)$; (right) shows how the $SPR(v, w)$ operation changes the tree, when w is an ancestor of v and $\mathsf{Sb}(v)$.

3 LOCAL SEARCH FOR THE COPHENETIC MEDIAN TREE PROBLEM

In this section we describe an efficient algorithm for approximating cophenetic median trees using a standard local search approach under the classic SPR tree edit operation.

3.1 *SPR*-Local search framework

Given a node $v \in V(S)\backslash\{\mathsf{Rt}(S)\}$, and a node $u \in V(\overline{S(v)})$, $SPR_S(v, u)$ is a tree obtained by the following modifications of the tree $S' = \overline{S(v)}$:

1. *If u is a root of S', then a new root w' is introduced, so that u is a child of w'. Otherwise, an edge $(\mathsf{Pa}(u), u)$ is subdivided by a new node w'.*
2. *Connect the pruned subtree $S(v)$ to the node w'.*

Further, we define the following sets of trees that can be obtained from S by performing SPR:

$$SPR_S(v) := \bigcup_u SPR_S(v, u); \qquad SPR_S := \bigcup_{v,u} SPR_S(v, u).$$

SPR_S is called an *SPR-neighborhood* of a tree S. It is easy to see from the definition that $|SPR_S| = O(n^2)$, where $n = |\mathsf{L}(S)|$.

Given a set of input trees $\mathcal{P} = \{G_1, ..., G_k\}$, the search space in an SPR local search problem could be viewed as a graph $\mathcal{T}$, where nodes represent all existing supertrees (candidate median trees) of $\mathcal{P}$. $\{S_1, S_2\}$ is an edge in $\mathcal{T}$, if S_1 could be transformed to S_2 with a single SPR operation.

At each iteration local search heuristic finds a candidate tree S' in the neighborhood of a current tree S, such that S' minimizes the cost function that we are interested in. In case $S \equiv S'$, the local search stops (reaches a local minimum). Otherwise, it proceeds to the next iteration with a tree S'. An instance (single iteration) of the SPR-based local neighborhood search problem could be formalized as follows:

Problem 3.1 (Cophenetic metric local neighborhood search).
Instance: An input set $\mathcal{P}$ and a candidate tree (supertree) S;
Question: Find a tree $S' = \arg\min_{S' \in SPR_S} \mathsf{d}_{\phi,p}(\mathcal{P}, S')$.

Naïve algorithm for the local search problems. Given two trees S and G, one can compute $\mathsf{d}_{\phi,p}(S, G)$ in $O(n^2)$ time for any p. Therefore, direct computation of the $\phi_p(\mathcal{P}, S')$ score for each $S' \in SPR_S$ would take $O(n^4 k)$ time, where $n = |\mathsf{L}(\mathcal{P})|$ and $k = |\mathcal{P}|$. Next, we show how to improve on this complexity under $p = 1$ (the *Manhattan* distance).

To fix the set up, let $\mathbf{G} \in \mathcal{P}$ be a fixed input tree, and let S_i be a supertree in the i-th iteration of the local search. Throughout the next section we refer to the restricted tree $S_i[\mathsf{L}(G)]$ as simply S.

3.2 Local search environment for cophenetic median trees

To design a faster algorithm for the cophenetic local search problem we examine the structure of the SPR-environment of a candidate median tree. We are interested in the structure of the cophenetic difference matrix $\Phi(T, S)$ for some $T = SPR_S(v, w)$. Let $U_T = (v = u_0, \ldots, u_t = w)$ be the path between v and w in T, and let u_h be the node closest to the root of S on that path (i.e., $u_h > u_i$ for all $0 \le i \le t, i \ne h$). Below we show the structure of the matrix $\Phi(S, T)$ by considering a few major cases that provably cover the whole matrix.

(i) $\mathbf{Sb}(v) \prec w$, i.e., the path U_T is a part of the path from v to $\mathsf{Rt}(S)$. This case is depicted in Figure 2 (right-hand side).
  (a) $\forall i \in C_v, j \in E_p : \phi_{i,j}(T) = \phi_{i,j}(S) - (t-p)$ for $1 \le p \le t-1$. This case characterizes the change in depths of LCAs between leaves in C_v and leaves in exit clusters of the path U_T. Note that while $\mathsf{LCA}_S(i, j) = u_p$, after regrafting we have $\mathsf{LCA}_T(i, j) = \mathsf{Pa}_T(w) = \mathsf{Pa}_T(v)$.
  (b) $\forall i \in C_w, j \in C_w \backslash E_1 : \phi_{i,j}(T) = \phi_{i,j}(S)+1$. This change is due to the fact that we add a new node, $\mathsf{Pa}_T(w)$, on the path from the nodes u_p (for $2 \le p \le t$) to the root. Note, however, that the depth of the node e_1 remains unchanged.

(ii) $\mathbf{Sb}_S(v) \succeq w$. This case is similar to the one considered above and it is depicted on the left-hand side of Figure 2.

(a) $\forall i \in C_v, j \in E_p$: $\phi_{i,j}(T) = \phi_{i,j}(S) + (p-2)$ for $2 \leq p \leq t$. Due to the observation that $\mathsf{LCA}_S(i,j) = u_1$, while after regrafting $\mathsf{LCA}_T(i,j) = \mathsf{Pa}_T(e_p)$.

(b) $\forall i \in C_{u_2}, j \in C_{u_2} \setminus E_t$: $\phi_{i,j}(T) = \phi_{i,j}(S) - 1$. We removed the node, $\mathsf{Pa}_S(v)$, from the paths from the nodes u_p (for $2 \leq p \leq t-1$) to the root. However, the depth of the node $e_t = w$ remains unchanged.

(iii) $\mathbf{Sb}(v) \nprec w, \mathbf{Sb}(v) \nsucceq w$. That is, u_h is some node on the path, which is neither w nor v.

(a) $\forall i \in E_1, j \in E_1$: $\phi_{i,j}(T) = \phi_{i,j}(S) - 1$. Node e_1 becomes one edge closer to the root.

(b) $\forall i \in C_w, j \in C_w$: $\phi_{i,j}(T) = \phi_{i,j}(S) + 1$. Node w becomes one edge further from the root.

(c) $\forall i \in C_v, j \in E_p$: $\phi_{i,j}(T) = \phi_{i,j}(S) + (p-h)$ for $1 \leq p \leq t, p \neq h$. For $p < h$, we have $\mathsf{LCA}_S(i,j) = u_p$ and $\mathsf{LCA}_T(i,j) = u_h$; as for $p > h$, we have $\mathsf{LCA}_S(i,j) = u_h$ and $\mathsf{LCA}_T(i,j) = \mathsf{Pa}_T(e_p)$.

(iv) For all three cases outlined above: $\forall i, j \in C_v$: $\phi_{i,j}(T) = \phi_{i,j}(S) - \delta_v(S) + \delta_w(S) + 1$. Since we regraft the subtree $S(v)$ above w, depths of all nodes inside this subtree increase by $(-\delta_v(S) + \delta_w(S) + 1)$; hence, the change in the cophenetic vector.

(v) Observe that for any other choice of i and j, the corresponding cophenetic value, $\phi_{i,j}$, is not affected.

Overall, the following clusters are involved in the changes in the cophenetic vector of S: i is one of the clusters in $\mathscr{C}_i = \{C_v, C_w, C_{u_2}, E_1\}$, and j appears in $\mathscr{C}_j = \{C_v, C_w, C_{u_2}, E_1, \ldots, E_t\}$. The key observation is that regardless of the form of U_T, there are only $O(t)$ pairs of clusters $(C_i, C_j) \in \mathscr{C}_i \times \mathscr{C}_j$ such that the respective cophenetic values are altered.

Let $d(C_i, C_j)$ be the value, such that $\forall (i,j) \in C_i \times C_j$, $\phi_{i,j}(T) = \phi_{i,j}(S) + d(C_i, C_j)$ according to the cases outlined above. For example, $d(C_v, C_v) = -\delta_v(S) + \delta_w(S) + 1$. Given that, Equation 1 shows how the cophenetic distance $\phi(S, G)$ is effected by an SPR operation. The equation has been adopted from the work on Manhattan path-difference median trees [26]. For technical reasons we define

$$\Delta_{i,j}(C_1, C_2) := \begin{cases} 0, & \text{if } i > j \text{ and } (j,i) \in C_1 \times C_2 \\ \Phi_{i,j}(S,G), & \text{otherwise.} \end{cases}$$

In most cases the fixed clusters C_1 and C_2 are clear from the context, and hence we use the shorthand notation, d and $\Delta_{i,j}$ for $d(C_1, C_2)$ and $\Delta_{i,j}(C_1, C_2)$ respectively. Below we provide the final equation.

$$\mathsf{d}_{\phi,1}(T,G) - \mathsf{d}_{\phi,1}(S,G) = \sum_{\substack{C_1 \in \mathscr{C}_i \\ C_2 \in \mathscr{C}_j}} \sum_{\substack{i \in C_1 \\ j \in C_2}} \left(|\Delta_{i,j} + d| - |\Delta_{i,j}|\right)$$

$$= \sum_{\substack{C_1 \in \mathscr{C}_i \\ C_2 \in \mathscr{C}_j}} \left(\begin{array}{c} d \cdot \#\{(i \in C_1, j \in C_2) | \Delta_{i,j} \geq -d)\} \\ -d \cdot \#\{(i \in C_1, j \in C_2) | \Delta_{i,j} < -d)\} \\ +2 \sum\limits_{\substack{i \in C_1, j \in C_2: \\ -d \leq \Delta_{i,j} < 0}} \Delta_{i,j} - 2 \sum\limits_{\substack{i \in C_1, j \in C_2: \\ 0 \leq \Delta_{i,j} < -d}} \Delta_{i,j} \end{array} \right). \quad (1)$$

3.3 Efficient algorithm

To make use of the above analysis we adopt the data structures developed in the work on Manhattan path-difference median trees [26]. In this section we briefly describe the resulting preprocessing idea.

Let $\mathscr{C}(S)$ be a set of all clusters in a tree S. For $\mathsf{L}_1, \mathsf{L}_2 \in \mathscr{C}(S)$, we define $\Sigma_{\geq}(\mathsf{L}_1, \mathsf{L}_2)$ to be a vector indexed from $-n$ to n, such that

$$\Sigma_{\geq}(\mathsf{L}_1, \mathsf{L}_2)[x] = \Sigma_{\geq}(\mathsf{L}_2, \mathsf{L}_1)[x] = \sum_{\substack{i \in \mathsf{L}_1, j \in \mathsf{L}_2: \\ i \leq j,\ \Delta_{i,j} \geq x}} \Delta_{i,j}(L_i, L_j)$$

Similarly, we define a vector $\#_{\geq}(\mathsf{L}_1, \mathsf{L}_2)$ indexed from $-n$ to n, such that

$$\#_{\geq}(\mathsf{L}_1, \mathsf{L}_2)[x] = \#\{(i \in \mathsf{L}_1, j \in \mathsf{L}_2 - \mathsf{L}_1) | i \leq j, \Delta_{i,j}(L_1, L_2) \geq x\}$$

It is not difficult to check that given such vectors it is possible to compute $\mathsf{d}_{\phi,1}(T,G) - \mathsf{d}_{\phi,1}(S,G)$ for an arbitrary $T \in SPR_S$ in $O(n)$ time using Equation 1. For example, let's consider some $T = SPR_S(v, w)$, such that the corresponding path U_T is a part of a path from v to the root (i.e., $v \prec w$). That means that if we choose $C_1 = C_v$ and $C_2 = E_1$, then $d(C_1, C_2) = -t + 1$ according to the analysis presented in Section 3.2, where $t \geq 2$ is the length of U_T in edges. We can now use the vectors defined above to find a part of the sum in Equation 1 that corresponds to the chosen clusters C_1 and C_2. That is, we observe the following relations:

- $\#\{(i \in C_1, j \in C_2) | \Delta_{i,j} \geq t-1\}$ is simply $\#_{\geq}(C_1, C_2)[t-1]$.
- $\#\{(i \in C_1, j \in C_2) | \Delta_{i,j} < t-1\} = (\#_{\geq}(C_1, C_2)[-n] - \#_{\geq}(C_1, C_2)]t-1])$.
- $\sum\limits_{\substack{i \in C_1, j \in C_2: \\ 0 \leq \Delta_{i,j} < t-1}} \Delta_{i,j} = \Sigma_{\geq}(C_1, C_2)[0] - \Sigma_{\geq}(C_1, C_2)[t-1]$.

Complexity analysis. An algorithm for computing vectors $\Sigma_{\geq}$ and $\#_{\geq}$ efficiently was presented in [26]. Although there the vectors were defined in a slightly different way, the algorithm can be adopted for our needs (we omit the technical details for brevity).

The time complexity for computing these vectors is $O(n^3)$ for a fixed input tree G. Having these vectors computed we can calculate the value $\mathsf{d}_{\phi,1}(T,G)$ in $O(n)$ for all $T \in SPR_S$. Given that $|SPR_S| = O(n^2)$, and the number of input trees is k, the overall time complexity is $O(kn^3)$.

4 EXPERIMENTAL EVALUATION

Here we evaluate the local search approach enabled by the algorithm described in the previous section as applied to the Manhattan cophenetic median tree problem. In our first study we evaluate the local search approach in terms of time that it takes to converge to a local minimum on artificially constructed datasets of different sizes. In the second study we apply the state-of-the-art local search heuristic to sufficiently large empirical datasets and compare obtained cophenetic median trees to supertrees obtained by using other popular supertree and median tree methods.

4.1 Scalability analysis

We compare the runtime of pure local search strategies (when a starting tree is chosen randomly) for the estimation of Manhattan median trees using the naïve and improved algorithms described in Sections 3.1 and 3.3 respectively.

Data sets. We estimate the runtime for randomly generated sets of input trees. We generated 12 random input sets with 10 trees in each over the number of taxa varying from 10 in the smallest dataset to 120 in the largest one, with a step of 10.

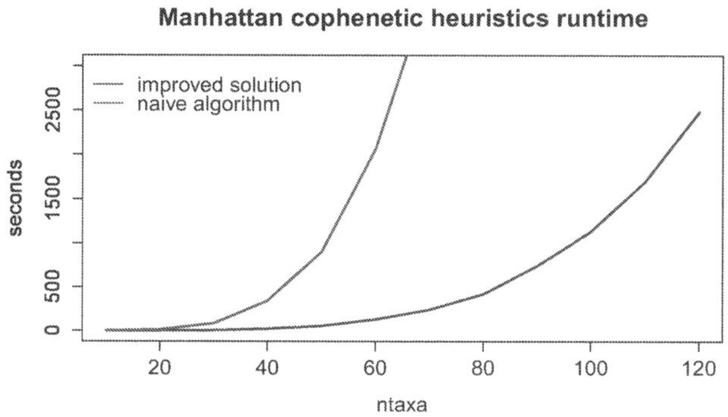

Figure 3: The growth of runtime until convergence with a gradual increase of the number of taxa in input datasets. Mean runtimes among five trials are presented.

Experimental setting. For each of the generated datasets we ran both the naïve and improved heuristics five times each. In Figure 3 we report the mean runtimes over the five trials.

Results. Figure 3 depicts that the runtime for the improved local search algorithm grows *substantially slower* than the runtime under the naïve algorithm. Without the improved algorithm the taxa limit for local search heuristic is reached already for 70 taxa. However, the presented here analysis and the resulting algorithm allows us to estimate cophenetic median trees for much larger instances, which we demonstrate in our second study.

4.2 Empirical study

In this section we compare heuristically estimated Manhattan cophenetic median trees to path-difference median trees and other supertrees constructed by using several highly recognized supertree methods. The study is conducted over two standard empirical datasets. The goal is to evaluate the applicability of the local search approach to the cophenetic median tree problem and to find relations between various supertree and median tree methods.

Data sets. Following the original work on path-difference median trees, we evaluate our cophenetic median tree heuristic on published baseline datasets [25, 26]

(i) *Cetartiodactyla*: contains 201 trees over 299 taxa overall [30];

(ii) *Marsupials*: contains 158 trees over 272 taxa overall [8].

These datasets are considerably large and serve as benchmarks for phylogenetic studies (see [3, 11, 21, 34]).

Methods. In order to obtain credible estimates for Manhattan cophenetic median trees (MCMT) we used the *hybrid heuristic* framework that was successfully applied to path-difference median trees outperforming other standard local search paradigms [26]. For comparison we use two path-difference median tree heuristics – one for Manhattan median trees (MMT) and another for Euclidean median trees (EMT).

Additionally, following the preceding studies [21, 25, 26], we include the following methods in our study: *modified min-cut* (MMC) algorithm that computes supertrees in polynomial time and was suggested for use on large-scale datasets [29]; two *triplet median tree heuristics* (TH) that approach the corresponding triplet median tree problem using SPR and TBR tree edit operations respectively [21]. Note that TBR (stands for tree bisection and reconnection) is an extension of the SPR operation, where the pruned subtree is allowed to be re-rooted before regrafting it. Finally, we include the classic *maximum parsimony with representation heuristic* (MRP). MRP was recognized as the most applied supertree method among practitioners [5]. Here we use the implementation of MRP heuristic in the popular software package, PAUP* [38], under the TBR branch swapping [21].

Experimental setting. To compare the methods under consideration we used the results of their execution over both datasets (each method was executed 10 times, except for MMC, which is a deterministic method). We further evaluated each of the generated supertrees with the respective input dataset using 6 relevant objectives: the Manhattan cophenetic distance, the Manhattan and Euclidean path-difference distances, triplet similarity (the objective function for triplet heuristics), the average maximum agreement subtree (MAST) similarity, and the parsimony score.

The best scores among the ten trials under each objective are presented in Table 1

Results. From Table 1 we observe that our objective function, the Manhattan cophenetic distance, significantly differs from others in terms of the distribution of scores across the methods. That is, as expected, the here introduced method, MCMT, performs best in terms of this objective. We also observe that the MRP and TH heuristics produce trees that are better in terms of cophenetic distance than the trees produced by path-difference median tree methods. On the other hand, MCMT produces trees that score better in terms of path-difference objectives than trees generated by MRP and TH heuristics. That is, we observe a rather asymmetric behavior for the three vector-based objectives and their respective median tree estimates (MMT, EMT, and MCMT).

4.3 Correlation with other cost functions

Cardona et.al. studied correlations between the cophenetic metrics and other popular tree comparison metrics including the path-difference distance and the classic Robinson-Foulds metric (RF) [9]. They have demonstrated that the Manhattan cophenetic distance (i) does not bare strong correlation with the Manhattan and Euclidean path-difference distances (Spearman correlation coefficient of ≈ 0.45), and (ii) has almost no significant correlation with the Robinson-Foulds distance (Spearman correlation coefficient of approximately ≈ -0.0008). As was mentioned in the introduction, the cophenetic distance is dependent on the LCA mappings, and therefore, can be expected to be more closely related to the cost functions originating from the gene tree parsimony (GTP) problem than the path-difference distance or RF. We consider the following GTP related cost functions: gene duplications (GD), deep coalescence (DC), and duplications with losses (DL). In fact, based on the formal definitions, the cophenetic distance is most closely related to the deep coalescence cost function, as both take into account the path-lengths between LCA mappings. In this section we test our hypothesis that the two cost functions are indeed correlated.

Experimental setting. In order to assess correlations between different cost function we follow the Cardona et.al. setting. That is,

Data set	Method	L_1 cophen.	L_1 PDD	L_2 PDD	Triplet-sim	MAST	Pars. score
Marsup 158 input trees 272 taxa	MMC	1,564,728	1,681,015	16,670.45	51.73 %	53.4 %	3901
	MRP	122,459	515,257	5,694.59	98.29 %	**71.6 %**	**2274**
	TH(SPR)	143,398	515,906	5,866.27	**98.99 %**	70.3 %	2312
	TH(TBR)	143,501	517,274	5,888.22	**98.99 %**	70.4 %	2317
	EMT	260,787	327,379	**4,380.77**	85.24 %	67.0 %	2869
	MMT	286,357	**323,909**	5,063.34	54.68 %	57.6 %	3817
	MCMT	**60,737**	372,719	4,974.58	90.90 %	64.8 %	3036
Cetartio 201 input trees 299 taxa	MMC	1,004,359	918,639	16,206.17	70.03 %	51.5 %	4929
	MRP	186,582	365,870	6,991.36	96.49 %	**65.2 %**	**2603**
	TH(SPR)	168,620	403,233	7,630.03	**97.28 %**	63.1 %	2754
	TH(TBR)	168,497	401,327	7,591.13	**97.28 %**	63.0 %	2754
	EMT	209,680	258,836	**5,639.24**	85.98 %	61.0 %	3394
	MMT	225,705	**258,424**	6,142.98	66.28 %	54.2 %	4218
	MCMT	**74,135**	288,411	6,620.88	87.80 %	58.1 %	3895

Table 1: Empricial evaluation of supertree methods over two published phylogenetic datasets. The best scores under each objective function are shown in bold.

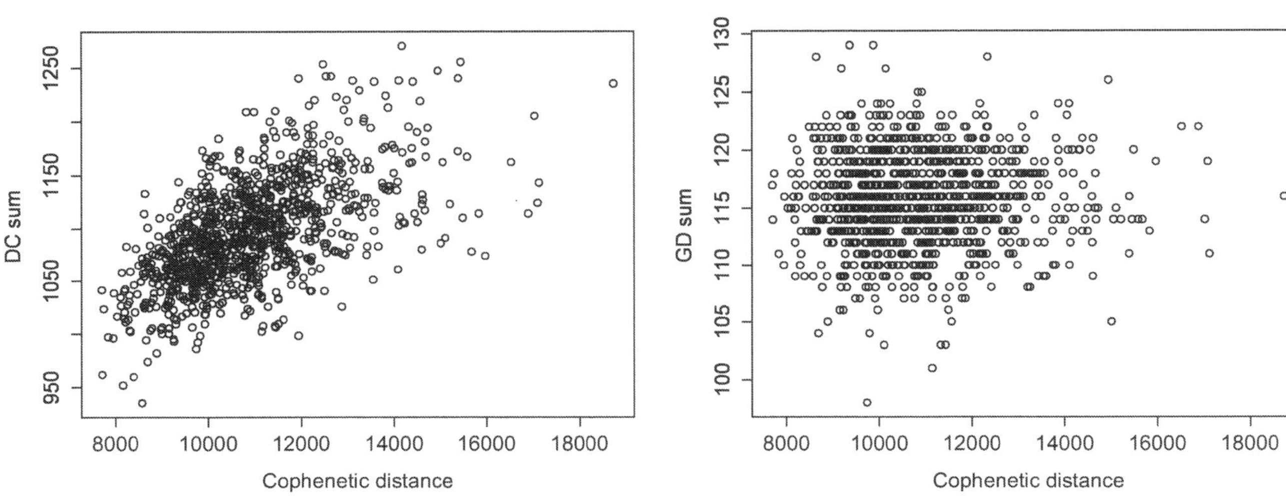

Figure 4: The figures depict the cophenetic distances between pairs of trees in comparison to the respective DC cost (left-hand side) and the GD cost (right-hand side).

we generated 1000 random pairs of bifurcating phylogenetic trees with 100 of labeled leaves each. The trees were drawn from the uniform distribution. Next, for each pair of trees, (T_1, T_2), we computed the Manhattan cophenetic distance as well as duplications, deep coalescence, and duplications with losses costs. Observe that the GD, DC, and DL cost functions are not symmetric. Thus, in order to compare it to the symmetric cophenetic distance, we computed the cost sums $C(T_1, T_2) + C(T_2, T_1)$, where $C \in \{GD, DC, DL\}$.

Based on the obtained scores for a thousand of tree pairs we computed Spearman correlation coefficients for each pair of cost functions (see Table 2). The data was also plotted on Figure 4 to emphasize the correlation patterns.

	DC sum	GD sum	DL sum
L_1 cophenetic	0.602	0.023	0.544
DC sum	-	0.331	0.975
GD sum	-	-	0.517

Table 2: Spearman correlation coefficients for the four LCA-based cost functions.

Results. Observe from Table 2 that the two most correlated cost functions are deep coalescence and duplications with losses. This was highly expected, since the DL cost function can be represented as a linear combination of DC and GD, where the DC cost is much more significant than the GD cost [41]. Further, in justification to our hypothesis, we observe a significant correlation between the Manhattan cophenetic distance and DC. Observe that the Spearman correlation for these two cost functions is higher than the respective correlation coefficient between the L_1 cophenetic distance and the path-difference distances. The observed correlation is further illustrated in Figure 4 (left-hand side) as opposed to the low correlation plot for the GD cost function (on the right-hand side).

5 CONCLUSION AND OUTLOOK

The problem of discordance in phylogenetic trees has been addressed by the means of the median tree approach for over 20 years [4, 5, 31]. Median tree methods employ various objective cost functions, which can be classified into mathematically informed costs, and biologically informed costs. Biological costs are based on evolutionary processes causing discordance between two trees (e.g., deep coalescences, gene duplications, and gene duplications with losses [14]), which are typically used when gene trees are compared with species trees [14]. In contrast, independent of any evolutionary causes, mathematical costs between two trees are measuring the amount of elementary evolutionary information that is common (or different) in these trees, and are thought to be applicable as a tool of error-correction and formal maximization of common information among the input trees [5]. Another distinction between mathematical and biological costs is that the former typically satisfy the properties of a metric [36], while the latter once are not symmetric and do not satisfy the triangle inequality [14]. Despite the differences between mathematical and biological costs, in the median tree setting the Manhattan cophenetic metric, a mathematical cost, and the deep coalescence cost function, a classic biological cost, showed to be strongly correlated in our experiments. This suggests that the cophenetic median tree methods may be used as a universal solution to the generalized supertree problem. Note also that as a metric, the cophenetic model provides valuable mathematical properties, which are not met by most of the biologically informed cost functions. The fact that the cophenetic metrics are not tied to a biological model also gives an advantage, as they can be naturally generalized for the comparison of weighted phylogenetic trees. Given the increasing interest in the time-annotated median trees [20], this property provides great applicability perspectives for the weighted cophenetic median trees.

In this work we presented a new method for median tree estimation based on the Manhattan cophenetic metric, and studied the correlations of this metric with other classic cost functions that have been applied and recognized in the context of median trees.

We devised an effective heuristic that enabled the computation of the first Manhattan cophenetic median tree estimates on sufficiently large phylogenetic datasets, which became only possible due to the efficient algorithm for the local neighborhood search that we put forward in this work. This algorithmic advancement allowed us to perform a first applicability study that evaluates the Manhattan cophenetic median tree heuristic against other supertree methods on benchmark datasets. The results of this study motivates much broader future investigations into the significance of cophenetic median trees from the evolutionary perspective.

Furthermore, the special properties of the cophenetic metrics, such as dependence on the LCAs, also indicate that it is possible to devise an efficient local search heuristic under the TBR edit operation [1, 12, 37], which will be feasible on large-scale datasets and complement our current work.

6 ACKNOWLEDGMENTS

We thank the four anonymous reviewers for their constructive comments. This material is based upon work supported by the National Science Foundation under Grant No. 1617626.

REFERENCES

[1] Benjamin L. Allen and Mike Steel. 2001. Subtree transfer operations and their induced metrics on evolutionary trees. *Annals of Combinatorics* 5 (2001), 1–15.

[2] Mukul S. Bansal, J. Gordon Burleigh, and Oliver Eulenstein. 2010. Efficient genome-scale phylogenetic analysis under the duplication-loss and deep coalescence cost models. *BMC Bioinformatics* 11 Suppl 1 (2010), S42. https://doi.org/10.1186/1471-2105-11-S1-S42

[3] Mukul S. Bansal, J. Gordon Burleigh, Oliver Eulenstein, and David Fernández-Baca. 2010. Robinson-Foulds Supertrees. *Algorithms for Molecular Biology* 5, 1 (2010), 1–12. https://doi.org/10.1186/1748-7188-5-18

[4] Bernard R. Baum. 1992. Combining Trees as a Way of Combining Data Sets for Phylogenetic Inference, and the Desirability of Combining Gene Trees. *Taxon* 41, 1 (1992), 3–10.

[5] Olaf R.P. Bininda-Emonds (Ed.). 2004. *Phylogenetic Supertrees: Combining Information to Reveal the Tree of Life.* Computational Biology, Vol. 4. Springer Verlag.

[6] Paola Bonizzoni, Gianluca Della Vedova, and Riccardo Dondi. 2005. Reconciling a gene tree to a species tree under the duplication cost model. *Theoretical computer science* 347, 1-2 (2005), 36–53.

[7] David Bryant. 1997. *Hunting for trees, building trees andcomparing trees: theory and method in phylogeneticanalysis.* Ph.D. Dissertation. Department of Mathematics, University of Canterbury, New Zeeland.

[8] Marcel Cardillo, Olaf R. P. Bininda-Emonds, Elizabeth Boakes, and Andy Purvis. 2004. A species-level phylogenetic supertree of marsupials. *Journal of Zoology* 264 (2004), 11–31. Issue 01. https://doi.org/10.1017/S0952836904005539

[9] Gabriel Cardona, Arnau Mir, Francesc Rosselló, Lucía Rotger, and David Sánchez. 2013. Cophenetic metrics for phylogenetic trees, after Sokal and Rohlf. *BMC Bioinformatics* 14, 1 (2013), 3. https://doi.org/10.1186/1471-2105-14-3

[10] Ruchi Chaudhary, Mukul S. Bansal, André Wehe, David Fernández-Baca, and Oliver Eulenstein. 2010. iGTP: a software package for large-scale gene tree parsimony analysis. *BMC Bioinformatics* 11 (2010), 574. https://doi.org/10.1186/1471-2105-11-574

[11] Duhong Chen, Oliver Eulenstein, David Fernández-Baca, and JGordon Burleigh. 2006. Improved heuristics for minimum-flip supertree construction. *Evolutionary Bioinformatics* 2 (2006).

[12] Duhong Chen, Oliver Eulenstein, David Fernández-Baca, and J Gordon Burleigh. 2006. Improved heuristics for minimum-flip supertree construction. *Evol Bioinform Online* 2 (2006), 347–56.

[13] James A Cotton and Mark Wilkinson. 2007. Majority-rule supertrees. *Syst Biol* 56, 3 (2007), 445–452. https://doi.org/10.1080/10635150701416682

[14] O. Eulenstein, S. Huzurbazar, and D.A. Liberles. 2010. *Evolution after Gene Duplication.* John Wiley, Chapter Reconciling Phylogenetic Trees.

[15] Peter Forster and Colin Renfrew. 2006. *Phylogenetic methods and the prehistory of languages.* McDonald Inst of Archeological.

[16] Henry Gee. 2003. Evolution: ending incongruence. *Nature* 425, 6960 (Oct 2003), 782. https://doi.org/10.1038/425782a

[17] Simon R. Harris, Edward J.P. Cartwright, M Estéée Török, Matthew T.G. Holden, Nicholas M. Brown, Amanda L. Ogilvy-Stuart, Matthew J. Ellington, Michael A. Quail, Stephen D. Bentley, Julian Parkhill, and Sharon J. Peacock. 2013. Whole-genome sequencing for analysis of an outbreak of meticillin-resistant Staphylococcus aureus: a descriptive study. *Lancet Infect Dis* 13, 2 (2013), 130–6. https://doi.org/10.1016/S1473-3099(12)70268-2

[18] Ruth. A. Hufbauer, Robin A. Marrs, Aaron K. Jackson, René Sforza, Harsh Pal Bais, Jorge M. Vivanco, and Shannan E. Carney. 2003. Population structure, ploidy levels and allelopathy of Centaurea maculosa (spotted knapweed) and C. diffusa (diffuse knapweed) in North America and Eurasia. In *Proceedings of the XI International Symposium on Biological Control of Weeds, Canberra Australia.* USDA Forest Service. Forest Health Technology Enterprise Team, Morgantown, WV., 121–126.

[19] Martyn Kennedy, Roderic DM Page, and R Prum. 2002. Seabird supertrees: combining partial estimates of procellariiform phylogeny. *The Auk* 119, 1 (2002), 88–108.

[20] Adam D. Leaché. 2010. The Timetree of Life. S. Blair Hedges and Sudhir Kumar, editors. *Integrative and Comparative Biology* 50, 1 (2010), 141–142. https://doi.org/10.1093/icb/icp110 arXiv:http://icb.oxfordjournals.org/content/50/1/141.full.pdf+html

[21] Harris T Lin, J Gordon Burleigh, and Oliver Eulenstein. 2009. Triplet supertree heuristics for the tree of life. *BMC Bioinformatics* 10, Suppl 1, Article S8 (2009). https://doi.org/10.1186/1471-2105-10-S1-S8

[22] Harris T. Lin, J. Gordon Burleigh, and Oliver Eulenstein. 2012. Consensus properties for the deep coalescence problem and their application for scalable tree search. *BMC Bioinformatics* 13 Suppl 10 (2012), S12. https://doi.org/10.1186/1471-2105-13-S10-S12

[23] Wayne P Maddison. 1997. Gene trees in species trees. *Systematic biology* 46, 3 (1997), 523–536.

[24] Wayne P. Maddison and L. Lacey Knowles. 2006. Inferring phylogeny despite incomplete lineage sorting. *Syst Biol* 55, 1 (2006), 21–30. https://doi.org/10.1080/10635150500354928

[25] Alexey Markin and Oliver Eulenstein. 2016. Path-Difference Median Trees. In *Bioinformatics Research and Applications: 12th International Symposium, ISBRA 2016, Minsk, Belarus, June 5-8, 2016, Proceedings*, Anu Bourgeois, Pavel Skums, Xiang Wan, and Alex Zelikovsky (Eds.). Springer International Publishing, Cham, 211–223. https://doi.org/10.1007/978-3-319-38782-6_18

[26] Alexey Markin and Oliver Eulenstein. 2017. Computing Manhattan Path-Difference Median Trees: a Practical Local Search Approach. *IEEE/ACM Transactions on Computational Biology and Bioinformatics* PP (2017). https://dx.doi.org/10.1109/TCBB.2017.2718507

[27] James O. McInerney, James A. Cotton, and Davide Pisani. 2008. The prokaryotic tree of life: past, present... and future? *Trends Ecol Evol* 23, 5 (May 2008), 276–81. https://doi.org/10.1016/j.tree.2008.01.008

[28] Serena Nik-Zainal and et al. 2012. The life history of 21 breast cancers. *Cell* 149, 5 (2012), 994–1007.

[29] Roderic D. M. Page. 2002. Modified Mincut Supertrees. In *Proceedings of the Second International Workshop on Algorithms in Bioinformatics (WABI '02)*. Springer-Verlag, London, UK, 537–552.

[30] Samantha A. Price, Olaf R. P. Bininda-Emonds, and John L. Gittleman. 2005. A complete phylogeny of the whales, dolphins and even-toed hoofed mammals (Cetartiodactyla). *Biological Reviews* 80, 3 (2005), 445–473. https://doi.org/10.1017/S1464793105006743

[31] Mark A Ragan. 1992. Phylogenetic inference based on matrix representation of trees. *Molecular phylogenetics and evolution* 1, 1 (1992), 53–58.

[32] Johannes J. Le Roux, Ania M. Wieczorek, Mohsen M. Ramadan, and Carol T. Tran. 2006. Resolving the native provenance of invasive fireweed (Senecio madagascariensis Poir.) in the Hawaiian Islands as inferred Poir.) in the Hawaiian Islands as inferred from phylogenetic analysis. *Diversity and Distributions* 12 (2006), 694–702.

[33] Charles Semple and Mike A. Steel. 2003. *Phylogenetics*. University Press, Oxford.

[34] S. Snir and S. Rao. 2010. Quartets MaxCut: A Divide and Conquer Quartets Algorithm. *IEEE/ACM TCBB* 7, 4 (2010), 704–718. https://doi.org/10.1109/TCBB.2008.133

[35] Robert R. Sokal and F. James Rohlf. 1962. The Comparison of Dendrograms by Objective Methods. *Taxon* 11, 2 (1962), 33–40. http://www.jstor.org/stable/1217208

[36] M. A. Steel. 1992. The complexity of reconstructing trees from qualitative characters and subtrees. *Journal of Classification* 9 (1992), 91–116.

[37] David L. Swofford. 1990. Phylogeny reconstruction. *Molecular Systematics* (1990), 411–501.

[38] David L. Swofford. 2002. PAUP*. Phylogenetic Analysis Using Parsimony (*and Other Methods). Version 4. Sinauer Associates, Sunderland, Massachusetts. (2002).

[39] Cuong Than and Luay Nakhleh. 2009. Species tree inference by minimizing deep coalescences. *PLoS Comput Biol* 5, 9 (2009), e1000501. https://doi.org/10.1371/journal.pcbi.1000501

[40] Martin F Wojciechowski, Michael J Sanderson, Kelly P Steele, and Aaron Liston. 2000. Molecular phylogeny of the "temperate herbaceous tribes" of papilionoid legumes: a supertree approach. *Advances in legume systematics* 9 (2000), 277–298.

[41] Louxin Zhang. 2011. From gene trees to species trees II: species tree inference by minimizing deep coalescence events. *IEEE/ACM Trans Comput Biol Bioinform* 8, 6 (2011), 1685–91. https://doi.org/10.1109/TCBB.2011.83

DeepCCI: End-to-end Deep Learning for Chemical-Chemical Interaction Prediction

Sunyoung Kwon
Electrical and Computer Engineering
Seoul National University
Seoul 08826, Korea

Sungroh Yoon*
Electrical and Computer Engineering
Seoul National University
Seoul 08826, Korea
sryoon@snu.ac.kr

ABSTRACT

Chemical-chemical interaction (CCI) plays a key role in predicting candidate drugs, toxicity, therapeutic effects, and biological functions. In various types of chemical analyses, computational approaches are often required due to the amount of data that needs to be handled. The recent remarkable growth and outstanding performance of deep learning have attracted considerable research attention. However, even in state-of-the-art drug analysis methods, deep learning continues to be used only as a classifier, although deep learning is capable of not only simple classification but also automated feature extraction. In this paper, we propose the first end-to-end learning method for CCI, named DeepCCI. Hidden features are derived from a simplified molecular input line entry system (SMILES), which is a string notation representing the chemical structure, instead of learning from crafted features. To discover hidden representations for the SMILES strings, we use convolutional neural networks (CNNs). To guarantee the commutative property for homogeneous interaction, we apply model sharing and hidden representation merging techniques. The performance of DeepCCI was compared with a plain deep classifier and conventional machine learning methods. The proposed DeepCCI showed the best performance in all seven evaluation metrics used. In addition, the commutative property was experimentally validated. The automatically extracted features through end-to-end SMILES learning alleviates the significant efforts required for manual feature engineering. It is expected to improve prediction performance in drug analyses.

CCS CONCEPTS

•Computing methodologies → Supervised learning by classification; Neural networks; •Applied computing → Bioinformatics;

GENERAL TERMS

Algorithms

*To whom correspondence should be addressed.

Permission to make digital or hard copies of all or part of this work for personal or classroom use is granted without fee provided that copies are not made or distributed for profit or commercial advantage and that copies bear this notice and the full citation on the first page. Copyrights for components of this work owned by others than ACM must be honored. Abstracting with credit is permitted. To copy otherwise, or republish, to post on servers or to redistribute to lists, requires prior specific permission and/or a fee. Request permissions from permissions@acm.org.
ACM-BCB'17, August 20-23, 2017, Boston, MA, USA.
© 2017 ACM. 978-1-4503-4722-8/17/08...$15.00
DOI: http://dx.doi.org/10.1145/3107411.3107451

KEYWORDS

chemical-chemical interaction; deep learning; neural network; CNN; commutative property

ACM Reference format:
Sunyoung Kwon and Sungroh Yoon. 2017. DeepCCI: End-to-end Deep Learning for Chemical-Chemical Interaction Prediction. In *Proceedings of ACM-BCB'17, August 20-23, 2017, Boston, MA, USA.*, , 10 pages.
DOI: http://dx.doi.org/10.1145/3107411.3107451

1 INTRODUCTION

Interaction is an action that occurs between two entities that may share similar functions or metabolic pathways [4, 41, 50]. Various interactions exist, such as protein-protein [15, 24, 47], compound-protein [58], miRNA-mRNA [33], and chemical-chemical interactions (CCI) [31].

Previous studies on computational approaches to CCI include the following: a study on compound synergism that predicts the therapeutic efficacy of molecule combinations, based on interactive chemicals [66]; toxicity related studies on predicting chemical toxicities and side effects based on the assumption that interacting chemicals are more likely to share a similar toxicity [6, 7]; targeted candidate drug discovery studies through which the new closest candidate drug to the commercialized target drug was proposed by connecting the interacting chemicals in the graphical aspects [8]; and a study in which a novel approach was developed for identifying biological functions of chemicals, based on the assumption that interactive chemicals participate in the same metabolic pathways [22]. As evidenced by the range of studies mentioned above, CCI has been used for many purposes. However, learning-based methods for CCI are hard to find. Instead, CCI is created from text mining, biological experiments, chemical-chemical similarities, and other information from chemical databases. We therefore propose a learning-based CCI prediction method in this paper.

The conventional learning-based chemical (drug) analyses can be divided into two stages, feature engineering and predicting activity, as shown in Figure 1. In drug analyses, features are also called descriptors, fingerprints, or molecular representations.

The feature engineering stage extracts informative features from chemicals. A significant amount of information has been manually designed by domain experts, ranging from simple counts (*e.g.*, the number of atoms, rings, and bonds) to topological properties (*e.g.*, atom pairs, shapes, and connectivities) [59]. Extracted features have been used in subsequent analyses and significantly affected prediction performance. Various works have been proposed to capture the essential properties of chemicals, and more than 5,000 diverse

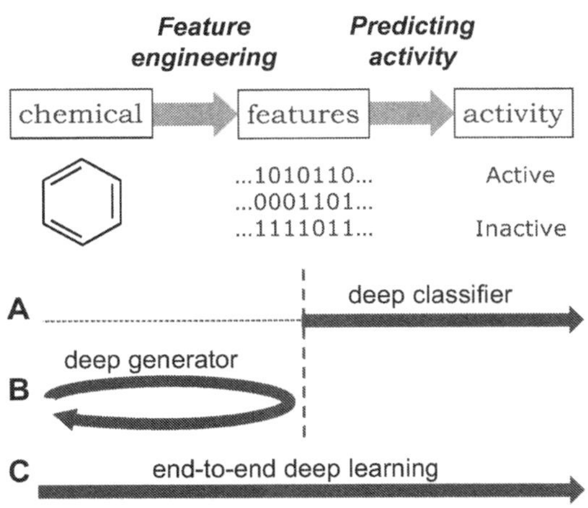

Figure 1: Two-stage chemical analysis: feature engineering and predicting activity. Three types of deep learning approaches are shown: (A) deep classifier, whereby deep learning is applied to the back-end, (B) deep generator, whereby deep learning is applied to the front-end, and (C) end-to-end deep learning, whereby deep learning is applied from the front-end to back-end (our approach).

features have been identified [59] (*e.g.*, PubChem, MACCS, and CDK fingerprint).

The predicting activity stage uncovers the relationship between the extracted features and biological activities, such as absorption, distribution, metabolism, excretion, and toxicity (ADMET) [57, 60]. To robustly learn relationships between chemicals and activities, and to handle a large amount of data, machine learning approaches (such as support vector machine (SVM) [10, 13] and random forest (RF) [55]) have been successfully applied.

Recently, the deep learning method has notably advanced to address challenging problems, such as natural language processing [3, 37, 54], speech and image recognition [12, 18, 20, 30, 67], and computational biology [14, 34–36, 44]. In addition, successful results of deep learning in drug fields [11, 38, 45, 58] have been achieved and attracted further attention. Deep learning approaches to drug analyses can be categorized in the following three cases (see Figure 1):

(A) **Deep classifier:** Deep learning is used as a back-end classifier for manually crafted chemical features. The deep learning based classifier has attracted considerable attention through the Kaggle 'Merck Molecular Activity Challenge' and its subsequent quantitative structure activity relationship (QSAR) predictions [11, 45]. The Kaggle competition and its subsequent predictions showed significant improvements in performance, by using the multi-task technique based on deep learning from the provided features. In addition, prediction of chemical-protein interaction [58] (for drug discovery, network pharmacology, and drug/protein target identification) showed boosted results by using deep learning from manually crafted chemical features. Although deep learning improves prediction performance, it has been used only as a classifier based on the well-crafted chemical features.

(B) **Deep generator:** Deep learning is used as a front-end generator for drug generation. Drug generation extracts the hidden features from the chemicals and then regenerates the chemicals from the extracted features. Generative deep models, such as a variational autoencoder [29] and a recurrent neural network [21], have been used for drug generation [17, 49]. Both models use the simplified molecular input line entry system (SMILES) [57] as input to extract the features and regenerate the SMILES string (or functionally similar SMILES string). Deep learning is only used as a deep generator between chemical strings and extracted features.

(C) **End-to-end deep learning:** Deep learning is used as an end-to-end learner which involves the entire process from feature engineering to predicting biological activity. It should extract hidden features from the original chemical inputs and then predict the biological activity by using the extracted features. However, owing to the considerable performance of using the crafted features and the difficulties of handling the original chemical input, the end-to-end learning framework has not been actively pursued.

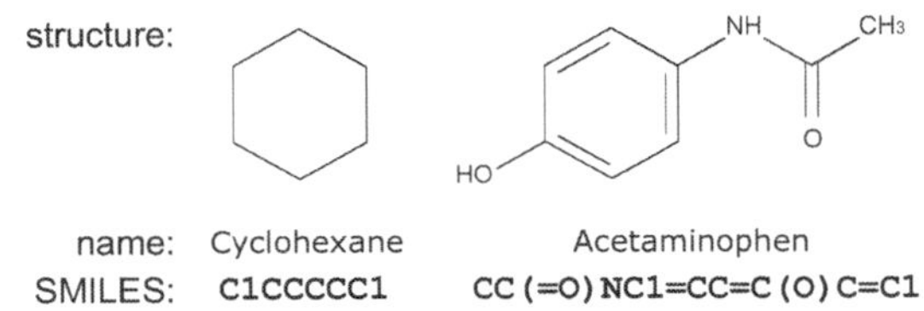

Figure 2: Examples of chemical compounds: 2D structure, name, and SMILES

Deep learning in drug (chemical) analyses is mainly used as a classifier; however, the original purpose of deep learning is not only for classification, but also for extracting hidden representations [39]. The hidden representations, extracted by deep learning, may have potentially important features that are unknown to domain experts. Therefore, we expect that end-to-end deep learning can improve prediction performance. For this reason, we propose an end-to-end deep learning framework, DeepCCI, for CCI prediction.

2 BACKGROUND

2.1 Representation of chemical compound

For end-to-end learning, it is important that the input contains all the latent feature information of the chemical compound. A considerable amount of chemical information exists, such as weight, molecular formula, rings, atoms, SMILES [65], and InChI [19]. Among the many pieces of information, SMILES represents the chemical structure as a line of ASCII characters. As shown in Figure 2, cyclohexane and acetaminophen are expressed as `C1CCCC1` and `CC(=O)NC1=CC=C(O)C=C1` respectively (`C` for carbon, `O` for oxygen, `=` for double bonds and `1` for the first ring). Atoms (*e.g.*, carbon, nitrogen, and oxygen), bonds (*e.g.*, single, double, and triple bonds), rings (*e.g.*, open ring, close ring, and ring number), aromaticitiy, and branching can be represented with SMILES. As a one-dimensional representation for the chemical structure, SMILES can be converted into a two- or three-dimensional chemical structure, which means that it contains sufficient structure information to derive higher dimensions. SMILES is also used for drug generation [17, 49] and for compound similarity [43].

It is generally known that structure is closely related to function [46, 53]. QSAR prediction, which exploits the relationship between the chemical structure and the biological activity, for identifying 'druglikeness'[1] and establishing metabolic pathways [27, 55]. As an expression of structure information, SMILES can be a means of clarifying the function of a chemical compound.

For these reasons, we used SMILES as a front-end input format for representing a chemical compound.

2.2 Convolutional neural networks

The convolutional neural network (CNN) [30], one of the most widely used deep learning architectures, has shown outstanding performance in one-dimensional biological sequences [1, 68] and linguistic sentences [25, 26], as well as in two-dimensional image processing [30, 32, 42].

Designed to analyze shift invariant spatial information, CNNs consist of convolution layers and pooling layers. At each convolution layer, learnable feature maps called filters scan the sub-regions across the sequence. Filters enable CNNs to discover locally correlated motifs regardless of their locations through local connectivity and parameter sharing. Then, each pooling layer summarizes non-overlapping sub-regions, and aggregates local features into more global features. We applied CNNs to capture the SMILES string specificity.

2.3 Commutative property

In mathematics, a commutative property means that changing the order does not affect the result (for example, 2+5=5+2).

As in indirect symmetric problems, such as distance or similarity between objects, predicting the interaction between objects A and B is independent of the ordering, namely $\mathcal{I}(A,B) = \mathcal{I}(B,A)$.

However, if the values $\mathbf{x}^A$ and $\mathbf{x}^B$ for objects A and B are simply concatenated, and then used for learning, the result can be different according to the input order

$$\begin{aligned}\mathcal{I}(\mathbf{x}^A,\mathbf{x}^B) &= w_1x_1^A + \cdots + w_nx^A + w_{n+1}x_1^B + \cdots + w_{2n}x_n^B \\ &\neq w_1x_1^B + \cdots + w_nx^B + w_{n+1}x_1^A + \cdots + w_{2n}x_n^A = \mathcal{I}(\mathbf{x}^B,\mathbf{x}^A).\end{aligned} \tag{1}$$

With this difference in mind, we designed a model that produces the same interaction probability regardless of the input order.

3 PROPOSED METHODOLOGY

Figure 3 shows the overview of the proposed DeepCCI. Our method presents end-to-end SMILES learning for CCI. It takes SMILES strings as inputs $\mathbf{x}^A$ and $\mathbf{x}^B$ for objects A and B, and then produces an interaction probability $\hat{y}$. The structure is divided into three stages. The first stage is for preprocessing SMILES inputs, the

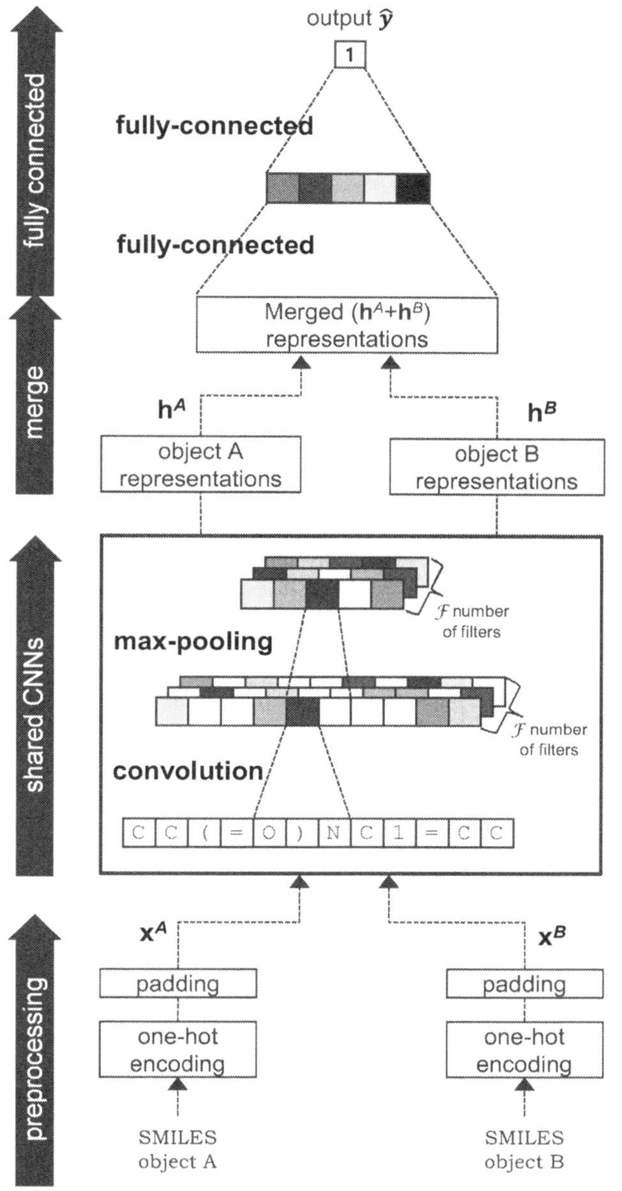

Figure 3: Overview of the proposed DeepCCI end-to-end methodology. Our method extracts hidden representations from SMILES learning and predicts the interaction through the extracted representations, using CNNs and fully connected layers. Inputs are one-hot encoded and zero padded (or truncated) to the maximum length. The preprocessed inputs are fed into shared 1D-CNNs for transforming into hidden representations. The transformed hidden representations for objects A and B are merged and then fed into two fully-connected layers to predict the interaction. The output is the predicted probability of the interaction between objects A and B.

[1] Druglikeness is a qualitative indicator to evaluate a drug-like molecule in terms of its bioavailability.

Algorithm 1 Pseudo-code of proposed DeepCCI

Input: $\mathbf{x}^A = (x_1^A, x_2^A, \cdots, x_\lambda^A)$ and $\mathbf{x}^B = (x_1^B, x_2^B, \cdots, x_\lambda^B)$ ▷ $\mathbf{x}^A$, $\mathbf{x}^B$: the encoded and padded/truncated inputs for objects A and B
Output: $\hat{\mathbf{y}}$ ▷ $\hat{\mathbf{y}}$: predicted probability of interaction
repeat
  $\mathbf{h} = \mathbf{Pool}(\sigma_r(\mathbf{Conv}(\mathbf{x})))$ ▷ shared CNNs described in Section 3.3
  $\hat{y} = \sigma_s(\mathbf{Fcl}(\sigma_r(\mathbf{Fcl}(\mathbf{h}^A + \mathbf{h}^B))))$ ▷ interaction prediction described in Section 3.4
  ▷ $\mathbf{h}^A$, $\mathbf{h}^B$: the outputs of shared CNNs from inputs $\mathbf{x}^A$,$\mathbf{x}^B$
  $\mathcal{L}(y, \hat{y}) = -y \log \hat{y} - (1 - y) \log(1 - \hat{y})$ ▷ learning objective to minimize the loss $\mathcal{L}(y, \hat{y})$
  $\mathbf{W} = \mathbf{W} - \Delta\mathbf{W}$ ▷ weights update $\Delta\mathbf{W}$ based on averaged $\mathcal{L}$ from mini-batch
until number of epoch reaches n_{epoch}

second stage is for learning latent hidden representations through 1D-CNNs, and the third stage is for interaction learning through merging and fully-connected layers. Algorithm 1 shows the overall procedure of DeepCCI.

3.1 Notations

The notations used in our paper are outlined below.

- $\mathcal{I}(A, B)$: interaction between objects A and B
- $\mathcal{X}$: SMILES character set, $\mathcal{X} = \{\text{C}, =, (,), \text{O}, \text{F}, 1, 2, \cdots\}$
- $\mathbf{x}$: SMILES string, $\mathbf{x}^A$ and $\mathbf{x}^B$ for objects A and B
- x_i: i-th character of $\mathbf{x}$, $\mathbf{x} = (x_1, x_2, \cdots, x_n)$, $x_i \in \mathcal{X}$
- h: hidden representations, $\mathbf{h}^A$ and $\mathbf{h}^B$ for objects A and B
- h_i: i-th element of h, $\mathbf{h} = (h_1, h_2, \cdots, h_n)$
- λ: maximum length of SMILES
- $\mathcal{F}$: number of filters
- k: length of filter (kernel size)
- $\mathbf{W}$: learning weights
- $\hat{y}$: predicted probability of interaction
- σ: activation function, σ_s for the sigmoid, σ_r for the rectified linear unit
- N: sample size, N_t for total sample, N_b for mini-batch size

3.2 Input Preprocessing

We used input $\mathbf{x} = (x_1, x_2, \cdots, x_n)$ which is represented by 65-character $x_i \in \mathcal{X}$ where $\mathcal{X} = \{\text{C}, =, (,), \text{O}, \text{F}, 1, 2, \cdots\}$, $|\mathcal{X}| = 65$ in the SMILES format. Input $\mathbf{x}$ should be converted into a numeric expression for learning.

For the numerical expression, we employ a widely used one-hot encoding scheme, which sets the corresponding single character to '1' and all the others to '0', thereby converting each character x_i into an $|\mathcal{X}|$-dimensional binary vector. An example of cyclohexane (C1CCCCC1) encoded $\mathbf{x}$ is as follows:

$$\{\text{C}, =,), (, \text{O}, \text{N}, 1, 2 \cdots\cdots\cdots\}$$

$$\mathbf{x} = \begin{bmatrix} x_1 \\ x_2 \\ x_3 \\ x_4 \\ x_5 \\ x_6 \\ x_7 \\ x_8 \end{bmatrix} = \begin{bmatrix} \text{C} \\ 1 \\ \text{C} \\ \text{C} \\ \text{C} \\ \text{C} \\ \text{C} \\ 1 \end{bmatrix} = \begin{bmatrix} [1,0,0,0,0,0,0,0,\cdots,0,0,0] \\ [0,0,0,0,0,0,1,0,\cdots,0,0,0] \\ [1,0,0,0,0,0,0,0,\cdots,0,0,0] \\ [1,0,0,0,0,0,0,0,\cdots,0,0,0] \\ [1,0,0,0,0,0,0,0,\cdots,0,0,0] \\ [1,0,0,0,0,0,0,0,\cdots,0,0,0] \\ [1,0,0,0,0,0,0,0,\cdots,0,0,0] \\ [0,0,0,0,0,0,1,0,\cdots,0,0,0] \end{bmatrix}$$

In general, SMILES strings are variable lengths depending on the complexity of the chemical structure. Chemical compounds of a complex structure have relatively longer SMILES strings compared to compounds of a simple structure. To effectively learn the hidden representations for SMILES, we limit the inputs to a certain maximum length, λ. If a sequence is shorter than the maximum length, zero values are pre-padded; otherwise, the sequence is truncated to the maximum length. After the padded or truncated processes, all input lengths are fixed to the maximum length, λ. According to the maximum length, the prediction performance is affected (see Figure 6A).

According to the encoding scheme and maximum length, input $\mathbf{x}$ is encoded into a $\lambda \times |\mathcal{X}|$-dimensional binary matrix. The input collection is represented by a $N_t \times \lambda \times |\mathcal{X}|$-dimensional binary tensor.

3.3 Modeling of Hidden Representations

To learn hidden representations $\mathbf{h}$ from preprocessed input $\mathbf{x}$ of SMILES strings, we used CNNs. The CNN architecture, used in our method, consists of a convolution layer and a pooling layer.

$$\mathbf{h} = \mathbf{Pool}(\sigma_r(\mathbf{Conv}(\mathbf{x}))) \tag{2}$$

The convolution layer plays a 'motif detector' role across the sequence. The preprocessed input $\mathbf{x}$ is convoluted with a set of learnable feature maps called filters (or kernels). Different filters may detect motifs of different chemical properties in the SMILES string. Scanning the local region across the input string with a parameter-shared filter may enable recognition of the shift-invariant local pattern.

The output shape of convoluted input $\mathbf{x}$ becomes an $\mathcal{F} \times (\lambda - k + 1)$-dimensional matrix, where $\mathcal{F}$ represents the number of filters, and k represents the filter length.

$$\mathbf{Conv}(\mathbf{x}) = (c_{f,i}) \in \mathbb{R}^{\mathcal{F} \times (\lambda - k + 1)}$$
$$c_{f,i} = \sum_{j=1}^{k} \sum_{s=1}^{|\mathcal{X}|} W_{f,j,s} x_{i+j,s} \tag{3}$$

where f and i are $1 \leq f \leq \mathcal{F}$ and $1 \leq i \leq (\lambda - k + 1)$, respectively. The parameters $\mathcal{F}$ and k of the CNN filter are decided through experiments (see Figure 6D and 6E).

After the convolution layer, each convoluted element is processed with the rectified linear unit (ReLU) [40]

$$\sigma_r(t) = max(0, t) \tag{4}$$

which is an activation function of non-saturating for positives and clamping to zero for negatives.

The pooling layer partitions the rectified responses with non-overlapping sub-regions and then outputs the maximum if it is max-pooling. It summarizes within the sub-regions and reduces the spatial size. The $\mathcal{F}$ dimension remains unchanged. The max-pooling length of 6 showed the best performance in our experiments (see Figure 6C)

To prevent overfitting and to produce generalization effects, we apply dropout [52] for the last CNN units.

For a symmetric problem, such as a tweets comparison, Keras use shared layers, which reuse the weights [9]. Likewise, we use shared CNNs to extract the hidden representations h^A and h^B for chemicals A and B from inputs $\mathbf{x}^A$ and $\mathbf{x}^B$.

3.4 Modeling of Interaction Between Chemicals

Unlike heterogeneous interactions, such as protein-chemical and miRNA-mRNA interaction, CCI is a homogeneous interaction between two chemicals. Homogeneous interaction between objects A and B should be the same regardless of their input order, $\mathcal{I}(A,B) = \mathcal{I}(B,A)$, thereby guaranteeing the commutative property described in Section 2.3. However, simple concatenating of the values of objects A and B cannot guarantee the property according to Equation 1.

To equally recognize $\mathcal{I}(A,B)$ and $\mathcal{I}(B,A)$, we strive to give the same weights $\mathbf{W}$ to both hidden representations $\mathbf{h}^A$ and $\mathbf{h}^B$ for objects A and B

$$\begin{aligned}\mathcal{I}(A,B) &\approx \mathbf{W}\mathbf{h}^A + \mathbf{W}\mathbf{h}^B \\ &= w_1 h_1^A + \cdots + w_n h_n^A + w_1 h_1^B + \cdots + w_n h_n^B \\ &= w_1 h_1^B + \cdots + w_n h_n^B + w_1 h_1^A + \cdots + w_n h_n^A \\ &= \mathbf{W}\mathbf{h}^B + \mathbf{W}\mathbf{h}^A \approx \mathcal{I}(B,A).\end{aligned} \tag{5}$$

Through the weight-sharing, we can guarantee the commutative property. The weight-sharing can be implemented by merging both hidden representations through summing process

$$\begin{aligned}\mathbf{W}\mathbf{h}^A + \mathbf{W}\mathbf{h}^B &= w_1 h_1^A + \cdots + w_n h_n^A + w_1 h_1^B + \cdots + w_n h_n^B \\ &= w_1 (h_1^A + h_1^B) + \cdots + w_n (h_n^A + h_n^B) \\ &= \mathbf{W}\left(\mathbf{h}^A + \mathbf{h}^B\right).\end{aligned} \tag{6}$$

The interaction between objects A and B, is learned with two fully-connected layers (Fcl) from summed representations.

$$\hat{y} = \sigma_s(\mathrm{Fcl}(\sigma_r(\mathrm{Fcl}(\mathbf{h}^A + \mathbf{h}^B)))) \tag{7}$$

where $\hat{y}$ is the predicted probability that an interaction will occur, σ_r is the ReLU in Equation (4) and σ_s is the sigmoid activation function

$$\sigma_s(t) = 1/(1 + \exp(-t)) \tag{8}$$

which make the output probability occur from zero to one.

The learning processes proceed to minimize the loss between the true label and the prediction $\mathcal{L}(y,\hat{y})$, where y is the true label and $\hat{y}$ is the predicted probability from Equation (7). For the loss function as the learning objective, we use the binary cross entropy

$$\mathcal{L}(y,\hat{y}) = -y\log\hat{y} - (1-y)\log(1-\hat{y}). \tag{9}$$

Table 1: Details of the datasets used in the experiments. The negative samples were randomly generated from negative-0 to balance them with the number of positives

type/dataset	CCI900	CCI800	CCI700
# of positives	9,812	75,908	171,665
# of negatives	9,812	75,908	171,665
total sample size	19,624	151,816	343,330

Weights are updated in mini-batch units; the loss for the batch unit is averaged by the mini-batch size.

$$\mathcal{L}(\mathbf{y},\hat{\mathbf{y}}) = \frac{1}{N_b}\sum_{i=1}^{N_b}\mathcal{L}(y_i,\hat{y}_i) \tag{10}$$

where N_b is the mini-batch size, and i represents the sample index.

In the fully-connected layers, we use 128 hidden nodes, batch normalization [23], and a dropout [52] rate of 0.25 for regularization. In our experiments, the entire learning was conducted with the Adam optimizer [28] (learning rate: 0.001, epoch: 100, and mini-batch size: 256). Most of these parameters and network structure were experimentally determined. An epoch of 100 showed stable convergence. We did not use early stopping.

4 EXPERIMENTAL RESULTS

4.1 Experimental Setup

4.1.1 Dataset. In our experiment, we used the CCI data (version 5.0) downloaded from the STITCH [31] database. Each interaction pair had a confidence score ranging from 0 to 999, which was derived from text-mining, experiments, similarity, and database. The higher the confidence score was, the greater the interaction probability was. The positive-900 (9,812 samples), positive-800 (75,908 samples), and positive-700 (171,665 samples) were generated from the samples with confidence scores more than 900, 800, and 700, respectively. The negative-0 (212,741 samples) were generated from the samples with confidence scores of zero.

According to the confidence score, three datasets were prepared: chemical-chemical interaction over 900 (CCI900), 800 (CCI800), and 700 (CCI700) as listed in Table 1. The total number of the positive-900, 800, and 700 samples were included in the CCI900, CCI800, and CCI700, respectively. The negatives were randomly selected from negative-zero (212,741) to balance them with the number of positives.

All three datasets were asymmetric, which means that only one each of the A-B pair and B-A pair was included; its opposite pair was not included in the dataset. Since methods of supporting the commutative property are advantageous to the symmetric dataset, we prepared the asymmetric dataset for a fair comparison.

4.1.2 Preparation of Input Representation. The representations of chemical compounds were prepared as two types: the SMILES string, and PubChem fingerprint [64]. The PubChem fingerprint is widely used descriptor. It has showed the best performance for

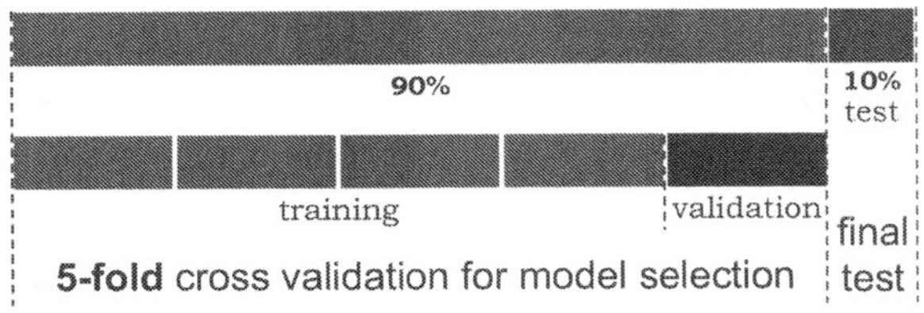

Figure 4: Dataset breakdown. The full dataset was randomly divided into the model selection set (90%) and final test set (10%). The model selection set was again partitioned into five sets, for 5-fold cross validation. Through the iterative validation, the model with hyperparameters, showing the best average performance, was selected.

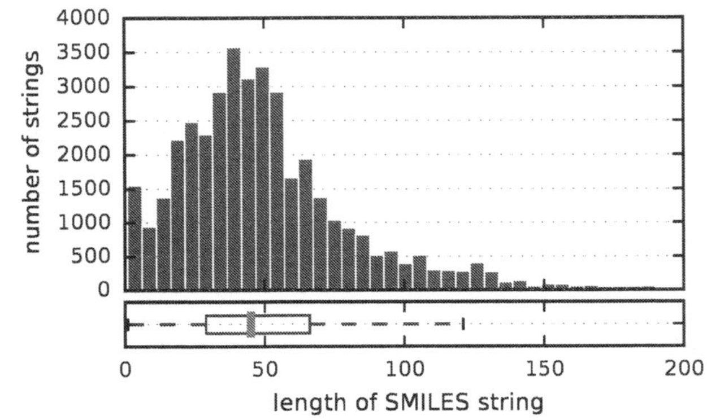

Figure 5: SMILES string length distribution based on CCI900: the median length is 45 and the average length is 53.5. The 91% of SMILES strings is less than 100 characters in length.

certain tasks [48, 63], although the performance of the molecular descriptor depends on the target problem and classifier.

Strings represented in SMILES were used as inputs for the proposed end-to-end deep learning method. Binary feature vectors represented in the PubChem fingerprint were used as inputs for the other methods. We prepared the PubChem fingerprint accordingly because it is difficult to handle the string in conventional machine learning methods, and the end-to-end learning performance had to be compared with a plain deep classifier (see Figure 1A).

The PubChem fingerprint represents the chemical properties as a 881-dimensional binary vector that has feature information, such as the presence or count of atoms, rings, and nearest neighbor patterns. We concatenated the fingerprints of two objects as a (2×881)-dimensional binary vector and then used it as the inputs for the learning algorithms tested.

From the chemical IDs listed in the STITCH database, we retrieved the SMILES string and PubChem fingerprint by using PubChemPy [56]. A representative example of cyclohexane is as follows:

- PubChem chemical ID: 8078
- SMILES string: C1CCCCC1
- Fingerprint: 1100000001100000000000000000000000 · · · (the 9-th bit is 1 if there are more than two carbon atoms and is 0 otherwise; the 10-th bit is 1 if there are more than four carbon atoms and is 0 otherwise)

4.1.3 Experimental Configuration. Our dataset consisted of training, validation, and test samples, as in the general learning experiments [2]. Figure 4 details the dataset. The full dataset was divided into two parts, one for model selection and the other for the independent test.

The goal of model selection was to find the optimal hyperparameters. Models with various sets of hyperparameters were trained and then iteratively validated through k-fold cross validation. Optimal hyperparameters, which showed the best average performance in terms of AUC, were selected. In our experiments, we used 5-fold cross validation.

The remaining test set was used to assess the generalization of the selected model, and compare its performance with other learning methods. Since the parameters were determined through training and validation independently of the test set, it could guarantee the fairness of the independent test.

Our experiments were run on Ubuntu 14.04 (3.5GHz Intel i7-5930K and GTX Titan X Maxwell (12GB)). For the implementation of deep learning, we used the Keras library package (version 1.1.1) [9].

4.1.4 Evaluation Metrics. For the performance comparison, we used seven different evaluation metrics:

- AUC: the area under the ROC curve, which is widely used in case of binary classification to show the overall performance of a binary classifier[2]
- ACC: accuracy, which is intuitively used metric to assess the performance[3]
- TPR: true positive rate, sensitivity or recall[4]
- TNR: true negative rate or specificity[5]
- PPV: positive predictive value or precision[6]
- NPV: negative predictive value[7]
- F1: F1 score[8]

4.2 Effects of Hyperparameter Variation

Five different hyperparameter variation experiments were performed to find the empirical optimal parameters.

As shown in Figure 5, the lengths of SMILES strings vary from 1 to over 200. Their median length is 45 and the average length is 53.5. The 84%, 91%, and 94% of SMILES strings are less than 80, 100, and 120 characters in length, respectively. The proposed method DeepCCI limits the SMILES strings to a certain maximum length, λ. The loss of information and dummy zeros according to the maximum length might affect the overall performance. Figure 6A depicts the performance of DeepCCI by varying the maximum

[2]The area under the ROC curve which plots $TPR(T)$ versus $FPR(T)$ with varying threshold T, where $FPR = 1 - TPR$
[3]$ACC = (TP + TN)/(TP + TN + FP + FN)$, where
TP: true positive, FP: false positive, FN: false negative, TN: true negative
[4]$TPR = TP/(TP + FN)$
[5]$TNR = TN/(TN + FP)$
[6]$PPV = TP/(TP + FP)$
[7]$NPV = TN/(TN + FN)$
[8]$F1 = 2TP/(2TP + FP + FN)$

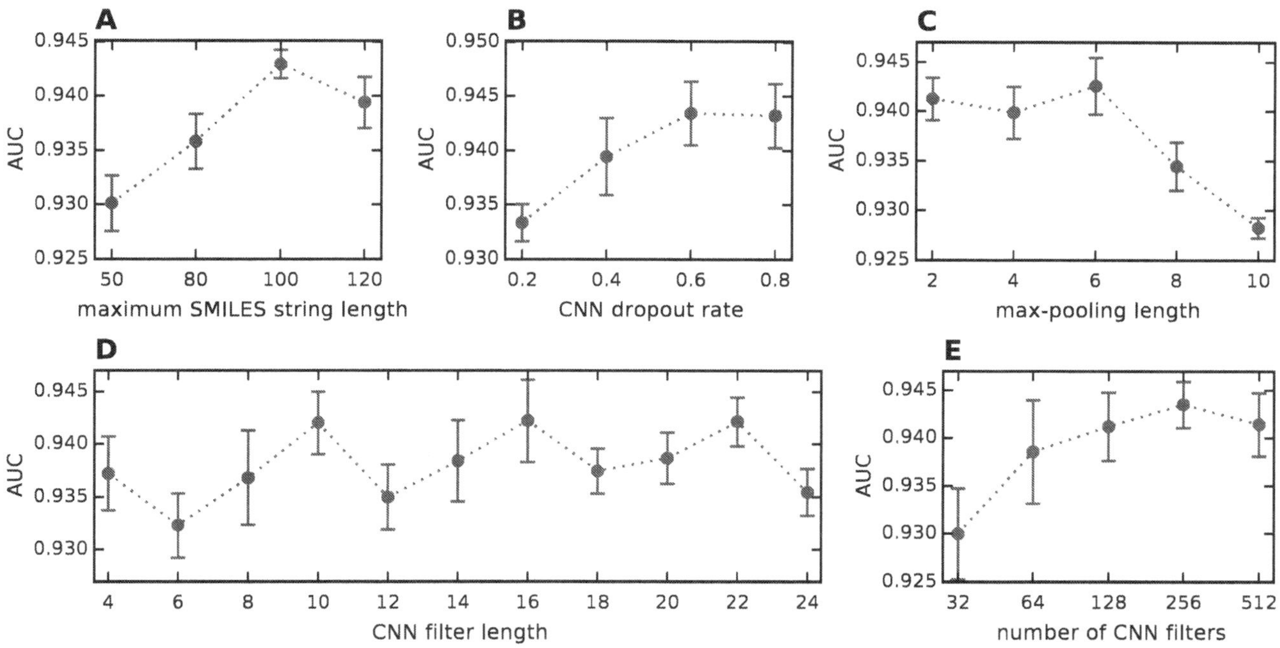

Figure 6: Hyperparameter optimization using 5-fold cross validation tested on CCI900. The baseline hyperparameters of the maximum SMILES string length, CNN dropout rate, max-pooling length, CNN filter length, and number of CNN filters are 100, 0.6, 6, 22, and 256, respectively. The performance changes as varying the (A) maximum SMILES string length from 50 to 120, (B) CNN dropout rate from 0.2 to 0.8, (C) max-pooling length from 2 to 10, (D) CNN filter length from 4 to 24, and (E) number of CNN filters from 32 to 512.

SMILES string length to 50, 80, 100 and 120. Among them, a maximum length of 100 shows the best performance in terms of AUC. In our experiments, the maximum length of 100 could mean that learning was achieved by reducing the computational burden while covering as much information as possible.

Figure 6B illustrates the performance as varying the CNN dropout rate from 0.2 to 0.8. Dropout as a regularization technique reduces overfitting by dropping out units in neural networks. In our validation experiments, a dropout rate of 0.6, meaning that 60% of units dropped out, showed the best performance and the lowest standard deviation.

The pooling layer summarized the adjacent features resulting abstract representations, and inputs were down-sampled, resulting in a smaller number of model parameters to learn [2]. A larger pooling length means a greater summary effect. In our experiments, pooling lengths of 2 and 6 showed similar performances in terms of AUC, as shown in Figure 6C. To achieve better summarization effects, we used the max-pooling with a length of 6 as the baseline parameter.

The key features of CNNs are a parameter sharing architecture and translation invariance characteristics, which are due to the use of filters (or kernels). The filter length depends on the characteristic of patterns to discover. The number of filters controls the capacity, depending on the complexity of the task. As shown in Figure 6D and 6E, we used the filter length of 22 and 256 filters as the baseline parameters. The filter lengths of 10, 16, and 22 (6 units apart) showed the highest AUC. The relatively longer molecule patterns compared to those of the PubChem fingerprint can be captured with these CNN filters. A PubChem fingerprint takes complicated neighbor patterns into consideration, but most of its features are targeted for short and simple patterns.

4.3 Performance Comparison with Other Methods

We compared our proposed method, DeepCCI, with a feedforward neural network (FFNN), which is a plain deep classifier described in Figure 1A, and the conventional machine learning methods of support vector machine (SVM) [61, 62], random forest (RF) [5, 55], and adaptive boosting (AdaBoost) [16]. SVM, RF, and AdaBoost were tested with default parameters. FFNN, which is a deep neural networks of three fully-connected layers (with 1,024 and 128 hidden units) was tested with ReLU for the hidden activation function and sigmoid for the output activation function, and the dropout rate of 0.25.

In the context of drug development, the high false positive rate means that there are more candidate chemicals to be screened, while the high false negative rate means that more chemicals, which should not be omitted in the screening list, are omitted. Therefore, both FP and FN rates should be properly controlled. We used seven evaluation metrics related to false positives and false negatives.

Table 2: Details of experimental results based on seven different evaluation metrics were obtained. The experiments were carried out on three dataset with five different methods. All values were the average of ten repeated experiments. The performances in terms of AUC and ACC are represented with bar plots in Figure 7.

data	methods	AUC	ACC	TPR	TNR	PPV	NPV	F1
CCI900	**DeepCCI**	**0.9483**	**0.8819**	**0.8823**	**0.8815**	**0.8770**	**0.8868**	**0.8796**
	FFNN	0.9313	0.8611	0.8424	0.8790	0.8696	0.8536	0.8557
	SVM	0.8399	0.7658	0.7225	0.8073	0.7830	0.7531	0.7509
	RF	0.9016	0.8217	0.8616	0.7836	0.7922	0.8554	0.8254
	AdaBoost	0.7742	0.7076	0.6865	0.7278	0.7071	0.7081	0.6966
CCI800	**DeepCCI**	**0.9904**	**0.9562**	**0.9703**	**0.9419**	**0.9439**	**0.9693**	**0.9569**
	FFNN	0.9776	0.9303	0.9339	0.9269	0.9279	0.9330	0.9308
	SVM	0.8711	0.7855	0.7678	0.8034	0.7980	0.7753	0.7820
	RF	0.9589	0.8918	0.9196	0.8638	0.8717	0.9144	0.8950
	AdaBoost	0.7994	0.7311	0.7014	0.7609	0.7470	0.7169	0.7235
CCI700	**DeepCCI**	**0.9932**	**0.9634**	**0.9773**	**0.9495**	**0.9507**	**0.9768**	**0.9639**
	FFNN	0.9862	0.9482	0.9509	0.9455	0.9457	0.9508	0.9483
	SVM	0.8808	0.7971	0.7655	0.8287	0.8184	0.7811	0.7899
	RF	0.9709	0.9134	0.9352	0.8918	0.8961	0.9323	0.9152
	AdaBoost	0.8082	0.7317	0.7114	0.7519	0.7410	0.7231	0.7259

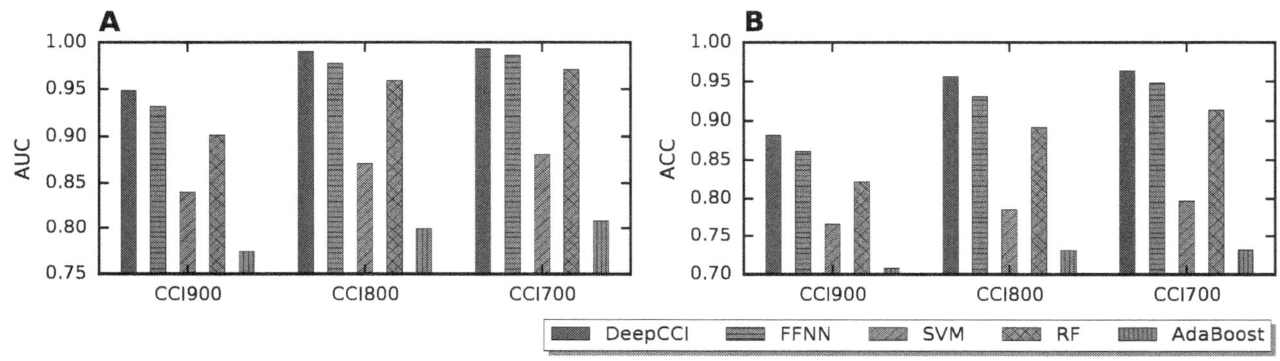

Figure 7: Visualized performance comparison in Table 2 for CCI900, CCI800, and CCI700 in terms of (A) AUC and (B) ACC.

Table 2 shows the overall detailed experimental results in terms of seven evaluation metrics, Figure 7 shows the visualized performance in terms of AUC and ACC with bar plots. All the values were averaged through ten repeated experiments and showed to be stable with a standard deviation of less than 0.004 in terms of AUC for all datasets. In all the metrics and datasets, DeepCCI showed the best performance, followed by FFNN and RF. AdaBoost and SVM showed unsatisfactory results, giving the accuracy of under 0.8 for all datasets. In terms of AUC, DeepCCI, FFNN, and RF were greater than 0.9 for all datasets, and DeepCCI outperformed the FFNN and RF by 1.82% (statistically significantly different, p-value[9] of 2.3E-09) and 5.17% (p-value of 1.7E-11), respectively for ICC900 dataset. The overall performance gradually increased as the dataset size increased.

[9] p-value from a t-test for ten repeated experimental results in terms of AUC of DeepCCI and the other method

The differences in performance between DeepCCI and FFNN could be interpreted as a result of the difference between the end-to-end SMILES and the crafted PubChem fingerprint. The end-to-end feature learning compared to the fingerprint showed better performance. We can surmise that potential key features are automatically extracted, which may be unknown to domain experts.

Figure 8 shows the experimental validation of the commutative property trained with CCI900 training data (order of A followed by B (A,B)) and tested with the switched order CCI900 training data (B followed by A (B,A)). DeepCCI showed the same training and test accuracy, on account of the effect of guaranteeing the commutative property. However, the test accuracy of FFNN, SVM, RF, and AdaBoost showed performance degradation by 18%, 17%, 21%, and 10% compared to the training accuracy. These results mean that the four methods recognized $\mathcal{I}(A,B)$ and $\mathcal{I}(B,A)$ independently and produced different prediction probabilities for them, whereas DeepCCI recognized them as the same.

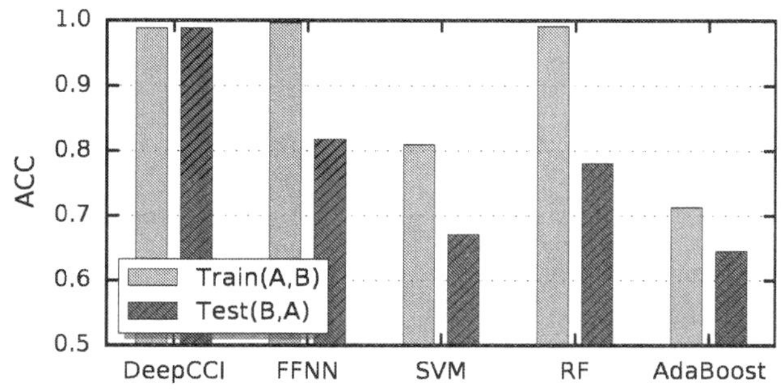

Figure 8: Experimental validation of the commutative property. Training accuracy for $\mathcal{I}(A,B)$ and test accuracy for switched order $\mathcal{I}(B,A)$.

5 DISCUSSION

In this paper, we proposed the first end-to-end deep learning method for CCI. It showed the best performance compared to a plain deep classifier and conventional machine learning methods.

Deep learning has shown remarkable success in chemical analyses and attracted considerable research attention. Despite the success and interest, the crafted features designed by domain experts continue to be used, even in state-of-the-art deep learning approaches. The objective of deep learning is not merely classification or regression from the crafted features, but automatically extracting meaningful features from the original input and analyzing them. For this reason, we have strived to perform end-to-end deep learning based on SMILES. Our approach showed better results than using the crafted PubChem fingerprint. With the CNN filters used in our experiments, we can capture relatively longer patterns that might otherwise be hard to discover with manually crafted PubChem fingerprints. We believe that patterns longer than 10 characters as well as short and simple patterns in a SMILES string play a particular role in biological reaction between chemicals. There are a variety of well-refined chemical features, and PubChem is one of the competent and widely used descriptors. Through a comparison with the PubChem, we confirmed the possibility of end-to-end SMILES learning, although we did not compare it with all descriptors.

Automatic feature learning alleviates the sophisticated efforts required for feature engineering of domain experts and it can enable discovery of meaningful features that are possibly unknown to domain experts. We expect that the proposed end-to-end SMILES learning is applied to other drug (chemical) analyses, such as QSAR prediction, chemical toxicology, and drug target prediction, and it will improve prediction performance.

In addition to presenting end-to-end SMILES learning framework, we guaranteed the commutative property in the prediction of CCI. Since CCI is a homogeneous interaction problem, it should produce the same interaction probability for $\mathcal{I}(A,B)$ and its converse, $\mathcal{I}(B,A)$. To guarantee the commutative property we used model sharing and merging hidden representations techniques and confirmed the property with experimental verification. We expect this technique can be applied to other homogeneous symmetric problems, such as protein-protein and gene-gene interactions, as well as other homogeneous comparisons.

The future revisions of DeepCCI may include the following improvements: We are planning to analyze how the features automatically extracted from shared CNNs affect the overall performance when they are applied to the conventional machine learning classifiers. As in other fingerprint-based approaches, deep learning-based hidden features may be used as a separate fingerprint for various classifiers. Instead of zero-padding, we may consider using a wildcard character in encoding as a special character, as was done in the idea of wildcard denoising [51]. All the zero values included in one-hot encoding may confuse the network, making it fail to recognize them as a padded region.

ACKNOWLEDGMENTS

The authors would like to thank the anonymous reviewers of this paper for their constructive comments and helpful suggestions. This work was supported in part by the National Research Foundation of Korea (NRF) grant funded by the Korea government (ICT and Future Planning) [No. 2015M3A9A7029735], in part by a grant of the Korea Health Technology R&D Project through the Korea Health Industry Development Institute (KHIDI), funded by the Ministry of Health & Welfare [HI14C3405030014 and HI15C3224] and in part by the Brain Korea 21 Plus Project in 2017.

REFERENCES

[1] Babak Alipanahi, Andrew Delong, Matthew T Weirauch, and Brendan J Frey. 2015. Predicting the sequence specificities of DNA-and RNA-binding proteins by deep learning. *Nature biotechnology* 33, 8 (2015), 831–838.

[2] Christof Angermueller, Tanel Pärnamaa, Leopold Parts, and Oliver Stegle. 2016. Deep learning for computational biology. *Molecular systems biology* 12, 7 (2016), 878.

[3] Dzmitry Bahdanau, Kyunghyun Cho, and Yoshua Bengio. 2014. Neural machine translation by jointly learning to align and translate. *arXiv preprint arXiv:1409.0473* (2014).

[4] Petko Bogdanov and Ambuj K Singh. 2010. Molecular function prediction using neighborhood features. *IEEE/ACM Transactions on Computational Biology and Bioinformatics (TCBB)* 7, 2 (2010), 208–217.

[5] Leo Breiman. 2001. Random forests. *Machine learning* 45, 1 (2001), 5–32.

[6] Lei Chen, Tao Huang, Jian Zhang, Ming-Yue Zheng, Kai-Yan Feng, Yu-Dong Cai, and Kuo-Chen Chou. 2013. Predicting drugs side effects based on chemical-chemical interactions and protein-chemical interactions. *BioMed research international* 2013 (2013).

[7] Lei Chen, Jing Lu, Jian Zhang, Kai-Rui Feng, Ming-Yue Zheng, and Yu-Dong Cai. 2013. Predicting chemical toxicity effects based on chemical-chemical interactions. *PLoS One* 8, 2 (2013), e56517.

[8] Lei Chen, Jing Yang, Mingyue Zheng, Xiangyin Kong, Tao Huang, and Yu-Dong Cai. 2015. The use of chemical-chemical interaction and chemical structure to identify new candidate chemicals related to lung cancer. *PloS one* 10, 6 (2015), e0128696.

[9] François Chollet. 2015. Keras: Deep Learning library for Theano and TensorFlow. https://github.com/fchollet/keras. (2015).

[10] Ryszard Czermiński, Abdelaziz Yasri, and David Hartsough. 2001. Use of support vector machine in pattern classification: Application to QSAR studies. *Molecular Informatics* 20, 3 (2001), 227–240.

[11] George E Dahl, Navdeep Jaitly, and Ruslan Salakhutdinov. 2014. Multi-task neural networks for QSAR predictions. *arXiv preprint arXiv:1406.1231* (2014).

[12] Li Deng and Roberto Togneri. 2015. Deep dynamic models for learning hidden representations of speech features. In *Speech and Audio Processing for Coding, Enhancement and Recognition*. Springer, 153–195.

[13] Jean-Pierre Doucet, Florent Barbault, Hairong Xia, Annick Panaye, and Botao Fan. 2007. Nonlinear SVM approaches to QSPR/QSAR studies and drug design. *Current Computer-Aided Drug Design* 3, 4 (2007), 263–289.

[14] Jesse Eickholt and Jianlin Cheng. 2013. DNdisorder: predicting protein disorder using boosting and deep networks. *BMC bioinformatics* 14, 1 (2013), 88.

[15] Andrea Franceschini, Damian Szklarczyk, Sune Frankild, Michael Kuhn, Milan Simonovic, Alexander Roth, Jianyi Lin, Pablo Minguez, Peer Bork, Christian

Von Mering, and others. 2013. STRING v9. 1: protein-protein interaction networks, with increased coverage and integration. *Nucleic acids research* 41, D1 (2013), D808–D815.

[16] Yoav Freund and Robert E Schapire. 1995. A desicion-theoretic generalization of on-line learning and an application to boosting. In *European conference on computational learning theory*. Springer, 23–37.

[17] Rafael Gómez-Bombarelli, David Duvenaud, José Miguel Hernández-Lobato, Jorge Aguilera-Iparraguirre, Timothy D Hirzel, Ryan P Adams, and Alán Aspuru-Guzik. 2016. Automatic chemical design using a data-driven continuous representation of molecules. *arXiv preprint arXiv:1610.02415* (2016).

[18] Alex Graves, Abdel-rahman Mohamed, and Geoffrey Hinton. 2013. Speech recognition with deep recurrent neural networks. In *Acoustics, speech and signal processing (icassp), 2013 ieee international conference on*. IEEE, 6645–6649.

[19] Stephen Heller, Alan McNaught, Stephen Stein, Dmitrii Tchekhovskoi, and Igor Pletnev. 2013. InChI-the worldwide chemical structure identifier standard. *Journal of cheminformatics* 5, 1 (2013), 7.

[20] Geoffrey Hinton, Li Deng, Dong Yu, George E Dahl, Abdel-rahman Mohamed, Navdeep Jaitly, Andrew Senior, Vincent Vanhoucke, Patrick Nguyen, Tara N Sainath, and others. 2012. Deep neural networks for acoustic modeling in speech recognition: The shared views of four research groups. *IEEE Signal Processing Magazine* 29, 6 (2012), 82–97.

[21] Sepp Hochreiter and Jürgen Schmidhuber. 1997. Long short-term memory. *Neural computation* 9, 8 (1997), 1735–1780.

[22] Le-Le Hu, Chen Chen, Tao Huang, Yu-Dong Cai, and Kuo-Chen Chou. 2011. Predicting biological functions of compounds based on chemical-chemical interactions. *PLoS One* 6, 12 (2011), e29491.

[23] Sergey Ioffe and Christian Szegedy. 2015. Batch normalization: Accelerating deep network training by reducing internal covariate shift. *arXiv preprint arXiv:1502.03167* (2015).

[24] Hawoong Jeong, Sean P Mason, A-L Barabási, and Zoltan N Oltvai. 2001. Lethality and centrality in protein networks. *Nature* 411, 6833 (2001), 41–42.

[25] Nal Kalchbrenner, Edward Grefenstette, and Phil Blunsom. 2014. A convolutional neural network for modelling sentences. *arXiv preprint arXiv:1404.2188* (2014).

[26] Yoon Kim. 2014. Convolutional neural networks for sentence classification. *arXiv preprint arXiv:1408.5882* (2014).

[27] T Kindt, S Morse, E Gotschlich, and K Lyons. 1991. Structure-based strategies for drug design and discovery. *Nature* 352 (1991), 581.

[28] Diederik Kingma and Jimmy Ba. 2014. Adam: A method for stochastic optimization. *arXiv preprint arXiv:1412.6980* (2014).

[29] Diederik P Kingma and Max Welling. 2013. Auto-encoding variational bayes. *arXiv preprint arXiv:1312.6114* (2013).

[30] Alex Krizhevsky, Ilya Sutskever, and Geoffrey E Hinton. 2012. Imagenet classification with deep convolutional neural networks. In *Advances in neural information processing systems*. 1097–1105.

[31] Michael Kuhn, Christian von Mering, Monica Campillos, Lars Juhl Jensen, and Peer Bork. 2008. STITCH: interaction networks of chemicals and proteins. *Nucleic acids research* 36, suppl 1 (2008), D684–D688.

[32] Steve Lawrence, C Lee Giles, Ah Chung Tsoi, and Andrew D Back. 1997. Face recognition: A convolutional neural-network approach. *IEEE transactions on neural networks* 8, 1 (1997), 98–113.

[33] Byunghan Lee, Junghwan Baek, Seunghyun Park, and Sungroh Yoon. 2016. deepTarget: end-to-end learning framework for microRNA target prediction using deep recurrent neural networks. *arXiv preprint arXiv:1603.09123* (2016).

[34] Byunghan Lee, Taehoon Lee, Byunggook Na, and Sungroh Yoon. 2015. DNA-level splice junction prediction using deep recurrent neural networks. *arXiv preprint arXiv:1512.05135* (2015).

[35] Taehoon Lee and Sungroh Yoon. 2015. Boosted Categorical Restricted Boltzmann Machine for Computational Prediction of Splice Junctions.. In *ICML*. 2483–2492.

[36] Michael KK Leung, Hui Yuan Xiong, Leo J Lee, and Brendan J Frey. 2014. Deep learning of the tissue-regulated splicing code. *Bioinformatics* 30, 12 (2014), i121–i129.

[37] Zachary C Lipton, John Berkowitz, and Charles Elkan. 2015. A critical review of recurrent neural networks for sequence learning. *arXiv preprint arXiv:1506.00019* (2015).

[38] Alessandro Lusci, Gianluca Pollastri, and Pierre Baldi. 2013. Deep architectures and deep learning in chemoinformatics: the prediction of aqueous solubility for drug-like molecules. *Journal of chemical information and modeling* 53, 7 (2013), 1563.

[39] Seonwoo Min, Byunghan Lee, and Sungroh Yoon. 2016. Deep learning in bioinformatics. *Briefings in Bioinformatics* (2016), bbw068.

[40] Vinod Nair and Geoffrey E Hinton. 2010. Rectified linear units improve restricted boltzmann machines. In *Proceedings of the 27th international conference on machine learning (ICML-10)*. 807–814.

[41] Ka-Lok Ng, Jin-Shuei Ciou, and Chien-Hung Huang. 2010. Prediction of protein functions based on function-function correlation relations. *Computers in Biology and Medicine* 40, 3 (2010), 300–305.

[42] Maxime Oquab, Leon Bottou, Ivan Laptev, and Josef Sivic. 2014. Learning and transferring mid-level image representations using convolutional neural networks. In *Proceedings of the IEEE conference on computer vision and pattern recognition*. 1717–1724.

[43] Hakime Öztürk, Elif Ozkirimli, and Arzucan Özgür. 2016. A comparative study of SMILES-based compound similarity functions for drug-target interaction prediction. *BMC bioinformatics* 17, 1 (2016), 128.

[44] Seunghyun Park, Seonwoo Min, Hyunsoo Choi, and Sungroh Yoon. 2016. deepMiRGene: deep neural network based precursor microRNA prediction. *arXiv preprint arXiv:1605.00017* (2016).

[45] Bharath Ramsundar, Steven Kearnes, Patrick Riley, Dale Webster, David Konerding, and Vijay Pande. 2015. Massively multitask networks for drug discovery. *arXiv preprint arXiv:1502.02072* (2015).

[46] Ambrish Roy, Alper Kucukural, and Yang Zhang. 2010. I-TASSER: a unified platform for automated protein structure and function prediction. *Nature protocols* 5, 4 (2010), 725–738.

[47] Jean-François Rual, Kavitha Venkatesan, Tong Hao, Tomoko Hirozane-Kishikawa, Amélie Dricot, Ning Li, Gabriel F Berriz, Francis D Gibbons, Matija Dreze, Nono Ayivi-Guedehoussou, and others. 2005. Towards a proteome-scale map of the human protein–protein interaction network. *Nature* 437, 7062 (2005), 1173–1178.

[48] Leander Schietgat, Bertrand Cuissart, Alban Lepailleur, Kurt De Grave, Bruno Crémilleux, Ronan Bureau, and Jan Ramon. 2013. Comparing chemical fingerprints for ecotoxicology. In *6èmes journées de la Société Française de Chémoinformatique*.

[49] Marwin HS Segler, Thierry Kogej, Christian Tyrchan, and Mark P Waller. 2017. Generating Focussed Molecule Libraries for Drug Discovery with Recurrent Neural Networks. *arXiv preprint arXiv:1701.01329* (2017).

[50] Roded Sharan, Igor Ulitsky, and Ron Shamir. 2007. Network-based prediction of protein function. *Molecular systems biology* 3, 1 (2007), 88.

[51] Xingjian Shi, Hao Wang, and Dit Yan Yeung. 2016. Collaborative Recurrent Autoencoder: Recommend while Learning to Fill in the Blanks. (2016).

[52] Nitish Srivastava, Geoffrey E Hinton, Alex Krizhevsky, Ilya Sutskever, and Ruslan Salakhutdinov. 2014. Dropout: a simple way to prevent neural networks from overfitting. *Journal of Machine Learning Research* 15, 1 (2014), 1929–1958.

[53] Andrew J Stuper, William E Brügger, and Peter C Jurs. 1979. *Computer assisted studies of chemical structure and biological function*. John Wiley & Sons.

[54] Ilya Sutskever, Oriol Vinyals, and Quoc V Le. 2014. Sequence to sequence learning with neural networks. In *Advances in neural information processing systems*. 3104–3112.

[55] Vladimir Svetnik, Andy Liaw, Christopher Tong, J Christopher Culberson, Robert P Sheridan, and Bradley P Feuston. 2003. Random forest: a classification and regression tool for compound classification and QSAR modeling. *Journal of chemical information and computer sciences* 43, 6 (2003), 1947–1958.

[56] Matt Swain. 2014. PubChemPy: a way to interact with PubChem in Python. http://pubchempy.readthedocs.io. (2014).

[57] Mahmud Tareq Hassan Khan. 2010. Predictions of the ADMET properties of candidate drug molecules utilizing different QSAR/QSPR modelling approaches. *Current Drug Metabolism* 11, 4 (2010), 285–295.

[58] Kai Tian, Mingyu Shao, Yang Wang, Jihong Guan, and Shuigeng Zhou. 2016. Boosting compound-protein interaction prediction by deep learning. *Methods* 110 (2016), 64–72.

[59] Roberto Todeschini and Viviana Consonni. 2009. *Molecular descriptors for chemoinformatics, volume 41 (2 volume set)*. Vol. 41. John Wiley & Sons.

[60] Han Van De Waterbeemd and Eric Gifford. 2003. ADMET in silico modelling: towards prediction paradise? *Nature reviews Drug discovery* 2, 3 (2003), 192–204.

[61] Vladimir Vapnik. 2013. *The nature of statistical learning theory*. Springer science & business media.

[62] Vladimir Naumovich Vapnik and Vlamimir Vapnik. 1998. *Statistical learning theory*. Vol. 1. Wiley New York.

[63] Qin Wang, Xiao Li, Hongbin Yang, Yingchun Cai, Yinyin Wang, Zhuang Wang, Weihua Li, Yun Tang, and Guixia Liu. 2017. In silico prediction of serious eye irritation or corrosion potential of chemicals. *RSC Advances* 7, 11 (2017), 6697–6703.

[64] Yanli Wang, Jewen Xiao, Tugba O Suzek, Jian Zhang, Jiyao Wang, and Stephen H Bryant. 2009. PubChem: a public information system for analyzing bioactivities of small molecules. *Nucleic acids research* 37, suppl 2 (2009), W623–W633.

[65] David Weininger. 1970. SMILES, a chemical language and information system. 1. Introduction to methodology and encoding rules. In *Proc. Edinburgh Math. SOC*, Vol. 17. 1–14.

[66] Jan Wildenhain, Michaela Spitzer, Sonam Dolma, Nick Jarvik, Rachel White, Marcia Roy, Emma Griffiths, David S Bellows, Gerard D Wright, and Mike Tyers. 2016. Systematic chemical-genetic and chemical-chemical interaction datasets for prediction of compound synergism. *Scientific Data* 3 (2016).

[67] Matthew D Zeiler and Rob Fergus. 2014. Visualizing and understanding convolutional networks. In *European conference on computer vision*. Springer, 818–833.

[68] Haoyang Zeng, Matthew D Edwards, Ge Liu, and David K Gifford. 2016. Convolutional neural network architectures for predicting DNA–protein binding. *Bioinformatics* 32, 12 (2016), i121–i127.

A Multi-view Deep Learning Method for Epileptic Seizure Detection using Short-time Fourier Transform

Ye Yuan
College of Information and Communication Engineering, Beijing University of Technology
Beijing 100124, China
yuanye91@emails.bjut.edu.cn

Guangxu Xun
Department of Computer Science and Engineering, State University of New York at Buffalo
Buffalo 14260, USA
guangxux@buffalo.edu

Kebin Jia
College of Information and Communication Engineering, Beijing University of Technology
Beijing 100124, China
kebinj@bjut.edu.cn

Aidong Zhang
Department of Computer Science and Engineering, State University of New York at Buffalo
Buffalo 14260, USA
azhang@buffalo.edu

ABSTRACT

With the advances in pervasive sensor technologies, physiological signals can be captured continuously to prevent the serious outcomes caused by epilepsy. Detection of epileptic seizure onset on collected multi-channel electroencephalogram (EEG) has attracted lots of attention recently. Deep learning is a promising method to analyze large-scale unlabeled data. In this paper, we propose a multi-view deep learning model to capture brain abnormality from multi-channel epileptic EEG signals for seizure detection. Specifically, we first generate EEG spectrograms using short-time Fourier transform (STFT) to represent the time-frequency information after signal segmentation. Second, we adopt stacked sparse denoising autoencoders (SSDA) to unsupervisedly learn multiple features by considering both intra and inter correlation of EEG channels, denoted as intra-channel and cross-channel features, respectively. Third, we add an SSDA-based channel selection procedure using proposed response rate to reduce the dimension of intra-channel feature. Finally, we concatenate the learned multi-features and apply a fully-connected SSDA model with softmax classifier to jointly learn the cross-patient seizure detector in a supervised fashion. To evaluate the performance of the proposed model, we carry out experiments on a real world benchmark EEG dataset and compare it with six baselines. Extensive experimental results demonstrate that the proposed learning model is able to extract latent features with meaningful interpretation, and hence is effective in detecting epileptic seizure.

CCS CONCEPTS

•Applied computing → Bioinformatics; •Computing methodologies → *Neural networks;* **•Information systems →** Data mining;

Permission to make digital or hard copies of all or part of this work for personal or classroom use is granted without fee provided that copies are not made or distributed for profit or commercial advantage and that copies bear this notice and the full citation on the first page. Copyrights for components of this work owned by others than ACM must be honored. Abstracting with credit is permitted. To copy otherwise, or republish, to post on servers or to redistribute to lists, requires prior specific permission and/or a fee. Request permissions from permissions@acm.org.
ACM-BCB'17, August 20–23, 2017, Boston, MA, USA.
© 2017 ACM.
ISBN 978-1-4503-4722-8/17/08...$15.00
DOI: http://dx.doi.org/10.1145/3107411.3107419

KEYWORDS

Deep learning; Epileptic seizure; Electroencephalogram; Feature extraction; Time-frequency analysis

1 INTRODUCTION

With the development of pervasive sensor technologies, tremendous opportunities are introduced to closely analyze patients' conditions. The advanced sensors, including implantable, wearable, and ambient sensors [20], allow to monitor continuously to prevent the serious outcomes caused by several medical diseases. The collected physiological data can be further used to recognize hidden patterns in biomedical applications to improve treatment [51]. Epilepsy, a serious chronic neurological disorder, affects approximately 50 million people worldwide [34]. Although anti-epileptic drugs do have some treatment effect, the disease may still result in serious physical injuries and even death [32, 45]. The major symptom of epilepsy is associated with recurrent and unpredictable epileptic seizures caused by sudden abnormal neuronal discharges in the brain [10]. According to previous studies, electroencephalogram (EEG) is one of the most effective methods to observe brain electrical activities by placing electrodes outside the skull (extra-cranial recording) or inside the skull (intra-cranial recording) [15]. Furthermore, with distributed continuous sensing, scalp EEG signals can be collected from a large number of input channels with high temporal resolution. This massive data can record synchronous activities of neurons in different brain areas. Therefore, epileptic seizure detection using multi-channel scalp epileptic EEG signals has gained great attention in neuro-informatics.

In clinical settings, visual inspection for epilepsy diagnosis requires scarce highly trained professionals in neurology. In addition, it is extremely laborious and time-consuming for physicians to identify epileptic patterns from long-term EEG readings [33]. These limitations have motivated researchers to develop automated seizure detection approaches via machine learning methods. Based on the categories of epileptic EEG signals [12], seizure detection can be regarded as a binary classification task for non-ictal and ictal states.

In general, the machine learning based seizure detection process consists of three steps, namely, preprocessing, feature extraction and classification [39]. Among these steps, feature extraction plays an important role since it aims to capture the meaningful and distinctive characteristics of EEG signals, which directly influences the final classification performance. Deep learning is a branch of machine learning that attempts to adopt a multi-layer neural network to automatically extract latent features from massive data. The initial concept of deep learning is an unsupervised greedy layer-wise training algorithm based on deep network [16]. By constructing a better representation with deep structure to learn a model, deep learning obtains high level features to enhance learning performance. There are mainly two steps in training a deep network: pre-training and fine-tuning. A greedy layer-wise unsupervised training method is adopted for pre-training using unlabeled data. The weights connected each layer are trained individually while fixing the others. This step is significantly different from traditional neural network training strategy. To improve performance, fine-tuning is then adopted in a supervised learning fashion by tuning the weights of all layers simultaneously using labeled data. Thus, the deep architecture transforms the features into a relative low dimension space, which enhances the ability of feature expression. Research has proved that the use of deep learning can achieve improved performance in a wide range of applications when compared to traditional hand-engineering approaches [3]. For this reason, numerous methods has been proposed to employ deep learning for seizure detection [23, 31, 44]. These unsupervised learning features are explored from unlabeled raw medical data [27, 28, 42], and have shown great promise in mining hidden seizure characteristics.

Despite promising results have been reported using such deep learning methods, there still exist several challenges that should be addressed. First, most traditional deep learning models independently feed each channel into seizure classifier and ignore the correlations between them, which leads to the failure to recognize the general signal patterns. Second, most of the channels in multi-channel EEG signals are irrelevant to brain related activities, including seizure onset [18, 25]. These irrelevant channels introduce lots of noise to data and could significantly reduce the performance of the learning methods. Third, it does not always yield good performance with conventional deep learning features with simple design, especially when confronted with unbalanced datasets or rare events which is a common issue in health informatics [1]. It is necessary to integrate knowledge from handcrafted engineering, such as signal processing, during the deep learning process to enhance the performance. Finally, the patterns of seizures in EEG signals may vary significantly across patients and even over time for the same patient, which makes it difficult to develop a cross-patient detector.

To tackle the aforementioned challenges, we propose a multi-view deep learning model to simultaneously extract the multiple latent features of multi-channel EEG signals from both intra and inter patient groups. Our model is described in Fig. 1. As the seizure state is related to an interval rather than a certain point of EEG signals, in this paper, we first slice the EEG signals of different patients into fixed-length pieces with a sliding window, and use short-time Fourier transform (STFT) as the preprocessing step to further capture the time-frequency information, denoted as EEG spectrogram representations. We then adopt stacked sparse denoising autoencoders (SSDA) to unsupervisedly learn multiple features by considering both intra and inter correlation of EEG channels, denoted as intra-channel and cross-channel features, respectively. Since the channel selection based techniques have been proven to be effective in bioinformatics [18, 25], we further extend this strategy and propose an SSDA-based channel selection procedure by integrating both zero-based and sample-based unsupervised information to derive a better understanding of the characteristics of seizure patterns. Finally, we merge the learned multi-features together and apply the fully-connected SSDA model with softmax classifier in a supervised fashion to jointly learn the cross-patient seizure detector. Our contribution can be summarized as:

- We develop an unsupervised feature learning method using the EEG spectrogram representation model as preprocessing. The generated 2-D time-frequency-based fragments are suitable for latent feature extraction using deep learning. This method also combines features from both signal handcrafted engineering and deep learning approaches.
- We develop an EEG channel selection procedure which uses an SSDA-based stimulus-response rate considering multiple unsupervised information to jointly determine the critical channel features. This results in a marked mitigation of the noise effect and a great reduction of data dimensionality.
- We propose a multi-view deep learning model that integrates both intra and inter correlation of EEG channels, i.e., cross-channel and intra-channel features, to explore hidden inherent seizure characteristics with meaningful interpretation in multi-channel EEG signals. The results show that the proposed model outperforms the baseline methods on different evaluation criteria.

The rest of the paper is organized as follows: Section 2 introduces the related works of seizure detection. Our proposed methodology is then described in Section 3. Section 4 presents and discusses the experimental results for our method followed by the conclusions in Section 5.

2 RELATED WORK

In recent years, there has been a growing interest in detecting epileptic seizure through deep learning methods. Pramod et al. [35] developed a patient-specific epileptic seizure detector using deep neural networks trained with dropout from EEG data. Some researchers applied deep belief networks (DBNs) to seizure detection. Turner et al. [46] applied DBNs to seizure detection in high resolution and multi-channel EEG data. Wulsin et al. [48] applied DBNs in a semi-supervised paradigm to model EEG waveforms for classification and anomaly detection, and the results showed that fast seizure detection are possible with sophisticated machine learning methods. There are some works related to convolution neural networks (CNNs)-based seizure detection approaches. Johansen et al. [19] developed a CNN model for detecting spikes in EEG of epileptic patients in an automated fashion. Antoniades et al. [2] considered deep learning for automatic feature generation from epileptic intracranial EEG data in time domain, and applied CNNs in a subject independent fashion. To increase the training ratio and overcome the curse of dimensionality, Li et al. [24] adopted a CNN-based method trained with accelerated proximal gradient algorithm

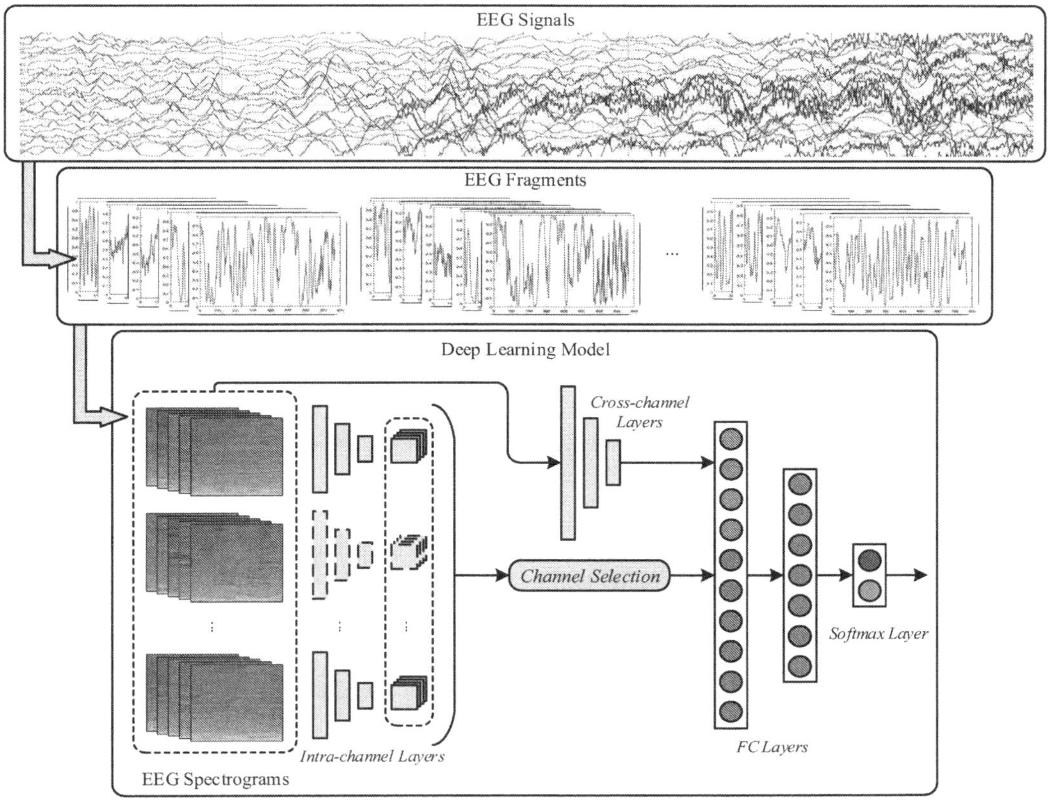

Figure 1: Schematic illustration of the overall approach pipeline.

for feature extraction and classification simultaneously. Moreover, stacked autoencoders were also used for analysis of epileptic EEG signals. Supratak et al. [43] developed a patient-specific seizure detector using stacked autoencoders and logistic classifier. This model investigated the possibility of utilizing unsupervised feature learning to automatically learn features from raw, unlabeled EEG data. Qi et al. [36] proposed a robust stacked autoencoder as a part of the deep network to jointly learn effective feature and classifier. The authors also proposed a maximum correntrpy criterion to reduce the effect of noise. To reduce the sample rate and enhance the efficiency of the vision detection, Yan et al. [50] proposed an EEG signal classification method based on sparse autoencoder and support vector machine. Lin et al. [26] proposed a framework for automatic detection of epileptic EEG using stacked sparse autoencoders, and the simulation results illustrated the effectiveness of the proposed framework. Majumdar. et al. [29] proposed a combined solution to the biomedical signal reconstruction and analysis, and use a semi-supervised stacked autoencoder to address this issue in a holistic fashion. With any strategy adopted, all the above discussed methods directly feed EEG signals as input into deep learning model without any handcrafted engineering knowledge assisted. These deep learning methods yielded good performance, however, they do not consider the irrelevant channels to seizure onset and ignore the correlations between EEG channels. With the help of signal processing and clinical knowledge, we propose to build a learning procedure to extract more meaningful interpretation from multi-channel EEG signals than traditional methods.

For the spectrogram representation, the time-frequency image-based features are also used to describe the non-stationary nature of EEG signals. These handcrafted representations contain richer features than raw signals. Recently, some existing approaches were proposed based on time-frequency image descriptors for epileptic seizure detection on EEG data. Kovacs et al. [22] proposed a rational discrete STFT to extract discriminative features in EEG data, and used alternating decision tree classifier to detect the seizure segments in presence of seizure-free segments. Şengür et al. [38] proposed a new texture descriptor to extract features from EEG time-frequency images, and employed support vector machine to detect epileptic seizures. Boubchir et al. [6, 7] developed a model using Haralickfis texture descriptor to describe visually the epileptic seizure patterns observed in time-frequency image of EEG signals. In order to improve the performance of EEG seizure detection and classification of non-stationary EEG signals, the optimal relevant translated features are selected according to maximum relevance and minimum redundancy criteria. Fu. et al. [11] presented a technique for seizure classification of EEG signals using Hilbert-Huang transform and support vector machine on time-frequency image. Some 2-D statistical features such as mean, variance, skewness and kurtosis of pixel intensity in the histogram were extracted. Samiee et al. [37] proposed a method based on an adaptive and localized time-frequency image representation of EEG signals relying on rational functions. The authors indicated that multi-layer perceptron was the optimal classifier compared with various classifiers such as naive Bayes, logistic regression, support vector machine, K-nearest neighbors. To improve the accuracy of epileptic EEG signal classification, Sivasankari et al. [41] introduced a model using time-frequency features extracted on the basis of three parameters, namely, standard deviation, correlation dimension, and Lyapunov exponents. Independent component analysis was incorporated as a preprocessing step and STFT is used for denoising the signal adequately. Tzallas. et al. [47] extracted features by measuring the signal segment fractional energy in specific time-frequency windows. The authors demonstrated the suitability of time-frequency analysis to classify EEG segments for epileptic seizures. To merge key instantaneous frequency descriptors, Boashash. et al. [5] presented an approach for EEG abnormalities detection and classification based on the features derived from EEG time-frequency representations. The authors combined signal related and image related features by calculating specific measurements such as instantaneous frequency, singular value decomposition, and morphometric features. With any strategy adopted, all the above discussed methods applied handcrafted feature engineering both in time-frequency representation and feature extraction. These appropriate features, however, is determined based on the specific case, which might not capture new patterns of seizure activity. In our proposed model, we employ a deep learning method to learn features that are complement to the handcrafted engineering, in order to improve the performance of seizure detection.

3 METHODOLOGY

3.1 EEG Segmentation

The proposed approach is designed to detect epileptic seizure in real-time. Since EEG signals cannot be explicitly segmented into sub-fragments associated with physiological meanings, we segment them into several slots of fixed length. In our model, we obtain EEG fragments by sliding a fix-length window through the entire signals parameterized by two predefined parameters: window length l and step length s. Fig. 2 shows an example of how to segment an EEG signal into fragments. Notice that increasing the segment length can improve the recognition accuracy, at the cost of the delay for real-time applications. Thus, the length of the sliding window is fixed to $l = 3seconds$ and the step length $s = 1second$.

3.2 EEG Spectrogram Representation

Considering the fact that the brain abnormality in EEG is reflected by frequency changes and increased amplitudes [14], combining signal processing knowledge improves seizure detection performance. Spectrogram representation is essential for extracting interpretable features in time-frequency domain. This enables the classifier to be more robust against amplitude changes and data shifting. In addition, spectrogram representation also provides an implicit way for noise cancellation of the signal over time.

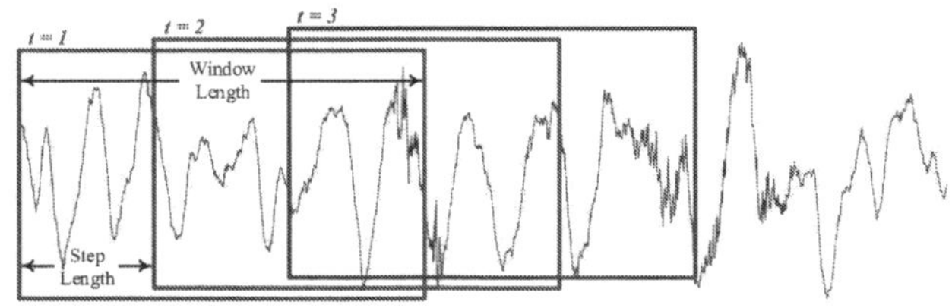

Figure 2: An example of EEG segmentation.

In our model, we use STFT to convert EEG fragments into EEG spectrogram representations in time-frequency domain. Formally, given EEG fragment $x(t)$ of one single-channel, the STFT of the signal in a continuous form is defined as [8]:

$$STFT_x(\tau, w) = \int_{-\infty}^{\infty} x(t)w(t-\tau)e^{-jwt}dt, \quad (1)$$

where $w(t)$ is the window function centered around zero, and τ denotes the time index to obtain time localization by taking Fourier transform of the windowed signal. STFT handles the non-stationarity by windowing, and thus taking the temporal variations into account. The spectrogram can be further calculated as the magnitude squared of the STFT to transform the complex values:

$$scalogram_x(\tau, w) = |STFT_x(\tau, w)|^2. \quad (2)$$

The resulting spectrogram is a matrix where time increases across the columns and frequency increases down the rows. In this way, by generating the EEG spectrogram representation, the frequency content in epileptic EEG signals can be described over time, which can be further learned as time-frequency images by the deep learning model. To demonstrate the basic idea of the proposed method, we adopt the Blackman window as the STFT window function in the following sections. We also examine different window functions as demonstrated later in Section 4.

3.3 Multi-view Deep Feature Extraction

In most cases, on the learning of seizure characteristics from EEG signals, only standard deep learning method with simple design is adopted to extract features. Using simple deep learning structure causes the inability of single feature to reach the robust and accurate results. To handle this problem, we propose to unsupervisedly extract high level and latent seizure features from different perspectives through the SSDA model [49]. Specifically, once the 2-D EEG spectrograms have been computed, a set of deep features can be automatically extracted by considering both intra and inter correlation of EEG channels, i.e., intra-channel features and cross-channel features. For instance, given a single-channel EEG spectrogram, we can regard it as a spectral image where various spatial features are extracted within each fragment. In this step, high dimensional raw features are integrated into low dimensional latent characteristics with meaningful interpretation.

In general, SSDA model is a multi-layer neural network consisting of several stacked basic denoising autoencoders (DA) with sparse constraint. DA is a single hidden layer model that attempts

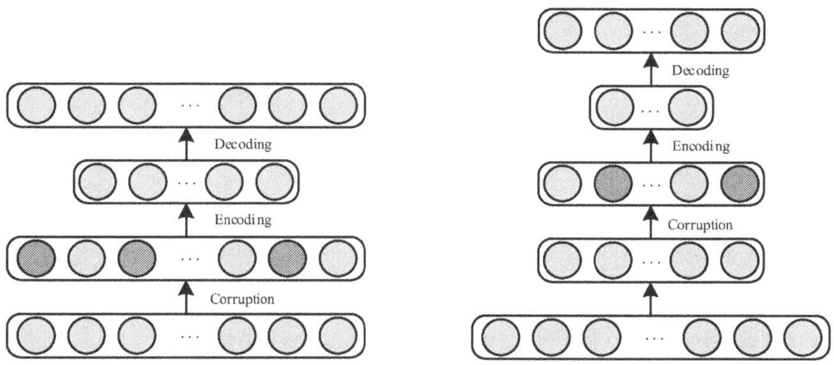

(a) The structure of DA network

(b) The structure of SSDA network

Figure 3: Deep model for EEG feature learning.

to let the output vector approximate the input vector by learning an encoder and a decoder, shown in Fig. 3(a). Different from the traditional autoencoder [17], DA adds random corruption to the input before encoding, sampling $\hat{x} \sim P_{corr}(\hat{x} \mid x)$, in order to enable the hidden layer to uncover more robust features. Formally, given a single input vector x, the output vector y can be expressed by the hypothesis function based on forward-propagation:

$$y = h_{W,b}(x) = f(W^{(l+1)} f(W^{(l)}\hat{x} + b^{(l)}) + b^{(l+1)}), \tag{3}$$

where $f(\cdot)$ is the activation function, $W^{(l)}$ and $b^{(l)}$ denote the weight matrix and bias in layer l, respectively.

The training objective for DA is to minimize the reconstruction error over training set. Given unlabeled training dataset $\{x^{(i)}, i = 1, 2, ..., m\}$ where $x^{(i)} \in \mathbb{R}^n$, by minimizing the reconstruction error between input $x^{(i)}$ and output $y^{(i)}$, the cost function in terms of parameters (W, b) is defined as:

$$J_{DA}(W,b) = \frac{1}{m}\sum_{i=1}^{m} \mathcal{L}_{\mathbb{H}}(x^{(i)}, h_{W,b}(x^{(i)})), \tag{4}$$

where $\mathcal{L}_{\mathbb{H}}$ represents the reconstruction error, which is measured by the cross-entropy loss:

$$\begin{aligned}\mathcal{L}_{\mathbb{H}}(x^{(i)}, h_{W,b}(x^{(i)})) = -\sum_{j=1}^{n}[x_j^{(i)} \log(h_{W,b}(x_j^{(i)})) \\ + (1 - x_j^{(i)}) \log(1 - h_{W,b}(x_j^{(i)}))].\end{aligned} \tag{5}$$

To combine the virtues of sparse coding and neural networks and avoid overfitting, we train a DA to minimize the cost function regularized by a sparsity penalty term:

$$J_{SDA}(W,b) = J_{DA}(W,b) + \frac{\lambda}{2}\|W\|^2 + \beta\sum_{j=1}^{s} KL(\rho \parallel \hat{\rho}_j), \tag{6}$$

where $J_{DA}(W, b)$ is the cost function defined in Equation 4, s is the number of hidden units. λ and β are the hyper-parameters that control the weight of the regularization constraint and sparsity constraint, receptively. Here $KL(\rho \parallel \hat{\rho}_j)$ is the Kullback-Leibler (KL) divergence to measure the difference between a Bernoulli random variable with mean ρ and a Bernoulli random variable with mean $\hat{\rho}_j$, defined as:

$$KL(\rho \parallel \hat{\rho}_j) = \rho \log\frac{\rho}{\hat{\rho}_j} + (1-\rho)\log\frac{1-\rho}{1-\hat{\rho}_j}, \tag{7}$$

where $\hat{\rho}$ is the average activation of hidden unit j (averaged over the training set), and ρ denotes the sparsity parameter which is a small value close to zero. Note that the regularization term is considered to decrease the magnitude of the weights and help prevent overfitting.

In this way, the SSDA model can be regarded as a deep stacked network, as shown in Fig. 3(b). The strategy for training the SSDA is using the greedy layer-wise method [4]. Specifically, the output hidden features extracted in the previous layer of SSDA is fed to the current layer as input. Thus, the parameters of each layer is trained individually while fixing the parameters of the other layers. For our model, P_{corr} is set as a binary mask on x which zeros out each entry independently with probability p. The activation function is defined as the sigmoid logistic function $f(z) = 1/(1 + \exp(-z))$. For further analysis, we extend the unsupervised SSDA framework by denoting the last hidden features learned from each channel and whole channels as the intra-channel features and the cross-channel features, receptively. This makes it well-suited to capture complex correlations across EEG time-frequency spectrograms in the low dimensional space, especially when working with relatively small dataset with few or unreliable labels.

3.4 Channel Selection

Channel selection is a special case of intra-channel feature extraction. In biology, brain related activities, which include epileptic seizure, are usually dominated by several specific areas of the brain. Thus in seizure detection, there exist some irrelevant channels which bring noise to the classification task. To filter out these irrelevant channels, in this section, we propose an SSDA-based channel selection method to determine the critical features by the partition of channels. This structure of channel selection can be easily integrated into the whole proposed deep learning framework. In our previous work [18, 25], we have shown the importance of channel selection in multi-channel EEG signals. This strategy involves using zero-stimulus method where an all-zero vector is used as input to the trained deep learning model. After this we measure the response rate, which is defined to be the distance between the value of resulting hidden units and random hidden units.

In our model, inspired by our previous work, we define a modified response rate considering both zero-based response and sample-based response with unsupervised information. Specifically, given the aforementioned training data and learned intra-channel SSDA model, we measure the proposed response rate of each channel c by calculating the weighted arithmetic mean:

$$R_c = w_1||h_z - \rho||^2 + \frac{w_2}{m}\sum_{i=1}^{m}||h_s(x^{(i)}) - \hat{\rho_s}||^2, \tag{8}$$

where h_z denotes the response stimulated by the all-zero vector, $h_s(x^{(i)})$ represents the response stimulated by the ith sample vector $x^{(i)}$, $\hat{\rho_s}$ is the average activation vector of the last learned SSDA hidden layer. Here $\{w_i, i = 1, 2\}$ where $w_i \in [0, 1]$ and $\sum w_i = 1$ denotes the weight constraint. Intuitively, both terms of Equation 8 represent the strength of response given the input data. The high value of R_c displays the salience of hidden units' activation in channel c. After the calculation, we rank the value of all channels and select the features from top u channels as the critical channel features. Here in the implementation, we fix u to be equal to half the number of EEG channels. In this way, the whole intra-channel layers are further established on the channel selection structure, which results in a marked mitigation of the noise effect and a great reduction of data dimensionality.

3.5 Learning and Detection

After extracting meaningful features, we concatenate the above-learned feature vectors together in a feature fusion fashion. Formally, given training sample $x^{(i)}$, the new fusion features of this sample is defined as:

$$x^{(i)}_{Fusion} = [x^{(i)}_1, x^{(i)}_2, ..., x^{(i)}_k] \in \mathbb{R}^{\sum_{j=1}^{k} n_j}, \tag{9}$$

where k denotes the feature index, and n_j is the dimensionality of each feature. In our model, the concatenated features are the combination of the intra-channel and cross-channel features mentioned above. Once the features are merged, we feed them into the fully-connected (FC) layers and adopt a softmax layer for classification.

Softmax regression is a supervised learning algorithm which generalizes logistic regression, a binary classification model, to a multi-class classification model. Formally, given the labeled training dataset $\{(x^{(i)}, y^{(i)}), i = 1, 2, ..., m\}$ where $x^{(i)} \in \mathbb{R}^n$ and $y^{(i)} \in \{1, 2, ..., k\}$, the hypothesis of softmax takes the form:

$$h_\theta(x^{(i)}) = \begin{bmatrix} p(y^{(i)} = 1|x^{(i)}; \theta) \\ \vdots \\ p(y^{(i)} = k|x^{(i)}; \theta) \end{bmatrix} = \frac{1}{\sum_{j=1}^{k} e^{\theta_j^T x^{(i)}}} \begin{bmatrix} e^{\theta_1^T x^{(i)}} \\ \vdots \\ e^{\theta_k^T x^{(i)}} \end{bmatrix}, \tag{10}$$

where $\theta = \begin{bmatrix}\theta_1^T & \theta_2^T & \cdots & \theta_k^T\end{bmatrix}^T$ denotes the parameters of the model, and term $1/\sum_{j=1}^{k} e^{\theta_j^T x^{(i)}}$ is for normalization. Thus, the cost function of softmax is described as:

$$J(\theta) = -\frac{1}{m}\left[\sum_{i=1}^{m}\sum_{j=1}^{k} 1\{y^{(i)} = j\} \log \frac{e^{\theta_l^T x^{(i)}}}{\sum_{l=1}^{k} e^{\theta_l^T x^{(i)}}}\right] + \frac{\lambda}{2}\sum_{i=1}^{k}\sum_{j=0}^{n} \theta_{ij}^2, \tag{11}$$

where $1\{\cdot\}$ is the indicator function and the second term is the regularization term which penalizes large values of the parameters. Notice that in the first term $e^{\theta_l^T x^{(i)}}/\sum_{l=1}^{k} e^{\theta_l^T x^{(i)}} = p(y^{(i)} = 1|x^{(i)}; \theta)$, which means the cost function of softmax is similar to logistic except the sum over the k. According to the deep learning mechanism, during the pre-training, the unlabeled data is used to train each layer individually. After that, the fine-tuning, which treats all layers as a single model, is adopted for supervised learning using labeled data. During the whole training step, the minibatch stochastic gradient descent is used to minimize the cost function. Note that we also use weight decay and momentum to accelerate gradient descent.

4 EXPERIMENTAL RESULTS

4.1 Dataset

The EEG data we use is an open access scalp EEG dataset collected at the Children's Hospital Boston [13, 40]. In this dataset, the multi-channel EEG signals are recorded from pediatric subjects with intractable seizures. The data is obtained from 23 patients, including 18 females and 5 males from age 2 to age 22, to characterize their seizures and assess the necessity of surgery for them. The beginning and end of each seizure are both annotated in the ground truth. Specifically, the EEG signals of each patient contains 23 channels (24 or 26 in a few cases), and the data of each channel is recorded at 256 Hz with 16-bit resolution.

Following the onset of a seizure, a set of EEG channels start to show rhythmic changes, which contains different time-frequency patterns. The rhythmic patterns can assist the seizure detector in distinguishing the ictal and non-ictal states. For example, Fig. 4 shows seizure samples of multi-channel scalp EEG signals from two different patients. The red bar marks the onset of a seizure, and both patients A and B start seizure at the 6th second. Fig. 4(a) illustrates the onset of a seizure of patient A. It can be seen that the onset of this seizure comes with the significant changes of EEG signals. In Fig. 4(b), the changes can still be observed between ictal and non-ictal states from patient B. However, the rhythmic patterns on EEG signals differ from patient A. Thus, the characteristics of seizures on EEG signals might vary significantly in different EEG channels across patients, and this variability makes the seizure detection problem even more difficult.

4.2 Baselines

Since it is a classification task, we adopt several widely used classification algorithms as the baseline methods, including standard SVM [9], neural network (NN) [30], and traditional deep learning method SSDA [49] as the first baseline group. For the sake of fairness and to avoid the curse of high dimensionality, it is necessary to reduce the dimensionality of the data before we send it to SVM, NN

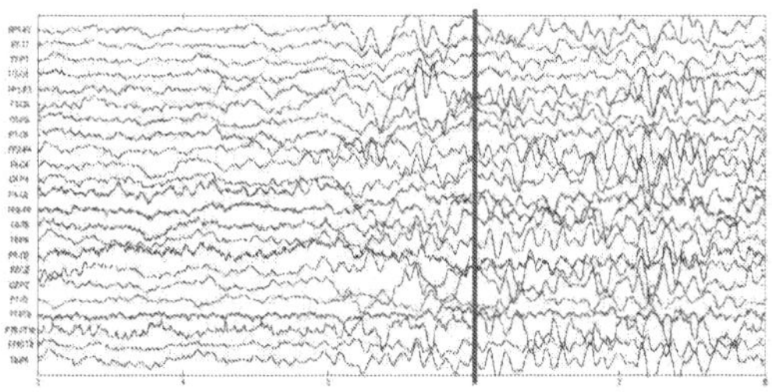

(a) The scalp EEG signals of patient A

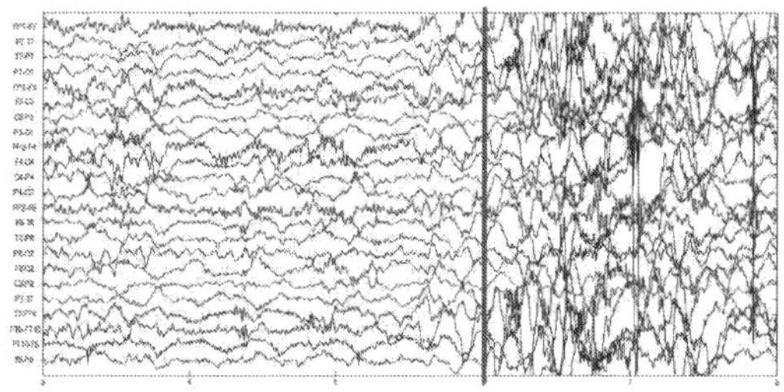

(b) The scalp EEG signals of patient B

Figure 4: Two samples of multi-channel scalp EEG signals.

and SSDA. Thus we employ principal component analysis (PCA) [21] as the data preprocessing mechanism, and we denote SVM with PCA as PSVM, NN with PCA as PNN, and SSDA with PCA as PSSDA. Moreover, since our proposed method is based on STFT, we denote the second baseline group as STFT-PSVM, STFT-NN, and STFT-SSDA to compare detection result. Notice that only SVM has no ability to reduce dimensions, thus PCA is still combined with SVM after the STFT step.

4.3 Evaluation Criteria

The evaluation criteria are calculated based on the confusion matrix of classification results. We present the definition of confusion matrix in Table 1. In order to demonstrate the effectiveness of our proposed method for epileptic seizure detection, we use *F1-score* and *Accuracy* to evaluate our model. *F1-score* is used to evaluate the results by taking into account both the precision and the recall, which is defined as:

$$F1\text{-}score = \frac{2 \times Prec \times Rec}{Prec + Rec}, \tag{12}$$

where $Prec = TP/(TP + FN)$ is denoted as the precision, and $Rec = TP/(TP + FP)$ is denoted as the recall. Based on the confusion matrix, *Accuracy* is defined as:

$$Accuracy = \frac{TP + TN}{TP + TN + FP + FN}. \tag{13}$$

Moreover, receiver operator characteristic (ROC) curves are plotted to generally capture how the number of correctly classified abnormal cases varies with the number of incorrectly classifying normal cases as abnormal cases. Since in most medical problems we usually care about the fraction of examples classified as abnormal cases that are truly abnormal, precision-recall (PR) curves are also plotted. In the experiments, we use area-under-the-curve (AUC), which measures the area under the ROC and PR curve respectively, to numerically evaluate the quality of each method. Notice that AUC scores are in the range of [0,1]. The higher AUC score, the better the performance.

4.4 Experiment Setup

To evaluate our method as a general seizure detecting algorithm, we combine 4302 EEG fragments from nine different patients as our experiment dataset, and randomly retain 3500 fragments as the training data and use the rest as the test data. As this is a binary classification problem, we denote the class label as interictal and ictal states for each EEG fragment according to the ground truth. During the process of signal acquisition, it is commonly found that an ictal state is usually 30-100 seconds long and surrounded by one hour long interictal signals, which means seizures are rare events and we have to deal with unbalanced data. Considering the rarity of seizure events, we trim our test data to balance the number of interictal fragments and ictal fragments. Notice that the training data is still imbalanced. Moreover, as the original sampling rate is 256 Hz and each file contains 23 channels of EEG signals, a 3-second long EEG fragment consists of 17664 raw data points.

To fit the input of our seizure detection problem, we use 23 2-hidden-layer SSDAs for intra-channel layers and a 3-hidden-layer SSDA for cross-channel layers. In each intra-channel SSDA, the first hidden layer consists of 100 hidden units and the second hidden layer consists of 50 hidden units. In cross-channel layers, we set 1000, 500 and 200 hidden units for the first, second and third layer, respectively. The fully-connected layers is a 2-hidden layer SSDA where the first and second hidden layers consist of 50 and 40 hidden units, respectively. We also scale each raw feature to a [0,1] range as data preprocessing.

4.5 Seizure Detection Performance

We compare the seizure detection performance of our proposed multi-view deep learning model (STFT-mSSDA) with the aforementioned baseline methods. We also implement the method that is purely based on intra-channel features which is denoted as STFT-cSSDA. The experimental results on the benchmark dataset are listed in Table 2. We can easily observe that both our STFT-cSSDA

Table 1: Confusion Matrix Definition

		Actual Class	
		Positive	Negative
Predicted Class	Positive	TP	FP
	Negative	FN	TN

and STFT-mSSDA methods outperform the baseline methods on all four different evaluation criteria. Our proposed STFT-mSSDA method has not only got significantly better accuracy and F1-score, but also obtained higher AUC-ROC and AUC-PR than the others.

Feature extraction is crucial for EEG classification. Given the results of both baseline groups, we can see that the performance of NN-based methods is worse than SVM-based methods both in time and time-frequency domain. The reason why NN-based method doesn't perform well is because the raw feature space is not suitable for NN-based method using gradient decent optimization algorithm, which is easy to reach a local minimum. The results of the second baseline group demonstrates that all the classifiers benefit from the EEG spectrogram representation. This is because by investigating the handcrafted features, noise interference is effectively reduced and classifiers can obtain more useful information in EEG time-frequency domain. Moreover, the standard SSDA-based method generates worse result than the others. This results from the low-quality features learned by simply applying traditional deep learning model on raw data. In contrast, given the results of STFT-mSSDA which utilizes SSDA method appropriately, we can conclude that the proposed method can successfully extract meaningful features from EEG signals.

Table 2: Detection Performance Comparisons

	AUC-ROC	AUC-PR	F1-score	Accuracy
PSVM	0.7283	0.6012	0.8826	0.8136
PNN	0.7754	0.5487	0.7515	0.6630
PSSDA	0.7166	0.3679	0.7627	0.6750
STFT-PSVM	0.7535	0.6356	0.9342	0.8850
STFT-NN	0.7314	0.5251	0.8212	0.7338
STFT-SSDA	0.6080	0.4985	0.8947	0.8195
STFT-cSSDA	0.9612	0.8507	0.9506	0.9242
STFT-mSSDA	**0.9833**	**0.9549**	**0.9605**	**0.9382**

Overall, as for the proposed STFT-cSSDA method, the relative improvements verify that the intra-channel features are playing an important role to identify seizure in EEG spectrograms. Moreover, based on the comparison between STFT-cSSDA and STFT-mSSDA, we arrive at a conclusion that cross-channel features provide complementary information towards intra-channel features and thus obtain more representative features from different perspectives than STFT-cSSDA, which is crucial for successful seizure detection.

Fig. 5 shows the ROC and PR curves of each method, respectively. We can observe that our STFT-mSSDA and STFT-cSSDA models perform better than the conventional classification techniques in terms of the ability of cross-patient seizure detection. In the ROC curve figure, the proposed STFT-mSSDA method achieves the best AUC of 0.9833 on the experiment data. And we can observe that, the true positive rate of the STFT-mSSDA model increases at a very fast speed in the beginning when the false positive rate is still close to zero, which means STFT-mSSDA is able to capture the important features to represent and separate interictal and ictal data points effectively. Furthermore, neither the precision nor recall take into account the number of true negatives, thus the PR curve is more persuasive than the ROC curve under the imbalanced data. In the PR curve figure, our method achieves the best AUC of 0.9549 compared with the methods such as STFT-SSDA, STFT-NN, STFT-PSVM and PSVM with AUC of 0.4985, 0.5251, 0.6356 and 0.6012, respectively.

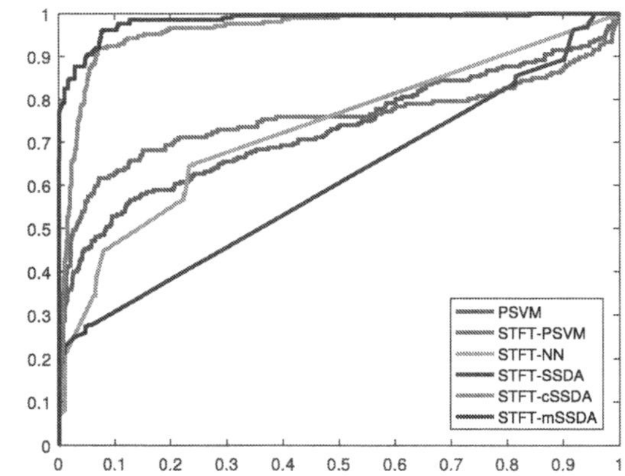

(a) ROC curves

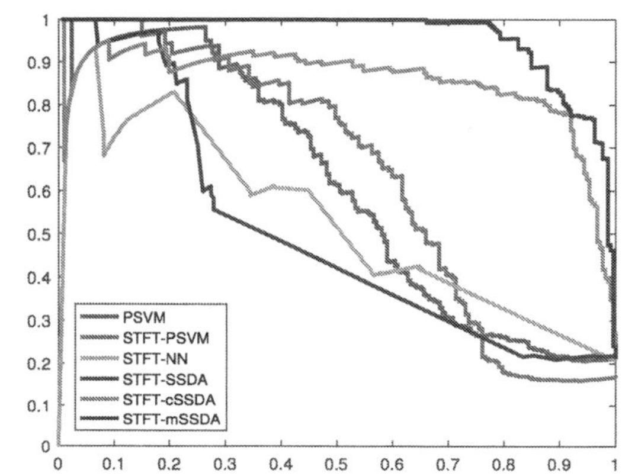

(b) PR curves

Figure 5: The ROC and PR curves of the proposed method and the baselines.

4.6 Analysis on Channel Selection

In this section, we conduct the experiment on both our proposed STFT-cSSDA and STFT-mSSDA models to discuss the effectiveness of our proposed channel selection method. We consider the strategy that selects all EEG channels for seizure detection, denoted as cSSDA(Full) and mSSDA(Full), respectively. Fig. 6 shows the performance comparisons on proposed models with different selected channels. The results reveal that by using the most significant features, the performance increase in terms of F1-score and accuracy. Specifically, the accuracy of our models using channel selection method averagely increases 2 percent compared with the full-channel selected models. Besides, as shown in Table 2 the good performance of these selected channels supports the effectiveness

Table 3: Comparative performance of proposed STFT-mSSDA with different window functions.

Window	AUC-ROC	AUC-PR	F1-score	Accuracy
Hann	0.9553	0.8761	0.9463	0.9163
Rectangular	0.9630	0.8880	0.9521	0.9252
Bartlett	0.9651	0.9049	0.9421	0.9123
Kaiser	0.9636	0.9041	0.9366	0.9013
Bartlett-Hann	0.9637	0.8998	0.9552	0.9312
Blackman-Harris	0.9704	0.9221	0.9452	0.9163
Bohman	0.9683	0.9271	0.9562	0.9322
Chebyshev	0.9676	0.9202	0.9373	0.9053
Flat Top	0.9516	0.8205	0.9368	0.9023
Gaussian	0.9567	0.8757	0.9391	0.9063
Tapered cosine	0.9526	0.8732	0.9485	0.9212
Blackman	**0.9833**	**0.9549**	**0.9605**	**0.9382**

of the proposed channel selection method. To sum up, the proposed method can select meaningful channels for the ultimate task of epileptic seizure detection.

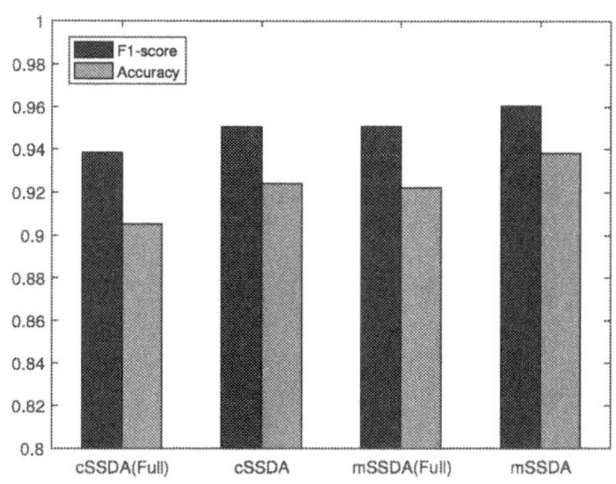

Figure 6: Performance comparisons on proposed models with different selected channels.

4.7 STFT Comparative Performance

We show the performance of the proposed method on our experiment dataset in various transform scenarios by using different STFT window functions in Table 3. From the given results, it is obvious that our proposed STFT-mSSDA model can still extract meaningful features from different STFT spaces and outperform the baseline methods, despite the influence of different window functions. And we can also see that Blackman window yield better performance than other window functions, which indicates that Blackman window can obtain more information from epileptic EEG signals.

5 CONCLUSIONS

In this paper, we design and evaluate our proposed multi-view deep learning model (STFT-mSSDA) for automated seizure detection using multi-channel scalp EEG signals. The proposed approach is a general, cross-patient model which is capable of extracting hidden inherent features considering both intra and inter correlation of EEG channels, denoted as intra-channel and cross-channel features, respectively. To integrate signal processing knowledge, we express the time-frequency information of EEG fragments via STFT, denoted as EEG spectrogram representation. The multiple latent features are learned from different perspectives through the SSDA model. The critical channels are selected according to our proposed SSDA-based response rate to reduce the dimension of intra-channel features. To train the seizure detector, the multi-view features are merged in a feature fusion fashion and are further fed into the fully-connected SSDA model with a softmax classifier. The proposed method has been tested on the CHB-MIT scalp EEG dataset and compared with several baseline methods. In general, the experimental results demonstrate the effectiveness and superiority of the proposed model in detecting epileptic seizures.

ACKNOWLEDGMENTS

This paper is supported by the Project for the National Natural Science Foundation of China under Grant No. 61672064, the China Scholarship Council Fund under Grant No. 201606540008.

REFERENCES

[1] Turkey N Alotaiby, Saleh A Alshebeili, Tariq Alshawi, Ishtiaq Ahmad, and Fathi E Abd El-Samie. 2014. EEG seizure detection and prediction algorithms: a survey. *EURASIP Journal on Advances in Signal Processing* 2014, 1 (2014), 183.

[2] Andreas Antoniades, Loukianos Spyrou, Clive Cheong Took, and Saeid Sanei. 2016. Deep learning for epileptic intracranial EEG data. In *Machine Learning for Signal Processing (MLSP), 2016 IEEE 26th International Workshop on*. IEEE, 1–6.

[3] Yoshua Bengio, Aaron Courville, and Pascal Vincent. 2013. Representation learning: A review and new perspectives. *IEEE transactions on pattern analysis and machine intelligence* 35, 8 (2013), 1798–1828.

[4] Yoshua Bengio, Pascal Lamblin, Dan Popovici, Hugo Larochelle, and others. 2007. Greedy layer-wise training of deep networks. *Advances in neural information processing systems* 19 (2007), 153.

[5] Boualem Boashash, Larbi Boubchir, and Ghasem Azemi. 2012. Improving the classification of newborn EEG time-frequency representations using a combined time-frequency signal and image approach. In *Information Science, Signal Processing and their Applications (ISSPA), 2012 11th International Conference on*. IEEE, 280–285.

[6] Larbi Boubchir, Somaya Al-Maadeed, and Ahmed Bouridane. 2014. Haralick feature extraction from time-frequency images for epileptic seizure detection and classification of EEG data. In *Microelectronics (ICM), 2014 26th International Conference on*. IEEE, 32–35.

[7] Larbi Boubchir, Somaya Al-Maadeed, and Ahmed Bouridane. 2014. On the use of time-frequency features for detecting and classifying epileptic seizure activities in non-stationary EEG signals. In *Acoustics, Speech and Signal Processing (ICASSP), 2014 IEEE International Conference on*. IEEE, 5889–5893.

[8] Leon Cohen. 1989. Time-frequency distributions-a review. *Proc. IEEE* 77, 7 (1989), 941–981.

[9] Corinna Cortes and Vladimir Vapnik. 1995. Support-vector networks. *Machine learning* 20, 3 (1995), 273–297.

[10] Robert S Fisher, Walter van Emde Boas, Warren Blume, Christian Elger, Pierre Genton, Phillip Lee, and Jerome Engel. 2005. Epileptic seizures and epilepsy: definitions proposed by the International League Against Epilepsy (ILAE) and the International Bureau for Epilepsy (IBE). *Epilepsia* 46, 4 (2005), 470–472.

[11] Kai Fu, Jianfeng Qu, Yi Chai, and Yong Dong. 2014. Classification of seizure based on the time-frequency image of EEG signals using HHT and SVM. *Biomedical Signal Processing and Control* 13 (2014), 15–22.

[12] Giorgos Giannakakis, Vangelis Sakkalis, Matthew Pediaditis, and Manolis Tsiknakis. 2015. Methods for seizure detection and prediction: an overview. *Modern Electroencephalographic Assessment Techniques: Theory and Applications* (2015), 131–157.

[13] Ary L Goldberger, Luis AN Amaral, Leon Glass, Jeffrey M Hausdorff, Plamen Ch Ivanov, Roger G Mark, Joseph E Mietus, George B Moody, Chung-Kang Peng, and H Eugene Stanley. 2000. Physiobank, physiotoolkit, and physionet. *Circulation* 101, 23 (2000), e215–e220.

[14] J Gotman, D Flanagan, J Zhang, and B Rosenblatt. 1997. Automatic seizure detection in the newborn: methods and initial evaluation. *Electroencephalography and clinical neurophysiology* 103, 3 (1997), 356–362.

[15] L John Greenfield, James D Geyer, and Paul R Carney. 2012. *Reading EEGs: a practical approach.* Lippincott Williams & Wilkins.

[16] Geoffrey E Hinton and Ruslan R Salakhutdinov. 2006. Reducing the dimensionality of data with neural networks. *science* 313, 5786 (2006), 504–507.

[17] Geoffrey E Hinton and Ruslan R Salakhutdinov. 2006. Reducing the dimensionality of data with neural networks. *science* 313, 5786 (2006), 504–507.

[18] Xiaowei Jia, Kang Li, Xiaoyi Li, and Aidong Zhang. 2014. A novel semi-supervised deep learning framework for affective state recognition on eeg signals. In *Bioinformatics and Bioengineering (BIBE), 2014 IEEE International Conference on.* IEEE, 30–37.

[19] Alexander Rosenberg Johansen, Jing Jin, Tomasz Maszczyk, Justin Dauwels, Sydney S Cash, and M Brandon Westover. 2016. Epileptiform spike detection via convolutional neural networks. In *Acoustics, Speech and Signal Processing (ICASSP), 2016 IEEE International Conference on.* IEEE, 754–758.

[20] Alistair EW Johnson, Mohammad M Ghassemi, Shamim Nemati, Katherine E Niehaus, David A Clifton, and Gari D Clifford. 2016. Machine learning and decision support in critical care. *Proc. IEEE* 104, 2 (2016), 444–466.

[21] Ian Jolliffe. 2002. *Principal component analysis.* Wiley Online Library.

[22] Peter Kovacs, Kaveh Samiee, and Moncef Gabbouj. 2014. On application of rational discrete short time fourier transform in epileptic seizure classification. In *Acoustics, Speech and Signal Processing (ICASSP), 2014 IEEE International Conference on.* IEEE, 5839–5843.

[23] Martin Längkvist, Lars Karlsson, and Amy Loutfi. 2014. A review of unsupervised feature learning and deep learning for time-series modeling. *Pattern Recognition Letters* 42 (2014), 11–24.

[24] Dazi Li, Guifang Wang, Tianheng Song, and Qibing Jin. 2016. Improving convolutional neural network using accelerated proximal gradient method for epilepsy diagnosis. In *Control (CONTROL), 2016 UKACC 11th International Conference on.* IEEE, 1–6.

[25] Kang Li, Xiaoyi Li, Yuan Zhang, and Aidong Zhang. 2013. Affective state recognition from EEG with deep belief networks. In *Bioinformatics and Biomedicine (BIBM), 2013 IEEE International Conference on.* IEEE, 305–310.

[26] Qin Lin, Shu-qun Ye, Xiu-mei Huang, Si-you Li, Mei-zhen Zhang, Yun Xue, and Wen-Sheng Chen. 2016. Classification of Epileptic EEG Signals with Stacked Sparse Autoencoder Based on Deep Learning. In *International Conference on Intelligent Computing.* Springer, 802–810.

[27] Fenglong Ma, Radha Chitta, Jing Zhou, Quanzeng You, Tong Sun, and Jing Gao. 2017. Dipole: Diagnosis Prediction in Healthcare via Attention-based Bidirectional Recurrent Neural Networks. In *Proceedings of the 23rd ACM SIGKDD International Conference on Knowledge Discovery and Data Mining.* ACM.

[28] Fenglong Ma, Chuishi Meng, Houping Xiao, Qi Li, Jing Gao, Lu Su, and Aidong Zhang. 2017. Unsupervised Discovery of Drug Side-Effects From Heterogeneous Data Sources. In *Proceedings of the 23rd ACM SIGKDD International Conference on Knowledge Discovery and Data Mining.* ACM.

[29] Angshul Majumdar, Anupriya Gogna, and Rabab Ward. 2016. Semi-supervised Stacked Label Consistent Autoencoder for Reconstruction and Analysis of Biomedical Signals. *IEEE Transactions on Biomedical Engineering* (2016).

[30] Warren S McCulloch and Walter Pitts. 1943. A logical calculus of the ideas immanent in nervous activity. *The bulletin of mathematical biophysics* 5, 4 (1943), 115–133.

[31] Piotr Mirowski, Deepak Madhavan, Yann LeCun, and Ruben Kuzniecky. 2009. Classification of patterns of EEG synchronization for seizure prediction. *Clinical neurophysiology* 120, 11 (2009), 1927–1940.

[32] Florian Mormann, Ralph G Andrzejak, Christian E Elger, and Klaus Lehnertz. 2007. Seizure prediction: the long and winding road. *Brain* 130, 2 (2007), 314–333.

[33] Florian Mormann, Ralph G Andrzejak, Christian E Elger, and Klaus Lehnertz. 2007. Seizure prediction: the long and winding road. *Brain* 130, 2 (2007), 314–333.

[34] World Health Organization. 2017. Epilepsy Fact Sheet. http://www.who.int/mediacentre/factsheets/fs999/en/. (2017).

[35] Siddharth Pramod, Adam Page, Tinoosh Mohsenin, and Tim Oates. 2014. Detecting Epileptic Seizures from EEG Data using Neural Networks. *arXiv preprint arXiv:1412.6502* (2014).

[36] Yu Qi, Yueming Wang, Jianmin Zhang, Junming Zhu, and Xiaoxiang Zheng. 2014. Robust deep network with maximum correntropy criterion for seizure detection. *BioMed research international* 2014 (2014).

[37] Kaveh Samiee, Peter Kovacs, and Moncef Gabbouj. 2015. Epileptic seizure classification of EEG time-series using rational discrete short-time Fourier transform. *IEEE transactions on Biomedical Engineering* 62, 2 (2015), 541–552.

[38] Abdulkadir Şengür, Yanhui Guo, and Yaman Akbulut. 2016. Time–frequency texture descriptors of EEG signals for efficient detection of epileptic seizure. *Brain Informatics* 3, 2 (2016), 101–108.

[39] Younghak Shin, Seungchan Lee, Minkyu Ahn, Hohyun Cho, Sung Chan Jun, and Heung-No Lee. 2015. Noise robustness analysis of sparse representation based classification method for non-stationary EEG signal classification. *Biomedical Signal Processing and Control* 21 (2015), 8–18.

[40] Ali Hossam Shoeb. 2009. *Application of machine learning to epileptic seizure onset detection and treatment.* Ph.D. Dissertation. Massachusetts Institute of Technology.

[41] K Sivasankari and K Thanushkodi. 2014. An improved EEG signal classification using neural network with the consequence of ICA and STFT. *Journal of Electrical Engineering and Technology* 9, 3 (2014), 1060–1071.

[42] Qiuling Suo, Hongfei Xue, Jing Gao, and Aidong Zhang. 2016. Risk Factor Analysis Based on Deep Learning Models. In *Proceedings of the 7th ACM International Conference on Bioinformatics, Computational Biology, and Health Informatics.* ACM, 394–403.

[43] Akara Supratak, Ling Li, and Yike Guo. 2014. Feature extraction with stacked autoencoders for epileptic seizure detection. In *Engineering in Medicine and Biology Society (EMBC), 2014 36th Annual International Conference of the IEEE.* IEEE, 4184–4187.

[44] Akara Supratak, Chao Wu, Hao Dong, Kai Sun, and Yike Guo. 2016. Survey on Feature Extraction and Applications of Biosignals. In *Machine Learning for Health Informatics.* Springer, 161–182.

[45] Shanbao Tong and Nitish Vyomesh Thakor. 2009. *Quantitative EEG analysis methods and clinical applications.* Artech House.

[46] JT Turner, Adam Page, Tinoosh Mohsenin, and Tim Oates. 2014. Deep belief networks used on high resolution multichannel electroencephalography data for seizure detection. In *2014 AAAI Spring Symposium Series.*

[47] Alexandros T Tzallas, Markos G Tsipouras, and Dimitrios I Fotiadis. 2009. Epileptic seizure detection in EEGs using time–frequency analysis. *IEEE transactions on information technology in biomedicine* 13, 5 (2009), 703–710.

[48] DF Wulsin, JR Gupta, R Mani, JA Blanco, and B Litt. 2011. Modeling electroencephalography waveforms with semi-supervised deep belief nets: fast classification and anomaly measurement. *Journal of neural engineering* 8, 3 (2011), 036015.

[49] Junyuan Xie, Linli Xu, and Enhong Chen. 2012. Image denoising and inpainting with deep neural networks. In *Advances in Neural Information Processing Systems.* 341–349.

[50] Bo Yan, Yong Wang, Yuheng Li, Yejiang Gong, Lu Guan, and Sheng Yu. 2016. An EEG signal classification method based on sparse auto-encoders and support vector machine. In *Communications in China (ICCC), 2016 IEEE/CIC International Conference on.* IEEE, 1–6.

[51] Guang-Zhong Yang and Magdi Yacoub. 2006. *Body sensor networks.* Vol. 1. Springer.

TUCUXI – An Intelligent System for Personalized Medicine: from Individualization of Treatments to Research Databases and Back

Alevtina Dubovitskaya
University of Applied Sciences Western Switzerland,
Swiss Federal Institute of Technology,
alevtina.dubovitskaya@epfl.ch

Thierry Buclin
University Hospital,
Lausanne, Switzerland
thierry.buclin@chuv.ch

Michael Schumacher
University of Applied Sciences Western Switzerland,
Sierre, Switzerland
michael.schumacher@hevs.ch

Karl Aberer
Swiss Federal Institute of Technology,
Lausanne, Switzerland
karl.aberer@epfl.ch

Yann Thoma
School of Eng. and Management,
Yverdon-les-Bains, Switzerland
yann.thoma@heig-vd.ch

ABSTRACT

Therapeutic Drug Monitoring (TDM) is a key concept in precision medicine. The goal of TDM is to avoid therapeutic failure or toxic effects of a drug due to insufficient or excessive circulating concentration exposure related to between-patient variability in the drug's disposition. We present *TUCUXI* – an intelligent system for TDM. By making use of embedded mathematical models, the software allows to compute maximum likelihood individual predictions of drug concentrations from population pharmacokinetic data, based on patient's parameters and previously observed concentrations. *TUCUXI* was developed to be used in medical practice, to assist clinicians in taking dosage adjustment decisions for optimizing drug concentration levels. This software is currently being tested in a University Hospital. In this paper we focus on the process of software integration in clinical workflow. The modular architecture of the software allows us to plug in a module enabling data aggregation for research purposes. This is an important feature in order to develop new mathematical models for drugs, and thus to improve TDM. Finally we discuss ethical issues related to the use of an automated decision support system in clinical practice, in particular if it allows data aggregation for research purposes.

CCS CONCEPTS

• **Information systems → Expert systems**; • **Applied computing → Health care information systems**;

KEYWORDS

Automated TDM, personalized medicine, clinical information system, data integration

Permission to make digital or hard copies of part or all of this work for personal or classroom use is granted without fee provided that copies are not made or distributed for profit or commercial advantage and that copies bear this notice and the full citation on the first page. Copyrights for third-party components of this work must be honored. For all other uses, contact the owner/author(s).
ACM-BCB'17, August 20-23, 2017, Boston, MA, USA
© 2017 Copyright held by the owner/author(s). 978-1-4503-4722-8/17/08...$15.00
DOI: http://dx.doi.org/10.1145/3107411.3107439

1 INTRODUCTION

Millions of people have to take a variety of medications every day. Unfortunately, treatments are not always effective in all patients. One reason for this is that different patients absorb, metabolize and eliminate drugs differently. Patients' response to a drug may depend on genetic makeup, age, body size, presence of kidney or liver diseases, drug-drug interactions, time of the day, etc. Therefore, the drug dose may be either insufficient and the patient will not benefit from the treatment, or excessive, which may cause serious toxicity. This is especially relevant to critical medications such as anti-cancer or anti-HIV drugs, which have both a narrow therapeutic range and a poorly predictable relationship between the dosage prescribed and the drug concentration exposure obtained in patients' blood.

For example, for the antiretroviral drug Rilpivirine used in the treatment of HIV patients, the target minimum concentration is 44ng/ml. However, it has been shown that on average four patients out of ten have Rilpivirine concentrations below the target. Therefore, a risk of insufficient efficacy exists in 40% of the patients treated with the standard dosage [2].

The problem of inappropriate dosing has been reported in medical literature [2, 4] and the TDM approach has been proposed as a corrective measure. TDM involves the measurement of drug concentrations in biological samples and the improvement of drug dosage to improve drug efficacy and reduce related toxicities [11, 16, 18]. TDM has evolved to become an important tool used for administration of antiarrhythmic and psychiatric drugs, anticonvulsants, anticancer agents, immunosuppressants, and antifungals [15].

Pharmacokinetic and pharmacodynamic (PKPD) models for numerous drugs are being developed by clinical pharmacologists to describe how the body handles a drug in terms of absorption, distribution, metabolism, and elimination (PK models). PD models then describe how a drug affects the body by linking the drug concentration profile to one or several efficacy metrics. PKPD models are ideally suited to summarize the background knowledge necessary to adjust the drug dosage in a given patient [15].

However, in everyday clinical practice, it is fairly difficult for a clinician to make use of these PKPD models available only in scientific literature, and to apply them in every specific patient's case. A consultation with a pharmacologist may not be arranged shortly and will require the pharmacologist to collect a sufficient amount of information on the patient's clinical history before issuing a valid recommendation for dosage adjustment. Still an appropriate correction of drug dosage may be of critical importance if concentration exposure is significantly away from the targets ensuring optimal treatment efficacy and tolerability.

In order to address these issues, an automation of TDM is proposed. Existing software for TDM computer assistance has been surveyed by Fuchs et al. [10]. However, an intelligent system integrated in everyday clinical practice, allowing precise and rapid evaluation and adjustment of drug dosages, and simultaneously making the data available for the development of new PKPD models, is still missing.

Our development had to address the following challenges:

- *Interdisciplinary collaboration.* Mathematical models developed by researchers in clinical pharmacology need to be embedded in a user-friendly software suitable to be used by medical doctors/pharmacologists.
- *Ergonomy.* The software has to efficiently help medical doctors and pharmacologists by being well suited to the actual processing flow of TDM requests faced daily.
- *Medical device certification.* According to current regulation, such a system is a medical device and as such needs to be certified in order to ensure proper functionalities without risks of harming patients.
- *Interoperability.* The software requires seamless insertion into the existing network of electronic medical records, laboratory information system and other medical application, thus raising issues related to different interfaces, data formats, comprehensive clinical data flow etc.
- *Data aggregation for research.* The collection of population data from daily use of the software would be ideally suited to improve existing models and to develop new PKPD models for drugs candidate to TDM. However, patients' data are sensitive, studies may have very different scopes, and data aggregation is time consuming.
- *Ethical issues.* Automated processing of TDM raises a question of medical liability regarding highly sensitive aspects of patients' management such as dosage decisions.

In this paper we present *TUCUXI*– a software that was developed and integrated into the clinical data flow in order to provide automated dosage evaluation and adjustment decisions to assist pharmacologists or medical doctors. The modular architecture of the software allows to plug in dedicated modules for data aggregation for research purposes. These data are to be used by researchers to improve or develop PKPD models for TDM.

The advantages of our solution are the following ones. First, it provides *personalized dosage adjustment advice* based on reference population PKPD data, patient's individual characteristics and concentrations previously observed, if available. Second, it *optimizes TDM procedures* and thus enables to process large numbers of requests; therefore it contributes to extend the use of TDM and the number of patients that may benefit from TDM services. Third, it provides an interface with other clinical applications, and could be easily *integrated into primary care and also used for medical research.* Finally, our solution also allows to *decrease the risk* of human mistakes.

The rest of the paper is organized as follows. In Section 2 we present current non-automatized processes of routine TDM in hospital settings and its difficulties. We describe the developed software in details in Section 3 along with its integration into the clinical data flow in Section 4. In Section 5 we discuss how the software enables data aggregation for research purposes. In Section 6 we discuss ethical issues related to the use of an automated software in clinical practice, to its validation, and to the aggregation of sensitive patients' medical data to improve TDM and therapeutic outcomes. We compare our software with currently existing solutions in Section 7 and we eventually express our conclusions about the evolution of TDM in Section 8.

2 TDM IN CLINICAL PRACTICE

Non-automated therapeutic drug monitoring, as currently practiced in most places, is a comprehensive and rather slow process. We studied the related procedures in actual medical practice at a University Hospital, where clinical pharmacologists work on a daily basis to provide dosage adjustment advice to medical doctors working either in the same hospital or elsewhere in the country.

The sequence diagram shown on Figure 1 (a) describes non – automated TDM[1]. The process begins when a patient starts receiving treatment with a drug considered to require TDM. In this case, after a couple of intakes, a blood sample is drawn to monitor the plasma concentration of the drug. The medical doctor in charge of the patient prescribes the test and requests to send the patient's sample together with appropriate data to the laboratory, where concentration measurements are performed (steps 1 – 5 of the diagram on Figure 1a). Then, next step (6): the data are transfered into a laboratory information system, where they are stored and will be accessed by the pharmacologist in charge of clinical interpretation of the measurement result, after its validation.

When the pharmacologist receives a request to interpret a drug concentration value, as already mentioned above, he needs to collect a certain amount of medical information regarding the patient's case. To do so, he may need to access multiple databases that store information about the the patient's clinical history, medication records, laboratory results, etc. (steps 7 – 12). The pharmacologist will also need to refer to PKPD models for the drug existing in the scientific literature (as step 15 indicates it). If any information about the patient is missing, a phone contact with the medical doctor that initiated the TDM request is also needed (steps 13 – 14).

When all the information is collected, the pharmacologist elaborates an interpretation of the laboratory result (16). At present, this is essentially made on an empirical basis. Some rare pharmacologists rely on models built up with custom tools (such as Excel), which can accommodate patient's medical characteristics and just one or sometimes two concentration measurements. Only a small minority of centers regularly use one of the commercially available dedicated software tools, considered of insufficient ergonomy for

[1] In order to simplify graphical representation of the processes on both sequence diagrams on the Figure 1 we do not show existing interfaces and proxies that can be modeled as boundary object and control objects and placed between actors and entity objects on the UML diagram.

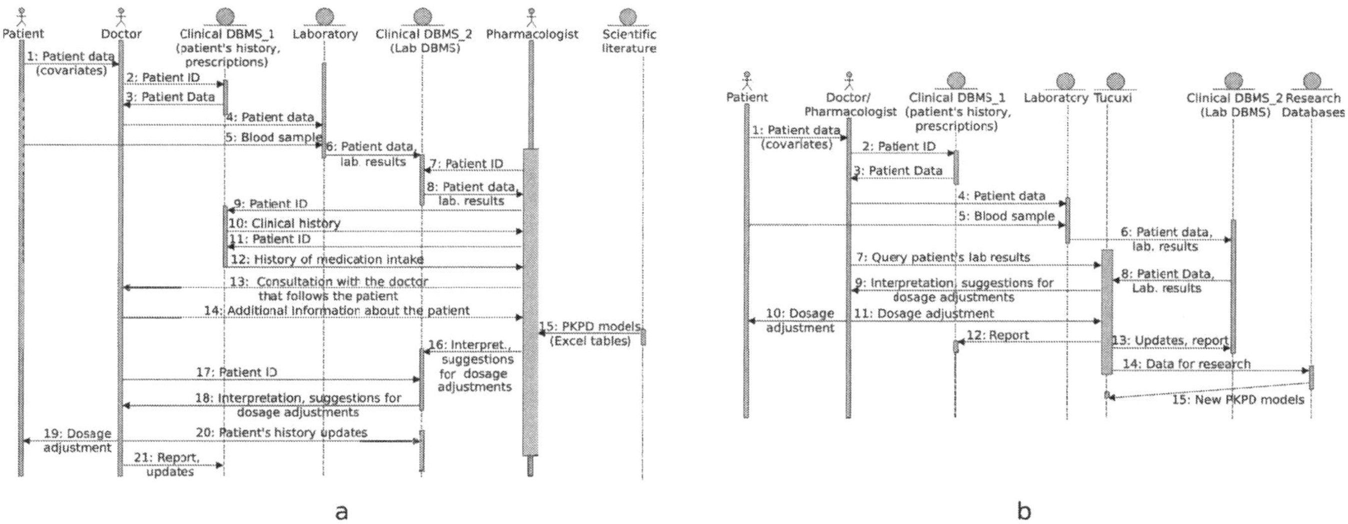

Figure 1: TDM in clinical practice: non-automatized process (a), *TUCUXI* (TDM software) integrated in clinical practice (b).

implementation in everyday routine [10]. The results and updates are sent to the hospital electronic medical record, which the physician that initiated the TDM request can now access (as presented by steps 16 – 21).

While working on each particular patient case, a pharmacologist has to access multiple sources of data, perform various estimations or calculations, switch contexts. Not only are current procedures slow and poorly efficient, but they also may increase the risk of human mistakes, which could significantly affect patient's condition.

When clinical pharmacologists are not available in the hospital, most laboratory results are sent without interpretation to the physicians that have requested TDM. Most physicians tend to translate TDM results into dosage adjustments according to an empirical trial-and-error strategy – which should not be entirely denigrated though, as it often fits clinical needs to a sufficient extent. In exceptional cases another institution will be contacted (such as the Hospital we are collaborating with). However, this may cause even longer delays due to the need to transfer the data, to clarify missing details about patient's history (due to the lack of interoperability between different hospitals, e.g., data stored in an hospital can only be accessed internally due to their sensitive nature), and to elaborate the pharmacological interpretation requested.

In order to optimize highlighted steps 7 – 20 of the diagram on Figure 1a, and to tackle the difficulties listed above, we propose to integrate a TDM software in the clinical data flow. The software provides an interface that guides the user through the TDM process, provides required information about the patient and employs PKPD models built up using population data and integrated into the software. This allows not only to interpret the current concentration value but also to predict future drug exposure, and to suggest a personalized dosage adjustment for the patient. Figure 1b presents the sequence diagram of the data flow using TDM software *TUCUXI* integrated in clinical practice. One can notice that the flow is simplified (steps 7 – 13), and also includes populating a research database for building up new PKPD models (steps 14 – 15).

3 TUCUXI AND EMBEDDED MATHEMATICAL MODELS

A software helping the clinicians in their daily practice can be conceived as a standalone software embedding a graphical user interface (GUI) or as a service hidden behind a client. We present here the GUI version, and we will discuss the service possibilities in Section 6.

3.1 Software Description

TUCUXI core capabilities can be segmented into three main parts:

(1) Computation of concentration percentiles and comparison with therapeutic targets, based on the patient's dosage regimen and clinical characteristics, as well as on reference PKPD data ;
(2) Computation of concentration predictions based on the same data confronted with the patient's observations ;
(3) Suggestion of dosage adjustments in order to drive the resulting concentration exposure into the therapeutic targets.

The general architecture is made of layers. The first layer is pure mathematics, implemented in a very optimized way. It ensures the three core capabilities listed above. The second layer (processing layer) is responsible for translating Domain Model Objects into mathematical objects and then calling the math functions. On top of this second layer the GUI exploits the processing layer and an interconnection module to create the final software.

The following subsection gives some insight corresponding to the three main mathematical software parts.

3.2 Mathematical Engine

3.2.1 Concentration calculation. Prediction of drug concentration can be done through model-free systems (e.g., Support Vector Machine [23]) based on population data, or through model-based systems. The model-free approach may be well suited for predicting concentration at a specific time (typically time of measure), but often suffers from limits of applicability (depending on the method, concentrations below zero could be calculated). The model-based approach is more suited for continuous curves, and is used by a majority of pharmacologists (also because it allows to *explain* the calculation in a physiological way).

The concept is to model the human body in terms of compartments exchanging substances. The drug concentration is typically measured in blood, so a central compartment corresponds to the entire blood veins and arteries. Models can have more than one compartment, and if such, the muscles are a typical second compartment. Taking a drug is seen as an input to a specific compartment, and the drug elimination corresponds to a flow leaving one of the compartments. Figure 2 represents a 2-compartment model for bolus injection.

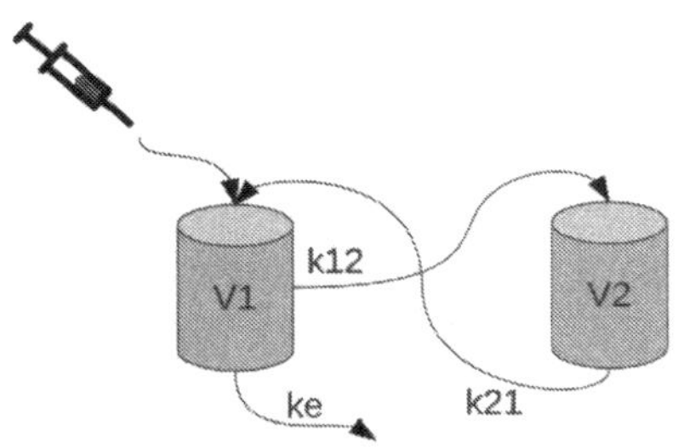

Figure 2: 2-compartment model

Constants ke, $k12$, $k21$ are used to describe the flow between the compartments. For example, here the differential equations are, for concentration $C1$ and $C2$, respectively in compartments $V1$ and $V2$:

$$\frac{dC_1}{dt} = k_{21}C_2 - k_{12}C_1 - k_eC_1,$$

$$\frac{dC_2}{dt} = k_{12}C_1 - k_{21}C_2.$$

It is to be noted that in this case, administrating a drug consists in adding a certain amount at the time of administration in compartment $V1$.

The constants are directly derived from population studies, typically published by pharmacologists for a specific set of patients. The equations presented above exploit so-called micro-constants that are calculated from macro-constants (clearance, volume, ...). Depending on the complexity of the differential equation, analytical solutions are available and more efficient in terms of computation time. For linear elimination models up to 3 compartments, such analytical solutions exist, but for other models (e.g. Michaelis-Menten [17]) only differential equations are available.

The macro-constants and the dosage history define exactly the prediction curve shape. The question is then about the way of evaluating these constants.

From a population pharmacokinetics study, the authors usually present parameters (macro-constants), their variability, consisting in inter-individual variability, an intra-individual variability, and the influence of patient covariates onto the parameters.

Based on this data, *TUCUXI* can first calculate predictions for the so-called *typical patient*. For each study, the average parameter values correspond to such a typical individual, and if no information is available about a patient, this calculation gives a first approximation of what could be the observed concentration based on the medical drug intakes.

If patient's covariates are known, the published models propose to adapt the average parameters thanks to update functions. This kind of adaptation is referred to as *a priori* calculations and results in a prediction reflecting more precisely the concentrations expected for a specific individual. Typical covariates are age, gender, or weight, but *TUCUXI* can handle any kind and number of covariates for a specific model.

Finally, the most accurate prediction is made when, in conjunction with covariates, the software "knows" the results of real concentration measurements done at specific times. The method currently implemented is based on a maximum likelihood function mixed with a Bayesian approach. It allows to take into account the population statistics as well as the measures, by exploiting the intra- and inter-individual variability. The resulting *a posteriori* prediction is the one used for the dosage adjustment.

3.2.2 Percentiles calculation. While prediction is at the core of *TUCUXI*, percentiles are essential in order to evaluate the normality of a patient response with respect to the population. Percentiles are calculated thanks to a Monte Carlo simulation exploiting the intra- and inter-individual variability. A particular attention was put on the implementation of this part of the software, as Monte Carlo simulations can be very slow. An in-depth optimization allows to calculate useful percentiles in around a second on a standard PC.

Typically these percentiles allow to evaluate the likelihood of a specific concentration measurement and will help the pharmacologists to better interpret the supplied result.

3.2.3 Dosage adjustment. Finally, *TUCUXI* not only calculates predictions and percentiles, but also can propose dosages adjustments. The software can issue recommendations on the amount of drug to be administrated, the interval between intakes, and on the infusion time in case of infusion intake. So, up to three values can be fitted to match the best treatment for a specific person. The goal is that concentration predictions actually match therapeutic targets. These targets can be of various types: (1) residual concentration (before the next intake), (2) peak concentration (typically 1 hour after the intake), (3) mean concentration, and (4) area under the curve (AUC). Fitness functions for each specific targets have been designed and are used to find the best combination of dose-interval-infusion. A score is therefore given to each combination and can be used to select the best candidates. It is to be noted that for each medical drug, a selection of discrete values is available so as to reduce the search space and more importantly to keep the treatment feasible. For instance, the authorized intervals are 8, 12, 24 and 36 hours and the doses correspond to the available drug formulations (e.g. pills, tablets, capsules), or possibly simple fractions of them (e.g. scored tablets).

3.3 Interface for Clinicians

TDM as performed every day in specialized institutions is based on custom tools and needs to be done rapidly in order not to cost too much time (and money for the institution). There is a real need for a software facilitating the clinicians' decisions. Therefore *TUCUXI* has been designed in close collaboration with pharmacologists. It reflects their thinking while performing TDM interpretation.

Figure 3 shows the GUI. The work flow is represented thanks to the buttons allowing to navigate through the various screens (or panels). Each button corresponds to a specific screen showing information related to a particular part of the process.

It is important to differentiate two use cases of the software:

(1) **Standalone.** A non-connected use where the user has to enter all the data by himself.
(2) **Connected.** A connection to an institutional database allows to retrieve a full set of data (cf. Section 4).

The two flows are run on the same GUI with the difference being that for the second use case the user mostly has to acknowledge the correctness of data instead of filling himself the forms. It is interesting to notice that the connected flow could be totally automated, except for the suggestions writing by the medical doctor. This automation corresponds to a server version without human interaction, as discussed later in Section 6.

The flow, corresponding to the current pharmacologists practice is decomposed into 9 panels, shown from left to right on the GUI (cf. Figure 3). They are described in the following lines, with some information about differences between the standalone and the connected flow.

(1) **Patient information.** This panel simply allows to check and complete if necessary administrative data about the patient. The most important part here is the birth date, as most of the models use this information as a covariate.
(2) **Medical drug selection.** For a standalone use, the user has to select the medical drug (the active substance), and the model to be used. This model can be dependent on the patient information (Caucasian or not, neonate, child or adult, for instance). For the connected use, the active substance is already defined, and only the model needs to be selected. This model selection could be automated in the future, based on patient data if available.
(3) **Dosages.** Past dosages are introduced within this panel. For a connected use, these fields can be fed from the electronic medical record.
(4) **Patient covariates.** Patient covariates are sensitive information. The models exploit them in order to more accurately predict the expected drug concentration. In standalone mode, the covariates used by the selected models are displayed and can be modified by the user, while in connected mode, most of these variables are automatically retrieved from the electronic medical record. The prediction curve displayed on this panel corresponds to the a priori prediction, with the corresponding percentiles.
(5) **Drug concentration measurements.** Observed concentrations are defined within this panel, or automatically fetched. From this panel up to the end of the flow, the prediction curve corresponds to the *a posteriori* prediction, taking into account the covariates and the past measurements.
(6) **Targets.** Before proposing an adjustment, the software allows to validate or modify the target concentrations. In most cases the default target values of the medical drug will be used, but if the physician has more patient's information that could affect the desired targets he can modify them.
(7) **Adjustment.** Based on all data filled up to this point, *TUCUXI* can propose an automatic drug dosage adjustment. Valid propositions are displayed in a list sorted by accuracy. The user can then select the most appropriate, which will be submitted as a recommendation and added to the list of dosages.
(8) **Validation.** After the selection of the best adjustment, the user can enter text that will be appended to the final report. Five different fields serve to guide the type of information required: expectedness, suitability, prediction, remonitoring and warning.
(9) **Report generation.** Finally, a report is automatically generated. It contains all data about the patient, a prediction curve, the kinetic parameters, and the text entered by the user. A PDF file can then be exported and potentially sent to the medical records database.

As *TUCUXI* is a medical device, ensuring that data are correct is highly important. In standalone mode, it is reasonable to make the assumption that the user is responsible of filling the data correctly. However, in connected mode, almost all data are automatically retrieved from a database. The user needs to acknowledge he went through all the panels in order to validate the interpretation. The validation status is shown on each flow button (see yellow circles in figure 3). These buttons can have three states: invalid, valid and validated. Data retrieved from the database is marked as valid, except if some fields cannot be correctly casted, and the user has to click on the circle to validate it. In figure 3 the validation and report panels can not be accessed because the user did not yet validate the first 7 panels. The development team took this decision based on the risk analysis of the software, in order to ensure the user is aware of the data used to predict concentrations and to propose adjustments.

4 TUCUXI INTEGRATION IN CLINICAL PRACTICE

Usually, the pharmacologist receives a list of pending requests for TDM interpretation. He selects a request from the list to analyze the concentration of the drug and evaluate the dosage adjustment called for. For each request he needs to query additional specific information about the corresponding patient. In this section we describe the process of integration of the TDM software presented in the previous section in clinical data flow. First, we show how the interoperability was achieved. Second, we present data structure and messages designed to exchange the data.

4.1 Interfaces for data exchange

In order to integrate the TDM software described in Section 3 into the clinical data flow presented above we had to define how to

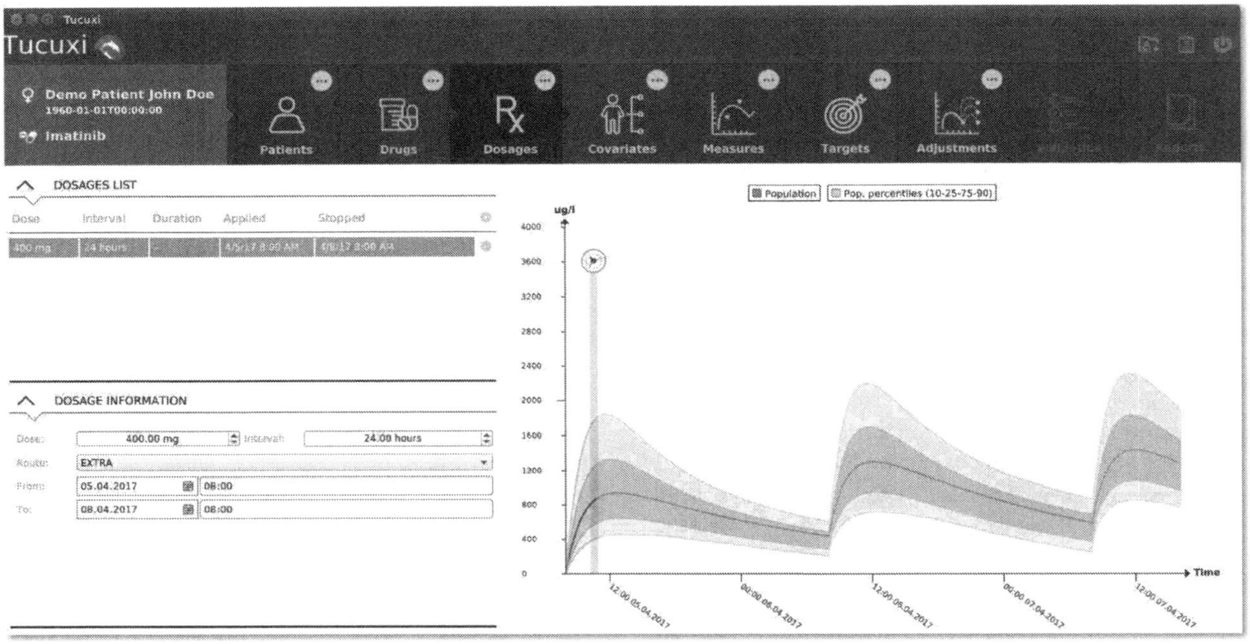

Figure 3: *TUCUXI* graphical user interface

exchange healthcare data between heterogeneous systems that support different data formats. Medical data are stored and exchanged between clinical databases in HL7 format. However, the software operates the data in XML format and produces the reports and graphs in PDF and PNG format. To solve this interoperability issue Mirth Connect [2] – an open source healthcare integration engine – has been used.

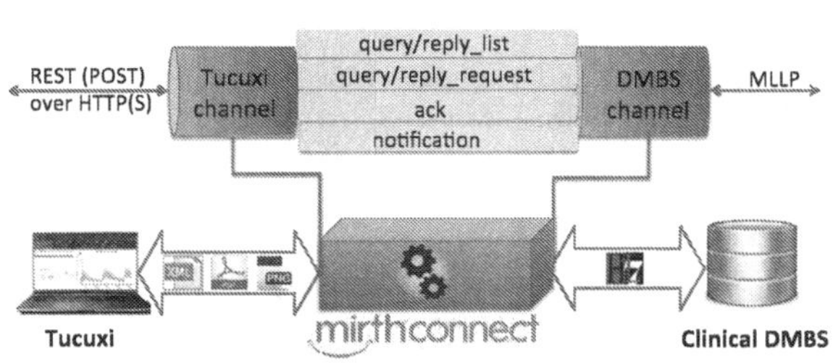

Figure 4: Communication between *TUCUXI* and the database of the medical institution

Figure 4 shows the actors involved in the process of data exchange and the formats of the data they use. We use a client-server architecture with a proxy to model communication between *TUCUXI* and clinical database management system (DMBS). We created two external channels for communications: one for *TUCUXI*-Mirth and one for DMBS-Mirth; and four channels were deployed on Mirth for the data transformations. To connect *TUCUXI* to another system there is no need to modify the software, only one Mirth channel may need to be adapted.

Communication between TDM software and proxy is done using a REST API. Sending a query or an update is initiated via an HTTP(S) request that encapsulates the corresponding message in XML format (cf. Figure 5). The client *TUCUXI* can send 2 types of query requests, an acknowledgment message (when a response is received) and a notification to update the DMBS. For each type of these messages the separate channel is deployed on the proxy and a message is filtered to the corresponding channel based on the message type. For all the messages sent by *TUCUXI* except the acknowledgment (there is no response for the ACK), the response will go through the same channel and will be transformed from HL7 format to XML. Transformations are defined separately using javaScript for each type of message.

Communication between Mirth and clinical DMBS is defined according to the Minimal Lower Layer Protocol (MLLP) – a standard for transmitting HL7 messages via TCP/IP.

We have implemented the data flow as shown on Figure 5. The sequence diagram that describes the data flow consists of the following steps:

(1) Obtaining the list of pending requests ;
(2) Obtaining the detailed data about specific request ;
(3) Individual dosage evaluation, adjustment proposition ;
(4) Sending results to the medical database.

At the source/destination of these channels we deployed a transformer using javaScript that perform the mapping and construct messages of each type required by the clinical flow. All the messages are received on an external channel that redirects the messages

[2]https://www.mirth.com

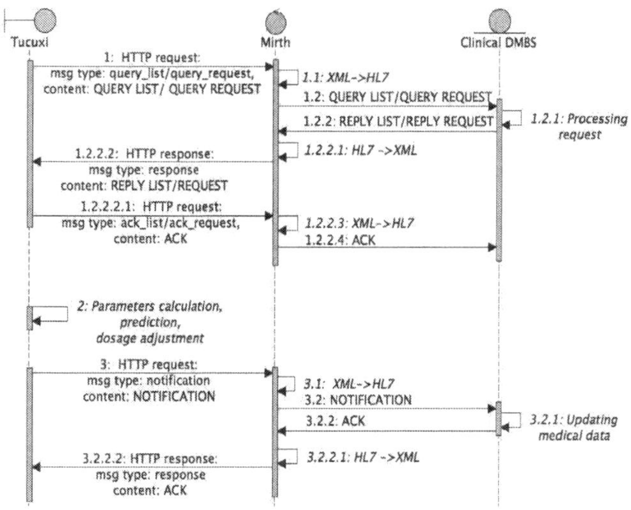

Figure 5: Communication diagram for the clinical data flow with *TUCUXI*

based on the filter defined with respect to the message header where the type of the message is specified.

4.2 Data structure and messages

In this subsection we present the content of the messages we constructed for data exchange between *TUCUXI* and a clinical database. Following the clinical flow of TDM we need to provide the user of the software (doctor, or pharmacologist) with the list of pending requests. A user can specify a time frame that will be an inclusion criteria for the requests based on their arrival date. According to standardized procedures of routine non-automated TDM in the hospital a code "CPCL" with the value "4CPCL" ("0CPCL") is used to tag whether request has (not) been already processed by a pharmacologist. Therefore in order to ask for the list of requests, a `QUERY LIST` message contains the time interval corresponding to the sampling arrival date/time and CPCL value: "0CPCL".

A `REPLY LIST` message is a list of pending requests and it contains, for each request, the following information:

- request Id – a unique identifier of the request within the clinical system ;
- CPCL code value ;
- information about the patient such as covariates (gender and age), as well as address and the patient identifier in the clinical system ;
- practitioner data: information about the doctor that prescribed the test, and the medical institution, if the sample is sent by another hospital ;
- sample data: identifier of the sample (identifier of the tube form the laboratory), the date/time of the sampling and sample arrival date/time in the laboratory ;
- information about the drug: code used in the system, active principle, brand name, Anatomical Therapeutic Chemical (ATC)[3] classification system code.

[3]www.whocc.no/atc_ddd_index/

This information allows the pharmacologist to ensure that the samples with the medications that require urgent analysis are validated on time.

To obtain more information about the request selected for validation, the `QUERY REQUEST` message is sent to the clinical database system. Multiple drugs can be measured in one sample and several samples can correspond to the same patient. Therefore, a `QUERY REQUEST` contains the patient unique identifier, request id and drug id. This combination uniquely identifies a request for validation of the drug.

`REPLY REQUEST` message in comparison to `QUERY LIST` contains extended information such as the following:

- dosages: start of the treatment or the date of last change of dosage, date/time of the last dose intake, current dosage, frequency of intake, route of administration, comments provided by the clinician ;
- sample results, containing observed concentration analyte and corresponding value and unit ;
- additional patient's covariates required for the drug model: bodyweight, renalfailure (y/n), lastcreatinine, hemodialysis (y/n), hemofiltration (y/n), gestationalage (for newborns), liverfailure (y/n), childpugh, heartfailure (y/n), lungfailure (y/n)), together with the value, unit and the date/time date of the covariate' s acquisition ;
- Timestamped clinical data such as clinical diagnosis, the adverse effects information (toxicity), indication that corresponds to the motivations to TDM, response.

While the `REPLY LIST` message contains the information that can help the clinician to review and choose next request to be validated, extended information from the `REPLY REQUEST` is used to fill in (or pre-fill) the panels (1)-(6) of the software. When a request is processed, and the report is generated, the `NOTIFICATION` message is sent to the clinical database with the following information:

- expectedness: the interpretation of the normality of the result by the analyst ;
- suitability of the treatment: the interpretation of the appropriateness of drug exposure by the analyst ;
- prediction: the recommendation of dosage adjustment by the analyst ;
- remonitoring: the recommendation for future monitoring by the analyst ;
- a priori and a posteriori parameters of the mathematical model ;
- some cautionary statement by the analyst and the timestamp of the interpretation ;
- image of the expected curve (in a binary format in base-64) ;
- report described in Section 3 generated automatically ;
- CPCL code with the value "4CPCL", corresponding to the validated request.

If any information about the patient has to be modified (due to a possible mistake originated from clinical database) it can be updated using a `NOTIFICATION` message.

When *TUCUXI* receives a `REPLY LIST` or a `REPLY REQUEST` message an `ACK` message is sent to the clinical database to acknowledge reception of the messages from clinical DBMS. Reception of `NOTIFICATION` is acknowledged by the clinical DMBS as well.

While constructing the messages with the the information listed above in HL7[4] v2.4 format, custom segments were introduced. Custom segments were used to express status of the request (validated or awaiting validation), information about drug and dosages, some clinical data, the report and the curve with the predicted concentration, as well as a priori and a posteriori parameters of the mathematical model. For each query/reply pairs we define so-called Conformance Statement – the information that identifies the query, specifies what items can be queried and describes what the response will look like.

5 FROM DROP OF BLOOD TO RESEARCH DATABASE AND BACK

Research studies that use retrospective medical data have become a major source of contributions to the biomedical science literature [12]. Therefore, data aggregation for the research purposes is a essential step towards enhancing clinical literature, e.g., by developing new PKPD models.

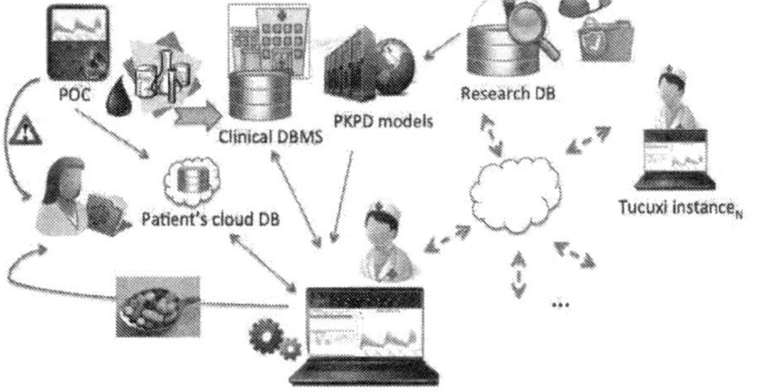

Figure 6: Connecting multiple instances of TDM software

Figure 6 shows the data flow in a healthcare system spanning from a patient bedside to the healthcare data aggregated in the cloud and used for the research purposes.

Characteristics of the data to be acquired for a research study are determined by the requirements of the study. Therefore, multiple databases need to be constructed. For this we need a system that will connect researchers and medical institutions and will allow them to collaborate with each other and will enable dynamic data aggregation. We assume that the number of data sources participating in the data aggregation should not be static as well as description of the data to be aggregated (could be adjusted during the process of data aggregation depending on the data availability) [6]. Dynamicity of such system will allow one to accelerate a notoriously time-consuming data collection process.

We developed a mutli-agent system for dynamic data aggregation for the research purposes. An agent is modeled as an instance of *TUCUXI* used by a doctor or in a hospital. It has been tested using anonymized TDM data and presented in detail in [6].

In clinical practice unless the patient provided a consent for sharing the data as they are, the data have to be anonymized. We also developed a privacy-preserving algorithm for distributed data aggregation for medical research [7] that can be used to ensure anonymity of the patients. However, anonymization may affect the utility of the data. To overcome this issue we are currently evaluating an algorithm that will allow to improve the data utility with the database growth while preserving patient's privacy.

Expanding TDM to a larger patients population by making it available at the Point-of-Care (POC) system will further advance the outcome of drug therapies. Key for widespread dosage adjustment is the availability of point-of-care devices able to measure plasma drug concentration in a simple, automated, and cost – effective fashion. Cappi et al. introduce and test such POC device. The authors present a portable, palm-sized transmission-localized surface plasmon resonance (T-LSPR) setup, comprised of off-the-shelf components and coupled with DNA-based aptamers specific to the antibiotic tobramycin [5]. Mobile version of the software e.g., running on the POC (cf. Figure 6) or on the tablet connected to POC, can be used to alert a patient in case of toxicity of inefficacy of the treatment and provide a recommendation to ask for medical assistance. Dosage adjustment can be made faster as there is no need to send the blood sample to a laboratory and to wait for the results to be transmitted back [5]. The results from POC could also be sent to the patient's cloud database, accessed by the clinician or pharmacologist and analyzed using TDM software.

6 DISCUSSION

In this section we discuss the ethical issues related to the use of automated software to manage patient's healthcare data.

6.1 Ethical issues

6.1.1 Decision making in medical domain. A piece of software like *TUCUXI* does not aim to replace physicians, but rather to provide assistance in TDM. Dosage individualization is suitable or even required for many drugs, but it is difficult and time consuming, the way it is done at present. Current tools such as Excel worksheets or non-ergonomic softwares are not well suited to manage heterogeneous patients' data in order to issue dosage adjustment decisions on a large scale. Moreover, the time required for a consultation with a clinical pharmacologist may delay important adjustments of the treatment. We think it is possible that clinicians use our software without consulting a specialist in pharmacology. For this we need to ensure "safety" of the software, i.e. its ability to detect unusual cases and to produce reports of no worse quality than those produced by trained clinical pharmacologists.

Before using any PKPD model for a given drug, the model will require approval by a trained pharmacologist after thorough testing. A semi- or fully-automated procedure may contribute to efficient validation of such drug models in the future. Certification of the whole software along with its reference PKPD database is required. Currently we are developing the necessary trials to make it a validated medical device according to applicable regulation.

6.1.2 Evaluation of TUCUXI as a TDM software. A recent review [19] describes four steps to implement pharmacometrics-based decision support tools, consisting of validating scientific components, defining technical options, considering regulatory aspects, and achieving efficient commercialization. Examples of

[4]http://www.hl7.org.

pharmacometrics-based decision tools that support monitoring of patients and individualization of treatment strategies in neonates, children and adults are presented. Concretely, the evaluation of a medical software such as *TUCUXI* requires several tasks:

(1) Verification of the **Correctness of implementation of mathematical models**, for instance, using automated mathematical validation of the software against NONMEM – the *de facto* standard for studies in pharmacokinetics [3].
(2) **Validation of data exchange** through a series of scripts aiming to obtain the list of pending TDM requests, run multiple times a day.
(3) While the first two tasks are being run automatically every day, thanks to scripting facilities, **clinical validation** requires a real validation in clinical practice. An evaluation protocol has been designed and is meant to be used after the first two tasks proved the correctness of the software.

6.1.3 Fully automated TDM. While the GUI version of *TUCUXI* is currently being tested, a next server version is under development. Its goal is to be able to propose an automated interpretation based on all data sent to the server. Basically it is meant to work as the GUI version, but automatically calculating predictions and dosage adjustments. A report will be generated, with graphs and a list of best dosage candidates for the specific patient. This server will allow to be integrated into an electronic patient infrastructure, as a service for analysis labs. Ethically speaking, a human should still be responsible to check the report and to choose the best dosage.

6.2 Patient's privacy

Having access to the population data is crucial for building new mathematical models, or improving characteristics and parameters of the existing ones. According to the current data protection legislation in US[5] and in Europe [9], as well as to the EU General Data Protection Regulation (GDPR) that will replace the European Data Protection Directive 95/46/EC starting from 25 May 2018[6], collecting and sharing personal data require signed consent from the patient to allow using his data for research purposes. Not all patients are willing to provide consent due to the risk of their data misuse [21, 22]. For example, if the healthcare data become publicly available insurance companies may infer that a person has a chronic disease susceptibility, and may refuse an application or reject the renewal of their insurance policy. An employer may try to infer healthcare information about potential employees and based on the sensitive information (a serious health condition or a chronic disease susceptibility) may discriminate the candidate [6]. As an alternative to the consent collection, the data can be anonymized: the patient's data to be used for the research must not be linked to the identity of a person to whom these data belong [8, 9].

How to ensure that the data that may belong to the same patient and were aggregated from different sources were properly anonymized? In [7] the authors proposed a privacy-preserving algorithm for independent release of medical data in distributed environment. However, one should take into account that absolute anonymization is only possible when no data are shared at all and, therefore, the privacy-utility trade-off needs to be found for every specific case. How to automatically adapt this trade-off for different databases? What is an acceptable risk of violation of patient's privacy? These questions still remain open.

[5]http://www.hhs.gov/hipaa/

[6]http://www.eugdpr.org/eugdpr.org.html

7 RELATED WORK

Fuchs at al in [10] present a review of twelve available clinical pharmacokinetic computer tools. The authors also describe the history and evolution of the software dedicated to monitoring and dosage adjustment staring from the software developed by Laboratory of Applied Pharmacokinetics at the University of Southern California (Los Angeles, CA, USA), launched in 1973 [14], and evolved to the *BestDose*[7] to the available[8] software packages such as *MwPharm* [20] and *TCIWorks* [25] that turned out to be the best ranked TDM programs according to the review [10].

MwPharm has the largest database of drugs with their pharmacokinetic properties and almost 300 population models embedded in the software. However, similarly to *BestDose* it is also a standalone TDM software. This means that the patient's data have to be manually inserted, and dosage adjustments are not automatically in patient's medical record, they will be stored in the local databases. However, according to [10] none of these programs, including *BestDose* and *TCIWorks* yet fulfills all of the requirements to clinical pharmokinetics computer program.

During last years (since the review of Fuchs et al. from 2013 [10]) few TDM software tools have been developed. *TDMx* is a novel web-based open-access support tool for optimising antimicrobial dosing regimens in clinical routine [24].*TDMx* is not a registered or certified medical device. As result of a research project, *TDMx* is provided for personal use only, the accuracy of the provided results can not be guaranteed[9]. Currently, *TDMx* is available for only 4 drugs (meropenem, piperacillin, amikacin and gentamicin).

NextDose is an online dose calculator that uses Bayesian nonparametric approach to propose dose regimens after concentration measurements become available. The software consists of three abstraction layers and provide a clear separation between the user interface, model controllers and the modeling software. *Doseme*[10] and *insightrx*[11] are recently available commercial software for TDM.

However, unlike *DoseMe* and *NextDose*, *TUCUXI* allows to calculate population, a priory and a posteriori percentiles. Moreover, the authors in [1] claim that presently available software (such as *DoseMe*, *insightrx* and *NextDose*) is still sufficiently complex and requires training to enable rapid use at the bedside by healthcare professionals. In contrast, *TUCUXI*– TDM software presented in this paper – has a very intuitive user interface, that makes the software easy to use by non-pharmacologists. It can be integrated in clinical practice, and can also be connected to the research database.

8 CONCLUSIONS

Therapeutic drug monitoring allows to individualize the dose and helps to ensure the best possible outcome for each patient [13].

[7]http://www.lapk.org/bestdose.php

[8]at the time of preparing the review, year 2013

[9]http://www.tdmx.eu/

[10]https://doseme.com.au/science-behind-doseme

[11]www.insight-rx.com

However, there is still a number of challenges that have to be overcome before individualized drug dosing based on TDM is widely used [1]. Software tools developed to automate the process of TDM are evolving. However, a solution with comprehensive clinical and research capabilities, showing simplicity, flexibility and user friendliness is still in demand [10].

In order to address this need and improve dosage adjustment procedures, *TUCUXI*, an intelligent automated system, spanning from the patient's bedside to research databases has been developed. This interactive tool is designed to guide a user through the process of TDM and, therefore, can be used not only by clinical pharmacologists but also by general practitioners and possibly by educated patients. We presented the functionalities of the system, user interface, as well as interfaces and messages developed to achieve interoperability with clinical DMBS and successful integration in clinical practice.

Correctness of mathematical models embedded in the software, as well of reliability of data exchange have already been verified. Currently real world trials to certify the software as medical device are being developed. Clinical validation by practitioners will follow. Moreover, *TUCUXI* software can be used to combine patient care and clinical research by exporting the data for developing new PKPD models. We also envisage the usage of a mobile TDM software embedded in a point-of-care "lab-on-chip" system, that will further advance the outcome of drug therapies. In this work, we also addressed a number of challenges and discussed ethical issues related to automation of therapeutic drug monitoring in patient care and medical research.

ACKNOWLEDGMENTS

This work was evaluated by the Swiss National Science Foundation, financed by the Swiss Confederation and funded by Nano-Tera.ch, in the framework of an RTD project ISyPeM2: developing therapeutic drug monitoring by designing a point-of-care system to measure drug concentration in blood samples and adjust dosage accordingly. The authors would like to thank all the software developers that allowed TUCUXI to be successful. They also wish to thank Séverine Petitprez for helpful discussions and anonymous reviewers for their comments.

REFERENCES

[1] Basma Al-Metwali and Hussain Mulla. 2017. Personalised dosing of medicines for children. *Journal of Pharmacy and Pharmacology* (2017).

[2] Manel Aouri, Catalina Barcelo, Monia Guidi, Margalida Rotger, Matthias Cavassini, Cédric Hizrel, Thierry Buclin, Laurent A Decosterd, Chantal Csajka, Swiss HIV Cohort Study, and others. 2017. Population Pharmacokinetics and Pharmacogenetics Analysis of Rilpivirine in HIV-1-Infected Individuals. *Antimicrobial Agents and Chemotherapy* 61, 1 (2017), e00899–16.

[3] AJ Boeckmann, LB Sheiner, and SL Beal. 1994. NONMEM users guide. *San Francisco: University of California San Francisco* (1994).

[4] Olivier Capitain, Andreaa Asevoaia, Michele Boisdron-Celle, Anne-Lise Poirier, Alain Morel, and Erick Gamelin. 2012. Individual fluorouracil dose adjustment in FOLFOX based on pharmacokinetic follow-up compared with conventional body-area-surface dosing: a phase II, proof-of-concept study. *Clinical colorectal cancer* 11, 4 (2012), 263–267.

[5] Giulia Cappi, Fabio M Spiga, Yessica Moncada, Anna Ferretti, Michael Beyeler, Marco Bianchessi, Laurent Decosterd, Thierry Buclin, and Carlotta Guiducci. 2015. Label-free detection of tobramycin in serum by transmission-localized surface plasmon resonance. *Analytical chemistry* 87, 10 (2015), 5278–5285.

[6] Alevtina Dubovitskaya, Visara Urovi, Imanol Barba, Karl Aberer, and Michael Ignaz Schumacher. 2016. A Multiagent System for Dynamic Data Aggregation in Medical Research. *BioMed Research International* 2016 (2016).

[7] Alevtina Dubovitskaya, Visara Urovi, Matteo Vasirani, Karl Aberer, and Michael Ignaz Schumacher. 2015. A Cloud-based eHealth Architecture for Privacy Preserving Data Integration. In *IFIP Advances in Information and Communication Technology (SEC 2015)*. Springer Science and Business Media.

[8] Khaled El Emam, Sam Rodgers, and Bradley Malin. 2015. Anonymising and sharing individual patient data. *bmj* 350 (2015), h1139.

[9] 2016. Regulation (EU) 2016/679 of the European Parliament and of the Council of 27 April 2016 on the protection of natural persons with regard to the processing of personal data and on the free movement of such data, and repealing Directive 95/46/EC (General Data Protection Regulation). *Official Journal of the European Union* L119/59 (May 2016). http://eur-lex.europa.eu/legal-content/EN/TXT/?uri=OJ:L:2016:119:TOC

[10] Aline Fuchs, Chantal Csajka, Yann Thoma, Thierry Buclin, and Nicolas Widmer. 2013. Benchmarking therapeutic drug monitoring software: a review of available computer tools. *Clinical pharmacokinetics* 52, 1 (2013), 9–22.

[11] Verena Gotta, Nicolas Widmer, Michael Montemurro, Serge Leyvraz, Amina Haouala, Laurent A Decosterd, Chantal Csajka, and Thierry Buclin. 2012. Therapeutic drug monitoring of imatinib: Bayesian and alternative methods to predict trough levels. *Clinical pharmacokinetics* 51, 3 (March 2012), 187–201. DOI: http://dx.doi.org/10.2165/11596990-000000000-00000

[12] Gregory William Hruby, James McKiernan, Suzanne Bakken, and Chunhua Weng. 2013. A centralized research data repository enhances retrospective outcomes research capacity: a case report. *Journal of the American Medical Informatics Association* 20, 3 (2013), 563–567.

[13] SH Jang, Z Yan, and JA Lazor. 2016. Therapeutic drug monitoring: A patient management tool for precision medicine. *Clinical Pharmacology & Therapeutics* 99, 2 (2016), 148–150.

[14] Roger W Jelliffe. 1991. The USC* PACK PC programs for population pharmacokinetic modeling, modeling of large kinetic/dynamic systems, and adaptive control of drug dosage regimens.. In *Proceedings of the Annual Symposium on Computer Application in Medical Care.* American Medical Informatics Association, 922.

[15] Ju-Seop Kang and Min-Ho Lee. 2009. Overview of therapeutic drug monitoring. *The Korean journal of internal medicine* 24, 1 (2009), 1–10.

[16] James J. Lee, Jan H. Beumer, and Edward Chu. 2016. Therapeutic drug monitoring of 5-fluorouracil. *Cancer Chemotherapy and Pharmacology* 78, 3 (2016), 447–464. DOI: http://dx.doi.org/10.1007/s00280-016-3054-2

[17] L. Michaelis and M. L. Menten. 1913. Die Kinetik der Invertinwirkung. 49 (1913), 333–369.

[18] J D Momper and J A Wagner. 2014. Therapeutic Drug Monitoring as a Component of Personalized Medicine: Applications in Pediatric Drug Development. *Clinical Pharmacology and Therapeutics* 95, 2 (2014), 138–140. DOI: http://dx.doi.org/10.1038/clpt.2013.227

[19] Fahima Nekka, Chantal Csajka, Mélanie Wilbaux, Sachin Sanduja, Jun Li, and Marc Pfister. 2017. Pharmacometrics-based decision tools facilitate mHealth implementation. *Expert Review of Clinical Pharmacology* 10, 1 (2017), 39–46. DOI: http://dx.doi.org/10.1080/17512433.2017.1251837 PMID: 27813436.

[20] Johannes H Proost and Dirk KF Meijer. 1992. MW/Pharm, an integrated software package for drug dosage regimen calculation and therapeutic drug monitoring. *Computers in biology and medicine* 22, 3 (1992), 155–163.

[21] Charles Safran, Meryl Bloomrosen, W Edward Hammond, Steven Labkoff, Suzanne Markel-Fox, Paul C Tang, and Don E Detmer. 2007. Toward a national framework for the secondary use of health data: an American Medical Informatics Association White Paper. *Journal of the American Medical Informatics Association* 14, 1 (2007), 1–9.

[22] Murat Sariyar and Irene Schlünder. 2016. Reconsidering Anonymization-Related Concepts and the Term "Identification" Against the Backdrop of the European Legal Framework. *Biopreservation and biobanking* 14, 5 (2016), 367–374.

[23] A. Simalatsar, R. Bornet, Wenqi You, Y. Thoma, and G. De Micheli. 2014. Safe Implementation of Embedded Software for a Portable Device Supporting Drug Administration. In *Bioinformatics and Bioengineering (BIBE), 2014 IEEE International Conference on.* 257–264. DOI: http://dx.doi.org/10.1109/BIBE.2014.55

[24] Sebastian G Wicha, Martin G Kees, Alexander Solms, Iris K Minichmayr, Alexander Kratzer, and Charlotte Kloft. 2015. TDMx: a novel web-based open-access support tool for optimising antimicrobial dosing regimens in clinical routine. *International journal of antimicrobial agents* 45, 4 (2015), 442–444.

[25] Daniel FB Wright and Stephen B Duffull. 2011. Development of a bayesian forecasting method for warfarin dose individualisation. *Pharmaceutical research* 28, 5 (2011), 1100–1111.

Interpretable Predictions of Clinical Outcomes with An Attention-based Recurrent Neural Network

Ying Sha
School of Biology,
Georgia Institute of Technology,
Atlanta, GA 30332,
United States
ysha8@gatech.edu

May D. Wang
Dept. of Biomedical Engineering,
Georgia Institute of Technology and
Emory University,
Atlanta, GA 30332,
United States
maywang@gatech.edu

ABSTRACT

The increasing accumulation of healthcare data provides researchers with ample opportunities to build machine learning approaches for clinical decision support and to improve the quality of health care. Several studies have developed conventional machine learning approaches that rely heavily on manual feature engineering and result in task-specific models for health care. In contrast, healthcare researchers have begun to use deep learning, which has emerged as a revolutionary machine learning technique that obviates manual feature engineering but still achieves impressive results in research fields such as image classification. However, few of them have addressed the lack of the interpretability of deep learning models although interpretability is essential for the successful adoption of machine learning approaches by healthcare communities. In addition, the unique characteristics of healthcare data such as high dimensionality and temporal dependencies pose challenges for building models on healthcare data. To address these challenges, we develop a gated recurrent unit-based recurrent neural network with hierarchical attention for mortality prediction, and then, using the diagnostic codes from the Medical Information Mart for Intensive Care, we evaluate the model. We find that the prediction accuracy of the model outperforms baseline models and demonstrate the interpretability of the model in visualizations.

CCS CONCEPTS

• **Applied computing → Life and medical sciences →Health informatics**; • **Computing methodologies → Artificial intelligence**

Permission to make digital or hard copies of all or part of this work for personal or classroom use is granted without fee provided that copies are not made or distributed for profit or commercial advantage and that copies bear this notice and the full citation on the first page. Copyrights for components of this work owned by others than ACM must be honored. Abstracting with credit is permitted. To copy otherwise, or republish, to post on servers or to redistribute to lists, requires prior specific permission and/or a fee. Request permissions from Permissions@acm.org.
ACM-BCB '17, August 20-23, 2017, Boston, MA, USA
© 2017 Association for Computing Machinery.
ACM ISBN 978-1-4503-4722-8/17/08...$15.00
http://dx.doi.org/10.1145/3107411.3107445

KEYWORDS

Health care; electronic health records; deep learning; recurrent neural networks; attention; interpretability; visualization.

1 INTRODUCTION

Health care is undergoing a revolution. The accumulation of big data in health care such as electronic health records (EHR) and claims data has enabled researchers to use machine learning techniques to learn from these data and build clinical decision support tools. Such capabilities facilitate timely and accurate predictions of medical risks of patients with regard to readmissions or deaths, and thus improve the quality and efficiency of clinical interventions. Several studies have demonstrated that health information technologies have improved the quality of health care [10; 11; 17].

Although healthcare data analytics offer promising opportunities for improving health care, key challenges remain unsolved regarding how to appropriately model healthcare data. Such data, such as EHR, have unique characteristics, including high dimensionality and temporal dependencies. With regard to the former, for example, a standard coding system of diagnosis, the International Classification of Diseases (ICD-9-CM), contains approximately 20,000 codes; and with regard to the latter, for example, the existence of one disease might increase the risk of one patient having certain diseases in the future. In addition, representing healthcare data is not a trivial task since medical histories vary greatly in length and contain hierarchical structures. That is, a typical healthcare record of one patient is a variable-sized set of discrete elements such as diagnostic codes with variable numbers.

An ideal model for healthcare data should not only appropriately model the unique structure of healthcare data but also maintain a balance between accuracy and interpretation. Conventional predictive models of clinical decision support rely heavily on feature engineering, such as ranking and selecting features based on certain criteria [12; 15; 31], which results in classifier-dependent features and task-specific models. An alternative to models that rely on feature engineering is deep learning, which has attracted considerable attention because of its impressive accuracy in a wide range of tasks [1; 20; 33] and its ability to generalize high-level representation of raw data even without domain knowledge [22]. However, resistance to and criticism of deep learning approaches still persist, which primarily results from its lack of interpretability. That is, to infer the importance of individual features on model outputs, people find it difficult to follow the reasoning of deep learning models. For clinical decision support, lack of model interpretability will meet resistance to such models by medical communities. Fortunately, the interpretability problem can be mitigated by the attention mechanism [5], which mimics the visual attention of human cognition by learning a set of attention weights that represent the relative importance of individual features on certain time steps or locations to the final prediction.

Researchers have recently begun to apply deep learning in health care. Some pioneer studies have focused on identifying patterns from healthcare data with deep learning. Lasko et al. were the first to apply deep learning in health care, and they demonstrated the capability of deep learning to generalize patterns from serum uric acid measurements with autoencoders [21]. Miotto et al. utilized denoising autoencoders to produce a compact and general representation of electronic health records that demonstrated better prediction accuracy when used in downstream analysis than the representation produced by conventional dimensional reduction approaches [26]. Some recent studies have characterized the temporal dependencies of EHR data using sophisticated gated recurrent neural networks, but these models suffer from lack of interpretation. Pham et al. used a sophisticated model built on long short-term memory (LSTM) to model the interaction between diagnosis and medication [30]. Nguyen et al. employed convolutional neural networks to extract "clinical motifs" from medical records and predict clinical outcomes [27]. Choi et al. were the first to introduce attention mechanism in health care, and they proposed a model that uses two recurrent neural networks (RNN) that separately produce attention weights [7]. Our work continues to explore the possibilities and advantages of introducing the attention mechanism to facilitate interpretation of prediction results.

To generate interpretable predictions of clinical outcomes, our work develops a gated recurrent unit (GRU)-based RNN with hierarchical attention (GRNN-HA). We use the GRNN-HA to address the following challenges: (1) handling the high dimensionality of medical codes, (2) modeling the temporal dependencies of healthcare events, (3) characterizing the hierarchical structure of healthcare data, and (4) improving the interpretability of predictive models. To handle the high dimensionality of medical codes, our model learns a low-dimensional representation of medical codes with word2vec [25]. To model temporal dependencies, we use bidirectional GRUs to encode temporal information from healthcare data. To characterize the hierarchical structure of healthcare data and to improve the interpretability of models, our model organizes visit- and code-level information hierarchically and learns hierarchical attention weights on both levels dependently to represent the visit- and code-level importance, respectively. We validate our model on MIMIC-III (Medical Information Mart for Intensive Care) [16], which is a publicly available database that contains rich information about critical care from a large hospital, and compare mortality predictions of our model to those of several baseline models. To illustrate the interpretable results generated by our model, we also provide visualizations.

2 METHODS

2.1 Recurrent Neural Networks and GRU

A recurrent neural network (RNN) belongs to a class of neural networks suitable for modeling sequential data, which is enabled by the recurrent structure of RNNs in which the activation of the hidden state of the current time step is dependent on that of the previous time step. Specifically, given a sequence x= ($x_1, x_2, \ldots, x_t$), an RNN updates its current hidden state h_t as

$$h_t = \phi(x_t, h_{t-1}),$$

in which ϕ is a nonlinear activation function that can be either as simple as sigmoid or as sophisticated as LSTM [14]. The purpose of introducing sophisticated activation functions is to overcome the vanishing gradient problem, which causes difficulties of training an RNN to capture long-term dependencies [2; 13].

To overcome the vanishing gradient problem, we apply a gated recurrent unit (GRU)-based RNN that encodes input sequences of variable length as vectors of fixed length. The GRU, proposed by Cho et al. [6], has been proven to outperform LSTM in a set of tasks [9]. Although similar to LSTM, GRU provides a simpler alternative, using two types of gates, the reset gate r_t and the update gate z_t, to control the information flow of hidden states without a separate memory gate. The reset gate determines part of the past information, which will remain in the current hidden state, and the update gate determines part of the new information, which will be added to the current hidden state. The detailed calculation of GRU is defined by the following equations:

$$r_t = \sigma(W_r x_t + U_r h_{t-1} + b_r),$$
$$z_t = \sigma(W_z x_t + U_z h_{t-1} + b_z),$$
$$\widetilde{h_t} = \tanh(W_h x_t + r_t \odot (U_h h_{t-1}) + b_h),$$
$$h_t = (1 - z_t) \odot h_{t-1} + z_t \odot \widetilde{h_t},$$

in which $\sigma(\cdot)$ is a sigmoid function, x_t is the sequence input at time t, h_t is the value of the hidden state at time t, and $\widetilde{h_t}$ is the candidate value of the hidden state at time t. The computation of candidate hidden states is similar to that of a traditional RNN, except that the information of h_{t-1} is gated by r_t. h_t is calculated as a linear interpolation between h_{t-1} and $\widetilde{h_t}$.

2.2 Low-dimensional Representation of Medical Codes

Motivated by considerable successful applications of word2vec [25] in learning word representations for a wide range of natural language processing (NLP) tasks [6; 18; 32], we extend word2vec to learn a representation of diagnostic codes in ICD-9. ICD codes are often sequential in healthcare datasets. For example, in the MIMIC data database, ICD codes assigned to different hospital admissions are chronically ordered, and the ICD codes assigned to one hospital admission are ordered based on priority. Because of the sequentiality of ICD codes, we observe an analogy between them and natural languages. That is, we can naturally view the sequence of ICD codes of one admission as a sentence and an ICD code as a word and then apply the continuous bag-of-words (CBOW) architecture of word2vec. CBOW constructs representations of words by optimizing the prediction of a center word from its context words. With w_O denoting a center word and w_I denoting a context word of the center word, the objective of CBOW is to maximize

$$p(w_O|w_I),$$

which is computed based on

$$p(w_O|w_I) = \frac{\exp({v'_{w_O}}^T v_{w_I})}{\sum_{O'=1}^{C} \exp({v'_{w_{O'}}}^T v_{w_I})},$$

in which v_w and v_w' are two vector representations of word w, respectively, and C is the number of words in the vocabulary. The vector representations of words learned by word2vec tend to retain the semantic meanings of words so that words with similar meanings are close to each other in the vector space.

2.3 Hierarchical Attention

Our work applies a hierarchical attention model with a similar structure to that proposed by [35] to predict the outcome of a patient based on longitudinal diagnostic codes. The architecture of the model is illustrated in Figure 1. Suppose that a patient has L hospital visits, each of which is assigned T diagnostic codes. We denote each diagnostic code as w_{it}, which represents the t-th ICD code in the i-th visit of this patient, with $i \in [1, L]$ and $t \in [1, T]$. We represent w_{it} with a low-dimensional vector through

$$x_{it} = V\, w_{it}, t \in [1, T],$$

in which V is an embedding matrix obtained through word2vec as described in 2.2. Then we encode each ICD code using a bidirectional GRU that summarizes the information of a sequence of ICD codes in one hospital visit from both directions through

$$\overrightarrow{h_{it}} = \overrightarrow{GRU}(x_{it}), t \in [1, T],$$
$$\overleftarrow{h_{it}} = \overleftarrow{GRU}(x_{it}), t \in [T, 1],$$

$$h_{it} = [\overrightarrow{h_{it}}, \overleftarrow{h_{it}}].$$

Bidirectional GRUs increase the amount of input information by enabling future information to be accessible by the current state. The purpose of introducing bidirectional GRUs is to mimic the behavior of a physician examining a patient's medical history both forwards and backwards.

Since each ICD code does not contribute equivalent information to one hospital visit, we introduce the code-level attention mechanism, which enables the model to pay more attention to informative ICD codes than other ICD codes. To implement the code-level attention mechanism, we first compute the hidden representation of h_{it}, denoted as u_{it}, to derive the attention of individual ICD codes α_{it} as the similarity of u_{it} and a code-level context vector u_c, and then encode each hospital visit v_i as a weighted sum of h_{it} through

$$u_{it} = \tanh(W_c h_{it} + b_c),$$
$$\alpha_{it} = \frac{\exp(u_{it}^T u_c)}{\sum_t \exp(u_{it}^T u_c)},$$
$$v_i = \sum_t \alpha_{it} h_{it}.$$

For each visit vector v_i, we also encode it with a bidirectional GRU as follows:

$$\overrightarrow{h_i} = \overrightarrow{GRU}(v_i),$$
$$\overleftarrow{h_i} = \overleftarrow{GRU}(v_i),$$
$$h_i = [\overrightarrow{h_i}, \overleftarrow{h_i}].$$

Similarly, since individual visits do not contribute equivalent information to predictions, we introduce the visit-level attention mechanism to render the model capable of focusing more on those visits that contribute more to the prediction of patient outcomes than other visits. To implement the visit-level attention mechanism, we introduce a visit-level context vector u_v and use it to calculate the visit-level attention α_i as follows:

$$u_i = \tanh(W_v h_i + b_v),$$

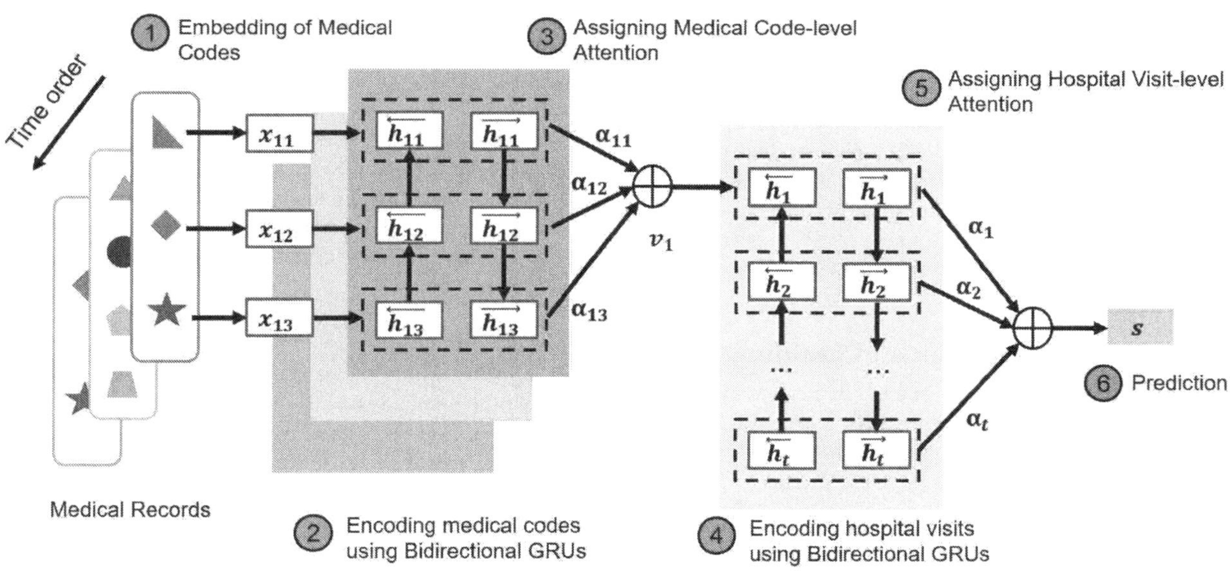

Figure 1: The architecture of the GRNN-HA model

$$\alpha_i = \frac{\exp(u_i^T u_v)}{\sum_i \exp(u_i^T u_v)},$$
$$s = \sum_i \alpha_i h_i.$$

Finally, to represent features, we use s and build a binary classifier as

$$\mathrm{p} = \mathrm{sigmoid}(Ws + b),$$

and we use the cross-entropy as our loss function, defined as

$$\mathrm{L} = \sum_i \mathrm{p_i} \times log\hat{\mathrm{p}}_\mathrm{i},$$

in which $\mathrm{p_i}$ is the predicted probability of a sample belonging to class i, and $\hat{\mathrm{p}}_\mathrm{i}$ is the true probability of the sample belonging to that class.

3 EXPERIMENTS

3.1 Description of Dataset

The dataset we use in this study comes from MIMIC-III (Medical Information Mart for Intensive Care), which is a freely accessible critical care database [16]. MIMIC-III contains data associated with 46,250 distinct patients admitted to the critical care units of a large tertiary hospital. The types of data include demographics, vital signs, diagnostic codes, and laboratory tests. Because of the wide availability of diagnostic codes in healthcare data and the ease of demonstrating the results produced by the model without excessive medical domain knowledge, we focus on diagnostics codes in this study. To ensure enough medical information about each patient, we include 7,537 patients who had at least two hospital admissions in MIMIC-III and then extract the diagnostic codes of each chosen patient. In addition, we maintain both the temporal order of diagnostic codes from multiple admissions and the priority-based order of diagnostic codes within one admission. We use these sequential diagnostic codes to predict mortality. Whether a patient died or not is recorded in MIMIC-III, and we find that 1,462 out of the selected 7,537 patients had died. To maintain the original proportion of mortality in both the training and test data, we use stratified sampling to set one-third of the dataset as a test set and the rest as a training set. We have repeated this stratified sampling three times to generate three sets of test and training data.

3.2 Model Implementation and Training

Here we describe the details of model implementation and training. We implement both the GRU-based RNN with hierarchical attention (GRNN-HA) and a GRU-based RNN without attention (GRNN) using keras 1.2.0 [8] with Theano 0.8.2 as the backend [3]. By training the CBOW version of word2vec on the training dataset, we obtain 200-dimentional representations of diagnostic codes. Then we use stratified sampling to set one-fifth of the training set for validation. We use the validation set to tune the hyperparameters of the models. The hyperparameters we have adjusted include the number of hidden units in GRUs at the visit and code levels. We vary the number of hidden units in GRUs over a range of 50 to 200 with a step size of 10. For model training, we minimize the loss function by using mini-batch stochastic gradient descent with a momentum of 0.9 and a batch size of 12. To evaluate the accuracy of mortality prediction given a relatively low mortality rate in our dataset, we use the Matthews correlation coefficient (MCC) in addition to commonly used measures, including the area under the receiver operating characteristic curve (AUROC) and the F1 score. MCC is an appropriate indicator of the quality of binary classification even when the sizes of both classes in a dataset significantly differ [24].

3.3 Baseline Models

Here we describe how we build our baseline models. To construct features for the baseline models, we derive n-grams from our data. An n-gram is a consecutive sequence of n items from sequential data such as text [4]. Because of their simplicity and ability to capture local contexts, N-gram-based features have been widely used in natural language processing [19; 23; 28]. To avoid model overfitting and computational infeasibility resulting from longer and more expressive n-grams, our study includes only the most frequent 5,000 unigrams and bigrams in the dataset to build a feature profile. After deriving the n-gram feature profile, we use either the number of occurrences of n-grams or the term frequency–inverse document frequency transformation (tf-idf) of n-grams as values for the feature profile. After constructing the features, we use logistic regression and support vector machines (SVM) as classifiers to build our baseline models. To select hyperparameters for the baseline models, we use a grid search over a parameter space through four-fold cross-validation on the training set. The hyperparameters of logistic regression include types of regularization and regularization parameters. We vary regularization over L1 and L2 and regularization parameter C over the logarithmic range of $[10^{-3}, 100]$. Likewise, the hyperparameters of SVM include gamma (the inverse of the standard deviation of kernel function) and regularization penalty parameter C when we use the Radial Basis Function (RBF) as the kernel function. When we use linear SVM as the kernel function, the hyperparameters of SVM include only regularization penalty parameter C. We choose gamma over the logarithmic range of $[10^{-2}, 1]$ and regularization penalty parameter C over the logarithmic range of $[10^{-2}, 10]$. We implement these baseline models with scikit-learn 0.18.1[29].

4 RESULTS

We show the results of mortality prediction on the MIMIC dataset by both the baseline and advanced methods in Table 1, in which "Logreg" is short for logistic regression. For all three metrics, the two advanced models, GRNN and GRNN-HA, demonstrate significantly better prediction results than those of the baseline models. Specifically, the average MCC of GRNN-HA is 11.71% higher than that of the highest average MCC of the baseline models. Even without the attention mechanism, the MCC of GRNN is still 7.32% higher than that of the highest average MCC of the baseline models. Using Steiger's test [34], which is a statistical test for comparing two dependent correlations, we find the two comparisons of MCC are both statistically significant ($p<0.05$). The superior results generated by the two GRNN-based advanced models demonstrate the advantages of utilizing word2vec to handle the high dimensionality of medical codes and GRNN for appropriate modeling of the temporal dependencies of healthcare data. Comparing the prediction results of two GRNN-based models, we find that GRNN-HA has higher MCC and F1 score values than GRNN. The AUROC of GRNN-HA is slightly lower than that of GRNN. Since AUROC is not sensitive for binary classification on imbalanced datasets, we argue that the prediction results of GRNN-HA are better than those of GRNN. That is, in our case, the attention mechanism is able to improve prediction results. In addition to producing accurate predictions, GRNN-HA generates interpretable results that are suitable for visualization. Figure 2 provides an example visualization for the results of the prediction about one patient in one of the test sets. This patient has three recorded hospital admissions, shown as three horizontal bars colored in blue of different intensities. The intensity of the color is proportional to the corresponding visit-level attention weight. The multiple diagnostic codes associated with each hospital admission are represented by lines of various lengths, the vertical order of which, from top to bottom, corresponds to the priority-based order of these codes. These lines, representing multiple diagnostics associated with one admission, are contained within the horizontal bar of the corresponding hospital admission. The length of a horizontal line is proportional to the attention weight of the diagnostic code to which the line corresponds.

From Figure 2, we observe that among the three hospital admissions, Visit 3, the last visit of this patient, dominates visit-level attention. This finding is reasonable because recent clinical conditions are usually more informative of a clinical outcome than early conditions. We also observe that two diagnostic codes, pneumonia and acute respiratory failure, dominate the code-level attention of the last hospital admission. To validate whether the interpretation of prediction by GRNN-HA is reasonable, we read the clinical notes linked to this patient and find out that the patient

Table 1: The results of mortality predictions

Model	MCC	F1 score	AUROC
Logreg + count	0.3664±0.0135	0.4604±0.0251	0.7884±0.0228
Logreg + tf-idf	0.3509±0.0203	0.4457±0.0330	0.7979±0.0094
SVM + count	0.3234±0.0241	0.4157±0.0679	0.7726±0.0267
SVM + tf-idf	0.3549±0.0218	0.4404±0.0227	0.7899±0.0118
GRNN + word2vec	0.4396±0.0486	0.5074±0.0613	**0.8650±0.0100**
GRNN-HA + word2vec	**0.4835±0.0585**	**0.5766±0.0623**	0.8603±0.0167

suffered mainly from acute respiratory failure, which is probably the consequence of multifocal pneumonia with suspected sepsis. Therefore, by assigning high attention weights of pneumonia and acute respiratory failure, GRNN-HA determines that this patient has a high risk of mortality, which is consistent with the clinical notes written by the medical experts.

To further evaluate the interpretability of the GRNN-HA model, we illustrate the distribution of attention weights of several representative and frequent diagnostic codes from the prediction results of the test dataset in Figure 3. Since the diagnostic codes receiving high attention weights tend to have more impact on the final prediction of mortality, we hypothesize that generally, diagnostic codes with high attention weights should represent diseases that are more life-threatening. Among the six diagnostic codes whose distribution we select to visualize, congestive heart failure and acute respiratory failure, which are life-threatening conditions, have attention weights with distribution shifted more to the right of the x-axis than the remaining ones (Figure 3a and 3c). The remaining conditions include chronic conditions such as diabetes mellitus and tobacco use disorder. Despite their risk to health, these conditions tend not to be determinants of mortality (Figure 3d and 3e). Although pneumonia receives a high attention weight in the example shown in Figure 2, most attention weights of pneumonia of patients from test set are below 0.2. This observation implies that GRNN-HA infers the attention weight of one diagnostic code in the context of medical history and suggests the potential of this model for personalized clinical decision support.

5 DISCUSSION

To predict mortality on diagnostic codes from the MIMIC 3 database, our work uses a GRU-based RNN with hierarchical attention. This model frees researchers from manual feature engineering that usually results in classifier-dependent features and task-specific models and achieves both high prediction accuracy and interpretability that make it suitable for clinical decision support. The interpretability of the model relies on attention weights, determined from relative importance of diagnostic codes on prediction, assigned to individual diagnostic codes and hospital visits. We notice that the attention weights for one specific condition form a distribution rather than a fixed value. This observation suggests that the model embraces the idea of personalized clinical decision support by inferring relative importance of one diagnostic code based on the context of the medical history of a patient. We envision an application scenario of the GRNN-HA model in which the GRNN-HA model scans the medical history of a new patient admitted into a hospital, generates a risk assessment, and provides an annotated visualization for physicians that can help them prioritize the order in which they will see patients.

We will address several limitations in our work in the future. First, the dataset may not be an optimal choice for our model to fully utilize longitudinal information because the MIMIC3 database contains limited longitudinal medical information of patients. That is, most of the patients in the dataset contain only two or three

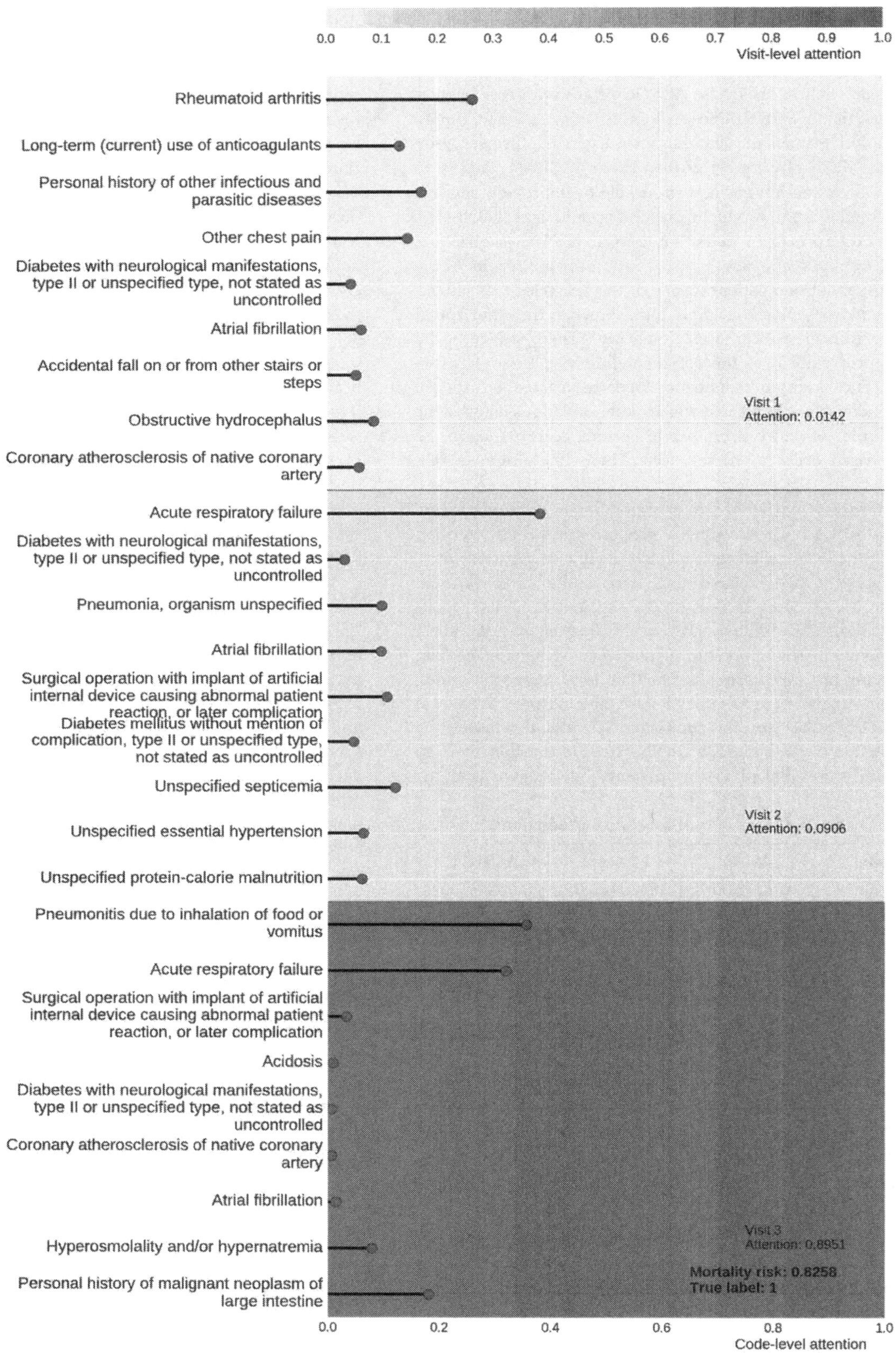

Figure 2: The visualization of the prediction result of a patient by GRNN-HA.

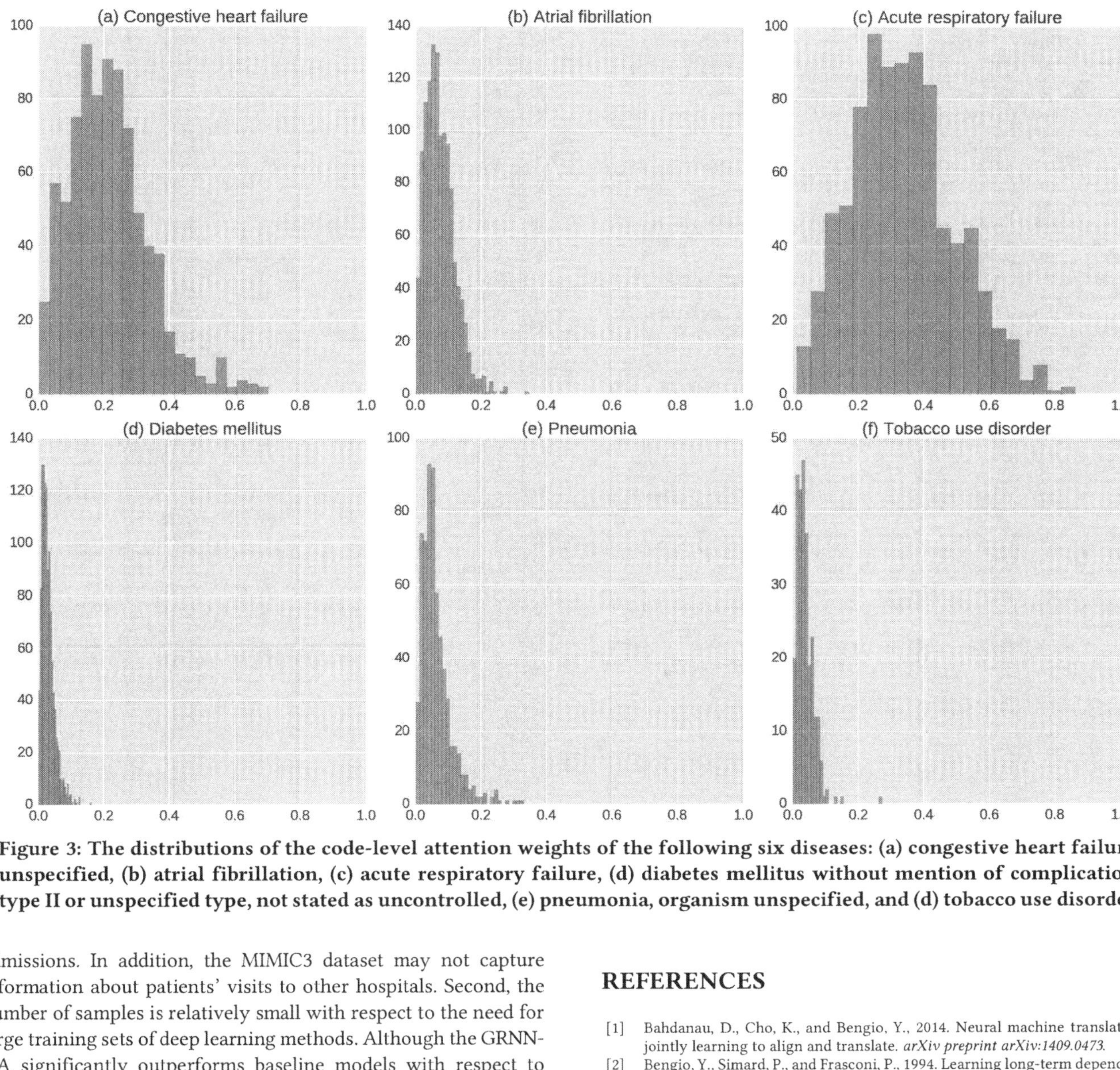

Figure 3: The distributions of the code-level attention weights of the following six diseases: (a) congestive heart failure, unspecified, (b) atrial fibrillation, (c) acute respiratory failure, (d) diabetes mellitus without mention of complication, type II or unspecified type, not stated as uncontrolled, (e) pneumonia, organism unspecified, and (d) tobacco use disorder.

admissions. In addition, the MIMIC3 dataset may not capture information about patients' visits to other hospitals. Second, the number of samples is relatively small with respect to the need for large training sets of deep learning methods. Although the GRNN-HA significantly outperforms baseline models with respect to available data, we still expect to see improvement in its prediction accuracy and more reasonable attention weights if we have a larger sample size and longer medical histories of patients. Finally, we analyze only diagnostic codes for ease of interpretation of results. In future work, we aim to extend our analysis over other data types such as vital signs and laboratory tests.

ACKNOWLEDGMENTS

The authors are grateful to Li Tong and Janani Venugopalan for their valuable comments and suggestions.

REFERENCES

[1] Bahdanau, D., Cho, K., and Bengio, Y., 2014. Neural machine translation by jointly learning to align and translate. *arXiv preprint arXiv:1409.0473.*

[2] Bengio, Y., Simard, P., and Frasconi, P., 1994. Learning long-term dependencies with gradient descent is difficult. *IEEE Transactions on neural networks 5*, 2, 157-166.

[3] Bergstra, J., Breuleux, O., Bastien, F., Lamblin, P., Pascanu, R., Desjardins, G., Turian, J., Warde-Farley, D., and Bengio, Y., 2010. Theano: A CPU and GPU math compiler in Python. In *Proc. 9th Python in Science Conf*, 1-7.

[4] Brown, P.F., Desouza, P.V., Mercer, R.L., Pietra, V.J.D., and Lai, J.C., 1992. Class-based n-gram models of natural language. *Computational linguistics 18*, 4, 467-479.

[5] Cho, K., Courville, A., and Bengio, Y., 2015. Describing multimedia content using attention-based encoder-decoder networks. *IEEE Transactions on Multimedia 17*, 11, 1875-1886.

[6] Cho, K., Van Merriënboer, B., Gulcehre, C., Bahdanau, D., Bougares, F., Schwenk, H., and Bengio, Y., 2014. Learning phrase representations using RNN encoder-decoder for statistical machine translation. *arXiv preprint arXiv:1406.1078.*

[7] Choi, E., Bahadori, M.T., Schuetz, A., Stewart, W.F., and Sun, J., 2016. RETAIN: Interpretable Predictive Model in Healthcare using Reverse Time Attention Mechanism. *arXiv preprint arXiv:1608.05745.*

[8] Chollet, F., 2015. Keras.

[9] Chung, J., Gulcehre, C., Cho, K., and Bengio, Y., 2014. Empirical evaluation of gated recurrent neural networks on sequence modeling. *arXiv preprint arXiv:1412.3555.*

[10] Free, C., Phillips, G., Watson, L., Galli, L., Felix, L., Edwards, P., Patel, V., and Haines, A., 2013. The effectiveness of mobile-health technologies to improve health care service delivery processes: a systematic review and meta-analysis. *PLoS Med 10*, 1, e1001363.

[11] Frisse, M.E. and Holmes, R.L., 2007. Estimated financial savings associated with health information exchange and ambulatory care referral. *Journal of biomedical informatics 40*, 6, S27-S32.

[12] He, D., Mathews, S.C., Kalloo, A.N., and Hutfless, S., 2014. Mining high-dimensional administrative claims data to predict early hospital readmissions. *Journal of the American Medical Informatics Association 21*, 2, 272-279.

[13] Hochreiter, S., 1998. The vanishing gradient problem during learning recurrent neural nets and problem solutions. *International Journal of Uncertainty, Fuzziness and Knowledge-Based Systems 6*, 02, 107-116.

[14] Hochreiter, S. and Schmidhuber, J., 1997. Long short-term memory. *Neural computation 9*, 8, 1735-1780.

[15] Jensen, P.B., Jensen, L.J., and Brunak, S., 2012. Mining electronic health records: towards better research applications and clinical care. *Nature Reviews Genetics 13*, 6, 395-405.

[16] Johnson, A.E., Pollard, T.J., Shen, L., Lehman, L.-w.H., Feng, M., Ghassemi, M., Moody, B., Szolovits, P., Celi, L.A., and Mark, R.G., 2016. MIMIC-III, a freely accessible critical care database. *Scientific data 3.*

[17] Jones, S.S., Rudin, R.S., Perry, T., and Shekelle, P.G., 2014. Health information technology: an updated systematic review with a focus on meaningful use. *Annals of internal medicine 160*, 1, 48-54.

[18] Karpathy, A. and Fei-Fei, L., 2015. Deep visual-semantic alignments for generating image descriptions. In *Proceedings of the IEEE Conference on Computer Vision and Pattern Recognition*, 3128-3137.

[19] Kešelj, V., Peng, F., Cercone, N., and Thomas, C., 2003. N-gram-based author profiles for authorship attribution. In *Proceedings of the conference pacific association for computational linguistics, PACLING*, 255-264.

[20] Krizhevsky, A., Sutskever, I., and Hinton, G.E., 2012. Imagenet classification with deep convolutional neural networks. In *Advances in neural information processing systems*, 1097-1105.

[21] Lasko, T.A., Denny, J.C., and Levy, M.A., 2013. Computational phenotype discovery using unsupervised feature learning over noisy, sparse, and irregular clinical data. *PloS one 8*, 6, e66341.

[22] LeCun, Y., Bengio, Y., and Hinton, G., 2015. Deep learning. *Nature 521*, 7553, 436-444.

[23] Marafino, B.J., Davies, J.M., Bardach, N.S., Dean, M.L., Dudley, R.A., and Boscardin, J., 2014. N-gram support vector machines for scalable procedure and diagnosis classification, with applications to clinical free text data from the intensive care unit. *Journal of the American Medical Informatics Association 21*, 5, 871-875.

[24] Matthews, B.W., 1975. Comparison of the predicted and observed secondary structure of T4 phage lysozyme. *Biochimica et Biophysica Acta (BBA)-Protein Structure 405*, 2, 442-451.

[25] Mikolov, T., Chen, K., Corrado, G., and Dean, J., 2013. Efficient estimation of word representations in vector space. *arXiv preprint arXiv:1301.3781.*

[26] Miotto, R., Li, L., Kidd, B.A., and Dudley, J.T., 2016. Deep Patient: An Unsupervised Representation to Predict the Future of Patients from the Electronic Health Records. *Scientific Reports 6.*

[27] Nguyen, P., Tran, T., Wickramasinghe, N., and Venkatesh, S., 2016. Deepr: A Convolutional Net for Medical Records. *arXiv preprint arXiv:1607.07519.*

[28] Pak, A. and Paroubek, P., 2010. Twitter as a Corpus for Sentiment Analysis and Opinion Mining. In *LREc.*

[29] Pedregosa, F., Varoquaux, G., Gramfort, A., Michel, V., Thirion, B., Grisel, O., Blondel, M., Prettenhofer, P., Weiss, R., and Dubourg, V., 2011. Scikit-learn: Machine learning in Python. *Journal of Machine Learning Research 12*, Oct, 2825-2830.

[30] Pham, T., Tran, T., Phung, D., and Venkatesh, S., 2016. DeepCare: A Deep Dynamic Memory Model for Predictive Medicine. In *Pacific-Asia Conference on Knowledge Discovery and Data Mining* Springer, 30-41.

[31] Rios, A. and Kavuluru, R., 2013. Supervised extraction of diagnosis codes from EMRs: role of feature selection, data selection, and probabilistic thresholding. In *Healthcare Informatics (ICHI), 2013 IEEE International Conference on* IEEE, 66-73.

[32] Rocktäschel, T., Grefenstette, E., Hermann, K.M., Kočiský, T., and Blunsom, P., 2015. Reasoning about entailment with neural attention. *arXiv preprint arXiv:1509.06664.*

[33] Sainath, T.N., Mohamed, A.-r., Kingsbury, B., and Ramabhadran, B., 2013. Deep convolutional neural networks for LVCSR. In *Acoustics, speech and signal processing (ICASSP), 2013 IEEE international conference on* IEEE, 8614-8618.

[34] Steiger, J.H., 1980. Tests for comparing elements of a correlation matrix. *Psychological bulletin 87*, 2, 245-251.

[35] Yang, Z., Yang, D., Dyer, C., He, X., Smola, A., and Hovy, E., 2016. Hierarchical attention networks for document classification. In *Proceedings of the 2016 Conference of the North American Chapter of the Association for Computational Linguistics: Human Language Technologies.*

Confused or not Confused?

Disentangling Brain Activity from EEG Data Using Bidirectional LSTM Recurrent Neural Networks

Zhaoheng Ni
The Graduate Center, City University of New York
New York, NY 10016, USA
zni@gradcenter.cuny.edu

Ahmet Cem Yuksel
The Graduate Center, City University of New York
New York, NY 10016, USA
ayuksel@gradcenter.cuny.edu

Xiuyan Ni
The Graduate Center, City University of New York
New York, NY 10016, USA
xni2@gradcenter.cuny.edu

Michael I Mandel
Brooklyn College, City University of New York
Brooklyn, NY 11210, USA
mim@mr-pc.org

Lei Xie*
Hunter College, City University of New York
New York, NY 10065, USA
lxie@iscb.org

ABSTRACT

Brain fog, also known as confusion, is one of the main reasons for low performance in the learning process or any kind of daily task that involves and requires thinking. Detecting confusion in a human's mind in real time is a challenging and important task that can be applied to online education, driver fatigue detection and so on. In this paper, we apply Bidirectional LSTM Recurrent Neural Networks to classify students' confusion in watching online course videos from EEG data. The results show that Bidirectional LSTM model achieves the state-of-the-art performance compared with other machine learning approaches, and shows strong robustness as evaluated by cross-validation. We can predict whether or not a student is confused in the accuracy of 73.3%. Furthermore, we find the most important feature to detecting the brain confusion is the gamma 1 wave of EEG signal. Our results suggest that machine learning is a potentially powerful tool to model and understand brain activity.

CCS CONCEPTS

•**Computing methodologies** → **Neural networks; Feature selection;** •**Applied computing** → *Bioinformatics;*

KEYWORDS

Confusion Detection, EEG, LSTM, Machine Learning

ACM Reference format:
Zhaoheng Ni, Ahmet Cem Yuksel, Xiuyan Ni, Michael I Mandel, and Lei Xie. 2017. Confused or not Confused?. In *Proceedings of ACM-BCB'17, August 20–23, 2017, Boston, MA, USA.*, 6 pages.
DOI: http://dx.doi.org/10.1145/3107411.3107513

*The corresponding author

Permission to make digital or hard copies of all or part of this work for personal or classroom use is granted without fee provided that copies are not made or distributed for profit or commercial advantage and that copies bear this notice and the full citation on the first page. Copyrights for components of this work owned by others than ACM must be honored. Abstracting with credit is permitted. To copy otherwise, or republish, to post on servers or to redistribute to lists, requires prior specific permission and/or a fee. Request permissions from permissions@acm.org.
ACM-BCB'17, August 20–23, 2017, Boston, MA, USA.
© 2017 ACM. ISBN 978-1-4503-4722-8/17/08...$15.00
DOI: http://dx.doi.org/10.1145/3107411.3107513

1 INTRODUCTION

1.1 Motivation

Brain fog is a constellation of symptoms that include reduced mental acuity and cognition, inability to concentrate and multitask, and loss of short-term and long-term memory. It is well distributed among not only patients with brain diseases but also healthy people [1]. Brain confusion, which is one of the symptoms of brain fog, can reduce people's concentration and cognition. Detecting and preventing brain confusion is very important and has many benefits. When a driver is confused, his/her cognition is reduced. This is very dangerous and can cause serious consequences. Another example is Massive Open Online Course (MOOC), which is an online course aiming at unlimited participation and open access via the web. Although there are several MOOC websites, the format still has shortcoming compared with traditional classes. Valerie et al. [2] showed that the lack of feedback is one of the main problems of student-teacher long distance communication. The students may feel confused about the lecture while the teacher doesn't notice and continues the lecture. If there is a practical approach to detect student's confusion immediately, it will help teachers understand better the students' status and react accordingly.

Electroencephalography (EEG) is an electro-physiological monitoring method to record electrical activity of the brain. In clinical contexts, EEG refers to the recording of the brain's spontaneous electrical activity over a period of time, as recorded from multiple electrodes placed on the scalp. It measures voltage fluctuations resulting from ionic currents within the neurons of the brain. EEG is most often used to diagnose epilepsy, which causes abnormalities in EEG readings. It is also used to diagnose sleep disorders, coma, encephalopathy, and brain death. Our motivation for choosing EEG signals as the data for detecting confusion in people's brains is that EEG signal is continuous and contains some patterns of status transitions. Our hypothesis is that when people are confused, their EEG signal will differ from normal. It is possible to build a model to analyze the continuous data and predict whether the subject is confused or not.

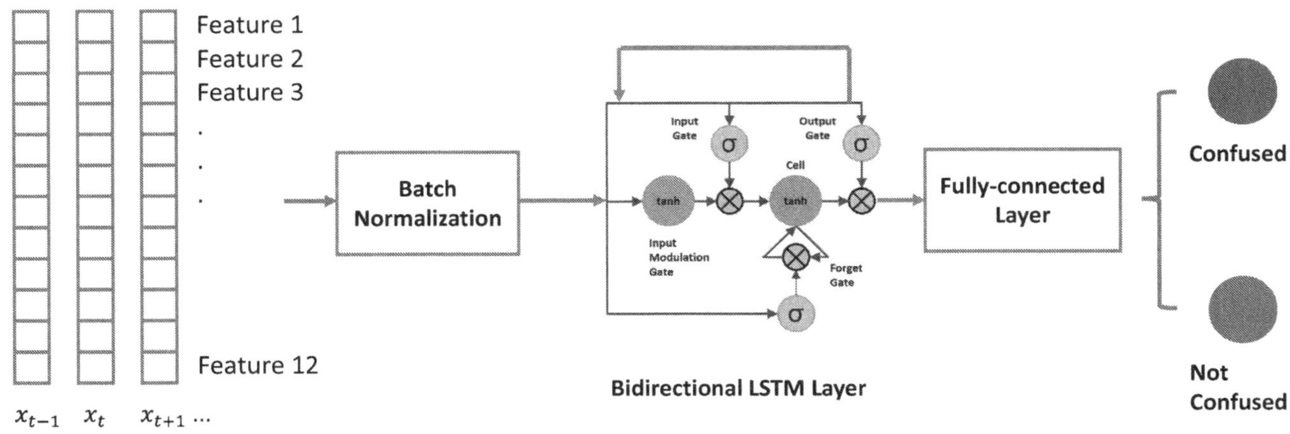

Figure 1: Framework of Bidirectional LSTM model.

1.2 Related Work

There is a general agreement that visual inspection of EEG waveforms patterns can reliably identify driver fatigue or drowsiness. There are many researchers applying machine learning methods to EEG data to accomplish different tasks, such as driver fatigue detection. Yeo et al. [3] used Support Vector Machines (SVMs) to detect the drowsiness of car drivers. Their results showed that extracting features from four EEG frequency bands achieved 99.3% accuracy. Besides drowsiness, Subashi et al. [4] applied SVM classifiers to predict if EEG signals represented epileptic seizures and achieved 100% accuracy. Wang et al. [5] showed the possibility of using EEG data to detect the confusion of students when they watch MOOC videos. They analyzed the EEG data using Gaussian Naive Bayes classifiers. The Gaussian Naive Bayes classifiers achieved a classification accuracy of 57%. The current paper explores methods to improve this confusion classification result on the same dataset.

Recently, deep learning has shown its power on many classification-related tasks compared with traditional machine learning approaches. Boureau et al. [6] proposed a Deep Belief Network (DBN) that can learn a high-level feature based on raw input and can capture higher-order dependencies between observed variables. Hajinoroozi et al. [7] applied DBNs to EEG signals to predict drivers' cognitive states. Classifiers using the features learned by DBNs outperformed those using Principal Component Analysis (PCA) features. Lee et al. [8] introduced convolutional DBNs to learn better feature representations and outperformed machine learning approaches using raw features. Due to the fact that the EEG signal is a time-series, however, detecting events in EEG signals using fixed-length features may be difficult.

Laurent et al. [2] proposed a Hidden Markov Model-based approach for mental state detection in EEG signals. Petrosiana et al. [9] showed that Recurrent Neural Networks can identify early signs of Alzheimer's disease in long-term EEG recordings. Few studies focus on detecting confusion from EEG signals using Deep Neural Networks (DNNs). Since LSTM Recurrent Neural Networks can easily analyze time-series data, the current study applies them to detecting confusion in EEG signal.

We utilize batch normalization, which has been shown to speed training of DNNs. Ioffe et al. [10] proposed a batch normalization layer, which uses mini-batch statistics to standardize features in deep neural networks which can achieve the same accuracy in much less time. Laurent et al. [11] showed that applying batch normalization, to Recurrent Neural Networks leads to a faster convergence of training.

1.3 Problem Statement

Given EEG data from 10 college students, our task is to predict their confusion using machine learning methods. The data is from the "EEG brain wave for confusion" data set, an EEG data from a Kaggle challenge [12]. 10 students were assigned to watch 20 videos, 10 of which were pre-labeled as "easy" and 10 as"difficult". Each video was about 2 minutes long. For "difficult" videos, the two-minute clip was taken abruptly from the middle of a topic to make the videos more confusing.

The students wore a single-channel wireless MindSet EEG device that measured activity over the frontal lobe. The MindSet measures the voltage between an electrode resting on the forehead and two electrodes (one ground and one reference) each in contact with an ear [13]. After each session, the student rated his/her confusion level on a scale of 1-7, where one corresponded to the least confused and seven corresponded to the most confused. These labels were quantized into two classes representing whether the students were confused or not. The two-class label serves as the target of our prediction task.

Since the confusion label is true or false, our problem is a two-class classification problem. In theory, many machine learning approaches can be applied to this task. To take advantage of EEG data's properties, we propose a confusion detection framework using LSTM Recurrent Neural Networks.

Table 1: Features extracted from MindSet. Table from [5]

Features	Description	Sampling rate	Statistic
Attention	Proprietary measure of mental focus	1 Hz	Mean
Meditation	Proprietary measure of calmness	1 Hz	Mean
Raw	Raw EEG signal	512 Hz	Mean
Delta	1-3 Hz of power spectrum	8 Hz	Mean
Theta	4-7 Hz of power spectrum	8 Hz	Mean
Alpha1	Lower 8-11 Hz of power spectrum	8 Hz	Mean
Alpha 2	Higher 8-11 Hz of power spectrum	8 Hz	Mean
Beta1	Lower 12-29 Hz of power spectrum	8 Hz	Mean
Beta 2	Higher 12-29 Hz of power spectrum	8 Hz	Mean
Gamma1	Lower 30-100 Hz of power spectrum	8 Hz	Mean
Gamma2	Higher 30-100 Hz of power spectrum	8 Hz	Mean

2 CONFUSION DETECTION FRAMEWORK

Based on the consideration that these data are continuous in time and the detection sample should not be too long to permit real-time processing, we propose a confusion detection framework as shown in Figure 1. The dataset provides EEG features organized by time. We then use Batch Normalization to normalize the value of each feature to have a mean of 0 and standard deviation of 1. We then train a Bidirectional LSTM model and evaluate its performance using 5-fold cross validation. We also test the contribution of each variable to the model and rank these contributions. The framework is designed as followed:

2.1 Feature Extraction

The EEG data can be downloaded from the Kaggle website [12], which provides open source data for various challenges. In the EEG dataset, 10 college students are asked to wear a wireless single-channel MindSet EEG device [13] that measured activity over the frontal lobe and to watch 10 2-minute long videos. The MindSet extracted the features that are shown in Table 1. "Attention" measures the mental focus of the student, and "Meditation" measures calmness. "Raw" is the average of the original EEG signals. The following features are values in different frequency regions of the power spectrum. The sampling frequency for the features extracted from the MindSet is 2 Hz. For each sample point, there are 14 features extracted from EEG signals, shown in Table 2.

"Subject id" ranges from 0 to 9, representing the subject of each recording, "video id" is the same for videos. We don't use them as features in our model. In the feature representations, we also have power spectrum for specific frequencies, which are all continuous data.

For each subject watching a video, features are extracted at a sampling frequency of 2 Hz. The final features are truncated to around one-minute long. So there are around 120 sample features for each data point. For models the only accept fixed-length features, we took the minimum number of samples (112 samples at last) and concatenated all the time steps to create a single feature vector. For the LSTM, the length of the time-series data is 112, each with a 12-dimension feature. In the end there are 100 data points, each with 112×12 features in total.

Table 2: Features with index.

F1	Attention
F2	Meditation
F3	Raw
F4	Delta
F5	Theta
F6	Alpha1
F7	Alpha2
F8	Beta1
F9	Beta2
F10	Gamma1
F11	Gamma2
F12	Predefined Label
F13	Subject id
F14	Video id

2.2 RNN-LSTM and Bidirectional LSTM

In RNNs, back propagation flows through many layers, passing through many stages of multiplication. During the training process, error messages flowing backward in time tend to either blow up, which may lead to oscillating weights, or vanish in which case they become too small to provide a learning signal.

Exploding gradients can be mitigated via truncation or squashing. Vanishing gradients are more difficult to fix. The Long Short-Term Memory RNN (LSTM) addresses this problem by introducing memory units to RNNs. The memory units help preserve the error signal so that it is large enough to be back propagated through time and layers, thereby opening a channel that links remote causes and effects. The architecture of the LSTM is shown in Figure 2.

Given an input sequence $X = (x_1, x_2, x_3, \dots, x_T)$, the hidden state in time t in RNN is defined as followed:

$$h_t = \Phi(W_h h_{t-1} + W_x x_t + b), \tag{1}$$

where $W_h \in \mathbb{R}^{d_h \times d_h}$, $W_x \in \mathbb{R}^{d_x \times d_x}$, $b \in \mathbb{R}^{d_h}$.

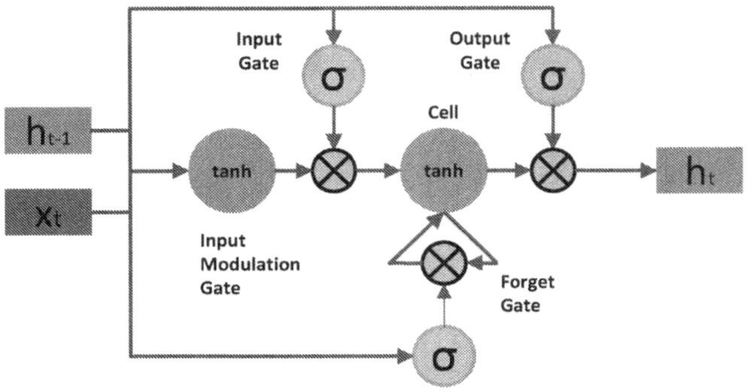

Figure 2: Architecture inside LSTM cell.

The architecture of the LSTM is defined as followed:

$$\begin{pmatrix} \tilde{f_t} \\ \tilde{i_t} \\ \tilde{o_t} \\ \tilde{g_t} \end{pmatrix} = W_h h_{t-1} + W_x x_t + b, \tag{2}$$

$$c_t = \sigma(\tilde{f_t}) \odot c_{t-1} + \sigma(\tilde{i_t}) \odot tanh(\tilde{g_t}), \tag{3}$$

$$h_t = \sigma(\tilde{o_t}) \odot tanh(c_t), \tag{4}$$

where $W_h \in \mathbb{R}^{d_h \times 4d_h}$, $W_x \in \mathbb{R}^{d_x \times 4d_x}$, σ is the logistic function, and the $\odot$ operation is the Hadamard product.

LSTM RNNs can learn long-term temporal dynamics that traditional RNNs cannot. Using its memory cells, it learns to forget previous memories and considering the current input, determines how much of the memory to be transferred to the next hidden state. In our case, since EEG features arrive over time, the LSTM can incorporate context information across time to improve performance.

While LSTMs predict the current output based on previous inputs, bidirectional LSTMs predict the current output based on both the past and the future. The basic idea is to predict the future based on the past and predict the past based on the future, then take the average of these two outputs as the finial output. In this way both future and past context information can be utilized to improve performance.

In our framework, we set the Bidirectional LSTM layer to have 50 neural units. The activation function in the LSTM layer is *tanh*. After the LSTM layer, the hidden states are fed into a fully connected layer with a sigmoid activation function, which produces output value between 0 and 1.

2.3 Batch Normalization

Training Deep Neural Networks is complicated by the fact that the distribution of the inputs to each layer changes during training, as the parameters of the previous layers change [14]. This slows down the training by requiring lower learning rates and careful parameter initialization, and makes it notoriously difficult to train models with saturating nonlinearities.

Recently, Ioffe et al. [10] proposed a Batch Normalization method which can be built as a sub-architecture into a model. Batch Normalization allows us to use much higher learning rates and be less careful about initialization. They showed that adding Batch Normalization to a state-of-the-art image classification model yields a substantial speedup in training. By further increasing the learning rates, removing Dropout, and applying other modifications afforded by Batch Normalization, their model matches the previous state of the art in only a small fraction of the number of training steps and then beats the state of the art in single-network image classification. Batch Normalization is defined as:

$$BN(x, \gamma, \beta) = \beta + \gamma \frac{x - \hat{\mathbb{E}}(x)}{\sqrt{V\hat{a}r(x) + \epsilon}} \tag{5}$$

where x is the vector that needs to be normalized. $\hat{\mathbb{E}}(x)$ and $V\hat{a}r(x)$ are the expectation and variance of the current mini-batch of x, respectively, ϵ is a constant added to the mini-batch variance for numerical stability, and β is a parameter to shift the normalized value.

In our framework, we normalize the training data in a feature-wise fashion (i.e., each feature dimension is normalized to have a mean of 0 and standard deviation of 1 across each batch of samples). The batch size is set to 20, which corresponds to our test data size. After Batch normalization, we put the normalized features into our Bidirectional LSTM model.

3 EXPERIMENTS

3.1 Baseline Models

To evaluate our framework's performance, we designed several baseline machine learning approaches, listed in Table 3.

Table 3: Baseline classification methods for classifying confusion.

Baseline Classification Methods
SVM (linear kernel)
SVM (rbf kernel)
SVM (sigmoid kernel)
K-Nearest Neighbors
Convolutional Neural Network
Deep Belief Network
RNN-LSTM

We apply three SVM classifiers using different kernel functions. We use grid search to tune the parameters C ranging in (1, 10, 100, 1000) and γ ranging in (10^{-3}, 10^{4}) for each kernel, respectively. We also apply a K Nearest Neighbor classifier as another baseline method. We use different K parameter values ranging from 2 to 5 and choose the highest accuracy as the final result. To compare the results of different neural networks, we use Convolutional Neural Network, Deep Belief Network, and a single-layer LSTM Recurrent Neural Network (RNN-LSTM) to classify the EEG data.

3.2 Variable Selection

To test which feature of the EEG dataset contributes the most to our model, we propose a variable selection method to find the most important feature in our Bidirectional LSTM model. Not putting all the features into the model, instead we leave one single feature out. Then we run the experiments with the remaining features. After we get the average accuracy across cross validation folds, we rank the accuracy from lowest to highest, providing the feature importance from highest to lowest.

4 RESULTS

4.1 Cross-Validation Results

To evaluate the models, we perform 5-fold cross validation. The result is shown in Table 4.

Table 4: Average accuracy for 5-fold cross validation.

Classification methods	Accuracy(%)
SVM (linear kernel)	67.2
SVM (rbf kernel)	51.3
SVM (sigmoid kernel)	51.0
K-Nearest Neighbors	51.9
Convolutional Neural Network	64.0
Deep Belief Network	52.7
RNN-LSTM	69.0
Bidirectional LSTM	73.3

The results show that the Bidirectional LSTM achieves the best performance compared to the other methods. Due to the nature of the dataset, the Deep Belief Network cannot approximate the data distribution with only 100 data points. Neither can the Convolutional Neural Network or K-Nearest Neighbors classifier. The SVM with linear kernel performs similarly to the RNN-LSTM, and outperforms the SVMs with more complex kernels. This result implies that the feature space is almost linearly separable. Classifying the data in this linear space is better than other spaces, which may cause overfitting.

Then we evaluated the robustness of the RNN-LSTM model and the Bidirectional LSTM model by analyzing the accuracy of each iteration of cross validation. The results are shown in Figures 3 and 4

The accuracy across the five folds of the RNN-LSTM model varies from 60 percent to 85 percent, while that of the Bidirectional LSTM model varies from 71 percent to 74 percent. These results show that the Bidirectional LSTM model not only outperforms all the other methods, but also is consistent.

4.2 Variable Selection

To find the feature that makes the most contribution to the model, we ran 12 experiments, each leaving out one feature. The accuracy of each of these classifiers is shown in Figure 5. From the rank among accuracies, we can see that losing feature 10, which is the gamma-1 feature, decreases the accuracy the most. The beta-2 and attention features also lead to large decreases in performance.

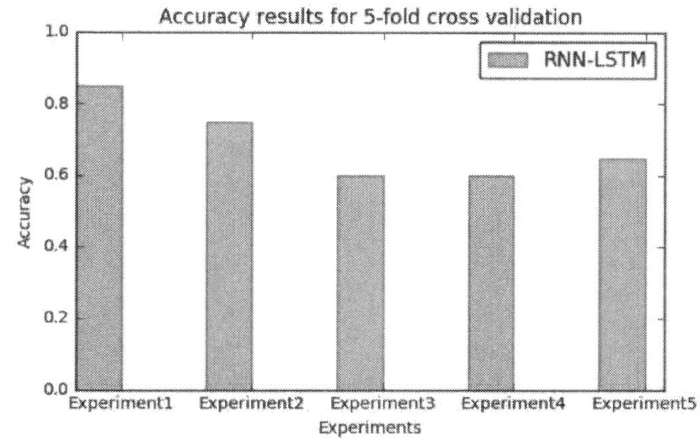

Figure 3: Accuracy variation of RNN-LSTM model.

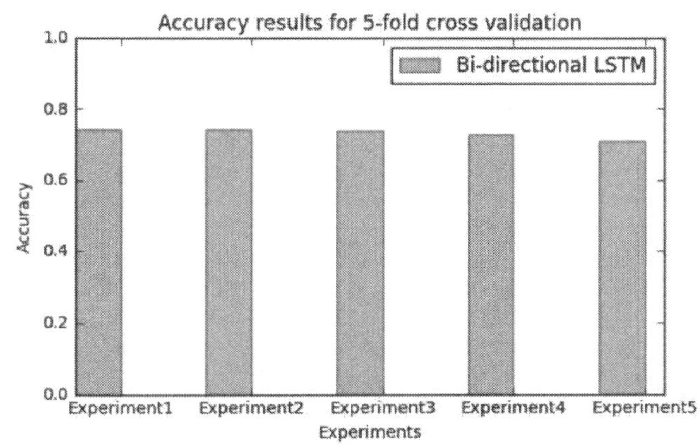

Figure 4: Accuracy variation of Bidirectional LSTM model.

Based on the rank of the features, we can select the most important features for the confusion detection system. In this way we can still maintain high accuracy and also make it possible for the system to detect confusion in real time.

We also found that the pre-defined video label contributed the least to our Bidirectional LSTM model's accuracy. The subjective judgment of video difficulty of the experiment designer is different from that of the students, a very interesting point. This can help teachers identify topics that students don't understand, while the teachers may think the class is easy for students.

For this specific dataset, it is hard to build a model from so few examples. Hence for deep neural networks such as the DBN and CNN it is hard to tune the parameters perfectly and easy to overfit. However, for the LSTM, though different time steps (i.e. feature for each 0.5 second) input to the LSTM share the same weights in the neural network, the forget gate can learn how to make use of previous hidden states. Bidirectional LSTMs make use of sequential information in both directions and learn a better representation. Adding context information helps us build a more robust and accurate model.

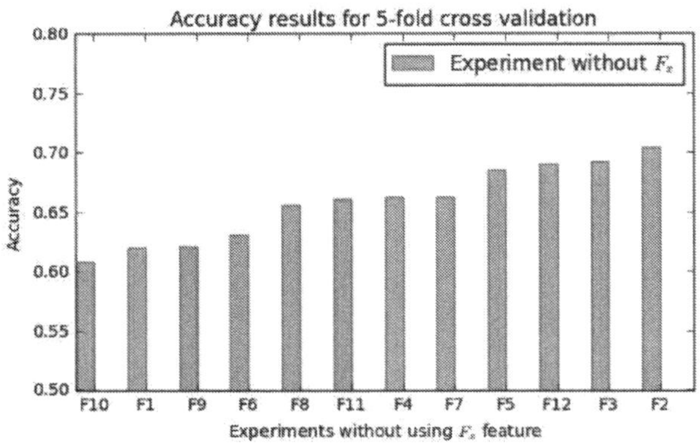

Figure 5: Accuracy without specific feature from 12 features. Ranked from lowest accuracy to highest.

5 CONCLUSIONS

We have proposed a Bidirectional LSTM Recurrent Neural Network framework to detect students' confusion when watching online course videos. The accuracy achieved by our model is higher than other machine learning approaches including a single-layer RNN-LSTM model and achieves the state-of-the-art result. The architecture of the Bidirectional LSTM model takes advantage of time-series features and helps improve performance. By analyzing the contribution of each feature to the model, we find the "gamma-1" and "attention" features are the most important in this task. We plan to validate our model on a larger EEG dataset. We also plan to apply our Bidirectional LSTM model on other EEG-related tasks, such as driver drowsiness detection.

ACKNOWLEDGMENTS

We appreciate reviewers constructive commends. This research was supported under National Institute of Health Grant R01LM011986.

REFERENCES

[1] Theoharis Constantin Theoharides, Julia M Stewart, and Erifili Hatziagelaki. Brain "fog," inflammation and obesity: key aspects of neuropsychiatric disorders improved by luteolin. *Frontiers in neuroscience*, 9:225, 2015.

[2] Laurent Vézard, Pierrick Legrand, Marie Chavent, Frédérique Faïta-Aïnseba, and Leonardo Trujillo. EEG classification for the detection of mental states. *Applied Soft Computing*, 32:113–131, 2015.

[3] Mervyn VM Yeo, Xiaoping Li, Kaiquan Shen, and Einar PV Wilder-Smith. Can SVM be used for automatic EEG detection of drowsiness during car driving? *Safety Science*, 47(1):115–124, 2009.

[4] Abdulhamit Subasi and M Ismail Gursoy. EEG signal classification using PCA, ICA, LDA and support vector machines. *Expert Systems with Applications*, 37(12):8659–8666, 2010.

[5] Haohan Wang, Yiwei Li, Xiaobo Hu, Yucong Yang, Zhu Meng, and Kai-min Chang. Using EEG to improve massive open online courses feedback interaction. In *AIED Workshops*, 2013.

[6] Y-lan Boureau, Yann L Cun, et al. Sparse feature learning for deep belief networks. In *Advances in neural information processing systems*, pages 1185–1192, 2008.

[7] Mehdi Hajinoroozi, Tzyy-Ping Jung, Chin-Teng Lin, and Yufei Huang. Feature extraction with deep belief networks for driver's cognitive states prediction from EEG data. In *Signal and Information Processing (ChinaSIP), 2015 IEEE China Summit and International Conference on*, pages 812–815. IEEE, 2015.

[8] Honglak Lee, Roger Grosse, Rajesh Ranganath, and Andrew Y Ng. Convolutional deep belief networks for scalable unsupervised learning of hierarchical representations. In *Proceedings of the 26th annual international conference on machine learning*, pages 609–616. ACM, 2009.

[9] AA Petrosian, DV Prokhorov, W Lajara-Nanson, and RB Schiffer. Recurrent neural network-based approach for early recognition of alzheimer's disease in EEG. *Clinical Neurophysiology*, 112(8):1378–1387, 2001.

[10] Sergey Ioffe and Christian Szegedy. Batch normalization: Accelerating deep network training by reducing internal covariate shift. *arXiv preprint arXiv:1502.03167*, 2015.

[11] Tim Cooijmans, Nicolas Ballas, César Laurent, Çağlar Gülçehre, and Aaron Courville. Recurrent batch normalization. *arXiv preprint arXiv:1603.09025*, 2016.

[12] Haohan Wang. EEG brain wave for confusion, 2016. Online: https://www.kaggle.com/wanghaohan/eeg-brain-wave-for-confusion.

[13] NeuroSky. NeuroSky's eSense meters and detection of mental state. 2009.

[14] César Laurent, Gabriel Pereyra, Philémon Brakel, Ying Zhang, and Yoshua Bengio. Batch normalized recurrent neural networks. In *Acoustics, Speech and Signal Processing (ICASSP), 2016 IEEE International Conference on*, pages 2657–2661. IEEE, 2016.

[15] Sepp Hochreiter and Jürgen Schmidhuber. Long short-term memory. *Neural computation*, 9(8):1735–1780, 1997.

Predicting the Effect of Point Mutations On Protein Structural Stability

Roshanak Farhoodi
UMass Boston
100 W.T. Morissey Blvd.
Boston, Massachusetts 02125
roshanak.farhoodi001@umb.edu

Max Shelbourne
Western Washington University
516 High Street
Bellingham, WA 98225
shelbom@wwu.edu

Rebecca Hsieh
Western Washington University
516 High Street
Bellingham, WA 98225
hsiehr@wwu.edu

Nurit Haspel
UMass Boston
100 W.T. Morissey Blvd.
Boston, Massachusetts 02125
nurit.haspel@umb.edu

Brian Hutchinson†
Western Washington University
516 High Street
Bellingham, WA 98225
brian.hutchinson@wwu.edu

Filip Jagodzinski
Western Washington University
516 High Street
Bellingham, WA 98225
filip.jagodzinski@wwu.edu

ABSTRACT

Predicting how a point mutation alters a protein's stability can guide drug design initiatives which aim to counter the effects of serious diseases. Mutagenesis studies give insights about the effects of amino acid substitutions, but such wet-lab work is prohibitive due to the time and costs needed to assess the consequences of even a single mutation. Computational methods for predicting the effects of a mutation are available, with promising accuracy rates. In this work we study the utility of several machine learning methods and their ability to predict the effects of mutations. We *in silico* generate mutant protein structures, and compute several rigidity metrics for each of them. Our approach does not require costly calculations of energy functions that rely on atomic-level statistical mechanics and molecular energetics. Our metrics are features for support vector regression, random forest, and deep neural network methods. We validate the effects of our *in silico* mutations against experimental $\Delta\Delta G$ stability data. We attain Pearson Correlations upwards of 0.69.

CCS CONCEPTS

•**Computing methodologies** → *Machine learning algorithms;*
•**Applied computing** → *Bioinformatics; Molecular structural biology;*

KEYWORDS

Machine Learning; Protein Structure; Mutation; Support Vector Regression; Random Forest; Deep Neural Network; Rigidity Analysis

† Brian Hutchinson has a joint appointment with Pacific Northwest National Laboratory, 1100 Dexter Ave N., Seattle, WA 98109.

Permission to make digital or hard copies of all or part of this work for personal or classroom use is granted without fee provided that copies are not made or distributed for profit or commercial advantage and that copies bear this notice and the full citation on the first page. Copyrights for components of this work owned by others than ACM must be honored. Abstracting with credit is permitted. To copy otherwise, or republish, to post on servers or to redistribute to lists, requires prior specific permission and/or a fee. Request permissions from permissions@acm.org.
ACM-BCB'17, August 20-23, 2017, Boston, MA, USA.
© 2017 ACM. 978-1-4503-4722-8/17/08...$15.00
DOI: http://dx.doi.org/10.1145/3107411.3107492

1 INTRODUCTION

The amino acid sequence of a protein determines its structure and as a result, its function. Even a single amino acid substitution can alter a protein's shape, which can be the cause of a debilitating disease. For example, mutations of α-galactosidase cause Fabry disease, a disorder that causes cardiac and kidney complications [14].

Wet-lab experiments can be used to engineer a protein with a specific mutation, and the mutant directly assessed to infer the effect of that amino acid substitution. The wild type and mutant proteins can be denatured to determine their relative unfolding rates, from which the free energy of unfolding ($\Delta\Delta G$) can be calculated; it is an indicator of whether a particular mutation is stabilizing or destabilizing, and to what degree. Existing experimental data about various mutations performed in physical proteins is available in the ProTherm database [23].

Unfortunately, conducting mutagenesis experiments on physical proteins is expensive and time consuming, and thus experimental data about the effects of mutations is limited. Therefore, computational methods can be helpful in estimating the effects of a mutation on a protein structure, and several computational methods have been developed in the past, with various degrees of success.

2 RELATED WORK

In this section we survey the existing experimental and computational work for predicting the effects of amino acid substitutions.

2.1 Experiments On Physical Proteins

Wet-lab experiments provide the gold standard for directly measuring the effect of mutations on a protein structure, measured by $\Delta\Delta G$ with respect to the wild type. Matthews *et al.* have generated many mutants of Lysozyme from the Bacteriophage T4 [2, 7, 12, 26–28]. They found that residues with high mobility or high solvent accessibility are much less susceptible to destabilizing substitutions. Although such studies provide precise, experimentally verified insights into the role of a residue based on its mutation, they are time consuming and cost prohibitive. Additionally, some mutations are so destabilizing that the mutant protein cannot be crystallized at all. Thus, only a small subset of all possible mutations can be studied explicitly.

2.2 Computational Approaches

To complement and inform mutation studies performed on physical proteins, computational methods have been developed over the years. These methods strive to predict the effects of mutations. Several have high prediction and accuracy rates in the 70-80% range.

Several computational methods for assessing the effects of mutations fix the atoms in the backbone of a protein and proceed to search for the best side-chain conformation, while others utilize rotamer side chain libraries to adjust a structure in response to an amino acid substitution [11, 19, 31]. Other approaches [24] rely on heuristic energy measurements to predict the stability of proteins in which side chains are perturbed. Yet another approach [15] estimates the folding free energy changes upon mutations using database-derived potentials. Prevost [32] used Molecular Dynamics simulations to study the effect of mutating Barnase, and concluded that the major contributions to the free energy difference arose from non-bonded interactions. Thus, progress has been made in predicting the effects of mutations on protein stability. However, many such methods rely on computationally intensive energy calculations and are therefore time intensive.

2.3 Combinatorial, Rigidity Based Methods

A first generation of rigidity-based mutation analysis tools are available, but the extent of the types of *in silico* mutations that they can perform are limited. Rigidity Analysis [16] is a combinatorial technique for identifying the flexible regions of biomolecules. Figure 1 depicts the cartoon and rigidity analysis results of PDB file 1hvr of HIV-1 protease. Rigidity analysis, which identifies rigid clusters of atoms, is distinguished from most other methods because it is fast. It does not rely on homologous protein data, nor costly all-atom energy calculations.

In our previous work we used rigidity analysis to probe how a mutation **to glycine** destabilizes a protein's structure. We compared the rigidity properties of the wild type structure to the rigidity properties of a mutant that we generated *in silico* using KINARI-Mutagen [18]. On input of a Protein Data Bank (PDB) structure file, KINARI-Mutagen identifies hydrogen bonds and hydrophobic interactions. The stabilizing interactions involving the atoms of the side chain being mutated to Glycine are removed from the protein's model. This is equivalent to computationally mutating a specific residue to Glycine, the smallest amino acid which has no side chain atoms that form stabilizing bonds.

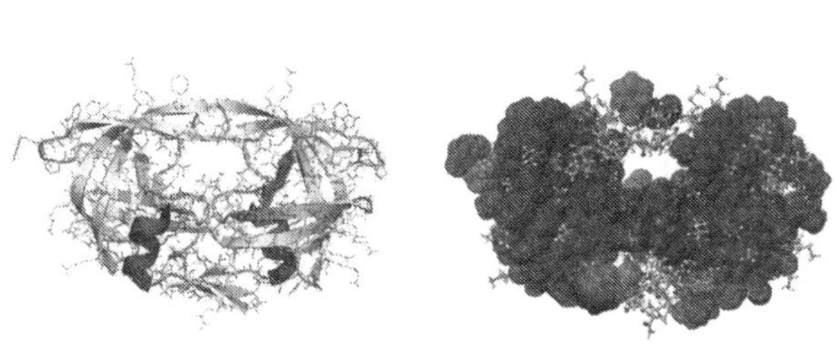

(a) Cartoon Representation (b) Rigidity Analysis

Figure 1: Rigidity analysis of PDB file 1hvr identifies sets of atoms belonging to rigid clusters. The largest rigid cluster is shown orange, which spans both halves of the protein. The larger rigid clusters are (cluster size : count) 11:6, 12:5, 15:2, 16:2, 19:2, 23:1 and 1371:1.

The effect of a mutation on the protein's structural stability can be correlated with its effect on a protein's rigidity. In our previous work [5, 17] we measured the effect of the mutation by recording the change in the size of the Largest Rigid Cluster (LRC) of the mutant versus the wild type (WT, non-mutated protein). The rationale was that the LRC is an indicator of the protein's rigidity or flexibility. Predictions were validated against experimentally derived $\Delta\Delta G$ unfolding measurements from the ProTherm [23] database. A negative $\Delta\Delta$G value for a mutant structure reveals that the mutant is less stable than the wild type, and thus the amino acid substitution is destabilizing.

2.4 Machine Learning Based Approaches

Machine learning (ML) is a branch of artificial intelligence involving algorithms that allow programs to classify, group, and learn from data. The regression problem proceeds via the following steps: a) represent a set of known data points as a set of *feature vectors* labeled by the corresponding output value, b) train a model that best maps inputs to the correct output, c) use the model to make predictions on a set of new (e.g. held out) data points. In Section 5 we detail each of the Support Vector Regression, Random Forest, and Deep Neural Network methods we used.

Machine learning and statistical methods have been developed to help predict the effects of mutations and to infer which residues are critical. Cheng *et al.* [10] used Support Vector Machines to predict with 84% accuracy the sign of the stability change for a protein due to a single-site mutation. Also, data of amino acid replacements that are tolerated within families of homologous proteins have been used to devise stability scores for predicting the effect of residue substitutions [35], which has been extended and implemented into an online web server [36].

In our previous work [17], we used an SVM-based model that combines rigidity analysis and evolutionary conservation, in addition to amino acid type and solvent accessible surface area, to a dataset of proteins with experimentally known critical residues. We achieved over 77% accuracy in predicting the sign of the change of stability for a single point mutation to Glycine and Alanine.

Brender, *et al* [9], have developed a scoring function that reasons about protein-protein interfaces. They used sequence- and residue-level energy potentials in conjunction with a Random Forest (RF) approach to achieve a Pearson correlation coefficient of approximately 80% between predicted and observed binding free-energy changes upon mutations. Jia, *et al* [20], have employed a variety of Machine Learning Tools to generate several models based on thermostability data for assessing the effects of single point mutations. They used 798 mutants from 51 different protein structures for which there is $\Delta\Delta G$ data, and attained accuracy rates ranging from 78-85% among SVM, RF, NBC, KNN, ANN, and PLS approaches, with the Random Forest Approach having the highest accuracy. Li, *et al* [25], developed a model based on the Random Forest algorithm for predicting thermostability changes due to amino acid substitutions. In their approach they relied on 41 features, and achieved accuracies of 79.9%, 78.2%, and 78.7% for single, double, and multiple point mutation.

3 MOTIVATION

As discussed above, existing experimental methods still provide only partial information about the effects of mutations. Computational methods can complement this information, but many existing methods are time consuming, or alternatively, their accuracy could be improved. There is a need for fast and reliable methods that can efficiently analyze the effect of a mutation of an amino acid on the structure of a protein. As already discussed, machine learning based methods have been used in the past by us and other researchers, and they are a promising avenue to explore further.

In this work, we present fast and efficient machine learning and graph theory based methods for predicting the effect of a mutation on a protein structure. Through rigidity analysis, support vector regression, random forests and deep neural networks, we predict the effect of a mutation on the $\Delta\Delta G$ of a protein. We validated our results by using experimental data from the ProTherm database. Our approach achieves strong performance in predicting the effect of a single point mutation on a protein structure, while being fast enough to run in a few minutes and sometimes seconds.

Several aspects of our work distinguish it from others. **Firstly, none of our features in use by our machine learning models require calculating energetics of various biophysical phenomena**. The calculation of our metrics does not require costly calculations based on statistical mechanics nor molecular energetics. Our features are strictly structure-based, which is a purposeful design decision to enable near real-time run-times. **Secondly, the number of data points that we use is far more than most others have used**. With 2,072 mutations for which we have experimentally derived data from ProTherm, our dataset far surpasses in size most others, many of which have fewer than 1,000. This dataset is far greater than we used in our previous work due to our recent expanded capabilities of generating mutations *in silico* [4]. **Lastly, the majority of our features in use by our models are derived from quick calculations detailing the rigidity properties of mutant, wild type pairs of protein structures**. With the exception of our past proof-of-concept work, nobody else has used rigidity metrics on a large scale to assess their use in enhancing models for predicting the effects of mutations.

4 DATA PREPARATION

Here we describe the source of our data, including how we processed the ProTherm $\Delta\Delta G$ values, how we generated *in silico* mutants, and the split of the data into training, development and testing sets for building our machine learning models. We enumerate our features and explain how each is normalized.

4.1 ProTherm Data, *in silico* mutants

We downloaded the entire ProTherm plain-text database, and identified 2,072 entries for single mutations with $\Delta\Delta G$ values. See Table 1 for a summary of the proteins and their mutations that we retained.

We used our in-house software, Protein Mutation High Throughput (ProMuteHT) [4], for quickly generating protein mutants *in silico*, with the mutations for which we had ProTherm stability data. That software is composed of several parts, including custom scripts and algorithms, integrated with off-the-shelf open access tools and libraries. It generates large-to-small (LTS) as well as small-to-large

Table 1: Summary of the data obtained from ProTherm.

Parsed Numerical Results	
Unique Proteins	44
Total Mutations	2,072
Mutated Residues that are Hydrophobic	892
Mutated Residues that are Aromatic	161
Mutated Residues that are Polar	432
Mutated Residues that are Charged	654
Mutated Residues with 0-30% SASA	932
Mutated Residues with 30-50% SASA	532
Mutated Residues with 50+ SASA% SASA	608

(STL) amino acid substitutions. For an LTS mutation ProMuteHT removes atoms from a PDB file to simulate a substitution. For example, mutating Leucine to Alanine involves removing from a protein structure file the CG, CD1 and CD2 atoms from the Leucine being mutated. When a small residue is mutated to a larger one, the STL module relies on the freely availably SCWRL 4.0 [22] software that makes predictions about a side chain's orientation. To account for the steric clashes that might arise due to replacing a small residue with a larger one, we used the NAMD [30] software to perform 500 energy minimization steps, requiring approximately 5 seconds.

The rigidity of each mutant and its wild type were analyzed using the publicly available rigidity software by Fox *et. al* [13]. The rigidity output data is of the form *rigid cluster size : count*, which offers the distribution of clusters and their sizes that were identified. We used the rigidity data for each mutant, wild type pair to calculate 6 different rigidity metrics. See [3] for a complete discussion explaining the motivation and utility of these metrics at inferring the effects of mutations.

4.2 Features and Data Split

From the ProTherm data and our rigidity calculations, we derived the following 60 features:

- WT SASA: how exposed to the surface a residue is.
- WT Secondary Structure: four features indicating whether the mutation took place in a sheet, coil, turn or helix.
- Temperature and pH at which the experiment for calculating $\Delta\Delta G$ was performed.
- Rigidity Distance (RD): one of *lm, sig1, sig2, sig3, sig4, sig5*. See [3] for a full explanation.
- WT Rigid Cluster Fraction: 24 features giving the fraction of atoms in the WT that belong to rigid clusters of size $2, 3, \ldots, 20$, 21-30, 31-50, 51-100, 101-1000 and 1001+, respectively.
- Mutation Rigid Cluster Fraction: 24 features giving the fraction of atoms in the mutation belonging to the same set of bins as above.
- Residue type: four binary features indicating whether the residue is Charged (D, E, K, R), Polar (N, Q, S, T), Aromatic (F, H, W, Y), or Hydrophobic (A,C,G,I,L,M,P,V).

These features along with their normalization scheme and range are summarized in Table 2.

Table 2: Feature summary.

Feat. #	Name	Norm.	Range
1	WT SASA	None	$[0, 1]$
2-5	WT Secondary Structure	None	$\{0, 1\}$
6	Temperature	0-1	$[0, 1]$
7	Potential of Hydrogen (pH)	pH	$\approx [-1, 1]$
8	Rigidity Distance (RD)	Standard	$\mathbb{R}$
9-32	WT Rigid Cluster Frac.	None	$[0, 1]$
33-56	Residue Rigid Cluster Frac.	None	$[0, 1]$
57-60	Residue Type	None	$\{0, 1\}$

Normalization "0-1" refers to the mapping

$$\frac{x_i - \min(x)}{\max(x) - \min(x)} \quad (1)$$

while "pH" normalization refers to a slight variant that maps pH of 0 to -1, 7 to 0 and 14 to 1:

$$\frac{x_i - 7}{7}. \quad (2)$$

Standardization refers to normalizing the feature to be zero-mean and unit-variance:

$$\frac{x_i - \mu}{\sigma} \quad (3)$$

We estimated the feature mean (μ) and standard deviation (σ) on the training set, and used these same values to transform the development and test sets. Our $\Delta\Delta G$ labels were also standardized prior to training using the training set statistics. The $\Delta\Delta G$ values fall in the range of [-5.02, 4.55] after standardization.

Our 2,072 data points were randomly split into a training set (1,438 data points), a development set (324 data points) and a test set (310 data points), under the constraint that all instances of each WT appear in a single dataset. **This constraint was used so that we can assess how well our methods generalize to new protein wild types, and means that our reported results are more pessimistic than they would be under an unconstrained random split.**

5 METHODS : SVR, RF, DNN

In this section, we provide more details about three popular machine learning methods, Random Forest, Support Vector Regression and Deep Neural Networks, that we used for predicting $\Delta\Delta G$. That is, we solve a regression problem: our objective is building a function that minimizes the difference between calculated (predicted) and actual observed target values for all data points in the training set.

5.1 SVR

Support Vector Machines are supervised learning models that are widely used for solving classification and regression problems. In case of Support Vector Regression (SVR), the aim is to minimize the generalization error bound in order to achieve strong generalization [6]. The generalization error bound is the combination of the training error and a regularization term that controls the complexity of hypothesis space [34]. SVR works based on generating a regression function in a high dimensional feature space where the input data are implicitly mapped using a *kernel function*. The kernel function can be linear or nonlinear (polynomial, sigmoid or radial basis).

The SVR model that we used in this work for $\Delta\Delta G$ prediction were implemented using Scikit-learn [29], which is a free machine learning library for the Python programming language. Scikit-learn offers a variety of easy to use clustering, classification and regression algorithms implementations.

We used grid search to tune the parameters of the model using our training and development sets. For the SVR model we tuned three main parameters; the penalty parameter of the error term (regularization constant) C, the kernel function and the kernel coefficient γ. Using the development set, we evaluated the prediction accuracy using values chosen from range of 0.1 to 1000 for C, examined RBF, linear and sigmoid as the kernel functions and changed γ values from 0.0001 to 1. The lowest error was achieved with C equal to 150, when the RBF kernel was used and γ was set to 0.1.

5.2 Random Forest

Random forests (RFs) work by utilizing the power of decision trees. A decision tree infers decision rules from the training data to carry out a regression or classification task. The decision rules are generated based on the value of a feature that yields the best split of the training data using a metric such as information gain or Gini impurity index. A random forest is an ensemble learning method that fits a number of decision trees on multiple random sub-samples of the training set and then use averaging to boost the accuracy of the prediction and control overfitting [8]. Each tree uses a sample size the same as the original training set. The method allows these samples to be the same as the original training set (Replicate) or to be drawn with replacement (Bagging).

The random forest model was also implemented using Scikit-learn. To tune the model parameters, we examined the prediction error while changing the number of estimators (trees in the forest) from 10 to 1000. The accuracy of the model did not show improvements when beyond 150 estimators were used. For resampling method, we used bagging (Bootstrap Aggregation), where each tree in the forest was trained using random subsamples from the training set chosen with replacement. Bagging showed over 30 percent improvement in accuracy compared to Replicate. For the rest of parameters such as maximum depth of the tree and minimum number of samples required to split an internal node we used Scikit-learn default values, but plan to include these parameters in our future tuning experiments.

5.3 DNN

A Deep Neural Network (DNN) is a supervised machine learning model in which the input undergoes multiple "hidden" layers of non-linear transformation before a prediction is made. This generalizes the standard, shallow neural network which has only a single hidden layer. Predictions, y, in our DNN are made according to the following:

$$y = W_{(L)}^T h_{(L)} + b_{(L)} \quad (4)$$

$$h_{(i)} = g\left(W_{(i-1)}^T h_{(i-1)} + b_{(i-1)}\right) \text{ for } i = 1, \ldots, L \quad (5)$$

where $h_{(0)}$ denotes the input x, and our model parameters are matrices $W_{(0)}, \ldots, W_{(L)}$ and vectors $b_{(0)}, \ldots, b_{(L)}$. The hidden activation function is denoted g; we explored two options: $g(z) = \tanh(z)$ and $g(z) = \text{ReLU}(z) = \max(0, z)$. Our model parameters are learned using first order optimization algorithms to minimize training set mean squared error (MSE).

We implemented our DNN using TensorFlow [1], an open-source machine learning toolkit. Our hyperparameters were tuned using a combination of random search and the Spearmint [33] tool. Spearmint is a Bayesian hyperparameter optimization tool, incrementally exploring the hyperparameter space with the objective of maximizing expected improvement.

We tuned several hyperparameters on the developed set: number of hidden layers (1 - 4), number of units per layer (10 - 100), learning rate (0.0001 - 0.5), weight initialization range (0.0001 - 0.1), activation function (tanh, ReLU), and the optimizer used for back-propagation (stochastic minibatch gradient descent, adam [21]).

6 RESULTS

The SVR, RF and DNN models were trained initially using the training set and the hyperparameters were tuned to optimize development set performance as described in Section 5. After the optimal parameters were identified, in a final round of training for SVR and RF, the samples in training set and development set were combined and used as the training set. For DNN, whose results were highly dependent on the initial random weight initialization, we omitted this step of combination and retraining, and simply used the best model trained on the training set alone. We repeated our experiments using the features mentioned in Section 4 for six configurations where in each configuration we included one RD measure for training. The prediction accuracy of the models on the test set was then evaluated using two metrics. We calculated Root Mean Square Error (RMSE) and the Pearson correlation coefficient between predicted and expected (actual) $\Delta\Delta G$ values. The prediction accuracy of the three models for each RD measure is presented in Table 3. As shown in the table, the RF model consistently outperformed the SVR and DNN models by having lower RMSE and higher correlation coefficients. The DNN performance typically falls in-between the other two. This relative ordering is fairly consistent regardless of the RD value used as a feature to train the models. Averaged over the six experiments (last rows of Table 3), the RF gives the best performance and the SVR gives the worst. While the RF RMSE and correlation variation over different RDs is rather small, RF generated the least RMSE (0.820) and highest correlation (0.694) when *sig2* was used in the feature set. With SVR and DNN *sig1* and lm showed the best performance among the RDs, respectively.

7 DISCUSSION

To assess the utility of our three models in predicting the values of $\Delta\Delta G$ due to point mutations, we compared the Pearson Correlation Coefficients of our Random Forest model (our highest scoring average) against equivalent coefficients for 12 other approaches that we found in the literature [20]. Our Pearson Correlation Coefficient value of 0.689 would rank our RF approach 9th of 12, with Prethemut, ProMaya, and ELASPIC having attained higher correlation coefficient values of 0.72, 0.74, and 0.77, respectively. Understandably, any such comparison must be taken with caution,

Table 3: Prediction accuracy (RMSE = Root Mean Square Error, C = Pearson Correlation)

RD	Accuracy Measure	SVR	RF	DNN
lm	RMSE	0.961	0.839	0.865
	C	0.534	0.673	0.647
sig1	RMSE	0.945	0.822	0.963
	C	0.555	0.691	0.528
sig2	RMSE	0.960	0.820	0.957
	C	0.534	0.694	0.537
sig3	RMSE	0.959	0.822	0.946
	C	0.539	0.692	0.551
sig4	RMSE	0.986	0.827	0.931
	C	0.500	0.687	0.571
sig5	RMSE	0.966	0.821	0.942
	C	0.524	0.694	0.557
Avg.	RMSE	0.963	0.825	0.934
	C	0.531	0.689	0.565

for example due to different data set sizes, different cross validation approaches, as well as data preprocessing. And although for this work we focused on a regression model rather than attempting a binary classification of the data, it is not uncommon in the literature for binary classification models to excluded neutral (0±0.5 $\Delta\Delta G$ kCal/mol) mutants. Any such similar pre-processing, which we did not do, might be employed by other methods and models attempting regression analyses, which might ultimately affect a ranking of different approaches.

Another important point worth reiterating is that none of our features were attained via direct calculations of energetic terms arising from changes in a protein's confirmation due to a mutation. Although we previously indicated that doing so was a conscious effort on our part aiming to minimize costly energy calculations, indeed excluding energy terms might be related to a possible limitation of our approach. Namely, an amino acid substitution on a protein structure might induce a destabilizing or stabilizing effect due to reasons that are not structure based, which our method would not be able to reason about because our features are all purely structural in nature.

8 CONCLUSIONS

We developed and present several machine learning based methods to predict the effects of mutations on the stability of a protein. In particular, our method predicts the change to the free energy of unfolding upon mutation ($\Delta\Delta G$), using a combination of graph based rigidity analysis and features like solvent accessible surface area (SASA), temperature, pH, and the type of mutated amino acid. We trained and tested our methods on an extensive dataset taken from the ProTherm database, which contains experimental information about point mutations. We show that our algorithm, especially the Random Forest (RF) based predictor, can predict the $\Delta\Delta G$ with high accuracy.

Our next steps involve developing methods to assess the effects of multiple point mutations. While many methods predict the effect of a single mutation on a protein structure, only very few of them assess how multiple amino acid substitutions affect a protein's structure and stability. Additionally, since our method is very fast and efficient, requiring as little as a few seconds to conduct a computational experiment, we are developing a server which will allow users to conduct hypothesis testing about the effects of mutations. We envision that our server will run in near real-time, and thus permit high-throughput studies, enabling screening a large number of amino acid substitutions and their effect on a protein's stability.

9 CONTRIBUTIONS

Roshanak conducted the RF and SVR analysis, Max performed the DNN analysis, and Rebecca preprocessed and aggregated the ProTherm data. Brian, Nurit, and Filip supervised the work. All authors contributed to the analysis of the results and the writing of the manuscript.

ACKNOWLEDGEMENTS

The work is supported in part by NSF grant CCF-1421871 (NH). BH and MS gratefully acknowledge the support of NVIDIA Corporation with the donation of the Titan X GPU used for this research.

REFERENCES

[1] M. Abadi, A. Agarwal, P. Barham, E. Brevdo, Z. Chen, C. Citro, G.S. Corrado, A. Davis, J. Dean, M. Devin, S. Ghemawat, I. Goodfellow, A. Harp, G. Irving, M. Isard, Y. Jia, R. Jozefowicz, L. Kaiser, M. Kudlur, J. Levenberg, D.Mané, R. Monga, S. Moore, D. Murray, C. Olah, M. Schuster, J. Shlens, B. Steiner, I. Sutskever, K. Talwar, P. Tucker, V. Vanhoucke, V. Vasudevan, F. Viégas, O. Vinyals, P. Warden, M. Wattenberg, M. Wicke, Y. Yu, and X. Zheng. 2015. TensorFlow: Large-Scale Machine Learning on Heterogeneous Systems. (2015). http://tensorflow.org/ Software available from tensorflow.org.

[2] T. Alber, S. Dao-pin, J.A. Wozniak, S.P. Cook, , and B.W. Matthews. 1987. Contributions of hydrogen bonds of Thr 157 to the thermodynamic stability of phage T4 lysozyme. *Nature* 330 (1987), 41–46.

[3] E. Andersson, R. Hsieh, H. Szeto, R. Farhoodi N. Haspel, and F. Jagodzinski. 2016. Assessing how multiple mutations affect protein stability using rigid cluster size distributions. In *Computational Advances in Bio and Medical Sciences (ICCABS), 2016 IEEE 6th International Conference on*. IEEE, 1–6.

[4] E. Andersson and F. Jagodzinski. 2017. ProMuteHT : A High Throughput Compute Pipeline for Generating Protein Mutants in silico. In *CSBW (Computational Structural Bioinformatics Workshop), in proc. of ACM-BCB (ACM International conference on Bioinformatics and Computational Biology)*.

[5] B. Akbal-Delibas, F. Jagodzinski, and N. Haspel. 2013. A Conservation and Rigidity Based Method for Detecting Critical Protein Residues. *BMC Structural Biology* 13(Suppl 1) (2013), S6.

[6] D. Basak, S. Pal, and D.C. Patranabis. 2007. Support vector regression. *Neural Information Processing-Letters and Reviews* 11, 10 (2007), 203–224.

[7] J.A. Bell, W.J. Becktel, U. Sauer, W.A. Baase, , and B.W. Matthews. 1992. Dissection of helix capping in T4 lysozyme by structural and thermodynamic analysis of six amino acid substitutions at Thr 59. *Biochemistry* 31 (1992), 3590–3596. Issue 14.

[8] L. Breiman. 2001. Random forests. *Machine Learning* 45, 1 (2001), 5–32.

[9] J. Brender and Y. Zhang. 2015. Predicting the effect of mutations on protein-protein binding interactions through structure-based interface profiles. *PLoS Computational Biology* 11, 10 (2015), e1004494.

[10] J. Cheng, A. Randall, and P. Baldi. 2006. Prediction of Protein Stability Changes for Single-Site Mutations Using Support Vector Machines. *PROTEINS: Structure, Function, and Bioinformatics* 62 (2006), 1125–1132.

[11] R.L. Jr. Dunbrack and M. Karplus. 1994. Conformational analysis of the backbone-dependent rotamer preferences of protein sidechains. *Nature Structural Biology* 1 (1994), 334–340. Issue 5.

[12] A.E. Eriksson, W.A. Baase, X.J. Zhang, D.W. Heinz, E.P. Baldwin, and B.W. Matthews. 1992. Response of a protein structure to cavity-creating mutations and its relation to the hydrophobic effect. *Science* 255 (1992), 178–183.

[13] N. Fox, F. Jagodzinski, and I. Streinu. 2012. Kinari-lib: a C++ library for pebble game rigidity analysis of mechanical models. *Minisymposium on Publicly Available Geometric/Topological Software* (2012).

[14] S.C. Garman and D.N. Garboczi. 2002. Structural basis of Fabry disease. *Molecular Genetics and Metabolism* 77, 1 (2002), 3–11.

[15] D. Gilis and M. Rooman. 1997. Predicting protein stability changes upon mutation usings database derived potentials : Solvent accessiblity determines the importances of local versus non-local interactions along the sequence. *Journal Molecular Biology* 272 (1997), 276–290. Issue 2.

[16] D.J. Jacobs, A.J. Rader, M.F. Thorpe, and L.A. Kuhn. 2001. Protein Flexibility Predictions Using Graph Theory. *Proteins* 44 (2001), 150–165.

[17] F. Jagodzinski, B. Akbal-Delibas, and N. Haspel. 2013. An Evolutionary Conservation & Rigidity Analysis Machine Learning Approach for Detecting Critical Protein Residues. In *CSBW (Computational Structural Bioinformatics Workshop), in proc. of ACM-BCB (ACM International conference on Bioinformatics and Computational Biology)*. 780–786.

[18] F. Jagodzinski, J. Hardy, and I. Streinu. 2012. Using rigidity analysis to probe mutation-induced structural changes in proteins. *Journal of Bioinformatics and Computational Biology* 10 (2012). Issue 3.

[19] J. Janin and S. Wodak. 1978. Conformation of amino acid side-chains in proteins. *Journal of Molecular Biology* 125 (1978), 357–386. Issue 3.

[20] L. Jia, R. Yarlagadda, and C.C. Reed. 2015. Structure Based Thermostability Prediction Models for Protein Single Point Mutations with Machine Learning Tools. *PloS One* 10, 9 (2015), e0138022.

[21] D. Kingma and J. Ba. 2014. Adam: A method for stochastic optimization. *arXiv preprint arXiv:1412.6980* (2014).

[22] G. Krivov, M. Shapovalov, and R.L. Dunbrack. 2009. Improved prediction of protein side-chain conformations with SCWRL4. *Proteins: Structure, Function, and Bioinformatics* 77, 4 (2009), 778–795.

[23] M.D. Kumar, K.A. Bava, M.M. Gromiha, P. Prabakaran, K. Kitajima, H. Uedaira, and A. Sarai. 2005. Protherm and Pronit : Thermodynamic databases for proteins and protein-nucleic acid interactions. *Nucleic Acids Research* 34 (2005), D204–D206.

[24] C. Lee and M. Levitt. 1991. Accurate prediction of the stability and activity effects of site-directed mutagenesis on a protein core. *Nature* 352 (1991), 448–451.

[25] Y. Li and J. Fang. 2012. PROTS-RF: a robust model for predicting mutation-induced protein stability changes. *PloS one* 7, 10 (2012), e47247.

[26] M. Matsumura, W.J. Becktel, and B.W. Matthews. 1988. Hydrophobic stabilization in T4 lysozyme determined directly by multiple substitutions of Ile 3. *Nature* 334 (1988), 406–410.

[27] B. Mooers, W.A. Baase, J.W. Wray, and B.W. Matthews. 2009. Contributions of all 20 amino acids at site 96 to the stability and structure of T4 lysozyme. *Protein Science* 18 (2009), 871–880. Issue 5.

[28] H. Nicholson, E. Soderlind, D.E. Tronrud, and B.W. Matthews. 1989. Contributions of left-handed helical residues to the structure and stability of bacteriophage T4 lysozyme. *Journal of Molecular Biology* 210 (1989), 181–193. Issue 1.

[29] F. Pedregosa, G. Varoquaux, A. Gramfort, V. Michel, B. Thirion, O. Grisel, M. Blondel, P. Prettenhofer, R. Weiss, V. Dubourg, J. Vanderplas, A. Passos, D. Cournapeau, M Brucher, M. Perrot, and E. Duchesnay. 2011. Scikit-learn: Machine Learning in Python. *Journal of Machine Learning Research* 12 (2011), 2825–2830.

[30] J.C. Phillips, R. Braun, W. Wang, J. Gumbart, E. Tajkhorshid, E. Villa, C. Chipot, R.D. Skeel, L. Kale, and K. Schulten. 2005. Scalable molecular dynamics with NAMD. *Journal of Computational Chemistry* 26, 16 (2005), 1781–1802.

[31] J.W. Ponder and F.M. Richards. 1987. Tertiary templates for proteins: Use of packing criteria in the enumeration of allowed sequences for different structural classes. *Journal of Molecular Biology* 193 (1987), 775–791. Issue 4.

[32] M. Prevost, S.J. Wodak, B. Tidor, and M. Karplus. 1991. Contribution of the hydrophobic effect to protein stability: analysis based on simulations of the Ile-96-Ala mutation in barnase. *Proceedings of the National Academy of Sciences* 88 (1991), 10880–10884. Issue 23.

[33] J. Snoek, H. Larochelle, and R.P. Adams. 2012. Practical Bayesian Optimization of Machine Learning Algorithms. In *Advances in neural information processing systems*. 2951–2959.

[34] M. Song, C.M. Breneman, J. Bi, N. Sukumar, K.P. Bennett, S. Cramer, and N. Tugcu. 2002. Prediction of protein retention times in anion-exchange chromatography systems using support vector regression. *Journal of Chemical Information and computer sciences* 42, 6 (2002), 1347–1357.

[35] C.M. Topham, N. Srinivasan, and T. Blundell. 1997. Prediction of the stability of protein mutants based on structural environment-dependent amino acid substitutions and propensity tables. *Protein Engineering* 10, 1 (1997), 7–21.

[36] C.L. Worth, R. Preissner, and L. Blundell. 2011. SDM-a server for predicting effects of mutations on protein stability and malfunction. *Nucleic Acids Research* 39 (2011), W215–W222. Issue Web Server Issue.

Synthesizing Species Trees from Unrooted Gene Trees: A Parameterized Approach

Jucheol Moon
Department of Computer Science
Iowa State University
Ames, Iowa 50010, USA
moon@iastate.edu

Oliver Eulenstein
Department of Computer Science
Iowa State University
Ames, Iowa 50010, USA
oeulenst@iastate.edu

ABSTRACT

Synthesizing species trees from a collection of smaller gene trees is a widely used approach for inferring credible species tree estimates. While corresponding computational problems are typically NP-hard, several of these problems have been effectively addressed by using the parameterized Strict Consensus Approach. This approach is limited to gene trees that are rooted. In practice, however, most gene trees are unrooted, and it is often difficult, if not impossible, to identify accurate rootings. Here, we address this stringent limitation by proposing efficient algorithms that adopt the parameterized Strict Consensus Approach to handle unrooted gene trees. Finally, we demonstrate the performance of our algorithms in a comparative study using empirical and simulated data sets.

CCS CONCEPTS

•Mathematics of computing → Trees; •Applied computing → Computational biology; Molecular evolution; Bioinformatics; •Theory of computation → *Design and analysis of algorithms;*

KEYWORDS

Guidance Tree based Unrooted Tree Fill-in; Guidance Tree based Tree Rooting; Pareto for Clusters; Strict Consensus Approach; Gene Duplication

1 INTRODUCTION

Phylogenetic tree inference of increasingly larger and more credible tree estimates is continuously enriching our fundamental knowledge about the evolutionary relationships of how evolutionary entities (e.g., molecular sequences, genomes, and species) have evolved over time. Through these relationships we are able to understand the general evolutionary principles of how evolutionary entities have evolved the way they are today. While these principles are already greatly benefitting our society and our economy (e.g., in the areas of epidemiology, vaccine development, and conservation biology) [19, 22, 23, 35, 43], they also allow us to predict how evolutionary entities may change in the future. Thus, phylogenetic trees can also be used as powerful predictive tools that are not only of fundamental importance to biology [13], but are also benefiting numerous applications in other research areas [25, 35].

Traditional phylogenetic tree inference approaches sample a single gene (gene family) for a set of species and construct the evolutionary history, or *gene tree*, of this gene. It is assumed that the gene tree is mimicking the evolution of the species, and, therefore, is identified with the species tree. However, gene trees for two distinct genes may differ due to complex evolutionary processes that affect the genomic locations differently (e.g., gene duplications, lateral transfer, or deep coalescence) [12, 36]. Therefore, identifying a gene tree with its species tree can result in largely misleading phylogenetic analyses. Furthermore, a gene might only have been sampled for a small number of species, and a small number of species in the resulting species tree can largely limit its benefit for phylogenetic analyzes [38].

In contrast, today's genomic data sets provide us with an unprecedented wealth of novel evolutionary information for credible phylogenetic studies. Such data sets provide us with thousands of genes (e.g., the human genome has about 21,000 genes [10, 15, 39]) sampled from across the species of interest, and make it possible to infer large-scale and credible phylogenetic species trees. However, inferring such phylogenetic tree estimates from genomic-sized data sets is one of the most complex and challenging problems in computational phylogenetics.

Median tree problems provide a powerful tool to synthesize large-scale species tree estimates from collections of discordant gene trees [5]. Given a collection of gene trees, *median tree problems* (also referred to as supertree problems [5]) seek a tree, called *median tree*, that is minimizing the overall distance to the input trees using a problem-specific measure. Median tree problems that are typically used in practice are NP-hard, and thus have been addressed by standard local search heuristics, which have produced some credible estimates of species trees [29, 47]. However, such heuristics are challenged to find a globally optimal species tree in a highly complex solution landscape whose size is double factorial in the size of the searched tree. In addition, this landscape has typically numerous local optima that can trap heuristic approaches [2].

Median tree problems, however, can be much more tractable and are better understood when their instances are *restricted* to gene trees whose leaf-genes are sampled from the same set of species [7]. While most median tree problems remain NP-hard in their restricted version, a class of such restricted problems has been effectively addressed using a parametrized approach, called *Strict Consensus Approach* [26, 34]. Most notably, this class includes the classic gene duplication [34], deep coalescence [26], and Robinson-Foulds [7] problems. It has been demonstrated that this approach

Permission to make digital or hard copies of all or part of this work for personal or classroom use is granted without fee provided that copies are not made or distributed for profit or commercial advantage and that copies bear this notice and the full citation on the first page. Copyrights for components of this work owned by others than ACM must be honored. Abstracting with credit is permitted. To copy otherwise, or republish, to post on servers or to redistribute to lists, requires prior specific permission and/or a fee. Request permissions from permissions@acm.org.
ACM-BCB'17, August 20-23, 2017, Boston, MA, USA.
© 2017 ACM. 978-1-4503-4722-8/17/08...$15.00
DOI: http://dx.doi.org/10.1145/3107411.3107450

can significantly improve on the scalability of such problems [26, 34].

In practice, however, the applicability of the Strict Consensus Approach has been severely limited due to its restriction to apply only to rooted gene trees that are sampled from the same set of species, while at the same time most available gene trees are sampled from various distinct sets of species [5] and are unrooted [21]. Motivated by the effectiveness of the Strict Consensus Approach, and in an effort to overcome its limitations, an efficient method has been developed that makes this approach applicable to unrestricted instances of rooted trees [32]. While this method is broadening the applicability of the Strict Consensus Approach, it is still limited to instances of rooted trees. However, the trees of most instances are inferred from molecular data, and standard phylogenetic inference methods, like maximum likelihood [16], maximum parsimony [17], or neighbor joining [44], only infer unrooted gene trees. Furthermore, it is often difficult, if not impossible, to identify accurate rootings [6, 8]. Recently, the first approach that makes the Strict Consensus Approach applicable to unrestricted and unrooted instances of phylogenetic trees has been introduced [33]. While this approach has shown promising initial results, its large runtime is typically prohibitive for inferring large-scale phylogenetic trees [33].

To overcome this stringent shortcoming, here, we introduce a substantially different approach together with efficient algorithms, and demonstrate that this approach allows large-scale phylogenetic tree inference using empirical published data sets.

1.1 Previous Work

The Strict Consensus Approach has been introduced in [26], which is applicable to a class of restricted median tree problems (i.e., problems where the input trees are restricted to a same leaf set) that satisfy the Pareto (for clusters) property [26, 50] and a substructure property [34]. The Pareto property has its roots in social choice theory [1], and various restricted median tree problems have been identified to satisfy this property [50].

A *cluster* for a node in a rooted tree is the set of all leaf-labels of the subtree rooted at this node. The set of clusters common to a collection $\mathcal{T}$ of restricted trees define the *strict consensus clusters* of $\mathcal{T}$ [45]. Strict consensus clusters form a rooted tree under the transitive reduction of the set-containment relationship between clusters, called the *strict consensus tree* of $\mathcal{T}$ [45].

When a collection of restricted trees that are rooted have clusters in common (i.e., the *strict consensus clusters* of these trees), then one would expect that an optimal species tree for these trees under any "reasonable" median tree problem would also contain these clusters. The Pareto property is formalizing this idea.

For a restricted median tree problem, when the strict consensus clusters of each instance are contained in the every corresponding solution, then this problem satisfies the *Pareto* property [50]. If there is at least one corresponding solution, then the problem satisfies a less stringent property referred to as the *weak Pareto* property [27]. Several restricted median tree problems are known to satisfy these properties, including the gene duplication problem [27], the deep coalescence problem [26], and the Robinson-Foulds problem [7]. While the first problem is only weak Pareto, the latter two problems are Pareto. Both versions of the Pareto property are not only valuable to practitioners for deciding which median tree problem might be most suitable for their analyses, but also, can lead to formal characterizations that reduce the complexity of such problems [26, 34]. Fig. 1 depicts an example, where the strict consensus tree of the input trees $T_1, \ldots, T_k$ is the tree G, which includes the multifurcation consisting of the *parent cluster* C_p and its *child clusters* $C_1, \ldots, C_l$. The optimal species tree, the tree S in the figure, refines this multifurcation based on the objective function of the applied median tree problem.

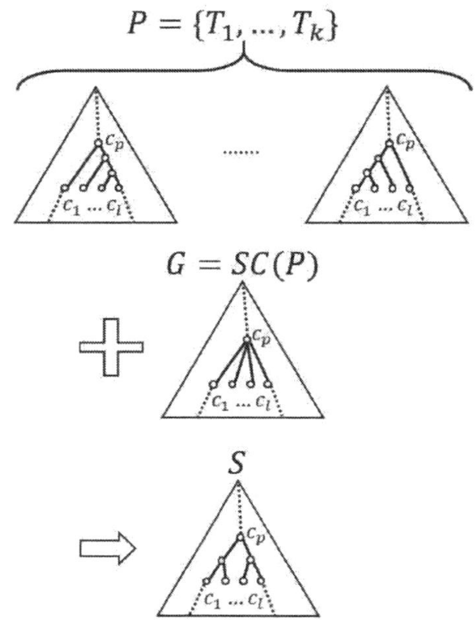

Figure 1: An illustration of the Strict Consensus Approach.
$P = \{T_1, \cdots, T_k\}$: input trees
G: the strict consensus tree of the input trees
S: the optimal species tree (a refinement of G)
$C_p, C_1, \cdots, C_l$: the common clusters of the input trees.

The Strict Consensus Approach refines all of the multifurcations of the strict consensus tree to reach an optimal solution. Each multifurcation is refined by solving a sub-instance of the original problem instance. Given a multifurcation, expressed as a parent and its child clusters, the corresponding *sub-instance* is computed by *trimming* the trees of the original instance to contain only clusters that are on a path between the parent cluster and its child clusters. Fig. 1 illustrates such a trimming for the parent cluster C_p and its child clusters $C_1, \ldots, C_l$, where the resulting sub-instance is depicted as a collection of subtrees of the input trees $T_1, \ldots, T_k$. Lastly, the refinements for each multifurcation of the strict consensus tree have to result in a solution of the corresponding restricted median tree problem, which is warranted if this problem is satisfying the substructure property that is formally described in Section 4 [34].

In summary, the Strict Consensus Approach is applicable to the median tree problems that are weak Pareto, or Pareto, and satisfy the substructure property. The restricted median tree problems that are known to satisfy these two properties are typically NP-hard, and the currently best-known algorithms solving them require exponential time in the size of the resulting median (species) tree. Consequently, the runtime of the Strict Consensus Approach is bound exponentially by the maximum node-degree of the strict consensus tree. In practice, if the size of sub-instances becomes prohibitive for the best known exact solution [9], then these instances often can be still effectively approached by using standard local search heuristics [48, 49]. It has been demonstrated that the Strict Consensus Approach can significantly improve on the accuracy and scalability of the gene duplication problem and the deep coalescence problem in their restricted version, when compared to the standard heuristics [26, 34].

To apply the Strict Consensus Approach to an unrestricted and rooted median tree problem, the Guidance tree based fill-in method has been introduced [32], which transforms a problem instance into the corresponding restricted and rooted one. Similarly, for an unrestricted and unrooted median tree problem, the Guidance tree based rooting and fill-in method has been described [33]. Given an instance of k unrestricted and rooted trees over n species, the algorithm to compute restricted and rooted trees requires $O(kn^2)$ time [32, 33]. For an unrestricted and unrooted problem instance, the algorithm is repeated for all edges of the Guidance tree, hence the overall process requires $O(kn^3)$ [33], which becomes prohibitive when computing large-scale median trees for thousands of species [33].

1.2 Our Contributions

Here we introduce a novel approach to adopt the Strict Consensus Approach to handle unrestricted and unrooted median tree problem instances of large size. This approach consists of new computational problems and efficient algorithms to solve them.

In detail, our approach transforms unrestricted and unrooted input trees into corresponding restricted and rooted ones. This transformation is guided by a special tree, called the *guidance tree*, that satisfies the *non-contradiction* property [42] to make this transformation possible. Existing methods, such as the Strict Consensus Merger(SCM) [18, 24], are available for the efficient construction of complex guidance trees that in practice often allow to break down instances into much smaller sub-instances [32].

The transformation of a collection of unrestricted and unrooted trees consists of two steps. First the trees are transformed into restricted trees by solving the "Guidance Tree based Fill-in Problem", which are then rooted by solving the "Guidance Tree based Rooting Problem". The *Guidance Tree based Fill-in Problem* seeks, for a given collection of unrestricted and unrooted trees $t_1, \ldots, t_k$ and a corresponding guidance tree G, a restricted version of the input trees $T_1, \ldots, T_k$ with an overall minimum number of nodes, such that (i) each restricted tree T_i displays one unrestricted tree t_i, and (ii) their strict consensus tree $SC(Q)$ is a refinement of, or identical to, the guidance tree G. The *Guidance Tree based Rooting Problem* seeks, for a given collection of restricted and unrooted trees $T_1, \ldots, T_k$ and a rooted guidance tree G', a rooted version of the input trees $T_1(e_1), \ldots, T_k(e_k)$ such that (i) each rooted tree $T_i(e_i)$ is the rooted version of one unrooted tree T_i and (ii) their strict consensus tree $SC(Q')$ is identical to the *rooted* guidance tree $G'(e_r)$.

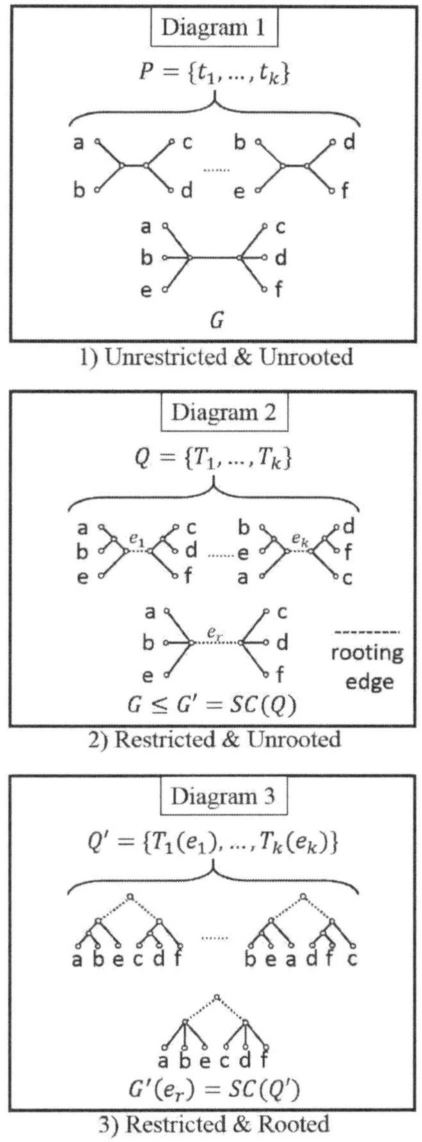

Figure 2: An illustration of the transformation from unrestricted and unrooted trees to the restricted and rooted trees. Diagram 1: Unrestricted → Diagram 2: Restricted Diagram 2: Unrooted → Diagram 3: Rooted

To solve the here introduced problems, the Guidance Tree based Fill-in Problem and the Guidance Tree based Rooting Problem, we describe efficient algorithms. Finally, we demonstrate the performance of our algorithms for the Strict Consensus Approach when applied to unrestricted and unrooted instances of the classical gene duplication problem, in comparison with standard heuristic approaches for this problem using simulated and published empirical data sets.

2 PRELIMINARIES AND BASIC DEFINITIONS

A *graph* G is an unordered pair (V, E) consisting of a non-empty node set $V(G)$, and an edge set $E(G)$. A *unrooted tree* T is an acyclic, connected, and undirected graph. The degree one nodes are called *leaves* and the remaining nodes are called *internal* nodes. The set of leaves in T is denoted by $\mathcal{L}(T)$, and the set of all internal nodes in T is denoted by $V_{int}(T)$. A *rooted tree* T is defined similar to an unrooted tree except that it has one distinguished node that leads a parent-child relationship on the nodes, called the *root* of T, denoted by $r(T)$.

Let $X \subseteq \mathcal{L}(T)$. The *subtree* of T induced by X, denoted by $T(X)$, is the minimal connected subtree of T that contains X. The *restricted subtree* of T induced by X, denoted by $T|X$ is the tree obtained from $T(X)$ by suppressing all nodes of degree two with the exception of the root for a rooted tree.

Let T be an unrooted tree. A *split* is an unordered bipartition of sets. The split in which parts are A and B is denoted by $A|B$. T *displays* a split $A|B$ if there is an edge in T whose removal gives trees T_1 and T_2 such that $A \subseteq \mathcal{L}(T_1)$ and $B \subseteq \mathcal{L}(T_2)$. A split $A|B$ is *full* if $A \cup B = \mathcal{L}(T)$. The set of all full splits displayed by T is denoted $\Sigma(T)$. Let $X \subseteq \mathcal{L}(T)$. The restriction of a split $\sigma \cap X$ is defined as $A \cap X|B \cap X$, $\Sigma(T|X) := \{x \cap X : \forall\sigma \in \Sigma(T) \wedge A \cap X \neq \emptyset \neq B \cap X\}$.

Let T be a rooted tree. We define $\leq_T$ to be the partial order on $V(T)$, where $x \leq_T y$ if y is a node on the path between $r(T)$ and x. If $x \leq_T y$, we call x a *descendant* of y, and y an *ancestor* of x. We also define $x <_T y$, if $x \leq_T y$ and $x \neq y$. If $\{x, y\} \in E(T)$ and $x \leq_T y$, then we call y the *parent* of x, denoted by $Pa_T(x)$, and x a *child* of y. The set of all children of y is denoted by $Ch_T(y)$. The *least common ancestor (LCA)* of $X \subseteq \mathcal{L}(T)$, denoted by $lca_T(X)$, is the unique smallest upper bound of X under $\leq_T$. For a node $v \in V(T)$, the subtree of T rooted at v is denoted by $T(v)$, the *cluster* of v by $C_T(v) := \mathcal{L}(T(v))$, and the set of all clusters of T by $\mathcal{H}(T)$.

Let T and T' be trees with the same leaves. We define $\leq$ to be the partial order on trees where $T \leq T'$ if $\Sigma(T) \subseteq \Sigma(T')$ for unrooted trees and $\mathcal{H}(T) \subseteq \mathcal{H}(T')$ for rooted trees. We say T' *refines* T if $T \leq T'$. Let $\mathcal{L}(t) \subseteq \mathcal{L}(T)$. A tree T *displays* tree t if $t \leq T|\mathcal{L}(t)$.

A *profile* is a collection of trees. Let $P = (t_1, \dots, t_k)$ be a profile, then its *leaves* is $\mathcal{L}(P) := \bigcup_i^k \mathcal{L}(t_i)$, and its *nodes cardinality* is $|P| := \sum_{i=1}^{k} |V(t_i)|$. A tree T is a *supertree* for P if $\mathcal{L}(T) = \mathcal{L}(P)$.

A tree T has the *non-contradiction* property if $T|\mathcal{L}(t_i) \leq t_i$ ($\forall i \in \{1, \cdots, k\}$). For example, if the supertree is a star tree it is satisfying the non-contradiction property for any input profile. A tree T is called *guidance tree* for P if T is a supertree for P and T has the non-contradiction property. A profile is called rooted (unrooted) if all trees in the profile are rooted (unrooted).

For each tree t in P we define its *span* $\langle t \rangle$, to be the set of all trees on $\mathcal{L}(P)$ displaying t. A *restricted span* $\langle t \rangle_G$ is the set of all trees on $\mathcal{L}(P)$ that display t and refine G. The *span* (*restricted span*) of P, denoted by $\langle P \rangle$ ($\langle P \rangle_G$), is the set of all profiles $Q = (T_1, \dots, T_k)$ where $T_i \in \langle t_i \rangle$ ($T_i \in \langle t_i \rangle_G$), $\forall i \in \{1, \cdots, k\}$. The *strict consensus splits (clusters)* of Q are the splits (clusters) common to the trees in Q, and the *strict consensus tree* of Q, denoted by $\mathcal{SC}(Q)$, is the tree that is defined exactly by these common splits (clusters).

3 GUIDANCE TREE BASED FILL-IN

We define the Guidance tree based unrestricted and unrooted profile fill-in problem and propose the efficient algorithm for solving this problem. For a given profile of unrestricted and unrooted trees $t_1, \dots, t_k$ and a corresponding guidance tree G, a restricted version of the input trees $T_1, \dots, T_k$ with an overall minimum number of nodes such that (i) each restricted tree T_i displays one unrestricted tree t_i and (ii) their strict consensus tree $\mathcal{SC}(Q)$ is a refinement of or identical to the guidance tree G.

PROBLEM 1. *(Guidance Tree based Fill-in Problem)*
Input: *An unrooted profile* $P = \{t_1, \cdots, t_k\}$ *such that* $\mathcal{L}(t_i) \subseteq \mathcal{L}(P)$ *and a guidance tree* G *for* P *such that* $\mathcal{L}(G) = \mathcal{L}(P)$ *and* $G|\mathcal{L}(t_i) \leq t_i$ ($\forall i \in \{1, \cdots, k\}$).
Output: *An unrooted profile* $Q \in \langle P \rangle_G$ *such that* $|Q| = \min_{Q' \in \langle P \rangle_G} |Q'|$.

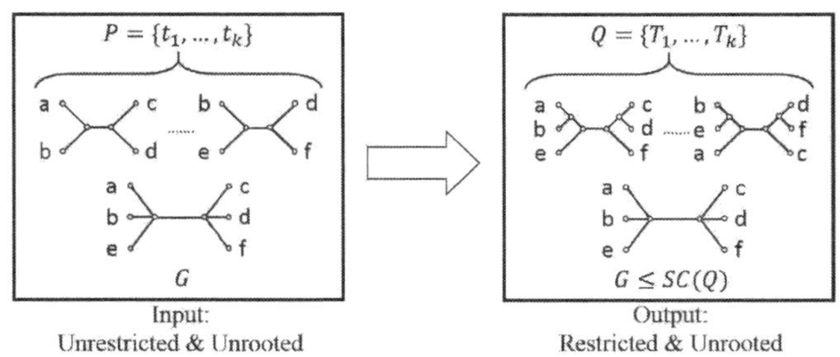

Figure 3: Schematic representation of the Guidance tree based unrestricted and unrooted profile fill-in problem. Unrestricted input trees are transformed into the corresponding restricted trees.

LEMMA 3.1. *Let* P *be an unrooted profile and* G *be a guidance tree for* P. *If* $Q \in \langle P \rangle_G$, *then* $G \leq \mathcal{SC}(Q)$.

PROOF. By the definition of the restricted span $\langle P \rangle_G$, $\forall T \in Q$ is a refined tree of G, hence, $G \leq \mathcal{SC}(Q)$. □

LEMMA 3.2. *Let* t *be a tree in an unrooted profile* P, *and* G *be a guidance tree for* P. *If* $T \in \langle t \rangle_G$, *then* $\Sigma(G) \cap (\Sigma(t) \setminus \Sigma(G|\mathcal{L}(t))) = \emptyset$ *and* $|\Sigma(T)| \geq |\Sigma(G)| + |\Sigma(t) \setminus \Sigma(G|\mathcal{L}(t))|$.

PROOF. For the first part, $\Sigma(G) \cap (\Sigma(t) \setminus \Sigma(G|\mathcal{L}(t))) = (\Sigma(G) \cap \Sigma(t)) \setminus \Sigma(G|\mathcal{L}(t)) = \Sigma(t) \cap (\Sigma(G) \setminus \Sigma(G|\mathcal{L}(t)))$. If $\mathcal{L}(t) = \mathcal{L}(G)$, then $\Sigma(G) \setminus \Sigma(G|\mathcal{L}(t)) = \emptyset$. Otherwise, $\Sigma(G) \cap \Sigma(t) = \emptyset$.

For the second part, let $f\colon \Sigma(\mathcal{T}) \times \mathcal{L} \to \Sigma(\mathcal{T}_{\mathcal{L}})$ be surjective function such that $\forall\sigma' \in \Sigma(\mathcal{T}_{\mathcal{L}}), \exists\sigma \in \Sigma(\mathcal{T}), \sigma' = \sigma \cap \mathcal{L}$ where $\mathcal{T}$ is a tree, $\mathcal{L} \subseteq \mathcal{L}(\mathcal{T})$ is a leaves, and $\mathcal{T}_{\mathcal{L}}$ is a tree on $\mathcal{L}$. From $T \in \langle t \rangle_G$, follows that $\Sigma(G) \subseteq \Sigma(T)$ and $f(\Sigma(T), \mathcal{L}(t)) = \Sigma(T|\mathcal{L}(t)) = \Sigma(t)$. Let $\Sigma = \Sigma(T) \setminus \Sigma(G)$, then $|\Sigma(T)| = |\Sigma(G)| + |\Sigma|$. From $\Sigma(t) = f(\Sigma(T), \mathcal{L}(t)) = f(\Sigma(G) \cup \Sigma, \mathcal{L}(t)) = \Sigma(G|\mathcal{L}(t)) \cup f(\Sigma, \mathcal{L}(t))$, it follows $\Sigma(t) \setminus \Sigma(G|\mathcal{L}(t)) \subseteq f(\Sigma, \mathcal{L}(t))$. Therefore, $|\Sigma| \geq |f(\Sigma, \mathcal{L}(t))| \geq |\Sigma(t) \setminus \Sigma(G|\mathcal{L}(t))|$ and $|\Sigma(T)| \geq |\Sigma(G)| + |\Sigma(t) \setminus \Sigma(G|\mathcal{L}(t))|$. □

A rooting in a tree T is defined by selecting an edge $e \in E(T)$ on which the root is to be placed. Such a rooted tree is denoted by $T(e)$, and e is the *rooting edge*. There exist a bijective mapping, denoted by $\mathcal{M} : V(T) \to V(T_e)$, between $V(T)$ and $V(T_e) \setminus \{r(T_e)\}$.

Algorithm 1 Guidance Tree based Fill-in(P, G)

```
Input:   An unrooted profile P = {t_1, ···, t_k} such that L(t_i) ⊂
         L(P) and a guidance tree G for P such that L(G) = L(P)
         and G|L(t_i) ≤ t_i (∀i ∈ {1, ···, k}).
Output:  An unrooted profile Q ∈ ⟨P⟩_G such that |Q| =
         min_{Q'∈⟨P⟩_G} |Q'|.
1:  for all t ∈ P do
2:      T = G
3:      Σ = Σ(t) \ Σ(G|L(t))
4:      for all σ ∈ Σ do                              ▷ let σ = A|B
5:          Pick arbitrarily v_b ∈ B
6:          e_b = (v_b, v'_b) ∈ E(T)                  ▷ v'_b ∈ V_int(T)
7:          v_lca = LCA_{T(e_b)}(A)
8:          for all v_a ∈ A do
9:              v = v_a
10:             Z = ∅
11:             while v ∉ Z & Pa_{T(e_b)}(v) ≠ v_lca do
12:                 Add v to Z
13:                 v = Pa_{T(e_b)}(v)
14:             end while
15:             if Pa_{T(e_b)}(v) = v_lca then
16:                 Add v to V_ch
17:             end if
18:         end for
19:         v_c ∈ V(T): mapped node of v_lca
20:         V_det ⊂ V(T): mapped nodes of V_ch
21:         Add v_new to V(T)
22:         Add (v_c, v_new) to E(T)
23:         for all v_det ∈ V_det do
24:             Remove (v_c, v_det) ∈ V(T)
25:             Add (v_new, v_det) to E(T)
26:         end for
27:     end for
28:     Add T to Q
29: end for
30: return Q
```

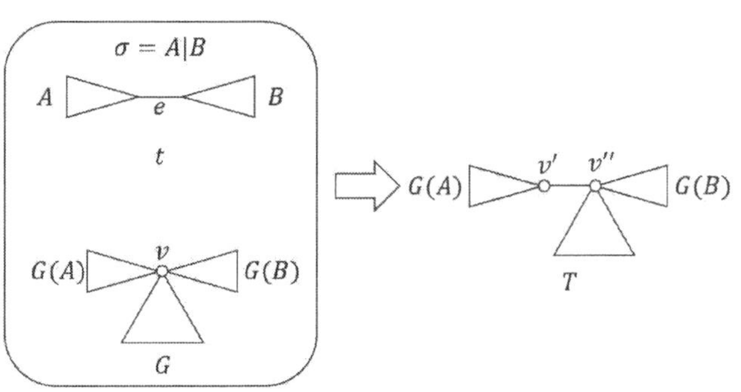

Figure 4: Schematic representation of the main idea of Algorithm 1. t: an input tree, $\sigma = A|B$: defined by removal of e G: the Guidance tree, T: the output tree G does not have an edge that defines $\sigma = A|B$, but T has the edge.

Lemma 3.3. *Let t be a tree in an unrooted profile P, and G be a guidance tree for P. If $\sigma = A|B \in \Sigma(t) \setminus \Sigma(G|\mathcal{L}(t))$, then $G(A)$ and $G(B)$ share a single node $v \in V(G)$.*

Proof. Suppose that $G(A)$ and $G(B)$ does not share a single node. If $G(A)$ and $G(B)$ are not connected, then there exists at least one split $\sigma' \in \Sigma(G)$ such that $\sigma' \cap \mathcal{L}(t) = \sigma$. This is a contradiction since $\sigma \in \Sigma(G|\mathcal{L}(t))$.

If $G(A)$ and $G(B)$ share more than one node, then $G(A)$ and $G(B)$ share at least one edge. Let $e \in E(G)$ be a shared edge and $\sigma_e = A_e|B_e \in \Sigma(G)$ be a split from removal of e, then $A \cap A_e \neq \emptyset$, $A \cap B_e \neq \emptyset$, $B \cap A_e \neq \emptyset$, and $B \cap B_e \neq \emptyset$. It follows $\sigma_e \cap \mathcal{L}(t) \in \Sigma(G|\mathcal{L}(t))$ and $\sigma_e \cap \mathcal{L}(t) \notin \Sigma(t)$. This is a contradiction since $\Sigma(G|\mathcal{L}(t)) \subsetneq \Sigma(t)$. □

Lemma 3.4. *Let T be an unrooted tree, $A, B \subset \mathcal{L}(T)$, and $A \cap B = \emptyset$. Suppose that $T(A)$ and $T(B)$ share a single node $v_c \in V(T)$. If $v_b \in B$ and $e_b = (v_b, v_{b'})$ where $e_b \in E(T)$, then $\mathcal{M}(v_c) = LCA_{T'}(A)$ where $T' = T(e_b)$.*

Proof. Let $V_A = \{\mathcal{M}(v) \mid v \in V(T(A))\}$ and $V_B = \{\mathcal{M}(v) \mid v \in V(T(B))\}$, then $V_A \cap V_B = \{\mathcal{M}(v_c)\}$. By the definition of the rooting, we observe that $v \leq_{T'} \mathcal{M}(v_c)$ for all node $v \in V_A$ and $\mathcal{M}(v_c) \leq_{T'} v$ for all node $v \in V_B \setminus \{\mathcal{M}(v_b)\}$. $\mathcal{M}(v_c)$ is the smallest upper bound of A under $\leq_{T'}$, hence, $\mathcal{M}(v_c) = LCA_{T'}(A)$. □

Proposition 3.5. *Algorithm 1 runs in $O(kn^2)$ time where k is the number of trees in a profile P and $n = |\mathcal{L}(P)|$.*

Proof. By Lemma 3.2, the number of splits in T (line 28), $|\Sigma(T)| = |\Sigma(G)| + |\Sigma(t) \setminus \Sigma(G|\mathcal{L}(t))|$, is the minimum among trees in $\langle t \rangle_G$. Lemma 3.3 guarantees that v_c (line 19) is the shared node between $G(A)$ and $G(B)$. The algorithm uses the temporary rooted tree $T(e_b)$ (line 7) to identify the v_c, which is guaranteed by Lemma 3.4.

By using the rooted tree $T(e_b)$, v_c is computable in $O(n)$ time since an lca operation (line 7) can be computed in constant time after an initial preprocessing step requiring $O(n)$ time [4, 21]. Every node (except the root) in $T(e_b)$ has a memory reference to its unique parent node. By using the memory reference to store the parent nodes of every node (except the root) and the data structure Q to determine which nodes have already been visited, the for-loops (lines 8 – 18) can be computable in $O(n)$. The for-loops (23 – 26) are also computable in $O(n)$ since $|V_{det}| < |n|$. Thus, the for-loop (lines 4 – 27) runs in time $O(n^2)$. The outer for-loop (lines 1 – 29) is executed k times, from which the desired runtime follows. □

4 GUIDANCE TREE BASED ROOTING

We define the Guidance tree based restricted and unrooted profile rooting problem and propose the efficient algorithm for solving this problem. For a given profile of restricted and unrooted trees $T_1, \ldots, T_k$ and a strict consensus tree G of the profile, a rooted version of the input trees $T_1(e_1), \ldots, T_k(e_k)$ such that (i) each rooted tree $T_i(e_i)$ is the rooting tree of one unrooted tree T_i and (ii) their strict consensus tree $\mathcal{SC}(Q')$ is identical to the *rooted* guidance tree $G(e_r)$.

Problem 2. *(Guidance Tree based Rooting Problem)*

Input: *An unrooted profile $Q = \{T_1, \cdots, T_k\}$ such that $\mathcal{L}(T_i) = \mathcal{L}(Q)$ and a rooting edge $e_r \in E(G)$ where $G = \mathcal{SC}(Q)$.*

Output: *A rooted profile $Q' = \{T_1(e_1), \cdots, T_k(e_k)\}$ such that $G(e_r) = \mathcal{SC}(Q')$ where $e_i \in E(T_i)$.*

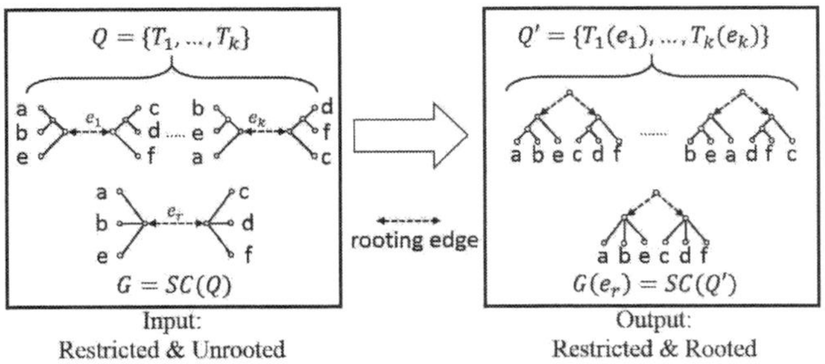

Figure 5: Schematic representation of the Guidance tree based restricted and unrooted profile rooting problem. Unrooted input trees are transformed into the corresponding rooted trees.

LEMMA 4.1. *Let $Q = \{T_1, \cdots, T_k\}$ be an unrooted profile, $G = \mathcal{SC}(Q)$, and $e_r \in E(G)$ be a rooting edge (defines σ_r). There exists an edge $e_i \in E(T_i)$ defines σ_r and $G(e_r) = \mathcal{SC}(Q')$ for the rooted profile $Q' = \{T_1(e_1), \cdots, T_k(e_k)\}$.*

PROOF. Since $\Sigma(S) \subseteq \Sigma(T_i)$ ($\forall i\{1, \cdots, k\}$), there is an edge $e_i \in E(T_i)$ that defines σ_r. If T be an unrooted tree and $e_r \in E(T)$ be a rooting edge (defines $\sigma_r = A_r|B_r$), then there exists a bijective function $f : \Sigma(T) \setminus \{\sigma_r\} \to \mathcal{H}\big(T(e_r)\big) \setminus \{\mathcal{L}(T), A_r, B_r\}$ such that $f(\sigma) = A \vee B$ where $\sigma = A|B$. $\mathcal{H}\big(\mathcal{SC}(Q')\big) \setminus \{\mathcal{L}(Q'), A_r, B_r\} = \cap_i \mathcal{H}\big(T_i(e_i)\big) \setminus \{\mathcal{L}(Q'), A_r, B_r\} = \cap_i \Big(\mathcal{H}\big(T_i(e_i)\big) \setminus \{\mathcal{L}(T_i), A_r, B_r\}\Big)$ $= \cap_i\{f(\sigma_j) : \forall \sigma_j \in \Sigma(T_i) \setminus \{\sigma_r\}\} = \{f(\sigma_j) : \forall \sigma_j \in \cap_i \Sigma(T_i) \setminus \{\sigma_r\}\} = \{f(\sigma_j) : \forall \sigma_j \in \Sigma(G) \setminus \{\sigma_r\}\}$. Hence, there exists $e_i \in E(T_i)$ defines σ_r and $G(e_r) = \mathcal{SC}(Q')$. □

Algorithm 2 Guidance Tree based Rooting(Q, G)

Input: An unrooted profile $Q = \{T_1, \cdots, T_k\}$ such that $\mathcal{L}(T_i) = \mathcal{L}(G)$ and a rooting edge $e_r \in E(G)$ where $G = \mathcal{SC}(Q)$.
Output: A rooted profile $Q' = \{T_1(e_1), \cdots, T_k(e_k)\}$ such that $G(e_r) = \mathcal{SC}(Q')$ where $e_i \in E(T_i)$.

```
1: G' = G(e_r)                        ▷ σ_r is defined by removal of e_r
2: σ_r = A_r|B_r
3: for all T ∈ Q do
4:     for all e ∈ E(T) do
5:         T' = T(e)                  ▷ σ is defined by removal of e
6:         σ = A|B
7:         if (A_r = A & B_r = B) || (A_r = B & B_r = A) then
8:             Add T' to Q'
9:             Break
10:        end if
11:    end for
12: end for
13: return Q'
```

PROPOSITION 4.2. *Algorithm 2 runs in $O(kn)$ time where k is the number of trees in a profile P and $n = |\mathcal{L}(P)|$.*

PROOF. Lemma 4.1 guarantees that there exists an split σ such that $\sigma = \sigma_r$ at line 7 and $\mathcal{SC}(Q') = G(e_r)$ at line 13. Assume σ is pre-computed when running Algorithm 1 and stored in a map data structure in the pair of edge key and split value. The σ which is defined by removal of e can be referenced in $O(c)$, hence, the for-loop (lines 4 – 11) runs in time $O(n)$. The outer for-loop (lines 1 – 29) is executed k times, from which the desired runtime follows. □

5 EXPERIMENTS

We demonstrate the applicability of our new approach that adopts the Strict Consensus Approach to handle unrooted and unrestricted instances. While the Strict Consensus Approach is applicable to various median tree problems, we are choosing here the classic gene duplication problem [14, 20]. This problem is NP-hard [28], $W[2]$-hard when parameterized by the gene duplication score [3] and hard to approximate better than a logarithmic factor [3]. While exact solutions for the gene duplication problem are coming into the reach of smaller phylogenetic studies (e.g., 22 taxa [9]), for large-scale studies such solutions remain out of reach. Therefore, effective local search heuristics have been proposed [2, 49], analyzed, and applied to compute large-scale median trees from gene trees [11, 30, 31, 37]. Duptree [49] is a standard implementation of these heuristics which we will use here for our comparative studies.

All experiments were performed on a workstation with an Intel® Xeon® CPU E7-8837 @2.66GHz with 128GB RAM.

5.1 Empirical Study

We evaluate the accuracy our new approach to solve the gene duplication problem in comparison with the program DupTree, using empirical data.

5.1.1 Data sets. Multiple sequence alignments for 12 genes, each sampled from subsets of 2849 amphibian species, were obtained from the data base Dryad repository (published in [40, 41]). These 12 genes are C-X-C chemokine receptor type 4 (CXCR4), histone 3a (H3A), sodium-calcium exchanger (NCX1), pro-opiomelanocortin (POMC), recombination-activating gene 1 (RAG1), rhodopsin (RHOD), seventh-in-absentia (SIA), solute-carrier family 8 (SLC8A3), tyrosinase (TYR), cytochrome b (cyt-b), and the subunits of the mitochondrial ribosome genes (12S/16S). We estimated unrooted gene trees for each of these alignments using the software RAxML version 8.2.9 [46]. The command we used was: raxmlHPC -s ⟨phylip alignment file⟩ -n ⟨output suffix⟩ -m GTRGAMMA. These estimates were completed in 27 hours using 10 threads of our workstation. Finally, we combined the 12 trees, which are unrestricted and unrooted, into a profile P.

5.1.2 Experimental Setting. For the DupTree approach we follow the procedure described in [8] to root the trees in profile P. In this procedure two rooting methods were used, midpoint rooting [6] and optimal re-rooting [8]. Then we run DupTree generating 500 estimates for each of the rooted profiles. The gene duplication scores for these estimates are summarized in the section A (midpoint rooting) and B (optimal re-rooting) of Fig. 6.

For our approach we computed the *unrooted guidance* tree G by using the SCM method [24] for the profile P. By applying our Algorithm 1 to P and G, we computed a restricted version of P. Then we computed a rooted profile of P for each edge of G using Algorithm 2.

Now we applied the Strict Consensus Approach to the restricted and rooted profiles generated from P by using G. Again, we were

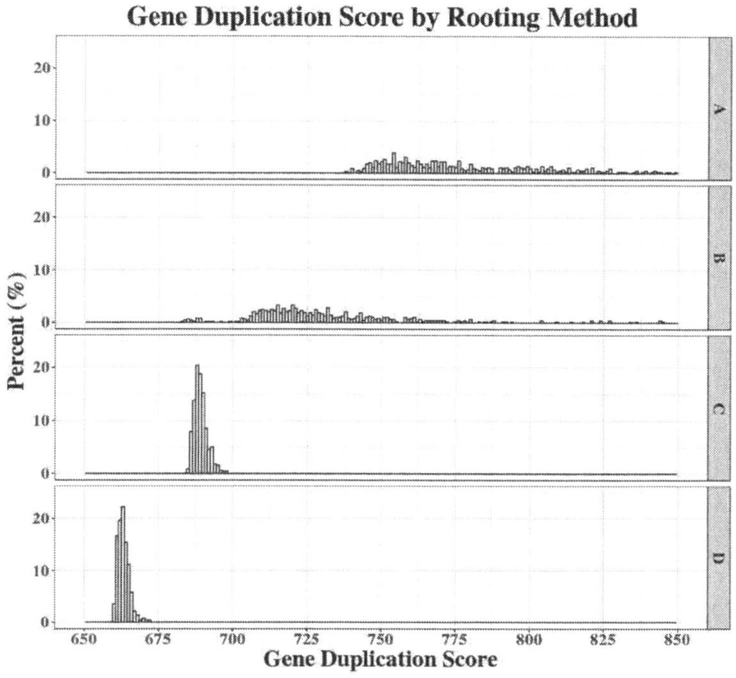

Figure 6: Gene duplication score comparison by the different rooting methods.
A: Gene trees midpoint rooting + DupTree heuristic.
B: Gene trees optimal re-rooting + DupTree heuristic.
C: Guidance tree rooting + Strict Consensus Approach (worst).
D: Guidance tree rooting + Strict Consensus Approach (best).

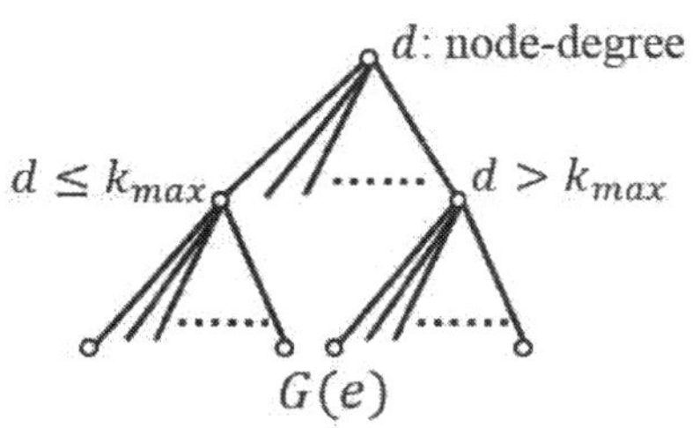

Figure 7: Schematic representation of node-degrees of internal nodes of a rooted guidance tree $G(e)$ and k_{max} value. The node-degree is equivalent to the number of taxa in the corresponding sub-problem. If the number of taxa of a corresponding sub-problem is larger than k_{max}, the sub-problem is addressed using the DupTree heuristic. Otherwise, the sub-problem is solved exactly.

running the Strict Consensus Approach on each of these profiles 500 times. The Strict Consensus Approach requires a value k_{max} that determines the maximum size (in the number of taxa) of the sub-problems that are solved exactly, while instances larger than k_{max} are addressed using the DupTree heuristic. Fig. 7 depicts an example for the usage of the value k_{max}. According to the ability of our workstation we set k_{max} to 9. To summarize the results we considered only the best and the worst gene duplication scores under the 500 runs performed for each edge in G, which are depicted in sections C (worst) and D (best) of Fig. 6.

Table 1: Descriptive statistics of the Gene duplication scores.
A: Gene trees midpoint rooting + DupTree heuristic.
B: Gene trees optimal re-rooting + DupTree heuristic.
C: Guidance tree rooting + Strict Consensus Approach (worst).
D: Guidance tree rooting + Strict Consensus Approach (best).

Group	Average	SD	Median	Min	Max	Range
A	785	42.8	771	738	1025	287
B	734	36.3	726	683	975	292
C	689	2.2	689	685	698	13
D	663	2.0	663	660	672	12

5.1.3 Results and Discussion. We observe that the distributions of the best and the worst guidance tree rootings, shown in Fig. 6, are narrow and bell-shaped, reflecting that most sub-instances were solved exactly. Note that under the assumption that every sub-instance is solved exactly, there would be only one score in each of the sections C and D. An increased number of heuristically solved instances would spread more widely in terms of scores. In detail, these phenomena can be explained by the distributions of the node-degrees of the guidance tree G, which has 251 multifurcations, where 9 of them have a node-degree larger than k_{max}. Therefore, 96.4% of sub-instances were solved exactly, and only 3.6% of them were addressed heuristically. The overall distributions demonstrate that the guidance tree rooting together with the Strict Consensus Approach improves significantly on the accuracy and the variance when compared with the DupTree results. The descriptive statistics of the gene duplication scores are summarized in Table 1. The average time to compute the scores for A is 30 seconds, and for B is 80 minutes, and for C and D are each 50 seconds. Note, the much longer computing time for B is caused by the frequent re-rooting procedure of DupTree that when terminating in a local minima will re-root the input trees to proceed [48].

5.2 Simulated Study

We evaluated the scalability of our approach when compared with DupTree for computing species trees by using simulated data sets with a maximum of 2744 taxa, where each instance contains 20 unrestricted and unrooted trees.

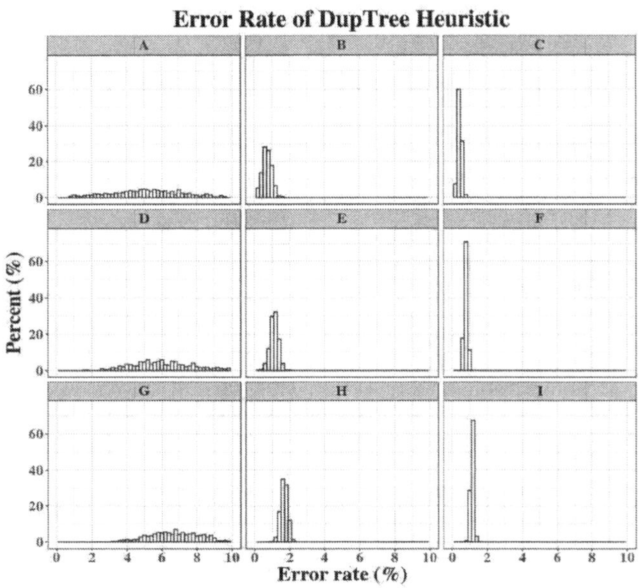

Figure 8: Error rate of DupTree heuristic by different taxa and scaffold factor.
Taxa=750 → A: Scaffold=25%, B: Scaffold=50%, C: Scaffold=75%
Taxa=1512 → D: Scaffold=25%, E: Scaffold=50%, F: Scaffold=75%
Taxa=2744 → G: Scaffold=25%, H: Scaffold=50%, I: Scaffold=75%

5.2.1 Data sets. For the simulation *back-bone trees* were created that are unrooted b-ary trees for $b \in \{5, 6, 7\}$, such that each of these trees has a special *center node* where the path lengths between the center node and every leaf are always 4. Consequently, the numbers of leaves of the back-bone trees are 750, 1512, and 2744. For each back-bone tree, an *intermediate profile* consisting of 20 restricted and unrooted trees was computed, where each tree in the profile is a random refinement of the back-bone tree. We then converted the intermediate profiles into profiles P_b for $b \in \{5, 6, 7\}$ of unrestricted and unrooted trees by replacing each tree T in each of intermediate profiles by the tree $T|A$ for an independent random set $A \subseteq \mathcal{L}(T)$. The probability that a leaf is selected for the subset A is called the *scaffold factor*. We produced profiles $P_{b,25}$, $P_{b,50}$, and $P_{b,75}$ for each scaffold factor 25%, 50%, and 75%, and we adopted the initial back-bone trees as the guidance trees G_b.

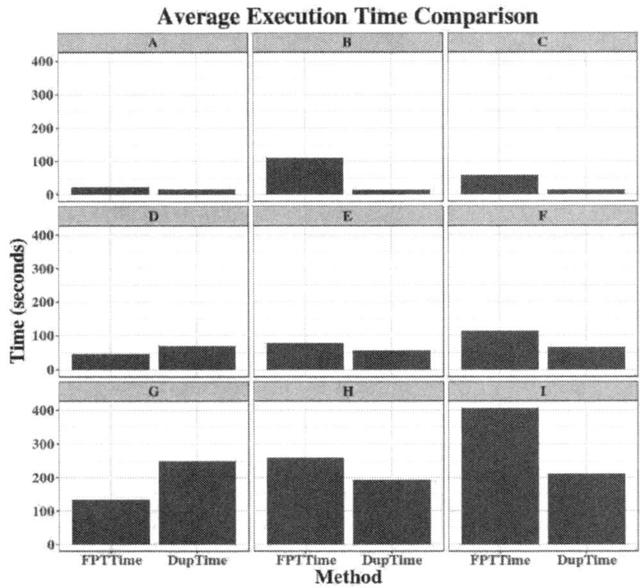

Figure 9: Average execution time of our approach (FTPTime) and DupTree heuristic (DupTime) by different taxa and scaffold factor.
Taxa=750 → A: Scaffold=25%, B: Scaffold=50%, C: Scaffold=75%
Taxa=1512 → D: Scaffold=25%, E: Scaffold=50%, F: Scaffold=75%
Taxa=2744 → G: Scaffold=25%, H: Scaffold=50%, I: Scaffold=75%

5.2.2 Experiment Setting. Algorithm 1 took $P_{b,s}$ and G_b as an input and produced the profile $Q_{b,s}$ of restricted and unrooted trees for each $b \in \{5, 6, 7\}$ and $s \in \{25, 50, 75\}$. Then we computed the *rooted guidance* tree G'_b by using the midpoint edge of G_b. Algorithm 2 took $Q_{b,s}$ and G'_b as an input and produced the profile $Q'_{b,s}$ of restricted and rooted trees. By repeating the described procedure 500 times, we produced a total number of 4500 instances of restricted and rooted trees and its rooted guidance tree. We set $k_{max} = 9$, and therefore, all sub-instances were solved exactly, since the node-degrees of the guidance trees are less than k_{max}. For the baseline method, we generated the unrestricted and rooted profile from $P_{b,s}$ by using the midpoint rooting, and then run DupTree to generate 500 estimates.

5.2.3 Results and Discussion. Our approach computed optimal species trees, while DupTree estimated these trees heuristically. Fig. 8 shows that the error rates of DupTree are increasing with an increasing number of taxa. Observe that the error rates are significantly higher scored for the 25% (A,D,G) scaffold factor than for the 50% (B,E,H) and 75% (C,F,I) scaffold factors. This suggests that the error rate of DupTree is greatly impacted by small scaffold factors. Fig. 9 shows that the gene duplication problem can be solved optimally in a reasonable time by using our approach.

CONCLUSION

There is an increased interest in making NP-hard median tree problems available for large-scale species tree construction. While it has been demonstrated that the Strict Consensus Approach can successfully synthesize such trees, it is only able to handle restricted median problems, which have largely limited applicability in practice. In this work, we introduced a novel approach that is overcoming these limitations by adopting the Strict Consensus Approach to handle unrestricted median tree problems. Our studies on empirical and simulated experiments demonstrate that our approach makes the Strict Consensus Approach a powerful tool for addressing large-scale supertree problems in their unrestricted version.

The performance of the Strict Consensus Approach depends on the choice of the guidance tree, and future research will focus on developing and analyzing new methods for constructing guidance trees. Further, while the approach is limited to median tree problems that are weak Pareto and satisfy the substructure property, many median tree problems have not been analyzed whether the satisfy these properties. Future studies will focus on such analyzes.

Acknowledgments

The authors would like to thank the three anonymous reviewers for their suggestions and comments. This material is based upon work supported by the National Science Foundation under Grant No. 1617626.

REFERENCES

[1] Kenneth J. Arrow. 1952. *Social Choice and Individual Values.* Yale University Press, New Haven, Connecticut, United States.

[2] Mukul S. Bansal and Oliver Eulenstein. 2013. Algorithms for genome-scale phylogenetics using gene tree parsimony. *IEEE/ACM Transactions on Computational Biology and Bioinformatics* 10, 4 (2013), 939–56. DOI: https://doi.org/10.1109/TCBB.2013.103

[3] Mukul S. Bansal and Ron Shamir. 2011. A Note on the Fixed Parameter Tractability of the Gene-Duplication Problem. *IEEE/ACM Transactions on Computational Biology and Bioinformatics* 8, 3 (2011), 848–50. DOI: https://doi.org/10.1109/TCBB.2010.74

[4] Michael A. Bender and Martin Farach-Colton. 2000. The LCA Problem Revisited. In *Proceedings of the Latin American Symposium on Theoretical Informatics.* Springer, New York, New York, United States, 88–94.

[5] Olaf R. Bininda-Emonds. 2004. *Phylogenetic Supertrees. Combining Information to Reveal the Tree of Life.* Springer Science & Business Media, New York, New York, United States.

[6] Laura M. Boykin, Laura S. Kubatko, and Timothy K. Lowrey. 2010. Comparison of methods for rooting phylogenetic trees: a case study using Orcuttieae (Poaceae: Chloridoideae). *Molecular Phylogenetics and Evolution* 54, 3 (2010), 687–700. DOI: https://doi.org/10.1016/j.ympev.2009.11.016

[7] David Bryant. 2003. A Classification of Consensus Methods for Phylogenetics. In *Discrete Mathematics and Theoretical Computer Science.* Vol. 61. American Mathematical Society, Providence, Rhode Island, United States, 163–185.

[8] J. Gordon Burleigh, Mukul S. Bansal, Oliver Eulenstein, Stefanie Hartmann, André Wehe, and Todd J. Vision. 2011. Genome-Scale Phylogenetics: Inferring the Plant Tree of Life from 18,896 Gene Trees. *Systematic Biology* 60, 2 (2011), 117–125. DOI: https://doi.org/10.1093/sysbio/syq072

[9] Wen-Chieh Chang, Pawe l Górecki, and Oliver Eulenstein. 2013. Exact Solutions for Species Tree Inference from discordant Gene Trees. *Journal of Bioinformatics and Computational Biology* 11, 05 (2013), 1342005. DOI: https://doi.org/10.1142/S0219720013420055

[10] International Human Genome Sequencing Consortium and others. 2004. Finishing the euchromatic sequence of the human genome. *Nature* 431, 7011 (2004), 931–945. DOI: https://doi.org/10.1038/nature03001

[11] James A. Cotton and Roderic D.M. Page. 2002. Going nuclear: gene family evolution and vertebrate phylogeny reconciled. *Proceedings of the Royal Society of London B: Biological Sciences* 269, 1500 (2002), 1555–1561. DOI: https://doi.org/10.1098/rspb.2002.2074

[12] James A. Cotton and Roderic D.M. Page. 2005. Rates and Patterns of Gene Duplication and Loss in the Human Genome. *Proceedings of the Royal Society of London B: Biological Sciences* 272, 1560 (2005), 277–83. DOI: https://doi.org/10.1098/rspb.2004.2969

[13] Theodosius Dobzhansky. 2013. Nothing in biology makes sense except in the light of evolution. *The american biology teacher* 75, 2 (2013), 87–91. DOI: https://doi.org/10.2307/4444260

[14] Oliver Eulenstein, Snehalata Huzurbazar, and David A. Liberles. 2010. *Evolution after Gene Duplication.* Wiley, Hoboken, New Jersey, United States, Chapter Reconciling Phylogenetic Trees, 185–206.

[15] Iakes Ezkurdia, David Juan, Jose Manuel Rodriguez, Adam Frankish, Mark Diekhans, Jennifer Harrow, Jesus Vazquez, Alfonso Valencia, and Michael L Tress. 2014. Multiple evidence strands suggest that there may be as few as 19 000 human protein-coding genes. *Human molecular genetics* 23, 22 (2014), 5866–5878. DOI: https://doi.org/10.1093/hmg/ddu309

[16] Joseph Felsenstein. 1981. Evolutionary trees from DNA sequences: A maximum likelihood approach. *Journal of Molecular Evolution* 17, 6 (1981), 368–376. DOI: https://doi.org/10.1007/BF01734359

[17] Walter M. Fitch. 1971. Toward Defining the Course of Evolution: minimum change for a specific tree topology. *Systematic Biology* 20, 4 (1971), 406–416. DOI: https://doi.org/10.1093/sysbio/20.4.406

[18] Markus Fleischauer and Sebastian Böcker. 2016. Collecting reliable clades using the Greedy Strict Consensus Merger. *PeerJ Computer Science* 4 (2016), e2172. DOI: https://doi.org/10.7717/peerj.2172

[19] Peter Forster and Colin Renfrew. 2006. *Phylogenetic methods and the prehistory of languages.* McDonald Inst of Archeological, Cambridge, England, United Kingdom.

[20] Morris Goodman, John Czelusniak, G. William Moore, A.E. Romero-Herrera, and Genji Matsuda. 1979. Fitting the Gene Lineage into its Species Lineage, a Parsimony Strategy Illustrated by Cladograms Constructed from Globin Sequences. *Systematic Biology* 28, 2 (1979), 132–163. DOI: https://doi.org/10.1093/sysbio/28.2.132

[21] Pawe l Górecki and Oliver Eulenstein. 2012. A Robinson-Foulds Measure to Compare Unrooted Trees with Rooted Trees. In *Proceedings of the International Symposium on Bioinformatics Research and Applications.* Springer, New York, New York, United States, 115–126.

[22] Simon R. Harris, Edward J.P. Cartwright, M Estéée Török, Matthew T.G. Holden, Nicholas M. Brown, Amanda L. Ogilvy-Stuart, Matthew J. Ellington, Michael A. Quail, Stephen D. Bentley, Julian Parkhill, and Sharon J. Peacock. 2013. Whole-genome sequencing for analysis of an outbreak of meticillin-resistant Staphylococcus aureus: a descriptive study. *The Lancet Infectious diseases* 13, 2 (2013), 130–136. DOI: https://doi.org/10.1016/S1473-3099(12)70268-2

[23] Ruth A. Hufbauer, Robin A. Marrs, Aaron K. Jackson, René Sforza, Harsh Pal Bais, Jorge M. Vivanco, and Shannan E. Carney. 2003. Population structure, ploidy levels and allelopathy of Centaurea maculosa (spotted knapweed) and C. diffusa (diffuse knapweed) in North America and Eurasia. In *Proceedings of the International Symposium on Biological Control of Weeds.* USDA Forest Service. Forest Health Technology Enterprise Team, Morgantown, WV., 121–126.

[24] Daniel H. Huson, Scott M. Nettles, and Tandy J. Warnow. 1999. Disk-Covering, a Fast-Converging Method for Phylogenetic Tree Reconstruction. *Journal of Computational Biology* 6, 3–4 (1999), 369–386. DOI: https://doi.org/10.1089/106652799318337

[25] Andrew P. Jackson. 2004. A reconciliation analysis of host switching in plant-fungal symbioses. *Evolution* 58, 9 (2004), 1909–23. DOI: https://doi.org/10.1554/03-661

[26] Harris T. Lin, J. Gordon Burleigh, and Oliver Eulenstein. 2012. Consensus Properties for the Deep Coalescence Problem and their Application for Scalable Tree Search. *BMC Bioinformatics* 13, 10 (2012), S12. DOI: https://doi.org/10.1186/1471-2105-13-S10-S1

[27] Harris T. Lin, Jucheol Moon, and Oliver Eulenstein. 2015. Consensus Properties of the Gene Duplication Problem for Enhanced Phylogenetic Inference. In *Proceedings of the International Conference on Bioinformatics and Computational Biology.* Curran Associates, Inc., Red Hook, New York, United States, 131–136.

[28] Bin Ma, Ming Li, and Louxin Zhang. 2000. From Gene Trees to Species Trees. *SIAM Journal on Computing* 30, 3 (2000), 729–752. DOI: https://doi.org/10.1137/S0097539798343362

[29] Wayne P. Maddison and L. Lacey Knowles. 2006. Inferring Phylogeny Despite Incomplete Lineage Sorting. *Systematic Biology* 55, 1 (2006), 21–30. DOI: https://doi.org/10.1080/10635150500354928

[30] Andrew P. Martin and Theresa M. Burg. 2002. Perils of paralogy: using HSP70 genes for inferring organismal phylogenies. *Systematic Biology* 51, 4 (2002), 570–587. DOI: https://doi.org/10.1080/10635150290069995

[31] Michael R. McGowen, Clay. Clark, and John Gatesy. 2008. The vestigial olfactory receptor subgenome of odontocete whales: phylogenetic congruence between gene-tree reconciliation and supermatrix methods. *Systematic biology* 57, 4 (2008), 574–590.

[32] Jucheol Moon and Oliver Eulenstein. 2016. Synthesizing Large-Scale Species Trees using Guidance Trees. In *Proceedings of the International Conference on Bioinformatics and Computational Biology.* Curran Associates, Inc., Red Hook, New York, United States, 103–108.

[33] Jucheol Moon and Oliver Eulenstein. accepted. Synthesizing Large-scale Species Trees using the Strict Consensus Approach. *Journal of Bioinformatics and Computational Biology* (accepted), in press.

[34] Jucheol Moon, Harris T. Lin, and Oliver Eulenstein. 2016. Consensus Properties and their Large-Scale Applications for the Gene Duplication Problem. *Journal of Bioinformatics and Computational Biology* 14, 03 (2016), 1642005. DOI:https://doi.org/10.1142/S0219720016420051

[35] Serena Nik-Zainal, Peter V. Loo, David C. Wedge, Ludmil B. Alexandrov, Christopher D. Greenman, King W. Lau, Keiran Raine, David Jones, John Marshall, Manasa Ramakrishna, Adam Shlien, Susanna L. Cooke, Jonathan Hinton, Andrew Menzies, Lucy A. Stebbings, Catherine Leroy, Mingming Jia, Richard Rance, Laura J. Mudie, Stephen J. Gamble, Philip J. Stephens, Stuart McLaren, Patrick S. Tarpey, Elli Papaemmanuil, Helen R. Davies, Ignacio Varela, David J. McBride, Graham R. Bignell, Kenric Leung, Adam P. Butler, Jon W. Teague, Sancha Martin, Goran Jönsson, Odette Mariani, Sandrine Boyault, Penelope Miron, Aquila Fatima, Anita Langerød, Samuel A.J.R. Aparicio, Andrew Tutt, Anieta M. Sieuwerts, Åke Borg, Gilles Thomas, Anne Vincent Salomon, Andrea L. Richardson, Anne-Lise Børresen-Dale, P. Andrew Futreal, Michael R. Stratton, and Peter J. Campbell. 2012. The Life History of 21 Breast Cancers. *Cell* 149, 5 (2012), 994–1007. DOI:https://doi.org/10.1016/j.cell.2012.04.023

[36] Roderic D.M. Page. 1998. GeneTree: comparing gene and species phylogenies using reconciled trees. *Bioinformatics* 14, 9 (1998), 819–820. DOI:https://doi.org/10.1093/bioinformatics/14.9.819

[37] Roderic D.M. Page. 2000. Extracting species trees from complex gene trees: reconciled trees and vertebrate phylogeny. *Molecular Phylogenetics and Evolution* 14 (2000), 89–106.

[38] Pekka Pamilo and Masatoshi Nei. 1988. Relationships between gene trees and species trees. *Molecular biology and evolution* 5, 5 (1988), 568–583.

[39] Elizabeth Pennisi. 2012. ENCODE project writes eulogy for junk DNA. *Science* 337, 6099 (2012), 1159–1161. DOI:https://doi.org/10.1126/science.337.6099.1159

[40] Robert A. Pyron and John J. Wiens. 2011. A large-scale phylogeny of Amphibia including over 2800 species, and a revised classification of extant frogs, salamanders, and caecilians. *Molecular Phylogenetics and Evolution* 61, 2 (2011), 543–583. DOI:https://doi.org/10.1016/j.ympev.2011.06.012

[41] Robert A. Pyron and John J. Wiens. 2011. Data from: A large-scale phylogeny of Amphibia including over 2800 species, and a revised classification of extant frogs, salamanders, and caecilians. (2011). http://datadryad.com/resource/doi:10.5061/dryad.vd0m7.

[42] Vincent Ranwez, Vincent Berry, Alexis Criscuolo, Pierre-Henri Fabre, Sylvain Guillemot, Celine Scornavacca, and Emmanuel J.P. Douzery. 2007. PhySIC: A Veto Supertree Method with Desirable Properties. *Systematic Biology* 56, 5 (2007), 798–817. DOI:https://doi.org/10.1080/10635150701639754

[43] Johannes J. Le Roux, Ania M. Wieczorek, Mohsen M. Ramadan, and Carol T. Tran. 2006. Resolving the native provenance of invasive fireweed (Senecio madagascariensis Poir.) in the Hawaiian Islands as inferred Poir.) in the Hawaiian Islands as inferred from phylogenetic analysis. *Diversity and Distributions* 12 (2006), 694–702.

[44] Naruya Saitou and Masatoshi Nei. 1987. The neighbor-joining method: a new method for reconstructing phylogenetic trees. *Molecular Biology and Evolution* 4, 4 (1987), 406–425. DOI:https://doi.org/10.1093/oxfordjournals.molbev.a040454

[45] Charles Semple and Mike A. Steel. 2003. *Phylogenetics.* Oxford University Press, Oxford, England, United Kingdom.

[46] Alexandros Stamatakis. 2014. RAxML version 8: a tool for phylogenetic analysis and post-analysis of large phylogenies. *Bioinformatics* 30, 9 (2014), 1312–1313. DOI:https://doi.org/10.1093/bioinformatics/btu033

[47] Cuong Than and Luay Nakhleh. 2009. Species Tree Inference by Minimizing Deep Coalescences. *PLOS Computational Biology* 5, 9 (2009), e1000501. DOI:https://doi.org/10.1371/journal.pcbi.1000501

[48] André Wehe, Mukul S. Bansal, J. Gordon Burleigh, and Oliver Eulenstein. 2008. DupTree: A program for large-scale phylogenetic analyses using gene tree parsimony. *Bioinformatics* 24, 13 (2008), 1540–1541. DOI:https://doi.org/10.1093/bioinformatics/btn230

[49] André Wehe and J. Gordon Burleigh. 2010. Scaling the gene duplication problem towards the Tree of Life: Accelerating the rSPR heuristic search. In *Proceedings of the International Conference on Bioinformatics and Computational Biology.* Curran Associates, Inc., Red Hook, New York, United States, 133–138.

[50] Mark Wilkinson, James A. Cotton, François-Joseph Lapointe, and Davide Pisani. 2007. Properties of Supertree Methods in the Consensus Setting. *Systematic Biology* 56, 2 (2007), 330–337. DOI:https://doi.org/10.1080/10635150701245370

Fleximer: Accurate Quantification of RNA-Seq via Variable-Length k-mers

Chelsea J.-T. Ju
Department of Computer Science
University of California, Los Angeles
chelseaju@ucla.edu

Ruirui Li
Department of Computer Science
University of California, Los Angeles
rrli@cs.ucla.edu

Zhengliang Wu
Department of Computer Science
University of California, Los Angeles
lanzhou522@gmail.com

Jyun-Yu Jiang
Department of Computer Science
University of California, Los Angeles
jyunyu.jiang@gmail.com

Zhao Yang
Department of Computer Science
University of California, Los Angeles
yz931129@gmail.com

Wei Wang
Department of Computer Science
University of California, Los Angeles
weiwang@cs.ucla.edu

ABSTRACT

The advent of RNA-Seq has made it possible to quantify transcript expression on a large scale simultaneously. This technology generates small fragments of each transcript sequence, known as sequencing reads. As the first step of data analysis towards expression quantification, most of the existing methods align these reads to a reference genome or transcriptome to establish their origins. However, read alignment is computationally costly. Recently, a series of methods have been proposed to perform a lightweight quantification analysis in an alignment-free manner. These methods utilize the notion of *k-mers*, which are short consecutive sequences representing the signatures of each transcript, to estimate the relative abundance from RNA-Seq reads. Current *k-mer* based approaches make use of a set of fixed size *k-mers*; however, the true signatures of each transcript may not exist in a fixed size. In this paper, we demonstrate the importance of *k-mers* selection in transcript abundance estimation. We propose a novel method, Fleximer, to efficiently discover and select an optimal set of *k-mers* with flexible lengths. Using both simulated and real datasets, we show that, with fewer *k-mers*, Fleximer is able to cover the similar amount of reads as Sailfish and Kallisto. The selected *k-mers* own more distinguishing features, and thus substantially reduce the errors in transcript abundance estimation.

CCS CONCEPTS

• **Applied computing → Molecular sequence analysis**; **Computational transcriptomics**; **Transcriptomics**; *Computational genomics*; *Bioinformatics*;

KEYWORDS

RNA-Seq; Suffix tree; Aho-Corasick algorithm; EM algorithm; Transcript quantification

Permission to make digital or hard copies of all or part of this work for personal or classroom use is granted without fee provided that copies are not made or distributed for profit or commercial advantage and that copies bear this notice and the full citation on the first page. Copyrights for components of this work owned by others than ACM must be honored. Abstracting with credit is permitted. To copy otherwise, or republish, to post on servers or to redistribute to lists, requires prior specific permission and/or a fee. Request permissions from permissions@acm.org.
ACM-BCB '17, August 20-23, 2017, Boston, MA, USA
© 2017 Association for Computing Machinery.
ACM ISBN 978-1-4503-4722-8/17/08...$15.00
https://doi.org/10.1145/3107411.3107444

1 INTRODUCTION

Gene expression profiling serves the means to study transcriptome. The knowledge acquired from expression studies aims to create a global picture of cellular function. In the past two decades, microarray and high-throughput sequencing are the popular technologies, providing a rapid measurement to quantify a large number of genes simultaneously. The sequencing-based technology that captures the snapshot of existing RNAs is referred to as RNA-Seq.

The advent of RNA-Seq poses substantial computational challenges, specifically in handling the massive amount of read data [27]. The traditional data analysis framework contains two components: read alignment and expression quantification. Millions of short reads generated by the sequencer are first aligned back to a reference genome or transcriptome to re-establish their origins. Several aligners include, but are not limit to, Tophat2 [13], MapSplice [26], and SpliceMap [2]. However, this alignment step requires a significant amount of computational resources [8]. Even with parallel computing, analyzing a reasonable size of RNA-seq experiment can still take hours [19]. Recently, alignment-free or pseudoalignment approaches have been developed to alleviate the computational burden [4, 19, 23, 28]. Instead of aligning reads back to their references, these approaches design k-mers to infer transcript abundances from read data. They have all demonstrated a rapid analysis, improving the running time from hours to minutes. The k-mer approach harbors the features and advantages of both microarray and RNA-Seq. A set of k-mers behaves similarly to the probes in a microarray chip, which is used to identify the corresponding sequences in cDNA sample pool. Unlike the measurement in a microarray, the amount of cDNA identified by these k-mers is unbounded in RNA-Seq. In addition, since the k-mer design is performed *in-silico*, it is easier to re-construct a different set of k-mers for new analyses than re-designing a microarray chip.

Sailfish [19] is the first implementation to use k-mers for transcript quantification. It indexes all k-mers that appear at least once in the transcriptome and counts their occurrences in RNA-Seq data. Based on these counts, it estimates the relative transcript abundance through the expectation-maximization (EM) algorithm. Further ameliorating the throughput, RNA-Skim [28] divides the transcriptome into clusters based on sequence similarity. For each cluster, it selects a set of k-mers that do not appear in any other clusters, denoting as *sig-mers* (signatures of a cluster). Since each cluster contains a unique set of k-mers, the quantification step can be performed independently for smaller groups of transcripts. Zhang and Wang [28] have shown that RNA-Skim requires less computational time to achieve the same accuracy. Kallisto [4] builds targeted de-Bruijn graphs on all k-mers to facilitate the quantification, and claims faster and more accurate performance than Sailfish. All of these methods use a fixed k, which is a predefined parameter. However, selecting the appropriate k is not intuitive for a new experiment, and the best k characterizing a transcript sequence varies for different transcripts. For these reasons, we focus on the discussion of how to select a set of k-mers that can best describe transcript sequences with flexible lengths.

A k-mer cannot be too short because it can randomly match to a read that comes from a different transcript than the k-mer origins. Shorter k-mers have a higher chance to be repeated in the genome. Moreover, this event also arises when a read contains sequencing errors or individual variations. The accidental mismatch scenario is similar to the "cross-hybridization" phenomenon in microarray [14]. On the other hand, since the quantification step requires an exact match between a k-mer and a segment of a read, a long k-mer is less robust to reads containing sequencing errors or individual variations. An optimal set of k-mers should be robust to sequencing errors and individual variations, and should also be able to describe the uniqueness of each transcript. Sailfish originally set the default value of k to be 20, but changed it to 31 according to its website [1]. The initial choice is based on the evaluations over a small range of k (15-25) without further optimization. RNA-Skim studies the overall accuracy of transcript abundances for different ks before setting it to 60 as the default option. Neither of them has provided any guidance in selecting the right k for a new experiment or species.

To overcome the limitation of a fixed k, our main contribution focuses on developing an efficient approach to identify and select an optimal set of k-mers with flexible lengths. Our method takes a predefined genomic or transcriptomic partition as an input. The partition can be based on sequence similarity, biological functions, or any other user-defined scheme. In order to discover k-mers that are unique to each cluster with all possible lengths, we rely on the structure and properties of a suffix tree. We use the Aho-Corasick algorithm to efficiently match the reads to a set of representative k-mers of variable sizes. Based on the read counts, we use the EM algorithm to estimate the relative expression abundance for each transcript. We evaluate the performance of our method, Fleximer, using both synthetic datasets and real RNA-Seq data. Results show that Fleximer is able to minimize the prediction errors, providing a more accurate transcript abundance estimation compare to existing k-mer based methods. Fleximer is implemented in C++11 and available at https://github.com/chelseaju/Fleximer.git.

2 METHODS

2.1 Fleximer Overview

The lightweight algorithms for RNA-Seq quantification start with identifying a set of *k-mers* in a transcriptome, followed by either counting the occurrence of *k-mers* in RNA-Seq reads, or directly counting the reads that contain these *k-mers*. Since we know the transcript origins of these *k-mers*, transcript abundance can be inferred from read counts or *k-mers* counts. We first partition a transcriptome Θ into a set of non-overlapping clusters θ_1, θ_2, .., θ_n based on sequence similarity, and select a special type of *k-mers*, named *sig-mers*, for each cluster. These *sig-mers* represent the discriminative short sequences of a cluster of transcripts and do not appear in any other clusters. Adopting the terminology introduced by RNA-Skim, a set of *sig-mers* s in cluster θ_i is defined as

$$\Omega(\theta_i) = \{s \mid s \in (k\text{-mers in } \theta_i), \forall \theta_j \in \Theta \setminus \theta_i, s \notin (k\text{-mers in } \theta_j)\}$$

The size of *k-mers* can have a predominant effect toward the accuracy of transcript abundance estimation. We conducted an experiment to examine the effects of different ks. Experimental details are described in Section 4.1. We compared the estimated abundance to true abundance using 14 sets of *sig-mers* from RNA-Skim, and six sets of *k-mers* from Kallisto, with different values of k. We observed that the best prediction for each transcript falls in different ks. Additionally, the accuracy varied largely among different sets of *sig-mers* for some genes. Motivated by these observations, our method aims to efficiently select a set of *sig-mers* with flexible lengths, and to accurately quantify transcript abundance using this set of *sig-mers* in RNA-Seq data. We divide our objective into four components, with the first two focusing on *sig-mer* generation and the last two addressing transcript quantification. Figure 1 shows an overview of our approach. We follow the partition scheme in RNA-Skim [28] to generate a set of non-overlapping clusters of transcripts based on sequence similarity. Given this set of clusters, the transcript sequences are inspected using a suffix tree data structure to identify the *sig-mers* of each cluster. We select a subset of *sig-mers* that are robust to read errors, and can best describe the signatures of each transcript. We then use the Aho-Corasick algorithm to efficiently determine the occurrence of *sig-mers* in each read. The presence of these *sig-mers* provides the information of transcripts where each read is potentially originated from. The counts of these potential transcripts are then distributed by the EM algorithm for expression quantification. In this section, we describe each component of Fleximer in detail, including a brief review of the suffix tree.

2.2 Background on Suffix Tree

Let t' be a string over the alphabet $\Sigma = \{A, C, G, T\}$, and "\$" be a unique character, such that $\$ \notin \Sigma$. This unique character is appended to the end of the string t' to guarantee that every suffix ends at a leaf in the tree. Therefore, we use the following notations: t denotes the entire string with a terminator ($t' + \$$), and $|t|$ denotes the size of t. The string t can be degenerated into $|t|$ suffixes, and stored into a compressed tree structure, known as the suffix tree. This suffix tree contains exactly $|t|$ leaves, which are labeled by the starting position of the corresponding suffix. Each internal node has at least two children. The label of an internal node is omitted for memory efficiency. Each edge is labeled with a non-empty substring of t; edges connecting from the same parent contains different starting characters. The edge labels can be concatenated through a path in the tree, forming a longer substring of t. Thus, any individual suffix of t can be recreated by traversing along a path from the root to a leaf and concatenating the labels of the edges along the way.

Multiple sequences can be stored in the same tree, forming a generalized suffix tree (GST) [3]. A GST can be constructed by appending different unique symbols at the end of each sequence to ensure no suffix is a substring of another. Alternatively, we can

[1] http://www.cs.cmu.edu/~ckingsf/software/sailfish/faq.html

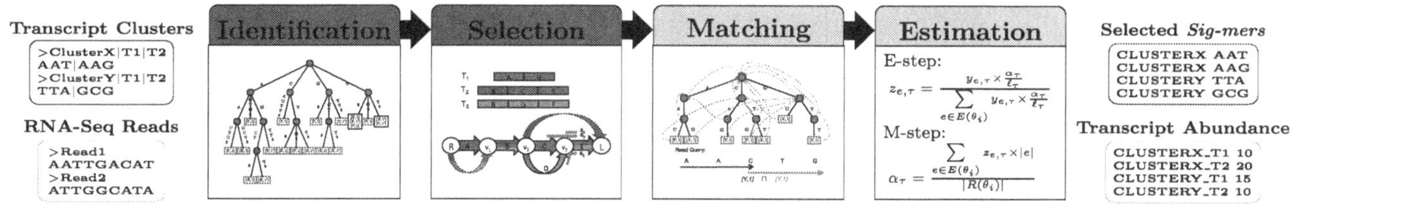

Figure 1: Fleximer Overview. Data input contains a predefined partition of a transcriptome, and RNA-Seq reads. The partition is stored in a specialized fasta format, where each entry represents one cluster. The header starts with a cluster name, follow by transcript names. The sequence field contains all transcript sequences in a cluster, separated by a special character "|". In *sig-mer* identification, we construct a suffix tree based on forward and reverse complementary sequences of all transcripts. We apply a post-order traversal on the suffix tree to identify all *sig-mers* with different lengths. We filter these *sig-mers* to keep only the optimal ones and use them to estimate the transcript expression in RNA-Seq data. In the matching step, we use the Aho-Corasick algorithm to determine the occurrence of *sig-mers* in each read. We then apply the EM algorithm to resolve the count of reads that are shared by multiple transcripts. The blue boxes denote the preparation stage for *sig-mer* generation, which only needs to be executed once. The green boxes denote the analysis stage, which applies to each RNA-Seq experiment.

concatenate these sequences into one long string, separated by a single terminator, and build a regular suffix tree for the resulting string. Regardless of using a single or multiple terminators, each leaf node stores sufficient information to retrieve the starting positions and sequence of origin for each suffix.

The construction of a suffix tree takes linear time and space respect to the total sequence size [6, 16, 24]. The most memory efficient implementation to handle genomic sequences is the Sadakane's compressed suffix tree [21, 25], which relies on several abstract data structures to reduce the memory footprint. It also preserves all the operations for a normal suffix tree. One of the abstract data structures is balanced parentheses [17], which represents the tree in pre-order. This structure can be further modified to retrieve node information in post-order. For these reasons, we implement our method using Sadakane's compressed suffix tree, which is available from Succinct Data Structure Library (SDSL) [2].

2.3 *Sig-mers* Identification in Fleximer

Given a set of n transcripts in a cluster θ_i, our first task is to identify the *sig-mers* that can characterize the uniqueness of a cluster. Suppose the average length of transcripts is m, the complexity of retrieving and examining all k-*mers* with length less than k is bounded by $O(nkm)$ (Supplementary A). In the human genome, there are over 20,000 protein coding genes, corresponding to more than 198,000 transcripts. The average length of a transcript is approximately 2,000 bp. Therefore, enumerating all possible substrings to check for their uniqueness is computationally intractable. The suffix tree is a powerful data structure for string searching algorithm, and it has been widely applied to a diverse range of biological sequence analyses [10, 11, 15]. Leveraging the suffix tree structure and properties, we apply a post-order traversal to identify all unique substrings.

We build a suffix tree based on all prefixes and suffixes of transcript sequences. We use both forward and reverse complementary sequences to construct the tree. There are two practical aspects to include the reverse complementary sequences. First, reads from the sequencing technology can be generated from the complementary strand. Second, suffixes of a reverse complementary sequence serve as the same mean as the prefixes of its forward sequence. If a substring is a *sig-mer*, then its reverse complementary sequence is also a *sig-mer*. In a suffix tree, if a substring from the root to any node appears only once in our transcript sequences, this path contains at least one *sig-mer*. We refer this node as a candidate. An internal node typically represents a substring that appears more than once in our transcript sequences. The path to any internal node contains a *sig-mer* only if all of the starting positions of this substring are located in the same cluster. These starting positions can be retrieved recursively from its descendants. Specifically, we use a bottom-up approach to examine each node through a post-order traversal.

The post-order traversal starts with the left subtree, followed by the right subtree, and the parent. We store the substring information of the nodes that have already been visited. This information does not include the actual sequence, but is sufficient to retrieve the cluster and sequence IDs, and the starting positions of a substring. At each internal node, we determine if it is a candidate by examining all substrings from its children. If all substrings come from the same cluster, then it is a candidate. Otherwise, the search process terminates for this branch, marking this node and its ancestors disqualified. Since the cluster information of a substring propagates from the leaves, all the ancestors of a disqualified node can be pruned. We use this anti-monotonic constraint to avoid further computation of its ancestors. Figure 2 uses a toy example to illustrate this idea to discover all *sig-mers*.

A substring from the root to a candidate node represents the longest *sig-mer* at this candidate. On the other hand, a substring from the root to the first character on the edge between the candidate node and its parent represents the shortest *sig-mer* for this candidate. In order to obtain *sig-mers* with all possible sizes, we need to append all prefixes of the edge label between the candidate and its parent to the path from the root to its parent. An example is illustrated in Figure 2.

2.4 *Sig-mers* Selection in Fleximer

The compressed suffix tree allows us to efficiently discover all *sig-mers* with different sizes. However, not all of them are necessary for the quantification stage. We select a set of representative *sig-mers* that possess three properties: 1) Be robust to sequencing errors and

[2]https://github.com/simongog/sdsl-lite/

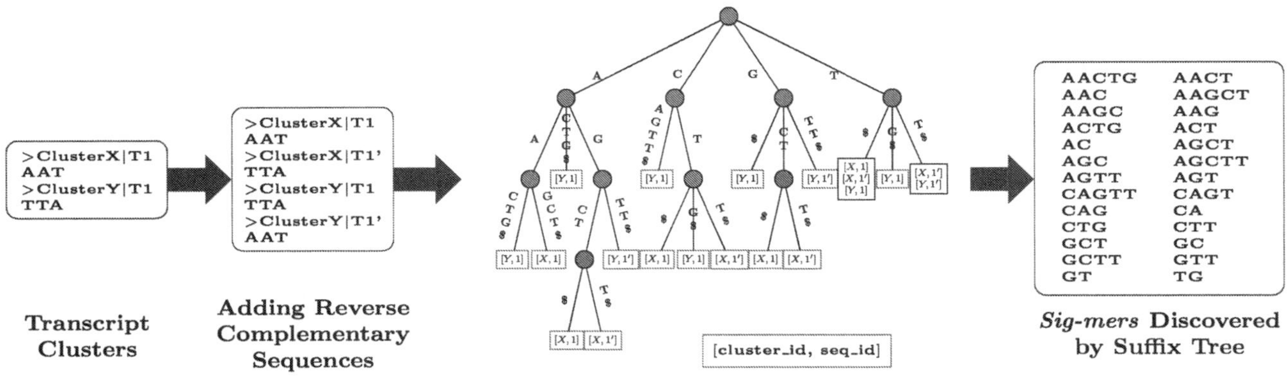

Figure 2: *Sig-mers* Identification. We use both forward and reverse complementary sequences of each transcript to construct a generalized suffix tree. Each leaf contains cluster and sequence IDs of a suffix. Each edge is labeled by a substring. The cluster and sequence IDs of an internal node are retrieved from its descendants through a post-order traversal. Candidates are highlighted in red. For example, substring *AGCT$* and *AGCTT$* appear uniquely in sequence 1 and 1' (reverse complementary of sequence 1) of cluster X, respectively. Thus, their nodes are candidates. Their parent is also a candidate since *AGCT* only appears in cluster X but not in cluster Y. However, their grandparent is not a candidate as *AG* appears in both cluster X and Y. The traversal process terminates here for this subtree. In order to generate all *sig-mers* with different sizes, we consider all prefixes of an edge label between a candidate and its parent. Therefore, *AGC* is also a *sig-mer* in addition to *AGCT*.

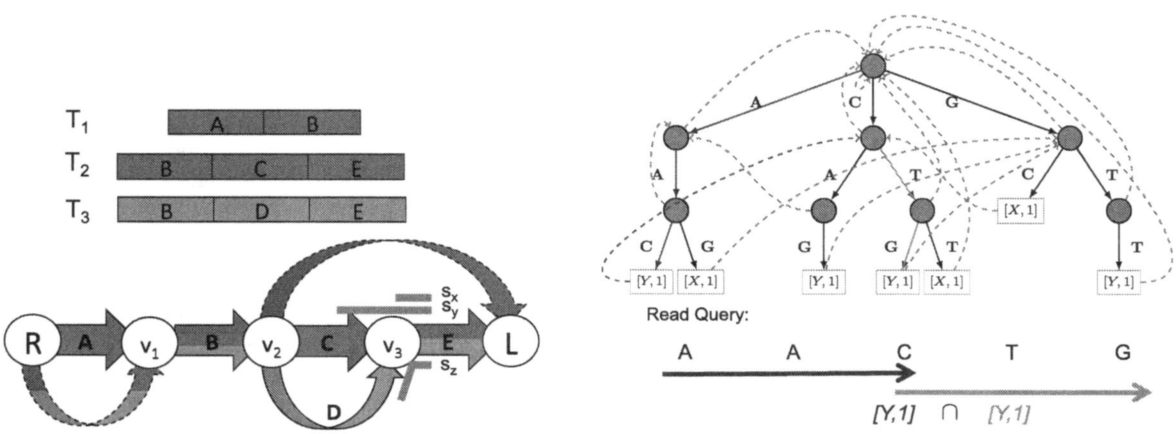

(a) *Sig-mer* Selection

(b) Read Matching

Figure 3: a) A cluster contains three transcripts, T_1, T_2, and T_3. The upper figure shows the composition of these transcripts. Each box represents either a unique or shared sequence segment. For example, segment B is shared by all transcripts, where segment A is unique to transcript T_1. If they are isoforms of the same gene, segment B can be interpreted as a common exon. Since a partition may include transcripts from more than one gene, we use the term 'segment' instead of the exon. A compact splicing graph can be constructed for all member transcripts in a cluster, as demonstrated in the lower figure. Each edge represents a segment, and each vertex indicates a transition point. Two virtual edges are included as dotted arrows from R to v_1 and from v_2 to L. In this graph, sequences of these three transcripts are depicted by three paths (blue, red, and gray) from R to L. *Sig-mers* can be viewed as a substring of an edge, denoted by the pink lines. *Sig-mers* span through a vertex are more powerful to determine the origin of a read, and thus are prioritized for selection. b) We use an automaton to facilitate the matching step between reads and a set of representative *sig-mers*. Each node consists a failure link to guide the search. Given a query "AACTG", we follow the path AAC (dark blue) and find the substring belongs to sequence 1 in cluster Y. Following the failure link, we can quickly find CTG (light blue), which also belongs to sequence 1 in cluster Y.

individual variations. 2) Characterize the uniqueness of each transcript. 3) Provide sufficient coverage across all transcript sequences. We will first discuss the optimal range of k for robustness.

In an ideal scenario where there are no sequencing errors and individual variations, *sig-mers* will match all reads that come from the same cluster. In reality, reads contain sequencing errors and individual variations. These reads are less likely to be recognized by long *sig-mers* since the matching process requires an exact match. On the other hand, these reads have a higher risk to be "matched" by short *sig-mers* that belong to other clusters. Therefore, a *sig-mer* cannot be too long or too short, with the optimal range depending on the sequencing error rate and the fraction of individual variations. In addition, the upper bound of k is constrained by the read length of an RNA-Seq experiment. Based on these considerations, we set the lower bound to 25bp, and the upper bound to 80% of a read length. *Sig-mers* are filtered based on their sizes.

After filtering, we use the concept of a splicing graph [9, 22] to guide the selection. Splicing graph is first introduced to predict and represent the choices of alternative splicing for a gene model [18]. It is a directed cyclic graph, in which vertices represent the splicing sites and edges are the exons or introns between two splicing sites. Two virtual vertices are added to the graph, root (R) and leaf (L), along with virtual edges, so that each transcript can be represented by a path that goes from R to L. Vertices with their indegree and outdegree equal to 1 are uninformative for delimiting alternative splicing event, and are often collapsed to obtain a more compact representation. Analogously, we can use a compact splicing graph to represent all member transcripts in a cluster. A cluster may contain transcripts from more than one gene, depending on the partitioning scheme. To incorporate this scenario, we broaden the definition of the edges and vertices. Edges represent different sequence segments that appear at least once in a cluster, and vertices represent transition points where the incoming edge covers a different set of transcripts from the outgoing edge. Figure 3a illustrates the compact splicing graph of a cluster with three member transcripts. A *sig-mers* can be viewed as a substring of an edge. As we observe from the graph, a *sig-mer* possesses higher discriminative power if it spans through a vertex. Considering three *sig-mers* s_x, s_y, and s_z in Figure 3a, s_x resides completely on segment E and is shared by two transcripts. Given a read that contains s_x, the origin of this read can be either one of these transcripts. On the other hand, s_y and s_z span through vertex v_3, and are unique to transcript T_2 and T_3, respectively. Since s_y and s_z are superstrings of s_x, reads containing s_y and s_z also contain s_x. However, s_y and s_z provide more specific information regarding the origin of these reads. Therefore, the selection process prioritizes *sig-mers* that span through a vertex.

The original proposal of splicing graph is constructed through ESTs (expressed sequence tags) or RNA-Seq reads assembly. Since we already know the starting positions of all *sig-mers*, we do not need to assemble these *sig-mers*. Instead, we order the *sig-mers* based on their starting positions. As we traverse through all starting positions in a sequential order, we pave all paths of a splicing graph. To provide a sufficient coverage for each transcript, we select additional *sig-mers* along the path, spaced by a small gap (e.g., 5bp) between two *sig-mers*. Since RNA-Seq reads may originate from transcripts in either forward or reverse direction, complementary sequences of the selected *sig-mers* are added to the final list.

2.5 RNA-Seq Reads Matching

The quantification stage starts with determining the potential transcript origins of each RNA-Seq read. We refer this set of potential transcripts as the "transcript profile" of a read. In the traditional framework, the transcript profile of a read is determined by aligning the read sequence to the reference transcriptome. In our setting, each *sig-mer* is associated with a transcript profile indicating its origins. We can construct the transcript profile for each read by taking the intersection of all transcript profiles associated with the *sig-mers* that appear in a read.

Discovering the occurrence of our representative *sig-mers* in RNA-Seq reads is equivalent to the keyword searching problem in computer science. A trivial approach is to index the representative *sig-mers* (keywords) with a hash table. Since we allow variable *sig-mer* sizes, the challenge lies on scanning through each read with different window sizes. Even with an efficient hashing function, such as rolling hash [12], the number of comparisons increases with the variety of window sizes. Assume that the read length is ℓ, and total length of *sig-mers* is M. The sizes of these *sig-mers* range from k_1 to k_d. The time complexity for constructing the hash is $O(M)$, and for searching *sig-mers* in one read is $O(\ell \times k_1) + \ldots + O(\ell \times k_d)$. The total time complexity would be $O(M + \ell \times \frac{k_1+k_d}{2} \times d)$.

A linear search solution is the Aho-Corasick algorithm [1], which constructs a finite state automaton for all *sig-mers*. This automaton is a keyword tree with additional links between internal nodes. These extra links allow fast transition between *sig-mer* matches without the need for backtracking. The complexity of building the automaton is $O(M)$ and for searching is $O(\ell + z)$ where z refers to the total number of occurrences of *sig-mers* in a read. Figure 3b illustrates the search using the Aho-Corasick algorithm.

2.6 Transcript Abundance Estimation

Since the transcriptome is partitioned into a set of non-overlapping cluster, each cluster can be quantified independently. After the *sig-mer* matching step, each read is associated with a transcript profile indicating its potential origins. Based on these profiles, we can group reads into their corresponding clusters. For each cluster θ_i, we use $\mathrm{R}(\theta_i)$ to represent the set of reads assigned to cluster θ_i, and $\mathrm{T}(\theta_i)$ to represent the set of transcripts in θ_i. Each transcript $\tau \in \mathrm{T}(\theta_i)$ is associated with a probability α_τ indicating its proportion of reads in cluster θ_i, and $\sum \alpha_\tau = 1$. If we know the exact origin of each read, we can form an indicator matrix Z, where $z_{r,\tau} = 1$ indicating that read $r \in \mathrm{R}(\theta_i)$ comes from transcript τ, and 0 otherwise. Since each read only comes from one transcript, α_τ can be estimated by $\sum z_{r,\tau} \ / \ |\mathrm{R}(\theta_i)|$, where $|\mathrm{R}(\theta_i)|$ is the total number of reads in θ_i. However, Z is not fully observed, and what we observed is the transcript profiles for each read, forming another indicator matrix Y. Similarly, $y_{r,\tau} = 1$ if τ is in the transcript profile of read r. Z is the hidden variable, and can be recovered from the observation Y. Therefore, we use the following likelihood function to estimate α:

$$\mathcal{L}(\alpha|Y) = \prod_{r \in \mathrm{R}(\theta_i)} \sum_{\tau \in \mathrm{T}(\theta_i)} y_{r,\tau} \frac{\alpha_\tau}{\ell_\tau} = \prod_{e \in \mathrm{E}(\theta_i)} \left(\sum_{\tau \in \mathrm{T}(\theta_i)} \frac{\alpha_\tau}{\ell_\tau} \right)^{|e|}$$

In this log-likelihood function, ℓ_τ is the effective length for transcript τ. We can improve the computation speed and memory by grouping reads with the same transcript profile into equivalence classes. The concept of the equivalence class is widely used in transcript abundance estimation [4, 19, 28]. We use $\mathrm{E}(\theta_i)$ to represent the set of equivalence classes in θ_i, and equivalence class $e \in \mathrm{E}(\theta_i)$ contains $|e|$ reads. We use the EM algorithm to compute the maximum likelihood estimates of α from our observed data Y. The algorithm alternates between allocating the fraction of counts of each equivalence class (E-step), and estimating the relative abundance given this allocation (M-step). More specifically, the E-step reconstruct the hidden variable Z as $z_{e,\tau} = \frac{y_{e,\tau} \times \frac{\alpha_\tau}{\ell_\tau}}{\sum_{e \in E(\theta_i)} y_{e,\tau} \times \frac{\alpha_\tau}{\ell_\tau}}$, and the M-step updates the probability through Z, $\alpha_\tau = \frac{\sum_{e \in E(\theta_i)} z_{e,\tau} \times |e|}{|R(\theta_i)|}$.The algorithm converges when the change of α is less than 10^{-7}. At convergence, read count of τ can be recovered through α_τ and $|R(\theta_i)|$. We report transcript abundance in three commonly used metrics: raw read count, RPKM (Reads Per Kilobase of transcript per Million mapped reads), and TPM (Transcripts Per Kilobase Million). Both RPKM and TPM are normalized measurements that account for sequencing depth and transcript length.

3 DATA

3.1 Reference Transcriptome

We used the gene annotation from Ensembl release 81 of Human Genome GRCh38 [5], which contained more than 22,000 protein-coding genes. Among these, there are 19,817 protein-coding genes located on the canonical chromosomes (chr1-21, X, Y, Mt). Our experiments focus only on the transcripts encoded by these genes, which correspond to 143,609 protein-coding transcripts.

Sequences of these transcripts were decomposed into k-mers and indexed by Sailfish and Kallisto. For RNA-Skim and Fleximer, these transcripts were first partitioned into non-overlapping clusters. Transcripts with high sequence similarity were placed in the same cluster. This partitioning scheme was adopted from RNA-Skim, resulting in 16,149 clusters. Details of this process were described in [28]. We used the specialized fasta format suggested in RNA-Skim to store the sequences. The header of each entry contains a cluster name and transcript names, separated by a special character "|". Similarly, the body of an entry contains transcript sequences in a cluster, separated by "|". Parameter settings of each software are described in Supplementary B.

3.2 Simulated Dataset

We used *polyester* [7] to generate 15 sets of single-end RNA-Seq reads for selected transcripts to evaluate the accuracy of different methods. We randomly selected 2-10 % of the protein-coding transcripts to be expressed in each sample. Each sample contained 3-97 millions of reads, with a read length of 75bp. Three different read depths were used: 10X, 20X, and 30X. We selected an empirical sequencing error model from *polyester* to simulate the protocol of Illumina Sequencing Kit v4. Each read was tagged with the name of the transcript where it originated. We computed the expected number of reads for each transcript by counting the transcript names in the raw read file. The expected RPKM and TPM were calculated from the expected read count.

3.3 Real Dataset

We included a public dataset provided by the Illumina Human BodyMap 2.0 Project (GSE30611). The samples contained individual and a mixture of 16 human tissues RNA, and were sequenced using Illumina HiSeq 2000 System. Among all these samples, we used six of the single-end data with 75bp in our evaluation: female brain, breast, and colon; male adrenal, lung, and liver. The Expression Atlas [20] provides gene expression information of highly-curated and quality-checked RNA-seq experiments, including all 16 human tissues of the Human BodyMap Project. We used the gene expression values reported in http://www.ebi.ac.uk/gxa/experiments/E-MTAB-513/ as our ground standard.

4 EXPERIMENTS AND RESULTS

4.1 Motivating Example

Current lightweight quantification methods use a fixed k; however, a set of fixed size k-*mers* may not be sufficient to capture the signature of each transcript. We evaluated the effect of different ks in abundance estimation for both Kallisto and RNA-Skim. Kallisto allows users to set k to be any odd integer up to 31; RNA-Skim does not have any restriction on the choice of k. For Kallisto, we indexed the transcriptome using 6 different ks. For RNA-Skim, we selected 14 sets of *sig-mers* with different ks. We used these k-*mers* to estimate the TPM of a simulated dataset containing 11,484 expressed transcripts. We computed the absolute differences between true and estimated TPM. A smaller value indicates a better estimation.

Among these sets of k-*mers*, we marked the k that gave the best prediction (smallest difference) for each transcript. Figure 4a shows the distribution of the best k. We also plotted three transcripts that displayed interesting estimation patterns over different ks in Figures 4b-d. The estimations fluctuate largely in RNA-Skim for these transcripts, indicating that this method is very sensitive to the choice of k. The variation is less severe in Kallisto; however, setting k to 21 produces the best prediction for ENST00000626009, but gives the worst prediction for both ENST00000265881 and ENST00000357370. These results indicate that the optimal k varies for different transcripts, and the selection of k has a substantial influence on the prediction accuracy.

4.2 k-*mers* Generation

Fleximer selects 6,299,554 *sig-mers* with sizes ranging from 25 to 60. Note that since the sequencing reads of our datasets were 75bp, we set the upper bound of k to 60. The distribution of the *sig-mers* size is illustrated in Figure 5a, where the frequencies are plotted in log-10 scale. The majority of the *sig-mers* reside on our lower bound; however, the rest of the *sig-mers* are equally distributed among this range. On the other hand, using the default parameters, RNA-Skim generates a set of 4,221,162 *sig-mers* with a fixed size of 60. Using the same fixed size of 31, Sailfish produces a set of 95,601,889 k-*mers* and Kallisto produces 94,945,357 k-*mers*. Figure 5b compares the number of k-*mers* generated in different methods. In terms of computational resources, Fleximer needs more time to identify a set of optimal *sig-mers* than other methods since the search space is much bigger. However, it is worth mentioning that this step only needs to be executed once. Sadakane's compressed suffix tree allows us to perform this step in less than 10G, which requires less memory than Sailfish and RNA-Skim.

4.3 Simulation Study

We evaluated the prediction accuracy using 15 simulated datasets. The accuracy metrics include Pearson correlation, rank correlation, and root-mean-square error (RMSE) (Supplementary C).

Figure 6 illustrates three metrics separately for different read depths. Each bar shows the mean and standard deviation over 5

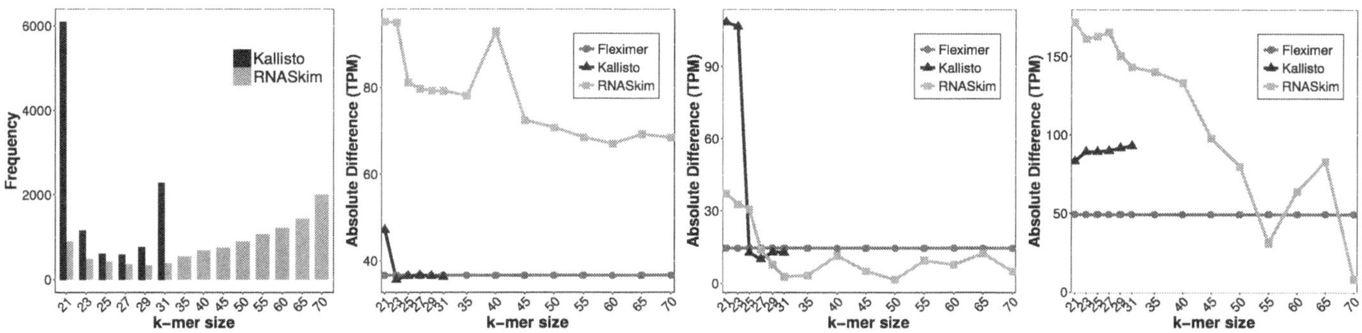

(a) Histograms (b) ENST00000265881 (c) ENST00000357370 (d) ENST00000626009

Figure 4: Evaluation of the TPM estimation over different sets of *k-mers*. a) The histogram shows the number of transcripts with the smallest error at different *k*s. b-d) Errors (absolute differences; smaller is better) at different *k*s for individual transcripts. Fleximer uses a wide range of *k*s, so the error is plotted as a single line.

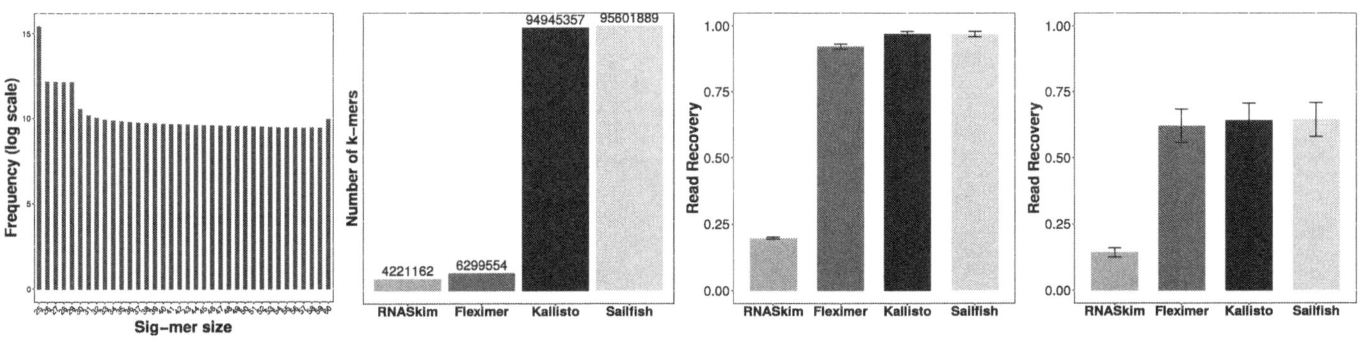

(a) Size Distribution (b) Number of *k-mers* (c) Simulated Studies (d) Human BodyMap

Figure 5: a) Distribution of *Sig-mers* sizes (25 to 60) in Fleximer b) Number of *k-mers* used in different methods for transcript abundance quantification. c-d) The average number of reads recovered by different sets of *k-mers* for simulated and real data, respectively. Error bars are included using one standard deviation.

datasets. Results indicate that Fleximer and Sailfish perform similarly with consistent Pearson and rank correlations. The Pearson correlations are slightly higher for Fleximer at different read depths. Higher correlation values are better as the predictions are in the same trend as the ground truth. On the other hand, lower residual errors are better as the predictions are closer to the ground truth. Fleximer presents the smallest RMSE among four methods. We also evaluated the running time as shown in Figure 7. Fleximer requires more time than others due to searching *sig-mers* of different sizes; however, it scales linearly with the number of reads. All experiments finish in less than 25 minutes (1500s). We further examined the utilization of our representative *sig-mers*. We calculated the fraction of reads recovered by each method. Figure 5c shows that Fleximer is able to cover more than 90% of the reads with fewer *k-mers* than Kallisto and Sailfish. The *sig-mers* Fleximer used are much more effective than the *sig-mer* set in RNA-Skim, which only recovers less than 30% of the reads.

4.4 Human BodyMap 2.0 Project

Simulated datasets could not capture all of the biases presented in a real RNA-Seq experiment; therefore, we evaluated the performance of different methods using six datasets from the Human BodyMap project. Figure 5d shows that on average, Fleximer is able to identify a similar amount of reads in these datasets as Sailfish and Kallisto (> 60%), but with less amount of *k-mers*. This result is consistent as demonstrated in the simulated studies.

Since we did not know the true abundance of each transcript, we used the estimated abundance reported in Expression Atlas as our ground standard. Expression Atlas provided expression values in RPKM on gene-level (instead of transcript-level). Two post-processing techniques are applied to normalize these values. First, we converted expression values reported in Expression Atlas to TPM. Second, we aggregated the expressions of all transcript isoforms estimated in each method to represent the gene expression. After normalization, we removed the non-protein coding genes from Expression Atlas and conducted the analyses on gene-level. Figure 8 shows an overall comparison of the number of expressed genes identified by each method, and Table 1 summarizes the comparison of expressed genes between each method and the ground standard. Expressed genes are defined as those with TPM greater than zero. Across six datasets, all methods identify a large number of shared expressed genes as demonstrated by the large overlap in six Venn diagrams. Each method identifies a few amount of unique genes that are not picked up by others. Among the four methods, RNA-Skim misses out the largest number of expressed genes reported in Expression Atlas (false negative). However, Sailfish and Kallisto pick up around 100 more genes than Fleximer that are not reported in Expression Atlas (false positive). We also experimented

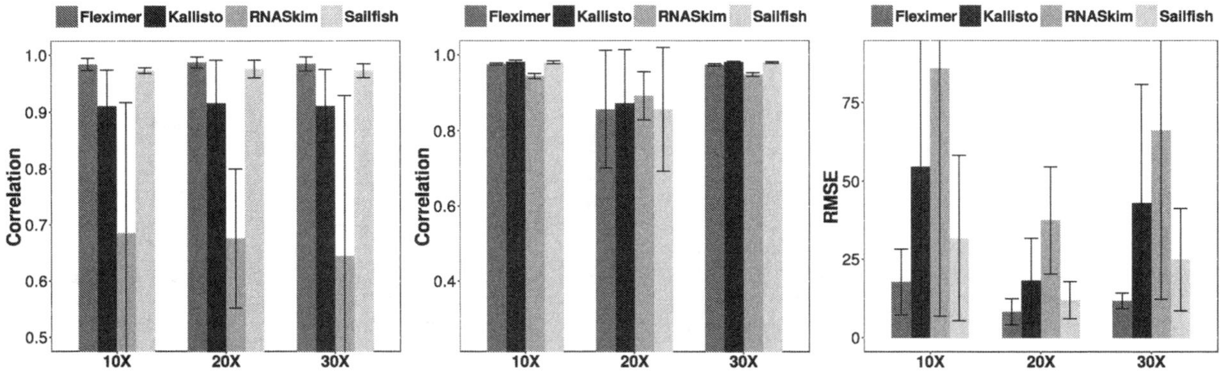

(a) Pearson Correlation (Higher is better)

(b) Rank Correlation (Higher is better)

(c) RMSE (Lower is better)

Figure 6: Accuracy Evaluations for Simulated Studies on Transcript-Level

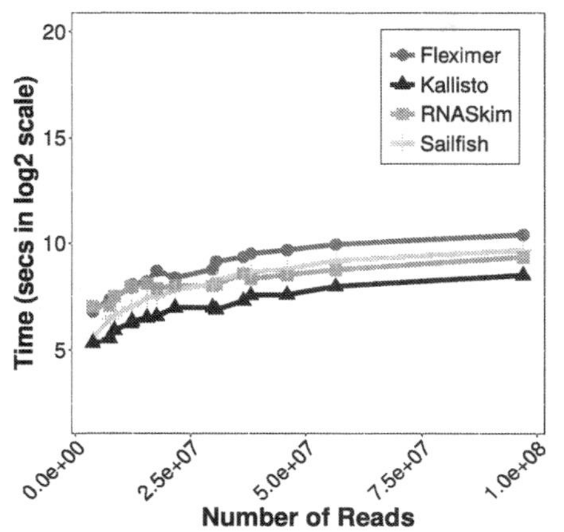

Figure 7: Running Time for Simulated Studies. Time is represented as seconds in the log-2 scale, where 10 represents to 1024 seconds (approximately 17 minutes).

with different thresholds in defining the expressed genes (i.e. 0.1, 0.5, and 1), and observed similar results as setting the TPM threshold to 0.

We further evaluated the prediction power of four different methods against the values reported in Expression Atlas using all genes. Figure 9 summarizes the average values of each accuracy metric over six datasets. Fleximer demonstrates the best accuracy, with the highest Pearson and rank correlations and the lowest RMSE.

5 CONCLUSION AND DISCUSSIONS

RNA-Seq has been the dominating technology in quantifying transcript abundance. The advent of this technology also comes with numerous computational challenges, especially in analyzing a large amount of data. Sailfish, RNA-Skim, and Kallisto have recently developed to aim for a rapid quantification using a pre-selected set of *k-mers*. These *k-mers* are of the same length, and present a limitation in characterizing different transcripts. We propose a novel method that allows selecting *k-mers* of flexible sizes.

Our approach leverages the properties and structure of a suffix tree to efficiently discover these *sig-mers*, and selects a subset of representative *sig-mers* for quantification. In order to determine the occurrences of these variable-length *sig-mers* in reads, Fleximer utilizes the Aho-Corasick algorithm to scan through reads in linear time. The final transcript abundance is estimated by the EM algorithm using the read counts. The results show that Fleximer is able to improve the accuracy of abundance estimations with fewer *sig-mers*. This observation is due to the fact that these variable-length *sig-mers* are capable of recognizing the signatures of each read in the RNA-Seq datasets. In addition, we only need a small set of *sig-mers* since they are unique enough to characterize different transcripts. In the future work, we would like to further improve the running time of our quantification step with parallel computing. We are also interested in exploring the possibilities of applying the idea of flexible *k-mers* to other sequencing applications.

ACKNOWLEDGMENTS

We thank Dr. Zhaojun Zhang and Dr. Farhad Hormozdiari for their comments and discussions, and Ms. Kim Vo for her proofreading. We would also like to thank the anonymous reviewers for their valuable comments and helpful suggestions. This work is supported by NIH R01GM115833, NSF DBI-1565137 and NSF IIS-1313606.

A RETRIEVING ALL *K-MERS*

Suppose the average length of a transcript is m, the complexity of retrieving and examining all *k-mers* with length less than and equal to k in one transcript is

$$\begin{aligned}\text{retrieve k-mers} &= m + (m-1) + (m-2) + \cdots + (m-k+1)\\ &= km - (1 + 2 + \cdots + (k-1))\\ &= km - (k \times (k-1)/2)\\ &= O(km)\end{aligned}$$

Given n transcripts, retrieving all *k-mers* is bounded by $O(nkm)$.

B SOFTWARE COMPARISON

B.1 Sailfish

The binary version of Sailfish-0.9.2 was downloaded. We followed the default setting of *k-mer* size for the indexing step (`--kmerSize = 31`). To conduct a fair comparison of all software, we used a

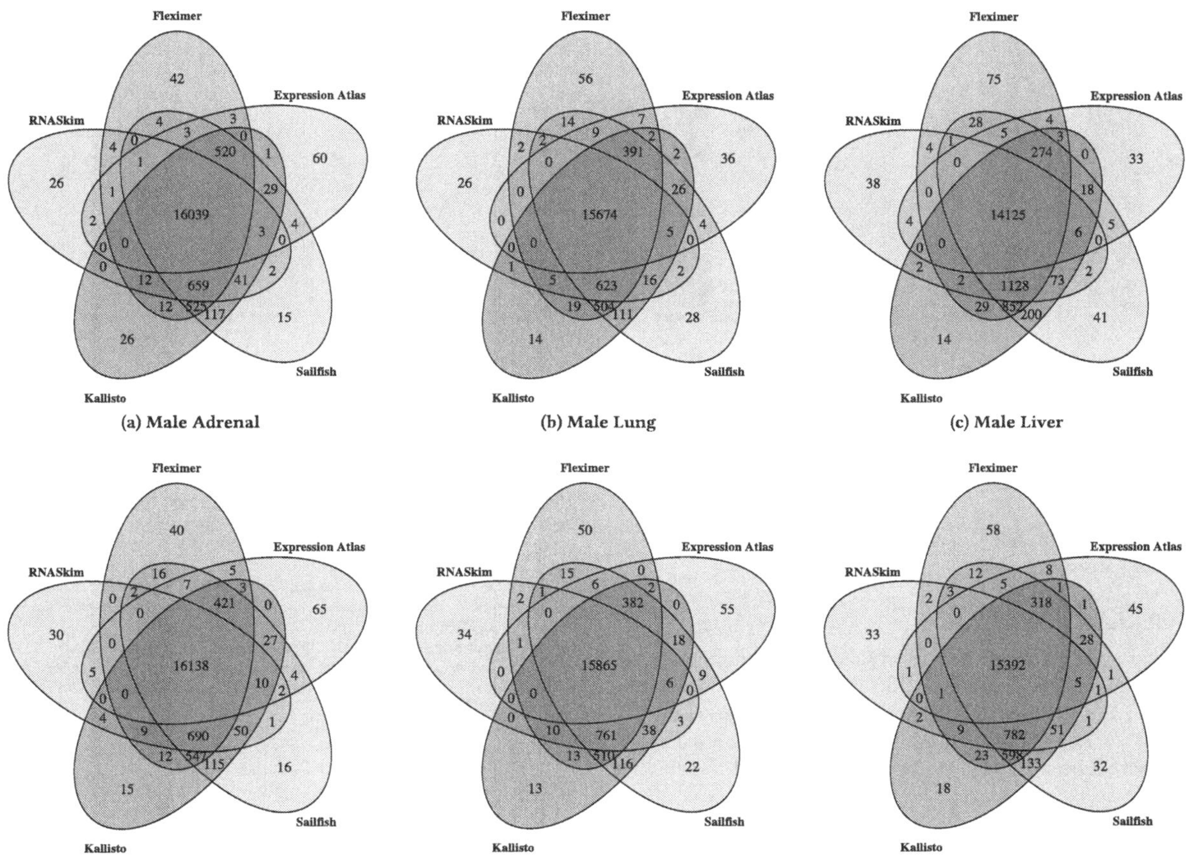

(a) Male Adrenal (b) Male Lung (c) Male Liver

(d) Female Brain (e) Female Breast (f) Female Colon

Figure 8: Evaluation of Human BodyMap. Venn diagrams showing the number of common and unique expressed genes identified by different methods.

Table 1: Comparison with Expression Atlas. True positives (TP) refer to expressed genes that are identified by each method and reported in Expression Atlas. False negatives (FN) refer to expressed genes that are reported in Expression Atlas but missed by each method. False positives (FP) refer to genes that are identified by each method but are not reported in Expression Atlas.

Method	Fleximer			RNA-Skim			Sailfish			Kallisto		
Evaluation	TP	FN	FP	TP	FN	FP	TP	FN	FP	TP	FN	FP
Male Adrenal	16567	99	1258	16046	620	744	16599	67	1363	16592	74	1392
Male Lung	16083	73	1225	15679	477	677	16109	47	1300	16100	56	1293
Male Liver	14411	66	2119	14135	342	1250	14433	44	2325	14426	51	2300
Female Brain	16574	113	1316	16155	532	786	16609	78	1437	16599	88	1442
Female Breast	16256	88	1362	15872	472	849	16286	58	1466	16273	71	1461
Female Colon	15725	82	1487	15400	407	883	15750	57	1612	15746	61	1616

single thread for both of the indexing and quantification steps (`--threads = 1`). All of our datasets contained single-end reads with a read length of 75bp; therefore, we used these parameters in the quantification stage: `-l -U --fldMean 75` and `--fldSD 1`.

B.2 Kallisto

The source code of Kallisto 0.43 was compiled with GCC/4.8.3. The suggested *kmer* size was the same as Sailfish. We set `--kmer-size=31` for indexing. For quantification, we used a single thread, `--threads=1`. To adjust for effective length, we used `--single -l 75 -s 1`.

B.3 RNA-Skim

The source code was compiled with GCC/4.7.2. We ran `rs_cluster` to generate the partition, with `-rs_length=60`. We ran `rs_index` and `rs_select` to generate a set of *sig-mers*. In the motivating example, `rs_length` was set to different values to evaluate the

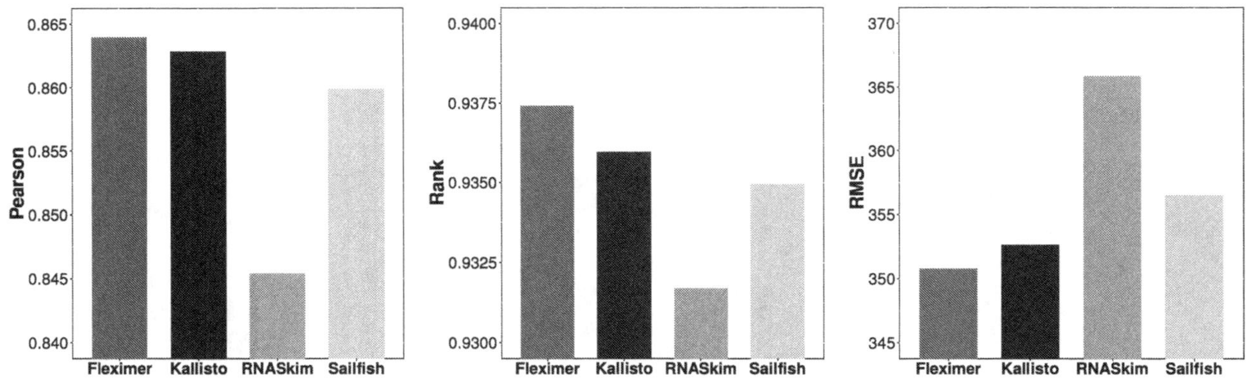

(a) Pearson Correlation (Higher is better)

(b) Rank Correlation (Higher is better)

(c) RMSE (Lower is better)

Figure 9: Accuracy Evaluations for Real Datasets on Gene-Level

effects of different ks. In both simulated and real studies, `rs_length` was set to 60 as suggested by RNA-Skim. We ran `rs_count` and `rs_estimate` using the default settings. We set `-num_threads=1` to enforce the software running on one thread.

C ACCURACY METRICS

We used Pearson, rank correlations, and Root Mean Squared Error (RMSE) to evaluate the accuracy of four different methods. Both of the Pearson and rank correlations were computed between the estimated abundance (TPM) and the true TPM. Given a list of n transcripts with estimated TPM of $x_1, x_2, \ldots, x_n$ and their true TPMs $y_1, y_2, \ldots, y_n$, the RMSE was calculated as $\sqrt{\frac{\sum_{i=1}^{n}(x_i - y_i)^2}{n}}$.

REFERENCES

[1] Alfred V. Aho and Margaret J. Corasick. 1975. Efficient string matching: an aid to bibliographic search. *Commun. ACM* 18, 6 (jun 1975), 333–340. https://doi.org/10.1145/360825.360855

[2] Kin Fai Au, Hui Jiang, Lan Lin, Yi Xing, and Wing Hung Wong. 2010. Detection of splice junctions from paired-end RNA-seq data by SpliceMap. *Nucleic acids research* 38, 14 (aug 2010), 4570–8. https://doi.org/10.1093/nar/gkq211

[3] Paul Bieganski, John Riedl, John V. Carlis, and Ernest F. Retzel. 1994. Generalized suffix trees for biological sequence data: applications and implementation. In *Proceedings of the Twenty-Seventh Hawaii International Conference on System Sciences HICSS-94*, Vol. 5. IEEE Comput. Soc. Press, 35–44. https://doi.org/10.1109/HICSS.1994.323593

[4] Nicolas L Bray, Harold Pimentel, Páll Melsted, and Lior Pachter. 2016. Near-optimal probabilistic RNA-seq quantification. *Nature biotechnology* 34, 5 (may 2016), 525–527. https://doi.org/10.1038/nbt.3519 arXiv:1505.02710

[5] Fiona Cunningham, M Ridwan Amode, Daniel Barrell, Kathryn Beal, Konstantinos Billis, Simon Brent, Denise Carvalho-Silva, Peter Clapham, Guy Coates, Stephen Fitzgerald, et al. 2015. Ensembl 2015. *Nucleic Acids Research* 43, D1 (jan 2015), D662–D669. https://doi.org/10.1093/nar/gku1010

[6] Martin Farach. 1997. Optimal Suffix Tree Construction with Large Alphabets. *38th IEEE Symp. on Foundations of Computer Science* (1997), 137–143.

[7] Alyssa C Frazee, Andrew E Jaffe, Ben Langmead, and Jeffrey T Leek. 2015. Polyester: simulating RNA-seq datasets with differential transcript expression. *Bioinformatics* 31, 17 (jun 2015), 2778–84. https://doi.org/10.1101/006015

[8] Manuel Garber, Manfred G Grabherr, Mitchell Guttman, and Cole Trapnell. 2011. Computational methods for transcriptome annotation and quantification using RNA-seq. *Nature methods* 8, 6 (jun 2011), 469–77. https://doi.org/10.1038/nmeth.1613

[9] Steffen Heber, Max Alekseyev, Sing-Hoi Sze, Haixu Tang, and Pavel A Pevzner. 2002. Splicing graphs and EST assembly problem. *Bioinformatics* 18 Suppl 1, 1 (2002), S181–S188. https://doi.org/10.1093/bioinformatics/18.suppl_1.S181

[10] Michael Höhl, Stefan Kurtz, and Enno Ohlebusch. 2002. Efficient multiple genome alignment. *Bioinformatics* 18, Suppl 1 (jul 2002), S312–S320. https://doi.org/10.1093/bioinformatics/18.suppl_1.S312

[11] Lars Kaderali and Alexander Schliep. 2002. Selecting signature oligonucleotides to identify organisms using DNA arrays. *Bioinformatics* 18, 10 (oct 2002), 1340–1349. https://doi.org/10.1093/bioinformatics/18.10.1340

[12] Richard M. Karp and Michael O. Rabin. 1987. Efficient randomized pattern-matching algorithms. *IBM Journal of Research and Development* 31, 2 (mar 1987), 249–260. https://doi.org/10.1147/rd.312.0249

[13] Daehwan Kim, Geo Pertea, Cole Trapnell, Harold Pimentel, Ryan Kelley, and Steven L Salzberg. 2013. TopHat2: accurate alignment of transcriptomes in the presence of insertions, deletions and gene fusions. *Genome biology* 14, 4 (apr 2013), R36. https://doi.org/10.1186/gb-2013-14-4-r36

[14] Hinanit Koltai and Carmiya Weingarten-Baror. 2008. Specificity of DNA microarray hybridization: characterization, effectors and approaches for data correction. *Nucleic acids research* 36, 7 (apr 2008), 2395–405. https://doi.org/10.1093/nar/gkn087

[15] Stefan Kurtz and Chris Schleiermacher. 1999. REPuter: fast computation of maximal repeats in complete genomes. *Bioinformatics* 15, 5 (may 1999), 426–427. https://doi.org/10.1093/bioinformatics/15.5.426

[16] Edward M. McCreight. 1976. A Space-Economical Suffix Tree Construction Algorithm. *J. ACM* 23, 12 (1976), 262–272. http://libeccio.di.unisa.it/TdP/suffix.pdf

[17] J. Ian Munro and Venkatesh Raman. 2001. Succinct Representation of Balanced Parentheses and Static Trees. *SIAM J. Comput.* 31, 3 (jan 2001), 762–776. https://doi.org/10.1137/S0097539799364092

[18] Herve Pagès, Daniel Bindreither, Marc Carlson, and Martin Morgan. 2013. SplicingGraphs: Create, manipulate, visualize splicing graphs, and assign RNA-seq reads to them. *R package version 1.14.0* (2013).

[19] Rob Patro, Stephen M Mount, and Carl Kingsford. 2014. Sailfish enables alignment-free isoform quantification from RNA-seq reads using lightweight algorithms. *Nature biotechnology* 32, 5 (may 2014), 462–4. https://doi.org/10.1038/nbt.2862

[20] Robert Petryszak, Tony Burdett, Benedetto Fiorelli, Nuno A Fonseca, Mar Gonzalez-Porta, Emma Hastings, Wolfgang Huber, Simon Jupp, Maria Keays, Nataliya Kryvych, et al. 2016. Expression Atlas update - An integrated database of gene and protein expression in humans, animals and plants. *Nucleic Acids Research* 44, D1 (jan 2016), D746–D752. https://doi.org/10.1093/nar/gkv1045

[21] Kunihiko Sadakane. 2007. Compressed Suffix Trees with Full Functionality. *Theory of Computing Systems* 41, 4 (2007), 589–607. http://web.stanford.edu/

[22] Michael Sammeth. 2009. Complete Alternative Splicing Events Are Bubbles in Splicing Graphs. *Journal of computational biology* 16, 8 (2009), 1117–1140. https://doi.org/10.1089/cmb.2009.0108

[23] Avi Srivastava, Hirak Sarkar, Nitish Gupta, and Rob Patro. 2016. RapMap: a rapid, sensitive and accurate tool for mapping RNA-seq reads to transcriptomes. *Bioinformatics* 32, 12 (oct 2016), i192–i200. https://doi.org/10.1101/029652

[24] Esko Ukkonen. 1995. On-line construction of suffix trees. *Algorithmica* 14, 3 (sep 1995), 249–260. https://doi.org/10.1007/BF01206331

[25] Niko Välimäki, Wolfgang Gerlach, Kashyap Dixit, and Veli Mäkinen. 2007. Compressed suffix tree —a basis for genome-scale sequence analysis. *Bioinformatics* 23, 5 (mar 2007), 629–30. https://doi.org/10.1093/bioinformatics/btl681

[26] Kai Wang, Darshan Singh, Zheng Zeng, Stephen J Coleman, Yan Huang, Gleb L Savich, Xiaping He, Piotr Mieczkowski, Sara a Grimm, Charles M Perou, James N MacLeod, Derek Y Chiang, Jan F Prins, and Jinze Liu. 2010. MapSplice: accurate mapping of RNA-seq reads for splice junction discovery. *Nucleic acids research* 38, 18 (oct 2010), e178. https://doi.org/10.1093/nar/gkq622

[27] Brian T Wilhelm and Josette-Renée Landry. 2009. RNA-Seq-quantitative measurement of expression through massively parallel RNA-sequencing. *Methods* 48, 3 (jul 2009), 249–57. https://doi.org/10.1016/j.ymeth.2009.03.016

[28] Zhaojun Zhang and Wei Wang. 2014. RNA-Skim: a rapid method for RNA-Seq quantification at transcript level. *Bioinformatics* 30, 12 (jun 2014), i283–i292. https://doi.org/10.1093/bioinformatics/btu288

A Sparse Latent Regression Approach for Integrative Analysis of Glycomic and Glycotranscriptomic Data

Xuefu Wang
Department of Statistics, Indiana University,Bloomington
wangxuef@indiana.edu

Sujun Li
School of Informatics and Computing, Indiana University, Bloomington
sujli@indiana.edu

Wenjing Peng
Department of Chemistry and Biochemistry, Texas Tech University
wenjing.peng@ttu.edu

Yehia Mechref
Department of Chemistry and Biochemistry, Texas Tech University
yehia.mechref@ttu.edu

Haixu Tang
School of Informatics and Computing, Indiana University, Bloomington
hatang@indiana.edu

ABSTRACT

Glycomics and glycotranscitomics have emerged as two key high-throughput approaches to interrogating the glycome within specific cells, tissues or organisms under specific conditions. Because the glycotransciptomic analysis utilizes the same experimental protocol as the whole-transcriptome sequencing (*RNA-seq*) that is commonly used in the genomic research, the glycotranscriptomic information can be conveniently extracted *in silico* for many biological samples from which RNA-seq data have been collected and made publicly available through large-scale projects such as The Cancer Genome Atlas (TCGA) proeject. However, the glycomic data collection is constrained by specialized analytical tools that are less accessible by biological researchers. In this paper, we present a Bayesian sparse latent regression (BSLR) model for predicting quantitative glycan abundances from glycotranscriptomic data. The model is built using the matched glycomic and glycotranscriptomic data collected in a same set of samples as training sets, and is then exploited to study the common properties of the training samples and to predict these properties (e.g., the glycan abundances) in similar samples from which only glycotranscriptomc data are available. The BSLR model assumes the glycomic and the glycotranscriptomic abundances are both modulated by a small number of independent latent variables, and thus can be constructed by using only a relatively small number of training samples. When tested on simulated data, we show our approach achieves satisfactory performance using only 10-20 training samples. We also tested our model on five cancer cell lines, and showed the BSLR model can accurately predict the glycan abundances from the transcription levels of glycan synthetic genes. Furthermore, the predicted glycan abundances can distinguish the metastatic cell line specifically targeting brain from the remaining breast cancer cell lines as well as the a brain cancer cell line, with only slightly lower power than the observed glycan abundances in glycomic experiments, indicating the BSLR prediction retains the variations of glycan abundances across different groups of samples from their glycotranscriptomic data.

Permission to make digital or hard copies of all or part of this work for personal or classroom use is granted without fee provided that copies are not made or distributed for profit or commercial advantage and that copies bear this notice and the full citation on the first page. Copyrights for components of this work owned by others than ACM must be honored. Abstracting with credit is permitted. To copy otherwise, or republish, to post on servers or to redistribute to lists, requires prior specific permission and/or a fee. Request permissions from permissions@acm.org.
ACM-BCB '17, August 20-23, 2017, Boston, MA, USA
© 2017 Association for Computing Machinery.
ACM ISBN 978-1-4503-4722-8/17/08...$15.00
https://doi.org/10.1145/3107411.3107468

CCS CONCEPTS

• **Applied computing → Life and medical sciences; Genetics; Transcriptomics;**

KEYWORDS

Bayesian model; transcriptomics; glycomics; sparse latent factor model; MCMC sampling; biomarker discovery

1 INTRODUCTION

The rapid progress of glycoscience in the past decade has revealed many examples where the recognition of specific glycans and glycoconjugates (glycoproteins and glycolipids) on cell surfaces is an initial and crucial step in cellular processes such as the development, inflammation and pathogen-host interaction [15]. Therefore, characterizing the glycans' roles in these processes is an important research topic towards the understanding of cell signaling pathways and their physiological and pathological consequences [14, 20]. The direct study of glycans is challenging in comparison with proteins and nucleic acids because of their complex structures, relatively low abundances in cells and template-free, step-wise manner of biological synthesis.

Two approaches were often used to interrogate the *glycome* (referred to as the whole collection of glycans) within specific cells, tissues or organisms under specific conditions. The glycomic approach attempts to profile the quantitative distribution of many glycan species in a complex sample through a single large-scale experiment. The glycans can be identified by the liquid chromatography-coupled mass spectrometry (LC-MS) analysis, from which the abundances of identified glycans can also be directly measured [9, 13, 16]. Alternatively, the interaction strengths between the glycan and their binding proteins (e.g., lectins) can be measured by using glycan arrays [5]. The second approach attempts to probe the activity of the glycan synthesis machinary (instead of the glycans) by measuring the expression levels of the transferases and transporters involved in the glycan synthesis pathway through transcriptomic profiling, an approach often referred to as *glycotranscriptomics* [10]. The glycomic data obtained by the first approach provide the global measurements of glycans; the data acquisition is, however, constrained by specialized analytical tools used in glycomic mass spectrometry, which have relatively low sensitivity, and are not easily accessible by biological researchers. On the other hand, while the early glycotranscriptomic studies focused on targeted profiling of the expression of glycan-related genes [11] (e.g., those encoding CAZy enzymes [2]), recent research adopted the whole transcriptome sequencing (RNA-seq) strategy [21] based on the next generation sequencing (NGS) techniques [17], which are well standardized and easily implemented for a variety of biological systems. In particular, in cancer genomics, RNA-seq data have been collected in many cell lines and tissue samples by large-scale projects such as The Cancer Genome Atlas (TCGA) project [18]. The glycotranscriptomic information on these samples can be conveniently extracted *in silico* from these publicly available RNA-seq data. Hence, it is highly desirable to develop novel informatics approaches that can predict quantitative glycan abundances from glycotranscriptomic data.

In theory, the change in glycan abundances (as measured by glycomic approaches) can be predicted from the change in the transcription levels of glycan synthesis genes (as measured by glycotranscriptomic approaches), because the glycans are ultimated synthesized by the enzymes encoded by these genes. In practice, however, it is often observed that the change in glycan abundances are not well correlated with the change in the transcription levels of the glycan synthesis genes [11]. This discrepancy may be explained by two factors. First, post-transcriptional regulations can be imposed on the transcripts of glycan synthesis genes. Some microRNAs were shown to be involved in such regulations in a recently paper [1]. Second, the relationship may be complex between the glycan abundances and the transcription levels of glycan synthetic genes, and thus can not be captured by straightforward linear models. Therefore, sophisticated machine learning (ML) models need to be developed to accurately predict glycan abundances from the glycotranscriptomic data with limited samples.

2 BAYESIAN SPARSE LATENT REGRESSION MODEL

2.1 Latent factor regression and likelihood

Suppose we have m samples, from which we acquire glycomic and glycotranscriptomc data. Let Y be a $n_Y \times m$ *glycomic* matrix, in which each column Y_i $(i = 1, 2, \ldots, m)$ is the vector of observed (and normalized) abundances of the n_Y glycan species in the sample i, as measured by using glycomic techniques, and X be a $n_X \times m$ *glycotranscriptomic* matrix, in which each column Y_i $(i = 1, 2, \ldots, m)$ is the vector of observed (and normalized) transcription level of the n_X glycan synthetic genes in the sample i, as measured by using glycotranscriptomic data. In each sample i, we assume the experimental measures (or *observations*), Y_i and X_i are modulated by the same k independent latent variables whose values are denoted as $F_i = (F_{i,1}, F_{i,2}, \ldots, F_{i,k})^t$, where k is a small number compared to the dimensions in each observation (i.e., the number of glycans or genes). Then we use the following latent regression model to integrate the observations:

$$X_i = A \cdot F_i + \zeta_i \quad (1)$$

$$Y_i = B \cdot F_i + \eta_i \quad (2)$$

$$i = 1, 2, ..., m$$

, where A and B are the *loading matrices* that are the same across all m samples, and ζ_i and η_i are the noise terms accounting for the variations that can not be explained by latent variables. Here, we assume that, although the dimensions in each observation (e.g., the abundances of glycans) are not independent, the latent variables are independent, and one of our goals is to model the dependence between the dimensions in each observation induced by the loading matrices.

Each equation in the above model represents a latent variable model involving two observation vectors from an individual; because we assume the two observations are modulated by the same set of latent variables, we can combine them in to a single latent variable model

$$\begin{bmatrix} Y_i \\ X_i \end{bmatrix} = L \cdot F_i + \epsilon_i \quad i = 1, 2, ..., m \quad (3)$$

, where $L = (B^t, A^t)^t$ and $\epsilon_i = (\zeta_i^t, \eta_i^t)^t$ represent the combined loading matrix and the error term, respectively. As discussed above, it is challenging to train the model by using conventional factor analysis methods, as we have only a small number of training samples (i.e., m is smaller than n_Y and n_X). To address this issue, we adopted a Bayesian framework as proposed in [19]. Models with different modifications have been used for various genomic studies, including gene translation, gene-environment interactions and oncogene deregulation [3, 4, 7, 8, 12].

Similar to the original framework, we further assume that the latent variables and the error terms both follow multivariate Gaussian distributions:

$$F_i \overset{i.i.d}{\sim} N(\mu_F, \Sigma_F) \quad \epsilon_i \overset{i.i.d}{\sim} N(0, \Sigma_\epsilon) \quad i = 1, 2, ..., m \quad (4)$$

, where Σ_F and Σ_ϵ are both diagonal matrices. Then the joint distribution of observable variables can be expressed as:

$$\begin{bmatrix} Y_i \\ X_i \end{bmatrix} \overset{i.i.d}{\sim} N(L\mu_F, L\Sigma_F L^t + \Sigma_\epsilon) \quad i = 1, 2, ..., m \quad (5)$$

We re-write $L\mu_F$ and $L\Sigma_F L^t + \Sigma_\epsilon$ as:

$$L\mu_F = \begin{bmatrix} \mu_Y \\ \mu_X \end{bmatrix} \quad L\Sigma_F L^t + \Sigma_\epsilon = \begin{bmatrix} \Sigma_Y & \Sigma_{YX} \\ \Sigma'_{YX} & \Sigma_X \end{bmatrix} \quad (6)$$

, where $dim(\mu_Y) = n_Y, dim(\Sigma_Y) = n_Y \times n_Y$ and $dim(\Sigma_X) = n_X \times n_X$. Let X_0 represent the transcription levels of the n_X glycan synthetic genes acquired from a new sample for which we attempt to predict the corresponding glycan abundances Y_0. A basic property of multivariate Gaussian distribution gives the conditional likelihood of Y_i, $f_{y|x}(Y_i|X_i, L, \Sigma_F, \Sigma_\epsilon)$ as:

$$Y_i|\{X_i, L, \Sigma_F, \Sigma_\epsilon\} \sim N(\mu_i, \Sigma_i) \quad \forall i = 0, 1, 2, ..m \quad (7)$$

where $\mu_i = \mu_Y + \Sigma_{YX}\Sigma_X^{-1}(X_i - \mu_X)$ and $\Sigma_i \equiv \Sigma_Y - \Sigma_{YX}\Sigma_X^{-1}\Sigma_{YX}^t$. We emphasize that this likelihood density formula is essential for our prediction algorithm shown later.

Notice that, by incorporating the latent factors, the modular property of glycan synthesis is represented by the loading matrix

L and the biological dependence among glycans is reflected by $L\Sigma_F L^t + \Sigma_\epsilon$ as in Eq[6].

2.2 Prediction of glycan abundances

Let our training data be the matrices $y = (y_1, y_2, ..., y_m)$ and $x = (x_1, x_2, ..., x_m)$, representing the observed matrices of glycan abundances and transcription levels of glycan synthetic genes, respectively, acquired from m samples. In this section, our primary goal is to construct a model that predicts Y_0, an unknown glycan abundances, from a new X_0, the transcription levels of glycan synthetic genes to be acquired in a new sample. The related model parameters are inferred from the training set $(y^t, x^t)^t$.

We start by scaling and centering each dimension of $(y^t, x^t)^t$. In this way, we can safely assume the mean values of all latent factors to be zero. Thus, it is reasonable to assign $\mu_F = \vec{0}$. For any diagonal matrix Σ_F, there exists a diagonal matrix Γ, $s.t.$ $\Sigma_F = \Gamma\Gamma^t$. Therefore, we can write $L\Sigma_F L^t = (L\Gamma)I_F(L\Gamma)^t = L'(L')^t$, where I_F is an identity matrix with $n_Y + n_X$ diagonal elements and $L' = L\Gamma$. Instead of solving for two matrices Σ_F and L, we solve for the matrix L' with respect to a set of latent factors whose covariance matrix is I_F. Under the sparsity assumption, the loading matrix L' for the independent latent factors should still be sparse. To achieve this, we set an *inclusion indicator*, $\mathcal{I}_{i,j}$, $s.t.$ $\forall i = 1, 2, ..., n_Y + n_X$ and $j = 1, 2, ..., k$:

$$L'_{i,j} \begin{cases} = 0 & \text{if } \mathcal{I}_{i,j} = 0 \\ \sim N(0, \sigma_L^2) & \text{if } \mathcal{I}_{i,j} = 1 \end{cases} \tag{8}$$

, where σ_L^2 is a parameter to be decided for specific data sets. Let $P(\mathcal{I}_{i,j} = 0) = \pi_j, i = 1, 2, ..., n_Y + n_X$. When $\pi_j, j = 1, 2, ..., k$ is close to 1, a large proportion of elements in L' will be exactly equal to zero. A *beta* prior distribution heavily favoring the right tail can be assigned for π_j for this purpose.

For the error term's Σ_ϵ, we can assume it is a diagonal matrix whose diagonal elements have an *inverse – gamma* distribution to ease our calculation, that is: $\Sigma_\epsilon = diag(\Psi)$, where $diag(v)$ is the diagonal matrix whose diagonal part is vector v and $dim(\Psi) = n_Y + n_X$. For $i = 1, 2, ..., n_Y + n_X$, $\Psi_i \sim inverse - gamma$. Hence, we have:

$$\begin{aligned} &\mathbb{E}(Y_0|X_0, y, x) \\ =&\mathbb{E}\Big[\mathbb{E}\Big(Y_0|y, x, X_0, L', \mathcal{I}, \pi, I_F, diag(\Psi)\Big)\Big] \\ =& \int \mu_0 f\Big(L', \mathcal{I}, \pi, I_F, diag(\Psi)|y, x\Big) d\Big(L', \mathcal{I}, \pi, I_F, diag(\Psi)\Big) \end{aligned} \tag{9}$$

, where $\mu_0 = \mu_Y + \Sigma_{YX}\Sigma_X^{-1}(X_0 - \mu_X)$ by Eq[6] and Eq[7]. There is no closed-form solution to get the posterior mean. However, when H sets of $\{L', \Sigma_F, diag(\Psi)\}$ are generated from the posterior distribution $f\Big(L', \mathcal{I}, \pi, I_F, diag(\Psi)|y, x\Big)$, we can use Monte Carlo method to approximate $\mathbb{E}(Y_0|X_0, y, x)$ by the average of constructed μ_0's:

$$\begin{aligned} \bar{Y}_0 = \frac{\sum_{h=1}^H \mu_0^{[h]}}{H} &= \frac{\sum_{h=1}^H [\mu_Y + \Sigma_{YX}^{[h]}(\Sigma_X^{[h]})^{-1}(X_0 - \mu_X)]}{H} \\ &= \frac{\sum_{h=1}^H \Sigma_{YX}^{[h]}(\Sigma_X^{[h]})^{-1}X_0}{H} \end{aligned} \tag{10}$$

, where $\{\Sigma_{YX}^{[h]}, \Sigma_X^{[h]}\}$ can be obtained from the hth sample $\{L^{[h]}, \Sigma_F^{[h]}, diag(\Psi)^{[h]}\}$ according to Eq[6]. And the last step in Eq[10] holds because $\mu_F = (\mu_Y^t, \mu_X^t)^t = \vec{0}$.

Finally, we re-write the posterior density function by the dependence relation between variables to aid our sampling procedure in Eq[11].

$$\begin{aligned} &f\Big(L', \mathcal{I}, \pi, I_F, diag(\Psi)|y, x\Big) \\ \propto& f\Big(y, x|L', \mathcal{I}, \pi, I_F, diag(\Psi)\Big) f\Big(L', \mathcal{I}, \pi, I_F, diag(\Psi)\Big) \\ =& \prod_{i=1}^N f\Big(y_i, x_i|L', \mathcal{I}, \pi, I_F, diag(\Psi)\Big) f(L'|\mathcal{I}) P(\mathcal{I}|\pi) f(\pi) f\Big(diag(\Psi)\Big) \end{aligned} \tag{11}$$

Here, various Markov Chain Monte Carlo (MCMC) sampling techniques can be used to meet different objectives of the inference (e.g., the speed, flexibility, etc.). The prior distributions and the likelihood function are summarized in Table 1.

Table 1: Summary of prior distributions. I_F is an identity matrix of size $k \times k$. Hyper parameters θ_1 through θ_4 are to be set with respect to a specific data set.

parameter/ variable	dimension(s)	prior and hyper parameters
π	$k \times 1$	$\pi_j \sim beta(\theta_1, \theta_2)$
$\mathcal{I}$	$(n_Y + n_X) \times k$	$\mathcal{I}_{i,j} \sim Bernoulli(\pi_j, 0, 1)$
Ψ	$n_Y + n_X$	$\Psi_i \sim inverse - gamma(\theta_3, \theta_4)$
L'	$(n_Y + n_X) \times k$	$L'_{i,j} \sim \pi_j(1 - \mathcal{I}_{i,j}) + (1 - \pi_j)N(0, \sigma_L^2)$
F_i	$k \times 1$	$F_j \sim N(0, I_F)$
ϵ_i	$(n_Y + n_X) \times 1$	$\epsilon_i \sim N\Big(0, diag(\Psi)\Big)$
$(Y_i^t, X_i^t)^t$	$(n_Y + n_X) \times 1$	$(Y_i^t, X_i^t)^t \sim N\Big(0, L'(L')^t + diag(\Psi)\Big)$

3 RESULTS

3.1 Simulated data

With simulated data, we show in this section that 1) the BSLR model returns posterior samples of loading matrices that well reconstruct the original (un-observed) data, and 2) given new partial observations (i.e., the expression levels of glycan synthesis genes), the BSLR model well predicts the values of the remaining variables (i.e., the abundances of glycans).

Goodness of fit of BSLR. The framework of BSLR model was originally proposed in [19], coincidentally, with the data also collected from cancer samples. Multiple papers adopted this framework and their inference algorithms based on MCMC sampling. However, to our best knowledge, no empirical results were reported to show the *goodness of fit* of the training data in the literature. We first generate a "known" 8×20 matrix that represents 20 samples' 8 latent factor values, and a "known" 1070×8 loading matrix (i.e., L') that represents the loadings of the same latent factors on the 1000 glycan synthesis genes and 70 N-Glycans. The multiplication of these two matrices is an "observable" 1070×20 matrix, representing "observed" abundances of the 1000 expressed genes (i.e., mRNAs) and 70 glycans across a total of 20 samples. During this simulation process, $(\theta_1, \theta_2, \theta_3, \theta_4, \sigma_L^2)$ are chosen as following: the parameters for the *beta* prior are set to be $\theta_1 = 4$ and $\theta_2 = 2$. This implies that, on average, we expect to see $\frac{4}{4+2} = \frac{2}{3}$ of the loadings in each column of L' equal to 0. For the $inverse - gamma$ distribution, we set $\theta_3 = 6$ and $\theta_4 = 0.5$. Correspondingly, σ_L^2 is set to be 1. This choice of θ_3, θ_4, and σ_L^2 is to guarantee a proper signal-to-noise ratio: When the jth latent factor has non-zero loading on the ith observable variable, the variance of the multiplication of the latent factor and its loading is:

$$\begin{aligned} Var(L'_{i,j}F_j|I_{i,j}=1) =& Var(L'_{i,j}|I_{i,j}=1)\mathbb{E}(F_j) + \mathbb{E}(L'_{i,j}|I_{i,j}=1)Var(F_j) + \\ &+ Var(L'_{i,j}|I_{i,j}=1)Var(F_j) \\ =& \sigma_L^2 = 1 \end{aligned}$$

The expected value of the variance of the ith error term ϵ_i is $\mathbb{E}(\Psi_i) = \frac{\theta_4}{\theta_3 - 1} = 0.1$, implying that the variance caused by the error term accounts for $\approx 10\%$ of the variance caused by a single pair of loading and latent factor.

From the observed 1070×20 matrix, our goal is to sample the possible loading matrices and factors through the BSLR model, which are then used to reconstruct the observable matrix. We used the *R* package *bfa* to conduct the MCMC sampling, following the details described in [6], in which a parameter expansion approach was proposed to improve the effective sample size of MCMC sampling. The reconstructed abundances of the glycan and gene expression values are plotted against their true (observed) values in Fig. 1 (a) when 8 latent factors were used. The Pearson correlation coefficient between the reconstructed and true values is $r^2 = 0.900$.

Prediction with the Bayesian sparse latent factor regression model. Once a BSLR model is learned using the glycomic and glycotransciptomic data obtained from training samples, we can predict the glycomic profile of a new sample (e.g., a cell line) from the glycotranscriptomic data obtained from the same sample, using MCMC sampling from the BSLR model, as shown in Eq[10] and Eq[6]. To evaluate the accuracy of the prediction, we simulate the expression levels of glycan synthesis genes and the abundances of glycans from 100 additional samples using the same procedure as described above for generating the observable matrix. The expression levels the genes data is then used to "predict" the abundances of glycans based on the BSLR model trained from the previous simulated data. We can compare the predicted with the true glycan abundances. When the number of latent factors is set to 8 (equal to the actual number of factors used in the simulation), the prediction is very accurate ($r^2 = 0.95$), as shown in Fig. 1 (b).

3.2 Cancer cell lines

Next, we tested the BSLR model on five cancer cell lines (including four breast cancer cell lines 213, 213BR, 361, and HTB-131, and one brain cancer cell line CRL-1620) in which the glycomic profiles and glycotranscriptomic data were acquired (each with three biological replicates) by using LC-MS and RNA-seq techniques, respectively [21].

Prediction of glycomic profiles from glycotranscriptomic data. We first evaluate the prediction accuracy using a respective analysis. We train a BSLR model using the glycan abundances and

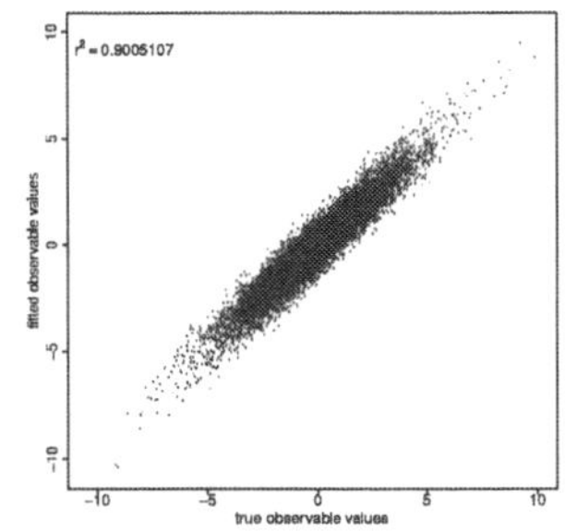

(a)Fitted values vs observed values on training samples in the simulation.

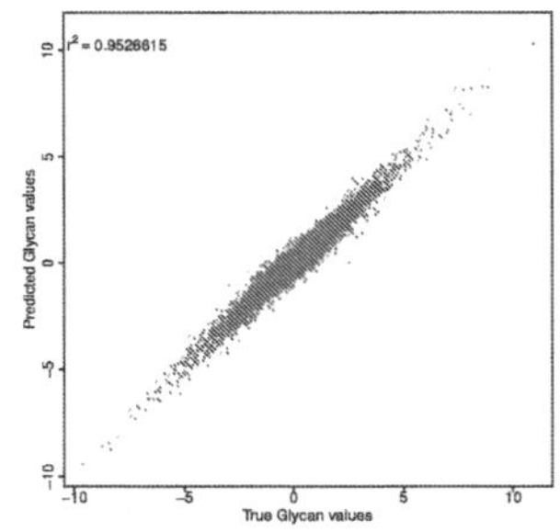

(b)Predicted values vs observed values in testing samples in the simulation.

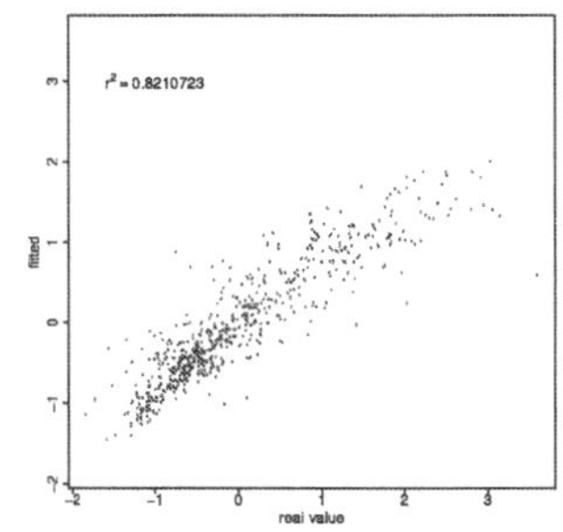

(c)Fitted values vs observed values on training samples in the cancer cell line data.

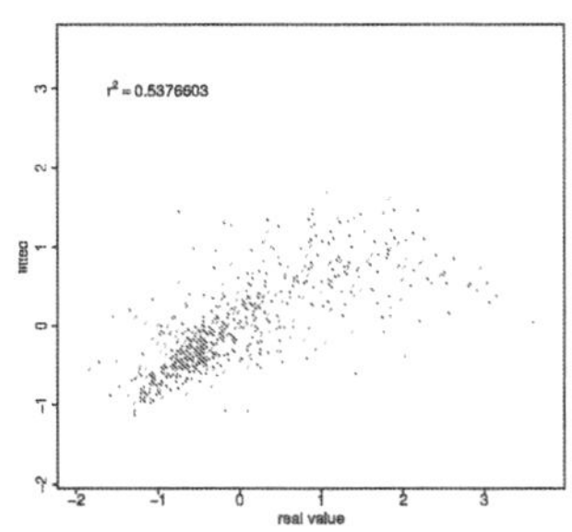

(d)Leave-one-out prediction vs observed values in the cancer cell line data.

Figure 1: The comparison of the true (x-axis) vs. predicted glycan abundances (y-axis) from gene expression levels on simulated (a-b) and cancer cell line data (c-d).

expression levels of glycan synthesis genes, measured in the full set of 15 samples (three replicates in each of five cell lines). We considered the BSLR model with up to 14 latent factors. We then use the model to predict the glycan abundances from the gene expression levels in each of the 15 samples, and compared the predicted glycan abundances with the observed glycan abundances. Due to the limited space, we only show results with 10 latent factors. As shown, in the scatter plot over 630 data points (42 glycans in each of the 15 samples) in Fig. 1 (c), the predicted values are close to the observed values when fitted with 10 latent factors ($r^2 = 0.821$). We then evaluate the prediction accuracy through the leave-one-out experiment, in which each time a BSLR model is trained on the glycomic and glycotranscriptomic data in 14 (out of 15) samples, and tested on the remaining sample. The predicted glycan abundances are compared with the true abundances over all 630 data points, as shown in the scatter plot (Fig. 1 (d)). From the results, we observe only on a small fraction of glycans the predictions deviate from the corresponding real values, while the overall prediction is also accurate ($r^2 = 0.538$). The reduced prediction accuracy is probably due to a lack of observations of highly abundant glycans in the leaving-one-out evaluation when building the model. When choosing the number of latent factors, we mainly consider the r^2 between the leave-one-out predictions and the true values. With similar r^2, we favor the smaller number of latent factors. (The r^2 for 6,8,12 and 14 latent factors are 0.524, 0.530, 0.538 and 0.537, respectively.)

We also estimated the covariance matrix $L\Sigma_F L^t + \Sigma_\epsilon$ in Eq[5] via the average of the sampled covariance matrices by the MCMC algorithm, from which we can estimate the Pearson correlation coefficient for each pair of glycan and glycan synthesis genes. Conceptually, if two Glycans are correlated well with the same subset of glycan synthesis genes, they are likely functionally linked, and the similar conclusion can be drawn for two glycan synthesis genes. Therefore, the matrix of correlation coefficients between glycans and genes (as shown in Fig. 2) can be used to group glycans/genes that are functionally correlated and affected by different latent factors. From Fig. 2, we can see the glycans and genes can be roughly grouped into four major clusters in terms of positive correlation or synthetic process. Notice, however, that it is not our intention to offer a definitive clustering scheme in this paper. The clustering method based on the interaction between glycan and genes should be addressed separately. **Glycan biomarker discovery using predicted glycan abundances.** We show that differential glycan abundances (on the glycomic profiles over 42 N-glycan species) can be observed across different breast cancer cell lines and the brain cancer cell lines by using the principal component analysis (PCA), as reported previously [21]. As shown in Fig. 3 (a), along the 2nd principal component (PC), all data points corresponding to 231BR exhibit much lower values than the other cell lines, whereas their 1st PC values overlap with the cell lines CRL-1620 and 361 (all close to 0). It is worth pointing out that, if we change the sign of the loading matrix in PCA, 231BR cell lines show greater values than other cell lines on the 2nd PC, but the distinction remains.

We show one example where we predict the glycan abundance using the leave-one-out approach, i.e., with the BSLR model trained on 14 samples, we predict the glycan abundances in the 15th sample (a 231BR cell line). Similarly, we conducted the PCA on the observed glycan abundances in the 14 training samples, and the rotation matrix from the PCA is then applied to the 15th sample's observed glycan abundances and and predicted glycan abundances, respectively. In Fig. 3 (b). since the signs do not affect the interpretation of the PCA results, we do not manually flip the signs here. The differential expression of glycans characterized by the 2nd principal component can still be observed from predicted glycan abundances from the BLSR model, indicating that the differential glycan biomarker between the 231BR and the other cells can be discovered from the predicted glycan abundances when only the glycotranscriptomic data are available. Even though we do not have a ground truth about the range of the 2nd principal component of breast cancer cell lines due to our sample size, the study provide us an insight on possible classification tool of a new cell line.

4 DISCUSSIONS

In this paper, we present a BSLR model for integrating glycotranscriptomic and glycomic data on a limited number of samples. Similar models were used in genomic data analysis where the number of samples is usually much smaller than the number of attributes. Moreover, glycotranscriptomic and glycomic data are regulated via a small number of pathway, modeled as latent factors in the BSLR model, which is not addressed by traditional dimension deduction approaches. We showed empirically that, the model can well re-construct observed glycomic data (i.e., glycan abundances) based on the observed glycotranscriptomic data when it is appropriately trained using match glycotranscriptomic and glycomic data acquired from a small number of samples. Our results also showed the predicted glycan abundances exhibited distinct patterns in different groups of cancer cell lines, similarly to that were obserseved on experimental glycomic data. Therefore, our method will be useful in glycomic biomarker discovery on clinical samples in which glycotranscriptomic data can be extracted from existing large-scale transcriptomic (RNA-seq) datasets.

A critical aspect of the BSLR model is the employment of the Bayesian approach that allows to learn sparse loading matrices from a small number of training samples. We showed here that it is useful for integrative glycotranscriptomic and glycomic data analysis, anticipating it is even more important for the cases where the number of attributes is greater (e.g., in metabolomics where hundreds to thousands of metabolites are simultaneously monitored). One limitation of the BSLR model is, however, that it is sensitive to the number of latent factors specified in the model. Our current method to determine the optimum number of latent factor relies on the r^2 as explained in 3.2. In the future, we plan to develop a fast algorithm to find such an optimum number, which can be the key for building accurate BSLR model at larger scale. We also plan to include more cancer cell line samples to the training set for the BSLR model as well.

5 ACKNOWLEDGEMENTS

This work is partially supported by NIH (1R01GM112490-01) and the Indiana University Initiative of Precesion Health.

REFERENCES

[1] Praveen Agrawal, Tomasz Kurcon, Kanoelani T Pilobello, John F Rakus, Sujeethraj Koppolu, Zhongyin Liu, Bianca S Batista, William S Eng, Ku-Lung Hsu, Yaxuan Liang, et al. 2014. Mapping posttranscriptional regulation of the human glycome uncovers microRNA defining the glycocode. *Proceedings of the National Academy of Sciences* 111, 11 (2014), 4338–4343.

[2] Brandi L Cantarel, Pedro M Coutinho, Corinne Rancurel, Thomas Bernard, Vincent Lombard, and Bernard Henrissat. 2009. The Carbohydrate-Active EnZymes database (CAZy): an expert resource for glycogenomics. *Nucleic acids research* 37, suppl 1 (2009), D233–D238.

[3] Carlos M Carvalho, Jeffrey Chang, Joseph E Lucas, Joseph R Nevins, Quanli Wang, and Mike West. 2008. High-Dimensional Sparse Factor Modeling: Applications in Gene Expression Genomics. *J. Amer. Statist. Assoc.* 103, 484 (2008), 1438–1456.

[4] Joseph R. Nevins Haige Shen Dan Merl, Joseph E. Lucas and Mike West. 2009. Trans-study projection of genomic biomarkers in analysis of oncogene deregulation and breast cancer. *The Oxford Handbook* (2009).

[5] Andreas Geissner and Peter H Seeberger. 2016. Glycan Arrays: From Basic Biochemical Research to Bioanalytical and Biomedical Applications. *Annual Review of Analytical Chemistry* 9, 1 (2016).

[6] Joyee Ghosh and David B Dunson. 2009. Default Prior Distributions and Efficient Posterior Computation in Bayesian Factor Analysis. *Journal of computational and graphical statistics : a joint publication of American Statistical Association, Institute of Mathematical Statistics, Interface Foundation of North America* 18, 2 (June 2009), 306–320.

[7] Joseph Lucas, Carlos Carvalho, Quanli Wang, Andrea Bild, Joseph R Nevins, Mike West, and Marina Vannucci. 2009. Sparse Statistical Modelling in Gene Expression Genomics. Cambridge University Press, Cambridge.

[8] Joseph Lucas, Carlos Carvalho, and Mike West. 2009. A bayesian analysis strategy for cross-study translation of gene expression biomarkers. *Statistical applications in genetics and molecular biology* 8, 1 (2009), Article 11–26.

[9] Yehia Mechref, Yunli Hu, Janie L Desantos-Garcia, Ahmed Hussein, and Haixu Tang. 2013. Quantitative glycomics strategies. *Molecular & Cellular Proteomics* 12, 4 (2013), 874–884.

[10] Alison Nairn and Kelley Moremen. 2015. Glycotranscriptomics. In *Glycoscience: Biology and Medicine*. Springer, 1475–1482.

[11] Alison V Nairn, Kazuhiro Aoki, Mitche dela Rosa, Mindy Porterfield, Jae-Min Lim, Michael Kulik, J Michael Pierce, Lance Wells, Stephen Dalton, Michael Tiemeyer,

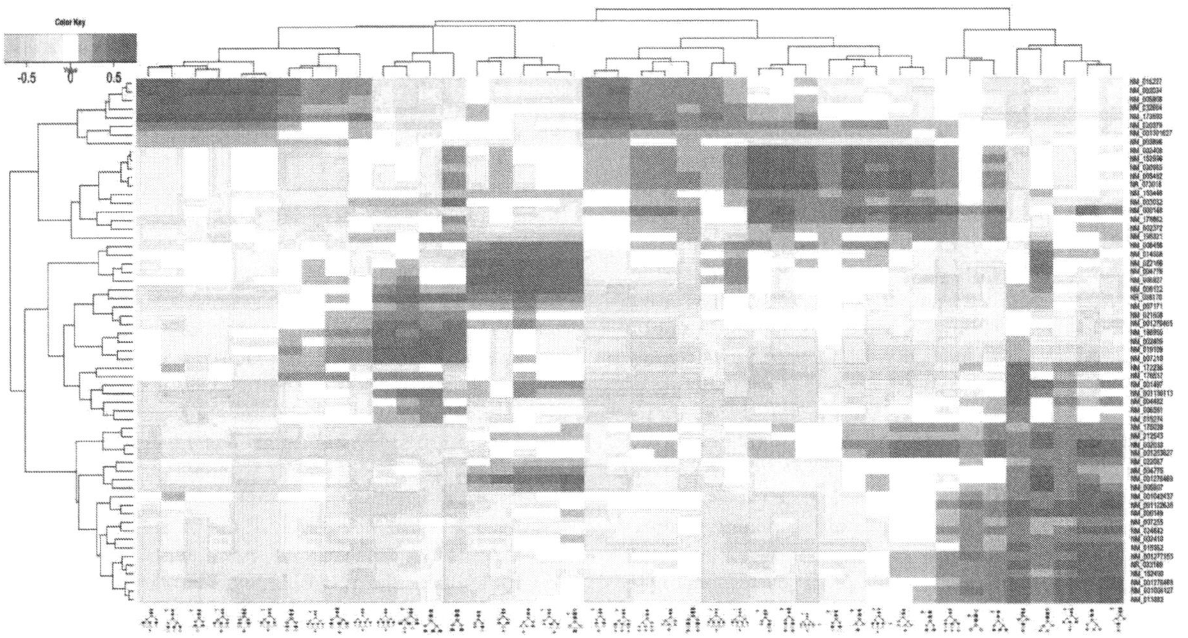

Figure 2: The heatmap illustration of the pairwise correlation coefficients between the glycans and the glycan synthesis genes based on the BSLR model built from the full set of data on cancer cell lines.

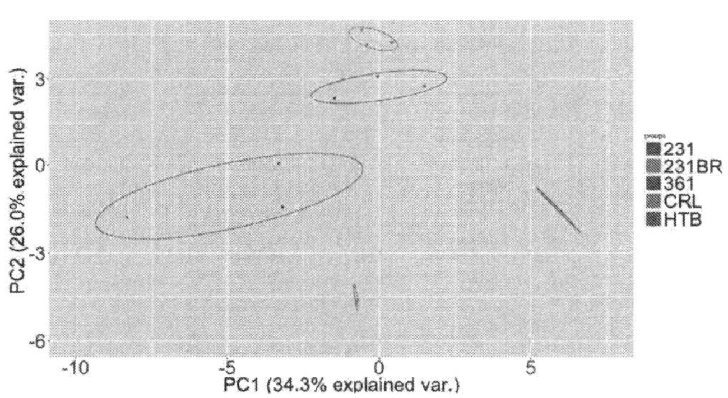

(a) PCA on complete Glycan data from 15 samples

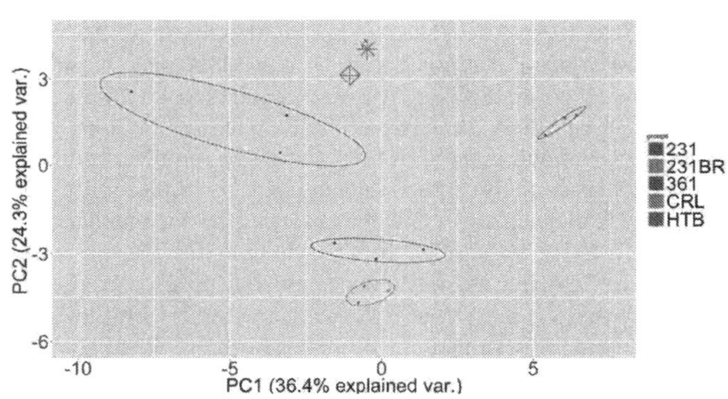

(b) PCA of 14 samples when leaving out a 231BR sample

Figure 3: PCA and prediction model are made with leave-one-out samples. The left-out sample's true and predicted principal components are then obtained via rotation matrix. ✳ represents the sample's true principal components, ⊠ represents the predicted.

et al. 2012. Regulation of Glycan Structures in Murine Embryonic Stem Cells: COMBINED TRANSCRIPT PROFILING OF GLYCAN-RELATED GENES AND GLYCAN STRUCTURAL ANALYSIS. *Journal of Biological Chemistry* 287, 45 (2012), 37835–37856.

[12] David M Seo, Pascal J Goldschmidt-Clermont, and Mike West. 2007. Of mice and men: Sparse statistical modeling in cardiovascular genomics. *The Annals of Applied Statistics* 1, 1 (June 2007), 152–178.

[13] Stevan A Springer and Pascal Gagneux. 2016. Glycomics: revealing the dynamic ecology and evolution of sugar molecules. *Journal of proteomics* 135 (2016), 90–100.

[14] Motoko Takahashi, Yasuhiko Kizuka, Kazuaki Ohtsubo, Jianguo Gu, and Naoyuki Taniguchi. 2016. Disease-associated glycans on cell surface proteins. *Molecular aspects of medicine* 51 (2016), 56–70.

[15] Ajit Varki. 2017. Biological roles of glycans. *Glycobiology* (2017), 27: 3–49.

[16] Ian Walsh, Sophie Zhao, Matthew Campbell, Christopher H Taron, and Pauline M Rudd. 2016. Quantitative profiling of glycans and glycopeptides: an informatics' perspective. *Current Opinion in Structural Biology* 40 (2016), 70–80.

[17] Zhong Wang, Mark Gerstein, and Michael Snyder. 2009. RNA-Seq: a revolutionary tool for transcriptomics. *Nature reviews genetics* 10, 1 (2009), 57–63.

[18] John N Weinstein, Eric A Collisson, Gordon B Mills, Kenna R Mills Shaw, Brad A Ozenberger, Kyle Ellrott, Ilya Shmulevich, Chris Sander, Joshua M Stuart, Cancer Genome Atlas Research Network, et al. 2013. The cancer genome atlas pan-cancer analysis project. *Nature genetics* 45, 10 (2013), 1113–1120.

[19] Mike West. 2002. Bayesian Factor Regression Models in the "Large p, Small n" Paradigm. *BAYESIAN STATISTICS* (2002), 000–000.

[20] Gherman Wiederschain. 2016. *Glycobiology and Human Diseases*. CRC Press.

[21] Norelle C Wildburger, Shiyue Zhou, Lauren G Zacharias, Roger A Kroes, Joseph R Moskal, Mary Schmidt, Parvin Mirzaei, Joy Gumin, Frederick F Lang, Yehia Mechref, et al. 2015. Integrated Transcriptomic and Glycomic Profiling of Glioma Stem Cell Xenografts. *Journal of proteome research* 14, 9 (2015), 3932–3939.

Use of Structural Properties of Underlying Graphs in Pathway Enrichment Analysis of Genomic Data

Pourya Naderi Yeganeh
College of Computing and Informatics,
University of North Carolina at Charlotte
9201 University City Boulevard
Charlotte, North Carolina 28213
pnaderiy@uncc.edu

M. Taghi Mostafavi
College of Computing and Informatics,
University of North Carolina at Charlotte
9201 University City Boulevard
Charlotte, North Carolina 28213
taghi@uncc.edu

ABSTRACT

Common methods for the functional inference of genomic data, such as Gene Sent Enrichment Analysis (GSEA) and Over Representation Analysis (ORA), often discard the interactions between the biomolecular entities. Recent studies have explored this issue through a variety of techniques and show that using evidence from the interactions produces a more relevant and insightful inference. In this article, we introduce a method, referred to as Causal Disturbance (Cdist), for enrichment analysis. Cdist utilizes the underlying graph of pathways in combination with experimental data to detect the pathway dysregulations. To test our methodology, we utilized a public microarray data from colorectal cancer. We show that Cdist identifies the dysregulated pathways of colorectal cancer that are not detectable by other conventional methods. Some of the detected pathways by Cdist, such as apoptosis and Ras signaling, are critical for their roles in cancer. We conclude that our method facilitates a more informative inference of the disease data by incorporating the topological features of the pathway graphs. Using these features will help to detect the pathway dysregulations that are not observable through conventional models.

CCS CONCEPTS

•**Applied computing** →*Biological networks; Bioinformatics;* Computational genomics;

1 INTRODUCTION

Complex diseases, such as cancer, incorporate various functional abnormalities for development and progression. Detection of these abnormalities is essential for understanding and tackling the diseases. Consequently, the system level inference of the experimental data is a formidable task for biomedical researchers. Enrichment analyses are among the most popular methods for inference of genomic data. Established in the late 90's and the early 2000's, enrichment analyses aim to detect the functional associations of experimental results with the manually annotated background knowledge [12, 16, 17, 20].

Permission to make digital or hard copies of all or part of this work for personal or classroom use is granted without fee provided that copies are not made or distributed for profit or commercial advantage and that copies bear this notice and the full citation on the first page. Copyrights for components of this work owned by others than ACM must be honored. Abstracting with credit is permitted. To copy otherwise, or republish, to post on servers or to redistribute to lists, requires prior specific permission and/or a fee. Request permissions from permissions@acm.org.
ACM-BCB'17, August 20–23, 2017, Boston, MA, USA.
© 2017 ACM. 978-1-4503-4722-8/17/08...$15.00
DOI: http://dx.doi.org/10.1145/3107411.3107488

ORA and GSEA are two major and widely used models of enrichment analysis [16]. Both use the annotated knowledge, in a categorized form, to investigate the experimental data. These models do not naturally account for the biological interactions. As a result, the causal nature of the entities is not analyzed, which often induces loss of information in the inference.

Cellular signals and information transmit through chains of biomolecular interactions and form the biological pathways. The signal transduction within the pathways imposes a causal paradigm between the entities and their functions. Position of the entities in the interaction network is integral to their functionality and effects. For instance, Jeong et al. in their paper [11] demonstrated that the number of interactions for each protein correlates with its lethality upon the removal from the protein protein interaction network.

Methods that account for the interactions of genes and proteins facilitate the inference and produce observations that are not feasible when interactions are disregarded. Related models have used graph theory for critical applications, including pathway discovery, enrichment analysis, and dimensionality reduction [6, 10, 17, 18, 21]. In the case of enrichment analysis, Algorithms SPIA - "signaling pathway impact analysis "- and EnrichNet detect pathways for diseases that are not identified by conventional methods such as ORA and GSEA[6, 17].

Our motivation is to devise a measurement that infuses the pathway graph structure with the enrichment analysis so that the genes with more structural importance are prioritized. Inspired by Pearl's causal networks models [15], we introduce an index for capturing the structural effects of the dysregulated genes in a pathway, denoted as causal disturbance (Cdist).

We extract Cdist based on the effect of the dysregulated genes on the total number of paths in the graph. This abstraction facilitates the capturing of structural dysregulation in a higher level scale compared to SPIA. We use additional statistical evidence from ORA to obtain a more precise and relevant inference, similar to the methodology used in SPIA [17]. Our model is designed to analyze genome wide experimental data with the pathways from publicly available databases.

2 METHODOLOGY

Problem Statement: We are interested in an enrichment model that prioritizes the nodes of a pathway, based on their effects on the pathway structure. An ideal model gives more enrichment value to the nodes that have more causal effect on the pathway activity due to their position in the graph. Figure 1 visualizes a hypothetical instance of this situation where the dysregulation of gene Y disconnects all of the graph nodes and might have more effects on the pathway activity compared to the dysregulation of gene X. We address this situation by directly evaluating the effects of the removal of each node on the underlying graph.

In a brief overview, we regard each pathway as a directed acyclic graph (DAG), where the dysregulation of each node deletes all the directed paths passing through the node. Each directed path in the DAG represents a chain of causal activities where one entity, e.g. gene, interacts with the others. We define *Cdist* as the fractions of the paths deleted after the removal of dysregulated genes from the graph. To evaluate the statistical significance of *Cdist* for each pathway, we use a sampling method to calculate the p-value for observing more extreme *Cdist*. We then combine the p-value of *Cdist* index (P_{Cdist}) with ORA p-value (P_{ORA}) to calculate an enrichment score for each pathway (P_{enp}). To evaluate our methodology, we utilized a colorectal cancer genomic expression data set by Hong et al., which was also used in the orignial SPIA paper [9, 17]. We compare P_{enp} with the p-values of SPIA and P_{ORA} to assess the utility of our introduced method.

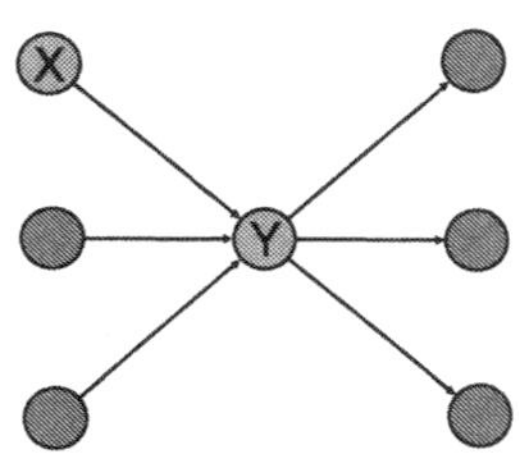

Figure 1: Enrichment analysis methods such as ORA and GSEA do not differentiate between the dysregulated genes based on their position in the pathway. In this example, the dysregulation of genes *X* and *Y* would yield the same statistical results in ORA or GSEA. However, the removal of *Y* disconnects more paths compared to the removal of *X* and is more likely to disturb the information flow in the graph.

2.1 Fundamentals and Definitions

We model each pathway, P_i, by using the graph notation $G_{P_i} = (V, E)$ where V is the set of nodes (biological entities) and E is the set of directed edges between the nodes, representing interactions among the entities. For the pathway graph G_{P_i}, the adjacency matrix is defined as

$$[A_{P_i}]_{j,k} = \begin{cases} 1 & \text{if } (v_j, v_k) \in E(G_i) \\ 0 & \text{otherwise} \end{cases} \tag{1}$$

To preserve the causal relationship between the nodes we choose to model the pathways as directed graphs. An ij path in a graph is a sequence of nodes $v_i, v_{i+1}, \ldots, v_j$, where for each v_k and v_{k+1}, $(i \leq k \leq j-1)$ we have $(v_k, v_{k+1}) \in E$. The number of paths of length k from a node i to a node j is obtained from the ij^{th} element of the matrix $A^k{}_{P_i}$. The count of all the paths with the length $\leq k$ (including zero) from a node i to a node j is the ij^{th} element of the following matrix sum.

$$A^* = \sum_{j=0}^{k} A^j \tag{2}$$

Moreover, we assume that each pathway graph is a directed acyclic graph (DAG). DAG modeling has been previously utilized for discovery of interaction networks and study of causal networks [10, 15]. DAGs provide several computational advantages. Any DAG with finite number of vertices has a finite number of paths. For a DAG of size n, the maximum path length is at most $n-1$ (because it has no loops) and the summation 2 converges because the numbers of the paths are finite. Equivalently, any DAG can be represented in an upper triangular form with zero on all the diagonal elements [14]; Therefore, all the eigenvalues are zero and the matrix geometric sum is convergent. Consequently, the formula 2 for a pathway DAG, G_{p_i}, can be modified to calculate the total number of paths in a DAG:

$$A^*_{P_i} = \sum_{j=0}^{\infty} A^j_{P_i} = (I - A_{P_i})^{-1} \tag{3}$$

$$Psum(G_{P_i}) = \sum_{j,k} [A^*_{P_i}]_{jk} \tag{4}$$

In the formula 3, the ij^{th} element of the matrix $A^*_{p_i}$ is total number of paths, obtained replacing $k = \infty$ in the formula 2. Subsequently, the formula 4 calculates the number of all paths in the graph by using element-wise summation of $A^*_{P_i}$.

As mentioned, the measurement for causal disturbance is defined as the ratio of all remaining paths after removal of dysregulated nodes. We can formulate this concept as following:

$$Cdist(P_i, S) = 1 - \frac{Psum(G_{p_i}[V_{p_i}/S])}{Psum(G_{p_i})} \tag{5}$$

In formula 5, $Cdist(P_i, S)$ denotes the causal disturbance of of a pathway P_i with respect to a set of nodes (S). $G_{p_i}[V_{p_i}/S]$ is the induced subgraph of G_{p_i} where all the nodes in S are removed from the graph. Equivalently, the causal disturbance of a pathway P_i with respect to a set of dysregulated genes (DE) is $Cdist(P_i, DE)$.

2.2 Statistical Pipeline

The probability of observing more extreme values for *Cdist* is calculated using multiple rounds of sampling (P_{Cdist}). The definition of *Cdist* allows for integration with other enrichment analysis method. This is inspired by the work of Tarca et al. in which they combine evidences from the genetic dysregulation magnitudes and enrichment analysis to produce a more informative inference [17]. Likewise, we use additional evidence from ORA by combining the p-values from Cdist and ORA in one unified test statistic. Additionally, we use false discovery rate methods for multiple hypothesis testing.

For each pathway P_i and a set of DE, we calculate *Cdist* using the formula 5. We define $P_{Cdist} = P(Cdist > C_0 \mid N_i)$ as the probability of observing a larger value of causal disturbance, given N_i dysregulated genes in the pathway. We calculate this p-value by repeatedly sampling a set random pathway nodes ,S, $|S| = |N_i|$, and calculating $Cdist(P_i, S)$. For each pathway, i, we use $N_i = |V(G_i) \cap DE|$. The probability of observing a more extreme value for causal disturbance is then calculated by using the formula $1 - cdf(Cdist(P_i, N_i))$ where $cdf(\,)$ is the cumulative distribution function. In our test on the experimental data we use 10^4 rounds of sampling each pathway. In addition, we incorporate evidence from ORA. First, we use the following formula to calculate ORA p-values for each pathway

$$P[X \geq N_i] \sim Hypergeometric(N_i, V_{G_i}, A, DE) \quad (6)$$

The left hand side indicates the probability of observing a larger number of dysregulated genes in a pathways, given N_i dysregulations. The right hand side is calculated based on hypergeometric testing. A represents the total number of genes in the reference array from input data. The formula 6 will be referred to as P_{ORA}. We then combine evidence from P_{Cdist} and P_{ORA} similar to the work describe by Tarca et al.[17]. For P_{Cdist} the null hypothesis is based on a fixed number of dysregulated genes in a pathway, while for P_{ORA} the null hypothesis is based on a fixed number of DE genes. P_{Cdist} is conditioned on the N_i and it is conditionally independent of P_{ORA}, which is observing a more number of dysregulated genes from DE. To show the independence of P_{ORA} and P_{Cdist} we have:

$$P\left(\frac{(Cdist_i(P_i, S) \geq C_0) \cap (X \geq |N_i|)}{DE, |S| = |N_i|}\right) = P\left(\frac{Cdist_i(P_i, S) \geq C_0}{|S| = |N_i|}\right) P\left(\frac{X \geq |N_i|}{DE}\right)$$

The left hand side represents the intersection probability for P_{Cdist} and P_{ORA}. On the right hand side, $P(X \geq |N_i| \mid DE)$ is P_{ORA}, and C_0 represents the observed causal disturbance based on the experimental evidence. A formal proof is obtained by rewriting the equation for different values of K in $P(\frac{X=K}{DE})$ and summation over different values of K by usin the mutual exclusivity of $P(\frac{X=K}{DE})$ for different K's. We use Fisher's method to unify the two independent probabilities P_{ORA} and P_{Cdist} in one test-statistic, which calculates the probability of observing more smaller values for product of the two evidences ($P[X_i \leq P_{Cdist} \cdot P_{ORA}]$). Chi-squared test with four degrees of freedom [2] estimates this p-value as follows:

$$\chi_4^2 \sim -2[ln(P_{Cdist}) + ln(P_{ORA})] \quad (7)$$

We use the p-values from formula 7, denoted as P_{enp}, as an indicator for pathway enrichment. P_{enp} is calculated for all processed pathways . To correct for multiple hypothesis testing, we use False Discovery Rate (FDR) method [1].

2.3 Experimental Validation

We use the pathway references annotated by Kyoto Encyclopedia of Genes and Genomes (KEGG) [12]. Importing and processing is done via KEGGgraph package [22]. This study uses the representation of one gene per node for KEGG pathways. Our methodology discards the non-gene encoded elements in the representation. Pathways are processed by eliminating self loops and removing edges to obtain a DAG subgraph. If the original graph is not a DAG, we use the following greedy steps to remove edges for obtaining a DAG.

(1) find the largest strong connected component in G_{p_i} that has node size more than 1.
(2) for each component remove 1 edge according to annotation index of the nodes
(3) repeat until the graph is DAG

Our analysis initially included 199 human pathways from KEGG including signaling, disease, organismal processes, and cellular processes. We excluded pathways with less than twenty number of interactions. 168 pathways passed this criteria for analysis. To investigate the validity of our approach, we examined all of the pathways for the ratio of edges removed to obtain the underlying DAG (Figure 4). We excluded from analysis the pathways with more than %10 of edges removed. Statistical processing and data analysis were all done using free available packages in R and Bioconductor [5]. We used colorectal cancer microarray samples by Hong et al. as our experimental dataset [9]. The data consists of 24 samples from 14 patients and 10 healthy controls. This data has been used by Tarca et al in the original SPIA article [17]. We excluded unannotated genes and modified the dysregulation p-values to $FDR \leq 0.1$ to identify DE genes. For comparison, we used SPIA algorithm on the experimental dataset [17]. To evaluate the statistical power of Cdist, we compared P_{enp}, P_{Cdist}, P_{ORA}, and SPIA p-values for KEGG Pathways.

3 RESULTS

The statistical criteria identifies 5322 dysregulated genes from 17227 array transcripts. Initially 199 KEGG annotated pathways were used for processing. A total 50 pathways were excluded for having more nodes than interactions, including 9 pathways without any annotated links. Also, 12 additional pathways were excluded because they had more than %10 of their links removed in the DAG processing. Finally, a total 137 KEGG annotated pathways were analyzed to obtain P_{enp}. In comparison, SPIA also analyzes 137 pathway, while 90 of which intersect with our pathway dataset.

The combined evidence, P_{enp}, detects 8 enriched pathways that are not detected when using ORA ($FDR \leq 0.05$)(Table 1). These results display how the incorporation of the graph structure detects pathway dysregulations that are not observable by ORA. The pathways apoptosis and RAS signaling are detectable using the combined evidence, which are frequently reported for their association with cancers including colorectal cancer [3, 7, 19]. As an example, figure 2 shows that the removal of the dysregulated nodes in apoptosis pathway deletes %98.6 of the directed paths.

Comparison with SPIA algorithm shows 10 pathway that are detected by P_{enp} and not by SPIA. Which includes cancer pathways apoptosis, notch signalling, and hedgehog signalling. In addition, Some of the KEGG annotated pathways are discarded by SPIA because of its algorithmic requirements. 14 of these pathways are detected as dysregulated using P_{enp} (Table 2), including many cancer related pathways. In addition, P_{enp}, does not identify 3 pathways detected by SPIA, which do not seem to be related to the colorectal cancer (Table 2).

To examine the computational behaviour of Cdist, we investigate the apoptosis pathways as it is detected by Cdist but not by SPIA and ORA. Cdist shows the removal of 44 DE genes (out of 126 genes) removes %98.6 of the total paths ($p - value < 0.0053$, Figure 2). Based on the DE genes, P_{ORA} is 0.187 which fails to identify the pathway as enriched (Table 1). Similarly, the significance level of

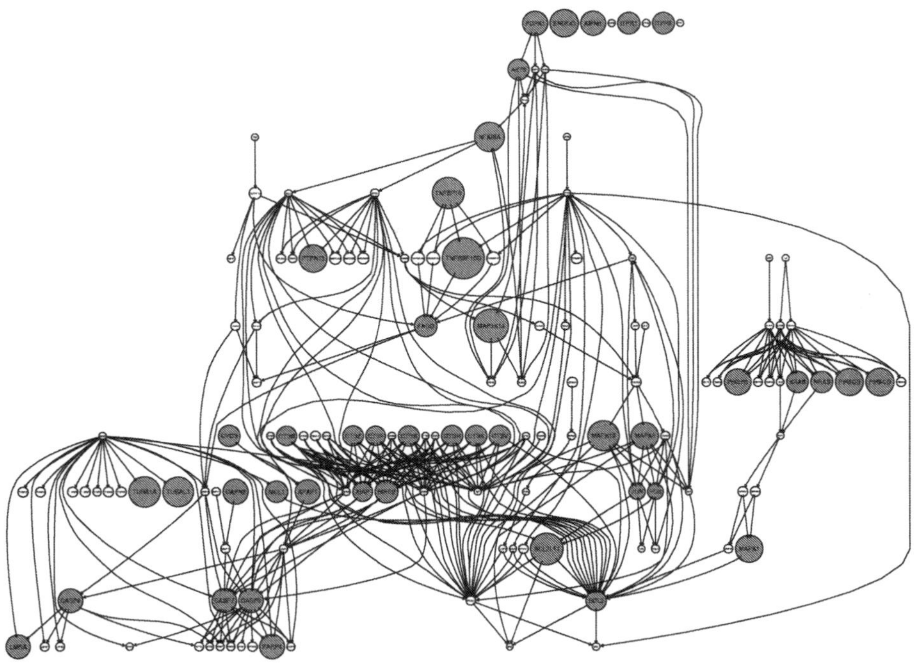

Figure 2: P_{enp} detects the apoptosis pathway dysregulation in the colorectal cancer dataset (FDR = 0.0371), while ORA and SPIA does not(P_{ORA} = 0.187, P_{SPIA} = 0.241). *Cdist* for this pathways is 0.986, which implies the 44 dysregulated genes (Out of 122) disturb the activity of %98.6 of the directed paths in this pathway (P_{Cdist} = 0.0053 at 10^4 sampling). Highlighted nodes are dysregulated genes. Node sizes are modified to display the gene names. Figure generated via R packages [5]

Figure 3: Null distribution of *Cdist* for apoptosis pathway in colorectal cancer. The plot is generated by 10^5 sampling rounds. Dysregulated genes exhibit causal disturbance index of 0.986 with respective p-value P_{Cdist} of 0.00489 as shown in the right hand side of the blue line.

apoptosis for SPIA is 0.241 (FDR) (Table 2). To illustrate the null distribution of Cdist in apoptosis pathway, we ran a 10^5 sampling round (figure 3), which yields a p-value of 0.00489 for P_{Cdist}. Figure 5 shows that the %95 confidence interval for P_{Cdist} falls in the significant region for sampling rounds (¿10^3).

4 DISCUSSION

In this manuscript, we showed how the combined structural evidence, P_{enp}, detect the KEGG pathways dysregulation in the colorectal cancer dataset. Some of which are not detected using ORA and SPIA (Table 2) [9, 12]. The detected pathways included known cancer pathways apoptosis, Notch signaling, and Ras signaling -which were not identified by the other methods (Figure 2,Table 2) [3, 19]. The results demonstrate that our methodology produces biologically relevant information by utilizing genetic interconnections (Table 2).

What distinguishes Cdist from its predecessors is that the algorithm utilizes the graph structure in a more global scale. As an example, SPIA uses evidence from the number of connections for each entity, which is closely related to the degree centrality [17]. In contrast, Cdist evaluates a dysregulated set in a pathway based on the number paths involved in the set. The formulation of Cdist is related to Katz centrality, with the dampening factor eliminated (Formula 3) [14]. Our results show that it is possible to improve

Table 1: The combined evidence (P_{enp}) identifies 8 pathways that are not detectable using ORA p-values (P_{ORA}). This table shows significant KEGG pathway enrichments ($FDR \leq 0.05$), using P_{enp}, in the test dataset [9]. ID represents KEGG identifier for the pathways. P_{Cdist} is the p-value for causal disturbance. $P^{\dagger}_{enp}$ is the corrected p-values using FDR. * indicates more sampling rounds are required to estimate a p-value

Name	ID	P_{ORA}	P_{Cdist}	P_{enp}	$P^{\dagger}_{enp}$
Ras sig...	04014	0.0375	0.0365	0.0104	0.0459
Cytokine-cyt...	04060	0.728	0.0012	0.00702	0.0356
Apoptosis	04210	0.187	0.0053	0.00786	0.0371
*Olfacto...	04740	0.9998	0	0	0
Breast cancer	05224	0.0456	0.0081	0.00329	0.0205
Pertussis	05133	0.0160	0.0536	0.00691	0.0356
Influenza A	05164	0.0145	0.0214	0.00282	0.0193
Hepatitis C	05160	0.384	0.0008	0.00279	0.0193

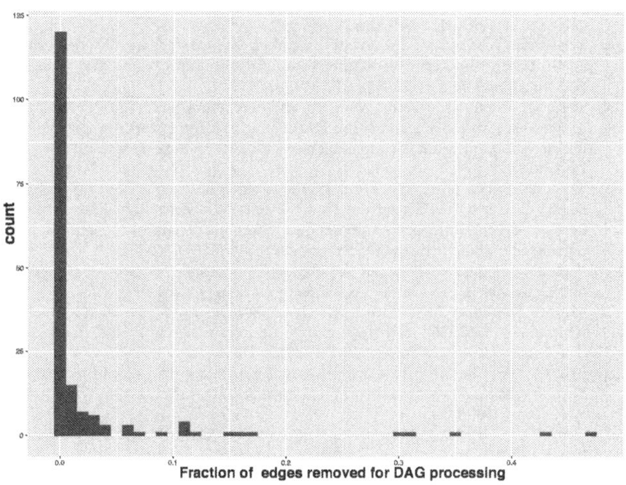

Figure 4: The process for extracting DAGs from pathways often preserves most of the edges. This plot shows the ratio of the edges removed from each pathway in DAG processing. Only 5 pathway are processed with more than 20% of their edges removed, while in 137 of 168 pathway with at least one annotated interaction less than 2% of edges needed to be removed to obtain a DAG.

the enrichment analysis by emphasizing on the interactions. P_{enp} produces a detailed inference compared other models, particularly by detection of well known cancer pathway, such as apoptosis and Ras signaling (Figure 2, Tables 1,2). The results also imply that the pathways' structures contain evidence regarding biological dysregulations. This observation is supported by the numerous researches that utilize the interaction to improve the inference [8, 11, 17, 18].

Pathways are known to have feedback loops that provide certain biological significance. This background might seem contrary to our assumption of DAG models for pathway graphs. However, as shown in figure 4, most of the pathways require only a few number of their edges removed in order to obtain a DAG. In particular, 94 out of 137 analyzed pathways are primarily DAG and do not need any edge removal, including many signalling pathways. In addition, DAGs are shown to be informative in the context of biological

Table 2: P_{enp} detects 32 (out of 137) pathways ($FDR \leq 0.05$). Out of 90 commonly analyzed pathways by SPIA and Cdist, 8 are detected by P_{enp} but not by SPIA (in bold) - including known cancer pathways. Similarly, P_{enp} does not detect 3 SPIA pathways (underlined). P_{enp} detects 14 pathways that are not annotated by SPIA. ID represents KEGG identifier. NA indicates not annotated. * indicates more sampling is needed to estimate a precise p-value

Name	ID	P_{enp}	SPIA
PPAR signaling...	03320	0.000821	0.000139
MAPK signaling...	04010	0.0134	0.00135
Cytokine-cytokine...	04060	0.0358	0.207
Apoptosis	04210	0.0371	0.241
Notch signaling...	04330	0.0328	0.107
Hedgehog sig...	04340	0.0134	0.98
Axon guidance	04360	0.00219	0.00065
Focal adhesion	04510	0.000154	2e-09
ECM-receptor...	04512	0.0103	2.36e-08
Fc gamma R-med...	04666	0.00241	0.00149
*Olfactory transduction	04740	0	1
Regulation of actin...	04810	0.000844	0.00546
Alzheimer's disease	05010	NA	9.71e-09
Parkinson's disease	05012	NA	3.68e-08
Huntington's disease	05016	NA	0.00135
Bacterial invasion...	05100	0.00291	0.0264
Salmonella infection	05132	0.047	0.0818
Pertussis	05133	0.0358	0.233
Hepatitis C	05160	0.0189	0.195
Influenza A	05164	0.0189	0.172
Pathways in cancer	05200	0.000192	0.000127
Small cell lung cancer	05222	0.107	0.00135
Glutamergic synapse	04724	0.225	0.0165
Pathogenic Escheria...	05130	0.145	0.0267
Ras signaling...	04014	0.0459	NA
Rap1 signaling...	04015	0.0381	NA
Hippo signaling...	04390	0.00241	NA
Hippo signaling...	04392	0.000822	NA
cGMP-PKG sig...	04022	0.0205	NA
Endocytosis	04144	1.95e-05	NA
Renin secretion	04924	0.034	NA
Choline meta...	05231	0.0103	NA
MicroRNAs in cancer	05206	0.0103	NA
Proteoglycans in cancer	05205	0.000844	NA
Breast cancer	05224	0.0205	NA
Non-alcoholic fatty...	04932	4.33e-06	NA
AGE-RAGE signaling...	04933	0.0223	NA
EGFR tyrosine kina...	01521	0.0371	NA

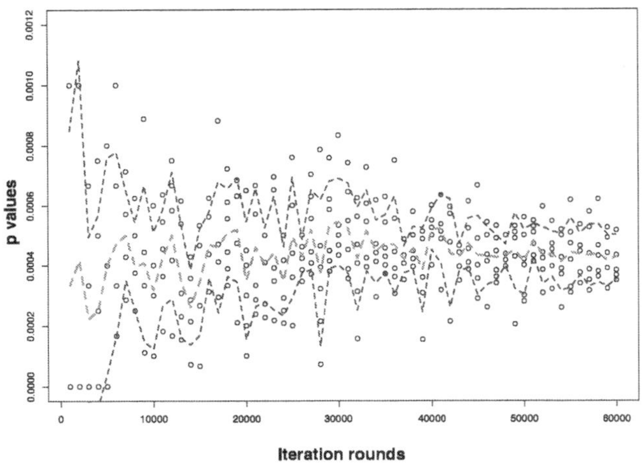

Figure 5: Repeated assessment of P_{Cdist} for apoptosis pathway. The x-axis is the sampling size (6 repeats). The calculation range is 1000 - 60000 (steps of 1000 increase). The orange line is the mean of p-values at the each iteration size. The gray bands display the 95% confidence interval.

networks, as they encompass several computational advantages [10, 14]. Nonetheless, designing similar models that analyze the cycles in pathway graphs is one of the objectives to be considered. The framework described in this study allows other centrality measures to be incorporated in the enrichment analysis, and possibly improving the power of the methodology. However, the choice of centrality measures and their validation remains to be seen. One advantage of the model presented in this article is its independence from subjective parameters in the computation of Cdist (formula 4), as it is the case in some centrality models such as Katz or Page-Rank [14]. The results discussed in this article show that causal disturbance serves as a proof of concept that the structural properties can be used as statistical evidence for enrichment analysis.

Integration of additional evidence is valuable for the improvement of Cdist. The possible additions include the dysregulation intensities and prioritization of genes based on their pathway specificity, as shown by Tarca et al. and Foroushani et al. [4, 17]. The framework presented in this study is compatible to be combined with predicted interactions, as explained by Ma et al. [13]. In addition, our model (Cdist) can be applied to the emerging targeted datasets in a personalized medicine context [23]. Evaluation of Cdist using synthetic models and larger datasets is an important topic of this study.

5 CONCLUSION

Pathway enrichment analysis using causal disturbance improves the inference to detect critical pathway dysregulations. The presented methodology facilitates biologically relevant inference by emphasizing on topological importance of an entity. This analysis models is applicable to any general genomic dysregulation data.

6 ACKNOWLEDGMENTS

We would like thank Dr. Erik Saule for his technical validation and comments on this research. We acknowledge the continuous support of College of Computing and Informatics at UNC Charlotte, financial and otherwise .

REFERENCES

[1] Yoav Benjamini and Yosef Hochberg. 1995. Controlling the false discovery rate: a practical and powerful approach to multiple testing. *Journal of the royal statistical society. Series B (Methodological)* (1995), 289–300.

[2] Allan Birnbaum. 1954. Combining independent tests of significance. *J. Amer. Statist. Assoc.* 49, 267 (1954), 559–574.

[3] Alberto Fernández-Medarde and Eugenio Santos. 2011. Ras in cancer and developmental diseases. *Genes & cancer* 2, 3 (2011), 344–358.

[4] Amir BK Foroushani, Fiona SL Brinkman, and David J Lynn. 2013. Pathway-GPS and SIGORA: identifying relevant pathways based on the over-representation of their gene-pair signatures. *PeerJ* 1 (2013), e229.

[5] Robert C Gentleman, Vincent J Carey, Douglas M Bates, Ben Bolstad, Marcel Dettling, Sandrine Dudoit, Byron Ellis, Laurent Gautier, Yongchao Ge, Jeff Gentry, and others. 2004. Bioconductor: open software development for computational biology and bioinformatics. *Genome biology* 5, 10 (2004), R80.

[6] Enrico Glaab, Anaïs Baudot, Natalio Krasnogor, Reinhard Schneider, and Alfonso Valencia. 2012. EnrichNet: network-based gene set enrichment analysis. *Bioinformatics* 28, 18 (2012), i451–i457.

[7] Douglas Hanahan and Robert A Weinberg. 2011. Hallmarks of cancer: the next generation. *cell* 144, 5 (2011), 646–674.

[8] Benjamin J Hescott, Mark DM Leiserson, Lenore J Cowen, and Donna K Slonim. 2010. Evaluating between-pathway models with expression data. *Journal of Computational Biology* 17, 3 (2010), 477–487.

[9] Yi Hong, Kok Sun Ho, Kong Weng Eu, and Peh Yean Cheah. 2007. A susceptibility gene set for early onset colorectal cancer that integrates diverse signaling pathways: implication for tumorigenesis. *Clinical Cancer Research* 13, 4 (2007), 1107–1114.

[10] Trey Ideker, Vesteinn Thorsson, Jeffrey A Ranish, Rowan Christmas, Jeremy Buhler, Jimmy K Eng, Roger Bumgarner, David R Goodlett, Ruedi Aebersold, and Leroy Hood. 2001. Integrated genomic and proteomic analyses of a systematically perturbed metabolic network. *Science* 292, 5518 (2001), 929–934.

[11] Hawoong Jeong, Sean P Mason, A-L Barabási, and Zoltan N Oltvai. 2001. Lethality and centrality in protein networks. *Nature* 411, 6833 (2001), 41–42.

[12] Minoru Kanehisa, Miho Furumichi, Mao Tanabe, Yoko Sato, and Kanae Morishima. 2017. KEGG: new perspectives on genomes, pathways, diseases and drugs. *Nucleic Acids Research* 45, D1 (2017), D353–D361.

[13] Jing Ma, Ali Shojaie, and George Michailidis. 2016. Network-based pathway enrichment analysis with incomplete network information. *Bioinformatics* 32, 20 (2016), 3165–3174.

[14] Mark Newman. 2010. *Networks: An Introduction.* Oxford University Press, Inc., New York, NY, USA.

[15] Judea Pearl. 2009. *Causality.* Cambridge university press.

[16] Aravind Subramanian, Pablo Tamayo, Vamsi K Mootha, Sayan Mukherjee, Benjamin L Ebert, Michael A Gillette, Amanda Paulovich, Scott L Pomeroy, Todd R Golub, Eric S Lander, and others. 2005. Gene set enrichment analysis: a knowledge-based approach for interpreting genome-wide expression profiles. *Proceedings of the National Academy of Sciences* 102, 43 (2005), 15545–15550.

[17] Adi Laurentiu Tarca, Sorin Draghici, Purvesh Khatri, Sonia S Hassan, Pooja Mittal, Jung-sun Kim, Chong Jai Kim, Juan Pedro Kusanovic, and Roberto Romero. 2009. A novel signaling pathway impact analysis. *Bioinformatics* 25, 1 (2009), 75–82.

[18] Fabio Vandin, Eli Upfal, and Benjamin J Raphael. 2011. Algorithms for detecting significantly mutated pathways in cancer. *Journal of Computational Biology* 18, 3 (2011), 507–522.

[19] AJM Watson. 2004. Apoptosis and colorectal cancer. *Gut* 53, 11 (2004), 1701–1709.

[20] Lingjie Weng, Fabio Macciardi, Aravind Subramanian, Guia Guffanti, Steven G Potkin, Zhaoxia Yu, and Xiaohui Xie. 2011. SNP-based pathway enrichment analysis for genome-wide association studies. *BMC bioinformatics* 12, 1 (2011), 99.

[21] Jeongah Yoon, Anselm Blumer, and Kyongbum Lee. 2006. An algorithm for modularity analysis of directed and weighted biological networks based on edge-betweenness centrality. *Bioinformatics* 22, 24 (2006), 3106–3108.

[22] Jitao David Zhang and Stefan Wiemann. 2009. KEGGgraph: a graph approach to KEGG PATHWAY in R and bioconductor. *Bioinformatics* 25, 11 (2009), 1470–1471.

[23] Qian Zhu, Aaron K Wong, Arjun Krishnan, Miriam R Aure, Alicja Tadych, Ran Zhang, David C Corney, Casey S Greene, Lars A Bongo, Vessela N Kristensen, and others. 2015. Targeted exploration and analysis of large cross-platform human transcriptomic compendia. *Nature methods* 12, 3 (2015), 211–214.

Seq2seq Fingerprint: An Unsupervised Deep Molecular Embedding for Drug Discovery

Zheng Xu
The University of Texas at Arlington
701 S. Nedderman Drive
Arlington, Texas 76019
zheng.xu@mavs.uta.edu

Sheng Wang
The University of Texas at Arlington
701 S. Nedderman Drive
Arlington, Texas 76019
sheng.wang@mavs.uta.edu

Feiyun Zhu
The University of Texas at Arlington
701 S. Nedderman Drive
Arlington, Texas 76019
feiyun.zhu@uta.edu

Junzhou Huang*
The University of Texas at Arlington
701 S. Nedderman Drive
Arlington, Texas 76019
jzhuang@uta.edu

ABSTRACT

Many of today's drug discoveries require expertise knowledge and insanely expensive biological experiments for identifying the chemical molecular properties. However, despite the growing interests of using supervised machine learning algorithms to automatically identify those chemical molecular properties, there is little advancement of the performance and accuracy due to the limited amount of training data.

In this paper, we propose a novel unsupervised molecular embedding method, providing a continuous feature vector for each molecule to perform further tasks, e.g., solubility classification. In the proposed method, a multi-layered Gated Recurrent Unit (GRU) network is used to map the input molecule into a continuous feature vector of fixed dimensionality, and then another deep GRU network is employed to decode the continuous vector back to the original molecule. As a result, the continuous encoding vector is expected to contain rigorous and enough information to recover the original molecule and predict its chemical properties. The proposed embedding method could utilize almost unlimited molecule data for the training phase. With sufficient information encoded in the vector, the proposed method is also robust and task-insensitive. The performance and robustness are confirmed and interpreted in our extensive experiments.

*This work was partially supported by U.S. NSF IIS-1423056, CMMI-1434401, CNS-1405985, and NSF CAREER grant IIS-1553687.

Permission to make digital or hard copies of all or part of this work for personal or classroom use is granted without fee provided that copies are not made or distributed for profit or commercial advantage and that copies bear this notice and the full citation on the first page. Copyrights for components of this work owned by others than ACM must be honored. Abstracting with credit is permitted. To copy otherwise, or republish, to post on servers or to redistribute to lists, requires prior specific permission and/or a fee. Request permissions from permissions@acm.org.
ACM-BCB '17, August 20-23, 2017, Boston, MA, USA
© 2017 Association for Computing Machinery.
ACM ISBN 978-1-4503-4722-8/17/08...$15.00
https://doi.org/10.1145/3107411.3107424

CCS CONCEPTS

• **Theory of computation → Unsupervised learning and clustering**; **Structured prediction**; • **Applied computing → Molecular sequence analysis**; **Sequencing and genotyping technologies**; *Bioinformatics*; Imaging;

KEYWORDS

Unsupervised Learning; Structured Prediction; Learning Representation; Sequence to Sequence Learning; Deep Learning; Drug Discovery; Virtual Screening; Molecular Representation; Imaging; Computational Biology

1 INTRODUCTION

In the most recent decade, every drug company with R&D department has carried out numerous initiatives for speeding up its drug discovery process [14]. Drug discovery is the process through which potential new medicines are identified. Modern drug discovery is usually implemented as drug compound selection, while, for every candidate chemical compound, the chemical drug properties, e.g., affinity, selectivity, metabolic stability, are biologically tested in the lab environment. Once all the properties pass the drug requirement tests, it will be selected as a new potential drug candidate. However, this process is excessively expensive and labor-intensive, and costs hundreds of million dollars each year.

Therefore, using machine learning methods to automatically predict the chemical properties has recently raised great interests in the drug discovery community [3, 5, 27, 35]. However, the majority of machine learning algorithms take fixed-length continuous feature vectors as inputs [55–57]. However, the nature of molecules makes it extremely hard to represent molecules with fixed-length vectors [11, 23, 44]. The readers might refer to Figure 1 to grab some intuition. As a simple example, we may consider H_2O (water) and O_2 (oxygen). They differ in atom types, numbers as well as bond types. One might find it is tricky to represent each molecule as a fixed-length vector. So a large class of research papers has been published to generate the fixed-length continuous vector representation for molecules. Overall, the choice of the representation of molecules is at the heart of the machine learning-based drug discovery [6, 8, 29, 34].

Table 1: Comparison among different types of fingerprint methods, in three different aspects: 1) if the design of the fingerprint requires biologists' expertise knowledge, 2) if the fingerprint has enough information to be reverted to original SMILE representation, and 3) if the fingerprint method requires many labeled data. DL is short for Deep learning while FP is short for FingerPrint.

Properties	Non-data driven Methods		Supervised DL FP [13, 26, 42]	Seq2seq FP (**ours**)
	Hash-based [17, 25, 28, 36]	Local feature[30, 37]		
Without biologist guide	✓	×	✓	✓
Revertible	×	×	×	✓
Less thirsty on label data	✓	✓	×	✓

Traditionally, the design of new fixed-length vector molecular representations, named **fingerprints**, is not data-driven and based on human expertise knowledge [7, 22, 32, 38, 39]. One type of those design is based on some hashing procedure, e.g., Extended Connectivity FingerPrint (ECFP) [36]. Those fingerprints are usually efficient in speed, but is much like a lossy compression in the imaging area [33, 50–52] and the operation is non-invertible. The other sort of non-data-driven fingerprint is based on local sub-structures of molecules. Biologists look for several highly related chemical molecular sub-structures for specific tasks and design the fingerprint feature vector accordingly. Representative works are [30, 37]. However, this kind of design obviously requires years of expertise experience and is highly task-sensitive. To sum up, the non-data-driven fingerprint is either limited in encoding enough information or highly lean to expensive and accurate human knowledge. Hence it has raised a great demand for the data-driven fingerprints, which does not require years of human guide and expensive biological experiments.

Observed the recent success of deep learning on imaging understanding [43, 47] or natural language processing [20, 31], there are a few attempts made in applying deep neural network to generate fingerprints. Among the most famous ones are the neural fingerprint [13] as well as [18, 26, 42, 46]. However, most supervised deep learning methods are data-hungry and usually completely fail when data scale is limited [53, 58], and unfortunately this is usually the case in the drug discovery due to the insane expensiveness of the lab experiment.

In this paper, we propose an unsupervised data-driven deep-learning-based molecular fingerprint method, named **seq2seq fingerprint**. To overcome the issues mentioned above, 1) the proposed method is data-driven, without any human expertise knowledge required. 2) the fingerprints generated by the proposed method are completely revertible to original molecular representations, ensuring the sufficiency of information encoded in the fingerprint vector. 3) the proposed method employs an unsupervised training on a **huge unlabeled** dataset, sufficiently releasing the horsepower of deep neural network. We illustrate a comparison among all mentioned fingerprint methods and our seq2seq fingerprint method.

Our fingerprint is designed based on a recent breakthrough model, called *sequence-to-sequence learning* (seq2seq learning). The seq2seq learning method comes from a seemingly unrelated area, English-to-French translation. The seq2seq learning method takes an English sentence as the input, encodes it into a *meaning* vector and then translates it back to a French sentence as the output. The crux of our method is similar, but differs in the way that we set both the input and output of the seq2seq learning as the same SMILE string, a text representation of a molecule. We map the SMILE string to a fixed-sized vector and then *translates* it back to the original SMILE string. The intermediate fixed-sized vector is extracted as the **seq2seq fingerprint**. Once the model is well-trained, the intermediate feature vector is considered to encode all the information to recover the original molecular representation. Hence, the seq2seq fingerprint is expected to capture the rigorous information with which we can accurately predict the molecular properties.

The benefits of the seq2seq fingerprint are three folds: 1) the training phase of seq2seq fingerprint is completely **label-free**, avoiding the costly and labor-intensive label acquiring procedure. 2) it is data-driven, eliminating the reliance on expert's subjective knowledge. 3) since the unlabeled data is almost unlimited in practice, we can fully utilize the power of deep learning, without suffering from the short supply of labeled data.

The technical contributions of this paper are summarized as: 1) the seq2seq fingerprint method is clearly the first attempt to apply the seq2seq learning method to perform drug discovery tasks, coupling two seemingly unrelated areas. 2) several important adaptations are made into the original seq2seq learning to suit drug discovery applications:

- GRU cell is used, instead of LSTM, to accelerate the training process,
- Attention Mechanism is employed to centralize the fingerprint space,
- Dropout layer is added to overcome the over-fitting issue during the training phase,
- An extra fingerprint extraction layer set is added to pull the fingerprint out.

3) extensive experiments confirm the superior performance on different tasks over the state-of-the-art methods.

The rest of the paper is organized as follows. We summarize several related work, in both drug discovery and sequence to sequence learning, in Section 2. In Section 3, we describe our entire pipeline in details. We show our experiment results in Section 4, demonstrating the superior performance of our method. We conclude and discuss the future direction of our paper in Section 5.

2 RELATED WORK

In this section, we present several related work. First, we introduce the initial representation of molecules, i.e., how the molecular data is persisted in the data store. Second, we list several state-of-the-art

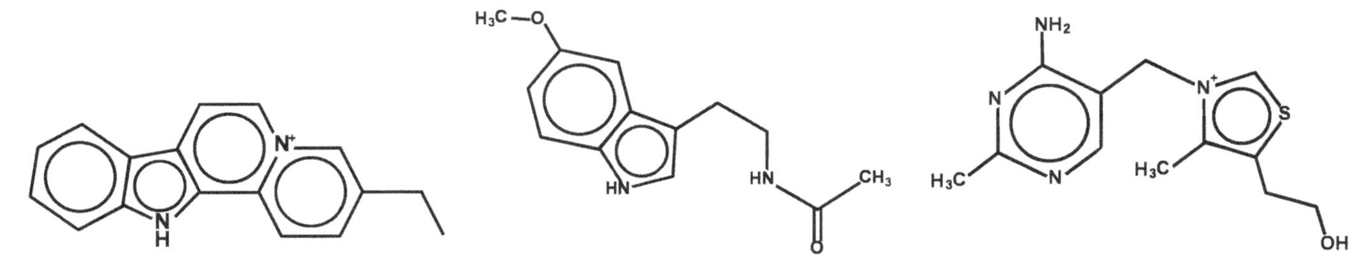

(a) Flavopereirin: CCc(c1)ccc2[n+]1ccc3c2Nc4c3cccc4 (b) Melatonin: CC(=O)NCCC1=CNc2c1cc(OC)cc2 (c) Thiamine: OCCc1c(C)[n+](cs1)Cc2cnc(C)nc2N

Figure 1: The examples of SMILE representations.

fingerprint methods, including the most recent ones using deep learning techniques. Last but not least, we briefly describe our cornerstone learning method, i.e., seq2seq learning, with several of its related work in language translation area.

2.1 SMILE Representations of Molecules

Initially, the molecules are represented through the Simplified Molecular-Input Line-Entry system (SMILE) [45], which is a line notation for describing the structure of chemical species using text strings. The SMILE system represents the chemical structures in a graph-based definition, where the atoms, bonds and rings are encoded in a graph. Simple examples of SMILE representations are 1) dinitrogen with structure $N \equiv N$ (N#N), 2) methyl isocyanate with structure $CH_3 - N = C = O$ (CN=C=O), where corresponding SMILE representations are included in the brackets. We show some more complex examples in Figure 1.

2.2 Fingerprint Methods

Hash-based Fingerprints. Many hash-based has been developed to generate unique molecular feature representation [17, 25, 28]. One of the most famous ones being Extended-Connectivity FingerPrint (ECFP) [36]. Circular fingerprints generate each layer's features by applying a fixed hash function to the concatenated features of the neighborhood in the previous layer. However, due to the non-invertible nature of the hash function, the hash-bashed fingerprint methods usually do not encode enough information and hence result in lower performance in the further predictive tasks.

Biologist-guided Local-Feature Fingerprints. Another mainstream of traditional fingerprint methods is designed based on the biological experiments and the expertise knowledge and experience, [30, 37]. Biologist look for several important task-related sub-structures (fragments), e.g., $CC(OH)CC$ for pro-solubility prediction, and count those sub-structures as local features to produce fingerprints. This kind of fingerprint methods usually work well for specific tasks, but generalize very poorly for other tasks.

Supervised Deep Learning-based Fingerprints. The growth of deep learning has provided the flexibility and performance to create the molecular fingerprint from data samples, without explicit human guide, [2, 13, 26, 40, 42]. The state-of-the-art work is the neural fingerprint [13]. The neural fingerprint mimics the process of generating circular fingerprint but instead the hash function is replaced by a non-linear activated densely connected layer. This method is based on the data-hungry deep neural network. To acquire enough labeled data, biologists need to perform a sufficiently large number of tests on chemical molecules, which is extremely expensive.

2.3 Encoder-Decoder Structured Neural Network

Variational Auto-Encoder. Variational Auto-Encoder (VAE) model [12] shares some similar structure as our method, which uses a *encoder* to encode the original representation to a vector or scalar then a *decoder* to decode the vector to original representation. The difference is that the VAE model puts the assumption that the embedded space follows some specific Gaussian distribution. In most recent months, the authors become aware of an unpublished VAE report in drug discovery [19]. However, there is no evidence and experimental results to support the Gaussian assumption on the embedded fingerprint space. Moreover, we still lack the evaluation on how the VAE will perform in the predictive tasks.

Generative Adversarial Network. Generative Adversarial Network (GAN) [21] has recently become popular in the machine learning area. A GAN is constructed by a *discriminator* and a *generator.* The discriminator acts as a cop to distinguish the training data samples from the samples generated from the generator. Hence, the learning process actually learns from both training data set and the generated fake data samples. It works well when the scale of data sample is limited. But such network is hard to train and we are not aware of any publicly available report that documents the attempt to adapt GAN into drug discovery.

Sequence to Sequence Model. The sequence to sequence model [41] has been recently used in English-to-French translation and demonstrated as a breakthrough success. The basic strategy of sequence to sequence learning is to map the input sequence, e.g., an English sentence, to a fixed-sized vector using one deep Long Short-Term Memory (LSTM) network, and then map the vector to the target sequence, e.g., the translated French sentence, with another deep LSTM network. The fixed-sized vector is considered as an intermediate representation and contains the *"meaning"* of sentences.

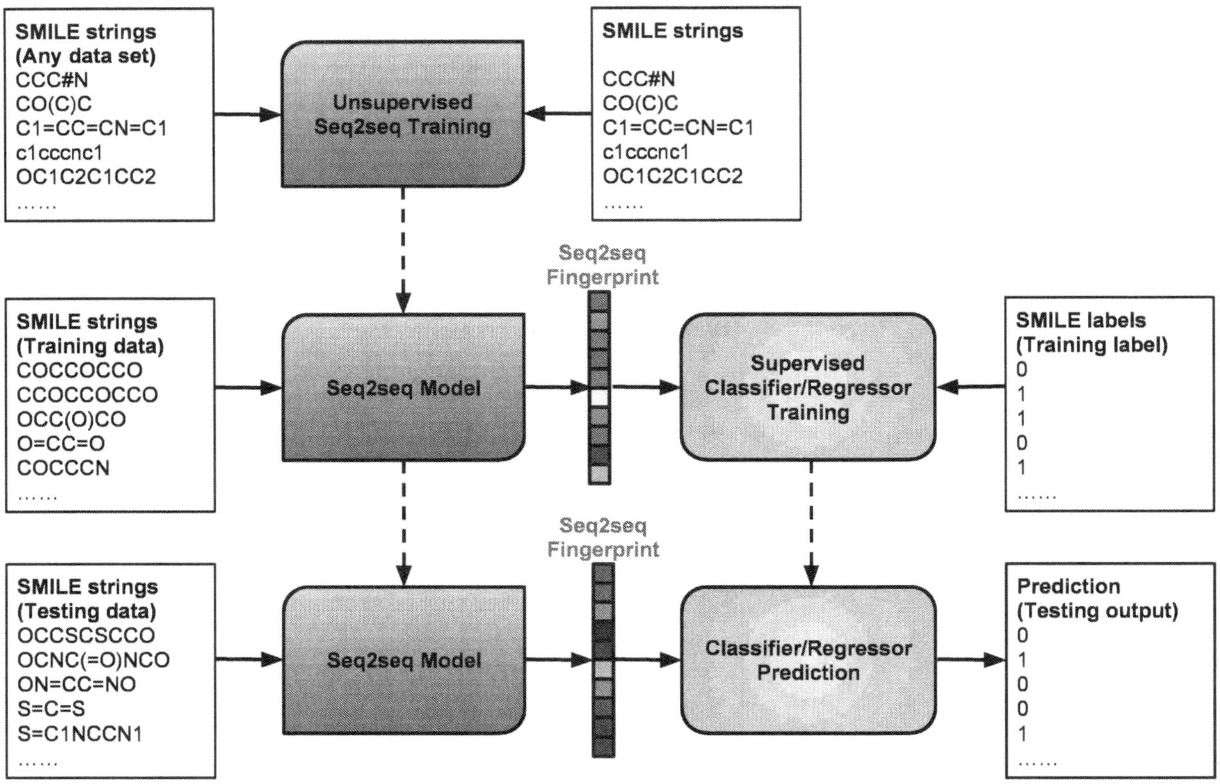

Figure 2: This figure shows how the entire pipeline works. 1) The seq2seq fingerprint model is trained on a large pool of unlabeled SMILE data. 2) The trained model is fed with SMILE strings to generate the seq2seq fingerprint. 3) Coupling the fingerprint and label, the pairs are fed into supervised classifiers/regressors to train a predictive model.

3 METHODOLOGY

In the sequel, we present the entire pipeline of the proposed method. First, we overview the entire pipeline with an introduction of the crux of our fingerprint method. Second, we detail each step of our method and our improvements and adaptations upon the original seq2seq learning method. Last, we discuss our methods to end this section.

3.1 Overview

The entire pipeline of our method consists of three steps: 1) we first train the seq2seq fingerprint model on a **huge** pool of unlabeled training data. 2) Then the trained model is used to generate the seq2seq fingerprint for the labeled data set. 3) The resulting fingerprints and their labels are fed to some supervised learning method to train a predictive model, e.g., Gradient Boosting, Multi-Layer Perceptron (MLP). An illustration of the pipeline is shown in Figure 2. As a result, the entire pipeline is able to **transfer** knowledge from a large number of unlabeled data samples to the supervised training on a relatively small labeled dataset and thus improve the final predictive performance.

The crux of our unsupervised seq2seq fingerprint method, **seq2seq fingerprint**, is to set both input and output sequences to the same SMILE string for each molecule in sequence-to-sequence learning for unsupervised training, or simply **translate the SMILE string to itself**. Since the intermediate vector is considered to maintain the "meaning" of the sequence, we thus extract the intermediate vector as the fingerprint. While the sequence to sequence learning [41] could in principle directly work with our idea, however, there are still many drawbacks yet to limit the application in the molecular predictive tasks.

First, at least in theory, our model can train on a pool of infinite molecular data. While the LSTM is famous for its slow training, the time invested in the training process on a large amount of data is absolutely unbearable. Second, the original sequence to sequence learning does not explicitly output the embedding vector, and therefore lacks an extra layer in order to output the fingerprint vector. Third, as argued in [4], when the length of the input sequence

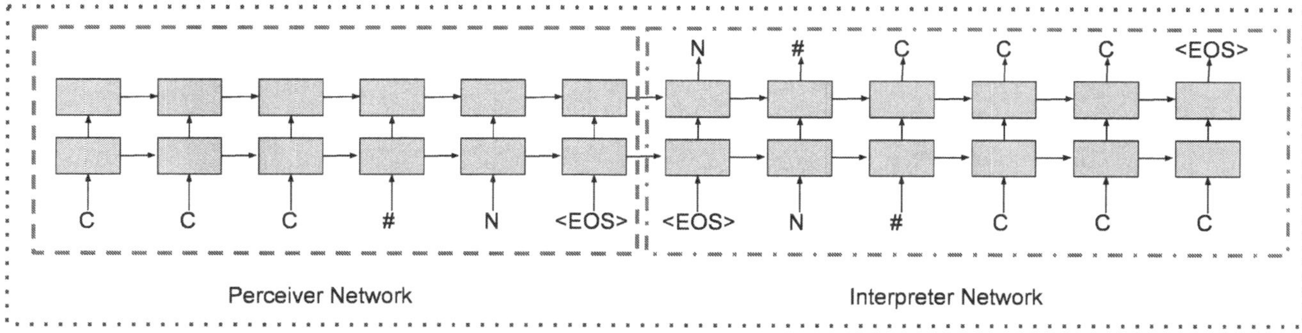

Figure 3: An example on how the unsupervised training works. The perceiver network understands the molecule SMILE representation, e.g., CCC#N, and encodes it into a fixed-length vector, i.e., seq2seq fingerprint. The interpreter network will then translate the fingerprint back to the sequence, e.g. N#CCC.

grows, the performance of the neural network decreases rapidly. However, SMILE representation usually contains several tens of characters (up to 250 characters), which is too long to be handled by the original sequence to sequence model. Finally, due to the large training data scale, the number of model parameters tends to be relatively smaller than demanded, yielding the over-fitting issue.

Here, we propose the seq2seq fingerprint, with various of improvement upon the original sequence-to-sequence learning [41] used in English-to-French translation to generate an effective fingerprint for drug discovery tasks. We detail each step in the following sub-sections.

3.2 Unsupervised Seq2seq Training

To train a fingerprint generator on a huge unlabeled dataset, we first employ a deep Gated Recurrent Unit (GRU) network, named *perceiver network*, to map the original molecular SMILE string to a fixed-sized vector, i.e., the seq2seq fingerprint. Then another deep GRU neural network, called *interpreter network*, is used to generate the original SMILE string back from the seq2seq fingerprint. A workflow illustration of our method is shown in Figure 3. In the following, we show, in the descent order of importance from the authors' perspective, the details we altered to adapt the drug discovery application.

GRU Units The Gated Recurrent Unit (GRU) is used in our experiment instead of LSTM. GRU is famous for its LSTM-like performance but faster training process. A GRU network computes a sequence of outputs $(s_1, \ldots, s_T)$ from the input sequences $(x_1, \ldots, x_T)$ by iterating

$$\begin{aligned} z_t &= \sigma_g(W_z x_t + U_z s_{t-1} + b_z) \\ r_t &= \sigma_r(W_r x_t + U_r s_{t-1} + b_r) \\ h_t &= \tanh(U_h x_t + W_h(s_{t-1} \circ r_t)) \\ s_t &= (1 - z_t) \circ h_{t-1} + z_t \circ s_{t-1}. \end{aligned} \quad (1)$$

A GRU cell has two gates: the update gate z and the reset gate r. Each gate has the trainable parameter W, U, b. The activation function σ for each gate is usually the sigmoid function. GRU also has the *"hidden memory" h*, which holds another set of trainable parameters U, W. In contrast with LSTM which has three gates, it has similar performance but faster training speed [10].

Attention Mechanism So far, the only connection between the perceiver and interpreter networks is the sharing hidden memory. When the sequence becomes longer, it becomes extremely challenging to pass the information from the perceiver to the interpreter network through the hidden memory. To address this issue, the attention mechanism is employed to establish a stronger connection and provide soft-alignment between the perceiver and interpreter networks. More details are referred to [4].

Dropout Layer One of the most favorable features in our model is the capability to use nearly unlimited molecular training data. However, the over-fitting issue will come to play if we grow our data unrestrictively. To enhance the generalizability of our model, we add dropout layer to each input, output gate and yet we do not add the dropout for the hidden memory transferring gate, following the practices in [54].

What do we inherit? While we improve the original sequence-to-sequence model from several aspects, we keep using the reverse technique introduced in [41], where the source sequence is mapped to the reverse sequence of the target. For example, instead of mapping a, b, c to α, β, γ, we map a, b, c to γ, β, α. This trick is observed to make it easier for the Stochastic Gradient Descent (SGD) algorithm to *"establish communication"* between the source and target sequences. Another important technique we keep is the *bucket training*, where all the training sequences are distributed into several buckets, and all the sequences in the same bucket are padded to the same length. This technique can parallel the training process on GPUs for acceleration.

3.3 Fingerprint Extraction

During the fingerprint extraction stage, we only feed-forward the *perceiver* network, leaving the interpreter network behind to save computational resources. Moreover, the original sequence to sequence model does not explicitly output the embedding vector, which brings us challenges to extract fingerprints we need. A fixed unit fully connected layer together with a GRU cell state concatenation layer is injected between the perceiver network and interpreter

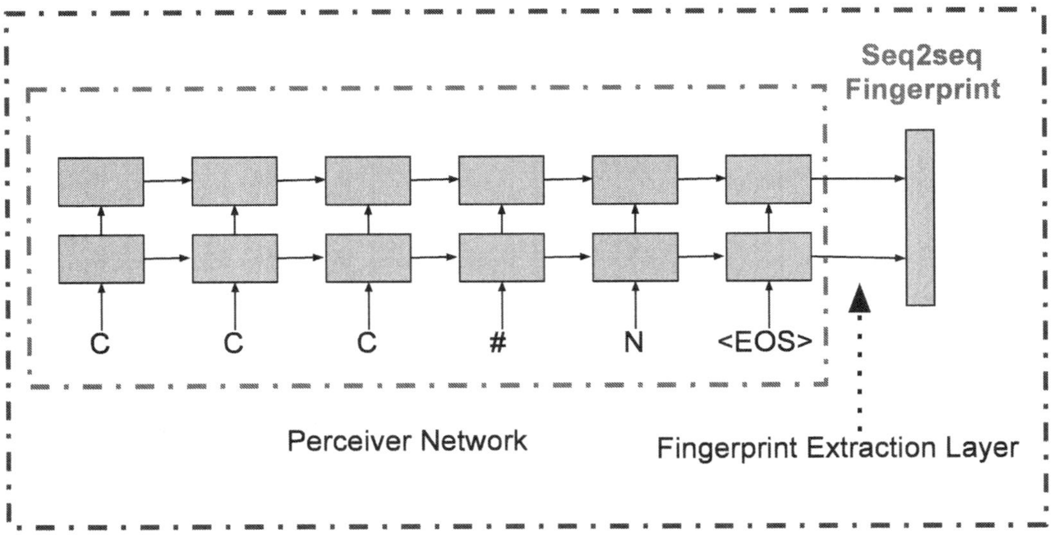

Figure 4: The illustration of how to extract the seq2seq fingerprint. Only the perceiver network is feed-forwarded with an extra fingerprint extraction layer to extract the resulting seq2seq fingerprint.

network to extract the seq2seq fingerprint from the network. The illustration of this process is in Figure 4.

3.4 Supervised Training on Labeled Data

Since our method embedded the molecular graph into a vector space with fixed dimension, the resulting fingerprint can be almost trained with almost all popular regressors or classifiers. Those methods include but not limited to linear Support Vector Machine (SVM), ν-support vector machine, and ensemble methods, e.g., AdaBoost, Extra Trees, etc. In our experiments, we investigate our fingerprints with three ensemble methods: AdaBoost, GradientBoost and Random Forest.

3.5 Discussion

Our method can indeed transfer knowledge from unlabeled data to the labeled data training. However, it is not technically semi-supervised, since the unlabeled data is not directly used in the supervised training. So we still name our fingerprint method as unsupervised.

4 EXPERIMENTS

In this section, we first detail the experimental setup, e.g., the data set description, hardware and software settings, etc. Then we report the recovery performance of the seq2seq fingerprint method, i.e., how the SMILE self-translation performance is. Finally, we show the superior performance on two predictive tasks for our seq2seq fingerprint method.

4.1 Experiment Setup

Unsupervised Train Dataset Our training data was collected from a combination of two large datasets: LogP and PM2-full datasets. Those datasets were obtained from National Center for Advancing Translational Sciences (NCATS) at National Institutes of Health (NIH). The training dataset contains 334,092 valid molecular SMILE representations.

Labeled Datasets We performed the classification on two smaller datasets:

- **LogP**: LogP dataset contains a total of 10,850 samples. Each sample contains a pair of a SMILE string and a water-octanol partition coefficient (LogP) value. A certain threshold of 1.88 is suggested by an NCATS expert. Samples with LogP value smaller than 1.88 will be classified as the negative samples, while the opposites are considered the positive samples.
- **PM2-10k**: PM2-10k dataset contains 10,000 pairs of SMILE strings and binary promiscuous class labels.

Comparison Methods We compared our seq2seq fingerprint method with two state-of-the-art methods: the ECFP [36] (circular fingerprint) and the neural fingerprint method [13]. The circular fingerprint is a hand-crafted hash-based feature. The neural fingerprint is constructed on a supervised deep graph convolutional neural network. The circular fingerprint was generated through RDKit [1] and we use Multi-Layer Perceptron for the future predictive task as suggested in [13]. We obtained the neural fingerprint from https://github.com/HIPS/neural-fingerprint and we carefully followed the authors' instructions to apply our datasets.

Infrastructure and Software The seq2seq fingerprint method was implemented through tensorflow package [1], and the trained models used in our experiments were trained on a workstation with Intel i7 6700K @ 4.00 GHz CPU, 16 Gigabytes RAM and a Nvidia GTX 1080 GPU. We performed the hyper-parameter grid search and the training process of the classifiers on the TACC

[1] http://www.rdkit.org

Table 2: The comparison of classification accuracy on the LogP data.

	Circular	Neural	Adaboost (Ours) 512	Adaboost (Ours) 768	Adaboost (Ours) 1024	GradientBoost (Ours) 512	GradientBoost (Ours) 768	GradientBoost (Ours) 1024	RandomForest (Ours) 512	RandomForest (Ours) 768	RandomForest (Ours) 1024
Mean	0.3674	0.6080	0.7044	0.6837	0.7342	0.7350	0.7149	**0.7664**	0.6895	0.6664	0.6845
StDev	0.0074	0.0135	0.0042	0.0097	0.0042	0.0060	0.0058	0.0043	0.0061	0.0100	0.0032

Table 3: The comparison of classification accuracy on the PM2-10k data.

	Circular	Neural	Adaboost (Ours) 512	Adaboost (Ours) 768	Adaboost (Ours) 1024	GradientBoost (Ours) 512	GradientBoost (Ours) 768	GradientBoost (Ours) 1024	RandomForest (Ours) 512	RandomForest (Ours) 768	RandomForest (Ours) 1024
Mean	0.3938	0.5227	0.5535	0.5561	0.6036	0.5741	0.5713	**0.6206**	0.5316	0.5282	0.5481
StDev	0.0114	0.0112	0.0132	0.0070	0.0147	0.0086	0.0151	0.0198	0.0110	0.0081	0.0088

Lonestar 5 cluster [2]. In addition to the traditional MPI package for distributed grid-search, we used a more flexible master-worker task distribution package for Python called *dgsearch*. The code for training the seq2seq fingerprint will become publicly available after the acceptance of this paper.

4.2 Seq2seq Fingerprint Recovery Performance

Throughout the entire experiment sections, we discuss three variants of our seq2seq fingerprint, varying in feature vector lengths as 512, 768, and 1024. Each model was trained for 24 hours. These three models differ only in the number of GRU layers and yet with the same Latent Dimension (LD). We report the training details and the recovery power of each fingerprint model in Table 4. The recovery performance is evaluated through the perplexity and Exact Match (EM) accuracy. The perplexity is calculated by the entropy of the probability distribution over the training set. The EM accuracy is the ratio between the exactly recovered SMILE strings and the total number of SMILEs in the test sets.

Table 4: The reconstruction performance with different number of GRU layers.

Model	Layer	LD	Perplexity	EM Accuracy
seq2seq-512	2	256	1.00897	94.24%
seq2seq-768	3	256	1.00949	92.92%
seq2seq-1024	4	256	1.01472	90.26%

Table 4 reveals a decreasing trend of recovery performance when we increase the layer number of stacked GRU cells. One might expect a deeper GRU network to have a better EM accuracy, which contrasts with the observation. The reason might be complex. First, the training of longer seq2seq fingerprint might take longer time to have better performance. Also, increasing the length of fingerprint actually expands the representation space of molecules, leaving more null spaces in the fingerprints. However, this observation does not indicate a longer fingerprint will decrease the performance in other tasks, as shown in the next subsection.

[2]https://www.tacc.utexas.edu/systems/lonestar

4.3 LogP Solubility and PM2 Promiscuous Classification

In this section, we report the classification performance of all three seq2seq models with fingerprint lengths 512, 768, and 1024, compared with the circular fingerprint [36] and neural fingerprint [13]. We use three ensemble classifiers for our seq2seq fingerprints: Adaboost [15], GradientBoost [16], and RandomForest [24]. We report the accuracy means and standard deviations of 5-fold classification cross validation on both LogP and PM2-10k data, in Table 2 and 3 respectively. All results are the 100-run averages to reduce the randomness. We also show the impact of seq2seq fingerprint length on the accuracy in Figure 5.

From the Table 2 and 3, we observe, on both data sets, our methods significantly outperform the circular and neural fingerprints, regardless of classifiers and fingerprint lengths. The circular fingerprint is hashing-based and abandons a large portion of information and is not invertible to original molecule, while our fingerprint is completely invertible and encodes rigorous information. One might argue if the ensemble classifiers will improve the performance of circular fingerprint. According to [13] and our preliminary experimental observation, the results will be worse if we switch the MLP classifier to ensemble classifiers, e.g., GradientBoost, due to the limited length and information of circular fingerprint. The neural fingerprint is a supervised deep learning-based algorithm, and it could be highly limited by the amount of labeled training data. While our method transfers knowledge from a fairly large amount of unlabeled data, our method could outperform the neural fingerprint method in classification tasks. Overall, our seq2seq fingerprints encode rigorous information for molecules and could train on a huge amount of data to achieve task-insensitive performance.

In Figure 5, however, despite the lower recovery performance of seq2seq-1024 fingerprint, it does always provide the best classification performance, while, surprisingly, the seq2seq-768 seems to always have lower classification performance. The longer fingerprints might have more information for ensemble classification methods, but might also bring in noise. While the noise takes the major effects, the performance might decrease. But when the information is encoded enough, the performance will boost.

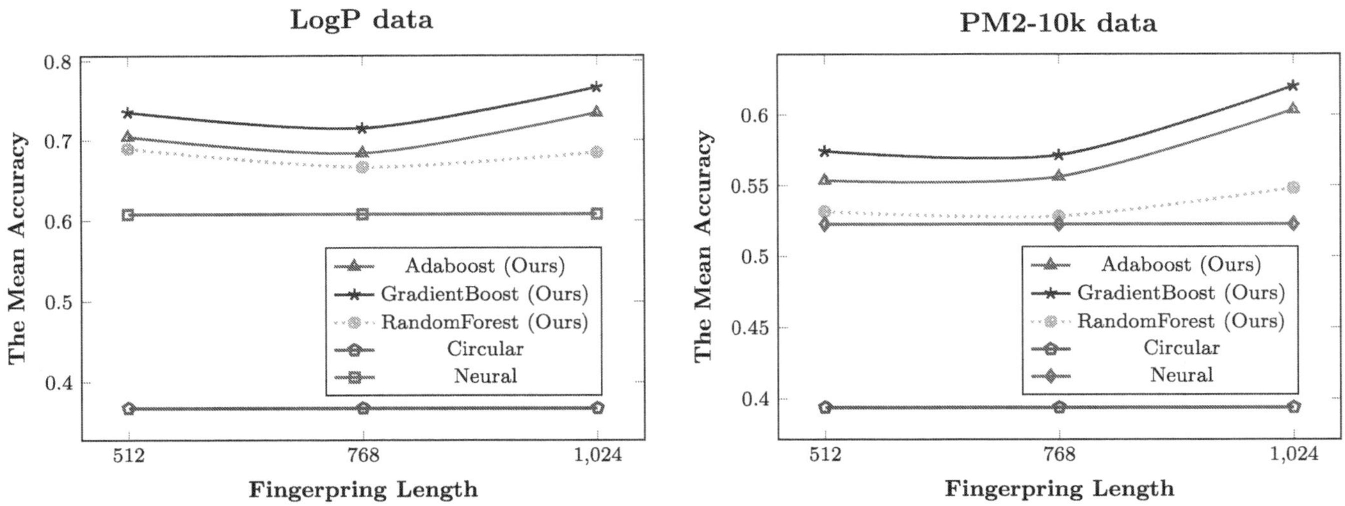

Figure 5: The mean accuracy of five methods. AdaBoost, GradientBoosting and RandomForest our methods. The circular and neural fingerprint are the state-of-the-art methods.

5 CONCLUSIONS

In this paper, we discuss a new unsupervised molecular representation system, called **seq2seq fingerprint**, based on the idea from the recent breakthrough on the English-to-French language translation, named sequence to sequence learning model. Our model translates the molecular SMILE string to the SMILE itself, while at the same time generates a fixed length fingerprint vector. The experiments on classification task demonstrate its superior performance. Also, the nature of our data-driven label-free model brings us even more benefits. 1) Our fingerprint system is completely unsupervised, meaning it will never be limited by the expensive label collection process. In fact, it could utilize each of every valid molecule, theoretically reaching the amount of infinite. 2) Contrast to the supervised learning models trained with very limited data samples, the seq2seq fingerprint is trained from a sufficiently large pool of samples, and therefore it is more robust to the specific task.

This seq2seq fingerprint is definitely not the end. It widely opens tons of new possibilities. Also due to the long training time, we might introduce efficient distributed training strategy [1, 48]. There are still many hyperparameters in our training algorithms, in the future, we might want to pick an optimal method for hyperparameter tuning [49]. Another quick future work would lie on how to embed some label information [9] to the fingerprint training to enhance its performance on the future machine learning task. Those type of semi-supervised learning could be a trend in the future drug discover tasks.

Acknowledgment The authors would like to thank NVIDIA for GPU donation and the National Cancer Institute for access to NCI's data collected by the National Lung Screening Trial. The authors would also like to thank Zhongxing Peng and Texas Advanced Computing Center (TACC) for generously providing computational resource for the preliminary experiments. The statements contained herein are solely of the authors and do not represent or imply concurrence or endorsement by NCI.

REFERENCES

[1] MartÃŋn Abadi and et.al. 2015. TensorFlow: Large-Scale Machine Learning on Heterogeneous Distributed Systems. (2015). http://download.tensorflow.org/paper/whitepaper2015.pdf

[2] Han Altae-Tran, Bharath Ramsundar, Aneesh S Pappu, and Vijay Pande. 2016. Low Data Drug Discovery with One-shot Learning. *arXiv preprint arXiv:1611.03199* (2016).

[3] Mark Ashton, John Barnard, Florence Casset, Michael Charlton, Geoffrey Downs, Dominique Gorse, John Holliday, Roger Lahana, and Peter Willett. 2002. Identification of Diverse Database Subsets using Property-Based and Fragment-Based Molecular Descriptions. *Molecular Informatics* 21, 6 (2002), 598–604.

[4] Dzmitry Bahdanau, Kyunghyun Cho, and Yoshua Bengio. 2014. Neural machine translation by jointly learning to align and translate. *arXiv preprint arXiv:1409.0473* (2014).

[5] Guy W Bemis and Mark A Murcko. 1996. The properties of known drugs. 1. Molecular frameworks. *Journal of medicinal chemistry* 39, 15 (1996), 2887–2893.

[6] Jeffrey M Blaney and J Scott Dixon. 2007. Distance geometry in molecular modeling. *Reviews in Computational Chemistry, Volume 5* (2007), 299–335.

[7] Frank R Burden. 1989. Molecular identification number for substructure searches. *Journal of Chemical Information and Computer Sciences* 29, 3 (1989), 225–227.

[8] Raymond E Carhart, Dennis H Smith, and R Venkataraghavan. 1985. Atom pairs as molecular features in structure-activity studies: definition and applications. *Journal of Chemical Information and Computer Sciences* 25, 2 (1985), 64–73.

[9] Guangliang Cheng, Feiyun Zhu, Shiming Xiang, Ying Wang, and Chunhong Pan. 2016. Semisupervised hyperspectral image classification via discriminant analysis and robust regression. *IEEE Journal of Selected Topics in Applied Earth Observations and Remote Sensing* 9, 2 (2016), 595–608.

[10] Junyoung Chung, Caglar Gulcehre, KyungHyun Cho, and Yoshua Bengio. 2014. Empirical evaluation of gated recurrent neural networks on sequence modeling. *arXiv preprint arXiv:1412.3555* (2014).

[11] Jörg Degen, Christof Wegscheid-Gerlach, Andrea Zaliani, and Matthias Rarey. 2008. On the Art of Compiling and Using'Drug-Like'Chemical Fragment Spaces. *ChemMedChem* 3, 10 (2008), 1503–1507.

[12] Carl Doersch. 2016. Tutorial on variational autoencoders. *arXiv preprint arXiv:1606.05908* (2016).

[13] David K Duvenaud, Dougal Maclaurin, Jorge Iparraguirre, Rafael Bombarell, Timothy Hirzel, Alán Aspuru-Guzik, and Ryan P Adams. 2015. Convolutional networks on graphs for learning molecular fingerprints. In *Advances in neural information processing systems*. 2224–2232.

[14] David Edwards. 2004. Accelerating Drug Development with Precision Dosing Techniques. In *PMPS*.

[15] Yoav Freund and Robert E Schapire. 1995. A desicion-theoretic generalization of on-line learning and an application to boosting. In *European conference on computational learning theory*. Springer, 23–37.

[16] Jerome H Friedman. 2001. Greedy function approximation: a gradient boosting machine. *Annals of statistics* (2001), 1189–1232.

[17] Robert C Glen, Andreas Bender, Catrin H Arnby, Lars Carlsson, Scott Boyer, and James Smith. 2006. Circular fingerprints: flexible molecular descriptors with applications from physical chemistry to ADME. *IDrugs* 9, 3 (2006), 199.

[18] Joseph Gomes, Bharath Ramsundar, Evan N Feinberg, and Vijay S Pande. 2017. Atomic Convolutional Networks for Predicting Protein-Ligand Binding Affinity. *arXiv preprint arXiv:1703.10603* (2017).

[19] Rafael Gómez-Bombarelli, David Duvenaud, José Miguel Hernández-Lobato, Jorge Aguilera-Iparraguirre, Timothy D Hirzel, Ryan P Adams, and Alán Aspuru-Guzik. 2016. Automatic chemical design using a data-driven continuous representation of molecules. *arXiv preprint arXiv:1610.02415* (2016).

[20] Ian Goodfellow, Yoshua Bengio, and Aaron Courville. 2016. *Deep Learning*. MIT Press. http://www.deeplearningbook.org.

[21] Ian Goodfellow, Jean Pouget-Abadie, Mehdi Mirza, Bing Xu, David Warde-Farley, Sherjil Ozair, Aaron Courville, and Yoshua Bengio. 2014. Generative adversarial nets. In *Advances in neural information processing systems*. 2672–2680.

[22] Osman F Güner. 2000. *Pharmacophore perception, development, and use in drug design*. Vol. 2. Internat'l University Line.

[23] Thomas A Halgren. 1996. Merck molecular force field. III. Molecular geometries and vibrational frequencies for MMFF94. *Journal of Computational Chemistry* 17, 5-6 (1996), 553–586.

[24] Tin Kam Ho. 1995. Random decision forests. In *Document Analysis and Recognition, 1995., Proceedings of the Third International Conference on*, Vol. 1. IEEE, 278–282.

[25] Ye Hu, Eugen Lounkine, and Jürgen Bajorath. 2009. Improving the Search Performance of Extended Connectivity Fingerprints through Activity-Oriented Feature Filtering and Application of a Bit-Density-Dependent Similarity Function. *ChemMedChem* 4, 4 (2009), 540–548.

[26] Steven Kearnes, Kevin McCloskey, Marc Berndl, Vijay Pande, and Patrick Riley. 2016. Molecular graph convolutions: moving beyond fingerprints. *Journal of computer-aided molecular design* 30, 8 (2016), 595–608.

[27] Xiao Qing Lewell, Duncan B Judd, Stephen P Watson, and Michael M Hann. 1998. Recap retrosynthetic combinatorial analysis procedure: a powerful new technique for identifying privileged molecular fragments with useful applications in combinatorial chemistry. *Journal of chemical information and computer sciences* 38, 3 (1998), 511–522.

[28] HL Morgan. 1965. The generation of a unique machine description for chemical structures-a technique developed at chemical abstracts service. *J. Chemical Documentation* 5 (1965), 107–113.

[29] Ramaswamy Nilakantan, Norman Bauman, J Scott Dixon, and R Venkataraghavan. 1987. Topological torsion: a new molecular descriptor for SAR applications. Comparison with other descriptors. *Journal of Chemical Information and Computer Sciences* 27, 2 (1987), 82–85.

[30] Noel M O'Boyle, Casey M Campbell, and Geoffrey R Hutchison. 2011. Computational design and selection of optimal organic photovoltaic materials. *The Journal of Physical Chemistry C* 115, 32 (2011), 16200–16210.

[31] Hao Pan, Zheng Xu, and Junzhou Huang. 2015. An effective approach for robust lung cancer cell detection. In *International Workshop on Patch-based Techniques in Medical Imaging*. Springer, 87–94.

[32] Robert S Pearlman and KM Smith. 2002. Novel software tools for chemical diversity. In *3D QSAR in drug design*. Springer, 339–353.

[33] Zhongxing Peng, Zheng Xu, and Junzhou Huang. 2016. RSPIRIT: Robust self-consistent parallel imaging reconstruction based on generalized Lasso. In *Biomedical Imaging (ISBI), 2016 IEEE 13th International Symposium on*. IEEE, 318–321.

[34] Anthony K Rappé, Carla J Casewit, KS Colwell, WA Goddard Iii, and WM Skiff. 1992. UFF, a full periodic table force field for molecular mechanics and molecular dynamics simulations. *Journal of the American chemical society* 114, 25 (1992), 10024–10035.

[35] Sereina Riniker and Gregory A Landrum. 2013. Similarity maps-a visualization strategy for molecular fingerprints and machine-learning methods. *Journal of cheminformatics* 5, 1 (2013), 43.

[36] David Rogers and Mathew Hahn. 2010. Extended-connectivity fingerprints. *Journal of chemical information and modeling* 50, 5 (2010), 742–754.

[37] Chetan Rupakheti, Aaron Virshup, Weitao Yang, and David N Beratan. 2015. Strategy to discover diverse optimal molecules in the small molecule universe. *Journal of chemical information and modeling* 55, 3 (2015), 529–537.

[38] Gisbert Schneider, Odile Clément-Chomienne, Laurence Hilfiger, Petra Schneider, Stefan Kirsch, Hans-Joachim Böhm, and Werner Neidhart. 2000. Virtual screening for bioactive molecules by evolutionary de novo design. *Angewandte Chemie International Edition* 39, 22 (2000), 4130–4133.

[39] Gisbert Schneider, Man-Ling Lee, Martin Stahl, and Petra Schneider. 2000. De novo design of molecular architectures by evolutionary assembly of drug-derived building blocks. *Journal of computer-aided molecular design* 14, 5 (2000), 487–494.

[40] Govindan Subramanian, Bharath Ramsundar, Vijay Pande, and Rajiah Aldrin Denny. 2016. Computational Modeling of β-secretase 1 (BACE-1) Inhibitors using Ligand Based Approaches. *Journal of Chemical Information and Modeling* 56, 10 (2016), 1936–1949.

[41] Ilya Sutskever, Oriol Vinyals, and Quoc V Le. 2014. Sequence to sequence learning with neural networks. In *Advances in neural information processing systems*. 3104–3112.

[42] Izhar Wallach, Michael Dzamba, and Abraham Heifets. 2015. AtomNet: a deep convolutional neural network for bioactivity prediction in structure-based drug discovery. *arXiv preprint arXiv:1510.02855* (2015).

[43] Sheng Wang, Jiawen Yao, Zheng Xu, and Junzhou Huang. 2016. Subtype Cell Detection with an Accelerated Deep Convolution Neural Network. In *International Conference on Medical Image Computing and Computer-Assisted Intervention*. Springer, 640–648.

[44] Lutz Weber, Sabine Wallbaum, Clemens Broger, and Klaus Gubernator. 1995. Optimization of the biological activity of combinatorial compound libraries by a genetic algorithm. *Angewandte Chemie International Edition in English* 34, 20 (1995), 2280–2282.

[45] David Weininger. 1970. SMILES, a chemical language and information system. 1. Introduction to methodology and encoding rules. In *Proc. Edinburgh Math. SOC*, Vol. 17. 1–14.

[46] Zhenqin Wu, Bharath Ramsundar, Evan N Feinberg, Joseph Gomes, Caleb Geniesse, Aneesh S Pappu, Karl Leswing, and Vijay Pande. 2017. MoleculeNet: A Benchmark for Molecular Machine Learning. *arXiv preprint arXiv:1703.00564* (2017).

[47] Zheng Xu and Junzhou Huang. 2015. Efficient lung cancer cell detection with deep convolution neural network. In *International Workshop on Patch-based Techniques in Medical Imaging*. Springer, 79–86.

[48] Zheng Xu and Junzhou Huang. 2016. Detecting 10,000 Cells in One Second. In *International Conference on Medical Image Computing and Computer-Assisted Intervention*. Springer, 676–684.

[49] Zheng Xu and Junzhou Huang. 2017. A General Efficient Hyperparameter-Free Algorithm for Convolutional Sparse Learning.. In *AAAI*. 2803–2809.

[50] Zheng Xu, Yeqing Li, Leon Axel, and Junzhou Huang. 2015. Efficient preconditioning in joint total variation regularized parallel MRI reconstruction. In *International Conference on Medical Image Computing and Computer-Assisted Intervention*. Springer, 563–570.

[51] Zheng Xu, Yeqing Li, and Junzhou Huang. 2016. Accelerated sparse optimization for missing data completion. In *Pattern Recognition (ICPR), 2016 23rd International Conference on*. IEEE, 1267–1272.

[52] Jiawen Yao, Zheng Xu, Xiaolei Huang, and Junzhou Huang. 2015. Accelerated dynamic MRI reconstruction with total variation and nuclear norm regularization. In *International Conference on Medical Image Computing and Computer-Assisted Intervention*. Springer, 635–642.

[53] Jiawen Yao, Xinliang Zhu, Feiyun Zhu, and Junzhou Huang. 2017. Deep Correlational Learning for Survival Prediction from Multi-modality Data. In *International Conference on Medical Image Computing and Computer Assisted Intervention (MICCAI)*.

[54] Wojciech Zaremba, Ilya Sutskever, and Oriol Vinyals. 2014. Recurrent neural network regularization. *arXiv preprint arXiv:1409.2329* (2014).

[55] Feiyun Zhu, Bin Fan, Xinliang Zhu, Ying Wang, Shiming Xiang, and Chunhong Pan. 2015. 10,000+ Times Accelerated Robust Subset Selection. In *Twenty-Ninth AAAI Conference on Artificial Intelligence*.

[56] Feiyun Zhu, Ying Wang, Bin Fan, Shiming Xiang, Geofeng Meng, and Chunhong Pan. 2014. Spectral unmixing via data-guided sparsity. *IEEE Transactions on Image Processing* 23, 12 (2014), 5412–5427.

[57] Feiyun Zhu, Ying Wang, Shiming Xiang, Bin Fan, and Chunhong Pan. 2014. Structured sparse method for hyperspectral unmixing. *ISPRS Journal of Photogrammetry and Remote Sensing* 88 (2014), 101–118.

[58] Xinliang Zhu, Jiawen Yao, Feiyun Zhu, and Junzhou Huang. 2017. WSISA: Making Survival Prediction from Whole Slide Pathology Images. In *IEEE Conference on Computer Vision and Pattern Recognition (CVPR)*. IEEE.

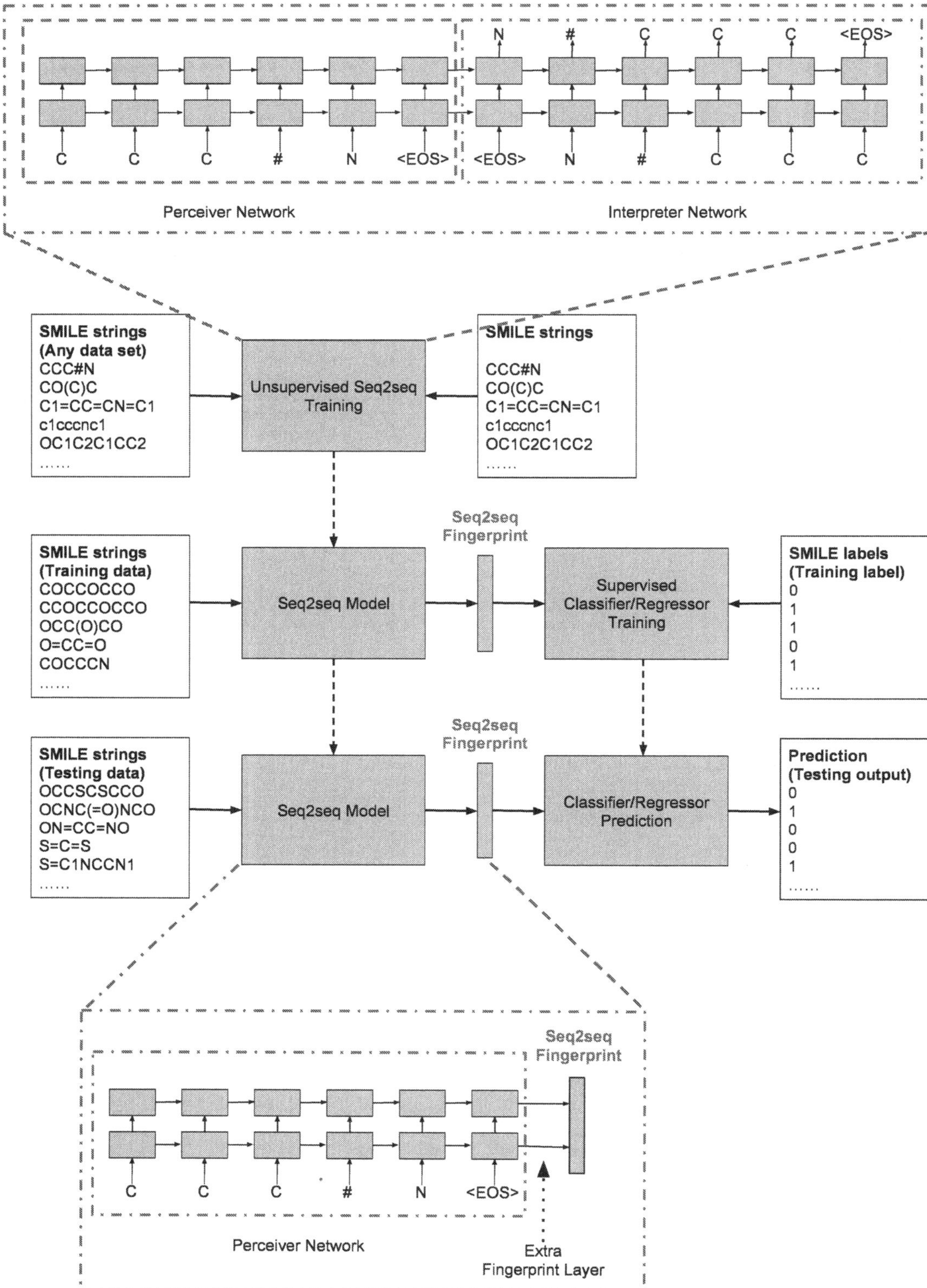

Figure 6: The illustration of overall pipeline for seq2seq fingerprint.

Detection of Differential Abundance Intervals in Longitudinal Metagenomic Data Using Negative Binomial Smoothing Spline ANOVA

Ahmed A. Metwally
Department of Bioengineering & Medicine
University of Illinois
Chicago, IL 60612, USA
ametwa2@uic.edu

Patricia W. Finn
Department of Medicine
University of Illinois
Chicago, IL 60612, USA
pwfinn@uic.edu

Yang Dai*
Department of Bioengineering
University of Illinois
Chicago, IL 60612, USA
yangdai@uic.edu

David L. Perkins*
Department of Medicine & Bioengineering
University of Illinois
Chicago, IL 60612, USA
perkinsd@uic.edu

ABSTRACT

Metagenomic longitudinal studies have become a widely-used study design to investigate the dynamics of the microbial ecological systems and their temporal effects. One of the important questions to be addressed in longitudinal studies is the identification of time intervals when microbial features show changes in their abundance. We propose a statistical method that is based on a semi-parametric Smoothing Spline ANOVA and negative binomial distribution to model the time-course of the features between two phenotypes. We demonstrate the superior performance of our proposed method compared to the two currently existing methods using simulated data. We present the analysis results of our proposed method in an analysis of a longitudinal dataset that investigates the association between the development of type 1 diabetes in infants and the gut microbiome. The identified significant species and their specific time intervals reveal new information that can be used in improving intervention or treatment plans.

KEYWORDS

Metagenomics, Microbiome, Differential Abundance, Longitudinal Studies, Smoothing Splines, Negative Binomial Distribution.

* Corresponding author.

Permission to make digital or hard copies of all or part of this work for personal or classroom use is granted without fee provided that copies are not made or distributed for profit or commercial advantage and that copies bear this notice and the full citation on the first page. Copyrights for components of this work owned by others than ACM must be honored. Abstracting with credit is permitted. To copy otherwise, or republish, to post on servers or to redistribute to lists, requires prior specific permission and/or a fee. Request permissions from Permissions@acm.org.

ACM-BCB '17, August 20-23, 2017, Boston, MA, USA.
© 2017 Association for Computing Machinery.
ACM ISBN 978-1-4503-4722-8/17/08...$15.00
http://dx.doi.org/10.1145/3107411.3107429

1 INTRODUCTION

The microbiome has been shown to be essential in not only understanding the interactions between the host genome and the body's microbial ecosystem but also the potential effects of those interactions on health and disease outcomes [1]–[3]. One of the objectives of the microbiome studies is to determine whether there is a particular microbial signature (e.g. taxa or genes) associated with a particular disease state and/or disease outcome. These biomarkers can play an important role in the development of preventative and therapeutic strategies. A major challenge in microbiome studies is the variability in microbial taxa among subjects, in addition to variability due to disease influences. A powerful strategy to address this challenge is the analysis of time series data in which the time intervals associated with temporal effects are identified.

Modeling metagenomic data for disease-association studies is an active area of research. The standard parametric models may reduce variance if the data follows the corresponding parametric distribution, but the models may be substantially biased if the data does not support that distribution. On the other hand, non-parametric models do not assume any prior distribution of the data and thus are not biased towards any distribution, but these models may suffer from a huge model variance [4].

Analyzing longitudinal metagenomic profile data is different from analyzing a single time point profile. An individual's microbiome evolves over time, but its composition has some dependency on its previous structure (i.e., Markov Process), despite the independence between samples. For longitudinal data, three types of differential abundance analysis can be proposed: (a) Treat data from each time point independently and detect features that have differential abundance between the phenotypes at individual time points [5]; (b) Identify features that have differential abundance during the time-course within a phenotype [6], [7]; (c) Model longitudinal metagenomic profiles and identify features that have differential abundance during certain time intervals. Correlating the features' differential time intervals with the time-specific clinical data may reveal information that can be used in improving intervention or treatment plans. To our knowledge, there are only two methods that can identify differentially abundant time-intervals for features, namely, MetaSplines [8] and MetaDprof [9].

MetaSplines is implemented as an R script within the metagenomeSeq package [10]. It starts by fitting a curve for the difference between the means of the read counts of a particular feature from two phenotypic groups across different time points. It uses the standard Smoothing Spline ANOVA (SS-ANOVA) approach [4], [11], [12], where the Gaussian distribution is assumed for the reads. The identification of a significant time interval is based on comparing the areas under the fitted curve to that of the null model, which is generated from the bootstrapping of the sample's group labels. This method is easy to use, and it handles time point inconsistencies in the samples collection, such as, variable sample collection times and the uneven number of time points among the subjects' longitudinal timeframe. However, it assumes the normality of metagenomic read counts, which are not suitable to be modeled by gaussian distribution. Additionally, MetaSplines has a relatively high false positive rate [9].

MetaDprof is also based on the standard SS-ANOVA which assumes the normality of the read count. The difference between the two methods is that MetaDprof fits a curve for each phenotypic/treatment group and compares the area between the two curves with the data generated by the permutation of the group labels. The identification of the significant time intervals is accomplished in two steps. Initially, MetaDprof tests whether the feature is globally significant or not. In the event that the feature is significant, it proceeds to identify significant time intervals. Compared to MetaSplines and Next-maSigPro [13], a tool for differential analysis of longitudinal RNAseq profiles, MetaDprof shows a high level of detection power. MetaDprof performs very well when the following criteria are met: a) the samples are equally spaced, b) the number of samples taken from each subject is equal, and c) the samples from subjects are collected at the same time points. In animal model studies, the sample collection process can be well controlled to meet the criteria. However, they rarely can be met for samples collected from humans, particularly when an invasive procedure is used, such as bronchoscopy to obtain a bronchoalveolar lavage (BAL) fluid samples.

Current advances leading to more affordable DNA sequencing strategies have unlocked the potential for performing time-series (longitudinal) analyses. This will provide further insight to the underlying mechanisms of health and disease. The DNA that is isolated from a biological sample is sequenced using either metagenomic shotgun (MGS) sequencing or 16S rRNA sequencing [14]. In the case of MGS, the sequence reads are processed by removing low-quality reads, short reads, and host genome reads [15]. High-quality microbial short reads are then assembled into longer sequences, i.e., "contigs" [16]. Then the microbial taxonomic profile can be constructed using pipelines, such as Kraken [17], or an ensemble method, such as WEVOTE [18]. The functional profile can also be generated by predicting the microbial genes [19] and annotating them by mapping to KEGG pathways [20]. The calculated read counts for each microbial feature [taxon (e.g., species) and gene] are then normalized to remove any bias due to the uneven sequencing depth prior to the downstream analysis [21].

In this work, we propose a new strategy to accurately identify the time intervals when the features are differentially abundant between two phenotypic groups. Our method has the ability to handle the inconsistencies and common challenges associated with human studies, such as variable sample collection times and uneven number of time points along the subjects' longitudinal study. The method employs a negative binomial distribution in conjunction with a semi-parametric SS-ANOVA to model the count reads. The method performs the significance testing based on unit time intervals.

2 METHODS

Longitudinal metagenomic profiling data can be processed and organized into a count matrix C, where (i,j) entry represents the number of reads mapped to feature i from sample j (Table I). To ease the notion, sample j could be considered to be taken from an individual at specific time point. However, in actuality, some of the samples may be missing at some time points. Since the number of mapped reads in each sample is affected by the sequencing depth, the metagenomic count data should be normalized using methods based on median-of-ratios scaling factor [22], Cumulative Sum Scaling [10], or Trimmed Mean of M-values [23].

Table I. An example of a metagenomic feature count table for *F* features and *S* samples.

	S_1	S_2	......	S_(*S*-1)	S_(*S*)
Feature_1	50	42	...	63	58
Feature _2	65	96	...	76	88
......	...	...	...	...	...
Feature_(*F*-1)	749	535	...	133	372
Feature _(*F*)	29	57	...	14	2

Our approach to the detection of metagenomic features with differential abundance intervals relies on two modeling components: the negative binomial distribution for modeling the mapped read counts for each feature and the semi-parametric SS-ANOVA technique for modeling the longitudinal profiles associated with different phenotypes. The two components are connected through the logit link. The overall framework of our approach is described in Algorithm 1. The details of each component are described in the next section.

Algorithm 1 Identify Differentially Abundant Time Intervals

Input: Metagenomic count matrix $\boldsymbol{C}$ with $\boldsymbol{F}$ features and $\boldsymbol{S}$ samples for time points $\boldsymbol{T}$.

Output: List $\boldsymbol{L}$ of the significant features with the corresponding significant time intervals.

```
For f from 1 to F do
    Model longitudinal counts using negative binomial SS-ANOVA
    Select regions where the fitted curve can be used for the significance testing
        start = max(start time of each class)
        end = min(end time of each class)
    Calculate the Area Ratio (AR) for each time interval
    Generate the empirical Area Ratio distribution
    Identify the significant time intervals
    If f has significant time intervals
        add f to L
End For
Return L
```

2.1 MODELING THE METAGENOMIC LONGITUDINAL DATA

We model the longitudinal metagenomic read counts by negative binomial distribution at each time point and fit a curve for each phenotypic group using a semi-parametric regression method based on a SS- ANOVA [4], [11], [12]. The negative binomial has been suggested for the metagenomic count data [24]. The list of the symbols and their definitions used in our model is provided in Table II. The random variable Y_{ftk} is assumed to follow a negative binomial distribution

$$Y_{ftk} \sim NB(\alpha, p(f,t,k) \qquad (1)$$

To model the time and phenotypic effect we use a general linear model with a logit link:

$$\zeta(f,t,k) = log\frac{p(f,t,k)}{1-p(f,t,k)} \qquad (2)$$
$$= \zeta_0(f) + \zeta_1(f,t) + \zeta_2(f,k) + \zeta_{12}(f,t,k)$$

The time and phenotype main effects satisfy the standard ANOVA side condition. From Eq. (2), we have

$$p(f,t,k) = \frac{e^{\zeta(f,t,k)}}{1+e^{\zeta(f,t,k)}} \qquad (3)$$

$$1 - p(f,t,k) = \frac{1}{1+e^{\zeta(f,t,k)}} \qquad (4)$$

Table II. Symbols and definitions used in our method.

Symbol	Definition
Y_{ftk}, y_{ftk}	Random variable and its value denote the number of mapped reads to a feature f at time point t from a sample in phenotype k
f, t, k	Feature, time point, and phenotype index, f=1,..., F; t=1,..., T; k=1, 2
$p(f,t,k)$	Probability of a read from a sample of group k at a time point t to be mapped to the feature f.
$NB(\alpha, p(f,t,k))$	Negative binomial distribution with number of failures $\alpha > 0$ and success probability $p(f,\ t,\ k)$
$\zeta(f,t,k)$	Mean of mapped reads to feature f of phenotype k at time point t.
$\zeta_0(f)$	Baseline log-transformed abundance of the feature without considering the effect of the time and phenotype.
$\zeta_1(f,t)$	The main time effect.
$\zeta_2(f,k)$	The main phenotype effect.
$\zeta_{1,2}(f,t,k)$	Interaction between time and phenotype.
$J(\zeta)$	Quadratic function quantifies the smoothness of ζ.
λ	Smoothing parameter controls the trade-off between the goodness of fit and the smoothness of ζ.

For a given time-course metagenomic count profiles y for feature f, we have

$$\mathcal{L} = \log L(Y = y \mid p, \alpha)$$
$$\cong \sum_{t=1}^{T}\sum_{k=1}^{2} y_{ftk} * \log\big(p(f,\ t,\ k)\big) + \alpha * \log(1 - p(f,t,k)) \qquad (5)$$

Using Eqs. (3)-(5), we have

$$\mathcal{L} \cong \sum_{t=1}^{T}\sum_{k=1}^{2}[y_{ftk} * \zeta(f,t,k) - (\alpha + y_{ftk})\log(1 + e^{\zeta(f,t,k)})] \qquad (6)$$

We seek the estimation of model parameters $(\alpha, p(f,t,k))$ by minimization of the minus log likelihood in Eq. (6). In order to control the smoothness of the function $\zeta(f,t,k)$, the quadratic function $J(\zeta)$ will be added to the minus log-likelihood together with the smoothing parameter λ for the trade-off between the goodness of fit and the smoothness of the spline curve:

$$min\ -\mathcal{L}\ + \lambda^* J(\zeta) \qquad (7)$$

In the objective function, $\mathcal{L}$ encourages the goodness of fit; J(ζ) is a quadratic function that quantifies the smoothness of ζ [4], i.e.,

$$J(\zeta) = \int (\zeta''(t))^2 \, dt \qquad (8)$$

where $\zeta''(t)$ is the second order derivative of $\zeta(t)$. λ controls the tradeoff between the goodness of fit and the smoothness of the spline. λ is determined using cross validation [4]. The solution to the optimization problem in Eq. (7) leads to the smoothing spline that fits the reads from the samples across multiple time points. With the estimated parameter $(\hat{\alpha}, \widehat{p(f,t,k)})$, we obtain the estimated mean of Y_{ftk} using $Var(Y_{ftk}) = \frac{\alpha p(f,t,k)}{(1-p(f,t,k))^2}$ and Eqs. (3), (4), i.e.,

$$E(\hat{Y}_{ftk}) = \hat{\alpha} e^{\zeta(f,t,k)} \qquad (9)$$

Connecting the values at each time point using Eq. (9) the fitted curve can be constructed in each group. The confidence intervals can be obtained for each feature using Eq. (9) and the variance of the NB distribution. We use the package "gss" [11] to solve Eq. (7) Figure 1.b illustrates the fitted curves for each phenotypic group.

2.2 INTERVAL SIGNIFICANCE TEST

In order to identify the time interval where a feature is different between the two groups, we utilize the two fitted curves to calculate the area ratio (AR) Eq. (10) between the two curves for each time interval of the T-1 time intervals.

$$AR\ (t, t+1) = \frac{|A^{k1}_{t,t+1} - A^{k2}_{t,t+1}|}{max(A^{k1}_{t,t+1}, A^{k2}_{t,t+1})} \qquad (10)$$

Then, we perform the bootstrapping procedure by permuting the sample labels to calculate the AR^b for the random samples. The procedure is repeated for B times. This is essential for calculating the p-value of each interval. The p-value is calculated using Eq. (11)

$$p\_value = \frac{\#(AR_b > AR)}{B} \qquad b \in \{1, \ldots, B\} \qquad (11)$$

The significant time intervals are those with p-value<0.05 after Benjamini Hochberg (BH) multiple testing correction [25] which adjusts for the number of time intervals per feature and for the number of features that are testing for Figure 1.c.

3 BENCHMARKING

We conducted a simulation benchmarking study to evaluate the performance of the proposed method in identifying the significant differential abundant time intervals of the metagenomic features with respect to the two previously described methods; MetaSplines and MetaDprof. We generated simulated data that mimics most of the metagenomic studies' configuration settings. The simulated data divides into two categories: (a) Datasets that mimic the ideal study settings, (b) Datasets that mimic the real samples collection settings.

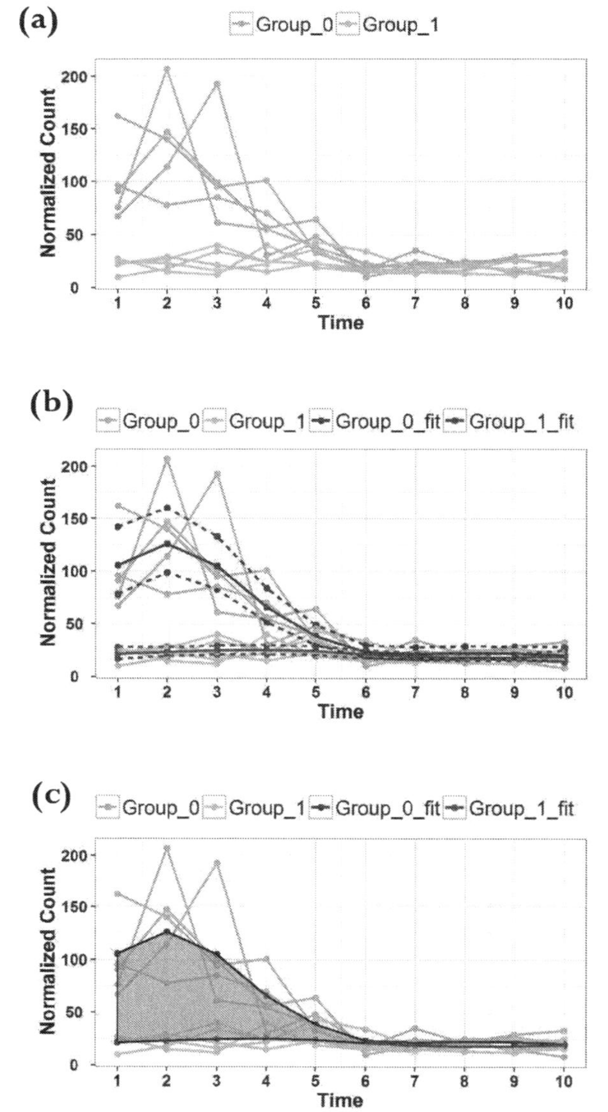

Figure 1 Illustration of how the proposed method works. (a) The longitudinal samples for one feature from two phenotypic groups. (b) The two fitted NB Smoothing Splines of two groups (The solid dark blue and dark red curves). The dashed curves show the 95% confidence interval. (c) The significant time intervals identified (the grey highlighted regions).

3.1 SIMULATIONS OF THE IDEAL STUDY SETTINGS

In this category, we simulated different datasets with an equal number of samples per subject; samples were taken at consistent time points and at each consecutive unit time. We used the R package "corcounts" [26] to simulate datasets that follow the NB distribution with a mean μ and a size factor $40/\mu$. In this regard, we followed the framework of generating simulated data, which was illustrated in MetaDprof [9].

Since longitudinal metagenomic profiles from the same individual are not completely independent [27], we assume that metagenomic count data from adjacent time points follow the first order autoregressive model [28] with a correlation $\rho \in [0,1]$; where ρ=0 means total independence between the samples' features count, and ρ=1 means complete correlation between the samples' features count. In our simulation study, we tested for ρ=0.2 and ρ=0.9. For each configuration setting, we generated datasets for consecutive time points per individual. We also tested for the effect of the number of samples (N=5, 15, and 30) per group at each time point. In order to evaluate the ability of the proposed method in identifying the significant time intervals regardless of where they occur on the time points, we generated four different configurations for the features.

(a) Features that show significant time intervals at the end of the study time course. The mean $\mu(t)$ of these features is modeled as depicted in Eq. (12) and illustrated in Figure 2.a

$$\mu(t) = \mathcal{N}(20,1) + \mathcal{N}(20,1) * (t-5) * I(t>5) \quad t = 1,2,\ldots\ldots,10 \tag{12}$$

where $\mathcal{N}$ (.,.), represents normal distribution and I(.) an indicator function.

(b) Features that show significant time intervals early in the study time course. The mean $\mu(t)$ of these features is modeled as depicted in Eq. (13) and illustrated in Figure 2.b.

$$\mu(t) = \mathcal{N}(20,1) + \mathcal{N}(20,1) * (6-t) * I(t<6) \quad t = 1,2,\ldots\ldots,10 \tag{13}$$

(c) Features that show significant time intervals in the middle of the study time course. The mean $\mu(t)$ of these features is modeled as depicted in Eq. (14) and illustrated in Figure 2.c

$$\mu(t) = \mathcal{N}(20,1) + 2 * \mathcal{N}(20,1) * (t-3) * I(t>3 \,\&t \le 5) + 2 * \mathcal{N}(20,1)(8-t) * I(t>5 \,\&t<8) \quad t = 1,2,\ldots\ldots,10 \tag{14}$$

(d) Features that do not show any significant time intervals. The mean $\mu(t)$ of these features is modeled as depicted in Eq. (15) and illustrated in Figure 2.d.

$$\mu(t) = \mathcal{N}(20,1) \qquad t = 1,2,\ldots,10 \tag{15}$$

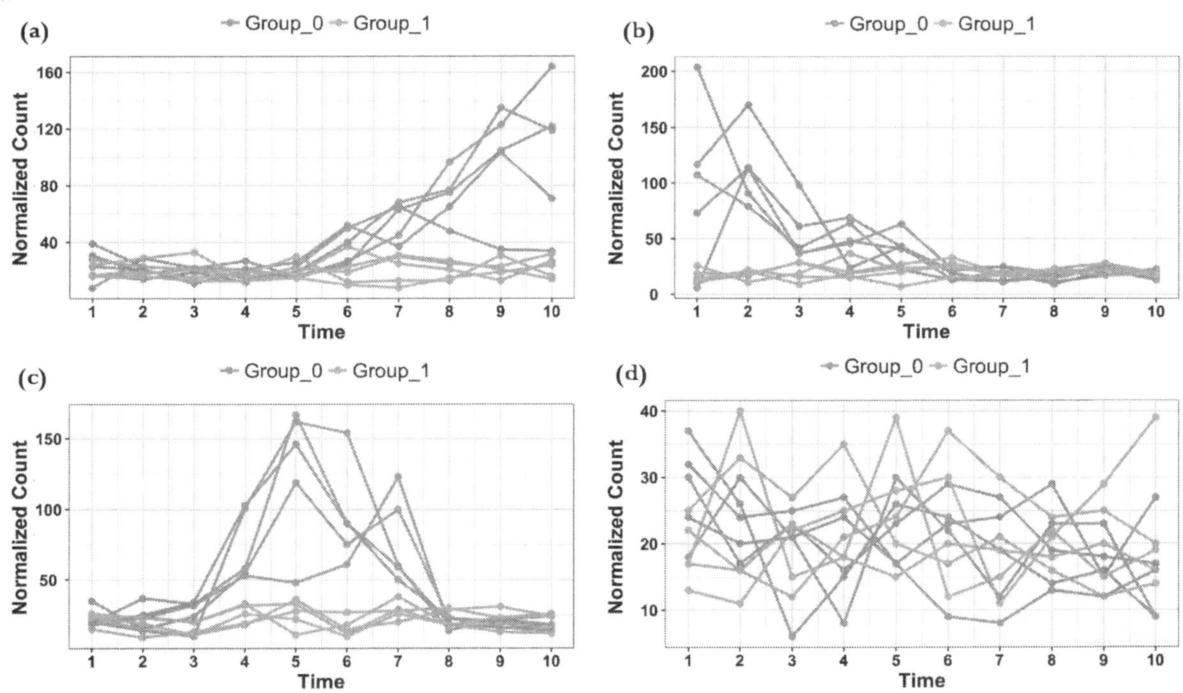

Figure 2. Simulated longitudinal datasets that mimic the ideal case settings of a metagenomic time-course study. Each sub-figure shows the normalized count of the same feature from many samples taken from multiple individuals. Each curve mimics longitudinal trajectories from an individual's normalized count of only one feature. Each sub-figure represents a specific pattern of the differential abundant time intervals: (a) Difference that occurs at the end of the study time period; (b) Difference that occurs early in the study time period; (c) Difference that occurs in the middle of the study time period; (d) No difference.

We simulated 200 features for each configuration (a)-(c) and 400 features for configuration (d). We compared the performance of the proposed method to those of MetaSplines and MetaDrpof. Furthermore, we included in the evaluation a semi-regression method that is based on fitting the splines using Locally Weighted Scatterplot Smoothing (LOWESS) [29] within the proposed framework. The latter evaluates the performance of the semi-parametric methods without regularization and assesses the ability of the proposed framework to incorporate other models.

Throughout all methods, we ran *B*=2000 permutations per unit interval in order to construct the AR empirical distribution of each time interval, and utilized an adjusted p-value of 0.05 as a cutoff for significant time intervals. For MetaSplines and MetaDprof, all other parameters were set to the defaults. Two performance metrics were used to benchmark the proposed method; $Sensitivity = \frac{TP}{TP+FN}$, and $Specificity = \frac{TN}{TN+FP}$. In this context, for each feature, "TP" indicates the number of the identified true positive time unit intervals, "FP" indicates the number of identified false positive time unit intervals, "TN" indicates the number of identified true negative time-unit intervals, and "FN" indicates the number of identified false negative time-unit intervals.

Table III shows the mean of the sensitivity and specificity of all the features of each method per configuration settings. With the exception of Configuration #3, our method outperforms all other methods. Increasing the number of subjects per group improved the performance irrespective of the used method with the proposed method being superior.

Table III. Performance evaluation of different methods using simulated data that mimics the ideal study settings. "Sens." denotes Sensitivity and "Spec." denotes Specificity. Values represent the mean of each configuration. Due to space limitations, the variance has been omitted, but in general it is very small.

		ρ=0.2						ρ=0.9					
		N=5		N=15		N=30		N=5		N=15		N=30	
		Sens.	Spec.	Sens.	Spec.	Sens.	Spec.	Sens.	Spec.	Sens.	Spec.	Sens.	Spec.
Config_1	**Proposed**	0.95	0.99	1	0.96	1	1	0.90	0.96	0.99	0.95	1	0.98
	MetaSplines	0.82	0.88	0.85	0.83	0.81	0.85	0.84	0.79	0.88	0.80	0.84	0.71
	MetaDprof	0.85	0.98	0.93	1	0.9	1	0.88	0.9	0.93	1	0.95	1
	LOWESS	0.94	0.92	1	0.81	1	0.7	0.87	0.98	0.98	0.82	1	0.86
Config_2	**Proposed**	0.96	0.98	1	0.95	1	0.96	0.95	0.97	0.96	0.91	1	0.95
	MetaSplines	0.86	0.98	0.82	0.88	0.82	0.91	0.9	0.86	0.84	0.86	0.82	0.70
	MetaDprof	0.84	0.95	0.87	0.93	0.89	1	0.90	0.93	0.95	0.90	0.94	1
	LOWESS	0.96	0.96	0.96	0.73	1	0.61	0.89	0.97	0.97	0.88	1	0.68
Config_3	**Proposed**	0.97	0.98	1	0.97	1	0.99	0.90	0.94	1	0.98	1	0.98
	MetaSplines	0.67	0.98	0.68	1	0.62	0.98	0.78	0.92	0.72	0.97	0.64	0.91
	MetaDprof	0.96	0.97	1	1	1	1	0.97	0.96	1	0.95	1	0.97
	LOWESS	1	0.62	1	0.42	1	0.42	0.94	0.72	1	0.53	1	0.47
Config_4	**Proposed**	-	0.97	-	0.99	-	0.98	-	0.97	-	0.99	-	1
	MetaSplines	-	0.82	-	0.67	-	0.53	-	0.93	-	0.55	-	0.46
	MetaDprof	-	0.96	-	0.98	-	0.97	-	0.98	-	0.92	-	0.97
	LOWESS	-	0.96	-	0.96	-	0.94	-	0.95	-	0.98	-	1

MetaSplines has a high false positive rate specifically when the differential abundance intervals come in the middle of the time course (Configuration #3). It also has many false positives when there are no differences (Configuration #4). MetaDprof shows a comparable level of specificity to the proposed method in most of the configurations, but the proposed method also maintains a higher level of sensitivity. On the other hand, LOWESS' high sensitivity is because it over fits which is the source of its lower specificity.

3.2 SIMULATIONS OF THE REAL STUDY SETTINGS

In this category of simulations, we tried to benchmark the proposed method using a simulated dataset that mimics the nature of samples collected from a human microbiome study, e.g., wherein the number of samples are not equal for all subjects, nor are they collected at consistent time points, etc.

We incorporated two classes: Class 1 includes 8 individuals, each individual has samples collected at 11 time points chosen randomly from 1 to 20. Class 2 includes 6 individuals, each with samples collected at 8 time points chosen randomly from 1 to 20. Similar to section 3.1, we assumed that the metagenomic longitudinal data follow the first order auto regressive model. We tested for ρ=0.2 and ρ=0.9. Furthermore, the generated features are divided into 4 configurations; (a) significant intervals that appear at the end of the time course Eq. (16), (b) significant intervals that appear at the beginning of the time course Eq. (17), (c) significant intervals that appear in the middle of the time course Eq. (18), and (d) no significant time interval Eq. (19).

$$\mu(t) = \mathcal{N}(20,1) + \mathcal{N}(20,1)(t-10) * I(t>10) \quad t = 1,2,\ldots,20 \tag{16}$$

$$\mu(t) = \mathcal{N}(20,1) + \mathcal{N}(20,1)(11-t) * I(t<11) \quad t = 1,2,\ldots,20 \tag{17}$$

$$\mu(t) = \mathcal{N}(20,1) + 2 * \mathcal{N}(20,1)(t-5) * I(t>5 \,\&t \le 10) + 2 * \mathcal{N}(20,1)(15-t) * I(t>10 \,\&t<15) \quad t = 1,2,\ldots,20 \tag{18}$$

$$\mu(t) = \mathcal{N}(20,1) \qquad t = 1,2,\ldots,20 \tag{19}$$

Table IV shows the sensitivity and specificity of the proposed method as well as MetaSplines and LOWESS. We could not compare the performance of MetaDprof because the available implementation of MetaDprof cannot handle the non-ideal study settings.

For most configuration settings, the proposed method outperforms MetaSplines and LOWESS. Very high sensitivity is always accompanied by high specificity in the proposed method. On the other hand, MetaSplines' high sensitivity is associated with low specificity. MetaSplines also has a high false positive rate when the feature does not have any significant time intervals across the time points, as shown in (Configuration #4) section at Table IV.

Table IV. Benchmarking in the real study settings. "Sens." denotes Sensitivity and "Spec." denotes Specificity. Values represent the mean of each configuration. Due to space limitations, the variance has been omitted, but in general it is very small.

		ρ=0.2		ρ=0.9	
		Sens.	**Spec.**	**Sens.**	**Spec.**
Config_1	**Proposed**	0.975	0.94	0.95	0.97
	MetaSplines	0.96	0.91	0.95	0.85
	LOWESS	0.97	0.93	0.93	0.95
Config_2	**Proposed**	0.92	1	0.93	1
	MetaSplines	0.95	1	0.91	0.90
	LOWESS	0.94	0.98	0.88	0.95
Config_3	**Proposed**	0.90	1	0.93	1
	MetaSplines	0.88	0.97	0.90	0.90
	LOWESS	1	0.63	0.92	0.71
Config_4	**Proposed**	-	1	-	1
	MetaSplines	-	0.88	-	0.64
	LOWESS	-	0.98	-	0.98

4 THE INFANT TYPE 1 DIABETES DATA

We applied the proposed method to a longitudinal metagenomic study that focuses on associating the dynamics of the gut microbiome to type 1 diabetes (T1D) development in infancy [30]. In that study, stool samples were collected from infants in monthly intervals from the day of birth to 3 years of age. Here we focus on 128 samples that have been sequenced using metagenomic shotgun sequencing. These samples come from 19 infants (11 seroconverted, 8 non-seroconverted). The 11 seroconverted infants are those who have a positive measurement of at least two of following autoantibodies: insulin autoantibodies (IAA), glutamic acid decarboxylase antibodies (GADA), islet antigen-2 antibodies (IA-2A), zinc transporter 8 antibodies (ZnT8A), and Islet cell antibodies (ICA). Four of these 11 infants developed T1D during the course of the study. The non-seroconverted infants are those who were consistently negative for the previously mentioned antibodies. Figure 3 shows the distribution of the stool sample collection time points from each of the 19 subjects. To identify significant time intervals during which the species were associated with the development of T1D, we labeled the samples T1D (4 seroconverted infants who developed T1D) and non-T1D (seroconverted infants who have not developed T1D plus the non-seroconverted). The sequence reads of all 128 samples were processed by removing short reads (<60 nt), low quality reads, and human DNA reads. Subsequently, species abundance was constructed for each sample using MetaPhlAn [31]. The aggregated taxonomic profiles of all 128 samples include 86 species.

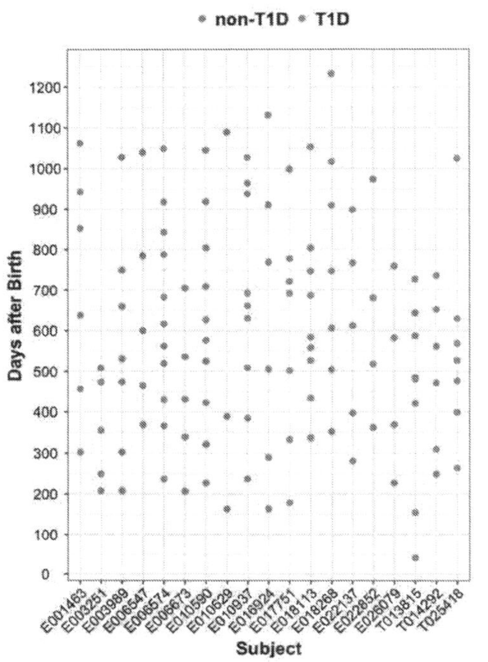

Figure 3. Distribution of the 128 stool samples collected from 19 infants.

Table V shows a summary of the differentially abundant species and their corresponding significant time intervals where the species were different between the non-T1D and the T1D groups (adjusted p-value < 0.05). Species such as *Streptococcus infantarius* was reported to have a higher abundance in the T1D group [30], but it is unclear when exactly it was significant. Using the proposed method, we were able to determine that *Streptococcus infantarius* became more abundant in the T1D group after the first year of life and up to the end of the study period (353-1049 days). Species such as *Bifidobacterium breve, Eubacterium rectale, Anaerostipes caccae*, and *Clostridium nexile* alternate in abundance between the T1D and non-T1D groups where no one group maintains a higher abundance throughout the study period. Figure 4 demonstrates the trajectories of the 6-different species that have significant time intervals. Correlating the clinical data with the identified significant species and their specific time intervals can reveal information that can be used in improving intervention or treatment plans.

Table V. Differentially abundant species and their estimated significant time intervals during the T1D study. The asterisk after the species name indicates that the corresponding species was reported in [30].

Species	Start (day)	End (day)	Dominant
Faecalibacterium prausnitzii	264	285	non-T1D
Enterococcus faecalis	686	695	non-T1D
	701	712	non-T1D
Ruminococcus obeum	211	216	non-T1D
	222	598	non-T1D
Ruminococcus torques	208	369	non-T1D
	893	1049	non-T1D
Bacteroides uniformis	208	361	non-T1D
Veillonella dispar*	368	555	non-T1D
Bacteroides dorei	394	861	non-T1D
Dorea formicigenerans	447	555	non-T1D
Haemophilus parainfluenzae	713	750	non-T1D
Bifidobacterium breve	256	307	non-T1D
	372	387	T1D
Anaerostipes caccae	489	710	non-T1D
	930	1049	T1D
Clostridium nexile	208	395	non-T1D
	400	875	T1D
Eubacterium rectale	208	302	non-T1D
	400	525	T1D
	563	1004	non-T1D
Lactobacillus acidophilus*	208	466	T1D
	713	913	T1D
Bacteroides ovatus	478	899	T1D
Streptococcus infantarius*	353	1049	T1D

5 CONCLUSIONS

We propose a statistical framework that models longitudinal metagenomics sequence reads of features (microbial taxa, genes, or biological functions) using a semi-parametric smoothing spline ANOVA method as the basis for fitting the longitudinal data. Our model uses the negative binomial distribution to model the sequencing reads and is designed to detect the time interval where a differential abundance is present. Our method has the ability to handle the inconsistencies and common challenges associated with human sample collection, such as variable collection times and uneven number of time points collected during a longitudinal study. We demonstrated the superior performance of our method in comparison to the two existing methods using various simulated data. We also presented analysis results of the proposed method to a longitudinal dataset that investigates the association between the development of type 1 diabetes in infants and their gut microbiome.

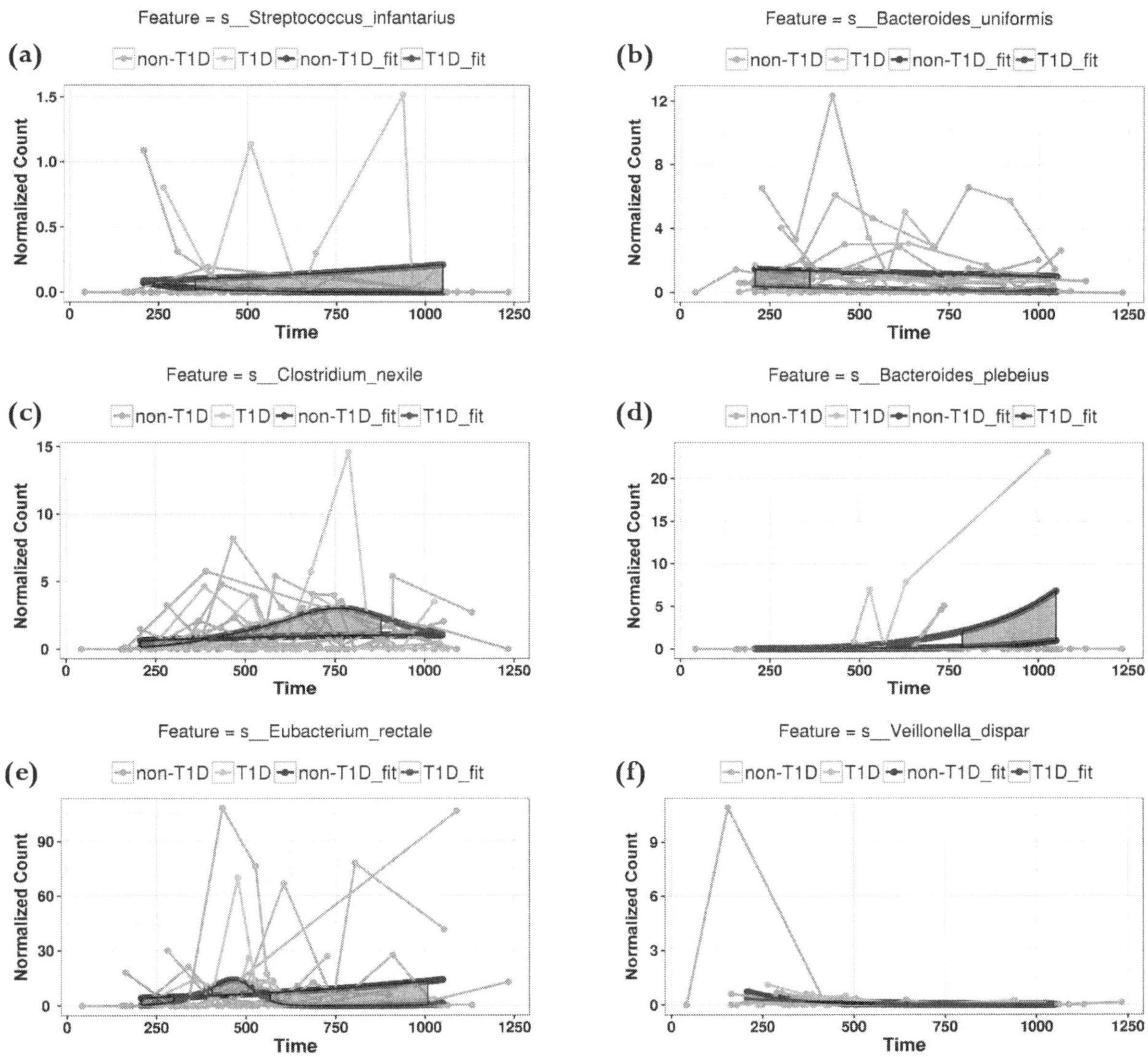

Figure 4. Trajectories of the significant time intervals of 6 species of the infant study. The solid dark red curve represents the smoothing splines fitting the T1D samples while the solid dark blue curve represents the non-T1D samples. The shaded area means the interval where the corresponding species was significantly abundant.

The identified significant bacterial species and their specific time intervals associated with development of T1D reveal new information that can be used in improving intervention or treatment plans. The running times of MetaSplines, MetaDprof, and the proposed method are comparable and vary with the change of the number of permutations used to construct the empirical distribution. It is noted that the current method treats all time points as reasonably spaced so the relationship of observations can be modeled using the smooth spline function. In the future, we plan to develop a strategy to detect time intervals that are not readily compatible for such an analysis.

ACKNOWLEDGMENTS

This work is supported by a UIC Chancellor's Research Award awarded to AM and UIC Center for Clinical and Translational Science (CCTS) grant UL1TR002003 to AM.

REFERENCES

[1] R. P. Dickson, J. R. Erb-Downward, C. M. Freeman, N. Walker, B. S. Scales, J. M. Beck, F. J. Martinez, J. L. Curtis, V. N. Lama, and G. B. Huffnagle, "Changes in the Lung Microbiome following Lung Transplantation Include the Emergence of Two Distinct Pseudomonas Species with Distinct Clinical Associations," *PLoS One*, vol. 9, no. 5, p. e97214, May 2014.

[2] I. Cho and M. J. Blaser, "The human microbiome: at the interface of health and disease.," *Nat. Rev. Genet.*, vol. 13, no. 4, pp. 260–70, Mar. 2012.

[3] K. J. Pflughoeft and J. Versalovic, "Human Microbiome in Health and Disease," *Annu. Rev. Pathol. Mech. Dis.*, vol. 7, no. 1, pp. 99–122, Feb. 2012.

[4] C. Gu, "Smoothing Spline ANOVA Models," 2012.

[5] E. K. Ganda, R. S. Bisinotto, S. F. Lima, K. Kronauer, D. H. Decter, G. Oikonomou, Y. H. Schukken, and R. C. Bicalho, "Longitudinal metagenomic profiling of bovine milk to assess the impact of intramammary treatment using a third-generation cephalosporin," *Sci. Rep.*, vol. 6, no. 1, p. 37565, Dec. 2016.

[6] F. Asnicar, S. Manara, M. Zolfo, D. T. Truong, M. Scholz, F. Armanini, P. Ferretti, V. Gorfer, A. Pedrotti, A. Tett, and N. Segata, "Studying Vertical Microbiome Transmission from Mothers to Infants by Strain-Level Metagenomic Profiling.," *mSystems*, vol. 2, no. 1, 2017.

[7] A. Y. Voigt, P. I. Costea, J. R. Kultima, S. S. Li, G. Zeller, S. Sunagawa, and P. Bork, "Temporal and technical variability of human gut metagenomes," *Genome Biol.*, vol. 16, no. 1, p. 73, Dec. 2015.

[8] J. N. Paulson, H. Talukder, and H. C. Bravo, "Longitudinal differential abundance analysis of microbial marker-gene surveys using smoothing splines," *bioRxiv*, p. 99457, 2017.

[9] D. Luo, S. Ziebell, and L. An, "An Informative Approach on Differential Abundance Analysis for Time-course Metagenomic Sequencing Data," *Bioinformatics*, vol. 334, p. btw828, Jan. 2017.

[10] J. N. Paulson, O. C. Stine, H. C. Bravo, and M. Pop, "Differential abundance analysis for microbial marker-gene surveys," *Nat. Methods*, vol. 10, no. 12, pp. 1200–1202, Sep. 2013.

[11] C. Gu, "Smoothing Spline ANOVA Models: R Package gss," *J. Stat. Softw.*, vol. 58, no. 5, pp. 1–25, 2014.

[12] G. Wahba, Y. Wang, C. Gu, R. Klein, and B. Klein, "Smoothing spline ANOVA for exponential families, with application to the Wisconsin Epidemiological Study of Diabetic Retinopathy: the 1994 Neyman Memorial Lecture," *Ann. Stat.*, vol. 23, no. 6, pp. 1865–1895, Dec. 1995.

[13] M. J. Nueda, S. Tarazona, and A. Conesa, "Next maSigPro: updating maSigPro bioconductor package for RNA-seq time series," *Bioinformatics*, vol. 30, no. 18, pp. 2598–2602, Sep. 2014.

[14] R. Ranjan, A. Rani, A. Metwally, H. S. McGee, and D. L. Perkins, "Analysis of the microbiome: Advantages of whole genome shotgun versus 16S amplicon sequencing," *Biochem. Biophys. Res. Commun.*, vol. 469, no. 4, pp. 967–977, Dec. 2015.

[15] J. R. Kultima, L. P. Coelho, K. Forslund, J. Huerta-Cepas, S. S. Li, M. Driessen, A. Y. Voigt, G. Zeller, S. Sunagawa, and P. Bork, "MOCAT2: a metagenomic assembly, annotation and profiling framework," *Bioinformatics*, vol. 32, no. 16, pp. 2520–2523, Aug. 2016.

[16] T. Namiki, T. Hachiya, H. Tanaka, and Y. Sakakibara, "MetaVelvet: an extension of Velvet assembler to de novo metagenome assembly from short sequence reads," *Nucleic Acids Res.*, vol. 40, no. 20, pp. e155–e155, Nov. 2012.

[17] D. E. Wood and S. L. Salzberg, "Kraken: ultrafast metagenomic sequence classification using exact alignments.," *Genome Biol.*, vol. 15, no. 3, p. R46, Jan. 2014.

[18] A. A. Metwally, Y. Dai, P. W. Finn, and D. L. Perkins, "WEVOTE: Weighted Voting Taxonomic Identification Method of Microbial Sequences," *PLoS One*, vol. 11, no. 9, p. e0163527, Sep. 2016.

[19] W. Zhu, A. Lomsadze, and M. Borodovsky, "Ab initio gene identification in metagenomic sequences," *Nucleic Acids Res.*, vol. 38, no. 12, pp. e132–e132, Jul. 2010.

[20] M. Kanehisa, S. Goto, M. Furumichi, M. Tanabe, and M. Hirakawa, "KEGG for representation and analysis of molecular networks involving diseases and drugs.," *Nucleic Acids Res.*, vol. 38, no. Database issue, pp. D355-60, Jan. 2010.

[21] M. Wallroth, "Normalization of metagenomic data A comprehensive evaluation of existing methods."

[22] M. I. Love, W. Huber, and S. Anders, "Moderated estimation of fold change and dispersion for RNA-seq data with DESeq2," *Genome Biol.*, vol. 15, no. 12, p. 550, Dec. 2014.

[23] M. D. Robinson, D. J. McCarthy, G. K. Smyth, L. Zhang, X. Cui, A. K. Benson, N. Yi, O. Adeola, C. Nakatsu, and K. Ajuwon, "edgeR: a Bioconductor package for differential expression analysis of digital gene expression data," *Bioinformatics*, vol. 26, no. 1, pp. 139–140, Jan. 2010.

[24] V. Jonsson, T. Österlund, O. Nerman, and E. Kristiansson, "Statistical evaluation of methods for identification of differentially abundant genes in comparative metagenomics," *BMC Genomics*, vol. 17, no. 1, p. 78, Dec. 2016.

[25] Y. Benjamini and Y. Hochberg, "Controlling the False Discovery Rate: A Practical and Powerful Approach to Multiple Testing on JSTOR," *J. R. Stat. Soc.*, vol. 57, no. 1, pp. 289–300, 1995.

[26] V. Erhardt, "corcounts," 2015. [Online]. Available: https://cran.r-project.org/web/packages/corcounts/corcounts.pdf. [Accessed: 22-Apr-2017].

[27] K. Faust, L. Lahti, D. Gonze, W. M. de Vos, and J. Raes, "Metagenomics meets time series analysis: unraveling microbial community dynamics.," *Curr. Opin. Microbiol.*, vol. 25, pp. 56–66, Jun. 2015.

[28] C. Chatfield, *The analysis of time series: an introduction*. 2016.

[29] W. S. Cleveland, "Robust Locally Weighted Regression and Smoothing Scatterplots," *J. Am. Stat. Assoc.*, vol. 74, no. 368, pp. 829–836, Dec. 1979.

[30] A. D. Kostic, D. Gevers, H. Siljander, T. Vatanen, T. Hyötyläinen, A.-M. Hämäläinen, A. Peet, V. Tillmann, P. Pöhö, I. Mattila, H. Lähdesmäki, E. A. Franzosa, O. Vaarala, M. de Goffau, H. Harmsen, J. Ilonen, S. M. Virtanen, C. B. Clish, M. Orešič, C. Huttenhower, M. Knip, R. J. DIABIMMUNE Study Group, and R. J. Xavier, "The dynamics of the human infant gut microbiome in development and in progression toward type 1 diabetes.," *Cell Host Microbe*, vol. 17, no. 2, pp. 260–73, Feb. 2015.

[31] N. Segata, L. Waldron, A. Ballarini, V. Narasimhan, O. Jousson, and C. Huttenhower, "Metagenomic microbial community profiling using unique clade-specific marker genes.," *Nat. Methods*, vol. 9, no. 8, pp. 811–4, Jun. 2012.

Cell Neighbor Determination in the Metazoan Embryo System

Zi Wang
The University of Tennessee
Knoxville, Tennessee, USA
zwang84@vols.utk.edu

Dali Wang *
Corresponding Author
The University of Tennessee
Knoxville, Tennessee, USA
dwang7@utk.edu

Husheng Li
The University of Tennessee
Knoxville, Tennessee, USA
hli31@tennessee.edu

Zhirong Bao
Sloan Kettering Institute
New York City, New York, USA
baoz@mskcc.org

ABSTRACT

Cell neighbor determination is a significant component in the simulation of a metazoan embryo system since it influences a number of fundamental biological processes, such as cell signaling, migration, and proliferation. Traditional approaches to find the neighbors of a cell such as Voronoi diagram successfully accomplish this goal, but are too time-consuming as the number of cells grows exponentially. In this paper, we propose a learning-based algorithm that determines the neighbors of specific cells in the metazoan embryo in real-time. We decrease the computational time by four orders of magnitude, and achieve an accuracy of 99.66%. For the verification purpose, the simulation results indicate that our model successfully reproduces the neighbor relationship in *C. elegans* Notch signaling pathways and cell-cell squeeze force modeling of the cell division process.

CCS CONCEPTS

• **Computer Application** → Life and Medical Sciences–Biology and genetics; • **Computing Methodologies** → Pattern Recognition–Design Methodology; Artificial Intelligence–Learning;

KEYWORDS

Cell Neighbor Determination; Metazoan Embryo System; Cell-Cell Signaling; Voronoi; Support Vector Machine

1 INTRODUCTION

Recent breakthroughs in cutting-edge live microscopy and 3D time-lapse imaging technologies allow biologists to observe the dynamics in diverse organisms and gather a tremendous amount of data with cellular resolution. Such data explosion promotes the research in specific developmental aspects, including but not limited to cell-cell signaling, cell migration, and proliferation. Recently, the regulatory mechanism of cell asymmetric division was discovered in [24]. A study analyzed the loss of function phenotypes of genes that functioning substantially during significant signaling processes during embryogenesis, and a multi-scale model was generated including a regulatory landscape of lineage differentiation [8, 9, 22]. In the above studies, to determine the neighbors of certain cells is a fundamental prerequisite. Signaling processes, especially those during early embryogenesis, are accomplished by a contacted interaction from one cell to another. The moving/dividing speed and direction of a cell are influenced to some extent by its neighbors that generate squeezing forces to it during its migration and division processes. Therefore, to obtain a correct neighbor relationship is the core of the success of the *in silico* simulation and *in vivo* experiment focusing on the above problems.

Voronoi diagram [6] is widely used for cell neighbor determination and its upstream applications, such as cell volume calculation and embryo segmentation in recent years [11, 15, 18]. By assigning every grid to the target point of (weighted) minimum distance with proper resolution, Voronoi diagram provides biologists with a sufficiently approximate solution to the above problems with the consideration of the complexity of a tissue. However, obtaining a Voronoi tessellation is not a computationally simple task, since it is difficult to derive an analytical solution. For a metazoan embryo (or similar situations), if we consider the asymmetric division of a cell, which leads to different volumes of the following generations, a weighted 3D Voronoi diagram has to be implemented, which makes things much worse. As a result, traversal approaches [3] are largely used for such kind of problems. The task becomes extremely time-consuming as the number of cells in the system grows exponentially.

Machine learning, especially its popular branch, deep learning, has been developing at a tremendous speed in recent years and opened new doors to a variety of fields [13, 14, 20, 23]. We are provided with unprecedented opportunities to consider the traditional neighbor determination problem with such completely new point of view. As mentioned above, cellular resolution, minute level embryogenesis data contain rich information that allows us to reduce the computational redundancy of the Voronoi approach in other perspectives. With properly extracted features and well-designed framework, we can train an efficient classifier to achieve real-time cell neighbor determination with very little accuracy loss. In this paper, we transform the neighbor determination problem

ACM acknowledges that this contribution was authored or co-authored by an employee, or contractor of the national government. As such, the Government retains a nonexclusive, royalty-free right to publish or reproduce this article, or to allow others to do so, for Government purposes only. Permission to make digital or hard copies for personal or classroom use is granted. Copies must bear this notice and the full citation on the first page. Copyrights for components of this work owned by others than ACM must be honored. To copy otherwise, distribute, republish, or post, requires prior specific permission and/or a fee. Request permissions from permissions@acm.org.
ACM-BCB '17, August 20-23, 2017, Boston, MA, USA
© 2017 Association for Computing Machinery.
ACM ISBN 978-1-4503-4722-8/17/08...$15.00
https://doi.org/10.1145/3107411.3107465

to a classification task. We preprocess the raw embryogenesis data as neighbor samples and label them, extract appropriate features and train the classifier. An accuracy of 99.66% is acquired from the simulation with *C. elegans* embryogenesis data.

The rest of this paper is organized as follows. In Section 2, a brief introduction to Voronoi diagram is given and its defects dealing with the cell neighbor determination problem are analyzed. Then we present a learning-based algorithm to achieve real-time neighbor determination to replace the Voronoi approach in the metazoan system in Section 3. Simulation results and discussions are provided in Section 4 and 5, respectively. Finally, we conclude the paper in Section 6.

2 VORONOI DIAGRAM

Voronoi diagram (Fig. 1(a)) is a unique space partition that contains certain points and a corresponding region with every point [17]. Suppose there is a set of target points $P = \{p_1, p_2, ..., p_n\}$ in the space. For each point x in the space that belongs to the region $dom(p_i)$, x is closer to p_i to any other p_s of P (Eq. (1)). Voronoi diagram and its variants are widely used in various fields, such as forest simulation [1], wireless sensor networks (WSNs) [10], and embryo segmentation (Fig. 1(b)) [21].

$$dom(p_i) = \{x \in R^m | d(x, p_i) < d(x, p_j), i \neq j\}, \quad (1)$$

where $d(x, p)$ is the Euclidean distance between x and p.

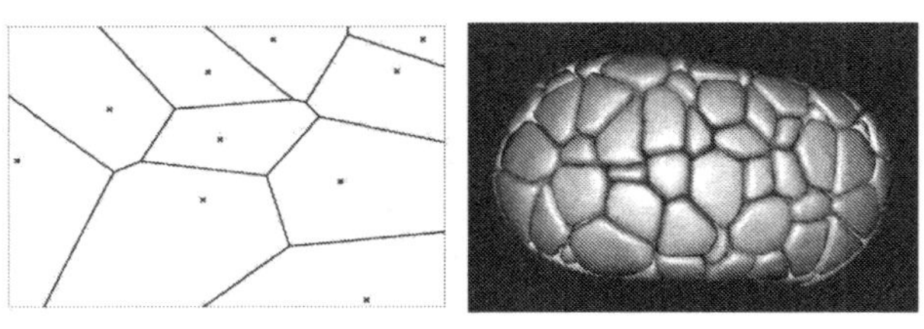

(a) 2D unweighted Voronoi diagram. (b) Embryo segmentation.

Figure 1: Voronoi diagrams.

Voronoi diagrams are usually generated with heuristic algorithms. The space is divided into small grids with proper resolution and the distances between a grid and each target point in the space are calculated and compared, and the grids are assigned to their nearest target points. Even though several preprocessing approaches that can reduce the computational complexity have been proposed [2], they have the following defects. (1) These algorithms focus on certain sub-problems derived from Voronoi diagrams, such as nearest neighbor query, path planning, and collision detection. Unfortunately, none of them solves our neighbor determination problem in the embryo system. (2) These algorithms require a preprocessing step as a prerequisite before reducing the computational complexity and a fixed Voronoi diagram is needed. However, in a metazoan embryo system, cells migrate, divide and squeeze with each other over time, which leads to highly dynamics of the Voronoi tessellation. Therefore, these approaches are not feasible under such situations. The most classical approach to obtain the Voronoi neighbor is Delaunay triangulation, which connects all the neighbor pairs in the whole diagram. Unfortunately, for a 3D weighted Voronoi diagram, there does not exist a way to obtain its Delaunay triangulation besides the heuristic approaches [12].

In conclusion, the Voronoi diagram, as an approach for neighbor determination, is not able to achieve fast processing. In a metazoan embryogenesis process, which contains hundreds to thousands of cells over hours to days of development, simulation time is much more valuable than that we spend to construct other pre-trained/processed built-in modules. As a result, a training/preprocessing expensive, but testing cheap framework for cell neighbor determination is required.

3 PROPOSED APPROACH

In this section, we present a learning-based approach to achieve the goal of cell neighbor determination. Our key idea is to transfer the cell neighbor determination problem into a classification task. We will discuss the general ideas about how to select features, and what kind of classifiers to choose for such task. The detailed implementation, performance and discussions are provided in Section 4 and 5, respectively.

3.1 Framework

The whole framework is described in Fig. 2. First of all, proper features are extracted from the raw embryogenesis data, and corresponding labels are assigned, indicating that under such circumstance, whether the two cells are neighbors (using 1) or not (using 0). Then we design/select an appropriate classifier and feed it with the samples. The performance is evaluated during the testing process and feedback is given to the classifier to adjust its hyperparameters. Finally, the well-trained model is built into specific real world problems to model more complicated tasks, such as cell-cell signaling and cell division.

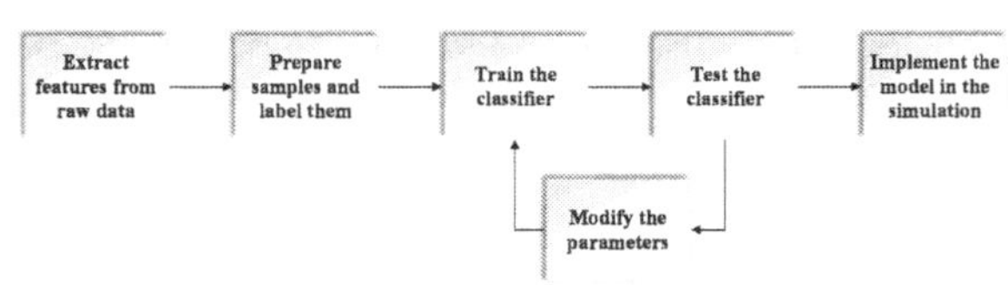

Figure 2: The framework of the proposed cell neighbor determination model.

3.2 Feature selection

To select proper features to train the classifier is the key for acquiring high accuracy. For the cell neighbor determination problem, an appropriate set of features can accurately provide sufficient information to describe the neighbor relationship between cells without redundancy. Here we list some of the features that can be the candidates for the neighbor determination problem. The feature selection details for specific problems are discussed in Section 4.1.

- Distance between two cells.
- Radius (or volume) of each cell.
- Length of each body axis (or volume) of the embryo.
- Distance between each cell to the eggshell.
- Total number of cells in the embryo.
- The distribution of the generations of the cells in the embryo.
- The intensity of pixels (if samples represented as images).

3.3 Classification

Two classical classifiers, namely, k-nearest neighbor (kNN) and support vector machine (SVM) [4], are implemented in our model. These algorithms are linear models that achieve a fast implementation for cell neighbor determination.

The kNN classifier aims to find the nearest k points to a testing sample. The result of the number of nearest neighbors is transferred as a maximum posterior probability (Eq. (2)) to determine whether the two cells are neighbors with each other given the situation described in the sample.

$$P(\omega_i|x) = \frac{p(x|\omega_i)P(\omega_i)}{p(x)} = \frac{K_i}{K}, \tag{2}$$

where $p(x|\omega_i) = K_iN_i/V$ is the probability density function (pdf) for each class, $P(\omega_i) = N_i/N$ is the prior probability, and $p(x) = K/(NV)$ is the normalization constant. K, K_i, N, N_i, V denote the total number of points in the space, the total number of points that belongs to ω_i in the space, the total number of samples, the total number of samples that belongs to ω_i, and the volume of the space, respectively.

The SVM classifier, also known as the large margin classifier, finds the best decision boundary that linearly separates the samples in the different classes. Such boundary holds largest minimum distances to both of the two classes by selecting proper support vectors. With SVM, the cell neighbor determination problem is transferred to an optimization problem that tries to minimize the loss function L (Eq. (3)).

$$L = C\sum_{n=1}^{N} \max(0, 1 - y_n w^T x_n) + \frac{1}{2}||w||^2, \tag{3}$$

where C is the hyperparameter, N is the total number of training samples, $y_n \in \{-1, 1\}$ depends on the specific label of the sample, w is the parameter of the classifier. The second term in Eq. (3), $1/2||w||^2$, is a regularization penalty and the Euclidean distance is used for this case.

4 EXPERIMENTS AND RESULTS

4.1 Simulation setup

Our simulation uses Nematode *C. elegans* as a study model. Because of its invariant cell lineage, fast developmental speed (only a few hours) from a zygote to hundreds of cells, *C. elegans* is a very suitable model for large-scale systematic quantitative analyses [8] and the existing data have been well formatted for further study. In our experiments, *C. elegans* embryogenesis data, which contain the locations, nucleus diameters, and names of each cell at certain time steps, are used as the raw dataset [16]. We cut off the dataset and reserve those from 0 to 350-cell stage. About 2 million samples are generated from 3D weighted Voronoi diagram as "correct answers" of the neighbor relationship. For both classifiers (kNN and SVM), 20% of the data are used for training and the rest for testing. The kNN approach is tested with different number of k (neighbors), and the SVM one uses a default linear kernel function. A 5-fold cross validation is implemented to guarantee the validity of the result. The runtime performance is tested on the hydra supercomputer from UTK's EECS department [7] with Matlab (R2015b).

We have discussed a number of candidates for the feature selection in Section 3.2. The distance of two cells, radius of each cell, and the total number of cells in the embryo are selected as the features in this experiment. Since the samples used for this simulation come from the same embryo, we ignore the embryo/eggshell related features, which share the same values among all the samples. Although we implement this simplified version of feature selection in our current model, we strongly believe that such model is without loss of generality, and can achieve as good accuracy as this simulation study by adding the missing features when dealing with the situation that embryo sizes vary.

During the very early stage of embryogenesis, asymmetric division commonly exists, especially in the germline cells. In Table 1, a list of the predefined ratio of volumes after asymmetric cell division in our simulation is provided. For other cells, the radii are calculated based on symmetric division.

Table 1: Volume ratios after asymmetric cell division during *C. elegans* early embryogenesis.

Cell Name	Daughter 1	Daughter 2	Ratio
P_0	AB	P_1	55:45
P_1	EMS	P_2	54:46
P_2	C	P_3	53:47
P_3	D	P_4	52:48

4.2 Runtime performance and accuracy

Running time is a significant factor when we build *in silico* models. The Voronoi approach iterates every grid in the 3D space, which is extremely time-consuming. What makes things worse is that such iteration has to be done three times with different orders of the axes to eliminate the miss of a neighbor pair where the Voronoi boundary is exactly along an axis. kNN compares the distances from a testing sample to all the training samples to find a certain number of nearest neighbors, while SVM optimizes a set of parameters and only a matrix multiplication is needed for a testing sample. Therefore, both kNN and SVM run at a much faster speed than the Voronoi approach. Due to the above internal properties of the two classifiers, as the number of cells increases, SVM should perform better than kNN on the running time.

Fig. 3 shows the running time comparison of the approaches using the Voronoi diagram, kNN, and SVM. The Voronoi approach is extremely time-consuming as the number of cells grows exponentially. But for the other two methods, the running times are controlled within a reasonable period of time. At the 350-cell stage, our proposed approaches increase the running speed by 10^4 times. Although SVM is more training expensive than kNN (training time at 350-cell stage: 370s vs. 18s), we care more about the simulation time, i.e., the testing time in our case, and SVM saves half time with the comparison to kNN (testing time at 350-cell stage: 72s vs 146s).

In our setup, the results generated from the Voronoi diagram are considered as the "correct answer" of the neighbor relationship, so the accuracy for the Voronoi approach is 100% at each stage as a reference. During early stages (0 to 100-cell), though kNN performs slightly better than SVM, neither classifier gives a satisfactory accuracy. But as the number of cells increases, the accuracy increases

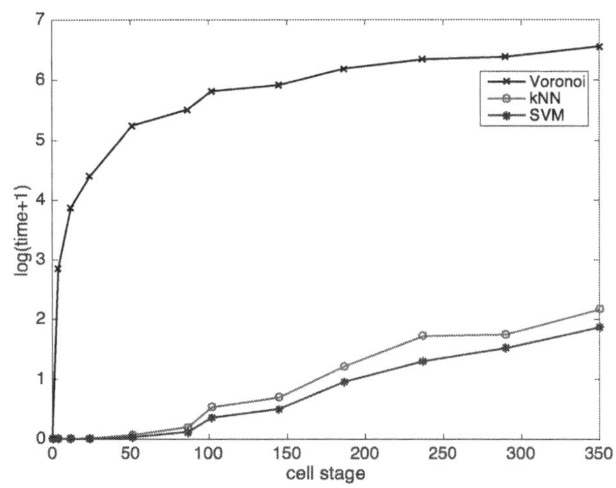

Figure 3: Running time comparison from 4 to 350-cell stage.

correspondingly, and SVM performs as good as kNN. When the simulation ends at 350-cell stage, the accuracies with kNN ($k = 5$) and SVM is 99.62% and 99.66%, respectively (Fig. 4).

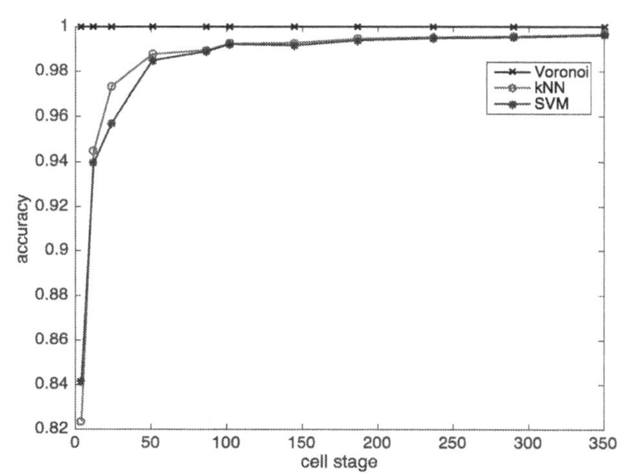

Figure 4: Accuracy comparison from 4 to 350-cell stage.

In conclusion, at the early stage (0 to 100-cell), there is no big difference of the running time, but kNN achieves higher accuracy. At late stage (100 to 350-cell), SVM performs as good as kNN on the accuracy, but can save half of the running time.

4.3 Verification and Visualization

To verify the validity of our proposed approach in specific problems, we implement it in *C. elegans* Notch signaling pathways, and the cell-cell squeeze model for cell division direction. The Notch signaling pathways play significant roles in *C. elegans* embryogenesis [19]. During four Notch signaling processes, certain cells interact in a contactable way to activate certain gene expressions, which leads to different cell fates in the AB-lineage. We test the neighbor relationships of the involved cells in the four Notch signaling pathways listed in Table 2. More specifically, signaling and receiving cells

Table 2: Cells involved in the four Notch signaling pathways in *C. elegans embryogenesis.*

#	Signaling cell	Receiving cell	Unsignaled cell*
1st	P_2	ABp	ABa
2nd	MS	ABalp,ABara	ABala,ABarp
3rd	ABalapp	ABplaaa	ABpraaa
4th	MSapa,MSapp	ABplpapp	ABprpapp

* The cells required not to be the neighbors of the signaling cell during certain Notch pathways.

are used for testing the neighbor relationship, while those listed in the "unsignaled cell" column are used for testing the algorithm that there does not exist a neighbor relationship between them and the signaling cells, which is exclusively required by each of the four Notch processes.

The neighbor relationship of the involved cells in the third and fourth Notch interactions are visualized via WormGUIDES [21] with the approach of Voronoi diagram, and our learning based approaches, respectively (Fig. 5). The results from Voronoi diagram are pre-examined to be consistent with the real world situations, and our approaches successfully capture the neighbor relationship in the Voronoi diagram (data not shown for the first two Notch cases).

Division/proliferation is one of the most fundamental cell behaviors, and the squeeze force between cells is a significant component that influences the division direction of a cell. Our model can be used for the determination of the neighbors of a dividing cell. A single cell-cell squeeze direction is then calculated by comparing the sum of the estimated cell radii and their spatial distance. Finally, we combine all the direction vectors associated with a squeeze distance k to obtain the composition direction. We test the model with *C. elegans* embryogenesis data from 4 to 350-cell stage and the whole system works well with our learning based cell neighbor determination approach. Some samples of the result (two daughters of ABal at AB8 stage) of the cell-cell squeeze direction during division process is presented in Table 3. The modeling framework for other division direction components, and the composition of them is beyond the scope of this paper.

5 DISCUSSIONS AND FUTURE WORK

5.1 Analysis of the accuracy rate

Accuracy is the most important issue we care about given that the proposed cell neighbor determination framework has largely increased the speed for calculating it. We consider the reasons for the errors in the following aspects. (1) The Voronoi diagram itself is an approximate approach for embryo segmentation. The real situation is that there exist gaps between cells, and the boundaries are not as sharp as those from Voronoi diagram, either. Moreover, technical errors might occur when the embryo boundary is not estimated properly. (2) The linear classification models have their own limitations, which make the decision boundaries not separate the samples well enough.

We divide the error into two categories, namely, false positive (FP, the two cells are not neighbors but the classifier believes they are.) and false negative (FN, the two cells are neighbors but the classifier

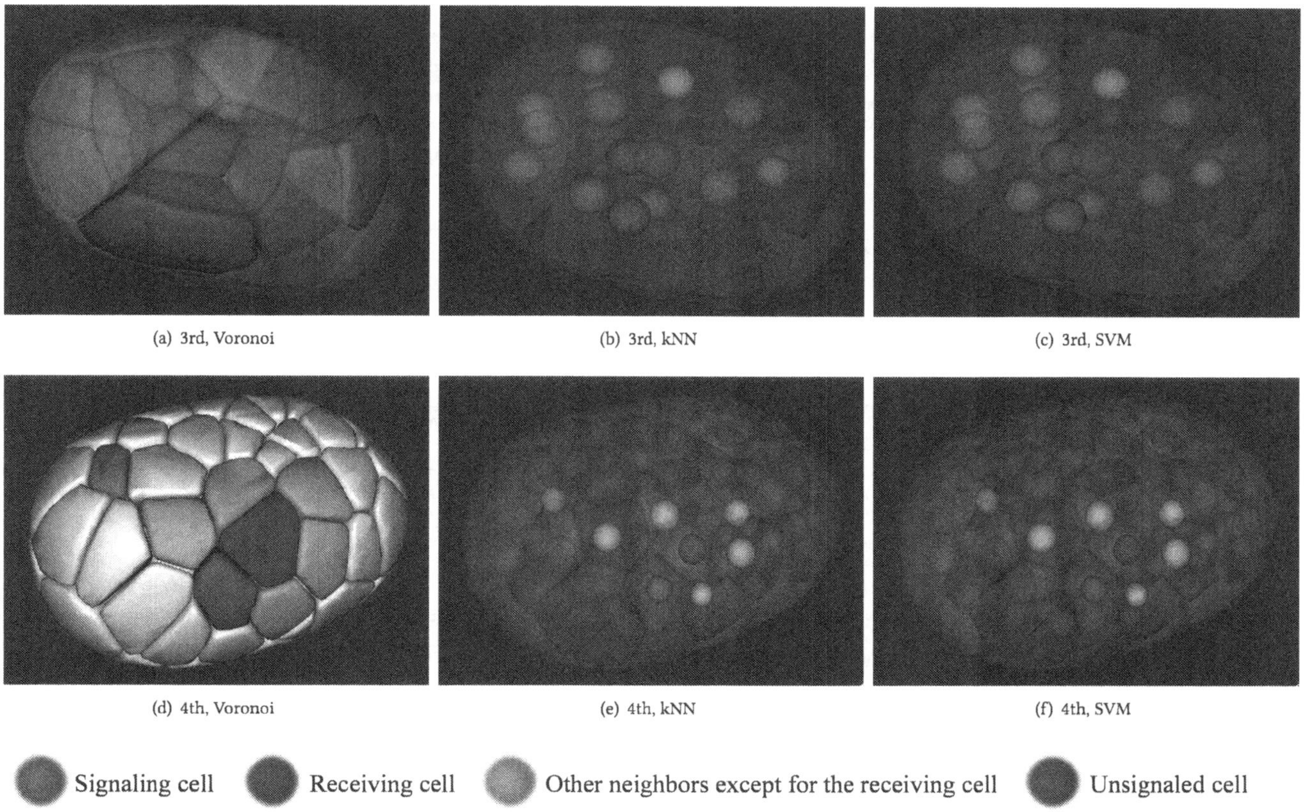

(a) 3rd, Voronoi (b) 3rd, kNN (c) 3rd, SVM

(d) 4th, Voronoi (e) 4th, kNN (f) 4th, SVM

Figure 5: The neighbor relationship from the Voronoi, kNN and SVM approaches during the 3rd and 4th Notch signaling pathways of *C. elegans* embryogenesis.

Table 3: Cell-cell squeeze direction of ABala and ABalp with their neighbors at AB8 stage.

Dividing cell	Location	Radius	Cell stage
ABala	(321, 181, 105)	92.52	16
ABalp	(334, 250, 90)	92.52	16

Dividing cell	Neighbor	Location	Distance	Radius	Squeeze dist	Division direction vector
ABala	ABalp	(334, 250, 90)	71.80	92.52	113.24	(-20.50, -108.83, 23.66)
	ABara	(254, 194, 65)	79.11	92.52	105.93	(89.72, -17.41, 53.57)
	ABarp	(220, 198, 130)	105.43	92.52	79.61	(76.27, -12.84, -18.88)
	ABplaa	(299, 238, 140)	70.41	46.26	68.35	(29.85, -77.34, -47.49)
ABalp	ABara	(254, 194, 65)	100.80	92.52	84.24	(66.86, 46.80, 20.89)
	ABala	(321, 181, 105)	71.80	92.52	113.24	(20.50, 108.83, -23.66)
	MSa	(276, 276, 55)	72.56	88.78	108.74	(86.92, -38.97, 52.45)
	ABplp	(251, 312, 120)	107.86	92.52	77.18	(59.40, -44.37, -21.47)
	ABplaa	(299, 238, 140)	62.20	46.26	76.56	(58.38, 20.02, -83.40)
	ABplap	(280, 245, 145)	77.24	46.26	61.52	(62.02, 5.74, -63.17)

believes they are not.) errors, and analyze them respectively. By counting the number of recognition errors during certain times (represent as cell stage), we find that the time intervals in which errors occur more frequently are centered around only a few cell stages, namely, 90, 190, and 350-cell stages (Fig. 6(a) and 6(b)). With further analysis of the number of cells in the embryo over time (Fig. 6(c)), we find that such time intervals are exactly the periods that the number of cells grows exponentially when the cells from the AB lineage divide extensively at similar times. As a result, the 3D geometry structure changes intensively, which leads to more errors.

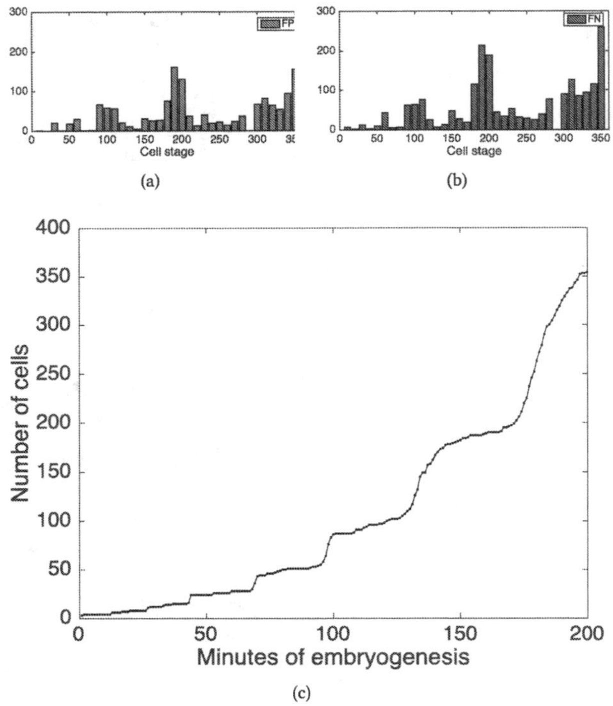

Figure 6: Distribution of the FP and FN results during embryogenesis simulation.

We count the number of neighbor determination errors in every cell pair in their cell cycles (Fig. 7(a)), and most errors happen less than three times (793 out of 859, 93% in FP results, 947 out of 1069, 89% in FN results). The frequency of these errors are presented in Fig. 7(b). We find out that most of the errors in certain cell pairs occur at a rate of less than 10% (696 out of 859, 81% in FP results, 839 out of 1069, 78% in FN results).

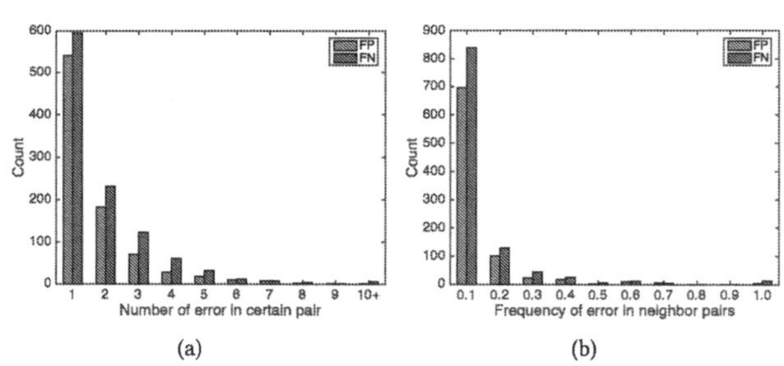

Figure 7: The number and frequency of errors of all cell pairs in FP and FN results.

An interesting spot in Fig. 7(b) is that there exists a slight increase of the frequency of errors in the interval from 90% to 100%. Therefore, we list these cell pairs, the number of errors, and the total number of time steps they exist simultaneously (both in their cell cycles) in the embryo, respectively (Table 4). It turns out that these high frequencies of errors occur when the two cells are not from the same generation, which means that one cell is just born, and the other is at the very end of her cell cycle. Therefore, the high frequency of errors results from the short time interval they exist in the embryo simultaneously, rather than the extensive errors generated from the classifier.

Table 4: Cell neighbor pairs with a high frequency of errors (90% to 100%) in FP and FN results.

Cell pair	Gens*	Error°	Existence†	Cat
Cpp,Cpaa	6,7	3	3	FP
Dap,Dppp	7,8	1	1	FP
P_4,MSppap	4,8	1	1	FP
ABalapapa, ABalpppaap	9,10	1	1	FP
MSppaaa, ABalaapaaa	9,10	3	3	FN
Cpap,Cpaaa	7,8	1	1	FN
ABalpp, ABplapa	6,7	1	1	FN
ABprpa, ABarapp	6,7	1	1	FN
ABplaaaaa, ABplaaaapp	9,10	3	3	FN
ABalapp, ABalapaa	7,8	1	1	FN
ABplaaap, ABalapapa	8,9	1	1	FN
Daa,Dppa	7,8	1	1	FN
Daa,Dppp	7,8	1	1	FN
ABarappaa, ABprpapaaa	9,10	2	2	FN
Caaaa,Cpaaaa	8,9	1	1	FN
ABaraaa, ABarapap	7,8	1	1	FN

* Generations of both cells.
° Number of errors occurring in their life cycles.
† Number of time steps of the existence in their life cycles.

It is worth noting that in Fig. 7(a), the total number of FN results is larger than that of FP ones (1069 vs. 859). To study the reason behind it, we count the thirty cells with the most number of errors in FP and FN results, respectively (Fig. 8(a) and 8(b)). Besides the fact that boundary cells close to the eggshell are more likely to be classified inaccurately in both cases, there exist a large number of errors that occur in peripheral cells with the largest weight around, which are the biggest ones near the eggshell, but are not the neighbors of the boundary cells, in the FN results. Further study indicates that the weighted Voronoi approach has a certain probability to generate wrong neighbor labels outside the embryo under the circumstance that the boundary of the eggshell is not estimated appropriately.

Analysis from AceTree [5] validates that for some of the boundary cells and peripheral cells, Voronoi approach gives a wrong segmentation, which leads to FN cases from the classifier, but is actually true results. Fig. 8(c) and 8(d) show an example in which the boundary cell ABalapaa and the peripheral cell ABalapp are not neighbors (at least they are separated by ABalapaa's posterior sister ABalapap). Under the situation that the peripheral cell ABalapp holds the largest weight near by, the Voronoi approach provides the classifier with a wrong label, while the classifier gives the correct answer, but is considered as an FN result. Further study of the 3D weighted Voronoi diagram shows that for the points with a large weight, encapsulated Voronoi tessellation is generated to nearby cells because of the distances calculated with the ratio of their different weights, even though they are actually not neighbors (Fig. 8(e)). Therefore, when the boundary of the eggshell is not estimated appropriately, a number of non-existent neighbor pairs are generated outside the embryo. On the other hand, learning-based approaches consider the distances between the features, which results in FN results that contradict those from the Voronoi approach, but is actually true.

5.2 Customization on different purposes

To assign different penalties on FP and FN results can improve the model, since they have different influences on the downstream applications. In the cell-cell squeeze model, it is reasonable to assume that the risk from FP results is much smaller than those from FN ones. This is because when we take the false neighbor pair from the FP results to calculate the squeeze force afterward, the sum of the radii of the two cells is very likely to be larger than the distance between them, and no extra force is generated to influence the division direction. Even if the force is unfortunately generated, since the embryo is a highly dynamic system, the extra vector from wrong results leads to a movement towards the direction of it, which is likely to be neutralized at the next time step when there does not exist FP result.

For the neighbor determination during signaling process, if various of cells contain certain receptor that can be activated by the same ligand through specific pathways, both FP and FN results lead to irreversible consequences. For example, during the first Notch signaling process, the germline cell P_2 expresses the Notch ligand APX-1/Delta, which can be received by both of the daughters of AB (ABa and ABp) with the receptor GLP-1/Notch. ABa and ABp are originally identical, but because of the anterior-posterior relationship, the posterior cell ABp is a neighbor of P_2 while ABa is not. As a result, the expression of the ref-1 family in ABp is induced and this leads to different cell fates of ABa and ABp. Suppose that both FP and FN results are wrongly generated from the model on the neighbor relationship of (P_2,ABa) and (P_2,ABp), respectively. It is obvious that a fate exchange will occur in the ABa and ABp cells. Under such circumstance, FP and FN results should be assigned with the same penalty. Therefore, for the signaling process, bad results on the neighbor relationship may have very large influences on the following processes. For the situations that regulatory mechanisms remain unknown, the operation to assign different penalties on FP and FN results should be treated cautiously.

5.3 Future work

Our immediate future work includes (1) designing new algorithms to increase the accuracy, and (2) incorporating this approach into downstream applications. Although in some cases, such as the cell-cell squeeze model, the recognition error is insignificant, under other situations, for example, cell-cell signaling, the requirement of accuracy is extraordinary strict, which requires more accurate neighbor determination models. Therefore, designing new frameworks with non-linear models, such as convolutional neural network, can further break through the limitations of the linear models above and reach higher accuracy.

As shown in Section 5, our approach greatly decreases the running time for the determination of the neighbor relationship. With such algorithm, it is now possible to build large multi-scale *in silico* embryogenesis simulation frameworks, which run in an acceptable period of time. Our second follow-up effort is to build this approach into general metazoan embryogenesis models [25, 26] to study fundamental developmental problems, such as cell fate differentiation, migration, and proliferation.

6 CONCLUSION

In this paper, we present a cell neighbor determination algorithm to discover the neighbor relationship in the metazoan embryo system. Our idea transfers the traditional Voronoi diagram approach into a classification problem, and takes kNN and SVM as the classifiers, which are trained by the "correct answers" generated from Voronoi. Simulation results show that our approach increases the running speed by 10^4 times with an accuracy of 99.66%. Our approach successfully models the neighbor relationship in *C. elegans* Notch signaling pathways and cell-cell squeeze forces prove its validity for the cell neighbor determination problem in metazoan developmental systems.

7 ACKNOWLEDGMENTS

We thank Anthony Santella for providing the Voronoi diagrams of *C. elegans* embryos. This study is supported by an NIH research project grants (R01GM097576 and 2R01GM097576). Research in the Bao lab is also supported by an NIH center grant to MSKCC (P30CA008748). Dr. Wang is also a Senior RD staff at Oak Ridge National Laboratory.

REFERENCES

[1] Begoña Abellanas, Manuel Abellanas, Arne Pommerening, Dolores Lodares, and Simón Cuadros. 2016. A forest simulation approach using weighted Voronoi diagrams. An application to Mediterranean fir Abies pinsapo Boiss stands. *Forest Systems* 25, 2 (2016), 062.

[2] Franz Aurenhammer. 1991. Voronoi diagrams-a survey of a fundamental geometric data structure. *ACM Computing Surveys (CSUR)* 23, 3 (1991), 345–405.

[3] Franz Aurenhammer and Herbert Edelsbrunner. 1984. An optimal algorithm for constructing the weighted Voronoi diagram in the plane. *Pattern Recognition* 17, 2 (1984), 251–257.

[4] Christopher M.. Bishop. 2006. *Pattern recognition and machine learning*. Springer.

[5] Thomas J Boyle, Zhirong Bao, John I Murray, Carlos L Araya, and Robert H Waterston. 2006. AceTree: a tool for visual analysis of Caenorhabditis elegans embryogenesis. *BMC bioinformatics* 7, 1 (2006), 275.

[6] Jonathan W Brandt and V Ralph Algazi. 1992. Continuous skeleton computation by Voronoi diagram. *CVGIP: Image understanding* 55, 3 (1992), 329–338.

[7] UTK EECS Department. 2017. UTK EECS Hydra Lab. https://www.eecs.utk.edu/resources/it/computing/hydra-lab-min-kao-421/. (2017).

[8] Zhuo Du, Anthony Santella, Fei He, Pavak K Shah, Yuko Kamikawa, and Zhirong Bao. 2015. The regulatory landscape of lineage differentiation in a metazoan embryo. *Developmental cell* 34, 5 (2015), 592–607.

[9] Zhuo Du, Anthony Santella, Fei He, Michael Tiongson, and Zhirong Bao. 2014. De novo inference of systems-level mechanistic models of development from live-imaging-based phenotype analysis. *Cell* 156, 1 (2014), 359–372.

[10] Jun Guo and Hamid Jafarkhani. 2016. Sensor deployment with limited communication range in homogeneous and heterogeneous wireless sensor networks. *IEEE Transactions on Wireless Communications* 15, 10 (2016), 6771–6784.

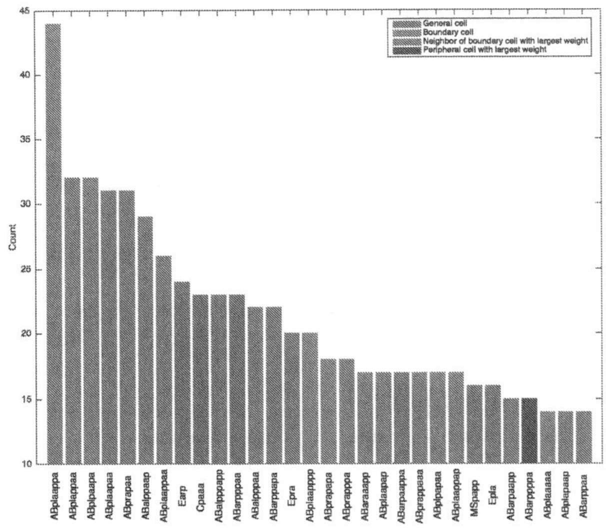

(a)

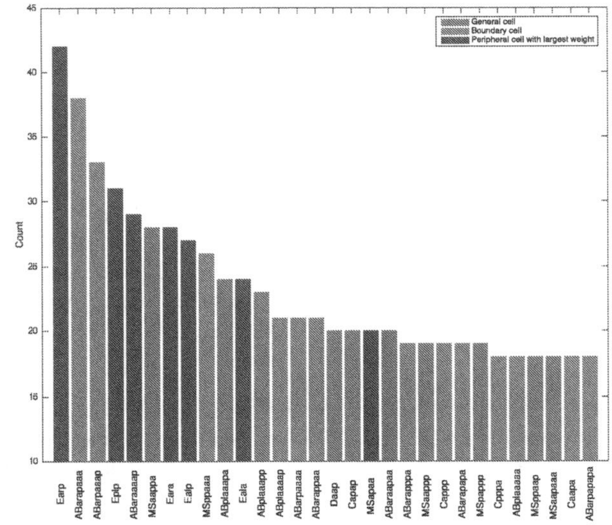

(b)

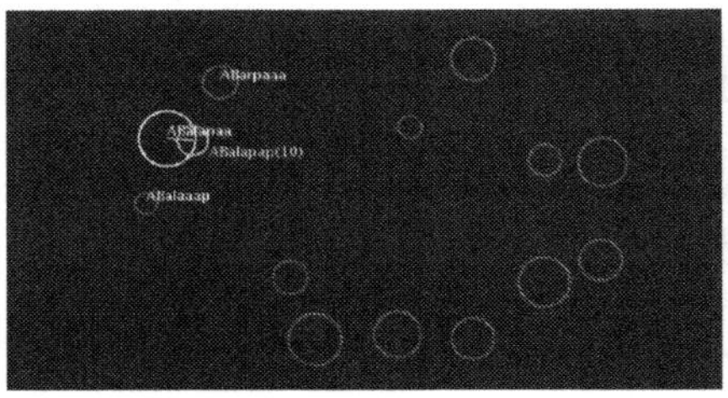

(c)

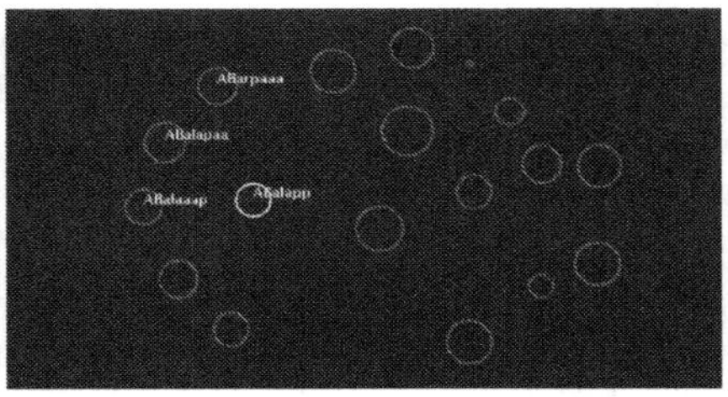

(d)

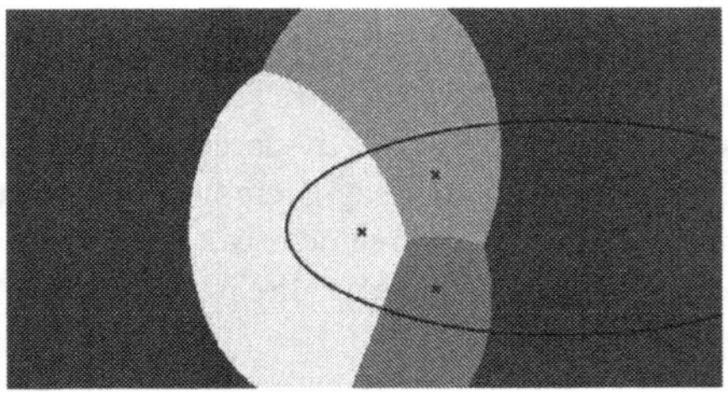

(e)

* Boundary cells: cells that are close to the eggshell.
° Peripheral cells: cells that are near the eggshell, but are not the neighbors of the boundary cells.

Figure 8: Top 30 cells with the most errors in FP and FN results, and analysis from AceTree.

[11] Jürgen Hench, Johan Henriksson, Martin Lüppert, and Thomas R Bürglin. 2009. Spatio-temporal reference model of Caenorhabditis elegans embryogenesis with cell contact maps. *Developmental biology* 333, 1 (2009), 1–13.
[12] Kenneth E Hoff III, John Keyser, Ming Lin, Dinesh Manocha, and Tim Culver. 1999. Fast computation of generalized Voronoi diagrams using graphics hardware. In *Proceedings of the 26th annual conference on Computer graphics and interactive techniques*. ACM Press/Addison-Wesley Publishing Co., 277–286.
[13] Tsung-Jung Hsieh, Hsiao-Fen Hsiao, and Wei-Chang Yeh. 2011. Forecasting stock markets using wavelet transforms and recurrent neural networks: An integrated system based on artificial bee colony algorithm. *Applied soft computing* 11, 2 (2011), 2510–2525.
[14] Alex Krizhevsky, Ilya Sutskever, and Geoffrey E Hinton. 2012. Imagenet classification with deep convolutional neural networks. In *Advances in neural information processing systems*. 1097–1105.
[15] Miguel A Luengo-Oroz, Louise Duloquin, C Castro, Thierry Savy, Emmanuel Faure, Benoit Lombardot, Paul Bourgine, Nadine Peyriéras, and Andrés Santos. 2008. Can voronoi diagram model cell geometries in early sea-urchin embryogenesis?. In *Biomedical Imaging: From Nano to Macro, 2008. ISBI 2008. 5th IEEE International Symposium on*. IEEE, 504–507.
[16] Julia L Moore, Zhuo Du, and Zhirong Bao. 2013. Systematic quantification of developmental phenotypes at single-cell resolution during embryogenesis. *Development* 140, 15 (2013), 3266–3274.
[17] A Okebe, B Boots, and K Sugihara. 2000. Concepts and applications of Voronoi diagrams. (2000).
[18] Nicolas Olivier, Miguel A Luengo-Oroz, Louise Duloquin, Emmanuel Faure, Thierry Savy, Israël Veilleux, Xavier Solinas, Delphine Débarre, Paul Bourgine, Andrés Santos, et al. 2010. Cell lineage reconstruction of early zebrafish embryos using label-free nonlinear microscopy. *Science* 329, 5994 (2010), 967–971.
[19] James R Priess. 2005. Notch signaling in the C. elegans embryo. *WormBook* 1 (2005), 1–16.
[20] Meenakshi Rawat, Karun Rawat, and Fadhel M Ghannouchi. 2010. Adaptive digital predistortion of wireless power amplifiers/transmitters using dynamic real-valued focused time-delay line neural networks. *IEEE Transactions on Microwave Theory and Techniques* 58, 1 (2010), 95–104.
[21] Anthony Santella, Raúl Catena, Ismar Kovacevic, Pavak Shah, Zidong Yu, Javier Marquina-Solis, Abhishek Kumar, Yicong Wu, James Schaff, Daniel Colón-Ramos, et al. 2015. WormGUIDES: an interactive single cell developmental atlas and tool for collaborative multidimensional data exploration. *BMC bioinformatics* 16, 1 (2015), 189.
[22] Anthony Santella, Ismar Kovacevic, Laura A Herndon, David H Hall, Zhuo Du, and Zhirong Bao. 2015. Digital development: a database of cell lineage differentiation in C. elegans with lineage phenotypes, cell-specific gene functions and a multiscale model. *Nucleic acids research* (2015), gkv1119.
[23] David Silver, Aja Huang, Chris J Maddison, Arthur Guez, Laurent Sifre, George Van Den Driessche, Julian Schrittwieser, Ioannis Antonoglou, Veda Panneershelvam, Marc Lanctot, et al. 2016. Mastering the game of Go with deep neural networks and tree search. *Nature* 529, 7587 (2016), 484–489.
[24] Kenji Sugioka, Kota Mizumoto, and Hitoshi Sawa. 2011. Wnt regulates spindle asymmetry to generate asymmetric nuclear β-catenin in C. elegans. *Cell* 146, 6 (2011), 942–954.
[25] Gerard Vanloo, Chung Ng, Kison Osborne, Kwai Wong, Ben Ramsey, Dali Wang, and Zhirong Bao. 2016. Using High Performance Computing to Model Cellular Embryogenesis. In *Proceedings of the XSEDE16 Conference on Diversity, Big Data, and Science at Scale*. ACM, 12.
[26] Zi Wang, Benjamin J Ramsey, Dali Wang, Kwai Wong, Husheng Li, Eric Wang, and Zhirong Bao. 2016. An Observation-Driven Agent-Based Modeling and Analysis Framework for C. elegans Embryogenesis. *PloS one* 11, 11 (2016), e0166551.

Predictive and Comparative Network Analysis of the Gut Microbiota in Type 2 Diabetes

Mostafa M Abbas
Qatar Computing Research Institute
(QCRI) Hamad Bin Khalifa University
Doha, Qatar
mohamza@hbku.edu.qa

Yasser EL-Manzalawy
College of Information Sciences and Technology
Pennsylvania State University
University Park, PA 16802
yme2@psu.edu

ABSTRACT

Metagenome-wide analysis studies provide a unique set of microbial features for biomarker discovery of associated disease as well as for studying diversity and dynamics of microbial communities under different conditions. Taxonomic classification of microbes in metagenomic samples quantifies what microbes are present and in what proportion. Despite the availably of several computational taxonomy profiling methods, this crucial step in metagenome-wide analysis remains very challenging and how using different taxonomy profiling methods might influence the outcome of the analysis is not well-studied. In this work, we consider three taxonomy profiling methods (MetaPhlAn2, Kraken, and EBI metagenomics pipeline) and examine their effect on the outcome of metagenome-wide analysis based on machine learning and comparative network approaches. Our results suggest that Kraken OTU-based data representation yields the best performing classifiers even using less number of features (e.g., OTUs). In addition, our preliminary results underscore the viability of leveraging multiple taxonomic classification methods in microbial network analysis. Finally, our analysis results are consistent with the current knowledge and reveal novel insights into interaction relationships between potential biomarkers in the gut microbiome associated with T2D.

CCS CONCEPTS

• **Computing methodologies** → **Machine learning algorithms**; • **Applied computing**→ Biological networks; Computational genomics

KEYWORDS

Metagenomics, Type 2 Diabetes, Predictive Analytics, Comparative Network Analysis

Permission to make digital or hard copies of all or part of this work for personal or classroom use is granted without fee provided that copies are not made or distributed for profit or commercial advantage and that copies bear this notice and the full citation on the first page. Copyrights for components of this work owned by others than ACM must be honored. Abstracting with credit is permitted. To copy otherwise, or republish, to post on servers or to redistribute to lists, requires prior specific permission and/or a fee. Request permissions from Permissions@acm.org.
ACM-BCB'17, August 20-23, 2017, Boston, MA, USA.
© 2017 Association of Computing Machinery.
ACM ISBN 978-1-4503-4722-8/17/08...$15.00.
DOI: http://dx.doi.org/10.1145/3107411.3107472

1 INTRODUCTION

The human gut microbiota contains a unique group of numerous microorganisms [1, 2]. Gut microbiota is a very complex and dynamic entity and is considered a major player in the development of many diseases including obesity [3], type 2 diabetes (T2D) [4], and cardiovascular [5]. A key goal of microbiome research is to define the structure and functional relationships between various organisms constituting the gut microbiome in healthy and active disease states [6]. Recent technological advances in next generation sequencing technology have substantially improved our capacity to explore the composition and dynamics of microbial communities from metagenomic samples.

Taxonomy profiling methods assign taxonomical labels or operational taxonomic units (OTUs) to metagenomic DNA reads [7, 8], thus enabling a metagenomic sample of millions of short DNA reads to be characterized by the abundance of OTUs corresponding to different microbes. Despite the availability of several computational tools for taxonomy profiling of metagenomic data (e.g., [9-12]), it is very challenging to assess the accuracy and the reliability of these tools partly due to the lack of well-studied benchmark datasets [13]. Existing taxonomy profiling comparative studies (e.g., [8, 14]) are often conducted using simulated data with very few samples.

Given the sequence classification profiles of metagenomic data, the analytic step of metagenomic data involves the application of statistical, machine learning, or comparative network approaches in order to test and/or derive testable hypotheses and to identify novel potential metagenomic biomarkers for different diseases [4]. In general, metagenome-wide analysis studies focus on one single approach (i.e., statistical, predictive, or comparative network analysis) and are limited to generating taxonomy profiles using one tool. To the best of our knowledge, understanding how using different taxonomy profiling methods could affect the conclusions of metagenome-wide analysis studies has not been addressed before.

Against this background, we analyze metagenomics data for the gut microbiota of 170 T2D samples as well as 174 healthy control samples using both machine learning and comparative network approaches to discover potential T2D biomarkers and characterize key changes in microbial communities and behavior of biomarkers in T2D patients. Our main contributions are threefold: i) we empirically examine how using different taxonomy profiling methods of metagenomics data could affect the outcome of predictive and comparative network analysis, respectively; ii) we propose a novel method for assessing taxonomy classification methods using the predictive performance of classifiers evaluated using the outcome of taxonomy classification methods as intermediate representation of metagenomics samples; iii) we propose biomarkers sub-networks as a tool for visualizing and analyzing nodes properties and interaction relationships between potential biomarkers detected using machine learning feature selection methods.

2 MATERIALS AND METHODS

2.1 Data

We considered 344 publicly available metagenomics samples from a recent metagenome-wide association study of gut microbiota in type 2 diabetes [4]. There were a total of 170 T2D patients and 174 non-diabetic controls. The high quality paired-end sequence read data were obtained from patient stool samples that were acquired using a two-stage strategy. An average of 31,972,726 sequence reads of length 75-90 bp are obtained per sample in the first stage while in the second stage, an average of 47,226,507 sequence reads were obtained per sample of length 90 bp.

Taxonomy profiles of samples were generated using two widely used taxonomy profiling tools, MetaPhlAn2 [15] and Kraken [9]. In addition, we used the taxonomy profiles of the samples downloaded from the European Bioinformatics Institute (EBI) metagenomics [16] (projects IDs SRP011011 and SRP008047). EBI metagenomics repository archives the profiles for only 323 samples (162 T2D and 161 non-diabetic control). MetaPhlAn2 profiles for all samples were downloaded from http://segatalab.cibio.unitn.it/tools/metaml. Kraken profiles were generated for all samples using a Kraken pre-built reference database which was constructed from complete bacterial, archaeal, and viral genomes in RefSeq (as of Dec. 8, 2014).

2.2 Taxonomy Profiling Methods

Marker-gene profiles of human microbiota provide a rich view of microbial diversity [10]. Taxonomy profiling methods determine what types of microbes are present in a metagenomic sample and in what proportion [7]. In general, taxonomy profiling methods could be categorized into two major approaches [8, 17]: i) supervised (or reference-based) approaches rely on the annotated sequences in a reference database for taxonomic assignment of a query sequence by the best matching sequence in the reference database; ii) unsupervised (or reference-free) approaches group reads into clusters, called operational taxonomy units (OTUs), and then relate each OTU to a taxonomy label using an OTU representative read. In what follows, we briefly summarize two supervised methods and one unsupervised method for metagenomic sequence profiling.

2.2.1 MetaPhlAn2. Metagenomic phylogenetic analysis version 2 (MetaPhlAn2) [15] is a program for profiling the composition of microbial communities (Bacteria, Archaea, Eukaryotes and Viruses) from metagenomic shotgun sequencing data with species level resolution. The program relies on a reference database of about 1M unique clade-specific marker genes identified from ~17,000 reference genomes.

2.2.2 Kraken. Kraken is one of the fastest tools for metagenomics sequence classification [9]. The program relies on an engineered database of marker genes or clade-specific genes. Kraken determines the taxonomic classification of each DNA read by mapping, using exact match, each k-mer extracted from the query read to the lowest common ancestor (LCA) of the genomes that contains that k-mer in the reference database.

2.2.3 EBI metagenomics pipeline. EBI metagenomics (EMG) is a publically available resource for analysis and archiving of metagenomic and meta-transcriptomic data [16]. EMG is partnering with the European Nucleotide Archive (ENA) [18] in order to provide a permanent metagenomics data repository. EMG provides an analysis workflow for producing rich taxonomic profiles as well as functional annotations. EMG analysis pipeline uses Greengenes reference database [19] and QIIME default closed-reference OTU picking protocol [20]. In this protocol, reads are clustered against a reference database and any reads that do not hit a sequence in the reference database are excluded from downstream analyses.

2.3 Predictive Analytics

The outcome of applying taxonomy profiling methods to metagenomics samples is an OTU abundance table, which lists the abundances of OTUs in the targeted metagenomic samples. We experimented with 5 supervised machine learning algorithms (Naïve Bayes (NB) [21], Logistic Regression (LR) [22], Support Vector Machine with linear kernel (SVML) [23], eXtreme Gradient Boosting (XGB) [24], and Random Forest (RF) [25]) to predict whether the metagenomic samples belong to T2D or control group. Briefly, to estimate the performance of a machine learning algorithm A for predicting T2D, we used the 10-fold cross-validation procedure where the data is stratified and randomly partitioned into 10 equal subsets. The performance of A is the average of 10 performance estimates each using one fold for testing and the remaining folds for training. The predictive performance of classifiers is reported using the following metrics [26]: Accuracy (ACC); Sensitivity (Sn); Specificity (Sp); Mathew Correlation Coefficient (MCC); and Area Under ROC Curve (AUC).

Due to high dimensionality of the data in the OTU space, applying supervised machine learning algorithms to metagenomic data using their OTU-based representation is often combined with some feature selection method [27, 28]. Following [29], we used embedded feature selection method based on a Random Forest classifier [25]. It should be noted that the top k selected features have been determined in each fold using training data only. In our experiments, we set k = 10, 20,..., 200.

2.4 Comparative Network Analysis

2.4.1 Network construction. Co-occurrence analysis of OTU abundance data for a group of samples (e.g., T2D or control samples) allows the identification of significance co-presence or mutual exclusion between OTUs [30]. Accurate identification of co-occurrence relationships between OTUs enables the construction of microbial interaction networks where nodes are OTUs and edges between nodes represent co-presence and/or mutual exclusion relationships between nodes.

We followed the protocol described in [31] to construct microbial interaction network models for healthy and T2D subjects using either MetaPhlAn2 or Kraken OTUs. Briefly, four similarity measures, Bray–Curtis and Kullback–Leibler dissimilarity, Pearson and Spearman correlation, are used to produce a distribution of all pair-wise scores. Using these distributions, thresholds were automatically selected such that each measure contributed 1000 positive and 1000 negative edges to the initial network. For each measure and each edge, 100 renormalized permutation and bootstrap scores were generated. Then, Brown's method [32] was used to merge method specific p-values and Benjamini Hochberg method [33] was used to adjust the p-values for multiple testing and only edges with merged p-values below 0.05 are kept.

2.4.2 Pairwise network comparisons. Healthy and T2D networks constructed using different OTU-based representations were compared at global, module, and node levels. At global level, we used Cytoscape "Network Analyzer" plugin [34] to characterize global topological properties of healthy and T2D networks. For module level comparisons, we used MCODE [35] to extract and visualize top highly-connected modules in healthy and T2D networks. Finally, potential biomarkers determined using our predictive analysis pipeline were projected into healthy and T2D networks and then relationships between potential biomarkers, in both types of networks, were inspected.

3 RESULTS AND DISCUSSION

3.1 Predictive Analytics of T2D Using Different Microbial Sequence Classification Methods

Table 1 reports the performance of different classifiers predicting T2D using OTU-based representation of 16S RNA reads obtained using MetaPhlAn2, Kraken, and EBI metagenomics pipeline. Using MetaPhlAn2 OTUs, the highest performance (AUC = 0.74) is observed using NB and RF classifiers. On the other hand, using Kraken identified OTUs, XGB classifier has AUC of 0.79. Moreover, two other classifiers, LR and RF, have AUC of 0.77 using only 40 and 30 OTUs, respectively. Finally, Table 1 shows that OTUs extracted using EBI metagenomics software pipeline cannot be used for developing good prediction models. The highest reported AUC using EBI derived OTUs is 0.66 using XGB or RF. Due to the poor predictive performance of all classifiers using EBI OTUs, we limited the rest of our experiments to MetaPhlAn2 and Kraken representations.

Despite discrepancies in classifiers performance using either MetaPhlAn2 or Kraken OTUs, both representations suggest discriminative OTUs that are in a good agreement. Table 2 lists the top 25 discriminative MetaPhlAn2 and Kraken OTUs as potential gut microbiota biomarker for type 2 diabetes. Results in Table 2 point to various members of butyrate- producing bacteria (e.g., Roseburia intestinalis and Faecalibacterium prausnitzii) as well as several opportunistic pathogens (e.g., Bacteroides fragilis) that have been linked with T2D [4]. Interestingly, we found that Alteromonadales (an order of Proteobacteria) is more abundant in T2D samples and is ranked high by our classifier after species from Roseburia genus. This finding is consistent with previous studies [36, 37] that showed that Proteobacteria is more enriched in T2D. Another interesting biomarker is bacteroides vulgatus ATCC 8482 strain. Bacteroides vulgatus is also commonly detected in higher numbers in healthy controls than in irritable bowel syndrome (IBS) [38].

An interesting observation regarding identified T2D metagenomics biomarkers in this study is that biomarkers associated with T2D are commonly linked to other related diseases (e.g., obesity and irritable bowel syndrome). We believe that developing classifiers for predicting disease association from metagenomic data should not be conducted in an isolated manner but instead metagenomics data from related diseases could be very helpful. Recent advances in machine learning including transfer learning [39], multi-task learning [40], and pre-training of deep learning neural network layers [41], facilitate the development of potentially better prediction models using data (labeled and/or unlabeled) from related classification tasks.

Finally, we noted that EBI metagenomics taxonomic assignment of the T2D dataset (projects IDs SRP011011 and SRP008047) could not serve as a good data representation for developing predictive models. We hope that this is not the case for other projects hosted in EMG and we plan to extend this study to include a broad range of metagenomic projects from EBI metagenomics. Nevertheless, we strongly recommend that, in the absence of a gold standard for taxonomic classification, EMG development team might have to revise their analysis pipeline to support more than one taxonomic classification method. Such an extension would be very helpful for comparing the analysis results not only over multiple projects hosted in EMG but also using different taxonomy profiling methods.

3.2 Comparative Networks Analysis of T2D Using Different Microbial Sequence Classification Methods

We built two co-occurrence networks for healthy and disease associated subjects and then analyzed the networks at global, local, and node levels. Similar to the machine learning approach, comparative network analysis is often reported using one sequence classification method. Due to the observed poor performance of the classifiers using EBI metagenomics OTUs, we constrained our comparative network analysis of gut microbiota in T2D and control samples to MetaPhlAn2 and Kraken OTU-based representations.

Table 1: Performance estimates, using 10-fold cross-validation, of different machine learning classifiers using three OTU-based representation of T2D dataset

Method	Classifier	No of features	ACC	Sn	Sp	MCC	AUC
MetaPhlAn2	NB	190	0.65	0.63	0.67	0.3	**0.74**
	LR	80	0.61	0.68	0.55	0.25	0.70
	SVML	130	0.63	0.56	0.7	0.29	0.64
	XGB	130	0.64	0.65	0.64	0.28	0.71
	RF	120	0.66	0.66	0.65	0.32	**0.74**
Kraken	NB	200	0.65	0.65	0.66	0.31	0.72
	LR	40	0.68	0.74	0.63	0.4	0.77
	SVML	60	0.7	0.71	0.68	0.44	0.70
	XGB	160	0.74	0.72	0.75	0.48	**0.79**
	RF	30	0.69	0.66	0.72	0.38	0.77
EBI	NB	60	0.57	0.55	0.59	0.14	0.62
	LR	60	0.59	0.47	0.72	0.2	0.65
	SVML	50	0.59	0.53	0.65	0.19	0.59
	XGB	50	0.59	0.58	0.6	0.19	**0.66**
	RF	90	0.59	0.56	0.62	0.19	**0.66**

3.2.1 Global topological properties of the networks. Table 3 reports several topological properties of healthy and T2D networks generated using either MetaPhlAn2 or Kraken OTU-based representations. For each OTU type, we used the log odd scores between T2D and healthy properties to quantify the change in each property in the T2D network relative to its corresponding property value in the healthy network. A log-odd score of zero indicates no change in the topological property of T2D network relative to the healthy network. A positive log-odd score indicates that this T2D property has a value larger than its corresponding value from the healthy network and vice versa for negative odd-scores. Table 3 shows that simple properties like number of nodes/edges and average number of neighbors cannot discriminate between T2D and healthy networks while degree distribution properties, network centralization, and diameter statistics are substantially different in T2D and healthy networks using either MetaPhlAn2 or Kraken representations. However, the log-odd scores of these discriminating properties, using either MetaPhlAn2 or Kraken representation, are not in agreement with each other in terms of the sign of the log-odd scores. For example, the log-odd scores of the network centralization are 0.43 and -0.26 for MetaPhlAn2 and Kraken representations, respectively. In other words, using MetaPhlAn2 OTUs, nodes in the T2D network are more close to each other than in the healthy network and hence the diameter of the healthy network is larger than the diameter of the T2D network. On the other side, using Kraken OTUs, nodes in the healthy network are closer to each other than in the T2D network and hence the diameter of the T2D network is larger than the diameter of the healthy network.

In summary, using either MetaPhlAn2 or Kraken derived OTUs, several topological properties of T2D and healthy networks suggest that gut microbial communities in T2D subjects have different compositions as well as co-occurrences and mutual exclusion relationships. To gain deeper insights into these differences, we consider comparative analysis at microbial communities (network modules) and nodes (potential biomarkers) levels.

3.2.2 Module-based analysis of networks. We applied MCODE, a Cytoscape plugin [35], to extract highly connected modules in the four networks considered in our experiments. Due to space limitation, we limit our analysis to the top module in each network. Fig. 1 shows the top module in T2D and healthy networks constructed from MetaPhlAn2 data representation. At the genus level, the top module in the healthy network involves positive and negative interactions among species from Akkermansia, Fusobacterium, Lachnospiraceae, Anaerostipes, and Clostridium. On the other hand, the top module in T2D network involves positive and negative interactions between species from only two families, Methanobacteriaceae and Fusobacteriaceae. We noted that negative correlations (red edges) are always between members of these two families which suggests antagonistic relationship between Methanobacteriaceae and Fusobacteriaceae.

Methanogens have been associated with various disease conditions including inflammatory bowel disease, colorectal cancer, anorexia or obesity [42]. Also, Fusobacteriaceae was found to be more abundant in morbidly obese patients with high insulin resistance [43].

Table 2: Top 25 ranked MetaPhlAn2 and Kraken OTUs. MetaPhlAn2 OTUs are reported the genus level and when not available the closest possible taxonomy (e.g., family or order) is reported

Rank	Top 25 MetaPhlAn2 OTUs	Top 25 Kraken OTUs
1	g--Roseburia	Roseburia intestinalis
2	g--Roseburia	Roseburia
3	g--Peptostreptococcaceae_noname	Roseburia intestinalis XB6B4
4	g--Haemophilus	Alteromonadales
5	g--Clostridium	Roseburia intestinalis M50/1
6	g--Eggerthella	Lachnospiraceae
7	g--Clostridium	Bacteroides vulgatus ATCC 8482
8	g--Peptostreptococcaceae_noname	Bacteroides vulgatus
9	g--Faecalibacterium	Faecalibacterium prausnitzii
10	f--Pasteurellaceae	Actinobacteridae
11	g--Faecalibacterium	Faecalibacterium
12	o--Bacteroidales	Butyrate producing bacterium SS3/4
13	g--Roseburia	Eubacterium rectale
14	g--Bacteroides	Unclassified Clostridiales
15	g--Veillonella	Butyrate producing bacterium SSC/2
16	g--Bacteroides	Parabacteroides distasonis
17	g--Erysipelotrichaceae_noname	Faecalibacterium prausnitzii L2/6
18	f--Lactobacillaceae	Bacteroidetes
19	o--Selenomonadales	Parabacteroides
20	o--Lactobacillales	Bifidobacterium
21	g--Erysipelotrichaceae_noname	Bacteroidetes Chlorobi group
22	g--Streptococcus	Unclassified Clostridiales miscellaneous
23	f--Bifidobacteriaceae	Bacteroidaceae
24	g--Coprobacillus	Bacteroides fragilis YCH46
25	p--Actinobacteria	Actinobacteria

Table 3: Properties of functional networks of T2D and healthy network constructed using MetaPhlAn2 and Kraken OTUs

	MetaPhlAn2			Kraken		
Network property	**T2D**	**Healthy**	**log-odd**	**T2D**	**Healthy**	**log-odd**
Nodes	514	482	0.03	303	282	0.03
Edges	1215	1038	0.07	919	940	-0.01
Density	0.009	0.009	0.00	0.02	0.024	-0.08
Centralization	0.141	0.052	0.43	0.056	0.102	-0.26
Diameter	11	15	-0.13	11	7	0.20
Clustering coefficient	0.597	0.608	-0.01	0.73	0.73	0.00
Degree distribution fitting slope	-0.439	-2.186	-0.70	-1.432	-0.786	0.26
Degree distribution fitting R2	0.236	0.445	-0.28	0.524	0.452	0.06
Avg. number of neighbors	4.728	4.307	0.04	6.066	6.667	-0.04

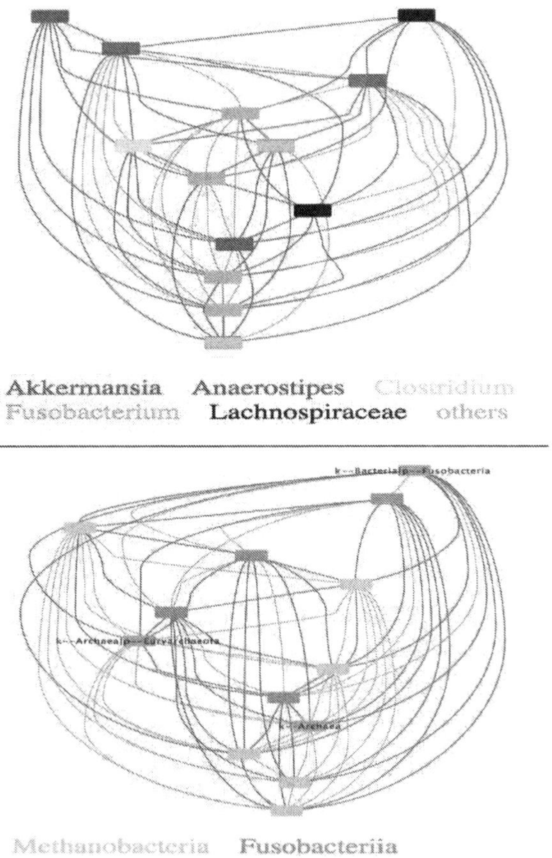

Figure 1: Top module in healthy (top) and T2D (bottom) MetaPhlAn2 based networks.

Surprisingly, our machine learning analysis does not link any member from Methanobacteriaceae and Fusobacteriaceae to T2D. This result suggests that comparative network analysis could complement the machine learning approach via detecting potential biomarkers not detected by machine learning methods due to small size of the data or the existence of hidden complex relationships between features.

Unlike MetaPhlAn2 top modules, Kraken top modules in T2D and healthy networks have only positive interactions between OTUs. The top module from healthy network involves only positive interactions between 18 different OTUs. The top module from T2D network involves only positive interactions between 14 OTUs, all of them belong to Prevotella. The second and third modules have only positive interactions between OTUs from Bifidobacterium and Bacteroidaceae, respectively. We noted that module-based comparative analysis of T2D and healthy network derived from MetaPhlAn2 and Kraken OTUs suggests differences between T2D and healthy networks at the module level. Moreover, several OTUs in the top module extracted from T2D network (e.g., Lachnospiraceae, Prevotella, and Bifidobacterium), using either MetaPhlAn2 or Kraken representation, have been recently linked with type 2 diabetes [4, 44].

3.2.3 Integrated machine learning and network analysis. Machine learning algorithms have been extensively applied to different network analysis problems including network construction [44], community detection [45], and link prediction [46]. On the other hand, how advances in network analysis can contribute to machine learning research is not well explored. A major limitation of machine learning models is the lack of human interpretability. Here, we propose biomarkers sub-networks as a tool for visualizing topological properties and interactions between biomarkers detected using black box machine learning classifiers.

Table 1 shows that RF and XGB classifiers achieve AUC of 0.77 and 0.79 using 30 and 160 Kraken OTUs, respectively. Unfortunately, the learned models are not human interpretable and must be treated as black boxes. In this experiment, we attempt to get more insights into the rule of the top 30 Kraken OTUs by mapping them into the healthy and T2D networks. First, we used Cytoscape Network Analyzer tool to map the size of the node to its degree (i.e., larger node size indicates higher node degree). Then, we mapped the top 30 OTUs on the network and generated a new network with these nodes only. This procedure produced 28 nodes clustered into 8 clusters in the healthy network and 29 nodes clustered into 7 clusters in the T2D network (See Fig. 2).

Several interesting observations can be made by comparing resultant clusters in the two networks. First, we noted that all interactions between nodes are positively correlated (green edges). Second, Bacteroides and Parabacteroides OTUs form cluster C1 in healthy network while in T2D they split into two clusters. Moreover, these OTUs tend to have higher node degrees in the healthy network. This suggests fewer interactions between Bacteroides and Parabacteroides in the gut of T2D patients. Third, we found that clusters C2 and C4 in healthy network formed from Roseburia and Faecalibacterium OTUs, respectively, are merged into one cluster via established interactions between Lachnospiraceae OTU and two Faecalibacterium OTUs. Reduction in the abundance of members of Lachnospiraceae family and faecalibacterium prausnitzii has been previously linked to T2D [4, 29].

To summarize, we introduced biomarkers sub-networks to visualize and analyze metagenomics biomarkers. Biomarkers sub-networks define interactions between biomarkers only (other OTUs are not considered) while node size and/or color encoded node properties (i.e., node degree or centrality) are determined over entire network. By visually inspecting biomarkers sub-networks derived from healthy and T2D networks, we identified interesting positive correlations between members of Lachnospiraceae family and faecalibacterium prausnitzii in T2D patients.

4 CONCLUSIONS

We explored how different taxonomy profiling methods could affect the outcome of predictive and network analysis studies applied to the human gut microbiota of T2D.

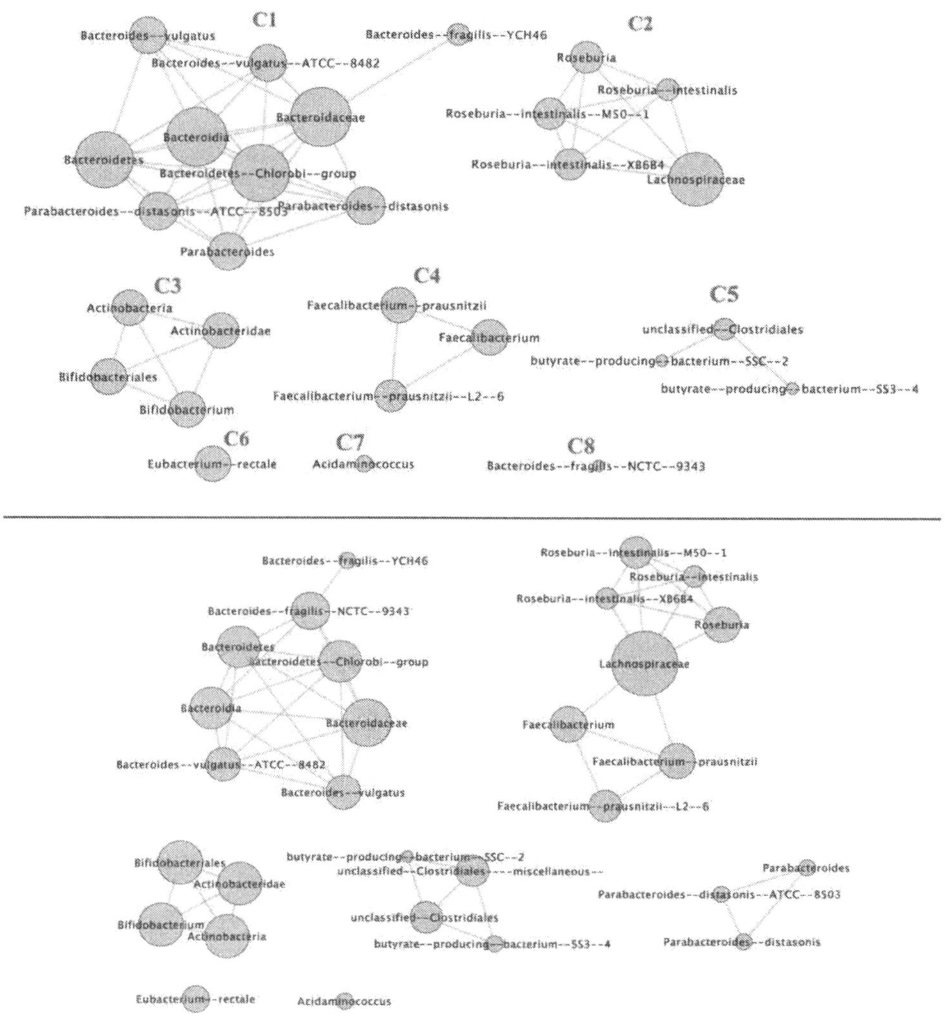

Figure 2: Biomarkers sub-networks from healthy (top) and T2D (bottom) Kraken based networks.

For predictive analysis studies, our results suggest that Kraken profiles yield best performing classifiers with substantially small number of features and hence identify a short list of discriminative features (only 30 potential biomarkers). For comparative network analysis, we found that network models constructed using either MetaPhlAn2 or Kraken have different global and local topological properties between healthy and T2D networks. Finally, we used the constructed network models as a powerful visualization tool to examine network properties (at node level) of machine learning identified biomarkers and to uncover co-presence and mutual exclusion interactions between these biomarkers under different conditions. Our ongoing work aims at: extending the study to include metagenomic data associated with other phenotypes; experimenting with more taxonomy profiling tools (e.g., [12-14]); developing software tools and workflows [47] for integrative machine learning and comparative network analysis of metagenomic data.

ACKNOWLEDGMENTS

This work has been supported in part by the Microbiome Center and the Center for Big Data Analytics and Discovery Informatics at the Pennsylvania State University.

REFERENCES

[1] C. A. Lozupone, J. I. Stombaugh, J. I. Gordon, J. K. Jansson, and R. Knight, "Diversity, stability and resilience of the human gut microbiota," *Nature*, vol. 489, no. 7415, pp. 220-230, 2012.

[2] J. C. Clemente, L. K. Ursell, L. W. Parfrey, and R. Knight, "The impact of the gut microbiota on human health: an integrative view," *Cell*, vol. 148, no. 6, pp. 1258-1270, 2012.

[3] R. E. Ley, P. J. Turnbaugh, S. Klein, and J. I. Gordon, "Microbial ecology: human gut microbes associated with obesity," *Nature*, vol. 444, no. 7122, pp. 1022, 2006.

[4] J. Qin, Y. Li, Z. Cai, S. Li, J. Zhu, F. Zhang, S. Liang, W. Zhang, Y. Guan, and D. Shen, "A metagenome-wide association study of gut microbiota in type 2 diabetes," *Nature*, vol. 490, no. 7418, pp. 55-60, 2012.

[5] W. W. Tang, and S. L. Hazen, "The contributory role of gut microbiota in cardiovascular disease," *The Journal of clinical investigation*, vol. 124, no. 10, pp. 4204-4211, 2014.

[6] K. P. Lemon, G. C. Armitage, D. A. Relman, and M. A. Fischbach, "Microbiota-targeted therapies: an ecological perspective," *Science translational medicine*, vol. 4, no. 137, pp. 137rv5-137rv5, 2012.

[7] R. G. Beiko, "Microbial malaise: how can we classify the microbiome?," *Trends in microbiology*, vol. 23, no. 11, pp. 671-679, 2015.

[8] W. Chen, C. K. Zhang, Y. Cheng, S. Zhang, and H. Zhao, "A comparison of methods for clustering 16S rRNA sequences into OTUs," *PloS one*, vol. 8, no. 8, pp. e70837, 2013.

[9] D. E. Wood, and S. L. Salzberg, "Kraken: ultrafast metagenomic sequence classification using exact alignments," *Genome biology*, vol. 15, no. 3, pp. R46, 2014.

[10] J. Ning, and R. G. Beiko, "Phylogenetic approaches to microbial community classification," *Microbiome*, vol. 3, no. 1, pp. 47, 2015.

[11] R. C. Edgar, "Search and clustering orders of magnitude faster than BLAST," *Bioinformatics*, vol. 26, no. 19, pp. 2460-2461, 2010.

[12] M. Ghodsi, B. Liu, and M. Pop, "DNACLUST: accurate and efficient clustering of phylogenetic marker genes," *BMC bioinformatics*, vol. 12, no. 1, pp. 271, 2011.

[13] D. Albanese, P. Fontana, C. De Filippo, D. Cavalieri, and C. Donati, "MICCA: a complete and accurate software for taxonomic profiling of metagenomic data," *Scientific reports*, vol. 5, pp. 9743, 2015.

[14] J. Lu, F. P. Breitwieser, P. Thielen, and S. L. Salzberg, "Bracken: Estimating species abundance in metagenomics data," *PeerJ Computer Science*, vol. 3, pp. e104, 2017.

[15] D. T. Truong, E. A. Franzosa, T. L. Tickle, M. Scholz, G. Weingart, E. Pasolli, A. Tett, C. Huttenhower, and N. Segata, "MetaPhlAn2 for enhanced metagenomic taxonomic profiling," *Nature methods*, vol. 12, no. 10, pp. 902-903, 2015.

[16] S. Hunter, M. Corbett, H. Denise, M. Fraser, A. Gonzalez-Beltran, C. Hunter, P. Jones, R. Leinonen, C. McAnulla, and E. Maguire, "EBI metagenomics—a new resource for the analysis and archiving of metagenomic data," *Nucleic acids research*, vol. 42, no. D1, pp. D600-D606, 2014.

[17] N. LaPierre, and H. Rangwala, "Predicting Clinical Phenotype Using OTU-Based Metagenome Representation." pp. 156-163.

[18] R. Leinonen, R. Akhtar, E. Birney, L. Bower, A. Cerdeno-Tárraga, Y. Cheng, I. Cleland, N. Faruque, N. Goodgame, and R. Gibson, "The European nucleotide archive," *Nucleic acids research*, pp. gkq967, 2010.

[19] T. Z. DeSantis, P. Hugenholtz, N. Larsen, M. Rojas, E. L. Brodie, K. Keller, T. Huber, D. Dalevi, P. Hu, and G. L. Andersen, "Greengenes, a chimera-checked 16S rRNA gene database and workbench compatible with ARB," *Applied and environmental microbiology*, vol. 72, no. 7, pp. 5069-5072, 2006.

[20] J. G. Caporaso, J. Kuczynski, J. Stombaugh, K. Bittinger, F. D. Bushman, E. K. Costello, N. Fierer, A. G. Peña, J. K. Goodrich, and J. I. Gordon, "QIIME allows analysis of high-throughput community sequencing data," *Nature methods*, vol. 7, no. 5, pp. 335-336, 2010.

[21] R. S. Michalski, J. G. Carbonell, and T. M. Mitchell, *Machine learning: An artificial intelligence approach*: Springer Science & Business Media, 2013.

[22] S. Le Cessie, and J. C. Van Houwelingen, "Ridge estimators in logistic regression," *Applied statistics*, pp. 191-201, 1992.

[23] V. Vapnik, *The nature of statistical learning theory*: Springer Science & Business Media, 2013.

[24] T. Chen, and C. Guestrin, "Xgboost: A scalable tree boosting system." pp. 785-794.

[25] L. Breiman, "Random forests," *Machine learning*, vol. 45, no. 1, pp. 5-32, 2001.

[26] P. Baldi, S. Brunak, Y. Chauvin, C. A. Andersen, and H. Nielsen, "Assessing the accuracy of prediction algorithms for classification: an overview," *Bioinformatics*, vol. 16, no. 5, pp. 412-424, 2000.

[27] Z. Liu, W. Hsiao, B. L. Cantarel, E. F. Drábek, and C. Fraser-Liggett, "Sparse distance-based learning for simultaneous multiclass classification and feature selection of metagenomic data," *Bioinformatics*, vol. 27, no. 23, pp. 3242-3249, 2011.

[28] D. Arndt, J. Xia, Y. Liu, Y. Zhou, A. C. Guo, J. A. Cruz, I. Sinelnikov, K. Budwill, C. L. Nesbø, and D. S. Wishart, "METAGENassist: a comprehensive web server for comparative metagenomics," *Nucleic acids research*, pp. gks497, 2012.

[29] E. Pasolli, D. T. Truong, F. Malik, L. Waldron, and N. Segata, "Machine learning meta-analysis of large metagenomic datasets: tools and biological insights," *PLoS Comput Biol*, vol. 12, no. 7, pp. e1004977, 2016.

[30] K. Faust, J. F. Sathirapongsasuti, J. Izard, N. Segata, D. Gevers, J. Raes, and C. Huttenhower, "Microbial co-occurrence relationships in the human microbiome," *PLoS Comput Biol*, vol. 8, no. 7, pp. e1002606, 2012.

[31] K. Faust, G. Lima-Mendez, J.-S. Lerat, J. F. Sathirapongsasuti, R. Knight, C. Huttenhower, T. Lenaerts, and J. Raes, "Cross-biome comparison of microbial association networks," *Frontiers in microbiology*, vol. 6, pp. 1200, 2015.

[32] M. B. Brown, "400: A method for combining non-independent, one-sided tests of significance," *Biometrics*, pp. 987-992, 1975.

[33] Y. Hochberg, and Y. Benjamini, "More powerful procedures for multiple significance testing," *Statistics in medicine*, vol. 9, no. 7, pp. 811-818, 1990.

[34] P. Shannon, A. Markiel, O. Ozier, N. S. Baliga, J. T. Wang, D. Ramage, N. Amin, B. Schwikowski, and T. Ideker, "Cytoscape: a software environment for integrated models of biomolecular interaction networks," *Genome research*, vol. 13, no. 11, pp. 2498-2504, 2003.

[35] G. D. Bader, and C. W. Hogue, "An automated method for finding molecular complexes in large protein interaction networks," *BMC bioinformatics*, vol. 4, no. 1, pp. 2, 2003.

[36] N. Larsen, F. K. Vogensen, F. W. van den Berg, D. S. Nielsen, A. S. Andreasen, B. K. Pedersen, W. A. Al-Soud, S. J. Sørensen, L. H. Hansen, and M. Jakobsen, "Gut microbiota in human adults with type 2 diabetes differs from non-diabetic adults," *PloS one*, vol. 5, no. 2, pp. e9085, 2010.

[37] H. Tilg, and A. R. Moschen, "Microbiota and diabetes: an evolving relationship," *Gut*, vol. 63, no. 9, pp. 1513-1521, 2014.

[38] I. Rangel, J. Sundin, S. Fuentes, D. Repsilber, W. Vos, and R. J. Brummer, "The relationship between faecal associated and mucosal associated microbiota in irritable bowel syndrome patients and healthy subjects," *Alimentary pharmacology & therapeutics*, vol. 42, no. 10, pp. 1211-1221, 2015.

[39] S. J. Pan, and Q. Yang, "A survey on transfer learning," *IEEE Transactions on knowledge and data engineering*, vol. 22, no. 10, pp. 1345-1359, 2010.

[40] T. Evgeniou, and M. Pontil, "Regularized multi--task learning." pp. 109-117.

[41] D. Erhan, Y. Bengio, A. Courville, P.-A. Manzagol, P. Vincent, and S. Bengio, "Why does unsupervised pre-training help deep learning?," *Journal of Machine Learning Research*, vol. 11, no. Feb, pp. 625-660, 2010.

[42] C. Bang, K. Weidenbach, T. Gutsmann, H. Heine, and R. A. Schmitz, "The intestinal archaea Methanosphaera stadtmanae and Methanobrevibacter smithii activate human dendritic cells," *PLoS One*, vol. 9, no. 6, pp. e99411, 2014.

[43] I. Moreno-Indias, L. Sánchez-Alcoholado, E. García-Fuentes, F. Cardona, M. I. Queipo-Ortuño, and F. J. Tinahones, "Insulin resistance is associated with specific gut microbiota in appendix samples from morbidly obese patients," *American Journal of Translational Research*, vol. 8, no. 12, pp. 5672, 2016.

[44] L. Li, Z. Wang, P. He, S. Ma, J. Du, and R. Jiang, "Construction and Analysis of Functional Networks in the Gut Microbiome of Type 2 Diabetes Patients," *Genomics, Proteomics & Bioinformatics*, vol. 14, no. 5, pp. 314-324, 2016.

[45] S. Fortunato, "Community detection in graphs," *Physics reports*, vol. 486, no. 3, pp. 75-174, 2010.

[46] M. Al Hasan, V. Chaoji, S. Salem, and M. Zaki, "Link prediction using supervised learning."

[47] J. Goecks, A. Nekrutenko, and J. Taylor, "Galaxy: a comprehensive approach for supporting accessible, reproducible, and transparent computational research in the life sciences," *Genome biology*, vol. 11, no. 8, pp. R86, 2010.

Bayesian Collective Markov Random Fields for Subcellular Localization Prediction of Human Proteins

Lu Zhu*
Bielefeld University
Bio-/Medical Informatics Department
International Research
Training Group 1906 (DiDy)
Bielefeld, NRW 33611, Germany
lzhu@techfak.uni-bielefeld.de

Martin Ester
Simon Fraser University
School of computing science
Burnaby, BC V5A 1S6, Canada
ester@cs.sfu.ca

ABSTRACT

Advanced biotechnology makes it possible to access a multitude of heterogeneous proteomic, interactomic, genomic, and functional annotation data. One challenge in computational biology is to integrate these data to enable automated prediction of the Subcellular Localizations (SCL) of human proteins. For proteins that have multiple biological roles, their correct *in silico* assignment to different SCL can be considered as an imbalanced multi-label classification problem. In this study, we developed a Bayesian Collective Markov Random Fields (BCMRFs) model for multi-SCL prediction of human proteins. Given a set of unknown proteins and their corresponding protein-protein interaction (PPI) network, the SCLs of each protein can be inferred by the SCLs of its interacting partners. To do so, we integrate PPIs, the adjacency of SCLs and protein features, and perform transductive learning on the re-balanced dataset. Our experimental results show that the spatial adjacency of the SCLs improves multi-SCL prediction, especially for the SCLs with few annotated instances. Our approach outperforms the state-of-art PPI-based and feature-based multi-SCL prediction method for human proteins.

KEYWORDS

Human protein subcellular localization; markov random field; transductive learning; imbalanced multi-label classification.

1 INTRODUCTION

Detailed molecular knowledge of the human proteome has become an important asset in the understanding of human biology and disease. Rapid advances in biotechnology have made available a variety of high-throughput experimentally obtained proteomics and interactomics datasets [14, 22], and knowledge of SubCellular Localization (SCL) of proteins can provide important insights for understanding their functions in cells and the mechanism of disease [12]. Owing to the annotation efforts of model organism databases, high-quality subcellular localization information for human proteins can be obtained from various curated sources. However, manually annotating a protein, especially determining the subcellular localization using the enormous data from heterogeneous source, is always a challenging and low-throughput task.A variety of computational methods have been developed for predicting the SCL of proteins for various organisms [3, 8] in the past decade. Nevertheless, there are relatively few efficient specific prediction tools for human proteins in the face of rapidly increasing numbers of newly identified proteins.

*Corresponding author

Permission to make digital or hard copies of all or part of this work for personal or classroom use is granted without fee provided that copies are not made or distributed for profit or commercial advantage and that copies bear this notice and the full citation on the first page. Copyrights for components of this work owned by others than ACM must be honored. Abstracting with credit is permitted. To copy otherwise, or republish, to post on servers or to redistribute to lists, requires prior specific permission and/or a fee. Request permissions from permissions@acm.org.
ACM-BCB'17, August 20–23, 2017, Boston, MA, USA.
© 2017 ACM. ISBN 978-1-4503-4722-8/17/08...$15.00
DOI: http://dx.doi.org/10.1145/3107411.3107412

Protein features, especially the sequence-based features, are always the essential part in various protein SCL predictors [4, 7, 10]. To carry out different functions, one protein can be located in different SubCellular Compartments (SCCs) simultaneously or at different times during different biological processes, e.g. protein trafficking. Sequence-based prediction methods have been successfully applied to genome-wide large-scale protein annotations and analysis. However it is hard to apply these methods to detect the translocation of proteins due to the fact that the primary sequences of the translocated protein are always about the same. The biological functions of proteins are carried out by interacting with other proteins. To interact, proteins (or any other molecules) must necessarily share a common SCC, or an interface between physically adjacent SCCs, transiently or conditionally. The SCL of a protein can therefore be inferred from the SCL of its interacting partners. Hence biological network information can complement feature-based approaches to SCL prediction.

Several methods have been developed which take advantage of Protein-Protein Interaction (PPI) networks to predict the SCL of proteins for different orgnisms using data integration from multiple data sources [13, 17, 21]. However, these approaches mainly focus on the co-localization (in the same SCL) of interacting proteins. The importance of the spatial adjacency among SCCs was underestimated. It was not investigated whether a protein SCL (e.g. plasma membrane) can be also inferred by its interacting partners in the adjacent SCLs (e.g. Extracellular and Cytoplasm). Secondly, for the proteins whose interacting partners are poorly annotated, the information of the adjacent SCLs can be used as the major prediction resource. In this study, we investigated whether the spatial adjacency among SCLs can improve PPI-based SCL prediction.

Conventional machine-learning approaches, such as supervised learning, predict protein SCLs by extracting information only from existing annotation. However, the number of unreviewed proteins increases at a remarkably faster rate than that of experimentally-annotated ones. It was shown that transductive leaning approaches are able to take advantage of the large number of available unknown data to improve the accuracy of classification [18, 23]. On the other hand, proteins are often annotated with multiple SCLs. The Multi-Labeled Datasets (MLDs) of protein SCLs are typically heavily imbalanced. The learning from an imbalanced multi-label classification is a well-known challenge in classification [6].

A Markov Random Field (MRF) is a graphical model of a joint probability distribution. Many problems in computer vision such as image segmentation, image restoration and systems biology such as identification of differentially expressed genes [24], protein function prediction [16] involve the solution of a probability distribution defined by a discrete MRF. In this paper, we propose a Bayesian Collective MRFs (BCMRFs) to predict the multi-SCLs of human proteins considering PPI network features, the proteins features, the spatial adjacency of SCCs and the imbalance of the dataset. The key contributions are summarized as follows:

(1) We introduce weighted MRFs based on the PPI network with label propagation to predict the SCL of the proteins in the network.
(2) We propose Collective MRFs, one MRF per SCL, which are trained collectively to exploit the spatial adjacency among SCLs.
(3) We show the transductive learning method is more efficient than supervised learning method.
(4) We discuss the drawbacks of the imbalance of SCL datasets for protein SCL prediction and show that it can be improved by balancing the minor class with the major class.
(5) We performed experiments evaluating the performance on a human protein SCL benchmark set. Our method outperforms the state-of-the-art methods including the PPI-based approache DC-kNN [17] and the feature-based approach Hum-mPLoc 3.0 [26].

The rest of the paper is organized as follows: In section 2 we introduce our MRFs and the corresponding learning procedure. section 3 details the experiment protocol and section 4 shows the experimental results. At last, we conclude our work along with the discussion of directions of future work.

2 THE BAYESIAN COLLECTIVE MRF MODEL

In this section, we firstly give basic definitions and notations of MRF, and the rational of using MRFs for protein SCL prediction. Then, we introduce our Bayesian Collective Markov Random Fields (BCMRFs) for predicting the multi-SCLs of human proteins. The BCMRFs are formed by interatively collecting and optimizing the labels from multiple binary Bayesian MRFs.

2.1 Markov Random Field (MRF) on protein SCL prediction

Markov Random Field is a graphical model of a joint probability distribution. It consists of an undirected graph $G = (X, E)$ in which the nodes X represent random variables $\mathbf{X} = X_1, X_2, ;X_n$, where each variable $X_i \in \mathbf{X}$ takes a value from the label set $\mathcal{L} = l_1, l_2, \ldots, l_k$. A labeling $\mathbf{x}$ refers to any possible assignment of labels to the random variables and takes values from the set $\mathcal{L}^n$.

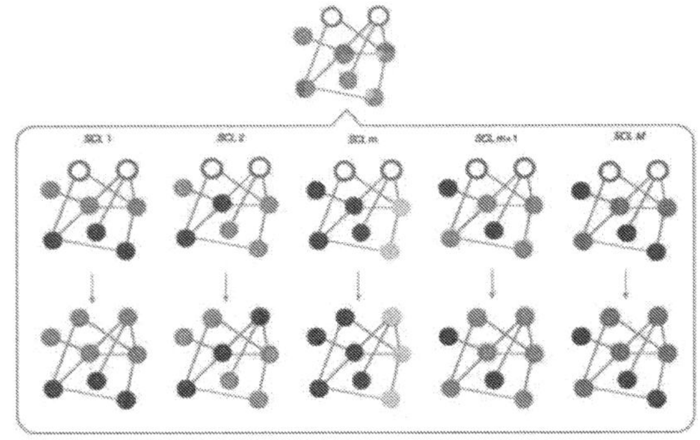

Figure 1: Multiple binary MRFs. The graph with multi-colored nodes on the top represents the general PPI network. Each node on the graph represents a protein associated with in total M SCL annotation terms. This network can be derived to M PPI networks for each single SCL term. The nodes are colored or in grey which represent 1 and 0 respectively if the SCL annotation of the protein is available for any of the M SCL terms. Otherwise, the node is not colored. And these nodes (proteins) are in need to be assigned with SCLs.

The posterior distribution $Pr(\mathbf{x}|\mathbf{D})$ over the labellings of the random field is a *Gibbs* distribution if it can be written in the form:

$$Pr(\mathbf{x}|\mathbf{D}) = \frac{1}{Z}\exp(-\sum_{c\in C}\phi_c(\mathbf{x}_c)) \quad (1)$$

where Z is a normalizing constant known as the partition function, and C is the set of all cliques. The term $\psi_c(\mathbf{x}_c)$ is known as the potential function of the clique c where $\mathbf{x}_c = x_i, i \in c$.

The corresponding Gibbs energy function E: $\mathcal{L}^n \longrightarrow \mathbb{R}$ maps any labelling $\mathbf{x} \in \mathcal{L}^n$to a real number $E(\mathbf{x})$ called its energy. Energy function are the negative logarithm of the posterior probability distribution of the labeling. Maximizing the posterior probability equals to minimizing the energy function and leads to the MLE or MAP solution, which is defined as $\mathbf{x} = argmin_{x\in L}E(\mathbf{x})$.

Energy functions can be decomposed into sum over unary(ϕ_i) and pairwise(ϕ_{ij}) potentials as:

$$E(\mathbf{x}) = \sum_{i\in v}\phi_i(x_i) + \sum_{(i,j)\in\varepsilon}\phi_{ij}(x_i, x_j) \quad (2)$$

where v is the set of all random variables and ε is the set of all pairs of interacting variables. However, the potential functions could be with more interacting variables[15].

As we described in Section 1, the SCLs of a protein can be inferred by the SCLs of its physically interacting proteins. A physical PPI network $G = (P, I)$ with N proteins, $N = |P|$, that are assigned in M different SCLs in total fullfills the definition and properties of a MRF. It's reasonable to apply MFRs on PPI network to predict the SCL(s) of a set of proteins in the network. Moreover, a PPI network in which each protein is labeled by single or multi SCLs can be considered as multi-label MRFs. Inspired by the statistical power of those MRF models, we applied MRFs to PPI network for solving protein SCL prediction problem.

Using the binary reference approach [9], for the SCL noted as $l_m, 1 \leq m \leq M$, the network is encoded in an N-dimensional vector $\mathbf{x} = \{x_1, \ldots, x_N\}$, where $x_i = 1$ if the protein $p_i, 1 \leq i \leq |P|$ is assigned with l_m, else $x_i = 0$. The multi-label classification problem is thus reduced to multiple binary classification problems (Figure 1). For each SCL, we build corresponding binary MRFs to predict SCL labeling of unknown proteins by maximizing the posterior probability distribution of the SCL labeling of proteins. The following elements are used in our MRFs model: (1) prior probability of any protein being located in l_m, (2) the number of interacting neighbors being located in l_m, (3) the number of interacting neighbors being located in the adjacent SCLs of l_m, and (4) the sequence-based features of protein.

Meanwhile, the quality of PPI data and the connectivity of PPI network are crucial for inferring the SCL of a protein by its interacting neighbors. However the confidence of PPIs varies from one to another depending on the method, and the size of experiment etc.[5]. To balance of having a high quality of PPI network and reduce the risk of losing valuable information by removing too many edges, we use the confidence scores of the PPIs to weight our MRFs. The detailed method is described in the following sections.

2.2 The weighted markov random field model

By definition, the posterior distribution $Pr(\mathbf{x})$ over the SCL labelings of the MRF is a *Gibbs* distribution which can be written in the form:

$$Pr(\mathbf{x}) = \frac{1}{Z}\exp(-E(\mathbf{x})) \tag{3}$$

where Z is a normalizing constant known as the partition function. $E(\mathbf{x})$ is the energy function of the MRFs which is defined as follows:

$$\begin{aligned} E(\mathbf{x}) = -(\sum_{i \in \mathcal{V}} \phi_i^S(x_i) + \sum_{i \in \mathcal{V}} \phi_i^F(x_i, F_i) + \sum_{i,j \in \varepsilon} \omega_{i,j}\phi_{ij}^P(x_i, x_j) \\ + \sum_{i,j \in \varepsilon} \omega_{i,j}\phi_{ij}^A(x_i, x_j, A_{ij})) \end{aligned} \tag{4}$$

with the unary potential

$$\phi_i^S = \begin{cases} 0 & x_i = 0 \\ \alpha & x_i = 1 \end{cases} \tag{5}$$

where α is the probability of a protein located in l_m. $\phi_i^F(x_i, F_i)$ is feature-based potential. F_i is a vector that includes the features for protein i. Conditional probability of a protein p_i being located in l_m given its features $Pr(x_i = 1|F_i)$.

$$\phi_i^F(x_i, F_i) = \begin{cases} 0 & x_i = 0 \\ \eta Pr(x_i = 1|F_i) & x_i = 1 \end{cases} \tag{6}$$

with

$$Pr(x_i = 1|F_i) = Pr(x_i = 1)\prod_{f=1}^{F} Pr(F_i^f | x_i = 1) \tag{7}$$

We includes thirty features which are generated from previous widely used sequence-based protein SCL predictor YLoc[4] into our model. These features include various types from simple amino acid composition to annotation information.Certain features are general such as protein size, number of small residues etc., while others specifically describing one certain SCL only. η is an unknown parameter associate to the ensemble of the 30 features F_i for protein i. The class priors and the feature probability distributions are estimated using the entropy-based supervised discretization of the training data. The final probabilities are obtained by normalizing the posterior such that the sum of all posterior is one. η together with other unknown parameters are estimated during parameters learning process.

ϕ^P is the pairwise potential of two proteins locating in l_m.

$$\phi_{ij}^P(x_i, x_j) = \begin{cases} 0 & (i,j) \notin \varepsilon \\ 0 & (i,j) \in \varepsilon \;\&\; x_i = x_j = 0 \\ \beta^{11} & (i,j) \in \varepsilon \;\&\; x_i = x_j = 1 \\ \beta^{10} & (i,j) \in \varepsilon \;\&\; x_i = 1 - x_j \end{cases} \tag{8}$$

where $\omega_{i,j}$ is a constant parameter , the confidential score of the PPI between P_i and P_j. $\phi_{ij}^A(x_i, x_j, A_{ij})$ is the potential which depends on if the protein p_i interacts with the proteins locating in the adjacent SCLs of l_m,

$$\phi_{ij}^A(x_i, x_j, A_{ij}) = \begin{cases} 0 & i,j \notin \varepsilon \\ \sum_{h=1}^{H} \mu_h A_{ij}^h & (i,j) \in \varepsilon \;\&\; x_i = 1 \end{cases} \tag{9}$$

where H is the total number of adjacent SCLs of SCL l_m. Given a set of H adjacent SCLs of SCL l_m, for each protein p_i which has N_{ne} of neighbors, we construct an $N_{ne} \times H$ binary matrix A, where the element A_{ij}^h is equal to 1 if protein p_i has an interacting neighbor p_j located in the adjacent SCL l_h and 0 otherwise. μ_h is an unknown parameter for the adjacent SCL l_h. The parameters $\alpha, \eta, \beta^{11}, \beta^{10}$, and μ are estimated during optimization.

2.3 Gibbs sampler and likelihood estimation

Energy functions are the negative logarithm of the posterior probability distribution of the SCL labeling. Maximizing the posterior probability equals to minimizing the energy function, which is defined as $\mathbf{x} = argmin_{x \in L}E(\mathbf{x})$. In this study we apply the approximation method Maximum pseudo-likelihood estimation(MPLE) to solve the maximization problem [1, 16]. Since the SCL datasets are usually highly imblanced, the posterior $Pr_\theta(x_i|\mathbf{x}_{-i})$ will tend to be overwhelmed by the majority classes (in this case negative examples in individual binary classifier). In order to deal with this problem, an imbalance coefficientis used to re-balance the influence on the joint likelihood by enhancing the minority classes [11]. Thus the re-balanced pseudo-likelihood function (PLF) can be written as

$$PLF(\mathbf{x}) = \prod_{i=1}^{N}(Pr(x_i|\mathbf{x}_{-i}))^{c_i^m} \tag{10}$$

where c_i is the imbalance coefficient

$$c_i^m = \begin{cases} \frac{n^-}{n^+} & x_i = 1 \\ 1 & x_i = 0 \end{cases} \tag{11}$$

where n^+ and n^- denote the numbers of positive samples and negative samples for the SCL l_m, respectively.

2.4 Collective MRFs

In our MRFs, each variable x_i in vector $\mathbf{x} = \{x_1, \ldots, x_N\}$, represents whether a protein being located to l_m or not. For protein p_i, it is possible that its neighbors located in adjacent SCLs are also unknown. To respect the property of MRF, we need to initialize the

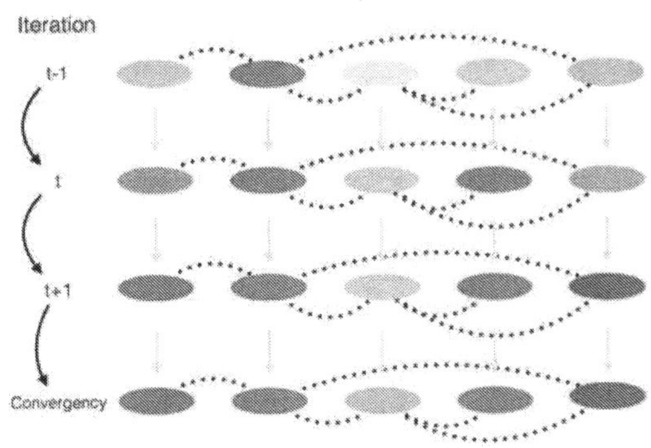

Figure 2: Collective MRFs. Each colored eclipse represents a MRF for one SCL term. The different shades of color represent the PLF value. The deeper the color is, the higher the PLF value calculated from this MRF is. The dotted line between eclipses represents the spatial relationship of SCLs.

labels of unknown proteins. Instead of using random labelings, we initialize in a more efficient way by the labeling results from the MRFs model without considering the adjacent SCLs. The results from the previous MRFs $MRF - l_m^t$ are collected and used in the next MRFs, such as $MRF - l_{m+1}^t, \ldots, MRF - l_M^t$. This process is repeated iteratively until the convergence of the pseudo-likelihood Equation 10. We name these MRFs as collective MRFs (see Figure 2 and algorithm 1).

Algorithm 1: Collective MRFs

Input: M partial labeled network for the M SCL terms
Output: M fully assigned network for the M SCL terms
for *each SCL terms* **do**
  Initialize the x_i values of unknown proteins using MRF model without adjacent SCLs potential ϕ^A (Equation 9).
end
while *not converge* **do**
  for *each SCL terms* **do**
    Optimize the $PLF^t(\mathbf{x})$.
    Calculate acceptance probability r comparing with the $PLF^{t-1}(\mathbf{x})$.
    if $r > r^*_{unif}$ **then**
      Update the labeling of $\mathbf{x}$ according to $PLF^t(\mathbf{x})$.
    end
  end
end

*: r_{unif} is a random variable follows uniform distribution.

3 EXPERIMENTAL SETUP

3.1 Dataset

A recently published high-quality human protein SCL benchmark set from the subcellular localization database Compartments [2] was used to evaluate the performance of our method. In total 9 SCLs including Cytosol, Endoplasmic Reticulum, Lysosome, Extracellular space, Golgi apparatus, Mitochondrion, Nucleus, Peroxisome and Plasma membrane are used for evaluation. The dataset was created from UniprotKB/Swiss-prot and Human Protein Atlas (HPA).

The corresponding protein sequences for generating the features from YLoc were retrieved from UniprotKB/Swiss-prot (version 2016.08). The PPI data were retrieved from the interactom browser - Mentha [5] (version 2016.09). It limits itself to direct physical PPIs curated by members of the International Molecular Exchange consortium (IMEx) [19]. Each PPI is associated with a reliability score which takes the evidienes such as experimental method, size of experiments and relevant literature into account [5]. In Figure 4 we notice a dramatic reduction of PPI size with a cutoff of reliability score 0.25. We consider that with this cutoff value, we can remove most of the low quality PPIs in the network. For the remaining PPIs, we use the reliability scores to weighted our MFRs. In the filtered connected PPI network, 5496 proteins are SCL-known while 1299 protein have no SCL annotation available. Figure 3 further shows the distribution of the SCLs of our human proteins data set. As can be seen, of the 5496 proteins, 4367 are single-SCL located proteins, 1129 have from 2 to 7 SCL annotations. As shown in the pie chart, the majority of single-SCL proteins locate in the nucleus which is consistent with the distribution of the overall proteins. For the proteins locate in 2 or more SCLs, nucleus shows less and less portion in the distribution. Therefore, the single-SCL protein plays more significant roles in shaping the overall distribution of the data set. Nevertheless, the multi-SCLs proteins which takes big percentage of the population can not be ignored.

3.2 Evaluation

To evaluate the prediction performance of our method, we perform 6 fold cross validation. For 1000 out of 5496 proteins, we mask their SCL labels, and treat them as unknown protein. Hence, 2299 proteins in the network are unlabeled. And the predicted label of these masked protein are used for performance evaluation. The dataset stratification was done by using R package "utiml" [20].
The traditional performance measures are difficult to apply for multiple SCL prediction. To better reflect the multi-label capabilities of classifiers, we use the popular multi-label measures including Precision (PRC), Recall (RCL), F1-score (F1), Average Precision (AP) and Hamming Loss (HL) [20]. Except HL, for all the rest of performance measures, the higher the measures, the better the prediction performance. To keep the consistency, we show the 1-HL instead of HL for the evaluation.

3.3 Comparison partners

In our experiments, in order to investigate the effects of different potentials described in section section 2, we build 4 versions of MRFs which include different combinations of potentials, such as MRFs with PPI only (M1) ,with PPI and SCL spatial adjacency (M2), with PPI and protein features (M3), and the MRFs with all three defined as Equation 4 (M4).

Moreover, we compared our MRFs with state-of-art SCL prediction methods, including:

- DC-kNN proposed by [17] provides the best SCLs predicting result for human proteins based on PPI. In their study, they reported the SCLs for 4366 human proteins with no

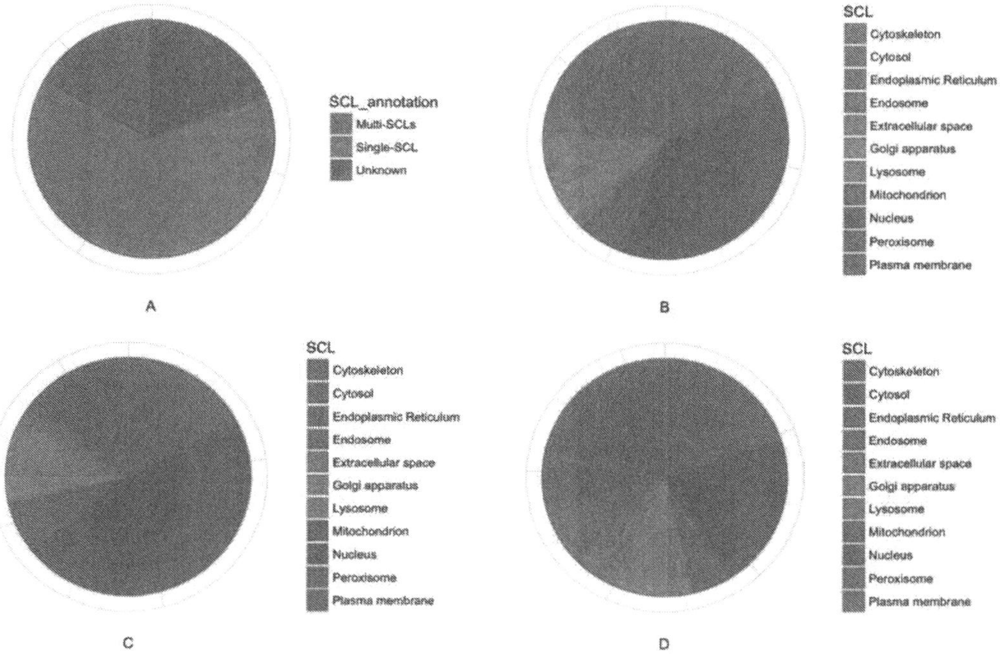

Figure 3: Information of our human protein data set. A. SCL annotation of proteins; B. Overall distribution of protein in SCL classes; C. Distribution of single-SCL protein; D. Distribution of multi-SCLs proteins.

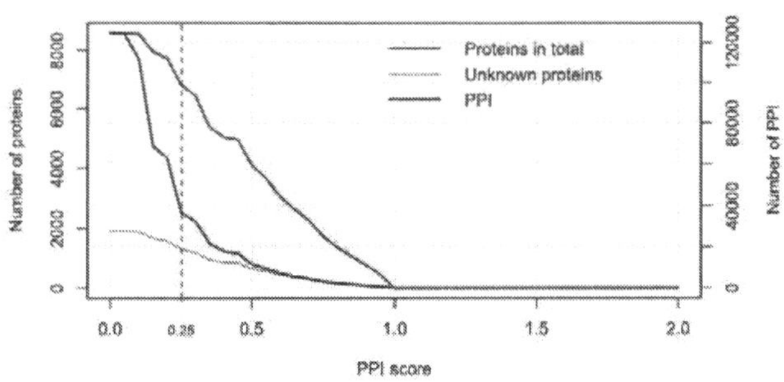

Figure 4: Protein-protein interactions of test dataset controlled by the confidential scores.

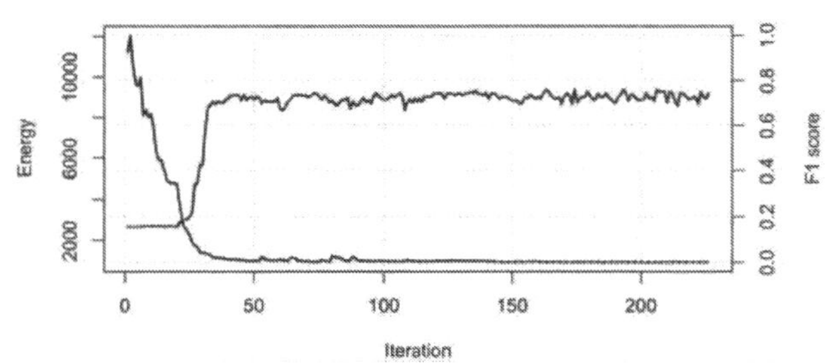

Figure 5: Relationship between the likelihood and prediction performance.

SCL previously known at the time in 2008 predicted by their method. From then to 2016, 1704 of these proteins has been reported in various SCLs. We collect the SCL annotations following the same criteria as their benchmark [17].

- Hum-mPLoc 3.0 is a most recent protein feature-based SCL predictor for human proteins [26]. The predicted SCLs of 5390 human proteins from their database are used for the comparison.

4 EXPERIMENTAL RESULTS

4.1 Likelihood and prediction performance

In our method, we minimize the energy function to correctly predict the SCL label of proteins. In other words, the higher the calculated conditional probability of a protein given its interacting neighbors for a certain SCL l_m, $1 \leq m \leq M$, the more confident that this protein locates in l_m, which infers that the overall prediction performance achieves for l_m should be positively correlated with the data likelihood. Figure 5 shows that the lower the energy (the negative logarithm of the likelihood) is, the higher the F1 score is which confirms the concept.

4.2 Effects of different potentials

To investigate the effect of the potential described for the prediction, we compare the performances including of the four versions of MRFs M1, M2, M3, M4.

4.2.1 Single-SCL prediction. We firstly compare the performance of the 4 models for each SCL class individually. **M2 VS M1** : Fig 6 shows that the spatial SCL adjacency relation of interacting proteins can improve the prediction for the majority of the SCL classes, expect Lysosome and Peroxisome. There are even the decrements of prediction performance. Firstly, these two SCL classes are highly imbalanced with few positive labels (see Figure 9). Moreover, we notice that the prediction on the SCL Cytosol is quite poor. Therefore, the MRFs of Lysosome and Peroxisome can not gain the correct information from their only spatial adjacent SCL Cytosol to increase their prediction performance. In order to put the spatial adjacency to good use, it is necessary to firstly improve the overall performance. Therefore, we integrated the potential based on protein features into MRF model (M3). With regard of Cytosol, it is an intracellular fluid which comprises most of the cellular organelles, and involved in many biological processes. The low performance could be due to its complication. The features can not improve the prediction performance. Finally, adding the SCL adjacency potential above on M3, we observe the improvement of prediction performance on most of the SCL classes.

4.2.2 Multi-SCLs prediction. As can be seen from Figure 7, M2 outperforms M1 which means additional spatial adjacency can improve the performance comparing with the simple SCL inference based on PPI only. However, the improvement is limited due to that M2 cannot efficiently gain correct knowledge from the adjacent SCLs which are poorly predicted. As expected, M3 significantly improve of prediction performance by adding the features of proteins on the model of M1. M4 can achieve the best performance of all. Comparing with M3 in particular, together with the observations of single-SCL predictions, we can conclude that the improvement is owing to that the model can efficiently gain the correct knowledge from the adjacent SCLs. However, in order to show a larger improvement of performance of the multi-SCLs prediction by adding the spatial adjacency on the proteins features in the model (M4 against M3), an additioanl tuning of parameters would be necessary.

4.3 A collective process improves the performance

To demonstrate how the collective MRFs can help to improve the performance of our SCL prediction, we show the changes of performance of M4 during the 21 iterations in Figure 8. Overall, the F1 scores gradually increase from initialization (iteration 1), single MRFs (iteration 2) and collective MRFs (from the 3rd iteration). The performances stay stable as the pseudo likelihood value of BCMRFs converge.

4.4 Transductive learning from imbalanced MLDs

Our human protein dataset is highly imbalanced since some of the labels are very frequent whereas most others are rarely used.

Table 1: F1 scores with/without imbalance correction.

Model	M1	M2	M3	M4
With imbalance coefficient	0.637	0.641	0.71	**0.732**
Without imbalance coefficient	0.616	0.632	0.701	0.722

Table 2: F1 scores for transductive VS conventional.

Model	M1	M2	M3	M4
Transductive learning	0.648	0.652	0.743	**0.759**
Conventional learning	0.602	0.647	0.684	0.692

The imbalance level of a MLD can be effectively measured by the imbalance ratio (*IRLbl*) [6]. Figure 9 shows that the SCLs such as Lysosome and Peroxisome are highly imbalanced compared to the other SCLs, with IRLbl of 22. 4 and 44.18 respectively.

Facing the imbalance problem, the popular solution is data resampling including under-sampling and over-sampling [6]. However, in our case the re-sampling techniques cannot be applied due to our method being highly sensitive to the topology of PPI network. The inference of SCL in this approach depends on the number of physical interactions. Under-sampling and over-sampling are based on the deletion of true interactions or repetition of existing interactions which can largely change the topology of the network and thus mislead the MRFs. Therefore, in this study we handle the imbalanced MLD problem by introducing imbalance coefficient (Equation 11). We compare the prediction performances of the BCMRFs with and without the imbalance coefficient. The results in Table 1 shows that the MRFs with the imbalance coefficient can improve the performance.

Furthermore, we compare the prediction results of the BCMRFs built on the complete PPI network including the unknown proteins against the BCMRFs built only on the sub-network of the annotated proteins. As we can see from Table 2, the MRFs of transductive learning outperforms the MRFs of the conventional learning.

4.5 Comparison with existing methods

To further demonstrate the performance of our method, we compare our BCMRFs with the only available PPI-based approach for predicting human protein SCLs, DC-*k*NN [17] and the state-of-art protein feature-based method Hum-mPLoc 3.0 [26]. DC-*k*NN is a physical PPI-based prediction method using a *k*-nearest neighbors classification with binary reference approach. Due to the unavailability of the program and of its prediction results, the dataset we use to compare our methods only contains 1704 human proteins (see subsection 3.3). For these 1704 human proteins, we evaluate the prediction results of DC-*k*NN and the results of our method. Table 3 shows that our method significantly outperforms DC-*k*NN overall.

Hum-mPLoc 3.0 [26] is the state-of-the-art feature-based SCL predictor specifically for human proteins. It predicts SCLs based on the amino acid sequence of proteins through modeling the hidden

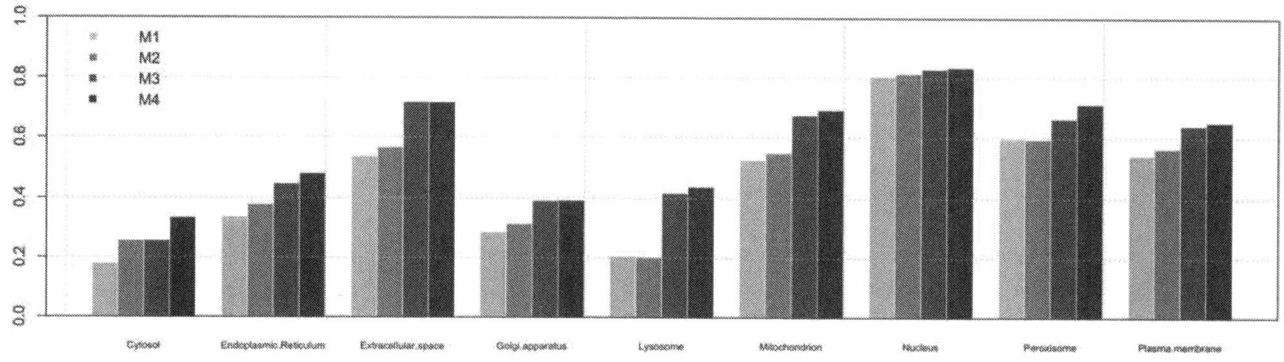

Figure 6: Comparison of four models for single label prediction.

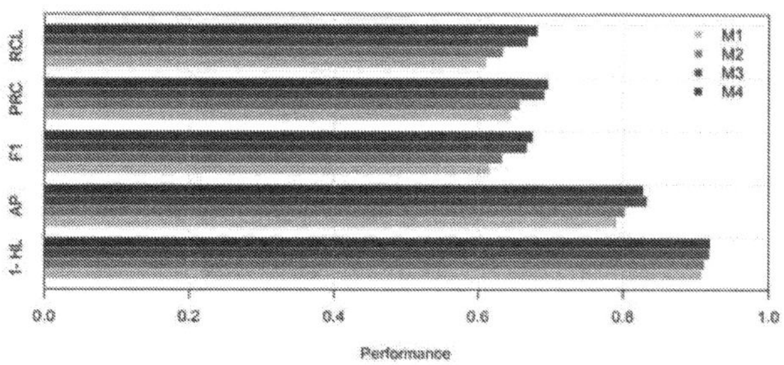

Figure 7: Performances of four models for multi-label classification.

correlations of gene ontology and functional domain features. The comparison of multi-SCL prediction results from Table 4 demonstrate that our method achieves better performance.

5 CONCLUSION AND FUTURE WORK

Protein subcellular localization prediction is an imbalanced multi-label classification problem. This paper proposes bayesian collective MRFs to predict multi-SCLs of human proteins. This is done by building the weighted MRFs based on the PPI network and then performing SCL label propagation to predict the SCLs of unknown proteins. We performed comprehensive experiments to evaluate the performance on human protein SCL datasets. The transductive learning from the re-balanced MLD proved to be more efficient to correctly assign SCLs. Owing to the collective MRFs which connect the binary MRFs by their spatial adjacency among SCLs, our method can achieve a higher performance for predicting the multi-SCLs comparing with the state-of-the-art methods of DC-*k*NN and Hum-mPLoc 3.0.

Interestingly, neither the present approach nor the previous state-of-the-art method for SCL prediction perform as effectively for human as for other organisms (such as bacteria: precision > 0.95 and recall >0.93 for single-SCL prediction) [25]. One explanation could be that the cell structures of the bacteria (5 and 6 SCCs in total) are much simpler than mammalian cells. The the activities of human cells, such as the interactions among proteins and with other molecules, the translocation of proteins, the functions of proteins, and the biological environment of the cell are also more complicated. Therefore, there may still be room for improvement of the SCL prediction of human proteins.

All PPI data used in this study are static data reported from different studies and techniques with a huge diversity. During different biological processes, one protein can play different roles and functions, for instance by interacting with different target proteins. However, the available PPI datasets do not differentiate them according to the biological contexts. Since a single protein cannot physically interact with tens or hundreds of partners at the same time, this presents a future challenge: can we determine which interactions occur simultaneously and which are mutually exclusive? And how can we explore this knowledge to make context-specific SCL predictions?

ACKNOWLEDGMENTS

The authors would like to thank Dr. William Duddy for the English corrections. The authors would also like to thank the anonymous referees for their valuable comments and helpful suggestions. This work is funded by the International DFG Research Training Group GRK 1906/1.

REFERENCES

[1] Barry C. Arnold and David Strauss. 1991. Pseudolikelihood Estimation: Some Examples. *SankhyĂĄ: The Indian Journal of Statistics, Series B (1960-2002)* 53, 2 (1991), 233–243. http://www.jstor.org/stable/25052695
[2] Janos X Binder, Sune Pletscher-Frankild, Kalliopi Tsafou, Christian Stolte, Seán I O'Donoghue, Reinhard Schneider, and Lars Juhl Jensen. 2014. COMPARTMENTS: unification and visualization of protein subcellular localization evidence. *Database : the journal of biological databases and curation* 2014 (jan 2014), bau012. DOI: http://dx.doi.org/10.1093/database/bau012
[3] Torsten Blum, Sebastian Briesemeister, and Oliver Kohlbacher. 2009. MultiLoc2: integrating phylogeny and Gene Ontology terms improves subcellular protein localization prediction. *BMC bioinformatics* 10 (jan 2009), 274. DOI: http://dx.doi.org/10.1186/1471-2105-10-274
[4] Sebastian Briesemeister, Jörg Rahnenführer, and Oliver Kohlbacher. 2010. YLoc– an interpretable web server for predicting subcellular localization. *Nucleic acids research* 38, Web Server issue (jul 2010), W497–502. DOI: http://dx.doi.org/10.1093/nar/gkq477
[5] Alberto Calderone, Luisa Castagnoli, and Gianni Cesareni. 2013. mentha: a resource for browsing integrated protein-interaction networks. *Nature methods* 10, 8 (aug 2013), 690–1. DOI: http://dx.doi.org/10.1038/nmeth.2561

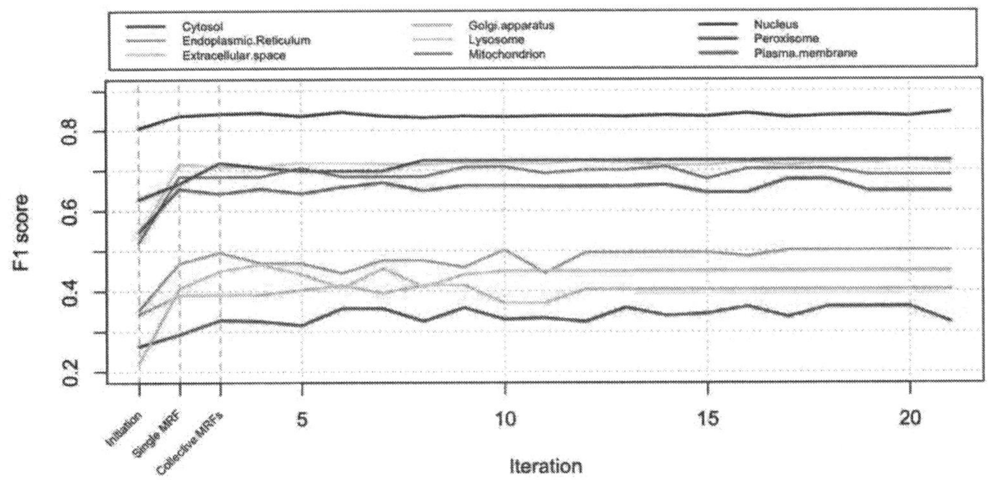

Figure 8: Performances of BCMRFs during iterations.

Table 3: Comparison with the method of DC-kNN - Multi-SCL prediction.

Method	Precision	Recall	F1 score	Average precision	Hamming loss
DC-kNN	0.502	0.472	0.474	0.672	0.119
BCMRFs	**0.674**	**0.621**	**0.633**	**0.899**	**0.073**

Table 4: Comparison with the method of Hum-mPLoc 3.0 - Multi-SCL prediction.

Method	Precision	Recall	F1 score	Average precision	Hamming loss
Hum-mPLoc 3.0	0.68	0.688	0.660	0.735	0.090
BCMRFs	**0.702**	0.67	**0.673**	**0.862**	**0.078**

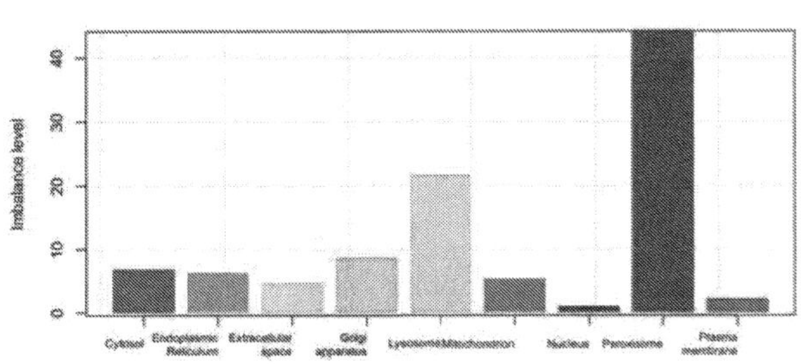

Figure 9: Imbalance level of each SCL class.

[6] Francisco Charte, Antonio Rivera, María José del Jesus, and Francisco Herrera. 2014. Concurrence among Imbalanced Labels and Its Influence on Multilabel Resampling Algorithms. Springer International Publishing, 110–121. DOI: http://dx.doi.org/10.1007/978-3-319-07617-1_10

[7] J. L. Gardy. 2003. PSORT-B: improving protein subcellular localization prediction for Gram-negative bacteria. *Nucleic Acids Research* 31, 13 (jul 2003), 3613–3617. DOI: http://dx.doi.org/10.1093/nar/gkg602

[8] Jennifer L Gardy and Fiona S L Brinkman. 2006. Methods for predicting bacterial protein subcellular localization. *Nature reviews. Microbiology* 4, 10 (oct 2006), 741–51. DOI: http://dx.doi.org/10.1038/nrmicro1494

[9] Shantanu Godbole and Sunita Sarawagi. 2004. Discriminative Methods for Multi-labeled Classification. Springer Berlin Heidelberg, 22–30. DOI: http://dx.doi.org/10.1007/978-3-540-24775-3_5

[10] Xiaotong Guo, Fulin Liu, Ying Ju, Zhen Wang, and Chunyu Wang. 2016. Human Protein Subcellular Localization with Integrated Source and Multi-label Ensemble Classifier. *Scientific Reports* 6, February (2016), 28087. DOI: http://dx.doi.org/10.1038/srep28087

[11] Jianjun He, Hong Gu, and Wenqi Liu. 2012. Imbalanced multi-modal multi-label learning for subcellular localization prediction of human proteins with both single and multiple sites. *PLoS ONE* 7, 6 (2012). DOI: http://dx.doi.org/10.1371/journal.pone.0037155

[12] Mien-Chie Hung and Wolfgang Link. 2011. Protein localization in disease and therapy. *Journal of cell science* 124, Pt 20 (oct 2011), 3381–92. DOI: http://dx.doi.org/10.1242/jcs.089110

[13] Jonathan Q Jiang and Maoying Wu. 2012. Predicting multiplex subcellular localization of proteins using protein-protein interaction network: a comparative study. *BMC bioinformatics* 13 Suppl 1, Suppl 10 (jan 2012), S20. DOI: http://dx.doi.org/10.1186/1471-2105-13-S10-S20

[14] T. S. Keshava Prasad, Renu Goel, Kumaran Kandasamy, Shivakumar Keerthikumar, Sameer Kumar, Suresh Mathivanan, Deepthi Telikicherla, Rajesh Raju, Beema Shafreen, Abhilash Venugopal, Lavanya Balakrishnan, Arivusudar Marimuthu, Sutopa Banerjee, Devi S. Somanathan, Aimy Sebastian, Sandhya Rani, Somak Ray, C. J. Harrys Kishore, Sashi Kanth, Mukhtar Ahmed, Manoj K. Kashyap, Riaz Mohmood, Y. I. Ramachandra, V. Krishna, B. Abdul Rahiman, Sujatha Mohan, Prathibha Ranganathan, Subhashri Ramabadran, Raghothama Chaerkady, and Akhilesh Pandey. 2009. Human Protein Reference Database -

2009 update. *Nucleic Acids Research* 37, November 2008 (2009), 767–772. DOI: http://dx.doi.org/10.1093/nar/gkn892

[15] Pushmeet Kohli, M. Pawan Kumar, and Philip H. S. Torr. 2007. P3 & Beyond: Solving Energies with Higher Order Cliques. In *2007 IEEE Conference on Computer Vision and Pattern Recognition*. IEEE, 1–8. DOI: http://dx.doi.org/10.1109/CVPR.2007.383204

[16] Yiannis A. I. Kourmpetis, Aalt D. J. van Dijk, Marco C. A. M. Bink, Roeland C. H. J. van Ham, and Cajo J. F. ter Braak. 2010. Bayesian Markov Random Field Analysis for Protein Function Prediction Based on Network Data. *PLoS ONE* 5, 2 (2010), e9293. DOI: http://dx.doi.org/10.1371/journal.pone.0009293

[17] Kiyoung Lee, Han-Yu Chuang, Andreas Beyer, Min-Kyung Sung, Won-Ki Huh, Bonghee Lee, and Trey Ideker. 2008. Protein networks markedly improve prediction of subcellular localization in multiple eukaryotic species. *Nucleic acids research* 36, 20 (nov 2008), e136. DOI: http://dx.doi.org/10.1093/nar/gkn619

[18] Noah Lee, Andrew F. Laine, and R. Theodore Smith. 2009. Bayesian Transductive Markov Random Fields for Interactive Segmentation in Retinal Disorders. Springer Berlin Heidelberg, 227–230. DOI: http://dx.doi.org/10.1007/978-3-642-03891-4_61

[19] Sandra Orchard, Samuel Kerrien, Sara Abbani, Bruno Aranda, Jignesh Bhate, Shelby Bidwell, Alan Bridge, Leonardo Briganti, Fiona Brinkman, Gianni Cesareni, Andrew Chatr-aryamontri, Emilie Chautard, Carol Chen, Marine Dumousseau, Johannes Goll, Robert Hancock, Linda I Hannick, Igor Jurisica, Jyoti Khadake, David J Lynn, Usha Mahadevan, Livia Perfetto, Arathi Raghunath, Sylvie Ricard-Blum, Bernd Roechert, Lukasz Salwinski, Volker Stümpflen, Mike Tyers, Peter Uetz, Ioannis Xenarios, and Henning Hermjakob. 2012. Protein interaction data curation: the International Molecular Exchange (IMEx) consortium. *Nature Methods* 9, 6 (2012), 626–626. DOI: http://dx.doi.org/10.1038/nmeth0612-626a

[20] Konstantinos Sechidis, Grigorios Tsoumakas, and Ioannis Vlahavas. 2011. On the Stratification of Multi-label Data. Springer Berlin Heidelberg, 145–158. DOI: http://dx.doi.org/10.1007/978-3-642-23808-6_10

[21] Chang Jin Shin, Simon Wong, Melissa J Davis, and Mark A Ragan. 2009. Protein-protein interaction as a predictor of subcellular location. *BMC systems biology* 3 (jan 2009), 28. DOI: http://dx.doi.org/10.1186/1752-0509-3-28

[22] Mathias Uhlen, Per Oksvold, Linn Fagerberg, Emma Lundberg, Kalle Jonasson, Mattias Forsberg, Martin Zwahlen, Caroline Kampf, Kenneth Wester, Sophia Hober, Henrik Wernerus, Lisa Björling, and Fredrik Ponten. 2010. Towards a knowledge-based Human Protein Atlas. *Nature Biotechnology* 28, 12 (dec 2010), 1248–1250. DOI: http://dx.doi.org/10.1038/nbt1210-1248

[23] Shibiao Wan, Man-Wai Mak, and Sun-Yuan Kung. 2017. Transductive Learning for Multi-Label Protein Subchloroplast Localization Prediction. *IEEE/ACM Transactions on Computational Biology and Bioinformatics* 14, 1 (jan 2017), 212–224. DOI: http://dx.doi.org/10.1109/TCBB.2016.2527657

[24] Zhi Wei and Hongzhe Li. 2007. A Markov random field model for network-based analysis of genomic data. *Bioinformatics* 23, 12 (2007), 1537–1544. DOI: http://dx.doi.org/10.1093/bioinformatics/btm129

[25] Nancy Y. Yu, James R. Wagner, Matthew R. Laird, Gabor Melli, Sébastien Rey, Raymond Lo, Phuong Dao, S Cenk Sahinalp, Martin Ester, Leonard J. Foster, Fiona S L Brinkman, S. Cenk Sahinalp, Martin Ester, Leonard J. Foster, and Fiona S L Brinkman. 2010. PSORTb 3.0: Improved protein subcellular localization prediction with refined localization subcategories and predictive capabilities for all prokaryotes. *Bioinformatics* 26, 13 (jul 2010), 1608–1615. DOI: http://dx.doi.org/10.1093/bioinformatics/btq249

[26] Hang Zhou, Yang Yang, and Hong-Bin Shen. 2016. Hum-mPLoc 3.0: prediction enhancement of human protein subcellular localization through modeling the hidden correlations of gene ontology and functional domain features. *Bioinformatics* (dec 2016), btw723. DOI: http://dx.doi.org/10.1093/bioinformatics/btw723

Differential Community Detection in Paired Biological Networks

Raghvendra Mall
Qatar Computing Research Institute,
Hamad Bin Khalifa University
Doha, Qatar
rmall@hbku.edu.qa

Ehsan Ullah
Qatar Computing Research Institute,
Hamad Bin Khalifa University
Doha, Qatar
eullah@hbku.edu.qa

Khalid Kunji
Qatar Computing Research Institute,
Hamad Bin Khalifa University
Doha, Qatar
kkunji@hbku.edu.qa

Fulvio D'Angelo
Institute for Cancer Genetics,
Columbia University Medical Center
New York, U.S.A.
fd2396@cumc.columbia.edu

Halima Bensmail
Qatar Computing Research Institute,
Hamad Bin Khalifa University
Doha, Qatar
hbensmail@hbku.edu.qa

Michele Ceccarelli
BioGeM, Institute of Genetic Research
"Gaetano Salvatore" &
Department of Science and
Technology, University of Sannio
Ariano Irpino & Benevento, Italy
m.ceccarelli@gmail.com

ABSTRACT

Motivation: Biological networks unravel the inherent structure of molecular interactions which can lead to discovery of driver genes and meaningful pathways especially in cancer context. Often due to gene mutations, the gene expression undergoes changes and the corresponding gene regulatory network sustains some amount of localized re-wiring. The ability to identify significant changes in the interaction patterns caused by the progression of the disease can lead to the revelation of novel relevant signatures.
Methods: The task of identifying differential sub-networks in paired biological networks (*A*:control,*B*:case) can be re-phrased as one of finding dense communities in a single noisy differential topological (DT) graph constructed by taking absolute difference between the topological graphs of A and B. In this paper, we propose a fast three-stage approach, namely Differential Community Detection (DCD), to identify differential sub-networks as differential communities in a de-noised version of the DT graph. In the first stage, we iteratively re-order the nodes of the DT graph to determine approximate block diagonals present in the DT adjacency matrix using neighbourhood information of the nodes and Jaccard similarity. In the second stage, the ordered DT adjacency matrix is traversed along the diagonal to remove all the edges associated with a node, if that node has no immediate edges within a window. Finally, we apply community detection methods on this de-noised DT graph to discover differential sub-networks as communities.
Results: Our proposed DCD approach can effectively locate differential sub-networks in several simulated paired random-geometric networks and various paired scale-free graphs with different power-law exponents. The DCD approach easily outperforms community detection methods applied on the original noisy DT graph and recent statistical techniques in simulation studies. We applied DCD method on two real datasets: a) Ovarian cancer dataset to discover differential DNA co-methylation sub-networks in patients and controls; b) Glioma cancer dataset to discover the difference between the regulatory networks of IDH-mutant and IDH-wild-type. We demonstrate the potential benefits of DCD for finding network-inferred bio-markers/pathways associated with a trait of interest.
Conclusion: The proposed DCD approach overcomes the limitations of previous statistical techniques and the issues associated with identifying differential sub-networks by use of community detection methods on the noisy DT graph. This is reflected in the superior performance of the DCD method with respect to various metrics like Precision, Accuracy, Kappa and Specificity. The code implementing proposed DCD method is available at https://sites.google.com/site/raghvendramallmlresearcher/codes.

Permission to make digital or hard copies of all or part of this work for personal or classroom use is granted without fee provided that copies are not made or distributed for profit or commercial advantage and that copies bear this notice and the full citation on the first page. Copyrights for components of this work owned by others than ACM must be honored. Abstracting with credit is permitted. To copy otherwise, or republish, to post on servers or to redistribute to lists, requires prior specific permission and/or a fee. Request permissions from permissions@acm.org.
ACM-BCB'17, August 20–23, 2017, Boston, MA, USA.
© 2017 ACM. ISBN 978-1-4503-4722-8/17/08...$15.00
DOI: http://dx.doi.org/10.1145/3107411.3107418

CCS CONCEPTS

•**Applied computing** → **Computational biology; Biological networks; Bioinformatics;** *Systems biology;* Recognition of genes and regulatory elements;

KEYWORDS

Network Comparisons; Differential sub-networks; Community detection; Systems biology

ACM Reference format:
Raghvendra Mall, Ehsan Ullah, Khalid Kunji, Fulvio D'Angelo, Halima Bensmail, and Michele Ceccarelli. 2017. Differential Community Detection in Paired Biological Networks. In *Proceedings of ACM-BCB'17, August 20–23, 2017, Boston, MA, USA.*, , 11 pages.
DOI: http://dx.doi.org/10.1145/3107411.3107418

1 BACKGROUND

In the modern era complex networks are ubiquitous. Their omnipresence is reflected in a myriad of domains including web graphs [6], road graphs [10], social networks [22, 40], financial networks

[4] and biological networks [20, 25, 41]. Here we focus on biological networks but the caveats introduced in this paper apply to networks in other domains.

In network biology, particularly in cancer research, comparisons are performed on gene regulatory networks [55] and DNA co-methylation networks [54] obtained from the gene expression and DNA methylation profiles of healthy and diseased tissues. The goal is to identify genes whose expression or methylation levels are significantly different between the conditions and can lead to discovery of novel molecular diagnostic and prognostic signatures. It was shown in [1, 8, 51] that the gene regulatory networks undergo some amount of localized re-wirings as cancer progresses.

One of the primary problems in cell biology is to infer regulatory networks, that capture the interactions between molecular entities from high-throughput data. An important challenge that needs to be addressed is how the cell changes its behaviour in response to changes in copy number or alterations such as driver somatic mutations or an external stimuli. The gene expression and methylation levels change due to the downstream effect of the de-regulation of the global behaviour of the cell in different conditions, for example different cancer subtypes [8]. Hence, it can be suggested that driver mutations regulate functional pathways described by different local re-wirings in the intrinsic gene regulatory networks.

The problem of detecting significant changes in paired biological networks is different from popular graph theory problems like graph isomorphism [44] and sub-graph matching [49] for which various graph matching and graph similarity algorithms [5, 28] exist and have been utilized in biological networks[43, 53]. This problem has primarily been addressed either in a statistical framework [19, 31, 35, 48] or from a community detection perspective [9, 13, 21, 30, 31, 52] in literature.

In statistics, a common statistic used to distinguish one graph from another is the Mean Absolute Difference (MAD), which is defined as: $d(A, B) = \frac{1}{N(N-1)} \sum_{i \neq j} |a_{ij} - b_{ij}|$. Here a_{ij} and b_{ij} are edge weights corresponding to the topological graphs of networks A and B. A topological graph captures first order interactions between the nodes in the network and can better apprehend subtle changes between two networks [47]. The Quadratic Assignment Procedure (QAP) [35] defined as: $Q(A, B) = \frac{1}{N(N-1)} \sum_{i=1} \sum_{j=1} a_{ij} b_{ij}$ is another statistic used to identify association between networks. These statistics are often used in permutation-based procedures to detect significant difference between two networks. Ruan et al [48] showed that these statistics are not always sensitive to subtle topological variations and proposed a Generalized Hamming Distance (GHD) based statistic to measure the distance between paired biological graphs which outperforms MAD and QAP.

The GHD permutation distribution follows a normal distribution under the null hypothesis that networks A and B are independent for scale-free networks whose power-law exponent α should strictly satisfy: $1 \leq \alpha \leq 2$ or $\alpha \geq 3$. They also generated closed-form expression for p-values and devised a differential sub-network identification technique, namely dGHD, where they iteratively remove least different node. This is unlike previous differential network analysis techniques [13, 14, 16] and generate p-values by comparing the remaining sub-networks. Recently, a Closed-Form approach was proposed in [31] which is faster and more accurate than the dGHD technique for identifying statistically significant changes between paired networks as differential sub-networks. However, these statistical techniques are still computationally expensive and suffer from strict restrictions on the exponent of power-law for scale-free graphs. It was shown in [36] that biological networks are scale-free and usually have power-law exponents that satisfies: $0 < \alpha \leq 2$ which is not always within the restrictions acceptable for dGHD and Closed-Form techniques.

The problem of community detection in graphs has received wide attention from several perspectives [3, 15, 27, 32–34, 42, 45, 46] and have also been applied to biological networks. Methods such as jActiveModules [9] and the Spinglass algorithm [45] have been applied to discover biologically meaningful modules such as protein complexes, disease associated clusters of genes, etc. as shown in [21, 52]. The problem of identifying differential sub-networks in paired biological networks can be re-formulated as one of finding heavy sub-networks, or dense modules, on a single differential topological (DT) graph obtained by taking the absolute difference in the edge weights between the topological graph of network A and the topological graph of network B i.e. $\mathrm{DT}(A, B)_{ij} = |a_{ij} - b_{ij}|$, $\forall i, j \in V$. This problem is equivalent to identifying communities in the DT graph. The notion of communities mean that nodes within one community are densely connected to each other and sparsely connected to nodes outside that community. Large-scale networks consist of several such communities. Hence, community detection is equivalent to finding dense block diagonals in the DT adjacency matrix. However, the DT graph can suffer from noise caused by interactions between nodes which are not part of differential sub-networks (referred further as *non-differential nodes*) and nodes which are part of differential sub-networks (referred further as *differential nodes*) which are just one hop away in either network A or B but not in both. This leads to spurious connections around the block diagonals present in the DT adjacency matrix. Community detection techniques like Louvain [3], Infomap [46] and Spectral [32] method can be applied to obtain the communities/modules with differential nodes with having perfect recall but suffer from very low precision due to false recognition of non-differential nodes as part of differential sub-networks.

The problem of identifying communities in the DT graph such that the nodes comprising the communities are part of differential sub-networks between paired biological networks (A, B) is unlike the traditional module based differential network analysis as shown in [13, 30]. In traditional module based differential network analysis, modules are detected at first in weighted gene co-expression networks (WGCNA) [13] obtained from gene expression data for case and controls. The modules are then compared using either Jaccard co-efficient (MOda) [30] or additional genetic marker data (WGCNA) [13] is utilized to differentiate the modules. The advantage of these methods is that by focusing on modules rather than on individual gene expressions, they can greatly alleviate the multiple-testing problem inherent in micro-array data analysis. However, our goal is to identify the difference between the paired biological networks as dense modules/communities rather than comparing the modules in the paired biological networks. For example, say minor localized changes within two modules in the original biological networks together form a differential sub-network. The method proposed in this paper will be able to identify these changes as a differential community which might otherwise not be detected by WGCNA or MOda.

In this paper, we propose a novel three-stage approach, namely Differential Community Detection (DCD), to identify differential sub-networks in paired biological networks as communities from the original nosiy DT graph. The proposed DCD method overcomes the restrictions on power-law exponents for scale-free graphs implied by statistical techniques and retains the advantage of greatly reducing the burden of multiple-testing from module based differential network analysis techniques. We applied our DCD method on two real datasets, an ovarian cancer dataset to discover differential DNA co-methylation sub-networks in patients and controls, and a glioma cancer dataset to discover the difference between the regulatory networks of IDH-mutant and IDH-wild-type.

2 METHOD

The proposed DCD approach consists of three primary stages: a) Ordering the DT graph - The proposed method re-orders the nodes of the DT graph to generate approximate block diagonals inherently present in the DT adjacency matrix. It utilizes the neighbourhood information from the DT graph for all the nodes and a notion of similarity based on the Jaccard index [29]. b) Denoising - In the second stage of DCD, the ordered yet noisy DT adjacency matrix is traversed along the diagonal to remove all the edges associated with a node, if that node has no immediate edges within a window. This is because the ordered DT adjacency matrix is already comprised of block diagonals and nodes which are not part of block diagonals are the ones causing spurious connections in the DT graph. We then pick out such nodes and remove all the edges associated with these nodes. c) Differential Community Detection - Finally, we apply community detection techniques like Louvain [3], Infomap [46] and Spectral [32] methods on this de-noised DT graph to discover the differential sub-networks as communities. Figure 1 illustrates all the steps involved in the DCD algorithm to locate differential sub-networks on a pair of simulated random-geometric (RG) networks.

2.1 Ordering the Noisy DT graph

The goal of first stage of DCD method is to detect sets of nodes which have higher similarity with each other in comparison to other nodes by following an iterative procedure to order the nodes in the adjacency matrix of the original DT graph $G(V, E)$. The total number of nodes in the DT graph is represented as $N = |V|$. This iterative process is essential as nodes are not usually ordered in the $G(V, E)$ and the inherent block diagonals have to be discovered. It is important to locate approximate block diagonals as it is a necessary condition for the second stage of DCD approach. We define $d(v_i, V^t)$ as degree of the node $v_i \in V^t$, where V^t represents the set of nodes to be investigated at iteration t. During the first iteration, we identify the node with highest degree i.e. $v^t_{max} = \arg_{max} d(v, V^t)$ using the topology of $G(V, E)$ and calculate its Jaccard similarity w.r.t. all the nodes. It is defined as:

$$J(v^t_{max}, v_i) = \frac{|n(v^t_{max}) \cap n(v_i)|}{|n(v^t_{max}) \cup n(v_i)|} \qquad (1)$$

Here v^t_{max} is the node with highest degree during iteration t, $v_i \in V$, $n(\cdot)$ represents the immediate neighbourhood set of a node and $|\cdot|$ represents the cardinality function. The Jaccard co-efficient of all the nodes that don't share a specified number of neighbours (θ) with v^t_{max} is set to 0. This threshold θ is a tunable parameter representing the minimum size of a block diagonal to be considered as a differential community in the DT graph. We then sort all the nodes having non-zero Jaccard similarity with v^t_{max} in decreasing order and break ties based on degree where higher degree nodes are placed closer to v^t_{max}. These ordered nodes and their corresponding edges results in the first approximate block diagonal ABD^t which is preserved in O_{DT}, representing the adjacency matrix of ordered noisy DT graph. ABD^t is an approximate block diagonal because nodes with spurious connections are still present and associated with ABD^t as highlighted in Figure 1d.

During further iterations ($t > 1$), an additional step is performed to re-order the nodes which are common between the ABD^{t-1} and ABD^t. The order of common nodes whose Jaccard similarity was higher with the previous v^{t-1}_{max} are unchanged and these nodes are removed from ABD^t. However, nodes which are common with ABD^{t-1} but have higher Jaccard similarity with v^t_{max} are removed from ABD^{t-1} while their order is retained in ABD^t. This iterative process is greedy by nature, as in any iteration t we compare only ABD^{t-1} with ABD^t, and stop when either all the nodes in the $G(V, E)$ are part of some approximate block-diagonal or degree of v^t_{max} is 0, which means we are left with only isolated nodes in the $G(V, E)$. Algorithm 1 summarizes this procedure.

Algorithm 1: Ordering Noisy DT graph

```
Data: Noisy DT graph G(V, E) and threshold θ.
Result: Ordered noisy DT adjacency matrix O_DT.
Initialize t = 1, V^t = V and an all zero adjacency matrix O_DT ∈ ℝ^{N×N}.
while V^t ≠ ∅ do
    Select node with highest degree as v^t_max from V^t.
    if d(v^t_max, V^t) = 0 then
        Break out of loop. // Only isolated nodes left in V^t.
    end
    Calculate J(v^t_max, v_i), ∀v_i ∈ V using Eq. 1.
    Set J(v^t_max, v_i) = 0, {∀v_i ∈ V | |n(v^t_max) ∩ n(v_i)| < θ}.
    Order v_i with non-zero J(v^t_max, v_i) in decreasing order.
    Ordered set of nodes and corresponding edges generate ABD^t.
    if t > 1 then
        Identify common nodes c as c = {v_i | v_i ∈ ABD^{t-1} ∩ v_i ∈ ABD^t}.
        Remove nodes and corresponding edges from ABD^{t-1} and its preserved copy
        in O_DT s.t. J(v^{t-1}_max, v_i) < J(v^t_max, v_i), ∀v_i ∈ c.
        Remove those nodes and corresponding edges from ABD^t s.t.
        J(v^{t-1}_max, v_i) > J(v^t_max, v_i), ∀v_i ∈ c.
        Keep remaining set of ordered nodes and their edges as ABD^t.
        /* A node can only be part of one approximate block diagonal.   */
    end
    Add ABD^t related info to O_DT.
    V^t = V^t \ s, such that s = {v_i ∈ ABD^t}.
    t = t + 1.
end
if V^t ≠ ∅ then
    // Still isolated nodes are left.
    Maintain isolated nodes v_i ∈ V^t as isolated in O_DT.
end
```

2.2 De-noising the DT graph

Once we have obtained O_{DT} as shown in Figure 1d, we prune out spurious edges associated with nodes which are falsely recognized as part of block diagonals in the previous step. We traverse the landscape of the O_{DT} matrix, for example in Figure 1d from left to right and bottom to up, along the diagonal. Since we have already identified approximate block diagonals (ABD's) in O_{DT}, our premise

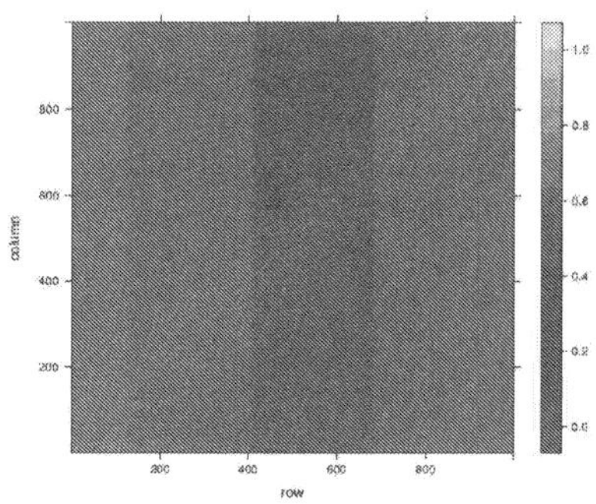

(a) Topological graph of A

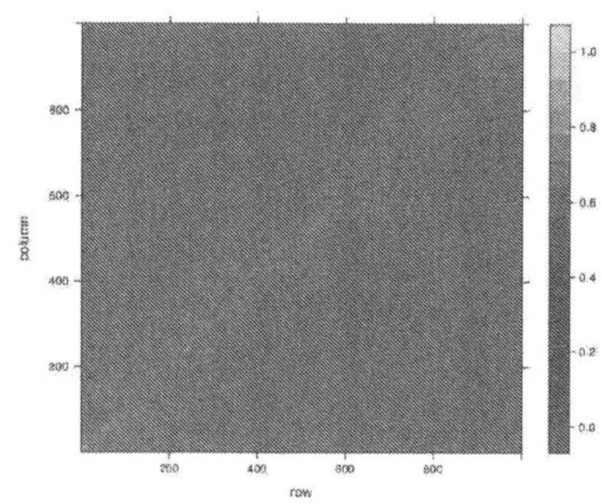

(b) Topological graph of B

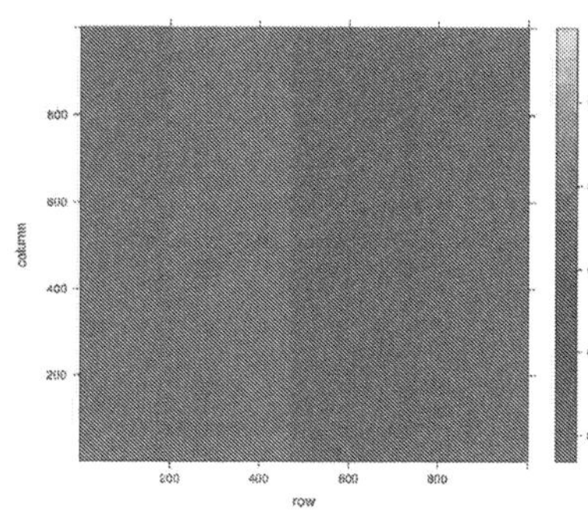

(c) Noisy DT graph

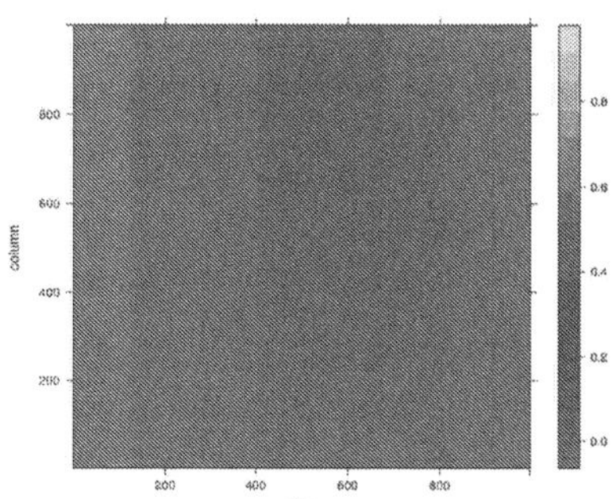

(d) Ordered noisy DT graph

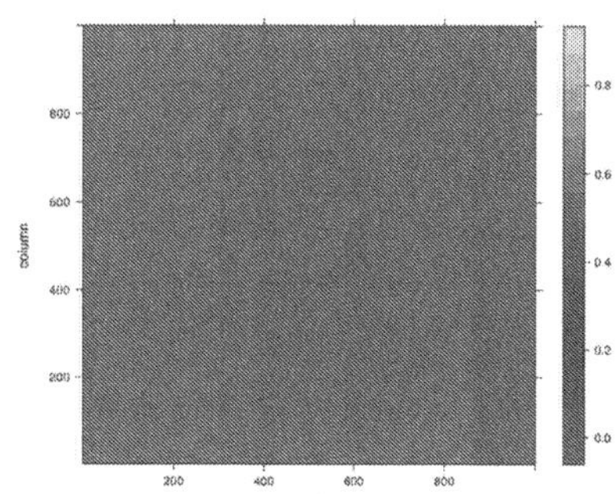

(e) Ordered de-noised DT graph

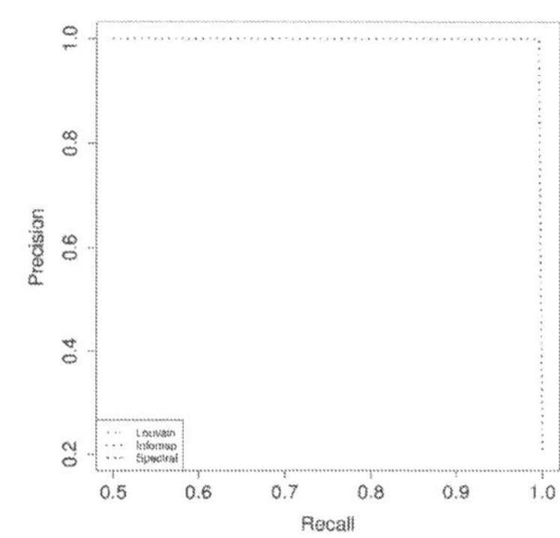

(f) Result on ordered de-noised DT.

Figure 1: Illustration of DCD method and its benefit over directly using community detection methods on noisy DT graph. Figures 1a and 1b correspond to the topological graphs of network A and B. Figure 1c shows the noisy differential topological (DT) graph obtained from topological graphs of A and B. Figure 1d illustrates the ordered noisy DT graph obtained from first stage of DCD approach. Figure 1e demonstrates the de-noised DT graph generated after the second stage of DCD method. Figure 1f showcases that 3 different community detection methods have identical performance while identifying the differential sub-networks from the de-noised DT graph.

is that if we traverse along the diagonal and pick a node v_i at random, there should be some immediate edges within θ to the left and to the right (below and above due to symmetry) in the landscape of O_{DT} for it to be a differential node in *ABD*. This means that $d(v_i, V_{i-\theta})$ and $d(v_i, V_{i+\theta})$ have to be non-zero at the same time. Here $V_{i-\theta}$ and $V_{i+\theta}$ represent the neighbourhood up to θ nodes to the left and right of v_i. A non-differential node can be part of *ABD* due to spurious connections with the differential set of nodes present in *ABD*. We then remove all the edges associated with such nodes from O_{DT} to generate the de-noised ordered DT graph i.e. D_{DT}. The proposed process leads to de-noised block diagonals *BD* in D_{DT} instead of having *ABD* as shown in Figure 1e. Algorithm 2 summarizes the de-noising procedure.

Algorithm 2: De-noising the DT graph

Data: Ordered DT adjacency matrix O_{DT} and parameter θ.
Result: De-noised ordered DT adjacency matrix D_{DT}.
Initialize an all 0 matrix $D_{\mathrm{DT}} \in \mathbb{R}^{N\times N}$, where nodes have same order as in O_{DT}.
for $i = 1$ **to** N **do**
  if $(i \leq \theta \;\&\; d(v_i, V_{i+\theta}) = 0)$ *or* $(i \geq N - \theta \;\&\; d(v_i, V_{i-\theta}) = 0)$ *or* $(d(v_i, V_{i+\theta}) = 0 \;\&\; d(v_i, V_{i-\theta}) = 0)$ **then**
    Set all edge-weights associated to v_i in O_{DT} to 0.
    // These nodes are non-differential nodes.
  end
  else
    Copy all edge-weights associated to v_i in O_{DT} to D_{DT}.
    /* Node v_i is part of a differential community. */
  end
end

2.3 Differential Community Detection

We can now run state-of-the-art community detection algorithms [3, 32, 46] to distinguish the *BD*'s in D_{DT} as differential communities in paired biological networks. The overall time complexity of proposed steps is $O(tN \log N + tEd_{\mu})$, where t is number of iterations in Algorithm 1, E represents number of edges and d_{μ} represents the average degree of a node in DT graph. Algorithm 3 provides an overview of the proposed DCD approach.

Algorithm 3: Differential Community Detection (DCD) approach for paired biological networks

Data: Paired biological networks (A,B) and threshold θ.
Result: Differential sub-networks identified as differential communities.
Create topological graphs for networks A and B.
Generate the noisy DT graph: $\mathrm{DT}(A, B)_{ij} = |a_{ij} - b_{ij}|, \forall i, j \in V$.
Use $G(V, E)$ and θ to generate O_{DT} as shown in Algorithm 1.
Use O_{DT} and θ to generate D_{DT} using Algorithm 2.
Use either Louvain [3], Infomap [46] or Spectral [32] community detection technique on D_{DT} to identify communities $\mathbb{C}_i \in \mathbb{C}, i = 1, \ldots, k$.
if $|\mathbb{C}_i| < \theta$ **then**
| Remove $\mathbb{C}_i$ from $\mathbb{C}$.
end
All remaining communities in $\mathbb{C}$ are marked as differential communities.
/* A differential community represents the set of nodes whose corresponding edges form the differential sub-networks. */

3 SIMULATED EXPERIMENTS & RESULTS

We performed multiple simulated experiments on paired random-geometric (RG) and paired scale-free networks under different experimental settings. All the experiments were repeated 10 times for each experimental setting.

In a RG network nodes are generated by uniformly sampling N points on $[0, 1]^2$. An edge is drawn between points if the euclidean distance between the points is less than a tuning parameter ν. This ν is a density parameter and controls the sparsity of the RG network where smaller values of ν result in sparse networks while larger values of ν result in dense networks. We used the same ν values as those used in the experiments in [31] for differential network analysis on paired RG networks. We performed two set of experiments on RG networks. In the first case, we generated RG network A_1 with $N = 1,000$ and $\nu = 0.15$. Network B is obtained by permuting first 100 nodes in network A. Thus, these first 100 nodes form the differential sub-network for the paired RG networks.

In the second case, we again used $N = 1,000$ and $\nu = 0.15$ to generate network A_2. We then create a small dense RG network with 100 nodes using $\hat{\nu} = 0.3$. Network B_2 was generated by replacing first 100 nodes in network A_2 with the small denser sub-network. These 100 nodes form the differential sub-network for the paired networks A_2 and B_2. Such a mechanism can appear in real-life networks, for example, in case of cancer the transcription activity of some set of genes might get enhanced or suppressed generating more or fewer edges in a sub-network of the gene or DNA methylation network. We performed similar set of experiments using density parameter $\nu = 0.3$ and permuting first 100 nodes, using density parameter $\nu = 0.3$ and adding more edges to first 100 nodes using revised density parameter $\hat{\nu} = 0.5$ on paired RG networks.

We also conducted experiments on undirected scale-free graphs, hereby referred as Power-Law (PL) networks, using $N = 1000$ and $E = 10,000$ with varying power-law exponents $\alpha = \{1, 1.5, 2\}$ respectively. We permuted the first 100 nodes of each PL network (A) to form the permuted network (B). The proposed DCD method has one tunable parameter θ. In Figure 2, we illustrate the effect of θ on the area under the precision-recall curve. From Figures 2a, 2b, 2e, 2f, 2i and 2j, we can observe that for smaller values of θ $(\{3, 5\})$, the area under precision-recall curves are relatively lower in comparison to those for higher values of θ. This is due to the fact that for smaller values of θ, we are allowing smaller sized communities to be distinguished as differential sub-networks. This can force to break the natural block diagonals inherently present in the DT graph and reduce the number of true positives (i.e. nodes which are actually part of differential sub-networks) leading to lower precision and recall. At the same time, smaller values of θ allow non-differential nodes with few spurious connections to differential nodes to be falsely identified as part of differential sub-networks resulting in lower precision. For higher values of θ $(\{7, 9\})$, the area under precision-recall curves shows less variance and converges to nearly perfect result (≈ 1) as depicted in Figures 2c, 2g,2h, 2k and 2l.

Table 1 encapsulates a comprehensive comparison of the proposed DCD approach, where the community detection technique used in DCD is either Louvain [3] or Infomap [46] or Spectral [32], with statistical techniques like dGHD [48] and Closed-Form [31] approach and direct application of community detection methods like Louvain, Infomap and Spectral on the noisy DT graph to detect differential sub-networks in the simulated experiments. We used the threshold $\theta = 7$ in the DCD approach for all comparisons as the area under precision-recall curves shows less variance and converges to nearly perfect value (≈ 1) in all the simulated experimental settings for this threshold as depicted in Figure 2. For nearly all PL graph experiments, if we directly apply community detection methods on the noisy DT graph, they identify all the nodes in the network as part of differential sub-network as depicted from evaluation metrics in Table 1. We set $\theta = 7$ for real experiments, as we observe the smallest variance and best performance of community detection methods for scale-free PL graphs at $\theta = 7$, as illustrated in Figure 2k. We utilize the Louvain method for all the real experiments as it is the fastest and has least variation in performance metrics for PL graphs as depicted in Figures 2i, 2j, 2k and 2l and Table 1.

4 APPLICATION TO CO-METHYLATION NETWORKS IN OVARIAN CANCER

We applied our proposed DCD approach, with parameter θ set to 7 for reasons explained above, on co-methylation networks generated from ovarian cancer dataset [50]. Thus, the smallest community in DT graph should comprise at least 7 nodes. The ovarian cancer dataset consists of methylation profiles for 27,578 CpG islands of 540 women, of which 266 cases were from post-menopausal women with ovarian cancer and 274 were healthy controls with similar age as that of cases. We compared case and control DNA co-methylation networks to identify differential sub-networks.

The pre-processed dataset was downloaded from GEO (repository number GSE19711). The original data was collected using Illumina Infinium 27k Human DNA methylation Beadchip v1.2. Since there were no missing or negative values for the intensity of the methylated (M) and unmethylated (U) alleles, beta values corresponding to each CpG probe were computed as: $\beta = \frac{M}{M+U}$ as in [48]. We followed the quality control procedure as originally introduced in [50]. Then principal component analysis (PCA) was applied to the beta values for detection and removal of outliers. After quality control, 243 case samples and 214 control samples remained for further analysis. Networks for case and control samples were created by treating each probe as a node. Edges between the nodes represent strong correlation and were inferred following [17]. Adjacency measure Ω_{ij} was computed for each pair of nodes (i and

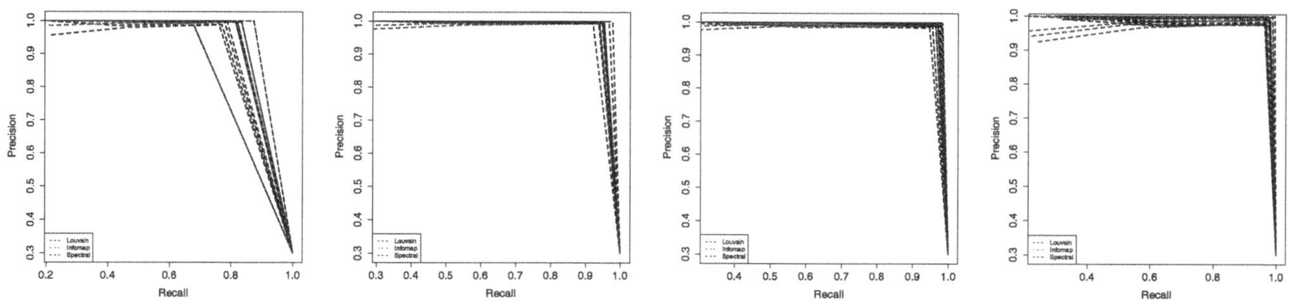

(a) $\theta = 3$, $\nu = 0.15$ (b) $\theta = 5$, $\nu = 0.15$ (c) $\theta = 7$, $\nu = 0.15$ (d) $\theta = 9$, $\nu = 0.15$

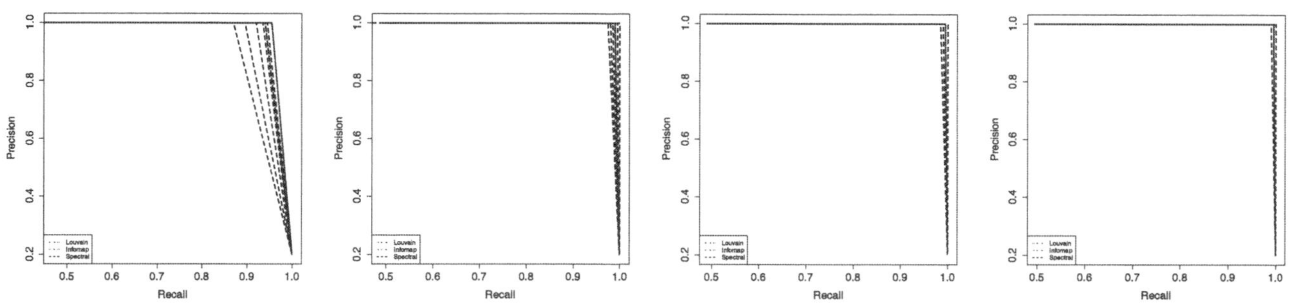

(e) $\theta = 3$, $\nu = 0.15$ & $\hat{\nu} = 0.3$ (f) $\theta = 5$, $\nu = 0.15$ & $\hat{\nu} = 0.3$ (g) $\theta = 7$, $\nu = 0.15$ & $\hat{\nu} = 0.3$ (h) $\theta = 9$, $\nu = 0.15$ & $\hat{\nu} = 0.3$

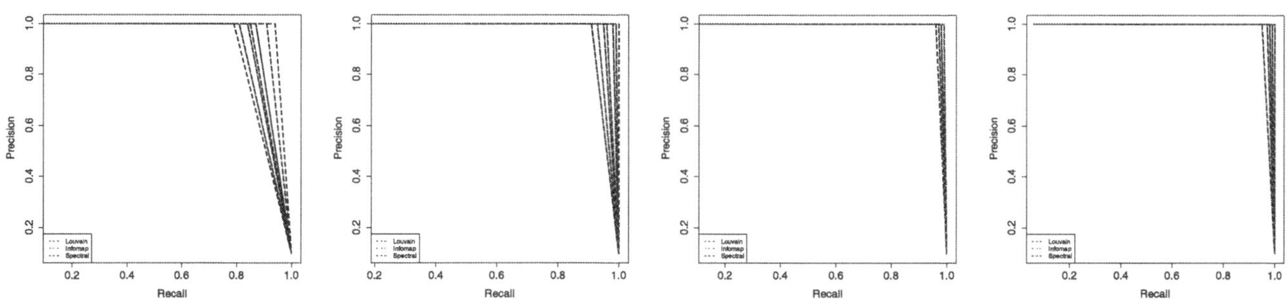

(i) $\theta = 3$, $\alpha = 1.5$ (j) $\theta = 5$, $\alpha = 1.5$ (k) $\theta = 7$, $\alpha = 1.5$ (l) $\theta = 9$, $\alpha = 1.5$

Figure 2: Area under the precision-recall curves for different values of threshold θ for 10 random runs of various experimental settings. We demonstrate the area under precision-recall curves using the proposed steps of DCD approach with either Louvain or Infomap or Spectral community detection method. Figures 2a,2b,2c and 2d show the role of parameter θ on precision-recall values for paired RG networks ($\nu = 0.15$) where first 100 nodes are permuted. Figures 2e,2f, 2g and 2h illustrate how the area under precision-recall curves vary with threshold θ for paired RG networks ($\nu = 0.15$) where the sub-network corresponding to first 100 nodes have higher density ($\hat{\nu} = 0.5$). Similarly, Figures 2i, 2j, 2k and 2l describes the role of variable θ on precision-recall values for paired PL networks ($\alpha = 1.5$) where the first 100 nodes are permuted. Detailed analysis of the role of θ on paired RG and PL networks is provided in the Results section.

j) as $\Omega_{ij} = \left|\frac{1+\text{cor}(\beta_i,\beta_j)}{2}\right|^b$, where $\text{cor}(\beta_i, \beta_j)$ represents Pearson's correlation coefficient between beta values observed at i^{th} and j^{th} CpG sites. The exponent b was set to 12 to emphasize more on higher positive correlations [55]. An edge exists if Ω_{ij} value was higher than 0.2. The resulting control network has 73, 145 edges and case network has 102, 799 edges. Each of these networks follows a scale-free network model as shown in Figure 3.

Our approach detected differential sub-networks comprising of a total of 1, 893 nodes. We used Louvain [3] method for detection of communities in the differential case and control sub-networks for reasons explained earlier. Nine pre-dominant communities were detected in the case differential sub-network out of which seven have similar topology in the control differential sub-network as shown in Figure 4. However, clusters C5 and C9 in the control

Graph	Parameters	Method	DT graph	AUC_ROC	Precision	Recall	Accuracy	Specificity	Kappa	Time
				Mean ± Sd	Mean ± Sd	Mean ± Sd	Mean ± Sd	Mean ± Sd	Mean ± Sd	Mean
RG:Permute	$\nu = 0.15$	**Closed-Form**	Noisy	0.935 ± 0.051	0.849 ± 0.037	0.846 ± 0.102	0.969 ± 0.011	0.983 ± 0.004	0.828 ± 0.068	0.078
RG:Permute	$\nu = 0.15$	**dGHD**	Noisy	0.926 ± 0.018	0.793 ± 0.021	0.878 ± 0.036	0.965 ± 0.005	0.974 ± 0.003	0.813 ± 0.026	1.0
RG:Permute	$\nu = 0.15$	**Louvain**	Noisy	0.5885 ± 0.012	0.3425 ± 0.007	**1.0 ± 0.0**	0.424 ± 0.017	0.114 ± 0.017	0.177 ± 0.024	**0.012**
RG:Permute	$\nu = 0.15$	**Infomap**	Noisy	0.589 ± 0.012	0.343 ± 0.006	**1.0 ± 0.0**	0.425 ± 0.016	0.115 ± 0.0168	0.178 ± 0.024	0.018
RG:Permute	$\nu = 0.15$	**Spectral**	Noisy	0.5884 ± 0.012	0.3425 ± 0.007	**1.0 ± 0.0**	0.424 ± 0.017	0.114 ± 0.017	0.177 ± 0.024	0.015
RG:Permute	$\nu = 0.15$	**DCD (Louvain)**	De-noised	**0.990 ± 0.007**	**1.0 ± 0.0**	0.980 ± 0.0176	**0.994 ± 0.004**	**0.986 ± 0.013**	**1.0 ± 0.0**	0.014
RG:Permute	$\nu = 0.15$	**DCD (Infomap)**	De-noised	**0.990 ± 0.008**	**1.0 ± 0.0**	0.980 ± 0.0176	**0.994 ± 0.005**	**0.986 ± 0.012**	**1.0 ± 0.0**	0.021
RG:Permute	$\nu = 0.15$	**DCD (Spectral)**	De-noised	**0.990 ± 0.007**	**1.0 ± 0.0**	0.980 ± 0.0176	**0.994 ± 0.004**	**0.986 ± 0.014**	**1.0 ± 0.0**	0.018
RG:Dense	$\nu = 0.15, \hat{\nu} = 0.3$	**Closed-Form**	Noisy	0.927 ± 0.048	0.839 ± 0.031	0.862 ± 0.098	0.969 ± 0.008	0.982 ± 0.005	0.825 ± 0.054	0.081
RG:Dense	$\nu = 0.15, \hat{\nu} = 0.3$	**dGHD**	Noisy	0.922 ± 0.022	0.806 ± 0.027	0.868 ± 0.045	0.966 ± 0.006	0.977 ± 0.004	0.816 ± 0.032	1.0
RG:Dense	$\nu = 0.15, \hat{\nu} = 0.3$	**Louvain**	Noisy	0.599 ± 0.008	0.349 ± 0.004	0.999 ± 0.002	0.440 ± 0.011	0.130 ± 0.011	0.199 ± 0.0015	**0.013**
RG:Dense	$\nu = 0.15, \hat{\nu} = 0.3$	**Infomap**	Noisy	0.602 ± 0.005	0.350 ± 0.003	0.999 ± 0.002	0.444 ± 0.007	0.134 ± 0.008	0.205 ± 0.011	0.020
RG:Dense	$\nu = 0.15, \hat{\nu} = 0.3$	**Spectral**	Noisy	0.600 ± 0.007	0.348 ± 0.004	**1.0 ± 0.0**	0.440 ± 0.011	0.131 ± 0.011	0.200 ± 0.015	0.016
RG:Dense	$\nu = 0.15, \hat{\nu} = 0.3$	**DCD (Louvain)**	De-noised	**0.998 ± 0.002**	**1.0 ± 0.0**	0.995 ± 0.005	**0.999 ± 0.001**	**0.997 ± 0.003**	**1.0 ± 0.0**	0.015
RG:Dense	$\nu = 0.15, \hat{\nu} = 0.3$	**DCD (Infomap)**	De-noised	**0.998 ± 0.003**	**1.0 ± 0.0**	0.995 ± 0.006	**0.999 ± 0.003**	**0.997 ± 0.002**	**1.0 ± 0.0**	0.0124
RG:Dense	$\nu = 0.15, \hat{\nu} = 0.3$	**DCD (Spectral)**	De-noised	**0.998 ± 0.003**	**1.0 ± 0.0**	0.995 ± 0.005	**0.999 ± 0.002**	**0.997 ± 0.002**	**1.0 ± 0.0**	0.019
RG:Permute	$\nu = 0.3$	**Closed-Form**	Noisy	0.877 ± 0.067	0.714 ± 0.075	0.789 ± 0.135	0.947 ± 0.016	0.975 ± 0.011	0.716 ± 0.099	0.083
RG:Permute	$\nu = 0.3$	**dGHD**	Noisy	0.724 ± 0.029	0.645 ± 0.049	0.577 ± 0.059	0.921 ± 0.007	0.971 ± 0.006	0.504 ± 0.051	1.0
RG:Permute	$\nu = 0.3$	**Louvain**	Noisy	0.909 ± 0.006	0.702 ± 0.013	**1.0 ± 0.0**	0.872 ± 0.008	0.730 ± 0.0149	0.818 ± 0.011	**0.013**
RG:Permute	$\nu = 0.3$	**Infomap**	Noisy	0.877 ± 0.011	0.698 ± 0.010	**1.0 ± 0.0**	0.842 ± 0.09	0.725 ± 0.022	0.807 ± 0.009	0.021
RG:Permute	$\nu = 0.3$	**Spectral**	Noisy	0.911 ± 0.007	0.708 ± 0.017	**1.0 ± 0.0**	0.876 ± 0.009	0.736 ± 0.018	0.823 ± 0.014	0.017
RG:Permute	$\nu = 0.3$	**DCD (Louvain)**	De-noised	**0.996 ± 0.001**	**1.0 ± 0.0**	0.992 ± 0.002	**0.998 ± 0.001**	**0.995 ± 0.002**	**1.0 ± 0.0**	0.016
RG:Permute	$\nu = 0.3$	**DCD (Infomap)**	De-noised	**0.996 ± 0.002**	**1.0 ± 0.0**	0.992 ± 0.002	**0.998 ± 0.002**	**0.995 ± 0.001**	**1.0 ± 0.0**	0.025
RG:Permute	$\nu = 0.3$	**DCD (Spectral)**	De-noised	**0.996 ± 0.001**	**1.0 ± 0.0**	0.992 ± 0.003	**0.998 ± 0.000**	**0.995 ± 0.003**	**1.0 ± 0.0**	0.02
RG:Dense	$\nu = 0.3, \hat{\nu} = 0.5$	**Closed-Form**	Noisy	0.979 ± 0.005	0.771 ± 0.061	0.930 ± 0.082	0.965 ± 0.012	0.969 ± 0.011	0.821 ± 0.062	0.09
RG:Dense	$\nu = 0.3, \hat{\nu} = 0.5$	**dGHD**	Noisy	0.848 ± 0.071	0.700 ± 0.038	0.731 ± 0.148	0.941 ± 0.010	0.964 ± 0.009	0.672 ± 0.078	1.0
RG:Dense	$\nu = 0.3, \hat{\nu} = 0.5$	**Louvain**	Noisy	0.758 ± 0.056	0.353 ± 0.086	**1.0 ± 0.0**	0.613 ± 0.090	0.310 ± 0.125	0.517 ± 0.113	**0.014**
RG:Dense	$\nu = 0.3, \hat{\nu} = 0.5$	**Infomap**	Noisy	0.752 ± 0.060	0.349 ± 0.092	**1.0 ± 0.0**	0.604 ± 0.097	0.302 ± 0.134	0.505 ± 0.121	0.023
RG:Dense	$\nu = 0.3, \hat{\nu} = 0.5$	**Spectral**	Noisy	0.750 ± 0.087	0.332 ± 0.047	**1.0 ± 0.0**	0.589 ± 0.099	0.286 ± 0.101	0.500 ± 0.175	0.02
RG:Dense	$\nu = 0.3, \hat{\nu} = 0.5$	**DCD (Louvain)**	De-noised	**1.0 ± 0.0**	**1.0 ± 0.0**	**1.0 ± 0.0**	**1.0 ± 0.0**	**1.0 ± 0.0**	**1.0 ± 0.0**	0.017
RG:Dense	$\nu = 0.3, \hat{\nu} = 0.5$	**DCD (Infomap)**	De-noised	**1.0 ± 0.0**	**1.0 ± 0.0**	**1.0 ± 0.0**	**1.0 ± 0.0**	**1.0 ± 0.0**	**1.0 ± 0.0**	0.027
RG:Dense	$\nu = 0.3, \hat{\nu} = 0.5$	**DCD (Spectral)**	De-noised	**1.0 ± 0.0**	**1.0 ± 0.0**	**1.0 ± 0.0**	**1.0 ± 0.0**	**1.0 ± 0.0**	**1.0 ± 0.0**	0.024
PL:Permute	$\alpha = 1$	**Closed-Form**	Noisy	0.797 ± 0.046	0.307 ± 0.007	0.799 ± 0.049	0.801 ± 0.018	0.349 ± 0.051	0.802 ± 0.022	0.09
PL:Permute	$\alpha = 1$	**dGHD**	Noisy	0.797 ± 0.023	0.294 ± 0.009	0.794 ± 0.027	0.787 ± 0.008	0.333 ± 0.045	0.784 ± 0.019	1.0
PL:Permute	$\alpha = 1$	**Louvain**	Noisy	0.500 ± 0.001	0.100 ± 0.001	**1.0 ± 0.0**	0.100 ± 0.001	0.001 ± 0.000	0.001 ± 0.000	**0.015**
PL:Permute	$\alpha = 1$	**Infomap**	Noisy	0.501 ± 0.002	0.101 ± 0.000	**1.0 ± 0.0**	0.101 ± 0.000	0.001 ± 0.000	0.001 ± 0.000	0.026
PL:Permute	$\alpha = 1$	**Spectral**	Noisy	0.500 ± 0.000	0.100 ± 0.001	**1.0 ± 0.0**	0.100 ± 0.001	0.001 ± 0.000	0.001 ± 0.000	0.019
PL:Permute	$\alpha = 1$	**DCD (Louvain)**	De-noised	**0.973 ± 0.012**	**1.0 ± 0.0**	0.945 ± 0.023	**0.995 ± 0.002**	**0.969 ± 0.014**	**1.0 ± 0.0**	0.018
PL:Permute	$\alpha = 1$	**DCD (Infomap)**	De-noised	**0.973 ± 0.011**	**1.0 ± 0.0**	0.945 ± 0.024	**0.995 ± 0.003**	**0.969 ± 0.015**	**1.0 ± 0.0**	0.03
PL:Permute	$\alpha = 1$	**DCD (Infomap)**	De-noised	**0.973 ± 0.013**	**1.0 ± 0.0**	0.945 ± 0.022	**0.995 ± 0.001**	**0.969 ± 0.013**	**1.0 ± 0.0**	0.022
PL:Permute	$\alpha = 1.5$	**Closed-Form**	Noisy	0.811 ± 0.045	0.311 ± 0.011	0.797 ± 0.051	0.807 ± 0.022	0.366 ± 0.015	0.810 ± 0.004	0.088
PL:Permute	$\alpha = 1.5$	**dGHD**	Noisy	0.809 ± 0.043	0.301 ± 0.009	0.791 ± 0.042	0.797 ± 0.015	0.344 ± 0.016	0.796 ± 0.007	1.0
PL:Permute	$\alpha = 1.5$	**Louvain**	Noisy	0.5 ± 0.0	0.1 ± 0.0	**1.0 ± 0.0**	0.1 ± 0.0	0.0 ± 0.0	0.0 ± 0.0	**0.016**
PL:Permute	$\alpha = 1.5$	**Infomap**	Noisy	0.5 ± 0.0	0.1 ± 0.0	**1.0 ± 0.0**	0.1 ± 0.0	0.0 ± 0.0	0.0 ± 0.0	0.026
PL:Permute	$\alpha = 1.5$	**Spectral**	Noisy	0.5 ± 0.0	0.1 ± 0.0	**1.0 ± 0.0**	0.1 ± 0.0	0.0 ± 0.0	0.0 ± 0.0	0.019
PL:Permute	$\alpha = 1.5$	**DCD (Louvain)**	De-noised	**0.989 ± 0.005**	**1.0 ± 0.0**	0.979 ± 0.010	**0.998 ± 0.001**	**0.988 ± 0.006**	**1.0 ± 0**	0.018
PL:Permute	$\alpha = 1.5$	**DCD (Infomap)**	De-noised	**0.989 ± 0.004**	**1.0 ± 0.0**	0.979 ± 0.010	**0.998 ± 0.000**	**0.988 ± 0.005**	**1.0 ± 0**	0.03
PL:Permute	$\alpha = 1.5$	**DCD (Spectral)**	De-noised	**0.989 ± 0.006**	**1.0 ± 0.0**	0.979 ± 0.009	**0.998 ± 0.001**	**0.988 ± 0.007**	**1.0 ± 0**	0.022
PL:Permute	$\alpha = 2$	**Closed-Form**	Noisy	0.825 ± 0.019	0.345 ± 0.015	0.825 ± 0.035	0.826 ± 0.007	0.402 ± 0.024	0.826 ± 0.004	0.085
PL:Permute	$\alpha = 2$	**dGHD**	Noisy	0.818 ± 0.027	0.327 ± 0.018	0.799 ± 0.050	0.816 ± 0.008	0.375 ± 0.031	0.817 ± 0.004	1.0
PL:Permute	$\alpha = 2$	**Louvain**	Noisy	0.5 ± 0.0	0.1 ± 0.0	**1.0 ± 0.0**	0.1 ± 0.0	0.0 ± 0.0	0.0 ± 0.0	**0.016**
PL:Permute	$\alpha = 2$	**Infomap**	Noisy	0.5 ± 0.0	0.1 ± 0.0	**1.0 ± 0.0**	0.1 ± 0.0	0.0 ± 0.0	0.0 ± 0.0	0.026
PL:Permute	$\alpha = 2$	**Spectral**	Noisy	0.5 ± 0.0	0.1 ± 0.0	**1.0 ± 0.0**	0.1 ± 0.0	0.0 ± 0.0	0.0 ± 0.0	0.019
PL:Permute	$\alpha = 2$	**DCD (Louvain)**	De-noised	**0.971 ± 0.017**	**1.0 ± 0.0**	0.941 ± 0.033	**0.994 ± 0.003**	**0.966 ± 0.020**	**1.0 ± 0.0**	0.018
PL:Permute	$\alpha = 2$	**DCD (Infomap)**	De-noised	**0.971 ± 0.018**	**1.0 ± 0.0**	0.941 ± 0.032	**0.994 ± 0.002**	**0.966 ± 0.021**	**1.0 ± 0.0**	0.03
PL:Permute	$\alpha = 2$	**DCD (Spectral)**	De-noised	**0.971 ± 0.016**	**1.0 ± 0.0**	0.941 ± 0.033	**0.994 ± 0.004**	**0.966 ± 0.019**	**1.0 ± 0.0**	0.022

Table 1: Comparison of proposed DCD approach with Closed-Form [31] and dGHD [48] statistical techniques and direct application of community detection methods like Louvain [3], Infomap [46] and Spectral [32] on nosiy DT graph to identify differential sub-networks in paired simulated networks for various settings. Here RG:Permute represents RG networks where first 100 nodes are permuted and form differential sub-network. Similarly, PL:Permute is used for experiments on PL graphs where first 100 nodes are permuted and constitute the differential sub-network. RG:Dense depicts RG networks, where first 100 nodes have higher density in network B in comparison to network A and make-up the differential sub-network. Time is represented as fraction w.r.t. the computational time of most expensive method (dGHD) and compared thoroughly amidst all the methods. Best results are highlighted in bold. The proposed DCD approach can robustly identify differential sub-networks in all simulated experimental settings. It performs the best for evaluation metrics: AUC_ROC (area under ROC curve), Precision, Accuracy, Kappa and Specificity.

differential sub-network splits into two clusters (C5 and C6) and (C8 and C9) in the case differential sub-network respectively.

We investigated the biological meaning of the sub-networks by identifying enriched Gene Ontology (GO) terms. We used R package `GOstats` [12] to identify Biological Processes (BP) and Molecular Functions (MF). The hypergeometric test detected 711 BP and 100 MF statistically significant terms enriched in the sub-networks at 5% significance level. The top three BPs were regulation of myeloid cell apoptotic process, myeloid cell apoptotic process, and establishment of protein localization to organelle. The top three MFs were protein binding, peroxidase activity and glycosaminoglycan binding. Furthermore, we identified 16 significantly enriched KEGG

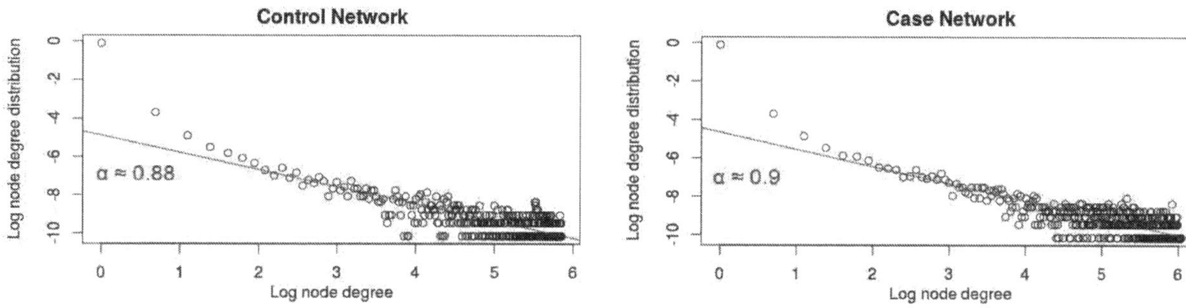

Figure 3: Degree distribution of nodes for control and case co-methylation networks. Since $\alpha < 1$ for both the networks, state-of-the-art statistical techniques cannot be applied on these paired networks for differential sub-network analysis.

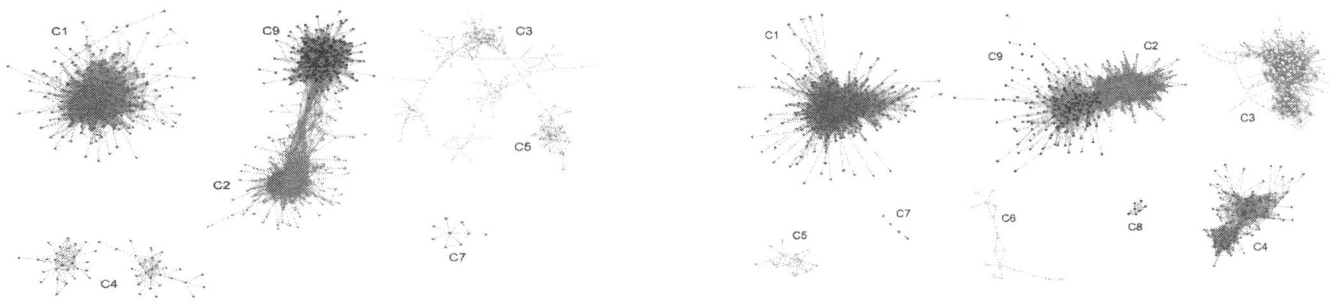

(a) Differential sub-networks in controls

(b) Differential sub-networks in case

Figure 4: DNA co-methylation differential sub-networks. Both the differential networks have the same number of nodes and clusters with similar topology have similar identification number. Cluster C7 is a special case. Even though it comprises of less than 7 nodes in the case sub-network, it consists of 9 nodes in control sub-network and has very different topology in the two sub-networks. As a result, it appears as a differential community of size greater than 7 in the de-noised DT graph. Clusters C5 in control differential sub-network splits into cluster C5 and C6 in case differential sub-network. Similarly, cluster C9 in the control differential sub-network breaks into cluster C9 and C8 in the case differential sub-network.

pathways at 5% significance level including transcriptional misregulation in cancer, hematopoietic cell lineage, and pathways in cancer using DAVID [18].

We detected probes with significant changes in mean methylation levels using the t-test. We found 5, 098 significantly differentially methylated CpGs at 5% significance level after FDR correction for multiple testing [2]. Table 2 summarizes the number of probes, differentially methylated probes (q_i), density ratio between control and case sub-networks (R_i), and distribution of enriched GO terms and KEGG pathways in the identified communities.

	C1	C2	C3	C4	C5	C6	C7	C8	C9	Total
Probes	825	364	198	155	21	17	11	8	294	1893
qi	5	363	22	140	18	0	1	2	245	5098
Ri	0.82	0.16	0.09	0.11	1.77	0	3.67	0	3.23	0.72
BP	628	542	452	378	195	118	136	124	495	711
MF	86	53	44	37	9	9	16	8	53	100
KEGG	6	4	1	3	0	0	0	0	4	16

Table 2: DNA co-methylation networks: a summary of different communities detected by DCD approach.

5 APPLICATION IN GLIOMA CANCER

We also applied the DCD approach, with parameter θ set to 7 for reasons explained earlier, on gene regulatory networks (GRN) generated from the TCGA pan-glioma dataset [31]. The TCGA pan-glioma dataset includes 1, 250 samples (463 IDH-mutant and 653 IDH-wild-type), 583 of which were profiled with Agilent microarray and 667 with RNA-Seq Illumina HiSeq (REF) downloaded from the TCGA portal. The batch effects between the two platforms were corrected using the COMBAT algorithm [23]. The final gene expression data includes 12, 985 genes and 1, 250 samples. From this data, we inferred the GRN for the two different glioma sub-types using the ARACNe [37] algorithm as in [31]. In our analysis, we compared the GRNs of IDH-mutant and IDH-wild-type to identify sub-networks of transcription factors (TFs) having a different regulatory program in these two major conditions.

The ARACNe networks were intersected with an active binding network based on the presence of binding sites in the promoter of a target gene. The active binding network is reconstructed for 2, 532 unique motifs corresponding to 1, 203 unique TFs [24, 26, 38]. A binding relationship is considered active if the TF motif signal is significantly (FDR < 0.05) over-represented in the target

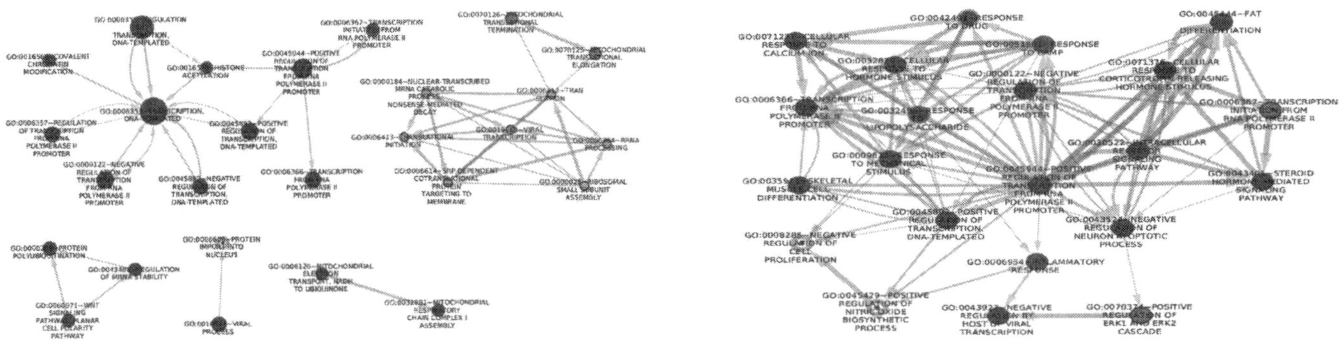

(a) Enrichment results for C_1 (b) Enrichment results for C_3

Figure 5: Comparison of enrichment results of IDH-mutant and IDH-wildtype for differential communities C_1 and C_3. Here the nodes correspond to the BPs and red circle size is proportional to number of genes in IDH-mutant associated with that BP. Similarly, the grey circle size in a node (BP) corresponds to the number of genes in IDH-wild-type related to that BP. Edge size corresponds to the number of genes that overlap between the two connected BPs. Green edges correspond to IDH-mutant while purple edges represent interaction between BPs in IDH-wild-type.

promoter region (∓ 5kbp TSS, hg19) and, in the same position (at least 1bp overlapping), chromatin state is classified as open by Hidden Markov Model proposed in [11]. The active binding network consists of 6, 652, 518 overlapping active sites resulting in 1, 959, 125 unique TF associations between 1, 203 TFs and 51, 705 targets.

The final pruned networks are then obtained by considering the common sub-network of active binding and functional ARACNE networks. They consists of 13, 683 unique connections for IDH-mutant and 14, 158 for IDH-wild-type between TF-TF and TF-target. The number of TFs was reduced to 457 when intersected with the 12, 895 genes of our combined expression matrix. We then apply the proposed DCD approach on the noisy DT graph $G(V, E)$ obtained by taking the absolute difference between the topological graphs of IDH-mutant and IDH-wild-type. The DCD technique discovered a total of 262 TFs as part of 7 differential communities using the Louvain [3] method in $G(V, E)$.

We further investigated these communities by considering the regulons of all the TFs associated with each such community C_i in the corresponding IDH-mutant and IDH-wild-type GRN. The regulon of a TF is defined as its neighbourhood in the GRN. We probed the regulons of all TFs present in a community to detect enriched GO terms using DAVID [23]. We found 15 and 17 statistically significant biological processes (BP) at a 5% significance level using the regulons of TFs in C_1 for IDH-mutant and IDH-wild-type GRNs respectively. We also located 50, 14, 9, 21, 51 and 40 significant BPs for C_2, C_3, C_4, C_5, C_6 and C_7 respectively in IDH-mutant GRN. Similarly, we unearthed 71, 11, 4, 20, 48 and 20 significant BPs for C_2, C_3, C_4, C_5, C_6 and C_7 respectively in IDH-wild-type GRN.

We utilized the output from DAVID for each C_i in the IDH-mutant and IDH-wild-type GRN as input to Enrichment Map tool [39] in Cytoscape. This tool provides a visualization for functional enrichment associated with BPs in C_i and allows comparison between enrichment results for two different conditions (IDH-mutant and IDH-wild-type). Figure 5a illustrates the difference between the enrichment results of C_1 in IDH-mutant and IDH-wild-type case. Similarly, Figure 5b compares the enrichment results of C_3 in IDH-mutant and IDH-wild-type.

Interestingly, the differential community C_1 is enriched with functions related to epigenetic changes such as Chromatin Modification and Histone Acetylation. Ceccarelli et al showed in [7] that the main difference between IDH-mutant and IDH-wild-type gliomas is the characteristic hyper-methylation phenotype (G-CIMP) which has a favourable prognosis both in high grade and low grade gliomas. Conversely, the C_3 reveals enrichments which are specific of IDH-wild-type gliomas such as proliferation and activation of inflammatory response. Therefore, the DCD approach is not only able to identify known but also potential novel enrichments which need to be investigated further, in the two pathological conditions. Additional supplementary information is provided at https://sites.google.com/site/raghvendramallmlresearcher/codes.

6 CONCLUSION

We propose a fast three-stage DCD approach to identify differential sub-networks in paired biological graphs. The proposed method performs node ordering using neighbourhood information of nodes and Jaccard similarity to detect approximate block-diagonals. It denoises the ordered noisy differential topological graph by traversing its landscape along the diagonal. Finally, differential sub-networks are identified using community detection algorithms. We showcased the effectiveness of proposed approach w.r.t. various statistical techniques and direct application of community detection methods for a myriad experimental settings using evaluation metrics like Precision, Accuracy, Kappa and Specificity. The DCD approach identified several meaningful biological processes and molecular functions on ovarian cancer dataset. Similarly, using DCD, we singled out some functional pathways that are different between the IDH-mutant and IDH-wild-type subtypes in case of glioma cancer.

REFERENCES

[1] Ahern, T., Horvath-Puho, E., Spindler, K., Sorensen, H., Ording, A., and Erichsen, R. Colorectal cancer, comorbidity, and risk of venous thromboembolism: assessment of biological interactions in a Danish nationwide cohort. *British Journal of Cancer 114*, 1 (2016), 96–102.

[2] Benjamini, Y., and Yekutieli, D. The control of false discovery rate in multiple testing under dependency. *Annals of Statistics 29* (2001), 1165–1188.

[3] Blondel, V. D., Guillaume, J.-L., Lambiotte, R., and Lefebvre, E. Fast unfolding of communities in large networks. *Journal of statistical mechanics: theory and experiment 2008*, 10 (2008), P10008.

[4] Boginski, V., Butenko, S., and Pardolas, P. M. Statistical analysis of financial networks. *Computational Statistics and Data Analysis 48*, 2 (2005), 431–443.

[5] Brandes, U., and Eriebach, T. Network Analysis: Methodological Foundations. *Springer 3418* (2005).

[6] Broder, A., Kumar, R., Maghoul, F., Raghavan, P., Rajagopalan, S., Stata, R., Tomkins, A., and Wiener, J. Graph structure in the web. *Comput. Netw. 33*, 1-6 (2000), 309–320.

[7] Ceccarelli, M., Barthel, F. P., Malta, T. M., Sabedot, T. S., Salama, S. R., Murray, B. A., Morozova, O., Newton, Y., Radenbaugh, A., Pagnotta, S. M., et al. Molecular Profiling Reveals Biologically Discrete Subsets and Pathways of Progression in Diffuse Glioma. *Cell 164*, 3 (Feb. 2016), 550–563.

[8] Ceccarelli, M., Cerulo, L., and Santore, A. De novo reconstruction of gene regulatory networks from time series data, an approach based on formal methods. *Methods 69*, 3 (Oct 2014), 298–305.

[9] Dittrich, M. T., Klau, G. W., Rosenwald, A., Dandekar, T., and Müller, T. Identifying functional modules in protein–protein interaction networks: an integrated exact approach. *Bioinformatics 24*, 13 (2008), i223–i231.

[10] Erath, A., Lchl, M., and Axhausen, K. Graph-theoretical analysis of the swiss road and railway networks over time. *Networks and Spatial Economics 9*, 3 (2009), 379–400.

[11] Ernst, J., and Kellis, M. Chromhmm: automating chromatin-state discovery and characterization. *Nature methods 9*, 3 (2012), 215–216.

[12] Falcon, S., and Gentleman, R. Using GOstats to test gene lists for GO term association. *Bioinformatics 23*, 2 (2007), 257–258.

[13] Fuller, T., Ghazalpour, A., Aten, J., Drake, T., Lusis, A., and Horvath, S. Weighted Gene Co-expression Network Analysis Strategies Applied to Mouse Weight. *Mammilian Genome 18*, 6 (2007), 463–472.

[14] Gill, R., Datta, S., and Datta, S. A statistical framework for differential network analysis from microarrya data. *BMC: Bioinformatics 11*, 1 (2010), 95.

[15] Girvan, M., and Newman, M. E. Community structure in social and biological networks. *Proc. of the national academy of sciences 99*, 12 (2002), 7821–7826.

[16] Ha, M., Baladandayuthapani, V., and Do, K. Dingo: differential network analysis in genomics. *Bioinformatics 31*, 21 (2015), 3413–20.

[17] Horvath, S., Zhang, Y., Langfelder, P., Kahn, R. S., Boks, M. P., van Eijk, K., van den Berg, L. H., and Ophoff, R. A. Aging effects on DNA methylation modules in human brain and blood tissue. *Genome biology 13*, 10 (2012), R97.

[18] Huang, D. W., Sherman, B. T., and Lempicki, R. A. Systematic and integrative analysis of large gene lists using david bioinformatics resources. *Nature protocols 4*, 1 (2009), 44–57.

[19] Hubert, L. J. Assignment methods in combinatorial data analysis. *Marcel Dekker 1* (1987).

[20] Ideker, T., Ozier, O., Schwikowski, B., and Siegel, A. Discovery regulartory and signalling circuits in molecular interaction networks. *Bioinformatics 18* (2002).

[21] Jiao, Y., Widschwendter, M., and Teschendorff, A. E. A systems-level integrative framework for genome-wide dna methylation and gene expression data identifies differential gene expression modules under epigenetic control. *Bioinformatics 30*, 16 (2014), 2360–2366.

[22] Jin, L., Chen, Y., Wang, T., Hui, P., and Vasilakos, A. Understanding user behavior in online social networks: a survey. *Communications Magazine, IEEE 51*, 9 (September 2013), 144–150.

[23] Johnson, W. E., Li, C., and Rabinovic, A. Adjusting batch effects in microarray expression data using empirical bayes methods. *Biostatistics 8*, 1 (2007), 118–127.

[24] Jolma, A., Yan, J., Whitington, T., Toivonen, J., Nitta, K. R., Rastas, P., Morgunova, E., Enge, M., Taipale, M., Wei, G., et al. Dna-binding specificities of human transcription factors. *Cell 152*, 1 (2013), 327–339.

[25] Keller, A., Bakes, C., Gerasch, A., Kaufmann, M., Kohlbacher, O., Meese, E., and Lenhof, H. A novel algorithm for detecting differentially regulated paths based on gene enrichment analysis. *Bioinfomatics 25*, 21 (2009), 2787–2794.

[26] Kulakovskiy, I. V., Vorontsov, I. E., Yevshin, I. S., Soboleva, A. V., Kasianov, A. S., Ashoor, H., Ba-Alawi, W., Bajic, V. B., Medvedeva, Y. A., Kolpakov, F. A., et al. Hocomoco: expansion and enhancement of the collection of transcription factor binding sites models. *Nucleic acids research 44*, D1 (2016), D116–D125.

[27] Lamirel, J.-C., Cuxac, P., Mall, R., and Safi, G. A new efficient and unbiased approach for clustering quality evaluation. *New Frontiers in Applied Data Mining* (2012), 209–220.

[28] Lena, P. D., Wu, G., Martelli, P., Casadio, R., and Nardini, M. C. An efficient tool for molecular interaction maps overlap. *BMC Bioinforma 14*, 1 (2013), 159.

[29] Levandowsky, M., and Winter, D. Distance between sets. *Nature 234*, 5323 (1971), 34–35.

[30] Li, D., Brown, J. B., Orsini, L., Pan, Z., Hu, G., and He, S. Moda: Module differential analysis for weighted gene co-expression network. *arXiv preprint arXiv:1605.04739* (2016).

[31] Mall, R., Cerulo, L., Bensmail, H., Iavarone, A., and Ceccarelli, M. Detection of statistically significant network changes in complex biological networks. *BMC Systems Biology 11*, 1 (2017), 32.

[32] Mall, R., Langone, R., and Suykens, J. A. Kernel spectral clustering for big data networks. *Entropy 15*, 5 (2013), 1567–1586.

[33] Mall, R., Langone, R., and Suykens, J. A. Self-tuned kernel spectral clustering for large scale networks. In *Big Data, 2013 IEEE International Conference on* (2013), IEEE, pp. 385–393.

[34] Mall, R., Langone, R., and Suykens, J. A. Multilevel hierarchical kernel spectral clustering for real-life large scale complex networks. *PloS one 9*, 6 (2014), e99966.

[35] Mantel, N. The detection of disease clustering and a generalized regression approach. *Cancer Research 27*, 2 (1967), 209.

[36] Marbach, D., Lamparter, D., Quon, G., Kellis, M., Kutalik, Z., and Bergmann, S. Tissue-specific regulatory circuits reveal variable modular perturbations across complex diseases. *Nature methods* (2016).

[37] Margolin, A. A., Nemenman, I., Basso, K., Wiggins, C., Stolovitzky, G., Favera, R. D., and Califano, A. Aracne: An algorithm for the reconstruction of gene regulatory networks in a mammalian cellular context. *BMC Bioinformatics 7*, S-1 (2006).

[38] Mathelier, A., Fornes, O., Arenillas, D. J., Chen, C.-y., Denay, G., Lee, J., Shi, W., Shyr, C., Tan, G., Worsley-Hunt, R., et al. Jaspar 2016: a major expansion and update of the open-access database of transcription factor binding profiles. *Nucleic acids research 44*, D1 (2016), D110–D115.

[39] Merico, D., Isserlin, R., Stueker, O., Emili, A., and Bader, G. D. Enrichment map: a network-based method for gene-set enrichment visualization and interpretation. *PloS one 5*, 11 (2010), e13984.

[40] Mislove, A., Marcon, M., Gummadi, K. P., Druschel, P., and Bhattacharjee, B. Measurement and analysis of online social networks. In *Proc. of the 7th ACM SIGCOMM Conference on Internet Measurement* (2007), IMC '07, ACM, pp. 29–42.

[41] Nacu, S., Critchley-Throne, R., Lee, R., and Holmes, S. Gene expression network analysis and applications to immunology. *Bioinformatics 23*, 7 (2007), 850–858.

[42] Orman, G. K., and Labatut, V. A comparison of community detection algorithms on artificial networks. In *International Conference on Discovery Science* (2009), Springer, pp. 242–256.

[43] Pržulj, N. Biological network comparison using graphlet degree distribution. *Bioinformatics 23*, 2 (2007), e177–e183.

[44] Ramana, M., Scheinerman, E., and Ullman, D. Fractional isomorphism of graphs. *Discrete Mathematics 132*, 1 (1994), 247–265.

[45] Reichardt, J., and Bornholdt, S. Statistical mechanics of community detection. *Physical Review E 74*, 1 (2006), 016110.

[46] Rosvall, M., and Bergstrom, C. T. Multilevel compression of random walks on networks reveals hierarchical organization in large integrated systems. *PloS one 6*, 4 (2011), e18209.

[47] Ruan, D. *Statistical methods for comparing labelled graphs.* PhD thesis, Imperial College London, 2014.

[48] Ruan, D., Young, A., and Montana, G. Differential analysis of biological networks. *BMC bioinformatics 16*, 1 (2015), 327.

[49] Shervashidze, N., Schweitzer, P., van Leeuwen, E. J., Mehlhorn, K., and Borgwardt, K. Weisfeiler-Lehman Graph Kernels. *Journal of Machine Learning Research 12* (2011), 2539–2561.

[50] Teschendorff, A. E., Menon, U., Gentry-Maharaj, A., Ramus, S. J., Weisenberger, D. J., Shen, H., Campan, M., Noushmehr, H., Bell, C. G., Maxwell, A. P., et al. Age-dependent DNA methylation of genes that are suppressed in stem cells is a hallmark of cancer. *Genome research 20*, 4 (2010), 440–446.

[51] Wallace, T., Martin, D., and Ambs, S. Interaction among genes, tumor biology and the environment in cancer health disparities: examining the evidence on a national and global scale. *Carcinogenesis 32*, 8 (2011), 1107–1121.

[52] West, J., Beck, S., Wang, X., and Teschendorff, A. E. An integrative network algorithm identifies age-associated differential methylation interactome hotspots targeting stem-cell differentiation pathways. *Scientific reports 3* (2013), 1630.

[53] Yang, Q., and Sze, S. Path matching and graph matching in biological networks. *Journal of Computational Biology 14*, 1 (2007), 56–67.

[54] Yang, X., Shao, X., Gao, L., and Zhang, S. Systematic dna methylation analysis of multiple cell lines reveals common and specific patterns within and across tissues of origin. *Human molecular genetics 24*, 15 (2015), 4374–4384.

[55] Zhang, B., Horvath, S., et al. A general framework for weighted gene co-expression network analysis. *Statistical applications in genetics and molecular biology 4*, 1 (2005), 1128.

TINTIN: Exploiting Target Features for Signaling Network Similarity Computation and Ranking

Huey Eng Chua, Sourav S. Bhowmick
Complexity Institute, Nanyang Technological University, Singapore
hechua|assourav@ntu.edu.sg

Lisa Tucker-Kellogg
Duke-NUS Medical School, National University of Singapore, Singapore
lisa.tucker-kellogg@duke-nus.edu.sg

ABSTRACT

Network similarity ranking attempts to rank a given set of networks based on its "similarity" to a reference network. State-of-the-art approaches tend to be general in the sense that they can be applied to networks in a variety of domains. Consequently, they are not designed to exploit domain-specific knowledge to find similar networks although such knowledge may yield interesting insights that are unique to specific problems, paving the way to solutions that are more effective. We propose TINTIN which uses a novel *target feature-based* network similarity distance for ranking similar signaling networks. In contrast to state-of-the-art network similarity techniques, TINTIN considers both topological *and* dynamic features in order to compute network similarity. Our empirical study on signaling networks from *BioModels* with real-world curated outcomes reveals that TINTIN ranking is different from state-of-the-art approaches.

1 INTRODUCTION

The *network similarity problem* scores the resemblance between a pair of related networks. We can broadly classify network similarity approaches for biological networks into two classes, namely *node mapping-based* and *network feature-based*. The former is based on graph isomorphism [15, 19] as node mappings are performed using different measures and the extent of the network similarity is dependent on the mappings. In contrast, the latter class of approaches do not assume the existence of such node mappings. These approaches [4, 17] generally employ network structure-based *local* or *global* measures to determine similarity between networks. Specifically, *global measures*, such as those based on network features, are derived from the entire biological network and tend to be biased as biological networks are inherently noisy and incomplete [17]. In contrast, *local measures*, which are typically derived from regions of networks that are well-studied, are deemed as more appropriate [17]. For instance, graphlet degree distribution (GDD) [17] and NETSIMILE [4] both use local measures to determine network similarity. A common theme that runs through these network feature-based approaches is their generality and applicability to other types of networks such as social networks. Consequently, they are not designed to exploit domain-specific knowledge to find similar networks, although such knowledge may yield interesting insights that are unique to specific problems. *In this paper, we present a novel network similarity technique called TINTIN, which is designed for signaling networks and leverages such domain-specific knowledge to identify networks that are similar in terms of target features.*

Signaling networks model biological systems as networks of interacting molecules. When biological processes are dysregulated due to diseases, the activities of downstream molecule(s) (referred to as *disease node(s)* in the paper) are affected and typically manifest themselves as phenotypic changes related to the disease. For instance, in the MAPK-PI3K network, the hyperactivity of activated ERK, a downstream molecule, is often linked to cell proliferation [21], a cancer hallmark. This has led to increasing popularity of targeted therapeutic strategies to tackle such diseases where drugs are designed to hit molecules in a signaling network crucial for tumor growth and progression [22]. These molecules (referred to as *targets*) modulate the disease node(s) directly (*e.g.*, MEK [21]) or indirectly (*e.g.*, Raf [21]).

In this paper, we exploit the network features associated with targets in a signaling network to compute similarity between signaling networks. Intuitively, in *target feature-based network similarity* problem we deem a pair of signaling networks as *similar* if their targets have *similar* characteristics. Hence, our network similarity technique called TINTIN (Target-based SIgnaling NeTwork SImilarity ComputatioN) is driven by similarity of features of targets that modulate specific disease-related nodes (disease nodes) associated with a pair of signaling networks. It takes as input (a) a *reference network* (e.g., Ras activation), its disease node (e.g., Ras) and an associated set of known targets; and (b) a set of *candidate networks* along with their disease nodes, known targets and features. It ranks these candidate networks based on their *degree of similarity* to the reference network w.r.t. the features of the known targets. TINTIN is potentially useful for several real-world applications such as network-based target prioritization [8][1] and clustering signaling networks based on the feature similarity of targets.

In summary, this paper makes the following key contributions: (a) We introduce the novel problem of *target feature-based network similarity* for signaling networks (Section 4). (b) We present TINTIN, a target-driven approach that is, to the best of our knowledge, the world's first algorithm to address this problem (Section 5). (c) We conduct an empirical study on real signaling networks and drug target data to analyze the similarities and differences of TINTIN's rankings compared to that of the state-of-the-art generic network similarity techniques (Section 6).

[1] In contrast to this work, the study in [8] does not focus on details of the network similarity problem. Instead, it *assumes* the existence of such a network similarity technique, which is utilized for target prioritization.

Permission to make digital or hard copies of all or part of this work for personal or classroom use is granted without fee provided that copies are not made or distributed for profit or commercial advantage and that copies bear this notice and the full citation on the first page. Copyrights for components of this work owned by others than ACM must be honored. Abstracting with credit is permitted. To copy otherwise, or republish, to post on servers or to redistribute to lists, requires prior specific permission and/or a fee. Request permissions from permissions@acm.org.
ACM-BCB'17, August 20–23, 2017, Boston, MA, USA.
© 2017 ACM. ISBN 978-1-4503-4722-8/17/08...$15.00
DOI: http://dx.doi.org/10.1145/3107411.3107470

2 RELATED WORK

Compared to generic *target-unaware* network similarity techniques such as GDD [17] and NETSIMILE [4], TINTIN differs in the following ways. First, the network similarity problems are defined differently in existing work. In GDD [17], two networks are deemed similar when they share similar *graphlet degree distribution* that is measured using the *GDD agreement* (topology-based feature); in NETSIMILE, network similarity is measured using a feature vector consisting of seven topological features. In contrast, we define similarity as the likelihood of two network sharing targets with similar topological and dynamic characteristics. Second, GDD was designed for undirected networks (*e.g.*, protein-protein interaction) and is not immediately applicable to directed networks such as cell signaling networks. Third, we consider a wider variety of network features inclusive of both *topological* and *dynamic* features. Both GDD and NETSIMILE use only topological features. Traditionally, the topological representation of signaling networks is considered static [12] as they capture specific observation under particular condition (*e.g.* equilibrium condition). Hence, topological characteristics (*e.g.*, betweenness centrality) that are derived from the network topology are static in nature as well. However, biological systems change with time and time-dependent response of molecular species are typically captured as dynamic time series data (*e.g.*, concentration-time profiles). Lastly, GDD and NETSIMILE are generic techniques. That is, they are not designed to exploit domain-specific knowledge (e.g., knowledge of disease nodes in a signaling network) to find similar networks. In contrast, our similarity measure is "disease node-aware" and is designed specifically for disease-related signaling networks.

3 BACKGROUND

In this section, we introduce key concepts necessary to understand this paper. We first describe the graphical representation of signaling networks and ordinary differential equation (ODE) models. Next, we introduce a recently proposed dynamic feature called *profile shape similarity distance* [5]. Lastly, we briefly describe a *target characterization* framework called TENET [6].

3.1 Graph Model of Signaling Networks

A biological signaling network describes biochemical reactions (with reactants and products) that affect the concentrations of molecular species in the network. Graphically, this reaction is typically represented as a directed hyperedge connecting one set of nodes to another set [14, 20]. Hence, a signaling network is naturally represented as a directed hypergraph $G = (V, E)$. Analysis of directed hypergraphs is generally more complex than graphs and many graph algorithms cannot be used directly on hypergraphs. Hence, hypergraphs are often transformed into graphs containing simple edges for analysis using techniques such as bipartite and substrate graph representation [14]. In this paper, we convert signaling network hypergraphs into bipartite graphs by adopting the method in [10]. We chose the bipartite graph representation as it retains the original structural information of the hypergraphs [14]. Note that the transformed bipartite graph is used to compute the topological features.

We refer to a node in a signaling network as a *candidate target* if when perturbed, it modulates the activity of a specific node (referred to as *disease node*). A *disease node* is a protein that is either involved in some biological processes which may be deregulated, resulting in manifestation of a disease, or be of interest due to its potential role in the disease. Given a signaling network $G = (V, E)$ and a disease node $x \in V$, let the set of nodes having a path leading to x be denoted as $V_x \subseteq V$. Then, the set of *candidate target* nodes in G relevant to x is denoted as $T_x \subseteq V_x$.

Each reaction (edge) in a signaling network is further annotated with dynamic information associated with the biochemical process. In signaling networks, numerous ordinary differential equations (ODEs) containing various reaction kinetics and initial concentrations for every species are used to model the production and consumption rates of different molecular species [2]. The determination of these reaction kinetics can be technically challenging. Hence, a large proportion of these kinetics are usually estimated using parameter estimation techniques [18]. Despite this uncertainty, these under-determined ODE systems can still model real, observable biological behaviour, providing valuable means for quantitative study. Note that ODE-based models of signaling networks are expected to grow further in the future and become an important and accepted way of representing biological knowledge [2]. In this paper, we use hypergraphs containing ODEs for simulation to obtain *concentration-time series profiles* (i.e., plots of concentration against time) of nodes.

3.2 Profile Shape Similarity Distance (PSSD)

In signaling networks, signal responses to perturbation are typically measured in terms of phosphoprotein concentrations dynamics represented as concentration-time profiles. There are certain considerations in comparing these phosphoprotein concentration-time profiles. In signaling networks, reactions occur at different and non-uniform rates [1] resulting in profiles with variable time delays. Hence, a distance measure based on one-to-one alignment on a time axis (Euclidean) is ineffective at detecting similarity in these profiles. A non-linear measure, such as *dynamic time warping* (DTW) distance, allows a more intuitive alignment between profiles [13] and is more suitable for biological time series data [1].

Definition 3.1. Given two discrete time series φ_u and φ_v, the ***dynamic time warping distance*** *between them is defined recursively as:*

$$\text{DTW}(\varphi_u, \varphi_v) = \xi(F(\varphi_u), F(\varphi_v)) + Min \begin{cases} \text{DTW}(\varphi_u, Rest(\varphi_v)) \\ \text{DTW}(Rest(\varphi_u), \varphi_v) \\ \text{DTW}(Rest(\varphi_u), Rest(\varphi_v)) \end{cases}$$

where $F(\varphi_u) = \{\varphi_{u[1]}\}$, $Rest(\varphi_u) = \{\varphi_{u[2]}, \varphi_{u[3]}, \cdots, \varphi_{u[n]}\}$, $\xi(\varphi_{u[i]}, \varphi_{v[j]}) = (\varphi_{u[i]} - \varphi_{v[j]})^2$ and $\varphi_{u[i]}$ is the value of φ_u at time point i [13].

Definition 3.2. Given a concentration-time profile ζ_u having n time points, denoted as $\varphi_u = \{\varphi_{u[0]}, \cdots, \varphi_{u[n]}\}$, let m be the median value of φ_u. The corresponding ***inverted profile*** *is denoted as $\varphi'_u = \{\varphi'_{u[0]}, \cdots, \varphi'_{u[n]}\}$ where $\varphi'_{u[i]} = 2 \times m - \varphi_{u[i]}$.*

Definition 3.3. Given a signaling network $H = (V_H, E_H)$, let φ_u, φ_v be the Z-normalized concentration-time profiles of $u, v \in V_H$. The ***profile shape similarity distance*** *[5] of u with respect to v is defined as:*

$$\Phi_{(u,v)} = Min(\text{DTW}(\varphi_u, \varphi_v), \text{DTW}(\varphi'_u, \varphi_v))$$

In summary, PSSD identifies the most relevant upstream regulators by assessing the similarity of the concentration-time series profiles of a target and its upstream regulators.

3.3 Target Characterization using TENET

In this paper, we leverage on a target characterization approach (TENET [6]) to generated the ground truth for assessing the performance of TINTIN. TENET is a network-centric, *in silico* target characterization system, which uses signaling networks having known targets from publicly-available signaling network repositories (e.g., *BioModels*) to learn for each network, a set of topological features that are predictive of targets and a *characterization model* that can be used to generate topological feature-based (TFB) rankings of targets. The characterization model specifies which topological features are important for discriminating the targets in a signaling network and how these features should be combined to quantify the likelihood of a node being a target. It generates different characterization models for different networks as it is unlikely for one characterization model to generalize the characteristics of known targets in all networks due to the complexity and diversity of signaling networks.

4 TARGET FEATURE-BASED NETWORK SIMILARITY PROBLEM

Network similarity measures the *similarity* between a pair of networks. In the literature, there are different strategies to measure such similarity for both directed (e.g., signaling networks) and undirected (e.g., PPI networks) networks. Hence, a set of networks can be *ranked* with respect to a *reference* network based on their similarity degrees to the latter. Formally, the *similarity-based network ranking problem* can be defined as follows.

Definition 4.1. Given a reference network G and a set of candidate networks $\mathcal{L} = \{L_1, \cdots, L_N\}$, the ***similarity-based network ranking problem*** *computes* ***network similarity distance*** *$D(G, L_i)$ between G and each $L_i \in \mathcal{L}$ and ranks them in ascending (or descending) order of $D(.)$. Given the networks L_i and L_j where $L_i, L_j \in \mathcal{L}$, L_i is more similar to G if $D(G, L_i) < D(G, L_j)$. The* ***best matched network*** *$L_k \in \mathcal{L}$ of G is the network with the smallest network similarity distance. That is, $\forall i\ D(G, L_k) < D(G, L_i)$.*

Recall that the network similarity distance in TINTIN is measured using target features. Hence, we now formally introduce it. The network similarity distance $D(G, L)$ between a pair of signaling networks, G and L, is based on similarity of the targets in G and L with respect to their network features. Table 1 lists the set of topological and dynamic features that we consider for computing $D(G, L)$ (referred to as *target features*). That is, given a reference network G and two candidate networks L_i and L_j, G is more *similar* to L_i if the feature distribution of the targets in G is more *similar* to that of the targets in L_i across all network features being considered.

Definition 4.2. Given a reference network G, its disease node x_G and an associated set of known targets T_G; a set of candidate networks $\mathcal{L} = \{L_1, \cdots, L_N\}$, their disease nodes $\bigcup_{i=1}^{|\mathcal{L}|} x_{\mathcal{L}[i]}$ and associated sets of known targets $\bigcup_{i=1}^{|\mathcal{L}|} T_{\mathcal{L}[i]}$; and a set of target features $\mathcal{X}$, the ***distribution similarity*** *of G and $\mathcal{L}_i$ for a target feature $\mathcal{X}_j$ is defined as*

Symbol	Description	Type
θ_u	Degree centrality of node u. The in, out and total degree centralities are denoted as $\theta_{in(u)}$, $\theta_{out(u)}$ and $\theta_{total(u)}$, respectively.	T
α_u	Eigenvector centrality of node u.	T
β_u	Closeness centrality of node u.	T
γ_u	Eccentricity centrality of node u.	T
δ_u	Betweenness centrality of node u.	T
π_u	Bridging coefficient of node u.	T
ζ_u	Bridging centrality of node u.	T
κ_u	Clustering coefficient of node u. The undirected, in, out, cycle and middleman clustering coefficients are denoted as $\kappa_{undir(u)}$, $\kappa_{in(u)}$, $\kappa_{out(u)}$, $\kappa_{cyc(u)}$ and $\kappa_{mid(u)}$, respectively.	T
μ_u	Proximity prestige of node u.	T
ω_u	Target downstream effect of node u [5].	T
$\Phi_{(u,v)}$	Profile shape similarity distance (PSSD) between nodes u and v [5].	D

Table 1: Target features. T: Topological, D: Dynamic

$$p_{G,\mathcal{L}_i,\mathcal{X}_j} = \mathcal{F}(\mathcal{G}(G, x_G, T_G, \mathcal{X}_j), \mathcal{G}(\mathcal{L}_i, x_{\mathcal{L}_i}, T_{\mathcal{L}_i}, \mathcal{X}_j)) \quad (1)$$

where $\mathcal{G}(G, x_G, T_G, \mathcal{X}_j)$ is a function that retrieves target feature $\mathcal{X}_j$ for a set of nodes T_G in a given network G with disease node x_G, and $\mathcal{F}(A, B)$ is a statistical function that computes the similarity of two distributions A and B. Then, the ***target feature-based similarity distance*** *between G and $\mathcal{L}_i$ is defined as*

$$D(G, \mathcal{L}_i) = C(\{p_{G,\mathcal{L}_i,\mathcal{X}_j} \mid 1 \leq j \leq |\mathcal{X}|\}) \quad (2)$$

where $C(Z)$ is a function that aggregates the set of items Z.

In this work, we use the target features specified in Table 1. Hence, the functions ($\mathcal{G}(G, x_G, T_G, \mathcal{X}_j)$) used for retrieving the target features correspond directly to the formula for computing these features. For example, to compute PSSD, we use the formula given in Definition 3.3. The formula for the remaining target features can be found in [6]. In particular, we use two statistical functions ($\mathcal{F}(A, B)$), namely, Wilcoxon Rank-Sum (Wilcoxon) and Kolmogorov-Smirnov (KS) statistical measures[2] to assess distribution similarity. Hence, distribution similarities are obtained as p-values. We use *Stouffer's method* (Stouffer) as the aggregation function ($C(Z)$) to aggregate the p-values in Equation 2. Note that Stouffer's method can be applied to combine dependent p-values by introducing some degree of dependence (correlation) between pairs by following the approach in [11]. A larger aggregated p-value implies the null hypotheses (a closer target feature-based similarity) are true for every test.

5 THE TINTIN ALGORITHM

Algorithm 1 outlines the TINTIN algorithm. Given a reference signaling network G, its disease node x_G and known targets T_G, a set of candidate networks $\mathcal{L}$, their disease nodes $x = \bigcup_{i=1}^{|\mathcal{L}|} x_{\mathcal{L}[i]}$ and known targets $T = \bigcup_{i=1}^{|\mathcal{L}|} T_{\mathcal{L}[i]}$, it identifies the best matched network $G_{best} \in \mathcal{L}$ of G and a ranked list of $\mathcal{L}$ in two phases. TINTIN provides an optional relaxation parameter p_r to configure the criteria for filtering out dissimilar networks.

[2] The Wilcoxon and KS tests are nonparametric and are suitable for features with distribution that are unknown a priori.

Algorithm 1 Algorithm TINTIN

```
Require: Reference network G and its disease node x_G and known targets
    T_G; set of candidate networks 𝓛, their disease nodes x and known
    targets T; relaxation parameter p_r (optional).
Ensure: Best matched network G_best and network ranked list r.
 1: X_best, P_best, H, Truth ←LEARNBESTVARIANT(𝓛,x,T)
 2: p_t ←LEARNPTHRESHOLD(Truth, P_best, p_r)
 3: G_best, r ←GETBESTNETWORK(G, x_G, T_G, 𝓛, X_best, p_t, H)
```

Algorithm 2 Procedure LEARNBESTVARIANT

```
Require: Set of training networks 𝓛, their disease nodes x and known
    targets T.
Ensure: Best feature type X_best; matrix of p-values for training networks
    using the best feature type P_best; matrix of all features values in all
    training networks H; and the ground truth Truth.
𝒜 ←INITIALIZE({X_all,X_T,X_D})
H ←EXTRACTFEATURES(𝓛,X_all)
Truth ←GETGROUNDTRUTH(𝓛,H)
for iteration i=1 to |𝓛| do
    for iteration j=i+1 to |𝓛| do
        for iteration k=1 to |𝒜| do
            M ←GETRELEVANTFEATURES(H,𝒜_k)
            P_W ←WILCOX(𝓛_i, 𝓛_j, M)
            P_KS ←KS(𝓛_i, 𝓛_j, M)
            PVal_i(k, 𝓛_j) ←COMBINEP(P_W,P_KS)
        end for
    end for
end for
for iteration i=1 to |𝒜| do
    for iteration j=1 to |𝓛| do
        Rank_{i,j} ←RANK(PVal, i, j)
    end for
    Distance_i ←SUM(SPEARMAN(Rank, i),KENDALL(Rank, i),Truth_i)
end for
X_best, P_best, H, Truth ←GETBESTVARIANT(Distance,PVal,𝒜)
```

The Learning Phase. In this phase, TINTIN learns the best variant for finding G_{best} (Lines 1-2 in Algorithm 1). In particular, three variants (Table 2) of TINTIN utilizing different feature sets (only topological features, only dynamic feature and combination of topological and dynamic features) are considered. We begin by identifying the *ground truth* (true order of the ranking) of the candidate networks. The ground truth reflects the *actual* similarity of the target characteristics of the networks based on prior knowledge or empirical results. Hence, it can either be provided by experts familiar with the candidate networks and its associated targets or generated automatically by using models that characterize the known targets in these networks. We adopt the latter strategy by utilizing TENET[6]. Specifically, in order to generate the ground truth, we exploit TENET in the following way. Given a reference network G and two candidate networks L_1 and L_2, L_1 is more similar to G if the characterization model of L_1 produces a better characterization of known targets in G compared to L_2. That is, the characterization model of L_1 achieves a larger AUROC (area under ROC curve) for known targets in G compared to that of L_2. Note that AUROC is typically used to assess classifier performance as the metric is robust for imbalanced datasets [9]. The ground truth can

Variant	All Features	T. Features	D. Features	Stouffer
TINTIN$_A$	√			√
TINTIN$_S$		√		√
TINTIN$_D$			√	√

√ marks inclusion in the variant. T.=Topological, D.=Dynamic

Table 2: Variants of our network similarity strategy.

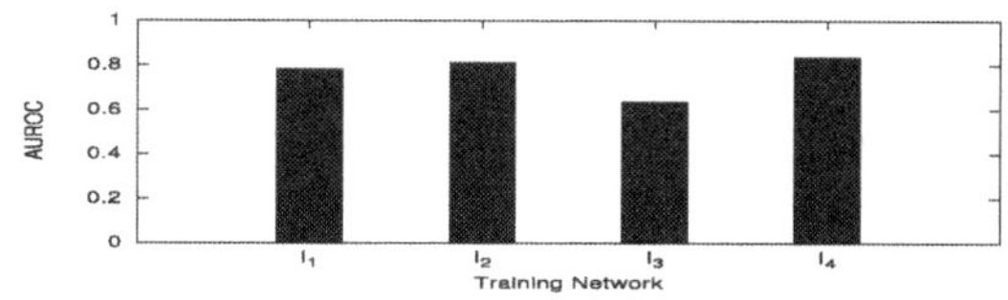

Figure 1: Ground truth found using AUROC.

be interpreted as the ordering of the candidate networks based on decreasing AUROC.

Next, all the features for targets in all candidate networks are extracted and the combined p-value for the Wilcoxon and the KS tests for each variant is computed. Then, for each candidate network $\mathcal{L}_i$, three ranked lists (denoted as r), each corresponding to one variant (see Table 2), are obtained by ordering the remaining candidate networks in decreasing order of the combined p-value. Next, the disagreement between r and the ground truth is measured using the *Spearman footrule distance* and *Kendall-Tau distance*, denoted as $\Upsilon(.)$ and $\Lambda(.)$, respectively. Given two complete rankings r_1 and r_2 of a set of N individuals, let $r_1(i)$ be the rank of $i \in N$ in the ranked list r_1. Then, the distances are calculated as:

$$\Upsilon(r_1, r_2) = \sum_{i \in N} |r_1(i) - r_2(i)|$$

$$\Lambda(r_1, r_2) = |\{i, j\} : r_1(i) < r_1(j) \text{ and } r_2(i) > r_2(j)|$$

For each variant, the Spearman footrule and Kendall-Tau distances for all the candidate networks are aggregated to obtain the overall distance. The best variant is the one yielding the least overall distance. Furthermore, this phase determines a p-value threshold (denoted as p_t) that shall be used to filter off dissimilar network (Algorithm 1, Line 2). First, it obtains a mapping between the combined p-values and "poor"[3] AUROC. Then, these combined p-values are averaged to obtain p_m. The value of p_t is set as the minimum of p_m and p_r since combined p-values less than p_t are removed.

The Ranking Phase. In the next phase, the TINTIN algorithm identifies the best matched network G_{best} and rank of the candidate networks with combined p-values greater than p_t. First, values of predictive topological features is extracted for G. Then, for each pair of $(G, \mathcal{L}_i)$, the Wilcoxon and KS tests are performed for each of these features and the p-values obtained are combined. Finally, the candidate networks with combined p-values greater than or equal to p_t are ranked in order of decreasing combined p-values to obtain r. The top-ranked network is G_{best}.

Observe that it is possible for our ranking strategy to return no best matched network if all the combined p-values are less than p_t. This indicates that none of the given candidate networks are similar. In this case, we can either explore additional candidate networks to identify G_{best} or relax p_t using p_r to obtain a suboptimal G_{best}.

THEOREM 5.1. *The worst-case time complexity of Algorithm 1 is* $O(|\mathcal{L}|(|\mathcal{L}| - 1)(\mathcal{G}(X_{all}) + |\mathcal{A}|(|V_{\mathcal{L}[i]}||V_{\mathcal{L}[j]}|)^2))$ *time in the worst*

[3] We deem AUROC<0.5 as "poor" since it indicates performance worse than random prioritization.

case, where $\mathcal{G}(X_{all})$ is the worst time complexity for extracting all features, $|V_{\mathcal{L}[i]}|$ is the number of nodes of the ith network in $\mathcal{L}$ and $|\mathcal{A}|$ is the number of TINTIN *variants.*

The proof of the above theorem is given in [7].

6 EXPERIMENTS

TINTIN is implemented using Java. In this section, we investigate its performance. All experiments are performed on a computer system using a 64-bit operating system with 8GB RAM and a dual core processor running at 3.60GHz.

Datasets. We use a reference network (I_0) and four candidate networks (I_1 to I_4) for our experiments as shown in Table 3. Note that although there are more than 600 curated signaling networks in *Biomodels*, we restrict our study to only five signaling networks. This is because we need to identify known targets of signaling networks for validating our experimental results. Unfortunately, to the best of our knowledge, there is no publicly available technique that can automatically identify known targets from signaling networks by analyzing biomedical literature. Hence, we are confined to manual target curation from a large volume of biomedical literature, a time-intensive process. Also, although larger signaling networks are desirable, to the best of our knowledge, no publicly-available large signaling networks (e.g., human cancer signaling network) contain dynamic information of *all* edges (ODEs), preventing us to exploit dynamic features such as PSSD. The targets of I_0 are curated from [16] (Ca^{2+}, EGF:EGFR, EGFR, activated EGFR and Ras) and from [3] (dimerized EGFR). The curated targets of the candidate networks are given in [7].

Best TINTIN variant. First, we identify the best variant of TINTIN. Specifically, we examine how various variants (Table 2) perform on the given set of candidate networks (I_1 to I_4). Then, we examine if the best performing variant for the candidate networks is also effective in identifying the best matched network for the reference network. Finally, we analyze their runtime performance.

Figure 2 reports the results. Interestingly, we observe that the variant using only dynamic feature performs better (smaller distance between ground truth and TINTIN ranking) than variants that either use only topological feature set or a combination of topological and dynamic feature sets. *This underscores the importance of considering dynamic feature. The best performing variant obtained from the learning phase (*LEARNBESTVARIANT*) is* TINTIN_D.

Next, we examine the effect of applying different variants on the reference network to validate if the learning phase yields the desired best performing variant. Indeed, TINTIN_D is the top performing variant for the reference network (Figure 2, top, reference network). In fact, majority of the TINTIN variants identify I_4 as the best matched network (Figure 2, middle).

In terms of the runtime performance (Figure 2, bottom), the learning process (Step 2) consumes the bulk of its execution time. Hence, learning can be performed offline to improve the runtime performance. The improvement is up to 2 orders of magnitude for certain variants (*e.g.*, TINTIN_S for comparison of networks with fewer than 100 nodes). In addition, we observe that the runtime performance is dependent on the size of the network, the types and number of features used by the variant. In subsequent experiments, we shall use TINTIN_D.

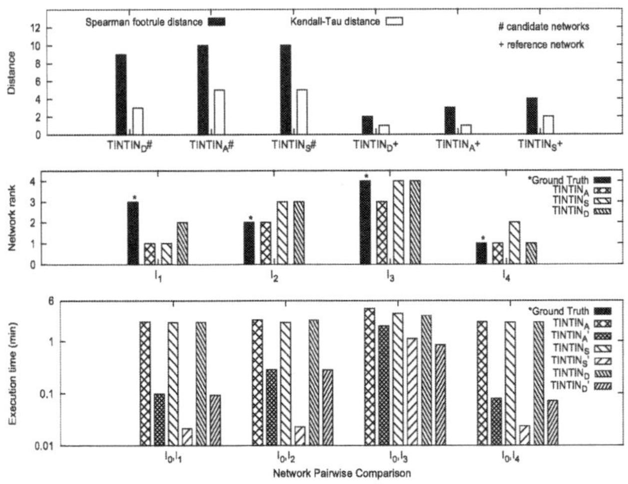

Figure 2: Performance of TINTIN variants. Top: distance between ground truth and rankings from variants in candidate networks and reference network, middle: individual network ranking, bottom: runtime performance.

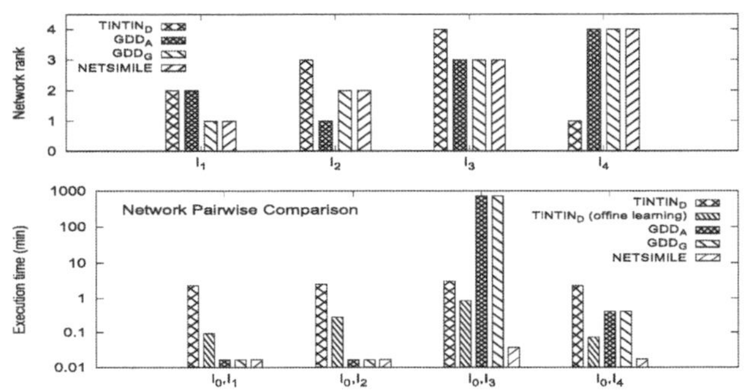

Figure 3: Performance of different network similarity-based ranking approaches.

Performance of the LEARNPTHRESHOLD procedure. In this set of experiments, we identify the threshold p-value p_t learnt from the candidate networks. Table 4 shows the combined p-values of each pair of candidate networks using TINTIN_D and the corresponding AUROC when applying the characterization model of one candidate network to another. p_t is the average combined p-value of the cells marked with $\sharp$. That is, $p_t = \frac{2.2x10^{-16}+2.2x10^{-16}+0.045}{3} = 0.01$. When we apply $p_t = 0.01$ to the ranked list of I_1 to I_4 obtained using TINTIN_D, we note that I_3 (AUROC=0.632, combined p-value=2.2x10^{-16}) is considered as a dissimilar network and filtered off. Note that p_t affects the number of networks being ranked, but not the actual rank of the network. Hence, it is possible to have no best matched network if the given set of candidate networks is considered dissimilar to the unseen network.

Comparison with state-of-the-art. Lastly, we compare TINTIN_D against GDD [17] and NETSIMILE [4] in terms of network ranking and runtime performance. We consider both the arithmetic and geometric versions of GDD which are denoted as GDD_A and GDD_D, respectively. Since these target-unaware network similarity approaches define similarity differently from TINTIN (Section 2), it is

Network notation	I_0	I_1	I_2	I_3	I_4
Data set (BioModel ID)	Ras activation (0000000161)	MAPK-PI3K (0000000146)	glucose-stimulated insulin secretion (0000000239)	endomesoderm gene regulatory (0000000235)	glucose metabolism (0000000244)
Disease node	$RasGTP_{PM}$	ERKPP	$ATP_{mitochondrial}$	Protein_E_Endo16	acetate
No. of nodes	46	36	59	622	47
No. of hyperedges	43	34	45	778	109
No. (%) of targets	5 (10.9%)	9 (25%)	6 (10.2%)	206 (33.1%)	16 (34%)

Table 3: Dataset.

	I_1 Model	I_2 Model	I_3 Model	I_4 Model
I_1	-	$6.52\text{x}10^{-4}$ [0.55]	$2.2\text{x}10^{-16}$ [0.47#]	0.128 [0.64]
I_2	$6.52\text{x}10^{-4}$ [0.62]	-	$2.2\text{x}10^{-16}$ [0.54]	0.045 [0.43#]
I_3	$2.2\text{x}10^{-16}$ [0.65]	$2.2\text{x}10^{-16}$ [0.60]	-	$2.2\text{x}10^{-16}$ [0.48#]
I_4	0.128 [0.61]	0.045 [0.51]	$2.2\text{x}10^{-16}$ [0.55]	-

Table 4: Summary of result for LEARNPTHRESHOLD procedure (Algorithm 1). The $(i,j)^{th}$ cell entry is of the form $x[y]$ where x is the combined p-value for the (I_i,I_j) pair and y is the AUROC when characterization model of I_j is applied to I_i. # refer to cases with low AUROC (i.e., AUROC<0.5).

Rank comparison	S	K
TINTIN,GDD_A	6	4
TINTIN,GDD_G	6	3
TINTIN,NETSIMILE	6	3

Rank comparison	S	K
GDD_A,GDD_G	2	1
GDD_A,NETSIMILE	2	1
GDD_G,NETSIMILE	0	0

Table 5: Summary of comparison of ranks obtained using different approach. S and K indicate Spearman footrule and Kendall-Tau distances, respectively.

not possible to have a good network ranking benchmark that can be used as ground truth for comparison. Instead, we compare the similarities and differences in the rankings derived from TINTIN as compared to that from other approaches. As observed in Figure 3 (top), our approach differs in ranking of networks I_1 to I_4 when compared to traditional target-unaware network similarity approaches. The differences in ranking is more significant when we compare TINTIN against target-unaware approaches (Table 5, left) versus a comparison among traditional target-unaware approaches only (Table 5, right). In particular, I_4 was ranked best by TINTIN and worst by the target-unaware approaches (Figure 3, top).

The runtime performance is affected by the network size (Figure 3, bottom), of which the most significant[4] impact is experienced by the GDD-based approaches. In particular, NETSIMILE performs the best and scales well even for larger networks. The order of the approaches in terms of runtime performance is NETSIMILE $\prec$ TINTIN_D (offline learning) $\prec$ TINTIN_D $\prec$ GDD. Hence, *our approach has moderate runtime performance and the ranks produced are markedly different from state-of-the-art approaches.*

7 CONCLUSIONS & FUTURE WORK

In this paper, we present TINTIN, a target feature-based signaling network similarity computation and ranking technique by exploiting the topological and dynamic characteristics of the targets. It is interesting to note that the empirical study highlights a single dynamic feature (PSSD) as being more important than a set of topological features in identifying the best matched network. This signals the importance of considering dynamic features in measuring network similarity. However, to the best of our knowledge, majority of the work on network feature focus on topological features instead. Hence, as part of future work, we intend to explore novel dynamic network features that could be used to study signaling networks. In addition, our empirical results demonstrate the differences in terms of network ranking of TINTIN compared to state-of-the-art target-unaware network similarity techniques.

[4]The runtime performance of GDD degrades by about 3 orders of magnitude when applied to I_3 (622 nodes) as compared to I_4 (47 nodes).

Acknowledgments. Huey Eng Chua and Sourav S Bhowmick were partially supported by MOE AcRF Tier-1 Grant RGC 1/13.

REFERENCES

[1] J. Aach et al. Aligning gene expression time series with time warping algorithms. *Bioinformatics*, 17(6):495-508, 2001.
[2] B. Aldridge et al. Physicochemical modelling of cell signalling pathways. *Nat. Cell Biol.*, 8(11):1195-1203, 2006.
[3] J. Bangham. Therapeutics: Cetuximab constricts conformational contortionist. *Nat. Rev. Cancer*, 5:421, 2005.
[4] M. Berlingerio et al. NetSimile: a scalable approach to size-independent network similarity. In *ASONAM*, 2013.
[5] H. Chua et al. PANI:A Novel Algorithm for Fast Discovery of Putative Target Nodes in Signaling Networks. In *ACM BCB*, 2011.
[6] H. Chua et al. TENET:Topological Feature-based Target Characterization in Signaling Networks. *Bioinformatics*, 31(20):3306-3314, 2015.
[7] H. Chua, et al. TAPESTRY: A Network Similarity Ranking-Based Approach For Prioritizing Nodes In Signaling Networks. http://www.ntu.edu.sg/home/assourav/TechReports/TAPESTRY-TR.pdf, Technical Report, 2015.
[8] H. Chua, et al. TAPESTRY: Network-centric Target Prioritization Nodes In Disease-related Signaling Networks. In *ACM BCB*, 2016.
[9] D. Cieslak et al. Start globally, optimize locally, predict globally: Improving performance on imbalanced data. In *ICDM*, 2008.
[10] J. Engelfiet, et al. A comparison of boundary graph grammars and context-free hypergraph grammars. *Inform. Comput.*, 84(2):163-206, 1990.
[11] J. Hartung. A note on combining dependent tests of significance. *Biom. J.*, 41(7):849-855, 1999.
[12] V. Janjić et al. Biological function through network topology: a survey of the human diseasome. *Brief. Funct. Genomics*, els037, 2012.
[13] E. Keogh et al. Derivative Dynamic Time Warping. In *SDM*, 2001.
[14] S. Klamt et al. Hypergraphs and cellular networks. *PLoS Comput. Biol.*, 5(5):e1000385, 2009.
[15] L. Meng, et al. Local versus global biological network alignment. *Bioinformatics* 32(20): 3155-3164, 2016.
[16] NCI drug dictionary. *http://www.cancer.gov/drugdictionary/*, National Cancer Institute, accessed in April 2015.
[17] N. Pržulj. Biological network comparison using graphlet degree distribution. *Bioinformatics*, 23(2):e177-e183, 2007.
[18] J. O. Ramsay et al. Parameter estimation for differential equations: a generalized smoothing approach. *J. R. Stat. Soc.: Series B*, Statistical Methodology, 69(5), 2007.
[19] J. Raymond et al. Maximum common subgraph isomorphism algorithms for the matching of chemical structures. *J. Comput. Aided Mol. Des.*, 16(7):521-533, 2002.
[20] A. Ritz et al. Signaling hypergraphs. *Trends Biotechnol.*, 32(7):356-362, 2014.
[21] P. Roberts et al. Targeting the Raf-MEK-ERK mitogen-activated protein kinase cascade for the treatment of cancer. *Oncogene*, 26(22):3291-3310, 2007.
[22] M. Vanneman et al. Combining immunotherapy and targeted therapies in cancer treatment. *Nat. Rev. Cancer*, 12(4), 2012.

Determining Optimal Features for Predicting Type IV Secretion System Effector Proteins for *Coxiella burnetii*

Zhila Esna Ashari Esfahani
School of EECS
Washington State University
Pullman, WA 99164-2752
zesnaash@eecs.wsu.edu

Kelly A. Brayton
Department of VMP
Washington State University
Pullman, WA 99164-7040
kbrayton@vetmed.wsu.edu

Shira L. Broschat
School of EECS
Washington State University
Pullman, WA 99164-2752
shira@eecs.wsu.edu

ABSTRACT

Type IV secretion systems (T4SS) are constructed from multiple protein complexes that exist in some types of bacterial pathogens and are responsible for delivering type IV effector proteins into host cells. Effectors target eukaryotic cells and try to manipulate host cell processes and the immune system of the host. Some work has been done to validate effectors experimentally, and recently a few scoring and machine learning-based methods have been developed to predict effectors from whole genome sequences. However, different types of features have been suggested to be effective. In this work, we gathered the features proposed in previous reports and calculated their values for a dataset of effectors and non-effectors of *Coxiella burnetii*. Then we ranked the features based on their importance in classifying effectors and non-effectors to determine the set of optimal features. Finally, a Support Vector Machine model was developed to test the optimal features by comparing them to a set of features proposed in a previous study. The outcome of the comparison supports the effectiveness of our optimal features.

General Terms

Algorithms; Proteins; Machine Learning

Keywords

Type IV secretion system; T4SS effectors; t-test; feature selection; SVM classifier

1 INTRODUCTION

Some bacterial pathogens have specific effector proteins that are translocated into host cells and manipulate the environment to be more hospitable for infection. Secretion systems in these bacteria are responsible for translocating these effectors into host cells. There are at least seven types of secretion systems in Gram-negative bacteria. Type III and type IV secretion systems (T3SS and T4SS) have been the subject of many studies in recent years.

Type IV secretion systems, which are the focus of this work, are multi-protein complexes and are related to the bacterial conjugation machinery. The T4SS delivers effector proteins to the host cell cytosol; however, effector molecules tend not to be similar from pathogen to pathogen, and the signals that direct a protein to the T4SS apparatus are not well understood [1]. As a result, recognition of these effectors is not simple and has become the subject of much recent research. The ability to accurately predict candidate effectors makes it easier to test and validate them experimentally. However, prediction of these effectors is complicated because many different factors have been suggested to be involved.

Previously, researchers have experimentally identified novel T4SS effectors by using fusion protein reporter assays in translocation studies [2]. To accelerate identification of T4SS effectors, researchers have been interested in predicting effector molecules. Some have used scoring methods [3] or machine learning algorithms [4-8] to predict the effectors. However, the effective characteristics and features of protein sequences that are suggested in these works have some differences, and most of them have been specific to a particular species of bacteria. Burstein et al. [6] considered *Legionella pneumophila* while Wang et al. [7] focused on *Helicobacter pylori*. Meyer et al.'s method [3] was first used with the effector dataset of *L. pneumophila*, strain Philadelphia, and then tested on some other genomes of α- and γ-proteobacteria.

Coxiella burnetii, the main focus of this work, is a Gram-negative pathogen that causes Q fever. Two studies have been published examining *C. burnetii* effectors [8, 9]. However, the first one did not use a machine learning approach, and the second one did not consider some of the main features of these effectors. Although a number of effectors have been identified for *C. burnetii* using different methods, not all effectors have been found. On the other hand, because the number of identified effectors is sufficient to test a machine learning model, it permits us to determine an optimal set of features that can be selected from those proposed not just for *C. burnetii* but also for other pathogens. This optimal set of features may, in turn, prove useful for identifying the best group of features for other T4SS effectors as well.

Permission to make digital or hard copies of all or part of this work for personal or classroom use is granted without fee provided that copies are not made or distributed for profit or commercial advantage and that copies bear this notice and the full citation on the first page. Copyrights for components of this work owned by others than ACM must be honored. Abstracting with credit is permitted. To copy otherwise, or republish, to post on servers or to redistribute to lists, requires prior specific permission and/or a fee. Request permissions from Permissions@acm.org.
ACM-BCB '17, August 20-23, 2017, Boston, MA, USA
© 2017 Association for Computing Machinery.
ACM ISBN 978-1-4503-4722-8/17/08...$15.00
http://dx.doi.org/10.1145/3107411.3107416.

2 METHODOLOGY

A diagram of the workflow that we followed for this project is shown in Fig. 1, which includes creating a dataset of effectors and non-effectors for *C. burnetii*, gathering together as many different features as we could find in the literature, calculating different feature values, performing a t-test for each feature for all elements in the dataset, filtering an effective set of features based on their calculated p-values, and, finally, building a machine learning model based on the selected features to compare results with results obtained using features previously used. Each step is described in detail in the sections that follow.

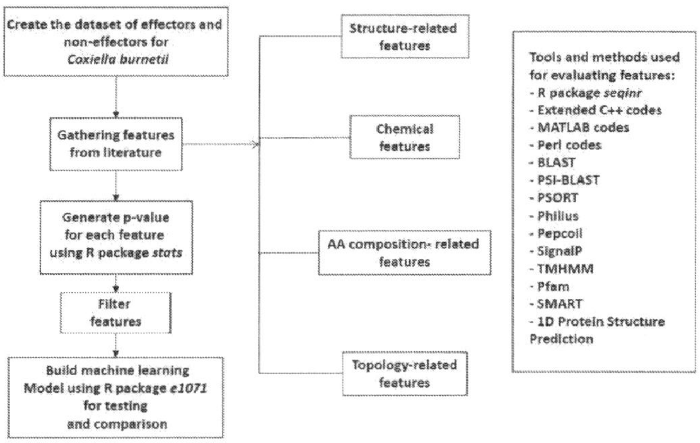

Figure 1: The steps used in this paper to identify optimal features for predicting *C. burnetii* effector proteins.

2.1 Dataset

As described earlier, the objective of our work is to identify the optimal features for predicting *C. burnetii* T4SS effector proteins. In order to accomplish this, we first needed a dataset of known and verified effectors and non-effectors. Thus, we searched through all the published literature to find previously recognized effectors for *C. burnetii* [2,4, 9-12] and used all those that were found. For our set of non-effectors we used the ones given in [4]. Our final dataset was composed of 86 effectors and 95 non-effectors.

2.2 Features

After finding our dataset, we made a thorough search of the literature for features previously used in supervised machine learning models and scoring algorithms for predicting not just *C. burnetii* T4SS effector proteins but effector proteins for other pathogens as well [3-8, 13]. The paper by Lifshitz et al. [8] describes features used to predict *C. burnetii* effectors. The work by Meyer et al. [3] targets *L. pneumophila* but indicates that the features can be considered for identification of other types of effectors as well. Zou et al. and Yu et al. [4, 5] also consider all types of T4SS effectors while Burstein et al. and Wang et al. [6, 7] focus on *L. pneumophila* and *H. pylori*, respectively. We considered all features that were reasonable for *C. burnetii*, and this resulted in the sets of features described below.

The first group of features consists, for the most part, of the chemical properties of proteins, and C++ code was developed to calculate values for these features for each protein sequence in our dataset. Also, the R package *seqinr* version 3.3.0 was used to obtain values for many of the different amino acid features that were considered.

First, the **total hydropathy**, **average hydropathy**, **C-terminal hydropathy,** and **N-terminal hydropathy** of the protein sequences were calculated and considered [3, 5, 13]. The hydrophobic and hydrophilic characteristics of the amino acid are shown by hydropathy index. The indices used in *seqinr* are from a paper written by Kyte and Doolittle [14] which proposed this index for the first time. We considered a length of 30 amino acids at the C-terminus or N-terminus in this work. Thus, the value used for each terminus represents the sum of the 30 index values for the 30 amino acids. The **isoelectric point** was also considered as suggested in [5]. The isoelectric point (pI) is the pH at which a particular molecule is neutral. **Molecular mass (Mr)**, which is the mass of a molecule, was used for the sequences in our database. Mr is calculated by determining the atomic mass of each amino acid multiplied by the number of amino acids of that element in the molecule, and then summing the results. **Total charge, C-terminal charge, and N-terminal charge** were the next features to be calculated. These features are also mentioned in [3, 13] for the purpose of finding T4SS effectors. The indices used in this work were taken from [13]. The next features used were **C-terminal basicity** and **N-terminal basicity** which are considered important features [3, 13].

The second group of features consists mainly of those related to the structure or composition of the protein sequences in our database. These are listed and described below.

The **length** of a protein sequence as suggested in [3, 8] and some **different combinations of amino acids** present in the sequence, suggested by Lifshitz et al. [8], are the next features that we considered. The combinations are as follows: 1) combined content of Isoleucine, Leucine, Valine, and Phenylalanine; 2) combined content of Aspartic and Glutamic acid; 3) combined content of Asparagine and Glutamine; 4) combined content of Arginine, Lysine, and Histidine; 5) combined content of Serine and Threonine; 6) combined content of Serine, Asparagine, Glutamic acid, and Lysine; and 7) combined content of Valine, Alanine, Glycine, and Isoleucine.

Next we calculated four sets of features that are vectors, i.e., features that are lists of features, and, as such, each vector element represents a separate feature: First, the **amino acid composition** for each sequence in the dataset has 20 features and represents the percentage of presence of each type of amino acid in the protein sequence. Second, we calculated the **dipeptide composition of amino acids** in each sequence, which has 400 features and represents the presence of different pairs of amino acids that are adjacent to each other in the sequence. Third and fourth, we extracted the **PSSM composition** having 400 features and **auto-covariance transformation of PSSM** having 160 features from calculating the PSSM profile, respectively, for each sequence. As mentioned in the introduction, these features were suggested in [4] for predicting T4SS effectors, and calculations were performed using the same procedure as described. A position-specific scoring matrix (PSSM) is a type of scoring matrix for amino acids for which scores are assigned to positions based on how close a sequence is to the sequences used to create the scoring matrix. PSI-BLAST was used for calculation of the PSSM for this paper.

Homology to known effectors using BLAST was the next feature that was calculated. This feature is suggested in [3, 6, 8], and the dataset of known effectors that was used for calculating the identity to our built dataset of *C. burnetii* effectors includes all the known effectors used in [3]. Also an e-value threshold of 0.01 was used as suggested in [3] for determining the similarity between sequences.

We calculated **protein subcellular localization** using a bioinformatics prediction tool called PSORT [16]. This feature predicts where a protein localizes in a cell and has been proposed as an important feature for T4SS prediction in [5]. The predicted locations within the cell are the outputs of the program, and they are in seven classes: cytoplasmic, cytoplasmic membrane, extracellular, extracellular secondary localization, periplasmic, outer membrane, and unknown.

Transmembrane prediction was also calculated in this paper using the Philius tool [17]. This feature is considered to be important for T4SS prediction [5], perhaps because a transmembrane protein can span a cell wall, and this allows it to transport other molecules into and out of the cell. The output classes of Philius are: globular, globular with signal peptide, transmembrane, and transmembrane with signal peptide.

Effector proteins in pathogens can contain eukaryotic protein domains that imitate the function of the host. The Pepcoil tool (www.bioinformatics.nl/cgi-bin/emboss/pepcoil) was used for the prediction of eukaryotic coiled-coil domains in our protein sequences. The two features **pepcoil hitcount** and **pepcoil length**, as suggested in [3, 6, 8], were extracted from the results for all our sequences.

The SignalP 3.0 Server [18] was used for finding the **presence of cleavage sites** and also **signal peptide probability** for our protein sequences, also considered in [5]. This server is designed for prediction of the presence of signal peptide cleavage sites in protein sequences for both Gram-positive and Gram-negative prokaryotes and also eukaryotes using artificial neural networks and hidden Markov models.

TMHMM Server v. 2.0 [19] was used for prediction of **transmembrane helices** in our protein sequences as suggested in [5, 6, 8].

As mentioned previously, eukaryotic protein domains can be found in effector proteins; other protein domains are indicators of effectors and non-effectors as well. We searched for **Ank, Coiled-Coil, DUF, TM (transmembrane), F-box, F-box like, U-box, Pkinase, LLR, TPR, Sel1, and Patatin domains** as proposed in [3, 13, 15]. To find these domains, the tools at the SMART and Pfam version 30.0 websites were used. Pfam is a database of protein families represented by multiple sequence alignments obtained using hidden Markov models (HMMs). SMART (a Simple Modular Architecture Research Tool) is also a database that allows the identification of protein domains using HMMs.

In addition to what has previously been described, we searched for several different types of protein motifs associated with effector proteins including **regulatory motifs (PmrA and CpxR motifs), NLS (nuclear localization signals), MLS (mitochondrial localization signals), Prenylation Domain (CaaX motif), and E-Block (EEXXE motif)** as suggested and described in [3, 6, 8, 21].

Finally, the last features we considered are some remaining protein topology features, the **percentages of alpha helices, beta strands, and coiled coils as the secondary structure** of our protein sequences as suggested in [7]. For predicting the secondary structure of our sequences, we used the 1D Protein Structure Prediction Server (biomine.ece.ualberta.ca/1D/1D.html) [20]. This server is designed for the prediction of secondary structure contents and classes as well as fold type prediction for given a protein sequence.

2.3 Feature Evaluation

After gathering and calculating values for all the features of interest, we focused on evaluating how important each feature is in determining whether or not a given *C. burnetii* protein sequence is a T4SS effector. For this purpose, we used the t-test. A t-test is used to determine whether there is a statistically significant difference between a statistical measure for two different populations. In our case, we used a t-test over all our dataset of effectors and non-effectors versus each computed feature as explained in section 2.2. The resulting p-values were stored for each feature. A p-value is commonly used in statistical hypothesis testing when two populations are under consideration. Our null hypothesis was that there was no difference between our two populations, effectors and non-effectors, and the p-value for each feature provided a measure of whether it was compatible with the null hypothesis. Thus, a smaller calculated p-value for a feature corresponded to a feature that was more effective in recognizing an effector protein, i.e., that feature rejected the null hypothesis. As we worked with a large number of features, we set a small threshold for our p-value to select the set of optimal features.

Prior to applying the t-test, we performed a correlation assessment between features to eliminate redundancy of information. The formulation for calculating the correlation between two vectors $x=(x_1,x_2,\ldots, x_n)$ and $y=(y_1,y_2,\ldots, y_n)$ is:

$$r = \frac{n\sum x_i y_i - (\sum x_i)(y_i)}{\sqrt{n(\sum {x_i}^2)-(\sum x_i)^2}\sqrt{n(\sum {y_i}^2)-(\sum y_i)^2}} \quad (1)$$

where the number of data pairs is shown by n. From this assessment we found that the maximum cleavage site probability and signal peptide probability had 96% correlation so we kept only the former. Also, the coiled-coil domain hitcount and coiled-coil domain length had a correlation of 97%, and again we kept the former.

Next, we performed the t-test over all the features using the following: calculate the sample mean and standard deviation, the test statistic (p-value), and the probability of observing the test statistic under the null hypothesis. To accomplish this, we used the R package *stats* version 3.2.2. We ranked all the features based on their calculated p-values and made a list of ranked features based on their effectiveness. We selected a threshold p-value of 0.009 on the basis of both the total number of features and the p-values for the most informative selected features, which were on the order of 10^{-20}. Then we filtered out features with p-values larger than this threshold, leaving the set of optimal features. Finally, an SVM classifier was used to measure the accuracy of our optimal features for prediction of effectors in comparison to a previously suggested set of features. Evaluations and comparisons were made for both sets. The results obtained are described in the next section.

3 RESULTS AND DISCUSSION

Ranking the calculated features based on their p-values allowed us to determine their relative significance. Feature selection filtering resulted in 289 optimal features. Differences in p-values for the 289 optimal features are shown in Fig. 2 for linear and logarithmic scales.

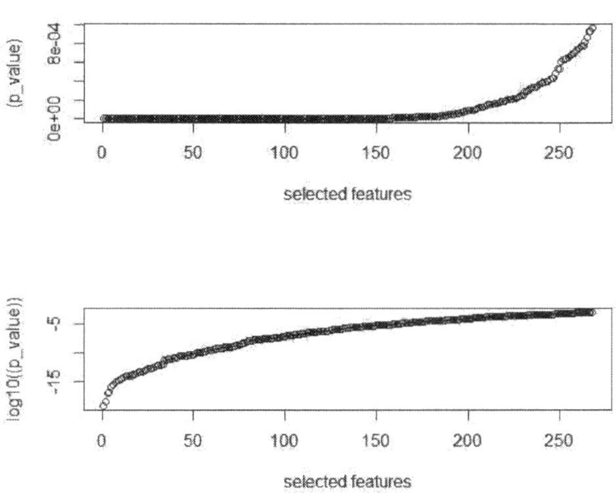

Figure 2: Change in p-values for optimal features; bottom figure gives top figure values in $\log_{10}$

The majority of the optimal features are from four vector features. These are the amino acid composition, dipeptide composition, PSSM composition, and auto-covariance transformation of PSSM. These four vector features are clearly important and account for all but 11 of the 289 features. Based on the calculations, the most significant feature is the sixth element of the PSSM composition and its p-value is on the order of 10^{-20}.

Table 1. Optimal features for effector prediction

Four vector features plus other top features selected
PSSM composition*
Amino acid composition*
Auto-covariance transformation of PSSM*
Dipeptide composition*
Identity to known effectors
Alpha helix secondary structure
Hydropathy of C-terminal
Average hydropathy
Hydropathy of N-terminal
Total hydropathy
Coiled coil domains
Coiled coil secondary structure
Subcellular localization
Beta strand secondary structure
Ank domains

* vector feature

The top nine features are all from the PSSM composition, indicating how important this scoring matrix is in predicting effector proteins. The eleven ranked non-vector features are shown in Table 1 following the vector features. As we can see in Table 1, identity to known effectors and percentage of alpha helices in secondary structure prediction of protein sequences is very important for finding *C. burnetii* effector proteins. Also, different types of hydropathy indices play important roles for this type of bacteria.

In order to demonstrate that our optimal features are effective, we needed to implement them in a machine learning model and compare them to other features. Therefore, we decided to compare a model using our optimal features and the features suggested in [3] which we refer to as DCASN features. As described in section 1, [3] talks about selection of T4SS effectors and was used for *C. burnetii* as well. In addition, all the features in its set of proposed features were considered in our work.

For our purpose we used an SVM machine learning algorithm. The reason for selecting an SVM as our classifier is that it is a faster and more flexible classifier than other well-known classifiers such as decision trees. Because an SVM uses kernels, it can be applied to complex data types, and it tries to find optimal boundaries for separation of data classes. Also, some classifiers such as decision trees are sensitive to large numbers of features and overfitting may occur. Finally, the focus of this paper is on feature selection and not on model development.

The R package *e1071* version 1.6.7 was used for creating the machine learning model, and its SVM tuning function was used to find the best parameters for the model based on our dataset, selecting the radial kernel and a C parameter of 1. We used two approaches for making the classifier model. Our first approach was based on training the SVM model over all the data in our dataset to have a more accurate model by making use of all our data and then testing it over a third of the data to find the training accuracy. For the second approach, we divided our dataset of known and unknown effectors into two parts consisting of training and testing data. Two-thirds of the data were kept for training and the remaining third was used for testing. We then applied our SVM algorithm using the optimal features and also using the DCASN features.

After implementing the machine learning models for each set of features, we used them with the test dataset, and confusion matrices were created to measure accuracy. The results are shown in Tables 2 and 3 for the optimal features and in Tables 4 and 5 for the DCASN features. In these tables, TP = true positive meaning that an effector was accurately predicted, FP = false positive meaning that an effector was inaccurately predicted, FN = false negative meaning that a non-effector was predicted to be an effector, and TN = true negative meaning that a non-effector was predicted accurately. Yes indicates an effector and No a non-effector. Tables 2 and 4 correspond to the first approach when all data were used for training, and Tables 3 and 5 correspond to the second approach when 2/3 data were used for training and 1/3 data was used for testing.

Table 2. Confusion matrix for training accuracy for SVM model using optimal features

		Predicted	
		Yes	No
Actual	Yes	TP = 29	FN = 3
	No	FP = 0	TN = 29

Table 3. Confusion matrix for testing accuracy for SVM model using optimal features

		Predicted	
		Yes	No
Actual	Yes	TP = 25	FN = 7
	No	FP = 4	TN = 25

Table 4. Confusion matrix for training accuracy for SVM model using DCASN features

		Predicted	
		Yes	No
Actual	Yes	TP = 17	FN = 4
	No	FP = 12	TN = 28

Table 5. Confusion matrix for testing accuracy for SVM model using DCASN features

		Predicted	
		Yes	No
Actual	Yes	TP = 13	FN = 6
	No	FP = 16	TN = 26

To measure the accuracy of our results, we used the metric given by Eq. (2). The results are shown in Table 6. Because our original dataset consisted of 86 effectors and 95 non-effectors and the proportions were maintained for both training and testing sets, we did not have skewed classes, and accuracy is a good measure for our comparisons.

$$\text{Accuracy} = \frac{\text{TP} + \text{TN}}{\text{TP} + \text{FP} + \text{TN} + \text{FN}} \tag{2}$$

Table 6. Comparison of accuracy of training and testing

	Our features	DCASN
Training	95.1%	73.8%
Testing	82.0%	63.9%

As we can see, for both approaches our optimal features have increased the accuracy of predicting effectors, which supports the effectiveness of our feature study.

4 CONCLUSIONS

In summary, we have determined the features that are most effective for predicting type IV secretion system effector proteins for *C. burnetii* bacteria. We found that four vector features play a large role. These are amino acid composition, dipeptide composition, PSSM composition, and auto-covariance transformation of PSSM. In particular, the first nine features of the 289 optimal features found are all PSSM composition values, indicating the importance of the PSSM. Of the 289 optimal features, only eleven are not vector features. Of these eleven, eukaryotic protein domains, hydropathy, and homology dominate.

To test the effectiveness of our work, we compared the success of our optimal features and features proposed in a previous work for recognizing T4SS effectors by means of a machine learning model. We used an SVM classifier to build a predictor, and the accuracy of the results of the predictions for the two groups of features shows the effectiveness of our feature selection.

Given the difficulty of predicting T4SS effectors, our approach can be used for different bacteria that have effector proteins with type IV secretion systems for invading host cells. In this way we will be able to determine the most effective features and characteristics that most effector protein sequences share. This might make it possible to construct a new and effective pipeline for predicting T4SS effectors for many different types of pathogens.

ACKNOWLEDGMENTS

This research was supported by National Institutes of Health grant R01AI042792 and by the Carl M. Hansen Foundation.

REFERENCES

[1] Daniel E. Voth, Laura J. Broederdorf, and Joseph G. Graham. 2012, Bacterial Type IV Secretion Systems: Versatile Virulence Machines. *Future Microbiol.* 7(2): 241–257. doi:10.2217/fmb.11.150.

[2] Daniel E. Voth, Paul A. Beare, Dale Howe, Uma M. Sharma, Georgios Samoilis, Diane C. Cockrell, Anders Omsland, and Robert A. Heinzen. 2010. The *Coxiella burnetii* Cryptic Plasmid Is Enriched in Genes Encoding Type IV Secretion System Substrate. *Journal of Bacteriology*, 193, 1493–1503.

[3] Damien F. Meyer, Christophe Noroy, Amal Moumene, Sylvain Raffaele Emmanuel Albina and Nathalie Vachiery. 2013. Searching algorithm for type IV secretion system effectors 1.0: a tool for predicting type IV effectors and exploring their genomic context. *Nucleic Acids Research, 41,* 9218–9229.

[4] Lingyun Zou, Chonghan Nan, and Fuquan Hu. 2013. Accurate prediction of bacterial type IV secreted effectors using amino acid composition and PSSM profiles. *Bioinformatics* 29, 3135–3142.

[5] L. Yu, Y. Guo, Y. Li, G. Li, M. Li, J. Luo, W. Xiong, and W. Qin. 2010. SecretP: identifying bacterial secreted proteins by fusing new features into Chou's pseudo-amino acid composition. *Journal of Theoretical Biology*, 267, 1-6.

[6] David Burstein, Tal Zusman, Elena Degtyar, Ram Viner, Gil Segal and Tal Pupko. 2009. Genome-Scale Identification of *Legionella pneumophila* Effectors Using a Machine Learning Approach. *PLoS Pathogens,* 5.

[7] Y. Wang, X. Wei, H. Bao, and S. Liu. 2014. Prediction of bacterial type IV secreted effectors by C-terminal features. *BMC Genomics,* 15-50.

[8] Ziv Lifshitz, David Burstein, Kierstyn Schwartz, Howard A. Shuman, Tal Pupko and Gil Segal. 2014. Identification of Novel *Coxiella burnetii* Icm/Dot Effectors and Genetic Analysis of Their Involvement in Modulating a MitogenActivated Protein Kinase Pathway. *Infection and Immunity,* 82, 3740–3752.

[9] Chen Chen, Simran Banga, Katja Mertens, Mary M. Weber, Ivana Gorbaslieva, Yunhao Tan, Zhao-Qing Luo, and James E. Samuel. 2010. Large-scale identification and translocation of type IV secretion substrates by *Coxiella burnetii. PNAS,* 107, 21755–21760.

[10] K. Carey, H. Newton, A. Luhrmann, and C. R. Roy. 2011. The *Coxiella burnetii* Dot/Icm System Delivers a Unique Repertoire of Type IV Effectors into Host Cells and Is Required for Intracellular Replication. *PLoS Pathogen,s* 7.

[11] Xiaoxiao Pan, Anja Lührmann, Ayano Satoh, Michelle A. Laskowski-Arce, and Craig R. Roy. 2008. Ankyrin Repeat Proteins Comprise a Diverse Family of Bacterial Type IV Effectors. *NIH Public Access 320,* 1651–1654.

[12] Daniel E. Voth, Dale Howe, Paul A. Beare, Joseph P. Vogel, Nathan Unsworth, James E. Samuel, and Robert A. Heinzen. 2009. The *Coxiella burnetii* Ankyrin Repeat Domain-Containing Protein Family Is Heterogeneous, with C-Terminal Truncations That Influence Dot/Icm-Mediated Secretion. *Journal of Bacteriology* ,191, 4232–4242.

[13] Svetlana Lockwood, Daniel E. Voth, Paul A. Beare, Wendy C. Brown, Robert A. Heinzen and Shira L. Broschat. 2011. Identification of *Anaplasma marginale* Type IV Secretion System Effector Proteins. *PLoS ONE,* 6.

[14] J. Kyte, RF Doolittle. 1982. A simple method for displaying the hydropathic character of a protein. *Journal of Molecular Biology* 157, 105–132.

[15] David Burstein, Francisco Amaro, Tal Zusman, Ziv Lifshitz, Ofir Cohen, Jack A Gilbert, Tal Pupko, Howard A Shuman, and Gil Segal. 2016. Genomic analysis of 38 *Legionella* species identifies large and diverse effector repertoires. *Nature Genetics,* 48.

[16] N.Y. Yu, J.R. Wagner, M.R. Laird, G. Melli, S. Rey, R. Lo, P. Dao, S.C. Sahinalp, M. Ester, L.J. Foster, F.S.L. Brinkman, 2010, PSORTb 3.0: Improved protein subcellular localization prediction with refined localization subcategories and predictive capabilities for all prokaryotes, *Bioinformatics,* 26(13):1608-1615.

[17] Reynolds SM, Käll L, Riffle ME, Bilmes JA, Noble WS, 2008, Transmembrane Topology and Signal Peptide Prediction Using Dynamic Bayesian Networks. *PLoS Comput Biol,* 4(11): e1000213. doi:10.1371/journal.pcbi.1000213.

[18] Jannick Dyrløv Bendtsen, Henrik Nielsen, Gunnar von Heijne and Søren Brunak, 2004. Improved prediction of signal peptides: SignalP 3.0. *Journal of Molecular Biology,* 340:783-795.

[19] A. Krogh, B. Larsson, G. von Heijne, and E.L.L. Sonnhammer, 2001. Predicting transmembrane protein topology with a hidden Markov model: Application to complete genomes, *Journal of Molecular Biology,* 305(3), 567-580.

[20] K Chen, LA Kurgan, 2007. PFRES: Protein Fold Classification by Using Evolutionary Information and Predicted Secondary Structure. *Bioinformatics,* 23(21), 2843-2850.

[21] Price CT, Al-Quadan T, Santic M, Jones SC, Abu Kwaik Y, 2010. Exploitation of conserved eukaryotic host cell farnesylation machinery by an F-box effector of Legionella pneumophila. *The Journal of Experimental Medicine,* 207(8): 1713-26. doi: 10.1084/jem.20100771.

Knowledge Rich Natural Language Queries over Structured Biological Databases*

Hasan M. Jamil
Department of Computer Science
University of Idaho, USA
jamil@uidaho.edu

ABSTRACT

Increasingly, keyword, natural language and NoSQL queries are used for information retrieval from both traditional and non-traditional databases such as web, document, GIS, legal, and health databases. While their popularity are undeniable for obvious reasons, their engineering is far from simple. In most part, semantics and intent preserving mapping of a well understood natural language query expressed over a structured database schema to a structured query language is still a difficult task, and research to tame the complexity is intense. In this paper, we propose a multi-level knowledge-based middleware to facilitate such mappings that separate the conceptual level from the physical level. We augment these multi-level abstractions with a concept reasoner and a query strategy engine to dynamically link arbitrary natural language querying to well defined structured queries. We demonstrate the feasibility of our approach by presenting a Datalog based prototype system, called *BioSmart*, that can compute responses to arbitrary natural language queries over arbitrary databases once a syntactic classification of the natural language query is made.

CCS CONCEPTS

•Information systems →Database query processing; Query languages for non-relational engines; *Data model extensions;* Relational database query languages; **•Computing methodologies →Natural language processing; Logic programming and answer set programming; •Applied computing →Bioinformatics;**

KEYWORDS

Query mapping; cooperative query answering; implied query response; logical implication; query semantics

ACM Reference format:
Hasan M. Jamil. 2017. Knowledge Rich Natural Language Queries over Structured Biological Databases. In *Proceedings of ACM-BCB'17, August 20–23, 2017, Boston, MA, USA.*, , 10 pages.
DOI: http://dx.doi.org/10.1145/3107411.3107442

*Research supported in part by National Science Foundation grants IIS 0612203 and DRL 1515550.

Permission to make digital or hard copies of all or part of this work for personal or classroom use is granted without fee provided that copies are not made or distributed for profit or commercial advantage and that copies bear this notice and the full citation on the first page. Copyrights for components of this work owned by others than the author(s) must be honored. Abstracting with credit is permitted. To copy otherwise, or republish, to post on servers or to redistribute to lists, requires prior specific permission and/or a fee. Request permissions from permissions@acm.org.
ACM-BCB'17, August 20–23, 2017, Boston, MA, USA.
© 2017 Copyright held by the owner/author(s). Publication rights licensed to ACM.
ISBN 978-1-4503-4722-8/17/08...$15.00
DOI: http://dx.doi.org/10.1145/3107411.3107442

1 INTRODUCTION

An overwhelming majority of scientific databases use traditional database query languages SQL and XQuery, and graphical query interfaces to grant access to their contents. As the information contents of these databases grow more complex in representation, interpretation and analysis, query interfaces needed to access them are also becoming increasingly complicated. Often time, the only convenient method is a predesigned graphical interface through which all accesses are facilitated even though it severely limits the usefulness of these rich information repositories. Although widely used in Life Sciences, these interfaces do not allow ad hoc or spontaneous queries, or investigative queries in ways a natural language interface (NLI) would allow. An encouraging sign is that NLIs are increasingly being used to provide non traditional query responses in various types of databases such as knowledge repositories [7, 13], text based information repositories [15, 29], biological and clinical databases [16, 36], Geographic Information Systems (GIS) databases [26] and of course traditional relational databases [27, 39] with limited scopes.

From the standpoint of end users in Life Sciences, flat view of data is perhaps the most acceptable of all formats while some forms of shallow nesting were also welcomed. Therefore, it can be argued that the relational data model fits well with the practice and end user psychology in this domain. While XML is creeping its way up in use, querying such data sets using languages such as XQuery or XPath is considered truly difficult still. Therefore, without an abstraction that flattens the nested structure of XML, the natural language processing (NLP) interfaces to such databases [27, 39] do not appear to have a serious influence. As argued in works such as BioBike [12], for over 40 years biologists have voted overwhelmingly not to embrace computer programming as a basic tool through which to look at their world that led to BioBike's development (and many other that followed, e.g., [16, 36]) that tried to use NLP as a means to gain access to needed information from the vast array of Life Sciences repositories. But the reality is that such a high level interface still remains illusive mostly because of the representation hurdles, highly interpretive nature of Life Sciences data[1], translation from natural language to database queries, and the inherent difficulty in processing NLP queries. A practical approach[2], we argue, is providing a flat relational view of complex data such as XML so that users can comprehend and query the

[1]Tool applications are essential to understand most biological data such as DNA sequences, protein structures, or pathways. Simple reading of the data usually does not reveal much.

[2]This is not to say that other data models are not useful, but to emphasize that flat relations make it possible to use powerful deductive query engines such as Prolog and XSB [38] without much effort as we demonstrate in this paper.

information repositories in the well understood model of flat relations as a middle ground. Once chosen, the question remains, how do we facilitate comprehension of a natural language query in a given context, device a strategy to compute its response, and implement the strategy as a traditional query over structured relations stored in local or remote information repositories?

Our goal in this paper is to show that a prudent design of multiple abstraction layers separating the lower level structural details from the upper levels aids in developing a powerful reasoning mechanism for the semantic characterization of database objects and their relationships. Once the natural language query's (NLQ) structural characterization is made, a reasoner can be used to analyze the layered representation to map the NLQ to a structured query that not only implements the intent of the upper level query, it does so in a cooperative manner which SQL or XQuery cannot do. By that we mean, we can now actually respond to queries in much the same way a human might do and thereby reflect a deeper semantic understanding of the queries and their true intents. The diagram in figure 1 shows a bird's eye view of the interrelationships between the components in different abstraction layers, the machineries involved, and the conceptual model how the entire system functions to produce near human response to NLQs.

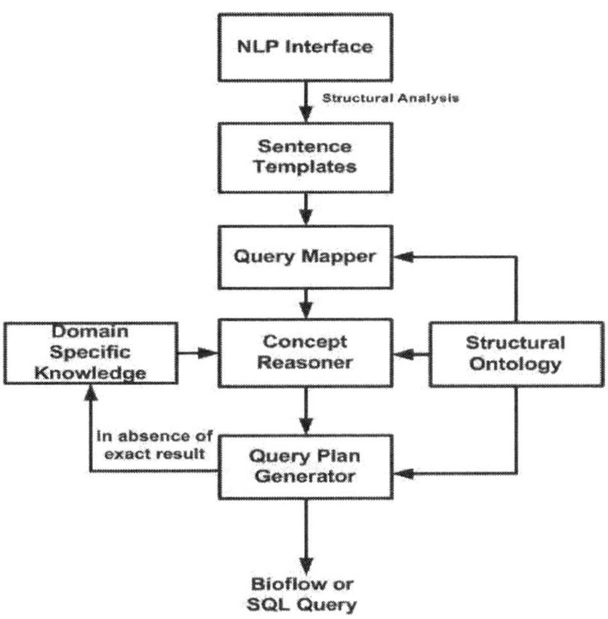

Figure 1: System components.

As a next logical step, we believe it is possible to extend this system toward a cooperative information repository that is capable of sensing the context of a query and carrying the context over an entire investigative session. To that end, we also envision a system where concepts are learned in a query session, and the interrelationship among them and the constraints they impose can be made to influence the candidate set of responses. In an early research on SmartBase [40], we have shown that monotonic inheritance of constraints (SQL's `where` clause conditions) related to concepts in a query to the next query as a logical conjunct simulates an increasingly smaller and focused world semantics in a practical and computable way yet offers a better and richer approach to interactive query processing and cooperative response than systems such as [32] or earlier research on cooperative query processing [10, 34]. We claim that contextual and knowledge rich NLP query processing remains as an extremely difficult proposition in contemporary approaches and the NLP model in the *BioSmart* system we propose in this paper can be adapted to include SmartBase query processing features to support a truly contextual NLQ interface.

1.1 A Motivating Example

Consider a protein/gene function database consisting of two base tables – *UniProt Protein Table* and *Entrez Gene Table* as shown in figures 2(a) and 2(b) respectively. Now consider answering queries of the form

(1) *"List all F-box domain protein 2 sequences"*, or
(2) *"What are the functions of UniProt proteins Q9UKT8 and Q9NVA1"*?

In a conventional relational database, these two natural language queries will most likely map to the following to two SQL queries to return the answer sets shown in figures 2(c) and 2(d) respectively.

```
select DNASequence
from Entrez as e, UniProt as u
where u.ProteinID=e.UniProtProteinID and
  ProteinName="F-box domain protein 2"

select Function
from UniProt
where ProteinID in {Q9UKT8, Q9NVA1}
```

The scientific fact here is that the UniProt protein Q60584, with corresponding gene name FBXW2, is a mouse protein. Functionally, Q60584 is identical to UniProt protein Q9UKT8 and have the same gene name, FBXW2, is a human protein. Furthermore, they also have almost identical DNA sequences. This similarity can be computed – (i) by homology of the two sequences corresponding to the UniProt IDs Q60584 and Q9UKT8 as shown in Entrez Gene Table, (ii) knowing that these two genes are orthologs, (iii) by determining that they have identical gene names in Entrez Gene Table, (iv) by consulting a ID mapping database such as GeneCard [1] and finding their equivalence, or (v) by consulting the Gene Ontology (GO) database [14], among many other ways. If such background knowledge is used, then it becomes possible to return the tables shown in figures 2(e) and 2(f) with an additional response in each table, as knowledge derived responses. Notice that such inferences are not directly possible in traditional relational databases, but these responses are valid, and useful. The BioBike system actually takes this approach.

In contrast, in BioBike, users must specifically perform a homolog computation in order to receive the responses shown in figures 2(e) and 2(f). The system only provides the computational means. The novelty of our system is that such knowledge is derived by the system on its own and no explicit requests need to be made. In a more recent work [21], it was shown that an ontology based logical query language ConLog can be used to non-intrusively capture semantic knowledge and query response generated without

ProteinName	ProteinID	Function
Putative replication	O85067	Plasmid maintenance
Ubiquinol-cytochrome c reductase	Q9NVA1	Cytoplasmic vesicle
F-box domain protein 2	Q60584	Substrate recognition

(a) Protein Table "UniProt"

GeneName	GeneID	UniProtProteinID	DNASequence	...
FBXW2	30050	Q60584	CTCTTTCTTTCG ...	...
repA1	1246500	O85067	ACCCTTGGAAACCC...	...
FBXW2	26190	Q9UKT8	CTCTTTCTTTCT ...	...
UQCC	55245	Q9NVA1	TTTTGGGGCCCCAAA...	...

(b) Gene Table "Entrez"

DNASequence
CTCTTTCTTTCG ...

(c) Query 1 Response

Function
Cytoplasmic vesicle

(d) Query 2 Response

DNASequence
CTCTTTCTTTCG ...
CTCTTTCTTTCT ...

(e) Enhanced Response 1

Function
Cytoplasmic vesicle
Substrate recognition

(f) Enhanced Response 2

Figure 2: Queries over UniProt and Entrez databases.

such explicit knowledge entailed response computation. In this paper, our goal is to show that a canonical representation, as shown in figures 3(a) through 3(e), can be used to compose queries in a logic based language such as Datalog without user intervention. More importantly, we show that natural language sentences can be classified into sentence structure templates, and these templates can be used to select appropriate query predicates to fire to compute intended responses. In the next few sections, we present a detailed discission how our approach works.

1.2 Related Research

Our research in this paper is mainly influenced by the BioBike project [12] at Virginia Commonwealth University with a goal to complement the data integration and querying language BioFlow [22] and analytic engine VisFlow [31] within our LifeDB project [8] and to support knowledge rich queries. The promise of knowledge rich query interfaces in Life Sciences inspired us to explore if systems could detect query intent, especially in exploratory settings such as in SmartBase in which we developed a contextual query processor capable of recognizing the query skyline [24] from a set of successive queries. Despite many such efforts, articulating application description by domain scientists in Biology to facilitate knowledge rich queries remain a significant challenge. This, we believe, is mainly due to a complex regiment of interpretive tools needed to analyze the raw data, the domain specific knowledge that leads to many alternative and approximate response to a query, and so on. From these standpoints an NLP interface seems to be very attractive for this community and BioBike stands out as an interesting model as it demonstrated its ability to respond to Biological queries in an intuitive way. In this paper, our goal is to fuse these two approaches to be able to respond to natural language queries over arbitrary biological databases.

While interesting in its approach, BioBike still seems to have encoded the query processing logic into the system in a way that did not support good enough abstractions that made it a less likely candidate for a viable architecture that designers could just adopt as a generalized engine for widespread use. To a large extent, it still remained a seriously hard wired programming application. Though NLP interfaces for traditional structured databases are extensively studied in the literature (e.g., [27, 39]), knowledge rich queries using NLP [23] have been rarely and tangentially explored. Mostly existing NLP systems map NLQs to structured queries only when the database structures, application domain and the interpretation of the data are known and well understood. Although NLP is being increasingly used to return possible answers [6, 11], we stand out in the way we conceptualize the database, represent them in a canonical form, and allow an intelligent and user specific analysis of the content of the database to map the NLQ to a target declarative query language. We are unaware of any system that follow this approach including BioBike.

The remainder of the paper is organized as follows. We discuss several expository examples and their executions to illustrate the functionalities of the system components just presented in section 2. The type of NLP queries we support are introduced in section 3 and demonstrate that the type of queries we support covers a wide class of queries, and they can be nested to pose more semantically rich queries. Our goal is to build a middleware that is capable of interpreting the problem description by recognizing the intent of the overall workflow, and offer a near NLP experience and return a more cooperative response than traditional databases. From this standpoint, we also highlight the salient features of our system that distinguishes it from the leading contemporary systems. In section 4, we discuss the heart of our system BioSmart, its concept reasoner that helps compute knowledge rich queries using domain specific knowledge. The method to incorporate application specific computational tools in Datalog are also discussed since custom designed and generic computational tools play a significant role in biological data processing. In section 4.4, we discuss Java specific calls to facilitate invocation of computational tools from XSB, the reasoning platform we use in BioSmart. In section 4.5, we discuss a more generic and more powerful approach to modeling external function calls in the form of a database engine using workflows. We summarize and discuss possible future research in section 5.

ConceptA	ConceptB
Gene	Protein

(a) Derivatives: der

TableX	TableY	ColumnX	ColumnY
Entrez	UniProt	UniProtProteinID	ProteinID

(b) Foreign Keys: forK

ConceptX	ConceptY	Relation
Gene	Gene	Ortholog, Paralog, Duplication

(c) Similar Concepts: simCon

Relation	Operation
Ortholog	BLAST, ORSCAN
Paralog	GENCODE

(d) Tools: cTool

ConceptName	TableName	Key	Attributes
Gene	Entrez	GeneID	GeneName, DNASequence, ...
Protein	UniProt	ProteinID	Function, ProteinName, ...

(e) Structural Ontology (sO)

Concept	PrimaryKey	AttributeName	AttributeValue
Gene	1246500	GeneName	repA1
Gene	1246500	UniProtProteinID	O85067
Gene	1246500	DNASequence	ACCCTTGGAAACCC...
Gene	1246500	GeneID	1246500
Gene	55245	GeneName	UQCC
Gene	55245	UniProtProteinID	Q9NVA1
Gene	55245	DNASequence	TTTTGGGGCCCCAAA...
Gene	55245	GeneID	55245
Protein	O85067	ProteinID	O85067
Protein	O85067	Function	Plasmid maintenance
Protein	O85067	ProteinName	Putative replication
Protein	Q9NVA1	Protein ID	Q9NVA1
Protein	Q9NVA1	Function	Cytoplasmic vesicle
Protein	Q9NVA1	ProteinName	Ubiquinol-cytochrome c reductase
...	...	...	...

(f) Canonical Database: canDB

Figure 3: Internal representations and meta data for knowledge rich queries.

2 BIOSMART SYSTEM

Representation and interpretation of biological data are complex, and analyzing them requires domain specific knowledge which may vary from user to user. To support such a fluid and knowledge driven querying environment, we offer a free-form NLP interface called *BioSmart*. In this interface, users may ask arbitrary queries that are parsable as a valid natural language sentence. We then categorize these sentences into several classes that fit into predefined syntactic templates[3]. These templates are then analyzed in the context of the underlying database structures and and assigned an interpretation entailed by its logical meaning. We expect the analysis to yield a query and a query execution plan in a declarative language such as SQL, Datalog, or BioFlow.

2.1 Overview of the System

Let us introduce the architecture of the NLQ engine we envision with the help of an example query Q below.

> *"Find the photosynthetic genes of cyanobacteria Prochlorococcus sp. strain (known also as MED4)".*

[3]We omit the discussion on specific mapping algorithms from NLQ to categorized templates in this paper for the sake of brevity. Instead, we mainly focus on how such templates once generated are interpreted to respond to queries.

Prochlorococcus is an extremely small Chl *b*-containing light-harvesting cyanobacterium antenna system sometimes constituting up to 50% of the photosynthetic biomass in the oceans [17]. So, the query above is interesting at many levels. First, although there is a fairly recent database on cyanobacteria called *CKB* [35], it is not so simple to dig out the information this query seeks from this database. The search term Prochlorococcus does not pull up any information from CKB. But, from the literature [17] we know that Prochlorococcus has two strains, MED4 and MIT9313 that are representatives of high and low-light adapted ecotypes, characterized by their low or high Chl *b/a* ratio, respectively. Furthermore, MED4 is more recently evolved and has about 1,686 protein coding genes while MIT9313 belongs to the most deeply branching lineage of Prochlorococcus with 2,200 genes. The Prochlorophyte Chlorophyll-Binding proteins (PCBs) responsible for photosynthesis in Prochlorococcus are encoded by a single gene in all the low *b/a* strains, whereas multigene families have been found in several high b/a strains. It is also known that pcb is a gene in the high light-adapted MED4, and pcb1 and pcb2 are two genes in low light-adapted MIT9313 strain for photosynthesis.

However, it is not possible to isolate these genes from CKB using pcb as the search term to know if their function is photosynthesis. To discover this knowledge, one must sift through to select all rows having pcb as a column, and link the gene names to either UniProt of KEGG databases to see if their functions include photosynthesis. Two such gene names are PMM0627, and pcbA or Pro0783 that are listed to have photosynthesis as their functions in KEGG and UniProt databases respectively. So the innocent looking query is not that simple at all to compute without knowing all these details from the literature in the first place and thus obviating the need for querying. Even when one wants to learn more, starting off with a wrong database or inappropriate search term may throw the search in a wrong direction. Finally, phylogenetically the closest relative of Prochlorococcus is the organism Synechococcus, and there is great deal of information on this organism that can be leveraged to learn details about photosynthetic genes of Prochlorococcus indirectly. Therefore, we believe the novelty of BioSmart is that given a query Q, a database D and a knowledgebase K, it computes the response A to the query as the entailment relation $D \cup K \models_Q A$, which to our knowledge no other leading databases or query answering system in Life Sciences do.

2.2 The Generative Process

The entailment relation we have introduced above is captured in the architecture of BioSmart shown in figure 1. The NLQs in BioSmart are accepted and parsed by its *NLP Interface* (NLI) and mapped to predefined sentence or query templates. It is possible that a sentence will be broken down into several such templates that capture the meaning. The *Query Mapper* (QM) component transforms the templates into a logical query using the information in the *Structural Ontology* (SO) in the context of the underlying database – identifies the tables, the analysis tools needed, and the possible joins needed to compute the query.

In the SO, we maintain concepts and their properties independent of their structural affiliation in tables or their specificity as objects in a table. For example, the two tables *Entrez* Gene Table and *UniProt* Protein Table in figures 2(a) and 2(b) will be described in SO as a meta-data table as shown in figure 3(e). The concepts in SO (e.g., Gene and Protein in column *ConceptName*) can now be linked to natural language concepts independent of their table affiliation, which now can actually be discovered from the table in figure 3(e) using column name *TableName*. Other components such as *Query Mapper* (QM), *Concept Reasoner* (CR) and *Query Plan Generator* (QPG) also use the services by and the information maintained in SO.

2.3 Query Mapping

The CR subsystem uses a set of axioms to discover how responses can be generated using the objects in the database for a given natural language sentence template. This component also discovers relationships that can be used to construct alternative responses, either directly or indirectly as well as any need for tool applications to find query responses. The interesting aspect of this component is that the axioms used in CR are not domain specific, and so, the system can be used for other domains as is. However, *domain/concept specific knowledge* (DSK) in the form of a knowledge base can be supplied as a plug-in to tailor the functionality and bring specificity to the system. Better or more richer the knowledgebase is, more sophisticated response it is capable of generating. The union of DSK, CR and SO serves as the knowledgebase K in the entailment relation $D \cup K \models_Q A$, and the response A is as rich as entailed by K.

The query specification generated by the CR is then forwarded to the QPG which in consultation with the SO transforms the specification into a set of database specific executable queries in a language of choice. QPG achieves this goal by using the *canonical representation* of the existing data sources. In the canonical representation, we represent the underlying database in a triple form similar to RDF [4]. All the tables from the user-specified database are broken up in a ⟨*concept, attribute type, attribute value*⟩ triple format. Concept is a combination of the concept types and the primary key for a conceptual object. Attribute type is the column name from the original data table and attribute value is the value stored in that column for a particular concept. Canonical representation of the data sources shown in the figures 2(a) and 2(b) is presented in figure 3(f). The steps involved in the mapping process is outlined in algorithm 1 at a very high level.

Algorithm 1: Mapping NLQ Q to executable knowledge rich query Q_e.

```
Input: A natural language query Q
Output: Executable declarative query Q_e
Perform syntactic analysis of Q to generate a parse tree T;
Perform structural analysis of T to match a sentence
template s ∈ S;
Generate logical equivalent L of s;
Apply DSK to L to generate conceptual plan C;
Generate executable script Q_e from C;
Execute Q_e;
if Q_e succeeds then
    Return result A;
    Exit;
else
    Try alternate mapping, if possible;
```

3 QUERY TYPES

Since interpretation of arbitrary natural language sentences are difficult, keeping in mind that most flat and structured databases use a set based model, natural language sentences that mimic select-project-join (SPJ) queries are our priority. Such queries have limited interpretive scopes in terms of what they allow. For example, queries are mostly about objects and their properties, and their relationships with other objects. Often, we need to construct complex objects by piecing together parts from various tables. We believe almost all such query structures can be admitted if we recognized three basic types of sentence structures – *iterative, conditional*, and *imperative* or *interrogative* natural language queries. Keeping the admissible sentence structures set simple and small, we actually follow SQL's footsteps in which complex and more expressive queries can be built by nesting simple structures arbitrarily. Thus, most of the biological queries potentially can be expressed by one of these types, or by a combination of them. In

BioSmart, we do so by allowing series of queries in succession in a context.

3.1 Iterative Queries

Consider expressing a query in English in two different but semantically equivalent ways.

> *"List the functions of all human genes"*

and,

> *"For all Homo sapiens genes, list their functions."*

These two seemingly two structurally different queries in English actually map identical structured queries in SQL, or at least can be expressed by a single query from table 2(a). But as a query type, these natural language queries ask to retrieve objects that satisfy certain properties (including empty properties). If we parse these queries in a syntax tree as shown in figure 4, we will discover that each of these query types roughly adhere to one of the parse tree structures in this figure, we call sentence templates. The queries above can be parsed to resemble the template shown in figure 4(a), or the iterative type.

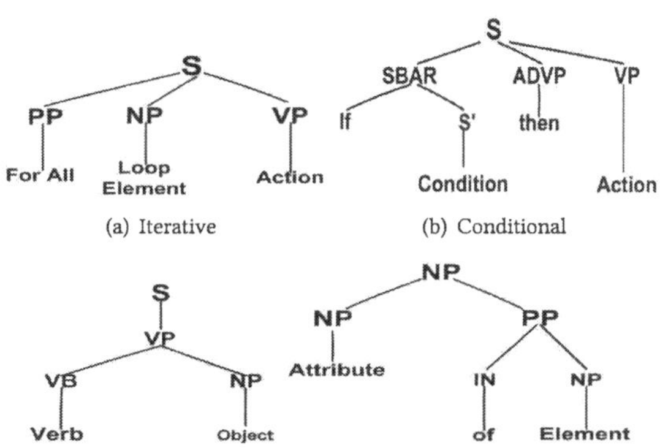

(a) Iterative (b) Conditional (c) Imperative (d) The noun phrase structure

Figure 4: Natural language query templates.

An iterative, or *loop*, type natural language query, and thus its template, starts with a prepositional phrase (PP), followed by a noun phrase (NP) and then a verb phrase (VP). The prepositional phrase usually includes the phrase "for all", or its variants. The noun phrase essentially points to the objects or entities we are to apply the verb phrase, i.e., properties or actions. The parse tree for the query

> *"For all genes of cyanobacteria find homologs"*

is shown in figure 5(a) which actually is an instance of the iterative query template in figure 4(a). In this query the NP is *all genes of cyanobacteria* and the VP is *find homologs.*

3.2 Conditional Queries

Iterative queries are not required to satisfy any constraint. In other words, they can be viewed as a simple projection query in SQL (i.e., `select from`), possibly with a simple `where` clause condition for the purpose of object or property identification. In contrast, a *conditional* query specifies an arbitrary precondition that the objects

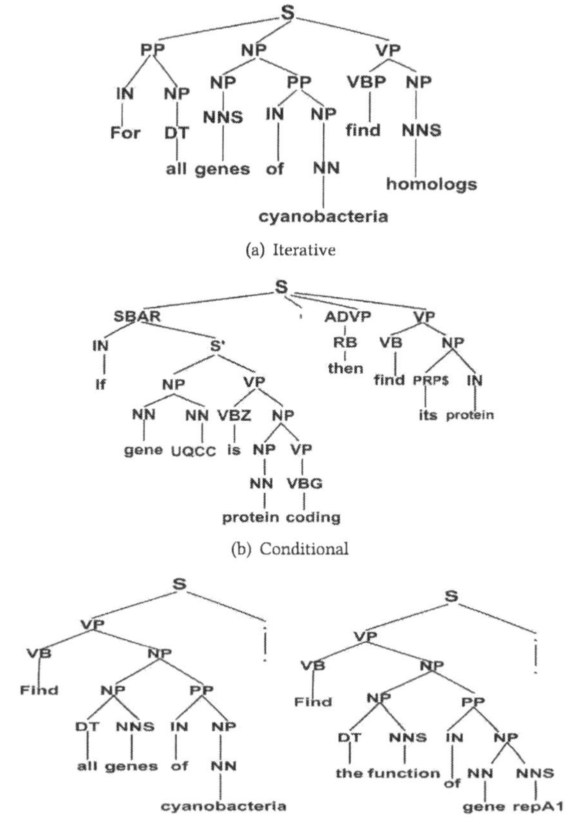

(a) Iterative

(b) Conditional

(c) Imperative (d) Parsed tree

Figure 5: Natural language query examples.

must satisfy in the form of an *if then* structure as shown in the query template in figure 4(b). In such queries, a NP-VP sequence follows the *if* condition (i.e., the S' subtree), and the VP following the NP captures the action clause, where the NP-VP sequence has a simple *subject-verb-object* sentence structure. The VP after the *then* has a *verb-object* imperative sentence structure. Figure 5(b) shows the parse tree for the query

> *"If gene UQCC is protein coding, then find its protein"*,

as an instance of the template in figure 4(b). In this example *"is protein coding"* is the VP for the *if* condition, and *"find its protein"* is the VP for the *then* inference.

3.3 Imperative Queries

Imperative sentences or queries are basically a verb phrase (VP) consisting of a verb (VB) and an object (NP) on which the verb is to be applied. The template representing an imperative query is shown in figure 4(c). These type of sentences are used as standalone queries or as a part of more complex iterative of conditional queries. Usually the object (NP) has a structure of the form *"attribute of element"* as in figure 4(d). As an example, consider the query

"List all genes of cyanobacteria",

and its parse tree in figure 5(c). Here the verb is *List* and the object is *genes of cyanobacteria* in conformance with the structure of figure 4(d). As discussed in section 2.1, we will be correct to return genes of Prochlorococcus and Synechococcus, and MED4 and MIT9313, such as pcb and pcbA.

4 KNOWLEDGE RICH QUERYING

The query identification and processing apparatus we have introduced earlier can now be leveraged to respond to the simple knowledge rich query

"Find the function of gene repA1"

in Escherichia coli. Though this query appears simple, as discussed in section 2.1, finding answer to it may require the use of multiple biological data sources and tools. A user can go to NCBI GenBank to find its function. Failing to find the answer in GenBank, she can find its UniProt ID P03066 and try to find its function from UniProt database, and a full annotation can also be obtained from GO database. In UniProt, the function for repA (Replication initiation protein) is listed as `plasmid replication`, and `copy control`, whereas GO annotation includes {`DNA replication, plasmid maintenance`}. In the event none of these databases produced any useful information, she could try to use NCBI BLAST search to find the orthologs of repA1 and then find the function of those orthologs.

Such approaches force users familiarity with all these details, and complex queries require even more complex and intricate interwoven knowledge. Moreover, different resources and tools have unique representation and naming policy which makes it even more difficult to find answers. For example, the GeneCards database assigns RPA1 as the ID for repA1, which is supposed to be an authoritative site for finding the IDs for repA1 in various databases. Apparently, repA1 gene symbol has been discontinued and replaced with the name RPA1. To aid biologists in such a confusing landscape, in BioSmart, we approach the computation of the query in several steps. We use the Stanford parser to first parse the query submitted to BioSmart NLI and attempt a mapping to one of the query templates in figure 4 as resulting in the imperative query parse tree in figure 5(d), with action *Find* on attribute *function* of element *gene repA1*.

4.1 Direct Concept Reconstruction

From the discussion in section 1.1 it may not have been apparent that we actually do not use the base tables in figure 2. Instead, we always use the derived tables in figure 3. In particular, all tables are collapsed into the canonical database form in figure 3(f) that allows reconstruction of the objects in any table using an object identifier, the primary key of each table represented as a concept. The remaining set of tables in figure 3 forms the DSK and SO components. The reconstruction process depends on the query type, and the complexity of the query and its interpretation assigned.

In the query above, the goal is to compute the *function* (a property) of a *gene* (a concept/object) named *repA1* (attribute value) corresponding to another property (i.e., *gene name*). QM uses this interpretation to map the properties to the attribute *AttributeName*, the concept to the attribute *Concept*, and attribute value to *AttributeValue*. Essentially, we are trying to compute the pair ⟨*function, AttributeValue*⟩ for the concept *gene* having ⟨*GeneName, repA1*⟩ as an entry in the canonical database *CanDB*. Logically, the response can be constructed by an equi-join of the *CanDB* table on the column *PrimaryKey* for the *Concept gene*. In general, the reconstruction is captured in the following CR rule,

```
1: res(Con, Pk, AttName, AttVal) :-
     canDB(Con, Pk, AttName, AttVal).
```

and with the conjunctive query below that is equivalent to the equi-join above.

```
? res('Gene', Pk, 'GeneName', 'repA1'),
    res('Gene', Pk, 'Function', Val).
```

If k number of attributes of a concept were needed to be computed, we would be required to write a k-way conjunctive query in this approach.

Obviously, this query will fail. But, had the query been,

```
? res('Gene', Pk, 'GeneName', 'repA1'),
    res('Gene', Pk, 'UniProtProteinID', Val).
```

it would have succeeded producing a binding 085067 for *Val*. It failed because the concept *gene* does not have a *function* in the base table *Entrez*, and consequently in the table *CanDB*. Therefore, the response remains empty unless CR tries an alternative evaluation.

4.2 Indirect Response Generation

The query above failed because concept *gene* does not have a property called *function*. Biologically, we know that genes encode proteins, and thus gene functions are manifest as protein functions, and thus are synonymous. Such knowledge are captured in the table *der* in figure 3(a). A transitive closure of this relationship captures what we can compute as substitutes for a given concept, as captured in the axioms in rules 3 and 4 below.

```
2: res(Con, Pk, AttName, AttVal) :-
     rel(Con, Der, Pk, PkD),
     res(Der, PkD, AttName, AttVal).
3: rel(Con, Der, PkC, PkD) :- der(Con, Der),
     sO(Con, TabC, KeyC, AttsC),
     member(ColC, AttsC),
     sO(Der, TabD, KeyD, AttsD),
     member(ColD, AttsD),
     forK(TabC, TabD, ColC, ColD),
     canDB(Con, PkC, ColC, ValC),
     canDB(Der, PkD, ColD, ValC).
4: rel(Con, Der, PkC, PkD) :-
     rel(Con, DerC, PkC, PkDC),
     sO(DerC, TabC, KeyC, AttsC),
     member(ColC, AttsC),
     sO(Der, TabD, KeyD, AttsD),
     member(ColD, AttsD),
     forK(TabC, TabD, ColC, ColD),
     canDB(DerC, PkDC, ColC, ValC),
     canDB(Der, PkD, ColD, ValC).
5: member(Mem, [Mem|_]).
6: member(Mem, [_|Tail]) :- member(Mem, Tail).
```

To reconstruct the extended object, for the property pair ⟨*function, AttributeValue*⟩ from the corresponding concept `Protein`, we need to establish the fact that `Protein` indeed is a substitute (in the *der* table in figure 3(a)), *UniProtProteinID* `085067` corresponds to *GeneID* `1246500` (in table *Entrez* in figure 2(b)), and that the *Protein* `085067` has the pair ⟨*Function, AttributeValue*⟩ in table *CanDB*, by virtue of table *UniProt* in figure 2(a). We do so in rule 2 above by asserting a transitive relationship between the concepts `Gene` and `Protein`, and making sure they are connected by a foreign key relationship.

The rules 3 and 4 are a bit involved, but are conceptually simpler. These rules basically say, two objects are connected by a derived relationship is they have a direct foreign key relationship (rule 3), or a transitive foreign key relationship between the concept *C* and *S* such that *C* has a direct foreign key relationship with some concept *D* in *der* table and a foreign key relationship between the derived concept *D* and some other concept *S*. The rules 5 and 6 are necessary axioms to test list memberships used in rules 3 and 4 to inspect the base tables have the required attributes. Adding rules 2 through 6 will now help us evaluate the subquery

```
res('Gene', Pk, 'Function', Val)
```

to be true with a binding `Plasmid maintenance` for the variable *Val*, essentially computing the *Function* for the gene `repA1`, via *ProteinID* `085067`, and *GeneID* `1246500`.

4.3 Interpretive Queries

The indirect responses in the previous section are actually a class of queries that use conceptual substitutions to derive responses, i.e., property of proteins for genes know that they are substitutable as captured in the table *der* as a derivative. In fact any such biological knowledge can be encoded in BioSmart by creating a new rule for the predicate *rel/4* to link objects or concepts through their identifying keys. The independence of the *rel/4* predicate from how the antecedent is represented, makes it possible to make the mapping algorithm abstract and generic. For example, Scandinavian males, especially 33%-45% Swedish males, carry the I1 haplotype. We could then link genes of an offspring to his geographic origin, or to someone in that region, to discover possible properties. In such cases too, the predicate *rel/4* can be leveraged to link seemingly unrelated pieces of information to derive knowledge.

But such relationships are required to be in one of the database tables as ground values. In other words, no new information is actually generated, they are only linked in a meaningful and informative way. In BioSmart, we do allow a third kind of queries that actually allows generation of new knowledge not available in the database as ground facts using computational tools or functions. Applications of such tools have the potential to reveal new relationship among the database objects previously unknown, or discover new properties of objects in it.

Aside from storing base facts in tables such as in PhylomeDB [19] or TreeBASE [44], we can actually apply computational tools to compute these relationships and infer new properties. For example, orthologs can be computed using BLAST like tools such as Ortholog-Finder [18] or ORCAN [45], and phylogeny construction tools such as MEGA [25] or PAUP [41]. New relationships can also be established using databases such as GeneCards [37] using ID mapping. In BioSmart, we allow such tool application based on background knowledge to link objects and then use the direct and indirect construction of properties using discovered relationships. For example, for the gene *repA1*, there are several orthologs that can be computed or retrieved from Entrez database or by using tools such as Ortholog-Finder or ORCAN: Gene ID `327491` in zebra fish, Gene ID `68275` in mouse, and Gene ID `417563` in chicken, each one of which could be used to decipher properties for the gene `repA1`. It is interesting to note that recent studies show that although `repA1` does not have paralogs in animals, it has paralogs in plants: `RPA1A` to `RPA1E` in Arabidopsis thaliana, and `RPA1B` in Glycin max, `RPA1C` in Sorghum bicolor, and so on [5]. This result is only available as of today in scientific literature, and not in any database, indicating that a text mining tool such as GeneView [42] may be appropriate to discover this knowledge.

Calling such external functions from logic based languages such as Datalog, Prolog or XSB, is application specific. In general, they are called *foreign* codes or functions, and have specific protocols for implementation. In BioSmart, we use XSB [38] as a reasoning platform for its set based processing strategy, and Interprolog [2, 9] Java API for procedure calls. Interface *javaMessage()* of Interprolog binds XSB predicates with Java procedures. The rule implementing interpretive queries thus take the form below.

```
7: res(Con, PkC, AttNameR, AttValR) :-
      res(Con, PkC, _, _), simCon(Con, RelCon, Reln),
      cTool(RelnO, Ops), member(RelnO, Reln),
      res(RelCon, PkR, AttNameR, AttValR),
      member(Op, Ops), applyOp(Op, PkC, PkR).
```

The rule 7 above basically asserts that we can derive the pair ⟨*AttNameR, AttValR*⟩ for an object *Con* with an identifier *PkC*, if it is related to another object via the relationship in *simCon* table and an external call to the tool *Op* can verify the stated relationship with the object *RelCon* with the identifier *PkR* having the pair ⟨*AttNameR, AttValR*⟩ as its property.

4.4 Computational Tool Integration

Predicate **applyOp()** in rule 7 above is a foreign function for XSB which is implemented procedurally in Java. It invokes different types of functions depending on the argument *Op*, i.e., it may access databases such as PhylomeDB, TreeBase or GeneCards, it may initiate a computation by running desktop tools such as MEGA or PAUP, or look up the information in an web accessible tool such as ORCAN. We use the *Interprolog* [2] API to switch between the XSB reasoner and the procedural Java environment. Interface *javaMessage()* of Interprolog binds XSB predicates with Java procedures. The general form of *javaMessage()* interface is shown bellow.

```
javaMessage(Target, Result, Exception,
   MessageName, ArgList, NewArgList)
```

Interface *javaMessage()* synchronously calls a method of a Java object *Target*, then waits for its *Result*, catching any *Exception* that may occur. *ArgList* specifies the arguments necessary for the function call, which must be of the proper Java-compatible types. *NewArgList* contains the same objects in *ArgList* reflecting possible state changes after the function has been processed. Here, *MessageName* is the invoked method of object *Target*.

A Java class called *MessageCaller* has been implemented to model the functions of *javaMessages* invoked by XSB. A method named *performOperation()* of *MessageCaller* calls online tools such as BLAST or ORCAN based on the operations specified (sent as the argument list *ArgList* by *javaMessage*). For example, to compute homology of genes by the online tool BLAST, method *performOperation()* uses the *NCBI BLAST Java Interface* [3]. Given the ID of a gene, BLAST returns the IDs of the orthologs as an XML file. We then parse the XML file to retrieve the *GeneIds* of the orthologous genes and send them back to XSB as *Result*. An alternative technique for sending results is to store them in a database table and use an XSB predicate to retrieve those results within the XSB reasoner.

To be precise, the **applyOp**(*Op, PkC, PkR*) call in XSB is handled by the *javaMessage()* operation as follows. XSB initiates the *javaMessage()* call with the instantiations *Target* to *MessageCaller*, *Result* to *PkR*, *MassageName* to *performOperation()*, and *ArgList* to ⟨*Op, PkC*⟩. *Exception* and *NewArgList* are returned by Java as appropriate. Note that, the argument *Op* depends on the adornment of the variable by XSB before the call and depends on the tool list *Ops* in the *cTool* predicate. Eventually, method *performOperation()* of class *MessageCaller* applies the appropriate tool to perform the intended operation expected in the **applyOp**(*Op, PkC, PkR*) predicate.

4.5 Accessing Online Tools and Databases

In BioSmart, we leverage another level of abstraction for the interpretive class queries that opens up the possibility of endless ways of computing them, and infer knowledge in unprecedented ways. That also means the Java *MessageCaller* will need to be implemented on a case by case, which we believe is a daunting task. To avoid such unique implementation for each call type, we have decided to use the power of the abstraction encoded into the BioFlow language introduced earlier. This language, and its variants, have been leveraged in our implementation of LifeDB and VisFlow. In BioFlow, tools, databases and online web interfaces are viewed as function calls and are abstracted uniformly. Therefore, depending on the invocation and the specific tool, it is capable of customizing the evaluation.

In most tool applications, database processing and web applications, some form of selection conditions are applied (input arguments to a function), and results are extracted (output of the operation) before and after the operations are performed. There is also some form of schema mismatch between the terminologies used in the XSB program and the target system. Without the abstraction, users and the Java application writers will need to be fully aware of these terminologies and resolve the disparities manually. The BioFlow syntax already includes the machineries needed for schema matching and wrapping, in addition to accessing remote sites. The statement to access deep web resources in BioFlow is the extract statement with the following syntax,

> extract $A_1, \ldots, A_k$
> using matcher μ wrapper ω filler ϕ
> from φ submit r where θ

where θ is the form condition, $A_1, \ldots, A_k$ is the projection list, μ is the schema matcher (e.g., PruSM [33]), ω is the wrapper (e.g., WebProspector [30]), ϕ is the form filler (e.g., iForm [43]), and φ is the web form address or the form function. Note that this statement returns a table by submitting columns from each row in r to the deep web database at φ. When a matcher, wrapper or filler isn't necessary, the corresponding clauses can be omitted. This statement can be constructed using the stepwise mapping of a resource such as d_1. Note that, in the case of a web service at φ, a form filler and a wrapper are not needed as the web service itself handles these functions, and no form conditions (θ) are necessary either. But a transformation function τ may be required to convert XML to flat list of attributes, which could be made available in BioSmart library and help BioFlow extract the target fields automatically with a statement similar to the one below.

> extract $A_1, \ldots, A_k$
> using matcher μ transformer τ
> from φ submit r

These features of BioFlow allow users to write applications without having to worry about the details of extraction methods, location, technology specific nuances, format, and schema heterogeneity. The adoption of BioFlow also allows us to implement complex workflows using the applications similar to VisFlow. Users now can conceptualize a complete workflow at the highest abstraction level keeping a global scheme in mind knowing that the underlying data management and integration apparatus will be able to map her application onto potentially heterogeneous resources correctly and efficiently without any loss in query semantics.

For the call **applyOp**(*BLAST, repA1, PkR*), we will construct the following BioFlow statement to execute.

> extract *GeneID*
> using matcher *PruSM* wrapper *FastWrap* filler *iForm*
> from *'http://blast.ncbi.nlm.nih.gov/Blast.cgi'*
> submit *ArgRel*

In the above expression, we will supply `repA1` as the lone tuple in the table *ArgRel*. In fact, BioFlow can process set of inputs and thus is capable of a set based processing which can be utilized to speed up XSB predicate evaluation using external functions.

5 SUMMARY AND FUTURE RESEARCH

While there is a great deal of opportunities and interests in non-traditional data management and querying using key word based, NoSQL or natural language over unstructured databases, querying of structured databases using these approaches are also equally interesting. In this paper, and in our earlier research, we have demonstrated that interesting knowledge rich queries can be answered using such approaches, especially in investigative applications. Our contention is that users need not go to unimaginable lengths to dig out information just because they did not know how to. The BioSmart system we propose demonstrates the opportunities that exist and what is possible.

The concept reasoner, and domain specific knowledgebase we have leveraged is one of the major tool boxes that make BioSmart actually smart. But the design of these components are manual, often application specific and tedious. However, it also makes it possible to apply BioSmart to other scientific domains just by changing these components. Opportunities exists to use ontologies such as GO and SnoMed CT [20] to help users frame effective natural language queries by allowing terminology independence. This will require mapping query terms to conceptual terms in the ontologies and use the standardized terms in the mapped queries. We are investigating an approach designing the CR and DSK components, at least partially, automatically from these components.

In Schema-Free SQL [28], meta information such as relation trees were used to aid query processors to tolerate mismatch or errors in schema information, and in ConLog [21] conceptual structures were leveraged to map queries properly to underlying scheme. In BioSmart the need for such a structure to appropriately select parts of schema to frame the queries is much greater. Currently, the engineering of this structure is application specific and manual. Developing a similar conceptual structure generation scheme at least semi-autonomously will significantly improve usability of BioSmart. These are some of the issues we plan to continue as our future research.

6 ACKNOWLEDGEMENT

The author acknowledges Saikat Dey's contributions toward the preliminary implementation of BioSmart in XSB as part of a directed research.

REFERENCES

[1] *GeneCards: The Human Gene Compendium.* http://www.genecards.org/. Accessed: June 16, 2017.
[2] *InterProlog 2.1.2: a Java front-end and enhancement for Prolog.* http://www.declarativa.com/interprolog/. Accessed: May 20, 2012.
[3] *NCBI BLAST Java Interface (Concordia University).* http://users.encs.concordia.ca/~f_kohant/ncbiblast/. Accessed: May 20, 2012.
[4] *Web Services Description Language (WSDL) Version 2.0.* http://www.w3.org/TR/wsdl20/. Accessed: June 15, 2012.
[5] B. Aklilu and K. Culligan. Molecular evolution and functional diversification of replication protein a1 in plants. *Frontiers in Plant Science*, 7(33), January 2016.
[6] N. Aletras, D. Tsarapatsanis, D. Preotiuc-Pietro, and V. Lampos. Predicting judicial decisions of the european court of human rights: a natural language processing perspective. *PeerJ Computer Science*, 2:e93, 2016.
[7] Y. Amsterdamer, A. Kukliansky, and T. Milo. A natural language interface for querying general and individual knowledge. *PVLDB*, 8(12):1430–1441, 2015.
[8] A. Bhattacharjee, A. Islam, M. S. Amin, S. Hossain, S. Hosain, H. M. Jamil, and L. Lipovich. On-the-fly integration and ad hoc querying of life sciences databases using LifeDB. In *20th International Conference on Database and Expert Systems Applications*, pages 561–575, Linz, Austria, August 2009.
[9] M. Calejo. InterProlog: Towards a declarative embedding of logic programming in Java. In *IEEE International Conference on Robotics and Automation*, pages 714–717. Springer, 2004.
[10] W. W. Chu. Cobase: A cooperative query answering facility for database systems. In *DEXA, Prague, Czech Republic, September 6-8*, pages 134–145, 1993.
[11] B. L. Cook, A. M. Progovac, P. Chen, B. Mullin, S. Hou, and E. Baca-Garcia. Novel use of natural language processing (NLP) to predict suicidal ideation and psychiatric symptoms in a text-based mental health intervention in madrid. *Comp. Math. Methods in Medicine*, 2016:8708434:1–8708434:8, 2016.
[12] J. Elhai, A. Taton, J. Massar, J. K. Myers, M. Travers, J. Casey, M. Slupesky, and J. Shrager. BioBIKE: A Web-based, programmable, integrated biological knowledge base. *Nucl. Acids Res.*, 37:W28–32, 2009.
[13] S. Ferré. Sparklis: An expressive query builder for SPARQL endpoints with guidance in natural language. *Semantic Web*, 8(3):405–418, 2017.
[14] Gene Ontology Consortium. Gene ontology: tool for the unification of biology. *Nat. Genet.*, 25:25–29, 2000.
[15] E. J. Goldsmith, S. Mendiratta, R. Akella, and K. Dahlgren. Natural language query in the biochemistry and molecular biology domains based on cognition search. *Nature*, 2008.
[16] T. Hamon, N. Grabar, and F. Mougin. Querying biomedical linked data with natural language questions. *Semantic Web*, 8(4):581–599, 2017.
[17] W. R. Hess, G. Rocap, C. S. Ting, F. Larimer, S. Stilwagen, J. Lamerdin, and S. W. Chisholm. The photosynthetic apparatus of Prochlorococcus: Insights through comparative genomics. *Photosynth Res*, 70(1):53–71, 2001.
[18] T. Horiike, R. Minai, D. Miyata, Y. Nakamura, and Y. Tateno. Ortholog-Finder: A tool for constructing an ortholog data set. *Genome Biology and Evolution*, 8(2):446, 2016.
[19] J. Huerta-Cepas, S. Capella-Gutiérrez, L. P. Pryszcz, M. Marcet-Houben, and T. Gabaldón. PhylomeDB v4: zooming into the plurality of evolutionary histories of a genome. *Nucleic Acids Research*, 42(Database-Issue):897–902, 2014.
[20] IHTSDO. *SNOMED-CT.* http://www.ihtsdo.org/snomed-ct. Accessed: May 14, 2016.
[21] H. Jamil. A natural language interface plug-in for cooperative query answering in biological databases. *BMC Genomics*, 13(Suppl 3):S4, 2012.
[22] H. M. Jamil, A. Islam, and S. Hossain. A declarative language and toolkit for scientific workflow implementation and execution. *International Journal of Business Process Integration and Management*, 5(1):3–17, 2010. IEEE SCC/SWF 2009 Special Issue on Scientific Workflows.
[23] S. W. Joseph and R. Aleliunas. A knowledge-based subsystem for a natural language interface to a database that predicts and explains query failures. In *Proceedings of the Seventh International Conference on Data Engineering, April 8-12, Kobe, Japan*, pages 80–87, 1991.
[24] D. Kossmann, F. Ramsak, and S. Rost. Shooting stars in the sky: An online algorithm for skyline queries. In *VLDB 2002, Proceedings of 28th International Conference on Very Large Data Bases, August 20-23, Hong Kong, China*, pages 275–286, 2002.
[25] S. Kumar, M. Nei, J. Dudley, and K. Tamura. MEGA: a biologist-centric software for evolutionary analysis of DNA and protein sequences. *Briefings in Bioinformatics*, 9:299–306, 2008.
[26] C. Lawrence and S. Riezler. NLmaps: A natural language interface to query openstreetmap. In *COLING, December 11-16, Osaka, Japan*, pages 6–10, 2016.
[27] F. Li and H. V. Jagadish. Understanding natural language queries over relational databases. *SIGMOD Record*, 45(1):6–13, 2016.
[28] F. Li, T. Pan, and H. V. Jagadish. Schema-free SQL. In *International Conference on Management of Data, SIGMOD 2014, Snowbird, UT, USA, June 22-27, 2014*, pages 1051–1062, 2014.
[29] C. D. Maio, G. Fenza, V. Loia, and M. Parente. Natural language query processing framework for biomedical literature. In *IFSA-EUSFLAT-15, Gijón, Spain., June 30.*, 2015.
[30] S. Mir, S. Staab, and I. Rojas. Web-prospector - an automatic, site-wide wrapper induction approach for scientific deep-web databases. In *BTW*, pages 87–106, 2009.
[31] X. Mou, H. M. Jamil, and R. Rinker. Visual orchestration and autonomous execution of distributed and heterogeneous computational biology pipelines. In *IEEE International Conference on Bioinformatics and Biomedicine, BIBM 2016, Shenzhen, China, December 15-18*, pages 752–757, 2016.
[32] A. Nandi and H. V. Jagadish. Qunits: queried units in database search. In *CIDR*, 2009.
[33] T. H. Nguyen, H. Nguyen, and J. Freire. PruSM: a prudent schema matching approach for web forms. In *CIKM*, pages 1385–1388, 2010.
[34] L. Novik, P. Godfrey, and J. Minker. An architecture for a cooperative database system. In *ADBy*, pages 3–24, 1994.
[35] A. P. Peter, K. Lakshmanan, S. Mohandass, S. Varadharaj, S. Thilagar, K. A. Abdul Kareem, P. Dharmar, S. Gopalakrishnan, and U. Lakshmanan. Cyanobacterial knowledgebase (CKB), a compendium of cyanobacterial genomes and proteomes. *PLOS ONE*, 10(8):1–12, 08 2015.
[36] L. Safari and J. D. Patrick. Restricted natural language based querying of clinical databases. *Journal of Biomedical Informatics*, 52:338–353, 2014.
[37] M. Safran, I. Dalah, J. Alexander, N. Rosen, T. Iny Stein, M. Shmoish, N. Nativ, I. Bahir, T. Doniger, H. Krug, A. Sirota-Madi, T. Olender, Y. Golan, G. Stelzer, A. Harel, and D. Lancet. GeneCards Version 3: the human gene integrator. *Database*, 2010(0):baq020–, 2010.
[38] K. Sagonas, T. Swift, and D. S. Warren. XSB as an efficient deductive database engine. *SIGMOD Rec.*, 23(2):442–453, 1994.
[39] D. Saha, A. Floratou, K. Sankaranarayanan, U. F. Minhas, A. R. Mittal, and F. Özcan. ATHENA: an ontology-driven system for natural language querying over relational data stores. *PVLDB*, 9(12):1209–1220, 2016.
[40] K. Z. Sultana, A. Bhattacharjee, M. S. Amin, and H. M. Jamil. A model for contextual cooperative query answering in e-commerce applications. In *8th International Conference on Flexible Query Answering Systems, Roskilde, Denmark, October 26-28*, pages 25–36, 2009.
[41] D. L. Swofford. *PAUP*: Phylogenetic Analysis Using Parsimony (*and Other Methods). Version 4.* Sinauer Associates, Sunderland, Massachusetts, 2003.
[42] P. Thomas, J. Starlinger, A. Vowinkel, S. Arzt, and U. Leser. GeneView: a comprehensive semantic search engine for PubMed. *Nucleic Acids Research*, 40(W1):W585–W591, 2012.
[43] G. A. Toda, E. Cortez, A. S. da Silva, and E. S. de Moura. A probabilistic approach for automatically filling form-based web interfaces. *PVLDB*, 4(3):151–160, 2010.
[44] R. A. Vos, H. Lapp, W. H. Piel, and V. Tannen. TreeBASE2: Rise of the Machines. *Nature Precedings*, (713), 2010.
[45] A. Zielezinski, M. Dziubek, J. Sliski, and W. M. Karlowski. ORCAN - a web-based meta-server for real-time detection and functional annotation of orthologs. *Bioinformatics*, ePub, 2017. doi: 10.1093/bioinformatics/btw825.

Discovering Inconsistencies in PubMed Abstracts through Ontology-Based Information Extraction

Nisansa de Silva
Department of Computer and Information Science
University of Oregon
Eugene, Oregon 97403, USA
nisansa@cs.uoregon.edu

Dejing Dou
Department of Computer and Information Science
University of Oregon
Eugene, Oregon 97403, USA
dou@cs.uoregon.edu

Jingshan Huang
School of Computing
University of South Alabama
Alabama 36688, USA
huang@southalabama.edu

ABSTRACT

Searching for a cure for cancer is one of the most vital pursuits in modern medicine. In that aspect microRNA research plays a key role. Keeping track of the shifts and changes in established knowledge in the microRNA domain is very important. In this paper, we introduce an *Ontology-Based Information Extraction* method to detect occurrences of inconsistencies in microRNA research paper abstracts. We propose a method to first use the Ontology for MIcroRNA Targets (*OMIT*) to extract triples from the abstracts. Then we introduce a new algorithm to calculate the *oppositeness* of these candidate relationships. Finally we present the discovered inconsistencies in an easy to read manner to be used by medical professionals. To our best knowledge, this study is the first ontology-based information extraction model introduced to find shifts in the established knowledge in the medical domain using research paper abstracts. We downloaded 36877 abstracts from the PubMed database. From those, we found 102 inconsistencies relevant to the microRNA domain.

CCS CONCEPTS

•**Computing methodologies** → **Information extraction; Ontology engineering;** *Language resources;* •**Applied computing** → **Bioinformatics;**

KEYWORDS

Ontology; Semantic Oppositeness; Information Extraction; miRNA; PubMed

1 INTRODUCTION

Second only to cardiovascular diseases in the rates of mortality caused by noncommunicable diseases, cancers claim 8.2 million lives worldwide each year [27]. Thus, research that could contribute to preventing or curing cancer is imperative. As the growth of cancer involves abnormal cell division, it is important to look at the agents that get involved in that process. MicroRNA (miRNA) is a small non-coding RNA molecule that plays a complementary role to mRNAs (messenger RNAs) in the gene regulation step of cell division [6]. It is possible to observe the presence of miRNA in plants, animals, and some viruses. Mainly they are involved in RNA silencing and post-transcriptional regulation of gene expression. This vital role played by miRNAs in gene expression is what makes them relevant and interesting for the pursuit of a cure for cancer.

In light of the potential importance of miRNA, an increasing quantity of research is being engaged upon its domain, albeit that not all studies are confirming studies. As such, some of the new studies about miRNA might either alter, or even completely disprove, some of the prior knowledge. Recognizing how this knowledge alters over the course of time is important for various analytical tasks. It is also vital to note these changes so that forthcoming studies would not mistakenly base their assumptions and start conditions on conclusions in a prior body of work that has since been disproved. It should be noted that, any changes in the foundation upon which some later research is done, (and conclusions drawn thereupon) will lead to a need for re-evaluation of that later research. This is due to the fact that, given that the aforementioned conclusions on which these new researches were based were found to be not valid anymore.

The objective of this study is to find such alterations in knowledge in the miRNA domain. For this, we need to have a source from which we obtain details of research about miRNA. The best source to get details about scientific research is through research papers which is the common method used in all sciences to publish new findings. In a research paper, the abstract is a fair summarization of the area of importance and the conclusions driven by the research which is being described in the said paper. Given that miRNA falls in the medical domain, an ideal source for searchable medical abstracts is PubMed [8], a free search engine, accessing primarily the MEDLINE database of references and abstracts on life sciences and biomedical topics. It is maintained by the United States National Library of Medicine (NLM) at the National Institutes of Health (NIH) as part of the Entrez system of information retrieval. As of 5 January 2017, PubMed has over 26.8 million records going back to 1966. of those, 13.1 million of PubMed's records are listed with their abstracts.

In addition to keeping records of research papers, PubMed also provides free access to a Medical Subject Headings (MeSH) [25] database. MeSH is a comprehensive controlled vocabulary for the purpose of indexing journal articles and books in the life sciences. Thus it facilitates searching for a particular subject within the medical domain. MeSH is created and updated by the United States National Library of Medicine (NLM).

Permission to make digital or hard copies of all or part of this work for personal or classroom use is granted without fee provided that copies are not made or distributed for profit or commercial advantage and that copies bear this notice and the full citation on the first page. Copyrights for components of this work owned by others than ACM must be honored. Abstracting with credit is permitted. To copy otherwise, or republish, to post on servers or to redistribute to lists, requires prior specific permission and/or a fee. Request permissions from permissions@acm.org.
ACM-BCB'17, August 20-23, 2017, Boston, MA, USA.
© 2017 ACM. 978-1-4503-4722-8/17/08...$15.00
DOI: http://dx.doi.org/10.1145/3107411.3107452

Based on the above observations and resources, we propose an ontology-based information extraction model to discover inconsistencies in PubMed abstracts. These inconsistencies are found when the knowledge extracted from one abstract disagrees with the knowledge extracted from another abstract. Thus it is an indication of the aforementioned shifts and improvements in the study of miRNAs. Ontology-Based Information Extraction (OBIE) is a subfield of information extraction where an ontology is used to guide the information extraction process [29]. Given that this study is focusing on the miRNA domain, we used the Ontology for MIcroRNA Targets (OMIT) [14] as the guiding ontology for the OBIE process. Because OMIT lacks relationship data, such that traditional OBIE methods were not applicable, we used the Open Language Learning for Information Extraction (OLLIE) [21]. OLLIE is unique in utilizing tree-like representations of the dependencies of the sentence, such that it is able to capture long-range relations. Once relationship information is extracted from the abstracts in the form of triples, we introduce a novel method to calculate the oppositeness between the said relationships on the basis of the semantic similarity measure of Wu and Palmer [30].

The key idea of our methodology is that the information in the PubMed abstracts in the miRNA domain are expressed in terms of concepts and relationships that exist between those concepts. An inconsistency would arise if the relationship that was extracted between given two concepts in a certain abstract is opposite to the relationship that was extracted between the same two concepts in a different abstract. As mentioned above, we use OBIE methods utilizing the OMIT ontology to extract the said concepts from the abstracts. In order to discover the relationships between the extracted concepts, we use OLLIE information extraction system. Our main contributions of are as follows:

- We introduce an ontology-based information extraction model to discover inconsistencies in PubMed abstracts.
- We propose a new methodology to incorporate open information extraction into ontology-based information extraction process in order to compensate for the lack of relationships in the domain ontology.
- We propose a semantic oppositeness measure to be used to calculate the oppositeness between two relationships. We illustrate how this novel semantic oppositeness measure is superior to the antonym method and to the naive similarity inverse method.

The rest of the paper is organized as follows. In Section 2, we first introduce the related works and background in information extraction, Ontologies and semantic similarity. We then introduce the methodology to prepare the data in Section 3. We present our method of creating final triples in Section 4 and the methodology to discover inconsistencies in Section 5. Results and discussion follows that in Section 6. The work is concluded in Section 7.

2 RELATED WORKS AND BACKGROUND

While important, research about extracting information from the abstracts of biomedical papers is limited to a very narrow area of topics. An example is the seminal work by Kulick, et al. [17] that extracted information on drug development and cancer genomics.

Information extraction is a process in artificial intelligence (AI) domain to acquire knowledge by looking for occurrences of a particular class of objects and looking for relationships among objects in a given domain. The objective of information extraction is to find and retrieve certain types of information from text. However, it does not attempt to comprehend natural language. Comprehending natural language is handled by the research area, *natural language understanding. Natural language understanding* is what chat bot AIs or personal assistant AIs attempt to do. Information extraction is also different from *information retrieval*, which retrieves documents or parts of documents related to a user query from a large collection of documents. *Information retrieval* is what search engines do. The main difference between *information retrieval* and *information extraction* is that the latter goes one step further by providing the required information itself, instead of a pointer to a document.

In an information extraction task, the input is either unstructured text or slightly structured, such as HTML or XML. Usually the output is a template set filled in with various information that the system was supposed to find. Thus, the information extraction process is a matter of analyzing document(s) and filling template slots with values extracted from document(s).

There are two main methods of information extraction in literature: (a) attribute-based extraction; and (b) relation extraction. In attribute-based extraction, the system assumes the entire text to be referring to a single object. Thus, the task is to extract attributes of said object. This is typically done using regular expressions. Relation extraction, on the other hand, extracts multiple objects, and relationships thereof from a document. One famously efficient way to do this is the FASTUS method by Hobbs et. al [12].

2.1 Ontologies and OBIE

An ontology is defined as "formal, explicit specification of a shared conceptualisation" [10] in information science. Ontologies are used to organize information in many areas as a form of knowledge representation. These areas include: artificial intelligence, linguistics [3, 4, 28], biomedical informatics [14], law [15], library science, enterprise bookmarking, and information architecture. In each of these use cases the ontology may model either the world or a part of it as seen by the said area's viewpoint [4].

2.1.1 *Ontology for MIcroRNA Targets (OMIT).*

The Ontology for MIcroRNA Targets (OMIT) [14] was created with the purpose of establishing data exchange standards and common data elements in the microRNA (miRNA) domain. Biologists and bioinformaticians can make use of OMIT to leverage emerging semantic technologies in knowledge acquisition and discovery for more effective identification of important roles performed by miRNAs (through their respective target genes) in humans' various diseases and biological processes. The OMIT has reused and extended a set of well-established concepts from existing bio-ontologies; e.g., Gene Ontology [1], Sequence Ontology [5], PRotein Ontology [24], and Non-Coding RNA Ontology (NCRO) [13].

2.1.2 *Ontology Based Information Extraction.*

Ontology-based information extraction (OBIE) is a subfield of information extraction. In this, ontologies are used to make the information extraction process more efficient and effective. In most cases, the output is also presented through an ontology. But that is not a requirement. As mentioned in 2.1, generally, ontologies are specified for particular domains. Given that information extraction is essentially concerned with the task of retrieving information for a particular domain as mentioned in the first paragraphs of Section 2, it is rational to conclude that an ontology that has formally and explicitly specified the concepts in that domain would be helpful in this process.

A more formal definition of OBIE was given by Wimalasuriya and Dou in [29]: "a system that processes unstructured or semi-structured natural language text through a mechanism guided by ontologies to extract certain types of information and presents the output using ontologies."

One most important component of an ontology for an OBIE system is the set of relationships present in the ontology. They are the ones that can be used to build extraction rules for the information extraction system. This is exactly the problem with OMIT. Even though it has a very extensive hierarchy of concepts and instances, it contains little to no relationships between the said entities. Thus some of the most powerful conventional OBIE methods cannot be used alongside OMIT. Later sections discuss how this study overcame this challenge.

2.2 Advanced Information Extraction Methods

Given that this study is involved in non-trivial information extraction, it is not possible just to be content with the basic Information Extraction (IE) techniques discussed in the beginning of Section 2. Thus, following advanced IE methodologies are used.

2.2.1 Open Information Extraction. The requirement of having pre-specified relations of interest is the main drawback of the traditional information extraction systems. Open Information Extraction systems solve this problem by extracting relational triples from text, by identifying relation phrases and associated arguments in arbitrary sentences without requiring a pre-specified vocabulary. Thus it is possible to discover important relationships that are not pre-specified.

Usually, Open Information Extraction systems automatically identify and extract binary relationships from sentences given the parsed text of the target language. The parsed text provides the dependency relationships between the various phrases of the sentence. The Open Information Extraction system used in this paper, OLLIE [21], is different from others in its genre due to the fact that it works on a tree-like representation (a graph with only small cycles) of the dependencies of the sentence, based on the Stanford's compression of the dependencies, while other Open Information Extraction systems operate on flat sequences of tokens. Thus OLLIE is uniquely qualified to capture even long-range relations.

Given that open information extraction does not depend on pre-configured rules, we are using Open Information Extraction as a bridge between OMIT, which is an ontology with little to no relations as described in section 2.1.1, and the conventional OBIE methods described in 2.1.2. More information on this, is discussed in Section 7.

2.2.2 Semantic Similarity Measure. Semantic similarity of two entities is a measure of the likeness of the semantic content of the said two entities. It is common to define semantic similarity using topological similarity by means of ontologies.

Using WordNet [22], Wu and Palmer proposed a method to give the similarity between two words in the 0 to 1 range [30]. The approach proposed by Jiang and Conrath measures the semantic similarity between word pairs using corpus statistics and lexical taxonomy [16]. By means of [26], the strengths of these algorithms were evaluated in [3]. According to that, we selected Wu and Palmer's implementation for the purposes of this paper.

A set of examples of word similarities are shown in Table 1. For the similarity with *Car*, the same word gets the perfect score of 1. *Truck* gets a higher score than *Ship*, because a *Truck* too, is a land vehicle, like a *Car*. However, *Ship* gets a higher score than *Book* because a *Ship* is a vehicle and a *Book* is not. *Book* gets a higher score than *Air* because the *Book* is solid and *Air* is not. *Air* gets a higher score than *Thought* because *Air* is a physical entity and a *Thought* is not.

Table 1: WORD SIMILARITIES USING WU AND PALMER METHOD

Word 1	Word 2	Similarity
Car	Car	1.0000
Car	Truck	0.9231
Car	Ship	0.7200
Car	Book	0.5217
Car	Air	0.3158
Car	Thought	0.2105

A useful observation from this is the fact that, no matter how dissimilar two words are, if both of those words exist in WordNet, this method will return a greater than zero value. Thus, there exists an inherent bias towards declaring that two words have a non-zero similarity; rather than declaring that there exists a difference. Thus, in the sections 5.2 and 4, we use dissimilar weights named "yes weight" (W_{yes}) and "no weight" (W_{no}), where W_{no} is larger than W_{yes} by a considerable amount.

2.3 Inconsistency Detection

Inconsistency finding in text is mostly a field researched in the NLP for education domain. This has brought to light a number methods. The first among them is based on the identification of coincident words and n-grams [19]. While this method is adequate for automatic text grading which is based on evaluating characteristics such as the fluency of the text, it is not suitable for the application in this study due to each of the abstracts being independent documents and not descriptions of or summarizations of a source document. The second method is the popular NLP technique Latent Semantic Analysis (LSA) [7, 9]. Here also, the vector representations of the students' documents are matched against that of a gold standard (i.e. correct text). This approach would have been very difficult to scale for this study where all abstracts are compared against each other. The third method is based on Information Extraction (IE) [2, 11, 23] it intends to capture the underlying semantics of the text. Given that the objective of this study matches well with that intention, we move in that direction. Out of the IE studies, the closest one to this study is the one proposed in [11].

But in many ways, our methodology is significantly different than that of [11]. That difference exists despite incremented inconsistency finding being common to the two approaches. The main difference is the fact that in [11], the inconsistencies were found by adding the discovered triplets to the existing ontology and running reasoners on it to see if the ontology has become inconsistent. This study, on the other hand, uses the ontology as a tool in information extraction, as per the concept of OBIE, and does the inconsistency detection outside.

3 DATA PREPARATION

3.1 Obtaining PubMed Abstracts

The first step was to obtain a list of relevant PubMedIDs. This was done by querying the on-line PubMed site with the header "miRNA". The PubMedIDs were then processed to remove duplicates, and they were then separated into easily manageable files with a maximum of 1000 IDs each.

These IDs are then used to extract the abstracts out of the PubMed system. One important thing to note here is the fact that even though PubMed has an option to query its system with an ID to supposedly return the relevant abstract, we found it to be inefficient for this study. The reason for this is the following: More often than not, the formatting of the free text was done in different ways, as shown in Fig. 1(a) and Fig. 1(b). Thus it proved that extracting the pure abstract out of this output would require some unnecessary effort. Instead, it was decided to use the XML interface provided by PubMed and extract the abstracts locally. This step corresponds to the "preprocessor" component of OBIE [29].

3.2 Creating OLLIE triples

The downloaded free text is then subjected to the open information extraction system introduced in [21], that was described in 2.2.1 by the name OLLIE. This process extracts triples in the form of binary relations from the free text and creates a set of possible triples as shown in Example 1. From this point onwards, this paper will refer to these triples as "OLLIE triples".

Code 1: Open Information Extraction Example

```
Nevertheless , we found that miR-31 was particularly up-
    regulated in HSCs but not in hepatocytes during
    fibrogenesis .
0.689: (miR-31; was particularly; up-regulated)
0.661: (miR-31; was particularly up-regulated in; HSCs)
```

The first line of the example shows the original sentence itself. Then each line has an extracted triple. The number leading the triple is the confidence that the OLLIE algorithm has of the triple being valid.

The remainder of the triple is of the format $(A; R; B)$ where A is the *subject* of the relation R, and B is the *object* of the relation R. Typically, in regular information extraction processes, that were explained in the leading paragraphs of Section 2, these relations (R) are fairly simple and would contain one to a few words. Similarly the Subject (A) and Object (B) are set out to be clear cut singular concepts. However, due to the openness of this methodology, which does not depend on any subject context-specific rule but the grammar rules of the language itself, the output of this step does not have those properties. Typically the relation name is just the text linking the subject and the object. Subject and object themselves are more often phrases rather than coherent concepts as expected. This is an issue that we rectify in a later step.

3.3 Creating Stanford XML files

The same free text obtained in Section 3.1 are sent through a system to extract other linguistic information. In this case we are using the methodology developed by Manning, et. al. [20]. The objective of this step is to extract the parse tree, get the lemmatized forms of each word, and get each sentence element separated. From this point onwards, this paper will refer to these outputs for each abstract as "Stanford XML".

3.4 Creating medical term dictionary

Before moving on to the next part of this study, some background data have to be generated pertaining to the abstracts. A very important part in an ontology-based information extraction system is the semantic lexicon [29]. WordNet is the primary lexicon in this system. But due to medical domain language being specific, a general lexicon such as WordNet is not enough to serve as the *Semantic Lexicon* for this system. Thus, a complementary lexicon has to be created with information specific to the medical domain. That is what is done in this step.

A good indication of how important a given term is in a certain domain is the frequency in which it is used within the domain. Therefore, the semantic information of term usage is vital to the following information extraction task and is not something that can be obtained via a generic lexicon such as WordNet. Given that the semantic information that is to be extracted is of the format of term frequencies, it was decided to follow the structure of the famous information retrieval algorithm TF-IDF [18].

Each abstract is considered a separate document, and the term frequency of each term in abstract is calculated. Then the inverse document frequency is calculated across abstracts. These two statistics are combined to calculate a semantic weight for each of the terms. Using the Stanford XML, the lemma of each term is extracted. Next, a triple consisting of the term (word), the lemma of the term, and its semantic weight is created for each term. Finally, the triples for each term (word) are output in to a dictionary file as an intermediate output.

4 CREATING FINAL TRIPLES

With the above intermediary outputs ready, we move on to the next step of creating triples. Triples are created on the basis of separate abstracts. Each of the OLLIE triple sets for a given abstract is read along side the corresponding Stanford XML. Each triple carries the triple information (*Subject;Relationship;Object*), confidence value, the relevant original sentence from the text abstract, and the sentence id.

4.1 Triple building

The first information extraction step is a gazetteer list approach as described in [29]. In this stage, a gazetteer list of MESH terms is made out of the OMIT ontology by extracting the concept tree rooted at *MESH term* concept and adding all the individuals present in that tree to the gazetteer list. One important thing to note here

1. Intervirology. 2016 Nov 23;59(2):111-117. [Epub ahead of print]

Nonstructural Protein 1 of Tick-Borne Encephalitis Virus Induces Oxidative Stress and Activates Antioxidant Defense by the Nrf2/ARE Pathway.

Kuzmenko YV(1), Smirnova OA, Ivanov AV, Starodubova ES, Karpov VL.

Author information:
(1)Engelhardt Institute of Molecular Biology, Russian Academy of Sciences, Moscow, Russia.

BACKGROUND: Infection with tick-borne encephalitis virus (TBEV) causes pathological changes in the central nervous system. However, the possible redox alterations in the infected cells that can contribute to the virus pathogenicity remain unknown.
OBJECTIVE: In the current study we explored the ability of TBEV nonstructural protein 1 (NS1) to induce oxidative stress and activate antioxidant defense via the nuclear factor (erythroid-derived-2)-like 2/antioxidant response element (Nrf2/ARE) pathway.
METHODS: HEK 293T cells were transfected with plasmid encoding NS1 protein, and the production of reactive oxygen species (ROS) was measured using oxidation-sensitive dyes, the activation of the ARE promoter was estimated using a reporter plasmid, and the expression of phase II detoxifying enzymes was quantified by measuring their mRNA levels using RT-qPCR.
RESULTS: A high level of ROS production was detected in cells transfected with NS1-expressing plasmid. In addition, this protein activated the promoter with an ARE and upregulated the transcription of ARE-dependent genes that encode phase II enzymes.
CONCLUSION: TBEV NS1 protein both triggers ROS production and activates a defense Nrf2/ARE pathway. These data suggest that a role of redox-mediated processes in TBEV-induced damage of the central nervous system should also be explored. These data can contribute to a better understanding of TBEV pathogenicity, further improvement of TBE treatment, and the development of vaccine candidates against this infection.

© 2016 S. Karger AG, Basel.

DOI: 10.1159/000452160
PMID: 27875810 [PubMed - as supplied by publisher]

(a) Sample abstract 1

1. Sci Rep. 2016 Nov 22;6:37370. doi: 10.1038/srep37370.

Effects of light-emitting diode irradiation on the osteogenesis of human umbilical cord mesenchymal stem cells in vitro.

Yang D(1), Yi W(1), Wang E(1), Wang M(1).

Author information:
(1)Department of Orthopaedics, Nanshan Hospital, Guangdong MedicalCollege, Shenzhen Guangdong, 518052, China.

The aim of this study was to examine the effects of light-emitting diode (LED) photobiomodulation therapy on the proliferation and differentiation of human umbilical cord mesenchymal stem cells (hUMSCs) cultured in osteogenic differentiation medium. HUMSCs were irradiated with an LED light at 620 nm and 2 J/cm(2) and monitored for cell proliferation and osteogenic differentiation activity. The experiment involved four groups of cells: the control group; the osteogenic group (osteo group); the LED group; the osteogenic + LED group (LED + osteo group). HUMSC proliferation was detected by performing a3-(4,5-dimethylthiazol-2yl)-2,5 diphenyltetrazolium bromide(MTT) assay. Osteogenic activity was evaluated by performing alkaline phosphatase (ALP) and Von Kossa staining, and osteopontin (OPN) gene mRNA expression was evaluated byreverse transcription polymerase chain reaction (RT-PCR). The hUMSCs in the LED + osteo group exhibited a significantly higher proliferation rate than the other subgroups. Additionally, there were greater numbers of ALP-positive cells and Von Kossa nodules in the LED + osteo group. OPN mRNA expression in the LED + osteo group was higher than other subgroups. In conclusion, low levels of LED light at a wavelength of 620 nm enhance the proliferation and osteogenic differentiation of hUMSCs during a long culture period.

DOI: 10.1038/srep37370
PMID: 27874039 [PubMed - in process]

(b) Sample abstract 2

Figure 1: Sample PubMed text abstracts

is the fact that some of the strings in the OMIT ontology are not in the same format that one would use in a text. An example would be *Technology, Pharmaceutical.* Entries such as this were changed to the normalized form; for example *Pharmaceutical Technology.* Next, the subject and the object of the triple are tested for occurrences of an individual now present in the gazetteer list. If any were present, the node list corresponding to the relevant subject or object is updated by appending the returned OMIT concept node to the end of the said list.

Next, Regular Expression (REGEX) based information extraction, is used. A base REGEX is built on the common usages of miRNA in abstracts and is matched to the counterparts in OMIT as per the descriptions in [29]. The base REGEX is then expanded to cover all common forms of mentions of miRNA in literature. This is further enhanced by adding other pairings of REGEX and OMIT concepts. All of these REGEXes are then used to find the corresponding OMIT concept nodes for each of the words that exist in the subject or the object of the triple (depending on which one is being examined at the time.) These results, too, are then added to the node list as explained above.

The relationship in the OLLIE triple is then analyzed against the corresponding elements in the Stanford XML. In the case of the relationship being a single word, the lemmatized form of the said word is extracted from the Stanford XML, and the relationship is replaced with that lemmatized form. Simplification is not done when the relationship is a phrase.

The above steps are reduction steps, in the sense that out of all the concepts in the English language, only the ones that are directly relevant to the miRNA domain are present in the OMIT ontology. Thus, the subject and/or object of some of the OLLIE triples will have empty node lists.

Next a triple each is created using every node in the object list for every node in subject list, utilizing the reduced or pure relationship from the original OLLIE triple. (As mentioned above, the relationship is only reduced when it is comprised of a single word.) This is an increment step, given the fact that the resulting number of triples is the multiplication of the number of elements in subject list and the object list of the original OLLIE triple. Thus, this also means that any OLLIE triple that was reduced to have an empty subject list or an empty object list will produce no triples in this step.

4.2 Triple simplification

Newly created triples are then sent through two simplification processes. An important point to note here is the fact that these simplifications happen on a sentence-by-sentence basis here. In this step, triples corresponding to one sentence have no effect on the triples corresponding to a different sentence.

The first simplification step goes through all the given triples and analyses the subject, the object, and the relationship. In the case where all three of them are equal for two given triples, a new merged triple is created with the same subject, object, and relationship along with the average value for the confidence.

The second simplification uses the concept hierarchical information from OMIT. Thus it belongs to the ideas of Ontology-Based Information Extraction discussed in 2.1.2. Here, the triple list is simplified, on the fact that some triples in the list, are ancestors of other triples in the list as defined in Definition 4.1.

Definition 4.1 (Triple Ancestor). A triple X is defined as the ancestor of another triple Y if and only if the following two conditions are satisfied: both triples have the same relationship; and the subject node and the object node of X are respectively ancestors of the subject node and object node of Y as defined by Definition 4.2.

Definition 4.2 (Node Ancestor). The ancestor relationship for nodes W and Z are defined as follows; a node W is the ancestor of a node Z if and only if, the node W is the same as node Z or the OMIT node of W is an ancestor of OMIT node of Z in the concept hierarchy of the OMIT ontology.

First the triple list is scanned from left to right to see if any triple would be the ancestor of one that is listed left of it. In the case where an ancestor is found, the ancestor is discarded and the descendant's confidence is set to the average of that of the original confidence value of the descendant and the confidence value of the ancestor. Then the triple list is scanned from right to left to see if any triple would be the ancestor of one that is listed right of it. The same simplification process used in the left to right scan is applied on the ancestors and descendants that are found.

The rationale of this process is the following: in the step in which we created the new triples out of OLLIE triples, we were doing string REGEX matching on the subjects and objects of the OLLIE triples and assigning nodes that correspond to a concept in OMIT. There are many cases in OMIT ontology where the name of an ancestor node is a substring of a descendant node. An example is, shown in Fig. 2 where the concept node with the name *"Cells"* has descendants with names such as *"Goblet Cells"* and *"Dendritic Cells"*. Thus a sentence that mentioned *"Goblet Cells"* such as *"The goblet cells are found in the intestinal tract"* that is expected to produce the triple *(Goblet Cells ; are found in ; Intestinal Tract)* will also produce the triple *(Cells ; are found in; Intestinal Tract).* From definition 4.1, it is evident that the latter triple is an ancestor of the former triple. Thus by the simplification process discussed above, the latter triple is removed and the confidence of the former triple is updated using the current confidence values of the former and latter triples. This makes sense because sentences are always relevant to the concept with the smaller granularity as shown in the above example.

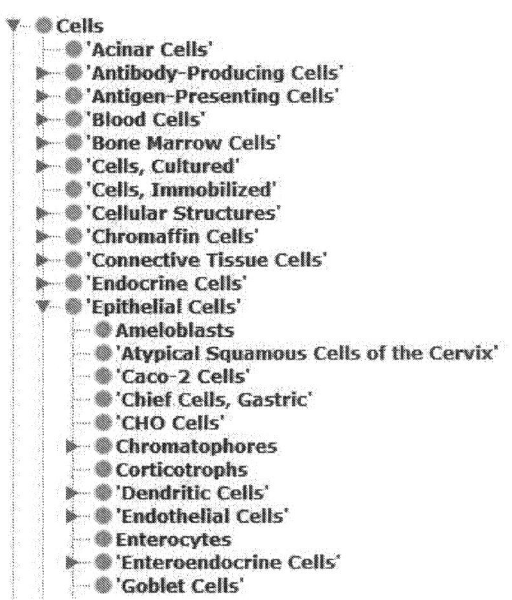

Figure 2: Part of OMIT hierarchy

Once the simplification process is finished for each sentence, all the resultant triples are added to a single list. Then that list is passed to a simplification process similar to that of the first step but with a slight change. Just like in the per sentence simplification, the process goes through all the given triples and analyses the subject, the object, and the relationship; but this time, it is done over the entire abstract. It should be noted that the second simplification, i.e. ancestor-based simplification is not done here. This is because of the possibility of losing a generalized claim when it exists in an abstract that also makes a specific claim. In the case where all three – subject, object and relationship – are equal for two given triples, a new merged triple is created. But this time, the new triple will carry both sentences (if they are different), and the confidence value is updated to the new value C_{new} according to Equation 1, where: the confidence in triple 1 is given by C_1 (Such that $0 < C_1 < 1$), the confidence in triple 2 is given by C_2 (Such that $0 < C_2 < 1$), the sentence count in triple 1 is given by S_1, and the sentence count in triple 2 is given by S_2. Sentence count is never zero.

$$C_{new} = \frac{C_1 * S_1 + C_2 * S_2}{S_1 + S_2} \quad (1)$$

The resultant triples of the above process are put in to a list. These are the final triples. The final triples are then written to a set of files as an intermediate output. A separate file is written for each separate abstract. By this point, some abstracts will have empty lists, because none of the OLLIE triples of those abstracts have survived the conversion to the final triples form, if the OLLIE triples from those abstracts lacked any information relevant to be extracted using the OMIT ontology. These abstracts will have empty files in their name.

5 DISCOVERING INCONSISTENCIES

From here onwards, we discuss the methodology used to find inconsistencies using the final triples, other resources, and intermediate files created in the previous sections.

5.1 Preparing to find inconsistencies

First order of business for finding inconsistencies is to load the intermediate files created at 4 and 3.4 for new triples and the dictionary respectively. Abstracts are read and data are loaded next. But instead of storing data with the distinct unit per abstract as we have been doing so far, a new minimum unit is introduced which has a unique entry for each triple. Which means a sentence with multiple candidate triples will be represented in corresponding multiple entries.

All the triple entries are loaded to a list. Each triple entry i is compared with each triple entry j such that i goes from 1 to the length of triple entry list while for each i, j goes from $i + 1$ to the length of triple entry list. This way, the triple entries are compared with the triple entries that follow them thus each pair of triple entries only gets compared once.

5.1.1 Initial filtering. Before the analysis begin, a couple of filters are applied. First filter makes sure that triple entries of the same abstract are not compared to each other because finding inconsistencies within the same abstract is not the objective of this study. Second filter is applied to handle the case where in some cases, a redacted article is found to have the exact same content as another legitimate article. In this case, one is dropped from the consistency checking. For the purpose of this study, it does not matter which one is dropped for the simple reason that if the legitimate article is dropped and the system end up finding an inconsistency with the redacted article against some third article, it is a simple matter of reconsulting the PubMed database to find the relevant legitimate article by way of the redacted article.

5.1.2 Cleaning the strings. The relation value of triple entry pairs that pass the filtering process are then put through a cleaning process. Special contractions such as "can't", "won't" are explicitly handled and simple contractions such as "don't", "hadn't" are scripturally handled. Next the relationship is split to the terms and when there exist a "not", it is handled as the negation of the following term. Following that, all the stop words are removed from the list and finally, using the lemmatization results loaded from the dictionary created at section 3.4, all words are stemmed to their basic lemma.

5.2 Calculating oppositeness of relationships

The two lists of cleaned strings that were created from the triple relationships are then evaluated against each other word by word. We define the item count of these lists as c_1 and c_2. Before going in to the oppositeness function, some simple comparisons are made to lighten the computing load.

When both the comparing words are exactly the same, the weight of the word is extracted from the dictionary that was created at section 3.4 and were loaded at the beginning of section 5.1. This is raised to the power of two and then multiplied by the constant "yes weight" (W_{yes}). The resultant value is added to the similarity amount ($simil_T$), the similarity number counter (s_n) is increased by one.

When either of the words is the direct simple negation of the other by the key word "not", (i.e.: "increased"-"not increased", "found"-"not found"), again the weight of the non negated word is extracted from the dictionary and raised to the power of two. The resultant value is then multiplied by the constant "no weight" (W_{no}). This value is added to the difference amount (dif_T), the difference number counter (d_n) is increased by one.

5.2.1 Oppositeness Function for words. Word pairs that are not handled by either of above situations need specialized work. First, the word pair is checked for similarity by the Wu and Palmer [30] semantic similarity measure (sim) discussed in section 2.2.2. We show this in equation 2.

$$simil = \frac{sim(w_1, w_2)}{c_1 + c_2} \tag{2}$$

Checking for oppositeness is not as straight forward. First it should be noted that a simple antonym system is ill-suited for the requirement of this study to be used in lieu of oppositeness. This is because while all relationship words that are antonyms to a given relationship word are in fact indicating an inconsistency, all words that indicate an inconsistency are not antonyms of each other. To overcome this, we need a value on a continuous scale similar to that of the similarity measure discussed above. Given that the word similarity is between 0 to 1 as mentioned in the section 2.2.2, it is possible to naïvely assume that just taking the complement of whatever the similarity value would be enough for finding the oppositeness. This, sadly, is not the case. What this means is, semantic difference, is not the same as semantic oppositeness.

We demonstrate this with the following example; assume we have the word *increase* in one hand and the words *expand, decrease, change,* and *cat* on the other hand to be checked against *increase* to see which one of the said words are the most contradictory in nature to the word *increase.* A simple antonym system will report *decrease* to be the antonym of *increase.* But it will report all the rest of the words under the umbrella term; not-antonym. Obviously, that is not an adequate result.

In comparison, a human would see these words and see that the word *cat* is irrelevant here. It is neither slimier nor different to *increase.* In fact the meaning is orthogonal to the meaning of *increase.* Next, the human might point out that the word *expand* is semantically similar to the word *increase.* Both of the words are discussing adding to an amount that already exists. The word *decrease,* the human might say, is the antonym of the word *increase.* Finally, *change* should sit somewhere between *increase* and *decrease* because it can go either way. However, *change* is not completely irrelevant to the meaning of *increase* like *cat* is. Thus it is possible to use this as the golden standard to order these words in a way that each of these (or at least the opposite words) are easily identifiable.

If one decides to use the naïve approach and take the inverse of calculated the similarities, one would get the result shown in Table 2.

Table 2: NAÏVE METHOD TO FIND OPPOSITENESS

	expand	*decrease*	*change*	*cat*
Similarity to *increase*	0.80	0.75	0.46	0.25
1−Similarity	0.20	0.25	0.54	0.75

If the words are sorted in the increasing difference according to the above calculated values, the word order is *expand, decrease, change,* and *cat.* This is not the desired outcome. If this method is used and a threshold is introduce to determine *decrease* as an opposite of *increase,* automatically *change* and *cat* also become opposites of *increase.* Given this issue, instead of the naïve approach, we introduce the following method.

First, for each of the pair of words, the lemma is extracted using the dictionary created at section 3.4. Let us call them L_1 and L_2. When the word does not exist in the dictionary, the word itself is used as its own lemma. For each lemma, all the synsets relevant for each of the word senses are extracted. Given that a word might have many senses, this is a *one to many* mapping.

For each synset, the list of antonym synsets are collected using WordNet's antonym feature. Given that a word sense can have many antonyms in various contexts, this is yet again a *one to many* mapping. All the retrieved antonym synsets for one original lemma are put into a single list. Each of the words in each of the synsets in the said list are then taken out to make a word list. Yet again this is a *one to many* mapping given that each synset has one or many words in them.

The resultant word list is then run trough a duplicate remover. This is the first reduction step in the antonym process so far. We name antonym list of L_1 as a_1 and the antonym list of L_2 as a_2. Number of items in a_1 is n while the number of items in a_2 is m. Next, each antonym of L_1 is checked for similarity against the original L_2 and the maximum difference is extracted as dif_1 as shown in equation 3. Similarly each antonym of L_2 is checked for similarity against the original L_1 and the maximum difference is extracted as dif_2 as shown in equation 4.

$$dif_1 = max(sim(L_2, a_1(1)), sim(L_2, a_1(2)), ..., sim(L_2, a_1(n))) \quad (3)$$

$$dif_2 = max(sim(L_1, a_2(1)), sim(L_1, a_2(2)), ..., sim(L_1, a_2(m))) \quad (4)$$

Once dif_1 and dif_2 are calculated, the overall difference, dif is calculated using equation 5.

$$dif = \frac{\frac{dif_1}{c_1} + \frac{dif_2}{c_1}}{2} \quad (5)$$

Table 3 shows the results of the dif values for the same example as table 2.

Table 3: OPPOSITENESS WITH ONLY dif

	expand	*decrease*	*change*	*cat*
dif to *increase*	0.63	1.0	0.72	0.25

If the words are sorted using dif in the increasing order, they would be *cat, expand, change, decrease.* We have gotten the expected order where first we have irrelevant word, then the most similar word, next the neutral word and finally the opposite word. However still, the spread of words is not optimum. This can be seen from the gap between each pair of words in the above sorted order. It is; 0.38, 0.09, 0.28 in order. What is needed is a way to magnify the difference value of the opposite word while shrinking the other differences so that the threshold line can be comfortably drawn.

With both the dif and $simil$ values at hand, it is possible to calculate the oppositeness fulfilling the above condition. Before moving on to the equation, it is prudent to look at the example on Table 2, once more. The words there are being compared to the word *increase*. As per the above discussion on the golden standard for this, the similarity measure correctly shows that *expand* and *decrease* are in the shared context of *increase*. Semantically, this implies that entities that can *increase* can also *expand* or *decrease*. They can also *change*, hence the value for *change* comes next. But it is not as close as the previous two because the word *change* can apply in a context that is very different from a context that is valid for *increase*. Finally there is the value for *cat* which is an irrelevant concept. What is observed from this is the fact that, more semantically similar the two words are, the difference value has to be magnified proportional to that closeness. When the two words becomes less similar, the difference value has to be penalized. Thus equation 6 is introduced to calculate oppositeness. Figure 3 shows the plot for the equation. $simil$ is the x variable and dif is the y variable.

$$oppo = dif_T^{(0.5*\frac{W_{no}}{W_{yes}}*simil_T+1)} \quad (6)$$

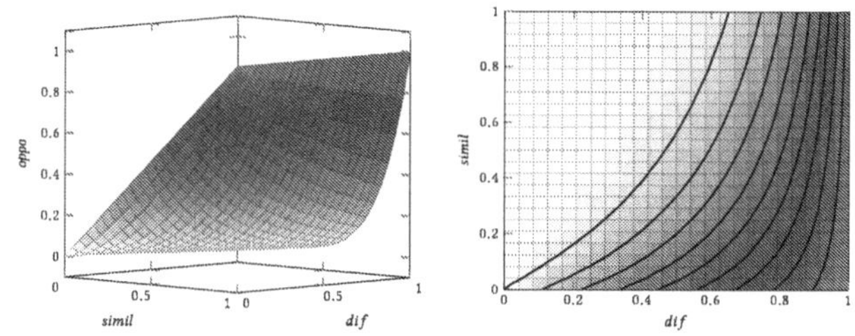

(a) 3D plot (b) Contour plot

Figure 3: Oppositeness function

As evident by Fig 3(a) and Fig 3(b), in higher word similarities ($simil_T$), the difference (dif_T) also have to be very high for the final *oppo* value to be high. in lower $simil_T$ range, *oppo* becomes closer and closer to being directly proportional to dif_T and achieves it when $simil_T$ becomes zero. This quality, in this example, effectively pushes *decrease* farther away from *increase* than others. Values after this transformation is shown in table 4.

Table 4: OPPOSITENESS WITH *oppo*

	expand	*decrease*	*change*	*cat*
oppo **to** *increase*	0.05	0.2	0.098	0.022
max scaled to 1	0.25	1	0.49	0.11

Again the word order in increasing oppositeness is; *cat, expand, change, decrease*. Scaled gap between the words are 0.14, 0.24, 0.51. Now the actual opposite word is placed clearly apart from the rest of the words. The difference between the near synonym *expand* and neutral word *change* is more prominent (distance 0.25 and 0.49 from *increase* compared to 0.63 and 0.72 in previous case). The irrelevant word *cat* is pushed more downwards.

The final *oppo* value is multiplied by −1 and is returned up as the oppositeness measure of the two words. The returned value is then multiplied by the weights of the two words extracted from the dictionary. If the value is greater than zero, the value is multiplied by the constant "yes weight" (W_{yes}). The resultant value is added to the similarity amount ($simil_T$), the similarity number counter (s_n) is increased by one.

If it is less than zero, value is then multiplied by the constant "no weight" (W_{no}) and −1. This value is added to the difference amount (dif_T), the difference number counter (d_n) is increased by one. Thus when the value is zero no change happens to any similarity/difference values or counters.

5.2.2 Finalizing the oppositeness of relationship strings. Once all the words in the two relationship strings have finished going through the above steps, both $simil_T$ and dif_T are normalized using a small constant ϵ with s_n and d_n as shown in equations 7 and 8.

$$simil_T = \frac{simil_T * (d_n + \epsilon) * W_{yes}}{s_n + d_n + 2 * \epsilon} \quad (7)$$

$$dif_T = \frac{dif_T * (s_n + \epsilon) * W_{no}}{s_n + d_n + 2 * \epsilon} \quad (8)$$

Finally, if $simil_T$ is greater than dif_T, $simil_T$ is returned as the similarity value of the two relationship strings. Otherwise dif_T multiplied by -1 is returned as the difference value of the two relationship strings.

5.3 Registering inconsistencies

The returned value by the above step for a given pair of relationship strings is then multiplied by -1 and put through a threshold test. If it passes the threshold, it is registered as an inconsistency.

For each abstract that gets involved in a potential inconsistency, PubMed was queried again to obtain the publication date and other relevant details. The reason for doing this at this stage is the fact that only a small portion of all abstracts are relevant for this stage and thus we can do a lesser amount of processing and data storage for the bearable cost trade off of few instances of XML fetching over the Internet.

Each of the inconsistencies that were found are written to an intermediate result file where a line holds; confidence (the difference value returned), PubMedIds of the contradicting abstracts along with the publication dates, subject and object of the relevant triple, relationship present in the triple in first abstract, relevant sentence id from the first abstract, relationship present in the triple in second abstract, relevant sentence id from the second abstract. An example of some lines from the said intermediate result file is shown at example 2.

Code 2: Intermediate inconsistency result example

```
0.8333333;24969691;2014/9/1;27601936;2016/9/7;Cells;
    Vimentin;increase;3;decrease;7
0.8333333;25435961;2015/1/1;26632856;2015/12/1;DNA;Cells;
    promote;7;breaks in;12
0.625;25004396;2014/6/15;26257392;2015/11/1;MIR152;Cells;
    were decreased in;3;be Interestingly increased in;10
```

5.4 Preparing inconsistency for analysis

This is the final stage of the methodology. First, the intermediate result file written the previous step is read. Then the Subject and Object of the inconsistent triples are checked against OMIT to see if either or both of them are of the type miRNA. The reason we pushed this check to this final step is for the fact that, this way, the intermediate file created before this step can potentially be used for other researches on inconsistencies in the medical abstracts in domains other than miRNA as well.

If either or both the subject and the object are indeed of the type of miRNA, then for each such inconsistency, the relevant OLLIE files are read and the contributing actual sentences are extracted using the sentence IDs. Then the information gained from the intermediate result file and the extracted sentences are reformatted to be more readable by humans. Here, finally the original OLLIE confidences are used. The final confidence Con_{fin} is calculated using the inconsistency confidence Con_{cont} calculated above, OLLIE confidence of triple 1 Con_1, OLLIE confidence of triple 2 Con_2, and the constant C as shown in Equation 9. C is selected $C > 1$.

$$Con_{fin} = C * Con_{cont} * Con_1 * Con_2 \quad (9)$$

The reformatted inconsistencies are then written to the final result file to be read and analyzed by human experts. An example of some lines from the said result file is shown in example 3.

Code 3: Final result file example

```
0.056045435

25738546
2015/5/1
( MIR214 ; was significantly increased in ; Tissues )
4
Our results revealed that miR-214 expression was
     significantly increased in the BC tissues compared
     with the adjacent benign tissues, and that the
     upregulation of miR-214 was significantly associated
     with the invasion ability of the BC cells.

27109339
2016/6/1
( MIR214 ; were significantly decreased in ; Tissues )
4
Our results revealed that the expression of miR-214 and
     miR-218 were significantly decreased in breast
     cancer tissues compared with adjacent tissues.
```

6 RESULTS AND DISCUSSION

In the PMID-extraction step we obtained 39149 relevant abstract IDs, from which 36877 were processed and downloaded as text files containing abstracts. Around 5.8% of extracted PubMed entries did not have an abstract section, and there were three possible situations. (1) When an entry had some graphs instead of an entire research paper, e.g., PMIDs 24324220, 24318653, 24311611, and 24303553. (2) When there was only a comment about the entry rather than a complete entry, e.g., PMIDs 24311611 and 24303553. (3) When the entry was empty except for the entry name, author names, and other metadata, e.g., PMID 24313780. Other than these three situations, each and every abstract from the remaining 94.2% of relevant IDs were downloaded for analysis.

All 36877 downloaded abstracts were processed to yield OLLIE triple files and Stanford XML files. These intermediate files were used to create the intermediate result file, where a total of 67481 unique subject-object pairs were detected. Then, 503 total inconsistencies were discovered from these subject-object pairs, involving 224 out of 36877 abstracts. This observation indicated that, the percentage of abstracts that contributed to inconsistencies was only 0.61% out of all considered.

After the reduction step (detailed in Section 5.4) was performed to keep only the inconsistencies that involved at least one miRNA entry, we ended up with 102 inconsistencies involving 95 abstracts. This outcome revealed that, out of 503 total inconsistencies, only 20.28% were relevant to miRNA. Abstracts participating in inconsistencies involving miRNA consisted of 0.26% of all downloaded abstracts and 42.41% of those abstracts that were found to be involved in inconsistencies of any kind.

7 CONCLUSION

The primary research contribution of this study was to use ontology-based information extraction to observe how inconsistencies rise in the literature in relation to previously established knowledge in a scientific field. This study successfully proposed a method to do that observation and succeeded in finding 503 such inconsistencies in a corpus of 39149 research paper abstracts. Since these inconsistencies are rooted in very domain specific medical jargon, they need to be analyzed by medical experts before getting incorporated into future studies.

This study had to face the problem of the ontology that was being used not having the relationship rules that most of the established OBIE systems use. Thus, this study came up with a novel way to solve this problem by involving open information extraction systems to extract the relationships and then using the conventional OBIE systems to do the information extraction. This methodology can be considered as a new way of doing OBIE in addition to the traditional and established methods discussed in [29].

Apart from the above two main contributions, this research also resulted in the creation of the the oppositeness measure introduced in the section 5.2 which would be useful in the natural language processing domain, especially for sentiment analysis.

For future work, one most basic thing that can be improved is in the preprocessing stage to include common medical acronyms that are used but are not defined in the first use. It is also possible to investigate the redacted articles mentioned in section 5.1.1 to see if the redaction was a result of an inconsistency. It is also possible to extend the *cleaning the strings* step and *creation of final triples* step using the already generated Stanford XML.

ACKNOWLEDGMENTS

Funding for this research was provided by the National Cancer Institute (NCI) at the National Institutes of Health (NIH), under the Award Number U01CA180982.

REFERENCES

[1] M. Ashburner, C. A. Ball, J. A. Blake, D. Botstein, and others. 2000. Gene ontology: tool for the unification of biology. The Gene Ontology Consortium. *Nature genetics* 25, 1 (May 2000), 25–29.

[2] E. Brent, C. Atkisson, and N. Green. 2010. Time-shifted online collaboration: Creating teachable moments through automated grading. In *Proceedings of Monitoring and assessment in online collaborative environments: Emergent computational technologies for e-learning support.* IGI Global, 55–73.

[3] N. H. N. D. de Silva. 2015. SAFS3 algorithm: Frequency statistic and semantic similarity based semantic classification use case. In *Proceedings of Advances in ICT for Emerging Regions (ICTer), 2015 Fifteenth International Conference on.* IEEE, 77–83.

[4] N. H. N. D. de Silva, A. S. Perera, and M. K. D. T. Maldeniya. 2013. Semi-supervised algorithm for concept ontology based word set expansion. In *Proceedings of Advances in ICT for Emerging Regions (ICTer), 2013 International Conference on.* IEEE, 125–131.

[5] K. Eilbeck, S. E. Lewis, C. J. Mungall, M. Yandell, and others. 2005. The Sequence Ontology: a tool for the unification of genome annotations. *Genome Biology* 6, 5 (2005), R44.

[6] Exiqon. 2016. What are microRNAs? (2016). Retrieved December 08, 2016 from http://www.exiqon.com/what-are-microRNAs

[7] P. W. Foltz, D. Laham, and T. K Landauer. 1999. Automated essay scoring: Applications to educational technology. In *Proceedings of World Conference on Educational Multimedia, Hypermedia and Telecommunications*, Vol. 1. 939–944.

[8] National Center for Biotechnology Information. 2017. PubMed Help. (March 2017). Retrieved April 22, 2017 from https://www.ncbi.nlm.nih.gov/books/NBK3827/

[9] M. Franzke and L. A Streeter. 2006. Building student summarization, writing and reading comprehension skills with guided practice and automated feedback. *Highlights from research at the University of Colorado, a white paper from Pearson Knowledge Technologies* (2006).

[10] T. R. Gruber. 1993. A Translation Approach to Portable Ontology Specifications. *Knowledge Acquisition* 5, 2 (June 1993), 199–220.

[11] F. Gutierrez, D. Dou, S. Fickas, D. Wimalasuriya, and H. Zong. 2016. A hybrid ontology-based information extraction system. *Journal of Information Science* 42, 6 (2016), 798–820.

[12] J. R. Hobbs, D. Appelt, J. Bear, D. Israel, and others. 1993. Fastus: A system for extracting information from text. In *Proceedings of the workshop on Human Language Technology.* Association for Computational Linguistics, 133–137.

[13] J. Huang, B. Eilbeck, K.and Smith, J. A. Blake, and others. 2016. The Development of Non-coding RNA Ontology. *International journal of data mining and bioinformatics* 15, 3 (Jan. 2016), 214–232.

[14] J. Huang, F. Gutierrez, H. J Strachan, D. Dou, and others. 2016. OmniSearch: a semantic search system based on the Ontology for MIcroRNA Target (OMIT) for microRNA-target gene interaction data. *Journal of biomedical semantics* 7, 1 (2016), 1.

[15] V. Jayawardana, D. Lakmal, N. de Silva, A. S. Perera, K. Sugathadasa, and B. Ayesha. Deriving a Representative Vector for Ontology Classes with Instance Word Vector Embeddings. In *Proceedings of Innovative Computing Technology (INTECH), 2017 Seventh International Conference on.* IEEE, to appear.

[16] J. J. Jiang and D. W. Conrath. 1997. Semantic similarity based on corpus statistics and lexical taxonomy. *10th International Conference on Research in Computational Linguistics, ROCLING'97* (1997).

[17] S. Kulick, A. Bies, M. Liberman, M. Mandel, and others. 2004. Integrated annotation for biomedical information extraction. In *Proceedings of the Human Language Technology Conference and the Annual Meeting of the North American Chapter of the Association for Computational Linguistics (HLT/NAACL).* 61–68.

[18] A. Leskovec, J.and Rajaraman and J. D. Ullman. 2014. *Mining of massive datasets.* Cambridge University Press.

[19] C. Y. Lin. 2004. Rouge: A package for automatic evaluation of summaries. In *Proceedings of the ACL-04 workshop: Text summarization branches out*, Vol. 8. Barcelona, Spain.

[20] C. D. Manning, M. Surdeanu, J. Bauer, J. Finkel, and others. 2014. The Stanford CoreNLP Natural Language Processing Toolkit. In *Proceedings of Association for Computational Linguistics (ACL) System Demonstrations.* 55–60.

[21] Mausam, M. Schmitz, S. Soderland, R. Bart, and O. Etzioni. 2012. Open Language Learning for Information Extraction.. In *Proceedings of the Joint Conference on Empirical Methods in Natural Language Processing and Computational Natural Language Learning (EMNLP-CoNLL).* 523–534.

[22] G. A. Miller, R. Beckwith, C. Fellbaum, D. Gross, and K. J. Miller. 1990. Introduction to WordNet: An on-line lexical database. *International journal of lexicography* 3, 4 (1990), 235–244.

[23] T. Mitchell, T. Russell, P. Broomhead, and N. Aldridge. 2002. Towards robust computerised marking of free-text responses. *Proceedings of International Computer Assisted Assessment Conference.*

[24] D. A. Natale, C. N. Arighi, W. C. Barker, J. A. Blake, and others. 2011. The Protein Ontology: a structured representation of protein forms and complexes. *Nucleic Acids Research* 39, suppl 1 (2011), D539–D545.

[25] U.S. National Library of Medicine. 2016. Medical Subject Headings. (2016). Retrieved November 25, 2016 from https://www.nlm.nih.gov/mesh/

[26] H. Shima. 2016. WordNet Similarity for Java (WS4J). (2016). Retrieved November 23, 2005 from https://code.google.com/p/ws4j/

[27] World Health Organization (WHO). 2017. NCD mortality and morbidity. (2017). Retrieved April 22, 2017 from http://www.who.int/gho/ncd/mortality_morbidity/en/

[28] I. Wijesiri, M. Gallage, B. Gunathilaka, M. Lakjeewa, and others. 2014. Building a WordNet for Sinhala. *Volume editors* (2014), 100–109.

[29] D. C. Wimalasuriya and D. Dou. 2010. Ontology-based Information Extraction: An Introduction and a Survey of Current Approaches. *Journal of Information Science* 36, 3 (June 2010), 306–323.

[30] Z. Wu and M. Palmer. 1994. Verbs Semantics and Lexical Selection. In *Proceedings of the 32Nd Annual Meeting on Association for Computational Linguistics (ACL '94).* Association for Computational Linguistics, Stroudsburg, PA, USA, 133–138.

TRuML: A Translator for Rule-Based Modeling Languages

Ryan Suderman
Los Alamos National Laboratory
Theoretical Division
P.O. Box 1663
Los Alamos, NM 87545
ryants@lanl.gov

William S. Hlavacek
Los Alamos National Laboratory
Theoretical Division
P.O. Box 1663
Los Alamos, NM 87545
wish@lanl.gov

ABSTRACT

Rule-based modeling languages, such as the Kappa and BioNetGen languages (BNGL), are powerful frameworks for modeling the dynamics of complex biochemical reaction networks. Each language is distributed with a distinct software suite and modelers may wish to take advantage of both toolsets. This paper introduces a practical application called TRuML that translates models written in either Kappa or BNGL into the other language. While similar in many respects, key differences between the two languages makes translation sufficiently complex that automation becomes a useful tool. TRuML accommodates the languages' complexities and produces a semantically equivalent model in the alternate language of the input model when possible and an approximate model in certain other cases. Here, we discuss a number of these complexities and provide examples of equivalent models in both Kappa and BNGL.

CCS CONCEPTS

• **Applied computing** → **Systems biology**; • **Computing methodologies** → *Simulation languages*;

KEYWORDS

Kappa; BNGL; rule-based modeling; systems biology; reaction network modeling; domain-specific languages

1 INTRODUCTION

Rule-based modeling is a recently developed framework for modeling dynamics of biochemical reaction networks [2]. Its strength lies in the ability to encode large numbers of (or infinite) reactions with individual rules. In essence, parts of molecules that do not participate in a particular reaction are omitted from the rule, a paradigm known in the rule-based modeling community as *don't care, don't write.* This is analogous to the representation of reactions in organic chemistry in which a reaction involving some functional group may occur regardless of the configuration of the functional groups neighboring structure (*e.g.* R-OH represents the set of all alcohols). Rule-based frameworks can thus be used to build relatively concise models that exhibit considerable combinatorial complexity [12]. In simple cases (where the number of distinct biochemical species can be enumerated), rule-based models can be converted to a reaction network or system of equations and simulated using traditional methods (*e.g.* the stochastic simulation algorithm (SSA) [7] or numerical integration techniques). For cases involving systems that can generate large numbers of (or infinite) species, alternative kinetic Monte Carlo approaches based on the SSA have been developed that directly apply rules to a mixture of objects representing specific molecular configurations [3, 11]. In these approaches, rules serve as event generators where their iterative application to some initial mixture generates a stochastic trajectory.

ACM acknowledges that this contribution was authored or co-authored by an employee, or contractor of the national government. As such, the Government retains a nonexclusive, royalty-free right to publish or reproduce this article, or to allow others to do so, for Government purposes only. Permission to make digital or hard copies for personal or classroom use is granted. Copies must bear this notice and the full citation on the first page. Copyrights for components of this work owned by others than ACM must be honored. To copy otherwise, distribute, republish, or post, requires prior specific permission and/or a fee. Request permissions from permissions@acm.org.
ACM-BCB'17, August 20-23, 2017, Boston, MA, USA.
© 2017 ACM. 978-1-4503-4722-8/17/08...$15.00
DOI: http://dx.doi.org/10.1145/3107411.3107471

2 RULE-BASED MODELING LANGUAGES

Underlying rule-based modeling frameworks are formal languages designed to encode biochemical interactions. Here, we are concerned with converting between two prominent rule-based modeling languages, the Kappa language [4] and the BioNetGen language (BNGL) [6]. These languages encode types of molecules and their interactions as human- and machine-readable plain text as a name and a list of *sites* that can interact with other molecules' sites or occupy one of a finite number of predefined states (see the grammars in Appendix A). For example, given a molecule, or *agent*, 'A' with a site 'b' that only engages in binding other sites and a site 's' that can occupy three distinct states (0, 1 or 2) or engage in binding, the BNGL encoding of the molecule type is

```
A(b,s~0~1~2)                (Ex. 1)
```

Writing rules involves constructing *patterns* composed of molecule types in which a subset of the molecule types' sites are present in some specified state (including binding state). To clarify the terminology used here: patterns refer to language constructs that are used to match some set of biochemical species and *complexes* or *molecules* refer to the biochemical species themselves or to the specific objects that make up a pattern. The left-hand side (LHS) elements of a rule (denoted by patterns to the left of an arrow operator) identify the *reactants*, the right-hand side (RHS) elements identify the *products*, and the difference between the two sides is the representation of some physical or chemical transformation . Rules can then be applied during the course of simulation when the rule's LHS matches (is *embedded* into) some biochemical species in the simulation mixture, precluding the need for *a priori* enumeration of the biochemical species that may arise. Consider a molecule 'C' with a single binding site 'b'. A binding rule between 'A' from Ex. 1 and 'C' written in BNGL could then be

```
A(b)+C(b) -> A(b!1).C(b!1) 1        (Ex. 2)
```

where '!1' denotes the bond ('1' is the bond label, local to the rule), the '+' operator denotes molecules that are not yet bound, the '.' operator denotes molecules that are a part of the same complex (regardless of whether an explicit bond is present), and the trailing '1' is the rule's rate constant. This rule applies to any molecule 'A' that is not bound on site 'b' regardless of the state of 's' or whether or not 's' is bound to another molecule. Assuming other rules may be present that govern interactions for the site 's' on 'A', some complexes that this rule could be applied to (*i.e.* that the 'A' molecule type in the rule's LHS matches) are

```
A(b,s~0)
A(b,s~1!1).A(b!1,s~0)
A(b,s~2!1).A(b!1,s~0!2).A(b!2,s~1)
```

3 TRANSLATION

Here, we introduce TRuML, a Translator for **Ru**le-based **M**odeling **L**anguages that translates BNGL models into Kappa models and vice versa. Each framework contains a number of analytical tools and features that the other does not[1] and modelers may wish to use both sets. The conversion can often be a nontrivial or error-prone exercise that is better left to automation. It is relevant to note that most of the difficult components to translate are semantic in nature, as the two languages are very similar lexically and syntactically. For clarity, our examples involve what we term *simple* rules and patterns that only involve agents or molecules and not other language features such as Kappa's *tokens* or BNGL's rule modifiers. To place our work in a broader context, work by Děd, *et al.* describes a third framework related to both Kappa and BNGL but operating at a higher level of abstraction to achieve the relation [5]. Additionally, the PySB framework for systems biology modeling in Python acts as a wrapper for features of both languages, facilitating use of rule-based modeling with other Python libraries for data analysis and visualization [10]. Outside of these examples, we are unaware of any other work that considers integration of or translation between these two rule-based modeling languages.

As a simple first example, we refer to Ex. 2 involving molecule 'A' and its interaction with molecule 'C'. BNGL and Kappa have nearly equivalent syntax for defining a molecule's name, its sites, and the states they may occupy (Grammars 1 & 3). However, one important distinction lies in the operators two languages use to connect multiple molecule . The Kappa equivalent to Ex. 2 is (under certain assumptions discussed in Section 3.3)

```
A(b),C(b) -> A(b!1),C(b!1) @ 1          (Ex. 3)
```

where the '@' symbol separates the rule's mechanism from its associated rate constant(s), distinct from BNGL's whitespace separation. Note that, in Kappa, the ',' operator connects all molecules types on one side of the rule, regardless of whether or not they are bound to each other. This difference from the '.' and '+' operators has connotations for model translation that will be discussed in Section 3.3.

More subtle translation issues involve language conventions that are not obvious simply by reading a model. One example involves under-the-hood rate modification in BNGL-compatible simulation engines in order to maintain consistency with the law of mass action. If symmetries exist in a rule's LHS then the rule's rate is divided by the number of symmetries to account for the resulting combinatorial effect. Another way of describing this (as patterns in rule-based modeling languages can be represented as graphs) is to say that the rate is divided by the number of members in the automorphism group of the BNGL rule's LHS. In contrast, automorphisms in Kappa rules must be explicitly accounted for. For example, given the BNGL rule:

```
A(b!1).A(b!1) -> A(b) + A(b) 1
```

the equivalent Kappa rule would be

```
A(b!1),A(b!1) -> A(b),A(b) @ 0.5
```

since there are two automorphisms in the rule's LHS.

3.1 Semantic objects

TRuML parses rule-based models written in either language and converts the plain-text representations into semantic classes that generate appropriate text in either BNGL or the Kappa language. For example, both Kappa and BNGL require molecule type definitions as in Ex. 1. A number of other features of the languages are directly analogous (see Appendix A.1 & Table 1). Some examples include:

- Initial conditions that specify numbers of biochemical species at the start of a simulation
- Observables[2] that track the number of a particular pattern throughout the simulation
- Expressions that represent both static[3] and dynamic[4] quantities. Kappa uses *variables* to define both, while BNGL distinguishes between static quantities (*parameters*) and dynamic quantities (*functions*)

3.2 Identical site names

One major difference between the two languages is the ability to define molecule types with identical sites in BNGL, which is not allowed in Kappa. In certain biological systems (*e.g.* mast cell signaling networks) the relevant molecules may exhibit multiple independent and functionally identical structures (*e.g.* antibodies with two antigen-binding *Fab* arms), and the BioNetGen software suite was designed to accommodate these cases by allowing identically named sites and appropriately scaling the rate constants using statistical factors. TRuML converts the BNGL molecule representation with identical sites to a similar Kappa representation with numbered sites that behave identically. For example, a bivalent antibody ('Ab') molecule and a trivalent antigen ('Ag') might be encoded in BNGL as follows:

```
Ab(Fab,Fab)
Ag(ep,ep,ep)                             (Ex. 4)
```

where the 'Fab' sites on an antibody bind the epitopes ('ep' sites) on an antigen molecule. TRuML renames the sites systematically

[1] See Appendix B

[2] BNGL has a certain type of observable that is incompatible with Kappa (Section 5)

[3] Examples of static quantities are interaction affinities or protein copy numbers

[4] Dynamic quantities are typically calculations involving the number of embeddings of some pattern at each time step in the simulation, such as the Michaelis-Menten approximation of enzyme activity

for translation to Kappa

```
Ab(Fab0,Fab1)
Ag(ep0,ep1,ep2)
```
(Ex. 5)

Rules must also be appropriately modified. A binding rule between free antigen and antibody (as defined in Ex. 4) in BNGL would be[5]:

```
Ab(Fab,Fab) + Ag(ep,ep,ep) -> \
 Ab(Fab!1,Fab).Ag(ep!1,ep,ep) 1
```
(Ex. 6)

whereas the equivalent statement in Kappa must consider all 6 site permutations from the translated molecule definitions (in Ex. 5) resulting:

```
Ab(Fab0,Fab1),Ag(ep0,ep1,ep2) -> \
 Ab(Fab0!1,Fab1),Ag(ep0!1,ep1,ep2) @ 1
Ab(Fab0,Fab1),Ag(ep0,ep1,ep2) -> \
 Ab(Fab0,Fab1!1),Ag(ep0!1,ep1,ep2) @ 1
Ab(Fab0,Fab1),Ag(ep0,ep1,ep2) -> \
 Ab(Fab0!1,Fab1),Ag(ep0,ep1!1,ep2) @ 1
...
```
(Ex. 7)

Note that the BNGL rule's rate will be scaled by a statistical factor by the simulation engine as there are 6 different interactions governed by this rule. Not coincidentally, our convention for translation to Kappa involves 6 rules that are applied using the unscaled rate.

Also affected are patterns that define observables in terms of identically named sites. These observables must have their Kappa equivalents multiplied by the number of automorphisms in the BNGL pattern, since the Kappa pattern will only have the trivial automorphism. While BNGL automatically adjusts rates to account for the automorphism group of a rule's LHS, the BNGL observable counts are not similarly scaled. As might be expected, translation becomes increasingly complex if identically named sites in one molecule can bind identically named sites in another such as the following rule where an antigen 'crosslinks' multiple antibodies, meaning it is already bound to at least one antibody when binding another antibody:

```
Ag(ep!+,ep) + Ab(Fab) -> \
 Ag(ep!+,ep!1).Ab(Fab!1) 1
```
(Ex. 8)

Here the '!+' notation means that a bond on this site is required for a pattern match, but the binding partner is irrelevant.

3.3 Molecularity

Perhaps most complex issue to handle in converting between Kappa and BNGL is molecularity (*e.g.* determining whether or not molecules are bound). Rules involving molecules in the same or distinct complexes are easily identified in BNGL syntax due to the dual '.' and '+' operators.[6] In Kappa this is a bit more difficult, as the absence of an explicit bond between two molecules does not preclude a pattern from matching two molecules that are a part of the same complex. For example, the Kappa pattern `A(b),A(b)` embeds into the complex `A(b,s~0!1),A(b,s~0!1)`.

This is termed *ambiguous molecularity* and modelers using the Kappa language are advised to avoid this if possible by including additional context into rules where this might occur. The rule in question could be rewritten as two rules to clarify the modelers' intentions:

```
A(b,s),A(b,s) -> A(b!1,s),A(b!1,s) @ 1
A(b,s!0),A(b,s!0) -> \
 A(b!1,s!0),A(b!1,s!0) @ 100
```
(Ex. 9)

If ambiguity is unavoidable, as in cases involving polymerization where rings must not form (Ex. 8), Kappa modelers may use the rate syntax "`k1 {k2}`" (see Grammar 2) at the expense of simulation performance as in the following rule:

```
A(b),A(b) -> A(b!1),A(b!1) @ 1 {100}
```
(Ex. 10)

The first number (k1) is the reaction rate when the molecule types on the rule's LHS match separate molecules (intermolecular association; the first rule in Ex. 9) and the second number in brackets (k2) is applied when the matched molecules are in the same complex (intramolecular association; the second rule in Ex. 9). TRuML detects this syntax and will appropriately construct two forms of the above rule in the BNGL syntax:

```
A(b)+A(b) -> A(b!1).A(b!1) 1
A(b).A(b) -> A(b!1).A(b!1) 100
```
(Ex. 11)

Note that the second rule's LHS contains an implicit bond as the two 'A' molecule types are connected with the '.' operator. When converting from BNGL to Kappa, it is not always obvious if intramolecular bonds can form. If TRuML cannot make this determination automatically, it will include two separate rules for each Kappa binding rule, one with each operator. The user may also specify the absence of any intramolecular bond formation when converting from Kappa to BNGL, and only the '+' operator will be used for binding rules.

Translating rules from BNGL to Kappa can be considerably more difficult, due to the nature of the BNGL '+' and '.' operators. Each rule translated into Kappa must guarantee that the molecularity constraints placed on the rule by the BNGL operators hold for the Kappa rule. As a result, some BNGL rules cannot be converted to Kappa rules. For example, BNGL models containing rules with greater than 2 '+' operators on either the LHS or RHS of the rule cannot be translated into Kappa. Furthermore, some rules such as the following fall outside the purview of Kappa's ambiguous molecularity rate notation and must be clarified by adding explicit binding context if possible:

```
A().B().C(a~0) -> A().B().C(a~1) 1
```

This notation cannot be translated when the implicitly bound pattern can match polymers of arbitrary size. TRuML therefore has a user-specified flag that tells the application if polymers or rings can form. This information will prevent potential infinite loops in the pattern disambiguation process.

4 RESULTS

In this section, we compare simulation results of translated models to the original models. These translations are equivalent in the sense

[5]The backslash is a line-continuation character

[6]The NFsim simulation engine currently does not check for product molecularity while the built-in BioNetGen SSA and numerical integration algorithms do. TRuML includes a flag for conversion to either of these implementations

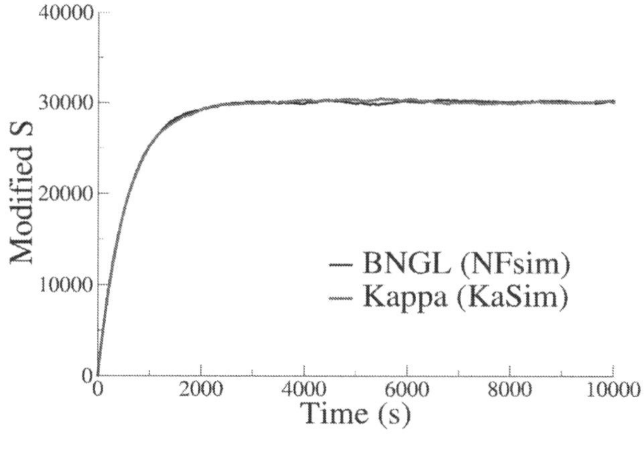

Figure 1: Dynamics for the number of modified substrate observables regardless of binding state in a Kappa futile cycle model (red) and its BNGL translation (black).

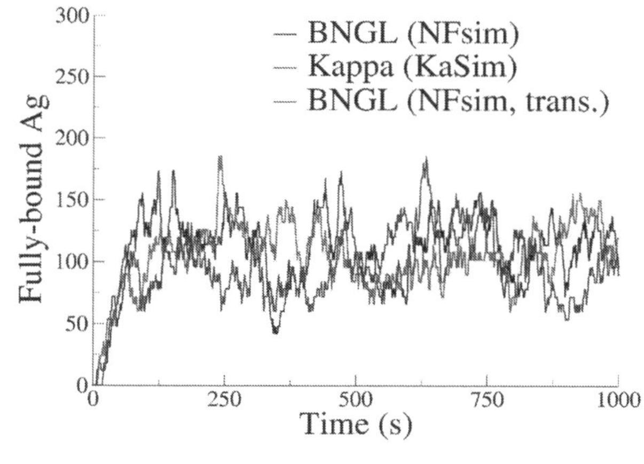

Figure 2: Dynamics for the fully-bound antigen observable "Ag(ep!+,ep!+,ep!+)" in a BNGL antigen-antibody model (black), its Kappa translation (red) and a second translation back into BNGL (blue). Note that this is the number of *patterns* (6x the number of actual molecules corresponding to this pattern).

that no information is lost in the encoding of the reaction network (no approximations are present in the translation). Both sets of results use Kappa's KaSim engine [1] and BNGL's NFsim engine [11] for simulation. Since both use stochastic simulation methods, the results shown from either language will not be identical, but will be statistically indistinguishable.

4.1 Futile cycle model

As a simple demonstration of TRuML, we developed a rule-based model of a futile cycle written in the Kappa language. It is composed of 3 molecule types: two enzymes (E1 & E2) and a substrate (S). One enzyme modifies the substrate and the other removes the modification, both according to the Michaelis-Menten model of enzyme kinetics. In Figure 1 we plot timecourse data from the original and translated models, revealing statistically equivalent simulation trajectories.

4.2 Antibody-antigen binding model

As a second example, we constructed a BNGL model of trivalent antigen molecules binding bivalent antibody molecules based on Ex. 4, Ex. 6, and Ex. 8. The BNGL model contains three rules and two molecule types, but because both molecule types have identical sites and the rules are capable of generating polymers, the resulting Kappa translation has a notably larger set of rules. To further demonstrate that equivalent models can be represented using different conventions, we then translated the Kappa model back into BNGL. The dynamics for fully-bound antigen from all three models are shown in Figure 2.

We also recorded the system state for each simulation after 1000 seconds of simulation time to analyze the distribution of aggregates formed. Each simulation generated between 125 and 135 unique molecular species (not counting the remaining antigen and antibody monomers) and between 350 and 380 total complexes, from a starting point of 6000 monomeric antigen molecules and 600 monomeric antibody molecules. We generated histograms for each trajectory (seen in Figure 3) and performed pairwise Kolmogorov-Smirnov tests on the distributions. All of the tests failed to distinguish between the distributions.

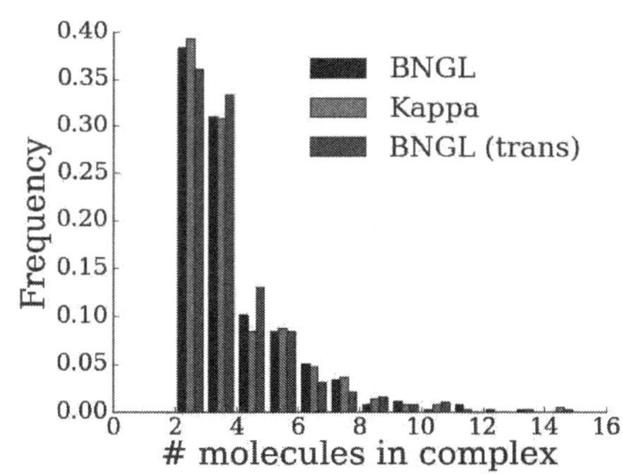

Figure 3: A histogram showing the frequency of aggregate size (omitting monomers) at the end of a 1000-second simulation for each antigen-antibody model. Colors match those in Figure 2

5 DISCUSSION

As with translating natural language, it is important to note that a statement in one language may have numerous equivalent statements in another. As a result, translating from one language to the other and back again may produce a model that appears distinct from the original despite its semantic equivalence. Furthermore, TRuML utilizes one particular (arbitrarily chosen) convention for translating between these rule-based modeling languages. An alternative approach to representing molecules with identically named sites in Kappa has been suggested, which involves a complex that does not dissociate [8]. Using this convention, the antigen molecule in Ex. 4 could be represented with the following molecule type and complex:

```
Ag(ep,x,y)
Ag(ep,x!1,y!2),Ag(ep,x!2,y!3),Ag(ep,x!3,y!1)
```

In addition to representing three identically named sites, this structure also preserves the implicit symmetry in its BNGL equivalent through its symmetric bonding structure. Certain rules could then be written in a more BNGL-like style, especially if the antibody molecule type follows a similar convention.

```
Ag(ep!1),Ab(Fab!1) -> Ag(ep),Ab(Fab) @ 1
```

Finally, both languages are capable of describing models that are impossible to exactly translate into the other language. Some of the issues involving rule structure resulting in incompatible models have already been discussed (*e.g.* implicit bonds that match polymers). However other features of both frameworks preclude exact translation as well. BNGL models can contain a specific type of observable called a *Species* observable, which tracks the number of complexes in the mixture that contain a particular pattern. This is typically used for determining the number of aggregates on-the-fly. On the other hand, Kappa models allow variables to take an infinite value. Encoding a rule that takes place instantly (in simulation time) is easily done by assigning it an infinite rate. Only an approximation of this can be reached in BNGL (typically by assignment of a very large rate constant).

As the readers may have noticed, the complexities in translating between BNGL and Kappa generally come when converting BNGL models with certain properties to Kappa models. Features that allow concise representation of certain types of systems in BNGL can occasionally result in Kappa models with considerably more rules upon translation. This is not to say that BNGL is more useful than Kappa (or vice versa) when considering the entire modeling framework associated with these languages. Indeed, Kappa is arguably more tractable for formal analysis as outlined in [8]. The occasionally non-trivial differences between these two languages make TRuML useful for systems biology modelers who wish to fully exploit the features of both the Kappa and BNGL frameworks.

A GRAMMARS AND OTHER SYNTAX

A.1 Definition Syntax

Syntax for defining equivalent features differs slightly between the two formalisms. Consider how the two languages represent

Feature	BNGL block	Kappa identifier
Agent signature	molecule types	%agent:
Initial condition	seed species	%init:
Static quantity	parameters	%var: | %obs:
Dynamic quantity	functions	%var: | %obs:
Observables	observables	%obs:
Rules	reaction rules	N/A

Table 1: Defining analogous features in BNGL and Kappa. The '|' symbol denotes that either Kappa identifier can be used.

mathematical expressions involving time-varying quantities:

```
begin functions
f = 1 + numUnboundA
end functions
```

where *numUnboundA* is defined in an observable block. The equivalent Kappa definition is simply the line:

```
%var: 'f' 1 + 'numUnboundA'
```

where *numUnboundA* is similarly defined as an observable. Table 1 defines equivalent features in BNGL and Kappa.

A.2 Grammars

Grammars describing patterns and simple rules in Kappa and BNGL are given in Extended Backus-Naur Form. Character sequences in single quotes are terminal symbols, and the grammars use the following non-terminal symbols defined by regular expressions:

- ⟨*integer*⟩ = [0-9]+
- ⟨*bName*⟩ = [a-zA-Z][a-zA-Z_0-9]*
- ⟨*kName*⟩ = [a-zA-Z][a-zA-Z_0-9+-]*
- ⟨*string*⟩ = .*
- ⟨*newline*⟩ = \n
- ⟨*ws*⟩ = [\t]

The grammars do not include treatment of whitespace (except for that needed to separate the products from the rate in BNGL) or the line continuation character (\) for simplicity.

⟨*pattern*⟩	::=	⟨*empty*⟩ | ⟨*agent*⟩, [{',', ⟨*agent*⟩}]
⟨*agent*⟩	::=	⟨*kName*⟩, '(', ⟨*siteList*⟩, ')'
⟨*siteList*⟩	::=	⟨*empty*⟩ | ⟨*site*⟩, [{',', ⟨*site*⟩}]
⟨*site*⟩	::=	⟨*kName*⟩, ⟨*siteState*⟩, ⟨*bond*⟩
⟨*siteState*⟩	::=	⟨*empty*⟩ | '~', ⟨*kName*⟩
⟨*bond*⟩	::=	⟨*empty*⟩ | '!', ⟨*integer*⟩ | '!_' | '?'

Grammar 1: Kappa patterns as defined in [1]

⟨*uniRule*⟩ ::= ['‘', ⟨*string*⟩, '’'], ⟨*pattern*⟩, '->', ⟨*pattern*⟩, '@', ⟨*rate*⟩, ⟨*newline*⟩

⟨*biRule*⟩ ::= ['‘', ⟨*string*⟩, '’'], ⟨*pattern*⟩, '<->', ⟨*pattern*⟩, '@', ⟨*rate*⟩, ⟨*rate*⟩, ⟨*newline*⟩

⟨*rate*⟩ ::= ⟨*expression*⟩, ['{', ⟨*expression*⟩ '}']

⟨*expression*⟩ ::= ? an algebraic expression in Kappa syntax ?

Grammar 2: A grammar for simple rules in Kappa (using patterns from Grammar 1) based on grammars in [1]

⟨*pattern*⟩ ::= '0' | ⟨*molecule*⟩, [{'.', ⟨*molecule*⟩}]

⟨*molecule*⟩ ::= ⟨*bName*⟩, ['(', ⟨*compList*⟩ ')']

⟨*compList*⟩ ::= ⟨*empty*⟩ | ⟨*component*⟩, [{',', ⟨*componentt*⟩}]

⟨*component*⟩ ::= ⟨*bName*⟩, ⟨*compState*⟩, ⟨*compBond*⟩

⟨*compState*⟩ ::= ⟨*empty*⟩ | '~', ⟨*bName*⟩

⟨*compBond*⟩ ::= ⟨*empty*⟩ | '!?' | '!+' | '!',⟨*integer*⟩

Grammar 3: BNGL patterns, based on the grammar defined in [9]. '0' denotes the empty pattern. Note that BNGL patterns only match molecules that are in the same complex.

⟨*uniRule*⟩ ::= [⟨*bName*⟩, ':'], ⟨*patternList*⟩, '->', ⟨*patternList*⟩, ⟨*ws*⟩, ⟨*rate*⟩, ⟨*newline*⟩

⟨*biRule*⟩ ::= [⟨*bName*⟩, ':'], ⟨*patternList*⟩, '<->', ⟨*patternList*⟩, ⟨*ws*⟩, ⟨*rate*⟩, ⟨*rate*⟩, ⟨*newline*⟩

⟨*patternList*⟩ ::= ⟨*empty*⟩ | ⟨*pattern*⟩, '+', ⟨*patternList*⟩

⟨*rate*⟩ ::= ? an algebraic expression in BNGL syntax ?

Grammar 4: A grammar for simple rules in BNGL using patterns from Grammar 3 and based on the grammar in [9].

B TOOLS FOR MODEL AND SIMULATION ANALYSIS

Both languages are accompanied by software that enables simulation and analysis of the model itself. Web resources can be found for both Kappa (http://dev.executableknowledge.org/) and BNGL (http://bionetgen.org/index.php/Main_Page)

B.1 Kappa

The program KaSim simulates models written in the Kappa language. In addition to the language describing the interactions between biomolecules, KaSim also contains a *perturbation* language exists that enables the modeler to specify modifications to the simulation state on-the-fly. One feature of the perturbation language is the ability to flag an observable in order to record the sequence of events that leads to its formation. Kappa models can also be analyzed without simulation (termed *static* analysis) using the KaSa program. KaSa can be used to build the *contact map*, which describes how molecules in the model may be connected to each other. Another is the influence map, which describes how the execution of a rule during simulation may affect the propensity of other rules to be executed.

B.2 BNGL

The BioNetGen software suite (or simply BioNetGen) has a number of methods for model simulation, and BNGL models typically contain an *actions* block with commands that engage simulation. Two methods require generating a *network file* (hence the name 'BioNetGen'), a process that enumerates all species a particular rule set can form, assuming polymerization cannot occur. The network file is interpreted either as a system of differential equations or a Markov chain and is simulated accordingly. The previously mentioned NFsim (Network-Free simulation) engine is used for on-the-fly generation of molecular species and is distributed with accompanying scripts for analyzing results in MATLAB. BioNetGen also contains visualization tools that generate graph-based images of the set of rules or visual model summaries.

ACKNOWLEDGMENTS

This work was supported by NIH/NIGMS grant R01 GM111510 and the Center for Nonlinear Studies at Los Alamos National Laboratory.

REFERENCES

[1] Pierre Boutillier, Jérôme Feret, Jean Krivine, and Lý Kim Quyên. 2017. *KaSim and KaSa Reference Manual.* http://dev.executableknowledge.org/docs/KaSim-manual-master/KaSim_manual.htm.

[2] Lily A. Chylek, Leonard A. Harris, Chang-Shung Tung, James R. Faeder, Carlos F. Lopez, and William S. Hlavacek. 2014. Rule-based modeling: a computational approach for studying biomolecular site dynamics in cell signaling systems. *Wiley Interdisciplinary Reviews. Systems Biology and Medicine* 6, 1 (2014), 13–36. DOI: https://doi.org/10.1002/wsbm.1245 arXiv:NIHMS150003

[3] Vincent Danos, Jérôme Feret, Walter Fontana, and Jean Krivine. 2007. Scalable Simulation of Cellular Signaling Networks. In *Programming Languages and Systems*. Springer Berlin Heidelberg, Berlin, Heidelberg, 139–157. DOI: https://doi.org/10.1007/978-3-540-76637-7_10

[4] Vincent Danos and Cosimo Laneve. 2004. Formal molecular biology. *Theoretical Computer Science* 325, 1 (2004), 69–110. DOI: https://doi.org/10.1016/j.tcs.2004.03.065

[5] T. Děd, D. Šafránek, M. Troják, M. Klement, J. Šalagovič, and L. Brim. 2016. Formal Biochemical Space with Semantics in Kappa and BNGL. *Electronic Notes in Theoretical Computer Science* 326 (2016), 27–49. DOI: https://doi.org/10.1016/j.entcs.2016.09.017

[6] James R. Faeder, Michael L. Blinov, and William S. Hlavacek. 2009. Rule-Based Modeling of Biochemical Systems with BioNetGen. In *Systems Biology*, Ivan V. Maly (Ed.). Humana Press, Totowa, NJ, 113–167. DOI: https://doi.org/10.1007/978-1-59745-525-1_5

[7] Daniel T Gillespie. 2007. Stochastic simulation of chemical kinetics. *Annual Review of Physical Chemistry* 58 (2007), 35–55. DOI: https://doi.org/10.1146/annurev.physchem.58.032806.104637

[8] Russ Harmer, Vincent Danos, Jérôme Feret, Jean Krivine, and Walter Fontana. 2010. Intrinsic information carriers in combinatorial dynamical systems. *Chaos* 20, 3 (2010), 1–16. DOI: https://doi.org/10.1063/1.3491100

[9] Justin S Hogg. 2013. Advances in Rule-based Modeling: Compartments, Energy, and Hybrid Simulation, with Application to Sepsis and Cell Signaling. (August 2013). http://d-scholarship.pitt.edu/19621/

[10] Carlos F Lopez, Jeremy L Muhlich, John A Bachman, and Peter K Sorger. 2013. Programming biological models in Python using PySB. *Molecular Systems Biology* 9, 646 (2013), 646. DOI: https://doi.org/10.1038/msb.2013.1

[11] Michael W Sneddon, James R Faeder, and Thierry Emonet. 2011. Efficient modeling, simulation and coarse-graining of biological complexity with NFsim. *Nature Methods* 8, 2 (2011), 177–183. DOI: https://doi.org/10.1038/nmeth.1546

[12] Ryan Suderman and Eric J. Deeds. 2013. Machines vs. Ensembles: Effective MAPK Signaling through Heterogeneous Sets of Protein Complexes. *PLoS Computational Biology* 9, 10 (2013).

HEMnet: Integration of Electronic Medical Records with Molecular Interaction Networks and Domain Knowledge for Survival Analysis

Edward W Huang*
ewhuang3@illinois.edu

Sheng Wang*
swang141@illinois.edu

Bingxue Li†
bingxueevalee@163.com

Ran Zhang†
dr_zhangran@163.com

Baoyan Liu‡
liuby@mail.cintcm.cn

Runshun Zhang‡
runshunzhang@139.com

Jie Liu†
dr.liujie@163.com

Xuezhong Zhou§
xzzhou@bjtu.edu.cn

Hongsheng Lin†
dr_linhs@163.com

ChengXiang Zhai*
czhai@illinois.edu

ABSTRACT

The continual growth of electronic medical record (EMR) databases has paved the way for many data mining applications, including the discovery of novel disease-drug associations and the prediction of patient survival rates. However, these tasks are hindered because EMRs are usually segmented or incomplete. EMR analysis is further limited by the overabundance of medical term synonyms and morphologies, which causes existing techniques to mismatch records containing semantically similar but lexically distinct terms. Current solutions fill in missing values with techniques that tend to introduce noise rather than reduce it. In this paper, we propose to simultaneously infer missing data and solve semantic mismatching in EMRs by first integrating EMR data with molecular interaction networks and domain knowledge to build the HEMnet, a heterogeneous medical information network. We then project this network onto a low-dimensional space, and group entities in the network according to their relative distances. Lastly, we use this entity distance information to enrich the original EMRs. We evaluate the effectiveness of this method according to its ability to separate patients with dissimilar survival functions. We show that our method can obtain significant (p-value < 0.01) results for each cancer subtype in a lung cancer dataset, while the baselines cannot.

*University of Illinois at Urbana-Champaign
†Guang'anmen Hospital, China Academy of Chinese Medical Sciences
‡National Data Center of Traditional Chinese Medicine, China Academy of Chinese Medical Sciences
§Beijing Jiaotong University

Permission to make digital or hard copies of all or part of this work for personal or classroom use is granted without fee provided that copies are not made or distributed for profit or commercial advantage and that copies bear this notice and the full citation on the first page. Copyrights for components of this work owned by others than ACM must be honored. Abstracting with credit is permitted. To copy otherwise, or republish, to post on servers or to redistribute to lists, requires prior specific permission and/or a fee. Request permissions from permissions@acm.org.
ACM-BCB'17, August 20-23, 2017, Boston, MA, USA.
© 2017 ACM. 978-1-4503-4722-8/17/08...$15.00
DOI: http://dx.doi.org/10.1145/3107411.3107422

1 INTRODUCTION

Electronic medical records (EMRs) were the focus of the American Recovery and Reinvestment Act, which was a high-priority initiative that devoted significant resources to improving EMR adoption rate in healthcare practices across the United States [1]. In fact, EMR adoption has been estimated to save more than $81 billion annually [14]. EMRs can also improve patient safety by alerting doctors to potentially harmful interactions that may result from prescribing multiple drugs [3]. Furthermore, with more accessible EMR databases, doctors can apply stronger statistical methods to accomplish previously infeasible tasks, such as **relationship mining** and **clinical prediction of survival** (CPS).

Relationship mining allows doctors to discover useful associations among entities in medical records, including novel drug usages and adverse drug events [13]. On the other hand, CPS allows doctors to predict a new patient's probability of survival, which would help hospitals optimize resource allocation and treatment planning. In particular, accurate survival estimates for terminally ill patients can prevent inappropriate therapies and avoid unnecessary toxicity [12].

Analyses such as the two aforementioned applications utilize patient features extracted from EMRs. These features include test results, clinical notes, symptoms, diagnoses, and medical history. However, there are two main challenges that frequently appear with these features:

(1) **Missing data.** Many methods assume the availability of all features. However, this assumption typically does not hold for many EMR databases. One reason is that doctors do not perform all existing medical tests on each patient. Other reasons include incomplete medical records or inconsistent text data in the form of clinical notes. Mean imputation, the most common method of filling missing values, has been shown to introduce noise rather than reduce it [25].
(2) **Semantic mismatch.** Patients with similar but distinct features may be judged to be dissimilar. In the traditional vector space model, in which each unique word in the vocabulary

Table 1: An example of the semantic mismatching problem in the traditional vector space model. The two patients in this table have similar cancer diagnoses (adenocarcinoma and adenosquamous carcinoma) and synonymous symptoms (halitosis and bad breath). Despite this, standard models do not judge the two patients to be similar.

	Adeno-carcinoma	Adenosquamous carcinoma	Halitosis	Bad breath
$patient_1$	✓	×	×	✓
$patient_2$	×	✓	✓	×

occupies a dimension, patient records require exact matches of features in order to be considered similar (Table 1). This problem of semantic mismatch has been addressed with methods such as word2vec, which trains similar representations for similar words [28]. However, this method has had limited success in the context of medical records (see **Related Work** for more details) [8].

Because of these challenges, existing models have been unable to effectively group similar EMRs together. Fortunately, genetic and protein interactome databases are rapidly growing due to advances in high-throughput experiments [35] and improved biocuration via text mining [15]. These interactomes typically take the form of molecular interaction networks. We can analyze the topologies of these networks and extract meaningful patterns. This analysis stems from the "guilt by association" rule, which loosely states that associated or interacting proteins in the network are more likely to be functionally related [31]. Our study applies this rule to a molecular interaction network in order to reveal implicit relationships among nodes with common neighbors. We also integrate medical records as well as existing domain knowledge into this network to help solve the primary EMR challenges of missing data and semantic mismatching.

Contributions:

We present the **HE**terogeneous **M**edical record **net**work (HEMnet), which consists of information derived from EMRs, molecular interaction networks, and domain knowledge. As far as we can tell, the HEMnet is the first to integrate medical records and molecular interactions into a single network.

We show that efficient node representations trained from the HEMnet can be used to enrich EMRs. Furthermore, we show that the enriched EMRs can better group similar patients whose records may otherwise be misinterpreted due to missing data and semantic mismatches.

Though we performed experiments in the context of EMR enrichment, the HEMnet is a general model that can be applied to many different tasks, including drug-gene relationship discovery and survival prediction.

2 DATA DESCRIPTION

The National Data Center of Traditional Chinese Medicine in Beijing, China has been collecting traditional Chinese medicine (TCM) EMRs since 2007, integrating them into a clinical data warehouse [44]. The data warehouse stores over 300,000 clinical cases and will continue to acquire patient records from six hospitals in subsequent years. Each hospital in the program has received roughly three million patient visits annually for a decade. In general, TCM data is a largely untapped resource, and provides an unprecedented opportunity to apply powerful mining algorithms to discover useful knowledge. Several interesting studies have already succeeded in detecting herb combinations for disease treatment [39], latent symptom phenotype regularities [41], and herb-symptom relationships [7]. Additionally, Li *et al.* showed that discovering knowledge from TCM data has a variety of significant clinical applications [23].

The data we used was curated from a hospital that also provides traditional Chinese medicine (TCM) services. In addition to the aforementioned benefits of TCM data, we chose this dataset for our experiments because semantic mismatches are even more prevalent in the TCM field [16]. Thus, if our method could yield strong results on this dataset, it would also work well for EMR datasets in most other domains. All patients in the data were diagnosed with some type of non-small-cell lung carcinoma (NSCLC), including adenocarcinoma, squamous-cell carcinoma, adenosquamous carcinoma, and papillary adenocarcinoma. In addition to TCM herb prescriptions, patients received standard western medical treatments.

In our experiments, we only considered the first visit that each patient made to the hospital. Overall, we selected 133 patients with high degrees of missing data. Patients in the dataset have six feature types: medical history, medical test results, prescribed herbs, prescribed drugs, symptoms, and syndromes. Here, syndromes denote "patterns" that are specific to TCM and have no direct western medical translation [9]. In total, there are 449 unique features in the dataset. On average, each record is missing 407 of the 449 possible features, which provided a unique challenge of both missing data and semantic mismatch.

In addition, the database contains each patient's survival information as the number of months before the final event. A patient's final event is either hospital discharge or death. The data is right-censored (i.e., if there is no recorded death event, then death occurred at some unknown time after hospital discharge).

3 HEMNET

We propose to create the heterogeneous medical record network (HEMnet) to address the challenges of EMR analysis by leveraging information from several external sources in order to supplement clinical data. We present its definition, the network embedding process, and how we used the resulting node representations to enrich the raw medical record feature matrix in the following sections.

3.1 Definition of HEMnet

The HEMnet is a network that consists of nodes and edges associated with different types of information. Formally, we define the HEMnet as a graph $G = (V, E, R)$, where V is the set of typed nodes (i.e., each node belongs to a specified type), E is the set of typed edges, and R is the set of edge types. An edge $e \in E$ in the HEMnet is an ordered triplet $e = \{u, v, r\}$, where $u, v \in V$ are typed nodes and $r \in R$ is the corresponding edge type.

In our study, we utilized four distinct categories of edges to create the HEMnet. The first three categories were drawn from external databases, while the last category drew directly from the EMR database.

(1) **Protein-protein interaction network.** This network is based on HumanNet, an external network of protein-encoding genes [21]. For a functional linkage between two proteins p_1 and p_2, we created a node for p_1, a node for p_2, and an undirected edge $\{p_1, p_2\}$ in the HEMnet. This is the molecular interaction network.
(2) **Herb targets.** This database contains herbs and the proteins they target, curated from expert knowledge and medical literature. We created a node h, a node p, and an undirected edge $\{h, p\}$ if an herb h targets a protein p. This is domain knowledge.
(3) **Herb-symptom dictionary.** This database is a TCM textbook consisting of herbs and the symptoms they treat, also curated from expert knowledge and medical literature. We created a node h, a node s, and an undirected edge $\{h, s\}$ if an herb h treats a symptom s in the dictionary. This is domain knowledge.
(4) **Electronic medical records.** We directly added co-occurrence edges from each medical record. For example, if a patient was diagnosed with cancer type c and prescribed a drug d, then we created a node c, a node d, and an undirected edge $\{c, d\}$. We repeated this for all elements in each patient's medical record.

Because of the sparsity of patient records, the external information was critical in discovering relationships among EMR entities that may have otherwise been hidden. Overall, $|V| = 11,911$, $|E| = 379,715$, and $|R| = 23$ for the HEMnet in our experiments. It is important to note that only 449 of the nodes were EMR features, and that the remaining nodes were proteins.

3.2 Network Embedding

The HEMnet uses a recently proposed embedding method, ProSNet [37], to infer relationships among its constituent nodes. ProSNet was originally developed to discover functionally similar proteins from large biological networks across multiple species. It takes a heterogeneous network as input, on which it performs a novel dimensionality reduction algorithm to optimize a low-dimensional vector representation for each node. The vectors of two nodes are co-localized in the low-dimensional space if the nodes are close to each other in the heterogeneous network. A key contribution is that ProSNet obtains low-dimensional vectors through a fast online learning algorithm instead of the batch learning algorithm used in previous works [36]. In each iteration, ProSNet samples a path from the heterogeneous network and optimizes the vectors based on this path instead of all pairs of nodes. Therefore, it can easily scale to large networks containing millions of edges and nodes, making it suitable for training on the HEMnet. In our experiments, we chose our vectors to be of the recommended number of 500 dimensions.

3.3 Feature Matrix Enrichment

After generating low-dimensional vector representations of nodes in the HEMnet, we can tackle the problem of missing data and semantic mismatches in the patient records.

We define the raw patient record matrix, M, to be an $n \times m$ matrix, where n is the number of patients and m is the number of features. In our experiments, $n = 133$ and $m = 449$. Each row consists of a patient record with binary, categorical, discrete, or continuous values, depending on the corresponding feature. For example, drugs may be continuous features because they are recorded as dosages, while metastasis sites are categorical features that may include multiple locations in the body. For our particular dataset, we binarized the categorical features.

In order to impute missing features in M, we propose to construct an $m \times m$ feature similarity matrix, S, where m is the number of features. Each entry S_{ij} is the absolute value of the cosine similarity between feature i and feature j's embedding vectors. Furthermore, we select a threshold such that any entry S_{ij} is set to 0 if S_{ij} is less than the threshold. In other words, we ignore negligible similarities between features. We empirically picked this threshold to be 0.3, as it resulted in the best performance in our experimental setting. After creating S, we generate the enriched patient record matrix M' with the following operation:

$$M' = M \times S \tag{1}$$

With this operation, we can simultaneously solve the problems of incomplete data and semantic mismatches for each patient by filling in missing features that are highly similar to existing features. For example, a patient that has "halitosis" in his or her patient record will receive a non-zero value for "bad breath", as these two symptoms are likely to have similar neighbors, and thus similar embedding vectors.

4 EXPERIMENTAL DESIGN

Typical cancer dataset studies might cluster patients based on a particular characteristic or set of characteristics (e.g., gene expression profiles) [4]. Thus, we identified features that discriminate patients who develop metastases (or die) from those who remain metastasis-free [38]. To this end, we clustered patients into two groups. Framing this as an unsupervised binary classification task in which a patient's medical record determines if he or she is likely to survive, a good clustering is thus one that has a cluster with a significantly better survival rate than the other.

In summary, our method generates the HEMnet, trains network embedding vectors, and then creates the enriched feature matrix M' (Figure 1). We compared the performance of our method with that of two baselines. The first baseline, which we refer to as the raw baseline, directly uses the raw feature matrix M. The second baseline, which we refer to as the mean imputation baseline, replaces each missing feature in M with the average of the available values to generate a dense feature matrix M_{mean}. We compared the performances of these three feature matrices in identical clustering tasks. In the following sections, we discuss cancer subtypes, the clustering process, and our evaluation methods.

4.1 Cancer Subtypes

Different cancer types are affected by different factors. For example, age has been shown to be negatively correlated with survival rates for patients with glioblastoma multiforme [5]. On the other hand, younger breast cancer patients statistically have worse prognoses than older patients [30]. Therefore, we separated the patients in our database into two groups: one of squamous-cell lung carcinoma (SCC) patients and the other of non-squamous-cell non-small-cell lung carcinoma (non-SQ NSCLC) patients (Figure 2). There were

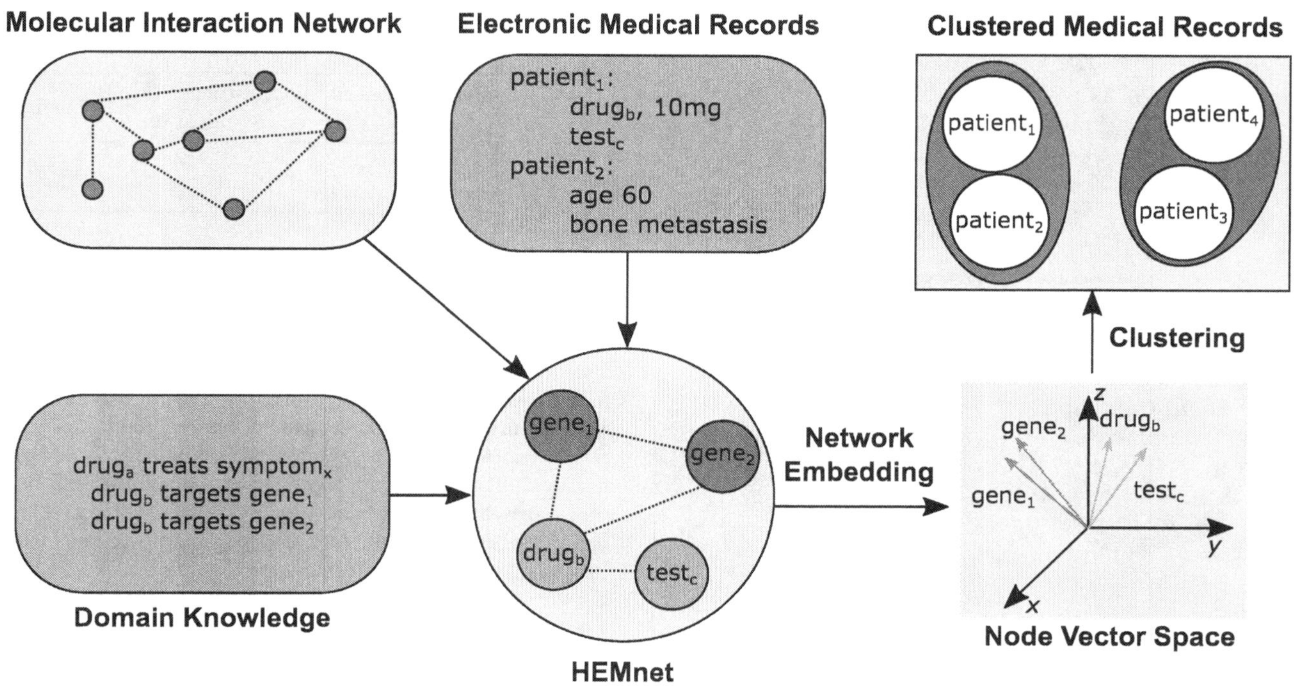

Figure 1: The pipeline for the HEMnet, our proposed heterogeneous information network consisting of electronic medical records, molecular interaction networks, and domain knowledge. We train network embedding vectors on the HEMnet, obtaining low-dimensional vector representations for each node. With these vectors, we enrich the original medical records and then cluster the patients into two groups.

43 SCC patients and 90 non-SQ NSCLC patients in our dataset. We performed experiments and analysis on these two cancer subtypes independently, but built the HEMnet with all available records.

4.2 Clustering

As stated in a previous section, we generated two clusters from each method's feature matrix. Note that the survival information was excluded from the clustering process. We did not necessarily use all features during clustering, but rather combinations of feature categories. For example, we clustered on feature matrices containing only drug features, feature matrices containing drug and medical history features, feature matrices containing all available features, etc. Using symptom and medical history features (a total of 57 features) yielded the best performance.

In addition, we performed dimensionality reduction with principal component analysis (PCA) to dampen the impact of highly correlated features. From the reduced feature matrix, we computed a dissimilarity matrix using pairwise cosine distance, which is commonly used to calculate the dissimilarity between two documents [33]. We ran k-means for two clusters on the resulting dissimilarity matrix.

4.3 Survival Analysis (Quantitative Evaluation)

In order to analyze the difference between the survival rates of two given clusters, we first computed the survival curves using the Kaplan-Meier estimator, one of the most frequently used methods in survival analysis [18]. After estimating the survival functions of both groups, we determined whether they were significantly different by comparing the two curves with the log-rank test [26]. The log-rank test computes a χ^2 statistic and a corresponding p-value to indicate if two survival functions are significantly different. We performed survival analysis with the R package `survival`[1]. Recall that a clustering is of high quality if one cluster possesses a significantly higher survival rate than the other.

When reporting the means of survival functions, we use a restricted mean. Since final events are not always deaths in the dataset, the corresponding survival curve estimates do not necessarily go to zero, which results in undefined means. Thus, we set the upper limit to be some constant u, so that the "restricted" mean signifies the number of months out of the first u months that each group is expected to experience [32].

4.4 Feature Analysis (Qualitative Evaluation)

Throughout our discussion, we denote the cluster with longer survival c_{long} and the cluster with shorter survival c_{short}. After obtaining c_{long}, we wished to identify the features that were responsible for its higher survival rate. Although we only used a subset of features during the clustering phase, we analyzed all features that occur in the EMRs. This is because all features were used in the HEMnet to train embedding vectors, so they may have indirectly impacted the clustering.

[1]https://CRAN.R-project.org/package=survival

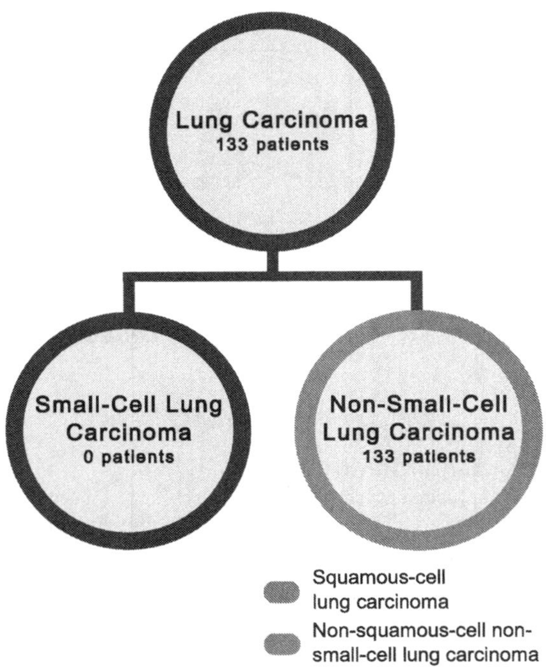

Figure 2: A diagram of the lung carcinoma subtypes in our data. All 133 patients were diagnosed with non-small-cell lung carcinoma (NSCLC). 43 of these patients were diagnosed with squamous-cell carcinoma (SCC) of the lung, while 90 patients were diagnosed with non-squamous-cell (non-SQ) non-small-cell lung carcinoma.

We identified interesting features by computing an unpaired t-test for each feature, where one set of samples came from c_{long} and the other set came from c_{short}. The features with significant p-values (< 0.01) were candidates for further exploration.

5 RESULTS AND DISCUSSION

We discuss the results of the survival and feature analyses below for each of the three methods. First, we discuss the SCC patients, then the non-SQ NSCLC patients.

5.1 The HEMnet substantially improves stratification on SCC patients

After clustering squamous-cell carcinoma patients into two groups using the HEMnet-enriched feature matrix, M', c_{long} had 28 patients and c_{short} had 15 patients (Figure 3a). By the log-rank test, c_{long}'s survival function was significantly better than c_{short}'s with a χ^2 statistic of 10.79 (p-value = 0.001020). We show the cluster summary statistics in Table 2, with $u = 33.3$.

In contrast, when clustering on the raw feature matrix, M, c_{long} had 25 patients and c_{short} had 18 patients (Figure 3c). Their survival functions were not significantly different at the 1% significance level, with a χ^2 statistic of 6.214 (p-value = 0.01267).

When clustering on the mean-imputed feature matrix, M_{mean}, c_{long} had 25 patients and c_{short} had 18 patients (Figure 3e). Here,

Table 2: SCC Patient Survival Time Statistics with HEMnet

	Cluster Size	Restricted Mean	Restricted Mean Standard Error	Median
c_{long}	28	20.7	2.01	22.7
c_{short}	15	11.0	1.60	11.0

the survival functions were not significantly different with a χ^2 statistic of 2.489 (p-value = 0.1147).

After computing an unpaired t-test for each feature, we received a p-value denoting how different the feature's values were in c_{long} from its values in c_{short} (Table 3). In the table, we place an asterisk after features that were identified by our method but not by the raw baseline. The mean imputation baseline only identified five features, all of which were identified by the raw baseline. In both the raw baseline and mean imputation baseline, "umbrella polypore" had a p-value of 0.01513, "sulphurweed" had a p-value of 0.01507, "sputum" had a p-value of 0.02150, and "*A. tataricus*" had a p-value of 0.01352. "Cough" had a p-value of 0.1056 in the raw baseline and a p-value of 0.3069 in the mean imputation baseline.

Our method missed one feature deemed significant by the raw baseline: "TNM staging system", which describes the stage of the cancer's progression [10]. Since there are many missing values in our data, the raw baseline failed to leverage a variety of features. However, our method does not have this limitation, and also achieved a more significant separation between the two clusters. Additionally, it missed no features identified by the mean imputation baseline.

Of all significant features, only "Karnofsky performance status" had a higher mean in c_{long} than in c_{short}. This is expected, as a higher KPS score indicates a relatively healthier cancer patient [19]. All other significant features had lower means in c_{long} than in c_{short}. This is reasonable for symptom features, as patients with longer survival rates generally have less severe symptoms. On the other hand, it might initially appear as if the herbs' higher values in c_{short} indicate their ineffectiveness. However, this can be explained by the fact that patients with more life-threatening conditions require higher dosages of treatments.

The raw baseline did not find "sputum" and "cough" to be symptoms that were statistically different between c_{long} and c_{short}, while our method did. However, they are very common symptoms in lung cancer patients, and tend to be more severe in patients with lower survival rates. Furthermore, the other three features that our method discovered were all herbs. We can interpret these features' higher values in c_{short} as potential herb-symptom relationships. In the herb-symptom dictionary, sulphurweed is listed as a treatment for both cough and sputum, while umbrella polypore treats only urinary tract-related symptoms and *A. tataricus* simply does not appear. Despite these relationships not appearing in the domain knowledge, the HEMnet was able to capture them in our method. In fact, a study showed that a naturally occurring compound derived from umbrella polypore mycelia induces apoptosis in human lung cancer cells [20]. Furthermore, a recent study showed that a polysaccharide isolated from *A. tataricus* inhibits the growth of cancer cells [42].

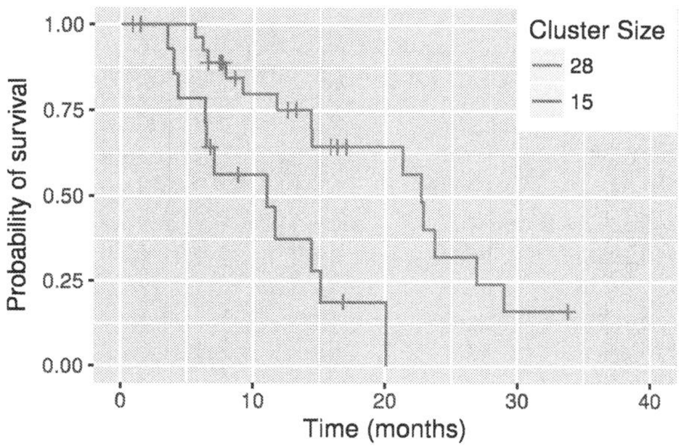

(a) SCC Patients with HEMnet (p-value = 0.001020)

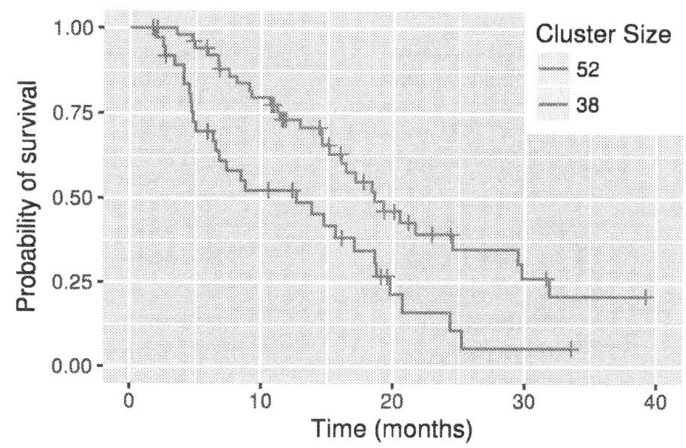

(b) Non-SQ NSCLC Patients with HEMnet (p-value = 0.003652)

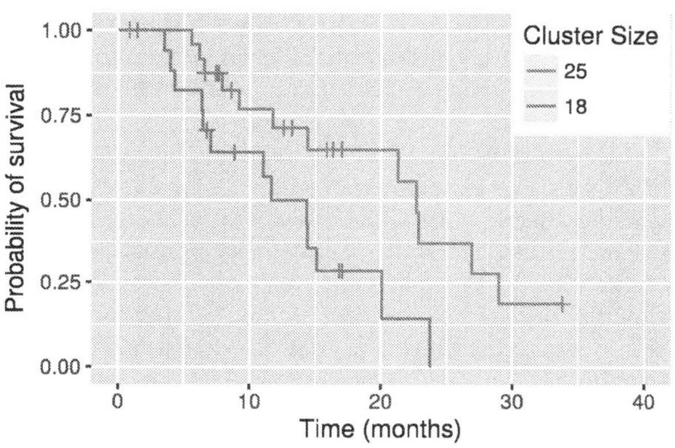

(c) SCC Patients with Raw Baseline (p-value = 0.01267)

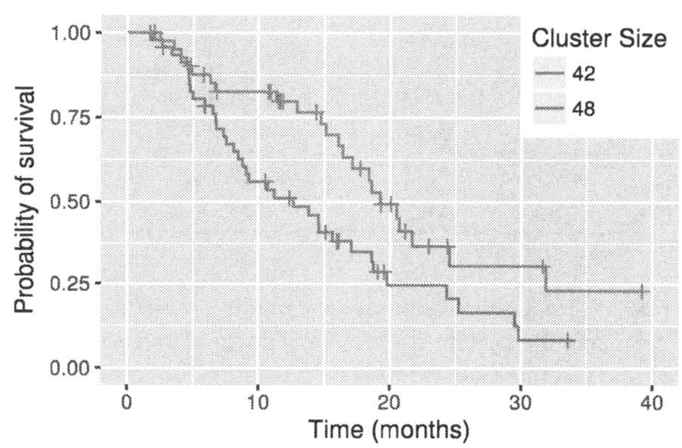

(d) Non-SQ NSCLC Patients with Raw Baseline (p-value = 0.02333)

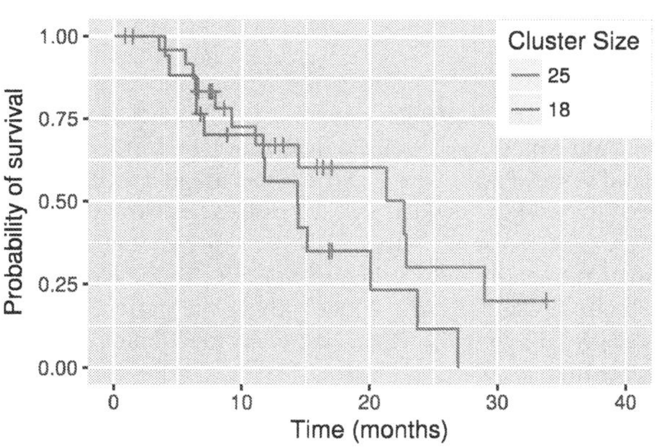

(e) SCC Patients with Mean Imputation Baseline (p-value = 0.1147)

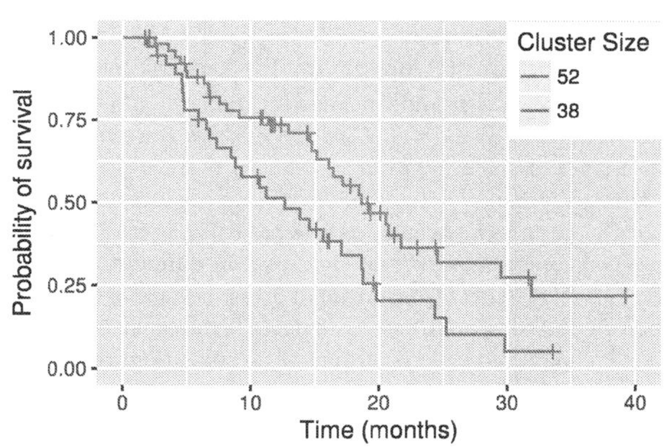

(f) Non-SQ NSCLC Patients with Mean Imputation Baseline (p-value = 0.01341)

Figure 3: A comparison of survival functions for two patient clusters in SCC patients (subfigures a, c, and e) and non-SQ NSCLC patients (subfigures b, d, and f). Subfigures a and b use HEMnet-enriched feature matrices, subfigures c and d use the raw feature matrices, and subfigures e and f use the raw feature matrices enriched by mean imputation.

Table 3: Significant SCC Patient Features with HEMnet (p-value < 0.01). Features not found to be significant by the raw baseline have asterisks. Feature means and standard deviations (SD) are shown.

Feature Name	p-value	c_{long} mean	c_{long} SD	c_{short} mean	c_{short} SD	Feature Type
Karnofsky performance status	4.427×10^{-7}	77.86	6.739	62.67	9.978	Medical Test
Loss of appetite	2.691×10^{-6}	0.2857	0.6999	1.600	0.8794	Symptom
Shortness of breath	2.440×10^{-4}	0.6786	0.8886	1.733	0.7717	Symptom
Fatigue	2.687×10^{-4}	0.4286	0.8207	1.467	0.8844	Symptom
S. tuberosa	1.407×10^{-3}	0.03571	0.1856	1.800	2.857	Herb
P. suffruticosa	2.730×10^{-3}	0	0	1.067	1.879	Herb
Umbrella polypore*	3.847×10^{-3}	0.1429	0.7423	1.267	1.806	Herb
Sulphurweed*	4.562×10^{-3}	0.1071	0.4087	1.667	2.891	Herb
Sputum*	5.015×10^{-3}	0.8214	0.7585	1.533	0.8844	Symptom
A. tataricus*	5.678×10^{-3}	0.1071	0.3093	3.667	6.925	Herb
Cough*	9.388×10^{-3}	1.321	0.8474	1.933	0.5735	Symptom

Table 4: Non-SQ NSCLC Patient Survival Time Statistics with HEMnet

	Cluster Size	Restricted Mean	Restricted Mean Standard Error	Median
c_{long}	52	23.9	2.67	18.6
c_{short}	38	14.1	2.18	12.7

Our method was able to capture meaningful herb-symptom relationships while the baselines were not. Thus, we have shown that the HEMnet can integrate external herb information in the form of herb-protein targets and protein-protein interaction information.

5.2 The HEMnet also substantially improves stratification on Non-SQ NSCLC patients

After clustering non-SQ NSCLC patients into two sets using the HEMnet-enriched feature matrix, M', c_{long} had 52 patients and c_{short} had 38 patients (Figure 3b). By the log-rank test, c_{long}'s survival function was significantly better than c_{short}'s with a χ^2 statistic of 8.449 (p-value = 0.003652). We show the cluster summary statistics in Table 4, with $u = 50.8$.

In contrast, when we clustered on the raw feature matrix, M, c_{long} had 42 patients and c_{short} had 48 patients (Figure 3d). Again, the survival functions were not significantly different at the 1% significance level, with a χ^2 statistic of 5.144 (p-value = 0.02333).

When we clustered on the mean-imputed feature matrix, M_{mean}, c_{long} had 52 patients and c_{short} had 38 patients (Figure 3f). The survival functions were not significantly different with a χ^2 statistic of 6.115 (p-value = 0.01341).

Again, we computed an unpaired t-test for each feature, receiving a p-value for each one to indicate significance (Table 5). Consistent with earlier results, "Karnofsky performance status" was the only feature to have a higher mean in c_{long} than in c_{short}.

In the raw baseline, "pamidronate disodium injection" had a p-value of 0.04887, "atelectasis" had a p-value of 0.01208, "white peony" had a p-value of 0.05991, "shortness of breath" had a p-value of 0.021107, "Chinese cinnamon" had a p-value of 0.06895, and "*A. asphodeloides*" had a p-value of 0.03629. Our method obtained p-values below 0.01 for each of these features. The mean imputation baseline did identify "pamidronate disodium injection" as a significant feature (p-value = 0.008043), but did not identify any herb features.

Because our method found several treatments to be significant, it allowed us to extract meaningful relationships. Pamidronate disodium injections are well-known treatments for patients with bone metastases [11], which was also a significant feature (p-value = 1.294×10^{-6}). Atelectasis and shortness of breath are common symptoms among lung cancer patients. White peony roots have been shown to inhibit tumor growth in non-small-cell lung cancer patients [17]. Lastly, a study has shown *A. asphodeloides* to have anti-tumor effects [2]. As with the SCC patients, our method captured these meaningful herb-symptom relationships while the baselines could not. We attribute this to the external information integrated into the HEMnet.

5.3 KPS Feature Significance

Because "Karnofsky performance status" had the lowest p-value for both cancer types with our method, we further explored its significance. Performance status scores are assigned to cancer patients in attempts to quantify their overall health and well-being. It is therefore reasonable that KPS was a discriminative feature for patients of both cancer subtypes. Specifically, the Karnofsky score runs from 100 to 0, where 100 is relatively perfect health and 0 is death [19]. In this dataset, Karnofsky performance scores were assigned in standard intervals of 10.

To test whether KPS can accurately classify patients by itself, we placed patients into c_{long} if they had a Karnofsky score greater than 60, and the rest into c_{short} (Figure 4). Although using only KPS significantly separated non-SQ NSCLC patients (p-value = 5.571×10^{-4}), the survival curves were not significantly different in SCC patients (p-value = 0.3655). Thus, we conclude that KPS alone cannot accurately predict a patient's survival rate, and that the HEMnet-enriched feature matrices leveraged a variety of features to achieve better clustering results.

Table 5: Significant Non-SQ NSCLC Patient Features with HEMnet (p-value < 0.01). Features not found to be significant by the raw baseline have asterisks. Feature means and standard deviations (SD) are shown.

Feature Name	p-value	c_{long} mean	c_{long} SD	c_{short} mean	c_{short} SD	Feature Type
Karnofsky performance status	5.570×10^{-8}	76.35	8.993	63.42	11.98	Medical Test
Pamidronate disodium injection*	2.196×10^{-7}	0.2115	0.8166	15.34	19.74	Drug
Bone metastasis	1.294×10^{-6}	0.03846	0.1923	0.4211	0.4937	Medical Test
Atelectasis*	1.250×10^{-3}	0.01923	0.1373	0.2105	0.4077	Symptom
TNM staging system	1.307×10^{-3}	7.346	2.472	8.632	0.6250	Medical Test
Distant metastasis	2.307×10^{-3}	0.3846	0.4865	0.6842	0.4648	Medical Test
White peony*	8.760×10^{-3}	1.115	2.584	2.789	3.894	Herb
Shortness of breath*	8.999×10^{-3}	0.6346	0.8555	1.105	0.9676	Symptom
Chinese cinnamon*	9.302×10^{-3}	0.03846	0.2747	0.4211	1.091	Herb
A. asphodeloides*	9.952×10^{-3}	0.05769	0.4120	1.158	3.273	Herb

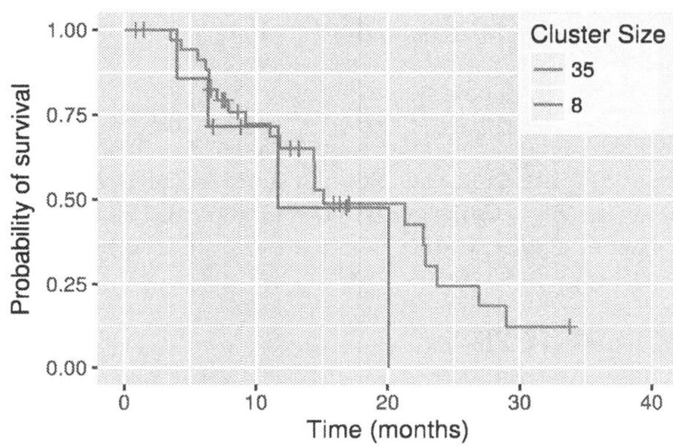

(a) SCC Patients (p-value = 0.3655)

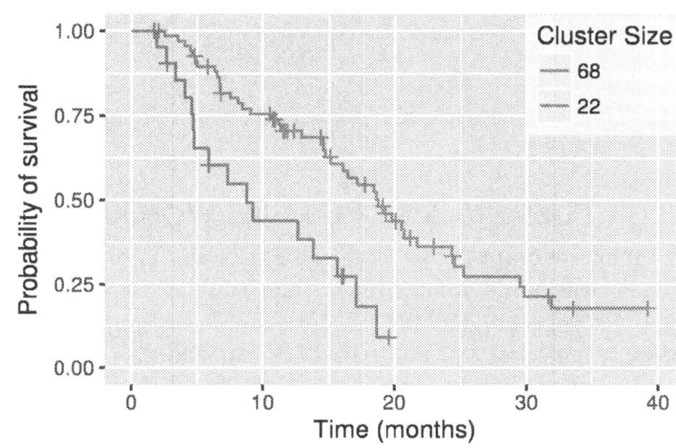

(b) Non-SQ NSCLC Patients (p-value = 5.571×10^{-4})

Figure 4: A comparison of survival functions when separating patients only by their Karnofsky performance score.

5.4 Parameter Tuning

The number of dimensions of each embedding vector, which was recommended to be 500 in the original ProSNet paper, is a parameter that requires tuning. In our experiments, we saw that optimal results were also achieved at 500 dimensions (Figure 5). Furthermore, 400 and 600 dimensions produced statistically significant results for both cancer subtypes.

6 RELATED WORK

Though our work is the first to utilize molecular interaction networks in conjunction with electronic medical records, it drew inspiration from many tasks and networks.

A previous study integrated genetics by linking EMR data to biobanked blood samples [27]. However, they use patient-matched DNA samples and patient genetic data rather than prior domain knowledge. Deep Patient is a previous work that also learns embedding vectors from EMRs [29]. However, they learn representations of patients rather than individual medical entities and do not use molecular information networks. Med2Vec is an algorithm that also learns efficient representations of medical concepts, but its joint optimization process relies on sequences of multiple visits [8], which is less applicable to inpatients. Word2vec, on which Med2Vec is based, provided the basis for much of the current research on learning efficient word embeddings [28]. However, it can only be applied to patient records directly and cannot incorporate molecular interaction networks or domain knowledge.

Many related works have implemented data mining techniques on heterogeneous networks such as bibliographic networks [40, 43], gene-phenotype networks [22], and social media networks [24]. However, none of these studies focused on EMR tasks. A previous study performed similarity searched within heterogeneous information networks [34]. It also exploited the idea of paths within a heterogeneous network, but instead used them for similarity computations rather than for vector optimization. Another previous work also trained embeddings on a network consisting of prior knowledge in order to enrich EMRs for clustering tasks [16]. However, they only used domain knowledge in the training network. Caballero and Akella also performed data imputation on EMR data [6]. However, they used an expectation-maximization method

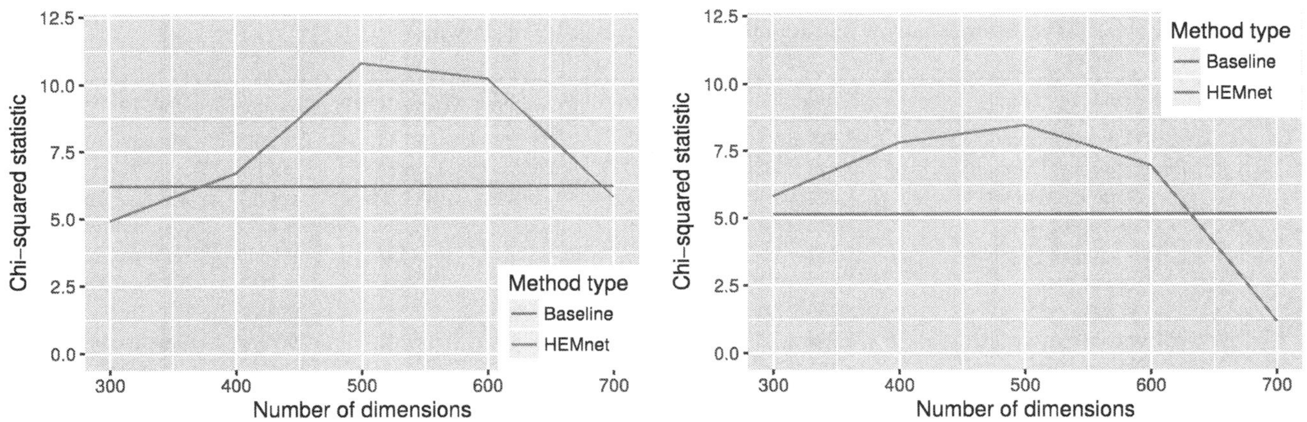

(a) SCC Patients

(b) Non-SQ NSCLC Patients

Figure 5: Results of tuning the number of dimensions to observe parameter sensitivity.

rather than prior information and domain knowledge to fill missing values.

7 CONCLUSIONS AND FUTURE WORK

In this paper, we proposed to integrate EMRs with molecular interaction networks and domain knowledge using a heterogeneous medical record network, HEMnet, to solve two challenges in analyzing EMRs, i.e., missing data and semantic mismatch. By extracting knowledge from molecular interaction networks and domain knowledge and then combining them with medical records, we created a network that allows for the training of accurate embedding vectors. We showed how we can use these vectors to enrich EMR databases, and then evaluated their performance based on survival prediction. Our method was able to perform better than the baseline feature matrices by successfully splitting patients of both cancer subtypes (squamous-cell lung carcinoma and non-squamous-cell non-small-cell lung carcinoma). We showed this via quantitative evaluation by performing survival analysis on the resulting cluster pairs of each cancer subtype. Lastly, we verified the effects of the HEMnet with qualitative analysis, studying the features and their differences between healthy and unhealthy clusters.

For future work, we plan to implement tasks for clinical prediction of survival (CPS). Given the framework proposed in this paper, we can attempt to predict a new patient's probability of survival by first grouping him or her into the most similar cluster, and then extrapolating the survival rate from the neighboring patient records (similar to the k-nearest neighbors algorithm). Furthermore, the HEMnet allows for even more sophisticated methods of feature discovery, including novel drug-drug interactions. This feature discovery will expand upon our current qualitative evaluation.

ACKNOWLEDGMENTS

This material is based on work supported by the National Science Foundation Graduate Research Fellowship Program under grant No. DGE-1144245. This research was also supported by NIGMS under grant 1U54GM114838 through funds provided by the trans-NIH Big Data to Knowledge (BD2K) initiative (www.bd2k.nih.gov). Our work also received support from National Key Technology R&D Program grants 2013BAI02B01 and 2013BAH06F03, National S&T Major Project of China grant 2013BAI13B04, and Special Research Project of TCMS by State Administration of Traditional Chinese Medicine grant 201407001.

REFERENCES

[1] The 111th United States Congress. 2009. American Recovery and Reinvestment Act. (2009). https://www.gpo.gov/fdsys/pkg/PLAW-111publ5/html/PLAW-111publ5.htm.

[2] Wenna Bao, Haifeng Pan, Min Lu, Yuan Ni, Rui Zhang, and Xingguo Gong. 2007. The apoptotic effect of sarsasapogenin from Anemarrhena asphodeloides on HepG2 human hepatoma cells. *Cell biology international* 31, 9 (2007), 887–892.

[3] David W Bates, Lucian L Leape, David J Cullen, Nan Laird, Laura A Petersen, Jonathan M Teich, Elizabeth Burdick, Mairead Hickey, Sharon Kleefield, Brian Shea, and others. 1998. Effect of computerized physician order entry and a team intervention on prevention of serious medication errors. *Jama* 280, 15 (1998), 1311–1316.

[4] David G Beer, Sharon LR Kardia, Chiang-Ching Huang, Thomas J Giordano, Albert M Levin, David E Misek, Lin Lin, Guoan Chen, Tarek G Gharib, Dafydd G Thomas, and others. 2002. Gene-expression profiles predict survival of patients with lung adenocarcinoma. *Nature medicine* 8, 8 (2002), 816–824.

[5] Peter C Burger and Sylvan B Green. 1987. Patient age, histologic features, and length of survival in patients with glioblastoma multiforme. *Cancer* 59, 9 (1987), 1617–1625.

[6] Karla Caballero and Ram Akella. 2015. Dynamic Estimation of the Probability of Patient Readmission to the ICU using Electronic Medical Records. In *AMIA Annual Symposium Proceedings*, Vol. 2015. American Medical Informatics Association, 1831.

[7] Jinpeng Chen, Josiah Poon, Simon K Poon, Ling Xu, and Daniel M Y Sze. 2015. Mining symptom-herb patterns from patient records using tripartite graph. *Evidence-Based Complementary and Alternative Medicine* 2015 (2015).

[8] Edward Choi, Mohammad Taha Bahadori, Elizabeth Searles, Catherine Coffey, Michael Thompson, James Bost, Javier Tejedor-Sojo, and Jimeng Sun. 2016. Multi-layer representation learning for medical concepts. In *Proceedings of the 22nd ACM SIGKDD International Conference on Knowledge Discovery and Data Mining*. ACM, 1495–1504.

[9] Steven Clavey. 1995. *Fluid physiology and pathology in traditional Chinese medicine*. Churchill Livingstone.

[10] James R Egner. 2010. AJCC cancer staging manual. *JAMA* 304, 15 (2010), 1726–1727.

[11] Donna Glover, Alan Lipton, Alan Keller, Antonius A Miller, Scott Browning, Robert J Fram, Sebastian George, Kenneth Zelenakas, Richard S Macerata, and John J Seaman. 1994. Intravenous pamidronate disodium treatment of bone metastases in patients with breast cancer. A dose-seeking study. *Cancer* 74, 11 (1994), 2949–2955.

[12] Stephan Gripp, Sibylle Moeller, Edwin BoìĹlke, Gerd Schmitt, Christiane Matuschek, Sonja Asgari, Farzin Asgharzadeh, Stephan Roth, Wilfried Budach, Matthias Franz, and others. 2007. Survival prediction in terminally ill cancer patients by clinical estimates, laboratory tests, and self-rated anxiety and depression. *Journal of Clinical Oncology* 25, 22 (2007), 3313–3320.

[13] Rave Harpaz, William DuMouchel, Nigam H Shah, David Madigan, Patrick Ryan, and Carol Friedman. 2012. Novel Data-Mining Methodologies for Adverse Drug Event Discovery and Analysis. *Clinical Pharmacology & Therapeutics* 91, 6 (2012), 1010–1021.

[14] Richard Hillestad, James Bigelow, Anthony Bower, Federico Girosi, Robin Meili, Richard Scoville, and Roger Taylor. 2005. Can electronic medical record systems transform health care? Potential health benefits, savings, and costs. *Health affairs* 24, 5 (2005), 1103–1117.

[15] Lynette Hirschman, Gully AP C Burns, Martin Krallinger, Cecilia Arighi, K Bretonnel Cohen, Alfonso Valencia, Cathy H Wu, Andrew Chatr-Aryamontri, Karen G Dowell, Eva Huala, and others. 2012. Text mining for the biocuration workflow. *Database* 2012 (2012), bas020.

[16] Edward W Huang, Sheng Wang, Runshun Zhang, Baoyan Liu, Xuezhong Zhou, and ChengXiang Zhai. 2016. PaReCat: Patient Record Subcategorization for Precision Traditional Chinese Medicine. In *Proceedings of the 7th ACM International Conference on Bioinformatics, Computational Biology, and Health Informatics*. ACM, 443–452.

[17] Jen-Yu Hung, Chih-Jen Yang, Ying-Ming Tsai, Hurng-Wern Huang, and Ming-Shyan Huang. 2008. Anti-proliferative activity of Paeoniflorin is through cell cycle arrest and the FAS/FAS ligand-mediated apoptotic pathway in human non-small cell lung cancer A549 cells. *Clinical and Experimental Pharmacology and Physiology* 35, 2 (2008), 141–147.

[18] Edward L Kaplan and Paul Meier. 1958. Nonparametric estimation from incomplete observations. *Journal of the American statistical association* 53, 282 (1958), 457–481.

[19] David A Karnofsky, Walter H Abelmann, Lloyd F Craver, and Joseph H Burchenal. 1948. The use of the nitrogen mustards in the palliative treatment of carcinoma. With particular reference to bronchogenic carcinoma. *Cancer* 1, 4 (1948), 634–656.

[20] Tae Hwan Kim, Ju Sung Kim, Zoo Haye Kim, Ren Bin Huang, and Ren Sheng Wang. 2014. Khz (Fusion of Ganoderma lucidum and Polyporus umbellatus Mycelia) induces apoptosis in A549 human lung cancer cells by generating reactive oxygen species and decreasing the Mitochondrial membrane potential. *Food Science and Biotechnology* 23, 3 (2014), 859–864.

[21] Insuk Lee, U Martin Blom, Peggy I Wang, Jung Eun Shim, and Edward M Marcotte. 2011. Prioritizing candidate disease genes by network-based boosting of genome-wide association data. *Genome research* 21, 7 (2011), 1109–1121.

[22] Yongjin Li and Jagdish C Patra. 2010. Genome-wide inferring gene–phenotype relationship by walking on the heterogeneous network. *Bioinformatics* 26, 9 (2010), 1219–1224.

[23] Yu-Bing Li, Xue-Zhong Zhou, Run-Shun Zhang, Ying-Hui Wang, Yonghong Peng, Jing-Qing Hu, Qi Xie, Yan-Xing Xue, Li-Li Xu, and Xiao-Fang Liu. 2015. Detection of herb-symptom associations from traditional Chinese medicine clinical data. *Evidence-Based Complementary and Alternative Medicine* 2015 (2015).

[24] Lu Liu, Jie Tang, Jiawei Han, Meng Jiang, and Shiqiang Yang. 2010. Mining topic-level influence in heterogeneous networks. In *Proceedings of the 19th ACM international conference on Information and knowledge management*. ACM, 199–208.

[25] Peng Liu, Lei Lei, Junjie Yin, Wei Zhang, Wu Naijun, and Elia El-Darzi. 2006. Healthcare data mining: Prediction inpatient length of stay. In *Intelligent Systems, 2006 3rd International IEEE Conference on*. IEEE, 832–837.

[26] Nathan Mantel. 1966. Evaluation of survival data and two new rank order statistics arising in its consideration. *Cancer chemotherapy reports. Part 1* 50, 3 (1966), 163–170.

[27] Catherine A McCarty, Rex L Chisholm, Christopher G Chute, Iftikhar J Kullo, Gail P Jarvik, Eric B Larson, Rongling Li, Daniel R Masys, Marylyn D Ritchie, Dan M Roden, and others. 2011. The eMERGE Network: a consortium of biorepositories linked to electronic medical records data for conducting genomic studies. *BMC medical genomics* 4, 1 (2011), 13.

[28] Tomas Mikolov, Kai Chen, Greg Corrado, and Jeffrey Dean. 2013. Efficient estimation of word representations in vector space. *arXiv preprint arXiv:1301.3781* (2013).

[29] Riccardo Miotto, Li Li, Brian A Kidd, and Joel T Dudley. 2016. Deep patient: An unsupervised representation to predict the future of patients from the electronic health records. *Scientific reports* 6 (2016).

[30] Asa J Nixon, Donna Neuberg, Daniel F Hayes, Rebecca Gelman, James L Connolly, Stuart Schnitt, Anthony Abner, Abram Recht, Frank Vicini, and Jay R Harris. 1994. Relationship of patient age to pathologic features of the tumor and prognosis for patients with stage I or II breast cancer. *Journal of Clinical Oncology* 12, 5 (1994), 888–894.

[31] Stephen Oliver. 2000. Proteomics: guilt-by-association goes global. *Nature* 403, 6770 (2000), 601–603.

[32] G Miller Rupert and JR Miller. 1981. Survival analysis. (1981).

[33] Amit Singhal. 2001. Modern information retrieval: A brief overview. *IEEE Data Eng. Bull.* 24, 4 (2001), 35–43.

[34] Yizhou Sun, Jiawei Han, Xifeng Yan, Philip S Yu, and Tianyi Wu. 2011. Pathsim: Meta path-based top-k similarity search in heterogeneous information networks. *Proceedings of the VLDB Endowment* 4, 11 (2011), 992–1003.

[35] Damian Szklarczyk, Andrea Franceschini, Stefan Wyder, Kristoffer Forslund, Davide Heller, Jaime Huerta-Cepas, Milan Simonovic, Alexander Roth, Alberto Santos, Kalliopi P Tsafou, and others. 2014. STRING v10: protein–protein interaction networks, integrated over the tree of life. *Nucleic acids research* (2014), gku1003.

[36] Sheng Wang, Hyunghoon Cho, ChengXiang Zhai, Bonnie Berger, and Jian Peng. 2015. Exploiting ontology graph for predicting sparsely annotated gene function. *Bioinformatics* 31, 12 (2015), i357–i364.

[37] Sheng Wang, Meng Qu, and Jian Peng. 2016. ProSNet: Integrating homology with molecular networks for protein function prediction. In *Pacific Symposium on Biocomputing. Pacific Symposium on Biocomputing*, Vol. 22. 27.

[38] Yixin Wang, Jan GM Klijn, Yi Zhang, Anieta M Sieuwerts, Maxime P Look, Fei Yang, Dmitri Talantov, Mieke Timmermans, Marion E Meijer-van Gelder, Jack Yu, and others. 2005. Gene-expression profiles to predict distant metastasis of lymph-node-negative primary breast cancer. *The Lancet* 365, 9460 (2005), 671–679.

[39] Huiming Xu, Yueming Wang, and Tiansong Zhang. 2014. Data Mining of Regularities and Rules of Compound Herbal Formulae for Nonalcoholic Fatty Liver Disease. *Chinese Journal of Information on Traditional Chinese Medicine* (2014), 21(8):38–41.

[40] Xiao Yu, Quanquan Gu, Mianwei Zhou, and Jiawei Han. 2012. Citation prediction in heterogeneous bibliographic networks. In *Proceedings of the 2012 SIAM International Conference on Data Mining*. SIAM, 1119–1130.

[41] Nevin L Zhang, Shihong Yuan, Tao Chen, and Yi Wang. 2008. Latent tree models and diagnosis in traditional Chinese medicine. *Artificial intelligence in medicine* 42, 3 (2008), 229–245.

[42] Yunxin Zhang, Qiusheng Wang, Tie Wang, Haikui Zhang, Ying Tian, Hong Luo, Shen Yang, Yuan Wang, and Xun Huang. 2012. Inhibition of human gastric carcinoma cell growth in vitro by a polysaccharide from Aster tataricus. *International journal of biological macromolecules* 51, 4 (2012), 509–513.

[43] Ding Zhou, Sergey A Orshanskiy, Hongyuan Zha, and C Lee Giles. 2007. Co-ranking authors and documents in a heterogeneous network. In *Data Mining, 2007. ICDM 2007. Seventh IEEE International Conference on*. IEEE, 739–744.

[44] Xuezhong Zhou, Shibo Chen, Baoyan Liu, Runsun Zhang, Yinghui Wang, Ping Li, Yufeng Guo, Hua Zhang, Zhuye Gao, and Xiufeng Yan. 2010. Development of traditional Chinese medicine clinical data warehouse for medical knowledge discovery and decision support. *Artificial Intelligence in Medicine* 48, 2 (2010), 139–152.

A Novel Approach for Classifying Gene Expression Data using Topic Modeling

Soon Jye Kho*
Knoesis Center, Wright State University
3640 Colonel Glenn Hwy
Dayton, Ohio 45431
soonjye@knoesis.org

Hima Bindu Yalamanchili*
Knoesis Center, Wright State University
3640 Colonel Glenn Hwy
Dayton, Ohio 45431
himay.87@gmail.com

Michael L. Raymer
Knoesis Center, Wright State University
3640 Colonel Glenn Hwy
Dayton, Ohio 45431
michael.raymer@wright.edu

Amit P. Sheth
Knoesis Center, Wright State University
3640 Colonel Glenn Hwy
Dayton, Ohio 45431
amit@knoesis.org

ABSTRACT

Understanding the role of differential gene expression in cancer etiology and cellular process is a complex problem that continues to pose a challenge due to sheer number of genes and inter-related biological processes involved. In this paper, we employ an unsupervised topic model, Latent Dirichlet Allocation (LDA) to mitigate overfitting of high-dimensionality gene expression data and to facilitate understanding of the associated pathways. LDA has been recently applied for clustering and exploring genomic data but not for classification and prediction. Here, we proposed to use LDA in clustering as well as in classification of cancer and healthy tissues using lung cancer and breast cancer messenger RNA (mRNA) sequencing data. We describe our study in three phases: clustering, classification, and gene interpretation. First, LDA is used as a clustering algorithm to group the data in an unsupervised manner. Next we developed a novel LDA-based classification approach to classify unknown samples based on similarity of co-expression patterns. Evaluation to assess the effectiveness of this approach shows that LDA can achieve high accuracy compared to alternative approaches. Lastly, we present a functional analysis of the genes identified using a novel topic profile matrix formulation. This analysis identified several genes and pathways that could potentially be involved in differentiating tumor samples from normal. Overall, our results project LDA as a promising approach for classification of tissue types based on gene expression data in cancer studies.

KEYWORDS

Topic modeling, Latent Dirichlet Allocation, Clustering, Classification, Machine learning, Cancer, Gene expression

*These authors contributed equally to this work

Permission to make digital or hard copies of all or part of this work for personal or classroom use is granted without fee provided that copies are not made or distributed for profit or commercial advantage and that copies bear this notice and the full citation on the first page. Copyrights for components of this work owned by others than ACM must be honored. Abstracting with credit is permitted. To copy otherwise, or republish, to post on servers or to redistribute to lists, requires prior specific permission and/or a fee. Request permissions from permissions@acm.org.
ACM-BCB '17, August 20-23, 2017, Boston, MA, USA
© 2017 Association for Computing Machinery.
ACM ISBN 978-1-4503-4722-8/17/08...$15.00
https://doi.org/10.1145/3107411.3107483

1 INTRODUCTION

Traditional diagnosis for cancer is based on clinical and morphological data, but these methods have been reported to have limitations in their diagnostic ability. [1, 12]. To overcome the limitations, cancer detection based on genomic data has been proposed [17, 18]. In recent years, with the wide employment of microarray and next-generation sequencing methods, increase in data volume poses both promise and challenges to researchers in identifying patterns and analyzing the data [15]. Although there has been a lot of research in the identification of differentially expressed genes associated with various types of cancer tissues, typically small sample size and high dimensionality of expression data continues to pose challenges to researchers. Understanding and interpretation of results remains a key challenge in analyzing gene expression data.

Topic modeling, a machine learning approach has shown promise in the fields of text mining and image retrieval, where it has been successfully implemented to extract information from high dimensional data [6, 14, 24]. Latent Dirichlet Allocation (LDA) is one of the most popular topic modeling approaches in text mining among others like Latent Semantic Indexing (LSI) and Probabilistic Latent Semantic Analysis (PLSA) [9, 11]. Since its emergence, researchers have implemented this approach in biomedical text mining as well [4, 25].

Given the successful implementation of topic models in discovering the useful structure of the documents, researchers are beginning to implement topic modeling approaches to analyze data other than document collections [8, 27]. Recently, there have been efforts to use topic modeling techniques in the field of bioinformatics to perform unsupervised analysis and obtain insights into high-dimensional -omics data [13, 16, 22, 23]. To gain better understanding into cancer classification and gene identification from such data, in this paper, we focus on the class prediction of breast cancer and lung cancer based on gene expression data using topic modeling.

We approached this study in three phases (Figure 1). In the first phase, we employed LDA as a clustering application. LDA has been successfully applied as a clustering algorithm for gene expression data in the past [28]. Here, we confirmed that LDA-derived document clusters based on our rank-based data transformation technique show clear separation between cancer and healthy tissue samples. In the second phase, we investigated the application of LDA as a classification algorithm. This involved optimizing several algorithmic parameters including the number of topics and algorithm passes with respect to classification of gene expression data. We used 10-fold cross validation to estimate classification effectiveness. We compared our results with alternative machine learning techniques including Support Vector Machine (SVM), Naive Bayes and Random Forest classification, as well as Principal Component Analysis (PCA) and Hierarchical Clustering for unsupervised learning. In the third phase, we additionally investigated the effectiveness of LDA in identifying genes differentially regulated between cancer and normal tissues. We explored the degree to which specific topics identified by the LDA algorithm correspond to gene regulatory pathways which vary between tumor and normal tissues.

The remaining of this paper is organized as follows. In Section 2, we review the related work of implementing LDA in gene expression data. In Section 3, we describe data collection and preprocessing while in Section 4 we describe our proposed method, evaluation techniques, results from two data sets and interpretation of identified differentially expressed genes.

2 RELATED WORK

One of the challenges in using LDA for genetic studies is the nature of the data. The input of topic modeling is typically a simplified bag-of-words representation of a corpus. However, gene expression data is numerical in nature, and thus needs to be transformed into text to provide appropriate input for the LDA algorithm. The most commonly used transformation method is scaling the matrix and interpreting the discrete values as gene/word occurrences. The higher the expression value, the higher the frequency of the gene in the bag of words [3, 19]. One limitation using this approach is genes that have zero expression value will not be present in the training corpus. Consequently, this transformation approach is suitable for clustering and feature reduction, but not for classification because the test set might have genes that are unseen by the trained model.

More recently, Zhao et al. [28] used a different transformation method for generating a corpus. For each gene, expression values were normalized to 0 (lower than median) or 1 (higher than median). The samples were then transformed into a bag-of-words, containing only genes with normalized value 1. This transformation method does not capture the deviation between samples. That is, two differentially expressed genes are treated the same regardless of the degree of deviation. Besides, this method is not feasible for imbalanced dataset as the cutoff point between two different classes could not be represented by median value. Rogers et al. [22] used Latent Process Decomposition (LPD), a derivative of LDA, to capture the continuous nature of gene expression data. No significant difference in terms of accuracy has been reported using LPD compared to classical approaches like pLSA [3].

To alleviate these limitations and broaden the range of applications using LDA, we propose a novel transformation strategy to generate bag of words. We adapted the gene ranking method from Wang et al. [26], which is described in detail in Section 3.2. The rationale behind this ranking is that relative ordering of gene expression is generally stable in a particular type of normal human tissue but is widely disturbed in a diseased tissue. Ranking method is able to capture the degree of deviation of gene expression across different samples and still enable gene interpretability of topics using topic profiles.

3 METHODS

3.1 Data Collection and Filtering

We obtained the mRNA-Seq data of 229 breast invasive carcinoma samples and 98 lung squamous cell carcinoma samples from The Cancer Genome Atlas (TCGA) data portal [1]. We artificially balanced the data using only the tumor samples with matched normals. Out of 229 breast cancer samples, 117 represent primary solid tumor and 112 represent solid normal tissue. Of the 98 lung cancer samples, half of the data (49) represent primary solid tumor and the other half (49) represent solid tissue normal. Both datasets have 60483 variables with an abundance of zero values – roughly 45% of the datasets. Genes that have zero expression value in more than 10% of samples were removed. This filtering step might remove some differentially expressed genes but such stringent threshold was used to prevent any bias (multiple bins having genes with exclusively zero expression value) that might arise in the preprocessing step. After filtering, a total of 23424 genes remained in the breast cancer data and 23996 genes remained in the lung cancer data.

3.2 Preprocessing

Here, we used a ranking approach to transform gene expression values into a bag-of-words. Within each sample, genes were sorted in ascending order based on their expression values. Expression values form a distribution that is divided into 20 bins. The performance of the algorithm is robust against the bin size (5, 10, 20, 30, 40 bins) and this is expected since the number of bins represents the relative ranking of expression level instead of absolute ranking (data not shown).

We chose 20 bins as a representative of the performed experiments. Actual expression values were then replaced with a quantized value (expression rank) based on its position. Value 1 indicates the group with lowest expression level and value 20 indicates the group with highest expression level. The combination of each gene with its corresponding expression rank (separated by a hyphen), generated a bag of words for each sample. For example, if gene BRCA1 was found in quantized bin 3 for a particular sample, the bag-of-words associated with that sample would include the word BRAC1-3 to represent the ranked and quantized expression of this gene. It is important to note that as a result of quantization, comparison between gene and word may not be absolute since one gene might represent many words across the samples. To extract gene-specific information from the LDA-derived model, it is thus necessary to develop a technique to reverse this one-to-many mapping and trace back genes from the corresponding words without deviating much from the expression rank (Section 4.2). After the transformation, the breast cancer data corpus had 229 documents and 23424 words within each document. The lung cancer data corpus had 98 documents and each document contained 23996 words.

[1] https://portal.gdc.cancer.gov/

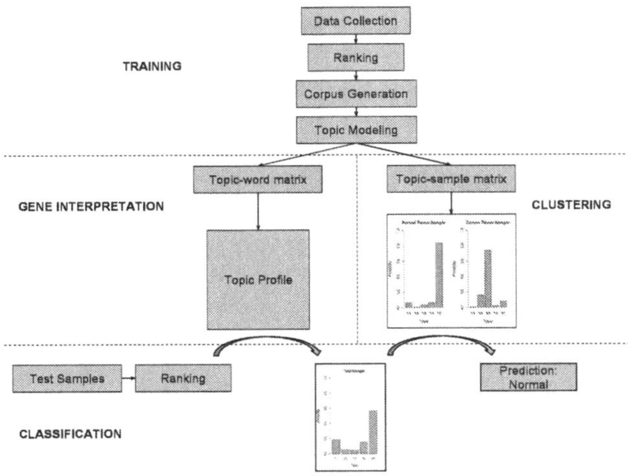

Figure 1: Flowchart of the proposed approach. Highlighted boxes represent the sequence of steps involved. Dashed lines divide the analysis into four groups: Training, Clustering, Classification and gene interpretation. Barplots represent the topic distribution of samples.

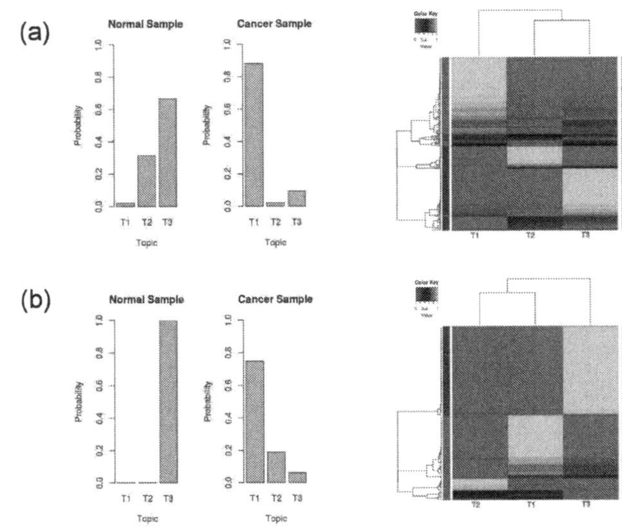

Figure 2: Topic probability distribution and Hierarchical clustering of samples using derived topic probability for (a) breast carcinoma and (b) lung squamous cell carcinoma. Bar plots represent average topic-sample probability for the 3 topics. Heat map shows the clustering of samples into two classes.

4 RESULTS AND ANALYSIS

For each dataset, LDA was implemented using an open-source Python library, Gensim [21]. The number of passes and number of topics were set to 10 and 3 respectively. These parameters were determined experimentally to provide the optimum performance (data not shown). The LDA algorithm produces two matrices: the topic-sample matrix, which expresses the computed probability of topics in a particular sample (document), and the topic-word matrix, containing the probability distribution over all available words for each topic. The LDA-derived matrices were utilized to perform analysis in 3 phases: clustering, classification and gene interpretation.

4.1 Clustering

Average topic distributions of samples from each class (normal and cancer) are depicted in Figure 2. This topic-sample matrix can be used for feature extraction/projection in a manner analogous to principal component analysis (PCA). Each column vector of the topic-sample matrix represents a single sample. There is one value in this vector for each topic, expressing the degree of association between the topic and the sample. Complete-linkage and euclidean-distance-based Hierarchical Clustering was applied on the topic-sample matrix to cluster the samples with similar probability distributions. The heatmap in Figure 2 shows that for both breast cancer and lung cancer data, samples were clearly grouped together into two classes, cancer and normal. Colors from red to green in the heatmap represent topic probabilities of the samples, ranging from 0 to 1.

The clustering result from LDA was compared with other conventional clustering and projection methods including hierarchical clustering and PCA. Hierarchical clustering was directly applied to the raw expression values for breast cancer (23424 genes) and lung cancer (23996 genes). PCA was first used to transform the original data into components that retain 90% of the variance. Hierarchical clustering was then applied on the transformed data. For both datasets, cluster purity and number of misclassified samples were calculated using Equation 1 to evaluate the clustering performance.

$$Purity = 1/N \sum_{i=0}^{k} max_j |c_i \cap t_j| \qquad (1)$$

Where N = number of data points, k = number of clusters, c_i = a cluster in K, t_j = classification that has the maximum count for cluster c_i.

Table 1 shows the clustering results of the three methods where the number of clusters (K) is fixed at 2, 3, and 4 clusters. Overall, LDA clusters align more closely to known cancer/healthy tissue labels than those obtained by PCA and Hierarchical Clustering. One advantage of LDA-based clustering for gene expression data may be its mutually non-exclusive assumption. Most non-fuzzy clustering approaches have a mutually exclusive/independence assumption that a sample/gene is restricted to only one cluster. This assumption might not be logical for gene expression data largely when a sample/gene share characteristics with more than one cluster (that is one gene can be involved in different pathways). Thus using LDA for clustering of gene data would reflect the complex interplay between genes and pathways and improve quality of the results.

Table 1: Clustering results of LDA-derived topic probabilities, PCA reduced features, and Hierarchical Clustering.

Method	K	Breast cancer		Lung cancer	
		No. of Misclassified Samples	Cluster Purity	No. of Misclassified Samples	Cluster Purity
Latent Dirichlet Allocation (LDA)	2	11	0.952	1	0.990
	3	11	0.952	1	0.990
	4	11	0.952	1	0.990
PCA	2	112	0.512	43	0.561
	3	112	0.512	43	0.561
	4	109	0.524	43	0.561
Hierarchical Clustering	2	112	0.511	48	0.510
	3	112	0.511	19	0.806
	4	112	0.511	15	0.847

4.2 Classification

In this section, we propose a novel approach to classification using LDA-based topic modeling, and explore the effectiveness of the proposed method in distinguishing gene expression patterns in breast and lung cancer tissues from those in healthy tissue. In contrast to the work by [3] where LDA is solely used as a feature extraction method and requires running LDA on both training and testing data, the approach proposed here applies the LDA algorithm only to the training data.

First, training of the LDA algorithm proceeds in the same manner as described previously for LDA-based clustering. For testing, LDA-derived topic-sample and topic-word matrices from the trained model are employed. To revert/collapse the genes from their corresponding words, expression rank and probabilities of all words representing a gene are taken and normalized over the entire probability distribution (Equation 2):

$$exp_g = \frac{\sum_{j=1}^{j} rank_g^j \times prob_g^j}{\sum_{j=1}^{j} prob_g^j} \tag{2}$$

where exp_g represents the collapsed expression rank of a gene g, j is the total number of words that representing gene g. $rank_g \in (rank_g^1, rank_g^2, ..., rank_g^j)$ is a vector of rank extracted from words and $prob_g \in (prob_g^1, prob_g^2, ..., prob_g^j)$ is the vector of corresponding probabilities for the words.

Combining the topic-word probabilities in this manner results in a new topic-gene matrix, in which each topic is associated with a specific rank value for each gene. The resulting topic profile facilitates subsequent classification.

To classify a test sample based on the trained LDA, we need to determine topic probability distribution of the test sample. First, the same pre-processing step described for clustering is applied to the test data, resulting in a bag-of-words based on ranked gene expression for each test sample. Then similarity (MSE) between testing data and each topic profile was calculated using Equation 3. The lower the MSE, the more similar the topic.

$$MSE = \sum_{g=1}^{g} (exp_g - bin_g)^2 \tag{3}$$

Where exp_g represents the collapsed expression rank of gene g in a topic profile and bin_g represents expression rank of gene g in test sample. Gaussian normalization was performed to reduce the range of the MSE, thus avoiding overflow errors in computation, without affecting the variation between topics and the softmax function (Equation 4) is applied to ensure that the probability distribution properly sums to 1.0 [5]. The probability distribution determined from similarity is used for prediction.

$$SoftmaxOutput = \frac{e^{sMSE}}{\sum_{k=1}^{k} e^{sMSE}} \tag{4}$$

The performance of our classification approach was compared with popular supervised methods including SVM, Naive Bayes and Random Forest classifiers using 10-fold cross validation. Traditional metrics for comparison like accuracy, precision, recall and F-measure were applied. As shown in Table 2, LDA achieves a competitive performance comparable to other algorithms.

4.3 Gene Interpretation

We utilized topic profiles from the two data sets to perform pathway analysis and disease annotation of differentially expressed genes within each topic. A list of differentially expressed genes (DEGs) is extracted by computing the difference in expression rank of each topic with a baseline.. For the experiments shown here, topic 3 was chosen as the baseline in both breast cancer and lung cancer datasets, since it shows the highest probability in normal samples (Figure 2). DEGs were then identified from all other topics (1 and 2 in this case). A threshold rank-difference of 5 was used to extract the significant genes and also limit the number of genes for further analysis. Thus, the extracted genes have at least 5 ranking changes between normal and tumor that could potentially represent significant dysregulation in our analysis.

We examined the pathway enrichment of the differentially expressed genes using DAVID Bioinformatics Resources 6.8 [2] [10] to explore the KEGG pathway database. Figures 3 and 4 show the number of genes and statistically enriched pathways in the topics for breast cancer and lung cancer, respectively.

The relevance of the identified differentially expressed genes was validated using the DAVID bioinformatics suite [10] and the

[2] https://david.ncifcrf.gov/home.jsp

Table 2: Classification results of our proposed approach and three supervised algorithms: SVM, Naive Bayes, and Random Forest.

	Breast cancer					Lung cancer			
	F-measure	Accuracy	Specificity	Sensitivity		F-measure	Accuracy	Specificity	Sensitivity
LDA	0.991	0.991	1.000	0.983	LDA	0.990	0.990	1.000	0.980
SVM	0.970	0.978	0.973	0.966	SVM	0.969	0.969	0.980	0.959
Naive Bayes	0.974	0.974	1.000	0.945	Naive Bayes	0.980	0.980	0.980	0.980
Random Forest	0.987	0.987	0.991	0.983	Random Forest	0.990	0.990	1.000	0.980

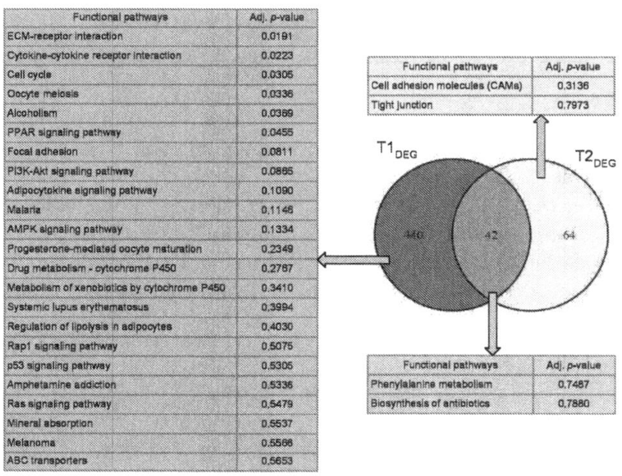

Figure 3: Functional annotation of dysregulated genes in breast cancer. Venn diagram of differentially expressed genes in Topic 1, in Topic 2 for breast cancer. Tables represent the affected pathways for each subset of genes, and their adjusted p-value. The lower the adjusted p-value, the higher the significance of pathway.

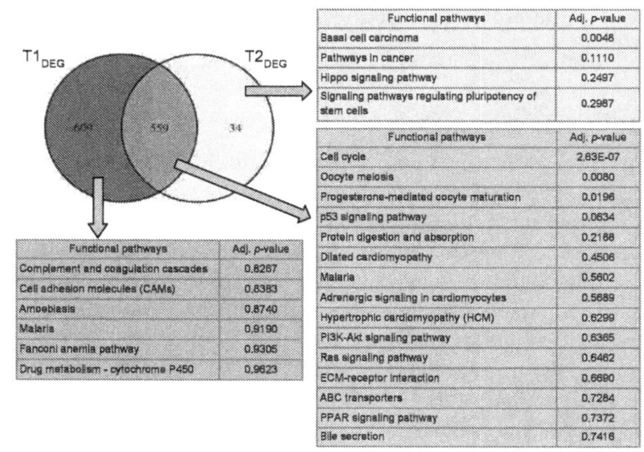

Figure 4: Functional annotation of dysregulated genes in lung cancer. Venn diagram of differentially expressed genes in Topic 1, in Topic 2 for Lung Cancer. Tables represent the affected pathways for each subset of genes, and their adjusted p-value. The lower the adjusted p-value, the higher the significance of the pathway.

NIH genetic association database (GAD) [2]. The DEGs were extracted by comparing the expression profile for normal and tumor samples. For each gene, its expression rank (exp_g) in topic profile matrix (~24000×3) was multiplied with respective topic probability distribution of normal group (3×1) and tumor group (3×1). This would generate two expression profiles: one for normal samples (~24000×1) and one for tumor samples (~24000×1). The difference in expression rank between these two profiles was computed. Top 250 DEGs was extracted both for breast cancer and lung cancer and annotated using DAVID Bioinformatics Resources 6.8 in terms of GAD disease. Table 3 shows the top 5 highly related diseases which are ranked ascendingly according to their adjusted p-value.

As expected, for the gene list extracted from breast cancer data corpus, 'breast cancer' is the disease with highest enrichment (lowest adjusted p-value) and for lung cancer data corpus, 'smoking cessation' and 'chronic obstructive pulmonary disease' are highly enriched.

Table 3: Top 5 annotated diseases, arranged in ascending order of adjusted p-value, from breast and lung cancer DEGs.

Breast Cancer	Adj. p-value	Lung Cancer	Adj. p-value
Breast cancer	2.7E-2	Cleft lip, cleft palate	3.7E-1
Alzheimer's disease	1.7E-1	Smoking cessation	4.0E-1
Chorioamnionitis	2.4E-1	Chronic obstructive pulmonary disease	9.2E-1
Colorectal cancer	3.6E-1	Breast cancer	9.5E-1
Lung cancer	4.3E-1	Leukemia, lymphocytic, chronic, B-cell	9.5E-1

5 DISCUSSION

Many approaches to diagnostic classification based on mRNA expression focus primarily on differential expression. The LDA-based approach described here differs in that the focus is primarily on co-expression. Just as textual LDA attempts to group co-occurring words into topics in order to explain the topic composition of a document, gene expression LDA can be used to identify co-regulated groups of genes that together explain the overall patterns of gene expression in healthy and disease states. In an unsupervised mode, this technique has shown a somewhat surprising ability to produce gene-collections (topics) that differ significantly between cancer and healthy tissues. Augmenting this technique with class labels results in an even more capable diagnostic classifier.

Here, our approach is only tested on gene expression data from next generation sequencing. Nevertheless, we expect it to work equally with similar data from different platforms or for different tasks such as disease subtype classification [7], survival analysis and treatment prognosis prediction [20]. We have shown that by using only gene expression data, the model was able to cluster the data into topics that are biologically coherent and meaningful. An interesting next step would be to include additional lifestyle and clinical metadata in the bag-of-words representing each sample. For example, by tagging clinical study data with labels such as smoker/non-smoker, male/female, adult/child, etc., associations between subject groups corresponding to these labels, disease state, and gene expression might further be identified. Understanding associated pathways and genomic etiology in these tasks is important in stratifying patients according to their risk and provide better diagnosis.

6 CONCLUSION

Overall our approach provides a novel direction for applying the LDA algorithm to identify and group differentially expressed genes between healthy and cancer tissues of various types. A novel technique for transformation of gene expression levels to words is presented and shown to be effective. Comparative evaluation of this approach with state-of-the-art pattern classification methods confirms the effectiveness of the proposed methodology. Differential gene expression patterns associated with lung and breast cancer were identified and validated as relevant using pathway analysis and the NIH's genetic association database. Next steps include testing the effectiveness of this LDA-based classification approach on genetic and epigenetic variation patterns and also testing the effectiveness of LDA as a supervised algorithm for the more complex problem of distinguishing among cancer subtypes.

ACKNOWLEDGMENTS

This work is partially funded by the Biomedical Sciences Ph.D. program at Wright State University.

REFERENCES

[1] F Azuaje. 1999. Interpretation of genome expression patterns: computational challenges and opportunities. *IEEE engineering in medicine and biology magazine: the quarterly magazine of the Engineering in Medicine & Biology Society* 19, 6 (1999), 119–119.
[2] Kevin G Becker, Kathleen C Barnes, Tiffani J Bright, and S Alex Wang. 2004. The genetic association database. *Nature genetics* 36, 5 (2004), 431–432.
[3] Manuele Bicego, Pietro Lovato, Barbara Oliboni, and Alessandro Perina. 2010. Expression microarray classification using topic models. In *Proceedings of the 2010 ACM Symposium on Applied Computing*. ACM, 1516–1520.
[4] Halil Bisgin, Zhichao Liu, Hong Fang, Xiaowei Xu, and Weida Tong. 2011. Mining FDA drug labels using an unsupervised learning technique-topic modeling. *BMC bioinformatics* 12, 10 (2011), S11.
[5] Christopher M Bishop. 2006. Pattern recognition. *Machine Learning* 128 (2006), 1–58.
[6] David M Blei and John D Lafferty. 2009. Topic models. *Text mining: classification, clustering, and applications* 10, 71 (2009), 34.
[7] Lars Bullinger, Konstanze Döhner, Eric Bair, Stefan Fröhling, Richard F Schlenk, Robert Tibshirani, Hartmut Döhner, and Jonathan R Pollack. 2004. Use of gene-expression profiling to identify prognostic subclasses in adult acute myeloid leukemia. *New England Journal of Medicine* 350, 16 (2004), 1605–1616.
[8] Xin Chen, Xiaohua Hu, Tze Yee Lim, Xiajiong Shen, EK Park, and Gail L Rosen. 2012. Exploiting the functional and taxonomic structure of genomic data by probabilistic topic modeling. *IEEE/ACM Transactions on Computational Biology and Bioinformatics (TCBB)* 9, 4 (2012), 980–991.
[9] Scott Deerwester, Susan T Dumais, George W Furnas, Thomas K Landauer, and Richard Harshman. 1990. Indexing by latent semantic analysis. *Journal of the American society for information science* 41, 6 (1990), 391.
[10] Glynn Dennis, Brad T Sherman, Douglas A Hosack, Jun Yang, Wei Gao, H Clifford Lane, and Richard A Lempicki. 2003. DAVID: database for annotation, visualization, and integrated discovery. *Genome biology* 4, 9 (2003), R60.
[11] Thomas Hofmann. 2001. Unsupervised learning by probabilistic latent semantic analysis. *Machine learning* 42, 1 (2001), 177–196.
[12] Halliday A Idikio. 2011. Human cancer classification: a systems biology-based model integrating morphology, cancer stem cells, proteomics, and genomics. *Journal of Cancer* 2, 1 (2011), 107–115.
[13] Lin Liu, Lin Tang, Wen Dong, Shaowen Yao, and Wei Zhou. 2016. An overview of topic modeling and its current applications in bioinformatics. *SpringerPlus* 5, 1 (2016), 1608.
[14] Wenhan Luo, Björn Stenger, Xiaowei Zhao, and Tae-Kyun Kim. 2015. Automatic Topic Discovery for Multi-Object Tracking.. In *AAAI*. 3820–3826.
[15] Vivien Marx. 2013. Biology: The big challenges of big data. *Nature* 498, 7453 (2013), 255–260.
[16] Tomonari Masada, Tsuyoshi Hamada, Yuichiro Shibata, and Kiyoshi Oguri. 2009. Bayesian multi-topic microarray analysis with hyperparameter reestimation. In *International Conference on Advanced Data Mining and Applications*. Springer, 253–264.
[17] Matthew Meyerson, Stacey Gabriel, and Gad Getz. 2010. Advances in understanding cancer genomes through second-generation sequencing. *Nature Reviews Genetics* 11, 10 (2010), 685–696.
[18] Iver Petersen. 2011. The morphological and molecular diagnosis of lung cancer. *Dtsch Arztebl Int* 108, 31-32 (2011), 525–531.
[19] Naruemon Pratanwanich and Pietro Lio. 2014. Exploring the complexity of pathway–drug relationships using latent Dirichlet allocation. *Computational biology and chemistry* 53 (2014), 144–152.
[20] Sridhar Ramaswamy, Ken N Ross, Eric S Lander, and Todd R Golub. 2003. A molecular signature of metastasis in primary solid tumors. *Nature genetics* 33, 1 (2003), 49–54.
[21] Radim Rehurek. 2008. Gensim. (2008).
[22] Simon Rogers, Mark Girolami, Colin Campbell, and Rainer Breitling. 2005. The latent process decomposition of cDNA microarray data sets. *IEEE/ACM transactions on computational biology and bioinformatics* 2, 2 (2005), 143–156.
[23] Janne Sinkkonen, Juuso Parkkinen, Janne Aukia, and Samuel Kaski. 2008. A simple infinite topic mixture for rich graphs and relational data. (2008).
[24] Min Song and Su Yeon Kim. 2013. Detecting the knowledge structure of bioinformatics by mining full-text collections. *Scientometrics* 96, 1 (2013), 183–201.
[25] Hongning Wang, Minlie Huang, and Xiaoyan Zhu. 2009. Extract interaction detection methods from the biological literature. *BMC bioinformatics* 10, 1 (2009), S55.
[26] Hongwei Wang, Qiang Sun, Wenyuan Zhao, Lishuang Qi, Yunyan Gu, Pengfei Li, Mengmeng Zhang, Yang Li, Shu-Lin Liu, and Zheng Guo. 2014. Individual-level analysis of differential expression of genes and pathways for personalized medicine. *Bioinformatics* (2014), btu522.
[27] Weizhong Zhao, James J Chen, Roger Perkins, Yuping Wang, Zhichao Liu, Huixiao Hong, Weida Tong, and Wen Zou. 2016. A novel procedure on next generation sequencing data analysis using text mining algorithm. *BMC bioinformatics* 17, 1 (2016), 1.
[28] Weizhong Zhao, Wen Zou, and James J Chen. 2014. Topic modeling for cluster analysis of large biological and medical datasets. *BMC bioinformatics* 15, 11 (2014), S11.

Differential Compound Prioritization via Bi-Directional Selectivity Push with Power

Junfeng Liu
Computer and Information Science, Indiana University - Purdue University Indianapolis
410 W. 10th St, HITS 5000
Indianapolis, Indiana 46202
liujunf@iupui.edu

Xia Ning
Computer and Information Science, Indiana University - Purdue University Indianapolis
410 W. 10th St, HITS 5011
Indianapolis, Indiana 46202
xning@iupui.edu

ABSTRACT

Effective *in silico* compound prioritization is critical to identify promising candidates in the early stages of drug discovery. Current methods typically focus on compound ranking based on one single property, for example, activity, against a single target. However, compound selectivity is also a key property that should be deliberated simultaneously so as to reduce the likelihood of undesired side effects of future drugs. In this paper, we present a novel machine-learning based differential compound prioritization method dCPPP. This dCPPP method learns compound prioritization models that rank active compounds well, and meanwhile, preferably rank selective compounds higher via a bi-directional push strategy. The bi-directional push is enhanced with push powers that are determined by ranking difference of selective compounds over multiple bioassays. Our experiments demonstrate that the dCPPP achieves an overall 19.221% improvement on prioritizing selective compounds over baseline models.

CCS CONCEPTS

• **Computing methodologies → Machine learning**; **Ranking**;
• **Applied computing → Bioinformatics**;

KEYWORDS

Prioritization/Ranking, Drug Discovery, Machine Learning

1 INTRODUCTION

Drug discovery is time-consuming and costly: it approximately takes at least 10 to 15 years and $500 million to $2 billion to fully develop a new drug [5]. To accelerate this process, *in silico* methods have been extensively developed as alternatives. *In silico* compound prioritization, which learns computational models to rank compounds in terms of their drug-like/disease-specific properties (e.g., efficacy, specificity), has been recently attracting increasing attention [3]. In this paper, we tackle the problem of differential compound prioritization for better ranking selective compounds.

Permission to make digital or hard copies of all or part of this work for personal or classroom use is granted without fee provided that copies are not made or distributed for profit or commercial advantage and that copies bear this notice and the full citation on the first page. Copyrights for components of this work owned by others than the author(s) must be honored. Abstracting with credit is permitted. To copy otherwise, or republish, to post on servers or to redistribute to lists, requires prior specific permission and/or a fee. Request permissions from permissions@acm.org.
ACM-BCB'17, August 20–23, 2017, Boston, MA, USA.
© 2017 Copyright held by the owner/author(s). Publication rights licensed to ACM.
ISBN 978-1-4503-4722-8/17/08...$15.00
DOI: http://dx.doi.org/10.1145/3107411.3107486

Current compound prioritization typically focuses on one single compound property [7], for example, biological activity. Biological activity of a compound can be initially tested in a target-specific bioassays by measuring whether the compound binds with high affinity to the protein target that it is aimed to affect. Activity is a critical property that a compound needs to exhibit in order to act efficaciously as a successful drug. Compound prioritization in terms of activity needs to rank most active compounds on top of less active compounds.

Compound selectivity is another key property that successful drugs need to exhibit [12]. Selectivity measures how a compound can differentially bind to only the target of interest with high affinity (i.e., high activity) while bind to other proteins with low affinities. Therefore, the compound selectivity prioritization needs to follow a combinatorial ranking criterion that 1). it ranks all the compounds well based on their activities; and meanwhile, 2). it ranks strongly selective compounds preferably higher, probably even higher than more active compounds that are not selective, in order to minimize the likelihood of undesirable side effectss of top drug candidates [10].

In this paper, we present an innovative machine learning method to conduct *in silico* compound prioritization that is able to achieve both the above goals, with a particular focus on better prioritizing selective compounds. This method consists of three components:

(1) A compound scoring function, which produces a score for each compound in a bioassay that will be used to rank the compound in the bioassay.
(2) An activity ranking model, which learns the compound scoring function and approximates the ranking structure among all compounds in a bioassay. The learning is via minimizing the pairwise ordering errors introduced by the scoring function.
(3) A bi-directional selectivity push strategy, which preferably pushes up selective compounds in the activity ranking model of a bioassay, and pushes down the compounds in the model that are selective in a different bioassay. This strategy leverages the ranking difference of selective compounds across multiple bioassays and alters the activity ranking by pushing selectivity-related compounds in two directions with specific powers.

These three components will be learned simultaneously within one optimization problem. This *d*ifferential *C*ompound *P*rioritization via bi-directional selectivity *P*ush with *P*ower method is denoted as dCPPP. Figure 1 presents the overall scheme of dCPPP. To the best of our knowledge, this is the first work in which the activity and selectivity are both tackled within one prioritization framework.

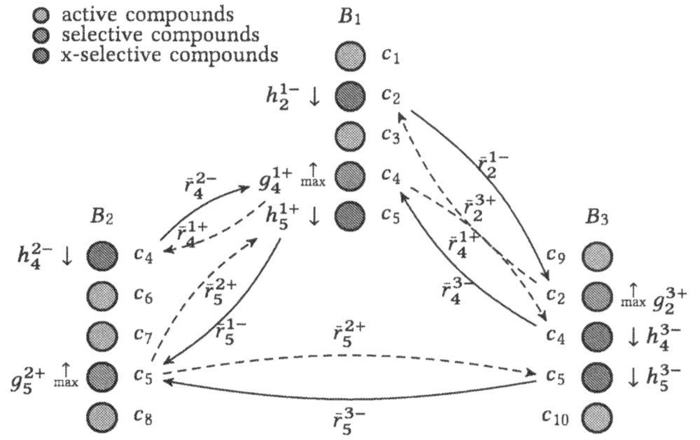

Figure 1: Overall scheme of dCPPP

Table 1: Notations

notations	meanings
$c/B/t$	compound/bioassay/target
c_i^{k+}/c_i^{k-}	selective/non-selective compound c_i in bioassay k (B_k)
$C_k/S_k/A_k/S_k^x$	all/selective/non-selective/x-selective compound set in B_k
$s_i^k/s_i^{k+}/s_i^{k-}$	score of $c_i/c_i^{k+}/c_i^{k-}$ in B_k
$r_i^k/r_i^{k+}/r_i^{k-}$	percentile ranking of $c_i/c_i^{k+}/c_i^{k-}$ in B_k
p_i^k	ranking position of c_i
R_i^{k+}/H_j^{k-}	reverse height of c_i^{k+}/ height of c_j^{k-}
g_i^{k+}/h_j^{k-}	push-up/push-down power for $c_i^{k+} \in S_k$/for $c_j^{k-} \in S_k$

2 RELATED WORK

2.1 *In Silico* Methods for Drug Discovery

A first step in drug discovery is to conduct bioassays that screen a large set of promising compounds. The outcomes from bioassays inform the following drug discovery steps. Classification and regression dominate the *in silico* methods in bioassay analysis, particularly in finding the relationship between the structures of chemical compounds and their bio-chemical properties, for example, Structure-Activity Relationship (SAR) and Structure-Selectivity Relationship (SSR). In these methods, compounds are typically represented by certain chemical fingerprints, for example, Extended Connectivity Fingerprints (ECFP)[1]. Compound activity and selectivity are used as a label/numerical target of the compounds. Popular methods include Support Vector Machines (SVM) [20], Bayesian matrix factorization [8], etc.

2.2 Structure-Activity-Relationship Modeling

A recent trend in SAR modeling is to leverage the information from multiple bioassays. In Ning *et al.* [15], the SAR classification methods first identify a set of targets related to the target of interest, and then employ various machine learning techniques (e.g., multi-task learning (MTL) [4]) to utilize activity information from these targets for a better SAR model. In Liu and Ning [13], assistance bioassays and assistance compounds are identified and incorporated intelligently to build models that can accurately prioritize active compounds in a bioassay. In the Target-Related Affinity Profiling method [6], the affinity profiles of compounds in a set of diverse bioassays are used as the fingerprints. These multi-assay based methods use multiple bioassays homogeneously and cannot utilize the differential signals for selectivity prioritization.

2.3 Structure-Selectivity-Relationship Modeling

Existing SSR methods include multi-step classification based approaches [19], in which compounds that are classified as active are further classified by a selectivity classifier; multi-class classification based approaches [21], in which compound activity and selectivity are considered as two classes in a common multi-class classifier; and multi-task based approaches [16], which incorporates both activity and selectivity models into one model to better differentiate activity and selectivity; etc. However, these methods cannot prioritize activity and selectivity simultaneously, or cannot leverage the prioritization structures among multiple bioassays to improve SSR modeling.

2.4 Learning to Rank

Learning to rank (LETOR) focuses on developing ranking models via learning, and has achieved tremendous success in information retrieval [14]. Existing LETOR methods fall into three categories: 1). pointwise methods, which learn individual scores that are used later for sorting; 2). pairwise methods, which model pairwise ranking relations; and 3). listwise methods, which model the full combinatorial structures of ranking lists [14]. A recent focus on LETOR is to improve the ranking performance on top of the ranking lists [1].

The idea of using LETOR approaches to prioritize compounds has also drawn some recent attention. For example, Agarwal *et al.* [2] developed bipartite ranking to well-separate active compounds from inactive ones in the ranking lists. However, LETOR for compound selectivity prioritization is still less developed.

3 DEFINITIONS AND NOTATIONS

A compound c is active in a bioassay B with protein target t if the IC_{50}[2] value of c for t is less than 1 μM. A compound c is selective in a bioassay B with protein target t if the following two conditions are satisfied [16]:

1). c is active for t; and 2). $\min_{\forall t_k \neq t} \frac{IC_{50}(c, t_k)}{IC_{50}(c, t)} \geq 50$.

In this paper, each bioassay has only one single protein target. Thus, activity/selectivity with respect to the bioassay and the target will be used interchangeably. A compound can be selective in at most one bioassay. A compound that is non-selective in a bioassay B_k but selective in another bioassay B_l is referred to as x-selective in B_k. Table 1 lists the notations that are used in this paper.

4 METHODS

4.1 Compound Scoring

In dCPPP, the compound prioritization uses a linear scoring function as follows,

$$\tilde{s}_i = \mathbf{w}^\top \mathbf{x}_i, \tag{1}$$

where $\mathbf{w}$ is a weight vector, $\mathbf{x}_i$ is the feature vector of the compound c_i, and $\tilde{s}_i$ is the score over compound c_i. Each compound in a

[1] Scitegic Inc, http://www.scitegic.com.

[2] https://www.ncbi.nlm.nih.gov/books/NBK91994/

bioassay is first scored using their features, and then ranked in a non-ascending order of their scores.

4.2 Activity Prioritization

The dCPPP method will produce a ranking of compounds in a bioassay that ranks compounds well based on their activities. That is, in general, active compounds will be ranked higher than less active ones. To quantitatively measure the activity ranking quality, we use a metric non-Concordance Index (denoted as nCI) as follows,

$$\text{nCI}(\{\tilde{s}_i^k\}, C_k) = \frac{1}{|\mathcal{P}_k|} \sum_{(c_i, c_j) \in \mathcal{P}_k} \mathbb{I}(\tilde{s}_i^k \leq \tilde{s}_j^k), \tag{2}$$

where $\mathcal{P}_k = \{c_i \succ c_j | c_i, c_j \in B_k\}$ is the set of all possible ordered compound pairs, $\mathbb{I}(x)$ is the indicator function ($\mathbb{I}(x)$ is 1 if x is true, 0 otherwise). In Equation 2, $c_i \succ c_j$ indicates that c_i is ranked higher than c_j in ground truth in B_k based on their IC_{50} values, $\tilde{s}_i^k \leq \tilde{s}_j^k$ indicates that compound c_i's predicted score is smaller than that of c_j, thus c_i is ranked lower than c_j.

Essentially, nCI represents the fraction of mis-ordered compound pairs by a certain ranking method. A lower nCI value indicates better ranking performance. Therefore, activity prioritization seeks a scoring function that can produce low nCI, and thus nCI over the predicted ranking is used as the loss for activity prioritization in dCPPP objective:

$$\mathcal{L}_c^k = \text{nCI}(\{\tilde{s}_i^k\}, C_k). \tag{3}$$

4.3 Bi-directional Selectivity Push with Power

To favor selective compounds in compound prioritization, two key questions need to be addressed. 1). how to enforce the selective compounds to go beyond the ordinary activity prioritization and get better ranked; and 2). how much the enforcement should be. To address the first question, we develop the bi-directional powered push scheme, which, for a target t, pushes t's selective compounds higher, and pushes t's x-selective compounds lower in compound ranking. To address the second question, we develop a scheme to determine push powers by comparing ranking difference of a compound in multiple bioassays.

4.3.1 Pushing up Selective Compounds. To push up selective compounds, dCPPP measures the ranking positions of selective compounds using their reverse height [2] and optimizes such positions.

Reverse height of a selective compound c_i^{k+} is the number of non-selective compounds ranked above c_i^{k+}, that is,

$$R_i^{k+} = R(c_i^{k+}) = \sum_{c_j \in A_k} \mathbb{I}(\tilde{s}_i^{k+} \leq \tilde{s}_j^{k-}), \tag{4}$$

where R_i^{k+} is the reverse height of c_i^{k+} in B_k, A_k is the set of non-selective compounds in B_k, and $\mathbb{I}(x)$ is the indicator function. Thus, to enforce higher ranking of selective compounds, it is to minimize the reverse heights of the selective compounds.

Push-up power for a selective compound c_i^{k+} decides how strongly c_i^{k+} should be pushed up in B_k, which depends on 1). how c_i is ranked in B_k; and 2). how c_i is ranked in other bioassays B_l's. Intuitively, if c_i is ranked high in B_l (i.e., c_i is very active but not selective to t_l), c_i should be pushed much higher in B_k and much lower in B_l. This is because c_i is very specific to t_k, and if c_i is selected for t_l, it will introduce low efficacy or side effects. Based on such intuition, we define the push-up power for c_i^{k+} as follows:

$$\begin{aligned} g_i^{k+} &= g(c_i^{k+}, B_k, \{B_l\} | \theta^{\uparrow}, \xi^{\uparrow}) \\ &= \exp\{\theta^{\uparrow}[(1 - \bar{r}_i^{k+}) + \max_{c_i \in A_l} \phi(\bar{r}_i^{l-}, \bar{r}_i^{k+} | \xi^{\uparrow})]\}, \end{aligned} \tag{5}$$

where $\theta^{\uparrow}$ is a parameter, and $\phi(x, y|\xi)$ is a thresholding function:

$$\phi(x, y|\xi) = (x - y + \xi)_+ = \max(x - y + \xi, 0) \tag{6}$$

In Equation 5, $\bar{r}_i^{k+}/\bar{r}_i^{l-}$ is the predicted percentile ranking of c_i in B_k/B_l from a respective baseline activity prioritization model, and $\xi^{\uparrow}$ is a thresholding parameter. Essentially, the push-up power considers if c_i^{k+} is ranked high enough in B_k (i.e., $1 - \bar{r}_i^{k+}$) and how differentially it is ranked in other bioassays (i.e., $\phi(\bar{r}_i^{l-}, \bar{r}_i^{k+} | \xi^{\uparrow})$). If the ranking positions of c_i^{k+} in B_k and other bioassays are not sufficiently different, the push-up power is exponentially large.

Selectivity Loss with Powered Push-up. To differentially push selective compounds up, we take the reverse heights of selective compounds enhanced by respective push-up powers in the dCPPP learning objective, that is,

$$\mathcal{L}_s^{k+} = \frac{1}{|S_k|} \sum_{c_i \in S_k} R_i^{k+} \cdot g_i^{k+}, \tag{7}$$

where $|S_k|$ is the size of S_k.

4.3.2 Pushing down x-Selective Compounds. To push down x-selective compounds, dCPPP measures the ranking positions of such x-selective compounds using their heights and optimize such positions.

Height of an x-selective compound c_j^{k-} is the number of compounds that are ranked below c_j^{k-}, that is,

$$H_j^{k-} = H(c_j^{k-}) = \sum_{c_i \in C_k} \mathbb{I}(\tilde{s}_i^k \leq \tilde{s}_j^{k-}) \tag{8}$$

where H_j^{k-} is the height of x-selective compound c_j^{k-} in B_k, C_k is the set of compounds in B_k, $\mathbb{I}(x)$ is the indicator function.

Push-down power for an x-selective compound c_j^{k-} determines how strongly c_j^{k-} should be pushed down in a bioassay B_k. We define the push-down power for c_j^{k-} in B_k as follows,

$$h_j^{k-} = h(c_j^{k-}, B_k, B_l | \theta^{\downarrow}, \xi^{\downarrow}) = \exp\{\theta^{\downarrow}[\bar{r}_j^{k-} + \phi(\bar{r}_j^{k-}, \bar{r}_j^{l+} | \xi^{\downarrow})]\} \tag{9}$$

where $\theta^{\downarrow}$ is a parameter, $\bar{r}_j^{k-}/\bar{r}_j^{l+}$ is the predicted percentile ranking of c_j from B_k's/B_l's baseline model ($c_j \in S_k^x, c_j \in S_l$). $\phi(\bar{r}_j^{k-}, \bar{r}_j^{l+} | \xi^{\downarrow})$ is thresholding function as defined in Equation 6, and $\xi^{\downarrow}$ is the thresholding parameter. Thus, if c_j is not ranked significantly higher in B_l than in B_k, the push-down power is large. Please note that c_j can be selective in only one bioassay, i.e., B_l. Therefore, only B_l is considered when pushing down c_j in B_k.

x-Selectivity Loss with Powered Push-down. To differentially push x-selective compounds down, we take the heights enhanced by their push-down powers in the dCPPP learning objective, that is,

$$\mathcal{L}_x^{k-} = \frac{1}{|S_k^x|} \sum_{c_j \in S_k^x} H_j^{k-} \cdot h_j^{k-}. \tag{10}$$

4.4 dCPPP Optimization Problem and Solutions

The overall optimization problem of dCPPP to learn a selectivity prioritization model (i.e., the scoring function as in Equation 1, parameterized by $\mathbf{w}$), which ranks selective compounds higher and x-selective compounds lower, is formulated as follows,

$$\min_{\mathbf{w}} \mathcal{L}^k = (1 - \alpha - \beta)\mathcal{L}_c^k + \alpha\mathcal{L}_s^{k+} + \beta\mathcal{L}_x^{k-}, \tag{11}$$

where α and β are two weighting parameters ($\alpha \in [0,1], \beta \in [0,1], \alpha + \beta \in [0,1]$). Thus, the dCPPP objective is a weighted combination of the loss on 1). activity prioritization ($\mathcal{L}_c^k$), 2). pushing up selective compounds ($\mathcal{L}_s^{k+}$), and 3). pushing down x-selective compounds ($\mathcal{L}_x^{k-}$). Since the indicator function is not continuous or smooth, we use the logistic loss as the surrogate function [18]:

$$\mathbb{I}(x \leq y) \approx \log[1 + \exp(-(x - y))]. \tag{12}$$

The surrogate function is continuous, smooth and differentiable. Thus, the loss $\mathcal{L}^k$ in Equation 11 with the surrogate function is differentiable, and thus we can use gradient descent methods to solve the optimization problem.

5 MATERIALS

5.1 Dataset

We constructed a set of bioassays from ChEMBL[3] following the protocol in Section 5.1.1 in order to have sufficient bioassays and sufficient active and selective compounds in each bioassay to reliably learn models. More details of the protocol are available online[4].

5.1.1 Dataset Generation. We first selected a set of 529 bioassays, denoted as $\mathcal{B}_s^{c_0}$, which are enriched with selective compounds, and meanwhile, the compound selectivity in these bioassays can be defined by other selected bioassays in $\mathcal{B}_s^{c_0}$. The bioassays in this initial set are all single-target binding bioassays and use IC_{50} to measure compound activities, and have at least 20 active compounds. Each compound in each of such bioassays has only one IC_{50} value. Among these 529 bioassays, 155 bioassays have more than 10 and less than 50 selective compounds. The $\mathcal{B}_s^{c_0}$ bioassays provide a closed space from which a subset of bioassays will be further constructed for the experiments.

The 529 $\mathcal{B}_s^{c_0}$ bioassays are further pruned in order to have reasonable number of compounds for dCPPP learning. After the pruning, all the bioassays retain all the selectivity related information (i.e., their own selective compounds and x-selective compounds), and have at around 100 compounds (if a bioasasy has more than 100 selective/x-selective compounds, all such compounds are retained). All the remaining bioassays and their compounds are used as the final dataset in our experiments. This set of pruned bioassays is denoted as $\mathcal{B}_s^c$.

5.1.2 Dataset Description. In the final dataset $\mathcal{B}_s^c$, 155 bioassays have $10 \sim 50$ selective compounds and less than 500 compounds in total. Note that if a bioassay in the final dataset has more than 100 compounds, these compounds have to be either selective compounds or x-selective compounds. Models with powered-push will be built for the set of these 155 bioassays, denoted as $\mathcal{B}_s^m$, and baseline models (i.e., without push) will be built for all the 529 $\mathcal{B}_s^c$ bioassays ($\mathcal{B}_s^m \subset \mathcal{B}_s^c$). Table 2 (the "before split" row) presents the data description for $\mathcal{B}_s^c$ and $\mathcal{B}_s^m$.

[3] https://www.ebi.ac.uk/chembl/, v.22_1, accessed on 12/08/2016)

[4] http://cs.iupui.edu/~liujunf/projects/selRank_2017/

Table 2: Dataset Description

	dataset	$\lvert\{B\}\rvert$	$\lvert\{c_i\}\rvert$	$\lvert C_k\rvert$	$\lvert A_k\rvert$	$\lvert S_k\rvert$	$\lvert S_k^x\rvert$
before split	$\mathcal{B}_s^c$	529	35,226	104.50	80.24	24.26	31.12
	$\mathcal{B}_s^m$	155	14,568	102.27	80.67	21.60	36.56
after split	$\mathcal{B}_s^m$	155	14,568	102.27	84.18	18.09	18.61

"{·}" represents a set. "| · |" represents the size of the corresponding set.

5.2 Compound Feature Generation

We used AFGen[5] to generate fingerprints from ChEMBL compound structures. Each dimension of the fingerprints represents a compound substructure, and the binary value at each dimension represents whether the corresponding substructure is present in the corresponding compound or not. For each bioassay, we calculated the pairwise Tanimoto similarity [22] of all its compounds, represented by the fingerprints, and used each row of the Tanimoto matrix as the feature representation of the corresponding compound, following the idea in [17]. Therefore, a same compound will have different features in different bioassays. This compound feature representation is unique compared to the existing compound fingerprint representations, and generated in a way that is dependent of computational tasks.

5.3 Experimental Protocol

We split each bioassay into five folds so that selective compounds are evenly split into the five folds. We conducted five-fold cross validation over the splits to evaluate the dCPPP performance. Note that once the data are split, the selectivity for any training compounds needs to be re-defined with respect to only the training (i.e., known) compounds of the bioassays. This is because that testing compounds are hold out as unknown compounds, and thus cannot be used to define selectivity. Similarly, the selectivity of the testing compounds (i.e., the ground-truth for performance evaluation) is also re-defined with respect to training data. In principle, the selectivity re-defined after data split will be different from that before data split. Table 2 (the "after split" row) presents the data description after the split. After the data split, all the 155 bioassays in $\mathcal{B}_s^m$ have selective compounds in at least one testing fold. The evaluation metrics are only calculated and averaged over testing folds which include selective compounds.

5.4 Evaluation Metrics

5.4.1 Reciprocal Selectivity Position Index (RSPI). Absolute ranking position is an important metric in compound prioritization. In real applications, typically, only the top few compounds will be of primary interest. Thus, we define a reciprocal selectivity position index, denoted as RSPI, to measure the average absolute reciprocal ranking positions of selective compounds in a ranking list:

$$\text{RSPI}(C_k) = \frac{1}{|S_k|} \sum_{c_i \in S_k} \frac{1}{\tilde{p}_i^k}, \tag{13}$$

where $\tilde{p}_i^k$ is the ranking position of a selective compound c_i in bioassay B_k predicted by a ranking model. The reciprocals are used to

[5] http://glaros.dtc.umn.edu/gkhome/afgen/overview

favor highly ranked compounds by up weighting the contribution of highly ranked selective compounds, and down weighting the contribution of lowly ranked selective compounds. Higher RSPI values indicate higher average absolute ranking positions for selective compounds and thus better performance of the ranking model.

5.4.2 Concordance Index (CI). Concordance Index (CI) is a popular metric that is used to evaluate the performance of ranking algorithms [9]. CI measures the fraction of correctly ordered pairs among all possible pairs and thus it is complementary to the nCI defined in Equation 2, that is,

$$\mathrm{CI}(C_k) = 1 - \mathrm{nCI}(C_k). \tag{14}$$

Higher CI values indicate better prediction overall (i.e., more concordant pairs are predicted correctly). In our experiments, we measure the CI values over all compounds C_k in a bioassay B_k. We also measure the CI values among only selective compounds S_k. In this case, the CI values are specifically denoted as CI and sCI, respectively.

6 EXPERIMENTAL RESULTS

In the results presented in this section, we use parameters $\theta^{\uparrow} = 0.5$ and $\theta^{\downarrow} = 0.5$. We tried combinations of various $\theta^{\uparrow}$ and $\theta^{\downarrow}$ values, and found that $\theta^{\uparrow} = 0.5$ and $\theta^{\downarrow} = 0.5$ give the best performance over all the evaluation metrics overall. The baseline model corresponds to dCPPP with ($\alpha = 0, \beta = 0$), that is, the standard ranking model without any push. The baseline model is denoted as dCPPP^0. If each bioassay uses its own optimal α and β values (i.e., the α and β value that together give the optimal RSPI performance for each bioassay), the corresponding optimal method is denoted as dCPPP*.

We also tried SVMRank [11] with Tanimoto kernel over AFGen features, and dCPPP over AFGen features as baselines. These two methods outperform dCPPP with tanimoto-similarity compound features at most by 4% but on average 8-fold slower. Thus, we use dCPPP over tanimoto-similarity compound features in the experiments.

6.1 Overall Performance

Table 3: Overall Performance Comparison

	RSPI	CI	sCI
dCPPP^0	0.411	0.635	0.506
dCPPP*	0.490	0.631	0.462
imprv (%)	19.221	-0.630	-8.696
best imprv (%)	95.463	1.724	38.523
p-value	8.10×10^{-23}	2.85×10^{-29}	1.12×10^{-32}

The column "RSPI", "CI" and "sCI" have the average RSPI, CI and sCI values. The row "dCPPP^0" has the average evaluations of dCPPP^0. The row "dCPPP*" has the average evaluations of dCPPP*. The row "imprv (%)" has the improvement of the average dCPPP* performance over the average dCPPP^0 performance. The row "best imprv (%)" has the average best improvement of dCPPP* over dCPPP^0 on each bioassay. The row "p-value" has the p-values comparing average results of dCPPP* and dCPPP^0.

Table 3 presents overall performance comparison between the dCPPP^0 and the optimal dCPPP* methods. For each bioassay, its optimal dCPPP* is the one which yields the best RSPI value, and its dCPPP^0 is the one that has the best RSPI value (and thus not the one that has the best CI due to different learning rates). Table 3 shows that on average, dCPPP* outperforms dCPPP^0 on RSPI significantly. The results demonstrate the superiority of the dCPPP method in prioritizing selective compounds.

6.2 Selective Compound Prioritization

Figure 2 presents the results of dCPPP in terms of RSPI over various α and β values (i.e., the parameters to weight the push-up and push-down terms, respectively, in dCPPP Equation 11). The values in these figures are the average respective evaluation metric values over all the bioassays in which both push-up for selective compounds and push-down for x-selective compounds are applied (i.e., bioassays in dataset $\mathcal{B}_s^m$).

Figure 2 presents the RSPI values of all the $\mathcal{B}_s^m$ bioassays. the best RSPI performance of dCPPP (RSPI = 0.458) is achieved at the parameter region $\alpha \in [0.4, 0.6], \beta \in [0.2, 0.4]$, that is, when both the push-up and push-down are applied, the selective compounds are most effectively to be ranked higher in the bioassays.

In particular, when α is increased from 0 (i.e., the push-up starts to take place), the RSPI values are significantly increased. This demonstrates the effectiveness of the push-up strategy in ranking selective compounds on top. However, the full-power push-up (i.e., $\alpha = 1.0$ and thus no ranking performance over non-selective compounds are considered in Equation 11) does not lead to optimal performance. This indicates that the prioritization of selective compounds over non-selective compounds is structurally constrained by the ordering among both selective and non-selective compounds together, and leveraging the information from non-selective compounds and their ordering structures is beneficial in improving selective compound prioritization.

On the other hand, push-down of x-selective compounds turns out to also have effects on prioritizing selective compounds. For example, ($\alpha = 0.4, \beta = 0.2$) (RSPI = 0.458) increases the RSPI performance over ($\alpha = 0.4, \beta = 0.0$) (RSPI = 0.453) in Figure 2. This may be due to the fact that the push-down exerts extra force on altering the overall ranking structures and thus better separates selective compounds from x-selective compounds. However, an over push-down (e.g., $\beta \geq 0.6$ with $\alpha = 0.4$) does not benefit selective prioritization any more. The reason could be that an overemphasis on x-selective becomes detrimental to the overall ranking structures among both selective and non-selective compounds.

For all the bioassays, we compared their RSPI values of dCPPP with ($\alpha = 0.4, \beta = 0.2$) with the respective values of dCPPP^0. The paired t-tests demonstrate the significance of the improvement from dCPPP on dCPPP^0 (p-values 2.11×10^{-25}).

6.3 Compound Ranking

Figure 3 and 4 present the CI values among all compounds and sCI among selective compounds over all the bioassays, respectively. In Figure 3, as α and β increase, the CI values decrease in general. This is anticipated as increasing α and β values will induce less emphasis on overall ranking structures as in Equation 11. However, dCPPP with ($\alpha = 0.2, \beta = 0.0$) slightly increases CI (CI = 0.636) from dCPPP^0 (CI = 0.635). This may be due to the fact that pushing up selective compounds may affect the ranking on other non-selective compounds and thus increase CI.

In Figure 4, the sCI performance among only selective compounds changes relatively irregularly. Specifically, with $\alpha \in [0.4, 0.6]$

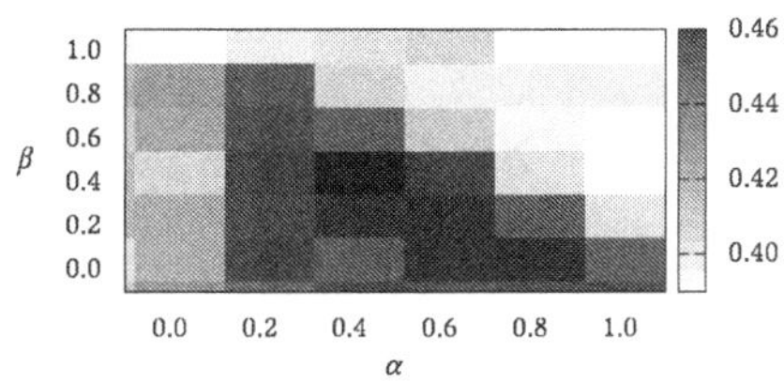

Figure 2: RSPI evaluation

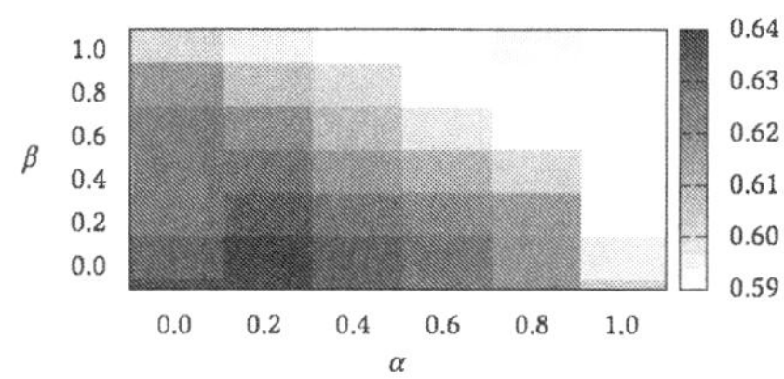

Figure 3: CI evaluation

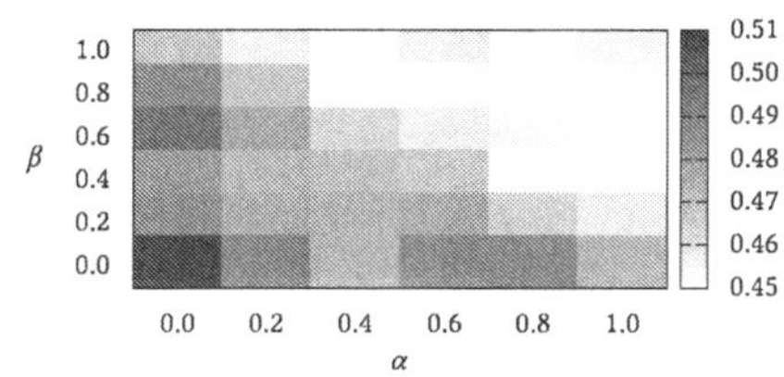

Figure 4: sCI evaluation

and $\beta \in [0.2, 0.4]$ (i.e., the optimal parameter region in which RSPI achieves the best), sCI is even below 0.5 (random ranking). This is because the selective compounds may be pushed into discordant orders compared to the ground truth. Note that the push-up power (Equation 5) is defined based on the difference of percentile rankings of a compound in multiple bioassays. Therefore, different selective compounds may receive different push powers within a bioassay due to their ranking positions among others bioassays. Together with the combinatorial influence from multiple x-selective compounds pushed-down at same time in the same bioassay, it is less likely that the selective compounds are pushed up but still in their original orders as before the push.

7 CONCLUSIONS

In this paper, we have developed a machine learning method dCPPP. In dCPPP, activity and selectivity prioritization are both tackled within one differential optimization model that involves collaborative information from multiple bioassays. A bi-directional powered push strategy is implemented in dCPPP, which pushes selective compounds up and x-selective compounds down in ranking. We have also conducted a comprehensive set of experiments and analysis on the ranking performance of dCPPP. Our experiments demonstrate that dCPPP is very effective in prioritizing selective compounds while maintaining a good activity ranking.

ACKNOWLEDGMENTS

This material is based upon work supported by the National Science Foundation under Grant Number IIS-1566219 and IIS-1622526. Any opinions, findings, and conclusions or recommendations expressed in this material are those of the author(s) and do not necessarily reflect the views of the National Science Foundation.

REFERENCES

[1] Shivani Agarwal. 2011. *The Infinite Push: A new Support Vector Ranking Algorithm that Directly Optimizes Accuracy at the Absolute Top of the List.* 839–850.

[2] Shivani Agarwal, Deepak Dugar, and Shiladitya Sengupta. 2010. Ranking Chemical Structures for Drug Discovery: A New Machine Learning Approach. *Journal of Chemical Information and Modeling* 50, 5 (2010), 716–731. DOI: https://doi.org/10.1021/ci9003865 arXiv:http://dx.doi.org/10.1021/ci9003865 PMID: 20387860.

[3] Euan A. Ashley. 2016. Towards precision medicine. *Nature Reviews Genetics* 17, 9 (16 Aug. 2016), 507–522. DOI: https://doi.org/10.1038/nrg.2016.86

[4] Rich Caruana. 1997. Multitask Learning. *Machine Learning* 28, 1 (1997), 41–75. DOI: https://doi.org/10.1023/A:1007379606734

[5] Joseph A DiMasi, Ronald W Hansen, and Henry G Grabowski. 2003. The price of innovation: new estimates of drug development costs. *Journal of Health Economics* 22, 2 (2003), 151 – 185. DOI: https://doi.org/10.1016/S0167-6296(02)00126-1

[6] S. L. Dixon and H. O. Villar. 1998. Bioactive diversity and screening library selection via affinity fingerprinting. *J Chem Inf Comput Sci* 38, 6 (1998), 1192–1203.

[7] Hanna Geppert, Martin Vogt, and Jürgen Bajorath. 2010. Current Trends in Ligand-Based Virtual Screening: Molecular Representations, Data Mining Methods, New Application Areas, and Performance Evaluation. *Journal of Chemical Information and Modeling* 50, 2 (2010), 205–216. DOI: https://doi.org/10.1021/ci900419k PMID: 20088575.

[8] Mehmet Gönen and Samuel Kaski. 2014. Kernelized Bayesian Matrix Factorization. *IEEE Trans. Pattern Anal. Mach. Intell.* 36, 10 (2014), 2047–2060. DOI: https://doi.org/10.1109/TPAMI.2014.2313125

[9] FRANK E. HARRELL, KERRY L. LEE, and DANIEL B. MARK. 1996. MULTIVARIABLE PROGNOSTIC MODELS: ISSUES IN DEVELOPING MODELS, EVALUATING ASSUMPTIONS AND ADEQUACY, AND MEASURING AND REDUCING ERRORS. *Statistics in Medicine* 15, 4 (1996), 361–387. DOI: https://doi.org/10.1002/(SICI)1097-0258(19960229)15:4<361::AID-SIM168>3.0.CO;2-4

[10] Ye Hu, Disha Gupta-Ostermann, and Jürgen Bajorath. 2014. Exploring compound promiscuity patterns and multi-target activity spaces. *Computational and structural biotechnology journal* 9, 13 (2014), 1–11.

[11] Thorsten Joachims. 2002. Optimizing Search Engines Using Clickthrough Data. In *Proceedings of the Eighth ACM SIGKDD International Conference on Knowledge Discovery and Data Mining (KDD '02)*. ACM, New York, NY, USA, 133–142. DOI: https://doi.org/10.1145/775047.775067

[12] Mazen W Karaman, Sanna Herrgard, Daniel K Treiber, Paul Gallant, Corey E Atteridge, Brian T Campbell, Katrina W Chan, Pietro Ciceri, Mindy I Davis, Philip T Edeen, and others. 2008. A quantitative analysis of kinase inhibitor selectivity. *Nature biotechnology* 26, 1 (2008), 127–132.

[13] Junfeng Liu and Xia Ning. 2017. Multi-Assay-based Compound Prioritization via Assistance Utilization: a Machine Learning Framework. *Journal of Chemical Information and Modeling* 57, 3 (2017), 484–498.

[14] Tie-Yan Liu. 2009. Learning to Rank for Information Retrieval. *Found. Trends Inf. Retr.* 3, 3 (March 2009), 225–331. DOI: https://doi.org/10.1561/1500000016

[15] Xia Ning, Huzefa Rangwala, and George Karypis. 2009. Multi-assay-based structure- activity relationship models: improving structure- activity relationship models by incorporating activity information from related targets. *Journal of chemical information and modeling* 49, 11 (2009), 2444–2456.

[16] Xia Ning, Michael Walters, and George Karypis. 2012. Improved Machine Learning Models for Predicting Selective Compounds. *Journal of Chemical Information and Modeling* 52, 1 (2012), 38–50. DOI: https://doi.org/10.1021/ci200346b arXiv:http://dx.doi.org/10.1021/ci200346b PMID: 22107358.

[17] Qichao Que and Mikhail Belkin. 2016. Back to the future: Radial basis function networks revisited. In *Proceedings of the 19th International Conference on Artificial Intelligence and Statistics*. 1375–1383.

[18] Cynthia Rudin. 2009. The P-Norm Push: A Simple Convex Ranking Algorithm That Concentrates at the Top of the List. *J. Mach. Learn. Res.* 10 (Dec. 2009), 2233–2271. http://dl.acm.org/citation.cfm?id=1577069.1755861

[19] Dagmar Stumpfe, Hanna Geppert, and Jürgen Bajorath. 2008. Methods for Computer-Aided Chemical Biology. Part 3: Analysis of Structure-Selectivity Relationships through Single-or Dual-Step Selectivity Searching and Bayesian Classification. *Chemical biology & drug design* 71, 6 (2008), 518–528.

[20] AnneMai Wassermann, Hanna Geppert, and Jurgen Bajorath. 2011. Application of Support Vector Machine-Based Ranking Strategies to Search for Target-Selective Compounds. In *Chemoinformatics and Computational Chemical Biology*, JÃijrgen Bajorath (Ed.). Methods in Molecular Biology, Vol. 672. Humana Press, 517–530. DOI: https://doi.org/10.1007/978-1-60761-839-3_21

[21] Anne Mai Wassermann, Hanna Geppert, and JÃijrgen Bajorath. 2009. Searching for Target-Selective Compounds Using Different Combinations of Multiclass Support Vector Machine Ranking Methods, Kernel Functions, and Fingerprint Descriptors. *Journal of Chemical Information and Modeling* 49, 3 (2009), 582–592. DOI: https://doi.org/10.1021/ci800441c arXiv:http://dx.doi.org/10.1021/ci800441c PMID: 19249858.

[22] Peter Willett, John M. Barnard, and Geoffrey M. Downs. 1998. Chemical Similarity Searching. *Journal of Chemical Information and Computer Sciences* 38, 6 (1998), 983–996. DOI: https://doi.org/10.1021/ci9800211

Understanding Sequence Conservation With Deep Learning

Yi Li
Dept of Computer Science, University of California, Irvine
Irvine, California 92697
yil8@uci.edu

Daniel Quang
Dept of Computer Science, University of California, Irvine
Irvine, California 92697
dxquang@uci.edu

Xiaohui Xie
Dept of Computer Science, University of California, Irvine
Irvine, California 92697
xhx@ics.uci.edu

ABSTRACT

Comparative genomics has been a powerful tool for identifying functional elements in the human genome. Millions of conserved elements have been discovered. However, understanding the functional roles of these elements still remain a challenge, especially in noncoding regions. In particular, it is still unclear why these elements are evolutionarily conserved and what kind of functional elements are encoded within these sequences. We present a deep learning framework, DeepCons, to further understand potential functional elements within conserved sequences. DeepCons is a convolutional neural net (CNN) that receives a short segment of DNA sequence as input and outputs the probability of the sequence of being evolutionary conserved. The CNN model utilizes hundreds of convolution kernels, which are analogous to sequence motifs, to extract features from DNA sequences during the training process. First, we train the model to discriminate 887,577 conserved elements from a matched number of nonconserved elements in the human genome. Then, we use visualization techniques to interpret how the model discriminates between the two classes of sequences, which provides indirect clues to the functional roles of conserved elements. Some kernels significantly match well-known regulatory motifs corresponding to transcription factors. Many kernels show positional biases relative to transcription start sites or transcription end sites. Most of the kernels do not correspond to any known functional element, suggesting that they might represent unknown categories of functional elements. We also utilize DeepCons to annotate how changes at individual nucleotides impact the conservation properties of the surrounding sequences, thereby providing an annotation of conserved sequences at an individual nucleotide level. The source code of DeepCons is publicly available at https://github.com/uci-cbcl/DeepCons.

KEYWORDS

Conserved Elements, Deep Learning, Regulatory Motifs

Permission to make digital or hard copies of all or part of this work for personal or classroom use is granted without fee provided that copies are not made or distributed for profit or commercial advantage and that copies bear this notice and the full citation on the first page. Copyrights for components of this work owned by others than ACM must be honored. Abstracting with credit is permitted. To copy otherwise, or republish, to post on servers or to redistribute to lists, requires prior specific permission and/or a fee. Request permissions from permissions@acm.org.
ACM-BCB '17, August 20-23, 2017, Boston, MA, USA
© 2017 Association for Computing Machinery.
ACM ISBN 978-1-4503-4722-8/17/08...$15.00
https://doi.org/10.1145/3107411.3107425

ACM Reference format:
Yi Li, Daniel Quang, and Xiaohui Xie. 2017. Understanding Sequence Conservation With Deep Learning. In *Proceedings of ACM-BCB '17, Boston, MA, USA, August 20-23, 2017,* 7 pages.
https://doi.org/10.1145/3107411.3107425

1 INTRODUCTION

Comparative genomics studies have shown that many sequence elements in the human genome are conserved across mammalian genomes. Many of these sequence elements lie in noncoding regions of the genomes. Some of these conserved sequences exhibit few nucleotide changes throughout millions of years mammalian evolution, suggesting strong purifying selection within these sequences [8, 28]. Studies based on human and rodent genomes estimate that about 5% bases of mammalian genomes are under negative selection, among which coding regions only account for 1.5% of the genome [28]. Previous studies and methods have focused on understanding the functional roles of conserved noncoding sequences. Nevertheless, the exact function of conserved non-coding sequences remains elusive.

Recent advances in deep learning [19] provide a new powerful method to study sequence conservation. Deep learning refers to algorithms that learn a hierarchical nonlinear representation of large datasets through multiple layers of abstraction (e.g. convolutional neural networks, multi-layer feedforward neural networks, and recurrent neural networks). It has achieved state-of-the-art performances on several machine learning applications such as speech recognition [12], natural language processing [30], and computer vision [18]. More recently, deep learning methods have also been adapted to solve genomics problems such as motif discovery [2, 24, 36], pathogenic variants identification [23], and gene expression inference [7].

In this paper we present a deep learning method for studying sequence conservation (DeepCons). DeepCons is a convolutional neural network trained to discriminate between conserved and non-conserved DNA sequences. One of the greatest strengths of neural networks is their ability to efficiently extract useful features from large datasets. Since conserved sequences are thought to be enriched for "functional" sequences relative to non-conserved sequences, by extension the neural network should also be learning features that differentiate functional sequence from non-functional sequences. After training, we can interpret the extracted features the model deems useful for predictions, thereby allowing us to indirectly draw insights into the functional role of individual conserved sequences.

2 METHODS

2.1 DeepCons

DeepCons is a convolutional neural network [19] composed of one input layer, three hidden layers and one output layer. The terminology we use here is very similar to the terminology used in previous genomics convolutional neural network methods, which include DeepsEA [36], DeepBind [2], Basset [16], and DanQ [24], and we direct readers to these methods for further reference. For a given DNA sequence x_i, DeepCons computes a probability $\hat{y}_i$ that measures the likelihood of x_i being conserved through five layers of transformation:

$$\hat{y}_i = \text{SIGMOID}_5(\text{DENSE}_4(\text{POOL}_3(\text{CONV}_2(\text{ONEHOT}_1(x_i))))) \quad (1)$$

The first input layer uses one hot encoding to represent each input DNA sequence as a 4-row binary matrix, with the number of columns equal to the length of the sequence. The second layer is a convolution layer composed of 1,000 length-10 and 500 length-20 convolution kernels with rectified linear units as the activation function. Each convolution kernel acts as a motif detector that scans across the length of a DNA sequence and produces different strengths of signals that are correlated to the underlying sequence patterns. To account for strandedness, each convolutional kernel also scans across each sequence's reverse complement. Different lengths of convolution kernels were combined to detect different lengths of motifs. The third layer is a global max pooling layer that takes the maximum output signals of each convolution kernel along the whole sequence and its respective reverse complement, producing a single score for each kernel representing the best motif match. The fourth layer is a fully connected dense layer of 1,500 hidden rectified linear units. The last layer applies a non-linear sigmoid transformation to produce a value between 0 and 1 that represents the probability of a sequence being conserved. DeepCons contains ~2.3 million parameters. Most of these parameters correspond to the edges connecting the max pooling and dense layers. Parameters are initialized with the Glorot uniform initializing algorithm [10].

Figure 1 shows the neural network architecture of DeepCons. With the ground truth label y_i of sequence x_i, cross-entropy is then used to calculate the loss:

$$\text{loss}_i = -(y_i log\hat{y}_i + (1 - y_i) log(1 - \hat{y}_i)) \quad (2)$$

DeepCons was trained using the standard back-propagation algorithm [26]. Parameters were iteratively updated with the Adagrad algorithm [9] using a mini-batch size of 128. Dropout [31] was used to perform model averaging and regularization. 25% dropout was applied to the convolutional layer and 50% dropout was applied to the fully connected dense layer. Model training was scheduled for 100 epochs but may early stop if the validation loss did not decrease for 10 epochs.

DeepCons is implemented with the Keras http://keras.io/ library using the Theano [5] backend. Training was performed on an Nvidia GTX TITAN Z graphics card. DeepCons is publicly available at https://github.com/uci-cbcl/DeepCons.

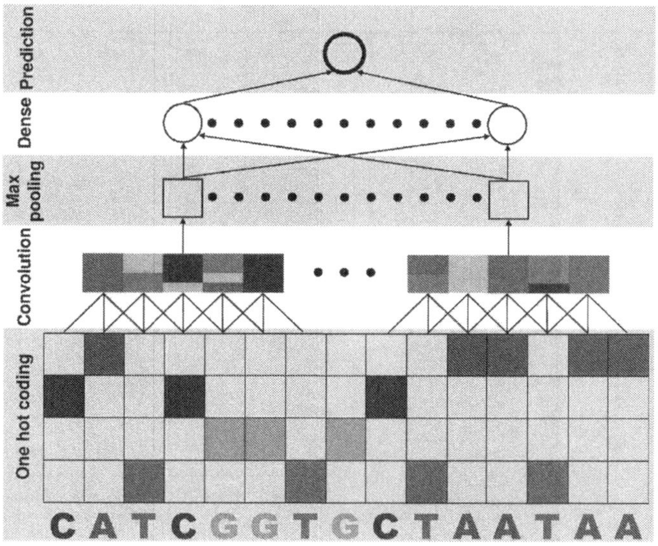

Figure 1: The neural network architecture of DeepCons.

2.2 Logistic regression

We also trained a baseline model using logistic regression (LR) for benchmarking purposes. Instead of using raw sequences as inputs, we first computed the counts of different k-mers of length 1-5 bp [24]. We then normalized the counts by subtracting the mean and dividing by the standard deviation and used these values as features. We also added a small L2 regularization of $1e$-6 to the cross entropy loss function of LR during training. LR was implemented with the scikit-learn [21] library.

3 RESULTS

3.1 Classifying conserved and non-conserved sequences

We first show that DeepCons can accurately discriminate between conserved and non-conserved sequences. To build the dataset of conserved sequences, we downloaded the 46-way phastCons conserved elements [28] under the mammal category from UCSC genome browser [14] based on the hg19 build of the human genome. The original conserved sequenced were further extended 5 bp on each end, and overlapping elements after extension were merged into one element. We excluded conserved sequences that overlap with repetitive sequences (http://www.repeatmasker.org/) or coding exons. We then filtered away conserved sequences that were either shorter than 30 bp or longer than 1,000 bp, leaving 887,577 sequences in the end. 75% of the nucleotides were preserved after the length filtering. To build the dataset of non-conserved sequences, we randomly sampled, without replacement, 887,577 sequences on hg19 using the bedTools shuffleBed utility [25], making sure to exclude repetitive sequences, coding exons and conserved sequences. We also ensured that both the conserved and non-conserved sequence sets share the same sequence length distribution. Each sequence is padded with capital N's to the maximum length of

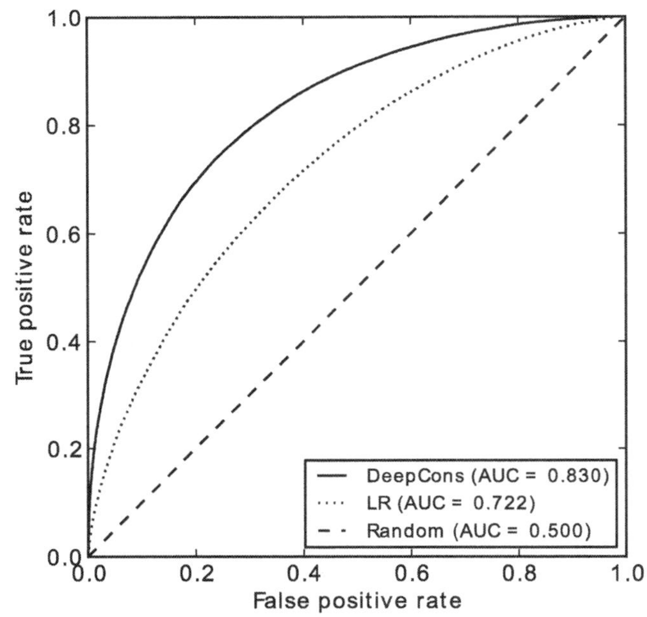

Figure 2: The receiver operating characteristic (ROC) curves of DeepCons and LR on classifying conserved and non-conserved sequences on the testing dataset.

1,000 bp. We randomly set aside ~80% for training (1,415,154 sequences), ~10% for validation (180,000 sequences) and ~10% for testing (180,000 sequences).

DeepCons achieved an accuracy of 74.9% and an area under the ROC curve (auROC) of 0.830 on the testing dataset. In comparison, the baseline LR model achieved an accuracy of 65.9% and an auROC of 0.722 on the testing dataset. Figure 2 shows the ROC of both methods on the testing dataset. DeepCons outperforms the baseline LR model significantly on classifying conserved and non-conserved sequences.

3.2 Known motifs

Previous results have shown that regulatory motifs are widely distributed within conserved noncoding elements across the human genome, such as the CTCF and the RFX family [34]. We observed similar results when examining the learned convolution kernels of DeepCons. Specifically, we converted the kernels from the convolution layer to position weight matrices, using the method described in DeepBind [2]. As a resource to the community, the position weight matrices are conveniently packaged together in minimal MEME format [3] in the DeepCons github repository. Then, we aligned these kernels to known motifs from the JASPAR database [20] using TOMTOM [11]. Of the 1,500 total kernels in the model, 69 kernels match known motifs significantly ($E < 10^{-2}$), including the CTCF and RFX families. The remaining kernels likely correspond to low level features, such as dinucleotide repeats [35], or motifs that lack proper matches in current databases. Figure 3 shows four examples of identified known motifs.

3.3 Positional bias

We observed that many of the convolution kernels display positional bias relative to TSS, TES and miRNA. Specifically, we downloaded RefSeq gene models[22] and obtained 4,000 bp sequences centered on the TSS or the TES of each gene. Then, we used CentriMo [4] to assess the positional bias of each kernel relative to TSS and TES. 264 and 779 kernels have significant ($E < 1e-5$) positional bias relative to TSS and TES, respectively, indicating these kernels have potential roles in transcriptional control and post-transcriptional regulation. Figure 4 shows the positional distributions of the top four biased kernels relative to TSS and TES. We note that the well known polyadenylation signal AATAAA and its reverse complement TTTATT are among the top four positional biased kernels relative to TES. These results are consistent with previous studies that reported motifs derived from conserved sequences display positional biases relative to TSS and TES [33].

In addition to positional biases relative to TSS and TES, we also observed several kernels have positional biases relative to miRNA. We downloaded all 1,881 human hairpin miRNA from miRBase [17] and used CentriMo [4] to test the positional bias of each kernel motif relative to miRNA. 122 kernels display significant ($E < 1e-5$) positional bias relative to the first 10 positions of miRNA. Previous studies have also reported that 95% of 8-mers discovered in conserved sequences match the first 10 positions of miRNA [33].

3.4 Strand bias

In addition to positional bias, we also observed the convolution kernels that are close to TES display strand bias. Specifically, for each of the top 100 positionally biased kernels relative to TSS and TES, we looked at the strand of the genes that the kernel is close to. Figure 5 shows the fractions of forward strand genes for each kernel. We found the fractions of forward strand genes is tightly distributed around 0.5 for kernels that positional biased to TSS, while the fractions significantly deviate from 0.5 for kernels that are positional biased to TES, suggesting those kernels also have strand bias and their RNA level regulatory effects.

3.5 Scoring sequences at nucleotide level resolution

Next, we sought to find out how the output of DeepCons depends on each individual nucleotide of the input sequence. For this purpose, we adopted saliency maps [27, 29]. Saliency maps are often used in image recognition tasks to highlight the relevancy of individual pixels to final predictions. In the context of conservation prediction, saliency maps may highlight transcription factor binding sites at single-nucleotide resolution. Unlike a simple PWM scan, saliency scores can take neighboring sequence context into account. The phyloP conservation score also similarly annotates individual; however, it ignores the effects of neighboring nucleotides. Using the same notation as Equation 1, the saliency, $S(x_i)$, is computed as the gradient of the predicted output with respect to the input sequence (treating the one hot coded matrix, x_i, as a vector):

$$S(x_i) = \nabla_{x_i} \hat{y}_i \tag{3}$$

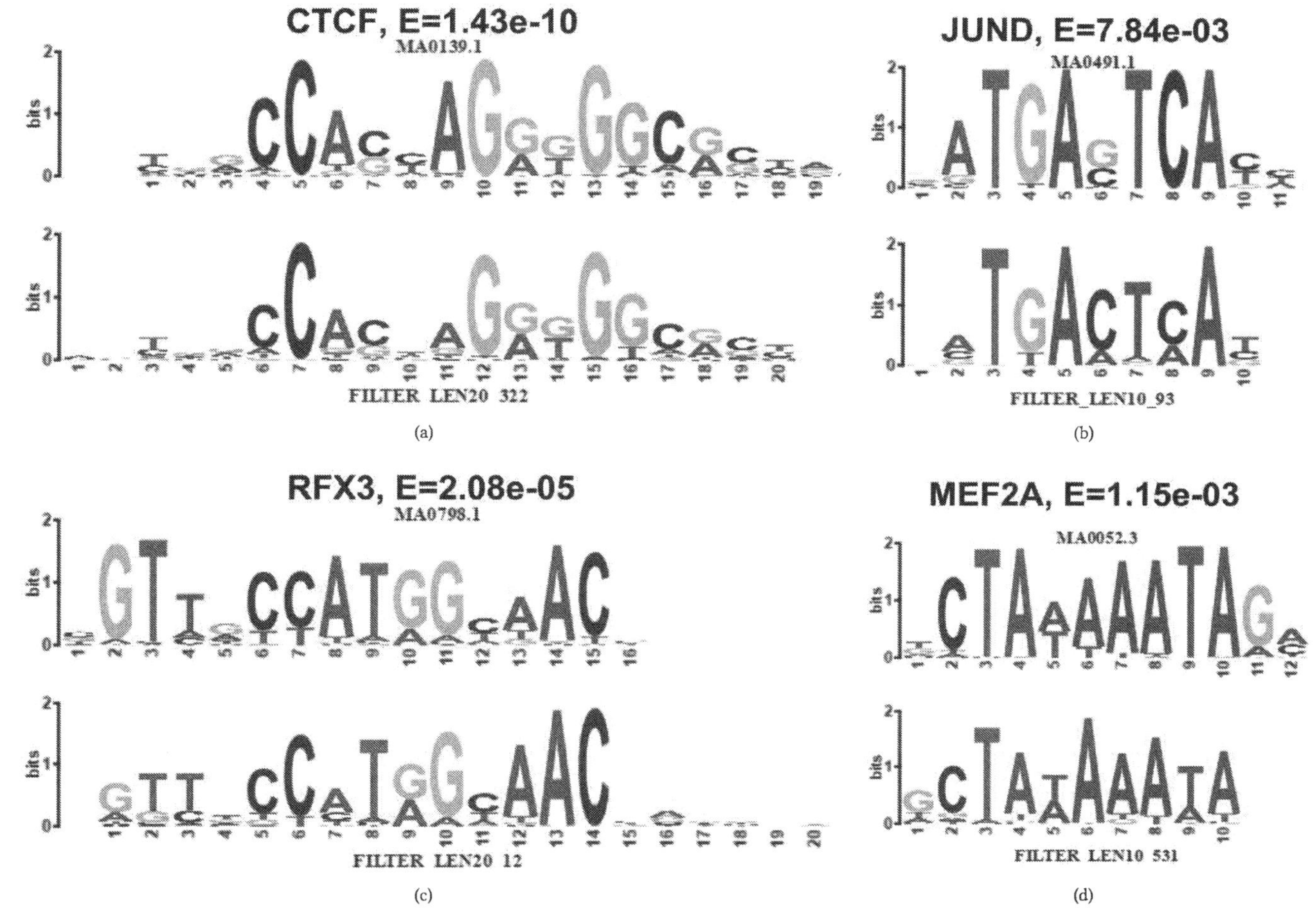

Figure 3: Four known motifs (top) aligned with convolution kernels (bottom). *E*-values, which are significance values corrected for multiple hypothesis testing that quantify similarity between query and target motifs, are displayed above the logos. (a)CTCF; (b)JUND; (c)RFX3; (d)MEF2A.

Figure 6 shows the saliency maps of four conserved sequences. The motifs of CTCF, JUND, RFX3 and MEF2A are clearly recovered in this example, demonstrating their relevancy to the final DeepCons output.

The saliency map provides an annotation of the input sequence at the individual nucleotide level, and offers a map on the importance of each nucleotide on the final conservation label of the entire input sequence. Since the conservation of a sequence is related to the functional significance of the sequence, the saliency map might provide an annotation on the function of individual nucleotides.

4 DISCUSSION

Comparative genomics is a powerful tool in finding functional elements across the human genome. However, our understanding of the functional roles of these conserved sequences remains incomplete, especially in noncoding regions. Here we present a deep learning approach, DeepCons, to understand sequence conservation by training a convolutional neural network to classify conserved and non-conserved sequences. The convolution kernels of the DeepCons model capture sequence motif information. We showed that some of these kernel motifs match motifs that are known to be widely distributed within conserved noncoding elements. We also show that many of the kernel motifs display positional bias relative to both transcription start sites (TSS), transcription end sites (TES) and miRNA, indicating their potential roles in transcriptional control and post-transcriptional regulation. Finally, some of the kernel motifs display strand bias relative to TES, suggesting their RNA level regulatory effects.

Although many of the learned convolution kernels match known motifs, the majority of the learned kernels do not seem to overlap with known motifs from existing databases. It is possible that some of these kernels might represent novel regulatory motifs, or new categories of functional elements not related to protein binding. It would be interesting to work with wet-lab biologists to further validate some of the discovered kernels.

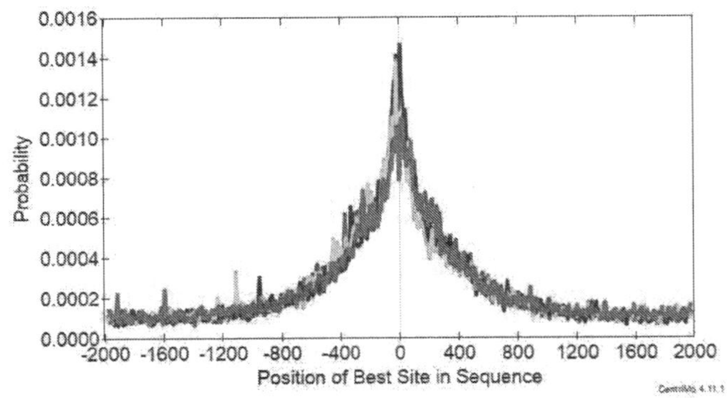

(a)

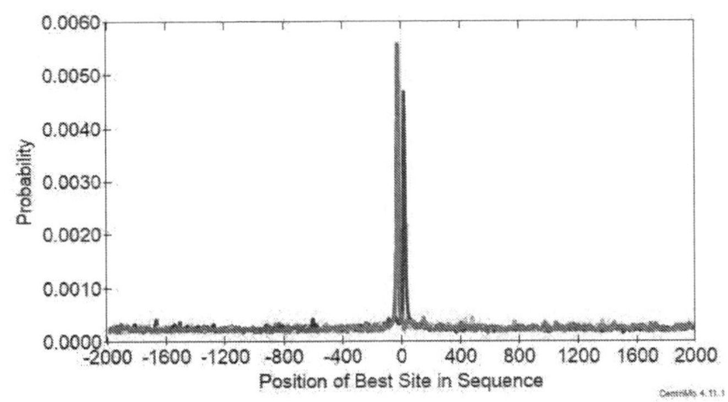

(b)

Figure 4: The positional distributions of the top four biased kernels relative to TSS and TES. (a)TSS; (b)TES.

Convolutional neural networks are very effective at finding local sequence patterns through their kernels, but they have limitations in discovering long range sequence patterns that might correspond to complex regulatory mechanisms. The size of the pattern mostly depends on the length of the convolution kernel, which typically ranges from a few bases to less than one hundred bases. Using multiple convolutional layers may help to capture broader ranges of sequence patterns, but interpreting kernels at top layers that are not directly connected to the input sequences remains difficult. Long short term memory (LSTM) networks [13], on the other hand, are specifically designed to capture long term sequential patterns, and have been widely applied to analysis natural languages [32]. However, an LSTM network is harder to train since its backpropagation step is equivalent to passing the error through dozens, even hundreds, of layers. We applied LSTM to classify conserved and non-conserved sequences, but due to the large training set the algorithm took prohibitively long time to run. In the future, we plan to investigate multi-GPU training schemes that are now supported by TensorFlow [1], and hopefully this solution will speed up training LSTM to within an acceptable time range. Interpreting LSTM networks trained on sequence data also requires novel methodologies.

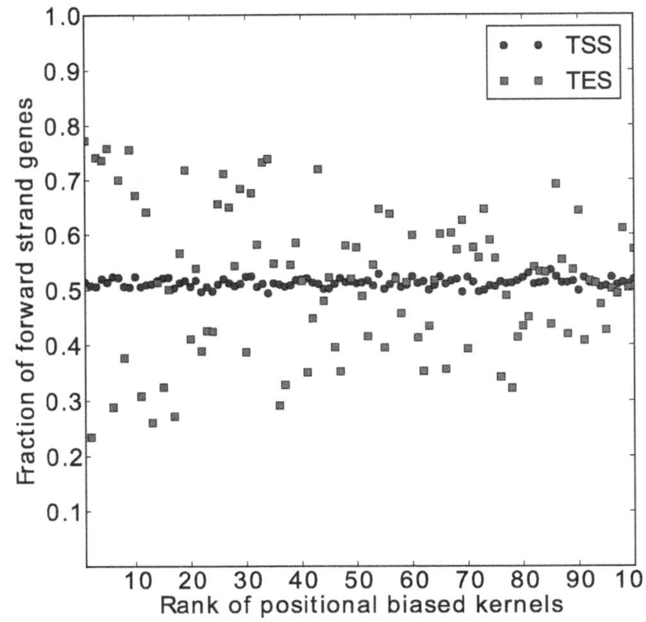

Figure 5: The strand bias of the top 100 positionally biased kernels relative to TSS and TES. The x-axis is the rank of each kernel. The y-axis is the fraction of forward strand genes that each kernel is positional biased to.

Visualizing the memory cell activities [15] may reveal some insights regarding long term sequence patterns.

In the current version of DeepCons, we selected the hyperparameters arbitrarily. Our choice of network architecture is by no means the most optimal. Although the DeepCons model greatly outperformed LR, this is an admittedly biased comparison. However, our choice of hyperparameters sufficiently demonstrated that the complexity of DNA sequence data is enough to justify a model as complex as a deep neural network. Hyperparameter tuning is a broad, ongoing field of research. One solution, which we have yet to implement, is to apply distributed computing hyperparameter tuning algorithms [6] to systematically search for optimal hyperparameter sets. Neural networks are known to be sensitive to initial parameters, but a thorough search over the parameter space is beyond the scope of this paper. Undoubtedly, as improvements in network architectural design are introduced, we can incorporate these changes to improve our method.

Since the conserved elements in the human genome might represent many different functional categories, it may also be interesting to group and cluster these elements into different categories for the purpose of both visualizing and understanding these elements. One promising solution is to apply a dimension reduction on the activations from the dense layer of DeepCons, and observe whether other non-coding elements such as long non-coding RNAs, TSSs, and TESs cluster together. Other clusters may correspond to functional elements that have yet to be properly characterized.

We finally demonstrate that DeepCons could be used to score sequence conservation at nucleotide level resolution. Since the

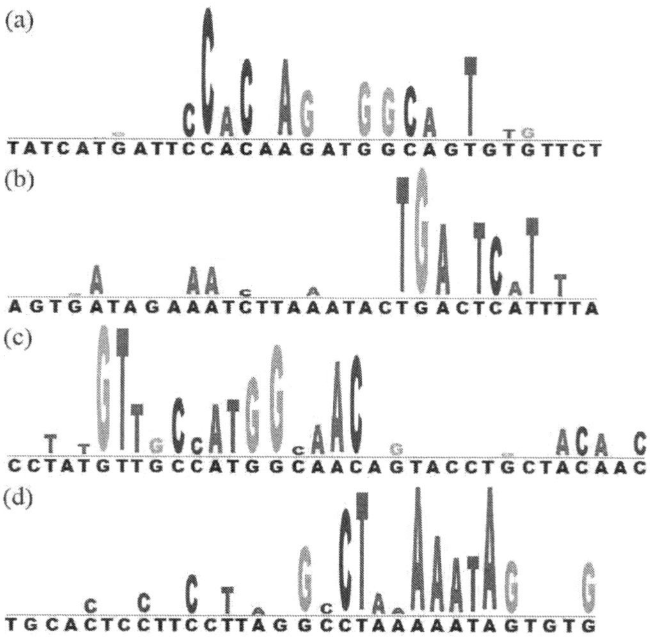

Figure 6: The saliency maps of four conserved sequences. The black letters below the gray line are the nucleotides of each sequence. The colored letters above the gray line are the nucleotides highlighted by their gradients, with the height proportional to the gradient. Negative gradients are clipped to zero. Four motifs are rediscovered in this example. (a)CTCF; (b)JUND; (c)RFX3; (d)MEF2A.

conservation of a sequence is suggestive of the underlying function of the sequence, the scoring of each individual nucleotide provided by DeepCons could serve the purpose of annotating the function of noncoding sequences in the human genome. In the past, many genetic variants associated with human disease and complex traits have been discovered, and the majority of these discovered variants are located in noncoding regions without functional annotations. The saliency map from DeepCons provides specific predictions on functional consequences of nucleotide changes, thereby offering an alternative framework for separating pathogenic variants from neutral ones.

ACKNOWLEDGEMENT

We acknowledge helpful discussions with Ali Mortazavi and Jason Ernst. This research is partially supported by NIH grant P50GM76516.

REFERENCES

[1] Martın Abadi, Ashish Agarwal, Paul Barham, Eugene Brevdo, Zhifeng Chen, Craig Citro, Greg S Corrado, Andy Davis, Jeffrey Dean, Matthieu Devin, and others. 2016. Tensorflow: Large-scale machine learning on heterogeneous distributed systems. *arXiv preprint arXiv:1603.04467* (2016).

[2] Babak Alipanahi, Andrew Delong, Matthew T Weirauch, and Brendan J Frey. 2015. Predicting the sequence specificities of DNA-and RNA-binding proteins by deep learning. *Nature biotechnology* (2015).

[3] Timothy L Bailey, Mikael Boden, Fabian A Buske, Martin Frith, Charles E Grant, Luca Clementi, Jingyuan Ren, Wilfred W Li, and William S Noble. 2009. MEME SUITE: tools for motif discovery and searching. *Nucleic acids research* (2009), gkp335.

[4] Timothy L Bailey and Philip Machanick. 2012. Inferring direct DNA binding from ChIP-seq. *Nucleic acids research* 40, 17 (2012), e128–e128.

[5] James Bergstra, Olivier Breuleux, Frédéric Bastien, Pascal Lamblin, Razvan Pascanu, Guillaume Desjardins, Joseph Turian, David Warde-Farley, and Yoshua Bengio. 2010. Theano: A CPU and GPU math compiler in Python. In *Proc. 9th Python in Science Conf.* 1–7.

[6] James Bergstra, Daniel Yamins, and David D Cox. 2013. Making a Science of Model Search: Hyperparameter Optimization in Hundreds of Dimensions for Vision Architectures. *ICML (1)* 28 (2013), 115–123.

[7] Yifei Chen, Yi Li, Rajiv Narayan, Aravind Subramanian, and Xiaohui Xie. 2016. Gene expression inference with deep learning. *Bioinformatics* (2016), btw074.

[8] Eugene V Davydov, David L Goode, Marina Sirota, Gregory M Cooper, Arend Sidow, and Serafim Batzoglou. 2010. Identifying a high fraction of the human genome to be under selective constraint using GERP++. *PLoS Comput Biol* 6, 12 (2010), e1001025.

[9] John Duchi, Elad Hazan, and Yoram Singer. 2011. Adaptive subgradient methods for online learning and stochastic optimization. *Journal of Machine Learning Research* 12, Jul (2011), 2121–2159.

[10] Xavier Glorot and Yoshua Bengio. 2010. Understanding the difficulty of training deep feedforward neural networks.. In *Aistats*, Vol. 9. 249–256.

[11] Shobhit Gupta, John A Stamatoyannopoulos, Timothy L Bailey, and William S Noble. 2007. Quantifying similarity between motifs. *Genome biology* 8, 2 (2007), R24.

[12] Geoffrey Hinton, Li Deng, Dong Yu, George E Dahl, Abdel-rahman Mohamed, Navdeep Jaitly, Andrew Senior, Vincent Vanhoucke, Patrick Nguyen, Tara N Sainath, and others. 2012. Deep neural networks for acoustic modeling in speech recognition: The shared views of four research groups. *IEEE Signal Processing Magazine* 29, 6 (2012), 82–97.

[13] Sepp Hochreiter and Jürgen Schmidhuber. 1997. Long short-term memory. *Neural computation* 9, 8 (1997), 1735–1780.

[14] Donna Karolchik, Angela S Hinrichs, Terrence S Furey, Krishna M Roskin, Charles W Sugnet, David Haussler, and W James Kent. 2004. The UCSC Table Browser data retrieval tool. *Nucleic acids research* 32, suppl 1 (2004), D493–D496.

[15] Andrej Karpathy, Justin Johnson, and Li Fei-Fei. 2015. Visualizing and understanding recurrent networks. *arXiv preprint arXiv:1506.02078* (2015).

[16] David R Kelley, Jasper Snoek, and John L Rinn. 2016. Basset: learning the regulatory code of the accessible genome with deep convolutional neural networks. *Genome research* 26, 7 (2016), 990–999.

[17] Ana Kozomara and Sam Griffiths-Jones. 2014. miRBase: annotating high confidence microRNAs using deep sequencing data. *Nucleic acids research* 42, D1 (2014), D68–D73.

[18] Alex Krizhevsky, Ilya Sutskever, and Geoffrey E Hinton. 2012. Imagenet classification with deep convolutional neural networks. In *Advances in neural information processing systems*. 1097–1105.

[19] Yann LeCun and Yoshua Bengio. 1995. Convolutional networks for images, speech, and time series. *The handbook of brain theory and neural networks* 3361, 10 (1995), 1995.

[20] Anthony Mathelier, Oriol Fornes, David J. Arenillas, Chih-yu Chen, Grégoire Denay, Jessica Lee, Wenqiang Shi, Casper Shyr, Ge Tan, Rebecca Worsley-Hunt, Allen W. Zhang, François Parcy, Boris Lenhard, Albin Sandelin, and Wyeth W. Wasserman. 2016. JASPAR 2016: a major expansion and update of the open-access database of transcription factor binding profiles. *Nucleic Acids Research* 44, D1 (2016), D110–D115. https://doi.org/10.1093/nar/gkv1176 arXiv:http://nar.oxfordjournals.org/content/44/D1/D110.full.pdf+html

[21] Fabian Pedregosa, Gaël Varoquaux, Alexandre Gramfort, Vincent Michel, Bertrand Thirion, Olivier Grisel, Mathieu Blondel, Peter Prettenhofer, Ron Weiss, Vincent Dubourg, and others. 2011. Scikit-learn: Machine learning in Python. *Journal of Machine Learning Research* 12, Oct (2011), 2825–2830.

[22] Kim D Pruitt, Garth R Brown, Susan M Hiatt, Françoise Thibaud-Nissen, Alexander Astashyn, Olga Ermolaeva, Catherine M Farrell, Jennifer Hart, Melissa J Landrum, Kelly M McGarvey, and others. 2014. RefSeq: an update on mammalian reference sequences. *Nucleic acids research* 42, D1 (2014), D756–D763.

[23] Daniel Quang, Yifei Chen, and Xiaohui Xie. 2014. DANN: a deep learning approach for annotating the pathogenicity of genetic variants. *Bioinformatics* (2014), btu703.

[24] Daniel Quang and Xiaohui Xie. 2016. DanQ: a hybrid convolutional and recurrent deep neural network for quantifying the function of DNA sequences. *Nucleic acids research* (2016), gkw226.

[25] Aaron R Quinlan and Ira M Hall. 2010. BEDTools: a flexible suite of utilities for comparing genomic features. *Bioinformatics* 26, 6 (2010), 841–842.

[26] David E Rumelhart, Geoffrey E Hinton, and Ronald J Williams. 1988. Learning representations by back-propagating errors. *Cognitive modeling* 5, 3 (1988), 1.

[27] Avanti Shrikumar, Peyton Greenside, Anna Shcherbina, and Anshul Kundaje. 2016. Not Just a Black Box: Learning Important Features Through Propagating Activation Differences. *arXiv preprint arXiv:1605.01713* (2016).

[28] Adam Siepel, Gill Bejerano, Jakob S Pedersen, Angie S Hinrichs, Minmei Hou, Kate Rosenbloom, Hiram Clawson, John Spieth, LaDeana W Hillier, Stephen

Richards, and others. 2005. Evolutionarily conserved elements in vertebrate, insect, worm, and yeast genomes. *Genome research* 15, 8 (2005), 1034–1050.

[29] Karen Simonyan, Andrea Vedaldi, and Andrew Zisserman. 2013. Deep inside convolutional networks: Visualising image classification models and saliency maps. *arXiv preprint arXiv:1312.6034* (2013).

[30] Richard Socher, Cliff C Lin, Chris Manning, and Andrew Y Ng. 2011. Parsing natural scenes and natural language with recursive neural networks. In *Proceedings of the 28th international conference on machine learning (ICML-11)*. 129–136.

[31] Nitish Srivastava, Geoffrey Hinton, Alex Krizhevsky, Ilya Sutskever, and Ruslan Salakhutdinov. 2014. Dropout: A simple way to prevent neural networks from overfitting. *The Journal of Machine Learning Research* 15, 1 (2014), 1929–1958.

[32] Ilya Sutskever, Oriol Vinyals, and Quoc V Le. 2014. Sequence to sequence learning with neural networks. In *Advances in neural information processing systems*. 3104–3112.

[33] Xiaohui Xie, Jun Lu, EJ Kulbokas, Todd R Golub, Vamsi Mootha, Kerstin Lindblad-Toh, Eric S Lander, and Manolis Kellis. 2005. Systematic discovery of regulatory motifs in human promoters and 3âĂš UTRs by comparison of several mammals. *Nature* 434, 7031 (2005), 338–345.

[34] Xiaohui Xie, Tarjei S Mikkelsen, Andreas Gnirke, Kerstin Lindblad-Toh, Manolis Kellis, and Eric S Lander. 2007. Systematic discovery of regulatory motifs in conserved regions of the human genome, including thousands of CTCF insulator sites. *Proceedings of the National Academy of Sciences* 104, 17 (2007), 7145–7150.

[35] J Omar Yáñez-Cuna, Cosmas D Arnold, Gerald Stampfel, Łukasz M Boryń, Daniel Gerlach, Martina Rath, and Alexander Stark. 2014. Dissection of thousands of cell type-specific enhancers identifies dinucleotide repeat motifs as general enhancer features. *Genome research* 24, 7 (2014), 1147–1156.

[36] Jian Zhou and Olga G Troyanskaya. 2015. Predicting effects of noncoding variants with deep learning-based sequence model. *Nature methods* 12, 10 (2015), 931–934.

SeqyClean: A Pipeline for High-throughput Sequence Data Preprocessing

Ilya Y. Zhbannikov*
Social Science Research Institute, Duke University
Durham, NC
27708-0420
ilya.zhbannikov@duke.edu

Samuel S. Hunter
Institute for Bioinformatics and Evolutionary Studies
University of Idaho
Moscow, ID 83844-3051
shunter@uidaho.edu

James A. Foster
Institute for Bioinformatics and Evolutionary Studies
University of Idaho
Moscow, ID 83844-3051
foster@uidaho.edu

Matthew L. Settles
UC Davis Genome Center
University of California
Davis, 95616
settles@ucdavis.edu

ABSTRACT

Modern high-throughput sequencing instruments produce massive amounts of data, which often contains noise in the form of sequencing errors, sequencing adaptors, and contaminating reads. This noise complicates genomics studies. Although many preprocessing software tools have been developed to reduce the sequence noise, many of them cannot handle data from multiple technologies and few address more than one type of noise. We present *SeqyClean*, a comprehensive preprocessing software pipeline. *SeqyClean* effectively removes multiple sources of noise in high throughput sequence data and, according to our tests, outperforms other available preprocessing tools. We show[1] that preprocessing data with *SeqyClean* first improves both de-novo genome assembly and genome mapping. We have used *SeqyClean* extensively in the genomics core at the Institute for Bioinformatics and Evolutionary STudies (IBEST) at the University of Idaho, so it has been validated with both test and production data. *SeqyClean* is available as open source software under the MIT License at http://github.com/ibest/seqyclean

Contact: ilya.zhbannikov@duke.edu

CCS CONCEPTS

• **Applied computing → Life and medical sciences → Bioinformatics**

KEYWORDS

Sequence analysis; data preprocessing; high-throughput dna sequencing

* Corresponding author
[1] On real-world data

Permission to make digital or hard copies of all or part of this work for personal or classroom use is granted without fee provided that copies are not made or distributed for profit or commercial advantage and that copies bear this notice and the full citation on the first page. Copyrights for components of this work owned by others than ACM must be honored. Abstracting with credit is permitted. To copy otherwise, or republish, to post on servers or to redistribute to lists, requires prior specific permission and/or a fee. Request permissions from Permissions@acm.org.
ACM-BCB'17, August 20-23, 2017, Boston, MA, USA.
© 2017 Association of Computing Machinery.
ACM ISBN 978-1-4503-4722-8/17/08...$15.00.
DOI: http://dx.doi.org/10.1145/3107411.3107446

1 INTRODUCTION

With the ability to easily outsource genome scale DNA sequencing and advances in modern computation tools, small labs are able to handle research tasks that were previously available only to large genome centers [1]. However, analysis of high-throughput DNA sequence data (HTS) still remains a non-trivial problem. Raw data from high-throughput sequencing machines contain various types of artificial inclusions (sequencing adapters, vectors, contaminants), and sequence errors caused by instrument imprecision. Therefore, there is a need for data preprocessing before later analysis tasks such as mapping and/or assembly. Aggressive preprocessing of HTS data, before mapping and/or assembly, in order to remove a majority of inclusions (vectors, adapters and contaminants) and potentially erroneous nucleotides is important because it can improve the quality, speed and reliability of analysis [2].

Preprocessing of HTS data can include a number of stages to identify and remove non-experimental artifacts. These include: (1) Identification and trimming of various kinds of DNA sequencing adapters. Sequencing technologies use known short sequences added during library preparation, known as adapters. Untrimmed adapters can lead to a fragmented genome assembly. (2) Filtering non-experimental contaminant sequences. Sequence contamination can come from many sources including, those derived from sample collection and preparation, lab equipment/reagents, or from the sequencing process. As an example, the Anolis Carolinensis k51:5946385 transcribed RNA sequence (GenBank ID GAGG011006923.1, ~5.3 kb) is most likely the sequence for Phi-X174 phage (99% identity, according to NCBI BLAST), a common spike-in library for Illumina sequencing. Had the reads been screened for this contaminant prior to assembly, this erroneous transcript would most likely not have been reported (3) Filtering and trimming BAC-vector remnants (it is very likely that plasmid and bacterial fragments are still present in raw library). (4) Read edges trimming of poor quality bases (low quality scores and 'N' bases) produced by instrument imprecision. (5) Combining/joining overlapping Illumina paired-end reads. Sequencing library fragments, which are shorter than the overall number of cycles being sequenced, can be overlapped and joined to produce a single, longer read.

Combining paired-end reads reduces data abundance and base redundancy, thereby potentially reducing analysis time and errors [2]. (6) Trimming poly A/T tails. When sequencing RNA samples poly A/T sequence is not a part of the original genome and may interfere with a read's ability to map. And finally, (7) Removing PCR duplicates, which do not convey any new information, but largely increase amount of data and thereby, analysis time.

1.1 Available sequence preprocessing software tools

Many of current sequence preprocessing tools have only some of the stages described above, or lack the ability to process multiple sequence data file formats from different sequencing technologies. Roche Life Sciences 454 systems and Life Technologies Ion Torrent/Proton systems use the SFF (Standard Flowgram Format), a binary file format [3], while Illumina, and others, use the FASTQ plain text file format to store both sequenced bases and quality information for each nucleotide and each read. FASTA/QUAL formats are similar but contain only sequence bases or quality scores (numeric) respectively. Table 1 provides a summary of file formats and capabilities for a representative set of other preprocessing applications. Briefly, the applications *Lucy* [4], *AlienTrimmer* [2], *Ea-Utils* [5], *AdapterRemoval* [6], *Skewer* [7], *Trimmomatic* [8], *Btrim* [9], Sickle [10], Picard [14], *PEAR* [15], *IeeHom*[16], *Cutadapt* [17] suites are examples of applications that perform multiple preprocessing stages, mostly adapter and quality trimming. *Lucy* is a preprocessing pipeline for quality, poly A/T and vector trimming. It was designed for lower-throughput Sanger sequence data and does not accept as input the modern SFF and FASTQ file formats or Illumina paired-end libraries. *AlienTrimmer* accepts both single-end and paired-end reads in FASTQ format, providing adapter and quality trimming. *AlienTrimmer* does not accept SFF files, requiring the user to first convert them to FASTQ format. *Btrim* performs quality and adapter trimming, but no vector and contaminants screening, poly-A/T removal or other preprocessing stages. *Ea-Utils* performs a number of stages, including quality, poly-A/T, adapter and vector and contaminants screening. It also accepts single- and paired-end reads and, moreover, it performs merging of overlapping paired-end reads. But does not process SFF binary files. *Skewer, Trimmomatic, AdapterRemoval* and *Sickle* perform adapter and quality trimming of single- and paired-end reads. *Picard* is a part of GATK suite for filtering for duplicated reads during data preprocessing before variant calling. *PEAR* and *IeeHom* are tools for merging overlapping paired-end reads. *IeeHom* also can perform adapter trimming. *Cutadapt* offers adapter trimming based on alignment. However, none of these applications incorporate all of the stages mentioned above into a single preprocessing pipeline. Therefore, there is a need for a universal preprocessing tool that incorporates all of the important preprocessing stages described above and is flexible enough to work on the most common types of data formats available.

In this paper we present *SeqyClean*, a comprehensive preprocessing software pipeline for high throughput sequence

Table 1: This table compares 8 different, commonly used data preprocessing tools to *SeqyClean*, indicating whether (X) or not they perform each of ten types of errors. See text for a discussion of which tools are included in this study, and for a definition of the types of error. * indicates that the corresponding tool allows this future, but only after splitting the input FASTQ-file into separate FASTA and QUAL (containing quality scores). Only *SeqyClean* handles and cleans all of these errors.

				Features						
Application	**SFF**	**FASTQ (single)**	**FASTQ (paired)**	**Contaminants**	**Vector**	**Adapter**	**Quality**	**Poly A/T**	**Overlap**	**Duplicates**
SeqyClean	**X**	**X**	**X**	**X**	**X**	**X**	**X**	**X**	**X**	**X**
Lucy	-	*X	-	-	X	-	X	X	-	-
Btrim	-	X	-	-	-	-	X	-	-	-
AlienTrimmer	-	X	X	X	X	X	X	-	-	-
AdapterRemoval	-	X	X	-	-	X	X	-	-	-
Skewer	-	X	X	-	-	X	X	-	-	-
Trimmomatic	-	X	X	-	-	X	X	-	-	-
Sickle	-	X	X	-	-	X	X	-	-	-
Ea-Utils	-	X	X	-	-	X	X	-	X	-
Picard	-	X	X	-	-	-	-	-	-	X
PEAR	-	X	X	-	-	-	-	-	X	-
IeeeHom	-	X	X	-	-	X	-	-	X	-
Cutadapt	-	X	X	-	-	X	-	-	-	-

data. The purpose of *SeqyClean* is to incorporate all of the sequence preprocessing stages (except error correction and removal of chimera sequences) together into one bioinformatics pipeline that works with the two most common sequence data formats, SFF and FASTQ files (both single-end and paired-end). *SeqyClean* successfully recognizes and removes technological components (sequencing adapters, primers, barcodes), contaminants and vectors. Further, *SeqyClean* provides quality trimming (without error correction), poly A/T trimming, overlapping of paired-end reads and PCR-duplicate detection and removal. Further, *SeqyClean* allows the user to choose which stages to perform and to adjust the default parameters within stages, as the experimental conditional may need. We show that *SeqyClean* greatly improves both genome de-novo assembly and genome mapping. *SeqyClean* has been extensively used in our lab with continued improvement and we believe that the research community can also benefit from its use.

2 METHODS

SeqyClean is an open-source software application that requires only the GNU C/C++ compiler installed and is available for download from the following link: http://github.com/ibest/seqyclean. A workflow comprises the following stages: (1) Input data preprocessing; (2) PCR-Duplicates removal; (3) Overlapping and adapter removal for paired-end reads; (4) Trimming poly A/T tails; (5) Vector trimming; (6) Contaminant removal; (7) Adapter trimming for single-end reads (454, Illumina single-end); (8) Quality trimming; (9) Establishing final trim points; (10) Generating output files and summary statistics. An advantage of *SeqyClean* is its modular structure, in which the user can specify different preprocessing strategies, rather than a strictly determined workflow. It also incorporates all of the preprocessing stages described in the Background section into single bioinformatics application, providing the most powerful sequence cleaning.

We describe each preprocessing stage in detail in the following sections. *SeqyClean* also has a number of additional utility functions that may be useful in preprocessing HTS data, such as minimum read length filtering, and conversion from the newer CASAVA v1.8 style FASTQ read IDs to the older pre-CASAVA 1.8 style read IDs. Refer to the user manual for additional information.

2.1 Removal PCR-duplicates from sequence data

During library preparation, the amount of DNA is typically amplified using a polymerase chain reaction (PCR) step. If library complexity is low, these duplicated templates are often sequenced multiple times, but because all of the sequenced reads originate from the same template they do not provide any additional information. Identification and removal of reads that are likely the result of PCR duplication reduces the pool of redundant sequence before assembly and mapping, which can potentially reduce both errors and analysis time. We define PCR duplicates as reads originating from the same parent molecule. For paired-end reads, PCR duplicates are identified if they share the same 35bp window (default) starting from base pair 10 (default) from the 5' end (70bp total must be an identical match, 35bp from each read) and ending at base 45 from the 5' end of each pair. For single-end reads (Roche 454 of single-end Illumina) 35bp must be identical. The window size, start position and maximum number of allowed duplicates can be adjusted by changing parameters 'startdw' (starting position, 10 by default) and 'sizedw' (window size, 35bp by default) and 'maxdup' (maximum number of duplicates to keep in preprocessed library (1 by default).

2.2 Poly A/T tail trimming for RNA sequence data

SeqyClean provides trimming of poly-A/T of RNA sequence data by implementing the approach previously introduced in the Lucy application [7]. The algorithm begins by searching for the first minimum occurrence of 10bp (by default) or longer of poly-T (or poly-A) fragment within the first initial search range of 50bp, from both the 5' and 3' ends of sequence, and then attempts to extend this poly-T (poly-A) seed outward, allowing for no more than the maximum (default=3) mismatches between every min span (default=10bp) consecutive T (A) bases in the search region.

2.3 Contaminant and vector detection and trimming

To identity contaminants and vectors we use exact *k*-mer matching, which works as follows: supplied contaminant references sequences are sampled into consecutive *k*-mers (15 bases long by default), each *k*-mer is stored in a hash table; Searching for a contaminant, or vector, is performed by sampling each read into consecutive *k*-mers (15bp length by default) and then performing a hash table lookup for each *k*-mer in a read. For flexibility, the distance (difference between starting position of the first *k*-mer and starting position of the second *k*-mer) between tandem *k*-mers in a read can be adjusted (default distance is one base). In the case of vector sequences, matches are first approximately found via consecutive *k*-mer matching, and then the exact coordinates are obtained by extending with a pairwise alignment between the read and corresponding region in a reference vector sequence. The read is trimmed of vector sequence if the match occupies less than 80% of the read and discarded otherwise. In case of contaminants screening the whole read is discarded as soon as it meets three (by default, can be adjusted) consecutive successful *k*-mer matches. In order to identify contaminant and vector sequences, reference sequence of expected contaminant/vectors must be provided in FASTA format.

2.4 Adapter identification and combining overlapping Illumina paired-end sequences

To trim adapters in single-end and SFF reads, we use the SSAHA algorithm [11] for detection of Roche 454 RL MID adapters in SFF files and Illumina Truseq adapters in single-end reads, by default; however the user can supply custom adapters. SSAHA is a hashing algorithm used for mapping reads, but implemented for use in adapter identification here.

In the case of paired-end reads, reads that contain adapter sequence will also contain a high quality, interior overlapping alignment where the overhangs are the adapter sequences. This technique is also described in *AdapterRemoval* and *Trimmomatic* and is based on the following assumption. If an adapter is found in one paired-end read, the corresponding adapter should also be present in the corresponding pair, while the interior sequences (non-adapter sequence) are reverse complements of each other. Otherwise, the read is free of adapter sequence. The algorithm is described as follows:

• First, the read pairs (read #1 and the reverse-complement of read #2) are fully overlapped (Fig. 1a) and an overlap score is computed according to the following equation:

$$Score = \frac{Number\ of\ matches}{Overlap\ length} \quad (1)$$

• Then reads are shifted by one base (to the exterior), relative to each other (Fig. 1b) and overlap scores are computed after each shift. If an overlap score reaches a pre-defined threshold (0.75 by default), the overlap position is recorded, the algorithm terminates and adapters are trimmed (Fig. 1c). Otherwise, the algorithm proceeds until the min overlap (=16 bases by default) is achieved.

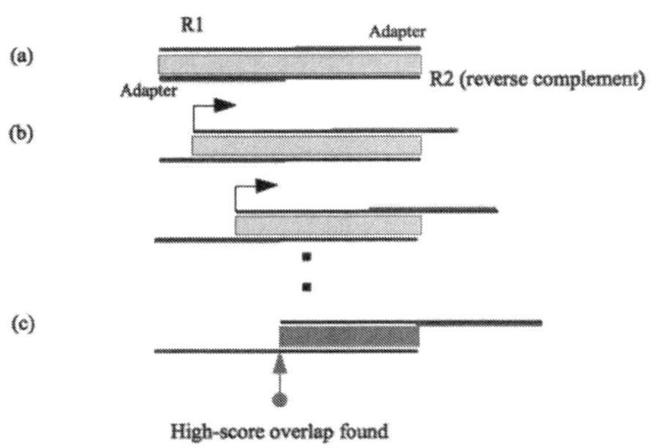

Figure 1: Detecting Illumina adapters by complete overlap: (a) Read 1 (R1) and reverse complement of read 2 (R2) are fully overlapped and scores are computed for all overlapping bases (solid blue region). Adapters in R1 and R2 are shown in red; (b) If scores are below the pre-defined threshold, reads are shifted by a single base relative to each other and scores are recomputed; (c) Shifting continues until the overlap with scores above the threshold is found or the overlap is more than minoverlap=16 bases (in this case adapters are considered as not found).

A potential benefit of the paired-end paradigm is the possibility to join paired-end reads into single, longer sequence with a length up to nearly twice the length of the individual reads, which can reduce assembly complexity. This is implemented as part of the paired-end adapter-trimming algorithm described previously, except it contains an additional consensus calling stage, in which the paired reads are combined into longer single read ('consensus read') with re-computed bases and quality scores. If disagreements are identified while constructing the consensus, the nucleotide call with the higher quality score is selected and the quality is set to the difference in quality scores between the two calls. In cases where quality scores are equal for unmatched calls, the residue for read #1 is reported with a quality of 2. The pseudo code is given below:

```
IF R1[i] != R2[i] THEN
    Cons.R.Qual[i] = |R1.Qual[i] – R2.Qual[i]|
    Cons.R[i] = R1.Qual[i] > R2.Qual[i] ? R1[i] : R2[i]
```

2.5 Quality trimming

SeqyClean utilizes the approach used in the *Lucy* quality and vector trimming application. Briefly, (1) the quality trimming algorithm searches for the longest region from both the 5' and 3' ends with average error lower than a predefined 'bracket_error' threshold. To do this, a sliding window is applied with size of 10 bp by default. Low-quality regions, which do not meet the criteria, are trimmed from each end; (2) At the next step, a quality algorithm identifies regions within a sequence that have high error rates. To do this, two types of windows are applied: first, a large window of 50 bp (default) is applied. Second, a smaller window of size 10 bp (default) is used to identify small low-quality regions that were missed using the larger window. (3) The largest high-quality region with average error lower than 'maximum_average_error' (MAE) is then chosen as a candidate for the final high quality range; (4) The last step is to check the last two bases from each end of the read. If they have an average error larger than the maximum_error_at_ends (MEE) parameter, trim them off. Parameters 'maximum_average_error' and 'maximum_error_at_ends' are each set to 0.01 (20 Phred) by default and represent the quality trimming threshold. In *SeqyClean* 'bracket_error' is set to 0.794 and the default maximum average error for both windows (50 and 10 bp) is also set to 0.794.

2.6 Final Trim Points

Trim points are positions on the 5' and 3' ends of the read and define the good-quality region that passed the quality trimming stage and are free from adapters, vector and polyA/T sequences.

2.7 Output files and summary statistics

This includes processed sequence data, and log files that record all parameters and flags used in preprocessing, summary statistics such as the number of discarded sequences, adapters found, etc., and statistics for each read (adapter position, read length, etc.)

2.8 Evaluation

We chose to evaluate *SeqyClean* by comparing de-novo genome assembly and mapping statistics using both original and processed reads. Our goals were to (1) identify a range of optimal quality parameters for general sequence preprocessing tasks; (2) compare the preprocessed datasets of *SeqyClean* to other tools and (3) explore effects of different preprocessing stages on de-novo assembly and mapping. We used the *QUAST* analytic tool [13] ver. 2.2 to extract statistics across all tests.

2.8.1 Datasets

Three HTS shotgun datasets were used in evaluation of *SeqyClean* and are summarized in Table 2.

Table 2: HTS datasets used

	Reads (bp)	Technology	Organism	Ref ID
1	621,578 (327,471,374)	Roche 454	*E. coli.* K-12/MG1655	NC000913.3
2	400,596 (2x100,149,00)	MiSeqPE250	*E. coli.* K-12/MG1655	NC000913.3
3	3,875,453 (2x968,863,250)	MiSeqPE250	*S. cerevisiae* W303	ALAV00000000.1

2.8.2 Preprocessing strategy for the goal #1

To identify the optimal quality error threshold, which includes 'maximum_average_error' (MAE) parameter and 'maximum_error_at_ends' (MEE) we conducted 39 preprocessing experiments on dataset #1 and dataset #3. We applied *SeqyClean* to these datasets using quality error thresholds ranging from 0.794 (Phred score of 1) to 0.000126 (Phred of 39, inclusive). A value of 0.794 indicates a 79.43% chance that the base was read incorrectly and a value of 0.000126 indicates a 0.0126% chance that a nucleotide base was read incorrectly. All other parameters were left at their defaults.

2.8.3 Optimal parameters for Roche 454 and Illumina preprocessing were estimated from de-novo genome assembly and mapping

We performed 39 de-novo assemblies of raw and *SeqyClean* processed (both Roche 454 and Illumina datasets, see above) using the *Roche GS De Novo Assembler (Newbler)* ver. 2.9 [3]. In addition, we also evaluated Roche's native clip points by supplying a library file to the assembler "as is", letting the assembler determine the optimal preprocessing strategy from clipping information encoded in the SFF file (only for 454 data). We used the following assembly assessment statistics: (1) N50; (2) total number of contigs; (3) average read length; (4) read coverage; (5) insertions/deletions (INDELs); (6) total length of the assembly. Mapping was performed with *Bowtie2* ver. 2.2.0 [12].

2.8.4 Comparison of SeqyClean to other preprocessing tools

We compared *SeqyClean* (ver. 1.9.9) to *Lucy* (ver. 1.2), *AlienTrimmer* (ver. 0.4.0), *Btrim* (ver. 0.2.0), and *Ea-Utils* (ver. 1.04.636), using the *E. coli* Roche 454 dataset (dataset 1). We also compared it to *AlienTrimmer*, *Ea-Utils*, *Skewer* (ver. 0.2.0), *Trimmomatic* (ver. 0.35), *AdapterRemoval* (ver. 2.1.6), and *Sickle* (ver. 1.33) using the *E.coli* Illumina data (dataset 2). We preprocessed each dataset using the default/suggested parameters provided by authors of each application. After preprocessing we performed de-novo assemblies. We compared the following assembly statistics: N50, number of large contigs (length of contig >= 1000 bp), total number of contigs, largest contig length, largest alignment and total length of the assembly. We also performed mapping with *Bowtie2* (ver. 2.2.0). Software parameters were left at their defaults. For mapping we compared the number of reads aligned for each application, assuming that higher percentage of aligned reads indicates better preprocessing.

2.8.5 Exploring effects of different preprocessing stages on genome de-novo assembly and mapping (goal #3)

We explored effect of the following preprocessing stages: de-duplication, quality and adapter trimming and merging paired-end reads. To do this we used *S. cerevisiae* W303 (dataset #3). We used *Roche GS De Novo Assembler (Newbler)* ver. 2.9 and *Bowtie2* ver. 2.2.0. Data set was preprocessed with *SeqyClean* ver. 1.9.9. Software parameters were left at their defaults.

3 RESULTS AND DISCUSSION

In this paper we introduced the *SeqyClean*, a comprehensive preprocessing tool that facilitates preprocessing of high-throughput sequence libraries. Data preprocessing is a necessary step before analyzing sequence data and *SeqyClean* is especially designed to perform this service. To test the *SeqyClean*, we determined optimal default parameters by determining the effects of quality and adapter trimming on genome assembly and mapping of typical datasets and then compared the effectiveness of *SeqyClean* to other pre-processing tools.

3.1 Comparison of SeqyClean to other preprocessing tools

We performed this test using two different technologies: Roche 454 pyrosequence library (dataset #1) and Illumina MiSeq library (dataset #2) in order to compare *SeqyClean* with best available sequence preprocessing tools.

3.1.1 De-novo assembling of the pyrosequence library preprocessed with SeqyClean and other tools (dataset #1)

According to the results (see Table 3), reads cleaned with SeqyClean and assembled with *Newbler* resulted in the largest N50 (111,928 bp). Assembly time was significantly lower in comparison to Lucy and raw data (10 minutes versus 3h 39min and 8 hours respectively). This indicates that the untrimmed artifacts (adapters) left in a library, introduce additional complexity to the assembler, which in turn, significantly increases of assembling time. Assembly from data preprocessed with *AlienTrimmer* and *Btrim* have N50 of 105,642 bp and 97,590 bp respectively, indicating second- and third-largest N50s.

Table 3: Assembly comparison: *SeqyClean* against other applications. Test library - *E.coli* 454 pyrosequence data (dataset #1: *E.coli* K-12/MG1655 454 pyrosequence data, 621,578 reads, 327,471,374 bases) sequenced on IBEST Genomic Core. Reference length: 4,641,652 bp.

Application	N50	Large (>1000bp)/Total Contigs	Total Length	Clock time HH:MM:SS
Lucy	86,508	168/1091	5,064,255	03:39:18
AlienTrimmer	105,642	164/1396	4,926,455	00:13:49
Btrim	97,590	176/548	4,723,675	00:04:02
Ea-utils	2,214	2561/3439	4,686,639	00:06:20
SeqyClean	**111,928**	**362/1294**	**5, 164,984**	**00:10:12**
Raw data	66,524	197/1379	4,927,210	08:37:28

Table 4: Assembly comparison: *SeqyClean* against other applications. Test library - *E.coli* Illumina library (dataset #2: *E.coli* K-12/MG1655 Illumina data (SRR519926, a 2 x 250 bp run, sequenced on an MiSeq)). Reference length: 4,641,652 bp.

Application	N50	Large (>1000bp)/Total Contigs	Total length	Clock time (HH:MM:SS)
AlienTrimmer	53,598	160/218	4,558,242	00:03:40
Ea-utils	59,473	131/183	4,556,869	00:20:24
Skewer	69,502	128/172	4,555,815	00:04:03
Trimmomatic	62,574	130/179	4,557,781	00:05:36
AdapterRemoval	62,382	134/180	4,556,466	00:04:22
Sickle	54,771	139/187	4,556,851	00:04:06
SeqyClean	**82,666**	**117/170**	**4,555,814**	**00:04:13**

Table 5: Comparison of *Bowtie2*-mapping: *SeqyClean* against other applications and raw data. Test library – dataset #1 (*E.coli* K-12/MG1655 454 pyrosequence data, 621,578 reads, 327,471,374 bases) sequenced on IBEST Genomic Core.

Application	Reads mapped/Reads total (%)	Total reads	Average read length
AlienTrimmer	86.42%	621,362	456.71
Lucy	85.89%	618,653	474.11
Btrim	91.02%	516,107	256.60
Ea-utils	81.11%	621,578	526.84
SeqyClean	88.40%	588,912	525.78

Among contig metrics, preprocessing with *Btrim* provides the smallest number of contigs (176 large/548 total) and *SeqyClean* provides the third smallest number (362 large/1294 total) of total contigs. Reads assembled from preprocessing with *Lucy* provide the second smallest total number of contigs (168 large/1091 total).

Preprocessing with *Ea-utils* and *Btrim* tools produced the closest total length to the reference (4,686,639 bp and 4,723,675 bp), and preprocessing with *SeqyClean* produced the fifth closest result (5,164,984 bp). Pre-processing with *SeqyClean* also produced the third smallest assembly time of 10 minutes, versus 4 (*Btrim*) and 6 minutes (*Ea-utils*). The assembly time for *Ea-utils* is lower in comparison to *SeqyClean*, but *Ea-utils* produced a very fragmented assembly (more than 3,000 contigs). *SeqyClean* outperforms the other preprocessing applications in terms of N50.

3.1.2 De-novo assembly of the *E. coli* paired-end library preprocessed with *SeqyClean* and other tools (dataset #2)

SeqyClean provided the largest N50 (82,666 bp Table 4) and outperformed the other applications among other parameters:

the number of contigs having lengths >=1,000bp (large contigs, according to *QUAST*),/total contigs (117/170); total length of large contigs (4,555,814 bp); total length of the assembly: 4,555,814 bp. *Skewer* produced the second-largest N50 (69,502 bp) and *Trimmomatic* the third (62,574 bp). Total assembly length was roughly the same for all tools. Also, data preprocessed with *SeqyClean* produced the smallest number of large/total contigs (117/130). Based on these results we can assume that the *SeqyClean* is at least comparable to these tools in terms of adapter and quality trimming.

3.1.3 Mapping of *E.coli* pyrosequence and Illumina libraries preprocessed with *SeqyClean* and other tools (dataset #1, 2)

As shown in Table 5, *SeqyClean* outperforms the other evaluated applications, except *Btrim*, providing second-highest percentage (88.40%) of mapped reads for 454 data. We assume this happens due to slightly better adapter removal with SSAHA algorithm, implemented in *SeqyClean*. All alignment tests ran quickly (from 0.5 to 1 min). The best results given by *Btrim*: 91.02%, *Lucy* provided 85.89% and *AlienTrimmer* provided 86.42%; and the worst, Ea-utils: 81.11%. For Illumina *E.coli* library (dataset #2), according to results shown in Table 6, *SeqyClean* provides the best results and outperforms other tools for post-processed paired-end reads (PE), unpaired single-end reads (SE, by 'single-end' we mean a situation when one read is lost its pair due to low quality of bases of it) and combined pair- and single-end reads (PE+SE). For quality trimming we used: MAE=20, MEE=20. Other parameters were left at their defaults. For other tools we used their recommended parameters.

SeqyClean outperforms other tools in PE+SE (combined paired- and single-end reads) test and provided 99.43% aligned sequences. *Trimmomatic* and *Sickle* provided only 92.83% and 89.50% of aligned reads (combined paired- and single-end reads). *SeqyClean* also slightly outperforms other tools in PE (paired-end) alignment tests, having 99.91% aligned reads against 99.89% from *Trimmomatic* and 95.60% from *Skewer*. In SE (single-end reads) alignment test, 97.25% reads were aligned, versus 66.73% from *Trimmomatic* and 43.95% from *Sickle*. The mapping test of raw reads resulted 76.15% of PE mapped/PE total. This may indicate better removal of TruSeq adapters in single- and, especially, in paired-end modes in comparison to other tools. A high number (more than 99%) of aligned paired-end reads that were preprocessed with other tools in comparison to low rate of alignment of single-end reads (66.73% for *Trimmomatic*, 43.95% for *Sickle*, other tools discard single-end reads) makes us to assume these tools do not perform comprehensive de-noising of single-end reads. *SeqyClean* performs de-noising both paired- and single-end reads. This potentially makes *SeqyClean* to be one of the leading applications for sequence preprocessing for subsequent analysis.

3.2 Effects of different preprocessing stages on de-novo assembly and mapping of *S.cerevisae* library

For this library (2x250bp paired-end data with 3,875,453 paired reads): the best assembly was seen from data preprocessed with all stages: de-duplication, combining paired reads, quality and adapter trimming, see Table 8. 3,966 reads were recognized and discarded as duplicates, 19.72% of total reads contained adapters, and roughly the same amount of reads were combined into longer single-end sequences. De-duplication and combining paired reads resulted in large effects on assembly speed and quality, requiring the shortest assembly time: 10 and 11hrs, in comparison to 32 and 47hrs in other tests since, de-duplication and combining paired reads decreased amount of data to assemble but still preserved enough for producing good quality assemblies.

Quality trimming also had a significant impact on assembly time and quality. N50 is 83,571bp against 80,595bp from data preprocessed with adapter trimming flag only. Assembly from data preprocessed with adapter and quality trimming flags also resulted in reduced assembly time: 32hrs versus 47hrs in comparison to adapter trimming only.

For the raw data, the assembler did not finish the task in a reasonable time, and the assembly process was stopped before results were generated.

The best mapping results were obtained from data preprocessed with all stages (de-duplication, merging overlapping paired reads, quality and adapter trimming), see Table 9. In this case there are 98.92% of mapped reads.

Without de-duplication (combining paired reads, quality and adapter trimming), there are 98.88% of reads properly mapped. Again, this may indicate that left duplicates had low quality thereby slightly decreasing mapping quality.

Without overlapping and de-duplication, mapping quality is still high in comparison to the two previous tests: 98.90% (which is slightly higher than from data preprocessed with merging overlapping reads option). This can indicate that even if we keep lower quality duplicates in a library, we can still have good results using the advantage of paired-end paradigm, where one pair support another (using the insert size) even if that pair not properly mapped. Or this might indicate that the library was of reasonably good quality and the mapper was able to soft-clip adapters where they existed.

With adapter trimming only we have 98.32% reads properly mapped, which indicates that quality trimming has no such great impact on mapping quality (19.72% reads with adapters were found). Again, in this case we may observe advantage of paired-end method.

Table 6: Comparison of *Bowtie2*-mapping: *SeqyClean* against other tools and raw data. Test library: *dataset #2, E.coli* K-12/MG1655 Illumina data (SRR519926, a 2 x 250 bp run, sequenced on a MiSeq)

Application	*PE+SE/Total PE+SE (Overall alignment rate%)	PE mapped/Total PE (Overall alignment rate, %)	SE mapped/Total SE (Overall alignment rate%)	Total reads, PE1/PE2/SE	Avg. read length, PE1/PE2/SE
AlienTrimmer	NA	628,734/632,259 (99.44%)	NA	315,744/315,744/NA	183.37/115.35 /NA
Ea-utils (fastq-mcf)	NA	637,468/640,206 (99.57%)	NA	319,676/319,676/NA	185.95/122.97/NA
Skewer	NA	637,828/ 640,098 (99.65%)	NA	319,254/319,254/NA	187.60/126.40/NA
Trimmomatic	599,405/645,673 (92.83%)	507,711/508,263 (99.89%)	91,694/137,410 (66.73%)	253,819/253,819/137,339	183.07/113.23/120.89
AdapterRemoval	NA	639,995/645,636 (99.13%)	NA	322,391/322,391/NA	187.90/120.54/NA
Sickle	631,627/ 704,390 (89.67%)	568,272/621,376 (91.45%)	36,484/83,014 (43.95%)	310,688/310,688/83,014	189.05/98.08 /154.51
SeqyClean	584,964/588,343 (99.43%)	480,196/480,616 (99.91%)	104,768/107,727 (97.25%)	239,989/ 239,989/107,613	188.09/118.32/154.51
Raw data	NA	610,084/801,192 (76.15%)	NA	400,596/400,596/NA	251/251/NA

PE – paired-end reads; SE – single-end reads; PE+SE – aligned combined PE and SE; PE – only PE, SE – only SE; NA – application does not report SE after cleaning.

Mapping of raw reads indicates only 92.67% of mapped reads. This is significant difference in comparison to the previous test: 5.65%. Thereby, adapter trimming significantly affects mapping quality even if 19.72% reads containing adapters were found.

3.3 Runtime and memory

Memory consumption directly depends on the size of reference contaminant FASTA data (more) and library size as well (less). Table 7 shows memory (RAM) footprints needed to store genomes of model organisms into a hash table. Using 2-bit DNA compression can significantly reduce memory consumption. In vector/contaminant trimming mode, the runtime of *SeqyClean* depends both on the reference and sample library size. Runtime depends on the size of the NGS library and on machine characteristics (4-24 cores, 8-128 GB of RAM) speed is: 1,251 reads/sec (799 sec for 106 reads) to process typical pyrosequence library (~600,000 – 1,000,000 reads) and 3,623 reads/sec (276 sec for 106 reads) to process typical Illumina library (~10,000,000 (MiSeq) ... ~200,000,000 (HiSeq) paired-end reads).

Table 7: Average memory usage for *SeqyClean* needed to store reference genome for different reference genome sizes (when the option vector trimming or option contaminants removal is turned on in additional to quality and adapter trimming)

Name	Genome size, bp	Memory usage
PhiX-174	5,386	11 MB
E.coli K-12	4,639,221	1.7 GB
S. cerevisiae	12,495,682	5.1 GB
Neurospora crassa	38,639,769	10 GB
Drosophila melanogaster	172,653,977	43 GB
Zebrafish	1.2×10^9	160 GB
Human	3.3×10^9	204 GB

Table 8: Evaluation of effect of different stages of pre-processing pipeline (adapter trimming, merging paired-end reads, duplicates screening and quality trimming) on de-novo assembly of *S.cerevisiae* Illumina MiSeq data (dataset #3, sequenced on IBEST Genomic Core). Note that assembly time is largest for raw data. Note: large contig has a length of >= 1000 bp.

Methodology				N50	Total length, (% of the reference)	Large/Total contigs	Assembling time (clock time) HH:MM:SS
De-dup	Merge	Qual	Adp				
X	X	X	X	85,803	11,631,506 (96%)	304/644	10:14:21
	X	X	X	79,076	11,569,355 (95%)	312/660	11:33:32
		X	X	73,443	11,569,413,	314/707	32:04:41
			X	70,595	11,560,405,	319/750	47:09:24

Table 9: Effect of different denoising stages on alignment of preprocessed *S.cerevisae* Illumina MiSeq data (dataset #3, sequenced on IBEST Genomic Core). Alignment was performed with *Bowtie2*.

Methodology				PE+SE mapped/Total PE+SE (%)
De-dup	Qual	Adp	Merge	
X	X	X	X	98.92
	X	X	X	98.88
		X	X	98.90
			X	98.32

4 CONCLUSIONS

Sequence quality greatly affects quality of analysis. With SeqyClean we preprocessed three different HTS libraries: *E.coli* Roche 454 (dataset #1), *E.coli* Illumina (dataset #2) and *S. cerevisiae* Illumina (dataset #3). We have shown that the quality of sequence data is greatly important for both genome assembly and genome mapping. In particular, adapter and quality trimming bring significant improvement of quality of assembly and mapping. As mapping quality increases false-positive INDELs and SNPs are reduced. Such false-positive variants can be mistakenly recognized as good, which leads to poor results. If the sequence library contains contaminants or vector sequence, it is necessary to perform vector and contaminant filtering in order to further improve the quality of analysis. Overall *SeqyClean* is a valuable improvement over existing preprocessing tools since it provides the most complete sequence preprocessing solution, offering all sequence preprocessing aspects. We are constantly working on optimization of the algorithms used in *SeqyClean*.

ACKNOWLEDGMENTS

This publication was made possible by NIH Grant P20RR16454 from the INBRE Program of the National Center for Research Resources.

REFERENCES

[1] Schatz M.C., Delcher A.L. and Salzberg S.L. 2010. Assembly of large genomes using second-generation sequencing, Genome Res, 20: 1165-1173.

[2] Criscuolo, A., Brisse, S. 2013. Alientrimmer: A tool to quickly and accurately trim off multiple short contaminant sequences from high-throughput sequencing reads. Genomics, 102(5-6):500-6. doi: 10.1016/j.ygeno.2013.07.011

[3] 454 Life Science, A. R. C. 2008. Point-and-click tools for assembly, mapping and amplicon variant analysis, http://454.com/products/analysis-software/index.asp.

[4] Chou, H., & Holmes, M. H. 2001. DNA sequence quality trimming and vector removal. Bioinformatics/computer Applications in The Biosciences, 17, 1093–1104.

[5] Erik Aronesty. 2013. Comparison of Sequencing Utility Programs. The Open Bioinformatics Journal, 7: 1-8.

[6] Schubert, M., Lindgreen S., Orlando L. 2016. AdapterRemoval v2: rapid adapter trimming, identification, and read merging, BMC Res Notes, 9:88.

[7] Hongshan Jiang, Rong Lei, Shou-Wei Ding and Shuifang Zhu. 2014. Skewer: a fast and accurate adapter trimmer for next-generation sequencing paired-end reads, BMC Bioinformatics, 15:182.

[8] Bolger, A. M., Lohse, M., & Usadel, B. 2014. Trimmomatic: A flexible trimmer for Illumina Sequence Data. Bioinformatics, 30(15):2114-20. doi: 10.1093/bioinformatics/btu170

[9] Kong, Y. 2011. Btrim: A fast, lightweight adapter and quality trimming program for next-generation sequencing technologies, Genomics, 98, 152-153.

[10] Joshi NA, Fass JN. 2011. Sickle: A sliding-window, adaptive, quality-based trimming tool for FastQ files (Version 1.29). Available at https://github.com/najoshi/sickle.

[11] Ning Z, Cox AJ and Mullikin JC, 2001. SSAHA: a fast search method for large DNA databases, Genome research, 11(10):1725-9.

[12] Langmead, B., & Salzberg, S. L. 2012. Fast gapped-read alignment with bowtie 2. Nat Meth, 9(4).

[13] Gurevich, A., Saveliev, V., Vyahhi, N., & Tesler, G. 2013. Quast: quality assessment tool for genome assemblies. Bioinformatics, 29(8), 1072-1075.

[14] Broad Institute. 2014. Picard: A set of command line tools (in Java) for manipulating high-throughput sequencing (HTS) data and formats such as SAM/BAM/CRAM and VCF, http://broadinstitute.github.io/picard/

[15] Zhang J., Kobert K., Flouri T., Stamatakis A. 2014. PEAR: a fast and accurate Illumina Paired-End reAd mergeR. Bioinformatics, 30 (5): 614-620.

[16] Renaud, G., Stenzel, U., & Kelso, J. 2014. IeeHom: adaptor trimming and merging for Illumina sequencing reads. Nucleic Acids Research, 42(18), e141. http://doi.org/10.1093/nar/gku699

[17] Martin, M. 2011. Cutadapt removes adapter sequences from high-throughput sequencing reads. EMBnet.journal. [Online] 17:1.

Distributed Memory Partitioning of High-Throughput Sequencing Datasets for Enabling Parallel Genomics Analyses

Nagakishore Jammula
Georgia Institute of Technology

Sriram P. Chockalingam
Georgia Institute of Technology

Srinivas Aluru
Georgia Institute of Technology

ABSTRACT

State-of-the-art high-throughput sequencing instruments decipher in excess of a billion short genomic fragments per run. The output sequences are referred to as *reads*. These read datasets facilitate a wide variety of analyses with applications in areas such as genomics, metagenomics, and transcriptomics. Owing to the large size of the read datasets, such analyses are often compute and memory intensive. In this paper, we present a parallel algorithm for partitioning large-scale read datasets in order to facilitate distributed-memory parallel analyses. During the process of partitioning the read datasets, we construct and partition the associated de Bruijn graph in parallel. This allows applications that make use of a variant of the de Bruijn graph, such as de novo assembly, to directly leverage the generated de Bruijn graph partitions. In addition, we propose a mechanism for evaluating the quality of the generated partitions of reads and demonstrate that our algorithm produces high quality partitions. Our implementation is available at github.com/ParBLiSS/read_partitioning.

1 INTRODUCTION

Since the inception of high-throughput sequencing (HTS) machines, the cost of sequencing has been declining and the throughput has been increasing exponentially [15]. For instance, using the recent HiSeq X Ten from Illumina, the current market leader, it is possible to generate, in a single day, the complete sequencing data of 45 human genomes for US$1000 each [8]. Moreover, the upcoming NovaSeq line of instruments are expected to bring this cost down to $100 per human genome. As a consequence of these revolutionary advances, HTS has found its use in a diverse range of applications beyond whole-genome sequencing. These include, among many others, genome resequencing, characterizing the transcriptome, cataloging of metagenomic samples, and providing personalized molecular diagnosis. See [6] and [15] for recent reviews on HTS and its applications.

Unfortunately, the large volumes of data generated from HTS experiments present significant computational challenges for downstream analysis pipelines. Analysis of such big datasets is compute intensive and requires a huge memory footprint. These challenges are expected to get more difficult, as more and more data becomes available in the future. Recent surveys note that many laboratories spend significantly more time and resources on the computational analysis of HTS data than on generating the data itself [12, 16]. Many investigators attempt to address the memory demands by resorting to shared-memory machines with a large memory capacity. However, the number of hardware threads available for computation in such machines is limited. The challenges posed by ever growing sequencing throughput and the limitations suffered by currently available sequence analysis methods provide the context for our proposed solution.

In this paper, we present an end-to-end distributed-memory parallel algorithm for partitioning HTS read datasets. The goal of partitioning a large-scale HTS read dataset is to enable fast analyses using distributed-memory parallel systems. Our algorithm comprises of the following steps: (1) Building a de Bruijn graph from the given set of input reads, (2) Compacting the de Bruijn graph to reduce its size, (3) Partitioning the resulting compacted graph using a graph partitioner, and (4) Generating a partition of the read dataset from the partitioning of the de Bruijn graph. We also propose an algorithm to evaluate the quality of the partitioned read datasets.

Excluding sequencing errors, the size of the de Bruijn graph is expected to track the cumulative length of the source DNA molecules from which the read dataset is generated. Every read traces a path in the de Bruijn graph and there are overlaps among paths traced by multiple reads. Based on these properties, our insight is that if we can generate a good partitioning of the de Bruijn graph associated with a set of reads, it can be translated into a good partitioning of the read set itself. We demonstrate that our solution produces high quality de Bruijn graph partitions, and as a consequence, high quality partitioning of read datasets, for an assortment of large-scale datasets. Such high quality partitioning enables fast distributed-memory parallel analyses of read datasets by keeping the communication necessary to execute the application low.

Since our approach leverages de Bruijn graph as an intermediate data structure, we are able to generate partitions of a set of reads without computing pairwise similarity among reads, which is known to be challenging both in terms of computation and memory. Variants of de Bruijn graph gained significant adoption for analyses of HTS reads, a prominent example being de novo genome assembly. State-of-the-art distributed-memory parallel assemblers use hashing to distribute the de Bruijn graph. This approach destroys data locality, and hence increases communication costs during downstream analyses. In contrast, our approach for partitioning the de Bruijn graph respects locality. Therefore, the partitioned de Bruijn graph we generate can be used by analyses that predominantly make use of some variant of the graph.

We present our proposed algorithms for de Bruijn graph and read set partitioning in Sections 4 and 5 respectively. Using real datasets, the respective sections also discuss the quality of the generated

Permission to make digital or hard copies of all or part of this work for personal or classroom use is granted without fee provided that copies are not made or distributed for profit or commercial advantage and that copies bear this notice and the full citation on the first page. Copyrights for components of this work owned by others than ACM must be honored. Abstracting with credit is permitted. To copy otherwise, or republish, to post on servers or to redistribute to lists, requires prior specific permission and/or a fee. Request permissions from permissions@acm.org.
ACM-BCB'17, August 20–23, 2017, Boston, MA, USA.
© 2017 ACM. 978-1-4503-4722-8/17/08...$15.00
DOI: 10.1145/3107411.3107491

partitions and the corresponding runtime incurred. Information about datasets and our methodology is provided in Section 3. Before we proceed to describe the proposed algorithms, we review the notations and relevant data structures used in this paper in Section 2.

2 BACKGROUND

2.1 Representation of Sequences

A DNA molecule is comprised of two strands. The forward strand of the molecule, defined in the 5′ to 3′ direction, is modeled as a sequence of characters from the alphabet set $\Sigma = \{A, C, G, T\}$. Given such a sequence of n characters, $s = s_1, \ldots, s_n$, its reverse complementary strand *i.e.,* the sequence in the 3′ to 5′ direction, is $\bar{s} = c(s_n), \ldots, c(s_1)$, where $c(x), x \in \Sigma$ is the mapping function : $c(A) \longrightarrow T, c(C) \longrightarrow G, c(G) \longrightarrow C, andc(T) \longrightarrow A$. A DNA molecule can be represented by the pair $(s, \bar{s})$ or only by the *canonical sequence* $\hat{s}$, which is the lexicographically smaller of the two strings s and $\bar{s}$ *i.e.,* $\min(s, \bar{s})$. Unless specified otherwise, we use the canonical representation by default.

A k-length DNA sequence is termed a k-mer. A k-molecule (e.g. $(m, \overline{m})$) and *canonical k-mer* (e.g. $\hat{m}$) are similarly defined. Given a read set R, the set of all the k-mers of R is represented by M^k. $\hat{M}^k$ denotes the set of canonical k-mers corresponding to M^k. In order to obtain M^k or $\hat{M}^k$, each read $r \in R$ of length l is decomposed into $(l - k + 1)$ k-mers, by sliding a window of length k along the read. *Coverage* of a read set R is defined as the average number of times a base in the source DNA molecule(s) appears in R. Most widely deployed HTS instruments from Illumina are capable of generating *paired-end reads.* A paired-end read consists of two reads which are sequenced from opposite ends of a longer DNA fragment, referred to as *insert.*

2.2 de Bruijn Graph

While many variants of *de Bruijn graph* have been proposed for analysis of short read datasets, we use a definition that closely resembles the one in [10]. We define *de Bruijn graph* as a graph with k-molecules (or equivalently the set of canonical k-mers $\hat{M}^k$) as its vertices. An edge is included between a pair of vertices u and v, if there is a $(k-1)$ length suffix-prefix overlap between a strand of u and a strand of v. In other words, for any edge between vertices u and v, the corresponding merged $(k+1)$-mer exists in M^{k+1}. An edge incident to a vertex u of the de Bruijn graph is called an *in-edge* (resp. *out-edge*) w.r.t. u if the corresponding $(k-1)$ length overlap includes the prefix (resp. suffix) of u. Note that a vertex u can have at most four *in-edges* and at most four *out-edges* incident to it, and hence a maximum of eight neighbors. The key difference between the above definition of *de Bruijn graph* and the one proposed in [10] is that an undirected edge representation is sufficient for our purposes.

2.3 Graph Partitioning

Let $\mathcal{G} = (V, E, W_v, W_e)$ be an undirected graph. Here, V is the set of vertices, E is the set of edges, and functions $W_v : V \longrightarrow \mathbb{R}$ and $W_e : E \longrightarrow \mathbb{R}$ define the vertex and the edge weights respectively. In the representation of an undirected graph $\mathcal{G}$, an edge between two vertices $u \in V$ and $v \in V$ appears twice in E, as two ordered pairs (u, v) and (v, u). Let $V_1, \ldots, V_m$ be a partition of $\mathcal{G}$'s set of vertices such that $V_i \cap V_j = \emptyset$ (for $i, j \in \{1, m\}$, $i \neq j$) and $V_1 \cup \ldots \cup V_m = V$. Then, the *balance* of the partition is defined as

$$\frac{\max_{1 \leq i \leq m} C(V_i)}{\sum_{1 \leq i \leq m} C(V_i)/m}$$

where $C(V_i)$ is the sum of the weights of all vertices $v_j \in V_i$. The *cut* of the partition is defined as the total sum of weights of edges between $u \in V_i$ and $v \in V_j$ for every pair $(V_i, V_j), 1 \leq i < j \leq m$.

The *graph partitioning* problem is defined as follows: Given $\mathcal{G}$, a positive integer $m \leq |V|$, and a parameter $\epsilon > 0$, find a partition $V_1, \ldots, V_m$ of the vertices of $\mathcal{G}$ that minimizes the *cut* of the partition, while bounding the *balance* of the partition to at most $(1 + \epsilon)$. We extend the definitions of cut and balance to read dataset partitioning in Section 5.4.

3 METHODOLOGY

Table 1 lists key properties of the datasets used in evaluating this work. All the three datasets, namely *Fish, Bird,* and *Snake*, were provided as part of the Assemblathon 2 competition [1]. These datasets are publicly available and the instructions for obtaining them are described in [1]. The sizes of the input read sets, for all the datasets, correspond to over $50X$ coverage based on the estimated length of the respective genomes.

Table 1: Datasets used for experimental evaluation

Dataset	Genome length (Giga base-pairs)	Dataset size (Giga bases)	Read length (Bases)
Fish	1.0 Gbp	52.7 Gb	101
Bird	1.2 Gbp	70.7 Gb	101
Snake	1.6 Gbp	84.1 Gb	121

We ran our experiments on a cluster with a 40 Gb QDR InfiniBand interconnect. Each node in the cluster has two 2.0 GHz 8-core Intel Xeon E5-2650 processors, for a total of 16 cores per node. The 16 cores in a node share 128 GB of main memory. For our experiments, we used up to 32 nodes in the cluster, for a total of 512 cores. Further, we used distributed-memory parallel programming with OpenMPI 1.8.6. For reporting performance results, each experiment was repeated three times. The maximum wall-times from all processes were collected for each run, and the minimum times amongst the repeats of an experiment are reported as they closely represent the capabilities of the system. Other details concerning experimental methodology are provided at appropriate places in the paper.

4 DE BRUIJN GRAPH PARTITIONING

4.1 Motivation

Estimating pairwise similarity among reads, for the purpose of partitioning a large set of reads, is known to be challenging both in terms of computation and memory. Therefore, we use the de Bruijn graph, constructed from the read set, to accomplish our end goal of read set partitioning. Excluding sequencing errors, the size of the de

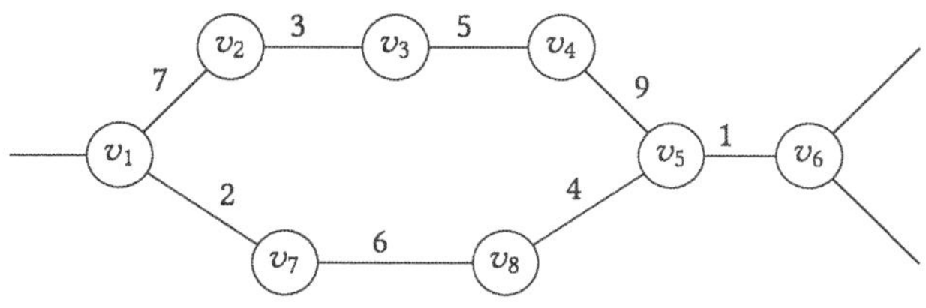

Figure 1: A fragment of the DBG. *in-edges* and *out-edges* are shown to the left and the right of a vertex respectively.

Bruijn graph is expected to be proportional to the cumulative length of the source DNA molecules from which the read set is generated. Therefore, the use of de Bruijn graph allows us to overcome both compute and memory limitations. Since reads trace paths in a de Bruijn graph, a high quality partitioning of the de Bruijn graph can be used to generate a high quality partitioning of the read set itself. Furthermore, the abundance of applications that make use of de Bruijn graph as a primary data structure, including de novo assembly, can directly leverage the partitioned de Bruijn graph.

Owing to their significance, the problems of de Bruijn graph construction and compaction received attention from several researchers. Majority of the proposed solutions are targeted at single-node machines, where multiple cores share the main memory. They are not suitable in the context of our proposed solution approach, which is meant for distributed-memory parallel systems. There are a few distributed-memory parallel solutions for compacting the de Bruijn graph. However, they cannot be leveraged due to the unique requirements of our solution approach. We need to explicitly keep track of the graph vertices, edges, and their weights. In this section, we present the data structures and the algorithms intended for constructing, compacting, and partitioning de Bruijn graphs.

4.2 Parallel Construction of de Bruijn Graph

We refer to a vertex u in the de Bruijn graph as a *branch* vertex if it has more than one *in-edge* or more than one *out-edge* incident to it. Otherwise, u is a *chain* vertex. If a chain vertex u has only one neighbor or has a *branch* vertex as one of its neighbors, then u is a *terminal* vertex. In the de Bruijn graph, a *chain* or a *unitig* is a sequence of vertices $\langle c_1, \dots, c_d \rangle$ that satisfies the following conditions: (a) c_{i+1} is a neighbor of c_i; (b) $c_i, 1 < i < d$ are chain vertices, and (c) c_1 and c_d are terminal vertices. The weight of a chain is the sum of weights of the edges between the vertices in the chain. For example, in the graph shown in Figure 1, v_2, v_3, v_4, v_7 and v_8 are chain vertices, whereas v_1, v_5 and v_6 are branch vertices. $\langle v_2, v_3, v_4 \rangle$ and $\langle v_7, v_8 \rangle$ are chains with weights 8 and 6 respectively.

To enable efficient manipulation of the de Bruijn graph, we represent the graph as a list of tuples $((u, v), w)$, where (u, v) is an ordered pair representing the edge between vertices u and v, and w is the edge weight *i.e.*, the number of times the corresponding merged $(k + 1)$-mer occurs in the read set. We classify an edge $((u, v), w)$ in the de Bruijn graph into one of two types: An edge (u, v) is a *chain* edge if both u and v are chain vertices. An edge (u, v) is a *branch* edge if either u or v is a branch vertex. Note that the edge type definitions are complementary to each other so that every edge in the graph belongs to exactly one of the two types. As an example, in the graph shown in Figure 1, $((v_2, v_3), 3)$, $((v_3, v_2), 3)$, $((v_3, v_4), 5)$, $((v_4, v_3), 5)$, $((v_7, v_8), 6)$, and $((v_8, v_7), 6)$ are chain edges, and the rest of the edges are branch edges.

Algorithm 1 constructs in parallel the de Bruijn graph for the input read set R by generating the two types of edges defined above. In Line 3, we make use of *KmerInd* [13] to build a distributed index of k-molecules. The entries in the index are of the form: $(u, [w_1, \dots, w_8])$. Here, the first element u is the k-molecule in its canonical representation, and the second element is an array of integers which contains, corresponding to each of u's eight possible neighbors, the number of times the respective $(k + 1)$-mer occurs in R. Line 6 ensures that the frequency of occurrence of every $(k + 1)$-mer in R is greater than a *threshold* parameter. This check enables filtering of low-frequency k-mers, which are produced due to sequencing errors. The value of this parameter is specified by the user.

Algorithm 1: Parallel construction of *de Bruijn graph*

Input: R, the set of reads
Output: Two distributed lists of edges: $\mathcal{C}$, *chain* edges, and $\mathcal{B}$, *branch* edges

1 **parallel** j = *processor's rank* **do**
2 Initialize $\mathcal{B}, \mathcal{C}, \mathcal{T}$ to empty list of tuples.
3 $\mathcal{I} \leftarrow$ Construct distributed index of k-molecules for R using *KmerInd* [13].
4 **for** $(u, [w_1, \dots, w_8]) \in \mathcal{I}$ **do**
5 Let $v_1, \dots, v_4$ be the k-molecules of the *in-edge* neighbors and $v_5, \dots, v_8$ be the corresponding *out-edge* neighbors (w.r.t the alphabet set Σ). Let w_i be the weight corresponding to edge (u, v_i).
6 **for** $1 \le i \le 8$ **do** Set w_i to 0 if $w_i < (k + 1)$-mer threshold.
7 $nbrs_i \leftarrow$ No. of non-zero elements in $[w_1, \dots, w_4]$.
8 $nbrs_o \leftarrow$ No. of non-zero elements in $[w_5, \dots, w_8]$.
9 **if** $((nbrs_i > 1) \lor (nbrs_o > 1))$ **then**
10 **for** $1 \le i \le 8$ **do** Append tuples $((u, v_i), w_i)$ and $((v_i, u), 0)$ to lists $\mathcal{B}$ and $\mathcal{T}$ respectively, if $w_i > 0$.
11 **else if** $((nbrs_i + nbrs_o) > 0)$ **then**
12 **for** $1 \le i \le 8$ **do** Append tuples $((u, v_i), w_i)$ to list $\mathcal{C}$, if $w_i > 0$.
13 **end**
14 **end**
15 Append $\mathcal{T}$ to $\mathcal{C}$, and sort the distributed list $\mathcal{C}$ in parallel.
16 Remove from $\mathcal{C}$ those edges that appear more than once and add them to $\mathcal{B}$.
17 **end**

Lines 7–13 in Algorithm 1 enable the segregation of edges into chain edges and branch edges, which together constitute the undirected de Bruijn graph. By counting the number of non-zero entries of the weight vector of an entry $(u, [w_1, \dots, w_8])$ (in Lines 7 and 8), it is possible to check if u is a chain or a branch vertex. Accordingly, the tuple $((u, v_i), w_i)$ is added either to the list $\mathcal{B}$, if u is a branch vertex (in Line 10), or to the list $\mathcal{C}$, if u is a chain vertex (in Line 12).

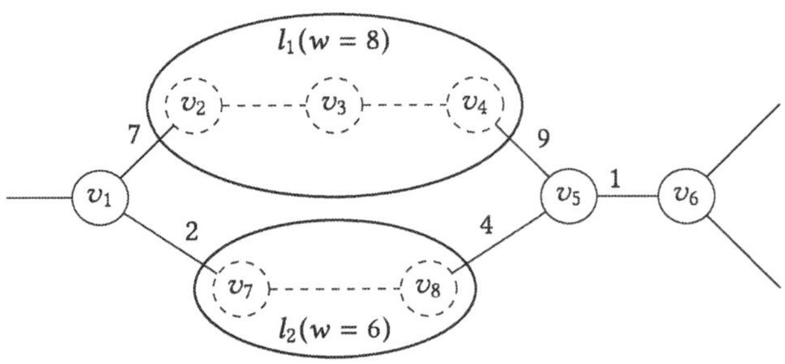

Figure 2: Compacted form of the de Bruijn graph fragment shown in Fig. 1. The chains $\langle v_2, v_3, v_4\rangle$ and $\langle v_7, v_8\rangle$ are replaced by labels l_1 and l_2 with weights 8 and 6 respectively.

However, since the index is distributed, it is not possible, with only locally available information, to verify if v_i is a branch vertex or a chain vertex. This implies that after adding all the tuples (i.e, at the end of the loop at Line 13), the branch edge list $\mathcal{B}$ does not include edges $((u, v), w)$, where v is a branch vertex and u is a chain vertex, whereas the chain edge list C includes edges $((u, v), w)$, where v is a branch vertex. In order to update the lists C and $\mathcal{B}$, a temporary list $\mathcal{T}$ containing edges $((u, v), w)$ such that v is a branch vertex is created (line 10). In Lines 15- 16, by making use of $\mathcal{T}$ and parallel sorting, the edges $((u, v), w)$ in C with v being a branch vertex are identified and moved from C to $\mathcal{B}$.

Categorization into branch and chain edges allows the algorithms described in the following subsections to label the chain vertices and subsequently compact the labeled chains to generate a significantly smaller graph. Note that the distributed index of k-molecules constructed by *KmerInd* recognizes *in-edges* and *out-edges* separately. However, as we mentioned in Section 2.2, an undirected edge representation of the de Bruijn graph suffices beyond this point for our purposes. Accordingly, the output lists of Algorithm 1 are comprised of only undirected edges.

4.3 Parallel Compaction of de Bruijn Graph

The next step in our solution is to compact the de Bruijn graph. De Bruijn graphs constructed from read sets are known to contain several long chains. De Bruijn graph based de novo assemblers make use of this observation to identify unambiguous segments in the graph. We leverage this observation to reduce the size of the graph, thus reducing the runtime and the memory requirements for subsequent steps.

The de Bruijn graph is compacted as follows: First, using the edge lists constructed in the previous subsection, Algorithm 2 labels all the chains in the graph. Algorithm 3 then replaces vertices in every chain by their chain label. Back to the example shown in Figure 1, the chains $\langle v_2, v_3, v_4\rangle$ and $\langle v_7, v_8\rangle$ are compacted and the resulting compact graph is shown in Figure 2.

Algorithm 2 describes the steps to label and compute weights of all the chains, where the weight of a chain is defined as the sum of the weights of all the edges that constitute the chain. Here, we make use of the fact that in the subgraph induced by only the chain edges, each chain is a connected component. This implies that labeling

Algorithm 2: Labeling of *de Bruijn graph chain* vertices

Input: Distributed list of chain edges C output by Algorithm 1
Output: $\mathcal{V}$, list of chain vertices. Each element in $\mathcal{V}$ is a tuple of three elements (u, l, w), where u is a chain vertex, l is the chain label, and w is the label weight.

1 **parallel** j = *processor's rank* **do**
2   Initialize $\mathcal{V}$ to an empty list of tuples.
  `// Attribute chain IDs (labels) to vertices`
3   Use the connectivity algorithm proposed in [5] to assign chain IDs to vertices in C. The output of this algorithm is $\mathcal{L}$, a distributed list of tuples (u, l). Here, u is a chain vertex and l is the ID of the chain to which u belongs to.
  `// Compute chain weights`
4   Initialize $\mathcal{T}$ to an empty list of tuples. $\mathcal{T}$ accommodates tuples of four elements (u, v, l, w), where u and v are graph vertices, l is a label, and w is the edge weight.
5   **for** $((u, v), w) \in C$ **do** Append tuple $(u, v, null, w)$ to $\mathcal{T}$.
6   **for** $(u, l) \in \mathcal{L}$ **do** Append tuple $(u, u, l, 0)$ to $\mathcal{T}$.
7   Parallel sort $\mathcal{T}$ by the first element of the tuple.
8   **foreach** *segment* T *of* $\mathcal{T}$ *s.t. every* $t \in T$ *has the same first element* **do**
9     $(u_t, v_t, l_t, w_t) \leftarrow$ tuple in T, whose label is not null.
10   Set l_t as the label for all the tuples of T
11   **end**
12   Parallel sort $\mathcal{T}$ by the label element of the tuple.
13   **foreach** *segment* T *of* $\mathcal{T}$ *s.t. every* $t \in T$ *has the same label* **do**
14     $w_s \leftarrow$ sum of the weight values of all the tuples in T.
15   Set w_s as the weight for all the tuples of T.
16   **end**
  `// Generate output list`
17   Parallel sort $\mathcal{T}$ by the first element of the tuple.
18   **foreach** *segment* T *of* $\mathcal{T}$ *s.t. every* $t \in T$ *has the same first element* **do**
19   Let (u_t, v_t, l_t, w_t) be the first element of T.
20   Append (u_t, l_t, w_t) to $\mathcal{V}$.
21   **end**
22 **end**

the chains is equivalent to labeling the connected components of the induced subgraph, which is accomplished as follows. Given the distributed list of chain edges, we use the parallel connectivity algorithm proposed in [5] (Line 3 in Algorithm 2) to identify the chain to which each chain vertex belongs to. The connectivity algorithm takes $log_2 L$ steps to complete this identification for all the chains, where L is the number of vertices in the longest chain.

After labeling all the chain vertices, the chain weights are computed as follows. In lines 4–11, a temporary distributed list of tuples $\mathcal{T}$ is created. Each tuple (u, v, l, w) in $\mathcal{T}$ corresponds to a chain edge (u, v) and includes the edge weight and u's chain label. $\mathcal{T}$ is then sorted in parallel by its label, and the total weight of the chain is computed as the sum of the weights of all tuples sharing the same label (lines 12–16). The final output from Algorithm 2 (prepared in lines 17–20) is $\mathcal{V}$, a distributed list of tuples, where each tuple corresponds to a chain vertex and contains the vertex ID (*i.e.*, the canonical k-mer representing the vertex), its chain label, and the chain weight.

Algorithm 3 uses outputs from both Algorithms 1 and 2 to complete the graph compaction. It outputs, for each edge in the compact de Bruijn graph, a tuple (u, v, we, wu), where u and v are the vertices in the compact graph, we is the edge weight and wu is the vertex weight of u. To construct the compact de Bruijn graph, Algorithm 3 starts with the distributed list of branch edges $\mathcal{B}$ from Algorithm 1. For each edge $((u, v), w) \in \mathcal{B}$, a tuple in the output format with zero vertex weight i.e., $(u, v, w, 0)$, is added to $\mathcal{E}$ (Line 3 in Algorithm 3). Recall that in a branch edge (u, v), either u or v should be a branch vertex, which in turn implies that either v or u can potentially be a chain vertex. Such entries in $\mathcal{E}$ are identified and the chain vertex is replaced by its corresponding label.

Lines 4–11 replace the vertex u in the tuples by its label, if u is a chain vertex. The vertex weights are updated with the corresponding label (chain) weights. Similarly, Lines 12–18 replace the vertex v by its label, if v happens to be a chain vertex. In both cases, the distributed list of vertex-label mapping $\mathcal{V}$ constructed in Algorithm 2 is used to match the vertex IDs. Finally, in Lines 19–23, the weights for edges and vertices of the compact graph are assigned.

4.4 Partitioning of Compacted de Bruijn Graph

We treat the compact de Bruijn graph output by Algorithm 3 as a standard graph data structure (as defined in Section 2.3) and find a partition for this graph. Graph partitioning is an important problem with applications in several domains and hence, has received significant attention from researchers over the years [2]. While the details of the various solution approaches proposed differ from one another, most of them adopt the multilevel graph partitioning paradigm first introduced in [7]. The key idea is to recursively coarsen the graph to reduce its size, partition the coarsest graph, and recursively uncoarsen the graph to its original size. Refinement is typically performed after every uncoarsening to improve the *cut*, defined in Section 2.3. Graph partitioning algorithms differ in the exact techniques they adopt for coarsening, partitioning, and uncoarsening.

We use a recently proposed distributed-memory graph partitioning algorithm called *KaHIP* [11] to partition the compacted de Bruijn graph output by Algorithm 3. *KaHIP* makes use of size-constrained label propagation algorithm during coarsening and uncoarsening phases, and coarse-grained evolutionary algorithm for partitioning the coarsest graph. In the context of the multilevel graph partitioning framework, the labeling of de Bruijn graph chains proposed in Algorithm 2 enables rapid compaction and un-compaction of the de Bruijn graph. As we will demonstrate in Section 4.5, this allows *KaHIP* to generate partitions significantly faster than if they were generated using the original de Bruijn graph. Use of domain knowledge about sequencing read sets and de Bruijn graphs enables realization of this efficient approach.

Algorithm 3: Parallel compaction of *de Bruijn graph*

Input: (a) $\mathcal{B}$, list of branch edges, output from Algorithm 1, and (b) $\mathcal{V}$, list of labeled chain vertices, output from Algorithm 2. Both lists are distributed.

Output: Compact *de Bruijn graph* as a distributed list of edges, $\mathcal{E}$. $\mathcal{E}$ includes tuples with four elements (u, v, we, wu), where u and v are the vertices of the compact graph, we is the edge weight, and wu is the node weight of u.

1 **parallel** *j = processor's rank* **do**
2 Initialize $\mathcal{E}$ to an empty list of tuples.
3 **for** $((u, v), w) \in \mathcal{B}$ **do** Append $(u, v, w, 0)$ to $\mathcal{E}$.
`// Replace chains in the graph by their labels`
4 **for** $(u, l, w) \in \mathcal{V}$ **do** Append $(u, l, null, w)$ to $\mathcal{E}$.
5 Parallel sort $\mathcal{E}$ by the tuple's first element.
6 **foreach** *segment E of $\mathcal{E}$ that share the same first element* **do**
7 $(u_t, l_t, null, wu_t) \leftarrow$ tuple t in E whose third element is null.
8 Set the first element of all the tuples in E to l_t.
9 Set the fourth element of all the tuples in E to wu_t.
10 Remove t from $\mathcal{E}$.
11 **end**
12 **for** $(u, l, w) \in \mathcal{V}$ **do** Append $(l, u, null, w)$ to $\mathcal{E}$.
13 Parallel sort $\mathcal{E}$ by the tuple's second element.
14 **foreach** *segment E of $\mathcal{E}$ that share the same second element* **do**
15 $(l_t, u_t, null, wv_t) \leftarrow$ tuple t in E whose third element is null.
16 Set the second element of all the tuples in E to l_t.
17 Remove t from $\mathcal{E}$.
18 **end**
`// Update weights`
19 Parallel sort $\mathcal{E}$ by the first element.
20 **foreach** *segment E of $\mathcal{E}$ that share the same first element* **do**
21 $sw \leftarrow$ sum of all the edge weights of $t \in E$.
22 **for** $t \in E$ **do** Add sw to wu of t.
23 **end**
24 **end**

4.5 Results and Analysis

In this section, for the three datasets listed in Table 1, we present quality and runtime results for the parallel algorithms to construct, compact, and partition a de Bruijn graph.

First, we evaluate the impact of compaction on reducing the size of the de Bruijn graph. Table 2 shows the compaction ratio obtained for all three datasets. It is computed as a ratio of the number of vertices in the de Bruijn graph before compaction to the number of vertices in the compact de Bruijn graph. We obtain a mean compaction ratio of 47 across the three datasets, implying that our proposed approach significantly reduces the size of the de Bruijn graph. For constructing the initial de Bruijn graph, we used a value of 5 for the *threshold* parameter. This implies a k-molecule u is filtered out, if all edges incident to u have a weight ≤ 4. For the parameter k, we used a value of 31. We used *KmerGenie* software [3] to estimate the optimal k-mer length. However, both of these parameters can be specified by users. Note that the compact de Bruijn graph produced by our algorithm can be used by de novo assemblers for rapid *unitig* (unambiguous segment) generation in distributed-memory parallel settings.

Table 2: Reduction in the size of the DBG due to compaction

Dataset	Plain graph (No. of vertices)	Compacted graph (No. of vertices)	Compaction ratio
Fish	733,774,187	16,672,988	44
Bird	1,208,521,390	25,740,770	47
Snake	1,361,026,568	27,199,895	50

Next, we present the *cut* and the *balance* values for the de Bruijn graph partitions generated by our algorithm. These measures, defined earlier in Section 2.3, serve as the quality indicators of a graph partition. A good graph partition has low cut value and a balance value close to 1. Table 3 shows the *cut* ratios computed for the partitions corresponding to the de Bruijn graphs of the three datasets. The *cut* ratio refers to the ratio of the sum of weights of edges cut to the sum of weights of all edges in the graph. The low cut ratio obtained for all the three datasets demonstrates that our solution produces high quality partitioning of de Bruijn graphs. All the partitions have a *balance* value of 1.03.

Table 3: Quality of de Bruijn graph partitioning

Dataset	Sum of weights of all edges in the graph	Sum of weights of edges cut	*Cut* ratio
Fish	13,593,910,042	19,252,245	1.42×10^{-3}
Bird	22,462,771,436	22,337,839	0.99×10^{-3}
Snake	29,754,489,857	47,197,297	1.59×10^{-3}

One of the input parameters for the graph partitioning algorithm is the number of desired partitions. One way to choose this parameter is to set it to the number of available compute nodes in the distributed system. However, if there are thousands of distributed nodes available in a system, then the output graph partitions will be too fragmented, which in turn increases the communication costs required to transfer neighboring regions of the graph among the nodes. Therefore, this parameter needs to be carefully selected for a given dataset.

We choose the number of partitions based on the available memory per node, as follows. Suppose, L_G is the approximate total length of the source DNA molecule(s), in Gbp, corresponding to a read dataset, and mem_b bytes are required for analysis, per base of the genome. Then, to analyze the dataset, $(L_G \times mem_b)$ GB of memory is required. However, if mem_n is the size of memory available per node in the distributed system, expressed in GB, at least $n_p = \left\lceil \frac{L_G \times mem_b}{mem_n} \right\rceil$ number of nodes are required to run the analysis. We select the number of desired partitions to be n_p because n_p partitions are sufficient to run the analysis using n_p nodes in the distributed system. This does not prevent the user from running the analysis using more than n_p compute nodes in the system. To run the analysis with more than n_p nodes, a partition is duplicated on multiple nodes and only a fraction of the partition is analyzed in a node. For example, to run the analysis with 128 partitions using 1024 nodes, each partition is duplicated in 8 nodes and each node processes only 1/8-th of the locally available partition. Such a duplication scheme incurs far less communication costs compared to processing as many partitions as the number of available nodes. With a conservative assumption of $mem_n = 32$ and $mem_b = 64$, the number of partitions for Fish, Bird, and Snake datasets are computed as 106, 142, and 168, respectively.

Finally, we present runtime and parallel scalability results of Algorithms 1, 2, and 3. Table 4 lists the runtime in seconds incurred by each of the algorithms individually (columns 2-4) and also the total runtime (column 5), for the Bird dataset. We present results by varying the number of available cores from 64 to 512. Note that the number of MPI processes used is the same as the number of cores. Our algorithms demonstrate good scalability across the board. The discrepancy in runtime (most notable in case of 64 cores) is due to interference from concurrently running jobs, while accessing the interconnection network and the parallel file system. With 512 cores, our solution is able to compute the compacted de Bruijn graph for a read set of size 71 Gbp in 2.7 minutes. We refer the reader to [11] for a demonstration of the parallel scalability of *KaHIP*. In our experiments, *KaHIP* took 4.3 minutes to partition the compacted de Bruijn graph for the Bird dataset using 512 cores. We also attempted to partition the initial (*i.e.*, un-compacted) de Bruijn graph generated by Algorithm 1 directly. *KaHIP* spent an order of magnitude more time to partition the initial de Bruijn graph, validating the merit behind our approach of compacting the de Bruijn graph prior to partitioning the graph.

Table 4: Runtime in seconds for the *Bird* dataset for de Bruijn graph construction (Algorithm 1), chain labeling (Algorithm 2) and compaction (Algorithm 3).

No. of cores	Algorithm 1 (s)	Algorithm 2 (s)	Algorithm 3 (s)	Total (s)
64	391	790	33	1214
128	159	309	11	479
256	76	180	6	262
512	45	115	3	163

5 READ DATASET PARTITIONING

5.1 Motivation

Algorithms 1, 2, and 3 described in the previous section facilitate partitioning of the de Bruijn graph corresponding to a read set R. Further, we demonstrated that the partitions generated are of very high quality. Since reads trace paths in the de Bruijn graph, high quality partitioning of the de Bruijn graph can be translated into a high quality partitioning of R. In this section, we describe the algorithm we developed for this purpose. The intuition behind our algorithm is to let the k-mers in a read vote for the partition to which the read should be assigned. We also describe a parallel algorithm we developed for evaluating the quality of read set partitioning and present corresponding results.

5.2 Parallel Partitioning of Reads

The parallel algorithm we designed for generating a partition for the read set based on the de Bruijn graph partitioning takes as its input the following: (a) the read set R, (b) the partition IDs assigned by the graph partitioner to vertices of the compact de Bruijn graph, (c) the list of de Bruijn graph vertices, and (d) the vertex to chain label mapping determined by Algorithm 2. The algorithm starts off by propagating the partition IDs assigned to the label vertices of the compact graph to the canonical k-mers that make up the corresponding chains. Using the mapping from canonical k-mers to partition IDs, a distributed index $\mathcal{D}$ is then constructed. Finally, the distributed index is used to compute the partition ID for a read r as the most frequently assigned partition ID for the k-mers in read r. In case of a *paired-end read*, our approach assigns the same partition ID to both reads. We accomplish this by subjecting the first read to the read partitioning algorithm and assigning the resulting partition ID to the second read as well.

5.3 Partitioning Quality Evaluation

If the true sequence of the source DNA molecule and the starting position for each read in the source DNA sequence are known, then it is possible to evaluate the quality of read partitioning against the truth. A good partitioning of the reads would place the reads derived from the same region in the source DNA within the same partition. However, even if the true source sequence is available, it is not possible to identify, for every read r, the exact position of r in the source sequence. Therefore, for the read sets given in Table 1, we use the local alignment of the reads against a reference genome as an approximation of the truth and evaluate the quality of the read partitioning against it.

We developed a parallel algorithm to evaluate the quality of a read partition using the alignment information of the read set R. It takes as its input the partition IDs assigned to reads by the proposed method and a SAM file, the standard file format to specify alignment data for a read set. We evaluate the partition quality using two measures called `intra-pairs` and `inter-pairs`, corresponding to the number of overlapping read pairs (as inferred from their alignment to the reference genome) that are assigned the same and different partition IDs, respectively. We consider two reads to overlap if they share at least one base in the reference. Note that this is a rather stringent requirement as no algorithm using only read information can reliably detect short overlaps, let alone a single base overlap. For every overlapping read pair, we determine if both constituent reads are placed in the same partition (`intra-pairs`) or in different partitions (`inter-pairs`).

5.4 Results and Analysis

We present results pertaining to the partitioning of the read sets. In order to evaluate the quality of read set partitioning, we make use of the local alignment of the reads to the reference sequence. For the three datasets used in our experiments, we used the submissions that were ranked the best in the Assemblathon 2 competition as the reference sequence [1]. We then mapped the read datasets to the corresponding reference sequence using BWA local alignment software [9]. We allowed an error rate of 2% while mapping the reads.

In order to enable interpretation of read partitioning quality results, we extend the definitions of *cut* and *balance*, defined for graph partitioning in Section 2.3, to read partitioning. We define *balance* of a read partitioning as the ratio of the size of the largest read partition to the average size of the partitions. *Cut* is defined as the number of overlapping pairs of reads that are assigned to different partitions (`inter-pairs`). *Cut ratio* is defined as the ratio of *cut* to the total number of overlapping read pairs *i.e.,* the sum of `intra-pairs` and `inter-pairs`. A lower cut ratio implies that fewer overlapping read pairs are assigned to different partitions, indicating a better quality partition.

Table 5 shows the total number of overlapping read pairs *i.e.,* `intra-pairs` + `inter-pairs` (column 2), `inter-pairs` (column 3), and cut ratio (column 4) for all the three datasets. The cut ratio shown in the table corresponds to the reads that are error-free *i.e.,* they map to the reference sequence with no errors. Cut ratio corresponding to 2% error rate (*i.e.,* all reads that map with up to 2% error rate are considered) for Fish, Bird, and Snake datasets is 2.15×10^{-2}, 1.42×10^{-2}, and 5.11×10^{-2}, respectively. The results demonstrate that a high quality partitioning of the de Bruijn graph translates into a high quality partitioning of the corresponding read set. Balance for the read partitioning of Fish, Bird, and Snake datasets is 1.02, 1.03, and 1.10, respectively.

Table 5: Read partitioning quality evaluation for all datasets

Dataset	No. overlapping read pairs	`inter-pairs`	Cut ratio
Fish	20,930,646,131	193,013,621	0.92×10^{-2}
Bird	14,302,047,674	304,849,664	2.13×10^{-2}
Snake	6,728,041,314	263,882,542	3.92×10^{-2}

Finally, we present runtime and parallel scalability results for the algorithm used to compute read partitioning from de Bruijn graph partitioning. The results shown in Table 6 for Bird dataset demonstrate that the algorithm scales nearly perfectly and takes less than 3.8 minutes using 512 cores. The end-to-end runtime for the Bird dataset using 512 cores is around 11 minutes. Therefore, our solution not only produces high quality partitions but is also fast and scalable.

Table 6: Runtime in seconds for the *Bird* dataset for computing read partitioning from de Bruijn graph partitioning.

No. of cores	64	128	256	512
Runtime (s)	2090	950	456	226

6 DISCUSSION

An alternative approach for partitioning a set of reads is to explicitly construct a read-similarity graph, where each vertex is a read and an edge between a pair of vertices implies similarity between the corresponding pair of reads. To evaluate the similarity between a pair of reads, a wide variety of measures have been proposed ranging from pair-wise alignments to alignment-free techniques [17], trading off accuracy for computational complexity. While the approach of read-similarity graph appears to be intuitive, constructing this graph using even the simplest of the available measures is computationally challenging. Partitioning the resulting graph is even more challenging owing to its size. In contrast, our proposed solution does not suffer from these challenges. This is because the size of the de Bruijn graph is expected to be a function of the length of the reference sequence rather than the size of the read set. Chains in the de Bruijn graph are amenable for easy identification and rapid compaction. Furthermore, the size of the compacted graph enables fast graph partitioning. The algorithm we proposed for evaluating the quality of read dataset partitioning can be used to evaluate the efficacy of alternative approaches for generating read set partitioning.

There are two prior works that discuss partitioning of read sets [4, 14], but with very different objectives that are less applicable in our context. In these works, the goal is not about partitioning the read sets into uniformly sized partitions. In [14], clusters of reads that give rise to distinct connected components in the de Bruijn graph are referred to as partitions. No restriction is imposed on the size of any single cluster. This poses a significant limitation for parallel processing, as the size of the largest cluster dictates the lower bound on the runtime. In [4], reads that potentially belong to a region of interest in the reference sequence are identified from a HTS dataset and segregated for subsequent targeted analysis, which the authors refer to as partitioning. Therefore, our work stands as the first demonstration of partitioning large-scale HTS read datasets to facilitate parallel genomics analyses.

After developing the proposed framework, we made use of openly available, efficient solutions for solving some subproblems in the framework, namely constructing a distributed index of k-molecules, computing the connectivity, and partitioning general graphs. Researchers have spent significant effort over the years to develop and improve solutions to these problems. By making use of the state-of-the-art methods available to solve these problems as components of our approach, we are able to devise an effective overall solution. In addition, the individual components can be replaced with better methods as they become available.

7 CONCLUSION

Analysis of large-scale datasets produced by modern day high-throughput sequencing (HTS) instruments poses significant computational and memory challenges. The attempt to address the memory aspect of the challenge using shared-memory machines has limited effectiveness due to the limitations on available memory and number of hardware threads available. To address these challenges, we proposed locality-sensitive partitioning of read sets that can be applied for communication-efficient distributed memory parallel analysis for many applications. Our solution facilitates scalable analysis of the partitioned read datasets in distributed-memory settings, thereby addressing the dual challenges of computation and memory.

As part of generating a partitioning of the read dataset, we construct and partition the de Bruijn graph corresponding to the read set. Partitions of de Bruijn graph can be directly used by applications that predominantly use a variant of the de Bruijn graph. We demonstrate that our proposed solution produces high quality de Bruijn graph and read set partitions for large-scale datasets. The partitioning algorithm is fast, scalable, and effective. Although demonstrated in the context of genomics datasets, it can be extended to applications in areas such as metagenomics and transcriptomics.

ACKNOWLEDGMENTS

This work is supported in part by the U.S. National Science Foundation under CCF-1360593.

REFERENCES

[1] Keith R Bradnam, Joseph N Fass, Anton Alexandrov, and others. 2013. Assemblathon 2: evaluating de novo methods of genome assembly in three vertebrate species. *GigaScience* 2, 1 (2013).
[2] Aydın Buluç, Henning Meyerhenke, Ilya Safro, and others. 2016. Recent advances in graph partitioning. In *Algorithm Engineering*. Springer, 117–158.
[3] Rayan Chikhi and Paul Medvedev. 2013. Informed and automated k-mer size selection for genome assembly. *Bioinformatics* (2013).
[4] Danai Fimereli, Vincent Detours, and Tomasz Konopka. 2013. TriageTools: tools for partitioning and prioritizing analysis of high-throughput sequencing data. *Nucleic acids research* 41, 7 (2013).
[5] Patrick Flick, Chirag Jain, Tony Pan, and Srinivas Aluru. 2015. A parallel connectivity algorithm for de Bruijn graphs in metagenomic applications. In *Proceedings of the SC*.
[6] Sara Goodwin, John D McPherson, and W Richard McCombie. 2016. Coming of age: ten years of next-generation sequencing technologies. *Nature Reviews Genetics* 17, 6 (2016), 333–351.
[7] Bruce Hendrickson and Robert W Leland. 1995. A Multi-Level Algorithm For Partitioning Graphs. *In Proceedings of the SC* (1995).
[8] Illumina Inc. 2017. An Introduction to Next-Generation Sequencing Technology. (2017). http://www.illumina.com/technology/next-generation-sequencing.html.
[9] Heng Li and Richard Durbin. 2009. Fast and accurate short read alignment with Burrows–Wheeler transform. *Bioinformatics* 25, 14 (2009), 1754–1760.
[10] Paul Medvedev, Konstantinos Georgiou, Gene Myers, and Michael Brudno. 2007. Computability of models for sequence assembly. In *International Workshop on Algorithms in Bioinformatics*. Springer, 289–301.
[11] Henning Meyerhenke, Peter Sanders, and Christian Schulz. 2015. Parallel Graph Partitioning for Complex Networks. In *Proceedings of the 2015 IEEE International Parallel and Distributed Processing Symposium*. 1055–1064.
[12] Paul Muir, Shantao Li, Shaoke Lou, and others. 2016. The real cost of sequencing: scaling computation to keep pace with data generation. *Genome biology* 17, 1 (2016).
[13] Tony Pan, Patrick Flick, Chirag Jain, and others. 2016. Kmerind: A flexible parallel library for k-mer indexing of biological sequences on distributed memory systems. In *Proceedings of the 7th ACM-BCB*. 422–433.
[14] Jason Pell, Arend Hintze, Rosangela Canino-Koning, and others. 2012. Scaling metagenome sequence assembly with probabilistic de Bruijn graphs. *Proceedings of the National Academy of Sciences* 109, 33 (2012), 13272–13277.
[15] Jason A Reuter, Damek V Spacek, and Michael P Snyder. 2015. High-throughput sequencing technologies. *Molecular cell* 58, 4 (2015), 586–597.
[16] Andrea Sboner, Xinmeng Jasmine Mu, Dov Greenbaum, and others. 2011. The real cost of sequencing: higher than you think! *Genome biology* 12, 8 (2011).
[17] Susana Vinga and Jonas Almeida. 2003. Alignment-free sequence comparison – a review. *Bioinformatics* 19, 4 (2003), 513–523.

Scalable Genomic Assembly through Parallel *de Bruijn* Graph Construction for Multiple K-mers

Kanak Mahadik, Christopher Wright, Milind Kulkarni, Saurabh Bagchi, Somali Chaterji
Purdue University, West Lafayette, IN, USA
{kmahadik,christopherwright,milind,sbagchi,schaterji}@purdue.edu

ABSTRACT

Extraordinary progress in genome sequencing technologies has led to a tremendous increase in the number of sequenced genomes. However, biologists have run into a computational bottleneck to assemble large and complex genomes quickly, due to the lack of scalable and parallel *de novo* assembly algorithms. Among several approaches to assembly, the iterative *de Bruijn* graph (DBG) assemblers, such as IDBA-UD, generate high-quality assemblies by sequentially iterating from small to large *k*-values used in graph construction. However, this approach is time intensive because the creation of the graphs for increasing *k*-values proceeds sequentially. For example, with just eight *k*-values, graph construction takes 96% of the total time to assemble a metagenomic dataset with 33 million paired-end reads. In this paper, we propose ScalaDBG, which transforms the sequential process of DBG construction for a range of *k* values, to one where each graph is built independently and in parallel. We develop a novel mechanism whereby the graph for the higher *k* value can be "patched" with contigs generated from the graph with the lower *k* value. We show that for a variety of datasets our technique can assemble complex genomes much faster than IDBA-UD (6.7X faster for the most complex genome in our dataset) while maintaining the same accuracy for the assembled genome. Moreover, ScalaDBG's multi-level parallelism allows it to *simultaneously* leverage the power of mighty server machines by using all their cores *and* of compute clusters by scaling out.

1 INTRODUCTION

With the rapid advancement of sequencing technologies projected to generate 2^{40} exabytes of data by 2025 just for the human genomes [16], there is a dire need for *de novo* assembly algorithms to play catch-up. A high latency genome assembly kernel, a fundamental step in all genomic analyses pipelines, is a bottleneck for the subsequent analyses kernels, negatively affecting the overall performance and impeding the extraction of knowledge from raw genomic datasets.

Currently the most popular de novo genome assembly method is the *de Bruijn Graph* (DBG) method [3], used by assemblers such as Velvet [17], ABySS [15], and ALLPATHS-LG [5].

Permission to make digital or hard copies of all or part of this work for personal or classroom use is granted without fee provided that copies are not made or distributed for profit or commercial advantage and that copies bear this notice and the full citation on the first page. Copyrights for components of this work owned by others than the author(s) must be honored. Abstracting with credit is permitted. To copy otherwise, or republish, to post on servers or to redistribute to lists, requires prior specific permission and/or a fee. Request permissions from permissions@acm.org.
ACM-BCB '17, August 20-23, 2017, Boston, MA, USA.
© 2017 Copyright held by the owner/author(s). Publication rights licensed to ACM.
978-1-4503-4722-8/17/08...$15.00
DOI: http://dx.doi.org/10.1145/3107411.3107482

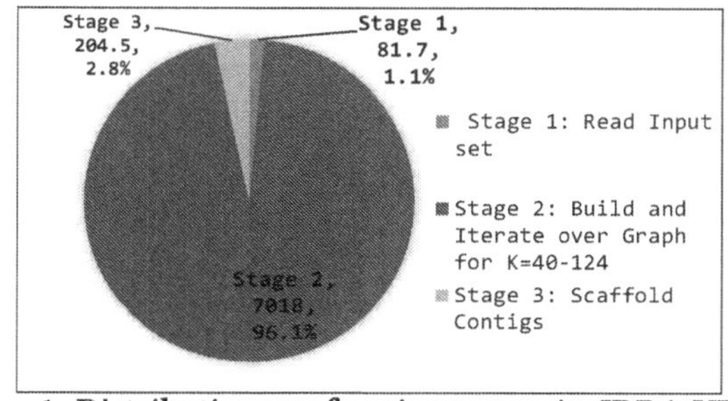

Figure 1: Distribution % of major stages in IDBA-UD, the time taken for each stage is provided in seconds for CAMI metagenomic dataset with 33 million paired-end reads of length 150, insert size 5kbp, 8 *k*-values : 40 – 124, **step-size** 12.

Characteristics of the DBG structure are highly dependent on the value of *k* selected for graph construction, with smaller *k*-values giving rise to *branching* of graphs and larger *k* values resulting in fragmented graphs [1, 7, 10, 12]. To achieve superior assemblies than a DBG built with a single *k*-value IDBA (Iterative DBG Assembler) [10], IDBA-UD [12], SOAPdenovo2 [7], and SPAdes [1] use multiple *k*-values, iteratively, to assemble the sequenced reads. Essentially, a DBG with a small *k*-value can be traversed to infer what longer sequences *might look like*, allowing a DBG with a larger *k*-value to incorporate this additional information to "patch up" gaps.

Unfortunately, while these solutions can leverage multiple *k*-values to generate higher quality assemblies, the time taken for assembly increases linearly with the number of different *k*-values being used. Figure 1 shows the time taken by IDBA-UD to execute the key stages of assembly: Reading the sequence file (stage 1), processing with multiple *k*-values—first building the graph and then iterating over the graph with $k = 40 - 124$ with a step size of 12 to generate the contigs (stage 2), and then, scaffolding (stage 3) to get the final assembly. We invoked IDBA-UD on a metagenomic dataset part of the CAMI benchmark with 33 million paired-end reads of length 150 and insert-size 5kbp. We used an Intel Xeon E5-2670 2.6 GHz node with 16 cores and 32 GB memory for the experiment. As shown in Figure 1, we found that the stage 2 of iterative graph-construction process, comprising of initial graph-build construction and iteration takes up 96.1% of the total workflow time. Clearly, the iterative graph-construction step dominates the total time taken for assembly.

The most common metric to assess assembly quality is *N50*[1]. We see in Table 1 that as the number of *k*-values in the range set is increased, the quality of the assembly improves. However,

[1] N50 is defined as the length of the smallest contig above which 50% of an assembly would be represented (or smallest scaffold if it is applied after scaffold construction). A higher N50 number indicates a better assembly.

k-value range (count)	step size	Total Time (sec)	N50	(%) improvement in N50	(%) increase in execution time
40-124 (2)	84	3165	3547	-	-
40-124 (4)	28	4954	8255	132	56.5
40-124 (8)	12	7100	10729	202	124.3

Table 1: Relationship between k-values, Quality of Assembly, and Runtime for IDBA-UD running CAMI medium-complexity metagenomic dataset

the total time taken also increases proportionately, *i.e.*, linearly in proportion with the number of different k values being used. This is an undesirable consequence of iterating through increasing numbers of k-values *sequentially*. Thus, although the N50 value of the assembly, when iterating using k-values of 40-124, with a step-size of 12, is $3X$ that of using k-values 40 and 124, it takes 124.3% higher time for constructing the final graph with these k-values.

To address this concern, we propose *ScalaDBG*, a new parallel assembly algorithm, which parallelizes stage 2 of Figure 1. The key insight behind ScalaDBG is that the graphs for multiple k-values need not be constructed serially. Instead, each graph construction can be done independently and in parallel. Accumulating the graph for the higher k-value, such as in IDBA-UD, introduces an apparent dependency on the graph with lower k-values. We remove this dependency, by introducing a *patching technique*, which can patch the higher k-valued graph (k_2) with contigs from the lower k-valued graph (k_1). Crucially, the first stage of construction of the k_1 graph and the k_2 graph can proceed in parallel and the relatively shorter stage of patching the k_2 graph with the contigs from the k_1 graph happens subsequently. Thus, the gaps in the higher k-valued graph are *cemented* from the contigs of the lower k-valued graph, with the branches of the lower k-valued graph removed. For a long list of k-values, ScalaDBG employs the divide-and-conquer approach according to the *tree reduction* pattern and identifies greater scope for parallel execution . ScalaDBG's technique is general and can be applied to parallelize any DBG-assembler that performs either single (Velvet) or multi-k value (IDBA, SPAdes) DBG construction, due to its modular design.

Several steps within the construction of a single DBG, such as k-mer counting, indexing, and lookup, occur in parallel. We borrow IDBA-UD's strategy for parallelizing graph construction for a *single* k-value. Thus, ScalaDBG exploits parallelism at 2 levels—a coarse-grained level (by constructing graphs with multiple k-values in parallel) and a fine-grained level (parallelizing the construction of each individual DBG). Thus, ScalaDBG can leverage the power of a robust server, with multiple processors and a large RAM, for *vertical scaling or scale-up*, as well as a cluster with multiple nodes, for *horizontal scaling or scale-out*. As a sample result, consider that IDBA-UD assembles the CAMI metagenomic dataset for a k-value range of $40 - 124$, with a step of 12 in ≈2.2 hours on a single node. With ScalaDBG, we assemble the same dataset in ≈1.1 hours on 8 such nodes, which is 2X faster.

We make the following technical contributions in this paper:

(1) We break the dependency in DBG creation for multiple k-values—from a purely serial process to one where the most time-consuming part (the DBG creation for individual k-values) is parallelized. This innovation can be applied out-of-the-box to most DBG-based assemblers.

(2) We develop a divide-and-conquer strategy for handling a long chain of k-values while efficiently utilizing all available machines in a cluster and all available cores on a machine.

(3) We develop a software package ScalaDBG that uses OpenMP for scale-up within one server and MPI for scale-out across multiple servers. The software package is available through https://github.com/purdue-dcsl/Scaladbg.

2 BACKGROUND

In this section, we provide background on the creation of DBGs using multiple k values and an overview of IDBA-UD.

2.1 Using Multiple k-values in Iterative Graph Assembly

Figure 2 shows the effect of using a small k ($k = 3$), and a larger k ($k = 4$) during DBG construction. Figure 2 (a) shows the graph constructed from read set with $k = 3$. The vertices are consecutive 3-mers of the read set. They are connected to each other if they have a 2-mer overlap. This graph has branching at vertex ACG due to repeating region in the genome *ACGT* and *ACGA*. The contig set generated by identifying maximal paths in the graph is *{AATGCCGT,ACGAA,ACGT,CGTACG}*. As the value of k is increased to 4, the branch disappears as the higher k-value can now distinguish between the repeat region in *ACGT* and *ACGA*. However, some reads such as *CCGTA* and *GTACG* are are not sampled from the genome sequence and so vertices and edges in the graph are missed. Hence *GTAC* and *TACG* cannot be connected. Thus, Figure 2 (b) with $k = 4$ has gaps in it. In general, DBG built using a lower k value has multiple branches, and DBG built using a higher k value has gaps. The contig set generated for $k = 4$ is *{TACGTAC, TACGAA, AATGCCGT}*. If we can take the graph built with $k = 4$ and augment it with the contigs from the $k = 3$ graph, then it is conceptually possible to arrive at the graph shown in Figure 2(c). In Figure 2(c), an edge is added between circled vertices *GTAC* and *TACG* due to presence of the substring *GTACG* in the contig set obtained using $k = 3$. After adding the edge, and traversing the composite graph, contigs longer than those created from both $k = 3$ and $k = 4$ are obtained : *{TACGTACG,TACGAA,AATGCCGT}*.

2.2 IDBA-UD

IDBA-UD is a de Bruijn graph assembler. It iterates on a range of k values from $k = k_{min}$ to $k = k_{max}$, with a step-wise increment of s. It maintains an accumulated de Bruijn graph H_k at each step. In the first step a de Bruijn graph $G_{k_{min}}$ is generated from the input reads. For $k = k_{min}$, H_k is equivalent to $G_{k_{min}}$. At any step, contigs for graph H_k are generated by considering all maximal paths in graph H_k. All vertices in any maximal path have an in-degree and out-degree equal to 1 except the vertices at the start and end of the path. All reads from the input set that are substrings of these contigs are removed, reducing the input size at each step. A read of length r generates $r - k + 1$ vertices. As k is increased each read will introduce fewer vertices. This reduction in input read set coupled with the fact that there are fewer vertices for larger k values, makes subsequent graph constructions less time consuming.

The inputs to the next step, where $k = k_{min} + s$ consist of the graph H_k, the remaining reads, and the contigs from H_k. Each path

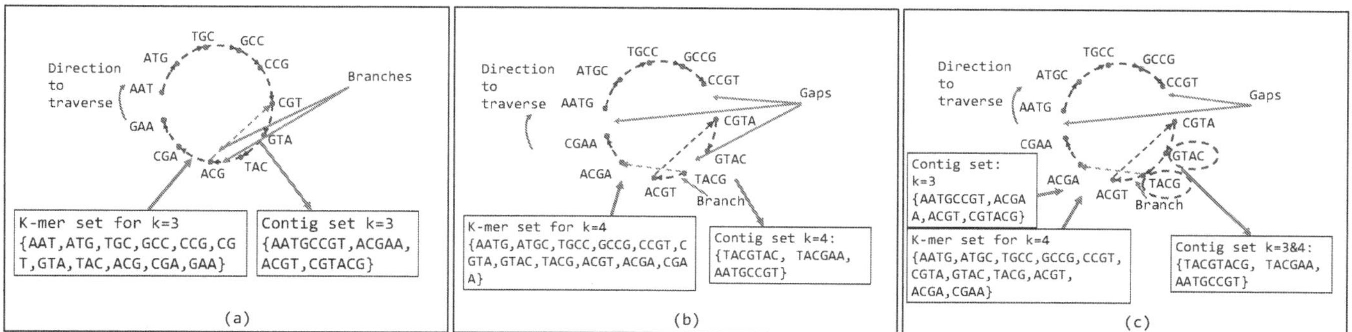

Figure 2: Desired Genome Sequence : AATGCCGTACGTACGAA, Read Set : *AATGC, ATGCC, GCCGT, TGCCG, CGTAC, TACGT, ACGTA, TACGA, ACGAA* De Bruijn Graph for $k = 3$ (sub-figure (a)) and $k = 4$ (sub-figure (b)). The final graph (sub-figure (c)) can be created by filling in some of the gaps in the $k = 4$ graph with contigs from the $k = 3$ graph. The vertices for which new edge is added (sub-figure (a)) are circled. Traversing this final graph results in the final contig set.

of length s in H_k is converted to a vertex. All such vertices are connected by an edge if the corresponding $(k + s + 1)$-mer exists in either the remaining reads or the contigs of H_k. This process is repeated for each subsequent iteration until $k = k_{max}$ is reached. Note that in this algorithm at iteration i, graph $H_{k_{min}+i*s}$ depends on graph $H_{k_{min}+(i-1)*s}$ obtained at iteration $i - 1$, the reduced read set, and the contigs obtained at the iteration $i - 1$.

This dependency forces IDBA-UD to operate sequentially on the chain of k-values, no matter how long the chain is. This is the crux of the problem that we address through ScalaDBG.

IDBA-UD also uses existing graph simplification strategies such as dead end removal and merging bubbles to get longer final contigs. In its dead end removal phase, IDBA-UD removes short simple paths leading to dead ends. In the bubble merging phase, several similar sequences are merged into one sequence. A *bubble* is formed when several similar paths have the same start and end vertex [17]. These bubbles can be formed due to errors in reads, generating similar paths with few differences. Bubble merging and dead end removal phases throw away vertices and edges from the graphs for simplification. At the end, scaffolding techniques are applied to the contigs of $H_{k_{max}}$ to get the final set of contigs.

3 DESIGN OF SCALADBG

In this section we describe the design details of ScalaDBG, considering the build phase (building a DBG) and the patch phase (patching a partial DBG with contigs from a lower k-value DBG).

3.1 Build Phase

To simplify the exposition, we describe our protocol first using just two different k values, $k1$ and $k2$, with $k1 < k2$. Figure 3 shows the stages of ScalaDBG for the two k values. In the build phase, DBGs are built for each k value in parallel, and the build module generates G_{k1} and G_{k2}. The graph construction is the most time consuming phase of the entire pipeline, with the construction of G_{k1} taking the most time.

Vertices in G_{k1} and G_{k2} are all $k1$-mers and $k2$-mers obtained from the original input read set I, respectively. Vertices and edges are established in G_{k1} and G_{k2} as per the definition of DBG. We denote the number of vertices in G_{k1} and G_{k2} as $|G_{k1}|$ and $|G_{k2}|$

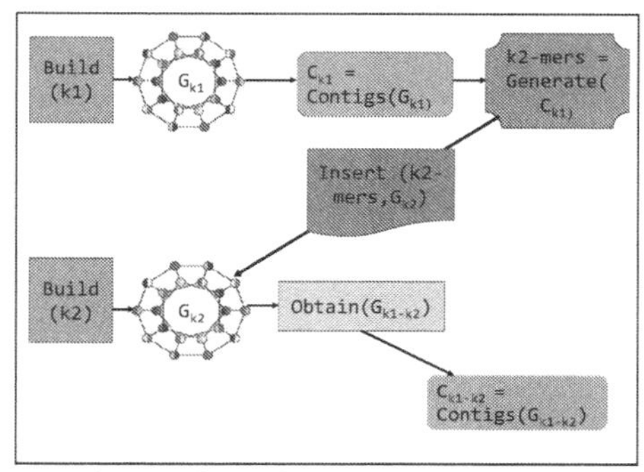

Figure 3: High Level Architecture Diagram of ScalaDBG. This shows the graph construction with only two different k values, $k1$ and $k2$ with $k1 < k2$. The graph G_{k2} is "patched" with contigs from G_{k1} to generate the combined graph G_{k1-k2}, which gives the final set of contigs. Different modules in ScalaDBG are highlighted by different colors.

respectively. Graph G_{k1} will typically be larger in size, in terms of vertices and edges, *i.e.*, $|G_{k1}| > |G_{k2}|$, since $k1 < k2$. Importantly, the creation of the DBGs for the two different k-values proceeds in parallel, unlike in all prior protocols. Now G_{k1} will have a higher number of branches than G_{k2}, while G_{k2} will have a higher number of gaps than G_{k1}. We generate contigs C_{k1} from G_{k1} by finding maximal paths according to standard practice (we use the IDBA algorithm specifically) but we do *not* yet proceed to generate C_{k2} from G_{k2}.

3.2 Patch Phase

We cannot simply create contigs from graph G_{k2} because it will have gaps relative to the graph G_{k1}. Therefore, our idea is to *patch* graph G_{k2}, *i.e.*, fill the gaps in the graph by bringing in more vertices and connecting the new vertices plus the existing vertices with additional edges. *The fundamental insight that we have is that contigs C_{k1} have the information to close some of these gaps.* We process C_{k1} by generating $k2$-mers from sequences in C_{k1}, *i.e.*, we generate all subsequences of length $k2$ from all contigs in the C_{k1} set. These $k2$-mers are inserted into the G_{k2} graph as vertices. The introduction of new vertices in the graph can result in the introduction of new edges. Two vertices u and v in the graph G_{k2} are connected by an edge if the last $(k2 - 1)$ nucleotides of the $k2$-mer represented by u are the same as the first $(k2 - 1)$ nucleotides of the $k2$-mer represented by v, and u and v are consecutive k-mers in the contig set C_{k1} or read set. The resulting graph is denoted as G_{k1-k2}. Thus, G_{k1-k2} is the aggregated graph obtained by filling gaps of G_{k2} using C_{k1}. The final contig set is generated from G_{k1-k2}.

3.3 Patching Multiple k Values in Parallel

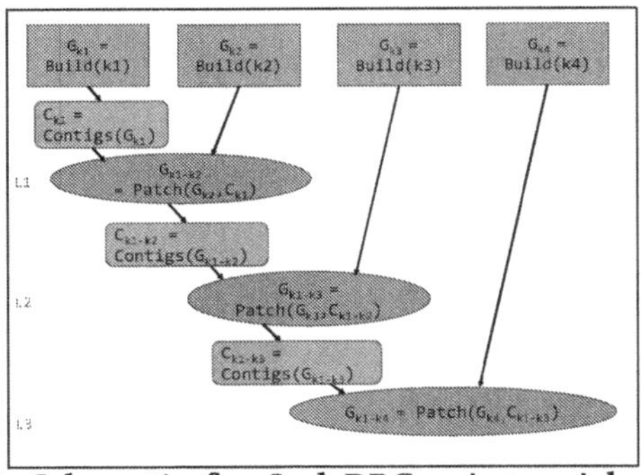

Figure 4: Schematic for ScalaDBG using serial patching, called ScalaDBG-SP

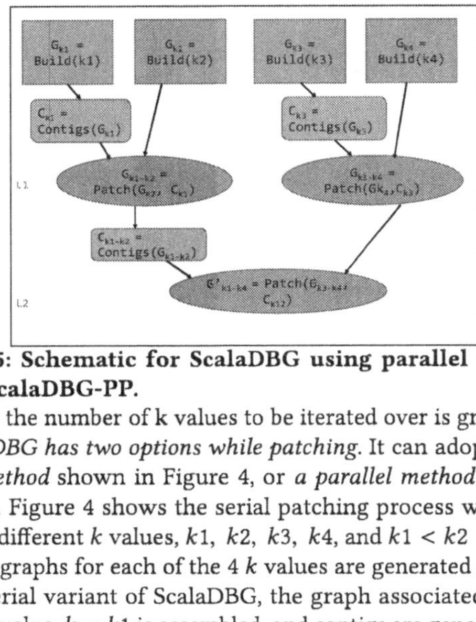

Figure 5: Schematic for ScalaDBG using parallel patching, called ScalaDBG-PP.

When the number of k values to be iterated over is greater than 3, *ScalaDBG has two options while patching.* It can adopt either *a serial method* shown in Figure 4, or *a parallel method* shown in Figure 5. Figure 4 shows the serial patching process when there are four different k values, $k1$, $k2$, $k3$, $k4$, and $k1 < k2 < k3 < k4$. Initially, graphs for each of the 4 k values are generated in parallel. In the serial variant of ScalaDBG, the graph associated with the lowest k value, $k = k1$ is assembled, and contigs are generated from the graph G_{k1}. The obtained contigs are used to patch the graph associated with the next higher k value ($k2$). Contigs are generated using the higher k valued graph. This process is repeated, serially for each increasing higher k value, until the graph associated with the highest k value in the chain is patched and assembled. The final set of contigs is generated from this final patched graph. Thus, the graph building for each separate k value occurs in parallel but the patching and generating contigs occurs serially. The advantage of the serial patching method is its simplicity, owing to the simple communication patterns between processes operating over the different k values. However, as the number of different k values increases, the number of serialized patching steps grows *linearly* with it. The serialized patching process starts dominating the total time of the workflow for ScalaDBG. To resolve this bottleneck, in the patch phase, ScalaDBG in the parallel mode allows multiple patch operations to occur in parallel.

The insight behind our parallel method is that multiple patch operations, which are independent of each other, can proceed in parallel. Thus, the patching process proceeds like a reduction tree. Figure 5 shows the parallel method of patching, where multiple patch processes occur in parallel, *e.g.*, the patching of graph G_{k2} with contigs from graph G_{k1} proceeds in parallel with the patching of graph G_{k4} with contigs from graph G_{k3}. Each pair of adjacent graphs is patched to generate a single graph. This process is repeated until there is only a single graph. Thus, patching proceeds according to the *tree reduction* parallel pattern. In this way, a long chain of k-values can be broken down, with both graph construction and patching happening in parallel. Thus, as the list of k values grows longer, ScalaDBG identifies greater scope for parallel construction while making use of more compute nodes. In the parallel patch method, the number of serialized patching steps grows only *logarithmically* with the number of different k values.

In the rest of the sections, we refer to ScalaDBG using serial patching as *ScalaDBG-SerialPatch* (or ScalaDBG-SP), and ScalaDBG using parallel patching as *ScalaDBG-ParallelPatch* (or ScalaDBG-PP). Between the serial and parallel patch methods, different pairs of graphs are merged with each other. Hence, the final contigs generated by the two methods may differ. In general, the assembly quality of the serial method is higher since the difference between k values associated with adjacent graphs is smaller and it has been shown that small jumps in the k-values leads to better quality aggregated DBGs [10].

4 CORRECTNESS OF SCALADBG METHODOLOGY

THEOREM 4.1 (EQUIVALENCE BETWEEN FINAL GRAPH OBTAINED IN ITERATIVE IDBA-UD AND SCALADBG- SP). *For a fixed iteration set of k-values starting from $k = kmin$ to $k = kmax$, the final graph obtained by ScalaDBG-SP and IDBA-UD is identical.*

PROOF. We use the principle of Mathematical Induction to establish the equivalence of the resulting graph in ScalaDBG- SP and IDBA-UD.

Initial Step Let R represent the initial read set input to ScalaDBG-SP and IDBA-UD. When $kmax = kmin$, the final graph obtained after the first iteration is the final graph. There is no patching involved. ScalaDBG-SP and IDBA-UD generate $kmin - 1$-mers from R and use the same build procedure to generate graph G_{kmin} which is the final graph.

Inductive Step For $kmax = K$, where $K > kmin$, the graph obtained using ScalaDBG-SP is identical to IDBA-UD. We denote this graph by G_K. We must prove, the statement is true for $kmax = K+1$.

The graph obtained by ScalaDBG-SP after constructing graphs from $k = kmin$ to $k = K$ in parallel, followed by serial patching is G_K. ScalaDBG-SP patches the graph G_{K+1} using contigs generated from G_K to get final graph P_{K+1}. IDBA-UD generates G_K at the end of $k = K$ iteration. After the next $K + 1$ iteration, it generates H_{K+1} as the final graph. We need to show that $P_{K+1} = H_{K+1}$.

As explained in Section 2, in IDBA-UD, to construct H_{K+1} from G_K , first potential contigs in G_K are constructed by identifying *maximal paths.* Let the contig set of G_K be denoted by C_G_K and R_K represent the read set of IDBA-UD at beginning of iteration $K + 1$. All reads in R_K that are substrings of a contigs in set C_G_K are removed. Let this new read set be denoted by R_{K+1}. Thus, $\{R_{K+1} = R_K - r\}, \forall r \in R_K$, r is a substring of a contig in C_G_K. In the construction of H_{K+1}, only the reads in R_{K+1} and the potential contigs of G_K stored in C_G_K are considered. H_{K+1} consists of vertices formed using edges in G_K where each edge (vi, vj) in G_K is converted into a vertex, representing a $(K + 1)$-mer, if the $(K + 1)$-mer is a substring of a contig in C_G_K.

ScalaDBG-SP starts with the original read set R and generates all $(K + 1)$-mers of the reads. Graph G_{K+1} is built using R. Contig set C_G_K (same graph will generate same contig set, inductive step) is built using G_K. Then ScalaDBG-SP extracts $K + 1$-mers from each contig in the set C_G_K and inserts it into G_{K+1}. Vertices and edges in H_{K+1} in IDBA-UD obtained by upgrading vertices in G_K are $(K + 1)$-mers of contigs in C_G_K. Hence ScalaDBG-SP is guaranteed to insert these vertices and edges as we create $(K + 1)$-mers from the contigs. All vertices and edges in P_{K+1} are formed using the original read set R and the contigs of G_K. Now R_{K+1} is a proper subset of R. So all vertices and edges inserted using R_{K+1} will be inserted by R. Hence all vertices and edges formed using $R_{K+1} + C\_G_K$ in H_{K+1} will be formed using $R + C\_G_K$ in P_{K+1}. Thus P_{K+1}, formed by patching together G_K and G_{K+1} is identical to H_{K+1}. From *Initial Step, Inductive Step* and principle of mathematical induction, IDBA-UD and ScalaDBG- SP generate identical graphs. □

Although the process of build and serial patch process of ScalaDBG essentially generates a graph identical to IDBA-UD, the assembly metrics of ScalaDBG- PP, ScalaDBG-SP and IDBA-UD differ. There are primarily two reasons for the differences : i) the out of order patching in ScalaDBG-PP and ii) the graph simplification procedures (bubble merging and dead end removal).

The order in which graphs built with different k values is significantly different for ScalaDBG- PP than ScalaDBG-SP, and IDBA-UD. While IDBA-UD iterates over the k values in an increasing order, with a maximum of *step-size* difference between the iterations, ScalaDBG-PP follows tree-style reduction to patch the graphs. Hence the difference in k values of two patched graphs will be higher, and the order of patching will also be different. The difference in output of ScalaDBG-SP, ScalaDBG-PP and IDBA-UD is also due to the graph simplification procedures applied before generating the contigs. The bubble merging and dead-end removal phases remove incorrect vertices and edges based on their multiplicity. The graphs obtained by ScalaDBG and IDBA-UD workflows have different multiplicity information for their vertices and edges. However, in our evaluation section, we will show that the difference is not statistically significant.

5 IMPLEMENTATION

We implement ScalaDBG using OpenMP (Version 4.0) (for parallelism within a node) and MPI (MVAPICH 2.2) (for parallelism across nodes in a cluster), compiled with GCC version 4.9.3.

In ScalaDBG- PP the work is split up into n chunks, where $n = number\_of\_kmers$. Each MPI process computes the $kmer\_size$ it will work on, and read the input files to build the DBG. The worker processes compute and send their DBGs to the Master. The Master process receives all other graphs and patches them in serial order, as shown at a high level in Figure 4. Intermediate graph representations are written and read from the Lustre Parallel File System.

In ScalaDBG- PP, the process is the same as ScalaDBG-SP, up through building a DBG. For the next stage we split up the processes with half receiving and half sending the DBG as shown in Figure 5. After a process sends its DBG, it is no longer used in the patching. This stage is repeated until there is only 1 process that receives, which will always be the Master. The Master will then complete the last assembly and perform contig generation.

6 EVALUATION

In this section we evaluate ScalaDBG in comparison to IDBA-UD in terms of the time taken to perform the assembly and the quality of the assembly. We used two different types of sequencing read sets - metagenomic and single cell sequencing, as they are typically assembled by the genomics community using the iterative de-bruijn graph approach.

6.1 Evaluation Setup and Data Sets

We performed our experiments on an Intel Xeon Infiniband cluster. Each node had Intel Xeon E5-2670, 2.6 GHz with 16 cores per node, and 32 GB of memory. The nodes were connected with QDR Infiniband. We used the latest version of IDBA-UD (1.1.1)[12]. We used the read sets listed in Table 2. We obtained the *S. aureus* and SAR 324 single-cell datasets from [9]. The metagenomics dataset was obtained from the CAMI benchmark [13]. In the case of metagenomic and single cell sequencing datasets, sequencing depths of different regions of a genome, or genomes from different organisms are exceedingly uneven. Hence multiple k-values are required for accurately assembling the datasets. So we evaluate ScalaDBG and IDBA-UD using these relevant datasets. The number of nodes in the cluster are equal to the number of different k-values in the configuration for ScalaDBG, while IDBA-UD can only run on a single node. ScalaDBG outputs contigs for a given dataset. Existing scaffolding techniques can be applied to these output contigs to get the final assembly. We only focus on evaluating the performance and accuracy metrics of the assembled contigs in the following experiments for IDBA-UD and ScalaDBG since our contribution is confined until that stage.

Name	Read Set Type	Read Length	# of reads	Characteristics
RM2	Real, Metagenomic	150 bp	33140480	PE,Insert size:5 kbp
SC -*S. aureus*	Real, Single Cell	100 bp	66,997,488	PE,Insert size:214bp
SC-SAR324	Real, Single Cell	100 bp	55,733,218	PE,Insert size:180bp

Table 2: Read Sets used in the Experiments. PE denotes Paired End reads

6.2 Performance Tests

Figures 6, 7, 8, and 9 show the time taken by IDBA, ScalaDBG-SP, and ScalaDBG-PP to generate contigs from the 3 different read sets mentioned in Table 2. The tests bring out the effect of different k-values on performance. For the metagenomic dataset we changed the step size to get three different configurations. We used step sizes of 28, 12, and 6 in the range 40 – 124 (we give step sizes in reverse order because this corresponds to an increasing number of k-values). For the single cell datasets, we used step sizes of 14, 6, and 3 in the range of 29 – 71. The lower and upper bounds of the range is lower for the single cell dataset since its reads are shorter in length. We also ran SAR324 in the range of 20 – 50 with step of 10, 5, and 2 to get 4, 7, 16 k values respectively.

The first 3 configurations have successively higher number of k-values: 4, 8,and 15, and are meant to evaluate the effect on quality of assembly and running time as the number of k values is increased. In addition the range extremes are held constant to obtain the information obtained from the two extreme k values. We ran ScalaDBG by matching the number of nodes in the cluster with the number of distinct k-values in the configuration to maximize scaling out performance for ScalaDBG. IDBA-UD on the other hand can only run on a single node. We report the overall execution times for both IDBA and ScalaDBG for generating the final contigs from the input readset.

We see that the speedup for ScalaDBG-PP and ScalaDBG-SP over IDBA increases with increase in the number of k values, for all the read sets. Speedup of ScalaDBG completely depends on the specific k values chosen. For the SAR324 dataset in the range of 20-50 with step size of 2, speedup of ScalaDBG- PP is 6.7X and speedup of ScalaDBG-SP is 3.1X over IDBA-UD. Of all the remaining readsets and configurations, ScalaDBG-PP achieves a maximum speedup of 3.3X for the SC-SAR324 readset in the $\{29 - 71\}$, step size 3 configuration. ScalaDBG- SP achieves a maximum speedup of 1.6X for RM2, SC-*S.aureus*, and SC-SAR324 readsets in the configurations processing 15 k values. For all the datasets and configurations, ScalaDBG is faster than IDBA-UD. Further, ScalaDBG-PP is faster than ScalaDBG-SP since it has higher parallelism during assembly for the patching process. Speedup of ScalaDBG-SP and ScalaDBG-PP over IDBA is higher for the larger readsets of RM2, SAR 324, and *S. aureus*.

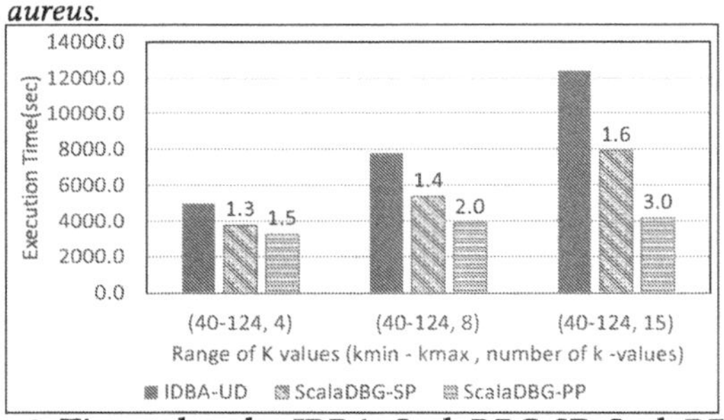

Figure 6: Time taken by IDBA, ScalaDBG-SP, ScalaDBG-PP on RM2 data set.

6.3 Accuracy

Table 3 show the accuracy metrics for assembling the datasets in Table 2 for the above performance tests. For the metagenomic dataset and SAR324 we only reported number of contigs, N50 and max contig length. The metagenomic dataset reference assemblies contain multiple genomes, while for SAR324 we could not obtain its reference genome, so we could not report the coverage, NGA50, and number of missassemblies for them. For SC-*S.aureus*, both IDBA-UD and ScalaDBG have NGA50 of 26379 and 3 missassemblies, coverage is 98.1 for IDBA-UD and 98.2 for ScalaDBG in all three configurations. Differences in the accuracy arise as a result of the

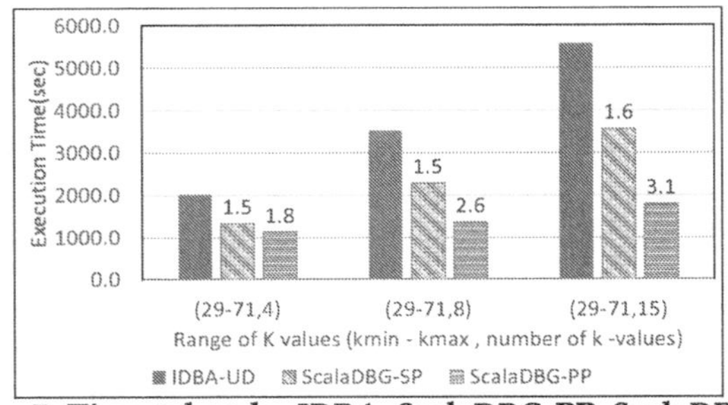

Figure 7: Time taken by IDBA, ScalaDBG-PP, ScalaDBG-PP for completing assembly on the SC-*S.aureus* dataset.

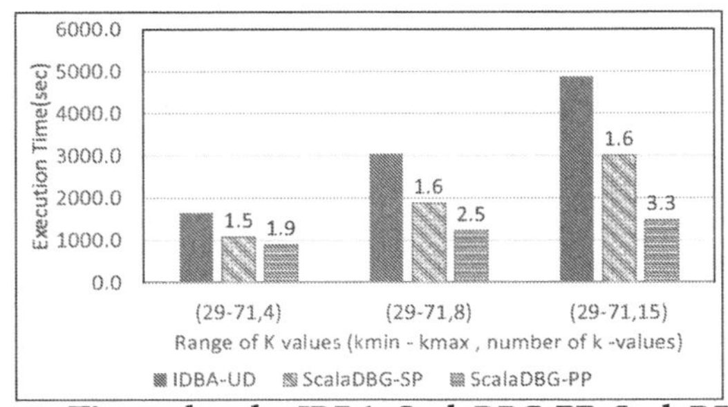

Figure 8: Time taken by IDBA, ScalaDBG-PP, ScalaDBG-PP for completing assembly on the SC-SAR324 dataset.

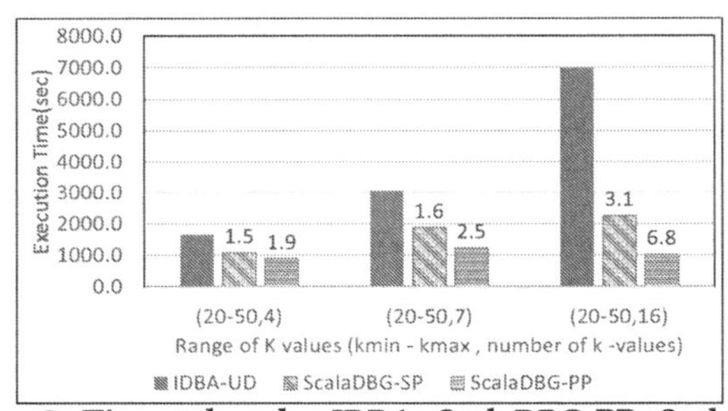

Figure 9: Time taken by IDBA, ScalaDBG-PP, ScalaDBG-PP for completing assembly on the SC-SAR324 dataset for range(20-50)

invocations of graph simplification and out of order patching, explained in Section 4. The results demonstrate that ScalaDBG and IDBA have comparable accuracy metrics in all cases. We performed the T-test and determined that the differences in the assembly metric N50 obtained for ScalaDBG-SP, ScalaDBG-PP and IDBA-UD are not statistically significant.

6.4 Scalability Tests

To evaluate the scaling out for ScalaDBG, we used the metagenomic dataset RM2. We varied the k values for ScalaDBG in the range of $\{40 - 124\}$ with a step size of 6. The range has 15 k-values. We increase the number of nodes in the cluster from 1 to 15, and measure the speedup achieved as shown in Figure 10. As can be seen, ScalaDBG achieves a speedup of 3X for the RM2 dataset , compared to the baseline version running on 1 node. It scales at nearly constant efficiency(slope of speedup curve) upto 8 nodes. The reduction in efficiency at 15 nodes is due the slightly imbalanced

Assembler	# Contigs	N50 (bp)	Max Contig Length	# Contigs	N50 (bp)	Max Contig Length
	RM2 k=40-124,4			**SC-*S.aureus* k=40-124,4**		
IDBA-UD	123807	2251	572031	400	24855	126604
ScalaDBG-SP	122427	2281	571953	377	24855	126604
ScalaDBG-PP	123037	2249	444176	370	24855	126604
	RM2 k=40-124,8			**SC-*S.aureus* k=40-124,8**		
IDBA-UD	121911	2457	563546	412	24855	126604
ScalaDBG-SP	121955	2582	573903	384	24855	126604
ScalaDBG-PP	121772	2408	444517	373	24855	126604
	RM2 k=40-124,15			**SC-*S.aureus* k=40-124,15**		
IDBA-UD	121720	2504	563546	413	24855	126604
ScalaDBG-SP	119814	2679	573903	393	24855	126604
ScalaDBG-PP	121568	2472	444518	374	24855	126604
	SC-SAR324 k=29-71,4			**SC-SAR324 k=20-50,4**		
IDBA-UD	733	61419	202281	1082	32119	131087
ScalaDBG-SP	709	64747	202281	1085	38257	131546
ScalaDBG-PP	705	62374	202281	1080	38257	131546
	SC-SAR324 k=29-71,8			**SC-SAR324 k=20-50,7**		
IDBA-UD	742	60700	202281	1088	33192	131087
ScalaDBG-SP	710	64747	202281	1087	38257	131546
ScalaDBG-PP	703	63904	202281	1078	38257	131546
	SC-SAR324 k=29-71,15			**SC-SAR324 k=20-50,16**		
IDBA-UD	747	60700	202281	7740	22977	131087
ScalaDBG-SP	723	64747	202281	8342	24254	131041
ScalaDBG-PP	712	64795	161406	8118	24254	131041

Table 3: Accuracy Comparison for Performance Tests on RM2, SC-*S.aureus* and SC-SAR324 datasets

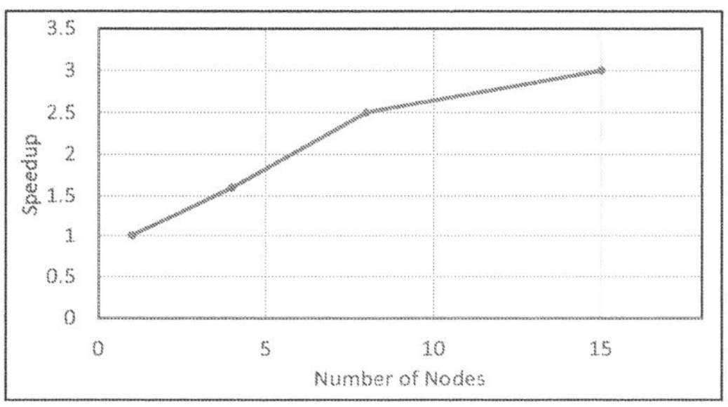

Figure 10: Scaling Results for ScalaDBG, speedup shown w.r.t ScalaDBG running on 1 node

parallel reduction tree of ScalaDBG-PP. The speedup demonstrates that ScalaDBG can scale out in a cluster and leverage the power of all its cores.

7 RELATED WORK

Efficient de-novo assembly applications have been proposed to deal with the tremendous increase in genomic sequences [1, 2, 4–8, 10–12, 14, 15, 17]. These assembly applications are either limited to scaling up on a single node, or cannot use multiple k values during the process of assembly. To our knowledge, there has been no previous work on parallelizing de bruijn graph construction for multiple K-mers on multiple nodes in a cluster.

Ray [2], ABySS [15], PASHA [6], and HipMer [4] can parallelize the assembly process for a single k value on multiple nodes in a cluster. However, they do not generate good quality assemblies for metagenomic and single cell datasets with uneven sequencing depths, unlike ScalaDBG. SGA [14], Velvet [17], SOAPdenovo [7], ALLPATHS-LG [5] can parallelize the assembly process on multiple cores of a single node. Metagenomic assemblers such as Metavelvet [8] also do not use multiple k values in assembly. IDBA, IDBA-UD, and SPAdes can utilize multiple k values. They are limited to scale on a single node. ScalaDBG can scale up, scale out, and also process multiple k-values.

8 CONCLUSION

Faster and cheaper sequencing technologies have led to a massive increase in the amount of sequencing data. Efficient assembly algorithms are key to uncovering knowledge within the data and make possible medical breakthroughs based on single cell and metagenomic datasets. Existing iterative methods of debruijn graph construction such as IDBA-UD, generate longer contigs but are completely sequential and suffer from significantly longer graph construction times. In this paper we presented a technique ScalaDBG that breaks this serial process of graph construction into a parallel process. Our technique is general, and can be easily extended to other DBG-based assembly algorithms.

REFERENCES

[1] Anton Bankevich, Sergey Nurk, Dmitry Antipov, Alexey A Gurevich, Mikhail Dvorkin, Alexander S Kulikov, Valery M Lesin, Sergey I Nikolenko, Son Pham, Andrey D Prjibelski, and others. 2012. SPAdes: a new genome assembly algorithm and its applications to single-cell sequencing. *Journal of Computational Biology* 19, 5 (2012), 455–477.

[2] Sébastien Boisvert, François Laviolette, and Jacques Corbeil. 2010. Ray: simultaneous assembly of reads from a mix of high-throughput sequencing technologies. *Journal of computational biology* 17, 11 (2010), 1519–1533.

[3] Phillip EC Compeau, Pavel A Pevzner, and Glenn Tesler. 2011. How to apply de Bruijn graphs to genome assembly. *Nature biotechnology* 29, 11 (2011), 987–991.

[4] Evangelos Georganas, Aydın Buluç, Jarrod Chapman, Steven Hofmeyr, Chaitanya Aluru, Rob Egan, Leonid Oliker, Daniel Rokhsar, and Katherine Yelick. 2015. HipMer: an extreme-scale de novo genome assembler. In *Proceedings of the International Conference for High Performance Computing, Networking, Storage and Analysis*. ACM, 14.

[5] Sante Gnerre, Iain MacCallum, Dariusz Przybylski, Filipe J Ribeiro, Joshua N Burton, Bruce J Walker, Ted Sharpe, Giles Hall, Terrance P Shea, Sean Sykes, and others. 2011. High-quality draft assemblies of mammalian genomes from massively parallel sequence data. *Proceedings of the National Academy of Sciences* 108, 4 (2011), 1513–1518.

[6] Yongchao Liu, Bertil Schmidt, and Douglas L Maskell. 2011. Parallelized short read assembly of large genomes using de Bruijn graphs. *BMC bioinformatics* 12, 1 (2011), 354.

[7] Ruibang Luo, Binghang Liu, Yinlong Xie, Zhenyu Li, Weihua Huang, Jianying Yuan, Guangzhu He, Yanxiang Chen, Qi Pan, Yunjie Liu, and others. 2012. SOAPdenovo2: an empirically improved memory-efficient short-read de novo assembler. *Gigascience* 1, 1 (2012), 18.

[8] Toshiaki Namiki, Tsuyoshi Hachiya, Hideaki Tanaka, and Yasubumi Sakakibara. 2012. MetaVelvet: an extension of Velvet assembler to de novo metagenome assembly from short sequence reads. *Nucleic acids research* 40, 20 (2012), e155–e155.

[9] University of California at San Diego. 2011. Single cell data sets. http://bix.ucsd.edu/projects/singlecell/nbt_data.html. (2011).

[10] Yu Peng, Henry CM Leung, Siu-Ming Yiu, and Francis YL Chin. 2010. IDBA–a practical iterative de Bruijn graph de novo assembler. In *Annual International Conference on Research in Computational Molecular Biology*. Springer, 426–440.

[11] Yu Peng, Henry CM Leung, Siu-Ming Yiu, and Francis YL Chin. 2011. Meta-IDBA: a de Novo assembler for metagenomic data. *Bioinformatics* 27, 13 (2011), i94–i101.

[12] Yu Peng, Henry CM Leung, Siu-Ming Yiu, and Francis YL Chin. 2012. IDBA-UD: a de novo assembler for single-cell and metagenomic sequencing data with highly uneven depth. *Bioinformatics* 28, 11 (2012), 1420–1428.

[13] Alexander Sczyrba, Peter Hofmann, Peter Belmann, David Koslicki, Stefan Janssen, Johannes Droege, Ivan Gregor, Stephan Majda, Jessika Fiedler, Eik Dahms, and others. 2017. Critical Assessment of Metagenome Interpretation- a benchmark of computational metagenomics software. *bioRxiv* (2017), 099127.

[14] Jared T Simpson and Richard Durbin. 2012. Efficient de novo assembly of large genomes using compressed data structures. *Genome research* 22, 3 (2012), 549–556.

[15] Jared T Simpson, Kim Wong, Shaun D Jackman, Jacqueline E Schein, Steven JM Jones, and İnanç Birol. 2009. ABySS: a parallel assembler for short read sequence data. *Genome research* 19, 6 (2009), 1117–1123.

[16] Zachary D Stephens, Skylar Y Lee, Faraz Faghri, Roy H Campbell, Chengxiang Zhai, Miles J Efron, Ravishankar Iyer, Michael C Schatz, Saurabh Sinha, and Gene E Robinson. 2015. Big data: astronomical or genomical? *PLoS Biol* 13, 7 (2015), e1002195.

[17] Daniel R Zerbino and Ewan Birney. 2008. Velvet: algorithms for de novo short read assembly using de Bruijn graphs. *Genome research* 18, 5 (2008), 821–829.

Co-MEAL: Cost-Optimal Multi-Expert Active Learning Architecture for Mobile Health Monitoring

Ramyar Saeedi
SCADS Lab, School of EECS
Washington State University
Pullman, Washington 99164
rsaeedi@eecs.wsu.edu

Keyvan Sasani
SCADS Lab, School of EECS
Washington State University
Pullman, Washington 99164
ksasani@eecs.wsu.edu

Assefaw H. Gebremedhin
SCADS Lab, School of EECS
Washington State University
Pullman, Washington 99164
assefaw@eecs.wsu.edu

ABSTRACT

Mobile health monitoring plays a central role in a variety of health-care applications. Using mobile technology, health-care providers can access clinical information and communicate with subjects in real-time. Due to the sensitive nature of health-care applications, these systems need to process physiological signals highly accurately. However, as mobile devices are employed in dynamic environments, the accuracy of a machine learning model drops whenever a change in configuration of the system occurs. Therefore, data mining and machine learning techniques that specifically address challenges associated with dynamic environments (e.g. different users, signal heterogeneity) are needed. In this paper, using *active learning* as an organizing principle, we propose a *cost-optimal multiple-expert* architecture to adapt a machine learning model (e.g. classifier) developed in a given context to a new context or configuration. More specifically, in our architecture, a system's machine learning model learns from experts available to the system (e.g. another mobile device, human annotator) while minimizing the cost of data labeling. Our architecture also exploits collaboration between experts to enrich their knowledge which in turn decreases both cost and uncertainty of data labeling in future steps.

We demonstrate the efficacy of the architecture using a publicly available dataset on human activity. We show that the accuracy of activity recognition reaches over 85% by labeling only 15% of unlabeled data. At the same time, the number of queries from human expert is reduced by up to 82%.

CCS CONCEPTS

•Human-centered computing →Ubiquitous and mobile computing systems and tools; •Applied computing →Health care information systems; •Computing methodologies →Active learning settings; •Hardware →Emerging architectures;

KEYWORDS

Mobile Health Monitoring; Wearables; Active Learning; Cost-Optimal; Time Series; Uncertainty; Query Strategy; Physical Activity Recognition; Collaborative; Multi-Expert; Accelerometer.

Permission to make digital or hard copies of all or part of this work for personal or classroom use is granted without fee provided that copies are not made or distributed for profit or commercial advantage and that copies bear this notice and the full citation on the first page. Copyrights for components of this work owned by others than ACM must be honored. Abstracting with credit is permitted. To copy otherwise, or republish, to post on servers or to redistribute to lists, requires prior specific permission and/or a fee. Request permissions from permissions@acm.org.
ACM-BCB'17, August 20–23, 2017, Boston, MA, USA.
© 2017 ACM. ISBN 978-1-4503-4722-8/17/08...$15.00
DOI: http://dx.doi.org/10.1145/3107411.3107430

1 INTRODUCTION

Mobile-health (M-health) is receiving growing attention due to its capacity to provide better and more efficient patient care. M-health technology refers to the use of smartphones, tablets, wearables, and implantable devices to deliver health care and preventive health services. The World Health Organization (WHO) describes M-health as "medical and public health practice supported by mobile devices" [1]. According to recent studies, 83 percent of physicians in the U.S. already use M-health technology [2, 3].

Health-care providers use M-health technology for a variety of goals: to access clinical information; to collaborate with care teams; to communicate with patients; and to conduct real-time health monitoring. On the other end, patients/users can use an M-health system to track their own health-data (e.g. Fitbit activity tracker), to access clinical records through patient/user portal, and to communicate with health-care providers [3–6].

Mobile devices considerably improve the quality and effectiveness of service, bringing especially high value for the elderly, patients with chronic conditions, athletes, and those requiring constant monitoring of their daily state [7–12]. Despite these enormous promises and potential use of M-health technology however, the utilization of mobile devices is currently largely limited to systems designed for controlled environments using passive supervised computational models. This has several undesirable consequences.

First, the accuracy of machine learning algorithms drops whenever the system's configuration changes (e.g. sensor calibration, device orientation, sensor location). For example, the training data may be collected using a smartphone located on waist, while the final data processing may be conducted on a Fitbit wristband. Second, sensor data, generated during personalized exercises or tasks, may be too specific or inadequate to be used as a training set for a new user/patient. Moreover, even for the same user, the physiological patterns may change over time. Third, a user's needs (e.g. number of events to detect) may change over time. For example, in a physical activity monitoring system, we may need to detect a new set of activities. Finally, supervised machine learning models are passive and as a result the system would necessarily fail or provide inaccurate outputs whenever a sensor failure or removal happens. Furthermore, a passive model is unable to leverage additional knowledge from a new point of view to detect events of interest in the mobile system.

Next generation mobile devices need to be context-aware and capable of adapting a machine learning model to the context at hand in order to generate appropriate feedbacks and make decisions (e.g. on-time alert, patient status). Such an adaptation is generally achieved in one or more of these ways: (i) using available knowledge including related data (e.g. other subjects), (ii) employing other points of view (e.g. another sensor), and (iii) using feedback from a human expert (e.g. physician). However, these ways may cause disturbance or interference in user's life and may incur expenses related to knowledge extraction [13–17].

Our aim in this work is to enable next generation mobile devices to actively update their machine learning models while minimizing the side-effects of system adaptation. In particular, we seek to design a system that exploits available sensory systems, smart environments, feedback from human experts, and related data. Such a system needs to be able to handle multiple sources of knowledge and update the associated computational models accordingly. Here, we call each source of knowledge an *expert* (a human expert is one type of expert).

In order to actively update a computational model whenever a new context is faced, the system needs to interact with the set of experts to access new labeled data [18–20]. The system should strive to minimize the cost of active learning from the experts while maintaining the system's accuracy. The cost associated with each expert may be defined in terms of user inconvenience, human expert's feedback cost, equipment's cost, power consumption, etc. Furthermore, an expert typically has only limited knowledge of user status or is uncertain in its knowledge. Considering expert uncertainty, a multi-expert system that implements *collaboration* between experts can result in lower overall cost and more accurate knowledge.

In this paper, we propose a *cost-optimal multi-expert active learning architecture* (Co-MEAL) targeted for M-health systems. The architecture is designed to meet a variety of requirements: a) avoid dependence on collecting lots of labeled data for each new configuration or context; b) minimize the total number of queries as well as queries from human experts in order to reduce the active learning cost; c) use the knowledge of different experts at the same time; d) allow for experts to collaborate to reduce both annotation cost and data labeling uncertainty; e) be able to add a new mobile device to the system for a more accurate decision making. We outline our specific contributions as follows.

a) Architecture. We propose a novel architecture for collaborative active learning for M-health systems. A key idea of the architecture is to minimize overall query cost while maintaining system's accuracy. Fig. 1 gives a high level overview of the architecture. The architecture is unpacked and discussed in detail in Section 2.

b) Problem Formulation. We formulate an optimization problem to model cost-optimal active learning in the multi-expert architecture. This formulation minimizes the cost of data annotation for informative instances. The formulation is presented in Section 3 along with formal definitions.

c) Algorithms. We have developed three algorithms corresponding to different aspects of the architecture. The first algorithm implements the overall functionality of the Co-MEAL architecture – it calls the other two algorithms as subroutines. The second algorithm is a knowledge transfer algorithm whose purpose is to initialize the learner of the system. The third algorithm is for finding the cost-optimal expert in each query phase of the active learning process. The algorithms are presented in Section 4.

d) Experimental Evaluation. We use a human physical activity dataset as a case study to validate the Co-MEAL architecture. We developed several scenarios to show the effects of active learning on the accuracy of a mobile monitoring system. These scenarios are used to show the applicability of the architecture for system reconfiguration as well as sensor integration to the system. We show that using the architecture increases the accuracy of physical monitoring by up to 45%. We also show that annotation cost is substantially reduced because of cost-optimal expert selection as well as collaboration between experts in the active learning phase. Our experimental evaluation along with details of the experimental set up are presented in Section 5.

2 SYSTEM ARCHITECTURE

A conventional mobile monitoring system is generally composed of several sensor nodes, a base station, and a back-end server. Each sensor node is attached to the body (a wearable or an implant device) to sample and preprocess physiological signals and transmit partial results (e.g. features) to the gateway. Moreover, sometimes additional sensors are placed in the environment (e.g. smarthome) to capture the context as well as the decision making process. The gateway is a more powerful unit, such as a smartphone, that performs data fusion for the health analytic system. The results are further transmitted, typically through the Internet, to a back-end server for storage, further processing, and clinical decision support from physicians and health-care experts.

With this description of conventional architecture of M-health systems as a background, our proposed reconfigurable architecture is constituted as depicted in Fig. 1. It consists of three main components: 1) databases (DB), 2) a data processing unit (DPU), and 3) an expert management unit (EMU). The DPU is the core intelligence of the M-health system. The DPU may be located entirely on the gateway or on both the gateway and the back-end server depending on the computational power of the gateway. The DB, the EMU, and the experts can be considered part of the back-end server.

The DPU communicates with the DB and the EMU whenever there is a need for system reconfiguration. The incoming data is sampled by the DPU, and then the DPU decides whether or not to request labels. If the learner is capable of classifying the data accurately using the labeled data in the current context, the active learning step is deactivated. The DPU has multiple submodules each of which is responsible for a different functionality in the reconfiguration phase. We discuss in the remainder of this section the details of each submodule, the Databases, and the EMU.

2.1 Learner Initialization

In active learning, a learner often begins with a small number of instances in the labeled training set L. However, an M-health system quite often may have to start with no labeled data at all. This requires more sophisticated strategies in the initialization phase of the active learning process. Meanwhile, for many applications of M-health, there may be data for *related* contexts. For example, in a physical activity monitoring system, the data from other subjects could be used to initialize the classifier of the system. In Section 4, we present an initialization algorithm which uses the related labeled data to build the first learner model.

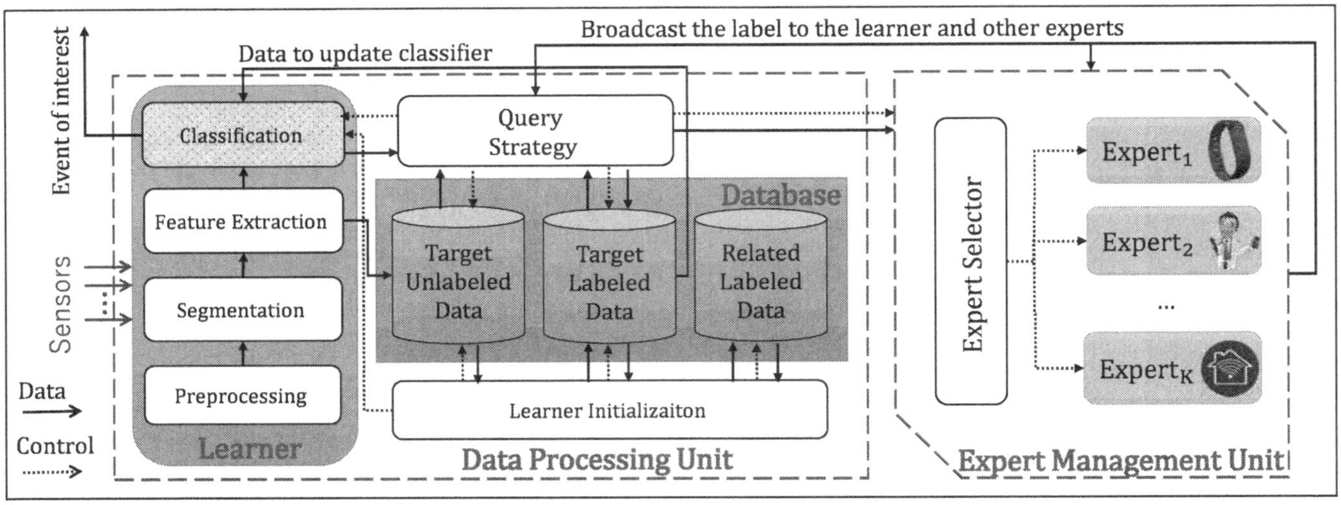

Figure 1: High-level illustration of the cost-optimal multi-expert active learning (Co-MEAL) architecture for M-health monitoring systems.

2.2 Query Strategy

In order to reduce annotation cost, we need a query strategy to select the best subset of unlabeled instances. The decision of whether or not to query an instance can be framed in several ways. One approach is to evaluate samples using some measure that shows how informative an instance is, since more informative instances are more likely to be queried [18]. For such a purpose, an entropy-based measure can be used. Entropy is an information-theoretic measure that represents the amount of information needed to encode a distribution. An informative data instance is defined as follows [18].

Definition 2.1 (Informative Instance). Let x be a vector that stands for an unlabeled data sample and $P_M(\ell_i|x)$ be the posterior probability under prediction model M. Then the data point x^*_H expressed below is the most informative data point:

$$x^*_H = \underset{x}{\operatorname{argmin}} \sum_i P_M(\ell_i|x) \log P_M(\ell_i|x) \quad (1)$$

where ℓ_i ranges over all possible labels.

Another query strategy is a committee-based algorithm. This approach involves maintaining a committee of models (e.g classifiers) which are all trained on the current labeled set L, but represent competing hypotheses. Each committee member is then allowed to vote on the labels of query candidates. The most informative instance is considered to be the one about which they most disagree. Different models should represent different regions of the feature space, and have some measure of disagreement among committee members [18].

In this paper, we use a hybrid query strategy of the above approaches that is based on a *random forest* classifier. The informativeness of an input instance is computed as the mean informativeness of the trees in the forest. The informativeness measure of a single tree is the fraction of samples of the same class in a leaf.

2.3 The Databases

A key component in our active learning architecture is a set of databases. Each database represents knowledge for a unique case. Below, we formally define a database.

Definition 2.2 (Database). A database (or dictionary) DB is an unordered set of instances. The ith instance is a q-dimensional vector denoted by DB_i, where q is number of features extracted from each intance. Each instance may or may not be labeled in the dictionary.

In our architecture, there are three types of dictionaries. The *target unlabeled data* dictionary stores the incoming streaming data in real-time. This data will be used both to initialize the system and to modify the classifier. The second database, *target labeled data*, gradually collects two kinds of information: (i) instances from the third database, *related labeled data*, and (ii) queries from the EMU. The database referred to as related labeled data is built based on related contexts and domains useful for initializing the classifier and decreasing the cost of queries.

2.4 The Expert Management Unit

In real-world health-care applications, labels may come from various sources, including different health-care experts, other mobile devices or even a smart environment. Furthermore, the knowledge provided by each expert is subject to uncertainty. For example, the performance of human annotators depends on factors such as level of expertise, experience, and concentration/distraction [21]. Additionally, experts may have more or less knowledge for different parts of the problem that has to be solved (e.g., different classes, different features). Another factor is the cost of data annotation by each expert. Therefore, it is necessary to design a system that is capable of interacting with multiple experts efficiently.

The multi-expert architecture we envision satisfies several unique properties. 1) The learning process relies on the collective intelligence of a group of experts. 2) The architecture could also provide a learning opportunity for experts. In particular, our system allows for each expert to update their knowledge based on the feedback from other experts in each round of query. 3) The expert selection submodule chooses the expert(s) in such a way that the query cost is minimized, while keeping the provided label for the queried instance accurate. 4) The architecture leverages different points of view from the experts to provide a more comprehensive model through the system's life time. For example, new class labels may arise during the life time, or a new sensor may be integrated into the mobile health system. 5) An expert can be part of the data processing unit. For example, in a multi-node mobile system, one node shares the label with the DPU whenever the node is confident. We present the algorithm we developed for expert selection in Section 4.

3 PROBLEM STATEMENT

In real applications, it is impossible to collect training data for every context. Furthermore, data collected for one setting (e.g. a subject, a sensor location) may no longer be suitable for a new setting. Therefore, there is a need to modify the machine learning algorithm (e.g. classifier) for accurate data processing. Given the initial related labeled database DB_R, the most relevant data instances can be selected to initiate the learner model. However, the initialized model may be inaccurate due the difference between the related data distribution and the current context. Whenever the user starts using the health monitoring system, context-specific unlabeled data is collected gradually throughout the system's life time and may well be different from the related labeled data.

The key idea behind our architecture is that the learner achieves continuously greater accuracy while minimizing the cost of annotation from the set of experts. The knowledge of the learner is used to select the cost-optimal expert for each query. Therefore, our goal is to actively update the machine learning algorithms using knowledge from experts.

An expert can be another sensor, a smart environment, a physician or the user. The query strategy submodule selects the top K informative instances in each query round, for a specified parameter K. The selected instances are passed to the expert selection submodule to find the cost-optimal, confident expert for each data instance. The expert selection needs access to the cost and uncertainty of each expert for data annotation. Also, the architecture is designed to update the expert knowledge on each round of query. We provide a formal definition of cost-optimal multi-expert active learning in the remainder of this section.

3.1 Problem Definition

Let $L = \{\ell_1, \ell_2, ..., \ell_k\}$ be a set of k labels that the system aims to recognize. Let $E = \{e_1, e_2, \dots, e_p\}$ be a set of p possible experts each of which has full or partial knowledge on the current labeled set L. We model the knowledge of each expert on each $\ell_i \in L$ using an *uncertainty score* vector. The formal definition of uncertainty score for each expert is as follows.

Definition 3.1 (Uncertainty Score). An uncertainty score vector $U = (u_1, u_2, \dots, u_k)$ for a given expert is a vector whose i^{th} entry stores a value in the range $[0, 100]$ (i.e. percentage) indicating the uncertainty of the expert on its prediction result on the label ℓ_i. A number close to 100 indicates highest uncertainty (lowest confidence) in prediction of a specific label.

In addition to uncertainty score, each expert has a query cost for each label. Our final goal is to minimized the overall cost of queries. We also assume that experts collaborate with each other to update their knowledge in the active learning process. We formally define the collaborative active learning (CAL) problem as follows.

Problem 1 (CAL Problem). *Suppose each instance of data is a q-dimensional vector, where q is the number of features. Let $X_U = \{x_1, x_2, \dots, x_n\}$ be the sequence of observations made by a learner device (e.g. smartphone), the labels of which are not yet known with certainty. Let $X_L = \{(x_{n+1}, y_{n+1}), (x_{n+2}, y_{n+2}), \dots, (x_{n+m}, y_{n+m})\}$ be the set of labeled data which are used to initialize the learner. This labeled data may come from related labeled data or partially trained learner. The collaborative active learning problem is to select a subset $X_S \subset X_U$ to query from the expert set E such that the overall cost of query is minimized and the overall knowledge of experts is maximized.*

3.2 Problem Formulation

The CAL problem can be formulated as an optimization problem as follows. Let β_i be a binary variable that determines whether or not the query strategy submodule selects x_i as an informative instance:

$$\beta_i = \begin{cases} 1, & \text{if label for } x_i \text{ is needed} \\ 0, & \text{otherwise.} \end{cases} \quad (2)$$

Let α_{ij} be a binary variable indicating whether or not the expert selection model requests the label for instance x_i from expert e_j. That is:

$$\alpha_{ij} = \begin{cases} 1, & \text{if label for } x_i \text{ is asked from } e_j \\ 0, & \text{otherwise} \end{cases} \quad (3)$$

And let c_{ij} be the query cost for instance x_i from expert e_j and p be the number of experts. Then, the Integer Linear Programming (ILP) formulation for the CAL problem is as follows:

$$\mathit{Minimize} \sum_{i=1}^{n} \sum_{j=1}^{p} \beta_i \alpha_{ij} c_{ij} \quad (4)$$

subject to:

$$\sum_{j=1}^{p} \alpha_{ij} \geq 1 \qquad \forall\, i \in \{i \mid \beta_i = 1\} \quad (5)$$

$$\beta_i \in \{0, 1\}, \ \alpha_{ij} \in \{0, 1\} \quad (6)$$

The objective function in (4) aims to minimize the total cost of the queries from the set of experts. The constraint (5) guarantees that each selected unlabeled data is asked from at least one expert and the constraint in (6) ensures that the variable β_i and α_{ij} take only binary values.

Algorithm 1 CollaborativeActiveLearning

Input: $M, DB_R, X_L, X_U, L = \{\ell_1, \ell_2, \ldots, \ell_k\}, K, u_{th}, E$
Output: Updated Learner M

```
(DB_L, M(x)) ← LearnerInitialization(X_U, DB_R, L)
X_L ← X_L ∪ DB_L, X_S ← ∅, count = 0
while u_M > u_th or count < |selectedFrom(X_U)| do
    (X, u) ← getInformativeInstances(K, X_U)
    for all x_i ∈ X do
        y_i ← ExpertSelection(x_i, E, M(x_i), u_th)
        X_S ← X_S ∪ (x_i, y_i)
    end for
    broadcastLabeledData(X_S) /*collaborative*/
    updateUncertaintyAll(X_S, E) /*collaborative*/
    X_L ← X_L ∪ X_S
    X_S ← ∅
    M ← UpdateLearner(X_L)
    count = count + K
end while
```

Algorithm 2 LearnerInitialization

Input: $DB_R, X_U, L = \{\ell_1, \ell_2, \ldots, \ell_k\}$
Output: DB_L, Learner $M(x)$

```
DB_L ← ∅, SIM ← ∅
(Centers_u, Clusters_u) = Clustering(X_U, k)
for all DB_Ri ∈ DB_R do
    SIM_i = cosSim(Centers_DBRi, Centers_u)
    SIM ← SIM ∪ SIM_i
end for
for all ℓ_i ∈ L do
    DB_ℓi ← argmax_ℓi SIM
    DB_L ← DB_L ∪ DB_ℓi
end for
M(X) ← Classifier(DB_L)
```

Algorithm 3 ExpertSelection

Input: x, E, semi-label $\mathcal{L}$, u_{th}
Output: label ℓ

```
u = 100
while u > u_th do
    E_conf ← ∅, C_conf ← ∅
    for all e_i ∈ E do
        if U_i(𝓛) ≤ u_th then
            add e_i to the E_conf /*confident experts*/
            add cost(e_i) to C_conf /*cost of experts*/
        end if
    end for
    expert ← argmin_{e_i ∈ E_conf} C_conf
    𝓛 ← label from expert for instance x
    u ← uncertainty of expert in labeling x
end while
ℓ = 𝓛
```

4 ALGORITHMS

The CAL problem is an ILP, which in general is known to be NP-Hard. We develop a greedy algorithm that finds an approximate solution.

Algorithm 1. The driver routine of our algorithm for solving the CAL problem is presented in psuedocode form in Algorithm 1. The algorithm takes as input the learner model $M(x)$, the dictionary of related labeled data DB_R, the dictionary of target labeled data X_L, the dictionary of target unlabeled data X_U, the label set L, the number of instances for each round of query K, the uncertainty threshold u_{th}, and the set E of experts. It gives as output an updated version of the model $M(x)$.

Algorithm 1 calls the routine LearnerInitialization (Algorithm 2) to initialize the learner based on the closest data instances to the current context in DB_R. It then adds this to the target labeled database X_L. The while-loop after the learner initialization represents the active learning phase. In each iteration of the while-loop, the most informative instances are selected via the function getInformativeInstances (recall the discussion about informative instances in Section 2.2), which returns the K most informative instances from the database of unlabeled data. Subsequently, the routine ExpertSelection (Algorithm 3) is called to find the label for each instance from the most-relevant, lowest-cost expert.

Then, the new labeled data are added to the target labeled database and the learner model $M(x)$ is updated. The function BroadcastLabeledData shares the new labeled data with the other experts. The function UpdateUncertaintyAll is run on each expert to update their knowledge and accordingly their uncertainty score. This process is repeated until we iterate over all the selected instances or the learner's uncertainty score falls below the threshold u_{th} for all $\ell_i \in L$. The learner built based on the enhanced target labeled data database is returned as the output of the algorithm (CAL).

Algorithm 2. The LearnerInitialization algorithm takes as input the dictionary of related labeled data DB_R, the dictionary of target unlabeled data X_U, and the label set L consisting of k elements. The algorithm finds k clusters for the unlabeled data. It then searches the entire database of related data DB_R to find the closest set of labeled data to each cluster. We used cosine similarity to measure the closeness of clusters and labeled data. The details are shown in Algorithm 2.

Algorithm 3. The ExpertSelection algorithm is a greedy algorithm. It takes as input the instance x, the set of experts E, a semi-label $\mathcal{L}$, and the uncertainty threshold u_{th}. The semi-label $\mathcal{L}$ is the most probable label for instance x. The goal of the algorithm is to find the least costly and most confident expert for the instance x. The set E_{conf} is the set of experts that are confident enough to detect the semi-label $\mathcal{L}$ at a given moment during the course of the algorithm. The semi-label $\mathcal{L}$ is updated in the course of the algorithm, and is deemed acceptable if the uncertainty score of the selected expert is lower than the threshold u_{th}. Further details are shown in Algorithm 3.

5 EXPERIMENTAL VALIDATION

We experimentally assess the efficacy of the proposed architecture using real human activity data. We implemented all of the algorithms we developed and simulated the proposed architecture in

Table 1: Statistical features extracted from each data segment.

Feature	Description
Amp	Amplitude of signal segment
Med	Median of signal segment
Mean	Mean value of signal segment
Max	Maximum amplitude of signal segment
P2P	Peak to peak amplitude
Var	Variance of signal segment
Std	Standard deviation
RMS	Root mean square power
S2E	Start to end value

Table 2: Uncertainty score of experts in E for all label $\ell_i \in L$.

	ℓ_1	ℓ_2	ℓ_3	ℓ_4	ℓ_5	ℓ_6	ℓ_7	ℓ_8
E1	00.01	00.02	00.01	00.01	00.01	00.03	00.01	00.20
E2	57.58	56.60	02.00	0.020	04.61	01.09	46.48	100.0
E3	100.0	80.36	100.0	04.33	01.19	02.60	100.0	100.0
E4	65.51	60.30	50.20	13.56	42.54	01.77	04.88	47.18
E5	60.69	60.69	56.84	82.61	02.41	13.86	30.31	28.00
E6	67.56	53.28	100.0	02.66	01.93	36.28	27.32	48.99
E7	54.55	75.76	02.33	01.20	30.48	04.09	12.50	74.12
E8	62.52	07.89	00.02	10.66	72.05	02.54	02.33	22.42

Python. We present our findings in this section. The section is organized as follows. We discuss our case study—physical activity monitoring—and describe the dataset we used in Section 5.1. We present the architecture design settings in Section 5.2. In Section 5.3, we show the benefits of using active learning on physical activity monitoring. In Section 5.4, we demonstrate results on cost evaluation of the architecture.

5.1 Case Study: Activity Monitoring

Activity recognition is an important research area in health monitoring systems because of its potential to enable novel context-aware applications in elderly care, fitness, education, sports, and patients with chronicle diseases. Various types of sensors have been proposed for such purposes, ranging from motion sensors such as accelerometers, gyroscopes, GPS sensors to combinations of different sensor modalities [22–24]. Because of the importance of physical activity monitoring, we chose an activity recognition dataset to show the efficacy of our proposed architecture.

Dataset Description. The dataset we used is publicly available at Data and Web Science Research Group, University of Mannheim [24]. Fifteen subjects, seven females and eight males, were asked to perform eight different daily activities: Walking, Running, Sitting, Standing, Stair down, Stair up, Jumping, and Lying. Subjects were asked to perform the activity set while carrying seven mobile devices located on chest, shin, forearm, thigh, upper-arm, head, and waist. Each subject performed each activity roughly 10 minutes except for jumping which is performed only for 100 seconds. Each mobile device is equipped with different types of sensors including tri-axial accelerometer and gyroscopes.

5.2 Architecture Design Settings

In this section, we describe the design settings of the Co-MEAL architecture we employed in our experiments.

5.2.1 Data Preparation. We applied a moving average filter on the activity data to remove high frequency noises from sensor data. After data filtering, a two-second sliding window was used for data segmentation. We consider 50% overlap between consecutive data segments.

A variety of features can be extracted from human activity data segments. Previous studies have identified statistical features that are effective for activity recognition [25, 26]. Table 1 lists the set of features that we extracted from individual data segments.

5.2.2 Classifiers and Query Strategy. A variety of classifiers can be used for activity detection. Previous studies have shown that K-NN, SVM, decision tree (DT), random forest (RF) classifiers are effective for activity recognition [27, 28]. In this work, we used RF for the learner model and sensor-based experts for two reasons. First, RF fits a number of decision tree classifiers on various sub-samples of the training data and uses averaging to improve the predictive accuracy to control over-fitting. Secondly, using RF, we already have a built-in query strategy for the active learning phase as we explained in Section 2.2.

5.2.3 Expert Initialization. For the purpose of simulation, we built a multi-expert EMU using the available sensor data for different locations. We also used the ground truth label as the least uncertain (most confident) expert in the EMU. In a real-world scenario, this expert can be a highly confident physician or the user in the monitoring system. We used the labeled data of other locations to simulate other experts.

To have more realistic scenario, each expert is trained in such a way that it is confidence over a subset of label set L. Therefore, each expert has imperfect knowledge over some of the labels. We initialize the uncertainty score of each expert based on their miss-classification for their own test data. Table 2 shows the expert set that we used along with their uncertainty score over the label set L. We set the uncertainty threshold to 20% for each expert in the expert selection procedure in all of the below experiments except for Section 5.4.1. We use the K-means clustering algorithm for the learner initialization.

5.3 Performance Evaluation Scenarios

To evaluate the performance of the Co-MEAL architecture, we used two different scenarios, a single sensor learning scenario and a multiple sensor learning scenario.

5.3.1 Single Sensor Learning. In this scenario, the assumption is that a single sensor is placed on human body as a learner (e.g. mobile phone on the waist). Our goal is to learn the sensor for a new context that is different compared to the available labeled data. We assume that we have training data for all the subjects in the related database except one subject. Therefore, the new context would be a new subject. The architecture actively retrains the learner for the excluded subject in the reconfiguration phase. We use the label of the excluded subject for accuracy evaluation.

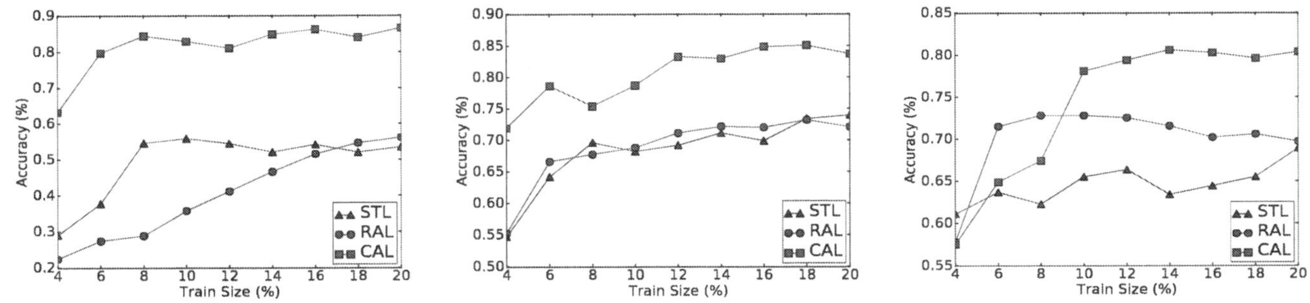

(a) Chest sensor learning. (b) Waist sensor learning. (c) Thigh sensor learning.

Figure 2: Single sensor learning scenario for different sensor locations.

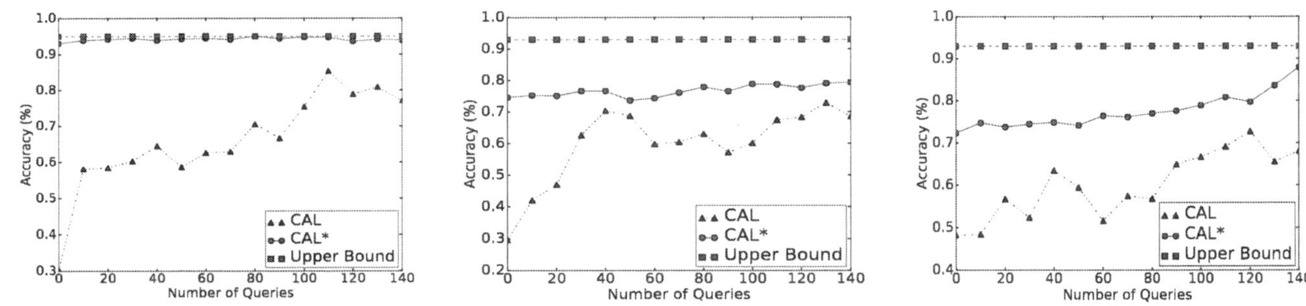

(a) No missing label. (b) One missing label. (c) Two missing label.

Figure 3: Multiple sensors (two sensors located on chest and waist) learning scenario.

After the learner initialization step, the query strategy submodule selects the top $K = 10$ informative instances in each query round and the EMU labels the selected instances. We compare the results of activity recognition accuracy with two learner models: 1) randomly select samples in the query procedure instead of informative samples (RAL) and 2) employ a simple transfer learning-based learner (STL) which uses the most relevant training data of other subjects. We run the experiment for all subjects and plot the average accuracy for all three algorithms. The results on are summarized in Fig. 2. The training data refers to the percentage of queries and the percentage of used training data for CAL/RAL and STL algorithms respectively.

Fig. 2 shows that using only 15% query, the accuracy of the proposed collaborative active learning algorithm CAL goes up to 88%. The accuracy of the STL algorithm fluctuates for most cases after adding a certain amount of training data from other subjects. After a point, the difference in distribution of training data and our context result in an uncertain learner for the STL algorithm. The RAL algorithm accuracy increases in the active learning process until a point that the added labeled data has no impact on the learner accuracy. The comparison of accuracy is shown in Fig. 2 for three different learner locations (Chest, Waist, and Thigh). The reported accuracy is the average for all subject in different runs.

5.3.2 Multiple Sensor Learning. Sometimes a user may need to integrate several sensors to the system for better performance or context-related data collection. Furthermore, one may need to classify more labels. We consider a learner with two sensor nodes located on different body parts. Each node is already trained on a subset of labels with high confidence. The union of the two label subsets may contain all or part of the label set L. Since in this case we additionally use previous knowledge of the learners, we call the set up CAL*, to distinguish it from our standard CAL algorithm.

The way data is collected for CAL* requires a bit of clarification. The subject will start using the system and the unlabeled data are labeled by both sensors in the system. Those samples for which one of the sensors is confident with their labeling decision are added to the target labeled database (X_L). The rest of unlabeled data are added to the target unlabeled data (X_U). The system also enhances the target labeled data using Algorithm 2.

We compare the results of the activity recognition accuracy obtained using CAL* with two other setups. (1) An active learning procedure without the knowledge of sensor nodes and where the system is built solely on actively selected queries (CAL). (2) The case in which the upper bound on accuracy is set using the same context training data (Upper Bound).

To compare the three setups, we consider three cases on the initial overall knowledge of the two learners: 1) cover all labels, 2) cover all labels except one, and 3) cover all labels except two labels. Fig. 3 shows using available knowledge of learners increases the initial activity recognition accuracy by up to 92%, 81%, and 88% for

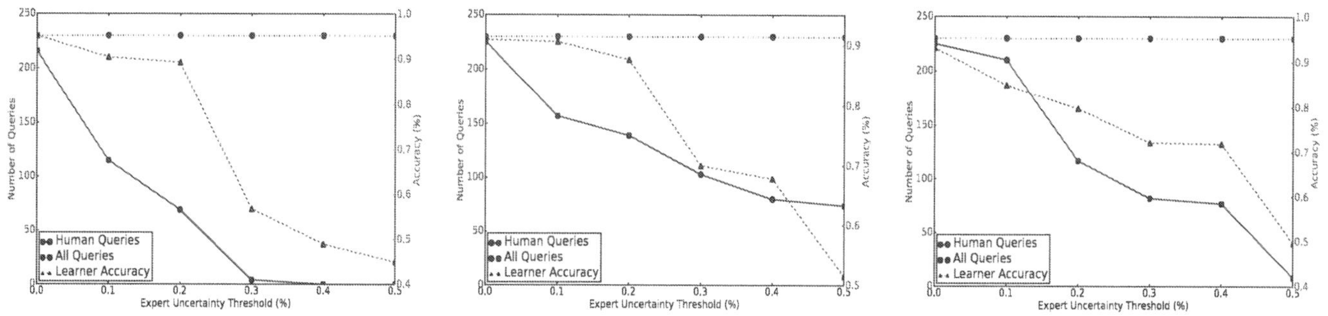

(a) Chest sensor (b) Upper arm sensor (c) Waist sensor

Figure 4: Expert uncertainty threshold versus activity recognition accuracy and number of queries (blue axes: number of queries, red axes: accuracy).

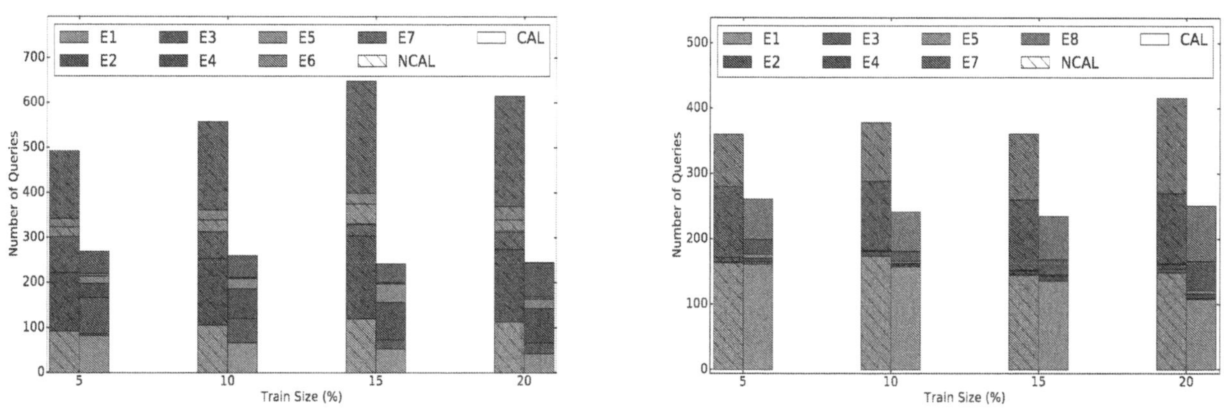

(a) The Waist and Ankle Sensor for Subject-1 (b) The Waist and Ankle Sensor for Subject-9

Figure 5: Comparison of non-collaborative and collaborative active learning in terms of total number queries. Each color corresponds to a different expert.

having knowledge on all labels, all labels except one label, and all labels except two labels, respectively. It can be seen that deficiency in knowledge on the label set raises the number of queries to get higher performances.

5.4 Query Cost Evaluation

In this section, we present results assessing the effects of uncertainty and the benefits of collaboration in the Co-MEAL architecture.

5.4.1 Effects of Uncertainty. Depending on how critical accurate decision making is to the application, we can control the quality of selected expert in the EMU unit. To show how uncertainty of each expert affects the number of queries in a real world application, we run the architecture with different uncertainty thresholds. Fig. 4 shows the effects of uncertainty on (i) the number of queries employed and (ii) the accuracy of activity recognition. Note that the plots in Fig. 4 use two vertical axes to show the two quantities simultaneously. In these experiments, we assumed that the most expensive data annotator is the subject, and we compared the number of human expert queries against all queries for different uncertainty score thresholds.

The lower the uncertainty score threshold is, the higher the number of expensive queries. However, even choosing uncertain experts, we still reach an acceptable data classification accuracy. We repeated the experiment for three different locations. We used 20% of the data in active learning process. We see that the EMU reduces the number of expensive queries by up to 40% while attaining an accuracy of greater than 80% for uncertainty score threshold lower than 0.2.

5.4.2 Benefits of Collaboration in Active Learning. As was shown in Table 2, we simulated a real world scenario using the available sensors on different locations as well as the ground truth labels. We defined a cost on each expert proportional to their confidence on the label set L. The expert set is sorted in a descending order based on their cost (E1 has the highest cost).

Fig. 5 shows the number of queries for both collaborative (CAL) and non-collaborative (NCAL) active leaning. NCAL is simply a variant of Algorithm 1 in which the lines 9 and 10 corresponding to collaboration between experts are deleted.

The training data size is the number of instance that are labeled by experts. As we can see, the total number of queries decreases for CAL compared to NCAL due to the use of the active learning process. As we go forward in time, experts' confidence increases in CAL, while the knowledge of experts remains the same for NCAL. We also see that the number of queries from expensive experts decreases for CAL. Therefore, the queries from inexpensive experts (e.g. E7, E8) increase, while using less queries from expensive experts (e.g. E1, E2).

6 RELATED WORK

There is no existing work against which a direct comparison with our approach can be made. But in a broader sense, reliable and reconfigurable design of health monitoring systems has been studied in a number of related works.

The **conventional approach** is to design reliable machine learning algorithms with vast amount of training data. In [29], a set of heuristics is presented for activity recognition with sensors displaced within a single body segment. The authors show that within certain limits and with modest quality degradation, activity recognition is tolerant to displacement. In [23], a location-aware activity monitoring is proposed for the purpose of accurate activity detection. Zappi et. al. investigate the effects of exploiting redundant sensors distributed on the body to use a subset of sensors in the presence of disorientation [28]. Allan et. al. investigate sensor heterogeneity in activity recognition systems [30]. A clustering based method is proposed to categorize different devices and then activity recognition is performed using a specific computational model for each category.

A shortcoming of the conventional approach is that it provides either limited degree of freedom (e.g. a certain amount of sensor displacement) or requires very large amount of training data to cover every situations (e.g displaced data, misplaced data) [28, 30, 31].

Transfer learning is another approach that recently has been used for system reconfiguration of health monitoring systems [32, 33]. Kyle et. al. propose three heterogeneous transfer learning techniques that reverse the typical transfer model and map the target feature space to the source feature space and apply them to activity recognition in a smart apartment [34]. In [35], the authors presente different algorithms for knowledge transfer in wearable systems. It is shown that knowledge transfer from the source domain to the target domain improves accuracy by 15%. In another work, a multi-view learning approach is presented for wearables with multiple sensors in which one of them acts as the source domain [36]. It is shown that by using an additional wearable node performance can be increased by up to 15%. Fallahzadeh et. al. [16] propose an uninformed cross-subject transfer learning algorithm that leverages cross-user similarities by constructing a network for data in source and target users and perform community detection to extract the core observations in the target data.

While transfer learning approaches offer advantages compared to conventional approaches, they still have several limitations: 1) they typically rely on sending the entire sensors' data to the back-end station to perform the knowledge transfer, 2) they are applicable for highly correlated contexts (e.g. similar user), and 3) even for similar contexts, knowledge transfer is inefficient for accurate data processing. Therefore, a system solely designed based on related knowledge can be inadequate for M-health monitoring systems.

Active learning approaches could help mitigate some of these limitations, and they have been used extensively in the broader literature of machine learning [37, 38]. However, active learning is rarely used in the context of health monitoring systems [39]. Longstaff et. al. [40] investigate the applicability of active learning for activity recognition. Active learning is compared with several semi-supervised learning methods including self-learning and co-learning. It is shown that active learning improves the system's accuracy the most. In [41], several active learning methods are designed and implemented for their applicability to the activity recognition task. The authors evaluated the methods using the CASAS smart home sensor data and present a crowd-sourcing application for annotation. Another active learning for activity recognition systems in single person smart homes is presented in [42]. This approach exploits clustering approaches to categorize in-home activities. Users only need to label each cluster as an activity as opposed to labeling all instances of all activities.

7 CONCLUSIONS

We explored the use of active learning for system reconfiguration of mobile sensory devices, focusing on mobile health monitoring. We targeted a design process that simultaneously addresses several challenges and scenarios: 1) The cost of data labeling through the learning process may be expensive. This cost may relate to interference in user's life, feedbacks from health-care experts, or equipment cost. 2) The suitable expert for each data instance may be unknown. And 3) the labels may be subject to uncertainty because of limited knowledge of experts.

To help address these challenges, we proposed a new architecture that manages a multi-expert M-health system. The architecture finds a cost-optimal and most-confident expert each time a query needs to be issued. At the same time, we considered collaboration among the experts in order to gain more accurate data labeling while minimizing the cost. We proposed new algorithms for the purpose of expert selection as well as system initialization for M-health systems. As part of the algorithms, we employed available clustering algorithms as well as ensemble classification methods.

We demonstrated the efficacy of the architecture and the developed algorithms using activity monitoring as a case study. Specifically, we considered accelerometer-based human activity recognition dataset. We showed that an accuracy of activity recognition as high as 85% can be achieved by labeling only 15% of unlabeled data. We also showed that annotation cost is substantially reduced because of cost-optimal expert selection as well as collaboration between experts in the proposed Co-MEAL architecture.

In future work, we plan to enhance the architecture to handle multi-modality sensory systems. We also plan to use the system in a real pilot study of an intervention system. In a separate future direction, we plan to integrate transfer learning and active learning approaches in order to further reduce the number of queries and increase learner's accuracy.

ACKNOWLEDGMENTS

This work was supported by a Research Fellowship from the Community Health Analytics Initiative (CHAI) at Washington State University and by the National Science Foundation CAREER Award IIS 1553528.

REFERENCES

[1] Misha Kay, Jonathan Santos, and Marina Takane. mHealth: New horizons for health through mobile technologies. *World Health Organization*, 3:66–71, 2011.

[2] Abu Saleh Mohammad Mosa, Illhoi Yoo, and Lincoln Sheets. A systematic review of healthcare applications for smartphones. *BMC medical informatics and decision making*, 12(1):67, 2012.

[3] Zachary W Adams, Erin A McClure, Kevin M Gray, Carla Kmett Danielson, Frank A Treiber, and Kenneth J Ruggiero. Mobile devices for the remote acquisition of physiological and behavioral biomarkers in psychiatric clinical research. *Journal of psychiatric research*, 85:1–14, 2017.

[4] Caroline Free, Gemma Phillips, Louise Watson, Leandro Galli, Lambert Felix, Phil Edwards, Vikram Patel, and Andy Haines. The effectiveness of mobile-health technologies to improve health care service delivery processes: a systematic review and meta-analysis. *PLoS Med*, 10(1):e1001363, 2013.

[5] Daniel F Hayes, Hugh S Markus, R David Leslie, and Eric J Topol. Personalized medicine: risk prediction, targeted therapies and mobile health technology. *BMC Medicine*, 12(1):37, 2014.

[6] Armin Shahrokni, Sanam Mahmoudzadeh, Ramyar Saeedi, and Hassan Ghasemzadeh. Older people with access to hand-held devices: Who are they? *Telemedicine and e-Health*, 21(7):550–556, 2015.

[7] Emanuela Marcelli, Alessandro Capucci, Gabriele Minardi, and Laura Cercenelli. Multi-sense cardiopatch: A wearable patch for remote monitoring of electro-mechanical cardiac activity. *Asaio Journal*, 63(1):73–79, 2017.

[8] Philip E Eggers, Eric A Eggers, and Benjamin Z Bailey. Wearable apparatus, system and method for detection of cardiac arrest and alerting emergency response, June 23 2016. US Patent 20,160,174,857.

[9] Javad Birjandtalab, Maziyar Baran Pouyan, Diana Cogan, Mehrdad Nourani, and Jay Harvey. Automated seizure detection using limited-channel eeg and non-linear dimension reduction. *Computers in Biology and Medicine*, 82:49–58, 2017.

[10] David Zakim and Matthias Schwab. Data collection as a barrier to personalized medicine. *Trends in pharmacological sciences*, 36(2):68–71, 2015.

[11] Ramin Fallahzadeh, Mahdi Pedram, Ramyar Saeedi, Bahman Sadeghil, Michael Ongl, and Hassan Ghasemzadeh. Smart-cuff: A wearable bio-sensing platform with activity-sensitive information quality assessment for monitoring ankle edema. 2015.

[12] Pio Alfredo Di Tore. Situation awareness and complexity: the role of wearable technologies in sports science. *Journal of Human Sport and Exercise*, 10(1proc):500–506, 2015.

[13] Rachel Lomasky, Carla E Brodley, Matthew Aernecke, David Walt, and Mark Friedl. Active class selection. In *European Conference on Machine Learning*, pages 640–647. Springer, 2007.

[14] Burr Settles, Mark Craven, and Lewis Friedland. Active learning with real annotation costs. In *Proceedings of the NIPS workshop on cost-sensitive learning*, pages 1–10, 2008.

[15] Hesam Sagha, José del R Millán, and Ricardo Chavarriaga. A probabilistic approach to handle missing data for multi-sensory activity recognition. In *Workshop on Context Awareness and Information Processing in Opportunistic Ubiquitous Systems at 12th ACM International Conference on Ubiquitous Computing*, number EPFL-CONF-151974, 2010.

[16] Ramin Fallahzadeh and Hassan Ghasemzadeh. Personalization without user interruption: Boosting activity recognition in new subjects using unlabeled data (an uninformed cross-subject transfer learning algorithm). In *International Conference on Cyber-Physical Systems (ICCPS)*. ACM/IEEE, 2017.

[17] Vincent Wenchen Zheng, Derek Hao Hu, and Qiang Yang. Cross-domain activity recognition. In *Proceedings of the 11th international conference on Ubiquitous computing*, pages 61–70. ACM, 2009.

[18] Burr Settles. Active learning literature survey. *Computer Science Technical Report 1648, University of Wisconsin, Madison*, (1-67):67, 2010.

[19] Wei Chu, Martin Zinkevich, Lihong Li, Achint Thomas, and Belle Tseng. Unbiased online active learning in data streams. In *Proceedings of the 17th ACM SIGKDD international conference on Knowledge discovery and data mining*, pages 195–203. ACM, 2011.

[20] Bo Wang and John Tsotsos. Dynamic label propagation for semi-supervised multi-class multi-label classification. *Pattern Recognition*, 52:75–84, 2016.

[21] Adrian Calma, Jan Marco Leimeister, Paul Lukowicz, Sarah Oeste-Reiß, Tobias Reitmaier, Albrecht Schmidt, Bernhard Sick, Gerd Stumme, and Katharina Anna Zweig. From active learning to dedicated collaborative interactive learning. In *ARCS 2016*, pages 1–8. VDE, 2016.

[22] Zelun Zhang and Stefan Poslad. Improved use of foot force sensors and mobile phone gps for mobility activity recognition. *IEEE Sensors Journal*, 14(12):4340–4347, 2014.

[23] Ramyar Saeedi, Navid Amini, and Hassan Ghasemzadeh. Patient-centric on-body sensor localization in smart health systems. In *Signals, Systems and Computers, 2014 48th Asilomar Conference on*, pages 2081–2085. IEEE, 2014.

[24] Timo Sztyler and Heiner Stuckenschmidt. On-body localization of wearable devices: an investigation of position-aware activity recognition. In *Pervasive Computing and Communications (PerCom), 2016 IEEE International Conference on*, pages 1–9. IEEE, 2016.

[25] H. Ghasemzadeh, E. Guenterberg, and R. Jafari. Energy-Efficient Information-Driven Coverage for Physical Movement Monitoring in Body Sensor Networks. *IEEE Journal on Selected Areas in Communications*, 27:58–69, 2009.

[26] Hassan Ghasemezadeh, Sarah Ostadabbas, Eric Guenterberg, and Alexandros Pantelopoulos. Wireless medical embedded systems: A review of signal processing techniques for classification. *IEEE Sensors Journal*, 2012, In Press.

[27] Yufei Chen and Chao Shen. Performance analysis of smartphone-sensor behavior for human activity recognition. *IEEE Access*, 5:3095–3110, 2017.

[28] Piero Zappi, Thomas Stiefmeier, Elisabetta Farella, Daniel Roggen, Luca Benini, and Gerhard Troster. Activity recognition from on-body sensors by classifier fusion: sensor scalability and robustness. In *Intelligent Sensors, Sensor Networks and Information, 2007. ISSNIP 2007. 3rd International Conference on*, pages 281–286. IEEE, 2007.

[29] Kai Kunze and Paul Lukowicz. Using acceleration signatures from everyday activities for on-body device location. In *Wearable Computers, 2007 11th IEEE International Symposium on*, pages 115–116. IEEE, 2007.

[30] Allan Stisen, Henrik Blunck, Sourav Bhattacharya, Thor Siiger Prentow, Mikkel Baun Kjærgaard, Anind Dey, Tobias Sonne, and Mads Møller Jensen. Smart devices are different: Assessing and mitigating mobile sensing heterogeneities for activity recognition. In *Proceedings of the 13th ACM Conference on Embedded Networked Sensor Systems*, pages 127–140. ACM, 2015.

[31] Ramyar Saeedi, Ramin Fallahzadeh, Parastoo Alinia, and Hassan Ghasemzadeh. An energy-efficient computational model for uncertainty management in dynamically changing networked wearables. In *International Symposium on Low Power Electronics and Design (ISLPED)*. IEEE/ACM, 2016.

[32] Sinno Jialin Pan and Qiang Yang. A survey on transfer learning. *IEEE Transactions on knowledge and data engineering*, 22(10):1345–1359, 2010.

[33] Sandeepkumar Satpal and Sunita Sarawagi. Domain adaptation of conditional probability models via feature subsetting. In *European Conference on Principles of Data Mining and Knowledge Discovery*, pages 224–235. Springer, 2007.

[34] Kyle Dillon Feuz and Diane J. Cook. Heterogeneous transfer learning for activity recognition using heuristic search techniques. *International Journal of Pervasive Computing and Communications*, 10(4):393–418, 2014.

[35] Ramyar Saeedi, Hassan Ghasemzadeh, and Assefaw H. Gebremedhin. Transfer learning algorithms for autonomous reconfiguration of wearable systems. In *IEEE International Conference on Big Data*. IEEE, 2016.

[36] Seyed Ali Rokni and Hassan Ghasemzadeh. Plug-n-learn: automatic learning of computational algorithms in human-centered internet-of-things applications. In *Proceedings of the 53rd Annual Design Automation Conference*, page 139. ACM, 2016.

[37] Akshay Gadde, Aamir Anis, and Antonio Ortega. Active semi-supervised learning using sampling theory for graph signals. In *Proceedings of the 20th ACM SIGKDD international conference on Knowledge discovery and data mining*, pages 492–501. ACM, 2014.

[38] Yi Yang, Zhigang Ma, Feiping Nie, Xiaojun Chang, and Alexander G Hauptmann. Multi-class active learning by uncertainty sampling with diversity maximization. *International Journal of Computer Vision*, 113(2):113–127, 2015.

[39] Andreas Holzinger. Interactive machine learning for health informatics: when do we need the human-in-the-loop? *Brain Informatics*, 3(2):119–131, 2016.

[40] Brent Longstaff, Sasank Reddy, and Deborah Estrin. Improving activity classification for health applications on mobile devices using active and semi-supervised learning. In *Pervasive Computing Technologies for Healthcare (PervasiveHealth), 2010 4th International Conference on-NO PERMISSIONS*, pages 1–7. IEEE, 2010.

[41] Salikh Bagaveyev and Diane J Cook. Designing and evaluating active learning methods for activity recognition. In *Proceedings of the 2014 ACM International Joint Conference on Pervasive and Ubiquitous Computing: Adjunct Publication*, pages 469–478. ACM, 2014.

[42] Enamul Hoque and John Stankovic. AALO: Activity recognition in smart homes using active learning in the presence of overlapped activities. In *Pervasive Computing Technologies for Healthcare (PervasiveHealth), 2012 6th International Conference on*, pages 139–146. IEEE, 2012.

Antidote Application: An Educational System for Treatment of Common Toxin Overdose

Jon B. Long
Metropolitan College, Boston University
808 Commonwealth Ave, Boston, MA
USA
longjb@me.com

Yingyuan Zhang
Metropolitan College, Boston University
808 Commonwealth Ave, Boston, MA
USA
zyy2013@bu.edu

Vladimir Brusic
School of Medicine and Bioinformatics Center, Nazarbayev University
Astana
Kazakhstan
vladimir.brusic@nu.edu.kz

Lou Chitkushev
Metropolitan College, Boston University
808 Commonwealth Ave, Boston, MA
USA
ltc@bu.wsu

Guanglan Zhang
Metropolitan College, Boston University
808 Commonwealth Ave, Boston, MA
USA
guanglan@bu.edu

ABSTRACT

Poisonings account for almost 1% of emergency room visits each year. Time is a critical factor in dealing with a toxicologic emergency. Delay in dispensing the first antidote dose can lead to life-threatening sequelae. Current toxicological resources that support treatment decisions are broad in scope, time-consuming to read, or at times unavailable. Our review of current toxicological resources revealed a gap in their ability to provide expedient calculations and recommendations about appropriate course of treatment. To bridge the gap, we developed the Antidote Application (AA), a computational system that automatically provides patient-specific antidote treatment recommendations and individualized dose calculations. We implemented 27 algorithms that describe FDA (the US Food and Drug Administration) approved use and evidence-based practices found in primary literature for the treatment of common toxin exposure. The AA covers 29 antidotes recommended by Poison Control and toxicology experts, 19 poison classes and 31 poisons, which represent over 200 toxic entities. To the best of our knowledge, the AA is the first educational decision support system in toxicology that provides patient-specific treatment recommendations and drug dose calculations. The AA is publicly available at http://projects.met-hilab.org/antidote/.

KEYWORDS

Medical informatics; Poison Control Centers; toxicology; toxicity; Decision Support

Permission to make digital or hard copies of all or part of this work for personal or classroom use is granted without fee provided that copies are not made or distributed for profit or commercial advantage and that copies bear this notice and the full citation on the first page. Copyrights for components of this work owned by others than the author(s) must be honored. Abstracting with credit is permitted. To copy otherwise, or republish, to post on servers or to redistribute to lists, requires prior specific permission and/or a fee. Request permissions from Permissions@acm.org.
ACM-BCB '17, August 20-23, 2017, Boston, MA, USA
© 2017 Copyright is held by the owner/author(s). Publication rights licensed to ACM.
ACM 978-1-4503-4722-8/17/08...$15.00
http://dx.doi.org/10.1145/3107411.3107415

1 INTRODUCTION

In medicine, drug information is presented in many forms such as FDA (the US Food and Drug Administration) approved package inserts, drug monographs, primary and tertiary literature, clinical decision support systems, and electronic drug information databases. In emergency situations due to poisoning, communication of salient drug information such as indication, dosing, and other essential information is important in the rapid delivery of lifesaving medical interventions.

Package inserts or drug monographs are the primary source for FDA approved drug dosing and drug use information. Though informative, they are not readily searchable, and consequently cumbersome to utilize in emergency situations. Primary literature, though peer reviewed, requires evaluation on the part of the reader for accuracy and appropriateness. Generic and toxicology focused clinical decision support systems (CDSS) and electronic drug databases do not include algorithms to combine drug information with patient specific treatment recommendations. Some CDSS do perform dose calculations, but to our knowledge none do both treatment recommendation and patient-specific dose calculation. This requires the user to manipulate patient information and calculate drug dosage, resulting in increased possibility of error and delays in antidote dispensing. A computational system that takes patient information into consideration, automatically provides treatment recommendations, and calculates individualized drug dosage will reduce medical error and "time to first dose."

Regional Poison Control Centers in the U.S. are an exceedingly useful tool that clinicians can rely on in a poisoning emergency. However, they are only available via telephone, which is dependent on the reliability of telecommunication providers. As of Dec 2015, the American College of Medical Toxicology listed only 177 licensed physicians in the Directory of Inpatient Medical Toxicology Services within the U.S. and most of them are clustered in major metropolitan areas (http://www.acmt.net/cgi/page.cgi/findtoxicologist.html). Licensed physicians who specialize in toxicology are either very few or non-existent in non-metropolitan areas.

There have been a few descriptions in the literature that describe the creation of clinical decision support systems that specifically address poisonings. In 1985, Rubens described a rule-based system that focuses on an in-home first response algorithm for accidental poisonings in children [1]. In 1994 Darmoni and coauthors described an expert system in toxicology developed for a regional hospital in France that focused on diagnosis of poisoning arising from medication overdose and gave general treatment recommendations with no patient specific dose calculations [2]. In 2010, a group in Malaysia developed a system that focused on poisoning diagnosis [3]. However none of these three expert systems are publically available.

To bridge the current gap in resources, we created the Antidote Application (AA), a computational system that automatically recommends individualized antidote treatment regimen and patient-specific doses for all age groups ranging from newborns to elderly adults. The AA was implemented in two formats: a standalone downloadable application for offline use (hereinafter referred to as Java AA) and an online web application (hereinafter referred to as Web AA). The AA hosts 27 algorithms for the treatment of common toxin exposure in North America. It covers the 29 antidotes recommended by Dart et al. [4], for treatment of poisonings by 31 specific toxins and 19 toxin classes. These specific toxins and toxin classes represent over two hundred toxic entities covered by this system. Phone numbers and links to regional PCCs and the federal adverse event reporting mechanism (FAER) are included in the AA. The AA represents a unique educational resource for treatment of common toxin overdose and is current as of May 2016.

2 MATERIALS AND METHODS

2.1 Implementation of Algorithms

In the AA, we implemented 27 algorithms for the treatment of common toxin exposure. The list of antidotes included in the AA was derived from an expert panel consensus document published in the Annals of Emergency Medicine in 2009 that recommends antidote formulary inclusions for hospitals as shown in the Antidotes and Poisons Table at http://projects.met-hilab.org/antidote/#/FAQ [4]. The formulary antidote recommendations are specific for North American Hospitals.

For dose calculations, the FDA approved dosing guidelines published by the manufacturers were used, whenever available. However, not all antidotes described by the expert panel had FDA approved indications and usage because some indications have been "grandfathered" as accepted practice after the FDA clarified the language on indications [5, 6]. Furthermore, the number of studies focusing on antidotes or medication poisonings in infants and children is small. At times the FDA approved indications can be so broad that there is debate on whether or not toxicity is an approved indication [7, 8]. For these antidotes, several off-label or unapproved-use algorithms reported in primary literature references were included in the AA in accordance with the FDA guidelines of the "Off-Label" use of marketed drugs [9]. We made every effort to avoid using tertiary literature because the survey of 17 major sources during AA development and implementation yielded inconsistencies in treatment recommendations. The treatment and dose recommendation in each algorithm in the AA is clearly labeled for its FDA approval status. The algorithms are verified using the drug dosing treatment guidelines found in the FDA approved antidote's drug monographs whenever available. In addition, we have implemented more advanced treatment guidelines as they became available through FDA approved amendments to the drug monographs. If no drug monograph is available to verify an antidote algorithm, guidelines from primary literature were obtained. Once an algorithm is verified, each permutation of the treatment and dose recommendations for all age groups and special populations were determined. Each antidote algorithm has distinct characteristics such as the indication, treatment thresholds, or hypersensitivity, which are specifically related to the treatment recommendations and dose calculations. All of these factors must be considered when determining the correct permutation of treatment and dose calculation for each individual patient.

Some medical antidotes described in the AA are used in multiple algorithms. These antidotes have multiple indications and each can be used under more than one poisoning scenario. For example, dimercaprol is used in two algorithms. It is used in conjunction with Ca-EDTA to treat lead poisoning and in the treatment of heavy metal (arsenic, gold or mercury) toxicity. At times multiple antidotes are recommended by one algorithm to treat a particular poisoning. One example is the Cyanide Antidote Package: Together amyl nitrite, sodium nitrite and sodium thiosulfate are indicated for use as a composite antidote in the treatment of cyanide poisoning. In the AA, the use of generic and trade names of antidotes follows medical convention of not capitalizing generic names and capitalizing brand names. For example, Tylenol is a brand name of acetaminophen.

2.2 User input data validation

To generate patient-specific dosing recommendations, users/trainees are required to enter a patient's age, weight, and height in the input boxes at the AA user interface. To minimize typographical errors, we implemented several data validation measures.

First, we implemented numeric data validation so that only numeric data and decimal points are allowed. In the Java AA, if any data other than numeric data and decimal points is entered, the user is notified that the data is invalid and is prompted to enter only numeric values. The Web AA ensures valid numeric data is to be entered by disabling all keyed entry other than numbers and decimal points.

Second, to validate if the values of a patient's height, weight, and age are in reasonable ranges, the user input values are compared to the 2000 CDC Growth Charts for the United States: Methods and Development document [10]. Values from the 3rd percentile in females (lower limit) to 97th percentile in males (upper limit) were used as boundaries for normal range. Census data for children from 0 to 24 months old had only the height in centimeters and weight in kg available. For all other age groups in the Census data the BMI (Body Mass Index) is available. The age range used to validate data is zero (a neonate) to 100 years old. The flowchart of the data validation algorithm is at http://projects.met-hilab.org/antidote/img/data_validation.png. The data validation subroutine is triggered every time a user inputs a set of patient values and clicks one of the begin buttons. If the BMI calculated based on the patient values are out of the normal range, the user is given an alert that the data is out of range and the option to override the alert or re-enter the data. As shown in Fig. 1, 900kg was entered as the value of patient weight. The resulting BMI, when compared to the BMI range from CDC Growth Charts, was flagged as out of range.

The default input units for weight and height are metric – kilograms (kg) and centimeters (cm). When a user sets the units to pound and inch, the weight and height values are automatically converted to corresponding metric values in kilograms and meters for BMI calculation. The BMI is calculated by using Quetelet Index formula described in 1832 by Adolphe Quetelet:

$$BMI = W/H^2 \tag{1}$$

where W denote patient's weight in kilograms and H height in meters.

The Body Surface Area (BSA) is calculated using the Gehan and George formula:

$$BSA\ (Gehan\ and\ George\ formula) = 0.0235H^{0.42246} * W^{0.51456} \tag{2}$$

where height (H) is in centimeters, and weight (W) is in kilograms [11]. The formula used in the calculation of some pediatric dosages is based on the Salisbury rule [11]. When a child's weight (W) is 30kg or less, the dose to be administered is equal to 2*W% of the adult dose, according to the Salisbury rule. If a patient weighs between 30 to 70 kg, the dose to be administered is equal to (30+W)% of the adult dose. For children weighing 70kg or more, the adult dose should be administered. For example if the patient weighs 20 kg administer 40% of the adult dose or if the patient weighs 50 kg administer 80% of the adult dose.

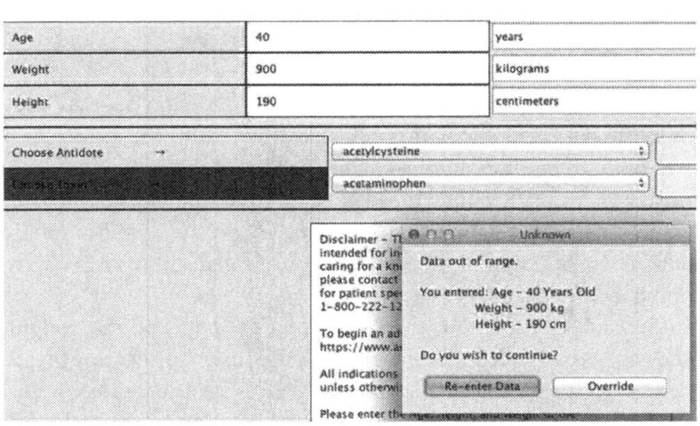

A)

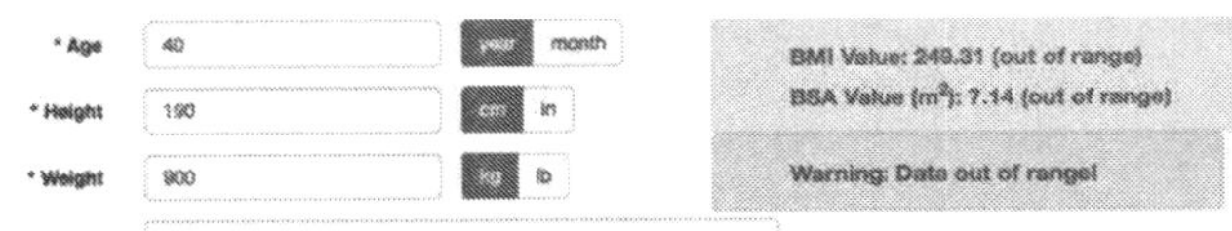

B)

Figure 1: Screenshots of the AA showing a data out of range message generated by the data validation function. A) Screenshot of the standalone Java AA. B) Screenshot of the web AA.

2.3 Description of the Treatment Algorithm

We implemented 27 algorithms that describe FDA approved use and evidence-based practices found in primary literature for the treatment of common toxin exposure. The flowcharts of all algorithms are available in Web AA. To illustrate the functioning of AA we present here one of the most complicated algorithms, the Acetylcysteine treatment algorithm. Acetylcysteine is used in the treatment of acetaminophen (brand name Tylenol®) overdose under FDA approved use. Because of the name similarity, to avoid confusion with the antidote acetylcysteine, the shorthand abbreviation of APAP is used to represent the toxin acetaminophen. In toxic concentrations, APAP saturates the glucuronide and sulfate conjugation pathways in the liver. It is then metabolized by the liver isozyme CYP2E1 to a potentially toxic intermediate metabolite that is quickly conjugated by hepatic glutathione to a nontoxic substance. As toxicity is sustained, glutathione reserves are depleted and the liver begins to build up highly toxic metabolites. If left untreated, liver dysfunction ensues [12].The mechanism of action for acetylcysteine is to replenish the glutathione reserves by acting as a glutathione substitute. It acts as a protectant until the liver can replenish the glucuronide and sulfate pathway reserves [12]. The major factors being considered in the treatment algorithm for APAP toxicity were weight, APAP blood levels, time the blood sample was taken, treatment threshold, and the time of overdose.

In 1975 Rumack and Mathew described a treatment threshold for APAP toxicity that is represented by its blood concentration in a log-linear fashion over time [13]. In those days, concentrations above the Rumack and Mathew line, the dashed line in Fig. 2, at any given time between 4 and 24 hours after APAP exposure were consistent with overdose. Liver dysfunction does not become noticeable until 4 hours after APAP exposure. Blood concentrations taken earlier than 4 hours post exposure can yield a false negative result [13-15]. In 1976 the FDA defined the treatment line that was 25% below the Rumack and Mathew line [15] (the solid line in Fig. 2). The treatment line, starting at 150μg/mL at 4 hours, is used in the U.S. hospitals to determine treatment of APAP overdose. The doses above 4 grams/day in adults and accordingly smaller doses in children have a high correlation with liver damage.

To automate the process of determination of treatment threshold at a specific time point, we derived mathematical equations based on the nomogram. Using two points on the treatment line (150μg/mL at 4hrs and 37.5μg/mL at 12hrs), we were able to use a pharmacokinetic first order rate equation to calculate the elimination rate constant. The following illustrates how the rate constant was derived.

$$C_t = C_0 e^{-(k)\Delta t} \tag{3}$$

$$\frac{C_t}{C_0} = e^{-(k)\Delta t} \tag{4}$$

$$ln\frac{C_t}{C_0} = -(k)\Delta t \tag{5}$$

$$-\frac{ln\frac{C_t}{C_0}}{\Delta t} = k \tag{6}$$

$$k = -\frac{ln\frac{37.5\ mcg}{150\ mcg}}{8hr} \tag{7}$$

$$k = 0.17329\ hr^{-1} \tag{8}$$

where denote the APAP plasma concentration at 4 hours post exposure and at time point t respectively, Δt denotes the time elapsed from 4 hours post ingestion to time point t, and k represents the elimination rate constant.

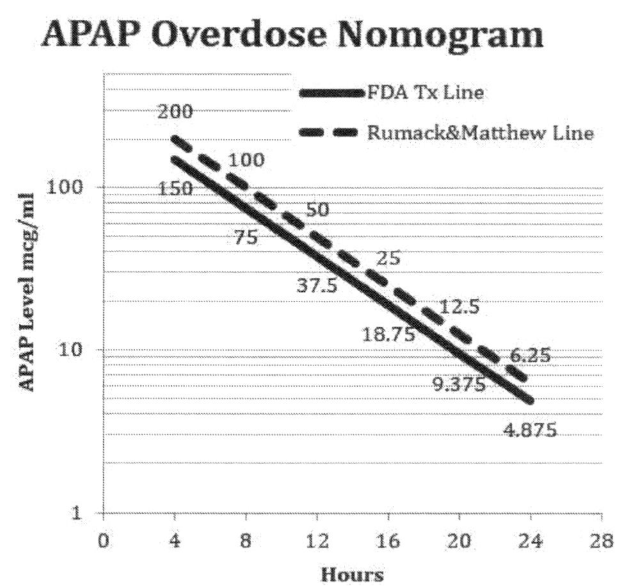

Figure 2: Acetaminophen overdose nomogram [14].

Next we calculate plasma threshold at a time ≥ 4 hours post APAP ingestion using the first order rate equation. This threshold is then compared to the APAP plasma concentration of the patient to determine if treatment is indicated.

If the APAP blood concentration observed at time point t (in hours post ingestion) is $\geq (150\mu g/ml)e^{-(0.17329)(t-4hours)}$, then treatment is indicated. For example an APAP concentration of 135mcg/ml at 5 hours post exposure is above the treatment threshold $(150mcg/ml)e^{-(0.17329)(5\ hours-4hours)}$ or 126µg/mL. Thus acetylcysteine therapy is indicated.

Oral dosing for acetylcysteine includes a loading dose of 140mg/kg PO once, followed by 70mg/kg every 4 hours for 17 doses. Intravenous dosing includes 150mg/kg (maximum of 15000mg) IV over 60 minutes followed by 50mg/kg (maximum 5000mg) IV over four hours followed by 100mg/kg (maximum 10000mg) IV over 16hours.

It is also suggested that activated charcoal should be administered orally to patients within 4 hours of suspected overexposure to APAP. This prevents further gastrointestinal absorption of APAP. Administration of activated charcoal 4 or more hours after exposure has little to no benefit [15].

In the algorithm that we implemented, there are a number of possible outcomes as shown in Fig. 3. The Data Validation flowchart connects to the flowchart in Fig. 3 A.

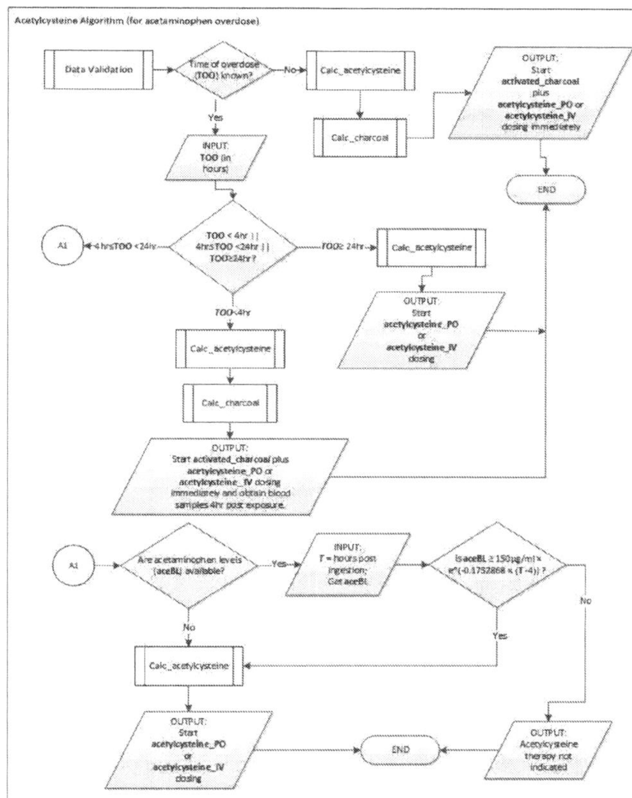

A)

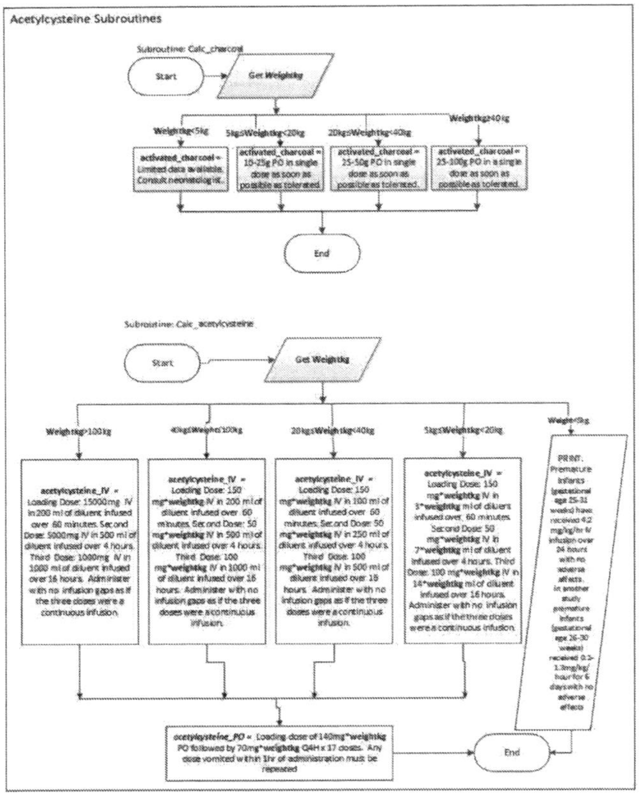

B)

Figure 3: Acetylcysteine algorithm and subroutines. A) The main program. B) The subroutines for dose calculation of activated charcoal and acetylcysteine.

3 RESULTS AND DISCUSSION

This section summarizes the key factors considered when choosing the programming language and architecture of the Java AA and Web AA. The Java AA may be downloaded from http://projects.met-hilab.org/antidote/antidote_application.jar. In the Mac and Windows OS, once downloaded the application may be ran by right clicking on the antidote_application.jar file in Finder. The security settings in the Mac and Windows OS will alert the user that the application is from an unidentified developer – this warning can be ignored. The application will begin by right clicking "open".

3.1 Standalone downloadable AA implementation

When considering a programming language for the standalone Antidote application, Java was an immediate favorite. There are a number of features that Java offers that are of great benefit to the AA. Java is platform independent, which means the code, can be written once and used on many different operating systems. Java programs are runnable on the Windows, Mac OS X, and Linux operating systems. Java is also object oriented, which allows code to be reused by other programs. This is of significant advantage and is used extensively in the Java AA. The parent Antidote class is a repository for many pieces of code used throughout the many child classes of the Java AA. For example the code for calculating doses based on body surface area (BSA) is located and called from the Antidote class. Java is relatively easy to learn and maintain. Since Java has a minimal number of keywords that are in natural-language syntax, Java is simpler to learn than some other languages. Also, as Java applications do not need to be rewritten for different platforms or operating systems, maintenance updates are easier to implement. Android, the mobile operating system is also based on Java. This is important as we plan to extend the AA project in the mobile application sphere.

The structure of the Java AA was kept very lean and simple. There is a parent class known as the Antidote class. The Antidote class contains instance variables and methods that are inherited by all of the child classes. The 27 child classes include the instance variables (attributes) and methods specific to each antidote algorithm. The graphical user interface class controls the flow of information between the user and the Java AA. The UML (Unified Modeling Language) diagram in Fig. 4 shows this relationship.

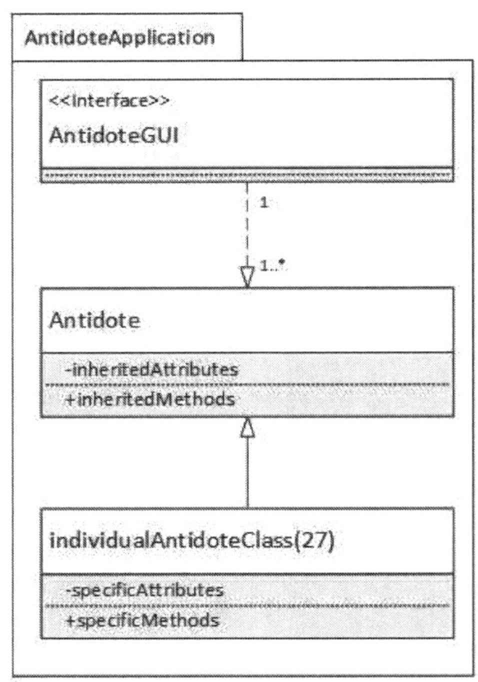

Figure 4: Antidote Application UML diagram.

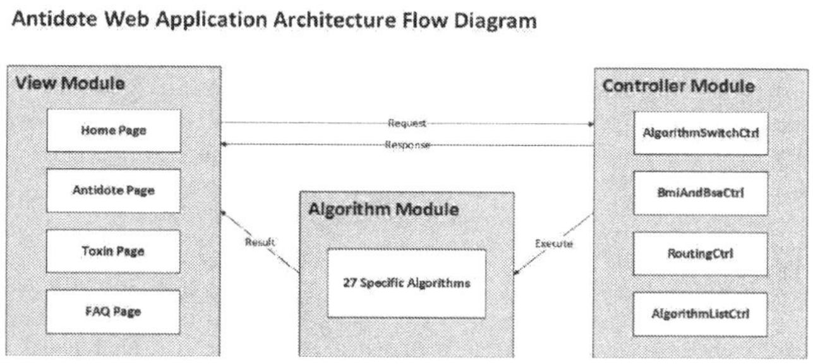

Figure 5: Architectural data flow diagram of the web AA.

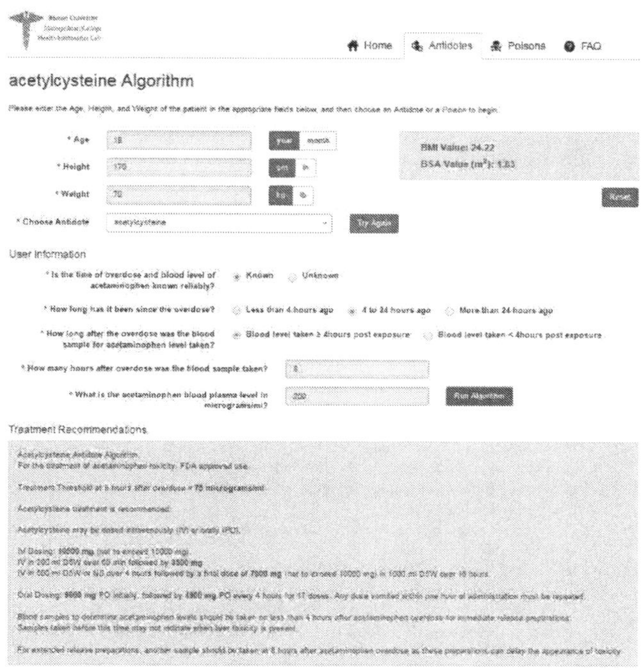

Figure 6: A screenshot showing the individualized treatment recommendation for acetylcysteine by the web AA.

When the Java AA is initiated, the antidote GUI interface is called and the user is presented with the main page of the program and prompted to enter the patient's age, weight, and height. The user is also prompted to select the algorithm of interest by choosing an antidote or the corresponding toxin if the user knows the cause of toxicity but unsure of the antidote. After user input data from the GUI is validated as described in section 2.2, the appropriate antidote class is called from the antidote class library. Any alerts or messages concerning the algorithm that need to be conveyed or if further data is required from the user, JOptionPane message or input windows are used from the javax.swing package. The return output in the form of a string is displayed in the text area of the GUI. At any point in time the user can select an antidote from the antidote dropdown scrollbar and click the references button to view the references of that particular antidote algorithm.

3.2 Web-based Antidote Application

The Web AA user interface, calculations and recommendations parallel the Java AA. Several web development technologies such as JavaScript, jQuery, HTML, CSS, Ajax, and AngularJS were employed. It is a client-side application, meaning that all computations are processed on the client's computer. The Web AA uses a Model-View-Controller (MVC) architecture, a software architectural pattern for implementing user interfaces. It divides a software application into three interconnected parts - the model consists of the application logic, the controllers are responsible for manipulating data, and views present the data generated by the user inputs and controller/model outputs. In the Web AA the model consists of the antidote algorithms, the views are the graphical representations, the controller manipulates the model and the view. The controller passes user inputs from the view to the model (antidote algorithms) and communicates the model outputs to the user. The separation into these distinct entities improves the extensibility and maintainability of the Web AA. Fig. 5 is a graphical representation the MVC relationship. Fig. 6 is a screenshot from the Web AA. It demonstrates the decision making process following the acetylcysteine algorithm (Fig. 3) for the treatment of acetaminophen toxicity. The patient was overdosed with APAP eight hours before the blood sample was taken. The acetaminophen blood plasma level was 200 μg/mL, which was above 75 μg/mL, the treatment threshold at 8 hours after overdose. Thus acetylcysteine treatment is recommended and individualized drug dosages, highlighted in red in Fig. 6, were calculated. Tutorials on how to use the web AA are available at http://projects.met-hilab.org/antidote/#/FAQ.

3.3 Discussion

We successfully implemented 27 algorithms for the treatment of common poison exposure in North America in both the Java AA and the Web AA. The Java AA is a robust, stable and easily maintainable system available offline as a standalone expert system. It is compatible with all leading operating systems e.g. MS Windows, Mac OS X, and Linux. It contains 31 classes, 200 methods, and 2831 lines of code. The average cyclomatic complexity is low (3.337) as well as the average nested block depth (1.45). The Java AA standalone system can be downloaded at http://www.met-hilab.org/files/antidote/antidote_application.jar.

The Web AA has the same cyclomatic complexity and average nested block depth as the Java AA. The Web AA contains 2443 lines of code, 34 classes and 200 methods. The web AA is publically available at http://projects.met-hilab.org/antidote/.

These 29 antidotes, 31 specific toxins and 19 toxin classes covered in AA are the essential antidotes that an expert panel of leading clinical toxicologists recommended to be stocked in North American hospitals. These specific toxins and toxin classes represent hundreds of toxic entities. Many of the antidotes in the AA have other clinically approved and unapproved indications. Atropine for instance is essential in advanced cardiac life support (ACLS) [16-18]. Sodium bicarbonate is used extensively for many other acute indications such as cardiac arrest, shock, severe dehydration, primary lactic acidosis, and severe diabetic acidosis, to mention a few [19].

4 CONCLUSIONS

The AA is a personalized treatment training system since it provides patient-specific treatment recommendations and dose calculations for all age groups ranging from newborns to elderly. All current electronic drug database systems provide incomplete information regarding the antidotes included in the AA. To verify this observation we reviewed 14 electronic toxicology databases and three quick reference antidote charts. In the area of toxicology, patient specific recommendations and calculations were largely non-existent. Some of the systems have links to calculators. While this is a step in the right direction, the calculations are not patient specific, which may result in unclear and possibly confusing treatment recommendations.

Both Java AA and Web AA provide guidance for reporting toxic exposures regionally and nationally as required by the national accrediting bodies and some states by providing the phone number to Poison Control and a link to the FAER. There is no federal law regarding the reporting of poisoning to Poison Control or the FAER. Some states, however, have adopted mandatory reporting of poisoning to Poison Control. Also, the Joint Commission, an independent organization authorized by the Centers for Medicare and Medicaid Services in the accreditation and certification of health organizations, requires the reporting of adverse events as a part of its core accountability measures [20]. The Joint Commission also requires that the toll-free Poison Control phone number be readily available throughout the hospital. Making these resources readily available assists healthcare organizations in complying with state law and support their accreditation effort. Of all of the electronic systems and quick reference charts reviewed in this work, only Medline Plus, a service of the U.S. National Library of Medicine, has both the Poison Control number and the link to the FAER.

Both AA systems have been thoroughly tested and all algorithms are fully referenced. Every effort was made to ensure that references are up-to-date and that the system is operationally robust.

This application can provide a rapid standard of practice solution in an emergency-poisoning situation during the waiting time – until poison control or a physician specializing in toxicology can respond. The time to first dose is critical in many poisoning situations. To the best of our knowledge, the AA is the first educational decision support system in toxicology that provides patient-specific treatment recommendations and drug dose calculations.

ACKNOWLEDGMENTS

Jon Long and Yingyuan Zhang were supported by the graduate assistantship from Metropolitan College, Boston University. We are thankful to Jeff Andre and Cheng-Hsien Lu for their advice in the implementation of the Antidote Application.

REFERENCES

[1] Catherine E. Rubens. 1985. A rule-based poison control expert system. *ACM SIGBIO Newsletter 7.1 (1985): 33-36*

[2] S. J. Darmoni, P. Massari, J.M. Droy, N. Mahe, T. Blanc, E. Moirot, and J. Leroy. 1994. SETH: an expert system for the management on acute drug poisoning in adults. *Computer methods and programs in biomedicine, 43(3-4), 171-176.*

[3] R. T. B. Batista-Navarro, D. A. Bandojo, .M. J. K. Gatapia, R. N. C. Santos, A. B. Marcelo, L. C. R. Panganiban, and P. C. Naval. 2010. ESP: An expert system for poisoning diagnosis and management. *Informatics for Health and Social Care, 35(2), 53-63.*

[4] R. C. Dart, S. W. Borron, E. M. Caravati, .D. J. Cobaugh, S. C. Curry, J. L. Falk, L. Goldfrank, S. E. Gorman, S. Groft, .K. Heard, and K. Miller. 2009. Expert consensus guidelines for stocking of antidotes in hospitals that provide emergency care. *Annals of emergency medicine, 54(3), 386-394.*

[5] U.S. Food and Drug Administration. 2009. *Indications.* Silver Spring, MD.

[6] U.S. Food and Drug Administration. 2015. *Federal Food, Drug, and Cosmetic Act. Code of Federal Regulations.* p. 201.57(a)(6).

[7] Hospira, Inc. 2009. *10% Calcium Chloride Injection, USP.*

[8] APP Pharmaceuticals, LLC 2009. *CALCIUM GLUCONATE - calcium gluconate injection, solution.*

[9] U.S. Food and Drug Administration. 2014. *"Off-Label" and Investigational Use Of Marketed Drugs, Biologics, and Medical Devices - Information Sheet. Silver Spring, MD.*

[10] R. J. Kuczmarski, C. L. Ogden, S. S. Guo, L. M. Grummer-Strawn, K. M. Flegal, Z. Mei, R. Wei, L. R. Curtin, A. F. Roche, and C. L. Johnson. 2002. 2000 CDC Growth Charts for the United States: methods and development. *Vital and health statistics. Series 11, Data from the national health survey 246 (2002): 1-190.*

[11] J. A. Lack and M. E. Stuart-Taylor. 1997. Calculation of drug dosage and body surface area of children. *British Journal of Anaesthesia, 78(5), 601-605.*

[12] M. Sutter. 2009. Goldfrank's manual of toxicologic emergencies. *Academic Emergency Medicine, 16(3), e7-e8.*

[13] B. H. Rumack and H. Matthew. 1975. Acetaminophen poisoning and toxicity. *Pediatrics, 55(6), 871-876.*

[14] A. Temple and J. Baggish. 2005. Guidelines for the management of acetaminophen overdose. *McNeil consumer and speciality pharmaceuticals.*

[15] B. H. Rumack, R. C. Peterson, G. G. Koch, and I. A. Amara. 1981. Acetaminophen overdose: 662 cases with evaluation of oral acetylcysteine treatment. *Archives of internal medicine, 141(3), 380-385.*

[16] Hospira, Inc. 2009. *Atropine Sulfate. Atropine Sulfate Package Insert. . Lake Forest, Illinois, U.S.*

[17] Meridian Medical Technologies, Inc. 2005. ATROPEN AUTO-INJECTOR - atropine sulfate injection. ATROPEN AUTO-INJECTOR - atropine sulfate injection Package Insert. *Columbia, Maryland, U.S.*

[18] M. E. Kleinman, L. Chameides, S. M. Schexnayder, R. A. Samson, M. F. Hazinski, D. L. Atkins, M. D. Berg, A. R. De Caen, E. L. Fink, E. B. Freid, and R. W. Hickey. 2010. Part 14: pediatric advanced life support. *Circulation, 122(18 suppl 3), pp.S876-S908.*

[19] Hospira, Inc. 2010. *SODIUM BICARBONATE- sodium bicarbonate injection, solution. . Lake Forest, Illinois, U.S.*

[20] The Joint Commission. 2010. *Facts about accountability measures. Available from: http://www.jointcommission.org/facts_about_accountability_measures/*

Automated Off-label Drug Use Detection from User Generated Content

Mengnan Zhao
College of Computing and Informatics
Drexel University
Philadelphia, Pennsylvania
mz438@drexel.edu

Christopher C. Yang
College of Computing and Informatics
Drexel University
Philadelphia, Pennsylvania
chris.yang@drexel.edu

ABSTRACT

Off-label drug use refers to using marketed drugs for indications that are not listed in their FDA labeling information. Such uses are very common and sometimes inevitable in clinical practice. To some extent, off-label drug uses provide a pathway for clinical innovation, however, they could cause serious adverse effects due to lacking scientific research and tests. Since identifying the off-label uses can provide a clue to the stakeholders including healthcare providers, patients, and medication manufacturers to further the investigation on drug efficacy and safety, it raises the demand for a systematic way to detect off-label uses. Given data contributed by health consumers in online health communities (OHCs), we developed an automated approach to detect off-label drug uses based on heterogeneous network mining. We constructed a heterogeneous healthcare network with medical entities (e.g. disease, drug, adverse drug reaction) mined from the text corpus, which involved 50 diseases, 1,297 drugs, and 185 ADRs, and determined 13 meta paths between the drugs and diseases. We developed three metrics to represent the meta-path-based topological features. With the network features, we trained the binary classifiers built on Random Forest algorithm to recognize the known drug-disease associations. The best classification model that used *lift* to measure path weights obtained F1-score of 0.87, based on which, we identified 1,009 candidates of off-label drug uses and examined their potential by searching evidence from PubMed and FAERS.

KEYWORDS

Off-label drug use; Online health community; Heterogeneous network; Meta path; Classification

Permission to make digital or hard copies of all or part of this work for personal or classroom use is granted without fee provided that copies are not made or distributed for profit or commercial advantage and that copies bear this notice and the full citation on the first page. Copyrights for components of this work owned by others than ACM must be honored. Abstracting with credit is permitted. To copy otherwise, or republish, to post on servers or to redistribute to lists, requires prior specific permission and/or a fee. Request permissions from Permissions@acm.org.
ACM-BCB'17, August 20-23, 2017, Boston, MA, USA.
© 2017 Association of Computing Machinery.
ACM ISBN 978-1-4503-4722-8/17/08...$15.00.
DOI: http://dx.doi.org/10.1145/3107411.3107475

1. INTRODUCTION

Off-label drug use refers to using marketed drugs for indications that are not listed in their FDA labeling information. Although FDA currently controls which medications can be brought to the market, they are not able to supervise and control if the medications are prescribed in accordance with the approved labels. Off-label drug uses are very common in clinical practice. Up to one-fifth prescriptions are off-label, and the number is even higher in certain diseases (e.g. psychiatric diseases), certain conditions (e.g. intensive care), and special subpopulations (e.g. pediatric and pregnant patients) [1]. Although physicians prescribe off-label drugs for the benefit of patients, and off-label drug uses deliver effective treatment and provide a pathway for clinical innovation in some cases, they could cause serious outcomes due to lacking scientific research and tests. For example, morphine has never received an FDA approval for pain treatment in pediatric patients, but it is extensively used in hospitalized practice. However, the misuse or overdose of such narcotic can cause addiction or death, especially in children.

As off-label drug use is inevitable to some degree, most healthcare related participants have the interest in gaining information about off-label uses in a timely manner. Healthcare providers and patients are concerned about the observation information of off-label drug uses in practice; pharmaceutical companies are required to provide the postmarketing surveillance reports of drug uses; biomedical and clinical researchers are interested in the novel, especially those successful, off-label drug uses to assess the potential benefits and risks [2]. Identifying the off-label drug uses could present a clue to the stakeholders to further the investigation on drug efficacy and safety.

Despite these needs and the wide practice of off-label drug uses, there is no regulatory agency that monitors such uses. FDA Adverse Event Reporting System (FAERS) [3] contains reports on the adverse event and medication error of approved drugs and therapeutic biologic products to support the FDA's postmarketing safety surveillance program, while FAERS does not designate the off-label uses particularly. Survey is another approach of detecting off-label uses from physicians but limited by many conditions such as the number of respondents, the quality and truthfulness of answers, and the cost. Therefore, the above factors raise the demand for a systematic way to detect off-label drug uses.

In this study, we focus on developing an automated approach to detect off-label drug uses from the health consumer contributed data. A variety of resources has been used to identify drug-disease associations, mainly including biomedical database, medical literature, EHR, and clinical note, and involving medical entities such as protein, compound, gene, pathway, and adverse drug reaction (ADR). While these data sources are useful in detecting off-label uses, they are mainly contributed by healthcare professionals and researchers. None of them capture the information offered by health consumers or patients. Meanwhile, the development of Web 2.0 not only breeds the various online social media sites like Facebook and Twitter, but also fosters online health communities (OHCs) such as MedHelp, PatientsLikeMe, and DailyStrength. OHCs have been growing in popularity across the world and provide a convenient way to exchange health information. It has been claimed that 80% of adults in US and 66% of adults in Europe seek online health advice [4]. 72% of Internet users said they searched online for health information in 2011 [5]. Taking MedHelp for instance, it empowers over 12 million people each month to seek and offer healthcare information on the site, which provides huge volumes of timely and valuable health-related information. With data coming from the OHC, we detected the most common three medical entities involved in user-generated contents: drugs, diseases, and adverse drug reactions (ADRs, and constructed a heterogeneous healthcare network. On the heterogeneous network, we determined the meta paths between drugs and diseases and extracted the meta-path-based topological features that are used for training a binary classification model to recognize the known drug-disease pairs and to predict the potential off-label drug-disease relationships.

2. RELATED WORK

A number of studies employed research methods such as survey and narrative interview to identify off-label uses. Conroy et al. [6] designed a prospective study to explore the use of unlicensed and off-label drugs in pediatric patients in European countries and found 39% of them involved off-label uses. Leslie & Rosenheck [7] investigated the off-label uses of antipsychotic drugs among patients who are enrolled in Medicaid by operating the retrospective analysis of administrative data, and found 57.6% patients received antipsychotics for off-label indications.

Recently, with the availability of online biomedical resources such as medical literature, pharmaceutical databases, electronic medical records (EMRs), and clinical text, a number of studies utilized automated methods to discover novel drug-indication/disease relationships to identify the off-label pairs. Mesgarpour et al. [8] focused on generating highly sensitive search strategies to detect off-label related documents in Excerpta Medica Database (EMBASE)-a major bibliographic database in biomedicine. Jung et al. [9] developed a predictive model to detect novel off-label uses from the clinical text. By utilizing NCBO Annotator, they tagged the words in the corpus of clinical notes first, and extracted the empirical relationships between drugs and indications from the population level rather than the textual level. In total, they calculated nine measures and used them as features to train a SVM classifier to predict novel off-label drug-indication pairs. Then they added extra 16 domain knowledge features from two pharmaceutical databases (Medi-Span and DrugBank) to develop a new SVM predictive model, and compared the performance of different feature sets [10]. In result, they discovered 6142 novel off-label pairs and validated 403 of them on MEDLINE literature and FAERS reports.

To unveil the drug-disease relationships that are critical for identifying off-label drug uses, previous studies have developed approaches based on natural language processing [11] and text mining [12]. Gottlieb et al. [13] calculated and ranked the similarity between potential drug-disease pairs with those in the gold standard set that they created by referring to several pharmaceutical databases, based on the assumption that similar drugs are indicated for similar diseases.

Additionally, some studies implemented heterogeneous network-based methods to discover novel drug-disease associations. Huang et al. [14] proposed a network propagation model to infer drug-disease associations, based on the integrated networks of three homogeneous networks and two heterogeneous, with the weights of edges assigned by knowledge from biomedical repositories. Chen et al. [15] also constructed a heterogeneous network of drug, disease, and protein, and predicted drug-disease associations by using a random walk based algorithm. Yu et al. [16] created a tripartite heterogeneous network of three types of nodes: diseases, drugs and protein complexes, with the weights of edges computed on a symmetrical conditional probability model. Moreover, heterogeneous network-based approaches have also been used to discover relationships between some other medical entities, such as drug-drug interactions [17], drug-targets [18], and multi drug-pathways [19]. For instance, Lee et al. [20] built a large heterogeneous network to discover drug-drug interactions (DDIs) by involving drugs, proteins, genes, pathways, side effects, targets and their interactions into the network.

3. OFF-LABEL DRUG USES DETECTION FROM ONLINE HEALTH COMMUNITIES

The previous studies render a promising way to unveil drug-disease relationships by heterogeneous network-based methods, based on which, we proposed a systematic method to identify off-label drug uses by using health consumer contributed data from OHCs, as illustrated in Figure 1. Firstly, we collected data from the OHC website to create the text corpus, and extracted the entities of diseases, drugs, and ADRs with lexicon based approach. Secondly, we constructed a heterogeneous healthcare network that contained three types of nodes (drug, disease, ADR) and six types of associations (drug-drug, disease-disease, ADR-ADR, drug-disease, drug-ADR, disease-ADR), determined the meta-paths, and utilized path count methods to measure the weights of associations between two nodes. Thirdly, we used the extracted weights as the features to train an effective classifier that distinguished known drug-disease pairs with those unknown, and then identified the off-label drug uses from the unknown pairs.

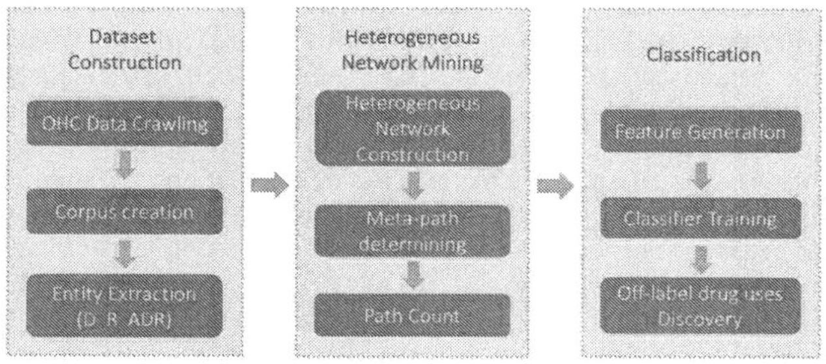

Figure 1: Flow of detecting off-label drug uses from OHC data

3.1 Dataset

In the current age, a large number of health consumers exchange health information on online health communities (OHCs). MedHelp (www.medhelp.org), as a pioneer in OHCs, has 176 health communities and empowers over 12 million visitors each month to discuss health related topics on the site. We collected the user generated data from MedHelp by implementing an automatic web crawler, with which, we retrieved all the posts and comments in the most popular 50 disease communities and obtained 70,960 threads (70,960 posts + 319,993 comments).

Within the extracted corpus, we identified the medical entities (i.e. drug, disease, ADR) by utilizing a lexicon-based approach, which has shown its advantage to OHC data in previous studies [21]. Unlike the pharmaceutical databases that include multiple medical entities (e.g. protein, compound, and gene), OHC data are mostly contributed by consumers without medical background talking about their diseases, the drugs they take, and the reactions or adverse reactions they experience. Therefore, we only employ the above three medical entities here.

For diseases and drugs, we utilized all their alternate names suggested in PharmGKB and UMLS and their abbreviations (e.g. OCD for Obsessive-Compulsive Disorder) to locate them, and tagged them with their UMLS-id. For example, the terms used to identify Parkinson included "parkinson" "parkinson disease" and "parkinson's disease", then all of those words were tagged with "C0030567".

However, the detection of ADR signals is more complicated than drugs and diseases in OHCs, because consumers use quite diverse and various expressions to describe the concepts and their adverse reactions. Thus, the standard medical lexicons managed by professionals are not applicable for analyzing user generated data. To address this problem, we resorted to Consumer Health Vocabulary (CHV) Wiki to create our ADR lexicon [21]. CHV Wiki connects the everyday expressions of healthcare-related topics with the professional expressions to bridge the communication gap between consumers and healthcare professionals [22]. For ADRs, it provides the preferred name of an ADR in UMLS and a list of its corresponding consumers' expressions. For example, "anorexia" is a professional expression of ADR, CHV Wiki extends it to "appetite lost" "appetite loss" "appetite lack" "no appetite" and several other common expressions of health consumers. Here we used all the expressions suggested by CHV Wiki to identify ADR signals in the corpus and tagged them with their UMLS-id. In result, we tagged 50 diseases, 1,297 drugs, and 185 ADRs on the corpus.

3.2 Heterogeneous network mining

3.2.1 Heterogeneous network construction

A heterogeneous network is defined as a graph consisting of nodes connected by links with at least two types of nodes or two types of links [23]. Most real-world networks are actually heterogeneous networks rather than homogeneous networks where the nodes and links are treated as the same type. Analysis based on homogeneous network may miss important semantic and schema-level information, while heterogeneous networks can deliver more essential, accurate and complete features, thus unveiling the underlying knowledge and patterns. Let $N = \{n_1, n_2, ..., n_k\}$ be a set of nodes and $L = \{l_1, l_2, ..., l_m\}$ be a set of links, then $G = (N, L)$ denotes the graph. In the graph G, each node $n_i \in N$ belongs to a particular type from γ; each link $l_i \in L$ belongs to a particular type from τ, and $|\gamma| > 1$ or $|\tau| > 1$, and can be directional or non-directional. Then $M_G = (\gamma, \tau)$ denotes the node types γ and link types τ in graph G.

By involving the medical entities we identified from the MedHelp corpus, we constructed a heterogeneous network that contains three types of nodes (disease(D), drug(R), ADR) and six types of links (drug-drug, disease-disease, ADR-ADR, drug-disease, drug-ADR, disease-ADR), as shown in Figure 2. That is, $N = \{d_1, \dots, d_k, r_1, \dots, r_m, adr_1, \dots, adr_n\}$, $\gamma = \{D, R, ADR\}$, and $\tau = \{L_{D-D}, L_{R-R}, L_{ADR-ADR}, L_{D-R}, L_{D-ADR}, L_{R-ADR}\}$. In this heterogeneous network, the interactions between two nodes, $w(n_i, n_j)$, were built on their co-occurrence in the same thread. Instead of inferring if a sentence contains use-to-treat relationship, we measured co-mention relationships at a population level by using co-occurrence-based indicators.

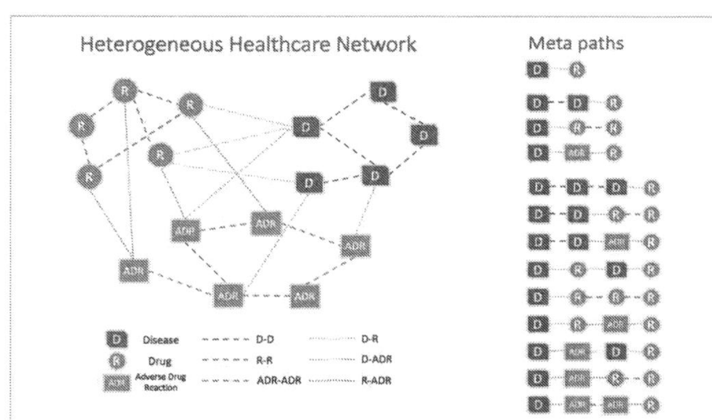

Figure 2: Heterogeneous healthcare network structure and meta-paths

3.2.2 Meta Path and Path Count

A meta path is a path defined on the network schema in the form of $A_1 \xrightarrow{L_1} A_2 \xrightarrow{L_2} \dots \xrightarrow{L_l} A_{l+1}$, which composes the relations between nodes in the heterogeneous network. Meta path-based approaches could describe the meta structure of the network and of the paths that derived from the network. To discover all the possible and reliable associations between diseases and drugs, we defined the topology between them using meta paths, and by limiting path length within three, we found 13 meta paths, as shown in Table 1:

Table 1: Meta paths

Length	Meta Path	Path structure
1	*D-R*	$d_i \overset{L_{D-R}}{\longleftrightarrow} r_j$
2	*D-D-R*	$d_i \overset{L_{D-D}}{\longleftrightarrow} d_k \overset{L_{D-R}}{\longleftrightarrow} r_j$
2	*D-R-R*	$d_i \overset{L_{D-R}}{\longleftrightarrow} r_k \overset{L_{R-R}}{\longleftrightarrow} r_j$
2	*D-ADR-R*	$d_i \overset{L_{D-ADR}}{\longleftrightarrow} adr_k \overset{L_{R-ADR}}{\longleftrightarrow} r_j$
3	*D-D-D-R*	$d_i \overset{L_{D-D}}{\longleftrightarrow} d_k \overset{L_{D-D}}{\longleftrightarrow} d_m \overset{L_{D-R}}{\longleftrightarrow} r_j$
3	*D-D-R-R*	$d_i \overset{L_{D-D}}{\longleftrightarrow} d_k \overset{L_{D-R}}{\longleftrightarrow} r_m \overset{L_{R-R}}{\longleftrightarrow} r_j$
3	*D-D-ADR-R*	$d_i \overset{L_{D-D}}{\longleftrightarrow} d_k \overset{L_{D-ADR}}{\longleftrightarrow} adr_m \overset{L_{R-ADR}}{\longleftrightarrow} r_j$
3	*D-R-D-R*	$d_i \overset{L_{D-R}}{\longleftrightarrow} r_k \overset{L_{D-R}}{\longleftrightarrow} d_m \overset{L_{D-R}}{\longleftrightarrow} r_j$
3	*D-R-R-R*	$d_i \overset{L_{D-R}}{\longleftrightarrow} r_k \overset{L_{R-R}}{\longleftrightarrow} r_m \overset{L_{R-R}}{\longleftrightarrow} r_j$
3	*D-R-ADR-R*	$d_i \overset{L_{D-R}}{\longleftrightarrow} r_k \overset{L_{R-ADR}}{\longleftrightarrow} adr_m \overset{L_{R-ADR}}{\longleftrightarrow} r_j$
3	*D-ADR-D-R*	$d_i \overset{L_{D-ADR}}{\longleftrightarrow} adr_k \overset{L_{D-ADR}}{\longleftrightarrow} d_m \overset{L_{D-R}}{\longleftrightarrow} r_j$
3	*D-ADR-R-R*	$d_i \overset{L_{D-ADR}}{\longleftrightarrow} adr_k \overset{L_{R-ADR}}{\longleftrightarrow} r_m \overset{L_{R-R}}{\longleftrightarrow} r_j$
3	*D-ADR-ADR-R*	$d_i \overset{L_{D-ADR}}{\longleftrightarrow} adr_k \overset{L_{ADR-ADR}}{\longleftrightarrow} adr_m \overset{L_{R-ADR}}{\longleftrightarrow} r_j$

Given the topological features determined by meta paths, the associations between D and R can be measured by the popular indicator – Path Count (PC), which counts the number of path instances between two objects under a given meta path, denoted as PC_P, where P is the given meta path. Here we developed two metrics to reveal the associations between two objects d_i and r_j $(d_i \in D, r_j \in R)$: given a meta path P, (1) Meta-Path-Indicator (MPI) indicates whether there exists a path $p \in P$ that associates d_i with r_j; (2) Path-Count-Indicator (PCI) counts the number of p that associates d_i with r_j.

$$MPI_P(d_i, r_j) = \begin{cases} 1, (\exists\, p \in P \Rightarrow d_i \overset{p}{\leftrightarrow} r_j = 1) \\ 0 \end{cases}$$

$$PCI_P(d_i, r_j) = \sum_{p \in P} 1, (d_i \overset{p}{\leftrightarrow} r_j = 1)$$

For example, $MPI_{D-R-R}(d_i, r_j) = 1$ denotes there is at least a path in the form of $d_i \overset{L_{D-R}}{\longleftrightarrow} r_k \overset{L_{R-R}}{\longleftrightarrow} r_j$ that connects d_i with r_j.

3.2.3 Association rule mining - lift

In the above equations for MPI and PCI, the weights of links were not taken into consideration. In order to incorporate more network information, here we utilized association rule mining to measure the weights of associations and embedded the results into the computation of Path Count to develop a new metric.

In association rule mining, let $I = \{I_1, I_2, \ldots, I_m\}$ be a set of items and let $T = \{T_1, T_2, \ldots, T_n\}$ be a set of transactions, where each transaction is a subset of items such that $T_i \subseteq I$. An itemset that contains k items is a k-itemset; the occurrence frequency of an itemset is the number of transactions that contain the itemset. The association rule is an implication in the form of $A \Rightarrow B$, where $A \subset I$, $B \subset I$ and $A \cap B = \emptyset$, which is deemed as an itemset. In this study, I denotes the whole set that contains diseases, drugs, and ADRs, or N in the heterogeneous network definition; T denotes the dataset of all threads and each thread represents a transaction; there are both 1-itemset ($\{D\}$, $\{R\}$, $\{ADR\}$) and 2-itemset ($\{D, D\}$, $\{R, R\}$, $\{ADR, ADR\}$, $\{D, R\}$, $\{D, ADR\}$, $\{R, ADR\}$) involved in our calculation. The goal is to mine and evaluate the associations presented in 2-itemset.

Support is a common indicator used in association rule mining, defined as the percentage of transactions that contain 1-itemset or 2-itemset, for instance:

$$support\ (n_i) = \frac{count(n_i)}{total\ threads}$$

$$support\ (n_i, n_j) = \frac{count(n_i \cup n_j)}{total\ threads}$$

in which, $count(n_i)$ is the number of threads that contain target n_i; $count(n_i \cup n_j)$ is the number of threads that contain both n_i and n_j; *total threads* denotes the total number of threads. Nevertheless, for the 2-itemset, *support* is appropriate only when the co-occurrence frequency of the items is high. However, when consumers mention a drug, they might discuss different aspects of drugs, so that threads that are related to ADR only occupy a small portion in all the threads. To address this problem, another indicator *lift* is often used. *Lift* is a measure based on probability and reflects the division of the actual probability and theoretical probability. For instance, when measuring the strength of rule $R \Rightarrow ADR$, lift not only takes account of $support(R \cup ADR)$ but also the the correlation between 1-itemset R and 1-itemset ADR, by calculating the ratio of the proportion of threads containing both R and ADR above those expected if R and ADR are independent of each other. For a direct link $A_1 \leftrightarrow A_2$, the equation for calculating $support\ (n_i, n_j)$ $(n_i \in A_1, n_j \in A_2)$ is:

$$lift(n_i, n_j) = \frac{support(n_i, n_j)}{support(n_i) \times support(n_j)}$$

Given a meta path P in the form of $A_1 \overset{L_1}{\rightarrow} A_2 \overset{L_2}{\rightarrow} \ldots \overset{L_l}{\rightarrow} A_{l+1}$, Path-Count-Lift (PCL) $PCL_P(n_1, n_l)$ $(n_1 \in A_1, \ldots, n_l \in A_l)$ is calculated by:

$$PCL_P(n_1, n_l) = \sum_{p \in P} lift(n_1, n_2) \times lift(n_2, n_3) \times \ldots \times lift(n_{l-1}, n_l), (n_1 \overset{p}{\leftrightarrow} n_l = 1)$$

Taking the meta path *D-D-R* for instance:

$$PCL_{D-D-R}(d_i, r_j) = \sum_{p \in P} lift(d_i, d_k) \times lift(d_k, r_j), (d_i \overset{p}{\leftrightarrow} r_j = 1)$$

in which, $d_i \overset{p}{\leftrightarrow} r_j = 1$ denotes there is a meth path p that associates d_i and r_j via $d_i \overset{L_{D-D}}{\longleftrightarrow} d_k \overset{L_{D-R}}{\longleftrightarrow} r_j$.

3.3 Classification

In order to recognize associations between drugs and diseases from all the possible pairs, we developed a supervised learning model by training a binary classifier. The outputs of the classifier were 'positive' or 'negative', indicating whether the predicted drug-disease pair could be a known pair or not. The inputs of the classifier came from the meta-path-based topological features. For each drug-disease pair, we constructed a set of features that were used to predict whether this pair is possibly to be a known association. Under the length of three, we defined 13 meta paths between drugs and diseases; with *MPI* or *PCI* or *PCL* on each meta path representing a feature, it created a set of 13 features. As the supervised learning model required both positive and negative labels, we built the gold standard dataset of known drug-disease pairs by referring to PharmGKB and DrugBank together, which suggested 2,087 known usages, and generated 28,000 negative instances randomly out of the unobserved associations between 50 diseases and 1,297 drugs.

In this work, we used a machine learning algorithm Random Forest as our classification method, which operates by constructing a multitude of decision trees that grow from bootstrap the training samples and outputs the labels based on the majority votes of the individual trees. In addition, considering there are much more negative instances than the positive in the dataset, we performed undersampling to avoid the imbalanced classification problem. Specifically, we divided the whole dataset into training (65%) and test (35%) sets firstly, then randomly split the negative pairs in the training set into 10 chunks. Each chunk and the positive training instances formed a sub-training set, where the classifier was trained and then tested on the hold-out test set.

3.4 Detection of off-label drug uses

Off-label drug uses are actually quite common in clinical practice and can be widely entrenched in certain clinical conditions. The document of medication providers such as EHRs and clinical notes provide the opportunity to detect off-label drug uses in an automated and scalable way. Meanwhile, from the perspective of medication receivers, they often talk about their drug uses and reactions on OHCs, which provides another resource to detect off-label uses. If the features extracted from user generated data enables us to recognize the known drug usages effectively, the other drug-disease pairs that present similar features with the known pairs are possibly to be off-label practices, in other words, the negative pairs that are falsely classified as "positive" are quite potential to be the off-label drug-disease usages. Therefore, the goal of this step is to identify the false positive (FP) predictions.

4. EXPERIMENTAL RESULTS

4.1 Classification results & evaluation

Evaluation of the classifier performance could indicate the effectiveness and accuracy of using network-based features to reveal drug-disease associations, furtherly, the effectiveness of identifying off-label drug-disease associations via this way [10]. In order to investigate the performance of different meta-path-based features, we did three experiments by using *MPI*, *PCI*, and *PCL* respectively. We trained the Random Forest classifiers on each sub-training set by performing 10-fold cross validation and evaluated the performance on the hold-out test set. Thus, we obtained 10 test results and took the average to represent the overall performance. Here, the classification performances were evaluated using Precision, Recall, and F1-score.

We trained and tested the Random Forest classifier with the *scikit-learn* tool in Python package [24]. The evaluation results of the binary classification were shown in Table 2. It is obvious that using MPI to represent the meta-path features obtained the worst results in all the three metrics, with F1-score equaling 0.639 in the test set. When incorporating the information about the number of meta paths between two objects, that is, using PCI to describe the meta-path features, the F1-score was improved by 18% compared with using MPI and achieved 0.754. Furtherly, after embodying the weights of links in the heterogeneous network and using PCL for features, the F1-score was improved by 36% compared with MPI and 15% with PCI. Besides, we obtained a very high Recall of 0.969, which means that among all the known drug-disease usages we classified 96.9% of them correctly. The Precision of 0.795 indicated that 79.5% of the predicted "positive" drug-disease pairs were indeed known usages, meanwhile, the other 21.5% were falsely classified as "positive" from the randomly generated negative pairs and might be the off-label pairs we were seeking. In summary, meta-path-based topological features have enabled us to develop successful supervised classification models for recognizing known drug-disease associations.

Table 2: Evaluation results of classification models built on different features

Feature	Dataset	Random Forest		
		Precision	Recall	F1 score
MPI	Training	0.670	0.713	0.692
	Test	0.618	0.663	0.639
PCI	Training	0.817	0.791	0.804
	Test	0.763	0.745	0.754
PCL	Training	0.897	0.971	0.932
	Test	0.795	0.969	0.870

As using PCL for features outperformed the other two indicators based on the evaluation results, we then applied the best trained classification model to the whole balanced dataset built by oversampling the minority class, to find all the possible off-label predictions. In result, we found 1,009 false-positive instances that might be potential candidates of off-label drug-disease associations, shown in Table 3.

Table 3: classification results of using PCL features

		Predicted	
		P	N
Actual	P	14480	300
	N	1009	26991

4.2 Validate results on PubMed and FAERS data

As the identified off-label usages have not been included in any pharmaceutical databases, the popular validation way is to find co-mention support from medical literature and reports [10]. The detected 1,009 potential candidates of off-label drug uses were checked for positive evidence in PubMed literature and FAERS reports. PubMed is a free resource developed and maintained by the National Center for Biotechnology Information (NCBI) and covers the titles and abstracts of more than 26 million biomedical publications, which can be accessed using the Entrez Programming Utilies (E-utilities). FAERS is the most important spontaneous reporting system as well as the primary data source for the study and identification of ADRs in United States. In PubMed, we found 407 of the novel predictions that have at least ten articles that both the drug and the disease were mentioned in the abstract; in FAERS, we only found 10 of the novel predictions that have at least ten reports co-annotating with both the drug and the disease. The reason why there was so less evidence in FAERS might be that: first, FAERS is designed for reporting adverse drug effects rather than off-label uses, therefore, if there is no ADR involved, people have no intension to report their situations to the system; second, people report ADRs spontaneously and voluntarily, which leads to a surprisingly low reporting rate because of the nature of passiveness, with a median of 6%; third, it usually takes FDA a long time to complete the whole process of collecting reports, investigating cases and releasing alerts, which limits the manner of timely for information.

5. CONCLUSIONS

Off-label drug uses are very common and sometimes inevitable in clinical practice. Although the stakeholders including healthcare providers, patients, researchers, and medication manufacturers have the interest to gain information about off-label drug uses comprehensively and timely, there is no regulatory agency supervising such usages yet, which raises the demand for a systematic way to detect and manage off-label drug uses. The documents of medication providers such as EHRs and clinical notes provide the resource of detecting off-label uses and have been exploited in some previous studies, meanwhile, the large volumes of data coming from medication receivers also render the opportunity to detect off-label uses in a systematic and scalable way. In this study, we developed an automated way to detect off-label uses based on heterogeneous network mining. With data collected from a popular OHC - MedHelp, we extracted the medical entities of diseases, drugs, and ADRs with lexicon-based approaches and constructed a heterogeneous healthcare network that contained three types of nodes and six types of edges. On the heterogeneous network, we determined 13 meta paths between drugs and diseases and developed three metrics to describe the meta-path-based topological features: Meta-Path-Indicator (MPI), Path-Count-Indicator (PCI), and Path-Count-Lift (PCL). Then we utilized these features as inputs for the Random Forest classifier to recognize the known drug-disease associations from all the possible pairs. Using MPI, PCI, and PCL for the features respectively, we conducted three classification experiments, and the classification model built on PCL achieved the best performance with F1-score reaching 0.87. The results showed that meta-path-based topological features could enable us to develop well-performed supervised classification models to recognize known drug-disease associations, furtherly, the other drug-disease pairs that present similar features with those known pairs are possibly to be the off-label practices, or the false-positive predictions are quite potential to be off-label drug-disease usages. Based on this hypothesis, we identified 1,009 candidates of off-label drug uses and examined them for positive support from PubMed and FAERS. In result, 407 of them were found evidence from at least ten articles in PubMed and 10 of them were found evidence from at least ten reports in FAERS.

6. ACKNOWLEDGEMENTS

This work was supported in part by the National Science Foundation under the Grant IIS-1650531 and DIBBs-1443019.

REFERENCES

[1]. Wittich, C. M., Burkle, C. M., & Lanier, W. L. (2012, October). Ten common questions (and their answers) about off-label drug use. In Mayo Clinic Proceedings (Vol. 87, No. 10, pp. 982-990). Elsevier.

[2]. Kao, J. (2016). White Paper: Pharmaceutical Regulation and Off-Label Uses.

[3]. Questions and Answers on FDA's Adverse Event Reporting System (FAERS). https://www.fda.gov/drugs/guidancecomplianceregulatoryinformation/surveillance/adversedrugeffects/

[4]. Barry, M. M., Domegan, C., Higgins, O., & Sixsmith, J. (2011). A literature review on health information seeking behaviour on the web: a health consumer and health professional perspective.

[5]. White, R. W., Tatonetti, N. P., Shah, N. H., Altman, R. B., & Horvitz, E. (2013). Web-scale pharmacovigilance: listening to signals from the crowd. Journal of the American Medical Informatics Association, 20(3), 404-408.

[6]. Conroy, S., Choonara, I., Impicciatore, P., Mohn, A., Arnell, H., Rane, A., ... & Rocchi, F. (2000). Survey of unlicensed and off label drug use in paediatric wards in European countries. Bmj, 320(7227), 79-82.

[7]. Leslie, D. L., & Rosenheck, R. (2012). Off-label use of antipsychotic medications in Medicaid. The American journal of managed care, 18(3), e109-17.

[8]. Mesgarpour, B., Müller, M., & Herkner, H. (2012). Search strategies to identify reports on "off-label" drug use in EMBASE. BMC medical research methodology, 12(1), 190.

[9]. Jung, K., LePendu, P., & Shah, N. (2013). Automated detection of systematic off-label drug use in free text of electronic medical records. AMIA Summits on Translational Science Proceedings, 2013, 94.

[10]. Jung, K., LePendu, P., Chen, W. S., Iyer, S. V., Readhead, B., Dudley, J. T., & Shah, N. H. (2014). Automated detection of off-label drug use. *PloS one*, *9*(2), e89324.

[11]. Fung, K. W., Jao, C. S., & Demner-Fushman, D. (2013). Extracting drug indication information from structured product labels using natural language processing. Journal of the American Medical Informatics Association, 20(3), 482-488.

[12]. Xu, R., & Wang, Q. (2013). Large-scale extraction of accurate drug-disease treatment pairs from biomedical literature for drug repurposing. BMC bioinformatics, 14(1), 181.

[13]. Gottlieb, A., Stein, G. Y., Ruppin, E., & Sharan, R. (2011). PREDICT: a method for inferring novel drug indications with application to personalized medicine. Molecular systems biology, 7(1), 496.

[14]. Huang, Y. F., Yeh, H. Y., & Soo, V. W. (2013). Inferring drug-disease associations from integration of chemical, genomic and phenotype data using network propagation. BMC medical genomics, 6(3), S4.

[15]. Chen, X., Liu, M. X., & Yan, G. Y. (2012). Drug–target interaction prediction by random walk on the heterogeneous network. Molecular BioSystems, 8(7), 1970-1978.

[16]. Yu, L., Huang, J., Ma, Z., Zhang, J., Zou, Y., & Gao, L. (2015). Inferring drug-disease associations based on known protein complexes. BMC medical genomics, 8(2), S2.

[17]. Yang, H., & Yang, C. C. (2016, October). Discovering Drug-Drug Interactions and Associated Adverse Drug Reactions with Triad Prediction in Heterogeneous Healthcare Networks. In Healthcare Informatics (ICHI), 2016 IEEE International Conference on (pp. 244-254). IEEE.

[18]. Yan, X. Y., Zhang, S. W., & Zhang, S. Y. (2016). Prediction of drug–target interaction by label propagation with mutual interaction information derived from heterogeneous network. Molecular BioSystems, 12(2), 520-531.

[19]. Soliman, T. H. A. (2014). Mining Multi Drug-Pathways via A Probabilistic Heterogeneous Network Multi-label Classifier. Bonfring International Journal of Research in Communication Engineering, 4(2), 10.

[20]. Lee, K., Lee, S., Jeon, M., Choi, J., & Kang, J. (2012, October). Drug-drug interaction analysis using heterogeneous biological information network. In Bioinformatics and Biomedicine (BIBM), 2012 IEEE International Conference on (pp. 1-5). IEEE.

[21]. Jiang, L., & Yang, C. C. (2015, March). Expanding Consumer Health Vocabularies by Learning Consumer Health Expressions from Online Health Social Media. In International Conference on Social Computing, Behavioral-Cultural Modeling, and Prediction (pp. 314-320). Springer International Publishing.

[22]. Zeng, Q. T., & Tse, T. (2006). Exploring and developing consumer health vocabularies. *Journal of the American Medical Informatics Association*, *13*(1), 24-29.

[23]. Han, J., Sun, Y., Yan, X., & Yu, P. S. (2010, July). Mining heterogeneous information networks. In Tutorial at the 2010 ACM SIGKDD Conf. on Knowledge Discovery and Data Mining (KDD'10), Washington, DC.

[24]. Pedregosa, F., Varoquaux, G., Gramfort, A., Michel, V., Thirion, B., Grisel, O., ... & Vanderplas, J. (2011). Scikit-learn: Machine learning in Python. *Journal of Machine Learning Research*, *12*(Oct), 2825-2830.

Circadian Rhythms in *Neurospora* Exhibit Biologically Relevant Driven and Damped Harmonic Oscillations

Hannah De los Santos
Rensselaer Polytechnic Institute
Institute for Data Exploration and Applications/Department of Mathematical Sciences
Troy, NY 12180
delosh@rpi.edu

Emily J. Collins
Rensselaer Polytechnic Institute
Department of Biological Sciences/Center for Biotechnology and Interdisciplinary Sciences
Troy, NY 12180
collie4@rpi.edu

Jennifer M. Hurley
Rensselaer Polytechnic Institute
Department of Biological Sciences/Center for Biotechnology and Interdisciplinary Sciences
Troy, NY 12180
hurlej2@rpi.edu

Kristin P. Bennett
Rensselaer Polytechnic Institute
Institute for Data Exploration and Applications/Department of Mathematical Sciences
Troy, NY 12180
bennek@rpi.edu

ABSTRACT

Circadian rhythms are endogenous cycles of approximately 24 hours reinforced by external cues such as light. These cycles are typically modeled as harmonic oscillators with fixed amplitude peaks. Using experimental data measuring global gene transcription in *Neurospora crassa* over 48 hours in the dark (i.e. with external queues removed), we demonstrate that many circadian genes frequently exhibit either damped harmonic oscillations, in which the peak amplitudes decrease each day, or driven harmonic oscillations, in which the peak amplitudes increase each day. By fitting extended harmonic oscillator models which include a damping ratio coefficient, we detected additional circadian genes that were not identified by the current standard tools that use fixed amplitude waves as reference, e.g. JTK_CYCLE. Functional Catalogue analysis confirms that our identified damped or driven genes exhibit distinct biological functions. The application of extended damped/driven harmonic oscillator models thus can elucidate, not only previously unidentified circadian genes, but also characterize gene subsets with expression patterns of biological relevance. Thus, expanded harmonic oscillators provide a powerful new tool for circadian system biology.

KEYWORDS

Circadian Rhythm; Damped Harmonic Oscillator; Driven Harmonic Oscillator; Harmonic Oscillator; Gene Transcription

Permission to make digital or hard copies of all or part of this work for personal or classroom use is granted without fee provided that copies are not made or distributed for profit or commercial advantage and that copies bear this notice and the full citation on the first page. Copyrights for components of this work owned by others than the author(s) must be honored. Abstracting with credit is permitted. To copy otherwise, or republish, to post on servers or to redistribute to lists, requires prior specific permission and/or a fee. Request permissions from permissions@acm.org.
ACM-BCB'17, August 20-23, 2017, Boston, MA, USA.
© 2017 Copyright held by the owner/author(s). Publication rights licensed to ACM.
978-1-4503-4722-8/17/08...$15.00
DOI: http://dx.doi.org/10.1145/3107411.3107420

1 INTRODUCTION

Circadian oscillations are self-sustaining approximately 24-hour molecular rhythms that can be reset by environmental factors, such as light and temperature, yet persist even in the absence of these cues. Fungal and animal cells share circadian oscillators of conserved regulatory architecture: a transcription-translation based negative feedback loop where a heterodimeric transcription-factor complex, "the positive arm," activates the transcription of a set of repressing proteins, "the negative arm" [2]. Circadian regulation of cellular functions stems from the influence of this molecular feedback loop. The current understanding of the mechanism underlying clock regulation over cellular functions is via transcriptional regulation, with the positive arm proteins regulating promoter activation of genes that do not encode proteins participating in the timekeeping loop itself, termed clock-controlled genes (ccgs).

Much of what is understood about the molecular circadian circuit comes from the clock model system *Neurospora crassa*, a bread mold whose well-defined clock shares a highly similar architecture with the mammalian circadian clock [8]. In *Neurospora*, the clock negative arm consists of the FRQ/FRH complex (FFC) and the positive arm consists of the WC-1 and WC-2 complex (WCC). The WCC binds to the *frq* promoter, initiating the transcription and translation of FRQ, which in turn forms the FFC. The FFC inhibits the activity of the WCC, decreasing *frq* expression. The resulting loss of the FFC releases the inhibition on the WCC, after which the cycle is reinitiated [5].

The circadian clock is a uniquely powerful regulator of gene expression and transcriptional regulation by the clock is evident for as many as 40% of genes in well-studied organisms [9]. While an understanding of direct clock control over cellular output is beginning to emerge, the networking of clock-controlled pathways to effect organismal physiology is poorly understood. What is known is that the consequences of chronically disrupting circadian regulation are severe. For example, chronic circadian disruption has been shown to lead to higher rates of cancer, diabetes, heart attack, and stroke in humans as well as in animal models [3]. To investigate the effects of circadian disruption, biologists often collect massive datasets quantifying temporal expression for tens of thousands of genes, transcripts, and proteins. Nowhere are these data sets as extensive as in *Neurospora*, for which multiple circadian transcriptomic data sets have been published [9, 16]. Importantly, *Neurospora* is also a model organism in the engineered overproduction of cellulases, which are enzymes essential for biofuel production [18]. Moreover, the production of cellulases is significantly influenced by the Neurospora circadian system, as circadian clocks coordinate cellular physiology for many fungal cells [20]. Therefore, a better understanding of which elements of the cellulase secretion pathway fall under circadian control could enable the maximization of production through manipulation of the clock.

Computational tools have been developed for identifying circadian oscillations in these large gene expression datasets [7, 10]. However, when distinctly circadian oscillations deviate from a typical sinusoidal waveform, they can be missed by the fixed amplitude models that these currently available tools utilize. Thus, a more biologically realistic mathematical model, e.g. the one proposed in Section 3, which can account for damped or driven oscillations, is needed to more thoroughly identify and characterize circadianly expressed genes.

2 DETECTION OF CIRCADIAN RHYTHMS

JTK_CYCLE is the most widely used algorithm for distinguishing between circadian and non-circadian expression data [7]. JTK_CYCLE uses the Jonckheere-Terpstra-Kendall (JTK) algorithm, which employs Kendall's τ rank correlation coefficent to determine how well the expression data match reference sinusoidal waves for a range of user-defined period lengths and phases. JTK_CYCLE provides the period, phase, amplitude, and p-values of cycling expression data. JTK_CYCLE and a later variant eJTK_CYCLE, which allows for non-sinusoidal reference waveforms, all assume that the amplitudes of the daily peaks are uniform across the time period.

Recent experimental evidence, however, demonstrates that under certain growth conditions, circadian genes in *Neurospora* (and likely oscillating genes in many other systems cultured without reinforcing entrainment cues (e.g. [11])) have peaks that decrease in amplitude each day, a phenomena known as damping. In [9], the core clock gene *frq* (NCU02265) clearly displayed this damping phenomena. To further verify this expression pattern, we performed a standard luciferase assay (see Methods). The resulting time course distinctly showed that *frq* expression mimics a damped harmonic oscillator (Figure 1). Thus, we hypothesized that many circadian genes may exhibit oscillatory damping and that standard detection methods such as JTK_CYCLE that assume fixed amplitudes at best do not report these daily amplitude changes and at worst fail to detect these genes as rhythmic. To test this hypothesis, we developed a novel circadian rhythm detection method based on models of harmonic oscillators from physics that allow the amplitudes to be decreased (damped) or increased (driven) over time.

3 DRIVEN AND DAMPED HARMONIC OSCILLATORS

Below, we first review simple harmonic oscillators and then discuss how this basic model was extended to account for damped and driven genes.

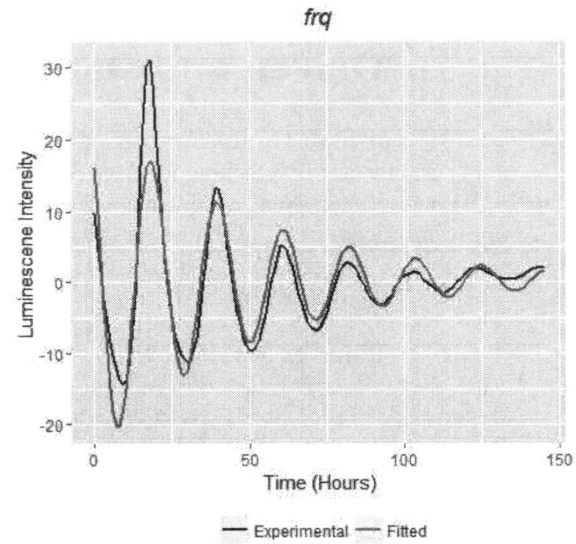

Figure 1: High resolution detrended and scaled luceriferase data tracking the levels of the core clock protein *frq* over six days demonstrates the pattern of a damped harmonic oscillator. Experimental data (detrended and scaled) is represented with a black line while the fitted extended harmonic oscillator is represented with a blue line.

The simple harmonic oscillator equation captures sinusoidal forms of varying amplitude and period, represented as follows:

$$x(t) = A\cos(\omega t + \phi) + y \tag{1}$$

where $x(t)$ represents the corresponding change in amplitude, A is the amplitude at time 0, ω is the radial frequency, t is time, ϕ is the phase shift, and y is the equilibrium value. This model is used in physics to describe oscillations in the ideal mass-spring problem, though it clearly has applications to oscillations in circadian rhythms.

This equation, however, fails to capture both the decaying and amplifying nature of oscillations in reality, where the ideal mass-spring problem faces friction and external added forces, respectively. In order to capture this nature, the first equation is changed as follows:

$$x(t) = Ae^{\frac{-\gamma t}{2}}\cos(\omega t + \phi) + y \tag{2}$$

where γ is the damping coefficient, and all other symbols retain their meaning from (1). This damping coefficient captures both driven and damped oscillations, with a positive value indicating damping and a negative value indicating driving. This equation is merely an extension of (1), as a damping coefficient value of 0 results in the simple harmonic oscillator.

4 METHODS

4.1 Oscillator Fitting Algorithms

Our method specifically fits the parameters of (2) by using nonlinear least squares. Given the experimental data points for each gene

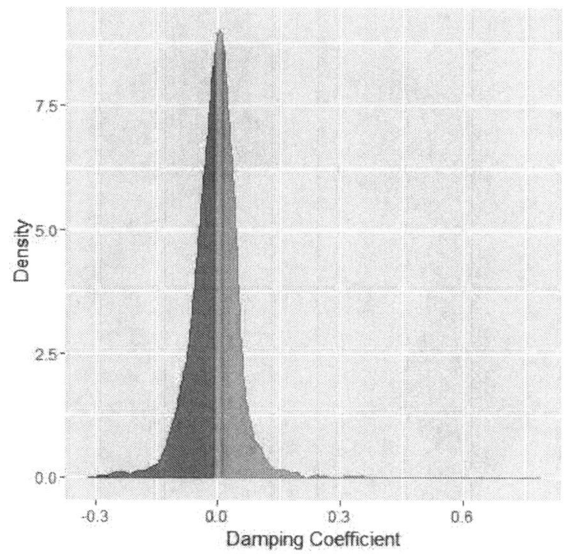

Figure 2: Density graph of the damping coefficients assigned to genes that were considered to be significantly rhythmic at a p-value less than .05. The left shaded region corresponds to driven genes (red), the middle to harmonic genes (orange), and the right to damped genes (blue). While the harmonic genes are well-represented in the dataset, it is the genes that display either damped or driven oscillations that dominate the circadian genes.

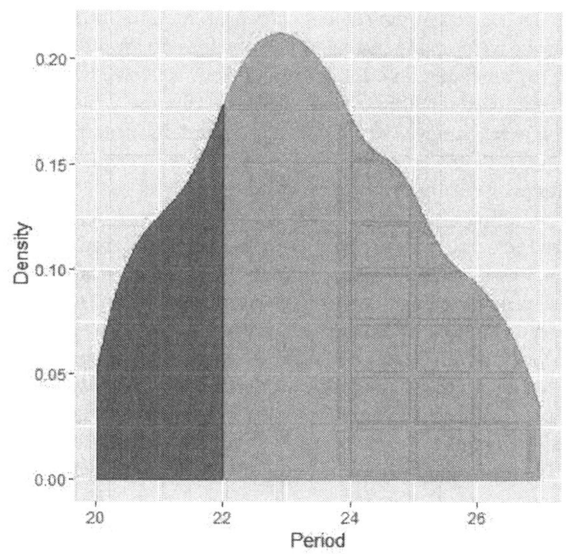

Figure 3: Density graph of periods considered to be significantly rhythmic at the p-value .05. The left shaded region corresponds to ultradian genes (red), the middle to circadian genes (orange), and the right to infradian genes (blue). The highest density of periods falls within the 22 to 24 hour window.

$(\mathbf{t}, \mathbf{x(t)}) = (t_1, x(t_1)), (t_2, x(t_2)), \ldots, (t_n, x(t_n))$ and parameters $\beta = (A, \gamma, \omega, y, \phi)$, this function minimizes residuals in the following manner:

$$\min_{\beta} \sum_{i=1}^{n} (x(t_i) - f(t_i, \beta))^2 \tag{3}$$

where n is the total number of data points and $f(t_i, \beta)$ represents the function for (2). A local solution is found using the `nl2sol` algorithm from the Port library, as implemented in `nls` function in R [13]. Problem (3) is nonconvex, so `nls` finds different local minima depending on the starting value. Thus, finding good starting values is necessary. The parameter starting values (denoted with subscript 0) are determined by prior knowledge and use of experimental values in the following manner:

$$A_0 = \max(x(t)) - \text{mean}(x(t))$$

$$\gamma_0 = \begin{cases} \frac{1}{\sqrt{1+(2\pi/\delta)^2}} & \text{if peak(1)} > \text{peak(2)} \\ -0.01 & \text{otherwise} \end{cases} \tag{4}$$

$$\omega_0 = \frac{2\pi}{22.5} \tag{5}$$

$$y_0 = \min(\mathbf{x}(t)) - \frac{\max(\mathbf{x}(t)) - \min(\mathbf{x}(t))}{2} \tag{6}$$

ϕ_0 is determined by partitioning the possible phase shift range into 12 pieces: $\frac{i\pi}{6}$ for $i = 0, \ldots, 11$. Using the other estimated starting values and this value of ϕ_0 at i, $x(t)$ at time points 2 and 3 (hour 4 and hour 6 as discussed below) are calculated using (2). Should the absolute value of the difference between these calculated values and the experimental values at those time points both be less than .1, the value of ϕ_0 at i is selected. The last i that satisfies this criteria is chosen.

The supports for (4), which are the vector of peaks within the experimental data and δ, the logarithmic decrement, are determined by the following:

$$\text{peak(k)} = \max(i-3, i-2, i-1, i, i+1, i+2, i+3),$$
$$\text{for } i = 4, \ldots, n-3 \text{ and } k = 1, \ldots, \text{number of peaks}$$

$$\delta = \frac{1}{n} \ln\left(\frac{x(t)}{x(t+T)}\right)$$

where i is the time point, k is the number of the peak, n is the number of time points in the series, and $t + T$ is the value at the next time point (in this case, time point 2).

We now consider our parameter choices. For (4), the logarithmic decrement δ estimates the amount of damping between two peaks. This method of estimation does not hold true for estimating γ in driven oscillators, and thus γ is set to a starting value of -.01 if the peak heights are non-decreasing.

The circadian period of *Neurospora crassa* [17] has been measured to be 22.5 hours. Thus we chose 22.5 hours for the starting value to determine circadian rhythms. Within (5), 22.5 represents this estimated period of the oscillation represented in hours.

For the *Neurospora* data, we chose a value of 0 for the equilibrium value (6), since the data for each gene is normalized to have mean 0 and standard deviation 1 over the time course.

Due to machine accuracy and experimental variation, finding an exact value of 0 for γ is unlikely. Therefore, we determined the range of γ for an oscillator to be considered harmonic as $(-.01, .01)$. Values of γ including and above .01 would be considered damped, while values including and below -.01 would be considered driven. We have also determined that a period in the range of [20,27) would be classified as circadian in order to be compatible with JTK_CYCLE. In the results section, we suggest alternative strategies for determining circadian rhythms that can exploit additional model parameters.

After the fitted parameters are determined by `nls`, we determine p-values for these fits using Kendall's τ rank correlation coefficient, which measures the concordance between two series of data. This is the same statistical test used in JTK_CYCLE. In this case, we seek to compare the fitted values, $\mathbf{y} = (y_1, ..., y_n)$, with the experimental data, $\mathbf{x} = (x_1, ..., x_n)$. Here n is the number of time points in the series. This is done using the following equation [7] [10]:

$$\tau(\mathbf{x}, \mathbf{y}) = \frac{\sum_{1 \leq i < j \leq n} \operatorname{sgn}(x_j - x_i) \cdot \operatorname{sgn}(y_j - y_i)}{\frac{1}{2}n(n-1)} \tag{7}$$

where $\operatorname{sgn}(x)$ is equal to 1 if x is positive and equal to -1 if x is negative. The numerator represents the number of pairs that vary concordantly minus the pairs that vary discordantly. The denominator represents the number of different pairs between the fitted values and experimental values, which allows τ to be normalized between -1 and 1. The distribution for the Kendall rank coefficient can be calculated explicitly for small samples. However, for larger samples, this can be approximated by the normal distribution, allowing for a simple p-value calculation. P-values were adjusted for multiple hypothesis testing using the Benjamini-Hochburg procedure. We used a .05 cutoff to determine significance.

For a baseline, we ran the JTK_CYCLE R script on the same data set. This run of JTK_CYCLE looked for periods between 20 and 26. To correct for multiple hypothesis testing, the output p-values were modified with the Benjamini-Hochburg procedure and significance was determined with an equivalent .05 cutoff.

4.2 *Neurospora* Time Course Data

We gathered data for this analysis from previous work investigating the extent to which the clock controls transcript levels in *Neurospora* [9]. For this publication, *Neurospora* was grown in constant dark conditions (DD) and triplicate time courses were run. During each time course, RNA was extracted from individual *Neurospora* cultures every 2 h over a period of 48 h. The extracted RNA from each sample was used to prepare Illumina libraries using standard protocols and the resultant libraries were subjected to Illumina high-throughput sequencing. The raw data were then normalized to fragments per kilobase of exon model per million mapped reads (FPKM) values [9]. A total of 9728 detected genes were detected using this analysis method. For our work, each gene was normalized to have mean 0 and standard deviation 1 over the time course and then each gene was analyzed using the methods described above.

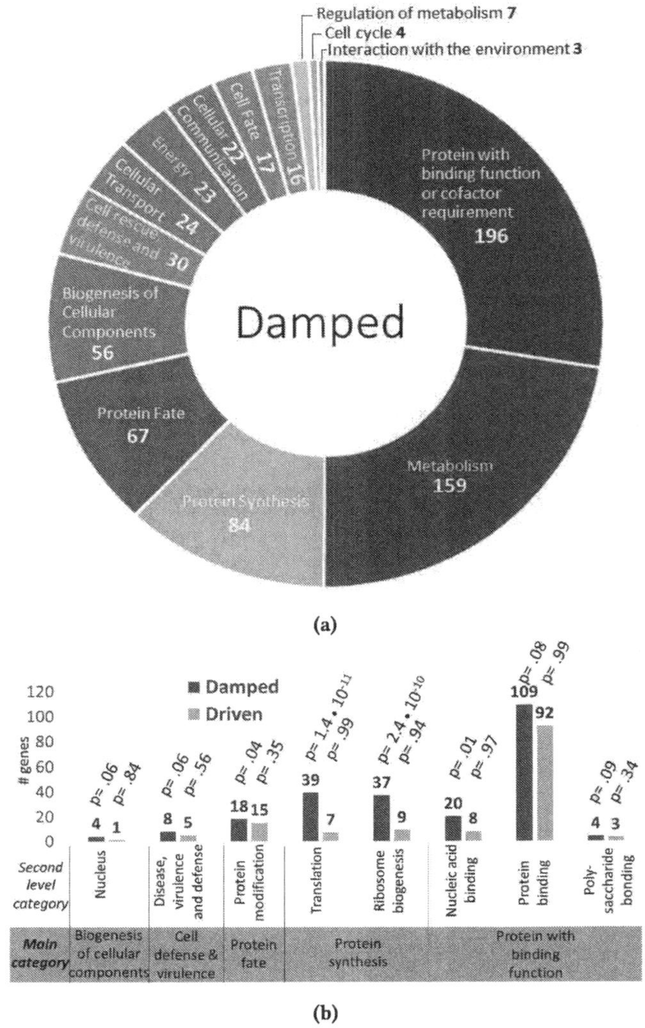

Figure 4: 4a: Primary functional categories of genes from the damped subset. Each color represents a distinct functional main category in the FunCat analysis with the name of the category labeled. The number of genes associated with each category from the damped subset is provided after the category name. 4b: Enriched second-level FunCat categories in the damped subset includes protein synthesis and proteins with binding function. Bar graphs represent the total number of genes from the driven (green) and damped (red) datasets in the secondary categories that have a significant enrichment for damped genes. P-values associated with each category and dataset are reported.

To demonstrate the damped nature of oscillatory rhythms, we tracked the expression level of the core clock gene *frq* using a standard Luciferase tracking assay. This assay was preformed and analyzed as described previously using strain X661-5a, in which the promoter of *frq* was fused to the codon optimized firefly *luciferase* gene [9]. In this way, luminescence levels represent the level of *frq* expression and therefore the phase of the clock. Due to the nature of the experiment, the data displayed a downwards linear trend

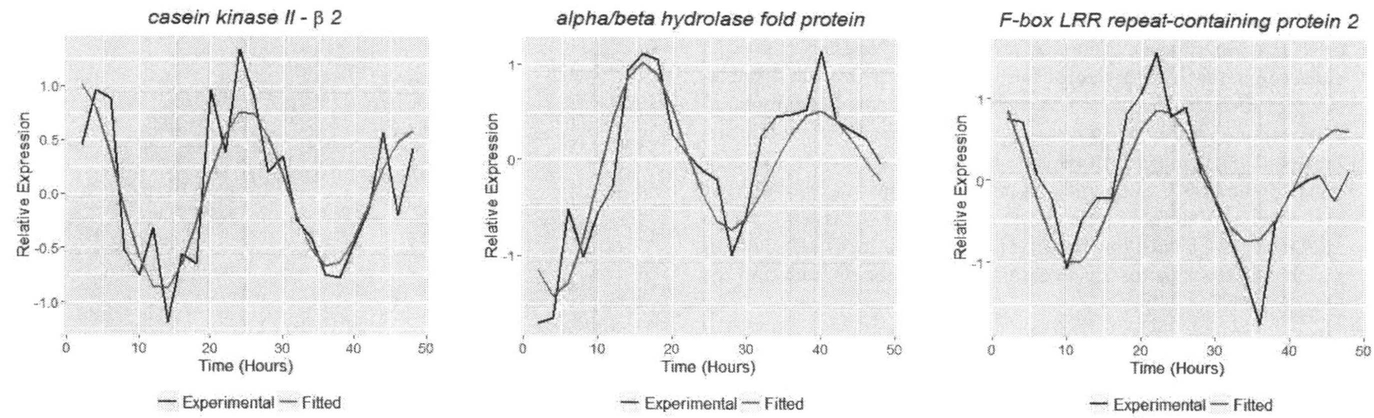

(a) (b) (c)

Figure 5: Examples of biologically relevant genes with damped harmonic oscillations missed under standard circadian analysis. Circadian proteins *casein kinase II subunit β-2* (5a), *alpha/beta hydrolase protein* (5b), and *F-box LRR repeat-containing protein 2* (5c) display a damped rhythm and are identified as rhythmic by the extended harmonic oscillator in this analysis but not by JTK_Cycle using identical statistical tests and significance. The figures provide both the experimental data (black) and the fitted models (blue).

over the six days. As such, the data was "detrended" by fitting a linear trend to the data by the method of linear least squares, which minimizes the squared residuals between the fitted data and the experimental data. This resulted in the intercept (a) and coefficient corresponding to the downwards trend over time (b) and was used to obtain the detrended results in the following manner:

$$x(t_i)_{detrended} = x(t_i) - (a + b * t_i) \text{ for } i = 1, \ldots, n$$

where $x(t)$ is the original value, t is the time point, and n is the total amount of time points. Detrending effectively makes the equilibrium value of the harmonic oscillator a constant. While we do see suspected drifts in the 48-hour RNA data, these shifts are relatively small. Thus we do not model equilibrium drift on any of the results for the 48-hour RNA data presented here.

5 RESULTS

Upon fitting each of the genes detected in the above described data set to (2), we found that 1819 genes of 9728 detected genes were considered to be significantly rhythmic, as compared the 994 given by JTK_CYCLE. 1624 of those genes were unique to the extended harmonic oscillator, indicating that JTK_CYCLE may have missed a large portion of genes by not accounting for damping or driving. Of these 1624 unique genes, 751 were driven, 587 were damped, and 286 were harmonic. This distribution of driven, damped, and harmonic genes is reflected in Figure 2. Periods of these genes were distributed such that the highest densities fell between 22 and 24, as expected from the known circadian period of *Neurospora* (Figure 3) [17].

To determine the biological functions of the genes we considered to be damped or driven, Functional Catalogue (FunCat) analysis was completed using the program FungiFun2 [12]. FunCat is a hierarchical category scheme to assign gene protein products to one or more functional annotations [15]. At the first level in the hierarchal description of each gene is a primary category function, e.g. metabolism or protein synthesis. Each primary category then contains second-level, third-level, etc. categories that further describe increasingly specific functional groups for a gene. Enrichment scores for categories represented in a dataset are then calculated by FungiFun2 as p-values considering the total number of genes possible for a category.

FunCat analysis of the 587 genes considered to be damped ($\gamma \geq 0.01$) identified a total of 14 primary categories (Figure 4a). Most numerous in this dataset are genes with protein binding function, followed by metabolic and protein synthetic genes. Second-level category enrichment reveals that genes involved in protein translation and ribosome biogenesis are the most statistically overrepresented categories in the damped gene dataset (Figure 4b). Among these damped genes is *ckβ2* (Figure 5a, ($\gamma = 0.02$)), a subunit of *casein kinase II*, which is a kinase demonstrated to be an essential component of clock function and output [21]. Another damped gene identified, *F-box LRR repeat-containing protein 2* (Figure 5c, ($\gamma = .03$)), is of interest as F-box proteins have been implicated in clock function as a primary mechanism for the temporal degradation of core clock proteins [6]. Finally, a third damped gene, *alpha/beta hydrolase protein* (Figure 5b, ($\gamma = .05$)), is characterized as a secondary metabolism gene product predicted to be involved in the breakdown of aromatic compounds [4].

Of the 751 genes considered to be driven, FunCat analysis identified 16 primary categories that were represented in the dataset

(Figure 6a). The most represented primary category was metabolism, followed by protein binding and protein fate. At the second-level, categories most enriched were vacuole biogenesis and several modes of metabolism, including fatty acid, carbohydrate and amino acid metabolism (Figure 6b). A particularly germane example of a driven gene with biological relevance is *endoglucanase* (Figure 7a, (γ = -.03)). *endoglucanase* is an enzyme necessary to the synergistic reactions that degrade biomass into compounds useful for industrial and biofuel applications [22]. Another driven gene of interest is *ubiquitin-protein ligase* (*uce-17*) (Figure 7b, (γ = -.04)), which functions primarily to target proteins for degradation by proteasomes [14, 22].

6 DISCUSSION

The inclusion of a parameter to capture the change in amplitude over time enabled the identification of previously overlooked circadian genes; granting a more in-depth insight into clock regulation over organismal output. Oscillators of fixed amplitude are limited in their scope and thereby miss oscillting genes which may be crucial to the regulation of *Neurospora crassa* behavior over circadian time. This is evidenced by genes which are identified by our analysis as circadian which were overlooked by JTK_CYCLE's algorithm; the genes identified in our data set, but not in JTK_CYCLE's, were largely comprised of driven and damped oscillators (Figure 3). Therefore, the addition of a parameter which allows for changes in oscillatory amplitudes provided inclusiveness as compared to current circadian gene identification packages (i.e. those that look at simply harmonic oscillations).

Moreover, the inclusion of this parameter has extended the understanding of circadian regulation as it has identified a previously unknown class of biologically relevant circadian genes. This feature is demonstrated by the functional categories associated with the damped or driven oscillations that were not recognized by JTK_CYCLE, underscoring the importance of utilizing an algorithm that can identify damped/driven rhythmic genes. Most strikingly at the primary category level, genes associated with protein synthesis were well represented in the damped subset, whereas genes associated with metabolism were present in greater numbers in the driven subset (Figure 4a and Figure 6a). Among the specific categories most enriched in the damped genes were those involving ribosomes, the cellular machinery to make proteins. The damping of protein synthesis genes suggests that over the experimental time course, circadian-influenced pathways were triggered by media nutrient depletion to decelerate protein synthesis as a means of conserving metabolites and slowing growth (Figure 4b). Alternative methods of resource and energy conservation include the damping of genes with nonessential secondary metabolism functions, like the above referenced *alpha/beta hydrolase protein* (Figure 5b).

A more direct example of potential damping effects on the clock lies in the gene *casein kinase II* (*ck2*) subunit β-2 (Figure 5a). The damping of *ck2* potentially represents a mechanism for not only the damping of genes under clock control, but the damping of the clock itself. The phosphorylating activities of *ck2* and its temporal incorporation into the afternoon-evening clock protein complex are

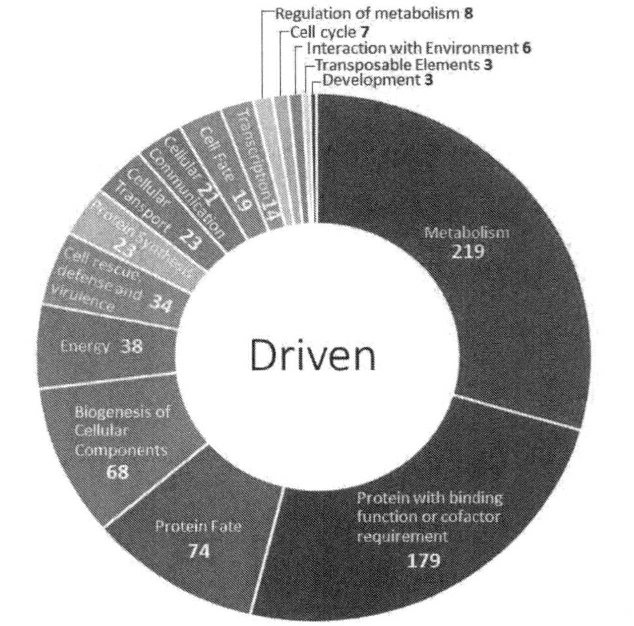

(a)

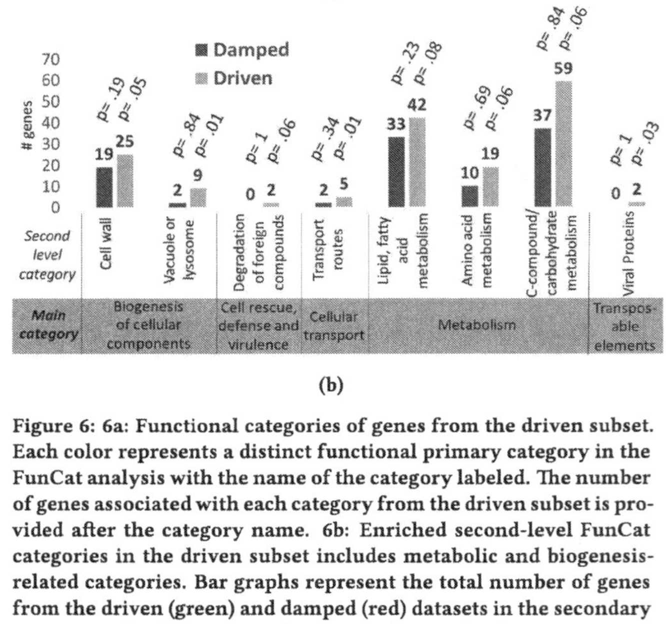

(b)

Figure 6: 6a: Functional categories of genes from the driven subset. Each color represents a distinct functional primary category in the FunCat analysis with the name of the category labeled. The number of genes associated with each category from the driven subset is provided after the category name. 6b: Enriched second-level FunCat categories in the driven subset includes metabolic and biogenesis-related categories. Bar graphs represent the total number of genes from the driven (green) and damped (red) datasets in the secondary categories that have a significant enrichment for driven genes. P-values associated with each category and dataset are reported.

essential to clock function and output in *Neurospora* [21]. If *ck2* expression and activity are directly damped by nutrient-sensing pathways, this could feed into the clock and in turn effect many genes under circadian control. Additionally, the effects of *ck2* damping could be widespread due to its additional phosphorylation targets which may alter cellular protein function, stability, and degradation.

f-box LRR repeat-containing protein 2 also presents a possible mechanism for overall clock damping (Figure 5c). F-box proteins are

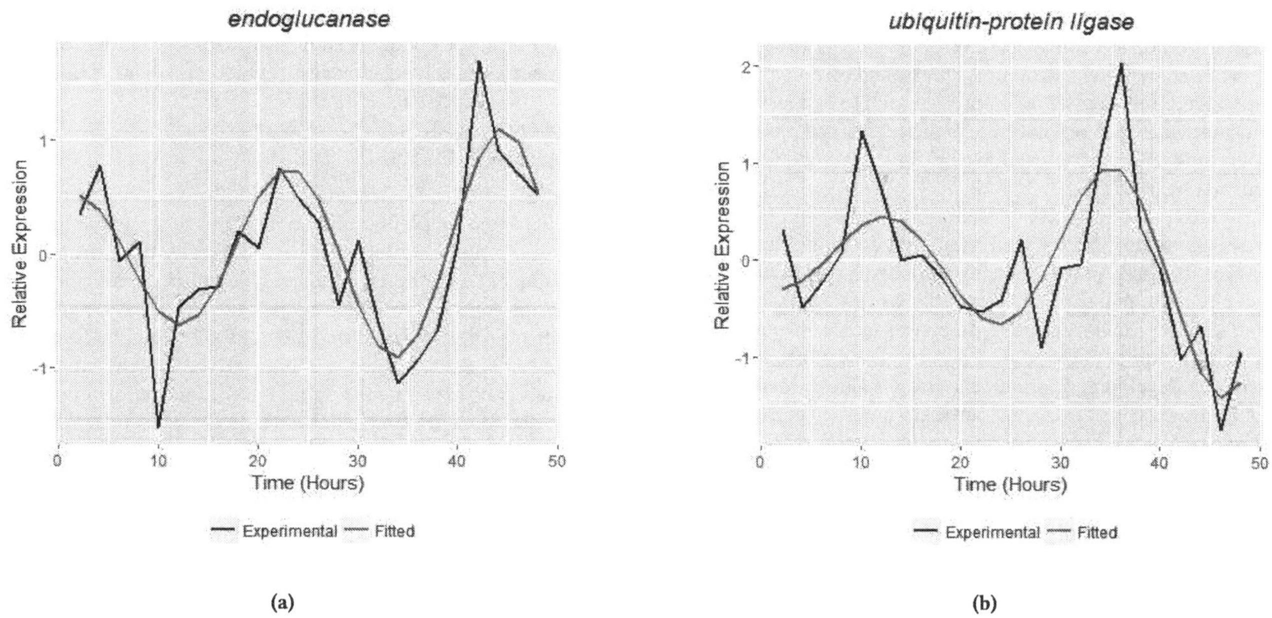

Figure 7: Examples of biologically relevant genes with driven harmonic oscillations missed under standard circadian analysis. Cellulase *endoglucanase* (7a) and degradation gene *ubiquitin-protein ligase* (7b) display a driven rhythm and are identified as rhythmic by the extended harmonic oscillator in this analysis but not by JTK_Cycle using identical statistical tests and significance. The figures provide both the experimental data (black) and the fitted models (blue).

known to facilitate the degradation of negative arm clock proteins in preparation for subsequent cycles of the transcription-translation negative feedback loop [6]. One could envision that the damping of *f-box LRR repeat-containing protein 2* may lead to more available negative arm protein causing increased inhibition of negative arm gene transcription, affecting clock gene expression with each oscillation.

Conversely, driven genes were most significantly composed of those categorized to aid in the breakdown and metabolism of sugars, lipids, and proteins or by the formation of lysosomes/vacuoles (Figure 6a). The circadian upregulation of metabolism genes may serve as an important survival mechanism to enhance pathways allowing the organism to be more resourceful; it may enable the metabolism of a more diverse array of intracellular substrates. The upregulation of the gene *uce-17* is further evidence of driven circadian expression aiding metabolic resourcefulness in nutrient-restricted conditions (Figure 7b). *uce-17* triggers degradation via the ubiquitin-proteasome pathway, potentially allowing the organism to recycle amino acids from existing proteins to generate proteins immediately essential to survival.

As an additional example of how driven genes may signify the organisms attempt to modify their environment to adapt to change, the well-documented cellulase gene, *endoglucanase*, was identified among the driven genes dataset (Figure 7a). This clock-driven regulation of a cellulase is of note as *Neurospora* is a commonly-used organism for components for ethanol biofuel production. Cellulases are enzymes that break down cellulose, the abundant starch giving structure to plant cell walls, into smaller sugars. They are produced by organisms like *Neurospora* as a means of digesting organic compounds into sugar metabolites and are utilized by bioengineers to ultimately produce fuels like ethanol from plant matter. *endoglucanase* cleaves the β-glycosidic bonds in cellulose to make the sugar chain accessible to other synergistic degradation enzymes [22]. Like many other genes important to metabolism, secretions of several cellulases are known to be circadian in *Neurospora* [16]. The driving of *endoglucanase* production suggests that pathways for cellulose degradation are circadianly amplified as the more easily metabolized compounds in the media are depleted, offering valuable information for implementing efficient biofuel production using *Neurospora*.

Our algorithm shows that to a great extent, genes that fall under circadianly regulation are damped or driven under artificial/experimental conditions. However, and surprisingly, the functions of circadianly damped and driven genes *Neurospora* are enriched in biologically germane processes, suggesting that damping/driving of circadian regulation may have biological relevance. Moreover, as we note that other circadian systems beyond fungal organisms display damping under artificial/experimental conditions and *Neurospora* has a molecular architecture that is conserved in mammalian clocks, this work argues that the damping/driving phenomena likely applies to clocks in higher eurkayotes. It is possible, perhaps probable, that the genes that can be damped or driven by the clock are linked to the diseases associated with chronic circadian rhythm disruption and therefore warrant study. The conserved cellular processes identified in our analyses (e.g. protein synthesis and carbon metabolism) further highlights the need for future research to better understand the mechanisms that regulate these processes and the influence that damping and driving can have on the circadian regulation of organismal behavior.

In summary, the preliminary biological results demonstrate that our development of a extended harmonic oscillator model is an important first step in the detection and analysis of damped and driven circadian genes. Moreover, this work demonstrates that state-of-the-art oscillating gene detection techniques are not always able to detect damped and driven genes, highlighting the need for the development of models that are able to identify these damping/driving rhythms. Thus, further studies with multiple synthetic and real datasets are underway to both optimize the detecting damped and driven oscillators as well as understand their importance in circadian regulation.

Our analysis revealed a few areas in which improvements should be made to further refine the harmonic oscillator model and the algorithm. For example, our current model assumes that the equilibrium value of the oscillators is constant. However, drifts downwards and or upwards have been noted in *in vivo* and *in vitro* datasets. While we followed the standard practice of "detrending" the luciferase data for *frq* (Figure 1) to remove a downward drift before circadian analysis, the model could be expanded to explicitly capture such drifts trends to further improve modeling of genes that exhibit potentially subtle upward or downward drifts (e.g Figure 7b). In addition, more robust algorithms could also further improve the results. For example, the underlying optimization problem (3) is non-convex and ill-conditioned; thus, the `nls` algorithm may get stuck in local minima or fail to converge.

We also observe that the definition of what constitutes a "circadian rhythm" under the proposed model should be further refined. As in the existing approach, JTK_CYCLE, we defined a gene as circadian if the period parameter is within the target range and the goodness of fit yields a significant p-value. The increased flexibility of the proposed model to account for damping or driving allows genes that are strongly damped or driven with very small oscillatory amplitudes (i.e. that exhibit roughly linear behavior) to be classified as circadian. Thus, the definition of "circadian" and the associated statistical tests should be refined to consider the damping coefficient and amplitude of the model as well.

Finally, we note that the presence of damped and driven harmonic oscillators, albeit under non-native conditions, indicates that a deeper understanding of the molecular mechanisms underlying circadian rhythms is needed. Prior investigations have lead to the creation of mathematical models that approximately represent the core mechanisms of the circadian clock; see for example [1, 19]. However, these models do not include a parameter to describe the damping of the core circadian oscillator under conditions without re-entraining cues. Our finding that this damping/driving phenomena may have biological relevance suggests that these models should be extended to incorporate this new aspect of the circadian clock. For example, one could utilize previously developed models of the molecular circadian clock to show that in the core clock, as well as in output, gene dynamics can be described by a dynamical equation corresponding to the damped harmonic oscillator equations. This modified model could provide insight into the molecular mechanism underlying circadian regulation. We leave this to future work.

7 CONCLUSION

Damped and driven harmonic oscillations diverge largely from simple harmonic oscillations, so much so that fixed amplitude detection methods cannot harness biologically relevant genes. The inclusion of the damping parameter, γ, within the simple harmonic oscillator equation provides an exponential decay or growth that explains the genes' functions over time, allowing the identification of additional circadian genes. Moreover, the categorization of these damped and driven genes demonstrates an important biological relevance to each expression pattern. The presence of functional distinctions between damped or driven genes supports a model where as nutrients become scarce, circadian output is influenced via damping or driving mechanisms to adapt clock control over behavior to environmental conditions to maximize organismal fitness. Computational results demonstrate that the proposed extended harmonic oscillator identifies circadian genes missed by fixed amplitude approaches and suggest that extended harmonic oscillators represent a powerful new class of methods for circadian biology.

ACKNOWLEDGMENTS

This work is supported by the National Science Foundation (#1331023 to K. Bennett), a Rensselaer Polytechnic Institute Presidential Fellowship (to H. De los Santos), the National Institutes of Health/ National Institute of Biomedical Imaging and Bioengineering (U01 EB022546 to J. Hurley) and an NIH T32 training grant (to E. Collins). We thank the Larrondo lab for their gift of the X661-5a strain. We thank the reviewers for their helpful suggestions.

REFERENCES

[1] Andrey A. Dovzhenok, Mokryun Baek, Sookkyung Lim, and Christian I. Hong. 2015. Mathematical modeling and validation of glucose compensation of the neurospora circadian clock. *Biophysical Journal* 108, 7 (apr 2015), 1830–1839. DOI: http://dx.doi.org/10.1016/j.bpj.2015.01.043

[2] Jay C. Dunlap. 1999. Molecular bases for circadian clocks. *Cell* 96, 2 (1999), 271–290.

[3] Jennifer A. Evans and Alec J. Davidson. 2013. Health consequences of circadian disruption in humans and animal models. *Prog Mol Biol Transl Sci* 119 (2013), 283–323.

[4] Dmitrij Frishman, Martin Mokrejs, Denis Kosykh, Gabi Kastenmller, Grigory Kolesov, Igor Zubrzycki, Christian Gruber, Birgitta Geier, Andreas Kaps, Kaj Albermann, Andreas Volz, Christian Wagner, Matthias Fellenberg, Klaus Heumann, and Hans-Werner Mewes. 2003. The PEDANT genome database. *Nucleic Acids Research* 31, 1 (2003), 207–211.

[5] Kevin K. Fuller, Jennifer M. Hurley, Jennifer J. Loros, and Jay C. Dunlap. 2014. *6: Photobiology and Circadian Clocks in Neurospora.* Springer Berlin Heidelberg, Berlin, Heidelberg, 121–148. DOI: http://dx.doi.org/10.1007/978-3-642-45218-5_6

[6] Qun He, Ping Cheng, Yuhong Yang, Qiyang He, Hongtao Yu, and Yi Liu. 2003. FWD1-mediated degradation of FREQUENCY in Neurospora establishes a conserved mechanism for circadian clock regulation. *The EMBO Journal* 22, 17 (2003), 4421–4430.

[7] Michael E. Hughes, John B. Hogenesch, and Karl Kornacker. 2010. JTK_CYCLE: an efficient nonparametric algorithm for detecting rhythmic components in genome-scale data sets. *Journal of Biological Rhythms* 25, 5 (2010), 372–380.

[8] Jennifer Hurley, Jennifer J. Loros, and Jay C. Dunlap. 2015. Chapter two-dissecting the mechanisms of the clock in Neurospora. *Methods in Enzymology* 551 (2015), 29–52.

[9] Jennifer M. Hurley, Arko Dasgupta, Jillian M. Emerson, Xiaoying Zhou, Carol S. Ringelberg, Nicole Knabe, Anna M. Lipzen, Erika A. Lindquist, Christopher G.

Daum, Kerrie W. Barry, and others. 2014. Analysis of clock-regulated genes in Neurospora reveals widespread posttranscriptional control of metabolic potential. *Proceedings of the National Academy of Sciences* 111, 48 (2014), 16995–17002.

[10] Alan L. Hutchison, Mark Maienschein-Cline, Andrew H. Chiang, SM Ali Tabei, Herman Gudjonson, Neil Bahroos, Ravi Allada, and Aaron R. Dinner. 2015. Improved statistical methods enable greater sensitivity in rhythm detection for genome-wide data. *PLoS Comput Biol* 11, 3 (2015), e1004094.

[11] Maren Keller, Jeannine Mazuch, Ute Abraham, Gina D. Eom, Erik D. Herzog, Hans-Dieter Volk, Achim Kramer, and Bert Maier. 2009. A circadian clock in macrophages controls inflammatory immune responses. *Proceedings of the National Academy of Sciences* 106, 50 (2009), 21407–21412.

[12] Steffen Priebe, Christian Kreisel, Fabian Horn, Reinhard Guthke, and Jrg Linde. 2015. FungiFun2: a comprehensive online resource for systematic analysis of gene lists from fungal species. *Bioinformatics* 31, 3 (feb 2015), 445–446. DOI: http://dx.doi.org/10.1093/bioinformatics/btu627

[13] R Core Team. 2015. *R: A Language and Environment for Statistical Computing.* R Foundation for Statistical Computing, Vienna, Austria. https://www.R-project.org/

[14] Patrick A. Robinson and Helen C. Ardley. 2004. Ubiquitin-protein ligases. *Journal of Cell Science* 117, 22 (2004). http://jcs.biologists.org/content/117/22/5191.short

[15] Andreas Ruepp, Alfred Zollner, Dieter Maier, Kaj Albermann, Jean Hani, Martin Mokrejs, Igor Tetko, Ulrich Güldener, Gertrud Mannhaupt, Martin Münsterkötter, and H Werner Mewes. 2004. The FunCat, a functional annotation scheme for systematic classification of proteins from whole genomes. *Nucleic Acids Research* 32, 18 (2004), 5539–45. DOI: http://dx.doi.org/10.1093/nar/gkh894

[16] Cigdem Sancar, Gencer Sancar, Nati Ha, François Cesbron, and Michael Brunner. 2015. Dawn- and dusk-phased circadian transcription rhythms coordinate anabolic and catabolic functions in Neurospora. *BMC Biology* 13 (feb 2015), 17. DOI: http://dx.doi.org/10.1186/s12915-015-0126-4

[17] Malcolm L. Sargent, Winslow R. Briggs, and Dow O. Woodward Hughes. 1966. Circadian Nature of a Rhythm Expressed by an Invertaseless Strain of Neurospora crassa. *Plant Physiology* 41, 8 (1966), 1343–1349.

[18] Chaoguang Tian, William T. Beeson, Anthony T. Iavarone, Jianping Sun, Michael A. Marletta, Jamie HD Cate, and N. Louise Glass. 2009. Systems analysis of plant cell wall degradation by the model filamentous fungus Neurospora crassa. *Proceedings of the National Academy of Sciences* 106, 52 (2009), 22157–22162.

[19] Yu-Yao Tseng, Suzanne M. Hunt, Christian Heintzen, Susan K. Crosthwaite, and Jean-Marc Schwartz. 2012. Comprehensive Modelling of the Neurospora Circadian Clock and Its Temperature Compensation. *PLOS Computational Biology* 8, 3 (03 2012), 1–13. DOI: http://dx.doi.org/10.1371/journal.pcbi.1002437

[20] Michael W. Vitalini, Renato M. de Paula, William D. Park, and Deborah Bell-Pedersen. 2006. The rhythms of life: circadian output pathways in Neurospora. *Journal of Biological Rhythms* 21, 6 (2006), 432–444.

[21] Yuhong Yang, Ping Cheng, and Yi Liu. 2002. Regulation of the Neurospora circadian clock by casein kinase II. *Genes & Development* 16, 8 (apr 2002), 994–1006. DOI: http://dx.doi.org/10.1101/gad.965102

[22] Ragothaman M. Yennamalli, Andrew J. Rader, Adam J. Kenny, Jeffrey D. Wolt, and Taner Z. Sen. 2013. Endoglucanases: insights into thermostability for biofuel applications. *Biotechnology for Biofuels* 6, 1 (jan 2013), 136. DOI: http://dx.doi.org/10.1186/1754-6834-6-136

Hybrid ODE/SSA Model of the Budding Yeast Cell Cycle Control Mechanism with Mutant Case Study

Mansooreh Ahmadian
Department of Computer Science
Virginia Tech
Blacksburg, Virginia
amadian@vt.edu

Shuo Wang
Department of Computer Science
Virginia Tech
Blacksburg, Virginia
wangshuo@cs.vt.edu

John Tyson
Department of Biological Sciences
Virginia Tech
Blacksburg, Virginia
tyson@vt.edu

Young Cao
Department of Computer Science
Virginia Tech
Blacksburg, Virginia
ycao@cs.vt.edu

ABSTRACT

The budding yeast cell cycle is regulated by complex and multi-scale control mechanisms, and is subject to inherent noise in a cell, resulted from low copy numbers of species such as critical mRNAs. Conventional deterministic models cannot capture this inherent noise. Although stochastic models can generate simulation results to better represent inherent noise in system dynamics, the stochastic approach is often computationally too expensive for complex systems, which exhibit multiscale features in two aspects: species with different scales of abundances and reactions with different scales of firing frequencies. To address this challenge, one promising solution is to adopt a hybrid approach. It replaces the single mathematical representation of either discrete-stochastic formulation or continuous deterministic formulation with an integration of both methods, so that the corresponding advantageous features in both methods are well kept to achieve a trade-off between accuracy and efficiency. In this work, we propose a hybrid stochastic model that represents the regulatory network of the budding yeast cell cycle control mechanism, respectively, by Gillespie's stochastic simulation algorithm (SSA) and ordinary differential equations (ODEs). Simulation results of our model were compared with published experimental measurement on the budding yeast cell cycle. The comparison demonstrates that our hybrid model well represents many critical characteristics of the budding yeast cell cycle, and reproduces more than 100 phenotypes of mutant cases. Moreover, the model accounts for partial viability of certain mutant strains. The last but not the least, the proposed scheme is shown to be considerably faster in both modeling and simulation than the equivalent stochastic simulation.

Permission to make digital or hard copies of all or part of this work for personal or classroom use is granted without fee provided that copies are not made or distributed for profit or commercial advantage and that copies bear this notice and the full citation on the first page. Copyrights for components of this work owned by others than the author(s) must be honored. Abstracting with credit is permitted. To copy otherwise, or republish, to post on servers or to redistribute to lists, requires prior specific permission and/or a fee. Request permissions from permissions@acm.org.
ACM-BCB'17, August 20-23, 2017, Boston, MA, USA.
© 2017 Copyright held by the owner/author(s). Publication rights licensed to Association for Computing Machinery.
ACM ISBN 978-1-4503-4722-8/17/08...$15.00
https://doi.org/10.1145/3107411.3107437

CCS CONCEPTS

• **Mathematics of computing** → *Numerical analysis*; *Ordinary differential equations*; Stochastic processes; *Probability and statistics*; • **Computing methodologies** → *Modeling and simulation*; *Model development and analysis*;

KEYWORDS

budding yeast cell cycle model; stochastic simulation algorithm (SSA); hybrid ODE/SSA method

1 INTRODUCTION

The budding yeast is a powerful yet economical model organism that provides researchers an economic system to understand cell functions and design principles. The budding yeast quickly replicates, thus is cheap to proliferate in laboratories and is easy to manipulate genetically. Hence, this system is well studied and a large amount of work [20, 22, 28, 31] has focused on the discovery of molecular mechanisms that control the budding yeast cell cycle. In particular, several mathematical models [6, 7, 16–18, 29, 30] have been proposed in order to address the complex regulatory network of the budding yeast cell cycle.

The conventional approach to model such a complex molecular mechanism is to formulate the time evolution of species' concentration by nonlinear ordinary differential equations (ODEs). ODE models consider the concentration of a species as a continuously varying quantity that evolves deterministically over time. However, this assumption is valid only if the number of molecules is sufficiently large so that molecular fluctuations within a cell can be ignored. ODE-based approaches, in spite of being computationally efficient, cannot model the intrinsic and extrinsic noise observed in wet-lab experiments [1, 21]. To explain this inherent randomness during cell growth and division of the budding yeast cell cycle, several stochastic models have been proposed [2, 3, 16, 18, 19, 33].

The early generation of stochastic models employs different techniques to introduce noise into deterministic models. One of these techniques is to add Gaussian noises to reaction rate equations [27]. This additive randomness can generate sufficient fluctuations of state variables, with sophisticated parameter estimation. However, Gaussian noises resulted from data fitting do not provide much knowledge about the sources of the observed molecular fluctuations in a system. There are also stochastic models developed for protein-protein interaction network [5, 24, 33]. Although these models can address the molecular fluctuations at the protein interaction level, they do not capture the main source of noise from gene expression levels. In fact, according to both experimental observations and theoretical analysis, the main sources of cell intrinsic noises are from gene regulatory network, rather than protein level interactions [21]. Reliability of stochastic models is contingent upon capturing noises at the gene expression level. To address this challenge, more comprehensive stochastic models, based on the framework of Gillespie's stochastic simulation algorithm (SSA) [9, 10], are introduced that take gene-protein regulatory network into accounts [1, 3, 18]. These models include the low abundance transcription dynamics and are successful in capturing the stochastic characteristics of molecular interactions at both gene and protein levels.

Gillespie's SSA yields accurate simulation for the dynamics of well-stirred chemical reaction systems. However, this algorithm is known to be computationally expensive as its time complexity scales with the number of reaction firings. To improve the efficiency of SSA, different approaches have been proposed, including a) optimization of data structures [8], b) approximation methods [11, 12, 25], and c) hybrid [13]. Among these approaches, the hybrid ODE/SSA method, originally proposed by Haseltine and Rawlings, is promising in modeling multi-scale chemical reaction networks. In this method, a system is divided into two subsets of fast and slow reactions, based on average propensities of the reactions. Fast reactions fire more frequently and are placed in the deterministic (ODE) regime. On the other hand, slow reactions are simulated using SSA, with a little modification to include the impact from the ODE regime. In this way, instead of a single mathematical representation for the whole system, we leverage the efficiency of deterministic approach for the fast subset, while maintaining the accuracy in noise by taking the fluctuations of low abundance molecules into account using the SSA.

Another interesting feature of this hybrid stochastic approach is that unpacking complex phenomenological rate laws of deterministic models may not be necessary. In fact, many deterministic budding yeast cell cycle models [6, 7, 17, 29, 30] use complex rate laws such as Michaelis-Menten (MM) equations, Hill functions, and zero-order ultra sensitivity, to model the protein regulatory system, while the original SSA framework proposed by Gillespie relies heavily on elementary chemical reactions (mass-action kinetics). Hence, to develop a stochastic model based on the deterministic approach, it is preferred to decompose the reactions with complex rate laws into elementary reactions. Kar et al [16] did the unpacking of complex MM rate laws for a simple three-variable deterministic model [30] of the budding yeast cell cycle. Nonetheless, that unpacking effort resulted in a complicated system with 19 species and 47 reactions. The cost of such conversion will be significantly higher for complex models with much more species. Moreover, the conversion introduces a set of new reactions which consequently increase the running time of numerical simulation. On the other hand, approximations were proposed [23] to directly convert the complex rate laws into propensity functions of reactions. This approximation approach, however, introduces uncertainties to the model [26]. In the hybrid ODE/SSA approach, deterministic rate laws at the protein-protein interaction level are directly applied to the fast subset of reactions. Zhen et al [19] implemented this approach for the same simple three-variable model of the budding yeast cell cycle and its performance is much more efficient than the full stochastic counterpart [16]. Numerical experiments show that the hybrid ODE/SSA method yields a 100-fold speedup in running time, while maintaining almost the same accuracy. It is worth noting that the state-of-the-art deterministic budding yeast cell cycle models [17, 18] include more species and reactions. With a larger network, the exact SSA will be more expensive. To cope with this increasing computational complexity, our previous work [32] adopts the hybrid ODE/SSA modeling approach, based on Chen et al's comprehensive deterministic model [6] with over 60 species and 100 reactions. This work shows that the hybrid model can accurately reproduce the critical characteristics of the budding yeast cell cycle, however, it does not study the phenotypes of mutant strains.

The main contribution of this work is to present a comprehensive analysis of both the deterministic and the hybrid ODE/SSA models. In particular, we study the phenotypes of 122 mutant strains and define a quantitative criteria to determine the (partial) viability of mutant cells. Simulation results demonstrate that our hybrid ODE/SSA model can reproduce important characteristics of the budding yeast cell cycle control mechanism observed in wet-lab experiments, including statistics of cell cycle times and cell volumes at division, as well as average population of many proteins. Moreover, our results show that the hybrid ODE/SSA model can match well with reported experimental results for the phenotypes of 103 out of the 122 mutant strains.

This paper is organized as follows. Sec. 2 describes the hybrid ODE/SSA method. Sec.3 explains the detailed procedure to convert the deterministic model into its hybrid ODE/SSA counterpart. Simulation results are shown in Sec. 4. The paper is concluded in Sec. 5.

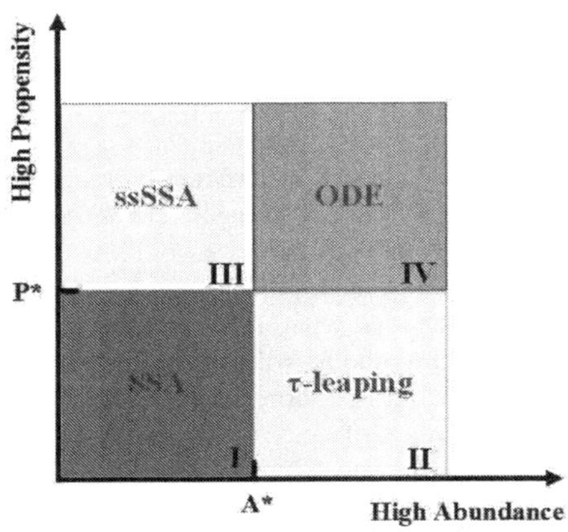

Figure 1: Partitioning a multi-scale system according to propensities of reactions and population of species [19].

2 BACKGROUND

As mentioned in the previous section, the main idea of the hybrid ODE/SSA modeling approach is to partition the set of reactions into two subsets of fast (S_{fast}), and slow (S_{slow}) ones, and generate solutions for each subset using appropriate numerical methods. Prior to explaining details of this hybrid approach, we first present the quantitative criterion to determine the slow and fast subsets.

Multi-scale systems are composed of species with various population scales, in addition to reactions with different scales of propensities. By using predefined thresholds for propensity A^* and population P^*, a system can be divided into four disjoint regions as shown in Fig. 1: a) region I that includes species with small populations and reactions with low propensities, b) region II that includes species with large populations and reactions with low propensities, c) region III with species that exhibit small populations and reactions with high propensities, and d) region IV that includes species with large populations and reactions with high propensities. By definition, regions I and IV can be clearly placed, respectively, into slow and fast subsets. However, the inclusion of regions II and III into fast and slow subsets depends on the partitioning strategy. One conservative strategy is to consider regions II and III within the slow subset and stochastically simulate all reactions in regions I, II, and III [13]. However, Liu et al [19] showed that if we put reactions in regions II and III into the "fast" subset, we may achieve a much better trade-off between efficiency and accuracy. Particularly, Liu et al discovered that we may put all reactions at the gene expression into region I, and then in the "slow" subset, while formulating reactions in all other regions by ODEs. Based on this observation, a hybrid cell cycle model [19] was constructed based on the same three-variable deterministic model. That hybrid model generates much more efficient simulation while maintaining similar accuracy as the complicated model [16].

Next, we present a step-by-step description for the hybrid ODE/SSA algorithm. Consider a well-stirred system with N species, denoted by $\mathcal{S} = \{S_1, \ldots, S_N\}$, which interact through M reaction channels in $\mathcal{R} = \{R_1, \ldots, R_M\}$. The reactions are partitioned into fast and slows subsets, such that $M{-}k$ reactions are formulated by ODEs in S_{fast}, and the remaining k slow reactions are simulated using the SSA in S_{slow}. Let $a_j(X(t), t)$ be the propensity function of the j-th reaction in S_{slow}, where $X(t) = (X_1(t), \ldots, X_N(t))$ is the state vector where each element $X_i(t)$ represents the number of molecules for species i at time t. Moreover, the state-change vector of the j-th reaction is $\boldsymbol{v}_j = (v_{j1}, \ldots, v_{jN})$, with v_{ji} represents the population change for species i when reaction j fires. In addition, let τ be the jump interval of the next slow reaction and μ be the index of the reaction that fires. The Hybrid ODE/SSA method in Algorithm 1 can be used to generate trajectories of state variables $X(t)$ as the time t moves forward. This algorithm only needs to simulate the firings of slow reactions, while integrating the fast subset of ODEs simultaneously in line 8. When a slow reaction fires, Algorithm 1 updates the corresponding state variables (in both fast and slow subsets). Our method does not implement the integral equation in line 7. Instead, we add the following equation to the ODE system:

$$\frac{dz}{dt} = a_0\left(X(t), t\right). \tag{1}$$

In each step, $z(t) = \log(r_1)$ is set as the initial value at time t. The algorithm numerically integrates (1) while solving the ODEs in line 7. The ODE integration stops when $z(t+\tau) = 0$, with τ denoting the solution of integral equation in line 7. At this time, the system variables are updated according to line 9. This procedure is repeated until Algorithm 1 reaches a stopping condition.

Algorithm 1 Hybrid Stochastic Simulation Algorithm

$HYBRID(S_{fast}, S_{slow}, X_0[1...N], t_0)$

1: $X \leftarrow X_0$
2: $t \leftarrow 0$
3: **while** $t < T$ **do**
4: Calculate the propensity function, a_i, for all reactions in slow subset $i = 1, ..., k$,
5: Calculate total propensity function: $a_0(X(t)) = \sum_{j=1}^{k} a_j(X(t))$,
6: Generate two uniform random variables r_1 and r_2 in $U(0, 1)$.
7: Integrate the ODE system until an event occurs at time $t + \tau$ such that
$$\int_t^{t+\tau} a_0(x(s))ds + log(r_1) = 0. \tag{2}$$
8: Select μ such that: $\sum_{i=1}^{\mu} a_i(x(t)) > r_2 a_0(x(t))$.
9: Update the state variables of S_{slow}: $X(t+\tau) \leftarrow X(t+\tau) + v_\mu$.
10: Update the time: $t \leftarrow t + \tau$.
11: **end while**

3 METHOD

We built our hybrid ODE/SSA cell cycle model based on the deterministic model proposed by Chen et al [6] for the budding yeast (*Saccharomyces Cerevisiae*). Since Chen's original model was formulated with normalized dimensionless concentrations, we have to convert the state variables from dimensionless concentrations into numbers of molecules for each species in a cell, so that we can compare corresponding numerical simulation results with wet-lab experimental measurements in Ball et al [1] and DiTalia et al [21]. In this section this conversion process is explained in details.

3.1 Conversion of concentration to the number of molecules

Without loss of generality, we use a simple example to explain the procedure for converting species' concentrations into numbers of molecules. Suppose we have the following reactions:

$$\emptyset \xrightarrow{k_s} P \xrightarrow{k_d} \emptyset, \tag{3}$$

where k_s and k_d are two constants that denote, respectively, the synthesis and degradation rates for protein P. Given that the ODE is formulated based on normalized concentration, the corresponding ODE for the reactions in (3) is given by:

$$\frac{d[P]_n}{dt} = k_s - k_d[P]_n, \tag{4}$$

where $[P]_n$ denotes the normalized concentration of protein P. To convert the normalized concentration $[P]_n$ to $[P]$, the actual concentration in a cell, we use a characteristic concentration C_P, such that $[P] = C_P[P]_n$. It is worth to note that C_P, as a scaling factor, cannot be arbitrarily chosen. For example, if P_1 and P_2 are involved in a reaction to form a complex P_3, then the characteristic concentration for these three species will have to be the same. This restriction prevents the possibility to choose different characteristic concentrations to match with experimental data. With this in mind, the number of molecules in a cell is calculated by

$$P = [P]N_AV(t) = C_P[P]_nN_AV(t), \tag{5}$$

where $V(t)$ is the volume of cell (in fL) and $N_A = 6.02\times10^{23}$ is the Avogadro number. One simplifying assumption made by some of the existing works, such as [2], is to consider a constant volume ($\approx 30fL$) for the budding yeast cell. However, this assumption obviously will lead to errors for the cell cycle model since the cell grows and divides in each round of cell cycle. In our model, we consider a varying volume $V(t)$ that changes proportionally with mass. That is, $V(t) = C_v \times [mass]$, where $C_v = V_0/M_0$ with $V_0 \approx 25\,fL$ and $M_0 \approx 1.2$. We assume that the cell grows exponentially with a growth rate μ, which can be formulated as

$$dV/dt = \mu V.$$

Thus, given that $[P] = P/V$, the differential equation for P can be formulated by:

$$\frac{dP}{dt} = V\frac{d[P]}{dt} + [P]\frac{dV}{dt} = V\frac{d[P]}{dt} + \mu P, \tag{6}$$

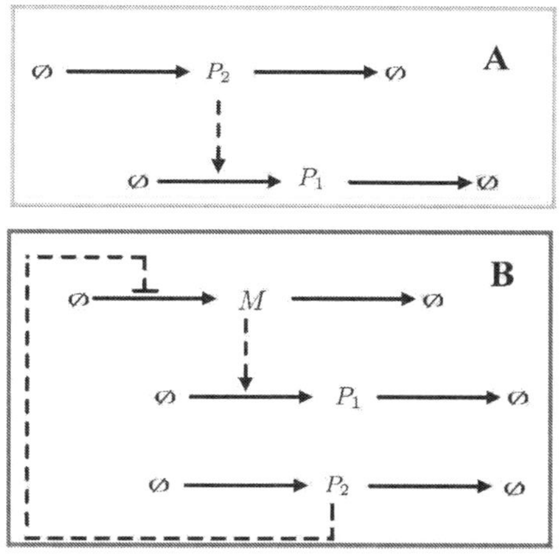

Figure 2: Example of a gene-protein regulatory network: (A) Synthesis and degradation of protein P_1 in protein-protein regulatory network. (B) Synthesis and degradation of protein P_1 in gene-protein regulatory network.

Using (5) and (6), we can rewrite (4) as:

$$\frac{dP}{dt} = k_s'[mass] - (k_d - \mu)P, \tag{7}$$

where $k_s' = k_sC_PN_A[P]_nC_v$. In (7), the ODE is based on the population of species P. This conversion procedure is applied to all equations of Chen's model to derive a deterministic model based on populations of species.

3.2 Adding mRNAs reaction network to the model

In the previous step, we scale the model to a population-based version, the next step is to include the dynamics of mRNAs in the model. Experimental results of the budding yeast cell cycle show a considerable variability with respect to populations of species, cell division times, and cell sizes before or after the division. The inclusion of mRNA dynamics in the model is critical to reproduce these observed variability. In our model, the protein regulation is modeled at the transcriptional level since transcriptional regulation is well studied in literature, while translational regulation is less known. In this section we again will explain the procedure of adding transcriptional regulation and mRNA dynamics to the model by a simple example. Fig. 2 (A) shows a simple protein-protein regulatory network consisted of proteins P_1 and P_2 that can be represented by the following ODE:

$$\frac{dP_1}{dt} = k_{s_{P_1}} f(P_2) - g(P_1, P_2)P_1, \tag{8}$$

where $f(P_2)$ and $g(P_1, P_2)$ are, respectively, the synthesis and degradation rate laws of protein P_1. Moreover, $k_{s_{P_1}}$ represents the background synthesis rate of P_1. We note that the above rate laws can be either traditional mass-action laws or any complex rate laws such as MM or Hill functions. After adding an mRNA species M to the model as shown in

Fig. 2 (B), equation 8 can be rewritten as:

$$\frac{dP_1}{dt} = k_{spm}M - g(P_1, P_2)P_1, \quad (9)$$

where the equation for M is formulated as

$$\frac{dM}{dt} = k_{sm}f(P_2) - k_{dm}M, \quad (10)$$

with k_{sm} and k_{dm} denoting, respectively, the synthesis and degradation rates of M. In addition, $k_{spm} = k_{sp}k_{dm}/f(P_2)$ is the synthesis rate of protein P_1 after adding mRNA M, which introduces a delay in synthesis of protein P_1. In transcriptional dynamics, mRNAs can be either regulated or unregulated. We note that (9) and (10) are general forms for a regulated mRNA. If $f(P_2) = 1$, (9) and (10) are then equations for unregulated mRNA.

As listed in Table 3, our model adds 11 unregulated and 8 protein-regulated mRNAs to the original deterministic model by defining appropriate synthesis and degradation rates for these mRNAs as well as translational rates from mRNAs to proteins. First, the degradation of an arbitrary mRNA is defined as $k_{dm} = \ln 2/t_m$, where t_m is the half-life time of a mRNA. In our model, mRNA half-life times are estimated based on reported experimental values [16]. If there is no half life time measurement for a mRNA, $t_m = 5$ minutes is considered, which is within a reasonable range for the half-life time of budding yeast mRNAs. Second, the synthesis rate k_{sm} is defined for regulated and unregulated mRNAs. For an unregulated mRNA, k_{sm} is chosen such that $\langle mRNA \rangle = k_{sm}/k_{dm}$ be close to the mean value of mRNA population measured in experiments. For a regulated gene, the total rate of mRNA synthesis is $\sum_{i=1}^{i=n} k_{sm,i}P_i$ where P_i and $k_{sm,i}$ are, respectively, the number of protein molecules and synthesis rate for the i-th protein that regulates the gene's expression. The rate constants, $k_{sm,i}, i = 1, \ldots n$, are chosen such that the number of mRNA molecules, averaged over a full cell cycle, approaches the mean number of mRNA molecules observed in experiments.

Furthermore, we add seven new ODEs into the model in order to capture the synthesis and degradation of proteins including $Cdc15_T$, $Tem1_T$, SBF_T, MBF_T, $Esp1_T$, $Mcm1_T$, and Apc_T. In fact, experimental data were not available for concentrations of many proteins at the time Chen's original model was developed [6]. However, measurements for many proteins are currently available [1, 21] and thus, corresponding changes have to be made. With this in mind, we add reactions for synthesis and degradation of these proteins. First, the degradation of a protein is estimated as $k_{dp} = \ln 2/t_p$, where $t_p = 15$ minutes is the estimated half-life time reported in literature [4]. Since transcription of these seven proteins are unregulated, we apply the same argument for (9) and (10) to these proteins.

3.3 Implementation

The aforementioned procedures in Sec. 3.1 and 3.2 yield a new deterministic model that 1) is based on the number of species, 2) includes many of important mRNAs, listed in Table 3, and 3) includes synthesis and degradation of seven proteins. ODEs resulted from the new deterministic model were solved using ODE solver *ode15s* in MATLAB. A hybrid ODE/SSA model can be naturally derived from the procedure, with all mRNA dynamics modeled in SSA and all other reactions modeled in ODEs. Numerical simulations of the hybrid ODE/SSA model are implemented in Fortran90. LSODAR is used for integrating the ODEs (the fast subsystem) and solve for the event equation (2). All simulations are executed in a Linux workstation with an Intel i7-3770 CPU and 16G memory. Simulation results of the hybrid ODE/SSA model are obtained for sufficiently large number of independent runs.

4 RESULTS AND DISCUSSION

In this section, we present a comprehensive performance analysis for both deterministic and hybrid models. Simulation results are compared with wet-lab experimental data, presented in Ball et al[1], which includes average populations for mRNAs. In addition, we use the dataset reported by Di Talia et al [21] that includes cell volumes at division, inter-division times, and average populations of proteins.

4.1 The model accurately describes the critical characteristics of the cell cycle

Fig. 3 demonstrates the oscillatory dynamics of selected proteins and mRNAs of the models for the wild-type cell. Figs. 3(A) and 3(B) show the deterministic trajectory of selected proteins and mRNAs molecule numbers, respectively. From Fig. 3(A), we can see that mass grows exponentially and when the Clb2 population drops below a threshold, the cell exits mitosis and the mass is divided asymmetrically between two newborn cells. This asymmetric division occurs according to the rule reported in Chen et al [7]. In fact, the mass of the smaller newborn cell, known as daughter cell, is $mass.f$, where $f = \exp(-1.026 + 32.k_g)$. Therefore, the mass of the larger cell, known as mother cell, will be $mass.(1 - f)$. In our model, the growth rate k_g is set to 7.25×10^{-3}. Furthermore, from Fig. 3(B) we can see that only CLB2 is regulated, while CDH1 and NET1 are unregulated. Such an observation stems from the fact that the number of Clb2 proteins increases with a delay, compared with other two unregulated mRNAs.

Figs. 3(C) and 3(D) show the time-course plots of the hybrid ODE/SSA model for the same proteins and mRNAs. In the hybrid ODE/SSA simulation, we do not follow the same division rule of the deterministic approach. Based on experimental observations [21], in glucose growing media, the ratio of mean volumes at birth of daughter and mother cells is 40:60. Therefore, in the hybrid stochastic simulation, $f = 0.4$. Compared with Fig. 3(A), Fig. 3(C) shows the randomness in populations of proteins, cycle times, and volumes of cells at division. Another interesting observation is that Fig. 3(D) exhibits more significant random behavior in comparison with Fig. 3(C). This is because all the reactions related to mRNAs are simulated by the SSA.

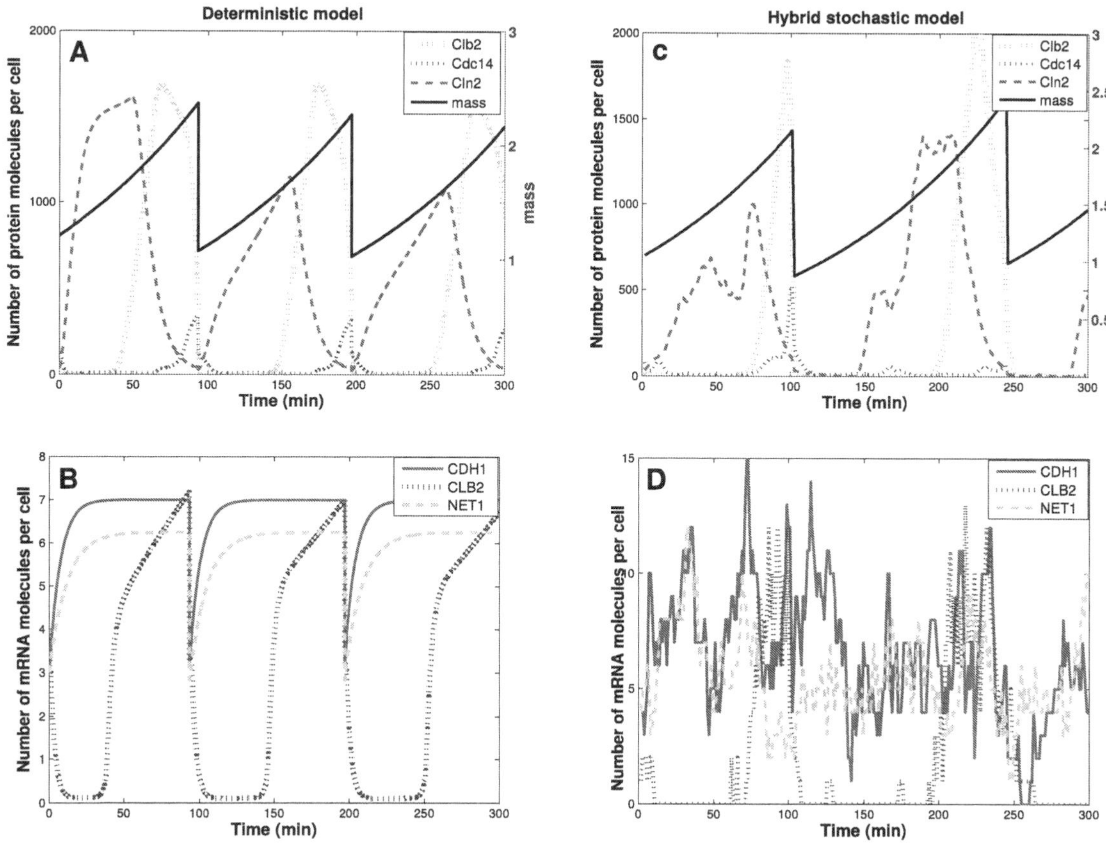

Figure 3: Oscillatory dynamics of selected proteins and mRNAs of deterministic and hybrid stochastic models: (A)-(B) Trajectories of selected proteins and mRNA simulated by the deterministic model. (C)-(D) Trajectories of selected proteins and mRNA simulated by the hybrid stochastic model.

Table 1: Statistics of deterministic and hybrid stochastic models compared with experimental data

Quantity	Mother Cell: (Mean,CV)			Daughter Cell : Mean (CV)		
	Deterministic model	Hybrid Model	Experimental data	Deterministic model	Hybrid Model	Experimental data
T_{div}	(83 , 0)	(87.5, 0.24)	(87 , 0.14)	(109.5 , 0)	(111.5 , 0.26)	(112.0 , 0.22)
T_{G1}	(18.85 , 0)	(20.9 , 0.31)	(16 , 0.5)	(32.6 , 0)	(33.8 , 0.5)	(37.0 , 0.5)
V_{birth}	(42.3 , 0)	(41.8 , 0.24)	(40 , 0.18)	(23.8 , 0)	(27.9 , 0.24)	(28.0 , 0.22)

Table 1 gives the statistics of critical cell cycle characteristics for both the deterministic and the hybrid ODE/SSA models. In particular, Table 1 shows statistics of cell cycle times, the times from division to budding (G1 time), and volumes at birth for both mother and daughter cells. From Table 1, we can see that our hybrid ODE/SSA model can reconstruct at least the first two moments of these stochastic characteristics in a cell cycle. The mean and coefficient of variation (CV = Standard Deviation/Mean) for these important metrics show very good agreement with experimental data. One notable difference is on the mean values of G1 times. Compared with experimental data, our hybrid model overestimates the average G1 time in mother cells and underestimates the average G1 time in daughter cells. Other than that all the rest measurements are in reasonable ranges.

The results shown in Table 1 validate our model and show that it can successfully capture various cell cycle features in exquisite details. The deterministic model also provides promising results for the mean values of critical characteristics. However, as expected, it cannot capture the variabilities in inter-division times and cell size.

To study the effect of transcriptional noise, the hybrid ODE/SSA model is simulated with all synthesis rates for mRNAs reduced to one third of their original levels and the synthesis rates for corresponding proteins increased by 3-fold. Thus the protein levels remain close to the original model while the mRNA levels reduce to one third. Fig. 4 shows its effect on the mean values and CVs of important cell cycle characteristics. While the mean of the cell cycle time does not change appreciably, the CV increases significantly.

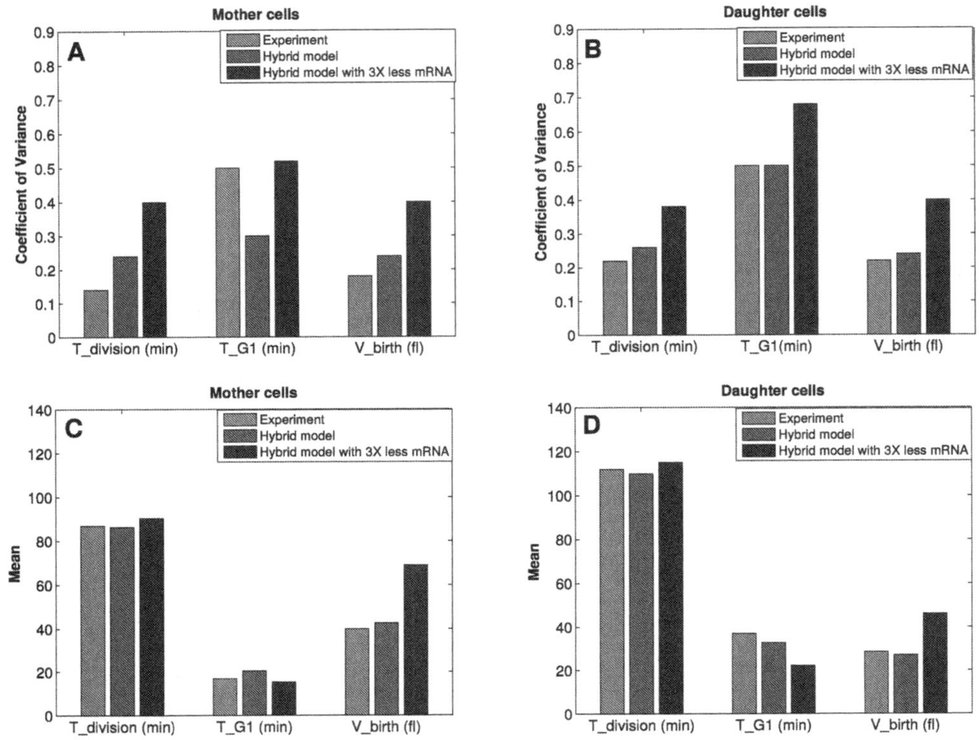

Figure 4: Effect of transcriptional activities on variability of the cell cycle characteristics. (A)-(B): Coefficient of variance of cycle time, G1 time and volume at birth for both mother and daughter cells. (C)-(D): Average cycle time, G1 time and volume at birth for both mother and daughter cells.

4.2 The model reproduces populations of proteins and mRNAs for wild-type cells

Table 2 presents the average populations of proteins. In Table 2 the protein populations generated by both deterministic and hybrid models are compared with experimental data [21]. To compare the statistics, in our simulation daughter and mother cells are counted separately and the mean values are reported in Table 2. We can see that both models can successfully generate the correct levels of mean values for proteins. In Table 3, the mRNA levels generated from both models are also compared with experimental data reported in Ball et al[1]. The results show that both models can successfully reproduce the mean values.

Table 2: Average number of protein molecules per cell compared with experimental data

Protein	Deterministic	Hybrid	Experiment
Cln2	950	1547	1500
Clb5	301	547	420
Clb2	822	881.49	650
CKI	942	1343	788
Swi5T	849	745.49	688
Tem1	973	667.26	573
Cdc15	338	238.40	238
Net1T	1752	1788.56	1590
Cdc55	4412	5060.12	5000
APC	405.39	611.04	500

4.3 The model conforms to the phenotype of more than 100 mutant strains

Prior to presenting the results of mutant tests, we elaborate the rules of viability in the hybrid model. In the original deterministic model, a cell is considered viable if following conditions are held: 1) the set of events, listed in [6], take place in a proper sequence, 2) the division occurs after budding, and 3) the cell mass does not exceed a predetermined threshold which is set particularly to 10 in Chen's model[6].

These three rules also apply to our hybrid stochastic model. In fact, a division that meets all those criteria is called a successful division, otherwise, it is considered as a failure. In a stochastic model, sometimes a cell won't divide. There is a probability of division, denoted by p. In numerical experiments, we can measure p by $\frac{\text{successful division}}{\text{successful division+failure}}$. From the measurement, a cell type is considered viable if this probability is greater than 0.7. This particular criteria can be explained as the following.

Table 3: Average molecule numbers of mRNAs compared with experimental data

mRNA	Deterministic	Hybrid	Experiment
mCdh1	6.64	6.67	-
mTem1	2.92	2.95	3.08
mCdc15	3.07	3.06	3.24
mCdc14	10.45	10.46	-
mNet1	5.8	5.85	6.25
mCdc55	6.72	6.67	-
mEsp1	3.09	3.10	3.29
mSBF	6.68	6.69	-
mMBF	6.69	6.71	-
mMcm1	5.64	5.75	5.95
mSic1	2.95	3.55	3.34
mCdc6	3.31	4.47	4.07
mSwi5	5.97	9.91	-
mAPC	6.63	6.68	-
mCln2	3.89	4.70	4.42
mClb5	4.20	7.35	-
mClb2	4.20	4.59	2.99
mCdc20	3.47	5.35	4.40
mPds1	4.88	6.76	-

Suppose there is an an initial population of N_0 cells. After one round of cell cycle, only pN_0 cells divide. So the next generation will have $(1+p)N_0$ cells ($2pN_0$ daughter cells and $(1-p)N_0$ mother cells that do not divide), although only $2pN_0$ cells have the potential to divide again (viable). For our analysis, we will only count those daughter cells that can divide. Thus $N_1 = 2pN_0$. Similarly, if we let N_k be the average number of cells after k cycles, we will have $N_k = (2p)^k N_0$. For a wild type cell, $p \approx 1$. After 20 cycles, we will have around $2^{20} \approx 10^6$ fold increase of population. In a wet-lab experiment, that increase will be very obvious and a small group of yeast cells will grow into a colony. If $p < 1$, we surely have to have $p > 0.5$, otherwise after every round, the number of viable cells will be even smaller than the previous round. For $0.5 < p < 1$, the criteria is tricky, we set up the criteria such that, after 20 rounds of cycles, the number of viable cells should have at least 1,000 fold increase. Thus we have $(2p^*)^{20} \approx 1000$. A simple estimation gives $p^* \approx \frac{\sqrt{2}}{2} \approx 0.7$.

From this argument, the choice of 0.7 seems a little arbitrary, since it is based on the assumption of 1,000 fold population increase after 20 rounds of cell cycles. What if we lower this criteria a little? It is easy to see that with $p = 0.65$, $N_{20} = (2p)^{20} \approx 190$, already significantly smaller than 10^3. Actually, in a wet-lab experiment, after 24 hours, yeast cells cannot go through 20 cycles. Wild type cells in glucose can have 16 cycles for mother cells in 24 hours. With $p = 0.7$, $N_{16} \approx 200$, and when $p = 0.65$, $N_{16} \approx 66$. Daughter cells take a little longer time to divide and many mutant cells take much longer time to divide. Overall, we think the criteria 0.7 is reasonable. Meanwhile we believe for $p < 0.65$ the cell type is clearly not viable, and for $p > 0.7$, the cell type is viable. If $0.65 \leq p \leq 0.7$, we may consider the cell type as partially viable.

Table 4: Performance comparison of the three models in terms of the number of consistent mutants.

Model	Number of consistent mutants
Chen	120/131
New deterministic	103/122
Hybrid stochastic	103/122

Based on this viability criteria, we assess the viability of 122 mutants of the budding yeast reported in Chen et al [6]. In contrast to the Chen model that only tracks the daughter cells, our model implements more realistic scenarios where both mother and daughter cells are tracked. Simulation results in Table 4 show that the proposed model successfully reproduces the phenotypes of 103 out of 122 mutant strains. Table 4 compares results of both deterministic and hybrid ODE/SSA simulations with the original model. To demonstrate the effect of randomness on mutant simulations, the simulation results of two mutants, namely *Cdc15-ts* **multicopy *CDC14*** and *Swi5Δ* ***GAL-CLB2***, are shown here. The first mutant is a temperature sensitive mutant of Cdc15 which can be rescued by multiple copies of ***CDC14*** genes, according to the experimental data [14]. The deterministic model in Fig. 5 (A) shows that cells consistently exit mitosis and divide. Using the hybrid ODE/SSA simulation, these mutants are viable with a probability of division $p \approx 0.73$, indicating that this mutant is viable. Nonetheless, some of the cells exit their cycle and stop dividing. To show this randomness, in Figs. 5(B) and (C), trajectories of a cell with the same initial values for *Cdc15-ts* **multicopy *CDC14*** are plotted from two independent simulation runs. In fact, Fig. 5(B) shows that the cell exits mitosis and divides successfully, while Fig. 5(C) demonstrates that the cell grows too large and never divides. On the other hand, experiments carried out by Toyn et al [15] show that the mutant strain of *Swi5Δ* ***GAL-CLB2*** is inviable. The computed probability of division for this mutant is $p \approx 0.29$ that implies the consistency of the model with experimental data. However, some of the cells eventually exit mitosis and divide successfully as shown in Fig. 5(E). For inviable cells, it is interesting to determine the phase in which cells are arrested. It is easy to observe from Figs. 5(D) and (F) that the abundance of Clb2 protein does not drop below the threshold, defined in Chen's model [6]. Thus, the cell is arrested in telophase.

As explained earlier, there are some mismatches between simulation results of our proposed hybrid ODE/SSA model and experimental data. In fact, 4 out of 19 inconsistencies already exist in Chen's original model. Hence, we do not expect our model to address these inconsistent cases. The remaining inconsistencies relate to *cdc15Δ* and *Sic1Δ* strains. The model requires more considerations to address the phenotypes of these mutant strains.

Here, we stress that the goal of this paper is to demonstrate the advantage of hybrid approach in modeling of a

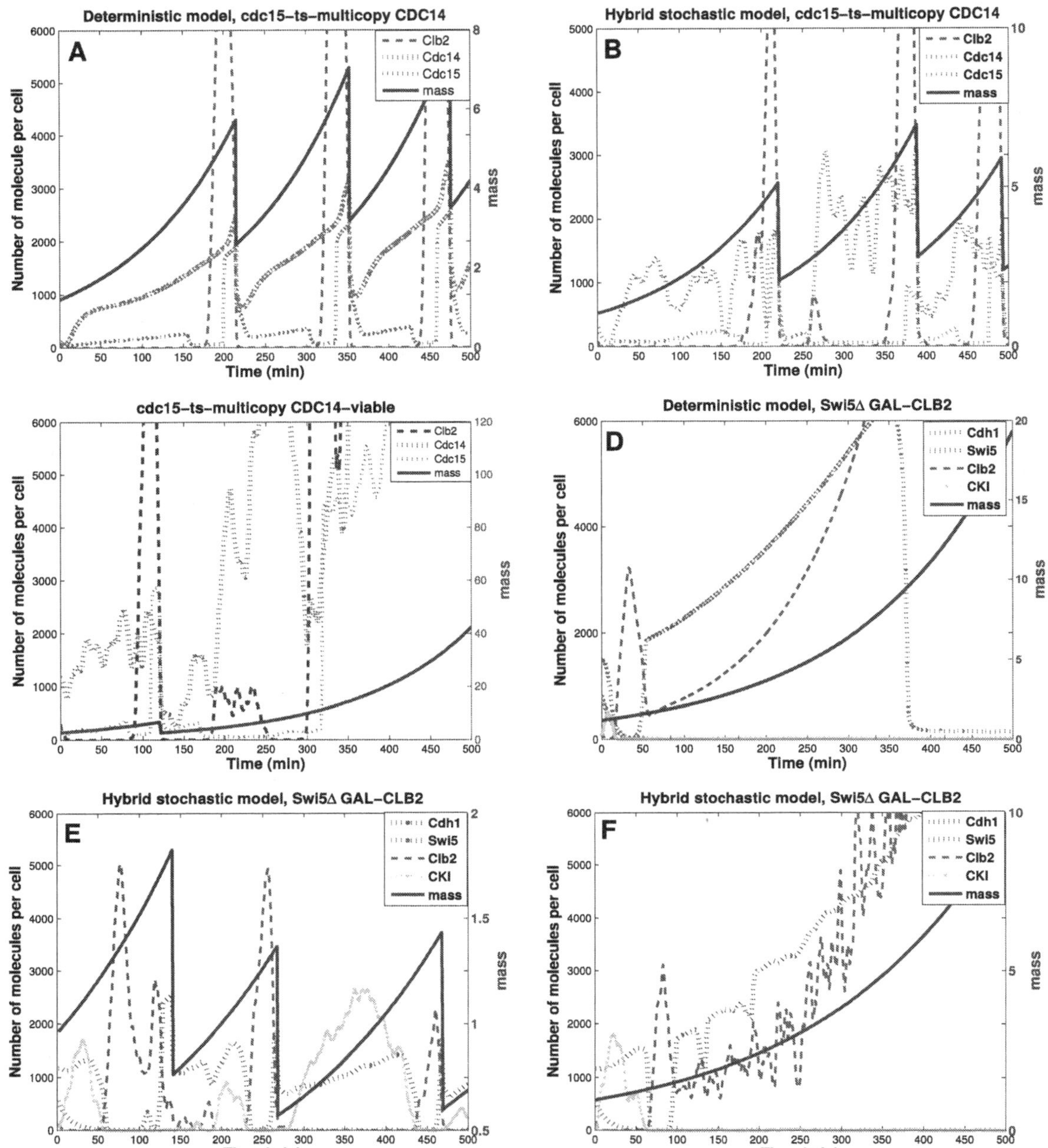

Figure 5: Trajectory of important species for selected mutant strains. (A) Trajectory of mutant *Cdc15-ts* multicopy *CDC14* generated by the deterministic model. (B)-(C) Trajectories of mutant *Cdc15-ts* multicopy *CDC14* generated by two independent runs of the stochastic model. (D) Trajectory of mutant *Swi5Δ GAL-CLB2* generated by the deterministic model. (E)-(F) Trajectories of mutant *Swi5Δ GAL-CLB2* generated by two independent runs of the stochastic model.

complex gene-protein regulatory network of the budding yeast. In our future work, we aim to reduce the number of inconsistencies observed in the model compared with the experimental data.

5 CONCLUSION AND DISCUSSION

In this paper, we present a hybrid ODE/SSA model to address the computational complexity of modeling molecular mechanisms that control the budding yeast cell cycle. The proposed hybrid method maintains the tradeoff between accuracy and efficiency by integrating deterministic and stochastic simulations for multi-scale system of the budding yeast. In order to incorporate the inherent molecular fluctuations of cell cycle in the model, we have enhanced the protein-protein regulatory network of the Chen's deterministic model to a gene-protein regulatory network where many of important mRNAs are included. We note that the proposed mRNA dynamics can be used to compare with RNA sequencing data. It will be a future direction of this work.

We have validated our proposed model by presenting comprehensive simulations. A set of 122 mutant strains have been simulated by both deterministic and hybrid ODE/SSA models. We have shown that results of the proposed model match very well with experimental data and reproduce the phenotypes of 103 out of 122 mutant cases. In addition, with manageable computational complexity, the proposed approach successfully reconstructs the first two moments of critical properties in the budding yeast cell cycle, such as cycle time, volume at division, and G1 time. The molecule abundance of proteins and mRNAs have also been captured in exquisite detail.

6 ACKNOWLEDGMENTS

This work was partially supported by the National Science Foundation under awards DMS-1225160, CCF-0953590, CCF-1526666, and MCB-1613741.

REFERENCES

[1] D. A. Ball, N. R. Adames, N. Reischmann, D. Barik, C. T. Franck, and J. J. Tyson. Measurement and modeling of transcriptional noise in the cell cycle regulatory network. *Cell Cycle*, 12(19):3203–3218, October 2013.

[2] D. A. Ball, T.-H. Ahn, P. Wang, K. C. Chen, Y. Cao, J. J. Tyson, J. Peccoud, and W. T. Baumann. Stochastic exit from mitosis in dudding yeast. *Cell Cycle*, 10(6):999–1009, March 2011.

[3] D. Barik, W. T. Baumann, M. R. Paul, B. Novak, and J. J. Tyson. A model of yeast cell-cycle regulation based on multisite phosphorylation. *Molecular System Biology*, 6(405):1–18, June 2010.

[4] A. Belle, A. Tanay, L. Bitincka, R. Shamir, and E. K. OShea. Quantification of protein half-lives in the budding yeast proteome. *Proceedings of the National Academy of Sciences of the United States of America.*

[5] S. Braunewell and S. Bornholdt. Superstability of the yeast cell-cycle dynamics: Ensuring causality in the presence of biochemical stochasticity. *Journal of Theoretical Biology*, 245(4):638 – 643, 2007.

[6] K. C. Chen, L. Calzone, A. Csikasz-Nagy, F. R. Cross, B. Novak, and J. J. Tyson. Integrative analysis of cell cycle control in budding yeast. *Molecular Biology of the Cell*, 15:3841–3862, August 2004.

[7] K. C. Chen, A. Csikasz-Nagy, B. Gyorffy, J. Val, B. Novak, and J. J. Tyson. Kinetic analysis of a molecular model of the budding yeast cell cycle. *Molecular Biology of The Cell*, 11(1):369–391, Jan 2000.

[8] M. A. Gibson and J. Bruck. Efficient exact stochastic simulation of chemical systems with many species and many channels. *The Journal of Physical Chemistry*, 104(2):1876–1889, February 2000.

[9] D. T. Gillespie. A general method for numerically simulating the stochastic time evolution of coupled chemical reactions. *Journal of Computational Physics*, 22(4):403–434, 1976.

[10] D. T. Gillespie. Exact stochastic simulation of coupled chemical reactions. *Journal of Physical Chemistry*, 81(25):2340–2361, 1977.

[11] D. T. Gillespie. Approximate accelerated stochastic simulation of chemically reacting systems. *Journal of Chemical Physics*, 115(4):1716–1733, July 2001.

[12] D. T. Gillespie and L. R. Petzold. Improved leap-size selection for accelerated stochastic simulation. *Journal of Chemical Physics*, 119(16):8229–8234, October 2003.

[13] E. L. Haseltine and J. B. Rawlings. Approximate simulation of coupled fast and slow reactions for stochastic chemical kinetics. *Journal of Chemical Physics*, 117(15):6959–6969, October 2002.

[14] S. L. Jaspersen, J. F. Charles, R. L. Tinker-Kulberg, and D. O. Morgan. A late mitotic regulatory network controlling cyclin destruction in saccharomyces cerevisiae. *Molecular Biology of The Cell.*

[15] T. JH, J. AL, D. JD, T. WM, and J. LH. The swi5 transcription factor of saccharomyces cerevisiae has a role in exit from mitosis through induction of the cdk-inhibitor sic1 in telophase. *Genetics.*

[16] S. Kar, W. T. Baumann, M. R. Paul, and J. J. Tyson. Exploring the roles of noise in the eukaryotic cell cycle. *PNAS*, 106(16):6471–6476, April 2009.

[17] P. Kraikivski, K. C. Chen, T. Laomettachit, T. Murali, and J. J. Tyson. From start to finish: computational analysis of cell cycle control in budding yeast. *System Biology and Applications*, 1(15016):1–9, December 2015.

[18] T. Laomettachit, K. C. Chen, W. T. Baumann, and J. J. Tyson. A model of yeast cell-cycle regulation based on a standard component modeling strategy for protein regulatory networks. *PLOS ONE*, pages 1–43, May 2016.

[19] Z. Liu, Y. Pu, F. Li, C. A. Shaffer, S. Hoops, J. J. Tyson, and Y. Cao. Hybrid modeling and simulation of stochastic effects on progression through the eukaryotic cell cycle. *Journal of Chemical Physics*, 136(3), January 2012.

[20] P. Lord and A. Wheals. Asymmetrical division of saccharomyces cerevisiae. *Journal of Bacteriology*, 142(3):808–818, June 1980.

[21] S. Di Talia, J. M. Skotheim, J. M. Bean, E. D. Siggia, and F. R. Cross. The effects of molecular noise and size control on variablility in the budding yeast cell cycle. *nature*, 448:947–952, August 2007.

[22] M. Miyata, M. Miyata, and M. Ito. The cell cycle in the fission yeast, schizosaccharomyces prombe. i. relationship between cell size and cycle time. *Cell Structure and Function*, 3(1):39–46, 1978.

[23] I. Mura and A. Csiksz-Nagy. Stochastic petri net extension of a yeast cell cycle model. *Journal of Theoretical Biology*, 254(4):850860, October 2008.

[24] S. R. Effects of stochasticity in models of the cell cycle: from quantized cycle times to noise induced oscillations. *Journal of Theoretical Biology*, 228(3):293–301, June 2004.

[25] C. V. Rao and A. P. Arkin. Stochastic chemical kinetics and the quasi-steady-state assumption: Application to the gillespie algorithm. *Journal of Chemical Physics*, 118(11):4999–5010, March 2003.

[26] M. Sabouri-Ghomi, A. Ciliberto, S. Kar, B. Novak, and J. J. Tyson. Antagonism and bistability in protein interaction networks. *Journal of Theoretical Biology*, 250(1):209–18, January 2008.

[27] A. Sveiczer, J. J. Tyson, and B. Novak. A stochastic, molecular model of the fission yeast cell cycle: role of the nucleocytoplasmic ratio in cycle time regulation. *Journal of Biophysical Chemistry*, (92):1–15, May 2001.

[28] J. J. Tyson. The coordination of cell growth and division–intentional or incidental? *BioEssays*, 2:72–77, February 1985.

[29] J. J. Tyson. Modeling the cell division cycle: Cdc2 and cyclin interactions. *PNAS*, 88(16):7328–7332, August 1991.

[30] J. J. Tyson and B. Novak. Regulation of the eukaryotic cell cycle: molecular antagonism, hysteresis, and irreversible transitions. *Journal of Theoretical Biology*, 210(2):249–263, May 2001.

[31] J. J. Tyson and B. Novak. Temporal organization of the cell cycle. *Current Biology*, 18(17):R759–R768, September 2008.

[32] S. Wang, M. Ahmadian, M. Chen, J. Tyson, and Y. Cao. A hybrid stochastic model of the budding yeast cell cycle control mechanism. *Proceedings of the 7th ACM International Conference on Bioinformatics, Computational Biology, and Health Informatics.*

[33] Y. Zhang, M. Qian, Q. Ouyang, M. Deng, F. Li, and C. Tang. Stochastic model of yeast cell-cycle network. *Physica D: Nonlinear Phenomena*, 219(1):35–39, July 2006.

RBFNN-based Modelling and Analysis for the Signal Reconstruction of Peripheral Nerve Tissue

Qichun Zhang
University of Essex
Wivenhoe Park
Colchester, Essex CO4 3SQ, UK
qichun.zhang@essex.ac.uk

Francisco Sepulveda
University of Essex
Wivenhoe Park
Colchester, Essex CO4 3SQ, UK
f.sepulveda@essex.ac.uk

ABSTRACT

This paper presents a novel modelling approach for complex nonlinear dynamic of the neural signal conduction along the myelinated or unmyelinated axons. Normally, this problem is described by the partial differential equation (PDE) combing cable equation, however the solution of the PDE approach is difficult to obtain and the interaction phenomena in nerve tissue is ignored. Based on radial basis function neural network (RBFNN), the membrane potential conduction can be restated by the dynamic of the weight vector while the shortcomings of the PDE approach can be fixed. Moreover, the neural signal prediction, the stimulation signal design and interaction characterization are further investigated using the presented model.

CCS CONCEPTS

• **Computing methodologies** → **Neural networks**; • **Hardware** → **Neural systems**; • **General and reference** → *Estimation*; • **Computer systems organization** → Embedded systems;

KEYWORDS

RBFNN, computational model, stimulation design, interaction characterization

1 INTRODUCTION

Modelling of the peripheral nerve tissue is a significant research topic. Moreover modelling is an effective approach to understand the generation of the action potential and the neural signal conduction. On the other hand, the accurate model is also an impressive tool to analyze the behaviour of the nerve fibres. From the view of the medical applications, modelling can be further considered as an essential guidance for the analysis and the design, such as the sensory rehabilitation of the next generation prosthesis [1, 2].

Since the Hodgkin-Huxley model [3] was presented in 1952, the associate membrane potential models have been developed by various approaches[4–6]. All of these existing results have been applied in many aspects such as neural encoding/decoding[7] etc. However, these mentioned results are mostly based on the analysis of the single myelinated/unmyelinated axon while the interaction [8] between the coupled axons in the nerve tissue has been ignored even this interaction phenomenon widely exists in vivo, for example, neuron and the (ephaptic) interaction [9]. Therefore, the interaction should be taken into account if we model the nerve tissue with multiple axons. Although the coupling factor[10] has been introduced to describe the mutual interaction, the computational complexity would be exploded with the increase of the number of investigated axons. In other words, the existing results can not be extended to the multi-axon case directly and the novel approach of modelling has to be developed.

Motivated by the modelling of stochastic distribution systems[11], the PDE description of the neural signal conduction can be restated by dynamic weights using RBFNN-based transformation. Due to the fact that RBFNN can estimate any nonlinear function, then the measured membrane potential of nerve tissue at any specified location can be represented by the weights of RBFNN. Along the nerve fibres, the conduction of neural signal with various locations can be described by the dynamics of the transformed weights. Based upon the data and system identification methods (RLS), the dynamics of the weights can be estimated by the linear state space format and the coefficient matrices can be identified. Similarly, the stimulation signal can also be rewritten by weights and the relationship between the membrane potential and stimulation can be further formulated by linear state space system with input vector. Once the model is obtained, the membrane potential at any location can be predicted using the initial weights. Moreover, the stimulation signal can be designed at any location to reshape the membrane potential. In addition, a novel approach is presented based on this model where the interaction can be further characterized.

As a summary, the contributions of this paper include as follows: 1) a novel RBFNN-based approach for modelling peripheral nerve tissue; 2) the potential applications of this model, such as nerve signal prediction and stimulation design; 3) a novel interaction characterization method.

2 MODELLING

2.1 Measurement and Dynamics of Membrane Potential

It has been shown that the measurement of the membrane potential should be formulated as the integral of the coupled axons' potentials [10]. Moreover, the nerve signal would be collected along the nerve fibre at various locations. In particular, the measurement and dynamics of membrane potential are shown in Figure 1 where the

Permission to make digital or hard copies of all or part of this work for personal or classroom use is granted without fee provided that copies are not made or distributed for profit or commercial advantage and that copies bear this notice and the full citation on the first page. Copyrights for components of this work owned by others than ACM must be honored. Abstracting with credit is permitted. To copy otherwise, or republish, to post on servers or to redistribute to lists, requires prior specific permission and/or a fee. Request permissions from permissions@acm.org.
ACM-BCB'17, August 20-23, 2017, Boston, MA, USA.
© 2017 ACM. 978-1-4503-4722-8/17/08...$15.00
DOI: http://dx.doi.org/10.1145/3107411.3107478

stimulation is applied to the nerve fibre at the same location of the membrane potential collection.

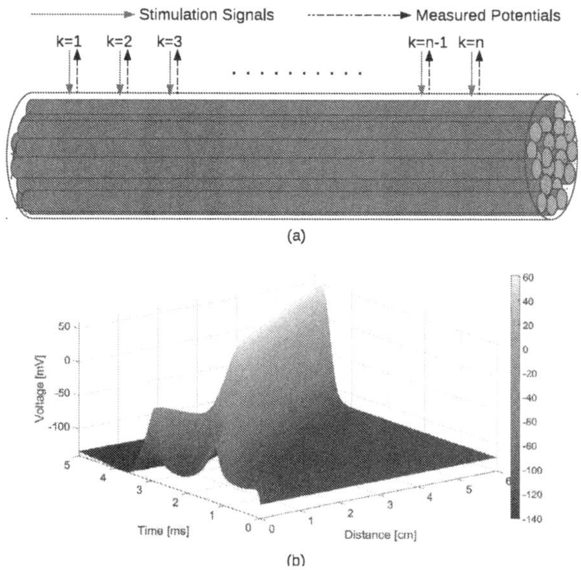

Figure 1: The problem description of this paper: (a) the signals are collected along the nerve fibre with multiple coupled axons where the index k denotes the location sampling; (b) the measured signal is shown by 3D mesh while the distance is discretized by k and the membrane potential is not with typical shape due to the neural interaction

2.2 Weight-based Transformation via RBFNN

Basically, the RBFNN can be used to approximate any nonlinear function such as the membrane potential with location sampling instance. Therefore, the membrane potential can be restated as follows:

$$V_k(t) = \sum_{i=1}^{m} w_{k,i} G_i + e_k \tag{1}$$

where the index k denotes the location sampling. w and G denote the weight and Gaussian radial basis function while m is the pre-specified number of radial basis functions. e stands for the approximation error and it is ignorable if value of m is sufficiently large and the weighs can be trained by data sets [12]. In order to illustrate this approximation, the transformation has been given in Figure 2

In other words, the membrane potential at location k can be represented by the m-dimensional weight vector which can be further denoted by the following vector.

$$W_k = \left[w_{k,1}, w_{k,2}, \ldots, w_{k,m}\right]^T \tag{2}$$

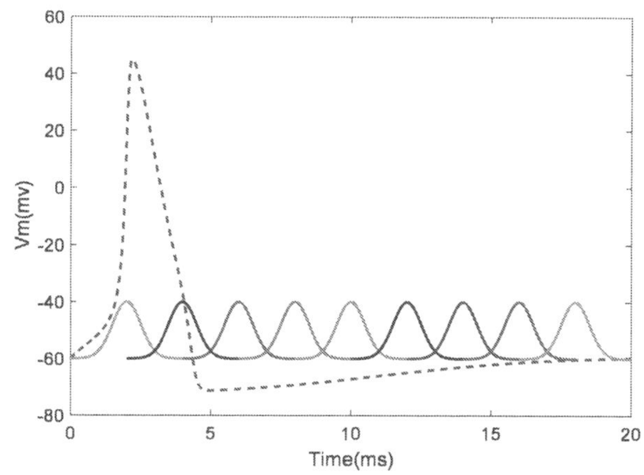

Figure 2: The approximation of the measured membrane potential via weights adjustment of RBFNN. (To make the illustration clear, all the Gaussian functions shown in figure are enlarged with different colours.)

Similarly, the stimulation signals can also be restated following the RBFNN transformation. Thus, we have

$$I_k(t) = \sum_{i=1}^{m} s_{k,i} G_i + e_k \tag{3}$$

where s denotes the weight of RBFNN. Then the weight vector can be expressed as follows.

$$S_k = \left[s_{k,1}, s_{k,2}, \ldots, s_{k,m}\right]^T \tag{4}$$

Notice that the numbers of the radial basis functions for these two transformation can be different which implies that the dimensions of W_k and S_k can be unmatched. However, in this paper, we select the same dimension for the simplicity of mathematical expression.

2.3 Weight-based Dynamics Description

Next, note that the membrane potential would be slightly changed by the conduction which means the weight vectors are different at different locations. Then the dynamics of the conduction can be described by the dynamics of the weight vectors which can be expressed as a general nonlinear function.

$$W_{k+1} = f(W_1, W_2, \ldots, W_k) \tag{5}$$

For more general situation, the stimulation signals should also be taken into account along with the investigated nerve fibre. Thus the nonlinear function should be further expressed as follows.

$$W_{k+1} = \bar{f}(W_1, W_2, \ldots, W_k, S_{k+1}) \tag{6}$$

To obtain the relationship between the weight vectors, the linearization operation can be considered to simplify the identification due to the fact that the structure of the general nonlinear function $\bar{f}$ is unknown. Then the dynamics can be suitably described by the following recursive format.

$$W_{k+1} = AW_k + BS_{k+1} \tag{7}$$

where A and B are coefficient matrices with appropriate dimension. Meanwhile, equation (1) can be rewritten by

$$V_k(t) = CW_k \tag{8}$$

while

$$C = [G_1, G_2, \ldots, G_m] \tag{9}$$

Combining equations (8) and (7), the complete RBFNN-based model is obtained as a representative of the nerve signal conduction.

Next, the system identification method should be used here to estimate the matrices A and B. As a results, we can obtain that

$$V_k(t) = TS_k \tag{10}$$

where T can be considered as a transfer function. It can be formulated by

$$T = C\left(\bar{I} - z^{-1}A\right)^{-1}B \tag{11}$$

while $\bar{I}$ denotes identity matrix and z^{-1} stands for backward shift operator.

Since the stimulation signal can also rewritten as the format of Equation (8), Equation (10) can be restated as follows.

$$CT^{-1}V_k(t) = CS_k = I_k(t) \tag{12}$$

with further expression

$$V_k(t) = CA\left(C^TC\right)^{-1}C^TV_{k-1}(t) + CB\left(C^TC\right)^{-1}C^TI_k(t) \tag{13}$$

Once the signals V_k, V_{k-1} and I_k are collected, the coefficient matrices A and B can be obtained since matrix C is known. In particular, the simplified form can be used to reduce the complexity if the weight vector can be collected for each location sampling. Then we can have

$$w_{k,i} = \sum_{j=1}^{m} a_{ij}w_{k-1,j} + \sum_{j=1}^{m} b_{ij}s_{k,j}, i = 1, \ldots, m \tag{14}$$

where a_{ij} and b_{ij} denote the elements of matrices A and B.

Rearranging Equation (14), it results in the standard form for parameter identification.

$$w_{k,i} = \theta_i^T\Phi_k, i = 1, \ldots, m \tag{15}$$

where

$$\theta_i = [a_{i1}, \ldots, a_{im}, b_{i1}, \ldots, b_{im}]^T \tag{16}$$

$$\Phi_k = \left[W_{k-1}^T, S_k^T\right]^T \tag{17}$$

Then the recursive least square (RLS) algorithm [13] can be used to estimate the parameter vector θ as follows.

$$\theta_i(l+1) = \theta_i(l) + \frac{P(l-1)\Phi_k\varepsilon(l)}{1 + \Phi_k^TP(l-1)\Phi_k} \tag{18}$$

$$\varepsilon(l) = w_{k,i} - \theta_i^T(l)\Phi_k \tag{19}$$

$$P(l) = \left(\bar{I} - \frac{P(l-1)\Phi_k}{1 + \Phi_k^TP(l-1)\Phi_k}\right)P(l-1) \tag{20}$$

where l is the index of the identification iteration.

Once the parameter vector θ_i estimation is completed, the modelling of peripheral nerve tissue is done.

2.4 Algorithm

Based on the materials mentioned above, the algorithm procedure is summarized by pseudocode as follows.Particularly, the matrices A and B are time-variant although they can be assumed as constant within a small segment.

Algorithm 1 Modelling Algorithm

Require: Data collection of stimulation signal I and membrane potential V
Input: I and V for each time and location sampling
Output: The coefficient matrices A and B

```
Initialization: Pre-specified the number of RBFs m and approximation error threshold e_th
for k ≤ n do
    Collect the time sampling data set of V and I at location index k
    while e ≥ e_th do
        e = || V_k − Σ_{i=1}^{m} w_{k,i} G_i ||
        e = || I_k − Σ_{i=1}^{m} s_{k,i} G_i ||  {Training the RBFNN via weights for membrane potential and stimulation signal}
    end while
    Format the weight vector W_k and S_k
    for i ≤ m do
        Estimate θ_i via RLS
    end for
    Rearrange the elements of the matrices A_k and B_k
    k = k + 1
end for
Rearrange the sequence of the matrices A and B
```

3 SIMULATION

Following the presented algorithm, the membrane potential can be transformed to weight vector since the RBFNN is used with training. For example, the membrane potential at $k = 50$ is shown by Figure 3 where all the simulation data is from the 3D mesh in Figure 1.

Based on the neural network, the training performance is given by Figure 4 which indicates that the performance with mean-square criteria. The estimation error decreases by the number increase of the epochs.

Notice that the computational loads would be drastically increased if the number of the basis functions are chosen as a large number. Without loss of the generality, the simple numerical example is given in this paper where we only pre-specified 5 basis functions. Although the accuracy of the weight transformation is weak, the performance and procedure of the presented algorithm can be demonstrated.

The stimulation signal is an intracellular current density of $0.1mA/cm^2$ and the duration is $0.2ms$, which is similar to the settings in [5]. When this stimulus is applied to one axon, the responses of other axons would achieve the action potential due to the neural interaction. Moreover, the measured membrane potentials at different location sampling are expressed by Table 1 via weights.

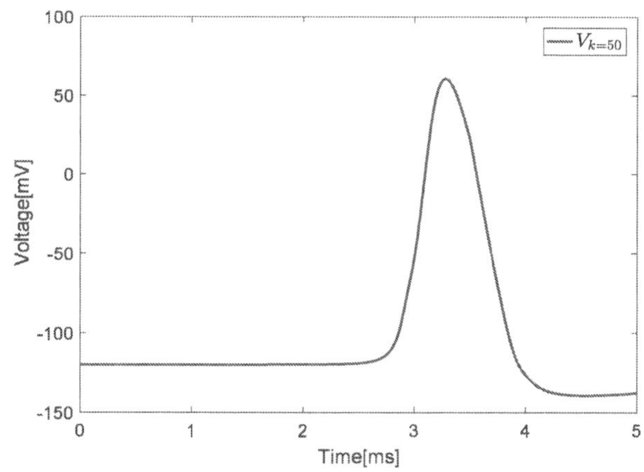

Figure 3: The membrane potential at location sampling k = 50

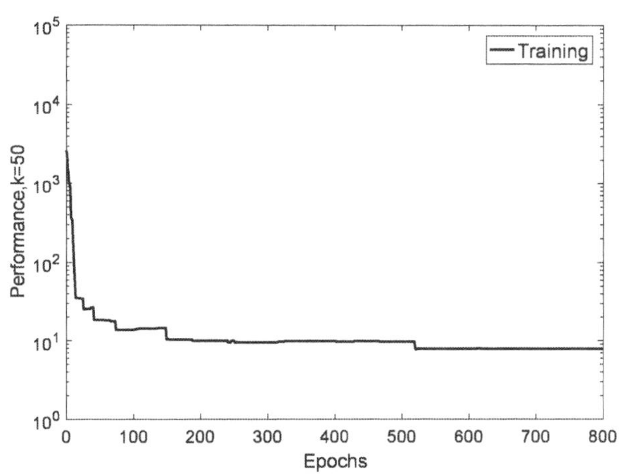

Figure 4: The training performance of the neural networks for membrane potential $V_{k=50}$. It shows that the accuracy would be improved if the network is sufficiently trained.

Table 1: Weight transformation of membrane potential

Sampling Index	Membrane Potential Weight Vector W	Stimulation Weight Vector S
k=0	0	-
k=1	3.7750 0.8900 5.0000 3.0450 0	0 0.0050 0 0 0
k=2	3.7800 0.8600 5.0000 3.0450 0	0
k=3	3.7950 0.8400 5.0000 3.0450 0	0
k=4	3.8150 0.8250 5.0000 3.0500 0	0
k=5	3.8450 0.8200 5.0000 3.0600 0	0
k=10	4.0100 0.8250 5.0000 3.0850 0	0
k=20	4.2150 0.9250 5.0000 2.6350 0	0
k=50	1.4200 4.9350 0 1.2400 3.3250	0
k=70	1.7800 5.0000 0 2.2900 4.9950	0
k=100	2.1300 0 3.5650 1.0800 4.5550	0

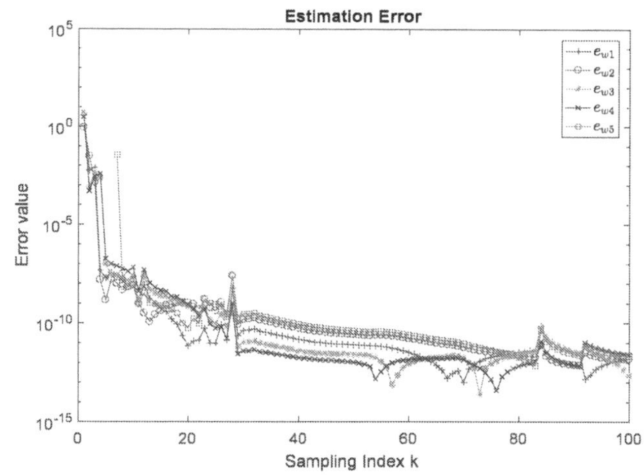

Figure 5: The estimation error of the weights for membrane potential at each location sampling.

From the adjustment of the weights, the conduction of the nerve signal is very clear, then the dynamics of these weights can be estimated following the presented algorithm. Notice that we assume $W_{k=0} = 0$ then the matrix B can be calculated directly based on the statics relationship between the membrane potential and stimulation with $k = 1$. Thus we have

$$B = \begin{bmatrix} 0 & 755 & 0 & 0 & 0 \\ 0 & 178 & 0 & 0 & 0 \\ 0 & 1000 & 0 & 0 & 0 \\ 0 & 609 & 0 & 0 & 0 \\ 0 & 0 & 0 & 0 & 0 \end{bmatrix}$$

Based upon RLS algorithm, the estimation error curves of the membrane potential weights are shown by Figure 5 while all the curves are convergent and the errors are very small. For example, the coefficient matrix A is obtained at $k = 100$.

$$A = \begin{bmatrix} 1, 5.6228e-12, 1.0059e-11, 1.0854e-12, -1.7648e-12 \\ 5.6230e-12, 1, -4.0032e-12, -4.1416e-13, 8.9930e-13 \\ 1.0059e-11, -4.0031e-12, 1, -3.2742e-13, 1.1375e-12 \\ 1.0853e-12, -4.1394e-13, -3.2732e-13, 1, 4.8573e-13 \\ -1.7651e-12, 8.9971e-13, 1.1377e-12, 4.8596e-13, 1 \end{bmatrix}$$

Therefore, the complete model can be formulated by $W_{k+1} = AW_k + BS_{k+1}$. Due to the fact that the membrane potentials are strong nonlinear, the estimated coefficient matrix A should be considered as a time-vary or interval-based time vary matrix which would improve the accuracy of the modelling.

4 DISCUSSIONS

4.1 Nerve Signal Prediction

It has been shown that the presented model is in discrete-time form based on the collection of the data with pre-specified locations. Is it possible to predict the membrane potential for any location along the nerve fibre? The solution will be discussed in this subsection.

At first, the derivative of the weight vector along the location can be replaced by the difference as follows.

$$\frac{\partial W}{\partial x} = \frac{W_{k+1} - W_k}{\Delta x} \tag{21}$$

where x and Δx denote the measurement of the location and the difference of the location, respectively.

Using Equation (21), the presented model can be further expressed by

$$\frac{\partial W}{\partial x} = \frac{1}{\Delta x}\left(A - \bar{I}\right) W(x) + \frac{1}{\Delta x} BS(x) \tag{22}$$

Note that the weight vector and stimulation are the functions in terms of the location.

Therefore, the weight vector for any location can be predicted with the initial values and the membrane potential are obtained based on the predicted weights. The presented analysis of the neural signal conduction reduces the cost of implementation because it is impossible to measure infinite location samplings.

4.2 Stimulation Design

Stimulation signal design is a significant challenge for neural medical applications, such as the sensory rehabilitation via next generation prosthesis. In particular, the response of the nerve fibre should be reproduced by electrical stimulation with pre-specified location.

Based on the presented model, the stimulation design can be transformed as the weights tracking control problem. Suppose that we have the reference weights for the location samplings which is denoted by $W_{ref,k}$.

To achieve the perfect tracking (the error converges to zero), the integrator should be introduced into the stimulation design which is defined as follows.

$$\varepsilon_{k+1} - \varepsilon_k = W_{ref,k} - W_k \tag{23}$$

Thus the model with the tracking integral can be formulated by

$$\begin{bmatrix} \varepsilon_{k+1} \\ W_{k+1} \end{bmatrix} = \bar{A} \begin{bmatrix} \varepsilon_k \\ W_k \end{bmatrix} + \bar{B} S_{k+1} + \begin{bmatrix} W_{ref,k} \\ 0 \end{bmatrix} \tag{24}$$

where

$$\bar{A} = \begin{bmatrix} I & -I \\ 0 & A \end{bmatrix}, \bar{B} = \begin{bmatrix} 0 \\ B \end{bmatrix} \tag{25}$$

Based on the control theory of linear system [14], the stimulation signal can be designed as a closed-loop input with linear gain matrix.

$$S_{k+1} = K \begin{bmatrix} \varepsilon_k \\ W_k \end{bmatrix} \tag{26}$$

where K should be selected to make the matrix $\bar{A} + \bar{B}K$ Hurwitz.

Notice that any existing design method from linear control system design can be applied here to design the stimulation signal such as PID[15], LQR[16], etc.

Moreover, in this paper we assume that the stimulation and the membrane potential are statics at same location. Also in practice, we only use one electrode as the stimuli at one single location sampling, which means that the model can be divided into two parts: The stimulation signal leads to a membrane potential response as a statics function; then the stimulated membrane potential can be considered as the initial value and recursively update as an autonomous system.

4.3 Interaction Characterization

The interactions between the coupled axons in nerve fibre cannot be ignored which has been discussed in Section I. Following the existing analysis in [10], this interaction can be characterized by the mutual coupling factor matrix based on the Hodgkin-Huxley model. In this paper, the interaction is implicit because it is impossible to collect the membrane potential separately for each individual axon. Therefore, a novel characterization approach is presented in this section.

Based upon the presented model with weight vector, the interaction has already been include in the transformed weight vector. In order to characterize the interaction, we only need to investigate the characterization of the weight vector. Following this basic idea, the covariance-like matrix of the weight vector can be defined as follows.

$$P_k = W_k W_k^T, Q_k = S_k S_k^T, \tag{27}$$

Which results in the following equation.

$$P_{k+1} = (AW_k + BS_{k+1})(AW_k + BS_{k+1})^T \tag{28}$$

$$= AP_kA^T + BQ_{k+1}B^T + AW_kS_{k+1}^TB^T + BS_{k+1}W_k^TA^T \tag{29}$$

Mostly, the stimulation signals are selected as zero, then the terms with S can be eliminated and the equation above can be expressed by

$$P_{k+1} = AP_kA^T \tag{30}$$

Moreover, the interaction can be considered as time-invariant which means that the dynamics of the weight vector will not affect the interaction characterization. Thus, we denote

$$\bar{P} = \lim_{k\to\infty} P_k \tag{31}$$

which leads to

$$\bar{P} = A\bar{P}A^T \tag{32}$$

It shows that the steady value of the matrix P can be selected to uniquely characterize the membrane potential, it can characterize the interaction naturally. As the matrix P is real symmetric matrix, the eigenvalue of $\bar{P}$ can be further describe this characterization for simplicity.

5 CONCLUSIONS

The modelling problem has been investigated for complex nonlinear dynamics of the nerve signal conduction along the myelinated or unmyelinated axons. Different from the existing PDE appraoch and the associated results, a novel approach has been presented based on the RBFNN while the membrane potential has been rewritten by the weight vector and the conduction of the nerve signal has been restated by the dynamics of the weights. In addition, the nerve signal prediction, the stimulation signal design and interaction characterization can also be discussed using the presented model, respectively. In particular, the contributions and novelties of this paper can be concluded as 1) a novel RBFNN-based approach for modelling peripheral nerve tissue; 2) the potential applications of this model, such as nerve signal prediction and stimulation design; 3) a novel interaction characterization method.

ACKNOWLEDGMENTS

This work is supported by UK's EPSRC-funded SenseBack project with grant number EP/M025977/1.

REFERENCES

[1] F. Kolbl, M. C. Juan, and F. Sepulveda. Impact of the angle of implantation of transverse intrafascicular multi-channel electrodes on axon activation. In *2016 IEEE Biomedical Circuits and Systems Conference (BioCAS)*, pages 484–487, Oct 2016.

[2] Stanisa Raspopovic, Marco Capogrosso, Francesco Maria Petrini, Marco Bonizzato, Jacopo Rigosa, Giovanni Di Pino, Jacopo Carpaneto, Marco Controzzi, Tim Boretius, Eduardo Fernandez, et al. Restoring natural sensory feedback in real-time bidirectional hand prostheses. *Science translational medicine*, 6(222):222ra19–222ra19, 2014.

[3] Alan L Hodgkin and Andrew F Huxley. A quantitative description of membrane current and its application to conduction and excitation in nerve. *The Journal of physiology*, 117(4):500, 1952.

[4] B Frankenhaeuser and AF Huxley. The action potential in the myelinated nerve fibre of xenopus laevis as computed on the basis of voltage clamp data. *The Journal of Physiology*, 171(2):302, 1964.

[5] F Rattay. The basic mechanism for the electrical stimulation of the nervous system. *Neuroscience*, 89(2):335–346, 1999.

[6] Sébastien Joucla and Blaise Yvert. Improved focalization of electrical microstimulation using microelectrode arrays: a modeling study. *PloS one*, 4(3):e4828, 2009.

[7] Liam Paninski, Jonathan Pillow, and Jeremy Lewi. Statistical models for neural encoding, decoding, and optimal stimulus design. *Progress in brain research*, 165:493–507, 2007.

[8] John W Clark and Robert Plonsey. A mathematical study of nerve fiber interaction. *Biophysical journal*, 10(10):937–957, 1970.

[9] György Buzsáki, Costas A Anastassiou, and Christof Koch. The origin of extracellular fields and currents - eeg, ecog, lfp and spikes. *Nature reviews neuroscience*, 13(6):407–420, 2012.

[10] Qichun Zhang and Francisco Sepulveda. A statistical description of pairwise interaction between the nerve fibres. In *Neural Engineering (NER), 2017 8th International IEEE/EMBS Conference on*. IEEE, 2017, in press.

[11] H. Wang. *Bounded Dynamic Stochastic Systems: Modelling and Control*. Advances in Industrial Control. Springer London, 2000.

[12] Steve A Billings and Guang L Zheng. Radial basis function network configuration using genetic algorithms. *Neural Networks*, 8(6):877–890, 1995.

[13] S Lawrence Marple. *Digital spectral analysis: with applications*, volume 5. Prentice-Hall Englewood Cliffs, NJ, 1987.

[14] Huibert Kwakernaak and Raphael Sivan. *Linear optimal control systems*, volume 1. Wiley-interscience New York, 1972.

[15] Karl Johan Åström and Tore Hägglund. *Advanced PID control*. ISA-The Instrumentation, Systems and Automation Society, 2006.

[16] Donald E Kirk. *Optimal control theory: an introduction*. Courier Corporation, 2012.

Reverse Engineering Gene Networks: A Comparative Study at Genome-scale

Sriram P. Chockalingam[†]
Institute for Data Engineering and Science
Georgia Institute of Technology
Atlanta, GA, USA
srirampc@gatech.edu

Maneesha Aluru[†]
School of Biology
Georgia Institute of Technology
Atlanta, GA, USA
maneesha.aluru@biology.gatech.edu

Hongqing Guo
Department of Genetics, Development, and Cell Biology
Iowa State University
Ames, IA, USA
hguo@iastate.edu

Yanhai Yin
Department of Genetics, Development, and Cell Biology
Iowa State University
Ames, IA, USA
yin@iastate.edu

Srinivas Aluru
School of Computational Science and Engineering
Georgia Institute of Technology
Atlanta, GA, USA
aluru@cc.gatech.edu

ABSTRACT

Motivation: Reverse engineering gene networks from expression data is a widely studied problem, for which numerous mathematical models have been developed. Network reconstruction methods can be used to study specific pathways, or can be applied at the whole-genome scale to analyze large compendiums of expression datasets to uncover genome-wide interactions. However, few methods can scale to such large number of genes and experiments, and to date, genome-scale comparative assessment of network reconstruction methods has largely been limited to simpler organisms such as *E. coli*.

Results: In this paper, we analyze 11,760 microarray experiments on the model plant *Arabidopsis thaliana* drawn from public repositories. We generate genome scale networks of Arabidopsis using three different methods – Pearson correlation, mutual information, and graphical Gaussian modeling – and analyze and compare these networks to test for their robustness in successfully recovering relationships between functionally related genes. We demonstrate that functional grouping of microarray experiments into different tissue types and experimental conditions is important to discover context-specific interactions. Our comparisons include benchmarking against experimentally confirmed interactions, the Arabidopsis network resource AraNet, and study of specific pathways. Our results show that networks generated by the mutual information based method have better characteristics in terms of functional modularity as measured by both connected component and sub-network extraction analysis with respect to gene sets selected from brassinosteroid and stress regulation pathways.

Availability: The classification datasets and constructed genome-scale networks are publicly available at the location http://alurulab.cc.gatech.edu/arabidopsis-networks

CCS CONCEPTS

• **Applied computing → Bioinformatics**; **Biological networks**; **Systems biology**;

KEYWORDS

Genome-scale Gene Networks; Arabidopsis Thaliana; Microarrays

1 INTRODUCTION

Reverse engineering gene networks from gene expression data obtained through microarray or RNA-seq experiments is a widely studied problem in systems biology. Several mathematical techniques have been proposed and applied that vary in the types of interactions they uncover, tradeoff between specificity and sensitivity, and the ability to scale to larger number of genes or expression profiles. Techniques that have been frequently utilized include Pearson correlation [18, 23], graphical Gaussian modeling (GGM) [17, 26, 29], information theory [3, 4, 11, 21, 32], and Bayesian networks [12, 22, 24, 31]. The bewildering array of network reconstruction methods spurred review articles [16, 27] and community efforts to assess performance on benchmark datasets [19, 20].

To date, comparative studies of gene network reconstruction methods have largely been limited to small network sizes and/or experiments, and the few studies conducted at the whole-genome scale were still limited to unicellular organisms such as *E. coli* and well below the scale of experiments analyzed here. In addition, many studies were performed in silico with synthetic networks and synthetically generated datasets, for convenience of validation. This is likely due to a number of factors, including the scaling limitations of the methods themselves, and the difficulty in establishing ground truth. For example, Soranzo *et al.* evaluate network construction

[†]The first two authors should be regarded as joint first authors.

Permission to make digital or hard copies of all or part of this work for personal or classroom use is granted without fee provided that copies are not made or distributed for profit or commercial advantage and that copies bear this notice and the full citation on the first page. Copyrights for components of this work owned by others than ACM must be honored. Abstracting with credit is permitted. To copy otherwise, or republish, to post on servers or to redistribute to lists, requires prior specific permission and/or a fee. Request permissions from permissions@acm.org.
ACM-BCB'17, August 20-23, 2017, Boston, MA, USA.
© 2017 ACM. 978-1-4503-4722-8/17/08...$15.00
DOI: http://dx.doi.org/10.1145/3107411.3107428

methods on synthetic datasets for 100 genes and genome-scale *E. coli* networks inferred from 445 experiments [27]. It has been shown that using the same network inference methods, quality of resulting networks from real data are not as good when compared to synthetic data [2].

We argue that an important use of network methods is to apply them to infer genome-scale networks from large gene expression data sets in public repositories, and utilize the resulting networks to develop biologically relevant hypotheses. By doing so, we can leverage already available big data and potentially reduce experimental costs in furthering knowledge of partially characterized pathways and predicting gene function. Many studies elaborate underlying complexities including the large number of genes, underdetermined nature of the problem, lack of comprehensive models for gene regulation, and lack of comprehensive information in expression data alone such as the effect of post-translations modifications. These complexities are further exacerbated at the genome-scale. Thus, it is not even clear how a particular inference method can be effectively utilized and what predictive power the inferred networks have for complex multicellular eukaryotic organisms such as plants. This work represents the first genome-scale comparative study on plants, and addresses the above questions using *Arabidopsis thaliana* microarray datasets.

Arabidopsis has long been a model organism in plant biology, and for studying complex multicellular organisms. During the past 40-50 years, it has been the focus of intense molecular, genetic, biochemical and physiological studies, and was the first plant genome to be fully sequenced. This led to the accumulation of a vast number of resources for manipulating and understanding its genome, and for testing new concepts in functional genomics. The availability of large-scale gene expression datasets in public repositories spurred the development of gene network models in Arabidopsis. Prior attempts to construct genome-scale networks of Arabidopsis include a Pearson correlation network of 6,206 genes from 1,094 microarrays [18], a 6,760 gene network from 2,045 microarrays using Pearson correlation and graphical Gaussian modeling [17], and a 15,495 gene network from 3,137 microarrays using mutual information [3]. Since the 2013 study, the available microarray datasets for Arabidopsis have more than quadrupled.

In this paper, we present a comparative study of network inference methods in the context of building Arabidopsis whole-genome networks. We make the following contributions:

- Demonstrate that functional grouping of experiments and building multiple networks based on these groupings is crucial when dealing with diverse and very large expression data sets,
- Compare network inference methods based on Pearson correlation, graphical Gaussian modeling, and mutual information,
- Propose network validation methods at genome-scale in the absence of clearly established ground truth, and
- Study efficacy of the resulting networks in brassinosteroid and dehydration stress pathways.

In addition, the classification datasets and the genome-scale networks we generated are a valuable resource for future Arabidopsis research.

2 METHODS

2.1 Datasets and Preprocessing

We collected all available Affymetrix Arabidopsis ATH1 microarray datasets from NASC, AtGenExpress, ArrayExpress and GEO public databases. After removal of duplicate entries, we obtained 13,386 CEL files in total, which is the largest number of Arabidopsis ATH1 expression profiles ever compiled (Table 1). These CEL files were grouped into 881 experiments, and include a combination of steady-state and time-series data generated from various Arabidopsis tissues, and under different developmental, treatment and environmental conditions.

Table 1: Microarray data collected from public databases. Columns show the database names, the number of experiments obtained from each database and the number of original CEL files that passed the quality control stage.

Database	Experiments	CEL Files	QC Filtered
ArrayExpress	543	7923	848
GEO	83	1270	102
NASC	211	2859	387
AtGeneExpress	44	1334	289
Total	881	13386	1626

We first performed manual inspection of all CEL files to remove GeneChips with irregular hybridization patterns. Quality control and normalization procedures (according to [3]) were then applied to the remaining CEL files to eliminate outliers and to render gene expression values comparable across all experiments. A total of 11,760 CEL files survived this process, and the entire dataset contained expression values of 22,810 probes, where each profile is a list of normalized expression values from all 11,760 microarray experiments. Filtering of probes sets and Arabidopsis gene annotations (TAIR version 10) were carried out as outlined in [3] (Figure 1).

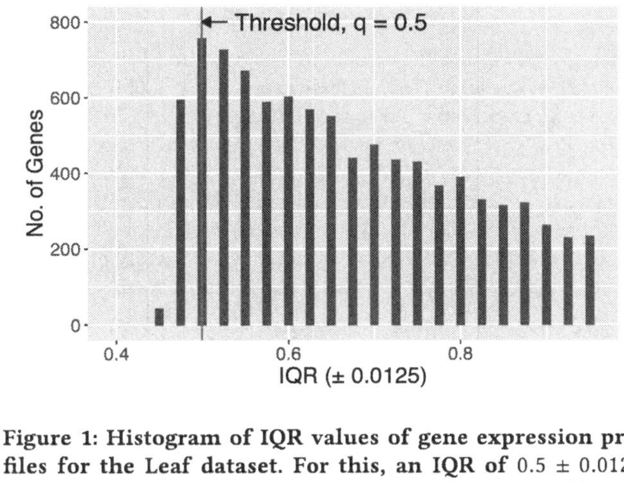

Figure 1: Histogram of IQR values of gene expression profiles for the Leaf dataset. For this, an IQR of 0.5 ± 0.0125 **shows the maximum value for number of genes, and hence the threshold** $q = 0.5$.

Probes with narrow range of expression profiles were eliminated using a threshold based on Inter-Quartile Range (IQR), a commonly used measure for gene expression profiles.

2.2 Network Reconstruction Methods

Marbach *et al.* (2012) [19] describe six different categories of methods for reverse engineering networks : regression, mutual information, correlation, Bayesian networks and methods that combine several different approaches. Among these, we chose for our comparative study, only those methods which have been previously been shown to work for tens of thousands of genes and for which a standard, empirically validated procedure to select the necessary parameters is established. The particular software for each specific method is dictated by the their ability to scale both to the problem size (~22,500 genes in Arabidopsis), and the number of gene expression datasets (11,760 in total) used in the study.

Three commonly used reconstruction methods fit these criteria – Pearson correlation, mutual Information (TINGe), and partial-correlation graphical Gaussian modeling (GeneNet). As Pearson correlation is not compute-intensive we developed our own code using the *pcor* function available in R statistical software. As far as we know, only these three methods have been used for construction of genome-scale gene networks for other plants also.

Let n denote the number of genes, with specific genes denoted by $g_1, g_2, \ldots, g_n$, and let m denote the number of gene expression datasets. The expression vector of gene g_i consisting of its expression values among the experiments is denoted by $x_i = (x_i(1), \ldots, x_i(m))$. Let D denote the gene expression matrix of size $n \times m$, whose i-th row corresponds to the expression vector of gene g_i. All the network construction methods discussed in this section assume that D is sampled from some joint probability distribution of n random variables, $\mathcal{X} = \{X_1, \ldots, X_n\}$.

2.2.1 Pearson Correlation Network. The sample Pearson correlation coefficient between two gene expression vectors x_i and x_j is defined as

$$r(x_i, x_j) = \frac{\sum_{k=1}^{m}(x_i(k) - \hat{\mu}_i)(x_j(k) - \hat{\mu}_j)}{\sqrt{\sum_{k=1}^{m}(x_i(k) - \hat{\mu}_i)^2}\sqrt{\sum_{k=1}^{m}(x_j(k) - \hat{\mu}_j)^2}}$$

where $\hat{\mu}_i$ and $\hat{\mu}_j$ are the sample means of x_i and x_j respectively. The $r(x_i, x_j)$ value lies in the closed range $[-1, 1]$ and is zero when there is no measurable linear correlation.

In a Pearson correlation network (that we term PearsonNet from here onwards), genes g_i and g_j are connected by an undirected edge if $|r(x_i, x_j)| > t$, a chosen threshold value. We estimated the value of t based on the plot of network density vs. threshold value, as suggested in [18]. Figure 2 shows, the network density plot for the leaf dataset and the threshold selection for its PearsonNet.

2.2.2 Mutual Information Network. For a pair or random variables $X_i \in \mathcal{X}$ and $X_j \in \mathcal{X}$, their joint entropy is defined as

$$\mathcal{H}(X_i, X_j) = -\sum_{k \in X_i}\sum_{l \in X_j} P_{ij}(k, l) \log P_{ij}(k, l)$$

where $P_{ij}(k, l)$ is the joint probability of the events $X_i = k$ and $X_j = l$ occurring together. If $P_{ij}(k, l) = 0$, the product is taken to be 0. In case of gene expression values, the possible events for X_i, corresponding to gene g_i, are 'down-regulated', 'up-regulated' and 'no-change'.

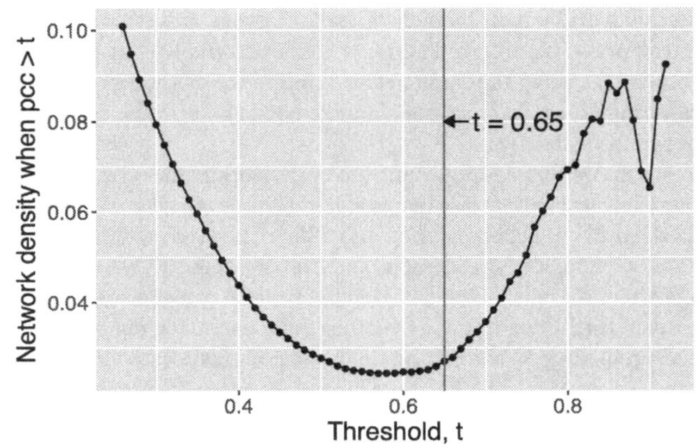

Figure 2: Plot shows network density of Pearson correlation network as a function of threshold for the leaf dataset. The minimum network density occurs around $r = 0.6$, and following [18] the threshold t is selected as the value to the right of the minimum, which in this case is 0.65.

Mutual Information (MI) between X_i and X_j, intended to measure the reduction in uncertainty in determining the expression level of gene g_i given the expression level of gene g_j, is defined as

$$I(X_i, X_j) = \mathcal{H}(X_i) + \mathcal{H}(X_j) - \mathcal{H}(X_i, X_j)$$

$I(X_i, X_j)$ is symmetric and non-negative and is zero if and only if X_i and X_j are independent. In the construction of MI-based network, an edge is added between g_i and g_j if $I(X_i, X_j)$ exceeds a threshold value.

While many MI-based network construction methods have been developed [4, 5, 11], we used the parallel MI-based network construction software TINGe [3] for our studies because of its ability to scale to thousands of genes. TINGe uses a B-spline estimator developed by [7] to compute pairwise MI values, and estimates the statistical significance of the computed MI values by permutation testing. TINGe also predicts and eliminates indirect interactions using the Data Processing Inequality (DPI), which states that if X_i, X_j and X_k form a Markov Chain in that order i.e., $X_i \to X_j \to X_k$, then $I(X_i, X_k) \leq I(X_i, X_j)$ and $I(X_i, X_k) \leq I(X_j, X_k)$. We ran TINGe on 16 nodes of a dual 8-core Intel Xeon cluster (256-way parallelism), with a p-value of 5×10^{-9}. We refer to the networks produced by the TINGe software as TINGeNet.

2.2.3 Graphical Gaussian Model. Graphical Gaussian models (GGM), also known as covariance selection models, are constructed under the assumption that the observed gene expression matrix D is drawn from a joint Gaussian distribution $\mathcal{N}(\mu, \Sigma)$ with the mean vector $\mu = (\mu_1, \ldots, \mu_n)^T$ and a positive definite covariance matrix $\Sigma = (\sigma_{ij}), 1 \leq i, j \leq n$. In a GGM, the strength of a pairwise correlation is characterized by the partial correlation matrix $\Pi = (\pi_{ij}), 1 \leq i, j \leq n$. Here, π_{ij} describes the extent to which X_i and X_j remain dependent given all other variables i.e., $\mathcal{X} \setminus \{X_i, X_j\}$. Results from standard graphical theory [9] show that the matrix

Π is related to the inverse of the standard correlation coefficient matrix $P = (\rho_{ij})$. Specifically, if $\Omega = P^{-1} = (\omega_{ij})$, then

$$\pi_{ij} = -\frac{\omega_{ij}}{\sqrt{\omega_{ii}\omega_{jj}}}$$

A GGM network has an edge for every non-zero partial correlation $\pi_{ij}, i \neq j$.

However, when $m < n$, as is often the case when analyzing gene expression data, the sample correlation matrix $\hat{P}$ is not positive definite and can not be inverted. The *GeneNet* software [26] overcomes this problem by using an analytic shrinkage estimator of the correlation matrix. Statistical significance of the computed partial correlation coefficient is assessed by fitting a mixture model to the observed partial correlation coefficients. Similar to [17], we used *GeneNet* to construct GGM based gene networks with a p-value of 5×10^{-9}.

All software runs were made on a cluster with each node having two 2.0 GHz 8-Core Intel Xeon E5 2650 processors and 128 GB of RAM, running RedHat Enterprise Linux. While software for Pearson correlation and GeneNet use only a single node, TINGe can run in parallel using multiple nodes of the cluster.

2.3 Network Validation and Comparative Assessment

If the ground truth is known, it would be straightforward to assess the quality of a predicted network by comparing the sets of edges between the true and predicted networks, and using standard statistical measures such as specificity, sensitivity, precision and recall, or the corresponding receiver operating characteristic (ROC) and precision-recall (PR) curves. Unfortunately, this is not the case and the experimentally confirmed interaction data for Arabidopsis is not as extensive as well studied unicellular organisms such as *E. coli* and Yeast.

We conducted network validation studies using two approaches. Our first approach is to validate the networks against as many experimentally confirmed interactions as available. For this purpose we used the Arabidopsis Transcriptional Regulatory Map (ATRM; [13]), which is a network of 790 genes and 1431 experimentally proven interactions between transcription factors (TF) and their target genes, created through systematic literature mining. Given the complexity of deciphering plant networks, we found that none of the methods directly captured even 10% of the interactions. To more comprehensively assess the quality of a generated network using the ATRM, we extracted all ATRM documented interactions where the corresponding genes are present in the same connected component of the network to be evaluated. We then computed the shortest path distance between each such pair and report mean and median of such distances. We also analyzed the shortest path distances by using the following cutoff measure: select a cutoff distance d and accept an ATRM interaction as being identified by the network if the shortest path distance between the corresponding genes is $\leq d$. We evaluate the variation in prediction accuracy with respect to an increase in the cutoff distance for all the networks. Note this result includes the number of interaction directly captured for the case of $d = 1$.

The ATRM network itself covers only about 3.5% of Arabidopsis genes. Also, validation against ATRM does not evaluate precision of the network and penalize for gene interactions predicted by the network that are incorrect. Hence, we developed a second approach to study functional modularity within the networks of genes and transcription factors experimentally characterized to be involved in specific pathways. A collection of brassinosteroid-regulated (BR) and RD26-regulated genes generated via microarray and/or RNA-seq experiments from Arabidopsis knockout mutants, and WT Arabidopsis treated with brassinosteroids, were used for this evaluation [30]. These datasets were supplemented with ChIP-ChIP data for Arabidopsis BES1/BZR1 target genes. To validate against this experimental data, we used GeNA [3] to extract context-specific subnetworks from the whole genome networks based on genes known to function in the specific pathway under consideration. With reference to a given set of seed genes, GeNA ranks other genes for their relevance using a page rank style algorithm. It then selects the minimum number of highest ranked genes that together with the seed genes form a connected subnetwork, and returns the subnetwork to the user. The quality of these subnetworks are then assessed against the experimental data. We expect that more precise the network is, better the agreement of the highest ranked genes with the experimentally verified genes. Note that if a method generates a complete network of all the genes, GeNA will simply report a random ranking of all the genes, leading to poor performance.

As another means to test the predictive power of network reverse engineering methods, we pitched their performance in pathway studies against AraNet [14, 15]. AraNet is a holistic, probabilistic network of *Arabidopsis Thaliana* genes constructed by integrating data from 18 different data sources including mRNA co-expression, domain co-occurrence, gene neighbourhoods, and ortholog information. Evidence from each data source is weighted, using a Bayesian Method, according to how well they can explain an interaction between a pair of genes. Each interaction, thus discovered, is given a log likelihood score (LLS) that represents how probable the interaction is a true functional association between the two genes. This provides an additional assessment of the predictive power networks based on gene expression data alone can provide.

3 RESULTS AND DISCUSSION

3.1 Network Reconstruction and Classification of Microarray Datasets

As is standard practice when reverse engineering genome-scale networks, we first applied each network reconstruction method to the entire dataset of 11,760 gene expression datasets. The resulting networks were very sparse (predicted a limited number of interactions) and fared poorly in network validation studies, uniformly across all three methods. For example, the mutual information based network on the entire dataset has 18,806 genes and 92,174 edges. When validated against the ATRM network, a mere 3.27% of the experimentally confirmed gene-gene interactions were directly found in the network. In case of PearsonNet and GeneNet, only 1.09% and 3.04% of the ATRM gene-gene interactions were found in the respective networks. Moreover, only 24.56% of the interactions were included in the mutual information based network, even when a shortest path length of up to 3 is allowed in the predicted network. Similarly for PearsonNet and GeneNet, respectively 4.44% and 21.42% interactions were included when we allow a path length of up to 3. If generous cut off distances are used to predict potential interactions, it will greatly increase the number of false positives, rendering the predictions useless in practice.

The key reason for this failure is gene interactions are specific to biological processes, and the signals are drowned out when included within a large number of unrelated experiments. Perversely, the quality of networks deteriorated with increase in data. This led us to perform a functional grouping of experiments and independently construct networks using experiments within each group. One approach to automatically generate such a grouping is through biclustering [10, 25]. In a recent survey, Eren *et al.* observed that the performance of biclustering algorithms degraded as the number of biclusters in the dataset increased, a serious concern when analyzing large gene expression datasets [10]. Hence, we adopted the painstaking but fruitful approach of classifying the experiments based on biological knowledge.

Spatial and temporal patterns of gene expression is a well-known phenomenon in eukaryotic organisms such as plants. Recent large-scale studies in maize have demonstrated this with modules that show tissue-specific expression of groups of genes in the maize genome [8]. We have also observed this within the collection of Arabidopsis microarray datasets used in this work. For example, certain probe sets showed a much more dynamic range of expression in specific tissues (Figure 3). This motivated us to classify microarray datasets into subsets based on different tissues and/or biological processes, and subject them to network construction separately (Table 2). As shown, we classified the 11,760 microarray experiments into five tissue-specific and seven process-specific categories. For process-specific classes, we manually classified datasets based on the description and the meta-data available for each experiment. In case of tissue-specific classes, we did an automatic preliminary classification by searching for specific keywords such as flower,

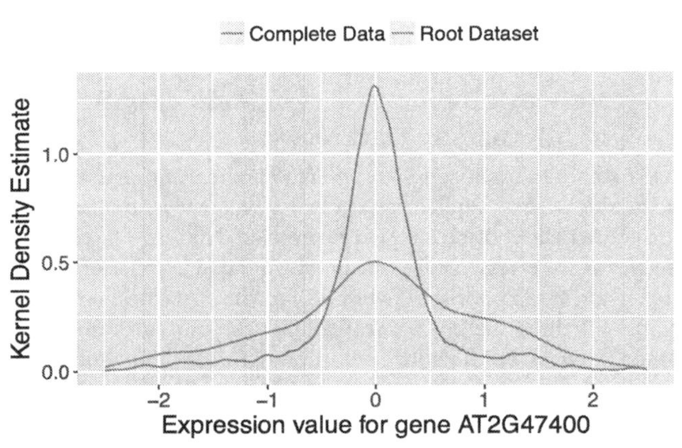

Figure 3: Kernel Density Estimate (KDE) of the normalized expression values for the gene AT2G47400 in complete dataset and root dataset. The gene AT2G47400 shows a wider range of expression in root dataset in comparison to the complete dataset.

Table 2: Classification of microarray experiments into process-specific and tissue-specific categories. For each category, the number of experiments, CEL files, and the total number of genes that survived the data filters are shown.

	Category	Experiments	CEL files	Genes
Process	Chemical	75	808	18026
	Development	190	2252	17827
	Hormone	116	1806	17646
	Light	64	1210	17895
	Metabolism	214	1535	17989
	Pathogen	69	1156	17486
	Stress	153	2476	19041
Tissue	Flower	69	764	17209
	Leaf	279	4268	17215
	Root	121	1939	17775
	Seedling	379	5234	17960
	Whole Plant	144	2359	18805

florescence, rosette, leaf, root and seedling in the experiment descriptions of microarray databases. Then, we manually examined each of the experiments and modified the classes as required.

To further confirm tissue and biological process-specificity of genes, we evaluated gene ontology terms associated with the genes present in specific datasets (for example, leaf, flower, and root). We used the topGO module in R package for this purpose, and the elimination method in topGO to select top 50 GO terms declared to be statistically significant by Fisher's Exact Test [1]. We performed comparisons of all pairs of genes that show wider range of expression values in different tissue-specific datasets, and also on pairs of genes that exhibit this property in the same tissue-specific dataset.

The results of topGO analyses suggest that specific datasets are enriched for genes involved in processes pathways unique to the corresponding tissue. For example, examination of the flower dataset shows inclusion of a large number of genes mediating regulation of flower development (p-value = 3.9×10^{-13}), petal formation (p-value = 4×10^{-12}), sepal formation (p-value = 4×10^{-12}), etc. Genes with these terms do not show a dynamic range of expression and/or are not significantly enriched in either the root or leaf tissue datasets, while genes involved in root hair development and elongation (p-value = 2×10^{-7}), nitrate and iron transport (p-value = 8.6×10^{-18}) are included only in the root dataset. On the other hand, flower and leaf datasets have certain common GO enriched terms such as pigment biosynthesis, and chloroplast organization, although each GO term contains a unique set of genes in the two tissue-types. Both these processes occur in the two tissues, and many of the genes listed in these GO categories are expected to be expressed in these two tissues (www.arabidopsis.org). However, microarray analysis of the compiled datasets suggests differential expression of these genes corresponding to a particular plant tissue or environmental condition. Thus, classification of datasets allowed for the recovery of genes specific to corresponding tissue or process, which was not possible by collective processing of the entire 11,760 microarray dataset.

Table 3: Summary of network properties of all the constructed union networks and AraNet. The characteristic path length (L) is the length of average shortest path computed over all pairs of genes in the network. Average clustering coefficient (C) is the average of clustering coefficient computed over all the nodes in the network. L_{random} and C_{random} are expected values for L and C for a random graph with the same number of nodes.

Properties	GeneNet			PearsonNet			TINGeNet			AraNet
	Process Union	Tissue Union	Full Union	Process Union	Tissue Union	Full Union	Process Union	Tissue Union	Full Union	
Nodes	15085	14330	15675	6712	7443	8429	20045	19247	20126	22667
Edges	1118750	787169	1813729	987625	1158046	1316408	638051	423813	905056	894877
Network Density	0.0098	0.0077	0.0147	0.0439	0.0418	0.0371	0.0032	0.0023	0.0045	0.0034
Avg. Node Degree	148.33	109.87	231.41	294.29	311.18	312.35	63.66	44.04	89.94	78.18
Diameter	13	13	12	11	11	10	6	6	5	11
Assortativity Coeff.	0.1319	0.0997	0.0997	-0.0004	0.1104	0.0936	0.0773	0.0419	0.0643	0.2704
Avg. Clustering Coeff. (C)	0.1094	0.0884	0.1295	0.6254	0.6410	0.6329	0.1026	0.1158	0.1102	0.2251
Characteristic Path Length (L)	2.9376	3.0159	2.8121	3.4354	3.3764	3.3301	2.9552	3.1663	2.7918	1.0236
L_{random}	1.9250	2.0365	1.7743	1.5501	1.5530	1.5737	2.3849	2.6063	2.2025	2.3006
C_{random}	0.00013	0.00014	0.00013	0.00029	0.00027	0.00023	0.00009	0.00010	0.000099	0.00008
L/L_{random}	1.5260	1.4809	1.5848	2.2162	2.1741	2.1161	1.2391	1.2149	1.2675	0.4449
C/C_{random}	841.54	631.42	1015.72	2156.55	2374.07	2667.27	1028.31	1129.17	1109.13	2551.25

3.2 Arabidopsis Whole Genome Networks

For each of the three network construction methods, we first generated 12 separate networks, one for each tissue-specific and process-specific dataset. We then constructed three union networks for each method, corresponding to graph union of all process-specific, all tissue-specific, and all networks, respectively (Table 3). Much of the network analyses we present here is done on these union networks. While all the genes are not simultaneously present in any single network, their union covers most of the genes in the Arabidopsis genome. The largest of the full union networks was generated by TINGe, and has 20,126 genes.

While quality of the networks is the main focus of this paper, we make a few remarks on run-time performance. Owing to its simplicity, the run-time for computing Pearson correlation networks is the lowest among the three methods. While GeneNet is faster than TINGe on a per processor basis, TINGe runs faster by being able to exploit the multiple processors available. By using 16 compute nodes, TINGe was able to run 2.5-6.5 times faster than GeneNet. Note that TINGe scales well to much larger number of nodes. Network construction times for the seedling dataset, the largest of all the classified datasets, are 28 minutes for PearsonNet, 83 minutes for TINGe, and 227 minutes for GeneNet, respectively. All the networks are made available for public use and can be opened in Cytoscape for further analysis.

3.3 Network Properties

Several network properties of the 9 union networks and AraNet are given in Table 3. The union networks constructed by Pearson correlation and GGM (GeneNet) contain more than one connected component, in which case the network properties of the largest component are shown. Union of MI-based (TINGe) networks always produced a connected network, and generated the largest network with respect to the number of nodes, except for the probabilistic functional network, AraNet. For the sake of comparison, the table also lists the clustering coefficients and characteristic path lengths in random networks of similar size, in which each pair of genes is equally likely to be connected.

There are significant differences between the networks constructed by the three different methods. Even so, all these networks sufficiently deviate from properties of random networks. Especially, with respect to the ratio C/C_{random}, all the networks show significant deviation from the clustering coefficient properties of random graphs. Pearson correlation networks have fewer nodes, but are denser compared to the other networks. This is because Pearson correlation method cannot distinguish between direct and indirect dependencies. In addition, many of the gene-gene interactions cannot be captured by considering only measures for linear correlations.

Both MI and GGM based methods are able to detect indirect dependencies, i.e., when activity of one of the genes is affected by another gene mediated via a third gene. Table 3 shows that both of these networks (especially the full union networks), show comparable network properties in terms of average clustering coefficient and characteristic path length. However, compared to GeneNet networks, TINGe networks include more number of genes while having smaller diameter. This is likely due to two reasons: The genes missing from GeneNet network may have failed to fit within the assumption of the underlying Gaussian distribution of GeneNet and the resulting missing connections increase the diameter of the network. Also, the way conditional independencies are evaluated to remove indirect edges is different – TINGe computes the probability distribution directly from the data, while GeneNet fits the data to a mixture distribution.

Union Networks generated by TINGe include a larger number of genes compared to both GeneNet and PearsonNet, but their network density and diameter is significantly smaller compared to other networks, indicating an ability of TINGe to grow the network by including more genes while adding relatively few edges. When the characteristic path length is comparable to, and the average clustering coefficient is significantly higher than, the expected values for a random graph, it is indicative of the small-world property [28]. Even though almost all the networks show significant deviation in the average clustering coefficient, the networks generated from TINGe show a characteristic path length comparable to that of the expected values for a random network of similar size. Therefore, the measure C/C_{random} indicates small-world property of networks constructed by TINGe compared to other networks.

AraNet has the largest number of nodes of any network presented here, and the network density is comparable to that of networks generated from TINGe. However, the characteristic path length is not comparable to that of a random network with same number of nodes. This is probably because AraNet is built by integrating multiple networks derived from different data sources and therefore some of the links predicted by a very few constituent networks could potentially be placed father from the hubs in the integrated network, resulting in path characteristics unlike a scale-free network.

3.4 Network Validation

3.4.1 Validation using Transcriptional Regulatory Map. An important mechanism to assess genome-scale networks is to test them against as many experimentally confirmed interactions as possible. For this purpose, we chose the Arabidopsis Transcriptional Regulatory Map [13], which documents 790 genes and 1431 interactions. Of these, at least 734 genes are present in at least one of the reverse-engineered networks. We selected the 1283 interactions involving these 734 genes for validation. As an interaction may not be directly present in the network being tested, we instead compute the shortest distance between the corresponding pair of genes (smaller values are better). We computed the mean and median of the shortest distances for each network over as many of the 1283 interactions as possible. Note that a TF and its target gene may not be connected in the network we are validating – either because the TF or gene is missing or because they are present in two different connected components. When computing the mean and median distances, we ignore such TF and target pairs.

Our analyses shows that the full union TINGeNet has the best average shortest distance (2.39) compared to other networks, followed by AraNet (2.54), PearsonNet (2.85), and GeneNet (2.86). With respect to the median shortest path distance, the full union TINGeNet again is better with a median distance of 2, while all other networks have a median distance of 3. For all the networks, the difference between mean and median is relatively small, which shows that the distribution of shortest path distances is not strongly skewed by a few outliers.

Table 4 shows the percentage of ATRM documented interactions captured by each union network where the corresponding gene pairs are within a distance of d. The cutoff value $d = 1$ estimates

Table 4: Validation using Arabidopsis Transcriptional Regulatory Map. For each of the full union networks, the table reports the percentage of experimentally confirmed interactions identified vs. cutoff distance.

Source Networks	Cut off Distance		
	1	2	3
PearsonNet	4.13	14.26	25.02
GeneNet	5.77	35.54	61.65
TINGeNet	9.43	50.66	97.11
AraNet	14.88	43.26	85.34

the number of interactions directly identified in the networks being tested. For $d = 1$, AraNet outperforms others by identifying 191 (14.88%) interactions. This is probably because AaraNet is a weighted integration of multiple different networks and a fundamental premise of such integration is that the deficiencies of a method will be addressed by some combination of the other methods. Among the genome-scale networks generated using a single methodology (PearsonNet, TINGeNet and GeneNet in our case), the full union TINGeNet achieves the best performance by identifying 121 (9.43%)interactions.

Clearly, increasing the cutoff distance will increase the number of interactions identified by a network. However, compared to AraNet, full union TINGeNet shows better improvement in accuracy with increased cutoff distance. With a cutoff distance of 2, the full union TINGeNet can identify 650 (50.66%) interactions, while AraNet identifies 555 (40.25%) interactions. Further increasing the cut off distance of 3, TINGeNet identifies 97.11 % of interactions, while the next best network AraNet identifies 85.34% of the interactions.

In case of PearsonNet and GeneNet networks, the improvement in accuracy is not in proportion to the increase in the cutoff distance. For example, with a cutoff distance of 3 in the PearsonNet full union network, only 25.02% of the interactions are present. The fact that more genes are missing in PearsonNet network compared to other networks most probably contributes to its poor performance. GeneNet networks show similar behavior, though they are slightly better in their accuracy compared to PearsonNet networks.

3.4.2 Classification and Components Analysis. To go beyond the relatively small number of experimentally confirmed interactions as summarized in the ATRM network, We developed two sets of experimentally identified genes involved in brassinosteroid regulation (BR) and dehydration stress, respectively. These sets, labeled BR8000 and RD26-8725 (RD26 is a dehydration induced NAC protein) based on the number of genes involved, contain differentially expressed genes experimentally identified by [30] through microarray and RNA-seq analysis of specific Arabidopsis BR and RD26 knockout mutants.

We used these gene sets to study functional modularity of networks as follows. We induced subgraphs from each of the genome-scale networks corresponding to BR8000 and RD26-8725 genes, and measured the number of connected components in the resulting subgraphs. Genes involved in the same biological process are expected to be cohesively grouped, and hence very few connected components would be expected in biologically relevant networks.

Table 5: Connected Component Analysis for different *TINGeNet* networks with respect to *BR8000* and *RD26-8725* gene sets. P-Value remain the same in all the cases because all the networks in empirical distribution have more connected components than the ones induced by the gene sets.

Gene List	Class	Genes	Edges	Components	Largest Component	Largest Comp. Edges	P-Value
BR8000	Development	5827	19779	309	5499	19759	8.33×10^{-7}
	Hormone	5707	18090	280	5415	18077	8.33×10^{-7}
	Stress	6281	25127	254	6016	25115	8.33×10^{-7}
	Root	5793	17775	337	5441	17759	8.33×10^{-7}
	Seedling	5874	17638	339	5525	17627	8.33×10^{-7}
	Whole plant	6167	21385	335	5820	21372	8.33×10^{-7}
RD26-8725	Development	6184	22392	325	5840	22372	8.33×10^{-7}
	Hormone	6056	19518	238	5813	19512	8.33×10^{-7}
	Stress	6664	35699	288	6370	35692	8.33×10^{-7}
	Root	6128	23593	332	5784	23580	8.33×10^{-7}
	Seedling	6242	20417	375	5852	20401	8.33×10^{-7}
	Whole plant	6561	28829	288	6269	28824	8.33×10^{-7}

In order to assess the statistical significance of the number of connected components found, we generated, similar to [3], a large collection of random networks with similar degree distribution and then computed the number of subcomponents in the subnetworks extracted from each of these random networks. We estimated the P-value to be the empirical probability that the same number of connected components occur in these generated random networks.

We first analyzed the effectiveness of microarray dataset classification on yielding networks of biological relevance. Since the MI-based method, TINGe, generates the largest network(s) from microarray data alone for any dataset-type, we performed connected component analysis on select tissue-specific and process-specific TINGe generated networks. Analysis of networks generated from development, stress, hormone, seedling, whole plant, and root datasets with respect to BR8000 shows that stress and hormone networks yield the lowest number of connected components, followed by development (Table 5). BRs are a class of steroid phytohormones known to be involved in plant development and biotic and abiotic stresses. Thus, these results are consistent with the function of BR-regulated genes in the plant. Furthermore, RD26 responsive genes appear to be similarly, but more closely associated in the stress and hormone networks suggesting that these cellular processes are in some way interconnected to each other. Consistent with this notion, recent studies show that there is a significant cross-talk between BR and drought stress pathways, which perhaps diverge at some point in a tissue-specific manner because with RD26-8725, the "whole plant" network induces fewer connected components versus the "development" network when compared to BR8000 [6, 13].

Having confirmed that the tissue and process-specific networks follow a priori knowledge, we conducted similar analyses with the larger union networks for better comparison of the three network inference methods and AraNet (Table 6). It is noteworthy that the results follow the network properties as shown in Table 3. As expected, networks generated with TINGe and AraNet have more of the BR8000 genes in their networks when compared to other networks, although TINGeNet shows far better connectivity for BR genes among the two networks with significantly fewer number of connected components and the largest percentage of genes included in its largest component. Although PearsonNet has fewer number of BR genes when compared to GeneNet, the number of connected components in the induced subgraphs is significantly less when compared to GeneNet indicating better network performance of Pearson correlation networks versus GeneNet with real datasets.

Despite the fact that AraNet contains the largest number of BR8000 genes in its network compared to all other union networks, the number of connected components are observed to be more than PearsonNet and TINGeNet. Moreover, the largest component from TINGe network(s) includes more than 99% of the BR genes present in the network, whereas the largest component from AraNet has 95% of the genes found.This is probably because AraNet is an integrated network of constitutent networks, and an analysis of large number of seed genes could potentially select genes from different constituent networks and thus potentially increase the chance that these constituent networks do not form a perfect connection. Also, note that in both AraNet and TINGe networks, almost all of the edges present in the subgraph are present in the largest component and hence most of the genes not connected to the largest component aremost likely present in the subgraph as single components. This suggests that even though AraNet has more genes in the network compared to the TINGe networks, the functionally related genes of BR8000 are not strongly associated within the network. TINGe networks, thus, are able to provide better functional cohesion in the network structure compared to the other networks. A similar trend is observed with the genes mediating drought stress (Table 6), with TINGe outperforming all other networks, and having greater association strength between genes of the same biological process. These results suggest that mutual information followed by Pearson correlation-based methods are better at predicting functional modularity of genes when large numbers of genes are analyzed.

Table 6: Connected Component Analysis of the union networks and AraNet with respect to *BR8000* and *RD26-8725* genes. Percent column shows the number of genes found in the largest component as a percentage of the total number of genes found.

Gene List	Method	Union Network	Genes	Edges	Components	Largest Component	Largest Comp. Edges	Percent	P-Value
BR8000	GeneNet	Tissues	3803	7893	930	2779	7789	73.07	1.00
	GeneNet	Conditions	4129	11360	804	3259	11286	78.93	1.00
	GeneNet	Full Union	4447	15703	791	3612	15652	81.22	1.00
	PearsonNet	Tissues	3510	167745	145	3348	167725	95.38	8.33×10^{-7}
	PearsonNet	Conditions	3381	149342	164	3203	149325	94.74	8.33×10^{-7}
	PearsonNet	Full Union	3977	198848	175	3787	198830	95.22	8.33×10^{-7}
	TINGeNet	Tissues	6349	73246	33	6316	73245	99.48	1.19×10^{-2}
	TINGeNet	Conditions	6619	97581	14	6606	97581	99.80	1.67×10^{-6}
	TINGeNet	Full Union	6646	136681	8	6639	136681	99.89	1.67×10^{-6}
	AraNet	N/A	7420	142284	325	7073	142260	95.32	8.33×10^{-7}
RD26-8725	GeneNet	Tissues	4164	8592	1032	2994	8441	71.90	1.00
	GeneNet	Conditions	4467	12797	869	3501	12698	78.37	1.00
	GeneNet	Full Union	4709	17890	801	3859	17839	81.95	1.00
	PearsonNet	Tissues	3820	272012	200	3590	271981	93.98	9.58×10^{-5}
	PearsonNet	Conditions	3720	256540	212	3475	256506	93.41	1.07×10^{-2}
	PearsonNet	Full Union	4253	319757	183	4059	319745	95.44	8.33×10^{-7}
	TINGeNet	Tissues	6737	88060	14	6724	88060	99.81	8.33×10^{-7}
	TINGeNet	Conditions	7020	114911	19	7002	114911	99.74	8.38×10^{-4}
	TINGeNet	Full Union	7049	162091	16	7034	162091	99.79	8.65×10^{-3}
	AraNet	NA	8062	231478	351	7703	231468	95.55	8.33×10^{-7}

3.4.3 Subnetwork Extraction. We next determined functional modularity of the union networks with a smaller but targeted set of 200 experimentally verified [30] BR-regulated transcription factors (designated as BTFs). Here, we use GeNA [3], a subnetwork extraction software which serially ranks each gene in the network with respect to its association with the given set of seed genes. We extracted the top 200 to 900 genes with respect to the BTFs, respectively, and assessed the percentage of these highly ranked genes predicted to be BR-regulated that are actually present in the set BR8000. Those not present in BR8000 are classified as wrong predictions. This is a more complex test of network modularity due to the multi-level regulation of eukaryotic genes and proteins as well as due to the fact that expression of the transcription factor and it target gene(s) is not well coordinated.

Results of subnetwork extraction (Figure 4) show that 80-90% of the BR-regulated genes are closely connected in the top 200 highly ranked genes. However, as we increase the number of top ranked genes in the extracted subnetwork from 200 to 900, the percentage decreases at least by 20-30% for all networks. TINGe, in general, outperforms other methods for almost all ranges of subnetwork sizes, while GeneNet performs the worst suggesting that more number of BR genes are closely and strongly associated with the BTFs in TINGeNet. This is consistent with results from the previous section. Figure 5 shows a more detailed analysis of the top 600 genes for all union networks.

PearsonNet performs best with smaller subnetworks where 90% of the genes in the top 200 ranked genes are BR-regulated. However, the percentage drops significantly as the subnetwork size increases

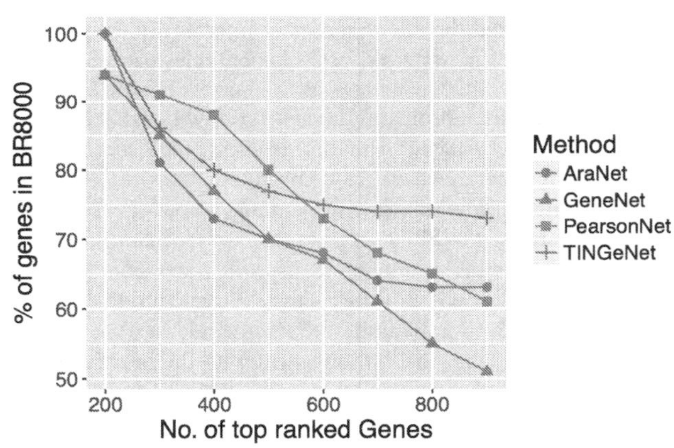

Figure 4: Percentage of the BR8000 genes found in the top ranked genes in subnetwork extracted from GeNA using 200 BTFs as the seed genes from the full union networks and AraNet.

from 200 to 900 genes, when compared to TINGeNet where the decline is more gradual. This is probably because subnetwork extraction algorithms can exploit the comparatively higher network density of PearsonNet networks to extract functionally related genes. However, since the number of genes covered by PearsonNet networks is smaller compared to other networks, the percentage of genes related to BR drops more rapidly with increase in number

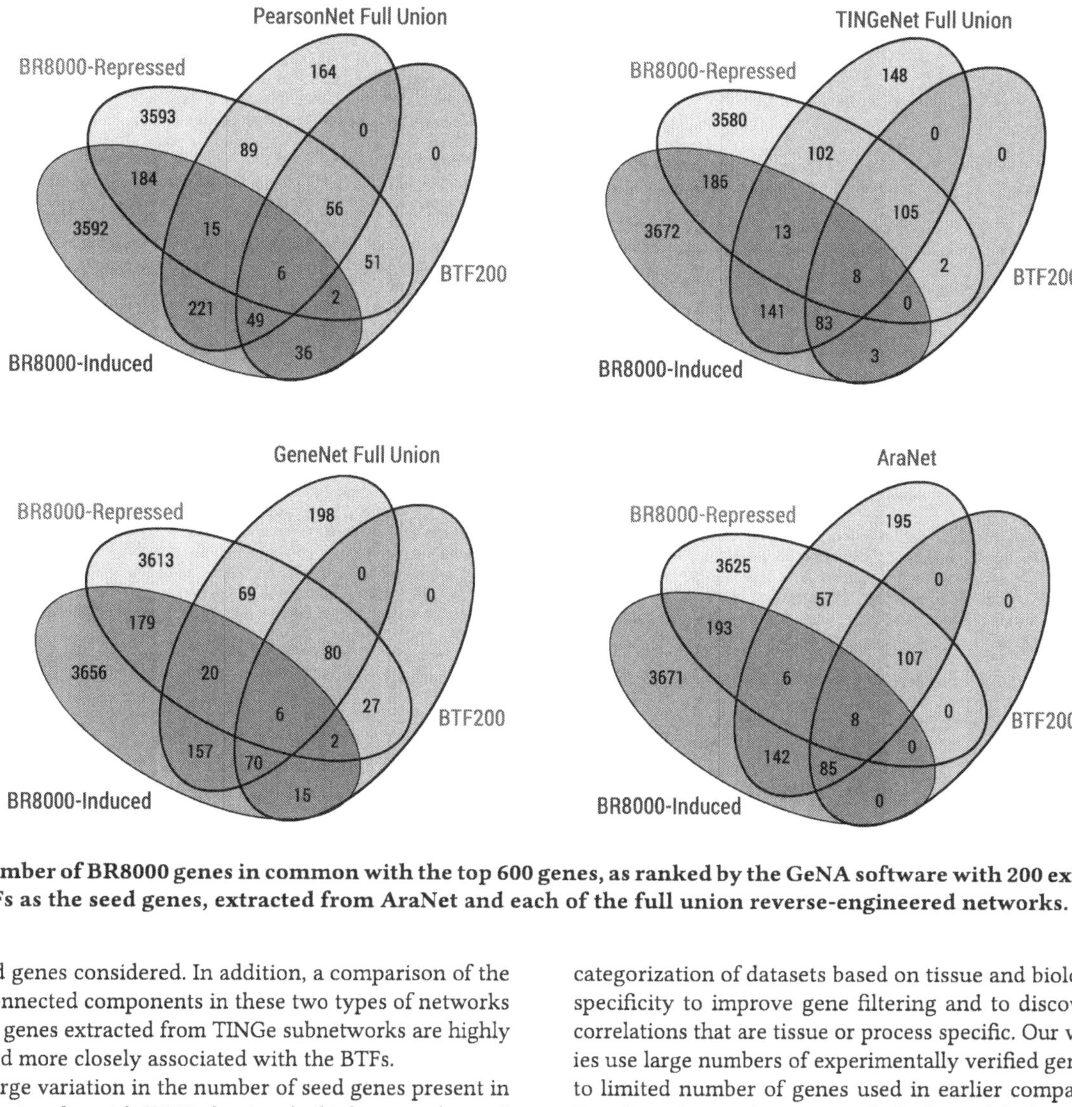

Figure 5: Number of BR8000 genes in common with the top 600 genes, as ranked by the GeNA software with 200 experimentally verified BTFs as the seed genes, extracted from AraNet and each of the full union reverse-engineered networks.

of top ranked genes considered. In addition, a comparison of the number of connected components in these two types of networks suggests that genes extracted from TINGe subnetworks are highly connected and more closely associated with the BTFs.

There is large variation in the number of seed genes present in the different networks, with TINGe having the highest number and PearsonNet having the least number of seed genes. With GeNA, the ranking of genes is sensitive to the number of seed genes as the quality of the subnetwork improves with increase in their number. To determine comparative network performance with the same number of seed genes, we repeated the tests using only those BTFs present in all networks as seed genes for subnetwork extraction. The results (not shown in the paper) are similar with TINGe performing better overall than all other networks and GeneNet performing the worst.

4 CONCLUSIONS AND FUTURE WORK

In this paper, we conducted a comparative study of network inference methods by constructing and analyzing whole-genome networks using Pearson correlation, graphical Gaussian modeling, and mutual information approaches. We demonstrated the need for categorization of datasets based on tissue and biological process-specificity to improve gene filtering and to discover gene-gene correlations that are tissue or process specific. Our validation studies use large numbers of experimentally verified genes as opposed to limited number of genes used in earlier comparative studies. Based on the results, we conclude that while linear interactions can be accurately uncovered by Pearson correlation, the networks become too dense due to direct edges between many indirect interactions. Overall, information theory based approaches seem to produce the best possible networks in terms of retaining functional modularity and keeping causal relations close if not directly connected. Our study constitutes the largest number of gene expression profiles ever collectively analyzed for Arabidopsis, and the largest Arabidopsis network constructed from microarray data to date. The tissue and process specific networks we generated are available to serve as a starting point for functional analysis of Arabidopsis genes.

Marbach *et al.* (2012) [19] found that a weighted aggregation of results from multiple network construction methods shows significant improvement over the results of the individual methods. However, estimating the appropriate weights requires an extensive empirical study that quantifies the performance of the methods, which we defer to future work.

ACKNOWLEDGMENTS

This research is supported in part by the National Science Foundation under IOS-1257631.

REFERENCES

[1] Adrian Alexa, Jörg Rahnenführer, and Thomas Lengauer. 2006. Improved scoring of functional groups from gene expression data by decorrelating GO graph structure. *Bioinformatics* 22, 13 (2006), 1600–1607.

[2] Jeffrey D. Allen, Yang Xie, Min Chen, Luc Girard, and Guanghua Xiao. 2012. Comparing statistical methods for constructing large scale gene networks. *PLoS One* 7, 1 (2012), e29348.

[3] Maneesha Aluru, Jaroslaw Zola, Dan Nettleton, and Srinivas Aluru. 2013. Reverse engineering and analysis of large genome-scale gene networks. *Nucleic Acids Research* 41, 1 (2013), e24.

[4] Katia Basso, Adam A Margolin, Gustavo Stolovitzky, Ulf Klein, Riccardo Dalla-Favera, and Andrea Califano. 2005. Reverse engineering of regulatory networks in human B cells. *Nature genetics* 37, 4 (2005), 382–390.

[5] Atul J Butte and Isaac S Kohane. 2000. Mutual information relevance networks: functional genomic clustering using pairwise entropy measurements. In *Proceedings of Pacific Symposium on Biocomputing*. 418–429.

[6] Yuhee Chung, Soon Il Kwon, and Sunghwa Choe. 2014. Antagonistic regulation of Arabidopsis growth by brassinosteroids and abiotic stresses. *Molecules and cells* 37, 11 (2014), 795–803.

[7] Carsten O Daub, Ralf Steuer, Joachim Selbig, and Sebastian Kloska. 2004. Estimating mutual information using B-spline functions–an improved similarity measure for analysing gene expression data. *BMC Bioinformatics* 5, 1 (2004), 118.

[8] Gregory S. Downs, Yong-Mei Bi, Joseph Colasanti, Wenqing Wu, Xi Chen, Tong Zhu, Steven J. Rothstein, and Lewis N. Lukens. 2013. A developmental transcriptional network for maize defines coexpression modules. *Plant Physiology* 161, 4 (2013), 1830–1843.

[9] David Edwards. 2012. *Introduction to graphical modelling*. Springer Science & Business Media, New York.

[10] Kemal Eren, Mehmet Deveci, Onur Küçüktunç, and Ümit V Çatalyürek. 2013. A comparative analysis of biclustering algorithms for gene expression data. *Briefings in Bioinformatics* 14, 3 (2013), 279–292.

[11] Jeremiah J Faith, Boris Hayete, Joshua T Thaden, Ilaria Mogno, Jamey Wierzbowski, Guillaume Cottarel, Simon Kasif, James J Collins, and Timothy S Gardner. 2007. Large-scale mapping and validation of *Escherichia coli* transcriptional regulation from a compendium of expression profiles. *PLoS Biology* 5, 1 (2007), e8.

[12] Nir Friedman, Michal Linial, Iftach Nachman, and Dana Pe'er. 2000. Using Bayesian networks to analyze expression data. *Journal of Computational Biology* 7, 3-4 (2000), 601–620.

[13] Jinpu Jin, Kun He, Xing Tang, Le Lv, Yi Zhao, Jingchu Luo, and Ge Gao. 2015. An Arabisopsis transcriptional regulatory map reveals distinct functiional and evolutionary features of novel transcription factors. *Mol. Bio. Evol.* 32, 7 (2015), 1767–1773.

[14] Insuk Lee, Bindu Ambaru, Pranjali Thakkar, Edward M Marcotte, and Seung Y Rhee. 2010. Rational association of genes with traits using a genome-scale gene network for Arabidopsis thaliana. *Nature Biotechnology* 28, 2 (2010), 149–156.

[15] Tak Lee, Sunmo Yang, Eiru Kim, Younhee Ko, Sohyun Hwang, Junha Shin, Jung Eun Shim, Hongseok Shim, Hyojin Kim, Chanyoung Kim, and others. 2014. AraNet v2: an improved database of co-functional gene networks for the study of Arabidopsis thaliana and 27 other nonmodel plant species. *Nucleic Acids Research* 43, D1 (2014), D996–D1002.

[16] Wei-Po Lee and Wen-Shyong Tzou. 2009. Computational methods for discovering gene networks from expression data. *Briefings in Bioinformatics* 10, 4 (2009), 408–423.

[17] Shisong Ma, Qingqiu Gong, and Hans J Bohnert. 2007. An Arabidopsis gene network based on the graphical Gaussian model. *Genome Research* 17, 11 (2007), 1614–1625.

[18] Linyong Mao, John L Van Hemert, Sudhansu Dash, and Julie A Dickerson. 2009. Arabidopsis gene co-expression network and its functional modules. *BMC Bioinformatics* 10, 1 (2009), 346.

[19] Daniel Marbach, James C Costello, Robert Küffner, Nicole M Vega, Robert J Prill, Diogo M Camacho, Kyle R Allison, Manolis Kellis, James J Collins, Gustavo Stolovitzky, and others. 2012. Wisdom of crowds for robust gene network inference. *Nature Methods* 9, 8 (2012), 796–804.

[20] Daniel Marbach, Robert J Prill, Thomas Schaffter, Claudio Mattiussi, Dario Floreano, and Gustavo Stolovitzky. 2010. Revealing strengths and weaknesses of methods for gene network inference. *Proceedings of the National Academy of Sciences* 107, 14 (2010), 6286–6291.

[21] Sanchit Misra, Kiran Pamnany, and Srinivas Aluru. 2015. Parallel Mutual Information Based Construction of Genome-Scale Networks on the Intel®Xeon Phi™ Coprocessor. *IEEE/ACM Transactions on Computational Biology and Bioinformatics* 12, 5 (2015), 1008–1020.

[22] Sanchit Misra, Md Vasimuddin, Kiran Pamnany, Sriram P Chockalingam, Yong Dong, Min Xie, Maneesha R Aluru, and Srinivas Aluru. 2014. Parallel Bayesian Network Structure Learning for Genome-Scale Gene Networks. In *Proceedings of the International Conference for High Performance Computing, Networking, Storage and Analysis, SC 2014*. IEEE, 461–472.

[23] Renuka R Nayak, Michael Kearns, Richard S Spielman, and Vivian G Cheung. 2009. Coexpression network based on natural variation in human gene expression reveals gene interactions and functions. *Genome Research* 19, 11 (2009), 1953–1962.

[24] Olga Nikolova and Srinivas Aluru. 2012. Parallel Bayesian network structure learning with application to gene networks. In *Proceedings of the International Conference for High Performance Computing, Networking, Storage and Analysis, SC 2012*. 63.

[25] Amela Prelić, Stefan Bleuler, Philip Zimmermann, Anja Wille, Peter Bühlmann, Wilhelm Gruissem, Lars Hennig, Lothar Thiele, and Eckart Zitzler. 2006. A systematic comparison and evaluation of biclustering methods for gene expression data. *Bioinformatics* 22, 9 (2006), 1122–1129.

[26] Juliane Schäfer and Korbinian Strimmer. 2004. An empirical Bayes approach to inferring large-scale gene association networks. *Bioinformatics* 21, 6 (2004), 754–764.

[27] Nicola Soranzo, Ginestra Bianconi, and Claudio Altafini. 2007. Comparing association network algorithms for reverse engineering of large-scale gene regulatory networks: synthetic versus real data. *Bioinformatics* 23, 13 (2007), 1640.

[28] Duncan J Watts and Steven H Strogatz. 1998. Collective dynamics of âĂŸsmall-worldâĂŹnetworks. *nature* 393, 6684 (1998), 440–442.

[29] Anja Wille, Philip Zimmermann, Eva Vranová, Andreas Fürholz, Oliver Laule, Stefan Bleuler, Lars Hennig, Amela Prelić, Peter von Rohr, Lothar Thiele, and others. 2004. Sparse graphical Gaussian modeling of the isoprenoid gene network in Arabidopsis thaliana. *Genome Biology* 5, 11 (2004), R92.

[30] Huaxun Ye, Sanzhen Liu, Buyun Tang, Jiani Chen, Zhouli Xie, Trevor M Nolan, Hao Jiang, Hongqing Guo, Hung-Ying Lin, Lei Li, and others. 2017. RD26 mediates crosstalk between drought and brassinosteroid signalling pathways. *Nature Communications* 8, 14573 (2017).

[31] Jing Yu, V Anne Smith, Paul P Wang, Alexander J Hartemink, and Erich D Jarvis. 2002. Using Bayesian Network Inference Algorithms to Recover Molecular Genetic Regulatory Networks.. In *Proceedings of the International Conference on Systems Biology*, Vol. 2002.

[32] Jaroslaw Zola, Maneesha Aluru, Abhinav Sarje, and Srinivas Aluru. 2010. Parallel information-theory-based construction of genome-wide gene regulatory networks. *IEEE Transactions on Parallel and Distributed Systems* 21, 12 (2010), 1721–1733.

Unsupervised Multi-View Feature Selection for Tumor Subtype Identification

Sultan Imangaliyev*
VU University Medical Center
Amsterdam, Netherlands
s.imangaliyev@vumc.nl

Evgeni Levin
Academic Medical Center
Amsterdam, Netherlands
e.levin@amc.uva.nl

ABSTRACT

Existing unsupervised feature selection algorithms are designed to extract the most relevant subset of features which can facilitate clustering and interpretation of the obtained results. However, these techniques are not directly applicable in many real-world situations in which one has access to datasets consisting of multiple views or dissimilar representations. By leveraging information from these different views one can obtain more robust and accurate results compared with single-view methods. In this paper Unsupervised Multi-View Feature Selection algorithm is used to simultaneously extract a relevant subset of features and to perform clustering that is consistent across different views. In the empirical evaluation of synthetic multi-view data we demonstrate the advantage of using the proposed algorithm over the use of its single-view analogue. We used the National Cancer Institute's NCI-60 panel dataset, exploiting information from various -omics representations to identify tumor subtypes based on very few requisite, biologically relevant features.

KEYWORDS

Unsupervised learning; Feature selection; Multi-view learning; Spectral clustering

1 INTRODUCTION

1.1 Background and Motivation

The general aim of the feature selection procedure is to extract a subset of relevant features that capture key information from a dataset. These selected features can be used to interpret results in a variety of ways such as dimensionality reduction, predictive value identification, and visualization of the data. While an abundance of literature has considered supervised feature selection over the past decades, recently unsupervised feature selection techniques have received significant attention. Unsupervised feature selection is particularly suitable when labeled data are not readily available. The methods that can process manifold information contained in the data have demonstrated exceptional results in such circumstances as Laplacian Score [10], Multi-Cluster Feature Selection [5], Joint Embedding Learning and Sparse Regression [12] algorithms.

Despite good performance, these techniques have displayed one fundamental limitation: they are not applicable in real-world situations when datasets often consist of multiple views or representations, *e.g.* various -omics profiles of patients, clinical records coupled with fMRI images, physiological parameters, and other such structured datasets. Frequently, individual biological data representations are not sufficient to reach an informative outcome and a model based on multiple views is vital in ensuring all available information is taken into account. This underprints the need for an unsupervised multi-view method capable of simultaneous analysis of multiple data representations of the underlying biological process from the same set of samples. Such a multi-view model should be able to investigate interactions of underlying biological processes from the same set of samples which would be otherwise missed by single-view methods.

This task can be accomplished via a co-regularization framework [28], that builds on the idea of agreement maximization among hypotheses constructed for different views. Within this framework, disagreement is taken into account by the so-called co-regularization term. This framework has been successfully used for various machine learning problems such as semi-supervised classification [14], regression [4], domain adaptation [8], preference learning [31], clustering [15].

In this paper a novel algorithm for Unsupervised Multi-View Feature Selection (UMVFS) is introduced which is naturally applicable to learning from datasets consisting of multiple diverse data representations. Computational cancer biology is a good example of an area in which multi-view unsupervised feature selection can provide benefits. Development of a tumor is a complex process involving multiple molecular interactions among miRNA, mRNA, DNA, peptides, signaling molecules, and drug activities. Recent advances in genomics facilitate the generation of multiple datasets referring to the same sample. Applying machine learning tools to those datasets can extract a subset of features which differentiate among multiple types of tumors across all views. This can help to develop fast diagnostic tools and aid cancer treatment. In this work a multi-view cancer NCI-60 dataset panel (available via the CellMiner web-based query tool [27]) is utilized to demonstrate applicability of UMVFS on biological data.

UMVFS is a learning algorithm that uses multiple views to jointly select features and perform clustering. The algorithm is empirically evaluated on synthetic multi-view datasets. We also demonstrate the applicability of UMVFS on biological data; the multi-view NCI-60 cancer panel dataset. Clustering performance of the model is evaluated using Normalized Mutual Information on synthetic datasets

*Corresponding author.

Permission to make digital or hard copies of all or part of this work for personal or classroom use is granted without fee provided that copies are not made or distributed for profit or commercial advantage and that copies bear this notice and the full citation on the first page. Copyrights for components of this work owned by others than ACM must be honored. Abstracting with credit is permitted. To copy otherwise, or republish, to post on servers or to redistribute to lists, requires prior specific permission and/or a fee. Request permissions from permissions@acm.org.
ACM-BCB'17, August 20-23, 2017, Boston, MA, USA.
© 2017 ACM. 978-1-4503-4722-8/17/08...$15.00
DOI: http://dx.doi.org/10.1145/3107411.3107413

and compared with the performance of the single-view unsupervised feature selection model. The relevance of selected features is compared with true features in the synthetic dataset analysis case and with existing scientific literature in the NCI-60 dataset analysis case.

1.2 Related work

Multiple studies have been published in which feature selection or clustering were applied separately or serially to multi-omics datasets with empirical evaluation of NCI-60 datasets. To the best of our knowledge, UMVFS is the first method which jointly extracts the relevant subset of features whilst simultaneously performing clustering that is consistent across different views within NCI-60 datasets. In this section we provide an overview of selected previous work applied to multi-omics NCI-60 datasets.

Our method has multiple advantages compared with other methods applied to this or similar datasets. UMVFS is the feature selection method unlike the Similarity network fusion method [32] applied on integration of mRNA, DNA methylation and miRNA expression data for five cancer datasets to identify subtypes with differential survival profiles. A multi-view unsupervised approach called Multiple Co-Inertia Analysis (MCIA) was used on transcriptome and proteome profiles [22]. Our method, compared with MCIA, imposes sparsity in the result, so that it selects fewer features than do methods that do not introduce regularization.

In order to extract important features from a quantitative proteome and kinome profile, hierarchical clustering and Elastic net were used separately to uncover protein signatures significantly associated with drug sensitivity and resistance [9]. Similarly, hierarchical clustering was firstly used to identify clusters; afterwards correlations were calculated between bioassays and corresponding PubChem assays to construct separate networks per cluster [6]. Another method integrates multi-view data using four steps by factorizing the membership matrices in a late integration manner [26]. All these methods exploit various multiple-step approaches which use separate objective functions one after another. Our method, on the contrary, performs both clustering and feature selection simultaneously, within a single objective function which is faster and more rigorous than carrying out two or more optimization steps.

Perhaps the most simplistic way to integrate multiple views is to concatenate features across all views by merging mRNA and miRNA datasets, and then later applying factor analysis combined with linear discriminant analysis to extract important features [20]. This approach is questionable due to possible overfitting caused by concatenating the features while ignoring differences among views. Another approach is to use Bayesian sparse factor analysis as has been done to analyze gene expression and drug sensitivity datasets by incorporating prior knowledge regarding gene-pathway and drug-pathway associations [21]. The UMVFS model is considered more versatile as it may be applied to integrate all types of -omics datasets even if domain-specific knowledge is limited.

A straightforward approach to solve a feature selection problem is to replace the unsupervised feature selection by a supervised one. Examples of such methods usually include classification coupled with a feature selection algorithm. It has been proposed to use the nearest shrunken centroid method [33] which computes centroid prototypes for each class and, following this, classification is applied to the nearest centroids in a LASSO manner. Besides LASSO, genetic algorithms may be used to perform classification directly on labels decoded from tumor tissue origins on DNA data [18, 19]. UMVFS is certainly preferable when working with real biomedical datasets, because it does not need classification labels. In addition, in comparison with all three above mentioned methods ours is multi-view, explicitly modeling interaction among multiple views.

The UMVFS algorithm addresses many disadvantages of the methods mentioned above. Namely, it is multi-view, allowing the inclusion of interaction among multiple data sources to improve overall performance. Next, it is unsupervised, therefore no labels need to be provided. Furthermore, it is sparse, thus it naturally performs feature selection simultaneously with clustering. Compared with other models, ours is closely related to the multi-view clustering concept [15], and it uses the idea of sparse spectral regression [12]. However, unlike multi-view clustering, it does perform feature selection and unlike sparse spectral regression, it is applicable in multi-view cases.

The UMVFS algorithm was utilized in our previous work [17], in which we used the National Institutes of Health Human Microbiome Project dataset to demonstrate the applicability of UMVFS to a metagenomics dataset. In that work we used clustering labels from previous work [13] to compute Normalized Mutual Information and we split views based on biological niche information of oral microbiology samples. In this article we use the same method, but on a truly multi-view datasets, meaning that views are originated from different -omics platforms.

2 MATERIALS AND METHODS

2.1 Mathematical formulation of the algorithm

Consider we are given a dataset containing multiple representations. Let $\mathbf{X}^{(v)} = \{\mathbf{x}_i^{(v)}\}_{i=1}^n$. Note that here superscript v denotes the representation for a single view. Let $\mathbf{A}^{(v)}$ denote an adjacency matrix of the graph constructed using the data representation in a view v. We can write the normalized Laplacian matrix as $\mathbf{L}^{(v)} = \mathbf{D}^{(v)-1/2}\mathbf{A}^{(v)}\mathbf{D}^{(v)-1/2}$, where $\mathbf{D}^{(v)}$ is the corresponding degree matrix.

Similarly to existing single view unsupervised feature selection techniques [12], our multi-view algorithm can take into account manifold structures in the data and it efficiently selects the most relevant features via sparse regularization. Consider the following standard spectral clustering algorithm [23] that solves the optimization problem

$$\begin{aligned} &\underset{\mathbf{Q}^{(v)}}{\operatorname{argmin}}\, tr\left(\mathbf{Q}^{(v)}\mathbf{L}^{(v)}\mathbf{Q}^{(v)^T}\right) \\ &\text{s.t.} \quad \mathbf{Q}^{(v)}\mathbf{Q}^{(v)^T} = \mathbf{I}, \end{aligned} \tag{1}$$

where $\mathbf{Q}^{(v)} \in \mathbb{R}^{m\times n}$ denotes the cluster assignment matrix. In spectral clustering the final cluster membership is obtained by applying the k-means algorithm on the rows of the matrix $\mathbf{Q}^{(v)}$.

Similarly to the approach taken in spectral regression and several unsupervised feature selection techniques, we regress each sample to its low dimensional embedding and enforce the sparsity by adding a regularization term. More concretely, we assume that $\mathbf{x}_i^{(v)}$ is centered and denote $\mathbf{W}^{(v)} = [\mathbf{w}_1^{(v)}, \mathbf{w}_2^{(v)}, \ldots, \mathbf{w}_m^{(v)}] \in \mathbb{R}^{d \times m}$ as the matrix of vectors $\{\mathbf{w}_i^{(v)}\}_{i=1}^m$. Then the minimization problem can be written as

$$\begin{aligned} &\underset{\mathbf{W}^{(v)}}{\operatorname{argmin}} \sum_{i=1}^{n} \left\| \mathbf{W}^{(v)^T} \mathbf{x}_i^{(v)} - \mathbf{q}_i^{(v)} \right\|_2^2 = \\ &= \left\| \mathbf{W}^{(v)^T} \mathbf{X}^{(v)} - \mathbf{Q}^{(v)} \right\|_2^2 + \lambda \left\| \mathbf{W}^{(v)} \right\|_{2,1}. \end{aligned} \tag{2}$$

By slightly overloading notation let us denote the $\bar{\mathbf{w}}_i^{(v)}$ as the i-th row of the matrix $\mathbf{W}^{(v)}$. Considering the task of feature selection we expect that only a small number of $\bar{\mathbf{w}}_i^{(v)}$ have nonzero elements. As a result, the corresponding features are selected since these feature are enough to regress original data to its low dimensional representation.

By defining the matrix $\mathbf{U} \in \mathbb{R}^{d \times d}$ as a diagonal matrix whose i-th element is $\mathbf{U}_{ii}^{(v)} = \frac{1}{2\left\|\bar{\mathbf{w}}_i^{(v)}\right\|_2}$ we can write $\left\|\mathbf{W}^{(v)}\right\|_{2,1}/2$ in a matrix notation as $tr(\mathbf{W}^{(v)^T}\mathbf{U}^{(v)}\mathbf{W}^{(v)})$ when $\bar{\mathbf{w}}_i^{(v)}$ is nonzero. Then, taking the derivative with respect to $\mathbf{W}^{(v)}$ we obtain

$$\mathbf{W}^{(v)} = (\mathbf{X}^{(v)}\mathbf{X}^{(v)^T} + \lambda \mathbf{U}^{(v)})^{-1}\mathbf{X}^{(v)}\mathbf{Q}^{(v)^T}. \tag{3}$$

So far we have formulated single-view task formulation. To take into account the agreement among the hypotheses constructed for different views, we use additional co-regularization term. For simplicity and demonstration purposes, we present a pairwise formulation of the algorithm. Let us consider the following objective

$$\begin{aligned} &\underset{\mathbf{W}^{(v)},\mathbf{U}^{(v)},\mathbf{W}^{(u)},\mathbf{U}^{(u)}}{\operatorname{argmin}} \quad tr\left(\mathbf{Q}^{(v)}\mathbf{L}^{(v)}\mathbf{Q}^{(v)^T}\right) + \\ &+ \nu\Big(\left\| \mathbf{W}^{(v)^T}\mathbf{X}^{(v)}(\mathbf{W}^{(u)^T}\mathbf{X}^{(u)})^T - \mathbf{Q}^{(v)}\mathbf{Q}^{(u)^T} \right\|_2^2 + \\ &+ \left\| \mathbf{W}^{(v)^T}\mathbf{X}^{(v)} - \mathbf{Q}^{(v)} \right\|_2^2 + \lambda tr(\mathbf{W}^{(v)^T}\mathbf{U}^{(v)}\mathbf{W}^{(v)}) \Big) \\ &\text{s.t.} \quad \mathbf{Q}^{(v)}\mathbf{Q}^{(v)^T} = \mathbf{I}, \mathbf{Q}^{(u)}\mathbf{Q}^{(u)^T} = \mathbf{I}. \end{aligned} \tag{4}$$

Substituting precomputed $\mathbf{W}^{(v)}$ and $\mathbf{W}^{(u)}$ matrices, opening the norms, and simplifying the equations by denoting

$$\begin{aligned} \mathbf{R}^{(v)} &= \mathbf{X}^{(v)^T}(\mathbf{X}^{(v)}\mathbf{X}^{(v)^T} + \lambda \mathbf{U}^{(v)})^{-1}\mathbf{X}^{(v)} \\ \mathbf{R}^{(u)} &= \mathbf{X}^{(u)^T}(\mathbf{X}^{(u)}\mathbf{X}^{(u)^T} + \lambda \mathbf{U}^{(u)})^{-1}\mathbf{X}^{(u)}, \end{aligned} \tag{5}$$

we end up with the following optimization problem that can be solved for each view given that the other view is fixed:

$$\begin{aligned} &\underset{\mathbf{Q}^{(v)}}{\operatorname{argmin}}\, tr\Big(\mathbf{Q}^{(v)}(\mathbf{L}^{(v)} + \nu(\mathbf{I} - \mathbf{R}^{(v)} + \\ &+ \gamma \mathbf{R}^{(v)}\mathbf{R}^{(u)}\mathbf{Q}^{(u)^T}\mathbf{Q}^{(u)}(\mathbf{R}^{(u)}\mathbf{R}^{(v)} - I) + \\ &\qquad + \mathbf{Q}^{(u)^T}\mathbf{Q}^{(u)}))\mathbf{Q}^{(v)^T}\Big) \\ &\text{s.t.} \quad \mathbf{Q}^{(v)}\mathbf{Q}^{(v)^T} = \mathbf{I}. \end{aligned} \tag{6}$$

Thus, we have three parameters to be tuned in the final implementation. The first one is λ controlling the influence of sparsity of the selected features, the second one is ν controlling the spectral regression part, and finally γ controlling the co-regularization between the views. The outline of the procedure of the UMVFS for pair-wise implementation on two views is listed in Table 1. Informally, we start by eigendecomposition of the Laplacian matrices constructed for each view and compute the corresponding weight matrices. Once the weights are computed we can estimate new co-regularized eigenvectors. We repeat the procedure several times and monitor the convergence by the difference in the value of the objective between consecutive iterations. We stop when the difference falls below a minimum threshold (*e.g.* 10^{-6}). The number of iterations rarely exceeds 50. Once the co-regularized eigenvectors for all views are computed we repeat the procedure for estimating new weight matrices and proceed until convergence.

Table 1: Procedure of UMVFS for pair-wise implementation on two views

Input:
- Multi-view datasets $\{\mathbf{x}_i^{(v)}\}_{i=1}^n$, $\{\mathbf{x}_i^{(u)}\}_{i=1}^n$;
- Hyperparameters λ, ν, γ;
- Dimensionality of embedding m;
- Number of total features in each view d, g;
- Selected feature score threshold s.

Stage one: Graph construction per each view v, u
1. Construct adjacency matrices $\mathbf{G}^{(v)}, \mathbf{G}^{(u)}$ and degree matrices $\mathbf{D}^{(v)}, \mathbf{D}^{(u)}$;
2. Construct graph Laplacians $\mathbf{L}^{(v)}$ and $\mathbf{L}^{(u)}$

Stage two: Alternative optimization
1. Compute initial $\mathbf{Q}^{(v)}, \mathbf{Q}^{(u)}$ by eigendecomposition of $\mathbf{L}^{(v)}$ and $\mathbf{L}^{(u)}$
2. Compute corresponding initial $\mathbf{W}^{(v)}$, $\mathbf{W}^{(u)}$
3. Alternatively update $\mathbf{Q}^{(v)}, \mathbf{Q}^{(u)}$,
   (a) Fix $\mathbf{R}^{(v)}, \mathbf{R}^{(u)}, \mathbf{Q}^{(u)}, \mathbf{L}^{(v)}$ and compute $\mathbf{Q}^{(v)}$;
   (b) Fix $\mathbf{R}^{(u)}, \mathbf{R}^{(v)}, \mathbf{Q}^{(v)}, \mathbf{L}^{(u)}$ and compute $\mathbf{Q}^{(u)}$;
   (c) Repeat steps a and b several times
4. Compute corresponding $\mathbf{W}^{(v)}$, $\mathbf{W}^{(u)}$ based on co-regularized $\mathbf{Q}^{(v)}, \mathbf{Q}^{(u)}$
5. Compute new $\mathbf{U}^{(v)}, \mathbf{U}^{(u)}$, based on new $\mathbf{W}^{(v)}$, $\mathbf{W}^{(u)}$
6. Repeat steps 3-5 until convergence

Stage three: Feature selection and clustering
1. Feature selection. Compute the scores for all features $\left\{\left\|\bar{\mathbf{w}}_i^{(v)}\right\|_2\right\}_{i=1}^d, \left\{\left\|\bar{\mathbf{w}}_i^{(u)}\right\|_2\right\}_{i=1}^g$. Sort these scores, select the values larger than s, extract their corresponding indices.
2. Clustering. Concatenate first m eigenvectors in set $\mathbf{Q}^{(v)}, \mathbf{Q}^{(u)}$ and run k-means with predefined number of clusters m.

Output:
- Selected feature score sets $\{r_i^{(v)}\}_{i=1}^{(s)}$, $\{r_i^{(u)}\}_{i=1}^{(s)}$;
- Joint clustering labels $\{q_i^{(v)}\}_{i=1}^n = \{q_i^{(u)}\}_{i=1}^n$.

2.2 Datasets

2.2.1 Synthetic datasets. Before testing the UMVFS algorithm on real-world datasets, we evaluated its performance by using synthetic datasets. We first used a multi-view dataset [15] which originally consisted of a thousand examples, three views of which each view contained only two features. To make the dataset suitable for a feature selection task, we added ninety-eight noisy features, resulting in a hundred features in each view. This expanded dataset contained two clusters only.

A second type of synthetic datasets was generated to assess the influence of the number of clusters as well as the number of noisy features. We used a scikit-learn implementation [25] of a synthetic data generator to generate a dataset with corresponding labels. Then we added additional noisy features and split the dataset into two views. Each view in these two-view synthetic datasets contains a thousand examples and twenty features in total. We varied the number of clusters between three and five to test a multi-cluster setting. At the same time we varied the number of useful features in each view between three and seven. Although in most biological datasets the number of examples is smaller than the number of features, these synthetic datasets were generated so that the number of examples is larger than the number of features. This ensures the receipt of a reliable estimation of Normalized Mutual Information (NMI), because NMI is an information theoretic based measure that tends to have larger variation when the ratio between the number of data points and the number of clusters is relatively small. Experiments on datasets with large number of examples allow the evaluation of the influence of the true features on the model's performance ignoring random variation of NMI results. A more realistic case is tested in the experiments applied to NCI-60 datasets.

2.2.2 NCI-60 datasets. In order to test the algorithm on a biological multi-view dataset we used NCI-60 datasets, available for downloading through the CellMiner tool [27]. CellMiner is a web application that facilitates systems biology through the retrieval and integration of the molecular and pharmacological datasets for the NCI-60 cell lines. It represents multiple biological views such as DNA, RNA, miRNA datasets from various platforms. We chose the following datasets:

- 162 features of reverse-phase protein lysate arrays (Proteomics data);
- 627 features of an oligonucleotide microchip for genome-wide miRNA profiling in human and mouse tissue (miRNA data);
- 47 features of specific oligonucleotide probes designed for each of the ATP-binding cassette transporters (ABC transporters) using DNAStar Primer Select (mRNA data);
- 422 features retrieved from 15000 probes for 723 human and 76 human viral miRNAs from the Agilent Human miRNA V2 GeneSpringGX platform (miRNA data);
- 626 features of the Spotted 70-mer OSU Transporter microarray (mRNA data).

Each dataset contains sixty examples referring to cell lines of leukemia (LE, six examples), melanomas (ME, ten examples) and carcinomas of ovarian (OV, seven examples), renal (RE, eight examples), breast (BR, five examples), prostate (PR, two examples), colon (CO, seven examples), lung (LC, nine examples) and the central nervous system (CNS, six examples) cancer. All datasets were scaled so that every feature has zero-mean and unit variance.

2.3 Experimental setup

2.3.1 General settings. Similarly to the experimental setup used in previous studies [12, 15], we tuned coefficients λ, γ and ν in our model via a grid search procedure. The other alternatives to grid search are random search [3], gradient-based optimization [3], and Bayesian optimization [29], but grid search was chosen due to its relative simplicity. To compute similarities, we used Gaussian kernel, where the standard deviation of the kernel is defined as equal to the median of the pair-wise Euclidean distances between the data points [15].

To measure the model performance, we used scikit-learn implementation [25] of NMI

$$NMI(U,V) = \frac{MI(U,V)}{\sqrt{H(U)H(V)}}, \tag{7}$$

where $MI(U,V)$ is the mutual information between two label assignments U and V, $H(U)$ and $H(V)$ are entropy measures for U and V respectively. This provides the mutual information [30] between obtained clustering (based on the selected subset of features) and true clustering (normalized by the cluster entropies). We report the results for each view and the co-regularized results based on concatenation of eigenvalues extracted from the co-regularized Laplacians [15]. For simplicity and demonstrative purposes, we ran the model on two views, but extension to multiple views is also possible.

To evaluate the influence of multi-view setting on model's performance, we compared the performance of UMVFS with the performance of Joint Embedded Learning via Spectral Regression (JELSR, [12]) as a baseline model. JELSR was shown to be superior to other single-view unsupervised feature selection models such as Laplacian Score [10], Spectral Feature Selection [35], Multi-Cluster Feature Selection [5], and Minimum Redundancy Spectral Feature Selection [36]. Since JELSR is the best of all single-view methods, we assume that using JELSR is sufficient for the comparison of performance between single-view and multi-view models. The aim of this study is to demonstrate the advantage of the use of multi-view model over a single-view model, therefore single-view JELSR was chosen as a good baseline model. We report four NMI measurements calculated on labels retrieved from both JELSR and UMVFS simulations. JELSR FC, JELSR V1, and JELSR V2 are the results of single-view model runs on, respectively: concatenated feature dataset, view one, and view two. UMVFS V12 is the result of a multi-view model run on both co-regularized views simultaneously.

2.3.2 Choice of tumor types in NCI-60 datasets. In order to model the influence of biological diversity on clustering results we performed three different experiments on NCI-60 datasets. During each experiment we subsampled datasets, selecting only those examples corresponding to a certain type of tumor. Subsampling was based on the epithelial or non-epithelial property of a tumor as provided by metadata available on the CellMiner website. We performed three experiments on various view combinations such as provided below:

(1) A mix of epithelial carcinomas of ovarian (OV, seven examples), renal (RE, eight examples), lung (LC, nine examples) cancers and non-epithelial melanoma (ME, ten examples) tumor examples;
(2) Only non-epithelial tumor cells of leukemia (LE, six examples), central nervous system (CNS, six examples) and melanoma (ME, ten examples);
(3) Only epithelial tumor cells of colon (CO, seven examples), renal (RE, eight examples) cancers and carcinomas of ovarian (OV, seven examples) cancer.

Other types of tumors such as breast cancer and prostate cancer are excluded from analysis due to insufficient number of samples for training to distinguish differences across tumor types. Also, lung cancer examples were excluded from the experiment 3 to achieve an equal number of clusters between experiments 2 and 3.

3 RESULTS AND DISCUSSION

3.1 Synthetic datasets

The results of UMVFS application to synthetic datasets are presented in Table 2. These results indicate that in datasets with an unequal number of useful features among views, NMI is usually higher by the views which have more truly important features. In all simulations UMVFS demonstrated better NMI in comparison with the single-view model. The synthetic dataset 1 [15] is imbalanced because its view 1 contains more useful information, which is reflected in a higher NMI. Adding additional, apparently noisier, view 2 did not improve the multi-view model's performance notably. On the contrary, the synthetic dataset 2 demonstrates relatively balanced NMI on single-view runs. It is apparent that information in each view is rather complementary than repetitive to each other. Hence, modelling both views in a multi-view fashion proves to be more beneficial than modelling them separately in a single-view setting. It is seen than NMI of UMVFS is roughly equal to the sum of NMI for JELSR of views 1 and 2. These results suggest that UMVFS is applicable and beneficial only in cases when both views contain complementary non-redundant information. It appears that co-regularization results in the modelling of clustering interactions among views, which are otherwise missed by a single-view approach. It also becomes clear that feature concatenation leads to inferior results in comparison with single view runs, because the amount of noise also increases with the number of total features. The number of selected features per each simulation for both JELSR and UMVFS are depicted in Figure 1.

This figure provides a comparison of how many real features were selected by JELSR and UMVFS. Since truly important features are known beforehand, this comparison allows to evaluate which features are selected as important ones, while in reality they are not important, *i.e.* which features are false positive important ones. On the contrary, if a truly important feature is not selected, such a feature can be called as a false negative important one. We observe that in most cases the UMVFS algorithm selects the useful features and disregards the noisy ones. In view combinations 1, 2, 6, 8 both JELSR and UMVFS select the same number of features. In view combination 8 the number of selected features for both views is exactly equal to the number of the true features. In view combinations 1, 2, 6 neither model selects all true features for one of the views (combinations 1 and 6) or for both of views (combination 2). We also observe that UMVFS gives better feature selection results in comparison with the single-view technique in several view combinations. Such view combinations are marked by inverse triangles (view combinations 3, 4, 5, 7). In combination 7 UMVFS selects all true features, while in combination 4 UMVFS selects extra false positive feature in view 2. In view combinations 3 and 5 neither JELSR or UMVFS selects all true features, but in combination 3 for view 2 UMVFS selects extra one true feature. Also, in combination 5 for view 1 UMVFS selects extra one true feature. These results suggest that both UMVFS and JELSR are rather strict in terms of feature selection and tend to select the false negative important features rather than false positive important ones.

The results for synthetic datasets suggest that the proposed UMVFS method performs well in three different tasks simultaneously. Firstly, it detects existing clusters as is shown by higher NMI values. Secondly, it efficiently uses complementary information contained in each view via a co-regularization procedure leading to a higher NMI than its single-view counterpart, JELSR. Finally, it selects only the relevant subset of features which is justified by the results of synthetic datasets in which we knew *a priori* which features are the true ones. Overall, results of the simulations on synthetic datasets demonstrate the advantage of UMVFS over JELSR and we suggest that in case of real-world datasets, such as NCI-60 datasets, UMVFS will remove noisy features jointly whilst revealing true clusters in a multi-view manner.

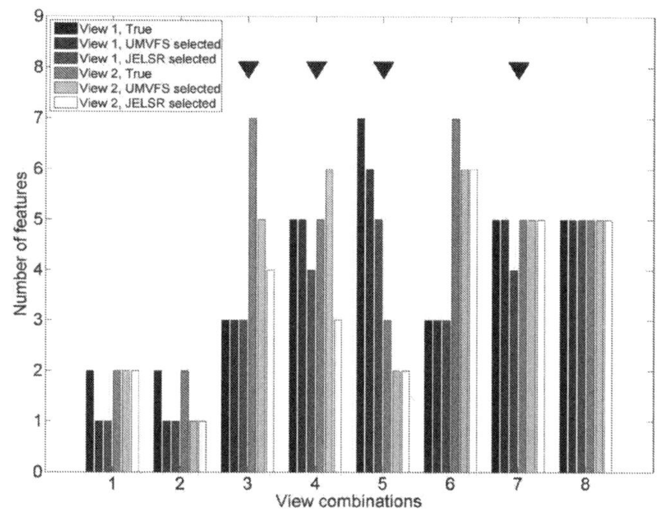

Figure 1: Comparison of the number of selected features between JELSR and UMVFS on synthetic data. The number of selected features per view combination in the experiments performed on the synthetic datasets compared between JELSR and UMVFS. Inverse triangles mark cases in which UMVFS selects more true features than JELSR. View combinations in this figure match view combinations shown in Table 2.

Table 2: NMI performance of the experiments performed on two synthetic datasets. JELSR - unsupervised single-view feature selection technique, UMVFS - unsupervised multi-view feature selection technique. V1 and V2 - single-view runs on views 1 and 2, V12 - co-regularized multi-view runs, FC - dataset obtained by feature concatenation of both views. First number in parentheses after data name indicates number of clusters; the second, number of examples. First number in parentheses after view name indicates total number of features; the second, number of useful features. NMI results in boldface emphasize the best performance, numbers in italics emphasize the second-best performance. View combinations in this table match view combinations shown in Figure 1.

Data	View 1	View 2	JELSR FC	JELSR V1	JELSR V2	UMVFS V12
Synth 1 (2,1000)	V1 (100,2)	V2 (100,2)	*0.92*	0.92	0.52	**0.94**
Synth 1 (2,1000)	V1 (100,2)	V2 (100,2)	*0.92*	0.92	0.49	**0.94**
Synth 2 (3,1000)	V1 (20,3)	V2 (20,7)	*0.22*	0.12	0.20	**0.28**
Synth 2 (3,1000)	V1 (20,5)	V2 (20,5)	*0.22*	0.20	0.17	**0.36**
Synth 2 (3,1000)	V1 (20,7)	V2 (20,3)	0.22	*0.23*	0.16	**0.35**
Synth 2 (4,1000)	V1 (20,3)	V2 (20,7)	0.26	0.19	*0.30*	**0.50**
Synth 2 (4,1000)	V1 (20,5)	V2 (20,5)	0.26	0.18	*0.27*	**0.45**
Synth 2 (5,1000)	V1 (20,5)	V2 (20,5)	0,31	0,25	0,24	**0,36**

3.2 NCI-60 datasets

Unlike synthetic datasets, with actual clinical datasets we have access neither to true clusters, nor to the number of true features for NCI-60 datasets. Therefore, measuring NMI becomes impossible, and in this section the main focus is given to the number of features selected after applying various combinations of views in three experiments. UMVFS still needs a number of clusters as an input parameter. We use the number of tumor types as the number of clusters, because the underlying biological assumption is that clustering would reveal the differences possibly caused by the tumor types.

We performed an exhaustive search among all ten possible combinations of views across all three experiments. The results of UMVFS for NCI-60 datasets are depicted in Figure 2. This figure demonstrates that UMVFS selects only a small subset of features and the percentage of selected features exceeds 25% only in a few rare cases. These cases are: Experiments 1 and 3 in view combination 5, Experiment 1 in view combination 6, Experiment 2 in view combination 7 and Experiment 1 in view combination 1. In these cases it is possible to reduce number of selected features by tuning λ, thereby controlling the influence of sparsity shrinkage. It is difficult to discern any pattern with respect to experiment number or view combination number. It is important, though, that in most other *view-experiment* combinations the model selects a very small fraction of features. Since UMVFS jointly optimizes feature sparsity and spectral regression, one can suggest that the selected features are sufficient to predict eigenvectors of the Laplacian matrix. The smaller subset of features is easier to interpret and in the NCI-60 dataset case these features may allow finding new biomarkers that discriminate among clusters of tumors.

For demonstration purposes, we provide a feature selection results for view combination 1, because there were fewer than ten selected features in each view. In this experiment the dataset from reverse-phase protein lysate arrays was combined with the ATP-binding cassette transporters mRNA dataset. Non-epithelial tumor cells of leukemia and lymphomas (LE, six examples), the central nervous system (CNS, six examples) and melanoma (ME, ten examples) were included, resulting in three types of tumors and thus three cluster simulations. The top six selected features of the proteomics-transcriptomics non-epithelial UMVFS run are shown in Table 3. The threshold of top six was selected based on better visualization of results in figures and a simpler interpretation of the results. It is important to note that these results are not based on a single-view, but on a multi-view model. Both views were co-trained and co-regularized; hence the results were reported per each view, although they were obtained in a single run of the multi-view model.

Table 3: The feature selection results from UMVFS for the joint protein and ABC transporters mRNA datasets. All feature importance coefficients were normalized so that the maximum value of the coefficient was set to 1.0.

	View 1, proteins		View 2, mRNA	
Rank	**Name**	**Score**	**Name**	**Score**
1	*EP300-16*	1.00	*ABCC12*	1.00
2	*PTPN6*	0.91	*ABCE1*	0.74
3	*EP300-20*	0.40	*ABCB7*	0.46
4	*EMS1*	0.26	*ABCC2*	0.35
5	*CDK4*	0.23	*ABCD2*	0.35
6	*KRT20*	0.22	*ABCB4*	0.25

To compare feature selection results of UMVFS and JESR, we also provide results of running JELSR model on the same protein and mRNA dataset, together with a joint dataset derived by concatenating features of the two datasets. These results are shown in Table 4. This table clearly shows that co-regularization has an effect on list of selected features. Unlike UMVFS results, JELSR selects different subset of features with different ranking and scores are distributed less equally across features, especially for the experiment performed on mRNA dataset only.

The results of clustering were also analyzed and they very closely coincide with the origins of tumor tissue. All CNS tumors were clustered together as were all LE examples. Out of ten melanoma examples nine were clustered together; the tenth (*ME:LOXIMVI*)

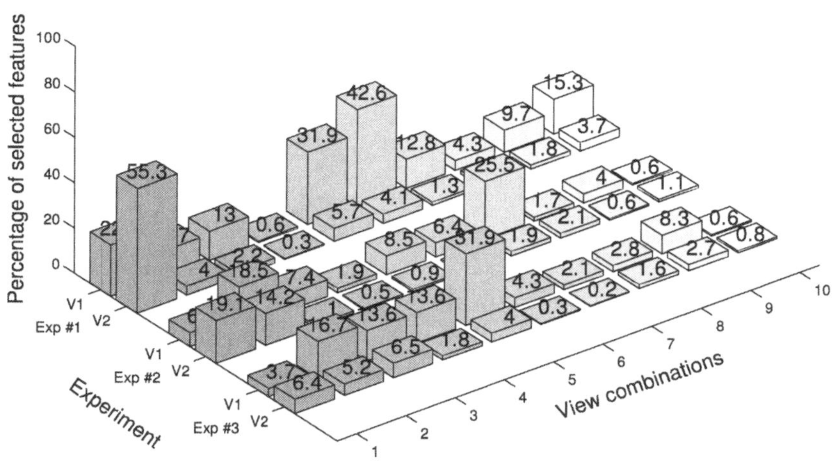

Figure 2: Percentage of selected features on NCI-60 data by UMVFS. The percentage of selected features per each view combination in the NCI-60 dataset experiments compared among three different experiments. In most of the view combinations and experiments the UMVFS model selects only a small subset of useful features.

Table 4: The feature selection results from JELSR for the dataset of concatenated features from protein and ABC transporters mRNA datasets, for the protein dataset separately, and for the ABC transporters mRNA dataset separately. All feature importance coefficients were normalized so that the maximum value of the coefficient was set to 1.0.

	View 1 and 2		View 1, proteins		View 2, mRNA	
Rank	Name	Score	Name	Score	Name	Score
1	*EP300-16*	1.00	*EP300-16*	1.00	*ABCC2*	1.00
2	*CDK4*	0.50	*CDK4*	0.50	*ABCF3*	0.99
3	*CTNNB1*	0.34	*CTNNB1*	0.34	*ABCB7*	0.01
4	*GTF2B*	0.22	*GTF2B*	0.17	*ABCD3*	0.01
5	*CDC2*	0.16	*CDC2*	0.14	*ABCE1*	0.01
6	*RIPK1*	0.03	*EP300-20*	0.01	*ABCB9*	0.01

was clustered in the group with CNS tumors. Feature-driven differences among the three clusters in the lysate arrays dataset view are visualized in Figure 3; while differences driven by features in the three clusters of the ATP-binding cassette transporters mRNA dataset view are visualized in Figure 4. Each subplot within the figures shows the box plot of the top six features grouped by cluster. For simplicity we marked cluster one as the CNS cluster, cluster two as the ME cluster and cluster three as the LE cluster. To emphasize differences, median points were connected with solid lines. Data were zero-mean unit-variance scaled; therefore values should be interpreted as z-scores. The absolute value of a z-score represents the distance between the raw data value and the population mean in units of the standard deviation. Z-score is negative when the raw data value is below the mean and positive when above. Compared with CNS and ME clusters, cluster LE has a much narrower distribution of selected feature values. The figures make evident that the combination of the selected features provides a distinct tumor profile per each cluster. Correct separation of examples based on tumor tissue origin assures that these features in combination are sufficient to cluster tumors based on their joint protein-mRNA interaction.

3.3 Biological relevance and interpretation

With reference to the results from the NCI-60 datasets, some of the selected features indicated in Table 3 have been reported in cancer literature as potential prognostic or therapeutic features in various types of cancer, including the tumor types used in the UMVFS simulations (leukemia, glioblastoma and melanoma). It is suggested [24] that *ABCB7* downregulation is a common pathway leading to the phenotype refractory anemia with ring sideroblasts. Primary melanoma and metastatic melanoma cell lines showed marked increase of *ABCE1* gene expression [11]. Scientific data [1] support the candidacy of *CDK4* as a proto-oncogene and suggest that deregulation of this checkpoint may represent a common step in the multistage progression of sporadic malignant melanomas. It is suggested [34] that *EP300* may serve as a potential therapeutic target for melanoma and other malignancies by promoting cellular responses to DNA damaging agents that are currently ineffective against some specific cancers. It was found [2] that the activity level of aberrant intron-retaining splice variant was lower in CD117+ acute myeloid leukemia patients at the stage of remission rather than at diagnosis, suggesting the involvement of post-transcriptional *PTPN6* processing in leukemogenesis. Not all selected features have been reported in the scientific literature for all types of tumors, perhaps because these types of tumors have not yet been thoroughly researched with respect to that set of genes or proteins.

We also note that using the tumor tissue types as classification labels might not be the superlative option for discovering cancer biomarkers from data, because the biological heterogeneity of tumors may prove to be an issue. We therefore recommend using clustering as a more appropriate method to discover biological insights in an unbiased manner. In the previous section we mentioned that *ME:LOXIMVI* was clustered in the same group with the

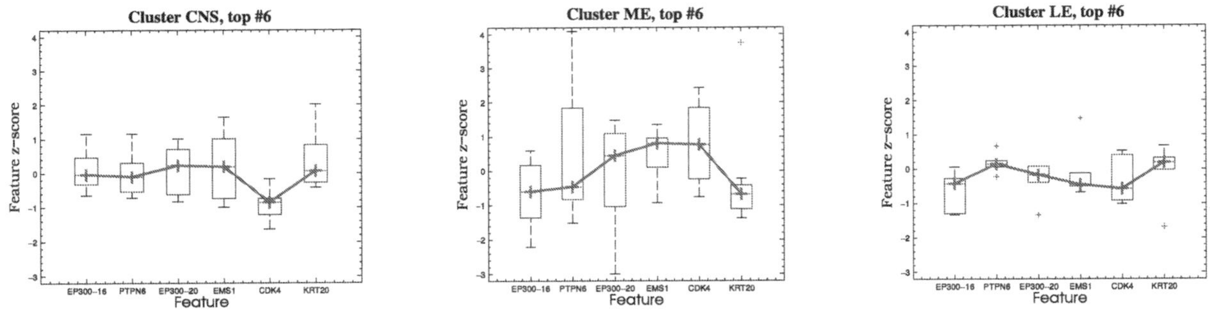

Figure 3: Box plots of the selected top six features of the reverse-phase protein lysate array dataset. Each subplot represents a profile of the features reported in Table 3 per specific tumor subtype. Red lines on the plot connect the median values of each feature.

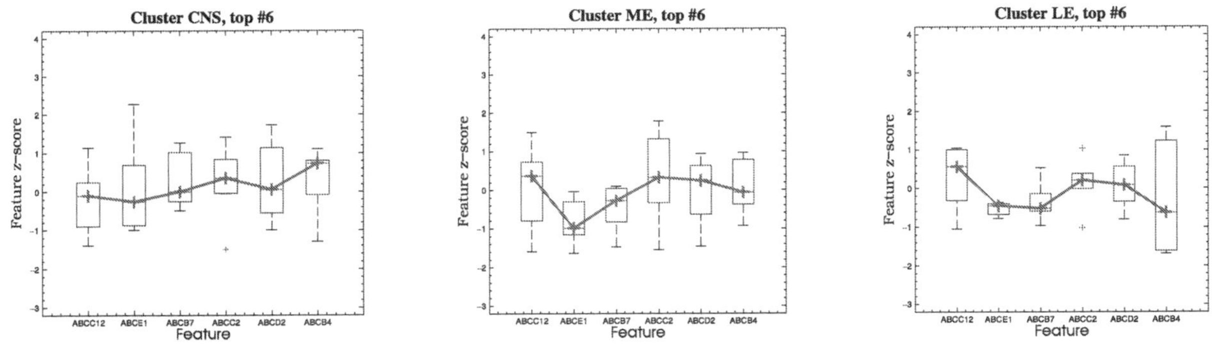

Figure 4: Box plots of the selected top six features of the ABC transporter mRNA dataset features. Each subplot represents a profile of the features reported in Table 3 per specific tumor subtype. Red lines on the plot connect the median values of each feature.

central nervous system tumors, although it is a melanoma example. Reference to NCI-60 metadata revealed that this is the only example of amelanotic melanoma, which is a type of skin cancer in which the cells do not make melanin. This difference from the other nine melanotic melanoma examples could provide explanation for such a clustering result. A similar tumor-specific clustering mismatch in NCI-60 panel has already been reported elsewhere. For example, it has been reported [9] that the estrogen receptor (ER)-negative breast cancer cell line Hs578T clustered with the stromal/mesenchymal cluster of glioblastoma and renal tumor cell lines. In contrast, the ER-positive breast cancer lines MCF-7 and T47D clustered to colon cancer lines displaying an epithelial phenotype.

In previously mentioned, Experiments 1, 2, 3 included cells extracted from patients with various types of cancer. As it was shown in Figure 2, despite the fact that view combinations are fixed, the number of selected features varies greatly among the three experiments. These differences may be explained by biological difference between epithelial and non-epithelial tissue. This was previously reported [7] where the authors' method distinguished cells with epithelial versus mesenchymal (non-epithelial) characteristics, because the epithelial to mesenchymal transition is implicated in the progression of malignancy in epithelial cancers such as breast and colon carcinomas. Similar observations were also made by other researchers [16]. Therefore, the UMVFS model can help to reveal additional information hidden in the complexity of domain knowledge. It is shown to be more advantageous compared with supervised methods.

4 CONCLUSIONS

In this paper we have proposed an Unsupervised Multi-View Feature Selection algorithm, a novel technique that simultaneously performs clustering and identifies the most relevant subset of features across different views. Unlike existing unsupervised single-view feature selection methods, our algorithm jointly uses information contained in different views and leads to more accurate results compared with those obtained by single-view techniques. Our algorithm is naturally suitable for application in the domain of computational biology where datasets with multi-view representations are frequent. We have demonstrated the efficacy of the algorithm on the NCI-60 dataset as well as on a synthetic dataset. In our experiments the proposed UMVFS algorithm successfully identified a biologically relevant subset of features and led to increased NMI performance in the case of the synthetic datasets.

In principle, UMVFS can be applied to any biological problem in which (a) labels are unknown, (b) the number of useful features is unknown and (c) phenomena could be described by multiple complementary representations. Therefore, we used NCI-60 cell panel data in a proof of principle study to demonstrate the power of UMVFS application in computational cancer biology.

Features extracted by UMVFS can be used to help biomedical specialists to perform more efficient diagnosis based on discovered biomarkers and provide guidance by patient stratification in a more realistic unsupervised way. Moreover, the proposed model can be used by other bioinformatics scientists who may be interested in adapting UMVFS to different scenarios, *e.g.* parallelization, implementation as a part of standard bioinformatics toolboxes, and publishing on-line as a web-based tool.

REFERENCES

[1] Jirina Bartkova, Jiri Lukas, Per Guldberg, Jan Alsner, Alexei F Kirkin, Jesper Zeuthen, and Jiri Bartek. 1996. The p16-cyclin D/CDK4-pRb pathway as a functional unit frequently altered in melanoma pathogenesis. *Cancer Research* 56, 23 (1996), 5475–5483.

[2] Alessandro Beghini, Carla B Ripamonti, Paolo Peterlongo, Gaia Roversi, Roberto Cairoli, Enrica Morra, and Lidia Larizza. 2000. RNA hyperediting and alternative splicing of hematopoietic cell phosphatase (PTPN6) gene in acute myeloid leukemia. *Human molecular genetics* 9, 15 (2000), 2297–2304.

[3] James Bergstra and Yoshua Bengio. 2012. Random search for hyper-parameter optimization. *The Journal of Machine Learning Research* 13, 1 (2012), 281–305.

[4] Ulf Brefeld, Thomas Gärtner, Tobias Scheffer, and Stefan Wrobel. 2006. Efficient co-regularised least squares regression. In *Proceedings of the International Conference on Machine learning*. ACM, New York, NY, USA, 137–144.

[5] Deng Cai, Chiyuan Zhang, and Xiaofei He. 2010. Unsupervised feature selection for multi-cluster data. In *Proceedings of the 16th ACM SIGKDD international conference on Knowledge discovery and data mining*. ACM, 333–342.

[6] Tiejun Cheng, Yanli Wang, and Stephen H Bryant. 2010. Investigating the correlations among the chemical structures, bioactivity profiles and molecular targets of small molecules. *Bioinformatics* 26, 22 (2010), 2881–2888.

[7] Aedín C Culhane, Guy Perrière, and Desmond G Higgins. 2003. Cross-platform comparison and visualisation of gene expression data using co-inertia analysis. *BMC Bioinformatics* 4, 1 (2003), 59.

[8] Hal Daume, Abhishek Kumar, and Avishek Saha. 2010. Co-regularization based semi-supervised domain adaptation. In *Advances in Neural Information Processing Systems 23*, J. Lafferty, C. K. I. Williams, J. Shawe-Taylor, R.S. Zemel, and A. Culotta (Eds.). 478–486.

[9] Amin Moghaddas Gholami, Hannes Hahne, Zhixiang Wu, Florian Johann Auer, Chen Meng, Mathias Wilhelm, and Bernhard Kuster. 2013. Global proteome analysis of the NCI-60 cell line panel. *Cell reports* 4, 3 (2013), 609–620.

[10] Xiaofei He, Deng Cai, and Partha Niyogi. 2005. Laplacian score for feature selection. In *Advances in neural information processing systems*. 507–514.

[11] Susanne Heimerl, Anja K Bosserhoff, Thomas Langmann, Josef Ecker, and Gerd Schmitz. 2007. Mapping ATP-binding cassette transporter gene expression profiles in melanocytes and melanoma cells. *Melanoma research* 17, 5 (2007), 265–273.

[12] Chenping Hou, Feiping Nie, Dongyun Yi, and Yi Wu. 2011. Feature selection via joint embedding learning and sparse regression. In *IJCAI Proceedings-International Joint Conference on Artificial Intelligence*, Vol. 22. 1324.

[13] Sultan Imangaliyev, Bart Keijser, Wim Crielaard, and Evgeni Tsivtsivadze. 2015. Personalized microbial network inference via co-regularized spectral clustering. *Methods* 83 (2015), 28–35.

[14] Balaji Krishnapuram, David Williams, Ya Xue, Alexander J Hartemink, Lawrence Carin, and Mário AT Figueiredo. 2004. On semi-supervised classification. In *NIPS*, Vol. 17. 721–728.

[15] Abhishek Kumar, Piyush Rai, and Hal Daume. 2011. Co-regularized multi-view spectral clustering. In *Advances in Neural Information Processing Systems*. 1413–1421.

[16] Kim-Anh Lê Cao, Pascal GP Martin, Christèle Robert-Granié, and Philippe Besse. 2009. Sparse canonical methods for biological data integration: application to a cross-platform study. *BMC bioinformatics* 10, 1 (2009), 34.

[17] Evgeni Levin, Sultan Imangaliyev, and Bart Keijser. 2013. Unsupervised Multi-View Feature Selection via co-regularization. In *NIPS Workshop on Machine Learning in Computational Biology*.

[18] Jane Jijun Liu, Gene Cutler, Wuxiong Li, Zheng Pan, Sihua Peng, Tim Hoey, Liangbiao Chen, and Xuefeng Bruce Ling. 2005. Multiclass cancer classification and biomarker discovery using GA-based algorithms. *Bioinformatics* 21, 11 (2005), 2691–2697.

[19] Kun-Hong Liu and Chun-Gui Xu. 2009. A genetic programming-based approach to the classification of multiclass microarray datasets. *Bioinformatics* 25, 3 (2009), 331–337.

[20] Yuanhua Liu, Valentina Devescovi, Suning Chen, and Christine Nardini. 2013. Multilevel omic data integration in cancer cell lines: advanced annotation and emergent properties. *BMC Systems Biology* 7, 1 (2013), 14.

[21] Haisu Ma and Hongyu Zhao. 2012. iFad: an integrative factor analysis model for drug-pathway association inference. *Bioinformatics* 28, 14 (2012), 1911–1918.

[22] Chen Meng, Bernhard Kuster, Aedín C Culhane, and Amin M Gholami. 2014. A multivariate approach to the integration of multi-omics datasets. *BMC Bioinformatics* 15, 1 (2014), 162.

[23] Andrew Y. Ng, Michael I. Jordan, and Yair Weiss. 2001. On spectral clustering: analysis and an algorithm. In *Advances in Neural Information Processing Systems 14*. 849–856.

[24] Maryam Nikpour, Christian Scharenberg, Anquan Liu, Simona Conte, Mohsen Karimi, Teresa Mortera-Blanco, Valentina Giai, Marta Fernandez-Mercado, Elli Papaemmanuil, Kari Högstrand, and others. 2013. The transporter ABCB7 is a mediator of the phenotype of acquired refractory anemia with ring sideroblasts. *Leukemia* 27, 4 (2013), 889–896.

[25] F. Pedregosa, G. Varoquaux, A. Gramfort, V. Michel, B. Thirion, O. Grisel, M. Blondel, P. Prettenhofer, R. Weiss, V. Dubourg, J. Vanderplas, A. Passos, D. Cournapeau, M. Brucher, M. Perrot, and E. Duchesnay. 2011. Scikit-learn: machine learning in Python. *Journal of Machine Learning Research* 12 (2011), 2825–2830.

[26] Angela Serra, Michele Fratello, Vittorio Fortino, Giancarlo Raiconi, Roberto Tagliaferri, and Dario Greco. 2015. MVDA: a multi-view genomic data integration methodology. *BMC bioinformatics* 16, 1 (2015), 1.

[27] Uma T Shankavaram, Sudhir Varma, David Kane, Margot Sunshine, Krishna K Chary, William C Reinhold, Yves Pommier, and John N Weinstein. 2009. CellMiner: a relational database and query tool for the NCI-60 cancer cell lines. *BMC genomics* 10, 1 (2009), 277.

[28] Vikas Sindhwani, Partha Niyogi, and Mikhail Belkin. 2005. A co-regularization approach to semi-supervised learning with multiple views. In *Proceedings of ICML workshop on learning with multiple views*. 74–79.

[29] Jasper Snoek, Hugo Larochelle, and Ryan P Adams. 2012. Practical Bayesian optimization of machine learning algorithms. In *Advances in neural information processing systems*. 2951–2959.

[30] Alexander Strehl and Joydeep Ghosh. 2003. Cluster ensembles—a knowledge reuse framework for combining multiple partitions. *The Journal of Machine Learning Research* 3 (2003), 583–617.

[31] Evgeni Tsivtsivadze, Tapio Pahikkala, Jorma Boberg, Tapio Salakoski, and Tom Heskes. 2010. Co-regularized least-squares for label ranking. In *Preference Learning*, Eyke Hüllermeier and Johannes Fürnkranz (Eds.). 107–123.

[32] Bo Wang, Aziz M Mezlini, Feyyaz Demir, Marc Fiume, Zhuowen Tu, Michael Brudno, Benjamin Haibe-Kains, and Anna Goldenberg. 2014. Similarity network fusion for aggregating data types on a genomic scale. *Nature methods* 11, 3 (2014), 333–337.

[33] Sijian Wang and Ji Zhu. 2007. Improved centroids estimation for the nearest shrunken centroid classifier. *Bioinformatics* 23, 8 (2007), 972–979.

[34] Gai Yan, Mark S Eller, Courtney Elm, Cecilia A Larocca, Byungwoo Ryu, Izabela P Panova, Beverley M Dancy, Erin M Bowers, David Meyers, Lisa Lareau, and others. 2013. Selective inhibition of p300 HAT blocks cell cycle progression, induces cellular senescence, and inhibits the DNA damage response in melanoma cells. *Journal of Investigative Dermatology* 133, 10 (2013), 2444–2452.

[35] Zheng Zhao and Huan Liu. 2007. Spectral feature selection for supervised and unsupervised learning. In *Proceedings of the 24th international conference on Machine learning*. ACM, 1151–1157.

[36] Zheng Zhao, Lei Wang, and Huan Liu. 2010. Efficient spectral feature selection with minimum redundancy. In *Proceedings of the Twenty-Fourth AAAI Conference on Artificial Intelligence*. AAAI Press, 673–678.

Computational Intractability Generates the Topology of Biological Networks

Ali Atiia
School of Computer Science
McGill University
atiia@cs.mcgill.ca

Corbin Hopper
School of Computer Science
McGill University
corbin.hopper@mail.mcgill.ca

Jérôme Waldispühl
School of Computer Science
McGill University
jeromew@cs.mcgill.ca

ABSTRACT

Virtually all molecular interactions networks, independent of organism and physiological context, have majority-leaves minority-hubs (mLmH) topology. Current generative models of this topology are based on controversial hypotheses that, controversy aside, demonstrate sufficient but not necessary evolutionary conditions for its emergence. Here we show that the circumvention of computational intractability provides sufficient and (assuming P≠NP) necessary conditions for the emergence of the mLmH property. Evolutionary pressure on molecular interaction networks is simulated by randomly labelling some interactions as 'beneficial' and others 'detrimental'. Each gene is subsequently given a benefit (damage) score according to how many beneficial (detrimental) interactions it is projecting onto or attracting from other genes. The problem of identifying which subset of genes should ideally be conserved and which deleted, so as to maximize (minimize) the total number of beneficial (detrimental) interactions network-wide, is NP-hard. An evolutionary algorithm that simulates hypothetical instances of this problem and selects for networks that produce the easiest instances leads to networks that possess the mLmH property. The degree distributions of synthetically evolved networks match those of publicly available experimentally-validated biological networks from many phylogenetically-distant organisms.

CCS CONCEPTS

• **Networks** → **Network design principles**; • **Applied computing** → **Biological networks**; **Systems biology**; **Bioinformatics**; • **Mathematics of computing** → *Combinatorial optimization*; • **Theory of computation** → *Complexity classes*; *Evolutionary algorithms*; • **Computing methodologies** → Parallel algorithms;

KEYWORDS

biological networks; computational intractability; Combinatorial optimization; evolutionary adaptations; systems biology; emergence

Permission to make digital or hard copies of part or all of this work for personal or classroom use is granted without fee provided that copies are not made or distributed for profit or commercial advantage and that copies bear this notice and the full citation on the first page. Copyrights for third-party components of this work must be honored. For all other uses, contact the owner/author(s).
ACM-BCB '17, August 20-23, 2017, Boston, MA, USA
© 2017 Copyright held by the owner/author(s).
ACM ISBN 978-1-4503-4722-8/17/08.
https://doi.org/10.1145/3107411.3107453

1 INTRODUCTION

Biological networks (BNs) are graphs where nodes and edges represent bio-molecules (protein, DNA, RNA, or metabolites) and interactions, respectively. A BN describes interactions in a given physiological context such as protein-protein, transcription factor-gene, small RNA-gene, or enzyme-metabolite interactions. Virtually all BNs, regardless of organism or physiological context [11, 25, 29, 32, 34, 38–40], are rich in loosely connected 'leaf' genes, with a small number of highly connected 'hub' genes. More precisely, the percentage of genes having degree d is exponentially inversely proportional to d. We refer to this topology as majority-leaves minority-hubs (mLmH). The scale [30] and quality [39] of experimentally-validated interaction networks has been exponentially increasing, but conclusive answers to fundamental questions about the emergence of their architectural properties remain elusive. The widely popular [27] scale-free (SF) model asserts that node degree frequencies in BNs follow a power-law distribution [5]. The veracity of this assertion and the design principles it later inspired [1, 6] has however been seriously questioned [10, 12, 18, 21, 36]. An important shortcoming of SF and other models [4] is that their respective higher-level abstractions do not account for any functional aspects in biological networks and as such provide no conclusive justification for the emergence of mLmH property [2]. Gene duplication has been suggested [7, 37] as a mechanism that leads to mLmH, but that does not explain 'intermediate states that necessarily exist in the context of actual populations' [23]. Key predictions of SF model in particular have been contradicted by experimental evidence [13, 16]. The highly-optimized tolerance (HOT) model aims to capture evolutionary pressure forces that result in the emergence of mLmH [8], arguing the latter is the result of 'trade-offs between yield, cost of resources, and tolerance to risks'. The fundamental question however still remains: on what basis can these trade-offs be considered universal? An explanatory model may well provide sufficient conditions, but they are not necessary unless there is a 'concrete underlying theory to support it' [35]. Simulated HOT systems are robust against 'designed-for uncertainties' [8], rendering the applicability of the model in biological context (where there is no design) problematic. In the absence of a convincing theory that justifies the emergence of mLmH (and rules out other plausible hypotheses), another radical hypothesis has also been proposed: system-level traits may be mere byproducts of non-adaptive evolutionary forces such as mutation and genetic drift [24, 26, 33]. The latter view effectively questions the scientific merit of systems biology itself.

In this work, we model the evolutionary pressure on BNs to rewire themselves as a computational optimization problem. An interaction between two genes can, at some point in evolutionary time, become advantageous or detrimental to the overall fitness of the organism. Under strong evolutionary pressure, it can become critical for the system to conserve (delete) some genes in order to fixate beneficial (cleanse detrimental) interactions. The optimization question is: which genes to conserve and which to delete so as to maximize (minimize to a threshold) the overall total number of beneficial (detrimental) interactions? If every gene is engaged in only beneficial (detrimental) interactions, the answer is clear and no optimization search is needed. However, some or all genes can be 'ambiguous': they are engaged in both beneficial and damaging interactions, and therefore a combinatorial optimization search is needed to identify the subset of genes that should ideally be conserved (deleted) so that the overall total number of beneficial interactions is maximal (minimal to a threshold).

Biological systems do not employ sophisticated search algorithms from one generation to the next: Nature's algorithm is simply successive iterations of random variation followed by non-random selection (RVnRS) [9]. However, the number of RVnRS iterations needed before a network's connectivity profile has been sufficiently transformed to a healthy state can, depending on the topology of the network, be hopelessly exponential. Our results show that simulating evolutionary pressure on a population of random networks, and repeatedly selecting those that produce easy instances of this problem (mainly, those having less ambiguous genes), leads to networks with mLmH property. The degree distribution of the evolved synthetic networks is compared against real BNs from various phylogenetically-distant organisms. The evolved networks quickly acquire mLmH property and end up having almost identical degree distribution to real networks of equal size (number of nodes and edges).

The presented results highlight the fact that system-level (software) traits can emerge after successive iterations of RVnRS over long stretches of evolutionary time. It is important to note that the implication here is not that natural selection acts directly on network topologies. Rather, the evolutionary advantageous mLmH topology is a soft property of the overall inter-connectivity among selected-for genes (alleles). The presented evolutionary algorithm simulates the variation part of the RVnRS process by introducing random changes to the interaction network's profile at each generation: (1) a gene may be invented and/or (2) two interacting (non-interacting) genes may cease (begin) to interact due to mutation. Evolutionary pressure is simulated by designating some interactions in the network as advantageous and others disadvantageous at a given point (generation) in evolutionary time, and we refer to such arbitrary designation as an 'Oracle advice' (OA). Subsequently, the fitness of the network as a whole is judged by the extent to which it can adapt to such pressure. Adaptability is quantified by how quickly the process of RVnRS can ultimately invent and/or alter the connectivity profile of genes in order to fixate (cleanse) beneficial (detrimental) interactions network-wide. Clearly the less ambiguous genes there are (on average over many instances of OAs) the faster RVnRS can transform the network away from a deleterious and into a healthier state (minimal damaging interactions).

The model is simple and general enough to avoid symbolic bloat and artificial complexity, but reasonably specific enough to capture the reality of BNs being constantly under pressure to change in response to changing environments. More importantly, it provides *sufficient* conditions for the emergence of mLmH and, because the inherent intractability of NP-hard problems is (assuming P≠NP) universally insurmountable, it explains why the emergence of mLmH is *necessary*. If BNs were more sparse (all genes of degree 1 in the extreme case), all genes are unambiguous under any scenario of evolutionary pressure but the genome size explodes (d specialty genes would be needed to carry out the function of a single gene performing d interactions). On the other hand, if they were more dense (less genes but higher connectivity per gene), the organism would drown in computational intractability: an exponential number of RVnRS iterations would be needed to ultimately invent the right set of genes whose *connectivity* maximizes (minimizes) beneficial (detrimental) interactions vis-à-vis the current evolutionary pressure scenario. The mLmH topology is the middle ground between the two extremes: essential functions are concentrated in hub genes that are unlikely to be detrimental in and of themselves. Regulating around them however, is where constant optimization is needed (e.g. micro-RNA regulation [15]). In the presence of an evolutionary pressure, such optimization (through iterations of RVnRS) can be done at minimal cost by experimenting with loosely connected leaf genes at the periphery of the network [20].

2 APPROACH

2.1 Evolutionary Pressure

A biological network of n genes $(g_1, g_2, \ldots, g_n)$ can be represent as an adjacency matrix $M = \lceil m_{jk} \rfloor$, $1 \leq j, k \leq n$ where $m_{jk} = +1, -1,$ or 0 implies, respectively, that g_j promotes, inhibits, or doesn't interact with g_k. At a given point in evolutionary time, some interactions may become detrimental to the overall fitness of the organism: g_j promotes (inhibits) g_k when the latter should in fact be inhibited(promoted). Conversely, some interactions can become critically advantageous: g_j promotes (inhibits) g_k when the latter should indeed be promoted (inhibited). Let matrix $A = \lceil a_{jk} \rfloor$ represent a hypothetical 'ideal' regulatory state, such that $a_{jk} \in \{+1, -1\}$ if $m_{jk} \neq 0$ and $a_{jk} = 0$ otherwise. We refer to A as an 'Oracle advice' (OA) on the network. While $m_{jk} \neq 0$ describes what the effect of g_j on g_k actually is, a_{jk} describes what that effect should *ideally* be. A beneficial (detrimental) interaction is one where $m_{jk} \times a_{jk} = 1$ ($m_{jk} \times a_{jk} = -1$). In other words, an interaction is beneficial (detrimental) if it is in agreement (disagreement) with what the Oracle says that interaction

BN	Biological Network
mLmH	Majority-leaves Minority-hubs topology
OA	Oracle Advice
NEP	Network Evolution Problem
RVnRS	Random Variation non-Random Selection

Table 1: Abbreviations

should ideally be. Assume for example that g_j promotes g_k, i.e. $m_{jk} = +1$, but the OA says that interaction should ideally be inhibitory instead, i.e. $a_{jk} = -1$, then $m_{jk} \times a_{jk} = -1$ implies the real disagrees with the ideal and the interaction is deemed detrimental.

The benefit (damage) score of each gene g_j, given an OA, is the sum of beneficial (detrimental) interactions that g_j is *projecting* onto (out-edges) or *attracting* from (in-edges) other genes. More precisely, the benefit score of g_j is defined as:

$$b_j = \sum_{k=1}^{n} m_{jk} \oplus a_{jk} + \sum_{k=1}^{n} m_{kj} \oplus a_{kj} \quad \text{where:}$$

$$m_{xy} \oplus a_{xy} = \begin{cases} 1 & \text{if} \quad m_{xy} \times a_{xy} > 0 \\ 0 & \text{otherwise} \end{cases}$$

and similarly the damage score is:

$$d_j = \sum_{k=1}^{n} m_{jk} \ominus a_{jk} + \sum_{k=1}^{n} m_{kj} \ominus a_{kj} \quad \text{where:}$$

$$m_{xy} \ominus a_{xy} = \begin{cases} 1 & \text{if} \quad m_{xy} \times a_{xy} < 0 \\ 0 & \text{otherwise} \end{cases}$$

An organism is clearly better off conserving a gene g_j if its benefit $b_j \neq 0$ and damage $d_j = 0$, and deleting g_j if $d_j \neq 0$ and $b_j = 0$. We refer to such genes as *unambiguous*. Clearly a degree-1 leaf gene g_k (i.e. it only interacts with one other gene) is always unambiguous. A degree-2 g_k can have one of four possible (b_k,d_k) values: 00, 01, 10, 11 with each digit representing an interaction (edge) and 0 or 1 implying the interaction is beneficial or detrimental, respectively, and as such g_k has a 50% chance of being unambiguous under a random OA (i.e. equal likelihood of an interaction being deemed beneficial or detrimental by the Oracle). As the degree d of g_k increases linearly, the probability of it being unambiguous under some OA decreases exponentially (namely, *prob.* $= 2^{1-d}$). The network evolution problem (NEP) is that of defining the following function f:

$$f : G \to \{0,1\} \text{ maximizing } \sum_{j=1}^{n} f(g_j) \times b_j \text{ s.t. } \left(\sum_{j=1}^{n} f(g_j) \times d_j \right) \leq t$$

NEP has previously been proved NP-hard [3]. Figure 1 (a) shows a hypothetical small interaction network of 5 genes, with promotional and inhibitory interactions denoted by arrows and bars, respectively. The network can equivalently be represented as an (adjacency) interaction matrix M (top matrix in Figure 1 (b)) where +1, -1 signify promotional, inhibitory interaction, respectively (notice m_{jk}=0 when no interaction exists between g_j and g_k). Against a hypothetical OA matrix A (middle matrix in Figure 1 (b)), where $a_{jk} \neq 0$ indicates what the interaction $m_{jk} \neq 0$ should ideally be, an interaction is deemed beneficial or detrimental (bottom matrix in Figure 1 (b)) when m_{jk} and a_{jk} are in agreement (i.e. $m_{jk} \times a_{jk} = 1$) or disagreement (i.e. $m_{jk} \times a_{jk} = -1$), respectively. The benefit (damage) score of g_j is the sum of beneficial (detrimental) interactions it is projecting onto (adding up absolute values along row j) or attracting from (along column j) other genes as shown in Figure 1 (c). Genes that have zero benefit or damage score (respectively g_5 and g_4 in this example) should unambiguously be conserved (deleted). However, among genes with non-zero benefit and damage scores, an optimization search is needed to determine the optimal action (conserve and delete) that maximizes (minimizes) the overall total number of beneficial (detrimental) interactions. Clearly the larger the number of such ambiguous genes, the harder the optimization task would be. Assuming a certain threshold of tolerable detrimental interactions = 2 for example, the optimal RVnRS trajectory (Figure 1 (d)) would be one that leads to the conservation of g_1, g_2 and g_4, and the deletion of g_3 and g_5.

2.2 Evolutionary Algorithm

Evolutionary pressure is simulated on a network by randomly generating OAs on all interactions. An evolutionary algorithm selects for networks that on average yield easier instances of the optimization problem. Instance difficulty is measured by (1) the percentage of genes that are unambiguous (benefit and/or damage = 0) and (2) the effective total benefits that are contributed by conserved genes in an optimal solution. Networks whose instances are easiest are considered fit, and a new generation of offspring networks are bred from the top performing networks. Offspring population are mutated before the next round of OA generation and instance evaluation starts. Figure 2 depicts the workflow of the algorithm. Individuals in the population are BNs, represented by their interaction matrix M. Individuals begin with either an empty network or one with randomly assigned edges. Mutation modifies connectivity between nodes by random edge reassignment to two randomly selected nodes, or by adding nodes and edges in simulations where network growth occurs. After mutation, the fitness of each network in the population is assessed based on the computational ease of the NEP instances that result from applying repeated evolutionary pressure (multiple OAs) on the network. Exact replicas are generated from the fittest 10% of the networks to create the next population networks. For a network of N nodes, the unambiguity metric U emphasizes sparsely connected nodes and is defined as the ratio of unambiguous nodes relative to the total number of nodes:

$$U = \frac{|\{g_i : b_i = 0 | d_i = 0\}|}{N}$$

The solution vector to an NEP instance is a sequence $(s_1, s_2, .., s_k)$ where $s_i \in \{0,1\}$ and $s_i = 1$ $(s_i = 0)$ implies

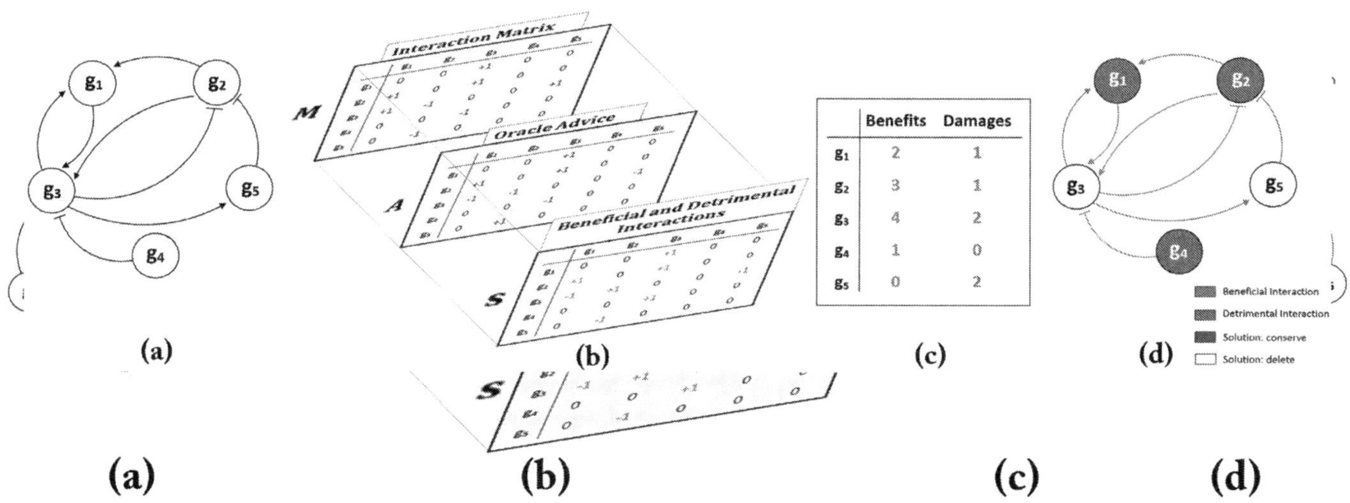

Figure 1: The network evolution problem. (a) A hypothetical molecular interaction network of five genes $g_1 \ldots g_5$ with some inhibitory or promotional interactions (bar- and arrow-terminated edges, respectively). (b) An equivalent representation of the network as an adjacency matrix (M). An Oracle advice (A) matrix indicates what the interactions in M should ideally be. For example the promotional interaction from g_1 to g_3 (from g_3 to g_5) is in agreement (disagreement) with what the Oracle says that interaction should be. Beneficial (in agreement) and detrimental (in disagreement) interactions are shown in the bottom matrix S in which s_{jk} obtained by multiplying each m_{jk} in M with a_{jk} in A. (c) Each gene g_j in the network is assigned a benefit (damage) value = the sum of beneficial (detrimental) interactions it projects onto (out-edge, adding absolute values along along row j in S) or attracts from (in-edge, adding absolute values along along column j in S) other genes. (d) Genes g_4, g_5 are unambiguous (totally beneficial, i.e. damage=0, or totally detrimental, i.e. benefit=0), while g_1, g_2 and g_3 are ambiguous (having both non-zero benefit/damage scores). Assuming a threshold 2 tolerable detrimental interactions, the optimal evolutionary trajectory would be to conserve g_1,g_2 and g_4 and delete g_3 and g_5.

'conserve' ('delete'). Accumulated benefits in an NEP instance's optimal solution is a multi-set $B = \{b_i : s_i = 1\}$, and the effective accumulated benefits $B_e = sum(set(B))$ (i.e. B_e is B normalized by the number of genes it takes to contribute a certain benefit value). For example, with $B1 = \{1, 1, 1, 2\}$ and $B2 = \{2, 3\}$, $sum(B1) = sum(B2)$, but $B1_e = 3$ while $B2_e = 5$. B_e reflects the effort (no. of genes conserved) needed to achieve a certain benefit. Generally, with a gene of degree d and assuming all its in- and out-edges are in agreement with the OA (i.e. a totally beneficial gene), it would single-handedly contribute $|d|$ to B_e. In the opposite extreme, if such a gene were broken into n specialty genes with degrees $(d_1, d_2.., d_n), d_i = 1 \forall i$, then B_e reduces down to 1 $((d_1 + d_2 \ldots d_n) \div n)$ assuming all such genes are beneficial. Let B_{tot} be the total benefit in a given NEP instance (the sum of gained benefits of conserved genes and lost benefits of deleted genes), the fitness of a given NEP instance S is measured as:

$$F(S) = U^{\alpha} \times \frac{B_e}{B_{tot}}$$

where $\alpha \in \approx \mathbb{R}^+$. In all simulations, we used $\alpha = 2$, which calibrated the opposing effects [20] of the the two selection criteria (instance size in U and effective total benefit in $\frac{B_e}{B_{tot}}$, further discussed in 3.1 and Figure 3). The larger a gene's degree is the more ambiguous it can be. Unambiguous genes do not need to be included in the computationally costly optimization search and can *apriori* be deemed beneficial (detrimental) and should therefore be conserved (deleted) regardless of the state of other genes. Mutations on unambiguous nodes will have a clear selection gradient since they are more likely to be totally beneficial or totally detrimental but not both. Although the problem is generally NP-hard, instances with small effective instance size (large number of unambiguous genes) are easier to satisfy. Clearly a very sparse network results most genes being unambiguous, but it also leads to an explosion of genome size since more genes are needed to fulfill a function that could have been handled by a single hub gene. While B_e measures the ability of a network to capture more benefits with less genes to conserve, normalizing it by the total benefits B_{tot} discourages networks that hemorrhage a large number of possible benefits lost to deleted genes.

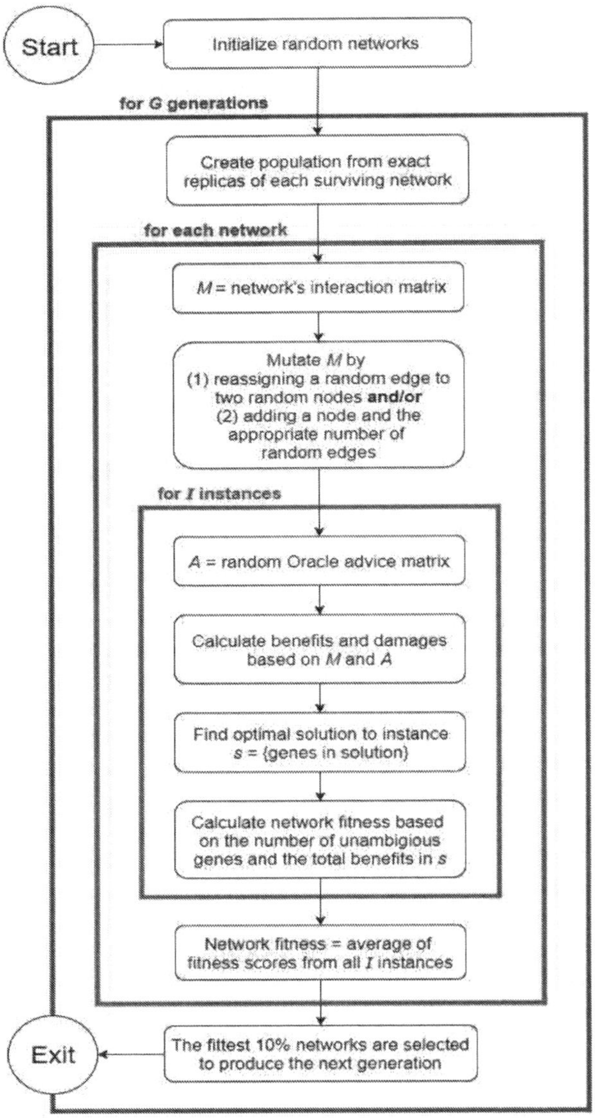

Figure 2: The algorithmic workflow of the evolutionary algorithm. Simulations begin with empty networks or seed networks that have randomly distributed edges. Each network is randomly mutated by reassigning one edge at each generation and, if growth is allowed, one node is also added along with as many randomly assigned edges as needed to maintain the desired edge:node ratio. An instance of the network evolution problem (NEP) is obtained by generating a random Oracle advice (OA) on all edges in the network. A network's fitness at each instance S is calculated following the $F(S)$ formula (Section 2.2). The 10% of networks with the highest average fitness over all instances are selected to breed a population of networks for the subsequent generation.

3 RESULTS

3.1 Adaptation

A population of random 400-node seed networks, each having an edge:node ratio matching that of the Yeast network (Table 2)[1], is subjected to successive rounds of RVnRS. The evolutionary algorithm mutates each network in the population by edge-reassignment only and subsequently selects the fittest networks (according to their $F(S)$ values) to breed the next population of networks. The networks are sorted according to fitness, and the top 10% are selected. Replicas are produced from each selected network bringing the population to its previous size. Figure 3 (a) displays the degree distribution of the fittest adapted network after 2000 mutate-select-breed generations (black dots) against 100 400-node randomly sampled subnetworks from Yeast. The connectivity of of the adapted network morphed into the mLmH property matching that of Yeast. Figure 3 (b) shows the change in the overall fitness score of the fittest network in the population at each generation (top) as well as the change in fitness score per metric (U^2 (left) and $\frac{B_e}{B_{tot}}$ (right) subplots). The fitness improves dramatically at the beginning and plateaus by generation 2000. The remaining fluctuations are largely due to variance in NEP as different instances may vary in fitness for the same network. U and $\frac{B_e}{B_{tot}}$ are balance the two competing forces of selecting for unambiguity (leaf nodes) and effective total benefits (hub nodes).

Figure 3 (c) depicts the percent of unambiguous nodes at the beginning and end of the simulation. The adapted network at generation 2000 has more leaf nodes contributing to the unambiguous 100:0 and 0:100 *benefit:damage* ratio groups. The random network exhibits 35.9% unambiguous nodes (solid red and green slices), whereas the evolved network results in 53.5% unambiguous nodes. The latter clearly produces NEP instances with small effective instance sizes. Figure 3(d) portrays the composition of the NEP solution. Adapted networks fit larger hubs into the solution due to the fact that the more leaf nodes a network has the less threshold damage is consumed and therefore hubs (which are likely to carry damaging interactions) are more likely to be conserved (i.e. part of the optimal solution) for their benefits and despite their damages. That implies that a hub involved in damaging interactions can still be tolerated while more experimentation in network composition (conserve/delete) and/or connectivity (mutations that affect interaction affinity) can take place [20]. Figure 3 (e) displays the change in degree distribution on a normal and a log-scaled (inset) plot. The seed networks at the first generation are created by randomly assigning edges resulting in an exponential degree distribution centred around the average degree. In stark contrast, adapted networks at generation 2000 display a heavy-tailed distribution with a few highly connected hubs. The model robustly evolves to mLmH topology despite unfavourable starting conditions. Very low degree (leaf) nodes dramatically increase in frequency, while more high-degree (hub) nodes emerge.

[1] The real BNs used in this study (Table 2) are publicly available in: http://cs.mcgill.ca/~malsha17/permlink/acmbcb17/

Network	no. nodes	no. edges	edge:node ratio
Plant [11]	2402	5486	2.3
Bacteria [29]	1014	1967	1.9
Yeast [40]	1647	2682	1.6
Worm [32]	2214	3659	1.7
Fly [38]	3058	5930	1.9
Human [39]	473	885	1.9
Bacteria Regulatory [14]	898	1481	1.6
Mouse Regulatory [22]	1436	3673	2.6

Table 2: Summary of real biological networks against which simulations were conducted with references to their sources. Bacteria Regulatory and Mouse Regulatory involve transcription-factor (TF)-gene, TF-TF or small RNA-gene interactions, while all other networks involve protein-protein interactions.

3.2 Adaptation with Growth

The same evolutionary algorithm is applied starting from a near empty seed network that grows in size over the generations. Networks in the population start with 4 nodes and periodically acquire new nodes and edges. Figure 4 illustrates simulated networks and their corresponding BNs that have the same edge:node ratio. The BNs are protein-protein interaction networks of 6 different organisms. The simulation is terminated when the simulation network reaches the size of 400 nodes. For comparison, 100 400-node subnetworks are sampled from the corresponding BN (colour dots in Figure 4). The degree distributions of simulated networks (black dots in Figure 4) closely match their corresponding BNs. The frequency of hubs in networks sampled from real BNs is comparable to those resulting from simulations, although the latter have lower probability of generating extremely highly connected hubs given their smaller size.

We considered whether the model can scale to larger networks by allowing the simulation to continue until the simulated network's size is equal to that of the corresponding BN, in contrast to previously described simulations (Figures 3 and 4) which terminated when networks' size reached 400 nodes. We performed four experiments in which the simulated networks were allowed to grow to a size equal to that of Bacteria, Worm, Bacteria Regulatory, or Mouse Regulatory networks (see Table 2 for their corresponding number of nodes/edges). The four experiments show the scalability of the model to larger networks, with the latter two further showing its scalability to the regulatory context (as opposed to all other networks which represent protein-protein interactions). Figure 5 shows the degree distribution of the the fittest network after multiple generations of mutate-and-select. The number of generations is approximately equal to that of the number of nodes in the corresponding BN. In contrast to the smaller-sized evolved networks depicted in Figure 4, the larger simulation networks shown in Figure 5 show an even smoother distribution particularly of hubs of degree ≥ 10.

4 METHODS

The simulation begins with a random network of 400 (adaptation) or 4 (adaptation with growth) nodes . The number of edges is defined by the chosen edge:node ratio that matches that of a given BN. Each individual network in the population is mutated once per generation. Mutation involves removing one randomly selected edge and replacing it with another edge between two random nodes. The interaction sign (promotional or inhibitory) is also assigned at random. The network must remain connected, meaning that no edge is removed if it severs one section of the network from the rest. After mutation, each network is assessed based on a number of NEP instances that is either fixed at 100 for the 400-node simulations, or varied proportional to $\sim$ 10% of the total nodes in the network for simulation of larger networks (Figure 5). For extremely small networks at early generations of adaptation-with-growth simulations of larger networks, a minimum of 10 NEP instances was generated. The threshold of tolerated damaging interactions in the solution is imposed at 5% of the sum of all damages in all simulations. The top 10% fittest networks represent the surviving population and are used to spawn the population of networks for the next generation by making an equal number of exact replicas from each of the four. The population size is kept constant at 40-64 networks throughout the generations.

For the adaptation-with-growth simulations (Section 3.2), a random node is added every 5 generations (in the 400-node networks shown in Figures 3 and 4) or at every generations (full-network simulations shown in Figure 5). In addition, the appropriate number of edges are added to maintain the edge:node ratio of the corresponding BN. The simulation proceeds to evolve for 2000 generations or until the desired network size is reached. In simulations where network size is capped at 400 nodes, the algorithm continues to evolve for 2000 more generations but with edge-reassignment mutation only. NEP instances were reduced to knapsack instances [3] and solved to optimality using a pseudopolynomial algorithm [28] implemented in C. Networks were encoded and manipulated using the NetworkX package [31].

5 DISCUSSION

Our simulation results show that computational intractability provides sufficient conditions for the emergence of the majority-leaves minority-hubs (mLmH) topology, irrespective of whether it follows a power-law distribution in a technical sense as has previously been intensely debated (see [21] and references therein). The fact that the intractability of NP-hard problems is (assuming P$\neq$NP) universally insurmountable renders it a necessary condition as well: it rules out the possibility of any other topology. A completely sparse network where each gene has only one interaction produces the easiest possible optimization instances (every gene can unambiguously be either beneficial or detrimental under any evolutionary pressure scenario). However, it also leads to a need for more genes since functions that could have been handled by one hub gene of degree d must now be handled by d specialty genes. This obviously leads to an explosion of genome size. Conversely, a highly dense network where the number of genes is minimized and interactions are handled

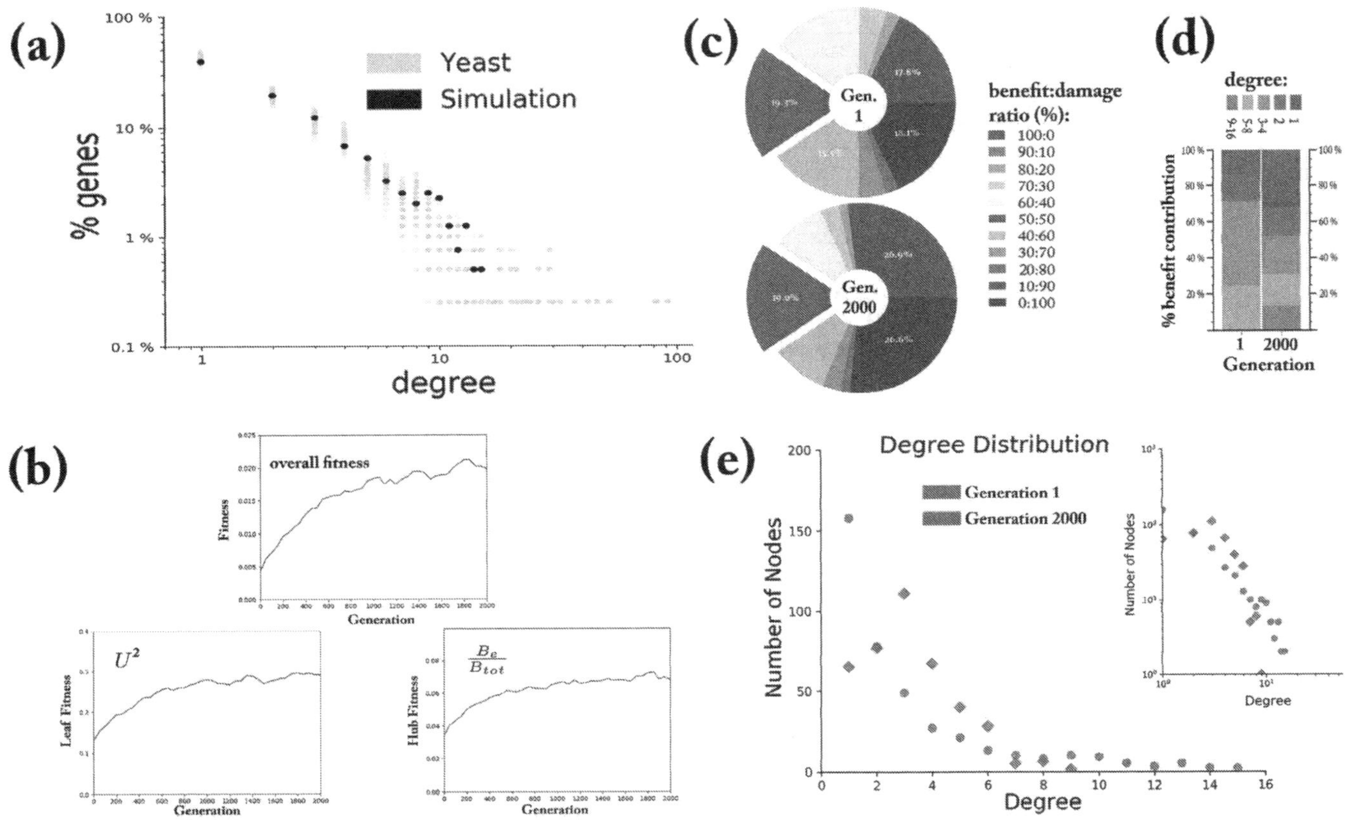

Figure 3: Adaptation of a random seed network. (a) starting from a network with the same edge:node ratio as the Yeast network, but with edges randomly assigned to nodes, the mLmH property emerges after 2000 generations of random mutation (random edge re-assignment) and random selection according to instance size and effective total benefits. (b) Improvement in fitness over the generations. The overall, U-only, and $\frac{B_e}{B_{tot}}$-only fitness per generation depicted in top, bottom-left, bottom-right subplots respectively. (c) The percentage of unambiguous genes in NEP increases over the course of simulated adaptation, resulting in easier instances with smaller effective instance sizes. Solid green (red) slices represent nodes with zero damage and non-zero benefit (zero benefit and non-zero damage). Top pie: the initial random network at generation 1 includes on average 35.9% unambiguous nodes; bottom pie: after 2000 generations, the network has on average 53.5% unambiguous nodes. (d) The percentage of benefits that nodes, grouped by degree range (legend, top), contribute to NEP solution before (generation 1 (left bar), random seed network) and after simulated adaptation (generation 2000, right bar). Larger nodes in adapted (generation 2000) network contribute a higher proportion of benefits due to the fact that the large number of damage-minimal leaves do not consume damage tolerance threshold thereby increasing the likelihood of (the more ambiguous and more tolerance-consuming) hubs to be in solution. The benefits in the solution for a random network (generation 1) are predominantly contributed by medium degree nodes. After 2000 generations, a marked increase in the contribution by the majority leaves (degree 1 and 2 particularly) and by high degree hubs of degree $\geq$ 5 is observed. (e) Initial random networks have exponential distributions. After simulated adaptation, mLmH topology emerges (more leaves and high-degree hubs in exchange for less medium-degree nodes); inset: the same plot in log scale.

by multi-purpose hub genes leads to an exponential search space: the number of iterations of random-variations and non-random selection [9] before the network has been optimally rewired into a healthier state (i.e. the right subset genes has been conserved, discovered, mutated or deleted to overcome a given evolutionary pressure) would be exponential in network size. The majority-leaves minority-hubs topology is the middle ground between these two extremes: concentrate essential functions in hubs genes [15], and respond to evolutionary pressure by experimenting (on the cheap) with loosely connected leaf genes at the periphery of the network [20]. Highly connected genes tend to perform essential functions

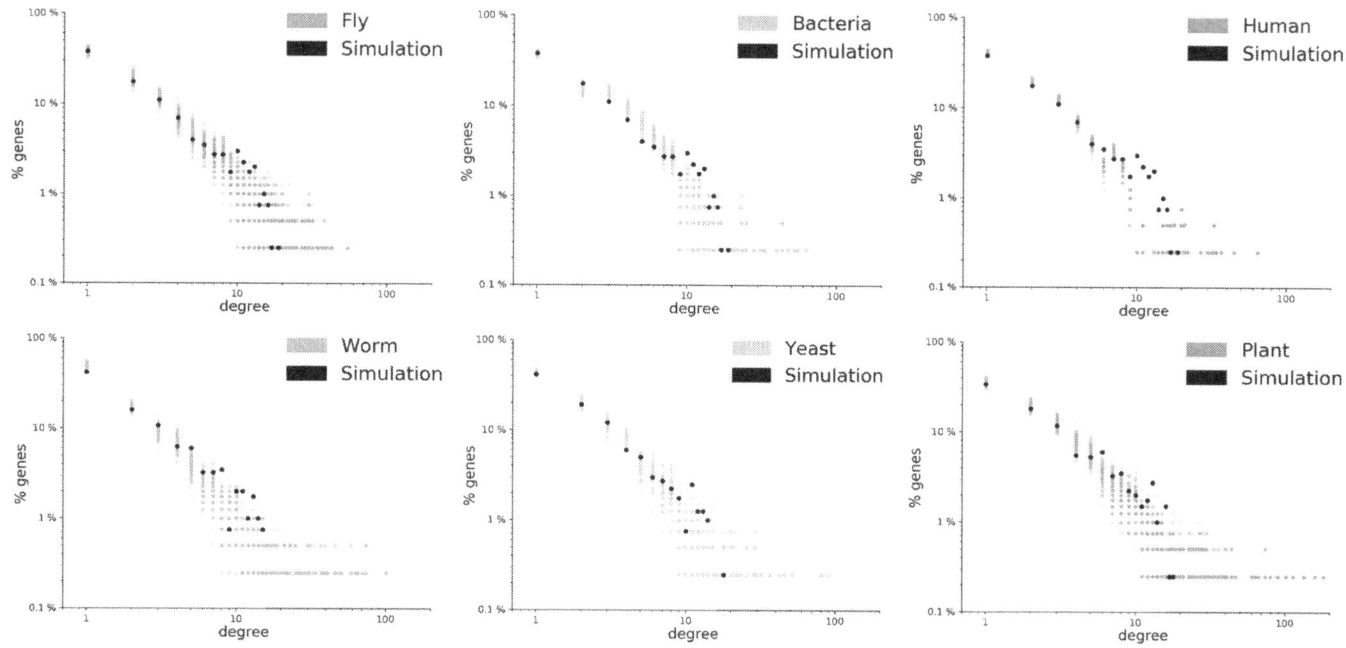

Figure 4: Adaptation with growth. Starting from a near empty network, evolution proceeds with mutations being random edge-reassignment as well as the addition of new nodes and edges. The size of the last network at algorithm termination is 400 nodes. The evolving networks are not mutated with additional edges when their edge:node ratio exceeds that of the corresponding BN of the same edge:node ratio. Shown here is the degree distribution of the fittest final network after 4000 generations of mutate-and-select (black dots), against the degree distribution of 100 400-node randomly sampled subnetworks from each corresponding BN (colour dots). In all cases, each evolved network's degree distribution closely follows its corresponding BN of the same edge:node ratio.

[19] and are unlikely to be detrimental in and of themselves. Regulating around them however (e.g. micro-RNA regulation [15]) is where the constant optimization is needed.

For the presented model to be applicable beyond explaining the emergence of mLmH, some limitations must be addressed. We have treated all interactions (edges) as equal, but in reality some interactions are more potent than others. Unfortunately there is no large-scale data as of yet that can inform meaningful assignment of edge weights (i.e. some $\pm\alpha \in \mathbb{R}$ instead of simply ± 1). Alternatively potency can be estimated based on the centrality of a given interaction (how many network shortest paths include it). We have also treated all genes (nodes) as equal, but in reality a gene's position matters [15, 20] and should be taken into account when attributing the magnitude of its benefit/damage scores. The benefit(damage) score of a central gene (many shortest paths pass through it) clearly has more positive (negative) impact on the network as a whole. Future work aims to overcome these limitations and apply its simulations as stress tests on experimentally-validated networks the coverage and accuracy of which is exponentially increasing [15, 17, 25, 34]. In this regard, we intend to ask the following question: what subset of pathways are involved in the hardest optimization instances under simulated evolutionary pressure? If the quick sands of computational intractability is the obstacle against Nature discovering a cancer-resistant regulatory network for example, the model may give a hint as to what subset of genes should combinatorially be optimized over (up- and down-regulation of genes). This can inform knockdown/out/in and RNA interference experiments, and is in sharp contrast with the dominant correlation-based cancer-target inference methods which, even if statistically sound, do not necessarily reveal underlying causation. The efficacy of the model in making such predictions can easily be falsified against previously known cancer-implicated sets of genes.

ACKNOWLEDGMENTS

Computations were made on the supercomputing cluster Guillimin from McGill University, managed by Calcul Québec and Compute Canada. The operation of these supercomputers is funded by the Canada Foundation for Innovation (CFI), ministère de l'Économie, de la Science et de l'Innovation du Québec (MESI) and the Fonds de recherche du Québec - Nature et technologies (FRQ-NT).

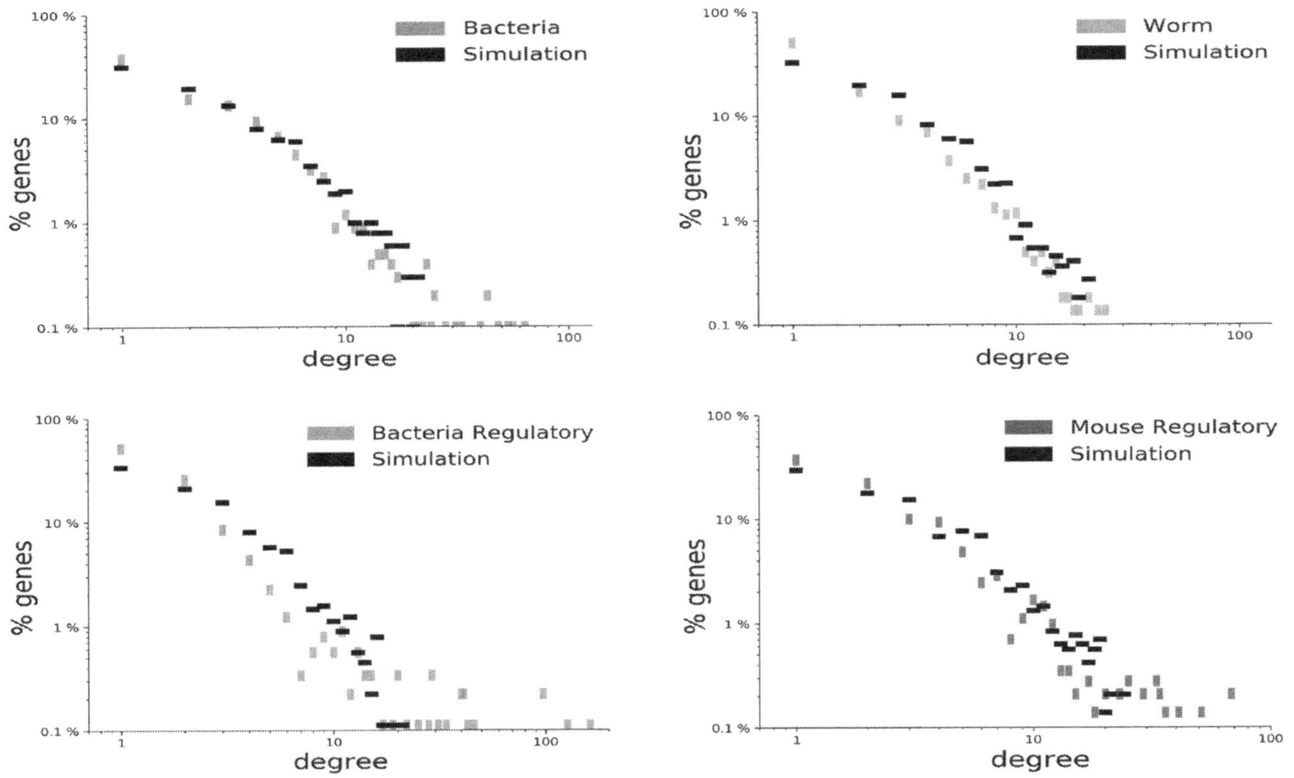

Figure 5: Scaling to larger networks and applicability to different physiological contexts. Networks start empty and undergo reassign-edge, add-node, add-edge mutations. An evolving network grows by adding one node, and one or more edges while maintaining its edge:node ratio equal that of its corresponding real BN. The simulation terminates when networks reach the same size (number of nodes) as that of the corresponding real BN. The final degree distribution of the fittest network is illustrated (horizontal black dashes) against that of the corresponding BN (vertical coloured dashes). Simulating against Bacteria and Mouse Regulatory networks (bottom row), which are comprised of TF-gene, TF-TF and (in Mouse only) small RNA-gene interactions as opposed to all other networks which are comprised of protein-protein interactions, further shows the applicability of the model to different physiological contexts.

REFERENCES

[1] Reka Albert, Hawoong Jeong, and Albert-Laszlo Barabasi. 2000. Error and Attack Tolerance of Complex Networks : Article : Nature. *Nature* 406, 6794 (July 2000), 378–382. https://doi.org/10.1038/35019019

[2] David L. Alderson and John C. Doyle. 2010. Contrasting Views of Complexity and Their Implications for Network-Centric Infrastructures. *IEEE Transactions on systems, man, and cybernetics-Part A: Systems and humans* 40, 4 (2010), 839–852.

[3] Ali Atiia and Jérôme Waldispühl. 2017. Computational Intractability Explains the Topology of Biological Networks. http://cs.mcgill.ca/~malsha17/permlink/paper1.pdf. (June 2017).

[4] Per Bak, Chao Tang, and Kurt Wiesenfeld. 1988. Self-Organized Criticality. *Physical review A* 38, 1 (1988), 364.

[5] Albert-László Barabási and Réka Albert. 1999. Emergence of Scaling in Random Networks. *Science* 286, 5439 (Oct. 1999), 509–512. https://doi.org/10.1126/science.286.5439.509

[6] Albert-László Barabási and Zoltán N. Oltvai. 2004. Network Biology: Understanding the Cell's Functional Organization. *Nature Reviews Genetics* 5, 2 (Feb. 2004), 101–113. https://doi.org/10.1038/nrg1272

[7] Ashish Bhan, David J. Galas, and T. Gregory Dewey. 2002. A Duplication Growth Model of Gene Expression Networks. *Bioinformatics* 18, 11 (Nov. 2002), 1486–1493. https://doi.org/10.1093/bioinformatics/18.11.1486

[8] J. M. Carlson and John Doyle. 1999. Highly Optimized Tolerance: A Mechanism for Power Laws in Designed Systems. *Physical Review E* 60, 2 (Aug. 1999), 1412–1427. https://doi.org/10.1103/PhysRevE.60.1412

[9] Anne-Ruxandra Carvunis, Thomas Rolland, Ilan Wapinski, Michael A. Calderwood, Muhammed A. Yildirim, Nicolas Simonis, Benoit Charloteaux, César A. Hidalgo, Justin Barbette, Balaji Santhanam, Gloria A. Brar, Jonathan S. Weissman, Aviv Regev, Nicolas Thierry-Mieg, Michael E. Cusick, and Marc Vidal. 2012. Proto-Genes and de Novo Gene Birth. *Nature* 487, 7407 (July 2012), 370–374. https://doi.org/10.1038/nature11184

[10] Aaron Clauset, Cosma Rohilla Shalizi, and Mark EJ Newman. 2009. Power-Law Distributions in Empirical Data. *SIAM review* 51, 4 (2009), 661–703.

[11] Arabidopsis Interactome Mapping Consortium. 2011. Evidence for Network Evolution in an Arabidopsis Interactome Map. *Science* 333, 6042 (July 2011), 601–607. https://doi.org/10.1126/science.1203877

[12] Evelyn Fox Keller. 2005. Revisiting "Scale-Free" Networks. *BioEssays* 27, 10 (2005), 1060–1068.

[13] Hunter B. Fraser, Aaron E. Hirsh, Lars M. Steinmetz, Curt Scharfe, and Marcus W. Feldman. 2002. Evolutionary Rate in the Protein Interaction Network. *Science* 296, 5568 (April 2002), 750–752.

https://doi.org/10.1126/science.1068696
[14] Socorro Gama-Castro, Heladia Salgado, Alberto Santos-Zavaleta, Daniela Ledezma-Tejeida, Luis Muñiz-Rascado, Jair Santiago García-Sotelo, Kevin Alquicira-Hernández, Irma Martínez-Flores, Lucia Pannier, Jaime Abraham Castro-Mondragón, Alejandra Medina-Rivera, Hilda Solano-Lira, César Bonavides-Martínez, Ernesto Pérez-Rueda, Shirley Alquicira-Hernández, Liliana Porrón-Sotelo, Alejandra López-Fuentes, Anastasia Hernández-Koutoucheva, Víctor Del Moral-Chávez, Fabio Rinaldi, and Julio Collado-Vides. 2016. RegulonDB Version 9.0: High-Level Integration of Gene Regulation, Coexpression, Motif Clustering and Beyond. *Nucleic Acids Research* 44, D1 (Jan. 2016), D133–D143. https://doi.org/10.1093/nar/gkv1156
[15] Mark B. Gerstein, Anshul Kundaje, Manoj Hariharan, Stephen G. Landt, Koon-Kiu Yan, Chao Cheng, Xinmeng Jasmine Mu, Ekta Khurana, Joel Rozowsky, Roger Alexander, Renqiang Min, Pedro Alves, Alexej Abyzov, Nick Addleman, Nitin Bhardwaj, Alan P. Boyle, Philip Cayting, Alexandra Charos, David Z. Chen, Yong Cheng, Declan Clarke, Catharine Eastman, Ghia Euskirchen, Seth Frietze, Yao Fu, Jason Gertz, Fabian Grubert, Arif Harmanci, Preti Jain, Maya Kasowski, Phil Lacroute, Jing Leng, Jin Lian, Hannah Monahan, Henriette O'Geen, Zhengqing Ouyang, E. Christopher Partridge, Dorrelyn Patacsil, Florencia Pauli, Debasish Raha, Lucia Ramirez, Timothy E. Reddy, Brian Reed, Minyi Shi, Teri Slifer, Jing Wang, Linfeng Wu, Xinqiong Yang, Kevin Y. Yip, Gili Zilberman-Schapira, Serafim Batzoglou, Arend Sidow, Peggy J. Farnham, Richard M. Myers, Sherman M. Weissman, and Michael Snyder. 2012. Architecture of the Human Regulatory Network Derived from ENCODE Data. *Nature* 489, 7414 (Sept. 2012), 91–100. https://doi.org/10.1038/nature11245
[16] Matthew W. Hahn, Gavin C. Conant, and Andreas Wagner. 2004. Molecular Evolution in Large Genetic Networks: Does Connectivity Equal Constraint? *Journal of Molecular Evolution* 58, 2 (Feb. 2004), 203–211. https://doi.org/10.1007/s00239-003-2544-0
[17] Heonjong Han, Hongseok Shim, Donghyun Shin, Jung Eun Shim, Yunhee Ko, Junha Shin, Hanhae Kim, Ara Cho, Eiru Kim, Tak Lee, and others. 2015. TRRUST: A Reference Database of Human Transcriptional Regulatory Interactions. *Scientific reports* 5 (2015).
[18] Raya Khanin and Ernst Wit. 2006. How Scale-Free Are Biological Networks. *Journal of computational biology* 13, 3 (2006), 810–818.
[19] Ekta Khurana, Yao Fu, Jieming Chen, and Mark Gerstein. 2013. Interpretation of Genomic Variants Using a Unified Biological Network Approach. *PLOS Computational Biology* 9, 3 (March 2013), e1002886. https://doi.org/10.1371/journal.pcbi.1002886
[20] Philip M. Kim, Jan O. Korbel, and Mark B. Gerstein. 2007. Positive Selection at the Protein Network Periphery: Evaluation in Terms of Structural Constraints and Cellular Context. *Proceedings of the National Academy of Sciences* 104, 51 (Dec. 2007), 20274–20279. https://doi.org/10.1073/pnas.0710183104
[21] Gipsi Lima-Mendez and Jacques van Helden. 2009. The Powerful Law of the Power Law and Other Myths in Network Biology. *Molecular BioSystems* 5, 12 (2009), 1482. https://doi.org/10.1039/b908681a
[22] Zhi-Ping Liu, Canglin Wu, Hongyu Miao, and Hulin Wu. 2015. RegNetwork: An Integrated Database of Transcriptional and Post-Transcriptional Regulatory Networks in Human and Mouse. *Database* 2015 (Jan. 2015). https://doi.org/10.1093/database/bav095
[23] Michael Lynch. 2007. The Evolution of Genetic Networks by Non-Adaptive Processes. *Nature Reviews Genetics* 8, 10 (Oct. 2007), 803–813. https://doi.org/10.1038/nrg2192
[24] Michael Lynch. 2007. The Frailty of Adaptive Hypotheses for the Origins of Organismal Complexity. *Proceedings of the National Academy of Sciences of the United States of America* 104, Suppl 1 (May 2007), 8597–8604. https://doi.org/10.1073/pnas.0702207104
[25] Shane Neph, Andrew B. Stergachis, Alex Reynolds, Richard Sandstrom, Elhanan Borenstein, and John A. Stamatoyannopoulos. 2012. Circuitry and Dynamics of Human Transcription Factor Regulatory Networks. *Cell* 150, 6 (2012), 1274–1286.
[26] Balázs Papp, Bas Teusink, and Richard A. Notebaart. 2009. A Critical View of Metabolic Network Adaptations. *HFSP journal* 3, 1 (2009), 24–35.
[27] Matjaž Perc. 2014. The Matthew Effect in Empirical Data. *Journal of The Royal Society Interface* 11, 98 (Sept. 2014), 20140378. https://doi.org/10.1098/rsif.2014.0378
[28] David Pisinger. 2005. Where Are the Hard Knapsack Problems? *Computers & Operations Research* 32, 9 (2005), 2271–2284.
[29] Seesandra V. Rajagopala, Patricia Sikorski, Ashwani Kumar, Roberto Mosca, James Vlasblom, Roland Arnold, Jonathan Franca-Koh, Suman B. Pakala, Sadhna Phanse, Arnaud Ceol, and others. 2014. The Binary Protein-Protein Interaction Landscape of Escherichia Coli. *Nature biotechnology* 32, 3 (2014), 285–290.
[30] Thomas Rolland, Murat Taşan, Benoit Charloteaux, Samuel J. Pevzner, Quan Zhong, Nidhi Sahni, Song Yi, Irma Lemmens, Celia Fontanillo, Roberto Mosca, and others. 2014. A Proteome-Scale Map of the Human Interactome Network. *Cell* 159, 5 (2014), 1212–1226.
[31] Daniel A. Schult and P. J. Swart. 2008. Exploring Network Structure, Dynamics, and Function Using NetworkX. In *Proceedings of the 7th Python in Science Conferences (SciPy 2008)*, Vol. 2008. 11–16.
[32] Nicolas Simonis, Jean-François Rual, Anne-Ruxandra Carvunis, Murat Tasan, Irma Lemmens, Tomoko Hirozane-Kishikawa, Tong Hao, Julie M. Sahalie, Kavitha Venkatesan, Fana Gebreab, Sebiha Cevik, Niels Klitgord, Changyu Fan, Pascal Braun, Ning Li, Nono Ayivi-Guedehoussou, Elizabeth Dann, Nicolas Bertin, David Szeto, Amélie Dricot, Muhammed A. Yildirim, Chenwei Lin, Anne-Sophie de Smet, Huey-Ling Kao, Christophe Simon, Alex Smolyar, Jin Sook Ahn, Muneesh Tewari, Mike Boxem, Stuart Milstein, Haiyuan Yu, Matija Dreze, Jean Vandenhaute, Kristin C. Gunsalus, Michael E. Cusick, David E. Hill, Jan Tavernier, Frederick P. Roth, and Marc Vidal. 2009. Empirically Controlled Mapping of the Caenorhabditis Elegans Protein-Protein Interactome Network. *Nature Methods* 6, 1 (Jan. 2009), 47–54. https://doi.org/10.1038/nmeth.1279
[33] Trevor R. Sorrells and Alexander D. Johnson. 2015. Making Sense of Transcription Networks. *Cell* 161, 4 (May 2015), 714–723. https://doi.org/10.1016/j.cell.2015.04.014
[34] Andrew B. Stergachis, Shane Neph, Richard Sandstrom, Eric Haugen, Alex P. Reynolds, Miaohua Zhang, Rachel Byron, Theresa Canfield, Sandra Stelhing-Sun, Kristen Lee, and others. 2014. Conservation of Trans-Acting Circuitry during Mammalian Regulatory Evolution. *Nature* 515, 7527 (2014), 365–370.
[35] Michael P. H. Stumpf and Mason A. Porter. 2012. Critical Truths About Power Laws. *Science* 335, 6069 (Feb. 2012), 665–666. https://doi.org/10.1126/science.1216142
[36] Reiko Tanaka, Tau-Mu Yi, and John Doyle. 2005. Some Protein Interaction Data Do Not Exhibit Power Law Statistics. *FEBS letters* 579, 23 (2005), 5140–5144.
[37] Alexei Vázquez, Alessandro Flammini, Amos Maritan, and Alessandro Vespignani. 2002. Modeling of Protein Interaction Networks. *Complexus* 1, 1 (2002), 38–44.
[38] Arunachalam Vinayagam, Jonathan Zirin, Charles Roesel, Yanhui Hu, Bahar Yilmazel, Anastasia A. Samsonova, Ralph A. Neumüller, Stephanie E. Mohr, and Norbert Perrimon. 2014. Integrating Protein-Protein Interaction Networks with Phenotypes Reveals Signs of Interactions. *Nature methods* 11, 1 (2014), 94–99.
[39] Xinping Yang, Jasmin Coulombe-Huntington, Shuli Kang, Gloria M. Sheynkman, Tong Hao, Aaron Richardson, Song Sun, Fan Yang, Yun A. Shen, Ryan R. Murray, Kerstin Spirohn, Bridget E. Begg, Miquel Duran-Frigola, Andrew MacWilliams, Samuel J. Pevzner, Quan Zhong, Shelly A. Trigg, Stanley Tam, Lila Ghamsari, Nidhi Sahni, Song Yi, Maria D. Rodriguez, Dawit Balcha, Guihong Tan, Michael Costanzo, Brenda Andrews, Charles Boone, Xianghong J. Zhou, Kourosh Salehi-Ashtiani, Benoit Charloteaux, Alyce A. Chen, Michael A. Calderwood, Patrick Aloy, Frederick P. Roth, David E. Hill, Lilia M. Iakoucheva, Yu Xia, and Marc Vidal. 2016. Widespread Expansion of Protein Interaction Capabilities by Alternative Splicing. *Cell* 164, 4 (Feb. 2016), 805–817. https://doi.org/10.1016/j.cell.2016.01.029
[40] Haiyuan Yu, Pascal Braun, Muhammed A. Yıldırım, Irma Lemmens, Kavitha Venkatesan, Julie Sahalie, Tomoko Hirozane-Kishikawa, Fana Gebreab, Na Li, Nicolas Simonis, Tong Hao, Jean-François Rual, Amélie Dricot, Alexei Vazquez, Ryan R. Murray, Christophe Simon, Leah Tardivo, Stanley Tam, Nenad Svrzikapa, Changyu Fan, Anne-Sophie de Smet, Adriana Motyl, Michael E. Hudson, Juyong Park, Xiaofeng Xin, Michael E. Cusick, Troy Moore, Charlie Boone, Michael Snyder, Frederick P. Roth, Albert-László Barabási, Jan Tavernier, David E. Hill, and Marc Vidal. 2008. High-Quality Binary Protein Interaction Map of the Yeast Interactome Network. *Science* 322, 5898 (Oct. 2008), 104–110. https://doi.org/10.1126/science.1158684

A Flexible and Robust Multi-Source Learning Algorithm for Drug Repositioning

Huiyuan Chen
Electrical Engineering and Computer Science
Case Western Reserve University
Cleveland, OH, 44106
hxc501@case.edu

Jing Li
Electrical Engineering and Computer Science
Case Western Reserve University
Cleveland, OH, 44106
jingli@cwru.edu

ABSTRACT

Drug repositioning is a promising strategy in drug discovery. New biomedical insights of drug-target-disease relationships are important in drug repositioning, and such relationships have been intensively studied recently. Most of the studies utilize network-based computational approaches based on drug and disease similarities. However, one common limitation of existing approaches is that both drug similarities and disease similarities are defined based on a single feature of drugs/diseases. In reality, the relationships between drug (or disease) pairs can be characterized based on many different features. Therefore, it is increasingly important to include them in drug repositioning studies. In this study, we propose a flexible and robust multi-source learning (FRMSL) framework to integrate multiple heterogeneous data sources for drug-disease association predictions. We first construct a two-layer heterogeneous network consisting of drug nodes, disease nodes and known drug-disease relationships. The drug repositioning problem can thus be treated as a missing link prediction problem on the heterogeneous graph and can be solved using Kronecker regularized least square (KronRLS) method. Multiple data sources describing drugs and diseases are incorporated into the framework using similarity-based kernels. In practice, a great challenge in such data integration projects is the data incompleteness problem due to the nature of data generation and collection. To address this issue, we develop a novel multi-view learning algorithm based on symmetric nonnegative matrix factorization (SymNMF). Extensive experimental studies show that our framework outperforms several recent network-based methods.

CCS CONCEPTS

• **Computing methodologies → Machine learning approaches**;

KEYWORDS

Drug Repositioning; Multi-View Learning; Heterogeneous Network

Permission to make digital or hard copies of all or part of this work for personal or classroom use is granted without fee provided that copies are not made or distributed for profit or commercial advantage and that copies bear this notice and the full citation on the first page. Copyrights for components of this work owned by others than the author(s) must be honored. Abstracting with credit is permitted. To copy otherwise, or republish, to post on servers or to redistribute to lists, requires prior specific permission and/or a fee. Request permissions from permissions@acm.org.
ACM-BCB'17, August 20–23, 2017, Boston, MA, USA.
© 2017 Copyright held by the owner/author(s). Publication rights licensed to ACM.
ISBN 978-1-4503-4722-8/17/08...$15.00
DOI: http://dx.doi.org/10.1145/3107411.3107473

1 INTRODUCTION

Traditional drug discovery using high-throughput screening could identify a new drug against a chosen target protein for a special disease. However, the whole screening process is still expensive, time consuming, and with high failure rates. A conservative estimate is that it takes on average 13.5 years and $1.8 billion to bring a new drug into the market [20]. Drug repositioning, exploiting new indications of approved drugs, is gaining increasing interests both in academia and pharmaceutical industry recently. For example, Minoxidil was originally used for hypertension, but was then approved for hair loss [10]. Drug repositioning provides a promising alternative strategy to reduce the total cost because existing drugs have already been approved by the U.S. Food and Drug Administration (FDA) with known toxicity information. A recent report has shown that among the 84 new drug products on the market in 2013, new clinical indications of existing drugs accounted for 20% [12]. Therefore, drug repositioning has played an important role in current drug development.

Recently, several network-based computational approaches for drug repositioning have been proposed [6, 7, 17, 19, 27, 28]. For example, a drug-disease network was constructed to predict novel indications of drugs and results were highly enriched in clinical trials [7]. In another study, a weighted heterogeneous network was applied to identify the connected communities of drugs and diseases using a network clustering approach [28]. Two network topology-based inference methods, ProbS and HeatS, were also introduced to predict new indications for different diseases [6]. DrugNet was another network-based prioritization approach simultaneously incorporating information about diseases, drugs and targets to perform drug-disease prioritization [19]. TL_HGBI was a three-layer heterogeneous network model that seamlessly integrated drug repositioning and drug-target prediction into one unified framework [27]. Similarly, MBiRW used a bi-random walk algorithm on a two-layer network to infer the potential drug-disease associations [17]. Most of those computational frameworks have utilized the guilt-by-association principle [1], which states that if two diseases share similar therapeutic profiles, then drugs for one disease could also treat the other with high possibility. However, most previous methods only incorporate one data source in calculating drug-drug similarity (*e.g.*, similarity based on chemical structures) and one data source for disease-disease similarity (*e.g.*, phenotype-based similarity), which may not be able to capture the complex interplay between drugs and diseases. In addition, for those non small molecule drugs (*e.g.*, Leuprolide), similarities cannot be measured based on chemical structures. In this case, other type of information (*e.g.*, drugs' side effects) may provide valuable insights in learning drug-disease relationships.

To overcome aforementioned limitations, we propose a novel **F**lexible and **R**obust **M**ultiple **S**ources Learning (FRMSL) framework to integrate distinct sources of biological datasets to better define similarities among drugs and among diseases. Our model can be viewed as a two-layer heterogeneous network, where the two layers representing drugs and diseases. Similarity kernels are defined for nodes within each layer based on multiple data sources. Links across layers are defined based on known drug indications. The drug repositioning problem is thus the same as the missing link prediction problem on the network. We solve the problem by utilizing Kronecker regularized least squares approach (KronRLS) [25]. It has been shown that integration of large-scale proteomic, genomic, transcriptomic and metabolic data into networks could provide new insights of molecular basis of complex human diseases [14]. However, due to the nature of data collection (*i.e.*, data were generated by different labs in different time), it is very unlikely that all datasets will be available for all drugs/diseases. Data incompleteness is always a significant challenge when merging them from different sources. To address this issue, we further develop a multi-view learning algorithm and subsequently solve the problem utilizing symmetric nonnegative matrix factorization (SymNMF). The basic idea is that missing information from one data source/view could be inferred by borrowing information from other sources/views. This can also be viewed as a network alignment algorithm for drug/disease layer, respectively, where each data source adds a sub-layer to one of the two layers and the SymNMF forces them to share a common network structure in terms of their weights (*i.e.*, similarities) . FRMSL is flexible because it can easily incorporate more data sources once they are available in the future. Extensive experimental studies have shown the benefits of multi-source learning and multi-view learning, and the proposed FRMSL greatly outperforms several state-of-the-art network-based methods. The rest of the paper is organized as follows. The theoretical derivations of the multi-source learning algorithm based on multiple kernels and multi-view learning for missing data imputation are introduced in Section 2. The description of datasets and experimental tests are presented in Section 3. We conclude our paper with a brief discussion in Section 4.

2 METHODS

In this section, we first formulate the drug repositioning task as a missing link prediction problem on a two-layer heterogeneous network, consisting of drugs and diseases. We choose to solve the problem by utilizing the Kronecker regularized least squares approach (KronRLS) [25]. We include a kernel fusion step to incorporate multiple data sources for each layer. The missing data imputations is then solved based on SymNMF. Finally we give a summary of our computational framework FRMSL.

2.1 Problem Formulation

Given a set of n drugs $C = \{c_1, c_2, \ldots, c_n\}$, a set of m diseases $D = \{d_1, d_2, \ldots, d_m\}$, and a set of known drug-disease relationships Y, (where $y_{ij} = 1$ if drug c_i can treat disease d_j, and $y_{ij} = 0$

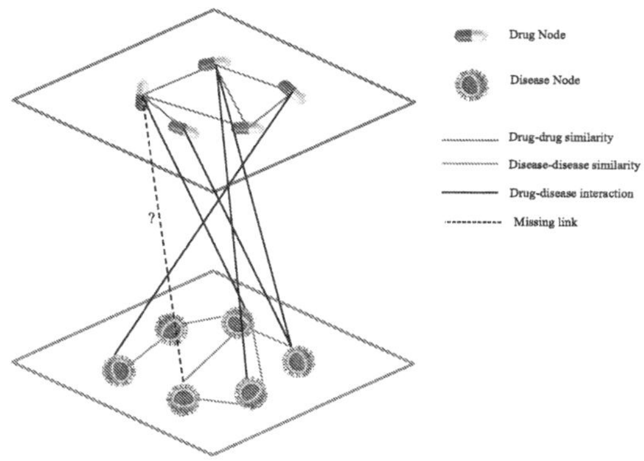

Figure 1: A heterogeneous network for drug repositioning

otherwise), we construct a two-layer heterogeneous network (Figure 1). The network consists of two types of nodes: drug nodes and disease nodes; three types of edges: drug-drug edges, disease-disease edges and drug-disease edges. The edges between the same type of nodes are labeled based on their similarities. Drug-disease edges are defined for all drug-disease pairs (i, j) with $y_{ij} = 1$. The goal of the drug repositioning problem is to predict missing links between the drug-layer and the disease-layer based on the information contained in the two-layer network. Although the two-layer heterogeneous network model is the same structure-wise as the models in some other studies [17, 26], our unique contribution in this study is the integration of multiple data sources and imputation of missing in one data source by borrowing information from other data sources.

2.2 KronRLS Algorithm

The missing link prediction problem can be solved using the regularized least square (RLS) approach in order to have good generalization power. Given a set of training data $S = \{(\boldsymbol{x}_i, y_i) : \boldsymbol{x}_i = (c_i, d_i); 0 \leq i \leq l\}$, the goal of the RLS algorithm is to find the mapping function $f : X \rightarrow Y$, by minimizing the following objective function:

$$\underset{f \in \mathcal{H}}{\operatorname{argmin}} \frac{1}{l} \sum_{i=1}^{l} (y_i - f(\boldsymbol{x}_i))^2 + \lambda \|f\|_{\mathcal{H}}^2 \tag{1}$$

where $\|f\|_{\mathcal{H}}^2$ is a Hilbert space norm of function f; λ is a trade-off between regression accuracy and the complexity of the function f in the Hilbert space. The representer theorem guarantees that Eq. (1) has a closed-form solution [21]:

$$f(\boldsymbol{x}) = \sum_{i=1}^{l} a_i K(\boldsymbol{x}, \boldsymbol{x}_i) \tag{2}$$

where $\boldsymbol{a} \in \mathbb{R}^l$ can be obtained by solving the following linear equation: $(\boldsymbol{K} + \lambda \boldsymbol{I})\boldsymbol{a} = \boldsymbol{y}$; and $\boldsymbol{K}$ is a pairwise instance kernel which represents the similarity between any two data points in the Hilbert space. In the current study, we define the pairwise instance kernel as the product of a drug-drug similarity kernel and a disease-disease similarity kernel, to incorporate information from both drugs and diseases. More specifically, for two instances $\boldsymbol{x}_i = (c_i, d_i)$ and $\boldsymbol{x}_j = (c_j, d_j)$, the kernel is defined as :

$$K(\boldsymbol{x_i}, \boldsymbol{x_j}) = K_c(c_i, c_j)K_d(d_i, d_j) \tag{3}$$

where K_c is a kernel to measure the similarity between drug c_i and drug c_j; K_d is a kernel to measure the similarity of diseases d_i and disease d_j. The drug-drug kernel K_c and the disease-disease kernel K_d can then be defined based on multiple sources (to be discussed in the next subsection).

To solve the optimization problem efficiently, we adopt the KronRLS algorithm [25], which further takes advantage of spectral decompositions of kernel matrices to speed up the calculation. Let $K_c = V_c\Lambda_c V_c{}^T$ and $K_d = V_d\Lambda_d V_d{}^T$ be the spectral decomposition of kernel K_c and K_d, respectively. Eq. (3) can be rewritten as Kronecker product kernel $K = K_c \otimes K_d = V\Lambda V^T$, where $V = V_c \otimes V_d$, $\Lambda = \Lambda_c \otimes \Lambda_d$, and $A \otimes B$ is the Kronecker product of two matrices A and B. Based on these transformations, one can get the prediction in the form of [25]

$$\hat{Y} = V_c Z^T V_d{}^T \tag{4}$$

where

$$vec(Z) = (\Lambda_c \otimes \Lambda_d)(\Lambda_c \otimes \Lambda_d + \lambda I)^{-1} vec(V_d{}^T Y^T V_c),$$

and $vec(\cdot)$ is the vectorization operator that stacks all columns of a matrix into a column vector.

2.3 Fusion Kernels Across Multiple Heterogeneous Sources

With increasing available biological datasets regarding drugs and diseases, drug-drug similarities and disease-disease similarities can be measured differently using different datasets. For example, one can define drug-drug similarities based on their chemical structures, or based on their side-effect profiles. Different datasets represent different aspects of drugs and/or their interplays with the human body system. Incorporating multiple heterogeneous sources can provide complementary and comprehensive understanding of a drug's mechanism of action (MoA). Furthermore, different datasets serve as different views of the same objects (*e.g.*, drugs or diseases), which can be used in missing data imputation as presented in next subsection.

For each data source, we will construct a similarity-based kernel (the details of datasets and kernels associated with them will be discussed in the next section). Given a set of kernels representing drug-drug similarities $k_C = \{K_c^{(1)}, K_c^{(2)}, \ldots, K_c^{(n_c)}\}$, and a set of kernels measuring disease-disease similarities $k_D = \{K_d^{(1)}, K_d^{(2)}, \ldots, K_d^{(n_d)}\}$, where n_c and n_d denote the numbers of kernels for drugs and diseases, we propose to combine them by a weighted sum linear convex function to obtain an overall drug kernel K_c^* and an overall disease kernel K_d^*, respectively [21]:

$$K_c^* = \sum_{i=1}^{n_c} \omega_c^i K_c^{(i)} \quad , \quad K_d^* = \sum_{j=1}^{n_d} \omega_d^j K_d^{(j)} \tag{5}$$

The ω_c^i and ω_d^j are corresponding convex weight parameters with the constraints $\sum_{i=1}^{n_c} \omega_c^i = 1$ and $\sum_{j=1}^{n_d} \omega_d^j = 1$. These values can be optimally trained using the cross-validation method on a training dataset. Alternatively, they can be assigned based on prior knowledge about relative reliability of different data sources.

2.4 Complete Kernels Across Multiple Heterogeneous Sources

As we discussed earlier, a significant challenge in data integration is data incompleteness. For example, one can define drug-drug similarities using their side-effect profiles. However, many drugs may not have their side-effect profiles recorded in databases (*e.g.*, SIDER[1]). Missing data points from a data source will lead to an incomplete kernel matrix with rows and columns missing. Previous studies have filled the missing rows and columns with zeros, primarily for computational convenience [25, 27, 28]. However, such a treatment can adversely affect prediction accuracy. Inspired by the idea of multi-view learning [16], we propose a novel framework to perform missing data imputation of multiple kernels based on symmetric nonnegative matrix factorization (SymNMF), which can also viewed as a network alignment algorithm that tries to align different kernels to a common clustering structure [16]. The algorithm is rooted in the guilt-by-association principle. For example, the weighted cluster structure of drug layer (Figure 1) should be highly aligned from both views of chemical structure and drugs side-effect profiles because similar drugs tend to have similar drugs side-effects [5]. Therefore, the missing components in one dataset can be inferred based on information from other datasets.

[1] http://sideeffects.embl.de/

Given a set of kernels $\{K^{(i)} : 1 \le i \le n_v; K^{(i)} \in \mathbb{R}^{N\times N}\}$ constructed from N instances, we first define an indicator matrix $M \in \mathbb{R}^{n_v\times N}$ with its elements defined as

$$M_{i,j} = \begin{cases} 1 & \text{if } j^{th} \text{ instance exists in view } i \\ 0 & \text{otherwise} \end{cases}$$

As a symmetric nonnegative matrix, a kernel matrix can be factorized into two matrices: $K^{(i)} \approx G^{(i)}G^{(i)T}$, $1 \le i \le n_v$, where $G^{(i)} \in \mathbb{R}^{N\times r}$ is the base of the kernel matrix $K^{(i)}$. Typically, $r \ll rank(K^{(i)})$. One can show that this factorization is equivalent to K-means-type clustering [9]. Our proposed network alignment algorithm is to jointly factorize all kernel matrices and push all the factors $G^{(i)}$ towards a consensus matrix G^* through regularization [16]. The objective function involving multiple kernels can then be written as:

$$\begin{aligned} \min_{\{G^{(i)}\}, G^*} \quad & O = \sum_{i=1}^{n_v} (\| W^{(i)}(K^{(i)} - G^{(i)}G^{(i)T})\|_F^2 + \alpha_i \| W^{(i)}(G^{(i)} - G^*)\|_F^2) \\ \text{s.t.} \quad & G^{(i)} \ge 0,\, G^* \ge 0,\, i = 1 \ldots n_v \end{aligned} \tag{6}$$

where the weighting parameters α_is control the relative alignment agreement between $G^{(i)}$ and the common matrix G^*. $W^{(i)} \in \mathbb{R}^{N\times N}$ is a diagonal matrix for incomplete view i, with the diagonal elements defined as :

$$W_{jj}^{(i)} = \begin{cases} 1 & \text{if } i^{th} \text{ view contains } j^{th} \text{ instance. } (M_{i,j} = 1) \\ \frac{\sum_{j=1}^N M_{i,j}}{N} & \text{otherwise} \end{cases}$$

Once the optimization problem is solved, the missing values in kernel $K^{(i)}$ can be approximated by the corresponding elements in $G^{(i)}G^{(i)T}$. However, because Eq. (6) is not jointly convex, an alternating optimization scheme has to be applied [16]. More specifically, the following two steps are iterated until the solution converges: (1) fixing $G^{(i)}$, minimize O over G^*; (2) fixing G^*, minimize O over $G^{(i)}$. We discuss these two steps in sequel.

2.4.1. Fixing $G^{(i)}$, minimize O over G^*.

The objective function $O(G^*)$ does not depend on $G^{(i)}$, we can find the optimal solution by taking the derivative $O(G^*)$ over G^*:

$$\begin{aligned} \frac{\partial O(G^*)}{\partial G^*} &= \sum_{i=1}^{n_v} \alpha_i(-2W^{(i)T}W^{(i)}G^{(i)} + 2W^{(i)T}W^{(i)}G^*) = 0 \\ \text{s.t.} \quad & G^* \ge 0, \quad i = 1, \ldots, n_v \end{aligned} \tag{7}$$

Solving the equation, we have an exact solution for G^*:

$$G^* = \frac{\sum_{i=1}^{n_v} \alpha_i W^{(i)T}W^{(i)}G^{(i)}}{\sum_{i=1}^{n_v} \alpha_i W^{(i)T}W^{(i)}} \ge 0 \tag{8}$$

With the constraint $G^{(i)} \geq 0$, the solution above is always nonnegative too.

2.4.2. Fixing G^*, minimize O over $G^{(i)}$.
When G^* is fixed, the objective function $O(G^{(i)})$ becomes a standard Sym-NMF problem with additional regularization [9]. Furthermore, because the calculation of $G^{(i)}$ does not depend on $G^{(i')}$ when $i' \neq i$, we can thus minimize the objective function $O(G^{(i)})$ with respect to $G^{(i)}$ for each view independently.

$$\begin{aligned} \frac{\partial O(G^{(i)})}{\partial G^{(i)}} = & -4{W^{(i)}}^T W^{(i)} K^{(i)} G^{(i)} + 4{W^{(i)}}^T W^{(i)} G^{(i)} {G^{(i)}}^T G^{(i)} \\ & + 2\alpha_i {W^{(i)}}^T W^{(i)} G^{(i)} - 2\alpha_i {W^{(i)}}^T W^{(i)} G^* \\ \text{s.t.} \quad & G^{(i)} \geq 0, , \quad i = 1, \dots, n_v \end{aligned} \tag{9}$$

Using the Karush-Kuhn-Tuvker (KKT) complementary condition [4], we can get:

$$\begin{aligned} & (-4{W^{(i)}}^T W^{(i)} K^{(i)} G^{(i)} + 4{W^{(i)}}^T W^{(i)} G^{(i)} {G^{(i)}}^T G^{(i)} \\ & + 2\alpha_i {W^{(i)}}^T W^{(i)} G^{(i)} - 2\alpha_i {W^{(i)}}^T W^{(i)} G^*) \odot G^{(i)} = 0 \end{aligned} \tag{10}$$

where $A \odot B$ denotes element-wise multiplication of two matrices A and B. Based on the fixed point equation above, we can derive the updating rule for $G^{(i)}$ as:

$$G^{(i)}_{j,k} \leftarrow G^{(i)}_{j,k} \frac{(2{W^{(i)}}^T W^{(i)} K^{(i)} G^{(i)} + \alpha_i {W^{(i)}}^T W^{(i)} G^*)_{j,k}}{(2{W^{(i)}}^T W^{(i)} G^{(i)} {G^{(i)}}^T G^{(i)} + \alpha_i {W^{(i)}}^T W^{(i)} G^{(i)})_{j,k}} \tag{11}$$

We will iteratively update variable G^* and $G^{(i)}$ using above updating rules until the objective function Eq.(6) converges. After obtaining a set of matrix factors $\{G^{(1)}, G^{(2)}, \dots, G^{(n_v)}\}$, we then reconstruct the incomplete kernel matrices by $K^{(i)} \approx G^{(i)} {G^{(i)}}^T$, $1 \leq i \leq n_v$.

3 EXPERIMENTS AND RESULTS

In this section, we first define similarity measures/kernels from multiple data sources for both drugs and diseases. We take those measures from recent literatures that have been shown effectiveness. We then evaluate the proposed FRMSL algorithm on a gold standard dataset and compare its performance with two state-of-the-art network-based methods published recently, as well as the KronRLS algorithm (without missing value imputation). Furthermore, we also investigate the performance of FRMSL on an independent test dataset. Finally, we present case study results on five complex human diseases to illustrate the practical usefulness of FRMSL in drug discovery.

3.1 Datasets

The dataset with known drug-disease associations used in this study is obtained from Gottlieb *et al.* [11], which consists of comprehensive drug-disease relationships from multiple datasets. There are in total 1, 933 known drug-disease interactions involving 593 drugs assembled from DrugBank[2] and 313 human diseases listed in the Online Mendelian Inheritance in Man (OMIM) database[3]. Additional information about drugs, including drug side-effects, drug target profiles and ligand-binding site, are extracted from SIDER, Uniprot[4] and PDB[5], respectively.

[2]https://www.drugbank.ca/
[3]https://www.omim.org/
[4]http://www.uniprot.org/
[5]http://www.rcsb.org/pdb/home/home.do

Based on different types of datasets, we define four distinct kernels to measure drug-drug similarities and three distinct kernels for disease-disease similarities. All of the similarity measures are finally normalized in the range of [0, 1]. Some of the similarity matrices are already positive definite when they are constructed and are obviously valid kernels (*e.g.*, the drug chemical structure similarity [18]). Even when a similarity matrix (symmetric, non-negative) is not strictly positive definite, one can add a small strictly positive definite kernel (e.g. $k'(x_i, x_j) = \delta_{ij}$) to eventually obtain a positive definite matrix [21]. The four drug-drug similarities are constructed as follows.

(1) Chemical structure similarity: Chemical properties of a drug are evidently related to its ultimate therapeutic effects [10]. In this article, chemical structures of drugs in Canonical SMILES form are downloaded from DrugBank. The Chemical Development Kit is then applied to compute the Tanimoto similarity score of two drugs using their corresponding 2D chemical fingerprints [23].

(2) Drug side-effect similarity: Drug side-effects, representing unintended consequences of drug activities, provide another measure of drug relationships in terms of their therapeutic effects. It has been shown that drug side-effect is an important factor and contributes significantly in revealing novel drug-target interactions [5]. In this work, drug side-effects are obtained from SIDER database. Each drug is then represented by a binary profile, in which the existence or absence of corresponding side effect keyword is encoded as 1 or 0. Finally, a cosine correlation coefficient is used to calculate the similarity score.

(3) Drug-target sequence similarity: Protein target information of drugs is another important feature that can be used to characterize drug relationships. For drugs with known protein targets, their similarities are measured based on the Smith-Waterman alignment scores of the amino acid sequences of their corresponding targets [22]. The similarity scores are further normalized based on the method in [2]. For drugs with more than one targets, the similarity score is the average of the scores computed from all the target proteins.

(4) Drug binding site similarity: Ligand binding sites are critical in defining relationships between drugs and their targets. We thus define a score to capture the binding site similarities among targets. Target protein structures are first downloaded from PDB. Then a binding similarity score is calculated based on the local structural alignment of two proteins using SMAP software [29]. Similarly, for drugs with multiple targets, the final similarity score is the average of the scores computed using all targets.

The three disease-disease similarities are constructed as follows.

(1) Phenotype similarity: Disease phenotypes are a reflection of interacting gene products and it has been shown that their similarities are positively correlated with gene functions. In this work, we adopt the phenotype similarity constructed by a text mining method [24], which are calculated based on the number of shared MeSH terms appearing in the medical description of diseases in OMIM database.

(2) Disease HPO similarity: The Human Phenotype Ontology (HPO) offers a standardized and controlled vocabulary reflecting phenotypic abnormalities of human diseases, and becomes a comprehensive resource for analyzing human disease phenotypes. The similarity between two diseases is computed based on the two HPO-term sets annotating the two diseases [8].

(3) Disease DO similarity: Disease Ontology is another comprehensive ontology representing disease classifications based on their etiology. A directed acyclic graph is first constructed for each disease based on their DO terms and the similarity score between the two diseases is measured based on their graph structures [15].

3.2 Experimental design

To systematically evaluate the performance of the proposed FRMSL algorithm, we first performed a five-fold cross-validation experiment on the gold standard dataset mentioned earlier, and compared its results with two recent network based algorithms, as well as the KronRLS algorithm (without missing data imputation). We used the receiver operating curve (ROC) and the area under the ROC curve (AUC) to evaluate the overall performance of different algorithms. Furthermore, using the trained models based on the gold standard dataset, we tested the performance of the four algorithms on an independent dataset. Finally, we showed that FRMSL could be used to detect novel drug-disease associations by utilizing all existing data.

3.3 Comparison with other methods

To see any improvement due to multi-view learning, we directly compared FRMSL with the KronRLS algorithm. For KronRLS, as a common practice, all the missing columns and rows in drug and disease kernels were filled with zeros. There are many parameters in FRMSL (KronRLS as well). In theory, one may find an optimal set of parameters using the grid search algorithm based on cross-validation experiments. But in this study, we chose these parameters based on prior experience, prior domain knowledge, or some uninformative priors. Although the final results of FRMSL may not be optimal, it still outperforms other algorithms (to be shown), which demonstrates its robustness and generalization power. In the experiments, we set $\lambda = 1$ in Eq. (1). For the parameters to fuse different kernels into one in Eq.(5), we simply chose the same weight for each kernel (*i.e.*, $W_c^i = 0.25$ for each drug kernel and $w_d^j = 0.33$ for each disease kernel). The same set of parameters were used for KronRLS for a fair comparison. For FRMSL, the regularization parameters $\{\alpha_i\}$ controls the level of consistency between each individual view/kernel and the common structure across all views. We chose them based on domain knowledge. Among the four drug kernels, the chemical structure, drug side-effect and drug binding sites similarity are all drug-centric (either drugs' intrinsic properties or drug-target local interaction property). On the other hand, the target sequence similarities based on global alignments of drug targets (e.g. K_{target}) may only be weakly associated with drugs' therapeutic effects. Therefore, we chose a higher penalty coefficient for G_{target} ($\alpha = 0.2$ for target sequence kernel and $\alpha = 0.1$ for the rest of the three kernels). This effectively forced the network represented by K_{target} to align more closely to other three kernels. For disease kernels, we used the same parameter ($\alpha = 0.1$) for all of them because no additional information about the relationships among phenotype, HPO and DO similarities was available.

Apparently, FRMSL performed much better than KronRLS (Fig.2, ROC 0.9295 vs 0.8356). Because the only difference between the two is the data imputation step, our results shows the effectiveness of the multi-view kernel completion approach. We also compared with two recent network-based approaches: TL_HGBI [27] and MBiRW [17]. TL_HGBI is a three-layer heterogeneous network that captures inter- and intra-relationships among drugs, targets and diseases. The target layer serves as a transfer layer to further improve the performance of drug repositioning with additional information on drug-target relationships. A random walk like algorithm across different layers of the heterogeneous network was developed to simultaneously predict new drug-disease and drug-target relationships. MBiRW is a more recent work that uses a two-layer network for drugs and diseases. The similarities among drugs and diseases were further adjusted by first clustering drugs and diseases. Finally, a Bi-Random walk algorithm was used to identify new drug-disease relationships. The five-fold cross-validation results (ROC curves and AUC values in Figure 2) show that all the three algorithms perform well on this dataset. The newly proposed approach FRMSL (AUC:0.9295) outperforms both TL_HGBI (AUC:0.8981) and MBiRW (AUC:0.9031), while the later two have almost identical performance.

Previous studies have found that the links with low drug-drug or disease-disease similarities provide little information for network inferences [25, 27]. All three methods have tried to handle this issue to some extend, but in different ways. For example, TL_HGBI tried to incorporate more information by adding an additional drug-target layer. It was shown that by randomly removing some known drug-target links in the graph, the performance

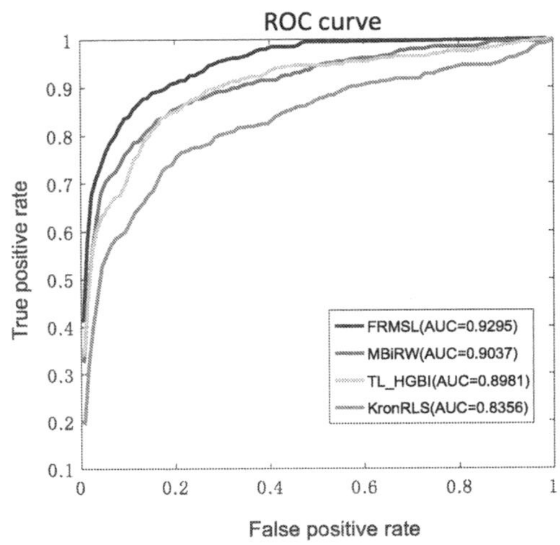

Figure 2: The ROC curves and AUC values for four methods.

gradually decreased [27], which supported the belief that drug-target information contributed to drug-disease prediction. However, it is hard to extend the model to include more data sources related to diseases or drugs. MBiRW handled this issue by first clustering drugs and diseases based on common drug indications. And similarities for drugs and diseases were adjusted if they were in the same cluster [17]. However, those clusters highly depended on the known drug-disease interactions. Also, although the original paper [17] has shown that MBiRW outperformed HGBI [26], results in the current study have shown that MBiRW and TL_HGBI had almost identical performance. FRMSL addressed this issue by incorporating multiple data sources and by imputing missing values using multi-view learning. It provides a better approach not only because it has better performance, but also because the framework can be easily extended to include more data sources.

3.4 Results on an independent test dataset

We also tested the four approaches for drug repositioning on an independent test set released recently by [19]. The drug-disease relationships in the new dataset were obtained mainly from recent literatures and KEGG database. After removing the repetitive drug-disease associations that were already in the gold standard dataset, 89 new associations were finally retained. We then utilized them to evaluate the performance of the four different algorithms. The overall results are presented in Table 1. None of the four algorithms performed as well as they did on the gold standard dataset, which is not surprising because the model was trained on the subset of the same data for cross-validation experiments. Nevertheless, FRMSL still outperforms the rest of three methods, which is consistent with the cross-validation results on the gold standard dataset. On the other hand, TH_HGBI achieves slightly better results than MBiRW. The KronRLS without imputation still performs the worst. Overall, results on the independent dataset has demonstrated that FRMSL is a promising method for novel drug-disease predictions.

Table 1: The AUC values on an independent dataset

Framework	FRMSL	MBiRW	TH_HGBI	KronRLS
AUC	0.8526	0.8317	0.8405	0.7810

4 DISCUSSION

Drug repositioning provides a promising alternative for drug discovery. In this article, we have proposed a novel flexible and robust algorithm based on multi-source learning to identify new indications for existing drugs. Distinct kernels are constructed first from multiple data sources to measure the similarities among drugs and among diseases. Furthermore, we have developed a multi-kernel completion algorithm to impute missing values by borrowing information from other data sources. We have also investigated the performance of the proposed algorithm FRMSL by comparing it with several other network-based drug repositioning methods. Both the five-fold cross-validation experiment and the test using an independent dataset have shown that FRMSL performs the best among all the approaches. Case studies on five human diseases have further demonstrated its effectiveness in practice. The performance of FRMSL can potentially be further improved by incorporating more data sources (*e.g.*, gene expression data, disease metabolic pathways, and general or disease specific protein-protein interaction (PPI) networks). The construction of FRMSL makes it very easy to integrate more data sources regarding drugs and diseases, which are increasingly available.

While the results of FRMSL are promising, the current framework can only assess the relationship between a single drug and a single disease. However, many human diseases (especially cancers) are extremely complex, involving multiple metabolic pathways. Therefore, the use of an individual drug, which usually binds to a single target protein, may not be always effective, for example, due to drug resistance. Recently, combinatorial drug therapy has been widely used to overcome drug resistance and to treat complex human diseases such as cancers [13]. Drug combinations, consisting of multiple agents, can possibly modulate activities of distinct signaling pathways simultaneously thus maximizing the therapeutic effect. For example, chlorpromazine and pentamidine do not show any anti-tumor activities when used separately in clinical trials, but their combination successfully inhibits the growth of tumor that is more effective than paclitaxel, a common anti-cancer chemotherapy drug [3].

We plan to address the drug combination prediction problem by extending our multiple sources learning framework in the future. One challenge is how to capture the relationships between multiple drugs and a disease in a graphic model. One possible solution is to first cluster drug compounds into different communities according to drugs' properties alone. These communities will be treated as one unit in evaluating their relationships with diseases. Another challenge in drug combination prediction is the administration of optimal doses of different components in treating diseases. It is known that different drug ratios can highly influence the kinetics of drugs [3] and limited training data is available with such information. Therefore, wet lab experimental test is an essential step to validate computational predictions, which cannot be achieved without collaborations with investigators with expertise in clinical medicine and drug discovery.

Acknowledgements

We would like to thank Dr. Wenhui Wang for helpful discussion of the project and Duan Li for running binding site similarity calculation and Dr. Ke Hu for general support in some of the experiments. Most of the computation was done on CWRU HPC clusters. This work has been supported in part by NIH grants R03HG008632 and R01DC012380.

REFERENCES

[1] Altshuler, D., Daly, M., and Kruglyak, L. Guilt by association. *Nature genetics 26*, 2 (2000), 135–138.

[2] Bleakley, K., and Yamanishi, Y. Supervised prediction of drug–target interactions using bipartite local models. *Bioinformatics 25*, 18 (2009), 2397–2403.

[3] Borisy, A. A., Elliott, P. J., Hurst, N. W., Lee, M. S., Lehár, J., Price, E. R., Serbedzija, G., Zimmermann, G. R., Foley, M. A., Stockwell, B. R., et al. Systematic discovery of multicomponent therapeutics. *Proceedings of the National Academy of Sciences 100*, 13 (2003), 7977–7982.

[4] Boyd, S., and Vandenberghe, L. *Convex optimization*. Cambridge university press, 2004.

[5] Campillos, M., Kuhn, M., Gavin, A.-C., Jensen, L. J., and Bork, P. Drug target identification using side-effect similarity. *Science 321*, 5886 (2008), 263–266.

[6] Chen, H., Zhang, H., Zhang, Z., Cao, Y., and Tang, W. Network-based inference methods for drug repositioning. *Computational and mathematical methods in medicine 2015* (2015).

[7] Chiang, A. P., and Butte, A. J. Systematic evaluation of drug-disease relationships to identify leads for novel drug uses. *Clinical pharmacology and therapeutics 86*, 5 (2009), 507.

[8] Deng, Y., Gao, L., Wang, B., and Guo, X. Hposim: an r package for phenotypic similarity measure and enrichment analysis based on the human phenotype ontology. *PloS one 10*, 2 (2015), e0115692.

[9] Ding, C., He, X., and Simon, H. D. On the equivalence of nonnegative matrix factorization and spectral clustering. In *Proceedings of the 2005 SIAM International Conference on Data Mining* (2005), SIAM, pp. 606–610.

[10] Dudley, J. T., Deshpande, T., and Butte, A. J. Exploiting drug–disease relationships for computational drug repositioning. *Briefings in bioinformatics* (2011), bbr013.

[11] Gottlieb, A., Stein, G. Y., Ruppin, E., and Sharan, R. Predict: a method for inferring novel drug indications with application to personalized medicine. *Molecular systems biology 7*, 1 (2011), 496.

[12] Graul, A., Cruces, E., and Stringer, M. The year's new drugs & biologics, 2013: Part i. *Drugs of today (Barcelona, Spain: 1998) 50*, 1 (2014), 51–100.

[13] Greco, F., and Vicent, M. J. Combination therapy: opportunities and challenges for polymer–drug conjugates as anticancer nanomedicines. *Advanced drug delivery reviews 61*, 13 (2009), 1203–1213.

[14] Hopkins, A. L. Network pharmacology: the next paradigm in drug discovery. *Nature chemical biology 4*, 11 (2008), 682–690.

[15] Li, J., Gong, B., Chen, X., Liu, T., Wu, C., Zhang, F., Li, C., Li, X., Rao, S., and Li, X. Dosim: An r package for similarity between diseases based on disease ontology. *BMC bioinformatics 12*, 1 (2011), 266.

[16] Liu, J., Wang, C., Gao, J., and Han, J. Multi-view clustering via joint nonnegative matrix factorization. In *Proceedings of the 2013 SIAM International Conference on Data Mining* (2013), SIAM, pp. 252–260.

[17] Luo, H., Wang, J., Li, M., Luo, J., Peng, X., Wu, F.-X., and Pan, Y. Drug repositioning based on comprehensive similarity measures and bi-random walk algorithm. *Bioinformatics* (2016), btw228.

[18] Mahé, P., Ralaivola, L., Stoven, V., and Vert, J.-P. The pharmacophore kernel for virtual screening with support vector machines. *Journal of Chemical Information and Modeling 46*, 5 (2006), 2003–2014.

[19] Martínez, V., Navarro, C., Cano, C., Fajardo, W., and Blanco, A. Drugnet: Network-based drug–disease prioritization by integrating heterogeneous data. *Artificial intelligence in medicine 63*, 1 (2015), 41–49.

[20] Paul, S. M., Mytelka, D. S., Dunwiddie, C. T., Persinger, C. C., Munos, B. H., Lindborg, S. R., and Schacht, A. L. How to improve r&d productivity: the pharmaceutical industry's grand challenge. *Nature reviews Drug discovery 9*, 3 (2010), 203–214.

[21] Scholkopf, B., and Smola, A. J. *Learning with kernels: support vector machines, regularization, optimization, and beyond*. MIT press, 2001.

[22] Smith, T. F., and Waterman, M. S. Identification of common molecular subsequences. *Journal of molecular biology 147*, 1 (1981), 195–197.

[23] Steinbeck, C., Hoppe, C., Kuhn, S., Floris, M., Guha, R., and Willighagen, E. L. Recent developments of the chemistry development kit (cdk)-an open-source java library for chemo-and bioinformatics. *Current pharmaceutical design 12*, 17 (2006), 2111–2120.

[24] Van Driel, M. A., Bruggeman, J., Vriend, G., Brunner, H. G., and Leunissen, J. A. A text-mining analysis of the human phenome. *European journal of human genetics 14*, 5 (2006), 535–542.

[25] van Laarhoven, T., Nabuurs, S. B., and Marchiori, E. Gaussian interaction profile kernels for predicting drug–target interaction. *Bioinformatics 27*, 21 (2011), 3036–3043.

[26] Wang, W., Yang, S., and Li, J. Drug target predictions based on heterogeneous graph inference. In *Pacific Symposium on Biocomputing. Pacific Symposium on Biocomputing* (2013), NIH Public Access, p. 53.

[27] Wang, W., Yang, S., Zhang, X., and Li, J. Drug repositioning by integrating target information through a heterogeneous network model. *Bioinformatics 30*, 20 (2014), 2923–2930.

[28] Wu, C., Gudivada, R. C., Aronow, B. J., and Jegga, A. G. Computational drug repositioning through heterogeneous network clustering. *BMC systems biology 7*, 5 (2013), S6.

[29] Xie, L., Xie, L., and Bourne, P. E. A unified statistical model to support local sequence order independent similarity searching for ligand-binding sites and its application to genome-based drug discovery. *Bioinformatics 25*, 12 (2009), i305–i312.

Tensor-Factorization-Based Phenotyping using Group Information: Case Study on the Efficacy of Statins

Jingyun Choi
Department of Computer Science and Engineering
Pohang University of Science and Technology
Pohang, Republic of Korea
jingyunc@postech.ac.kr

Yejin Kim
Department of Creative IT Engineering
Pohang University of Science and Technology
Pohang, Republic of Korea
yejin89@postech.ac.kr

Hun-Sung Kim
Department of Medical Informatics, College of Medicine
The Catholic University of Korea
Seoul, Republic of Korea
cadiz74@catholic.ac.kr

In Young Choi*
Department of Medical Informatics, College of Medicine
The Catholic University of Korea
Seoul, Republic of Korea
iychoi@catholic.ac.kr

Hwanjo Yu†
Department of Computer Science and Engineering
Pohang University of Science and Technology
Pohang, Republic of Korea
hwanjoyu@postech.ac.kr

ABSTRACT

To automatically extract medical concepts from raw electronic health records (EHRs), several applications based on machine learning techniques have been proposed. Among the various techniques, tensor factorization methods have attracted considerable attention because tensor representations can capture interactions among high-dimensional EHRs. Most of the existing tensor factorization methods for computational phenotyping are only designed to derive individual phenotypes that approximate the original data. However, deriving grouped phenotypes is desirable because patients form natural groups of interest (i.e., efficacy of treatment and disease categories). In this paper, we propose Supervised Non-negative Tensor Factorization with Multinomial Logistic Regression (SNTFL) to derive grouped phenotypes that are discriminative. We define a discriminative constraint to derive grouped phenotypes and jointly optimize a multinomial logistic regression during the tensor factorization process. Our case study on a hyperlipidemia dataset demonstrates that our proposed method obtains better discrimination on patient groups compared to the baselines and successfully discovers meaningful patient subgroups.

*Corresponding Author
†Corresponding Author

Permission to make digital or hard copies of all or part of this work for personal or classroom use is granted without fee provided that copies are not made or distributed for profit or commercial advantage and that copies bear this notice and the full citation on the first page. Copyrights for components of this work owned by others than ACM must be honored. Abstracting with credit is permitted. To copy otherwise, or republish, to post on servers or to redistribute to lists, requires prior specific permission and/or a fee. Request permissions from permissions@acm.org.
ACM-BCB '17, August 20-23, 2017, Boston, MA, USA
© 2017 Association for Computing Machinery.
ACM ISBN 978-1-4503-4722-8/17/08...$15.00
https://doi.org/10.1145/3107411.3107423

CCS CONCEPTS

• **Applied computing** → **Health care information systems**; **Health informatics**; • **Computing methodologies** → *Factorization methods*;

KEYWORDS

Computational phenotyping, Joint learning, Representation learning

1 INTRODUCTION

Electronic health records (EHRs) include various types of information, such as patient demographics, medical histories, drug prescription histories, vital signs, immunizations, clinical notes, laboratory results and so on. In recent years, EHRs have become important sources of data, and many studies have used EHRs to solve healthcare problems, such as clinical decision making [29], predictive modeling [23, 35], patient management [15], and early disease detection [33]. However, the use of EHRs faces some challenges. First, EHRs contain heterogeneous (e.g., numerical laboratory results and clinical narrative notes), noisy, irregular and sparse data, which make analyses of EHRs difficult. The greatest challenge is that EHRs do not easily map to medical concepts that clinical researchers directly use or need. To address these challenges, we need to extract meaningful medical concepts that clinical researchers directly use from the raw EHR data. The process of transforming the raw EHR data into meaningful medical concepts (i.e., phenotypes) is called phenotyping. However, clinical researchers and domain experts must spend substantial time and effort to obtain specific medical concepts from the complicated EHRs [13, 26]. For example, in the eMERGE Network [26], collaborative efforts between clinical researchers and IT experts are required for phenotyping. To reduce this time and effort, computational phenotyping has been introduced and widely used in many studies [5, 11, 12, 14, 17, 18, 21, 24, 27, 31, 34, 36].

Computational phenotyping is the process of automatically extracting phenotypes from EHR data using machine learning techniques. Computational phenotyping uses various machine learning techniques, such as deep learning methods [5, 14, 18], probabilistic graphical models [27] and dimensionality reduction methods [11, 12, 17, 21, 31, 34, 36]. Deep learning methods are used to obtain phenotypes because such methods can obtain insights from the heterogeneous EHR data [5, 14, 18, 24]. For example, a modified deep learning method is applied to clinical time series data for discovering and detecting characteristic patterns of physiology [5]. A probabilistic graphical model is used to cluster patients' longitudinal trajectories [27]. Some studies have been conducted to develop phenotyping methods based on dimensionality reduction, such as matrix factorization [21, 36] and tensor factorization [11, 12, 17, 31, 34]. For example, PACIFIER [36], which densifies the extremely sparse EHR data by performing matrix completion, was proposed based on matrix factorization. However, matrix factorization has difficulty taking into account the multidimensional structure that would be lost when analyzing the multidimensional structure of the data by collapsing some of the modes [25]. In contrast to matrix factorization, tensor factorization can handle multidimensional structures and capture complex interactions among high-dimensional EHR data. Due to this advantage, computational phenotyping via tensor factorization has attracted considerable attention [11, 12, 17, 31, 34]. For example, Marble [12] extracts concise phenotypes and chronic disease phenotypes that represent the baseline characteristics of the overall population. Rubik [31] extracts phenotypes using additional auxiliary information, such as prior knowledge. These methods aim to derive "individual" phenotypes that approximate the original data as closely as possible.

However, it is desirable to derive "grouped" phenotypes because patients form natural groups of interest (i.e., efficacy of treatment and disease categories). For example, assume that patients belong to either group A, B, or C (i.e., high, moderate, and low efficacy of treatments, respectively). Each patient group has its own characteristics and consists of subgroups of its own patients. Therefore, we need to derive grouped phenotypes that have discriminative characteristics on each patient group rather than individual phenotypes. An example of grouped phenotypes is shown in Table 1. Phenotypes 1, 2, and 3 have discriminative characteristics on patient group A (i.e., high-efficacy group) compared to patient groups B and C (Table 1). This property also means that the high-efficacy group consists of subgroups that are represented as phenotypes 1, 2, and 3. Deriving grouped phenotypes rather than individual phenotypes is beneficial because such a group-based phenotyping can provide insights on subgroups within each patient group.

Table 1: Example of grouped phenotypes. Phenotypes 1, 2, and 3 have discriminative characteristics on patient group A compared to patient groups B and C.

Patient group A (e.g., high efficacy)	Patient group B (e.g., moderate efficacy)	Patient group C (e.g., low efficacy)
Phenotype 1	Phenotype 4	Phenotype 6
Phenotype 2	Phenotype 5	Phenotype 7
Phenotype 3		

Two methods have recently been proposed to derive discriminative phenotypes for better prediction performance [17, 34]. These methods can derive discriminative phenotypes when there are two patient groups. However, there is still a limitation: these methods cannot be used if there are more than three patient groups.

Therefore, this paper proposes SUPERVISED NON-NEGATIVE TENSOR FACTORIZATION WITH MULTINOMIAL LOGISTIC REGRESSION (SNTFL) to derive grouped phenotypes that are discriminative regardless of the number of patient groups. Our main contributions are as follows:

(1) We propose a novel tensor factorization method, SNTFL, to derive grouped phenotypes that have discriminative characteristics on each patient group regardless of the number of patient groups.
(2) Our case study on a hyperlipidemia dataset demonstrates that our method discovers meaningful subgroups of patients.

The remainder of this paper is organized as follows. First, we introduce the preliminaries of tensor factorization and describe our proposed method. Next, we explain the data analysis procedure using SNTFL and evaluate our method on a hyperlipidemia dataset. Finally, we draw our conclusions.

2 PRELIMINARIES

We first present the preliminaries on tensors, and then we introduce tensor factorization and multinomial logistic regression.

2.1 Notation

Table 2: Notation

Symbol	Description
a	scalar
$\mathbf{a}$	vector (bold lowercase character)
$\mathbf{A}$	matrix (bold uppercase character)
$\mathcal{X}$	tensor
$\mathbf{X}_{(k)}$	k-mode matricization of a tensor
R	number of latent factors
K	number of modes
C	number of classes
$\circ$	outer product of vectors
$\otimes$	Kronecker product
$\odot$	Khatri-Rao product
$\mathbf{A}^T$	transpose of $\mathbf{A}$
$\langle \mathbf{A}, \mathbf{B} \rangle$	sum of element-wise products of two matrices, where $\mathbf{A}$ and $\mathbf{B}$ have the same size

We summarize the notations used in this paper (Table 2). We use bold lowercase characters for vectors, bold uppercase characters for matrices and bold script font for tensors. We represent the i-th row of matrix $\mathbf{A}$ as $\mathbf{A}_{i*}$, the j-th column as $\mathbf{A}_{*j}$, and the (i, j)-th element as $\mathbf{A}_{ij}$. We represent the k-th element of vector $\mathbf{a}$ as $\mathbf{a}_k$. The definitions for the tensor and algebraic operations are as follows:

DEFINITION 1. *Tensor. A tensor is a multidimensional array that can represent multiple attributes. The order of a tensor is the number of dimensions, and each dimension of a tensor is a mode. Vectors (first-order tensors) and matrices (second-order tensors) are special cases of tensors. A K-order tensor is denoted by* $\mathcal{X} \in \mathbb{R}^{I_1 \times I_2 \times \cdots \times I_K}$*, where* I_k *is the size of mode k. A K-order tensor is a rank-one tensor if it can be defined as the outer product of K vectors.*

Definition 2. *k-mode matricization. A K-order tensor* $\mathcal{X}$ *can be unfolded into a matrix by reordering the elements of* $\mathcal{X}$*. This process is called the k-mode matricization, also referred to as unfolding, of* $\mathcal{X}$*. The k-mode matricization is denoted by* $\mathbf{X}_{(k)} \in \mathbb{R}^{I_k \times (\prod_{j \neq k} I_j)}$*. For example, given a third-order tensor* $\mathcal{X} \in \mathbb{R}^{I_1 \times I_2 \times I_3}$*, the 1-mode matricization is* $\mathbf{X}_{(1)} \in \mathbb{R}^{I_1 \times (I_2 I_3)}$*.*

Definition 3. *Kronecker product. Given* $\mathbf{A} \in \mathbb{R}^{I \times J}$ *and* $\mathbf{B} \in \mathbb{R}^{K \times L}$*, the Kronecker product generates a matrix of size (IK) × (JL).*

$$\mathbf{A} \otimes \mathbf{B} = \begin{bmatrix} A_{11}\mathbf{B} & \cdots & A_{1J}\mathbf{B} \\ \vdots & \ddots & \vdots \\ A_{I1}\mathbf{B} & \cdots & A_{IJ}\mathbf{B} \end{bmatrix}$$

Definition 4. *Khatri-Rao product. Given* $\mathbf{A} \in \mathbb{R}^{I \times R}$ *and* $\mathbf{B} \in \mathbb{R}^{J \times R}$*, where* $\mathbf{A}$ *and* $\mathbf{B}$ *have the same number of columns, the Khatri-Rao product generates a matrix of size (IJ) × R.*

$$\mathbf{A} \odot \mathbf{B} = \begin{bmatrix} \mathbf{A}_{*1} \otimes \mathbf{B}_{*1} & \cdots & \mathbf{A}_{*R} \otimes \mathbf{B}_{*R} \end{bmatrix}$$

2.2 Tensor factorization

Tensor factorization is a dimensionality reduction method that is widely used in various fields, such as signal processing [19], computer vision [30] and bioinformatics [9], because it can analyze complex data sets that contain high dimensionality. Tensor factorization aims to approximate the observed tensor using the low-dimensional space. This process is equivalent to minimizing the difference between an observed tensor and a reconstructed tensor from the factor matrices.

CANDECOMP/PARAFAC (CP) decomposition [4, 10] is one of the most common tensor factorizations. CP decomposition approximates the observed tensor as a sum of rank-one tensors. Given a K-order tensor $\mathcal{X}$ and rank R, which indicates the number of latent factors, CP decomposition factorizes the K-order tensor $\mathcal{X}$ into K factor matrices, $\mathbf{U}^{(1)} \in \mathbb{R}^{I_1 \times R}, \ldots, \mathbf{U}^{(K)} \in \mathbb{R}^{I_K \times R}$. This process can be expressed as follows: $\mathcal{X} \approx \sum_{r=1}^{R} \mathbf{U}^{(1)}_{*r} \circ \cdots \circ \mathbf{U}^{(K)}_{*r}$. Each factor matrix $\mathbf{U}^{(k)} \in \mathbb{R}^{I_k \times R}$ represents the latent feature vectors for the k-th mode of the observed tensor $\mathcal{X}$. For example, given a third-order tensor $\mathcal{X} \in \mathbb{R}^{I_1 \times I_2 \times I_3}$, CP decomposition finds three factor matrices, $\mathbf{U}^{(1)} \in \mathbb{R}^{I_1 \times R}$, $\mathbf{U}^{(2)} \in \mathbb{R}^{I_2 \times R}$, and $\mathbf{U}^{(3)} \in \mathbb{R}^{I_3 \times R}$, that approximate $\mathcal{X}$ (Figure 1).

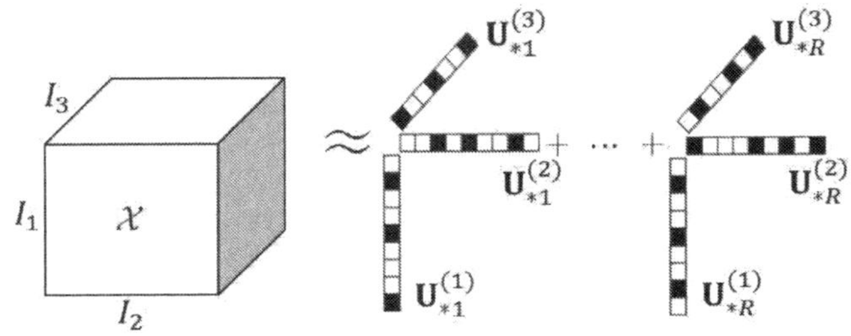

Figure 1: CP decomposition of a third-order tensor $\mathcal{X}$. The outer product of three vectors ($\mathbf{U}^{(1)}_{*r}$, $\mathbf{U}^{(2)}_{*r}$ and $\mathbf{U}^{(3)}_{*r}$) from factor matrices is a third-order rank-one tensor. The CP decomposition approximates $\mathcal{X}$ as a sum of R rank-one tensors.

2.3 Non-negative tensor factorization

Non-negative tensor factorization (NTF) decomposes a non-negative tensor into factor matrices that consist of non-negative elements. Given rank R and a K-order tensor $\mathcal{X}$, NTF minimizes the following objective function:

$$\min_{\mathbf{U}^{(1)},\ldots,\mathbf{U}^{(K)}} \left\| \mathcal{X} - \sum_{r=1}^{R} \mathbf{U}^{(1)}_{*r} \circ \mathbf{U}^{(2)}_{*r} \circ \cdots \circ \mathbf{U}^{(K)}_{*r} \right\|_F^2 \quad \text{s.t.} \quad \mathbf{U}^{(k)} \geq 0, \text{ for } k = 1, \ldots, K. \tag{1}$$

This non-negativity constraint simplifies the interpretation of factor matrices when analyzing non-negative data [7].

2.4 Multinomial logistic regression

Multinomial logistic regression is an extension of binomial logistic regression for solving multiclass classification problems. In the multiclass classification problem, we are given N data points, $\{\mathbf{s}^1, \ldots, \mathbf{s}^N\}$, and their corresponding class labels, $\{y^1, \ldots, y^N\}$, $y^n \in \{1, \ldots, C\}$, where C is the total number of classes. Assume that each data point has d features and belongs to one group among C groups. The label information of the data points is represented by $\mathbf{Y} \in \mathbb{R}^{N \times C}$, which is an indicator matrix. $\mathbf{Y}_{nc}$ is set to 1 if the n-th data point belongs to the c-th group and to 0 otherwise. Let $\mathbf{W} \in \mathbb{R}^{d \times C}$ be the coefficient of the multinomial logistic regression. Given $\mathbf{W}$, the probability that the n-th data point $\mathbf{s}^n \in \mathbb{R}^{1 \times d}$ belongs to the c-th group is calculated as $\frac{exp(\mathbf{s}^n \mathbf{W}_{*c})}{\sum_{b=1}^{C} exp(\mathbf{s}^n \mathbf{W}_{*b})}$. $\mathbf{W}$ is estimated by minimizing the negative log-likelihood function:

$$-\sum_{n \in N} \sum_{c=1}^{C} \mathbf{Y}_{nc} log \frac{exp(\mathbf{s}^n \mathbf{W}_{*c})}{\sum_{b=1}^{C} exp(\mathbf{s}^n \mathbf{W}_{*b})}. \tag{2}$$

One of the most widely used methods for optimizing Eq. (2) is iterative reweighted least squares (IRLS) [22].

3 PROPOSED METHOD

We propose a novel tensor factorization method, SNTFL, to derive grouped phenotypes that are discriminative. We first i) formulate SNTFL by incorporating a discriminative constraint to derive grouped phenotypes. Then, we ii) jointly optimize a multinomial logistic regression during the tensor factorization process. Finally, we iii) obtain grouped phenotypes and latent representations of patients to the phenotypes.

3.1 Problem formulation

SNTFL is an extension of NTF for deriving grouped phenotypes that have discriminative characteristics on each patient group. Our objective is to improve the discrimination among patient groups; thus, we use the group information (i.e., labels) of patients to achieve this goal. First, given a K-order tensor $\mathcal{X}$, we assume that the first mode of $\mathcal{X}$ denotes the patient. Then, each row of the patient factor matrix $\mathbf{U}^{(1)}$ represents the latent representation of a patient. The main idea is to exploit the group information of patients for making the rows of $\mathbf{U}^{(1)}$ discriminative on the labels. When approximating $\mathcal{X}$, factor matrices influence each other. If each row of $\mathbf{U}^{(1)}$ has discriminative characteristics, then the columns (i.e., the latent feature vectors) of other factor matrices also contain discriminative characteristics. These columns from all factor matrices except $\mathbf{U}^{(1)}$ are used as phenotypes such that we can derive grouped phenotypes that are discriminative. Therefore, we should minimize the difference between the observed K-order tensor and a reconstructed tensor from the factor matrices while simultaneously generating the discriminative latent representations of patients. We formulate the objective function of SNTFL as follows:

$$\min_{\mathbf{U}^{(1)},\dots,\mathbf{U}^{(K)}} \frac{1}{2}\left\| \mathcal{X} - \sum_{r=1}^{R} \mathbf{U}^{(1)}_{*r} \circ \mathbf{U}^{(2)}_{*r} \circ \cdots \circ \mathbf{U}^{(K)}_{*r} \right\|_F^2 + \lambda\Omega(\mathbf{U}^{(1)}) \quad \text{s.t.} \quad \mathbf{U}^{(k)} \geq 0, \text{ for } k = 1, \dots, K, \tag{3}$$

where $\Omega(\mathbf{U}^{(1)})$ is a discriminative constraint to derive grouped phenotypes that are discriminative and λ controls the weight of the discriminative constraint.

We can rewrite the objective function of SNTFL in terms of the unfolded tensor as

$$\min_{\mathbf{U}^{(k)}} \frac{1}{2}\left\| \mathbf{X}_{(k)} - \mathbf{U}^{(k)}\mathbf{G}^T \right\|_F^2 + \lambda\Omega(\mathbf{U}^{(1)}) \quad \text{s.t.} \quad \mathbf{U}^{(k)} \geq 0, \text{ for } k = 1, \dots, K, \tag{4}$$

where $\mathbf{G} = \mathbf{U}^{(K)} \odot \cdots \odot \mathbf{U}^{(k+1)} \odot \mathbf{U}^{(k-1)} \odot \cdots \odot \mathbf{U}^{(1)}$.

Next, we define the discriminative constraint using a multinomial logistic regression. Assume that we have N patients and that each patient belongs to one group among C groups. The latent representation for the n-th patient is $\mathbf{U}^{(1)}_{n*} \in \mathbb{R}^{1\times R}$. To represent the group information of the n-th patient, we use an indicator matrix $\mathbf{Y} \in \mathbb{R}^{N\times C}$. $\mathbf{Y}_{nc}$ is set to 1 if the n-th patient belongs to the c-th group and to 0 otherwise. Let $\mathbf{P} \in \mathbb{R}^{N\times C}$ refer to probabilities, where each element denotes the probability that a certain patient belongs to one group among C groups. We incorporate the multinomial logistic regression in the tensor factorization process. Let $\mathbf{W} \in \mathbb{R}^{R\times C}$ be the coefficient of the multinomial logistic regression. Given $\mathbf{W}$, the probability that the n-th patient belongs to the c-th group is calculated as

$$\mathbf{P}_{nc} = \frac{exp(\mathbf{U}^{(1)}_{n*}\mathbf{W}_{*c})}{\sum_{b=1}^{C} exp(\mathbf{U}^{(1)}_{n*}\mathbf{W}_{*b})}. \tag{5}$$

Using Eq. (5), we can define the discriminative constraint as

$$\Omega(\mathbf{U}^{(1)}) = -\sum_{n\in N}\sum_{c=1}^{C} \mathbf{Y}_{nc} log \mathbf{P}_{nc}. \tag{6}$$

Based on this discriminative constraint, the latent representations of patients should be more discriminative. Taken together, SNTFL minimizes the difference between the observed K-order tensor and the reconstructed tensor from the factor matrices; simultaneously, it minimizes the discriminative constraint to obtain the discriminative latent representations of patients and to improve discrimination among patient groups.

3.2 Joint optimization

We apply an alternating minimization approach to solve the optimization problem in Eq. (3). When solving a subproblem to update the k-th factor matrix $\mathbf{U}^{(k)}$, the other factor matrices are fixed. The objective function in Eq. (3) also contains a standard bound-constrained optimization problem. For this reason, we adopt the projected gradient method [20] to obtain factor matrices that consist of non-negative elements.

For the patient mode, we optimize each row of $\mathbf{U}^{(1)}$ (Algorithm 1) because each latent representation corresponds to the different group information. The gradient of the objective function with respect to $\mathbf{U}^{(1)}_{n*}$ is

$$\nabla_{\mathbf{U}^{(1)}_{n*}} = -(\mathbf{X}_{(1)})_{n*}\mathbf{G} + \mathbf{U}^{(1)}_{n*}\mathbf{G}^T\mathbf{G} - \lambda\sum_{c=1}^{C} \mathbf{Y}_{nc}(\mathbf{W}^T_{*c} - \mathbf{P}_{n*}\mathbf{W}^T). \tag{7}$$

To update $\mathbf{U}^{(1)}_{n*}$, we adopt the projected gradient method:

$$\mathbf{U}^{(1)}_{n*} \leftarrow P[\mathbf{U}^{(1)}_{n*} - \alpha\nabla_{\mathbf{U}^{(1)}_{n*}}], \tag{8}$$

where $P[\mathbf{A}]$ is a function that projects all the negative elements of $\mathbf{A} \in \mathbb{R}^{I\times J}$ to zero with $P[\mathbf{A}] = \begin{cases} \mathbf{A}_{ij} & \text{if } \mathbf{A}_{ij} > 0 \\ 0 & \text{otherwise} \end{cases}$, $i \in \{1, \dots, I\}$ and $j \in \{1, \dots, J\}$. α is the step size for the update rule. We use the Armijo rule [3] to adaptively determine α, which is adjusted until the following condition is satisfied:

$$(1-\sigma)\langle\nabla_{\mathbf{U}^{(1)}_{n*}}, \Delta_n\rangle + \frac{1}{2}\langle\Delta_n, \Delta_n\nabla^2_{\mathbf{U}^{(1)}_{n*}}\rangle \leq 0, \tag{9}$$

where $\nabla^2_{\mathbf{U}^{(1)}_{n*}} = \mathbf{G}^T\mathbf{G} - \lambda\sum_{c=1}^{C} \mathbf{Y}_{nc}(\mathbf{W}(\mathbf{P}^T_{n*}\mathbf{P}_{n*} - diag\{\mathbf{P}_{n*}\})\mathbf{W}^T)$ and $\Delta_n = P[\mathbf{U}^{(1)}_{n*} - \alpha\nabla_{\mathbf{U}^{(1)}_{n*}}] - \mathbf{U}^{(1)}_{n*}$. σ is the parameter of this condition. A common choice of σ is 0.01 [20].

Algorithm 1 Subproblem 1 solver to update $\mathbf{U}^{(1)}$

Input: $\mathbf{U}^{(1)}$, $\mathbf{G}$, maximum iterations l_{max}, weight λ, group information $\mathbf{Y}$
Output: $\mathbf{U}^{(1)}$

```
for l = 1 : l_max do
    if convergence then
        break
    end if
    for n = 1 : N do
        Set ∇_{U^(1)_n*} using Eq. (7)
        U^(1)_n* ← P[U^(1)_n* − α∇_{U^(1)_n*}]
    end for
end for
return U^(1)
```

If $k \neq 1$, then the gradient of the objective function with respect to $\mathbf{U}^{(k)}$ is

$$\nabla_{\mathbf{U}^{(k)}} = -\mathbf{X}_{(k)}\mathbf{G} + \mathbf{U}^{(k)}\mathbf{G}^T\mathbf{G}. \tag{10}$$

With the gradient $\nabla_{\mathbf{U}^{(k)}}$, $\mathbf{U}^{(k)}$ is updated (Algorithm 2) as

$$\mathbf{U}^{(k)} \leftarrow P[\mathbf{U}^{(k)} - \alpha\nabla_{\mathbf{U}^{(k)}}], \tag{11}$$

where $P[\mathbf{A}]$ is a function that projects all the negative elements of $\mathbf{A} \in \mathbb{R}^{I \times J}$ to zero with $P[\mathbf{A}] = \begin{cases} \mathbf{A}_{ij} & \text{if } \mathbf{A}_{ij} > 0 \\ 0 & \text{otherwise} \end{cases}$, $i \in \{1, \ldots, I\}$ and $j \in \{1, \ldots, J\}$. α is the step size. The condition of the Armijo rule for selecting α is

$$(1 - \sigma)\langle \nabla_{\mathbf{U}^{(K)}}, \Delta \rangle + \frac{1}{2}\langle \Delta, \Delta \mathbf{G}^T \mathbf{G} \rangle \leq 0, \quad (12)$$

where $\Delta = P[\mathbf{U}^{(k)} - \alpha \nabla_{\mathbf{U}^{(k)}}] - \mathbf{U}^{(k)}$.

Algorithm 2 Subproblem 2 solver to update $\mathbf{U}^{(k)}$ $(k \neq 1)$

Input: $\mathbf{U}^{(k)}$, $\mathbf{G}$, maximum iterations l_{max}
Output: $\mathbf{U}^{(k)}$
for $l = 1 : l_{max}$ **do**
  if convergence **then**
    break
  end if
  Set $\nabla_{\mathbf{U}^{(k)}}$ using Eq. (10)
  $\mathbf{U}^{(k)} \leftarrow P[\mathbf{U}^{(k)} - \alpha \nabla_{\mathbf{U}^{(k)}}]$
end for
return $\mathbf{U}^{(k)}$

The entire algorithm for SNTFL is presented in Algorithm 3. SNTFL takes four inputs: a K-order tensor $\mathcal{X}$, rank R, weight λ of the discriminative constraint and group information $\mathbf{Y}$ of patients. The algorithm starts by initializing the factor matrices with non-negative values. After initialization, a subproblem to update the k-th factor matrix $\mathbf{U}^{(k)}$ is solved with the other fixed factor matrices. In the case of the patient mode, the first mode of $\mathcal{X}$, Algorithm 1 is used to update $\mathbf{U}^{(1)}$ due to the discriminative constraint. Otherwise, Algorithm 2 is used. After updating $\mathbf{U}^{(1)}$, a common multinomial logistic regression is optimized to update the coefficient $\mathbf{W}$. We use IRLS [22] to optimize the multinomial logistic regression. Our proposed alternating optimization algorithm using the projected gradient method decreases the value of the objective function in Eq. (3) until convergence is reached.

Algorithm 3 Optimization algorithm for SNTFL

Input: tensor $\mathcal{X}$, rank R, weight λ, group information $\mathbf{Y}$
Output: $\mathbf{U}^{(1)}, \ldots, \mathbf{U}^{(K)}$
Initialize $\mathbf{U}^{(1)}, \ldots, \mathbf{U}^{(K)}$ with non-negative values
repeat
  for $k = 1 : K$ **do**
    $\mathbf{G} = \mathbf{U}^{(K)} \odot \cdots \odot \mathbf{U}^{(k+1)} \odot \mathbf{U}^{(k-1)} \odot \cdots \odot \mathbf{U}^{(1)}$
    if $k = 1$ **then**
      $\mathbf{U}^{(1)} \leftarrow$ solve subproblem 1 using Algorithm 1
      Update $\mathbf{W}$ for multinomial logistic regression
    else
      $\mathbf{U}^{(k)} \leftarrow$ solve subproblem 2 using Algorithm 2
    end if
  end for
until convergence
return $\mathbf{U}^{(1)}, \ldots, \mathbf{U}^{(K)}$

3.3 Phenotype discovery using SNTFL

For our case study, we use a hyperlipidemia dataset from EHRs from Seoul St. Mary's Hospital [16]. Each patient is classified into three groups according to the efficacy of a statin (i.e., high-efficacy group, moderate-efficacy group and low-efficacy group). This group information of patients is used for the discriminative constraint. We construct a third-order tensor with patient, trait (i.e., patient's demographics and past medical history before taking a statin) and statin modes. The tensor values are the numbers of co-occurrences between trait and statin for each patient. The constructed tensor is decomposed using SNTFL (Figure 2).

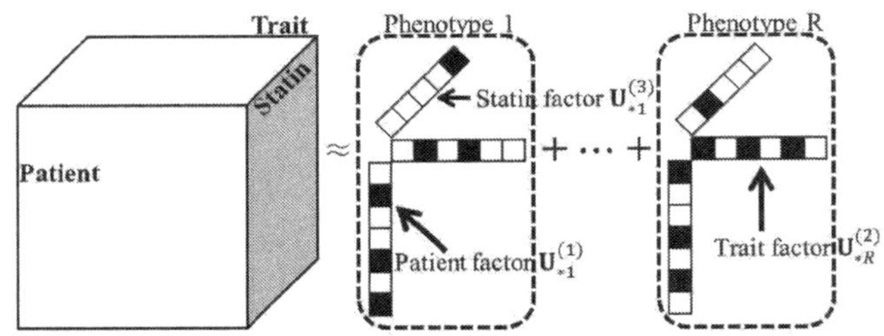

Figure 2: Generating phenotypes using SNTFL. Each phenotype consists of the patient factor $\mathbf{U}^{(1)}_{*r}$, the trait factor $\mathbf{U}^{(2)}_{*r}$ and the statin factor $\mathbf{U}^{(3)}_{*r}$.

We define a phenotype as a set of traits and an associated statin that can occur together in a patient. $\mathbf{U}^{(2)}_{*r}$ represents how much the certain traits are involved in the r-th phenotype. $\mathbf{U}^{(3)}_{*r}$ represents the certain statin that is involved in the r-th phenotype. For example, the r-th phenotype is defined using $\mathbf{U}^{(2)}_{*r}$ and $\mathbf{U}^{(3)}_{*r}$. The patient factor matrix $\mathbf{U}^{(1)}$ is used as the latent representation of patients. Each row of $\mathbf{U}^{(1)}$ expresses the latent representation of a patient. $\mathbf{U}^{(1)}_{n*}$ represents the degree to which the n-th patient is involved in R phenotypes. After decomposing the observed tensor, a multinomial logistic regression is trained on $\mathbf{U}^{(1)}$ to define grouped phenotypes. According to the magnitudes of the coefficients in the multinomial logistic regression, the phenotypes of each group are defined. We use MATLAB software and MATLAB Tensor Toolbox Version 2.5 [2] from Sandia National Laboratories to represent tensors and to compute tensor operations.

4 EXPERIMENTAL DESIGN

4.1 Dataset and preprocessing

We used a hyperlipidemia dataset from EHRs from Seoul St. Mary's Hospital between January 1, 2010, and December 31, 2012 [16]. This dataset includes patient demographics, past diagnoses and prescription histories before taking a statin, lab test results at the first and second visits (3 to 6 months) for statin prescription, and statins. We selected 4,970 patients who took one statin from among 17 statins and who had low-density lipoprotein cholesterol (LDL-C) levels at the first visit and second visit. We calculated the percent reduction in LDL-C (ΔLDL-C) between the first and second visits using $100\% \times \frac{(first\ visit - second\ visit)}{first\ visit}$. The patients belonged to one of three groups according to the efficacy of a statin: high-efficacy ($\triangle$LDL-C>50%), moderate-efficacy (10%$\leq\triangle$LDL-C$\leq$50%), and low-efficacy ($\triangle$LDL-C<10%) groups. The proportion of each group was imbalanced – 25.94% (1,289), 53.14% (2,641) and 20.92% (1,040) for each group, respectively; the majority of patients belonged to the moderate-efficacy group. To balance the number of patients in each group, we randomly selected the same number of patients from each group (i.e., 1,040 patients from each group, for 3,120 patients in total). We represented the data as the number of co-occurrences between trait (i.e., patient's demographics and past diagnoses/prescription histories before taking a statin) and statin of each patient. This co-occurrence is a natural representation to describe the interaction between a trait and statin. For example, patient 1, who received atorvastatin (10 mg), was a woman in her 50s and diagnosed with diabetes mellitus prior to taking a statin (Figure 3). We binned numerical attributes (e.g., LDL-C and age) and transformed it to a binary type (0 for absence and 1 for presence). Then, the trait consisted of 144 attributes: gender (2), binned age group (7), diagnosis histories (17), prescription histories (7) and binned lab test results (111). Thus, the constructed tensor size for the analysis was 3,120 patients by 144 traits by 17 statins.

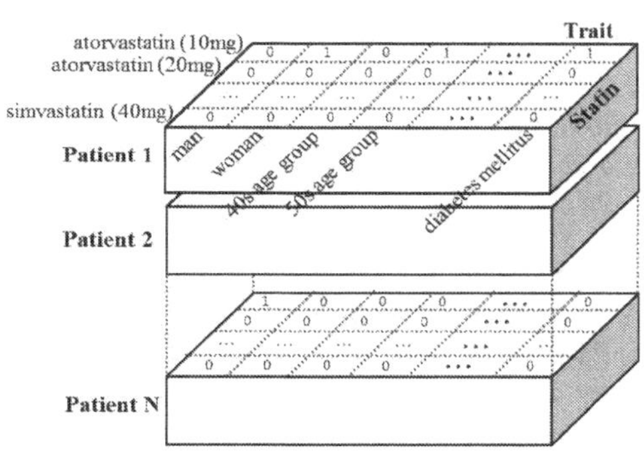

Figure 3: Constructed tensor from EHR data.

4.2 Analysis procedure

We summarize the design of our experiment in Figure 4. We used the constructed tensor that had a size of 3,120 patients by 144 traits by 17 statins (step 1), derived phenotypes using SNTFL with the training set (step 2), generated latent representations of new patients using the test set (step 3), and predicted the new patient's group using a multinomial logistic regression (step 4). We present the phenotype discovery (analysis 1) and prediction evaluation (analysis 2) results.

Specifically, to generate a new patient's latent representation (i.e., each row of new patient factor matrix $\tilde{\mathbf{U}}^{(1)}$), we projected the new patient's data $\tilde{\mathcal{X}}$ onto the space of derived phenotypes, $\mathbf{U}^{(2)}$ and $\mathbf{U}^{(3)}$. Given $\tilde{\mathcal{X}}$, $\mathbf{U}^{(2)}$ and $\mathbf{U}^{(3)}$, we calculated the $\tilde{\mathbf{U}}^{(1)}$ that best approximated $\tilde{\mathcal{X}} \approx \sum_{r=1}^{R} \tilde{\mathbf{U}}^{(1)}_{*r} \circ \mathbf{U}^{(2)}_{*r} \circ \mathbf{U}^{(3)}_{*r}$. Finally, we used the rows of $\tilde{\mathbf{U}}^{(1)}$ as features to predict the new patient's group (step 4-2). The prediction model was trained on $\mathbf{U}^{(1)}$, which was generated from the training set (step 4-1).

4.3 Measures and baselines

We used two types of area under the classification receiver operating characteristic curves (AUCs) as metrics to evaluate the prediction results of clinical diagnosis: MacroAUC, which is the average AUC of all the classes, and MicroAUC, which is the globally calculated AUC regardless of classes. We compared our proposed method with the following three baseline methods.

(1) NTF: Basic CP model [4, 10].
(2) CP-APR: Non-negative CP alternating Poisson regression model [6].
(3) SNTFL ($\lambda = 0$) : SNTFL with $\lambda = 0$.

All the methods were repeated ten times for stratified random sampling. We randomly selected 2,184 of all patients as the training set (70%) and the remainder as the test set (30%). We report the average Macro AUC and Micro AUC after ten repetitions.

5 RESULTS AND DISCUSSION

5.1 Tuning the weight of discriminative constraint

We studied the effect of λ to determine how it affected the prediction result of SNTFL. We first varied the number R of phenotypes from 30 to 70, and then we performed SNTFL with various values of λ. For each R, we varied λ from 0 to 0.006 to evaluate the sensitivity of SNTFL to the discriminative constraint. We calculated the average MicroAUC over 10 trials (Figure 5). The average MicroAUC first increased, reached its maximum value when $\lambda = 0.005$ and then decreased. When R was 70, the average MicroAUC was the greatest with $\lambda = 0.005$. The best average MicroAUC was 0.7592 when $R = 70$ and $\lambda = 0.005$.

5.2 Phenotype discovery

Using SNTFL with $\lambda = 0.005$ and $R = 50$, we derived 50 phenotypes. Among these phenotypes, we first filtered out phenotypes that were not statistically significant (i.e., p-values < 0.05 of a multinomial logistic regression). Then, a physician (HSK) removed phenotypes that were not clinically meaningful. To observe discriminative characteristics on each patient group and obtain insights on subgroups within each patient group, we present representative phenotypes from the 19 selected phenotypes (Figures 6, 7 and 8). For each patient group, three representative phenotypes with the largest coefficient $\mathbf{W}$ of the multinomial logistic regression are reported. We visualized the involvement of the traits and reported an associated statin on each phenotype. For the interpretability, we removed small non-zero values of the trait factor matrix of less than 0.01 and the statin factor matrix of less than 0.001.

For the high-efficacy group, the three phenotypes were as follows (Figure 6):

(1) "Men over 60 with metabolic diseases" (Figure 6a)
(2) "Women over 70 with metabolic diseases" (Figure 6b)
(3) "Mid-aged men with heart disease and prediabetes" (Figure 6c)

The first dominant phenotype in the high-efficacy group is the "men over 60 with metabolic diseases" phenotype (Figure 6a), which means a patient group in which male patients over 60 are diagnosed with metabolic diseases (i.e., diabetes mellitus, hypertension and

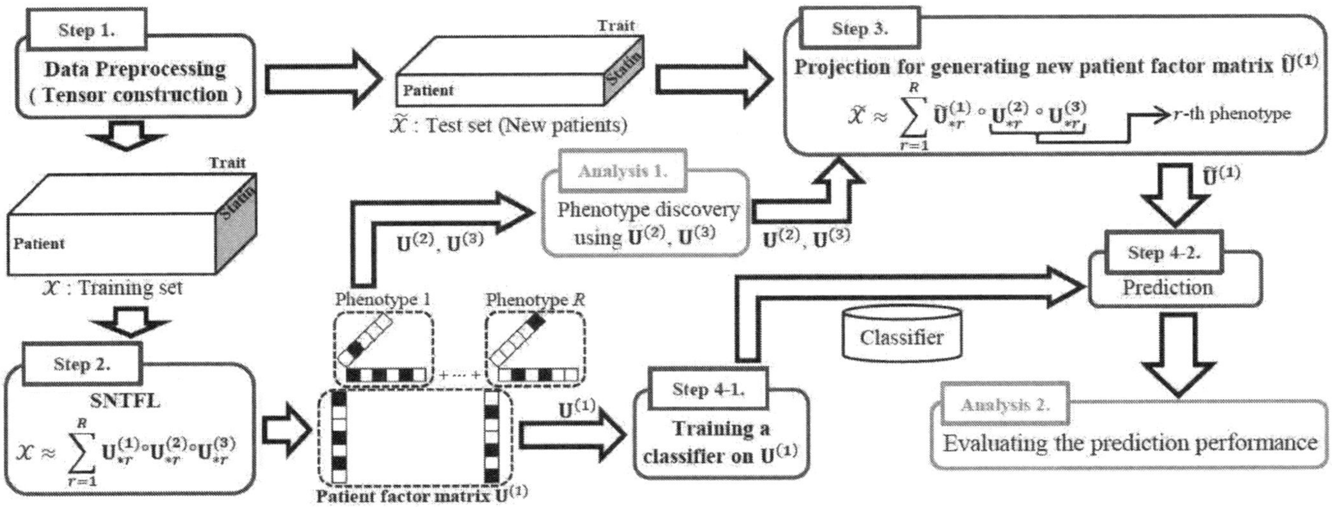

Figure 4: Design of the experiment. We first constructed a tensor (step 1), derived phenotypes using SNTFL (step 2), generated latent representations of new patients (step 3), and predicted the new patient's group using a multinomial logistic regression (step 4). We present the phenotype discovery (analysis 1) and prediction evaluation results (analysis 2).

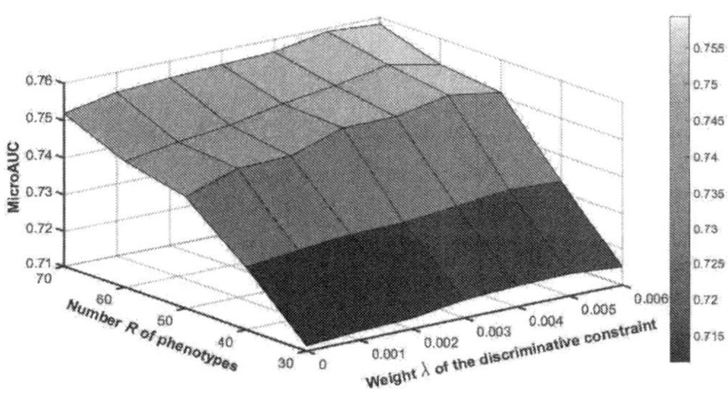

Figure 5: Effect of the weight λ on the average MicroAUC of SNTFL with R from 30 to 70 over 10 trials.

heart disease) before taking a statin, have abnormal lab results (i.e., LDL, A1C, AST and glucose) at the first visit, and take rosuvastatin (10 mg). The abnormal results of the A1C and glucose tests, which are used to screen for and diagnose diabetes [1], support the fact that the patient is diagnosed with diabetes prior to taking a statin. This finding is inconsistent with statin guidelines and statin therapy. According to the domain knowledge, rosuvastatin (10 mg) is known to reduce LDL-C levels by up to 50% [1, 28]. If we want to lower LDL-C levels by more than 50%, rosuvastatin (20~40 mg) is recommended for patients according to statin guidelines [1, 28]. However, patients who take high doses of statins may be more likely to develop kidney problems [8]. Therefore, this result is very valuable because we can recommend that elderly male patients with metabolic diseases take a relatively low dose of rosuvastatin when they are highly associated with this phenotype.

The second phenotype is the "women over 70 with metabolic diseases" phenotype (Figure 6b). This group consists of female patients over 70. Patients with metabolic diseases have abnormal levels in the A1C and glucose tests, which are associated with diabetes [1], and take rosuvastatin (10 mg). Similar to the "men over 60 with metabolic diseases" phenotype (Figure 6a), this result is also not consistent with statin therapy [1, 28]. Although patients take rosuvastatin (10 mg), their LDL-C levels decrease by more than 50%. From this finding, we can recommend that elderly female patients with metabolic diseases take rosuvastatin (10 mg) rather than rosuvastatin (20~40 mg) if they are highly associated with this result.

Third, the "mid-aged men with heart disease and prediabetes" phenotype (Figure 6c) represents a patient group that consists of mid-aged men with prediabetes and heart disease. After taking atorvastatin (20 mg), which is known to lower LDL-C levels by up to 50% [1, 28], their LDL-C levels decrease by more than 50%. In the case of atorvastatin, high doses (40~80 mg) are recommended to lower LDL-C levels by more than 50% according to statin guidelines [1, 28]. However, we can recommend that patients take a relatively low dose of atorvastatin when they are highly associated with this phenotype.

We also reported three phenotypes of the moderate-efficacy group (Figure 7), as follows:

(1) "Mid-aged men with diabetes mellitus and hypertension" (Figure 7a)
(2) "Mid-aged patients with diabetes mellitus and hypertension" (Figure 7b)
(3) "Patients over 50 with diabetes mellitus and hypertension" (Figure 7c)

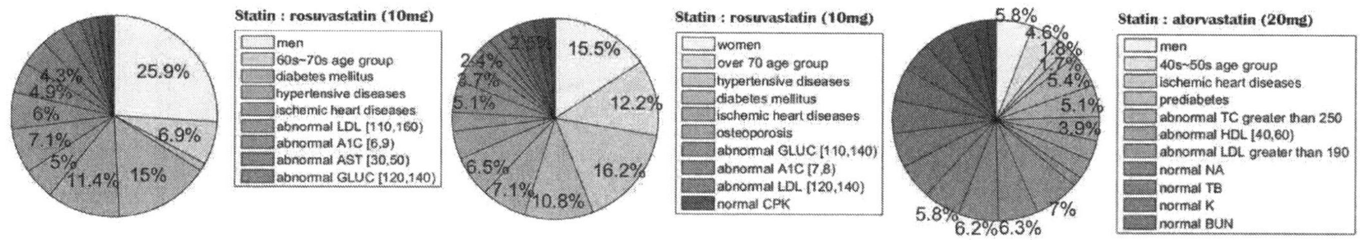

(a) Men over 60 with metabolic diseases. (b) Women over 70 with metabolic diseases. (c) Mid-aged men with heart disease and prediabetes.

Figure 6: Three representative phenotypes of the high-efficacy group (GLUC: glucose, TC: total cholesterol, NA: sodium, TB: total bilirubin, K: potassium, BUN: blood urea nitrogen).

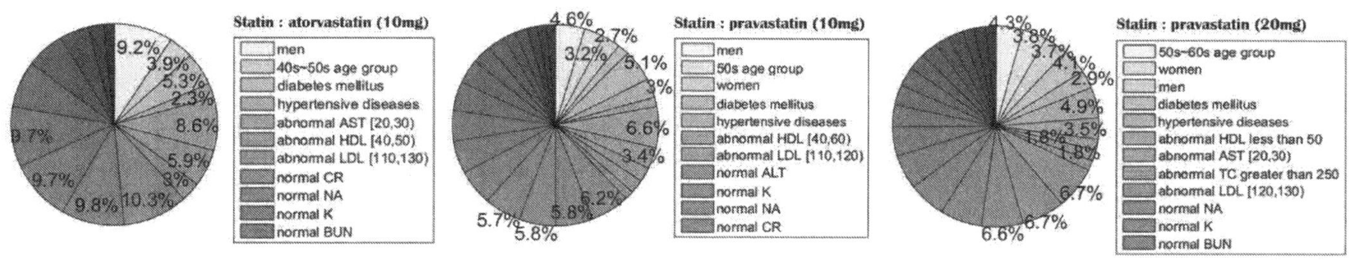

(a) Mid-aged men with diabetes mellitus and hypertension. (b) Mid-aged patients with diabetes mellitus and hypertension. (c) Patients over 50 with diabetes mellitus and hypertension.

Figure 7: Three representative phenotypes of the moderate-efficacy group (CR: creatinine, NA: sodium, K: potassium, BUN: blood urea nitrogen, TC: total cholesterol).

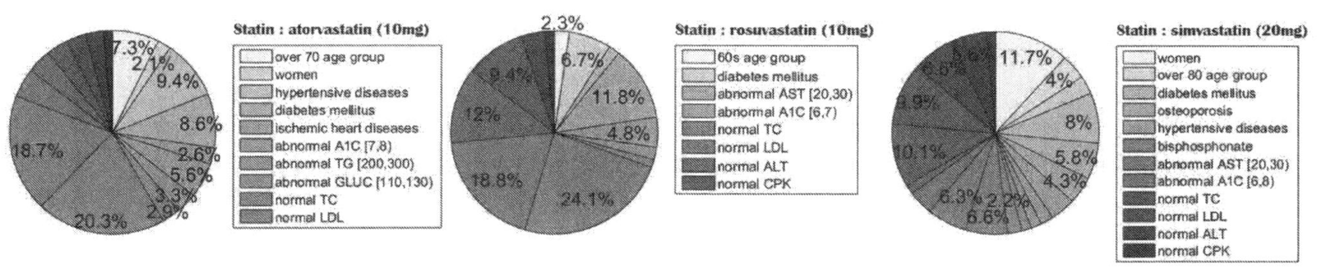

(a) Women over 70 within normal LDL levels. (b) Patients over 60 within normal LDL levels. (c) Women over 80 within normal LDL levels.

Figure 8: Three representative phenotypes of the low-efficacy group (GLUC: glucose, TC: total cholesterol).

Each subgroup within the moderate-efficacy group takes atorvastatin (10 mg), pravastatin (10 mg) and pravastatin (20 mg), respectively. According to statin therapy, atorvastatin (10 mg) [1, 28] is expected to reduce LDL-C levels by up to 50%. Additionally, pravastatin (10 mg) and pravastatin (20 mg) are known to lower LDL-C levels by up to 30% [28]. Each phenotype's expected efficacy is consistent with statin therapy.

Finally, we reported three phenotypes of the low-efficacy group (Figure 8), as follows:

(1) "Women over 70 within normal LDL-C level" (Figure 8a)
(2) "Patients over 60 within normal LDL-C level" (Figure 8b)
(3) "Women over 80 within normal LDL-C level" (Figure 8c)

Phenotypes within the low-efficacy group represent patient groups in which patients have a normal LDL-C level (LDL-C<100 mg/dL) [32] prior to taking a certain statin. Consequently, unlike statin therapy, these phenotypes show that the efficacy is lower than the efficacy expected according to statin guidelines regardless of the traits of patients and types of prescribed statins.

These results demonstrate the various advantages of using our proposed method. First, we can easily observe discriminative characteristics on each patient group. In contrast to the high-efficacy group (Figure 6) and the moderate-efficacy group (Figure 7), phenotypes within the low-efficacy group (Figure 8) represent patients within their normal LDL-C level (LDL-C<100 mg/dL) and TC level (TC<200 mg/dL) [32] before taking a statin. Compared to the phenotypes of the moderate-efficacy group (Figure 7), the phenotypes within the high-efficacy group (Figure 6) are associated with a specific condition, such as metabolic diseases, and represent the patients whose percent reduction in LDL-C is higher than expected. According to statin guidelines, taking atorvastatin (40~80 mg) or rosuvastatin (20~40 mg) is recommended to reduce more than 50 percent of ΔLDL-C [1, 28]. However, patients who take high doses of statins may be more likely to develop kidney problems, such as acute kidney injury [8]. From our findings, we can recommend a low dosage of statin, such as atorvastatin (20 mg) or rosuvastatin (10 mg), rather than atorvastatin (40~80 mg) or rosuvastatin (20~40 mg) when patients are highly associated with particular phenotypes (Figures 6a, 6b and 6c) of the high-efficacy group. The phenotypes of the moderate-efficacy group represent the patients whose percent reduction in LDL-C is in accordance with statin therapy [1, 28]. According to the results, our proposed method can discover the high efficacy of a statin in specific conditions, such as metabolic diseases, as well as the expected efficacy of a statin, as known according to statin guidelines. Moreover, we can easily obtain insights on subgroups within each patient group. For example, we observed two different subgroups of patients with metabolic diseases within the high-efficacy group (Figures 6a and 6b).

However, it is impossible to conduct a numerical analysis for the efficacy of each statin because we cannot conclude that a statin only has an influence on reducing LDL-C levels. Therefore, a clinical study must be conducted to determine how much each statin decreases LDL-C levels rather than data-driven approaches such as our proposed method.

5.3 Accuracy

To evaluate the extent to which our proposed method obtains better discrimination on several groups compared to the baselines, the derived phenotypes and the latent representations of patients were evaluated on a classification task of predicting a new patient's group. We compared SNTFL ($\lambda = 0.005$) to three baselines with varying R. The results indicated that the latent representations of SNTFL ($\lambda = 0.005$) obtained better diagnostic accuracy than the baselines (Figures 9, 10). For all values of R, SNTFL ($\lambda = 0.005$) achieved the best prediction result in the two metrics.

In terms of MicroAUC (Figure 9), the best average MicroAUC was 0.7592 using SNTFL ($\lambda = 0.005$, $R = 70$) but only 0.7148 using CP-APR ($R = 70$); i.e., SNTFL achieved an increase of almost 0.0444. For NTF ($R = 70$) and SNTFL ($\lambda = 0$, $R = 70$), the best average MicroAUC was 0.7388 and 0.7519, respectively. When R was 50, a significant difference in the average MicroAUC between SNTFL ($\lambda = 0$) and SNTFL ($\lambda = 0.005$) was observed; i.e., the average MicroAUC of SNTFL ($\lambda = 0.005$) was approximately 0.0125 higher than the average MicroAUC of SNTFL ($\lambda = 0$).

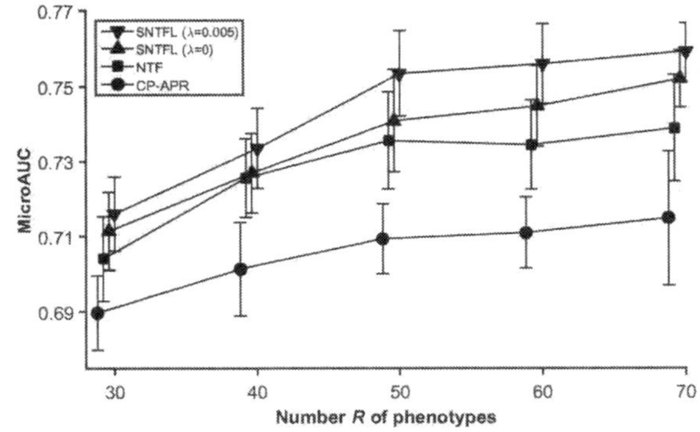

Figure 9: Effect of the number R of phenotypes on the average MicroAUC over 10 trials. Bars: ±1 s.d., n = 10.

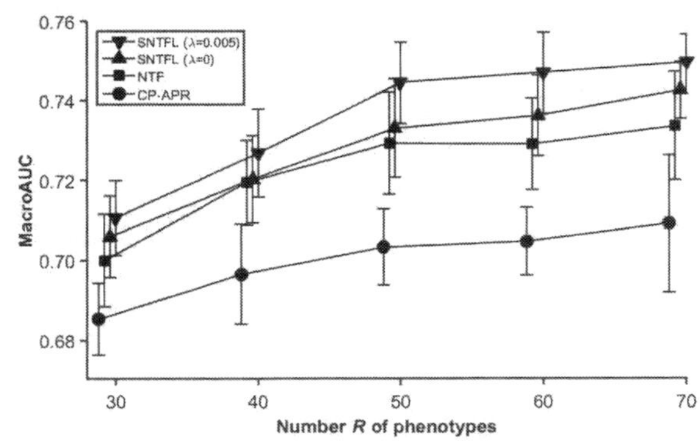

Figure 10: Effect of the number R of phenotypes on the average MacroAUC over 10 trials. Bars: ±1 s.d., n = 10.

The best average MacroAUC was 0.7494 using SNTFL ($\lambda = 0.005$, $R = 70$) (Figure 10). This result was 0.0402 higher than the best average MacroAUC of CP-APR ($R = 70$). For NTF ($R = 70$) and SNTFL ($\lambda = 0$, $R = 70$), the best average MacroAUC was 0.7335 and 0.7425, respectively.

These results indicate that the classification model of SNTFL was more predictive than the classification model of the baselines. This means that the grouped phenotypes and the latent representations from SNTFL have discriminative characteristics on each patient group rather than from the baselines. From these results, we infer that using the group information of patients and optimizing a multinomial logistic regression during the tensor factorization process made the phenotypes and latent representations discriminative. Conversely, the baselines obtained inferior accuracy because the baselines aimed only to derive individual phenotypes that approximate the original data as closely as possible.

6 CONCLUSION

In this paper, a novel tensor factorization method, named SNTFL, is proposed to derive grouped phenotypes that are discriminative regardless of the number of patient groups. We define a discriminative constraint to improve discrimination among patient groups and design an algorithm that optimizes a multinomial logistic regression during the tensor factorization process. To evaluate the effectiveness of SNTFL, we conduct a case study on a hyperlipidemia dataset. Consequently, our method derives grouped phenotypes that have discriminative characteristics on each patient group and achieves better diagnostic accuracy than the baselines. Moreover, SNTFL successfully discovers meaningful patient subgroups.

ACKNOWLEDGMENTS

This work was partly supported by a grant from the Korea Health Technology R&D Project through the Korea Health Industry Development Institute (KHIDI) funded by the Ministry of Health & Welfare, Republic of Korea (No. HC15C1362), and Institute for Information & communications Technology Promotion (IITP) grant funded by the Korea government (MSIP) (No.2014-0-00147, Basic Software Research in Human-level Lifelong Machine Learning (Machine Learning Center)).

REFERENCES

[1] American Diabetes Association. 2017. Standards of Medical Care in Diabetes-2017 Abridged for Primary Care Providers. *Clinical Diabetes* 35, 1 (2017), 5–26.

[2] B. W. Bader, T. G. Kolda, et al. 2012. MATLAB Tensor Toolbox Version 2.5. Available online. (January 2012). http://www.sandia.gov/~tgkolda/TensorToolbox/

[3] D. P. Bertsekas. 1999. Nonlinear programming. In *Belmont: Athena scientific.* 1–60.

[4] J. D. Carroll and J. J. Chang. 1970. Analysis of individual differences in multidimensional scaling via an N-way generalization of "Eckart-Young" decomposition. *Psychometrika* 35, 3 (1970), 283–319.

[5] Z. Che, D. Kale, W. Li, M. T. Bahadori, and Y. Liu. 2015. Deep computational phenotyping. In *Proceedings of the 21th ACM SIGKDD International Conference on Knowledge Discovery and Data Mining. ACM.* 507–516.

[6] E. C. Chi and T.G. Kolda. 2012. On tensors, sparsity, and nonnegative factorizations. *SIAM J. Matrix Anal. Appl.* 33, 4 (2012), 1272–1299.

[7] A. Cichock, A. H. Phan R. Zdunek, and S.I. Amari. 2009. Nonnegative matrix and tensor factorizations: applications to exploratory multi-way data analysis and blind source separation. *John Wiley & Sons* (2009).

[8] C. R. Dormuth and et al. 2013. Use of high potency statins and rates of admission for acute kidney injury: multicenter, retrospective observational analysis of administrative databases. *Bmj* 346, f880 (2013).

[9] M. Dyrby, D. Baunsgaard, R. Bro, and S. B. Engelsen. 2005. Multiway chemometric analysis of the metabolic response to toxins monitored by NMR. *Chemometrics and Intelligent Laboratory Systems* 76, 1 (2005), 79–89.

[10] R. A. Harshman. 1970. Foundations of the PARAFAC procedure: Models and conditions for an "explanatory" multi-modal factor analysis. In *UCLA Work Papers Phonet*, Vol. 16. 1–84.

[11] J. C. Ho, J. Ghosh, S. R. Steinhubl, W. F. Stewart, J. C. Denny, B. A. Malin, and J. Sun. 2014. Limestone: High-throughput candidate phenotype generation via tensor factorization. *Journal of biomedical informatics* 52, 6 (2014), 199–211.

[12] J. C. Ho, J. Ghosh, and J. Sun. 2014. Marble: high-throughput phenotyping from electronic health records via sparse nonnegative tensor factorization. In *Proceedings of the 20th ACM SIGKDD international conference on Knowledge discovery and data mining. ACM.* 115–124.

[13] G. Hripcsak and D. J. Albers. 2013. Next-generation phenotyping of electronic health records. Journal of the American Medical Informatics Association. *Journal of the American Medical Informatics Association* 20, 1 (2013), 117–121.

[14] D. Kale, Z. Che, Y. Liu, and R. Wetzel. 2014. Computational discovery of physiomes in critically ill children using deep learning. In *DMMI Workshop, AMIA.*

[15] D. Kansagara, H. Englander, A. Salanitro, D. Kagen, C. Theobald, M. Freeman, and S. Kripalani. 2011. Risk prediction models for hospital readmission: a systematic review. *Jama* 306, 15 (2011), 1688–1698.

[16] H. S. Kim, H. Lee, B. Park, S. Park, H. Kim, S. H. Lee, and et al. 2016. Comparative analysis of the efficacy of low-and moderate-intensity statins in Korea. *International journal of clinical pharmacology and therapeutics* 54, 11 (2016), 864.

[17] Y. Kim, R. El-Kareh, J. Sun, H. Yu, and X. Jiang. 2017. Discriminative and distinct phenotyping by constrained tensor factorization. *Scientific Reports* 7 (2017).

[18] T. A. Lasko, J. C. Denny, and M. A. Levy. 2013. Computational phenotype discovery using unsupervised feature learning over noisy, sparse, and irregular clinical data. *PloS one* 8, 6 (2013), e66341.

[19] L. D. Lathauwer and B. D. Moor. 1998. From matrix to tensor: Multilinear algebra and signal processing. In *Institute of Mathematics and Its Applications Conference Series.* 1–16.

[20] C. J. Lin. 2007. Projected gradient methods for nonnegative matrix factorization. *Neural computation* 19, 10 (2007), 2756–2779.

[21] C. Liu, F. Wang, J. Hu, and H. Xiong. 2015. Temporal phenotyping from longitudinal electronic health records: A graph based framework. In *Proceedings of the 21th ACM SIGKDD International Conference on Knowledge Discovery and Data Mining. ACM.* 705–714.

[22] T. P. Minka. 2003. A comparison of numerical optimizers for logistic regression. *Unpublished draft* (2003).

[23] R. Miotto, L. Li, B. A. Kidd, and J. T. Dudley. 2016. Deep patient: An unsupervised representation to predict the future of patients from the electronic health records. *Scientific reports* 6 (2016).

[24] R. Miotto, F. Wang, S. Wang, X. Jiang, and J. T. Dudley. 2017. Deep learning for healthcare: review, opportunities and challenges. *Briefings in Bioinformatics* (2017), bbx044.

[25] M. Mørup. 2011. Applications of tensor (multiway array) factorizations and decompositions in data mining. *Wiley Interdisciplinary Reviews: Data Mining and Knowledge Discovery* 1, 1 (2011), 24–40.

[26] K. M. Newton, P. L. Peissig, A. N. Kho, S. J. Bielinski, R. L. Berg, V. Choudhary, M. Basford, C. G. Chute, I. J. Kullo, R. Li, J. A. Pacheco, L. V. Rasmussen, L. Spangler, and J. C. Denny. 2013. Validation of electronic medical record-based phenotyping algorithms: results and lessons learned from the eMERGE network. *JAMIA* 20, e1 (2013), e147–e154.

[27] P. Schulam, F. Wigley, and S. Saria. 2015. Clustering Longitudinal Clinical Marker Trajectories from Electronic Health Data: Applications to Phenotyping and Endotype Discovery. In *AAAI.* 2956–2964.

[28] N. J. Stone and et al. 2014. 2013 ACC/AHA Guideline on the Treatment of Blood Cholesterol to Reduce Atherosclerotic Cardiovascular Risk in Adults. *Circulation* 129, 25 suppl 2 (2014), S1–S45.

[29] K. B. Wagholikar, K. L. MacLaughlin, M. R. Henry, R. A. Greenes, R. A. Hankey, H. Liu, and R. Chaudhry. 2005. Clinical decision support with automated text processing for cervical cancer screening. *Journal of the American Medical Informatics Association* 19, 5 (2005), 833–839.

[30] H. Wang and N. Ahuja. 2004. Compact representation of multidimensional data using tensor rank-one decomposition. *vectors* (2004).

[31] Y. Wang, R. Chen, J. Ghosh, J. C. Denny, A. Kho, Y. Chen, B. A. Malin, and J. Sun. 2015. Rubik: Knowledge guided tensor factorization and completion for health data analytics. In *Proceedings of the 21th ACM SIGKDD International Conference on Knowledge Discovery and Data Mining. ACM.* 1265–1274.

[32] Williams and Lippincott. 2002. Third report of the National Cholesterol Education Program (NCEP) expert panel on detection, evaluation, and treatment of high blood cholesterol in adults (Adult Treatment Panel III) final report. *Circulation* 106, 25 (2002), 3143–3143.

[33] J. Wu, J. Roy, and W. F. Stewart. 2010. Prediction modeling using EHR data: challenges, strategies, and a comparison of machine learning approaches. *Medical care* 48, 6 (2010), S106–S113.

[34] K. Yang, X. Li, H. Liu, J. Mei, G. Xie, J. Zhao, and F. Wang. 2017. TaGiTeD: Predictive Task Guided Tensor Decomposition for Representation Learning from Electronic Health Records. In *Thirty-First AAAI Conference on Artificial Intelligence.*

[35] J. Zhou, J. Sun, Y. Liu, J. Hu, and J. Ye. 2013. Patient risk prediction model via top-k stability selection. In *SIAM conference on data mining (SIAM).*

[36] J. Zhou, F. Wang, J. Hu, and J. Ye. 2014. From micro to macro: data driven phenotyping by densification of longitudinal electronic medical records. In *Proceedings of the 20th ACM SIGKDD international conference on Knowledge discovery and data mining. ACM.* 135–144.

Infer Cause of Death for Population Health Using Convolutional Neural Network

Hang Wu
Georgia Institute of Technology and Emory University
U.A. Whitaker Building, Suite 4236
Atlanta, GA 30332
hangwu@gatech.edu

May D. Wang
Georgia Institute of Technology and Emory University
U.A. Whitaker Building, Suite 4236
Atlanta, GA 30332
maywang@gatech.edu

ABSTRACT

In biomedical data analysis, inferring the cause of death is a challenging and important task, which is useful for both public health reporting purposes, as well as improving patients' quality of care by identifying severer conditions. Causal inference, however, is notoriously difficult. Traditional causal inference mainly relies on analyzing data collected from experiment of specific design, which is expensive, and limited to a certain disease cohort, making the approach less generalizable.

In our paper, we adopt a novel data-driven perspective to analyze and improve the death reporting process, to assist physicians identify the single underlying cause of death. To achieve this, we build state-of-the-art deep learning models, convolution neural network (CNN), and achieve around 75% accuracy in predicting the single underlying cause of death from a list of relevant medical conditions. We also provide interpretations for the black-box neural network models, so that death reporting physicians can apply the model with better understanding of the model.

CCS CONCEPTS

• **Computing methodologies** → **Causal reasoning and diagnostics**; **Neural networks**;

KEYWORDS

Causal Inference, Deep Learning, Interpretability

ACM Reference format:
Hang Wu and May D. Wang. 2017. Infer Cause of Death for Population Health Using Convolutional Neural Network. In *Proceedings of ACM-BCB'17, August 20-23, 2017, Boston, MA, USA.*, , 10 pages.
DOI: http://dx.doi.org/10.1145/3107411.3107447

1 INTRODUCTION

Physicians and medical examiners are faced with the challenges of inferring causes of death in their death reporting routine. When a death case occurs in hospital, for example, a physician will file a death certificate to the state agency, summarizing the demographics, a sequence of up to 20 medical conditions relevant to the death, coded using ICD-10 standards, and a single underlying cause of death the physician thinks most probable. These mortality data are finally aggregated and recorded by the national vital statistics system of the national center for health statistics (NCHS).

With more and more such death certificates available, it is natural for us to wonder: can we utilize the large-scale observational datasets, to build a causal inference model that can identify the cause of death based on the observations?

Causal inference, which aims to uncover the mechanism behind observations or predict the effect of an intervention to the system, is an important task in biomedical data analysis. Identifying the causes of diseases and deaths will facilitate public health reporting process, and improve individual's quality of care by guiding design of treatment for diseases.

Such causal inference tasks are notoriously difficult, as for each patient, we can only observe one of all the potential outcomes, and to determine the causal effect, we need to compare the observed ones against all others with some approximation schemes. Several biomedical studies have studied the causal structures inside patients with one type of disease, and design random or non-random experiments to analyze the causal effects. These studies provide great insight into the diseases they studied, but there are certain limitations to it: collecting experimental data is expensive and time-consuming; moreover, in a general hospital setting, physicians and nurses might be dealing with a combination of complicated medical conditions, and need to prioritize the treatment and resource allocation, which requires better understanding of the effect of combination of medical conditions, and current studies on one type of disease might be insufficient.

In this study, we take a novel approach, to study death certificates data and build predictive model to assist physicians in identifying the single underlying cause of death.

To predict the single cause of death, given the input as a sequence of conditions, poses several challenges: 1) The input sequence of conditions is highly unstructured, so if we are to use traditional one-hot vector to represent each of the conditions, we will be dealing with large dimension of inputs, and succeeding feature extraction will require large computation resources. 2) Since essentially we are selecting one medical condition out of a list of conditions, and each death certificate will be different, we need to seek a model that can adaptively process inputs of different lengths, and predict accordingly.

To address such challenges, inspired by the recent success of deep learning, we propose to apply deep learning, specifically convolutional neural networks, to build our causal inference model. Deep learning has shown great performance in processing raw data

Permission to make digital or hard copies of all or part of this work for personal or classroom use is granted without fee provided that copies are not made or distributed for profit or commercial advantage and that copies bear this notice and the full citation on the first page. Copyrights for components of this work owned by others than ACM must be honored. Abstracting with credit is permitted. To copy otherwise, or republish, to post on servers or to redistribute to lists, requires prior specific permission and/or a fee. Request permissions from permissions@acm.org.
ACM-BCB'17, August 20-23, 2017, Boston, MA, USA.
© 2017 ACM. 978-1-4503-4722-8/17/08...$15.00
DOI: http://dx.doi.org/10.1145/3107411.3107447

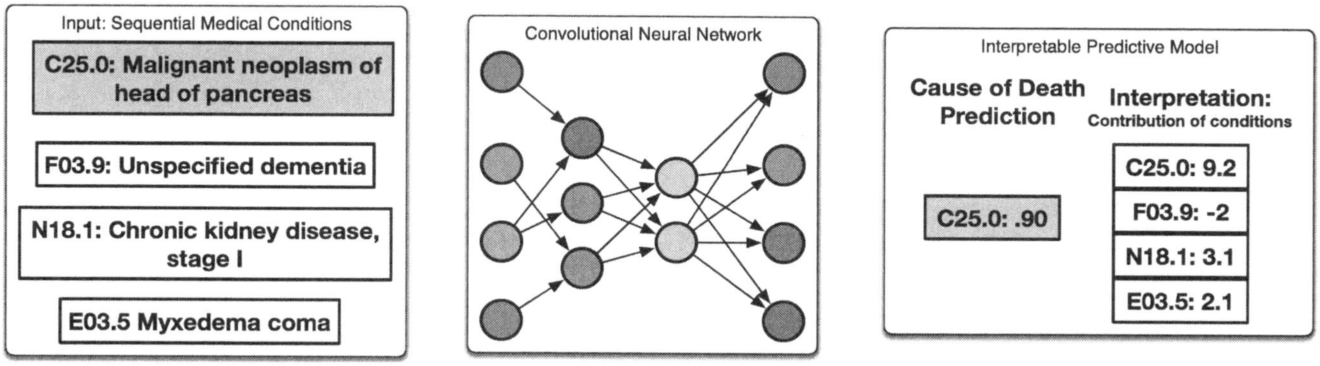

Figure 1: *Overall Architecture.* In this paper, we analyze a causal inference task originating from the death reporting process. In the process, for each of the death case, the physician will select a sequence of medical conditions, coded in ICD-10 standard, that is most relevant to death, and identify one condition as the underlying cause of death. To predict the cause of death using the sequence as input, we build a convolutional neural network, and provide interpretations of the model's prediction for physicians.

in various formats and obtain trainable representation specific to the tasks, and deep learning structures can be configured to adapt to inputs of different shapes [8].

Our model will facilitate the further analysis of causality modeling in several aspects: 1) although our current model is build on NCHS mortality data, it is directly transferrable to analyzing more specific electronic health records data (EHR) during hospital admission. By parsing EHR to a sequence of observed conditions format, we can identify the most likely cause of death, which can help physicians attend more to important conditions, thus improving the quality of care. 2) another advantage with deep learning models lie in the distributed representations of the input medical conditions, and such representation is universal and can be applied to other data analysis tasks to understand the relationships between them better.

The overall model structure is presented in Fig. 1.

Our contribution in this paper is mainly two-fold:

- We designed a convolutional neural network (CNN) model to identify the underlying cause of death from a list of relevant medical conditions using death certificates data, and achieved about 75% accuracy, a significant performance improvement over the conventional methods.
- We illustrated how we can interpret the black-box deep learning models, so that physicians can understand and choose whether to adopt the machine prediction.

In the rest of the paper, we first review related work on cause of death, causal inference, and deep learning models. We present our model in Section 3, with experiment results in Section 4. We then show how we can interpret the black-box algorithms, followed by discussions and conclusions.

2 RELATED WORK

2.1 Causes of Death

Understanding causes of death has been a big challenge in biomedical research, as discerning new risk factors for death can help physicians understand the mechanism of death and certain disease, so to improve the quality of care for patients.

Previous research mainly focuses on discovering the cause of death for patients with specific disease types, or discovering new factors that can be identified as cause of death. The Emerging Risk Factors Collaboration studied the risk factors associated with diabetes [4] and Khorana et al. studied for the cancer patients with chemotherapy [16]. Other studies include causes of death for neonatal deaths [22], Alzheimer's death [30], and sclerosis [43].

Back in 1986, Israel et al [13] first pointed out the potential multiple cause-of-death data, and with the popularity of statistical data analysis methods, the dataset gained more popularity in the healthcare research community. Redelings et al. [36] analyzed the associations of cause-of-death conditions, and Jiang et al. [15] analyzed the evolution of causes with a topic model approach. Some researchers also look in to the subgroups of patients associated with certain diseases, for example, McCoy et al. on asthma [26], Melamed et al. on sepsis [27]. Yet these studies mostly take on an association analysis approach and few have focused on the problem of causal identification.

2.2 Causal Inference

Causal inference plays a vital role in analyzing biomedical observational study, as it can help determine the treatment effect of certain drugs or procedures [19, 42]. Rubin et al. [39] was the first to analyze the causal inference problem in such experiment problems, and the paper mainly discussed the difference between random experiments and non-random experiments. Such experiments aim to discover the effect of a binary treatment, and the term "random/ non-random" refers to whether the assignment of treatment depends on the patients' conditions or not. In a random design experiment, since the treatment is assigned randomly, it's straightforward to analyze the treatment effect by comparing populations with treatment to populations without treatment. However, most of biomedical experiments are non-random observational studies, so it's crucial to identify the causal structure, or design special algorithms to account for the cofounding effects in such studies.

Identify causal structure mainly builds on the causal graph framework proposed by Pearl et al. [34], where variables/ features are represented as nodes, and edges indicate causal relationships. Under this framework, when the causal structure is specified beforehand, often by domain experts, structural equation model (SEM) [2, 32] can analyze the causal effects of intervention on certain variables.

Oftentimes, such structure is unknown or incomplete, thus, a series of work is conducted to learn the causal structure. Constraint-based algorithm, such as PC algorithm [44], learns the graph by exploiting conditional dependence relationship between variables. Score-based method [3] designs an evaluation metric to score each potential causal structure, and finds the one with highest score.

On the other hand, to analyze the treatment effect from observation studies, we could also adopt the potential outcomes framework [40]. Two popular approaches are matching [31, 41, 46] and propensity score. By matching, we find a pair of two instances, that receive opposite treatment, while are most similar in other features. In this way, the difference between them after treatment can be used as an estimate for the treatment effect. Propensity score works by reweighing instances to convert an observation study to a pseudo-random experiment and work with random experiment [1, 38].

2.3 Deep Learning and CNN

The past decade has witnessed the success of deep learning, enabled by effective training algorithm [9, 18], high performance computing structure including GPU, and large-scale labeled datasets [5]. Deep learning has shown great capabilities in image classification [20], image segmentation[24], text analysis [48], and reinforcement learning [29].

Recently, biomedical researchers are applying deep learning to biomedical data analysis [10]. Liu et al. analyzed brain imaging with deep learning, to achieve early diagnosis of Alzheimer's disease; Esteva et al. used deep learning to classify a skin cancer dataset containing about 130,000 images and beat human physician accuracy[7]; Suo et al. [47] applied deep belief nets to derive risk factors from electronic health records.

CNN was originally proposed to address image classification [23], initially dealing digit recognition. It revived as the standard practice of image classification around 2012, with the success of AlexNet beating human accuracy. Then CNN showed great success in other image processing tasks, such as image segmentation [24] and human action recognition [14]. CNN then was also applied to sentence classification [17] and inspired several follow-ups [6, 11]. Another direction of work uses recurrent neural network [21], and showed better capabilities in text generation [48], and text conversion to other modalities [25].

3 MODEL

3.1 Problem Formulation

In the death reporting scenario, a physician will first select several conditions, coded by ICD-10 codes [1], as the conditions most relevant to death. The conditions are then recorded as they are sequential observed. Among these conditions, one of them will be predicted as the cause of death, based on physicians' expertise and the understanding of the death case.

In this paper, we are interested in automating the latter part of the process, identifying the one cause of death from the list of conditions. Mathematically, suppose we have a vocabulary of ICD-10 conditions V, with the total number denoted as $|V|$. We are given a dataset of $\{x_i, y_i\}, i = 1, ..., N$, where $x_i = [c_{i,1}, ..., c_{i,i_k}]$ is the sequence of i_k relevant conditions recorded, and y_i is the identified cause of death. We are interested in learning a classifier as $f(x_i) = y_i \in V$, essentially a multi-class classification problem, with input being a list of items also from the vocabulary V.

The sequential and discrete nature of the ICD-10 conditions in our case presents a strong analogy with natural language. We can regard each ICD-10 condition as a word, and physicians use a sequence of ICD-10 conditions to describe a death case, which is similar to a human sentence describing a concept. So our problem can be considered as a sentence classification problem. However, we should note a profound difference between our problem and sentence classification: traditional sentence classification generally deals with binary classification (e.g., positive sentiment vs. negative sentiment), or a few classes that indicate the topic of the sentence (e.g., religious, movie, news, etc.). In our cause of death identification, we are dealing with thousands of ICD-10 vocabulary as the final class label, which means the final classification probability could be sparsely distributed among the vocabulary, posing a computational challenge.

In light of the recent success in deep learning in text classification cases, we adopt the convolutional neural network (CNN) framework to our application, and made necessary modifications.

3.2 Convolutional neural network(CNN) for sentence classification

Applying CNN to sentence classification is proposed by [17], and has thus been extensively studied and applied in the literature. Here, we first review the basics of the CNN framework, and then introduce the model we modified.

For a sequence $x = [c_1, ..., c_k]$, where each condition $c_j \in \mathbb{R}^{|V|}$ is one-hot vector encoding representation, we first apply a word embedding to obtain a distributed representation for it [28] in a lower dimensional space $\mathbb{R}^D$. Equivalently, we are learning a weight matrix $W \in \mathbb{R}^{|V|\times D}$, so that we embed each condition c_j as the jth row of the matrix, with the simple matrix multiplication $v_j = c_j W$.

After the embedding, we concatenate all the embedding vectors, and obtain the initial representation for the sequence as

$$v = v_1 \oplus v_2 \oplus ... v_k$$

. The convolution operator is applied to a segment of the sequence, determined by the window size. For example, for a window of size of H, the convolution uses a filter $m \in \mathbb{R}^{H\times D}$, and the result of this convolution to a segment $v_{i:i+H-1} = [v_i, v_{i+1}, ..., v_{i+H-1}]$ is

$$z_i = f(m * v_{i:i+H} + b_0)$$

, where $*$ is the convolution operator, b_0 a scalar bias term, and f a nonlinear transformation, such as Tanh and ReLU. The rationale for a convolution operation lies in that conditions that occur closely in

[1] Starting FROM 1999, NCHS has switched from ICD-9 to ICD-10 coding system.

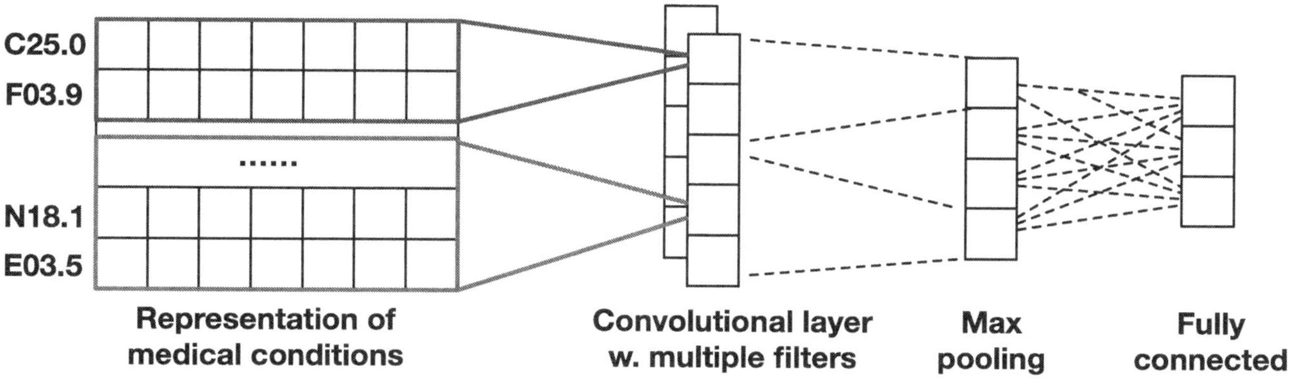

Figure 2: *Model architecture.* The convolution neural network architecture we used in the project is from Kim et al. [17], which contains a 1D convolution layer and a max pooling, followed by a fully connected layer as logit outputs.

the sequence should share some characteristics and be correlated to each other, as we would expect in the 2D image case.

We can further apply a pooling operation to the obtained feature map $[z_1, ..., z_k]$, which finds the maximum or average among all the z_js. The intuition is that for each filter, we find the most important features, and this operation naturally handles variable length sequences.

In practice, we can apply several convolution filters to obtain several corresponding features. These intermediate features can be passed again to convolution filters then nonlinear transformation, and the stacking of these layers compose a deep neural network structure, which some describes as Parrellel-CNN.

In the ultimate layer, for the hidden feature vector $u \in \mathbb{R}^{D_1}$, we apply a fully connected layer to obtain the final output $y = g(u^T Q + b_1)$. The parameter $Q \in \mathbb{R}^{D_1 * |V|}$ maps the hidden feature to a distribution over all the vocabulary V, and the condition with maximum probability is predicted as the cause of death.

An illustration of the model architecture is shown in Fig. 2.

3.3 Proposed method: convolutional neural network with dynamic computation graph

A challenge of the above vanilla CNN structure lies in the final parameter matrix Q, as computing a soft-max distribution over the whole vocabulary of codes can result in sparse entries, and makes the inference more difficult.

To overcome such challenge, we note that instead of predicting over the whole vocabulary, we only need to select one condition out of the input sequence, which has a length significantly smaller than the total vocabulary. Moreover, each of the sentence has a potential different length, so this requires that we dynamically build a neural network for each of the input.

The new "Define by Run" paradigm of deep learning framework has enabled us to build such dynamic neural networks. In brief, instead of specifying a static network structures before any input is fed, now we take a particular training sample, a sequence in our case, and define the network structure from this input to its output. This is also the same for testing phase, where we dynamically construct a network architecture for each test sample, potentially of various shapes. Although this practice seems more tedious in terms of computation, it supports dynamically sized data, such as our sequences of medical conditions with variable lengths, and also reduces the complexity of computation in computation graph implementation.

3.4 Regularization

Deep neural networks tend to overfit the data, thus, in our implementation, we imposed following three regularization techniques

Batch Normalization (BN). Batch Normalization (BN) [12] works on the intuition that during the training of neural network, because of the changes of the network parameters, the distribution of the nonlinearity activation function also shifts accordingly. Mathematically, for each dimension x_k of the D dimension input feature $x = [x_1, ..., x_D]$, the new normalized feature is

$$\hat{x}_k = \frac{x_k - \mathbb{E}[x_k]}{\sqrt{Var[x_k]}}$$

, where the expectation and variance are computed for each mini-batches.

Reducing such shift in covariates can accelerate the convergence in training, and sometimes has the benefit as regularization.

Dropout (DO). Dropout [45] is one of the most successful regularization techniques. In brief, the weights of a proportion of the hidden neurons in the network layers are chosen to be 0s during training. For example, in the ultimate layer of our network, we have the final output computed as $y = g(u^T Q + b_1)$. Instead of applying Q directly, we randomly generated as mask matrix M_Q, where each entry of it is a Bernoulli variable with specified probability p in $(0, 1)$, often set to 0.5 as suggested by literature [17, 45].

The output is then

$$\hat{y} = g(u^T (Q. \times M_Q) + b_1)$$

, where $.\times$ denotes the element-wise multiplication.

During test, we scale the learned weight matrices by p as $\hat{Q} = pQ$, and use them without dropout to predict unseen sentences.

Early Stopping (ES). Early stopping is also widely used as a regularization technique for almost any types of machine classifiers, that rely on sub-gradient methods as training algorithms. It attracts wide popularity in training deep neural networks as it can help save a great amount of computation time while preserving considerable test performance.

We first partition a small proportion of the training set as our development set, and train classifiers on the rest of the training set. Once we observe the test performance on development set is worse than the training performance on the rest, and the test performance exceeds a threshold we set beforehand, we can conclude that the training might already overfit the data, and terminate the training process.

3.5 Discussion: CNN Vs. Bag of Words

Traditional sentence processing mainly use the bag-of-n–grams method to represent the sentence [50], where each dimension is the term frequency times inverse document requency (tf-idf) for the n gram for the sentence. With features extracted, off-the-shelf classification methods, such as naive Bayes, support vector machine, can be applied to classify the sentences.

Despite its simplicity, there are several disadvantages of this approach compared to CNN: 1) the n -gram tend to be really sparse, and even infeasible to compute, when the n is large; 2) the one-hot representation of these n–grams ignore the shared parts between all n–grams, as well as the distributed representations obtained by embedding words; 3) training such models requires first loading all data into RAM to process the TFIDF matrix, so we cannot adopt mini-batch training techniques here, making the model less scalable.

4 EXPERIMENTS & RESULTS

4.1 Dataset overview

For the experiments, we pick the death certificates in the United States from Year 2014, which contains approximately 2 million records of death cases [33]. After preprocessing, removing identical records and filter out records with length less than 3, we obtain 1,499,128 records.

The ICD-10 codes, in the format of A123.4, observe a hierarchy structure, where the digits before the dot can be regarded a coarse high-level classification of the condition.To save computation, we here use the coarse version, and as a result, we obtain a vocabulary of input conditions of 1610 and a total of 1180 possible classes as causes of death.

4.2 Configurations for CNN

For our method, we experiment both static and dynamic constructed CNN. The static constructed one is referred to as *CNN-static*. As for the dynamic version, we can either train the network as a static structure, and when testing, only selects ones that are present in the input, or we can use a dynamic structure in both training and testing phase. These two versions are referred to *CNN-dyn-eval* and *CNN-dynamic* respectively.

The network structure we used is specified as follows:

```
Input -> Embedding Layer -> Convolution & Pooling
-> Batch Normalization -> Dropout
-> Fully Connected Layer -> Output
```

The embedding dimension is set to 128, and three kernel sizes for the convolution layers are 3,5,7. Dropout probability is set to .5 as suggested in [17] and maximum norm of parameters are set to 3.0. Our model is built with PyTorch [8], and adapted from open source implementations [2].

4.3 Baseline methods

For the baselines, we implemented two types of baseline algorithms: traditional BoW classification, and shallow classifiers built on embeddings.

For the bag-of-words feature extraction, we first construct a count matrix X, where $X[i, j]$ denotes the count of word j appearing in the document i. Then tf-idf transform, short for "term frequency times inverse document frequency" is applied to X to obtain the final feature matrix. We used bag-of-words, instead of more expressive n-gram, because it would require much more than the computation power we have available right now. We then apply naive Bayes (NB), support vector machine (SVM), and logistic regression (RF) to the feature matrix, and obtain predictions.

For shallow classifiers, we use the architectures shown below

```
Input -> Embedding Layer -> Vector Averaging
-> Fully Connected Layer -> Output
```

After we embed all the medical conditions of a sequence, we average them as the vector representation as the sentence, then use a fully connected layer to obtain the final output. We use cross entropy loss (equivalent to a logistic regression model), and multi margin loss (equivalent to a support vector machine model), and also implemented the three variants w./o. dynamic graph in PyTorch.

4.4 Experiment Settings

We randomly partition the data into training, development, and test sets with ratio 7.9:.1:1. The hyper-parameters were selected based on the performance on the development set and then tested on the test set. We also reported the model performance with and without early stopping using development set.

In naive Bayes, we don't have a parameter to tune, and we tune the regularization parameter for SVM, and the number of trees for RF. As for CNN, we mainly tune the kernel sizes. The results were reported by averaging 3 runs of experiments.

BoW classifiers are run in CPU with 60 GB RAM and we used implementation of this pipeline from Scikit-Learn [35]. CNN and shallow learners are trained with NVIDIA K80 GPU. We use a mini-batch of 64 for training, and we set the maximum number of epochs to 2 (the number of iterations over the whole training data). We used Adam with adaptive learning rate as the sub-gradient optimization method. Both training with and without early stopping are tested. Training such networks averaged to about 5 hours under our configurations, while testing a single case using a trained model takes about seconds.

[2]https://github.com/Shawn1993/cnn-text-classification-pytorch

Table 1: Classification Results

Classifier Name	Test Loss	Test Accuracy	Test Micro F1	Test Cohen Kappa
CNN-static	0.799±0.009	75.481±0.345	8.4e-06±3.8e-08	8.3e-06±3.8e-08
CNN-static-es	0.902±0.017	73.681±0.346	8.2e-06±3.8e-08	8.1e-06±4.0e-08
CNN-dyn	3.996±0.861	68.261±0.362	7.6e-06±4.0e-08	7.5e-06±3.9e-08
CNN-dyn-es	3.765±0.400	51.946±1.130	5.8e-06±1.3e-07	5.6e-06±1.2e-07
CNN-dyn-eval	**0.738±0.007**	**75.787±0.179**	**8.4e-06±2.0e-08**	**8.3e-06±1.8e-08**
CNN-dyn-eval-es	0.826±0.044	73.184±1.254	8.1e-06±1.4e-07	8.0e-06±1.4e-07
LR	1.011±0.007	66.762±0.298	7.4e-06±3.3e-08	7.3e-06±2.9e-08
LR-es	1.007±0.024	66.706±0.681	7.4e-06±7.6e-08	7.3e-06±7.6e-08
LR-dyn	0.852±0.014	66.946±0.431	7.4e-06±4.8e-08	7.3e-06±4.9e-08
LR-dyn-es	0.886±0.015	66.326±0.720	7.4e-06±8.0e-08	7.2e-06±8.0e-08
LR-dyn-eval	0.842±0.012	67.295±0.514	7.5e-06±5.7e-08	7.4e-06±6.0e-08
LR-dyn-eval-es	0.881±0.006	66.633±0.297	7.4e-06±3.3e-08	7.3e-06±3.1e-08
SVM	1.285±0.056	64.597±1.042	7.2e-06±1.2e-07	7.0e-06±1.2e-07
SVM-es	2.039±1.116	62.812±2.312	7.0e-06±2.6e-07	6.8e-06±2.6e-07
SVM-dyn	14.588±1.857	44.984±1.771	5.0e-06±2.0e-07	4.8e-06±2.3e-07
SVM-dyn-es	13.007±2.572	45.068±2.111	5.0e-06±2.3e-07	4.9e-06±2.3e-07
SVM-dyn-eval	13.800±1.670	47.377±1.891	5.3e-06±2.1e-07	5.1e-06±2.4e-07
SVM-dyn-eval-es	11.253±2.384	48.081±2.345	5.3e-06±2.6e-07	5.2e-06±2.8e-07
LR-BoW	6.486±0.000	8.3±0.000	8.3e-02±0.0e+00	0.0e+00±0.0e+00
NB-BoW	4.864±0.000	8.3±0.000	8.3e-02±0.0e+00	0.0e+00±0.0e+00

4.5 Evaluation Metrics

To evaluate the performance of the algorithms, we adopt common evaluation metrics for multi-class classification.

Accuracy (ACC). Accuracy (ACC) measures the percentage of the sequences that are predicted correct.

Cross Entropy Loss. For a classifier with logits as output, the classification cross entropy loss is defined as

$$Loss(logit, class) = -logit[class] + log(\sum_{j=1}^{C} exp(logit[j]))$$

, where *class* is the true class of the sample, and *logit* is a vector containing the logits for all the classes.

F1. To account for the potential imbalance between false-negative and false-positives, F1 measure computes the harmonic average of precision and recall. F1 is in the range of [0, 1] and the higher, the better predictive power. In the case of multi-class classification, we compute for each class an F1 measure, and then use the average of these F1s as the final metric.

Cohen's kappa. Cohen's kappa is a statistical that measures the inter-rater agreement between two classification output, defined as

$$\kappa = 1 - \frac{1 - p_o}{1 - p_e}$$

, where p_o is the accuracy we mentioned above, and p_e is the probability of agreement by chance. A perfect agreement will have $\kappa = 1$, and $\kappa < 0$ indicates a no agreement other than by chance.

4.6 Results & Discussion

We can see that Bag-of-Words classification techniques fail to capture the causal inference in our case, giving a poor classification performance. By examining the classification output, the classifier simply outputs the class that has the highest frequency, thus resulting in an identical output in all runs. This most likely results from the feature extraction process, where Bag-of-Words only consider the frequency of words.

Between the shallow classifiers and CNN, we can see that CNN obtained the highest classification accuracy, and the lowest loss with dynamic evaluation configuration, beating all other models with lowest variance.

Models with dynamic neural network structure in training and testing phase have a varied performance, and in the case of CNN and LR, it has the benefit of improving classification performance slightly, while in SVM, the benefit is not observed.

Early stopping as a regularization decrease the number of batches from about 21000 to about 9000 in all three models, saving almost

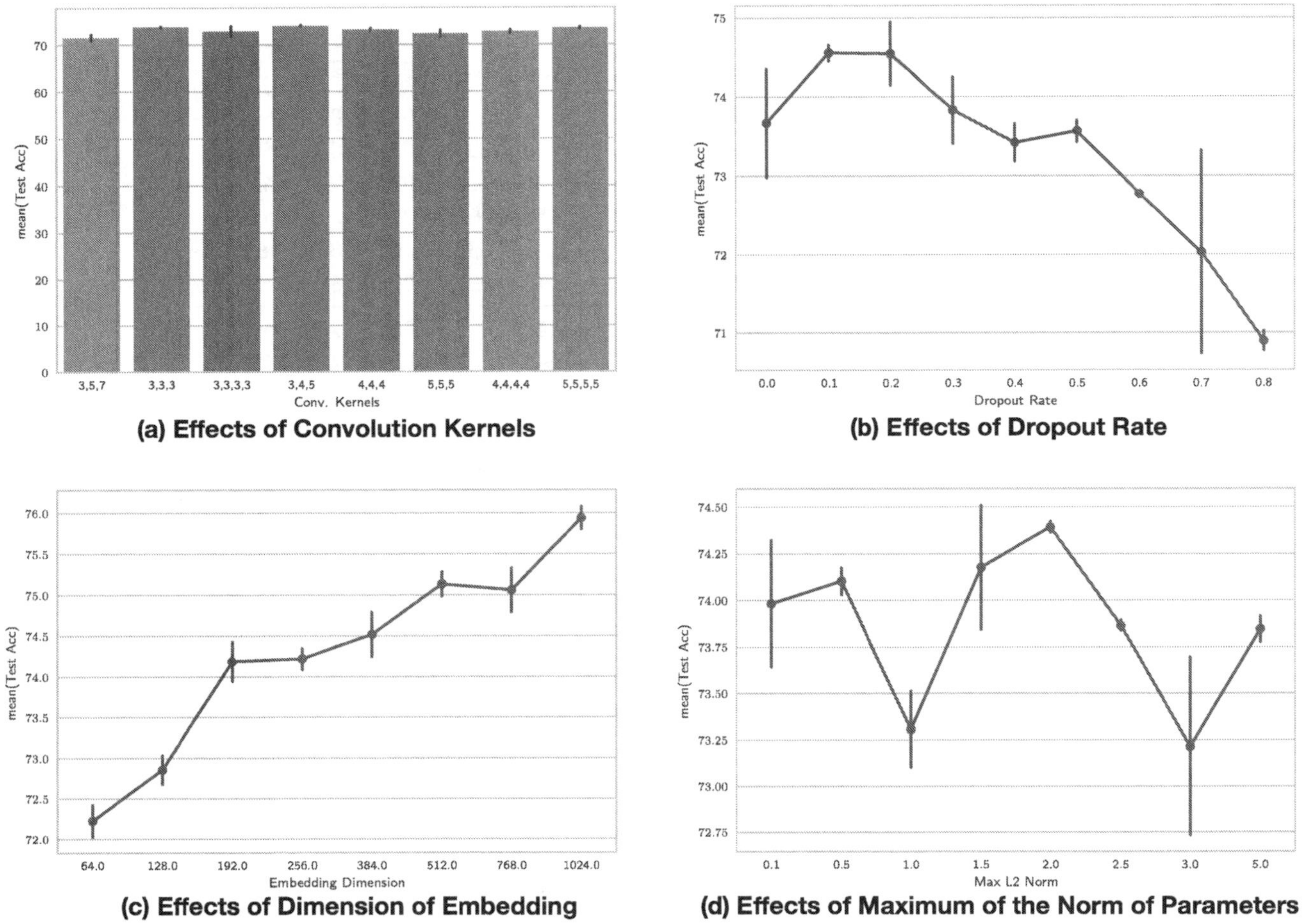

Figure 3: *Parameter Analysis.* We varied several key parameters of the CNN model and overall, the scale or the pattern of influence is not clearly shown from our experiments. The Y-axis is the accuracy on test sets with error bars and X-axis is the parameter we analyzed.

half of the running time, however, most of models with early stopping have a worse performance than the ones without early stopping, indicating that simply comparing development set training accuracy might not be a sufficient criterion for model overfitting, but just the oscillation behavior in the local minima region.

While some algorithms present performance in terms of accuracy and loss, all algorithms perform poorly evaluated with Cohen-Kappa's and microF1, mainly because of the fact that we are dealing with an extreme large number of classes. Take microF1 as an example, it's an average of the F1 value for each of the classes. For some of the classes, it may only have one or two samples, if the algorithm predicts these few samples wrong, its precision will be zero, thus a zero F1 score, significantly decreasing the final averaged microF1. In future, it may be of interest to design algorithms that can achieve high F1 in such classification case, as classification with extremely large number of classes itself is an interesting research question.

4.7 Parameter Analysis

Deep learning models have seemingly a large number of parameters to tune, in our case, such as the convolution kernels, the maximum norm, the dropout rate, and the dimension of embedding. Here we briefly show the effect of varying these parameters on the final prediction accuracy.

The base model is the standard static version of CNN, and we vary these four parameters, and plot the prediction accuracy on the test set with standard deviation as error bars.

From the figure, we can see that although there are several parameters to set, with a good model architecture, the specific values of these parameters don't influence the final outcome much. Except with the dimension of embedding medical conditions, we found that as the size of embedding dimension increases, the test performance slightly increases.

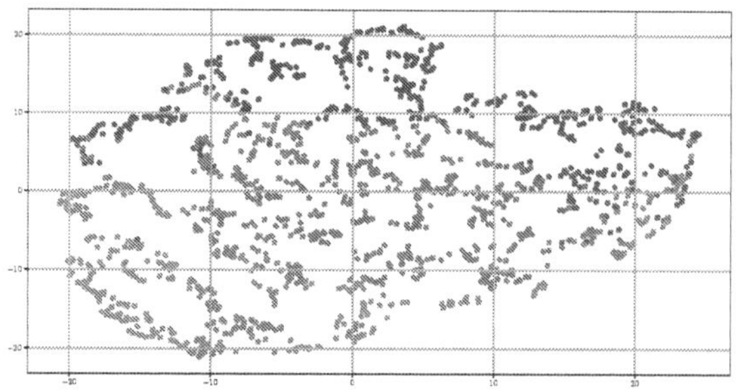

Figure 4: Embedding Visualization. After dimension reduction with kernel PCA, and t-SNE visualization, we plot the embeddings of medical conditions. We label the points with colors using the clustering results on the original embeddings. We can see the embedding vectors are scattered in the 2 dimensional data, and nicely clustered in five groups.

4.8 Analyzing Embeddings of Medical Conditions

One side-product of our model is the distributed representations of medical conditions, which we visually present in Fig. 4, using t-Distributed Stochastic Neighbor Embedding (t-SNE) [49] following a dimension reduction using kernal PCA to a three dimensional space.

The color of these dimension reduced points are obtained by running K-means clustering the embedding matrix of size (1610, 128), with number of clusters set to 5. We can see the embedding vectors are scattered in the 2 dimensional data, and nicely clustered in five groups.

To understand the embedding better, we also show some of the clustering results, with top conditions in each cluster 5. We conjecture the embedding of medical conditions reflect two characteristics, the likelihood of each condition causing death, and the physiological relationship between them, so we may not see a very clear pattern of the clustering results. For example, cluster 5 mainly consists of circulatory related conditions, while cluster 2 contains a few more severe diseases.

5 INTERPRETATION OF CAUSE IDENTIFICATION

Right now there are no golden standards as to explain the cause of death, and physicians mainly fill the death certificates speaking from their own perspective. The collection of death certificates from across the nation is thus a good resource to distill the knowledge in understanding cause of death, by training such supervised learning model. To help physicians really understand why our model gives predictions for causes given each sequences, we need to give proper interpretations for the black-box models, i.e., to provide relation between the input sequence and the final selected condition.

5.1 LIME-Local Interpretable Model-Agnostic Explanations

In this section, we briefly introduce the Local Interpretable Model-Agnostic Explanations model proposed [37], which can explain any type of black-box predication algorithms. To understand which parts of the input are contributing to the final prediction, the model perturbs the input around its neighbors, and analyzes the classifier's predictions on these perturbed instances with a sparse linear model. Then the weights from the linear model indicates how important the corresponding part is to the final predictions.

5.2 Case study

Here we showcase how the model will explain an unseen instance. we synthesize a patient history and the resulting sequence is

'I50,J44,I25,T82,Y83,I73,I10,J96,I64,K21,F17'

The explain model then outputs the top most likely cause of death as I25, as well as why certain conditions are more likely to cause the death, explained by the input conditions. We show such explanation in Fig. 6.

Because of the constraint of the data, we now can only pinpoint these ICD10 conditions, which admittedly, is still limited.

If we are to have a more complete dataset, where we have the complete history of patients, as well as the identified cause of death, we are then able to train a deep learning model predicting cause of death using the whole medical history. With the model and our explainer, we can understand in a greater detail about death cases. When a new patient is admitted to hospital, we can use such model to understand, which condition is the most likely cause of death, and which symptoms are contributing to this causality sequence.

Another interesting application of such interpretation model is that we can provide several predictive models for physicians, as well as their interpretations, and ask physicians to choose the one that matches human knowledge more. Running these tests will help us choose an accurate model that is more interpretable.

6 CONCLUSION & FUTURE WORK

In this paper, we showed how a modern deep learning architecture, CNN, can be adapted to identify the cause of death. The model shows significant improvement over the traditional baselines, and can handle even larger scale datasets than traditional methods. We also provide human understandable interpretation for the model, so that death reporting physicians.

The current work is limited by the dataset itself, and we are working

There are several ways our current work can be extended: First, we may deploy the model in a general EHR setting, where we can identify the most probable potential causes of death, so as to alert physicians and nurses to attend to more critical conditions. Second, there are medical ontologies specified by domain experts, which record all the viable causal relations between medical conditions. We can seek to integrate the guidance and constraint from these constraints into our models, and reach a model derived both from data and human knowledge. Moreover, it will be interesting to see how other deep learning architectures will perform in this task and other causal inference problems.

J69.X: Pneumonitis	J96.X: Respiratory failure, not elsewhere classified	I42.X: Cardiomyopathy	A41.X: Other sepsis
T42.X: Poisoning by, adverse effect of and underdosing of antiepileptic, sedative-hypnotic and antiparkinsonism drugs	K76.X: Other diseases of liver	G93.X: Other disorders of brain	I50.X: Heart failure
R26.X: Abnormalities of gait and mobility	G30.X: Alzheimer's disease	E83.X: Other disorders of fluid, electrolyte and acid-base balance	E88.X: Other and unspecified metabolic disorders
I69: Sequelae of cerebrovascular disease	T50.X: Poisoning by, adverse effect of and underdosing of diuretics and other and unspecified drugs, medicaments and biological substances	F03.X: Unspecified dementia	J80: Acute respiratory distress syndrome
J44.X: Other chronic obstructive pulmonary disease	F17.X: Nicotine dependence	C34.X: Malignant neoplasm of bronchus and lung	C15.X: Malignant neoplasm of esophagus
I49.X: Other cardiac arrhythmias	R13.X: Aphagia and dysphagia	E66.X: Overweight and obesity	R64: Cachexia
I10.X: Essential (primary) hypertension	R62.X: Lack of expected normal physiological development in childhood and adults	I11.X: Hypertensive heart disease	K65.X: Peritonitis
I99.X: Other and unspecified disorders of circulatory system	K92.X Other diseases of digestive system	M13.X: Other arthritis	C92: Myeloid leukemia

Figure 5: Clustering of Embedding. We perform K-means clustering with K=8 on the embeddings and plot for each of the cluster, the top conditions that are closest to its centroid.

Predicted Cause: I25 Chronic ischemic heart disease			Predicted Cause: J44 Other chronic obstructive pulmonary disease			Predicted Cause: E14 Unspecified diabetes mellitus		
I25	Chronic ischemic heart disease	4.90	J44	Other chronic obstructive pulmonary disease	4.39	J44	Other chronic obstructive pulmonary disease	-1.1
I50	Heart failure	0.68	T82	Complications of cardiac and vascular prosthetic devices, implants and grafts	-1.11	I25	Chronic ischemic heart disease	0.99
T82	Complications of cardiac and vascular prosthetic devices, implants and grafts	-0.64	I25	Chronic ischemic heart disease	-0.91	I50	Heart failure	-0.15
I25	Other chronic obstructive pulmonary disease	-0.34	I50	Heart failure	-0.19	T82	Complications of cardiac and vascular prosthetic devices, implants and grafts	-0.007

Figure 6: Interpretation. We use LIME on our CNN, and obtain the interpretation of the model for top three likely causes of death. For each of the likely cause, we show the contribution of each input medical condition to the final condition, where the absolute values indicate the scale of the contribution, and the sign indicates a positive or negative contribution.

ACKNOWLEDGEMENT

This work was supported in part by grants from the National Center for Advancing Translational Sciences of the National Institutes of Health (NIH) under Award UL1TR000454, National Science Foundation Award NSF1651360, the US Department of Health and Human Services (HHS) Centers for Disease Control and Prevention (CDC) HHSD2002015F62550B, and Microsoft Research and Hewlett Packard. The content is solely the responsibility of the authors and does not necessarily represent the official views of the National Institutes of Health nor National Science Foundation. The authors thank Paula Braun and Mark Braunstein for their valuable insights on the project, as well as helpful comments from Ying Sha and Janani Venugopalan.

REFERENCES

[1] Ralph B Agostino. 1998. Tutorial in biostatistics: propensity score methods for bias reduction in the comparison of a treatment to a non-randomized control group. *Stat Med* 17, 19 (1998), 2265–2281.
[2] Kenneth A Bollen and J Scott Long. 1993. *Testing structural equation models.* Vol. 154. Sage.
[3] David Maxwell Chickering. 2002. Optimal structure identification with greedy search. *Journal of machine learning research* 3, Nov (2002), 507–554.
[4] Emerging Risk Factors Collaboration and others. 2011. Diabetes mellitus, fasting glucose, and risk of cause-specific death. *N Engl J Med* 2011, 364 (2011), 829–841.
[5] Jia Deng, Wei Dong, Richard Socher, Li-Jia Li, Kai Li, and Li Fei-Fei. 2009. Imagenet: A large-scale hierarchical image database. In *Computer Vision and Pattern Recognition, 2009. CVPR 2009. IEEE Conference on.* IEEE, 248–255.
[6] Cícero Nogueira Dos Santos and Maira Gatti. 2014. Deep Convolutional Neural Networks for Sentiment Analysis of Short Texts.. In *COLING.* 69–78.
[7] Andre Esteva, Brett Kuprel, Roberto A Novoa, Justin Ko, Susan M Swetter, Helen M Blau, and Sebastian Thrun. 2017. Dermatologist-level classification of skin cancer with deep neural networks. *Nature* 542, 7639 (2017), 115–118.

[8] PyTorch Group. 2017. PyTorch: Tensors and Dynamic neural networks in Python with strong GPU acceleration. http://www.pytorch.org. (2017). Accessed: 2017-04-21.

[9] Geoffrey E Hinton, Simon Osindero, and Yee-Whye Teh. 2006. A fast learning algorithm for deep belief nets. *Neural computation* 18, 7 (2006), 1527–1554.

[10] Andreas Holzinger and Igor Jurisica. 2014. Knowledge discovery and data mining in biomedical informatics: The future is in integrative, interactive machine learning solutions. In *Interactive knowledge discovery and data mining in biomedical informatics*. Springer, 1–18.

[11] Baotian Hu, Zhengdong Lu, Hang Li, and Qingcai Chen. 2014. Convolutional neural network architectures for matching natural language sentences. In *Advances in neural information processing systems*. 2042–2050.

[12] Sergey Ioffe and Christian Szegedy. 2015. Batch normalization: Accelerating deep network training by reducing internal covariate shift. *arXiv preprint arXiv:1502.03167* (2015).

[13] Robert A Israel, Harry M Rosenberg, and Lester R Curtin. 1986. Analytical potential for multiple cause-of-death data. *American journal of epidemiology* 124, 2 (1986), 161–81.

[14] Shuiwang Ji, Wei Xu, Ming Yang, and Kai Yu. 2013. 3D convolutional neural networks for human action recognition. *IEEE transactions on pattern analysis and machine intelligence* 35, 1 (2013), 221–231.

[15] Hanyu Jiang, Hang Wu, and May D Wang. 2017. A Topic Model View on Causes of Death in the United States, 1999 to 2014. In *Biomedical and Health Informatics (BHI), 2017 IEEE-EMBS International Conference on*. IEEE.

[16] AA Khorana, CW Francis, E Culakova, NM Kuderer, and GH Lyman. 2007. Thromboembolism is a leading cause of death in cancer patients receiving outpatient chemotherapy. *Journal of Thrombosis and Haemostasis* 5, 3 (2007), 632–634.

[17] Yoon Kim. 2014. Convolutional neural networks for sentence classification. *arXiv preprint arXiv:1408.5882* (2014).

[18] Diederik Kingma and Jimmy Ba. 2014. Adam: A method for stochastic optimization. *arXiv preprint arXiv:1412.6980* (2014).

[19] Samantha Kleinberg and George Hripcsak. 2011. A review of causal inference for biomedical informatics. *Journal of biomedical informatics* 44, 6 (2011), 1102–1112.

[20] Alex Krizhevsky, Ilya Sutskever, and Geoffrey E Hinton. 2012. Imagenet classification with deep convolutional neural networks. In *Advances in neural information processing systems*. 1097–1105.

[21] Siwei Lai, Liheng Xu, Kang Liu, and Jun Zhao. 2015. Recurrent Convolutional Neural Networks for Text Classification.. In *AAAI*, Vol. 333. 2267–2273.

[22] Joy E Lawn, Simon Cousens, Jelka Zupan, Lancet Neonatal Survival Steering Team, and others. 2005. 4 million neonatal deaths: when? Where? Why? *The lancet* 365, 9462 (2005), 891–900.

[23] Yann LeCun, Yoshua Bengio, and others. 1995. Convolutional networks for images, speech, and time series. *The handbook of brain theory and neural networks* 3361, 10 (1995), 1995.

[24] Jonathan Long, Evan Shelhamer, and Trevor Darrell. 2015. Fully convolutional networks for semantic segmentation. In *Proceedings of the IEEE Conference on Computer Vision and Pattern Recognition*. 3431–3440.

[25] Junhua Mao, Wei Xu, Yi Yang, Jiang Wang, Zhiheng Huang, and Alan Yuille. 2014. Deep captioning with multimodal recurrent neural networks (m-rnn). *arXiv preprint arXiv:1412.6632* (2014).

[26] Lucie McCoy, Matthew Redelings, Frank Sorvillo, and Paul Simon. 2005. A multiple cause-of-death analysis of asthma mortality in the United States, 1990–2001. *Journal of Asthma* 42, 9 (2005), 757–763.

[27] Alexander Melamed and Frank J Sorvillo. 2009. The burden of sepsis-associated mortality in the United States from 1999 to 2005: an analysis of multiple-cause-of-death data. *Critical Care* 13, 1 (2009), R28.

[28] Tomas Mikolov, Ilya Sutskever, Kai Chen, Greg S Corrado, and Jeff Dean. 2013. Distributed representations of words and phrases and their compositionality. In *Advances in neural information processing systems*. 3111–3119.

[29] Volodymyr Mnih, Koray Kavukcuoglu, David Silver, Alex Graves, Ioannis Antonoglou, Daan Wierstra, and Martin Riedmiller. 2013. Playing atari with deep reinforcement learning. *arXiv preprint arXiv:1312.5602* (2013).

[30] Pekka K Mölsä, RJ Marttila, and UK Rinne. 1986. Survival and cause of death in Alzheimer's disease and multi-infarct dementia. *Acta Neurologica Scandinavica* 74, 2 (1986), 103–107.

[31] Stephen L Morgan and Christopher Winship. 2014. *Counterfactuals and causal inference*. Cambridge University Press.

[32] Bengt Muthén. 1984. A general structural equation model with dichotomous, ordered categorical, and continuous latent variable indicators. *Psychometrika* 49, 1 (1984), 115–132.

[33] NCHS. 2017. Mortality Data, Vital Statistics NCHS' Multiple Cause of Death Data, 1959 to 2015. (2017). http://www.nber.org/data/vital-statistics-mortality-data-multiple-cause-of-death.html

[34] Judea Pearl. 2009. *Causality*. Cambridge university press.

[35] F. Pedregosa, G. Varoquaux, A. Gramfort, V. Michel, B. Thirion, O. Grisel, M. Blondel, P. Prettenhofer, R. Weiss, V. Dubourg, J. Vanderplas, A. Passos, D. Cournapeau, M. Brucher, M. Perrot, and E. Duchesnay. 2011. Scikit-learn: Machine Learning in Python. *Journal of Machine Learning Research* 12 (2011), 2825–2830.

[36] Matthew D Redelings, Matthew Wise, and Frank Sorvillo. 2007. Using multiple cause-of-death data to investigate associations and causality between conditions listed on the death certificate. *American journal of epidemiology* 166, 1 (2007), 104–108.

[37] Marco Tulio Ribeiro, Sameer Singh, and Carlos Guestrin. 2016. Why Should I Trust You?: Explaining the Predictions of Any Classifier. In *Proceedings of the 22nd ACM SIGKDD International Conference on Knowledge Discovery and Data Mining*. ACM, 1135–1144.

[38] Paul R Rosenbaum and Donald B Rubin. 1983. The central role of the propensity score in observational studies for causal effects. *Biometrika* (1983), 41–55.

[39] Donald B Rubin. 1974. Estimating causal effects of treatments in randomized and nonrandomized studies. *Journal of educational Psychology* 66, 5 (1974), 688.

[40] Donald B Rubin. 2005. Causal inference using potential outcomes: Design, modeling, decisions. *J. Amer. Statist. Assoc.* 100, 469 (2005), 322–331.

[41] Donald B Rubin. 2006. *Matched sampling for causal effects*. Cambridge University Press.

[42] Donald B Rubin. 2007. The design versus the analysis of observational studies for causal effects: parallels with the design of randomized trials. *Statistics in medicine* 26, 1 (2007), 20–36.

[43] AD Sadovnick, K Eisen, GC Ebers, and DW Paty. 1991. Cause of death in patients attending multiple sclerosis clinics. *Neurology* 41, 8 (1991), 1193–1193.

[44] Peter Spirtes, Clark N Glymour, and Richard Scheines. 2000. *Causation, prediction, and search*. MIT press.

[45] Nitish Srivastava, Geoffrey E Hinton, Alex Krizhevsky, Ilya Sutskever, and Ruslan Salakhutdinov. 2014. Dropout: a simple way to prevent neural networks from overfitting. *Journal of Machine Learning Research* 15, 1 (2014), 1929–1958.

[46] Elizabeth A Stuart. 2010. Matching methods for causal inference: A review and a look forward. *Statistical science: a review journal of the Institute of Mathematical Statistics* 25, 1 (2010), 1.

[47] Qiuling Suo, Hongfei Xue, Jing Gao, and Aidong Zhang. 2016. Risk Factor Analysis Based on Deep Learning Models. In *Proceedings of the 7th ACM International Conference on Bioinformatics, Computational Biology, and Health Informatics*. ACM, 394–403.

[48] Ilya Sutskever, James Martens, and Geoffrey E Hinton. 2011. Generating text with recurrent neural networks. In *Proceedings of the 28th International Conference on Machine Learning (ICML-11)*. 1017–1024.

[49] Laurens Van der Maaten. 2014. t-distributed stochastic neighbor embedding (t-SNE). (2014).

[50] Florian Wolf, Tomaso Poggio, and Pawan Sinha. 2006. Human document classification using bags of words. (2006).

Automated Breast Cancer Diagnosis Using Deep Learning and Region of Interest Detection (BC-DROID)

Richard Platania*
Louisiana State University
Baton Rouge, Louisiana 70803
rplata1@lsu.edu

Shayan Shams*
Louisiana State University
Baton Rouge, Louisiana 70803
sshams2@cct.lsu.edu

Seungwon Yang
Louisiana State University
Baton Rouge, Louisiana 70803
seungwonyang@lsu.edu

Jian Zhang
Louisiana State University
Baton Rouge, Louisiana 70803
zhang@csc.lsu.edu

Kisung Lee
Louisiana State University
Baton Rouge, Louisiana 70803
lee@csc.lsu.edu

Seung-Jong Park
Louisiana State University
Baton Rouge, Louisiana 70803
sjpark@cct.lsu.edu

ABSTRACT

Detection of suspicious regions in mammogram images and the subsequent diagnosis of these regions remains a challenging problem in the medical world. There still exists an alarming rate of misdiagnosis of breast cancer. This results in both over treatment through incorrect positive diagnosis of cancer and under treatment through overlooked cancerous masses. Convolutional neural networks have shown strong applicability to various image datasets, enabling detailed features to be learned from the data and, as a result, the ability to classify these images at extremely low error rates. In order to overcome the difficulty in diagnosing breast cancer from mammogram images, we propose our framework for automated breast cancer detection and diagnosis, called BC-DROID, which provides automated region of interest detection and diagnosis using convolutional neural networks. BC-DROID first pretrains based on physician-defined regions of interest in mammogram images. It then trains based on the full mammogram image. The resulting network is able to detect and classify regions of interest as cancerous or benign in one step. We demonstrate the accuracy of our framework's ability to both locate the regions of interest as well as diagnose them. Our framework achieves a detection accuracy of up to 90% and a classification accuracy of 93.5% (AUC of 92.315%). To the best of our knowledge, this is the first work enabling both automated detection and diagnosis of these areas in one step from full mammogram images. Using our framework's website, a user can upload a single mammogram image, visualize suspicious regions, and receive the automated diagnoses of these regions.

KEYWORDS

mammogram; breast cancer; deep learning; automated diagnosis; convolutional neural network; object detection

*These authors contributed equally to this work.

Permission to make digital or hard copies of all or part of this work for personal or classroom use is granted without fee provided that copies are not made or distributed for profit or commercial advantage and that copies bear this notice and the full citation on the first page. Copyrights for components of this work owned by others than ACM must be honored. Abstracting with credit is permitted. To copy otherwise, or republish, to post on servers or to redistribute to lists, requires prior specific permission and/or a fee. Request permissions from permissions@acm.org.
ACM-BCB'17, August 20-23, 2017, Boston, MA, USA.
© 2017 ACM. 978-1-4503-4722-8/17/08...$15.00
DOI: http://dx.doi.org/10.1145/3107411.3107484

1 INTRODUCTION

Breast cancer is the most common and fatal cancer among adult women [36]. According to National Cancer Institute, approximately one in eight women will develop an invasive form of this cancer at some point in their lives [26]. Frequent screenings through mammograms can help detect early signs of breast cancer. However, there is still difficulty in recognizing troublesome areas, and applying a correct diagnosis, through these images alone. For example, breast cancer overdiagnosis is estimated to be 22~31% of all diagnosed breast cancers, costing several billions of dollars annually in healthcare spending [28]. In order to alleviate the misdiagnosis rate of mammogram screenings, further image analysis must be performed in order to provide physicians with an aid in diagnosis.

Existing methods for breast cancer detection and diagnosis have improved upon physician-only detection and diagnosis. Current works can be divided into two categories. The first focuses upon mass detection or segmentation in mammogram images. This aids the physician by pinpointing potential suspicious regions in the mammogram that may have been overlooked. While typical computer-aided detection (CAD) has shown little to no improvement in this category [22], more advanced machine learning and deep learning techniques have shown promise towards the detection and segmentation tasks [7–10, 17, 29]. The second category aims to diagnose breast cancer from mammogram images (or the masses). Some works have utilized more traditional machine learning methods for this task [38], while others have moved towards deep learning [3–5, 11, 23]. However, existing works have failed to combine these two tasks into one tool that simultaneously provides region of interest detection and diagnosis of mammogram images with visualization.

In order to further automate and improve upon the detection and diagnosis of breast cancer, we propose an automated diagnosis tool for mammograms, called BC-DROID, that uses deep learning for two outcomes; it detects and localizes any regions containing abnormalities and provides a diagnosis based on these regions. A simplified workflow diagram of BC-DROID is given in Figure 1. Given any mammogram image, our tool will provide visualization of regions of interest and the resulting diagnosis. As a result, our unique contribution consists of using a single model to both detect regions of interest and diagnose them, from complete mammogram

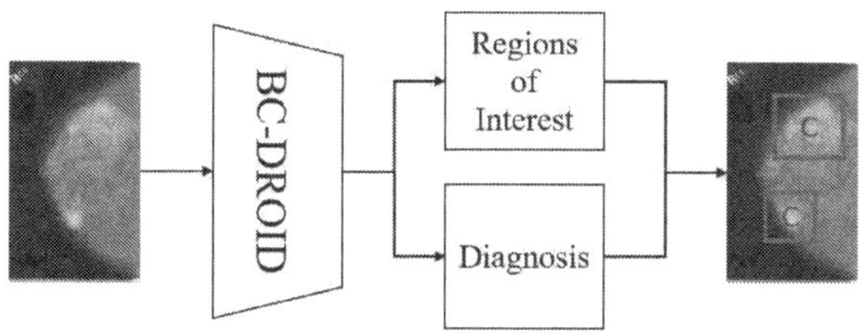

Figure 1: A diagram depicting the process of BC-DROID. Given a single mammogram image, it will detect regions of interest and diagnose them as cancer or benign.

images. The resulting model is made available through an efficient, easy-to-use website.

The remainder of the paper is organized as follows. First, we give some background of breast cancer screening with mammography and convolutional neural networks for object detection and classification. Next, we describe related works. Following, we describe our methodology, which includes details regarding our dataset, convolutional neural network model, and automated diagnosis tool. We then give results showing the accuracy of our work and its ability to detect and diagnose abnormalities in mammograms. Finally, we conclude and discuss future works.

2 BACKGROUND

2.1 Breast Cancer Screening with Mammography

Since its inception in 1913, mammography has been used for early detection and diagnosis of breast cancer by radiologists. It gained a wide acceptance by incorporating general purpose x-ray tubes, films, and techniques such as breast compression and use of fine-grain intensifying screens in the 1950s. Follow-up studies during this time showed a significant reduction in breast cancer mortality rate by almost one-third of women who had mammography screening [14, 37]. Mammography techniques improved significantly with the introduction of screen-film mammography (SFM) and magnification mammography in the 1970s. SFM, which is the gold standard for breast cancer detection, allowed rapid processing, shorter exposure to radiation, and sharper high contrast images for increased 'see-through' examination. FDA approved digital mammography (DM) systems in 2000 for efficient storing and analysis of mammograms using computers. It is reported that the overall diagnostic accuracy between SFM and DM was similar. However, DM showed significantly higher accuracy in women under 50 with dense breasts, and lower recall rate than SFM [24, 30].

Other screening technologies such as untrasound and breast magnetic resonance imaging (MRI) have been adopted in the 2000s as adjunctive screening tools along with a traditional mammography for women who have higher risk of developing breast cancer. Ultrasound screening was effective in women who have dense breast tissue and negative mammograms. MRI screening showed higher sensitivity for women with high-risk of developing hereditary breast cancer [19, 21]. However, it was also reported that both technologies-untrasonic and MRI-yielded high false-positive rates as well [21].

Recently, the 3D mammography technology, also known as digital breast tomosynthesis, emerged. It facilitated layer-by-layer examination of the breast, which enabled viewing of fine details that might have been unrecognizable in traditional mammograms. Further, the integrated 2D and 3D mammography increased cancer detection rate by 51% across all ages compared to that of 2D mammography, at the same time reducing false positive recalls [6, 16]. Multiple institutions such as Society of Breast Imaging, American Cancer Society, and American College of Radiology recommend a periodic screening for breast cancer (e.g., annual screening from age 40 for women at average risk, and age between 25 and 30 for women with BRCA1 or BRCA2 mutation carriers or with family history of breast cancer). However, controversy exists about the starting age of periodic mammography [18, 21].

2.2 Convolutional Neural Networks

Convolutional neural networks begin with (typically) at least several convolution layers and end with one or more fully connected layers. Between the convolution layers often lies pooling layers that perform subsampling on the data to reduce training overheads. Sometimes, between the convolution layers, there are also normalization layers, but they have not seen significant usage in recently developed models. The entire network will take as input an image of size (h,w,c), where h is the height, w is the width, and c is the number of channels in the image. These channels typically refer to different colors (RGB), so typically c has a value of three. Each convolution layer has many filters, the size of which is smaller than the input, that independently perform the convolutions across the image. These filters learn patterns across the entire image. As the input is passed through the network, the convolution layers perform convolutions on the image.

Because CNNs assume that the input is an image, they have several important structural changes compared to a traditional neural network. Neurons in neighboring layers exhibit a local connectivity pattern, ensuring that filters learn to detect patterns based on spatial locality. Many filters are stacked, producing a 3D volume of neurons that is capable of detecting many different patterns. Each filter scans the entire image for patterns. However, in order for a filter to detect a pattern across the whole image, weight sharing is used. This ensures that the model does not need to individually learn to detect a certain pattern at different positions in the image. Instead, a filter learns a certain pattern that it can detect across the whole image.

3 RELATED WORKS

3.1 Mammogram-based Classification Tasks

Deep learning has shown substantial applicability to medical image analysis in recent years. Furthermore, many of these efforts have been towards utilizing mammography data for classification tasks. Peterson et. al. and Kallenberg et. al. utilized unlabeled mammogram images and unsupervised deep learning for the classification of breast tissue segmentation, percentage mammographic density (PMD) score, and mammographic texture (MT) score [17, 29]. They employ a convolutional neural network (CNN) and sparse autoencoder for these tasks. As a result of this unsupervised learning, they aimed to better determine future cancer risk in patients. Other similar works have made use of CNNs for classification of regions of interest or mass lesions in mammograms. Arevalo et. al. use supervised learning with CNNs for representation learning and classification of breast mass lesions as benign or malignant [3, 4]. In a similar manner, Lévy et. al. trained a CNN for classification of breast mass lesions [23]. Abbas also utilizes deep learning for the classification of breast mass from predefined regions of interest [2]. Some works still make use of more traditional methods of image analysis, such as the work of Zhang et. al., which uses Fourier transforms and principal component analysis, followed by a support vector machine (SVM), to classify regions of interest [38]. While these works focus on classifying cancer risk based on full images, they do not detect and localize masses in the image. However, there exists the issue that these works rely on a predetermined region of interest, whereas our work is capable of processing the entire image with automated extraction of these regions. Two additional works leverage multiple image views, as seen in Figure 2, by training multiple CNNs (one for each view). Carreiro et. al. uses a CNN that has been pretrained on the ImageNet dataset [33] to estimate the risk of a patient developing breast cancer[5]. Since the images contained in the ImageNet dataset are vastly different than those in mammogram datsets, it is better to pretrain a model based on mammogram data. Our work pretrains the CNN based on regions of interest. Similar to the previously mentioned work, Geras et. al. classify based on risk, but instead use high-resolution images the network is not pretrained [11]. Our work, unlike these multi-view mammogram works, does not require multiple views of the breast for performing detection and classification.

3.2 Region of Interest Detection in Mammograms

Region of interest detection requires using the entire mammogram image. Processing the entire image is a much more challenging process. While the regions of interest may only be a few hundred pixels on any side, the whole image tends to have thousands of pixels. However, it is important to consider these full images since, in order to fully automate the diagnosis process, the regions of interest should be required to be predefined by an expert source (i.e., a physician). To date, there are a limited number of deep learning related works that utilize the entire mammogram image. Dhungel et. al. extended their previously mentioned works to include a deep belief network (DBM) capable of generating candidate regions of interest [7]. Unlike our work, which only looks at the image once, they require processing multiple scales of the same image, which further increases the complexity and time involved in analysis. Furthermore, their work focuses solely on the detection of masses and ignores the classification of these masses as cancerous or benign. Also operating on the full image, Ertosum et. al. train two CNNs [10]. The first CNN classifies a mammogram as containing or not containing a mass. Following this, the second CNN identifies and localizes the mass. Similar to the previously mentioned work, they do not classify them as malignant or benign. Because of the computational challenges involved, works related to region of interest detection are limited. Unlike the other works, BC-DROID is able to detect regions of interest and classify them from full mammogram images.

3.3 Convolutional Neural Networks for Object Detection and Classification

Convolutional neural networks (CNN) have played a major role in both object detection and classification of image data. Their popularity has sparked an influx in their applicability to many domains. Additionally, competitions, such as ILSVRC [33], push deep learning experts towards development of newer, more impressive CNN models [20, 34, 35]. Of particular difficulty is object detection. In general, it requires more time and complexity to train a model for this task when compared to classification. This is because techniques for this task tend to revisit the image multiple times or explore multiple different scales of the image. Several works have been created with the goal of reducing the time and complexity of object detection [12, 13, 25, 31, 32].

For this work, we make use of the techniques described in the YOLO paper[31]. YOLO allows for object detection and classification while processing the image only once, as is implied by it's name, You Only Look Once. This significantly reduces the time required for our task. Since we are dealing with processing large-scale images through our web-based tool, speed is important.

4 METHODS

4.1 Mammogram Data

This work uses the Image Retrieval in Medical Applications (IRMA) version of the Digital Database for Screening Mammography (DDSM) dataset, as well as some additional metadata provided directly by the original DDSM dataset [15, 27]. There are 2,620 cases, divided into three diagnoses: normal, benign, and cancer. Each case includes an overview file, four mammogram images, and zero to four overlay files. The overview file provides information such as the date of the experiment, age of the patient, and list of the image files. Each overlay file is associated with one image. It describes the number of abnormalities found in the image as well as the shape and location of the abnormalities. If there are no abnormalities in an image, there is no associated overlay file. Examples of the mammogram images are provided in Figure 2. It is worth noting the low quality of some images, as is visible in Figure 2(d). In total, there are 10,480 images, many of which have a size around 3,000 x 5,000 pixels. For further information regarding the DDSM dataset, see the official website[1].

4.2 Automated Regions-of-Interest Detection and Diagnosis using Mammogram

4.2.1 Data preprocessing. There were several steps taken to preprocess data and improve the training process. In order to remove unnecessary noise, such as the words visible in Figure 2, much of the black portion of the images was trimmed. This was done by flipping all right view images to left and trimming from right to left while the mean pixel value remained near zero (black). Several more common approaches were taken to reduce overfitting the model and improve overall accuracy. For example, each image was rotated five times at random angles and randomly mirrored across the y-axis. Following this, for n pixels, each pixel p_i was normalized

[1]http://marathon.csee.usf.edu/Mammography/Database.html

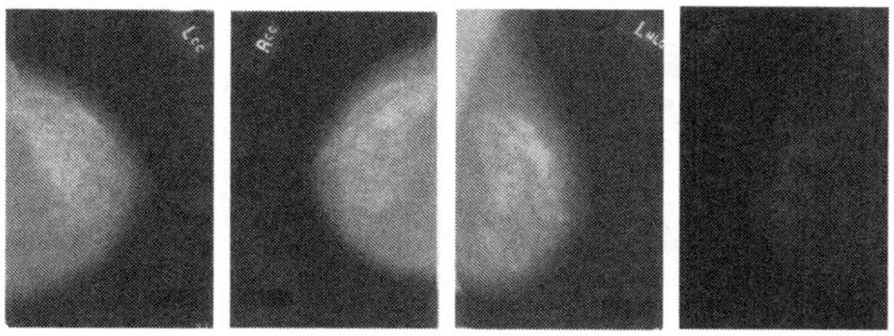

(a) LEFT_CC (b) RIGHT_CC (c) LEFT_MLO (d) RIGHT_MLO

Figure 2: Sample mammogram data from DDSM showing four different views of breast. Each figure may have noise as seen by the writing in the corners. Some images are also of low contrast, such as that seen in (d).

as follows:

$$p_i = p_i - \frac{\sum_{j=0}^{n} p_j}{n} \tag{1}$$

Note that it is important that the majority of unimportant, dark pixels were removed from the images prior to this step. Otherwise, they drastically affected the image mean and overall reduced the image quality.

Further processing was required for extracting the regions of interest from the mammograms for pretraining our model. To this end, the overlay files provided with the DDSM dataset were used. Since the regions of interest defined in these files take many shapes, we cropped the region such that the crop was the smallest possible square that contained the entire region. The extracted regions were then resized to 128 × 128 for pretraining.

4.2.2 Model for Region-of-Interest Detection and Diagnosis. We adapt the object-detection model proposed in YOLO [31] to identify region of interest (ROI) (and label the region as benign or cancer) for mammogram images. Our adapted model takes a mammogram image as input and outputs multiple predictions. In particular, we impose a $k \times k$ grid on the image. For each grid cell, the model predicts the following:

- A confidence value (c). It indicates the confidence that a region of interest (ROI) exists with respect to the grid cell. Similar to YOLO, we define the confidence to be the probability that the grid cell contains the center of a ROI, multiplied by the IOU (intersection over union) ratio of the ROI and the grid cell area.
- The coordinates (x and y) of the center of the ROI, relative to the grid cell. A grid cell is only responsible for the ROI whose center is inside the grid cell. Hence, $0 \leq x \leq 1$ and $0 \leq y \leq 1$.
- The width (w) and the height (h) of the ROI, relative to the size of the image.
- A class label vector (P). Because we consider diagnosis between two classes: benign and cancerous, the vector is of length 2, each element representing the probability of the corresponding class.

In summary, the model makes 7 predictions ($c, x, y, w, h, P[0], P[1]$) per grid cell. The total number of values predicted by the model is $7k^2$. Note that, the prediction for each of the values is based on the whole image, not the part of the image in the corresponding grid cell.

The deep neural network model for making these predictions has two main parts. The first part is a stack of 3 × 3 convolution layers, of which the first six are followed by 2 × 2 pooling layers. Convolution layers function as feature extractors that generate a high-level representation of the mammogram image and pooling layers provide invariance to small sequence shifts to the left or right and reduce the dimension of the input to the next layer. This CNN and its configuration are shown on the left in Figure 3. The second part is the last three fully connected layers. The last layer has $7k^2$ neurons and its outputs are the predictions described above. The full model is shown on the right side of Figure 3.

4.2.3 Pretraining CNN on regions of interest . After preprocessing the mammogram images, data augmentation and extracting the regions of interest, we generate 25,000 cropping of the area of interests and use them to pretrain the CNN part of the model. The pretraining process uses a modified version of the model, where the last fully connected layer is changed to have only two neurons. The modified model is trained to classify the cropping of the area of interests into two classes: benign or cancerous. After pretraining, the learned weights for the CNN part of the model are extracted and will be used as the initialization values for the CNN part in the main training process.

4.2.4 Training model on entire image. If a grid cell contains the center of a ROI, we say that the ROI is *presented* at that grid cell. Given an image in the training set, for each grid cell that has a ROI presented, we can calculate the true values for the predictions. Denote by $(\hat{c}, \hat{x}, \hat{y}, \hat{w}, \hat{h}, \hat{P})$ these true values. The goal of the training is to fit the predictions to the true values. Similar to YOLO [31], we use squared error in the fitting and for each grid cell i, we have the following loss functions:

$$\mathcal{L}_{coo}^{i} = \begin{cases} (x_i - \hat{x}_i)^2 + (y_i - \hat{y}_i)^2, & \text{ROI present} \\ 0, & \text{otherwise} \end{cases} \tag{2}$$

$$\mathcal{L}_{box}^{i} = \begin{cases} (\sqrt{w_i} - \sqrt{\hat{w}_i})^2 + (\sqrt{h_i} - \sqrt{\hat{h}_i})^2, & \text{ROI present} \\ 0, & \text{otherwise} \end{cases} \tag{3}$$

$$\mathcal{L}_{cls}^{i} = \begin{cases} \sum_j (P_i[j] - \hat{P}_i[j])^2, & \text{ROI present} \\ 0, & \text{otherwise} \end{cases} \tag{4}$$

These loss functions count prediction error only if a ROI is presented in the grid cell. Hence, the corresponding predictions are trained by the ROIs presented at that grid cell in the training dataset. If in a training example, the grid cell has no ROI, this example won't have any effect for training the above predictions for the cell. On the other hand, the empty case, i.e., grid cell with no ROI presented does affect the training of the confidence prediction for the cell:

$$\mathcal{L}_{cnf}^{i} = \begin{cases} (c_i - \hat{c}_i)^2, & \text{ROI present} \\ \beta(c_i - \hat{c}_i)^2, & \text{otherwise} \end{cases} \tag{5}$$

If there is a ROI at the grid cell i, $\hat{c}_i$ = IOU ratio of the ROI and the cell. If no ROI is presented, $\hat{c}_i = 0$. For any grid cell, there are many more

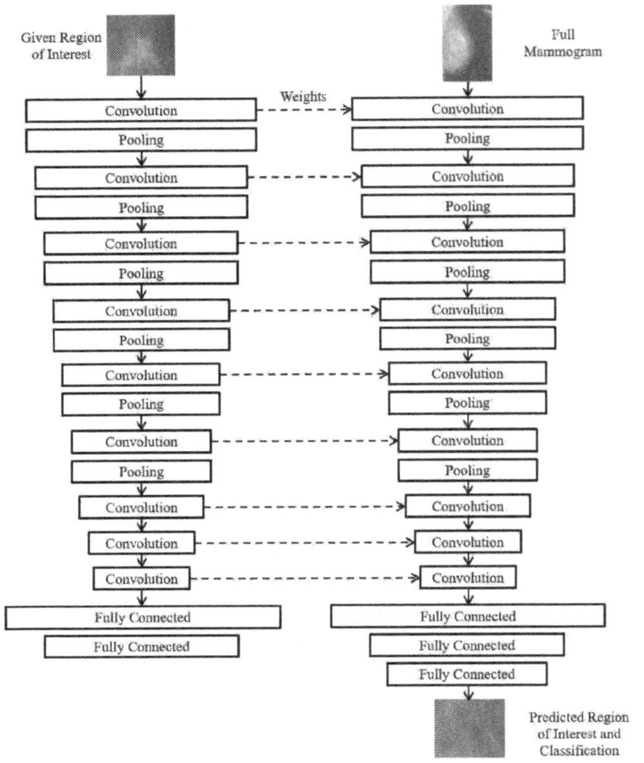

Figure 3: The left represents the pretraining of the model on the regions of interest. The weights from the convolutional layers are then used to initialize the model for training on the whole image.

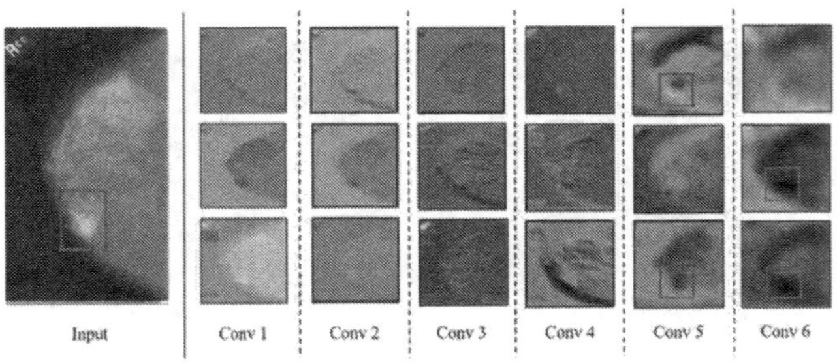

Figure 4: Activations of the first six convolution layers with respect to the given input image. The red rectangle indicates a region of interest. We can observe the convolution layers responding strongly to the region of interest, especially in the later convolution layers (Conv 5 and Conv 6).

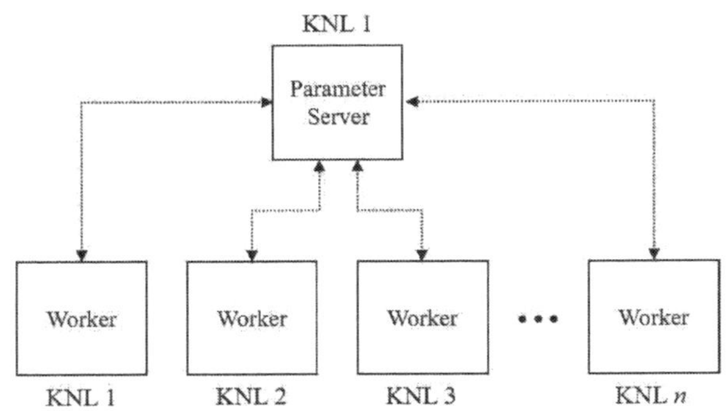

Figure 5: Our training architecture. We define one parameter server on the first Knight's Landing (KNL) node. More workers are defined based on the total number of KNL nodes.

training examples without ROI than examples with ROI. $0 < \beta < 1$ is used to balance the two cases in training.

The total loss sums up the above losses for each grid cell and then sums over all the grid cells:

$$\sum_{i=1}^{k^2} \alpha(\mathcal{L}_{coo}^i + \mathcal{L}_{box}^i) + \mathcal{L}_{cls}^i + \mathcal{L}_{cnf}^i \quad (6)$$

where α is a parameter similar to β that balances errors between location regression and the others. For our experiments, we found the best values for α and β to be 5 and 0.4, respectively.

To train the model, we minimize the total loss defined above by adjusting the neural network weights. The training uses whole mammogram images, not the ROI cropping. Stochastic gradient descent (SGD) is utilized for the minimization. The weights of the CNN part are initialized by the weights from pretraining. Figure 3 depicts the process of extracting the weights from the pretraining step and using them to initialize the CNN part in the main training. It is worth noting that the weights of the fully connected layers are initialized randomly, not by transferring those from the fully connected layers in the pretrained model.

4.2.5 Inference. To locate the ROI for a testing image, the model is applied to the image to obtain the prediction values (c, x, y, w, h, P) for each grid cell. Given a threshold τ, if $\max cP > \tau$ at a grid cell, then there is a ROI with location and size given by (x, y, w, h), and the class/diagnosis of the ROI is given by $\arg\max_i cP[i]$.

4.2.6 Hardware and software configuration. We used TensorFlow version one [1] for developing our model. Training was distributed among four Intel's Knight landings hosts (Intel Xeon Phi Processor 7230F (16GB, 1.30 GHz, 64 cores)) with one parameter server and four workers. An illustrated depiction of this setup is given in Figure 5. The batch size is 16 and the learning rate was increased from 10^{-4} to 10^{-3} for the first 20 epochs and then with 10^{-3} until 80 epochs. After that, we started decreasing the learning rate to 10^{-4} and then 10^{-5}.

4.2.7 Diagnosis of mammogram image through web-based application. In an effort to make our tool easily available and easy to use, it is available through our website[2]. An example screenshot of the site operating on a mammogram image is given in Figure 6. Since one of the aspect of this work is the applicability as a good assistant to physicians and radiologists, the network is designed to be fast even on a desktop. As a result, our network can process and infer a full mammogram image in 1.25 seconds on a desktop

[2]https://biglearning.cct.lsu.edu/

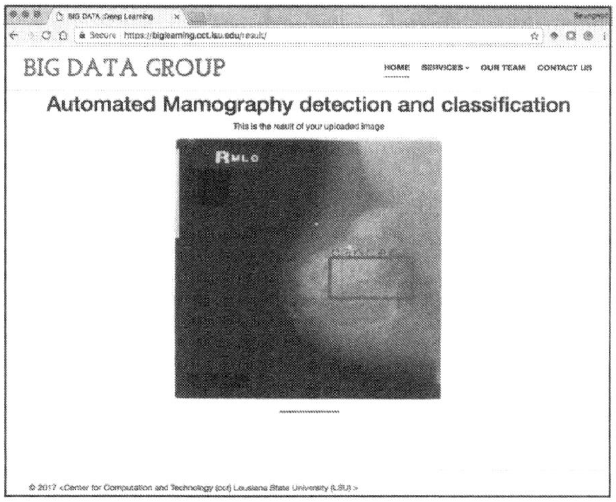

Figure 6: Screenshot of our website providing automated detection and diagnosis of mammogram image.

with 4 cores CPU and 16 GB of RAM, however since one goal is supporting data streaming, the model can scale up and scale out on GPUs. If there is a GPU available on the machine, our model will send the matrix and vector calculation to the available GPUs on the machine. It also is capable of having different parameter server and workers to scale out on different nodes. As a result, our network supports data streaming. The link is available, and the website will soon be available to the public, enabling researchers to stream their images and get the detection and diagnosis results in a very short time, since BC-DROID is supported by HPC platforms with multiple nodes and GPUs.

5 RESULTS

We present our results in two sections. First, we evaluate BC-DROID with respect to correctly detecting regions of interest in mammogram images. Then, we highlight the classification accuracy of these abnormal regions as cancerous or benign. Since to the best of our knowledge we are the first group doing mass classification and region of interest detection in one process, it is difficult to directly compare our detection results with previous works. Thus, for a fair comparison, we divide our result into two sections, detection and classification. We directly compare the classification results with other works. Since some of these works are using BIRADS score or using different data set, we chose the best accuracy score that they obtained for classification.

5.1 Region of Interest Detection

To measure how well our tool detects regions of interest in the images, we first define our accuracy metric. For detection accuracy we use the intersection of union (IOU) or The Jaccard index which is the percentage of overlap between our predicted region of interest and the actual region of interest. Given overlap IOU, which is the percentage of overlap between our predicted region of interest and the actual region of interest, and a threshold t, which defines

Table 1: Region of Interest detection accuracy with varying overlap percentage thresholds.

Overlap Threshold t	100%	75%	50%	25%
Accuracy a	53%	56%	84%	90%

Table 2: Classification results.

Specificity	Sensitivity	Accuracy	Precision	Recall
93%	94%	93.5%	93.39%	93%

the required value of o for correct detection, we can compute our accuracy a as follows:

$$a = \begin{cases} 1, & \text{if } IOU \geq t \\ IOU, & \text{otherwise} \end{cases} \tag{7}$$

In other words, if the percentage of overlap between the actual and predicted abnormal regions is above the defined threshold, we correctly detected the region for that particular threshold. Otherwise, if it is below the threshold, we used the calculated IOU score as accuracy score. Table 1 shows the accuracy results using this evaluation metric. When the required overlap between the actual and predicted regions is 100%, our tool has an accuracy of 53%. This score improves as we decrease the threshold. At 25% threshold, we get an accuracy of 90%. In practice, a threshold as low as 25% would still be indicative of the abnormal region in question.

For visualization of this region of interest detection process, we provide Figure 4. This displays the first six convolution layer activations with respect to an example input image. As expected, the earlier layers are very representative of the input image. The activations in the later layers, specifically the sixth, become much more sparse and localized. These localized activations become representative of the regions of interest in the original input. This process depicts our model properly learning to identify regions of interest. As it is shown in Figure 4, deeper CNN layers are concentrating on picking up features representing the region of interest. For better visualization we trace the region of interest for the input image.

We provide a further visualization in Figure 7. The provided mammogram image is an example of a cancer case. The left image depicts the region of interest as defined by the DDSM dataset. Note that the actual region of interest is not a rectangular shape. Instead, a rectangular box was drawn around the region such that it was minimal and fit the entire region. The image on the right shows our predicted region of interest. Both regions of interest (the actual and predicted) are indicative of the same region in the mammogram image.

5.2 Breast Cancer Classification

Here, we present our results concerning breast cancer classification. Table 2 summarizes our accuracy related results. Additionally, we provide Figure 8, which plots our ROC curve for breast cancer classification. The curve was drawn according to 100 different thresholds for classification. The AUC associated with this curve is

Table 3: Classification comparison with other works using AUC. Their best reported AUC for classification tasks using mammograms was used. If AUC was unavailable, accuracy is used instead.

Paper	Classification Task	Best Reported Result
[17]	Mammographic Texture	61% AUC
	Mammographic Density	62% AUC
[10]	Mass or No Mass	85% Accuracy
[29]	Mammographic Texture	70% AUC
	Breast Cancer Diagnosis	60% AUC
[3, 4]	Breast Cancer Diagnosis	86% AUC
[11]	Breast Cancer Diagnosis	76.5% AUC
[23]	Breast Cancer Diagnosis	92.9% Accuracy
[2]	Breast Cancer Diagnosis	91% AUC
BC-DROID	Breast Cancer Diagnosis	92.315% AUC

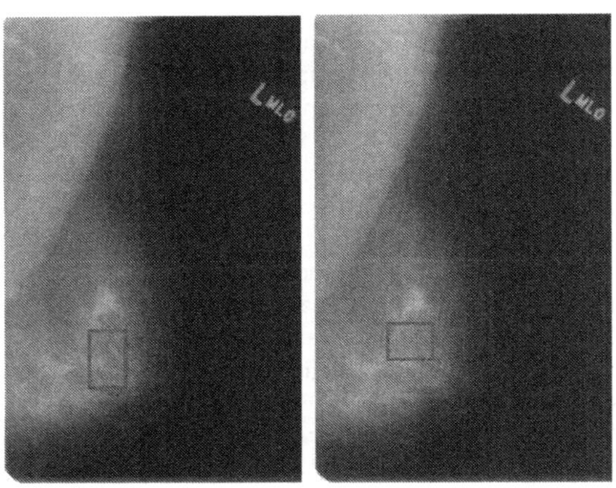

(a) Actual (b) Predicted

Figure 7: A comparison between the actual region of interest, as dictated by a physician, and the region of interest predicted by our automated diagnosis tool.

92.315%. To our best knowledge, these results are the highest of any similar works relating to classification of mammograms as cancer or benign.

We compare our results with related works in Table 3. We reported other works' AUC if available. Otherwise, we substituted in classification accuracy. Since many works differ in classification task, we briefly describe the task of each work in the second column. Tasks included either classifying mammographic texture score (MT), classifying mammographic density (MD) score, determining if an image contains a mass, or diagnosing breast cancer. Of these works, BC-DROID reports the best AUC (and accuracy when compared to works with no AUC).

6 CONCLUSION AND FUTURE WORKS

In this work, we presented our tool, BC-DROID, for automated detection and diagnosis of breast cancer using mammogram images

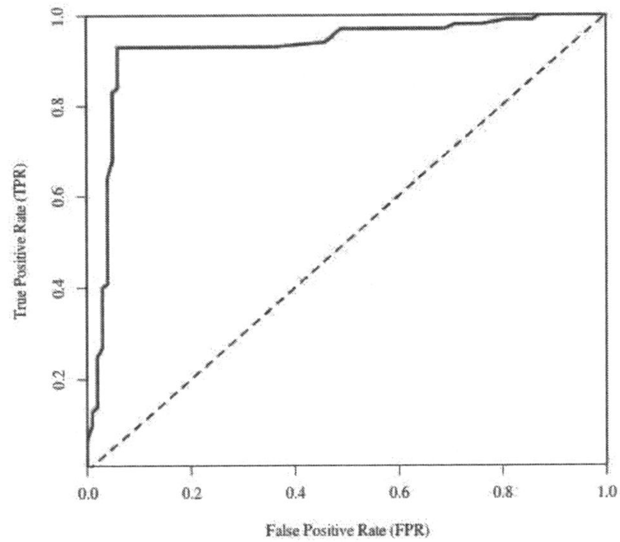

Figure 8: The ROC curve for our classification results. The associated AUC is 92.315%.

advanced deep learning techniques. We demonstrated the effectiveness of BC-DROID's detection of suspicious areas and further diagnosis as benign or malignant compared to related works. Our tool is made available through an easy to use web interface, allowing users to upload mammogram images and visualize areas of interest in the image, along with their associated diagnoses. Through this work, we provide physicians with an automated diagnosis that can assist them in making a more conclusive diagnosis. By doing so, this can reduce the rate of false positive diagnoses. Furthermore, it can pinpoint previously unnoticed worrisome areas, lowering the rate of undiagnosed breast cancer. In future work, we are going to frequently update the website with more accurate and faster versions of the pipeline to enable researchers and physicians to have better detection and diagnosis assistance. We plan to migrate our service to an improved High Performance Computing (HPC) system using multiple GPUs and computation nodes in order to enable BC-DROID as a streaming service. This will make it possible to process hundreds of images simultaneously and in a very short period of time. In addition, we plan to extend our technique to other medical imaging data, such as X-ray, fMRI, or others.

ACKNOWLEDGMENTS

This work was partially funded by NIH grants (P20GM103458-10, P30GM110760-03, P20GM103424), NSF grants (MRI-1338051, CC-NIE-1341008, IBSS-L-1620451), LA Board of Regents grants (LEQSF(2016-19)-RD-A-08 and ITRS), and IBM faculty awards.

REFERENCES

[1] Martín Abadi, Ashish Agarwal, Paul Barham, Eugene Brevdo, Zhifeng Chen, Craig Citro, Greg S Corrado, Andy Davis, Jeffrey Dean, Matthieu Devin, and

others. 2016. Tensorflow: Large-scale machine learning on heterogeneous distributed systems. *arXiv preprint arXiv:1603.04467* (2016).

[2] Qaisar Abbas. 2016. DeepCAD: A Computer-Aided Diagnosis System for Mammographic Masses Using Deep Invariant Features. *Computers* 5, 4 (2016), 28.

[3] J. Arevalo, F. A. GonzÃąlez, R. Ramos-PollÃąn, J. L. Oliveira, and M. A. Guevara Lopez. 2015. Convolutional neural networks for mammography mass lesion classification. In *2015 37th Annual International Conference of the IEEE Engineering in Medicine and Biology Society (EMBC)*. 797–800. DOI: https://doi.org/10.1109/EMBC.2015.7318482

[4] John Arevalo, Fabio A. GonzÃąlez, RaÃžl Ramos-PollÃąn, Jose L. Oliveira, and Miguel Angel Guevara Lopez. 2016. Representation learning for mammography mass lesion classification with convolutional neural networks. *Computer Methods and Programs in Biomedicine* 127 (2016), 248 – 257. DOI: https://doi.org/10.1016/j.cmpb.2015.12.014

[5] Gustavo Carneiro, Jacinto Nascimento, and Andrew P. Bradley. 2015. *Unregistered Multiview Mammogram Analysis with Pre-trained Deep Learning Models.* Springer International Publishing, Cham, 652–660. DOI: https://doi.org/10.1007/978-3-319-24574-4_78

[6] Stefano Ciatto, Nehmat Houssami, Daniela Bernardi, Francesca Caumo, Marco Pellegrini, Silvia Brunelli, Paola Tuttobene, Paola Bricolo, Carmine FantÃš, Marvi Valentini, Stefania Montemezzi, and Petra Macaskill. 2013. Integration of 3D digital mammography with tomosynthesis for population breast-cancer screening (STORM): a prospective comparison study. *The Lancet Oncology* 14, 7 (2013), 583 – 589. DOI: https://doi.org/10.1016/S1470-2045(13)70134-7

[7] N. Dhungel, G. Carneiro, and A. P. Bradley. 2015. Automated Mass Detection in Mammograms Using Cascaded Deep Learning and Random Forests. In *2015 International Conference on Digital Image Computing: Techniques and Applications (DICTA)*. 1–8. DOI: https://doi.org/10.1109/DICTA.2015.7371234

[8] Neeraj Dhungel, Gustavo Carneiro, and Andrew P. Bradley. 2015. *Deep Learning and Structured Prediction for the Segmentation of Mass in Mammograms.* Springer International Publishing, Cham, 605–612. DOI: https://doi.org/10.1007/978-3-319-24553-9_74

[9] N. Dhungel, G. Carneiro, and A. P. Bradley. 2015. Deep structured learning for mass segmentation from mammograms. In *2015 IEEE International Conference on Image Processing (ICIP)*. 2950–2954. DOI: https://doi.org/10.1109/ICIP.2015.7351343

[10] M. G. Ertosun and D. L. Rubin. 2015. Probabilistic visual search for masses within mammography images using deep learning. In *2015 IEEE International Conference on Bioinformatics and Biomedicine (BIBM)*. 1310–1315. DOI: https://doi.org/10.1109/BIBM.2015.7359868

[11] Krzysztof J Geras, Stacey Wolfson, S Kim, Linda Moy, and Kyunghyun Cho. 2017. High-Resolution Breast Cancer Screening with Multi-View Deep Convolutional Neural Networks. *arXiv preprint arXiv:1703.07047* (2017).

[12] Ross Girshick. 2015. Fast r-cnn. In *Proceedings of the IEEE International Conference on Computer Vision.* 1440–1448.

[13] Ross Girshick, Jeff Donahue, Trevor Darrell, and Jitendra Malik. 2016. Region-based convolutional networks for accurate object detection and segmentation. *IEEE transactions on pattern analysis and machine intelligence* 38, 1 (2016), 142–158.

[14] Richard H Gold, Lawrence W Bassett, and Bobbi E Widoff. 1990. Highlights from the history of mammography. *Radiographics* 10, 6 (1990), 1111–1131.

[15] Michael Heath, Kevin Bowyer, Daniel Kopans, and Richard Moore. The digital database for screening mammography.

[16] Nehmat Houssami, Petra Macaskill, Daniela Bernardi, Francesca Caumo, Marco Pellegrini, Silvia Brunelli, Paola Tuttobene, Paola Bricolo, Carmine Fantò, Marvi Valentini, and others. 2014. Breast screening using 2D-mammography or integrating digital breast tomosynthesis (3D-mammography) for single-reading or double-reading–Evidence to guide future screening strategies. *European Journal of Cancer* 50, 10 (2014), 1799–1807.

[17] M. Kallenberg, K. Petersen, M. Nielsen, A. Y. Ng, P. Diao, C. Igel, C. M. Vachon, K. Holland, R. R. Winkel, N. Karssemeijer, and M. Lillholm. 2016. Unsupervised Deep Learning Applied to Breast Density Segmentation and Mammographic Risk Scoring. *IEEE Transactions on Medical Imaging* 35, 5 (May 2016), 1322–1331. DOI: https://doi.org/10.1109/TMI.2016.2532122

[18] Oeffinger KC, Fontham EH, Etzioni R, and et al. 2015. Breast cancer screening for women at average risk: 2015 guideline update from the american cancer society. *JAMA* 314, 15 (2015), 1599–1614. DOI: https://doi.org/10.1001/jama.2015.12783 arXiv:/data/journals/jama/934597/jsc150008.pdf

[19] Mieke Kriege, Cecile T.M. Brekelmans, Carla Boetes, Peter E. Besnard, Harmine M. Zonderland, Inge Marie Obdeijn, Radu A. Manoliu, Theo Kok, Hans Peterse, Madeleine M.A. Tilanus-Linthorst, Sara H. Muller, Sybren Meijer, Jan C. Oosterwijk, Louk V.A.M. Beex, Rob A.E.M. Tollenaar, Harry J. de Koning, Emiel J.T. Rutgers, and Jan G.M. Klijn. 2004. Efficacy of MRI and Mammography for Breast-Cancer Screening in Women with a Familial or Genetic Predisposition. *New England Journal of Medicine* 351, 5 (2004), 427–437. DOI: https://doi.org/10.1056/NEJMoa031759 arXiv:http://dx.doi.org/10.1056/NEJMoa031759 PMID: 15282350.

[20] Alex Krizhevsky, Ilya Sutskever, and Geoffrey E Hinton. 2012. Imagenet classification with deep convolutional neural networks. In *Advances in neural information processing systems.* 1097–1105.

[21] Carol H Lee, D David Dershaw, Daniel Kopans, Phil Evans, Barbara Monsees, Debra Monticciolo, R James Brenner, Lawrence Bassett, Wendie Berg, Stephen Feig, Edward Hendrick, Ellen Mendelson, Carl D'Orsi, Edward Sickles, and Linda Warren Burhenne. 2010. Breast Cancer Screening With Imaging: Recommendations From the Society of Breast Imaging and the ACR on the Use of Mammography, Breast MRI, Breast Ultrasound, and Other Technologies for the Detection of Clinically Occult Breast Cancer. *Journal of the American College of Radiology* 7, 1 (Jan. 2010), 18–27.

[22] Constance D Lehman, Robert D Wellman, Diana SM Buist, Karla Kerlikowske, Anna NA Tosteson, and Diana L Miglioretti. 2015. Diagnostic accuracy of digital screening mammography with and without computer-aided detection. *JAMA internal medicine* 175, 11 (2015), 1828–1837.

[23] Daniel Lévy and Arzav Jain. 2016. Breast Mass Classification from Mammograms using Deep Convolutional Neural Networks. *arXiv preprint arXiv:1612.00542* (2016).

[24] John M Lewin, R Edward Hendrick, Carl J DâĂŹOrsi, Pamela K Isaacs, Lawrence J Moss, Andrew Karellas, Gale A Sisney, Christopher C Kuni, and Gary R Cutter. 2001. Comparison of full-field digital mammography with screen-film mammography for cancer detection: Results of 4,945 paired examinations 1. *Radiology* 218, 3 (2001), 873–880.

[25] Wei Liu, Dragomir Anguelov, Dumitru Erhan, Christian Szegedy, Scott Reed, Cheng-Yang Fu, and Alexander C Berg. 2016. SSD: Single shot multibox detector. In *European Conference on Computer Vision.* Springer, 21–37.

[26] Howlader N, Noone AM, Krapcho M, Miller D, Bishop K, Kosary CL, Yu M, Ruhl J, Tatalovich Z, Mariotto A, Lewis DR, Chen HS, Feuer EJ, and Cronin KA (eds). 2017. SEER Cancer Statistics Review, 1975-2014, National Cancer Institute. (2017).

[27] JÃžlia E. E. Oliveira, Mark O. Gueld, Arnaldo de A. AraÃžjo, Bastian Ott, and Thomas M. Deserno. 2008. Toward a standard reference database for computer-aided mammography. (2008). DOI: https://doi.org/10.1117/12.770325

[28] Mei-Sing Ong and Kenneth D Mandl. 2015. National expenditure for false-positive mammograms and breast cancer overdiagnoses estimated at $4 billion a year. *Health affairs* 34, 4 (2015), 576–583.

[29] Kersten Petersen, Mads Nielsen, Pengfei Diao, Nico Karssemeijer, and Martin Lillholm. 2014. *Breast Tissue Segmentation and Mammographic Risk Scoring Using Deep Learning.* Springer International Publishing, Cham, 88–94. DOI: https://doi.org/10.1007/978-3-319-07887-8_13

[30] Etta D. Pisano, Constantine Gatsonis, Edward Hendrick, Martin Yaffe, Janet K. Baum, Suddhasatta Acharyya, Emily F. Conant, Laurie L. Fajardo, Lawrence Bassett, Carl D'Orsi, Roberta Jong, and Murray Rebner. 2005. Diagnostic Performance of Digital versus Film Mammography for Breast-Cancer Screening. *New England Journal of Medicine* 353, 17 (2005), 1773–1783. DOI: https://doi.org/10.1056/NEJMoa052911 arXiv:http://dx.doi.org/10.1056/NEJMoa052911 PMID: 16169887.

[31] Joseph Redmon, Santosh Divvala, Ross Girshick, and Ali Farhadi. 2016. You Only Look Once: Unified, Real-Time Object Detection. In *The IEEE Conference on Computer Vision and Pattern Recognition (CVPR).*

[32] Shaoqing Ren, Kaiming He, Ross Girshick, and Jian Sun. 2015. Faster r-cnn: Towards real-time object detection with region proposal networks. In *Advances in neural information processing systems.* 91–99.

[33] Olga Russakovsky, Jia Deng, Hao Su, Jonathan Krause, Sanjeev Satheesh, Sean Ma, Zhiheng Huang, Andrej Karpathy, Aditya Khosla, Michael Bernstein, Alexander C. Berg, and Li Fei-Fei. 2015. ImageNet Large Scale Visual Recognition Challenge. *International Journal of Computer Vision (IJCV)* 115, 3 (2015), 211–252. DOI: https://doi.org/10.1007/s11263-015-0816-y

[34] Karen Simonyan and Andrew Zisserman. 2014. Very Deep Convolutional Networks for Large-Scale Image Recognition. *CoRR* abs/1409.1556 (2014). http://arxiv.org/abs/1409.1556

[35] Christian Szegedy, Wei Liu, Yangqing Jia, Pierre Sermanet, Scott Reed, Dragomir Anguelov, Dumitru Erhan, Vincent Vanhoucke, and Andrew Rabinovich. 2015. Going deeper with convolutions. In *Proceedings of the IEEE Conference on Computer Vision and Pattern Recognition.* 1–9.

[36] Yew-Ching Teh, Gie-Hooi Tan, Nur Aishah Taib, Kartini Rahmat, Caroline Judy Westerhout, Farhana Fadzli, Mee-Hoong See, Suniza Jamaris, and Cheng-Har Yip. 2015. Opportunistic mammography screening provides effective detection rates in a limited resource healthcare system. *BMC Cancer* 15, 1 (2015), 405. DOI: https://doi.org/10.1186/s12885-015-1419-2

[37] A Van Steen and R Van Tiggelen. 2007. Short history of mammography: a Belgian perspective. *JBR BTR* 90, 3 (2007), 151.

[38] Yu-Dong Zhang, Shui-Hua Wang, Ge Liu, and Jiquan Yang. 2016. Computer-aided diagnosis of abnormal breasts in mammogram images by weighted-type fractional Fourier transform. *Advances in Mechanical Engineering* 8, 2 (2016), 1687814016634243. DOI: https://doi.org/10.1177/1687814016634243 arXiv:http://dx.doi.org/10.1177/1687814016634243

A Physiological Thermal Regulation Model with Application to the Diagnosis of Diabetic Peripheral Neuropathy

Viktor Chekh, PhD
Blackmagic Design Pty Ltd
Colorado Spring, Colorado
viktorc@blackmagicdesign.com

Peter Soliz, PhD
VisionQuest BioMedical LLC
Albuquerque, New Mexico
psoliz@visionquest-bio.com

Mark Burge, MD
Department of Internal Medicine
University of New Mexico Health Science Center
Albuquerque, New Mexico
MBurge@salud.unm.edu

Shuang (Sean) Luan, PhD
Department of Computer Science
University of New Mexico
Albuquerque, New Mexico
sluan@cs.unm.edu

ABSTRACT

Diabetes afflicts an estimated over 400 million people worldwide. People with diabetes are at the risk of a wide range of devastating complications including diabetic peripheral neuropathy, which is commonly referred to as the "diabetic foot" and most often affects the lower extremities (i.e., leg and foot) and can lead to amputations. In this paper, we present a computer aided diagnostic system for diabetic foot. At the core of our system is an improved thermoregulation model that characterizes the thermal recovery process of the extremities of the body (e.g., foot) after a cold stress. The model consists of a series of differential equations which is developed based on physiological characterizations and yet also exhibits analytical solutions. The model has been shown to be accurate and robust. Based on the new thermal regulation model, we have developed a 2D Bayesian classifier. We have applied the classifier to a cohort of 49 subjects (35 with no diabetic peripheral neuropathy and 14 with diabetic peripheral neuropathy). The classifier can accurately diagnose 93% of the subjects with diabetic peripheral neuropathy with a false positive rate of only 6%. This significantly outperforms current clinical diagnostic methods which may miss 61% of the patients with diabetic peripheral neuropathy.

CCS CONCEPTS

• **Applied Computing → Life and Medical Sciences**; *Health informatics*

KEYWORDS: thermal infrared imaging; diabetic peripheral neuropathy; diabetic foot; bio-heat transfer; thermoregulation; vasodilation; vasoconstriction

ACM Reference Format

Viktor Chekh, Peter Soliz, Mark Burge, and Shuang Luan. 2017. A Physiological Thermal Regulation Model with Application to the Diagnosis of Diabetic Peripheral Neuropathy. In *Proceedings of ACM BCB, Boston, Massachusetts, USA, August 2017, 6 pages.* DOI: 10.1145/3107411.3107512

1 INTRODUCTION

Diabetic patients are at risk for a wide range of complications including heart disease, kidney disease (nephropathy), ocular diseases (diabetic retinopathy), and diabetic peripheral neuropathy (hereafter DPN), i.e., nerve damage [1][2][3]. Neuropathy most often affects the lower extremities (i.e., leg and foot) and can lead to serious pathological consequences, including amputation. It is estimated that 50% of people with diabetes have some degree of neuropathy. Fifteen percent of them will develop a foot ulcer during the lifetime [2][4][5][6]. Foot ulcers are the main cause for 85% of lower extremity amputation in patients with diabetes [7][8][9][10].

Studies have shown that neuropathy is a factor in the impairment of blood flow in the diabetic foot [12][13]. Patients with long-standing neuropathy have poor regulatory mechanisms and microcirculatory dysfunction [14][15]. This condition is linked to neuropathic complications that alter the regulatory mechanisms controlling blood flow in the extremities (e.g., foot), which has been confirmed by laser Doppler studies [16][17][18].

The key to preventing the advanced stages of DPN is early detection and intervention. Traditional techniques for diagnosing peripheral neuropathy are clinically based on sensory examination. Examples of these tests include Semmes-Weinstein monofilament testing [19][20][21], i.e., a monofilament wire used to exert about 10 grams of force against a location on plantar surface of the foot for 1 second. Others include a tuning fork [20][21], pinprick sensation [20][21][22], vibration perception threshold [20][21][23]

Permission to make digital or hard copies of all or part of this work for personal or classroom use is granted without fee provided that copies are not made or distributed for profit or commercial advantage and that copies bear this notice and the full citation on the first page. Copyrights for components of this work owned by others than ACM must be honored. Abstracting with credit is permitted. To copy otherwise, or republish, to post on servers or to redistribute to lists, requires prior specific permission and/or a fee. Request permissions from Permissions@acm.org.
ACM-BCB '17, August 20-23, 2017, Boston, MA, USA
© 2017 Association for Computing Machinery.
ACM ISBN 978-1-4503-4722-8/17/08..$15.00
http://dx.doi.org/10.1145/3107411.3107512

[24]. These tests are simple, noninvasive, and aim to determine if a patient has lost sensation in the feet. The patients who for example, cannot reliably detect the location of a monofilament are considered to have lost sensation due to onset of neuropathy. Many of these tests unfortunately present significant inter- and intra-observer variability leading to low sensitivity and low specificity [20][21]. Further DPN affects the foot non-uniformly, i.e., one region of a diabetic foot may be normal while another region may neuropathic. It is impossible for a physician to exhaustively test every point on the foot plantar. Due to these, studies have revealed that physicians may miss the diagnosis of diabetic peripheral neuropathy in as many as 61% of patients. An objective and quantitative means for reliable and early (possibly pre-clinical) diagnosis of peripheral neuropathy and the risk of foot ulcers is still lacking.

In our previous ACM-BCB paper [29], we have presented a new system for early quantitative detection of diabetic neuropathy based on thermal imaging and analytical techniques. The key to our system is to use infrared imaging to quantitatively measure the thermal response of the feet of diabetic patients following cold provocation. The technique is based on the observation that exposure of the foot to a cold stress leads to reduced blood flow in the foot. Once the cold stress is removed, our thermoregulation will respond by increasing the blood flow to carry more heat into the foot and thus allowing it to recover to normal core body temperature. An individual suffering from neuropathy will have impaired blood flow and poor thermoregulation, and therefore recovers slowly from the cold stress. The speed of the recovery process can then be used to calculate the body's ability of thermal regulation and therefore quantitatively diagnose the degree of DPN.

In our previous research [29][31][32], we have provided an overall design for our system including experimental set up, image processing and temperature change extraction, a thermal response model that was inspired by control theory, and finally a very small scale clinical study based on only 8 subjects (4 normal control and 4 DPN).

At the core of our computer aided diagnosis system for diabetic foot is its thermal response model that characterizes the foot temperature change following a cold stress. In our previous work, our model is completely based on control theory and doesn't characterize the physiology process of our experiment. As a result, we have trouble generalizing our previous model [29] to a larger data set that was subsequently acquired.

In this paper, we present an improved thermal regulation model based on physiologic characterization of the body's response to external heat stress under different scenarios. This new model consists of a series of differential equations that all exhibit analytical solutions. Compared to our old model in [29], our new model is not only more general but also more stable and robust due to its built-in physiology characteristics. We have applied our new model to cohort of 49 subjects (35 without DPN and 14 with DPN.) We can correctly classify 93% of the diabetic foot subjects with a false positive rate of only 6%. This significantly improves the current clinical diagnostic methods which may miss 61% of the patients with diabetic peripheral neuropathy [30].

The rest of the paper is organized as follows. Section 2 gives a brief overview of our computer aided diagnosis system. Section 3 presents the new thermal regulation model based on physiology characterizations. Section 4 discusses our experimental results. Section 5 concludes the paper and discusses some of the ongoing and future research directions.

2 THE COMPUTER AIDED DIAGNOSTIC SYSTEM

Our CAD system has the following key components [29]:

(1) **An IRB approved imaging protocol:** After an initial medical exam by the physician, the subject's foot was placed in cold water at 55°F (~13°C) for 5 minutes. Then a FLIR SC305 IR Camera (specs: 320×240 resolution, 8 Hz frame rate, 14-bit pixel dynamic range, 0.05°C thermal sensitivity, and 7.5-13 μm range) was used to record the foot temperature recovery for 15 minutes.

(2) **Image processing and segmentation** [31]: The recorded infrared video was segmented and registered and the temperature recovery curve for each point on the foot was extracted. (See Figure 1 for an example of the temperature recovery curves.)

(3) **Thermal regulation model for parameter extraction:** The temperature recovery curve was exported to the thermal regulation model and the thermal regulation characteristics (e.g., speed of thermal response) was calculated.

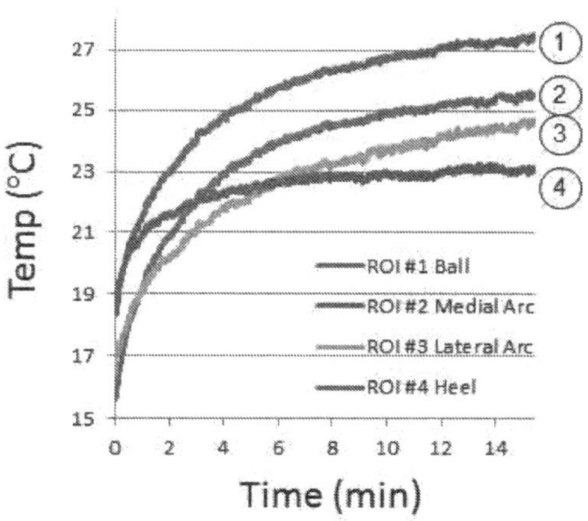

Figure 1. Sample set of temperature curves extracted for 6 ROIs.

(4) **Classification and diagnosis:** Based on the thermal regulation characteristics calculated in (3), the CAD system provided a diagnosis such as whether or not the patient is suffering from DPN.

3 THE NEW THERMAL REGULATION MODEL

3.1 The Penne's Bio-heat Equation

Any discussions on the thermal regulation and bio-heat transfer between the human body and its surrounding environment starts with the Penne's Equation [25]. The Pennes' Bio-heat Equation is the partial differential equation that describes the surface tissue temperature change [25][26][27][28]:

$$\begin{cases} V\rho c\dfrac{\partial T}{\partial t} = \nabla(\chi\nabla T) + (\rho c)_b\omega_b(T_b - T) \\ \quad +(\rho c)_e\omega_e(T_e - T) + +q_m + q_{rad} + q_{vap} \\ V_e(\rho c)_e\dfrac{\partial T_e}{\partial t} = (\rho c)_e\omega_e(T - T_e) - q_{rad} - q_{vap} \end{cases}$$

In the above equation, V $[m^3]$ is the volume, T [°K] is temperature, c $[J * \text{kg}^{-1} * °\text{K}^{-1}]$ is heat capacity, ρ $[kg * m^{-3}]$ is density, and χ $[J * m^2 * sec^{-1} * °\text{K}^{-1}]$ is surface thermal conductivity. The variables with subscript are related to tissue. The subscripts b and e stand for blood and environment, correspondently; $\omega_b[m^3 * sec^{-1}]$ represents blood perfusion, and $\omega_e[m^3 * sec^{-1}]$ is environment (air) perfusion. q_{rad} $[J * sec^{-1}]$ is the radiant heat, q_m $[J * sec^{-1}]$ is metabolic volumetric heat, and q_{vap} $[J * sec^{-1}]$ (always negative) is the evaporative heat.

The Penne's equation is a general equation and is developed to accommodate all possible situations and accounted for temperature changes due to diffusion, blood perfusion, and metabolic heat generation, evaporation, radiation, conduction, and convection. The equation is too complicated to be useful straightforwardly and must be customized to the settings of specific applications.

In our previous work [29], we have presented a detailed examination of the individual terms in the Penne's equation based on the typical clinical setting and the biological features of the human foot, and determined that for our computer-aided diagnostic system (see Section 2), the equation can be simplified to the following ordinary differential equation:

$$\frac{dT}{dt} = -r_b(T - T_b) - r_e(T - T_e) \qquad (Eq. 1)$$

In this ODE, $r_e = \frac{(\rho c)_e}{V\rho c}\omega_e$ $[sec^{-1}]$ is the characteristic of the body (foot) with respect to the external media, $r_b = \frac{(\rho c)_b}{V\rho c}\omega_b$ $[sec^{-1}]$ accounts for all the biological and thermal dynamical parameters responsible for the heat transfer between the blood and body. The goal of this paper is to resolve the above ODE with a correct physiological interpretation while at the same time exhibit analytical solutions that can be used in our diagnostic system.

3.2 The New Thermal Regulation Model

Let $T_A = \frac{T_e r_e + T_b r_b}{r_e + r_b}$ and $r(t) = r_e + r_b$, then Equation 1 can be transformed to:

$$\frac{dT}{dt} = -r(t)(T - T_A) \qquad (Eq. 2)$$

where T_A [°K] is the asymptotic recovery temperature and $r(t)$ $[sec^{-1}]$ is the thermoregulation characteristic. The key for resolving the Equation 2 is to come up with a meaningful model for the thermal regulation function $r(t)$, while at the meantime guarantee that the equation exhibits an analytical solution.

To understand our modeling of $r(t)$, let us first look at the physiological response of the body in contact with a cold stress. Assuming our body is at temperature T_b and the cold stress object is at temperature T_e, depending on the temperature difference $T_b - T_e$, different type of thermal response could be triggered, which we termed 0th order, 1st order, 2nd order thermal regulations models.

0th order model: For the simplest situation where the temperature difference is small, no thermal regulation is activated, i.e., no dilation or constriction of the blood vessels, and the temperature of the body $T(t)$ is only affected by the heat exchange between the tissue and the cold object. Clearly in this situation $r(t)$ should be a constant, i.e., $r(t) = k$. Equation 2 becomes $\frac{dT}{dt} = -k(T - T_A)$, where k is a constant implying that no thermal regulation is activated. This is obviously the well-known Newton's Law of Cooling, which states that the rate of heat loss of an object is inverse proportional to the difference in temperatures between the object and its ambient environment, i.e., $\frac{dT}{dt} \propto -(T - T_A)$, or $\frac{dT}{dt} = -k(T - T_A)$, where the constant k $[sec^{-1}]$ depends on the heat transfer coefficient, heat capacity and the surface area of the object. Newton's Law of Cooling has a simple analytical solution:

$$T(t) = T_A + (T(0) - T_A)e^{-kt}$$

where $T(0)$ is the initial temperature of the object at time 0.

1st order model: As the temperature difference increases, the body part in contact with the cold stress will be cooled down much quicker. The body part that is cooled down will get less blood to preserve the heat of the human body under the cold stress [33]. Thus, the cold stress activates thermal regulation and constricts the blood vessels (i.e., vasoconstriction). When the cold stress is removed, the recovery process begins and the dilation of the blood vessels begins (i.e., vasodilation), so that more heat can be carried to the cooled body parts. As the cooled body parts warmed up to the core body temperature, the blood vessels also gradually dilate to their normal diameter and completes the recovery process.

Clearly, one would expect that the thermoregulation $r(t)$ to have the shape as depicted in Figure 2. In other words, one would expect a strong thermal regulation response immediately after the cold stress is removed followed by a gradual decay as the cooler body parts recovers to the normal core body temperature. In our research, data indicate that utilization of $r(t) = k(1 + Qe^{-st})$ provides the best fit, which has the general shape as shown in Figure 2, and its ODE: $\frac{dT}{dt} = -k(1 + Qe^{-st})(T - T_A)$ also has an analytical solution:

$$T(t) = T_A + (T(0) - T_A)e^{-k\left(t + \frac{Q}{s}(1 - e^{-st})\right)}.$$

In Section 4, we will discuss the physiological meanings of the parameter Q which is related to the amplitude of initial thermal regulation response, and s $[sec^{-1}]$ which is the speed of thermal regulation. It is also worthwhile to point out that when $s = 0$, $r(t) = kQ$, which is a constant and therefore our 1st order model includes the 0th order model.

2nd order model: As the temperature difference further increases, we arrive at the extreme situations where a cold injury could occur. The situation is often referred to as hunting response or Lewis reaction [34][35][36][37][38]. Physiologically, to prevent cold injury, the recovery process will suddenly vasodilate that immediately increases the blood flow. The vasodilation is then followed by vasoconstriction because the dilation so strong and dramatic and "overshoots".

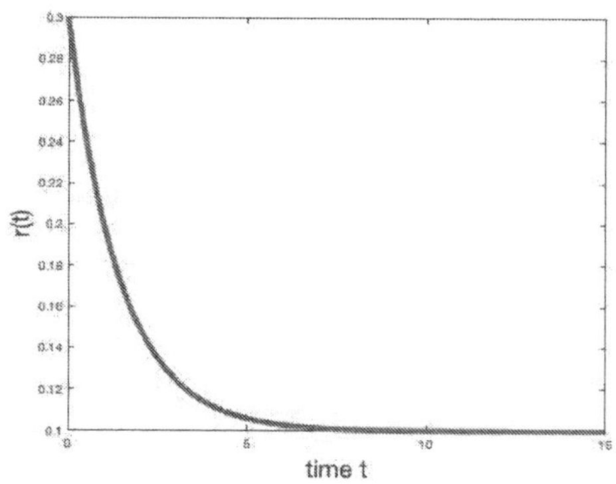

Figure 2. Illustrating the process of vasodilation in the 1st order model.

Clearly, one would expect $r(t)$ to be of the general shape as shown in Figure 3, i.e., a strong vasodilation response that overshoots followed a gradual vasoconstriction decay to restore the normal vessel diameters. We have decided to use $r(t) = k\left(1 + Qe^{-s_1 t}(1 + s_2 - s_1 s_2 t)\right)$, which has the shape as shown in Figure 3.

The ODE:

$$\frac{dT}{dt} = -k\left(1 + Qe^{-s_1 t}\left(1 + s_2 - s_1 s_2 t\right)\right)\left(T - T_A\right)$$

has the analytical solution:

$$T(t) = T_A + (T(0) - T_A)e^{-k\left(t + \frac{Q}{s_1}\left(1 - e^{-s_1 t} + s_2 t e^{-s_1 t}\right)\right)},$$

where the parameter Q is the amplitude of thermal regulation, s_1 $[sec^{-1}]$ is the speed of the initial vasodilation, and s_2 $[sec^{-1}]$ is the speed of the secondary vasoconstriction.

Observe that when $s_2 = 0$, $r(t) = k(1 + Qe^{-s_1 t})$, thus the second order model includes the 1st order model and is a generalization. In fact, it is possible to continue to extend our thermal response model further to the nth order. We omit the details here, since it is irrelevant to the following discussions.

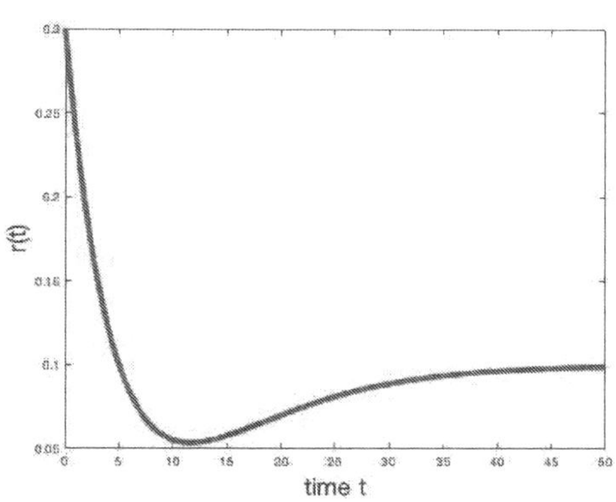

Figure 3. Illustrating the process of vasodilation followed by vasoconstriction in the 2nd order model.

3.3 Model Verification

It is important to realize that in our imaging protocol, the 1st order model should be used because the cold-water stress is only enough to activate thermal regulation but not severe enough to induce any cold injury.

We have applied our thermal regulation models to the collected temperature recovery data to verify the accuracy and robustness of the model. Depending on which model is used either linear least square (e.g., 0th order model) or non-linear least square (e.g., 1st and 2nd order models) will be used for curve fitting.

Recall that for each subject, we have 15 minutes of recorded temperature recovery data. We will perform two types of verifications: full range and truncated range. Take 0th order model $T(t) = T_A + (T(0) - T_A)e^{-kt}$ as an example, by **full range interpolation**, we will find the parameter k minimizing the error between the calculated temperature function $T(t)$ and the collected experimental data. By **truncated range verification**, instead of giving the curve fitting function the full 15 minutes of experimental data, we will only give it the truncated experimental data, e.g., removing the first 1.5 minutes of data to calculate $T(t)$. The removed 1.5 minutes of data will then be compared to the extrapolated data from the calculated $T(t)$. The rationale for the truncated range verification is that if the error between the removed data and the extrapolated data is small, then the model is both accurate and robust.

As expected, our 0th order model (i.e., Newton's Law of Cooling) will not work well because it doesn't incorporate thermal regulation. As can be seen from the Figure 4, there is significant amount of error when fitting the experimental data with the 0th order model. This error is even more pronounced when the fitting was performed using the truncated data, and the error can be as high as 1.2°C. We have also tried to use the thermal regulations parameters extracted from the 0th model for classification, and as expected this does not yield a good classifier.

Figure 5 shows the curve fitting result when using our 1st order model with the same data set. For full range interpolation, the 1st order model provides a tight fit to the experimental data. When truncated data was used, the error for the 1st order model is only 0.11 °C in comparison to the 1.2 °C for (2). The mean error for the 1st order model is less than 0.05 °C, which is within the sensitivity of the camera itself.

We attribute the success of the 1st model to its built-in physiological interpretation.

4 RESULTS

We have collected the temperature recovery curves of 49 subjects (35 subjects with no diagnosis of DPN and 14 subjects with diagnosed DPN).

Two parameters extracted from our thermal regulation models have been used as classifiers. These two parameters are amplitude of thermal regulation and speed of thermal regulations.

Recall that in the 1st order model (see Section 3.2 for details), the thermal regulation is:

$$r(t) = k(1 + Qe^{-st}).$$

Observe that $\frac{dr}{dt} = -kQs\, e^{-st}$. Since k, Q, and s are all nonnegative parameters, $\frac{dr}{dt} \le 0$, indicating that the function is decreasing implying that the strength of thermal regulation decreases as the time t increases when the cooled body part recovers to the core body temperature.

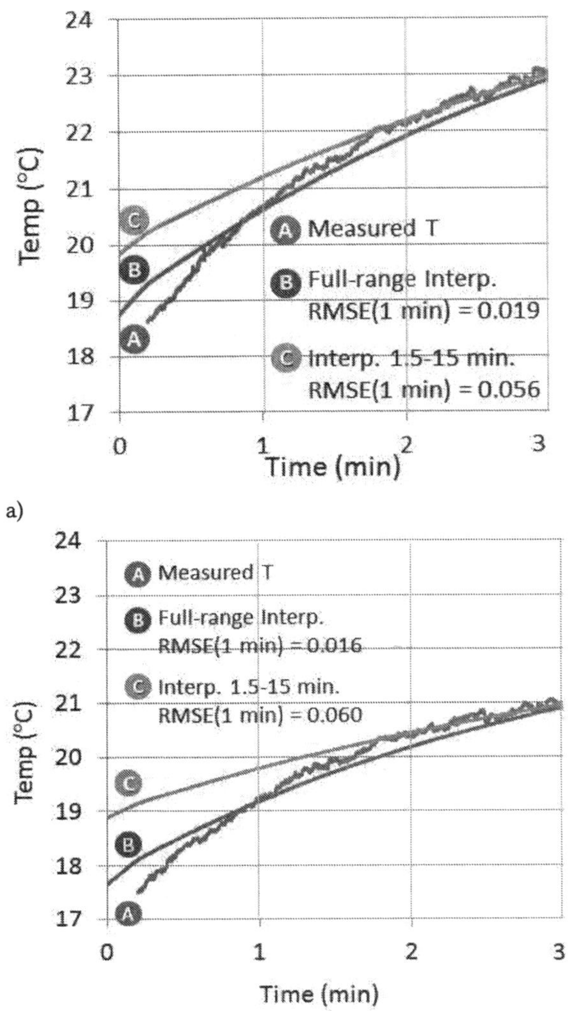

Figure 4. Extrapolation of the experimental data (A) with the Newton's Law of Cooling for a full 0-15 min. range (B), and without first 1.5 min (C) for the internal arch a), and for the heel b).

The magnitude of $\frac{dr}{dt}$, i.e., $|\frac{dr}{dt}| = kQs\, e^{-st}$ is the indicator of how fast the strength of thermal regulation is decreasing, i.e., how effective the cooled body part is recovering to the normal core body temperature. $|\frac{dr}{dt}|$ can be viewed as consisting of a linear component kQ and an exponential component se^{-st}, both components will determine how fast the body thermal regulates. We define $A_r = kQ$ (also equal to $r(0) - r(\infty)$) to be the **amplitude of thermal regulation** and s to be the **speed of thermal regulation**. For healthy patients, we expect their thermal regulation to be stronger (i.e., a larger amplitude kQ) and a quicker response (i.e., a faster speed s).

As mentioned previously, peripheral neuropathy does not affect the diabetic foot uniformly. The problematic areas which are strongly damaged with diabetes, i.e. the areas of DPN, are generally different on the foot for different patients. In other words, for a DPN patient, some regions of the foot can still have normal thermal regulation. Therefore, to use the amplitude of the speed of thermal regulations as a diagnostic classifier, one will need to use the minimum amplitude (i.e., min kQ) or the minimum speed (i.e., min s) over the entire foot or over an entire region of interest. If any point in the region of interest has bad thermal regulation, then the subject will be classified as DPN.

In our diagnostic system, we have successfully used the amplitude and the speed to construct a 2D naïve Bayesian classifier. The results are shown in Table 1.

Diagnosis	Controls	DPNs
No DPN	33	1
DPN	2 (5.7%)	14 (92.9%)

Table 1. Classification using both the amplitude and the speed of thermal regulation.

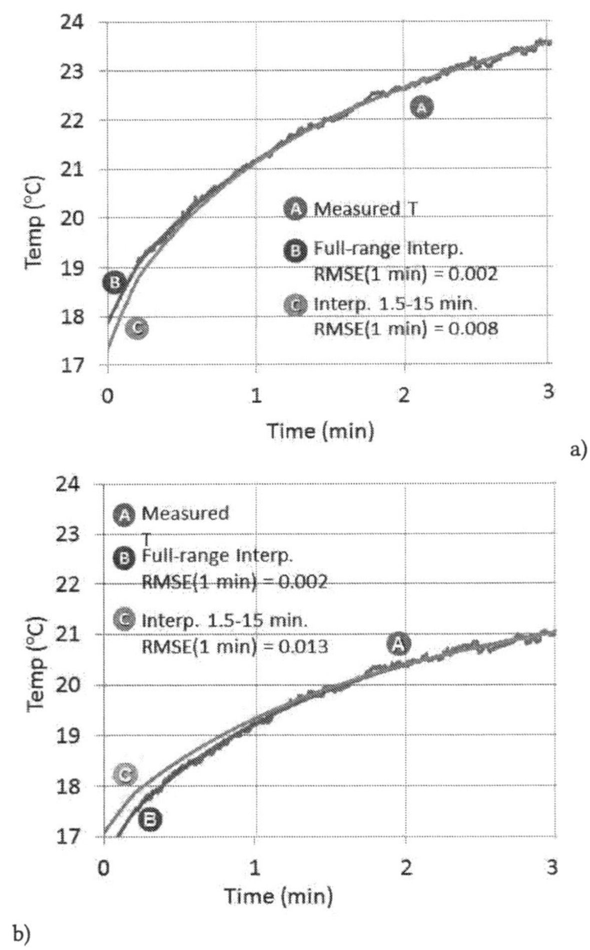

Figure 5. Extrapolation of the experimental data (A) with the thermoregulation model for a full 0-15 min. range (B), and without first 1.5 min (C) for the internal arch a), and for the heel b).

We have also performed cross validations for our Bayesian classifier. Since our data set is small, we first performed the leave-one-out cross-validation, and the loss is 0.0816. Since our data is highly asymmetric, i.e., with many subjects without DPNs, we have also performed stratified 2-fold cross validation, and the loss is 0.102.

5 CONCLUSIONS AND FUTURE WORK

We have presented an improved thermoregulation model that is developed based physiologic characteristics. The model has been applied to the problem of computer aided diagnosis of diabetic peripheral neuropathy, commonly referred to as the diabetic foot. Our studies have demonstrated that the new model is robust, accurate, and have produced Bayesian classifiers that have a 93% accuracy and only an 6% false positive rate.

As with any clinical studies, the burden of verification is almost always limited by the amount of clinical data that is available. Our current study was based on 49 subjects. For future research, we would like to collect more data, especially more DPN subjects.

ACKNOWLEDGMENTS

This work was supported by NIH DK093192, NIH 1R21CA197325-01, and NSF CBET-0853157.

REFERENCES

[1] Boulton AJM: The diabetic foot: a global view. Diabete Metab Res Rev 16:S2–S5, 2000

[2] Palumbo P J, Melton L J. Peripheral vascular disease and diabetes. In: Harris, Hamman, editors. Diabetes in America. 1st ed. Washington, D.C.: US Government Printing Office; 1985.

[3] Mancini L, Ruotolo V: The diabetic foot: epidemiology. Rays 22:511–523, 1997.

[4] Palubo P, Melton L. Peripheral vascular disease and diabetes. In: Hamman R, editor. Diabetes in America. Washington, DC: Government Printing Office; 1985. p. 1-21

[5] Reiber G E, Boyko E J, Smith D C. Lower extremity foot ulcers and amputations in diabetes. In: Harris, Cowie, Stern, Boyko E J, Reiber G E, Bennet, editors. Diabetes in America. 2nd ed. Washington, D.C.: US Government Printing Office; 1995. p. 402-428.

[6] Ramsey S D, Newton K, Blough D, McCulloch D K, Sandhu N, Reiber G E, et al. Incidence, outcomes, and cost of foot ulcers in patients with diabetes. Diabetes Care 1999; 22(3):382-7.

[7] Reiber G E, Boyko E J, Smith D C. Lower extremity foot ulcers and amputations in diabetes. In: Harris, Cowie, Stern, Boyko E J, Reiber G E, Bennet, editors. Diabetes in America. 2nd ed. Washington, D.C.: US Government Printing Office; 1995. p. 402-428.

[8] Pecoraro R E, Reiber G E, Burgess E M. Pathways to diabetic limb amputation. Basis for prevention. Diabetes Care 1990; 13(5):513-21.

[9] Morbach S, Lutale J, Viswanathan V, Mollenberg J, Ochs H, Rajashekar S, et al. Regional differences in risk factors and clinical presentation of diabetic foot lesions. Diabet Med 2004;21:91-5.

[10] Viswanathan V, Snehalatha C, Sivagami M, Seena R, Ramachandran A. Association of limited joint mobility and high plantar pressure in diabetic foot ulceration in Asian Indians. Diabetes Res Clin Pract 2003;60:57-61.

[11] American Diabetes Association Fast Facts Data and Statistics about Diabetes 2013.

[12] Flynn M, Edmonds M, Tooke J, Watkins P. Direct measurement of capillary blood flow in the diabetic neuropathic foot. Diabetologia 1988; 31:652-6..

[13] Rayman G, Williams S, Spencer P, Smaje L, Wise P, Tooke J. Impaired microvascular hyperaemic response to minor skin trauma in type 1 diabetes. Br Med J 1986; 292:1295-8.

[14] Flynn M, Tooke J. Diabetic neuropathy and the microcirculation. Diabet Med 1995; 12:298-301.

[15] Cobb J, Claremont D. Noninvasive measurement techniques for monitoring of microvascular function in the diabetic foot. Int J Low Extrem Wounds 2002;1:161-9.

[16] Cobb JE. An in-shoe laser Doppler sensor for assessing plantar blood flow in the diabetic foot [dissertation] in DEC. Bournemouth (UK): Department of Design, Engineering, and Computing, Bournemouth University; 2000.

[17] Belcaro G, Vasdekis S, Rulo A, Nicolaides AN. Evaluation of skin blood flow and venoarteriolar response in patients with diabetes and peripheral vascular disease by laser Doppler flowmetry. Angiology 1989 ;40:953-957.

[18] Bornmyr S, Svensson H, Lilja B, Sundkvist G. Skin temperature changes and changes in skin blood flow monitored with laser Doppler flowmetry and imaging: a methodological study in normal humans. Clin Physiol Funct Imaging 1997;17:71-82.

[19] Miranda-Palma B, Sosenko J, Bowker J, Mizel M, Boulton A. A comparison of the monofilament with other testing modalities for foot ulcer susceptibility. Diabetes Res Clin Pract 2005;70:8-12.

[20] Busko M. Common Tests May Miss Pediatric Diabetic Neuropathy. Medscape Medical News [serial online]. Apr 11 2014;Accessed Apr 23 2014. Available at http://www.medscape.com/viewarticle/823521.

[21] Hirschfeld G, von Glischinski M, Blankenburg M, et al. Screening for peripheral neuropathies in children with diabetes: a systematic review. Pediatrics. Apr 7 2014;[Medline].

[22] Boulton A.J.M. *et al.* Comprehensive Foot Examination and Risk Assessment. A report of the Task Force of the Foot Care Interest Group of the American Diabetes Association, with endorsement by the American Association of Clinical Endocrinologists. *Diabetes Care,* 31(8), 1679-1685, 2008.

[23] Young MJ, Breddy JL, Veves A, Boulton AJ: The prediction of diabetic neuropathic foot ulceration using vibration perception thresholds: a prospective study. Diabetes Care 17:557–560, 1994.

[24] Armstrong DG, Lavery LA, Vela SA, Quebedeaux TL, Fleischli JG: Choosing a practical screening instrument to identify patients at risk for diabetic foot ulceration. Arch Intern Med 158:289–292, 1998.

[25] Pennes, H.H. (1948) Analysis of tissue and arterial temperatures in the resting human forearm. Journal of Applied Physiology, 1, 93-122.

[26] L.Nilsson: Blood Flow, Temperature, and Heat Loss of Skin Exposed to Local Radiative and Convective Cooling. J. Invest. Dermatol 88: 586-593, 1987.

[27] Chen M.M., Holmes K.R. Microvascular contributions in tissue heat transfer. Ann. N.Y.Acad.Sci., 1980, 325; 137-150.

[28] A.Lakhssassi, E.Kengne, H.Semmaoui. Modifed Pennes' equation modelling bio-heat transfer in living tissues: analytical and numerical analysis. Natural Science, Vol.2, No.12, 1375-1385 (2010).

[29] Chekh V, Luan S, Burge M, Carranza C, Soliz P. McGrew E, and Barriga S. Quantitative Early Detection of Diabetic Foot. *Proc. ACM-BCB 2013.*

[30] Gawish H. Diabetic Foot Scope of the Problem. *Egyptian Society of Diabetic foot.*

[31] Chekh V, Soliz P, Luan S, McGrew E, Barriga S, Burge M, and Luan S. Computer Aided Diagnosis of Diabetic Peripheral Neuropathy. *SPIE Medical Imaging 2014*

[32] G. Iven, V. Chekh, S. Luan, A. Mueen, P. Soliz, W. Xu, M. Burge, Non-contact Sensation Screening of Diabetic Foot Using Low Cost Infrared Sensors, 27th International Symposium on Computer-based Medical Systems (CBMS), 2014

[33] J. Oberle, M. Elam, T. Karlsson and B. Gunnar Wallin. Temperature-dependent interaction between vasoconstrictor and vasolidator machanisms in human skin. Acta Physiol. Scand. 1988, 132, p. 459-469.

[34] Lewis T (1930) Observations upon the reactions of vessels of the human skin to cold. Heart 15: 1031-1034.

[35] Li X, Tokura H & Midorikawa T (1994) The effects of two different types of clothing on seasonal cold acclimation of thermophysiological responses. Int J Biometeorol 38: 40-43.

[36] Livingstone SD (1976) Changes in cold-induced vasodilatation during Arctic exercises. J Appl Physiol 40(3): 455-457.

[37] Shin-ichi Sawada, Shunichi ARAKI and Kazuhito Yokoyama. Changes in Cold-induced Vasodilatation, Pain and Cold Sensation in Fingers Caused by Repeated Finger Cooling in a Cool Environment. Industrial Health 2000, 38, 79–86

[38] Catherine O'Brien. Reproducibility of the cold-induced vasodilation response in the human finger. J Appl Physiol 98: 1334–1340, 2005

An Out-of-Core GPU based Dimensionality Reduction Algorithm for Big Mass Spectrometry Data and Its Application in Bottom-up Proteomics

Muaaz Gul Awan
Department of Computer Science
Western Michigan University
4601 Campus Drive
Kalamazoo, Michigan 49009
muaazgul.awan@wmich.edu

Fahad Saeed*
Department of Computer Science
Western Michigan University
4601 Campus Drive
Kalamazoo, Michigan 49009
fahad.saeed@wmich.edu

ABSTRACT

Modern high resolution Mass Spectrometry instruments can generate millions of spectra in a single systems biology experiment. Each spectrum consists of thousands of peaks but only a small number of peaks actively contribute to deduction of peptides. Therefore, pre-processing of MS data to detect noisy and non-useful peaks are an active area of research. Most of the sequential noise reducing algorithms are impractical to use as a pre-processing step due to high time-complexity. In this paper, we present a GPU based dimensionality-reduction algorithm, called G-MSR, for MS2 spectra. Our proposed algorithm uses novel data structures which optimize the memory and computational operations inside GPU. These novel data structures include *Binary Spectra* and *Quantized Indexed Spectra (QIS)*. The former helps in communicating essential information between CPU and GPU using minimum amount of data while latter enables us to store and process complex 3-D data structure into a 1-D array structure while maintaining the integrity of MS data. Our proposed algorithm also takes into account the limited memory of GPUs and switches between *in-core* and *out-of-core* modes based upon the size of input data. G-MSR achieves a peak speed-up of 386x over its sequential counterpart and is shown to process over a million spectra in just 32 seconds. The code for this algorithm is available as a GPL open-source at GitHub at the following link: https://github.com/pcdslab/G-MSR.

CCS CONCEPTS

• **Applied computing** → **Computational proteomics**; *Bioinformatics*; • **Computing methodologies** → *Massively parallel algorithms*;

*Corresponding author.
Permission to make digital or hard copies of all or part of this work for personal or classroom use is granted without fee provided that copies are not made or distributed for profit or commercial advantage and that copies bear this notice and the full citation on the first page. Copyrights for components of this work owned by others than ACM must be honored. Abstracting with credit is permitted. To copy otherwise, or republish, to post on servers or to redistribute to lists, requires prior specific permission and/or a fee. Request permissions from permissions@acm.org.
ACM-BCB '17, August 20-23, 2017, Boston, MA, USA
© 2017 Association for Computing Machinery.
ACM ISBN 978-1-4503-4722-8/17/08...$15.00
https://doi.org/10.1145/3107411.3107466

KEYWORDS

BigData, GPU, Proteomics, Out-of-Core, Data Reduction, Mass Spectrometry

1 INTRODUCTION AND BACKGROUND

With the advent of high resolution and more sensitive mass spectrometers, MS based proteomics has become a go-to method for systems biology research. It has found its applications in detection, treatment and determination of phenotypes of cancer [21], protein sequencing and quantization [10], profiling of exosomes [18], study of toxicology [12] [14] and in evolutionary biology [22].

For the above mentioned uses of MS based proteomics, protein sequencing and quantization is the core step. This process involves breaking down a protein into peptides and separating them based on their masses followed by fragmentation and quantization in a mass spectrometer [1]. The resultant spectra contain mass-to-charge ratios of these fragments along with their corresponding intensities which are referred to as *peaks*. These MS2 spectra can be large in number where each spectrum can have up to 4000 peaks [4].

For peptide sequencing MS2 spectra can then be processed through two types of peptide sequencing algorithms: i) denovo algorithms or ii) database search algorithms. Both algorithms have to sift through large number of combinatorial possibilities to deduce a peptide for a given spectra. In our previous studies we [4] [2] have shown that 90% of the peaks in a given spectra are not helpful in peptide deduction. However, classifying peaks as useful/non-useful *before* peptide deduction is a difficult problem which has led to the development of complex pre-processing algorithms [16][4]. Pre-processing of MS data has been studied under three major categories i.e. clustering [19], noise reduction [9] and quality assessment [5]. Algorithms from all categories have a common goal of assisting in peptide deduction by improving the quality of peptide spectral matches using standard peptide deduction algorithms. Several existing algorithms [16][15][9] are able to isolate and remove about 60% to 70% of the useless peaks which results in speeding up the process of peptide deduction. However, many of these compute intensive algorithms require more time for pre-processing than actual processing of peptide deduction; defeating the purpose of their design. A detailed review of these algorithms can be found in [4].

In our previous work, we introduced MS-REDUCE, a pre-processing algorithm [4]. It is shown to bring down pre-processing time from days to minutes. To the best of our knowledge, MS-REDUCE is the fastest known sequential noise/data reduction algorithm for MS2 spectra. But even with MS-REDUCE the pre-processing time forms a significant portion of proteomics pipeline. This calls for the introduction of many-core devices such as GPUs to solve this problem. GPUs with their thousands of cores have the capability of performing thousands of calculations concurrently thus speeding up the process manifolds. However, the performance of most GPU-based algorithms is limited by the memory-related bottlenecks [7]. Typical memory bottlenecks in GPU include large transfer times[11], limited in-core memory [7] and the toll incurred by the irregular memory accesses when large data structures are used [3][6].

In this paper we present a GPU based dimensionality reduction algorithm for MS2 spectra and we call it G-MSR. We introduce two novel data structures i.e. *Binary Spectra* and *Quantized Indexed Spectra (QIS)* which solves the memory-bottleneck problems and achieves large speed up over MS-REDUCE. G-MSR is effectively an out-of-core algorithm since it is capable of processing datasets larger than the size of GPU's in-core memory. Using the novel data structures and careful parallel design we were able to achieve a peak speed-up of 386x over MS-REDUCE without loss of any accuracy.

1.1 Overview of MS-REDUCE

The algorithm first introduced in [4] operates in three steps: 1) Spectral Classification, 2) Quantization and 3) Weighted Sampling stage. Given a spectrum s and a reduction factor $0 < R \leq 1$, MS-REDUCE outputs a reduced spectrum s' such that the size of reduced spectrum is approximately $R*|s|$. The core step of MS-REDUCE is the weighted sampling step, in which a reduced spectrum s' is constructed such that the following total peak equation is satisfied.

$$\sum_{i=1}^{n}(\frac{x_i}{100} * q_i) = p'$$

here x_i is the sampling weight for i-th quantum, q_i is the number of peaks in quantum i, p' represents total peaks in reduced spectrum and n is the number of quanta for given spectrum. Details of remaining steps can be found in [4]. Flow of MS-REDUCE algorithm can be observed in Fig. 2 A).

1.2 CUDA Programing Model

With the introduction of CUDA programing environment GPUs have become easier to program and have offered a new platform in the realm of parallel computing [3] [20]. A GPU houses several Streaming Multiprocessors (SM) with each SM containing multiple CUDA cores. In modern GPUs with compute capability 3.0 and later, each SM can have up to 192 CUDA cores. Using CUDA programing environment the intricacies of hardware architecture are hidden from a programmer; instead she can focus on parallelizing the problem. GPUs employ SIMT model which combines the usual SIMD with multiple threading. Threads in CUDA environment are organized in a two level hierarchy of grids and thread blocks. A grid consists of multiple blocks and each block contains several threads. Each thread within a block has a unique thread and a block id. Threads within a block can communicate via a shared memory and local thread synchronizations. Inter block communication is performed through global memory and block synchronizations. The global memory is 100x slower than the shared memory but the smaller size of shared memory limits its utilization to a user controlled cache [17].

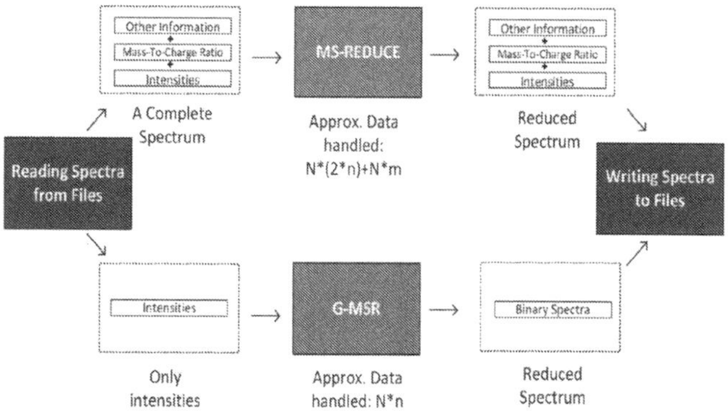

Figure 1: Here N denotes the number of spectra, n the size of largest spectrum and m the size of other information. Transferring only intensities to GPU for processing can conserve more than 50% of scarce in-core memory. G-MSR outputs the newly introduced Binary Spectra(defined in section: 2.1.2).

2 GPU BASED MS-REDUCE (G-MSR)

2.1 In-Core G-MSR

We have designed G-MSR to operate only on peak intensities. This preserves PCIe bandwidth since we only transfer intensities after rounding them off to the nearest integer. This does not have any effect on the quality as shown in our subsequent quality assessment experiments. Fig. 1 shows the difference in the amount of data handled by MS-REDUCE and G-MSR. In this paper, the word spectra or spectrum will refer to the arrays of peak-intensities.

2.1.1 Sorting and Intensity Spread Calculation. The calculation of average intensity spread (I_{avg}) requires sorting of intensities which forms a bottleneck [4]. To counter this we recently proposed a array sorting algorithm called GPU-ArraySort. It is a highly scalable algorithm for sorting large number of arrays making full use of GPU's resources [3]. We refer to the GPU-ArraySort Kernel as *Kernel-1*. Next, the intensity spread kernel i.e. *Kernel-2* calculates intensity spread for each spectrum and calculates I_{avg}. Pseudo code for Kernel 2 is given in Algo. 1.

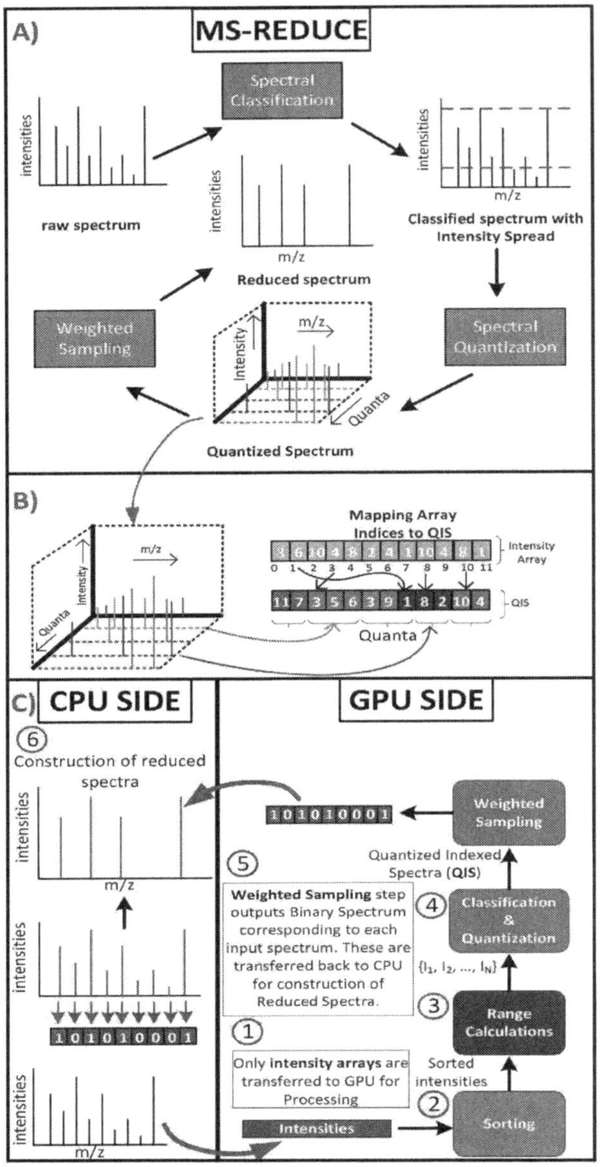

Figure 2: A) Shows the work flow of MS-REDUCE. B) Shows the construction of QIS from 3-D quantized spectrum from MS-REDUCE. C) Shows the work flow of G-MSR, blocks with same color represent processing in same kernel. A copy of actual spectra is maintained on the CPU for construction of reduced spectra.

2.1.2 Spectral Classification, Quantization and Sampling. Spectral Classification, Quantization and Sampling steps are boxed together in one single kernel function; we call it *Kernel-3*. Output of this kernel is a list of Binary Spectra. Binary Spectra provides a way of communicating this information between CPU and GPU necessary for constructing reduced spectrum from Binary Spectrum, as shown in Fig. 2.

Definition 2.1. Given a spectrum $s_i = \{p_1, p_2, p_3, \ldots, p_n\}$ a Binary Spectrum B_i for the corresponding reduced spectrum s_i' is defined as, $B_i = \{e_j = 1 | p_j \in s_i'\} \cup \{e_j = 0 | p_j \notin s_i'\}$.

As shown in Fig. 2 A), quantization step yields a complex 3-D data structure. Maintaining and accessing 3-D data structures inside GPU's memory can be very inefficient. To tackle this problem we introduce a novel data structure, Quantized Indexed Spectrum (QIS) to represent a quantized spectrum in a simple 1-D array. QIS helps avoiding irregular memory accesses and uses 50% less data, resulting in efficient, in-core memory usage. Fig. 2 B) shows the construction of QIS from intensity array. QIS can be formally defined as:

Definition 2.2. Given a spectrum s_i of size n, if after quantization, s_i has m quanta, then its QIS is given by $Q_i = \{l_1, l_2, l_3, \ldots, l_n\}$. Here l_x represents a peak index. Starting and ending offsets of quanta are stored in a separate array $p = \{st_1, e_1, st_2, e_2, \ldots, st_m, e_m\}$ where st_y is the offset where quantum y starts and e_y is where quantaum y ends.

The *Sampling* step involves determining the sampling weights for satisfying the peak equation. Peak-indices in QIS are sampled across all quanta based on these sampling weights. From the sampled-indices a Binary Spectrum is constructed using the array $O = \{0_1, 0_2, 0_3, \ldots 0_k\}$ of size same as s_i. And placing 1s at each index sampled before. Fig. 2 B) shows the process of constructing reduced spectra from Binary Spectra on CPU side.

2.2 Out-of-Core G-MSR

The out-of-core algorithm estimates the amount of memory required to process a given dataset. Depending on the total in-core memory of given GPU it then divides the dataset into parts and processes them in passes. However, because of data dependencies processing has to be performed in phases.

2.2.1 Phase 1. After moving the first chunk of spectra in the GPU memory, Kernel-1 is launched followed by Kernel-2 to calculate I_{avg}. The array of I_i for each chunk is stored on CPU temporarily. Then the process is repeated for remaining chunks, till I_i for all spectra and their sum is available on CPU. I_{avg} value for complete dataset is calculated on CPU and copied back.

2.2.2 Phase 2. In phase 2, each chunk of spectra along with its corresponding I_i array is copied to GPU and Kernel-3 is launched. The process repeats till all the chunks have been processed. Fig. 3 shows the flow of out-of-core execution.

Algorithm 1 Per thread Pseudo code for Kernel 2

Require: An array A of intensities and array S containing spectrum sizes. Subscript i wherever used, represents unique spectrum
Ensure: Array B containing binary spectrum of A
  for each thread i **do**
    $R_i \leftarrow$ SUM(Max10Peaks) - SUM(Min10Peaks)
    $R_{avg} \leftarrow$ Average(R)
  end for

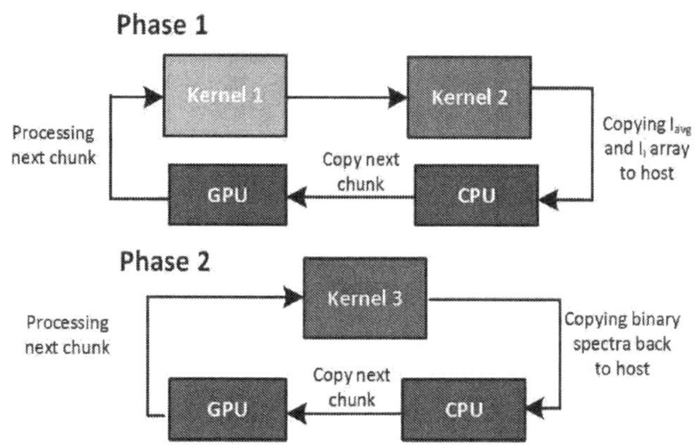

Figure 3: The figure showing the flow for out-of-core processing, phase 1 and phase 2 have been shown separately.

Algorithm 2 Per thread Pseudo code for Kernel 3

Require: An array A of intensities, Average Intensity Spread R and array of Intensity Spread R
Ensure: Array B containing binary spectrum of A
  for each thread i **do**
    $C_i \leftarrow$ getClass(A_i, R_i)
    $Q_i \leftarrow$ getTotalQuanta(C_i)
    for each $a_j \in A_i$ **do**
      $a_j \leftarrow$ getQuantum(a_j)
    end for
    $q_j \in qS \leftarrow$ quantaSizes(A_i)
    $B \leftarrow 0$
    for each $q_j \in qS$ **do**
      $q_j \leftarrow$ getSampleRate(q_j)
      B[getSample(q_j)] $\leftarrow 1$
    end for
  end for

3 TIME COMPLEXITY ANALYSIS

GPU-ArraySort uses insertion sort for sorting small sized bins. If p CUDA threads are used for sorting a spectrum of size n, its time complexity would be $O(\frac{n^2}{p})$, we can extend this for N spectra and B CUDA blocks to get $O(\frac{N*n^2}{B*p})$ for the sorting step. Intensity Spread calculation and Classification steps are constant time processes and take $O(N)$ for N spectra, while using a total of B threads across all CUDA blocks, both of these steps can be performed in $O(\frac{N}{B})$. The Quantization step takes $O(n)$ time for a spectrum of size n. For N spectra this would take $O(N * n)$, and when using B threads across all blocks it becomes $O(\frac{N*n}{B})$. The Random Sampling step has an execution time of $O(s * n)$ where s is the rate of sampling and its value varies from 0 to 1. While using a total of B threads across all blocks and for N spectra it becomes $O(\frac{s*N}{B})$. Combining all of the above time complexities and replacing $l = p * (2 + n + n * s)$, we get:

$$O(\frac{N * (n^2 + l)}{B * p}) \quad (1)$$

4 PERFORMANCE EVALUATION

We evaluated the performance of G-MSR from two different aspects. First was a time based analysis to determine the amount of speed-up obtained over the serial version. Second was a quality assessment experiment to see how the number of high quality peptide spectral matches (PSMs) varied when treating the spectra with G-MSR. We also evaluate the performance of G-MSR while using it as a tool for reductive proteomics for high resolution instruments.

4.1 Data Generation

For all the experiments, we made use of the thirteen datasets we used before in [4] and [19]. Naming conventions for all thirteen data sets are same as in [4].

4.2 Experiment Setup

For all the experiments we made use of a Linux server running Ubuntu Operating System, version 14.01. The server houses two Intel Xeon E5-2620 Processors, clocked at 2.40 GHz with a total RAM of 48 GBs. The system has an NVIDIA Tesla K-40c GPU with a total of 2880 CUDA Cores and 12 GBs of RAM. CUDA version 7.5 and GCC version 4.8.4 were used for compilation.

4.3 Scalability and Time Analysis

For this experiment, we used the appended UPS2 dataset which had over a million spectra. Timing experiments were performed with increasing datasizes to cover the out-of-core cases. Results for scalability studies can be observed in Fig. 5. In Fig. 5, when N is small and is almost equal to B we get huge speed ups. But as the number of spectra increase and the number of concurrent threads reach their limit we observe a decrease in speed up in accordance with Eq. 1. Also term l in Eq. 1 increases when reduction factor is increased. This explains higher speed ups for lower reduction factors.

4.4 Quality Assessment

We used the same method of quality assessment as discussed in [4]. For our experiments we set the FDR value of interest to 5% i.e. any PSM having FDR value below 5% is an acceptable match, we call them effective matches. Fig. 6 shows

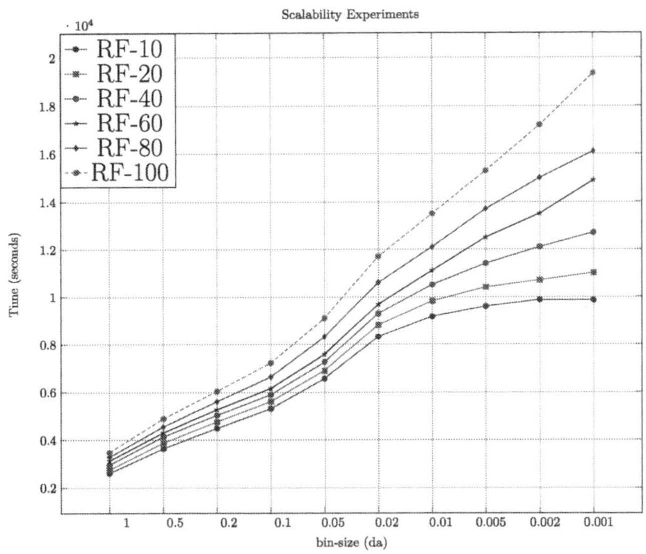

Figure 4: Timing plots of peptide deduction process using Tide with hiXcorr algorithm. Here RF is the reduction factor. An increasing RF makes the process more scalable.

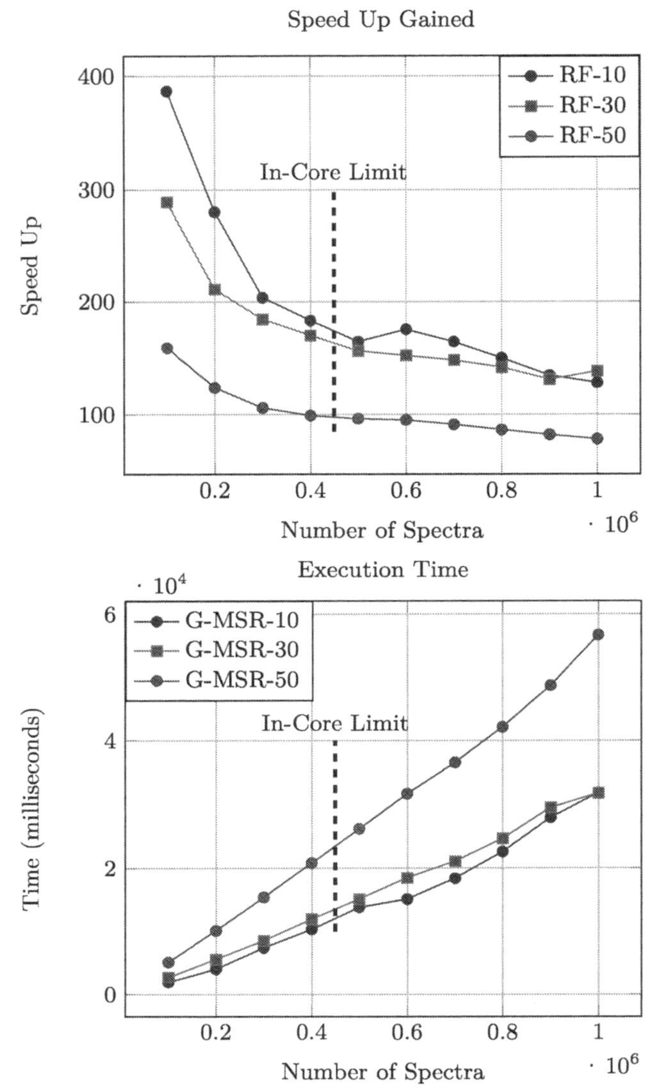

Figure 5: Top figure shows the speed up achieved by G-MSR over MS-REDUCE and the bottom figure shows the execution times for G-MSR operating at reduction factors of 10, 30 and 50. The vertical line represents the point where in-core memory is filled.

percentage of effective matches with varying reduction factors for both algorithms. G-MSR and MS-REDUCE gave almost same percentages of effective matches.

4.5 Reductive Proteomics for high resolution instruments

In high resolution mass spectrometery data, number of bins created can be quite large which can lead to large processing times for all sorts of peptide deduction algorithms [13].

Pre-processing of spectra with G-MSR will reduce the size of spectrum and hence the processing time for peptide deduction. We performed peptide deduction for UPS2 dataset after preprocessing it with G-MSR at different reduction factors. For this experiment Tide [8] integrated with hiXcorr [13] was used for peptide deduction. Fig. 4 shows that with smaller reduction factors the performance of peptide deduction algorithm becomes more scalable even with increasing resolution.

5 DISCUSSION AND CONCLUSION

Modern day multi- and many-core devices are changing the way scientists tackle computationally complex problems. Theoretically intractable problems with complex approximate solutions are now being solved in acceptable times using modern high performance computing devices. In the field of bioinformatics datasets may range from a few gigabytes to several terabytes. These large datasets not only provide computational bottlenecks but an added problem of data management inside the limited in-core memories of these devices. In this paper we presented a GPU based data reduction algorithm for MS2 spectra called G-MSR. We introduced two novel data structures called Quantized Indexed Spectrum (QIS) and Binary Spectrum which helped minimize the use of GPU memory and making memory accesses more localized and thus enabled the processing of large data sets in a single pass with maximum efficiency. Binary spectra allowed us to process spectra by just copying the required information on to the GPU while storing the actual spectra on CPU Memory.

Our proposed strategy is capable of processing datasets which exceed the memory limits of a GPU using an out-of-core technique. Our experiments show a peak speed-up of

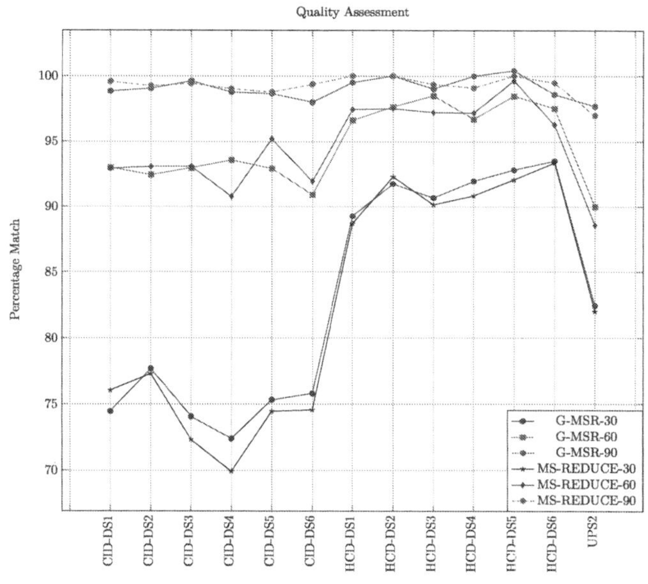

Figure 6: Quality assessment plots of MS-REDUCE and G-MSR. Numerical values in legend are the reduction factors. X-axis is the data set labels and Y-axis is the PSM percentage with FDR greater than 5%.

386x as compared to the serial version of the algorithm. And finally we introduce G-MSR to be used as a pre-processing step in reductive proteomics for high resolution instruments for high throughput processing.

ACKNOWLEDGMENTS

This research was supported by the National Institute Of General Medical Sciences (NIGMS) of the National Institutes of Health (NIH) under Award Number R15GM120820. The content is solely the responsibility of the authors and does not necessarily represent the official views of the National Institutes of Health. This work was supported in part by National Science Foundation grants NSF CRII CCF-1464268 and NSF CAREER ACI-1651724. We would also like to acknowledge the donation of a K-40c Tesla GPU from NVIDIA which was used for all GPU based experiments performed in this paper.

REFERENCES

[1] Ruedi Aebersold and Matthias Mann. 2003. Mass spectrometry-based proteomics. *Nature* 422, 6928 (2003), 198–207.
[2] Muaaz Gul Awan and Fahad Saeed. 2015. On the sampling of big mass spectrometry data. In *The International Society for Computers and Their Applications (ISCA)*.
[3] Muaaz Gul Awan and Fahad Saeed. 2016. GPU-ArraySort: A parallel, in-place algorithm for sorting large number of arrays. In *Parallel Processing Workshops (ICPPW), 2016 45th International Conference on Parallel Processing*. IEEE, 78–87.
[4] Muaaz Gul Awan and Fahad Saeed. 2016. MS-REDUCE: An ultrafast technique for reduction of Big Mass Spectrometry Data for high-throughput processing. *Bioinformatics* (2016), btw023.
[5] Marshall Bern, David Goldberg, W. Hayes McDonald, and John R. Yates IIII. 2004. Automatic Quality Assessment of Peptide Tandem Mass Spectra. *Bioinformatics* 20 (2004).
[6] Daniel Cederman and Philippas Tsigas. 2009. Gpu-quicksort: A practical quicksort algorithm for graphics processors. *Journal of Experimental Algorithmics (JEA)* 14 (2009), 4.
[7] Sankua Chao, James R Green, and Jeffrey C Smith. 2014,. Evaluation of a GPGPU-based de novo Peptide Sequencing Algorithm. *Journal of Medical and Biological Engineering* 34, 5 (2014,).
[8] Benjamin J. Diament and William Stafford Noble. 2011. Faster SEQUEST Searching for Peptide Identification from Tandem Mass Spectra. *Journal of Proteome Research* 10, 9 (July 2011), 3871–3879.
[9] Jiarui Ding, Jinhong Shi, Guy G Poirier, and Fang Xiang Wu. 2009. A novel approach to denoising ion trap tandem mass spectra. *Proteome Science* 7, 9 (March 2009).
[10] Jimmy K Eng, Ashley L McCormack, and John R Yates. 1994. An approach to correlate tandem mass spectral data of peptides with amino acid sequences in a protein database. *Journal of the American Society for Mass Spectrometry* 5, 11 (1994).
[11] Yusuke Fujii, Takuya Azumi, Nobuhiko Nishio, Shinpei Kato, and Masato Edahiro. 2013. Data transfer matters for GPU computing. In *Parallel and Distributed Systems (ICPADS), 2013 International Conference on*. IEEE, 275–282.
[12] Linnet K. 2013. Toxicological Screening and Quantitation Using Liquid Chromatography/Time-of-Flight Mass Spectrometry. *Journal of Forensic Science and Criminology* 1, 1 (2013).
[13] Hyunwoo Kim, Hosung Jo, Heejin Park, and Eunok Paek. 2015. HiXCorr: a portable high-speed XCorr engine for high-resolution tandem mass spectrometry. *Bioinformatics* (2015), btv490.
[14] Luc Alexis Leuthold, Jean-François Mandscheff, Marc Fathi, Christian Giroud, Marc Augsburger, Emmanuel Varesio, and Gerard Hopfgartner. 2006. Desorption electrospray ionization mass spectrometry: direct toxicological screening and analysis of illicit Ecstasy tablets. *Rapid Communications in Mass Spectrometry* 20, 2 (2006), 103–110.
[15] Nedim Mujezinovic, Gunther Raidl, James R. A. Hutchins, Jan-Michael Peters, Karl Mechtler, and Frank Eisenhaber. 2006. Cleaning of raw peptide MS/MS spectra: Improved protein identification following deconvolution of multiply charged peaks, isotope clusters, and removal of background noise. *Proteome Science* 6 (2006).
[16] Nedim Mujezinovic, Georg Schneider, Michael Wildpaner, Karl Mechtler, and Frank Eisenhaber. 2010. Reducing the haystack to find the needle: improved protein identification after fast elimination of non-interpretable peptide MS/MS spectra and noise reduction. *BMC Genomics* 11 (2010).
[17] Nvidia. 2016. CUDA Toolkit Documentation v7.5. (2016). http://docs.nvidia.com/cuda/index.html#axzz42Wi4k0Qc
[18] Trairak Pisitkun, Rong-Fong Shen, and Mark Knepper. 2004. Identification and proteomic profiling of exosomes in human urine. *Proceedings of the National Academy of Sciences of the United States of America* 101, 36 (2004).
[19] Fahad Saeed, Jason D. Hoffert, and Mark A. Knepper. 2013. CAMS-RS: Clustering Algorithm for Large-Scale Mass Spectrometry Data Using Restricted Search Space and Intelligent Random Sampling. *IEEE/ACM transactions on computational biology and bioinformatics* 11, 1 (2013), 128–141.
[20] Jason Sander and Edward Kandrot. 2010. *CUDA by Example*.
[21] Henk MW Verheul. 2014. Mass spectrometry-based proteomics: from cancer biology to protein biomarkers, drug targets, and clinical applications. American Society of Clinical Oncology.
[22] Boyang Zhao, Trairak Pisitkun, Jason D. Hoffert, Mark A. Knepper, and Fahad Saeed. 2012. CPhos: A program to calculate and visualize evolutionarily conserved functional phosphorylation sites. *Proteomics* 12, 22 (2012), 3299–3303.

Building Applications for Interactive Data Exploration in Systems Biology

Bjørn Fjukstad
Department of Computer Science
UiT The Arctic University of Norway

Vanessa Dumeaux
Department of Biology
Concordia University

Karina Standahl Olsen
Department of Community Medicine
UiT The Arctic University of Norway

Eiliv Lund
Department of Community Medicine
UiT The Arctic University of Norway

Michael Hallett
Department of Biology
Concordia University

Lars Ailo Bongo
Department of Computer Science
UiT The Arctic University of Norway

ABSTRACT

The significant increase in the rate of data generation by the systems biology community creates a need for interactive exploration tools to explore the resultant datasets. Such tools need to combine advanced statistical analyses, prior knowledge from biological databases, and interactive visualizations with intuitive user interfaces. Each specific research question potentially requires a specialized user interface and visualization methods. Although some features are application-specific, the underlying components of the data analysis tool can be shared and reused.

Our approach for developing data exploration tools in systems biology builds on the microservice architecture that separates an application into smaller components which can communicate using language-agnostic protocols. We show that this design is well suited for bioinformatics applications where different tools written in different languages by different research groups is the norm. Packaging each service in a software container enables re-use and sharing of key components between applications, reducing development, deployment, and maintenance time.

We demonstrate the viability of our approach through a web application, entitled MIxT blood-tumor, for exploring and comparing transcriptional profiles from blood and tumor samples in breast cancer patients. The application integrates advanced statistical software, up-to-date information from biological databases, and modern data visualization libraries.

Permission to make digital or hard copies of all or part of this work for personal or classroom use is granted without fee provided that copies are not made or distributed for profit or commercial advantage and that copies bear this notice and the full citation on the first page. Copyrights for components of this work owned by others than the author(s) must be honored. Abstracting with credit is permitted. To copy otherwise, or republish, to post on servers or to redistribute to lists, requires prior specific permission and/or a fee. Request permissions from permissions@acm.org.
ACM-BCB'17, August 20-23, 2017, Boston, MA, USA.
© 2017 Copyright held by the owner/author(s). Publication rights licensed to ACM.
978-1-4503-4722-8/17/08...$15.00
DOI: http://dx.doi.org/10.1145/3107411.3107481

KEYWORDS

Interactive data exploration, software containers, visualization, microservices, systems biology, breast cancer.

INTRODUCTION

In recent years the biological community has generated an unprecedented amount of data. While the cost of data collection has drastically decreased, data analysis continue to represent a large fraction of the total cost of these studies.[9] Data analysis tools, especially those designed specifically for the project at hand, provide clear benefit to the human experts who are interpreting data and deriving results.

Often in systems biology studies, the ability to explore newly generated data relative to prior knowledge located in third-party databases and software systems is key. This includes, for example, entities such as the Gene Ontology (GO),[1] the Kyoto Encyclopedia of Genes and Genomes (KEGG),[2] and the Molecular Signatures Database (MSigDB)[3] that together catalog the function of nearly every gene, gene product, pathway or cellular process. These tools, and most bioinformatics databases in general, offer interfaces for data retrieval.

Data analysis in systems biology is greatly reliant on programming languages especially tailored to these domains, providing easy direct access to specific algorithms and statistical routines. The R statistical programming language provides developers open access to thousands of libraries through repositories such as CRAN[4] or Bioconductor[5]. Similarly, other languages such as Python and Go have bioinformatic extensions including BioPython[2] and biogo[6] respectively, providing domain specific routines. Although tremendously helpful, different tools and languages are used in different domains of systems biology for many reasons. This creates a

[1] geneontology.org.
[2] kegg.jp.
[3] software.broadinstitute.org/gsea/msigdb.
[4] cran.r-project.org.
[5] bioconductor.org.

need for novel approaches to integrate the different libraries between the programming languages and tools.

A microservice architecture structures an application into small reusable, loosely coupled parts. These communicate via lightweight programming language-agnostic protocols such as HTTP, thus making it possible to write single applications in multiple programming languages. This way the most suitable programming language is used for each specific part. To build a microservice application, developers bundle each service in a software container. Containers are built from configuration files which describe the operating system, software packages and their associated versions. Several software container implementations exist including Rkt[6] but Docker,[7] is perhaps the most broadly used. Initiatives such as BioContainers[8] now provide containers pre-installed with different bioinformatics tools. While the enabling technology is available, the microservices approach is not yet widely adopted in bioinformatics.[11]

From our experience we identified a set of components and features that are central to building data exploration applications.

(1) A low-latency language-independent approach for integrating, or embedding, statistical software, such as R, directly into a data exploration application.
(2) Low latency language-independent interface to online reference databases in biology that users can query to explore analyses.
(3) A simple method for deploying and sharing the components of an application between projects.

In this paper, we describe a novel approach for building data exploration applications in systems biology via a sample web application, MIxT (Matched Interactions across Tissues) using high-throughput gene expression profiles of breast cancer tumor data with matched profiles from the patients blood.

METHODS

In this section we first motivate our microservice approach based on our experiences developing the MIxT web application. We describe the process from initial data analysis to the final application, highlighting the importance of language-agnostic services to facilitate the use of different tools in different parts of the application. We then generalize the ideas to a set of principles and services that can be reused and shared between applications, and show their design and implementation.

Motivating Example

The aim of the Matched Interactions Across Tissues (MIxT) study was to identify genes and pathways in the primary breast tumor that are tightly linked to genes and pathways in the patient blood cells.[3] We generated and analyzed expression profiles from blood and matched tumor cells in 173 breast cancer patients included in the Norwegian Women and Cancer (NOWAC) study. The MIxT analysis starts by identifying sets of genes tightly co-expressed across all patients in each tissue. Each group of genes or modules were annotated based on a priori biological knowledge about gene functionality. Focus was placed on the relationships between tissues by asking if specific biologies in one tissue are linked with (possibly distinct) biologies in the second tissue, and this within different subgroup of patients (i.e. subtypes of breast cancer).

We built an R package, mixtR,[9] with the statistical methods and static visualizations for identifying associations between modules across tissues. To make the results more easily accessible we built a web application that interfaces with the R package, but also online databases to retrieve relevant metadata. To make it possible to easily update or re-implement parts of the system without effecting the entire application, it was developed using a microservice architecture. The software containers allowed the application to be deployed on a wide range of hardware, from local installations to cloud systems.

Design Principles

Our experience can be generalized into the following design principles for building applications in bioinformatics:

Principle 1: Build applications as collections of language-agnostic microservices. This enables re-use of components and does not enforce any specific programming language on the user interfaces or the underlying components of the application.

Principle 2: Use software containers to package each service. This has a number of benefits: it simplifies deployment, ensures that dependencies and libraries are installed, and simplifies sharing of services between developers.

Microservice Design and Implementation

In the rest of the section we describe how we designed and implemented two microservices in Kvik[4] which we later used to build the MIxT web application.

Compute Service. The main goal of a data exploration application in systems biology is to help users discover interesting patterns in a biological dataset. Because of the complexity of biological data and analyses, we need specialized software to help find these patterns. Because these tools are built to provide specialized analyses, they often don't provide a reusable interface outside the programming environment they are built in.

We have built a compute service that provides an open interface directly to the R programming language, thus providing access to a wealth of algorithm and statistical analysis packages that exists within the R ecosystem. Application developers can use the compute service to execute specialized analyses and retrieve results either as plain text or binary data such as plots. By interfacing directly with R, developers

[6]coreos.com/rkt.
[7]docker.com.
[8]biocontainers.pro.

[9]Available online at github.com/vdumeaux/mixtR.

can modify input parameters to statistical methods directly from the user-facing application.

The compute service offers three main operations to interface with R: i) to call a function with one or more input parameters from an R package, ii) to get the results from a previous function call, and iii) a catch-all term that both calls a function and returns the results. We use the same terminology as OpenCPU[8] and have named the three operations Call, Get, and RPC respectively. These three operations provide the necessary interface for applications to include statistical analyses in the applications.

The compute service is implemented as an HTTP server that communicates with a pre-set number of R processes to execute statistical analyses. At initiation of the compute service, a user-defined number of R worker sessions are launched for executing analyses (default is 5). The compute service uses a round-robin scheduling scheme to distribute incoming requests to the workers. We provide a simple FIFO queue for queuing of requests. The compute service also provides the opportunity for applications to cache analysis results to speed up subsequent calls.

Database Service. To interpret data, experts regularly exploit prior knowledge via database queries and the primary scientific literature. There are a wealth of online databases, some of which provide open APIs in addition to web user interfaces that application developers can make use of. While the databases can provide helpful information, there are some limitations associated with their integration into interactive data exploration applications: i) the APIs are not fast enough to use in interactive applications where the application has to perform multiple database queries, ii) some databases put restrictions on the number of database queries, and iii) there is no uniform way for storing additional database metadata to identify database versions and query parameters.

To alleviate application developers of these challenges, we built an database service that provides a solution to the three. The service provides low latency, minimizes the number of queries to remote databases, and stores additional metadata to capture query parameters and database information. The database service provides an open HTTP interface to biological databases for retrieving meta-data on genes and processes. We currently have packages for interfacing with E-utilities,[10] MSigDB, HGNC, and KEGG.

Both the compute and the databases service in Kvik build on the standard *net/http* package in the Go programming language.[11] The database service use the *gocache*[12] package to cache any query to an online database. In addition we deploy each service as Docker containers.[13]

[10] eutils.ncbi.nlm.nih.gov.

[11] golang.org

[12] github.com/fjukstad/gocache.

[13] Available at hub.docker.com/r/fjukstad/kvik-r and hub.docker.com/r/fjukstad/db.

MATCHED INTERACTIONS ACROSS TISSUES (MIXT)

We show the viability of the microservices approach in Kvik by describing the MIxT web application for exploring and comparing transcriptional profiles from blood and tumor samples. We conduct an initial evaluation to illustrate that we can built interactive applications using the microservices provided by Kvik.

Analysis Tasks

The web application provides functionality to perform six data analysis tasks (A1-A6):

A1: Explore co-expression gene sets in tumor and blood tissue. Users can explore gene expression patterns together with clinicopathological variables (e.g. patient or tumor grade, stage, age) for each module. In addition we enable users to study the underlying biological functions of each module by including gene set analyses between the module genes and known gene sets.

A2: Explore co-expression relationships between genes. Users can explore the co-expression relationship as a graph visualization. Here genes are represented in the network with nodes and edges represent statistically significant correlation in expression between the two end-points.

A3: Explore relationships between modules from each tissue. We provide two different metrics to compare modules, and the web application enables users to interactively browse these relationships. In addition to providing visualizations the compare modules from each tissue, users can explore the relationships, but for different breast cancer patient groups.

A4: Explore relationships between clinical variables and modules. In addition to comparing the association between modules from both tissues, users also have the possibility to explore the association with a module and a specific clinical variable. It is also possible to explore the associations after first stratifying the tumors by breast cancer subtype (an operation that is common in cancer related studies to deal with molecular heterogeneity).

A5: Explore association between user-submitted gene lists and computed modules. We want to enable users to explore their own gene lists to explore them in context of the co-expression gene sets. The web application must handle uploads of gene lists and compute association between the gene list and the MIxT modules on demand.

A6: Search for genes or gene lists of interest. To facilitate faster lookup of genes and biological processes, the web application provides a search functionality that lets users locate genes or gene lists and show association to the co-expression gene sets.

Design and Implementation

From these six analysis tasks we designed and implemented MIxT as a web application that integrates statistical analyses and information from biological databases together with interactive visualizations. Figure 1 shows the system architecture of MIxT which consists of three parts i) the web application itself containing the user-interface and visualizations; ii) the compute service performing the MIxT analyses developed in an R package, delivering data to the web application; and iii) the database service providing up-to-date information from biological databases. Each of these components run within Docker containers making the process of deploying the application simple.

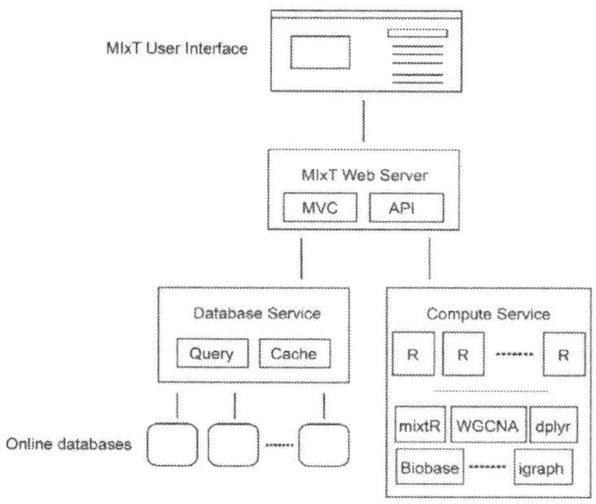

Figure 1: The architecture of the MIxT system. It consists of a web application, the hosting web server, a database service for retrieving metadata and a compute service for performing statistical analysis. Note that only the web application and the R package are specific to MIxT, the rest of the components can be reused in other applications.

We structured the MIxT application with a separate view for each analysis task. To explore the co-expression gene sets (**A1**), we built a view that combines both static visualizations from R together with interactive tables for gene overlap analyses. Figure 2 shows the web page presented to users when they access the co-expression gene set 'darkturquoise' from blood. To explore the co-expression relationship between genes (**A2**) we use an interactive graph visualization build with Sigmajs[14]. We have built visualization for both tissues, with graph sizes of 2705 nodes and 90 348 edges for the blood network, and 2066 nodes and 50 563 edges for the biopsy network. To visualize relationships between modules from different tissues (**A3**), or their relationship to clinical variables (**A4**) we built a heatmap visualization using the d3[15] library. We built a simple upload page where users can specify their gene sets (**A5**). The file is uploaded to the web application which redirects it to the compute service that runs the analyses. Similarly we can take user input to search for genes and processes (**A6**).

The web application is hosted by a custom web server. This web server is responsible for dynamically generating the different views based on data from the statistical analyses and biological databases, and serve these to users. It also serves the different JavaScript visualization libraries and style sheets.

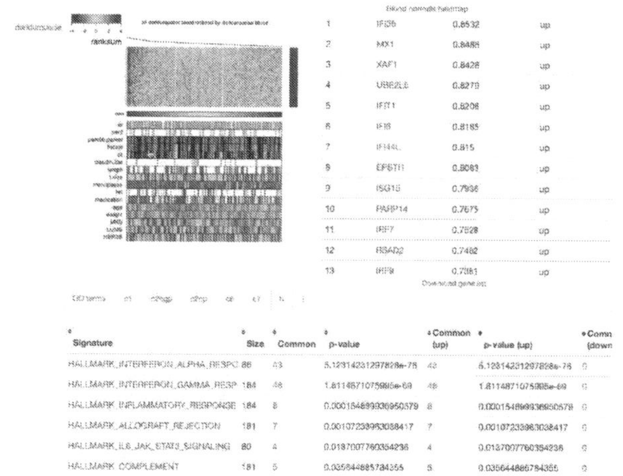

Figure 2: MIxT module overview page. The top left panel contains the gene expression heatmap for the module genes. The top right panel contains a table of the genes found in the module. The bottom panel contains the results of gene overlap analyses from the module genes and known gene sets from MSigDB.

Evaluation

To investigate if it is feasible to implement parts of an application as separate services, we evaluate the response times for a set of queries to each of the two supporting services.

To evaluate the database service we measure the query time for retrieving information about a specific gene with and without caching.[16] This illustrates how we can improve performance in an application by using a database service rather than accessing the database directly. We use a AWS EC2 *t2.micro*[17] instance to host and evaluate the database service. The results in Table 1 confirm a significant improvement in response time when the database service caches the results from the database lookups. In addition by serving the results out of cache we reduce the number of queries to the online database down to one.

Table 1: Time to retrieve a gene summary for a single gene, comparing different number of concurrent requests.

	1	2	5	10	15
No cache	956ms	1123ms	1499ms	2147ms	2958ms
Cache	64ms	64ms	130ms	137ms	154ms

We evaluate the compute service by running a benchmark consisting of two operations: first generate a set of 100

[14]sigmajs.org.
[15]d3js.org.
[16]More details online at github.com/fjukstad/kvik/tree/master/db/benchmark.
[17]See aws.amazon.com/ec2/instance-types for more information about AWS EC2 instance types.

random numbers, then plot them and return the resulting visualization.[18] We use two *c4.large* instances on AWS EC2 running the Kvik compute service and OpenCPU base docker containers. The servers have caching disabled. Table 2 shows the time to complete the benchmark for different number of concurrent connections. We see that the compute service in Kvik performs better than the OpenCPU[19] alternative. We believe that speedup is because we keep a pool of R processes that handle requests. In OpenCPU a new R process is forked upon every request that results in any computation executed in R. Other requests such as retrieving previous results do not fork new R processes.

Table 2: Time to complete the benchmark with different number of concurrent connections.

	1	2	5	10	15
Kvik	274ms	278ms	352ms	374ms	390ms
OpenCPU	500ms	635ms	984ms	1876ms	2700ms

RELATED WORK

In this section we discuss different methods that facilitates building applications using a microservices approach.

Integrate Statistical Analyses

OpenCPU is a system for embedded scientific computing and reproducible research.[8] Similar to the compute service in Kvik, it offers an HTTP API to the R programming language to provide an interface with statistical methods. It allows users to make function calls to any R package and retrieve the results in a wide variety of formats such as JSON or PDF. OpenCPU provides a JavaScript library for interfacing with R, as well as Docker containers for easy installation, and has been used to build multiple applications.[20]. The compute service in Kvik follows many of the design patterns in OpenCPU. Both systems interface with R packages using a hybrid state pattern over HTTP. Both systems provide the same interface to execute analyses and retrieve results. Because of the similarities in the interface to R in Kvik we provide packages for interfacing with our own R server or OpenCPU R servers.

Shiny is a web application framework for R[21] It allows developers to build web applications in R without having to have any knowledge about HTML, CSS, or Javascript. While it provides an easy alternative to build web applications on top of R, it cannot be used as a service in an application that implements the user-interface outside R.

Renjin is a JVM-based interpreter for the R programming language.[1] It allows developers to write applications in Java that interact directly with R code. This makes it possible to use Renjin to build a service for running statistical analyses on top of R. One serious drawback is that existing R packages must be re-built specifically for use in Renjin.

Visualization

Cytoscape is an open source software platform for visualizing complex networks and integrating these with any type of attribute data.[10] Through a Cytoscape App, cyREST, it allows external network creation and analysis through a REST API[7], making it possible to use Cytoscape as a service. To bring the visualization and analysis capabilities to the web applications the creators of Cytoscape have developed Cytoscape.js[22], a JavaScript library to create interactive graph visualizations. Another alternative for biological data visualization in the web browser is BioJS It provides a community-driven online repository with a wide range components for visualizing biological data contributed by the bioinformatics community.[5] BioJS builds on node.js[23] providing both server-side and client-side libraries. In MIxT we have opted to build the visualizations from scratch using sigma.js and d3 to have full control over the appearance and functionality of the visualizations.

Kvik and Kvik Pathwys

We have previously built a system for interactively exploring gene expression data in context of biological pathways.[4] Kvik Pathways is a web application that integrates gene expression data from the Norwegian Women and Cancer (NOWAC) cohort together with pathway images from the Kyoto Encyclopedia of Genes and Genomes (KEGG). We used the experience building Kvik Pathways to completely re-design and re-implement the R interface in Kvik. From having an R server that can run a set of functions from an R script, it now has a clean interface to call any function from any R package, not just retrieving data as a text string but in a wide range of formats. We also re-built the database interface, which is now a separate service. This makes it possible to leverage its caching capabilities to improve latency. This transformed the application from being a single monolithic application into a system that consists of a web application for visualizing biological pathways, a database service to retrieve pathway images and other metadata, and a compute service for interfacing with the gene expression data in the NOWAC cohort. We could then re-use the database and the compute service in the MIxT application.

DISCUSSION

There are different arguments for reusing and sharing microservices over libraries in bioinformatics applications, that would justify the cost of hosting an maintaining a set of distributed microservices. We argue that applications that require large computational or storage resources can benefit from the microservices approach because the applications can share the underlying compute infrastructure between

[18] More details at github.com/fjukstad/kvik/tree/master/r/benchmarks.
[19] Built using the *opencpu-server* Docker image.
[20] opencpu.org/apps.html.
[21] shiny.rstudio.com.
[22] js.cytoscapejs.org.
[23] nodejs.org.

multiple applications and users. This makes it possible to deploy an application on a lightweight system that uses a common service for computation and storage. In addition, benefits such as using different programming languages for a single application, and packaging a microservice as a software container, help to outweigh the operational burden related to using microservices to build applications.

We have used this approach to build different web applications and command line tools, but out of space constraints we only showcase one application in this paper. We have reused the microservices for running statistical analyses and fetch biological metadata, and share these between applications. This makes it possible for multiple applications to use one or more powerful servers for hosting the services. In the case of statistical analyses we simply install the necessary R packages for each application on the compute service and run it as we would for one single application.

Future work

We intend to address few points we aim to address in future work, both in the MIxT web application as well as the supporting microservices. The first issue is to improve the user experience in the MIxT web application. Since it is executing many of the analyses on demand, the user interface may seem unresponsive. We are working on mechanisms that gives the user feedback when the computations are taking a long time, but also reducing analysis time by optimizing the underlying R package. The database service provides a sufficient interface for the MIxT web application. While we have developed the software packages for interfacing with more databases, these haven't been included in the database service yet. In future versions we aim to make the database service an interface for all our applications. We also aim to improve how we capture data provenance. We aim to provide database versions and meta-data about when a specific item was retrieved from the database. One large concern that we haven't addressed in this paper is security. In particular one security concern that we aim to address in Kvik is the restrictions on the execution of code in the compute service. We aim to address this in the next version of the compute service, using methods such as AppArmor[24] that can restrict a program's resource access. In addition to code security we will address data access, specifically put constraints on who can access data from the compute service. We also aim to explore different alternatives for scaling up the compute service. Since we already interface with R we can use the Sparklyr[25] or SparkR[26] packages to run analyses on top of Spark.[12] Using Spark as an execution engine for data analyses will enable applications to explore even larger datasets.

CONCLUSIONS

We have designed an approach for building data exploration applications in systems biology that is based on a microservice architecture. Using this approach we have built a web application that leverages this architecture to integrate statistical analyses, interactive visualizations, and data from biological databases. While we have used our approach to build an application in systems biology, we believe that the microservice architecture can be used to build data exploration systems in other disciplines as well.

ACKNOWLEDGMENTS

We would like to thank Andrew Bogecho and the System Staff at the School of Computer Science at McGill University for maintaining the compute infrastructure used to run the MIxT system.

This work has been funded by The European Research Council (ERC-AdG 232997 TICE), and The Canadian Cancer Society Research Institute (INNOV2-2014-702940).

REFERENCES

[1] Alexander Bertram. 2013. Renjin: The new R interpreter built on the JVM. In *The R User Conference, useR! 2013 July 10-12 2013 University of Castilla-La Mancha, Albacete, Spain*, Vol. 10. 105.

[2] Peter JA Cock, Tiago Antao, Jeffrey T Chang, Brad A Chapman, Cymon J Cox, Andrew Dalke, Iddo Friedberg, Thomas Hamelryck, Frank Kauff, Bartek Wilczynski, and others. 2009. Biopython: freely available Python tools for computational molecular biology and bioinformatics. *Bioinformatics* 25, 11 (2009), 1422–1423.

[3] Vanessa Dumeaux, Bjørn Fjukstad, Hans Fjosne E, Jan-Ole Frantzen, Marit Muri Holmen, Enno Rodegerdts, Ellen Schlichting, Anne-Lise Børresen-Dale, Lars Ailo Bongo, Eiliv Lund, and Michael T. Hallett. 2017. Interactions between the tumor and the blood systemic response of breast cancer patients. *Under review* (2017).

[4] Bjørn Fjukstad, Karina Standahl Olsen, Mie Jareid, Eiliv Lund, and Lars Ailo Bongo. 2015. Kvik: three-tier data exploration tools for flexible analysis of genomic data in epidemiological studies. *F1000Research* 4 (2015).

[5] John Gómez, Leyla J García, Gustavo A Salazar, Jose Villaveces, Swanand Gore, Alexander García, Maria J Martín, Guillaume Launay, Rafael Alcántara, Noemi Del Toro Ayllón, and others. 2013. BioJS: an open source JavaScript framework for biological data visualization. *Bioinformatics* (2013), btt100.

[6] R Daniel Kortschak and David L Adelson. 2014. bíogo: a simple high-performance bioinformatics toolkit for the Go language. *bioRxiv* (2014). DOI:https://doi.org/10.1101/005033 arXiv:http://biorxiv.org/content/early/2014/05/12/005033.full.pdf

[7] Keiichiro Ono, Tanja Muetze, Georgi Kolishovski, Paul Shannon, and Barry Demchak. 2015. CyREST: Turbocharging Cytoscape Access for External Tools via a RESTful API. *F1000Research* 4 (2015).

[8] Jeroen Ooms. 2014. The OpenCPU System: Towards a Universal Interface for Scientific Computing through Separation of Concerns. *arXiv preprint arXiv:1406.4806* (2014).

[9] Andrea Sboner, Xinmeng Jasmine Mu, Dov Greenbaum, Raymond K Auerbach, and Mark B Gerstein. 2011. The real cost of sequencing: higher than you think! *Genome biology* 12, 8 (2011), 125.

[10] Paul Shannon, Andrew Markiel, Owen Ozier, Nitin S Baliga, Jonathan T Wang, Daniel Ramage, Nada Amin, Benno Schwikowski, and Trey Ideker. 2003. Cytoscape: a software environment for integrated models of biomolecular interaction networks. *Genome research* 13, 11 (2003), 2498–2504.

[11] Christopher L Williams, Jeffrey C Sica, Robert T Killen, and Ulysses GJ Balis. 2016. The growing need for microservices in bioinformatics. *Journal of Pathology Informatics* 7 (2016).

[12] Matei Zaharia, Mosharaf Chowdhury, Michael J Franklin, Scott Shenker, and Ion Stoica. 2010. Spark: Cluster Computing with Working Sets. *HotCloud* 10, 10-10 (2010), 95.

[24] wiki.ubuntu.com/AppArmor.

[25] spark.rstudio.com.

[26] spark.apache.org/docs/latest/sparkr.html.

Mining Faces from Biomedical Literature using Deep Learning

Mitchell Dawson
Visual Geometry Group
Dept. of Engineering Science
University of Oxford
mdawson@robots.ox.ac.uk

Andrew Zisserman
Visual Geometry Group
Dept. of Engineering Science
University of Oxford
az@robots.ox.ac.uk

Christoffer Nellåker
Nuffield Dept. of Obstetrics & Gynaecology
University of Oxford
christoffer.nellaker@bdi.ox.ac.uk

ABSTRACT

Gaining access to large, labelled sets of relevant images is crucial for the development and testing of biomedical imaging algorithms. Using images found in biomedical research articles would contribute some way towards a solution to this problem. However, this approach critically depends on being able to identify the most relevant images from very large sets of potentially useful figures. In this paper a deep convolutional neural network (CNN) classifier is trained using *only* synthetic data, to rapidly and accurately label raw images taken from biomedical articles. We apply this method in the context of detecting faces in biomedical images; and show that the classifier is able to retrieve figures containing faces with an average precision of 94.8%, from a dataset of over 31,000 images taken from articles held in the PubMed database. The utility of the classifier is then demonstrated through a case study, by aiding the mining of photographs of patients with rare genetic disorders from targeted articles. This approach is readily adaptable to facilitate the retrieval of other categories of biomedical images.

CCS CONCEPTS

• **Computing methodologies → Machine learning; Supervised learning by classification; Neural networks;**

KEYWORDS

Biomedical Data Mining; Image Classification; Deep Learning; Convolutional Neural Network; Computer Vision; Machine Learning

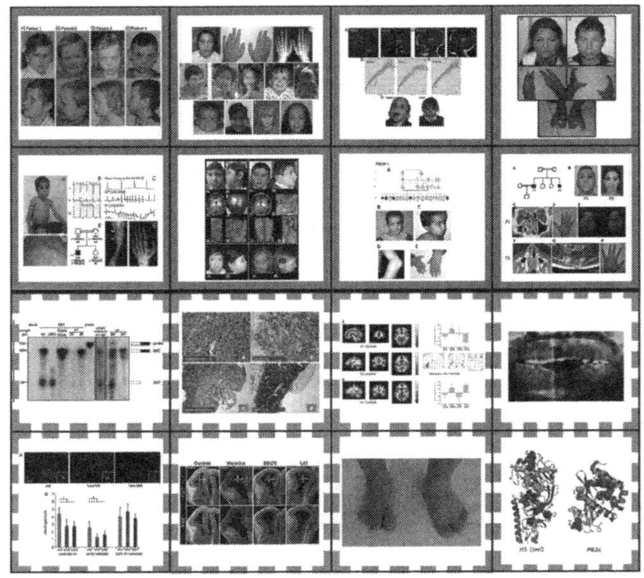

Figure 1: Examples of figures, containing faces (green solid borders) and not containing faces (orange dashed borders), taken from research articles held in the PubMed database. Many of the figures are composite in nature: they combine images of faces alongside other body parts, X-ray imaging, molecular structures, graphs and charts etc. Citations for these figures can be found at http://bit.ly/2rOu3wv. All copyrights remain the property of the original owners.

1 INTRODUCTION

Over the past few years, the volume and diversity of electronic resources available to biomedical scientists has dramatically increased. This has led to opportunities for researchers to leverage data mining techniques to make significant progress in fields such as protein-protein interactions, gene function and drug discovery (Fleuren and Alkema 2015).

Research in the sector of biomedical data mining has largely focused on the retrieval and extraction of information from the *text* of research articles or patient records (Gonzalez et al. 2016). However, figures and images contained in these articles can also constitute a valuable resource for biomedical scientists. These figures often provide a representation of a concept more clearly and entirely than a written description could. Although, to be utilised in the development and testing of medical imaging algorithms, images must often be explicitly labelled.

Extracting images from articles is now easier than ever before with the development of open source software projects such as xPDF[1], and the related rendering library Poppler[2]. The Poppler library was recently used to develop PDFFigures 2.0: a software solution which is able to extract figures and tables alongside their respective captions from research articles, with a precision and recall of over 90% (Clark and Divvala 2016).

Several research groups have also shown means to collect, categorise and store biomedical images in a way that is easily searchable (Demner-Fushman et al. 2012; Xu et al. 2008). These image databases

Permission to make digital or hard copies of all or part of this work for personal or classroom use is granted without fee provided that copies are not made or distributed for profit or commercial advantage and that copies bear this notice and the full citation on the first page. Copyrights for components of this work owned by others than the author(s) must be honored. Abstracting with credit is permitted. To copy otherwise, or republish, to post on servers or to redistribute to lists, requires prior specific permission and/or a fee. Request permissions from permissions@acm.org.
ACM-BCB'17, August 20-23, 2017, Boston, MA, USA.
© 2017 Copyright held by the owner/author(s). Publication rights licensed to ACM.
978-1-4503-4722-8/17/08...$15.00
DOI: http://dx.doi.org/10.1145/3107411.3107476

[1]xPDF: http://www.foolabs.com/xpdf
[2]Poppler: https://poppler.freedesktop.org/

frequently employ captions or textual information to allow the user to query-by-search-term and/or employ a 'bag of visual-words' approach to include query-by-example capabilities (Koike and Takagi 2009; Lehmann et al. 2005). However, these databases often only include a comparatively tiny subset of all the figures contained in biomedical articles.

There now exist tools that are able to classify real images with very high levels of performance. In the field of image classification, and in a variety of other computer vision tasks, deep convolutional neural networks (CNNs) achieve state-of-the-art results (Krizhevsky et al. 2012). A CNN is a type of artificial neural network built using multiple connected layers of non-linear feature extractors (LeCun et al. 1989). This type of classifier would provide a fast and accurate method of determining amongst a collection of biomedical figures, which ones are most likely to contain faces.

Training a deep CNN to robustly classify a wide variety of images typically requires the use of huge sets of labelled training data (Krizhevsky et al. 2012). This creates a causality dilemma. To train a CNN, one must first possess a large dataset of biomedical images labelled by whether they contain a face or not. However, if it were already possible to accurately and rapidly label images in this way, there would be no need to build a classifier originally. Furthermore, collecting a sufficient number of figures that contain faces from the biomedical literature to effectively train a CNN is currently impractical.

In this paper, we show that this problem can be resolved by training a classifier using *only* synthetic images, designed to mimic common biomedical figures. Our approach is inspired by research in the fields of text localisation (Gupta et al. 2016; Jaderberg et al. 2014) and object detection in natural images (Rozantsev et al. 2015), which have shown that synthetic images may be used for training purposes in lieu of domain specific data.

We demonstrate this approach by training a classifier to label whether figures contain images of human faces; and show that although the classifier is trained on synthetic images, it is capable of adapting to the domain of real images taken from biomedical articles. In testing, the classifier is able to determine whether an image contains a face with an average precision of 94.8% on a dataset of over 31,000 images taken from real biomedical articles. We also present a case study to exhibit how the classifier can be used to help mine images of patients with rare genetic disorders.

2 TRAINING A CLASSIFIER USING SYNTHETIC DATA

This section describes our method for training a CNN classifier to be able to label biomedical figures by whether they contain an image of a face. Our approach is to train the classifier using only synthetic figures, fabricated from images taken from an internet search engine, which resemble figures found in the biomedical literature.

The classifier is trained in two stages, using a bootstrap approach. In the first stage, an *initial* classifier is trained using synthetic images, and its performance assessed on a synthetic evaluation set. The misclassified images from this evaluation set are then analysed to identify visual themes which reoccur amongst the failure cases of the initial classifier. A second, larger, synthetic dataset is then generated that specifically includes more examples of images exhibiting these themes. In the second stage, this larger set is used to retrain the classifier. The success of this bootstrapping approach is then measured by evaluating the initial and final classifier on a synthetic test set.

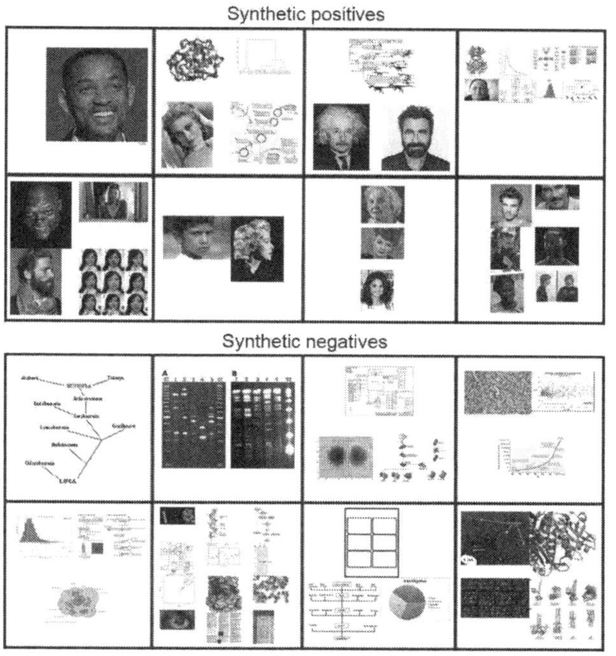

Figure 2: Examples of the synthetic grid figures produced using images downloaded from the Bing search engine. These images were used in training the initial classifier. Top: examples of positive training images; bottom: examples of negative training images.

2.1 Generating Synthetic Data

Figures found in biomedical articles can often be divided into a small number of themes (photographs, tables, X-ray imaging, graphs etc.). Furthermore, to adhere to journals' editorial guidelines, researchers will frequently concatenate individual images, as shown in Fig. 1, to form compound grid-like figures. Therefore, to ensure our classifier is able to adapt to the domain of real biomedical images, we train it on synthetic grid-like images composed of sub-images which are representative of the categories often found in biomedical literature.

To generate this synthetic data, we first compiled a list of search queries which were used to download images from the Bing search engine[3]. To collect facial photographs, 37 search terms such as 'face', 'adult face', and 'child face' were used. To collect non-facial images, representative of figures found in biomedical papers, we used 56 terms such as 'line-graph', 'protein structure', and 'brain scan'. Images were downloaded and categorised by whether they contained a face or not. This produced a dataset of 'positive' and 'negative' labelled images, which were further separated into training, validation and evaluation partitions. The images were then

[3]Bing Images: http://www.bing.com/images

pasted onto white backgrounds in 18 different tiled configurations, chosen to mimic the most common sub-panel arrangements found in a sample of figures taken from real biomedical research articles. Examples are shown in Fig. 2.

In total, 9,610 images were downloaded, of which 1,849 contained at least one face. These images were used to produce the initial dataset of synthetic grid images, as well as the initial synthetic evaluation set of 19,516 images. The statistics of the training and validation split of the initial dataset are given in Table 1. We ensure the synthetic datasets are balanced, with roughly half of synthetic figures containing at least one image of a face. This helps to prevent the classifier from learning a bias towards the larger class of images.

2.2 Training and Evaluating the Initial Classifier

The initial classifier was trained using the synthetic dataset generated as described in section 2.1. The CNN implemented in this paper is based upon the VGG-M architecture (Chatfield et al. 2014) and is constructed using MatConvNet, a Matlab-based framework for implementing CNNs (Vedaldi and Lenc 2015). The classifier used was pre-trained on the ILSVRC 2012 dataset to classify images into one of 1,000 object categories, as part of the ImageNet challenge (Russakovsky et al. 2015). Pre-training involves using a CNN initialised with a set of weights which have been found to be useful in another image classification task (Sharif Razavian et al. 2014). These weights can then be fine-tuned to tackle the new task, typically requiring much less training data than if the parameters were initialised randomly. Additionally, we made a simple architectural change to the CNN, reducing the final fully-connected layer of the network from 1,000 nodes (corresponding to the object categories in the ImageNet challenge) to 2 nodes (corresponding to 'does not contain face' or 'does contain face'). The pre-trained VGG-M was fine-tuned on the synthetic training data using stochastic gradient descent to minimise a cross entropy loss objective function.

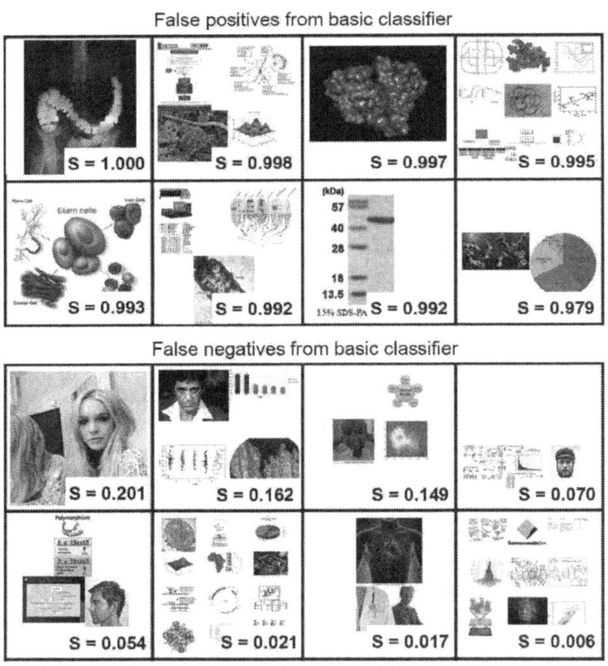

Figure 3: Examples of synthetic grid images which were misclassified by the initial classifier. Common themes amongst the false negative images include: black and white photographs; faces in profile; small images of faces; and people with irregular poses or facial expressions. Common themes amongst the false positives include: X-ray images; protein and crystal structures; and images of bacteria and cells.

Table 1: Summary of the number of images in the initial and final synthetic datasets, and the synthetic and real test sets.

Dataset	Train		Val		Test	
	Pos	Neg	Pos	Neg	Pos	Neg
Initial Syn	28,865	28,865	9,597	9,597	24,884	24,884
Final Syn	74,165	74,165	24,368	24,368		
Real	–	–	–	–	725	30,731

We evaluated the initial classifier on an initial evaluation set of synthetic images to direct the training of an improved classifier. For each image, I, the CNN outputs a score, $S(I)$, where $0 < S(I) < 1$, corresponding to the classifier's confidence that an image contains a face. The performance of the initial classifier was measured by ranking every image in the evaluation set by its respective score. Observing images in this way allowed the identification of themes which were present amongst those images that were classified incorrectly by the initial classifier. Examples of the highest ranked false positives and lowest ranked false negatives are shown in Fig. 3.

2.3 Creating the Final Synthetic Dataset and Synthetic Test Set

Identifying common themes amongst the images which were missed, or misclassified, by the initial classifier, guided the creation of a second dataset (examples of themes are given in the caption of Fig. 3). This final synthetic dataset, used to retrain the CNN classifier, is over 2.5 times larger than the initial.

We created the final synthetic dataset by expanding the set of search terms from the original set of 93 used to download images from Bing. We added 46 new search phrases relating to faces (e.g. 'greyscale faces', 'side profile of face'), and 26 associated to other biomedical entities (e.g. 'X-ray imaging', 'cells under microscope'). This resulted in an image pool of 37,801 images, of which 23,268 contained at least one face. The final synthetic training dataset and synthetic test set (see Table 1) were then generated using these images, through the method described in section 2.1.

2.4 Training and Evaluating the Final Classifier

We use the final synthetic dataset to retrain the CNN, employing the same regime as described for the initial classifier in section 2.2. The performance of the initial and final classifiers is compared on the synthetic test set using receiver operating characteristic (ROC) and precision-recall (PR) curves. It is depicted in Fig. 4 that, although both classifiers perform well on this test set, the final

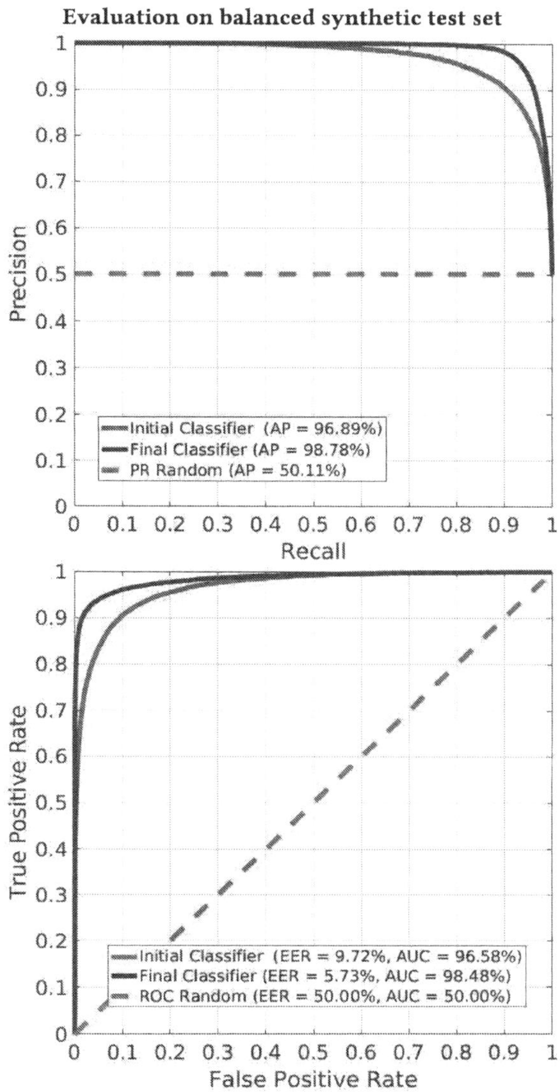

Figure 4: PR and ROC curves displaying the performance of the initial and final classifiers on a balanced test set of 49,768 synthetic grid images. The final classifier outperforms the initial on the test statistics of average precision, equal error rate, and area under ROC curve.

classifier achieves considerably better results than the initial. The initial and final classifiers achieve an average precision of 96.58% and 98.48%, and an equal error rate of 9.72% and 5.73% respectively. This indicates a marked reduction in the classification error.

In these experiments we have fine-tuned all layers of the network. To measure the effectiveness of this approach, we repeated the above experiments, fine-tuning only the last layer of the pre-trained network. We found the difference in results to be negligible for the initial classifier, and notably worse for the final classifier, indicating that training all layers of the network is a more effective approach, given a suitably large training dataset.

Table 2: Results of testing the initial and final classifiers on the synthetic and real test sets. The average precision (AP) and area under receiver operating characteristic curve (ROC AUC) are reported.

Dataset	Classifier AP (%)		Classifier ROC AUC (%)	
	Initial	Final	Initial	Final
Syn. Test	96.89	98.78	96.58	98.48
Real	59.26	**94.80**	96.10	**99.66**

3 TESTING THE CLASSIFIER ON REAL BIOMEDICAL FIGURES

In this section, we test the final classifier on a collection of real figures taken from biomedical articles. Up to this point, the CNN classifiers have been tested on synthetically generated figures, and it has been shown that the final classifier is able to outperform the initial classifier on these images. However, the true test of the classifier is whether it is able to accurately determine whether figures taken from *real* biomedical articles contain an image of a face.

The dataset collected for testing the classifier consists of 31,456 figures from research papers held in the PubMed database. These images were gathered from 3,875 distinct articles, each of which relates to one of 72 biomedical search terms. The figures were extracted using open source software provided by xPDF[4], and display a wide variation in lighting, pose, occlusion, facial morphology and size. We further ensure that the images used to generate our synthetic data are disjoint from these real figures. Examples of the images extracted from biomedical articles are shown in Fig. 1.

Aside from being comprised of real images, this dataset also differs from the synthetic training set by being heavily unbalanced. Although balanced datasets were used in training to avoid introducing biases into the classifier, only 725 (2.3%) of the figures in the real test set contain one or more photographs of a face. This is representative of the actual ratio of face images obtained by mining, and so provides a realistic test of the classifier's performance on unbalanced data.

3.1 Results on Real Biomedical Figures

It can be seen in Fig. 5, that the final classifier achieves a high average precision of 94.8% on the real unbalanced test set. This level of performance is sufficient to ensure the classifier would be of pragmatic use in determining amongst a set of biomedical figures, which contain faces.

As described in section 2.2, each image, I, is assigned a score, $S(I)$, by the classifier, representing the classifier's confidence that the figure contains a face. In practice, once the images in a dataset have been classified, they can be ranked in descending order according to the value of $S(I)$. The highest ranked images often include a very high proportion of correctly classified images which contain faces.

The CNN can also be used as a simple binary classifier to determine, amongst a batch of images, which contain a face. The PR curve shown in Fig. 5 can be used to determine a decision threshold

[4]xPDF: http://www.foolabs.com/xpdf

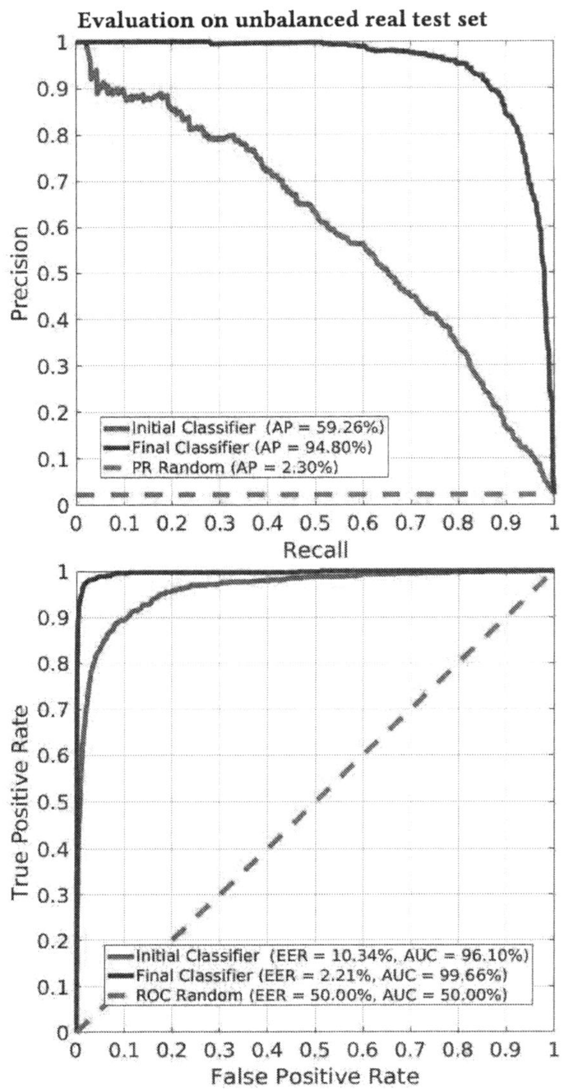

Figure 5: PR and ROC curves displaying the performance of the initial and final classifiers on 31,456 real images (725 containing one or more faces) extracted from biomedical research articles. The final classifier appreciably outperforms the initial on the test statistics of average precision, equal error rate, and area under ROC curve.

for binary classification, based on the precision and recall requirements of a user. A decision threshold, T, is a fixed constant, such that images with $S(I) \geq T$ are classified as containing faces. If the decision threshold is set at $T \approx 0.63$, the classifier achieves a precision and recall of 69% and 95% respectively, meaning that 95% of all images containing a face are retrieved, and 69% of retrieved images are true positives. Alternatively, if a higher decision threshold of $T \approx 0.91$ is chosen, the precision and recall of the classifier are both approximately equal to 89%.

Fig. 5 also highlights the effectiveness and necessity of the bootstrapping approach used to create the final classifier. In contrast to the performance of the final classifier, the initial classifier achieves an average precision of only 59.3% when tested on real figures. One reason for this is that the real dataset is heavily unbalanced towards negative examples, so the rate at which false positive errors are committed by the classifiers is amplified. Retraining the CNN with a much larger dataset, and including more image themes which were originally missed, or misclassified, appears to have helped make the classifier more robust against false positive errors.

4 CASE STUDY – RARE GENETIC DISORDERS

One direct application of this research is to aid further study in the field of rare disease phenotyping. In 2014, Ferry et al. demonstrated that machine learning techniques can be used to recognise craniofacial morphologies to help narrow the diagnostic search space for patients with suspected rare genetic disorders (Ferry et al. 2014). The accuracy of such machine learning approaches critically depends on sourcing large numbers of facial images of patients with genetic disorders to train algorithms and models. This is currently difficult as the use of patient images in medical research is subject to a number of patient consent and ethical considerations, as well as data protection laws. One solution to this problem could be to use images of patients taken from biomedical articles. In reported case studies of patients with rare or novel disorders, clinicians have already sought consent for publication, which makes further analyses of such published images uncontroversial from an ethical standpoint.

We test the efficacy of the classifier by retrieving images of patients with rare genetic disorders from published biomedical articles. Specifically, we aim to collect images of patients with one of ten rare genetic disorders, chosen for their relevance to the paper by Ferry et al. The articles are collected from several journals known to publish research articles in the field of rare disorders. A full list of the disorders is given in Table 3.

4.1 Obtaining Faces of Patients with Rare Genetic Disorders

We began by obtaining a list of candidate articles using the PubMed E-utilities API [5]. This resulted in a list of 1,176 articles, each potentially containing images of patients, for which the corresponding PDF document was obtained.

Next, we extracted the images from each of the candidate articles, and prepared them for analysis by the CNN classifier. Aside from the legitimate numbered figures found within papers, the image extraction software often retrieved small regions of white space, which had been used as padding by authors formatting their work. Other small images commonly found included copyright stamps, and the logos of journals and institutions. These small images comprised a non-trivial proportion of the images initially retrieved, particularly from older papers. Given that numbered figures used in research papers need to be large enough to convey meaningful information, images with a height or width of under 50 pixels were immediately discarded from further analysis. This resulted in a dataset of 3,124 images, each relating to one of ten search terms.

[5]Entrez E- utilities: https://www.ncbi.nlm.nih.gov/books/NBK25497/

Table 3: Summary of classifier results on figures taken from articles relating to ten rare genetic disorders. We report the number of images found for each disorder; how many images actually contained faces; how many images the classifier predicted contained faces; and how many face images the classifier missed. The classifier greatly reduces the search space for face images with almost no missed positives

Search term	Images	GT faces	Classified +ves	Missed +ves
Angelman	615	43	54	1
Apert	68	5	8	0
Cutis Laxa	210	26	40	1
Fragile X	854	20	24	0
Kabuki	61	13	14	0
Noonan	450	32	46	0
Prader-Willi	275	27	34	0
Rubinstein-Taybi	87	16	16	0
Treacher Collins	223	8	10	0
Williams-Beuren	281	13	20	0
Total	**3,124**	**203**	**266**	**2**

4.2 Results on Case Study Images

As shown in Table 3, of the 3,124 images found, 203 (6.5%) actually contained a face. The final classifier predicted that 266 of the 3,124 images contained a face, missing only two positive examples. In this experiment, the decision threshold of the final classifier was set using the equal error rate found during the real image testing described in section 3. Under this regime, the classifier achieves an overall precision of 76% (201/266), and an overall recall of 99% (201/203). Most importantly, the classifier was able to reduce the search space of potentially relevant figures by over 91% from 3,124 to 266.

A small minority of the figures retrieved by the classifier, whilst containing faces, did not contain faces of patients with the particular disorder of interest. In several examples, images of healthy relatives of individuals with a disorder were retrieved. These images were included in case reports to contrast the facial morphology displayed by the patient. In other examples, articles discussed multiple syndromes, or explicitly dismissed the target disorder as a potential diagnosis.

Despite these instances, the performance of the classifier in this case study provides proof of concept that this approach can be used to aid the mining of images of patients with rare genetic disorders. Furthermore, such a pipeline could be easily scaled to accrue more images by targeting articles from a wider array of journals, relating to a greater variety of rare disorders.

5 CONCLUSION

In this paper, we have demonstrated that a deep convolutional neural network can be trained using *only* synthetic images to classify whether figures extracted from biomedical research articles contain faces. Our implementation consists of a two-stage bootstrapping approach. First, an initial classifier is trained using synthetic images designed to mimic real biomedical figures. Then, by identifying themes in the images missed by the initial classifier, a larger dataset of synthetic images, which includes more of these hard examples, is generated and used to retrain the classifier. This strategy led to considerable improvement in classification precision and recall when tested on synthetic images, and real images taken from biomedical articles. It was also shown that this approach is able to assist in the mining and labelling of biomedical figures to identify potentially relevant patient photographs for rare disease phenotyping research.

The approach developed in this paper is particularly suitable for cases where a specific category of image, that may exhibit some intra-class variation, needs to be retrieved, and sufficiently many examples from the image category can be obtained either through internet search engines or other means. We have demonstrated the approach for the case of faces, but the method could be readily adapted to retrieve other categories of biomedical images, for example: electrophoresis gels, hands, mice, protein structures, cell cultures, human tissues, X-ray images, etc.

ACKNOWLEDGMENTS

This research was financially supported by the EPSRC programme grant Seebibyte EP/M013774/1, the EPSRC Systems Biology DTC EP/G03706X/1, and the MRC Grant MR/M014568/1.

REFERENCES

K. Chatfield, K. Simonyan, A. Vedaldi, and A. Zisserman. 2014. Return of the Devil in the Details: Delving Deep into Convolutional Nets. In *Proc. BMVC*.

C. Clark and S. Divvala. 2016. PDFFigures 2.0: Mining figures from research papers. In *JCDL*. 143–152.

D. Demner-Fushman, S. Antani, M. Simpson, and G. Thoma. 2012. Design and development of a multimodal biomedical information retrieval system. *JCSE* 6, 2 (2012), 168–177.

Q. Ferry, J. Steinberg, C. Webber, D. R. FitzPatrick, C. P. Ponting, A. Zisserman, and C. Nellåker. 2014. Diagnostically relevant facial gestalt information from ordinary photos. *eLIFE* (Jun 2014). DOI: 10.7554/eLife.02020.

W. Fleuren and W. Alkema. 2015. Application of text mining in the biomedical domain. *Methods* 74 (2015), 97–106.

G. Gonzalez, T. Tahsin, B. Goodale, A. Greene, and C. Greene. 2016. Recent advances and emerging applications in text and data mining for biomedical discovery. *Brief. Bioinform.* 17, 1 (2016), 33–42.

A. Gupta, A. Vedaldi, and A. Zisserman. 2016. Synthetic Data for Text Localisation in Natural Images. In *Proc. CVPR*.

M. Jaderberg, K. Simonyan, A. Vedaldi, and A. Zisserman. 2014. Synthetic Data and Artificial Neural Networks for Natural Scene Text Recognition. In *Workshop on Deep Learning, NIPS*.

A. Koike and T. Takagi. 2009. Classifying biomedical figures using combination of bag of keypoints and bag of words. In *CISIS*. 848–853.

A. Krizhevsky, I. Sutskever, and G. E. Hinton. 2012. ImageNet Classification with Deep Convolutional Neural Networks. In *NIPS*. 1106–1114.

Y. LeCun, B. Boser, J. S. Denker, D. Henderson, R. E. Howard, W. Hubbard, and L. D. Jackel. 1989. Backpropagation Applied to Handwritten Zip Code Recognition. *Neural Computation* 1, 4 (1989), 541–551.

T. Lehmann, M. Güld, T. Deselaers, D. Keysers, H. Schubert, K. Spitzer, H. Ney, and B. Wein. 2005. Automatic categorization of medical images for content-based retrieval and data mining. *Comput Med Imaging Graph* 29, 2 (2005), 143–155.

A. Rozantsev, V. Lepetit, and P. Fua. 2015. On rendering synthetic images for training an object detector. *Comput Vis Image Und* 137 (2015), 24–37.

O. Russakovsky, J. Deng, H. Su, J. Krause, S. Satheesh, S. Ma, S. Huang, A. Karpathy, A. Khosla, M. Bernstein, A.C. Berg, and F.F. Li. 2015. ImageNet Large Scale Visual Recognition Challenge. *IJCV* (2015).

A. Sharif Razavian, H. Azizpour, J. Sullivan, and S. Carlsson. 2014. CNN features off-the-shelf: an astounding baseline for recognition. In *CVPRW*. 806–813.

A. Vedaldi and K. Lenc. 2015. MatConvNet: Convolutional neural networks for MATLAB. In *Proc. ACMM*.

S. Xu, J. McCusker, and M. Krauthammer. 2008. Yale Image Finder (YIF): a new search engine for retrieving biomedical images. *Bioinformatics* 24, 17 (2008), 1968–1970.

A Correlation Network Model Utilizing Gait Parameters for Evaluating Health Levels

Elham Rastegari
College of Information Science and Technology
University of Nebraska Omaha, USA
erastegari@unomaha.edu

Hesham H. Ali
College of Information Science and Technology
University of Nebraska Omaha, USA
hali@unomaha.edu

ABSTRACT

Healthcare is moving rapidly from the long-standing reactive treatment approach to the early detection and preventative era. However, to fully embrace this trend, new approaches need to be developed. A step in this direction is to explore how to leverage data collected from wearables sensors to help in assessing health levels. This would pave the way for continuously monitoring individuals, which, in turn, lead to helping physicians diagnose diseases in the early stages. However, a major missing piece in moving forward with this concept is the lack of a sophisticated data analytics model. In this study, we propose a new correlation network model in which several aspects associated with health levels can be identified using population analysis. The proposed model is based on identifying various mobility parameters associated with groups under study, then a correlation network is developed based on the specified parameters. In such network, each node corresponds to a person and two nodes are connected by an edge if the corresponding individuals share similar mobility profiles. We show that various network properties reflect health information of the groups under study. To test the proposed model, we use gait parameters collected from three various groups, healthy younger people, geriatrics and Parkinson's disease patients. Obtained results show that the proposed model is very promising and can be a starting point towards a robust population analysis technique for utilizing mobility data in assessing health levels and predicting potential health hazards.

KEYWORDS

Correlation network, mobility and health, gait parameters, population analysis, geriatrics, Parkinson's Disease

1 INTRODUCTION

Mobility has been always considered as one of the important factors that has great influence on individuals' health and quality of life. In fact, mobility and health are inter-correlated. An alteration in the mobility level of an individual will likely affect health level and a change in the health condition of an individual is likely to impact on the mobility level.

Permission to make digital or hard copies of all or part of this work for personal or classroom use is granted without fee provided that copies are not made or distributed for profit or commercial advantage and that copies bear this notice and the full citation on the first page. Copyrights for components of this work owned by others than ACM must be honored. Abstracting with credit is permitted. To copy otherwise, or republish, to post on servers or to redistribute to lists, requires prior specific permission and/or a fee. Request permissions from Permissions@acm.org.
ACM-BCB '17, August 20-23, 2017, Boston, MA, USA
© 2017 ACM. ISBN 978-1-4503-4722-8/17/08....$15.00
http://dx.doi.org/10.1145/3107411.3107487

In recent years, mobility has been predominantly studied using gait analysis. More than 3400 publications with "gait" in the title have been reported between 2012 and 2013 [20]. A great number of experiments have been successful in capturing and analysing gait parameters to track the evolution of various diseases, including aging-related diseases, neurological disease such as Parkinson's Disease (PD) , and systemic diseases such as cardiopathies [20]. Therefore, we have enough evidences to claim that continuously monitoring individuals' mobility and gait patterns will provide us precious information associated with health. In this work, our focus is on utilizing gait parameters in particular to assess health levels of individuals.

Monitoring gait patterns seamlessly and continuously over time will help physicians diagnose diseases in the early stages. It will also help in assessing treatment options and recommending the best treatment. Evaluating mobility continuously and in a timely manner to prevent further irregularities in walking and gait functional abilities is introduced as one of the major difficulties for healthcare providers [32]. Traditional gait measurement approaches such as infrared cameras and pressure sensor platforms necessitate individuals to come to the gait-monitoring laboratories. Therefore, traditional approaches do not support the idea of continuously monitoring gait.

Portability and affordability of wearable sensors along with improved accuracy and capability of monitoring gait during daily activities make them highly effective devices for clinical gait analysis [20]. However, there is still a lack of a sophisticated and robust model that could assess individuals' health levels over time by utilizing gait patterns and help diagnose diseases in the early stages or provide an objective measure of the amount of progress a person has made over a period of time. In this study, we propose a correlation network model to fill this gap. Correlation networks have been implemented and validated in multiple research areas, particularly in Bioinformatics research [5].

Utilizing gait parameters for health assessment relies on population analysis. Many aspects of health-related assessments are based on comparing individual's data points with as many data points as possible in various populations with various health levels. Clinical diagnosis and treatment evaluation would be very difficult without population comparisons. Therefore, in constructing the proposed correlation network model, there is an absolute need of having access to the gait parameters and other related parameters from different populations.

Variability of gait, stride length, stride time, cadence, and asymmetry are some of the gait parameters that have been studied in the context of clinical decision making [9, 14, 30]. These gait parameters should be selected carefully to be used in creating an accurate correlation network model. Our proposed correlation network model will utilize discriminating gait parameters between groups of our interest to find correlation between each pair of subjects. Then, a network model will be created in which each person is modelled by a node and two nodes have an edge if their corresponding subjects have highly correlated gait parameters. Using graph tools and algorithms, we will be able to identify clusters, gateway vertices, transitions and cliques.

Our primary goal in this study is to be able to identify various groups with common health conditions and track each individual's health status over time using gait parameters and other differentiating parameters such as age, gender, and genetic background. The proposed model can also be used in tracking changes associated with the mobility parameters of each individual to assess progress of treatments or potential degradation in health for early detection purposes. This would allow for the ability to assign/reassign each individual dynamically to a group or subpopulation with similar mobility patterns or health levels. In this study, we evaluate gait parameters associated with three groups of people (healthy control, geriatrics, and patients with PD) who participated in a study conducted by Barth and his colleagues [3] to show the feasibility and importance of the model. Our proposed model will be explained in the next section which will be followed by a section explaining each step of the model in the context of our case study. Then, results will be provided and discussed.

2 PROPOSED CORRELATION NTWORK MODEL

In this section, we introduce the correlation network model. Then, in the following section, we will explain how this model works using a case study. The diagram in Figure 1 shows our proposed correlation network model.

First step in the correlation network model is to identify groups of people with health conditions affecting walking and gait patterns. Although there is still a lack of comprehensive knowledge regarding all health conditions that impact on walking and gait patterns, a great number of these health conditions are already identified. Moreover, once these groups are identified and a model is built, the model will be flexible enough to add newly identified populations with various health conditions.

The second step is to identify gait parameters that are significantly different between groups identified from the first step and gait parameters that are significantly different between control healthy population and populations identified from the first step.

In the third step, we need to determine those discriminating gait parameters that can be captured using wearable sensors. Variability of gait, stride length, stride time, cadence, and asymmetry are some of the gait parameters that have been studied in the context of clinical decision making using wearable mobility and gait monitoring devices [9, 14, 30].

Different types of wearable monitoring devices, including accelerometers, gyroscopes, magnetometers, force sensors, extensometers, and goniometers have been utilized to capture different signals that describe the human gait [20]. A decision is needed to be made regarding the type and the number of sensors so they provide us our desired gait parameters identified in the previous step.

At this point, data needs to be collected in an appropriate approach using the knowledge acquired from all previous steps. Then, an accurate and robust step/stride detection algorithm is needed. Several algorithms for step/stride detection from accelerometer-derived data have been proposed based on peak detection methods [7, 15, 24] or based on template matching methods [3, 29]. Since the accuracy of the later steps in this model highly depends on this step, a very accurate step/stride segmentation algorithm should to be selected.

In the next step, gait parameters identified from previous steps need to be extracted. Then, in order to examine parameters and find the significantly different parameters between two or more groups, we need to run a simple t-test or ANOVA. A post hoc test can provide us groups' pairwise comparisons. Once statistical analysis is done, a vector will be created using the significantly different parameters. The order of the parameters in the vector should be the same for all of the subjects. If other differentiating parameters such as age, gender, and genetic background are available, they can also be added to each subject's vector.

Taking the vectors of gait parameters from the previous step, a pairwise Pearson correlation will be performed. A threshold needs to be set for the correlation values. Two subjects are considered highly correlated if their corresponding vectors of parameters have a correlation above the predefined threshold.

Using the correlation values, a network model will be created in which each vertex represents a subject and two subjects are connected by an edge if the correlation value between them is above the threshold. Some characteristics of this network will be of our interest, including clusters, cliques, transitions, and gateway vertices.

Partitioning of elements into subsets is called clustering so two criteria are satisfied: homogeneity (similarity of the elements inside a cluster), and separation (low similarity of the elements from different clusters) [27]. Clusters help us to identify different groups of people with different health conditions. Plus, if we add a new individual to the model and it is placed in a particular category, it is very likely that this individual's health status follows the overall health status of people in that category. A clique is defined as a maximal complete sub-graph [17, 23], which is subset of elements where there is a pairwise connection between all elements. Existence of a clique in the proposed correlation network can be interpreted as a group with highly consistent gait parameters. Individuals inside a clique are highly likely to have very similar health condition. Gateway nodes are representing elements that change between state [6]. In this study, if a vertex has connections to more than one group (belongs to more than one cluster), this vertex is called a gateway vertex, showing that the individual associated with the gateway vertex is in a transition between two health conditions. This property would help both individuals and physicians to diagnose diseases in the early stages.

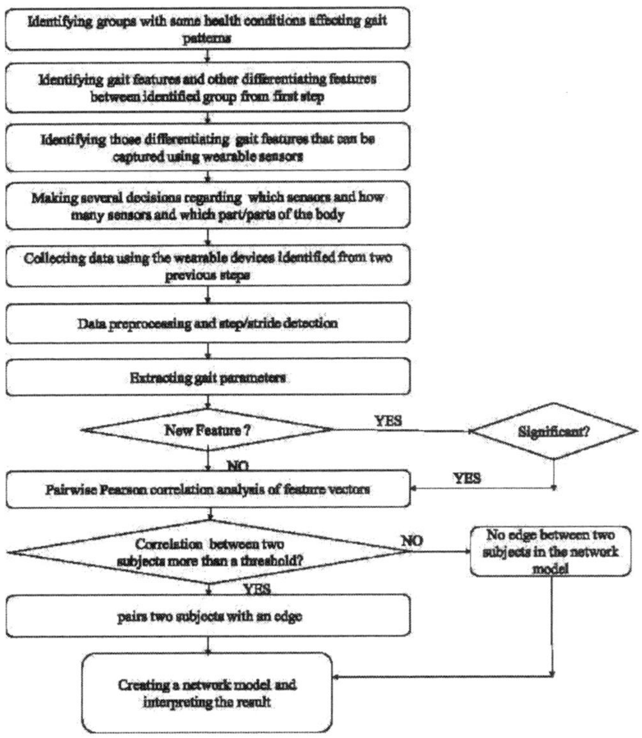

Figure 1. Proposed correlation network model for assessing individuals' health level by utilizing gait parameters

3. A CASE STUDY

In order to explain how the proposed model would work, we apply the correlation network model to a case study.

3.1 Aging and Parkinson's Disease

Gait irregularities has been already identified as the symptoms of a great number of health conditions, including aging, PD, Multiple Sclerosis, and Amyotrophic Lateral Sclerosis, just to name a few. Here, PD and aging were selected as health conditions affecting gait due to the limited data set we had.

Gait depends on the power, strength, and action of multiple organs, including neurologic sensory, cardiovascular system and musculoskeletal system. Aging would affect these organs and consequently gait. Altered gait in elderlies has been reported in many studies [13, 14, 16, 28].

PD is a neurological condition decreasing the dopamine level. This condition leads to muscle function and mobility impairment. Gait deficiencies in PD can be divided into two types: episodic and continuous [8]. Continuous changes refer to changes in the gait patterns that are persistent all the time, while episodic gait changes occur time to time and include start hesitation, festination and freezing of gait [26]. Altered gait in patients with PD either with or without freezing gait has been reported as an issue affecting these patients' quality of life [4, 8, 19, 22].

3.2 Gait Parameters Discriminating between Healthy, Geriatric and PD Groups

3.2.1 Gait Parameters Discriminating between Healthy Younger individuals and Geriatrics. Shorter step length, shorter single support time, less power and motion at ankle and less hip flexion-extension have been reported as altered gait parameters in elderlies compared to younger individuals [13]. It has also been reported that older adults walk significantly slower than younger adults due to reduction in stride length and increased double support stance time [28]. Sue Lord and his colleagues developed a model for gait in older adults, and identified five factors explaining almost 80% of gait variance in this population, among them asymmetry and variability accounts for 30% of variance [16].

Furthermore, healthy older adults show significantly greater step and stride time variability as well as less symmetry of the acceleration in the anterior-posterior direction compared to healthy young individuals [14]. Galit Yogev and his colleagues also reported gait asymmetry as a significant gait parameter in both elderly fallers and patients with PD [30]. Since stride time, variability and symmetry alterations are identified gait parameters associated with aging, and the fact that these parameters can be extracted from accelerometer-derived data [14, 33], these parameters are considered as differentiating gait parameters between healthy group and geriatrics in our study.

3.2.2 Gait Parameters Discriminating between Healthy Individuals and Patients with PD. In this study, our focus is on the continuous changes in gait patterns that could differentiate individuals with PD from healthy adults. Some of the reported gait parameters in individuals with PD are including longer double limb support [4, 19], shorter stride length [4, 19], greater stride time [11], increased left-right gait asymmetry [22, 26, 30], and higher gait variability [1, 2, 10]. Variability changes and higher average stride length in patients with PD have been reported for both PD patients in the early stages of disease and those in the advanced stages of disease [1, 12]. Since greater stride time, higher variability and less symmetry are reported as gait parameters associated with PD, and these parameters can be extracted from accelerometer-derived data [10, 11, 22], these parameters are considered as discriminating gait parameters between healthy younger group and patients with PD.

3.3 Participants and Protocol

We used accelerometers-derived data from a publically available data set collected by Barth and his colleagues [3]. This data set includes gait data of three groups of people: healthy people, geriatrics, and people with PD. A total number of fifteen subjects participated in the study, five from each group. The experiment was conducted under two protocols. We selected the data associated with the free-walk protocol in which data was collected from subjects' left and right ankles using SHIMMER while they were walking two minutes around the hospital with comfortable speed. SHIMMER is a flexible inertial sensing platform, including accelerometer and gyroscope. We used the initial 40 seconds of the two-minute walk for our analysis. Accelerometer's X, Y, and Z axes represents signals in Anterior-Posterior (AP), Vertical, and Medio-Lateral (ML) directions, respectively. Table 1 shows Subjects' information. Average of the Unified Parkinson's Disease Rating Scale (UPDRS) and Hohen and Yahr (H&Y) scale are shown for PD patients. These two scales show how the symptoms of PD progress. Figure 2 shows left and right ankles' acceleration signals of three individuals from three groups in the AP direction.

Table 1. Subjects' Characteristics

	Control	PD	Geriatrics
Number of subjects	5	5	5
Gender (M/F)	3:2	3:2	2:3
Age	64 (10)	72 (6.3)	81 (5.9)
UPDRS III		20.8 (6.1)	
H & Y		2.6 (0.5)	

3.4 Preprocessing and Stride Segmentation

We calibrated the data based on the guideline provided by the authors of [3]. In order to identify strides from both legs, we used a peak detection algorithm. Data from z-axis of gyroscope has been used for step/stride segmentation with the characteristic peak in the middle of swing phase [24, 25]. The stride segmentation algorithm was implemented as described in the study by Salarian and his colleagues [25] and peaks were identified using the conditions applied in the study by Barth et al. [3]. Compared to the Gold standard, we acquired F-measures of 97.5%, 96% and 95% for healthy, geriatrics, and PD groups, respectively. Missed strides were included and miss-identified strides were removed using Gold standard data and post processing.

3.5 Extracting Gait Parameters associated with Aging and PD

Gait parameters extracted from acceleration-derived data are listed in Table 2. This table shows different measures of variability, symmetry and magnitude of acceleration. Vector magnitude, representing intensity, was included as a gait parameter since it is reported as one of the metrics for continuous gait monitoring using accelerometers [31]. Variability of acceleration was also extracted, since it is reported as a differentiating gait parameter between fit and frail older adults [18] and might be useful in differentiating geriatrics and healthy population. Another added gait parameter used in our study was mean of the maximum acceleration per stride. This parameter was included because we observed obvious differences between three groups regarding this parameter. In Figure 2, this parameter differences between three subjects from three groups can be seen.

$$\textbf{Symmetry} = \frac{\mathrm{Min}(Fl, Fr)}{Max\ (Fl, Fr)}$$

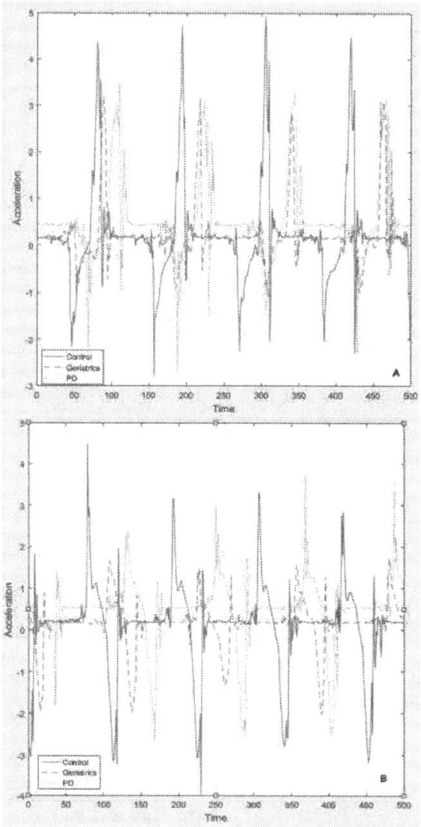

Figure 2. (A) and (B) Left and right ankle acceleration signal of one subject from each group

We used standard deviation (std) and Coefficient of Variation (CV) to calculate variability measures. To measure symmetry, differences between left and right ankle acceleration were calculated using the following equation, in which Fl is the value of the gait parameter F associated with the left ankle sensor and Fr is the value of the same gait parameter associated with the right ankle sensor.

3.6 Significantly Different Gait Parameters between Groups Using Statistical Analysis

We performed one-way ANOVA (alpha = 0.05) to compare all of the extracted parameters associated with three groups of individuals. All assumptions for ANOVA were satisfied. Then, a post hoc analysis was done for group's pairwise comparison. No significant difference was found between three groups regarding stride time variability and stride time symmetry, while all other parameters were found to be significantly different among three groups. Table 3 shows the results of groups' post hoc comparison. All of the significantly different parameters between two groups or between all three groups were taken to the next step for correlation analysis.

Table 2. Gait Parameters Extracted from Accelerometer Data

Parameter	What this parameter measures	Axis
Avg_StrideTime [11, 14]	Average stride Time	-
Acc_Var	Standard deviation of stride_to_stirde acceleration (stride-to-stride acceleration variability)	X, Y, Z
Std_StrideTime [9, 14]	Standard deviation of Stride time (variability)	-
CV_StrideTime [11, 14]	Stride time coefficient of variation	-
Avg_RMS	Magnitude of acceleration	X, Y, Z
MaxAcc_perStride	Mean value of maximum magnitude of acceleration per stride	X, Y, Z
Avg_VecMag [31]	Vector magnitude of acceleration in all directions (Intensity)	-
StrideTime_Sym [14]	Stride time symmetry between left and right leg	-
VecMag_Sym	vector magnitude symmetry between left and right leg	-

The healthy control group shows significantly shorter mean stride time compared to geriatrics and geriatrics show greater mean stride time compared to the PD group. Variability of vertical acceleration for the patients with PD was significantly greater than of the geriatrics. Healthy individuals had significantly greater mean of vector magnitude of acceleration and RMS of acceleration in the AP and vertical direction compared to the geriatric group. The same gait parameters were significantly greater for patients with PD compared to geriatrics. Vector magnitude symmetry was significantly greater for the healthy group compared to the geriatrics. Mean of the strides' maximum acceleration in the AP direction was significantly different between all three groups. Mean of the same parameter in the vertical and ML direction were lower for the geriatric group compared to the PD group.

3.7 Correlation Analysis the Network Model

Once significant discriminating parameters are extracted, a correlation analysis between subjects from all groups was done in which correlation between each pair of subjects is calculated considering the identified significant parameters' vector. While t-test, ANOVA, and post-hoc analysis identifies differences in the mean value of each gait parameter associated with the groups, correlation analysis considers all of the parameters together and examine how similar two subjects are regarding their gait patterns. In this study, a threshold of 95 % correlation with the significance value of 0.05 was set to create the network model.

Table 3. Results of groups' pairwise comparison regarding all parameters using ANOVA and post hoc analysis

Parameters	Control vs Geriatrics		Control vs PD		Geriatrics vs PD	
	Mean difference	p-value	Mean difference	p-value	Mean difference	p-value
Avg_StrideTime	-0.23**	0.004	0.53	0.621	o.18*	0.021
Acc_Var_X	0.037	0.075	0.41	0.059	0.003	0.960
Acc_Var_Y	0.049	0.063	-0.19	0.603	-0.68*	0.011
Acc_Var_Z	0.077	0.051	0.02	0.681	0.056	0.091
Std_StrideTime	-.082	0.144	-0.032	0.711	-0.05	0.450
CV_StrideTime	-2.97	0.364	-0.566	0.961	2.40	0.506
Avg_VecMag	0.04**	0.004	-0.21	0.119	-0.62***	0.000
Avg_RMSX	0.37***	0.000	0.039	0.728	-0.34***	0.000
Avg_RMSY	0.43***	0.001	-0.14	0.278	-0.58***	0.000
Avg_RMSZ	0.19*	0.040	0.33	0.882	-0.16	0.091
MaxAcc_perStrideX	1.67***	0.000	0.72*	0.020	-0.95***	0.001
MaxAcc_perStrideY	1.87***	0.000	0.38	0.562	-1.48**	0.004
MaxAcc_perStrideZ	1.01	0.140	-0.46	0.616	-1.48*	0.027
VecMag_Sym	0.42	0.323	0.83*	0.030	0.41	0.341
StrideTime_Sym	0.016	0.542	0.028	0.245	0.009	0.231

* $P < 0.05$, significant difference between two groups
** $p < 0.01$, significant difference between two group
*** $p < 0.001$, significant difference between two groups

In order to be able to interpret the created network, we assigned numbers one to five, six to ten, and eleven to fifteen to the healthy individuals, geriatrics, and patients with PD, respectively. Resulted network is shown in Figure 3 in which pink nodes (1-5) represent healthy subjects, blue nodes (6-10) represent geriatrics and green nodes (11-15) represent patients with PD. Two clusters can be observed in the network, meaning that there are at least two groups of people with different health conditions. Considering the numbers assigned to the vertices, it is observed that healthy individuals are all clustered together while geriatrics and patients with PD are somehow clustered together. However, a distinction between geriatrics and patients with PD still can be observed. Existing a clique, including pink vertices (1-5), indicates that gait parameters of this group of individuals are pretty consistent and they are very likely to have very similar health conditions and as we know they are all from healthy group.

As it is observed, an obvious gateway vertex is vertex 6, which belongs to two clusters of healthy individuals and individuals with health issues. One possible explanation is that this subject is in a transition between two health conditions. Since we know this vertex is associated to an individual from the geriatric group, this individual is in a transition between healthy condition and geriatrics' health condition.

In general, when we observe gateway vertices, if we have previous health information of the individuals associated with these vertices and previous network model, we can easily identify the transition direction between two health conditions.

This network will be dynamic once we have enough gait data from each individual over time. So, as time goes by, this network structure will change depending on changes in individuals' health levels that would be affecting their gait parameters.

4. DISCUSSION

The findings demonstrate that the correlation network model built using gait parameters of healthy people, geriatrics and patients with PD could reveal precious information regarding individuals' health condition. Our results show that the gait parameters used was selected appropriately so they discriminate between healthy individuals and individuals with some health issues. Two clusters were found, one consisting of vertices associated with healthy individuals and the other one consisting of vertices associated with two other groups. A distinction still can be observed between geriatrics and PD groups. However, this distinction is not entirely clear since cluster separation is limited. This might be due to the limited number of subjects and parameters. This lack of clear distinction might be also due to less difference in the gait patterns of individuals from these two groups. Further investigation is needed to explain this lack of a clear distinction between geriatrics and patients with PD in our study.

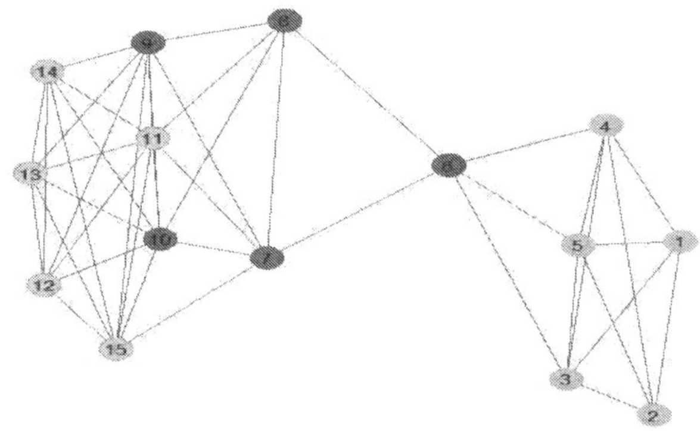

Figure 3: Network model in which pink nodes (1-5) represent control healthy subjects, blue nodes (6-10) represent geriatrics and green nodes (11-15) represent patients with PD

A gateway vertex (vertex number 6) can be observed in the created correlation network. This might be due to a transition of the associated individual between two health conditions. We do not have any information about this individual's detailed health condition to examine potential hypotheses. However, we cannot reject the fact that changes in the health levels happen over a period of time and a person who is in a transition from one health condition to a different health condition can be associated with more than one group at different times. Therefore, the gait parameters of this individual may be similar to those found in more than one group.

This model provides healthcare providers a tool to track individuals' health over time and make better decisions in diagnosis and treatment. We made this model with the information that was available for us to demonstrate the feasibility of the model. However, in the future, this model should be able to compare each mobility parameters of individuals over time as well as to previously recorded parameters of other groups with different health conditions in order to assign/reassign each individual to the most similar cluster, using a similarity measure.

Limitations. The total number of subjects were fifteen, five from each group. This number limits generalization or validation of our results. We will apply this model to the other data set provided by the same group and use the results to generalize and validate the model using triangulation.

Another limitation of this study is that subjects were not age-matched. Therefore, it is not that much clear whether the distinction between the gait patterns is due to aging or due to the health issues. Data was not normalized based on BMI since we did not have BMI information and this is another limitation of this study. However, we can still claim that no matter why three groups under study had different gait patterns, the proposed correlation network could identify healthy individuals from other two groups only using gait parameters. It will be of our future work to examine the proposed model with a data set of BMI and age-matched individuals from various groups. Data will be collected in more details, including age, gender, genetic background, whether subjects have been under medications or not, types of medication and other information that could enrich the proposed model and add to its accuracy.

Although mean age of the individuals in the healthy group was 64 and that of the geriatric group was 84, these two groups were considered as two different groups due to the existing significant age difference and reported several significantly different gait parameters between elderlies above 81 years old and those between 60 and 65 years old [21].

5 CONCLUSIONS

A correlation network model is proposed in this study. This model employs mobility parameters collected from individuals belong to differ groups. The model should help physicians and healthcare providers to diagnose disease in the early stages and to make the best decision regarding treatment approaches by long-term monitoring individuals' mobility patterns. Each step of the model is explained in details using a case study. A correlation network was created using gait parameters of three various groups of people: healthy younger, geriatrics and patients with PD. The findings demonstrate that correlation network model built using only gait parameters of the three mentioned groups could reveal precious information regarding individuals' health condition. This is the first major attempt to use population analysis to in developing mobility-based system to assess health levels and potentially predict health hazards. This represents an important step towards the development of an advanced data analytics approach for utilizing data collected seamlessly and continuously in health assessment.

REFERENCES

[1] Baltadjieva, R., Giladi, N., Gruendlinger, L., Peretz, C., & Hausdorff, J. M. (2006). Marked alterations in the gait timing and rhythmicity of patients with de novo Parkinson's disease. European Journal of Neuroscience, 24(6), 1815–1820.

[2] Barbe, M. T., Amarell, M., Snijders, A. H., Florin, E., Quatuor, E.-L., Schönau, E., ... Timmermann, L. (2014). Gait and upper limb variability in Parkinson's disease patients with and without freezing of gait. Journal of Neurology, 261(2), 330–342.

[3] Barth, J., Oberndorfer, C., Pasluosta, C., Schülein, S., Gassner, H., Reinfelder, S., ... Eskofier, B. M. (2015). Stride Segmentation during Free Walk Movements Using Multi-Dimensional Subsequence Dynamic Time Warping on Inertial Sensor Data. Sensors, 15(3), 6419–6440.

[4] Bond, J. M., & Morris, M. (2000). Goal-directed secondary motor tasks: Their effects on gait in subjects with Parkinson disease. Archives of Physical Medicine and Rehabilitation, 81(1), 110–116.

[5] Cooper, K. D., Pawaskar, S., & Ali, H. H. (2015). Identification of Biologically Significant Elements Using Correlation Networks in High Performance Computing Environments. In International Conference on Bioinformatics and Biomedical Engineering (pp. 607–619). Springer.

[6] [Cooper, K. M., Bonasera, S., & Ali, H. (2015). Identifying aging genes in the aging mouse hypothalamus using gateway node analysis of correlation networks. In 6th International Conference on Bioinformatics Models, Methods and Algorithms, BIOINFORMATICS 2015. SciTePress.

[7] Derawi, M. O., Bours, P., & Holien, K. (2010). Improved cycle detection for accelerometer based gait authentication. In Intelligent Information Hiding and Multimedia Signal Processing (IIH-MSP), 2010 Sixth International Conference on (pp. 312–317). IEEE.

[8] Giladi, N., Hausdorff, J. M., & Balash, Y. (2013). Episodic and continuous gait disturbances in Parkinson's disease 22. Scientific Basis for the Treatment of Parkinson's Disease, 417.

[9] Hausdorff, J. M., Schaafsma, J. D., Balash, Y., Bartels, A. L., Gurevich, T., & Giladi, N. (2003). Impaired regulation of stride variability in Parkinson's disease subjects with freezing of gait. Experimental Brain Research, 149(2), 187–194.

[10] Hausdorff, Jeffrey M. (2009). Gait dynamics in Parkinson's disease: common and distinct behavior among stride length, gait variability, and fractal-like scaling. Chaos: An Interdisciplinary Journal of Nonlinear Science, 19(2), 026113.

[11] Hausdorff, Jeffrey M., Cudkowicz, M. E., Firtion, R., Wei, J. Y., & Goldberger, A. L. (1998a). Gait variability and basal ganglia disorders: Stride-to-stride variations of gait cycle timing in parkinson's disease and Huntington's disease. Movement Disorders, 13(3), 428–437.

[12] Hausdorff, Jeffrey M., Lertratanakul, A., Cudkowicz, M. E., Peterson, A. L., Kaliton, D., & Goldberger, A. L. (2000). Dynamic markers of altered gait rhythm in amyotrophic lateral sclerosis. Journal of Applied Physiology, 88(6), 2045–2053.

[13] Jo, J., S, O., & 3rd, D. R. (1996). Effects of age on the biomechanics and physiology of gait. Clinics in Geriatric Medicine, 12(4), 659–678.

[14] Kobsar, D., Olson, C., Paranjape, R., Hadjistavropoulos, T., & Barden, J. M. (2014). Evaluation of age-related differences in the stride-to-stride fluctuations, regularity and symmetry of gait using a waist-mounted tri-axial accelerometer. Gait & Posture, 39(1), 553–557.

[15] Libby, R. (2008). A simple method for reliable footstep detection on embedded sensor platforms. Sensors (Peterborough, NH), 116.

[16] Lord, S., Galna, B., Verghese, J., Coleman, S., Burn, D., & Rochester, L. (2013). Independent Domains of Gait in Older Adults and Associated Motor and Nonmotor Attributes: Validation of a Factor Analysis Approach. The Journals of Gerontology: Series A, 68(7), 820–827.

[17] Luce, R. D., & Perry, A. D. (1949). A method of matrix analysis of group structure. Psychometrika, 14(2), 95–116.

[18] Moe-Nilssen, R., & Helbostad, J. L. (2005). Interstride trunk acceleration variability but not step width variability can differentiate between fit and frail older adults. Gait & Posture, 21(2), 164–170.

[19] Morris, M. E., Iansek, R., Matyas, T. A., & Summers, J. J. (1996). Stride length regulation in Parkinson's disease. Brain, 119(2), 551–568.

[20] Muro-de-la-Herran, A., Garcia-Zapirain, B., & Mendez-Zorrilla, A. (2014). Gait Analysis Methods: An Overview of Wearable and Non-Wearable Systems, Highlighting Clinical Applications. Sensors, 14(2), 3362–3394.

[21] Murray, M. P. (1959). Walking patterns in healthy old men. J. Gerontology, 24, 169–178.

[22] Plotnik, M., & Hausdorff, J. M. (2008). The role of gait rhythmicity and bilateral coordination of stepping in the pathophysiology of freezing of gait in Parkinson's disease. Movement Disorders, 23(S2), S444–S450.

[23] Provan, K. G., Fish, A., & Sydow, J. (2007). Interorganizational networks at the network level: A review of the empirical literature on whole networks. Journal of Management, 33(3), 479–516.

[24] Sabatini, A. M., Martelloni, C., Scapellato, S., & Cavallo, F. (2005). Assessment of walking features from foot inertial sensing. IEEE Transactions on Biomedical Engineering, 52(3), 486–494.

[25] Salarian, A., Russmann, H., Vingerhoets, F. J. G., Dehollain, C., Blanc, Y., Burkhard, P. R., & Aminian, K. (2004). Gait assessment in Parkinson's disease: toward an ambulatory system for long-term monitoring. IEEE Transactions on Biomedical Engineering, 51(8), 1434–1443.

[26] Schaafsma, J. D., Balash, Y., Gurevich, T., Bartels, A. L., Hausdorff, J. M., & Giladi, N. (2003). Characterization of freezing of gait subtypes and the response of each to levodopa in Parkinson's disease. European Journal of Neurology, 10(4), 391–398.

[27] Shamir, R., Sharan, R., & Tsur, D. (2004). Cluster graph modification problems. Discrete Applied Mathematics, 144(1–2), 173–182.

[28] Patla, A. E., & Walt, S. E. (1990). Biomechanical W hng Pattern Changes in the Fit and Healthy Elderly. Phys Ther, 70, 340-347.

[29] Ying, H., Silex, C., Schnitzer, A., Leonhardt, S., & Schiek, M. (2007). Automatic step detection in the accelerometer signal. In 4th International Workshop on Wearable and Implantable Body Sensor Networks (BSN 2007) (pp. 80–85). Springer.

[30] Yogev, G., Plotnik, M., Peretz, C., Giladi, N., & Hausdorff, J. M. (2007). Gait asymmetry in patients with Parkinson's disease and elderly fallers: when does the bilateral coordination of gait require attention? Experimental Brain Research, 177(3), 336–346.

[31] Youn, I.-H., Khazanchi, D., Youn, J.-H., & Siu, K.-C. (2016). Multidimensional Mobility Metric for Continuous Gait Monitoring using a Single Accelerometer. Int'l Conf. Healht informatics and Medical Systems.

[32] Zijlstra, W., & Aminian, K. (2007). Mobility assessment in older people: new possibilities and challenges. European Journal of Ageing, 4(1), 3–12.

[33] Zijlstra, W., & Hof, A. L. (2003). Assessment of spatio-temporal gait parameters from trunk accelerations during human walking. Gait & Posture, 18(2), 1–10.

Study of Antidepressant Molecular Structure Leading to Safer Dosing

Meera Garg
Charter School of Wilmington
Wilmington, Delaware USA
mgarg321@gmail.com

ABSTRACT

What type of structures for various drugs enhance their metabolism and efficacy when they bind to CYP enzymes in the body, and how can we predict the binding inhibition of antidepressants with CYP2D6?

KEYWORDS

Safer Dosing; Molecular Structure; Antidepressant

1 INTRODUCTION

In this study the structures of 16 molecules with known pKi values for CYP2D6 inhibition were evaluated in silico and quantified using molecular descriptors. The 16 molecules had similar structures, as they were all either SSRIs, SNRIs, or other molecularly similar drugs. The role of the molecular structure of the drugs in predicting the inhibition of the CYP2D6 enzyme was evaluated. This was done using a mathematical model that established a linear relationship between a drug's predicted pKi values and the drug's molecular structure. After measuring the effect that different molecular descriptors had on the accuracy of the predicted pKi values, the math model was limited to 4 descriptors that provided reasonably good fit to predict a drug's pKi inhibition: pKi = 2.56272 + (-0.68072 logS) + (2.49311 PC+) + (-1.48765 SlogP) + (-0.09520 TPSA). Using this model, the predicted pKi values for the 16 molecules in the test set were calculated, and they were cross-validated against the known pKi values for each of the molecules. The model was then used to predict the pKi values for 3 antidepressants whose pKi values for inhibiting 2D6 were unknown. Knowing this is imperative for physicians, as incorrect dosed medications can lead to deadly synergy between various drugs (drug-drug interactions).

Permission to make digital or hard copies of part or all of this work for personal or classroom use is granted without fee provided that copies are not made or distributed for profit or commercial advantage and that copies bear this notice and the full citation on the first page. Copyrights for third-party components of this work must be honored. For all other uses, contact the Owner/Author.
ACM-BCB '17, August 20-23, 2017, Boston, MA, USA
© 2017 Copyright is held by the owner/author(s).
ACM ISBN 978-1-4503-4722-8/17/08.
http://dx.doi.org/10.1145/3107411.3108179

REFERENCES

[1] Jin, X., Potter, B., Luong, T., Nelson, J., Vuong, C., Potter, C., & Marcsisin, S. R. (2016). Pre clinical Evaluation of CYP2D6 Dependent Drug-Drug Interactions Between Primaquine and SSRI/SNRI Antidepressants. Malaria Journal, 15, 280.

[2] Cytochrome P450. (2016, March 14). Retrieved March 19, 2016, from https://ghr.nlm.nih.gov/geneFamily/cyp

Supervised Machine Learning Approaches Predict and Characterize Nanomaterial Exposures: MWCNT Markers in Lung Lavage Fluid

Naveena Yanamala
EAB/NIOSH/CDC,
1095 willowdale Rd, MS 3030
Morgantown, WV - 26505, USA
+1 – 304-285-6313
wqu1@cdc.gov

Marlene S. Orandle
PPRB/NIOSH/CDC,
1095 willowdale Rd,
Morgantown, WV - 26505, USA
+1 – 304-285-6020
yjj6@cdc.gov

Vamsi K. Kodali
PPRB/NIOSH/CDC,
1095 willowdale Rd, MS 3030
Morgantown, WV - 26505, USA
+1 – 304-285-5928
ywu0@cdc.gov

Lindsey M. Bishop
PPRB/NIOSH/CDC,
1095 willowdale Rd,
Morgantown, WV - 26505, USA
+1 – 304-285-6313
lbishop921@gmail.com

Patti C. Zeidler-Erdely
PPRB/NIOSH/CDC,
1095 willowdale Rd,
Morgantown, WV - 26505, USA
+1 – 304-285-5881
paz9@cdc.gov

Jenny R. Roberts
ACIB/NIOSH/CDC,
1095 willowdale Rd,
Morgantown, WV - 26505, USA
+1 – 304-285-5727
jur6@cdc.gov

Vincent Castranova
West Virgina University,
School of Pharmacy, PO Box 9530
Morgantown, WV – 26506, USA
+1 – 304-293-8236
vcastran@hsc.wvu.edu

Aaron D. Erdely
PPRB/NIOSH/CDC,
1095 willowdale Rd,
Morgantown, WV - 26505, USA
+1 – 304-285-5903
efi4@cdc.gov

ABSTRACT

Globally, carbon nanotubes (CNT) make up 30% of the total engineered nanomaterial market. Within that 30%, multi-walled carbon nanotubes (MWCNT) make up 94% of the total. Recent experimental evidence points towards significant pulmonary toxicity of MWCNTs such as inflammation, sub-pleural fibrosis and granuloma formation, associated with CNTs. Although numerous studies explore the adverse potential of various CNTs, their comparability is often limited. This is due to differences in administered dose, physico-chemical characteristics (e.g. agglomeration/aggregation state, metal impurities, stiffness, length) of the CNTs studied, exposure methods employed, as well as the differences in the end points monitored. In this study, we attempted to address the problem of identifying protein markers consistent across different MWCNT studies through the application of a sparse supervised classification methods. A panel of proteins measured in bronchoalveolar lavage collected from mice at various post-exposure time points and concentrations exposed to two different pristine or as-produced MWCNT, their polymer coated counterparts, or a well-studied reference material, MWCNT-7, were analyzed.

The main objective was to take advantage of the power of sparse classification methods in identifying a small number of highly predictive and correlated markers (4 to 7, out of a panel of 52 proteins) that can distinguish exposure to MWCNT and/or be attributable to MWCNT toxicity in mice. Using this approach, we identified a small subset of proteins clearly distinguishing each exposure. MDC/CCL22, in particular, was associated with various MWCNT exposures and was independent of exposure route tested i.e., oropharyngeal aspiration versus inhalation exposure. The approaches presented in this study could enable comparison not only within a class of engineered nanomaterials but between various classes of nanomaterials. This study thus serves as a "proof of concept" that can be expanded to future nanomaterial risk profiling studies by informing decisions related to dose- and time-response relationships and to generate relevant experimental conditions.

Keywords

Fibrosis markers; Computational toxicology; Nanotoxicology; Predictive models; Support vector machines.

Disclaimer

The findings and conclusions in this report are those of the authors and do not necessarily represent the views of the National Institute for Occupational Safety and Health.

Permission to make digital or hard copies of part or all of this work for personal or classroom use is granted without fee provided that copies are not made or distributed for profit or commercial advantage and that copies bear this notice and the full citation on the first page. Copyrights for third-party components of this work must be honored. For all other uses, contact the Owner/Author.
ACM-BCB '17, August 20-23, 2017, Boston, MA, USA
© 2017 Copyright is held by the owner/author(s).
ACM ISBN 978-1-4503-4722-8/17/08.
http://dx.doi.org/10.1145/3107411.3108181

Prokaryotic Autolysin Database Construction*

Brandon A Saiz
University of Tampa
Tampa, Fl USA
bsaiz123@gmail.com

Padmanabhan Mahadevan
University of Tampa
Tampa, Fl USA
pmahadevan1@gmail.com

ABSTRACT

Databases are valuable resources that are capable of collecting and disseminating sizeable quantities of data with the purpose of furthering research done in that particular field. Currently, there are databases for organismal genomes and classes of proteins, but currently there is no database for bacterial autolysins in particular. Autolysins such as LytA in *Streptococcus pneumoniae* are of vital importance as it allows the bacterium to evade antimicrobial peptides (Kietzman et. al, 2015). Additionally autolysins have been found to promote horizontal gene transfer in S. pneumoniae, as well as promoting sporulation in Bacillus subtilis (Allocati et. al, 2015). While some methods currently exist to manipulate autolysin expression, such as a broth with 2% choline, a large scale computational analysis of these proteins may provide more insight to these mechanisms (Balachandran et al, 2001).

11,458 proteomes encompassing all available *Streptococcus (n=9,341), Bacillus (n=1,003)*, and *Listeria (n=1,114)* were obtained from GenBank, and 5 autolytic domains including amidase 3 and glucosaminidase were detected using hmmer with an E-value threshold of 10^-5. Resulting 68,748 output files were analyzed indicating 35,319 positive results containing at least one detected domain. This revealed that certain domains such as Glucosaminidase and LysM are highly conserved having been detected in 98.6%, 93.6%, and 99.9% of *Streptococcus, Bacillus*, and *Listeria* proteomes respectively, whereas others were noticeably more prevalent in a particular genus such as amidase 2 (75.5% *Streptococcus*, 92.1% *Bacillus*, 76.5% *Listeria*). Additionally, the proteomic locus of each detected domain has been recorded. Currently we aim to organize and compile data into a useful database using SQLite. Additionally, more genera are expected to be added to eventually encompass all bacterial proteomes. Moreover we aim to determine associated domains using hmm scan.

KEYWORDS

Prokaryote;Autolysin;Antibiotic Resistance;Virulence Factors

ACM Reference format:

Brandon A Saiz, Padmanabhan Mahadevan. 2017. Prokaryotic Autolysin Database Construction. *In Proceedings of ACM-BCB '17, Boston, MA, USA, August 20-23, 2017,* 1 page.
DOI: http://dx.doi.org/10.1145/3107411.3108183

REFERENCES

[1] Allocati, N., Masulli, M., Ilio, C. D., & Laurenzi, V. D. (2015). Die for the community: an overview of programmed cell death in bacteria. Cell Death and Disease,6(1). doi:10.1038/cddis.2014.570

[2] Balachandran, P., Hollingshead, S. K., Paton, J. C., & Briles, D. E. (2001). The Autolytic Enzyme LytA of Streptococcus pneumoniae Is Not Responsible for Releasing Pneumolysin. Journal of Bacteriology,183(10), 3108-3116. doi:10.1128/jb.183.10.3108-3116.2001

[3] Kietzman, C. C., Gao, G., Mann, B., Myers, L., & Tuomanen, E. I. (2016). Dynamic capsule restructuring by the main pneumococcal autolysin LytA in response to the epithelium. Nature Communications,7, 10859. doi:10.1038/ncomms10859

Permission to make digital or hard copies of part or all of this work for personal or classroom use is granted without fee provided that copies are not made or distributed for profit or commercial advantage and that copies bear this notice and the full citation on the first page. Copyrights for third-party components of this work must be honored. For all other uses, contact the Owner/Author.
ACM-BCB '17, August 20-23, 2017, Boston, MA, USA
© 2017 Copyright is held by the owner/author(s).
ACM ISBN 978-1-4503-4722-8/17/08.
http://dx.doi.org/10.1145/3107411.3108183

The Fate of Retrotransposed Processed Genes in *Arabidopsis Thaliana*

Basma Abdelkarim
University of Ottawa
451 Smyth Rd, Ottawa, ON
Canada, K1H 8L6
+1 (613) 737-8899 #73255
babde007@uottawa.ca

Vincent Maranda
University of Ottawa
75 Laurier Ave E, Ottawa, ON
Canada, K1N 6N5
vmara023@uottawa.ca

Guy Drouin
University of Ottawa
75 Laurier Ave E, Ottawa, ON
Canada, K1N 6N5
+1 (613) 562-5800 #6052
guy.Drouin@uottawa.ca

ABSTRACT
Processed genes are functional genes that are generated as a result of retrotransposition of mRNA molecules into loci where recruited or pre-existing promoter elements support their transcription. Here, we investigate the fate of previously identified Arabidopsis thaliana processed genes. We found that six A. thaliana processed genes originated in the common ancestor of five Brassicaceae species. Ka/Ks analysis of these processed genes, and of their parental genes, show that they experienced similar selective pressures. Furthermore, the expression of processed genes is not correlated to the presence of CAATT and TATA-boxes, or nearby genes. Most of these processed genes are likely to have gained expression through recruitment of novel promoter sequences. However, the selective pressure acting on their expression level has not yet been adapted.

Keywords
Comparative genomics; Processed genes; Plants.

1. RESULTS
We found that six A. thaliana processed genes originated in the common ancestor of five Brassicaceae species (Figure 1). Ka/Ks analysis of these processed genes, and of their parental genes, show that they experienced similar selective pressures. These Ka/Ks ratios are significantly negatively correlated to the expression level of the parental genes, but not of processed genes. Moreover, the processed genes are expressed in similar tissues as their parental genes. Furthermore, the expression of processed genes is not correlated to the presence of CAATT and TATA-boxes, or nearby genes.

Our results suggest that the A. thaliana processed genes evolve relatively slowly and have been conserved for about 30 million years to produce more of the same product, and in the same tissues, as their parental genes. Most of these processed genes are likely to have gained expression through recruitment of novel promoter sequences. However, the selective pressure acting on their expression level has not yet been adapted.

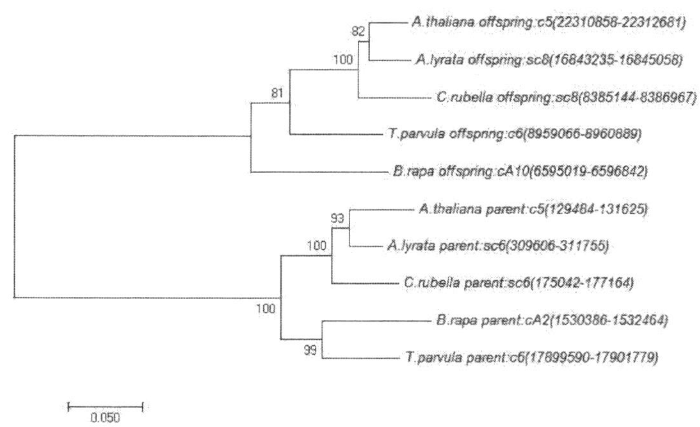

Figure 1. Phylogenetic tree of At5g01320 gene sequences. The scale bar represents 5% nucleotide divergence.

Permission to make digital or hard copies of part or all of this work for personal or classroom use is granted without fee provided that copies are not made or distributed for profit or commercial advantage and that copies bear this notice and the full citation on the first page. Copyrights for third-party components of this work must be honored. For all other uses, contact the Owner/Author.
ACM-BCB '17, August 20-23, 2017, Boston, MA, USA
© 2017 Copyright is held by the owner/author(s).
ACM ISBN 978-1-4503-4722-8/17/08.
http://dx.doi.org/10.1145/3107411.3108186

Super-enhancer Dynamics throughout Myogenesis

Basma Abdelkarim
University of Ottawa
451 Smyth Rd, Ottawa, ON
Canada, K1H 8L6
+1 (613) 737-8899 #73255
babde007@uottawa.ca

Theodore Perkins
Ottawa Hospital Research Institute
501 Smyth Rd, Ottawa, ON
Canada, K1H 8L6
+1 (613) 737-8899 #79795
tperkins@ohri.ca

ABSTRACT

Genome-wide ChIP-seq analysis of transcription factor binding and histone marks has uncovered large regulatory domains, known as super-enhancers, that consist of clusters of active enhancers within 12.5 kb of each other. Super-enhancers are characterized by high abundance of H3K27ac histone marks, disproportionate binding of master regulators and coactivators, and drive the expression of important cell identity genes. The algorithm, Rank Ordering of Super-Enhancers (ROSE), was developed to identify SEs based on their characteristics and has been extensively used, on various cell types. Less attention has been aimed at understanding how super-enhancers change in different cellular contexts, and in particular, during the differentiation of stem cells. We use ROSE, in conjunction with other tools, to investigate the dynamics of super-enhancers across myogenesis. Using ChIP-seq data for various transcription factors and stage-matched RNA-seq data, we characterize several super-enhancer regions and their associated genes in myoblasts and myotubes, finding them to be largely stage-specific.

Keywords

Bioinformatics, ChIP-seq, Big data, Genomics, Epigenetics, Super-enhancers.

1. RESULTS

Using peak files for MyoD, Pbx1 and Tead4 for myoblasts, and MyoG, Pbx1 and Tead4 for myotubes, we identified super-enhancers in both myoblasts (Figure 1) and myotubes which were majorly stage-specific. However, we also found a few super-enhancer regions that were shared between the two stages.

Permission to make digital or hard copies of part or all of this work for personal or classroom use is granted without fee provided that copies are not made or distributed for profit or commercial advantage and that copies bear this notice and the full citation on the first page. Copyrights for third-party components of this work must be honored. For all other uses, contact the Owner/Author.
ACM-BCB '17, August 20-23, 2017, Boston, MA, USA
© 2017 Copyright is held by the owner/author(s).
ACM ISBN 978-1-4503-4722-8/17/08.
http://dx.doi.org/10.1145/3107411.3108187

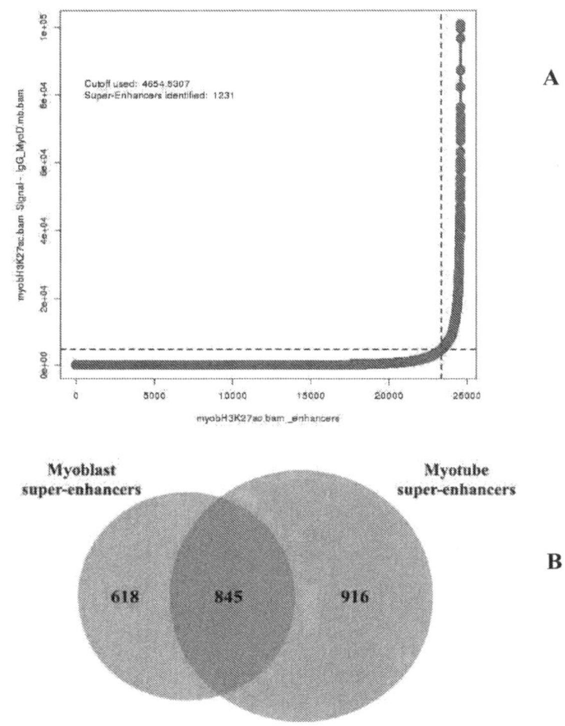

Figure 1. A) Rank ordering of super-enhancers binding MyoD in myoblasts, based on H3K27ac signal with mathematically calculated cut-off differentiating typical enhancers from super-enhancers. B) Overlap between myoblast and myotube super-enhancers

2. FUTURE DIRECTIONS

The next step is to have a deeper look at these regions and their associated genes to identify the processes that are distinct for each stage. In addition, we will be analysing RNA-seq data for both myoblasts and myotubes to investigate differential gene expression patterns between the two stages and to characterize super-enhancer dynamics throughout myogenesis. Later we plan to add more myogenic stages to the analysis to obtain a wider view of super-enhancer remodelling during cell development. In addition, we plan to compare super-enhancer dynamics in myogenesis with those in diseased muscle cells like muscular dystrophy or Rhabdomyosarcoma.

Varsimlab: A Docker-based Pipeline to Automatically Synthesize Short Reads with Genomic Aberrations

Abdelrahman Hosny
University of Connecticut
Storrs, CT 06268
abdelrahman@engr.uconn.edu

Fatima Zare
University of Connecticut
Storrs, CT 06268
fatemeh.zare@uconn.edu

Sheida Nabavi
University of Connecticut
Storrs, CT 06268
sheida.nabavi@uconn.edu

ABSTRACT

Individuals of a species have similar characteristics but they are rarely identical because of the genomic variations. One of the important genomic variations is structural variation (SV), including copy number variation (CNV), which is a result of amplifications or deletions of genomic regions. It has been shown that SV plays an important role in phenotypic diversity and evolution. A Genome encompasses other aberrations such as Single Nucleotide Polymorphism (SNP) and small insertions and deletions (Indels). Although genetic variations contribute to our uniqueness, they can comprise critical developmental genes leading to gene dosage imbalances, new genes creation, and gene structures reshaping that ultimately may result in disease. Understanding the mechanisms of structural variation formation helps us better understand human phenotypic diversity, evolution and diseases susceptibility.

Computational tools have been developed for genomic variation detection using next-generation sequencing (NGS) data. However, with no prior knowledge about variants in real samples, the tools that are used for detection and analysis have been hindered by the lack of a gold standard benchmark. Some multi-variant simulators have been developed for whole genome sequencing (WGS) data such as SInC and SCNVSim. However, they are not easy to use and technical skills are required to run them. Moreover, those simulators only apply genomic variations to a reference file; and other software tools, such as ART simulator, need to be used to generate the sequenced short reads. We have developed a user-friendly automated pipeline, VarSimLab, which offers an integrated web-based suite to simulate structural variations and also to generate WGS and WES short reads. It utilizes some of the existing tools and packages them into a standard Docker image; an open source technology used to package applications and their dependencies into a standardized software container. VarSimLab automates the process of simulating tumor genotypes such as SNPs, Indels, CNVs, transition/transversion, ploidy and tumor sub-clone and generating short reads. Thanks to the Docker technology, the pipeline is platform-independent and super easy for non-technical scientists to use from a web browser. VarSimLab is designed to grow as a full suite of integrated tools to analyze genomic aberrations.

Permission to make digital or hard copies of part or all of this work for personal or classroom use is granted without fee provided that copies are not made or distributed for profit or commercial advantage and that copies bear this notice and the full citation on the first page. Copyrights for third-party components of this work must be honored. For all other uses, contact the Owner/Author.
BCB'17, August 20-23, 2017, Boston, MA, USA
© 2017 Copyright is held by the owner/author(s).
ACM ISBN 978-1-4503-4722-8/17/08.
http://dx.doi.org/10.1145/3107411.3108188

General Terms

Next Generation Sequencing, Simulation

Keywords

Docker; Structural Variations; Copy Number Variation; Reproducibility

ACKNOWLEDGMENTS

This work was supported by a grant from the National Institutes of Health (NIH, R00LM011595, PI: Nabavi).

An Advanced Workflow for Metabolite Annotation*

Neda Hassanpour
Department of Computer Science
Tufts University, Medford, MA, US
Neda.Hassanpour@tufts.edu

Nicholas Alden
Department of Chemical and Biological Engineering
Tufts University, Medford, MA, US
Nicholas.Alden@tufts.edu

Kyongbum Lee
Department of Chemical and Biological Engineering
Tufts University, Medford, MA, US
Kyongbum.Lee@tufts.edu

Soha Hassoun
Department of Computer Science
Tufts University, Medford, MA, US
soha@cs.tufts.edu

ABSTRACT

Metabolomics is an expanding field of 'omics' that involves the identification and quantification of small molecules in cells, tissues and other complex biological samples. Metabolomics is emerging as a strong tool for disease treatments and drug developments. A major challenge in realizing the full potential of metabolomics to globally characterize metabolism lies in processing and analyzing the collected data. Obtaining meaningful biological information depends on reliably and efficiently resolving the chemical identities of the detected data features (unique mass and associated fragmentation spectrum in the case of mass spectrometry experiments). We propose in this poster a novel metabolomics data processing workflow to enhance the accuracy and performance of metabolite identification.

* Permission to make digital or hard copies of part or all of this work for personal or classroom use is granted without fee provided that copies are not made or distributed for profit or commercial advantage and that copies bear this notice and the full citation on the first page. Copyrights for third-party components of this work must be honored. For all other uses, contact the Owner/Author.
ACM-BCB '17, August 20-23, 2017, Boston, MA, USA
© 2017 Copyright is held by the owner/author(s).
ACM ISBN 978-1-4503-4722-8/17/08.
http://dx.doi.org/10.1145/3107411.3108189

Development of a Polymer-Theoretic Approach to Describing Constraints on Reactions Between Antipeptide Antibodies and Intrinsically Disordered Peptide Antigens: Implications for B-Cell Epitope Prediction

Salvador Eugenio C. Caoili
Department of Biochemistry and Molecular Biology, College of Medicine, University of the Philippines Manila
Room 101, Medical Annex Building, 547 Pedro Gil Street, Ermita, Manila 1000, Philippines
badong@post.upm.edu.ph

ABSTRACT

B-cell epitope prediction aims to support translational applications as exemplified by peptide-based vaccine design. This entails selection of immunizing peptide sequences that tend to be intrinsically disordered and thus appropriately described within the framework of polymer theory. A fully extended hexapeptide sequence spans a typical antibody footprint; but disordered peptides are flexible rather than rigid, such that their B-cell epitopes may vary in length according to the diversity of conformations assumed upon binding by antibodies. Hence, peptides were modeled herein as worm-like chains, using an interpolated approximation of the radial probability density distribution function to estimate the probability that the ends of a peptidic sequence are separated by a distance less than or equal to a typical antibody footprint diameter. The results suggest that the epitopes are likely to be no more than 17 residues long, which is consistent with available structural data on immune complexes consisting of antipeptide antibodies bound to cognate peptide antigens. For such antigens, B-cell epitope prediction thus could proceed with initial scanning for intrinsically disordered sequences of length up to a physico-chemically plausible maximum value (e.g., 17 residues), with analysis of progressively longer subsequences to identify nonredundant sets of putative epitopes (e.g., based on predicted affinity).

CCS CONCEPTS

• **Information systems → Chemical and biochemical retrieval**; • **Applied computing → Chemistry; Molecular sequence analysis; Molecular structural biology; Health informatics; Bioinformatics**;

Permission to make digital or hard copies of part or all of this work for personal or classroom use is granted without fee provided that copies are not made or distributed for profit or commercial advantage and that copies bear this notice and the full citation on the first page. Copyrights for third-party components of this work must be honored. For all other uses, contact the owner/author(s).
ACM-BCB'17, August 20–23, 2017, Boston, MA, USA.
© 2017 Copyright held by the owner/author(s).
ACM ISBN 978-1-4503-4722-8/17/08.
https://doi.org/10.1145/3107411.3108190

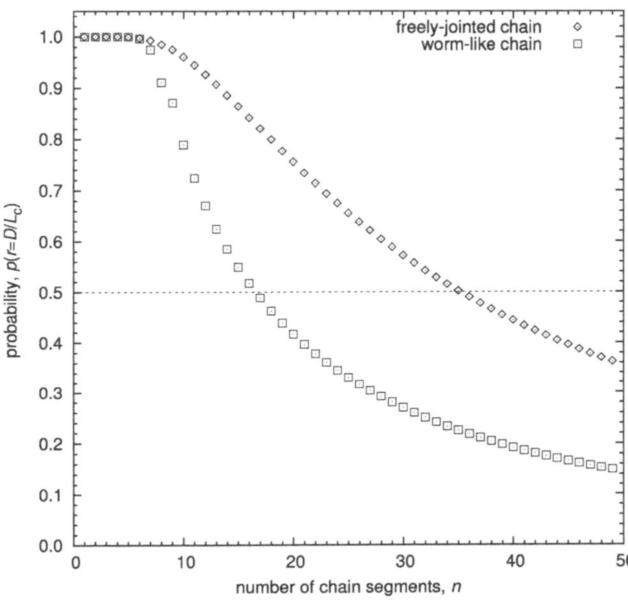

Figure 1: Estimated probability of peptide end-to-end distance ≤ 20 Å (antibody footprint diameter) for chain segment length = 3.8 Å and persistence length = 4.0 Å for worm-like chain.

KEYWORDS

B-cell epitope prediction; antipeptide antibodies; peptide antigens; intrinsically disordered peptides; polymer theory; worm-like chains

ACKNOWLEDGMENTS

This work was supported by an Angelita T. Reyes Centennial Professorial Chair grant awarded to the author.

REFERENCES

[1] N. B. Becker, A. Rosa, and R. Everaers. 2010. The radial distribution function of worm-like chains. *Eur Phys J E Soft Matter* 32, 1 (May 2010), 53–69. [DOI:10.1140/epje/i2010-10596-0] [PubMed:20517631].

[2] H. X. Zhou. 2004. Polymer models of protein stability, folding, and interactions. *Biochemistry* 43, 8 (Mar 2004), 2141–2154. [DOI:10.1021/bi036269n] [PubMed:14979710].

Development of Nicotinic Acetylcholine Receptor nAChR α7 Binding Activity Prediction Model: Coupling Machine Learning with Competitive Molecular Docking

Huixiao Hong[1*], Carmine Leggett[2], Suguna Sakkiah[1]

[1]Division of Bioinformatics and Biostatistics, National Center for Toxicological Research, U.S. Food and Drug Administration, 3900 NCTR Road, Jefferson, AR 72079, USA; [2]Division of Nonclinical Science, Office of Science, Center for Tobacco Products, U.S. Food and Drug Administration, Silver Spring, MD 20993, USA

*Correspondence should be addressed to Dr. Huixiao Hong at huixiao.hong@fda.hhs.gov

ABSTRACT

Despite the well-known adverse health effects associated with tobacco use, addiction to nicotine found in tobacco products causes difficulty in quitting among users. Nicotinic acetylcholine receptors (nAChRs) are the physiological targets of nicotine and facilitate addiction to tobacco products. The nAChR α7 receptor subtype plays an important role in addiction; therefore, predicting the binding activity of tobacco constituents to nAChR α7 would contribute to methods assessing the addictive potential of tobacco constituents. Among the receptor-ligand complexes obtained from the Protein Data Bank (PDB), we found that there were two distinct clusters of binding-pocket conformations for nAChR α7. One template was selected from each cluster to construct the 3D structures of human nAChR α7 using homology modeling. The competitive docking model was developed for determination of the structure of nAChR α7 bound with a chemical. To develop a prediction model of human α7 binding activity, we used a training data set of extracted 930 chemicals assessed for human α7 binding from the two databases, PubChem and ChEMBL. We also extracted 1448 chemicals evaluated for rat α7 binding from the same databases as the external testing data set. Based on the competitive docking results, the winning docking scores were partitioned to identify the key residues that play important roles in the receptor-ligand binding for each chemical. Our previously published algorithm, Decision Forest (DF), which combines multiple Decision Tree models was used to train the human α7 binding activity prediction model based on the partitioned docking scores. Five-fold cross validations were conducted to estimate the performance of the DF models. The DF model was tested using the external testing data set and then was used to predict the potential human α7 binding activity for the 5275 tobacco constituents of unknown activity. The human α7 binding activity data for 84 of the 5275 tobacco constituents were experimentally measured to confirm the prediction results. The overall prediction accuracy, sensitivity and specificity were 77.4%, 57.7% and 86.2%, respectively, demonstrating that the developed predictive model of human α7 binding activity could be a useful tool for high-throughput screening of potential addictive tobacco constituents.

Disclaimer: The findings and conclusions in this abstract are not a formal dissemination of information by the US Food and Drug Administration (FDA) and do not represent Agency position or policy.

Permission to make digital or hard copies of part or all of this work for personal or classroom use is granted without fee provided that copies are not made or distributed for profit or commercial advantage and that copies bear this notice and the full citation on the first page. Copyrights for third-party components of this work must be honored. For all other uses, contact the Owner/Author.

ACM-BCB '17, August 20-23, 2017, Boston, MA, USA

© 2017 Copyright is held by the owner/author(s).

ACM ISBN 978-1-4503-4722-8/17/08.
http://dx.doi.org/10.1145/3107411.3108191

Automated Next Generation Sequencing Bioinformatics Pipelines for Pathogen Discovery and Surveillance

Margaret Okomo-Adhiambo
Centers for Disease Control and Prevention
Atlanta, GA, USA
gfv3@cdc.gov

Edward Ramos
CSRA Inc.
Atlanta, GA, USA
yqd9@cdc.gov

Reagan Kelly
CSRA Inc.
Atlanta, GA, USA
ylb9@cdc.gov

Yatish Jain
CSRA Inc.
Atlanta, GA, USA
nnw8@cdc.gov

Roman Tatusov
CSRA Inc.
Atlanta, GA, USA
yqy9@cdc.gov

Anna Montmayeur
CSRA Inc.
Atlanta, GA, USA
xda8@cdc.gov

Gregory Doho
CSRA Inc.
Atlanta, GA, USA
iqy1@cdc.gov

Rachel L. Marine
Centers for Disease Control and Prevention
Atlanta, GA, USA
loz7@cdc.gov

Terry Fei Fan Ng
Centers for Disease Control and Prevention
Atlanta, GA, USA
ylz9@cdc.gov

Adam Retchless
Centers for Disease Control and Prevention
Atlanta, GA, USA
ymw8@cdc.gov

Steve Oberste
Centers for Disease Control and Prevention
Atlanta, GA, USA
mbo2@cdc.gov

Paul Rota
Centers for Disease Control and Prevention
Atlanta, GA, USA
par1@cdc.gov

Xin Wang
Centers for Disease Control and Prevention
Atlanta, GA, USA
gqe8@cdc.gov

Agha N. Khan
Centers for Disease Control and Prevention
Atlanta, GA, USA
akk3@cdc.gov

ABSTRACT

Next-generation sequencing (NGS) has become a vital tool in clinical microbiology, with numerous applications in infectious disease diagnostics, outbreak investigations, and public health surveillance. Although the NGS technology enables comprehensive pathogen detection in a relatively short time at a low cost, the enormous amount of genomics data generated creates a critical challenge of effectively organizing, archiving, analyzing, and reporting the results within a clinically relevant timeframe. Automated pipelines provide the first step in standardizing NGS data processing and reporting, thus eliminating the common bottlenecks in bioinformatics analyses, and providing rapid turnaround. Here, we present the Viral NGS Pipeline optimized for identification and whole genome assembly of viruses, and the Bacterial Meningococcus Genome Analysis Platform (BMGAP), designed for genotypic characterization of meningitis pathogens. These respective pipelines have been used to analyze more than 11,000 clinical samples and isolates. The pipelines are deployable on both standalone and cloud-based servers, enabling their accessibility to internal CDC users, as well as external partners, including state public health laboratories and other collaborators worldwide. These automated pipelines have the potential to contribute to the development of unbiased NGS-based clinical assays for pathogen detection that demand rapid turnaround times, and are expected to play a key role in infectious disease surveillance in the future.

Permission to make digital or hard copies of part or all of this work for personal or classroom use is granted without fee provided that copies are not made or distributed for profit or commercial advantage and that copies bear this notice and the full citation on the first page. Copyrights for third-party components of this work must be honored. For all other uses, contact the Owner/Author.
ACM-BCB '17, August 20-23, 2017, Boston, MA, USA.
© 2017 Copyright is held by the owner/author(s).
ACM ISBN 978-1-4503-4722-8/17/08.
http://dx.doi.org/10.1145/3107411.3108192

CCS CONCEPTS

• **Applied computing** → Computational biology; Molecular sequence analysis; Genomics; Bioinformatics

KEYWORDS

Next-generation sequencing (NGS); automated bioinformatics pipelines; pathogen molecular detection; infectious disease surveillance

ACM Reference Format:

M. Okomo-Adhiambo, E. Ramos, R. Kelly, Y. Jain, R. Tatusov, A. Montmayeur, G. Doho, R.L. Marine, T.F.F. Ng, A. Retchless, S. Oberste, P. Rota, X. Wang, and A.N. Khan. 2017. Automated Next Generation Sequencing Bioinformatics Pipelines for Pathogen Discovery and Surveillance. Poster Abstract. *In Proceedings of ACM-BCB '17, August 20-23, 2017, Boston, MA, USA,* 1 page.
http://dx.doi.org/10.1145/3107411.3108192

Protein Classification using Modified *N-gram* and *Skip-gram* Models

Extended Abstract

S M Ashiqul Islam*
Institute of Biomedical Studies, Baylor University
1301 S University Parks Dr
Waco, Texas 76798
s_islam@baylor.edu

Christopher Michel Kearney
Department of Biology, Baylor University
1301 S University Parks Dr
Waco, Texas 76798
chris_kearney@baylor.edu

Ankan Choudhury
Department of Biology, Baylor University
1301 S University Parks Dr
Waco, Texas 76798
ankan_choudhury@baylor.edu

Erich J Baker†
Department of Computer Science, Baylor University
One Bear Place #97356
Waco, Texas 76798
Erich_Baker@baylor.edu

ABSTRACT

Machine Learning (ML)-based classification of protein characteristics from primary sequences is an important tool for exploring candidate proteins in targeted drug discovery, mutational analysis, and functional identification. However, ML feature selection requires extensive manual curation and knowledge of protein chemistry, interactions, and micro-environment of the proteins of interest. Current approaches include amino acid composition strategies, specific motif analysis or Quantitative Structure Activity Relationship (QSAR)-based feature generation methods. In contrast, we propose an automated generalized feature generation method based on Natural Language Processing (NLP), using a modified combination of *N-Gram* and *Skip-Gram* models (m-NGSG). Optimal parameters are selected using an adapted grid search algorithm, enabling a high-throughput global application of our approach. A meta-comparison of logistic regression mediated classification approaches exploiting m-NGSG with other published models illustrates enhanced functional and structural binary and multi-class classification accuracy in every instance. The lack of dependence on detailed physicochemical knowledge makes the m-NGSG approach ideal for the exploration of protein characteristics recalcitrant to previous approaches without any loss in predictive accuracy. A further test on prediction quality of m-NGSG on cationic channel blockers with 70% sequence identity from Arthropods demonstrated 94.10% and 92.30% accuracy on the training and test set, respectively. The latter study demonstrates the applicability of m-NGSG model on a functional classification of proteins employing a novel dataset.Thus, without the requirement of expert intervention for optimal feature selection, it is hoped that this automated feature generation approach will reduce the time needed to employ ML classification strategies for prediction of protein characteristics.

*The first author
†The principal investigator.

Permission to make digital or hard copies of part or all of this work for personal or classroom use is granted without fee provided that copies are not made or distributed for profit or commercial advantage and that copies bear this notice and the full citation on the first page. Copyrights for third-party components of this work must be honored. For all other uses, contact the owner/author(s).
ACM-BCB '17, August 20-23, 2017, Boston, MA, USA
© 2017 Copyright held by the owner/author(s).
ACM ISBN 978-1-4503-4722-8/17/08.
https://doi.org/10.1145/3107411.3108193

CCS CONCEPTS

• **Computing methodologies → Natural language processing; Information extraction; Supervised learning by classification;** • **Applied computing → Molecular sequence analysis;**

KEYWORDS

machine learning,natural language processing, *n-grams,skip-grams*, protein sequence analysis,feature generation, channel blocker toxins

ACM Reference format:
S M Ashiqul Islam, Christopher Michel Kearney, Ankan Choudhury, and Erich J Baker. 2017. Protein Classification using Modified *N-gram* and *Skip-gram* Models. In *Proceedings of ACM-BCB '17, Boston, MA, USA, August 20-23, 2017,* 1 pages.
https://doi.org/10.1145/3107411.3108193

Self-Tuning Spectral Clustering for Full-length Viral Quasispecies Reconstruction with PacBio Long Reads†

Xiaoli Jiao
Laboratory of Human Retrovirology and Immunoinformatics, Leidos Biomedical Research, Inc. Frederick National Laboratory for Cancer Research, Frederick, MD 21702
jiaox3@mail.nih.com

Hiromi Imamichi
Laboratory of Immunoregulation National Institute of Allergy and Infectious Diseases, National Institutes of Health, Bethesda, Maryland 20892
himamichi@mail.nih.gov

Tauseef Rehman
Virus Isolation and Serology Laboratory, Leidos Biomedical Research, Inc. Frederick National Laboratory for Cancer Research, Frederick, MD 21702
trehman@mail.nih.gov

Rishub Nahar
Laboratory of Human Retrovirology and Immunoinformatics, Leidos Biomedical Research, Inc. Frederick National Laboratory for Cancer Research, Frederick, MD 21702
rishub.nahar@nih.gov

Robin L. Dewar
Virus Isolation and Serology Laboratory, Leidos Biomedical Research, Inc. Frederick National Laboratory for Cancer Research, Frederick, MD 21702
rdewar@mail.nih.gov

H. Clifford Lane
Laboratory of Immunoregulation National Institute of Allergy and Infectious Diseases, National Institutes of Health, Bethesda, Maryland 20892
CLANE@niaid.nih.gov

Tomozumi Imamichi
Laboratory of Human Retrovirology and Immunoinformatics, Leidos Biomedical Research, Inc. Frederick National Laboratory for Cancer Research, Frederick, MD 21702
timamichi@mail.nih.gov

Brad T. Sherman
Laboratory of Human Retrovirology and Immunoinformatics, Leidos Biomedical Research, Inc. Frederick National Laboratory for Cancer Research, Frederick, MD 21702
bsherman@mail.nih.gov

ABSTRACT

Rapidly evolving RNA viruses prevail within a host as a collection of closely related variants, referred to as viral quasi-species. Uncovering the genetic diversity (i.e., inferring viral haplotypes and their proportions in the population) of an RNA virus can significantly benefit the study of disease progression, antiviral drug design, vaccine design and viral pathogenesis. Recent advances in PacBio single-molecule sequencing offers sufficient throughput and contiguous long reads (>10kb) covering the full length of most genes and RNA viral genomes, providing a potential to reliably profile the viral populations. However, the relatively high error rate (2~15%) in the long-read data requires novel analysis methods to deconvolute sequences derived from complex viral mixtures. We examined samples containing complex mixtures of near-full-length HIV-1 genomes, single molecules sequenced as near-full-length (9kb) amplicons directly from PCR products, and developed a novel signature-based self-tuning spectral clustering method called SigClust to accurately determine the identity (above 99.5%) and relative abundances of viral genomes in the mixtures. Results on real HIV-1 and influenza benchmark data sets demonstrate efficacy and superior performance of SigClust.

†The full version of the author's guide is available as acmart.pdf document

Permission to make digital or hard copies of part or all of this work for personal or classroom use is granted without fee provided that copies are not made or distributed for profit or commercial advantage and that copies bear this notice and the full citation on the first page. Copyrights for third-party components of this work must be honored. For all other uses, contact the Owner/Author.
ACM-BCB '17, August 20-23, 2017, Boston, MA, USA
© 2017 Copyright is held by the owner/author(s).
ACM ISBN 978-1-4503-4722-8/17/08.
http://dx.doi.org/10.1145/3107411.3108194

CCS CONCEPTS

• **Applied computing** → Sequencing and genotyping technologies; • **Life and medical sciences** → Computational biology

KEYWORDS

Viral Quasispecies; Clustering; Next Generation Sequencing; Pacbio long reads

Best Setting of Model Parameters in Applying Topic Modeling on Textual Documents

Wen Zou*
Division of Bioinformatics and Biostatistics,
National Center for Toxicological Research,
U.S. FDA
Jefferson, Arkansas
wen.zou@fda.hhs.gov

Weizhong Zhao
Division of Bioinformatics and Biostatistics,
National Center for Toxicological Research,
U.S. FDA
Jefferson, Arkansas
weizhong.zhao@fda.hhs.gov

James J Chen
Division of Bioinformatics and Biostatistics,
National Center for Toxicological Research,
U.S. FDA
Jefferson, Arkansas
jamesj.chen@fda.hhs.gov

Roger Perkins
Division of Bioinformatics and Biostatistics,
National Center for Toxicological Research,
U.S. FDA
Jefferson, Arkansas
roger.perkins@fda.hhs.gov

ABSTRACT

Probabilistic topic modeling is an active research field in machine learning and has been mainly used as an analytical tool to structure large textual corpora for data mining. It offers a viable approach to structure huge textual document collections into latent topic themes to aid text mining. Latent Dirichlet Allocation (LDA) [1] is the most commonly used topic modelling method across a wide number of technical fields. However, model development can be arduous and tedious, and requires burdensome and systematic sensitivity studies in order to find the best set of model parameters. In this study, we use a heuristic approach to estimate the most appropriate number of topics. Specifically, the rate of perplexity change (RPC) as a function of numbers of topics is proposed as a suitable selector [2]. We test the stability and effectiveness of the proposed method for three markedly different types of grounded-truth datasets: *Salmonella* next generation sequencing, pharmacological side effects, and textual abstracts on computational biology and bioinformatics (TCBB) from PubMed [1]. Then we describe extensive sensitivity studies (in Figure 1) to determine best practices for generating effective topic models. To test effectiveness and validity of topic models, we constructed a ground truth data set from PubMed that contained 41 health related themes including negative controls, and mixed it with a data set of unstructured documents. The results show that obtaining the most useful model and tuning to desired sensitivity versus specificity, requires an iterative process wherein preprocessing steps, the type of topic modeling algorithm, and the algorithms model parameters are systematically varied. Models need to be compared with both qualitative, subjective assessments and quantitative, objective assessments, and care is required that Gibbs sampling in model estimation is sufficient to assure stable solutions. With a high quality model, documents can be rank-ordered in accordance with probability of being associated with complex regulatory query string, greatly lessoning text mining work. Importantly, topic models are agnostic about how words and documents are defined, and thus our findings are extensible to topic models where samples are defined as documents, and genes, proteins or their sequences are words.

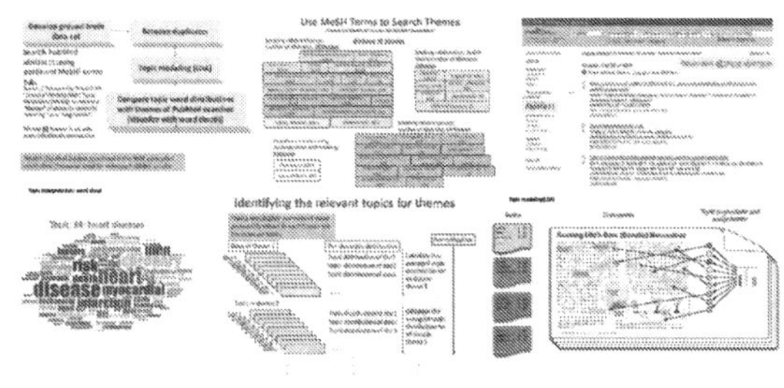

Figure 1: Workflow of experiment.

KEYWORDS

Topic Modeling, LDA, Parameter Setting, Text Mining

ACM Reference format:
Wen Zou, Weizhong Zhao, James J Chen, and Roger Perkins . 2017. Best Setting of Model Parameters in Applying Topic Modeling on Textual Documents. In *Proceedings of ACM-BCB '17, Boston, MA, USA, August 20-23, 2017,* 1 pages.
https://doi.org/10.1145/3107411.3108195

*Corresponding author.
[1] https://www.ncbi.nlm.nih.gov/pubmed/

Permission to make digital or hard copies of part or all of this work for personal or classroom use is granted without fee provided that copies are not made or distributed for profit or commercial advantage and that copies bear this notice and the full citation on the first page. Copyrights for third-party components of this work must be honored. For all other uses, contact the owner/author(s).
ACM-BCB '17, August 20-23, 2017, Boston, MA, USA
© 2017 Copyright held by the owner/author(s).
ACM ISBN 978-1-4503-4722-8/17/08.
https://doi.org/10.1145/3107411.3108195

REFERENCES

[1] David M. Blei, Andrew Y. Ng, and Michael I. Jordan. 2003. Latent dirichlet allocation. *Journal of machine Learning research* 3 (January 2003), 993–1022.
[2] Weizhong Zhao, James J Chen, Roger Perkins, Zhichao Liu, Weigong Ge, Yijun Ding, and Wen Zou. 2015. A heuristic approach to determine an appropriate number of topics in topic modeling. *BMC Bioinformatics* 16, 13 (December 2015), S8.

Neopepsee: Accurate Genome-level Prediction of Neoantigens by Harnessing Sequence and Amino Acid Immunogenicity Information

Sora Kim
Yonsei University
College of Medicine
Seoul, 03722 Korea
sora15@yuhs.ac

Han Sang Kim
Yonsei University
College of Medicine
Seoul, 03722 Korea
modeerfhs@yuhs.ac

Sangwoo Kim
Yonsei University
College of Medicine
Seoul, 03722 Korea
swkim@yuhs.ac

ABSTRACT
In cancer genomics, next generation sequencing data are usually used to detect somatic driver mutations for identifying the cause of tumorigenesis. However, non-driver somatic mutations, or passenger mutations, can also play an important role in cancer cell survival and treatment by generating aberrant short peptide sequences as known as 'neoantigens'. Tumor-specific mutations form novel immunogenic peptides called neoantigens, which could be important to the recent promising outcomes of cancer immunotherapy, including immune checkpoint blockade. Many studies have tried to identify various sequence characteristics for prediction of immunogenicity; however, practical applications rely on a single predicted value (MHC-I binding affinity) with an arbitrary cut-off. Here, we developed Neopepsee, a method that applies a machine learning to predict personal neoantigen with next generation sequencing data. Neopepsee not only automates the entire computational procedure for immunogenicity prediction from raw data but also improves accuracy by harnessing 10 different features for classification, including conventional MHC-I and T-cell receptor binding affinity and amino acid characteristics (e.g., hydrophobicity, polarity and charge). Additionally, we found that protein sequence similarity to known pathogenic epitopes is a novel strong feature for classification. Tests with validated epitope datasets and independently proven neoantigens confirmed the remarkable improvement in accuracy. Application of Neopepsee to 224 public stomach adenocarcinoma data predicted neoantigens, whose burden is strongly correlated with patient prognosis. By providing a convenient platform with better accuracy, Neopepsee will be of many uses in cancer immunotherapy research, such as in developing predictive biomarkers and in designing personalized cancer vaccines.

Permission to make digital or hard copies of part or all of this work for personal or classroom use is granted without fee provided that copies are not made or distributed for profit or commercial advantage and that copies bear this notice and the full citation on the first page. Copyrights for third-party components of this work must be honored. For all other uses, contact the Owner/Author.
ACM-BCB '17, August 20-23, 2017, Boston, MA, USA
© 2017 Copyright is held by the owner/author(s).
ACM ISBN 978-1-4503-4722-8/17/08.
http://dx.doi.org/10.1145/3107411.3108196

General Terms
Algorithms; Measurement

Keywords
Immunoinformatics; cancer; genomics; NGS; neoantigen

ACKNOWLEDGMENTS
This work was supported by the Brain Korea 21 PLUS Project for Medical Science, Yonsei University. The authors thank Dong-Su Jang (Medical Illustrator, Department of Research Affairs, Yonsei University College of Medicine, Seoul, South Korea) for his help in creating the medical illustrations. The research was supported by the Basic Science Research Program through the National Research Foundation of Korea (NRF) funded by the Ministry of Science, ICT & Future Planning (No. 2015R1C1A1A01053638).

Novel Unsupervised Named Entity Recognition Used in Text Annotation Tool (OntoMate) At Rat Genome Database

Omid Ghiasvand
Medical College of Wisconsin,
Milwaukee, WI

Mary Shimoyama
Medical College of Wisconsin,
Milwaukee, WI

ABSTRACT

In model organism databases, one of the important tasks is to convert free text in biomedical literature to a structured data format. Curators in the Rat Genome Database (RGD), the primary source of rat genomic, genetic, and physiological data, spend considerable time and effort curating functional information for genes, QTLs, and strains from the literature. To increase curation efficiency and prioritize literature for data extraction OntoMate was developed at RGD. This tool tags Pubmed abstracts with genes, gene names, gene mutations, organism name and terms from 16 ontologies/vocabularies, including synonyms and aliases, used to represent functional information. In this project, we have used an unsupervised tagging method to reduce human effort for creating training data. In this approach, a machine learning tool based on decision tree classification techniques has been developed. Mentions that are uniquely belong to a semantic type play positive sample roles, and those with semantic types other than desired group are assumed to be negative samples. An interface allows the user to create a complex query incorporating terms from any of the ontologies, gene symbols, organisms, dates and other parameters. The results return abstracts along with all tagged parameters indicated in the query, along with children of the ontology terms chosen. Results can be further filtered by the user through a panel that lists organisms, genes and diseases with number of paper returned. Abstracts and papers are provided in rank order by relevance to the query. The tool is fully integrated into curation software so citations and abstracts can be automatically entered into the RGD database and given ID and genes and ontology terms in the tags can be checked to create annotations linked to the paper. The system was built with a scalable and open architecture, and literature is updated daily. This tool uses Solr indexing technology and categorizes papers based on a relevance score. It indexes and tags more than 27 million abstracts. With the use of bioNLP tools, RGD has added more automation to its curation workflow.

CCS CONCEPTS

• **Artificial Intelligence** → Natural Language Processing – *Language parsing and understanding, Text analysis.*

KEYWORDS

Text Mining; Annotation, Ontology; Machine Learning; Classification; Unsupervised; Curation.

ACM Reference format:

Omid Ghiasvand, Mary Shimoyama 2017. Novel Unsupervised Named Entity Recognition Used in Text Annotation Tool (OntoMate) At Rat Genome Database. In *Proceedings of ACM-BCB '17, August 20-23, 2017, Boston, MA, USA*, 1 page.
DOI: http://dx.doi.org/10.1145/3107411.3108198

Permission to make digital or hard copies of part or all of this work for personal or classroom use is granted without fee provided that copies are not made or distributed for profit or commercial advantage and that copies bear this notice and the full citation on the first page. Copyrights for third-party components of this work must be honored. For all other uses, contact the Owner/Author.
ACM-BCB '17, August 20-23, 2017, Boston, MA, USA
© 2017 Copyright is held by the owner/author(s).
ACM ISBN 978-1-4503-4722-8/17/08.
http://dx.doi.org/10.1145/3107411.3108198

Bias and Noise Cancellation for Robust Copy Number Variation Detection

Fatima Zare*
University of Connecticut
Storrs, Connecticut 06269
fatemeh.zare@uconn.edu

Sardar Ansari
University of Michigan
Ann Arbor, Michigan 48109
sardara@umich.edu

Kayvan Najarian
University of Michigan
Ann Arbor, Michigan 48109
kayvan@umich.edu

Sheida Nabavi
University of Connecticut
Storrs, Connecticut 06269
Sheida.nabavi@uconn.edu

ABSTRACT

High-throughput next generation sequencing (NGS) technologies have created an opportunity for detecting copy number variations (CNVs) more accurately. In this work, we introduce a novel preprocessing pipeline to improve the detection accuracy of CNVs in heterogeneous NGS data such as cancer whole exome sequencing data. We employ several normalizations to reduce biases due to GC contents, mappability and tumor contamination. We also utilize the Taut String method as an efficient effective smoothing approach to reduce noise.

CCS CONCEPTS

• **Applied computing → Bioinformatics**;

KEYWORDS

Copy Number Variation; Whole-Exome Sequencing; Signal Processing; Taut String; Cancer; Normalization; Denoising

1 INTRODUCTION

Copy number variations (CNVs) are a critical and common source of variation in the human genome. In general, CNV detection consists of two major parts: preprocessing and segmentation. The aim of the preprocessing part is reducing noise and biases for better identification of CNV regions in the segmentation part. We have developed a new comprehensive pipeline for preprocessing the readcount data, which is divided into 5 blocks: 1) filtering low quality readcount data; 2) removing GC bias from both tumor and normal readcount data; 3) calculating the ratios of tumor and normal readcounts for each genomic window and removing mappability bias; 4) eliminating noise from the normalized readcount data using Taut String (TS) [1, 2]; 5) eliminating the effects of the tumor contamination by normalizing the denoised ratios using the expectation maximization (EM) algorithm. The outputs of the preprocessing pipeline (the normalized readcount ratios) then input a segmentation algorithm for the detection of CNVs. We used the circular binary segmentation (CBS) method for segmentation [3].

*Corresponding author. This study was supported by a grant from the National Institutes of Health (NIH, R00LM011595, PI: Nabavi)

Permission to make digital or hard copies of part or all of this work for personal or classroom use is granted without fee provided that copies are not made or distributed for profit or commercial advantage and that copies bear this notice and the full citation on the first page. Copyrights for third-party components of this work must be honored. For all other uses, contact the owner/author(s).
ACM-BCB '17, August 20-23, 2017, Boston, MA, USA
© 2017 Copyright held by the owner/author(s).
ACM ISBN 978-1-4503-4722-8/17/08...$15.00
https://doi.org/10.1145/3107411.3108199

2 RESULT AND DISCUSSION

To evaluate the performance of each block of the proposed pipeline, we computed sensitivity, false discovery rate and specificity of CNV detection before and after applying the preprocessing steps using 10 breast cancer tumors from the cancer genome atlas (TCGA). In overall, by using the proposed preprocessing steps, the sensitivity of detecting amplifications improves from 50.99% to 72.75% and the sensitivity of detecting deletions improves from 60.37% to 84.30%. The performance of the CNV detection method is mostly affected by the denoising block. The denoising block improves the performance of detection for amplifications from 58.57% to 70.15% and from 68.74% to 80.04% for deletions. Removing noise by TS and discrete wavelet transform (DWT) improves the overall performance of a CNV detection method. DWT has shown good performance on denoising readcount data and has been used by a few tools. We compared the performance of DWT and TS methods in terms of reducing noise and computational time. For noisy signal, the one-norm between constructed and original signal is equal to 7.56 for TS, while it is equal to 8.45 for DWT. One reason for the better performance of TS is associated with the regression method which is used in its denoising algorithm. Also, the TS shows less runtime compared to DWT. On average, DWT took 30.73 seconds while TS took only 5.51 seconds. To conclude this study, we can say that preprocessing the readcount data is essential in precise detection of CNVs; and advanced normalization and noise cancellation methods from other fields, such as signal processing and statistics, can be utilized for an effective preprocessing.

REFERENCES

[1] Ashwin Belle, Sardar Ansari, Maxwell Spadafore, Victor A Convertino, Kevin R Ward, Harm Derksen, and Kayvan Najarian. 2016. A Signal Processing Approach for Detection of Hemodynamic Instability before Decompensation. *PloS one* 11, 2 (2016), e0148544.

[2] P Laurie Davies and Arne Kovac. 2001. Local extremes, runs, strings and multiresolution. *Annals of Statistics* (2001), 1–48.

[3] Adam B Olshen, ES Venkatraman, Robert Lucito, and Michael Wigler. 2004. Circular binary segmentation for the analysis of array-based DNA copy number data. *Biostatistics* 5, 4 (2004), 557–572.

Applying Bayesian Changepoint Model and Hierarchical Divisive Model for Detecting Anomalies in Clinical Decision Support Alert Firing

Soumi Ray
Brigham and Women's Hospital and
Harvard Medical School 75 Francis St
Boston, MA 02115
443-765-5333
sr278@bwh.harvard.edu

Adam Wright
Brigham and Women's Hospital and
Harvard Medical School 75 Francis St
Boston, MA 02115
617-732-7063
awright@bwh.harvard.edu

ABSTRACT
Clinical Decision Support (CDS) Systems are widely used to support efficient evidence-based care and have become an important aspect of healthcare. CDS systems are complex, and sometimes malfunction or exhibit anomalous behavior [4]. We have previously shown how anomaly detection models can be used to successfully identify malfunctions in CDS systems [3]. We have extended this work and applied two new anomaly detection models on CDS alert firing data from a large health system.

1. METHODS

Hierarchical Divisive Changepoint Model: The hierarchical divisive changepoint model estimates the number of changepoints and the positions at which they occur in time series observations using hierarchical divisive clustering algorithm. The algorithm estimates multiple changepoints without a priori knowledge of the number of changepoints [2].

Bayesian Changepoint Model: The Bayesian changepoint procedure provides the probability of each point being a changepoint rather than specific locations of changepoints. Bayesian changepoint method provides probability estimates: posterior probability of a position being a changepoint. We can call a position a changepoint by deciding a threshold for the posterior probability [1].

2. RESULTS

Alerts originating from the electronic health record used at Partners HealthCare (PHS) were employed in this study. We examined an alert that suggests that aspirin be ordered for patients with coronary artery disease who are either not taking it or are not on any other antiplatelet therapy. The hierarchical model detected the start date of this anomaly with a delay of 2 days as shown in Figure 1. The Bayesian changepoint model was able to detect the start date of the anomaly with a delay of 1 day, shown in Figure 2. The Bayesian model was able to detect successfully the exact end date of this anomaly while hierarchical model was able to detect this anomaly with a 12 days delay.

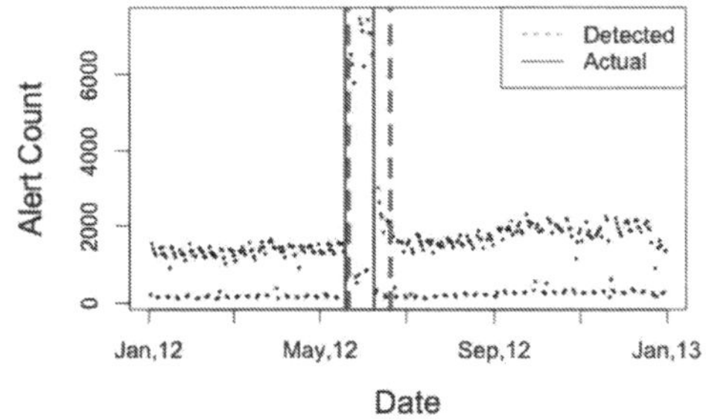

Figure 1: Hierarchical Model

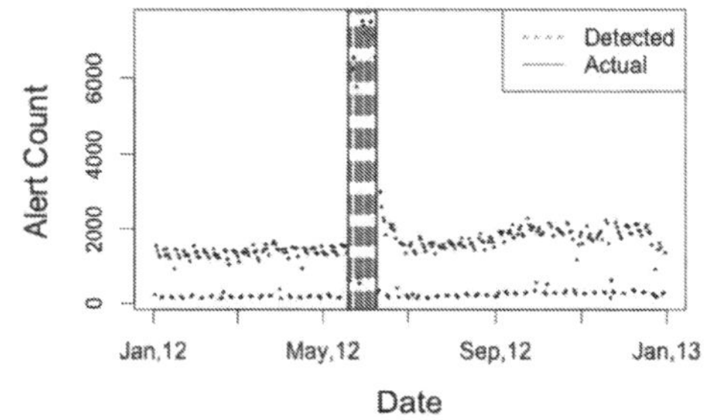

Figure 2: Bayesian Model

This work was supported by National Library of Medicine of the National Institutes of Health grant number R01LM011966. The content is solely the responsibility of the authors and does not necessarily represent the official views of the National Institutes of Health.

Permission to make digital or hard copies of part or all of this work for personal or classroom use is granted without fee provided that copies are not made or distributed for profit or commercial advantage and that copies bear this notice and the full citation on the first page. Copyrights for third-party components of this work must be honored. For all other uses, contact the Owner/Author.
ACM-BCB '17, August 20-23, 2017, Boston, MA, USA
©2017 Copyright is held by the owner/author(s).
ACM ISBN978-1-4503-4722-8/17/08.
http://dx.doi.org/10.1145/3107411.3108200

3. REFERENCES

[1] Erdman, C. and Emerson, J.W. 2007. bcp: An RPackage for Performing a Bayesian Analysis of Change Point Problems. *Journal of Statistical Software.* 23, 3 (2007).

[2] James, N.A. and Matteson, D.S. 2014. ecp: An RPackage for Nonparametric Multiple Change Point Analysis of Multivariate Data. *Journal of Statistical Software.* 62, 7 (2014).

[3] Ray, S. and Wright, A. 2016. Detecting Anomalies in Alert Firing within Clinical Decision Support Systems using Anomaly/Outlier Detection Techniques. *BCB.* (2016), 185–190.

[4] Wright, A. et al. 2016. Analysis of clinical decision support system malfunctions: a case series and survey. *Journal of the American Medical Informatics Association.* 23, 6 (Oct. 2016), 1068–1076.

Preconditioned Random Forest Regression: Application to Genome-Wide Study for Radiotherapy Toxicity Prediction

Sangkyu Lee
Memorial Sloan Kettering Cancer Center
New York, NY
lees14@mskcc.org

Sarah Kerns
University of Rochester Medical Center
Rochester, NY
Sarah_Kerns@URMC.Rochester.edu

Barry Rosenstein
Icahn School of Medicine at Mount Sinai
New York, NY
Barry.Rosenstein@mssm.edu

Harry Ostrer
Albert Einstein College of Medicine
Bronx, NY
harry.ostrer@einstein.yu.edu

Joseph O. Deasy
Memorial Sloan Kettering Cancer Center
New York, NY
DeasyJ@mskcc.org

Jung Hun Oh
Memorial Sloan Kettering Cancer Center
New York, NY
OhJ@mskcc.org

ABSTRACT

Urinary toxicity after radiotherapy (RT) limits the quality of life of prostate cancer patients, and clinically actionable prediction has yet to be achieved. We aim to exploit genome-wide variants to accurately identify patients at higher congenital toxicity risk. We applied preconditioned random forest regression (PRFR) to predict four urinary symptoms. For a weak stream endpoint, the PRFR model achieved an area under the curve (AUC) of 0.7 on holdout validation. Preconditioning enhanced the performance of random forest. Gene ontology (GO) analysis showed that neurogenic biological processes are associated with the toxicity. Upon further validation, the predictive model can be used to potentially benefit the health of prostate cancer patients treated with radiotherapy.

KEYWORDS

Radiotherapy, Genome Wide Association Studies, Random Forests

Urinary toxicity after RT can arise due to radiation spill to surrounding normal tissues, and single nucleotide polymorphisms (SNPs) were identified as risk factors [1]. We apply PRFR [2] on genome-wide data to achieve strong predictive power by combining small effects of multiple SNPs. We studied 368 prostate cancer patients who received RT at the Mount Sinai Hospital and were examined for 4 urinary symptoms (frequency, urge, nocturia, and weak stream (WS)) after RT. Samples was split to training (2/3) and validation (1/3) sets with matching event rates. We chose the SNPs with association Chi-square p-value < 0.001. PRFR predicted WS with the highest AUC on holdout validation (0.70), followed by frequency (0.64), nocturia (0.54), and urge (0.53). For the WS endpoint, when the training data changed over 5-fold cross validation, the PRFR method significantly outperformed the random forest, least absolute shrinkage and selection operator (LASSO), and preconditioned LASSO (figure 1). We performed GO enrichment analysis for biological processes on the 241 genes that were found from the 75% top variable importance SNPs of the WS model, where PRFR performance was optimal (figure 1). ClueGO identified 11 groups of GO terms from these genes (figure 2). The most prominent group, consisting of 9 terms, was related to neurogenesis (p = 5.8E-6).

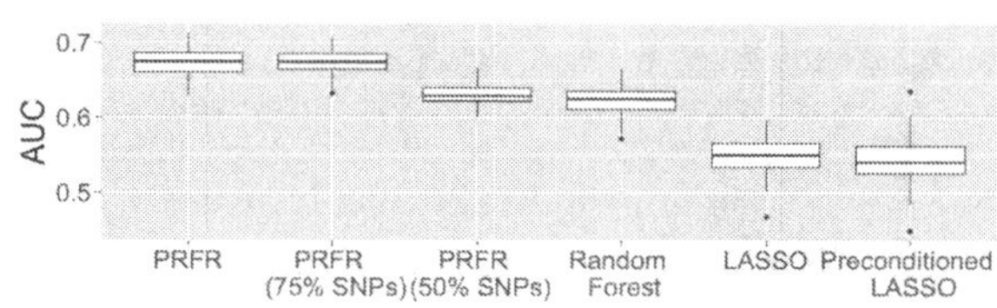

Figure 1: Validation AUC for WS endpoint.

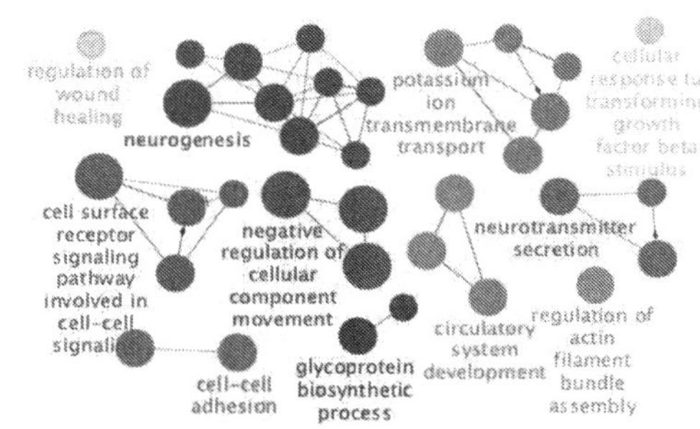

Figure 2: Overrepresented GO terms in the genes that were associated with WS endpoint.

REFERENCES

[1] S. L. Kerns, N. N. Stone, R. G. Stock, L. Rath, H. Ostrer, and B. S. Rosenstein. 2013. A 2-stage genome-wide association study to identify single nucleotide polymorphisms associated with development of urinary symptoms after radiotherapy for prostate cancer. *J Urol* 190, 1 (2013), 102–8.

[2] J. Oh, S. Kerns, H. Ostrer, S. Powell, B Rosenstein, and J. Deasy. 2017. Computational methods using genome-wide association studies to predict radiotherapy complications and to identify correlative molecular processes. *Sci. Rep.* 7 (2017), 43381.

Permission to make digital or hard copies of part or all of this work for personal or classroom use is granted without fee provided that copies are not made or distributed for profit or commercial advantage and that copies bear this notice and the full citation on the first page. Copyrights for third-party components of this work must be honored. For all other uses, contact the owner/author(s).
ACM-BCB '17, August 20-23, 2017, Boston, MA, USA
© 2017 Copyright held by the owner/author(s).
ACM ISBN 978-1-4503-4722-8/17/08.
https://doi.org/10.1145/3107411.3108201

Outlier Genes as Biomarkers of Breast Cancer Survivability in Time-Series Data

Naveen Mangalakumar
University of Windsor
401 Sunset Avenue
Windsor, ON, Canada
mangalan@uwindsor.ca

Abed Alkhateeb
University of Windsor
401 Sunset Avenue
Windsor, ON, Canada
alkhate@uwindsor.ca

Huy Quang Pham
University of Windsor
401 Sunset Avenue
Windsor, ON, Canada
pham118@uwindsor.ca
University of Dalat,
01 Phu Dong Thien Vuong,
Dalat, Vietnam
huypq@dlu.edu.vn

Luis Rueda
University of Windsor
401 Sunset Avenue
Windsor, ON, Canada
lrueda@uwindsor.ca

Alioune Ngom
University of Windsor
401 Sunset Avenue
Windsor, ON, Canada
angom@uwindsor.ca

ABSTRACT

Studying gene expression through various time intervals of breast cancer survival may provide new insights into the recovery from the disease. In this work, we propose a hierarchical clustering method to separate dissimilar groups of gene time-series profiles, which have the furthest distances from the rest of the profiles throughout different time intervals. The isolated outliers can be used as potential biomarkers of Breast Cancer survivability.

Keywords Breast cancer; survival; biomarker genes; machine learning; clustering, time series

1. INTRODUCTION

Despite the fast increase in the breast cancer rates nowadays, the survival rates have also increased, not the only due to the improvement in the treatments. To the best of our knowledge, this work is the first time-series model that is built on the survival time of the patient after the treatment.

2. RESOURCES AND METHODS

We used the METABRIC dataset and extracted only the patients who survived after breast cancer treatment. The time series data was created by partitioning the time axis (survival time in months) into bins of length six months, starting from 0-6 up to 49-55 month intervals, and then, for each gene, we average its expression level over all patients who appear in a survival bin.

Gene expressions throughout those time points are cubic spline interpolated to create a trending profile for each gene. After universally aligning the profiles to minimize the vertical area between each pair of profiles, we cluster the genes using hierarchical clustering based on minimized vertical distances [1]. An appropriate number of clusters was chosen based on the profile alignment and agglomerative clustering (PAAC) index as well as visual observations of the clusters.

3. EXPERIMENTAL RESULTS

We identified 24 genes (obtained as singleton clusters), which can be considered as potential biomarkers of breast cancer survivability. Of these, PSAP, CD81, and EEF1A1 have been previously reported in the literature to play some role in breast cancer.

Figure 1 shows the background cluster, where the majority of the profiles are clustered, i.e., the profiles trends over the time-points with different gene expressions. Figures 2 to 4 show the trends of each of the profile trends of three relevant biomarkers PSAP, CD81, and EEF1A1.

4. CONCLUSION

Our study suggests that the combination of proper clustering, distance function and index validation for clusters is a suitable model to identify genes as informative biomarkers of breast cancer survivability.

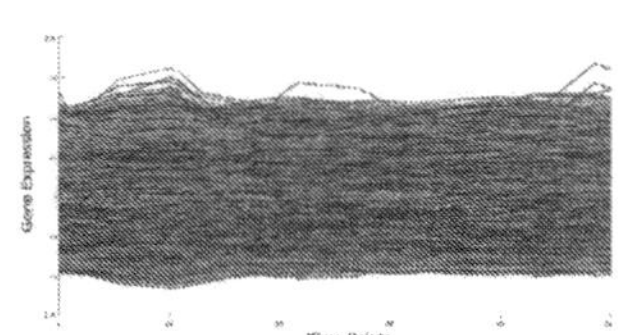

Figure 1: Background Cluster

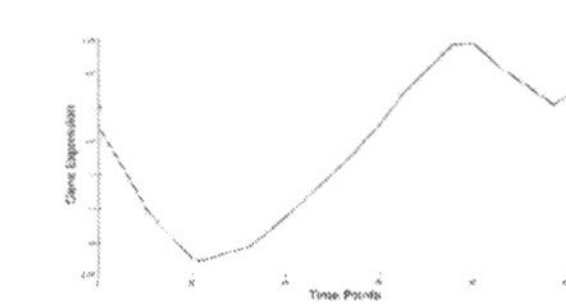

Figure 2: CD81 gene profile in outlier Cluster

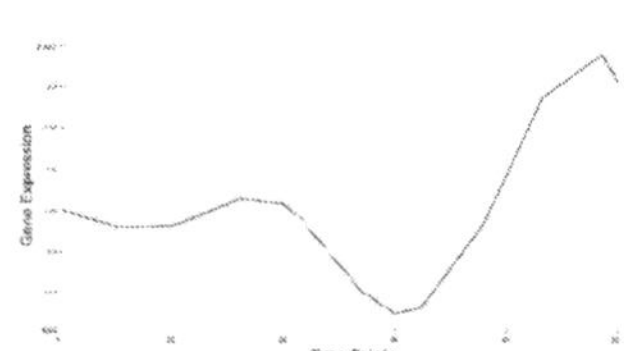

Figure 3: EEF1A1 gene profile in Outlier Cluster

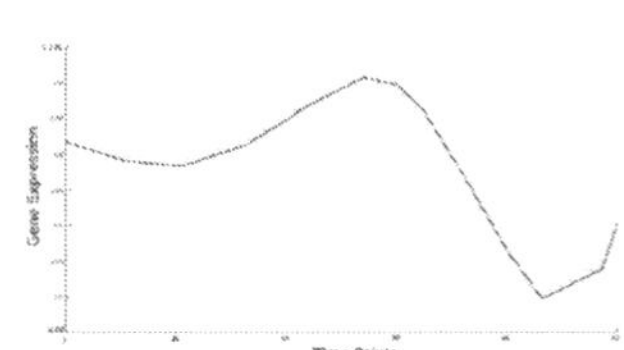

Figure 4: PSAP gene profile in outlier Cluster

5. ACKNOWLEDGMENTS

This work has been partially supported by the Natural Sciences and Engineering Research Council of Canada (NSERC), and the Windsor Essex County Cancer Centre Foundation (WECCCF) via a Seeds4Hope grant.

6. REFERENCES

[1] Alkhateeb, Abed, et al. "Obtaining biomarkers in cancer progression from outliers of time-series clusters." Bioinformatics and Biomedicine (BIBM), 2015 IEEE International Conference on. IEEE, 2015.

Permission to make digital or hard copies of part or all of this work for personal or classroom use is granted without fee provided that copies are not made or distributed for profit or commercial advantage and that copies bear this notice and the full citation on the first page. Copyrights for third-party components of this work must be honored. For all other uses, contact the Owner/Author.
ACM-BCB '17, August 20-23, 2017, Boston, MA, USA
© 2017 Copyright is held by the owner/author(s).
ACM ISBN 978-1-450347228/17/08.
http://dx.doi.org/10.1145/3107411.3108202

Pisces: An Accurate and Versatile Single Sample Somatic and Germline Variant Caller

Tamsen Dunn
Illumina Inc.
5200 Illumina Way
San Diego, CA 92122
tdunn@illumina.com

Gwenn Berry
Illumina Inc.
5200 Illumina Way
San Diego, CA 92122
gberry@illumina.com

Dorothea Emig-Agius
Illumina Inc.
5200 Illumina Way
San Diego, CA 92122
dagius@illumina.com

Yu Jiang
Illumina Inc.
5200 Illumina Way
San Diego, CA 92122
yjiang2@illumina.com

Anita Iyer
Illumina Inc.
5200 Illumina Way
San Diego, CA 92122
aiyer@illumina.com

Nitin Udar
Illumina Inc.
5200 Illumina Way
San Diego, CA 92122
nudar@illumina.com

Michael Strömberg
Illumina Inc.
5200 Illumina Way
San Diego, CA 92122
mstromberg@illumina.com

ABSTRACT

We present Pisces, a tumor-only variant caller exclusively developed at Illumina for detecting low frequency mutations from next generation sequencing data. Pisces has been an integral part of the Illumina Truseq Amplicon workflow since 2012, and is available on BaseSpace and on the MiSeq sequencing platforms. Pisces has been available to the public on github, since 2015. (https://github.com/Illumina/Pisces)

CCS CONCEPTS

• **Applied computing~Computational genomics**

KEYWORDS

Pisces; single sample; somatic; germline; variant caller; tumor only

1 SUMMARY

A method for robustly and accurately detecting rare DNA mutations in tumor samples is critical to cancer research. Because many clinical tissue repositories have only FFPE-degraded tumor samples, and no matched normal sample from healthy tissue available, being able to discriminate low frequency mutations from background noise in the absence of a matched normal sample is of particular importance to research. Current state of the art variant callers such as GATK and VarScan focus on germline variant calling (used for detecting inherited mutations following a Mendelian inheritance pattern) or, in the case of FreeBayes and MuTect, focus on tumor-normal joint variant calling (using the normal sample to help discriminate low frequency somatic mutations from back ground noise).

The Pisces variant calling team have developed Pisces as a method for single-sample variant calling for tumor-only and germline samples. We have made available a suite of variant calling tools, including a ReadStitcher, Variant Phaser, and Variant Quality Recalibration tool, to be used along with the core variant caller, Pisces. In our poster, we describe the Pisces variant calling tools and core algorithms.

Permission to make digital or hard copies of part or all of this work for personal or classroom use is granted without fee provided that copies are not made or distributed for profit or commercial advantage and that copies bear this notice and the full citation on the first page. Copyrights for third-party components of this work must be honored. For all other uses, contact the owner/author(s).
ACM-BCB '17, August 20-23, 2017, Boston, MA, USA
© 2017 Copyright is held by the owner/author(s).
ACM ISBN 978-1-4503-4722-8/17/08.
http://dx.doi.org/10.1145/3107411.3108203

Nirvana: Clinical Grade Variant Annotator*

Michael Stromberg
Illumina Inc. 5200 Illumina way, San Diego, CA.
mstromberg@illumina.com

Rajat Roy
Illumina Inc. 5200 Illumina way, San Diego, CA.
rroy1@illumina.com

Julien Lajugie
Illumina Inc. 5200 Illumina way, San Diego, CA.
jlajugie@illumina.com

Yu Jiang
Illumina Inc. 5200 Illumina way, San Diego, CA.
yjiang2@illumina.com

Haochen Li
Illumina Inc. 5200 Illumina way, San Diego, CA.
hli2@illumina.com

Elliott Margulies
Illumina Inc. 5200 Illumina way, San Diego, CA.
emargulies@illumina.com

ABSTRACT

Sequencing an individual genome typically produces approximately three million variants compared to the human reference genome. The consequence for each variant depends on the location and nature of the variant and is a key question for genetic analysts performing clinical diagnosis. Variant annotation describes how a variant affects the sample's genome. These annotations include the functional consequence on the different transcripts for a gene or in proximal regulatory regions. Annotation also includes additional data on what is known about a given variant that can help in understanding its relevance to a given line of investigation. Often this data is provided by different sources and contain allele frequencies for different populations, clinical implications, relevance to cancer types, additional studies, etc. Ultimately this information helps clinicians interpret variants when providing a diagnosis.

The three most widely used open source annotation tools are VEP, SnpEff and AnnoVar. VEP is widely considered to be most accurate of the three, but is also slower than both SnpEff and AnnoVar. When annotating the variants from a 30x genome (NA12878), VEP finished in 18 hours whereas SnpEff 4.3g and AnnoVar finish in 15 min and 67 min respectively using one core.

We present Nirvana, an open source clinical variant annotator, that is both accurate (over 99.9% concordance with VEP) and fast (takes 7 min to annotate NA12878). Nirvana is used in all of Illumina's relevant analysis pipelines and is tested rigorously to ensure adherence to clinical standards.

KEYWORDS

Bioinformatics; variant annotation; clinical; genetic diagnosis.

Permission to make digital or hard copies of all or part of this work for personal or classroom use is granted without fee provided that copies are not made or distributed for profit or commercial advantage and that copies bear this notice and the full citation on the first page. Copyrights for components of this work owned by others than ACM must be honored. Abstracting with credit is permitted. To copy otherwise, or republish, to post on servers or to redistribute to lists, requires prior specific permission and/or a fee. Request permissions from Permissions@acm.org.
ACM-BCB '17, August 20-23, 2017, Boston, MA, USA
© 2017 Copyright is held by the owner/author(s).
ACM ISBN 978-1-4503-4722-8/17/08.
http://dx.doi.org/10.1145/3107411.3108204

Streptomyces clavuligerus Constraint-Based Modeling and Gene Expression Analysis for Clavulanic Acid Production

Leon F. Toro
Instituto de Biología
Universidad de Antioquia
A.A 1226
+57 4 2198513
lfelipe.toro@udea.edu.co

Laura Pinilla-Mendoza
Instituto de Biología
Universidad de Antioquia
A.A 1226
+57 4 2198513
laura.pinilla@udea.edu.co

Rigoberto Ríos-Estepa
Departamento de Ingeniería Química
Universidad de Antioquia
A.A 1226
+57 4 2198568
rigoberto.rios@udea.edu.co

ABSTRACT

In this work, we use a high-resolution transcriptome of *S. clavuligerus* cultured on a chemically defined medium and the corresponding measured metabolic fluxes as experimental constraints to identify through an expanded genome-scale metabolic model the different metabolic process associated to primary/secondary metabolism based on available *omics* integration algorithms. The predicted fluxes showed to be in agreement with the corresponding gene expression data associated providing a detailed interpretation compared to traditional constrained-based methods (FBA and pFBA). In general, the observed patterns in intracellular fluxes coincided with reactions that have been identified as important precursors for secondary metabolism mainly those involved in clavulanic acid synthesis.

Keywords: *Streptomyces clavuligerus*, gene expression, genome scale metabolic model, clavulanic acid, integration data.

1. INTRODUCTION

Streptomyces clavuligerus (Sclav) produce secondary metabolites with diverse biological activities; among them, clavulanic acid (CA), cephamycin C (CephC) and other compounds with a clavam. CA is a potent inhibitor of β-lactamase enzymes produced by gram-positive and gram-negative bacteria [1].

On the other hand, genome-scale metabolic models (GSMMs) allow the interpretation of experimental data related to defined metabolic states [2]. Additionally, *omics* data can be integrated with GSMM by improving their predictive power, increasing the accuracy of the model predictions [2]. In this study, gene expression was integrated by algorithms of *omics* data in a GSMM to identify more precisely network-wide reaction fluxes in *Sclav* growth on a limited defined media.

2. METHODOLOGY

2.1 Microorganism and cultivation conditions

Mycelium stock of *Streptomyces clavuligerus* ATCC 27064 strain was used as inoculum. The chemically defined medium GSPG [1] was evaluated in 250 ml baffled flasks; 50 mL of medium (28°C, 220 rpm, pH 6.8) The quantification of glycerol, CA, phosphate, amino acids, ammonia and biomass were performed according to [1].

Permission to make digital or hard copies of part or all of this work for personal or classroom use is granted without fee provided that copies are not made or distributed for profit or commercial advantage and that copies bear this notice and the full citation on the first page. Copyrights for third-party components of this work must be honored. For all other uses, contact the Owner/Author.
ACM-BCB '17, August 20-23, 2017, Boston, MA, USA
© 2017 Copyright is held by the owner/author(s).
ACM ISBN 978-1-4503-4722-8/17/08.
http://dx.doi.org/10.1145/3107411.3108205

2.2 Transcriptomic Data Integration into the Sclav_iLT1021 Model

The Sclav_iLT1021 model (reconstructed by L. Toro) was used for *in silico* analysis, it accounts for 1021 ORFs, 1360 metabolites and 1494 reactions. For gene expression data integration, iMAT and GIMME algorithms were used [2]. Finally, to examine the impact of transcriptome integration into GSMM, FBA and pFBA was performed to establish differences in intracellular fluxes.

3. RESULTS AND DISCUSSION

3.1 Flask Cultivation

Fermentations performed with GSPG medium, reached a maximum CA concentration of 21.0±0.5 mg·L^{-1} (75 h). Specific growth rate was 0.0213 h^{-1}.

3.2 Constraint-based Analysis Integrating Gene Expression

GSMM was quantitatively constrained in the uptake and secretion rates for the measured metabolites. The reaction activity obtained by iMAT analysis resulted in 106 active reactions involved mainly in central carbon pathway, amino acid metabolism such as L-glutamate and L-proline and secondary metabolism including CA and CephC. Reactions associated to lowly expressed genes included pathways such as glyoxylate shunt, starch, sucrose and pyrimidine metabolism. Fluxes associated to fructose-bisphosphate aldolase (FBA) and 6-phosphofructokinase (FBP) were predicted as active (iMAT and GIMME) favouring the PPP pathway through 6-phosphogluconate-dehydrogenase (PGDH). iMAT showed to be the most reliable integrative method due to positively associated fluxes to CephC synthesis coinciding with the gene expression data and not over-estimated the fluxes associated to PPP unlike the FBA and pFBA

4. CONCLUSIONS

In general, through RNA-seq integration data a flux mapping that closely matches with cellular phenotype of *S. clavuligerus* growth was obtained. The comparison with the phenotype vector resulted by FBA approach, corroborate that the biological systems function under suboptimal conditions resulting in wrong predictions when only uptake/excretion rates were used as constraints and the growth rate optimization was proposed.

5. REFERENCES

[1] Romero J, Liras P, Martin, JF. Dissociation of cephamycin and clavulanic acid biosynthesis in *Streptomyces clavuligerus*. *Applied Microbiology and Biotechnology.*, 1984;*20*(5), 318-325.

[2] Kim MK, Lun DS. 2014. Methods for integration of transcriptomic data in genome-scale metabolic models. *Computational and structural biotechnology journal*, 11(18), 59-65.

Notch Signaling plays an Important Role in mTEC Specification during Fetal Thymus Development

Dong Liu[1], Anastasia I. Kousa[2], Simon R. Tomlinson[3], Prof. C. Clare Blackburn[4]

[1]MRC Centre for Regenerative Medicine, SCRM Building, The University of Edinburgh, Edinburgh Bioquarter, 5 Little France Drive, Edinburgh, EH16 4UU, UK, s0905405@sms.ed.ac.uk

[2]MRC Centre for Regenerative Medicine, SCRM Building, The University of Edinburgh, Edinburgh Bioquarter, 5 Little France Drive, Edinburgh, EH16 4UU, UK, s1148079@sms.ed.ac.uk

[3]MRC Centre for Regenerative Medicine, SCRM Building, The University of Edinburgh, Edinburgh Bioquarter, 5 Little France Drive, Edinburgh, EH16 4UU, UK, simon.tomlinson@ed.ac.uk

[4]MRC Centre for Regenerative Medicine, SCRM Building, The University of Edinburgh, Edinburgh Bioquarter, 5 Little France Drive, Edinburgh, EH16 4UU, UK, cblackbu@staffmail.ed.ac.uk

ABSTRACT

Thymic epithelial cells (TECs) are a vital element of the thymic microenvironments that direct T cell differentiation and repertoire selection, and are thus indispensable for development of a functional immune system. TECs are thought to derive from a bipotent thymic epithelial progenitor cell (TEPC) that differentiates into the functionally distinct cortical (c) and medullary (m) TEC sub-lineages. TEC differentiation is orchestrated by the transcription factor FOXN1. However, the precise mechanisms regulating TEC differentiation, and divergence of the cTEC and mTEC sub-lineages is not yet understood. Here, we have used bioinformatics analysis in conjunction with experimental validation to investigate the molecular regulation of the early development and specification of the thymic epithelium. Our data demonstrate an important role for Notch signaling pathway in mTEC specification during fetal thymus development.

Permission to make digital or hard copies of part or all of this work for personal or classroom use is granted without fee provided that copies are not made or distributed for profit or commercial advantage and that copies bear this notice and the full citation on the first page. Copyrights for third-party components of this work must be honored. For all other uses, contact the Owner/Author.

ACM-BCB '17, August 20-23, 2017, Boston, MA, USA

© 2017 Copyright is held by the owner/author(s).

ACM ISBN 978-1-4503-4722-8/17/08.
http://dx.doi.org/10.1145/3107411.3108206

KEYWORDS

Thymus; thymic epithelial cell; stem cell; progenitor cell; lineage divergence; differentiation; cell fate regulation; Notch signaling

Analysis of 16S Genomic Data using Graphical Databases

Olivia M. Ahern
University of Rhode Island
Graduate School of Oceanography
Narragansett, Rhode Island 02882
olivia_ahern@uri.edu

Rebecca J. Stevick
University of Rhode Island
Graduate School of Oceanography
Narragansett, Rhode Island 02882
rstevick@my.uri.edu

Li Yuan
University of Rhode Island
Department of Computer Science and Statistics
Kingston, Rhode Island 02881
li_yuan@my.uri.edu

Noah M. Daniels*
University of Rhode Island
Department of Computer Science and Statistics
Kingston, Rhode Island 02881
noah_daniels@uri.edu

1 INTRODUCTION

Since the Human Genome Project was completed in 2003, many data scientists have developed algorithms in order to store and query high volumes of genomic data. The most common data storage techniques employed in these algorithms are flat files or relational databases. While sophisticated indexing techniques can accelerate queries [5], an alternative is to store biological sequence data directly in a way that supports efficient queries. Here we introduce a new algorithm that aims to compress the redundant information and improve the performance of query speed with the help of graphical databases, which have been commercial available since the mid-late 2000s. A graphical database stores information using nodes and relationships (edges).

Our approach is to identify subsequences that are common among many sequences, and to store these as "common nodes" in the graphical database. This is accomplished for sequencing data as follows: split the whole sequence into k-mers: if a given k-mer is common to enough sequences, then it is labeled as a *common segment*; if a k-mer is unique (or common to too few sequences), then it is labeled as a *single segment*. Thus, common nodes and single nodes are formed from common segments and single segments, respectively. These two kinds of nodes are connected by edges in the graphical database, allowing each original sequences to be reconstructed by following edges in the graph.

This graphical database model allows for fast taxonomic queries of 16S rDNA. When queried, the database can first attempt to find common nodes that match the query sequence, and subsequently follow edges to single nodes to refine the search. This approach is analogous to that of "compressive genomics" [2, 4] except that the compression is implicit in the graphical database storage model.

Beyond simple sequence queries, this graphical database representation also supports variability analysis [1], which identifies highly variable vs. conserved regions of 16S sequence. Regions of low variability correspond to common nodes, while regions of high variability correspond to a variety of paths through single nodes. Figure 1 illustrates common and single nodes, and a corresponding plot of variability.

Benchmarking of sequence search indicates that query time in graphical databases is significantly faster than in flat files or relational databases. Implementation of graphical databases in genomic data analysis will allow for accelerated search, and may lend itself to other forms of efficient analysis, such as tetramer frequency analysis, which is useful in metagenomic binning [3].

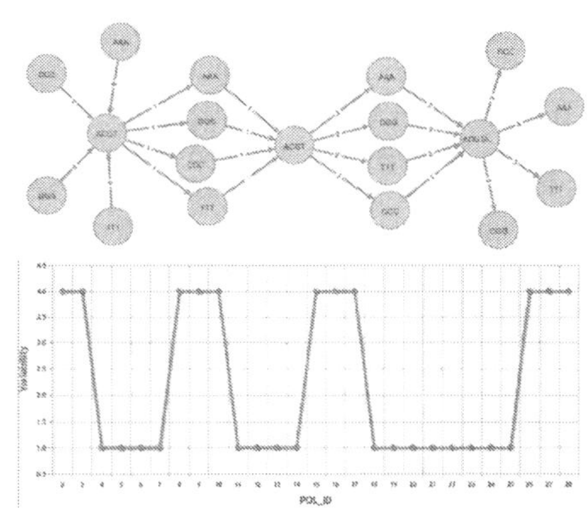

Figure 1: Example of common and unique nodes in a 16S rDNA dataset. The variability plot depicts the number of nodes found at each position in sequence. Common nodes correspond to low variability.

*to whom correspondence should be addressed

Permission to make digital or hard copies of part or all of this work for personal or classroom use is granted without fee provided that copies are not made or distributed for profit or commercial advantage and that copies bear this notice and the full citation on the first page. Copyrights for third-party components of this work must be honored. For all other uses, contact the owner/author(s).
ACM-BCB'17, August 20–23, 2017, Boston, MA, USA.
© 2017 Copyright held by the owner/author(s). ISBN 978-1-4503-4722-8/17/08.
DOI: http://dx.doi.org/10.1145/3107411.3108208

REFERENCES

[1] Josselin Bodilis, Sandrine Nsigue-Meilo, Ludovic Besaury, and Laurent Quillet. 2012. Variable copy number, intra-genomic heterogeneities and lateral transfers of the 16S rRNA gene in Pseudomonas. *PloS one* 7, 4 (2012), e35647.

[2] Noah M Daniels, Andrew Gallant, Jian Peng, Lenore J Cowen, Michael Baym, and Bonnie Berger. 2013. Compressive genomics for protein databases. *Bioinformatics* 29, 13 (2013), i283–i290.

[3] Hsin-Hung Lin and Yu-Chieh Liao. 2016. Accurate binning of metagenomic contigs via automated clustering sequences using information of genomic signatures and marker genes. *Scientific reports* 6 (2016).

[4] Po-Ru Loh, Michael Baym, and Bonnie Berger. 2012. Compressive genomics. *Nature biotechnology* 30, 7 (2012), 627–630.

[5] Jared T Simpson and Richard Durbin. 2010. Efficient construction of an assembly string graph using the FM-index. *Bioinformatics* 26, 12 (2010), i367–i373.

High Dimensional Ensemble Neuronal Activity Pattern Analysis: Visualization and Wave Detection Focused

Varshini Guddanti
Northern Illinois University
1425 W Lincoln Hwy
DeKalb, IL 60115
vguddanti@niu.edu

Shawn Horvatic
Northern Illinois University
1425 W Lincoln Hwy
DeKalb, IL, USA 60115
sbhorvatic@gmail.com

Jie Zhou
Northern Illinois University
1425 W Lincoln Hwy
DeKalb, IL, USA 60115
jzhou@niu.edu

Yujia Hu
University of Michigan
500 S State St
Ann Arbor, MI 48109
henryhu@umich.edu

Bing Ye
University of Michigan
500 S State St
Ann Arbor, MI 48109
bingye@umich.edu

ABSTRACT

Neuron activities are the source of behavior in living beings and understanding the neuron circuitry has been one of the most interesting areas of neuroscience in the recent past. As a part of it, analyzing the spatiotemporal synchronized neuronal ensemble consecutive firings, such as the calcium ion waves *in vivo,* will shed light on the underlying mystery of neuronal ensembles. However, manual analysis of waves is prone to human error due to the complex high dimension of images, and may also be limited by the subjective observation of the neuroscientist. Subsequently, to date there has been limited progress in high dimensional ensemble neuronal waves analysis computationally or manually despite the fast growing of the imaging techniques. Here we present a novel way of employing 3D and 4D image wave detection methods to analyze the neuronal ensemble waves in the entire *Drosophila M.* Larval Ventral Nerve Cord (VNC). We focus on the computational methods that reduce the high dimension of the data and extract the wave information from non-wave firings.

KEYWORDS

High-dimensional neuronal activity; Wave; Drosophila Larva; Ventral Nerve Cord; Dimensionality Reduction; Calcium Imaging

Permission to make digital or hard copies of part or all of this work for personal or classroom use is granted without fee provided that copies are not made or distributed for profit or commercial advantage and that copies bear this notice and the full citation on the first page. Copyrights for third-party components of this work must be honored. For all other uses, contact the Owner/Author.
ACM-BCB '17, August 20-23, 2017, Boston, MA, USA
© 2017 Copyright is held by the owner/author(s).
ACM ISBN 978-1-4503-4722-8/17/08.
http://dx.doi.org/10.1145/3107411.3108209

1 INTRODUCTION

Despite growing research in neuroscience, the dynamics of neuron firing patterns are still not known to the fullest. With improvement in the ensemble neuronal activity analysis methods, we can understand brain functionality and predict the behaviors. As wave is one of those important neural activities, wave analysis can provide insights for the behavior patterns.

Apart from the current methods, the presented work aims at filling the gap in both technical capability and neuroscience by designing and implementing algorithms to accurately identify waves from 3D and 4D calcium activity recordings with focus on wave analysis which yield insightful information about spontaneous and evoked activities.

2 APPROACH AND RESULTS

We employ both 3D and 4D analysis for the detection of the organized waves in high dimensional ensemble activity. Under the 3D image analysis process, after pre- processing the images, peak detection algorithms are applied to the calcium signal of the larva VNC. Using the detected peaks, patterns of spatiotemporal synchronized waves are identified. Under the 4D wave analysis, a 3D image registration followed by a novel dimensionality reduction technique, converting 4D to 3D is performed. Thereupon, waves are detected by tracking the brightest point using min-max localization. The waves commonly detected from both 3D analysis and 4D analysis are considered as true waves.

We tested our methods on more than 100 recordings of neural activities using genetically encoded calcium indicator on the entire VNC analyzing both spontaneous and evoked activities. Our preliminary study suggests that our techniques are promising for wave analysis, evidenced by effective peak detection and the comparison between waves detected under different experimental conditions.

Tumor Neoantigens Derived from RNA Sequence Analysis

Shaojun Tang[1*], Suthee Rapisuwon[2], Anton Wellstein[2], Subha Madhavan[1]

[1] Innovation Center for Biomedical Informatics, Georgetown University Medical Center, Washington, DC, USA

[2] Lombardi Comprehensive Cancer Center, Department of Oncology, Georgetown University, Washington, DC, USA

ABSTRACT

Successful treatment of cancers with Immune Checkpoint Inhibitors (ICIs) has been associated with the mutational load of tumors. The biological rationale for this association between mutational load and ICI response is that neoantigens are generated by mutations in protein coding sequences that provide a steady flow of neoantigens to prime the immune system for the production of antigen-specific tumor-infiltrating lymphocytes (TILs). It is thought that mutant protein fragments will lead to altered MHC/peptide recognition and immune cell activation; ICI treatment enhances TIL functionality. Neoantigens are also relevant for an alternative, cell-based immunotherapeutic approach, i.e. Adoptive Cell Transfer (ACT). This concept of neoantigens derived from DNA mutations has led to an intense line of investigation to uncover relevant neoantigens. However, there has been mixed success with the current neoantigen discovery approach based on DNA mutation analysis of tumor samples by exome sequencing of genomic DNA. The current concept of neoantigens derived from mutant DNA ignores an alternative mechanism that can also generate neoantigens in cancers: Posttranscriptional editing of primary RNA. Here we propose to use full-length Single Molecule Real Time (SMRT) RNAseq to uncover pathologically edited mRNAs in cancers and complement the discovery of pathologic mRNA. We will discuss the respective algorithms and propose the combination with identification of candidate neoantigen peptides by mass spectrometry.

Permission to make digital or hard copies of part or all of this work for personal or classroom use is granted without fee provided that copies are not made or distributed for profit or commercial advantage and that copies bear this notice and the full citation on the first page. Copyrights for third-party components of this work must be honored. For all other uses, contact the Owner/Author.
ACM-BCB '17, August 20-23, 2017, Boston, MA, USA
© 2017 Copyright is held by the owner/author(s).
ACM ISBN 978-1-4503-4722-8/17/08.
http://dx.doi.org/10.1145/3107411.3108210

Challenges in Prediction of different Cancer Stages using Gene Expression Profile of Cancer Patients

Sherry Bhalla
Bioinformatics Centre
CSIR-Institute of Microbial Technology
Sector 39 A Chandigarh
160036 India
+918968834420
sherry@imtech.res.in

Suresh Sharma
Centre for Systems Biology and Bioinformatics, Panjab University
Sector 14 Chandigarh
160014 India
+91-172-2534529
ssharma@pu.ac.in

Gajendra Pal Singh Raghava
1. Bioinformatics Centre
CSIR-Institute of Microbial Technology
Sector 39 A Chandigarh
India
2. Indraprastha Institute of Information Technology, Delhi
Okhla Industrial Estate,Phase I
New Delhi, India - 110020
+91-011-26907444
raghava@imtech.res.in
raghava@iiitd.ac.in

ABSTRACT

Despite the plethora of gene expression based cancer biomarkers in the scientific literature, a few make their way to the clinic[1]. In the past, several efforts have been made to predict cancer biomarkers with very limited success so far. One of the challenges in the field of cancer biology is to predict cancer at an early stage. The success of various therapies to treat cancer patients depends on correct identification of stage or progression of cancer. Despite the tremendous progress in the field of genomics and proteomics, the performance of stage classification has not improved substantially. Recently our group also developed CancerCSP, a server with prediction models for discriminating early and late stage of clear cell renal cancer (ccRCC) samples based on the gene expression profile. We achieved maximum accuracy of 72.64% with ROC value 0.81, despite the fact that we tried state of- the-art techniques to improve the performance of our models. This raises the question, why the models fail to discriminate ccRCC patients in the early and late stage with high accuracy. In this poster, the analysis is carried out on ccRCC samples obtained from The Cancer Genome Atlas (TCGA) data portal to understand the reasons for the failure of the stage classification models. Firstly, we performed bin-wise analysis of top 20 genes that can discriminate (single gene-based models using threshold) early and late stage samples with highest ROC. A significant overlap was observed in the expression of each gene in early and late stage samples. Though the number of early and late stage samples varied in different gene expression bins, this was not sufficient to classify both types of samples with high accuracy. As an example, the gene NR3C2 had maximum ROC of 0.67 at expression (log RSEM) of 7.61. There were nearly 70% early stage patients above this threshold that made it an average expression marker but the presence of nearly 55% of late stage patients above this threshold increased the false positives. Secondly, we performed hierarchical clustering of ccRCC samples using 64- gene expression features selected using Weka showed weak concordance with pathological stage. The k-means clustering of patients into four groups showed four separable clusters, but these clusters were not associated with the pathological stage. These observations led to the conclusion that the molecular parameters do not always comply with histopathological features. The third analysis was done to identify patients, which were not predicted correctly by any of the four machine-learning algorithms (SVM, Random Forest, SMO and Naïve Bayes). Many samples were not predicted correctly by any of the four machine-learning methods. The false positives and false negatives belonged to explicit clusters obtained through clustering. This further points out to the interspersed nature of the data to differentiate between histopathological stages of cancer. We reach the conclusion that expression profile of genes is not adequate to classify different stages of cancer samples.

Permission to make digital or hard copies of part or all of this work for personal or classroom use is granted without fee provided that copies are not made or distributed for profit or commercial advantage and that copies bear this notice and the full citation on the first page. Copyrights for third-party components of this work must be honored. For all other uses, contact the Owner/Author.
ACM-BCB '17, August 20-23, 2017, Boston, MA, USA
© 2017 Copyright is held by the owner/author(s).
ACM ISBN 978-1-4503-4722-8/17/08.
http://dx.doi.org/10.1145/3107411.3108211

General Terms

Algorithms, Reliability

Keywords

ccRCC; Renal Cancer; Biomarkers; Gene Expression; Machine Learning

NGSPipes: Fostering Reproducibility and Scalability in Biosciences*

Bruno Dantas
ISEL, Polythenic Institute of Lisbon, Portugal

Calmenelias Fleitas
ISEL, Polythenic Institute of Lisbon, Portugal

Alexandre Almeida
ISEL, Polythenic Institute of Lisbon, Portugal

João Forja
ISEL, Polythenic Institute of Lisbon, Portugal

Alexandre P. Francisco†
INESC-ID / IST, University of Lisbon, Portugal

José Simão†
INESC-ID / ISEL, Polythenic Institute of Lisbon, Portugal

Cátia Vaz†
INESC-ID / ISEL, Polythenic Institute of Lisbon, Portugal

ABSTRACT

Biosciences have been revolutionised by NGS technologies in last years, leading to new perspectives in medical, industrial and environmental applications. And although our motivation comes from biosciences, the following is true for many areas of science: published results are usually hard to reproduce, delaying the adoption of new methodologies and hindering innovation. Even if data and tools are freely available, pipelines for data analysis are in general barely described and their setup is far from trivial. NGSPipes addresses these issues reducing the efforts necessary to define, build and deploy pipelines, either at a local workstation or in the cloud. NGSPipes framework is freely available at http://ngspipes.github.io/.

CCS CONCEPTS

• **Applied computing** → **Bioinformatics**; • **Computer systems organization** → *Cloud computing*; • **Software and its engineering** → *Domain specific languages*;

KEYWORDS

scientific workflows; reproducible science; domain specific languages; decentralised computing

ACM Reference format:

Bruno Dantas, Calmenelias Fleitas, Alexandre Almeida, João Forja, Alexandre P. Francisco, José Simão, and Cátia Vaz. 2017. NGSPipes: Fostering Reproducibility and Scalability in Biosciences. In *Proceedings of ACM-BCB '17, Boston, MA, USA, August 20-23, 2017,* 1 pages.
https://doi.org/10.1145/3107411.3108213

*This work was partly supported by national funds through FCT – Fundação para a Ciência e Tecnologia, under projects BacGenTrack (TUBITACK/0004/2014), NEUROCLINOMICS2 (PTDC/EEI-SII/1937/2014), PRECISE (SAICTPAC/0021/2015) and UID/CEC/500021/2013.

†These authors contributed equally to this work.

Permission to make digital or hard copies of part or all of this work for personal or classroom use is granted without fee provided that copies are not made or distributed for profit or commercial advantage and that copies bear this notice and the full citation on the first page. Copyrights for third-party components of this work must be honored. For all other uses, contact the owner/author(s).
ACM-BCB '17, August 20-23, 2017, Boston, MA, USA
© 2017 Copyright held by the owner/author(s).
ACM ISBN 978-1-4503-4722-8/17/08.
https://doi.org/10.1145/3107411.3108213

Most scientific experiments that employ next-generation sequencing (NGS) rely on running a series of intertwined computational analysis and visualization tasks on large amounts of data. These so called analysis *pipelines*, or more generally workflows, start with voluminous raw sequences and can end with detailed structural, functional, and evolutionary results. Pipelines involve the use of multiple software tools and data resources in a staged fashion, with the output of one tool being passed as input to the next one [2]. Although there are several pipeline frameworks, with some being HPC capable, most of them cannot be easily installed and configured, are available as centralized services, and are most of the times only available to users with some kind of specialized IT support.

NGSPipes allows automatic tool configuration, and the precise description of pipelines, while avoiding specialized configurations [1]. It relies on (i) an easy to learn domain-specific language (DSL), (ii) a tool annotation language and repositories of tools, (iii) a rich interface pipeline editor and (iv) two execution engines. Tool repositories reference remote Docker containers with tools and include files with information for automatic execution of each tool. Note that pipeline and tools specifications are decoupled from data sources and real tools, leading to a more flexible and decentralized framework. The DSL has simple constructs capable of capturing the dependence between tools and express sequential or parallel processing. Once specified, a pipeline can be executed either on a workstation or on a compatible cloud environment. Both engines analyse the pipeline description and transform it to a *deployable* format, determining resource requirements of each tool based on the *tool configuration* present in the repository. Local execution relies on a virtual machine for isolation. Cloud-based execution relies on a remote cluster running Apache Mesos, a widely used, distributed and fault tolerant system to manage multitentant clusters, with native support for Docker images. Pipelines are executed as a set of Chonos' jobs. Both engines support multi-core, but the latter supports also multi-task and data parallelism.

REFERENCES

[1] Bruno Dantas, Calmenelias Fleitas, Alexandre P. Francisco, José Simão, and Cátia Vaz. 2017. Beyond NGS data sharing and towards open science. *CoRR* abs/1701.03507 (2017). http://arxiv.org/abs/1701.03507
[2] Jeremy Leipzig. 2016. A review of bioinformatic pipeline frameworks. *Briefings in Bioinformatics* 18, 3 (2016), 530–536.

Dynamic Phylogenetic Inference for Sequence-based Typing Data*

Alexandre P Francisco
INESC-ID / IST, University of Lisbon, Portugal

Marta Nascimento
INESC-ID / IST, University of Lisbon, Portugal

Cátia Vaz
INESC-ID / ISEL, Polythenic Institute of Lisbon, Portugal

ABSTRACT

Typing methods are widely used in the surveillance of infectious diseases, outbreaks investigation and studies of the natural history of an infection. And their use is becoming standard, in particular with the introduction of High Throughput Sequencing (HTS). On the other hand, the data being generated is massive and many algorithms have been proposed for phylogenetic analysis of typing data, such as the goeBURST algorithm. These algorithms must however be run whenever new data becomes available starting from scratch. We address this issue proposing a dynamic version of goeBURST algorithm. Experimental results show that this new version is efficient on integrating new data and updating inferred evolutionary patterns, improving the update running time by at least one order of magnitude.

CCS CONCEPTS

• **Theory of computation** → *Dynamic graph algorithms*; • **Applied computing** → *Computational biology*; • **Mathematics of computing** → Graph algorithms;

KEYWORDS

phylogenetic inference; phylogenetic trees; dynamic algorithms; sequence-based typing data

ACM Reference format:
Alexandre P Francisco, Marta Nascimento, and Cátia Vaz. 2017. Dynamic Phylogenetic Inference for Sequence-based Typing Data. In *Proceedings of ACM-BCB '17, Boston, MA, USA, August 20-23, 2017,* 1 pages.
https://doi.org/10.1145/3107411.3108214

DYNAMIC GOEBURST

Sequence-based typing methods are fundamental in epidemiological and genetic studies [4]. On the other hand, the introduction of High Throughput Sequencing (HTS) technology, and the decrease in costs of using it, have contributed to large repositories of typing data, creating the need of developing efficient and scalable methods that are suitable for large scale phylogenetic analyses [3, 5]. Since most methods are distance-based, their running time is dominated by the computation of pairwise distances among taxa, leading to at least quadratic running time [5]. We propose here a dynamic version of the goeBURST algorithm [1].

The problem solved by goeBURST can be stated as a graphic matroid, with the solution following a classic greedy approach. Its running time is then $O(\ell \min\{n^2, m \log n\})$, where n is the number of taxa, m is the number of pairs for which the distance is defined, and ℓ is the number of loci under analysis. Usually we consider all-pairs Hamming distance [2], leading to $O(\ell n^2)$ running time.

The dynamic version of goeBURST allows the addition of a new taxa to a previously computed minimum spanning tree (MST) without the need of running goeBURST algorithm from scratch. Although there are well know dynamic algorithms for computing and updating MSTs, they are not directly usable in this context due to distance updating and tie breaking rules. The basic process of adding a new edge to a MST can be done by checking if that edge creates a cycle and, in that case, removing the heaviest edge from that same cycle. Since goeBURST has some specific tie breaking rules regarding the number of locus variants, we have implemented two versions for dynamic updating: dynamic goeBURST algorithm with tie breaking rules and without (relying only on edge weights/distances). The dynamic algorithm with tie breaking rules is more complex because adding a taxon can change the entire tree. This is due to the fact that the overall number of locus variants for all taxa will vary causing a possible change on the tie breaking rule applied before. Adding a new taxon takes linear time on average for real data, being dominated by the time for processing n edges and pairwise comparisons. We achieve this running through the use of efficient data structures, namely for MST representation.

Experimental results were obtained with the *Streptococcus pneumoniae* MLST dataset available at https://pubmlst.org, with the number of taxa varying from $n = 10$ to $n = 1000$ and running times averaged over 500 executions. The update time for adding a new taxon grows linearly with the number of taxa on the tree, while the static goeBURST takes quadratic time for computing the tree, as expected. In particular, static goeBURST takes more than 1500 ms to add 1000 taxa, while both dynamic versions take less than 150 ms to add a new taxon to a previously computed 999 taxa MST.

*This work was partly supported by national funds through FCT – Fundação para a Ciência e Tecnologia, under projects BacGenTrack (TUBITACK/0004/2014), PRECISE (SAICTPAC/0021/2015) and UID/CEC/500021/2013.

Permission to make digital or hard copies of part or all of this work for personal or classroom use is granted without fee provided that copies are not made or distributed for profit or commercial advantage and that copies bear this notice and the full citation on the first page. Copyrights for third-party components of this work must be honored. For all other uses, contact the owner/author(s).
ACM-BCB '17, August 20-23, 2017, Boston, MA, USA
© 2017 Copyright held by the owner/author(s).
ACM ISBN 978-1-4503-4722-8/17/08.
https://doi.org/10.1145/3107411.3108214

REFERENCES

[1] Alexandre P Francisco, Miguel Bugalho, Mário Ramirez, and João A Carriço. 2009. Global optimal eBURST analysis of multilocus typing data using a graphic matroid approach. *BMC Bioinformatics* 10, 1 (2009), 152.
[2] R. W. Hamming. 1950. Error Detecting and Error Correcting Codes. (1950), 147–160 pages.
[3] Marta Nascimento, Adriano Sousa, Mário Ramirez, Alexandre P Francisco, João A Carriço, and Cátia Vaz. 2017. PHYLOViZ 2.0: providing scalable data integration and visualization for multiple phylogenetic inference methods. *Bioinformatics* 33, 1 (2017), 128–129.
[4] D Ashley Robinson, Edward J Feil, and Daniel Falush. 2010. *Bacterial population genetics in infectious disease.* John Wiley & Sons.
[5] Naruya Saitou. 2013. *Introduction to evolutionary genomics.* Springer.

Classification and Prediction of Antimicrobial Peptides Using N-gram Representation and Machine Learning

Manal Othman
George Mason University
Manassas, VA 20110
mothman@gmu.edu

Sujay Ratna
George Mason University
Manassas, VA 20110
sratna03@gmail.com

Anant Tewari
George Mason University
Manassas, VA 20110
anant.tewari98@gmail.com

Anthony M. Kang
George Mason University
Manassas, VA 20110
minsukusa@gmail.com

Katherine Du
George Mason University
Manassas, VA 20110
dukatherine@hotmail.com

Iosif I. Vaisman
George Mason University
Manassas, VA 20110
ivaisman@gmu.edu

ABSTRACT

Current antibiotic treatments for infectious diseases are drastically losing effectiveness, as the organisms they target have developed resistance to the drugs over time. In the United States, antibiotic-resistant bacterial infections annually result in more than 23,000 deaths, the morbidity rates are much higher. A promising alternative to current antibiotic treatments are antimicrobial peptides (AMPs), short sequences of amino acid residues that have been experimentally identified to inhibit the propagation of pathogens. In this study, we demonstrated that an N-gram representation of AMP sequences using reduced amino acid alphabet combined with machine learning (ML) methods provide a simple and efficient AMP classification with performance comparable to the more complex algorithms.

All AMP sequences were retrieved from public data sources. Our AMP set consists of 7760 sequences, regardless of AMP subclass. We also used class-specific AMP sets (antibacterial, antiviral, antifungal, and antiparasitic). We created a raw negative set consisting of 20258 non-antimicrobial peptides (non-AMPs) using sequence fragments from annotated protein sequence databases.

Models for all AMP against non-AMP sequences classification achieved a maximum accuracy of 85.0% using frequency N-gram analysis, and the RF model with 10-fold cross-validation. The datasets ranged from 200 to 7760 sequences per class.

Classification using more specific classes of AMPs was conducted next. First, classification of ABPs against non-ABP sequences achieved an accuracy of up to 100% depending on a ML algorithm and alphabet reduction used. ABP against AVP sequences classification yielded a maximum accuracy of 81.8% AVP against non-AVP - 80.7% and AVP against AFP - 80.5%.

The common trends present across multiple experiment series include the following: Random Forest frequently outperforms other algorithms. The optimal size of the reduced alphabet is either 3 or 4 letters. Reduction to 2 letters leads to a significant drop in accuracy, reduction to 5 or more letters does not provide any noticeable gains in classification accuracy.

The results of this study indicate that N-gram based classification of AMPs is a promising approach with a strong potential for providing important insights into understanding AMP mechanisms and computationally designing new AMPs.

CCS Concepts

[Bioinformatics Applications]: Bioinformatics and Computational Biology.

KEYWORDS

N-gram, Antimicrobial Peptides, Machine Learning, Reduced Alphabet.

ACKNOWLEDGMENTS

This work was supported in part by Princess Nourah bint Abdulrahman University, College of Medicine and GMU ASSIP Program.

Permission to make digital or hard copies of part or all of this work for personal or classroom use is granted without fee provided that copies are not made or distributed for profit or commercial advantage and that copies bear this notice and the full citation on the first page. Copyrights for third-party components of this work must be honored. For all other uses, contact the Owner/Author.
ACM-BCB '17, August 20-23, 2017, Boston, MA, USA
© 2017 Copyright is held by the owner/author(s).
ACM ISBN 978-1-4503-4722-8/17/08.
http://dx.doi.org/10.1145/3107411.3108215

Network Analysis Identifies Regulatory Hotspots in Regions of Chromosome Interactions

Anastasiya Belyaeva
Massachusetts Institute of Technology
Cambridge, MA
belyaeva@mit.edu

Saradha Venkatachalapathy
National University of Singapore
Singapore
saradhavpathy@gmail.com

Mallika Nagarajan
National University of Singapore
Singapore
mallikanc@gmail.com

G.V. Shivashankar
National University of Singapore
Singapore
shiva.gvs@gmail.com

Caroline Uhler*
Massachusetts Institute of Technology
Cambridge, MA
cuhler@mit.edu

ABSTRACT

The three-dimensional structure of the genome plays a key role in regulatory control of the cell. Chromosomes are organized non-randomly inside the nucleus and form a network of interactions. Recent experimental methods such as Hi-C have been used to probe the 3D architecture of the genome, giving average pairwise contact frequencies between chromosomes [1, 3]. However, deducing the spatial organization of chromosomes from this data remains a challenge due to high levels of noise and technical bias. Here, we propose a novel framework that leverages 1D features of the genome (e.g. gene expression) in combination with Hi-C data to identify interacting regions in the genome. First, we find domains of high average interaction in Hi-C maps using a large average submatrix algorithm [4]. Then we construct a weighted network with genomic regions as nodes and interactions as edges, where the edge weights are given by the correlation between genomic features. Individual interacting clusters are determined using weighted correlation clustering on the network [2]. In addition to recapitulating known organizational patterns of chromosome interactions, we validate our predictions using fluorescence in situ hybridization (FISH). We uncover two types of intermingling clusters - active and inactive clusters based on enrichment for RNA polymerase II and H3K9me3, respectively. We show that active clusters are hotspots for transcription factor binding. Our method provides a quantitative framework that allows to couple features of the 1D genome with 3D interactions to uncover the guiding principles of genome spatial organization and regulatory control.

CCS CONCEPTS

• **Applied computing → Recognition of genes and regulatory elements**; *Bioinformatics*; • **Computing methodologies** → *Network science*; • **Mathematics of computing** → Graph algorithms;

*Corresponding author.

Permission to make digital or hard copies of part or all of this work for personal or classroom use is granted without fee provided that copies are not made or distributed for profit or commercial advantage and that copies bear this notice and the full citation on the first page. Copyrights for third-party components of this work must be honored. For all other uses, contact the owner/author(s).
ACM-BCB '17, August 20-23, 2017, Boston, MA, USA
© 2017 Copyright held by the owner/author(s).
ACM ISBN 978-1-4503-4722-8/17/08.
https://doi.org/10.1145/3107411.3108216

KEYWORDS

chromosome intermingling, 3D FISH, network and clustering analysis, Hi-C, epigenetics

ACM Reference format:

Anastasiya Belyaeva, Saradha Venkatachalapathy, Mallika Nagarajan, G.V. Shivashankar, and Caroline Uhler. 2017. Network Analysis Identifies Regulatory Hotspots in Regions of Chromosome Interactions. In *Proceedings of ACM-BCB '17, Boston, MA, USA, August 20-23, 2017,* 1 pages.
https://doi.org/10.1145/3107411.3108216

REFERENCES

[1] Job Dekker and Leonid Mirny. 2016. The 3D Genome as Moderator of Chromosomal Communication. *Cell* 164, 6 (2016), 1110–1121. https://doi.org/10.1016/j.cell.2016.02.007
[2] Micha Elsner and Warren Schudy. 2009. Bounding and comparing methods for correlation clustering beyond ILP. *Proceedings of the NAACL HLT Workshop on Integer Linear Programming for Natural Language Processing* June (2009), 19–27. https://doi.org/10.3115/1611638.1611641
[3] Erez Lieberman-aiden, Nynke L Van Berkum, Louise Williams, Maxim Imakaev, Tobias Ragoczy, Agnes Telling, Ido Amit, Bryan R Lajoie, Peter J Sabo, Michael O Dorschner, Richard Sandstrom, Bradley Bernstein, M A Bender, Mark Groudine, Andreas Gnirke, John Stamatoyannopoulos, and Leonid A Mirny. 2009. Comprehensive Mapping of Long-Range Interactions Reveals Folding Principles of the Human Genome. *Science* 326, October (2009), 289–293.
[4] Andrey A. Shabalin, Victor J. Weigman, Charles M. Perou, and Andrew B. Nobel. 2009. Finding large average submatrices in high dimensional data. *Annals of Applied Statistics* 3, 3 (2009), 985–1012. https://doi.org/10.1214/09-AOAS239 arXiv:0905.1682

Machine Learning Model for Identifying Gene Biomarkers for Breast Cancer Treatment Survival

Ashraf Abou Tabl
University of Windsor
401 Sunset Avenue, Windsor, ON, Canada
aboutaba@uwindsor.ca

Abed Alkhateeb
University of Windsor
401 Sunset Avenue, Windsor, ON, Canada
alkhate@uwindsor.ca

Waguih ElMaraghy
University of Windsor
401 Sunset Avenue, Windsor, ON, Canada
wem@uwindsor.ca

Alioune Ngom
University of Windsor
401 Sunset Avenue, Windsor, ON, Canada
angom@uwindsor.ca

ABSTRACT

Studying the breast cancer survival genes information will help to enhance the treatment and save more patents life by identifying the genes biomarker to recommend the proper treatment type. That is why it is now a great challenge for researchers to have more research on breast cancer specially with the great enhancement in the fields of bioinformatics, data mining, and machine learning techniques which were a new revolution in the cancer treatment.

Keywords Breast cancer, survival, biomarker gens, treatment, machine learning, classification, feature selection.

1. INTRODUCTION

The survival rates are increased due to the improvement in the treatments and utilizing bioinformatics and new technologies.

2. RESOURCES AND METHODS

A dataset contains the survival information and treatments methods for 1980 female breast cancer patient is used for building the prediction model, the gene expression are the features of the learning model [1], where the combination of the survival and treatments information are the classes. A hierarchal model that consists of hybrid feature selection and classification method are utilized to differentiate a class from the rest of the classes.

3. EXPERIMENTAL RESULTS

The results show that a few number of gene biomarkers (gene signature) at each node which can determine the class with accuracy around 99% for survival living / deceased based on treatments which is vital to ensure that the patients will have the best potential response to a specific therapy. This signatures will be used as a predictor of survival in breast cancer.

4. ACKNOWLEDGMENTS

This work has been partially supported by the Natural Sciences and Engineering Research Council of Canada (NSERC), and the Windsor Essex County Cancer Centre Foundation (WECCCF) Seeds4Hope program.

Permission to make digital or hard copies of part or all of this work for personal or classroom use is granted without fee provided that copies are not made or distributed for profit or commercial advantage and that copies bear this notice and the full citation on the first page. Copyrights for third-party components of this work must be honored. For all other uses, contact the Owner/Author.
ACM-BCB '17, August 20-23, 2017, Boston, MA, USA
© 2017 Copyright is held by the owner/author(s).
ACM ISBN 978-1-4503-4722-8/17/08.
http://dx.doi.org/10.1145/3107411.3108217

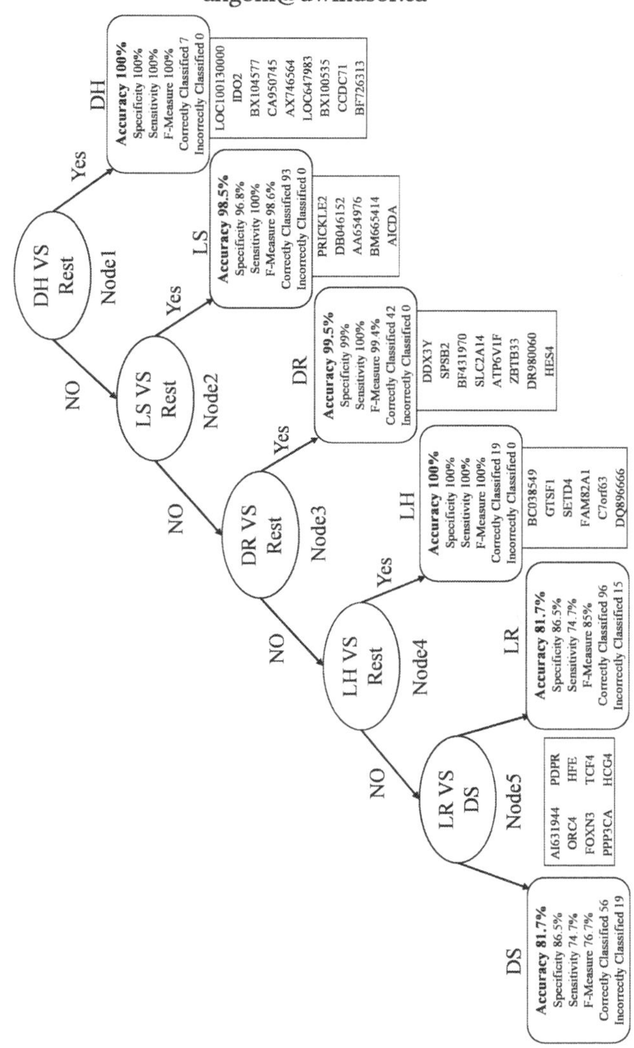

Figure 1: Multi-Class Classification Model with performance measures

5. REFERENCES

[1] Pereira B. et al., The somatic mutation profiles of 2,433 breast cancers refine their genomic and transcriptomic landscapes. Nature communications. 2016 May 10;7.

Genome-Wide Association Study (GWAS) for the Infliximab Responsiveness in Korean Inflammatory Bowel Disease Patients

Zewon Park
zpark1@korea.kr

Ko-woon Choi
choikowoon@korea.kr

Doo Won Seo
realize17@korea.kr

Sunae Ryu
sunae04@korea.kr

Jong Gu Lee
alclrl1@korea.kr

Woo Yong Oh
wy01@korea.kr

Ministry of Food and Drug Safety, National Institute of Food and Drug Safety Evaluation

Clinical Research Division, NIFDS, MFDS, Osong Health Technology Administration Complex, 187, Osongsaengmyeong 2-ro, Osong, Cheongju, 28159, Korea
+82-43-719-5262

Abstract

Inflammatory bowel disease (IBD) subdividing into Crohn's disease (CD) and ulcerative colitis (UC) is a chronic intestinal inflammatory disorder. Infliximab (IFX) as an anti-TNF-α has been prescribed for treatment of IBD patients. However, some patients show no response or a loss of response to this agent. In this study, we investigated to identify genetic variants associated with response to IFX. A total of 148 IBD patients from Yonsei University Health System who received IFX were classified according to subtypes of IBD except 12 patients unsuitable for this study. We also categorized the patients into three groups by IFX response; response (sustained response, loss of response), nonresponse. Whole exome sequencing (WES) was performed and identified on average 35,000 variants including silent, missense and nonsense mutation in each sample. We performed GWAS using the WES data to find out genetic variants associated with response to IFX. We identified only missense variants with suggestive evidence of association. In CD patients, AEBP1 (rs2537188) was associated with nonresponse and PLA2R1 (rs35771982, rs3749117) and IDO2 (rs10109853) were associated with loss of response. In UC patients, AMACR (rs10941112, rs3195676) was associated with loss of response. Furthermore, we will investigate *in vitro* study at the cellular level for the functional analysis of those genetic variants.

Keywords

Inflammatory bowel disease (IBD); Infliximab; Response to drug; Whole exome sequencing; GWAS

Permission to make digital or hard copies of part or all of this work for personal or classroom use is granted without fee provided that copies are not made or distributed for profit or commercial advantage and that copies bear this notice and the full citation on the first page. Copyrights for third-party components of this work must be honored. For all other uses, contact the Owner/Author.
ACM-BCB '17, August 20-23, 2017, Boston, MA, USA
© 2017 Copyright is held by the owner/author(s).

ACM ISBN 978-1-4503-4722-8/17/08.
http://dx.doi.org/10.1145/3107411.3108218

Pipeline for Workflow

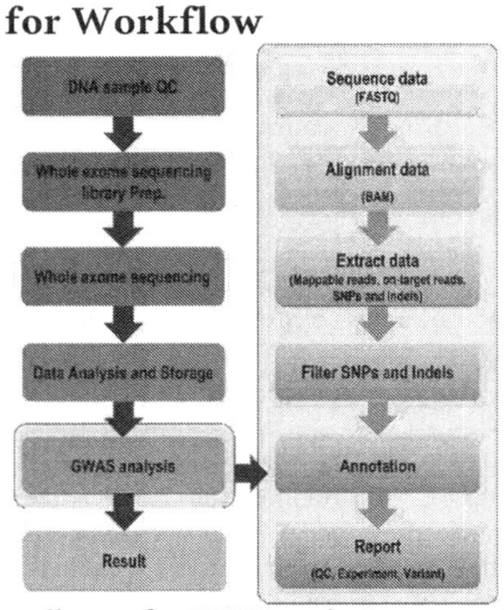

Figure 1. Overall steps for GWAS analysis using whole exome sequencing.

Results

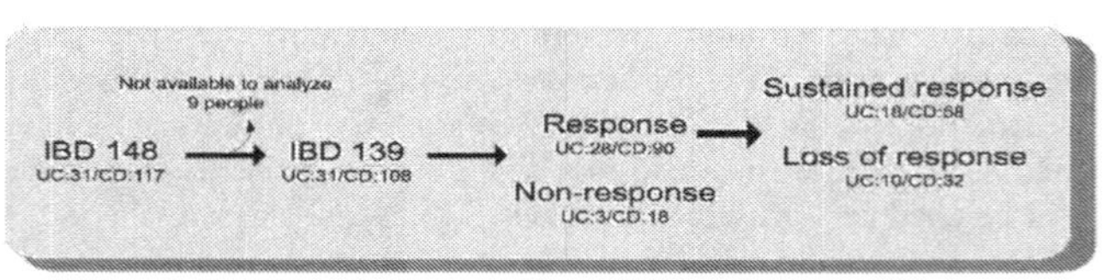

Figure 2. Patient classification according to Infliximab responsiveness for WES and GWAS.

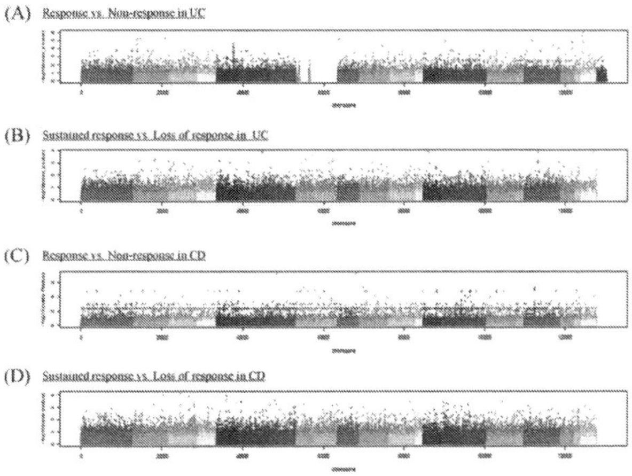

Figure 3. Manhattan plots for GWAS of infliximab responsiveness in IBD patients.

Disease	Group	CHR	SNP	Gene	Ref. Allele	Alt. Allele	Effect of variant	Amino acid change	p-value
CD	Response vs. Non-response	7	rs2537188	AEBP1	C	A	Missense	P273T	5.06e-08
	Sustained response vs. Loss of response	8	rs10109853	IDO2	C	T	Missense	R248W	5.43e-04
		2	rs35771982	PLA2R1	G	C	Missense	H300D	6.19e-04
		2	rs3749117	PLA2R1	T	C	Missense	M292V	6.34e-04
UC		5	rs10941112	AMACR	C	T	Missense	G175D	6.65e-04
		5	rs3195676	AMACR	C	T	Missense	V9M	7.45e-04

Table 1. Candidate SNPs and regions. (p<0.001)

rs2537188 genotype (AEBP1)			
Group	CC	CA+AA	Total
Response	49 (54%)	41 (46%)	90 (100%)
Non-response	8 (44%)	10 (56%)	18 (100%)

rs10109853 genotype (IDO2)			
Group	CC	CT+TT	Total
Sustained response	22 (38%)	36 (62%)	58 (100%)
Loss of response	23 (72%)	9 (28%)	32 (100%)

rs35771982 genotype (PLA2R1)			
Group	GG	GC+CC	Total
Sustained response	36 (62%)	22 (38%)	58 (100%)
Loss of response	8 (25%)	24 (75%)	32 (100%)

rs3749117 genotype (PLA2R1)			
Group	TT	TC+CC	Total
Sustained response	36 (62%)	22 (38%)	58 (100%)
Loss of response	8 (25%)	24 (75%)	32 (100%)

rs10941112 genotype (AMACR)			
Group	CC	CT+TT	Total
Sustained response	1 (6%)	17 (94%)	18 (100%)
Loss of response	6 (60%)	4 (40%)	10 (100%)

rs3195676 genotype (AMACR)			
Group	CC	CT+TT	Total
Sustained response	1 (6%)	17 (94%)	18 (100%)
Loss of response	6 (60%)	4 (40%)	10 (100%)

Table 2. Genotype frequencies of the polymorphisms located in the genes studied in IBD patents.

Conclusion

- We performed a GWAS for the infliximab responsiveness in 139 Korean IBD patients.
- As a results, some SNPs(rs2537188, rs10109853, rs35771982, rs3749117, rs10941112, rs3195676) were expected the cause of difference in infliximab responsiveness.
- In our further study, we will elucidate the molecular and functional mechanisms of those SNPs as well as AEBP1, IDO2, PLA2R1 and AMACR related SNPs .

ACKNOWLEDGMENTS

This research was supported by a grant 16181MFDS446 from Ministry of Food and Drug Safety in 2016

Integrating Prior Information with Bayesian Feature Selection

Ali Foroughi pour, Lori A. Dalton
Electrical and Computer Engineering Department
The Ohio State University
2015 Neil Ave.
Columbus, Ohio 43210
foroughipour.1@osu.edu,dalton@ece.osu.edu

ABSTRACT

Biomarker discovery aims to find biomarkers involved in biological mechanisms of a disease under study that can be further utilized for diagnosis, prognosis, drug development, etc. Although current high throughput technologies provide a deluge of data per point, research is usually constrained to small samples, impeding reliable biomarker discovery. Given the ongoing research on biomarker discovery during the past decades there exists an incredibly useful, but still limited, prior knowledge on cancer biology, such as small gene sets already known to be involved in cancer. This information, if properly integrated with feature selection, could potentially help to detect new biomarkers. However, most current methods used for biomarker discovery cannot easily be extended to account for such prior knowledge.

Recent work proposes a hierarchical Bayesian framework for feature selection which places priors on both the identity of all features and identity-conditioned feature distribution. Various models are obtained based on this framework, including dependent good dependent bad (DGDB) model [3]. An approximate solution of DGDB has been used with a set selection heuristic [2] to successfully find genes involved in colon cancer and multiple sclerosis [3, 4]. While the approximate solution only relies on training data, we propose a new algorithm that takes advantage of previously known biomarkers to find additional biomarkers, hereafter called Informed Approximate 3MNC-DGDB (IA-3MNC). In three synthetic simulations we illustrate (a) IA-3MNC outperforms many popular feature selection algorithms, and (b) prior knowledge helps to correctly detect additional biomarkers, particularly under small samples. We apply IA-3MNC to colon cancer and breast cancer datasets deposited on gene expression omnibus [1] with accession numbers GSE1456 and GSE41850, respectively. Top 20 selected genes of IA-3MNC and top 10 enriched pathways are listed in Tabs. 1 and 2, respectively, where enrichment analysis is done using PANTHER [5, 6]. Many of highly ranked genes and pathways are suggested to be involved in cancer.

CCS CONCEPTS

• **Computing methodologies → Feature selection**; • **Mathematics of computing → Bayesian computation**; • **Theory of computation → Bayesian analysis**;

Permission to make digital or hard copies of part or all of this work for personal or classroom use is granted without fee provided that copies are not made or distributed for profit or commercial advantage and that copies bear this notice and the full citation on the first page. Copyrights for third-party components of this work must be honored. For all other uses, contact the owner/author(s).
ACM-BCB'17, August 20–23, 2017, Boston, MA, USA.
© 2017 Copyright held by the owner/author(s). 978-1-4503-4722-8/17/08.
DOI: http://dx.doi.org/10.1145/3107411.3108219

Table 1: Top 20 Genes of IA-3MNC

Breast Cancer				Colon Cancer			
DCT	MPHOSPH10	HDGFRP3	NAGA	NBLA00301	RYR3	GAGE1,12,4,5,6,7	RSPO2
PHTF1	MUC5AC	HMMR	CCT8	EPHA7	SCN7A	ASB5	TRIM10
ZNF192	KIAA0649	ZNF227	DGUOK	CPNE4	MYH11	SEMG2	OCR1
CEACAM7	PCSK6	HTR2C	SON	LOC100133920 LOC286297	PDK4	CCDC7	ARHGEF12
ZP2	ABCA11P	BICD2	LONP1	LOC100507186	KCNIP4	NBLA00301	S100A7

Table 2: Top 10 Pathways of IA-3MNC

Breast Cancer		Colon Cancer	
Pathway Name	P-value	Pathway Name	P-value
Ubiquitin proteasome p.w.	$1.31E-05$	Cadherin sig. p.w.	$1.86E-04$
p53 p.w.	$5.71E-04$	Blood coagulation	$1.43E-03$
Huntington disease	$1.61E-03$	Wnt sig. p.w.	$1.89E-03$
Heme biosynthesis	$1.95E-03$	Gonadotropin-releasing hormone receptor p.w.	$2.21E-03$
FAS sig. p.w.	$2.22E-03$	Ionotropic glutamate receptor p.w.	$2.30E-03$
Gonadotropin-releasing hormone receptor p.w.	$3.83E-03$	Het. G-prot. sig. p.w.-Gi alpha & Gs alpha med. p.w.	$6.10E-03$
Cell cycle	$6.47E-03$	Synaptic vesicle trafficking	$8.50E-03$
DNA replication	$8.35E-03$	p53 p.w. feedback loops 2	$9.89E-03$
Angiogenesis	$9.45E-03$	MYO sig. p.w.	$1.09E-02$
De novo purine biosynthesis	$1.02E-02$	Activin beta sig. p.w.	$1.09E-02$

KEYWORDS

feature selection; Bayesian analysis; biomarker discovery; prior construction

ACM Reference format:
Ali Foroughi pour, Lori A. Dalton. 2017. Integrating Prior Information with Bayesian Feature Selection. In *Proceedings of ACM-BCB'17, August 20–23, 2017, Boston, MA, USA.*, , 1 pages.
DOI: http://dx.doi.org/10.1145/3107411.3108219

REFERENCES

[1] R. Edgar, M. Domrachev, and A. E. Lash. 2002. Gene Expression Omnibus: NCBI gene expression and hybridization array data repository. *Nucleic Acids Res.* 30, 1 (2002), 207–210.
[2] A. Foroughi pour and L. A. Dalton. 2014. Optimal Bayesian feature selection on high dimensional gene expression data. In *Proceedings of the 2014 IEEE Global Conf. on Signal and Information Processing*. 1402–1405.
[3] A. Foroughi pour and L. A. Dalton. 2016. Multiple sclerosis biomarker discovery via Bayesian feature selection. *In Proceedings of the 7th ACM Int. Conf. on Bioinformatics, Computational Biology, and Health Informatics*, 540–541.
[4] A. Foroughi pour and L. A. Dalton. 2017. Robust feature selection for block covariance Bayesian models. *To appear in the proceedings of 42nd Int. Conf. on Acoustics, Speech and Signal Processing*.
[5] H. Mi, X. Huang, A. Muruganujan, and et. al. 2017. PANTHER version 11: Expanded annotation data from gene ontology and Reactome pathways, and data analysis tool enhancements. *Nucleic Acids Res.* 45, 1 (2017), 183–189.
[6] H. Mi and P. Thomas. 2009. PANTHER pathway: an ontology-based pathway database coupled with data analysis tools. *Protein Networks and Pathway Analysis* (2009), 123–140.

An Integrated Reconciliation Framework for Domain, Gene, and Species Level Evolution

Lei Li
Department of Computer Science & Engineering
University of Connecticut
Storrs, CT 06269
lei.li@uconn.edu

Mukul S. Bansal
Department of Computer Science & Engineering
University of Connecticut
Storrs, CT 06269
mukul.bansal@uconn.edu

ABSTRACT

The majority of genes in eukaryotes consist of multiple *protein domains* that can be independently lost or gained during evolution. This gain and loss of protein domains, through domain duplications, transfers, or losses, has important evolutionary and functional consequences for genes. Yet, most computational methods for studying gene evolution view genes as the basic unit of evolution and assume that evolutionary processes such as duplications and losses act on entire genes, rather than on parts of genes. Specifically, even though it is well understood that domains evolve inside genes and genes inside species, there do not exist any computational frameworks to simultaneously model the evolution of domains, genes, and species and account for their inter-dependency.

Here, we develop a *three-tree* model of domain evolution that explicitly captures the interdependence of domain-, gene-, and species-level evolution. Our model extends the classical phylogenetic reconciliation framework, which infers gene family evolution by comparing gene trees and species tree, by explicitly accounting for domain-level events. The new model decouples domain-level events from gene-level events and provides a much more fine-grained view of gene family and domain family evolution that is easy to interpret. Specifically, we (i) introduce the new three-tree computational framework, (ii) prove that the associated optimization problem is NP-hard, (iii) devise an efficient heuristic solution for the problem, (iv) apply our algorithm to a large dataset of about 4000 domain trees and 7000 gene trees from 12 fly species, and (v) demonstrate the impact of using our new computational framework by comparing the inferred evolutionary histories against those obtained using existing approaches. Our experimental results show that using the new three-tree model has a significant impact on the inference of both domain-level and gene-level events, and on the inference of domain content in ancestral genes and gene content in ancestral species, compared to existing approaches.

CCS CONCEPTS

• **Applied computing** → **Computational biology**; *Molecular evolution*;

Permission to make digital or hard copies of part or all of this work for personal or classroom use is granted without fee provided that copies are not made or distributed for profit or commercial advantage and that copies bear this notice and the full citation on the first page. Copyrights for third-party components of this work must be honored. For all other uses, contact the owner/author(s).
ACM-BCB '17, August 20-23, 2017, Boston, MA, USA
© 2017 Copyright held by the owner/author(s).
ACM ISBN 978-1-4503-4722-8/17/08.
https://doi.org/10.1145/3107411.3108220

KEYWORDS

Protein domains, Gene family evolution, Phylogenetic reconciliation

ACM Reference format:
Lei Li and Mukul S. Bansal. 2017. An Integrated Reconciliation Framework for Domain, Gene, and Species Level Evolution. In *Proceedings of ACM-BCB '17, Boston, MA, USA, August 20-23, 2017,* 1 pages.
https://doi.org/10.1145/3107411.3108220

Assessing the Impact of Uncertain Gene Tree Rooting on Phylogenetic Reconciliation Using a Simulation Framework

Soumya Kundu
Department of Computer Science and Engineering
University of Connecticut
Storrs, CT 06269
soumya.kundu@uconn.edu

Mukul S. Bansal
Department of Computer Science and Engineering
University of Connecticut
Storrs, CT 06269
mukul.bansal@uconn.edu

ABSTRACT

Evolutionary trees are fundamental to the study of evolution. The two main types of evolutionary trees are gene trees and species trees. A *gene tree* shows the evolutionary history of a chosen gene family, while a *species tree* shows the evolutionary history of a chosen collection of species. Duplication-Transfer-Loss (DTL) reconciliation is one of the most effective techniques for studying the evolution of gene families and inferring evolutionary events such as gene duplications, horizontal gene transfers, and gene losses. Given a gene tree and the corresponding species tree, DTL reconciliation compares the gene tree with the species tree and reconciles any differences between the two by proposing gene duplication, horizontal gene transfer, and gene loss events [2].

DTL reconciliations are generally computed using a parsimony framework where each evolutionary event is assigned a cost and the goal is to find a reconciliation with minimum total cost. The resulting optimization problem is called the *DTL-reconciliation problem*. While standard formulations of the DTL-reconciliation problem require the gene tree and the species tree to be rooted, gene trees can be notoriously difficult to root accurately, and consequently, the gene trees used for DTL reconciliation are often unrooted. When provided with an unrooted gene tree, existing DTL reconciliation algorithms and software first find a root for the unrooted gene tree and then use the resulting rooted gene tree for the reconciliation. The approach employed for rooting unrooted gene trees is to compute the reconciliation cost for each possible rooting of the unrooted gene tree and then choose a rooting that yields the minimum reconciliation cost [1].

However, there is little understanding of the accuracy of DTL reconciliation methods in rooting gene trees. Moreover, gene trees reconciled by DTL reconciliation often have multiple optimal rootings, leading to a great amount of uncertainty regarding their true roots [3]. In the absence of biological data regarding the true root of a gene tree, simulation provides a powerful technique for evaluating the performance of such a rooting method. Furthermore, varying the different parameters, such as the rates of different evolutionary events, used to simulate the evolution of a gene tree can help us identify the conditions under which DTL reconciliation might perform well. Ultimately, the ability to accurately identify the root of a gene tree will allow biologists to construct accurate evolutionary histories and properly understand how genes and species evolve, directly benefiting our understanding of biology.

Currently, multiple simulation frameworks with the ability to simulate gene family evolution exist [4, 5]. However, there are several factors that are crucial to the accurate simulation of gene family evolution, especially for prokaryotic gene families, that no existing simulation framework accounts for. In this work, we address this limitation by constructing a simulation framework for gene family evolution that accurately simulates horizontal gene transfers by accounting for both additive and replacing transfers, along with multi-gene transfers, and by improving the implementation of biased gene transfers. We use the new simulation framework to generate a large collection of gene trees and species trees, for different combinations of the parameter settings, and use these trees to test the accuracy of DTL reconciliation in identifying the true root of the gene trees under different evolutionary scenarios.

Permission to make digital or hard copies of part or all of this work for personal or classroom use is granted without fee provided that copies are not made or distributed for profit or commercial advantage and that copies bear this notice and the full citation on the first page. Copyrights for third-party components of this work must be honored. For all other uses, contact the owner/author(s).
ACM-BCB '17, Boston, MA, USA
© 2017 Copyright held by the owner/author(s). 978-1-4503-4722-8/17/08.
DOI: 10.1145/3107411.3108221

CCS CONCEPTS

•**Applied computing → Computational biology;** *Molecular evolution;*

KEYWORDS

Gene family evolution, gene tree rooting, phylogenetic reconciliation, simulation framework, horizontal gene transfer

ACM Reference format:
Soumya Kundu and Mukul S. Bansal. 2017. Assessing the Impact of Uncertain Gene Tree Rooting on Phylogenetic Reconciliation Using a Simulation Framework. In *Proceedings of ACM-BCB '17, Boston, MA, USA, August 20-23, 2017,* 1 pages.
DOI: 10.1145/3107411.3108221

REFERENCES

[1] Mukul S. Bansal, Eric J. Alm, and Manolis Kellis. 2012. Efficient algorithms for the reconciliation problem with gene duplication, horizontal transfer and loss. *Bioinformatics* 28, 12 (2012), 283–291.

[2] Jean-Philippe Doyon, Celine Scornavacca, K. Yu. Gorbunov, Gergely J. Szöllosi, Vincent Ranwez, and Vincent Berry. 2010. An Efficient Algorithm for Gene/Species Trees Parsimonious Reconciliation with Losses, Duplications and Transfers. In *RECOMB-CG (Lecture Notes in Computer Science)*, Eric Tannier (Ed.), Vol. 6398. Springer, 93–108.

[3] Soumya Kundu and Mukul S. Bansal. 2017. On the Impact of Uncertain Gene Tree Rooting on Duplication-Transfer-Loss Reconciliation. In *ISBRA 2017 (Lecture Notes in Computer Science)*, Zhipeng Cai, Ovidiu Daescu, and Min Li (Eds.), Vol. 10330. Springer, L–LI.

[4] Diego Mallo, Leonardo De Oliveira Martins, and David Posada. 2016. SimPhy: Phylogenomic Simulation of Gene, Locus, and Species Trees. *Systematic Biology* 65, 2 (2016), 334–344.

[5] Joel Sjöstrand, Lars Arvestad, Jens Lagergren, and Bengt Sennblad. 2013. GenPhyloData: realistic simulation of gene family evolution. *BMC Bioinformatics* 14, 209 (2013).

Overlap Graph Reduction for Genome Assembly using Apache Spark

Alexander J. Paul
Bioinformatics and Computational Biology Program
Saint Louis University
St. Louis, MO 63103
apaul7@slu.edu

Dylan Lawrence
Computational and Systems Biology Program
Washington University in St. Louis
St. Louis, MO 63130
dylan.lawrence@wustl.edu

Tae-Hyuk Ahn
Department of Computer Science
Saint Louis University
St. Louis, MO 63103
ahnt@slu.edu

ABSTRACT

The advent of third-generation long-range DNA sequencing and mapping techniques has permitted nearly perfect or very high quality *de novo* assemblies of genomes. However, most overlap graph *de novo* assemblers still require large amounts of computer memory to resolve the large genome graphs. Here, we apply string graph reduction algorithms for genome assembly using Apache Spark on a distributed cloud computing platform.

CCS CONCEPTS

• **Applied computing** → **Life and medical sciences**; *Computational genomics* • **Mathematics of computing**→ Graph algorithms

KEYWORDS

genome assembly, overlap-layout-consensus, apache spark

1 INTRODUCTION

De novo genome assembly programs stitch together fragmented reads of DNA from an organism. Generally, de Bruijn graphs are a suitable approach for high-throughput short reads and overlap-layout-consensus (OLC) algorithm assemblers handle relatively long reads [1]. The assembly of the reads using OLC still struggles when the overlap graph is very large and the Layout step that tries to simplify and reduce the graph requires a vast amount of shared machine memory. Apache Spark is a new framework for fast and efficient data processing [2]. Using the Spark GraphX library, we have applied and tested several string graph reduction algorithms with a very large sample data set for efficient genome assembly on distributed cloud computing platform.

2 GRAPH REDUCTION AND BENCHMARK

3.1. Transitive edge reduction (TER)

Transitive edge reduction is a method of reducing complexity in graphs and helps provide clearer contigs when running OLC. In TER we eliminate extraneous paths in the graph. Formally, TER states that an edge of the graph G from a -> b may be removed if and only if the graph G' with edge a -> b removed still contains a path leading from a to b.

3.2. Composite edge contraction (CEC)

Composite edge contraction (CEC) is another method of reducing complexity. To simplify the overlap graph, a simple vertex, r, along with its only in-arrow edge (u, r) and only out-arrow edge (r,w), are replaced by a composite edge (u,w) in the overlap graph.

3.3. Benchmark

We have validated the scalability of the Layout module using the Spark GraphX library in the Amazon cloud using a sample dataset. This dataset was assembled by the proposed Spark algorithms using 15 virtual machines in 0.5 hours. Compared to the OLC based Omega [3] assembler's run time of 7.5 hours, the Spark based approach greatly improved the Layout step's runtime.

3 CONCLUSION

This work has focused on solving the computationally expensive task of genome assembly Layout. Apache Spark has enabled us to reduce the complexity and runtime of assembling large genomes.

ACKNOWLEDGMENTS

This work is supported in part by startup funds from Saint Louis University and the award NSF CRII-1566292.

REFERENCES

[1] Li, Z., Chen, Y., Mu, D., Yuan, J., Shi, Y., Zhang, H., Gan, J., Li, N., Hu, X., Liu, B., Yang, B. and Fan, W. Comparison of the two major classes of assembly algorithms: overlap-layout-consensus and de-bruijn-graph. *Brief Funct Genomics*, 11, 1 (Jan 2012), 25-37.

[2] Zaharia, M., Chowdhury, M., Franklin, M. J., Shenker, S. and Stoica, I. Spark: cluster computing with working sets. In *Proceedings of the Proceedings of the 2nd USENIX conference on Hot topics in cloud computing* (Boston, MA, 2010). USENIX Association, [insert City of Publication],[insert 2010 of Publication].

[3] Haider, B., Ahn, T. H., Bushnell, B., Chai, J. J., Copeland, A. and Pan, C. L. Omega: an Overlap-graph *de novo* Assembler for Metagenomics. *Bioinformatics*, 30, 19 (Oct 1 2014), 2717-2722.

Permission to make digital or hard copies of part or all of this work for personal or classroom use is granted without fee provided that copies are not made or distributed for profit or commercial advantage and that copies bear this notice and the full citation on the first page. Copyrights for third-party components of this work must be honored. For all other uses, contact the Owner/Author.
ACM-BCB '17, August 20-23, 2017, Boston, MA, USA
© 2017 Copyright is held by the owner/author(s).
ACM ISBN 978-1-4503-4722-8/17/08.
http://dx.doi.org/10.1145/3107411.3108222

A Cross-Platform System Architecture for Form Design and Data Analytics for Public Health

Blake Camp, Jaya Mandivarapu, Jay Mehta, Nagashayana Ramamurthy, James Wingo, Anu G. Bourgeois, Xiaojun Cao, and Rajshekhar Sunderraman
Department of Computer Science, Georgia State University, Atlanta, GA 30302
abourgeois@gsu.edu

ABSTRACT

The CDC's Epi-Info is widely-used by epidemiologists and public health researchers to collect and analyze public health data, especially in the event of outbreaks. As it exists today, Epi-Info runs only on the Windows platform and is made of separate code-bases for several different devices and use-cases. Software portability has become increasingly important over the past few years. In this poster, we present a cross-platform architecture for Epi-Info. To simplify and expedite future development, the cross-platform system architecture uses Electron, AngularJS, and Python with the capability of running on virtually any desktop or laptop computer. Additionally, the code can be easily deployed to the Web, and has the potential to be a viable solution for several mobile use-cases.

Keywords: Epi-Info, Cross-Platform, Public Health

1. INTRODUCTION

The CDC's Epi-Info Software Suite [1] allows the creation of forms, data-entry, and sophisticated analytics. Epi-Info as it exists today, is not Mac-compatible, with separate code-bases for each type of device: desktop, mobile, web, cloud. However, it is often necessary for developers to rapidly deliver new modules, which can be challenging for current Epi-Info, particularly when resources are stretched and time is scarce. In this work, we propose a cross-platform system architecture for Epi-Info. We explore a platform-agnostic architecture with a web-based form-designer, NoSQL databases, and fast offline/online analytics.

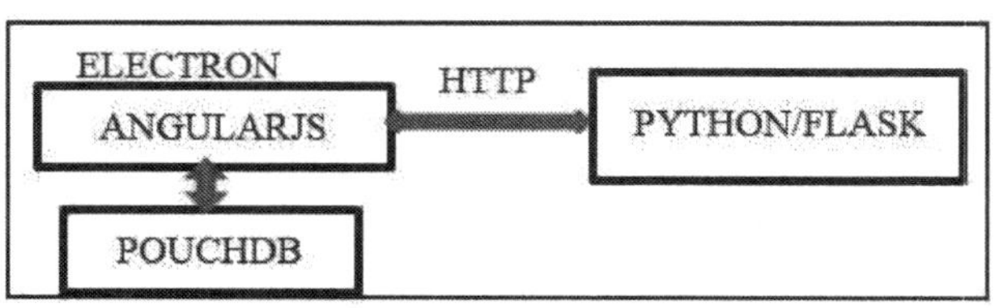

Figure 1. A Cross-Platform Architecture for Epi-Info.

This work is supported through a collaboration with US Centers for Disease Control and Prevention (funded through Broad Agency Announcement No. 2016-N-17812).

Permission to make digital or hard copies of part or all of this work for personal or classroom use is granted without fee provided that copies are not made or distributed for profit or commercial advantage and that copies bear this notice and the full citation on the first page. Copyrights for third-party components of this work must be honored. For all other uses, contact the Owner/Author.
ACM-BCB '17, August 20-23, 2017, Boston, MA, USA
© 2017 Copyright is held by the owner/author(s).
ACM ISBN 978-1-4503-4722-8/17/08.
http://dx.doi.org/10.1145/3107411.3108223

2. CROSS-PLATFORM ARCHITECITURE

As shown in Figure 1, our cross-platform system architecture takes advantages of the emerging technologies such as Electron, PouchDB, Python, UI and Form-Designer. Electron [2] has recently emerged as a viable cross-platform solution for many use-cases. It allows for the creation of native desktop applications using familiar web-technologies like JavaScript, HTML, and CSS. This was appealing, as it would undoubtedly accelerate UI development. Python is adopted for our analytics Module because of its ease-of-use and vast library of third-party modules which further facilitate faster development. Consequently, we needed Electron to serve as a GUI for our python application. The application is a Python/Flask app loaded into the Electron Shell. Flask serves the Angular application, and Angular communicates directly with the embedded PouchDB. Analytics requests are sent to the Python module via a simple HTTP connection.

PouchDB is an open-source NoSQL JavaScript database inspired by Apache CouchDB that is designed to run well within the browser. It enables our application to store data locally while offline, then synchronize it with CouchDB when online. Python is extremely popular among data and machine-learning scientists, and is also platform agnostic, suitable for our cross-platform needs. For the UI and Form-Designer, Electron enables us to use familiar web-technologies like AngularJS [3], HTML, and CSS.

3. RESULTS AND DISCUSSION

We have successfully generated executables for Linux, Mac, and Windows using a single code-base. We have found the NoSQL database to be well-suited to storing highly unstructured form schemas while Angular offering a drag-and-drop form designer. In addition, we have experimented that the architecture is well suited to handle datasets less than 300MB in size: roughly 50k records, with 200 features. In such a case, the conversion from NoSQL to a Pandas DataFrame will take less than 10 seconds, depending upon the machine, on a single core.

4. REFERENCES

[1] Epi-Info, https://www.cdc.gov/epiinfo/index.html
[2] Electron, https://github.com/electron/electron
[3] AngularJS, https://angularjs.org/

Deep Residual Nets for Improved Alzheimer's Diagnosis

Aly Valliani
Swarthmore College
aavalliani@gmail.com

Ameet Soni
Swarthmore College
soni@cs.swarthmore.edu

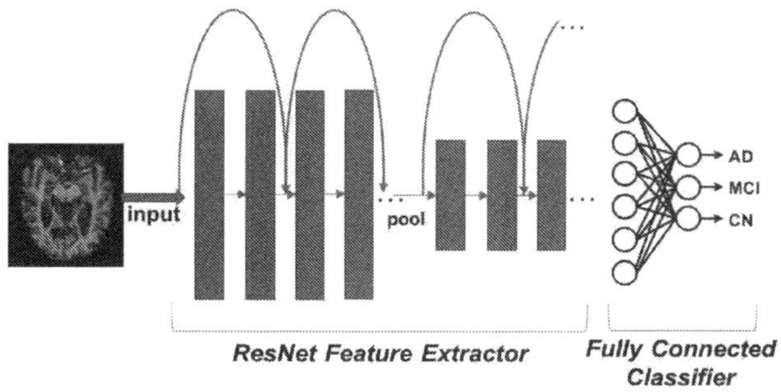

Figure 1: An overview of our approach.

ABSTRACT

We propose a framework that leverages deep residual CNNs *pretrained* on large, non-biomedical image data sets. These pretrained networks learn cross-domain features that improve low-level interpretation of images. We evaluate our model on brain imaging data and show that pretraining *and* the use of deep residual networks are crucial to seeing large improvements in Alzheimer's Disease diagnosis from brain MRIs.

1 INTRODUCTION AND METHODS

Alzheimer's Disease (AD) is a neurodegenerative disorder affecting millions of people. Early diagnosis is difficult as early signs of Alzheimer's are difficult to differentiate from other cognitive declines due to aging. Brain imaging remains an underutilized resource for aiding diagnosis and automated approaches remain limited due to the small size of image data sets.

We propose the use of *pretrained residual network* models for predicting Alzheimer's Disease from brain images to overcome current limitations in the field [1, 3]. Specifically, we utilize the state-of-the-art ResNet [2] network trained on millions of natural images, thus overcoming the limitation of data size. The residual architecture allows for the learning of "very deep" networks, which are empirically more accurate and easier to optimize.

Residual neural networks are a variant of Convolutional Neural Neteworks (CNNs) that employ shortcut connections (Fig. 1) to allow input from lower layers of the network to be available to nodes at higher layers. If a typical layer aims to learn a latent representation $F(x)$, a residual block models $H(x) = F(x) + x$ (see He et al. [2]). This allows multiple pathways for gradients to flow through the network, enabling the training of deeper networks without the burden of vanishing gradients.

We construct a deep residual network consisting of 18 layers modeled after the ResNet-18 architecture. We use the *pretrained* weights learned on the ImageNet data set. To account for task-specific differences, we only take the convolutional layers as filters, add two fully-connected layers (1000 and 100 hidden units respectively), and fine-tune the entire network on MRI images.

Permission to make digital or hard copies of part or all of this work for personal or classroom use is granted without fee provided that copies are not made or distributed for profit or commercial advantage and that copies bear this notice and the full citation on the first page. Copyrights for third-party components of this work must be honored. For all other uses, contact the owner/author(s).
ACM-BCB '17, August 20-23, 2017, Boston, MA, USA
© 2017 Copyright held by the owner/author(s).
ACM ISBN 978-1-4503-4722-8/17/08.
https://doi.org/10.1145/3107411.3108224

Model	AD vs. CN	3-way
Baseline CNN	73.8%	49.2%
ResNet	77.5%	50.8%
Pretrained ResNet	78.8%	56.1%
Pretrained ResNet + augmentation	**81.3%**	**56.8%**

Table 1: Accuracy on 2-way and 3-way diagnosis

2 RESULTS AND DISCUSSION

We ran experiments on 660 median axial brain slices from the Alzheimer's Disease Neuroimaging Initiative (188 diagnosed as Alzheimer's Disease (AD), 243 as Mild Cognitive Impairment (MCI), and 229 as Cognitively Normal (CN)) using an 80/20 train/test split. Table 1 shows the test-set accuracy on classifying AD vs. CN and the more difficult 3-way classification (AD vs. MCI vs. CN).

First, we trained two networks – the proposed approach above (pretrained ResNet) and a baseline single-layer CNN to approximate existing approaches [1, 3]. Our results show a large improvement in accuracy over the baseline CNN model on both tasks; thus we can conclude **the ResNet structure successfully adapts to the MRI domain and improves prediction**.

Next, we assess the relative importance of pretraining by comparing a randomly initialized ResNet and a pretrained ResNet (rows 2 and 3). The results show that **pretraining on non-medical images improves performance**, though the relative importance of the residual architecture and pretraining differs in the two tasks.

Lastly, a key method for regularizing networks and simulating more data is the use of real-time data augmentation (affine transformations of the data through rotations, flips and translations during training). The last two rows in Table 1 examine a pretrained ResNet without and with data augmentation, respectively. **Data augmentation improves accuracy on both tasks**.

REFERENCES

[1] Ashish Gupta, Murat Ayhan, and Anthony Maida. 2013. Natural Image Bases to Represent Neuroimaging Data. In *Proceedings of the 30th International Conference on Machine Learning*. Atlanta, Georgia, USA, 987–994.

[2] Kaiming He, Xiangyu Zhang, Shaoqing Ren, and Jian Sun. 2015. Deep Residual Learning for Image Recognition. (2015). arXiv:1512.03385

[3] A. Payan and G. Montana. 2015. Predicting Alzheimer's Disease: a neuroimaging study with 3D convolutional neural networks. (Feb. 2015). arXiv:1502.02506

Integrative Sufficient Dimension Reduction Methods for Multi-Omics Data Analysis*

Extended Abstract

Yashita Jain
Center for Bioinformatics and Computational Biology
University of Delaware
yashita@udel.edu

Shanshan Ding
Applied Economics and Statistics
Center for Bioinformatics and Computational Biology
University of Delaware
sding@udel.edu

ABSTRACT

With the advent of high throughput genome-wide assays it has become possible to simultaneously measure multiple types of genomic data. Several projects like TCGA, ICGC, NCI-60 has generated comprehensive, multi-dimensional maps of the key genomic changes like MiRNA, MRNA, proteomics etc. from cancer samples[2, 4]. These genomic data can be used for classifying tumour types[5]. Integrative analysis of these data from multiple sources can potentially provide additional biological insights, but methods to do any such analysis are lacking.

One of the widely used solutions to handle high dimension data is by removing redundant information in the integrated sample. Most of the expressed genes are overlapped and can be projected onto lower dimension, and then be used to classify different tumor types, without the loss of any/much information. Sufficient dimension reduction (SDR) [1], a supervised dimension reduction approach, can be ideal to achieve such a goal. In this paper, we propose a novel integrative SDR method that can reduce dimensions of multiple data types simultaneously while sharing common latent structures to improve prediction and interpretation. In particular, we extend the sliced inverse regression (SIR) technique, a major SDR method, to integrate multiple omits data for simultaneous dimension reduction.

SIR is a supervised dimension reduction method that assumes that the outcome variable Y depends on the predictor variable X through d unknown linear combinations of the predictor[3]. The predictor variable is replaced by its projection into a lower dimension subspace of the predictor space without the loss of information. The aim is to find the intersection of all the subspaces δ called the central susbspace (CS) of the predictor space satisfying the property

$$Y \perp\!\!\!\perp X | P_{\delta} X. \tag{1}$$

To integrate multiple types of data, we propose and implement a new integrative sufficient dimension reduction method extending SIR[3], called integrative SIR. The main idea is that we take into account all the multi-omics data information simultaneously while finding a basis matrix for each data type with some sharing latent structures. Finally, we get d dimension data which is much smaller than the original data dimension. The reduced dimension d was achieved by cross validation.

To demonstrate the integrated analysis of multi-omics data, we applied and compared conventional SIR and integrative SIR to analyze MRNA, MiRNA and proteomics expression profile of a subset of cell lines from the NCI-60 panel. The data used is taken from [6]. The outcomes we have to classify are CNS, Leukemia and Melanoma tumor types. We pre-screened 400 variables from each data type with the criteria of high variance. To find classification error, we performed random forest classification after we applied to each method with leave-one-out cross-validation. As a result, we found out that integrative SIR leads to less classification error as compared to conventional SIR.

To summarize, we proposed a new integrative SIR method, a supervised dimension reduction technique for integrative analysis of multi-omics data types. Unlike conventional SDR methods, the new approach can reduce the dimensions of multiple omics data simultaneously while sharing common latent structures across data types without losing any information in prediction. By efficiently capturing the common information, our numerical study shows that integrative SIR classifies tumor types more accurately as compared to conventional SDR methods.

*Produces the permission block, and copyright information

Permission to make digital or hard copies of part or all of this work for personal or classroom use is granted without fee provided that copies are not made or distributed for profit or commercial advantage and that copies bear this notice and the full citation on the first page. Copyrights for third-party components of this work must be honored. For all other uses, contact the owner/author(s).
ACM-BCB'17, August 20-23, 2017, Boston, MA, USA.
© 2017 Copyright held by the owner/author(s).
978-1-4503-4722-8/17/08.
DOI: http://dx.doi.org/10.1145/3107411.3108225

CCS CONCEPTS

•**Mathematics of computing** →**Dimensionality reduction;**

KEYWORDS

integrative genomic analysis; supervised learning; sufficient dimension reduction; sliced inverse regression; bioinformatics

REFERENCES

[1] R Dennis Cook. 1996. Graphics for regressions with a binary response. *J. Amer. Statist. Assoc.* 91, 435 (1996), 983–992.
[2] Amin Moghaddas Gholami et al. 2013. Global Proteome Analysis of the NCI-60 Cell Line Panel. *Cell Reports* 4, 3 (2013), 609 – 620. https://doi.org/10.1016/j.celrep.2013.07.018
[3] Ker-Chau Li. 1991. Sliced inverse regression for dimension reduction. *J. Amer. Statist. Assoc.* 86, 414 (1991), 316–327.
[4] Hongfang Liu, D'Andrade, et al. 2010. mRNA and microRNA expression profiles of the NCI-60 integrated with drug activities. *Molecular cancer therapeutics* 9, 5 (2010), 1080–1091.
[5] Jun Lu, Getz, et al. 2005. MicroRNA expression profiles classify human cancers. *nature* 435, 7043 (2005), 834–838.
[6] Chen Meng et al. 2016. Dimension reduction techniques for the integrative analysis of multi-omics data. *Briefings in bioinformatics* 17, 4 (2016), 628–641.

Predicting Breast Cancer Outcome under Different Treatments by Feature Selection Approaches

Huy Quang Pham
University of Dalat,
01 Phu Dong Thien Vuong,
Dalat, Vietnam
huypq@dlu.edu.vn

Luis Rueda
University of Windsor
401 Sunset Avenue
Windsor, ON, Canada
lrueda@uwindsor.ca

Alioune Ngom
University of Windsor
401 Sunset Avenue
Windsor, ON, Canada
angom@uwindsor.ca

ABSTRACT
Gene expression data have been studied in many researches to reveal the underlying mechanism of diseases. In this study, we applied feature selection techniques on breast cancer patients in the METABRIC Study to predict whether patients will be disease free or not, under different treatments. Our models yield excellent prediction results. Thus, the genes obtained by those models might help reveal the mechanisms of the disease, and these potential gene biomarkers can become targets for new therapies.

General Terms
Algorithms; Performance; Reliability.

Keywords
Breast cancer; survival, treatment; machine learning; classification; feature selection; bio-marker.

1. DATA
We applied feature selection techniques to predict whether patients will be disease free or not when treated with one of four types of treatments: chemotherapy (CT), hormone therapy (HT), radiation therapy (RT), or none of them (NONE). We used the Molecular Taxonomy of Breast Cancer International Consortium dataset [1] (METABRIC) containing 1904 patient gene expression profiles and 24369 genes. The data distribution is given in Table 1.

Table 1. Data distribution versus treatments

Data	#Disease Free	#Recurred
CT	26	19
HT	284	121
RT	174	54
NONE	82	207

2. METHODS AND RESULTS
The initial gene set for feature selection and classification were collected from literature including: (1) those significantly correlated to growth inhibitory effects of paclitaxel, tamoxifen, methotrexate, epirubicin, doxorubicin, and 5-fluorouracil [1]; (2) 173 genes from [2] which include 40 driver-genes; and (3) those whose mutual information versus the classes are in the top 100.

We have applied the following approaches: (1) Minimum Redundancy and Maximum Relevance (mRMR) for feature selection and support vector machines (SVM) for classification, denoted as mRMR_SVM; (2) mRMR for feature selection and Random Forest for classification, denoted as mRMR_RF; and, (3) using AFS [3] for feature selection, and SVM for classification, denoted AFS_SVM. The performances of these approaches are shown in Table 2. They are evaluated both in terms of accuracy (ACC), and Mathews correlation coefficient (MCC).

Table 2. Prediction performance

Data	Method	ACC	MCC	# Genes
CT	mRMR_SVM	**1.000**	**1.000**	6
	mRMR_RF	0.778	0.424	5
	AFS_SVM	**0.978**	**0.955**	7
HT	mRMR_ SVM	0.775	0.417	10
	mRMR_RF	0.785	0.445	21
	AFS_SVM	**0.798**	**0.484**	15
RT	mRMR_ SVM	**0.886**	**0.669**	9
	mRMR_RF	0.851	0.552	15
	AFS_SVM	0.864	0.594	6
NONE	mRMR_SVM	0.813	0.515	16
	mRMR_RF	**0.827**	**0.544**	7
	AFS_SVM	0.820	0.535	6

3. ACKNOWLEDGMENTS
This work has been partially supported by the Natural Sciences and Engineering Research Council of Canada (NSERC grants #RGPIN/2016-05017 and #RGPIN/05084-2014), and the Windsor Essex County Cancer Centre Foundation (WECCCF) Seeds4Hope grant #814221.

4. REFERENCES
[1] Mucaki EJ, Baranova K, Pham HQ *et al.* Predicting Outcomes of Hormone and Chemotherapy in the Molecular Taxonomy of Breast Cancer International Consortium (METABRIC) Study by Biochemically-inspired Machine Learning (version 3). F1000Research, 2017.

[2] Pereira, Bernard, et al. "The somatic mutation profiles of 2,433 breast cancers refines their genomic and transcriptomic landscapes." Nature communications 7, 2016.

[3] Huy Quang Pham, Alioune Ngom, and Luis Rueda. "A new feature selection approach for optimizing prediction models, applied to breast cancer subtype classification". Bioinformatics and Biomedicine (BIBM), 2016 IEEE International Conference on. IEEE, 2016.

Permission to make digital or hard copies of part or all of this work for personal or classroom use is granted without fee provided that copies are not made or distributed for profit or commercial advantage and that copies bear this notice and the full citation on the first page. Copyrights for third-party components of this work must be honored. For all other uses, contact the Owner/Author.
ACM-BCB '17, August 20-23, 2017, Boston, MA, USA
© 2017 Copyright is held by the owner/author(s).
ACM ISBN 978-1-4503-4722-8/17/08.
http://dx.doi.org/10.1145/3107411.3108226

Breaking Ties in Weighted Interactomes

Ibrahim Youssef
Biology Department, Reed College, Portland, OR 97202
Biomedical Engineering Dept, Cairo University, Giza, Egypt
youssefi@reed.edu

Anna Ritz
Biology Department
Reed College
Portland, OR 97202
aritz@reed.edu

ABSTRACT

Automatic signaling pathway reconstruction methods using protein-protein interactomes are hindered by the unit/coarsely-weighted edges that lead to many paths sharing the same cost. We propose to use gene expression as an orthologous dataset from the pathway of interest to re-prioritize tied paths. The proposed method promotes/demotes paths based on the number of inferred true pathway edges. In general, it can be applied to any signaling pathway reconstruction method that outputs an ordered list of paths, trees, or other subgraphs.

1 INTRODUCTION

Multiple computational methods have emerged to automatically reconstruct signaling pathways (SPs) from interactomes built from protein-protein interactions (PPIs). PathLinker [4] is one such SP reconstruction method that uses a weighted interactome and a known set of receptors and transcriptional regulators (TRs) of a specific SP to compute a set of shortest paths from the interactome PPIs that connect receptors to TRs. Though PathLinker showed promising results, we observed that a substantial number of the returned paths share the same path cost due to ties in the interactome weighted edges, and that this is not restricted only to the PathLinker interactome, but it is more pronounced in other interactomes such as the popular HIPPIE network [1], where 50% of the interactions share the same edge weight).

Contributions. We propose a framework which re-prioritizes PathLinker paths using an orthologous dataset relevant to the pathway of interest. Using the Wnt SP from the NetPath database [2] as a case study, we apply gene expression data from colon cancer samples, a disease that is known to dysregulate Wnt signaling [3], to the paths to "break" ties.

2 METHODS

Given a graph G with nodes V (proteins) and edges E (interactions), PathLinker outputs a ranked list of the k shortest paths, $\mathcal{P} = [P_1, P_2, \ldots, P_k]$, where a path $P_i \subset E$ is comprised of edges and it starts at a receptor and ends at a TR, with a path cost of w_i.

Path Reordering. Our method returns a subset of the paths $\mathcal{P}' \subseteq \mathcal{P}$ that are likely to contain true positive edges according to an orthologous dataset. For every node $v \in V$, we assign a binary classification label $y_v \in \{0, 1\}$ that is 1 if v is predicted to be a positive and 0 otherwise. Each edge $(u, v) \in E$ is then assigned a score $s_{uv} = y_u y_v$. We compute a total score $\mathcal{S}$ for each $P_i \in \mathcal{P}$: $\mathcal{S}(P_i) = \sum_{(u,v) \in P_i} s_{uv}$. The retained paths $\mathcal{P}'$ are those having non-zero scores, implying that at least one interaction connecting two proteins is predicted by the classifier to be a positive: $\mathcal{P}' = \{P_i : \mathcal{S}(P_i) > 0\}$. Then, $\mathcal{P}'$ is partitioned into ties: $\mathcal{P}' = [P_{w_1}, \ldots, P_{w_n}]$, where $P_{w_j} \subseteq \mathcal{P}'$ is the group of paths sharing the same path cost w_j, and $w_j < w_{j+1}$ for $1 \leq j < n$ for n distinct costs. Paths $P_i \in P_{w_j}$ within each group are reordered according to $\mathcal{S}(P_i)$.

Classification Scheme. We used a support vector machine (SVM) classifier with a polynomial kernel of the third degree trained with the nodes gene expression values. A 2-fold cross validation (CV) scheme was used to test the trained SVM model.

Permission to make digital or hard copies of part or all of this work for personal or classroom use is granted without fee provided that copies are not made or distributed for profit or commercial advantage and that copies bear this notice and the full citation on the first page. Copyrights for third-party components of this work must be honored. For all other uses, contact the owner/author(s).
ACM-BCB '17, August 20-23, 2017, Boston, MA, USA
© 2017 Copyright held by the owner/author(s).
ACM ISBN 978-1-4503-4722-8/17/08.
https://doi.org/10.1145/3107411.3108228

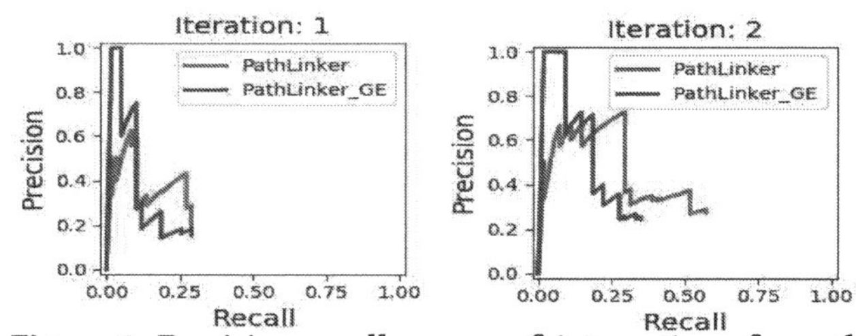

Figure 1: Precision-recall curves of interactions from the original paths (red) and the re-ordered paths (blue).

3 RESULTS AND CONCLUSION

Figure 1 shows the precision-recall (PR) curves for the original PathLinker (in red) and the proposed algorithms (in blue) for the two CV iterations. The proposed method has higher precision at the early recall values, meaning that the first shortest paths contain more true positives and have less negatives. This is because some positives were ranked higher (promoted) and some negatives were ranked lower (demoted) or removed completely.

In conclusion, many interactome edges tend to have equal weights leading to ties in the ranked outputs. Using gene expression data as a post-processing method improves the precision of the output by re-prioritizing paths that are relevant to Wnt signaling. Importantly, the precision increases at low values of recall, denoting that there are more positives earlier in the ranked list of interactions. Future work includes building a more sophisticated predictor of signaling relevance from gene expression data and applying our method to other interactomes and signaling reconstruction algorithms.

REFERENCES

[1] G. Alanis-Lobato et al. 2017. HIPPIE v2.0: enhancing meaningfulness and reliability of protein-protein interaction networks. *Nucleic Acids Research* 45 (2017), D408–D414.
[2] K. Kandasamy et al. 2010. NetPath: a public resource of curated signal transduction pathways. *Genome Biol.* 11, 1 (Jan 2010), R3.
[3] D. M. Muzny et al. 2012. Comprehensive molecular characterization of human colon and rectal cancer. *Nature* 487, 7407 (Jul 2012), 330–337.
[4] A. Ritz et al. 2016. Pathways on demand: automated reconstruction of human signaling networks. *npj Systems Biology and Applications* 2 (2016), 16002.

Microbiome Dynamics as Predictors of Lung Transplant Rejection

Ahmed Metwally[1,2], Christian Ascoli[2], Kalista Andropolis[2], Ravi Ranjan[2], Yang Dai[1], Thomas Ferkol[4], Patricia Finn[2], David Perkins[1,2,3]

[1] Department of Bioengineering, University of Illinois, Chicago, IL, USA
[2] Department of Medicine, University of Illinois, Chicago, IL, USA
[3] Department of Surgery, University of Illinois, Chicago, IL, USA
[4] Washington University School of Medicine, St. Louis, MO, USA
E-mail: ametwa2@uic.edu

ABSTRACT

Lung transplantation offers the only treatment for multiple chronic diseases. Transplantation is dependent upon successful resistance to organ rejection. For children, a vulnerable population, the five and ten-year survival for lung transplants is only 52% and 29%, respectively. The reason for this low survival rate is primary due to chronic lung graft rejection in the form of Bronchiolitis Obliterans Syndrome (BOS). Our hypothesis is that the changes in the composition of the pulmonary microbiome are associated with the development and progression of graft rejection which is in turn related to detrimental cardiopulmonary outcomes and poor overall survival in lung transplant recipients. Samples were obtained from 6 pediatric lung transplant patients over multiple time points. Bronchoalveolar lavage (BAL) samples were collected at approximately 7 time points for each subject. The DNA isolated from BAL is sequenced on an Illumina MiSeq machine. The longitudinal taxonomic profiles demonstrate the phylum Proteobacteria to be the most abundant across all samples. This suggests that certain members of this phylum may indicate a core microbiome in the lung graft. The association between Pseudomonas aeruginosa overgrowth and clinically suspected infection requiring antibiotic therapy was evaluated throughout the study period employing a Smoothing Splines ANOVA on the microbial taxonomic time series' profile. Overgrowth of Cellulomonas is associated with infection during the early days after the lung transplantation. Conversely, Bradyrhizobium, Acetobacter, and Coriobacterium are more abundant in the non-infected subjects. We also propose MetaLonDA, an R package that can be used to accurately detect metagenomic features (species, genes) relating to the phenotype or disease status, and accurately detect the starting and ending time points when the differences arise. It is able to handle sampling at different time points, unequal number of time points among the subjects, and long gap between longitudinal time points.

Permission to make digital or hard copies of part or all of this work for personal or classroom use is granted without fee provided that copies are not made or distributed for profit or commercial advantage and that copies bear this notice and the full citation on the first page. Copyrights for third-party components of this work must be honored. For all other uses, contact the Owner/Author.
ACM-BCB '17, August 20-23, 2017, Boston, MA, USA.
© 2017 Copyright is held by the owner/author(s).
ACM ISBN 978-1-4503-4722-8/17/08.
http://dx.doi.org/10.1145/3107411.3108229

Analysis of Controls in ChIP-seq

Aseel Awdeh
University of Ottawa
75 Laurier Ave E
Ottawa, ON K1N6N5
aseel.awdeh@gmail.com

Theodore J. Perkins
Ottawa Hospital Research Institute
501 Smyth Road
Ottawa, ON K1H8L6
tperkins@ohri.ca

ABSTRACT

The chromatin immunoprecipitation followed by high throughput sequencing (ChIP-seq) method, initially introduced a decade ago, is widely used by the scientific community to detect protein/DNA binding and histone modifications across the genome in various cell lines. Every experiment is prone to noise and bias, and ChIP-seq experiments are no exception. To alleviate bias, incorporation of control datasets in ChIP-seq analysis is an essential step. The controls are used to detect background signal, whilst the ChIP-seq experiment captures the true binding or histone modification signal. However, a recurrent issue is the existence of noise and bias in the controls themselves, as well as different types of bias in ChIP-seq experiments. Thus, depending on which controls are used, peak calling can produce different results (i.e., binding site positions) for the same ChIP-seq experiment. Consequently, generating "smart" controls, which model the non-signal effect for a specific ChIP-seq experiment, could enhance contrast and thus increase the reliability and reproducibility of the results. Our analysis aims to improve our understanding of ChIP-seq controls and their biases. We use unsupervised clustering and dimensionality reduction techniques to compare 160 controls for the K562 cell line in the ENCODE project, finding distincting groupings of controls which correlate to experimental characteristics. To customize a control for each ChIP-seq experiment, we use LASSO regression to fit a sparse set of controls to each of 500 ChIP-seq experiments (again, from ENCODE data for the K562 cell line). We look at how many controls are selected, which controls are used per ChIP-seq experiment, and how they are related to the different ChIP-seq experiment characteristics. Perhaps most surprisingly, we find that the LASSO models are not particularly sparse, often including half of the possible controls to model any given ChIP-seq. Cross-validation as well as testing with smaller sets of candidate controls proves that such large numbers of controls are beneficial for modeling ChIP-seq background distributions. We also observe clusters of ChIP-seq experiments that tend to rely on clusters of controls, and we look at the experimental characteristics that tend to cause a given control to be useful in modeling the background of a given ChIP-seq experiment. Through these analyses, we attempt to answer largely-unstudied questions regarding how much control data and of what types are useful in ChIP-seq analysis, and how suitable controls can be matched to ChIP-seq datasets.

Permission to make digital or hard copies of part or all of this work for personal or classroom use is granted without fee provided that copies are not made or distributed for profit or commercial advantage and that copies bear this notice and the full citation on the first page. Copyrights for third-party components of this work must be honored. For all other uses, contact the owner/author(s).
ACM-BCB'17, , August 20-23, 2017, Boston, MA, USA.
© 2017 Copyright held by the owner/author(s).
ACM ISBN 978-1-4503-4722-8/17/08.
https://doi.org/10.1145/3107411.3108230

CCS CONCEPTS

• **Applied computing → Sequencing and genotyping technologies; Computational genomics; Bioinformatics;**

REFERENCES

[1] Laura Arrigoni, Andreas S Richter, Emily Betancourt, Kerstin Bruder, Sarah Diehl, Thomas Manke, and Ulrike Bönisch. 2015. Standardizing chromatin research: a simple and universal method for ChIP-seq. *Nucleic acids research* (2015), gkv1495.

[2] Yuval Benjamini and Terence P Speed. 2012. Summarizing and correcting the GC content bias in high-throughput sequencing. *Nucleic acids research* (2012), gks001.

[3] Yiwen Chen, Nicolas Negre, Qunhua Li, Joanna O Mieczkowska, Matthew Slattery, Tao Liu, Yong Zhang, Tae-Kyung Kim, Housheng Hansen He, Jennifer Zieba, and others. 2012. Systematic evaluation of factors influencing ChIP-seq fidelity. *Nature methods* 9, 6 (2012), 609–614.

[4] ENCODE Project Consortium and others. 2004. The ENCODE (ENCyclopedia of DNA elements) project. *Science* 306, 5696 (2004), 636–640.

[5] Christoffer Flensburg, Sarah A Kinkel, Andrew Keniry, Marnie E Blewitt, and Alicia Oshlack. 2014. A comparison of control samples for ChIP-seq of histone modifications. *Frontiers in genetics* 5 (2014), 329.

[6] Naozumi Hiranuma, Scott Lundberg, and Su-In Lee. 2016. CloudControl: Leveraging many public ChIP-seq control experiments to better remove background noise. In *Proceedings of the 7th ACM International Conference on Bioinformatics, Computational Biology, and Health Informatics.* ACM, 191–199.

[7] Mehran Karimzadeh, Carl Ernst, Anshul Kundaje, and Michael M Hoffman. 2016. Umap and Bismap: quantifying genome and methylome mappability. *bioRxiv* (2016), 095463.

[8] Stephen G Landt, Georgi K Marinov, Anshul Kundaje, Pouya Kheradpour, Florencia Pauli, Serafim Batzoglou, Bradley E Bernstein, Peter Bickel, James B Brown, Philip Cayting, and others. 2012. ChIP-seq guidelines and practices of the ENCODE and modENCODE consortia. *Genome research* 22, 9 (2012), 1813–1831.

[9] Ben Langmead, Cole Trapnell, Mihai Pop, and Steven L Salzberg. 2009. Ultrafast and memory-efficient alignment of short DNA sequences to the human genome. *Genome biology* 10, 3 (2009), R25.

[10] Heng Li and Richard Durbin. 2009. Fast and accurate short read alignment with Burrows–Wheeler transform. *Bioinformatics* 25, 14 (2009), 1754–1760.

[11] Georgi K Marinov, Anshul Kundaje, Peter J Park, and Barbara J Wold. 2014. Large-scale quality analysis of published ChIP-seq data. *G3: Genes| Genomes| Genetics* 4, 2 (2014), 209–223.

[12] Clifford A Meyer and X Shirley Liu. 2014. Identifying and mitigating bias in next-generation sequencing methods for chromatin biology. *Nature Reviews Genetics* 15, 11 (2014), 709–721.

[13] Ryuichiro Nakato and Katsuhiko Shirahige. 2016. Recent advances in ChIP-seq analysis: from quality management to whole-genome annotation. *Briefings in bioinformatics* (2016), bbw023.

[14] Parameswaran Ramachandran, Gareth A Palidwor, and Theodore J Perkins. 2015. BIDCHIPS: bias decomposition and removal from ChIP-seq data clarifies true binding signal and its functional correlates. *Epigenetics & chromatin* 8, 1 (2015), 33.

[15] Joel Rozowsky, Ghia Euskirchen, Raymond K Auerbach, Zhengdong D Zhang, Theodore Gibson, Robert Bjornson, Nicholas Carriero, Michael Snyder, and Mark B Gerstein. 2009. PeakSeq enables systematic scoring of ChIP-seq experiments relative to controls. *Nature biotechnology* 27, 1 (2009), 66–75.

[16] Mingxiang Teng and Rafael A Irizarry. 2016. Accounting for GC-content bias reduces systematic errors and batch effects in ChIP-Seq peak callers. *bioRxiv* (2016), 090704.

[17] Reuben Thomas, Sean Thomas, Alisha K Holloway, and Katherine S Pollard. 2016. Features that define the best ChIP-seq peak calling algorithms. *Briefings in bioinformatics* (2016), bbw035.

SeqAnt: Cloud-Based Whole-Genome Annotation and Search

Alex V. Kotlar
Emory University School of Medicine
615 Michael St NE Atlanta, GA, USA
akotlar@emory.edu

Cristina E. Trevino
Emory University School of Medicine
615 Michael St NE Atlanta, GA, USA
c.e.trevino@emory.edu

Michael E. Zwick
Emory University School of Medicine
615 Michael St NE Atlanta, GA, USA
mzwick@emory.edu

David J. Cutler
Emory University School of Medicine,
615 Michael St NE Atlanta, GA, USA
djcutle@emory.edu

Thomas S. Wingo
Atlanta VA Medical Center,
1670 Clairmont Rd Decatur, GA, USA
thomas.wingo@emory.edu

ABSTRACT

Describing, prioritizing, and selecting alleles from large sequencing experiments remains technically challenging. SeqAnt (https://seqant.emory.edu) is the first online, cloud-based application that makes these tasks accessible for non-programmers, even for terabyte-sized experiments containing thousands of whole-genome samples. It rapidly describes the alleles found within submitted VCF files, and then indexes the results in a natural-language search engine, which enables users to locate alleles of interest in milliseconds using normal English phrases. Our results show that SeqAnt decreases processing time by orders of magnitude and that its search engine can be used to precisely identify alleles by phenotype, genomic structure, and population genetics characteristics.

CCS CONCEPTS

• **Applied computing → Life and medical sciences -> Bioinformatics**

KEYWORDS

Genomics; bioinformatics; big data; search; network architecture

2 EXPERIMENTAL AND COMPUTATIONAL DETAILS

2.1 SeqAnt Annotation and Search Architecture

SeqAnt's open-source annotator uses the LMDB database to scale to N threads. SeqAnt's Lucene-based search engine indexes n-grams for flexible queries. Submitted VCF files are distributed to N computational nodes in AWS and processed (Figure 1).

Permission to make digital or hard copies of part or all of this work for personal or classroom use is granted without fee provided that copies are not made or distributed for profit or commercial advantage and that copies bear this notice and the full citation on the first page. Copyrights for third-party components of this work must be honored. For all other uses, contact the Owner/Author.
ACM-BCB '17, August 20-23, 2017, Boston, MA, USA
© 2017 Copyright is held by the owner/author(s).
ACM ISBN 978-1-4503-4722-8/17/08.
http://dx.doi.org/10.1145/3107411.3108231

RESULTS AND DISCUSSION

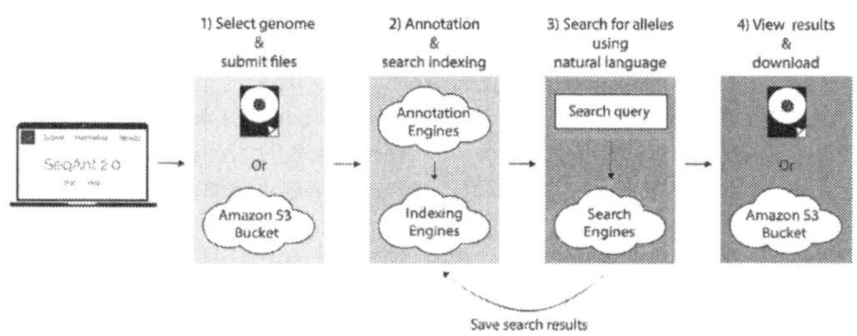

Figure 1: Seqant Architecture

3.1 Annotation Performance

Online, SeqAnt was the only program able to annotate the full 1000 Genomes Phase 3 VCF file ($8.5x10^7$ alleles, 800GB, 3.67 hours). Offline, on an i3.2xlarge EC2 instance, SeqAnt was 57x faster than ANNOVAR[1] and 425x faster than VEP[2].

3.2 Search Performance

The query "exonic" returned exonic variants, with a transition / transversion ratio consistent with coding regions (2.92, Query #1, Table 1). The query "cadd > 20 maf < 0.001 pathogenic expert review missense" returned rare, predicted deleterious alleles (Query #2, Table 1). This query could be written using partial words ("pathogen"), possessive nouns ("expert's"), different tenses ("reviews"), and synonyms ("nonsynonymous") without changing results. The query "early-onset breast cancer" returned alleles in *BRCA1* and *BRCA2* (Query #3, Table 1).

Table 1: SeqAnt online search performance with Phase 3

Query	Time(s)	Alleles	Tr/Tv
1	0.15 ± 0.04	993,330	2.92
2	0.12 ± 0.02	65	1.71
3	0.04 ± 0.02	4,335	2.48

References

[1] Yang, H. & Wang, K 2015. Genomic variant annotation and prioritization with ANNOVAR and wANNOVAR. *Nat Proc* 10, 1556-1556 (2015)

[2] McLaren, W. et al. 2016. The Ensembl Variant Effect Predictor. *BMC Bioinformatics* 17, 102 (2016).

A Tool for Predicting the Dark Side of Enzymes

Linfeng Liu
Tufts University
161 College Avenue
Medford, MA
+1(339)224-8906
linfeng.liu@tufts.edu

Soha Hassoun
Tufts University
161 College Avenue
Medford, MA
+1(617)627-5177
soha.hassoun@tufts.edu

ABSTRACT
Early studies considered enzymes as specific catalysts following the classical rule, "one enzyme, one activity". Evidence, however, suggests that some enzymes have a promiscuous (dark) side and act on substrates other than the preferred substrate [1]. The ability to predict products due to enzyme promiscuity can yield beneficial results across many areas in biotechnology, including discovering novel pathways to synthesize target molecules, and identifying derivatives in of ingested foreign chemicals. In our group, we have recently used enzyme promiscuity to annotate measurements collected via untargeted metabolomics from a biological sample. We were able to experimentally validate our finding, thus providing the first demonstration of predicting and verifying *in vivo* enzyme promiscuity [2]. To this end, it would be advantageous to have a reliable tool for predicting metabolic derivatives due to promiscuous enzymes.

In this work, we create a tool, PROXIMAL II, that generalizes the methodology in PROXIMAL [3]. PROXIMAL II allows the end user to specify a query molecules and a set of reactions and then predict potential derivative products. We construct biotransformation operators lookup table using Reaction Center, Difference Region, and Matched Region (RDM) patterns [4] and molecular substructures. The RDM patterns specify local regions of similarities/differences for reactant-product pairs based on chemical structure [5]. For each potential R pattern matched for the query molecule, a set of transformations are looked up in the table and applied to the query molecule, thus generating a set of possible transformed molecules. PROXIMAL II will provide a variety of predicting capabilities, based on EC number, KEGG reaction number, or organism.

Permission to make digital or hard copies of part or all of this work for personal or classroom use is granted without fee provided that copies are not made or distributed for profit or commercial advantage and that copies bear this notice and the full citation on the first page. Copyrights for third-party components of this work must be honored. For all other uses, contact the Owner/Author.
ACM-BCB '17, August 20-23, 2017, Boston, MA, USA
© 2017 Copyright is held by the owner/author(s).
ACM ISBN 978-1-4503-4722-8/17/08.
http://dx.doi.org/10.1145/3107411.3108232

General Terms
Algorithms

Keywords
Biotransformation operators; Enzyme promiscuity

REFERENCES

[1] R. A. Jensen, *Annual Reviews in Microbiology* **1976**, *30*, 409-425.

[2] N. Hassanpour, N. Alden, K. Lee and S. Hassoun, **In preparation.**

[3] M. Yousofshahi, S. Manteiga, C. Wu, K. Lee and S. Hassoun, *BMC systems biology* **2015**, *9*, 94.

[4] M. Oh, T. Yamada, M. Hattori, S. Goto and M. Kanehisa, *Journal of chemical information and modeling* **2007**, *47*, 1702-1712.

[5] M. Hattori, Y. Okuno, S. Goto and M. Kanehisa, *Journal of the American Chemical Society* **2003**, *125*, 11853-11865.

Pathway Enrichment Analysis for Untargeted Metabolomics

Vladimir Porokhin
Tufts University
Department of Computer Science
vporok01@eecs.tufts.edu

Xinmeng Li
Tufts University
Department of Computer Science
xinmeng.li@tufts.edu

Soha Hassoun
Tufts University
Department of Computer Science
soha@cs.tufts.edu

KEYWORDS

Metabolomics; *in silico* fragmentation; metabolite annotation; pathway enrichment; mass spectrometry

ABSTRACT

Metabolomics-based studies have provided critical insights across many applications and now offer researchers an opportunity to collect information about thousands of small molecules in-bulk through untargeted metabolomics. However, taking advantage of this new development requires accurate identification of metabolites and their biological significance in a given sample, which unfortunately remains difficult. Pathway enrichment is a powerful method that can aid in addressing those tasks, but existing techniques intended for gene enrichment analysis are not directly applicable to untargeted metabolomics.

In this poster we address the following problem: given a network model of the biological sample and a likelihood score of observing metabolites (nodes) within the network, compute the enrichment of pathways within the network model. We approach this challenge as an optimization problem, where a solution is defined as a particular assignment of mass features to candidate metabolites. The method generates possible assignments of features to compounds using *in silico* fragmentation tools (e.g., MetFrag [1], CFM-ID [2], and CSI:FingerID [3]) and spectral database (e.g., MassBank [4]) and then attempts to iteratively improve a possible solution.

By developing this method, we enable the use of pathway enrichment as an effective way of metabolite identification in untargeted metabolomics.

Permission to make digital or hard copies of part or all of this work for personal or classroom use is granted without fee provided that copies are not made or distributed for profit or commercial advantage and that copies bear this notice and the full citation on the first page. Copyrights for third-party components of this work must be honored. For all other uses, contact the Owner/Author.
ACM-BCB '17, August 20-23, 2017, Boston, MA, USA
© 2017 Copyright is held by the owner/author(s).
ACM ISBN 978-1-4503-4722-8/17/08.
http://dx.doi.org/10.1145/3107411.3108233

REFERENCES

[1] Wolf, S., et al., *In silico fragmentation for computer assisted identification of metabolite mass spectra.* BMC Bioinformatics, 2010. **11**: p. 148.
[2] Allen, F., R. Greiner, and D. Wishart, *Competitive fragmentation modeling of ESI-MS/MS spectra for putative metabolite identification.* Metabolomics, 2015. **11**(1): p. 98-110.
[3] Dührkop, K., et al., *Searching molecular structure databases with tandem mass spectra using CSI: FingerID.* Proceedings of the National Academy of Sciences, 2015. **112**(41): p. 12580-12585.
[4] Horai, H., et al., *MassBank: a public repository for sharing mass spectral data for life sciences.* J Mass Spectrom, 2010. **45**(7): p. 703-14.

Towards the Design of Matrix Metalloproteinases (MMP) Antibody Sequences

Xinmeng Li
Tufts University
161 College Avenue
Medford, MA
+1(339)674-8882
xinmeng.li@tufts.edu

James Van Deventer
Tufts University
4 Colby Street
Medford, MA
+1(617)627-6339
james.van_deventer@tufts.edu

Soha Hassoun
Tufts University
161 College Avenue
Medford, MA
+1(617)627-5177
soha.hassoun@tufts.edu

ABSTRACT

Matrix metalloproteinases (MMPs) are a family of enzymes dependent on metal ion cofactors that cleave the proteins found in the extracellular matrix and proteins involved in signalling processes in humans. These proteins play many important roles in normal physiology and development, but under pathological conditions, disregulated MMP activity can lead to cancer progression, undesired inflammation, and numerous other conditions [1]. Biological inhibitors of MMPs in the form of antibodies offer an appealing method for disrupting MMP enzyme activity, as antibodies are capable of potently, specifically inhibiting individual MMPs [2] in ways that traditional small molecules cannot [3]. The key challenge in establishing antibody-based inhibition as a general strategy for interfering with the pathologic functions of MMPs is the lack of fundamental information relating the amino acid sequences of inhibitory antibodies to their unique properties as inhibitors.

In this poster, we present a method for analyzing protein sequences to uncover salient features of sequences of antibodies capable of binding to and inhibiting MMPs. The method consists of the following steps. First, we number antibody sequences [4] and divide them into frameworks [6], scaffolds that shape the antibodies' overall structures, and complementarity determining regions (CDRs) [5], peptide loops that directly contact the target MMP or other biological target. Second, we extract frameworks and CDRs [7] from the sequences. Third, we identify the most distinguishing features of antibody utilizing feature selection and machine learning algorithms. We expect to find distinct features of antibodies that bind or inhibit MMPs with this method. Distinct features can be further experimentally evaluated by altering the features unique to MMP-binding or MMP-inhibiting antibodies to assess their importance.

Permission to make digital or hard copies of part or all of this work for personal or classroom use is granted without fee provided that copies are not made or distributed for profit or commercial advantage and that copies bear this notice and the full citation on the first page. Copyrights for third-party components of this work must be honored. For all other uses, contact the Owner/Author.

ACM-BCB '17, August 20-23, 2017, Boston, MA, USA
© 2017 Copyright is held by the owner/author(s).
ACM ISBN 978-1-4503-4722-8/17/08.
http://dx.doi.org/10.1145/3107411.3108234

General Terms

Algorithms; Design; Experimentation.

Keywords

Metrix metalloproteinases; Antibody; Sequence analysis.

REFERENCES

[1] Kessenbrock, K., C.-Y. Wang, and Z. Werb, Matrix metalloproteinases in stem cell regulation and cancer. Matrix biology, 2015. 44: p. 184-190.

[2] Devy, L., et al., Selective inhibition of matrix metalloproteinase-14 blocks tumor growth, invasion, and angiogenesis. Cancer research, 2009. 69(4): p. 1517-1526.

[3] Vandenbroucke, R.E. and C. Libert, Is there new hope for therapeutic matrix metalloproteinase inhibition? Nature reviews Drug discovery, 2014. 13(12): p. 904-927.

[4] Dunbar, J. and C.M. Deane, ANARCI: antigen receptor numbering and receptor classification. Bioinformatics, 2015: p. btv552.

[5] Al-Lazikani, B., A.M. Lesk, and C. Chothia, Standard conformations for the canonical structures of immunoglobulins. Journal of molecular biology, 1997. 273(4): p. 927-948.

[6] Brochet, X., M.-P. Lefranc, and V. Giudicelli, IMGT/V-QUEST: the highly customized and integrated system for IG and TR standardized VJ and VDJ sequence analysis. Nucleic acids research, 2008. 36(suppl 2): p. W503-W508.

[7] Marcatili, P., A. Rosi, and A. Tramontano, PIGS: automatic prediction of antibody structures. Bioinformatics, 2008. 24(17): p. 1953-1954.

ProSol DB: A Protein Solubility Database

Sara A. Amin
Tufts University
161 College Avenue
Medford, MA
sara.amin@tufts.edu

Venkatesh Endalur Gopinarayanan
Tufts University
4 Colby Street,
Medford, MA
Venkatesh.Endalur_Gopinarayanan@tufts.edu

Nikhil U. Nair
Tufts University
4 Colby Street
Medford, MA
Nikhil.Nair@tufts.edu

Soha Hassoun
Tufts University
161 College Avenue
Medford, MA
Soha.hassoun@tufts.edu

ABSTRACT

Engineering non-native synthesis pathways in microbial hosts has shown promise in producing commercially useful molecules. The selection of highly soluble protein sequences to implement catalyzing reactions along synthesis pathways can be facilitated by predicting the solubility of protein sequences in the host. Current solubility predictors apply machine-learning algorithms, such as Support Vector Machines (SVM) and Neural Networks (NN), to predict solubility using protein sequence features such as hydrophilicity, net charge and α-helix. Features are then used to build classifiers [1, 2], one-layered logistic regression models [3], or more sophisticated multi-layered models [4, 5] that determine protein solubility.

We present in this poster a database, referred to as Protein Solubility Database (*ProSol DB*), that allows for quick lookup of predicted solubility values using Enzyme Commission (EC) numbers. We used *ccSOL omics* [6] to compute solubility prediction scores for various proteins from *UniProtKB* in *Escherichia coli*. *ProSol DB* serves as a source of identifying protein sequences with high predicted solubility scores eliminating the need of recurring calls to protein solubility predictors. Combining the *ProSol* DB with synthesis pathway tools can assist in avoiding experimental efforts spent on expressing low solubility enzymes when more soluble alternatives are identified. This work promises to expedite the design-build-test cycle of metabolic engineering efforts.

Keywords

ProSol DB; Protein Solubility; Metabolic Engineering

Permission to make digital or hard copies of part or all of this work for personal or classroom use is granted without fee provided that copies are not made or distributed for profit or commercial advantage and that copies bear this notice and the full citation on the first page. Copyrights for third-party components of this work must be honored. For all other uses, contact the Owner/Author.
ACM-BCB '17, August 20-23, 2017, Boston, MA, USA
© 2017 Copyright is held by the owner/author(s).
ACM ISBN 978-1-4503-4722-8/17/08.
http://dx.doi.org/10.1145/3107411.3108235

ACKNOWLEDGMENTS

This work was supported by the National Science Foundation (NSF) under Grant CISE 1421972

REFERENCES

[1] Wilkinson, D.L. and R.G. Harrison, *Predicting the solubility of recombinant proteins in Escherichia coli.* Bio/technology (Nature Publishing Company), 1991. **9**(5): p. 443-448.

[2] Bertone, P., et al., *SPINE: an integrated tracking database and data mining approach for identifying feasible targets in high-throughput structural proteomics.* Nucleic acids research, 2001. **29**(13): p. 2884-2898.

[3] Diaz, A.A., et al., *Prediction of protein solubility in Escherichia coli using logistic regression.* Biotechnology and bioengineering, 2010. **105**(2): p. 374-383.

[4] Smialowski, P., et al., *PROSO II–a new method for protein solubility prediction.* Febs Journal, 2012. **279**(12): p. 2192-2200.

[5] Magnan, C.N., A. Randall, and P. Baldi, *SOLpro: accurate sequence-based prediction of protein solubility.* Bioinformatics, 2009. **25**(17): p. 2200-2207.

[6] Agostini, F., et al., *ccSOL omics: a webserver for solubility prediction of endogenous and heterologous expression in Escherichia coli.* Bioinformatics, 2014. **30**(20): p. 2975-2977.

Building a Molecular Taxonomy of Disease

Jisoo Park
Tufts University
161 College Avenue
Medford, Massachusetts 02155
jisoo.park@tufts.edu

Benjamin J. Hescott
Tufts University
161 College Avenue
Medford, Massachusetts 02155
hescott@cs.tufts.edu

Donna K. Slonim
Tufts University
161 College Avenue
Medford, Massachusetts 02155
slonim@cs.tufts.edu

KEYWORDS

Disease Ontology, Disease Taxonomy, Disease-gene association, Molecular Disease Hierarchy

ACM Reference format:
Jisoo Park, Benjamin J. Hescott, and Donna K. Slonim. 2017. Building a Molecular Taxonomy of Disease. In *Proceedings of ACM-BCB '17, Boston, MA, USA, August 20-23, 2017,* 1 pages.
https://doi.org/10.1145/3107411.3108236

1 INTRODUCTION

The advent of high throughput technologies contributes to the rapid growth of molecular-level knowledge about human disease. However, existing disease taxonomies tend to focus on either physiological characterizations of disease or the organizational and billing needs of hospitals. Most fail to fully incorporate our rapidly increasing knowledge about molecular causes of disease. More modern disease taxonomies would presumably be built based on the combination of clinical, physiological, and molecular data. In this study, we analyzed our ability to infer disease relationships from molecular data alone. This approach may provide insights into how to ultimately build more modern taxonomies of disease.

2 RESULTS

We developed a new technique we call Parent Promotion to infer hierarchical relationships between disease terms using disease-gene association data. We compare the performance of our method with both an established ontology inference method (CliXO) [3] and a minimum weight spanning tree approach. Evaluation of these methods is not trivial because there is no gold standard. We address this problem by comparing our inferred disease hierarchies to two existing disease hierarchies known to be somewhat suitable for molecular analyses and comparisons [1]: the Medical Subject Headings (MeSH) [4] category C forest of diseases, and the Disease Ontology (DO) [2, 5]. We introduce several evaluation metrics suitable for cross-ontology comparisons.

Our comparison provides insights about the inference algorithms, evaluation metrics, impact of molecular data on the performance of the inference methods, and the current molecular content of parts of MeSH and the DO. Our results suggest that the Parent Promotion method performs well in most cases. We observed that performance across MeSH trees is correlated between inference methods, suggesting that disease relationships in some MeSH categories are inherently easier to learn than others. Inferred relationships are more consistent with those in smaller disease trees (or networks) than larger ones, with some notable exceptions that may correlate with higher molecular content. The exceptions include some MeSH disease trees containing well-studied diseases, such as the Endocrine System Disease tree, containing diabetes and ovarian and pancreatic cancer; or the Respiratory Tract Disease tree, containing asthma and COPD. We also observed that adding more molecular data improves the performance of all inference methods. Finally, by examining inferred edges connecting pairs of disease terms not previously known to be connected, we discovered novel yet plausible disease relationships that may suggest new therapies.

Permission to make digital or hard copies of part or all of this work for personal or classroom use is granted without fee provided that copies are not made or distributed for profit or commercial advantage and that copies bear this notice and the full citation on the first page. Copyrights for third-party components of this work must be honored. For all other uses, contact the owner/author(s).
ACM-BCB '17, August 20-23, 2017, Boston, MA, USA
© 2017 Copyright held by the owner/author(s).
ACM ISBN 978-1-4503-4722-8/17/08.
https://doi.org/10.1145/3107411.3108236

3 CONCLUSIONS

Our experiments provide insights about inferring relationships between disease terms using disease genes alone. They imply that disease gene information can form an important part of the foundation of modern disease taxonomies. Our results also suggest future work, including exploration of the prospect of novel disease term discovery from molecular data, and an investigation of methods to combine molecular data with anatomical and clinical knowledge.

ACKNOWLEDGMENTS

We thank Michael Kramer for providing implementation of CliXO along with thoughtful advice, Inbar Fried for comments about measurement for network (ontology) alignment, and members of the Tufts Bioinformatics and Computational Biology group for helpful feedback and comments. We gratefully acknowledge the support of NIH R01 HD 076140.

REFERENCES

[1] Susan Desmond-Hellmann, Charles L. Sawyers, et al. 2011. *Toward Precision Medicine: Building a knowledge network for biomedical research and a new taxonomy of disease.* Technical Report. National Research Council.
[2] Pan Du, Gang Feng, Jared Flatow, Jie Song, Michelle Holko, Warren A. Kibbe, and Simon M. Lin. 2009. From disease ontology to disease-ontology lite: statistical methods to adapt a general-purpose ontology for the test of gene-ontology associations. *Bioinformatics* 25, 12 (2009), i63–i68.
[3] Michael Kramer, Janusz Dutkowski, Michael Yu, Vineet Bafna, and Trey Ideker. 2014. Inferring gene ontologies from pairwise similarity data. *Bioinformatics* 30 (2014), i34–i42.
[4] Henry J. Lowe and G. Octo Barnett. 1994. Understanding and Using the Medical Subject Headings (MeSH) Vocabulary to Perform Literature Searches. *JAMA* 271, 14 (April 1994), 1103–1108.
[5] Lynn Marie Schriml, Cesar Arze, Suvarna Nadendla, Yu-Wei Wayne Chang, Mark Mazaitis, Victor Felix, Gang Feng, and Warren Alden Kibbe. 2011. Disease Ontology: a backbone for disease semantic integration. *Nucleic Acids Research* 40, Database issue (2011), D940–D946.

Network Analysis of Correlated Mutations in Influenza

Uday Yallapragada
School of Systems Biology
George Mason University
Manassas, VA 20110
uyallapr@gmu.edu

Iosif I. Vaisman
School of Systems Biology
George Mason University
Manassas, VA 20110
ivaisman@gmu.edu

ABSTRACT

Influenza A Virus (IAV) is remarkably adept at surviving in human populations. IAV thrives even among populations with wide spread access to vaccines and anti-viral drugs, and continues to be a major cause of morbidity and mortality. Correlated mutations are an important factor in IAV's evolution and are critical for host adaptation and pathogenicity. Large sets of publicly available sequences of IAV combined with its rapid and complex evolutionary dynamics present interesting opportunities and unique challenges to analyze correlated mutations in influenza proteomes. In this work, we performed a comprehensive analysis of correlated mutations in IAV using a network theory approach where residues in each protein act as nodes in the graph and edges in the graph are created based on inter-residue correlated mutations. Our approach used 'maximal information coefficient' (MIC) to compute correlations between residues and the edges connect nodes if their MIC exceeds a threshold (Fig 1). We created a modular and robust pipeline and applied it to multiple datasets of H1N1, H3N2, H5 and H7N9 subtypes. We studied structural dynamics of IAV sub-systems based on topological properties of their networks resulting in several important conclusions. The main finding is that correlated mutation networks in IAV are sub-type and host specific and the differences for various subtypes and hosts are significant (Fig 2 & Fig 3). We identified nodes with highest degree along with edges and triplets with strongest weight for each network. To contextualize our results, we performed entropy analysis to gain a global view of sequence variation and computed solvent accessibility profiles to identify statistical differences in correlation profiles between surface and buried residues. To understand the extent of co-variation between the 10 proteins in IAV sequences, we created visualizations of protein correlation graphs where the proteins acts as nodes and the strength of connections between the nodes depends on the number of correlated mutations between residues of connected proteins (Fig 4). A web application and visualization tools to explore the results and search for correlated mutations were developed.

Keywords

Network Analysis; Correlated Mutations; Influenza

General Terms

Algorithms

Permission to make digital or hard copies of part or all of this work for personal or classroom use is granted without fee provided that copies are not made or distributed for profit or commercial advantage and that copies bear this notice and the full citation on the first page. Copyrights for third-party components of this work must be honored. For all other uses, contact the Owner/Author.
ACM-BCB '17, August 20-23, 2017, Boston, MA, USA
© 2017 Copyright is held by the owner/author(s).
ACM ISBN 978-1-4503-4722-8/17/08.
http://dx.doi.org/10.1145/3107411.3108237

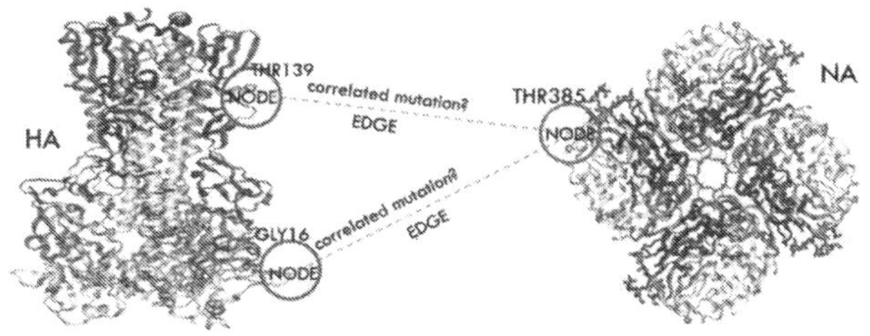

Figure 1 - Creating a network based on correlated mutations

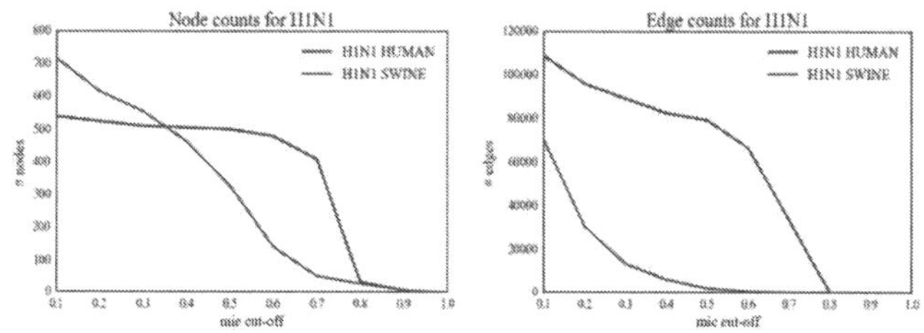

Figure 2: Node and edge counts for different MIC thresholds for H1N1 Human and Swine

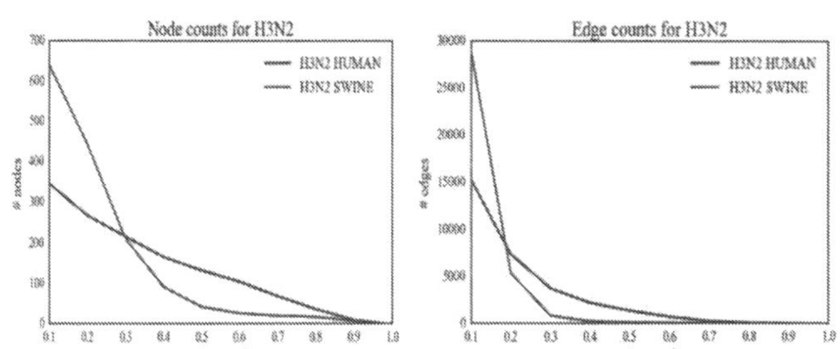

Figure 3: Node and edge counts for different MIC thresholds for H3N2 Human and Swine

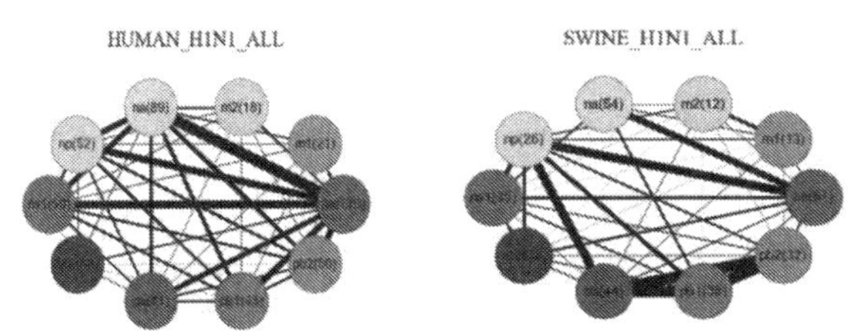

Figure 4: Protein Correlation Graphs for Human H1N1 and Swine H1N1

ACM-BCB '17 Tutorial: Robotics-inspired Algorithms for Modeling Protein Structures and Motions

Kevin Molloy
George Mason University
4400 University Dr.
Fairfax, Virginia 22030

David Morris
George Mason University
4400 University Dr.
Fairfax, Virginia 22030

Amarda Shehu*
George Mason University
4400 University Dr.
Fairfax, Virginia 22030

ABSTRACT

With biomolecular structure recognized as central to understanding mechanisms in the cell, computational chemists and biophysicists have spent significant efforts on modeling structure and dynamics. While significant advances have been made, particularly in the design of sophisticated energetic models and molecular representations, such efforts are experiencing diminishing returns. One of the culprits is low exploration capability. The impasse has attracted AI researchers to offer adaptations of robot motion planning algorithms for modeling biomolecular structures and motions. This tutorial introduces students and researchers to robotics-inspired treatments and methodologies for understanding and elucidating the role of structure and dynamics in the function of biomolecules. The presentation is enhanced via an open-source software developed in the Shehu Computational Biology laboratory. The software allows researchers to integrate themselves in a new research domain and drive further research via plug-and-play capabilities. The hands-on approach in the the tutorial benefits both students and senior researchers keen to make contributions in computational structural biology.

CCS CONCEPTS

•**Applied computing → Computational biology; Molecular structural biology; Bioinformatics;**

KEYWORDS

Computational structural biology, protein structure, structural rearrangements, robotics-inspired treatments

ACM Reference format:
Kevin Molloy, David Morris, and Amarda Shehu. 2017. ACM-BCB '17 Tutorial: Robotics-inspired Algorithms for Modeling Protein Structures and Motions. In *Proceedings of ACM-BCB'17, August 20–23, 2017, Boston, MA, USA.*, 1 pages.
DOI: http://dx.doi.org/10.1145/3107411.3107493

This tutorial introduces students and researchers to robotics-inspired treatments and methodologies put forth for the purpose of elucidating the role of structure and dynamics in the biological function of key macromolecules, such as proteins and RNA. This community has gained maturity, and a rich body of literature is now available, attesting to the efficacy of robotics-inspired methods for biomolecular modeling. The tutorial places the presentation of topics in a practical context, demonstrating to participants how they can use a plug-and-play software developed in the Shehu laboratory to understand the capabilities of robotics-inspired algorithms, utilize them for their studies of structure and structural dynamics, and even develop their own novel algorithms via the plug-and-play functionality. The tutorial is structured as follows:

The audience is introduced to the current understanding and limitations therein on the role of biomolecular structure and dynamics for molecules. The introduction focuses on aspects of central importance in macromolecular modeling: (i) size and dimensionality of the conformational space of a molecular system and (ii) ruggedness and other properties of the energy landscape underlying this space. The exposition is enhanced by pointing to specific classes in the software that realize conformation, structure, and energy model.

The tutorial then highlights mechanistic analogies between articulated robotic chains and biomolecules. The analogies are employed to introduce key sampling-based methods and their adaptations from the robot motion planning problem to problems on modeling structures, folding, and other motions in proteins and RNA. Participants are shown mechanistic analogies in the software, as well as popular representation-aware variation/perturbation operators.

Key methods are then introduced by both making use of slides and referring to the software. Tree-based methods are presented first, followed by roadmap-based methods. Selected RRT-, EST-, and PRM-based methods are demonstrated in action, employing the software, both to better understand these methods and their capabilities. The software demos emphasize the ability of developers to obtain novel variants of algorithms via the plug-and-play feature.

The tutorial (i) introduces the audience to the current state of the art in robotics-inspired approaches for protein and RNA modeling; (ii) highlights recent robotics-inspired methods for structural characterization of biomolecules; (iii) spurs further interactions to promote cross-pollination of ideas, lead towards more powerful robotics-inspired treatments, invite more researchers to contribute to important problems in computational structural biology, and in turn allow further progress. The showcase and demoing of the software alongside each of the introduced topics provide a practical context in support of the above objectives.

1 ACKNOWLEDGMENTS

This work is supported in part by NSF IIS CAREER Award No. 1440581.

*Corresponding Author: amarda@gmu.edu

Permission to make digital or hard copies of part or all of this work for personal or classroom use is granted without fee provided that copies are not made or distributed for profit or commercial advantage and that copies bear this notice and the full citation on the first page. Copyrights for third-party components of this work must be honored. For all other uses, contact the owner/author(s).
ACM-BCB'17, August 20–23, 2017, Boston, MA, USA.
© 2017 Copyright held by the owner/author(s). ISBN 978-1-4503-4722-8/17/08.
DOI: http://dx.doi.org/10.1145/3107411.3107493

Computational Modeling of Protein-RNA Interactions

Yaron Orenstein
Computer Science and Artificial Intelligence Laboratory
Massachusetts Institute of Technology
Cambridge, MA 02139
United States
yaronore@mit.edu

ABSTRACT

Protein-RNA interactions, mediated through both RNA sequence and structure, play vital role in all cellular processes. In recent years, technologies have been developed to measure these interactions in high-throughput manner. Researchers would like to infer accurate models from the experimental data in order to predict new interactions and better understand the underlying binding mechanism. In this tutorial, I will present the main computational challenges in incorporating RNA structure information into computational algorithms and models. I will describe in detail two state-of-the-art methods to infer structure-based models from experimental data and discuss their strengths and weakness. I will conclude with open problems in the field.

KEYWORDS

Protein-RNA binding; RNA structure; RNA regulation.

Permission to make digital or hard copies of part or all of this work for personal or classroom use is granted without fee provided that copies are not made or distributed for profit or commercial advantage and that copies bear this notice and the full citation on the first page. Copyrights for third-party components of this work must be honored. For all other uses, contact the Owner/Author.
ACM-BCB '17, August 20-23, 2017, Boston, MA, USA
© 2017 Copyright is held by the owner/author(s).
ACM ISBN 978-1-4503-4722-8/17/08.
http://dx.doi.org/10.1145/3107411.3107495

Stochastic Process Model and Its Applications to Analysis of Longitudinal Data

Ilya Y. Zhbannikov*
Social Science Research Institute
Duke University, Durham, NC, USA
ilya.zhbannikov@duke.edu

Konstantin G. Arbeev
Social Science Research Institute
Duke University, Durham, NC, USA
konstantin.arbeev@duke.edu

ABSTRACT

Longitudinal [1] studies are widely used in medicine, biology, population health and other areas related to bioinformatics. A broad spectrum of methods for joint analysis of longitudinal and time-to-event (survival) data has been proposed the in last few decades. The Stochastic process model (SPM) represents one possible framework for modelling joint evolution of repeatedly measured variables and time-to-event outcome typically observed in longitudinal studies. SPM is applicable for analyses of longitudinal data in many research areas such as demography and medicine and allows researchers to utilize the full potential of longitudinal data by evaluating dynamic mechanisms of changing physiological variables with time (age), allowing the study of differences, for example, in genotype-specific hazards. SPM allows incorporation of available knowledge about regularities of aging-related changes in the human body for addressing fundamental problems of changes in resilience and physiological norms. It permits evaluating mechanisms that indirectly affect longitudinal trajectories of physiological variables using data on mortality or onset of diseases. In this tutorial we explain the basic concepts of SPM, its current state and possible applications, corresponding software tools and show practical examples of analysis of joint analysis of longitudinal and time-to-event data with this methodology.

CCS CONCEPTS

• **Applied computing → Life and medical sciences → Bioinformatics**

KEYWORDS

Stochastic process model; quadratic hazard; longitudinal data; life tables; risk factors

* Corresponding author

[1] Permission to make digital or hard copies of all or part of this work for personal or classroom use is granted without fee provided that copies are not made or distributed for profit or commercial advantage and that copies bear this notice and the full citation on the first page. Copyrights for components of this work owned by others than ACM must be honored. Abstracting with credit is permitted. To copy otherwise, or republish, to post on servers or to redistribute to lists, requires prior specific permission and/or a fee. Request permissions from Permissions@acm.org.
ACM-BCB'17, August 20-23, 2017, Boston, MA, USA.
© 2017 Association of Computing Machinery.
ACM ISBN 978-1-4503-4722-8/17/08...$15.00.
DOI: http://dx.doi.org/10.1145/3107411.3107496

ACKNOWLEDGMENTS

This work was supported by the National Institute on Aging of the National Institutes of Health (NIA/NIH) under Award Numbers P01AG043352, R01AG046860, and P30AG034424. The content is solely the responsibility of the authors and does not necessarily represent the official views of the NIA/NIH.

REFERENCES

[1] Akushevich I., Kulminski A. and Manton K. 2005. Life tables with covariates: Dynamic model for Nonlinear Analysis of Longitudinal Data. Mathematical Population Studies, 12(2), pp.: 51-80.
[2] Akushevich I. et al. 2012. New stochastic carcinogenesis model with covariates:an approach involving intracellular barrier mechanisms, Math Biosc, 236(1):16-30.
[3] Allison D.B., Faith M.S., Heo M., Kotler D.P. 1997. Hypothesis concerning the U-shaped relation between body mass index and mortality, Am. J. Epidemiol., 146 (4), pp. 339–349.
[4] Arbeev, K.G., et al. 2009. Genetic model for longitudinal studies of aging, health and longevity and its potential application to incomplete data. Journal of Theoretical Biology. 258(1): p. 103-111.
[5] Manton K.G., Stallard E., Singer B.H. 1992. Projecting the future size and health status of the U.S. elderly population. Int J Forecast 8:433–458.
[6] Witteman J.C.M., Grobbee D.E., Valkenburg H.A. et al.,1994. J-shaped relation between change in diastolic blood pressure and aortic atherosclerosis. Lancet 343:504–507.
[7] Woodbury M.A., Manton K.G. 1977. Random-Walk of Human Mortality and Aging.. Theoretical Population Biology, 11:37-48.
[8] Yashin, A.I., Manton K.G., Vaupel J.W. 1985. Mortality and aging in a heterogeneous population: a stochastic process model with observed and unobserved variables. Theor Pop Biology, 27.
[9] Yashin, A.I., Manton, K.G., Stallard, E. 1986. Dependent competing risks: a stochastic process model, J. Math. Biol. 24, p: 119.
[10] Yashin, A.I. et al. 2007(a). Health decline, aging and mortality: how are they related? Biogerontology, 8(3), 291–302.
[11] Yashin, A.I. et al. 2007(b). Stochastic model for analysis of longitudinal data on aging and mortality. Mathematical Biosciences, 208(2), 538 – 551.
[12] Yashin A.I. et al. 2008. Model of hidden heterogeneity in longitudinal data. Theoretical Population Biology 73, pp. 1–10.

Analyzing the eICU Collaborative Research Database

Alistair E. W. Johnson
Massachusetts Institute of Technology
77 Massachusetts Avenue
Cambridge, MA, USA
aewj@mit.edu

Tom J. Pollard
Massachusetts Institute of Technology
77 Massachusetts Avenue
Cambridge, MA, USA
tpollard@mit.edu

Leo A. Celi
Massachusetts Institute of Technology
77 Massachusetts Avenue
Cambridge, MA, USA
lceli@mit.edu

Roger G. Mark
Massachusetts Institute of Technology
77 Massachusetts Avenue
Cambridge, MA, USA
rgmark@mit.edu

ABSTRACT

Patients in hospital intensive care units (ICUs) are physiologically fragile and unstable, generally have life-threatening conditions, and require close monitoring and rapid therapeutic interventions. Staggering amounts of data are collected in the ICU daily: multi-channel waveforms sampled hundreds of times each second, vital sign time series updated each second or minute, alarms and alerts, lab results, imaging results, records of medication and fluid administration, staff notes and more. Reducing the barriers to data access has the potential to accelerate knowledge generation and ultimately improve patient care.

In this interactive tutorial we introduce the eICU Collaborative Research Database: a large, publicly available database created by the MIT Laboratory for Computational Physiology in partnership with the Philips eICU Research Institute. The database contains routinely collected data from over 200,000 admissions to intensive care units across the United States, with representation from over 12% of US ICU beds. The data facilitates a breadth of research studies, such as investigations into treatment efficacy, discovery of clinical markers in illnesses, and the development of decision support models.

Participants in the tutorial gain an overview of the eICU Collaborative Research Database, in particular being introduced to its structure, content, and limitations. Following this overview, participants explore a demo version of the database using a laptop in a hands-on project. This exercise requires minimal technical expertise and gives an insight into the type of study that can be carried out using the database. We also highlight the growing online community centered around secondary analysis of this data. All tutorial materials are open source and publicly available.

The eICU Collaborative Research Database offers an unparalleled insight into ICU care. Access to the database is granted to legitimate researchers who request it, following completion of a training course in human subjects research and acceptance of a data use agreement. We anticipate that the research community will use this unique resource to further human knowledge in the field of critical care.

KEYWORDS

Critical care; data mining; electronic health record

ACM Reference format:

A. E. W. Johnson, T. J. Pollard, L. A. Celi, and R. G. Mark. 2017. Analyzing the eICU Collaborative Research Database. In *Proceedings of the 8th ACM International Conference on Bioinformatics, Computational Biology, and Health Informatics. ACM New York, NY, USA.*

Permission to make digital or hard copies of part or all of this work for personal or classroom use is granted without fee provided that copies are not made or distributed for profit or commercial advantage and that copies bear this notice and the full citation on the first page. Copyrights for third-party components of this work must be honored. For all other uses, contact the Owner/Author.
ACM-BCB '17, August 20-23, 2017, Boston, MA, USA
© 2017 Copyright is held by the owner/author(s).
ACM ISBN 978-1-4503-4722-8/17/08.
http://dx.doi.org/10.1145/3107411.3107494

Instrumenting the Health Care Enterprise for Discovery in the Course of Clinical Care

Shawn Murphy MD, Ph.D.
Massachusetts General Hospital, Partners Healthcare,
and Harvard Medical School
Boston, MA
murphy.shawn@mgh.harvard.edu

ABSTRACT

Objectives: Although patients may have a wealth of imaging, genomic, monitoring, and personal device data, it has yet to be fully integrated into clinical care.

Methods: We identify three reasons for the lack of integration. The first is that "Big Data" is poorly managed by most Electronic Medical Record Systems (EMRS). The data is mostly available on "cloud-native" platforms that are outside the scope of most EMRS, and even checking if such data is available on a patient often must be done outside the EMRS. The second reason is that extracting features from the Big Data that are relevant to healthcare often requires complex machine learning algorithms, such as determining if a genomic variant is protein-altering. The third reason is that applications that present the big data need to be modified constantly to reflect the current state of knowledge, such as instructing when to order a new set of genomic tests. In some cases, the applications need to be updated nightly.

Results: A new architecture for the EMRS is evolving which could unite Big Data, machine learning, and clinical care through a microservice-based architecture which can host applications focused on quite specific aspects of clinical care, such as managing cancer immunotherapy.

Conclusion: Informatics innovation, medical research, and clinical care go hand in hand as we look to infuse science-based practice into healthcare. Innovative methods will lead to in a new ecosystem of Apps interacting with healthcare providers to fulfill a promise that is still to be determined.

CCS Concepts/ACM Classifiers

Life and medical sciences, Genomics, Consumer health, Health care information systems, Health informatics, Medical information policy, Medical records

Author Keywords

Personal Device Data; Machine Learning; i2b2; SMART Apps; Artificial Intelligence

BIOGRAPHY

Dr. Murphy is the Chief Research Information Officer at Partners HealthCare, is a Professor of Neurology and Biomedical Informatics at Harvard Medical School, and serves as Associate Director for the Laboratory of Computer Science at the Massachusetts General Hospital. He received his BS in Chemistry from the University of Notre Dame, and his Ph.D. in

Pharmacology and Physiology and MD from the University of Chicago. Dr. Murphy's research interests include the creation of query methods for healthcare data that enable them to be directly used by scientists even when the data is extremely large. Dr. Murphy has created Informatics for Integrating Biology and the Bedside (i2b2), a high impact and widely accepted open source project that focuses on the integration of highly diverse phenotypic, imaging, and genomic data such that new discoveries can be visualized and produced from secondary use of routinely collected healthcare data and be applied to new methods of providing clinical decision support in a learning healthcare system.

Permission to make digital or hard copies of part or all of this work for personal or classroom use is granted without fee provided that copies are not made or distributed for profit or commercial advantage and that copies bear this notice and the full citation on the first page. Copyrights for third-party components of this work must be honored. For all other uses, contact the owner/author(s).
ACM-BCB'17, August 20-23, 2017, Boston, MA, USA.
© 2017 Copyright is held by the owner/author(s).
ACM ISBN 978-1-4503-4722-8/17/08.
DOI: http://dx.doi.org/10.1145/3107411. 3121000

Challenges of Drug Design

Dagmar Ringe
Brandeis University
Waltham, MA 02454

ABSTRACT

Computational drug design is highly dependent on the model being used for docking and fitting of structure. Those models are derived mainly from X-ray structures and hopefully represent the physiologically relevant form of the protein in solution. And here is the conundrum: the conditions from which the crystals are derived are usually far from physiological in terms of ionic strength, pH, identity of salts, and presence of other additives, and temperature at which the data were acquired. Even with a molecule bound, the conformations observed may not be the correct ones, partly because of adjustment of the proteins to a molecule not representative of substrate, and partly because there are too many structures of complexes in which the small molecule has been fitted incorrectly. So far, there has been some progress on all of these issues and we can explore ways to address them further, partly at the experimental level and partly at the computational level.

Keyword

Drug design

BIOGRAPHY

Dagmar Ringe is the Harold and Bernice Davis Professor in Aging and Neurodegenerative Disease, Department of Biochemistry and Department of Chemistry, and Rosenstiel Basic Medical Sciences Research Center at Brandeis University. She has been working for over 30 years on the development of methods for the identification of function for proteins of unknown function and methods for drug design, employing a combination of X-ray crystallography, site-directed mutagenesis, kinetics, organic synthesis, computational methods to identify active sites and to probe the mechanisms of action of enzymes and the role of protein dynamics in protein function. There are a number of areas to which these methods have been applied. The most recent efforts are aimed at an understanding of the functions of proteins associated with neurodegenerative diseases, with a view toward determining the functions of gene products associated with such diseases, and the search for and design of specific inhibitors or activators as potential drugs to treat these diseases. We have developed a structural method to find binding sites in proteins, the MCSC method, based on the interactions of small probe molecules to the surface. The method is the basis for fragment-based drug discovery, and has been developed into a computational one.

Permission to make digital or hard copies of part or all of this work for personal or classroom use is granted without fee provided that copies are not made or distributed for profit or commercial advantage and that copies bear this notice and the full citation on the first page. Copyrights for third-party components of this work must be honored. For all other uses, contact the owner/author(s).
ACM-BCB'17, August 20-23, 2017, Boston, MA, USA.
© 2017 Copyright is held by the owner/author(s).
ACM ISBN 978-1-4503-4722-8/17/08.
DOI: http://dx.doi.org/10.1145/3107411.3107464

Genome-scale Estimation of the Tree of Life

Tandy Warnow
University of Illinois at Urbana-Champaign
Urbana, Illinois 61801
warnow@illinois.edu

ABSTRACT

Estimating the Tree of Life is one of the grand computational challenges in Science, and has applications to many areas of science and biomedical research. Despite intensive research over the last several decades, many problems remain inadequately solved. For example, multiple sequence alignment, maximum likelihood gene tree estimation, and species tree estimation from genome-scale data are problems that are not yet adequately addressed for large complex datasets. In this talk, I will describe the current state of the art for these problems, what is understood about these problems from a mathematical perspective, and identify some of the open problems in this area where mathematical research, drawing from graph theory, combinatorial optimization, and probability and statistics, is needed.

CCS Concepts/ACM Classifiers

Applied computing~Molecular evolution

Author Keywords

Phylogenetics; phylogenomics; incomplete lineage sorting; horizontal gene transfer; gene trees; species trees.

BIOGRAPHY

TANDY WARNOW is a Founder Professor of Computer Science at the University of Illinois. She received her PhD in Mathematics at UC Berkeley, under the supervision of Gene Lawler, and then spent a year as a postdoc with Mike Waterman and Simon Tavare at the University of Southern California. Her awards include the National Science Foundation Young Investigator Award (1994), the David and Lucile Packard Foundation Award in Science and Engineering (1996), a Radcliffe Institute for Advanced Study Fellowship (2003), and a John Simon Guggenheim Memorial Foundation Fellowship (2011). She was elected a Fellow of the Association for Computing Machinery (ACM) in 2016 and of the International Society for Computational Biology (ISCB) in 2017.

REFERENCES

[1] http://tandy.cs.illinois.edu/PhylogenomicsProject.html

Permission to make digital or hard copies of part or all of this work for personal or classroom use is granted without fee provided that copies are not made or distributed for profit or commercial advantage and that copies bear this notice and the full citation on the first page. Copyrights for third-party components of this work must be honored. For all other uses, contact the owner/author(s).
ACM-BCB'17, August 20-23, 2017, Boston, MA, USA.
© 2017 Copyright is held by the owner/author(s).
ACM ISBN 978-1-4503-4722-8/17/08.
DOI: http://dx.doi.org/10.1145/3107411.3107463

Highlights Talks at ACM BCB 2017

It is our great pleasure to have eight highlights talks in the program of the *2017 ACM Conference on Bioinformatics, Computational Biology, and Health Informatics, ACM-BCB'17.* These invited talks are based on journal articles that have been published in the prior 18 months, and represent some of the most interesting and exciting work in our field. The following lists the accepted highlight papers, in the order the talks appear in the program schedule:

- *Osmanbeyoglu, Hatice U., Eneda Toska, Carmen Chan, José Baselga, and Christina S. Leslie. "Pancancer modelling predicts the context-specific impact of somatic mutations on transcriptional programs." Nature Communications 8 (2017): 14249.*
- *Héliou, Amélie, Dominik Budday, Rasmus Fonseca, and Henry van den Bedem. "Fast, clash-free RNA conformational morphing using molecular junctions." Bioinformatics (2017): btx127.*
- *Trieu, Tuan, and Jianlin Cheng. "3D genome structure modeling by Lorentzian objective function." Nucleic acids research 45, no. 3 (2017): 1049-1058.*
- *Wang, Sheng, Siqi Sun, Zhen Li, Renyu Zhang, and Jinbo Xu. "Accurate de novo prediction of protein contact map by ultra-deep learning model." PLoS computational biology 13, no. 1 (2017): e1005324.*
- *Tuncbag, N., Gosline, S.J., Kedaigle, A., Soltis, A.R., Gitter, A. and Fraenkel, E., 2016. Network-based interpretation of diverse high-throughput datasets through the Omics Integrator software package. PLoS computational biology, 12(4), p.e1004879.*
- *Zeng, Chun, Francesca Mulas, Yinghui Sui, Tiffany Guan, Nathanael Miller, Yuliang Tan, Fenfen Liu et al. "Pseudotemporal Ordering of Single Cells Reveals Metabolic Control of Postnatal β Cell Proliferation." Cell Metabolism 25, no. 5 (2017): 1160-1175.*
- *Stanfield, Zachary, Mustafa Coşkun, and Mehmet Koyutürk. "Drug Response Prediction as a Link Prediction Problem." Scientific reports 7 (2017): 40321.*
- *Michael, Drew G., Ezekiel J. Maier, Holly Brown, Stacey R. Gish, Christopher Fiore, Randall H. Brown, and Michael R. Brent. "Model-based transcriptome engineering promotes a fermentative transcriptional state in yeast." Proceedings of the National Academy of Sciences 113, no. 47 (2016): E7428-E7437.*

Highlights talk speakers were given the option of inclusion of a 1-page abstract of their highlights talk in the conference proceedings. For all highlights talk presenters who availed themselves of this option, their abstract follows this overall summary page. We thank our Highlights Talks Track co-chairs, Chris Bailey-Kellogg (Dartmouth University), Terri Gaasterland (UCSD), and Mona Singh (Princeton University) for reviewing submissions and putting together such a strong set of talks.

Amarda Shehu
ACM-BCB'17 Program Chair
George Mason University, USA

Tamer Kahveci
ACM-BCB'17 Program Chair
University of Florida, USA

Giuseppe Pozzi
ACM-BCB'17 Program Chair
Politecnico di Milano, Italy

Model-based transcriptome engineering

Michael Brent
Washington University
Saint Louis, MO
brent@wustl.edu

ABSTRACT

The ability to rationally manipulate the transcriptional states of cells would be of great use in medicine and bioengineering. We have developed an algorithm, NetSurgeon, which uses genome wide gene-regulatory networks to identify interventions that force a cell toward a desired expression state. We first validated NetSurgeon extensively on existing datasets. Next, we used Net-Surgeon to select transcription factor deletions aimed at improving ethanol production in Saccharomyces cerevisiae cultures that are catabolizing xylose. We reasoned that interventions that move the transcriptional state of cells using xylose toward that of cells producing large amounts of ethanol from glucose might improve xylose fermentation. Some of the interventions selected by NetSurgeon successfully promoted a fermentative transcriptional state in the absence of glucose, resulting in strains with a 2.7-fold increase in xylose import rates, a 4-fold improvement in xylose integration into central carbon metabolism, or a 1.3-fold increase in ethanol production rate. We conclude by presenting an integrated model of transcriptional regulation and metabolic flux that will enable future efforts aimed at improving xylose fermentation to prioritize functional regulators of central carbon metabolism.

CCS Concepts/ACM Classifiers

- Genomics
- Computational genomics
- Systems biology

Author Keywords

Gene regulatory networks; transcriptome engineering; Saccharomyces cerevisiae; ethanol; xylose

BIOGRAPHY/BIOGRAPHIES

After completing his PhD in Computer Science at MIT, Professor Brent served as Assistant and Associate Professor of Cognitive Science at the Johns Hopkins University, where his research focused on computational modeling of how children learn language.

He brought these interests to Washington University in St. Louis in 1999, where he developed a second research program in computational biology and eventually phased out computational linguistics. From 2001 to 2008 he focused on computational and molecular methods for improving the accuracy of genome annotation. Since 2008, Professor Brent has focused on computational and molecular methods for mapping and modeling gene regulation networks.

Professor Brent was elected Fellow of the American Association for the Advancement of Science (AAAS) in 2012.

Permission to make digital or hard copies of part or all of this work for personal or classroom use is granted without fee provided that copies are not made or distributed for profit or commercial advantage and that copies bear this notice and the full citation on the first page. Copyrights for third-party components of this work must be honored. For all other uses, contact the owner/author(s).
ACM-BCB'17, August 20-23, 2017, Boston, MA, USA.
© 2017 Copyright is held by the owner/author(s).
ACM ISBN 978-1-4503-4722-8/17/08.
DOI: http://dx.doi.org/10.1145/3107411.3107454

Analysis of Single Cells on a Pseudotime Scale along Postnatal Pancreatic Beta Cell Development

Francesca Mulas
UCSD, CA
fmulas@ucsd.edu

Chun Zeng
UCSD, CA
c2zeng@ucsd.edu

Yinghui Sui
UCSD, CA
y3sui@ucsd.edu

Tiffany Guan
UCSD, CA
tiffguan@gmail.com

Nathanael Miller
UCLA, CA and BU, MA
nmiller0@bu.edu

Yuliang Tan
UCSD, CA
yuliangtan@gmail.com

Fenfen Liu
UCSD, CA
f2liu@ucsd.edu

Wen Jin
UCSD, CA
w8jin@ucsd.edu

Andrea C. Carrano
UCSD, CA
acarrano@ucsd.edu

Mark O. Huising
UC Davis, CA
mhuising@ucdavis.edu

Orian Shirihai
UCLA, CA and BU, MA
shirihai@me.com

Gene W. Yeo
UCSD, CA
geneyeo@ucsd.edu

Maike Sander
UCSD, CA
masander@ucsd.edu

ABSTRACT

Single-cell RNA-seq generates gene expression profiles of individual cells and has furthered our understanding of the developmental and cellular hierarchy within complex tissues. One computational challenge in analyzing single-cell data sets is reconstructing the progression of individual cells with respect to the gradual transition of their transcriptomes. While a number of single-cell ordering tools have been proposed, many of these require knowledge of progression markers or time delineators. Here, we adapted an algorithm previously developed for temporally ordering bulk microarray samples [1] to reconstruct the developmental trajectory of pancreatic beta-cells postnatally. To accomplish this, we applied a multi-step pipeline to analyze single-cell RNA-seq data sets from isolated beta-cells at five different time points between birth and post-weaning. Specifically, we i) ordered cells along a linear trajectory (the Pseudotime Scale) by applying one-dimensional principal component analysis to the normalized data matrix; ii) identified annotated and de-novo gene sets significantly regulated along the trajectory; iii) built a network of top-regulated genes using protein interaction repositories; and iv) scored genes for their network connectivity to transcription factors [2]. A systematic comparison showed that our approach was more accurate in correctly ordering cells for our data set than previously reported methods and allowed for direct comparisons with external data sets. Importantly, our analysis revealed never before seen changes in beta-cell metabolism and in levels of mitochondrial reactive oxygen species. We demonstrated experimentally a role for these changes in the regulation of postnatal beta-cell proliferation. Our pipeline identified maturation-related changes in gene expression not captured when evaluating bulk gene expression data across the developmental time course. The proposed methodology has a broad applicability beyond the context here described and could be used to examine the trajectory of other single cell types along a continuous course of cell state changes.

KEYWORDS

Single-cell; Pseudotime ordering; RNA-Seq; Dimensionality reduction; Beta cell; Pancreas.

REFERENCES

[1] L. Zagar, F. Mulas, S. Garagna, M. Zuccotti, R. Bellazzi and B. Zupan. Stage prediction of embryonic stem cell differentiation from genome-wide expression data. *Bioinformatics* 27 (2011), 2546-2553.

[2] F. Mulas, E. Del Fabbro, B. Zupan and R. Bellazzi. Interest propagation for knowledge extraction and representation. *Stud Health Technol Inform* 186 (2013), 182-186.

Permission to make digital or hard copies of part or all of this work for personal or classroom use is granted without fee provided that copies are not made or distributed for profit or commercial advantage and that copies bear this notice and the full citation on the first page. Copyrights for third-party components of this work must be honored. For all other uses, contact the Owner/Author.
ACM-BCB '17, August 20-23, 2017, Boston, MA, USA
© 2017 Copyright is held by the owner/author(s).
ACM ISBN 978-1-4503-4722-8/17/08.
http://dx.doi.org/10.1145/3107411.3107458

Drug Response Prediction as a Link Prediction Problem

Zachary Stanfield
Case Western Reserve University
Cleveland, OH 44106
United States
zachary.stanfield@case.edu

Mustafa Coşkun
Case Western Reserve University
Cleveland, OH 44106
United States
mustafa.coskun@case.edu

Mehmet Koyutürk
Case Western Reserve University
Cleveland, OH 44106
United States
mehmet.koyuturk@case.edu

ABSTRACT

Drug response prediction is a well-studied problem in which the molecular profile of a given sample is used to predict the effect of a given drug on that sample. Effective solutions to this problem hold the key for precision medicine. In cancer research, genomic data from cell lines are often utilized as features to develop machine learning models predictive of drug response. Molecular networks provide a functional context for the integration of genomic features, thereby resulting in robust and reproducible predictive models. However, inclusion of network data increases dimensionality and poses additional challenges for common machine learning tasks. To overcome these challenges, we here formulate drug response prediction as a link prediction problem. For this purpose, we represent drug response data for a large cohort of cell lines as a heterogeneous network. Using this network, we compute "network profiles" for cell lines and drugs. We then use the associations between these profiles to predict links between drugs and cell lines. Through leave-one-out cross validation and cross-classification on independent datasets, we show that this approach leads to accurate and reproducible classification of sensitive and resistant cell line-drug pairs, with 85% accuracy. We also examine the biological relevance of the network profiles.

Permission to make digital or hard copies of part or all of this work for personal or classroom use is granted without fee provided that copies are not made or distributed for profit or commercial advantage and that copies bear this notice and the full citation on the first page. Copyrights for third-party components of this work must be honored. For all other uses, contact the Owner/Author.
ACM-BCB '17, August 20-23, 2017, Boston, MA, USA
© 2017 Copyright is held by the owner/author(s).
ACM ISBN 978-1-4503-4722-8/17/08.
http://dx.doi.org/10.1145/3107411.3107459

CCS CONCEPTS

• **Data Mining** → Data integration • **Networks** → Network proximity; Link prediction • **Machine Learning** → Cross validation; Classification

KEYWORDS

Drug response, cancer cell line, protein-protein interaction network, random walk with restart, machine learning

ACM Reference format:

Z. Stanfield, M. Coskun, and M. Koyuturk. 2017. Drug Response Prediction as a Link Prediction Problem. In *Proceedings of ACMBCB conference, Boston, MA USA, August 2017 (ACMBCB'17)*, 1 page, DOI: *10.1145/3107411.3107459*

Fast, Clash-Free RNA Conformational Morphing using Molecular Junctions

A. Héliou
LIX, Ecole Polytechnique
Université Paris-Saclay
Palaiseau, France
amelie.heliou@polytechnique.edu

Dominik Budday
Chair of Applied Dynamics
University of Erlangen-Nuremberg
Erlangen, Germany
dominik.budday@fau.de

Rasmus Fonseca
Department of Molecular and Cellular Physiology
Stanford University
Stanford, California, USA
rfon@stanford.edu

Henry van den Bedem*
SLAC National Accelerator Laboratory
Stanford University
Menlo Park, California, USA
vdbedem@stanford.edu

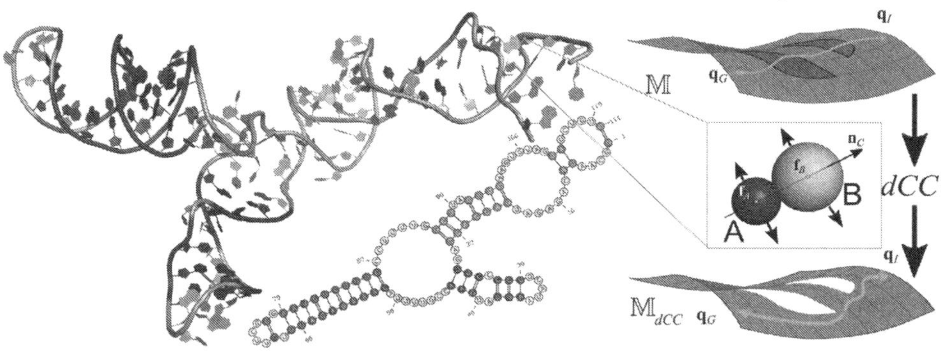

Figure 1: RNA 3D and 2D representations. Helices are color-coded and flexible single stranded regions are shown in gray. The blue plane represents the secondary-structure constraint conformational manifold, $\mathbb{M}$, defined by Watson-Crick pairs (blue lines in 2D representation). Red patches represent sterically unfeasible regions. Moving directly from an initial conformation, q_I, to a goal, q_G, will frequently result in clashing atoms. Dynamic Clash-avoiding Constraints (dCC) prevent atoms A and B from approaching, but allows motion in directions orthogonal to n_c or jointly along n_c. The clash regions are absent in a lower-dimensional manifold $\mathbb{M}_{dCC}$ (cut-out) defined by the dCC, resulting in a clash-free path between q_I and q_G.

ABSTRACT

Non-coding ribonucleic acids (ncRNA) are functional RNA molecules that are not translated into protein. They are extremely dynamic, adopting diverse conformational substates, which enables them to modulate their interaction with a large number of other molecules. The flexibility of ncRNA provides a challenge for probing their complex 3D conformational landscape, both experimentally and computationally. Despite their conformational diversity, ncRNAs mostly preserve their secondary structure throughout the dynamic ensemble. Here we present a kinematics-based procedure to morph an RNA molecule between two 3D conformations, while avoiding interatomic clashes. We represent an RNA as a kinematic linkage, with fixed groups of atoms as rigid bodies and rotatable bonds as degrees of freedom. Our procedure maintains RNA secondary structure by treating hydrogen bonds between base pairs as constraints. The constraints define a lower-dimensional, secondary-structure constraint manifold in conformation space (Fig 1), where motions are largely governed by molecular junctions of unpaired nucleotides. We furthermore introduce temporary, dynamic Clash Constraints (dCC) between atoms in close contact, which instantaneously redirect the conformational search toward sterically favorable conformations by defining a clash-free submanifold of the constraint manifold. In addition to relieving clashes, the dCC mimic transient interactions, coupling motions between distant parts of the linkage. **Results.** On a large benchmark set, we show that our morphing procedure compares favorably to peer algorithms, and can approach goal conformations to within a low all-atom RMSD by directing fewer than 1% of its atoms. Our results suggest that molecular junctions can modulate 3D structural rearrangements, while secondary structure elements guide large parts of the molecule along the transition to the correct final conformation.

Source code and binaries are available from https://github.com/ExcitedStates/KGS

*To whom correspondence should be addressed

Permission to make digital or hard copies of part or all of this work for personal or classroom use is granted without fee provided that copies are not made or distributed for profit or commercial advantage and that copies bear this notice and the full citation on the first page. Copyrights for third-party components of this work must be honored. For all other uses, contact the owner/author(s).
ACM-BCB '17, August 20-23, 2017, Boston, MA, USA
© 2017 Copyright held by the owner/author(s).
ACM ISBN 978-1-4503-4722-8/17/08.
https://doi.org/10.1145/3107411.3107460

Network-based Interpretation of Diverse High-Throughput Datasets through the Omics Integrator Software Package

Amanda J. Kedaigle
Massachusetts Institute of Technology, mandyjoy@mit.edu

ABSTRACT

High-throughput 'omic' methods reveal many aspects of cellular state and biological responses to perturbations. However, no single data type is capable of fully representing the cellular activity. Beyond the list of molecules from each data type, there is a necessity to consider multiple data jointly and reconstruct the relations between these molecules with personalized network-based approaches. We introduced the Omics Integrator software that integrates a variety of 'omic' data as input and identifies putative underlying molecular pathways. The approach applies an advanced network optimization algorithm to a network of thousands of molecular interactions to find high-confidence, interpretable subnetworks that best explain the data. Omics Integrator also provides an elegant framework to incorporate not only positive data, but also negative evidence. Incorporating negative evidence allows Omics Integrator to avoid unexpressed genes and avoid being biased toward highly-studied hub proteins, except when they are strongly implicated by the data. The tool has been applied in several examples, including data derived from Huntington's Disease and glioblastoma multiforme models, to identify novel pathways and nodes through which biological perturbations cause changes in the cell.

Omics Integrator software is available on GitHub at https://github.com/fraenkel-lab/OmicsIntegrator, or as a web tool at http://fraenkel.mit.edu/omicsintegrator

CCS Concepts/ACM Classifiers

- Applied computing~Biological networks;
- Applied computing~Systems biology;
- Applied computing~Computational transcriptomics;
- Applied computing~Computational proteomics;
- Mathematics of computing~Graph algorithms;
- Human-centered computing~Graph drawings

Author Keywords

bioinformatics; network biology; network optimization

Highlighted Paper: Tuncbag N, Gosline SJC, Kedaigle A, Soltis AR, Gitter A, Fraenkel E (2016). Network-based interpretation of diverse high-throughput datasets through the Omics Integrator software package, PLOS Comp Bio, 12(4):e1004879. http://journals.plos.org/ploscompbiol/article?id=10.1371/journal.pcbi.1004879

Permission to make digital or hard copies of part or all of this work for personal or classroom use is granted without fee provided that copies are not made or distributed for profit or commercial advantage and that copies bear this notice and the full citation on the first page. Copyrights for third-party components of this work must be honored. For all other uses, contact the owner/author(s).
ACM-BCB'17, August 20-23, 2017, Boston, MA, USA.
© 2017 Copyright is held by the owner/author(s).
ACM ISBN 978-1-4503-4722-8/17/08.
DOI: http://dx.doi.org/10.1145/3107411.3107461

3D Genome Structure Modeling by Lorentzian Objective Function

Tuan Trieu
Department of Electrical Engineering
and Computer Science
University of Missouri, Columbia, MO 65211 USA
tatrz9@mail.missouri.edu

Jianlin Cheng
Department of Electrical Engineering
and Computer Science
University of Missouri, Columbia, MO 65211 USA
chengji@missouri.edu

ABSTRACT

Reconstructing 3D structure of a genome from chromosomal conformation capturing data such as Hi-C data has emerged as an important problem in bioinformatics and computational biology in the recent years. In this talk, I will present our latest method that uses Lorentzian function to describe distance restraints between chromosomal regions, which will be used to guide the reconstruction of 3D structures of individual chromosomes and an entire genome. The method is more robust against noisy distance restraints derived from Hi-C data than traditional objective functions such as squared error function and Gaussian probabilistic function. The method can handle both intra- and inter-chromosomal contacts effectively to build 3D structures of a big genome such as the human genome consisting of a number of chromosomes, which are not possible with most existing methods.

We have released the Java source code that implements the method (called LorDG) at GitHub (https://github.com/BDM-Lab/LorDG), which is being used by the community to model 3D genome structures. We are currently further improving the method to build very high-resolution (e.g. 1KB base pair) 3D genome and chromosome models.

CCS CONCEPTS • Bioinformatics → Genomics

KEYWORDS

3D genome; modeling; optimization; Lorentzian function; chromosomal conformation capturing; Hi-C

ACM Reference format:

T. Trieu and J. Cheng. 2017. 3D Genome Structure Modeling by Lorentzian Objective Function. In *Proceedings of the 8th ACM Conference on Bioinformatics, Computational Biology, and Health Informatics, Boston, MA, USA, August 2017*, 1 page.

Permission to make digital or hard copies of part or all of this work for personal or classroom use is granted without fee provided that copies are not made or distributed for profit or commercial advantage and that copies bear this notice and the full citation on the first page. Copyrights for third-party components of this work must be honored. For all other uses, contact the Owner/Author.
ACM-BCB '17, August 20-23, 2017, Boston, MA, USA
© 2017 Copyright is held by the owner/author(s).
ACM ISBN 978-1-4503-4722-8/17/08.
http://dx.doi.org/10.1145/3107411.3107455

Folding Large Proteins by Ultra-Deep Learning*

Jinbo Xu
Toyota Technological Institute at Chicago, USA
jinboxu@gmail.com

ABSTRACT

Ab initio protein folding is one of the most challenging problems in computational biology. The popular fragment assembly method mainly can only fold some small proteins. Recently contact-assisted folding has made some progress, but it requires accurate contact prediction, which by existing methods can only be achieved on some proteins with a very large number (>500 or 1000) of sequence homologs. To deal with proteins without so many sequence homologs, we have developed a novel deep learning model for contact prediction by concatenating two deep residual neural networks (ResNet), which performed the best in 2015 computer vision challenges. The first ResNet conducts convolutional transformation of 1-dimensional features and the second conducts convolutional transformation of 2-dimensional information including output of the first one. Experimental results suggest that our deep learning method greatly outperforms existing contact prediction methods and doubles the accuracy of pure co-evolution methods on proteins without many sequence homologs. Our method is ranked 1st in terms of the total F1 score in the latest CASP competition (i.e., CASP12), although back then (May-July 2016) our method was not fully implemented. Our predicted contacts also lead to much more accurate contact-assisted folding. Blindly tested in the weekly benchmark CAMEO (which can be interpreted as fully-automated CASP) since October 2016, our fully-automated web server implementing this method successfully folded many large hard targets (up to 600 residues) without good templates and many sequence homologs. Our large-scale benchmark indicates that ab initio folding (based upon predicted contacts) now can correctly fold more than 2/3 of randomly-chosen proteins. We have also applied this method to membrane protein contact prediction, which produces very good results in terms of both contact prediction accuracy and folding. An important finding is that even trained by only non-membrane proteins, our deep model works very well on membrane protein contact prediction and folding. This is because our deep model learns to predict contacts by making use of contact occurrence patterns (which are shared between membrane and non-membrane proteins) instead of sequence similarity. This method can also be extended to protein-protein interaction prediction, protein complex prediction and protein docking. Our web server implementing this method is publicly available at http://raptorx.uchicago.edu/ContactMap/. For technical and result details, please see our papers [1-2].

Permission to make digital or hard copies of part or all of this work for personal or classroom use is granted without fee provided that copies are not made or distributed for profit or commercial advantage and that copies bear this notice and the full citation on the first page. Copyrights for third-party components of this work must be honored. For all other uses, contact the Owner/Author.
ACM-BCB '17, August 20-23, 2017, Boston, MA, USA
© 2017 Copyright is held by the owner/author(s).
ACM ISBN 978-1-4503-4722-8/17/08.
http://dx.doi.org/10.1145/3107411.3107456

ACKNOWLEDGMENTS

This work was supported by NIH R01GM089753, NSF BIO-1564955 and GPU hardware grant from Nvidia Inc.

REFERENCES

[1] S. Wang, S. Sun, Z. Li, R. Zhang and J. Xu. Accurate De Novo Prediction of Protein Contact Map by Ultra-Deep Learning Model. PLoS Computational Biology, January 2017
[2] S. Wang, Z. Li, Y. Zhou and J. Xu. Folding Membrane Proteins by Deep Transfer Learning. Cell Systems, 2017 (accepted). A conference version also appears at RECOMB 2017.

The 2017 Computational Structural Bioinformatics Workshop

Nurit Haspel*
University of Massachusetts Boston
100 Morrissey Blvd.
Boston, Massachusetts 02125
nurit.haspel@umb.edu

Amarda Shehu
George Mason University
4400 University Dr.
Fairfax, Virginia 22030
amarda@gmu.edu

Kevin Molloy
George Mason University
4400 University Dr.
Fairfax, Virginia 22030
kmolloy1@gmu.edu

ABSTRACT

The rapid accumulation of macromolecular structures presents a unique set of challenges and opportunities in the analysis, comparison, modeling, and prediction of macromolecular structures and interactions. This workshop aims to bring together researchers with expertise in bioinformatics, computational biology, structural biology, data mining, optimization and high performance computing to discuss new results, techniques, and research problems in computational structural bioinformatics.

CCS CONCEPTS

•**Applied computing → Computational biology; Molecular structural biology; Bioinformatics;**

KEYWORDS

Computational structural biology, structural bioinformatics, computational biology

ACM Reference format:
Nurit Haspel, Amarda Shehu, and Kevin Molloy. 2017. The 2017 Computational Structural Bioinformatics Workshop. In *Proceedings of ACM-BCB'17, August 20–23, 2017, Boston, MA, USA.*, , 1 pages.
DOI: http://dx.doi.org/10.1145/3107411.3108166

This year CSBW was co-located with ACM-BCB 2017. A total of 18 original research articles were submitted for review to CSBW 2017. Each submission received at least 3 reviews, and 12 submissions were selected for presentation at CSBW 2017 and publication in the workshop companion proceedings of AMC-BCB 2017.

In "Automated Protein Chain Isolation from 3D Cryo-EM Data and Volume Comparison Tool," Michael Nissenson, Jing He, and Dong Si present a method to automate and so reduce the time it takes to manually isolate volumetric 3D cryo-EM protein density map data surrounding known protein structures. In "Gaussian Mixture Models with Constrained Flexibility for Fitting Tomogram Tiltseries," the authors, Kasra Manavi, Sahba Tashakkori, and Lydia Tapia present a Gaussian Mixture Model to fit flexible, coarse-grained models of molecular systems to projections from low-resolution tomogram tiltseries. In "Geometry Analysis for Protein Secondary Structures Matching Problem," Kamal Al Nasr, Feras Yousef, Christopher Jones, and Ruba Jebril present a new scoring function to improve the accuracy of a popular algorithm for finding the topology of secondary structures of a protein within a cryo-EM density map. In "A Method for Characterization of β-strand twist from a 3-dimensional Image of a protein," Tunazzina Islam, Michael Poteat, and Jing He present a method to address the difficult problem of detecting the twist of a β-strand in a cryo-EM density map. In "A Graph Based Method for the Prediction of Backbone Trace from Cryo-EM Density Maps," Peter Collins and Dong Si present a method to reconstruct the backbone trace corresponding to a high-resolution cryo-EM density map.

In "Investigating Rigidity Properties of Protein Cavities", Stephanie Mason, Brian Chen, and Filip Jagodzinski show via a structural analysis of cavities in 8,000 protein chains that cavity size correlates with many cavity rigidity metrics and can be a useful tool to better understand and predict specificity of ligand binding, and molecular docking. In "ProMuteHT : A High Throughput Compute Pipeline for Generating Protein Mutants in silico," Erik Andersson and Filip Jagodzinski present a computational pipeline to reduce manual intervention when performing *in-silico* amino-acid substitutions in a given protein structure, opening the way to *in-silico* mutagenesis.

In "Statistical Analysis of Computed Energy Landscapes to Understand Dysfunction in Pathogenic Protein Variants," Wanli Qiao, Tatiana Maximova, Erion Plaku, and Amarda Shehu present a method that identifies basins in protein energy landscapes and so elucidates mechanisms via which sequence mutations impact biological function. In "Geometric Sampling Framework for Exploring Molecular Walker Energetics and Dynamics," Bruna Jacobson, Jon David, Mitch Malone, Kasra Manavi, Susan R. Atlas, and Lydia Tapia present a robotics-inspired method to model the motion of kinesin along a microtubule. In "Evolving Conformation Paths to Model Protein Structural Transitions," Emmanuel Sapin, Kenneth De Jong, and Amarda Shehu present an evolutionary algorithm to model slow structural rearrangements in proteins.

In "Computational Modeling of pH-dependent gp120-CD4 Interactions in Founder and Chronic HIV Strains," Jonathan Howton and Joshua Phillips present a computational pipeline for analyzing the pH sensitivity of protein-protein interactions and elucidate transmission-critical interactions between the HIV gp120 and host CD4 proteins. In "Feature-Based and String-Based Models for Predicting RNA-Protein Interaction," Donald Adjeroh, Jun Tan, and Jie Lin present two supervised learning algorithms to predict RNA-Protein interactions from structure and sequence data. In "Ranking Protein-Protein Binding Using Evolutionary Information," Roshanak Farhoodi, Bahar Akbal-Delibas, and Nurit Haspel present a method to re-rank docked protein complexes based on machine learning and evolutionary information.

*Corresponding author

Permission to make digital or hard copies of part or all of this work for personal or classroom use is granted without fee provided that copies are not made or distributed for profit or commercial advantage and that copies bear this notice and the full citation on the first page. Copyrights for third-party components of this work must be honored. For all other uses, contact the owner/author(s).
ACM-BCB'17, August 20–23, 2017, Boston, MA, USA.
© 2017 Copyright held by the owner/author(s). ISBN 978-1-4503-4722-8/17/08.
DOI: http://dx.doi.org/10.1145/3107411.3108166

Computational Modeling of pH-dependent gp120-CD4 Interactions in Founder and Chronic HIV Strains

Jonathan Howton
jh6w@mtmail.mtsu.edu
Middle Tennessee State University
Department of Computer Science
Murfreesboro, TN 37130, USA

Joshua L. Phillips*
Joshua.Phillips@mtsu.edu
Middle Tennessee State University
Department of Computer Science
Murfreesboro, TN 37130, USA

ABSTRACT

Human Immunodeficiency Virus has been studied for several decades, but a consistently effective vaccine has not yet been produced. While most experimental and computational work in this area has been performed under slightly basic conditions (eg. blood/plasma), viral transmission events often occur under highly acidic conditions (eg. vaginal mucosa). Environmental pH can greatly affect protein structure and epitope exposure to either inhibit or facilitate transmission. We develop a computational pipeline for analyzing the pH sensitivity of protein-protein interactions, and use the pipeline to analyze the transmission-critical interaction between the HIV gp120 and host CD4 proteins. The interaction between gp120 and CD4 is found to be stronger at low pH for all strains tested, which is consistent with previous work and supports the accuracy of the introduced pipeline. Also, early transmitted founder (TF) strains are found to generally bind CD4 better at low pH and are more pH sensitive than systemically circulating chronic control (CC) strains.

CCS CONCEPTS

• **Applied computing → Molecular structural biology**;

KEYWORDS

HIV; protein-protein interaction; environmental factors; vaccines; antibodies; molecular modeling; gp120; CD4

1 INTRODUCTION

More than thirty years after the discovery of Acquired Immune Deficiency Syndrome (AIDS), there is still no vaccine against the Human Immunodeficiency Virus (HIV) that causes the disease [17]. Since HIV has a very high mutation rate, antigenic regions which are targeted by host antibodies vary greatly across HIV virions even within a single host. Therefore, most vaccine research has focused on inducing so-called broadly neutralizing antibodies (bnAbs). The bnAbs are able to target regions of the virus that must be conserved due to functional requirements [4], most of which are found on the gp120 extracellular subunit of the viral envelope protein (Env) that is responsible for binding CD4 on the surface of host T-Cells to begin infection [31]. Vaccines have been produced from Env fragments that have been computationally optimized to (potentially) invoke the production of bnAbs [11]. Results from these vaccines have varied from successful [3] to unsuccessful [19]. A possible explanation for this inconsistency is that the bnAbs are isolated from the blood, which has a slightly basic pH, while HIV is often transmitted at the mucosa, which are highly acidic. Since protein structure and protein-protein interactions are typically affected by pH, it is likely that the structure of Env and its affinity for other proteins, such as CD4 and bnAbs, is altered. In addition, experimental and computational studies have shown that pH impacts both Env conformation and CD4 binding [29]. In particular, trimeric Env proteins were found to bind CD4 better under acidic conditions, Env surface charge was more complimentary (negative) to the host CD4 surface (positive), and the unbound to bound conformational change was electrostatically more preferable at mucosal pH levels.

Since HIV mutates rapidly within the host, we anticipate that strains in a chronic infection, so called chronic control (CC) strains, will likely have adapted to the systemic pH, and will be less efficient at binding CD4 under acidic conditions when compared to transmitted founder (TF) strains. Consequently, bnAbs produced in chronically infected individuals might be less likely to neutralize HIV transmission at the mucosa. Therefore, it is important to study gp120-CD4 binding under mucosal pH because this conserved interaction is an important target for vaccine production. However, the large variation in gp120 sequence across HIV strains makes experimental studies prohibitive, but computational modeling can help fill this gap in a predictive capacity.

We describe the implementation of a computational modeling pipeline capable of quickly creating and analyzing models of unbound gp120 and the gp120-CD4 interaction for a large number of Env sequences across a wide pH range. A dataset of TF and CC pairs, spanning HIV clades B and C, is used to validate the pipeline and explore several contingent hypotheses: 1) that the Env-CD4 interaction would be strongest at low pH, 2) that the Env protein from TF strains would bind CD4 better under low pH compared to CC strains, and 3) that the Env-CD4 interaction would be more pH sensitive in TF strains. Data obtained from the pipeline is also used to elucidate potential mechanisms responsible for differences between HIV classes.

*The corresponding author

Permission to make digital or hard copies of all or part of this work for personal or classroom use is granted without fee provided that copies are not made or distributed for profit or commercial advantage and that copies bear this notice and the full citation on the first page. Copyrights for components of this work owned by others than the author(s) must be honored. Abstracting with credit is permitted. To copy otherwise, or republish, to post on servers or to redistribute to lists, requires prior specific permission and/or a fee. Request permissions from permissions@acm.org.
ACM-BCB'17, August 20-23, 2017, Boston, MA, USA.
© 2017 Copyright held by the owner/author(s). Publication rights licensed to ACM.
978-1-4503-4722-8/17/08...$15.00
DOI: http://dx.doi.org/10.1145/3107411.3107506

2 BACKGROUND

2.1 HIV Variant Subclasses

In most clinical HIV infections, a single TF virion is responsible for the transmission event [16]. TF viruses share common traits that distinguish them from chronic control (CC) strains, and these traits likely enhance TF virus fitness for crossing the mucosal barrier and promoting productive initial infection [23]. Since TF virions are often transmitted at acidic mucosa, it is expected that TF strains are better adapted for transmission at low pH relative to CC strains.

Clades B and C are subgroups of the HIV-1 group major [30]. Clade C is the most prevalent clade of HIV globally, and is the most common in China, India, and Africa, while clade B is most prevalent in America and Europe [1]. Clade C is less virulent [1], which causes a slower progression and a longer asymptomatic period and increases opportunities for transmission [25].

2.2 Previous gp120-CD4 Electrostatic Modeling

The gp120 protein was previously modeled using several solved gp120 fragment crystal structures [29]. Partial atomic charges and protonation states were calculated across pH and salinity ranges using the PDB2PQR [7] and the PROPKA3.0 [28] framework. The APBS [2] tool was used to determine surface charge density. Similar approaches have been used to examine protein-protein interactions in available crystal structures [20]. The surface potentials of the CD4 protein and the CD4 binding site of gp120 were found to be complementary at low pH. Also, comparisons between bound and unbound conformations predicted that gp120 exhibits a lower solvation energy for the bound conformation at low pH, effectively priming Env for binding to CD4. Binding assays and electrophoretic measurements using trimeric Env confirmed this hypothesis, suggesting complementary charge density modulated by environmental pH as the primary mechanism. These calculations were facilitated by crystal structures, so only a limited number of sequences could be compared. Also, electrostatic contributions to the binding energy could not be quantified since CD4 is not present in most structures.

Two tools exist for extending the approach above for modeling unsolved gp120 structures. The first is MODELLER: software for homology modeling of protein structures [8, 26]. The second is FRODAN: software for computationally efficient geometric simulation of protein structures which can adapt modeled protein structures to target conformations while preserving stereochemical constraints [10]. There are several solved gp120 structures, such as 1RZK [14] and 2B4C [13], but all models have CD4, an antibody, or both bound. The only unbound model available is 2BF1, which is the simian immunodeficiency virus (SIV) gp120 subunit [5]. Despite HIV/SIV sequence differences, 2BF1 provides a reasonable template for unbound structural alignments with HIV gp120 as evidenced in the study above [29]. APBS [2] can then be used to directly calculate the electrostatic contribution to the binding energy, ΔG_e, of the gp120-CD4 complex across a wide pH range.

3 METHODS

3.1 gp120 Sequences

One TF sequence and one CC sequence were analyzed from each of 24 individuals. Of these 24 pairs of sequences, 18 pairs were B clade sequences, and 6 were C clade sequences. TF sequences were defined as sequences collected within the first 6 months of infection, while CC sequences were collected after this initial period. Additional sequence details including accession numbers and sequence alignments can be found in [12].

3.2 Pipeline Configuration and Automation

Bash 4.1.2, Python 3.4, and R 3.4.0 scripts were used to automate the modeling and analysis of all sequences within the dataset. The pipeline is initialized using sequences and target structures and proceeds in the stepwise fashion desribed below.

3.2.1 Structural Modeling. The analyzed sequences do not have solved structures, so MODELLER [26] was used with a preconstructed set of seven template gp120 structures to produce a set of homology models. The template structures used were 1G9M [18], 1RZK [14], 2B4C [13], 2NY7 [32], 3JWD [22], 3JWO [22], and 3LQA [6]. Ten homology models were produced for each tested sequence to account for natural structural variations in the flexible, variable-loop regions. Ten models were sufficient to assess statistical significance between the different Env classes and sensitivity conditions in this study. However, attempts to discriminate differences between individual Env sequences may require an order of magnitude or more increase in the number of models.

To determine the binding energy of the complex, the electrostatic energy of the complex and the individual components of the complex must be determined. FRODAN is used to adjust the core structure of the models to the three conformations (unbound, bound, and CD4-complex) while preserving stereochemical constraints similar to the approach used by [24]. 2BF1 was the target used to produce the unbound conformations. The bound and CD4-complex conformations were produced using target 1RZK.

3.2.2 Electrostatic Binding Energy and Charge Density. Charge and protonation data were determined for all models across a wide range of pH using PDB2PQR 2.0.0 [7] and PROPKA 3.0 [21, 28]. The tested pH range was from 3 to 9 in increments of 0.1. PQR files were generated over the pH range for all model conformations.

Electrostatic energy for each structure was calculated for all of the PQR files using APBS 1.4 [2] to solve the full non-linear Poisson-Boltzmann equation. For each set, the number of grid points, coarse mesh lengths, fine mesh lengths, and known center were calculated using the APBS [2] psize tool. The counter ion (e.g. NaCl) concentration was set to 0.155M for ions with a +1 charge and for ions with a -1 charge. The calculations were carried out with 310K as the system temperature. Surface potential data were saved in DX format for each molecule within a set at whole number pH values.

Binding energies were calculated in two ways. First, the standard bound form binding energy was calculated by subtracting the electrostatic energies of both the CD4 molecule and the bound conformation of gp120 from the electrostatic energy of the gp120-CD4 complex at a given pH. Second, the unbound form binding energy was calculated by subtracting the electrostatic energies of both the CD4 molecule and the unbound conformation of gp120 from the electrostatic energy of the gp120-CD4 complex at a given pH. The solvation energy difference was found by subtracting the electrostatic energy of the bound gp120 conformation from the electrostatic energy of the unbound gp120 conformation.

3.2.3 Statistical Analysis. Binding energy sensitivity was determined as the binding energy at low-pH (3.5, 3.6, 3.7, 3.8, 3.9, 4.0, 4.1, 4.2, 4.3, 4.4, and 4.5) subtracted from the binding energy at high-pH (7.0, 7.1, 7.2, 7.3, 7.4, 7.5, 7.6, 7.7, 7.8, 7.9, and 8.0), respectively. This produces 11 binding energy sensitivity values for each of the 10 models within each sequence. Individual sequence sensitivity was determined by pooling the 11 sensitivities from all 10 models within a sequence and creating a boxplot from these values. Group sensitivity was determined by finding the median sensitivity across the 10 models within each sequence. The 11 median sensitivity values for each sequence were then pooled with the sensitivity values from all sequences within a corresponding group to produce group sensitivity boxplots. The pH sensitivity of solvation energy differences between the bound and unbound conformations was calculated similarly, but solvation energy differences at the indicated pH values were used in place of binding energies. Significant differences between median values for these and all subsequent results were determined using the Mann-Whitney test.

Whole molecule charge density was calculated as the sum of all charges determined by APBS divided by the total solvent accessible surface area, which was determined using VMD [15]. The median charge density was determined within each group at pH 4, 5, 7, and 8. Residue-specific charge density was calculated as the sum of all charges determined by APBS that were on the surface of the residue, divided by the solvent accessible surface area of the residue. VMD [15] was used to assign electrostatic charge coordinates to corresponding residues and to determine the solvent accessible surface area of each residue.

To determine pH sensitivity of whole molecule charge density, first charge density differences were determined by subtracting the unbound charge density from the bound charge density at each pH value. These charge density differences were directly compared. The sensitivity was calculated as this value at pH 4 subtracted from this value at pH 7, this value at pH 5 subtracted from this value at pH 8, or the average of these two sensitivities.

3.2.4 Sequence Alignment-Based Model Fitting. Next, identification of sequence motifs which correlate with differences between residue-specific surface charge density was performed. Clustal Omega [27] was used to align all analyzed sequences. Within each group tested, charges were assigned to alignment positions in two ways as described in [12]. Groups were compared by subtracting each assigned value from the corresponding value in the other group. The top 1% of residues were identified as residues that had an absolute sensitivity difference larger than 1% of the absolute sum of residue sensitivity differences in a given comparison.

4 RESULTS

The pH sensitivity of gp120 charge density was found to be significantly more sensitive in the CC strains when compared to TF strains (Figure 1a). Additionally, B clade strains were found to be significantly more sensitive than C clade strains (Figure 1b).

When the unbound structure was not considered, the gp120-CD4 interaction was significantly more favorable (lower binding

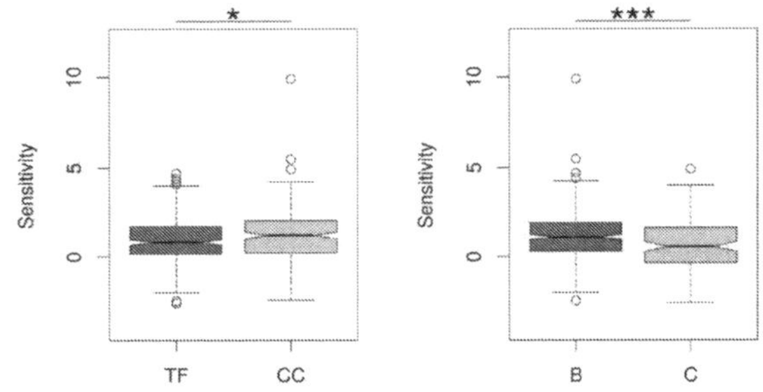

(a) TF vs CC (b) B vs C

Figure 1: Charge density sensitivity comparisons between (a) TF and CC classes and (b) B and C clades. (* $p < 0.05$, *** $p < 0.001$)

energy values) for TF strains than CC strains at many pH values between pH 4 and 6.5 (Figure 2a). However, there was no significant difference when comparing the pH sensitivity of this interaction (Figure 2a inset boxplot). Considering the energy contribution of the unbound to bound conformational change altered the shape of the binding energy curve, this calculation suggests that CC strains bind CD4 better at pH values between 6.5 and 8.5. However, this was only significant at pH 7.9, 8, and 8.1 (Figure 2b). The binding energy in TF strains was found to be significantly more sensitive to pH than CC strains when considering this conformational change (Figure 2b inset boxplot). These results appear to be most representative within the B clade (data not shown; reported in [12]).

The unbound binding energy calculation was used to compare B and C clades within each class (Figure 3). Within the TF class, the only significant difference was at pH 9, though there was a general trend of C binding CD4 better at pH values above 6.5 (Figure 3a). There was no significant difference in sensitivity within TF (Figure 3a inset boxplot). Within the CC class, the only significant difference found was at pH 3.7 (Figure 3b). However, CD4 binding was found to be significantly more pH sensitive in C clade when compared to B clade (Figure 3b inset boxplot).

The difference in solvation energy between the bound and unbound conformations was used to determine the conformation that was most energetically favorable at each pH. A difference above zero indicates that the bound conformation is more favorable, while a value below zero indicates that the unbound conformation is more favorable. Within B clade, the CC class had a significantly more positive solvation energy difference than the TF class at many pH values above 6, as well as pH 4.7 and 4.8 (Figure 4a). This conformation preference was found to be significantly more sensitive to pH in the TF class (Figure 4a inset boxplot). Within the CC class, there were no significant differences in solvation energy difference at any pH value between B and C clades, though there was a trend of B clade being more positive at pH values from 5 to 8 (Figure 4b). The conformation preference was found to be significantly more pH sensitive in C clade (Figure 4b inset boxplot).

Residue-specific charge density pH sensitivity was determined and the difference in sensitivity between corresponding groups was calculated as described above. The most significant difference in binding energy between TF and CC strains was found within B

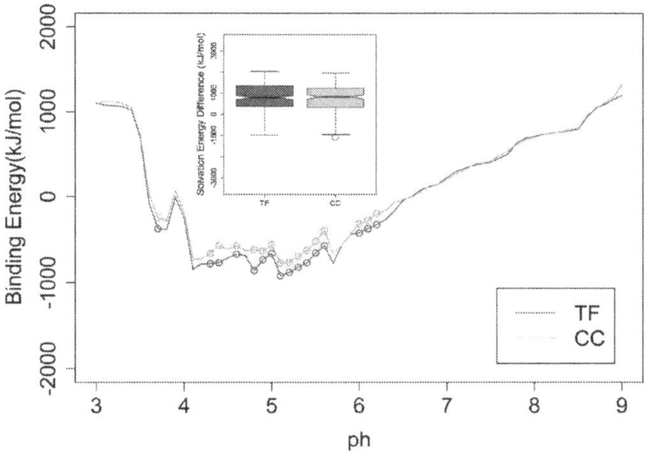

(a) Bound Calculation

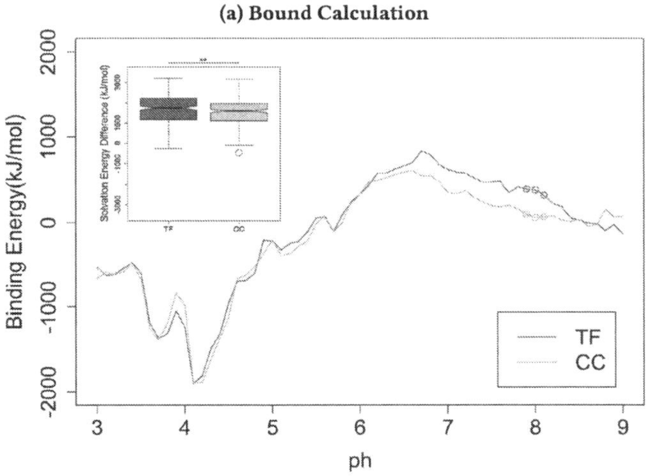

(b) Unbound Calculation

Figure 2: Median binding energy comparison between TF and CC strains across pH range using (a) bound calculation and (b) unbound calculation. Significantly different binding energies are identified by corresponding points. Boxplots compare pH sensitivity of binding energy between TF (left) and CC (right). ($p < 0.01$)**

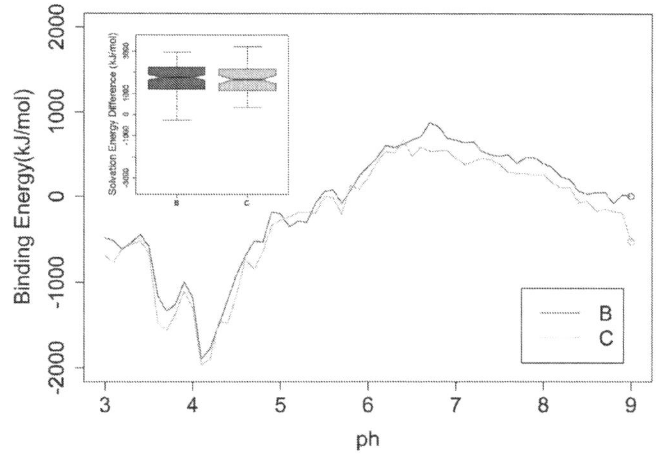

(a) Within TF

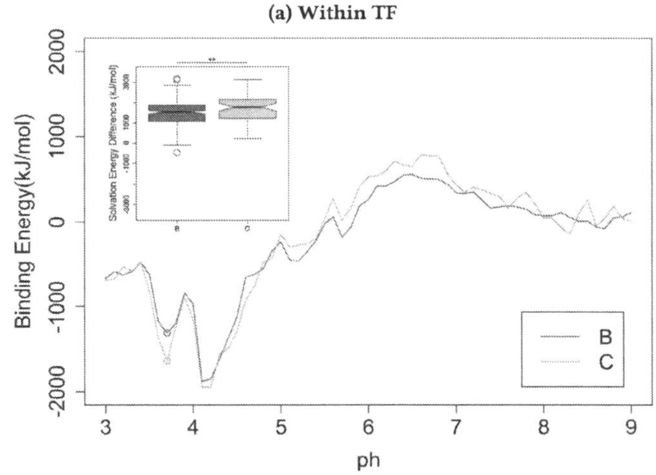

(b) Within CC

Figure 3: Median binding energy comparison between B and C clades across pH range using the unbound calculation (a) within the TF class and (b) within the CC class. Significantly different binding energies are identified by corresponding points. Boxplots compare pH sensitivity of binding energy between B (left) and C (right). ($p < 0.01$)**

clade, so the residue sensitivity was compared within this clade. Differences were found at residues 343 and 402. However, for 402 these differences only occur in a single TF and a single CC strain, and is not representative of the groups overall (see [12]).

Residues with the largest sensitivity difference were also identified by comparing B and C clades within the CC class. Only a single residue was identified (474), and it was also poorly representative of the overall sequences as indicated by low bit scores (see [12]).

5 DISCUSSION

Though AIDS and HIV have been studied for several decades, a viable vaccine has yet to be produced. Since the significance of the acidic pH of the typical mucosal transmission site has been broadly overlooked, we constructed a pipeline to analyze the pH sensitivity of the gp120-CD4 interaction in TF and CC strains.

The charge density of CC strains was found to be more pH sensitive than TF strains (Figure 1a). Also, the surface charge of B clade sequences was significantly more sensitive to pH than that of C clade sequences (Figure 1b). While no difference between CC and TF strains nor B and C clades was reported in previous work [29], these difference are most likely due to the increased number of sequences analyzed here.

Calculations using the bound conformation found TF strains to bind CD4 significantly better than CC strains at low pH (Figure 2a). At high pH values, CC was found to bind CD4 better in the calculation using the unbound gp120 conformation (Figure 2b). Additional analysis (data not shown, see [12]) showed that this was

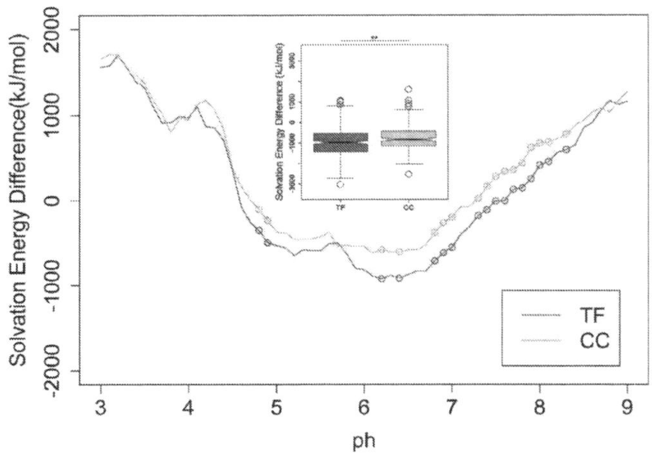

(a) TF vs CC Within B Clade

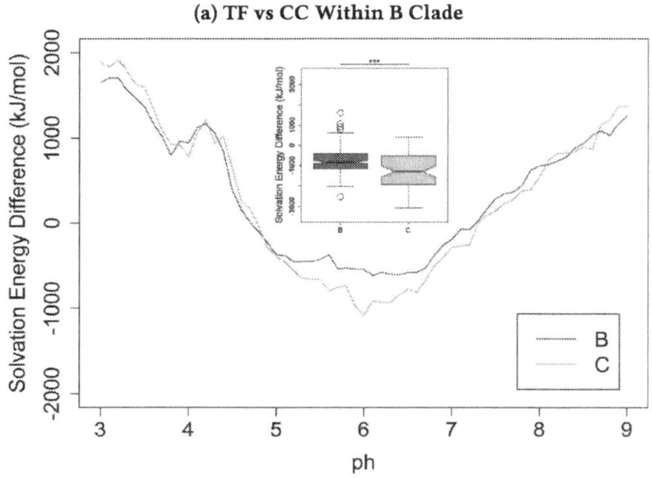

(b) B vs C Within CC Class

Figure 4: Median solvation energy difference between bound and unbound conformations across pH range compared between (a) TF and CC classes within B clade and (b) B and C clades within the CC class. Significantly different binding energies are identified by corresponding points. Boxplots compare pH sensitivity of binding energy between B (left) and C (right). ($p < 0.01$, *** $p < 0.001$)**

found to be significant within B clade while the CC class within B clade also significantly prefers the unbound conformation at both high and low (but not intermediate) pH. These results suggest that the increased CD4 binding at low pH in TF strains is not due to increased pressure to assume the bound conformation, but is more likely due to a more favorable interaction between gp120 and CD4. Conversely, the increased binding ability of CC strains at higher pH values appears to be influenced by an increased preference to assume the bound conformation.

Using the unbound calculation, there was a trend within class TF in which C clade bound CD4 better at pH values above 6.5 (Figure 3a). Additional analysis (see [12]) revealed that B clade preferred the unbound conformation over C clade from pH 5 to 7 within the overall group and within the CC class, but C clade prefers the unbound conformation within class TF from pH 6 to 8. The trend within class TF suggests that C clade may bind better at higher pH due to a preference for the bound conformation. However, this is based upon an observed trend, so a larger number of C clade samples would be needed to evaluate its significance. Regardless, across all binding energy calculations, gp120 bound CD4 better at low pH, consistent with previous experimental results [29].

When calculating sensitivity with the bound gp120 conformations, no significant differences could be found between TF and CC (Figure 2). However, when using the unbound conformation for the calculation, the TF gp120-CD4 interaction was significantly more sensitive to pH (Figure 2b), particularly within B clade [12]. This was consistent with previous experimental results [29]. Additionally, the preference for the bound conformation was significantly more pH sensitive for TF strains within the B clade (Figure 4a). This suggests that the increased binding energy pH sensitivity of the TF strains within B clade is due to the effect of pH on the gp120 conformation, and that modeling of the unbound conformation was integral to these results.

Within the CC class, CD4 binding was found to be significantly more sensitive in C clade when using the unbound conformation (Figure 3b). Also within CC, the preference for the bound conformation was found to be significantly more sensitive in C clade (Figure 4b). These results suggest that within the CC class, pH affects CD4 binding through the conformational shift in C clade.

Efforts to understand a mechanism of binding sensitivity identified a few residues that may contribute to the observed differences (see results and additional data reported in [12]). Unfortunately, sequence comparisons did not indicate any clear sequence difference that could contribute to the observed sensitivity differences.

Overall, this work shows the importance of the pH sensitivity mechanism and its potential role in the gp120-CD4 interaction. Several subclass-specific mechanisms were identified using the pipeline even though residue-specific pH sensitivity provided no additional insights. This is particularly important for HIV vaccine research because the CD4 binding site is an important vaccine target, and pH has been shown to affect antibody binding at the mucosa [9]. Additionally, bnAbs typically target the CD4 binding site of gp120 [31]. Investigations into the pH sensitivity of gp120-bnAb interactions using the pipeline are currently ongoing.

Additionally, this work shows the effectiveness of the proposed pipeline for analyzing pH sensitivity for protein-protein interactions. The pipeline builds upon previous approaches for computing electrostatic potential across a range of environmental conditions [20, 29] by integrating high-throughput structural modeling, conformational search, and targeted docking for a large set of sequences [8, 10, 24]. Computed gp120-CD4 binding energy sensitivities were also consistent with previous work [29].

REFERENCES

[1] Kevin K Ariën, Guido Vanham, and Eric J Arts. 2007. Is HIV-1 evolving to a less virulent form in humans? *Nature Reviews. Microbiology* 5, 2 (2007), 141–51. DOI: https://doi.org/10.1038/nrmicro1594

[2] N A Baker, D Sept, S Joseph, M J Holst, and J A McCammon. 2001. Electrostatics of nanosystems: application to microtubules and the ribosome. *Proceedings of the National Academy of Sciences of the United States of America* 98, 18 (2001), 10037–41. DOI: https://doi.org/10.1073/pnas.181342398

[3] Dan H Barouch, Kathryn E Stephenson, Erica N Borducchi, Kaitlin Smith, Kelly Stanley, Anna G McNally, Jinyan Liu, Peter Abbink, Lori F Maxfield, Michael S Seaman, Anne-Sophie Dugast, Galit Alter, Melissa Ferguson, Wenjun Li, Patricia L Earl, Bernard Moss, Elena E Giorgi, James J Szinger, Leigh Anne Eller, Erik A Billings, Mangala Rao, Sodsai Tovanabutra, Eric Sanders-Buell, Mo Weijtens, Maria G Pau, Hanneke Schuitemaker, Merlin L Robb, Jerome H Kim, Bette T Korber, and Nelson L Michael. 2013. Protective efficacy of a global HIV-1 mosaic vaccine against heterologous SHIV challenges in rhesus monkeys. *Cell* 155, 3 (Oct 2013), 531–9. DOI: https://doi.org/10.1016/j.cell.2013.09.061

[4] Dennis R Burton, Pascal Poignard, Robyn L Stanfield, and Ian A Wilson. 2012. Broadly neutralizing antibodies present new prospects to counter highly antigenically diverse viruses. *Science (New York, N.Y.)* 337, 6091 (Jul 2012), 183–6. DOI: https://doi.org/10.1126/science.1225416

[5] Bing Chen, Erik M Vogan, Haiyun Gong, John J Skehel, Don C Wiley, and Stephen C Harrison. 2005. Structure of an unliganded simian immunodeficiency virus gp120 core. (2005). DOI: https://doi.org/10.1038/nature03327

[6] Ron Diskin, Paola M Marcovecchio, and Pamela J Bjorkman. 2010. Structure of a clade C HIV-1 gp120 bound to CD4 and CD4-induced antibody reveals anti-CD4 polyreactivity. *Nature Structural Molecular Biology* 17, 5 (May 2010), 608–13. DOI: https://doi.org/10.1038/nsmb.1796

[7] Todd J. Dolinsky, Paul Czodrowski, Hui Li, Jens E. Nielsen, Jan H. Jensen, Gerhard Klebe, and Nathan A. Baker. 2007. PDB2PQR: Expanding and upgrading automated preparation of biomolecular structures for molecular simulations. *Nucleic Acids Research* 35, SUPPL.2 (2007), 522–525. DOI: https://doi.org/10.1093/nar/gkm276

[8] Narayanan Eswar, Ben Webb, Marc A. Marti-Renom, M.S. Madhusudhan, David Eramian, Min-Yi Shen, Ursula Pieper, and Andrej Sali. 2002. *Comparative protein structure modeling using modeller.* John Wiley & Sons, Inc. DOI: https://doi.org/10.1002/0471250953.bi0506s15

[9] Kelly M. Fahrbach, Olga Malykhina, Daniel J. Stieh, and Thomas J. Hope. 2013. Differential Binding of IgG and IgA to Mucus of the Female Reproductive Tract. *PLOS ONE* 8, 10 (10 2013), 1–11. DOI: https://doi.org/10.1371/journal.pone.0076176

[10] Daniel W. Farrell, Kirill Speranskiy, and M. F. Thorpe. 2010. Generating stereochemically acceptable protein pathways. *Proteins: Structure, Function and Bioinformatics* 78, 14 (2010), 2908–2921. DOI: https://doi.org/10.1002/prot.22810

[11] Will Fischer, Simon Perkins, James Theiler, Tanmoy Bhattacharya, Karina Yusim, Robert Funkhouser, Carla Kuiken, Barton Haynes, Norman L Letvin, Bruce D Walker, Beatrice H Hahn, and Bette T Korber. 2007. Polyvalent vaccines for optimal coverage of potential T-cell epitopes in global HIV-1 variants. *Nature Medicine* 13, 1 (Jan 2007), 100–6. DOI: https://doi.org/10.1038/nm1461

[12] Jonathan Howton. 2017. *A Computational Electrostratic Modeling Pipeline for Comparing pH-dependent gp120-CD4 Interactions in Founder and Chronic HIV Strains.* Master's thesis. Middle Tennessee State University, Murfreesboro, TN. http://jewlscholar.mtsu.edu/xmlui/handle/mtsu/5324

[13] Chih-Chin Huang, Min Tang, Mei-Yun Zhang, Shahzad Majeed, Elizabeth Montabana, Robyn L Stanfield, Dimiter S Dimitrov, Bette Korber, Joseph Sodroski, Ian A Wilson, Richard Wyatt, and Peter D Kwong. 2005. Structure of a V3-containing HIV-1 gp120 core. *Science (New York, N.Y.)* 310, 5750 (Nov 2005), 1025–8. DOI: https://doi.org/10.1126/science.1118398

[14] C C Huang, M Venturi, S Majeed, M J Moore, S Phogat, M Y Zhang, D S Dimitrov, W A Hendrickson, J Robinson, J Sodroski, R Wyatt, H Choe, M Farzan, and P D Kwong. 2004. Structural basis of tyrosine sulfation and VH-gene usage in antibodies that recognize the HIV type 1 coreceptor-binding site on gp120. *Proc Natl Acad Sci U S A* 101, 9 (2004), 2706–2711. DOI: https://doi.org/10.1073/pnas.0308527100

[15] William Humphrey, Andrew Dalke, and Klaus Schulten. 1996. VMD – Visual Molecular Dynamics. *Journal of Molecular Graphics* 14 (1996), 33–38.

[16] Brandon F Keele, Elena E Giorgi, Jesus F Salazar-Gonzalez, Julie M Decker, Kimmy T Pham, Maria G Salazar, Chuanxi Sun, Truman Grayson, Shuyi Wang, Hui Li, Xiping Wei, Chunlai Jiang, Jennifer L Kirchherr, Feng Gao, Jeffery A Anderson, Li-Hua Ping, Ronald Swanstrom, Georgia D Tomaras, William A Blattner, Paul A Goepfert, J Michael Kilby, Michael S Saag, Eric L Delwart, Michael P Busch, Myron S Cohen, David C Montefiori, Barton F Haynes, Brian Gaschen, Gayathri S Athreya, Ha Y Lee, Natasha Wood, Cathal Seoighe, Alan S Perelson, Tanmoy Bhattacharya, Bette T Korber, Beatrice H Hahn, and George M Shaw. 2008. Identification and characterization of transmitted and early founder virus envelopes in primary HIV-1 infection. *Proceedings of the National Academy of Sciences of the United States of America* 105, 21 (2008), 7552–7. DOI: https://doi.org/10.1073/pnas.0802203105

[17] Bette Korber and S. Gnanakaran. 2011. Converging on an HIV Vaccine. *Science* 333, 6049 (2011), 1589–1590. DOI: https://doi.org/10.1126/science.1211919

[18] P D Kwong, R Wyatt, S Majeed, J Robinson, R W Sweet, J Sodroski, and W A Hendrickson. 2000. Structures of HIV-1 gp120 envelope glycoproteins from laboratory-adapted and primary isolates. *Structure (London, England : 1993)* 8, 12 (Dec 2000), 1329–39. http://www.ncbi.nlm.nih.gov/pubmed/11188697

[19] Hua-Xin Liao, Mattia Bonsignori, S Munir Alam, Jason S McLellan, Georgia D Tomaras, M Anthony Moody, Daniel M Kozink, Kwan-Ki Hwang, Xi Chen, Chun-Yen Tsao, Pinghuang Liu, Xiaozhi Lu, Robert J Parks, David C Montefiori, Guido Ferrari, Justin Pollara, Mangala Rao, Kristina K Peachman, Sampa Santra, Norman L Letvin, Nicos Karasavvas, Zhi-Yong Yang, Kaifan Dai, Marie Pancera, Jason Gorman, Kevin Wiehe, Nathan I Nicely, Supachai Rerks-Ngarm, Sorachai Nitayaphan, Jaranit Kaewkungwal, Punnee Pitisuttithum, James Tartaglia, Faruk Sinangil, Jerome H Kim, Nelson L Michael, Thomas B Kepler, Peter D Kwong, John R Mascola, Gary J Nabel, Abraham Pinter, Susan Zolla-Pazner, and Barton F Haynes. 2013. Vaccine induction of antibodies against a structurally heterogeneous site of immune pressure within HIV-1 envelope protein variable regions 1 and 2. *Immunity* 38, 1 (Jan 2013), 176–86. DOI: https://doi.org/10.1016/j.immuni.2012.11.011

[20] Aaron C. Mason and Jan H. Jensen. 2008. Protein-protein binding is often associated with changes in protonation state. *Proteins: Structure, Function and Genetics* 71, 1 (2008), 81–91. DOI: https://doi.org/10.1002/prot.21657

[21] Mats H M Olsson, Chresten R Søndergaard, Michal Rostkowski, and Jan H Jensen. 2011. PROPKA3: Consistent Treatment of Internal and Surface Residues in Empirical pKa Predictions. *Journal of Chemical Theory and Computation* 7, 2 (2011), 525–537. DOI: https://doi.org/10.1021/ct100578z

[22] Marie Pancera, Shahzad Majeed, Yih-En Andrew Ban, Lei Chen, Chih-chin Huang, Leopold Kong, Young Do Kwon, Jonathan Stuckey, Tongqing Zhou, James E Robinson, William R Schief, Joseph Sodroski, Richard Wyatt, and Peter D Kwong. 2010. Structure of HIV-1 gp120 with gp41-interactive region reveals layered envelope architecture and basis of conformational mobility. *Proceedings of the National Academy of Sciences of the United States of America* 107, 3 (Jan 2010), 1166–71. DOI: https://doi.org/10.1073/pnas.0911004107

[23] Nicholas F Parrish, Feng Gao, Hui Li, Elena E Giorgi, Hannah J Barbian, Erica H Parrish, Lara Zajic, Shilpa S Iyer, Julie M Decker, Amit Kumar, Bhavna Hora, Anna Berg, Fangping Cai, Jennifer Hopper, Thomas N Denny, Haitao Ding, Christina Ochsenbauer, John C Kappes, Rachel P Galimidi, Anthony P West, Pamela J Bjorkman, Craig B Wilen, Robert W Doms, Meagan O'Brien, Nina Bhardwaj, Persephone Borrow, Barton F Haynes, Mark Muldoon, James P Theiler, Bette Korber, George M Shaw, and Beatrice H Hahn. 2013. Phenotypic properties of transmitted founder HIV-1. *Proceedings of the National Academy of Sciences of the United States of America* 110, 17 (2013), 6626–33. DOI: https://doi.org/10.1073/pnas.1304288110

[24] Joshua L. Phillips and S. Gnanakaran. 2015. A data-driven approach to modeling the tripartite structure of multidrug resistance efflux pumps. *Proteins: Structure, Function and Bioinformatics* 83, 1 (2015), 46–65. DOI: https://doi.org/10.1002/prot.24632

[25] Indianara Rotta and Sérgio Monteiro de Almeida. 2011. Genotypical diversity of HIV clades and central nervous system impairment. *Arquivos de Neuro-psiquiatria* 69, 6 (Dec 2011), 964–72. http://www.ncbi.nlm.nih.gov/pubmed/22297889

[26] A Sali and T L Blundell. 1993. Comparative protein modelling by satisfaction of spatial restraints. *Journal of Molecular Biology* 234, 3 (1993), 779–815. DOI: https://doi.org/10.1006/jmbi.1993.1626

[27] Fabian Sievers, Andreas Wilm, David Dineen, Toby J Gibson, Kevin Karplus, Weizhong Li, Rodrigo Lopez, Hamish McWilliam, Michael Remmert, Johannes Söding, Julie D Thompson, and Desmond G Higgins. 2011. Fast, scalable generation of high-quality protein multiple sequence alignments using Clustal Omega. *Molecular Systems Biology* 7, 1 (2011). DOI: https://doi.org/10.1038/msb.2011.75

[28] Chresten R. Søndergaard, Mats H M Olsson, Michał Rostkowski, and Jan H. Jensen. 2011. Improved treatment of ligands and coupling effects in empirical calculation and rationalization of pKa values. *Journal of Chemical Theory and Computation* 7, 7 (2011), 2284–2295. DOI: https://doi.org/10.1021/ct200133y

[29] Daniel J. Stieh, Joshua L. Phillips, Paul M. Rogers, Deborah F. King, Gianguido C. Cianci, Simon A. Jeffs, Sandrasegaram Gnanakaran, and Robin J. Shattock. 2013. Dynamic electrophoretic fingerprinting of the HIV-1 envelope glycoprotein. *Retrovirology* 10, 1 (2013), 33. DOI: https://doi.org/10.1186/1742-4690-10-33

[30] Barbara S Taylor, Magdalena E Sobieszczyk, Francine E McCutchan, and Scott M Hammer. 2008. The challenge of HIV-1 subtype diversity. *The New England Journal of Medicine* 358, 15 (Apr 2008), 1590–602. DOI: https://doi.org/10.1056/NEJMra0706737

[31] R Wyatt, P D Kwong, E Desjardins, R W Sweet, J Robinson, W A Hendrickson, and J G Sodroski. 1998. The antigenic structure of the HIV gp120 envelope glycoprotein. *Nature* 393, 6686 (Jun 1998), 705–11. DOI: https://doi.org/10.1038/31514

[32] Tongqing Zhou, Ling Xu, Barna Dey, Ann J Hessell, Donald Van Ryk, Shi-Hua Xiang, Xinzhen Yang, Mei-Yun Zhang, Michael B Zwick, James Arthos, Dennis R Burton, Dimiter S Dimitrov, Joseph Sodroski, Richard Wyatt, Gary J Nabel, and Peter D Kwong. 2007. Structural definition of a conserved neutralization epitope on HIV-1 gp120. *Nature* 445, 7129 (Feb 2007), 732–7. DOI: https://doi.org/10.1038/nature05580

Analysis of β-strand Twist from the 3-dimensional Image of a Protein

Tunazzina Islam
Department of Computer Science
Old Dominion University
Norfolk, VA 23529
tislam@cs.odu.edu

Michael Poteat
Old Dominion University
Norfolk, VA 23529
mpote001@odu.edu

Jing He
Department of Computer Science
Old Dominion University
Norfolk, VA 23529
jhe@cs.odu.edu

ABSTRACT

Electron cryo-microscopy (Cryo-EM) technique produces density maps that are 3-dimensional (3D) images of molecules. It is challenging to derive atomic structures of proteins from 3D images of medium resolutions. Twist of a β-strand has been studied extensively while little of the known information has been directly obtained from the 3D image of a β-sheet. We describe a method to characterize the twist of β-strands from the 3D image of a protein. An analysis of 11 β-sheet images shows that the Averaged Minimum Twist (AMT) angle is larger for a close set than for a far set of β-traces.

CCS CONCEPTS

- **Pattern Recognition** → **Models** → Geometric; Structural;
- **Simulation and Modeling** → General

KEYWORDS

Protein, β-strand; secondary structure; image; pattern, twist

1 INTRODUCTION

3-dimensional (3D) molecular images of large biological assemblies are produced and archived in the Electron Microscopy Data Bank (EMDB) [12]. As of April 2017, EMDB contains 4730 entries of 3D images (density maps) of molecules. Most of the 3D images with a higher than 10Å resolution are produced using cryo-electron microscopy (cryo-EM). This technique is particularly suitable for structure determination of large molecular assemblies that are often challenging for traditional methods such as X-ray crystallography and Nuclear Magnetic Resonance (NMR). Some recently solved atomic structures from high resolution images include the complex of β-galactosidase and inhibitor (2.2Å resolution) [5], bacteriophage Sf6 (2.9Å resolution) [26], and P22 bacteriophage (3.3Å resolution) [10]. EMDB is linked with Protein Data Bank (PDB). It is possible to obtain a data set that contains both 3D images (from the EMDB) and their corresponding atomic models (from the PDB).

Although atomic structures are being routinely solved from density maps with sufficient quality, it is computationally challenging to derive atomic structures from density maps at medium resolutions (5-10 Å). Existing approaches require fitting a known atomic structure into the Cryo-EM density map [18; 24; 25]. De novo methods do not rely on template structures; rather, rely on the intrinsic relationship among secondary structures to construct the backbone of the protein [1-3; 6].

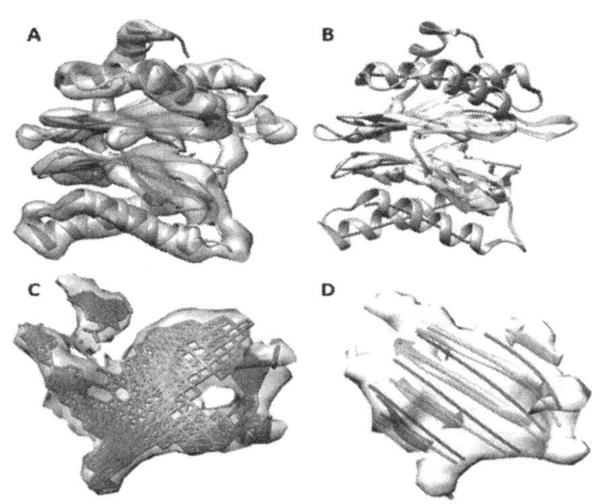

Figure 1: 3D image of cryo-electron microscopy density map, the atomic structure of a protein chain, and segmented secondary structures based on characteristic density patterns. (A): The density map (gray) extracted from Electron microscopy Data Bank 1733 (6.8 Å resolution) superimposed on its atomic structure (ribbon; PDB 3C91 chain H). (B): Segmented helices (represented as red sticks) and two β-sheets (yellow density), using SSETracer [19]. (C): The iteratively derived Bézier surface (blue) from β-sheet image (gray) that corresponds to sheet Q. (D): Two sets of β-traces (green and red lines) that were derived from the Bézier surface are superimposed on the atomic structure of β-strands (ribbon) and the image.

Permission to make digital or hard copies of all or part of this work for personal or classroom use is granted without fee provided that copies are not made or distributed for profit or commercial advantage and that copies bear this notice and the full citation on the first page. Copyrights for components of this work owned by others than ACM must be honored. Abstracting with credit is permitted. To copy otherwise, or republish, to post on servers or to redistribute to lists, requires prior specific permission and/or a fee. Request permissions from Permissions@acm.org.
ACM-BCB '17, August 20-23, 2017, Boston, MA, USA
© 2017 Association for Computing Machinery.
ACM ISBN 978-1-4503-4722-8/17/08...$15.00
http://dx.doi.org/10.1145/3107411.3107507

Major secondary structures such as helices and β-sheets are visible in density maps of medium resolutions. An α-helix often appears as a cylinder in a density map of medium resolutions. Various methods have been developed to evaluate cylindrical character in the 3D image [4; 8; 11; 13; 17; 19; 23]. Recently a deep learning method was developed using a convolutional neural network [13]. A β-sheet may appear as a thin layer of density (Fig. 1A). Each β-sheet is composed of multiple β-strands with an inter-strand distance of 4.5Å-5Å. A β-strand possesses a right-handed twist [7], resulting in a non-flat structure of a β-sheet [9; 16]. This property may be visible in a medium-resolution image. Although a β-sheet is not as characteristic as a helix in an image, computational methods exist to detect major region of a β-sheet [4; 19; 23]. Fig. 1B shows an example of detected β-sheet region (yellow) using SSETracer [19].

Due to the spacing of β-strands (about 4.5-5Å), it is almost impossible to distinguish the location of β-strands from a density map with lower than 5Å resolution. We previously showed that right-handed twist of β-sheet is effective in elimination of wrong candidate sets of β-strands [21]. We recently have showed that it is also possible to predict β-strand traces from β-barrel images utilizing the nature of barrels [22]. However, it is still an open question as to how to distinguish the best candidate among a pool of candidate β-strands that are all right-handed twisted to slightly different levels. An important question is how to measure twist angles accurately for a set of lines. Twist angles are slightly different when measured at different locations of the lines. We previously used one angle at the central region of a pair of lines [20]. In this paper, we sample many angles along a pair of lines and analyze the behavior of twist angles for two types of sets: sets close and far from the realistic positions of the β-strands.

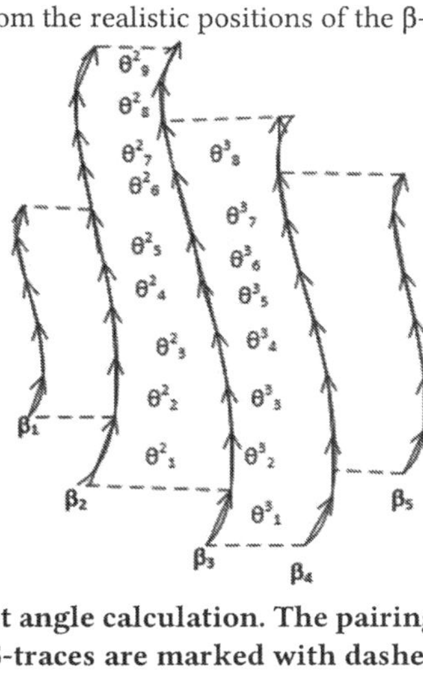

Figure 2: Twist angle calculation. The pairing length of two neighboring β-traces are marked with dashed lines.

2 METHOD

2.1 Computing twist angles from 3D image of a β-sheet

In order to represent twist angles precisely, a 3D image of the β-sheet was first converted to a surface using iterative Bézier fitting [15] or a polynomial fitting [21]. Once the surface is optimized, a set of lines was generated from the surface to mimic traces of β-strands. We refer to the set of such generated lines as β-traces. One set of β-traces may differ from another set by orientation or by translation. It is important to distinguish the set that is closest to the actual set representing the atomic structure of β-strands.

Let β-strand traces be $\beta_1, \beta_2, \ldots, \beta_m$, and let θ_j^i be the angle formed by β_i and β_{i+1} at location j of $\beta_i, 1 \leq i < m, 1 \leq j \leq n_i$. As an example, the angles formed by β_1 and β_2 along the strands are $(\theta_1^1, \theta_2^1, \ldots, \theta_{n_1}^1)$. We divided a line of β-trace into consecutive vectors of certain length, and calculated the angle formed by two vectors from adjacent traces, as illustrated in Fig. 2. The longest pairing length of a pair of β-traces was determined for each two neighboring traces. Note that the longest pairing length is often different from the individual length of each trace due to the relative position of the two lines. Since longer pairs of β-strands are major components of a β-sheet, we used the two longest pairs of β-traces to calculate an overall twist angle of a set of β-traces. Note that since the level of twist is often different at different locations of a β-sheet, a consistent measure of twist is needed to compare the level of twist created by different sets of β-traces. We define an averaged minimum twist (AMT), τ, for each set of β-traces as in (1). The idea of AMT is that the region with the minimum twist is the most stable spot for a pair of β-traces, and the two longest pairs formed by β_{i_1}, β_{i_1+1}, and β_{i_2}, β_{i_2+1}respectively were used for representing the major region of a β-sheet.

$$\tau = \frac{1}{2}\left(min_{k_1} \sum_{j_1=k_1}^{k_1+p} \frac{\theta_{j_1}^{i_1,}}{p} + min_{k_2} \sum_{j_2=k_2}^{k_2+q} \frac{\theta_{j_2}^{i_2,}}{q}\right) \quad (1)$$

Here, p and q are parameters, for which we used 4 in this paper. The choice of p and q is related to the length of the vector in angle calculation.

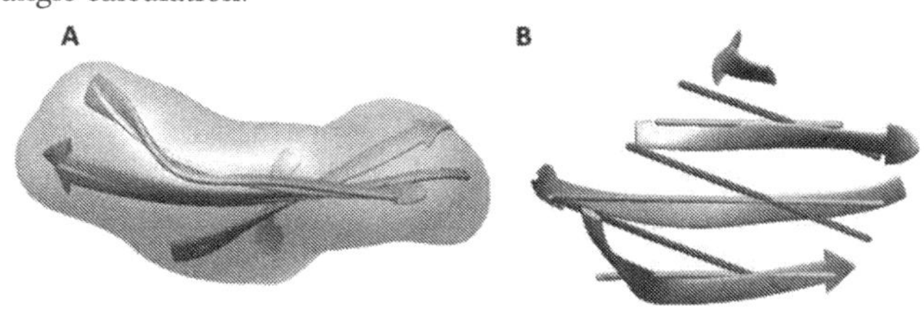

Figure 3: Twist analysis for β-strand splines, the close set, and the far set of β-traces. (A): The 3D image (gray) of β-sheet A of 1A12 (PDB ID), the atomic structure of β-strands (ribbon), and the β-strand splines (yellow lines) derived from the atomic structure. (B): The atomic structure (ribbon), the close set (green) and the far set of β-traces (red) derived from the 3D image of the β-sheet. Two different views of the same β-sheet are shown in (A) and (B) respectively.

2.2 Twist calculation using splines of β-strands

Given the atomic structure of a protein, one way to calculate the twist angle is to use two vectors, one from each of two neighboring β-strands [9]. The vector is defined by the two mid-points of consecutive C-N bonds along the β-strand. In order to characterize the AMT of a set of lines that precisely represent β-strands, we derived splines for β-strands. A cubic spline of a β-strand was calculated using mid-points of C-N bonds on the β-strand. Once the splines were generated, AMT was calculated. Note that the process of generating β-strand splines is different from the process of generating β-traces. One uses the atomic structure of β-strands, while the other uses 3D image of the β-sheet. In order to generate a robust AMT for β-strand splines, we measured the AMT three times and took an average. Each pass of the AMT was calculated by shifting the beginning of the line by one, two, or three points on the line.

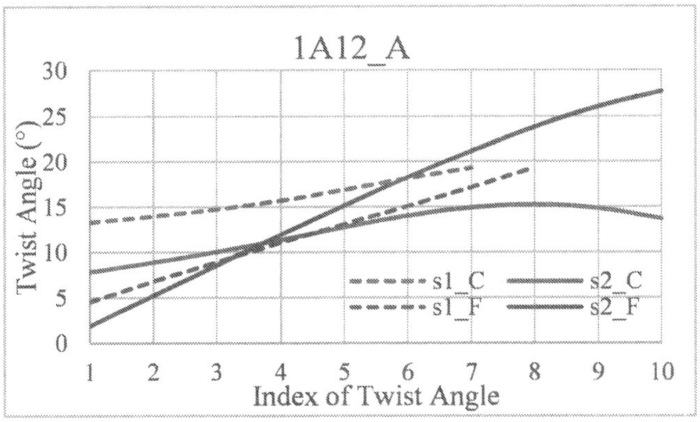

Figure 4: Twist angles along a pair of β-traces. Twist angles of the two longest pairs of β-traces in 1A12 (PDB ID) sheet A. The longest pair (S2) and the second longest pair (S1) of β-traces are shown for the close set (green) and far set (red).

3 RESULTS

Ten β-sheet images were generated using atomic structures of the β-sheets and Chimera [14] to a 10Å resolution. The data set represents small to large β-sheets, each of which has three to nine β-strands. StrandTwister was used to generate candidate sets of β-traces. StrandTwister only returns β-traces that have right-handed twist. The close set of β-traces aligns better with the atomic structure of β-strands than the far set, since it is selected based on the smallest overall distance between atoms of β-strands and the β-traces [21]. As an example, the close set of 1A12 sheet A appears to align much better than the far set with a visual inspection in Fig. 3.

3.1 Twist angles along a pair of β-traces

The magnitude of twist is often different at different locations of a β-strand. We investigated twist angles measured along a pair of β-traces for both the close set and the far set. Since most short pairs are near the edge, the most challenging region of the β-sheet, we focused on the longest pairs. For each set, the twist angles of two longest pairs are calculated. In the case of 1A12 sheet A, as shown in Fig. 4, the longest pair has twist angles between 7.8° and 15.3° for the close set, and between 1.9° and 27.7° for the far set. Note that both pairs are on the same surface, but they show different levels of twist depending on where they are located on the surface due to twist of the surface. In this case, the region with the smallest twist is on the left side of the curve for the close set (solid green curve). This is the similar region with the smallest twist in the far set (solid red curve) (Fig. 4). If we compare the smallest twist of the longest pair between the close set and the far set, the close set would have bigger twist.

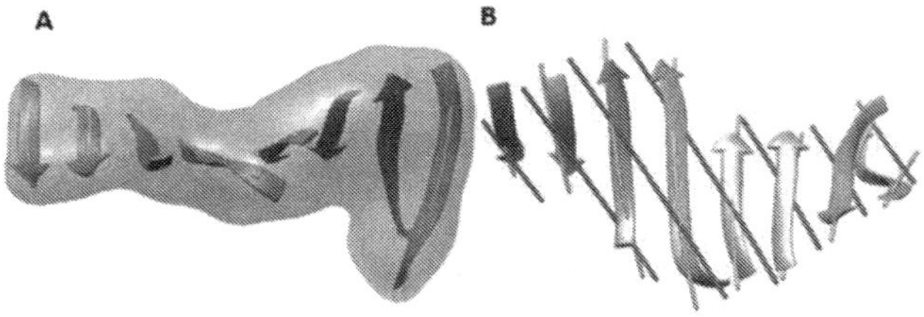

Figure 5: Twist analysis of β-strand splines, the close set, and the far set of β-traces 1DTD (PDB ID) sheet A. Colors and lines are annotated as in Fig. 3.

1DTD sheet A has eight β-strands. For the close set of 1DTD, as shown as green lines in Fig. 5B, the twist angles of the longest pair of β-traces (longest blue line in Fig. 6) are between 7° and 14°. The second longest pair (blue line in Fig. 6) has twist angles between 11° and 18°. Twist angles along a pair of β-traces show the challenge of twist analysis. The longest pair in a close set does not always have larger twist angles than the longest pair in a far case. In fact the two lines may cross (longest solid line and longest dashed line) indicating that in certain regions one has bigger twist than the other. However, if both the longest and the second longest pairs are considered, solid lines in Fig. 6 appear to out-twist corresponding dashed lines if AMT is calculated. Fig. 7 shows two sets of β-traces for 1ATZ sheet A.

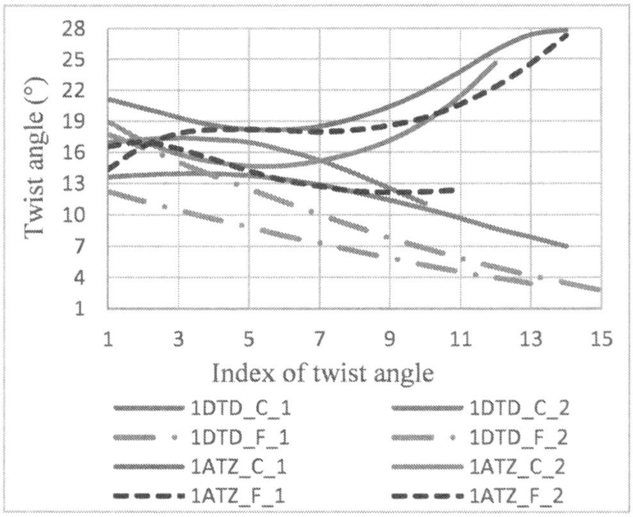

Figure 6: Twist angles along a pair of β-traces. Twist angles were calculated for the longest and the second longest pair of β-traces for a close set (solid lines) and a far set (dashed lines) in two cases: 1DTD sheet A (green lines) and 1ATZ sheet A (blue lines).

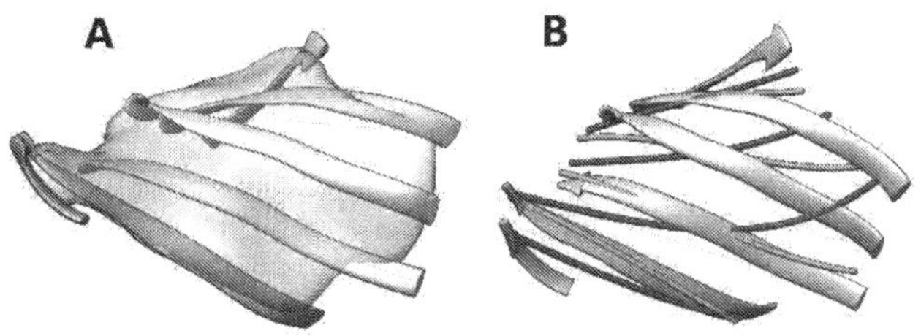

Figure 7: The close set and the far set of β-traces for 1ATZ (PDB ID) sheet A. Annotation method for color and lines is as in Fig. 3.

3.2 Twist characterization for simulated β-sheet images

In order to distinguish two sets of β-traces, we defined AMT to characterize the regional twist of a β-sheet. As an example for 1A12 sheet A, The AMT shows 11.98° for the close set, larger than that of the far set of 7.36° in Table 1. We observed similar pattern for β-sheet A of 1DTD that has eight β-strands. The close set (green lines in Fig. 5B) has an AMT of 10.75°, and the far set (red lines in Fig. 5B) has an AMT of 4.07° in Table 1. In all the eleven cases, we observed that the close set of β-traces shows larger AMT than the far set (Table 1 column 4 and 5).

Table 1: Average Minimum Twist angle of three sets of lines: the set of β-strand splines, two sets of β-traces.

ID[a]	Str[b]	AMT std[c]	AMT close[d]	AMT far[e]	AMT diff[f]
1B3A_B	3	27.22	9.76	4.69	5.07
1A12_A	4	27.24	11.98	7.36	4.62
1AOP_A	5	24.12	2.81	1.28	1.53
1AKY_A	5	23.40	7.54	6.16	1.38
1ATZ_A	6	16.70	16.62	12.37	4.25
1CHD_SH1	7	12.97	6.40	1.79	4.61
1ELU_B	7	21.02	7.76	3.88	3.88
1D5T_A	7	16.34	10.88	8.09	2.79
1DTD_A	8	13.21	10.75	4.07	6.68
1QNA_C	9	22.99	16.62	8.12	8.50
EMD1733-3C91_H_Q	5	21.69	9.70	8.97	0.73

a. the PDB/EMDB and sheet ID of the protein;
b. number of strands in a β-sheet;
c. average of minimum twist angle (in degrees) for splines c β-strands;
d. average minimum twist angle (in degrees) for a close set;
e. average minimum twist angle (in degrees) for a far set;
f. difference (in degrees) between d and e.

The difference of AMT between a close set and a far set is shown in column 6 of Table 1. We analyze three cases that are shown in Fig. 1, Fig. 3, and Fig. 5. The difference of AMT shows 0.73° (EMD1733 chain H Sheet Q), 4.62° (1A12_A), and 6.68° (1DTD_A). A visual examination of the three cases show that the smallest difference in AMT of 0.73° corresponds to similar orientation and position between the close set and far set (Fig. 1D). In this case, the two sets are mostly different by a translation with the orientations being similar. The largest difference in AMT of 6.68° correlates with the large difference between the close set and the far set, particularly at major region where longest lines are located (Fig. 5B). By relating the difference of AMT (column 6 of Table 1) with visual examination for the three cases (shown in Fig. 1, Fig. 3, and Fig. 5), we observed that the measurement of AMT was able to distinguish the level of closeness between sets across different cases.

3.3 Twist characterization for a β-sheet image of a cryo-EM density map

The cryo-EM density map (EMD-1733) was downloaded from EMDB, and the corresponding structure 3C91 (PDB ID) was downloaded from PDB. Chain H of 3C91 was used as a mask to isolate the density region corresponding to the chain in Fig. 1A. SSETracer [19] was used to detect the location of α-helices (red lines in Fig. 1B) and β-sheet (yellow in Fig. 1B). Since the two β-sheet regions detected by SSETracer are naturally separate, we used one of them (sheet Q of chain H) in this case study. Iterative Bézier fitting was performed to derive a surface (blue in Fig. 1C) for the 3D image of sheet Q [15]. Two sets of β-traces were constructed on the Bézier surface. One set of β-traces (green lines in Fig. 1D), referred to the close set, appears to align better with the atomic structure (ribbon in Fig. 1D) than the other set (red lines in Fig. 1D), referred to the far set. We tested if the two sets can be distinguished using the estimation we defined in (3). We observed that by quantifying twist at the stable region of a pair of β-traces, a close set of β-traces shows bigger twist than a far set. The close set has an AMT of 9.70°, slightly larger than 8.97° for the far set Table 1. A visual examination between the two sets show similar orientation between the two sets in Fig. 1D, yet AMT detected slight difference between the two. Since β-strand splines were derived directly from atomic structure of β-strands, they are expected to align with β-strands quite accurately. A measure of the AMT for β-strand splines shows 21.69° in Table 1. We observe that the AMT of β-strand splines is even larger than that of the close set. This case study suggests that AMT might be suitable for distinguishing a set of β-traces that aligns well with the atomic structure of β-strands.

4 CONCLUSIONS

β-strands are naturally twisted. Given the 3D image of a β-sheet, there are many ways to generate β-traces from the image to satisfy the inter-trace distance of 4.5 to 5Å. Multiple sets of β-traces need to be generated using a reference surface that captures the overall shape of the 3D image. One set of β-traces may differ from another set mostly by orientation or by translation. We investigated a method to distinguish a close set from a far set, and observed from 11 test cases that the AMT is larger for a close set of β-traces than for a far set. This suggests that AMT can be a potential measure to identify most accurate β-traces from a pool of candidates. Additional measures may be combined for accurate detection of β-strands from medium-resolution images of β-sheets.

ACKNOWLEDGMENTS

The work in this paper was supported in part by NSF DBI-1356621, NIH R01-GM062968, Modeling and Simulation Scholarship (to TI) and Honors College Undergraduate Research Scholarship (to MP) of Old Dominion University.

REFERENCES

[1] ABEYSINGHE, S., JU, T., BAKER, M.L., and CHIU, W., 2008. Shape modeling and matching in identifying 3D protein structures. *Computer Aided-design 40*, 708-720.

[2] AL NASR, K., RANJAN, D., ZUBAIR, M., CHEN, L., and HE, J., 2014. Sovling the secondary structure matching problem in cryo-EM de novo modeling using a constrained K-shortest path graph algorithm. *IEEE/ACM Trans Comput Biol Bioinform 11*, 2, 419-429.

[3] AL NASR, K., RANJAN, D., ZUBAIR, M., and HE, J., 2011. Ranking valid topologies of the secondary structure elements using a constraint graph. *J Bioinform Comput Biol 9*, 3 (Jun), 415-430.

[4] BAKER, M.L., JU, T., and CHIU, W., 2007. Identification of secondary structure elements in intermediate-resolution density maps. *Structure 15*, 1 (Jan), 7-19.

[5] BARTESAGHI, A., MERK, A., BANERJEE, S., MATTHIES, D., WU, X., MILNE, J.L.S., and SUBRAMANIAM, S., 2015. 2.2 Å resolution cryo-EM structure of β-galactosidase in complex with a cell-permeant inhibitor. *Science 348*, 6239, 1147-1151.

[6] BISWAS, A., RANJAN, D., ZUBAIR, M., ZEIL, S., NASR, K.A., and HE, J., 2016. An Effective Computational Method Incorporating Multiple Secondary Structure Predictions in Topology Determination for Cryo-EM Images. *IEEE/ACM Transactions on Computational Biology and Bioinformatics 14*, 3, 578-586.

[7] CHOTHIA, C., 1973. Conformation of twisted beta-pleated sheets in proteins. *J Mol Biol 75*, 2 (Apr 5), 295-302.

[8] DAL PALU, A., HE, J., PONTELLI, E., and LU, Y., 2006. Identification of Alpha-Helices from Low Resolution Protein Density Maps. *Proceeding of Computational Systems Bioinformatics Conference(CSB)*, 89-98.

[9] HO, B.K. and CURMI, P.M., 2002. Twist and shear in beta-sheets and beta-ribbons. *J Mol Biol 317*, 2 (Mar 22), 291-308.

[10] HRYC, C.F., CHEN, D.-H., AFONINE, P.V., JAKANA, J., WANG, Z., HAASE-PETTINGELL, C., JIANG, W., ADAMS, P.D., KING, J.A., SCHMID, M.F., and CHIU, W., 2017. Accurate model annotation of a near-atomic resolution cryo-EM map. *Proceedings of the National Academy of Sciences 114*, 12 (March 21, 2017), 3103-3108.

[11] JIANG, W., BAKER, M.L., LUDTKE, S.J., and CHIU, W., 2001. Bridging the information gap: computational tools for intermediate resolution structure interpretation. *J Mol Biol 308*, 5 (May), 1033-1044.

[12] LAWSON, C.L., BAKER, M.L., BEST, C., BI, C., DOUGHERTY, M., FENG, P., VAN GINKEL, G., DEVKOTA, B., LAGERSTEDT, I., LUDTKE, S.J., NEWMAN, R.H., OLDFIELD, T.J., REES, I., SAHNI, G., SALA, R., VELANKAR, S., WARREN, J., WESTBROOK, J.D., HENRICK, K., KLEYWEGT, G.J., BERMAN, H.M., and CHIU, W., 2011. EMDataBank.org: unified data resource for CryoEM. *Nucleic Acids Res 39*, suppl 1 (Jan), D456-464.

[13] LI, R., SI, D., ZENG, T., JI, S., and HE, J., 2016. Deep convolutional neural networks for detecting secondary structures in protein density maps from cryo-electron microscopy. In *2016 IEEE International Conference on Bioinformatics and Biomedicine (BIBM)*, 41-46.

[14] PETTERSEN, E.F., GODDARD, T.D., HUANG, C.C., COUCH, G.S., GREENBLATT, D.M., MENG, E.C., and FERRIN, T.E., 2004. UCSF Chimera—A visualization system for exploratory research and analysis. *Journal of Computational Chemistry 25*, 13, 1605-1612.

[15] POTEAT, M. and HE, J., 2017. An Iterative Bezier Method for Fitting Beta-shheet Component of a Cryo-EM Density Map. *Mol. Based Math. Biol 5*, 31-39.

[16] RICHARDSON, J.S. and RICHARDSON, D.C., 1985. Interpretation of electron density maps. *Methods Enzymol 115*, 189-206.

[17] RUSU, M. and WRIGGERS, W., 2012. Evolutionary bidirectional expansion for the tracing of alpha helices in cryo-electron microscopy reconstructions. *J Struct Biol 177*, 2 (Feb), 410-419.

[18] SCHRÖDER, G.F., BRUNGER, A.T., and LEVITT, M., 2007. Combining Efficient Conformational Sampling with a Deformable Elastic Network Model Facilitates Structure Refinement at Low Resolution. *Structure 15*, 12, 1630-1641.

[19] SI, D. and HE, J., 2013. Beta-sheet Detection and Representation from Medium Resolution Cryo-EM Density Maps. *BCB'13: Proceedings of ACM Conference on Bioinformatics, Computational Biology and Biomedical Informatics*(September 22-25), 764-770.

[20] SI, D. and HE, J., 2014. Orientations of beta-strand traces and near maximum twist. In *Proceedings of the Proceedings of the 5th ACM Conference on Bioinformatics, Computational Biology, and Health Informatics* (Newport Beach, California2014), ACM, 2660835, 690-694.

[21] SI, D. and HE, J., 2014. Tracing beta-strands using strandtwister from cryo-EM density maps at medium resolutions. *Structure 22*, 11, 22(11):1665-1676.

[22] SI, D. and HE, J., 2017. Modeling Beta-Traces for Beta-Barrels from Cryo-EM Density Maps. *Biomed Res Int 2017*, 1793213.

[23] SI, D., JI, S., AL NASR, K., and HE, J., 2012. A machine learning approach for the identification of protein secondary structure elements from electron cryo-microscopy density maps. *Biopolymers 97*, 9 (Sep), 698-708.

[24] TRABUCO, L.G., VILLA, E., MITRA, K., FRANK, J., and SCHULTEN, K., 2008. Flexible fitting of atomic structures into electron microscopy maps using molecular dynamics. *Structure 16*, 5 (May), 673-683.

[25] WRIGGERS, W. and BIRMANNS, S., 2001. Using situs for flexible and rigid-body fitting of multiresolution single-molecule data. *J Struct Biol 133*, 2-3 (Feb-Mar), 193-202.

[26] ZHAO, H., LI, K., LYNN, A.Y., ARON, K.E., YU, G., JIANG, W., and TANG, L., 2017. Structure of a headful DNA-packaging bacterial virus at 2.9 Å resolution by electron cryo-microscopy. *Proceedings of the National Academy of Sciences 114*, 14 (April 4, 2017), 3601-3606.

ProMuteHT : A High Throughput Compute Pipeline for Generating Protein Mutants *in silico*

Erik Andersson
Western Washington University
516 High Street
Bellingham, WA 98225
ander625@wwu.edu

Filip Jagodzinski
Western Washington University
516 High Street
Bellingham, WA 98225
filip.jagodzinski@wwu.edu

ABSTRACT

Understanding how an amino acid substitution affects a protein's structure is fundamental to advancing drug design and protein docking studies. Mutagenesis experiments on physical proteins provide a precise assessment of the effects of mutations, but they are time and cost prohibitive. Computational approaches for performing *in silico* amino acid substitutions are available, but they are not suited for generating large numbers of protein variants needed for high-throughput screening studies. We present **ProMuteHT**, a program for high throughput *in silico* generating user-specified sets of mutant protein structures with single or multiple amino acid substitutions. We combine our custom mutation algorithm with side chain homology modeling external libraries, and generate energetically feasible mutant structures. Our efficient command-line invocation syntax requires only a few arguments to specify large datasets of mutant structures. We achieve quick run-times due to our hybrid approach in which we limit the use of costly energy calculations when mutating from a large to a small amino acid. We compare our mutant structures with those generated by FoldX, and report faster run-times. We show that the mutants generated by **ProMuteHT** are of high quality, as determined via all-atom and mutated residue RMSD measurements for existing mutant structures in the PDB.

CCS CONCEPTS

•**Applied computing → Molecular structural biology;** *Bioinformatics;*

KEYWORDS

Mutagenesis; in silico; Modeling; Protein Structure

1 INTRODUCTION

Knowing to what extent a mutation affects a protein's stability can aid in drug design studies that aim to deliver pharmaceutical solutions for combating diseases caused by protein mutants [24]. Protein-compound interactions play a vital role in drug design studies, and generating *in silico* mutants is a major component driving such work [20].

One approach for studying the effects of a mutation is to perform *in vitro* experiments by engineering amino acid substitution directly in a physical protein, and then solving the structure via X-ray crystallography. However, that is impractical because some variants are difficult to crystallize. Moreover if a large set of mutant variants must be assessed, working with physical proteins is prohibitive because a single experiment to infer the role of just one mutation can be costly and may take weeks, or more, of wet-lab work. Alternatively, it is possible to infer the effect of a mutation in a physical protein without the need to resolve the structure. Free energy of unfolding experiments that use denaturants involve measuring the extent to which the wild type (WT), non-mutated, protein denatures relative to the mutant, and a quantitative assessment of the effects of the mutation(s) is attained via the Schellman equation [25]. However that approach, too, involves wet-lab work, and assessing the effect of more than a small handful of mutations is impractical.

To help complement and inform mutation studies performed on physical proteins, computational methods are available. Some methods reason about the effects due to changes to side-chain conformations [9, 15, 23], others rely on heuristic energy functions or database-derived potentials [10, 18], while others still leverage insights from large data sets of homologous proteins [5, 27, 28]. Machine learning (ML) approaches developed for this need exhibit great variety as well, with some relying on Vector Machine methods [7, 14], while others utilize Random Forest and similar approaches [6, 13, 16, 19].

Most of these computational methods do not output structure files of protein mutants, in spite of a need by protein docking and drug design studies for many structures for high throughput screening purposes. Moreover, the majority of prediction and modeling methods are most suited for generating and assessing structures with single amino acid substitutions. It is because of these limitations of existing tools that we have developed a stand-alone program that efficiently generates many protein mutants *in silico*.

2 RELATED WORK

Generating and modeling mutations in protein structures has been done a variety of ways over the years. Some tools require extensive human intervention, while others include near-automated capabilities. In this section we survey a handful of tools for modeling and generating amino acid substitutions.

Permission to make digital or hard copies of all or part of this work for personal or classroom use is granted without fee provided that copies are not made or distributed for profit or commercial advantage and that copies bear this notice and the full citation on the first page. Copyrights for components of this work owned by others than the author(s) must be honored. Abstracting with credit is permitted. To copy otherwise, or republish, to post on servers or to redistribute to lists, requires prior specific permission and/or a fee. Request permissions from permissions@acm.org.
ACM-BCB'17, August 20-23, 2017, Boston, MA, USA.
© 2017 Copyright held by the owner/author(s). Publication rights licensed to ACM.
978-1-4503-4722-8/17/08...$15.00
DOI: https://doi.org/10.1145/3107411.3116251

In early work, amino acid substitutions were simulated not by altering protein structure files, but by modifying energy and structure parameters of simulations of proteins. Motivated by a need to predict how mutations influence molecular functions, You, *et. al* [29], indirectly studied the effects of mutations on bacteriophage T7 molecules by altering molecule parameters in their simulations. In such studies, no structure files were ever generated.

More recent tools for generating mutant structures with amino acid substitutions are available. PyMol [8] offers a rich set of Graphical User Interface (GUI) tools for generating amino acid substitutions. A user manually modifies individual residues with the aid of a rotomer library and a visual guide showing possible steric clashes due to the choice of the side chain selected. This approach is amenable to creating only a small set of mutants, as each one has to be created by-hand. Another tool, Swiss PDB viewer [12], is unfortunately not available in Linux, and thus cannot be integrated into a custom compute pipeline for generating large sets of mutants.

A few tools for generating mutants afford components of automation, but they still require a more-than-desired amount of human intervention. Some of these are dependent on costly energy calculations which reduces their applicability when thousands of mutants are needed. One such tool is the `buildmodel` command in the FoldX software suite [26]. The FoldX server and applications were developed around an empirical force field for evaluating the effects of mutations. The main component of the software calculates free energy values for a macromolecule using a linear combination of 9 empirical energy terms, including hydrogen bond energies, energies due to steric clashes, and energies arising from van der Waal forces. The `buildmodel` option in FoldX is a relatively new feature of the suite of tools, and requires composing a list by-hand of all mutations that are needed. Most importantly, when multiple mutations in a single structure are *in silico* generated, the energy terms for the force field are calculated for each substitution, which creates a computational bottleneck when many *in silico* amino acid substitutions in a single structure are sought.

3 MOTIVATION

Thus, existing tools are available for *in silico* creating protein structures with amino acid substitutions. In the case of those tools that require a user to manually interact with a GUI, they are not practical for creating large sets of mutant structures. Alternatively, there exist tools for generating good mutant structures, but they nonetheless have limitations. For example FoldX requires creating a mutation list file by hand. In addition, most tools rely on energy and force field calculations, which prevents them from being used to generate massive sets of mutants with multiple mutations each, despite a need for such structures across different research efforts. For example, upwards of 10^5 simulation steps are commonly used to generate and score decoys for studying protein-protein docking interactions [11], while machine learning approaches for studying protein-ligand interactions are dependent on vast counts of complexes for screening drug targets [1].

In this work we present a new, hybrid compute pipeline for generating *in silico* mutations, whose reliance on costly energy calculations we reduce as much as possible. We are motivated by a need to generate large sets of mutant structures. To that effect, we have developed **ProMuteHT**, with two main goals in mind :

(1) Ease of specifying which mutants should be generated
(2) Reducing the need on energy calculations to improve performance when scaling to generate upwards of hundreds of thousands of mutant structures.

4 METHODS - COMPUTE PIPELINE

There are several components to our mutant generation process, summarized in Figure 1. Upon input of user-supplied parameters informing what *in silico* mutations are desired, PDB and FASTA file are fetch and preprocessed. The mutant generation step includes invoking one of two modules for each mutation that is specified, depending on whether the mutation is from a large to a small amino acid, or small to large amino acid. All mutant structure files are energy minimized to account for unfavorable energetic terms that might have been introduced during the *in silico* mutation.

4.1 Parameter Input, and Preprocessing

There are several command-line input formats accepted by **proMuteHT**. One permits a user to specify a comma-separated list of residue numbers, and/or range of amino acids, as well as the specific amino acid substitution(s) to be performed. The general syntax is of the following form:

$$\texttt{PDBID chain}_s\texttt{:chain}_e\ \texttt{res}_s\texttt{:res}_e\texttt{,res}_n\{^*X\}\ \texttt{subs}$$

where PDBID is the 4 alphanumeric structure ID from the Protein Data Bank [3], $\texttt{chain}_s$ and $\texttt{chain}_e$ are used to specify the chain(s) in the protein on which mutations should be generated, $\texttt{res}_s$ and $\texttt{res}_e$ are used to specify a range of residues to be mutated, and $\texttt{res}_n$ are individual residues delimited by comma(s). Providing a single letter amino acid abbreviation in the residue designation portion of the command permits specifying combinatorial *n*-wise sets. The use of the : permits specifying ranges (inclusive), while the optional

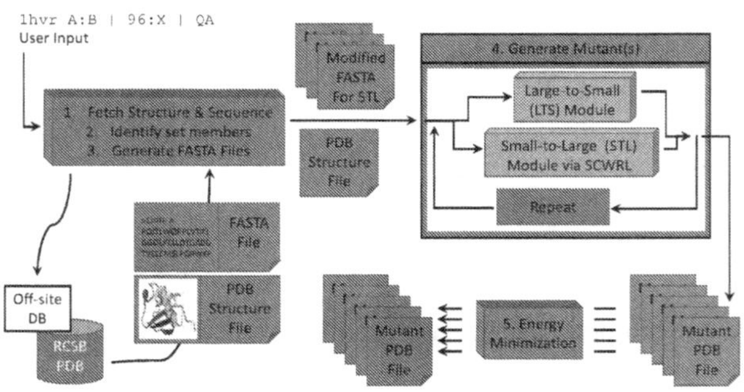

Figure 1: ProMuteHT fetches a protein structure and its FASTA file from the PDB (1), enumerates a mutant list per the user's input parameters (2), processes the FASTA file as needed by SCWRL [17] when a small-to-large mutation is required (3), and iteratively generates mutant files (4) which then are energy minimized (5).

parameters X and * designate *all*, and *hold fixed*. The subs field indicates which amino acid substitutions should be performed, what we call the *targets*, and consists of the single letter abbreviations for the 20 naturally occurring amino acids, as well as the lower case characters pol, char, and phobic to specify amino acids that are polar (Gln, Asn, His, Ser, Thr, Tyr, Cys, Met, Trp), charged (Arg, Lys, Asp, and Glu), and hydrophobic (Ala, Ile, Leu, Phe, Val, Pro, and Gly). Consider the below two invocations:

$$\texttt{1hvr A:B 96:X A} \tag{1}$$

$$\texttt{2ped A:A 3,10:16 phobic} \tag{2}$$

Invocation (1) specifies mutate chains A through B of PDB structure 1hvr, residues 96 through the end (residue 99), to residues Alanine, and would result in a total of $2_c \times 4_r \times 1_t = 8$ mutants, where the c, r, t subscripts refer to the number of chains, residues, and targets. Invocation (2) specifies mutate chain A of PDB structure 2ped, residues 3, and 10 through 16, and mutate each of them systematically to the hydrophobic residues, for a total of $1_c \times 8_r \times 7_t = 56$ mutants. More intricate examples are give in Section 5.1.

When the input parameters are parsed, checks are performed for the values provided by the user. A warning message is output and the program terminates whenever any of the following occurs:

- The PDB ID supplied does not adhere to the 4 alphanumeric character format in use by the Protein Data Bank
- There is no entry in the PDB for the provided ID
- The specified chain (or a chain in a range specified), and/or residues do not exist in the PDB structure file
- There is ambiguity in the formatting of the syntax specifying which mutants to generate.

If the input arguments would result in more than 250 mutants being generated, the user is prompted to confirm continue.

4.2 Generating Mutants

ProMuteHT is composed of several parts, including custom scripts and our in-house developed software, integrated among off-the-shelf open access tools and libraries. In an effort to reduce as much as possible the need for force field calculations, we have identified the following two broad types of amino acid substitutions :

(1) large-to-small (LTS) amino acid substitutions
(2) small-to-large (STL) amino acid mutations.

Our iterative program for generating mutant PDB structure files is made up of LTS and STL modules for performing these tasks. In the case that multiple mutations in a single structure are desired, they are performed one-after-the-other. The output structure that results from invoking either the LTS or STL module is the input structure for the next amino acid substitution in the list of mutations being performed *in silico* (*Repeat* step in Figure 1).

The LTS module removes atoms from a PDB file to simulate large-to-small amino acid substitutions. No energy minimization of any kind is involved. See Figure 2 for a schematic. As an example, mutating Valine or Leucine to Alanine involves removing the CG1 and CG2 atoms from Valine, and CG, CD1 and CD2 atoms from the Leucine structure file. Mutating Valine or Leucine to Glycine involves removing all of the side chain atoms, including the CB

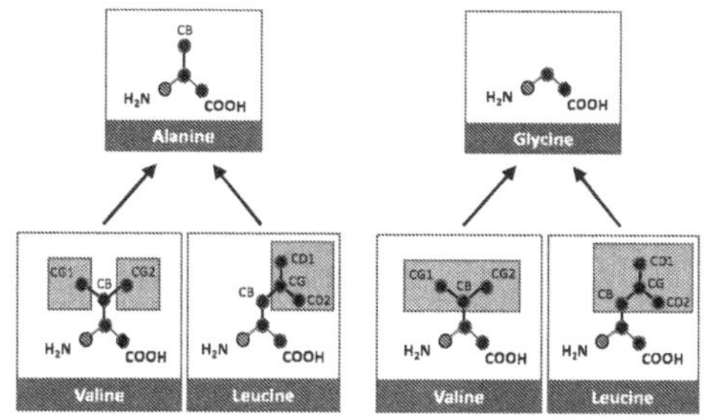

Figure 2: Large-to-small (LTS) mutations in ProMuteHT do not require energetics calculations. The *in silico* mutation involves retaining only the atoms of the target, smaller, residue. To mutate Valine or Leucine to Alanine, we remove the carbon atoms at the γ and δ positions (yellow boxes).

atom. The CB, CG1, etc. are the $C\beta$, $C\gamma$, etc. atom nomenclature terms in use in PDB files. Other LTS mutations, for example to Serine, follow a similar methodology. Although a void is created when this procedure is performed, especially when mutating a core residue from a large to a small one (Phenylalanine to Glycine, for example), the energy minimization step (Section 4.3) addresses this.

When a small residue is mutated to a larger one, the STL module is invoked. It relies on the freely available SCWRL 4.0 [17] software that makes predictions about a side chain's orientation. SCWRL uses rotamer libraries [4] based on kernel density estimates to make predictions about side chain confirmations. Among several other metrics, it is dependent on a hydrogen bonding function and a van der Waals interaction potential. **Although SCWRL is fast, we want to minimize its use nonetheless because even brief energy calculations can amount to lengthy delays when tens of thousands of mutations are being performed.** SCWRL's input is a PDB file, and the corresponding FASTA sequence with edits specifying desired side chain replacements. In Step 3 of the compute pipeline (Figure 1), a modified FASTA file is generated for any mutant desired which requires a small-to-large mutation. For example, if the FASTA sequence of the wild type is GAGGAFN, and the third residue's side chain is being mutated to aspartic acid, then the modified FASTA file would be edited to contain GAdGAFN (we underline the changes).

In the case of multiple-chain proteins, we do not use SCWRL as-is, because in those cases it often cannot make a side chain replacement. In that case, our software extracts each chain in the PDB file, and uses SCWRL to mutate the residue in the chain where the mutation is being performed. **ProMuteHT** then combines the un-mutated chain(s) and the altered one, and the end product is a multi-chain protein with the desired mutation.

4.3 Energy Minimization

Performing energy minimization is especially necessary when a small-to-large mutation is involved. That is because SCWRL does not take into account steric clashes that arise due to the introduction of new side chain atoms into the space occupied by the smaller residue's fewer atoms. Although mutating a large residue to a small one using our LTS module does not introduce steric clashes, there is nonetheless a void introduced, so energy minimization is performed in those cases, too. We rely on the NAMD [22] software to perform 200 energy minimization steps, requiring a few seconds of computation time, depending on the protein's size. We chose 200 steps from empirical experiments in which we observed that most structures by that time had settled enough so that high velocity atoms were no longer present.

5 RESULTS

To demonstrate the utility of **ProMuteHT**, we tallied its run-times, assessed the quality of the mutants generated, and also compared our approach with the mutation engine in FoldX. We used a quad core Intel Xeon E5-2620 processors at 2.0GHz, with 16GB of RAM.

5.1 ProMuteHT v.s. FoldX, Speed

In Table 1 we show four invocations of **ProMuteHT** for generating data sets with 13, 171, 342, and 418 mutants. The *real* run-times were measured using the linux *time* command.

Table 1: Run Times for sample invocations of ProMuteHT.

Invocation	# res	# muts	run-time (s)
`1hhp A:A 3,7,10:20 G`	99	13	21.9
`1crn A:A 12:30 pol`	46	171	220
`1pef A:A X:X X`	18	342	407
`1hvr A:B 20:30 X`	198	418	586

To compare the run-times of **ProMuteHT** with FoldX, we invoked both programs to generate two sets of mutants from PDB files 1hhp (99 residues) and 1pef (18 residues). We created by hand the required *mutant-file.txt* parameter files for specifying in FoldX what mutations to generate. We found that to be prohibitive, because not only must the target residue be specified, but FoldX also requires that the parameter file specify the non-mutated residue at the substitution point. In comparison, the commands for invoking our software for generating the equivalent mutants are the following:

```
1hhp A:A 19G*,20:25 A      (3)
1pef A:A X:X G             (4)
```

Invocation (3) specifies mutate chain A of structure 1hhp, residues 20 through 25 to an Alanine, paired with residue 19 being mutated to a Glycine. This generated the following 6 mutants:

- $Mutant_1$: res. 19 mutated to Glycine, and 20 to Alanine
- $Mutant_2$: res. 19 mutated to Glycine, and 21 to Alanine
- $Mutant_2$: res. 19 mutated to Glycine, and 22 to Alanine
- $Mutant_3$: res. 19 mutated to Glycine, and 23 to Alanine
- $Mutant_4$: res. 19 mutated to Glycine, and 24 to Alanine
- $Mutant_5$: res. 19 mutated to Glycine, and 25 to Alanine

Invocation (4) specifies mutate all residues in Chain A of 1pef to a Glycine. The mutants for 1hhp and 1pef are shown in Table 2. The run-times reveal that **ProMuteHT** has far overall lower run-times than FoldX when generating the same mutants. We suspect that is because the `buildmode` of FoldX relies heavily on energy calculations, and that even in the case of a small protein (1pef), the computations required are non-trivial. However our *in silico* LTS mutation process does not rely on energy calculations except for a brief minimization run after all substitutions have been performed. Although the speedup is only 2-3X, such a speedup would become significant if thousands of mutants were being generated.

Table 2: FoldX vs ProMuteHT run times for *in silico* generating two sets of mutants with 5 and 18 structures each.

protein	# muts	mutants (comma delimited)	Run-Times (s) FoldX	Run-Times (s) ProMuteHT
1hhp	6	L19G and K20A, L19G and E21A, L19G and E22A, L19G and L23A, L19G and L24A, L19G and D25A	82.5	12.3
1pef	18	E1G, Q2G, L3G, L4G, K5G, A6G, L7G, E8G, F9G, L10G, L11G, K12G, E13G, L14G, L15G, E16G, K17G, L18G	66.5	32

5.2 ProMute v.s. FoldX, Quality

To validate the quality of the amino acid substitutions performed by **ProMuteHT**, we generated several mutants whose structures we then compared to actual mutant structures in the PDB. We also compared the quality of our structures to those generated by FoldX.

We searched the PDB and selected 20 wild type, mutant pairs, involving substitutions to all possible naturally occurring amino acids. Eleven of those entries include 2lzm as the wild type. That is because Matthews *et al.* have generated and resolved the structures of many variants of Lysozyme from Bacteriophage T4 [2, 21]. We used **ProMuteHT** to *in silico* mutate the wild type of each pair, performing the same mutation that exists in the mutant structure. For each generated mutant, actual mutant pair, we measured the all-atom Root Mean Squared Deviation (RMSD), for both the full structure and the mutated residues only.

The run-times and comparative results of *in silico* mutating single amino acids are shown in Table 3. The **RMSD all** column lists the all-atom RMSD measurements for the mutants generated by FoldX (FX) and **ProMuteHT** (PM) for the entire structure compared to the known PDB mutant structure. The **RMSD res** column lists the all-atom RMSD measurements for the mutants generated by FoldX (FX) and **ProMuteHT** (PM) for just the atoms of the residue that was mutated. Yellow, red, and green entries for the PM columns identifies mutant structures we generated that were equally as good, worse, or better than those generated by FoldX, when compared to the actual mutant structures available in PDB files. Notice that even in those cases where our generated structures were not as good as those generated by FoldX, the RMSD values are nonetheless similar. When the RMSD measurements were calculated using only the mutated residue's atoms, the quality of the mutants generated by **ProMuteHT** was overall higher than those generated

Table 3: The quality of variants output by ProMuteHT was assessed by comparing *in silico* generated mutants with mutant structures from the PDB with equivalent mutations. Res=residue in the polypeptide chain, AA=Amino Acid for the wild type and Mutant for the indicated Res, and ASA=Accessible Surface Area. RMSD=Root Mean Squared Deviation between the actual (from PDB) and *in silico* generated mutants. Colors specify structures output by ProMuteHT (PM) that were worse (red), the same (yellow), or of better (green) quality than those generated by FoldX (FX).

WT Structure				Mutant		RMSD all		RMSD res	
PDB	res	AA	ASA	AA	PDB	FX	PM	FX	PM
1lz1	56	I	0.3	A	2hec	0.21	0.21	0.04	0.04
2lzm	149	V	0.0	C	237l	0.17	0.19	0.05	0.04
1lz1	110	V	60.1	D	1gfu	0.22	0.26	0.91	1.10
2lzm	105	Q	32.5	E	1l98	0.22	0.25	0.21	0.14
1lz1	54	Y	8.1	F	1wqq	0.21	0.22	0.77	0.06
1lz1	59	I	1.6	G	2hee	0.22	0.22	0.03	0.03
2lzm	157	T	41.8	H	1l09	0.08	0.11	0.85	1.12
2lzm	99	L	0	I	1l92	0.13	0.15	0.26	0.07
2lzm	120	M	16.4	K	232l	0.19	0.22	0.21	0.17
2lzm	6	M	0	L	230l	0.20	0.22	0.68	0.35
2lzm	99	L	0	M	1l93	0.13	0.15	1.10	1.06
2lzm	2	V	0	N	1gfe	0.22	0.24	0.85	1.36
2lzm	3	I	10.7	P	1l96	0.21	0.24	0.21	0.17
2rn2	48	E	10.8	Q	1rdb	0.19	0.23	0.18	0.17
1lz1	2	V	0	R	1gfg	0.22	0.25	0.85	0.77
2lzm	42	A	0	S	206l	0.15	0.15	0.04	0.03
1lz1	56	I	0.3	T	1oua	0.22	0.41	0.08	0.15
2lzm	44	S	57.5	W	216l	0.90	0.96	0.01	0.10
1lz1	56	I	0.3	V	2bqd	0.23	0.26	0.11	0.10
1lz1	110	V	60.1	Y	1gft	0.27	0.31	0.03	1.31

by FoldX, indicated by the green entries. Also notice that some residues were deeply buried (low Accessible Surface Area), and when mutating them from small to large amino acids, the *in silico* generated structures nonetheless had good alignment with the actual mutant structures from the PDB. **Overall, the quality of the mutant structures generated by ProMuteHT is comparable – and often better – to the quality of the structures generated by FoldX, while our run times are better** (Section 5.1).

We also assessed the quality of mutants generated by **ProMuteHT** when multiple amino acid substitutions were performed *in silico*. As with our validation of mutants with single mutations, we compared the mutants we generated with PDB files containing corresponding mutations done in physical proteins. We identified 10 wild type, mutant pairs in the PDB, and *in silico* mutated the wild type structures to have the amino acid substitutions of the mutants in the PDB. As we did when assessing the quality of performing single *in silico* mutations, we calculated the all-atom RMSD values between the actual and generated mutant files. We also tallied the run-times of both FoldX and **ProMuteHT** (Table 4). The RMSD values all are below 1Å, and indeed for several structures with mutations at residues that are buried, the RMSD alignment between our generated and actual mutant structures were below 0.5Å. The run-times show that **ProtMuteHT** was faster (often twice as fast) than FoldX. We show in Figure 3 the alignment for the generated (from wild type 2lzm) and 190l (actual) mutant, both with 3 substitutions.

6 CONCLUSIONS

We have developed **ProMuteHT** for generating single and multiple amino acid substitutions *in silico*. With the aim of reducing compute times in the case that large numbers of mutants need to be generated, our goal from the onset was to limit the use of energy and force field calculations, especially when performing amino acid substitutions that did not produce steric clashes, which occurs when mutating from a large to a small residue. This approach has enabled us to achieve considerable speedup over FoldX, while still generating quality mutant structures. Our software also provides a simple command-line syntax to facilitate easily specifying which mutants to generate.

A limitation of our current implementation is mutating multiple amino acids in different chains of a multi-chain protein. We are prevented from currently doing this because of the choice of syntax for specifying which mutations should be *in silico* generated.

In on-going work, we are expanding and modifying the syntax of the input parameters to provide a user an even richer set of mutation options that they might specify. Also, we are extending the **ProMuteHT** software to leverage multiple cores to expedite the generation of mutants even more. Extensions to our software will also provide the user with options to specify parameters for the energy minimization portion of the compute pipeline. Lastly, the software is being deployed onto a web-server, which will provide an easy-to-use Graphical User Interface enabling generating many mutants with just a few mouse clicks. The **ProMuteHT** software is available from the authors for non-commercial use.

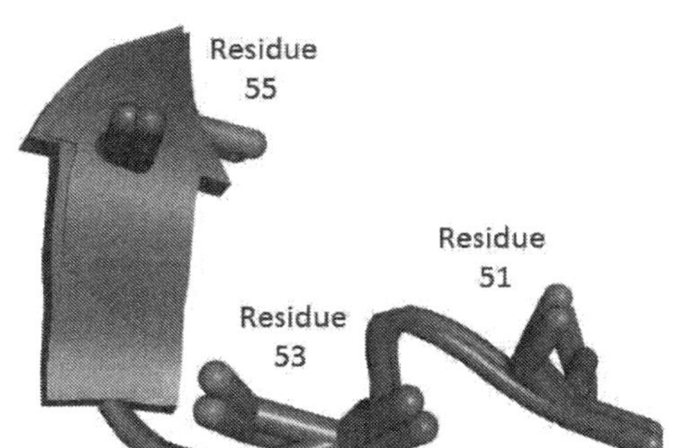

Figure 3: Aligning a mutant generated *in silico* by ProMuteHT (blue) with an actual mutant structure with equivalent mutations (magenta) shows a very good match. Amino acids substitutions performed were N53, N55A, and V57A in input PDB wild type structure 2lzm. The generated mutant achieved an RMSD of 0.20Å with the pdb file 190l which contains the actual mutations.

Table 4: Run-time and performance quality measurements for generating mutants with multiple amino acid substitutions. We used all-atom RMSD of the entire structure to measure the quality of the generated mutant when compared to the actual PDB mutant structure with equivalent mutations. Run-times are in seconds. SS=Secondary Structure, and ASA=Accessible Surface Area.

PDB WT	Mutant	Mutations	SS	ASA	all-atom RMSD	Run-times (s)	
						FoldX	ProMuteHT
1LZ1	1LHM	C 77 A, C 95 A	T, H	14.67, 1.28	0.203	3.4	1.7
4LYZ	1HEN	I 55 V, S 91 T	T, H	0.43, 0.43	0.407	3.1	1.3
4LYZ	1HEQ	T 40 S, S 91 T	S, H	0.07, 0.43	0.416	3.2	1.6
2LZM	1L49	A 98 V, T 152 S	H, H	0.00, 0.00	0.211	5.1	1.9
2LZM	1L89	L 99 A, F 153 A	H, H	0.00, 0.05	0.250	7.1	2.6
4LYZ	1HEP	T 40 S, I 55 V, S 91 T	S, T, H	0.07, 0.43, 0.43	0.424	6.7	2.5
2LZM	190L	N 53 A, N 55 A, V 57 A	C, T, S	85.72, 78.55, 44.24	0.202	7.3	2.4
2LZM	1L50	A 98 V, V 149 C, T 152 S	H, H, H	0.00, 0.07, 0.00	0.195	6.8	2.2
2LZM	1L51	A 98 V, V 149 I, R 152 S	H, H, H	0.00, 0.07, 0.00	0.225	7.2	2.3
451C	1DVV	F 7 A, V 13 M, F 34 Y, E 43 Y, V 78 I	T, T, T, T, H	1.89, 54.33, 39.66, 59.42, 6.90	0.869	9.6	3.1

REFERENCES

[1] Pedro J Ballester and John BO Mitchell. 2010. A machine learning approach to predicting protein–ligand binding affinity with applications to molecular docking. *Bioinformatics* 26, 9 (2010), 1169–1175.

[2] Jeffrey A Bell, Wayne J Becktel, Uwe Sauer, Walter A Baase, and Brian W Matthews. 1992. Dissection of helix capping in T4 lysozyme by structural and thermodynamic analysis of six amino acid substitutions at Thr 59. *Biochemistry* 31, 14 (1992), 3590–3596.

[3] Frances C Bernstein, Thomas F Koetzle, Graheme JB Williams, Edgar F Meyer, Michael D Brice, John R Rodgers, Olga Kennard, Takehiko Shimanouchi, and Mitsuo Tasumi. 1977. The protein data bank. *European Journal of Biochemistry* 80, 2 (1977), 319–324.

[4] M J Bower, F E Cohen, and R L Jr Dunbrack. 1997. Prediction of protein side-chain rotamers from a backbone-dependent rotamer library: a new homology modeling tool. *J Mol Biol* 267, 5 (1997), 1268–1282.

[5] Jeffrey R Brender and Yang Zhang. 2015. Predicting the effect of mutations on protein-protein binding interactions through structure-based interface profiles. *PLoS Comput Biol* 11, 10 (2015), e1004494.

[6] Yana Bromberg and Burkhard Rost. 2008. Comprehensive in silico mutagenesis highlights functionally important residues in proteins. *Bioinformatics* 24, 16 (2008), i207–i212.

[7] J. Cheng, A. Randall, and P. Baldi. 2006. Prediction of Protein Stability Changes for Single-Site Mutations Using Support Vector Machines. *PROTEINS: Structure, Function, and Bioinformatics* 62 (2006), 1125–1132.

[8] Warren L DeLano. 2002. The PyMOL molecular graphics system. (2002).

[9] R.L. Jr. Dunbrack and M. Karplus. 1994. Conformational analysis of the backbone-dependent rotamer preferences of protein sidechains. *Nature Structural Biology* 1 (1994), 334–340. Issue 5.

[10] D. Gilis and M. Rooman. 1997. Predicting Protein Stability Changes Upon Mutation Using Database-dervied Potentials: Solvent Accessibility Determines the Importance of Local Versus Non-Local Interactions Along the Sequence. *Journal of Molecular Biology* 272, 2 (1997), 276–290.

[11] Jeffrey J Gray, Stewart Moughon, Chu Wang, Ora Schueler-Furman, Brian Kuhlman, Carol A Rohl, and David Baker. 2003. Protein–protein docking with simultaneous optimization of rigid-body displacement and side-chain conformations. *Journal of molecular biology* 331, 1 (2003), 281–299.

[12] Nicolas Guex and Manuel C Peitsch. 1997. SWISS-MODEL and the Swiss-Pdb Viewer: an environment for comparative protein modeling. *electrophoresis* 18, 15 (1997), 2714–2723.

[13] Maximilian Hecht, Yana Bromberg, and Burkhard Rost. 2015. Better prediction of functional effects for sequence variants. *BMC genomics* 16, 8 (2015), S1.

[14] F. Jagodzinski, B. Akbal-Delibas, and N. Haspel. 2013. An Evolutionary Conservation & Rigidity Analysis Machine Learning Approach for Detecting Critical Protein Residues. In *CSBW (Computational Structural Bioinformatics Workshop), in proc. of ACM-BCB (ACM International conference on Bioinformatics and Computational Biology)*. 780–786.

[15] J Janin and S Wodak. 1978. Conformation of amino acid side-chains in proteins. *J Mol Biol* 125 (1978), 357–386.

[16] Lei Jia, Ramya Yarlagadda, and Charles C Reed. 2015. Structure Based Thermostability Prediction Models for Protein Single Point Mutations with Machine Learning Tools. *PloS one* 10, 9 (2015), e0138022.

[17] Georgii G Krivov, Maxim V Shapovalov, and Roland L Dunbrack. 2009. Improved prediction of protein side-chain conformations with SCWRL4. *Proteins: Structure, Function, and Bioinformatics* 77, 4 (2009), 778–795.

[18] C. Lee and M. Levitt. 1991. Accurate prediction of the stability and activity effects of site-directed mutagenesis on a protein core. *Nature* 352 (1991), 448–451.

[19] Yunqi Li and Jianwen Fang. 2012. PROTS-RF: a robust model for predicting mutation-induced protein stability changes. *PloS one* 7, 10 (2012), e47247.

[20] Sushil Kumar Mishra, Jan Adam, Michaela Wimmerovaffi, and Jaroslav Kocffha. 2012. In silico mutagenesis and docking study of Ralstonia solanacearum RSL lectin: performance of docking software to predict saccharide binding. *Journal of chemical information and modeling* 52, 5 (2012), 1250–1261.

[21] Blaine HM Mooers, Walter A Baase, Jonathan W Wray, and Brian W Matthews. 2009. Contributions of all 20 amino acids at site 96 to the stability and structure of T4 lysozyme. *Protein Science* 18, 5 (2009), 871–880.

[22] James C Phillips, Rosemary Braun, Wei Wang, James Gumbart, Emad Tajkhorshid, Elizabeth Villa, Christophe Chipot, Robert D Skeel, Laxmikant Kale, and Klaus Schulten. 2005. Scalable molecular dynamics with NAMD. *Journal of computational chemistry* 26, 16 (2005), 1781–1802.

[23] J.W. Ponder and F.M. Richards. 1987. Tertiary templates for proteins: Use of packing criteria in the enumeration of allowed sequences for different structural classes. *Journal Molecular Biology* 193 (1987), 775–791. Issue 4.

[24] Boris Reva, Yevgeniy Antipin, and Chris Sander. 2011. Predicting the functional impact of protein mutations: application to cancer genomics. *Nucleic Acids Research* (2011).

[25] John A Schellman. 1987. The thermodynamic stability of proteins. *Annual review of biophysics and biophysical chemistry* 16, 1 (1987), 115–137.

[26] Joost Schymkowitz, Jesper Borg, Francois Stricher, Robby Nys, Frederic Rousseau, and Luis Serrano. 2005. The FoldX web server: an online force field. *Nucleic acids research* 33, suppl 2 (2005), W382–W388.

[27] C.M. Topham, N. Srinivasan, and T. Blundell. 1997. Prediction of the stability of protein mutants based on structural environment-dependent amino acid substitutions and propensity tables. *Protein Engineering* 10, 1 (1997), 7–21.

[28] C.L. Worth, R. Preissner, and L. Blundell. 2011. SDM-a server for predicting effects of mutations on protein stability and malfunction. *Nucleic Acids Research* 39, Web Server Issue (2011), W215–W222.

[29] Lingchong You and John Yin. 2002. Dependence of epistasis on environment and mutation severity as revealed by in silico mutagenesis of phage T7. *Genetics* 160, 4 (2002), 1273–1281.

String-Based Models for Predicting RNA-Protein Interaction

Donald Adjeroh, Maen Allaga, Jun Tan
West Virginia University
donald.adjeroh@mail.wvu.edu

Jie Lin, Yue Jiang
Fujian Normal University
Fuzhou, China

Ahmed Abbasi
University of Virginia

Xiaobo Zhou
Wake Forest University Health Sciences

ABSTRACT
In this work, we study string-based approaches for the problem of RNA-Protein Interaction (RPI). We apply string algorithms and data structures to extract effective string patterns for prediction of RPI, using both sequence information (protein and RNA sequences), and structure information (protein and RNA secondary structures). This led to different string-based models for predicting interacting RNA-protein pairs. We show results that demonstrate the effectiveness of the proposed string-based models, including comparative results against state-of-the-art methods.

General Terms
Algorithms, Theory

Keywords
RNA protein interaction; RPI; *k*-mers; suffix trees; richness.

1. INTRODUCTION
The interaction between proteins and RNA is known to be an important cellular process. RNA interaction with malfunctioning proteins has been implicated in cell misregulation, leading to serious diseases [1, 3]. Yet, we still lack a complete understanding of the characteristics of a protein or of an RNA that allow them to interact. Even less is known about those characteristics that play a significant role in the formation of new protein-RNA complexes. Various groups have thus studied interactions for specific pairs of protein and RNA, even without knowing the general properties that facilitate or inhibit such interactions. Starting with experimentally known interacting RNA-protein pairs, computational methods, such as machine learning can be brought to bear on the problem, by attempting to predict possible RNA-protein interactions based on information from the already known interacting RNAs and proteins [2, 3].

Permission to make digital or hard copies of all or part of this work for personal or classroom use is granted without fee provided that copies are not made or distributed for profit or commercial advantage and that copies bear this notice and the full citation on the first page. Copyrights for components of this work owned by others than ACM must be honored. Abstracting with credit is permitted. To copy otherwise, or republish, to post on servers or to redistribute to lists, requires prior specific permission and/or a fee. Request permissions from Permissions@acm.org.
ACM-BCB '17, August 20-23, 2017, Boston, MA, USA
© 2017 Association for Computing Machinery.
ACM ISBN 978-1-4503-4722-8/17/08…$15.00
http://dx.doi.org/10.1145/3107411.3107508

The protein or RNA secondary structure describes how the molecules are bound together in a three dimensional space, and therefore can play a crucial role in characterizing the interaction process. The RNA secondary structure describes how some nucleotides in the single stranded RNA are paired to form potentially complicated structures, such as stems, loops, and hairpins. Some methods have been developed to predict RNA secondary structure based on the nucleotide sequences. Thermodynamic methods are the most popular amongst these methods [4, 5]. These mainly rely on the notion of free energy, and building secondary structures based on the minimum free energy principle [4]. On the other hand, protein secondary structures describe how the amino acids are positioned in a three dimensional space. Various approaches have been used to describe the protein secondary structure. A popular approach is by using the dihedral angles (φ and ψ) between the amino acids. Dihedral angles define the angles of rotation between two planes, in this case, the planes are defined by the bonds between three adjacent amino acids [6]. Ramachandran codes are derived from Ramachandran plots (which are 2D charts describing the distribution of the dihedral angles), by reducing information in the plot to some clusters [6, 7, 8]. Another approach is the protein blocks, which describe protein secondary structures based on the folds formed by five consecutive amino acids and then clustering these folds [9].

Earlier methods for RNA-Protein interaction prediction focused on sequence data, building features based on only sequence information, for RNA and protein individually, or combining both sequences to extract representative features [3]. Recently, secondary structures were shown to be important in the interaction process, and are now being included in the prediction [10]. In this work, we consider different representations for proteins and RNAs. We consider sequence and structural information for both protein and RNA. For the sequences, we use the traditional 4-letter alphabet for RNA (A, C, G, U), but a 7-letter reduced alphabet for protein. For structures, we use the Ramachandran codes for protein structure representation. These have been used in previous work on studying protein structures [6, 7]. However, this work represents the first time Ramachandran codes are being used for protein-RNA interaction studies. RNA secondary structures have been used earlier in RNA alignment and Protein-RNA interaction prediction. In this work, we consider string-based representations for both the RNA secondary structure, and the protein secondary structure, in addition to the traditional protein and RNA sequences.

Armed with these representations, we build two different prediction models using a string-based approach. Here, we built a feature space based on *k*-grams (i.e., *k*-length substrings, also called *k*-mers in the biology literature). We analyze the sequences of Protein-RNA pairs to determine the *k*-mers that tend to appear in interacting pairs, and those that are often found in non-interacting pairs. We then used these *k*-mer pairs as our descriptors (feature set) for predicting RNA-protein interaction. We applied this approach on both sequence-based information and structure-based information, after representing the structural information as strings.

The reminder of this paper is organized as follows: Section 2 provides some background, and discusses previous work on predicting Protein-RNA interaction. Section 3 describes the proposed string-based approach. Section 4 presents the results, including comparison with the state-of-the-art. Section 5 concludes the paper.

2. BACKGROUND & RELATED WORK

The importance of RNA-Protein interaction comes from the key role it plays in regulating cellular processes. Researches have shown interest in RNA-Protein interactions primarily driven by the need to understand how cells work, including cell localization and other fundamental processes [10]. Studies have shown that some cases of RNA-Protein interaction are related to some important diseases [1]. Clearly, the problem of prediction is closely related the issue of representing the RNAs and proteins. Success in identifying and extracting the information that is most relevant to protein-RNA interaction will no doubt lead to improved computational prediction of such interactions.

Methods for addressing the RNA-Protein Interaction (RPI) problem can be traced to those that have been used to study the related problem of protein-protein interaction (PPI). The Protein-Protein interaction problem is well studied due to the importance of proteins in all cell processes, including coding and decoding genes. Shen et. al [11] were among the first to predict protein-protein interaction using only sequence information. They used a simplified 7-character alphabet to represent protein sequences and built a Support Vector Machine (SVM) prediction model using a high quality database containing 16,443 experimentally validated entries. They were not only able to predict Protein-Protein interaction, but also to build a protein interaction network that shows the relationships and connections between different proteins based on their interactions [11]. For other related work on protein-protein interaction see [12, 13, 14].

Muppirala et. al. [3] explored RNA and protein sequences separately. They build a 599-dimensional feature space, with 343 features extracted from protein and 256 features from RNA. Similar to Shen et. al. [11], the 343 protein features were extracted by first considering the 7-class reduced protein alphabet, whereby the 20 amino-acids are clustered into 7 groups based on their dipole moments and their side-chain volumes. To conserve locality information, the notion of triads was used to extend the feature space to 7x7x7 features for protein, and 4x4x4 features for RNA. Two classification models (SVM and Random Forests) were deployed to build the prediction scheme. The models were trained using two datasets, namely, RPI369 and RPI2241. The Random Forest model trained with RPI2241 obtained the most accurate results among other trained models, achieving 89.6% in accuracy, with 0.89 and 0.90 for precision and recall, respectively.

In [15], Wang et. al. applied *k*-mer approach by finding the pairs of protein amino acids and RNA nucleotides that tends to appear together. They worked with a reduced protein alphabet, the 20 amino acids were grouped based on their charge and polarity. The new alphabet consisted of 4 groups representing the 20 amino acids. Then, they considered protein 4-mers and RNA 3-mers. This allowed them to preserve some locality information, which was indicated to have high impact on the prediction process. The feature space consisted of a 4094-dimensional space (4^3 features for protein, and 4^3 features for RNA). This high dimensional space requires relatively large datasets for training. Thus, they selected only 500 features that showed the highest impact on the prediction, and adopted the naive-Bayes classifier as the basic classification method. They tested the method on different datasets, including RPI369, RPI2241 and NPInter. The accuracy achieved for these three datasets were 75%, 74% and 77.6%, respectively.

RPI-Pred [10] was developed by Suresh et. al. to predict the interaction between non-coding RNA and proteins. They included information from both sequences and secondary structures, building a features-vector of 132 features. Here, they used 20 features to describe the RNA considering 4 different nucleotides and 5 secondary structure elements including stem, hairpin, loop, bulges. They used 112 features to characterize proteins, following the reduced 7-class alphabet for amino acids, and the extracted 16 protein blocks [9]. They introduced a new dataset, namely, RPI1807 and used this for training. They tested their method using three datasets, namely, RPI369, RPI2241 and NPInter. Using SVM as the prediction scheme, they achieved an accuracy of 92%, 84% and 86.9% using RPI369, RPI2241 and NPInter, respectively.

Lu et. al. [16] followed a different approach in predicting RNA-Protein interaction. The core difference in their work is in how they extracted their features. RNA secondary structures were predicted using Vienna RNA package. Additionally, they used hydrogen bonding information, then using the Fourier transform they extracted a feature set for both RNA and protein to form the feature vector for each RNA and protein. They included the first ten terms of the Fourier series for each information type. They built a training dataset containing 649 non-redundant protein-RNA pairs (322 of these were interacting pairs, and the remaining 327 were non-interactive pairs). They trained a scoring matrix which gives a score for each protein-RNA pair. Based on the assigned score, they predict the interaction between protein and RNA. The method achieved a 77% accuracy on the NPInter dataset.

Recently, the problem of RNA-Protein interaction has been considered from the viewpoint of complete structural representations. Zhang et al. [17] developed a deep learning model to define the preferences of RNA Binding Protein (RBP) structural representations. They used information from predicted RNA tertiary structures to study the problem of RNA-Protein interaction. This helped them to define a 3D representation for RPI complexes, which were then used to describe the binding preferences.

For both RNA and protein, their sequences and secondary structures can each be expressed in the form of strings [18, 19]. In this work, we take advantage of efficient string algorithms and data structures to extract discriminative feature sets and build prediction models that can predict RNA-Protein interaction. The other contribution is the development of a prediction model built on Ramachandran codes for protein structures, and enhanced descriptors of RNA secondary structure elements. In this work, we used both Support Vector Machines (SVM) and Random Forests (RF) to explore the influence of classification schemes on the prediction performance.

3. STRING-BASED MODELS

In this work, we will use information from both sequences and secondary structures. Before we discuss our string-based approach, we first describe how the information from the protein and RNAs are represented.

3.1 Representing RNAs

For RNA sequences, although a nucleotide can be any of A, U, C and G nucleotides, some RNAs are not completely known and they include X at some positions denoting that the nucleotide at this position is unknown, therefore the alphabet for RNA sequences is extended to 5 characters (A, U, C, G, X). This alphabet will be used to encode RNA sequences in this work. We also use information from the RNA secondary structure. In this work, when the RNA structure is unknown, we will use RNAFold (part of the Vienna RNA suite of programs [4, 20]) to predict the structure. The method implements a free energy model to predict the secondary structure for a given RNA sequence. To describe the RNA secondary structure, we use the RNA secondary structure elements (SSE) -- see Figure 1 (taken from [18]). For simplicity, we consider only the five basic types, namely, Single strands, Stem (or stack), Loop, Internal Loop and Bulges. The RNA secondary structure is thus represented as a string -- sequence of basic SSEs.

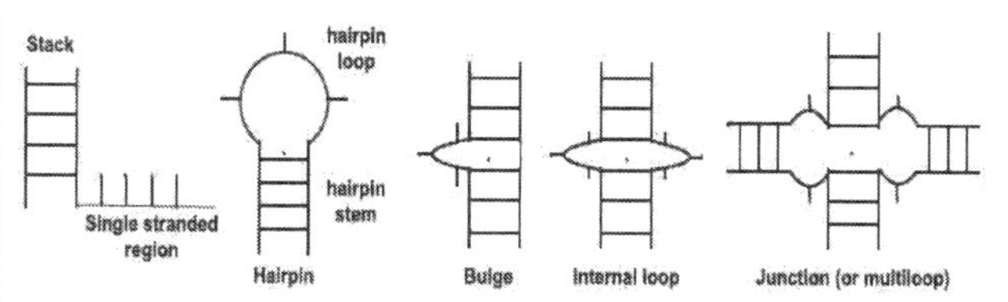

Figure 1: RNA secondary structure elements [18].

3.2 Representing Protein

Given the chemical similarity between amino acids, we can group amino acids into different groups and use the groups, rather than the individual amino acids, to represent protein sequences. Grouping the amino acids can be done based on various criteria. In this work, we follow [3, 10], where amino acids were classified based on their dipole moments and their side chain volumes. This way the original 20 amino acids are be classified into 7 groups: I: {Ala, Gly, Val}, II: {Ile, Leu, Phe, Pro}, III: {Tyr, Met, Thr, Ser}, IV: {His, Asn, Gln, Trp}, V: {Arg, Lys}, VI: {Asp, Glu} and VII: {Cys}. The protein secondary structure is defined by the positions of consecutive molecules in 3D space. The positions can be described by the dihedral angles between each three consecutive molecules, denoted Omega (ω), phi (φ) and psi (ψ). Due to the limitation in ω angle, usually only φ and ψ angles are considered in describing the protein secondary structure. Ramachandran et. al. [21] studied the relationship between φ and ψ and presented 2D plots (now called Ramachandran plots), showing the density of the joint occurrences of these angles. This density can be used to derive protein secondary structure representations by clustering the values from the Ramachandran plot, then replacing the values of (φ, ψ) pairs by their cluster representative. To represent protein structure, Suresh et al [10] used 16-character protein blocks. In this work, we will use a 7-symbol alphabet representing 7 clusters from the Ramachandran plot. See [6, 7]. Hence, the protein representation used will consist of a 7-character alphabet for amino acid groups (for the sequence), and another 7-character alphabet from the Ramachandran codes (for the protein secondary structure).

3.3 String-based Approach

Although the feature-based approach is powerful and contains a lot of information about RNA and protein, it does disregard important local information. This local information could be important in the prediction process. When an RNA bonds to a protein, it is not just an amino acid and a nucleotide that are involved, but a set of neighboring nucleotides against a set of amino acids.

Furthermore, the secondary structures should be compatible to allow RNA-Protein bonding. These observations suggest that we could consider small portions or *k*-grams (*k*-mers) of sequences and structures when building the feature vector rather than looking for individual molecules. This will typically lead to a very large dimensional feature space. Consider for instance, the 5-mer strings under a 25-character alphabet (using the RNA representation presented earlier). This means we have more than $25^5 \approx 9.8\times10^6$ possible different 5-mers to consider for RNA only, besides the $49^5 \approx 2\times10^8$ 5-mers for proteins. This is a huge feature space that will be very difficult to handle with current computational limitations. Thus, we need to reduce the feature space dimensionality. A quick observation is that this feature space will be very sparse, as most combinations of the RNA and protein symbols will not occur in practice.

Reducing feature space dimensionality means we need to carefully select some *k*-mers and drop the rest. Not all *k*-mer strings hold the same amount of information. Thus, to enhance prediction accuracy, we need to identify the *k*-mers that have the most influence on the prediction of interacting or non-interacting RNA-protein pairs. Hence, we look for the *k*-mer strings that appear mostly in the positive pairs and those that appear mostly in the negative pairs, and then construct a feature vector based on these.

3.4 Suffix trees for protein and RNA strings

The naive approach to find the most occurring substrings is to count each of them within the dataset. The running time for this approach will be $O(nk)$ for *each* *k*-mer, where n is the total number of all characters in the dataset. This means we need to hold a large dictionary of all possible substrings, the size of this dictionary would be in $O(\alpha^k)$, where α is the alphabet size (in our case, $\alpha=25$ for RNA and $\alpha=49$ for protein). We need to find a better approach to study the distribution of *k*-mers, i.e. a memory- and time-efficient method to find the *k*-mers that contribute most in the interaction process. An improved approach will be to go over the database to first determine all the *k*-mers that actually occurred, and then use standard linear-time pattern matching algorithms to determine their respective number of occurrences. Overall, this will be $O(kn^2)$ time worst case.

A better approach will be to use suffix trees and suffix arrays [19, 22-25] to provide a better tool to find the most occurring substrings within positive pairs and negative. The suffix tree requires an $O(n)$ time and space for construction. After construction, we can traverse the $O(n)$ nodes of the suffix tree to determine the occurrence counts of all substrings in $O(n)$ time. Thus, this is the time required to count all the *k*-mers in the string, independent of *k*. The power in using the suffix tree to find the distribution of *k*-mers is that we don't need to maintain a large dictionary. We built suffix trees counting occurrences of each substrings of length 2 to 5 for RNA sequence and secondary structure, and protein sequence and secondary structure. That is, we constructed four suffix trees, one for each type of string representation we used, namely: RNA sequence, RNA secondary structure elements represented as strings, protein sequence, protein secondary structure represented as a sequence of Ramachandran codes.

3.5 Richness for protein and RNA substrings

In general, the *k*-mers that tend to occur more in positive pairs (i.e., interacting RNA-protein pairs) would provide more information in deciding on a positive pair than other *k*-mers that appeared equally in both positive and negative pairs. Similarly for *k*-mers that appeared more in negative pairs. With this observation, we should look for more than just occurrence counts. The richness could be a better measure of the contribution of a *k*-mer to the interaction between RNA-protein pairs. Given a *k*-mer, say β, let:

$\gamma_+(\beta)$ = #occurrences of β in the positive pairs.

$\gamma_-(\beta)$ = #occurrences of β in the negative pairs.

The *k*-mer richness is simply defined as:

$$R(\beta) = (\gamma_+(\beta)+1)/(\gamma_-(\beta)+1).$$

Thus, *k*-mers with richness greater than 1 appear more in positive pairs (positive *k*-mers), while a richness value near zero means the *k*-mer appeared mostly in the negative pairs (negative *k*-mer). Richness values close to 1 are associated with *k*-mers that appear equally in both positive and negative pairs, hence they provide less discrimination ability between interacting and non-interacting pairs.

Given the foregoing, we now construct four suffix trees for positive dataset, and another four suffix trees for the negative dataset. We extracted pairs that appeared only in positive pairs or only in negative pairs as they hold the most discriminative information for interaction prediction. To provide some perspective on the feature space generated, we used the RPI1807 dataset (see Section 4.1 on datasets), to build suffix trees of depth five and computed the distributions for *k*-mers up to length 5. RNA 4-mers appeared for as many as 18,020 times in positive pairs and 16,894 in negative pairs, while for 5-mers, the number drops to 3,700 appearances in positive pairs and 3,494 negative pairs. Obviously, the numbers drop as the *k*-mer length increases. Protein 4-mers occurred about 1,134 times in positive pairs, and 443 times in negative pairs. As mentioned, the direct *k*-mer count distribution may not be the best way to capture the information carried by the *k*-mers. Thus, we considered the richness as the main factor to compare *k*-mers and build the feature vector. Figure 2 shows the RNA *k*-mer richness (log scale) for the RPI1807 dataset above. In this chart, positive log values imply *k*-mers that appear more in the positive pairs, while negative values correspond to those that appear more in the negative pairs. Thus, a simple threshold can be used to select the positive *k*-mers and the negative *k*-mers, while avoiding those that are less discriminative (those close to 0).

3.6 String-based Models

Based on the foregoing, we then consider string-based prediction models that combine the extracted RNA and protein *k*-mers. Our models consider different combinations of the identified *k*-mers that pass the richness threshold. We consider 5 models based on these combinations, viz: QQ: RNA sequence *k*-mers in combination with protein sequence *k*-mers; SS: RNA secondary structure *k*-mers and protein secondary structure *k*-mers, QS: RNA sequence *k*-mers and protein secondary structure *k*-mers, and SQ: RNA secondary structure *k*-mers and protein sequence *k*-mers. The final model (QSQS) combines *k*-mers from the first four models, thus exploiting info from RNA sequence, and RNA structure, protein sequence, and protein structure.

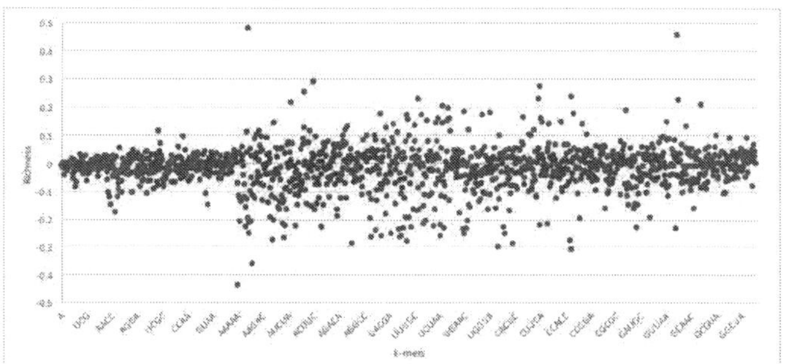

Figure 2: RNA sequence *k*-mer richness (log values) using the RPI1807 dataset. Not all *k*-mers are shown.

4. EXPERIMENTS & RESULTS

4.1 Datasets and Setup

We performed experiments to test the performance of the proposed methods, using some known datasets. Classification was performed using both SVM and Random Forests (RF) using Weka, version 3.6.13. SVM parameters were set as $C=2^5$, $\gamma=2^{-7}$ for the string-based models. For RF, the number of decision trees was set to 200. We used the RPI1807 dataset from [10] to construct our models, and set parameters. The dataset has 1,807 positive pairs (1807 protein and 1078 RNA chains), and 1436 negative pairs (including 1436 protein and 493 RNA chains). Then, we evaluated the models on the RPI369 and RPI2241 datasets reported in [3]. Both were obtained from the PRIDB dataset of RNA-protein complexes [26] extracted from the protein databank (PDB). RPI2241 includes complexes with rRNA, ncRNA and mRNA, and this is more challenging.

4.2 Performance Measurement

We evaluated our approaches using 10-fold cross-validation. To measure the performance, we used precision (PRE), recall (REC), accuracy (ACC), and F-measure (FSC), viz: PRE=TP/(TP+FP), REC=TP/(TP+FN), ACC=(TP+TN)/(TP+TN+FP+FN), FSC=2*(PRE*REC)/(PRE+REC), where, TP is true positive (the count of correctly classified positive pairs), FP is false positive (the count of wrongly classified positive pairs), TN is true negative (count of correctly classified negative pairs), and FN is false negative (count of wrongly classified negative pairs). We also computed the area under the curve (AUC) (with values in [0 1], with 1 indicating perfect prediction).

4.3 Results

Table 1 shows the results of our proposed string-based models. Columns 2 and 3 show results for the QSQS model, using both SVM and RF. Clearly, RF is doing much better than SVM using our approach. Thus, subsequent results in this work are reported only for the RF classifier.

Table 1: Results for the proposed string-based models

Metric	QSQS (SVM)	QSQS (RF)	QQ	SS	QS	SQ
#*k*-mers	7,030	7,030	4,680	2,350	3,255	2,955
AUC	0.75	0.98	0.93	0.66	0.64	0.95
PRE	0.79	0.93	0.93	0.79	0.78	0.91
REC	0.74	0.93	0.93	0.67	0.65	0.89
FSC	0.73	0.93	0.98	0.61	0.58	0.89
ACC (%)	74.00	93.35	93.19	66.98	65.15	89.29

As expected, the QSQS model achieved the best result. This is due to its use of more detailed information from both structure and sequence. The results of using only sequences (QQ model) were very close to using all available info. This could be due to the fact that secondary structure is determined by the sequence. Interestingly, using *k*-mers from only the secondary structures (SS model) led to a significant performance drop (ACC=66.98%). The table shows that sequences provide a key information for RPI prediction. Though secondary structures can help when combined with sequences, they lack precision when used independently.

4.4 Comparison with State-of-the-Art

We compared our models with two recent approaches reported in [10] and [3]. Table 2 shows the comparative results using the RPI2241 dataset. Our string-based model (QSQS) had an accuracy of 86.5%, performing better than RPI-Pred (84.0%) and close to RPISeq-SVM (87.1%).

Table 2: Comparative analysis of proposed string-based models on RPI2241 dataset

Metric	String - Based	RPI-Pred[10]	RPISeq-SVM[3]	RPISeq-RF [3]
AUC	0.92	0.89	0.97	0.92
PRE	0.86	0.88	0.87	0.89
REC	0.86	0.78	0.88	0.90
FSC	0.86	0.83	0.87	0.90
ACC (%)	86.5	84.0	87.1	89.6

Table 3 shows the results when using the RPI369 dataset. The string-based method outperformed all three competing methods (ACC= 96.38%). The proposed models were more consistent over different datasets. Our string-based had an accuracy of at least 86.52% over each dataset.

Table 3: Comparative analysis of proposed string-based models on RPI369 dataset

Metric	String-Based	RPI-Pred[10]	RPISeq-SVM[3]	RPISeq-RF [3]
AUC	0.98	0.95	0.81	0.81
PRE	0.96	0.89	0.73	0.75
REC	0.96	0.89	0.73	0.78
FSC	0.96	0.89	0.73	0.77
ACC (%)	96.38	92.0	72.8	76.2

5. CONCLUSION

We have introduced different string-based models for predicting RPI. We used the Ramachandran codes to represent protein secondary structure, and developed an innovative *k*-mers approach using powerful string data structures to address the problem of RPI prediction. The string-based approach maintained locality information which plays a key role in interaction between RNA and protein. Our approach showed comparable performance with the state-of-the-art methods on one dataset, while outperforming the methods on a second dataset.

Further improvement could be obtained by finding better ways to integrate the sequence and structure information, and intelligent fusion of the feature-based and string-based approaches. The string-based approach can also explore longer substrings (the *k*-mers), or perhaps inexact *k*-mers. Computing the *k*-mer richness by considering the sequence and structure information jointly, rather than separately, could lead to further improvements.

6. ACKNOWLEDGMENTS

Part of this work is supported by funds from the NSF (IIS-1552860, IIS-1553109), and from the NIH (1R01GM123037-01).

7. BIBLIOGRAPHY

[1] Jankowsky, E., & Harris, M. E. (2015). Specificity and nonspecificity in RNA–protein interactions. Nature Reviews Molecular Cell Biology, 16(9), 533–544.

[2] Khalil, A. M., & Rinn, J. L. (2011). RNA-protein interactions in human health and disease. Seminars in Cell & Developmental Biology, 22(4), 359–65.

[3] Muppirala, U. K., Honavar, V. G., & Dobbs, D. (2011). Predicting RNA-protein interactions using only sequence information. BMC Bioinformatics, 12(1), 489.

[4] Hofacker, I. L. (2003). Vienna RNA secondary structure server. Nucleic Acids Research, 31(13), 3429–31.

[5] Zuker, M., & Stiegler, P. (1981). Optimal computer folding of large RNA sequences using thermodynamics and auxiliary information. Nucleic Acids Research, 9(1), 133–48.

[6] Lo, W.-C. et al. (2007). Protein structural similarity search by Ramachandran codes. BMC Bioinformatics, 8, 307.

[7] Tan J. & Adjeroh D. (2015). Text encoding for protein structure representation. Proc., 45th, Symp. Interface: Com-puting Science & Statistics, Morgantown, WV, Jun 10-13.

[8] Hooft, R. W., Sander, C., & Vriend, G. (1997). Objectively judging the quality of a protein structure from a Ramachandran plot. CABIOS, 13(4), 425–430.

[9] Brevern, A. G. De, Etchebest, C., & Hazout, S. (2000). Bayesian probabilistic approach for predicting backbone structures in terms of protein blocks. Proteins, 287:271–287.

[10] Suresh, V., Liu, L., Adjeroh, D., & Zhou, X. (2015). RPI-Pred: predicting ncRNA-protein interaction using sequence and structural information. Nucleic Acids Research, 43(3), 1370–1379.

[11] Shen, J., Zhang, J., Luo, X., Zhu, W., et al. (2007). Predicting protein-protein interactions based only on sequences information. PNAS, 104(11), 4337-4341.

[12] Koh, G., et al. (2012). Analyzing protein-protein interaction networks. Journal of Proteome Research, 11(4), 2014-2031.

[13] Epusz, T., Yu, H., & Paccanaro, A. (2012). Detecting overlapping protein complexes in protein-protein interaction networks. Nature Methods, 9(5), 471-472.

[14] Reynolds, C., et al. (2009). ProtorP: A protein-protein interaction analysis server. Bioinformatics, 25(3), 413-414.

[15] Wang, Y., Chen, X., Liu, Z.-P., et al. (2012). De novo prediction of RNA-protein interactions from sequence information. Molecular BioSystems, 133–142.

[16] Lu, Q., Ren, S., Lu, M., Zhang, Y., et al. (2013). Computational prediction of associations between long non-coding RNAs and proteins. BMC Genomics, 14(1), 651.

[17] Zhang S, et al. (2016). J. A deep learning framework for modeling structural features of RNA-binding protein targets. Nucleic Acids Research, 44(4), p. e32.

[18] Beal, R., & Adjeroh, D. (2015). Efficient pattern matching for RNA secondary structures. Theoretical Computer Science, 592, 59-71.

[19] Gusfield, D. (1997). Algorithms on Strings, Trees, and Sequences: Computer Science and Computational Biology. Cambridge University Press, New York.

[20] Hofacker, I. L., et al. (2002). Secondary structure prediction for aligned RNA sequences. JMB, 319(5), 1059–66.

[21] Ramachandran GN, et al. (1966). Stereochemical criteria for polypeptide and protein chain conformations. III. Helical and hydrogen-bonded polypeptide chains. Biophys J. 6:849-72.

[22] Ukkonen, E. (1995). On-line construction of suffix trees. Algorithmica, 14(3), 249–260.

[23] Manber, U., & Myers, G. (1993). Suffix arrays: A new method for on-line string searches. SIAM Journal on Computing, 22(5), 935.

[24] Adjeroh, D., Bell, T. C., & Mukherjee, A. (2008). The Burrows-Wheeler Transform: Data Compression, Suffix Arrays, and Pattern Matching, Springer, New York.

[25] Adjeroh D., & Nan, F. (2010). Suffix-Sorting via Shannon-Fano-Elias Codes, Algorithms 2010, 3(2), 145-167.

[26] Lewis, B., Walia, R., et al. (2011). PRIDB: A protein-RNA interface database. NAR, 39(Database), D277-D282.

Ranking Protein-Protein Binding Using Evolutionary Information and Machine Learning

Roshanak Farhoodi
University of Massachusetts Boston
100 Morrissey Blvd.
Boston, Massachusetts 02125
rfarhoodi@gmail.com

Bahar Akbal-Delibas
Kadir Has University
Kadir Has Caddesi, Cibali
Istanbul, Turkey
bahar.delibas@khas.edu.tr

Nurit Haspel*
University of Massachusetts Boston
100 Morrissey Blvd.
Boston, Massachusetts 02125
nurit.haspel@umb.edu

ABSTRACT

Discriminating native-like complexes from false-positives with high accuracy is one of the biggest challenges in protein-protein docking. The relationship between various favorable intermolecular interactions (e.g., Van der Waals, electrostatic, desolvation forces, etc.) and the similarity of a conformation to its native structure is commonly agreed, though the precise nature of this relationship is not known very well. Existing protein-protein docking methods typically formulate this relationship as a weighted sum of selected terms and tune their weights by introducing a training set with which they evaluate and rank candidate complexes. Despite improvements in recent docking methods, they are still producing a large number of false positives, which often leads to incorrect prediction of complex binding. Using machine learning, we implemented an approach that not only ranks candidate complexes relative to each other, but also predicts how similar each candidate is to the native conformation. We built a Support Vector Regressor (SVR) using physico-chemical features and evolutionary conservation. We trained and tested the model on extensive datasets of complexes generated by three state-of-the-art docking methods. The set of docked complexes was generated from 79 different protein-protein complexes in both the rigid and medium categories of the Protein-Protein Docking Benchmark v.5. We were able to generally outperform the built-in scoring functions of the docking programs we used to generate the complexes, attesting to the potential of our approach in predicting the correct binding of protein-protein complexes.

CCS CONCEPTS

• **Computing methodologies → Machine Learning; Supervised learning; Support vector machines**; *Neural networks*; • **Applied computing → Computational biology; Molecular structural biology; Bioinformatics**;

KEYWORDS

Protein-Protein docking, machine learning, evolutionary conservation, SVR

*Corresponding author

Permission to make digital or hard copies of all or part of this work for personal or classroom use is granted without fee provided that copies are not made or distributed for profit or commercial advantage and that copies bear this notice and the full citation on the first page. Copyrights for components of this work owned by others than ACM must be honored. Abstracting with credit is permitted. To copy otherwise, or republish, to post on servers or to redistribute to lists, requires prior specific permission and/or a fee. Request permissions from permissions@acm.org.
ACM-BCB'17, August 20–23, 2017, Boston, MA, USA.
© 2017 ACM. ISBN 978-1-4503-4722-8/17/08...$15.00
DOI: http://dx.doi.org/10.1145/3107411.3107497

ACM Reference format:
Roshanak Farhoodi, Bahar Akbal-Delibas, and Nurit Haspel. 2017. Ranking Protein-Protein Binding Using Evolutionary Information and Machine Learning. In *Proceedings of ACM-BCB'17, August 20–23, 2017, Boston, MA, USA.*, , 6 pages.
DOI: http://dx.doi.org/10.1145/3107411.3107497

1 INTRODUCTION

Proteins play a major role in nearly any vital biological function [14, 21]. Proteins often bind to other proteins as part of their function, to form *protein complexes* [13]. In order to understand many of the important roles proteins play, we must have good understanding of their structure and function [14, 17, 24].

Computational docking methods aim to compute the correct bound form of two or more molecules. Protein-protein docking methods take two (or more) protein structures and try to predict the structure of the complex formed by them. This is a highly challenging task because even for rigid body docking, the search space spans the three translational and three rotational degrees of freedom for the other protein. Therefore, the search space grows exponentially with the size of the input proteins [25]. To make the problem more tractable, some docking programs allow the user to add a-priori knowledge like interacting residues [9, 11] or an initial conformation which is the basis for a local search [22].

Protein-Protein Scoring Functions: Most docking algorithms apply a geometric search for the correctly bound complex, followed by a ranking/scoring stage where a scoring function aims to distinguish native-like candidates from false positives. Scoring functions are designed to favor conformations with low binding energy, good geometric fit, clusters of conserved residues on the binding interfaces, and more. Over the past 20 years several scoring functions have been developed for ranking putative docked complexes. These scoring functions combine geometric complementarity with physical and chemical interactions [9, 11, 15, 20, 22]. These functions often use a combination of Van der Waals (VdW) energy, electrostatic interactions and desolvation terms. The combination and weighing of the terms differs among different methods. A recent docking refinement method by our group [2, 3] uses a scoring function that also includes an evolutionary traces (ET) term [30]. The assumption is that binding interfaces tend to be conserved due to their evolutionary importance.

Modern docking algorithms are often successful in predicting the correctly bound complex of their input proteins but many times the highest ranking docking candidates are still often false positives [15, 16]. A recent large-scale benchmarking of many current docking methods revealed that most physics-based scoring functions still fail to accurately predict the binding affinity of complexes [17]. In other words, the top scoring candidates are not always the closest ones to the native complex. Furthermore, even the most accurate scoring functions cannot always accurately estimate the least RMSD (lRMSD) of a docked structure with respect to its native conformation, since their aim is to provide relative ranking of a set of docked structures. Therefore, more work is needed to improve the existing scoring functions or design new methods.

It is generally agreed that there is a relationship between various scoring terms (e.g., Van der Waals, electrostatic, desolvation forces, etc.) and the similarity of a docked complex to its native structure [4]. However, the exact form of this relationship is unknown. Therefore, docking algorithms often formulate this relationship as a weighted sum of selected energetic, biochemical or geometric terms and adjust their weights against a training set [24]. Yet, the general inaccuracy of the rankings may suggest that the relationship between the scoring function terms and lRMSD of a conformation may be more complex than a weighted sum. For this reason, many docking algorithms provide an additional, sometimes optional, refinement stage, where selected putative complexes are being refined and re-ranked in order to improve the geometric fit and the binding energy of the candidate complexes.

Machine Learning for Docking: In recent years there has been an increasing use of machine learning based methods in bioinformatics. Support Vector Machines (SVM) are one of supervised learning methods that are widely used in solving classification problems. An SVM model is a representation of the training samples as points in space that are mapped so that different classes are separated by a gap that is as wide as possible. To classify new samples, features of the new data is used to map the samples into the same space and their class label is determined based on which side of the gap they fall on. SVMs can also be used to do nonlinear classification by using a kernel, where the samples are mapped into high-dimensional feature spaces to achieve separation of the target classes [10]. SVMs can be modified to suit regression problems, where they are referred to as Support Vector Regression (SVR) methods. Inspired by statistical learning theory, support vector methods aim at minimizing the training error while trying to keep the complexity of the function to be learned under control. SVR learns the nonlinear mapping between the feature values and the output values of the given training set in the form of a function, and this function can be later used to do prediction of target values. SVMs, SVRs and other similar kernel methods have been successfully used in bioinformatics applications including protein interaction prediction in the context of interaction networks [6], ranking of predicted protein structures [28], protein function classification [8] and protein ligand docking [18]. To the best of our knowledge, there are not many machine learning methods applied to protein-protein docking. In this work we use an SVR model as our scoring function in protein complex similarity prediction.

This Contribution: The objective of this paper is two-fold: first, based on our previous work [1, 5, 12], we describe a new SVR based machine learning approach, to predict the lRMSD of a set of candidate complexes with respect to their native conformation. Our method includes evolutionary conservation information in addition to physico-chemical interactions. Through a set of cross validation experiments, the SVR model showed comparable performance with the best performing method from our previous work, a multilayer neural network, while being much faster (The comparisons are not shown in this paper). Additionally, our SVR prediction model shows comparable and often better performance than the built-in scoring functions of three well-known docking methods, which were used to produce the protein complexes.

Second, in our previous work we used smaller sets of protein complexes including mostly near-native complexes of lRMSD range (0-7Å) [12]. That set provided only a partial sampling of the conformational space of docking candidates, which often span a very wide range of RMSDs from the native complex. In this paper, in order to conduct a more extensive analysis, we used complexes with much wider RMSD ranges. We also used a larger and more diverse set of 79 complexes from both the easy and medium categories of the Protein-Protein Docking Benchmark v.5 [29]. Our experiments can be used as a guiding tool for building the right training dataset and employing an accurate model in the studies that rely on identifying the best docking candidate complexes.

2 METHODS

2.1 Generating the Complexes

We initially selected 81 protein-protein dimers from the easy (rigid) and medium categories in the Protein-Protein Docking Benchmark v.5 [29] for which the corresponding evolutionary trace files were available in the ET Server [23]. Then, we generated docking results for each of these input complexes with PyDock [9], coarse RosettaDock [22] (without refinement) and a version of ClusPro [20] which generates the candidate complexes using the PIPER scoring function [19], without the clustering phase (S. Vajda, personal communication). For each protein, we retained the top-ranking 100 complexes generated by each one of the three docking algorithms, as ranked by that docking program's built-in scoring function. The lRMSD distribution of the generated candidates with respect to the native complex is shown in Table 1 and Figures 1-2.

To generate VdW and electrostatic values for our scoring function, we added hydrogen atoms using CHARMM [7] followed by 500 steps of energy minimization using NAMD [27] to resolve collisions without creating large changes to the complexes. Following these stages, two complexes were excluded due to problems in the calculation of the evolutionary trace values. The remaining 79 complexes were used to produce the results below.

2.2 Training Dataset

The training datasets contain 6,400 complexes (100 complexes for each protein) generated for the following 44 proteins from the easy category and 20 proteins from the medium category of the Protein-Protein Docking Benchmark v.5 [29]. The easy complexes are: 1Z5Y, 2AJF, 1GLA, 1JTD, 1YVB, 2GTP, 1EWY, 3A4S, 1J2J, 1T6B, 1US7, 1OC0, 1ZHI, 1OYV, 1H9D, 2I25, 2VDB, 1ZHH, 2HLE, 1EFN, 1B6C, 2OOB, 2O8V, 1Z0K, 1PVH, 4H03, 3BIW, 3VLB, 1GL1, 2YVJ, 2A9K, 2AYO, 2FJU, 2G77, 2J0T, 2SNI, 3PC8, 1R0R, 4M76, 7CEI, 2GAF, 2B42, 1GXD, 2A5T

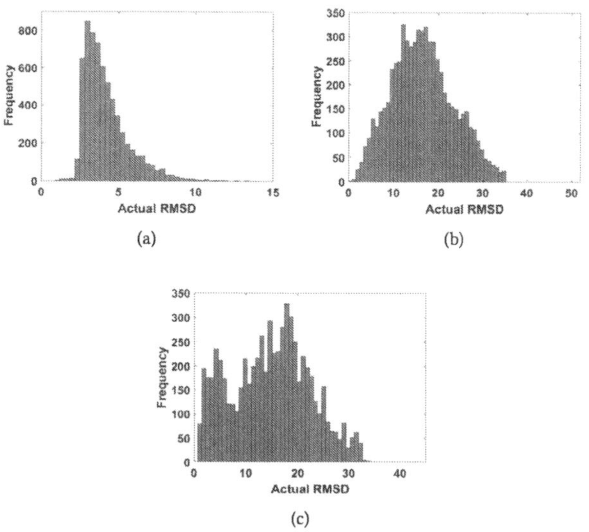

Figure 1: RMSD (Å) distribution with respect to the native complex of training datasets generated by (a) RosettaDock, (b) pyDock and (c) ClusPro.

The complexes from the medium category are: 1GRN, 2HRK, 1LFD, 3CPH, 2Z0E, 1XQS, 1R6Q, 3DAW, 4IZ7, 1WQ1, 2CFH, 1CGI, 1I2M, 1ZM4, 1NW9, 1HE8, 1MQ8, 2OZA, 3S9D, 4FZA.

2.3 Test Dataset

The test set includes 1,000 complexes (100 complexes for each protein) from the following 10 proteins in the easy category: 3D5S, 3K75, 2HQS, 1JTG, 1GPW, 1XD3, 2A1A, 4CPA, 1FFW, 1S1Q, and 500 complexes from the following 5 proteins in the medium category: 1SYX, 1JIW, 1M10, 3BX7, 3AAD.

Table 1: Training and test datasets statistics summary: minimum, mean, maximum and standard deviation of the least RMSD (lRMSD) values of the samples in each dataset and the methods used to generate the samples (Tr=Training, Te=Testing, N=Number of proteins in each set)

Set	Range	Mean	Std	Method	N
Tr 1	1.1–14.41	4.2	1.49	Rosetta	64
Tr 2	0.74–51.78	17.05	7.59	pyDock	64
Tr 3	0.75–44.37	14.91	7.79	Cluspro	64
Tr 4	0.74–51.78	15.98	7.77	pyDock-Cluspro	64
Te 1	0.77–11.44	3.84	1.38	Rosetta	15
Te 2	1.47–31.55	14.85	5.71	pyDock	15
Te 3	0.66–27.67	12.71	6.76	Cluspro	15
Te 4	0.66–31.55	13.78	6.25	pyDock-Cluspro	15

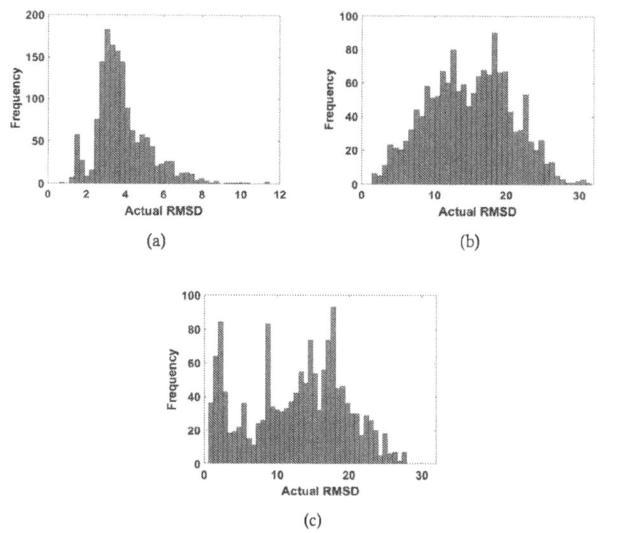

Figure 2: RMSD (Å) distribution with respect to the native complex of the test datasets generated by (a) RosettaDock, (b) pyDock, and (c) ClusPro.

2.4 Features

Our prediction methods approximate the relationship between 16 different features and the lRMSD of a protein complex with respect to its native structure. The majority of these features are used as scoring function terms by multiple docking and refinement methods [9, 19]. Additionally, we have an evolutionary conservation based feature (ICAR) [4]. The features are as follows:

- Van der Waals (VdW): The VdW force for interface atoms (defined as the atoms within at most 6Å to the adjacent chain atoms) is computed using a soft Lennard-Jones potential [2].
- Electrostatic: Computed for interface atoms, based on Coulomb's law as explained in [2].
- Interface Conserved Atom Ratio (ICAR): the ratio of the evolutionarily conserved interface atoms to the total interface size, see [4].
- Complex Category: The numeric representation of the protein category, as defined in the Protein-Protein Docking Benchmark v.5 [29].
- The fraction of interface atoms belonging to a residue type: Hydrophobic (A, C, G, I, L, M, P, V); Positively Charged (H, K, R); Negatively Charged (D, E); Polar (N, Q, S, T); Aromatic (F, H, W, Y).

2.5 Prediction Method: SVR

We used the training complexes represented with the above 16 features to train the SVR model. Eight of these features consist of continuous values and were initially scaled to the range of [0..1]. The remaining eight features, that are used to represent the eight different protein categories, have been used as binary categorical features. The lRMSD values of the training samples have been scaled to the range of [0..1] as well. After several exploratory rounds of parameter tuning and cross validation (exhaustive grid search), we chose RBF (Radial Basis Function) as the kernel for the SVR model with kernel coefficient (gamma) equal to 0.01. The penalty term for the error was chosen to be 0.9. After the model was implemented using the module provided by Scikit-learn [26] and trained using the training sets, the models were then used to predict the output value of the given test structures, where the resulting values were re-scaled to represent the final predicted lRMSD value.

3 RESULTS AND DISCUSSIONS

In this section, we discuss the prediction accuracy of the models by comparing predicted and actual lRMSDs of the samples in our test datasets, as well as describing our cross-validation experiments for comparing different datasets that we used to train the SVR models. Last but not least, we compared the performance of SVR with the scoring functions of Rosetta, pyDock and ClusPro using two objective metrics that will be described in next subsections. We mainly aimed at comparing the predictive power of SVR in protein complex ranking with other well-known methods. We first conducted a set of experiments to compare the prediction accuracy of the models when trained using each of our datasets. In these experiments we measured the errors and Pearson correlations of the actual and predicted RMSD values. Then, a set of 5-fold cross validation tests were conducted to unbiasedly examine the accuracy of the models using randomly selected training and testing sets. Finally, we examined how SVR stands in ranking the top 100 structures for each of the candidate complexes generated by Rosetta, pyDock and ClusPro when compared to those methods' rankings.

3.1 Performance Testing

We tested the performance of our method against complexes from the easy and medium category of the protein-protein benchmark [29]. The medium difficulty complexes are harder to predict, since they model possible conformational changes upon binding. Each of the test sets had a total of 1,500 candidates from 15 proteins that we had randomly selected for testing (see Test Datasets above). The Pearson correlation coefficients of the predicted and actual lRMSD values and the error of these experiments for each test protein is listed in Table 2. The lowest average prediction error of 1.15Å was observed with the structures generated by RosettaDock and the highest average error of 6.09Å was returned by the ClusPro dataset. Despite having proteins with medium difficulty, we were able to obtain prediction errors within less than one standard deviation of the lRMSD distribution, and the correlation coefficients were all above 0.33.

Finally, our goal is to make our method agnostic to the docking method used to generate the complexes. We trained the model using the dataset that we built by combining the structures generated by pyDock and ClusPro. We kept the RosettaDock out of this experiment since it is a local search method as opposed to the FFT-based search used by both ClusPro and PyDock, and hence the lRMSD range is much lower, which would result in a vastly different conformational space. The test results using this 4th dataset are shown in Table 2. The average prediction error of 5.82Å was returned, which not surprisingly is approximately midway between the ClusPro and pyDock separate predictions.

Looking at the prediction results, it is worth highlighting that the correlation coefficients of the actual and predicted RMSD values as well as the prediction accuracy of models vary from case to case for a given protein due to the diversity of the distribution of features and RMSD values for each protein. Also, a general observation worth noting is that the prediction errors of the models trained with samples generated using RosettaDock were on average smaller compared to the models trained with samples generated by pyDock and ClusPro. We attribute this to having considerably more samples with lower lRMSD values in training and test datasets generated by RosettaDock due to its local sampling nature, while the complexes obtained by pyDock and ClusPro had a much wider spread over the higher ranges of lRMSD values.

Table 2: SVR Prediction errors and Pearson correlations using complexes from the rigid+medium category generated by Rosetta, pyDock and ClusPro and a combined set of pyDock and ClusPro(Err=Error, Co=Pearson correlation, C. and D.=ClusPro and pyDock)

	Rosetta		pyDock		ClusPro		C. and D.	
PDB	**Err**	**Co**	**Err**	**Co**	**Err**	**Co**	**Err**	**Co**
3D5S	0.87	0.58	6.53	0.33	13.07	0.3	10.43	0.08
3K75	0.79	0.25	5.9	0.34	2.87	0.15	4.68	0.04
2HQS	1.47	0.64	6.68	0.17	5.99	0.23	6.11	0.17
1JTG	1.91	0.01	5.7	0.23	8.35	0.08	7.11	0.27
1GPW	0.99	0.44	4.65	0.57	8.92	0.2	6.86	0.6
1XD3	0.71	0.38	7.45	0.63	12.43	0.19	10.28	0.6
2A1A	1.42	0.4	6.16	0.67	5.35	0.74	5.73	0.76
4CPA	0.7	0.37	4.8	0.77	2.57	0.49	3.01	0.65
1FFW	0.64	0.16	4.71	0.34	3.98	0.13	4.19	0.3
1S1Q	0.96	0.21	2.82	0.53	2.58	0.64	2.82	0.67
1SYX	0.51	0.4	3.67	0.07	2.71	0.63	3.46	0.21
1JIW	0.9	0.2	5.57	0.16	6.62	0.07	6.23	0.07
1M10	2.46	0.36	6.27	0.18	4.21	0.3	5.13	0.41
3BX7	1.42	0.64	6.01	0.26	6.18	0.91	6.11	0.49
3AAD	1.44	0.13	4.64	0.51	5.53	0.73	5.17	0.49
Avg.	1.15	0.34	5.44	0.38	6.09	0.37	5.82	0.39

3.2 Model Comparison by Cross Validation

In order to analyze the performance of the models in an unbiased fashion and to demonstrate that characteristics of individual protein complexes in our test sets is not in any way favoring the prediction, we conducted 5- fold cross validation experiments. We combined the training/test datasets and randomly divided the samples into training and testing sets, where 80 percent of total samples were used for training and the remaining samples were set aside for testing. This was repeated in an iterative manner for 5 times such that no samples generated for a particular protein could fall in both training and testing sets.

The prediction errors and correlation coefficients for the four datasets are summarized in Table 3. Similarly, the lowest average error of 1.34Å and highest average correlation of 0.47 were generated by RosettaDock complexes. Average prediction errors of 6.57Å 7.6Å and 7.17Å were produced by pyDock, ClusPro and the combined dataset respectively. The prediction error was similar to the test sets reported above, with a slightly lower but still positive correlation.

Table 3: 5-fold cross validation SVR results using the structures in medium category generated by Rosetta, pyDock and ClusPro.

	Rosetta		pyDock		ClusPro		C. and D.	
Fold	**Err**	**Co**	**Err**	**Co**	**Err**	**Co**	**Err**	**Co**
1	1.25	0.33	6.41	0.29	6.52	0.42	6.69	0.33
2	1.22	0.47	6.83	0.34	7.98	0.18	7.4	0.27
3	1.25	0.43	6.33	0.28	6.21	0.39	6.67	0.22
4	1.79	0.36	7.24	0.4	9.26	0.08	8.3	0.21
5	1.21	0.59	6.05	0.29	8.03	0.15	6.75	0.27
Avg.	1.34	0.47	6.57	0.32	7.6	0.24	7.17	0.26

3.3 Comparing SVR with the Scoring Functions

Finally, we compared the predictive ability of our model with the built-in scoring functions used by the docking methods to rank the candidate complexes. For each complex, we compared the relative ranking of the 100 docking candidates based on the docking method's scoring function against the predicted lRMSD produced by our model. As a ground truth we ranked the candidate complexes by their lRMSD from their native complex. In order to conduct an objective comparison for the ranking performance of the SVR and the other 3 docking methods, two measurements are used: (1) the number of correctly identified top ten structures for each complex, and (2) each method's ranking of a structure against its real ranking is compared and the root mean square error in ranking is calculated.

Tables 4, 5 and 6 present how RosettaDock, pyDock and ClusPro ranked the 100 solutions for each protein. In these set of experiments, SVR performed better than pyDock and ClusPro in identifying top-10 complexes, and had lower average ranking error. Our model performs slightly worse than RosettaDock in average ranking error. RosettaDock achieved lower ranking error in 73 percent of the cases, but the difference is rather small (25.57 for RosettaDock vs. 26.98 for SVR). Finally, SVR and RosettaDock identified, on average, the same number of top-10 complexes, but our model was able to identify more top-10 complexes in six out of the 15 test cases, whereas RosettaDock identified more top-10 complexes in four out of the 15 cases.

4 CONCLUSIONS

We presented a machine learning approach to predict and rank protein-protein docking candidates. A major challenge in protein-protein docking is that existing scoring functions still produce a large number of false positive candidates, which are high-ranking complexes with high RMSD with respect to the native complex.

Table 4: Comparison of Rosetta and SVR by the number of best structures included in their top-10, and by their error in ranking, medium category.

	Error in ranking		# of detected top-10	
PDB	**Rosetta**	**SVR**	**Rosetta**	**SVR**
3D5S	20.68	20.78	3	**5**
3K75	30.06	30.46	0	**1**
2HQS	11.06	17.87	6	4
1JTG	32.46	34.34	2	1
1GPW	23.5	24.42	3	3
1XD3	26.26	**24.66**	3	1
2A1A	20.68	24.54	1	**2**
4CPA	19.2	24.38	0	1
1FFW	40.04	**37.06**	0	0
1S1Q	23.44	27.38	1	1
1SYX	29.92	**26.58**	0	0
1JIW	24.5	30.52	0	0
1M10	24.34	25.76	3	1
3BX7	18.78	19.68	2	**3**
3AAD	38.7	**36.24**	0	1
Avg.	25.57	26.98	1.6	1.6

Table 5: Comparison of pyDock and SVR by the number of best structures included in their top-10, and by their error in ranking, medium category.

	Error in ranking		# of detected top-10	
PDB	**pyDock**	**SVR**	**pyDock**	**SVR**
3D5S	33.6	40.68	3	0
3K75	31.9	**28.36**	3	**6**
2HQS	35.72	**23**	1	**3**
1JTG	31.46	**27.88**	4	1
1GPW	28.2	**20.6**	4	3
1XD3	32.22	**18.42**	1	**3**
2A1A	30.4	**22.12**	3	**5**
4CPA	30.6	**15.54**	0	**2**
1FFW	33.52	39.04	2	0
1S1Q	38.5	**19.42**	0	**4**
1SYX	35.54	37.68	0	0
1JIW	30.58	32.16	1	**2**
1M10	36.36	37.34	0	**1**
3BX7	24.24	25.62	2	1
3AAD	29.36	**23.78**	1	**2**
Avg.	32.15	27.44	1.67	2.2

We trained our prediction model on a large number of protein-protein docking candidates with a wide range of RMSDs and complex types. Our features include amino acid type, physico-chemical interactions and evolutionary conservation on the binding interface. We showed that our ranking and predictive ability was comparable to, and in most cases better than, existing scoring functions. Initial results (not shown) demonstrate that the addition of evolutionary

Table 6: Comparison of ClusPro and SVR by the number of best structures included in their top-10, and by their error in ranking, medium category.

	Error in ranking		# of detected top-10	
PDB	**ClusPro**	**SVR**	**ClusPro**	**SVR**
3D5S	36.5	**26.66**	0	**1**
3K75	37.74	**34.04**	0	**1**
2HQS	34.28	**26.7**	1	**6**
1JTG	33.78	34.7	0	1
1GPW	36.02	**29.96**	1	0
1XD3	29.32	33.46	1	0
2A1A	30.32	**14.92**	2	**5**
4CPA	34.76	44.92	1	1
1FFW	34.76	**30.22**	1	0
1S1Q	35.84	**16.76**	0	**3**
1SYX	37.6	**22.7**	2	**3**
1JIW	32.08	33.72	2	0
1M10	33	39.56	1	0
3BX7	33.6	**15.18**	2	**4**
3AAD	34.54	**18.94**	3	2
Avg.	33.59	29.75	0.87	1.67

conservation contributes to the better performance of the model in all of our test cases, and especially when the binding interface is not known and the full conformational space is explored. This is the subject of current work. Future work includes incorporating the ranking function into a docking scheme. Most docking programs first perform geometric search, followed by a ranking stage. Incorporating a scoring phase in the search will allow us to filter out implausible candidates and make the search more effective.

Acknowledgements

The work was funded in part by NSF grant no. CCF-1421871 (NH). Some of the computations were carried out on the UMB research cluster and on the Massachusetts Green High Performance Computing Center (MGHPCC) cluster.

REFERENCES

[1] B. Akbal-Delibas, R. Farhoodi, M. Pomplun, and N. Haspel. 2016. Accurate refinement of docked protein complexes using evolutionary information and deep learning. *Journal of Bioinformatics and Computational Biology* 14, 3 (2016), 1642002.

[2] B. Akbal-Delibas, I. Hashmi, A. Shehu, and N. Haspel. 2012. An evolutionary conservation-based method for refining and reranking protein complex structures. *J Bioinform Comput Biol* 10, 3 (2012).

[3] B. Akbal-Delibas and N. Haspel. 2013. A conservation and biophysics guided stochastic approach to refining docked multimeric proteins. *BMC Structural Biology* 13, Suppl 1 (2013), S7.

[4] B. Akbal-Delibas, M. Pomplun, and N. Haspel. 2014. AccuRMSD: a machine learning approach to predicting structure similarity of docked protein complexes. In *Proceedings of the 5th ACM Conference on Bioinformatics, Computational Biology, and Health Informatics*. ACM, 289–296.

[5] B. Akbal-Delibas, M. Pomplun, and N. Haspel. 2015. Accurate Prediction of Docked Protein Structure Similarity. *J. Comp. Biol.* 22, 9 (2015), 892–904.

[6] Asa Ben-Hur and William Stafford Noble. 2005. Kernel methods for predicting protein-protein interactions. *Bioinformatics* 21, suppl 1 (2005), i38–i46.

[7] B Brooks, R.E. Bruccoleri, B.D. Olafson, D.J. States, S. Swaminathan, and M. Karplus. 1983. CHARMM: A program for macromolecular energy, minimization, and dynamics calculations. *J Comput Chem* 4, 2 (1983), 187 - 217.

[8] C.Z Cai, W.L Wang, L.Z Sun, and Y.Z Chen. 2003. Protein function classification via support vector machine approach. *Mathematical Biosciences* 185, 2 (2003), 111 - 122. DOI:https://doi.org/10.1016/S0025-5564(03)00096-8

[9] T.M-K. Cheng, T.L. Blundell, and J. Fernandez-Recio. 2007. pyDock: Electrostatics and desolvation for effective scoring of rigid-body protein–protein docking. *Proteins: Structure, Function, and Bioinformatics* 68, 2 (2007), 503–515.

[10] N. Cristianini and J. Shawe-Taylor. 2000. *An introduction to Support Vector Machines and other kernel-based learning methods*. Cambridge University Press.

[11] C. Dominguez, R. Boelens, and A. Bonvin. 2003. Haddock: A protein-protein docking approach based on biochemical or biophysical information. *J. Am. Chem. Soc.* 125, 1 (2003), 1731–1737.

[12] R. Farhoodi, B. Akbal-Delibas, and N. Haspel. 2015. Accurate Prediction of Docked Protein Structure Similarity Using Neural Networks and Restricted Boltzmann Machines. In *CSBW (Computational Structural Bioinformatics Workshop), in conjunction with IEEE-BIBM 2015*.

[13] D.S. Goodsell and A.J. Olson. 2000. Structural symmetry and protein function. *Annu. Rev. Biophys. Biomol. Struct.* 29, 1 (2000), 105–153.

[14] J.J. Gray. 2006. High-resolution protein–protein docking. *Current opinion in structural biology* 16, 2 (2006), 183–193.

[15] I. Halperin, B. Ma, H. Wolfson, and R. Nussinov. 2002. Principles of docking: an overview of search algorithms and a guide to scoring functions. *Proteins: Structure, Function, and Bioinformatics* 47, 4 (2002), 409–443.

[16] J. Janin. 2010. Protein–protein docking tested in blind predictions: the CAPRI experiment. *Molecular BioSystems* 6, 12 (2010), 2351–2362.

[17] P. L. Kastritis and A. M. Bonvin. 2010. Are Scoring Functions in Protein-Protein Docking Ready To Predict Interactomes? Clues from a Novel Binding Affinity Benchmark. *J. Proteome Res.* 9, 5 (2010), 2216–2225.

[18] Mohamed A Khamis, Walid Gomaa, and Walaa F Ahmed. 2015. Machine learning in computational docking. *Artificial intelligence in medicine* 63, 3 (2015), 135–152.

[19] D. Kozakov, R. Brenke, S.R. Comeau, and S. Vajda. 2006. PIPER: An FFT-based protein docking program with pairwise potentials. *Proteins: Structure, Function, and Bioinformatics* 65, 2 (2006).

[20] D. Kozakov, D.R. Hall, B. Xia, K.A. Porter, D. Padhorny, C. Yueh, D. Beglov, and S. Vajda. 2017. The ClusPro web server for protein-protein docking. *Nature Protocols* 12 (2017), 275–288.

[21] A.M. Lesk. 2008. *Introduction to Bioinformatics* (3rd ed.). Oxford UniversityPress.

[22] S. Lyskov and J. J. Gray. 2008. The RosettaDock server for local protein-protein docking. *Nucleic Acids Res.* 36, S2 (2008), W233–W238.

[23] I. Mihalek, I. Res, and O. Lichtarge. 2006. Evolutionary Trace Report Maker: a new type of service for comparative analysis of proteins. *Bioinformatics* 22, 13 (2006), 1656–7.

[24] Iain H Moal, Mieczyslaw Torchala, Paul A Bates, and Juan Fernández-Recio. 2013. The scoring of poses in protein-protein docking: current capabilities and future directions. *BMC bioinformatics* 14, 1 (2013), 286.

[25] I.S. Moreira, P.A. Fernandes, and M.J. Ramos. 2010. Protein–protein docking dealing with the unknown. *J. Comput. Chem.* 31, 2 (2010), 317–342.

[26] F. Pedregosa, G. Varoquaux, A. Gramfort, V. Michel, B. Thirion, O. Grisel, M. Blondel, P. Prettenhofer, R. Weiss, V. Dubourg, J. Vanderplas, A. Passos, D. Cournapeau, M. Brucher, M. Perrot, and E. Duchesnay. 2011. Scikit-learn: Machine Learning in Python. *Journal of Machine Learning Research* 12 (2011), 2825–2830.

[27] J.C. Phillips, R. Braun, W. Wang, J. Gumbart, E. Tajkhorshid, E. Villa, C. Chipot, R.D. Skeel, L. Kale, and K. Schulten. 2005. Scalable molecular dynamics with NAMD. *Journal of computational chemistry* 26, 16 (2005), 1781–1802.

[28] J. Qiu, W. Sheffler, D. Baker, and W.S. Noble. 2008. Ranking predicted protein structures with support vector regression. *Proteins: Structure, Function, and Bioinformatics* 71, 3 (2008), 1175–1182. DOI:https://doi.org/10.1002/prot.21809

[29] T. Vreven, I.H. Moal, A. Vangone, B.G. Pierce, P.L. Kastritis, M. Torchala, R. Chaleil, B. Jiménez-García, P.A. Bates, J. Fernandez-Recio, and others. 2015. Updates to the Integrated Protein–Protein Interaction Benchmarks: Docking Benchmark Version 5 and Affinity Benchmark Version 2. *Journal of molecular biology* 427, 19 (2015), 3031–3041.

[30] A. Wilkins, S. Erdin, R. Lua, and O. Lichtarge. 2012. Evolutionary trace for prediction and redesign of protein functional sites. *Methods Mol Biol.* 819 (2012), 29–42.

Evolving Conformation Paths to Model Protein Structural Transitions

Emmanuel Sapin
Dept of Computer Science
George Mason University
4400 University Dr.
Fairfax, Virginia 22030
esapin@gmu.edu

Kenneth De Jong
Dept of Computer Science
George Mason University
4400 University Dr.
Fairfax, Virginia 22030
kdejong@gmu.edu

Amarda Shehu*
Dept of Computer Science
George Mason University
4400 University Dr.
Fairfax, Virginia 22030
amarda@gmu.edu

ABSTRACT

Proteins are dynamic biomolecules. A structure-by-structure characterization of a protein's transition between two different functional structures is central to elucidating the role of dynamics in modulating protein function and designing therapeutic drugs. Characterizing transitions challenges both dry and wet laboratories. Some computational methods compute discrete representations of the energy landscape that organizes structures of a protein by their potential energies. The representations support queries for paths (series of structures) connecting start and goal structures of interest. Here we address the problem of modeling protein structural transitions under the umbrella of stochastic optimization and propose a novel evolutionary algorithm (EA). The EA evolves paths without reconstructing the energy landscape, addressing two competing optimization objectives, energetic cost and structural resolution. Rather than seek one path, the EA yields an ensemble of paths to represent a transition. Preliminary applications suggest the EA is effective while operating under a reasonable computational budget.

CCS CONCEPTS

•**Applied computing → Molecular structural biology;**

KEYWORDS

protein modeling, structural transition, energy landscape, conformation path, stochastic optimization, evolutionary algorithm

ACM Reference format:
Emmanuel Sapin, Kenneth De Jong, and Amarda Shehu. 2017. Evolving Conformation Paths to Model Protein Structural Transitions. In *Proceedings of ACM-BCB'17, August 20–23, 2017, Boston, MA, USA.*, 6 pages.
DOI: http://dx.doi.org/10.1145/3107411.3107498

1 INTRODUCTION

We have known for decades that proteins undergo fast vibrations and slower structural rearrangements/transitions [8]. Structural transitions allow a protein to access different three-dimensional structures with which to interact with different molecular partners, thus modulating its biological function [11]. A detailed structure-by-structure characterization of a protein's transition between two different functional structures is central to elucidating the role of dynamics and mutation-altered dynamics in (dys)function and the design of novel therapeutic drugs [20].

Rapid advances have occurred in the wet laboratory, most notably by single-molecule methods that can resolve one or more intermediate structures in a transition of interest [6, 7, 9]. Advances have also been made in the dry laboratory, but at the moment no single wet- or dry-laboratory method can provide a detailed, structure-by-structure characterization of transitions on any protein of interest [13]. Challenges are due to disparate spatio-temporal scales; the start and goal structures may differ by several angstroms (Å), and the transition may occur over several milliseconds.

An important concept in protein dynamics is the energy landscape, which organizes structures by their potential energies. A protein energy landscape is rich in iso-energetic minima that are separated by energetic barriers. Different functional structures that allow a protein to interact with different molecular partners correspond to basins (broad neighborhoods of local minima), and a structural transition can be represented as a series of structures that allow the protein to hop from one basin to another [2, 5].

Two canonical approaches to modeling protein structural transitions are Molecular Dynamics (MD) and the Monte Carlo (MC). In MD, repeated applications of Newton's second law of motion and numerical integration allow following small-timescale motions of the atoms constituting a protein of interest. Due to the dependency of numerical integration on small time steps, an MD simulation is likely to converge rapidly to a local minimum near the start structure of the sought transition. The MC approach does away with integration and employs instead biased random walks in the energy landscape. This results in higher exploration capability, though the walks also converge to nearby local minima. Many "enhanced sampling" techniques are proposed to increase the exploration capability of MD or MC approaches [13].

A complementary group of methods aim to increase exploration capability by constructing discrete representations (a tree or a graph) of the protein energy landscape that support queries for series of intermediate structures that detail a start-to-goal transition of a protein of interest. Some of the earliest work originated in a subcommunity of scientists that took inspiration from mechanistic analogies between modeling protein motions and planning robot motions [28]. Often, such methods are referred to as robotics-inspired.

*Corresponding Author

Permission to make digital or hard copies of all or part of this work for personal or classroom use is granted without fee provided that copies are not made or distributed for profit or commercial advantage and that copies bear this notice and the full citation on the first page. Copyrights for components of this work owned by others than ACM must be honored. Abstracting with credit is permitted. To copy otherwise, or republish, to post on servers or to redistribute to lists, requires prior specific permission and/or a fee. Request permissions from permissions@acm.org.
ACM-BCB'17, August 20–23, 2017, Boston, MA, USA.
© 2017 ACM. ISBN 978-1-4503-4722-8/17/08...$15.00
DOI: http://dx.doi.org/10.1145/3107411.3107498

Robotics-inspired methods rely on sampling conformations to generate new structures (a conformation is a chosen representation of a molecular structure). Tree-based methods generate such samples as part of the process of growing a tree (vertices are the samples). The growth of the tree is biased so as to propagate from the start to the goal structure with low-energy intermediate structures. The result is a local (discrete) representation of the energy landscape (the tree), that may not correspond to the lowest-cost path that connects the given start and goal structures. On the other hand, graph-/roadmap-based methods first generate samples and then embed them in a nearest-neighbor graph where each sample is connected to its nearest neighbors. These methods are more likely to capture the lowest-cost path (as well as support multiple path queries between any structures of interest), but the nonlocal view comes at a higher computational cost (many samples/structures). Advances have been made in roadmap-based modeling of protein structural transitions, and the reader is referred to [28] for a review of the state of the art. For instance, some roadmap-based methods can model transitions between start and goal structures as far as 13Å away from each-other [14, 15, 17–19].

Tree- and roadmap-based methods seek the lowest-cost path to represent a transition; the notion of cost captures that of the work that has be to done for a protein to "go over" the energetic barriers. Similar-cost paths may exist, considering the multidimensionality of the landscape; however, finding the lowest-cost path is challenging by itself. In roadmap-based methods, path resolution (the maximal distance between two consecutive structures) is not an explicit objective alongside cost, and sampling more structures is seen as the only way to improve path resolution. Tree-based methods can directly control resolution by generating a child structure that is low in energy and close to its parent in the tree. The cost of the path connecting the root (the start structure) to a leaf deemed close to the goal structure is not directly controlled.

In this paper we treat both path cost and path resolution as objectives when seeking paths to represent a structural transition. Specifically, we cast the problem of modeling protein structural transitions as a stochastic optimization problem; to the best of our knowledge, this is a novel approach. We propose an evolutionary algorithm (EA) that evolve paths that are both low in cost and high in resolution. The EA directly controls both path cost and resolution and yields an ensemble of paths to better represent a structural transition in the multidimensional protein energy landscape. We now relate details of the proposed EA.

2 METHODS

Several building blocks employed in the proposed EA have been developed and analyzed by us in prior work on memetic EAs for capturing structured, sample-based representations of protein energy landscapes [25–27]. A key building block is the exploitation of experimentally-known structures of a protein to select a representation of a structure (a conformation). Briefly, the experimentally-known structures of a protein (of the wildtype form and mutated versions/variants) are subjected to principal component analysis (PCA). PCA yields a new basis whose axes are ordered by the amount of variance they capture in the structure data. The axes are also referred to as principal components (PCs). The top m PCs that collectively capture a threshold variance are selected as variables with which to represent a conformation. Typically, a threshold of 80–90% results in $m \in [10, 25]$, which is over a hundred-fold reduction over the number of Cartesian coordinates (were one to use such coordinates of all the atoms in a protein). Further details can be found in Ref. [4].

Path Representation. The proposed EA evolves path individuals utilizing only two given structures. These structures are projected onto the start and goal conformations. A path is represented as an ordered (start-to-goal directed) list of conformations.

Path Cost The fitness/cost of a path sums up the energy increase between structures corresponding to consecutive conformations in the path. This path cost formulation considers only the amount of work needed for a protein to "climb" energy barriers separating local minima in the landscape (and has been employed in robotics-inspired methods [10, 15]).

Path Resolution This is measured here as the maximum distance (via the Euclidean distance function) between two consecutive conformations. A complementary, valid consideration is to make use of the root-mean-square-deviation (rmsd) [16]. However, rmsd is a computationally-costly measurement due to the need to align the two structures. In addition, the conformations in a path are not yet structures (but rather points in the m–dimensional space of PCs extracted from experimentally-known structures).

Relationship between Cost and Resolution. Fig. 1 illustrates the relationship between path cost and resolution. A low-resolution path may erroneously report that the cost of a basin-basin transition is low, ignoring the separating barrier. Fig. 1(a) juxtaposes the lowest-resolution path (no intermediate structures) in such a scenario to a path that follows the landscape more closely and as a result has higher cost. Fig. 1(b) illustrates another scenario, where the start and goal structures reside on nearby barriers separated by a basin. These two examples illustrate that a low-resolution path is easy to compute (fewer intermediate structures) but associates an inaccurate, possibly low energetic cost with a transition. On the other hand, as the resolution of a path improves due to more intermediate structures, the path cost may increase due to the path following the landscape more closely.

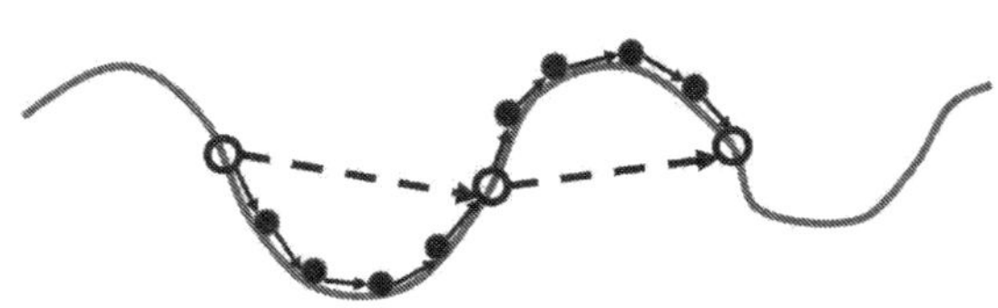

Figure 1: The first pair of structures (empty circles) can be connected via a path with no intermediate structures. A higher-resolution path with intermediate structures (black dots) would correctly take into account the basin in the cost of the transition. The second pair of structures (empty circles) can be connected via a path with no intermediate structures, missing the barrier. A higher-resolution path would contain intermediate structures in the barrier and consider that in the cost of the transition.

Initial Population. $n_$points are obtained by linear interpolation between the given start and end conformations. Each resulting conformation undergoes a transformation, which converts a conformation to an all-atom protein structure that corresponds to a local minimum in the all-atom Rosetta energy landscape [12]. The transformation relies on the Rosetta *relax* function, which is stochastic; repeating it N times allows us to obtain an initial population of N different paths. The transformation of a conformation to an all-atom structure corresponding to a local minimum is also a building block developed and analyzed in prior work [3].

Variation Operator. Successive generations evolve the population of paths as follows. For every two consecutive conformations in a path, a variation operator yields a new mid-point/conformation, which is converted to a (local minimum) all-atom structure utilizing the transformation summarized above. The variation operator is not explicitly yielding a path offspring but rather additional conformations from a path individual. The burden of providing offspring paths is passed on to the selection operator.

Selection Operator. The selection operator takes all conformations (existing ones in the paths and new ones obtained from the variation operator) and inserts them into a nearest-neighbor graph (nngraph). The nngraph connects a point to others within a ball of radius ϵ; ϵ is measured via the Euclidean distance function. N consecutive applications of Dijkstra's path search algorithm on the nngraph yield the N paths that initialize the next generation. After each application, the points utilized in the found path are removed from the graph, and the next application of Dijkstra's is carried out in the induced subgraph. This mechanism yields N low-cost non-redundant paths.

Evolutionary Pressure. ϵ decreases or increases to apply pressure to find high-resolution paths. At the first generation (after the initial population), ϵ is set to $d/(x+i*0.1)$, where d is the Euclidean distance between the start and goal conformations, $x = 1$, and $i = 1$. If a path is found, i is incremented, and this process continues until a path cannot be found (we adapt Dijkstra's to consider dynamic neighbors that disappear as ϵ decreases). If a path is not found, the path that is reported is the one found at the prior attempt, and this is the value of i that is employed in the next application of Dijkstra's in the induced subgraph to find another path. The last successful value of i (yielding the Nth path) is recorded and in the next generation ϵ is initialized to a lower value by incrementing the last successful value of i. This process provides pressure for the EA to find both low-cost and high-resolution paths. Note that while in the initial population all paths have the same length in terms of the number of conformations, the paths obtained in subsequent generations have variable lengths. Also note that the so-described selection operator circumvents the issue of comparing two paths to determine which one is better. The latter is non-trivial due to the complex relationship between cost and resolution. Cost and resolution are treated as different optimization objectives by the EA, and the selection operator is key to addressing both.

Implementation Details. The EA is implemented in C++ and run on a 16 core Red Hat Linux box with 3.2 GHz HT Xeon CPU and 8GB RAM. The cores allow to parallelize the transformation of conformations into structures. $m = 10$, $N = 15$, and $n\_points = 10$. In Section 3, the resolution of paths is converted to rmsd [16] and reported in Å due to domain-specific insight on what rmsds correspond to low or high values. The EA operates under a fixed computational budget, tallying up the number of energy evaluations in the transformations of conformations to structures. For most of the applications described in Section 3, the budget is 100,000 fitness evaluations. On a protein of 166 amino acids, the total running time of the EA is about 38 CPU hours; a significant portion of this time is devoted to conduct N lowest-cost path searches in each generation.

3 RESULTS

We analyze the performance of the proposed EA on four variant sequences of the H-Ras enzyme, which is a central enzyme to cell growth regulation. Specifically, we apply the EA to the WT sequence, two oncogenic variants, G12C and Q61L, and a syndrome-causing variant Y32CC118S. The naming convention `[AACode1][Position][AACode2]` for a single-mutant variant indicates that the amino acid `AACode1` (using one-letter codes) at position `Position` in the WT is replaced with the amino acid `Code2` in the particular variant. Additional mutations are joined in order of positions, as in the Y32CC118S variant we consider here.

The EA is run to obtain paths connecting two different biologically-relevant structures of H-Ras that correspond to the on/active state and the off/inactive states. The start structure used to represent the on state is obtained from the Protein Data Bank (PDB) [1] under PDB entry id `1qra`. The goal structure selected to represent the off state is obtained from the PDB entry with id `4q21`.

For each of the test cases, the computational budget of the EA is fixed to 100,000 fitness evaluations, which is 10 times less than that used in the roadmap-based method in [25] to which we compare the quality of the computed paths. Specifically, the 15 lowest-cost paths obtained by the proposed EA with this budget are compared to the top paths found by the roadmap-based method in [25].

We relate the following results. First, we compare the top paths found by the EA to those found by the roadmap-based method in [25] on H-Ras WT in terms of both cost and resolution. We then draw these paths and further demonstrate that the proposed EA has not reached saturation; when provided a higher computational budget, it is able to further improve the quality of paths. Finally, we show the performance of the EA on the other three H-Ras variants.

3.1 Comparative Analysis on H-Ras WT

Table 1 compares the cost and resolution of ten top paths found by the proposed EA (Columns 1-4) to those of the top ten paths found by the roadmap-based method in [25] (Columns 5-6). Paths are ordered from high to low costs. The proposed EA is run under two regimes, under a budget of 100,000 fitness evaluations (Columns 3-4) and then a budget of 200,000 fitness evaluations (Columns 1-2). These budgets are 1/10 and 1/5, respectively, the budget employed by the roadmap-based method in [25]. All paths obtained by the roadmap-based method have the same resolution, as this is imposed in the construction of the nngraph prior to answering path queries. As described in Section 2, the paths obtained by the proposed EA have varying resolution.

The comparison in Table 1 shows that the proposed EA obtains very high-resolution (0.133Å and 0.129Å under the two budgets) paths with much less computational budget (and so fewer generated structures) than the roadmap-based method. The resolutions even with the more modest budget are better than the roadmap-based method. As described in Section 2, path costs at higher resolutions typically increase due to the high ruggedness of protein energy landscapes. Taken altogether, these results demonstrate that the proposed EA is able to find paths with better resolution than the roadmap-based method while operating under a smaller computational budget.

Table 1: Top ten paths obtained by each algorithm.

Proposed EA 200K fitness evals		Proposed EA 100K fitness evals		Roadmap-based [25] 1M fitness evals	
Cost	Res	Cost	Res	Cost	Res
487	0.129	554	0.133	588	0.145
301	0.134	296	0.146	546	0.145
291	0.139	292	0.143	504	0.145
288	0.152	149	0.162	470	0.145
271	0.157	148	0.172	408	0.145
267	0.150	129	0.172	395	0.145
263	0.172	123	0.172	376	0.145
251	0.143	113	0.195	324	0.145
248	0.158	112	0.190	306	0.145
236	0.172	109	0.192	266	0.145

Table 1 also shows that the EA is able to further improve the quality of paths when afforded more fitness evaluations (and so allowed to evolve paths over more generations). Specifically, the average value over the resolutions of of the paths improves from 0.168Å (when the budget is 100, 000 fitness evaluations) to 0.151Å when the budget is doubled. Comparing Columns 1 to 3 makes it clear that the higher resolutions invariably increase the costs of paths. Specifically, the average path cost increases from 170.33REUs to 260.07REUS when the budget is doubled. This supports the relationship between path cost and resolution that is illustrated in Section 2 and motivates the recasting of the path computation problems as a multi-objective optimization problem. With paths following the rugged landscape more closely, path costs are expected to increase.

The actual paths found by the proposed EA under the two computational budgets are drawn in Figure 2. Panel (a) draws the paths in the final generation of the proposed EA restricted to a budget of 100, 000 fitness evaluations, and panel (b) does so when the budget is doubled. The paths are drawn by connecting consecutive structures with edges, with the start structure on the right of each panel and the goal structure on the left. Conformations are drawn as dots, using their coordinates along the top two PCs. Conformations generated by the EA but not utilized in the top paths are also drawn and color-coded by the Rosetta all-atom energy values of their corresponding structures. Comparison of panels (a) and (b) in Figure 2 clearly reveals that under the higher computational budget, the top paths phenotypically converge to a narrower region of the fitness landscape and thus capture the sought structural transition more accurately.

3.2 Comparative Analysis on Pathogenic Variants

Figure 3 shows the paths in the last generation of the proposed EA for each of the three other test cases that are oncogenic variants of H-Ras. The resolutions are generally worse in comparison to what the EA can find for the WT sequence, which helps reduce the total cost of a path, as described earlier (the resolutions are better than those found by the roadmap-based EA on the WT sequence). The lower resolutions for these three variants in comparison to what the proposed EA finds on the WT sequence point to possibly more complex landscapes where more applications of the variation operator may be needed to uncover local minima in higher-energy regions. Visual comparison of the generated conformations (color-coded projections) across the WT and these three variants suggests higher-energy regions separating the start and goal structures sought to be connected by the path-evolving EA for G12C and Y32CC118S, but a possibly higher-energy, off basin (left of the panels in Fig. 3).

4 CONCLUSION

We have presented a novel algorithm that, to the best of our knowledge, is the first to cast and address the problem of modeling protein structural transitions as a multi-objective optimization problem. Specifically, this paper makes the case that both energetic cost and resolution, which are ineffectively treated at the moment by other methods, are key to the quality of a modeled structural transition.

The proposed algorithm is an EA, as EAs are effective at addressing hard optimization problems. Moreover, unlike previous adaptations of EAs for structure-related problems in computational structural biology, the proposed EA evolves paths rather than molecular structures. The EA also relies on a novel selection operator to address both path cost and path resolution as competing objectives.

The evaluation demonstrates the capability of the proposed EA to improve over state-of-the-art, landscape-reconstructing, roadmap-based methods [25]. The analysis on th H-Ras WT also shows the ability of the proposed EA to further improve the quality of its solutions with larger computational budgets. The emphasis on lower computational budgets is due to the potential of path-evolving EAs to obtain and then compare the structural dynamics of various forms of a protein in a large-scale setting. This would allow elucidating mutation-altered dynamics and its impact in dysfunction.

The results suggest that treating the problem of modeling protein structural transitions as a multi-objective one is reasonable and can result in novel research directions. It is worth noting that while EAs have garnered attention and momentum in *de-novo* protein structure prediction [21–24], this paper proposes for the first time an EA to address the problem of modeling transitions between known structures. Moreover, evolving individuals with complex representations, such as paths, is of interest in evolutionary computation and is likely to spur further research on effective variation and selection operators.

5 ACKNOWLEDGMENTS

This work is supported in part by NSF CCF No. 1421001 and NSF IIS CAREER Award No. 1144106.

REFERENCES

[1] H. M. Berman, K. Henrick, and H. Nakamura. 2003. Announcing the worldwide Protein Data Bank. *Nat Struct Biol* 10, 12 (2003), 980–980.

[2] J. D. Bryngelson, J. N. Onuchic, N. D. Socci, and P. G. Wolynes. 1995. Funnels, pathways, and the energy landscape of protein folding: a synthesis. *Proteins: Struct Funct Genet* 21, 3 (1995), 167–195.

[3] R. Clausen, B. Ma, R. Nussinov, and A. Shehu. 2015. Mapping the Conformation Space of Wildtype and Mutant H-Ras with a Memetic, Cellular, and Multiscale Evolutionary Algorithm. *PLoS Comput Biol* 11, 9 (2015), e1004470.

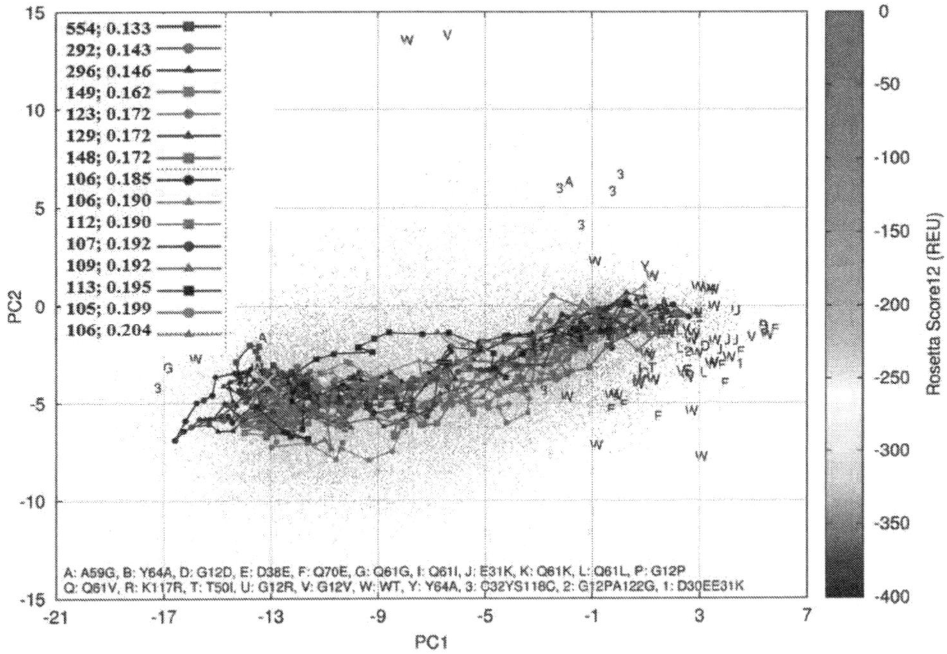

(a) 100, 000 fitness evaluations

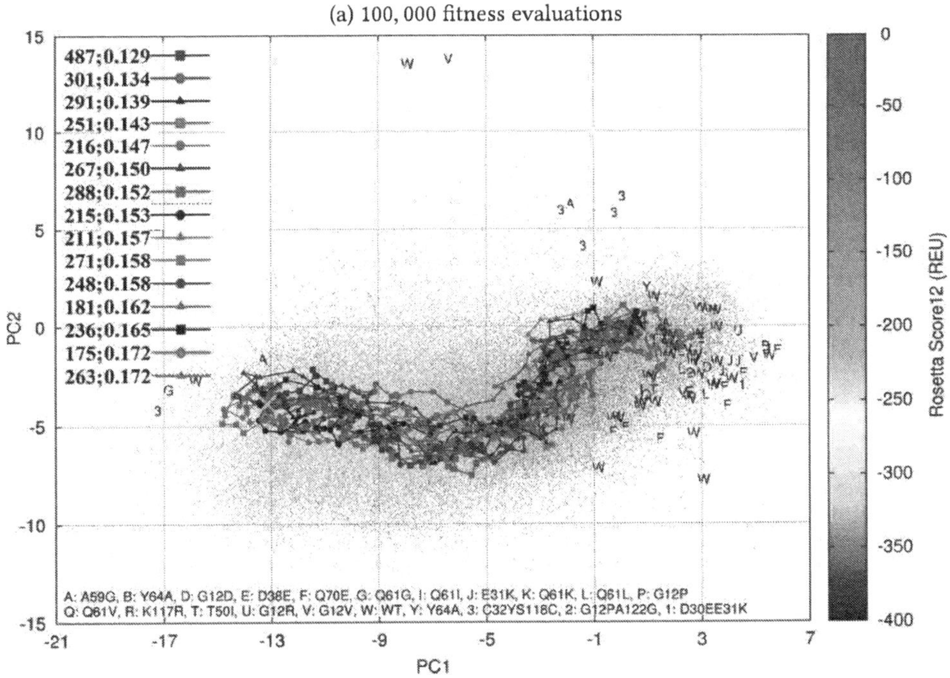

(b) 200, 000 fitness evaluations

Figure 2: The EA is allowed a computational budget of (a) 100, 000 or (b) 200, 000 fitness evaluations; the paths in the last generation are shown in each setting, drawing an edge between two consecutive structures. Dots show conformations. Dots outside the drawn paths are color-coded and note conformations generated during the execution of the algorithm but not selected by the selection operator. The blue-to-red color-coding scheme encodes low-to-high energy values measured with the all-atom Rosetta energy function (score12). The text annotations indicate projections of experimentally-known structures. The legend in each plot lists the path costs in Rosetta energy units (REUs) and their resolutions in angstroms (Å).

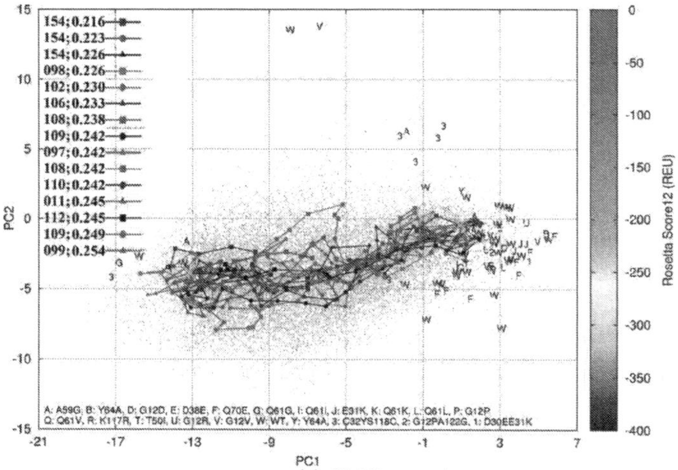

(a) G12C

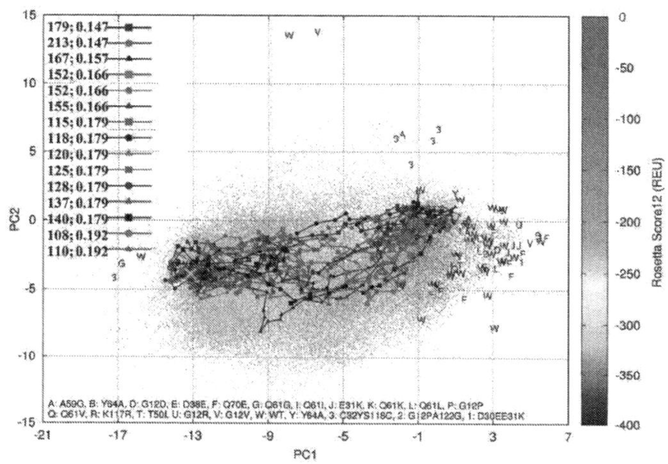

(b) Q61L

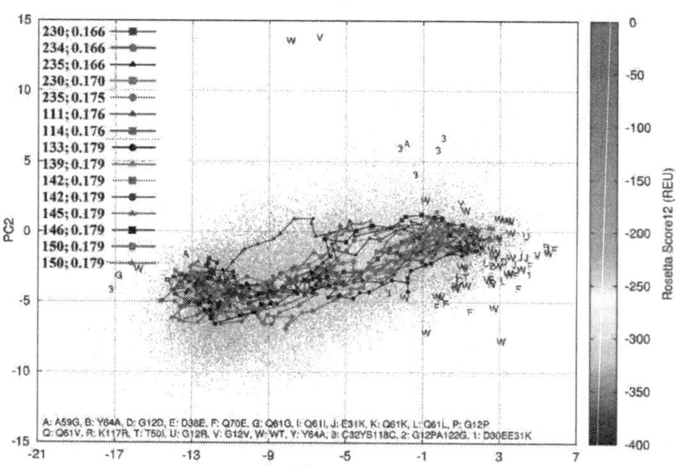

(c) Y32CC118S

Figure 3: The paths obtained by the proposed EA in the last generation (with a budget of 100, 000 fitness evaluations) are shown here for three more test cases. The same plotting style is followed as in Fig. 2.

[4] R. Clausen and A. Shehu. 2015. A Data-driven Evolutionary Algorithm for Mapping Multi-basin Protein Energy Landscapes. *J Comp Biol* 22, 9 (2015), 844–860.

[5] H. Frauenfelder, S. G. Sligar, and P. G. Wolynes. 1991. The energy landscapes and motion on proteins. *Science* 254, 5038 (1991), 1598–1603.

[6] A. Gall, C. Ilioaia, T. P. Krüger, V. I. Novoderezhkin, B. Robert, and R. van Grondelle. 2015. Conformational Switching in a Light-Harvesting Protein as Followed by Single-Molecule Spectroscopy. *Biophys J* 108, 11 (2015), 2713–2720.

[7] W. J. Greenleaf, M. T. Woodside, and S. M. Block. 2007. High-Resolution, Single-Molecule Measurements of Biomolecular Motion. *Annu Rev Biophys Biomol Struct* 36 (2007), 171–190.

[8] K. A. Henzler-Wildman, V. Thai, M. Lei, M. Ott, M. Wolf-Watz, T. Fenn, E. Pozharski, M. A. Wilson, G. A. Petsko, M. Karplus, C. G. Hübner, and D. Kern. 2007. Intrinsic motions along an enzymatic reaction trajectory. *Nature* 450, 7171 (2007), 838–844.

[9] J. Hohlbein, T. D. Craggs, and T. Cordes. 2014. Alternating-laser excitation: single-molecule FRET and beyond. *Chem Soc Rev* 43, 4 (2014), 1156–1171.

[10] L. Jaillet, J. Cortés, and T. Siméon. 2010. Sampling-based path planning on configuration-cost costmaps. *IEEE Trans Robot* 26, 4 (2010), 635–646.

[11] K. Jenzler-Wildman and D. Kern. 2007. Dynamic personalities of proteins. *Nature* 450, 7172 (2007), 964–972.

[12] A. Leaver-Fay, M. Tyka, S. M. Lewis, O. F. Lange, J. Thompson, R. Jacak, K. Kaufman, P. D. Renfrew, C. A. Smith, W. Sheffler, I. W. Davis, S. Cooper, A. Treuille, D. J. Mandell, F. Richter, Y. E. Ban, S. J. Fleishman, J. E. Corn, D. E. Kim, S. Lyskov, M. Berrondo, S. Mentzer, Z. Popovifj, and et. al. 2011. ROSETTA3: an object-oriented software suite for the simulation and design of macromolecules. *Methods Enzymol* 487 (2011), 545–574.

[13] T. Maximova, R. Moffatt, B. Ma, R. Nussinov, and A. Shehu. 2016. Principles and Overview of Sampling Methods for Modeling Macromolecular Structure and Dynamics. *PLoS Comput Biol* 12, 4 (2016), e1004619.

[14] T. Maximova, E. Plaku, and A. Shehu. 2015. Computing Transition Paths in Multiple-Basin Proteins with a Probabilistic Roadmap Algorithm Guided by Structure Data. In *Intl Conf on Bioinf and Biomed (BIBM)*. IEEE, Washington, D.C., 35–42.

[15] T. Maximova, E. Plaku, and A. Shehu. 2016. Structure-guided Protein Transition Modeling with a Probabilistic Roadmap Algorithm. *IEEE/ACM Trans Comput Biol & Bioinform* 13, 5 (2016), 1–14.

[16] A. D. McLachlan. 1972. A mathematical procedure for superimposing atomic coordinates of proteins. *Acta Crystallogr A* 26, 6 (1972), 656–657.

[17] K. Molloy, R. Clausen, and A. Shehu. 2016. A Stochastic Roadmap Method to Model Protein Structural Transitions. *Robotica* 34, 8 (2016), 1705–1733.

[18] K. Molloy and A. Shehu. 2013. Elucidating the Ensemble of Functionally-relevant Transitions in Protein Systems with a Robotics-inspired Method. *BMC Struct Biol* 13, Suppl 1 (2013), S8.

[19] K. Molloy and A. Shehu. 2015. Interleaving Global and Local Search for Protein Motion Computation. In *LNCS: Bioinformatics Research and Applications*, R. Harrison, Y. Li, and I. Mandoiu (Eds.), Vol. 9096. Springer International Publishing, Norfolk, VA, 175–186.

[20] Colm Ó'Dúnlaing, Micha Sharir, and Chee K. Yap. 2014. Protein Conformational Dynamics. In *Advances in Experimental Medicine and Biology*, K.-L. Han, X. Zhang, and M.-J. Yang (Eds.). Springer International Publishing, Switzerland, 488.

[21] B. Olson, K. A. De Jong, and A. Shehu. 2013. Off-Lattice Protein Structure Prediction with Homologous Crossover. In *Conf on Genetic and Evolutionary Computation (GECCO)*. ACM, New York, NY, 287–294.

[22] Brian Olson and Amarda Shehu. 2012. Efficient basin hopping in the protein energy surface. In *IEEE Intl Conf on Bioinf and Biomed (BIBM)*, Jean Gao, Werner Dubitzky, Cathy Wu, Michael Liebman, Reda Alhaij, Lyle Ungar, Anastasia Christianson, and Xiaohua Hu (Eds.). IEEE, Philadelphia, PA, 119–124.

[23] B. Olson and A. Shehu. 2012. Evolutionary-inspired probabilistic search for enhancing sampling of local minima in the protein energy surface. *Proteome Sci* 10, Suppl 1 (2012), S5.

[24] B. Olson and A. Shehu. 2014. Multi-Objective Optimization Techniques for Conformational Sampling in Template-Free Protein Structure Prediction. In *Intl Conf on Bioinf and Comp Biol (BICoB)*. Las Vegas, NV.

[25] E. Sapin, D. B. Carr, K. A. De Jong, and A. Shehu. 2016. Computing energy landscape maps and structural excursions of proteins. *BMC Genomics* 17, Suppl 4 (2016), 456.

[26] E. Sapin, K. A. De Jong, and A. Shehu. 2016. A Novel EA-based Memetic Approach for Efficiently Mapping Complex Fitness Landscapes. In *Conf on Genetic and Evolutionary Computation (GECCO)*. ACM, 85–92.

[27] E. Sapin, K. A. De Jong, and A. Shehu. 2017. From Optimization to Mapping: An Evolutionary Algorithm for Protein Energy Landscapes. *IEEE/ACM Trans Comput Biol & Bioinform* (2017). in press.

[28] A. Shehu and E. Plaku. 2016. A Survey of omputational Treatments of Biomolecules by Robotics-inspired Methods Modeling Equilibrium Structure and Dynamics. *J of Artif Intell Res* 597 (2016), 509–572.

Statistical Analysis of Computed Energy Landscapes to Understand Dysfunction in Pathogenic Protein Variants

Wanli Qiao*
Dept of Statistics
George Mason University

Tatiana Maximova
Dept of Computer Science
George Mason University

Erion Plaku
Dept of Electrical Engineering and Computer Science
The Catholic University of America

Amarda Shehu†
Dept of Computer Science
George Mason University

ABSTRACT

The energy landscape underscores the inherent nature of proteins as dynamic systems interconverting between structures with varying energies. The protein energy landscape contains much of the information needed to characterize protein equilibrium dynamics and relate it to function. It is now possible to reconstruct energy landscapes of medium-size proteins with sufficient prior structure data. These developments turn the focus to tools for analysis and comparison of energy landscapes as a means of formulating hypotheses on the impact of sequence mutations on (dys)function via altered landscape features. We present such a method here and provide a detailed evaluation of its capabilities on an enzyme central to human biology. The work presented here opens up an interesting avenue into automated analysis and summarization of landscapes that yields itself to machine learning approaches at the energy landscape level.

CCS CONCEPTS

•**Applied computing → Molecular structural biology;**

KEYWORDS

protein energy landscape, dysfunction, mutation, basins, barriers, saddle points, landscape analysis

ACM Reference format:

Wanli Qiao, Tatiana Maximova, Erion Plaku, and Amarda Shehu. 2017. Statistical Analysis of Computed Energy Landscapes to Understand Dysfunction in Pathogenic Protein Variants. In *Proceedings of ACM-BCB'17, August 20–23, 2017, Boston, MA, USA.*, 6 pages.
DOI: http://dx.doi.org/10.1145/3107411.3107499

1 INTRODUCTION

Proteins switch between different shapes/structures to interact with different molecular partners [15]. These motions, if visualized, correspond to hops in a high-dimensional energy landscape that organizes structures by their potential energies. An energy landscape can reveal basins and barriers, with basins corresponding to thermodynamically-stable and semi-stable structural states, and barriers corresponding to higher-energy regions that slow down basin-to-basin diffusions and regulate the structural rearrangements that allow a protein to interact with different molecules [6].

Obtaining detailed representations of biomolecular energy landscapes is central to elucidating the structural dynamics that regulates the function or dysfunction of a biomolecule [15]. Some of the most complex human disorders, including cancer, are driven by DNA mutations that percolate to protein dysfunction [18]. While it is known that mutations percolate to dysfunction by changing the energy landscape and in turn the structural dynamics of a protein, quantifying changes to the landscape and dynamics of a protein in response to a mutation remains elusive [11]. Due to the disparate spatio-temporal scales involved, currently, neither wet- nor dry-laboratory techniques can fully reconstruct energy landscapes [21].

Recent algorithmic efforts circumvent the issue of disparate spatio-temporal scales by exploiting information available in resolved structures of healthy and diseased forms (pathogenic variants) of a protein [4]. Several stochastic optimization algorithms have been proposed and shown to reconstruct energy landscapes of various medium-size proteins with reasonable computational budgets (no more than a few CPU days) [3, 5, 12, 13, 22].

These algorithms, whether employing concepts from evolutionary search strategies (thus operating under the umbrella of evolutionary computation) or concepts adapted from robot motion planning (thus often referred to as robotics-inspired algorithms), effectively sample new structures (ranging anywhere from 50K to 1M structures depending on the energy function employed) of a protein sequence under consideration in a carefully-selected, low-dimensional variable space; the latter is extracted via Principal Component Analysis (PCA) of known structures. Some of these (robotics-inspired) algorithms integrate the latest AMBER energy functions, yielding detailed, sample-based representations of AMBER energy landscapes (containing thousands of new structures) that allow understanding the role of stable and semi-stable states and transitions between them in (dys)function [12, 13].

As a result of these recent algorithmic developments, it is now possible to reconstruct detailed energy landscapes of medium-size proteins with sufficient prior structure data. These developments allow us to turn our focus from computing to mining protein energy landscapes. Specifically, given the ability to compute landscapes

*Corresponding Author: wqiao@gmu.edu
†Corresponding Author: amarda@gmu.edu

Permission to make digital or hard copies of all or part of this work for personal or classroom use is granted without fee provided that copies are not made or distributed for profit or commercial advantage and that copies bear this notice and the full citation on the first page. Copyrights for components of this work owned by others than ACM must be honored. Abstracting with credit is permitted. To copy otherwise, or republish, to post on servers or to redistribute to lists, requires prior specific permission and/or a fee. Request permissions from permissions@acm.org.
ACM-BCB'17, August 20–23, 2017, Boston, MA, USA.
© 2017 ACM. ISBN 978-1-4503-4722-8/17/08...$15.00
DOI: http://dx.doi.org/10.1145/3107411.3107499

of variants of a protein effectively on demand and to do this in a comprehensive fashion, for the WT and many pathogenic variants, the goal is to develop computational tools for analysis and comparison of energy landscapes. The latter is necessary to quantify and summarize energy landscape features altered by mutations and then formulate thermodynamics-based hypotheses on the impact of sequence mutations on (dys)function.

In this paper, we present such a landscape analysis method. The method analyzes computed samples (representing structures of a protein sequence) and automatically identifies basins and ridges in the landscape comprised by the samples. Visualization of detected basins and ridges allows qualitatively comparing landscapes of healthy and pathogenic variants of a protein. More importantly, the method exposes the deepest point in a basin, which, alongside with saddle points allow us to define quantitative landscape descriptors. The latter, as we demonstrate here, open the way for landscape mining techniques to summarize landscapes, compare them, and even relate landscape features to wet-laboratory measurements of biological mechanisms impacted by mutations.

In Section 1.1, we provide a better context for the landscape analysis method proposed here via a background and summary of related work. The method is described in detail in Section 2, and evaluated on variants of H-Ras, a cell-growth regulating enzyme central to human biology and health. Our evaluation in Section 3 draws several mechanisms of interest by which oncogenic and non-oncogenic mutations alter features of the energy landscape and in turn impact the wildtype structural dynamics. An interesting avenue is also related on how automated landscape analysis opens the way for machine learning approaches to operate over energy landscapes. The paper concludes in Section 4 with a summary and description of future directions of work.

1.1 Related Work

Let $e(x)$ be an energy function defined on the domain $D \subseteq \mathbb{R}^d$ ($d \geq 1$). Denote $e_{\min} = \min_{x \in D} e(x)$ and $e_{\max} = \max_{x \in D} e(x)$. For $c \in [e_{\min}, e_{\max}]$, let the *lower-level set* $L(c) = \{x \in D : e(x) \leq c\}$. $L(c)$ may contain components with separate boundaries. The concept of a *basin*, though not explicitly defined in current literature, can be related to each component, but basins may have hierarchical structure (a smaller basin can be a subset of a larger basin). This structure ought to be revealed by a landscape analysis method but only emerges when iteratively decreasing the energy level c. As energy decreases, a basin shkrinks until it disappears or gets split into more components with separate boundaries; i.e., more basins. The method we propose detects these scenarios.

Other concepts relate to *barriers* or *ridges*, which are collections of local maxima on paths between basins; *saddles* are critical points on these paths. Statistical analyses of ridges exist in literature [16, 19]. The identification of basins is strongly connected to ridges, but here we focus on basins, leaving ridge detection to future research.

Problems related to landscape analysis arise in other disciplines. The vast amount of cosmological data exhibits complex network-like spatial structures, consisting of clusters, filaments, walls, and voids. Persistent diagrams are employed to extract topological summarization of cosmological data [23]. Here, however, the focus is on geometric features of spatial data (in particular, basins). A related method, proposed in [1], analyzes a nearest-neighbor graph of structures, seeking critical points in the graph in a discrete manner. Basins are represented by local minima. In contrast, our approach analyzes the smoothed energy landscape. Therefore, the method we propose is robust against both the ruggedness of the energy landscape and the non-uniform sampling density that is often expected from stochastic optimization methods. Additionally, the basins identified by our method are sub-regions of the landscape and have clear boundaries that facilitate visualization.

2 METHODS

The SoPriM algorithm [12] and its faster version, SoPriMp [10], leverage known structures to obtain an ensemble of structures that provide a discrete, sample-based representation of the energy landscape of a protein sequence of interest. The algorithms feasibly provide detailed representations of landscapes of many medium-size proteins [13]. Both algorithms do not directly operate in the structure space of a protein, so as to circumvent the dimensionality issue, but instead compute samples that represent structures in a low-dimensional variable space (of principal components – PCs). Fast transformations between the variable space and the all-atom structure space allow the algorithms to obtain low-energy all-atom structures. We refer the reader to work in [10] for more details. Here we employ SoPriMp (due to its higher exploration capability [10]) to provide the proposed landscape analysis method with samples (points in the variable space) corresponding to computed all-atom structures with associated Amber ff14SB energies.

The proposed method explicitly reconstructs the landscape by finding basins and saddles. Here we limit the application to automated analysis of 3D samples, using as observations the PC1, PC2 coordinates of the SoPriMp-computed samples and the Amber ff14SB energy values of the structures corresponding to the samples. In principle, all the variables employed by SoPriMp can be used (all selected principal components, which typically range from 10 to 25), but the number of variables determines the dimensionality of the space; increasing dimensionality adds to the computational cost associated with the analysis. It is worth noting that cases where SoPriMp can be employed to obtain sample-based representations of energy landscapes, the top two PCs capture more than 50% of the structural variance, and the top three capture well above 70% of the variance. In this paper, we demonstrate that a coarse and fast analysis can still be very valuable to extract features of a landscape. The emphasis on reasonable computational costs is due to our objective to apply this algorithm in a comparative analysis setting, where we screen dozens or more variants of a protein in search of energetic features that help us summarize, categorize, and elucidate the impact of mutations on dysfunction.

Finding Basins and Saddles

We refer to the method as Basin_Finder, though the method finds basins and saddles separating basins. The method first finds the α-convex hull [17, 20] of the PC1-PC2 sample locations and then defines a 2D grid over the samples in the hull; the distance between adjacent grid points is a parameter δ_1. The collection of the resulting grid points is denoted as $S_{\max}$. The energy of each grid point is estimated via the Nadaraya-Watson (NW) kernel regression [14]. At each grid point x, the energy estimate is the weighted average of the observed sample energies in a small neighborhood (bandwidth h) around x. We note that kernel regression is a smoothing technique that is central in spatial data analysis (the amount of smoothing is controlled by h). In particular, energy landscapes reconstructed with all-atom energy functions, such as Amber ff14SB here, are overly rugged [11]. Kernel regression is a mechanism to reduce the ruggedness and also address non-uniform density of samples.

Let the minimum and maximum (estimated) energy on S_{max} be c_{max} and c_{min}, respectively. The method then iteratively decreases the energy level c, starting from c_{max} by a small step δ_2, detecting when basins split, and storing detected basins and basin-separating saddle points in a list Ω for further visualization and quantitative analysis. A recursive implementation of the proposed Basin_Finder method is shown in pseudocode in Algo 1. The initial arguments are S_{max}, c_{max}, and the list Ω, which is initially empty.

On any given collection S of grid points, the method calculates the (possibly more than 1) k boundaries of S using the α-convex hull (lines 3-4). If S is one component, the method proceeds to identify possible hierarchical structure emerging at lower-energy levels, decreasing c by δ_2 (line 6) and updating the grid locations that meet the energetic threshold (line 7) before calling itself recursively (lines 12-13). If instead S contains $k > 1$ components with separate boundaries, a basin splitting event has been detected (lines 8-9). The newly identified basins $S_1 \dots S_k$ (line 8) are added to the list Ω (line 11). Possible saddle points emerging at the boundaries of neighboring basins are also identified (line 10) and added to the list Ω. The minimum distance between vertices on polygonal boundaries of different basins S_i, S_j is computed, and if this distance is not above a threshold d_th (S_i, S_j are deemed neighboring), the middle point of the minimum-length line is estimated to be the saddle point saddle$_{ij}$. The method terminates when no more grid locations are left (lines 1-2).

Algo. 1 Basin_Finder(S, c, Ω)

```
1:  if S = ∅ then
2:      return
3:  ∂S ← bd(S)          //boundary of S using the α-convex hull
4:  k ← nb(∂S)          //number of separated boundaries in ∂S
    //no basin splitting detected
5:  if k = 1 then
6:      c ← c − δ2                                  //lower energy
7:      S_k ← subset of S with energy ≤ c //update lower-level set
    //basin splitting detected
8:  else
9:      {S_1, ..., S_k}     //subsets of S with separate boundaries
                            //are new basins
10:     saddle_i,j ← saddle point between neighboring basins S_i, S_j
11:     Ω ← Ω ∪ {S_1 ... S_k} ∪ {saddle_ij}
12: for 1 ≤ i ≤ k do
13:     Basin_Finder(S_i, c, Ω)  //seek further hierarchical structure
```

For clarity, the pseudocode in Algo 1 does not show some modifications we make to lower computational costs. Since the basins in which we are most interested are in the low-energy regions of the landscape, the dense boundaries in the high-energy regions can be both distracting and consuming of computational time. So, the method is adjusted via a cutoff point c_0. If $c \leq c_{min} + c_0$, the method is run without any adjustment. If $c > c_{min} + c_0$, we make use of a threshold n_0, such that, if the number of grid points within any basin S_i is less than n_0, we do not dig further into S_i for any hierarchical structure in it.

The value of δ_2 also has an impact on computational costs. We balance between keeping computational costs reasonable and capturing the exact moment when a basin splits. Instead of always lowering the energy level by δ_2 (line 6), we first perform a jump test by decreasing the energy by $m\delta_2$ for some moderately large m. If the resulting lower level set at the level $c - m\delta_2$ splits into smaller basins, it means we have missed the important moment of splitting; so, we revert back to $c - \delta_2$. Otherwise, we conclude that no interesting events occur between the current energy level c and $c - m\delta_2$. We then directly move down to the level $c - m\delta_2$ and continue with the jump test until the test fails. Again, jumps are only applied for $c > c_{min} + c_0$, because the computational costs decrease with $c \leq c_{min} + c_0$ (in general, computation time correlates negatively with c). It is still possible that some very small and shallow basins can quickly appear and then disappear in a jump between c and $c - m\delta_2$. In this sense, the parameter m has a similar effect as n_0 in terms of ignoring small basins. This approach recognizes that it is best to apportion computational costs and thus keep all the details in the region with energy level $c \leq c_{min} + c_0$.

Implementation Details

Basin_Finder is implemented in R and uses $\delta_1 = 0.1$, $\delta_2 = 0.3$, $m = 50$, $c_0 = 200$, $n_0 = 100$, $\alpha = 0.15$ (parameter for α-convex hull), and d_th $= 20 \cdot \alpha$. Different values of h are analyzed (see Section 3). Gaussian kernel is used in the NW regression. On each of the test cases related in Section 3, the method takes anywhere from 12-24 CPU hours to complete on ARGO, a research computing cluster provided by the Office of Research Computing at George Mason University. Compute nodes used for testing are Intel Xeon E5-2670 CPU with 2.6GHz base processing speed and 3.5TB of RAM.

3 RESULTS

First we relate 2D landscapes obtained via the method described in Section 2. We do so for the H-Ras WT and several diseased variants and draw larger observations into what mechanisms the different mutations employ to alter the energy landscape with implications for dysfunction. Second, we extract quantitative descriptors of basins and basin-separating saddles detected automatically by the method proposed in Section 2 and showcase how such descriptors can be correlated to wet-laboratory measurements that allow us to relate specific characteristics of mutation-altered landscapes to biological mechanisms in which H-Ras participates.

3.1 Visualization and Qualitative Comparison of 2D Landscapes

All the landscapes reconstructed by our method on variants of H-Ras add specific energetic features to the schematic shown in Fig. 1. Fig. 1 summarizes the presence of two large basins, one corresponding to the GTP-activated state (also known as On), and the other to the GDP-activated state (also known as Off). A saddle point in the schematic denotes the presence of a barrier separating the two basins. The GTP-activated basin is larger, and contains many structures reported by different wet laboratories, such as those with PDB ids 1QRA, 1CTQ, 3L8Y, 2RGD, 3K8Y, and more. The latter three structures represent allosteric states of H-Ras, denoted as Reactive (R) and Tardy (T). Interconversion between the R- and T-states is reported in [8] and suggested to be more important than the On to Off interconversion for dysfunction in oncogenic variants. Visual comparison of landscapes reconstructed (with contour lines denoting detected basins) shows that changes from mutations impact the size of basins, the appearance or disappearance of basins within basins, elevation of existing barriers, and/or separation/split of basins.

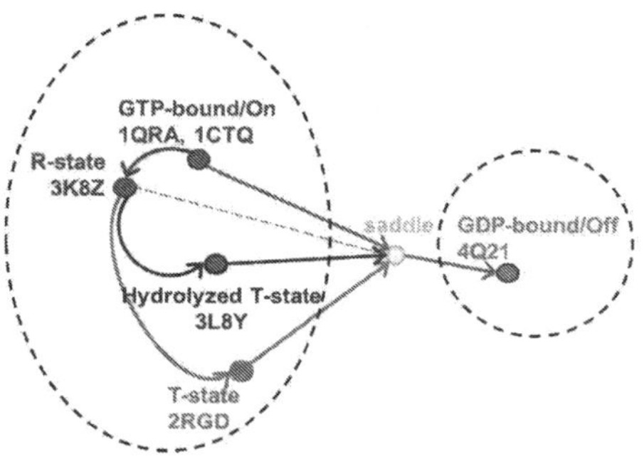

Figure 1: Known and putative Ras state interconversions.

Reconstructed landscapes of representative variants are shown in Fig. 2. We first draw attention to the impact of the bandwidth value by showing the landscape of H-Ras WT at two different such values (top panel of Fig. 2). Lower bandwidth values provide more detail, detecting narrow basins, as well as basins within basins. Higher bandwidth values may miss some of these details; for instance, the GTP-activated structures of H-Ras, under PDB ids 1QRA and 1CTQ occupy their own narrow basin (within the larger On basin), which is smoothed away at the higher bandwidth value (see top panel of Fig. 2). The hydrolyzed T-state (represented by the structure with PDB id 3L8Y) is within the larger, GTP-activated basin but appears to be just outside the basin at the higher bandwidth value (due to basin narrowing by the kernel regression). The R- and T-states (PDB ids 3K8Z, 2RGD, 3L8Y) reside within one basin, validating work in [8] that reports interconversions of these structures. In contrast, the interconversion of the R- and T-states into the GTP-activated forms needs external energy, as correctly reproduced in our work in the form of an energy barrier. However, the hydrolyzed T-state appears to be just outside the basin at the higher bandwidth value (due to basin narrowing by the kernel regression). We have determined that bandwidth values ≥ 0.8 remove too many important energetic features, whereas the high level of detail obtained when using values ≤ 0.5 makes visualization difficult. For this reason, all 2D landscapes shown and visually compared in the rest of the analysis are those obtained with a bandwidth value of 0.7.

In Fig. 2 we also show landscapes of select oncogenic (middle panel) and non-oncogenic but syndrome-causing (bottom panel) variants. Comparison of landscapes (using the WT landscape as baseline) allows making the following observations (also holding for other variants not shown here). In oncogenic variants, the barrier between the On and Off basins typically rises (Q61L illustrates this mechanism). The Off basin shrinks or disappears (see Q61L and F28L). The On basin splits, separating the R- and T-states (see Q61L). We note that the rigidification of H-Ras (due to barrier elevation or shrinkage or disappearance of the Off basin) is validated by prior work [3]. A novel feature that prior work does not capture is the separation of the R- and T-states (due to basin splitting) in oncogenic variants. This, together with wet-laboratory work suggesting that the R-to-T interconversion in H-Ras is central to function suggests an interesting mechanism via which oncogenic mutations percolate to dysfunction, by essentially disrupting the allosteric switch. On syndrome-causing variants, changes over the WT are less drastic (see bottom panel of Fig. 2) but degeneracy emerges. The Off basin leaks into other regions (K5N and Q22R are illustrative examples), or both the Off and On basins degenerate, even merging with one another and spilling over much of the landscape (see Q22R). The degeneracy suggests an interesting mechanism for dysfunction via delay of the On-to-Off diffusion (by, for instance, internal diffusions within the larger, degenerate Off basin).

3.2 Landscape Mining

We now compare landscape descriptors with biochemical parameters of several catalytic activities of Ras measured in the wet laboratory and reported in [2, 7]. These include GTP activation, GAP sensitivity, (MEK, ERK) activation of the RAF-kinase pathway and AKT activation of the PI3K-kinase pathway, GTP/GDP dissociation, GEF activity of SOS1, intrinsic GTP hydrolysis, GAP-regulated hydrolysis, and RAF1-RBD binding affinity. We number these as P0 through P9 (so, P2-P4 for the three kinase pathways). In [2, 7], these parameters are reported for the WT, 2 oncogenic variants (G12V and F28L) and 12 non-oncogenic but syndrome-causing variants (K5N, V14I, Q22E, Q22R, P34L, P34R, T58I, G60R, Y71H, K147E, E153V, F156L). We curate and normalize these parameters (not shown) to allow the following correlation-based analysis.

All 15 variants characterized in [2, 7] are subjected to SoPriMp and the method presented here. We extract descriptors related to spatial and energetic distances of known states of H-Ras (these states are related in Fig. 1) to the saddle point separating the On and Off basins. Each state can be mapped to the global minimum of the basin containing it, or alternatively, the location and energy of the known wet-lab structure representing it; we relate results with the latter, as results are similar. For instance, the spatial distance d(On, Saddle) is measured via Euclidean distance in PC1-PC2 space between the canonical structure representing this basin (PDB id 1QRA) and the saddle point detected by the proposed landscape analysis method. The energetic distance dE(On, Saddle) measures the height of the barrier (dE(Saddle) - E(On)). So, each landscape is summarized with these 10 descriptors. Each descriptor across 15 variants is compared with each biochemical parameter reported for these variants and Pearson correlations are measured.

Table 1 lists comparisons resulting in correlations ≥ 0.5. These yield many insights. We highlight a few. Work in [2, 7] reveals that intrinsic hydrolysis (named P7 by us) is higher in the variants over the WT. Table 1 shows that this occurs due to elevated barriers of all

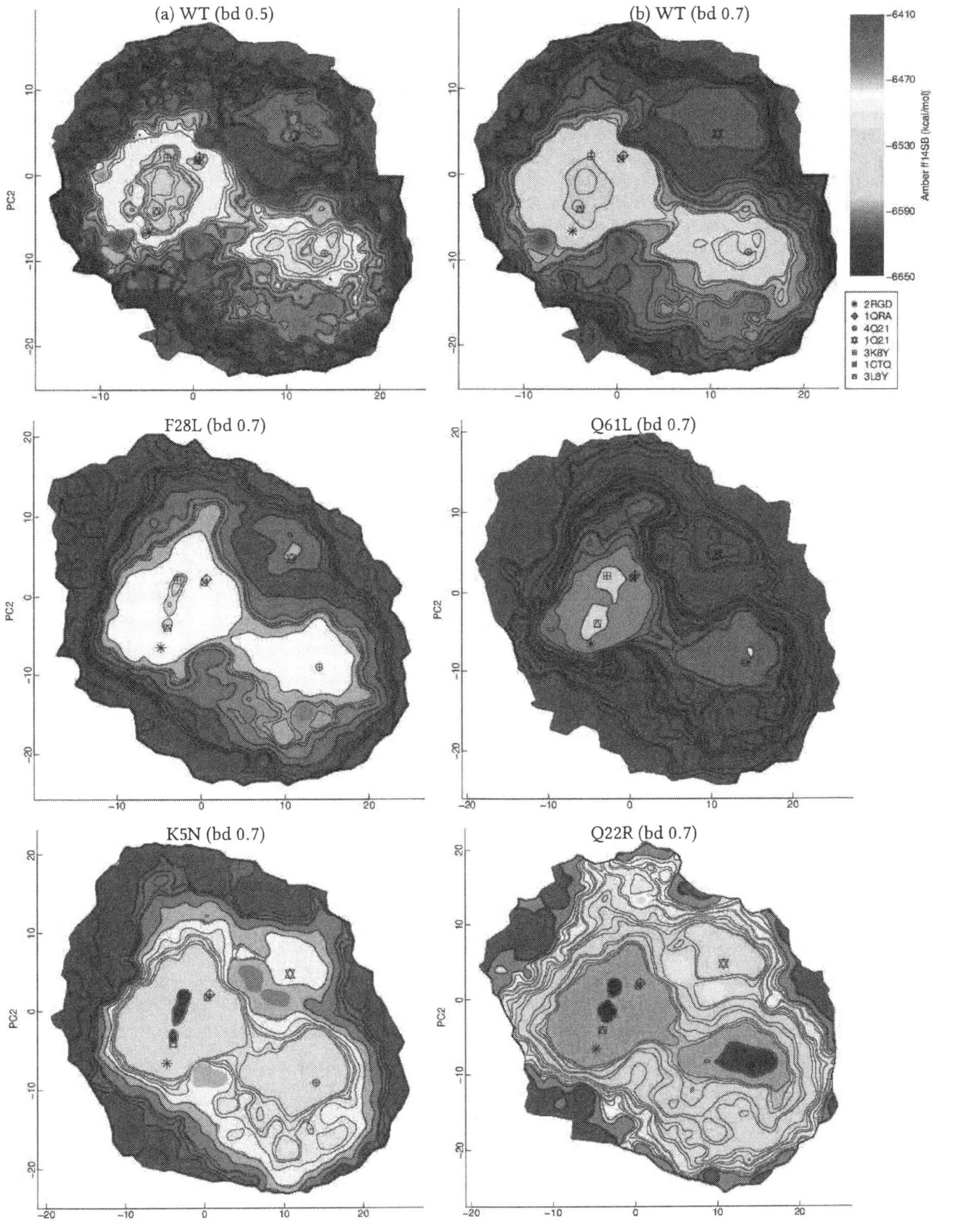

Figure 2: Top panel: landscape of WT at two bandwidth values. Landscapes of selected oncogenic (middle panel) and syndrome-causing (bottom panel) variants are also shown. The color coding-scheme is based on Amber ff14SB energy values estimated for every grid point as described in Section 2. Symbols that annotate projections of select experimentally-known structures are also shown.

states (positive correlations), movement of the Off state away from the saddle point (positive correlation), and movement of all other states towards saddle point (negative correlations). This suggests that equilibrium diffusions from the various states within the On basin to the Off basin directly relate to intrinsic hydrolysis; thus, this activity is perturbed in pathogenic variants by changing landscape features. GAP-catalyzed (as opposed to intrinsic) hydrolysis (P8) is another activity impacted by mutations. Table 1 shows correlations of 0.50 and 0.53 between P8 and Off-to-saddle and hydrolyzed T-to-saddle barrier height variations, which suggests a specific role of these states in GAP-catalyzed hydrolysis. A prior study relating FoldX energies (FoldX is a protein design algorithm) of specific structures to biochemical parameters in [2, 7] could only obtain two correlations, 0.65 for intrinsic hydrolysis and 0.43 for GAP-activated hydrolysis [9]. The highest correlations we obtain are −0.85 and 0.58, respectively. In addition, Table 1 shows that spatial and energetic distances of states from the On-to-Off saddle point correlate well with parameters measuring GTP activation (P0) and ERK activation of the RAF-kinase pathway (P3). These results show that the On and R-states are important for activation of this pathway, and suggest that the increased barrier heights between the GTP-activated states and the saddle point delay activation and so increase the amount of unbound GTP in pathogenic variants.

Table 1: Measured landscape descriptors and biochemical parameters (reported in [2, 7]) with correlations ≥ 0.5. T-* indicates hydrolyzed T-state.

State	d(State, Saddle)	dE(State, Saddle)
On	P7(-0.84), P3(0.53)	-
Off	P7(0.83)	P7(0.58), P0(0.54), P8(0.50)
T-	P7(-0.79)	P0(0.62)
R-	P7(-0.85), P3(0.51)	P7(0.61), P0(0.51)
T*-	P7(-0.82)	P7(0.62), P0(0.54), P8(0.53)

4 CONCLUSION

This paper evaluates a new line of research on mining energy landscapes of protein variants as a means of elucidating how mutations associated with various disorders alter the landscape. This is now possible due to a method that obtains detailed sample-based representations of energy landscapes of medium-size proteins with experimentally-resolved structures and a novel method, described here, that can reconstruct landscapes thus facilitating visualization, as well as automatically extract basins and saddles from them.

Visual comparison of reconstructed landscapes of pathogenic H-Ras variants validates prior dry- and wet-lab work and reveals novel mechanisms via which mutations percolate to dysfunction. The quantitative analysis suggests that a simple correlation-based investigation can reveal insights into which structures and interconversions can be related to specific Ras activities. Many more quantitative descriptors can be extracted from the list of basins and saddles that the proposed method extracts from a reconstructed landscape. This opens the way for learning from computed landscapes and macroscopic observations made in the wet laboratory. Altogether, the results suggest the approach of an exciting stage where one can compute and then mine landscapes of protein variants to learn *in-silico* models of how mutations impact function, as well as elucidate the role of specific structures and structural rearrangements in key biological activities.

5 ACKNOWLEDGMENTS

This work is supported in part by NSF CCF No. 1421001 and NSF IIS CAREER Award No. 1144106.

REFERENCES

[1] F. Cazals, T. Dreyfus, D. Mazauric, A. Roth, and C.H. Robert. 2015. Conformational ensembles and sampled energy landscapes: Analysis and comparison. *J. of Computational Chemistry* 36, 16 (2015), 1213–1231.
[2] I. C. Cirstea et al. 2013. Diverging gain-of-function mechanisms of two novel KRAS mutations associated with Noonan and cardio-facio-cutaneous syndromes. *Human Molecular Genetics* 22, 2 (2013), 262–270.
[3] R. Clausen, B. Ma, R. Nussinov, and A. Shehu. 2015. Mapping the Conformation Space of Wildtype and Mutant H-Ras with a Memetic, Cellular, and Multiscale Evolutionary Algorithm. *PLoS Comput Biol* 11, 9 (2015), e1004470.
[4] R. Clausen and A. Shehu. 2014. A Multiscale Hybrid Evolutionary Algorithm to Obtain Sample-based Representations of Multi-basin Protein Energy Landscapes. In *Conf on Bioinf and Comp Biol (BCB)*. ACM, Newport Beach, CA, 269–278.
[5] R. Clausen and A. Shehu. 2015. A Data-driven Evolutionary Algorithm for Mapping Multi-basin Protein Energy Landscapes. *J Comp Biol* 22, 9 (2015), 844–860.
[6] H. Frauenfelder, S. G. Sligar, and P. G. Wolynes. 1991. The energy landscapes and motion on proteins. *Science* 254, 5038 (1991), 1598–1603.
[7] L. Gremer et al. 2011. Germline KRAS mutations cause aberrant biochemical and physical properties leading to developmental disorders. *Human Mutation* 32, 1 (2011), 33–43.
[8] C. W. Johnson and C. Mattos. 2013. The allosteric switch and conformational states in Ras GTPase affected by small molecules. *Enzymes* 33, Pt. A (2013), 41–67.
[9] C. Kier and C. Serrano. 2014. Structure-energy-based predictions and network modelling of RASopathy and cancer missense mutations. *Mol Syst Biol* 10, 5 (2014), 727–.
[10] T. Maximova, D. Carr, E. Plaku, and A. Shehu. 2016. Sample-based Models of Protein Structural Transitions. In *Conf Bioinf and Comp Biol (BCB)*. ACM, Seattle, WA, 128–137.
[11] T. Maximova, R. Moffatt, B. Ma, R. Nussinov, and A. Shehu. 2016. Principles and Overview of Sampling Methods for Modeling Macromolecular Structure and Dynamics. *PLoS Comput Biol* 12, 4 (2016), e1004619.
[12] T. Maximova, E. Plaku, and A. Shehu. 2015. Computing Transition Paths in Multiple-Basin Proteins with a Probabilistic Roadmap Algorithm Guided by Structure Data. In *Intl Conf on Bioinf and Biomed (BIBM)*. IEEE, Washington, D.C., 35–42.
[13] T. Maximova, E. Plaku, and A. Shehu. 2016. Structure-guided Protein Transition Modeling with a Probabilistic Roadmap Algorithm. *IEEE/ACM Trans Comput Biol & Bioinform* 13, 5 (2016), 1–14.
[14] E. A. Nadaraya. 1964. On estimating regression. *Theory of probability and its applications* 9, 1 (1964), 141–142.
[15] R. Nussinov and P. G. Wolynes. 2014. A second molecular biology revolution? The energy landscapes of biomolecular function. *Phys Chem Chem Phys* 16, 14 (2014), 6321–6322.
[16] U. Ozertem and D. Erdogmus. 2011. Locally defined principal curves and surfaces. *Journal of Machine Learning Research* 12 (2011), 1249–1286.
[17] B. Pateiro-Lopez. 2008. *Set estimation under convexity type restrictions*. Ph.D. Dissertation. Universidad de Santiago de Compostela.
[18] I. A. Prior, P. D. Lewis, and C. Mattos. 2012. A comprehensive survey of Ras mutations in cancer. *Cancer Res* 72, 10 (2012), 2457–2467.
[19] W. Qiao and W. Polonik. 2016. Theoretical analysis of nonparametric filament estimation. *Annals of Statistics* 44, 3 (2016), 1269–1297.
[20] H. Rodriguez-Casal. 2007. Set estimation under convexity type assumptions. *Annales de l'I.H.P.- Probabilites & Statistiques* 43 (2007), 763–774.
[21] D. Russel, K. Lasker, J. Phillips, D. Schneidman-Duhovny, J. A. Veláquez-Muriel, and A. Sali. 2009. The structural dynamics of macromolecular processes. *Curr Opin Cell Biol* 21, 1 (2009), 97–108.
[22] E. Sapin, D. B. Carr, K. A. De Jong, and A. Shehu. 2016. Computing energy landscape maps and structural excursions of proteins. *BMC Genomics* 17, Suppl 4 (2016), 456.
[23] R. van de Weygaert et al. 2011. Alpha, betti and the megaparsec universe: on the topology of the cosmic Web. *Transactions on Computational Science XIV* 6970 (2011), 60–101.

Automated Protein Chain Isolation from 3D Cryo-EM Data and Volume Comparison Tool

Michael Nissenson[1], Dong Si[1*]
[1]University of Washington Bothell, 18115 Campus Way NE, Bothell, WA, USA, dongsi@uw.edu

ABSTRACT

In electron cryo-microscopy (cryo-EM), manual isolation of volumetric protein density map data surrounding known protein structures is a time-consuming process that requires constant expert attention for multiple hours. This paper presents a tool, Volume Cut, and an algorithm to automatically isolate the volumetric data surrounding individual protein chains from the entire macro-molecular complex that runs in just minutes. This tool can be used in the data collection and data pre-processing steps to generate good training datasets of single chain volume-structure pairs, which can be further used for the study of protein structure prediction from experimental 3D cryo-EM density maps using data mining and machine learning. Additionally, an application of this tool was explored in depth that compares the cut experimental cryo-EM data with simulated data in an attempt to find irregularities of experimental data for the purpose of validation. The source for both tools can be found at https://github.com/nissensonm/VolumeCut/.

CCS CONCEPTS

Applied computing → Life and medical sciences → Bioinformatics; Computing methodologies →Machine learning

KEYWORDS

Protein; Electron cryo-microscopy; 3D density map; volume isolation; validation; data preprocessing; Hausdorff distance

ACM Reference format:

2017. Automated Protein Chain Isolation from 3D Cryo-EM Data and Volume Comparison Tool. In *Proceedings of Computational Structural Bioinformatics, Boston, MA, USA, August 2017 (CSBW), 6 pages.*
DOI: 10.1145/3107411.3107500

1 Introduction

Electron cryo-microscopy (cryo-EM) is used to study large, complex molecules such as viruses at near-atomic resolutions [1, 2]. A large repository of cryo-EM data is publically available online for free at the EMDataBank , a unified data resource for 3D Electron Microscopy [3]. Cryo-EM data is generated as volumetric density maps that can be incredibly hard to interpret at the individual protein structure level [4]. As a result, to efficiently interpret cryo-EM density maps, machine learning and image processing techniques are usually applied to help predict protein structures for molecules with unknown compositions [4–14]. However, accurate protein structure prediction from cryo-EM maps typically requires an abundant, balanced set of training data. While many training data sets do exist, they are often either imbalanced or, in the case of some types of proteins such as membranes, there is a deficiency in the quality or amount of data available [15, 16]. If there is a deficiency or imbalance in data, this then requires additional data to be collected or created manually to have a sufficiently high quality set of training data.

Currently, generating good cryo-EM training data requires manual isolation of experimental volume voxels surrounding individual protein true structure chains. Isolating volume data manually can take hours as all data that is not near a protein chain has to be removed by hand using a data visualization tool, such as Volume Eraser in UCSF Chimera [17]. Manual isolation using the Volume Eraser tool requires the user to individually remove regions of space by highlighting them with a sphere. Using the Volume Eraser tool, we have found that with some practice, data isolation takes anywhere from forty-five minutes for smaller chains to over an hour for longer, more complex chains. The Volume Cut tool we propose in this paper aims to significantly reduce the time required to isolate data, with typical run times in seconds rather than minutes or hours, while simultaneously automating the process to minimize user input. Figure 1 is an example of how complex it can be to cut away volumetric data of one chain from the very large scale cryo-EM density map.

There are additional applications of using the Volume Cut tool beyond generating training data. A second application compares the experimental volume isolated by Volume Cut against simulated data at the same resolution in order to validate the quality of experimental cryo-EM density map in the region surrounding a specified chain. The second tool outlined in this paper was named Volume Compare as it compares the experimental data against simulated data in an attempt to measure how accurate or noisy the experimental data is. The performance of Volume Cut and the validation results of Volume Compare are discussed in the results section.

Permission to make digital or hard copies of all or part of this work for personal or classroom use is granted without fee provided that copies are not made or distributed for profit or commercial advantage and that copies bear this notice and the full citation on the first page. Copyrights for components of this work owned by others than ACM must be honored. Abstracting with credit is permitted. To copy otherwise, or republish, to post on servers or to redistribute to lists, requires prior specific permission and/or a fee. Request permissions from Permissions@acm.org.
ACM-BCB'17, August 20-23, 2017, Boston, MA, USA.
© 2017 Association of Computing Machinery.
ACM ISBN 978-1-4503-4722-8/17/08...$15.00.
DOI: http://dx.doi.org/10.1145/3107411.3107500

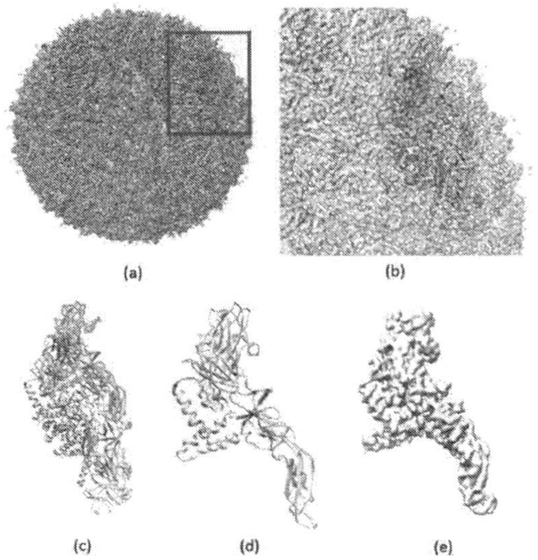

Figure 1: Volume Cut isolating the volume voxels surrounding chain A from PDB-5IRE (Zika Virus) and EMD-8116 (resolution 3.8 Å). (a) The entire EMD-8116 map. (b) Zoomed in region near where PDB-5IRE is aligned in EMD-8116. (c) PDB-5IRE with chain A highlighted. (d) Chain A from PDB-5IRE as cut and written by Volume Cut tool. (e) The density volume around Chain A cut from EMD-8116 and written by Volume Cut tool.

2 Method

Figure 2 shows the flowchart of how both Volume Cut and Volume Compare tools are intended to be used together. Sections that are bold require user input or action. Please note that both tools require input for protein structures to be in Protein Data Bank (PDB) format and cryo-EM density maps in Medical Research Council (MRC) format.

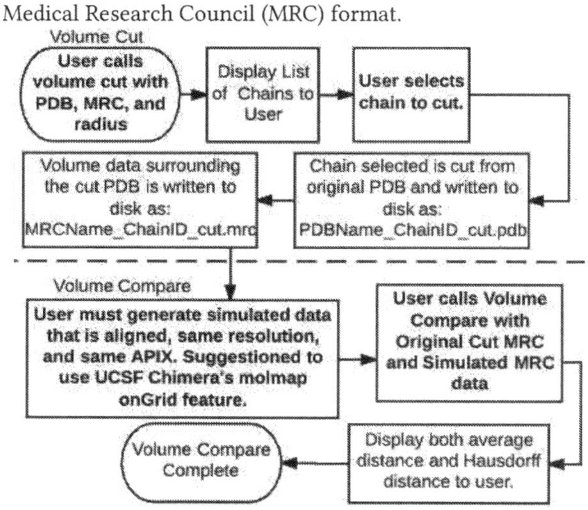

Figure 2: The flow of how the tools are intended to be used and what data is written at which step in the process. Boxes with bold text require user interaction.

2.1 Volume Cut

The program is expected to be supplied with the MRC file for the entire cryo-EM density volume, the fitted PDB file, a radius parameter to define how much volume to cut away around the single backbone chain, and the stated resolution of the MRC density map file. The radius parameter defines the distance around the backbone that will be cut.

On startup, the user is first prompted to select which chain they wish to cut. Once the chain is selected, the individual protein structure chain is written to disk as a PDB file named as *PDBFileName_chainID_Cut*. Then, from the selected chain, the locations of all carbon alpha atoms are stored. Line segments are then interpolated between consecutive carbon alpha atoms. At every interval of 0.1Å along the interpolated line, new coordinates are generated. This creates a backbone trace along the entire protein chain. A sphere is then defined around each coordinate that was generated, and the volume is cut from those spheres. Figure 3 shows a visual example of how the volume region is cut. Note that Figure 3(b) and 3(c) are not to scale and that the spheres are much more compact than what is illustrated.

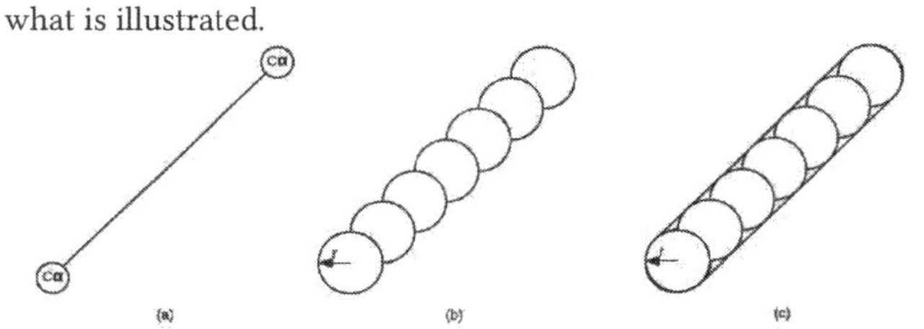

Figure 3: How the volume region is cut along the backbone. Cα are carbon alpha atoms. *r* is the user defined radius. (a) A line is interpolated between consecutive Cα atoms. (b) Points are chosen from the interpolated line at regular intervals of 0.1 Å. A sphere is defined at each point. (c) The spheres are close enough that they effectively form a cylinder that traces the backbone.

If the resolution of the density map is lower than 5 Å, the volume surrounding alpha helices is cut differently. Rather than generating the coordinates along the carbon alpha atom backbone, a line is instead interpolated through the center of the alpha helix as shown in Figure 4(b). Coordinates are then generated every 0.1 Å along the interpolated axis line of the helix. This change was done to better match how volume densities near alpha helices are represented at medium resolutions. Typically, volume voxels surrounding alpha helices at medium resolution appear as relatively straight rods, which is why they are cut from the center to better match that shape [18]. Figure 4 shows how data is cut surrounding alpha helices at both high and medium resolutions. Beta sheets are cut using the standard method of tracing along the carbon alpha backbone because they are typically found as continuous plates that trace along the backbone [18].

An output MRC density file with the same dimensions as the input MRC file is initialized to all zeroes for the voxel values. If the Euclidian distance from the generated carbon alpha backbone trace to a density voxel in the input MRC file falls within the radius set by the user, then the density voxel is stored in the output MRC file. Once all coordinates on the generated carbon alpha backbone trace have been iterated through, the output MRC file for the single chain is written to disk as *MRCFileName_chainID_Cut.*

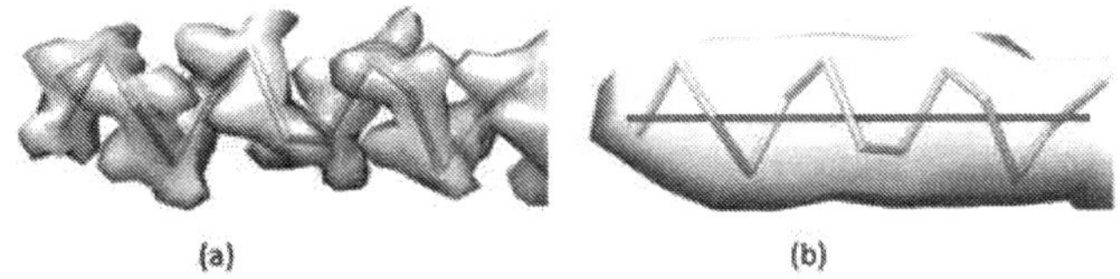

Figure 4: The difference between high and medium resolution cuts near alpha helices using simulated data. Both volumes were cut with a 2.5 Å radius. (a) At a resolution of 3 Å, the volume is cut surrounding lines interpolated between carbon alpha atoms. (b) At a resolution of 7 Å, the volume is cut surrounding a trace down the center of the alpha helix.***Performance Improvements.*** There are two algorithms that are used to speed up the runtime significantly, reducing the average runtime from minutes to seconds.

The first algorithm is concerned with how spheres surrounding the generated coordinates are defined. Originally, to define a sphere, it was necessary to calculate the distance from the generated coordinate (the center of the sphere) against all other coordinates in the MRC file to find which coordinates were inside the sphere's radius. This is inefficient because a vast majority of the coordinates in the MRC file are outside the sphere. A majority of the coordinates that are too far can be ruled out immediately by inscribing each sphere inside a cube. The cube is defined by taking two corner points as defined in equation 1.

$$P_{corner} = < Cx \pm r, Cy \pm r, Cz \pm r > \quad (1)$$

Where P_{corner} is the two corner points of the cube, C is the coordinate that was generated, and r is the user defined radius. By adding or subtracting the radius to the stored coordinate, the smallest possible cube that can inscribe the sphere can be defined. Figure 5 shows a 2D example of how inscribing the sphere can save computation time. Any coordinates that fall outside that cube are eliminated and their distances are not checked as the sphere will be entirely contained within the cube.

The second performance increase involves storing a set of flags for each discrete point in the MRC file. When the MRC file is written for a given point, the corresponding flag is set as well. When the flag has been set for a specific point in the MRC file, then the distance calculation to see if a coordinate is within the sphere should not be calculated again as the volume data will be written regardless. This prevents additional expensive, relative to checking the corresponding flag, distance calculations.

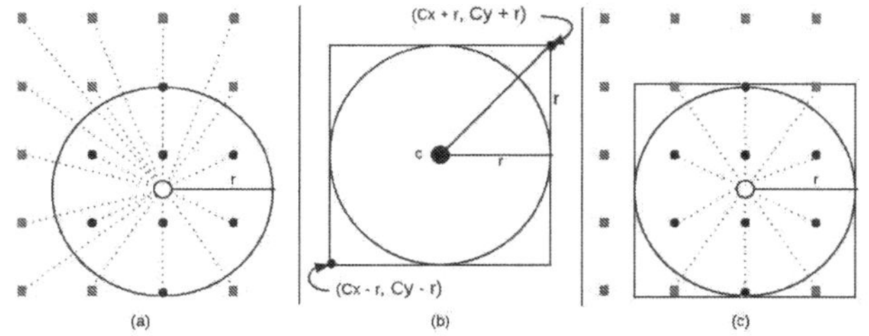

Figure 5: A 2D demonstration showing how inscribing a circle inside a square reduces the total number of calculations needed to find all points inside a circle. For a 3D point cloud, just add an extra dimension. If the Euclidian distance from the center to a point is less than the radius, then the point is inside the circle. Dotted lines indicate a distance calculation. Red squares indicate points outside circle, black dots indicate points inside circle. (a) With no boundaries, the distance to center of the circle must be calculated for all points. (b) Define a square that can inscribe the circle by finding two corners of the square. (c) With the circle inscribed, only need to check the points inside the square.

2.2 Generating Simulated Data

To use the Volume Comparison tool, simulated data for the cut protein chain must first be generated. The simulated data acts as a "ground truth" to compare the cut experimental volume voxel data against. This simulated data must be the same resolution and dimensions as the MRC file for the cut experimental cryo-EM density map. This can be done quickly and easily through UCSF Chimera's molmap onGrid feature [17]. Note that this step was run on windows, but it should work for any system that has Chimera installed. This step was automated by creating the following script to generate the simulated data:

volume #1 expandSinglePlane true style surface
volume #1 step 1
molmap #0 ***Resolution*** *onGrid #1*
volume #2 expandSinglePlane true style surface
volume #2 save simulated_data.mrc

The script is saved as "GenerateSimulatedData.cmd". The only parameter that needs to be modified is the resolution (bolded above) of the MRC file. The cut PDB and MRC files should be placed in the same directory as the script, then run chimera with the following parameters:

chimera --nogui --silent ***pdb_name****.pdb* ***mrc_name****.mrc GenerateSimulatedData.cmd*

Replace the bolded pdb_name and mrc_name with the correct file names. This will generate simulated data for the resolution specified and save the data as *simulated_data.mrc* in the folder chimera was called from.

2.3 Volume Comparison

The Volume Comparison tool started as a way to measure the accuracy of the Volume Cut tool. However, after reviewing the results it generated, it quickly became apparent that there were more applications than just using it to test Volume Cut. Section 2.4 explores how this tool was used to measure the accuracy of Volume Cut.

The Volume Comparison tool works by comparing the experimentally generated MRC data that was isolated with Volume Cut against simulated data generated based on the cut PDB chains. First, the values of the volume voxels for both the simulated and experimental data are normalized between 0 and 1. A threshold of 0.25 is then taken to filter out a majority of the noise. All points that were under the threshold are no longer considered for the following steps.

The one-sided Hausdorff distance from the simulated data to the points on the original cut volume is used to compare the point cloud sets. Measuring the Hausdorff distance is a relatively efficient way of computing the difference in shape between two point cloud data sets [19]. Figure 6 shows how the one-sided Hausdorff distance is calculated.

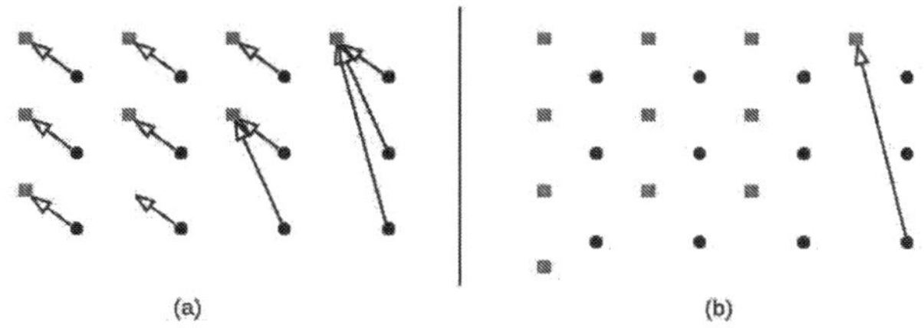

Figure 6: How the one-sided Hausdorff distance is calculated with two 2D point clouds. The black circles represent the first point cloud set. The red squares represent the second set. (a) Step 1: Find Euclidian distance for each point in the black point cloud to their nearest neighbor in the red set. (b) Step 2: Take the maximum distance found in step 1, which is the one-sided Hausdorff distance.

The one-sided Hausdorff distance is calculated by:

$$D_h(X,Y) = \max_{x \in X}[d(x,Y)] \quad (2)$$

$$d(x,Y) = \min_{y \in Y} \|x - y\| \quad (3)$$

X and Y are point cloud sets, x and y are individual points from X and Y, D_h is the Hausdorff distance, and $\|x\|$ is the Euclidian norm. The Hausdorff distance is useful for measuring the similarity of shape between two point clouds, with the smaller the Hausdorff distance indicating a greater degree of similarity. The one-sided Hausdorff distance is used over the two-sided Hausdorff distance because the simulated data is used as a ground truth for how the data should be distributed for a given resolution. We are only interested in how dissimilar the experimental data is from the ground truth's shape, not the other way around.

Ultimately, what the Hausdorff distance tells us is how dissimilar the experimental data is from the simulated data. The higher the Hausdorff number, the more dissimilar it is, and more likely it is that there is a problem with the experimental data.

2.4 Accuracy of Volume Cut Tool

The accuracy of the Volume Cut tool was measured using the Volume Comparison tool. First, data was simulated from true PDB structures using the method outlined in section 2.2. This generates a density map that follows a PDB's structure with no noise or missing data present. Second, the Volume Cut tool is run on the simulated data with a variety of different radii. All of the isolated, cut data generated by Volume Cut should have a one-sided Hausdorff distance of 0 when compared against the original simulated data. A one-sided Hausdorff distance of 0 verifies that each point from the cut data has a corresponding point that exactly matches the original simulated data, which confirms the cuts are accurate. If the one-sided Hausdorff distance is not 0, then the cut is imperfect, and something has gone wrong. The accuracy was verified using the eleven PDB chains in Table 1 in section 3.2; all eleven chains (with simulated density data) had a one-sided Hausdorff distance of 0.

3 Results

Eleven different chains from nine different PDB-EMD combinations were selected to show the results of both tools. They were chosen because they represented a diverse set of macro-molecular sizes with relatively similar EMDB resolutions. All tests were conducted in Ubuntu 14.04 on machines with 3.4GHz Intel i7-3770 processors and 16GB RAM.

3.1 Volume Cut

Run times for Volume Cut ranged from a couple seconds for files that were less than one hundred MB to approximately one hundred and ten seconds for MRC files that approached 2 GB in size. One aspect of Volume Cut that is important to consider is that care needs to be taken when specifying the radius to cut. If the radius is too small, some information will be lost. If the radius is too large, information from neighboring chains will also be included. Figure 7 shows results of cutting the same chain with different radii. If getting all the data for a chain is most important, then choose a larger radius. If getting no data from a neighboring chain is more important, choose a smaller radius. The radius should be modified based on what the cut data is to be used for. Generally speaking, we have found that a radius of 2.5 provides a good balance between getting most of the data surrounding secondary structures without too much extra data from nearby chains.

3.2 Volume Compare

The runtime of the Volume Compare tool ranges from a couple seconds to approximately two minutes for MRC files that approach 2 GB in size. Our results seem to indicate that the Volume Compare tool was able to detect when significant irregularities between simulated data created from protein structures and experimental EMDB data were present.

Note that for the Volume Cut step, a radius of four was selected. A larger radius was chosen to guarantee that all data was selected from a chain. Further, the extra data that was cut from nearby chains should not cause a significant change in the results. This is because the one-sided Hausdorff distance measures from the simulated data to its nearest neighbor in the experimental data. If the simulated data finds its nearest neighbor in a separate chain, then it is likely that the data is missing from the original chain; this would cause the Hausdorff distance to rise, which is the desired result as it will help to highlight problems with the experimental data.

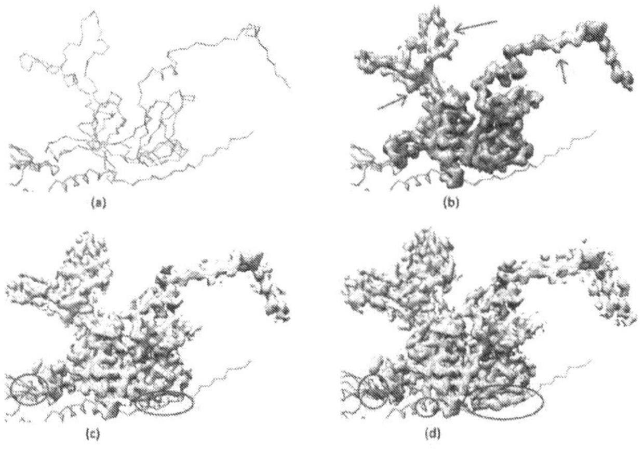

Figure 7: **An example showing the effect different radii have on Volume Cut, running with chain C from PDB-3J6B and EMD-2566. PDB-3J6B chain C is shown in green, part of chain M from PDB-3J6B is shown in orange, and EMD-2566 is shown cut with different radii. Regions circled in red indicate data from other chains that were cut. Red arrows indicate regions where volume is missing. (a) Entire chain C from PDB-3J6B and part of chain M with no volume information. (b) Radius 2 misses some volume around secondary structures. (c) Radius 3 gets most of the information for chain C and some data from surrounding chains. (d) Radius 4 gets all information from chain C and a large amount of extra data from surrounding chains.**

The results from table 1 show a fairly stable range of values from four to six for the one-sided Hausdorff distance. Having a non-zero Hausdorff distance is expected as experimental data will always have some amount of noise. As a result, the suggested way to use this data is to compare a large amount of data with similar resolutions together, and then look for outliers.

Chain E from PDB-3J7Y and EMD-2762 shows a fairly standard result of 5.39 Å for the Hausdorff Distance. This is within the expected range. Figure 8 provides both the experimental volume voxel data (grey) and the simulated data (yellow). Visual inspection shows they are fairly similar, with a small amount of noise present in the experimental data.

Table 1: **Comparing simulated data to the cut volume voxel data.**

PDB	EMDB	Chain	Resolution (Å)	One-Sided Hausdorff Distance
1QHD	1461	A	3.8	6.16
3C5B	5003	A	4.5	4.69
3J4U	5764	C	3.5	4.24
3J4U	5764	N	3.5	4.12
3J5P	5778	A	3.275	25.51
3J6B	2566	C	3.2	5.00
3J6B	2566	I	3.2	5.92
3J7L	6000	A	3.8	4.90
4CI0	2513	A	3.36	5.39
3J7Y	2762	E	3.4	5.39
5IRE	8116	A	3.8	5.83

The result that stands out as an outlier from our result set is chain A from PDB-3J5P with EMB-5778. The Hausdorff distance of 25.51 Å is significantly higher than the other results. The reason why their values are so different can be seen in figure 9. From visually examining the data, it becomes clear that there is missing data in EMD-5778 near the bottom left corner of the EMB map.

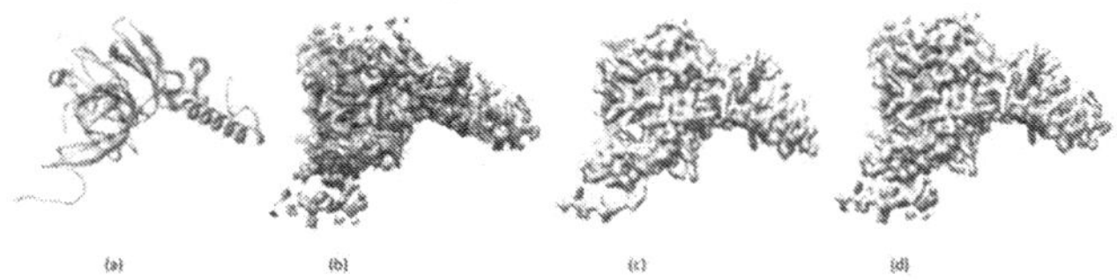

Figure 8: **Experimental and simulated data used by Volume Compare. Both simulated and experimental data are fairly similar, and have an average Hausdorff number of 5.38 Å as a result. All data is shown at a normalized threshold level of 0.25. (a) Chain E of PDB-3J7Y (b) Cut Volume Data from EMD-2762 around just PDB-3J7Y (c) Simulated data surrounding PDB-3J7Y (d) Yellow simulated data overlaid on top of grey experimental data**

Further, it appears that the resolution reported of 3.275 Å for EMD-5778 may not be accurate [20]. The difference in resolution appears evident by looking at the relatively detailed, intricate structure of the simulated data when compared with the less detailed experimental data. While this is certainly not conclusive proof that the reported resolution is not correct, it is still worth pointing out the difference.

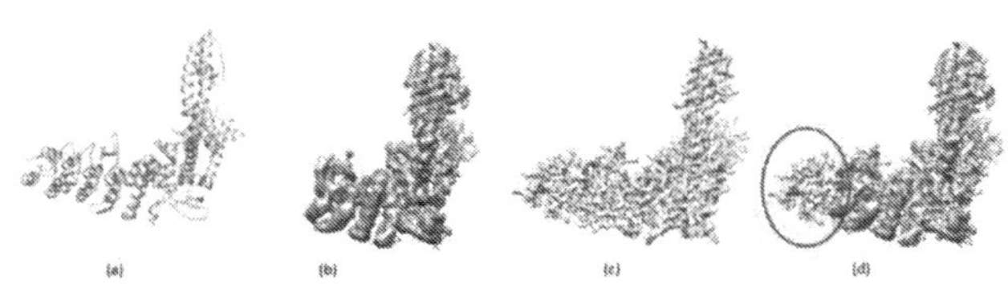

Figure 9: **Experimental and simulated data used by Volume Compare. As the experimental data is missing voxels found in the simulated data, there is a relatively high Hausdorff number of 25.52 Å. All data is shown at a normalized threshold level of 0.25. (a) Chain A of PDB-3J5P (b) Cut Volume Data from EMD-5778 from area around PDB-3J5P using Volume Cut (c) Simulated data surrounding PDB-3J5P (d) Yellow simulated data overlaid on grey experimental data. The region missing from the experimental data is highlighted with a red circle.**

There has been significant work done in the past to verify the integrity of data submitted to EMDB [21, 22]. However, the focus has generally been on verifying that the stated resolution of EMDB data was correct. Comparatively, there appears to be relatively little work done that compares experimental volume data surrounding the fitted protein structures to simulated data that at the same resolution in an attempt to find irregularities of the cryo-EM density.

4 Conclusion

This paper has presented two tools. The first was the Volume Cut tool which can isolate the volume data surrounding an individual chain when provided with a protein structure (PDB) and EMDB (MRC) cryo-EM density file. The first use of Volume Cut is to efficiently and accurately generate training data (3D density map and true structure pair) to help with applying data mining and machine learning techniques on 3D cryo-EM density maps. Volume Cut reduces the time and effort required to isolate volume data from hours of skilled, expert attention, to an automated process that takes just minutes to complete. It can also be set up to autonomously handle large batches of files with very little input from a user. As a result, this tool is capable of opening the door to a wealth of new training data set that would otherwise be locked behind weeks or months of painstaking work to prepare.

The second use of Volume Cut is to provide data to be fed into the second tool presented in this paper, the Volume Compare tool. Volume Compare, when combined with Volume Cut, can quickly find experimental cryo-EM data in a large data set that is either incomplete or inaccurate. Currently, Volume Compare is limited to just finding large irregularities within a set of data. This causes smaller irregularities that may be present to be lost. Further, it does not immediately tell the user where the data is missing; the user must visually examine the volume data to see what caused the unusually high distance. Future work with the tool could go towards finding other metrics that provide additional information to the user at a glance. A future extension of this work could be to create an automated end-to-end pipeline to get a very rough sense of quality or number of irregularities found within the EMDB.

5 Acknowledgement

This work was supported by the Graduate Research Award from the Computing and Software Systems division of University of Washington Bothell and the startup fund 74-0525.

6 References

[1] Mancini, E.J. et al. 2000. Cryo-electron microscopy reveals the functional organization of an enveloped virus, Semliki Forest virus. *Molecular Cell*. 5, 2 (Feb. 2000), 255–266.

[2] Daban, J.-R. 2011. Electron microscopy and atomic force microscopy studies of chromatin and metaphase chromosome structure. *Micron (Oxford, England: 1993)*. 42, 8 (Dec. 2011), 733–750.

[3] EMDataBank: *http://www.emdatabank.org/*. Accessed: 2017-04-30.

[4] Jiang, W. et al. 2001. Bridging the information gap: computational tools for intermediate resolution structure interpretation. *Journal of Molecular Biology*. 308, 5 (May 2001), 1033–1044.

[5] Si, D. et al. 2012. A machine learning approach for the identification of protein secondary structure elements from electron cryo-microscopy density maps. *Biopolymers*. 97, 9 (Sep. 2012), 698–708.

[6] Li, R. et al. 2016. Deep convolutional neural networks for detecting secondary structures in protein density maps from cryo-electron microscopy. *2016 IEEE International Conference on Bioinformatics and Biomedicine (BIBM)* (Dec. 2016), 41–46.

[7] Si, D. and He, J. 2014. Combining image processing and modeling to generate traces of beta-strands from cryo-EM density images of beta-barrels. *Conference proceedings: ... Annual International Conference of the IEEE Engineering in Medicine and Biology Society. IEEE Engineering in Medicine and Biology Society. Annual Conference*. 2014, (2014), 3941–3944.

[8] Si, D. and He, J. 2014. Tracing beta strands using StrandTwister from cryo-EM density maps at medium resolutions. *Structure (London, England: 1993)*. 22, 11 (Nov. 2014), 1665–1676.

[9] Zhao, J. et al. 2013. TMaCS: A hybrid template matching and classification system for partially-automated particle selection. *Journal of Structural Biology*. 181, 3 (Mar. 2013), 234–242.

[10] Scheres, S.H.W. 2012. RELION: Implementation of a Bayesian approach to cryo-EM structure determination. *Journal of Structural Biology*. 180, 3 (Dec. 2012), 519–530.

[11] Scheres, S.H.W. 2015. Semi-automated selection of cryo-EM particles in RELION-1.3. *Journal of Structural Biology*. 189, 2 (Feb. 2015), 114–122.

[12] Ma, L. et al. 2012. RENNSH: A Novel alpha-Helix Identification Approach for Intermediate Resolution Electron Density Maps. *IEEE/ACM Transactions on Computational Biology and Bioinformatics*. 9, 1 (Jan. 2012), 228–239.

[13] Langlois, R. et al. 2014. Automated particle picking for low-contrast macromolecules in cryo-electron microscopy. *Journal of Structural Biology*. 186, 1 (Apr. 2014), 1–7.

[14] Albert, N. and Dong, S. 2017. Genetic Algorithm Based Beta-Barrel Detection for Medium Resolution Cryo-EM Density Maps. (Honolulu, Hawaii, 2017).

[15] Cheng, J. et al. 2008. Machine learning methods for protein structure prediction. *IEEE reviews in biomedical engineering*. 1, (2008), 41–49.

[16] Jia, J. et al. 2016. iSuc-PseOpt: Identifying lysine succinylation sites in proteins by incorporating sequence-coupling effects into pseudo components and optimizing imbalanced training dataset. *Analytical Biochemistry*. 497, (Mar. 2016), 48–56.

[17] Pettersen, E.F. et al. 2004. UCSF Chimera--a visualization system for exploratory research and analysis. *Journal of Computational Chemistry*. 25, 13 (Oct. 2004), 1605–1612.

[18] Baker, M.L. et al. 2007. Identification of secondary structure elements in intermediate-resolution density maps. *Structure (London, England: 1993)*. 15, 1 (Jan. 2007), 7–19.

[19] Girardeau-Montaut, D. et al. 2005. *Change Detection on Points Cloud Data Acquired with a Ground Laser Scanner*.

[20] Liao, M. et al. 2013. Structure of the TRPV1 ion channel determined by electron cryo-microscopy. *Nature*. 504, 7478 (Dec. 2013), 107–112.

[21] Scheres, S.H.W. and Chen, S. 2012. Prevention of overfitting in cryo-EM structure determination. *Nature Methods*. 9, 9 (Sep. 2012), 853–854.

[22] Henderson, R. et al. 2012. Outcome of the first electron microscopy validation task force meeting. *Structure (London, England: 1993)*. 20, 2 (Feb. 2012), 205–214.

A Graph Based Method for the Prediction of Backbone Trace from Cryo-EM Density Maps

Peter Collins
University of Washington Bothell
Bothell, WA, USA
peterc16@uw.edu

Dong Si*
University of Washington Bothell
Bothell, WA, USA
dongsi@uw.edu

ABSTRACT

Cryo-electron microscopy (Cryo-EM) is able to achieve high resolution density maps. These density maps are near atomic resolution and individual atoms can be seen as well as large secondary structure elements. However, it is challenging to extract the backbone structure information automatically and efficiently. This paper presents a novel method for creating a backbone trace and predicting locations of Cα atoms for high resolution density maps. It is a graph based method utilizing density along a backbone trace and features of secondary structure elements to find the optimal backbone trace and Cα atom locations. The method is mostly automatic requiring an initial user determined threshold value and primary secondary structure type. We tested our method on fifteen simulated maps at 3Å resolution and four experimental cryo-EM density maps between 2.6-3.1Å resolution. The result shows that our method is able to generate a complete Cα backbone trace when the density map is not missing data at near atomic resolution.

CCS CONCEPTS

• **Applied computing → Bioinformatics**; • **Mathematics of computing →** ***Graph algorithms***;

KEYWORDS

Cryo-electron microscopy; Cryo-EM; Density map; Carbon-Alpha; Graph; Backbone Trace

1 INTRODUCTION

Cryo-electron microscopy (cryo-EM) is a method of generating three dimensional (3D) density maps for protein molecules [4, 6, 27]. Recently, high resolution cryo-EM maps have become available, allowing for more features to be detected [2, 12]. Specifically, the backbone of proteins and Cα atoms. Cα atoms are the most significant atom in determining the structure of a protein. The linked series of Cα atoms are known as the protein Cα backbone trace.

Secondary structures, such as α-helices and β-sheets, are the most identifying features of lower resolutions cryo-EM maps. There are many methods for identifying secondary structures at medium resolution [1, 5, 8, 10, 11, 15, 17–24, 26]. These features are still visible at higher resolutions and are useful in predicting Cα atom locations. α-helices typically have Cα atoms in close proximity while β sheets have Cα atoms farther apart. α-helices tend to have strong density towards the helix axis because the Cα atoms are closer together. This makes it more difficult to detect individual Cα atoms. These structures are important at high resolutions and are useful in determining the backbone structure. They also help during placement of Cα atoms along the backbone trace.

Pathwalking is a method that models backbone structures and Cα atoms locations on high-resolution cryo-EM data using a Traveling Salesman Problem solver. Ludtke et al. [13] use a skeletonization algorithm and secondary structures to create a Cα trace for the density map. This creates a protein backbone prediction as well as identifying secondary structures [3]. Both of these methods require user intervention. In Wang et al. [25], the backbone structure and side-chain density are used to create a sequence for the density map. This uses the Monte Carlo method which is computationally expensive and has difficulty when proteins have a large number of β sheets.

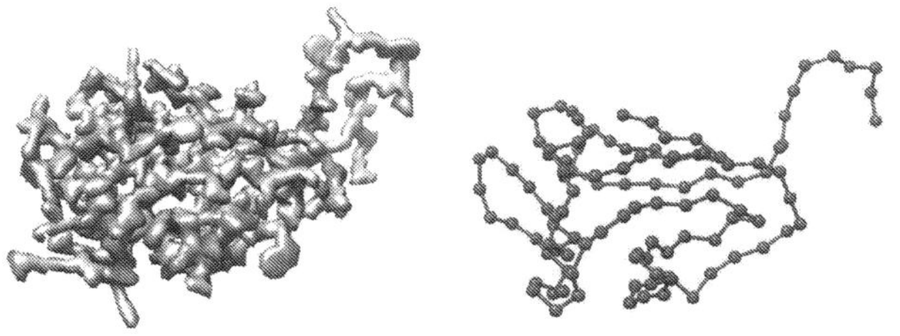

Figure 1: Cryo-EM density map of a protein (left) with the backbone trace and predicted Cα locations (right).

This paper presents a method for predicting Cα atom locations from a high resolution cryo-EM density map. Figure 1 shows the cryo-EM density and predicted Cα backbone trace. It uses the greater detail in high resolution data and the secondary structure features to create a trace of the protein backbone and predict Cα atom locations along the predicted backbone. The method is mostly automatic requiring two initial values to trace the entire chain and predict Cα locations.

Permission to make digital or hard copies of all or part of this work for personal or classroom use is granted without fee provided that copies are not made or distributed for profit or commercial advantage and that copies bear this notice and the full citation on the first page. Copyrights for components of this work owned by others than ACM must be honored. Abstracting with credit is permitted. To copy otherwise, or republish, to post on servers or to redistribute to lists, requires prior specific permission and/or a fee. Request permissions from permissions@acm.org.
ACM-BCB'17, August 20-23, 2017, Boston, MA, USA.
© 2017 Association for Computing Machinery.
ACM ISBN 978-1-4503-4722-8/17/08...$15.00
http://dx.doi.org/10.1145/3107411.3107501

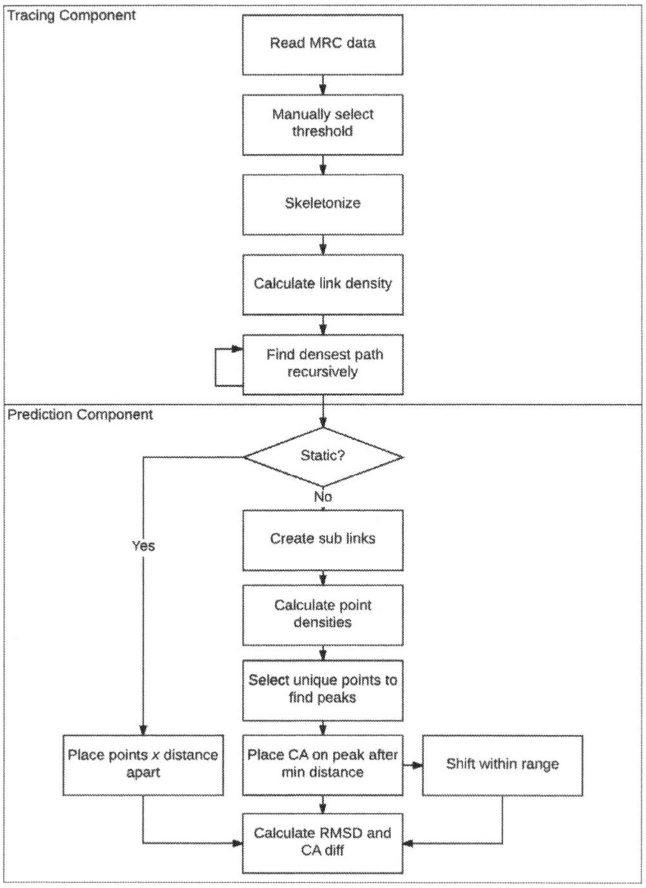

Figure 2: Flow chart of backbone tracing to CÅ prediction using static and dynamic components.

2 METHODS

There are two components, tracing and prediction, for this method, shown in figure 2. The tracing component builds a continuous end-to-end path of the protein chain. The prediction component places $C\alpha$ atoms along the trace using either static or dynamic prediction.

2.1 Tracing Component

The tracing component operates on the density map of a protein chain. First, a threshold value is found for the density map so the entire true structure has a density around it. This is a manually selected value based off observation of the density map and true structure using UCSF Chimera [16]. Then the density map is transformed into a logical matrix where values above the threshold are 1 and below are 0.

The logical matrix is passed into the skeletonizing code which creates a list of nodes and links [9]. As part of this process, any branches shorter than 8Å are cut which removes many side chains that exist for the protein. Links are a set of connected points that form a possible backbone sub-trace. Nodes are beginning and ending points of the links. Nodes have multiple connections to other nodes forming paths through the graph.

The density of each link is calculated. Using two consecutive link points, create a vector between them to define the center axis of a cylinder with radius of 3Å. This defines all voxels in the density map within range of the current link. Cylinder density is calculated by dividing the sum of all voxel values within the cylinder by the volume. Repeat for all points in the link. Sum all cylinder densities to find the link density. Repeat this process, outputting every link and its density.

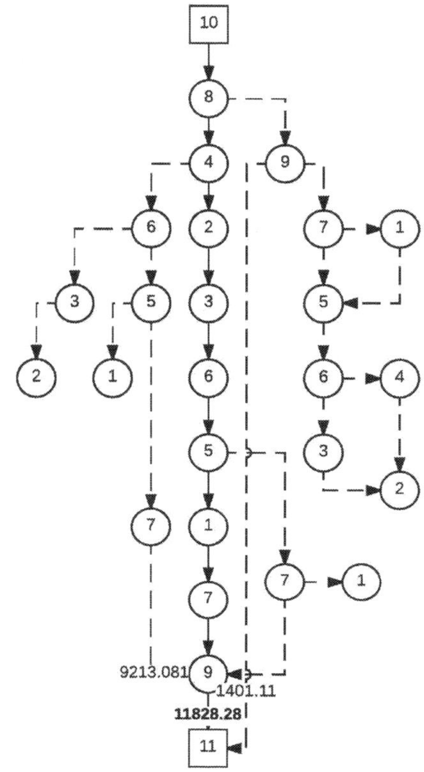

Figure 3: Graph of the routes through the skeleton for PDB 1ewf_A01. Dotted lines represent false branches. The solid line is the final backbone trace. Square boxes represent start/end points and the values above them are the density of the specific trace along that route.

Our method finds the highest density path out of all possible paths. Each node is connected to a few other nodes forming a graph. The graph edges correspond to links from the previous step. Starting at the root node (classified as an end point), recursively walk through the graph summing weights of all the visited links. Once a node is visited, it may not be revisited. The end condition is when there are no unvisited nodes left stemming from the current node. Once all possible routes are visited, the route with the highest density is selected as the final trace result. Figure 3 illustrates how the root node is node 10 and it can only visit node 8. Node 8 can visit either node 4 or 9 etc. Each path is visited and a density for the path is stored. The path with the highest density value is chosen which corresponds to the path node 10->8->4->2->3->6->5->1->7->9->11.

The final trace is a single continuous path from beginning to end of the protein chain. This defines an approximate backbone trace of the protein but does not include location of atoms within the trace. The trace is used in the prediction component to determine the location of $C\alpha$ along or near the trace.

2.2 Prediction Component

The prediction component uses two strategies, static and dynamic distance, for predicting placement of $C\alpha$ atoms along the trace. The number of amino acids in the protein sequence determines which method to use. If the number of amino acids is less than 180 the static distance is used and if greater than 180 the dynamic distance is used. Two methods are used because as the number of amino acids in the sequence increase, the static distance method accumulates significant error. The choice to use 180 as the point to swap from static to dynamic was determined after testing both methods and observing that 180 appeared to be the breakpoint.

2.2.1 Static Distance Placement. Static distance placement uses a distance value (units are in Å) set before execution. The major secondary structures in the protein determine distance value. These are defined as Alpha, Beta, or Alpha_Beta and have values 2.85, 3.2, and 3.15 respectively. These values are approximations determined after observing many different true structures and measuring the distance between $C\alpha$ atoms for different secondary structures. The value is used to place $C\alpha$ atoms on the backbone trace. The backbone trace is assumed to follow the densest area of the backbone and $C\alpha$ atoms are assumed to be the densest locations. Therefore, the $C\alpha$ locations are predicted to be points on the backbone trace.

The backbone trace is a list of three-dimensional coordinates called trace points. Between each trace point, ten additional points are inserted at equal distances along a vector between the trace points. The first point in the trace is assumed to be a $C\alpha$ because the beginning and end of a trace have to be $C\alpha$ atoms in the true structure. Next, iterate through all points and calculate the distance between the last predicted $C\alpha$ atom location and the current point until no more points are available. The distance is the Euclidean length of the vector that connects two points. If the distance is within an offset range of the static distance, select the point as the next predicted $C\alpha$ location. The offset range is added to handle inconsistencies in the backbone trace and is set to 0.2Å. After fully iterating through the points, the process needs to be repeated but starting from the other end of the trace. The first trace point at this end is assumed to be a $C\alpha$ atom. The output is two backbone traces with predicted $C\alpha$ atom locations.

2.2.2 Dynamic Distance Placement. Dynamic distance placement uses a variable value dependent on the difference of predicted vs actual $C\alpha$ atoms. This method requires the density map and voxel information.

The method creates five points between trace points from the tracing component. The dynamic approach uses a smaller number than static distance placement because the spacing between voxels is larger than the distance between points which causes duplicate density values for points in a small area. The density of each point is then calculated as the summation of voxels values within 1Å radius of the point divided by the area of the sphere around the point. Duplicate values can occur because multiple points contain the same voxels (due to voxel spacing in the density map). Duplicates are removed to create a list of density points for the backbone trace.

Density points follow a signal type pattern of sharp peaks and valleys, see figure 7. The peaks correspond to high density areas (atoms) and valleys to low density areas (between atoms). Assuming density is highest near $C\alpha$ atoms, then all peaks are possible $C\alpha$ atoms.

The method iterates through density points starting at the first peak and finds the next peak greater than the minimum distance (initially set to 2.5Å) from the previous $C\alpha$ atom. Then $C\alpha$ atoms are continually placed until no more density points are available. The difference between number of predicted vs actual $C\alpha$ atoms is then calculated. The minimum distance is then increased by 0.1Å and the density points are iterated through again. The value is increased until the number of predicted vs actual $C\alpha$ atoms is larger than the previous iteration. The difference must be less than 0 because the backbone trace is always shorter than the true structure using the current skeletonization technique. The final result is one predicted $C\alpha$ atom set.

The second set shifts the predicted locations to the densest voxel within a 1.0Å radius of the predicted location. The minimum distance value in the previous iteration can force a predicted $C\alpha$ to be farther from its true location. The shift is to counteract the slight offsets. Again, the assumption is that the density is greatest near $C\alpha$ atoms which is why the shift is towards the densest point in range. The result is the second predicted $C\alpha$ atom set.

Once the two sets are complete, calculate the RMSD and percentage of $C\alpha$ within 3Å\5Å of their actual locations.

3 RESULTS

The method was tested using fifteen simulated density maps and four real density maps. The simulated density maps were generated using *pdb2mrc* from EMAN [14]. The simulated density maps were generated at a resolution of 3Å with a spacing of 1Å/pixel. The results were measured using the root-mean-square deviation (RMSD), number of predicted vs actual $C\alpha$, and percentage of predicted $C\alpha$ within 3Å and 5Å of the real location.

This method uses Matlab to execute and was ran on i5 2.4GHz processor with 16GB of RAM. Our method takes a varying amount of time that is dependent on the number of nodes/links found during the skeletonization process. On this configuration, the process took anywhere from one minute up to ten minutes depending on the density map being processed. No parallelization took place to improve performance.

$$RMSD = \sqrt{\frac{1}{N}\sum_{i=1}^{N}\delta_i^2} \quad (1)$$

The RSMD is the average distance between two sets of atoms. Specifically, between atoms of the true structure and predicted locations. The value shows how close the $C\alpha$ atoms in the predicted chain match with the actual locations. Lower RMSD signals better predictions. δ_{i} is the distance between the ith predicted $C\alpha$ atom

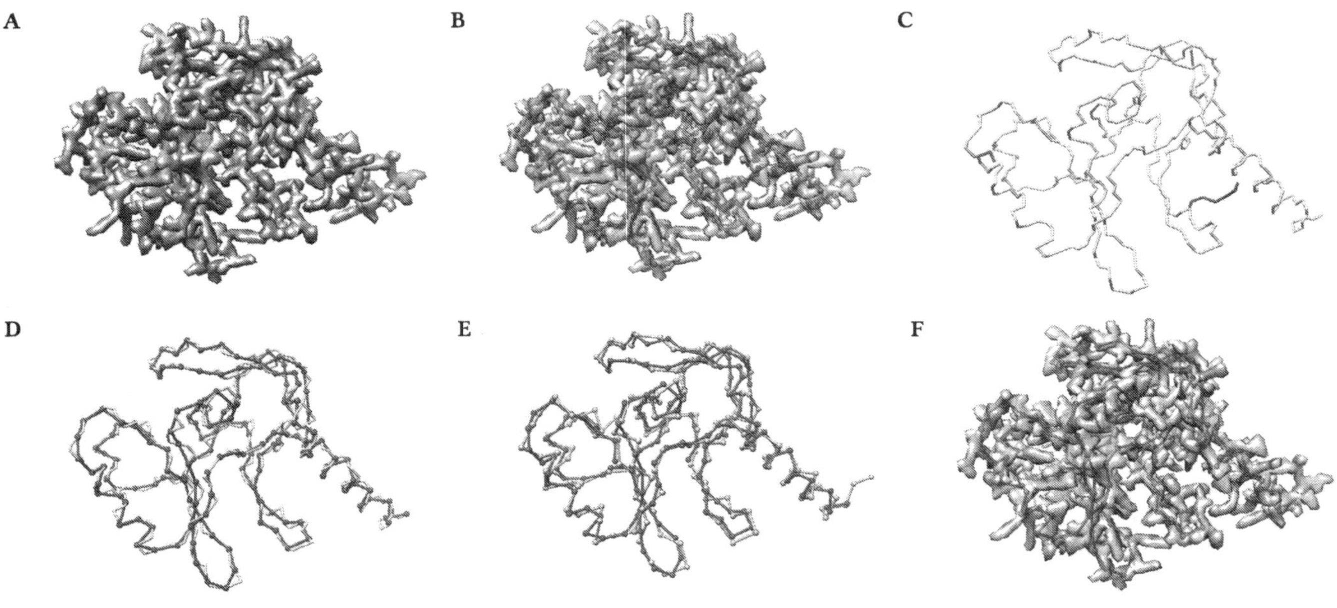

Figure 4: Results using the static distance placement (PDB 3f9x_D00). (A) is the density map. (B) is the skeleton for the density. (C) is the trace (yellow) found from the skeleton(red). (D) is the predicted Cα on the trace. (E) and (F) show the predicted Cα on the true structure and density map respectively.

and the corresponding Cα atom on true structure. N is the total number of predicted Cα.

3.1 Performance on density maps

Each method was measured and the best Cα atom set was selected for each test data. Our method achieved low RMSD on simulated data. Using dynamic Cα distance during prediction improved accuracy on larger protein structures (larger than 180 amino acids). For real and simulated data, predicted Cα atom locations covers a high percentage of the total structure.

The real data contains both α-helices and beta sheets. The density differences are very apparent and cause issues when skeletonizing the densities at a single threshold. This is especially true for the real data vs the simulated data. Table 2 shows the different results from taking the entire chain, α-helices and β-sheets, vs separating them into separate density maps for analysis.

3.1.1 Simulated density maps. Table 1 shows the results for simulated density maps. The PDB ID contains the specific chain and CathDB domain ID. The table shows RMSD for both the static (S) and dynamic (D) Cα atom placement methods depending on which was used. Figure 4 shows the results at different steps of the tracing and prediction process for PDB 3f9x_D00. The results for this PDB can be found in row 11 of table 1. The RMSD for this result was 1.76 with an average RMSD of 2.32 for static placement method. Part (E) in figure 4 shows the predicted Cα atom along with the true structure. Figure 5 shows the result when the dynamic Cα atom placement method is used. Even with the increased number of Cα the result is very good with most of the error coming from skipped Cα atom placement which will be discussed in further detail in the Discussion section.

3.1.2 Real density maps. An example of our method on real data is shown in table 2 which include results for rota-virus VP6 at 2.6Å resolution [7]. Our method was ran on the entire chain and then the chain was split into two segments. One segment contains mostly β sheets and was tested separately. The results show that when working with a mix of α-helices and β sheets the type of secondary structure elements drastically affect the performance. α-helices and β-sheets in real experimental map often have different density levels. α-helices are not modeled particularly well at the thresholds where β strands appear. This is the current challenge in real experimental data. Figures 5(b), row 3 with RMSD of 10.55, and 5(c), row 2 with RMSD of 4.11, show how the trace and predictions are able to predict Cα atoms close to the actual but there are many missed Cα especially along the α-helices. The average RMSD for the four real data tests was 6.32 which is higher than for simulated data.

3.2 Static vs. Dynamic Distance Usage

The static and dynamic distance work better for different length protein chains. In general, static distances work best for protein chains that contain less than 180 amino acids. Figure 4 shows results at different steps using a static placement.

The dynamic distance method works best for protein chains that contain over 180 amino acids. The longer the chain, the more chance that offset error can accumulate if static distance is used. As Cα atoms are placed at static distances, if they are placed slightly off from the actual location then the next predicted point will potentially be shifted incorrectly as well. This error accumulates for

Table 1: Results of simulated data. Mix of static and dynamic placement determined by the number of Cα in the chain. The RMSD is measured for either static (S) or dynamic (D) methods determined by number of Cα in the protein chain.

PDB ID	Modeled Cα	Native Cα	Diff in Cα	RMSD (D)	RMSD (S)	% Cα in 3Å	% Cα in 5Å
1ewf_A01	177	180	-3	3.92	-	98.89	100
1pjx_A00	308	314	-6	4.08	-	99.36	100
1rwh_A02	270	271	-1	2.34	-	98.89	100
1uzk_A01	45	45	0	-	2.31	97.78	100
1yfq_A00	341	342	-1	3.22	-	99.42	99.71
2bmo_A02	121	129	-8	-	2.14	96.12	97.67
2dpf_A00	110	111	-1	-	2.56	94.59	96.40
2o9s_A00	66	67	-1	-	2.42	94.03	97.01
2vxn_A00	249	249	0	5.02	-	98.39	99.20
3dha_A01	244	245	-1	3.66	-	99.59	100
3f9x_D00	163	161	2	-	1.76	98.14	99.38
3goe_A00	78	80	-2	-	2.49	97.5	100
3i07_B01	51	51	0	-	1.50	98.04	100
3puc_A00	93	98	-5	-	2.51	93.88	96.94
3ulj_B00	90	90	0	-	3.25	96.67	98.89
Average				3.48	2.32	97.42	99.01

Table 2: Results of real data. The β is a partial of the entire chain which only contains β-sheets without the α-helices. The other is the full chain including the α-helices.

EMD_PDB ID	Resolution(Å)	Modeled Cα	Native Cα	Diff in Cα	RMSD (D)	RMSD (S)	% Cα in 3Å	% Cα in 5Å
6272_3j9s_A (α)	2.6	142	144	-2	6.03	-	97.22	97.92
6272_3j9s_A (β)	2.6	195	196	-1	4.11	-	100	100
6272_3j9s_A	2.6	357	397	-40	10.55	-	96.47	98.23
8362_5t62_N	3.1	188	193	-5	4.58	-	91.71	99.48
Average					6.32		96.35	98.91

each successive placement and for longer chains this causes greater error. The dynamic placement of Cα atoms work better for longer chains because previous Cα placement does not have as large an impact. Instead, it looks for the next highest density location along the trace. Figure 5(a) shows how dynamic placement works well when a large number of Cα atoms are in the chain.

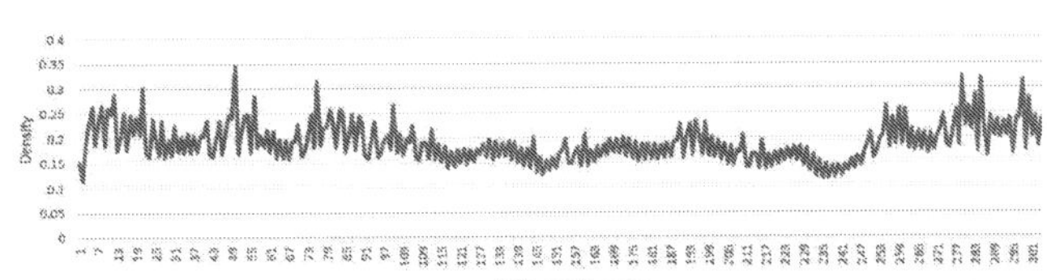

Figure 6: Real data 6272_3j92_A. Graph shows the density value for each point in the backbone trace.

3.3 Graphed Density

Graphing the density of points along the trace followed a pattern that was useful in determining location of Cα atoms for dynamic distances. The dynamic placement method places a predicted Cα within a range from the previous location. The graphed density shows the peaks in density along the trace and is used to determine a possible location for the next Cα. This follows the assumption that the densest regions occur around the Cα atom. The density graph is more uniform for simulated, see figure 7, vs real data, see figure 6, which shows the variability in real data.

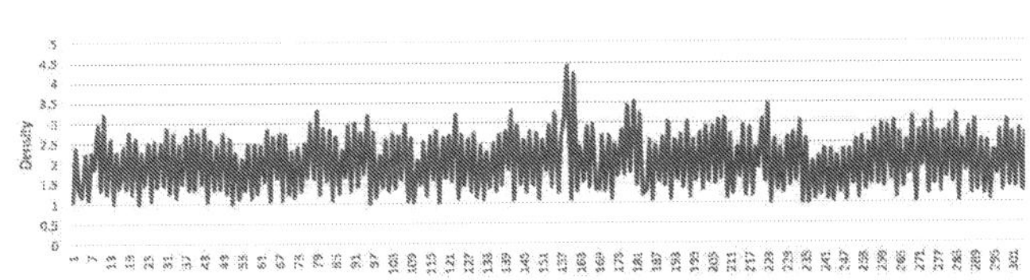

Figure 7: Simulated data 1ewf_A01. Graph shows the density value for each point in the backbone trace.

A

B

C

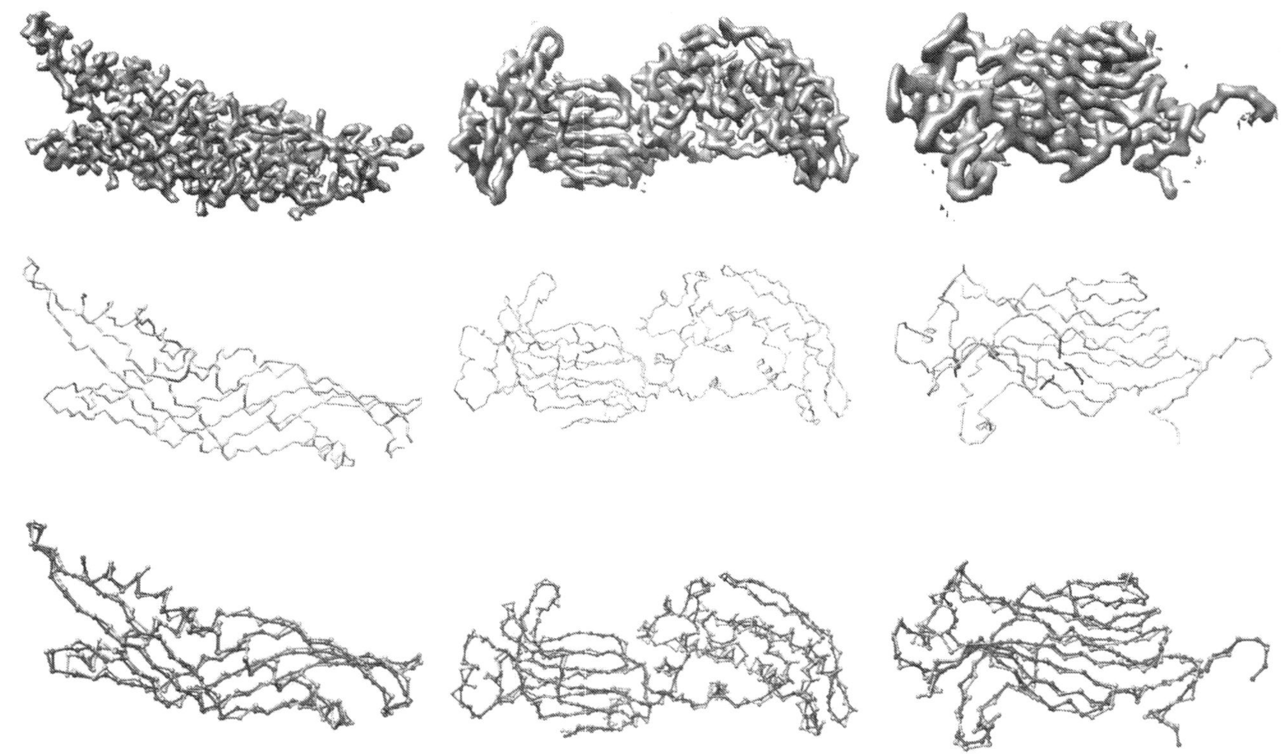

(a) 1ewf_A01 (b) 6272_3j9s_A (c) 6272_3j9s_A β

Figure 5: Example outputs from tests. (A) is the original density map. (B) is the trace route (yellow) with unused links from the skeleton (red). (C) is the predicted Cα locations (red) with the true structure (blue).

One interesting phenomenon observed was the fact that density is most likely to be greatest at a location that was next to the Cα atom and not directly on it. The observation is that the carbon-oxygen bond next to the Cα atom appears to have a stronger density in many situations. Density appears greatest at interactions between atom types where their electrons meet. Therefore, there will most likely be some error when method rely on locations with strong density.

4 DISCUSSION

A potential way to improve results is to have more than one threshold for different parts of the density map. α-helices are not modeled particularly well at the thresholds where β strands appear. Multiple thresholds at high resolution would get more information about α-helices while maintaining β strands. The current skeletonizing code only finds a full trace when there are not large gaps in the density map. β strands appear less dense than α-helices so the threshold must be lower to get the full skeleton. This causes the α-helices to lose their distinct shape in high resolution data. If a high resolution can be used for the α-helices and a lower for the β strand, their results can be combined which could lead to higher accuracy.

A current issue with the skeletonization is a tendency to place the trace along helical structures' central axes. This causes the predicted number of Cα atoms along portions of the trace to be less than the actual. When placing the Cα atom, there is a minimum distance between one and the next. Therefore, if one Cα is placed off center this can shift the next predicted location/. Figure 8 shows an example of the trace following the central axis and missing a Cα atom. A solution is to shift the points closer to the actual locations then measure the distance between them. If this distance is larger then some value, a Cα atom needs to be inserted which could improve the accuracy.

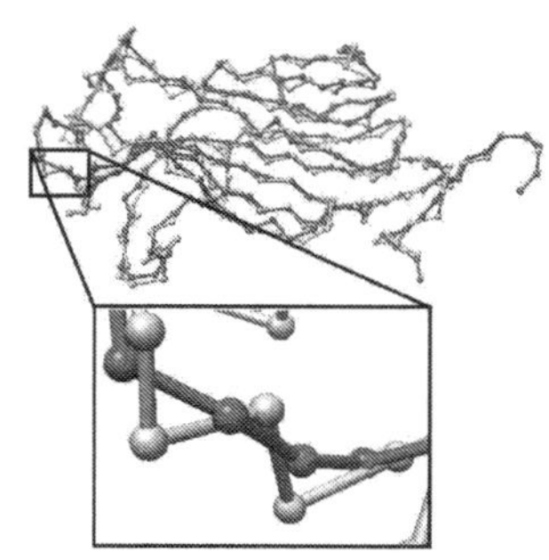

Figure 8: Example of Cα being skipped

We attempted to compare our method against the results from Pathwalking but were unable to to successfully complete results. This was due to unfamiliarity with the Pathwalking system and lack of understanding of the different parameters effects on the result.

5 CONCLUSION

In summary, we proposed a fast and automatic approach that works well in creating a trace of the backbone structure in a protein chain and predicting Cα locations from the trace. High resolution cryo-EM density maps show enough detail to make this approach feasible. We proposed a graph based method that looks at the density along a trace which produces a pattern that can be used to predict Cα atom locations. We also used the secondary structures to determine placement of Cα with the static placement method.

The densities being greater near the carbon-oxygen bonds instead of directly on the Cα can be looked at in the future for adjusting placement of Cα atoms. Also, shifting the predicted location based off local density shapes could improve the accuracy of the model. In order to address the skipped Cα, the distance between predictions could be used. If the distance between consecutive points is too high it could mean that a Cα needs to be inserted along the trace.

6 ACKNOWLEDGEMENTS

This work was supported by the Graduate Research Award from the Computing and Software Systems division of University of Washington Bothell and the startup fund 74-0525.

REFERENCES

[1] Matthew L. Baker, Tao Ju, and Wah Chiu. 2007. Identification of Secondary Structure Elements in Intermediate-Resolution Density Maps. *Structure* 15, 1 (Jan. 2007), 7–19. https://doi.org/10.1016/j.str.2006.11.008

[2] Alberto Bartesaghi, Alan Merk, Soojay Banerjee, Doreen Matthies, Xiongwu Wu, Jacqueline L. S. Milne, and Sriram Subramaniam. 2015. 2.2 ÅĚ resolution cryo-EM structure of Îš-galactosidase in complex with a cell-permeant inhibitor. *Science* 348, 6239 (June 2015), 1147. https://doi.org/10.1126/science.aab1576

[3] Muyuan Chen, Philip R. Baldwin, Steven J. Ludtke, and Matthew L. Baker. 2016. De Novo modeling in cryo-EM density maps with Pathwalking. *Journal of Structural Biology* 196, 3 (Dec. 2016), 289–298. https://doi.org/10.1016/j.jsb.2016.06.004

[4] Wah Chiu, Matthew L. Baker, Wen Jiang, Matthew Dougherty, and Michael F. Schmid. 2005. Electron Cryomicroscopy of Biological Machines at Subnanometer Resolution. *Structure* 13, 3 (March 2005), 363–372. https://doi.org/10.1016/j.str.2004.12.016

[5] A Dal Palu, J He, E Pontelli, and Y Lu. 2006. Identification of a-helices from low resolution protein density maps'. In *Computational Systems Bioinformatics Conference*. 89–98.

[6] Niels Fischer, Piotr Neumann, Andrey L. Konevega, Lars V. Bock, Ralf Ficner, Marina V. Rodnina, and Holger Stark. 2015. Structure of the E. coli ribosome-EF-Tu complex at <3 A resolution by Cs-corrected cryo-EM. *Nature* 520, 7548 (April 2015), 567–570. http://dx.doi.org/10.1038/nature14275

[7] Timothy Grant and Nikolaus Grigorieff. 2015. Measuring the optimal exposure for single particle cryo-EM using a 2.6 ÅĚ reconstruction of rotavirus VP6. *eLife* 4 (May 2015), e06980. https://doi.org/10.7554/eLife.06980

[8] Wen Jiang, Matthew L. Baker, Steven J. Ludtke, and Wah Chiu. 2001. Bridging the information gap: computational tools for intermediate resolution structure interpretation1. *Journal of Molecular Biology* 308, 5 (May 2001), 1033–1044. https://doi.org/10.1006/jmbi.2001.4633

[9] Michael Kerschnitzki, Philip Kollmannsberger, Manfred Burghammer, Georg N Duda, Richard Weinkamer, Wolfgang Wagermaier, and Peter Fratzl. 2013. Architecture of the osteocyte network correlates with bone material quality. *Journal of Bone and Mineral Research* 28, 8 (2013), 1837–1845. https://doi.org/10.1002/jbmr.1927

[10] Yifei Kong and Jianpeng Ma. 2003. A Structural-informatics Approach for Mining Îš-Sheets: Locating Sheets in Intermediate-resolution Density Maps. *Journal of Molecular Biology* 332, 2 (Sept. 2003), 399–413. https://doi.org/10.1016/S0022-2836(03)00859-3

[11] R. Li, D. Si, T. Zeng, S. Ji, and J. He. 2016. Deep convolutional neural networks for detecting secondary structures in protein density maps from cryo-electron microscopy. In *2016 IEEE International Conference on Bioinformatics and Biomedicine (BIBM)*. 41–46. https://doi.org/10.1109/BIBM.2016.7822490

[12] Zheng Liu, Fei Guo, Feng Wang, Tian-Cheng Li, and Wen Jiang. 2016. 2.9ÅăÅĚ Resolution Cryo-EM 3D Reconstruction of Close-Packed Virus Particles. *Structure* 24, 2 (Feb. 2016), 319–328. https://doi.org/10.1016/j.str.2015.12.006

[13] Steven J. Ludtke, Matthew L. Baker, Dong-Hua Chen, Jiu-Li Song, David T. Chuang, and Wah Chiu. 2008. De Novo Backbone Trace of GroEL from Single Particle Electron Cryomicroscopy. *Structure* 16, 3 (March 2008), 441–448. https://doi.org/10.1016/j.str.2008.02.007

[14] Steven J. Ludtke, Philip R. Baldwin, and Wah Chiu. 1999. EMAN: Semiautomated Software for High-Resolution Single-Particle Reconstructions. *Journal of Structural Biology* 128, 1 (Dec. 1999), 82–97. https://doi.org/10.1006/jsbi.1999.4174

[15] Albert Ng and Dong Si. 2017. *Genetic Algorithm Based Beta-Barrel Detection for Medium Resolution Cryo-EM Density Maps*. Springer International Publishing, Cham, 174–185. https://doi.org/10.1007/978-3-319-59575-7_16

[16] Eric F. Pettersen, Thomas D. Goddard, Conrad C. Huang, Gregory S. Couch, Daniel M. Greenblatt, Elaine C. Meng, and Thomas E. Ferrin. 2004. UCSF ChimeraâĂŤA visualization system for exploratory research and analysis. *Journal of Computational Chemistry* 25, 13 (2004), 1605–1612. https://doi.org/10.1002/jcc.20084

[17] Mirabela Rusu and Willy Wriggers. 2012. Evolutionary bidirectional expansion for the tracing of alpha helices in cryo-electron microscopy reconstructions. *Journal of Structural Biology* 177, 2 (Feb. 2012), 410–419. https://doi.org/10.1016/j.jsb.2011.11.029

[18] Dong Si. 2016. Automatic Detection of Beta-barrel from Medium Resolution Cryo-EM Density Maps. In *Proceedings of the 7th ACM International Conference on Bioinformatics, Computational Biology, and Health Informatics*. ACM, Seattle, WA, USA, 156–164.

[19] Dong Si and Jing He. 2013. Beta-sheet Detection and Representation from Medium Resolution Cryo-EM Density Maps. In *Proceedings of the International Conference on Bioinformatics, Computational Biology and Biomedical Informatics (BCB'13)*. ACM, New York, NY, USA, Article 764, 7 pages. https://doi.org/10.1145/2506583.2506707

[20] D. Si and J. He. 2014. Combining image processing and modeling to generate traces of beta-strands from cryo-EM density images of beta-barrels. In *2014 36th Annual International Conference of the IEEE Engineering in Medicine and Biology Society*. 3941–3944. https://doi.org/10.1109/EMBC.2014.6944486

[21] Dong Si and Jing He. 2014. Orientations of Beta-strand Traces and Near Maximum Twist. In *Proceedings of the 5th ACM Conference on Bioinformatics, Computational Biology, and Health Informatics (BCB '14)*. ACM, New York, NY, USA, 690–694. https://doi.org/10.1145/2649387.2660835

[22] Dong Si and Jing He. 2014. Tracing Beta Strands Using StrandTwister from Cryo-EM Density Maps at Medium Resolutions. *Structure* 22, 11 (Nov. 2014), 1665–1676. https://doi.org/10.1016/j.str.2014.08.017

[23] Dong Si and Jing He. 2017. Modeling Beta-Traces for Beta-Barrels from Cryo-EM Density Maps. *BioMed Research International* 2017 (2017), 1–9. https://doi.org/10.1155/2017/1793213

[24] Dong Si, Shuiwang Ji, Kamal Al Nasr, and Jing He. 2012. A Machine Learning Approach for the Identification of Protein Secondary Structure Elements from Electron Cryo-Microscopy Density Maps. *Biopolymers* 97, 9 (2012), 698–708. https://doi.org/10.1002/bip.22063

[25] Ray Yu-Ruei Wang, Mikhail Kudryashev, Xueming Li, Edward H. Egelman, Marek Basler, Yifan Cheng, David Baker, and Frank DiMaio. 2015. De novo protein structure determination from near-atomic-resolution cryo-EM maps. *Nature Methods* 12, 4 (April 2015), 335–338. https://doi.org/10.1038/nmeth.3287

[26] Zeyun Yu and Chandrajit Bajaj. 2008. Computational Approaches for Automatic Structural Analysis of Large Biomolecular Complexes. *IEEE/ACM Trans. Comput. Biol. Bioinformatics* 5, 4 (Oct. 2008), 568–582. https://doi.org/10.1109/TCBB.2007.70226

[27] Z HONG ZHOU. 2011. ATOMIC RESOLUTION CRYO ELECTRON MICROSCOPY OF MACROMOLECULAR COMPLEXES. *Advances in protein chemistry and structural biology* 82 (2011), 1–35. https://doi.org/10.1016/B978-0-12-386507-6.00001-4

Investigating Rigidity Properties of Protein Cavities

Stephanie Mason
Western Washington University
516 High Street
Bellingham, WA 98225
stephanie.mason@wwu.edu

Tim Woods
Western Washington University
516 High Street
Bellingham, WA 98225
woodst@wwu.edu

Brian Chen
Lehigh University
19 Memorial Drive West
Bethlehem, PA 18015
chen@cse.lehigh.edu

Filip Jagodzinski
Western Washington University
516 High Street
Bellingham, WA 98225
filip.jagodzinski@wwu.edu

ABSTRACT

Cavities in proteins facilitate a variety of biochemical processes. The shapes and sizes of cavities are factors that contribute to specificity in ligand binding, and docking with other biomolecules. A deep understanding of cavity properties may enable new insights into protein-protein interactions, ligand binding, and structure-based drug design studies. In this work we explore how biological properties such as size and residue membership of protein cavities correlate with the flexibility of the cavity as computed using an efficient graph theoretic rigidity algorithm. **We hypothesize that various rigidity properties of protein cavities are dependent on cavity surface area.** In this work we enumerate a set of cavity rigidity metrics, and demonstrate their use in characterizing over 120,000 cavities from approximately 2,500 chains. We show that cavity size indeed does correlate with some – but not all – cavity rigidity metrics.

CCS CONCEPTS

•**Computing methodologies** → ; •**Applied computing** → *Molecular structural biology; Bioinformatics;*

KEYWORDS

Protein; Cavity; Rigidity

1 INTRODUCTION

Many biological functions performed by proteins are known to be dependent on the size, structure, and placement of a protein's cavities. For example, ligand binding sites are strongly correlated with the largest and deepest cavity in a protein, and the specific geometry of a cavity has relevance for ligand design studies[18]. Figure 1 shows a few cavities for typical chains. The size and geometry of cavities has proven useful in making predictions about protein-protein interactions and protein druggability [10, 16]. Such inferences depend on a large body of training data relating to cavity properties. Where the space of such properties can be expanded to reflect new biophysical characteristics like molecular rigidity, the capability of all inference building algorithms can be enhanced.

Our specific goal is to describe a qualitative and quantitative survey of the rigidity properties of a large set of protein cavities. We leverage the speed of rigidity analysis [12], which builds a mechanical model of a protein from which an associated graph containing nodes, hinges, and bars is constructed. This enables us to calculate structural information about cavities for a large set of proteins in a reasonable amount of time, which we then analyze to infer whether or not over-arching trends are discernible. The rigidity analysis approach that we have chosen is different from other approaches, which either require time and labor intensive work on physical proteins, or else require computationally expensive energetics calculations.

We define several metrics of interest: cavity surface area, residues in cavities, rigid clusters in cavities, and the total number of atoms which are members of rigid clusters that are part of a cavity. New tools for exploring these metrics may provide insights on how cavities are affected by mutations, and how cavities facilitate drug-ligand binding, and protein-protein interactions. In the long term, understanding the relationship between protein cavities and rigidity

(a) lysozyme, 2lzm

(b) HIV-1 protease, 1hhp

Figure 1: A cavity can be in a deep cleft of a protein (a), or can be near a biomolecule's surface (b). Identified cavities are shown purple. Secondary structures are red and yellow (α helix and β sheets). Rendered in PyMol.

Permission to make digital or hard copies of all or part of this work for personal or classroom use is granted without fee provided that copies are not made or distributed for profit or commercial advantage and that copies bear this notice and the full citation on the first page. Copyrights for components of this work owned by others than the author(s) must be honored. Abstracting with credit is permitted. To copy otherwise, or republish, to post on servers or to redistribute to lists, requires prior specific permission and/or a fee. Request permissions from permissions@acm.org.
ACM-BCB'17, August 20-23, 2017, Boston, MA, USA.
© 2017 Copyright held by the owner/author(s). Publication rights licensed to ACM.
978-1-4503-4722-8/17/08...$15.00
DOI: http://dx.doi.org/10.1145/3107411.3107502

analysis can lead to new approaches for *in silico* experiments useful for making predictions about protein function and how it is affected by such variables as residue mutations, drug/ligand binding, or environmental factors. By performing this large scale assessment we begin to understand generalized relationships and create a basis for more complex, detailed computations and biological insights.

2 RELATED WORK

In vitro studies investigating the roles of protein cavities have been conducted on a variety of biomolecules. The scope and breadth of such studies highlights the importance of that work. Experiments elucidating the roles of cavities have been conducted *in vitro* on a variety of physical proteins.

For example, Musah *et al.* have studied the binding thermodynamics of cytochrome *c* [19]. They report on the binding of a small molecule to mutant structures, and reveal that cavities exhibit strong specificity for heterocyclic cations. Among 18 X-ray resolved structures with bound molecules, they showed that cavities induced by the mutations were able to exclusively bind specific molecules. This shows that changes to a cavity's configuration can drastically affect the binding properties of molecules.

In other work, Bade *et al*, have studied cytotoxic T lymphocytes and peptide-human leukocyte antigen complexes [1]. They explored the role of a single amino acid substitution, and identified six pockets which play a specificity role in restricting antigen binding. They showed that antigen polymorphism affects which cavities the antigen is compatible with.

In other research highlighting the important role of cavities, synthetic C peptides were engineered to study drug targets of the HIV-1 gp4 envelope protein [4]. Crystal structures of the core of gp41 were resolved, and showed that 3 C helices pack against a central coiled coil when the protein is in its function-activation conformation. The helices make strong contacts with hydrophobic cavities on the surface of the coiled coil.

Binda, *et al.*, studied monoamine oxidase B (MAO B), which due to its role in a variety in neurological disorders, is a common target for antidepressants and neuroprotective drugs [3]. Several beta helices and coils at various positions of the oxidase were identified to play key roles in the protein's binding affinity with substrates. The active site was identified as a 420 $\mathring{A}^2$ hydrophobic cavity interconnected with a second cavity of almost the same size. This has yielded understanding of the catalytic mechanism of the oxidase, and drug design studies consider the induced fit of ligand-enzyme interactions [2].

In yet other work, Elliott *et al.* studied the serpin family of serine proteinase inhibitors to improve understanding of their roles in the inflammatory, coagulation, and fibrinolytic cascades [7]. They identified five cavities as potential drug targets which were hypothesized to be associated with conformational changes of the proteinase inhibitor family of molecules. The ability of the serine proteinase inhibitors to undergo structural rearrangements enables them to perform their functions, which causes a host of adverse medical conditions such as cirrhosis, thrombosis, and angioedema. Knowledge of the cavities involved has enabled the rational design of drug agents to prevent conformational transitions and pharmacologically control the debilitating diseases they cause.

Computational approaches have also been developed, which aim to identify protein cavities to enable predicting drug binding sites. Such tools often leverage insights from machine learning. SCREEN utilizes a Random Forest approach to identify druggable cavities, analyzing surface cavities of nonreduntant proteins crystallized with drugs [20]. MetaPocket 2.0 is a popular web services that predicts drug binding sites with approximately 75% accuracy [22]. Fpocket detects and identifies ligand binding pockets through use of alpha spheres and Voronoi tessellation [9].

These studies show how knowledge of protein cavities has far reaching implications across a variety of research efforts. Due to the labor intensive work needed to conduct studies in physical proteins, research efforts most often focus on a single protein or a class of proteins. Thus, knowledge gained about the characteristics and roles of specific cavities applies only to the biomolecules being investigated. A few large scale studies have been conducted, in which the properties of protein cavities have been categorized by their function in relation to their size [16, 18]. There is a close relationship between the size of cavities and the active site of proteins, with a majority of proteins binding ligands at their largest cavity [16]. Additionally, the number of cavities correlates with the size of the protein. However, even though the largest cavity is the binding site in most cases, certain methods of measuring cavities have revealed there is no correlation between the size of the protein and the size of the active site.

3 METHODS

Our computational pipeline includes several steps (Figure 2). For each protein in our data set of PDB structures, we identify the residues in the cavities on the molecule's surface and calculate the rigidity properties of each protein. We generate a data set which aggregates structural information from a PDB file, the information output by the cavity detection program, and the rigidity analysis.

We analyzed 2,497 non-redundant chains from a randomly selected group of PDBs, all of which were resolved using X-ray crystallography. From these structures we used a cavity detection radius of 1 solvent Radii, and eliminated all cavities smaller than $1\mathring{A}^2$. We were left with a list of 123,872 cavities.

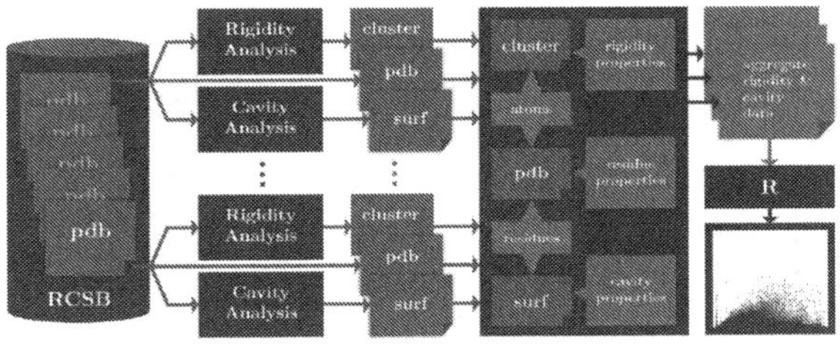

Figure 2: Computation pipeline. We identify cavities among protein chains in PDBs. We use an efficient rigidity analysis approach to identify rigid clusters of atoms in a protein. The structure (pdb), rigidity (cluster), and cavity (surf) files are aggregated to generate details of the rigidity properties of the cavities. From the aggregate metrics we plot various cavity-rigidity-atom properties.

3.0.1 *Identifying Cavities.* The software *VASP-E* [5] was used to identify cavities and to calculate their surface areas. The surface area is the sum of the areas of all triangles defined to be on the surface based on the molecular surface area [6]. Molecular surfaces are defined as C1-smooth surfaces that surround the atoms of a protein. It is generated conceptually by rolling a ball around the surface, and defined by the region of space that ball cannot occupy. [17] The residues that participate in each cavity were also identified as the set of amino acids closest to the cavity surface. Specifically, the surface is defined as a mesh of triangles and every triangle has an atom of the structure closest to it. That atom is part of some amino acid, which is added to a list. Consider the following output of the cavity calculation program:

```
Pocket 0 (area: 23.60): (2,4,5,7,12,45,46,47)
Pocket 1 (area: 12.34): (11,13,15,16,17)
Pocket 2 (area: 6.04): (18,19,20)
```

Three pockets are identified, with IDs 0, 1 and 2, with cavity surface areas of 23.60, 12.34, and 6.04 $\mathring{A}^2$. The largest pocket (ID 0) has participating residues 2, 4, 5, 7, 12, 45, 46, and 47, the second largest pocket has participating residues 11, 13, 15, 16, and 17, and so forth. From among the proteins that we studied, the largest cavity was 6,257 $\mathring{A}^2$. We did not include any cavities with surface area less than 1 $\mathring{A}^2$ because this represents the geometry of an amino acid.

3.0.2 *Rigidity Analysis.* Rigidity analysis [13, 14, 21] is a fast graph-based method that provides information about the flexibility of proteins, which are known to contain regions of varying degrees of rigidity [15]. In rigidity analysis, atoms and their chemical interactions are used to construct a mechanical model of a molecule. A

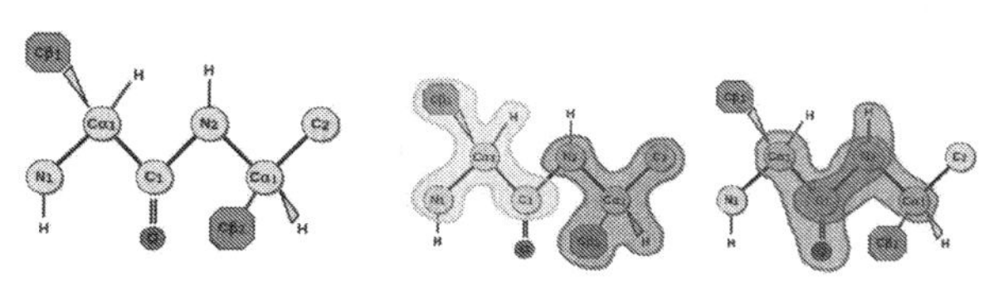

(a) Atoms and bonds (b) rigid bodies

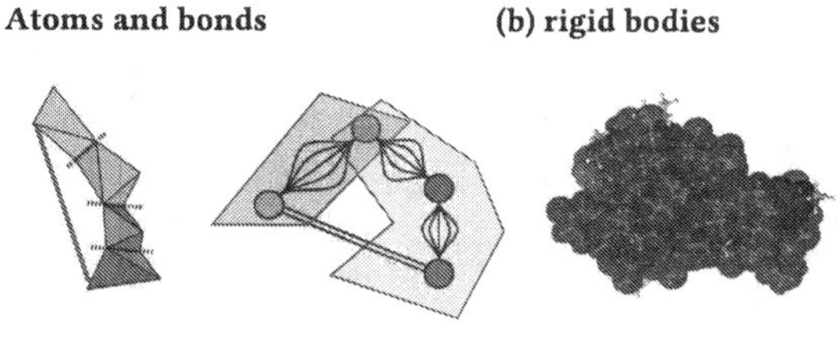

(c) model (d) analysis (e) rigid clusters

Figure 3: Rigidity Analysis: atoms from a PDB file and bonds among them (a) are analyzed to determine rigid bodies (b), the smallest rigidity components in a molecule. A mechanical model (c) representing the degrees of freedom among the rigid bodies is converted to an associated graph (d) on which rigidity analysis is performed. Its output is used to identify rigid clusters of atoms in the protein (e).

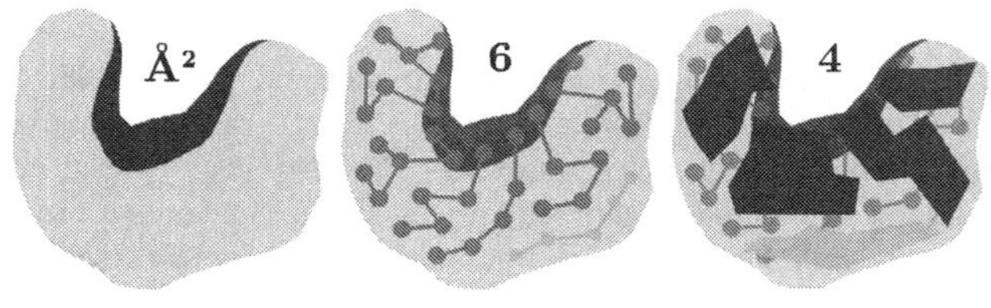

(a) Area (b) Member Residues (c) Rigid Clusters

Figure 4: Structure Based Metrics. The properties of protein cavities that we are exploring are the surface area (a), the number of residues participating in the cavity (b, which has six residues) and the number of rigid clusters participating in the cavity (c, which has four rigid clusters).

graph is constructed from the model in which each body is associated to a node, a hinge between two bodies to five edges, and a bar is associated to an edge. Pebble game algorithms [11] are used to analyze the rigidity of the graph. The results are used to infer the rigid and flexible regions of the protein. See Figure 3 for an overview of rigidity analysis.

We use the freely available KINARI rigidity software [8] to calculate the rigidity properties of each protein in our data set. The rigidity analysis output is an XML file containing the identified rigid clusters of atoms. The following is a sample output of the rigidity analysis of a protein; it identifies atoms 2 and 3 (the IDs from the PDB file) as being members of the rigid body with ID 0.

```
<body id="0">
 <pointSet>
  <point id="2"/>
  <point id="3"/>
 </pointSet>
</body>
```

3.0.3 *Aggregation of Data.* Rigidity data files contain information about atom IDs and clusters; PDB files contain information about residue IDs and atom IDs; and cavity data files contain information about residue IDs and rigid clusters. None of these files individually contain comprehensive information about rigidity properties and residue properties of the protein. In order to associate the rigid clusters with the cavities, the residue identities from the cavity surfaces are cross referenced with a PDB file to identify the alpha carbon associated with that residue. The atom IDs of a rigid cluster are scanned, and if the alpha carbon exists in that rigid cluster it is associated with the cavity.

The output of our aggregation step is a tabular summative record of all cavities at least 1$\mathring{A}^2$ in size. A sample output below, lists from left-to-right the protein ID, chain ID, cavity ID, cavity surface area, count of residues, count of rigid clusters, and total atoms in those rigid clusters.

```
1e9w A 0 23.6024493 16 6 63
1e9w A 1 17.0409083 17 3 45
```

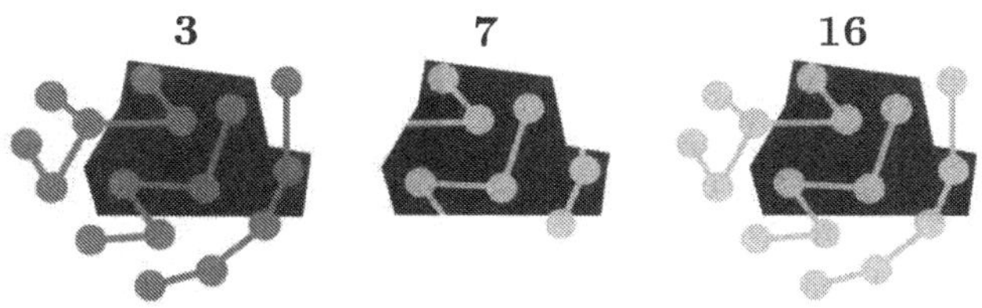

(a) Residues (b) Atoms (c) Residue Atoms

Figure 5: Rigidity Based Metrics. The rigid cluster metrics we tally include the count of residues in a rigid cluster (a, count of 3), the count of atoms in a rigid cluster (b, count of 7), and the count of atoms among the residues that have membership in a rigid cluster, irrespective if the atoms are themselves part of the rigid cluster or not (c, count of 16).

4 CAVITY / RIGIDITY METRICS

The aggregate data, along with the rigidity, cavity, and PDB data, permit us to define a number of metrics for exploring the rigidity properties of the proteins in our data set. The cavity-rigidity metrics that we explore are the following:

- $C_{resCount}$: number of residues in a cavity
- $C_{rigidClustCount}$: number of rigid clusters in a cavity
- $C_{clusterAtomCount}$: count of atoms in the rigid clusters that have membership in a cavity

We are particularly interested in exploring how the surface area of a cavity correlates with other metrics, including the cavity-rigidity metrics, because the size of a cavity is known to determine structural and functional properties of a protein [10, 16]. Because rigidity analysis is quick, identifying relationships between cavities and their rigidity properties has the potential to complement existing studies at a fraction of the computation time, and without the need for laborious wet lab work. Ultimately we aim to quantify the cavity-rigidity relationships to improve cavity analysis software and research. We identify two broad types of metrics: those that are structure based, and those that are rigidity based. We describe both in the following two subsections.

4.0.1 Structure Based Metrics. Several properties of cavities we are exploring are from a biological context, and are taken directly from existing PDB data. These include surface area of protein cavities having size greater than 1 Å^2 (Figure 4a), and the number of residues that participate in a cavity (Figure 4b).

4.0.2 Rigidity Based Metrics. We identify three rigidity metrics of cavities. We tally the count of residues in a rigid cluster (Figure 5a), the count of atoms in a rigid cluster (Figure 5b), and the count of atoms among all of the residues participating in a rigid cluster, irrespective if the atoms themselves are members of the rigid cluster or not (Figure 5c). The implications of these particular properties of cavities are still largely unexplored, and these metrics are the foundation that will permit us in future work to quantify how properties of atoms in rigid clusters relate to cavity size.

5 RESULTS

Following through with our motivation to explore the rigidity properties of protein cavities, we enumerated the relationship among several of the metrics in Section 4. For each pair of metric correlations we explored, we generated a plot. We discuss these here.

5.0.1 Residue count versus cavity surface area. As a validation step, we plotted the surface area of cavities versus the number of residues in those cavities (Figure 6). Although the 20 naturally occurring amino acids are composed of different numbers of atoms and are therefore different sizes, on average a cavity composed of more residues is expected to be larger than one composed of fewer residues. A linear relationship (correlation coefficient: 0.975) for cavity size versus the number of residues in a cavity follows this logic. Subsequent graphs containing these metrics have very similar overall shapes attributable to this linear relationship.

5.0.2 Rigid cluster count versus cavity surface area and residue count. The correlation coefficient between the rigid cluster count of a cavity and the size of the cavity (Figure 7) was 0.761. **The plot suggests that a small number of rigid clusters will not dominate a large cavity.** There are only a few isolated cases where a large cavity surface area contains a low count of rigid clusters, and these cases are isolated from the behavior of the majority of the cavities plotted.

We observed that **for a particular cavity surface area, the counts of rigid clusters that have membership in that cavity fall predominantly within a lower and upper limit**. For example, in the upper plot in Figure 7, cavity surface areas of approximately 1,000Å^2 are composed of between 30 and 150 rigid clusters, but most of the rigid clusters are between 30 and 100 atoms. Similarly, for cavities greater than 1,000Å^2, there are no cases where 1 or 2 rigid clusters only are members of those cavities. There are a handful of outlier cases where a large cavity is made up of a small count of rigid clusters (the line of outliers along the left side of the top and bottom of Figure 7). A few examples of these proteins are

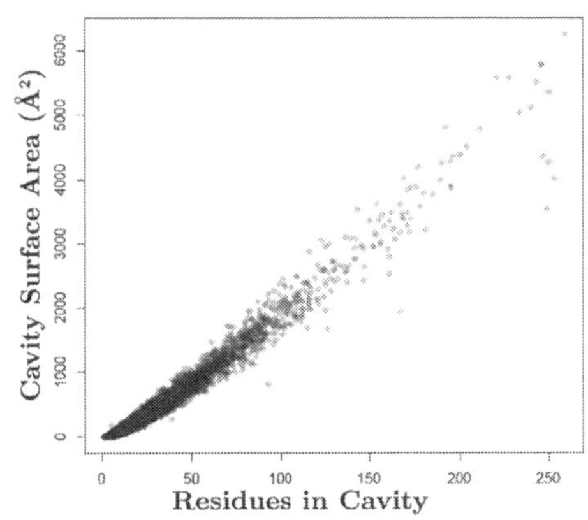

Figure 6: Validation of our Calculations, Residue Count vs Cavity Surface Area. The surface area of cavities has a linear relationship with the number of residues participating in the cavity, with a correlation coefficient of 0.975.

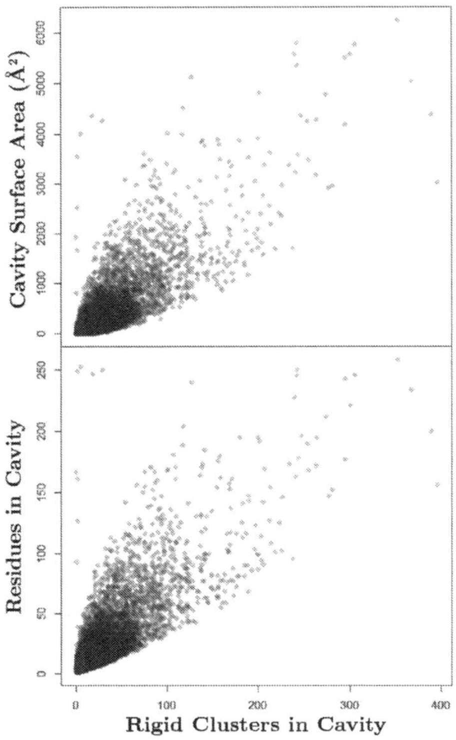

Figure 7: Rigid Cluster Count vs Cavity Surface Area and Residue Count. With the exception of a select number of proteins containing unusual characteristics (the points along the left hand side of the graphs, specifying large cavities dominated by single rigid clusters), the ranges of the count of rigid clusters in a cavity falls within a distinct range, which grows wider as cavities increase in size. The correlation coefficients for cavity surface area and residue count versus rigid cluster count are 0.761 and 0.769 respectively.

PDB structures 1rea, 1tgl, 1tia, and 1tic. Our preliminary investigation into these particular proteins reveals that they all have a large, shallow concave surface, and that there is a single rigid cluster that consumes the entire cavity.

5.0.3 Total Atoms in Rigid Clusters versus cavity surface area, residue count, and rigid cluster count. For smaller cavities (less than 1,000Å^2, or approximately 50 residues), there does not exist a discernible correlation between the total atoms in the rigid clusters that are members of a cavity and the number of residues in the cavity. This can be seen in the dense placing of points at the bottom of the graphs for total atoms in rigid clusters versus cavity surface area/residues/rigid clusters in the cavity (Figure 8), and in the low correlation coefficients of 0.128 for residue count and 0.109 for cavity surface area. However, **in cavities with sizes greater than 1,000Å^2, it is more likely that those cavities contain smaller rigid clusters**. This can be seen in each of the subplots in Figure 8, where there are far more points to the left of 4,000 for each Cavity size than there are to the right of 4,000. The relationship between

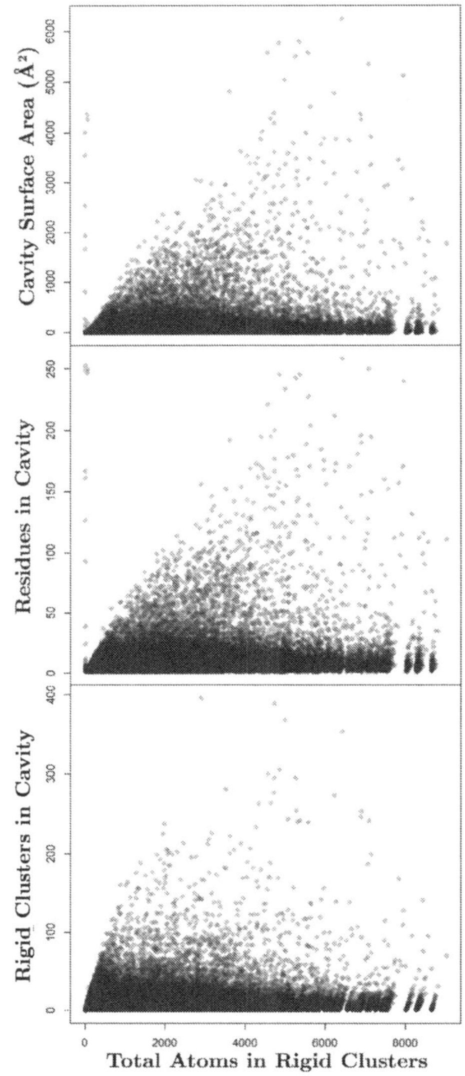

Figure 8: Total Atoms in Rigid Clusters vs Rigid Clusters in Cavity, Residues in Cavity, and Cavity Surface Area. While there is no correlation between these metrics (having corelation coefficients of 0.109 for cavity surface area, 0.128 for residues in cavity, and -0.103 for rigid clusters versus total atoms in rigid clusters), there is a heavier distribution of smaller rigid clusters (fewer total atoms) for cavities larger than 1000Å^2 or which have more than 50 residues. Under this threshold there is an even spread of rigid cluster sizes.

rigid clusters and their atom counts likely affects some of the outcomes of how rigid clusters are correlating with the size of the cavity/residues in the cavity.

5.0.4 Rigid cluster count versus cavity surface area versus total rigid atoms. A three dimensional graph (Figure 9) of our metrics best shows how a relationship exists between the size of cavities, the number of rigid clusters participating in those cavities, and the

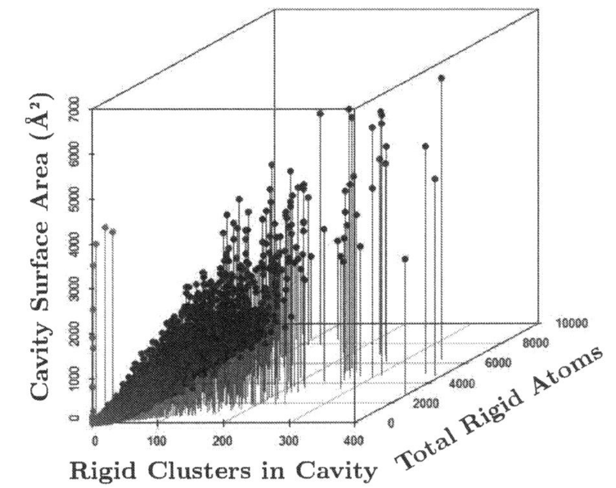

Figure 9: Rigid Cluster Count vs Cavity Surface Area vs Total Atoms in Rigid Clusters. Larger surface areas coincide with higher rigid cluster counts/more overall rigid atoms.

number of atoms contained in those rigid clusters. There are more rigid clusters associated with bigger cavities, and these rigid clusters grow larger as the cavity surface area increases. This suggests that larger rigid clusters are correlated with larger cavities. There are strong limits on the range of how many rigid clusters exist in a cavity of a given size, as well as a limit on the range of how large those rigid clusters can be. There are some exceptions to these ranges where there is low rigid cluster count to cavity surface area ratio.

6 CONCLUSION

A large scale assessment of the rigidity properties of protein cavities is our ultimate goal. We have enumerated a series of cavity rigidity metrics and demonstrated their use in exploring a small subset of available PDB data. Of the correlations among the rigidity and cavity metrics that we explored, we were able to identify several interesting relationships. As expected, the number of rigid clusters has a positive correlation with cavity size (Figure 7). Additionally we observed that for small cavities, no correlation exists between the size of rigid clusters and the size of the cavity; cavities smaller than approximately 1,000Å^2 were composed of both small and large rigid clusters from among the proteins that we studied. However, for larger cavities, we observed that they are composed predominantly of rigid clusters composed of residues with less than 4,000 total atoms (Figure 8). Our initial hypothesis that rigidity properties of cavities vary with cavity surface area is true.

For future work, we will explore the correlations that exist among cavity size and other rigidity and biological properties. For example, how counts of the different types of amino acids that are participating in rigid clusters of a cavity correlate with surface area. Additionally we will investigate how secondary and tertiary structures of protein cavities interact with rigidity metrics. Many of our outliers, on cursory inspection, had similar features such as a large, shallow cavities. Creating more selective data sets that contain similar structures (for example, proteins with largest cavities over a certain threshold, or classes of proteins such as transmembrane proteins with beta-barrels or alpha helix domains) and looking in close detail at their rigidity analysis/cavity data may lead to useful insights that are not apparent in an overview study. There are also statistical analyses that need to be performed on our existing data to better quantify the relationships. Finally, we plan to analyze the majority of the more than 120,000 protein structures in the PDB.

REFERENCES

[1] C. Bade-Doeding, T. Huyton, B. Eiz-Vesper, and R. Blasczyk. 2011. The composition of the F pocket in HLA-A* 74 generates C-terminal promiscuity among its bound peptides. *Tissue antigens* 78, 5 (2011), 378–381.

[2] C. Binda, M. Li, F. Hubálek, N. Restelli, D. Edmondson, and A. Mattevi. 2003. Insights into the mode of inhibition of human mitochondrial monoamine oxidase B from high-resolution crystal structures. *Proceedings of the National Academy of Sciences* 100, 17 (2003), 9750–9755.

[3] C. Binda, P. Newton-Vinson, F. Hubálek, D.E. Edmondson, and A. Mattevi. 2002. Structure of human monoamine oxidase B, a drug target for the treatment of neurological disorders. *Nature structural & molecular biology* 9, 1 (2002), 22–26.

[4] D. Chan, C.T. Chutkowski, and P.S. Kim. 1998. Evidence that a prominent cavity in the coiled coil of HIV type 1 gp41 is an attractive drug target. *Proceedings of the National Academy of Sciences* 95, 26 (1998), 15613–15617.

[5] B.Y. Chen. 2014. Vasp-e: Specificity annotation with a volumetric analysis of electrostatic isopotentials. *PLoS Comput Biol* 10, 8 (2014), e1003792.

[6] B.Y. Chen and B. Honig. 2010. VASP: a volumetric analysis of surface properties yields insights into protein-ligand binding specificity. *PLoS Comput Biol* 6, 8 (2010), e1000881.

[7] P. R. Elliott, X.Y. Pei, T.D. Dafforn, and D.A. Lomas. 2000. Topography of a 2.0 Å structure of α1-antitrypsin reveals targets for rational drug design to prevent conformational disease. *Protein Science* 9, 7 (2000), 1274–1281.

[8] N. Fox, F. Jagodzinski, and I. Streinu. 2012. KINARI-lib: a C++ library for pebble game rigidity analysis of mechanical models. *Minisymposium on Publicly Available Geometric/Topological Software* (2012).

[9] V. Le Guilloux, P. Schmidtke, and P. Tuffery. 2009. Fpocket: an open source platform for ligand pocket detection. *BMC bioinformatics* 10, 1 (2009), 168.

[10] N. Huang and M.P. Jacobson. 2010. Binding-site assessment by virtual fragment screening. *PLoS One* 5, 4 (2010), e10109.

[11] D.J. Jacobs and B. Hendrickson. 1997. An algorithm for two-dimensional rigidity percolation: the pebble game. *J. Comput. Phys.* 137, 2 (1997), 346–365.

[12] D.J. Jacobs, A.J. Rader, L.A. Kuhn, and M.F. Thorpe. 2002. Protein flexibility predictions using graph theory. *Journal of Molecular Graphics and Modelling* 2 (2002), 195–207.

[13] D.J. Jacobs, A.J. Rader, M.F. Thorpe, and L.A. Kuhn. 2001. Protein Flexibility Predictions using Graph Theory. *Proteins 44* (2001), 150–165.

[14] D.J. Jacobs and M.F. Thorpe. 1995. Generic rigidity percolation: the pebble game. *Physical review letters* 75, 22 (1995), 4051.

[15] A.G. Ladurner and A.R. Fersht. 1997. Glutamine, alanine or glycine repeats inserted into the loop of a protein have minimal effects on stability and folding rates. *Journal of Molecular Biology* 273, 1 (1997), 330 – 337.

[16] R.A. Laskowski, N.M. Luscombe, M.B. Swindells, and J.M. Thornton. 1996. Protein clefts in molecular recognition and function. *Protein science: a publication of the Protein Society* 5, 12 (1996), 2438.

[17] B. Lee and F.M. Richards. 1971. The interpretation of protein structures: estimation of static accessibility. *Journal of molecular biology* 55, 3 (1971), 379IN3–400IN4.

[18] J. Liang, C. Woodward, and H. Edelsbrunner. 1998. Anatomy of protein pockets and cavities: measurement of binding site geometry and implications for ligand design. *Protein science* 7, 9 (1998), 1884–1897.

[19] R. Musah, G.M. Jensen, S.W. Bunte, R.J. Rosenfeld, and D.B. Goodin. 2002. Artificial protein cavities as specific ligand-binding templates: characterization of an engineered heterocyclic cation-binding site that preserves the evolved specificity of the parent protein. *Journal of molecular biology* 315, 4 (2002), 845–857.

[20] M. Nayal and B. Honig. 2006. On the nature of cavities on protein surfaces: application to the identification of drug-binding sites. *Proteins: Structure, Function, and Bioinformatics* 63, 4 (2006), 892–906.

[21] I.R. Tsang and I.J. Tsang. 1999. Cluster size diversity, percolation, and complex systems. *Physical Review E* 60, 3 (1999), 2684.

[22] Z. Zhang, Y. Li, B. Lin, M. Schroeder, and B. Huang. 2011. Identification of cavities on protein surface using multiple computational approaches for drug binding site prediction. *Bioinformatics* 27, 15 (2011), 2083–2088.

Geometric Sampling Framework for Exploring Molecular Walker Energetics and Dynamics

Bruna Jacobson
Department of Computer Science
University of New Mexico
Albuquerque, New Mexico 87131-0001
bjacobson@unm.edu

Jon Christian L. David
Department of Computer Science
University of New Mexico
Albuquerque, New Mexico 87131-0001
jdavid@cs.unm.edu

Mitchell C. Malone
Department of Computer Science
University of New Mexico
Albuquerque, New Mexico 87131-0001
mmalone1@unm.edu

Kasra Manavi
Department of Computer Science
University of New Mexico
Albuquerque, New Mexico 87131-0001
kazaz@cs.unm.edu

Susan R. Atlas
Department of Physics and Astronomy
Department of Computer Science
University of New Mexico
Albuquerque, New Mexico 87131-0001
susie@sapphire.phys.unm.edu

Lydia Tapia
Department of Computer Science
University of New Mexico
Albuquerque, New Mexico 87131-0001
tapia@cs.unm.edu

ABSTRACT

The motor protein kinesin is a remarkable natural nanobot that moves cellular cargo by taking 8 nm steps along a microtubule molecular highway. Understanding kinesin's mechanism of operation continues to present considerable modeling challenges, primarily due to the millisecond timescale of its motion, which prohibits fully atomistic simulations. Here we describe the first phase of a physics-based approach that combines energetic information from all-atom modeling with a robotic framework to enable kinetic access to longer simulation timescales. Starting from experimental PDB structures, we have designed a computational model of the combined kinesin-microtubule system represented by the isosurface of an all-atom model. We use motion planning techniques originally developed for robotics to generate candidate conformations of the kinesin head with respect to the microtubule, considering all six degrees of freedom of the molecular walker's catalytic domain. This efficient sampling technique, combined with all-atom energy calculations of the kinesin-microtubule system, allows us to explore the configuration space in the vicinity of the kinesin binding site on the microtubule. We report initial results characterizing the energy landscape of the kinesin-microtubule system, setting the stage for an efficient, graph-based exploration of kinesin preferential binding and dynamics on the microtubule, including interactions with obstacles.

KEYWORDS

Molecular walkers; kinesin; motion planning; OBPRM; energy landscape; protein-protein interaction; motor protein

ACM acknowledges that this contribution was authored or co-authored by an employee, or contractor of the national government. As such, the Government retains a nonexclusive, royalty-free right to publish or reproduce this article, or to allow others to do so, for Government purposes only. Permission to make digital or hard copies for personal or classroom use is granted. Copies must bear this notice and the full citation on the first page. Copyrights for components of this work owned by others than ACM must be honored. To copy otherwise, distribute, republish, or post, requires prior specific permission and/or a fee. Request permissions from permissions@acm.org.
ACM-BCB'17, August 20-23, 2017, Boston, MA, USA.
© 2017 ACM. 978-1-4503-4722-8/17/08...$15.00
DOI: http://dx.doi.org/10.1145/3107411.3107503

1 INTRODUCTION

The motor protein kinesin-1 (henceforth referred to as kinesin) is a molecular walker responsible for intracellular cargo transport. The full protein structure contains two catalytic domains (heads) responsible for procession; a neck linker that connects the heads to its stalk; and a long coiled-coil structure that binds to the cargo. The protein walks on microtubule tracks [25, 28]. Microtubules are composed of 13 protofilament chains of α and β tubulin heterodimer subunits (see Figure 1a). Normally kinesins walk along a single protofilament on microtubules, however sidestepping is known to occur under certain conditions [12].

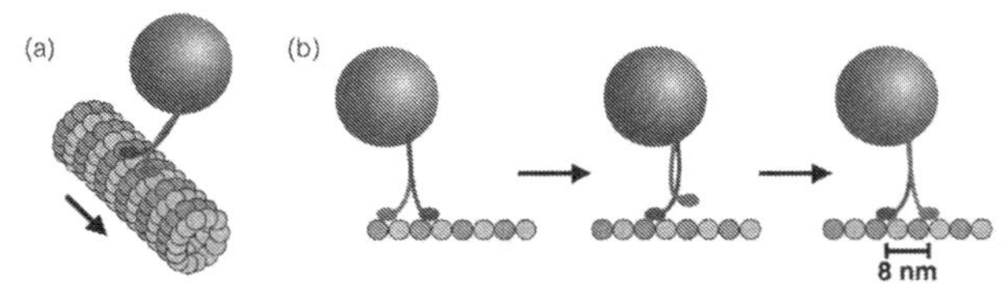

Figure 1: (a) Illustration of kinesin walking along a microtubule comprised of 13 protofilaments. Green and yellow disks represent α and β tubulin heterodimers. Kinesin is shown in red and purple. The blue bead attached to the stalk represents the cargo. (b) Hand-over-hand kinesin walk. The catalytic domains or heads (red and purple) bind to the microtubule and alternate leading position during the walk, in a hand-over-hand fashion.

A kinesin catalytic head consumes one ATP molecule to take each 8-nm hand-over-hand step in one-dimensional transport along the microtubule [30], Figure 1b. There is currently a large body of experimental and theoretical work on the biophysical, biochemical, and dynamical properties of kinesin. However, the molecular details of how kinesin transforms the chemical energy from ATP hydrolysis into a mechanical step are not yet fully understood.

The interaction of the kinesin catalytic heads with the microtubule as it walks can be characterized as protein binding and unbinding events. During each step the kinesin catalytic head binds to a microtubule subunit, the α-β tubulin heterodimer. Binding sites on the microtubule correspond to low energy configurations of the microtubule-kinesin complex.

The goal of the present work is to develop a model of the kinesin-tubulin interaction energy landscape to enable full dynamical simulations. We utilize the Probabilistic Roadmap Method (PRM) [15], a method originally developed for identifying robotic motions. Specifically, we apply the PRM variant, Obstacle-based Probabilistic Roadmap Method (OBPRM) [3], that samples configurations on surfaces prior to connecting nearby configurations with weighted edges. The resulting roadmap enables the study of kinesin interactions with the microtubule surface through the sampling of potential binding sites and possible trajectories. The roadmap is generated by creating a three-dimensional model of the kinesin head and microtubule system based on their protein crystal structures, and efficiently sampling the conformational space of the interacting molecules. For each sampled conformation, we compute the all-atom energy of the interacting system to determine the energy landscape explored by the kinesin head as it executes diffusive motion before binding to the microtubule.

2 RELATED WORK

The energy landscape around the microtubule has been investigated in the context of the kinesin walk via several physics-based methods. In [11], the authors used Brownian dynamics coupled with a Poisson-Boltzmann approach to study the eletrostatics-induced bias of the kinesin head search to the binding site on the microtubule. Their method did not include van der Waals energy terms, which are important when the two molecules are in close proximity. A multiscale Poisson-Boltzmann method was applied in [16] to compute the electrostatic interaction between kinesin and the microtubule. In this work, the authors included a van der Waals energy term, but the Poisson-Boltzmann electrostatics component used precomputed regular grids with fine sampling only in the vicinity of assumed binding sites, causing potential loss of ruggedness detail elsewhere on the microtubule surface.

Simulation and modeling of macromolecular interactions have been extensively discussed in [17]. A comprehensive review of robotics-inspired methods for protein folding is given in [21]. Motion planning algorithms have been extensively applied to molecular simulations [2, 19], including protein folding pathways [22, 23, 27]. In particular, simulation of receptor-ligand binding has been carried out using OBPRMs [3, 4]. These techniques have been shown to be successful at capturing kinetic information for RNA [26] and proteins [27].

3 METHODS

3.1 Models

The starting models for kinesin and tubulin were obtained from the Protein Data Bank. We used the kinesin/microtubule structure from PDB ID 4LNU. This structure represents one kinesin head bound to a tubulin heterodimer [8]. Additional chains, nucleotides, other ligands, and water in the original 4LNU structure were removed using Pymol [10]. The resulting structure has 3 chains: A, B, and K, representing α-tubulin, β-tubulin, and the kinesin head, respectively. The head is composed of 309 amino acids and 4,824 atoms, and the α-β tubulin heterodimer has 870 amino acids and 13,464 atoms. The final structure is shown in Figure 2.

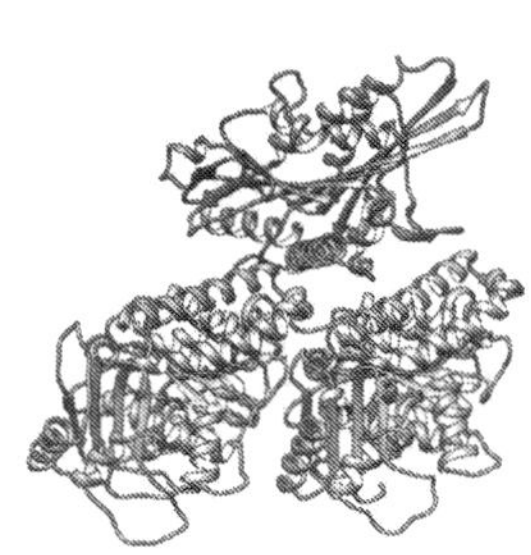

Figure 2: Protein structure from the Protein Data Bank used in this work, PDB ID 4LNU. Additional chains, nucleotides, ligands and water have been removed. The kinesin head is shown in blue and the microtubule heterodimer in tan.

To construct the microtubule patch, we used a 3D electron microscopy (EM) map from [24], and the crystal structure of the tubulin heterodimer for the microtubule subunits. Several copies of 4LNU were fit to the EM map using the rigid fit feature in Chimera [20]. We then created a 3-by-3 patch of heterodimers (9 total) to model the microtubule surface. The patch is comprised of 7,830 amino acids and 121,176 atoms. In the cleaned model of 4LNU, the α-β tubulin heterodimer is aligned to the central heterodimer in the 3-by-3 patch, placing the kinesin head into a bound state relative to the microtubule model, shown in Figure 3.

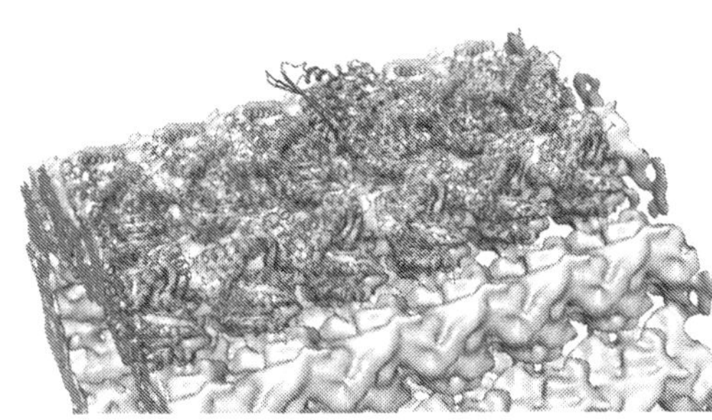

Figure 3: Fitting PDB structure of microtubule heterodimer and kinesin head to EM map of microtubule.

Once the microtubule patch has been created, as a single structure with a kinesin bound to the middle of the patch, hydrogens were added via Chimera (Figure 4, left). Then the kinesin and microtubule patch structures were separated into two PDB files. To apply OBPRM to the molecules, it is necessary to generate three-dimensional geometric structure models that capture protein surface ruggedness. Geometric models were created for the kinesin and patch structures via the *Multiscale Models* option in Chimera to make models (with parameter resolution set to 8), with results as shown in Figure 4 (right).

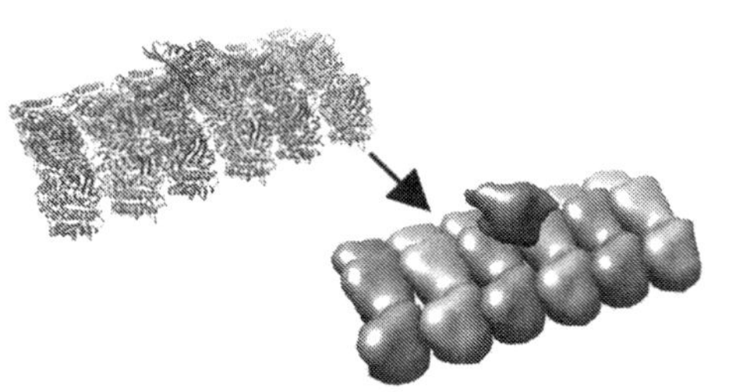

Figure 4: Left: Microtubule patch with a bound kinesin head resulting from EM fit. Right: Geometric model obtained by generating a 3D model of the protein structure.

The geometric centers of mass of the models of the kinesin head and the microtubule patch were found using the IVCON package [7]. These values were recorded and the 3D modeling tool Blender [5] was used to center them. Centering is done by translating the two models (of kinesin head and microtubule patch) such that both geometric centers of mass are set to the origin of the coordinate system. If x_{iv}, y_{iv}, and z_{iv} are the geometric centers of mass as reported by IVCON, then the translation vector used in Blender is: $x = -x_{iv}$, $y = z_{iv}$, and $z = -y_{iv}$, since IVCON and Blender use different coordinate systems. It is important to note that the geometric center of mass of the geometric model is not the same as the center of mass of the PDB structure. All calculations were performed with respect to the geometric center of mass.

3.2 Generating Configurations with OBPRM

We use OBPRM to create configuration samples of the kinesin head. Before sampling begins, we restrict configuration generation to a sampling region on the microtubule surface with dimensions $x \in [-70, 75]$, $y \in [-20, 150]$, and $z \in [-125, 125]$ Å. The three dimensions correspond to longitudinal length (around the microtubule curvature, x), vertical distance from the microtubule (height, y), and length parallel to the microtubule long axis (z). Two initial configurations are chosen randomly within this sampling region, such that one configuration is in collision with the microtubule and the other configuration is not. By connecting the two configurations' geometric centers we create a vector that points outwards in a random direction.

Binary search is performed along this vector to find the configuration of the kinesin head where the microtubule and kinesin head surfaces are within a given positional resolution but not in collision. This configuration and the vector are used in order to guide the creation of new samples at 5 Å intervals along the vector. We take one kinesin head sample towards the minus end of the vector (into the microtubule), and four samples toward the plus end of the vector (outside the microtubule). For each of these samples we perform a random rotation of the kinesin head with respect to its native bound position, for which the pitch (α), yaw (β), and roll (γ) angular values are all restricted to $[-5°, 5°]$. The procedure is repeated until 100,000 configurations have been generated. The positions of the center of mass of the resulting samples are illustrated in Figure 5. It should be noted that retention of the configuration along the vector toward the microtubule surface is not standard in OBPRM, and may produce configurations in collision, which have high energy. We chose to generate and retain these samples because it is important to identify binding configurations, possibly in tight proximity to the microtubule surface. Since each sample is subsequently evaluated energetically, possible high-energy samples can be easily identified and disregarded when low energy paths are followed.

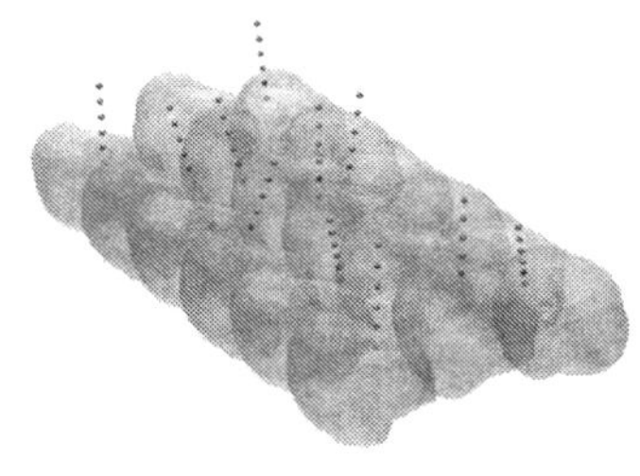

Figure 5: Illustration of OBPRM sampling of kinesin head. Example configurations are samples along vectors as shown, at 5 Å intervals. Green dots: Position of the center of mass of the kinesin head, which is treated as a rigid body. Blue dots: Samples on the surface of the microtubule. Red dots: Samples within the microtubule. The direction of the line is chosen randomly. Rotations are randomly chosen within $[-5°, 5°]$ for all three rotational degrees of freedom.

3.3 Energy calculations

Once all configurations of the kinesin head and the microtubule have been generated, we compute the interaction energies between the two molecules at each configuration. We use our in-house software *Molecular Docking Game* (MDG) to move the kinesin head to each configuration [1]. Both the kinesin head and microtubule patch are kept rigid.

The interaction energy is given by the sum of the electrostatic energy and the van der Waals energy, as represented by the non-bonded energy terms in molecular dynamics force fields [6, 29]. The terms are computed for intermolecular interactions only.

The electrostatic energy between atom i in the kinesin head and atom j in the microtubule, U_{ij}, is:

$$U_{ij} = \frac{q_i q_j}{4\pi\epsilon_0 r_{ij}}, \tag{1}$$

where $q_{i(j)}$ is the charge of atom $i(j)$, and r_{ij} is the distance between the atoms. The van der Waals interaction between atom i in the kinesin head and atom j in the microtubule, V_{ij}, is:

$$V_{ij} = \epsilon_{ij} \left[\left(\frac{\sigma_{ij}}{r_{ij}} \right)^{12} - 2 \left(\frac{\sigma_{ij}}{r_{ij}} \right)^{6} \right], \tag{2}$$

where the parameter ϵ_{ij} is the depth of the potential well, and σ_{ij} is the distance at which the potential between the atoms vanishes. The total energy for the system is:

$$E = \sum_{i=1}^{K} \sum_{j=1}^{M} \left(U_{ij} + V_{ij} \right), \tag{3}$$

where the sum over i runs over all K atoms in the kinesin head, and the sum over j is over all M atoms in the microtubule.

MDG uses the Amber94 [29] force field parameters to compute energies. These energies are calculated for atoms out to a maximum distance of 12 Å. The electrostatic and van der Waals energies have discontinuities at the 12 Å cutoff, going to zero for intermolecular atomic pairs whose distance is greater than 12 Å.

3.4 Roadmap Connectivity

We construct a graph such that each node i is connected to all nodes j whose distance between i and j is less than or equal to $k = 5$ Å. All edges are bidirectional. The edge weight W_{ij} is defined as the energy difference between the nodes:

$$W_{ij} = E_j - E_i. \tag{4}$$

The connected component of this roadmap includes the kinesin bound state. To simulate how kinesin navigates the energy landscape on the microtubule by finding low energy paths to the bound state, we use Dijkstra's algorithm to find the lowest weighted path to the known native state, where the initial and final states are defined for each run.

4 RESULTS

We used OBPRM from the Parasol Motion Planning Library from Texas A&M University to generate the 100,000 configurations in parallel on a Dell PowerEdge R620 with an Intel Xeon E5-2670, 2.6 GHz processor. This machine has 24 nodes, 16 cores per node, 4GB of RAM per core, and runs Scientific Linux OS.

Both the kinesin head and the microtubule are treated as rigid bodies. The microtubule is held fixed, and the six degrees of freedom of the center of mass of the kinesin head, three spatial and three rotations, are stored for each configuration. For the points that are not in collision, the node density is nearly 0.32 nodes/Å^3, which results in an average shortest distance between nodes of about 0.9 Å. In the connected roadmap there are 99,999 nodes and 6,375,848 total edges, with on average 127.5 edges per node.

MDG is used for the energy calculations. The 6-dimensional degrees of freedom of the configurations, and the atomic positions (PDB files) of all molecules are used as input. A supercomputer cluster with 24 nodes, 16 cores per node, and 4GB of RAM per core was used to compute the energies, to sample kinesin positions and to connect nodes in the roadmap.

Timing results for sampling, energy, and connectivity calculations are shown in Table 1.

Table 1: Timing Results for Sampling, Energy, and Connectivity Calculations.

	Sampling	Energy	Connectivity
CPU-time (s)	3.191×10^2	1.304×10^7	2.083×10^2

By construction, some configurations are generated in collision with the microtubule (Figure 6). The distribution of energies found with the MDG that are lower than 2000 kcal/mol is shown in Figure 7. A few energy values, as high as 10^{28} kcal/mol, were found; however these correspond to unphysical configurations in collision. In Figure 8, we show the distribution of positive and negative energy values along the length of the microtubule patch. The periodic peaks on the histograms are out of phase by about $\pi/2$, showing an increase in positive energies (possibly related to collision) when there is a decrease in negative energies. Peaks in negative energies occur at ≈ 40 Å intervals in the z axis, coinciding with the region where the α and β tubulins are joined along a single protofilament.

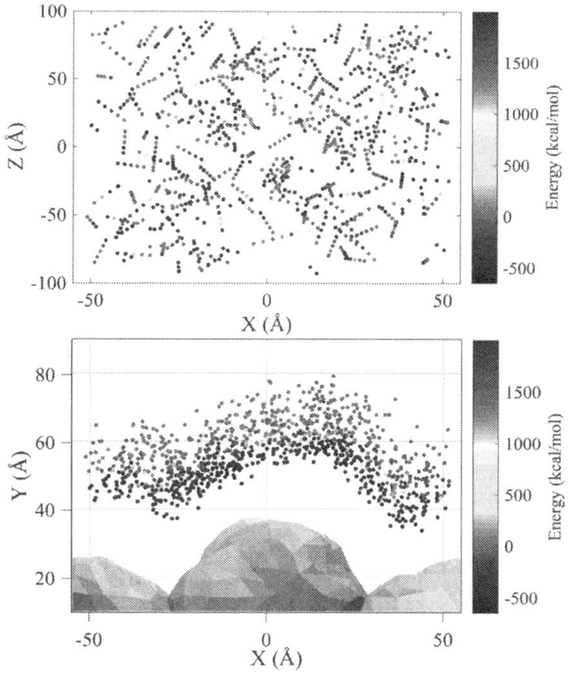

Figure 6: First 1000 configurations generated using the methodology described in the text. Top: Two-dimensional *xz* (top) view of the microtubule surface. The kinesin head is sampled by moving its center of mass 5 Å along lines started at random positions on the microtubule. The transition from collision to non-collision states is identified by the configuration energy value, as the points on a line move from high energies (red) to low energies (blue). Bottom: Same data shown in *xy* plane.

This periodic effect for low energy regions is also seen in the energy plot on the xz plane, Figure 9. Here we see a concentration of low energy values (< -500 kcal/mol) at the intersection of α and β tubulins along a protofilament.

We also observe that some low energy clusters are broader than others. The clusters where binding positions exist (near -80, 0, and 80 Å in the z axis) are narrower than clusters where binding of kinesin to the microtubule does not occur (near z = -40 Å and z = 40 Å).

To understand how the low energy regions influence kinesin stepping, we examined whether lowest weighted Dijkstra pathways connecting random nodes choose to visit these regions. We analyzed two lowest-weighted Dijkstra paths in this energy landscape. The

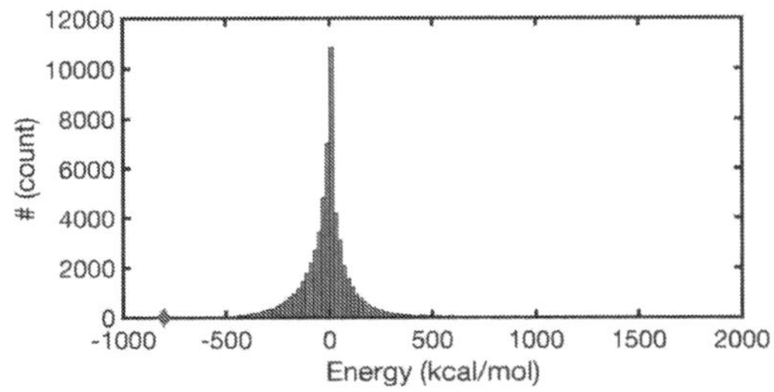

Figure 7: Energy distribution histogram for kinesin and microtubule system. Only energy values less than 2000 kcal/mol are shown, but a few high energy values (as high as 10^{28} kcal/mol) also appear for collisions. The bound state energy is shown as the red diamond at $E_{bound} = -803.35$ kcal/mol. The location of the peak at zero energy is due to the large number of configurations for which all kinesin and microtubule atoms are separated by a distance greater than 12 Å.

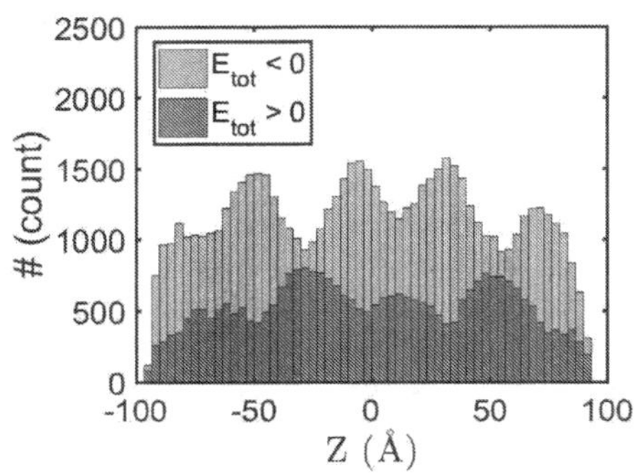

Figure 8: Histogram of positive (red) and negative (blue) energies along the microtubule axis. There are more negative energy values overall, but peaks in negative energies correspond to troughs in positive energy and vice-versa, with ≈ 40 Å spacing. High positive energy values are due to collisions between the kinesin head and the microtubule.

first connects a random initial state with zero energy (the black ∘ in Figure 10) to the first microtubule bound state (positioned at the black × in Figure 10). The second Dijkstra pathway starts from this bound state and ends at a second bound state about 80 Å away, toward the minus z axis (the black ◁ in Figure 10).

As shown in Figure 10, the Dijkstra pathway tends to stay along a single protofilament and visits every low energy region on the protofilament between the start and end states. The path takes the kinesin head away from the microtubule surface in between these regions when passing through a high energy barrier.

5 DISCUSSION AND CONCLUSIONS

We have shown that motion planning methods allied to a physics-based model are successful in locating the low energy configurations in the interaction energy landscape of two macromolecules.

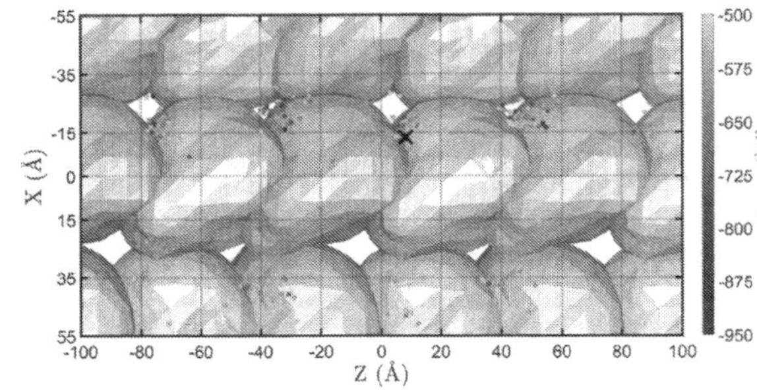

Figure 9: Low energy configurations on the microtubule surface. Each point corresponds to the position of the center of mass of the kinesin head. The black × at $x = -13.33$ Å, $z = 8.28$ Å corresponds to the position of the center of mass of the native bound state of the kinesin head. Note the periodic pattern of the location of low energy valleys, at approximately every 40 Å along the protofilament.

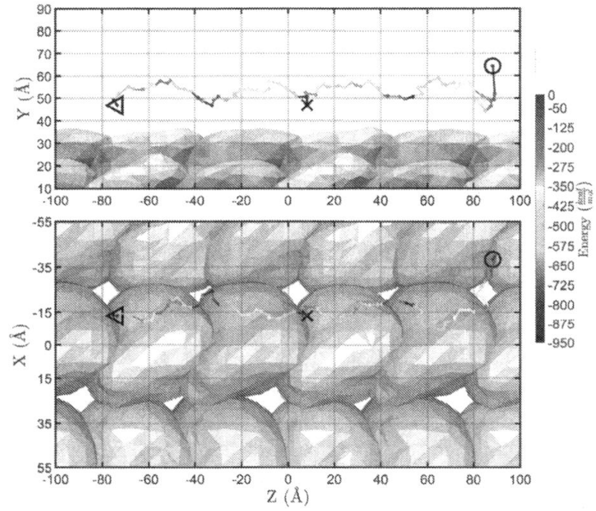

Figure 10: Two-dimensional yz (top) and xz (bottom) views of two Dijkstra runs showing lowest-weighted paths from $x = -38.31$ Å, $y = 64.33$ Å, $z = 88.44$ Å (shown as a black ∘), to a kinesin-microtubule bound state at $x = -13.33$ Å, $y = 46.76$ Å, $z = 8.28$ Å (shown as a black ×), and from this bound state (×) to a second bound state at $x = -13.33$ Å, $y = 46.76$ Å, $z = -73.52$ Å (shown as a black ◁). At the initial point, the kinesin head is far from the microtubule and the interaction energy is zero. Note that both paths visit all low energy regions along the same protofilament between the start and goal (see Figure 9 for location of low energy basins).

These locations are associated with targets for protein-protein binding. Our simulations corroborate experimental evidence that a kinesin head without nucleotides (ATP or ADP) has strong interactions with binding sites on the microtubule [9]. These strong interaction regions, the low energy basins, appear at the native binding sites, but also exist in between binding sites, showing a periodic pattern at approximately every 40 Å along each protofilament. Since the kinesin step is 8 nm in length, the appearance of these low energy states in between step locations supports the possibility of a substep. Such 4-nm substeps have been proposed in models [13] but so far they have eluded experimental detection, due to the need to observe fast time scales at high spatial resolution. However, more recent experiments have been approaching this limit, and previously undetected states of the protein during its walk have now been observed [14, 18]. Our lowest weighted Dijkstra pathways demonstrated a low energy pathway along a single protofilament. This reflects experimentally observed behavior that finds progression along a single protofilament instead of sidestepping [25]. In addition, all low energy regions along the protofilament are visited, further indicating that these low energy regions may indeed correspond to substeps. To investigate this possibility, we plan to perform a kinetic analysis to compute lifetimes of the kinesin head at the intermediate low energy regions, with longer lifetimes suggestive of metastable substep positions. The application of motion planning methods for the kinesin walk may prove particularly important when considering that the microtubule is in reality decorated with stabilizing proteins (such as tau protein), and crowded with other molecular walkers. For these situations, motion planning will enable studies of how kinesin avoids colliding with these obstacles and continues its walk by switching to an adjacent protofilament.

6 ACKNOWLEDGEMENTS

The authors are thankful to Torin Adamson for his assistance in setting up and running some of the computational models. We also thank the Center for Advanced Research Computing (CARC) at UNM for providing computational resources and support. This work is supported by the National Science Foundation (NSF) (S.R.A.) and under NSF Grant Nos. CCF-1518861, IIS-1528047, IIS-1553266 (L.T., CAREER) and National Institutes of Health Grant P50GM085273 to the New Mexico SpatioTemporal Modeling Center. Any opinion, findings, and conclusions or recommendations expressed in this material are those of the authors and do not necessarily reflect the views of the National Science Foundation.

REFERENCES

[1] Torin Adamson, John Baxter, Kasra Manavi, April Suknot, Bruna Jacobson, Patrick Gage Kelley, and Lydia Tapia. 2014. Molecular Tetris: Crowdsourcing Molecular Docking Using Path-Planning and Haptic Devices. In *Proceedings of the Seventh International Conference on Motion in Games (MIG '14)*. ACM, New York, NY, USA, 133–138. DOI: https://doi.org/10.1145/2668084.2668086

[2] Ibrahim Al-Bluwi, Thierry Siméon, and Juan Cortés. 2012. Motion planning algorithms for molecular simulations: A survey. *Computer Science Review* 6, 4 (2012), 125 – 143.

[3] Nancy M. Amato, O. Burchan Bayazit, Lucia K. Dale, Christopher Jones, and Daniel Vallejo. 1998. OBPRM: An Obstacle-Based PRM for 3D Workspaces. In *Proc. Int. Wkshp. on Alg. Found. of Rob. (WAFR)*. 155–168.

[4] O. Burchan Bayazit, Guang Song, and Nancy M. Amato. 2001. Ligand Binding with OBPRM and User Input. In *IEEE Int. Conf. on Rob. and Auto.* 954–959.

[5] Blender Online Community. 2017. *Blender - a 3D modelling and rendering package.* Blender Foundation, Blender Institute, Amsterdam. http://www.blender.org

[6] Bernard R. Brooks, Robert E. Bruccoleri, Barry D. Olafson, David J. States, S. Swaminathan, and Martin Karplus. 1983. CHARMM: A program for macromolecular energy, minimization, and dynamics calculations. *Journal of Computational Chemistry* 4, 2 (1983), 187–217.

[7] John Burkardt, John F Flanagan, Zik Saleeba, Martin van Velsen, Gert van der Spoel, Philippe Guglielmetti, and Tomasz Lis. 2014. *IVCon - a 3D graphics file converter package.* http://ivcon-tl.sourceforge.net/

[8] Luyan Cao, Weiyi Wang, Qiyang Jiang, Chunguang Wang, Marcel Knossow, and Benoît Gigant. 2014. The structure of apo-kinesin bound to tubulin links the nucleotide cycle to movement. *Nature Comm.* 5 (2014), 1–9.

[9] R.A. Cross. 2016. Review: Mechanochemistry of the kinesin-1 ATPase. *Biopolymers* 105, 8 (2016), 476–482.

[10] Warren L. DeLano. 2002. The PyMOL molecular graphics system. (2002).

[11] Barry J. Grant, Dana M. Gheorghe, Wenjun Zheng, Maria Alonso, Gary Huber, Maciej Dlugosz, J. Andrew McCammon, and Robert A. Cross. 2011. Electrostatically Biased Binding of Kinesin to Microtubules. *PLoS Biol* 9, 11 (2011), e1001207.

[12] Gregory J. Hoeprich, Andrew R. Thompson, Derrick P. McVicker, William O. Hancock, and Christopher L. Berger. 2014. Kinesin's Neck-Linker Determines Its Ability to Navigate Obstacles on the Microtubule Surface. *Biophysical Journal* 106, 8 (2014), 1691–1700.

[13] Changbong Hyeon and José N. Onuchic. 2007. Mechanical control of the directional stepping dynamics of the kinesin motor. *Proceedings of the National Academy of Sciences* 104, 44 (2007), 17382–17387.

[14] Hiroshi Isojima, Ryota Iino, Yamato Niitani, Hiroyuki Noji, and Michio Tomishige. 2016. Direct observation of intermediate states during the stepping motion of kinesin-1. *Nature Chemical Biology* (2016).

[15] Lydia E. Kavraki, Petr Švestka, Jean-Claude Latombe, and Mark H. Overmars. 1996. Probabilistic roadmaps for path planning in high-dimensional configuration spaces. *IEEE Trans. Robot. Automat.* 12, 4 (August 1996), 566–580.

[16] Lin Li, Joshua Alper, and Emil Alexov. 2016. Multiscale method for modeling binding phenomena involving large objects: application to kinesin motor domains motion along microtubules. *Scientific Reports* 6 (2016), 23249.

[17] Tatiana Maximova, Ryan Moffatt, Buyong Ma, Ruth Nussinov, and Amarda Shehu. 2016. Principles and overview of sampling methods for modeling macromolecular structure and dynamics. *PLoS Comput Biol* 12, 4 (2016), e1004619.

[18] Keith J. Mickolajczyk, Nathan C. Deffenbaugh, Jaime Ortega Arroyo, Joanna Andrecka, Philipp Kukura, and William O. Hancock. 2015. Kinetics of nucleotide-dependent structural transitions in the kinesin-1 hydrolysis cycle. *Proc. Nati. Acad. Sci. (USA)* 112, 52 (2015), E7186–E7193.

[19] Brian Olson, Kevin Molloy, and Amarda Shehu. 2011. In search of the protein native state with a probabilistic sampling approach. *Journal of Bioinformatics and Computational Biology* 9, 03 (2011), 383–398.

[20] E.F. Pettersen, T.D. Goddard, C.C. Huang, G.S. Couch, D.M. Greenblatt, E.C. Meng, and T.E. Ferrin. 2004. UCSF Chimera–A visualization system for exploratory research and analysis. *J. Comput. Chem.* 25 (October 2004), 1605–1612. Issue 13.

[21] Amarda Shehu and Erion Plaku. 2016. A survey of computational treatments of biomolecules by robotics-inspired methods modeling equilibrium structure and dynamics. *Journal of Artificial Intelligence Research* 57 (2016), 509–572.

[22] Guang Song and Nancy M. Amato. 2000. A motion planning approach to folding: from paper craft to protein folding. In *Proc. IEEE Int. Conf. Robot. Autom. (ICRA)*. 948–953.

[23] Guang Song, Shawna Thomas, Ken A. Dill, J. Martin Scholtz, and Nancy M. Amato. 2003. A path planning-based study of protein folding with a case study of hairpin formation in protein G and L. In *Proc. Pacific Symposium of Biocomputing (PSB)*. 240–251.

[24] Haixin Sui and Kenneth H. Downing. 2010. Structural basis of interprotofilament interaction and lateral deformation of microtubules. *Structure* 18, 8 (2010), 1022–1031.

[25] Karel Svoboda, Christoph F. Schmidt, Bruce J. Schnapp, and Steven M. Block. 1993. Direct observation of kinesin stepping by optical trapping interferometry. *Nature* 365, 6448 (1993), 721–727.

[26] Xinyu Tang, Shawna Thomas, Lydia Tapia, David P. Giedroc, and Nancy M. Amato. 2008. Simulating RNA folding kinetics on approximated energy landscapes. *J. Mol. Biol.* 381 (2008), 1055–1067.

[27] Lydia Tapia, Xinyu Tang, Shawna Thomas, and Nancy M. Amato. 2007. Kinetics analysis methods for approximate folding landscapes. *Bioinformatics* 23, 13 (2007), i539–i548.

[28] Ronald D. Vale, Thomas S. Reese, and Michael P. Sheetz. 1985. Identification of a novel force-generating protein, kinesin, involved in microtubule-based motility. *Cell* 42, 1 (1985), 39–50.

[29] Junmei Wang, Romain M. Wolf, James W. Caldwell, Peter A. Kollman, and David A. Case. 2004. Development and testing of a general amber force field. *Journal of Computational Chemistry* 25, 9 (2004), 1157–1174.

[30] Ahmet Yildiz, Michio Tomishige, Ronald D. Vale, and Paul R. Selvin. 2004. Kinesin walks hand-over-hand. *Science* 303, 5658 (2004), 676–678.

Gaussian Mixture Models with Constrained Flexibility for Fitting Tomographic Tilt Series

Kasra Manavi
University of New Mexico
Albuquerque, New Mexico 87131
kazaz@cs.unm.edu

Sahba Tashakkori
University of New Mexico
Albuquerque, New Mexico 87131
stashakkori@unm.edu

Lydia Tapia
University of New Mexico
Albuquerque, New Mexico 87131
tapia@cs.unm.edu

ABSTRACT

Electron Microscopy (EM) has become an invaluable part of modern structural biology. As the limits of EM techniques are explored, issues arise with model reconstruction and fitting, especially at resolutions lower than 10 Å where structural detail is lost. In this paper, we introduce methods to model and fit molecular structures into low resolution EM datasets (20-40 Å resolution). First, we use Gaussian Mixture Models (GMMs) to describe molecular systems with high flexibility and enable efficient conformation sampling. Then, GMM parameters are optimized to best describe the model molecular structure. Finally, these GMMs are placed into a fitting procedure to generate a conformation of the GMM that fits an input set of tilt series tomograms, a set of 2D images of a 3D molecule taken at a variety of angles. We evaluate our method by fitting a model of the IgE-FcϵRI complex to a variety of simulated single tilt axis datasets. This work was done in preparation for analysis of larger aggregate structures of IgE.

KEYWORDS

Molecular Structural Biology; Flexible Fitting; EM Tomography

1 INTRODUCTION

Fitting a known structure to experimentally imaged molecules is critical to understanding molecular conformations. One such tool to image molecules, Electron Microscopy (EM), has become an essential part of understanding cellular function [13]. EM is performed by preparing a sample and placing it into an electron microscope. The microscope produces an image (tomogram) of the sample. A tomogram can be thought of as a 2D image of a 3D object where the intensity of the image pixel is proportional to the density of the 3D object. Electron Tomography (ET) is a technique that utilizes a series of EM tomograms to produce a 3D reconstruction of the molecular structure. Tomograms of a sample are captured from a variety of angles and are then combined to produce a 3D density map. These tomograms can be collected in an ordered fashion (e.g., single/dual axis tilt series) or an unordered fashion (e.g., single molecule imaged in solution). EM and ET are becoming cornerstones of modern structural biology research, but several challenges remain, including model fitting and reconstruction evaluation [9].

Permission to make digital or hard copies of all or part of this work for personal or classroom use is granted without fee provided that copies are not made or distributed for profit or commercial advantage and that copies bear this notice and the full citation on the first page. Copyrights for components of this work owned by others than ACM must be honored. Abstracting with credit is permitted. To copy otherwise, or republish, to post on servers or to redistribute to lists, requires prior specific permission and/or a fee. Request permissions from permissions@acm.org.
ACMBCB '17, August 2017, Boston, MA, USA
© 2017 Association for Computing Machinery.
ACM ISBN 978-1-4503-4722-8/17/08...$15.00
https://doi.org/10.1145/3107411.3107504

Depending on the type of sample, density map reconstruction can be challenging. This step, required before an atomic model can be fit, can suffer from issues including distortions in tomogram alignment and the missing wedge problem [15]. Distortions in alignment occur when the tomograms of a dataset are clustered and aligned to produce an averaged tomogram from a given perspective. The quality of the clustering/alignment results are highly dependent on the size of the input dataset and tomogram quality. The missing wedge problem occurs during reconstruction of a tilt series, a set of projections captured by rotating the sample about an axis. If the angle range is narrow, portions of the sample are not imaged, resulting in a loss of information that elongate reconstructions.

In addition to the challenge of reconstruction, fitting structural models, typically all-atom structures, to reconstructed density maps can be difficult. Resolution of a density map is important to the type of fitting technique used. At high resolution (< 10 Å), all-atom fitting techniques work well, but lower resolutions (20-40 Å) still pose a challenge to existing methods due to a lack of detail [26]. This is particularly true for larger asymmetric molecular systems that are typically imaged at lower resolutions.

In order to address both the issues of reconstruction quality and fitting at lower resolutions, we propose a method that uses a flexible reduced-resolution molecular model for fitting directly to a series of tomograms. These tomograms depict images of a static molecular structure at a series of angles which can be efficiently fit with our GMM by comparing projections of our reduced-resolution molecular model at corresponding angles of the tomograms. In order to represent flexibility of the model that may exist in the imaged molecule, we use a multi-body GMM with constrained flexible joints. GMM fit evaluation is performed against all tomograms in the dataset, thus enabling evaluation of a conformation of the GMM against experimental data. While this method does not directly provide all-atom structures, it provides a quick assessment of the imaged molecule and the reasonableness of the conformation.

Our motivation for this approach is determination of structures of large molecular assemblies, specifically antibody/antigen aggregates critical to the understanding of the human allergic immune response. As a first step toward this goal, we focus on one component of these assemblies, the large antibody complex (IgE-FcϵRI). These molecules are potentially highly dynamic, so we are inspired by static images such as datasets captured via Cryo EM where samples are flash frozen before imaging. To evaluate our construction procedure, we generate a GMM of IgE-FcϵRI and assess how well the GMM can model a variety of datasets by optimizing parameters of the GMM. We then evaluate our fitting technique by generating a set of IgE-FcϵRI conformations under a variety of conditions and attempting to fit them to the known native conformation. We show that our GMM is flexible enough to model a variety of datasets and is capable of fitting tilt series data.

2 RELATED WORK

Projection Matching. Several computational geometry methods have been used to model volumes from projection information and vice versa [2, 17, 19, 27]. For example, the optimal packing/covering problems have been solved using Phi-functions which were developed to evaluate the interaction of geometric objects [2]. Another example is shadow art, the idea of occluding light from a source to produce an image. One such method uses light sources and a desired shadow art as input and produces a sculpture that is capable of generating the scene [17]. This work has been expanded to model shadow theater where shadow art is generated by the pose of a single or multiple performance artists [27]. Another similar method turns 2D silhouettes from different perspectives into 3D models [19].

EM and Structure Determination. Integrating comparative modeling and EM data to produce atomic models is reviewed in [25]. Fitting structures to reconstructed 3D EM data can be broken down into two main methodologies, rigid and flexible [7]. Most six degree of freedom rigid fitting is done using methods like geometric techniques [4], GMMs [12], or Zernike descriptors [6]. Flexible fitting focuses on using molecular simulation methods [14, 23], robotic motion planning techniques [1], as well as statistical techniques [5, 22] to determine candidate conformations. GMMs have been applied to other aspects of EM analysis, including reconstruction of single particles imaging [11] and structural dynamic evaluation [10].

Antibody Structure. Antibodies are immunological molecules which identify and target foreign threats to the body. Immunoglobulin (Ig) proteins have been determined to be highly flexible and can form asymmetrical structures [3, 21]. The structures obtained from X-ray diffraction analysis show that IgG is composed of three major structural subunits: two identical binding arms (Fab arms) and a membrane bound constant domain [20]. Since antibodies are known to have very flexible and dynamic structures, populations of different conformations have been found to co-exist in images [24, 28]. Therefore, commonly used methods such as X-ray crystallography, which rely on molecular averaging, often do not reflect protein dynamics and flexibility [29]. In contrast, EM can be used to reconstruct unique and independent samples [20].

3 METHODS

To generate a semi-flexible reduced resolution model of a molecular system, we start with an all-atom molecular structure. This structure is decomposed into rigid subunits, and Principal Component Analysis (PCA) is applied to these subunits to generate a GMM. Flexibility between rigid regions is added, and GMM subunits are refined to complete the model construction. This process is outlined in Figure 1. The resulting model is used to fit tomographic tilt series. In this paper, evaluation focuses on the IgE-FcϵRI complex [16]. The model was constructed using available PDB structures (1OAU, 2VWE, 1O0V, 1F6A) and is composed of 1,709 amino acids (13,477 atoms total) [16].

3.1 Model Construction

To begin model construction, we identify rigid subunits of the model by performing rigidity analysis of the all-atom model using Kinari-Web [8]. If a sequence of residues is considered flexible, we identify the rigid subunits at the termini of the flexible sequence.

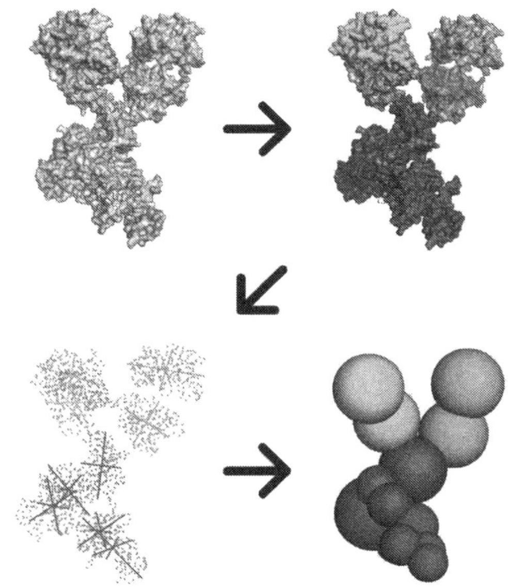

Figure 1: Process of taking an all-atom structure and generating a GMM. First, the atomic model (*top left*) is decomposed into rigid subunits (*top right*). The rigid subunits are then processed using PCA (*bottom left*). The results of PCA are then used to construct a GMM (*bottom right*).

If both ends of the sequence are associated with the same subunit, the sequence is considered a rigid part of that subunit. For our IgE model, ten rigid subunits were classified into five regions outlined in Table 1.

Structural Subunit	Chain & Residues	Region
FcϵRIα 1	A 5-84	1
FcϵRIα 2	A 88-169	1
Constant 1	H 256-355, I 256-355	1
Constant 2a	H 364-462	1
Constant 2b	I 364-462	1
Constant 3	H 469-571, I 469-571	1
Fab 1 - C terminal	H 151-247, L 140-234	2
Fab 1 - N terminal	H 21-144, L 26-127	3
Fab 2 - C terminal	I 151-247, M 140-234	4
Fab 2 - N terminal	I 21-144, M 26-127	5

Table 1: IgE-FcϵRI subunits calculated from rigidity analysis. A flexible region is considered part of a rigid region if both ends of the region are associated with the same structural subunit.

After rigid subunits have been identified, we convert the decomposed subunits into a GMM representation. This is done by performing PCA on the atom positions of each subunit structure identified by rigidity analysis decomposition (Figure 1, *bottom left*).

If the difference between the lowest and highest eigenvalues of the PCA is high, the subunit is divided. From our data we used a ratio of 1.8x or larger as a cutoff for division. For the IgE complex, subunits 1 and 2 of FcϵRIα and constant subunits 2a and 2b were split along their principle component.

Using the results of PCA, molecular subunits are converted to a GMM description with Gaussian functions centered at the subunit's mean μ with standard deviation σ set to the square root of the largest subunit eigenvalue. For each subunit, we include a σ-scaling factor to compensate for potential differences in model resolution, discussed in Section 3.2. This construction method is applied to all subunits of the IgE complex, resulting in a model composed of fourteen Gaussian functions (Figure 1, *bottom right*).

To capture flexibility that may exist between rigid subunits, we incorporate distance constraints into the GMM. Specifically, distances between GMM subunits that are linked together via non-rigid portions of the protein backbone are maintained. If a flexible region is found to connect rigid subunits during rigidity analysis, the α-carbons of the amino acids on both termini of the flexible regions are stored with their associated GMM subunit. These points are evaluated for distance when a new GMM conformation is generated. The distance must be less than $n{\cdot}d$, where n is the number of amino acids in the flexible region and d is the average distance between α-carbons. For our IgE-FcϵRI complex model, we use the average distance between the α-carbons of the flexible regions.

In the IgE complex, there are six flexible regions that connect molecular subunits. Each Fab arm is connected to the constant domain, resulting in two distance constraints. Fab arms are composed of two subunits connected together by two flexible regions, resulting in two distance constraints per arm. This results in six distance constraints total, outlined in Table 2.

Class	Subunits	Chain & Residues	Length
Arm Linker	Con 1, Fab 1C	H 248-255	8
Arm Linker	Con 1, Fab 2C	I 248-255	8
Fab Short	Fab 1C, Fab 1N	H 145-150	6
Fab Long	Fab 1C, Fab 1N	L 128-139	12
Fab Short	Fab 2C, Fab 2N	I 145-150	6
Fab Long	Fab 2C, Fab 2N	M 128-139	12

Table 2: Flexible regions between rigid antibody subunits. Con 1 represents the Constant subunit and Fab subunits are labeled "Fab *XY*", *X* being the arm index (1 or 2) and *Y* being the termini (N or C). Length is in number of residues in the flexible region.

3.2 GMM Refinement and Fitting

In this section we discuss how we refine GMM parameters to tailor our GMMs to a particular experiment (Algorithm 1). We then outline how we minimize GMM conformation to identify a best fit to the provided EM tilt series (Algorithm 2).

When tomograms and density maps are generated, various levels of image and post processing are applied to prepare the data for reconstruction/fitting. Depending on the parameterization of these processes, results can differ from experiment to experiment. This can alter the ability of the GMM to represent the data. In order to capture these differences, we introduce Algorithm 1 which performs parameter refinement, a method that produces a GMM that is tailored to a particular dataset that can also be used to fit other datasets from the same experiment.

Algorithm 1 GMM Parameter Refinement

Input. GMM model c_{init}, dataset projections P, parameter ranges R and maximum iteration count $iter_{max}$
Output. conformation c_{opt} optimized to match P

1: $c_{cur} \leftarrow c_{init}$
2: $o_{cur} \leftarrow EvalOverlap(c_{cur}, P)$
3: **for** $iter = 0$; $iter \leq iter_{max}$; $iter{+}{+}$ **do**
4: $\quad v_{cur} \leftarrow EvalParams(c_{cur}, R, o_{cur})$
5: $\quad c_{cur} \leftarrow UpdateParams(c_{cur}, v_{cur})$
6: $\quad o_{cur} \leftarrow EvalOverlap(c_{cur}, P)$
7: **end for**
8: $c_{opt} \leftarrow c_{cur}$

To generate a GMM specific to a given dataset, each parameter of the GMM needs to be optimized (positions and σ-scales) with respect to the input dataset. Parameter refinement begins with evaluating the initial GMM quality (line 2). To determine the quality of the match between a conformation and a dataset, we compare projections of the GMM and dataset from the same perspective. Projections are generated and compared as seen in Figure 2. Corresponding pixel values of the projections are evaluated using the OR and XOR operators. The OR operator provides us with the number of pixels in the projections occupied by both the GMM (u) and the part of the dataset visualized as the non-black pixels in the last row of Figure 2. The XOR operator provides us with the number of pixels that are occupied by either GMM or dataset but not both (x), representing the differences in projections (red and blue pixels in the last row of Figure 2). The overlap score is the proportion of pixels that overlap in the union, $((u - x) / u)$.

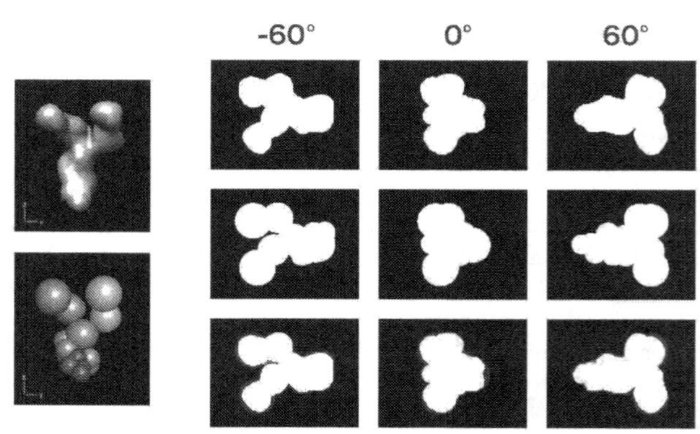

Figure 2: Comparison of tilt series to evaluate overlap score. Molecular data (*top left*) and GMM (*bottom left*) orthogonally projected at angles {-60,0,60} (*top/middle rows, right*). Projections from the same perspective are overlaid and evaluated for OR and XOR (*bottom row, right*).

To perform GMM parameter refinement, we use a binary search scheme over a range of values (R) centered at the initial parameter values of the input GMM (C_{init}). For each iteration, every parameter is evaluated for overlap score at 3 values, at the upper and lower bounds of the range and the middle (line 4). The overlap scores are compared and the parameter values with the highest overlap scores are used to update the saved values and the ranges for the next iteration (line 5). The process is iterated for a specified number of times ($iter_{max}$), and the resulting GMM parameter values are returned.

Algorithm 2 GMM conformation Fitting

Input. GMM model conformation c_{init} and tilt series projections t, maximum iteration count $iter_{max}$, window averaging width w and local minima detection interval i

Output. conformation c_{min} that is the best fit of t

1: $c_{cur} \leftarrow c_{init}$
2: $c_{best} \leftarrow c_{cur}$
3: $so_{cur} \leftarrow EvalSubOverlap(c_{cur})$
4: $so_{best} \leftarrow so_{cur}$
5: **for** $iter = 0; iter \leq iter_{max}; iter{+}{+}$ **do**
6: $\quad c_{new} \leftarrow UpdateGMM(c_{cur}, t)$
7: $\quad IsCollisionFree \leftarrow CollisionResolution(C_{new})$
8: $\quad IsDCSatisfied \leftarrow DCSatisfaction(c_{new})$
9: $\quad$**if** $InLocalMin(w, i)$ **then**
10: $\quad\quad c_{cur} \leftarrow Resample(c_{new})$
11: $\quad$**else**
12: $\quad\quad$**if** $!IsCollisionFree \,||\, !IsDCSatisfied$ **then**
13: $\quad\quad\quad c_{cur} \leftarrow Resample(c_{new})$
14: $\quad\quad$**else**
15: $\quad\quad\quad c_{cur} = c_{new}$
16: $\quad\quad$**end if**
17: $\quad$**end if**
18: $\quad so_{cur} = EvalSubOverlap(c_{cur})$
19: $\quad$**if** $EvalNewMax(so_{cur}, so_{best}) == True$ **then**
20: $\quad\quad c_{best} = c_{cur}$
21: $\quad\quad so_{best} \leftarrow so_{cur}$
22: $\quad$**end if**
23: **end for**

At this point, we have a GMM for fitting a tilt series. Our procedure for conformational fitting is described in Algorithm 2. To begin fitting, we start by generating a GMM conformation to fit. Preparation of the initial GMM conformation for minimization can be performed using a variety of methods including rigid body fitting, user specified conformations, or using a sampling-based methods. For the IgE-FcϵRI-complex, we evaluate the procedure with an analysis of minimizing a wide variety of initial GMM conformations. We evaluate and score the fit of a given conformation directly to the tilt series by generating projections of our GMM conformation and individual subunits and compare the projections to their tilt series counterpart (line 3).

The overlap scores of the individual subunits are stored to a list used to monitor minimization progress. For each iteration, we evaluate changes in overlap score for each subunit. At a given positional resolution, all subunits are translated each axis in both directions (6 evaluations total) and overlap scores are calculated. If necessary, i.e., for evaluating a multi-component subunit, orientation is evaluated in a similar fashion to positions using rotation. The results of position and orientation evaluation are used to generate a new conformation c_{new} (line 6). The new conformation is resolved of any collisions and evaluated for distance constraint satisfaction.

To avoid getting stuck in local minima, we monitor the progress of the score throughout the minimization process. We do this by calculating the current average overlap score by averaging the last w overlap scores of the minimization. We evaluate progress by adding the current average overlap score to the list of previously averaged overlap scores and calculate the differences between consecutive average scores (deltas). If the most recent delta values of the local minima interval, i, are less than or equal to zero, the conformation is considered to be in a local minima (line 9) and is resampled. For resampling, individual subunit overlap scores are evaluated and the worst performing subunit is resampled. If the new conformation is not considered in a local minima, the new sample c_{new} is validated (line 12). If c_{new} is collision free and satisfies all distance constraints, it is assigned to c_{cur}. If not, the conformation is resampled.

Once a new conformation is generated, c_{cur} is updated and compared to the current best conformation and is stored if the overlap score is better (lines 18-21). The best scoring conformation is returned.

4 EXPERIMENTS

4.1 GMM Parameter Refinement

To evaluate whether or not our GMM model is robust enough to fit datasets of varying quality, we refine the parameters of our GMM to a variety of tilt series collected from simulated density maps of the native conformation of IgE-FcϵRI. Density maps were generated at three resolutions (20, 30, and 40 Å) using the molecular modeling software Chimera [18]. Density maps are rendered at a specified isolevel, producing an image of the surface of a density map that has been thresholded at the isolevel value. Higher isolevel values render surfaces that represent higher density volumes in the map. For lower isolevel values, the surface is typically larger since the lower threshold results in an increase of volume to render. As mentioned previously, values can vary between density maps so isolevel values for rendering are evaluated empirically on a per dataset basis. For our evaluation, the maps were rendered at two isolevel values (0.09 and 0.06), resulting in six datasets.

To generate projections for GMM parameter refinement, we rotate our sample molecule along the X and Y axis (dual-axis). Rotations about the X axis were generated over 180° in 10° intervals (18 angles total). Rotations about the Y axis were generated over 360° in 10° intervals (36 angles total). All combinations of X and Y angle values are evaluated, resulting in a total of 648 projections.

For our experiments, two rounds of ten iterations refinement were used (Algorithm 1). The first round started with an initial conformation, and the second started with the results of the first round (Figure 3). We observed that two rounds of refinement provided an exceptional increase in model quality, but more rounds did not significantly improve the result.

From the results, GMM is able to model a variety of density maps and isosurface values well. Overlap scores of the initial GMM range from ~70-85% to the different datasets. After refinement, our six different datasets all produced GMM parameters with overlap scores between 91% and 95%, Figure 3. This increase in overlap

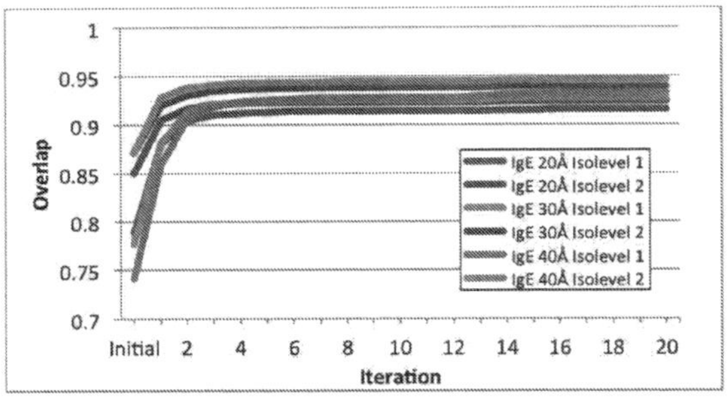

Figure 3: Refinement of the IgE-FcϵRI complex GMM parameters. Score (Y-axis) is shown over multiple iterations (X-axis) for two rounds of optimization.

shows how robust our GMM can be in dealing with various EM datasets and that we can produce GMMs tailored to fit particular datasets.

4.2 GMM Tilt Series Fitting

In this section we present results on tilt series fitting using our GMM and density map projections. We use single axis projection sets where rotation is performed about the Y-axis. We evaluate datasets generated from three angle ranges [-45°, 45°], [-60°, 60°] and [-90°, 90°]. These represent 90°, 120° and 180° of total range, respectively. We used the 30 Å density map of our default antibody conformation rendered at an isosurface value of 0.09 to generate our projections. Collision was detected using a σ-scale value of 1.5 and a distance of 3.5 Å was used as D, the distance-per-residue for distance constraints. Positional and orientation resolutions values were 1.0 Å and 1.0°, respectively. Fifty runs of each experiment were performed.

To evaluate our method, we fit GMM conformations to tilt series of the native state density map. We setup three conditions to model potential variation in the initial base position. Each condition allows a different amount of angle change in the base position. In the first condition, (No Change), we leave the IgE-FcϵRI complex base alone and just sample the Fab arms. This is considered the condition with the highest quality start states. In the second condition (Small), we randomly sample the IgE-FcϵRI complex base along the Y and Z axes within an angle range of [-30°, 30°] and then sample the Fab arms. The final condition (Large) is the same as the second but the angle range is [-60°, 60°] and models the condition with the lowest quality start states.

To determine the quality of the fitting, we used a scoring scheme to quantify the fit given subunit positions. The Root Mean Squared Distance (RMSD) of each GMM subunit is calculated, and a cutoff value of 8.0 Å (determined from subunit RMSD distributions) is used to determine if a given subunit is properly placed. Average RMSD values are reported in Table 3 and the number of properly located subunits is shown in Figure 4.

Table 3 demonstrates that as total angle range increases, RMSD decreases. Greater visibility, as provided by a larger number and range of tomograms, improves fitting quality. We see this trend in all conditions of the starting conformation. We also observe that starting condition does have an impact on fit quality. Sampling the base with no angle change performs the best and as base sampling range increases the fit is worse.

For the smallest total angle range of 90° (Fig 4a), we see that only a small number of conformations (~17%) produced place more than half of their subunits in the correct location. Figure 4b demonstrates that increasing the angle range to 120° increases overall

Tilt Series	No Change	Small	Large
90°	51.45 ± 22.26	57.56 ± 27.24	63.36 ± 27.41
120°	45.86 ± 19.69	54.83 ± 26.59	56.60 ± 23.81
180°	23.53 ± 12.27	26.58 ± 12.78	38.17 ± 22.36

Table 3: Average RMSD (Å) with variance of the fitted GMM conformations to the native GMM conformation. Rows are angle range of the tilt series and the average RMSD values for different starting conditions.

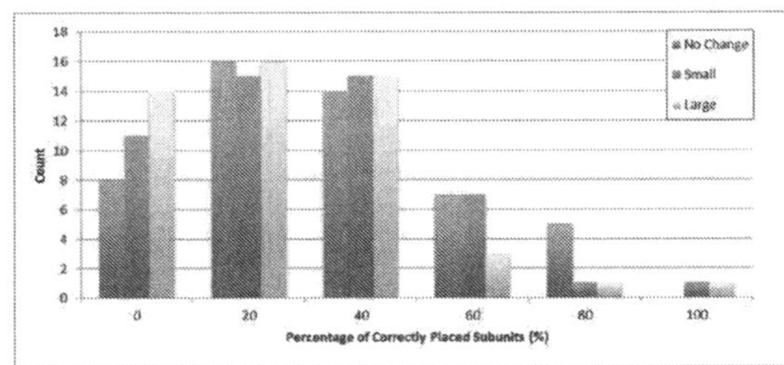

(a) 90° Angle Range

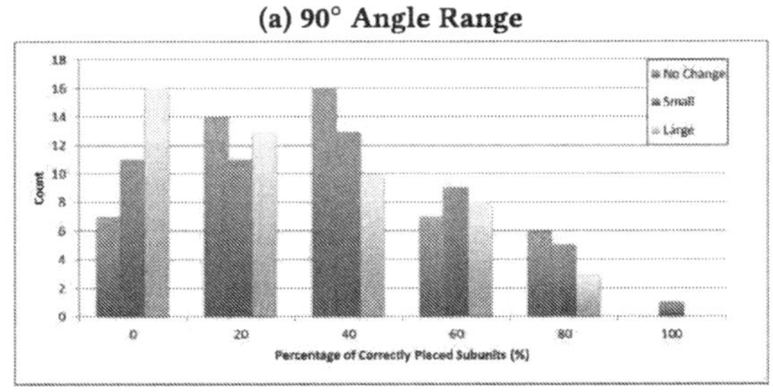

(b) 120° Angle Range

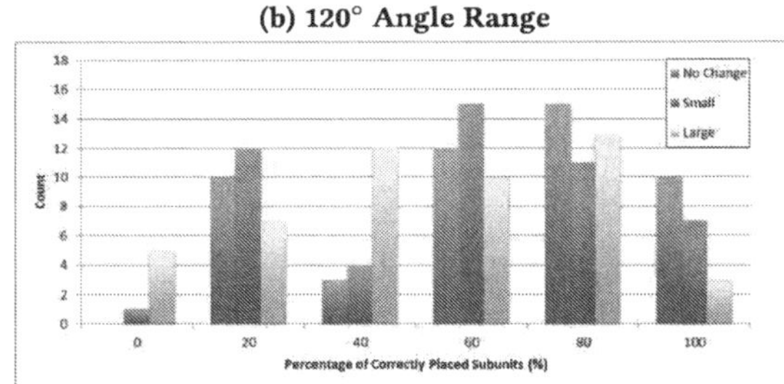

(c) 180° Angle Range

Figure 4: Evaluation of correctly placed subunits for three experiments with different angle ranges. The number of generated conformations (Y-axis) is plotted versus percentage of correctly placed subunits (X-axis). No Change, Small, and Large represent the amount of variation in the position of the base.

conformation quality. This is observed in the increase of conformations with correctly placed subunits, where ~26% of results placed more than half of the subunits correctly. This trend is continued in Figure 4c where the largest angle range of 180° produces the largest percentage of correctly positioned conformations (~64%). Of these correct conformations, about 13% have all subunits in the structure correctly positioned.

5 DISCUSSION AND CONCLUSION

In this paper, we presented a method for flexible fitting of GMM models to projections from tilt series. We performed this by generating a GMM representation of atomic models of the IgE-FcϵRI complex. We showed that our GMM can represent a range of tomogram resolutions. We also showed that the our GMM parameters can be refined to be compatible with a wide array of datasets. We then used our GMM to fit tilt series projections directly and evaluated our method's ability to perform flexible fitting. From our fitting results, we are able to see that the minimization scheme we implemented works better with more information and performs better when the initial conformation is closer to the conformation described by the tilt series. For future work, our goal is to work with our experimental collaborators who produce cryo EM tilt series and begin fitting their datasets.

ACKNOWLEDGMENTS

This work was supported in part by the National Science Foundation (NSF) under Grant Numbers IIS-1528047, IIS-1553266 (Tapia, CAREER), and CCF-1518861 and by National Institutes of Health Grant P50GM085273 to the New Mexico SpatioTemporal Modeling Center. The authors would like to thank the University of New Mexico Center for Advanced Research Computing for the computational resources they provided, as well as Bridget Wilson and Niels Volkmann for their discussions and input.

REFERENCES

[1] Kamal Al Nasr and Jing He. 2009. An Effective Convergence Independent Loop Closure Method Using Forward Backward Cyclic Coordinate Descent. *International Journal of Data Mining and Bioinformatics* 3, 3 (2009), 346–361.

[2] J. Bennell, G. Scheithauer, Y. Stoyan, and T. Romanova. 2010. Tools of mathematical modeling of arbitrary object packing problems. *Annals of Operations Research* 179, 1 (2010), 343–368.

[3] L Bongini, D Fanelli, F Piazza, P De Los Rios, S Sandin, and U Skoglund. 2005. Dynamics of antibodies from cryo-electron tomography. *Biophysical Chemistry* 115, 2 (2005), 235–240.

[4] Pablo Chacón and Willy Wriggers. 2002. Multi-resolution contour-based fitting of macromolecular structures. *Journal of Molecular Biology* 317, 3 (2002), 375–384.

[5] Pilar Cossio and Gerhard Hummer. 2013. Bayesian analysis of individual electron microscopy images: Towards structures of dynamic and heterogeneous biomolecular assemblies. *Journal of Structural Biology* 184, 3 (2013), 427 – 437.

[6] Juan Esquivel-Rodríguez and Daisuke Kihara. 2012. Fitting Multimeric Protein Complexes into Electron Microscopy Maps Using 3D Zernike Descriptors. *The Journal of Physical Chemistry B* 116, 23 (2012), 6854–6861.

[7] Juan Esquivel-Rodríguez and Daisuke Kihara. 2013. Computational methods for constructing protein structure models from 3D electron microscopy maps. *Journal of Structural Biology* 184, 1 (2013), 93–102.

[8] Naomi Fox, Filip Jagodzinski, Yang Li, and Ileana Streinu. 2011. KINARI-Web: a server for protein rigidity analysis. *Nucleic acids research* 39, suppl 2 (2011), W177–W183.

[9] Richard Henderson, Andrej Sali, Matthew L Baker, Bridget Carragher, Batsal Devkota, Kenneth H Downing, Edward H Egelman, Zukang Feng, Joachim Frank, Nikolaus Grigorieff, and others. 2012. Outcome of the first electron microscopy validation task force meeting. *Structure* 20, 2 (2012), 205–214.

[10] Slavica Jonić and Carlos Óscar Sánchez Sorzano. 2016. Coarse-graining of volumes for modeling of structure and dynamics in electron microscopy: Algorithm to automatically control accuracy of approximation. *IEEE Journal of Selected Topics in Signal Processing* 10, 1 (2016), 161–173.

[11] Paul Joubert and Michael Habeck. 2015. Bayesian inference of initial models in cryo-electron microscopy using pseudo-atoms. *Biophysical Journal* 108, 5 (2015), 1165–1175.

[12] Takeshi Kawabata. 2008. Multiple Subunit Fitting into a Low-Resolution Density Map of a Macromolecular Complex Using a Gaussian Mixture Model. *Biophysical Journal* 95, 10 (2008), 4643 – 4658.

[13] Catherine L. Lawson, Matthew L. Baker, Christoph Best, Chunxiao Bi, Matthew Dougherty, Powei Feng, Glen van Ginkel, Batsal Devkota, Ingvar Lagerstedt, Steven J. Ludtke, Richard H. Newman, Tom J. Oldfield, Ian Rees, Gaurav Sahni, Raul Sala, Sameer Velankar, Joe Warren, John D. Westbrook, Kim Henrick, Gerard J. Kleywegt, Helen M. Berman, and Wah Chiu. 2011. EMDataBank.org: unified data resource for CryoEM. *Nucleic Acids Research* 39 (2011), D456 – D464.

[14] Steffen Lindert, Nathan Alexander, Nils Wötzel, Mert Karakaş, Phoebe L. Stewart, and Jens Meiler. 2012. EM-Fold: De Novo Atomic-Detail Protein Structure Determination from Medium-Resolution Density Maps. *Structure* 20, 3 (2012), 464 – 478.

[15] Vladan Lučić, Friedrich Förster, and Wolfgang Baumeister. 2005. Structural studies by electron tomography: from cells to molecules. *Annu. Rev. Biochem.* 74 (2005), 833–865.

[16] Avanika Mahajan, Dipak Barua, Patrick Cutler, Diane S. Lidke, Flor A. Espinoza, Carolyn Pehlke, Rachel Grattan, Yuko Kawakami, Chang-Shung Tung, Andrew R. M. Bradbury, William S. Hlavacek, and Bridget S. Wilson. 2014. Optimal Aggregation of FcϵRI with a Structurally Defined Trivalent Ligand Overrides Negative Regulation Driven by Phosphatases. *ACS Chemical Biology* 9, 7 (2014), 1508–1519.

[17] Niloy J. Mitra and Mark Pauly. 2009. Shadow Art. *ACM Trans. Graph.* 28, 5 (Dec. 2009), 156:1–156:7.

[18] Eric F. Pettersen, Thomas D. Goddard, Conrad C. Huang, Gregory S. Couch, Daniel M. Greenblatt, Elaine C. Meng, and Thomas E. Ferrin. 2004. UCSF Chimera–A visualization system for exploratory research and analysis. *Journal of Computational Chemistry* 25, 13 (2004), 1605–1612.

[19] Alec Rivers, Frédo Durand, and Takeo Igarashi. 2010. 3D Modeling with Silhouettes. *ACM Trans. Graph.* 29, 4 (2010), 109:1–109:8.

[20] Sara Sandin, Lars-Göran Öfverstedt, Ann-Charlotte Wikström, Örjan Wrange, and Ulf Skoglund. 2004. Structure and flexibility of individual immunoglobulin G molecules in solution. *Structure* 12, 3 (2004), 409–415.

[21] Erica Ollmann Saphire, Robyn L Stanfield, MD Max Crispin, Paul WHI Parren, Pauline M Rudd, Raymond A Dwek, Dennis R Burton, and Ian A Wilson. 2002. Contrasting IgG structures reveal extreme asymmetry and flexibility. *Journal of Molecular Biology* 319, 1 (2002), 9–18.

[22] Sjors H.W. Scheres. 2012. RELION: Implementation of a Bayesian approach to cryo-EM structure determination. *Journal of Structural Biology* 180, 3 (2012), 519 – 530.

[23] Gunnar F. Schröder, Axel T. Brunger, and Michael Levitt. 2007. Combining Efficient Conformational Sampling with a Deformable Elastic Network Model Facilitates Structure Refinement at Low Resolution. *Structure* 15, 12 (2007), 1630 – 1641.

[24] Huimin Tong, Lei Zhang, Allan Kaspar, Matthew J Rames, Liqing Huang, Gary Woodnutt, and Gang Ren. 2013. Peptide-conjugation induced conformational changes in human IgG1 observed by optimized negative-staining and individual-particle electron tomography. *Scientific Reports* 3 (2013), 1089:1–1089:9.

[25] Maya Topf and Andrej Sali. 2005. Combining electron microscopy and comparative protein structure modeling. *Current Opinion in Structural Biology* 15, 5 (2005), 578 – 585.

[26] Elizabeth Villa and Keren Lasker. 2014. Finding the right fit: chiseling structures out of cryo-electron microscopy maps. *Current Opinion in Structural Biology* 25 (2014), 118–125.

[27] Jungdam Won and Jehee Lee. 2016. Shadow Theatre: Discovering Human Motion from a Sequence of Silhouettes. *ACM Trans. Graph.* 35, 4 (July 2016), 147:1–147:12.

[28] Lei Zhang and Gang Ren. 2012. IPET and FETR: Experimental Approach for Studying Molecular Structure Dynamics by Cryo-Electron Tomography of a Single-Molecule Structure. *PLOS ONE* 7, 1 (2012), 1–19.

[29] Xing Zhang, Lei Zhang, Huimin Tong, Bo Peng, Matthew J Rames, Shengli Zhang, and Gang Ren. 2015. 3D structural fluctuation of IgG1 antibody revealed by individual particle electron tomography. *Scientific Reports* 5 (2015), 9803:1–9803:13.

Geometry Analysis for Protein Secondary Structures Matching Problem

Kamal Al Nasr*
Department of Computer Science, Tennessee State University, Nashville, TN 37209
kalnasr@tnstate.edu

Feras Yousef
Department of Mathematics, The University of Jordan, Amman 11942, Jordan
fyousef@ju.edu.jo

Christopher Jones
Department of Computer Science, Tennessee State University, Nashville, TN 37209
cjone141@my.tnstate.edu

Ruba Jebril
Department of Computer Science, Tennessee State University, Nashville, TN 37209
rjebril@my.tnstate.edu

ABSTRACT

De novo modeling is a promising computational approach to model the structure of proteins using Cryo-Electron Microscopy data. Not all data produced is within a resolution that enables us to visualize the atomic-structure of the molecule. However, information like secondary structure locations is detectable. At an intermediate step in *de novo* modeling, the matching between these locations and the amino acid sequence segments that underlie these secondary structure elements needs to be addressed. Many tools have been developed to address this matching problem including DP-TOSS. In this paper, we propose a recast of DP-TOSS that incorporates a geometry-based analytical function to improve accuracy. A test of 15 proteins shows that our analytical function has a positive impact on the accuracy of DP-TOSS.

KEYWORDS

Cryo-EM; Protein Secondary Structure Elements; Geometry Analysis; Protein Geometry

1 INTRODUCTION

Three-dimensional (3D) structural information of biological systems such as proteins, macromolecular assemblies, and protein inhibitor complexes is crucial to understanding structure-function relationships. To date, the gap between the number of known protein sequences and the determined structures is astronomical. The main three biophysics techniques used to determine the structure of proteins are X-ray crystallography, Nuclear Magnetic Resonance (NMR), and Cryo-Electron Microscopy (cryo-EM). Although X-ray crystallography and NMR are the dominant techniques for protein structure determination, they suffer from numerous limitations [1-3]. Among these limitations are the required amount of the sample, non-crystallization, and the stability of the structures. These limitations become troublesome for macromolecule machines and some protein molecules such as viral capsids, ribosomes, and membrane proteins. In contrast, cryo-EM has proved to be a powerful biophysics technique that is capable of imaging the macromolecular machines in their native environment. Further, it does not suffer from the crystallization problem. Therefore, it can determine the structure of protein types that are hard to resolve using conventional methods. These difficult to image proteins, such as membrane bound proteins account for nearly 50% of contemporary drug targets. In addition, cryo-EM is expected to be the main workhorse to capture the molecular interaction between large complexes within cells [4, 5]. Cryo-EM produces volumetric images in which most are at sub/nanometer resolution (>5Å). It is challenging to determine atomic structures from images generated at sub/nanometer resolution using current technologies. In addition, the number of prospective sub/nanometer cryo-EM images is rapidly growing with the greatly improved detectors that are now available. Therefore, computational methods are critically important to address this significant problem. The development of powerful and automatic computational methods would greatly advance the role of cryo-EM as a complement to traditional diffraction methods.

The computational methods used to model the 3D structure of proteins can be divided into three classes: *ab initio*, comparative, and *de novo* modeling techniques. When the target protein molecule adopts a similar structure to that of an experimentally determined molecule, comparative modeling can be used [6-8]. The existence of an appropriate template (i.e., a pre-determined protein molecule) is crucial for the success of this modeling method. Otherwise, *ab initio* modeling is used. The *ab initio* approach models the structure of the target protein molecule using its sequence. Most *ab initio* methods use knowledge-based and physics-based potentials that may govern protein folding to guide the modeling process [9-11]. Due to the difficulty of the problem

*Corresponding author

Permission to make digital or hard copies of all or part of this work for personal or classroom use is granted without fee provided that copies are not made or distributed for profit or commercial advantage and that copies bear this notice and the full citation on the first page.
Copyrights for components of this work owned by others than the author(s) must be honored. Abstracting with credit is permitted. To copy otherwise, or republish, to post on servers or to redistribute to lists, requires prior specific permission and/or a fee. Request permissions from Permissions@acm.org.
ACM-BCB '17, August 20-23, 2017, Boston, MA, USA.
© 2017 Copyright is held by the owner/author(s). Publication rights licensed to ACM.
ACM ISBN 978-1-4503-4722-8/17/08...$15.00
DOI: http://dx.doi.org/10.1145/3107411.3107505

and the astronomical size of the search space, *ab initio* methods are restricted to small protein molecules. A third approach, called *de novo*, is to use the images produced by cryo-EM to model the structure of the protein. The huge size of the images, structural details to consider, and the computational costs are still challenges which must be overcome.

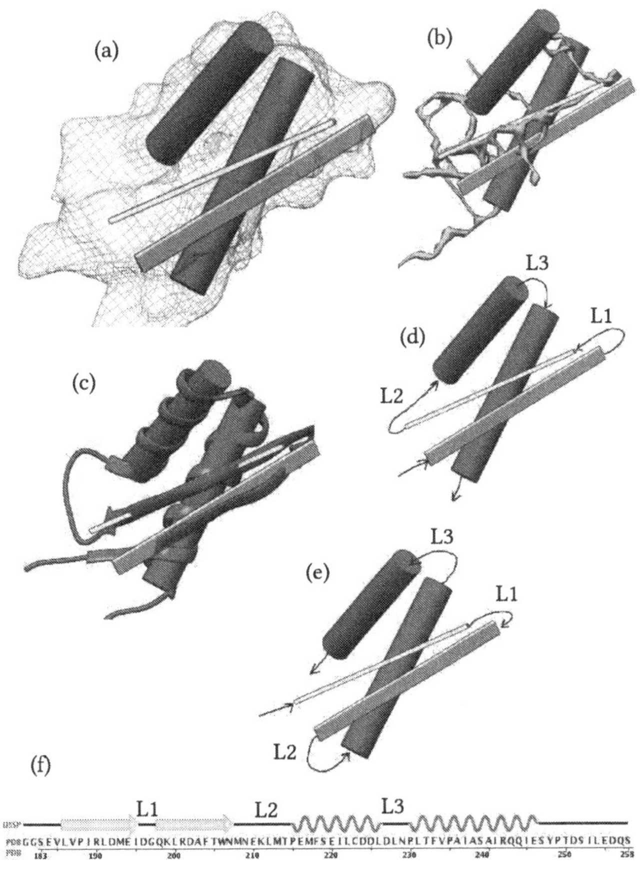

Figure 1: An example of topology determination problem. a) the cryo-EM density map and the extracted SSEs-V for protein 5L7B (PDB ID). b) the skeleton and the SSEs-V are superimposed. The skeleton is usually used to visualize the connections between the SSEs-V. c) the native structure is overlaid with the SSEs-V to show the correct topology. d) a schematic representation of the correct topology. e) a schematic representation of one example of wrong topologies. f) the sequence of the protein and its DSSP showing the SSEs-S.

Many *de novo* modeling approaches have been proposed [12-18]. Wu et al. [17] used a geometry filter followed by an energetics-based evaluation. The energy evaluation is carried out by a knowledge-based pair-wise potential function to evaluate fold candidates. One drawback of their work is the time required to accomplish the search process. It is not suitable for medium or large proteins. Baker et al. [12, 18] have used Gorgon in a semi-automatic approach to build the structures of the molecules. Gorgon [12] solves the topology determination problem first and then, with user intervention, the model of the molecule is built. The modeling process greatly depends on user-system interaction and is not automatic. Further, the systems is shown to be insufficient with large molecules [19, 20]. Lindert et al. [13, 14] proposed a *de novo* folding approach called EM-Fold. EM-Fold uses a Monte Carlo sampling to address the topology problem. A Monte Carlo refinement process is then used to improve the placement of secondary structure elements (SSEs). In a subsequent step, the loops and side chains are added by Rosetta's iterative side-chain repacking and backbone reconstruction protocols which generate a model at atomic resolution [21]. Although this method can work with a large solution space, the stochastic nature of the approach may miss the packing of the protein.

At sub/nanometer resolution range, the atomic structure of the protein cannot be derived directly from the volumetric image. In contrast, the spatial description of some features is visible. For instance, the location and the orientation of major secondary structure elements on the image (SSEs-V) such as helices and β-strands are detectable (Fig. 1) [22-26]. On the other hand, the locations of the secondary structures from the sequence of the protein (SSEs-S) are predictable with accuracy around 80% [27, 28]. An early step in *de novo* modeling is to find the correct matching between SSEs-V and SSEs-S. The order and the direction of assigning the SSEs-S to SSEs-V is called protein topology determination. Topology determination is challenging and is proven to be NP-Hard [29]. The total number of possible topologies is $\binom{M_\alpha}{N_\alpha} N_\alpha!\, 2^{N_\alpha} \binom{M_\beta}{N_\beta} N_\beta!\, 2^{N_\beta}$, where N_α is the number of helical SSEs-V, M_α is the number of helical SSEs-S, N_β is the number of β-strands SSEs-V, M_β is the number of β-strands SSEs-S, and M_α and M_β are assumed to be equal or larger than N_α and N_β respectively. To construct the backbone of the protein, the correct topology of the SSEs has to be determined first and then the backbone of the protein can be modeled for further optimization [13, 14, 30, 31]. Due to factors such as the resolution of the image and the inaccuracy of detecting SSEs-V and SSEs-S, some *de novo* methods find top topologies and then evaluate the constructed models [12, 30]. Few approaches have been attempted to address the topology problem of the SSEs [12, 13, 32]. One approach uses Gorgon to find the topology [12, 13, 17, 32]. Another approach uses geometry and energetic-based screening [17]. Recently, a version of a dynamic programming algorithm, called DP-TOSS, which finds the best-K topologies has been proposed [20, 29]. DP-TOSS translates the problem into a constraint graph problem and find the topologies using a dynamic programming algorithm. DP-TOSS uses the skeleton of the cryo-EM image to discover the connections of SSEs-V and, therefore, finds the topology of the protein. In this paper, we propose a recast to the scoring function used by DP-TOSS. The recast is based on a geometry analysis carried on protein crystal structures similar to the one used in [17]. The new finding will be incorporated with the current method used in DP-TOSS to determine the topology of protein's secondary structures.

2 METHODS AND APPROACHES

2.1 Definitions and Notations

The topology determination problem relies on two sources of information. One source contains the detected SSEs-V, such as helix and strand sticks, from the volumetric image (Fig. 1 (a)). The other source contains the SSEs-S (Fig. 1 (f)). Let $SQ_i, i = 1,2,3, \ldots, M_H + M_\beta$ be the segments of amino acid sequence for the helices and β-strands of a protein. Due to the linear nature of the protein sequence, the sequence segments have a fixed order $(SQ_1, SQ_2, \ldots, SQ_{M_H+M_\beta})$. Let $\{D_1, D_2, \ldots, D_{N_H+N_\beta}\}$ be the set of sticks detected from cryo-EM image. In the context of this paper, we assume $M_x > N_x$, where x is H or β, although vice versa is possible. The topology determination problem can be described as a problem to find a permutation γ of $\{1,2, \ldots, N_H + N_\beta\}$ such that assigning SQ_i to $D_{\gamma(i)}, i = 1,2, \ldots, N_H + N_\beta$ matches the native topology of the protein. In the assignment, each SQ_i is assigned to $D_{\gamma(i)}$ in one of the two opposite directions. The total number of possible topologies is $\binom{M}{N} N!\, 2^N$.

We use a weighted directed layered-graph G_{TOP} to address the topology determination problem introduced in DP-TOSS [20]. For details, we refer the reader to [29] and [20]. We briefly outline the main idea of the graph approach here. The number of regular nodes in the graph is $M \times N \times 2$, where M is the number of the SSEs-S and N is the number of the SSEs-V. Each node represents one possible assignment between one SSE-S and one SSE-V in a specific direction. For example, a node (i, j, t) denotes an assignment of sequence segment SQ_i to stick D_j in t direction and a node (i, j, t') denotes the same assignment in the other direction (Fig, 2). Two special nodes $START$ and END are added.

A path in G_{TOP} begins at $START$ node and ends at END node. When approached in this manner the problem of enumerating the best topologies becomes the problem of enumerating the best paths. Not every path is a valid. For example, those paths that visit the same column more than once are not valid paths, since no stick of the SSEs-V can be assigned to multiple sequence segments. An example of a valid path is shown in magenta thick lines and a non-valid path is shown in red dashed lines (Fig. 2). Ideally, the shortest path will represent the true topology of SSEs. However, due to the inaccuracy in the prediction of the SSEs-S and/or detection of the SSEs-V, the true topology is expected to be near the top shortest topologies. The edge weights in the graph are assigned by tracing the skeleton. For any possible edge, the weight of the edge is the absolute difference between the virtual length of the loop that is connecting the SSEs-S and the virtual length of the trace detected on the skeleton that is connecting the SSEs-V. The edge is impossible with weight=∞, if the virtual length of the loop is shorter than the Euclidean distance between the two ends of the assigned SSEs-V. The virtual length of the loop is calculated by multiplying the number of amino acids and 3.8Å (the distance between any two consecutive Cα atoms in an extended structure). The running time complexity of the algorithm to find the shortest valid path in the topology graph is $O(D^2 N^2 2^N)$, where $D = M - N$, M is the number of the SSEs-S, N is the number of the SSEs-V, and $M \geq N$.

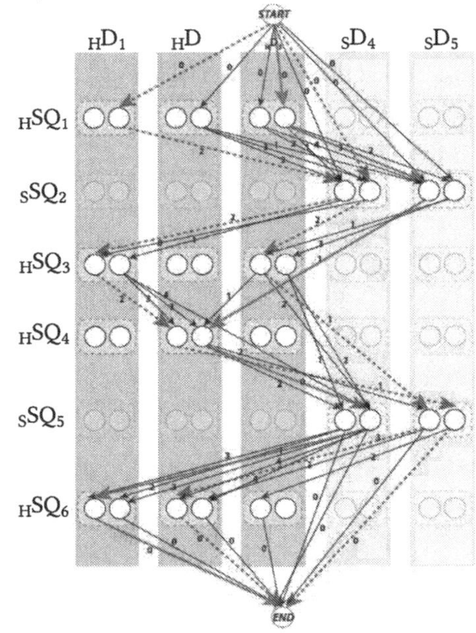

Figure 2: An example of a topology graph. The weights were restricted to integers to save the space in drawing. Rows are SSEs-S and columns are the SSEs-V. Each shaded column can be assigned in either of two possible directions. Blue columns are helical SSEs-V and can only be assigned to helical SSEs-S. Green columns are β-strand SSEs-V and can only be assigned to a β-strand SSEs-S. Two examples of invalid paths are shown in red dashed lines. The shortest path is shown in magenta solid lines. The transparent nodes are nodes that are invalid where the sequence segment is assigned to a stick of different type. Only possible edges are shown.

2.2 Geometry Analysis

In this paper, we propose an update to the current scoring function used in DP-TOSS. The revised scoring function is based on an analysis performed on a total of 110,120 loop structures extracted from a database of 4,006 protein structures obtained from protein database (PDB) based on cullpdb_pc20_res2.0_R0.25 PISCES's list [33]. Three vectors were defined as shown in Fig. 3(a) to describe the packing of a loop and its neighboring SSEs. Two vectors to describe the geometry of the SSEs and one vector to describe the geometry of the connecting loop, V_1, V_3 and V_2 respectively. V_1 and V_3 can be any secondary structures, helices or strands. For helices, the vector is defined by the two points calculated from the center mass of the first and last triangle that is calculated by the backbone atoms (N, Cα, C) of the first and last amino acid respectively. The Cα atom of the first and last amino acids defines the vector of a β-strand. The end of the first SSE and the start of the second SSE define Loop vector, V_2. Any packing that is missing any of the atom's coordinate involved in calculating any one of the vectors was excluded. Two packing angles were defined, dihedral angle φ and packing angles η such that $\eta = \theta_1 + \theta_2$. The normal quantile–quantile plots, shown in Fig. 3(b), show that our data were approximately normally distributed for the dihedral angle φ (Fig. 3(c)) and the sum of the two packing angles η (Fig. 3 (d)), with a skewness of (0.282) and a kurtosis of (0.098) for φ and a skewness of (0.206) and a kurtosis of (0.082) for η [34]. Hence, the independent angles φ and η exhibit a bivariate normal distribution. Thus, we define the scoring function using matrix notation as:

$$f(\varphi,\eta) = A\exp\left(\frac{-1}{2}(\mathbf{x}-\mathbf{\Lambda})^T \mathbf{\Sigma}^{-1}(\mathbf{x}-\mathbf{\Lambda})\right),$$

where A is a normalization scaling factor,

$\mathbf{x} = \begin{pmatrix}\varphi \\ \eta\end{pmatrix}$, $\mathbf{\Lambda} = \begin{pmatrix}\Lambda_1 \\ \Lambda_2\end{pmatrix}$ is a mean vector and

$\mathbf{\Sigma} = \begin{pmatrix}\Sigma_{11} & \Sigma_{12} \\ \Sigma_{21} & \Sigma_{22}\end{pmatrix}$ is a 2x2 covariance matrix.

The analytical scoring function, $f(\varphi,\eta)$, can be evaluated continuously against dihedral angle φ and packing angles η. In our scoring function, there were six parameters ($\Lambda_1, \Lambda_2, \Sigma_{11}, \Sigma_{12}, \Sigma_{21}$, and Σ_{22}), which were determined to be (-4.501, 203.207, 5581.972, 0, 0, and 2103.773). These values of the parameters were used in the score calculation for each viable topology candidate.

The links in the topology graph in DP-TOSS are changed based on the analysis. The weight of a link in DP-TOSS evaluates how likely two SSEs-S are to be assigned to two SSEs-V. The current weight of each link is calculated by tracing the skeleton between the two SSEs-V if two SSEs-S are assigned to them in a particular direction. The new score proposed for a link is: $w((i,j,t),(i',j',t')) = f_{skel} - f(\varphi,\eta)$, where f_{skel} is the skeleton trace score.

3 RESULTS AND DISCUSSION

A set of 15 Cryo-EM density maps and their associated skeletons were used to evaluate the performance of our approach. The density maps are synthesized to 10Å resolution using the structure of the protein and the *molmap* command in Chimera package [35]. The proteins selected for the synthesized maps are either helical or β-containing. It is still a challenging problem to detect β-strands SSEs-V from the sub/nanometer resolution data. Therefore, all SSEs-V were extracted from the native protein structures when aligned with the density maps. The two ends of each SSE-V were calculated by the center mass of the two end triangles of the first and last three alpha-carbon atoms. To mimic the current challenges of detecting SSEs-V from cryo-EM data, we only extracted the data for helices longer than five amino acids and beta-strands longer than two amino acids. The true location of the helical SSEs-S was generated from the PDB file of the protein structure. Finally, the skeletons were obtained using Skel-EM [19, 36].

The topologies were ranked using the original and updated scoring functions. The correctness evaluation of the two tests was carried out by comparing the produced topologies with the correct topology of each protein obtained from the PDB. The rank of the true topology is then reported in Table 1. A failure is reported (N/A in Table 1) if DP-TOSS could not find the true topology within the top 100 topologies. We used the same skeleton and same SSEs-V sticks for both tests.

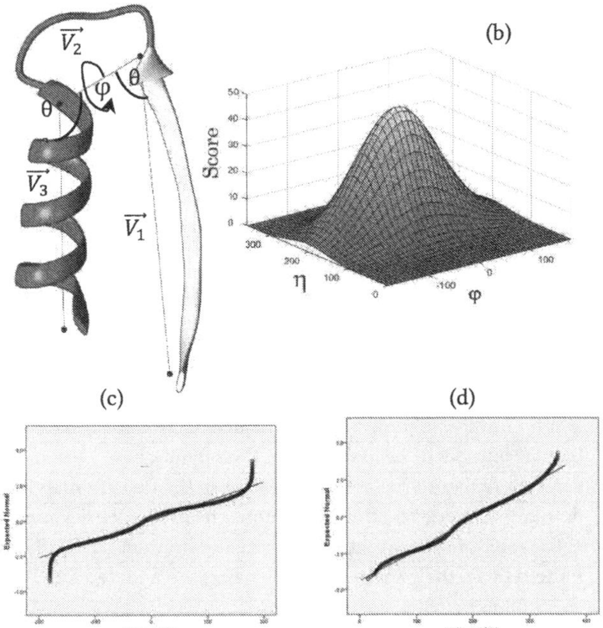

Figure 3: The geometry of consecutive secondary structures. a) the three vectors describe the geometry of the secondary structures and the loop. b) a schematic representation of the scaled bivariate normal distribution of the dihedral angle (φ) and the sum of two packing angles (η). c) the normal Q-Q plot of dihedral angle (φ). d) Normal Q-Q plot of the sum of the two packing angles (η).

Table 1 shows the performance of DP-TOSS before and after incorporating the geometry function, f(φ,η). In general, the performance of DP-TOSS was improved in terms of ranking the correct topology within the first 100. Some tests show unchanged performance. For example, tests such as 1FLP (row 1), 3HJL (row 8) and 1OZ9 (row 10) have the rank unchanged. For most of the tests, the performance was improved noticeably. In some cases, the recast has improved the native (correct) topology by improving its rank to higher positions. For example, the rank of 3ACW (row 5) has moved from position 32 to position 7. Similarly, the rank of 4OXW (row 11) has moved from position 6 to position 1. The ultimate goal is to have the native topology for all proteins in rank 1 or near top. In addition, the geometry function could substantially improve the performance of DP-TOSS for β-strand containing proteins. For example, the native topologies of the last three proteins were not within top 100 when ranked using DP-TOSS. After using the geometry function, the rank of these topologies has been substantially improved.

Table 1: The performance of the recast of DP-TOSS scoring function

No	PDB ID	αSSEs-S[a]	βSSEs-S[b]	αSSEs-V[c]	βSSEs-V[d]	Rank DP-TOSS[e]	Rank DP-TOSSg[f]
1	1FLP	7	0	6	0	1	1
2	1NG6	9	0	7	0	2	2
3	2XB5	13	0	10	0	11	2
4	1BZ4	5	0	5	0	1	1
5	3ACW	17	0	15	0	32	7
6	1A7D	6	0	4	0	12	2
7	3ODS	21	0	16	0	7	1
8	3HJL	20	0	20	0	1	1
9	1ICX	6	7	4	7	31	12
10	1OZ9	5	8	5	7	2	2
11	4OXW	5	3	4	3	6	1
12	1YD0	5	3	4	3	31	5
13	2Y4Z	6	2	6	2	N/A	14
14	4YOK	1	16	1	14	N/A	37
15	4R9A	1	13	0	10	N/A	27

a: total number of helices in the sequence.
b: total number of beta-strands in the sequence.
c: total number of helices extracted from the density map (cryo-EM image).
d: total number of β-strands extracted from the density map.
e: the rank of the correct topology using original DP-TOSS scoring function
f: the rank of the correct topology using the updated DP-TOSS scoring function when $f(\varphi, \eta)$ is incorporated.

This is important when structure evaluation takes place. In general, *de novo* modeling constructs the structural configuration for top-K topologies and further evaluate them using energy calculation. If the native/correct topology is not within the top-K positions, the using of the intensive energy calculation is useless. Thus, our effort to try to guarantee that the correct topology will always be reported within the top ranks.

4 CONCLUSIONS

Cryo-EM has recently become a major structure determination technique. More data is being produced every year. Most of the data is not clear enough to visualize the backbone of the protein molecule. However, secondary structure information can be computationally processed from sub/nanometer resolution. Several tools have been introduced to model protein structure using cryo-EM data. Most of the tools resolve the problem of matching between SSEs-V and SSEs-S. Some of these tools use the skeleton of the cryo-EM data (i.e., density map) to reduce the search space and to derive the protein structure. DP-TOSS is a dynamic-programming based computational tool capable of finding the correct topology of large proteins. DP-TOSS uses a scoring function to weight the edges of a layered graph. The current scoring function used in DP-TOSS is based on the traces of the skeleton.

In this paper, we proposed an initial recast to DP-TOSS's scoring function. We have analyzed a large database of protein structures and derived a scoring term that describes the packing of secondary structure elements. The current scoring function of DP-TOSS was updated accordingly. A test of 15 proteins showed that the proposed geometry term has improved the performance of DP-TOSS. However, a more careful analysis of other geometry features should improve the DP-TOSS in terms of accuracy and its capability to work with larger proteins.

ACKNOWLEDGMENTS

This work was supported by the US National Science Foundation (NSF) Research Initiation Award (RIA) (HRD: 1600919).

REFERENCES

[1] H. Zheng, K. B. Handing, M. D. Zimmerman, I. G. Shabalin, S. C. Almo, and W. Minor. 2015. X-ray crystallography over the past decade for novel drug discovery – where are we heading next? *Expert Opinion on Drug Discovery*, 10, 9 (2015), 975-989.

[2] A. R. Pearson and A. Mozzarelli. 2011. X-ray crystallography marries spectroscopy to unveil structure and function of biological macromolecules. *Biochimica et Biophysica Acta (BBA) - Proteins and Proteomics*, 1814, 6 (2011), 731-733.

[3] A.-H. Emwas. 2015. The Strengths and Weaknesses of NMR Spectroscopy and Mass Spectrometry with Particular Focus on Metabolomics Research. Methods in Molecular Biology. Springer New York. 161-193.

[4] K. Mitra and J. Frank. 2006. Ribosome dynamics: insights from atomic structure modeling into cryo-electron microscopy maps. *Annual Review of Biophysics and Biomolecular Structure*, 35 (2006), 299-317.

[5] J. Frank. 2009. Single-particle reconstruction of biological macromolecules in electron microscopy – 30 years. *Quarterly Reviews of Biophysics*, 42, 03 (2009), 139-158.

[6] A. Fiser. 2010. Template-Based Protein Structure Modeling. *Methods in Molecular Biology*. Humana Press. 73-94.

[7] M. Källberg, H. Wang, S. Wang, J. Peng, Z. Wang, H. Lu, and J. Xu. 2012. Template-based protein structure modeling using the RaptorX web server. *Nat. Protocols*, 7, 8 (2012), 1511-1522.

[8] Y. J. Huang, B. Mao, J. M. Aramini, and G. T. Montelione. 2014. Assessment of template-based protein structure predictions in CASP10. *Proteins: Structure, Function, and Bioinformatics*, 82 (2014), 43-56.

[9] D. E. Kim, D. Chivian, and D. Baker. 2004. Protein structure prediction and analysis using the Robetta server. *Nucleic Acids Res*, 32, Web Server issue (2004), W526-531.

[10] K. T. Simons, C. Kooperberg, E. Huang, and D. Baker. 1997. Assembly of protein tertiary structures from fragments with similar local sequences using simulated annealing and Bayesian scoring functions. *Journal of Molecular Biology*, 268, 1 (1997), 209-225.

[11] B. Adhikari, D. Bhattacharya, R. Cao, and J. Cheng. 2015. CONFOLD: Residue-residue contact-guided ab initio protein folding. *Proteins: Structure, Function, and Bioinformatics*, 83, 8 (2015), 1436-1449.

[12] M. L. Baker, S. S. Abeysinghe, S. Schuh, R. A. Coleman, A. Abrams, M. P. Marsh, C. F. Hryc, T. Ruths, W. Chiu, and T. Ju. 2011. Modeling protein structure at near atomic resolutions with Gorgon. *Journal of Structural Biology*, 174, 2 (2011), 360-373.

[13] S. Lindert, N. Alexander, N. Wötzel, M. Karaka, Phoebe L. Stewart, and J. Meiler. 2012. EM-Fold: De Novo Atomic-Detail Protein Structure Determination from Medium-Resolution Density Maps. *Structure*, 20, 3 (2012), 464-478.

[14] S. Lindert, R. Staritzbichler, N. Wötzel, M. Karakas, P. L. Stewart, and J. Meiler. 2009. EM-fold: De novo folding of alpha-helical proteins guided by intermediate-resolution electron microscopy density maps. *Structure*, 17, 7 (2009), 990-1003.

[15] J. He, Y. Lu, and E. Pontelli. 2004. A Parallel Algorithm for Helix Mapping between 3-D and 1-D Protein Structure using the Length Constraints. *Lecture Notes in Computer Science*, 3358 (2004), 746-756.

[16] A. Dal Palu, E. Pontelli, J. He, and Y. Lu. 2006. A constraint logic programming approach to 3D structure determination of large protein complexes. In *Proceedings of the 2006 ACM Symposium on Applied Computing*. ACM, New York, NY, 131-136.

[17] Y. Wu, M. Chen, M. Lu, Q. Wang, and J. Ma. 2005. Determining protein topology from skeletons of secondary structures. *Journal of Molecular Biology*, 350, 3 (2005), 571-586.

[18] S. S. Abeysinghe and T. Ju. 2009. Interactive skeletonization of intensity volumes. *Vis. Comput.*, 25, 5-7 (2009), 627-635.

[19] K. Al Nasr, C. Liu, M. Rwebangira, L. Burge, and J. He. 2013. Intensity-Based Skeletonization of CryoEM Gray-Scale Images Using a True Segmentation-Free Algorithm. *IEEE/ACM Trans. Comput. Biol. Bioinformatics*, 10, 5 (2013), 1289-1298.

[20] K. Al Nasr, D. Ranjan, M. Zubair, L. Chen, and J. He. 2014. Solving the Secondary Structure Matching Problem in Cryo-EM De Novo Modeling Using a Constrained K-Shortest Path Graph Algorithm. *Computational Biology and Bioinformatics, IEEE/ACM Transactions on*, 11, 2 (2014), 419-430.

[21] F. DiMaio, M. D. Tyka, M. L. Baker, W. Chiu, and D. Baker. 2009. Refinement of protein structures into low-resolution density maps using rosetta. *Journal of Molecular Biology*, 392, 1 (2009), 181-190.

[22] D. Si, S. Ji, K. Al Nasr, and J. He. 2012. A machine learning approach for the identification of protein secondary structure elements from cryoEM density maps. *Biopolymers*, 97 (2012), 698-708.

[23] K. Lasker, O. Dror, M. Shatsky, R. Nussinov, and H. J. Wolfson. 2007. EMatch: discovery of high resolution structural homologues of protein domains in intermediate resolution cryo-EM maps. *IEEE/ACM Transactions on Computational Biology and Bioinformatics*, 4, 1 (2007), 28-39.

[24] M. L. Baker, T. Ju, and W. Chiu. 2007. Identification of secondary structure elements in intermediate-resolution density maps. *Structure*, 15, 1 (2007), 7-19.

[25] A. Del Palu, J. He, E. Pontelli, and Y. Lu. 2006. Identification of Alpha-Helices from Low Resolution Protein Density Maps. *Proceeding of Computational Systems Bioinformatics Conference(CSB)* (2006), 89-98.

[26] D. Si and J. He. 2014. Tracing Beta Strands Using StrandTwister from Cryo-EM Density Maps at Medium Resolutions. *Structure*, 22, 11 (2014), 1665-1676.

[27] G. Pollastri and A. McLysaght. 2005. Porter: a new, accurate server for protein secondary structure prediction. *Bioinformatics*, 21, 8 (2005), 1719-1720.

[28] D. T. Jones. 1999. Protein secondary structure prediction based on position-specific scoring matrices. *Journal of Molecular Biology*, 292, 2 (1999), 195-202.

[29] K. Al Nasr, D. Ranjan, M. Zubair, and J. He. 2011. Ranking Valid Topologies of the Secondary Structure elements Using a constraint Graph. *Journal of Bioinformatics and Computational Biology*, 9, 3 (2011), 415-430.

[30] K. Al Nasr, L. Chen, D. Si, D. Ranjan, M. Zubair, and J. He. 2012. Building the initial chain of the proteins through de novo modeling of the cryo-electron microscopy volume data at the medium resolutions. In *Proceedings of the ACM Conference on Bioinformatics, Computational Biology and Biomedicine*. ACM, New York, NY, 490-497.

[31] K. Al Nasr, W. Sun, and J. He. 2010. Structure prediction for the helical skeletons detected from the low resolution protein density map. *BMC Bioinformatics*, 11, Suppl 1 (2010), S44.

[32] S. Abeysinghe, T. Ju, M. L. Baker, and W. Chiu. 2008. Shape modeling and matching in identifying 3D protein structures. *Computer-Aided Design*, 40, 6 (2008), 708-720.

[33] G. Wang and R. L. Dunbrack Jr. 2003. PISCES: a protein sequence culling server. *Bioinformatics*, 19, 12 (2003), 1589-1591.

[34] D. P. Doane and L. E. Seward. 2011. Measuring Skewness: A Forgotten Statistic? *Journal of Statistics Education*, 19, 2 (2011).

[35] E. F. Pettersen, T. D. Goddard, C. C. Huang, G. S. Couch, D. M. Greenblatt, E. C. Meng, and T. E. Ferrin. 2004. UCSF Chimera—A visualization system for exploratory research and analysis. *Journal of Computational Chemistry*, 25, 13 (2004), 1605-1612.

[36] K. Al Nasr, C. Liu, M. Rwebangira, and L. I. Burge. 2013. A Graph Approach to Bridge the Gaps in Volumetric Electron Cryo-microscopy Skeletons. Lecture Notes in Computer Science. Springer Berlin Heidelberg. 211-223.

ParBio'17 – 6th Workshop on Parallel and Cloud-based Bioinformatics and Biomedicine

Mario Cannataro
University "Magna Græcia"
Catanzaro, Italy 88100
cannataro@unicz.it

John A., Springer
Purdue University
West Lafayette, Indiana 47907-2021
jaspring@purdue.edu

ABSTRACT

The 6th International Workshop on Parallel and Cloud-based Bioinformatics and Biomedicine (ParBio 2017) aims to bring together scientists in the fields of high performance and cloud computing, computational biology and medicine, to discuss, among the others, the organization of large scale biological and biomedical databases, the parallel and service-based implementation of bioinformatics and biomedical applications, and problems and opportunities of moving biomedical and health applications on the Cloud.

KEYWORDS

Bioinformatics; Biomedicine; Parallel Computing; Cloud Computing; Analysis Pipeline;

1 WORKSHOP SUMMARY

Due to the availability of high-throughput platforms (e.g. next generation sequencing, microarray and mass spectrometry) and clinical diagnostic tools (e.g. medical imaging), a recent trend in Bioinformatics and Biomedicine is the increasing production of experimental and clinical data. Considering the complex analysis pipeline of the biomedical research, the bottleneck is more and more moving toward the storage, integration, and analysis of experimental data, as well as their correlation and integration with publicly available data banks.

While Parallel Computing and Grid Computing [3, 5] may offer the computational power and the storage to face this overwhelming availability of data, Cloud Computing [2] is a key technology to hide the complexity of computing infrastructures, to reduce the cost of the data analysis task, and especially to change the overall model of biomedical research and health provision.

Parallel computing can be used for basic pre-processing [4] and for more advanced analysis, such as parallel statistical and data mining analysis. Moreover, novel parallel architectures (e.g. CELL processors, GPUs, FPGA, hybrid CPU/FPGA) coupled with emerging programming models, may overcome the limits posed by conventional computers to the mining and exploration of large amounts of data. On the other hand, these technologies yet require great investments by biomedical and clinical institutions and are based on a traditional model where users often need to be aware and face different management problems, such as hardware and software management, data storage, software ownership, and not scalable costs (different professional-level applications in the biomedical domain have high starting costs that prevent many small laboratories to use them).

The Cloud Computing technology, that is able to offer scalable costs and increased reachability, availability and easiness of application use, and also the possibility to enforce collaboration among scientists, is already changing the business model in different domains and now it is used also in the bioinformatics and biomedical domains. However, many problems remain to be solved, such as availability and safety of the data, privacy-related issues, availability of software platforms for rapid deployment, execution and billing of biomedical applications [2]. Data integration of data coming from different data sources (e.g. hospitals) [6] and efficient data visualization [1], are other emerging issues.

The *ParBio 2017* workshop aims to bring together scientists in the fields of high performance and cloud computing, computational biology and medicine, to discuss, among the others, the organization of large scale biological and biomedical databases, the parallel/service-based implementation of bioinformatics and biomedical applications, and problems and opportunities of moving biomedical and health applications on the cloud. The workshop focuses on research issues, problems and opportunities of moving biomedical and health applications on the cloud, and discusses about parallel and distributed management and analysis of molecular and clinical data, that more and more need to be integrated and analyzed in a joint way.

Permission to make digital or hard copies of part or all of this work for personal or classroom use is granted without fee provided that copies are not made or distributed for profit or commercial advantage and that copies bear this notice and the full citation on the first page. Copyrights for third-party components of this work must be honored. For all other uses, contact the owner/author(s).
ACM-BCB '17, August 20-23, 2017, Boston, MA, USA
© 2017 Copyright held by the owner/author(s).
ACM ISBN 978-1-4503-4722-8/17/08.
https://doi.org/10.1145/3107411.3108170

REFERENCES

[1] Giuseppe Agapito, Pietro Hiram Guzzi, and Mario Cannataro. 2013. Visualization of protein interaction networks: problems and solutions. *BMC bioinformatics* 14, 1 (2013), S1. https://doi.org/10.1186/1471-2105-14-S1-S1
[2] Barbara Calabrese and Mario Cannataro. 2015. Cloud computing in healthcare and biomedicine. *Scalable Computing: Practice and Experience* 16, 1 (2015), 1–18. https://doi.org/10.12694/scpe.v16i1.1057
[3] Mario Cannataro, Antonio Congiusta, Carlo Mastroianni, Andrea Pugliese, Domenico Talia, and Paolo Trunfio. 2004. Grid-Based Data Mining and Knowledge Discovery. In *Intelligent Technologies for Information Analysis*. Springer, 19–45. https://doi.org/10.1007/978-3-662-07952-2_2
[4] Mario Cannataro, Pietro Hiram Guzzi, Tommaso Mazza, Giuseppe Tradigo, and Pierangelo Veltri. 2005. Preprocessing of mass spectrometry proteomics data on the grid. In *CBMS 2005*. IEEE. https://doi.org/10.1109/CBMS.2005.87
[5] Mario Cannataro and Domenico Talia. 2003. Towards the next-generation Grid: a pervasive environment for knowledge-based computing. In *ITCC 2003*. IEEE. https://doi.org/10.1109/ITCC.2003.1197569
[6] Mario Cannataro, Domenico Talia, Giuseppe Tradigo, Paolo Trunfio, and Pierangelo Veltri. 2008. SIGMCC: A system for sharing meta patient records in a Peer-to-Peer environment. *FGCS* 24, 3 (2008), 222–234. https://doi.org/10.1016/j.future.2007.06.006

GPU-PCC: A GPU Based Technique to Compute Pairwise Pearson's Correlation Coefficients for Big fMRI Data

Taban Eslami
Department of Computer Science
Western Michigan University
Kalamazoo, MI
taban.eslami@wmich.edu

Muaaz Gul Awan
Department of Computer Science
Western Michigan University
Kalamazoo, MI
muaazgul.awan@wmich.edu

Fahad Saeed*
Department of Computer Science
Western Michigan University
Kalamazoo, MI
fahad.saeed@wmich.edu

ABSTRACT

Functional Magnetic Resonance Imaging (fMRI) is a non-invasive brain imaging technique for studying the brain's functional activities. Pearson's Correlation Coefficient is an important measure for capturing dynamic behaviors and functional connectivity between brain components. One bottleneck in computing Correlation Coefficients is the time it takes to process big fMRI data. In this paper, we propose GPU-PCC, a GPU based algorithm based on vector dot product, which is able to compute pairwise Pearson's Correlation Coefficients while performing computation once for each pair. Our method is able to compute Correlation Coefficients in an ordered fashion without the need to do post-processing reordering of coefficients. We evaluated GPU-PCC using synthetic and real fMRI data and compared it with sequential version of computing Correlation Coefficient on CPU and existing state-of-the-art GPU method. We show that our GPU-PCC runs 94.62× faster as compared to the CPU version and 4.28× faster than the existing GPU based technique on a real fMRI dataset of size 90k voxels. The implemented code is available as GPL license on GitHub portal of our lab at https://github.com/pcdslab/GPU-PCC.

CCS CONCEPTS

• **Computing methodologies** → **Massively parallel algorithms**; • **Applied computing** → *Health informatics*;

KEYWORDS

fMRI, time series, Pearson's Correlation Coefficient, GPU, CUDA

1 INTRODUCTION

Functional Magnetic Resonance Imaging (fMRI) is a non-invasive brain imaging technique for studying the brain functional activities [2]. This technology helps researchers and physiologists to find the facts related to human behavior and psychology and is based on Blood Oxygen Level Dependent (BOLD) contrast. fMRI data includes a sequence of images taken by a scanner through time while subject performs one or more tasks. The data acquired from an fMRI experiment includes a number of cubic elements called voxels. Changes in voxel intensity across time reveals the hemodynamics change in the brain [7]. A time series data set is extracted from each voxel and used for further analysis. Pearson's Correlation Coefficient has become popular in fMRI study to analyze functional connectivity of different regions in the brain [13, 15]. This measure reveals linear dependency between pairs of elements. For a pair of variables (x, y), Pearson's Correlation Coefficient is calculated using the following equation:

$$\rho_{xy} = \frac{\sum_{i=1}^{T}(x_i - \bar{x})(y_i - \bar{y})}{\sqrt{\sum_{i=1}^{T}(x_i - \bar{x})^2}\sqrt{\sum_{i=1}^{T}(y_i - \bar{y})^2}} \tag{1}$$

In this equation x and y are two T dimensional variables. In case of fMRI data, x and y corresponds to two individual voxels and T shows the length of time series of each voxel. Pearson's Correlation Coefficient ρ_{xy} is a real value in range -1 and 1 [5]. Absolute value of 1 indicates strong perfect linear relationship among variables while value 0 indicates no linear relationship and -1 shows perfect negative linear relationship among them. Computing pairwise correlations is computationally expensive for large number of data (like fMRI data), so multiple approaches have been proposed based on parallel computing techniques to accelerate the computations. Gembris et al. [4] proposed a GPU based method that computes pairwise Correlation Coefficients among elements by reformulating the Pearson's correlation equation to minimize the number of necessary divisions:

$$\rho_{xy} = \frac{T\sum_{i=1}^{T}x_iy_i - \sum_{i=1}^{T}x_i \cdot \sum_{i=1}^{T}y_i}{\sqrt{T\sum_{i=1}^{T}x_i^2 - (\sum_{i=1}^{T}x_i)^2}\sqrt{T\sum_{i=1}^{T}y_i^2 - (\sum_{i=1}^{T}y_i)^2}} \tag{2}$$

Wang et al.[13] proposed a parallel method for computing pairwise Correlation Coefficients over multiple time windows. They used a controller worker method with Message Passing Interface (MPI). In another work, Liu et al. developed a general framework for computing all pairwise Correlation Coefficients on Intel Xeon Phi clusters [8]. Based on the symmetric property of Pearson's Correlation Coefficient ($corr(x, y) = corr(y, x)$), pairwise Correlation Coefficients among N elements can be presented by an array containing N(N-1)/2 elements which corresponds to the upper triangle above the main diagonal part of the correlation matrix. The main diagonal is disregarded since it shows the correlation of each element with itself which is always one. Fig. 1 shows an example of the desired elements of the correlation matrix and their orders in the array. In this order, the first $N-1$ elements of the array show the

*To whom correspondence should be addressed.
Permission to make digital or hard copies of all or part of this work for personal or classroom use is granted without fee provided that copies are not made or distributed for profit or commercial advantage and that copies bear this notice and the full citation on the first page. Copyrights for components of this work owned by others than ACM must be honored. Abstracting with credit is permitted. To copy otherwise, or republish, to post on servers or to redistribute to lists, requires prior specific permission and/or a fee. Request permissions from permissions@acm.org.
ACM-BCB '17, August 20-23, 2017, Boston, MA, USA
© 2017 Association for Computing Machinery.
ACM ISBN 978-1-4503-4722-8/17/08...$15.00
https://doi.org/10.1145/3107411.3108173

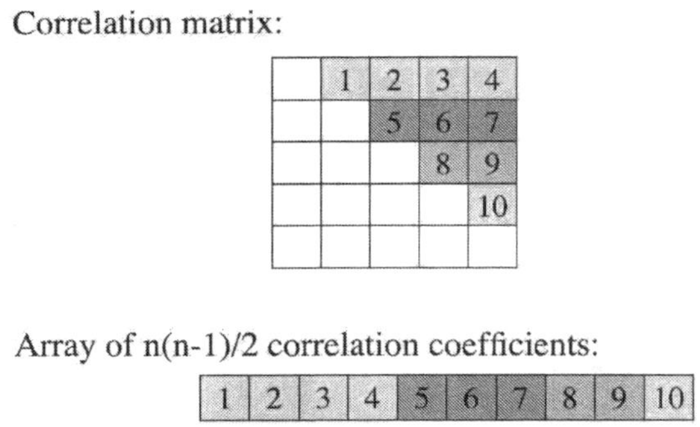

Figure 1: The order of desired Correlation Coefficients of a 5×5 correlation matrix

Pearson's Correlations between the first variable and all other variables, the next $N-2$ elements show the correlation of the second variable with all others and so on. Liang et al [6] developed a tool using GPU for constructing gene co-expression networks based on computing N(N-1)/2 Pearson Correlation Coefficients. The order of resulting correlation coefficients in that approach is different from Fig. 1; also they applied a different strategy for distributing work among threads. Based on the symmetric property, a hybrid CPU-GPU framework for computing Correlation Coefficient using General Matrix-Matrix Multiplication (GEMM) is proposed by Wang et al [14]. In this approach, they normalize the time series of each voxel v using the following equation[1]

$$u_i = \frac{v_i - \bar{v}_i}{\|v_i - \bar{v}_i\|_2} \tag{3}$$

and $U = (u_1, u_2, ..., u_n)$ aggregates all normalized vectors. The correlation matrix can be constructed by multiplying matrix U to its transpose ($U \times U^T$). Since the size of correlation matrix may be larger than GPU memory, they divide matrix U into smaller blocks and compute matrix multiplication of each block with others. Using this strategy, this approach can handle correlation matrices of any size. If data contains N vectors and each block contains d vectors, there will be $B = \lceil \frac{N}{d} \rceil$ blocks. Considering the symmetric property, two blocks are multiplied to each other once which results in B(B+1)/2 block multiplications. The number of computed elements is greater than N(N-1)/2 and their order is different than what we showed in Fig. 1. A post processing step is needed in their implementation to eliminate redundant elements and reorder the elements. The post processing part runs on CPU.

In this paper, we first perform a preliminary experiment for computing vector of Correlation Coefficients by performing Matrix-Vector multiplication using CUDA built-in functions. In order to exploit fine-grained thread level parallelism, we proposed an approach called GPU-PCC in which we designed our own kernel to compute Pearson's Correlation Coefficients without using built-in functions. Our proposed technique normalizes the data and computes their multiplications using massive number of GPU cores. The design of our parallel strategy allows us to compute the Correlation Coefficients in the desired order and without redundancies; eliminating the needs for post-processing strategies. This results in highly scalable parallel strategy with increasing number of elements.

[1] $u_i = \frac{v_i - \bar{v}_i}{|v_i - \bar{v}_i|}$ is the equation that is mentioned in their paper [14] but we found that equation 3 is used in their implementation

1.1 GPU architecture, CUDA programming model and cuBLAS library

Graphics Processing Unit (GPU) were originally designed to satisfy the demand for higher quality graphics in video games to create more realistic 3D environment [12]. Recently GPU's have found multitude of high performance applications which can exploit high latency and high throughput of enormous number of GPU cores [1, 3]. A GPU is made up of an array of streaming multiprocessors (SMs). Each SM contains multiple streaming processors or cores. Hundreds of threads run on the same core concurrently based on SIMT (Single Instruction Multiple Threads) strategy. A warp is a group of 32 threads which execute the same instruction at the same time on the SM. Compute Unified Device Architecture (CUDA) is a programming model interface created by NVIDIA for programming graphic cards. CUDA programmers define functions called kernel which is executed on device. A kernel is defined using a number of GPU threads which execute the kernel's code in parallel. Parallel invocations of kernel are grouped into blocks which are distributed among available SMs. Each block has up to three dimensions and contains maximum 1024 threads. A grid consists of multiple blocks in one or two dimensions. The NVIDIA CUDA Basic Linear Algebra Subroutines (cuBLAS) library is the GPU version implementation of BLAS (Basic Linear Algebra Subprograms) library which performs vector and matrix operations like Matrix-Vector multiplication and Matrix-Matrix multiplication [11].

2 PROPOSED METHODS

As stated earlier, after normalizing the data, Pearson's Correlation Coefficient among two variables can be computed by multiplying their corresponding normalized vectors. It worth mentioning that the normalization step is performed much faster than the multiplication step so we leave this step to be performed on CPU.

Assume that data is stored in an $N \times M$ matrix called U, which N corresponds to the number of data points and M corresponds to the length of each data point. In case of fMRI data, N is the number of voxels and M is to the length of time series. In this section we present our preliminary experiment and proposed method to compute the ordered array of Correlation Coefficients without the need of post-processing re-ordering of elements.

2.1 Preliminary experiment of performing Matrix-Vector multiplication using CUDA built-in function

In order to obtain the desired order of Correlation Coefficients, this approach first computes the Correlation Coefficient between the first element and all other elements. This can be performed by multiplying the first row of matrix U to all other rows. We consider the transpose of all the rows except the first row as another matrix, so correlation between the first element and rest of elements can be computed by performing Matrix-Vector multiplication. Similarly,

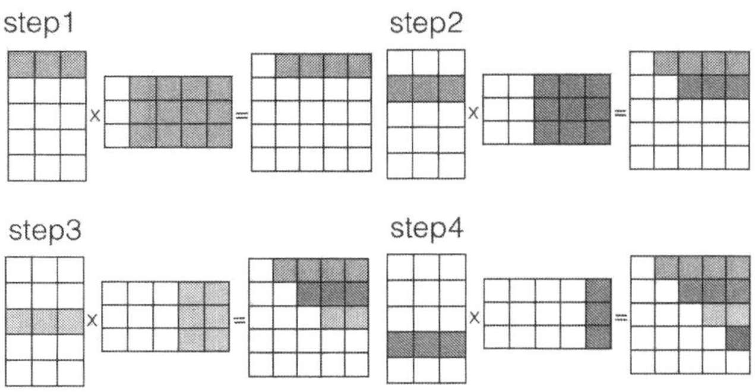

Figure 2: Example of performing Matrix-Vector multiplication, step i computes $n - i$ elements of the final result

the correlation between the second element and the rest of elements can be computed in the same way, but this time we multiply the second row with a matrix containing all rows except the first two rows. We don't consider the first row because correlation between the first and second elements has been computed in previous step. In step i, row i of matrix U is multiplied to the matrix consisting of column $i+1$ to column N of matrix U^T. We continue performing this procedure until multiplying $(N-2)$th vector to $(N-1)$th vector. The procedure of this method is illustrated using an example in Fig. 2. Algorithm 1 shows the pseudocode of this method.

```
Algorithm 1: Matrix-Vector multiplication
Input: Matrix U containing N elements each of length M
output: Array R containing N(N − 1)/2 Correlation Coefficients
Normalize each vector of matrix U using equation 3
for i = 1 to N − 1
    Multiply row i of matrix U to the matrix containing column
      i + 1 to N of U^T
    Add the N − i computed elements to array R
Return R
```

Matrix-Vector multiplication is implemented efficiently in cuBLAS library and we used that in our implementation (cublasSgemv function [11]). In order to minimize the latency of transferring data between host and device, instead of copying the $N - i$ computed elements back to the CPU in each iteration, we store them in a GPU array until there is not enough space in GPU memory. Once there is no more space all computed elements are transferred to the CPU and next iteration starts. This approach is successful in computing the Correlation Coefficients in order. To exploit fine-grained thread level parallelism, we propose an approach called GPU-PCC in which we designed our own kernel to compute Pearson's Correlation Coefficients.

2.2 GPU-PCC method

In this method normalized data is initially copied to GPU global memory in row-major order. We launch blocks of 512 threads and consider multiple groups per block. Each group of threads is responsible to perform a vector dot product in order to compute a Correlation Coefficient between two vectors. We used vectorized load by using float2 data type for reading data from global memory to increase bandwidth and decrease latency [9]. In order to access global memory efficiently and have coalesced memory access, we considered 16 consecutive threads in each block as a group. Threads of each group request consecutive values from memory which causes loading 128 bytes aligned data in one transaction. Since each block contains 512 threads and each 16 threads belong to one group, there are $\frac{512}{16} = 32$ groups per block which causes computing 32 Correlation Coefficients simultaneously. After each group finishes performing dot product of two vectors (we explain about the dot product process soon), it stores the result at index k of resulting vector R. Index k is computed based on the following equation:

$$k = blockIdx.x \times 32 + threadIdx.x/16 \tag{4}$$

Based on value of k, threads of each group can compute the index of vectors that they should multiply to each other (i and j) using the following equations:

$$i = n - 2 - \left\lfloor \frac{\sqrt{-8 \times k + 4 \times n \times (n-1) - 7}}{2} - 0.5 \right\rfloor \tag{5}$$

$$j = k + i + 1 - \frac{n \times (n-1)}{2} + \frac{(n-i) \times ((n-i)-1)}{2} \tag{6}$$

Equations 5 and 6 guarantee that for any index k of the resulting array, we pick the right vectors to compute their correlations and in this way the resulting array will have the correct order. Starting from the beginning of vectors i and j, each thread multiplies two corresponding consecutive values of vector i and j which results in 32 simultaneous multiplications per group. This process continuous to the next 32 elements of the vectors until all of their elements are multiplied to each other. A local variable in each thread stores the sum of products performed by that thread. In order to compute the result of dot product, the partial sums of 16 threads in each group should be added to each other. Since we have to add the values of 16 consecutive threads and these values are in thread's registers, we used shuffle warp reduce technique introduced in [10] for computing global sum. This technique allows exchanging data among threads in the same warp without needing to use shared memory. After computing the global sum, the result of dot product will be stored at index k of vector R. Fig. 4 shows the process of vector dot product and Algorithm 2 shows the pseudo code of the kernel. Since we use float2 data type in our implementation and it needs $M/2$ load instructions, in cases that M is not even, we add a zero element at the end of each vector. This does not change the result of dot product (we don't consider these additional zeros in normalization step because it will change the result of correlation). If the size of resulting array R is larger than GPU memory, we call the kernel multiple times. Each kernel call continues the computation until there is not enough space in global memory of the GPU to store the results. Otherwise, the computed elements are copied to host and new kernel call starts to continue the computation. Fig. 3 shows the work flow of GPU-PCC. Empirical analysis of the implemented code showed that time-efficiency improved when L1 cache was enabled. Usually L1 cache can be enabled at compile time depending on the device properties.

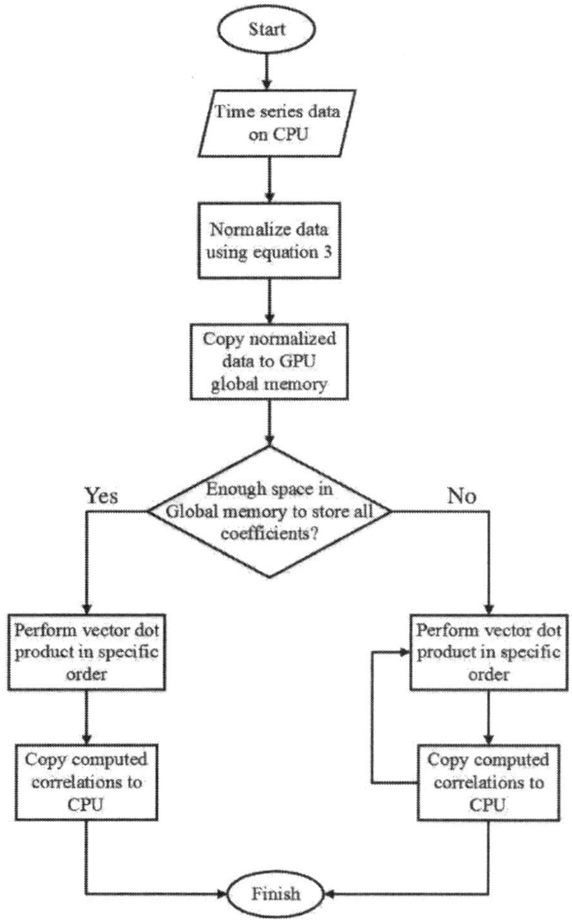

Figure 3: The work flow of GPU-PCC algorithm

Algorithm 2: GPU-PCC kernel

Input: Array U containing $N \times M$ normalized elements located in GPU memory
output: Array R containing $N(N-1)/2$ Correlation Coefficients
$thread\_groupId = threadIdx.x/16$
$thread\_local\_offset = threadIdx.x\%16$
$k = blockIdx.x \times 32 + thread\_groupId$
$i = n - 2 - \lfloor \frac{\sqrt{-8 \times k + 4 \times n \times (n-1) - 7}}{2} - 0.5 \rfloor$
$j = k + i + 1 - \frac{n \times (n-1)}{2} + \frac{(n-i) \times ((n-i)-1)}{2}$
$iter = m/32$
$local\_sum = 0$
$float2\ data1, data2$
$for\ l = 1\ to\ iter$
    $data1 = U[i \times m/2 + l * 16 + thread\_local\_offset]$
    $data2 = U[j \times m/2 + l * 16 + thread\_local\_offset]$
    $local\_sum += data1.x \times data2.x + data1.y \times data2.y$
$if\ m\%32\ != 0$
    continue the multiplication for the rest of elements
sum = adding up $local\_sum$ of threads in a group using shuffle instruction
$if\ thread\_local\_offset = 0$
    $R[k] = sum$

3 PERFORMANCE EVALUATION

All the experiments reported in this section are performed on a linux server with Ubuntu Operating System version 14.01. The server consists of two Intel Xeon E5 2620 processors with clock speed 2.4 GHz, 48 GBs RAM and NVIDIA Tesla K40c Graphic Processing Unit. This GPU contains 15 Streaming Multiprocessors each consists of 192 CUDA cores and 11520 MBytes global memory.

We evaluated the performance of GPU-PCC by comparing it with three other approaches. The first approach is the experiment we performed using Matrix-Vector multiplication; second one is the sequential version of Pearson's Correlation Coefficient computation on CPU. We used the code that is implemented by Wang et al [14][2]. In this implementation after normalizing data using equation 3, N(N-1)/2 vector dot products are computed on CPU. No math library is used in this implementation. We compiled the sequential code using g++ compiler version 4.8.4. The third approach that we compared our method was implemented by Wang et al [14][2]. This approach computes Correlation Coefficients by performing Matrix-Matrix multiplication on GPU (refer to section I for more details of this approach). To reorder computed elements and eliminate redundant ones, the results are post processed on CPU. So for comparing the running time of other methods with this approach, we considered both matrix multiplication and post processing steps. All reported running times in this section measure the execution time of pairwise Pearson Correlation Coefficients in desired order. The execution starts from normalizing data to performing last multiplication (For our proposed approaches to finish copying the last chunk from GPU to CPU and for Wang's approach after finishing the postprocessing to reorder computed coefficients). All the experiments for each dataset are repeated multiple times and the minimum running time is reported. We performed our experiments using synthetic and real fRMI data sets. Synthetic data sets were created with N = 20000, 30000, 40000, 50000, 60000, 70000, 80000, 90000, 100000 and M = 300. For each vector, we generated uniformly random floating point numbers in range −2 and 2 as intensity of each voxel. For real data set, we used Orangeburg dataset (www.nitrc.org/projects/fcon_1000/). The dataset contains resting state fMRI data of 20 healthy subjects, 15 female and 5 male with age range 20-55. The data were acquired using 1.5 Tesla scanner. Subject were asked to close their eyes during acquisition. We picked one of the subjects randomly for our experiments. Table 1, Fig. 5 and Fig. 6 compare the running time of different approaches. Based on the results shown in Table 1 and Fig. 5, GPU-PCC and Matrix-Vector multiplication using CUDA built-in functions show better performance than the other two approaches and GPU-PCC shows superior results. Fig. 7 shows the achieved speedups of these two methods on synthetic data. Based on the results, the achieved speedup over Wang's method for the Matrix-Vector multiplication using CUDA built-in functions is around 2 and for GPU-PCC is

[2] https://github.com/BNAplatform-organization/PAGANI-toolkit/tree/master/src/BNAPlatform-win64-cuda7.0-20151118/src/CorMat

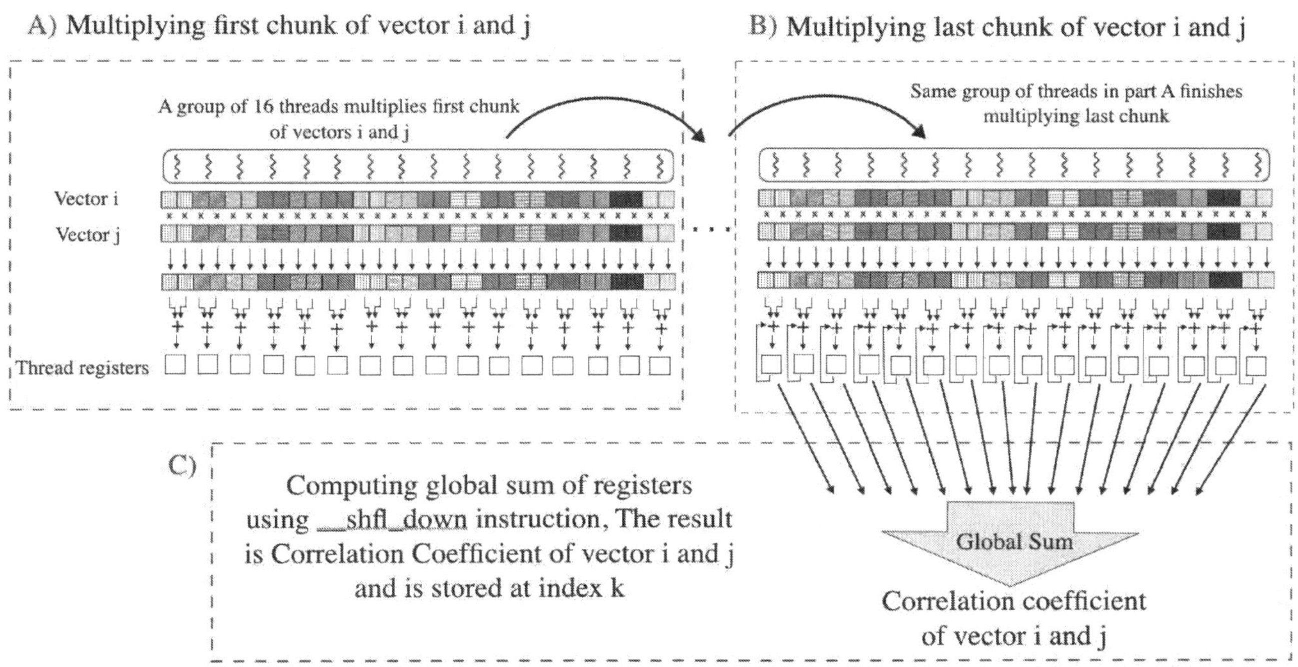

Figure 4: Example of performing vector dot product of two normalized rows (i and j) of matrix U. Multiplication of i and j is performed by a group of 16 threads. Each thread multiplies two consecutive corresponding elements of i and j, adds the results and stores it in its register. Elements that are processed with the same thread are shown using the same pattern in figure. Part A shows the multiplication of first chunk of two vectors each chunk containing 32 elements (since there are 16 threads in group each working on two elements). Part B shows the same process for the last chunk of the vectors. After multiplying the first chunk, each thread needs to update its register value by adding the new result to it. In part C, all the elements in thread registers are summed using warp shuffling technique and stored at index k (equation 4).

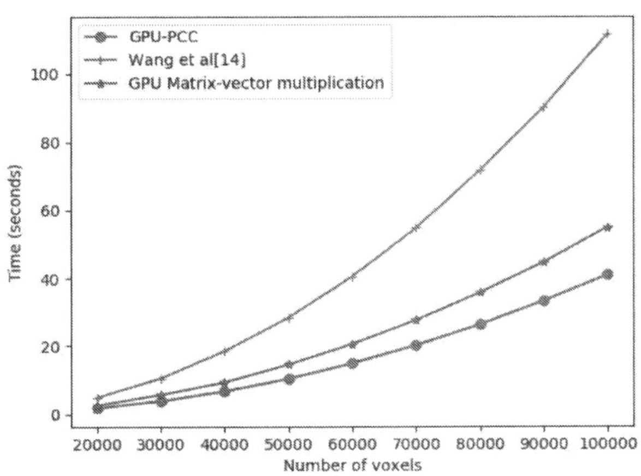

Figure 5: Running time comparison of our proposed methods and Wang's method

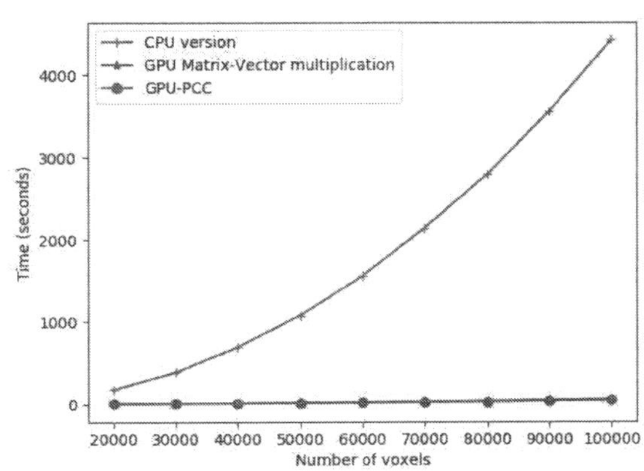

Figure 6: Running time comparison of our proposed methods and CPU version

around 2.7. The speedups are around 70 and 100 over CPU version respectively. Table 2 shows the running time comparisons on real data. On real dataset, Matrix-Vector Multiplication using CUDA built-in functions runs 65.12× faster than CPU version and 2.95× faster than Wang's technique. Our GPU-PCC runs 94.62× faster as compared to the CPU version and 4.28× faster than the Wang's method. It worth mentioning that we didn't find specific optimization in the sequential and the postprocessing codes and we used the

Table 1: Comparing running time (Seconds) of different approaches on synthetic fMRI data

Size of N	*Mat-Vec mult*	*GPU-PCC*	*Wang et al[14]*	*CPU version*
20000	2.5	1.69	4.83	172.412
30000	5.37	3.76	10.45	387.89
40000	9.26	6.62	18.39	689.49
50000	14.45	10.28	28.35	1077.28
60000	20.49	14.8	40.49	1554.23
70000	27.55	20.11	54.61	2140.32
80000	35.64	26.22	71.68	2787.92
90000	44.63	33.14	90.06	3553.47
100000	54.89	40.88	111.47	4415.22

Table 2: Comparing running time (Seconds) of different approaches on real fMRI data

Size of N	*GPU Mat-vec mult*	*GPU-PCC*	*Wang et al[14]*	*CPU version*
90112	30.31	20.86	89.45	1973.85

default CPU optimizations without using any optimization flags. Optimization of those codes could result in better running time.

4 CONCLUSION

Pearson's Correlation Coefficient is a well-known technique that measures the functional connectivity between brain voxels. Since there are thousands of voxels in one fMRI experiment, using traditional CPU based methods are very time consuming. Parallel computing techniques will be essential for processing data- and compute-intensive operations for big brain research especially in the context of precision and personal medicine. Exploiting the symmetric property of the Pearson's Correlation, we can reduce the number of coefficients that need computation from N^2 to N(N-1)/2. Thereafter, we first did an experiment by performing Matrix-Vector multiplication using CUDA built-in function and then proposed a method called GPU-PCC which can compute ordered correlations and do not require further post-processing. We compared our implemented methods with a sequential C++ implementation and also with a GPU based technique based on General Matrix-Matrix Multiplication (GEMM). Both real and synthetic fMRI data sets were used in evaluation. We show that our proposed HPC method outperforms existing state-of-art methods and is around 94× faster than the CPU versions and 4.28× faster than the GPU based techniques for similar GPU devices and data set.

ACKNOWLEDGMENT

This material is based in part upon work supported by the National Science Foundation under Grant Numbers NSF CRII CCF-1464268 and NSF CAREER ACI-1651724. Any opinions, findings, and conclusions or recommendations expressed in this material are those of the author(s) and do not necessarily reflect the views of the National Science Foundation. We would also like to acknowledge the donation of a K-40c Tesla GPU from NVIDIA which was used for all GPU based experiments performed in this paper.

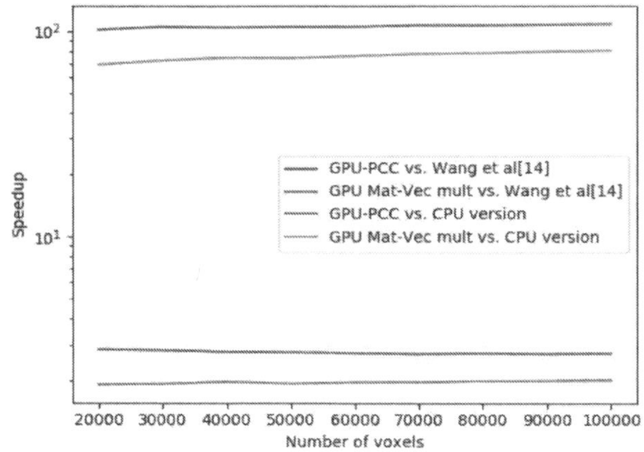

Figure 7: Speedup gained by our proposed methods over Wang's method and CPU version

REFERENCES

[1] Muaaz Gul Awan and Fahad Saeed. 2016. GPU-ArraySort: A parallel, in-place algorithm for sorting large number of arrays. In *Parallel Processing Workshops (ICPPW), 2016 45th International Conference on*. IEEE, 78–87.

[2] R Cameron Craddock, Rosalia L Tungaraza, and Michael P Milham. 2015. Connectomics and new approaches for analyzing human brain functional connectivity. *GigaScience* 4, 1 (2015), 1.

[3] Anders Eklund, Mats Andersson, and Hans Knutsson. 2012. fMRI analysis on the GPU-possibilities and challenges. *Computer methods and programs in biomedicine* 105, 2 (2012), 145–161.

[4] Daniel Gembris, Markus Neeb, Markus Gipp, Andreas Kugel, and Reinhard Männer. 2011. Correlation analysis on GPU systems using NVIDIA's CUDA. *Journal of real-time image processing* 6, 4 (2011), 275–280.

[5] Joseph Lee Rodgers and W Alan Nicewander. 1988. Thirteen ways to look at the correlation coefficient. *The American Statistician* 42, 1 (1988), 59–66.

[6] Meimei Liang, Futao Zhang, Gulei Jin, and Jun Zhu. 2015. FastGCN: a GPU accelerated tool for fast gene co-expression networks. *PloS one* 10, 1 (2015), e0116776.

[7] Martin A Lindquist and others. 2008. The statistical analysis of fMRI data. *Statist. Sci.* 23, 4 (2008), 439–464.

[8] Yongchao Liu, Tony Pan, and Srinivas Aluru. 2016. Parallel pairwise correlation computation on intel xeon phi clusters. In *Computer Architecture and High Performance Computing (SBAC-PAD), 2016 28th International Symposium on*. IEEE, 141–149.

[9] Justin Luitjens. 2013. UDAf Pro Tip: Increase Performance with Vectorized Memory Access. (Dec. 2013). https://devblogs.nvidia.com/parallelforall/cuda-pro-tip-increase-performance-with-vectorized-memory-access/

[10] Justin Luitjens. 2014. Faster Parallel Reductions on Kepler. (Feb. 2014). https://devblogs.nvidia.com/parallelforall/faster-parallel-reductions-kepler/

[11] NVIDIA. 2017. cuBLAS. (March 2017). http://docs.nvidia.com/cuda/cublas/index.html#axzz4VJn7wpRs

[12] Jason Sanders and Edward Kandrot. 2010. *CUDA by example: an introduction to general-purpose GPU programming*. Addison-Wesley Professional.

[13] Yida Wang, Jonathan D Cohen, Kai Li, and Nicholas B Turk-Browne. 2014. *Full correlation matrix analysis of fmri data*. Technical Report. Technical report, Princeton Neuroscience Institute.

[14] Yu Wang, Haixiao Du, Mingrui Xia, Ling Ren, Mo Xu, Teng Xie, Gaolang Gong, Ningyi Xu, Huazhong Yang, and Yong He. 2013. A hybrid CPU-GPU accelerated framework for fast mapping of high-resolution human brain connectome. *PloS one* 8, 5 (2013), e62789.

[15] Hui Zhang, Jie Tian, and Zonglei Zhen. 2007. Direct measure of local region functional connectivity by multivariate correlation technique. In *2007 29th Annual International Conference of the IEEE Engineering in Medicine and Biology Society*. IEEE, 5231–5234.

Ensemble Convolution Neural Network with a Simple Voting Method for Lung Tumor Detection

Allison M Rossetto
University of Massachusetts Lowell
1 University Avenue
Lowell, Massachusetts 01854
Allison_Rossetto@student.uml.edu

Wenjin Zhou
University of Massachusetts Lowell
1 University Avenue
Lowell, Massachusetts 01854
Wenjin_Zhou@uml.edu

ABSTRACT

Lung cancer is the leading cause of cancer deaths in the United States. Approximately 225, 000 people each year are diagnosed with lung cancer in the US alone. Early detection is a crucial part of giving patients the best chance of recovery. Current methods suffer from high false positive rates. Deep learning gives us an opportunity to increase the accuracy of the automated initial diagnosis. Here we present an ensemble of Convolution Neural Networks (CNN) that is built from two individual CNNs: one uses unprocessed images and the other images smoothed with a Gaussian filter. The ensemble method decreases the number of false positives in the automated labeling of the scans using a voting system. If both CNNs have the same output, a negative (0) or a positive (1) cancer prediction, the voting system outputs that prediction. However, if the CNNs do not have the same output then the voting system outputs a negative (0) prediction. Our ensemble method has an average accuracy of 85.91% and false positive rate of 0.50%. This is a decrease in the false positive rate of approximately 99.47% from current methods. This is a great improvement over the currently used methods and shows that our method has promise as an initial diagnosis technique.

CCS CONCEPTS

• **Computing methodologies** → **Neural networks**; • **Applied computing** → *Health informatics*;

KEYWORDS

Lung Tumors, Cancer, Automated Diagnoses, Deep Learning, Convolutional Neural Networks, False Positive Rate

1 INTRODUCTION

Lung cancer is the leading cause of cancer deaths in the United States with over 225, 000 people being diagnosed every year [3]. Early detection is a crucial part of increasing the chance of patient survival. Automated initial diagnosis techniques are an essential part of increasing early detection. Current screening methods which include chest x-rays, CT scans, and PET scans do not do very well when used alone as they tend to suffer from very high false positive rates some of which have been reported to be as high as 95% [5, 13]. Due to the nature of the screening methods, normal tissues or non-cancerous masses can be misidentified as cancer. Sometimes cancerous tumors can also be missed, though this is much less likely.

Low-dose CT has been found to be one of the best screening methods available but they also have a high false positive rate [14]. The high rates of false positive diagnoses can lead to unnecessary treatments and procedures which waste time, money, and resources. They also cause undue stresses to patients and families as well as being detrimental to patient health. Our goal is to increase the accuracy of identification as well as the decrease the false positive rate of the diagnoses by providing a deep learning method that can give an accurate initial diagnosis.

Deep learning gives us an opportunity to increase the accuracy of the early detection by providing an accurate, automated initial diagnosis of medical scans. Deep learning has been applied to the problem of cancer diagnosis before in many different ways. An approach proposed by Yang, Yu, and Wang used geometric transformations on CT images before classification as cancerous or not via convolution neural network (CNN) [15]. They found the image transformations were useful in the classification process, however, this method required data that suspected tumors already be identified. Another application of a CNN based deep learning method by Ciompi, et al. tried to classify lung tumors by their type [4]. The system did fairly well in identifying most of the kinds of tumors but again needed the tumors to be identified in scans before classification. Roth, Lu, et al. developed a method to improve upon initial computer-aided detection methods using a deep convolutional network [12]. Their method introduces a second tier, consisting of a deep network, on top of a preexisting automated detection system to try to decrease the high false positive rate of the detection system. This did improve the false positive rates, reducing it by around 30%, however, this method only works in conjunction with another prediction system.

Here we are addressing the problem of using deep learning to give an initial diagnosis of lung CT scans as either cancerous or not. These CT scans do not require tumor locations identified in the CT scans before training which makes this problem different than many of the others addressed by previous works. To do this, we have developed an ensemble of Convolution Neural Networks (CNN) and pre-processing pipeline. We use both unsmoothed and smoothed images in separate networks. We then combine the resulting predictions from each of the networks using a simple voting system. The voting system is designed to decrease the number of false positives by outputting non-consensus values between the

Permission to make digital or hard copies of all or part of this work for personal or classroom use is granted without fee provided that copies are not made or distributed for profit or commercial advantage and that copies bear this notice and the full citation on the first page. Copyrights for components of this work owned by others than ACM must be honored. Abstracting with credit is permitted. To copy otherwise, or republish, to post on servers or to redistribute to lists, requires prior specific permission and/or a fee. Request permissions from permissions@acm.org.
ACM-BCB'17, August 20–23, 2017, Boston, MA, USA.
© 2017 ACM. ISBN 978-1-4503-4722-8/17/08...$15.00
DOI: http://dx.doi.org/10.1145/3107411.3108174

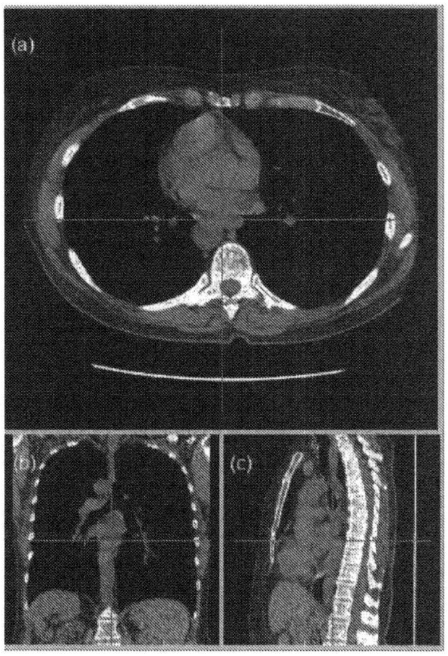

Figure 1: Sample view of a cancer positive patient CT image from the dataset showing a (a) top, (b) front, and (c) side view.

two CNNs as a negative prediction, it does not false negatives into account at this time.

2 METHODS

We have used the lung cancer imaging database provided by the Kaggle Data Science Bowl 2017 [1]. This is a large dataset with CT scans for 1397 patients, which is a total of 248, 580 images. Each patient dataset is diagnosed as positive(1) or negative(0) for cancer. The locations of the tumors in the CT scans are not labeled nor is any other patient data provided. The slice thickness, image quality, and scanning parameters vary from patient to patient. Figure 1 shows a sample view of one of the CT scans from the dataset.

We use both the unaltered images and images smoothed with a Gaussian filter as inputs to the two CNNs. We have implemented the ensemble using the Matlab Neural Network Toolbox [6]. The pipeline is shown in Figure 2. Our method differs from others by using two separate networks with different inputs. We also differ by getting our final predictions using our simple voting system, which reduces false positives, rather than taking an average value [7] to produce predictions. An average value is not a good fit for this method because we only use two CNNs and the output of the CNNs are binary, not fractional values. We give the details of the pipeline and the voting mechanisms as well as details on the metrics we used to evaluate our method in the following subsections.

2.1 Image Preprocessing

In order to implement our method efficiently in Matlab, we first preprocessed all our images by converting them from their original DICOM format to a PNG format. We do this in order to utilize the ability of Matlab to process certain image types (JPG and PNG) using an image data storage object [8]. This allows Matlab to process the images for the CNN without having to import them all into the memory at the same time. The image data store object enables us to build our networks with much more data than we would have been able to use with the images in the DICOM format. We have chosen the PNG format because of the lossless nature of the format. No other processing or modifications were done to the images in this step.

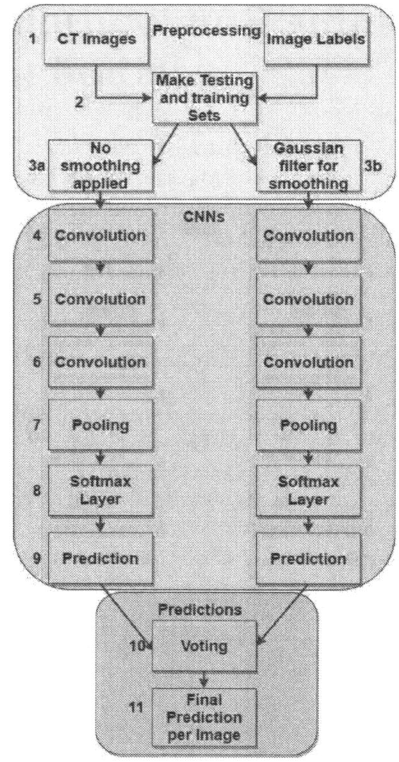

Figure 2: This image shows the pipeline of the CNN ensemble. One network has the smoothed images, processed with a Gaussian filter, as the input while the other uses the unmodified, unsmoothed images. The architecture of the two CNNs is otherwise the same. The predictions of each network are combined using a simple consensus voting mechanism to obtain the final predictions for each image.

2.2 Pipeline of CNN Ensemble

The pipeline can be broken into three main parts: preprocessing (steps 1-3), the CNNs (steps 4-9), and the prediction (steps 10-11) Here we explain each step, as seen in Figure 2, in detail.

(1) The medical scans and the labels for the images (positive or negative for cancer) are imported into the system for training and testing.
(2) Randomized testing and training sets are created for the CNNs. We use a data split of 50% for training (which is approximately 124, 290 images from 700 patients). The rest of the data was used to create test sets of 10, 848 images each (60 patients per test set).

(3) (a) The images are passed to the unsmoothed CNN without further processing. (b) A Gaussian filter is applied to the testing and training images to create the smoothed training-testing set. The smoothing step helps to reduce noise that can be present in the CT scans, especially for those scans that are of lower quality.
(4) The input data for each of the CNNs is then fed into the first convolution layer which uses twenty $20x20$ convolutions to processes the images and gives us feature activation for the images.
(5) This is then sent to the second convolution layer which uses ten $10x10$ convolutions to further convolve the features.
(6) The final convolution layer uses five $5x5$ convolution to give us the final convoluted features of the data.
(7) The convolved features then go into the maximum pooling layer. The pooling layer calculates the maximum value of the feature over a region of the image so we can use the features for classification.
(8) The features resulting from the convolution and pooling of the features of each CNN are then input into their respective softmax layers. The softmax layer calculates the normalized exponential function to calculate the output activation function. This function is calculated as:

$$P(c_r|x,\theta) = \frac{P(x,\theta|c_r)p(c_r)}{\sum_{j=1}^{k} P(x,\theta|c_j)p(c_j)} = \frac{exp(a_r(x,\theta)}{\sum_{j=1}^{k} exp(a_j(x,\theta)}$$

Where $P(c_r)$ is the class prior probability, $P(x,\theta|c_r)$ is the conditional probability of the given class r, and $a_r = ln(P(x,\theta|c_r)P(c_r))$ [2]
(9) The final layer of the CNNs is the prediction layer that outputs the predicted value for each image.
(10) The voting mechanism is applied at this point. The voting system works by either giving the output agreed on by the two CNNs or it outputs a negative. This is described in more detail in the Subsection 2.3.
(11) The final prediction for each image is then output from the voting system.

2.3 The Voting Scheme

The voting system we use is a simple one designed to try to reduce the number of false positives but not the number of false negatives. Our system has two possible outputs: a negative cancer prediction (represented by a 0) and a positive cancer prediction (represented by a 1). The voting system evaluates the predictions to find those that agree, that is it checks for matching predictions and then outputs this matching value for these predictions. Non-matching predictions are considered unsure so we default to a negative (0) output. The mechanism can be explained as the following two cases:

- **Case 1: The predictions are in agreement.** If both CNNs have the same output, a negative (0) or a positive (1) cancer prediction, this consensus prediction is output by the voting system.
- **Case 2: The predictions are not in agreement.** If the two CNNs do not agree (i.e. one outputs a negative (0) and the other a positive (1)) the ensemble outputs a negative (0) prediction.

The reasoning behind this voting scheme is a simple one: we want to avoid false positives. We attempt to do this by decreasing the number of questionable positive outputs using Case 2. There is some risk that it may increase the false negative rate because we default to a negative output. However, because the main concern from the current methods [5, 13] is a high false positive rate, our focus at this point is on decreasing this rate.

2.4 Accuracy Evaluation

We use several different metrics in order to evaluate the accuracy of our model. We have calculated the accuracy, precision, recall, F_1 score, and the Matthews Correlation Coefficient (MCC) [10]. The accuracy gives the overall percentage of how many correct prediction our model outputs. The precision is a measurement of true versus false positives which gives us a measure of how many of our positive predictions are correct. The recall, also called sensitivity, gives us a measurement of the positive predictions to the actual positives. The F_1 score is a quality measure that combines the precision and recall measures into one value. The Matthews Correlation Coefficient gives us a measure of the quality of our binary classifier. The formulas for each of these are given below. We also use the following abbreviations in the rest of this paper: tp is the number of true positives, tn is the number of true negatives, fp is the number of false positives, and fn is the number of false negatives.

The accuracy of the models is calculated using the formula:

$$accuracy = \frac{tp + tn}{tp + tn + fp + fn}$$

We calculate the accuracy of the individual CNNs, the unsmoothed and the smoothed, in addition to the overall accuracy after voting.

The precision is the ratio of true positives and the total positive predictions. This is calculated as:

$$Precision = \frac{tp}{(tp + fp)}$$

The recall is the ratio of true positives and the total, actual positives. This is calculated as:

$$Recall = \frac{tp}{(tp + fn)}$$

The F_1 score [10] is a combination of these two measures. It is calculated as:

$$F_1 = 2 * \frac{Recall * Precision}{Recall + Precision}$$

where recall and precision are calculated as above.

The F_1 score ranges from 0 to 1, where 1 is the best possible score.

The Matthews Correlation Coefficient (MCC) score [10] is calculated as:

$$MCC = \frac{(tp/n) - sp}{\sqrt{ps(1-s)(1-p)}} = \frac{(tp)(tn) - (fp)(fn)}{\sqrt{(tp + fp)(tp + fn)(tn + fp)(tn + fn)}}$$

where n is the total number of predictions, $s = (tp + fn)/n$, $p = (tp + fp)/n$, tp is the number of true positives, tn is the number of true negatives, fp is the number of false positives, and fn is the number of false negatives.

The MCC gives us an alternate measure of accuracy by providing a measure of the quality of the predictions. The values returned are between −1 and 1, where 1 is a perfect prediction, 0 is no better than a random prediction, and −1 would be a model that always output the opposite of the actual value. An MCC value between 0.4 and 0.6 is considered a strong classifier while an MCC value of over 0.7 is considered a very strong classifier.

We also use a few more statistics in this work: thestandard deviation, the false negative rate, and the false positive rate.

The standard deviation (SD) is calculated as:

$$SD = \frac{\sum_{i=1}^{n}(x_i - \overline{x})^2}{n-1}$$

where n is the total number of networks, x_i is the metric value for network i, and $\overline{x}$ is the average value of the metric.

The False Positive Rate (FPR) [10] is calculated as:

$$FPR = fp/(tn + fp)$$

The False Negative Rate (FNR) [10] is calculated as:

$$FPR = fn/(tp + fn)$$

3 RESULTS AND DISCUSSION

The CNNs were built and tested using three Nvidia GTX 1080 GPUs. We present our results in four subsections: the unsmoothed image model, smoothed image model, the ensemble, and a comparison of the three methods. The three sets of networks were trained and tested using randomly generated training and testing sets. Each network was trained using one of five training and testing sets. Each training set was 50% of the total data (approximately 124, 290 images from 700 patients). The remaining 50% of the data was used to build five testing sets of 10, 848 images from 60 patients. The networks built for each model type are numbered 1 through 5. Corresponding numbered networks from each of the different models were trained and testing using the same data. We present these results in the following subsections.

3.1 Unsmoothed Image Model

Table 1 shows the accuracy values for the unsmoothed image model. We can see that we have a very consistent accuracy from this model. The average accuracy is 87.53% with a standard deviation of 0.01. The precision value and the recall values are also consistent. The average precision is 82.06% (standard deviation = 0.03) and the average recall is 71.43% (standard deviation = 0.03). The F_1 score is also good at an average value of 0.77 (standard deviation = 0.01). We can also see we have a high average value for our MCC of 0.7 (standard deviation =0.02) which indicates that our classifier does a good job of classification.

Table 2 shows the breakdown of each network's true and false predictions. We can see that both the number of false positives and false negatives are relatively low but not at an optimal level.

3.2 Smoothed Image Model

Table 3 shows the accuracy values for the smoothed image model. The average runtime is about 5.5 times longer than that for the unsmoothed model. The smoothed model has similar results to the unsmoothed model. We expect the results to be similar, though the smoothed model will do better with more noisy results.

The average accuracy for this model is 86.15% (standard deviation = 0.02). The average precision and recall are 81.42% (standard deviation = 0.03) and 65.32% (standard deviation = 0.06) respectively. The recall value would indicate that for this model there are a higher number of false negatives for this model than our unsmoothed model discussed in the previous subsection. We can see this in Table 4. The table also shows that this model has fewer false positives per network than the unsmoothed model for all of the networks expect Network 3. This model also has a good, average F_1 with an average value of 0.72 (standard deviation = 0.04). The average MCC value is 0.66 (standard deviation = 0.05) which indicates that this model is a good classifier.

Table 1: Accuracy and quality metrics with runtimes for the unsmoothed model networks with five training and testing sets[a].

Network	Accuracy	Precision	Recall	F_1	MCC	Runtime
1	87.71%	79.55%	75.43%	0.77	0.71	8643.21s
2	87.62%	83.08%	69.95%	0.76	0.70	8649.25s
3	88.32%	86.57%	68.90%	0.77	0.71	8887.48s
4	89.08%	84.66%	74.41%	0.79	0.74	11124.58s
5	86.84%	78.36%	73.09%	0.76	0.69	7315.14s

[a] $Accuracy = (tp + tn)/(tp + tn + fp + fn)$, $Precision = tp/(tp + fp)$, $Recall = tp/(tp + fn)$, $F_1 = 2 * (recall * precision)/(recall + precision)$, **and the Matthews Correlation Coefficient is** $MCC = (tp)(tn) - (fp)(fn)/\sqrt{(tp + fp)(tp + fn)(tn + fp)(tn + fn)}$ **Runtime is the time recorded by the GPU at run time in seconds.**

Table 2: The number of true positive, false positive, true negatives, and false negatives for each of the unsmoothed model networks.

Network	True Positives	False Positives	True Negatives	False Negatives
1	2287	588	7228	745
2	2121	432	7384	911
3	2089	324	7492	943
4	2256	409	7407	776
5	2216	612	7204	816

3.3 Ensemble Method

Table 5 shows the accuracy values for the voting ensemble method. We have an average accuracy of 85.91% (standard deviation = 0.02). We can see in Table 5 that the accuracies are very consistent. The precision value is also very high and consistent with the ensemble. The average precision was 96.83% (standard deviation = 0.01). The recall, however, was not as high. The average recall value was 52.89% (standard deviation = 0.06). This happens with precision and recall though, as there tends to be a tradeoff between the two metrics [10]. The ensemble is a strong classifier with an MCC value of 0.65 (standard deviation = 0.04).

Table 3: Accuracy and quality metrics with runtimes for the smoothed model networks with five training and testing sets[b].

Network	Accuracy	Precision	Recall	F_1	MCC	Runtime
1	83.23%	78.43%	55.18%	0.65	0.59	49040.01s
2	88.36%	85.23%	70.58%	0.77	0.72	49029.02s
3	85.21%	78.99%	64.12%	0.71	0.64	49588.17s
4	87.64%	85.10%	67.61%	0.75	0.70	48359.33s
5	86.34%	79.33%	69.13%	0.74	0.67	45912.30s

[b] $Accuracy = (tp + tn)/(tp + tn + fp + fn)$, $Precision = tp/(tp + fp)$, $Recall = tp/(tp + fn)$, $F_1 = 2 * (recall * precision)/(recall + precision)$, and the Matthews Correlation Coefficient is $MCC = (tp)(tn) - (fp)(fn)/\sqrt{(tp + fp)(tp + fn)(tn + fp)(tn + fn)}$ Runtime is the time recorded by the GPU at run time in seconds.

Table 4: The number of true positive, false positive, true negatives, and false negatives for each of the unsmoothed model networks.

Network	True Positives	False Positives	True Negatives	False Negatives
1	1673	460	7356	1359
2	2140	371	7445	892
3	1944	517	7299	1088
4	2050	359	7457	982
5	2096	546	7270	936

The ensemble does very well with the number of false positives, as we can see from Table 6. The false positive rate for this mode, which is calculated as the number of false positives over the total number of samples, is between 0.37% and 0.38%. This is an enormous drop from the high rate of 95% reported by the currently used methodologies [5, 13]. However, the false negatives are higher for this model than the other two model we have previously discussed, though they are under 18% which is not high enough to be a major concern. The runtime is much longer for this model (average 57861.28s) than either of the other models (averages of 8923.93s and 48385.77s, respectively).

Table 5: Accuracy and quality metrics with the runtime of the ensemble networks with five different training and testing sets[c].

Network	Accuracy	Precision	Recall	F_1	MCC	Runtime
1	82.54%	97.28%	43.54%	0.60	0.58	57240.42s
2	85.34%	97.46%	51.66%	0.63	0.64	57242.94s
3	86.50%	97.52%	53.07%	0.69	0.66	57678.26s
4	87.73%	97.12%	57.82%	0.72	0.69	57891.13s
5	87.46%	94.80%	58.34%	0.72	0.69	59253.65s

[c] $Accuracy = (tp + tn)/(tp + tn + fp + fn)$, $Precision = tp/(tp + fp)$, $Recall = tp/(tp + fn)$, $F_1 = 2 * (recall * precision)/(recall + precision)$, and the Matthews Correlation Coefficient is $MCC = (tp)(tn) - (fp)(fn)/\sqrt{(tp + fp)(tp + fn)(tn + fp)(tn + fn)}$. Runtime is the time recorded by the GPU at run time in seconds.

Table 6 shows that our number of false positives is very low with this model. The number of false positives stays under 100 for 10, 848 images. Our average false positive rate for the ensemble is 0.50% (standard deviation = 0.002). This is a significantly lower than the false positive rates reported by the current methods [5, 13].

Table 6: The number of true positive, false positive, true negatives, and false negatives for each of the ensemble networks.

Network	True Positives	False Positives	True Negatives	False Negatives
1	1430	40	7524	1854
2	1584	41	7283	1482
3	1609	41	7775	1423
4	1753	52	7764	1279
5	1769	97	7719	1263

3.4 Comparison of the models

Here we compare the three models used for the classification of the CT images. Table 7 shows the comparisons of the results for the three models. We can see that using the ensemble with the voting gives us a very large increase in the average precision. This is because our simple voting model drops the number of false positives significantly. The ensemble method has the lowest false positive rate by far of the three models. The ensemble is a strong classifier with an average MCC value of 0.65 and an F_1 score of 0.68. This is slightly lower but still very close to the best score, that of the unsmoothed model.

Table 8 shows the average false positive and false negative rates for each of the models. The ensemble has an average false positive rate of 0.07% while the unsmoothed and smoothed models have average false positives rates of 6.05% and 5.77% respectively. The ensemble false positive rate is decreased by 99.93% from the 95% rate reported for current methods [5, 13]. This low false positive rate for the ensemble method is due to our voting system.

The false negative rate is, however, higher for the ensemble than for our other two methods. We can see in Table 8 that there is an increase in the false negative rate rate the voting method. This in an increase of 70.38% over the unsmoothed model and an increase of 35.84% over the smoothed model. This is because of the simple nature of our voting method, which discounts false negatives in favor of reducing false negatives, causes a tradeoff in the voting system. Therefore, we will address the false negative rate by implementing a more complex voting mechanism in future work. According to the U.S. Preventive Services Task Force, the false negative rate for cancer from CT scans is around 20% [9], however this measure varies greatly in different studies and has been reported as much higher and much lower. False negative rates also vary by lung cancer types, with false negatives being very common in cases of mesothelioma [11]. Thus, our false negative rate is about 20% higher than current screening methods but, because our false positive rate is so much lower it this indicates we have taken an interesting step towards reducing false diagnoses.

Another tradeoff between the three models obviously comes in the runtime. The runtime for the ensemble significantly longer than either of the individual models. We can see from Table 7, the average runtime for the ensemble method is around 16 hours. The unsmoothed model has an average runtime of around 2.5 hours which is about 6.5 times faster than the ensemble method. However, because the overhead is in training, there is still justification for using this despite the long runtime because the false positives are one of the biggest concerns in the diagnosis.

Table 7: Comparison of the average accuracy, precision, recall, and runtimes of the unsmoothed, smoothed, and ensemble methods[d].

Network	Average Accuracy	Average Precision	Average Recall	Average F_1	Average MCC	Average Runtime
Unsmoothed	87.91%	82.44%	72.35%	0.77	0.71	8923.93s
Smoothed	86.15%	81.42%	65.32%	0.72	0.66	48385.76s
Voting	85.91%	96.83%	52.89%	0.68	0.65	57861.278s

[d] $Accuracy = (tp + tn)/(tp + tn + fp + fn)$, $Precision = tp/(tp + fp)$, $Recall = tp/(tp + fn)$, $F_1 = 2 * (recall * precision)/(recall + precision)$, **and the Matthews Correlation Coefficient is** $MCC = (tp)(tn) - (fp)(fn)/\sqrt{(tp + fp)(tp + fn)(tn + fp)(tn + fn)}$. **Runtime is the time recorded by the GPU at run time in seconds.**

Table 8: Comparison of False Positive Rate (FPR) and False Negative Rate (FNR) of the three models[e].

Network	Average False Positive Rate	Average False Negative Rate
Unsmoothed	6.05%	27.65%
Smoothed	5.77%	34.68%
Voting	0.70%	47.11%

[e] $False\ Positive\ Rate = (fp)/(tn + fp)$ **and** $False\ Negative\ Rate = (fn)/(tp + fn)$. **Runtime is the time recorded by the GPU at run time in seconds. The averages of each of these metrics are calculated by taking a simple average of the values from the individual networks for each model.**

4 CONCLUSIONS

Automated initial diagnosis is an important part of addressing the serious problem of lung cancer deaths in the US and around the world. Accurate and swift early detection is needed to help increase patient survival. Our method contributes to the movement towards accurate, automated initial diagnosis techniques by showing that the false positive rates that plague current methods can be significantly decreased. As we stated earlier, the false positive rates in the currently used diagnosis methods are very high, as high as 95% in some cases [5, 13]. The false positive rate of our ensemble method has an average value of 0.50%. This is a decrease in the false positive rate of approximately 99.47% which is a great improvement over the currently used methods.

We see that our simple voting method doesn't significantly increase the accuracy over that of our individual unsmoothed and smoothed models. However, it does significantly decrease the number of false positives and greatly increases the precision of the model. The voting method specifically targets the false positives but it doesn't do anything about the false negatives. Therefore, the false negatives are not decreased during voting. Since the false negative rates with this particular model are higher than those seen clinically [9], an alternative method for dealing with them is needed.

As part of our future work, we will develop and implement a more complex, weighted voting system. The weighted voting system would allow us to try to reduce both the false positives and false negatives. Such a voting system would evaluate the likelihood of a prediction being a false positive or false negative based on previous testing results. These weights could be updated given more data to give us a more accurate result. This would allow us to determine a positive or a negative diagnosis as a final prediction when the individual CNNs do not output the same prediction value rather than merely defaulting to a negative prediction. Further tuning and of the model architecture may also increase the accuracy which in turn will help us reduce our false prediction rates when implemented in conjunction with the voting system. We are also looking into incorporating other methods to increase the overall accuracy of identification.

REFERENCES

[1] 2017 (accessed April, 2017). *Kaggle Data Science Bowl 2017.* https://www.kaggle.com/c/data-science-bowl-2017
[2] Christopher M Bishop. 2006. *Pattern recognition.*
[3] Centers for Disease Control and Prevention. 2013 (accessed April, 2017). *1999 to 2013 Cancer Incidence and Mortality Data.* https://nccd.cdc.gov/uscs/
[4] Francesco Ciompi, Kaman Chung, Sarah J. van Riel, Arnaud Arindra Adiyoso Setio, Paul K. Gerke, Colin Jacobs, Ernst Th. Scholten, Cornelia Schaefer-Prokop, Mathilde M. W. Wille, Alfonso Marchiano, Ugo Pastorino, Mathias Prokop, and Bram van Ginneken. 2016. Towards automatic pulmonary nodule management in lung cancer screening with deep learning. *CoRR* abs/1610.09157 (October 2016). http://arxiv.org/abs/1610.09157
[5] Jennifer M Croswell, David F Ransohoff, and Barnett S Kramer. 2010. Principles of cancer screening: lessons from history and study design issues. In *Seminars in oncology*, Vol. 37. Elsevier, 202–215.
[6] Howard Demuth and Mark Beale. 2009. Matlab neural network toolbox userŠs guide version 6. The MathWorks Inc. (2009).
[7] Debapriya Maji, Anirban Santara, Pabitra Mitra, and Debdoot Sheet. 2016. Ensemble of Deep Convolutional Neural Networks for Learning to Detect Retinal Vessels in Fundus Images. *CoRR* 1603.04833 (March 2016). arXiv:arXiv:1603.04833v1
[8] Mathworks. 2016. *Matlab 2016b.* Mathworks Inc., Natick, MA.
[9] Virginia A Moyer. 2014. Screening for lung cancer: US Preventive Services Task Force recommendation statement. *Annals of internal medicine* 160, 5 (2014), 330–338.
[10] David Martin Powers. 2011. Evaluation: from precision, recall and F-measure to ROC, informedness, markedness and correlation. (December 2011).
[11] M Patricia Rivera, Atul C Mehta, and Momen M Wahidi. 2013. Establishing the diagnosis of lung cancer: Diagnosis and management of lung cancer: American College of Chest Physicians evidence-based clinical practice guidelines. *CHEST Journal* 143, 5_suppl (2013), e142S–e165S.
[12] Holger R Roth, Le Lu, Jiamin Liu, Jianhua Yao, Ari Seff, Kevin Cherry, Lauren Kim, and Ronald M Summers. 2016. Improving Computer-Aided Detection Using Convolutional Neural Networks and Random View Aggregation. *IEEE transactions on medical imaging* 35, 5 (May 2016), 1170–1181.
[13] Divakar Sharma, Thomas G Newman, and Wilbert S Aronow. 2015. Lung cancer screening: history, current perspectives, and future directions. *Arch Med Sci* 11, 5 (May 2015), 1033–1043.
[14] National Lung Screening Trial Research Team and others. 2011. Reduced lung-cancer mortality with low-dose computed tomographic screening. *N Engl J Med* 2011, 365 (August 2011), 395–409.
[15] He Yang, Hengyong Yu, and Ge Wang. 2016. Deep Learning for the Classification of Lung Nodules. *CoRR* arXiv:1611.06651 (November 2016). https://arxiv.org/abs/1611.06651

Fuzzy Prediction of Incipient Alzheimer's Disease cases from Mild Cognitive Impaired cases

Oriehi E. D. Anyaiwe
Gautam B. Singh
oanyaiwe@oakland.edu
singh@oakland.edu
Department of Computer Science and Engineering
Oakland University
MI, 48309, USA

ABSTRACT

Naturally, aging impedes all the functional systems of the body. However, the severity and time of manifestation of these changes differ and due to the effect of both epigenetics and heredity factors. Alzheimer's disease (AD) which can be defined as a pathological lost of memory and cognitive abilities as a result of brain degeneration, injury to the brain or actions of protein biomarkers is the concern of this paper. We presents a *fuzzy criteria* for the identification and prediction (prognosis) of acute cognitive impairment cases from mild impaired cases based on the distance values determined between ions generated by Mass Spectrometer surface enhanced laser desorption/ionization assay procedures. The result obtained augments current clinical techniques by way of introducing additional use of Mass Spectra data. It also solves the problems associated with diagnosing AD through longitudinal follow-up practices and bridges the gap between protein biomarkers discovery and AD diagnosis.

KEYWORDS

Alzheimer's Disease; diagnose; Mild Cognitive Impairment (MCI); incipient tAD; Fuzzy Criteria; prognosis.

1 INTRODUCTION

Every individual is susceptible to a degree of forgetfulness and memory loss due due to aging, stress, or lack of frequent use of particular information. Though this could be in variant degrees, severe cases are awkward as well as awful. The term *Dementia* disease (DD) refers to the loss of memory and other mental abilities that are severe enough to affect ones daily life. There are over eight types of DD with *Alzheimer's* disease (AD) being the most common. AD could be caused by generalized degeneration of the brain, brain injuries or onset by protein biomarkers and is currently suffered by over five million people in the US [1] and most prominent with age.

Permission to make digital or hard copies of all or part of this work for personal or classroom use is granted without fee provided that copies are not made or distributed for profit or commercial advantage and that copies bear this notice and the full citation on the first page. Copyrights for components of this work owned by others than ACM must be honored. Abstracting with credit is permitted. To copy otherwise, or republish, to post on servers or to redistribute to lists, requires prior specific permission and/or a fee. Request permissions from permissions@acm.org.
ACM-BCB'17, August 20–23, 2017, Boston, MA, USA.
© 2017 ACM. 978-1-4503-4722-8/17/08...$15.00
DOI: http://dx.doi.org/10.1145/3107411.3108176

At this point in time, there exists no cure for AD. Early *diagnosis* is the key to better care, management and sometimes cure. In practice, early diagnosis is hampered by the lack of diagnostic tools or devices for the disease. Related works available in literature attempts solving the problem of AD diagnosis from other angles; they either pinpoint biological factors (pathology) that increase/reduce the risk of AD [2] or establish potential biomarker for AD [3]. Our work augments these studies, in that, it actually identifies respondents risks of AD with a generalize-able framework.

In our previous works ([4], [5] and [6]), we developed classification models that directly discriminates elements of Mass Spectrometer *Saliva* data based on three stages of AD. The data used was generated through surface enhanced laser desorption/ionization (MS-SELDI) assay procedure. By extension, the models built the parameter for easy, fast and reliable diagnosis of AD.

In the models, we categorized the severity of AD into three stages; *control/normal group* (*CON*) for aged protein source donors with no cognitive impairment, *mild cognitive impairment* group (*MCI*) and *acute or total cognitive impairment* group (*tAD*). The protein source sample (PSS) used is *saliva* and the functionality of the models are independent of clinical data or longitudinal study reports and there are easy to apply and yields instant outputs without any dependent on autopsy results.

The science of Proteomics is not new, with it individual proteins can be identified from complex mixtures [11]. Other advantages of proteomics includes protein identification and protein biomarker discovery through the further studies of differentially expressed ions generated by high-throughput assay techniques.

The foundation of the functionality of the models described in [4]–[6] is the same. They hypothesized that average *intra-class* distance between protein spectra is significantly less than the *inter-class* distances. Such that mining (or machine learning) a pool of mass spectra (a collection of *differentially* expressed ions) will generate inherent pattern in the dataset for classification purposes and the diagnosis of AD, but this task is formidable since each data point is a *matrix* and available supervised learning algorithms do *vector-to-vector* discrimination. Hitherto, further studies of SELDI ions typically involves the use of algorithms (e.g [11]-[14]) to match the properties of generated peptide ions to those that exists in theoretical and/or public peptide data base, upon this, inferences are made.

An immediate consideration upon the realization of the goal of these models [4]–[6] is that the severity of *tAD* stage is downplayed when it is combined with *MCI* for analysis. A descriptive x-ray of

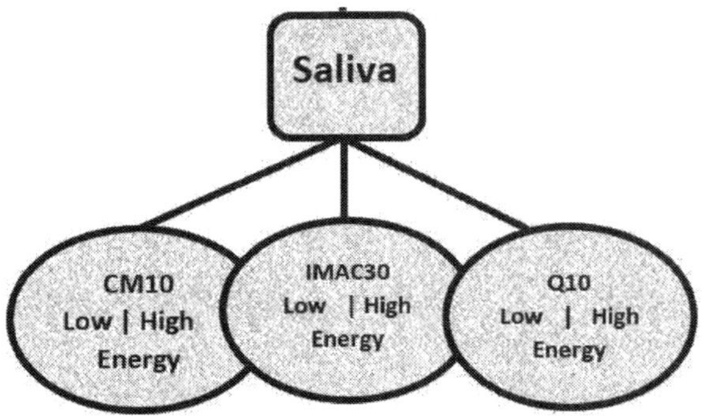

Figure 1: Tree representation of the Data Set
Data set: showing the names of proteinChips (CM10, IMAC30 & Q10) and laser energy levels (low & high) of MS-SELDI analysis of saliva

this scenario is presented in subsection *2.3*. This work discriminate and identify early or incipient AD from age-associated cognitive impairment (*MCI*) cases. The methodology is described in section 2, section 3 covers the results and discussion, while conclusion is presented in section 4.

2 METHODOLOGY

In our previous works mentioned [4] (*eKNN*) and [5] (*WMDC*), we developed classification models for the classification of Mass Spectrometer surface enhanced laser desorption/ionization (MS-SELDI) Saliva data set towards the diagnosis of Alzheimer's disease (AD). In this work, we review and present benefits of exploring these models algorithm by way of developing the parameter for AD prognoses. In particular, by the sensitivity analysis done in subsection 2.3 we fault the idea of combining *MCI* and *tAD* elements to form the **predisposed** category against *CON* elements as the **non-disposed** category. Our interest here is in identifying incipient cases of *tAD* from *MCI* or relapse from *MCI* to *CON* stage. The methodology uses the vectors contained in *CON* and *tAD* data points as a basis and benchmark to identify the level of neural degeneration expressed in any given test (*MCI*) data point using a *fuzzy criteria*.

Generally, it is less invasive obtaining saliva compared to serum, this is one of the reasons for saliva as the PSS, the data set tree is shown in Fig. ??. Another argument for using saliva as the analyte is akin to that made for cerebrospinal fluid (CSF) in improving early detection, differential diagnosis and tracking of disease progression in AD since CSF is in direct contact with the brain [10]. SELDI assay procedures were carried out and stored under three proteinChips; CM10, IMAC30 and Q10 and further partitioned by low and high laser energy bombardment levels.

The final output of an MS-SELDI analysis is usually a collection n differentially expressed peaks i.e, observed ions that were selected from the pool of generated spectrum based on their properties e.g. their p-values.

As a pre-processing step, both *eKNN* and *WMDC* model reduces each SELDI result from an *n-by-m* matrix to an *n-by-2* matrix and thereafter, examine and classify them based on the evidence of their constituent vectors under the model's underlying classification principle. A summary of the model's classification principles is given below, it suffices to say that they form a larger part of the basis for the methodology of this work.

2.1 eKNN Classification Model

eKNN is an abbreviation for *exponential* k-nearest neighbor classification model [4]. The model adopted *Euclidean* distance function with an *exponential* bias for the differences between the mass values of any two subsequent vectors. Thus, the distance between any two vectors a and b was defined to be

$$dist_{(a,b)} = \sqrt{(e^{(m_a - m_b)^2} - 1)^2 + (I_a - I_b)^2} \quad (1)$$

Where m and I respectively represents the mass (M/Z) and intensity values of the vectors a and b of a test data point (matrix). For a collection C (Eq. 2) *eKNN* finds and utilizes $min(C)$ i.e. the minimum value in C. The bias was necessitated to blow up $(m_a - m_b)$ values so as to lay emphasis on values obtained from determining the differences between the intensity values $(I_a - I_b)$ in particular.

$$C = \{dist_{(a,b)}), (dist_{(a,c)}), (dist_{(a,c)}) \cdots, (dist_{(a,z)})\} \quad (2)$$

Consider Fig. 2 and the illustrations of Eq. 3, notice that the intensity values expressed in plot-*B* are equal $(I_a = I_b)$ however, these peaks are expressed for different mass values, learning them and using any information gleaned from that exercise will lead to wrong conclusions. Thus, we hit the difference of their mass values with the exponential function and blow up the corresponding distance value obtained with them so that it wont be a choice to be considered for use by *eKNN*. An advantage of this is that it remarkably discourages the use of any two peaks with different mass values (however small their distance apart is) and favors using peaks expressed on the same mass values. We used $K = 1$ in *eKNN* model.

$$dist_{(a,b)} = \begin{cases} \sqrt{(I_a - I_b)^2} & m_a = m_b \\ Eq.\ 1 & m_a \neq m_b;\ I_a \neq I_b \\ \sqrt{(e^{(m_a - m_b)^2} - 1)^2} & I_a = I_b \end{cases} \quad (3)$$

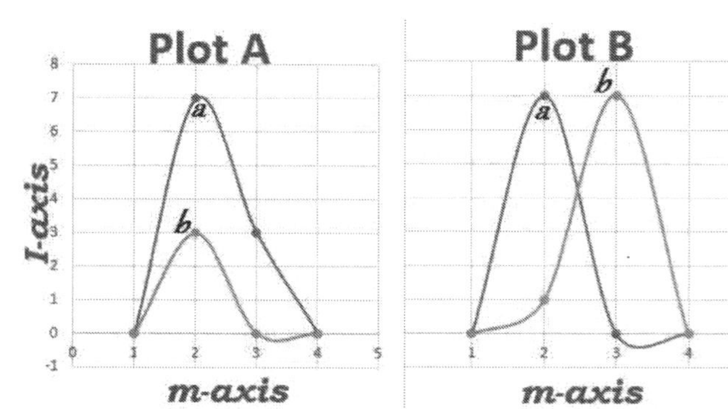

Figure 2: Choice of Peaks by location

Jackknife sampling method was used to select subsequent test data points from the data set, then a distance *hit table* (Table 1) was generated to keep count of the stage label of the vectors contained in the train data set that were closest to each of the n-vectors in the test data point using Eq. 1. The classification iteration concludes by classifying the test data to the stage label with the highest counts. For instance, the test data TEST1 was classified as *MCI* while TEST2 is *tAD* based on majority votes. Additional details, including performance rating is given in [4]

Table 1: Hit Table

	CON	MCI	tAD
TEST1	44	**75**	60
TEST2	49	57	**73**

2.2 WMDC Model

The weighted Manhattan distance classifier (*WMDC*) [5] has a similar approach to *eKNN*, but the underlying distance function is the *Manhattan* distance formulae (Eq. 4). The validation of evidence (distance between vectors) upon which the classification is based on, is determined individually for each vector contained in a test data point using Eq. 5.

$$d_m(u,v) = |m_1 - m_2| + |I_1 - I_2| \tag{4}$$

$$significance = \frac{1}{d_m} \tag{5}$$

Where d_m is the distance or the measure of the length of projections of the *line segments* between the two vectors $v = (m_1, I_1)$ and $u = (m_2, I_2)$ onto the coordinates axes of a 2-dimensional space. The final step in classifying a test data is still based on majority votes, where the votes are substitutions made with stage labels of vectors of the train data sets that were most significant to vectors of the test data point. A pseudocode of the algorithm, its performance and analysis is found in [5].

2.3 Sensitivity Analysis of eKNN & WMDC Results

Table 2: Analysis Results

Energy Level	Low	High
ProteinChips		
CM10	55%	88%
IMAC30	55%	87%
Q10	60%	90%

Table 2 shows in percentage the number of correctly classified instances using WMDC with respect to the proteinChips and energy levels used in the SELDI experiment (a similar table exists for eKNN). Using the confusion matrix Table 3, for Q10-High-energy value (90%) of Table 2, 0.075 was established as the probability for committing *type II error* by [5].

Table 3: Q10 High Energy (90%)

	CON	MCI	tAD
CON	19	1	0
MCI	2	17	1
tAD	1	1	18

In the analysis two classes were created; *non disposed* (NO) and *predisposed* (YES) class. The *non disposed* class was made up of by only the control group data points while a combination of the mild and totally impaired data points constituted the *predisposed* class. While this seems to be true, it is not entirely correct, it hides the grave differences between an *MCI* person and a *tAD* patient, it is like equating road and air accidents.

By definition, a *type II error* is committed if an actual YES is classified to be a NO by the model while a *type I error* is committed if an actual NO was classified to be a YES. To this end and judging from Table 3 a *type II error* cannot be committed when classifying elements of the *CON* stage, using the same argument a *type I error* will never be committed with *tAD* data points but on the other hand, the chances of committing any of the error types exists for any given *MCI* data point (see Fig. 3).

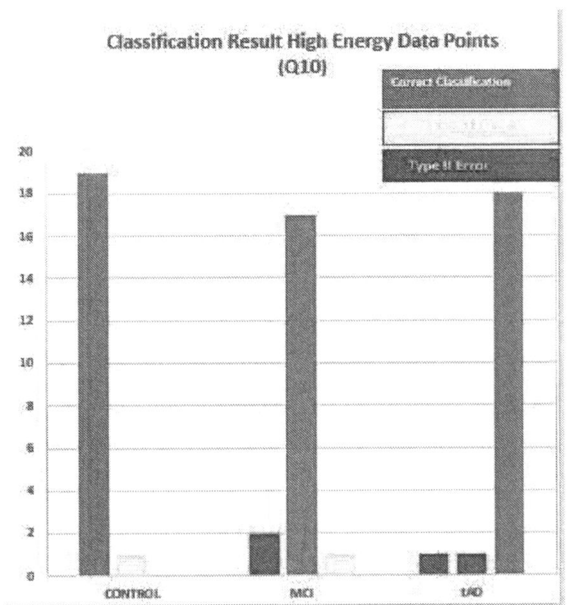

Figure 3: Error Types using Table 3

2.4 Fuzzy Criteria

From the previous subsection, we can itemize the following deductions

- *CON* and *tAD* are the extreme left and right cases
- A different form of error is created when the classification results obtained for *MCI* data points is combined with either those of *CON* or *tAD*

Ordinarily, not all cases of forgetfulness is Alzheimer's case. We now present a simple and succinct fuzzy criteria to identify incipient cases of *AD* from *mild cognitive impaired* cases based on a generalized concept gained from the standards developed in [4], [5] and the deductions above.

First, reconstruct the strata of the data set; the *CON* and *tAD* data points constitute the *train* data set but each of them maintains its 'extreme' position while *MCI* data points becomes the test data set. To 'evaluate' the status of subsequent test data points we either adopt the principle used in *eKNN* or *WMDC* model and evaluate all the vectors in the test data point. Thereafter, we adopt *fuzzy* criteria for final classification and forecast of risk of incipient AD.

Definition: Let n be the number of differentially expressed ions in a test data point, with c and t the number of ions in the test data that are respectively most significant to the vectors *CON* and *tAD* in the train data pool, so that $n = c + t$. Then the *fuzzy* criteria is a function defined by

$$fuzzyCriteria = \max\left(\frac{c}{n}, \frac{t}{n}\right) \tag{6}$$

The *fuzzy* criteria partitions the n vectors of a test data into two sets $\frac{c}{n}$ and $\frac{t}{n}$ which represents the level neural degradation and categorizes a test data as *incipient tAD* if the output of Eq. 6 is $\frac{t}{n}$ and *relapsing* otherwise.

3 RESULT AND DISCUSSION

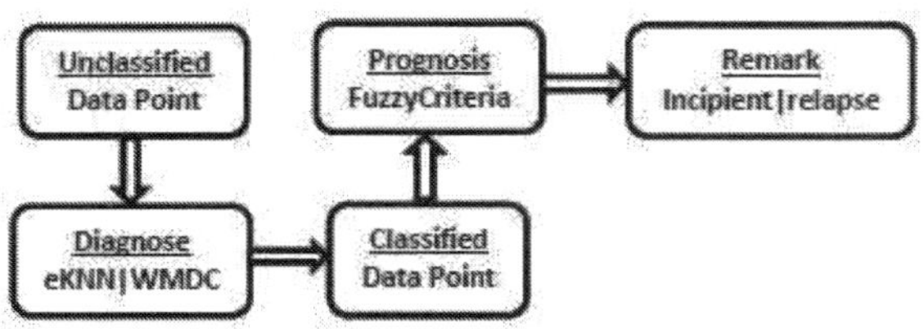

Figure 4: Fuzzy Criteria Steps

Fig. 4 is a snapshot of the pipeline of this model. At the beginning an unclassified data point is fed into *eKNN* or *WMDC* model for classification in the diagnose step. Classified outputs of the diagnose step is then fed as input into the fuzzy model and a prognosis remark is generated.

As a consequence of the *level* of homogeneity expressed by the data points generated under low energy laser beam, the classification results obtained with *eKNN* and *WMDC* for them was not very satisfactory. Thus, we only focused on the other set of data points generated under high energy bombardment here.

Also, four *CON* data points that were previously considered as *MCI* data points in [4] and [6] in error, are re-introduced as *MCI* data points. We prefixed these new data points with *special* to differentiate them.

The output of the prognosis step remarks each data point as being *incipient* or *relapse* which conveys the degree (in percentage) of evaluated brain degeneration. Each row of Table 4 is an evaluation result of a test data point. With the number (n) of *differentially* expressed peaks/ions contained in such a test data point is known (e.g, in CM10 high energy data points n is 29), the sum of the cell entries under *CON* and *tAD* for each row of the table should equal $n = 299$ in this case. Applying Eq. 6, we obtained the entries under *Remarks*; *incipient*, if the output of Eq. 6 is $\frac{t}{n}$ and *relapse* if the output is $\frac{c}{n}$. For instance,

Table 4: Fuzzy Prediction Result

S/N	REF_NUMBER	CON	tAD	Remarks
1.	635_SpotA_#11A	123	176	incipient
2.	635_SpotC_#14A	142	157	incipient
3.	450_SpotG_#19B	153	146	relapse
4.	450_SpotH_#16B	160	139	relapse
5.	451_SpotD_#13B	155	144	relapse
6.	454_SpotG_#15B	144	155	incipient
7.	454_SpotA_#18B	144	155	incipient
8.	454_SpotE_#11B	138	161	incipient
9.	**Special_20A**	208	91	**CON**
10.	**Special_20B**	219	80	**CON**
11.	**Special_17A**	213	85	**CON**
12.	**Special_17B**	212	86	**CON**
13.	635_SpotF_#12A	154	145	relapse
14.	634_SpotF_#19A	159	140	relapse
15.	633_SpotD_#15A	150	149	Approx
16.	633_SpotE_#18A	142	157	incipient
17.	632_SpotC_#12B	122	177	incipient
18.	454_SpotF_#13A	150	149	Approx
19.	450_SpotC_#14B	142	158	relapse
20.	450_SpotF_#16A	153	146	relapse

$$degree_{\{incipient/relapse\}} = \max\left(\frac{c}{n}, \frac{t}{n}\right) \times 100 \tag{7}$$

the degree of incipient for the first test data (S/N=1) is $176/299 \times 100 = 59\%$. In the same manner, the 9th test data is 70% a member of the control group (as expected). By fuzzy criteria, the degree of membership of the 15th and 18th test data points is approximately equal (50.2 vs 49.8), hence the categorization as *Approx* under remarks.

Once again, the introduction of the *special* data points with serial numbers 9 -to-12 serve as control to mark failure/success of the fuzzy criteria. Notice that with a wide margin or degree, they were categorized correctly (as showing minor degradation). This scenario as a matter of fact, adds credibility to the classification results presented for *eKNN* and *WMDC* as well as identifying the significant value of the outcomes of *fuzzy* criteria (Eq. 6).

4 CONCLUSION

The non scientific clinical follow-up procedures (such as, the Six Item Cognitive Impairment Test, Mini Mental State Examination, or Clock Drawing Test) that are the only approaches currently in use for the diagnosis of Alzheimer's disease leaves much to be desired. However, owing to the fact that not all cases of forgetfulness can be termed AD we have developed a platform for actually identifying and quantifying neural degeneration due to Alzheimer's disease using saliva MS-SELDI assay results. The idea is simple and easy to adopt and yields accurate, clear and generalize-able outcomes.

Collaborating with bio-pharmaceutical companies and medical institutions in other to acquire larger data set as well as following-up and validating obtained results or patterns are concerns for future works.

REFERENCES

[1] Alzheimer's Association. http://www.alz.org/facts/overview.asp. [Accessed 3 July 2016].

[2] Hiroko H. Dodge, Jian Zhu, et al. *Risk of incident clinical diagnosis of Alzheimerfis disease-type dementia attributable to pathology-confirmed vascular disease*; Alzheimerfis & Dementia, vol. 13, pp. 613-623, 2017.

[3] Jose Luis Molinuevo, Kaj Blennow, et. al. *The clinical use of cerebrospinal fluid biomarker testing for Alzheimer's disease diagnosis: A consensus paper from the Alzheimer's Biomarkers Standardization Initiative*; Alzheimerfis & Dementia, vol. 10, pp. 808fi?!817, 2014.

[4] O. E. D. Anyaiwe, S. B. Gautam, et. al. *eK-NN Classification of Mass Spectra Data for Diagnosing Alzheimer's Disease*, ACM SigBio, 2017.

[5] O. E. D. Anyaiwe, G. D. Wilson, et al. *Weighted Manhattan Distance Classifier; SELDI Data for Alzheimer's Disease Diagnosis*, IEEE CEC Transactions, 2017.

[6] O. E. D. Anyaiwe, S. B. Gautam, and G. D. Wilson. *Classification By Clustering: Saliva MS-SELDI Data for Alzheimer's Disease Diagnosis*, SDPC 2017.

[7] Tierney M. C., Fisher R. H., et al. *Toward a definite diagnosis of Alzheimer's disease*; Comprehensive Psychiatry, vol. 33, pp 282-290, 1992.

[8] Jellinger K. A. (1996) *Diagnostic accuracy of Alzheimerfis disease: a clinicopathological study.* Acta Neuropathol. 91, 219fi?!220, 1996.

[9] Galasko D., Hansen L. A., Katzman R., et al. *Clinical-neuropathological correlations in Alzheimerfis disease and related dementias.* Arch. Neurol. 51, 888fi?!895, 1994.

[10] Blennow K, Vanmechelen E, Hampel H. *CSF total tau, Abeta42 and phosphorylated tau protein as biomarkers for Alzheimer's disease*, Mol Neurobiol 24:87fi?!97, 2001.

[11] Marina Spivak. *Analysis of Mass Spectrometry Data for Protein Identification in Complex Biological Mixtures.* (Doctoral dissertation, New York University), 2010.

[12] Chuen Seng Tan, Alexander Ploner, Andreas Quandt, Janne Lehtio and Yudi Pawitan. *Finding regions of significance in SELDI measurements for identifying protein biomarkers.* 2006: Bioinformatics.

[13] J. K. Eng, A. L. McCormack, and J. R. Yates. *An approach to correlate tandem mass spectral data of peptides with amino acid sequences in a protein database.* 1994: Journal of the American Society for Mass Spectrometry.

[14] J. K. Eng, B. Fischer, J. Grossman, and M. J. MacCoss. *A fast SEQUEST cross correlation algorithm.* 2008: Journal of Proteome Research.

Using GenotypeAnalytics to Analyze Pharmacogenomic Datasets

Giuseppe Agapito
Data Analytics Research Center, Department of Medical and Surgical Sciences, University "Magna Græcia"
Catanzaro, Italy 88100
agapito@unicz.it

Pietro, Hiram Guzzi
Data Analytics Research Center, Department of Medical and Surgical Sciences, University "Magna Græcia"
Catanzaro, Italy 88100
hguzzi@unicz.it

Mario Cannataro
Data Analytics Research Center, Department of Medical and Surgical Sciences, University "Magna Græcia"
Catanzaro, Italy 88100
cannataro@unicz.it

ABSTRACT

The identification of multiple allelic variants with the conditions of patient's could be allow to better understand the reason due to the different response to the same treatments of patients affected by the same disease. To evaluate the different response of patients we analyzed datasets obtained by using Affymetrix DMET. The Affymetrix DMET (Drug Metabolizing Enzymes and Transporters) microarray platform offers the possibility to determine the ADME (Absorption, Distribution, Metabolism, and Excretion) gene variants of a patient and correlate them with drug-dependent adverse events. Therefore, using DMET data may reveal important information to clinicians about possible correlations among drug response, and allelic variants, in cases-controls studies. To provide an easy and effective support to this analysis we developed GenotypeAnalytics, a software service RESTFull based, ables to automatically extract association rules from DMET datasets and convey to the user the best rules able to discriminate among the two different class of patients, i.e. tox, no-tox, or respond not-respond. GenotypeAnalytics is able to perform an automatic analysis of DMET dataset, without that users have to set-up the data preprocessing step as well as handle specialised hardware. The only interaction with the tool are i) upload the input file to analyze and, ii) set-up the level of relevance of the mined association rules. Finally, we present a case study to highlight the usefulness of GenotypeAnalytics when analyzing huge court of patients.

CCS CONCEPTS

• **Applied computing → Life and medical sciences**;

KEYWORDS

Bioinformatics,Genomics

1 INTRODUCTION

One of the problem related to drug-development and to clinical practice is the variability of the response to the same drug. Pharmacogenomic is a relatively novel discipline based on the rationale that this variability is due to different variants on the genome of patients. [5, 15]. In particular, it has been shown that a set of genes, defined to as drug absorption, distribution, metabolism and excretion genes (ADME-genes) [13] are related to such processes [6–8, 10, 12, 14, 16].Such genes present known Single Nucleotide Polymorphisms (SNPs), e.g. variants on the sequence of nucleotides, related to different drug responses [4, 11], or differences on the component of each pair of genes present in humans, allelic variants.

The DMET (Drug Metabolism Enzymes and Transporters) platform developed by Affymetrix is employed to identify in human samples the allelic variants, in ADME genes. From a computer science point of view, the result of a DMET experiment is a $n \times m$ matrix of alleles, where n is the number of probes ($n = 1936$ in the current DMET plate) and m is the number of samples (patients). Each cell of such table contains a string value including two alleles symbols i.e. $''a_1/a_2''$, where $a_1, a_2 \in A = \{A, C, G, T, -\} \in ''NoCall''$ symbol.

Existing approaches of analysis of DMET data, span from preprocessing of raw data, e.g. Affymetrix-power-tools, Affymetrix-DMET-Console, to the correlation of variants with respect to different patient conditions, e.g. DMET-Analyzer [9], Cloud4snp [1] and DMET-Miner [3].

Main limitation of these softwares are the need to configure many parameters of preprocessing or to handle specialised hardware. Conversely, RESTful services are known to help user making many details transparent to end-user. Consequently we developed GenotypeAnalytics, a RESTful service to analyze such data, GenotypeAnalytics improve the performances of DMET-Miner by using optimized data structures that give good performance results in rule extraction also with massive DMET datasets.

In summary, GenotypeAnalytics is an RESTFul web service able to efficiently read and manage data produced by the Affymetrix DMET platform. Also, GenotypeAnalytics can extract relevant knowledge by computing frequent item sets in an efficient way, as well as mining association rules [2] that link allelic variants in more than one probe with the health status of patients (e.g. subjects responding or not responding to drugs).

2 DMET DATA.

The DMET datasets obtained by using Affymetrix DMET is arranged as a $m \times n$ SNP DMET table. In particular, m is the number of probes (in the current version of the DMET chip is equals to 1936), whereas n is the number of subjects (patients) gathered together for the class of membership i.e. Healthy and Diseased, Responding or NotResponding. Without loose in generality we can suppose that from $i to p$ patients belong to class A while, from $p + 1 to n$ belong to class B. Finally, each cell (i, j) contains the allele recognized

Permission to make digital or hard copies of all or part of this work for personal or classroom use is granted without fee provided that copies are not made or distributed for profit or commercial advantage and that copies bear this notice and the full citation on the first page. Copyrights for components of this work owned by others than ACM must be honored. Abstracting with credit is permitted. To copy otherwise, or republish, to post on servers or to redistribute to lists, requires prior specific permission and/or a fee. Request permissions from permissions@acm.org.
ACM-BCB'17, August 20-23, 2017, Boston, MA, USA.
© 2017 Association for Computing Machinery.
ACM ISBN 978-1-4503-4722-8/17/08...$15.00
https://doi.org/10.1145/3107411.3108177

to the *ith* probe and at the *jth* sample RDG iteratively fills each element of the table (i,j), where i is the probe identifier (for current DMET platform, $m = 1936$) and j is the sample (e.g. patient) identifier. An example of synthetic SNP DMET dataset is reported in Table 1.

Table 1: A simple DMET SNP microarray data set. *S* **and** *P* **respectively refer to sample and probe identifiers.**

Probes \ Samples	S_1	S_2	S_3	…	S_N
P_1	G/A	A/G	A/G	…	T/T
P_2	G/A	A/G	A/G	…	T/C
⋮	⋮	⋮	⋮	…	⋮
P_M	G/A	A/G	A/G	…	T/C

To extract relevant rules, we need to convert the input DMET dataset into a transaction database. The conversion of DMET dataset includes the following steps: *i)* loading and transposing of the input DMET dataset and (let see e.g. Table 1) obtaining a $n \times m$ table of alleles named AllelesTable *AT*. In this way, each row of the *AT* represents a transaction, where all detected SNPs are the items of the transaction. Table 2 shows the transformed matrix *AT* for the input dataset of Table 1.

Table 2: The AllelesTable *TA* **obtained transposing the input DMET microarray dataset.** *S* **and** *P* **respectively refer to sample and probe identifiers.**

Samples \ Probes	P_1	P_2	…	P_M
S_1	G/A	G/A	…	G/A
S_2	A/G	A/G	…	A/G
S_3	A/G	A/G	…	A/G
⋮	⋮	⋮	⋮	⋮
S_N	T/T	T/C	…	T/C

ii) Table 2 is then used to extract frequent itemsets. Thus, to explain the overall process, we here recall the central concepts that we use in the following. Let $I = \{i_1, i_2, \ldots, i_n\}$ be a set of items (alleles), where an item is identified by a specific SNP into a cell (i,j) of *AT*.

Let T the set of transactions, formally a transaction over I is a couple $T = (tid, I)$, where tid is the transaction identifier, and I is an item or itemset. The number of items present in a transaction is defined as *transaction width.* A transaction T_j contains an itemset J, if J is a subset of T_j, this is $J \subset T$.

Let $D = \{t_1, t_2, \ldots, t_m\}$ be a set of transactions, called *DMET-Dataset D* hereafter. Each transaction in D is identified by an unique *ID* of the corresponding sample or patient.

Now we may start the mining phase by performing the following steps:

(1) pruning all the item that present a support value lower than the specified minimum frequency threshold.
(2) add all the frequent items to the FP-Tree.
(3) mine association rules from the FP-Tree.

The power of frequent item sets extraction concerns with the ability to discover interesting relationships hidden in large data sets. This feature relies on a crucial property of the itemset also known as *Support.* Support refers to the number of transactions that contain a particular item or item set. Formally, the Support $S(\cdot)$ of an item X, $S(X)$ can be defined as follows: $S(X) = |\{\forall t_i \subset X \wedge t_i \in T\}|$, where $|\cdot|$ denotes the cardinality of the set. In other words, $S(X)$ is the fraction of transactions in T containing the item/item-set X.

Association models extract rules that express the relationships among items into frequent itemsets. For example, a rule belonging to the frequent itemsets composed by the following elements $\{A/A, G/C, C/T\}$ might be stated as: **IF** $(A/A \wedge G/C)$ **THEN** C/T that can be read as: if A/A and G/C are included in a transaction, then C/T likely should also be included; this rule, for example, may be related to a complex disease such as cancer or diabetes.

3 THE GENOTYPEANALYTICS PLATFORM

We have designed and built GA as a web-based platform for the client-server model for the analysis and storage of data produced by using SNP-microarray by implementing the analysis methodology described in the previous section. Using the client-server protocol allows the user to access the services provided by the platform even remotely through the use of a web browser. Specifically, the client layer provides the user with a simplified platform access interface, while the server layer, via the web, allows the client to communicate and interact with the logic of the application that does not reside locally. In this way, data analysis is transparent for the user who does not have to worry about maintaining and managing high-performance hardware to process these huge data queues. Lastly, the client-server model is efficient and scalable because it allows multiple user data requests to be met at the same time. GA has been developed by using Java v8.0, REST, and HTML5, and it is compatible with all the known operating systems. Figure 1 shows the web platform's top architecture that allows remote access to the SNP microarray data analysis service.Below is a description of the main functions of the platform modules as web services.

- *Internet Access Protocols*: The internet access module should provide the tools needed to transfer information from client to server and vice versa. We implemented our software by using REST technology, since REST exploits the potential of the HTTP protocol, such as security and addressing mechanisms.
- *Data Encryption/Decription*: The data encryption/decryption module is crucial to allow researchers to safely transfer sensitive information, avoiding compromising the privacy of patients. To ensure that communications between client servers run safely, communications occur on HTTPS protocol, a variant of the HTTP protocol to which the Secure Socket Layer (SSL, Security Layer) is added.

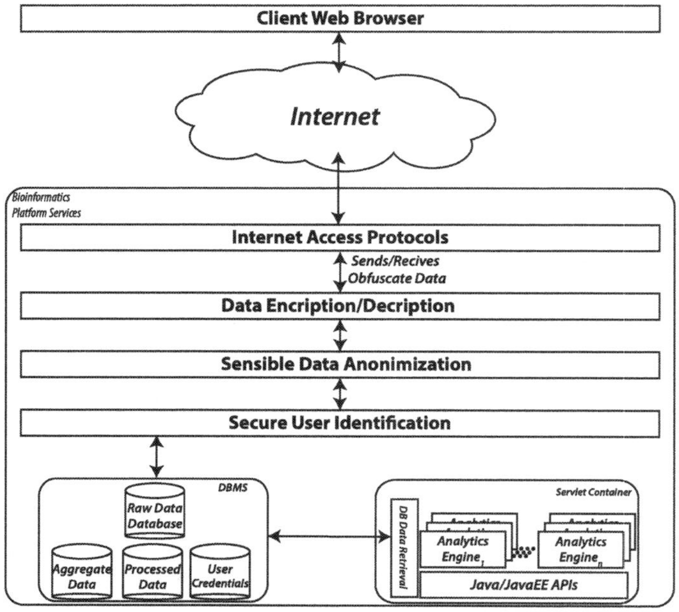

Figure 1: The GenotypeAnalytics Platform.

- *Sensible Data Anonymization*: Data anonymization is indispensable if you want to allow researchers to store data from their products to help shape a digital catalog (for example, the SNP mutation catalog). Anonymization is a process that allows us to modify data so that the subject's identity can not be identified.
- *DBMS*: The DBMS (Database Management System) manages the database and is perfectly integrated with the web server client architecture. The DBMS memorizes the user's SNP data prior to storing the aggregate data reusable for future analysis. Lastly, the DBMS handles user access credentials to the properly encrypted platform.
- *User Identification*: Allows only registered users to access to their area and manage their data (for example, make them public within the platform). The first step for using platform services is that the user logs onto the platform by defining their user profile. For subsequent accesses, you will only have to authenticate by providing your credentials on the platform's login page.
- *DBDataRetrieval*: is a software module developed using JDBC (Java DataBase Connectivity). JDBC is a Java library, consisting of a set of APIs that provide a layer of access to the DataBase. Then DBDataRetrieval lets us to submit client and server requests to the DBMS, ensuring scalability and efficiency in data management.
- *AnalyticsEngines*: The engine objective is to provide a web interface to the algorithms offered by the platform. Enabling the user to locate and use the algorithms using the HTTP protocol.

4 CASE STUDY

Here we show the use of GenotypeAnalytics through an example. Figure 2 shows the web interface of the software. Initially the user has to choose the file containing the DMET dataset and to upload the dataset into the system. Then the user has only to select the minimum values of support and confidence parameters. The system preprocesses the dataset automatically. At the end of the computation the system notifies the user by sending an email.

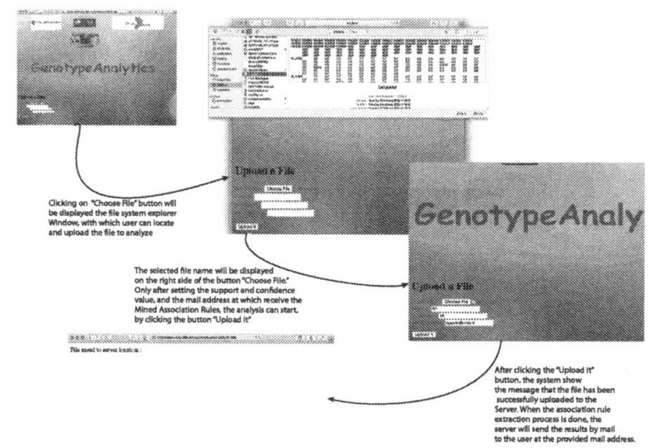

Figure 2: The interface of GenotypeAnalytics

GenotypeAnalytics implements an optimized version of the mining algorithms that outperforms the previous DMET-Miner. Figure 3 shows the improvements of GenotypeAnalytics with respect to DMET-miner when analysing a DMET dataset of 45 patients (45 columns, 1936 rows).

5 CONCLUSIONS

GenotypeAnalytics is a platform for services to support data analysis in pharmacogenomic. GenomeAnalytics could support researcher and medical doctors to identify new molecular markers that can be

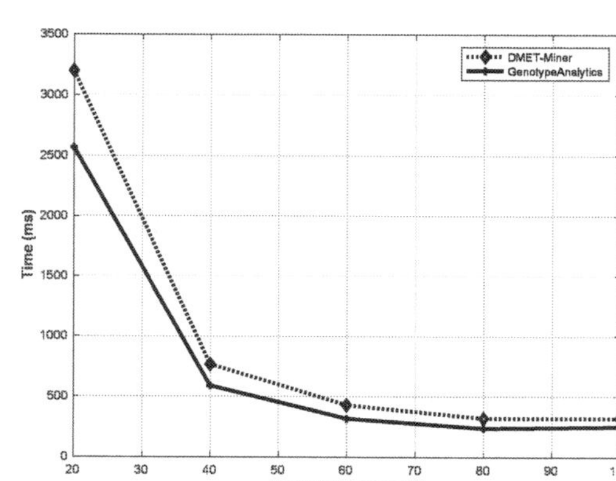

Figure 3: Execution Times of GenotypeAnalytics compared to DMET-Miner

used clinically. Possible new molecular markers can be used to understand which SNPs are responsible for a particular pathology, or what are the SNPs that negatively or positively influence drug responses in subjects with the same pathology and subjected to the same therapy. The plastform makes data analysis simple and effective through the implementation of methods ranging from statistics to data mining analysis of data generated by microarrays. Thanks to an automated system tuning process, the users will only have to send the data they intends to analyze by specifying the level of significance and await the results, allowing the researchers to identify multiple genetic variants that affect complex pathologies in humans.

ACKNOWLEDGMENTS

This work has been partially funded by the following research project funded by the Italian Ministry of Education and Research (MIUR): "BA2Know-Business Analytics to Know" (PON03PE_00001_1).

REFERENCES

[1] Giuseppe Agapito, Mario Cannataro, Pietro Hiram Guzzi, Fabrizio Marozzo, Domenico Talia, and Paolo Trunfio. 2013. Cloud4snp: distributed analysis of snp microarray data on the cloud. In *Proceedings of the International Conference on Bioinformatics, Computational Biology and Biomedical Informatics*. ACM, 468.

[2] Giuseppe Agapito, Mario Cannataro, Pietro Hiram Guzzi, and Marianna Milano. 2015. Using GO-WAR for mining cross-ontology weighted association rules. *Computer methods and programs in biomedicine* 120, 2 (2015), 113–122.

[3] Giuseppe Agapito, Pietro H Guzzi, and Mario Cannataro. 2015. DMET-Miner: Efficient discovery of association rules from pharmacogenomic data. *Journal of biomedical informatics* 56 (2015), 273–283.

[4] Mariamena Arbitrio, Maria Teresa Di Martino, Vito Barbieri, Giuseppe Agapito, Pietro Hiram Guzzi, Cirino Botta, Eleonora Iuliano, Francesca Scionti, Emanuela Altomare, Stefania Codispoti, et al. 2016. Identification of polymorphic variants associated with erlotinib-related skin toxicity in advanced non-small cell lung cancer patients by DMET microarray analysis. *Cancer chemotherapy and pharmacology* 77, 1 (2016), 205–209.

[5] Mariamena Arbitrio, Maria Teresa Di Martino, Francesca Scionti, Giuseppe Agapito, Pietro Hiram Guzzi, Mario Cannataro, Pierfrancesco Tassone, and Pierosandro Tagliaferri. 2016. DMET (Drug Metabolism Enzymes and Transporters): a pharmacogenomic platform for precision medicine. *Oncotarget* 7, 33 (2016), 54028.

[6] Maria T. Di Martino, Mariamena Arbitrio, Pietro H. Guzzi, Emanuela Leone, Francesco Baudi, Eugenio Piro, Tullia Prantera, Iole Cucinotto, Teresa Calimeri, Marco Rossi, Pierangelo Veltri, Mario Cannataro, Pierosandro Tagliaferri, and Pierfrancesco Tassone. 2011. A peroxisome proliferator-activated receptor gamma (PPARG) polymorphism is associated with zoledronic acid-related osteonecrosis of the jaw in multiple myeloma patients: analysis by DMET microarray profiling. *British Journal of Haematology* (2011), 529–533. https://doi.org/10.1111/j.1365-2141.2011.08622.x

[7] Maria Teresa Di Martino, Mariamena Arbitrio, Emanuela Leone, Pietro Hiram Guzzi, Maria Saveria Rotundo, Domenico Ciliberto, Vera Tomaino, Fernanda Fabiani, Danilo Talarico, Pasquale Sperlongano, Patrizia Doldo, Mario Cannataro, Michele Caraglia, Pierfrancesco Tassone, and Pierosandro Tagliaferri. 2011. Single nucleotide polymorphisms of ABCC5 and ABCG1 transporter genes correlate to irinotecan-associated gastrointestinal toxicity in colorectal cancer patients: A DMET microarray profiling study. *Cancer Biology and Therapy* 12, 9 (November 1 2011), 780–787.

[8] Maria Teresa Di Martino, Pietro Hiram Guzzi, Daniele Caracciolo, Luca Agnelli, Antonino Neri, Brian A Walker, Gareth J Morgan, Mario Cannataro, Pierfrancesco Tassone, and Pierosandro Tagliaferri. 2015. Integrated analysis of microRNAs, transcription factors and target genes expression discloses a specific molecular architecture of hyperdiploid multiple myeloma. *Oncotarget* 6, 22 (2015), 19132–47.

[9] Pietro Guzzi, Giuseppe Agapito, Maria Di Martino, Mariamena Arbitrio, Pierfrancesco Tassone, Pierosandro Tagliaferri, and Mario Cannataro. 2012. DMET-Analyzer: automatic analysis of Affymetrix DMET Data. *BMC Bioinformatics* 13, 1 (2012), 258. https://doi.org/10.1186/1471-2105-13-258

[10] Pietro Hiram Guzzi, Giuseppe Agapito, and Mario Cannataro. 2014. coresnp: Parallel processing of microarray data. *IEEE Trans. Comput.* 63, 12 (2014), 2961–2974.

[11] Pietro H Guzzi, Giuseppe Agapito, Marianna Milano, and Mario Cannataro. 2015. Methodologies and experimental platforms for generating and analysing microarray and mass spectrometry-based omics data to support P4 medicine. *Briefings in bioinformatics* (2015), bbv076.

[12] Pietro H Guzzi and Mario Cannataro. 2010. μ-CS: An extension of the TM4 platform to manage Affymetrix binary data. *BMC bioinformatics* 11, 1 (2010), 315.

[13] Jing Li, Luyong Zhang, Hang Zhou, Mark Stoneking, and Kun Tang. 2011. Global Patterns of Genetic Diversity and Signals of Natural Selection for Human ADME Genes. *Human Molecular Genetics* 20, 3 (2011), 528–540. https://doi.org/10.1093/hmg/ddq498

[14] Giuseppe Lombardi, Enrica Rumiato, Roberta Bertorelle, Daniela Saggioro, Patrizia Farina, Alessandro Della Puppa, Fable Zustovich, Franco Berti, Valeria Sacchetto, Raffaella Marcato, et al. 2013. Clinical and Genetic Factors Associated With Severe Hematological Toxicity in Glioblastoma Patients During Radiation Plus Temozolomide Treatment: A Prospective Study. *Am J Clin Oncol. doi* 10 (2013), 1097.

[15] Urs A Meyer. 2000. Pharmacogenetics and adverse drug reactions. *The Lancet* 356, 9242 (2000), 1667–1671.

[16] Enrica Rumiato, Elisa Boldrin, Alberto Amadori, and Daniela Saggioro. 2013. DMET (Drug-Metabolizing Enzymes and Transporters) microarray analysis of colorectal cancer patients with severe 5-fluorouraci-induced toxicity. *Cancer Chemotherapy and Pharmacology* 72, 2 (2013), 483–488. https://doi.org/10.1007/s00280-013-2210-1

Discovery of Regular Domains in Large DNA Data Sets

Francesca Bertacchini
Department of Engineering Mechanics, Energy and Management
University of Calabria, Italy
francesca.bertacchini@unical.it

Eleonora Bilotta
Department of Physics
University of Calabria, Italy
eleonora.bilotta@ unical.it

Pietro Pantano
Department of Physics
University of Calabria, Italy
piepa@ unical.it

ABSTRACT

To analyze [1] large DNA data sets, we hypothesized that the organization of repeated bases within DNA follows rules similar to Cellular Automata (CA). These sequences could be defined as regular domains. By considering DNA strings as a finite one-dimensional cell automated, consisting of a finite (numerable) set of cells spatially aligned on a straight line and adopting a color code that transforms the DNA bases (A, C, T, G) in numbers, we analyzed DNA strings in the approach of computational mechanics. In this approach, a regular domain is a space-time region consisting of sequences in the same regular language (the particular rule of system evolution, which gives rise to a formal language) that creates patterns computationally homogeneous and simple to describe. We discovered that regular domain exists. Results revealed the exact number of strings of given lengths, establishing their limit in length, their precise localizations in all the human chromosomes and their complex numerical organization. Furthermore, the distribution of these domains is not at random, nor chaotic neither probabilistic, but there are numeric attractors around which the number of these domains are distributed. This leads us to think that all these domains within the DNA are connected to each other and cannot be casually distributed, but they follow some combinatorics rules.

KEYWORDS

Cellular Automata; DNA Regular Domains; DNA automatic segmentation

1 INTRODUCTION

The study of artificial systems to understand better biological ones is one of the main theme of contemporary research into Genomics [1]. Until some time ago attempts were made to create artificial systems that could imitate biological models by building life-like systems [2-3]. In this paper, mathematical models such as Cellular Automata are used to provide a tool to understand real biological systems like DNA. While other methods have been settled in other sectors of the simulation and the analysis of biological and artificial data [5-8], we developed a computer programs by Mathematica [9] that enables efficient access and analysis of large DNA data sets, together with the statistical measures that assess relationships among members of these large data sets. In particular, we used Cellular Automata systems as a filter to:

1. Create 64 types of sequences that is possible to get by combining the basic DNA bases (A, C, T, G);
2. Locate long sequences composed of repetitions of triplets of DNA bases.
3. Locate these sequences within all the DNA chromosomes;

Get the statistical measures of all the 64 types of sequences, clustering them into family of related sequences.

2 CELLULAR AUTOMATA AND REGULAR DOMAINS

According to Wolfram [4], a one-dimensional cellular automaton (CA) is a set of N adjacent sites whose values are either 0s or 1s. Given a site i at time t, its value at time t+1 will be a function, denoted r of the same site's value and the value of its neighbors. The lattice starts out with an initial configuration (IC) of cell states (0s and ls) and this configuration changes at discrete time steps during which all cells are updated simultaneously according to the CA's rule r. A two-dimensional space-time pattern results from state change of sites during time. If, given a site, only the site's value and the value of the two closer neighbors influence the state transition of the that site, we can said that the radius r of the neighborhood is 1. If r=2 then the next value of the site will be influenced by its own value, the two neighbors on the left and the two neighbors on the right. A CA's rule is given by the set of local transition rules for a site. For elementary CA having r=1, the number of local rules is 8 (or 23). Consequently, there are 256 (or 28) evolution rules. We will use periodic boundary conditions (PBC): a site at the extreme boundary of the lattice has the other extreme as a neighbor.

To analyze regular domains we use the approach of computational mechanics, developed in works [10-12]. According to this approach that contains in itself aspects of nonlinear dynamics and the theory of computation, patterns that manifest themselves in natural processes are analyzed through formal models of computation. In fact, CA connections with computation

†The full version of the author's guide is available as acmart.pdf document
[1]It is a datatype.

Permission to make digital or hard copies of all or part of this work for personal or classroom use is granted without fee provided that copies are not made or distributed for profit or commercial advantage and that copies bear this notice and the full citation on the first page. Copyrights for components of this work owned by others than ACM must be honored. Abstracting with credit is permitted. To copy otherwise, or republish, to post on servers or to redistribute to lists, requires prior specific permission and/or a fee. Request permissions from Permissions@acm.org.
ACM-BCB '17, August 20-23, 2017, Boston, MA, USA
© 2017 Association for Computing Machinery.
ACM ISBN 978-1-4503-4722-8/17/08...$15.00
http://dx.doi.org/10.1145/3107411.3110419

theory have long been investigated [13-14]. In contrast, computational mechanics treats CAs from the perspective of physical science, trying to discover and characterize typical behavior patterns of an CA. Of crucial importance in AC dynamics are the regular domains introduced in [10]. Informally, a regular domain is a spatially and temporally homogeneous pattern that can be described by a finite automaton, where a pattern is repeated with the same organizational structures. In CAs, in addition to characterizing emerging space structures, regular domains are fixed or periodic points in the model space. They have the following characteristics:

(a) Temporal invariance or periodicity:

(b) Spatial homogeneity.

3 THE LANGUAGE OF REGULAR DOMAINS

We can build a language on regular domains, such in [3].

Let $S = \{0,1,\dots,k-1\}$, be an alphabet representing the possible states of a cell in the CA and let λ_m be a string of length m composed of symbols in S. Let Ω be the set of all possible strings (or words) composed of symbols in S. Then

$$\Omega = \{\lambda_m \ / \ \lambda_m = s_1 s_2 \cdots s_n, s_i \epsilon S\} \qquad (1)$$

Now consider the function:

$$f_{mod\ h}: \Omega \to \Omega \qquad (2)$$

The function shifts the characters of λ_m by h positions. The boundary conditions mean that a character originally in position $i < h$ will shift to position $m + i$. In this way, the length of the string is still m. In brief, function f defines a translation of *length* h or a *translation module h*. If we consider two strings λ_m , ρ_m of the same length, and an application (2) such that:

$$\rho_m = f_{mod\ h}(\lambda_m) \qquad (3)$$

the characters belonging to string ρ_m will be shifted by h positions with respect to the characters in string λ_m. For example, with h=3, the characters of $\rho_m = 032120$ shift by 3 positions with respect to $\lambda_6 = 120032$. Now consider a string λ_m composed of the concatenation of n substrings λ_h , such that:

$$\lambda_m = \lambda_h \lambda_h \cdots \lambda_h \qquad (4)$$

where $m = hn$. Now consider a 1D CA with k possible states for each of its m cells. The overall state can thus be described by a string λ_m, as in (1). After time p, we observe (3):

$$\rho_m = f_{mod\ s}(\lambda_m)$$

Where ρ_m is the state of the CA after time p. The characters of the string have shifted by h positions. In this case, we say that λ_m is a *regular domain module s*, with p phases π_i, where $i = 0,1,\cdots,p-1$ and p is the period of the regular domain. Obviously, each phase can be represented by a string of length m over the alphabet S. Let c_s be the set of all phases of the regular domain. The Shift Velocity for the domain is given by:

$$v_s = \frac{s}{p} \qquad (5)$$

Suppose that for each phase there exist a set of strings c_h^i in the form given in (4). Thus:

$$\pi_s = c_h^i c_h^i \cdots c_h^i \qquad (6)$$

In this case, the c_h^i are the generating strings for the different phases and we can restrict our analysis to these strings alone. If each of the generating strings is made up of a single character, we say it is *periodic*. When all the phases for a regular domain are the same, we say it is *homogeneous*. Obviously, a rest state generates a homogeneous domain.

4 THE COMPUTATIONAL PROCEDURE

It is well known that the triads of bases A, C, G, and T can generate all the amino acids encoding the proteins. These possible triads are 64 (4^3), and all of these possible combinations are shown in Table.1.

Table 1: Table listing all possible triads that can be generated from the DNA bases

AAA	AAC	AAG	AAT	ACA	ACC	ACG	ACT
AGA	AGC	AGG	AGT	ATA	ATC	ATG	ATT
CAA	CAC	CAG	CAT	CCA	CCC	CCG	CCT
CGA	CGC	CGG	CGT	CTA	CTC	CTG	CTT
GAA	GAC	GAG	GAT	GCA	GCC	GCG	GCT
GGA	GGC	GGG	GGT	GTA	GTC	GTG	GTT
TAA	TAC	TAG	TAT	TCA	TCC	TCG	TCT
TGA	TGC	TGG	TGT	TTA	TTC	TTG	TTT

For simplicity, we can establish a visual correspondence between these triads and the corresponding colour sequences, using the following convention, obtaining the result displayed in Fig. 1:

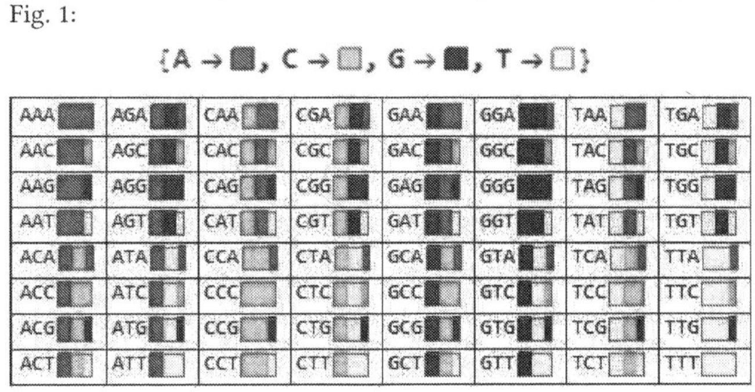

Figure 1: Figure listing all possible triads that can be generated from the DNA bases.

So we started the computational procedure to analyse large DNA data sets, in search of large sequences of repeated bases within DNA. The pipeline of the algorithms we have developed is as follows:

a. Construction of strings composed of 64 DNA triplets of different lengths, these strings are the regular domains of the used model;

b. Connection to the GenBank database for accessing the collection of all publicly available DNA sequences, through the Mathematica language "GenomeData";
c. "GenomeLookup" command language to match the sequences of interest within the DNA structures;
d. Statistical analysis of the found sequences;
e. Automation of the process for different lengths of domains or for domain composition.
f. Localization of the domains within the chromosome.

Graphical representations of the results by Mathematica.

5 RESULTS

Using the definitions introduced for CAs, we can define a regular domain with a sequence of repeated patterns. In particular, we can build regular domains by repeating the previously introduced triads several times. Fig. 2 shows the construction of regular domains by repeating 21 times the 64 triads of the DNA.

Are regular domains contained in the whole DNA? Consider that the probability that a single regular domain exists in some genome position is equal to $p_d \approx \frac{3080419480}{4^{63}}$, where the numerator is the number of bases of all chromosomes, and the denominator is the probability that a given domain manifests itself by considering an orderly sequence of 63 events with four different possible events. Then:

$$p_d \approx \frac{3080419480}{4^{63}} \approx \frac{3.08 \ x\ 10^9}{8.51\ x\ 10^{37}} \approx 3.62\ x\ 10^{-29}$$

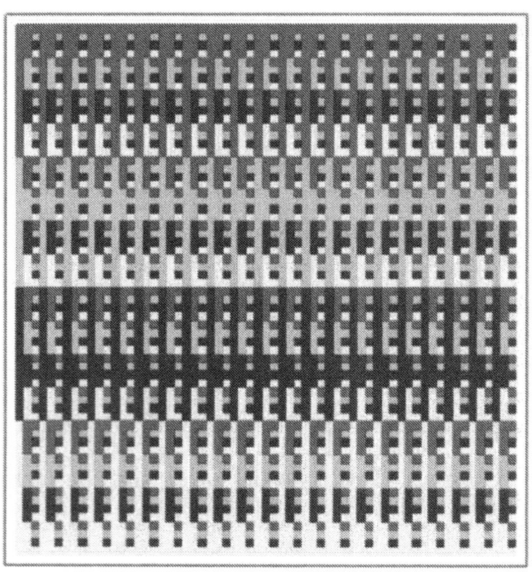

Figure 2. By repeating the 64 triads of the DNA 21 times on the horizontal dimension, we obtain strings of regular domains existing in the DNA. In this image, the all the strings have been collected on the vertical dimension

Thus the probability that a regular domain of this size is present within the chromosome is completely negligible, being p_d a very small number. So we could expect that such regular domains are completely absent in the genome. Actually, this is not exactly in these terms. In fact, if we consider the string: "AAAAAAAAAAAAAAAAAAAAAAAAAAAAAAAAAAAA AAAAAAAAAAAAAAAAAAAAAAAAAAA", it appears in 9 chromosomes, a total of 111 times within the whole DNA, with the distribution shown in Table 2

Table 2: Number of occurrences of the string: "AAAAAAAAAAAAAAAAAAAAAAAAAAAAAAAAAAA AAAAAAAAAAAAAAAAAAAAAAAAAAAA" in 9 chromosomes.

Chromosome	Occurrences
Chromosome1	7
Chromosome2	1
Chromosome4	16
Chromosome6	21
Chromosome7	11
Chromosome12	29
Chromosome15	17
Chromosome18	3
Chromosome X	6

Contrary to what it would be reasonable to expect, this behavior is not only specific to the sequence considered, but is quite common to the 64 domains we have investigated, as shown in Fig.4, where single-domain repetitions are reported.

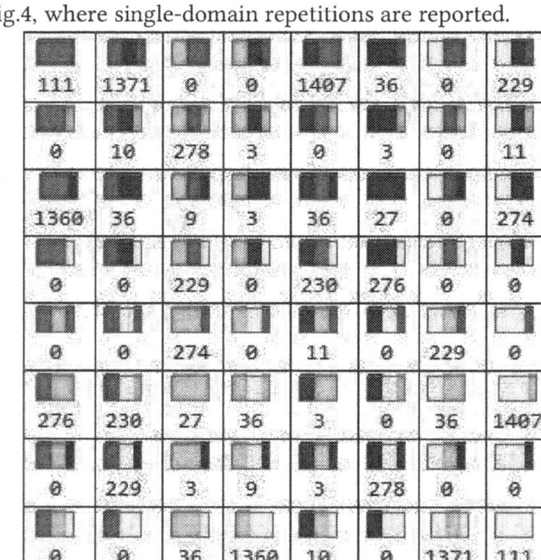

Figure 3. In this Figure, single-domain sequences, together with their occurrences in DNA are reported.

A plot with the number of repetitions within the DNA on the x-axis for the 64 triplets is visualized in Fig. 4. As it is possible to see, some triplets show a very high number of occurrences, others are between 101 and 1000, the most part are between 1 and 100.

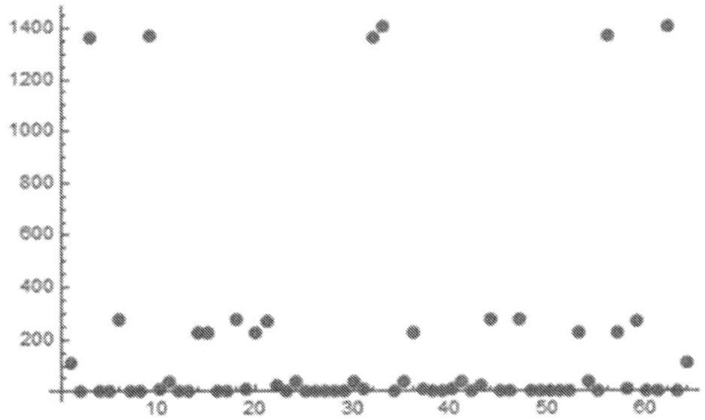

Figure 4. Plot of the occurrences of the 64 regular domains obtained by repeating the triplets of DNA.

We observe that there is a fine structure: that is, the blocks are organized around particular numbers: therefore not only the regular domains of 63 letters are present many times within the DNA but the strings follow particular trends, that is, some numbers are privileged compared to others. To further analyse data, we eliminate the 24 domains that are not present in the chromosomes, focusing our attention on the discovered domains. We divide this data into four families, according to the length of the regular domains. So we have found domains that are between 1 and 9, between 10 and 100, between 101 and 1000, over 1000. The results are shown in Table 3.

Table 3: The four families of regular domains discovered in the DNA sequences

Between 1 and 9	Between 10 and 99	Between 100 and 999	Over 1000
9	10	111	1360
3	36	276	1371
3	27	230	1360
3	36	229	1407
9	36	278	1371
3	36	229	1407
3	11	274	
3	10	230	
	36	276	
	27	278	
	36	229	
	11	229	
		274	
		111	

This means that strings of a certain length are not randomly distributed but there is some relationship in the distributions. Then the distribution of 63-character strings, obtained by repeating 21 times the same tern, are not randomly distributed but are equal to a particular number or are in a small circle of that number. It is important to note that these numbers do not appear individually, but always in pairs. Numbers 3 and 36 are repeated 6 times, 229 is repeated 4 times. Equivalence between these numbers creates symmetries between domains.

6 LARGER OR SMALLER DOMAINS OF LENGTH 63

This result contradicts a simple criterion of randomness. It does not change if we consider distributions of all 64 domains, ranging from 48 to 63 bases. Here again, we look at particular numbers that represent attractors in these distributions. The number of these domains in the DNA chromosomes is given in Table 4.

Table 4: The four families of regular domains discovered in the DNA sequences

Domain Length	Domain numbers
48	2, 22, 23, 24, 32, 34, 36, 38, 43, 59, 76, 77, 80, 132, 133, 135, 272, 276, 281, 327, 362, 363, 364, 389, 499, 2293, 3276, 3280, 3303
51	1, 5, 10, 12, 14, 15, 19, 22, 51, 56, 58, 59, 92, 102, 104, 106, 123, 169, 251, 253, 257, 332, 334, 1097, 2820, 2852
54	0, 1, 2, 6, 8, 9, 10, 22, 30, 40, 42, 43, 44, 45, 80, 81, 244, 245, 311, 312, 313, 520, 2396, 2399, 2435
57	0, 2, 3, 4, 5, 7, 8, 28, 30, 31, 39, 62, 63, 239, 240, 258, 296, 297, 300, 2010, 2015, 2048
60	0, 1, 4, 16, 18, 19, 33, 46, 48, 157, 234, 235, 285, 286, 288, 1666, 1674, 1706
63	0, 3, 9, 10, 11, 27, 36, 111, 229, 230, 274, 276, 278, 1360, 1371, 1407

It's interesting to note how these numbers decrease as the domain length increases (this also because the number of domains present decreases) and that these numbers change depending on the length of the domain. As in the previous section, we can see which types of symmetries are located between chromosomes that have the same number of domains present.

It can be noticed that, as the length of the domain grows, the total of domains present in the chromosomes tends to decrease. Domains of length 48 and 51 are present in all chromosomes; while domains of length 54, 57, 60 and 63 are absent in chromosomes 6, 12, 22 and 24, respectively. If we analyse how often these numbers are repeated, we note that even in these cases they always appear in pairs, with rare exceptions, always in multiples of 2.

Let us consider domains longer than those so far analyzed, made of 93, 123, 153, 183 and 213 bases. Even in these cases, we still find regular domains. We found 18 domains of length equal to 93, 123, 153, 183, while only 12 domains of length equal to 213 bases, although the probability of finding domains of this size would be completely insignificant. Let us now analyse the domains made of 213 bases. These 12 domains are made up of the following repeated 71 times:

"ACC"&"ATC"&"ATG"&"CAC"&"CAT"&"CCA"&"GAT"&"GGT"&"GTG"&"TCA"&"TGA"&"TGG". Let's see how many times these domains appear in the DNA. In this case too, we observe the presence of attractors: in fact the numbers that appear are 42 (repeated 2 times, 43 repeating 4 times and 130 repeating 6 times). In the following table how many times these domains appear in the genome depending on their length. The symmetries between the backs are interesting: e.g. TCA and TGA are obtained by substituting C by G; ATC and ATG are obtained in the same way, while CAT and GAT are obtained from the previous ones through equal parallels.

7 INCREASING THE LENGTH OF THE DOMAINS BY BASES REVERSAL

The longest composite strings that appear in the DNA consisting of repetition of triplets have a maximum length of 603 characters and result from the repetition for 213 times of the following strings:

"ACC", "CAC", "CCA", "GGT", "GTG", "TGG". So these domains appear only once. In fact, if we carefully analyse these strings, the first 3 appear in Chromosome 2, strand -1, respectively at positions

{114135903 and 114136532}, {114135902 and 114136531}, {114135904 and 114136533}.

It is obvious that they refer to a single string that begins with CAC and ends with CCA. Below the string with some term before and after its beginning.

CATCACCATC
ACCACCACCACCACCACCACCACCACCACCACCACCACCA
CCACCACCACCACCACCACCACCACCACCACCACCACCAC
CACCACCACCACCACCACCACCACCACCACCACCACCACC
ACCACCACCACCACCACCACCACCACCACCACCACCACCA
CCACCACCACCACCACCACCACCACCACCACCACCACCAC
CACCACCACCACCACCACCACCACCACCACCACCACCACC
ACCACCACCACCACCACCACCACCACCACCACCACCACCA
CCACCACCACCACCACCACCACCACCACCACCACCACCAC
CACCACCACCACCACCACCACCACCACCACCACCACCACC
ACCACCACCACCACCACCACCACCACCACCACCACCACCA
CCACCACCACCACCACCACCACCACCACCACCACCACCAC
CACCACCACCACCACCACCACCACCACCACCACCACCACC
ACCACCACCACCACCACCACCACCACCACCACCACCACCA
CCACCACCACCACCACCACCACCACCACCACCACCACCAC
CACCACCACCACCACCACCACCACCACCACCACCACCACC
ACCACCACCACCACCACCACCACCACCACCA ACACCACCA

The other three domains have been found in Chromosome 2 as well, but in strand 1, between positions: {128814618 and 128815247}, {128814619 and 128815248}, {128814619 and 128815248} respectively.

These also refer to single strings. Even in this case, there is the presence of symmetries that induce us to think that the distributions of these repeated strings are not at random. If we analyse the previous string, we find that the right domain continues to grow. We increase the search range of 30 other positions on the right, getting the following string:

CATCACCATCACCACCACCACCACCACCACCACCACC
ACCACCACCACCACCACCACCACCACCACCACCACCACCA
CCACCACCACCACCACCACCACCACCACCACCACCACCAC
CACCACCACCACCACCACCACCACCACCACCACCACCACC
ACCACCACCACCACCACCACCACCACCACCACCACCACCA
CCACCACCACCACCACCACCACCACCACCACCACCACCAC
CACCACCACCACCACCACCACCACCACCACCACCACCACC
ACCACCACCACCACCACCACCACCACCACCACCACCACCA
CCACCACCACCACCACCACCACCACCACCACCACCACCAC
CACCACCACCACCACCACCACCACCACCACCACCACCACC
ACCACCACCACCACCACCACCACCACCACCACCACCACCA
CCACCACCACCACCACCACCACCACCACCACCACCACCAC
CACCACCACCACCACCACCACCACCACCACCACCACCACC
ACCACCACCACCACCACCACCACCACCACCACCACCACCA
CCACCACCACCACCACCACCACCACCACCACCACCACCAC
CACCACCACCACCACCACCACCACCACCACCACCACCACC
AC**CAACACCACCACCACCACCACCATCACCATCATTT**
CCACCA

This last regular domain is even longer than that previously found. The same happens for the second domain. In the first case, the maximum length of these two domains is 630 bases, resulting by repeating "CAC" for 210 times. Likewise, it happens for the second string, maintaining this form of complementarity with their respective pairs. The possibility that such a domain is exclusively formed on probabilistic bases is at least one order of magnitude smaller than the smallest order of magnitude in the physical universe that is equal to the Plank's constant. Finally, it is important to note that domains may be even longer, as seen from the previous string, but small differences interpose to change their regularity.

8 SELF-REPRODUCING DOMAINS

May we hypothesize that the mechanisms of self-production is at the basis of the large repeated sequences formation within the same chromosome and between different chromosomes? To test this hypothesis, we start by testing the distribution of domains in the chromosomes. Let us represent with a vector the 64 domains present within the chromosomes. It appears. It is as follows:

{9, 0, 24, 0, 0, 8, 0, 0, 24, 5, 7, 0, 0, 4, 4, 0, 0, 8, 4, 4, 8, 0, 1, 7, 0, 1, 1, 0, 0, 6, 4, 24, 24, 0, 6, 4, 5, 1, 1, 5, 7, 1, 1, 8, 0, 0, 8, 0, 0, 0, 0, 0, 4, 7, 0, 24, 4, 5, 8, 0, 0, 24, 0, 9}

A summary list of the results is as follows:

- 25 of these domains never appear;
- 7 domains appear only in one chromosome;
- 8 domains appear in 4 different chromosomes;
- 4 domains appear in 5 different chromosomes;
- 2 domains appear in 6 different chromosomes;
- 4 domains in 7 different chromosomes;
- 6 domains in 8 different chromosomes;
- 2 domains in 9 different chromosomes;
- 6 domains in all 24 chromosomes.

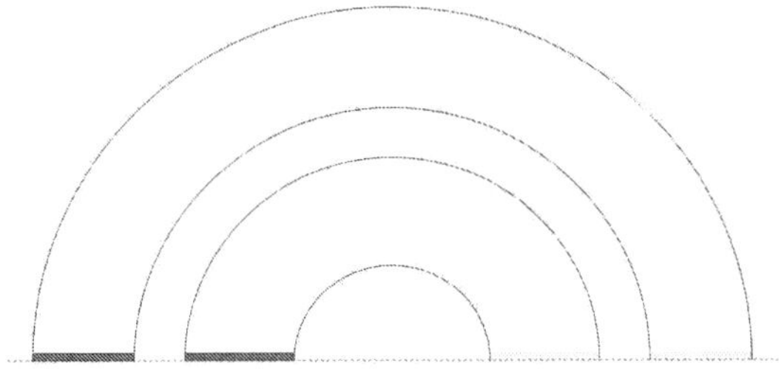

Figure 5. Complementation and Reflection for the domains of Chromosome 4.

To highlight the process of self-replication, we provide an example found within the chromosome 4. Two identical domains of length 68 and 72 are coupled with a second pair, long 72 and 68, showing a clear correlation. This inverse symmetry is also manifested by comparing the distances between the beginning of two first different domains that are {81055655, 81055651}, and the end of two different domains {81055651, 81055655}. The difference between the first and the second value is related to the fact that the second domain of the first pair is longer than 4 bases. This result allows us to say that the self-replication mechanism is not at random. Instead, it is elegantly regulated as A and T are pairs of complementary bases, and this symmetry is maintained in the replication process. Figure 5 shows this symmetry of complementation and reflection with respect to both pairs.

9 CONCLUSIONS

In this work, adopting the model of a language built on Cellular Automata, we hypothesized that triple repetitions, formed by the 4 bases of DNA could exist. We built a series of programs that allowed us to access all DNA sequences, filtered them through the searched sequences, discovered and analyzed them, locating their position in the Human chromosomes. We divided these sequences into 4 families, according to their occurrences. We also found interesting sequences that are repeated in pairs, with interesting complementation and reflection processes. Although further investigations need to be carried out, we believe that this method, with the help of the cellular automata and regular domains methodology illustrated in this paper, allows to analyse DNA strings more effectively.

REFERENCES

[1] J. Craig. Venter. 2013. *Life at the speed of light: from the double helix to the dawn of digital life.* New York, Penguin Books, 2013

[2] E. Bilotta, A. Lafusa and P. Pantano. 2003. Life-like self-reproducers. *Complexity*, 9, 1 (Sep. 2003), 38-55, DOI: 10.1002/cplx.10118

[3] Eleonora Bilotta and Pietro Pantano (Eds.). 2010. *Cellular Automata and Complex Systems: Methods for Modeling Biological Phenomena*, Hersey, IGI Global, 2010..

[4] Stephen Wolfram. 1984. Universality and complexity in cellular automata. *Physica D: Nonlinear Phenomena*, 10, 1-2 (Jan.1984), 1-35, DOI: 10.1016/0167-2789(84)90245-8

[5] E. Bilotta, P. Pantano and S. Vena. 2017. Speeding up cellular neural network processing ability by embodying memristors. *IEEE TNNLS*, 28, 5 (Feb. 2017), 1228-1232, DOI: 10.1109/TNNLS.2015.2511818

[6] M. C. Lombardo, R. Barresi, E. Bilotta, F. Gargano, P. Pantano, M. Sammartino. 2016. Demyelination patterns in a mathematical model of multiple sclerosis. *J. Math. Biol.*, (Dec. 2016), 1-45, DOI: 10.1007/s00285-016-1087-0

[7] M. Abdechiri, K. Faez, H. Amindavar and E. Bilotta. 2017 The chaotic dynamics of high-dimensional systems. *Nonlinear Dynamics* 87, 4 (Mar. 2017), 2597-2610, DOI: 10.1007/s11071-016-3213-3

[8] F. Bertacchini, E. Bilotta and P. Pantano. 2017. Shopping with a robotic companion. *Comp. Hum. Behav.* In Press, (2017), DOI: 10.1016/j.chb.2017.02.064.

[9] Stephen Wolfram. 2015. *An Elementary Introduction to the Wolfram Language.* Wolfram Media, Incorporated, 2015.

[10] James E., Hanson, and James P. Crutchfield. 1991. The attractor–basin portrait of a cellular automaton. *J. Stat. Phys.* 66.5 (May 1991), 1415-1462, DOI: 10.1007/BF01054429

[11] James P. Crutchfield and James E., Hanson. 1993. Attractor vicinity decay for a cellular automaton. *Chaos* 3, 2, (Feb. 1993), 215-224, DOI: 10.1063/1.165986

[12] James P. Crutchfield and James E., Hanson. 1993. Turbulent pattern bases for cellular automata. *Physica D: Nonlinear Phenomena*, 69.3-4 (Dec.1993), 279-301, DOI: 10.1016/0167-2789(93)90092-F.

[13] Stephen Wolfram. 1984. Computation theory of cellular automata. *Comm. Math. Phys.*, 96, 1, (Mar.1984), 15-57, DOI: 10.1007/BF01217347

[14] K. Culik II, L. P. Hurd, and S. Yu. 1990. Computation theoretic aspects of cellular automata. *Physica D*, 45, 1-3, (Sep.1990), 357-378, DOI: 10.1016/0167-2789(90)90194-T.

CNB-MAC'17 – The Fourth International Workshop on Computational Network Biology: Modeling, Analysis, and Control

Byung-Jun Yoon
Texas A&M University
College Station, TX, USA
bjyoon@ece.tamu.edu

Xiaoning Qian
Texas A&M University
College Station, TX, USA
xqian@ece.tamu.edu

Tamer Kahveci
University of Florida
Gainesville, FL, USA
tamer@cise.ufl.edu

ABSTRACT

The Fourth International Workshop on Computational Network Biology: Modeling, Analysis, and Control (CNB-MAC 2017) is held in Boston, MA, on August 20. As in previous years, the workshop is organized in conjunction with the 8th ACM Conference on Bioinformatics, Computational Biology, and Health Informatics (ACM-BCB 2017), the flagship conference of the ACM SIGBio. The primary goal of the workshop is to provide an international scientific forum for presenting recent advances in computational network biology that involve modeling, analysis, and control of biological systems and system-oriented analysis of large-scale OMICS data.[1]

KEYWORDS

Computational network biology; network modeling; network analysis; network intervention; OMICS data analysis.

1 INTRODUCTION

Next-generation high-throughput profiling technologies have enabled more systematic and comprehensive studies of living systems. Network models play crucial roles in understanding the complex interactions that govern biological systems, and their interactions with external environment. The inference and analysis of such complex networks and network-based analysis of large-scale measurement data have already shown strong potential for unveiling the key mechanisms of complex diseases as well as for designing improved therapeutic strategies. At the same time, the inference and analysis of complex biological networks pose new exciting challenges for computer science, signal processing, control, and statistics.

The Fourth International Workshop on Computational Network Biology: Modeling, Analysis, and Control (CNB-MAC 2017) is held in Boston, MA, August 20, 2017, in conjunction with ACM-BCB 2017, the flagship conference of ACM SIGBio. The first, the second, and the third CNB-MAC workshops have been successfully held in conjunction with ACM-BCB 2014, ACM-BCB 2015, ACM-BCB 2016, respectively, attracting researchers working in the emerging field of computational network biology.

The workshop aims to provide an international scientific forum for presenting recent advances in computational network biology that involve modeling, analysis, and control of biological systems under different conditions, and system-oriented analysis of large-scale OMICS data. CNB-MAC 2017 features original research papers that report new research findings that have not been published elsewhere, highlights that present advances in the field that have been reported in recent journal publications, and posters for rapid dissemination of the latest research findings relevant to computational network biology. The main emphasis of the workshop lies on rigorous mathematical or computational approaches in studying biological networks, analyzing large-scale OMICS data, and investigating mathematical models for human-microbiome-environment interactions.

Selected original research papers accepted for presentation at CNB-MAC 2017 will be published in special issues of the workshop's partner journals, which include: BMC Bioinformatics, BMC Genomics, BMC Systems Biology, and IET Systems Biology. An overview of the original research papers presented at CNB-MAC 2016 can be found in [1].

ACKNOWLEDGMENTS

We would like to thank the National Science Foundation for providing travel grants to outstanding student authors, whose work has been accepted for presentation at CNB-MAC 2017, through the award CCF-1743820. We also would like to thank the CNB-MAC 2017 technical program committee (TPC) members who have thoroughly reviewed the manuscripts submitted to the workshop to ensure the quality of the papers that will be included in the partner journals' special issues. The list of CNB-MAC 2017 TPC members can be found at https://cnbmac.org/cnbmac2017-committee/

REFERENCES

[1] Byung-Jun Yoon, Xiaoning Qian, and Tamer Kahveci. "Selected research articles from the 2016 International Workshop on Computational Network Biology: Modeling, Analysis, and Control (CNB-MAC)." *BMC Bioinformatics*, 18(Suppl 4): 159, 2017. DOI: 10.1186/s12859-017-1521-3

[1] Permission to make digital or hard copies of part or all of this work for personal or classroom use is granted without fee provided that copies are not made or distributed for profit or commercial advantage and that copies bear this notice and the full citation on the first page. Copyrights for third-party components of this work must be honored. For all other uses, contact the Owner/Author.
ACM-BCB '17, August 20-23, 2017, Boston, MA, USA
© 2017 Copyright is held by the owner/author(s).
ACM ISBN 978-1-4503-4722-8/17/08.
http://dx.doi.org/10.1145/3107411.3108167

Bayesian Graphical Models for Computational Network Biology

Yang Ni
The University of Texas at Austin
Austin, Texas
yangni87@gmail.com

Peter Müller
The University of Texas at Austin
Austin, Texas
pmueller@math.utexas.edu

Lin Wei
NorthShore University HealthSystem
Evanston, Illinois
kylin9wei@gmail.com

Yuan Ji
NorthShore University HealthSystem
University of Chicago
Evanston, Illinois
koaeraser@gmail.com

ABSTRACT

We first review the use of Bayesian graphical models to model complex molecular networks with an emphasis on *reciprocal graphical models* (RG) which remain curiously under-used in biostatistics and bioinformatics literature. RG's strictly contain chain graphs as a special case and are suitable to model reciprocal causality such as feedback mechanism in molecular networks. We then extend the RG approach in [1] to modeling molecular networks by integrating DNA-, RNA- and protein-level data. We apply the extended RG method to The Cancer Genome Atlas (TCGA) multi-platform ovarian cancer data and reveal several interesting findings.

KEYWORDS

Directed graph, undirected graph, chain graph, reciprocal graph, causality.

REFERENCES

[1] Yang Ni, Yuan Ji, and Peter Mueller. 2016. Reciprocal Graphical Models for Integrative Gene Regulatory Network Analysis. *arXiv preprint arXiv:1607.06849* (2016).

Permission to make digital or hard copies of part or all of this work for personal or classroom use is granted without fee provided that copies are not made or distributed for profit or commercial advantage and that copies bear this notice and the full citation on the first page. Copyrights for third-party components of this work must be honored. For all other uses, contact the owner/author(s).
ACM-BCB'17, August 20–23, 2017, Boston, MA, USA.
© 2017 Copyright held by the owner/author(s). ISBN 978-1-4503-4722-8/17/08.
DOI: http://dx.doi.org/10.1145/3107411.3110405

Detangling PPI Networks to Uncover Functionally Meaningful Clusters

Sarah Hall-Swan Jake Crawford Rebecca Newman Lenore J. Cowen*
Department of Computer Science
Tufts University
Medford, MA 02140

ABSTRACT

We compare computational methods for decomposing a PPI network into non-overlapping modules. A method is preferred if it results in a large proportion of nodes being assigned to functionally meaningful modules, as measured by functional enrichment over terms from the Gene Ontology (GO). We compare the performance of three popular community detection algorithms with the same algorithms run after the network is pre-processed by removing and reweighting based on the diffusion state distance (DSD) between pairs of nodes in the network. We call this "detangling" the network. In almost all cases, we find that detangling the network based on the DSD distance reweighting provides more meaningful clusters.

KEYWORDS

PPI Networks; Protein Function Prediction; Community Detection; Diffusion State Distance

1 INTRODUCTION

Clustering of protein-protein interaction networks is one of the most common approaches to predicting modules of genes and proteins that work together in functional roles [11]. However, the low network diameter and dense interconnection structure in these networks confounds a notion of local neighborhood in these networks; it is difficult to partition a network into clusters representing local neighborhoods when the network best resembles a tangled hairball, and most nodes are close to all other nodes in shortest path distance, a problem termed the "ties in proximity problem" by Arnau et al [1]. There are nonetheless many notions of clustering that have been developed for the so-called "community detection" problem in biological or social networks; many of them seek to maximize the *modularity* of the clusters, a quantity defined by Girvan and Newman [6] that measures the relative denseness of interconnections within a cluster as compared to the connection of that cluster to the rest of the network, or alternatively the *conductance* of the clusters [13]. Other clustering methods have been proposed based on random walks, successive removal of cut edges, spectral embeddings and so on [5, 7, 8].

In 2013, Cao et al. introduced a new distance measure called Diffusion State Distance, or DSD, designed to be a more fine-grained distance measure for protein-protein interaction networks [4]. In contrast to the typical shortest path metric, which measures distance between pairs of nodes by the number of hops on the shortest path that joins them in the network, DSD was shown to spread out the pairwise distances, making for a more fine-grained notion of graph local neighborhood. We hypothesized that re-embedding the PPI network by first reweighting its edges according to their DSD distance in the original network might lead to better clusters. Before we can test this hypothesis, however, we need to think about how to measure the overall quality of a set of clusters: only then can we talk about once method producing *better* clusters than some other method.

*To whom correspondence should be addressed: lenore.cowen@tufts.edu

Permission to make digital or hard copies of part or all of this work for personal or classroom use is granted without fee provided that copies are not made or distributed for profit or commercial advantage and that copies bear this notice and the full citation on the first page. Copyrights for third-party components of this work must be honored. For all other uses, contact the owner/author(s).
ACM-BCB'17, August 20–23, 2017, Boston, MA, USA.
© 2017 Copyright held by the owner/author(s). ISBN 978-1-4503-4722-8/17/08.
DOI: http://dx.doi.org/10.1145/3107411.3110409

2 MEASURING QUALITY OF A CLUSTERING

In the current study, we consider the problem of separating the yeast protein-protein association network (as downloaded from the STRING database [12]) into non-overlapping clusters. Some proposed ways to measure the quality of a clustering are purely graph-theoretic, based on minimizing quantities such as *modularity* or *conductance*. In this study, instead, we wish to judge the quality of the clustering we obtain by how "meaningful" the clusters are biologically– where the standard way to measure this would be based on measuring functional enrichment of the resulting clusters. In this study, we measure functional enrichment of the clusters over the GO using the FuncAssociate tool [2], with appropriate multiple testing correction for the number of clusters in our set.

However, while it is easy to declare one particular cluster to be known to be meaningful if it is enriched for at least one biological function, it is not immediately clear how to use this to compare the overall quality of different clusterings, particularly when the number and distribution of cluster sizes is different across the different clustering algorithms. We look at which statistics are best at measuring the overall quality of a clustering. In particular, observe that the *percentage of enriched clusters* is not a good statistic: any algorithm that picks off small good clusters around the periphery of the network, and then puts all the remaining nodes into a giant single cluster in the center will score all but one of its clusters enriched (the large center cluster), for a very large percentage of enriched clusters. Restricting the maximum size of a cluster (as we do for some of the experiments) can ameliorate this behavior to a large extent, but we still are faced with the need to find a meaningful overall statistic even when the distribution of cluster sizes is highly non-comparable.

Because we are restricting ourselves to *non-overlapping* clusterings, we choose as the main statistic by which we judge the quality of a clustering to be *the number (or percent) of network nodes that are placed within enriched clusters.* We note that this statistic can be measured across clusterings with different numbers of clusters, size of clusters, and different cluster size distributions. However, even this statistic is most meaningful when comparing clusterings when the number of clusters and their ranges of sizes are approximately matched. Some of the algorithms we test allow greater or lesser control in setting maximum or minimum cluster sizes or the number of clusters that are output in the clustering; we discuss how we would recommend setting these parameters in such a way as to make the resulting clusterings more meaningful for the biological networks we study, and also more comparable.

3 EXPERIMENTS AND RESULTS

We implemented three popular methods (Louvain [3], Walktrap [10] and Spectral Clustering [9]) for clustering biological or social networks in two modes: in the first mode, we ran each method directly on the STRING network with the original edge weights, and in the second mode, we first ran DSD to detangle the network, and then ran each method. The detangling process is as follows: considering the weighted PPI network (with edge weights from STRING confidence values), we compute the DSD distance matrix to produce distances between all network nodes. We then create a new graph with edges between only pairs of nodes whose DSD distance is below a threshold, with edge weights inversely proportional to their DSD distance. We considered each method in the setting where there was no restriction on maximum cluster size, and also in the setting where the maximum size of any cluster was bounded by 100 nodes.

Figure 1 compares median cluster sizes over 10 runs of the Louvain algorithm (with cluster sizes restricted to 3-100 nodes, randomly reordering the nodes for each run) directly on the yeast PPI network and on the DSD-detangled network. In this case, "detangling" with DSD means removing edges between nodes with a DSD distance > 5.0, and including edges between nodes with a DSD distance ≤ 5.0 but reweighting the edges with the reciprocal of their DSD distance in the original network.

For all three methods, in all cases but one, we find that running DSD first to detangle the network results in a larger percentage of nodes placed within enriched clusters. The exception is the Walktrap algorithm, when modified to produce clusters of size between 3 and 100 nodes. We find that this algorithm does comparably (or even very slightly better) for most parameter settings when run directly on the PPI network without first running DSD. We further discuss parameter settings that influenced the resulting number of clusters and their sizes in the network, and make recommendations for each method. In nearly all settings, we can advocate that reweighting the network using DSD as a pre-processing step for decomposing protein-protein networks into functionally coherent communities produces more meaningful clusters.

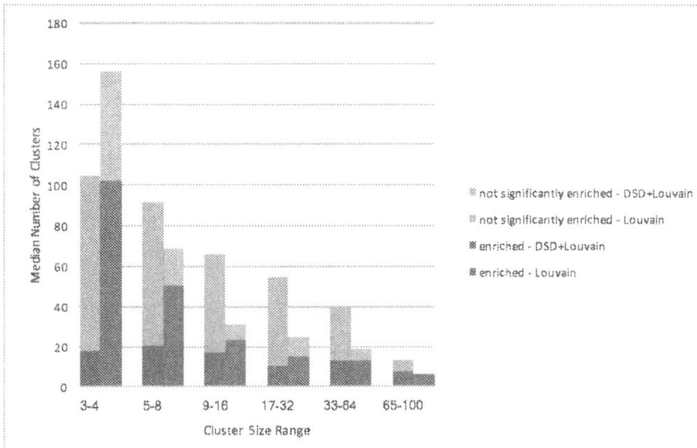

Figure 1: This figure compares median cluster sizes running Louvain (with cluster sizes restricted to 3-100) directly on the PPI network with Louvain running on the DSD-detangled network (again with cluster sizes restricted to 3-100), with an edge removal threshold of 5.0. The overall median% enriched clusters is 24.4% for Louvain directly, and 46.3% for DSD+Louvain, while the percentage of nodes in enriched clusters is 31.3% for Louvain directly and 48.7% for DSD+Louvain.

REFERENCES

[1] V. Arnau, S. Mars, and I. Marin. 2005. Iterative cluster analysis of protein interaction data. *Bioinformatics* 31 (2005), 364–378.

[2] Gabriel F Berriz, John E Beaver, Can Cenik, Murat Tasan, and Frederick P Roth. 2009. Next generation software for functional trend analysis. *Bioinformatics* 25, 22 (2009), 3043–3044.

[3] Vincent D Blondel, Jean-Loup Guillaume, Renaud Lambiotte, and Etienne Lefebvre. 2008. Fast unfolding of communities in large networks. *Journal of statistical mechanics: theory and experiment* 2008, 10 (2008), P10008.

[4] Mengfei Cao, Hao Zhang, Jisoo Park, Noah M. Daniels, Mark E. Crovella, Lenore J. Cowen, and Benjamin Hescott. 2013. Going the distance for protein function prediction. *PLOS One* 8 (2013), e76339.

[5] Santo Fortunato. 2010. Community detection in graphs. *Physics reports* 486, 3 (2010), 75–174.

[6] Michelle Girvan and Mark EJ Newman. 2002. Community structure in social and biological networks. *Proceedings of the National Academy of Sciences USA* 99, 12 (2002), 7821–7826.

[7] Steve Harenberg, Gonzalo Bello, L Gjeltema, Stephen Ranshous, Jitendra Harlalka, Ramona Seay, Kanchana Padmanabhan, and Nagiza Samatova. 2014. Community detection in large-scale networks: a survey and empirical evaluation. *Wiley Interdisciplinary Reviews: Computational Statistics* 6, 6 (2014), 426–439.

[8] Jure Leskovec, Kevin J Lang, and Michael Mahoney. 2010. Empirical comparison of algorithms for network community detection. In *Proceedings of the 19th international conference on World Wide Web*. ACM, 631–640.

[9] Andrew Y Ng, Michael I Jordan, Yair Weiss, and others. 2001. On spectral clustering: Analysis and an algorithm. In *NIPS*, Vol. 14. 849–856.

[10] Pascal Pons and Matthieu Latapy. 2006. Computing communities in large networks using random walks. *J. Graph Algorithms Appl.* 10, 2 (2006), 191–218.

[11] Jimin Song and Mona Singh. 2009. How and when should interactome-derived clusters be used to predict functional modules and protein function? *Bioinformatics* 25, 23 (2009), 3143–3150.

[12] Damian et al. Szklarczyk. 2015. STRING v10: protein–protein interaction networks, integrated over the tree of life. *Nucleic Acids Research* 43, D1 (2015), D447–D452.

[13] Deepak Verma and Marina Meila. 2003. A comparison of spectral clustering algorithms. *University of Washington Tech Rep UWCSE030501* 1 (2003), 1–18.

SMILE: A Novel Procedure for Subcellular Module Identification with Localization Expansion

Lixin Cheng
Computer Science & Engineering
The Chinese University of Hong Kong
Hong Kong
lxcheng@cse.cuhk.edu.hk

Pengfei Liu
Computer Science & Engineering
The Chinese University of Hong Kong
Hong Kong
pfliu@cse.cuhk.edu.hk

Kwong-Sak Leung
Computer Science & Engineering
The Chinese University of Hong Kong
Hong Kong
ksleung@cse.cuhk.edu.hk

ABSTRACT

We propose a novel procedure, Subcellular Module Identification with Localization Expansion (SMILE), to identify super modules that consist of several subcellular modules performing specific biological functions among cell compartments. These super modules identified by SMILE are more functionally diverse and have been verified to be more associated with known protein complexes and biological pathways compared with the modules identified from the global protein interaction networks in both the ComPPI and InWeb_InBioMap protein interaction datasets. Our results reveal that subcellular localization is a principal feature of functional modules and offers important guidance in detecting biologically meaningful results.

KEYWORDS

Module identification; super module; protein interaction network; subcellular localization; cell compartment

Computational clustering methods help identify functional modules in protein–protein interaction networks, since proteins usually cluster together to participate in the same biological pathways or specific functions [1-4]. However, cell compartmentalization is overlooked by previous standard procedures, despite a large number of exciting results emerging from analyses at the global cellular level [1,5,6]. In fact, eukaryotic cells are composed of several subcellular compartments that enable the cell to implement various metabolic activities simultaneously, and proteins need to target appropriate compartment to interact with each other and to form compound functional complexes in the signaling pathways for specialized biological processes and functions [7,8]. Therefore, identifying modules consisting of closely interacted proteins localized in a specific compartment is expected to generate more biologically meaningful results, as cells can naturally be decomposed into several compartments. Additionally, we should note that proteins are interacting spatially to form a dynamic cellular network. Some proteins are localized in multiple compartments and may not directly interact with each other in the same compartment, but they still work toward similar cellular functionalities and hence should belong to the same modules. For instance, transmembrane receptor proteins tend to interact with cytoplasmic proteins as well as with extracellular ligands in signal transduction cascades [9]. Hence, highly overlapped protein modules, either from the same or different compartments, need to be merged to achieve the final super modules.

Permission to make digital or hard copies of part or all of this work for personal or classroom use is granted without fee provided that copies are not made or distributed for profit or commercial advantage and that copies bear this notice and the full citation on the first page. Copyrights for third-party components of this work must be honored. For all other uses, contact the Owner/Author.
ACM-BCB '17, August 20-23, 2017, Boston, MA, USA
© 2017 Copyright is held by the owner/author(s).
ACM ISBN 978-1-4503-4722-8/17/08.
http://dx.doi.org/10.1145/3107411.3110415

We introduce a novel procedure, Subcellular Module Identification with Localization Expansion (SMILE), to identify subcellular modules from each cell compartment with localization extension. Our results demonstrate that it outperforms the conventional clustering method with respect to protein complex detection and biological pathway annotation, especially for the novel modules exclusively identified by SMILE.

The SMILE procedure has three steps: first, constructing subcellular networks based on localization annotation; second, identifying clusters with high cohesiveness from each subnetwork; and third, combining highly overlapped clusters (Fig. 1).

(1) Subnetwork construction. Suppose the input PPI network is $G = (P, E)$, where P is the set of proteins and E is the set of interactions among proteins. Each protein P is annotated to one or more than one compartment. Based on the information of subcellular localization, we can easily extract the subnetwork among proteins. For compartment C_i, we can define its corresponding subnetwork to be $G_i = (P_i, E_i)$, where P_i is the subset of proteins in compartment C_i and E_i is the subset of interactions in compartment C_i.

(2) Module identification in each subnetwork. Calculate the cohesiveness of $f(V_i)$ in compartment $C_i$using ClusterONE [1]. Let V_i denote the set of clusters in the subnetwork of G_i, $w^{in}(V_i)$ denote the number of interactions contained within the cluster, $w^{out}(V_i)$ denote the number of interactions coming out of the cluster, and $p|V_i|$ is a penalty term aiming to model the uncertainty of unchecked interactions in the subnetwork, the cohesiveness of V_i is defined as follow

$$f(V_i) = \frac{w^{in}(V_i)}{w^{in}(V_i)+w^{out}(V_i)+p|V_i|} \quad (1)$$

(3) Merging. The final step is to merge highly overlapped modules to generate super modules. Let A and B represent two clusters of proteins from different subnetwork, respectively. Their similarity is measured by overlap score, which is defined as:

$$\omega(A,B) = \frac{|A \cap B|^2}{|A||B|} \quad (2)$$

where $|A|$ and $|B|$ are the size of the two clusters and $|A \cap B|$ is the number of the overlapping proteins annotated with both subcellular locations.

Lastly, we combine subcellular modules concurrently from different subnetworks with the overlap score ω larger than a user-specified threshold. The threshold is set as 0.5 by default, which implies more than 70% of the members of the two modules being compared are overlapped if they have the same size. Such merges are performed concurrently. Specifically, given a set of clusters, the procedure first calculates the overlap scores ω_{ij} for each pair of clusters and constructs an adjacent matrix in which each row i (or column j) represents a cluster, and two clusters are overlapped if they have substantially high ω_{ij}. The overlapped clusters are then merged into a big group defined as super module. Mathematically, the super modules are

$$\{S(W) \mid W_{ij} = I(\omega_{ij} > \Omega), W \in R^{n*n}\} \quad (3)$$

where $S()$ is the function to find the connected components from an adjacent matrix W, I() is the identity function, n is the total number of subcellular modules, and Ω is the specified threshold of overlap score ω. Essentially, a super module is the maximal connected subcellular modules among all subnetworks.

We found SMILE outperforms the conventional procedure of ClusterONE and MCL based on two protein complex reference sets, CORUM and PCDq, on two PPI networks ComPPI and InWeb_IM. Three measurements, Sensitivity, Positive Predictive Value, and Accuracy, were used to assess the quality of the identified module sets with respect to protein complex prediction. Then, we examined the biological relevance of the detected modules by performing overrepresentation analysis of pathway associations. We found super modules, especially the novel ones, consist of more proteins in the biological pathways on all the four resources on both PPI networks of ComPPI [5] and InWeb_IM [10]. Besides, two case studies showed that the novel modules exclusively identified by SMILE in ComPPI also tend to involve in the Bcl-2 and the SNARE gene families, respectively.

Overall, SMILE is superior in identifying super modules, either overlapped with global modules or not, with higher biological relevance and functional significance. Not limited to ClusterONE and MCL, SMILE is also applicable to other module identification algorithms depending on users' preference, since it provides more meaningful biological data by evaluating how within compartment or cross-compartment protein interactions altered or propagated within proteomic datasets. Furthermore, SMILE can be easily applied to other types of network studies to capture modules with multiple components like lncRNA and mRNA [11].

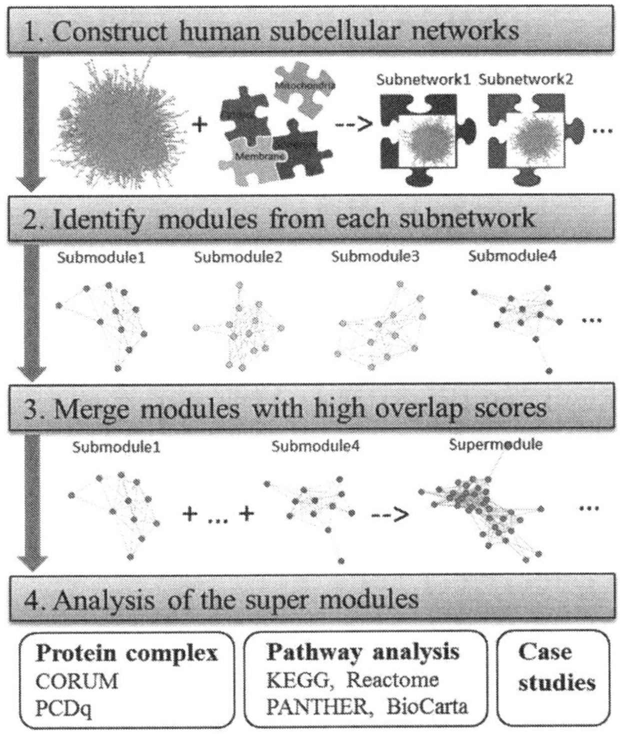

Figure 1: The flowchart of SMILE.

ACKNOWLEDGMENTS

This work was supported by The Chinese University of Hong Kong Direct Grant and Research Grants Council of Hong Kong GRF Grant [414413].

REFERENCES

[1] Nepusz, T., Yu, H. and Paccanaro, A. 2012. Detecting overlapping protein complexes in protein-protein interaction networks, *Nature methods*, 9, 471-472.

[2] Wang, Y. and Qian, X. 2014. Functional module identification in protein interaction networks by interaction patterns, *Bioinformatics*, 30, 81-93.

[3] Li, X., et al. 2010. Computational approaches for detecting protein complexes from protein interaction networks: a survey, *BMC Genomics*, 11 Suppl 1, S3.

[4] Pizzuti, C. and Rombo, S.E. 2014. Algorithms and tools for protein-protein interaction networks clustering, with a special focus on population-based stochastic methods, *Bioinformatics*, 30, 1343-1352.

[5] Veres, D.V., et al. 2015. ComPPI: a cellular compartment-specific database for protein-protein interaction network analysis, *Nucleic Acids Res*, 43, D485-493.

[6] Zhang, B., et al. 2013. Integrated systems approach identifies genetic nodes and networks in late-onset alzheimer's disease. *Cell*, 153(3), 707-720.

[7] An, S., et al. 2008. Reversible compartmentalization of de novo purine biosynthetic complexes in living cells, *Science*, 320, 103-106.

[8] Hao, N. and O'Shea, E.K. 2011. Signal-dependent dynamics of transcription factor translocation controls gene expression, *Nature structural & molecular biology*, 19, 31-39.

[9] Papin, J.A., et al. 2005. Reconstruction of cellular signalling networks and analysis of their properties, Nature reviews. *Molecular cell biology*, 6, 99-111.

[10] Li, T., et al. 2017. A scored human protein-protein interaction network to catalyze genomic interpretation, *Nature methods*, 14, 61-64.

[11] Cheng, L., et al. 2016. CrossNorm: a novel normalization strategy for microarray data in cancers. *Scientific reports*, 6.

Overlapping Functional Modules Detection in PPI Network with Pairwise Constrained Nonnegative Matrix Tri-Factorization

Guangming Liu
Beijing Key Lab of Traffic Data Analysis and Mining
Beijing Jiaotong University
Beijing, China 100044
guangmingliu@bjtu.edu.cn

Bianfang Chai
Department of Information Engineering
Hebei GEO University
Hebei, China 050031
chaibianfang@163.com

Kuo Yang
Beijing Key Lab of Traffic Data Analysis and Mining
Beijing Jiaotong University
Beijing, China 100044
yangkuo@bjtu.edu.cn

Xuezhong Zhou*
Beijing Key Lab of Traffic Data Analysis and Mining
Beijing Jiaotong University
Beijing, China 100044
xzzhou@bjtu.edu.cn

Jian Yu†
Beijing Key Lab of Traffic Data Analysis and Mining
Beijing Jiaotong University
Beijing, China 100044
jianyu@bjtu.edu.cn

ABSTRACT

Uncovering functional modules from PPI networks will help us to better understand the mechanism of cellular. Numerous computational algorithms have been designed to identify functional modules automatically in the past decades. However, most community detection methods are unsupervised models and the known protein complexes have not been considered by them. In this paper, we propose a novel semi-supervised model named pairwise constrains nonnegative matrix tri-factorization (PCNMTF), which takes full advantage of the usable well known complexes to find overlapping functional modules based on protein module indicator matrix and module correlation matrix simultaneously from PPI networks. The experiment results demonstrate that PCNMTF gains more precious functional modules by integrating PPI network and known protein complexes than state-of-art methods.

KEYWORDS

overlapping functional module detection, PCNMTF, pairwise constraints

1 INTRODUCTION

Non-negative matrix factorization (NMF) is a broadly used matrix decomposition approach has been successfully applied in functional module detection. Nevertheless, the physical meaning of the two factorized matrices are ambiguous. Luckily, non-negative matrix tri-Factorization (NMTF) has been proposed to assign a clear physical meaning to each matrix. Wang et al. [3] use NMTF to co-cluster multi-type relational data simultaneously, Zhu et al. [4] use NMTF to analyze both user-level and tweet-level sentiments on social media and Pei et al. [1] utilize NMTF to detect community structure in social networks. All these three works are unsupervised methods. We propose a novel semi-supervised model named pairwise constrained non-negative matrix tri-Factorization (PCNMTF) which combines the topological structureand known protein complexes together to detect functional modules.

The main contributions of this work include: 1) We present a novel semi-supervised functional module detection model PCNMTF which makes full use of known protein complexes; 2) We add a Frobenius constraint on community relationship matrix **G** to make the solution stable; 3) Different from existing NMF and NMTF methods, the membership of proteins is decided not only based on the indicator matrix but also in terms of the module relationship matrix.

*Corresponding author
†Corresponding author

Permission to make digital or hard copies of part or all of this work for personal or classroom use is granted without fee provided that copies are not made or distributed for profit or commercial advantage and that copies bear this notice and the full citation on the first page. Copyrights for third-party components of this work must be honored. For all other uses, contact the owner/author(s).
ACM-BCB'17, August 20–23, 2017, Boston, MA, USA.
© 2017 Copyright held by the owner/author(s). 978-1-4503-4722-8/17/08.
DOI: http://dx.doi.org/10.1145/3107411.3110414

2 FUNTIONAL MODULE DETECTION

2.1 PCNMTF

The main idea in this work is to use pairwise constraints as a penalty term rather than simply to incorporate the prior information into the original PPI network. The objective function of PCNMTF is defined as follow:

$$\min_{F\geq 0, G\geq 0} J(F,G) = \left\| A - FGF^T \right\|_F^2 + \alpha \left\| G \right\|_F^2 + \beta Tr(F^T LF) \tag{1}$$

where $A = [a_{ij}] \in \mathbb{R}_+^{n\times n}$ denote the adjacency matrix of PPI network, $F \in \mathbb{R}_+^{n\times k}$ is a $n \times k$ matrix representing the module membership of proteins (k is the maximum possible number of protein modules) in each module, $G \in \mathbb{R}_+^{k\times k}$ is a $k \times k$ symmetric matrix denoting the correlations between any module pairs, α is a smoothing parameter and β is the parameter used to balance the tradeoff between prior knowledge and topological structure of PPI network. Then the updating rules of protein indicator matrix $\mathbf{F}$ and module relationship matrix $\mathbf{G}$ are given as follows:

$$F = F \otimes \frac{2AFG + \beta MF}{2FGF^TFG + \beta DF} \tag{2}$$

$$G = G \otimes \frac{F^TAF}{F^TFGF^TF + \alpha G} \tag{3}$$

where $\otimes$ means the element-wise multiplication between two matrices.

2.2 Overlapping module detection

The element f_{ij} denotes the membership strength how protein i serves to module j. For protein i, we first assign it to module c to which it most likely to belong when module c is to meet $c = arg\max_c f_{ic}$. Furthermore, in addition to module c, we also consider clustering protein i into another module j if the following conditions are satisfied in the mean time: $f_{ij} \geq \omega$ and $u_{cj} > 0$.

3 EXPERIMENTS

3.1 Data Sets

We introduce two common synthetic networks: GN8 network and the LFR networks and two human related PPI networks: one is derived from DIP human subset and the other is HPRD. The protein complex database CORUM and PCDq are employeed as ground-truth.

3.2 Performance of our PCNMTF

The performance of seven other well known state-of-art NMF-based community detection methods are employed to compare with our method. The compared five methods include NMF, PCNMF, SNMF, PCSNMF, NMTF, NMTFJAC and NMFADJ. The NMI [2] used to evaluate the performance of module detection methods. Fig. 1 (a) and Fig. 1 (b) display the NMI of different algorithms with various percentage prior information. The PCNMTF has the best performance. The Precision, Recall and F-measure of the compared algorithms on both two PPI networks showed in Fig. 2, then we can find that the proposed algorithm PCNMTF outperforms other compared methods by means of all these three metrics.

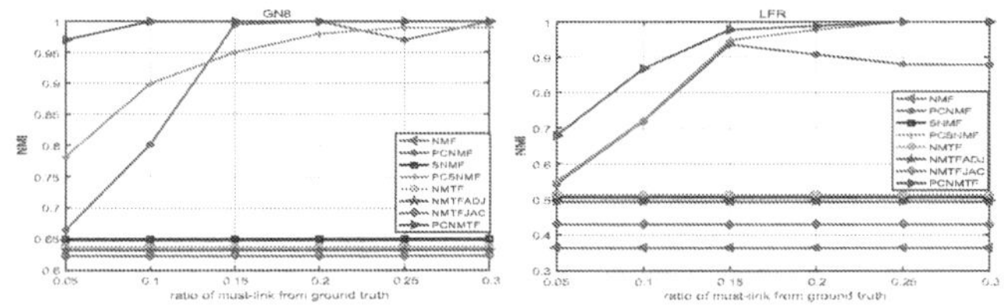

(a) GN8 (b) LFR

Figure 1: The NMI of different methods with different percentage of must-link constraints derived from ground-truth.

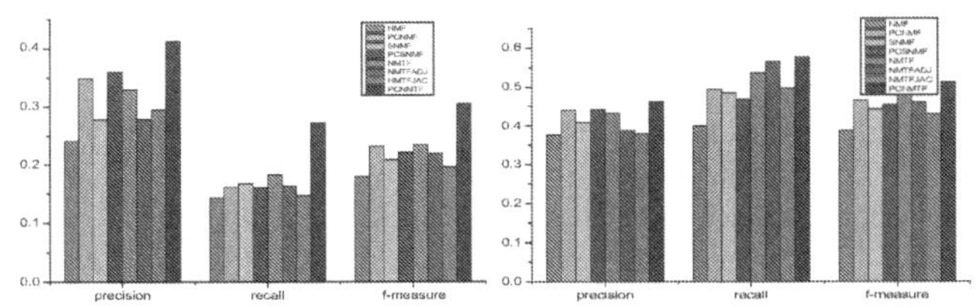

(a) DIP(CORUM) (b) HPRD(CORUM)

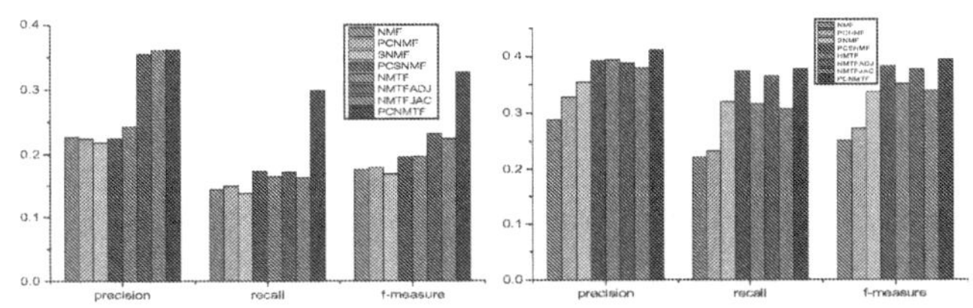

(c) DIP(PCDq) (d) HPRD(PCDq)

Figure 2: The precision, recall and f-measure of compared methods on DIP and HPRD.

4 CONCLUSIONS

In this manuscript, we propose a novel semi-supervised model called Pairwise Constrained Non-negative Matrix Tri-Factorization (PCNMTF) to detect protein overlapping functional modules from PPI networks. The experiments are executed on synthetic networks and two real human related PPI networks, DIP and HPRD, and PCNMTF shows superior performance in finding functional modules since we use hand-curated complexes from CORUM. In future, we will consider to introduce other biological data, such as gene expression data and GO functional annotations, into our model to get more accurate protein functional modules in nature.

REFERENCES

[1] Yulong Pei1 Nilanjan Chakraborty and Katia Sycara. 2015. Nonnegative matrix tri-factorization with graph regularization for community detection in social networks. (2015).

[2] Filippo Radicchi, Claudio Castellano, Federico Cecconi, Vittorio Loreto, and Domenico Parisi. 2004. Defining and identifying communities in networks. *Proceedings of the National Academy of Sciences of the United States of America* 101, 9 (2004), 2658–2663.

[3] Hua Wang, Feiping Nie, Heng Huang, and Chris Ding. 2011. Nonnegative matrix tri-factorization based high-order co-clustering and its fast implementation. In *Data Mining (ICDM), 2011 IEEE 11th International Conference on*. IEEE, 774–783.

[4] Linhong Zhu, Aram Galstyan, James Cheng, and Kristina Lerman. 2014. Tripartite graph clustering for dynamic sentiment analysis on social media. In *Proceedings of the 2014 ACM SIGMOD international conference on Management of data*. ACM, 1531–1542.

Heuristic Algorithms for Feature Selection under Bayesian Models with Block-diagonal Covariance Structure

Ali Foroughi pour
The Ohio State University
2015 Neil Avenue
Columbus, Ohio 43210
foroughipour.1@osu.edu

Lori A. Dalton
The Ohio State University
2015 Neil Avenue
Columbus, Ohio 43210
dalton@ece.osu.edu

ABSTRACT

Many bioinformatics studies aim to identify markers, or features that can be used to discriminate between distinct groups. In problems where strong individual markers are not available, or where interactions between gene products are of primary interest, it may be necessary to consider combinations of features as a marker family. To this end, recent work proposes a hierarchical Bayesian framework for feature selection that places a prior on the set of features we wish to select and on the label-conditioned feature distribution. While an analytical posterior under Gaussian models with block covariance structures is available, the optimal feature selection algorithm for this model remains intractable since it requires evaluating the posterior over the space of all possible covariance block structures and feature-block assignments. To address this computational barrier, prior work proposes a simple suboptimal algorithm, 2MNC-Robust, with robust performance across the space of block structures. Here, we present three new heuristic feature selection algorithms that outperform 2MNC-Robust on synthetic data. Enrichment analysis on real cancer data indicates that they also output many of the genes and pathways linked to the cancers under study.

CCS CONCEPTS

• **Computing methodologies** → **Feature selection**; • **Applied computing** → **Bioinformatics**; • **Theory of computation** → *Bayesian analysis*;

KEYWORDS

Feature selection; Bayesian learning; Biomarker discovery; Heuristic search algorithms

EXTENDED ABSTRACT

Many bioinformatics studies aim to identify predictive biomarkers that can be used to establish diagnosis or prognosis, or to predict a drug response. This problem can often be framed as a feature selection task, where the goal is to identify a list of features (molecular biomarkers) that can discriminate between groups of interest based on high-dimensional data from microarray, RNA-seq, or other high-throughput technologies.

Initially, exploratory studies are often conducted on small samples to generate a shortlist of biomarker candidates before a large-sample validation study is performed. However, such studies have too often been unsuccessful at producing reliable and reproducible biomarkers [1]. Biomarker discovery is inherently difficult, given the large number of features, highly complex interactions between genes and gene products, enormous variety of dysfunctions that can occur, and many sources of error in the data. As a result, feature selection algorithms are often implemented without much consideration of the particular demands of the problem. For instance, variants of t-test are perhaps the most widely implemented selection strategies in bioinformatics, but can only detect strong individual features, and fail to take correlations into account.

Given that molecular signaling is often inherently multivariate, there is a need for methods that can account for correlations and extract combinations of features as a marker family. Wrapper methods do this by ranking sets of features according to some objective function, usually the error of a classifier. However, methods based on classifier error are computationally expensive, and may not necessarily produce the best markers; indeed, strong features can be excluded if they are correlated with other strong features. Furthermore, analysis downstream from feature selection may include gene set enrichment analysis, where the hope is to identify known pathways or other biological mechanisms that contain a statistically significant number of genes in the reported gene set, or may involve the development of new pathways and gene networks. We are thus motivated to develop methods that not only select markers useful for discrimination, but select all relevant markers, even individually weak ones.

To address this, recent work proposes a hierarchical Bayesian framework for feature selection, labeling features as "good" or "bad", where good features are those we wish to select, i.e., biomarkers. Under independent features, Optimal Bayesian Filtering reports a feature set of a given size with a maximal expected number of true good features (CMNC-OBF) [2]. CMNC-OBF is extremely fast and enjoys particularly excellent performance when markers are individually strong with low correlations, but, like all filter methods, may miss weak features that are of interest due to high correlations with strong features [2, 4]. Assuming good and bad features are separately dependent, 2MNC-Robust proposes an approximation of the posterior on good features and ranks features

Permission to make digital or hard copies of part or all of this work for personal or classroom use is granted without fee provided that copies are not made or distributed for profit or commercial advantage and that copies bear this notice and the full citation on the first page. Copyrights for third-party components of this work must be honored. For all other uses, contact the owner/author(s).
ACM-BCB '17, August 20-23, 2017, Boston, MA, USA
© 2017 Copyright held by the owner/author(s).
ACM ISBN 978-1-4503-4722-8/17/08.
https://doi.org/10.1145/3107411.3110412

by evaluating all sets of size 2 [3]. 2MNC-Robust is computationally manageable and generally improves upon CMNC-OBF in the presence of correlations.

Though both algorithms have robust performance across Bayesian models with different block-diagonal covariance structures [4], performance can be improved in the presence of correlation. To this end, we propose three new feature selection algorithms: (1) REcursive MArginal posterior INflation (REMAIN), which uses an iterative strategy to update the approximate posterior used in 2MNC-Robust, (2) POsterior FActor-Constrained (POFAC), which uses a novel scoring function inspired by Bayes factors to improve overall rankings, and (3) Sequential Partition Mustering (SPM), which attempts to detect the underlying block structure of the data.

In the full paper, we discuss the interpretation and effect of various input parameters to the proposed algorithms, show that these algorithms have comparable computation time to 2MNC-Robust, and provide simulations showing the strengths and weaknesses of each algorithm relative to performance on synthetic Gaussian data with block-diagonal covariance matrices and on synthetic microarray data. In general, the proposed algorithms outperform CMNC-OBF, 2MNC-Robust and many other popular feature selection algorithms. CMNC-OBF is very good at selecting individually strong features, and under non-informative priors typically performs similarly to Bhattacharyya distance under Gaussian distributions with estimated moments. Under small sample sizes, or cases where correctly labeling good features is more difficult, REMAIN tends to output very few features resulting in even better performance, however note that OBF can also enjoy this characteristic if implemented using the unconstrained MNC objective instead of CMNC. SPM is a more complex algorithm that can perform poorly when the sample size is small, possibly due to over-fitting or sensitivity to the prior, but has great performance when sample size is large. Finally, POFAC is an interesting option, enjoying competitive performance across all sample sizes. POFAC outperforms 2MNC-Robust with only slightly higher computation cost.

We apply CMNC-OBF, REMAIN, POFAC, and SPM to breast cancer microarray data from [5], with 119 relapse free patients in class 0 and 40 patients with relapses in class 1. The top five genes selected by CMNC-OBF, REMAIN and POFAC are provided in Tab. 1. Note SPM outputs feature blocks, not a feature ranking. The top three pathways from enrichment analysis on the gene sets selected by all four algorithms is provided in Tab. 2. Many of these genes and pathways have suggested involvement in breast cancer. In particular, PHTF1, ZNF192, and MUC5AC have been documented in the literature, DCT and ZP2 are high-profile biomarkers, and the gonadotropin-releasing hormone receptor pathway, ubiquitin proteasome pathway, CCKR signaling map, and integrin signalling pathway have also been linked to breast cancer.

In the full paper, we provide a complete discussion of these results, as well as similar analyses on colon cancer and acute myeloid leukemia datasets. In general, CMNC-OBF tends to find individually strong markers that already have known involvement in cancer, and might miss biomarkers that are individually weak but heavily correlated with strong biomarkers. Hence, CMNC-OBF may tend to produce strongly annotated genes and pathways, but might not be as useful for discovery. POFAC and REMAIN tend to find genes that are individually strong or highly correlated with individually strong biomarkers. These algorithms might be more useful in identifying genes directly involved in cancer, or genes that directly interact with them. SPM is specifically designed to find all genes correlated with individually strong biomarkers. Hence, it tends to report large gene sets, and may be particularly useful for identifying and hypothesizing which biological functions are affected in the cancer under study.

Table 1: Top Genes of Breast Cancer

Rank	CMNC-OBF	REMAIN	POFAC
1	DCT	DCT	DCT
2	PHTF1	ZNF192	PHTF1
3	ZNF227	ZP2	MUC5AC
4	ZP2	PCSK6	HUWE1
5	CEACAM7	CEACAM7	MLANA

Table 2: Top Pathways of Breast Cancer

Algorithm	Pathway	P-value
CMNC-OBF	Gonadotropin-releasing hormone receptor pathway	$4.93E-05$
	p53 pathway	$8.34E-05$
	Ubiquitin proteasome pathway	$1.26E-04$
REMAIN	Ubiquitin proteasome pathway	$3.33E-07$
	Angiogenesis	$3.40E-04$
	FAS signaling pathway	$7.23E-04$
POFAC	CCKR signaling map	$3.82E-05$
	p53 pathway	$2.61E-04$
	Ubiquitin proteasome pathway	$4.18E-04$
SPM	Ubiquitin proteasome pathway	$6.25E-07$
	Integrin signalling pathway	$1.72E-06$
	Pyrimidine Metabolism	$2.87E-05$

ACKNOWLEDGMENTS

The work of LAD is supported by the National Science Foundation (CCF-1422631 and CCF-1453563).

REFERENCES

[1] Eleftherios P. Diamandis. 2010. Cancer biomarkers: Can we turn recent failures into success? *Journal of the National Cancer Institute* 102, 19 (2010), 1462–1467.

[2] Ali Foroughi pour and Lori A. Dalton. 2015. Optimal Bayesian feature filtering. In *Proceedings of the 6th ACM Conference on Bioinformatics, Computational Biology and Health Informatics*. 651–652.

[3] Ali Foroughi pour and Lori A. Dalton. 2016. Multiple sclerosis biomarker discovery via Bayesian feature selection. *In Proceedings of the 7th ACM International Conference on Bioinformatics, Computational Biology, and Health Informatics*, 540–541.

[4] Ali Foroughi pour and Lori A. Dalton. 2017. Robust feature selection for block covariance Bayesian models. *To appear in the proceedings of 42nd International Conference on Acoustics, Speech and Signal Processing (ICASSP).*

[5] Yudi Pawitan, Judith Bjöhle, Lukas Amler, Anna-Lena Borg, Suzanne Egyhazi, Per Hall, Xia Han, Lars Holmberg, Fei Huang, Sigrid Klaar, Edison T. Liu, Lance Miller, Hans Nordgren, Alexander Ploner, Kerstin Sandelin, Peter M. Shaw, Johanna Smeds, Lambert Skoog, Sara Wedrén, and Jonas Bergh. 2005. Gene expression profiling spares early breast cancer patients from adjuvant therapy: derived and validated in two population-based cohorts. *Breast Cancer Research* 7, 6 (2005), 953–964.

Feature Selection with Interactions in Logistic Regression Models using Multivariate Synergies for a GWAS Application

Easton Li Xu
Department of Electrical and Computer Engineering
Texas A&M University, College Station, TX
xulimc@gmail.com

Xiaoning Qian
Department of Electrical and Computer Engineering, Texas A&M University
College Station, TX
xqian@ece.tamu.edu

Qilian Yu
Department of Electrical and Computer Engineering, University of California, Davis
Davis, CA
dryu@ucdavis.edu

Han Zhang
Department of Electrical and Computer Engineering, University of California, Davis
Davis, CA
hanzh@ucdavis.edu

Shuguang Cui
Department of Electrical and Computer Engineering, University of California, Davis
Davis, CA
sgcui@ucdavis.edu

ABSTRACT

Identifying "synergistic" interactions with respect to the outcome of interest can help accurate phenotypic prediction and understand the underlying mechanism of system behavior. Many statistical measures for estimating synergistic interactions have been proposed in the literature for such a purpose. However, except for empirical performances, there is still no theoretical analysis on the power and limitation of these synergistic interaction measures.

In this paper, we provide a rigorous theoretical analysis on how the information-theoretic multivariate synergy helps with identifying genetic risk factors via synergistic interactions. When genotype-phenotype relationships can be modeled with logistic regression, it is shown that the multivariate synergy depends on a small subset of the interaction parameters in the model, sometimes on only one interaction parameter. We further conduct the experiments over both a simulated data set and a real-world Genome-Wide Association Study (GWAS) data set to show the effectiveness.

CCS CONCEPTS

• **Theory of computation** → **Theory and algorithms for application domains**; *Machine learning theory*; Models of learning;

KEYWORDS

Genotype-phenotype association, feature selection, genome-wide association study, synergistic interaction, mutual information

Permission to make digital or hard copies of part or all of this work for personal or classroom use is granted without fee provided that copies are not made or distributed for profit or commercial advantage and that copies bear this notice and the full citation on the first page. Copyrights for third-party components of this work must be honored. For all other uses, contact the owner/author(s).
ACM-BCB '17, August 20-23, 2017, Boston, MA, USA
© 2017 Copyright held by the owner/author(s).
ACM ISBN 978-1-4503-4722-8/17/08.
https://doi.org/10.1145/3107411.3110406

1 INTRODUCTION

Understanding genotype-phenotype relationships is one of the most critical problems to help identify "causal" risk factors or biomarkers, further develop accurate phenotypic prediction models, and derive effective therapeutic strategies. In statistical learning, risk factor or biomarker identification problems can be formulated as feature selection or feature screening [1–3] to identify a subset of profiled variables or features that are significantly associated with the system behavior of interest in a statistical sense.

To find important features considering interactive effects, one possible solution is to derive a full Logistic Regression model that incorporates the interactive effects as feature multiplication terms [4]. However, the model complexity can increase exponentially and hence requires a large number of samples to generate reproducible results.

The primary goal of this work is to establish rigorous mathematical theories for feature screening and selection approaches with the consideration of interactive effects under a specific system model based on logistic regression [2, 3], which has been arguably the most popular model for biomarker identification and phenotypic classification, for example, in Genome-Wide Association Studies (GWAS). We derive a family of interactive measures that can provide accurate detection of such cooperative interactions. We theoretically prove that such interactive measures can indeed be approximated by quadratic functions of the parameters of the cooperative interactions in logistic regression. Finally, we apply our results in both simulated datasets and a real-world GWAS dataset to demonstrate the effectiveness of these information theoretic measures.

2 SYSTEM MODEL

Consider d independent binary variables $X_1, X_2, \ldots, X_d$ and a binary outcome variable Y. The profiled variables are assumed to have the probability distribution $\Pr(X_i = +1) = p_i$ and $\Pr(X_i = -1) = q_i$ with $p_i, q_i > 0$, $p_i + q_i = 1$ for

$1 \leq i \leq d$, and the conditional probability of the outcome variable Y is assumed to take the following form:

$$\begin{aligned}\Pr(Y = 1|X_1, X_2, \ldots, X_d) \\ &= \sigma\left(\beta_\emptyset + \sum_{\emptyset \subset S \subseteq \{1,2,\ldots,d\}} \beta_S \prod_{i \in S} X_i\right), \\ \Pr(Y = -1|X_1, X_2, \ldots, X_d) \\ &= 1 - \Pr(Y = 1|X_1, X_2, \ldots, X_d),\end{aligned}$$

where $\sigma(x) := 1/(1+e^{-x})$ is the sigmoid function and $\{\beta_S : S \subseteq \{1, 2, \ldots, d\}\}$ is a family of real parameters. For any subset S of $\{1, 2, \ldots, d\}$, parameter β_S measures the amount of the cooperative interaction among the variables X_i's ($i \in S$). We can estimate the cooperative interactions among candidates X_i's and Y via the help of multivariate synergy, which is first suggested in [5] and recently proposed for interaction and association studies in bioinformatics by Anastassiou [6]. Precisely, for any n random variables $Z_1, Z_2, \ldots, Z_n$, the multivariate synergy $\mathscr{S}$ of these variables is defined to be

$$\begin{aligned}&\mathscr{S}(Z_1; Z_2; \ldots; Z_n) \\ &\triangleq (-1)^n \sum_{1 \leq i \leq n} H(Z_i) + (-1)^{n-1} \sum_{1 \leq i < j \leq n} H(Z_i, Z_j) \\ &\quad + \cdots + (-1)H(Z_1, Z_2, \ldots, Z_n),\end{aligned}$$

where H is the Shannon entropy [7, 8].

3 RESULTS

The main theoretical result that we establish is to show why such a multivariate synergy can help risk factor identification with interactions. It shows that for any subset S of $\{1, 2, \ldots, d\}$, the multivariate synergy of $X_S \triangleq \{X_i : i \in S\}$ and Y is approaching a quadratic function over parameter β_S of the cooperative interaction corresponding to S.

THEOREM 1. *For any subset $S \subseteq \{1, 2, \ldots, d\}$,*

$$\begin{aligned}&\mathscr{S}(X_S; Y) = \frac{1}{8}\left(\prod_{i \in S} 4p_i q_i\right) \\ &\cdot \left[\beta_S + \sum_{S \subset G \subseteq \mathcal{I}} \left(\beta_G \prod_{i \in G \setminus S} (p_i - q_i)\right)\right]^2 + O(C^4).\end{aligned}$$

The above theorem shows that the multivariate synergy depends only on the interaction parameters β_G for $G \supset S$ approximately, when C is small enough.

COROLLARY 2. *Assume that each profiled variable X_i is uniformly distributed. For any set $S \subseteq \{1, 2, \ldots, d\}$, we have*

$$\mathscr{S}(X_S; Y) = \frac{1}{8}\beta_S^2 + O(C^4).$$

From this corollary, it is clear that the multivariate synergy mainly depends on β_S when C is small enough. Hence, estimating the multivariate synergy can help identify interactions without inferring the full logistic regression model.

COROLLARY 3. *Assume that there is no interaction of orders higher than m, i.e., $\beta_G = 0$ if $|G| > m$. For any set $S \subseteq \{1, 2, \ldots, d\}$ with order m, we have*

$$\mathscr{S}(X_S; Y) = \left(\frac{1}{8}\prod_{i \in S} 4p_i q_i\right)\beta_S^2 + O(C^4).$$

This result tells us that the highest-order multivariate synergy mainly depends on β_S when C is small enough. This indeed guarantees that when the sample size is large enough, we can correctly estimate the highest-order interactions in logistic regression without actually learning the full model.

Based on the above results, we find that the multivariate synergy has a monotonic relationship with the magnitude of the interactive effects in the full logistic regression model. We propose an **adjusted multivariate synergy**, which directly reflects the interactive effect in the logistic regression model with the normalization to adjust for the interference:

DEFINITION 4. **Adjusted Multivariate Synergy:**

$$\mathscr{S}_{adj}(X_S; Y) \triangleq \frac{8\mathscr{S}(X_S; Y)}{\prod_{i \in S} 4p_i q_i}. \quad (1)$$

The experiments show the adjusted multivariate synergy achieves an excellent empirical performance in risk factor identification with interactions over both simulated data and real-world GWAS data on Type 1 Diabetes.

ACKNOWLEDGEMENTS

Easton Li Xu, Qilian Yu, Han Zhang, and Shuguang Cui have been supported in part by DoD with grant HDTRA1-13-1-0029, by grant NSFC-61328102/61629101, and by NSF with grants DMS-1622433, AST-1547436, ECCS-1508051/1659025, and CNS-1343155. Xiaoning Qian has been supported in part by NIH/NIDDK with grant R21DK092845, by JDRF with grant 1-PNF-2014-151-A-V, and by NSF with grant CCF-1553281.

REFERENCES

[1] Yvan Saeys, Iñaki Inza, and Pedro Larrañaga. 2007. A review of feature selection techniques in bioinformatics. *Bioinformatics* 23, 19 (Oct. 2007), 2507–2517.
[2] Jerome Friedman, Trevor Hastie, and Robert Tibshirani. 2001. *The elements of statistical learning.* Springer series in statistics, Vol. 1. Springer, Berlin, Germany.
[3] Kevin P. Murphy. 2012. *Machine Learning: A Probabilistic Perspective.* MIT press, Boston, MA.
[4] Michael Lim and Trevor Hastie. 2015. Learning interactions via hierarchical group-lasso regularization. *J. Comput. Graph. Stat.* 24, 3 (Jul. 2015), 627–654.
[5] Gal Chechik, Amir Globerson, Mike J. Anderson, Eric D. Young, Israel Nelken, and Naftali Tishby. 2002. Group redundancy measures reveal redundancy reduction in the auditory pathway. In *Proceedings of Advances in neural information processing systems*, Vancouver, BC, 173–180.
[6] Dimitris Anastassiou. 2007. Computational analysis of the synergy among multiple interacting genes. *Mol. Syst. Biol.* 3, 83 (Jan. 2007), 1–8.
[7] Claude E. Shannon. 2001. A mathematical theory of communication. *ACM SIGMOBILE Mobile Comput. Commun. Rev.* 5, 1 (Jan. 2001), 3–55.
[8] Thomas M. Cover and Joy A. Thomas. 2012. *Elements of information theory.* John Wiley & Sons, Hoboken, NJ.

Simulating Variance Heterogeneity in Quantitative Genome Wide Association Studies

Ahmad Al Kawam
Electrical & Computer Engineering
Texas A&M University
College Station, TX 77843
ahmad.alkawam@tamu.edu

Mustafa Alshawaqfeh
Electrical & Computer Engineering
Texas A&M University
College Station, TX 77843

James Cai
Veterinary Integrative Biosciences
Texas A&M University
College Station, TX 77843

Erchin Serpedin
Electrical & Computer Engineering
Texas A&M University
College Station, TX 77843

Aniruddha Datta
Electrical & Computer Engineering
Texas A&M University
College Station, TX 77843

ABSTRACT

Variance heterogeneity in genome wide association studies (vGWAS) is a recent approach that is gaining interest due to its ability to detect non-additive interactions in the genome. Recent studies have found that in the presence of a non-additive interaction, such as a gene-gene or a gene-environment interaction, variance heterogeneity is introduced in at least one of the interacting loci. As opposed to typical GWAS analysis techniques, vGWAS tests the variance at each targeted location to identify the genotypes that cause a significant differentiation in the variance. The development of vGWAS methods to perform this task is an ongoing process in this relatively new field. In order to contribute to this process, in this work we introduce a mathematical framework and algorithm for simulating quantitative vGWAS data. An accurate simulation process is essential for the development and evaluation of vGWAS methods through establishing a ground truth for comparison. The presented simulation model accounts for both haploid and diploid genotypes under different modes of dominance. We used this simulation process to assess the performance of existing quantitative vGWAS detection algorithms. Finally, we use this assessment to point out the challenges these methods face, in hope of motivating the development of more advanced methods.

KEYWORDS

Variance Heterogeneity, Genome Wide Association Studies, GWAS Simulation

1 INTRODUCTION

Over the past decade, GWAS analysis has been able to uncover associations between genomic loci and a wide range of phenotypic traits and diseases. Due to their high computational complexity, GWAS analysis has faced challenges when accounting for non-additive genetic associations such as gene-gene (GxG) and gene-environment (GxE) interactions. vGWAS attempts to resolve these challenges by resorting to a one-dimensional genome-wide scan that tests for variance differentiation between genotypes at the targeted genetic loci. This difference in variance has been found to be linked to non-additive effects.

Using this approach, several studies have been proposed to detect non-additive interactions for a variety of traits. For example, in one study, vGWAS identified an interaction between a locus that affects body mass and the physical activity of the individual [7]. Another study identified several variance controlling loci located in regions that increase the individual's susceptibility to various complex neurological disorders such as schizophrenia and Parkinson disease [2]. Finally, a third study confirmed the existence of two GxG and GxE interaction loci in lymphoblastoid cell lines [6].

Over the past few years, there has been a steady increase of vGWAS analysis methods in the specialty literature. However, the most predominant method for testing for variance heterogeneity is Levene's (Brown-Forsythe) test. Recent methods [2, 5] have relied on regression models to locate loci with statistically significant variance differentiation. These regression models exhibit an advantage over the typical Brown-Forsythe test as they are able to account for both mean and variance differentiation as well as population-specific effects.

However, these vGWAS analysis models lack reliable and consistent simulation procedures to enable the objective assessment and comparisons of competing algorithms. Therefore, vGWAS simulation presents itself as a fundamental tool for GWAS analysis. Simulation provides researchers with three important features: 1) Control over the input genotypes, 2) Predictability of the output values, and 3) Consistency across different runs. Unlike lab experiments, simulation is reliable and inexpensive especially for testing under different genetic conditions.

In this work, we present a mathematical framework for simulating vGWAS data and a simulation algorithm that implements that framework. The algorithm is applicable to either haploid or diploid genotypes. It also takes into account the effects of multiple vGWAS loci using an additive model. This work aims to motivate the evaluation of current vGWAS methods and hopes to motivate the development of more advanced methods.

Permission to make digital or hard copies of part or all of this work for personal or classroom use is granted without fee provided that copies are not made or distributed for profit or commercial advantage and that copies bear this notice and the full citation on the first page. Copyrights for third-party components of this work must be honored. For all other uses, contact the owner/author(s).
ACM-BCB '17, August 20-23, 2017, Boston, MA, USA
© 2017 Copyright held by the owner/author(s).
ACM ISBN 978-1-4503-4722-8/17/08.
https://doi.org/10.1145/3107411.3110407

2 METHODS

In order to simulate vGWAS data, two steps should be performed. In the first step, a population of genotypes is simulated. The main focus of this step is to generate a realistic population through controlling several genetic and evolutionary parameters. The second step of the simulation entails assigning numerical values to the genotype profiles in this population. This is done through a model that creates a mapping between the genotypes at user-defined genetic loci and the resulting phenotype values. In our work, we propose a model for calculating phenotype values based on either haploid or diploid genotypes. We extend our model to account for the effects of multiple vGWAS loci using an additive model.

We based our phenotype calculation on Eq. 1, which relates the phenotype value to the subject's genotype state at the targeted loci in the presence of a normally distributed residual variance:

$$y = \mu + g\alpha + \epsilon, \quad \epsilon \sim N(0, \sigma_E^2) \tag{1}$$

where y denotes the phenotype value, μ stands for the baseline mean value, $g \in \{0, 1\}$ represents the genotype state and α is the mean shift. ϵ represents the residual effects. In our vGWAS model, ϵ is decomposed into two parts, a part that is affected by the individual's genotype, and a remaining residual variance due to non-genetic environmental effects as shown in Eq. 2:

$$\sigma_E = \sigma + g\phi, \tag{2}$$

where σ denotes the baseline standard deviation, g represents the genotype state, and ϕ is the standard deviation shift due to the minor allele.

In addition, we developed a simulation algorithm that implements the presented mathematical framework. As an input, the algorithm uses genotype profiles which could be generated using population simulators or by using real data extracted from genotype experiments. In addition to genotypes, the algorithm requires information about the phenotype affecting loci, such as their number, minor allele frequency, and mean and variance effect sizes. The algorithm then employs the mathematical framework to calculate the phenotype values based on genetic loci that meet the user's specifications.

3 RESULTS AND DISCUSSION

To evaluate our simulation procedure, we conducted two sets of experiments. In the first set, we generated and visualized all the modes of variation supported by our tool to demonstrate its ability to mimic realistic patterns. In the second set of experiments, we used common GWAS and vGWAS approaches to recover the loci generated using our algorithm.

The aim of the first experiment is to verify that the generated phenotype values are in accordance with values observed in realistic vGWAS studies. We generated six sets of genotypes, three of which correspond to haploid genotypes and the other three to diploid genotypes. Using these genotypes, we simulated three types of effects: pure variance effects, pure mean effects, and mixed mean and variance effects. We observed the phenotype distributions of the generated sets and concluded that all of the simulated effects produce phenotype values that are in accordance with the desired and intended behavior.

In the second set of experiments, we simulated genotypes based on realistic settings and then used GWAS and vGWAS analysis methods to recover the simulated loci. We generated genotypes that present similar characteristics to those observed in arabidopsis thaliana [1, 3, 4]. We generated three diploid chromosomes, each containing a single phenotype affecting locus. The first locus exhibited mean effects and no variance effects. Similarly, the second locus presented variance effects and no mean effects. The third locus had a total effect size that is comparable to the effect sizes of the first two loci. However, these effects were divided equally between mean and variance effects.

To recover the simulated signals, we used three methods: 1) We used Plink's 'assoc' function which is used in typical GWAS analysis and mainly attempts to detect mean effects. 2) The Brown-Forsythe test which is generally used for vGWAS analysis since it measures the significance of the variance effects. Lastly, 3) we implemented the dglm association method described in [2] which attempts to recover both mean and variance effects simultaneously.

Upon the analysis of the results, we determined that the Plink association test and the dglm method were able to recover the mean-affecting locus on the first chromosome. However, this locus was not detected by the Brown-Forsythe test which only checks for variance effects. On chromosome two, the Brown-Forsythe test and the dglm method both recovered the variance-affecting locus, which has gone unnoticed by the Plink association. Lastly, the locus on the third chromosome resulted in a mild significance using the Plink and Brown-Forsythe tests. Only the mixed-effect dglm method was able to recover a significant signal at that locus. Therefore, using typical analysis techniques, loci with mixed variance and mean effects can potentially go undetected. This demonstrates the advantage of the most recent regression methods that account for both mean and variance effects, such as Hulse et al. (2013).

We hope that these results would motivate the development of more advanced methods that account for the combined mean and variance effects.

REFERENCES

[1] Susanna Atwell, Yu S Huang, Bjarni J Vilhjálmsson, Glenda Willems, Matthew Horton, Yan Li, Dazhe Meng, Alexander Platt, Aaron M Tarone, Tina T Hu, et al. 2010. Genome-wide association study of 107 phenotypes in Arabidopsis thaliana inbred lines. *Nature* 465, 7298 (2010), 627–631.

[2] Amanda M Hulse and James J Cai. 2013. Genetic variants contribute to gene expression variability in humans. *Genetics* 193, 1 (2013), 95–108.

[3] Sung Kim, Vincent Plagnol, Tina T Hu, Christopher Toomajian, Richard M Clark, Stephan Ossowski, Joseph R Ecker, Detlef Weigel, and Magnus Nordborg. 2007. Recombination and linkage disequilibrium in Arabidopsis thaliana. *Nature genetics* 39, 9 (2007), 1151–1155.

[4] Yan Li, Yu Huang, Joy Bergelson, Magnus Nordborg, and Justin O Borevitz. 2010. Association mapping of local climate-sensitive quantitative trait loci in Arabidopsis thaliana. *Proceedings of the National Academy of Sciences* 107, 49 (2010), 21199–21204.

[5] Lars Rönnegård and William Valdar. 2011. Detecting major genetic loci controlling phenotypic variability in experimental crosses. *Genetics* 188, 2 (2011), 435–447.

[6] Wen-Hua Wei, John Bowes, Darren Plant, Sebastien Viatte, Annie Yarwood, Jonathan Massey, Jane Worthington, and Stephen Eyre. 2016. Major histocompatibility complex harbors widespread genotypic variability of non-additive risk of rheumatoid arthritis including epistasis. *Scientific Reports* 6 (2016).

[7] Jian Yang, Ruth JF Loos, Joseph E Powell, Sarah E Medland, Elizabeth K Speliotes, Daniel I Chasman, Lynda M Rose, Gudmar Thorleifsson, Valgerdur Steinthorsdottir, Reedik Mägi, et al. 2012. FTO genotype is associated with phenotypic variability of body mass index. *Nature* 490, 7419 (2012), 267–272.

Sparse Tensor Decomposition for Haplotype Assembly of Diploids and Polyploids*

Abolfazl Hashemi
Department of Electrical and Computer Engineering
University of Texas at Austin, USA
abolfazl@utexas.edu

Banghua Zhu
Electronic Engineering Department
Tsinghua University, China
13aeon.v01d@gmail.com

Haris Vikalo
Department of Electrical and Computer Engineering
University of Texas at Austin, USA
hvikalo@ece.utexas.edu

1 EXTENDED ABSTRACT

Technological advancements in DNA sequencing enabled routine studies of genetic variations and the effects those variations have on an individual's health. Full information about variations in an individual's genome is given by haplotypes, ordered lists of single nucleotide polymorphisms (SNPs) on the individual's chromosomes [22]. Haplotype information is critical for a wide range of applications [8, 11, 21]. In order to reconstruct haplotypes using short reads obtained by high-throughput DNA sequencing, one needs to partition the reads into K clusters, each containing the reads that sample one of the chromosomes. If there were no sequencing errors in the reads, performing such a clustering task would be easy. However, sequencing errors make the origin of a read unclear and therefore render haplotype assembly difficult. Majority of haplotype assembly methods consider the minimum error correction (MEC) formulation where the goal is to find the smallest number of nucleotides in reads that need to be changed so that the corrected reads are consistent with having originated from precisely K chromosomes [5, 14, 17, 18, 25]. It is known that finding optimal solution to the MEC formulation of the haplotype assembly problem is NP-hard [5, 7]. Exact methods such as branch-and-bound schemes [24?] and dynamic programing techniques [12, 14] struggle to remain accurate and practically feasible at high coverages. This has motivated a number of heuristics such as those in [1–3, 9, 10, 13, 15, 15, 19].

In addition to studies of diploids, advancements in sequencing also enabled studies of genetic variations of polyploid organisms. However, with the exception of HapCompass [1], SDhaP [9] and BP [19], the above listed methods are restricted to haplotype assembly of diploid genomes. Other recent techniques capable of reconstructing haplotypes for both diploid and polyploid genomes include HapTree [4], a Bayesian method for finding the maximum likelihood haplotype shown to outperform HapCompass and SDhaP [16], and H-PoP [25], the state-of-the-art dynamic programming method that significantly outperforms the schemes developed in [1, 4, 9] in terms of accuracy, memory consumption, and speed. Note that majority of existing polyploid assembly methods are generally not capable of reconstructing haplotypes with polyallelic variant sites.

We present a unified framework for haplotype assembly of diploid and polyploid genomes that relies on sparse tensor decomposition. Let us represent nucleotides numerically using alphabet $\mathcal{A} = \{(1,0,0,0), (0,1,0,0), (0,0,1,0), (0,0,0,1)\}$ and organize reads into a binary tensor which can be thought of as being obtained by multiplying a matrix $\mathbf{U}$ that encodes unknown origin of the reads and a tensor $\underline{\mathbf{V}}$ that consists of strain sequences. This representation is illustrated in Fig. 1 where n and k denote number of reads and size of population, respectively, and where m is the haplotype block length.

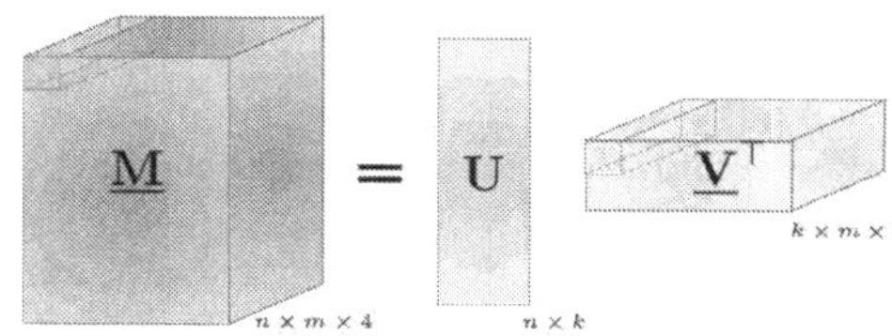

Fig. 1. *Representing population sequences and sequencing reads using tensors. Horizontal slices of tensor $\underline{\mathbf{V}}^T$ are population sequences while matrix $\mathbf{U} \in \{0,1\}^{n\times k}$ assigns each of the n horizontal slices of $\underline{\mathbf{M}}$ (reads) to one of the k strains, i.e., the ith row of $\mathbf{U}$ is an indicator of the origin of the ith read.*

A sequencing device provides a noisy sampled version of $\underline{\mathbf{M}}$ which we denote by $\underline{\mathbf{R}}$; one can think of $\underline{\mathbf{R}}$ as being a tensor collecting sequencing reads, which are erroneous and incomplete samples of haplotypes. One can show (details omitted for brevity) that the strain reconstruction problem can readily be formulated as the optimization

$$\min_{\mathbf{U},\underline{\mathbf{V}}} \ \frac{1}{2}\left\|\mathcal{P}_\Omega(\underline{\mathbf{R}} - \mathbf{U}\underline{\mathbf{V}}^\top)\right\|_F^2, \tag{1}$$

where $\|.\|_F$ denotes the Frobenius norm of its argument and $\mathcal{P}_\Omega$ is a sampling operator that describes the pattern of missing entries in $\underline{\mathbf{R}}$. Although the objective function in (1) is convex in each of the factors when the other factor is fixed, the objective is generally nonconvex which makes (1) computationally challenging. Note that tensor and matrix factorization have received a lot of attention in recent years [6, 23].

We propose an iterative procedure for finding tensor decomposition that exploits underlying structural properties of the factors in (1) to perform decomposition at a low computational cost. The algorithm, which we refer to as AltHap, thus assembles haplotypes in an iterative fashion, alternating between two computationally

*This work is funded by the National Science Foundation under grants CCF 1320273 and CCF 1618427.

Permission to make digital or hard copies of part or all of this work for personal or classroom use is granted without fee provided that copies are not made or distributed for profit or commercial advantage and that copies bear this notice and the full citation on the first page. Copyrights for third-party components of this work must be honored. For all other uses, contact the owner/author(s).
ACM-BCB'17, August 20–23, 2017, Boston, MA, USA.
© 2017 Copyright held by the owner/author(s).
978-1-4503-4722-8/17/08.
DOI: http://dx.doi.org/10.1145/3107411.3110417

Table 1. Performance of AltHap on simulated polyallelic triploid data set with haplotype block length $m = 1000$. The simulations were conducted on a single core Intel Xeon E5-2690 v3 (Haswell) with 2.6 GHz and 64 GB DDR4-2133 RAM.

Error rate	Coverage	CPR	MEC	t(sec)
0.002	20	0.952	2346	232.07
0.01	20	0.855	7272	235.86
0.05	20	0.939	9120	236.73

tractable optimization tasks. It should be noted that while state-of-the-art haplotype assembly methods for polyploids assume haplotypes may only have biallelic sites, the proposed method is capable of reconstructing polyallelic haplotypes. Since polyallelic variants are common in plants, this is of importance for applications such as crop cultivation [20].

Performance of AltHap on simulated triploid with polyallelic variant sites is shown in Table 1. In particular, the performance is expressed in terms of the minimum error correction (MEC) scores and correct phasing rate (CPR) that the algorithm achieves for a given sequencing coverage and data error rate.

REFERENCES

[1] D. Aguiar and S. Istrail. 2012. HapCompass: a fast cycle basis algorithm for accurate haplotype assembly of sequence data. *J. Comput. Biol.* 19, 6 (2012), 577–590.

[2] V. Bansal and V. Bafna. 2008. HapCUT: an efficient and accurate algorithm for the haplotype assembly problem. *Bioinformatics* 24, 16 (2008), i153–i159.

[3] V. Bansal, A.L. Halpern, N. Axelrod, and V. Bafna. 2008. An MCMC algorithm for haplotype assembly from whole-genome sequence data. *Genome research* 18, 8 (2008), 1336–1346.

[4] E. Berger, D. Yorukoglu, J. Peng, and B. Berger. 2014. HapTree: A Novel Bayesian Framework for Single Individual Polyplotyping Using NGS Data. *PLoS Comput. Biol.* 10, 3 (2014).

[5] P. Bonizzoni, R. Dondi, G.W. Klau, Y. Pirola, N. Pisanti, and S. Zaccaria. 2016. On the Minimum Error Correction Problem for Haplotype Assembly in Diploid and Polyploid Genomes. *J. Comput. Biol.* 23, 9 (2016), 718–736.

[6] E.J. Candès and B. Recht. 2009. Exact matrix completion via convex optimization. *Found. Comput. math.* 9, 6 (2009), 717–772.

[7] R. Cilibrasi, L. Van Iersel, S. Kelk, and J. Tromp. 2005. On the complexity of several haplotyping problems. In *Algorithms in Bioinformatics*. Springer, 128–139.

[8] A.G. Clark. 2004. The role of haplotypes in candidate gene studies. *Genetic epidemiology* 27, 4 (2004), 321–333.

[9] S. Das and H. Vikalo. 2015. SDhaP: Haplotype assembly for diploids and polyploids via semi-definite programming. *BMC Genomics* 16:260 (April 2015).

[10] J. Duitama, G.K. McEwen, T. Huebsch, S. Palczewski, S. Schulz, and et al. 2011. Fosmid-based whole genome haplotyping of a HapMap trio child: evaluation of Single Individual Haplotyping techniques. *Nucleic acids research* (2011), gkr1042.

[11] R.A. Gibbs, J.W. Belmont, P. Hardenbol, T.D. Willis, F. Yu, and et al. 2003. The international HapMap project. *Nature* 426, 6968 (2003), 789–796.

[12] D. He, A. Choi, K. Pipatsrisawat, A. Darwiche, and E. Eskin. 2010. Optimal algorithms for haplotype assembly from whole-genome sequence data. *Bioinformatics* 26, 12 (2010), i183–i190.

[13] J.H. Kim, M.S. Waterman, and L.M. Li. 2007. Diploid genome reconstruction of Ciona intestinalis and comparative analysis with Ciona savignyi. *Genome research* 17, 7 (2007), 1101–1110.

[14] V. Kuleshov. 2014. Probabilistic single-individual haplotyping. *Bioinformatics* 30, 17 (2014), i379–i385.

[15] S. Levy, G. Sutton, P.C. Ng, L. Feuk, A.L. Halpern, and et al. 2007. The diploid genome sequence of an individual human. *PLoS biology* 5, 10 (2007), e254.

[16] E. Motazedi, R. Finkers, C. Maliepaard, and D. de Ridder. 2017. Exploiting next-generation sequencing to solve the haplotyping puzzle in polyploids: a simulation study. *Brief. Bioinform.* (2017), bbw126.

[17] M. Patterson, T. Marschall, N. Pisanti, L. Van Iersel, L. Stougie, and et al. 2015. WhatsHap: Weighted haplotype assembly for future-generation sequencing reads. *J. Comput. Biol.* 22, 6 (2015), 498–509.

[18] Y. Pirola, S. Zaccaria, R. Dondi, G.W. Klau, N. Pisanti, and P. Bonizzoni. 2015. HapCol: accurate and memory-efficient haplotype assembly from long reads. *Bioinformatics* (2015), btv495.

[19] Z Puljiz and H Vikalo. 2016. Decoding genetic variations: Communications-inspired haplotype assembly. *IEEE/ACM Trans. Comput. Biol. Bioinform.* (2016).

[20] S. Renny-Byfield and J.F. Wendel. 2014. Doubling down on genomes: polyploidy and crop plants. *American J. botany* 101, 10 (2014), 1711–1725.

[21] P.C. Sabeti, D.E. Reich, J.M. Higgins, H.Z.P. Levine, D.J. Richter, and et al. 2002. Detecting recent positive selection in the human genome from haplotype structure. *Nature* 419, 6909 (2002), 832–837.

[22] R. Schwartz and et al. 2010. Theory and algorithms for the haplotype assembly problem. *Communications in Info. & Sys.* 10, 1 (2010), 23–38.

[23] R. Sun and Z.Q. Luo. 2016. Guaranteed matrix completion via non-convex factorization. *IEEE Trans. Info. Theory* 62, 11 (2016), 6535–6579.

[24] R. Wang, L. Wu, Z. Li, and X. Zhang. 2005. Haplotype reconstruction from SNP fragments by minimum error correction. *Bioinformatics* 21, 10 (2005), 2456–2462.

[25] M. Xie, Q. Wu, J. Wang, and T. Jiang. 2016. H-PoP and H-PoPG: Heuristic partitioning algorithms for single individual haplotyping of polyploids. *Bioinformatics* (2016), btw537.

Intrinsically Bayesian Robust Classifier for Single-Cell Gene Expression Time Series in Gene Regulatory Networks

Alireza Karbalayghareh
Texas A&M University
College Station, Texas 77843, USA
alireza.kg@tamu.edu

Ulisses Braga-Neto
Texas A&M University
College Station, Texas 77843, USA
ulisses@tamu.edu

Edward R. Dougherty
Texas A&M University
College Station, Texas 77843, USA
edward@ece.tamu.edu

ABSTRACT

This paper studies expression-based classification under the assumption that single-cell measurements are sampled at a sufficient rate to detect regulatory timing. Observations are expression trajectories. In effect, classification is performed on data generated by an underlying gene regulatory network. Network regulation is modeled via a Boolean network with perturbation, regulation not being fully determined owing to inherent biological randomness, and we assume a partially known Gaussian observation model belonging to an uncertainty class of models. We derive the intrinsically Bayesian robust classifier to discriminate between wild-type and mutated networks based on expression trajectories. We test it using the mammalian cell-cycle model, discriminating between wild-type and mutated networks. Tests examine all model aspects, including trajectory length, perturbation probability, and the hyperparameters governing the prior distribution over the uncertainty class.

KEYWORDS

Intrinsically Bayesian robust classifier; Optimal Bayesian classifier; Bayesian trajectory classifier; Single-cell expression trajectory; Gene regulatory network; Boolean network; Bayesian partially observed Boolean dynamical system

1 INTRODUCTION

Phenotype classification is a salient issue for translational genomics. Both expression microarray and RNA-Seq measurements have received much interest; however, both suffer from a lack of specificity. First, pathway timing is not reflected in the data and, second, expressions are averaged across groups of cells, so that individual cell responses are not detectable. New technologies are being developed for profiling individual cells, whose expression levels can be measured at various time points. Given single-cell measurements sampled with a sufficient rate to detect regulatory timing, classification could be done on data reflecting an underlying gene regulatory network.

In [7], we introduced the Bayes classifier for the state trajectories of probabilisitic Boolean networks (PBNs) and Boolen networks with perturbations (BNps). In [6] and [5], we assumed an observation model on the state dynamics of BNps, from which the expression values of the genes are obtained. As the parameters of the model were all unknown and the network functions were partially known, we proposed an expectation-maximization (EM) - based algorithm to estimate these parameters and functions, and then plugged them into the Bayes classifier. In this paper we extend single-cell trajectory classification to the Bayesian framework by applying the intrinsically Bayesian robust (IBR) classifier [2] to the trajectories.

Unlike [5], we assume that the parameters have uncertainty and put prior distributions on them. Instead of class-conditional densities, we derive the effective class-conditional densities, which are the key parts of the IBR classifier. There are two classes: wild-type ($S = 0$) and mutated ($S = 1$). We introduce a Bayesian version of the partially observed Boolean dynamical system (POBDS), proposed in [4], as our observation model. We use a beta prior distribution for the prior probability of the class $S = 0$ and also for the gene perturbation probability. Since the observation model given the states is Gaussian, we employ a normal-gamma distribution as the prior distribution of the mean and precision (inverse of variance) of the Gaussian model.

We assume that the underlying Boolean networks for both the wild-type and mutated classes are known and the only uncertain parameter at the state level is the perturbation probability, which is governed by a beta prior. We define a Bayesian partially-observed Boolean dynamical system (BPOBDS) as the model for the gene-expression data. Gene expressions come from Gaussian distributions whose parameters are uncertain. These are governed by prior distributions whose parameters are a function of the hidden Boolean states.

2 METHODS

If $y_j(k)$ is the expression value of the j-th gene at time k, then the observation model can be written as

$$p\left(y_j(k)|\theta_j(k),\lambda_j(k)\right) \sim \mathcal{N}(\theta_j(k),\lambda_j(k)^{-1}),$$

for all $j = 1,2,\cdots,n$ and $k = 1,2,\cdots$, where $\theta_j(k)$ and $\lambda_j(k)$ respectively denote the mean and precision of the Gaussian distribution. We employ the normal-gamma prior distribution for $\theta_j(k)$ and $\lambda_j(k)$:

$$\begin{aligned} p(\lambda_j(k)) &\sim \text{Gamma}(\alpha_0,\beta_0), \\ p(\theta_j(k)|\lambda_j(k),x_j(k)) &\sim \mathcal{N}\left(\mu_j(k),(\kappa_0\lambda_j(k))^{-1}\right), \\ \text{where } \mu_j(k) &= \mu_0+\delta_0 x_j(k), \end{aligned}$$

where α_0, β_0, κ_0, μ_0, and δ_0 are the known positive hyperparameters, and $x_j(k)$ is the hidden Boolean state of gene j at time k,

Permission to make digital or hard copies of part or all of this work for personal or classroom use is granted without fee provided that copies are not made or distributed for profit or commercial advantage and that copies bear this notice and the full citation on the first page. Copyrights for third-party components of this work must be honored. For all other uses, contact the owner/author(s).
ACM-BCB '17, August 20-23, 2017, Boston, MA, USA
© 2017 Copyright held by the owner/author(s).
ACM ISBN 978-1-4503-4722-8/17/08.
https://doi.org/10.1145/3107411.3110408

whose values at each time are determined by the Boolean functions governing the network [6]. The intuition behind the prior is that when a gene j at time k is on and off, that is, $x_j(k) = 1$ and 0, the hyper-mean of expression for that gene is respectively $\mu_j(k) = \mu_0 + \delta_0$ and $\mu_j(k) = \mu_0$ at time k. μ_0 is the baseline expression level and δ_0 is the expression coefficient. The hyperparameters α_0, β_0, and κ_0 determine the level of uncertainty, by which we can control the variance of the outputs. We assume the same values of hyperparameters for all the genes at all times.

Intrinsically robust Bayesian classification pertains to the situation in which the feature-label distribution is unknown but belongs to an uncertainty class Θ of feature-label distributions governed by a prior distribution π. Given a classifier ψ, from the perspetive of mean-square error, the best error estimate minimizes the MSE between its true error (a function of θ) and an error estimate. This Bayesian minimum-mean-square-error (MMSE) estimate is given by the expected true error, $\widehat{\varepsilon}(\psi) = \mathrm{E}_\theta[\varepsilon(\psi, \theta)]$, where $\varepsilon(\psi, \theta)$ is the error of ψ on the feature-label distributin parameterized by θ and the expectation is taken relative to the prior distribution $\pi(\theta)$ [1].

An IBR classifier minimizes the Bayesian MMSE estimate, that is, the expected true error. If $\psi(\mathbf{x}) = 0$ if $\mathbf{x} \in R_0$ and $\psi(\mathbf{x}) = 1$ if $\mathbf{x} \in R_1$, where R_0 and R_1 partition the sample space, then [2]

$$\widehat{\varepsilon}(\psi) = \mathrm{E}_\pi[c] \int_{R_1} f_\Theta(\mathbf{x}|0)\, d\mathbf{x} + (1 - \mathrm{E}_\pi[c]) \int_{R_0} f_\Theta(\mathbf{x}|1)\, d\mathbf{x},$$

where

$$f_\Theta(\mathbf{x}|y) = \int_{\Theta_y} f_{\theta_y}(\mathbf{x}|y)\, \pi\left(\theta_y\right) d\theta_y$$

is the *effective class-conditional density* for class y, Θ_y being the space for θ_y, and an IBR classifier is given pointwise by

$$\psi_{\mathrm{IBR}}(\mathbf{x}) = \begin{cases} 0 & \text{if } \mathrm{E}_\pi[c] f_\Theta(\mathbf{x}|0) \geq (1 - \mathrm{E}_\pi[c]) f_\Theta(\mathbf{x}|1), \\ 1 & \text{otherwise.} \end{cases}$$

Returning to expression trajectories, given the expressions of n genes at m consecutive time points, the problem is to optimally classify this observed trajectory $\mathcal{Y}$ to the class 0 (wild-type) or class 1 (mutated). The IBR classifier for the trajectories is

$$\psi_{\mathrm{IBR}}(\mathcal{Y}) = \begin{cases} 0 \text{ if } \mathrm{E}[c] p(\mathcal{Y}|S=0) \geq \\ \qquad (1 - \mathrm{E}[c]) p(\mathcal{Y}|S=1) \\ 1 \text{ otherwise} \end{cases},$$

where $p(\mathcal{Y}|S = s)$ is the effective class-conditional density of the trajectory $\mathcal{Y}$ in the class $S = s$, for $s = 0, 1$, and c is the prior probability of the class $S = 0$, assumed to be governed by a beta prior. The main body of the full paper is devoted to evaluating the effective class-conditional densities of the trajectories.

Once an analytic representation of the IBR classifier is found, it is applied to the 10-gene mammalian cell-cycle gene regulatory network depicted in Figure 1. The Boolean functions of the corresponding wild-type network ($S = 0$) are given in [8]. According to [3], a mutation leading to cancer is when the gene p27 is shut down and cannot be activated by its regulating genes ($S = 1$). We analyze the effects of the hyperparameters and m on classification error by considering various hyperparameter combinations.

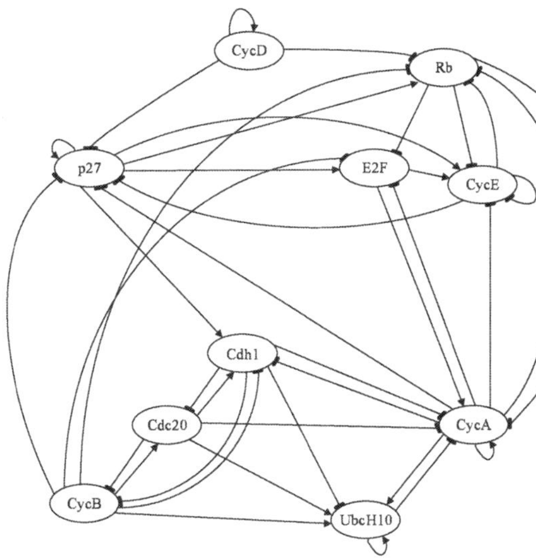

Figure 1: Mammalian cell-cycle gene regulatory network [6].

REFERENCES

[1] L. A. Dalton and E. R. Dougherty. 2011. Bayesian Minimum Mean-Square Error Estimation for Classification Error-Part I: Definition and the Bayesian MMSE Error Estimator for Discrete Classification. *IEEE Transactions on Signal Processing* 59, 1 (Jan 2011), 115–129.

[2] L. A. Dalton and E. R. Dougherty. 2013. Optimal classifiers with minimum expected error within a Bayesian framework—Part I: Discrete and Gaussian models. *Pattern Recognition* 46, 5 (2013), 1301 – 1314.

[3] A. Fauré, A. Naldi, C. Chaouiya, and D. Thieffry. 2006. Dynamical analysis of a generic Boolean model for the control of the mammalian cell cycle. *Bioinformatics* 22, 14 (2006), e124–e131.

[4] M. Imani and U. M. Braga-Neto. 2017. Maximum-Likelihood Adaptive Filter for Partially Observed Boolean Dynamical Systems. *IEEE Transactions on Signal Processing* 65, 2 (Jan 2017), 359–371.

[5] A. Karbalayghareh, U. Braga-Neto, and E. R. Dougherty. 2017. Classification of Gaussian trajectories with missing data in Boolean gene regulatory networks. In *2017 IEEE International Conference on Acoustics, Speech and Signal Processing (ICASSP)*. 1078–1082.

[6] A. Karbalayghareh, U. Braga-Neto, and E. R. Dougherty. Submitted. Classification of Gene Expression Trajectories from Incomplete and Noisy Data. *IEEE/ACM Transactions on Computational Biology and Bioinformatics* (Submitted).

[7] A. Karbalayghareh, U. Braga-Neto, J. Hua, and E. R. Dougherty. 2016. Classification of State Trajectories in Gene Regulatory Networks. *IEEE/ACM Transactions on Computational Biology and Bioinformatics* PP, 99 (2016), 1–1.

[8] X. Qian and E. R. Dougherty. 2008. Effect of Function Perturbation on the Steady-State Distribution of Genetic Regulatory Networks: Optimal Structural Intervention. *IEEE Transactions on Signal Processing* 56, 10 (Oct 2008), 4966–4976.

Constraints on signaling networks logic reveal functional subgraphs on Multiple Myeloma OMIC data

Bertrand Miannay
LS2N, UMR 6004, École Centrale de Nantes
CRCINA, INSERM, CNRS, Université d'Angers, Université de Nantes
Nantes, France
bertrand.miannay@ec-nantes.fr

Stéphane Minvielle
CRCINA, INSERM, CNRS, Université d'Angers, Université de Nantes
Nantes, France

Olivier Roux
LS2N, UMR 6004, École Centrale de Nantes
Nantes, France

Florence Magrangeas
CRCINA, INSERM, CNRS, Université d'Angers, Université de Nantes
Nantes, France

Carito Guziolowski
LS2N, UMR 6004, École Centrale de Nantes
Nantes, France
carito.guziolowski@ls2n.fr

1 INTRODUCTION

The exponential increase of biological data (genomic, transcriptomic, proteomic) and of biological interaction knowledge in Pathway Databases allow modeling cellular regulatory mechanisms. Modeling biological mechanisms is done, most of the time, using boolean or ordinary differential equation representation. Those approaches have shown their efficiency in cellular phenomena study, disease research, and bio-production optimization. However, those modeling approaches cannot take into account the large amount of data. This limitation requires that the researcher preselects the OMIC data and network, adding bias in the analysis. A classical way to perform OMIC data preselection is to use differentially expressed genes, this leads to select genes which expression levels are highly heterogeneous by imposing a fix threshold when their activation threshold may be specific for each of them. As a consequence the selected pathways may not be specific for the biological problematic. A common way to perform network preselection consists on choosing specific pathways according to the type of data and the biological problematic. However, this network preselection approach can hide unsuspected pathways reducing the possibility to discover new ones.

In this study, we propose a method, based on graph coloring approaches by looking for *perfect* colorations which maximize the agreement between the molecular species *active* or *inactive* states and the directionality of the pathways reactions according to their activator or inhibitor control role. We correlate the graph coloring models that maximize the perfectness notion and in this way built correlated graph *components*. After adding experimental data, our method is able to identify components of interest. We present an application of this method with transcriptomic data from myeloma cells (MC) of 602 MM patients and from normal plasma cells (NPC) of 9 healthy donors. MM is a hematologic malignancies representing 1% of all cancer with a survival rate of 49.6% after 5 years.

Permission to make digital or hard copies of part or all of this work for personal or classroom use is granted without fee provided that copies are not made or distributed for profit or commercial advantage and that copies bear this notice and the full citation on the first page. Copyrights for third-party components of this work must be honored. For all other uses, contact the owner/author(s).
ACM-BCB'17, August 20–23, 2017, Boston, MA, USA.
© 2017 Copyright held by the owner/author(s). ISBN 978-1-4503-4722-8/17/08.
DOI: http://dx.doi.org/10.1145/3107411.3107411

2 METHOD AND IMPLEMENTATION

We propose a *perfect colorations* modeling framework which confronts a regulatory network with transcriptomic data. The perfect colorations identification is implemented in Answer Set Programming (ASP).

2.1 Modeling perfect coloring with ASP

2.1.1 *Instantiation.*

Graph a graph is composed of a set of nodes and edges.
Target a target is a node with at least one predecessor.

2.1.2 *Candidate solutions generation.*

Colored Graph A colored graph is a graph in which all nodes will be associated to a sign: up standing for "+" and down for "-".

2.1.3 *Definitions.*

Local consistent node coloring A node colored in a consistent way will be a node where its color is explained by at least one of its direct predecessor in the graph. Same sign if the predecessor is an activator and oppositive sign if this is an inhibitor.
Imperfect target coloring An imperfect node coloring happens when a node is colored with a sign not explained by at least one of its direct predecessors in the graph.
Imperfect weighted regulator An imperfect weighted regulator p is a direct predecessor of a node n that does not explain consistenly the color of n. The weight of this rule will be the weight of the edge from p to n.

2.1.4 *Optimization constraints.* Our method identifies graph colorings which minimize conflicts between target and predecessors, that is, it finds *perfect graph colorings* with minimal conflicts. In order to do this we apply 3 minimizations.

Inconsistency minimization: The first optimization will select the colored graphs with the minimal number of inconsistent targets.
Imperfect target coloring minimization: The second optimization aims to reduce the solutions space to the graph with the minimal number of imperfect targets.
Imperfect weighted regulator minimization: The last optimization will minimize the sum of imperfect weighted regulators.

2.2 Component identification

A *component* is defined as a set nodes which are color-correlated. Given a set of perfect colorations, we can build a correlation matrix for all nodes. Two nodes which are positively or negatively correlated will be incorporated in the same component.

2.3 Maximal similarity

Due to the perfect coloring framework and the fact that our model is based on a two-signs coloring, the nodes of a component C_i will have exactly two coloring configurations, we denote them by C_i^1 and C_i^2. C_i^1 will be the exact reverse of C_i^2 (the reverse of up is down and vice versa). We represent a dataset by a set of nodes with a fixed coloration. The maximal similarity (MS) computes the maximum, with respect to the size, of the intersection between the dataset of observations and each coloring configuration divided by the number of nodes observed in the component:

$$MS_i = \frac{max(|obs_i \cap C_i^1|, |obs_i \cap C_i^2|)}{|obs_i|}$$

where i stands for the analyzed component and obs_i the colorations of nodes in the component C_i.

2.4 Space solution reduction

A coloring model and its reverse represents the same coloring perfectness, therefore, it is possible to instantiate a node with a fixed color to reduce to half the solution space size.

To furthermore reduce the complexity of the candidate solution space, we propose 3 graph reduction methods which can be applied successively over the graph prior to the perfect coloring ASP solving. These methods identify and merge nodes that will be in the same component. First reduction will aim to identify then merge nodes which are candidates to have a sign correlation in consistent solutions. The second reduction looks for correlated nodes candidates colored graph with minimized imperfect coloring. The last reduction will reduce the edges number by balancing their weights.

3 APPLICATION

3.1 Data and graph

We worked with gene expression profiles (GEP) issued from myeloma cells (MC) of 602 MM patients and from normal plasma cells (NPC) of 9 healthy donors. For each GEP, we identified the over/under-expressed genes by comparison to NPC mean expression with a 1.2-fold. Then, we use the PID-NCI database to generate a graph by extracting the downstream events from three signaling pathways (IL6/IL6-R, IGF1/IGF1-R and CD40) to the differentially expressed genes. The obtained subgraph from NCI-PID 2012, contained 2269 nodes, 2683 edges and connected 529 differentially expressed genes.

3.2 Perfect colorations

The graph reduction allowed to reduce the graph to 194 subcomponents and 389 edges. The perfect colorations method identified 16384 coloring models. We can notice that the optimization results are the same for the initial and reduced graphs. However, the computation time of the original graph is larger than the reduced graph in 2 magnitude orders (72min, 12 sec *vs* 14 sec).

3.3 Components identification, validation and specification

From those perfect colorations we identified 15 components. Due to the fact that only two components are composed of more than one gene, we focused mainly on those components C^2 (422 nodes and 167 genes) and C^6 (1832 nodes and 349 genes). For each gene expression profile n and each selected component c, we computed the maximal similarity: MS_c^n.

In order to validate the similarity computing, we compared MS between real and randomized datasets with a Welch's t-test. Both components have a p-value lower than 0.05, allowing us to conclude to a statistical significance.

To identify specific component between MC and NPC, we compared the MS between the MC and NPC for each validated component with a Welch's t-test. C^2 was the only component with a significant p-value (0.019),allowing us to conclude to a statistically different between MC and NPC.

3.4 Biological results

We analyzed the genes set included in C^2 and C^6 using a Gene Ontology Enrichment Analysis. The genes included in C^2 seem associated with cell death pathways: the three first biological processes are linked to cell death which is strongly implicated in cancer disease while C^6 does not look associated to oncogenic pathways.

4 CONCLUSION

We proposed a method that imposes constraints to model graph coloration on biological signaling and regulatory networks. This method can reduce a regulatory network to subparts called components in the context of the *perfect coloring* constraints. Moreover, by using observations, we can select some of those components based on the maximal similarity between components configurations and those observations.

Using our method we were able to identify 15 components from a subgraph of the PID-NCI signaling and regulatory network. One of these components (C^2) is strongly associated to cell death pathways, this biological process is robustly associated to cancer.

When comparing GEP from myeloma cells and healthy donors with the 15 components, we observed that C^2 was having a significant statistical specificity.

Our method seems efficient to identify and select functional components specific to the gene expression profiles used in our study taking into account the computational complexity that represents analyzing large-scale networks. As a perspective of this work, we wish to improve the subcomponent identification in order to be able to compute larger regulatory networks, and potentially full databases. Another research line will be to apply this method to other data.

Protein-Protein Interaction Extraction Using Attention-Based Convolution Neural Networks

Hao Zhang
State Key Laboratory of Symbolic Computation and Knowledge Engineering of Ministry of Education, College of Computer Science and Technology, Jilin University, Changchun 130012, CHN
hzhanght@163.com

Mary Qu Yang
1. MidSouth Bioinformatics Center and Joint Bioinformatics Ph.D. Program of UALR-UAMS,2801 S. Univ. Ave, Little Rock, AR, 72204 USA
mqyang@ualr.edu
2. Department of Genetics, Yale University
333 Cedar St., New Haven, CT 06520 USA
mary.yang@yale.edu

Xiaoyue Feng
State Key Laboratory of Symbolic Computation and Knowledge Engineering of Ministry of Education, College of Computer Science and Technology, Jilin University, Changchun 130012, CHN
fengxy@jlu.edu.cn

William Yang
Department of Computer Science, Carnegie Mellon University
School of Computer Science
5000 Forbes Ave
Pittsburgh, PA 15213 USA.
wyang1@andrew.cmu.edu

Weida Tong
Division of Bioinformatics and Biostatistics,
National Center for Toxicological
United States Food and Drug Administration,
3900 NCTR Road
Jefferson, AR 72079 USA
Weida.Tong@FDA.HHS.GOV

Renchu Guan*
1.State Key Laboratory of Symbolic Computation and Knowledge Engineering of Ministry of Education, College of Computer Science & Technology, Jilin University, Changchun 130012, CHN
2. MidSouth Bioinformatics Center & Joint Bioinformatics Ph.D. Program of UALR-UAMS, University of Arkansas, Little Rock, AR 72204 USA
* Corresponding Author:
guanrenchu@jlu.edu.cn

ABSTRACT

Protein-protein interaction (PPI) is a physical contact established between two or more protein molecules resulting from biochemical events, which are discoverable in almost all cellular processes, such as metabolism, signaling, regulation, and proliferation. PPI extraction is a method for relation extraction in the biocuration process. However, the rapid growth in the volume of biomedical literature makes manual PPI annotation barely possible. Consequently, designing and implementing effective and efficient models that can automatically discover and extract PPIs from huge amounts of biomedical literature has become a hot topic in current biomedical research. In this paper, we focus primarily on binary interaction extraction. If there are more than two protein entities in a sentence, we consider each pair of entities. Popular approaches for this task can be categorized based on the type of method used: co-occurrence, pattern, feature, and kernel. Here, the kernel method has been the most commonly used of the four. Kernel methods can help to overcome failure problems associated with a kernel function and to help researchers learn latent feature representations. However, these traditional methods for PPI extraction are almost entirely based on linguistic knowledge, and their performance greatly depends on the proficiency of natural language processing (NLP) tools. In addition, traditional features used in the PPI extraction are not fully capable of grasping the semantics of sentences.

During the recent resurgence in neural network research, deep neural-network-based approaches for the relation extraction task have performed well in a variety of biomedical research areas, such as cell differentiation and skin cancer identification. Furthermore, a neural-network-based method can automatically learn the semantics of sentences and help alleviate noise in data.

In this paper, we propose an attention-based convolutional neural network for PPI discovery. Given a sentence S with a pair of labeled protein entities, we consider PPI extraction as a binary classification problem. If the sentence expresses interaction between the two entities, we will output true, and vice versa. A tokenized sentence is the input of the deep neural network. First, the representation layer transfers all tokens into real-value vectors representing the semantics of the token. Then, the convolution layer is used to encode the contextual information represented by n-grams. Next, we adopt attention mechanisms which can grasp every piece of information about the target relation by intuitively reconciling the relational proportionality of every phrase and interaction and learning the sentence representation. Finally, we compute a score for the two labels by calculating the dot product between the sentence representation

Permission to make digital or hard copies of part or all of this work for personal or classroom use is granted without fee provided that copies are not made or distributed for profit or commercial advantage and that copies bear this notice and the full citation on the first page. Copyrights for third-party components of this work must be honored. For all other uses, contact the Owner/Author.
ACM-BCB '17, August 20-23, 2017, Boston, MA, USA
© 2017 Copyright is held by the owner/author(s).
ACM ISBN 978-1-4503-4722-8/17/08.
http://dx.doi.org/10.1145/3107411.3110418

and relation representation. We adopt a margin-based loss function and utilize stochastic gradient descent to minimize the loss function. Pre-trained word embedding is beneficial for training our neural network. We use all PMC (PubMed Central Open Access subset) data to train word embedding with word2vec, and initialize the word representation layer with this pre-trained word embedding.

To examine the effectiveness of our model, we use the most common corpora for PPI extraction, AIMed, BioInfer, HPRD50, IEPA, and LLL in our experiments. These corpora differ in many ways, such as scope of annotated entity types, coverage of entities, and direction of interactions. We perform 10-fold document level cross-validation on each corpus. In order to directly compare the results, the document-level split for each corpora is the same, and we adopt the same data format used in previous studies. To evaluate the performance, we choose F1-score and AUC for evaluation metrics.

The experiment results demonstrate that our attention-based CNN outperforms other methods in all corpora except HPRD50 when compared to other models by F1 score. With the AIMed dataset, we achieve an F1 score of 65.5% by our attention-based CNN, with 4.7% improvement, compared to the hybrid method, and with 9.3% improvement, compared to the best single kernel APG on this dataset. With the BioInfer, HPRD50, and LLL datasets, our attention-based CNN also outperforms the aforementioned state-of-the-art methods with improvements of 1.0%, 3.0% and 2.3%, respectively. When we compare our model with other models by AUC score, we achieve our best experimental results in all corpora except BioInfer. With the AIMed dataset, we achieve an AUC score of 89.5% by our attention-based CNN, with 2.7% improvement, compared to the hybrid method, and with 4.9% improvement, compared to the best single kernel APG on this dataset. With the IEPA, HPRD50, and LLL datasets, our attention-based CNN outperforms the aforementioned methods with improvements of 0.7%, 0.2% and 0.2%, respectively. Moreover, the attention-based CNN achieves a much better performance on all five corpora than does the classical CNN. Hence, it can be found that attention-based pooling is more effective than max-pooling. Additionally, we use our model to extract representative trigrams from the five corpora. Most trigrams include some important information regarding protein-protein interactions. For example, there are some representative words indicating the protein-protein interaction, such as binding, interaction, activation, and so on.

Based on the experimental results above, it can be concluded that our model alleviates the accumulation of errors by avoiding using traditional biomedical NLP tools like those used in the kernel-based method. Pre-trained word embedding by word2vec using biomedical full-text provides domain knowledge for the task. However, the proposed attention-based CNN needs a large number of labeled sentences to help further improve its performance. Distant supervision provided large amounts of annotated sentences by aligning the PPI knowledge base with the biomedical literature. We will develop a new neural-network model suited for protein-protein extraction by distant supervision in our future research.

General Terms

Algorithms, Verification.

Keywords

Convolution neural network; word2vec; attention mechanism; protein-protein interaction.

ACKNOWLEDGMENTS

Dr. Mary Yang and Dr. Renchu Guan were supported in part by the United States National Institutes of Health (NIH) Academic Research Enhancement Award 1R15GM114739 and National Institute of General Medical Sciences (NIH/NIGMS) 5P20GM103429, United States Food and Drug Administration (FDA) HHSF223201510172C through Arkansas Research Alliance (ARA) BAA-15-00121 and Arkansas Science and Technology Authority (ASTA) Basic Science Research 15-B-23 and 15-B-38. William Yang was supported in part by the United States National Institutes of Health (NIH) KUH Research Traineeship Award 5R25DK101408 and United States National Science Foundation (NSF) ICERT Research Traineeship Award #1359304.

The authors are grateful for the support of the NSF-C (National Natural Science Foundation of China) grants #61602207, 61572228 and 61472158, the Science Technology Development Project of Jilin Province, China grant #20160101247JC, the Premier Discipline Enhancement Scheme project of the city government of Zhuhai, the Premier Key-Discipline Enhancement Scheme project of the provincial government of Guangdong (Canton), and the Scholarship Council of China.

Investigation of Model Stacking for Drug Sensitivity Prediction

Kevin Matlock
Department of Electrical and Computer Engineering, Texas Tech University
1012 Boston Ave
Lubbock, Texas 79409
kevin.matlock@ttu.edu

Carlos De Niz
Department of Electrical and Computer Engineering, Texas Tech University
1012 Boston Ave
Lubbock, Texas 79409
carlos.de-niz@ttu.edu

Raziur Rahman
Department of Electrical and Computer Engineering, Texas Tech University
1012 Boston Ave
Lubbock, Texas 79409
raziur.rahman@ttu.edu

Souparno Ghosh
Department of Mathematics and Statistics, Texas Tech University
1108 Memorial Circle
Lubbock, Texas 79409
souparno.ghosh@ttu.edu

Ranadip Pal*
Department of Electrical and Computer Engineering, Texas Tech University
1012 Boston Ave
Lubbock, Texas 79409
ranadip.pal@ttu.edu

ABSTRACT

A requirement for precision medicine is the accurate prediction of the sensitivity of a given drug on an individual patient. A very common method for this prediction is the use of Random Forest built on Genomic Features such as gene expression. However, effective drug sensitivity prediction requires the use of multiple heterogeneous dataset but it is rare that all such information is available for all drug and cell line combinations. To effectively incorporate all available data into a drug sensitivity prediction problem requires the use of stacking multiple models, built using a variety of different methods and data. In this article we investigate stacking in the context of drug sensitivity prediction.

First, we examine basic models utilized in drug sensitivity prediction including the Random Forest, Neural Network, and K-Nearest Neighbor approach. To stack individual models we utilize a linear stacking method built utilizing a held-out validation set. We then investigate which form of stacking is most effective in improving accuracy. The two forms of stacking investigate are vertical stacking, in which our training samples are split and then stacked, and horizontal stacking, where our features are split before stacking. From a theoretical standpoint we have shown that horizontal stacking outperforms vertical stacking, especially as the sample size becomes large. Our theory is then proven utilizing both synthetically generated data, as well as data extracted from the Cancer Cell Line Encyclopedia. Despite having the best individual predictor, vertical stacking consistently underperformed compared to horizontal stacking.

Finally, we build a stacked model utilizing data extracted from a variety of sources. Gene Expression for individual cell lines are taken from the GDSC database, drug target data is data mined from Pubchem and physical features are extracted utilizing PaDEL-Descriptor software. Using this data we aim to predict the Area Under the Curve value for individual drug-cell line combinations. We examine the performance of individual and stacked models. We note that stacking models built on two heterogeneous datasets provide superior performance to stacking different models built on the same dataset. It is also noted that stacking provides a noticeable reduction in the bias of our predictors when the dominant eigenvalue of the principle axis of variation in the residuals is significantly higher than the remaining eigenvalues. [1]

*Corresponding author

Permission to make digital or hard copies of part or all of this work for personal or classroom use is granted without fee provided that copies are not made or distributed for profit or commercial advantage and that copies bear this notice and the full citation on the first page. Copyrights for third-party components of this work must be honored. For all other uses, contact the owner/author(s).
ACM-BCB'17, August 20-23, 2017, Boston, MA, USA.
© 2017 Copyright held by the owner/author(s). 978-1-4503-4722-8/17/08.
DOI: http://dx.doi.org/10.1145/3107411.3110413

CCS CONCEPTS

•Applied computing → Bioinformatics; •Computing methodologies → *Ensemble methods;*

KEYWORDS

Drug Sensitivity Prediction, Stacking, Bias

[1]This work was supported by NIH grant R01GM122084-01.

A Bayesian Approach to Determine the Composition of Heterogeneous Cancer Tissue

Ashish Katiyar
Department of Electrical and Computer Engineering, Texas A&M University
College Station, TX 77843-3128
ashish.katiyar13@tamu.edu

Anwoy Mohanty
Division of Genetics, Department of Medicine, Brigham and Women's Hospital and Harvard Medical School
P.O. Box 1212
Boston, MA 02115
amohanty@broadinstitute.org

Chao Sima, Jianping Hua, Rosana Lopes
Center for Bioinformatics and Genomic Systems Engineering, TEES/Texas A&M University
College Station, TX
simachao@tamu.edu

Aniruddha Datta
Department of Electrical and Computer Engineering, Texas A&M University
College Station, TX 77843-3128
datta@ece.tamu.edu

Michael L. Bittner
Translational Genomics Research Institute
Phoenix, AZ
mbittner@tgen.org

ABSTRACT

Cancer Tissue Heterogeneity is an important consideration in cancer research as it can give insights into the causes and progression of cancer. It is known to play a significant role in cancer cell survival, growth and metastasis. Determining the compositional breakup of a heterogeneous cancer tissue can also help address the therapeutic challenges posed by heterogeneity. This necessitates a low cost, scalable algorithm to address the challenge of accurate estimation of the composition of a heterogeneous cancer tissue. In this paper, we propose an algorithm to tackle this problem by utilizing the data of accurate, but high cost, single cell line cell-by-cell observation methods in low cost ensemble observation method for heterogeneous cancer cell mixtures to obtain their composition in a Bayesian framework. The algorithm is analyzed and validated using synthetic data and experimental data obtained from mixtures of cancer cell lines.

KEYWORDS

Cancer Tissue Heterogeneity; Bayesian Modeling; Metropolis; Kernel Density Estimation

1 INTRODUCTION

Cancer tissue heterogeneity is a very important aspect in cancer research. It is a phenomena observed in almost all kinds of cancers and poses challenges in effective therapy design as stated in [2]. It is a cause of acquired drug resistance. In addition, a treatment approach mentioned in [1] requires close monitoring of the ratio of subpopulations of a heterogeneous cancer tissue. Hence determining the composition of heterogeneous cancer tissue is crucial.

Permission to make digital or hard copies of part or all of this work for personal or classroom use is granted without fee provided that copies are not made or distributed for profit or commercial advantage and that copies bear this notice and the full citation on the first page. Copyrights for third-party components of this work must be honored. For all other uses, contact the owner/author(s).
ACM-BCB'17, August 20–23, 2017, Boston, MA, USA.
© 2017 Copyright held by the owner/author(s). ISBN 978-1-4503-4722-8/17/08.
DOI: http://dx.doi.org/10.1145/3107411.3110410

There was an accurate but high cost optical approach suggested in [5] to determine the composition of a heterogeneous cancer tissue by making cell-by-cell red, green and blue fluorescence measurements. In the proposed algorithm, we aim to reduce the cost of this optical approach by determining heterogeneity using low cost and simple ensemble optical observations. For a setup like in [5], this would be the addition of red, green and blue intensities due to all the cells in the heterogeneous mixture. To achieve this, we extend the methods based on gene expression profiles suggested in [3], [4] so that the ensemble optical measurements can be used instead of gene expression measurements to determine the compositional breakup of the tissue under observation. The proposed algorithm requires the expensive cell-by-cell observation of individual subpopulations only once and can then be used to determine the composition of any number of heterogeneous cancer tissues composed of those subpopulations.

2 ALGORITHM

Let us assume that we need to study heterogeneous cancer tissues composed of a given set of n different cell lines. Let there be m different quantitatively measured attributes. These attributes are chosen such that they are independent and the different cell lines have dissimilar attribute profiles. The first step of the algorithm is to profile each of these n cell lines individually by making cell-by-cell observations for them. To do this, we measure the value of the m attributes for individual cells of a particular cell line. We do this separately for all the n different cell lines. From these observations, we estimate the sample mean, $\hat{\mu_{ij}}$, and sample standard deviation, $\hat{\sigma_{ij}}$, of the jth attribute of ith cell line for $1 \leq i \leq n$ and $1 \leq j \leq m$. This is the expensive one time procedure. An important consideration here is that the experiment setup should remain consistent for the next step of the algorithm too. Hence a proper protocol for experimentation is important.

The next step of the algorithm analyses a given heterogeneous cancer tissue. Assume the true composition of the tissue is given by $N = (N_1, N_2, \ldots, N_n)$ where N_i represents the number of cells of ith cell line present in the tissue. N is not known and needs to be estimated. In this step, we measure the ensemble attribute value of the m attributes for the given heterogeneous cancer tissue which is a low cost process. The ensemble measurements are assumed to be arising from the summation of the attributes of individual cells in the mixture. Note that the attribute values of individual cells are not observed. Let the vector of observed ensemble attributes be E_{sum}. The objective of the algorithm is to take E_{sum}, $\hat{\mu_{ij}}$ and $\hat{\sigma_{ij}}$ as inputs and give an accurate estimate of N as the output. The algorithm is independent of the distribution of attribute values of cell lines. The estimate of N is represented by $\hat{N}$.

The algorithm requires the different attributes to be independent and assumes that the contribution of different cells from a particular cell line in the ensemble observation are identically distributed. In addition, we assume that the cells do not interact with each other. With these assumptions we use the Central Limit Theorem to estimate the likelihood of N for the observed E_{sum} and given μ and σ presented in Equation 1.

$$P(E_{sum}|N,\mu,\sigma) \approx \prod_{j=1}^{m} \frac{1}{\sqrt{2\pi(\sum_{i=1}^{n} N_i\sigma_{ij}^2)}} e^{-\frac{(E_{sumj}-\sum_{i=1}^{n}\mu_{ij}N_i)^2}{2\sum_{i=1}^{n}N_i\sigma_{ij}^2}} \quad (1)$$

where E_{sumj} is the jth component of E_{sum} vector. Maximizing this likelihood is difficult to solve analytically. Hence, we use a Bayesian approach to estimate N. We assume a uniform prior for all the components of N_i. Evaluating the posterior directly from the expression is infeasible. To address this issue, we use the Metropolis algorithm to draw samples from the posterior distribution followed by Kernel Density Estimation to estimate the distribution from the drawn samples. The output of the algorithm, $\hat{N}$, is the maximum a posteriori probability (MAP) estimate of N.

3 RESULTS

The performance of the algorithm is evaluated for synthetic data and experimental data. For synthetic data, the analysis is done for a two cell and two attribute system to demonstrate the performance of the algorithm for varying parameters like similarity of attribute profile for the two cell lines and standard deviation of attributes. Here, we present the result to demonstrate the effect of similarity of attribute profile on the confidence interval of posterior probability measure. We demonstrate the algorithm by generating samples from an exponential distribution with mean $\mu_{11} = \mu_{22} = 100$ and $\mu_{21} = \mu_{12} = k\mu_{11}$, where k controls the similarity of the attribute profiles. We generate 2000 samples for both the cell lines to perform the profiling of attributes. Then, we simulate the heterogeneous cancer tissue composed of 2000 cells of Cell Type 1 and 3000 cells of Cell Type 2 and generate the ensemble observation for the same. The posterior probability is presented in Figure 1.

The algorithm is also evaluated for experimental data where mixtures of three cell lines HCT116, A2058 and SW480 were used to simulate a heterogeneous cancer tissue. We use red, green and blue fluorescence as attributes. Mixture 1 was approximately mixed in the ratio [1/3 1/3 1/3] and Mixture 2 was approximately mixed in the ratio [7/20 3/20 1/2]. Each mixture is perturbed and imaged under three different conditions: untreated, treated with Lapatinib

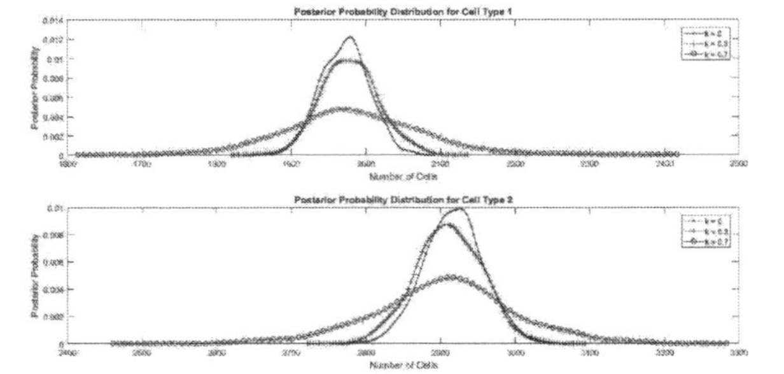

Figure 1: Posterior Probability Distribution of N when the elements of the attribute vector are Exponentially distributed

Experiment	$\hat{N}_{cbc}$	$\hat{N}_{ens}$
Untreated Mixture 1	[3314 3710 2070]	[3418 3543 14]
Untreated Mixture 2	[1466 757 1557]	[1509 688 1979]
Lapatinib Mixture 1	[2440 3812 2060]	[2613 3630 1287]
Lapatinib Mixture 2	[1558 691 1782]	[1494 679 2804]
Temsirolimus Mixture 1	[2756 3833 1991]	[2794 3855 98]
Temsirolimus Mixture 2	[1767 741 1490]	[1668 772 2397]

Table 1: Number of cells in the mixture obtained by cell-by-cell analysis and ensemble analysis

and treated with Temsirolimus. Hence, overall there are six test cases. Due to factors such as multiplication of cells at different rates in the time between mixing and imaging, inaccuracy of the mixing equipment and the imaging process not capturing the true ratio, we compare the results of the algorithm ($\hat{N}_{ens}$) with the results obtained from [5] ($\hat{N}_{cbc}$) instead of the ratio that they were originally mixed in. These results are mentioned in Table 1. We observe that there are inaccuracies in the estimation of number of cells of SW480 cell line. To understand the discrepancy we looked at the cell-by-cell data for the mixture too and the reason is determined to be a difference in the mean of blue attribute in the attribute profiling experiment and the mixture experiment.

This algorithm can estimate the composition of a heterogeneous cancer tissue which can have a big impact in cancer therapy design.

REFERENCES

[1] Robert A. Gatenby, Ariosto S. Silva, Robert J. Gillies, and B. Roy Frieden. 2009. Adaptive Therapy. *Cancer Research* 69, 11 (2009), 4894–4903. https://doi.org/10.1158/0008-5472.CAN-08-3658 arXiv:http://cancerres.aacrjournals.org/content/69/11/4894.full.pdf

[2] Nicholas McGranahan and Charles Swanton. 2015. Biological and Therapeutic Impact of Intratumor Heterogeneity in Cancer Evolution. *Cancer Cell* 27, 1 (January 2015), 15–26. https://doi.org/10.1016/j.ccell.2014.12.001

[3] A. K. Mohanty, A. Datta, and V. Venkatraj. 2014. A Model for Cancer Tissue Heterogeneity. *IEEE Transactions on Biomedical Engineering* 61, 3 (March 2014), 966–974. https://doi.org/10.1109/TBME.2013.2294469

[4] A. K. Mohanty, A. Datta, and V. Venkatraj. 2016. A Conjugate Exponential Model for Cancer Tissue Heterogeneity. *IEEE Journal of Biomedical and Health Informatics* 20, 2 (March 2016), 699–709. https://doi.org/10.1109/JBHI.2015.2410279

[5] C. Sima, J. Hua, R. Lopes, A. Datta, and M. L. Bittner. 2016. Detecting Cell Growth and Drug Response in Heterogeneous Populations: A Dynamic Imaging Approach. In *2016 IEEE 16th International Conference on Bioinformatics and Bioengineering (BIBE)*. 121–128. https://doi.org/10.1109/BIBE.2016.55

CAME 2017 – 6th Workshop on Computational Advances in Molecular Epidemiology

Yury Khudyakov
Division of Viral Hepatitis
Centers of Disease Control and Prevention
Atlanta, GA 30329
yek0@cdc.gov

Ion Mandoiu
Computer Science & Engineering Department
University of Connecticut
Storrs, CT 06269
ion@engr.uconn.edu

Pavel Skums
Department of Computer Science
Georgia State University
Atlanta, GA 30303
pskums@gsu.edu

Alexander Zelikovsky
Department of Computer Science
Georgia State University
Atlanta, GA 30303
alexz@cs.gsu.edu

Welcome to the *6th Workshop on Computational Advances in Molecular Epidemiology*, held on August 20, 2017 in Boston, MA in conjunction with the *8th ACM Conference on Bioinformatics, Computational Biology, and Health Informatics (ACM-BCB)*.[1]

Molecular epidemiology is essentially an integrative scientific discipline that considers molecular biological processes in specific epidemiological settings. It relates molecular biological events to etiology, distribution and prevention of disease in human populations. Over years, molecular epidemiology has become extensively fused with mathematical and computational science and immensely benefitted from this tight association. The CAME workshop aims to provide a forum for presentation and discussion of the latest computational research in molecular epidemiology. This multidisciplinary workshop brings together field practitioners of molecular epidemiology, molecular evolutionists, population geneticists, medical researchers, bioinformaticians, statisticians and computer scientists interested in the latest developments in algorithms, mining, visualization, modeling, simulation and other methods of computational, statistical and mathematical analysis of genetic and molecular data in the epidemiological context.

This year's workshop builds upon 5 prior editions successfully held in Atlanta (Nov. 12-15, 2011, in conjunction with the *2011 IEEE International Conference on Bioinformatics and Biomedicine*), New Orleans (June 12-14, 2013, in conjunction with the *3rd IEEE International Conference on Computational Advances in Bio and Medical Sciences*), Miami Beach (June 2-4, 2014, in conjunction with the *4th IEEE International Conference on Computational Advances in Bio and Medical Sciences*), Norfolk, Virginia (June 7-10, 2015, in conjunction with the *11th International Symposium on Bioinformatics Research and Applications*), and Atlanta (October 13-15, 2016, in conjunction with the *6th IEEE International Conference on Computational Advances in Bio and Medical Sciences*). The workshop program includes 21 invited talks spanning four sessions.

The first session features six talks devoted to computational methods for transmission network inference. Topics include phylogenetic methods for inference of genetic relatedness between viral populations, reconstruction of transmission networks from next-generation viral sequencing (NGS) data as well as combined genetic and epidemiological data, agent-based simulation of quasispecies evolution, and the use of inferred networks for guiding intervention strategies.

The second session is comprised of four talks on molecular surveillance, including overviews of current state-of-the-art in molecular surveillance of HCV, quality control of molecular diagnostic systems, and algorithms for incidence estimation and differentiation between recent and chronic infections.

The third session includes six talks at the interface between molecular epidemiology and immunology. Topics include computational methods for epitope prediction, profiling the T and B cell receptor repertoires using NGS modeling stochastic effects in immune responses, and understanding the role played by the immune system in molecular evolution of pathogens.

The last session has five talks on software systems for managing and visualizing molecular epidemiology data and machine learning methods for reducing biases in NGS data, predicting drug resistance, and large-scale screening of drug combinations.

As for previous editions of CAME, speakers will be invited to submit full length articles to special issues of premier journals in the field. This year both *BMC Bioinformatics* and *Infection, Genetics and Evolution: Journal of Molecular Epidemiology and Evolutionary Genetics of Infectious Diseases (MEEGID)* have agreed to publish special issues devoted to works presented at the workshop.

We would like to thank Workshop Co-chairs Jianlin Cheng, Bhaskar Dasgupta, and Lydia Tapia for the opportunity to organize CAME 2017 in conjunction with the *8th ACM-BCB*. Last but not least, we would like to thank all speakers for presenting their work at the workshop.

[1]Permission to make digital or hard copies of part or all of this work for personal or classroom use is granted without fee provided that copies are not made or distributed for profit or commercial advantage and that copies bear this notice and the full citation on the first page. Copyrights for third-party components of this work must be honored. For all other uses, contact the Owner/Author.
ACM-BCB '17, August 20-23, 2017, Boston, MA, USA
© 2017 Copyright is held by the owner/author(s).
ACM ISBN 978-1-4503-4722-8/17/08.
http://dx.doi.org/10.1145/3107411.3108168

A Workshop on Microbiomics, Metagenomics, and Metabolomics

Soha Hassoun
Tufts University
161 College Avenue
Medford, MA
+1(617)627-5177
soha.hassoun@tufts.edu

Curtis Huttenhower
Harvard University
655 Huntington Avenue
Boston, MA
+1(617) 432-4912
chuttenh@hsph.harvard.edu

ABSTRACT

Microbiota are ecological communities of microorganisms found throughout nature. In humans and animals, microbiota communities can reside on or within the body, and exist in a commensal or mutualistic relationship with their host to impact physiological functions and play critical roles in the host's development. These microbial communities can be very complex. One such example is the intestinal microbiota, comprising hundreds of species that interact with other microorganisms in the community as well as their host. Recent studies have demonstrated that microbiota impacts a wide range of physiological processes, including digestion, development of the immune system, and inflammation. Further, significant alterations in the intestinal microbiota composition has shown to correlate with several diseases, including obesity diabetes, cancer, asthma, and even autism spectrum disorder. Characterizing the microbiota and understanding its relation to health and disease stand to significantly improve human health.

Efforts to characterize microbiota have greatly benefited from technical advances in DNA sequencing. In particular, low-cost culture-independent sequencing has made metagenomic and metatranscriptomic surveys of microbial communities practical, including bacteria, archaea, viruses, and fungi associated with the human body, other hosts, and the environment. The resulting data have stimulated the development of many new computational approaches to meta'omic sequence analysis, including metagenomic assembly, microbial identification, and gene, transcript, and pathway metabolic profiling. Further, recent advances in untargeted metabolomics have stimulated the development of many tools that enhance the functional profiling of microbial communities.

Through invited talks, this workshop will highlight recent advances computational methods for metagenomics and metabolomics, and present pressing challenges. A hands-on tutorial will provide an introduction to computational metagenomics. This workshop is timely, and will broaden the scope of the conference to cover such pressing important topics.

Permission to make digital or hard copies of part or all of this work for personal or classroom use is granted without fee provided that copies are not made or distributed for profit or commercial advantage and that copies bear this notice and the full citation on the first page. Copyrights for third-party components of this work must be honored. For all other uses, contact the Owner/Author.
ACM-BCB '17, August 20-23, 2017, Boston, MA, USA
© 2017 Copyright is held by the owner/author(s).
ACM ISBN 978-1-4503-4722-8/17/08.
http://dx.doi.org/10.1145/3107411.3108172

Author Index

www.ingramcontent.com/pod-product-compliance
Lightning Source LLC
LaVergne TN
LVHW080105011026
849160LV00013B/1030
* 9 7 8 1 4 5 0 3 5 6 7 3 2 *